G000293070

EasyRead London

First published 2001 by

Philip's, a division of
Octopus Publishing Group Ltd
2–4 Heron Quays, London E14 4JP

Second edition 2003
Second impression with revisions 2004

ISBN-10   0-540-08468-9
ISBN-13   978-0 540-08468-5

© Philip's 2004

Ordnance Survey®

This product includes mapping data licensed from
Ordnance Survey® with the permission of the
Controller of Her Majesty's Stationery Office.
© Crown copyright 2004. All rights reserved. Licence
number 100011710

Contents

II	Key to map pages
IV	Administrative and Postcode boundaries
VI	Route planning
X	Key to map symbols
1	Street maps
228	Keys to enlarged map pages and symbols
229	Enlarged street maps
271	Index
410	List of numbered locations
423	Hospitals
424	Shopping, theatres, cinemas
426	Central London buses
428	Local rail and London Underground
430	Places of interest

Digital Data

The exceptionally high-quality mapping found in this atlas is available as digital data in TIFF format, which is easily convertible to other bit mapped (raster) image formats.

The index is also available in digital form as a standard database table. It contains all the details found in the printed index together with the National Grid reference for the map square in which each entry is named

For further information and to discuss your requirements, please contact Philips on
020 7644 6932 or james.mann@philips-maps.co.uk

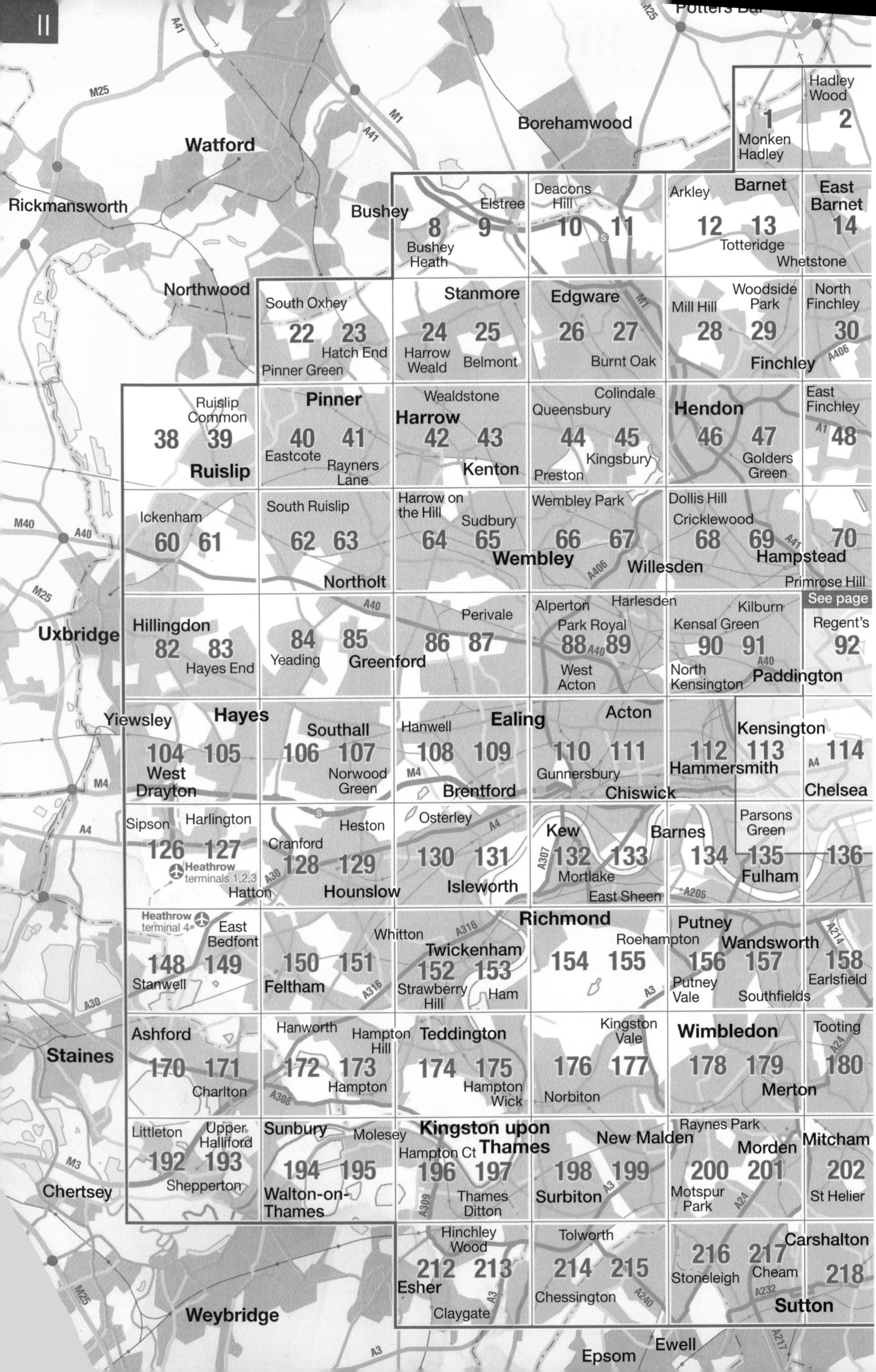

Potters Bar

M25

Watford

M1 A41

Borehamwood

Hadley Wood

1 Monken Hadley

2

Rickmansworth

Bushey

Elstree 8 9

Deacons Hill 10 11

Arkley 12 **Barnet** 13

East Barnet 14

Totteridge

Whetstone

M25 M40 A40 M25 M4 A4 A30 M3

Northwood

South Oxhey 22 23 Hatch End Pinner Green

Stanmore 24 25 Harrow Weald Belmont

Edgware 26 27 Burnt Oak

Mill Hill 28 Woodside Park 29 **Finchley**

North Finchley 30 A406

Ruislip Common 38 39 **Ruislip**

Pinner 40 41 Eastcote Rayners Lane

Wealdstone **Harrow** 42 43 **Kenton**

Colindale Queensbury 44 45 Kingsbury Preston

Hendon 46 47 Golders Green

East Finchley A1 48

Ickenham 60 61

South Ruislip 62 63 **Northolt**

Harrow on the Hill 64 Sudbury 65 **Wembley**

Wembley Park 66 67 A406 **Willesden**

Dollis Hill Cricklewood 68 69 A41

Hampstead 70 Primrose Hill

Uxbridge

Hillingdon 82 83 Hayes End

84 85 Yeading **Greenford**

Perivale 86 87

Alperton Park Royal 88 A40 89 West Acton

Harlesden Kilburn Kensal Green 90 91 North Kensington **Paddington**

Regent's 92 See page

Yiewsley **Hayes** 104 105 West Drayton

Southall 106 107 Norwood Green

Hanwell 108 109 **Brentford**

Ealing 110 111 Gunnersbury **Chiswick**

Acton 112 113 **Hammersmith**

Kensington A4 114 **Chelsea**

Sipson Harlington 126 127 Heathrow terminals 1,2,3

Cranford 128 129 Hatton

Heston 130 131 **Isleworth**

Osterley A4 **Hounslow**

Kew 132 133 Mortlake East Sheen

Barnes 134 A205

Parsons Green 135 **Fulham**

136

Heathrow terminal 4 East Bedfont 148 149 Stanwell

150 151 **Feltham** A316

Whitton A316 **Twickenham** 152 153 Strawberry Hill Ham

Richmond 154 155

Roehampton **Putney** 156 157 Putney Vale Southfields **Wandsworth**

A214 158 Earlsfield

Ashford 170 171 Charlton

Hanworth 172 173 Hampton Hill Hampton A308

Teddington 174 175 Hampton Wick

Kingston Vale 176 177 Norbiton

Wimbledon 178 179 **Merton**

Tooting A24 180

Littleton Upper Halliford 192 193 Shepperton M3

Sunbury 194 195 Molesey **Walton-on-Thames**

Kingston upon Thames 196 197 Hampton Ct Thames Ditton A809

New Malden 198 199 **Surbiton** A3

Raynes Park 200 201 **Morden** Motspur Park A24

Mitcham 202 St Helier

Chertsey

Weybridge

Hinchley Wood 212 213 **Esher** Claygate A3

Tolworth 214 215 Chessington A240

216 217 Stoneleigh Cheam A232

Carshalton 218 **Sutton**

Ewell Epsom

A217

Key to map pages

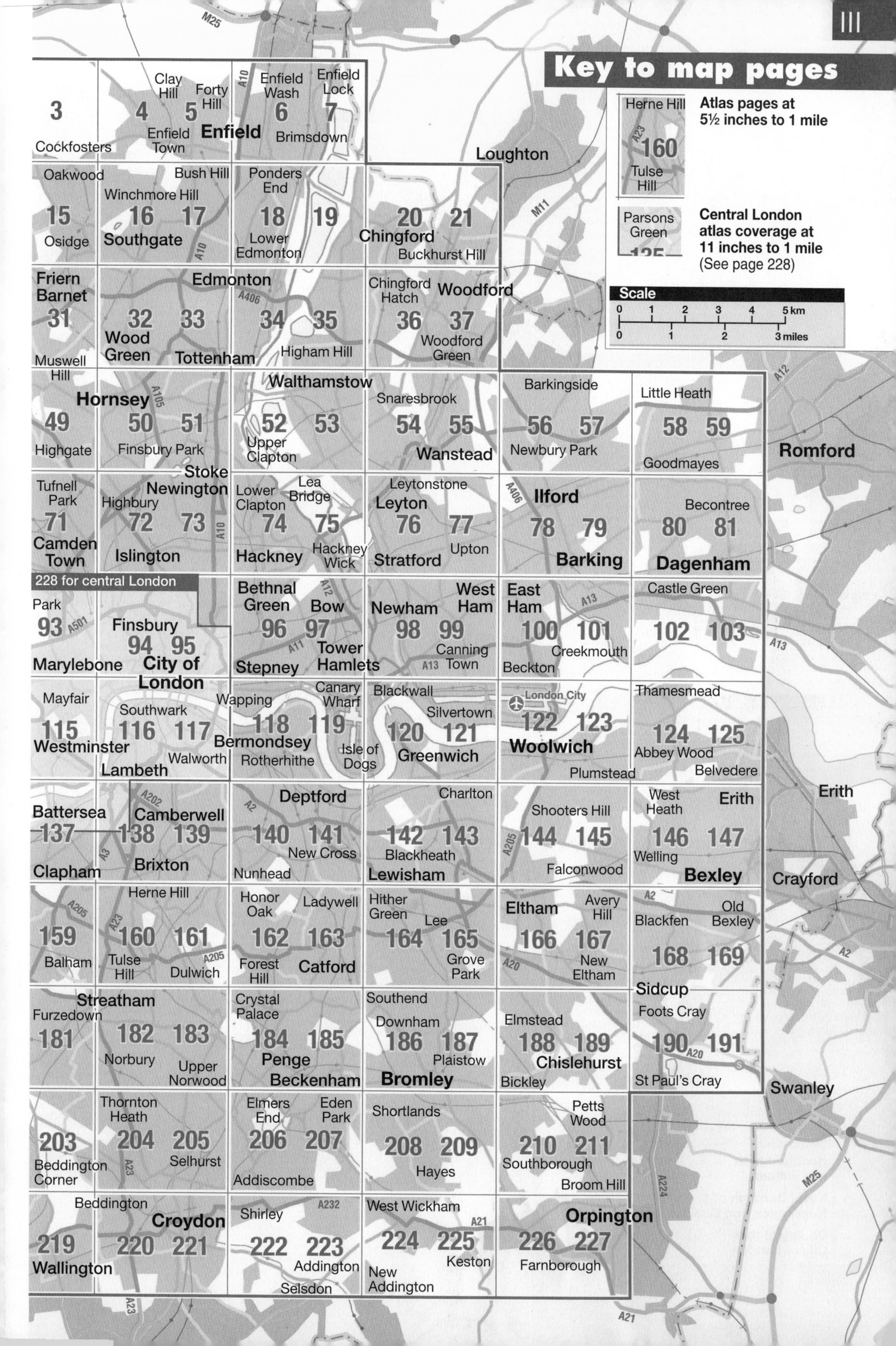

M25

Clay Hill **4** Forty Hill **5** Enfield Town **Enfield**

Enfield Wash **6** Enfield Lock **7** Brimsdown

3 Cockfosters

A10

Loughton

M11

Oakwood **15** Osidge Winchmore Hill **16** **17** Southgate

A10

Ponders End **18** **19** Lower Edmonton

Chingford **20** **21** Buckhurst Hill

Friern Barnet **31** Muswell Hill

Edmonton **32** **33** Wood Green Tottenham

A406

34 **35** Higham Hill

Chingford Hatch **36** **37** Woodford Green Woodford

Hornsey **49** **50** **51** Highgate Finsbury Park

A105

Walthamstow **52** **53** Upper Clapton

Snaresbrook **54** **55** **Wanstead**

Barkingside **56** **57** Newbury Park

Little Heath **58** **59** Goodmayes

Romford

A12

Tufnell Park **71** Camden Town

A10

Highbury **72** **73** Islington **Stoke Newington**

Lower Clapton **74** **75** **Hackney** Lea Bridge Hackney Wick

Leytonstone **76** **77** **Stratford** **Leyton** Upton

A406

Ilford **78** **79** **Barking**

Becontree **80** **81** **Dagenham**

228 for central London

Park **93** A501

Finsbury **94** **95** **City of London** **Marylebone** **Stepney**

Bethnal Green **96** **97** Bow **Tower Hamlets**

A12

Newham **98** **99** Canning Town A13

West Ham East Ham **100** **101** Creekmouth Beckton

A13

Castle Green **102** **103**

A13

Mayfair **115** Westminster Southwark **116** **117** **Bermondsey** Walworth **Lambeth**

Wapping **118** **119** Rotherhithe Isle of Dogs

Canary Wharf

Blackwall **120** **121** **Greenwich** Silvertown

London City **122** **123** **Woolwich** Plumstead

Thamesmead **124** **125** Abbey Wood Belvedere

Erith

Battersea ~~137~~ A202 **Camberwell** ~~138~~ **139** **Brixton** Clapham

A3

Deptford **140** **141** New Cross Nunhead

Charlton **142** **143** Blackheath **Lewisham**

A205 Shooters Hill **144** **145** Falconwood

A205

West Heath **146** **147** Welling **Erith**

Crayford

A205 Herne Hill **159** **160** Tulse Hill **161** Dulwich Balham

A23 A205

Honor Oak **162** Ladywell **163** Forest Hill **Catford**

Hither Green **164** Lee **165** Grove Park

Eltham **166** Avery Hill **167** New Eltham

A20

A2 Blackfen **168** Old Bexley **169**

Bexley

A2

Streatham Furzedown **181** **182** **183** Norbury Upper Norwood

Crystal Palace **184** **185** **Penge** **Beckenham**

Southend Downham **186** **187** Plaistow **Bromley** Bickley

Elmstead **188** **189** **Chislehurst**

Sidcup Foots Cray **190** A20 **191** St Paul's Cray

Swanley

A224

Thornton Heath **203** **204** **205** Selhurst Beddington Corner

A23

Elmers End **206** Eden Park **207** Addiscombe

Shortlands **208** **209** Hayes

Petts Wood **210** **211** Southborough Broom Hill

M25

Beddington **219** **220** **221** **Croydon** Wallington

Shirley **222** **223** Addington Selsdon

A232

West Wickham **224** **225** New Addington Keston

A21

Orpington **226** **227** Farnborough

A21

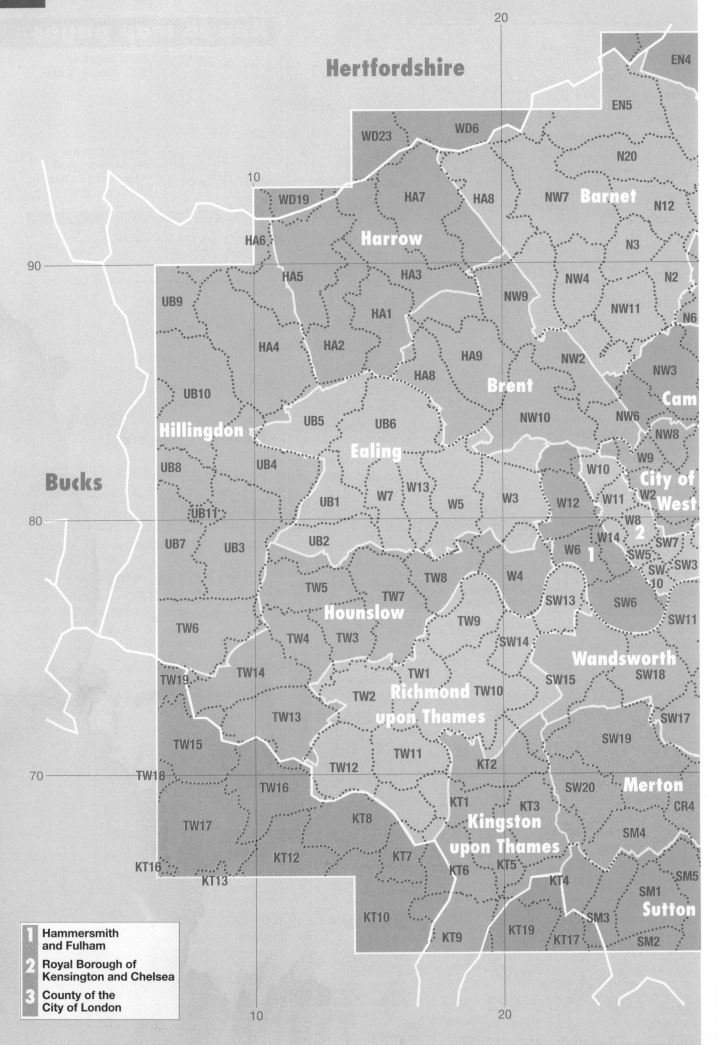

IV

Hertfordshire

Bucks

EN4
EN5
N20
N12
N3
N2
N6

WD23
WD6
WD19
HA6
HA7
HA8
NW7
Barnet
Harrow
HA5
HA3
NW4
NW11
HA1
NW9
UB9
HA4
HA2
HA9
NW2
NW3
HA8
Brent
Cam
Hillingdon
UB5
UB6
NW10
NW6
UB10
NW8
UB8
UB4
Ealing
W9
W10
City of
UB11
UB1
W7
W13
W5
W3
W12
W11
W2
West
UB7
UB3
UB2
W6
W14
W8
2
SW7
SW5
TW5
TW8
W4
SW3
SW10
SW13
SW6
Hounslow
TW7
1
SW11
TW6
TW4
TW3
TW9
SW14
TW1
SW15
Wandsworth
SW18
TW19
TW14
TW2
Richmond
TW10
SW17
TW13
upon Thames
SW19
TW15
TW11
KT2
SW20
Merton
CR4
TW18
TW16
KT1
KT3
TW17
KT8
Kingston
SM4
KT16
KT12
KT7
upon Thames
SM5
KT13
KT6
KT5
KT4
SM1
KT10
SM3
Sutton
KT9
KT19
KT17
SM2

1 Hammersmith
and Fulham

2 Royal Borough of
Kensington and Chelsea

3 County of the
City of London

20
10
90
80
70
10
20

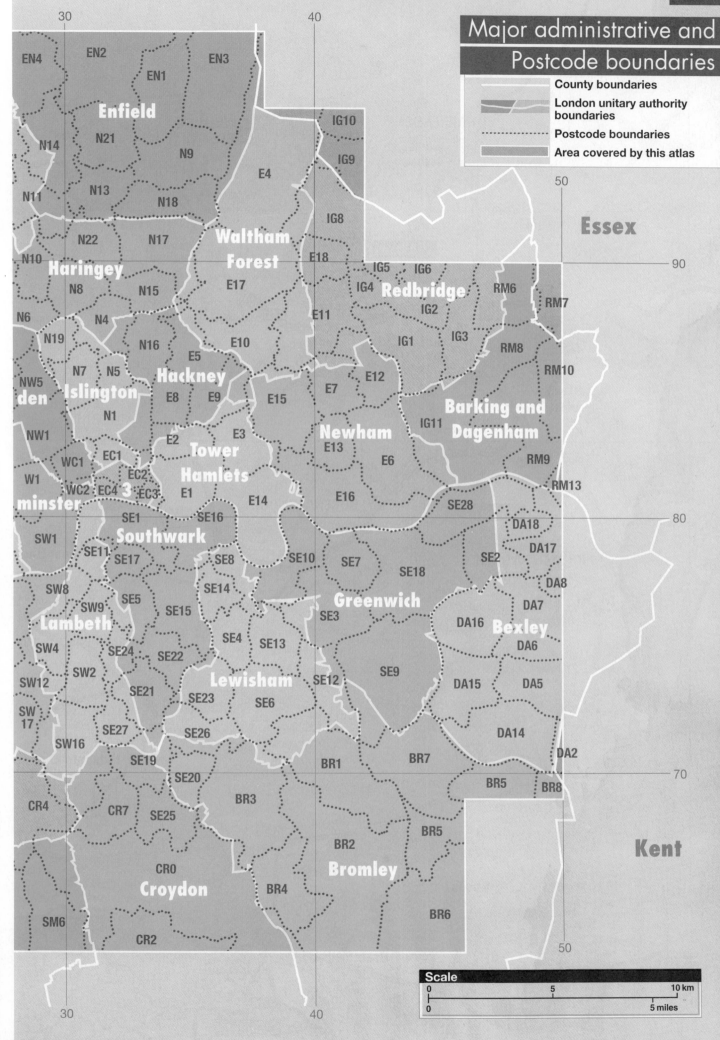

Major administrative and Postcode boundaries

County boundaries
London unitary authority boundaries
Postcode boundaries
Area covered by this atlas

Essex

Kent

Enfield

EN4 EN2 EN1 EN3

N14 N21 N9

N11 N13 N18

N22 N17 Waltham Forest E18 IG10 IG9

N10 Haringey E17 IG8

N8 N15 IG5 IG6 Redbridge RM6 RM7

N6 N4 IG4 IG2 RM8 RM10

N19 N16 E10 E5 IG1 IG3

N7 N5 Hackney E12 RM9 RM13

NW5 E8 E9 E15 E7 Barking and Dagenham

den Islington N1 E2 E3 Newham IG11

NW1 Tower E13 E6

WC1 EC1 Hamlets E16 SE28

W1 WC2 EC2 EC4 EC3 E1 E14 DA18

minster SE1 SE16 SE2 DA17

SW1 Southwark DA8

SE11 SE17 SE8 SE10 SE7 SE18 DA7

SW8 SE5 SE14 Greenwich DA16 Bexley DA6

SW9 SE15 SE3 DA15 DA5

Lambeth SE4 SE13 SE9

SW4 SE24 SE22 DA14

SW2 Lewisham SE12 DA2

SW12 SE21 SE23 SE6

SW17 SE27 SE26 BR1 BR7 BR5 BR8

SW16 SE19

SE20 BR3 BR5

CR4 CR7 SE25 BR2 Bromley

CR0 BR4 BR6

SM6 Croydon CR2

Scale
0   5   10 km

0   5 miles

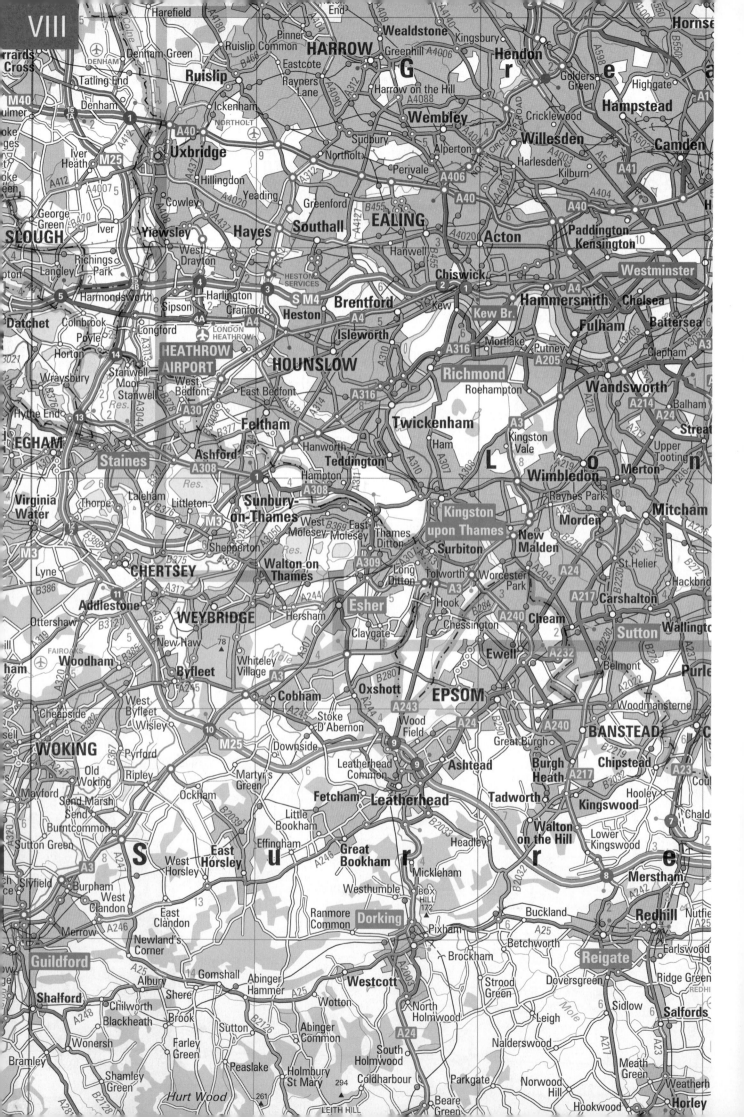

Key to map symbols

Roads

 Motorway with junction number

Primary route
– single, dual carriageway

A road – single, dual carriageway

B road – single, dual carriageway

Through-route
– single, dual carriageway

Minor road
– single, dual carriageway

Road under construction

Rural track, private road or narrow road in urban area

Path, bridleway, byway open to all traffic, road used as public path

Tunnel, covered road

Congeston Charge Zone boundary
Roads within the zone are outlined in red

Gate or obstruction, car pound

P   **P&R**   Parking, park and ride

Crooked Billet   Junction name

Pedestrianised or restricted access area

Public transport

Railway with station, private railway station

London Underground station, Docklands Light Railway station

Tramway or miniature railway with Tramlink station

Bus, coach station

Scale

5½ inches to 1 mile   1:11520

0	220 yds	440 yds	660 yds	½ mile

0	250m	500 m	750 m	1km

Emergency services

 Ambulance, police, fire station

 Hospital, accident and emergency entrance

General features

Market, public amenity site

Information centre, post office

VILLA   **House**   Roman, non-Roman antiquity

100   .304   House number, spot height – metres

Christian place of worship

Mosque, synagogue

Other place of worship

Houses, important buildings

Woods, parkland / common

 Adjoining page number

Leisure facilities

Camp site, caravan site

Golf course, picnic site, view point

Boundaries

Postcode boundaries

Westminster   County and unitary authority boundaries

Water features

Barking Creek   Water name

Tidal water

River or canal – minor, major

Stream

Water

Abbreviations

Acad	**Academy**	Coll	**College**	Drv Rng	**Golf Driving**	LC	**Level Crossing**	Pl Fld	**Playing Field**	Stad	**Stadium**
Allot Gdns	**Allotments**	Ct	**Court**		**Range**	Liby	**Library**	Pal	**Royal Palace**	Sw Pool	**Swimming Pool**
Bndstd	**Bandstand**	Crem	**Crematorium**	Gn	**Green**	Mkt	**Market**	PH	**Public House**	Tenn Cts	**Tennis courts**
Btcl	**Botanical**	Crkt	**Cricket**	Gd	**Ground**	Meml	**Memorial**	Recn Gd	**Recreation**	TH	**Town Hall**
Bwg Gn	**Bowling**	Ent	**Enterprise**	Hort	**Horticultural**	Mon	**Monument**		**Ground**	Trad Est	**Trading Estate**
Cemy	**Cemetery**	Ex H	**Exhibition Hall**	Ind Est	**Industrial Estate**	Mus	**Museum**	Resr	**Reservoir**	Univ	**University**
Ctr	**Centre**	Fball	**Football**	Inst	**Institute**	Nat Res	**Nature Reserve**	Ret Pk	**Retail Park**	YH	**Youth Hostel**
C Ctr	**Civic Centre**	Gdns	**Gardens**	Int	**Interchange**	Obsy	**Observatory**	Sch	**School**		
CH	**Club House**	Glf C	**Golf Course**	Ct	**Law Court**	Pav	**Pavilion**	Sh Ctr	**Shopping Centre**		
Ctry Pk	**Country Park**	Glf Crs	**Golf Course**	L Ctr	**Leisure Centre**	Pk	**Park**	Sp	**Sports**		

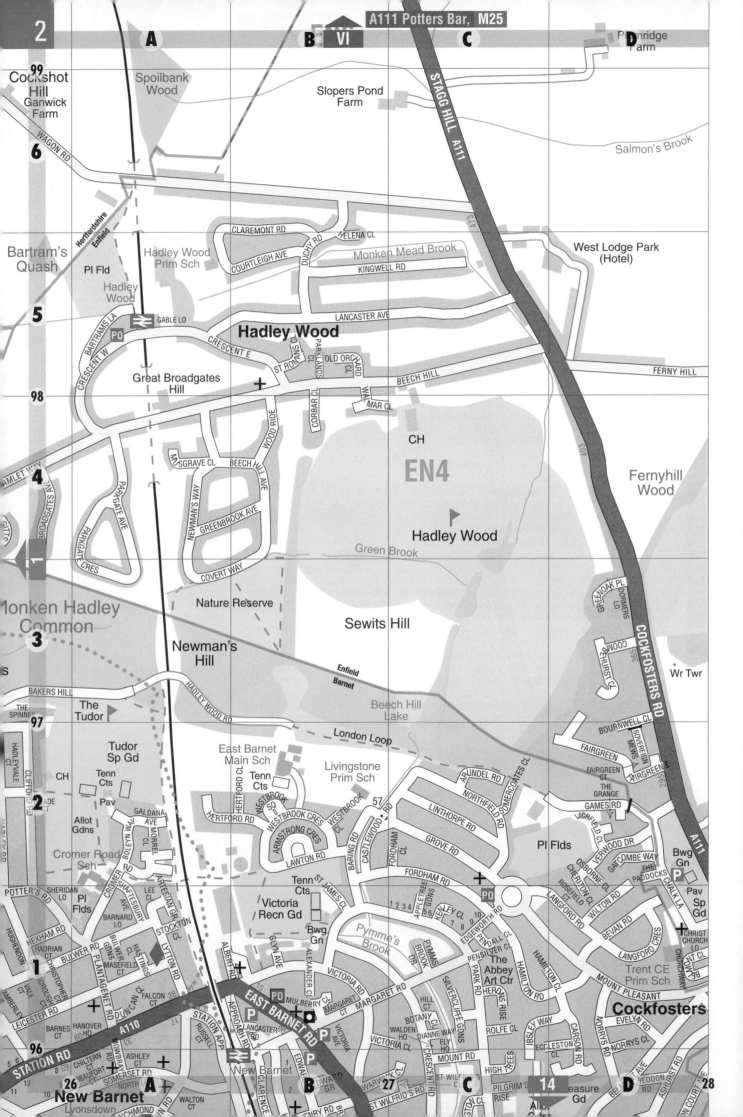

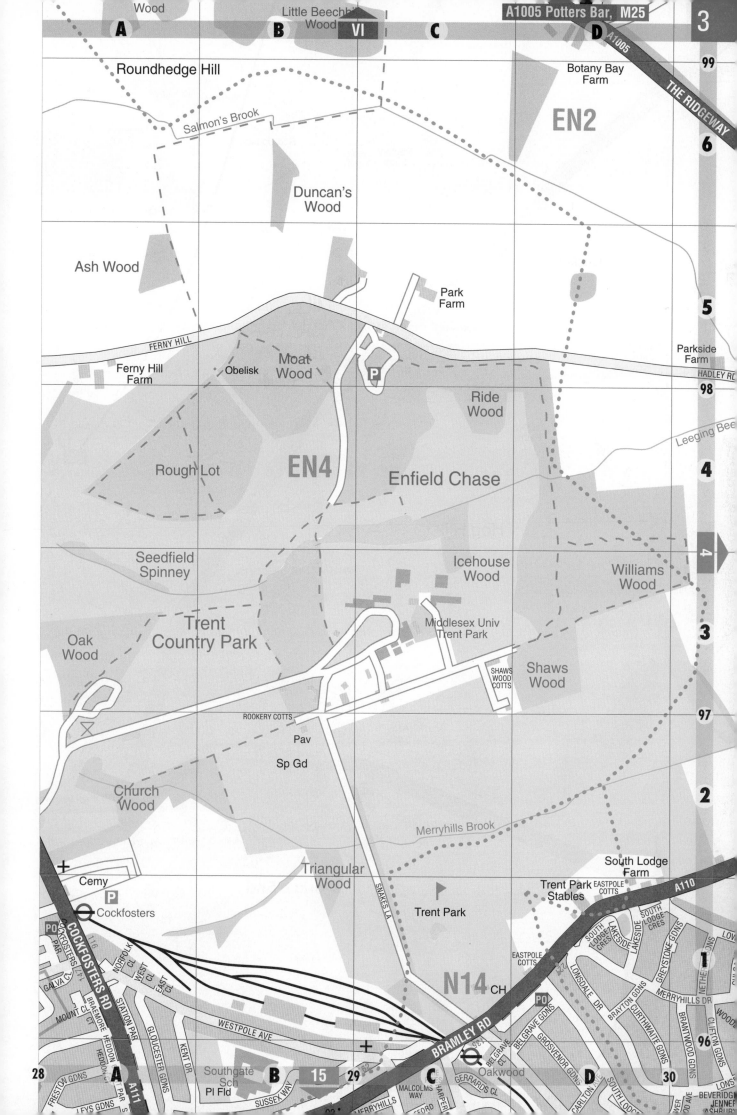

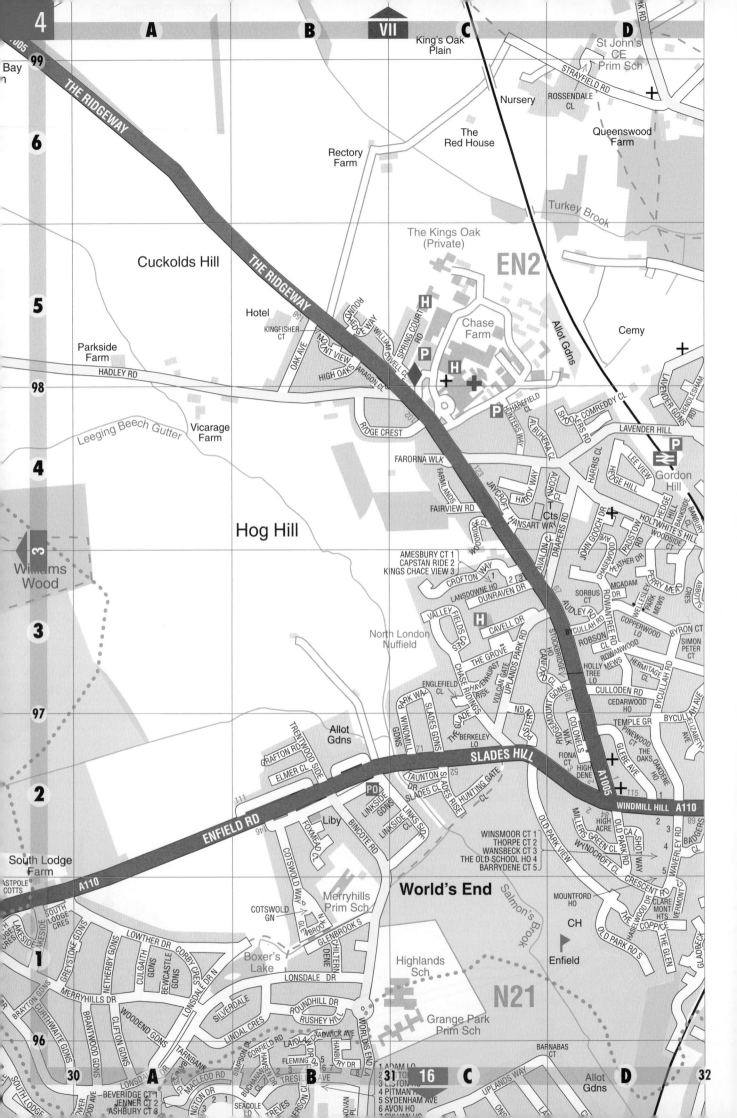

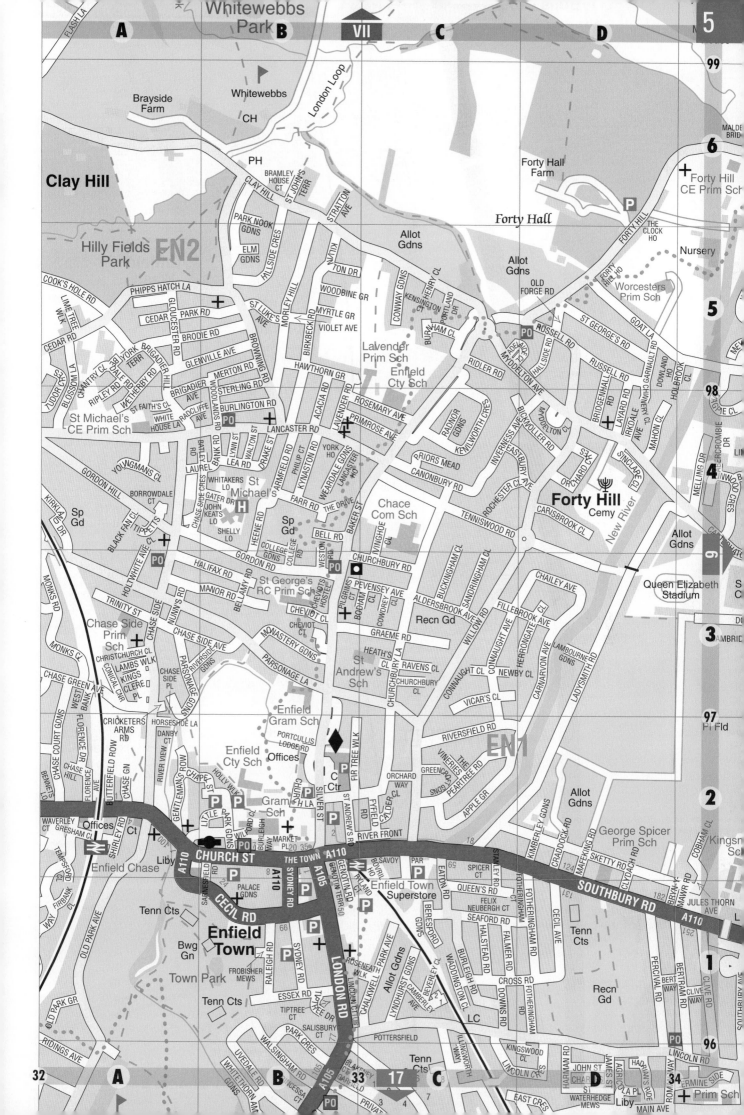

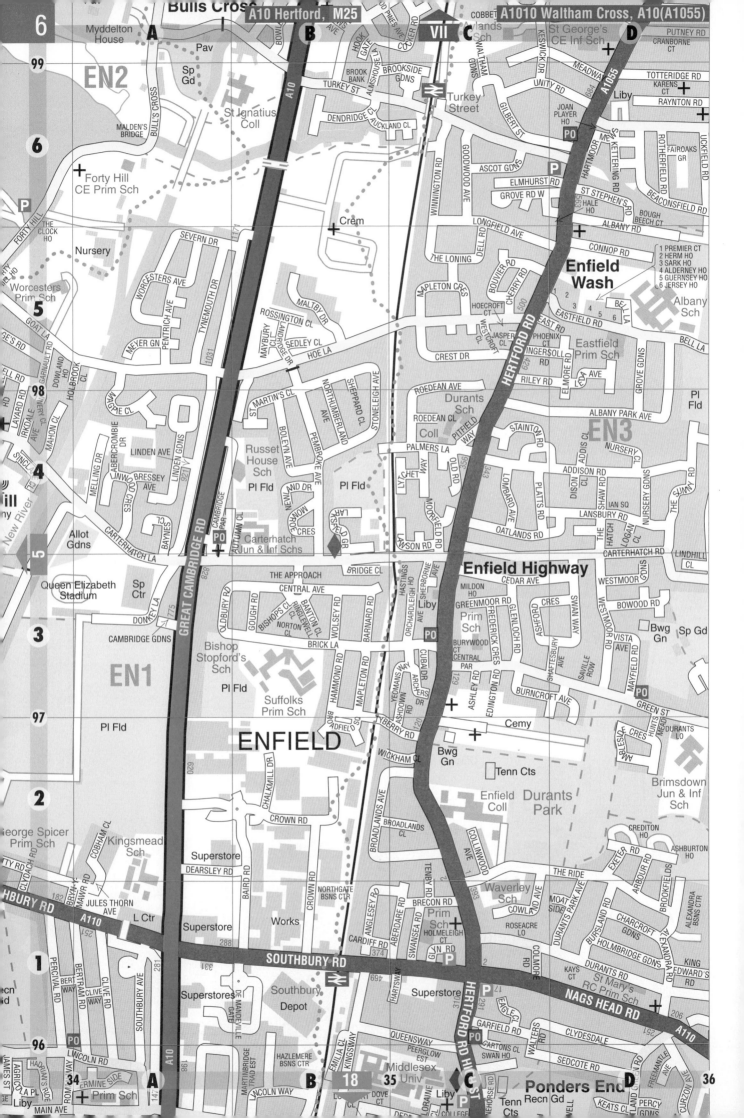

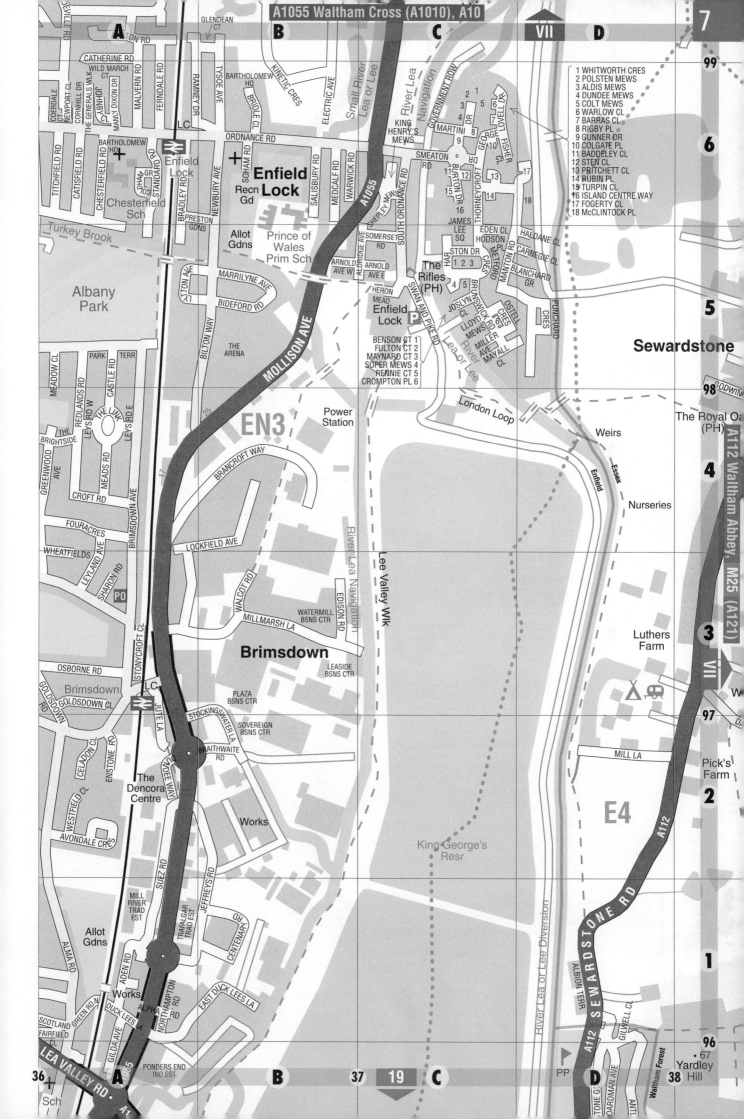

A B C D

1 WHITWORTH CRES
2 POLSTEN MEWS
3 ALDIS MEWS
4 DUNDEE MEWS
5 COLT MEWS
6 WARLOW CL
7 BARRAS CL
8 RIGBY PL
9 GUNNER DR
10 COLGATE PL
11 BADDELEY CL
12 STEN CL
13 PRITCHETT CL
14 RUBIN PL
15 TURPIN CL
16 ISLAND CENTRE WAY
17 FOGERTY CL
18 McCLINTOCK PL

SEVILLE RD
GLENDEAN CT
ASTON RD
CATHERINE RD
WILD MARCH CT
MALVERN RD
MANLY DIXON DR
FERNDALE RD
RAMNEY DR
TYSOE AVE
BARTHOLOMEW HO
BRIDLE CL
KINETIC CRES
ELECTRIC AVE
Small River Lea or Lee
River Lea Navigation
GOVERNMENT ROW
NEWPORT CL
CORNHILL DR
THE GENERALS WLK
ABNHO
COERDALE
TITCHFIELD RD
CATISFIELD RD
CHESTERFIELD RD
BARTHOLOMEW HO
STANDARD RD
GR
HAM
LC

Enfield Lock
Chesterfield Sch
ORDNANCE RD
SOHAM RD
SALISBURY RD
MEDCALF RD
WARWICK RD
KING HENRY'S MEWS
SMEATON RD
MARTINI
GEORGE
FISHER CL
LOVELL DR
DR
BURTON DR
THORNEYCROFT
SHEPLEY MEWS
JAMES LEE SQ
HAR STON DR
EDEN CL
HODSON PL
HALDANE CL
CARNEGIE CL
METFORD CRES
BLANCHARD GR

Enfield
Lock
Recn
Gd

Turkey Brook

Albany
Park

Allot
Gdns
Prince of Wales
Prim Sch

MARRILYNE AVE
BIDEFORD RD
THE ARENA
BILTON WAY
MOLLISON AVE
ARNOLD AVE W
ALDRIDGE AVE
ARNOLD AVE E
SOMERSET RD
HERON MEAD
SWAN AND PIKE RD

Enfield
Lock
P
BENSON CT 1
FULTON CT 2
MAYNARD CT 3
SOPER MEWS 4
RENNIE CT 5
CROMPTON PL 6

The Rifles
(PH)

JOSLYN CL
BRUNSWICK CRES
LLOYD MEWS
OSTELL CRES
MILLER AVE
MAYALL CL
PUNCHARD CRES

River Lea or Lee

MEADOW CL
REDLANDS RD
PARK TERR
CASTLE RD
THE LINK
LEYS RD W
LEYS RD E
MEADS RD
GREENWOOD AVE
THE BRIGHTSIDE
CROFT RD
FOURACRES
WHEATFIELDS
LEYLAND AVE
SHARON RD
BRIMSDOWN AVE
PO

EN3

Power
Station

BRANCROFT WAY
LOCKFIELD AVE
WALCOT RD
MILLMARSH LA
WATERMILL BSNS CTR
EDISON RD
River Lea Navigation
Lee Valley Wlk

London Loop

Weirs

Enfield
Essex
Sewardstone

98
GODWIN
The Royal Oak
(PH)

Nurseries

Luthers
Farm

Brimsdown

LEASIDE BSNS CTR

PLAZA BSNS CTR
SOVEREIGN BSNS CTR
JUTE LA
STOCKINGSWATER LA
BRAITHWAITE RD
STONYCROFT CL
LC

OSBORNE RD
GOLDSDOWN CL
GOLDSDOWN RD
CELADON CL
ENSTONE RD
WESTFIELD CL
AVONDALE CRES
The Dencora Centre
DUNDEE WAY

Works

MILL LA

Pick's
Farm

E4

King George's
Resr

A112 Waltham Abbey, M25 (A121)

5
4
3
VII
W
97

Allot
Gdns
SUEZ RD
ALMA RD
ADEN RD
GILDA AVE
DUCK LEES LA
NORTHAMPTON RD
ALPHA RD
TRAFALGAR TRAD EST
CENTENARY RD
JEFFREYS RD
EAST DUCK LEES LA
MILL RIVER TRAD EST

Works

SEWARDSTONE RD
A112
ALBION TERR
River Lea or Lee Diversion
2
1

SCOTLAND GREEN RD N
FAIRFIELD CL
GREEN RD N
STONE GR
BOARDMAN AVE
GILLVELL CL
ANTL
Waltham Forest

PP

67
Yardley
Hill

96

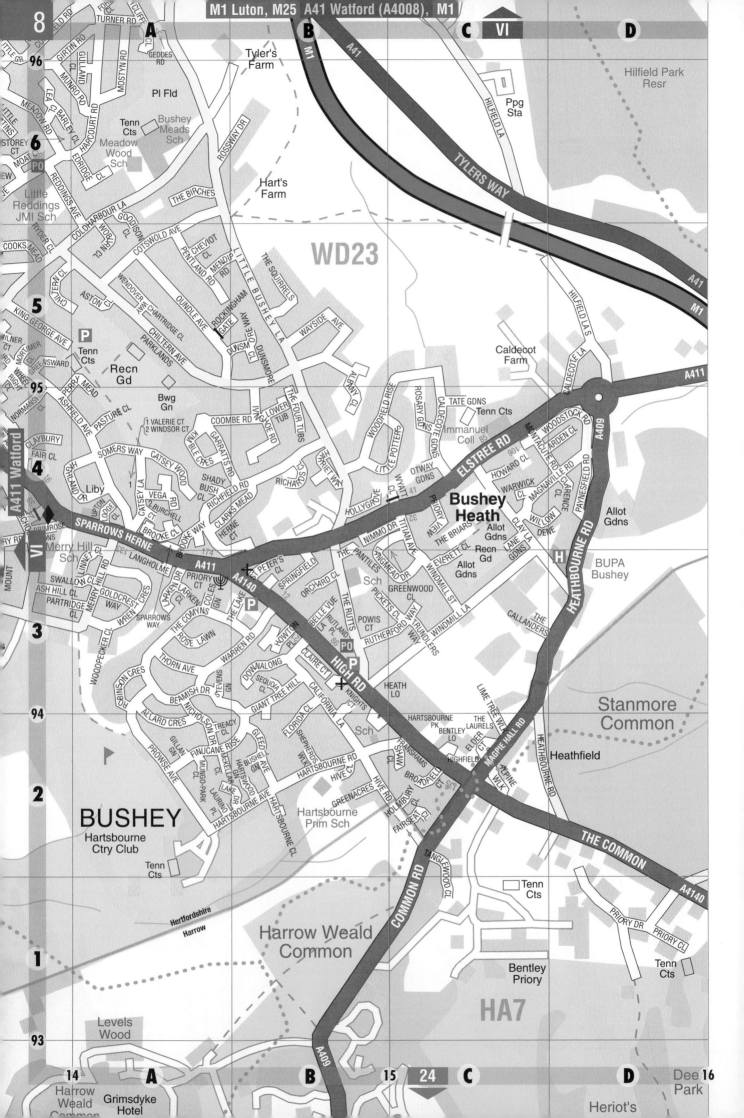

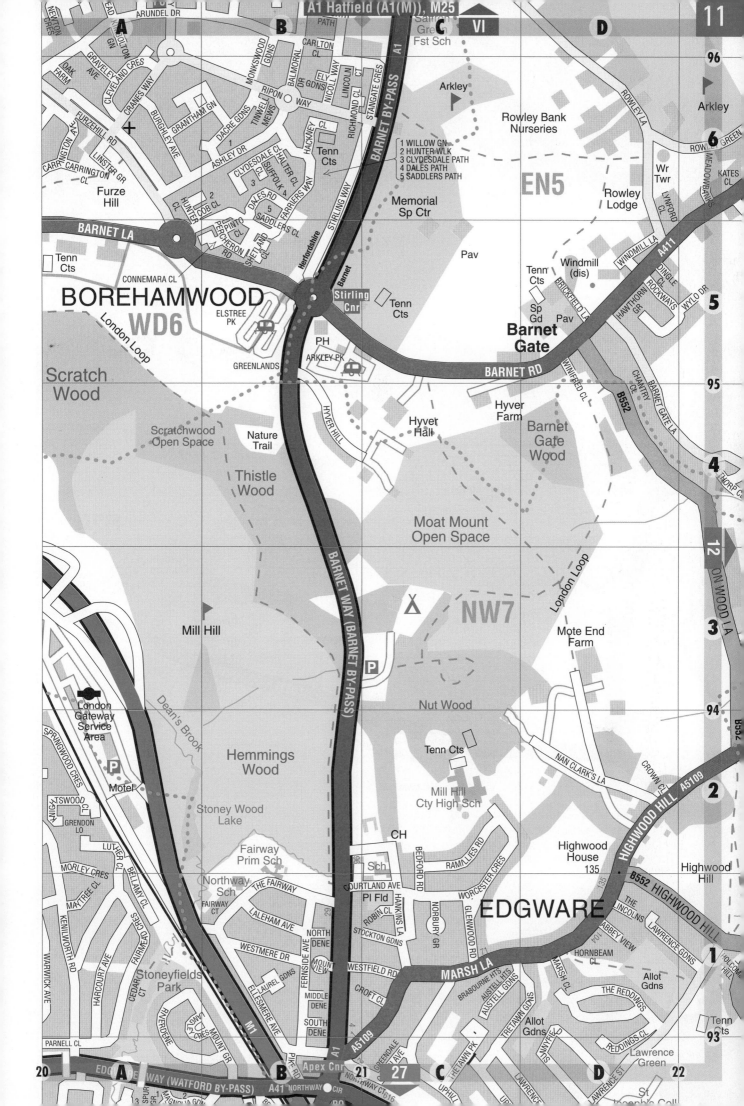

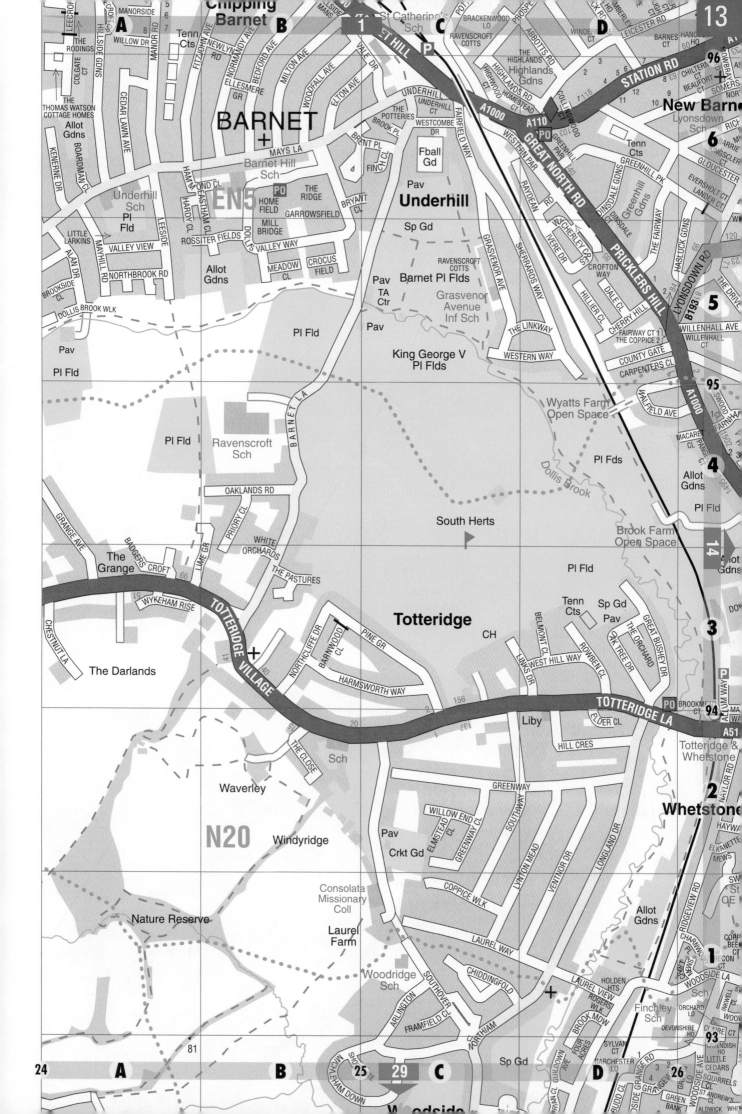

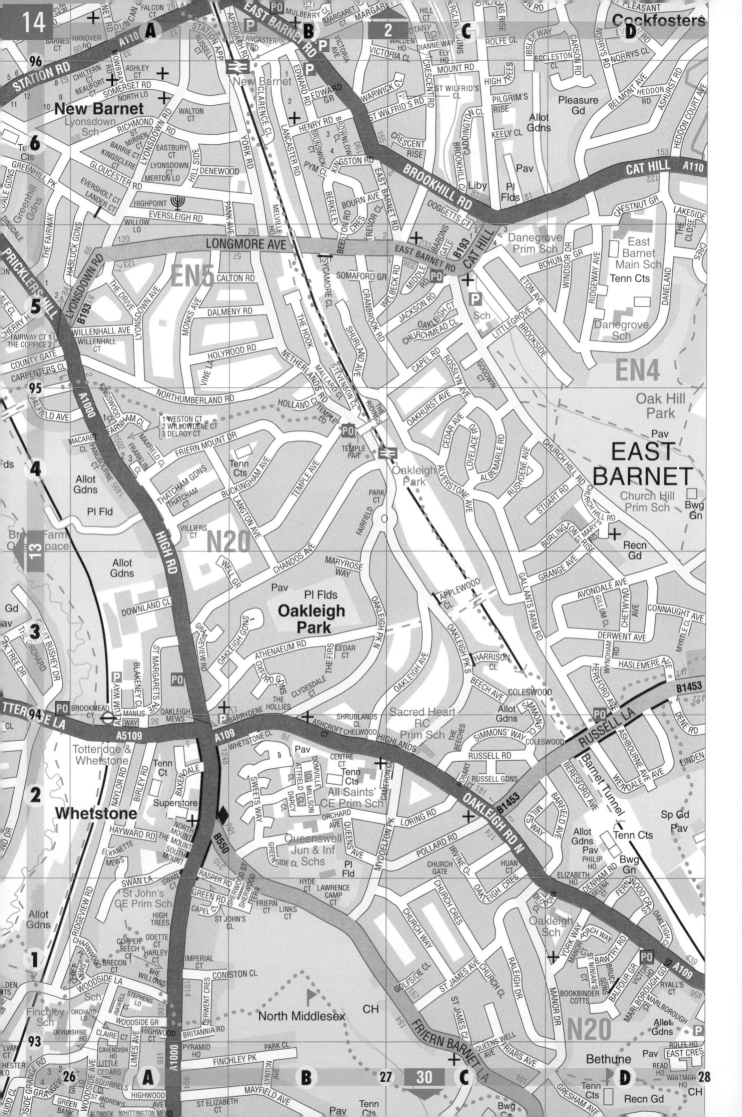

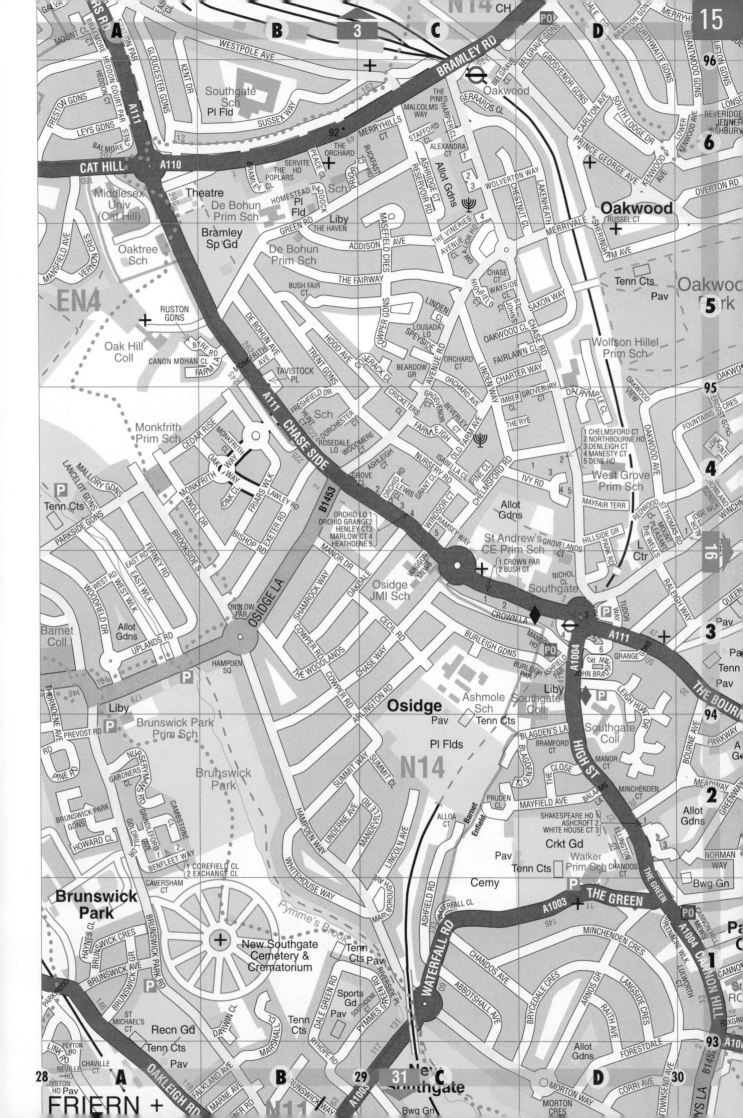

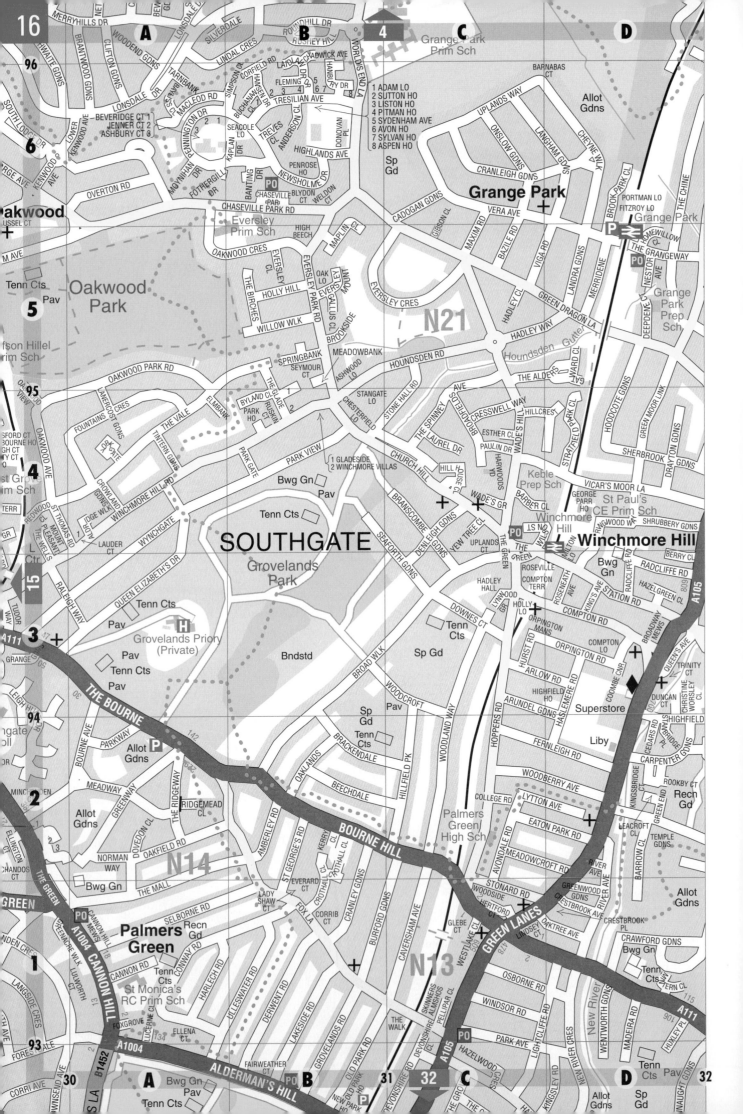

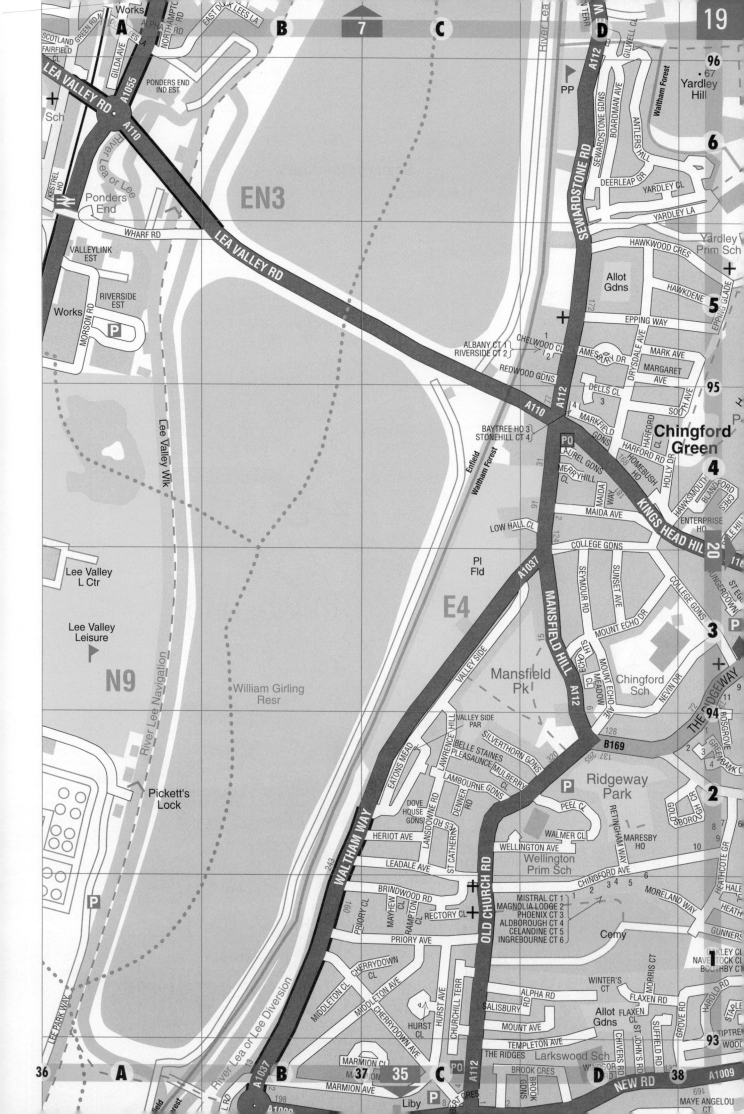

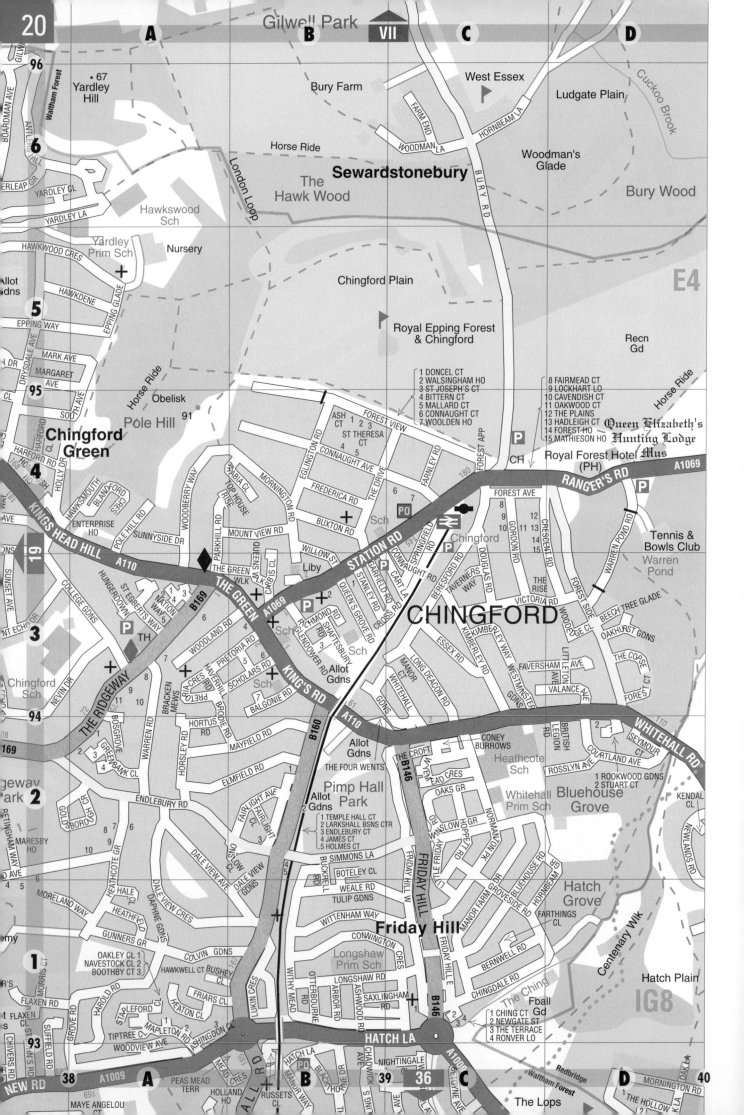

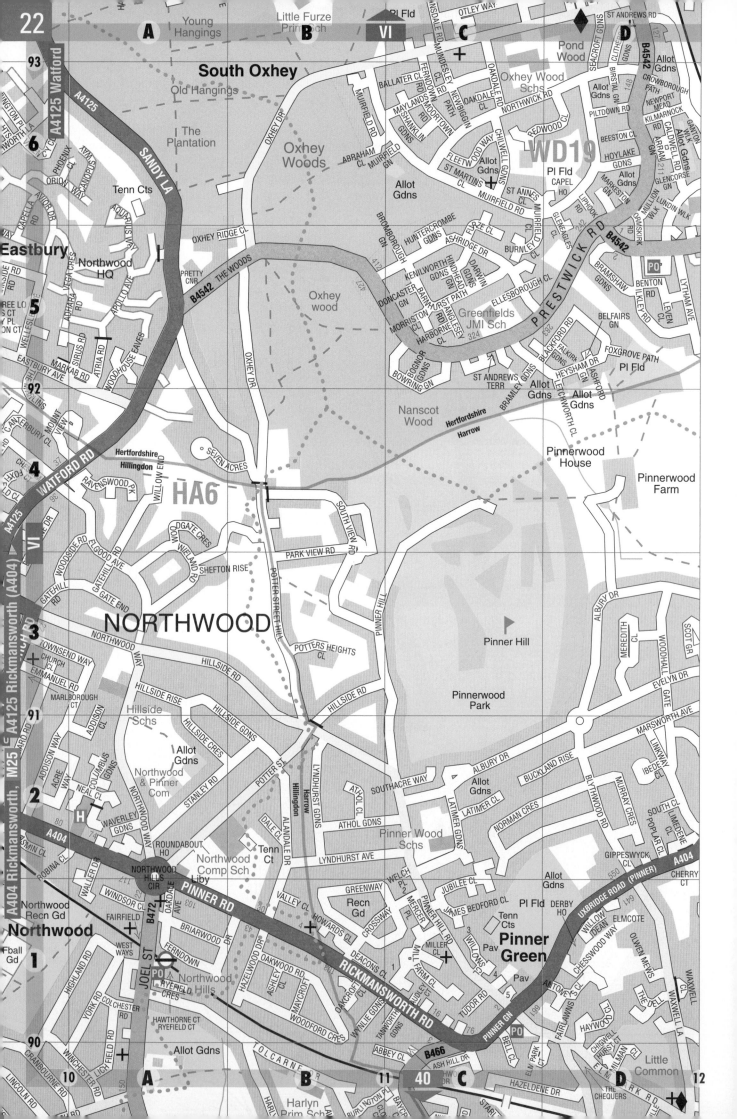

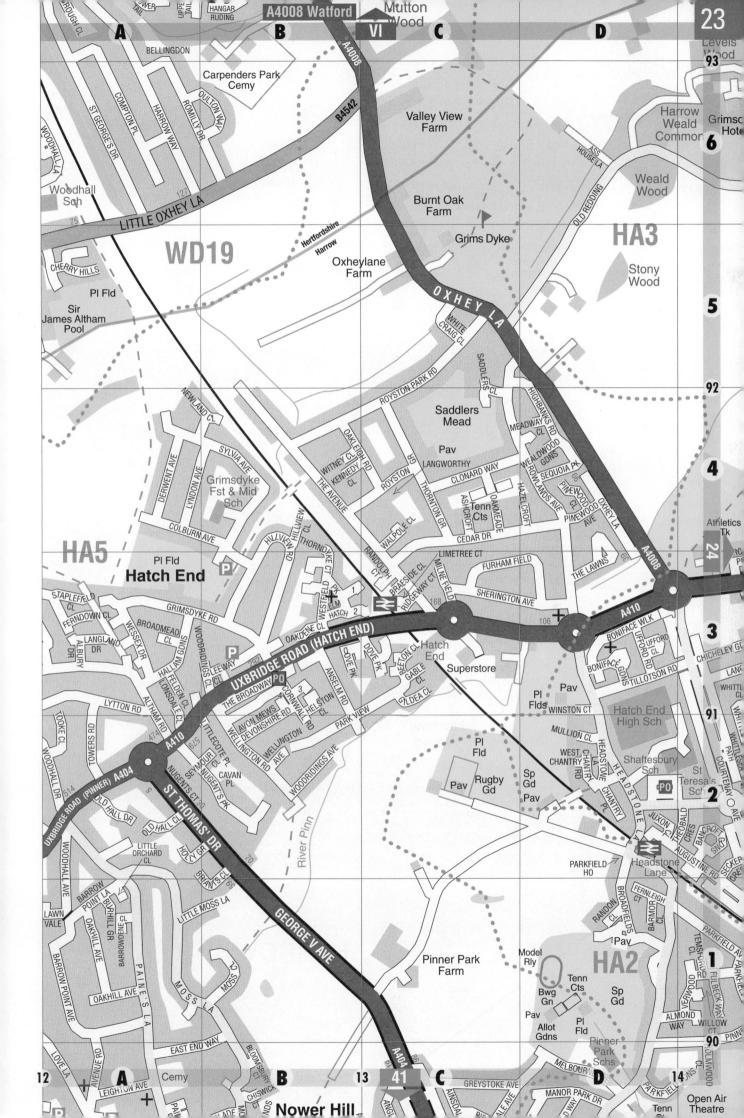

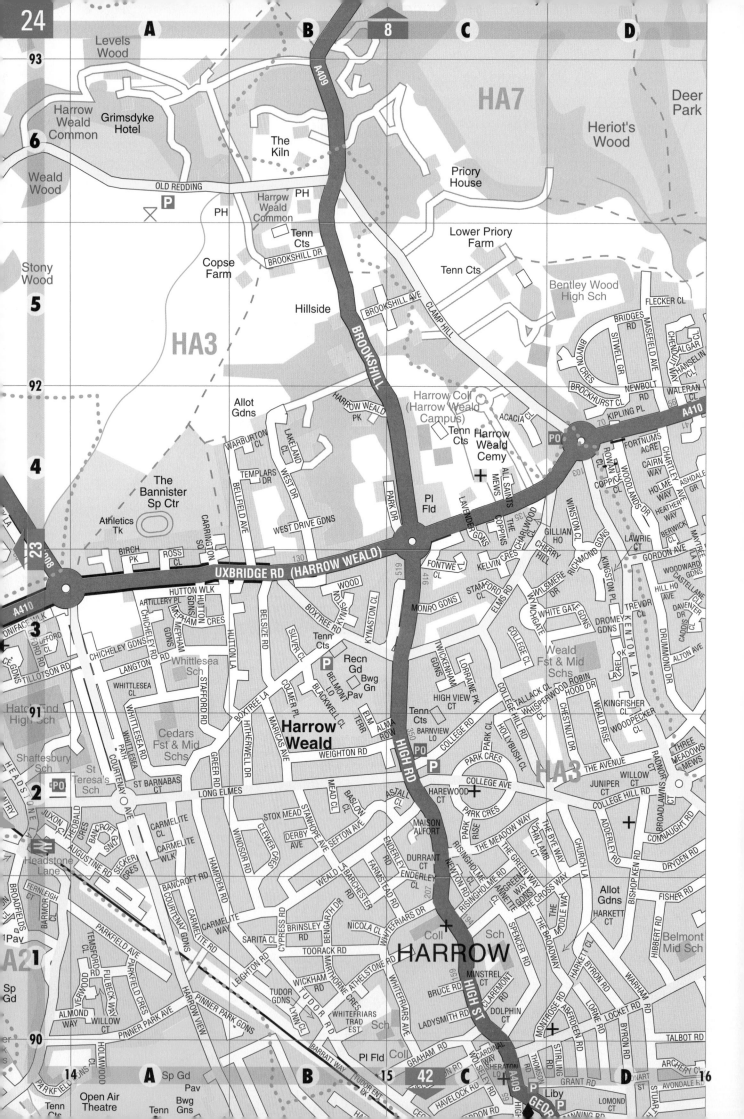

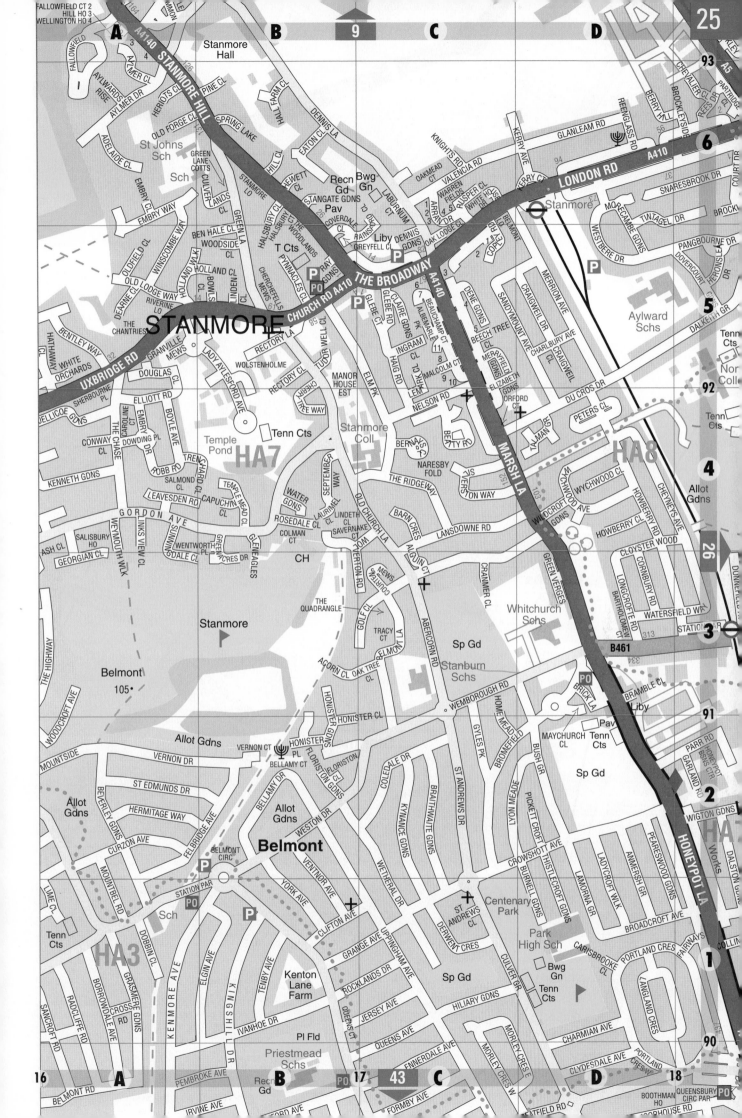

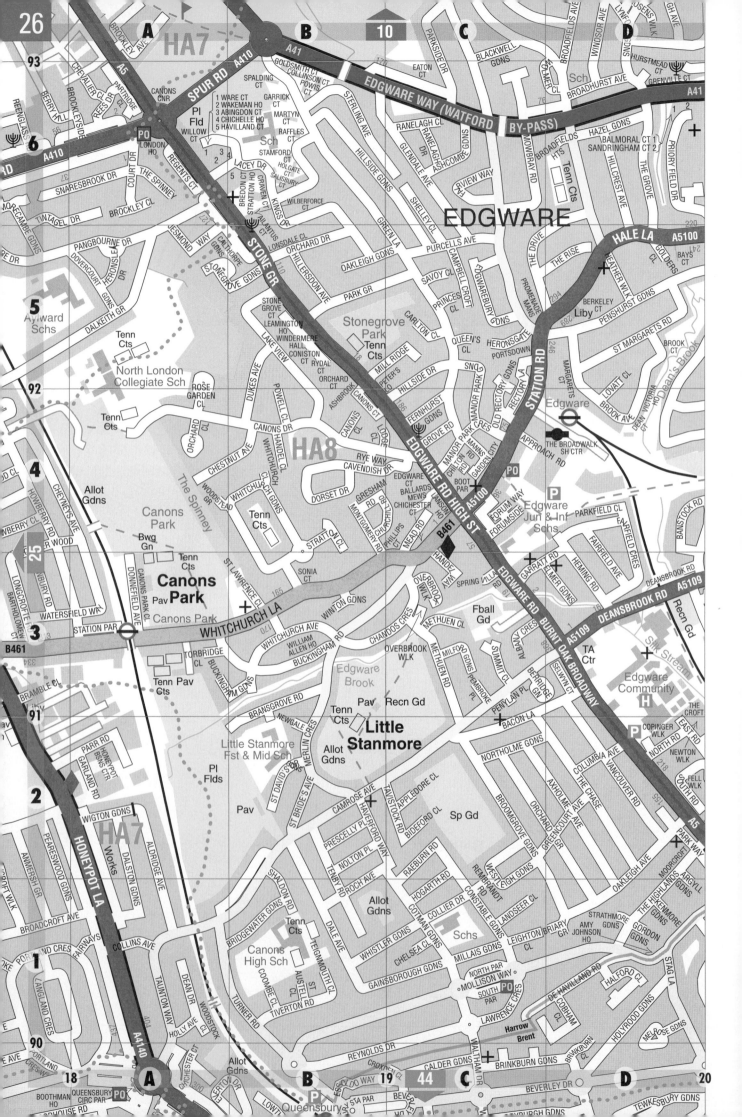

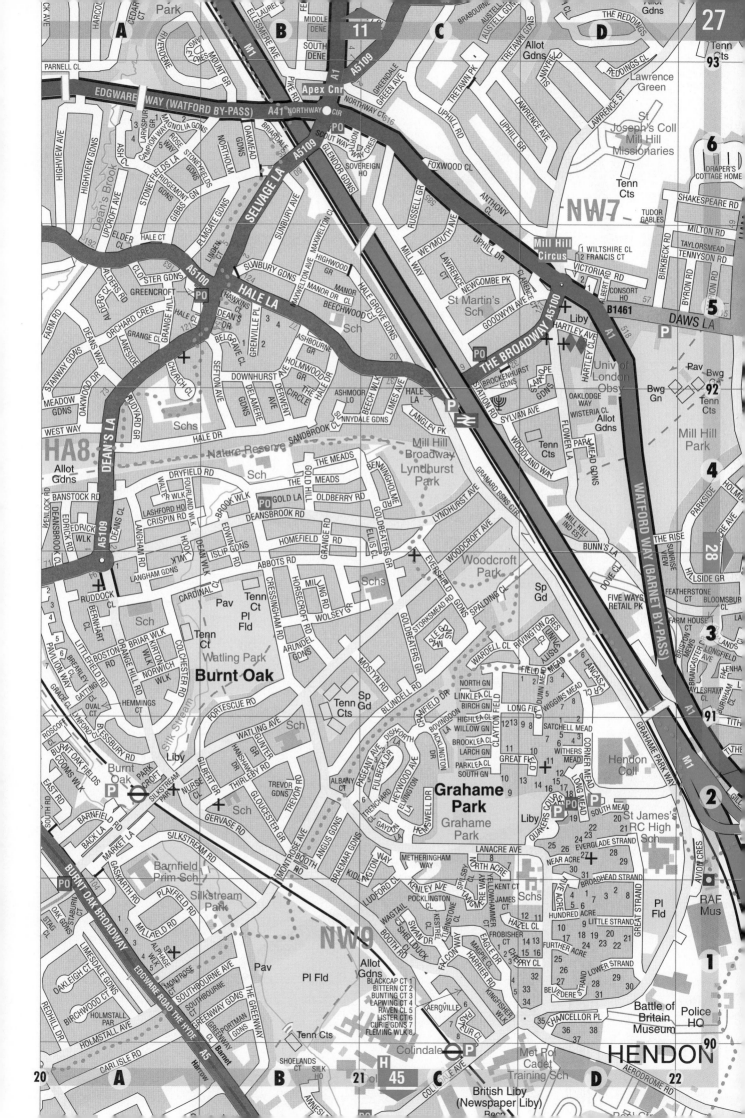

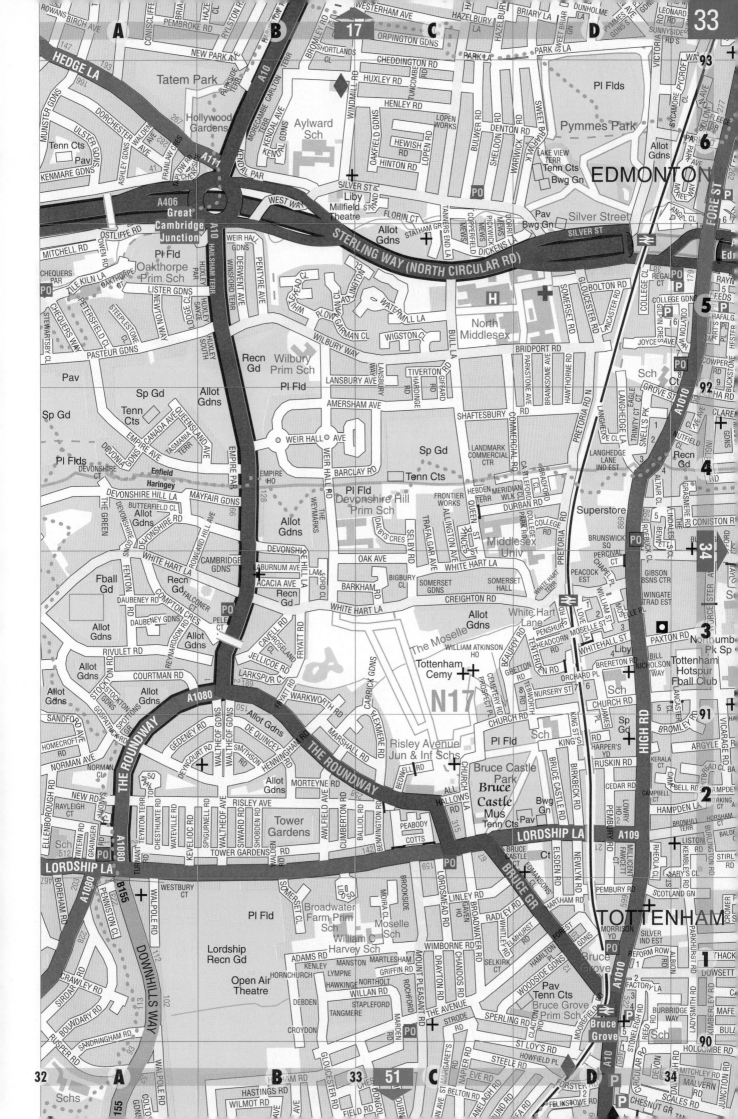

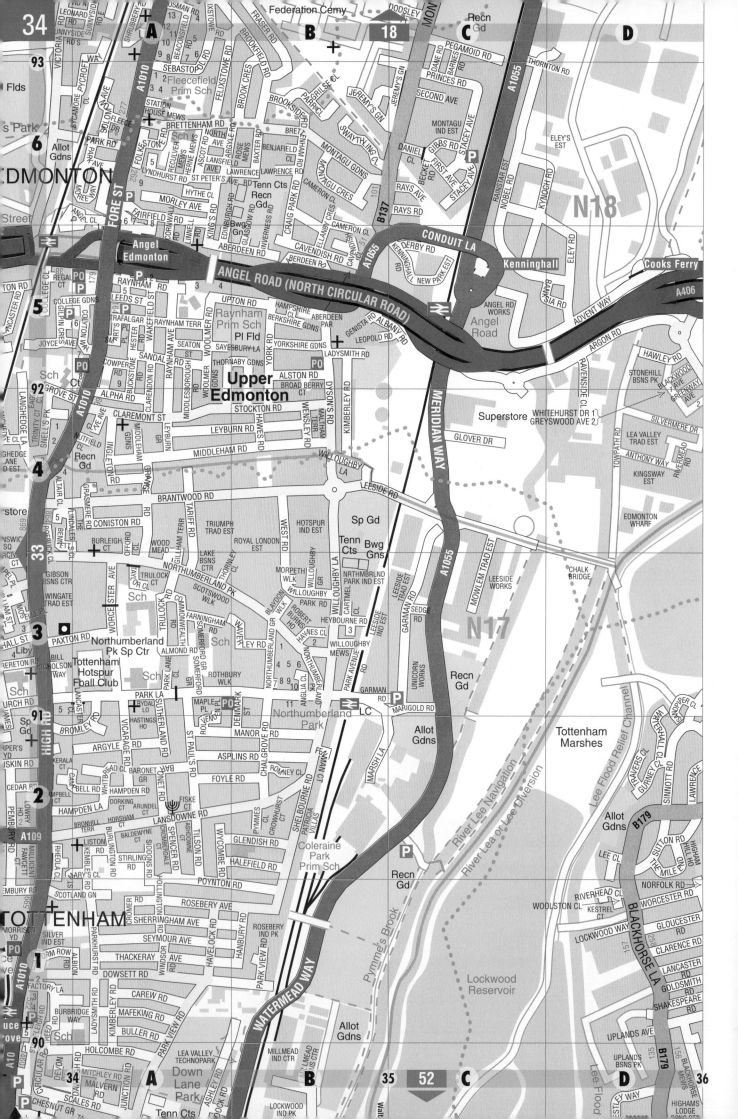

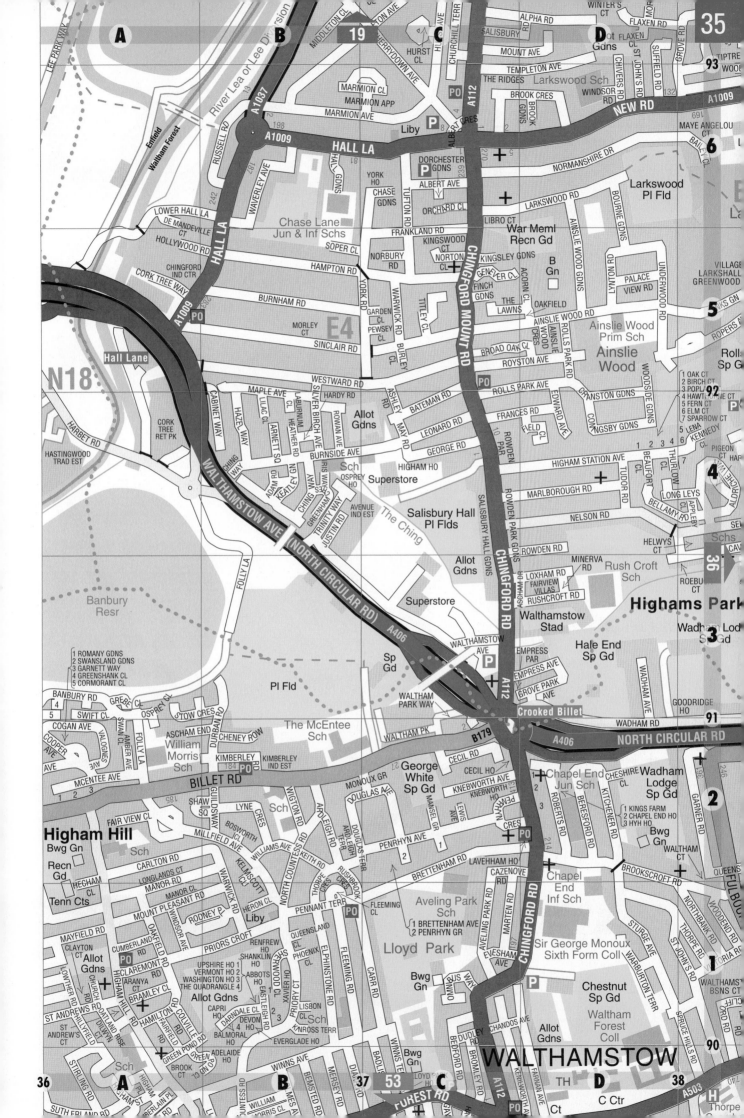

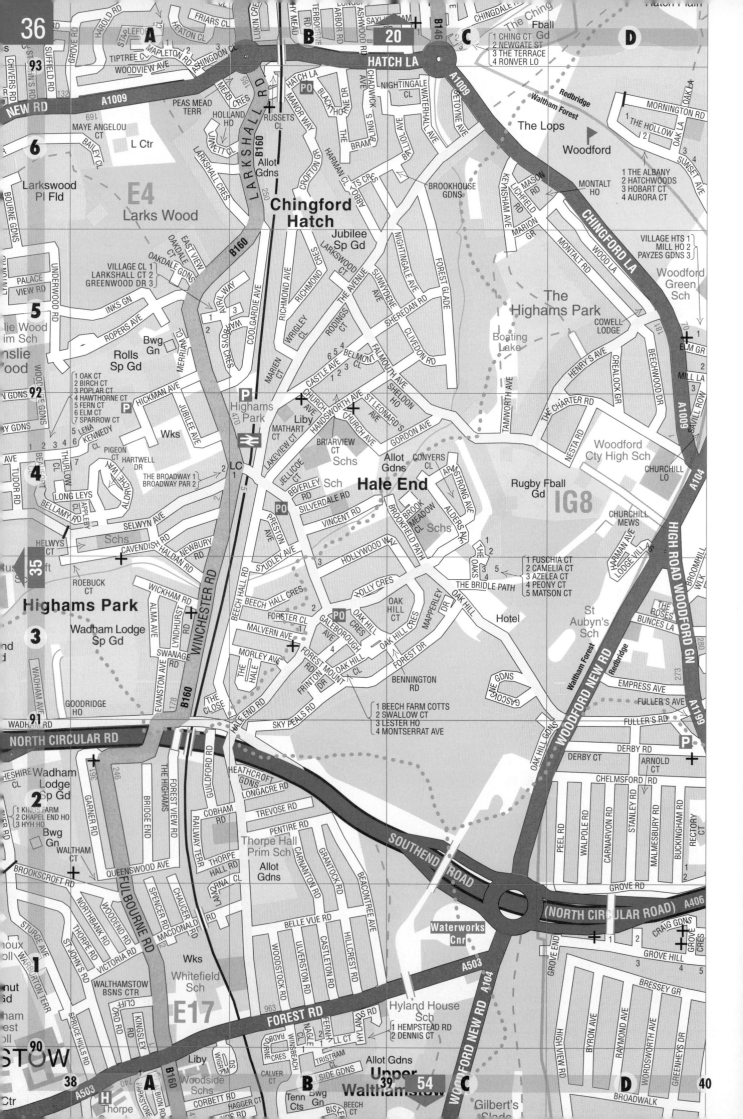

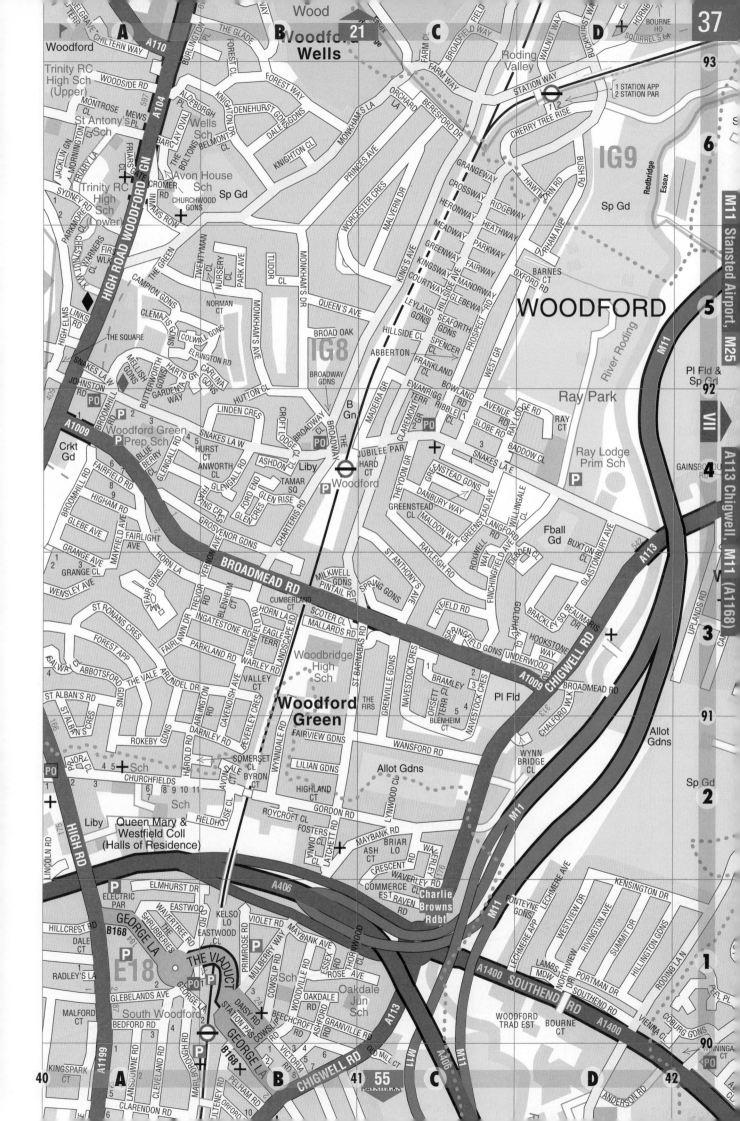

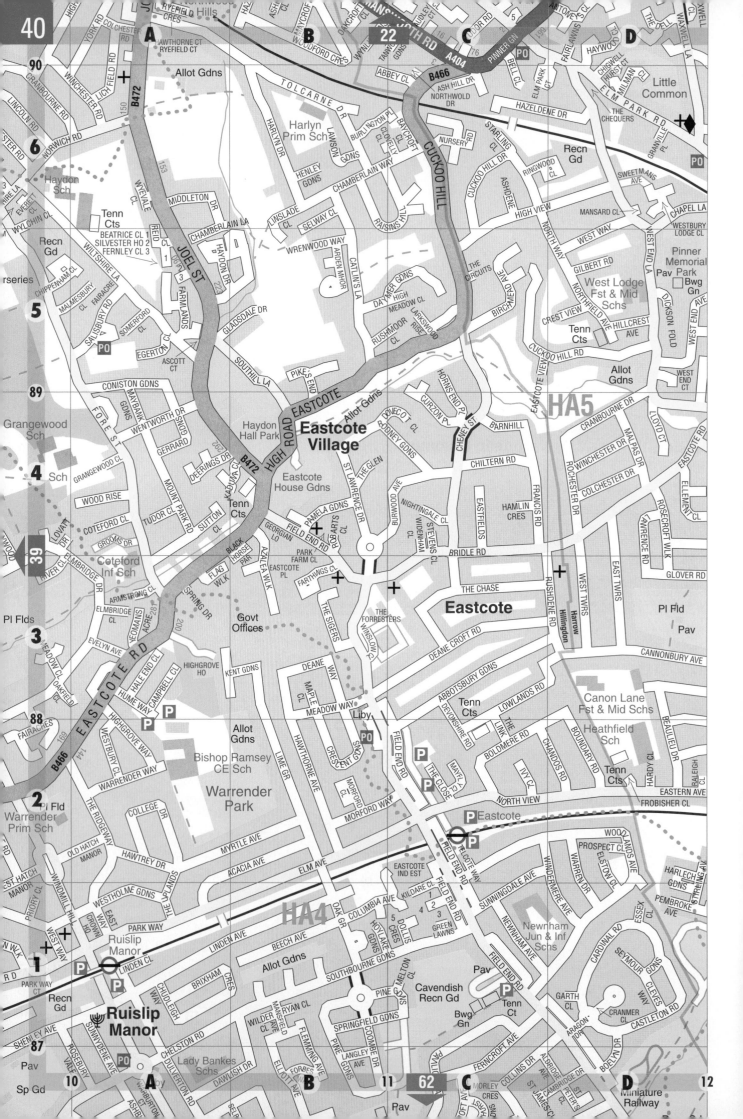

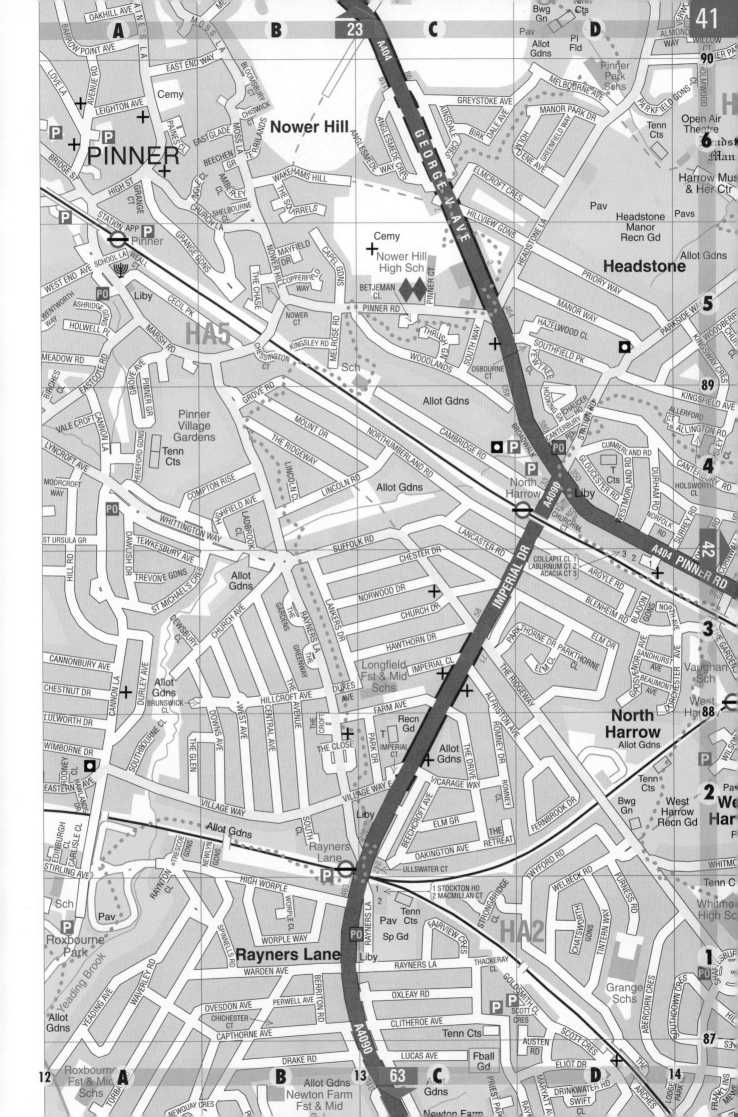

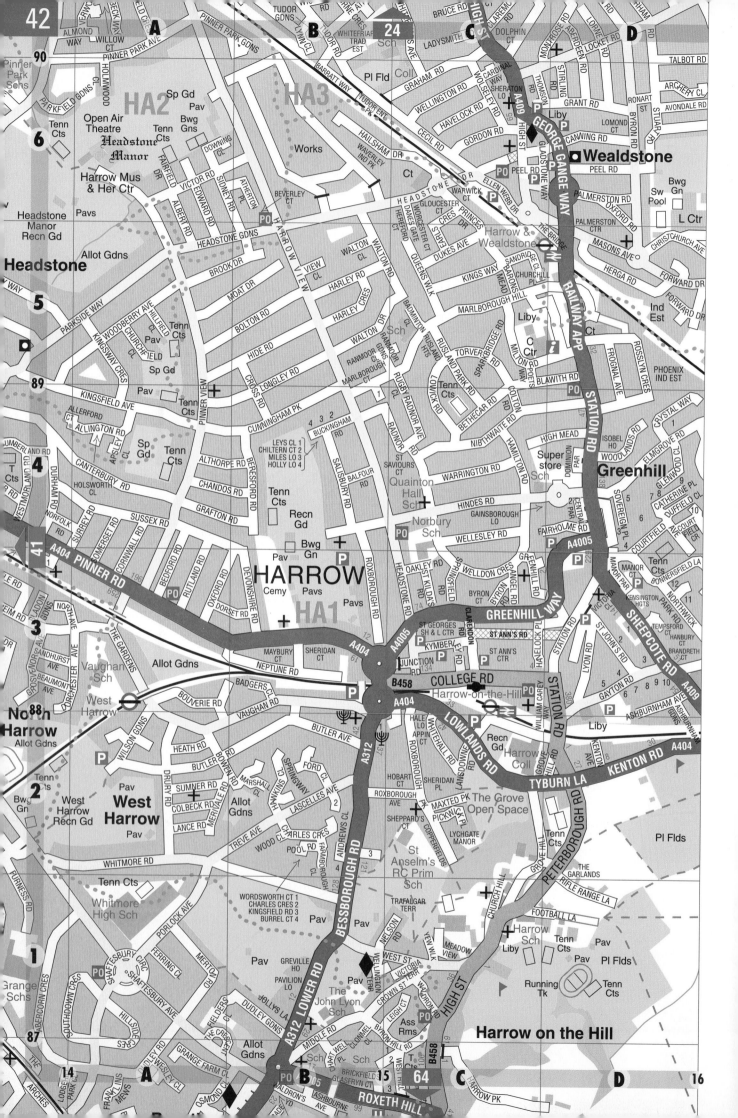

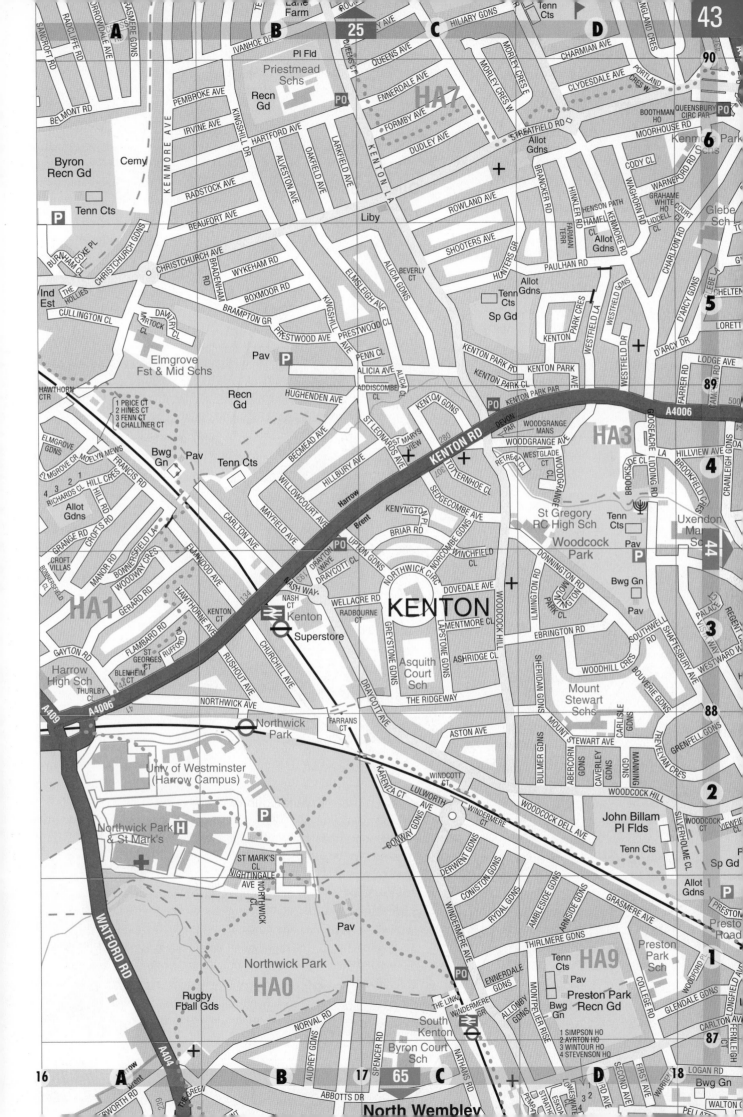

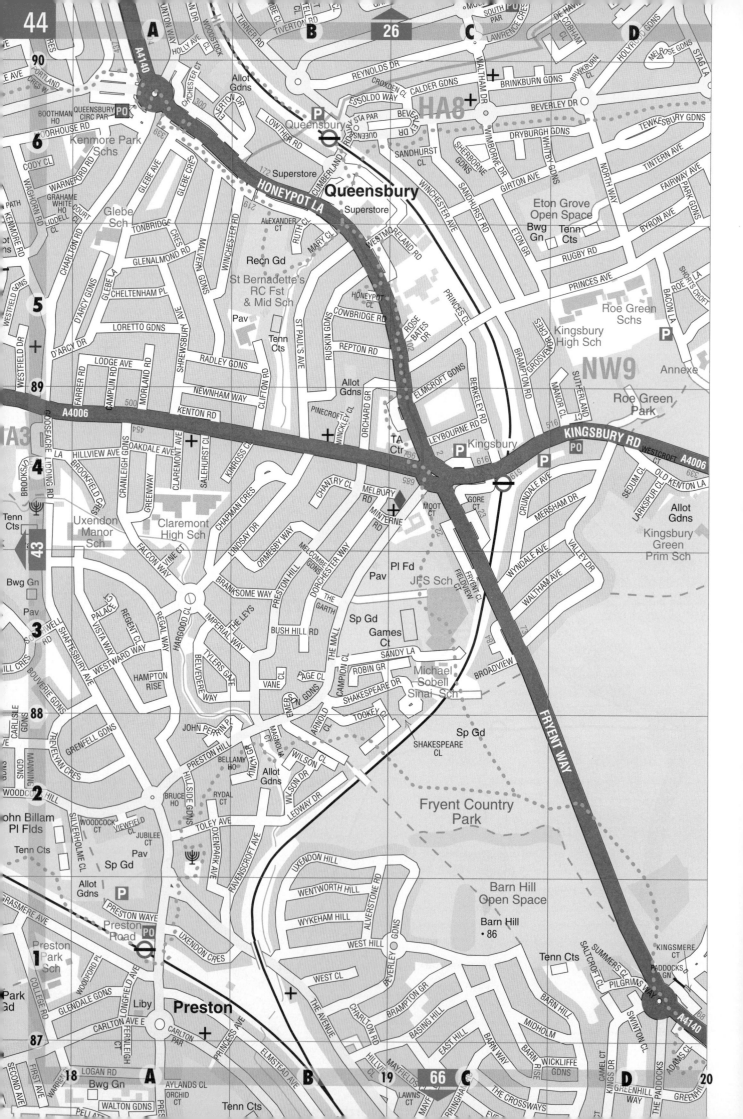

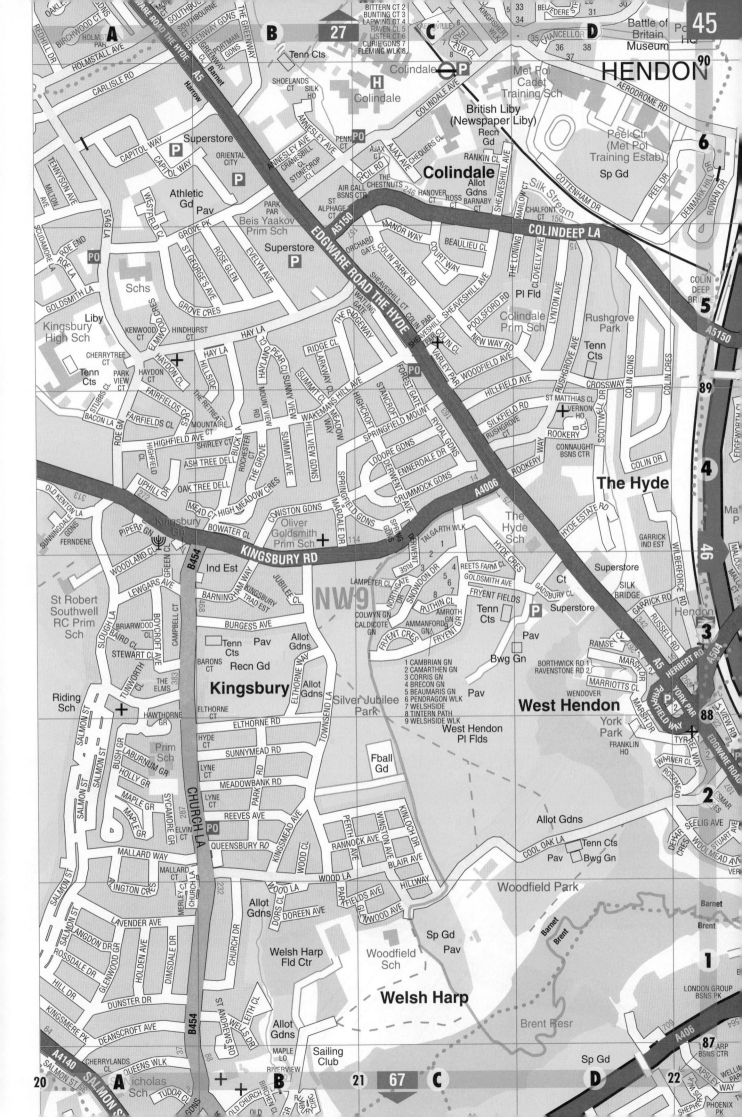

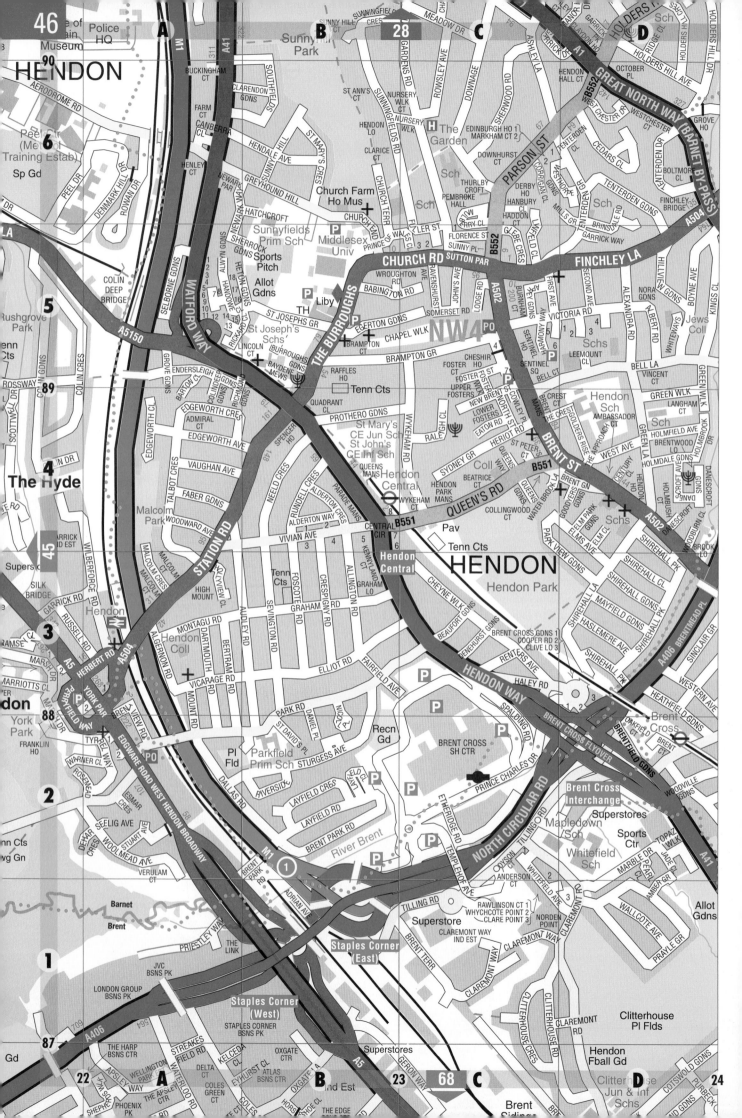

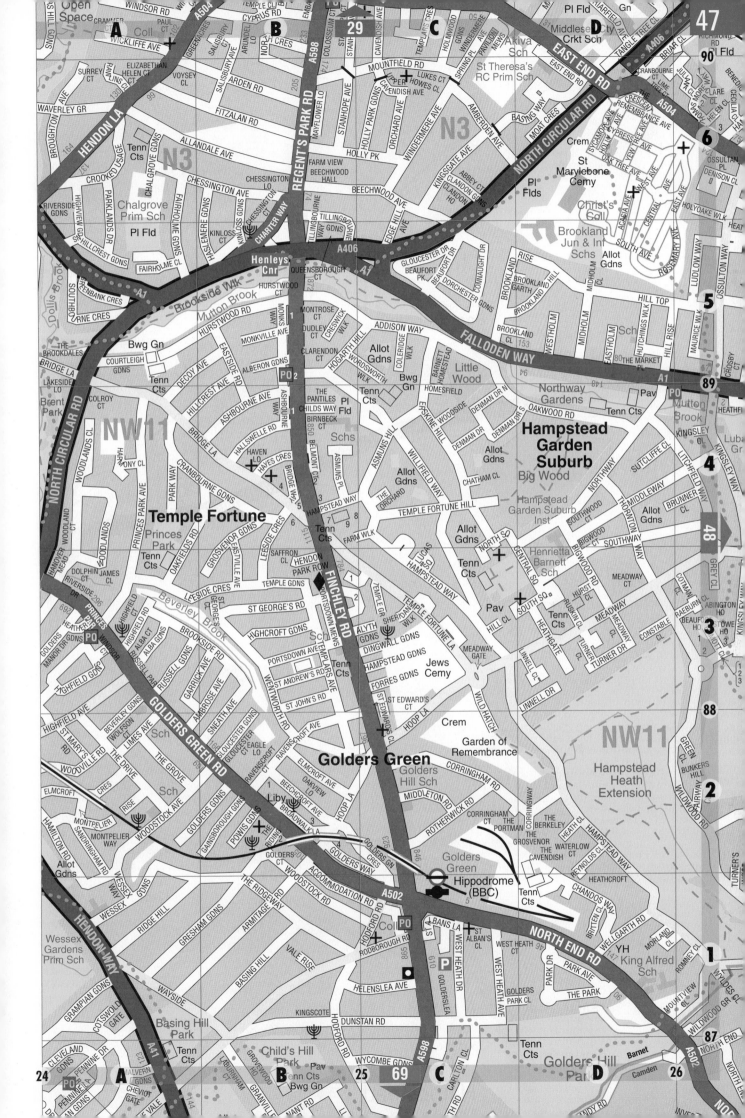

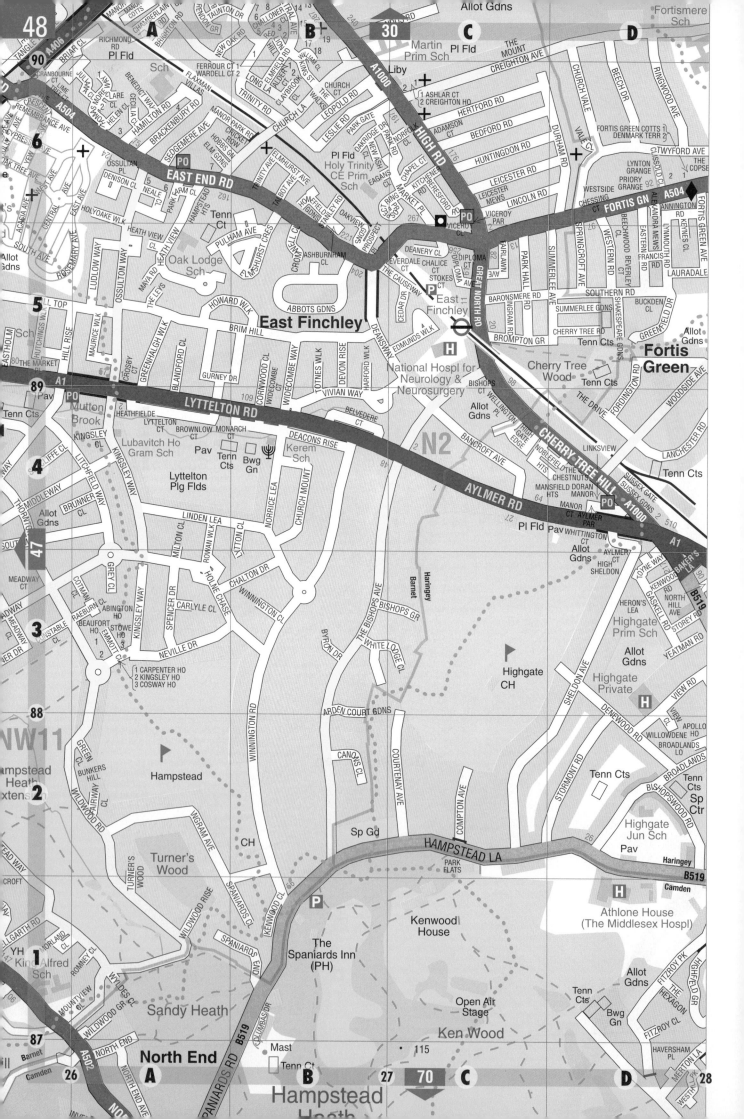

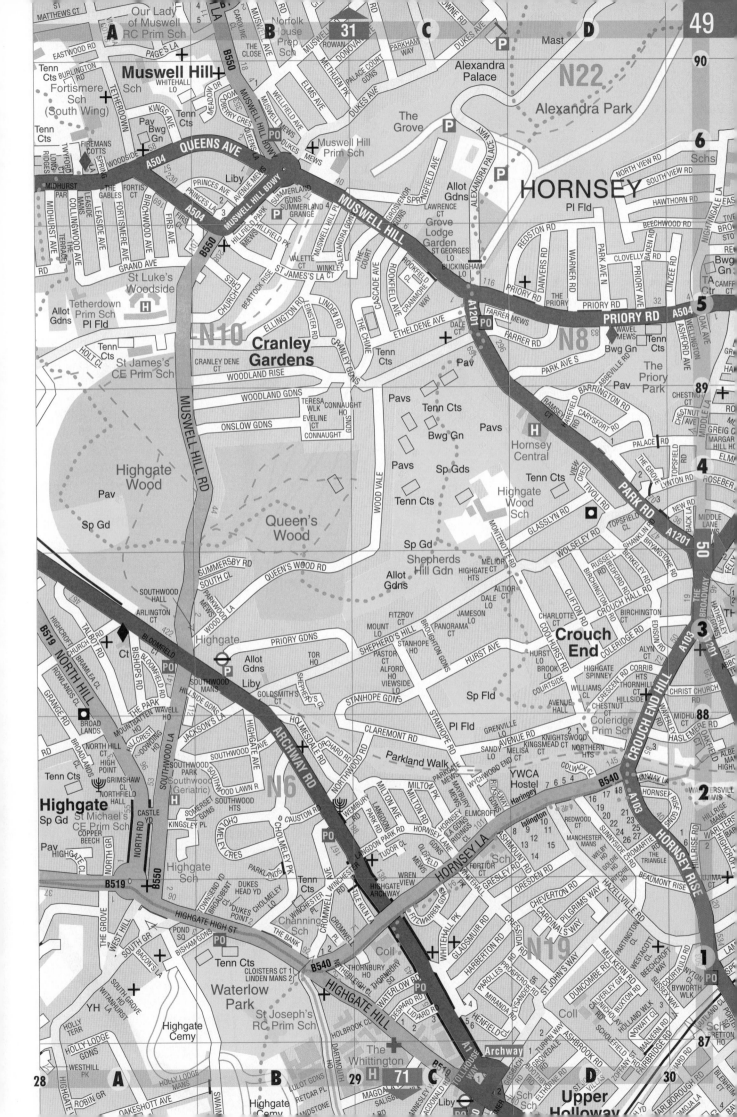

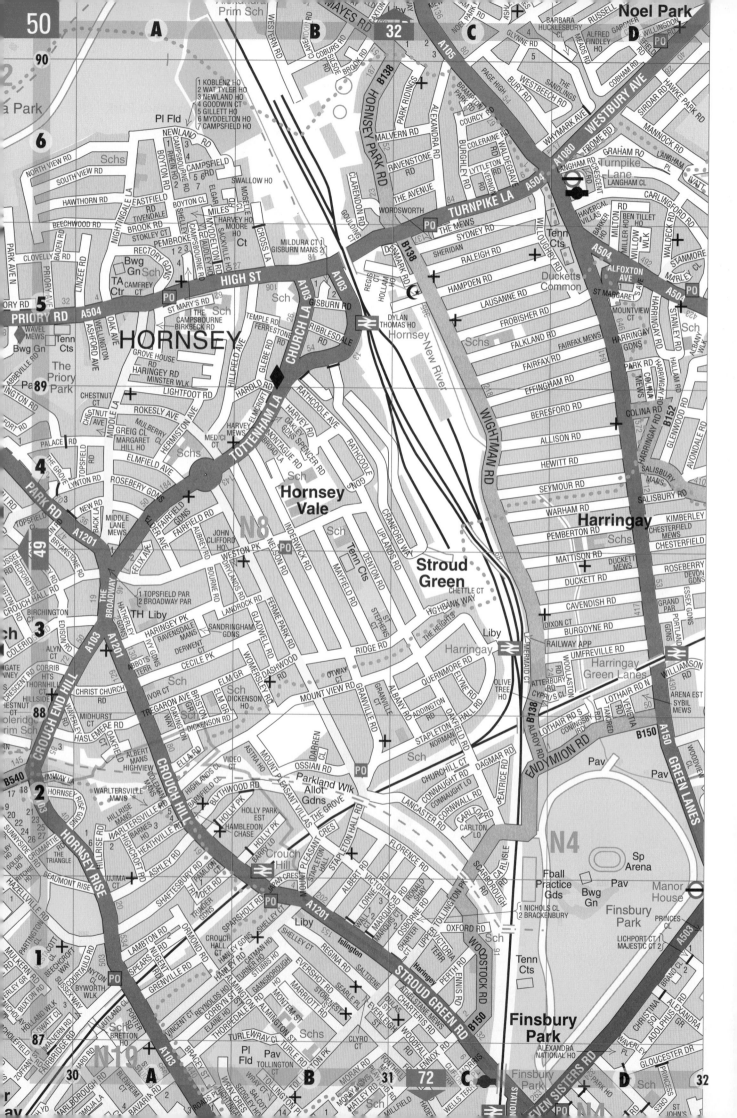

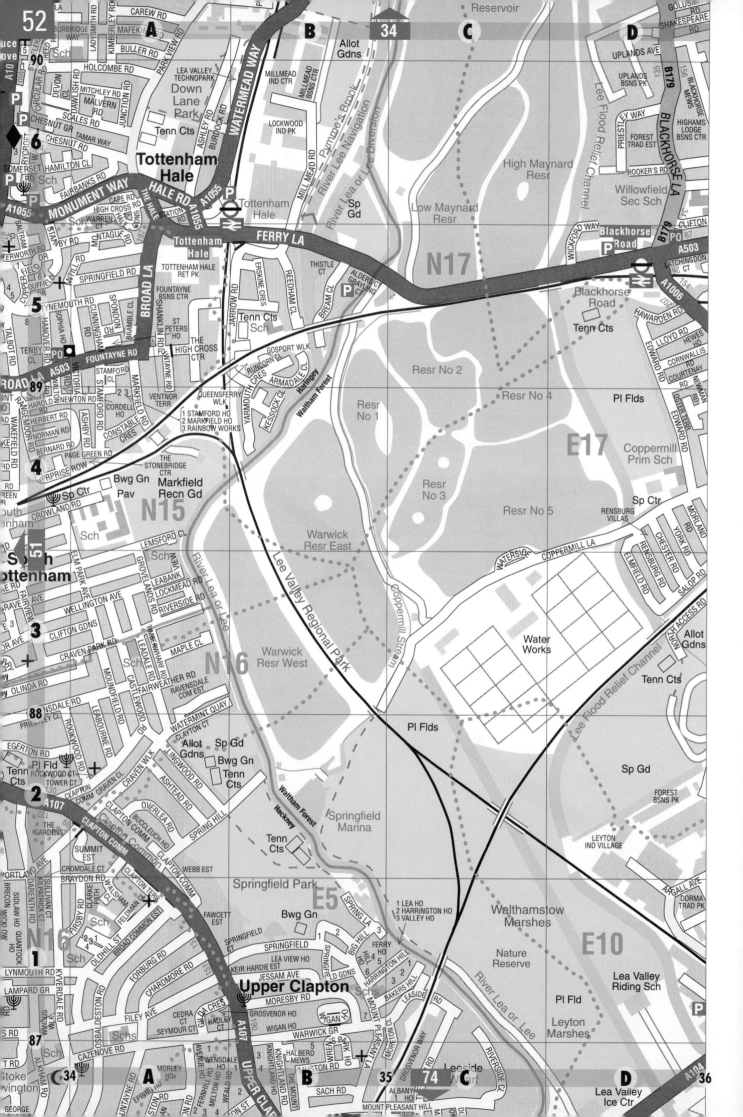

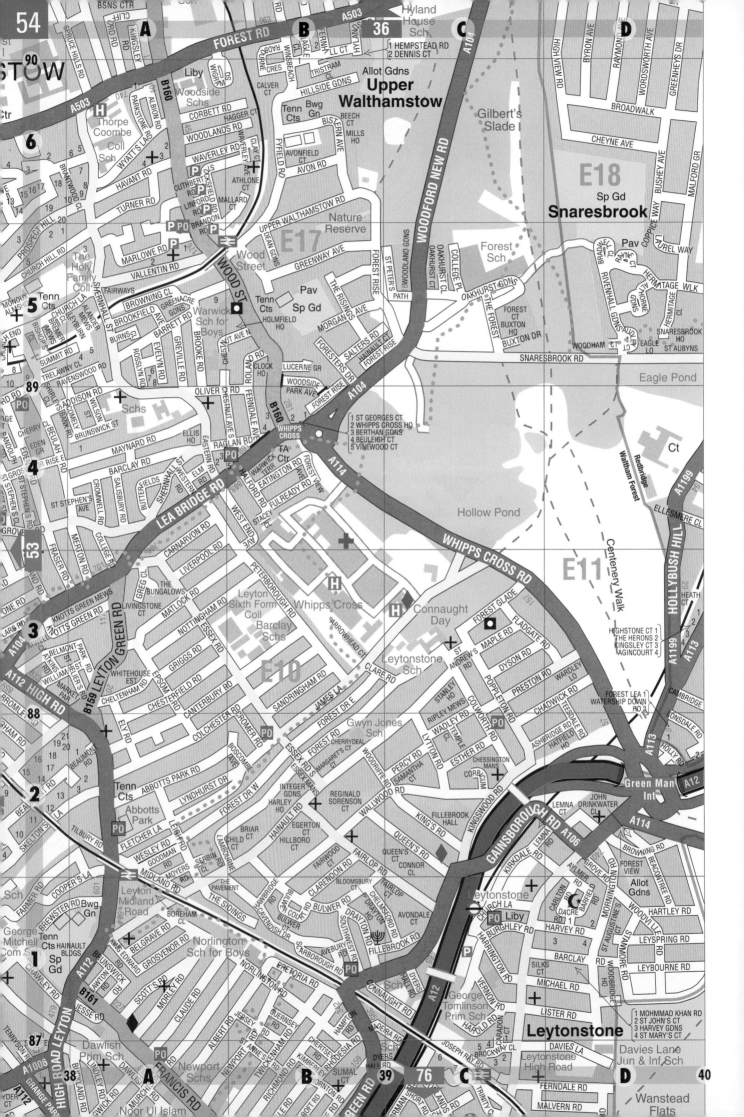

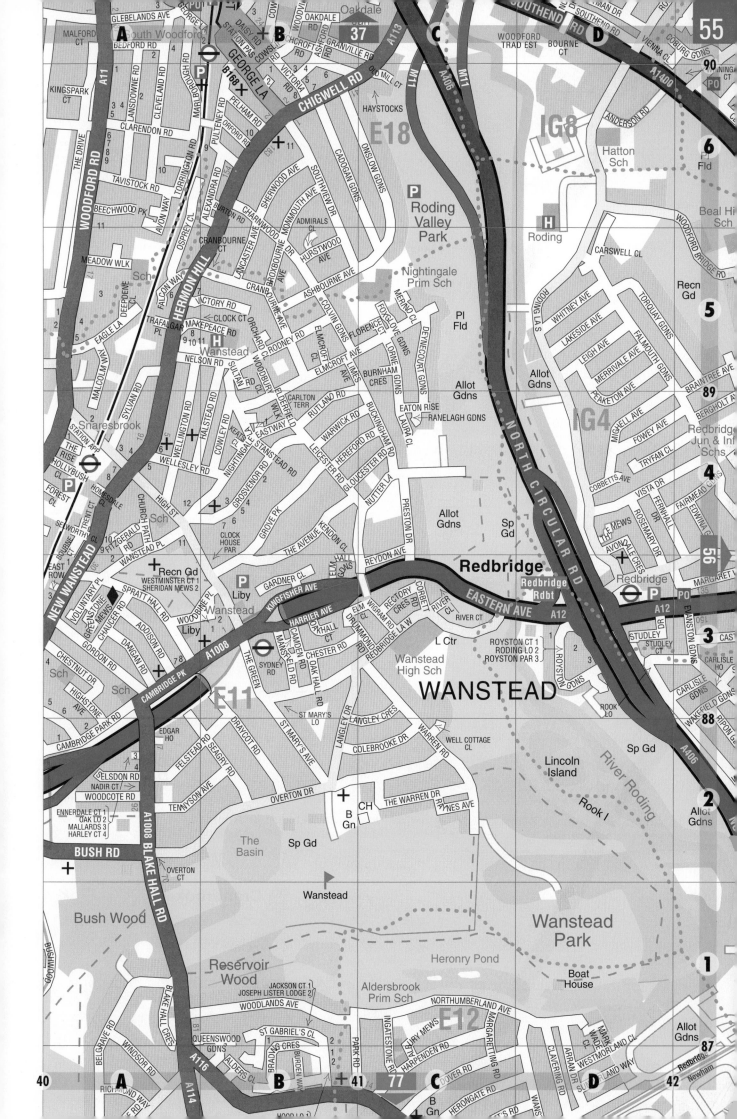

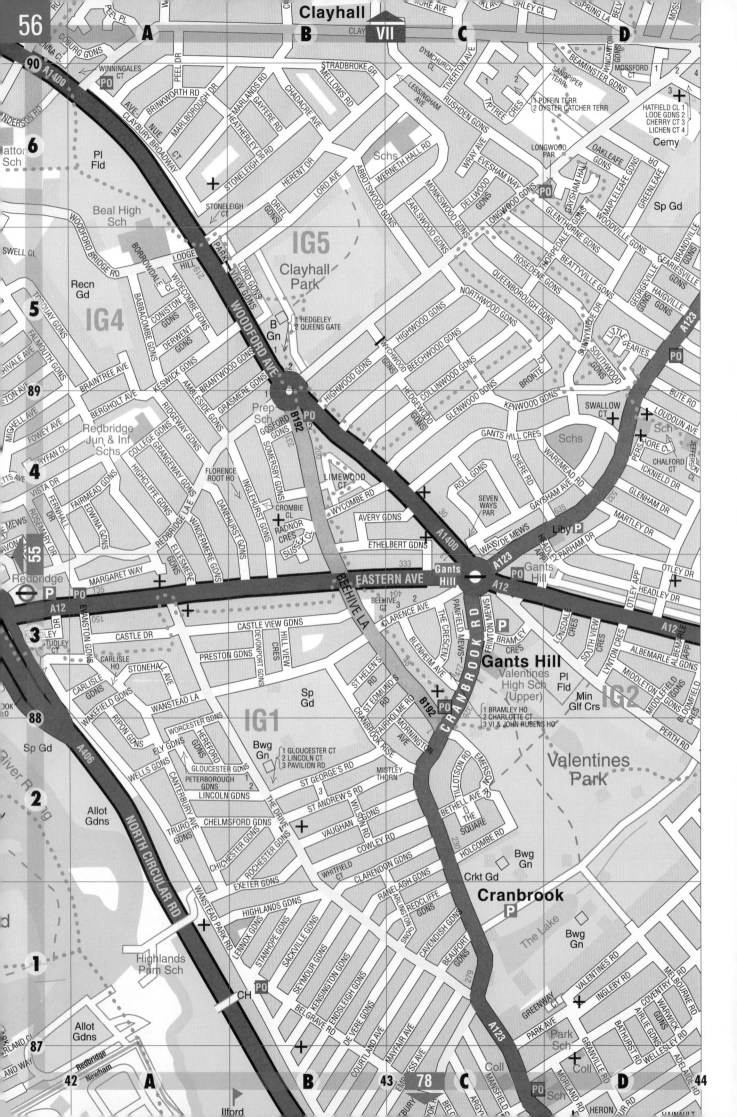

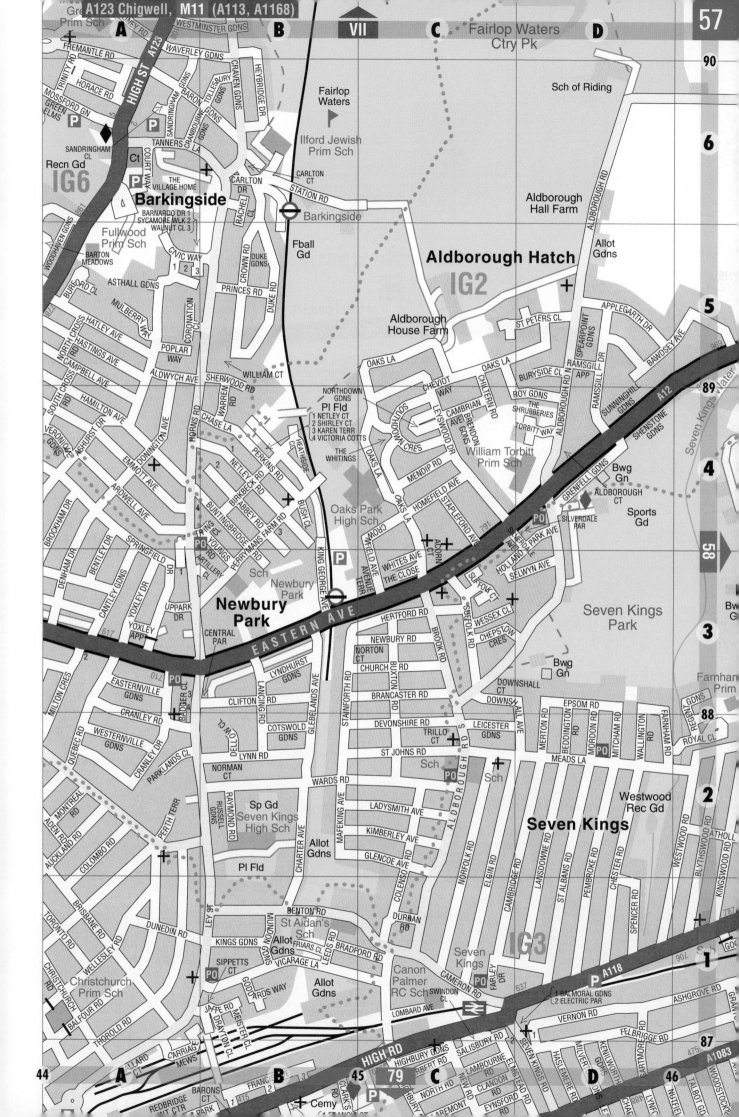

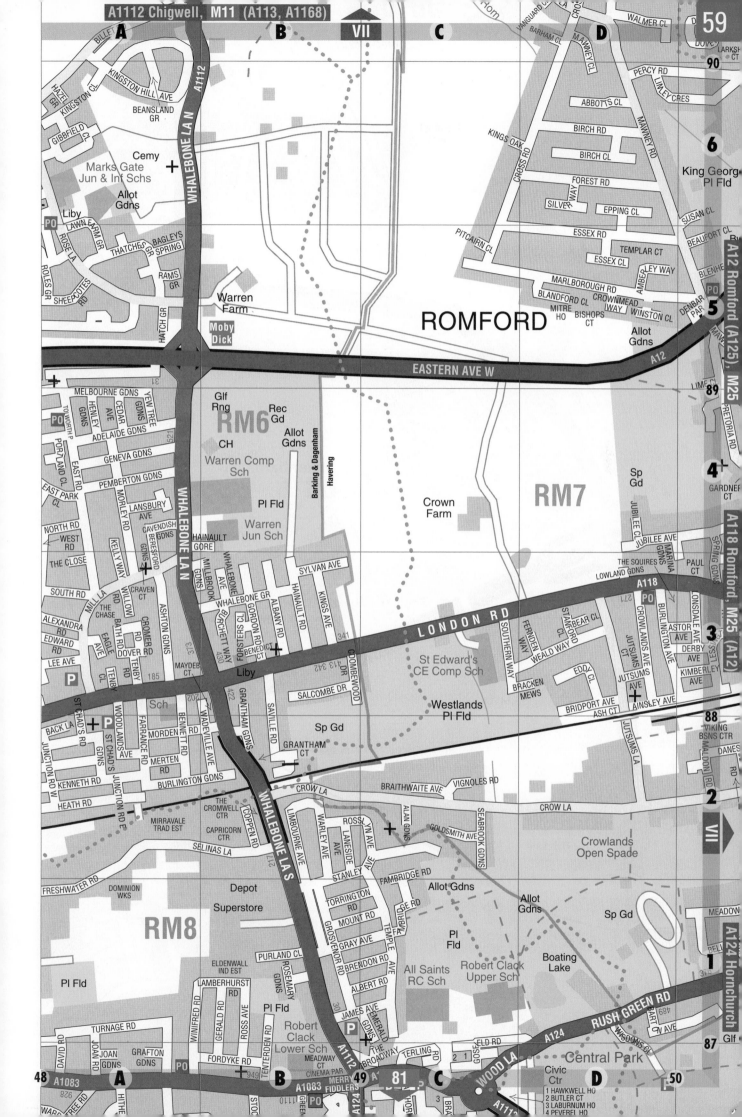

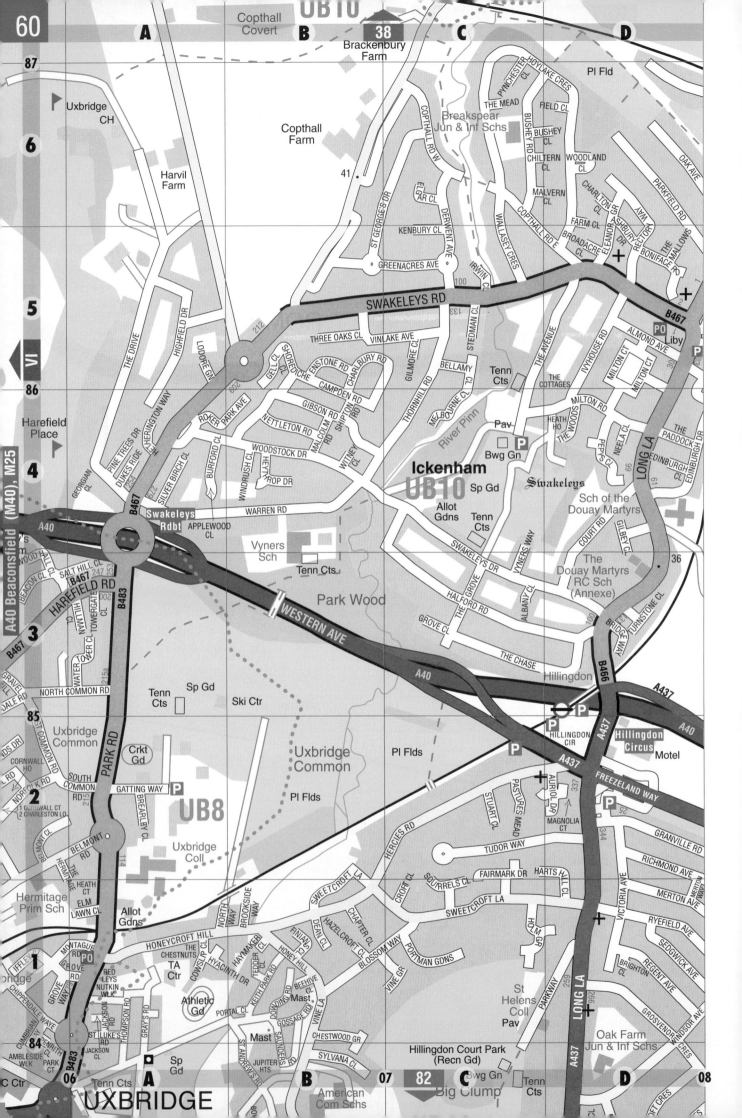

A Ruislip

B 39 NGSEND

C Ruislip

D Recn Gd

Mar

87

STATION PARI
BEAUFORT RD 2

HARWELL CL

SEAFORD CL

WHITSTABLE CL

WOOD LA

POOLE CL

HELFORD CL

WILLOW GR

SHENLEY AVE

ROSEBURY VALE

Pav

Sp Gd

THE GREENWAY

Drv Rng

CH

CORDINGLEY RD

CHICHESTER

HAMBLE CL

SHERLEYS CT 1
MASTERS CT 2

GARDEN CL

CRANLEY

EVERSLEY CRES

GROSVENOR VALE

COURTFIELD GDNS

DENBIGH CL

CORNWALL RD

HATHERLEIGH RD

KINGSWEAR RD

SALCOMBE W

6

BUCKLAND CT

West Ruislip

West Ruislip

LYMINGTON DR

BEMBRIDGE

HERON CT

KESTREL CT

FALCON CT

POND GN

Sacred Heart RC Prim Sch

45

BEECHWOOD AVE

RUISLIP CT

RALEIGH CL

WEST END RD

Allot Gdns

WILLOW

SEATON GDNS

HIGH TREES

Tenn Cts

NARBOROUGH CL

HASLAM CL

CRANSTON CL

MELVILLE CL

BLENHEIM CRES

MERLIN CT

Recn Gd

CROSIER WAY

WESTFIELD WAY

ROXBURN WAY

New Pon Pl Flds

5

Pav

HEACHAM AVE

PENTLAND WAY

FINCHAM

AYLSHAM DR

TAYFIELD CL

THORPLAND AVE

HERLWYN AVE

Pav

West Ruislip Sch

TWEEDDALE GR

1

2

1 ANNANDALE GR
2 NITHSDALE GR

Works

LAWN CL

ALMOND

BELL CL

A4180

PO

86

CHURCH PL Min Rly

COMMUNITY CL

WILLOWTREE CL

AUSTIN'S LA

HA4

Ruislip Gardens

Ickenham

LAWRENCE DR

KEMPTON CL

CROSIER RD

UB10

Ruislip Gardens Prim Sch

STAFFORD RD

BROMLEY CRES

HATHAWAY CL

TREVOR CRES

Allot Gdns

CLOVELLY CL

CLOVELLY AVE

GLEBE AVE

GLEBE CL

ST GILES AVE

Allot Gdns

ACORN GR

BEDFORD RD

CLYFFORD RD

4

35

Glebe Prim Sch

MILVERTON DR

BURNHAM AVE

SUSSEX RD

TAVISTOCK RD

Allot Gdns

LEA CRES

Yeading Brook

62

Tenn Cts

Pl Flds

Ickenham Manor

Long Lane Farm

3

Northolt Aerodrome

85

Ickenham Marsh

2

Freezeland Covert

WESTERN AVE A437

Allot Gdns

North Hillingdon

Recn Gd

WESTERN AVE

WESTON RD

A40

1

Allot Gdns

LYNHURST RD

OAKLEIGH RD

LYNHURST CRES

Gutteridge Wood

Yeading Brook

UB4

RYEFIELD AVE

FLORISTON RD

BERKELEY RD

MIDHURST GDNS

PO

Ten Acre (Nature Reserve)

84

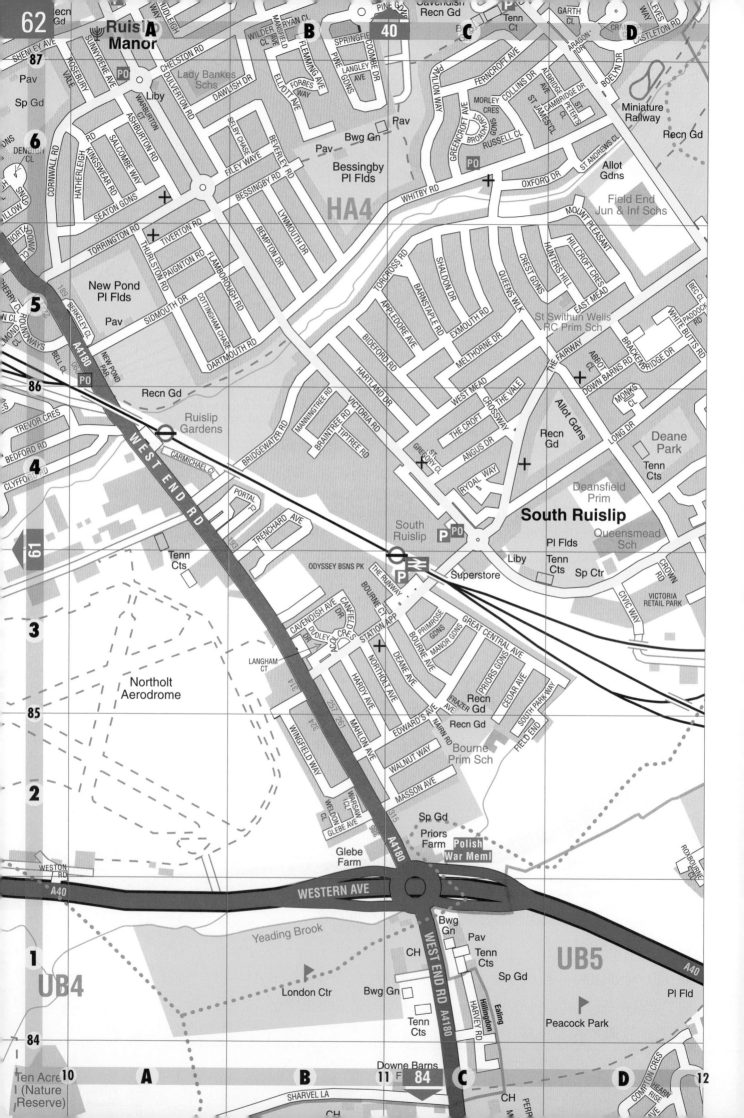

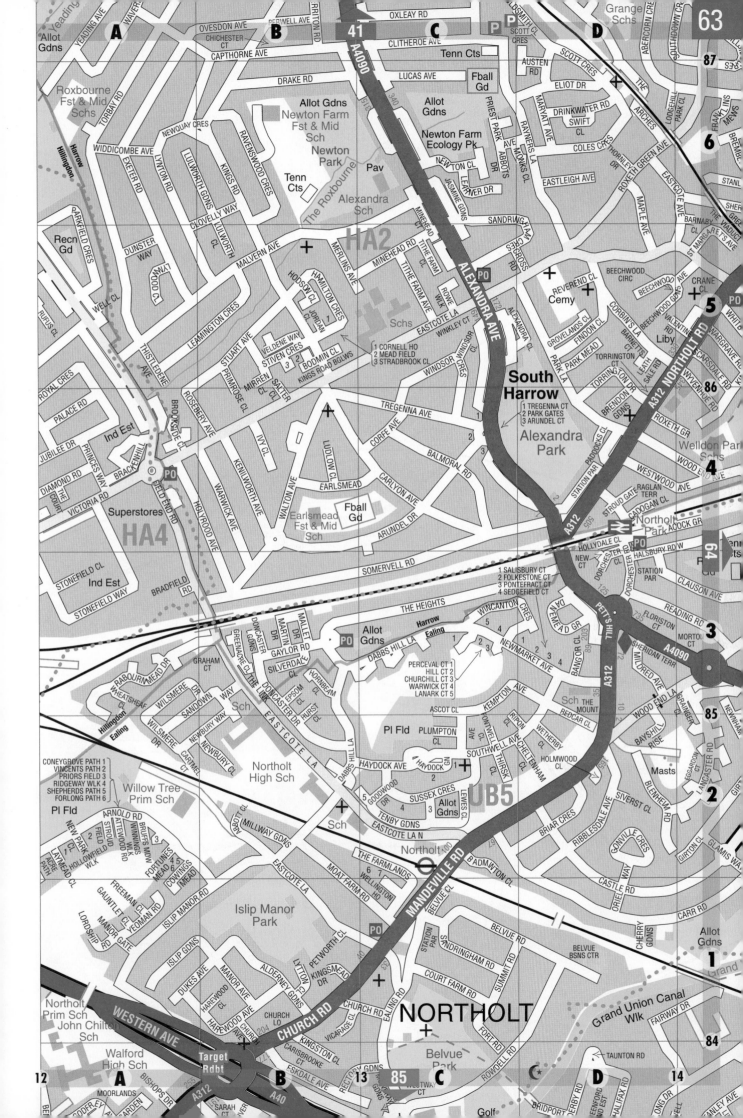

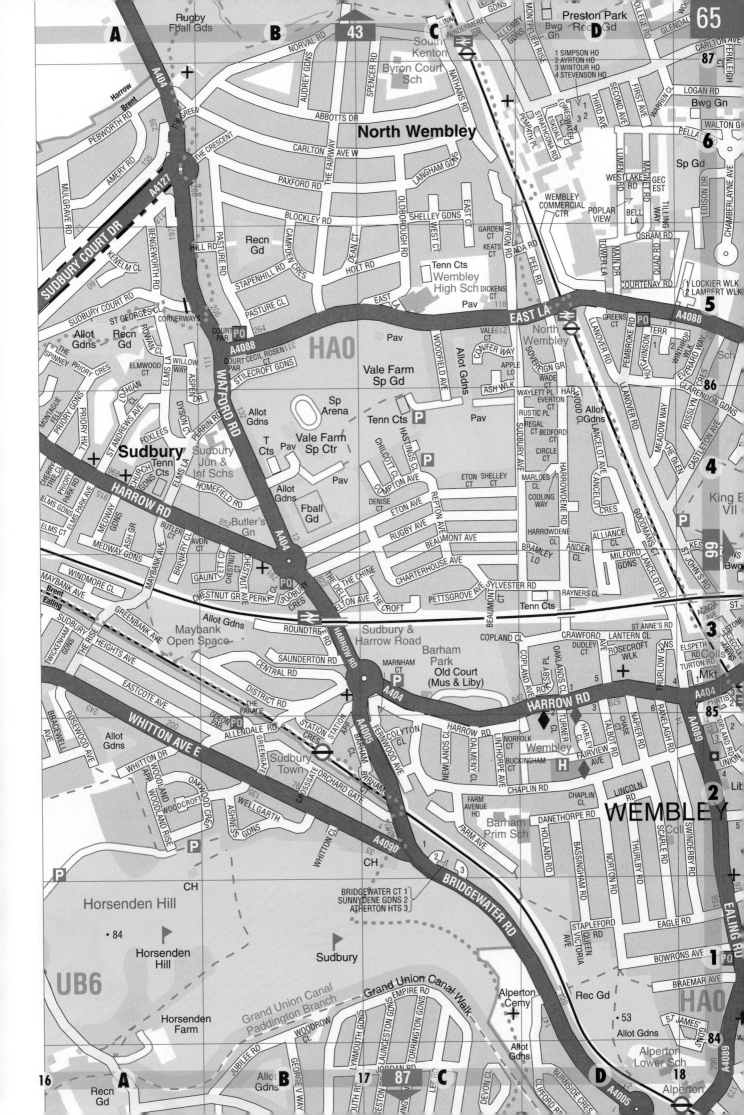

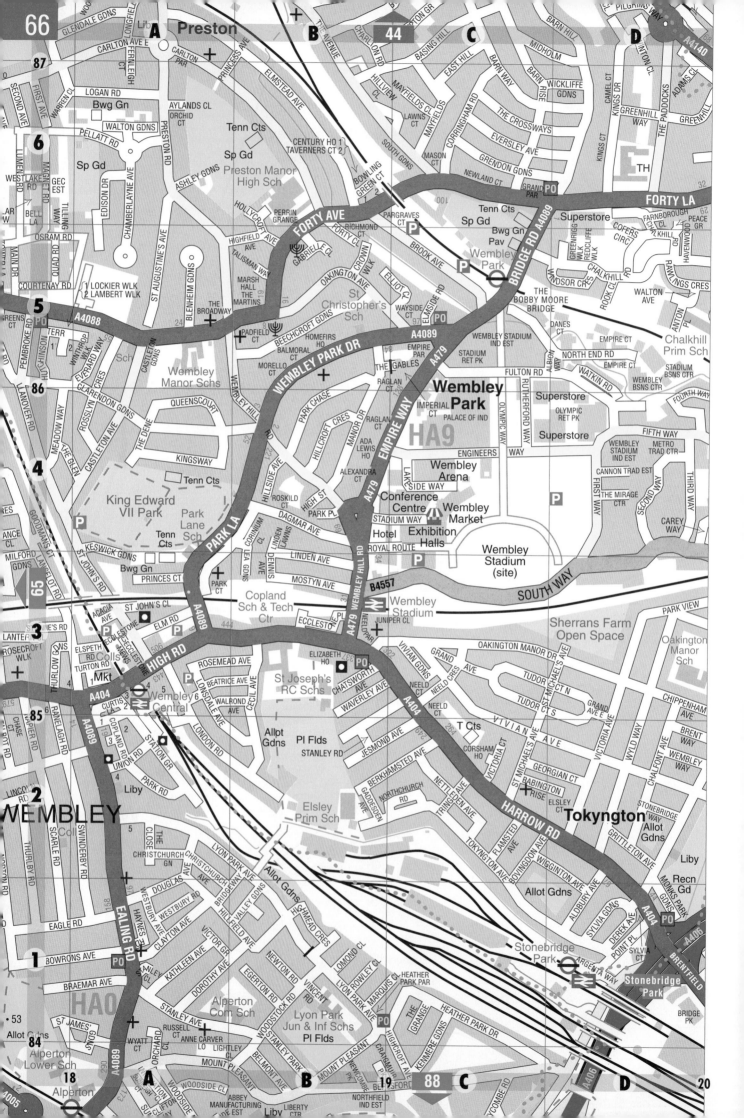

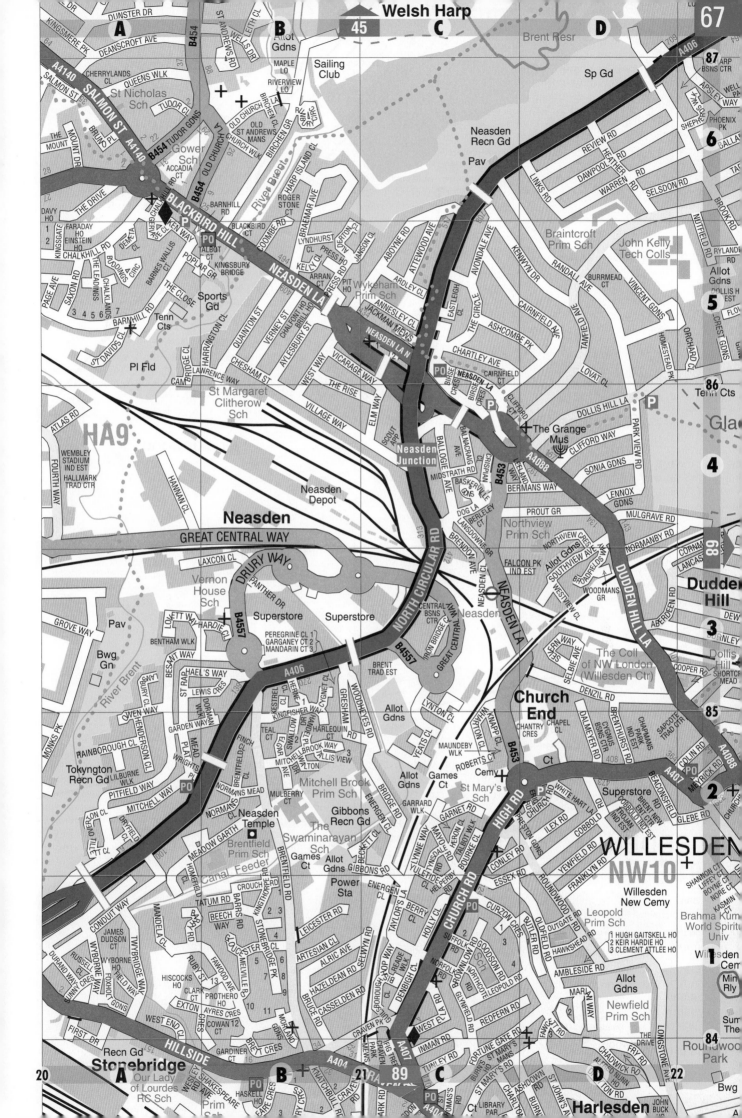

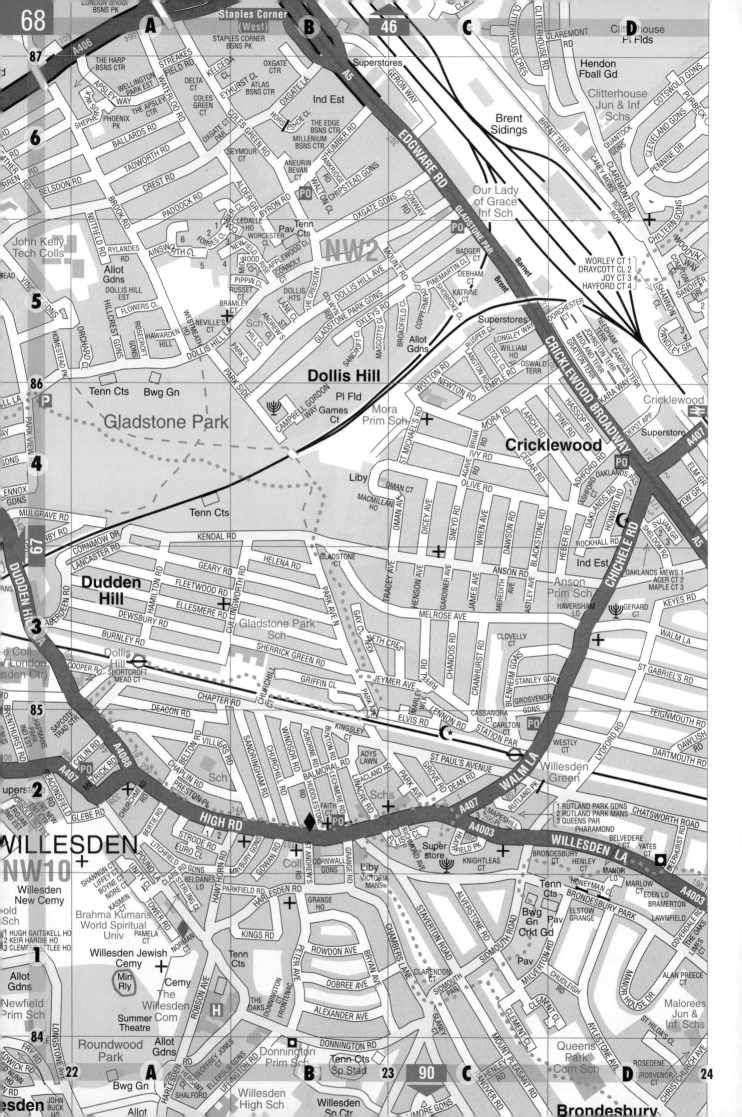

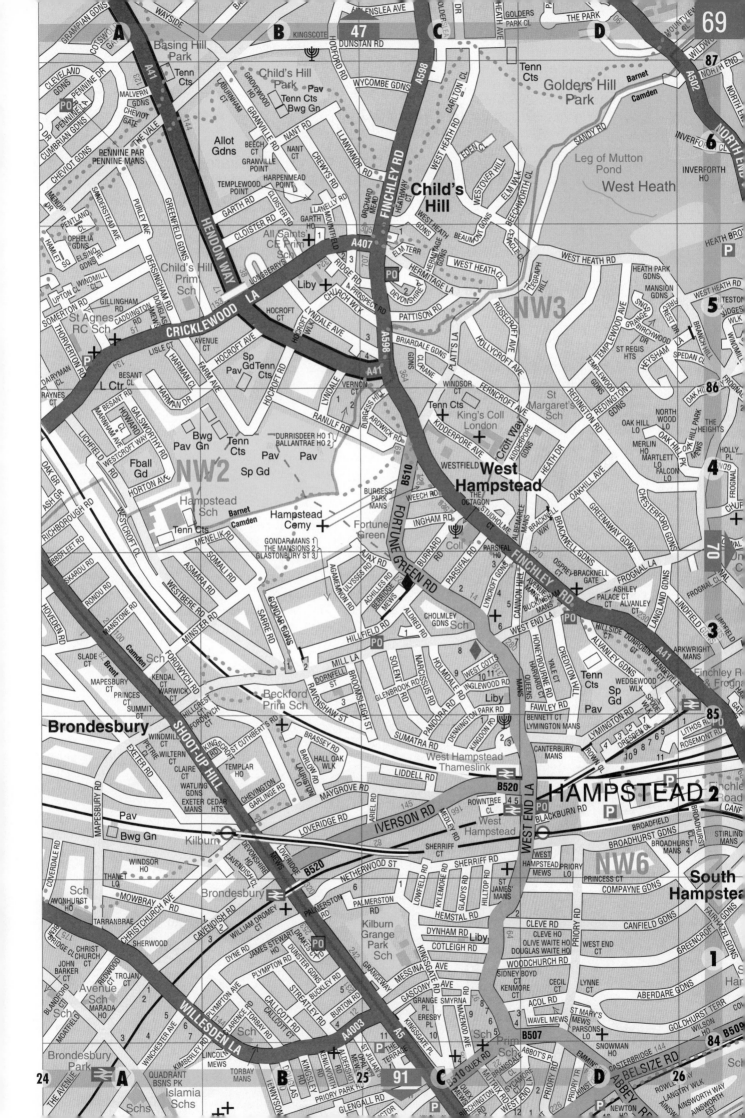

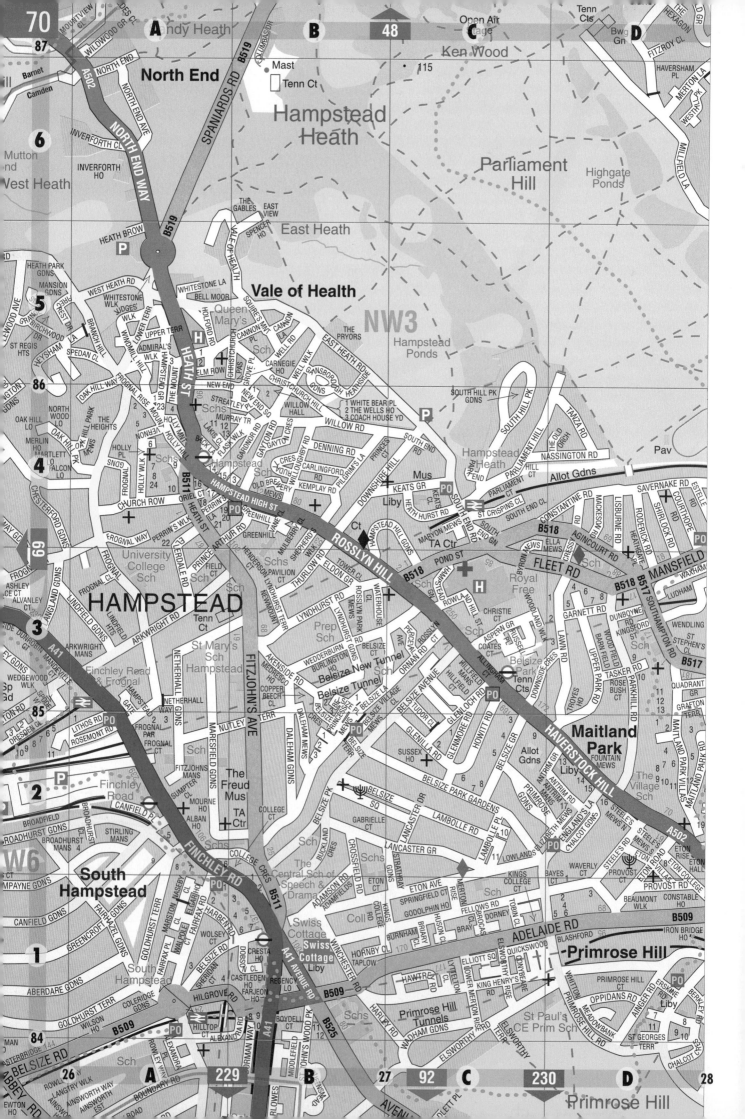

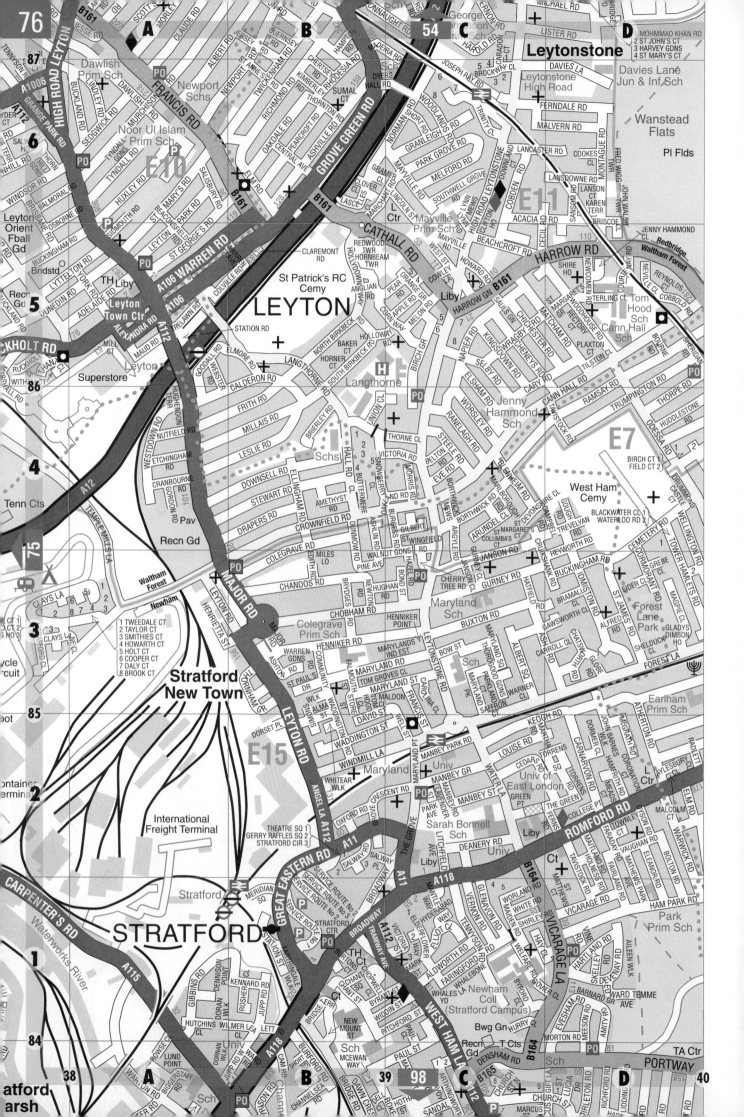

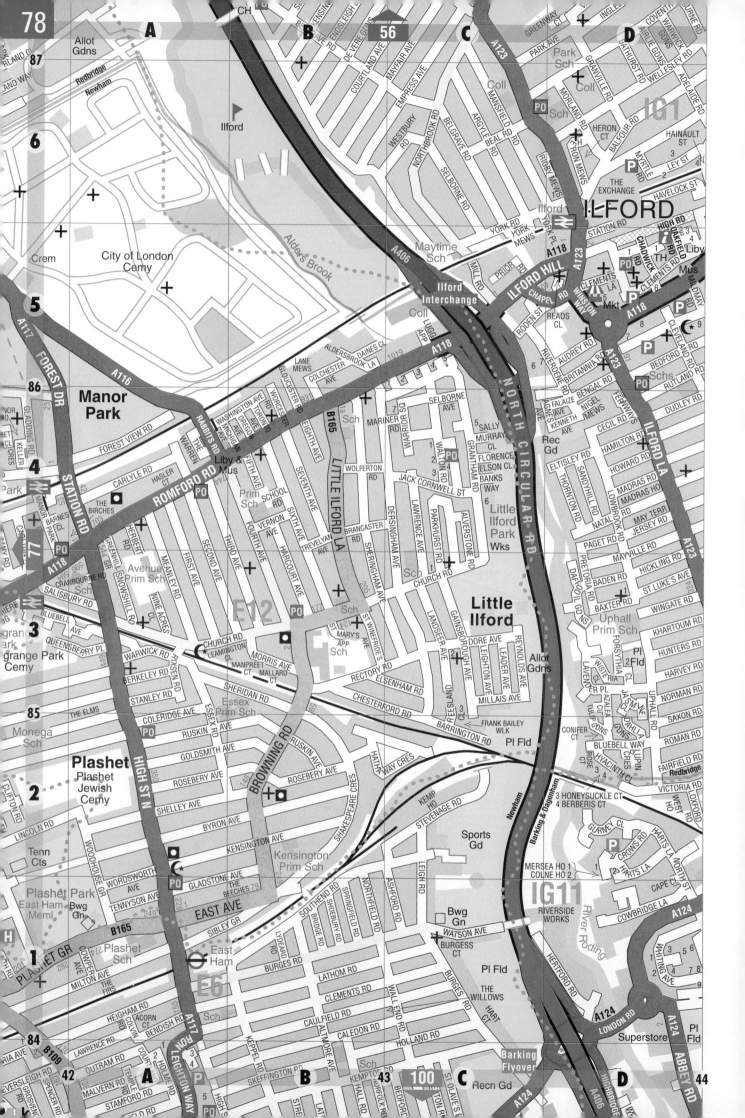

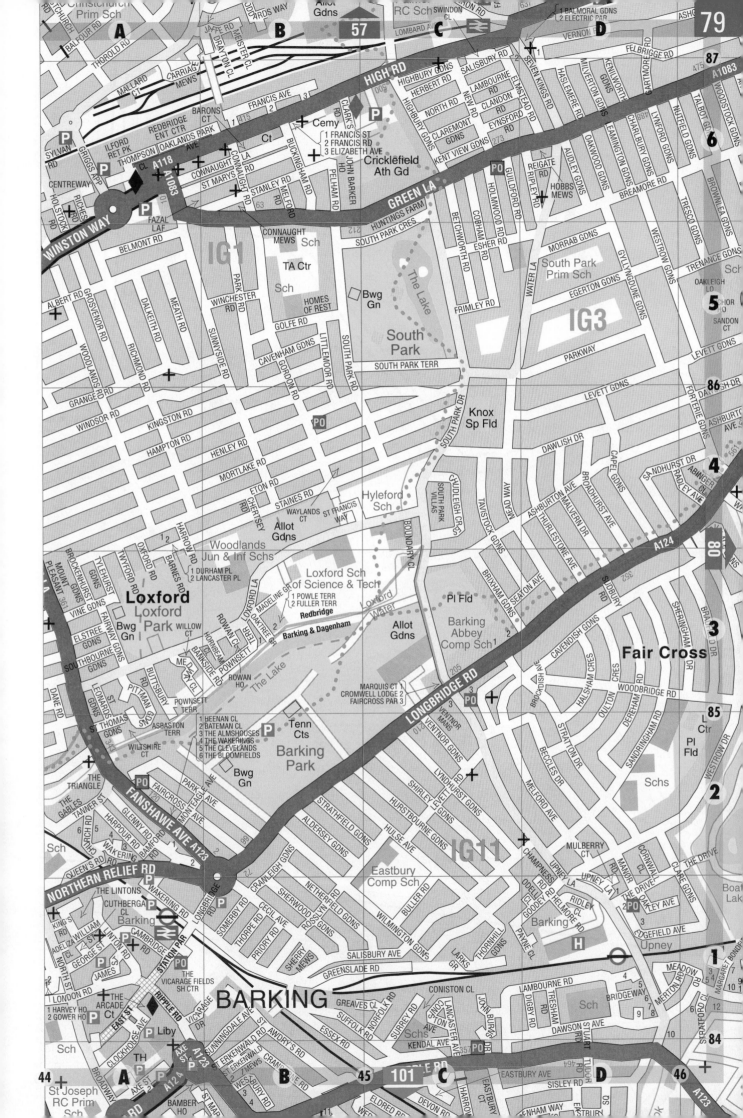

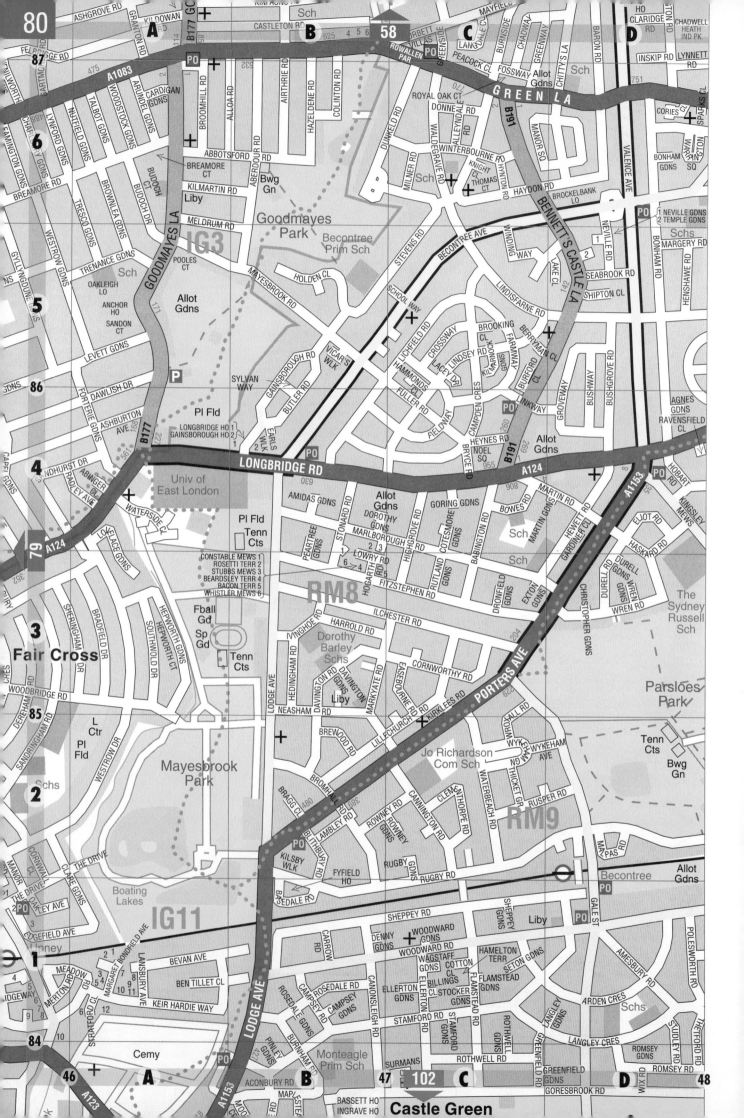

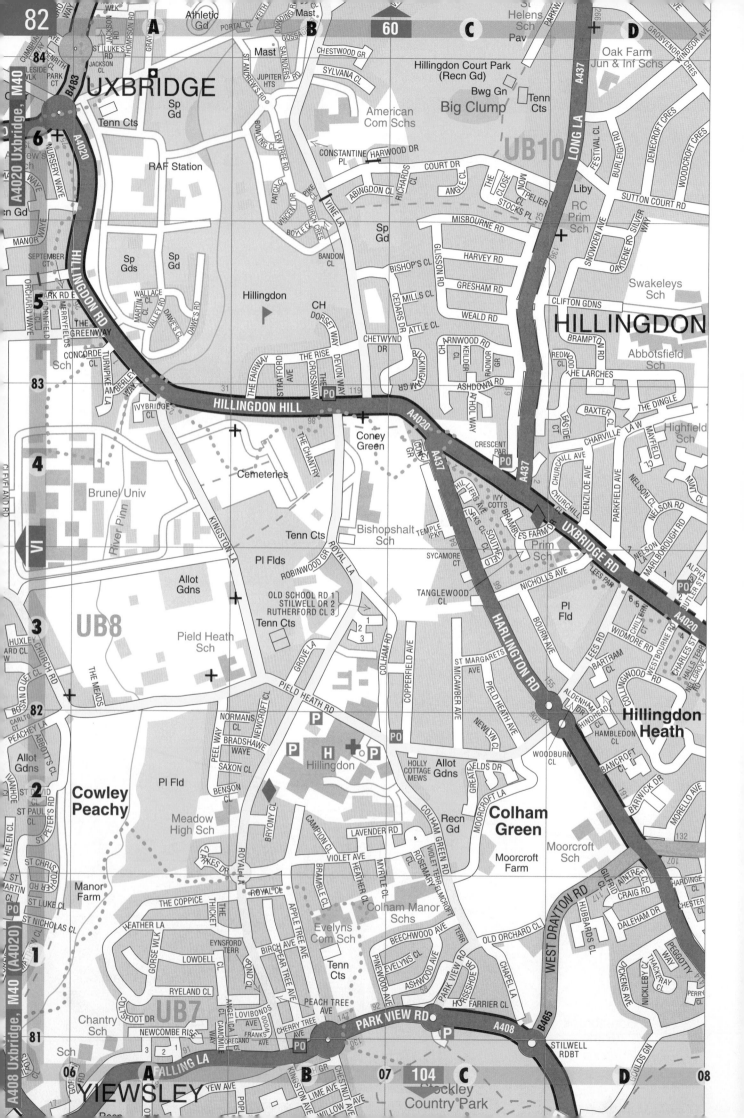

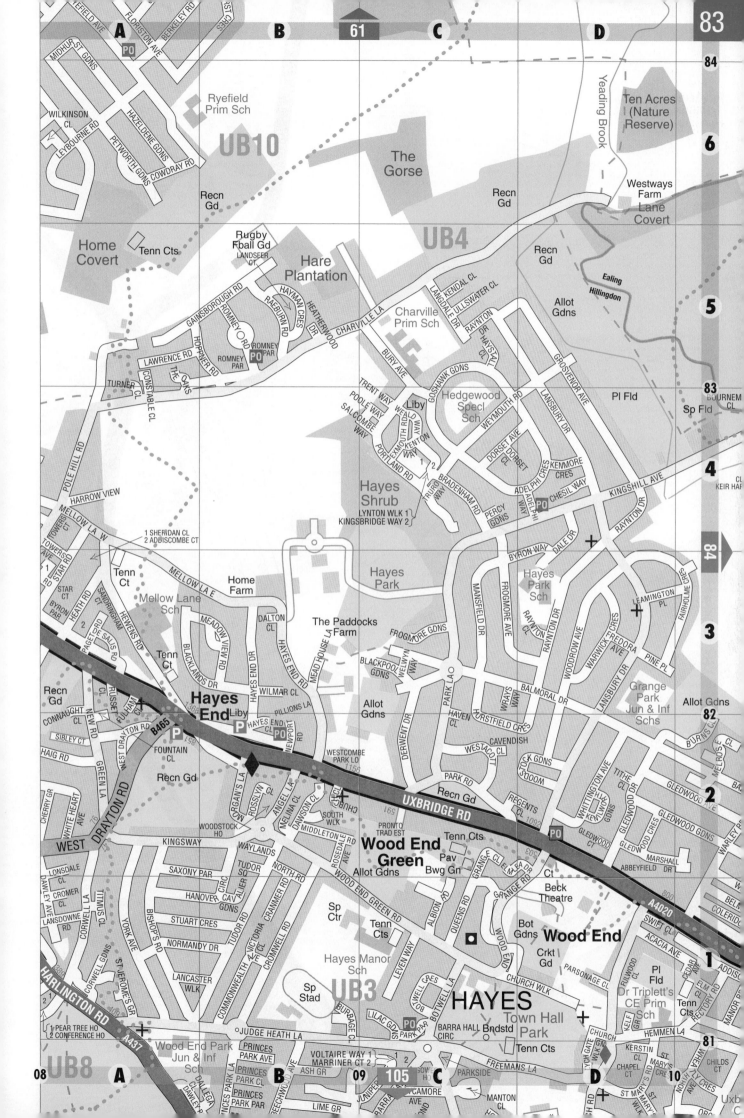

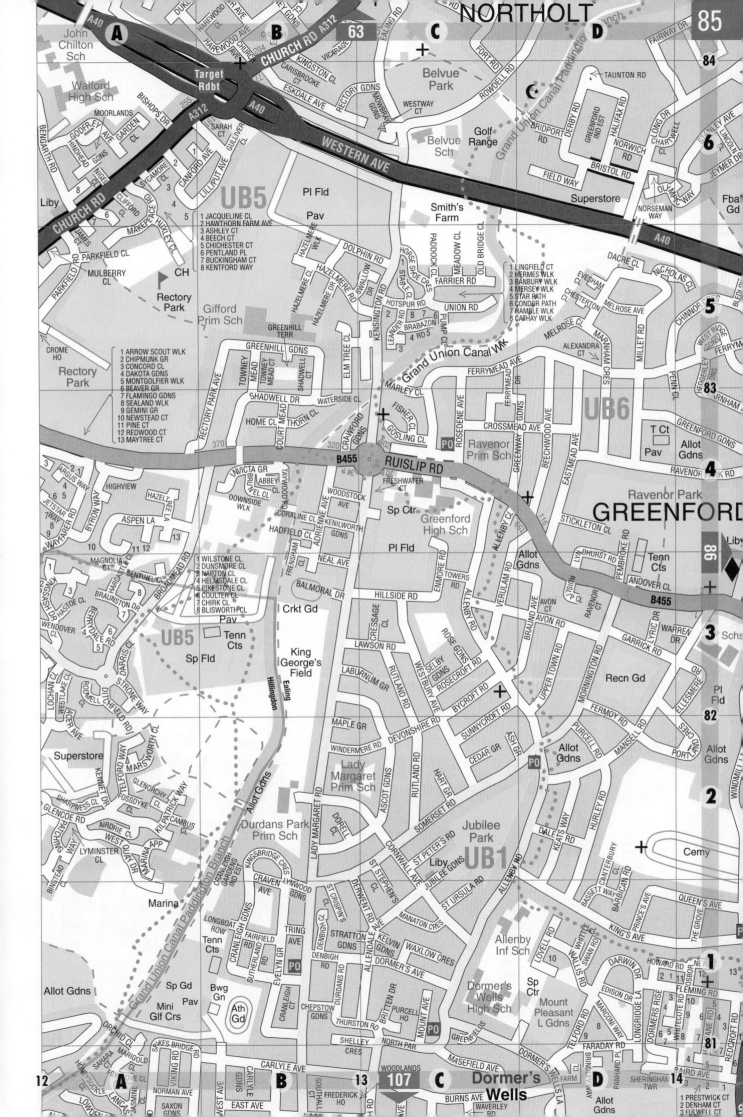

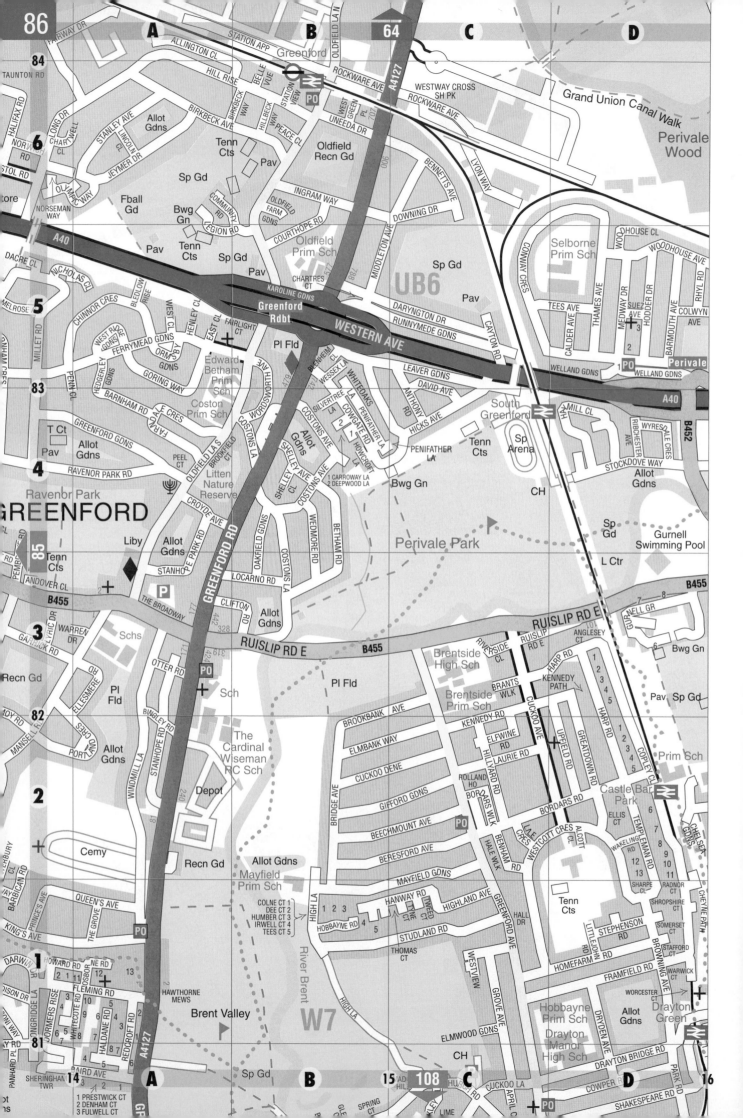

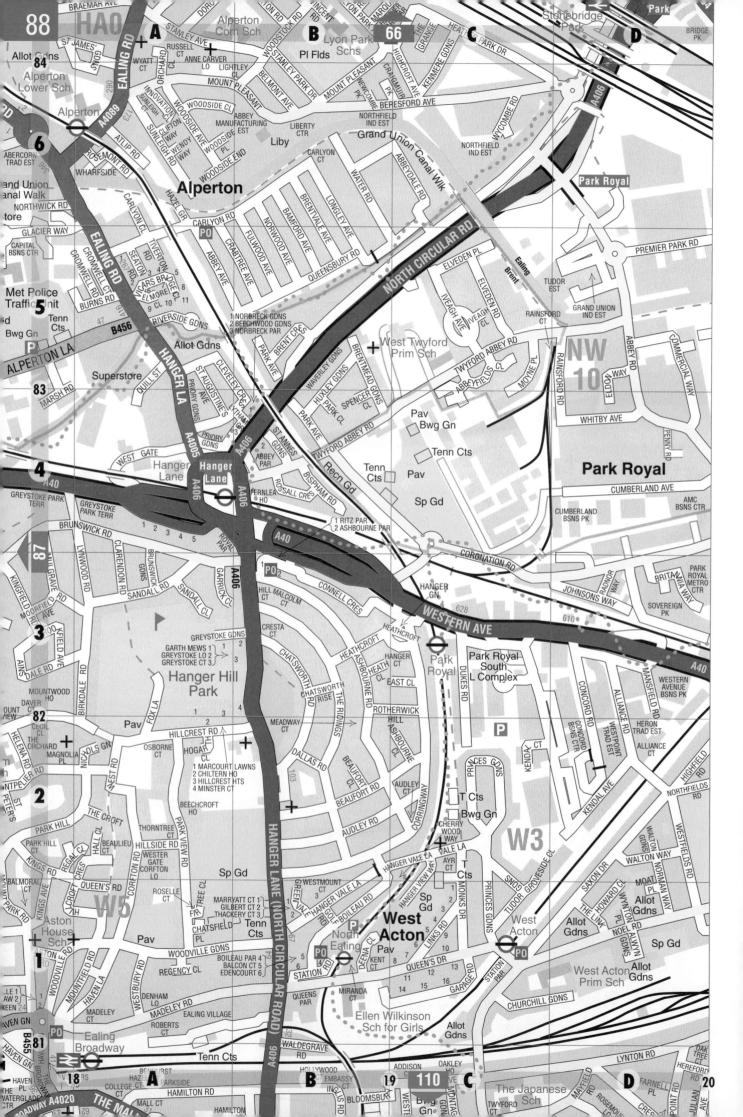

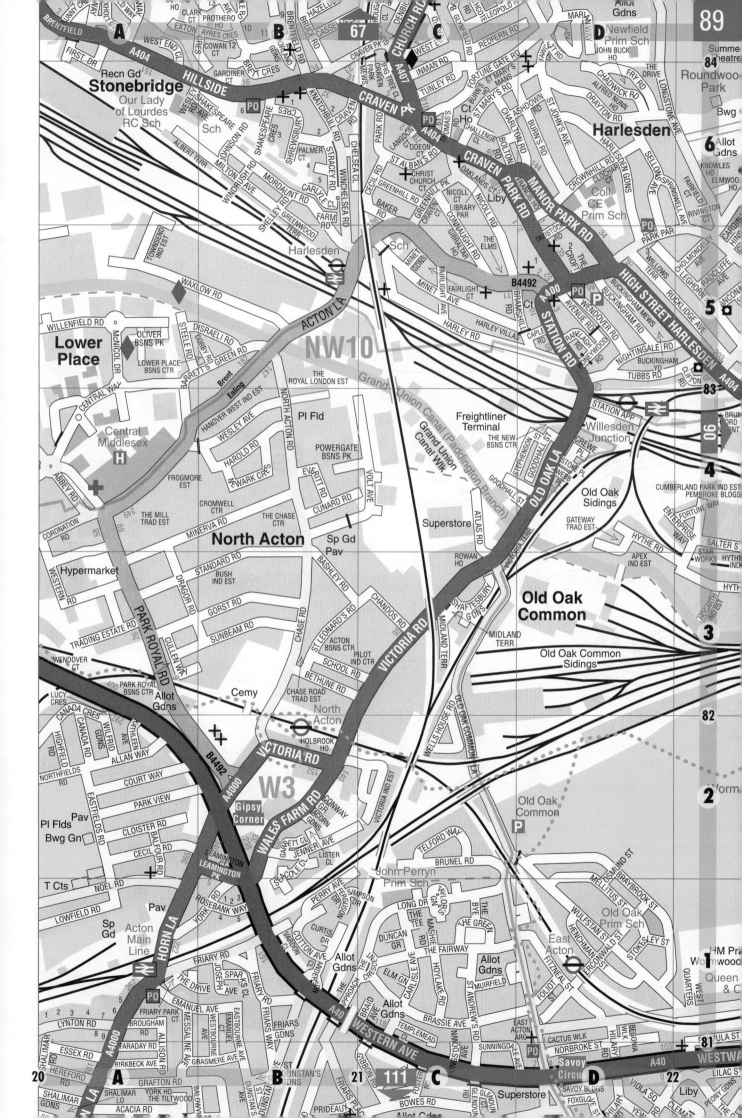

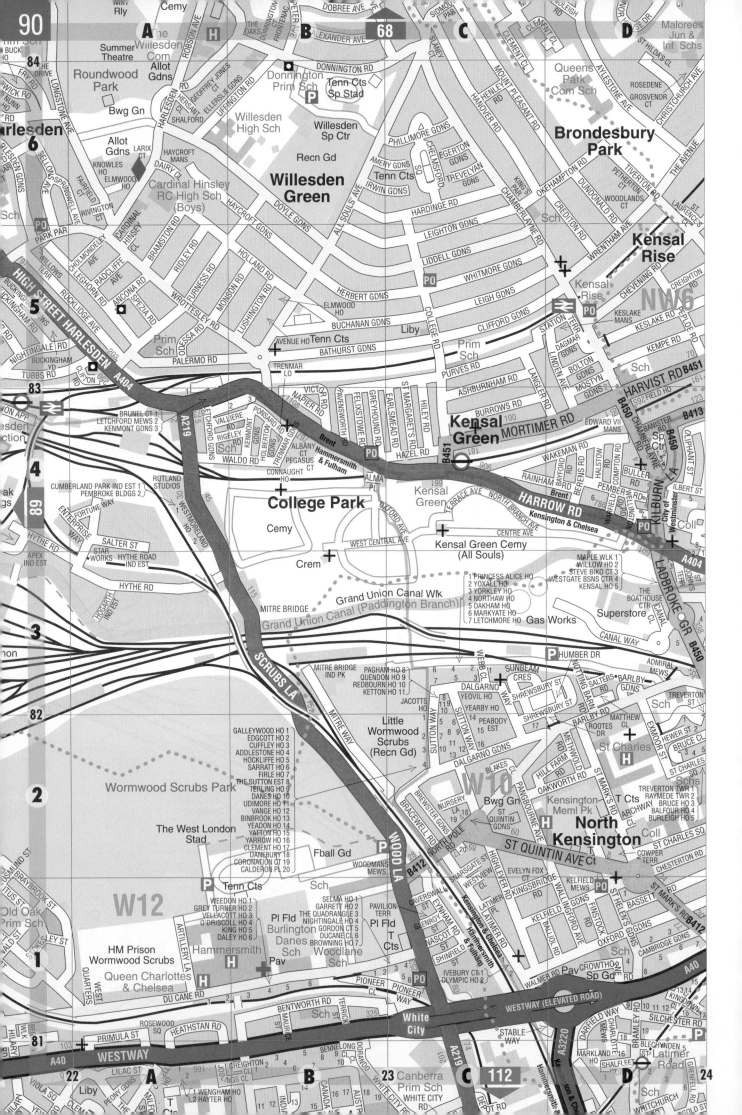

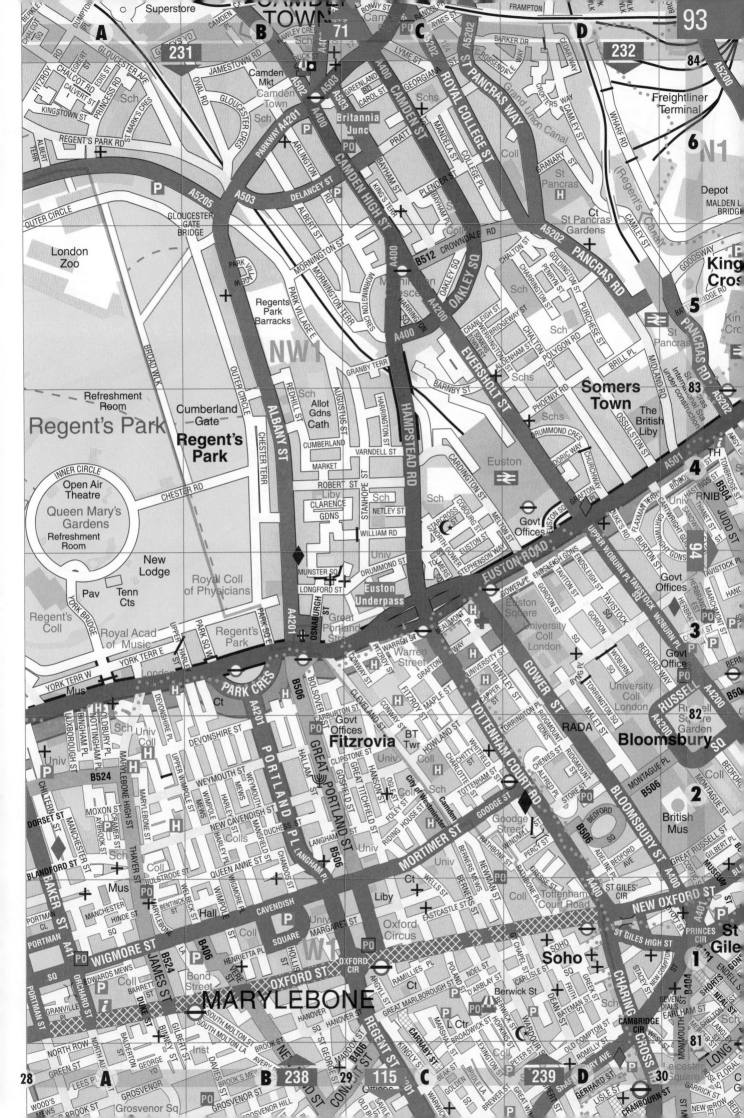

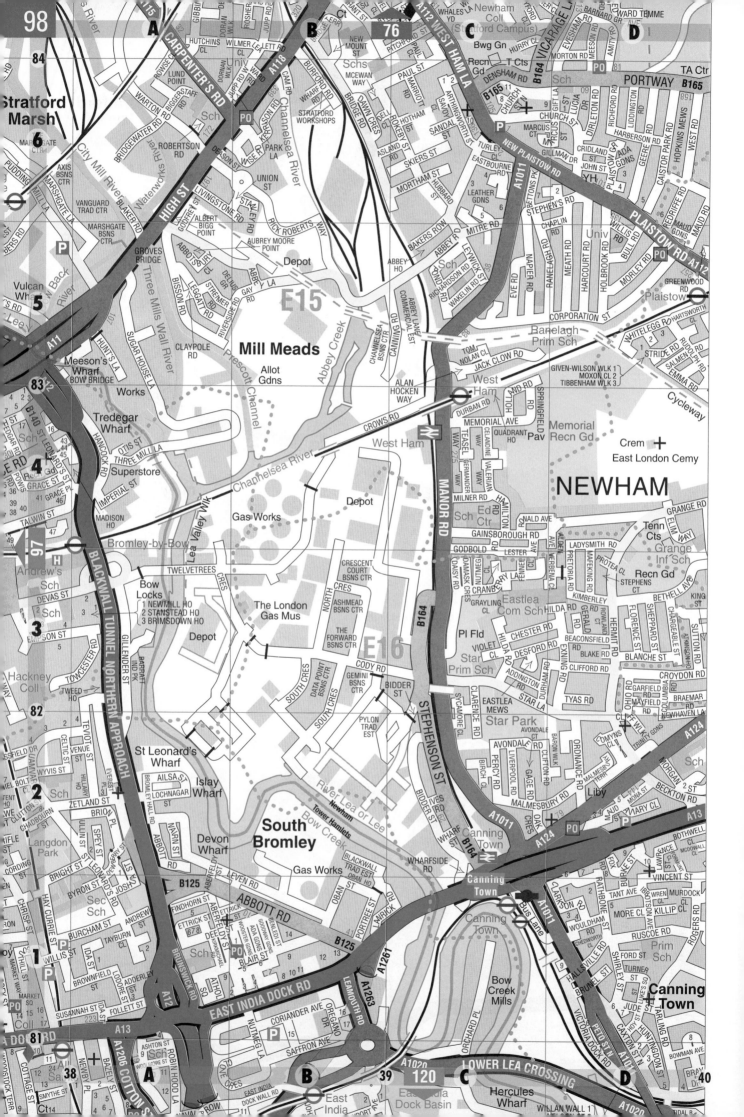

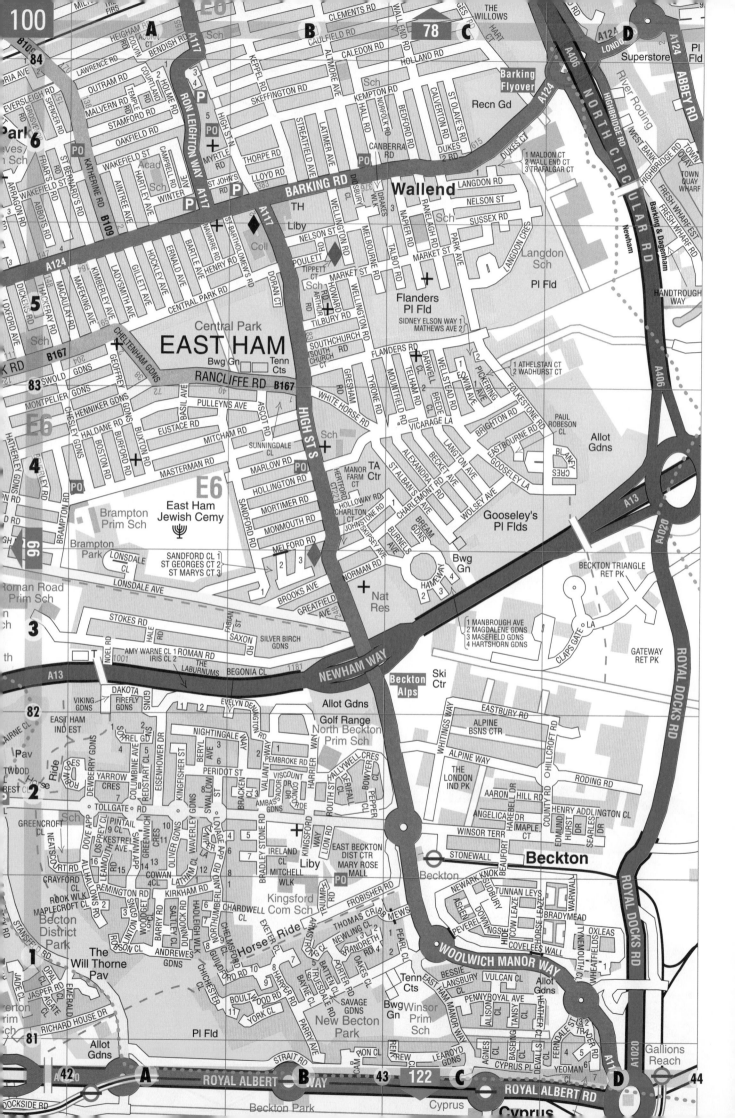

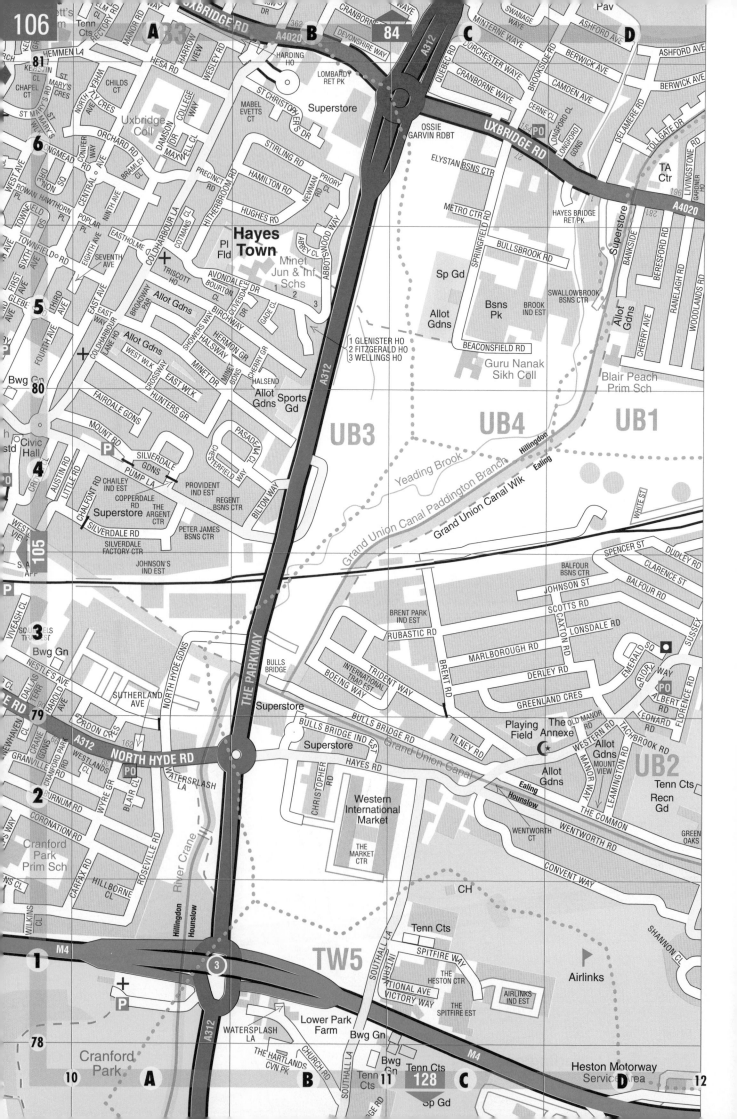

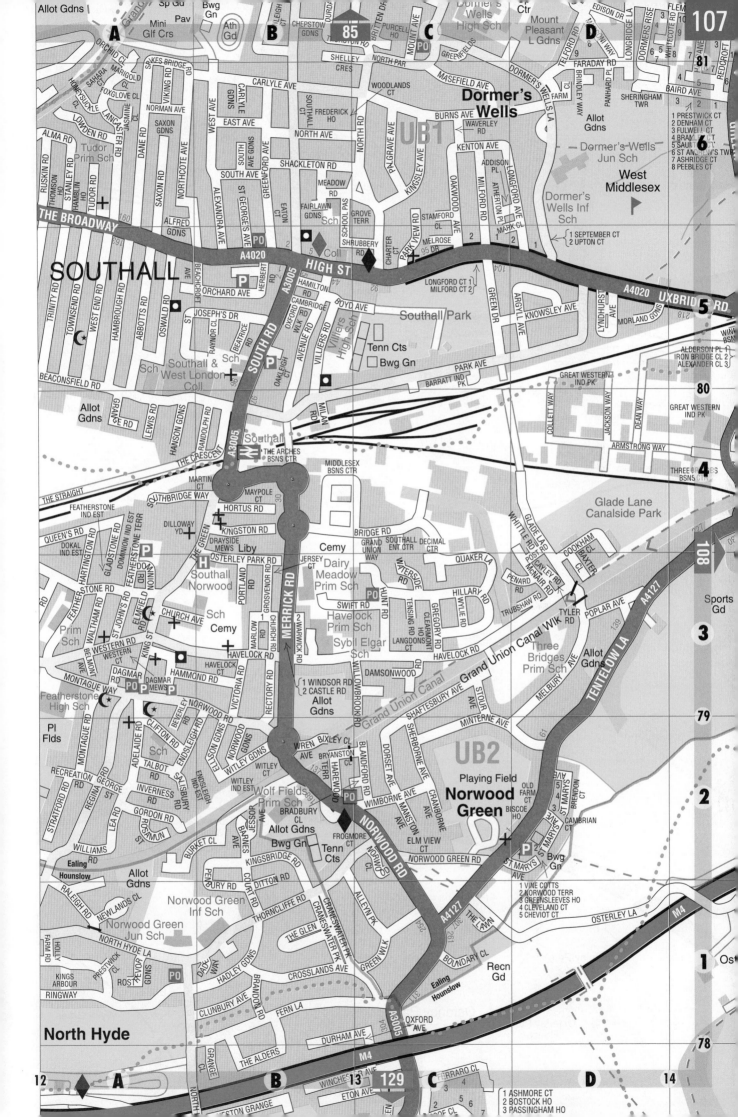

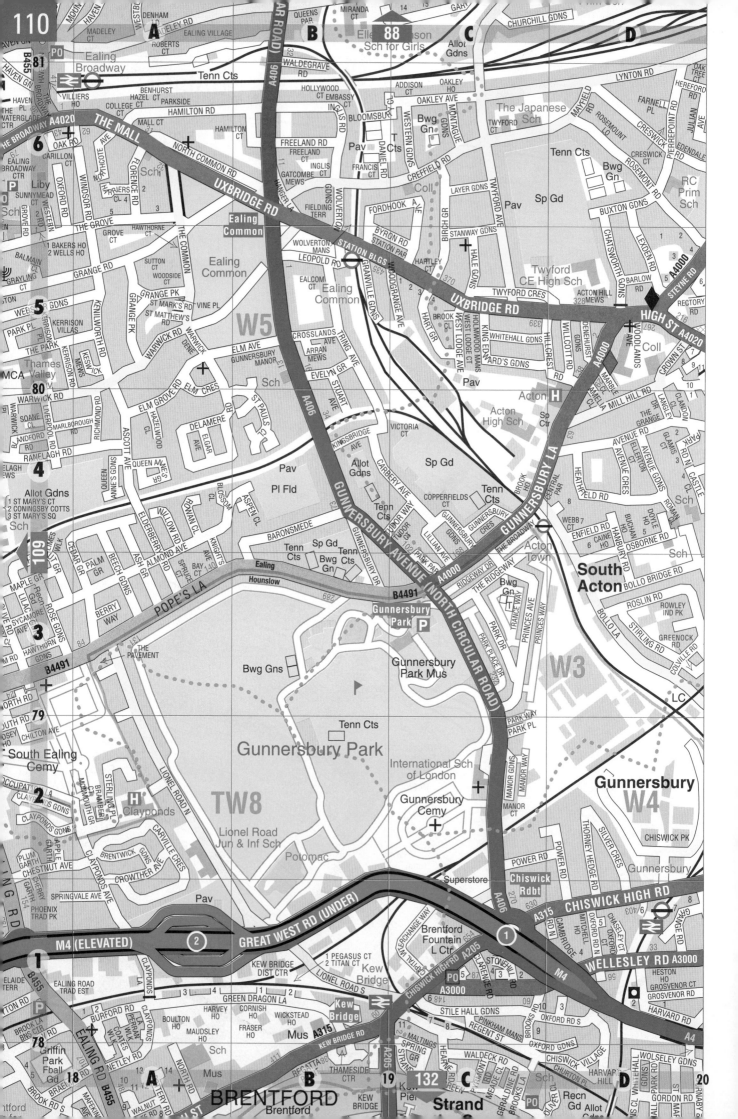

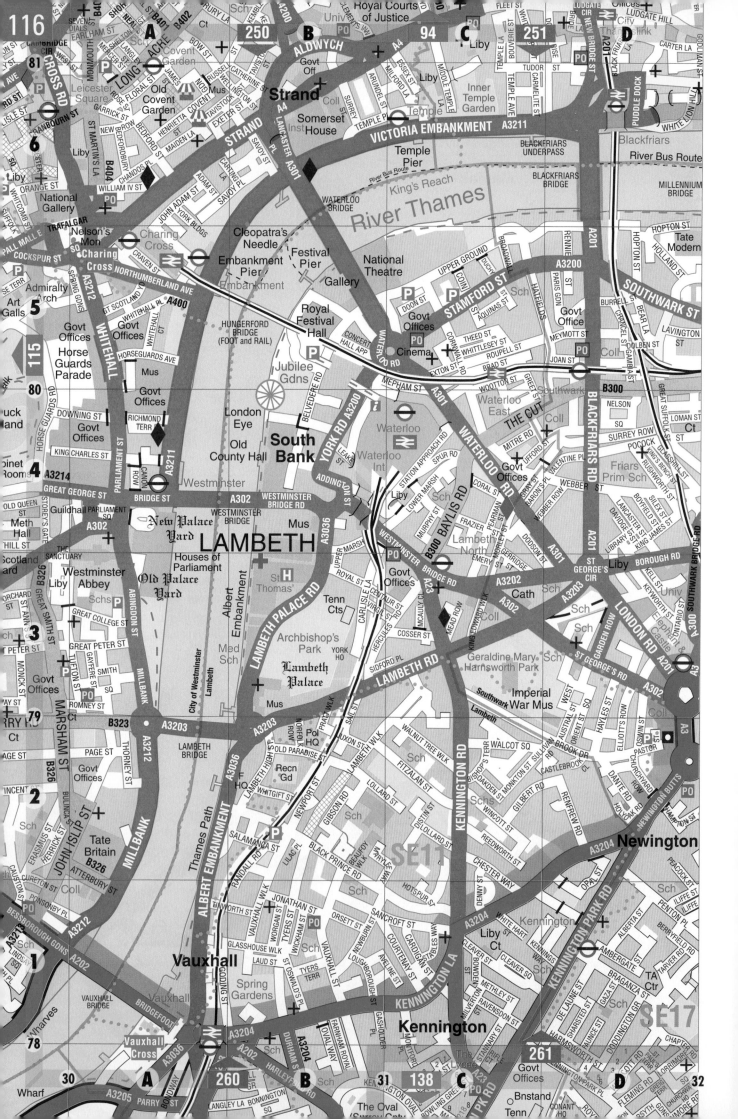

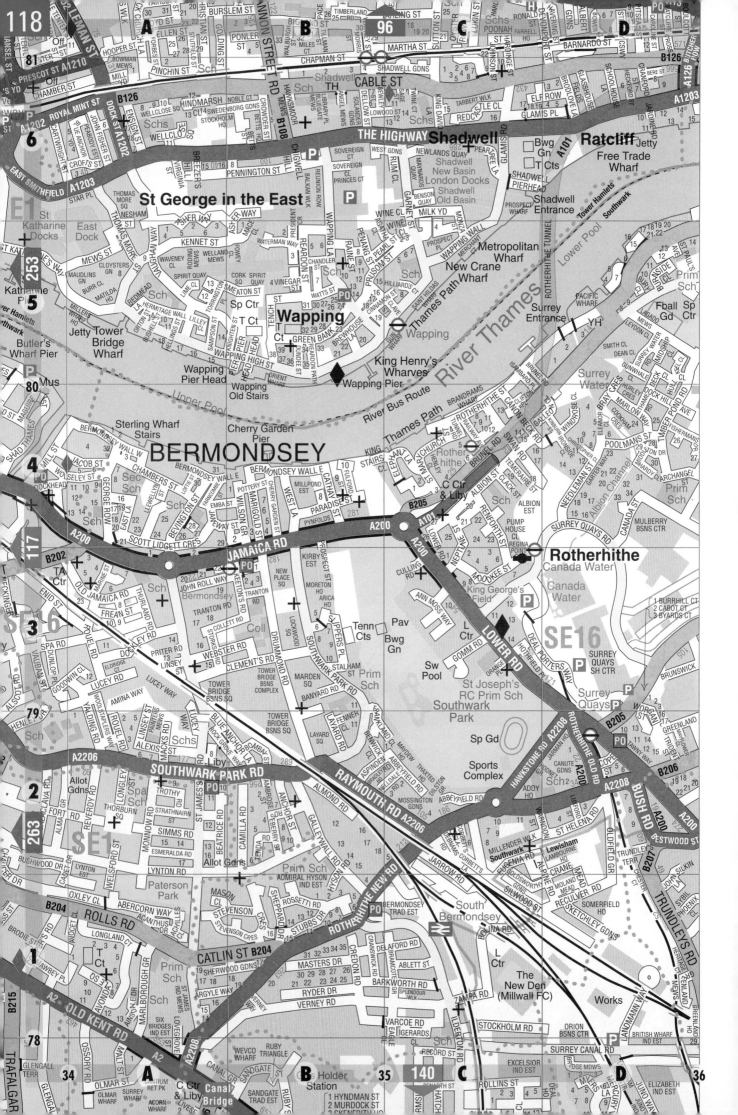

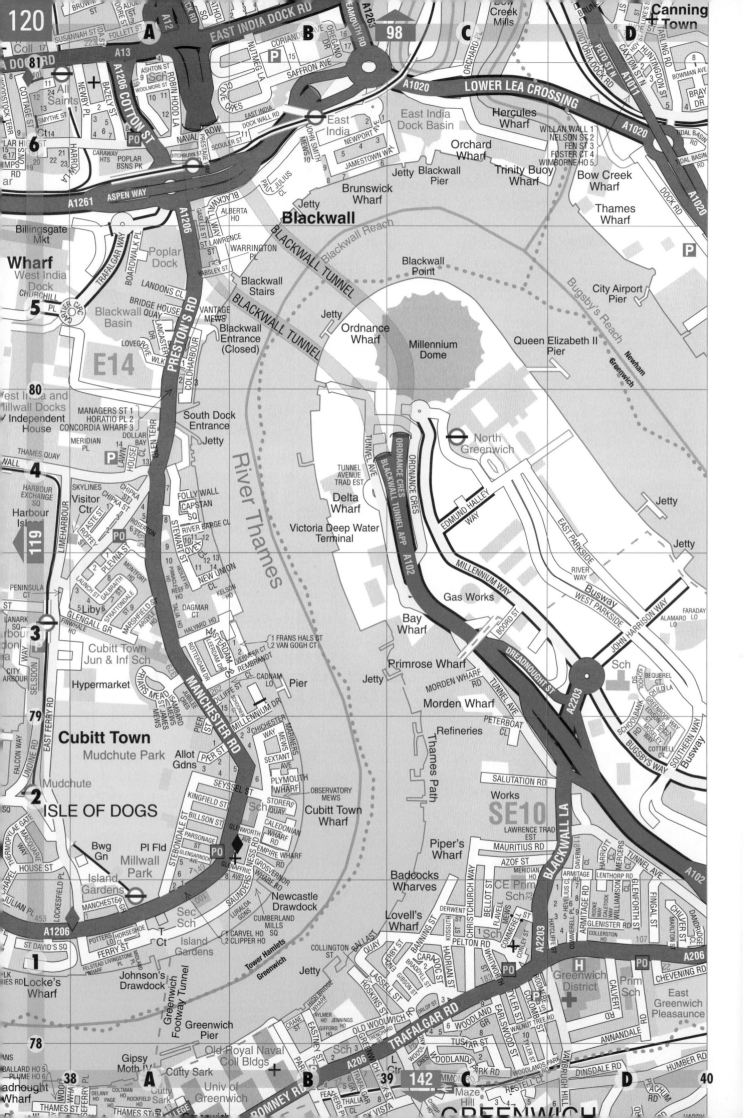

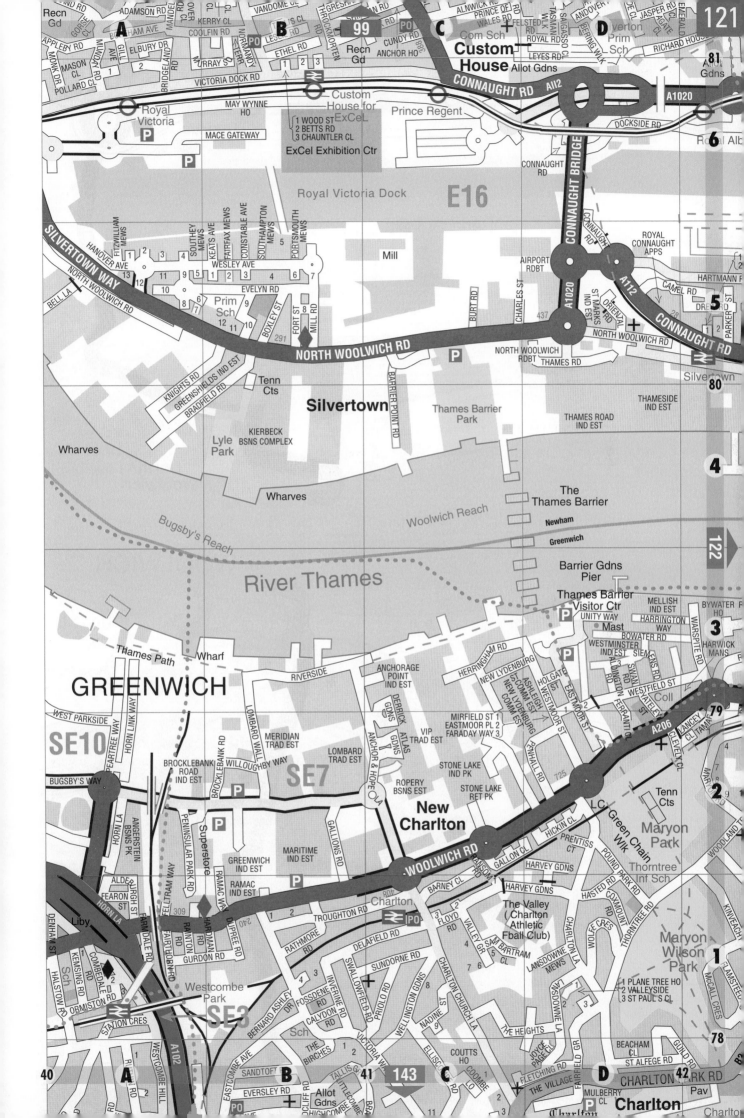

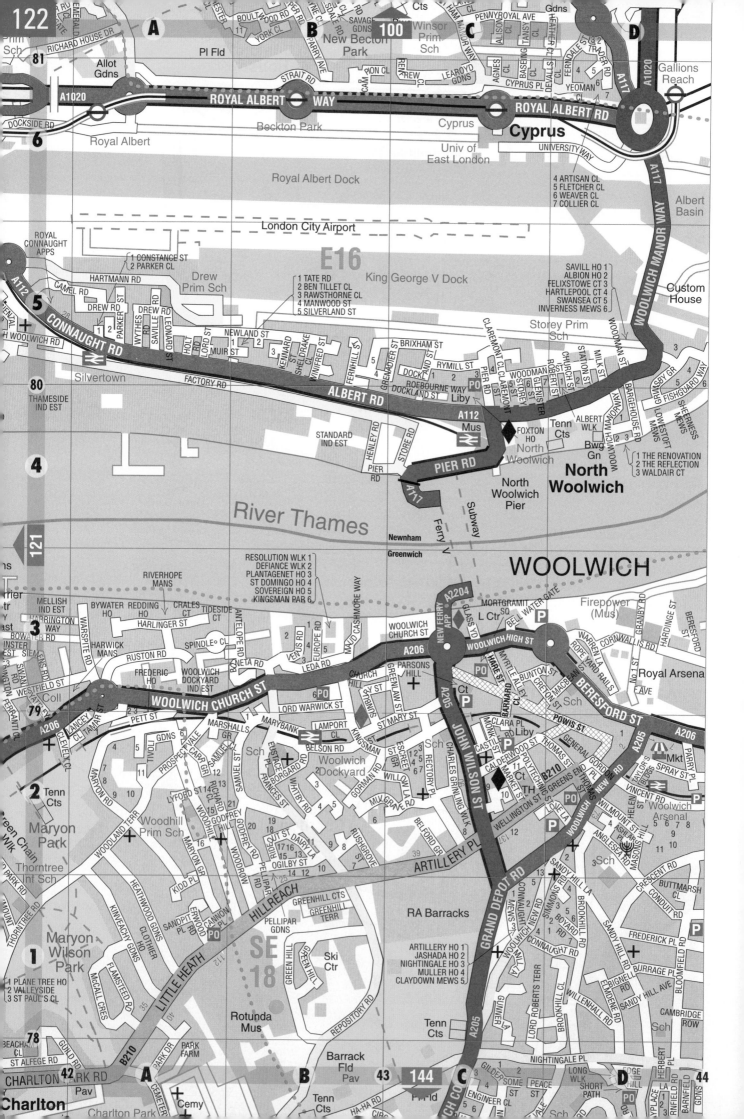

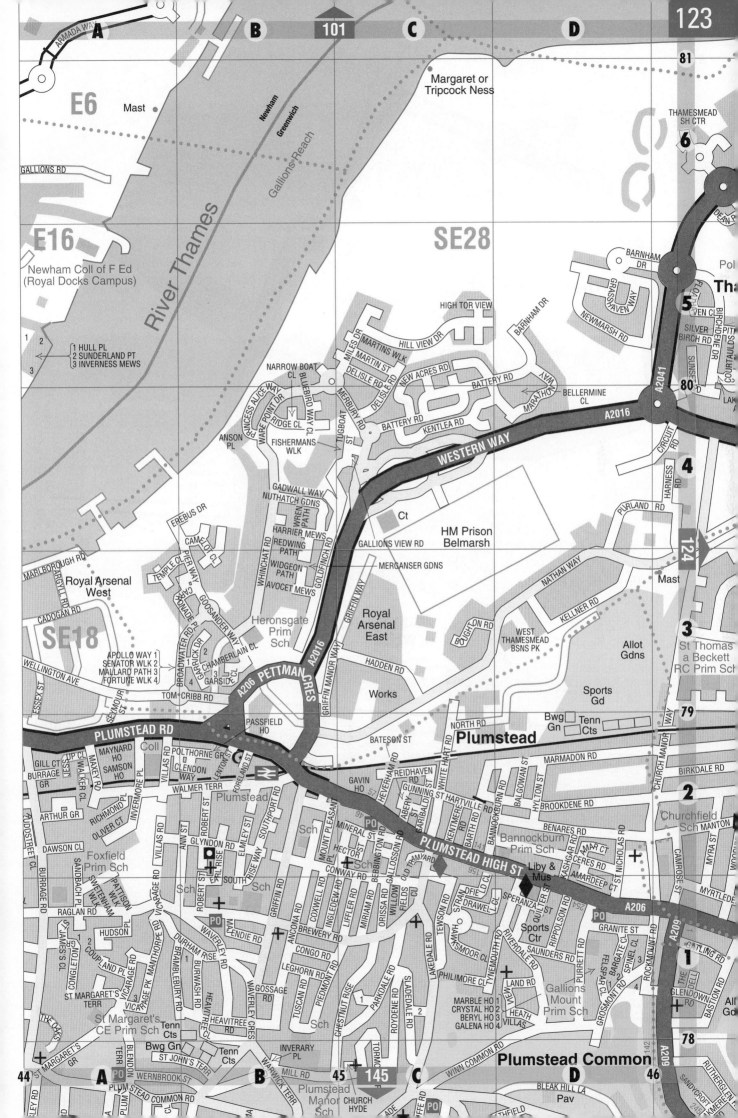

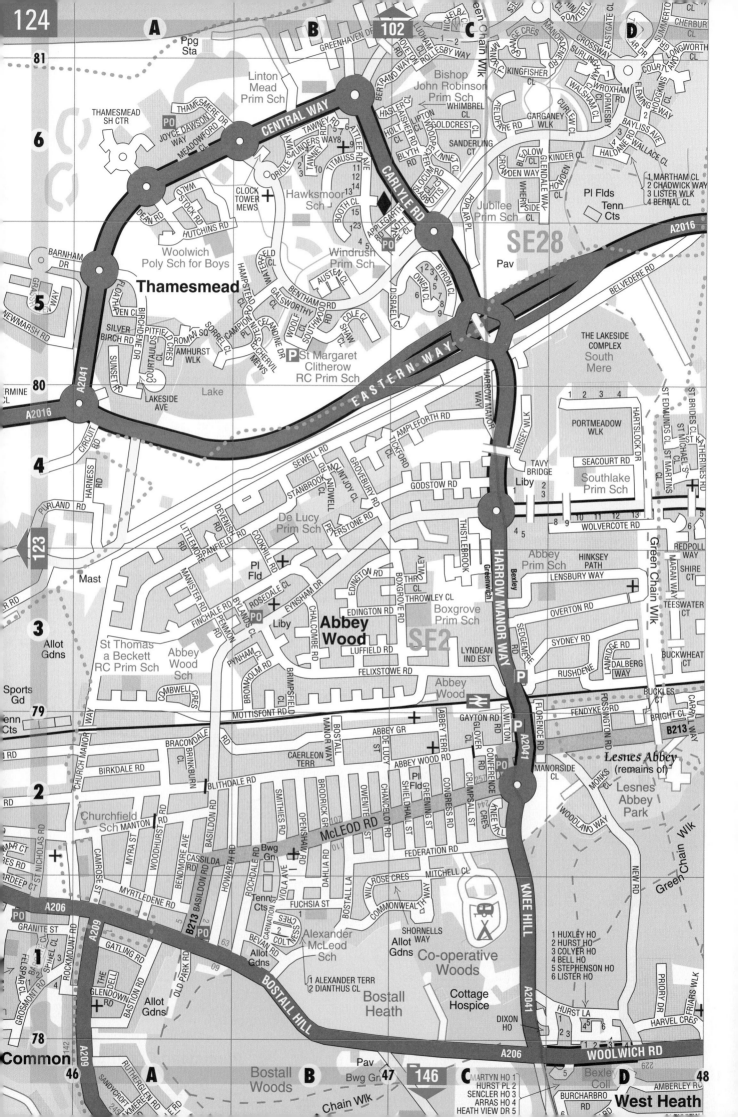

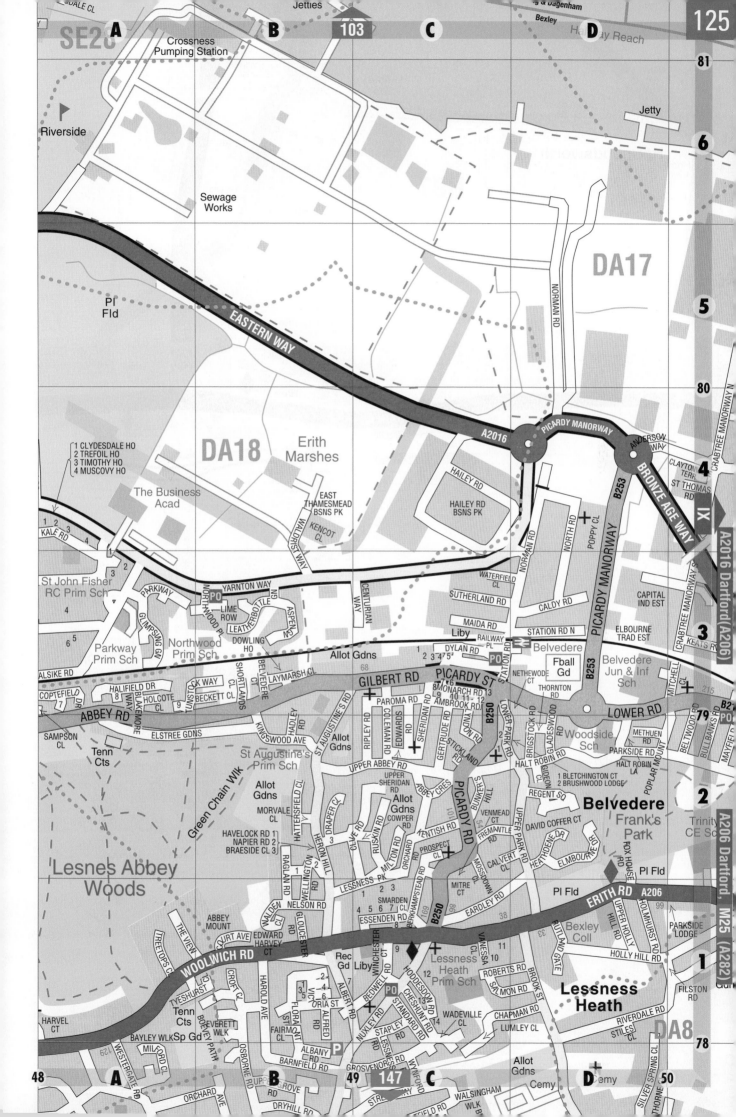

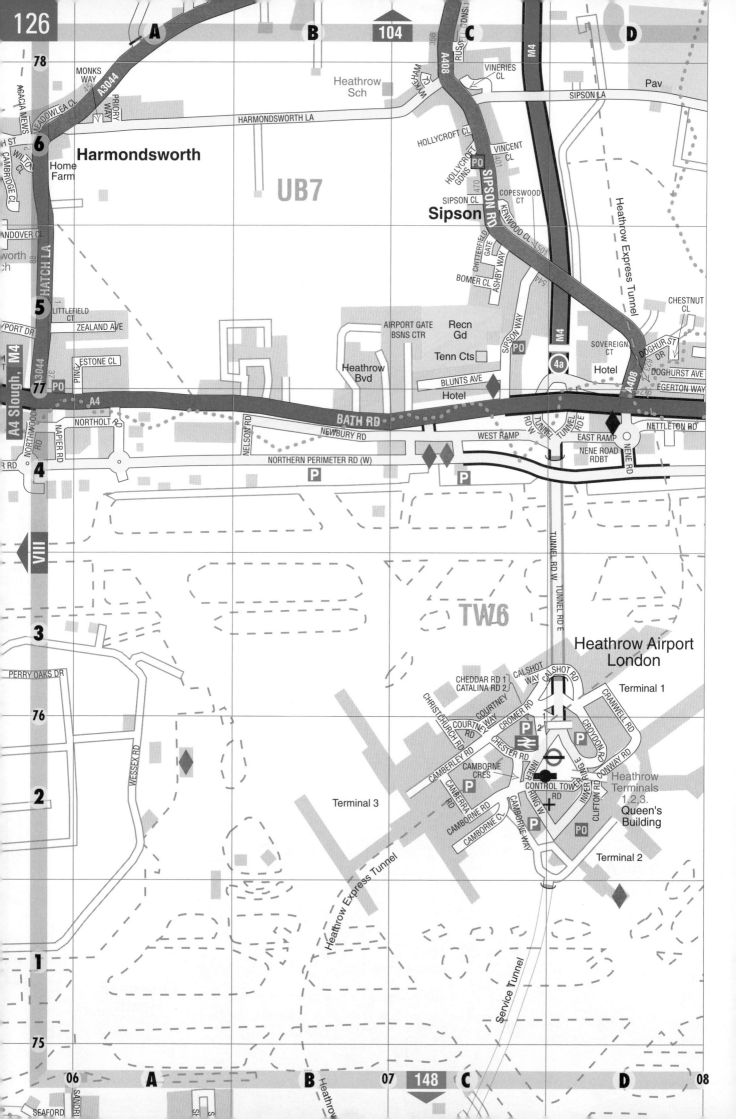

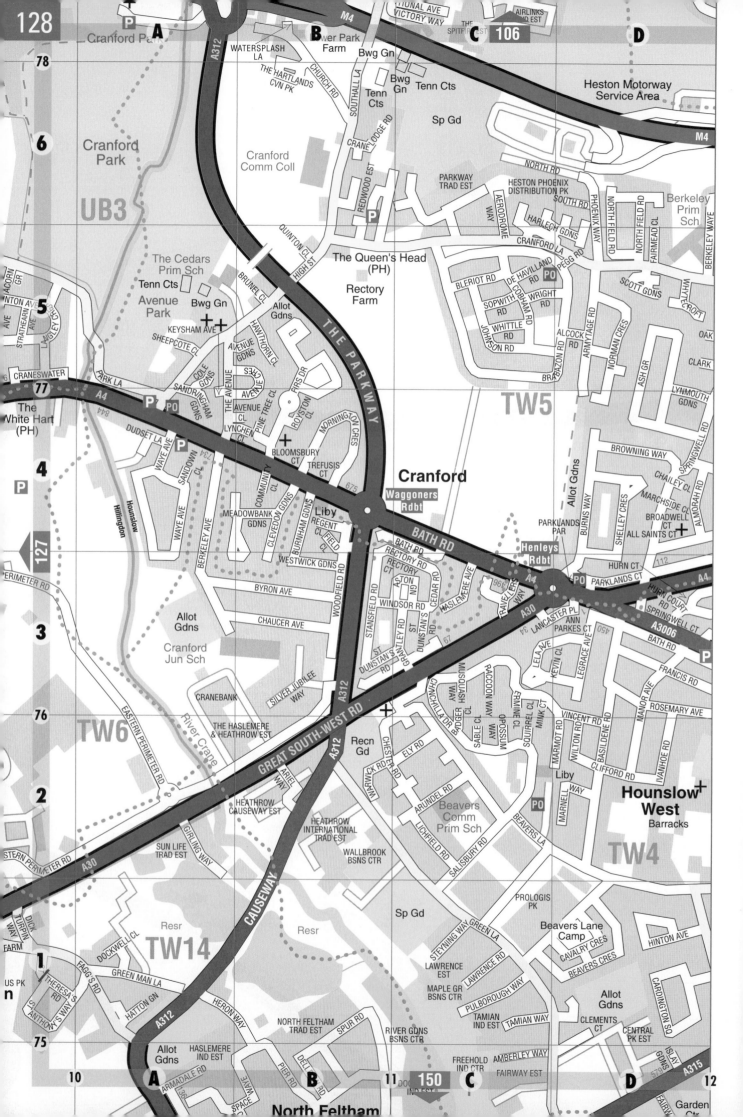

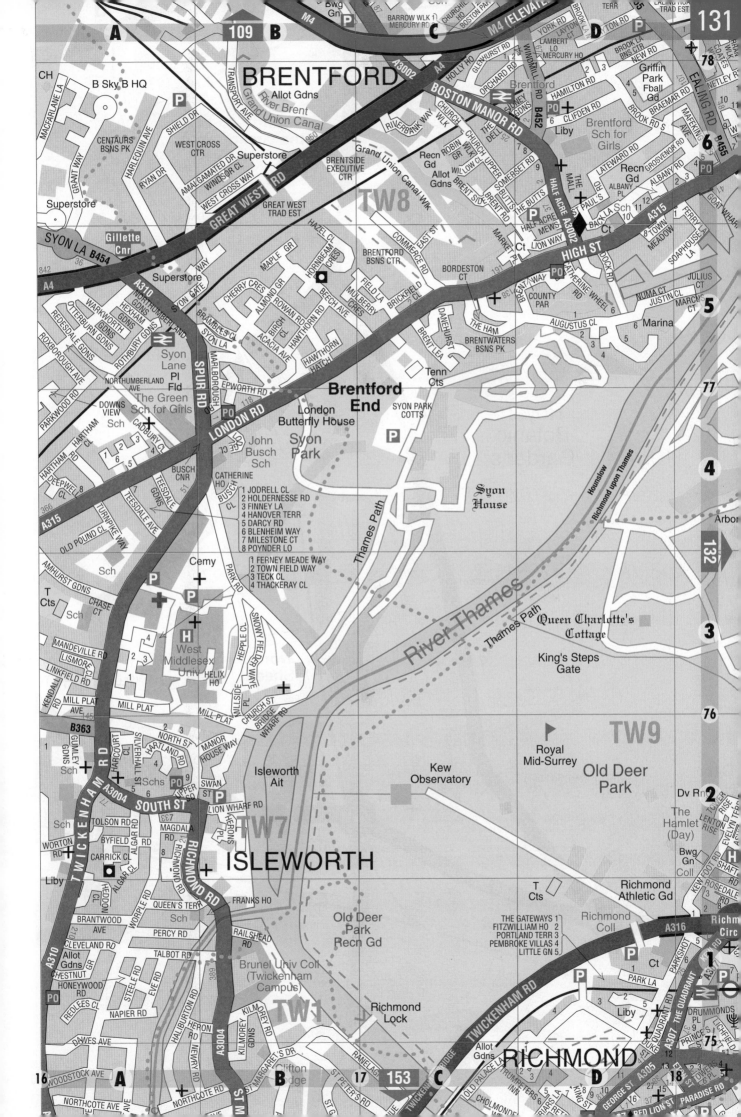

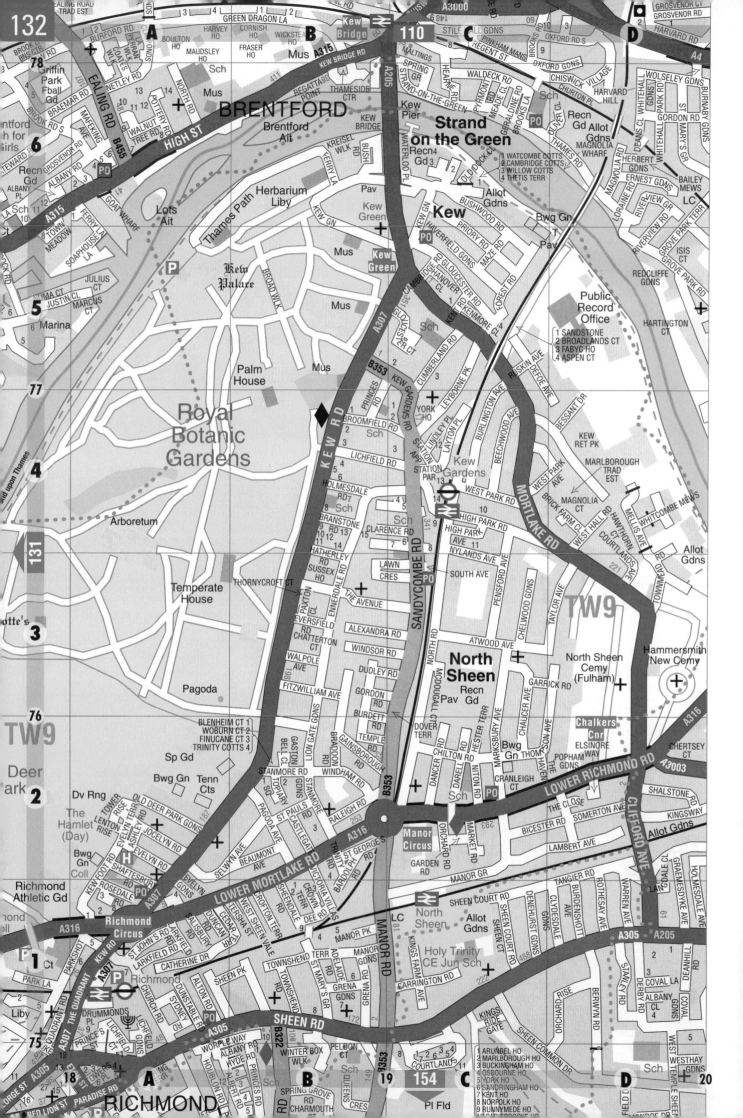

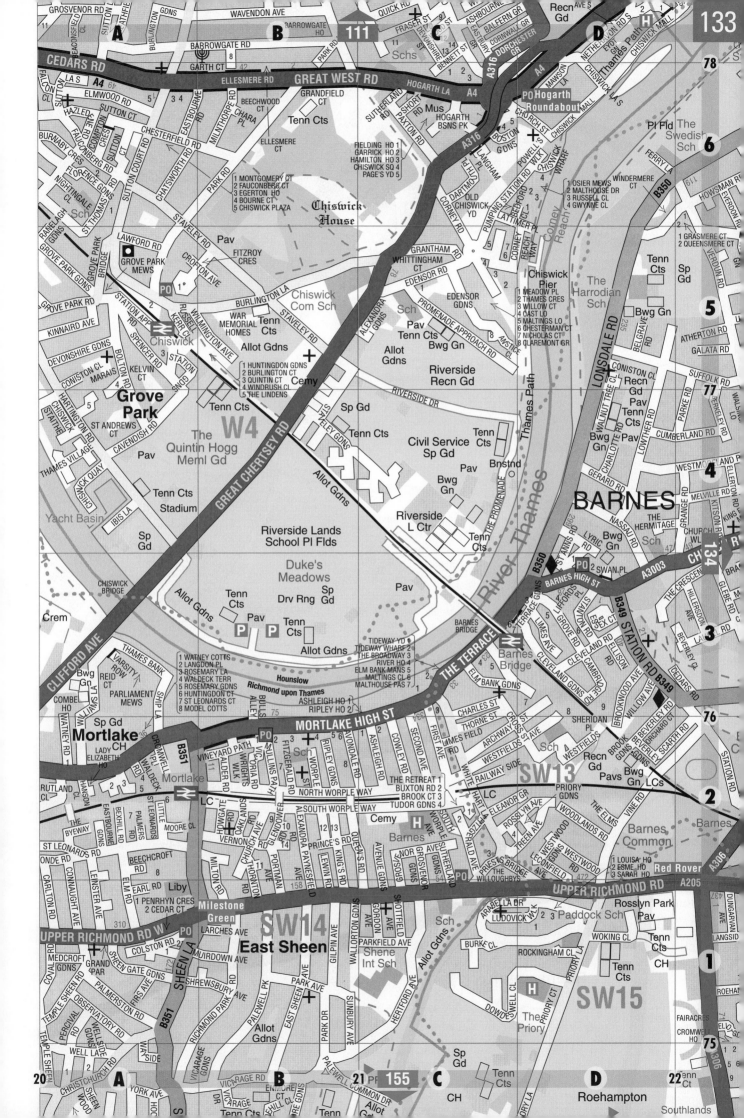

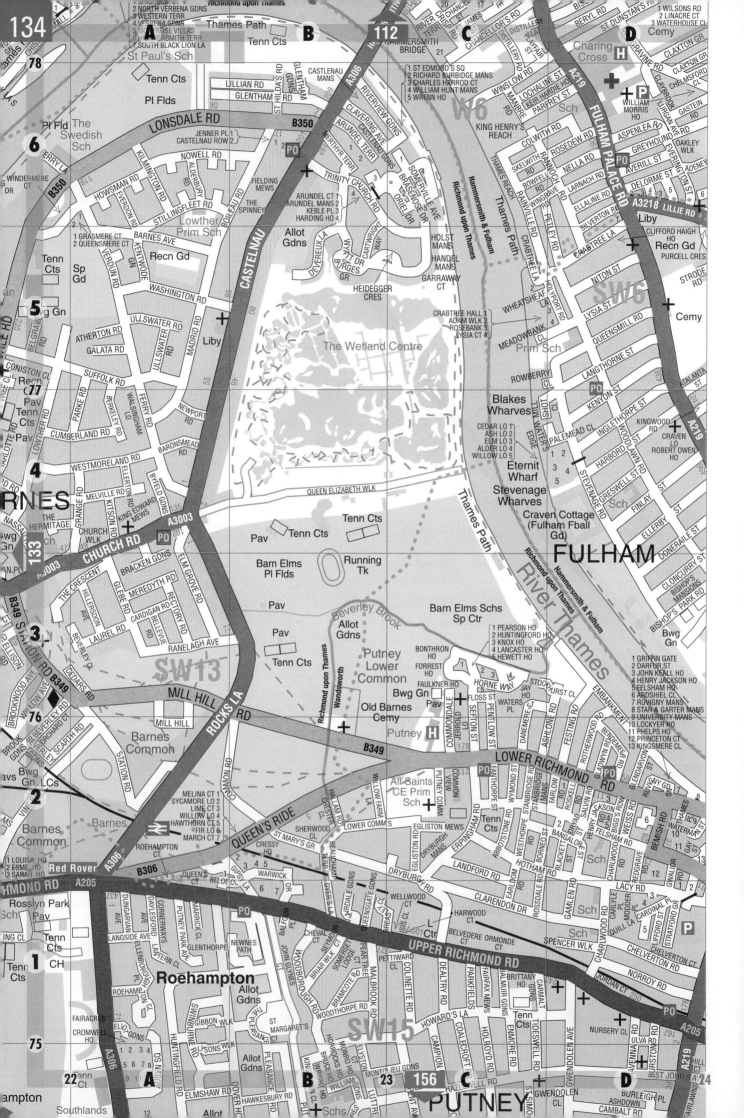

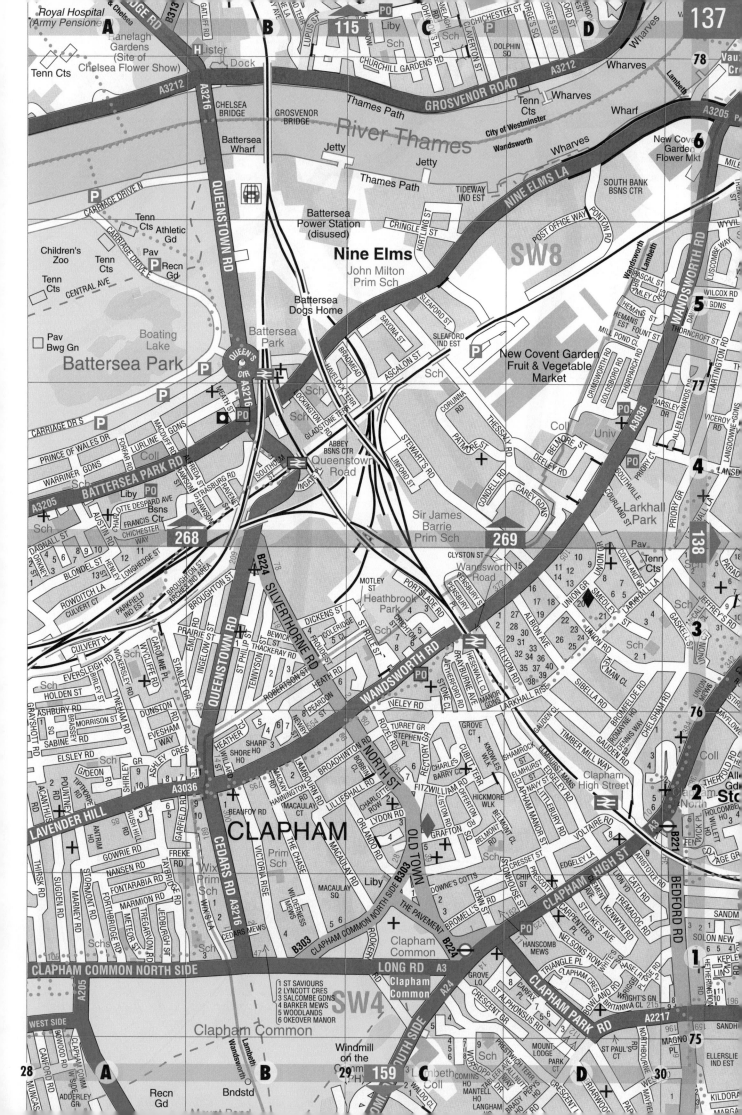

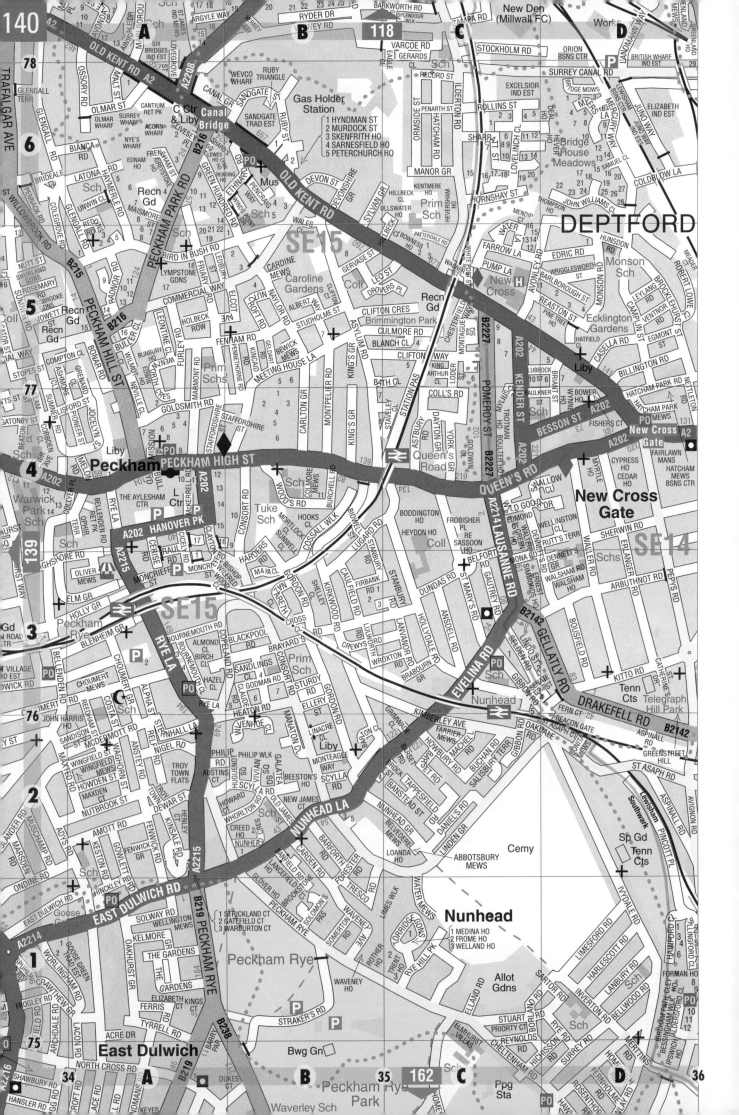

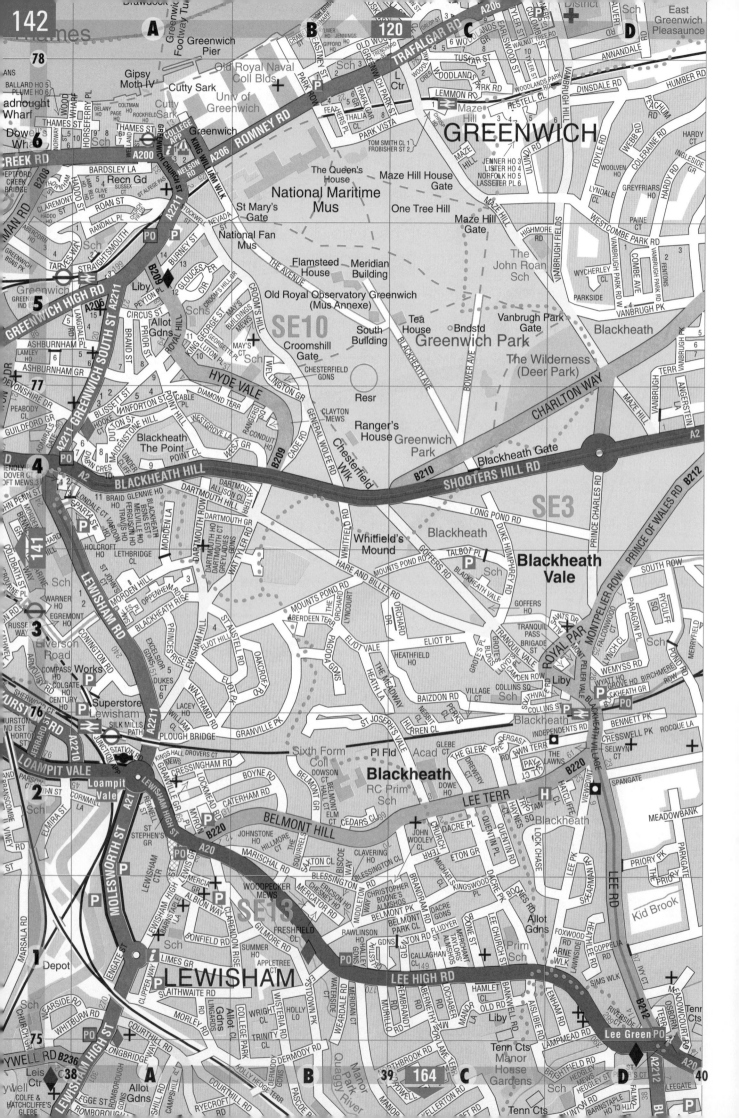

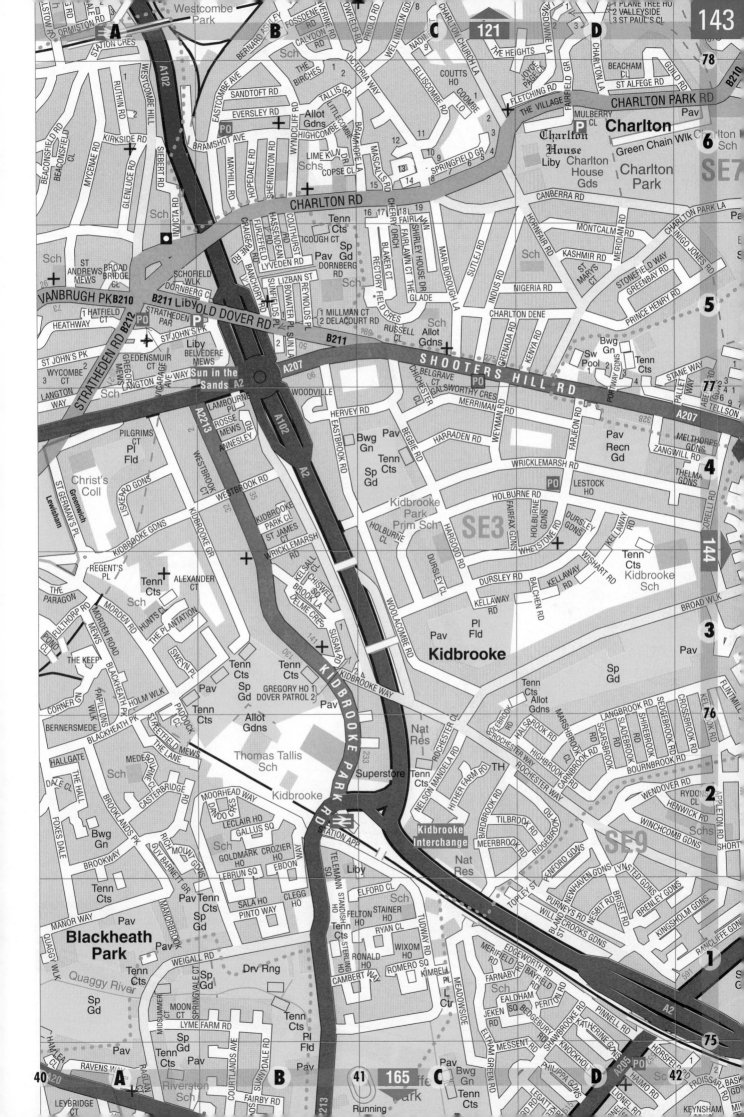

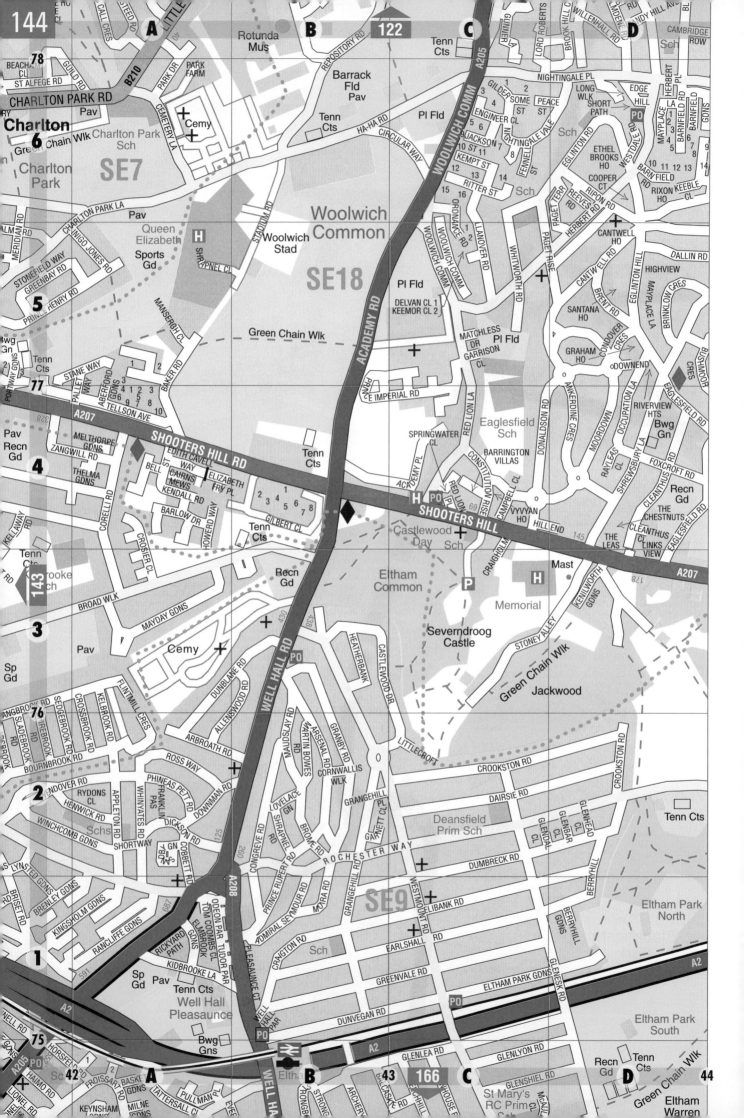

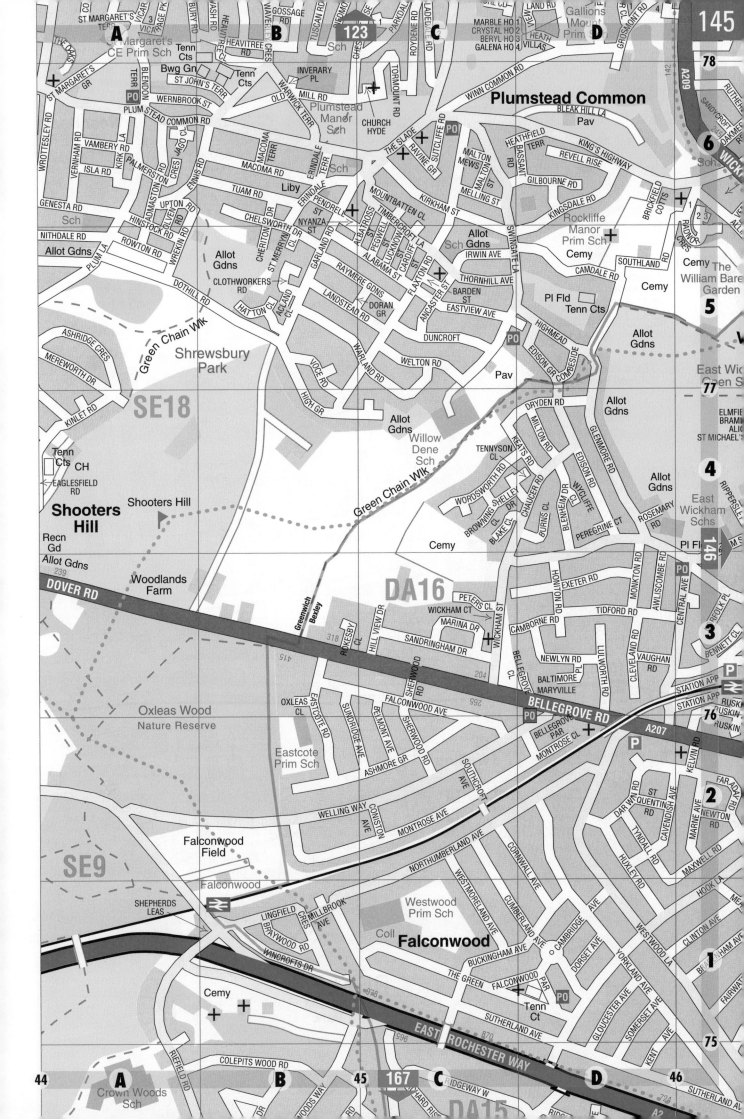

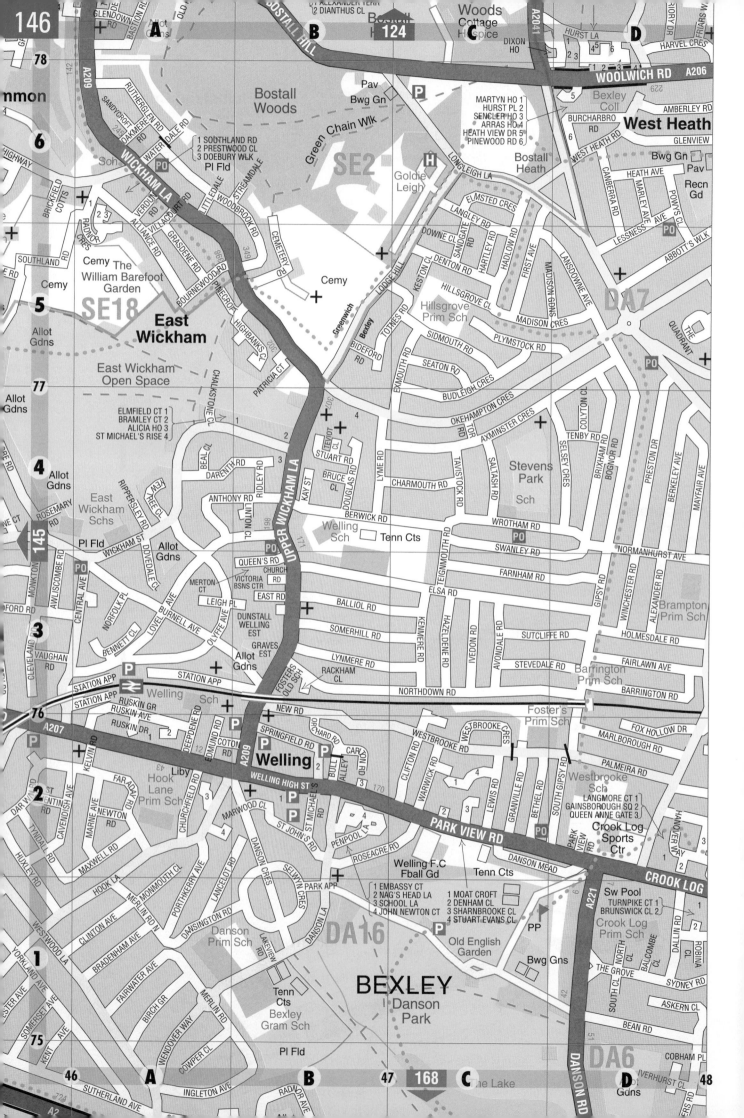

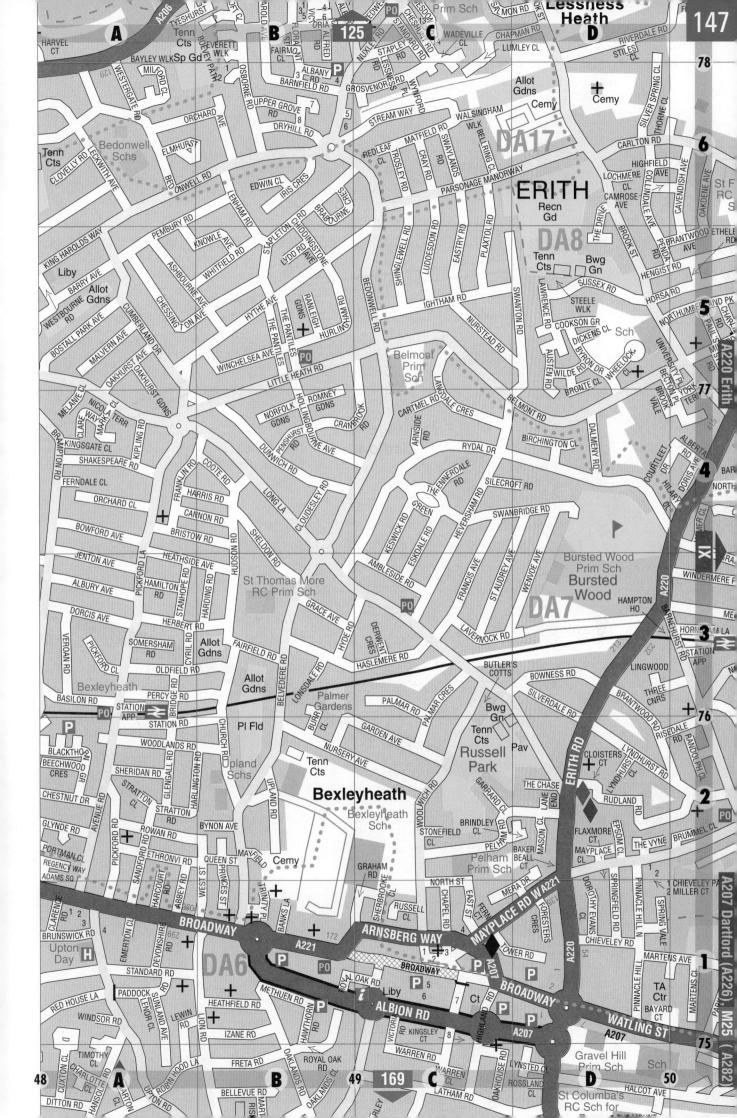

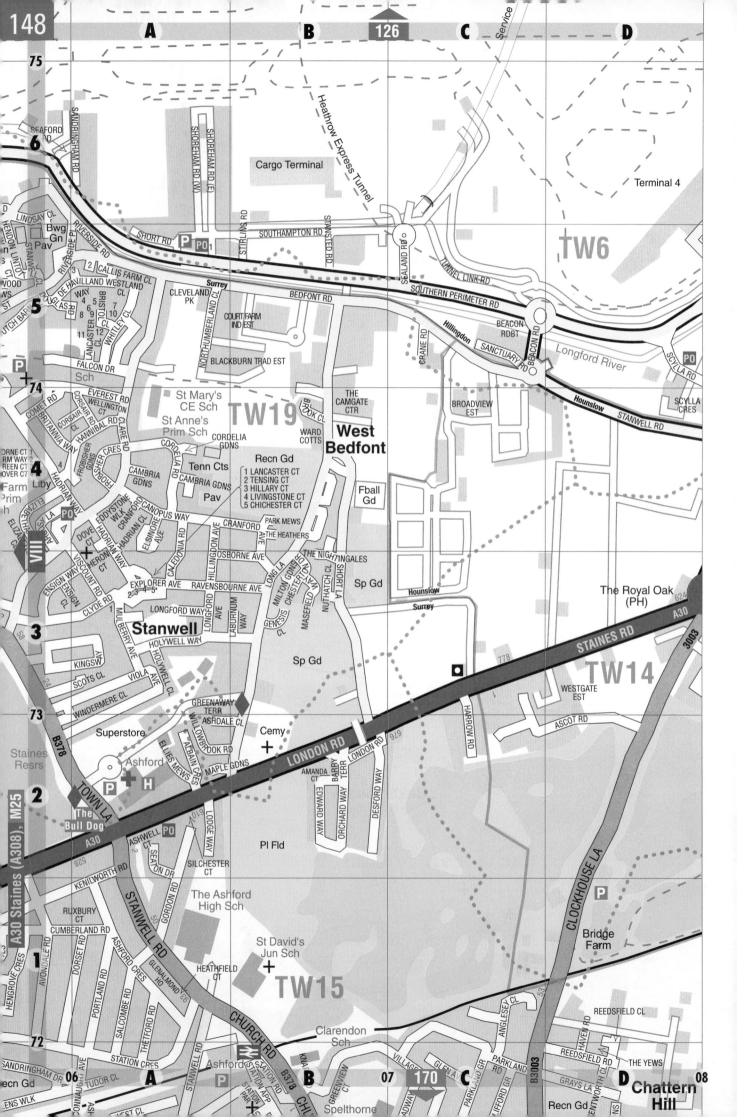

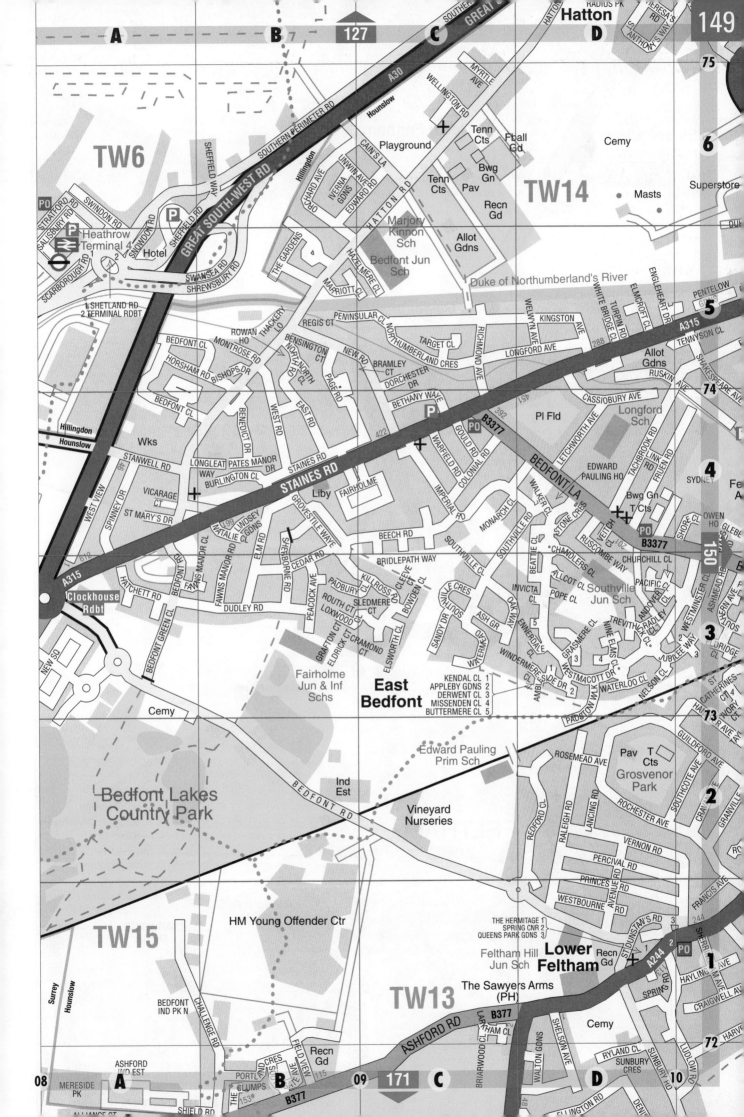

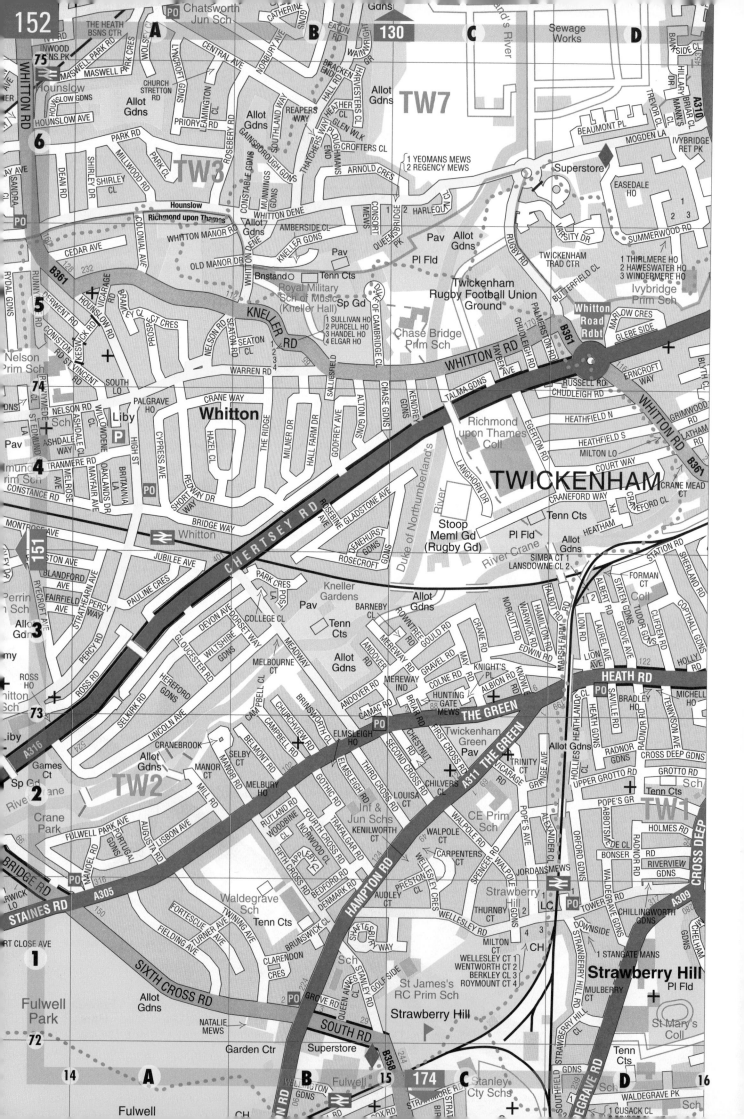

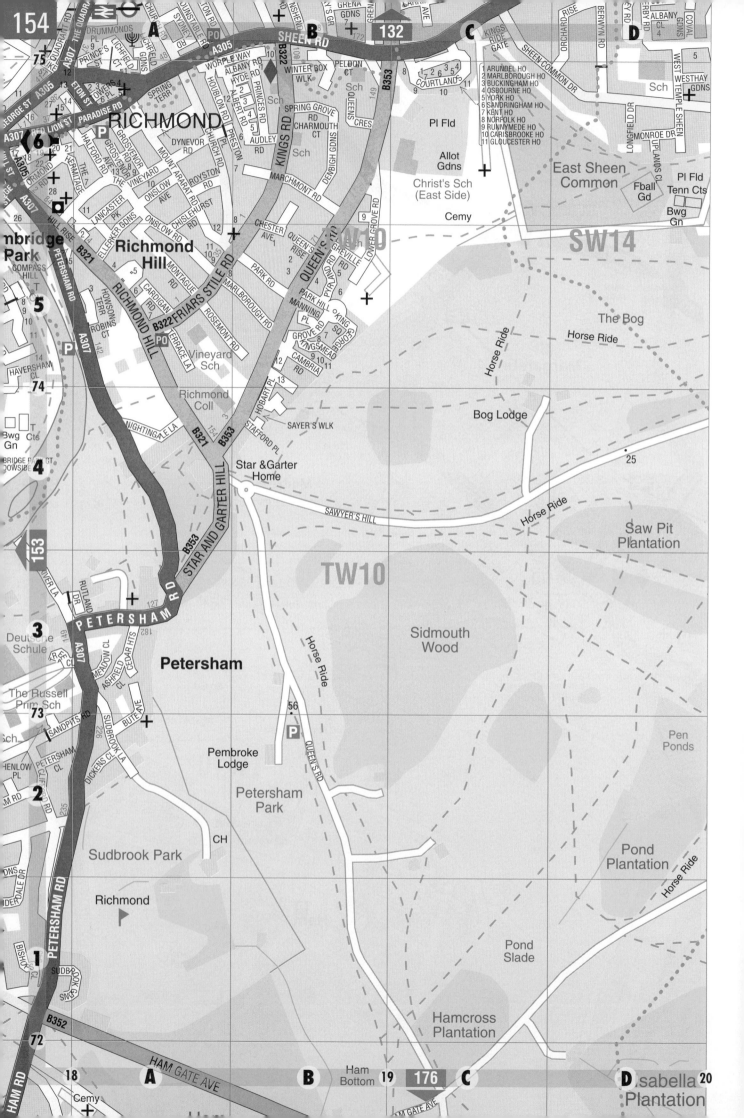

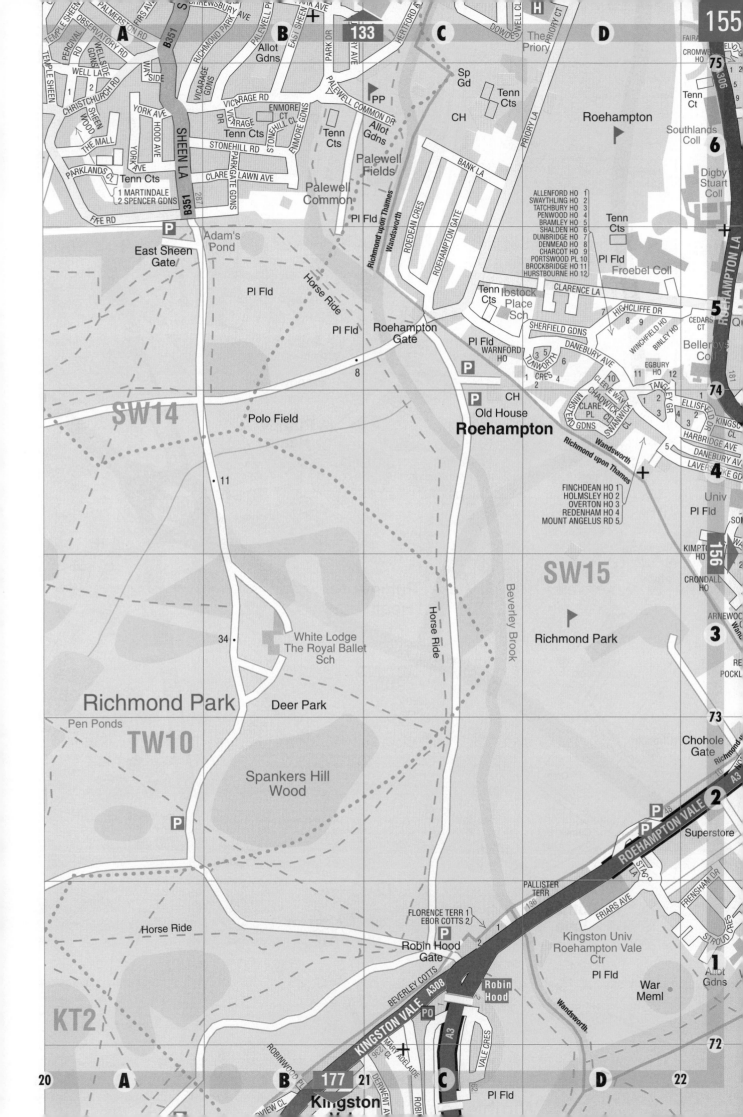

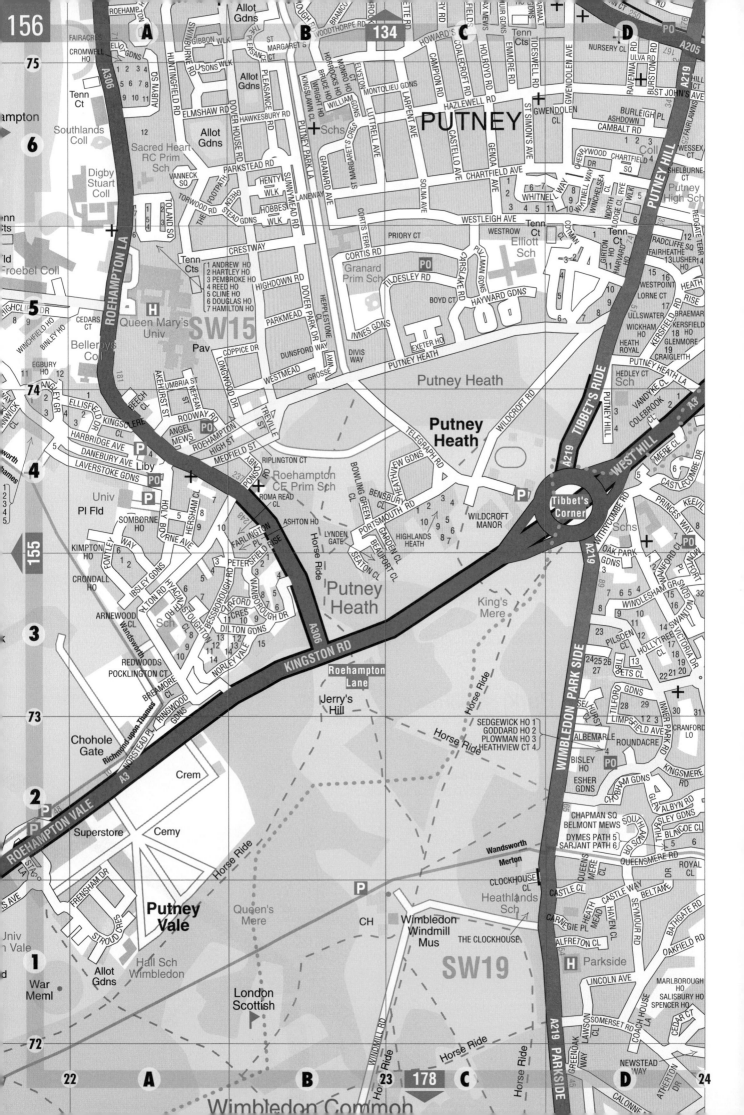

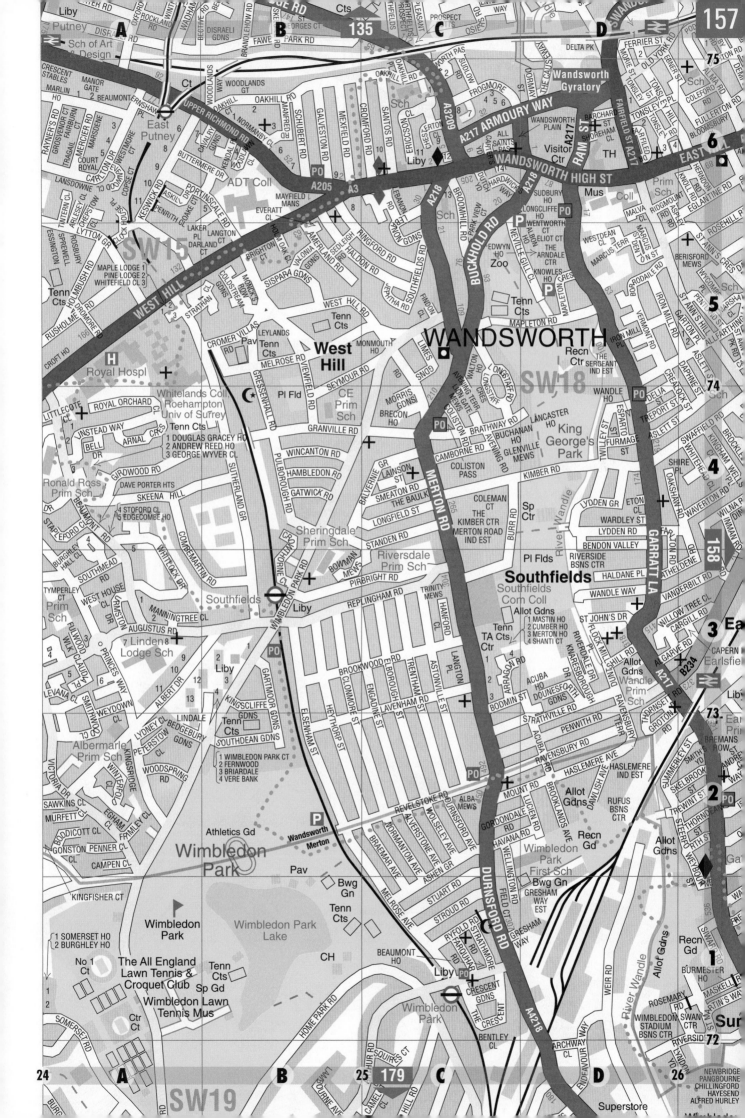

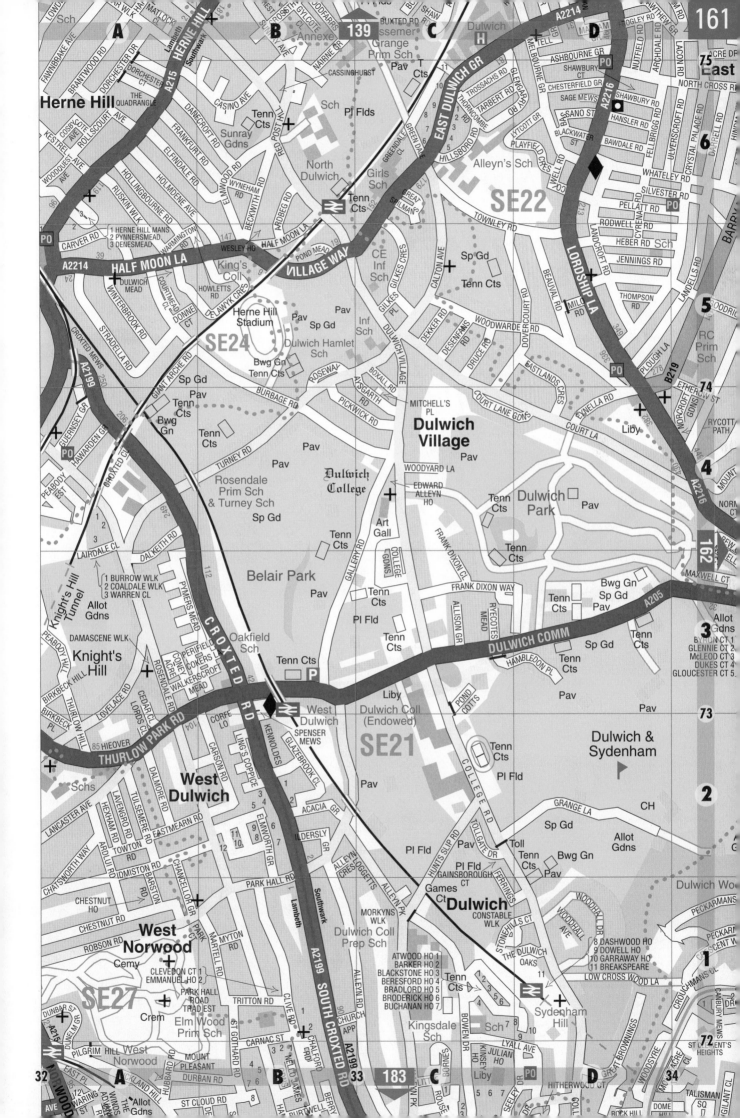

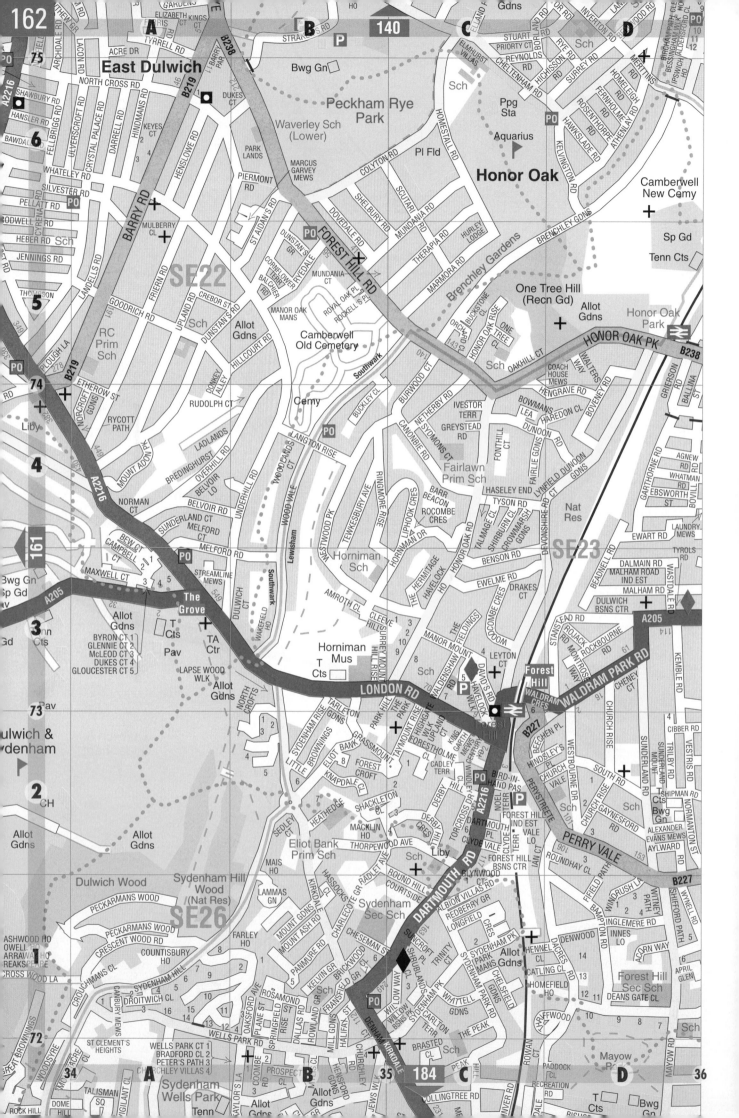

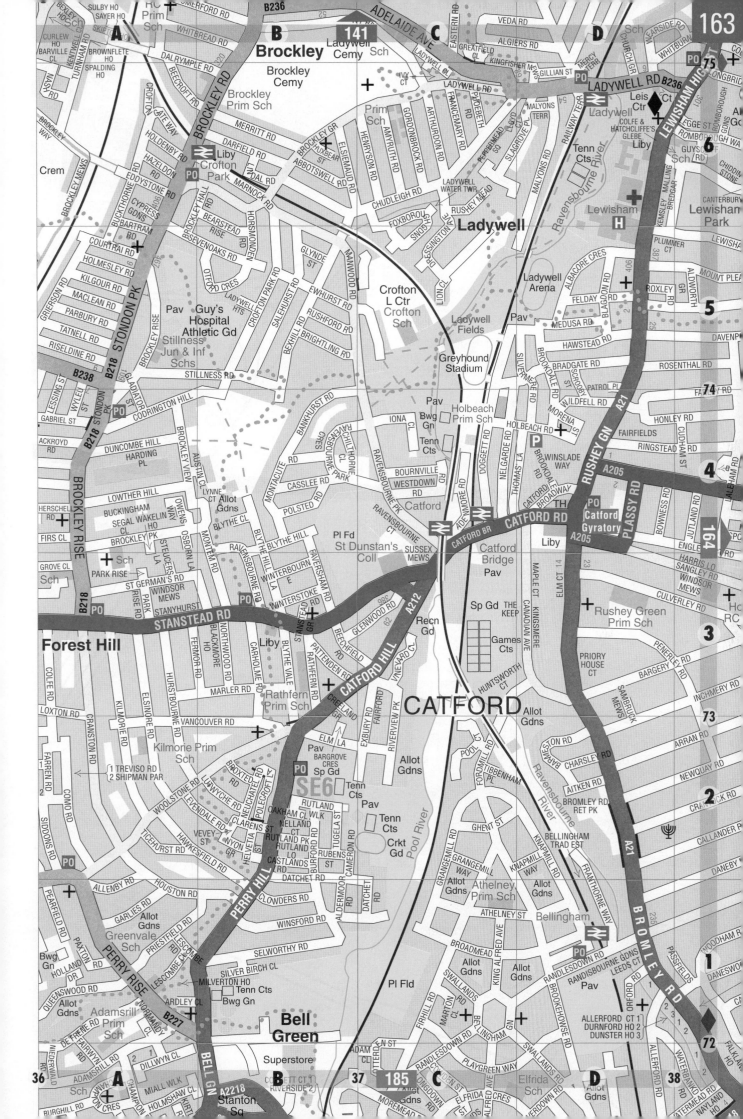

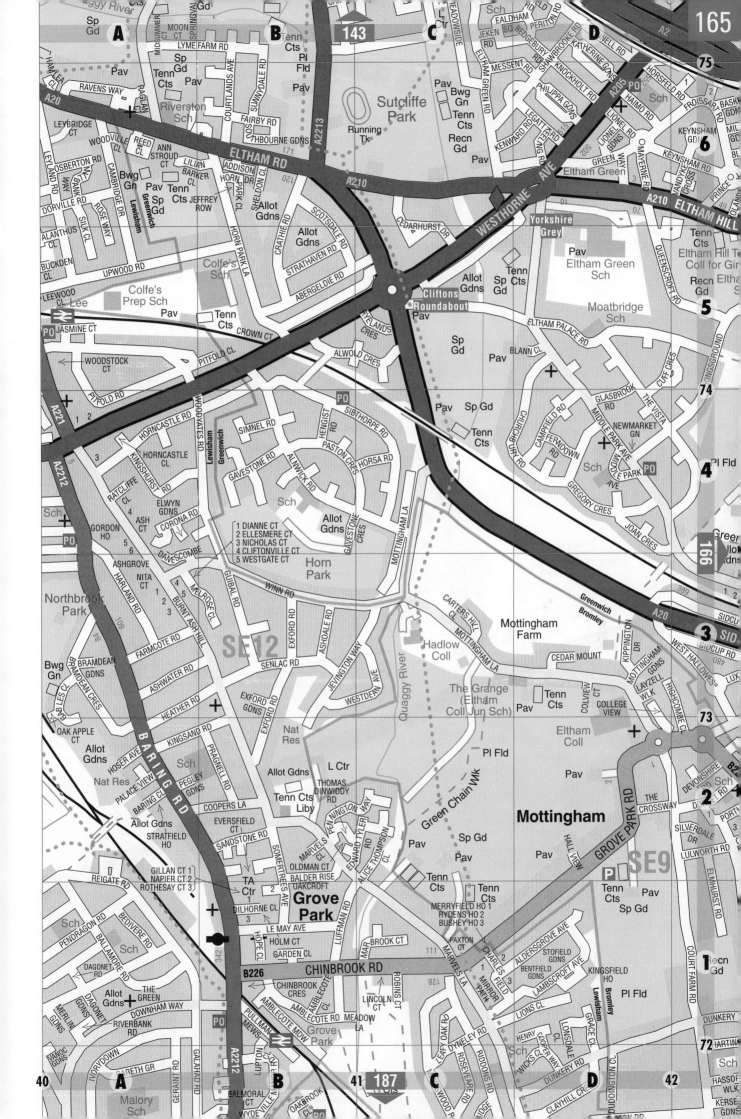

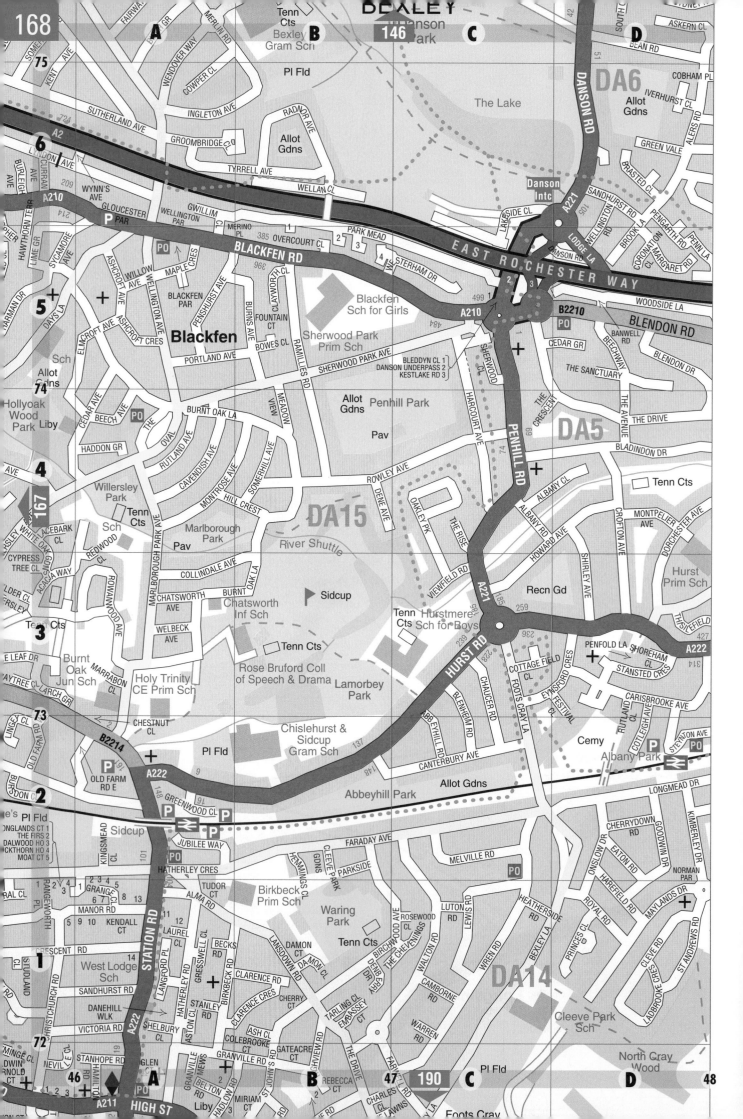

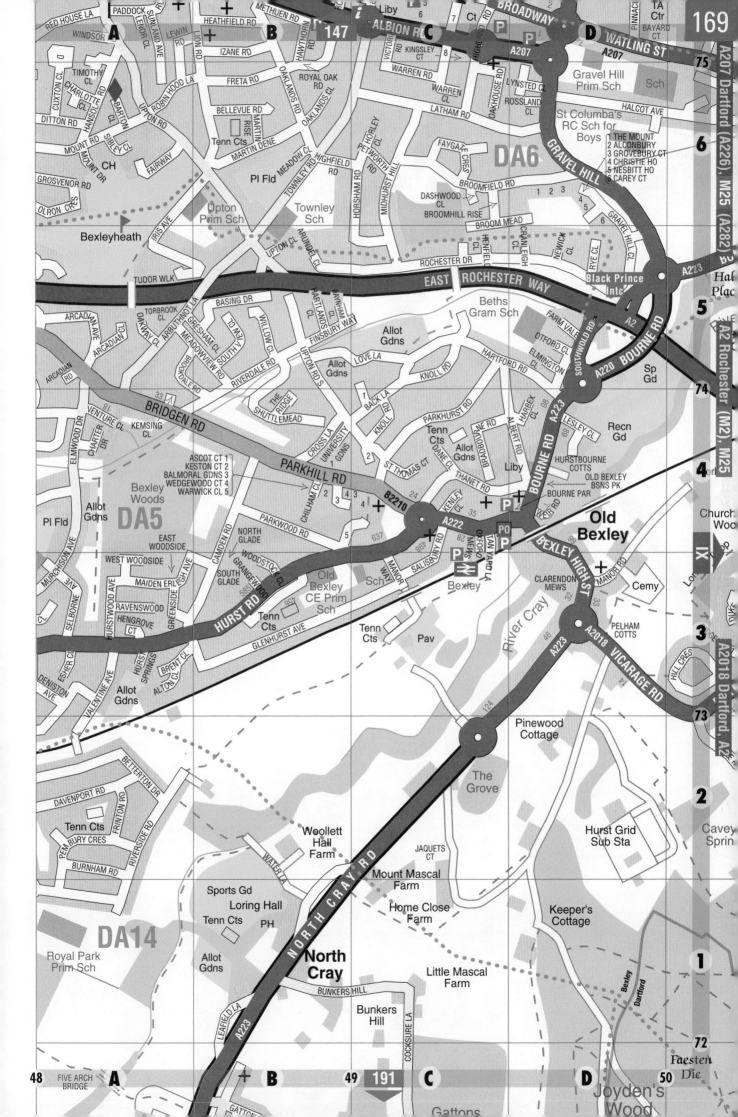

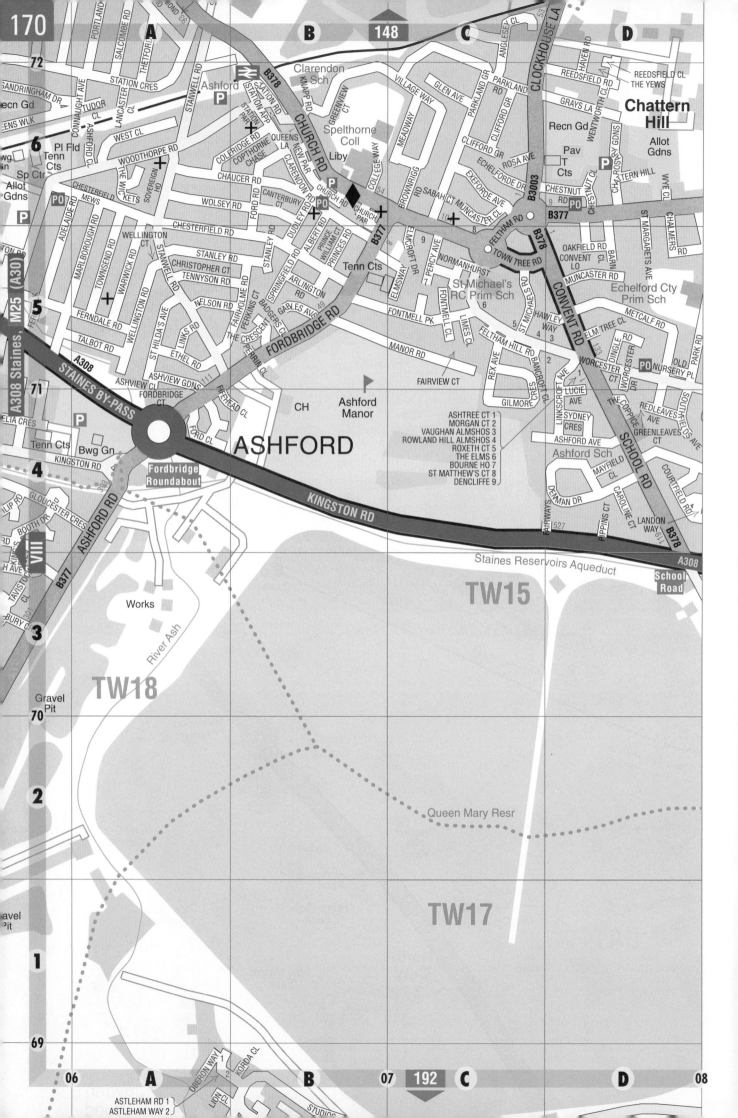

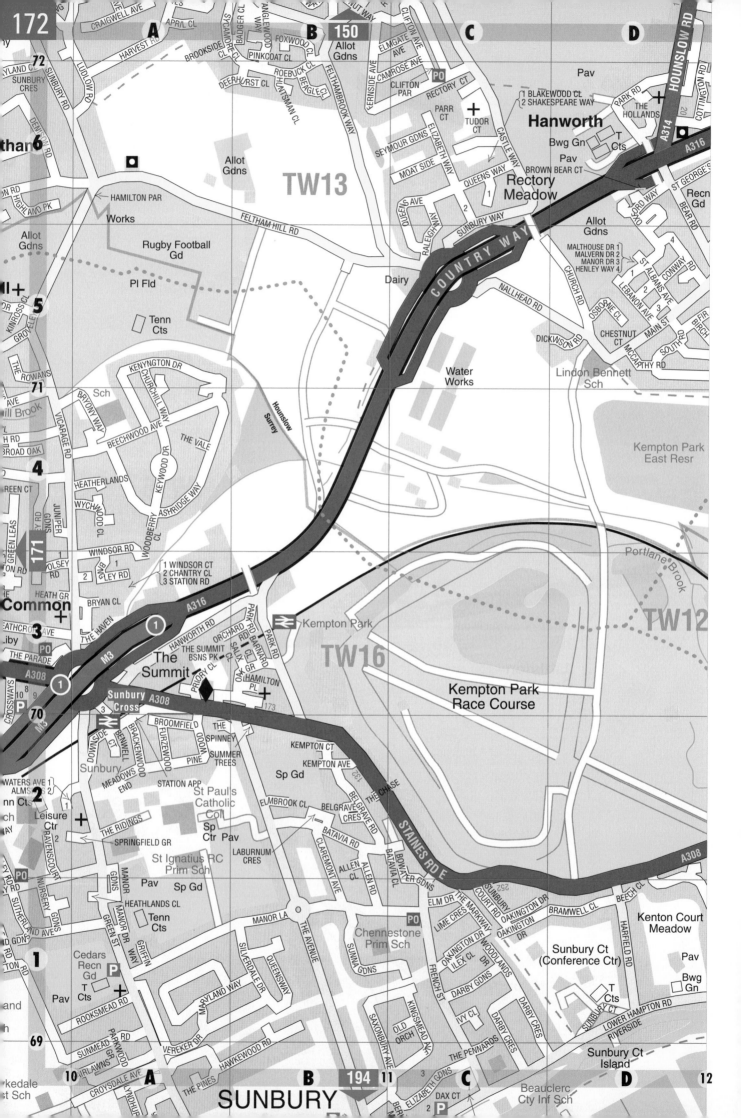

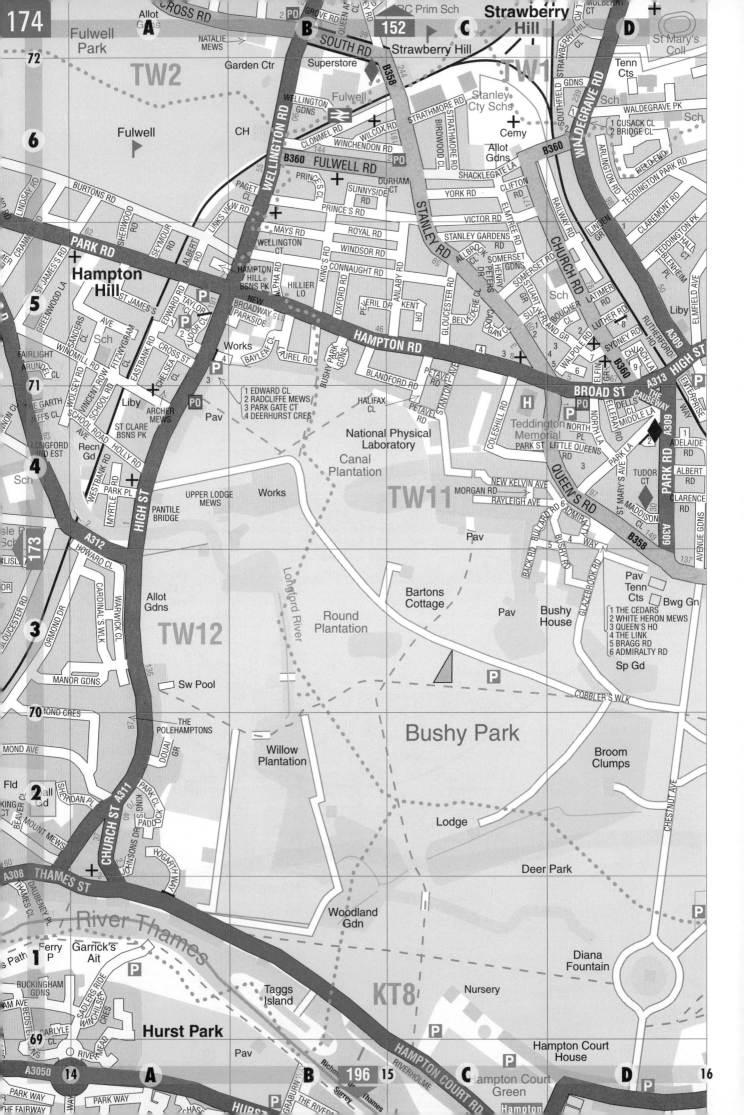

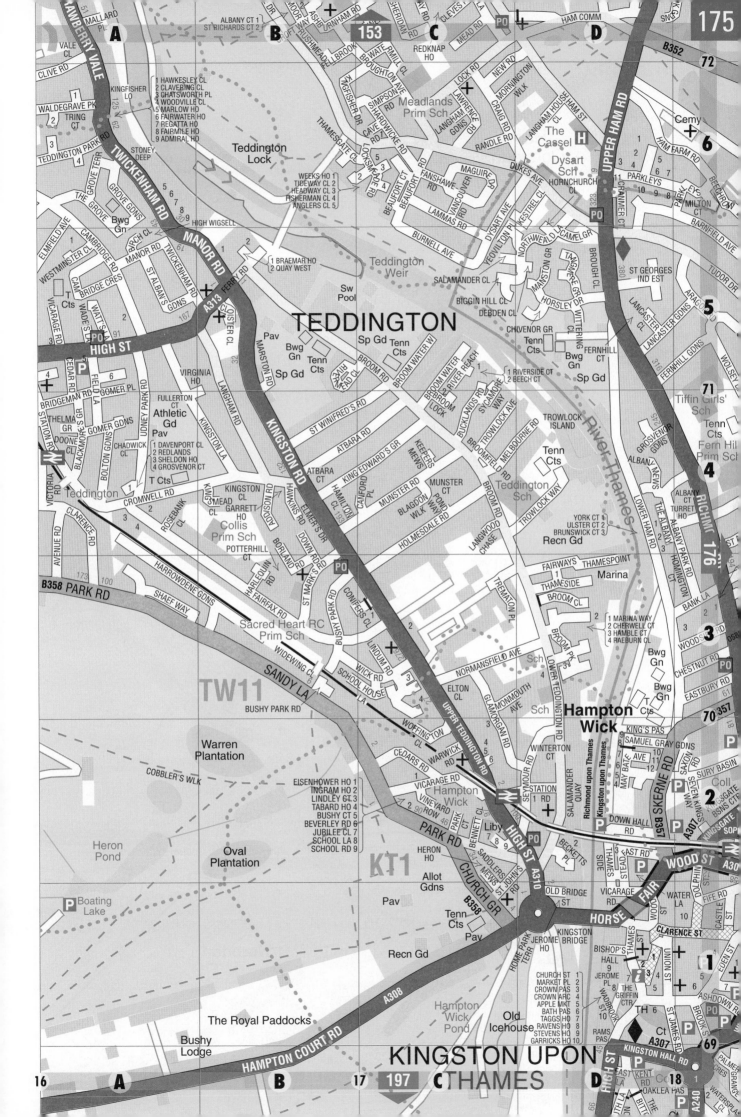

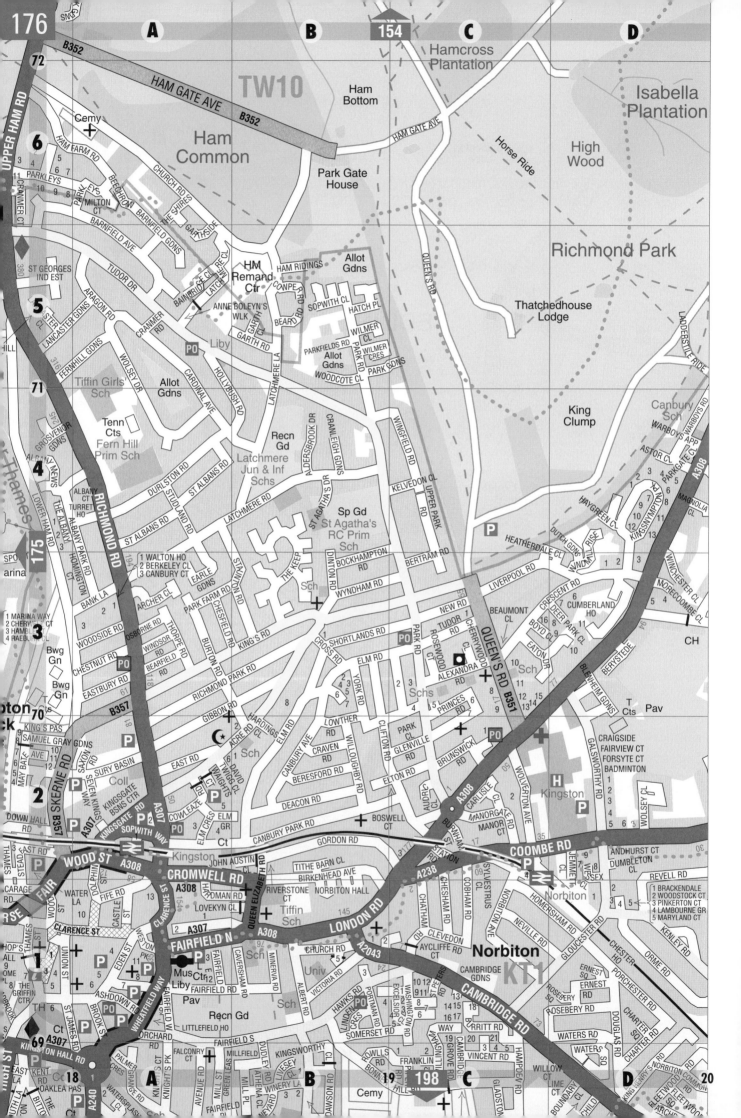

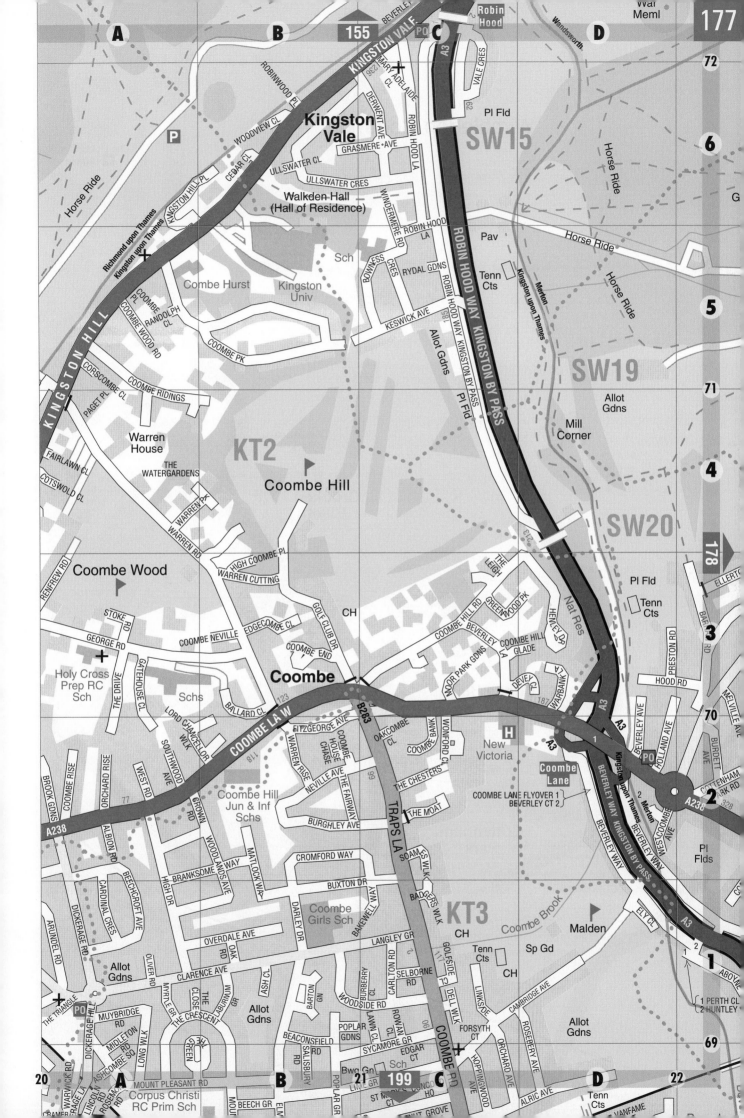

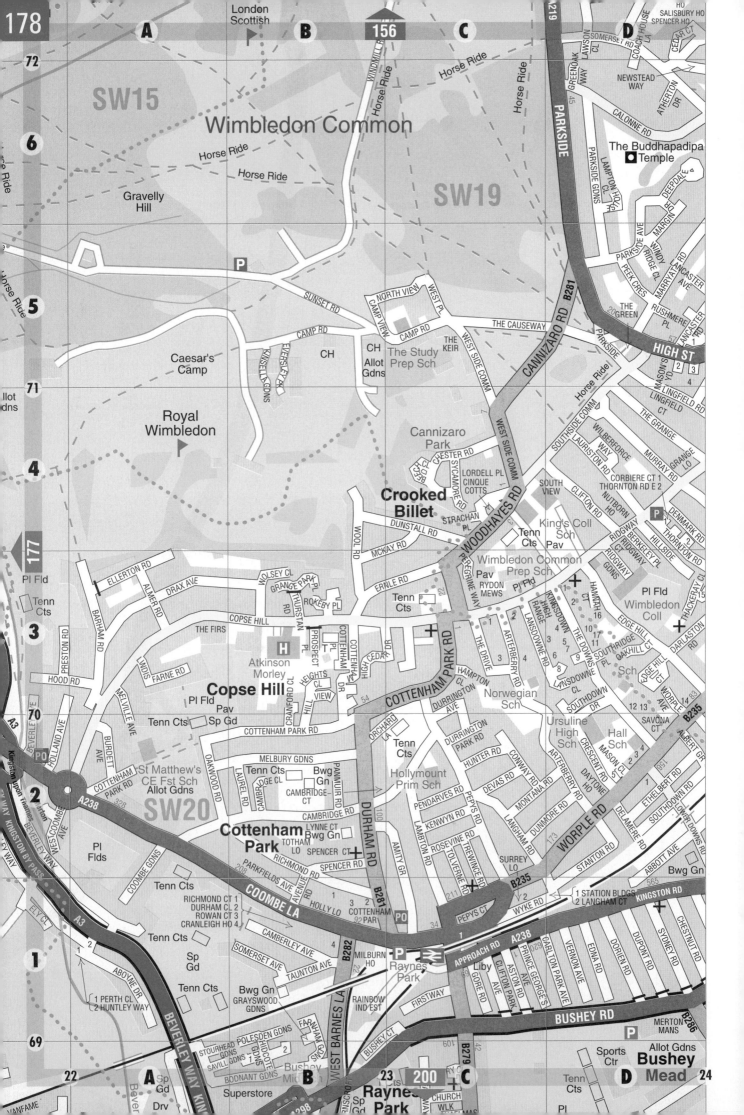

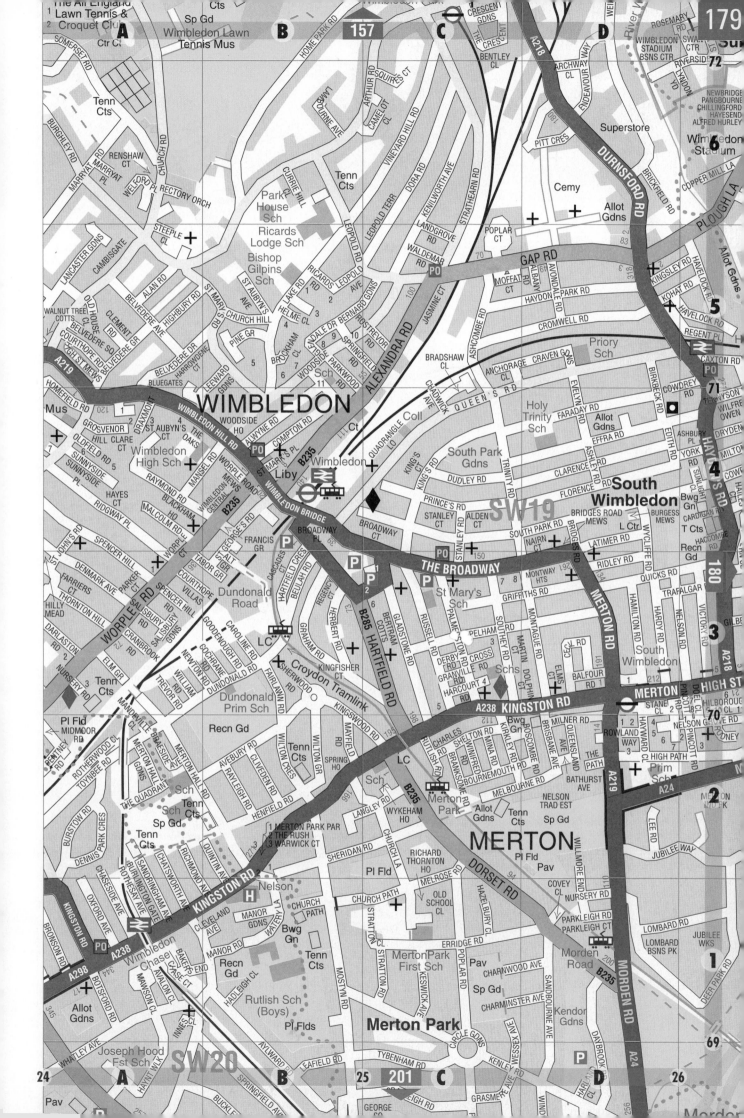

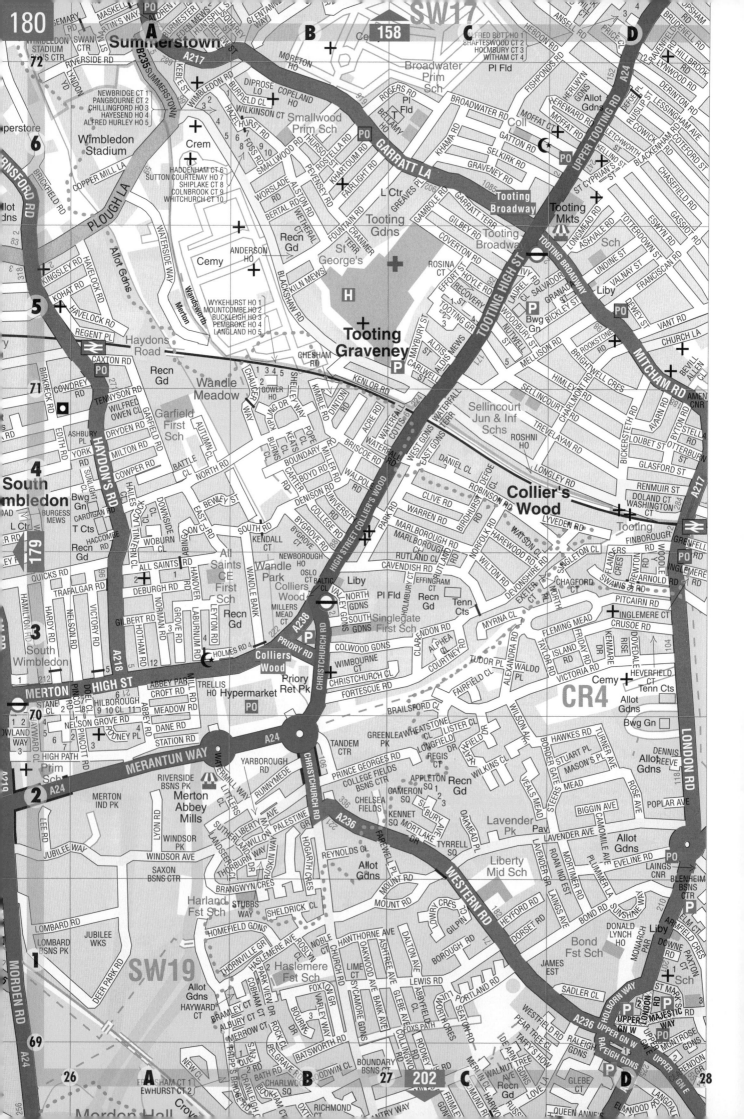

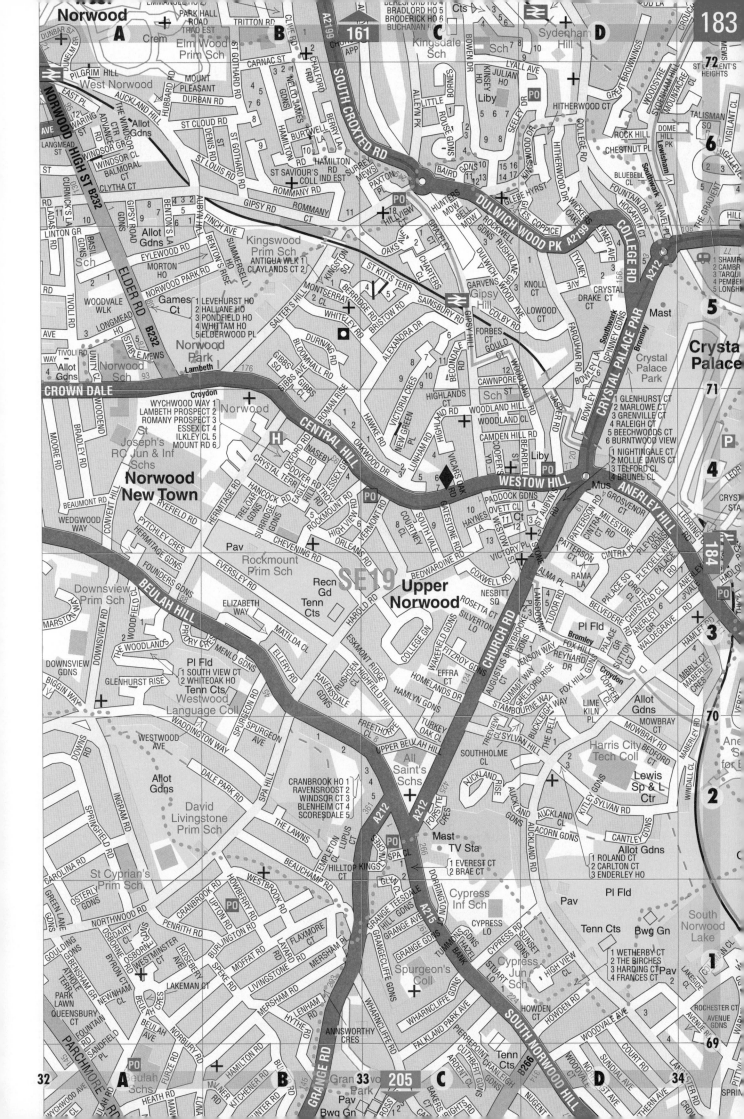

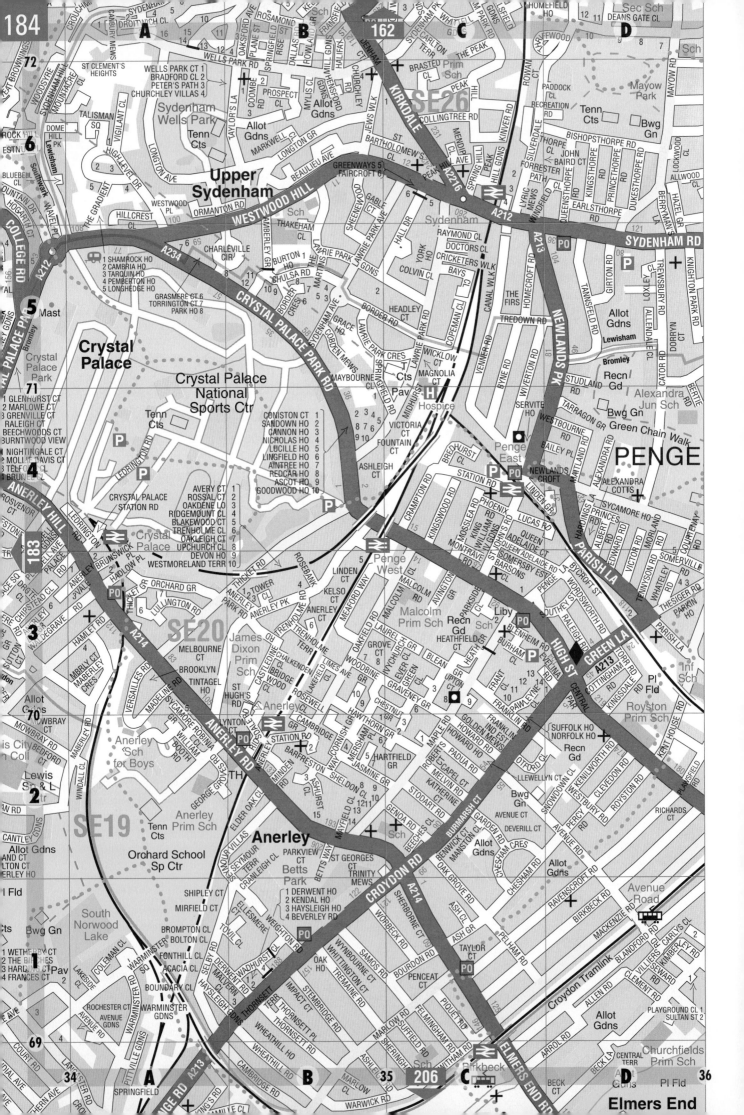

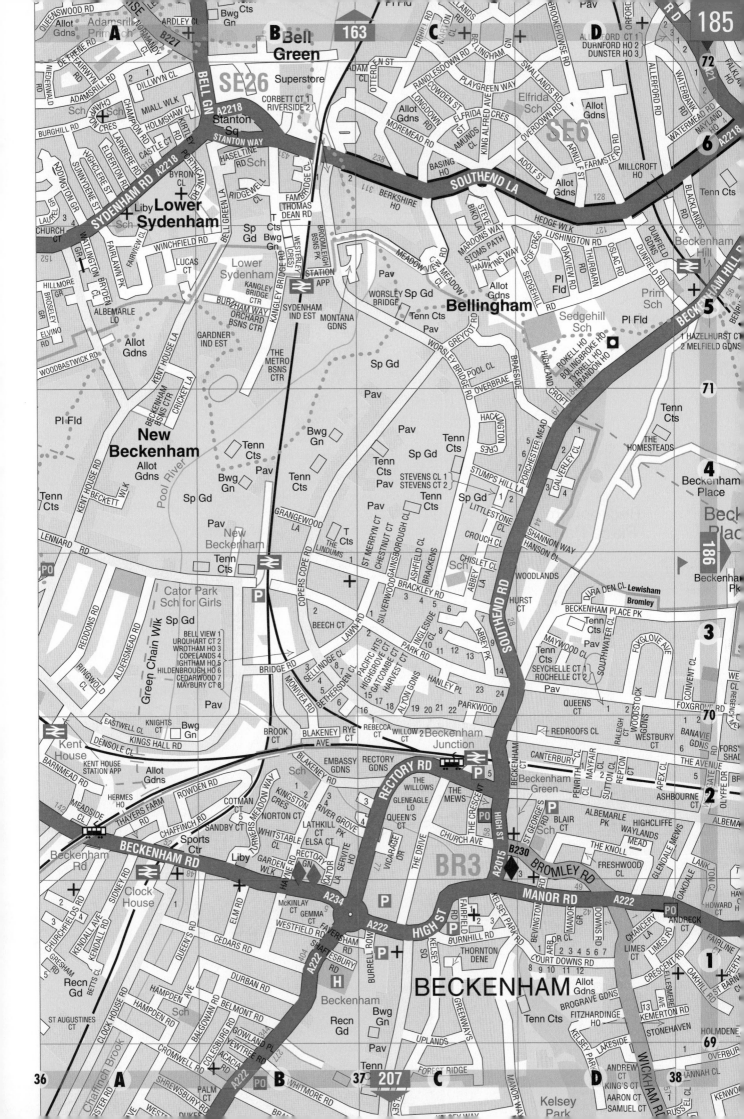

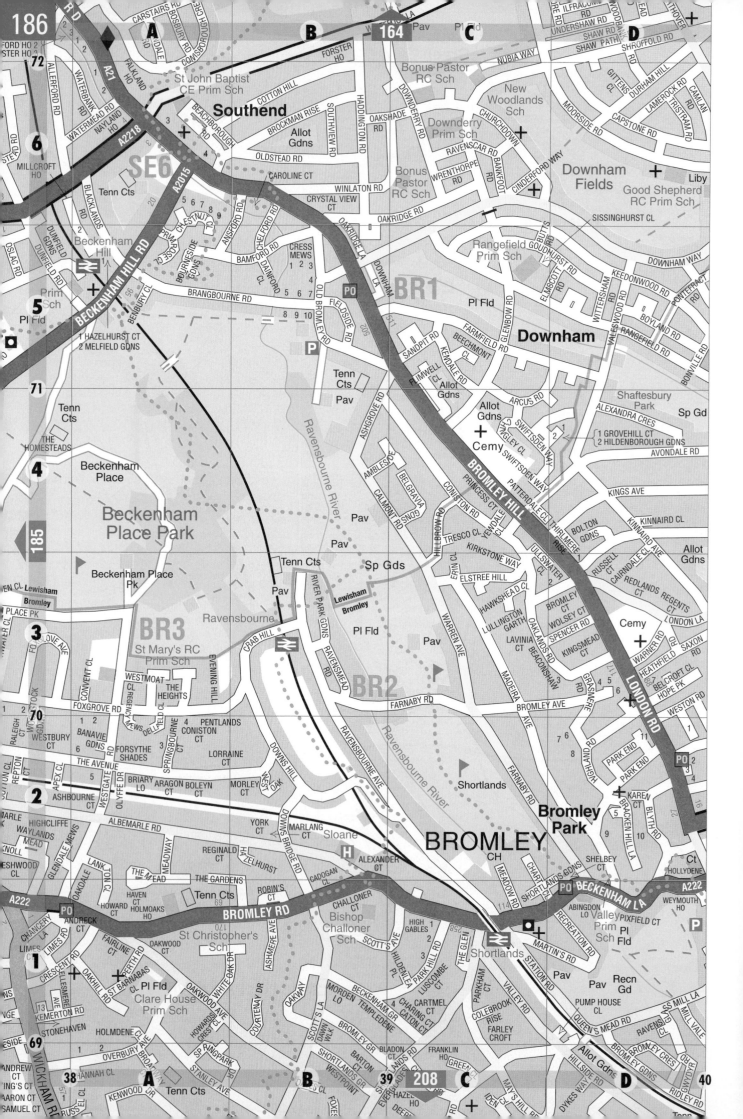

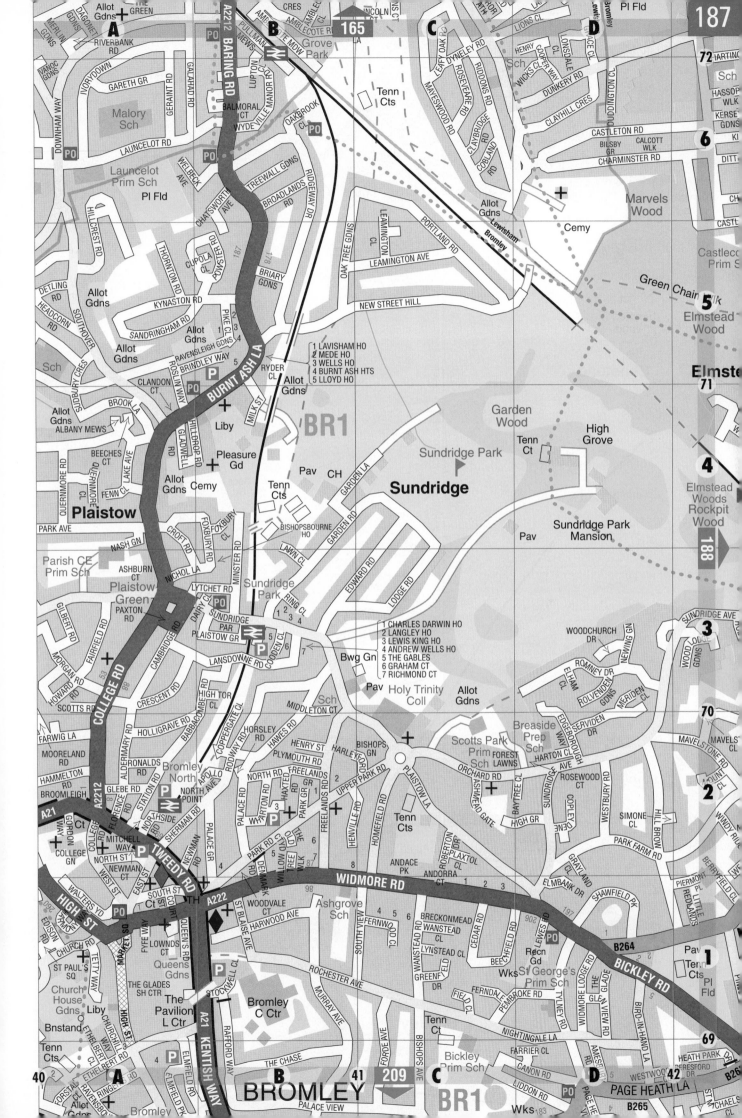

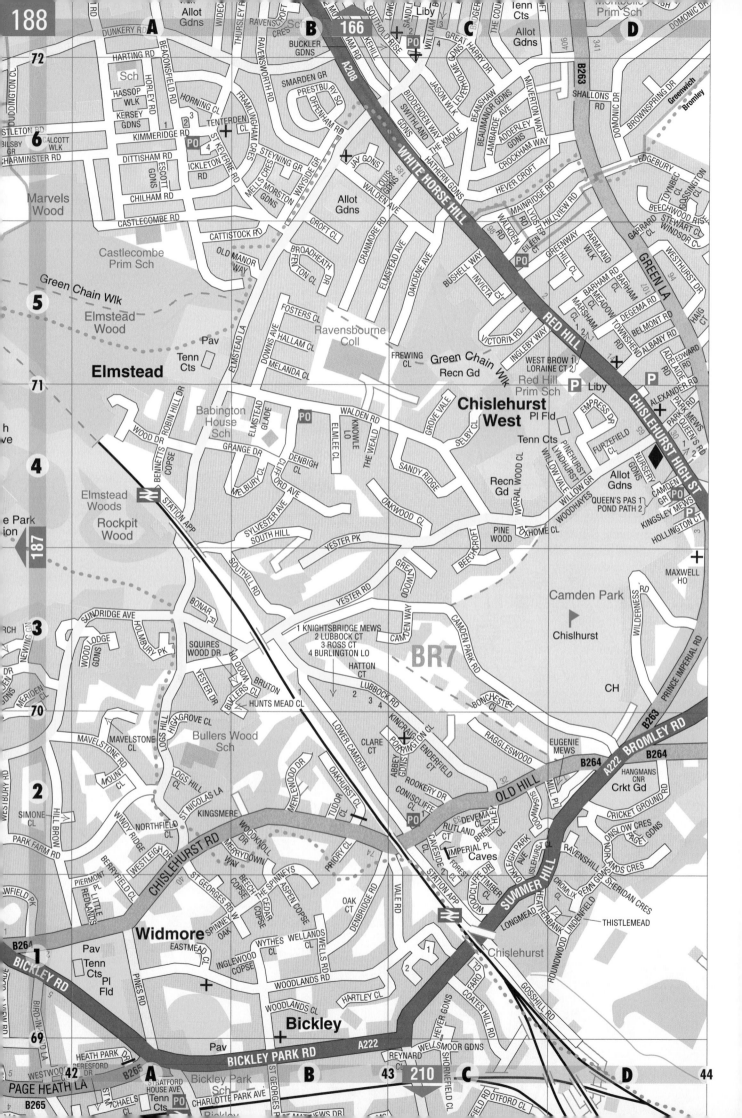

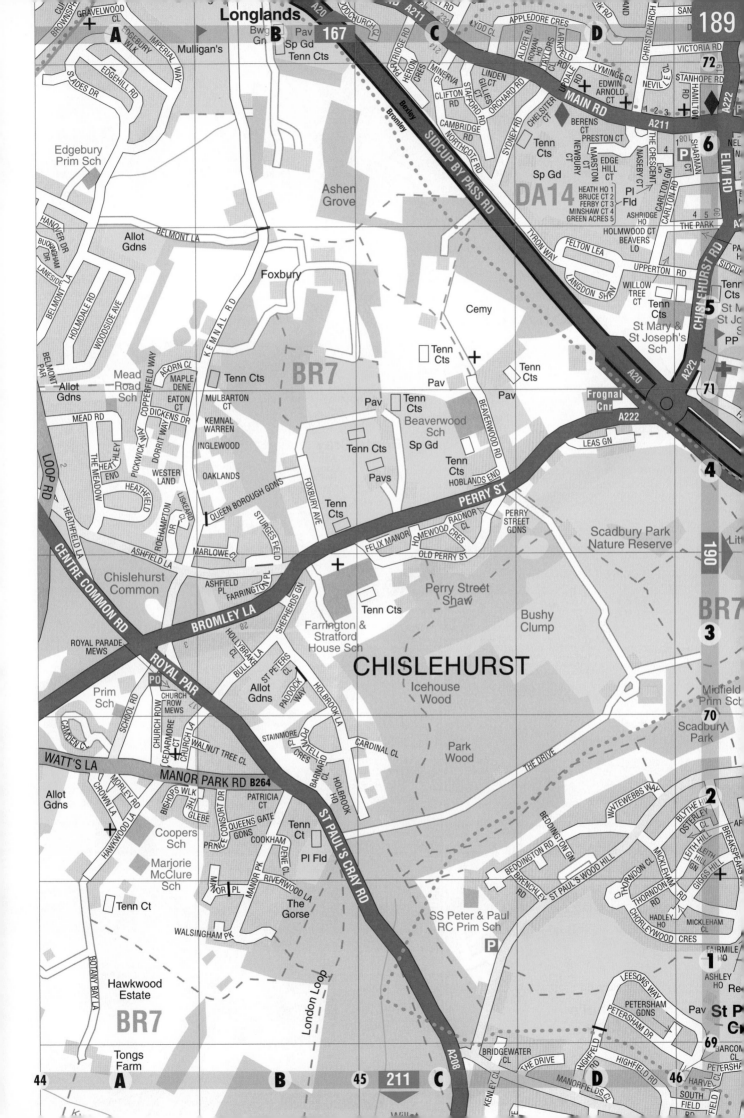

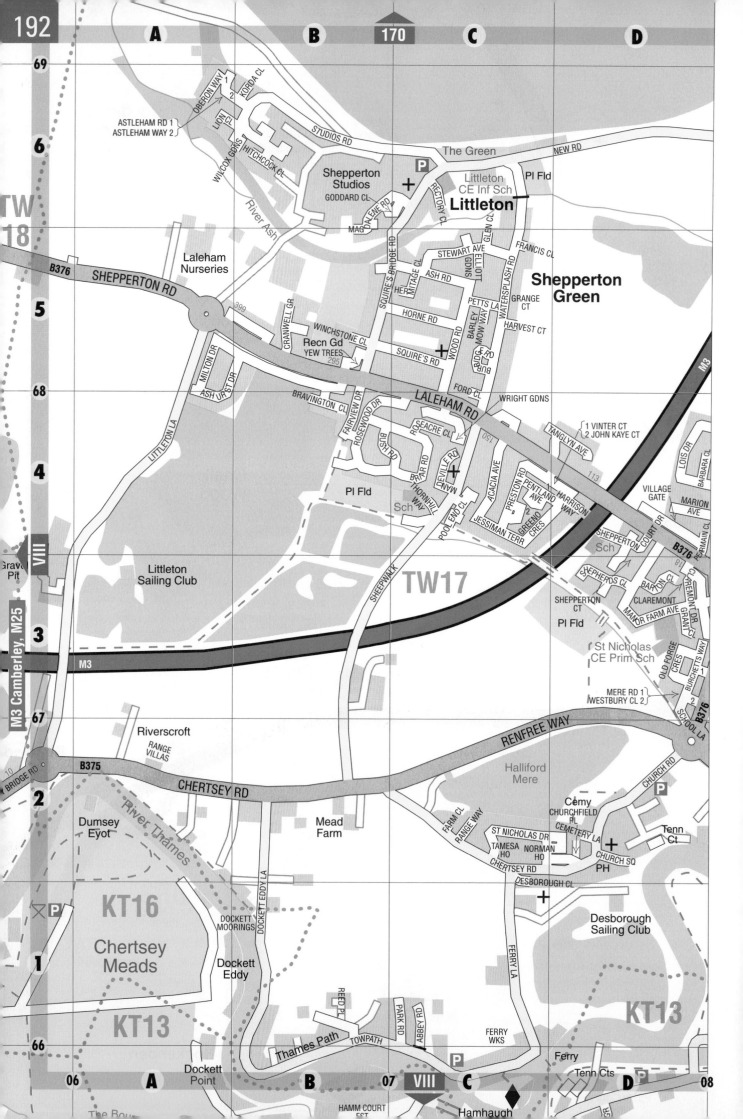

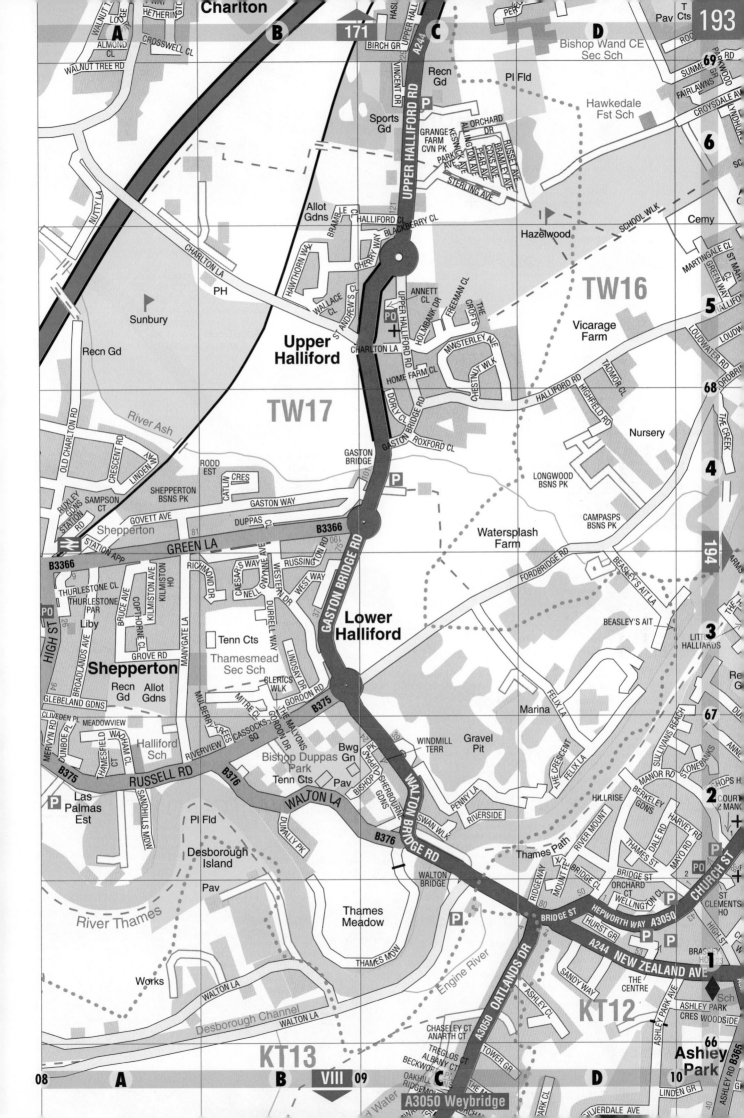

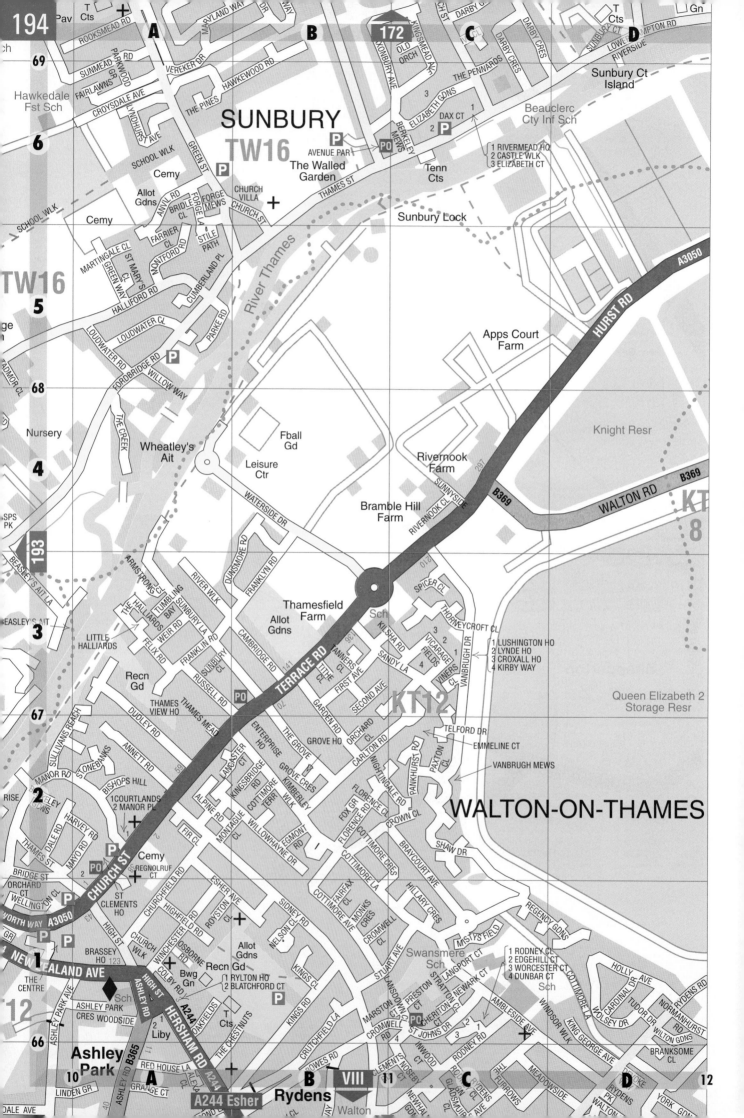

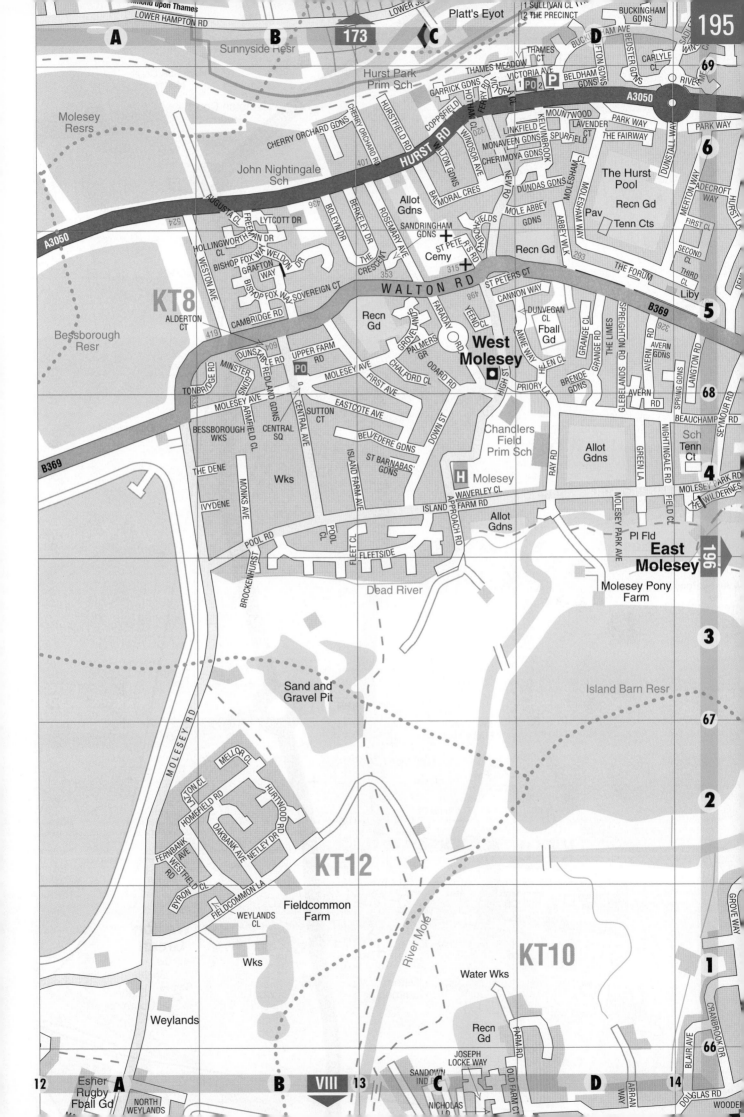

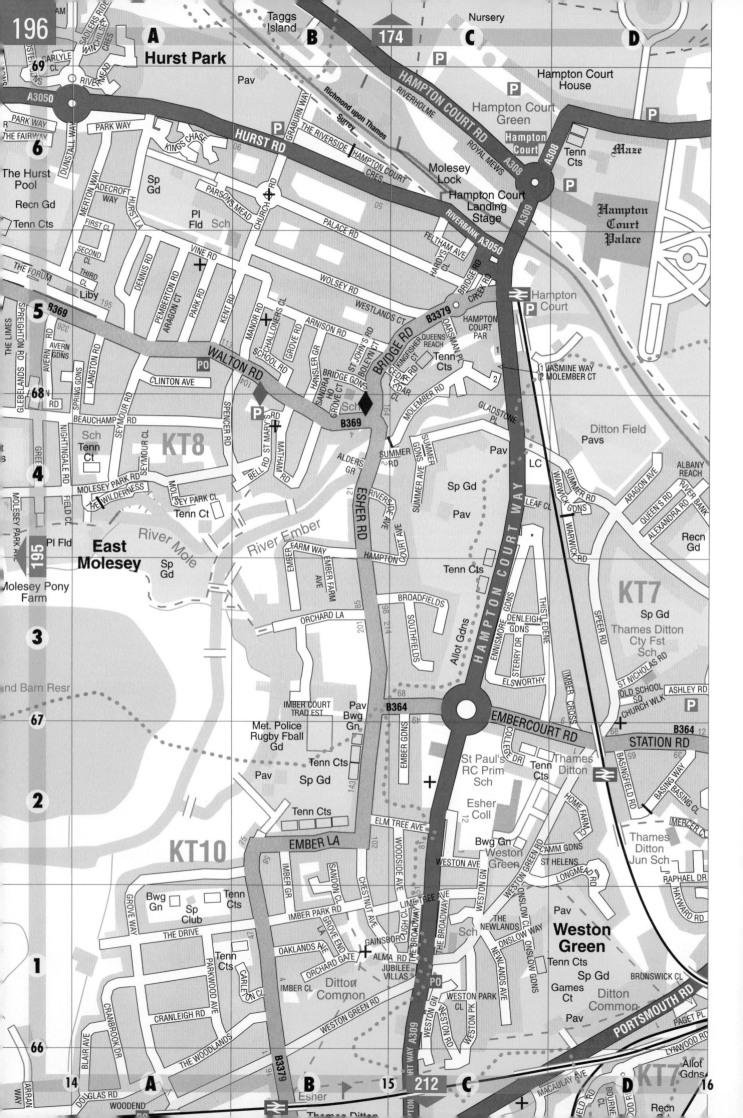

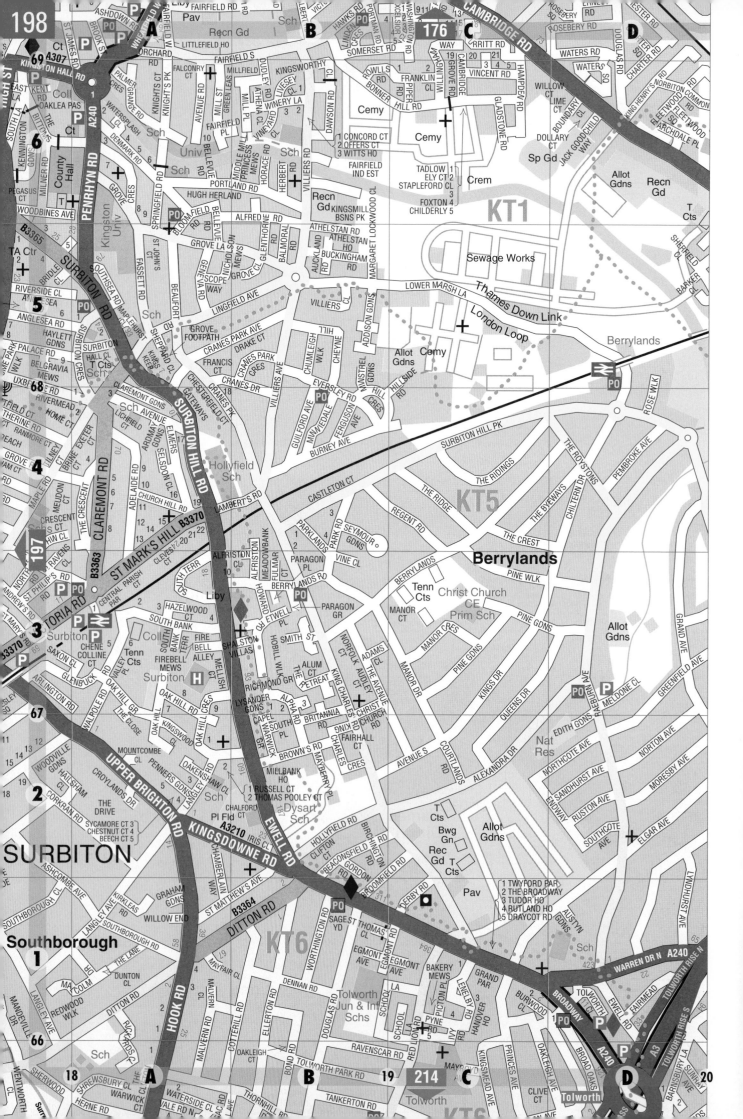

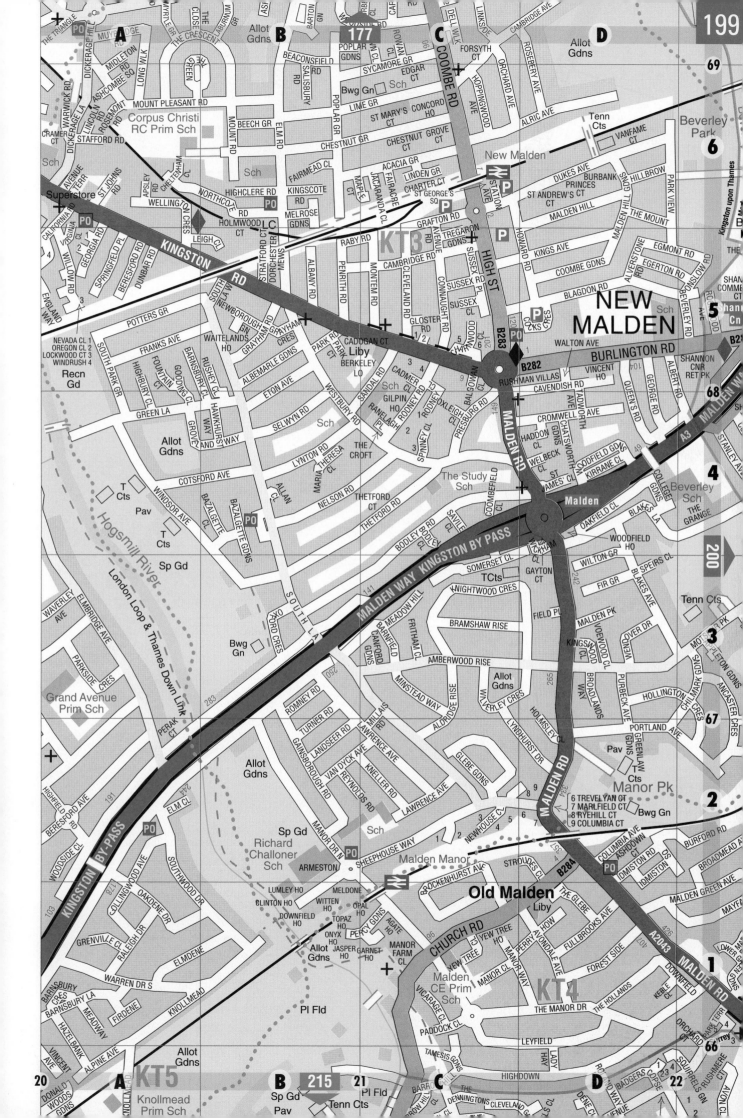

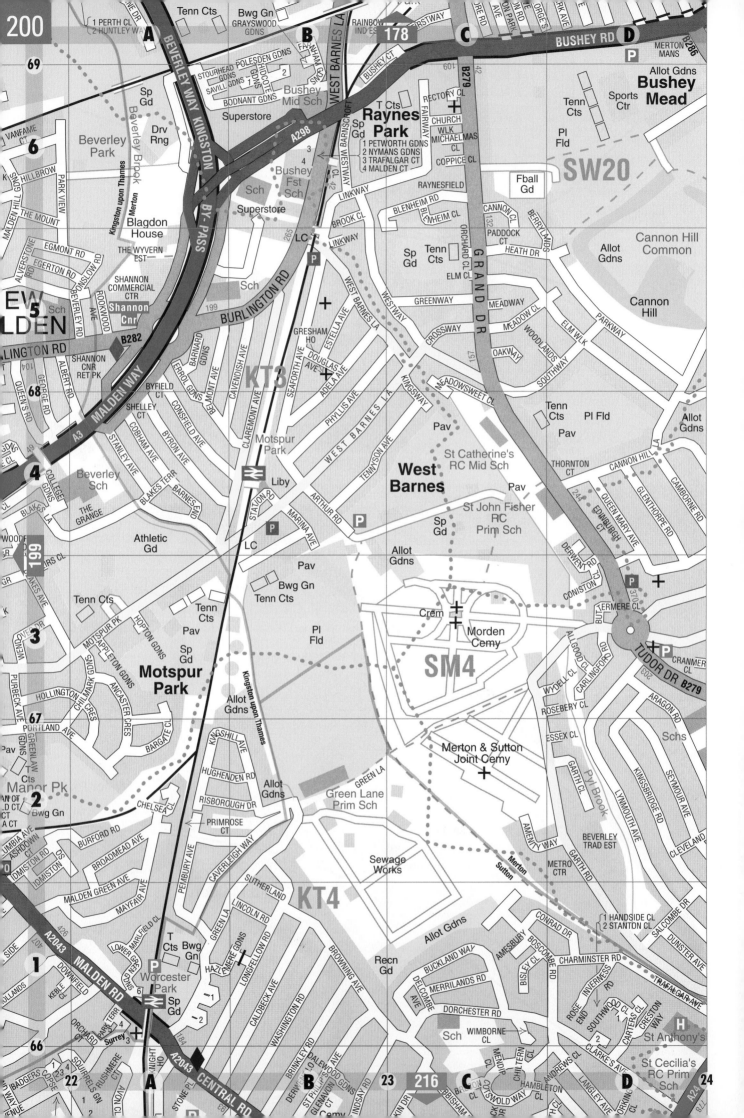

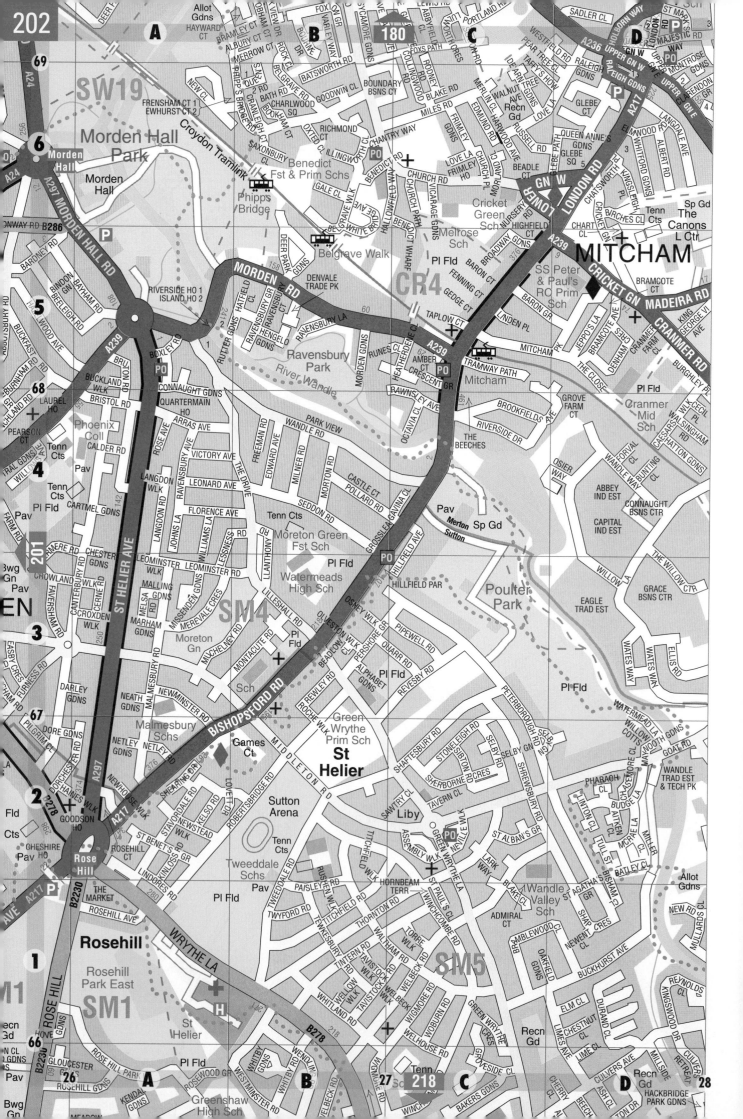

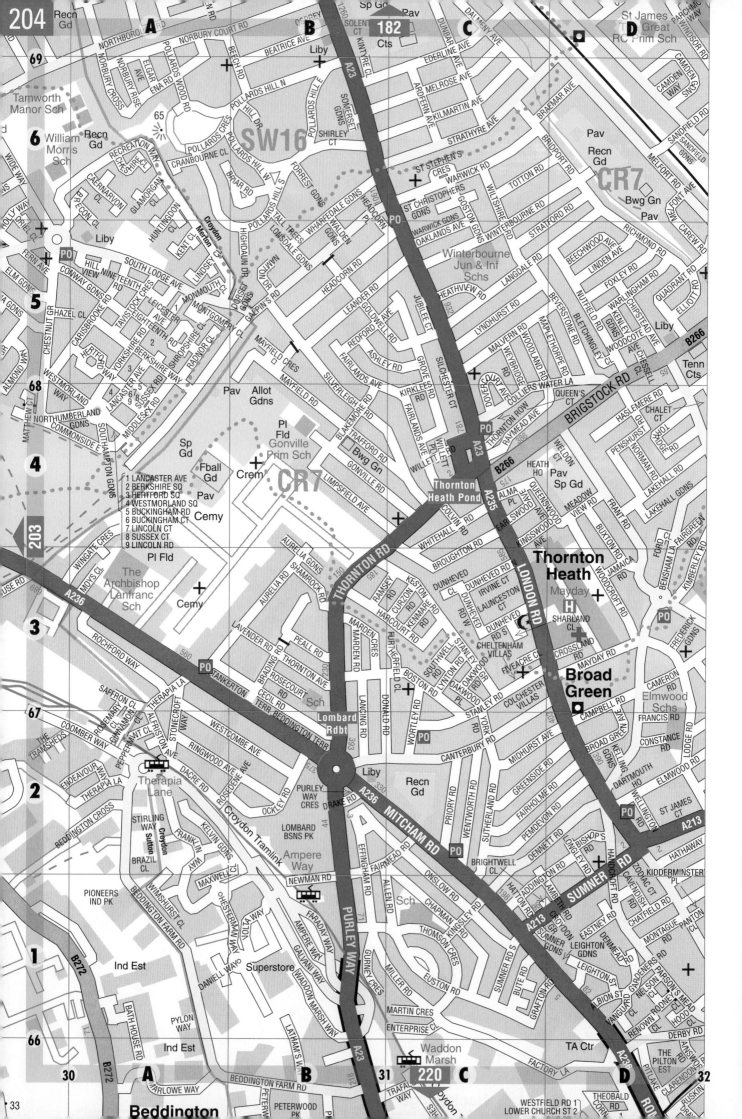

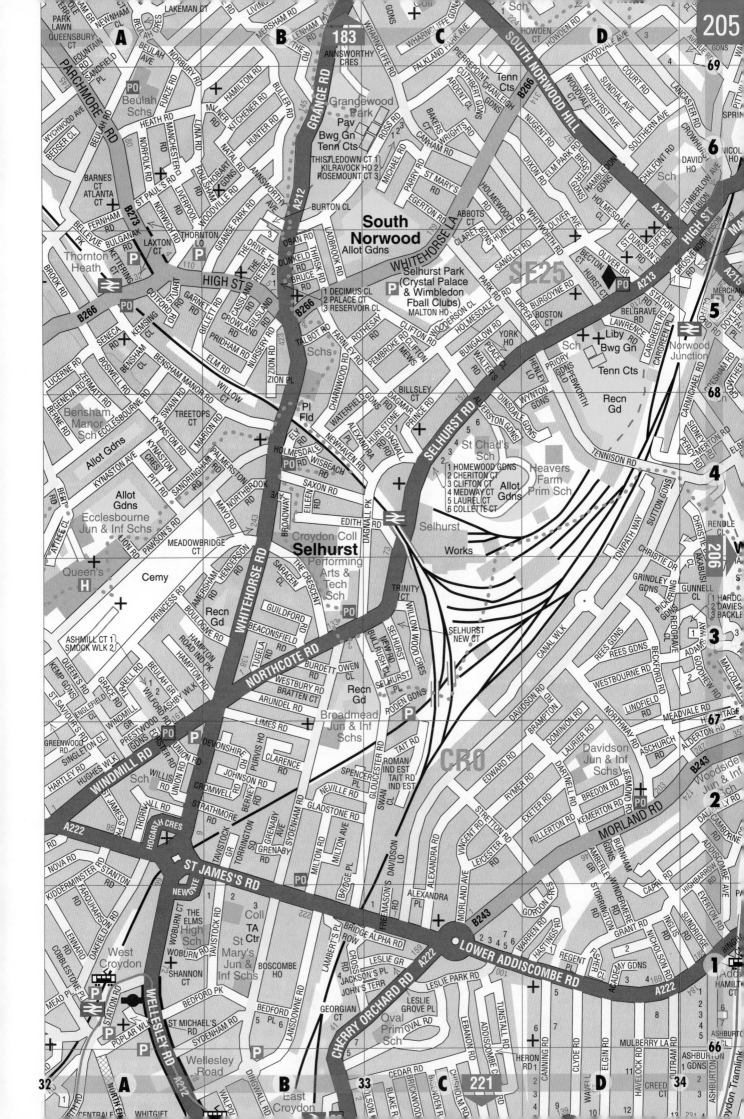

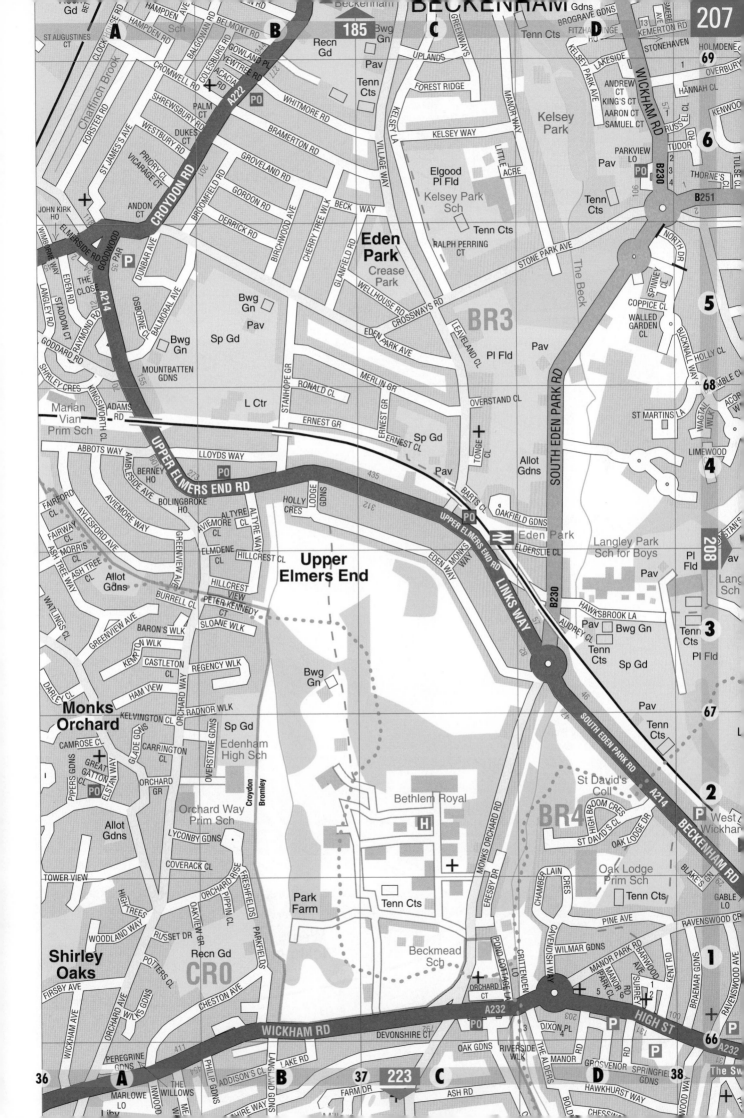

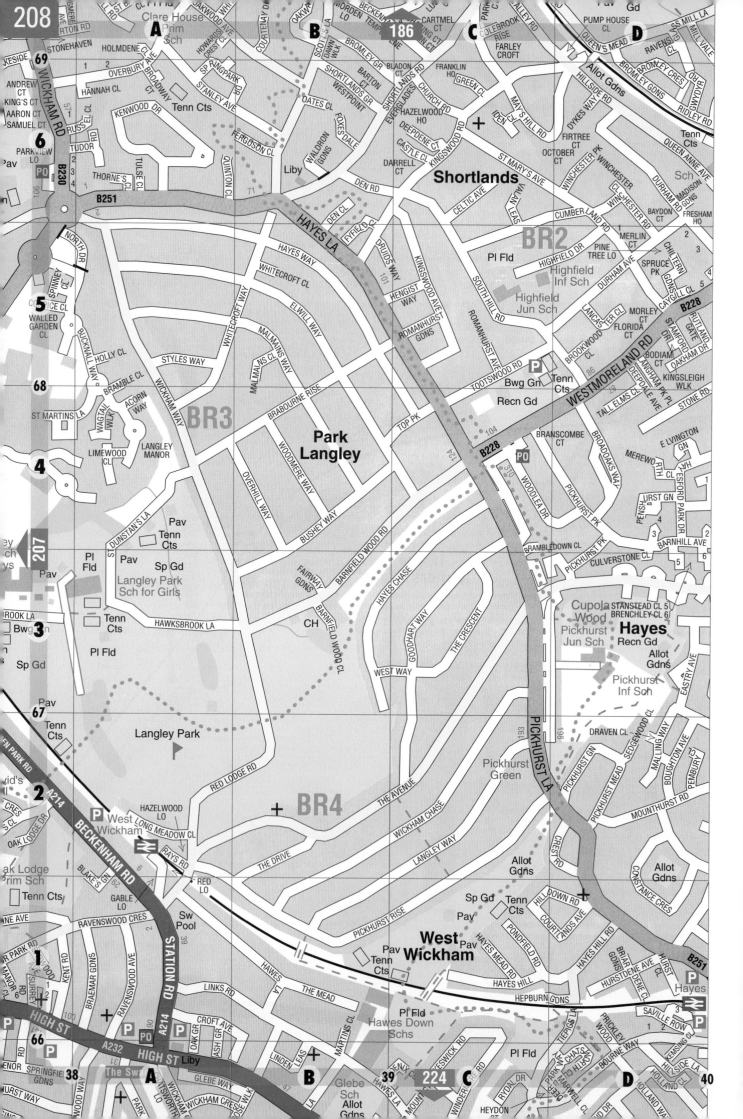

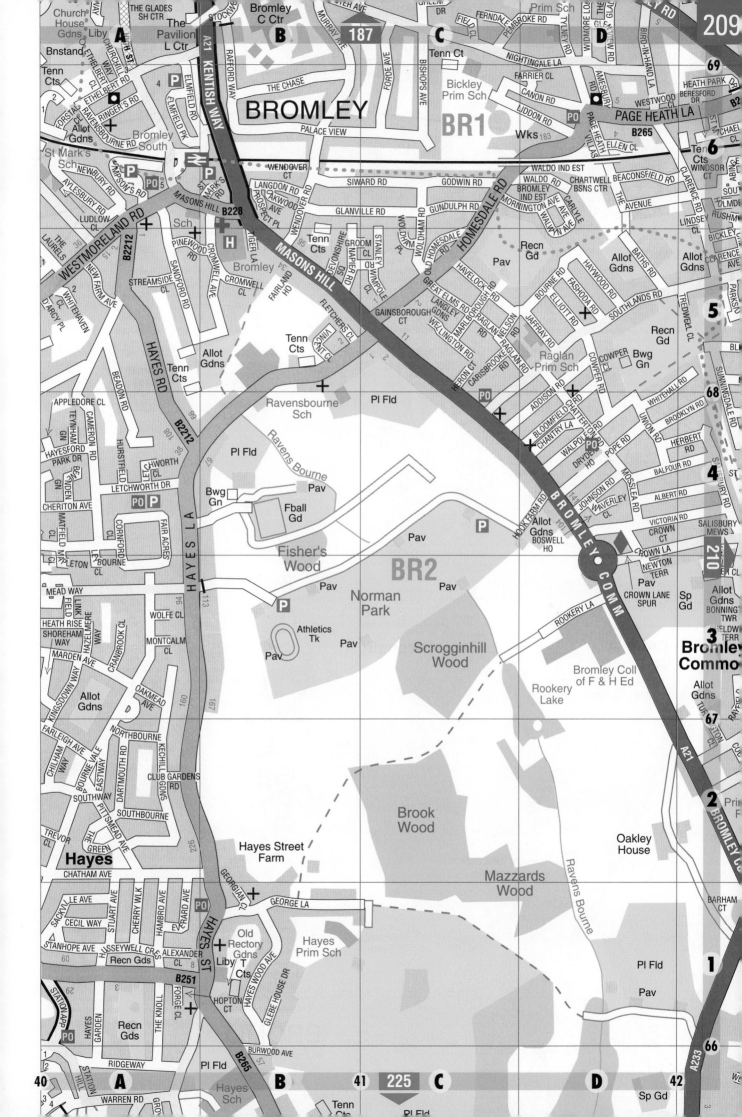

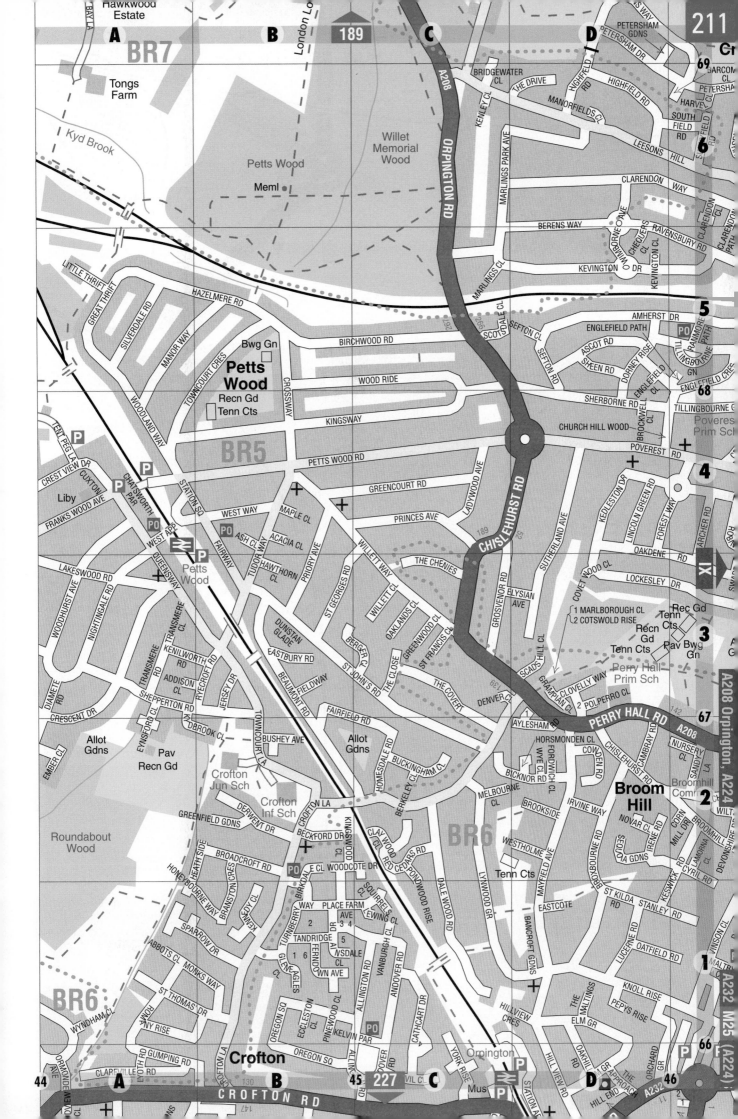

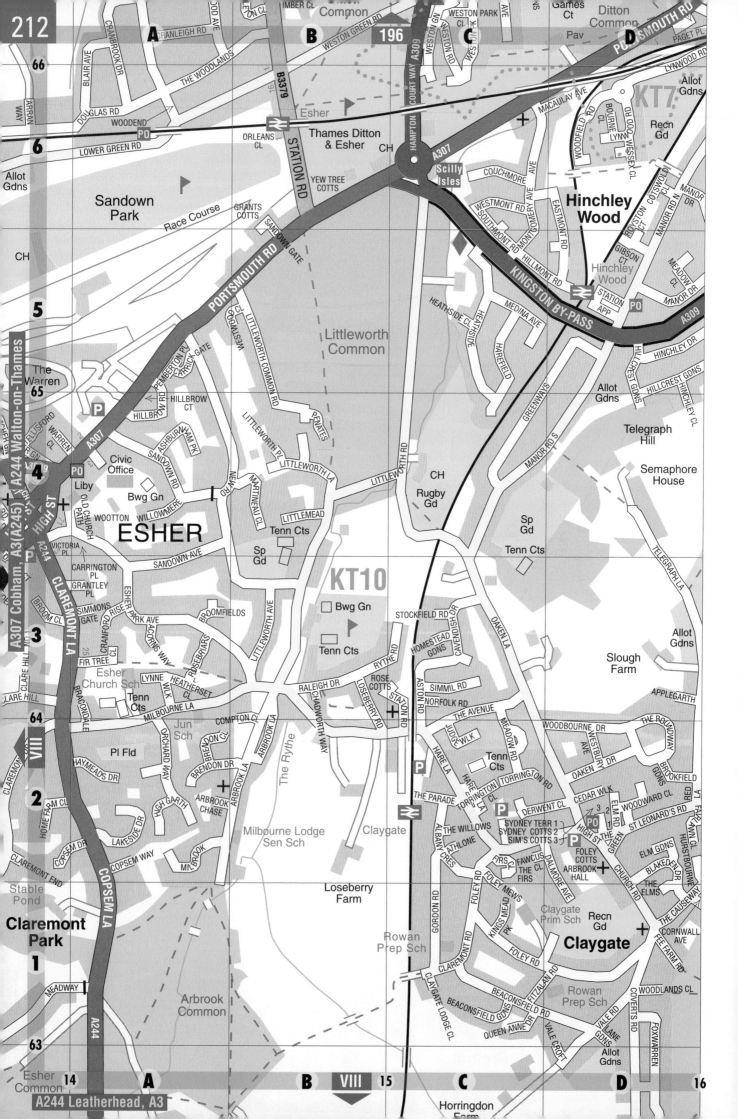

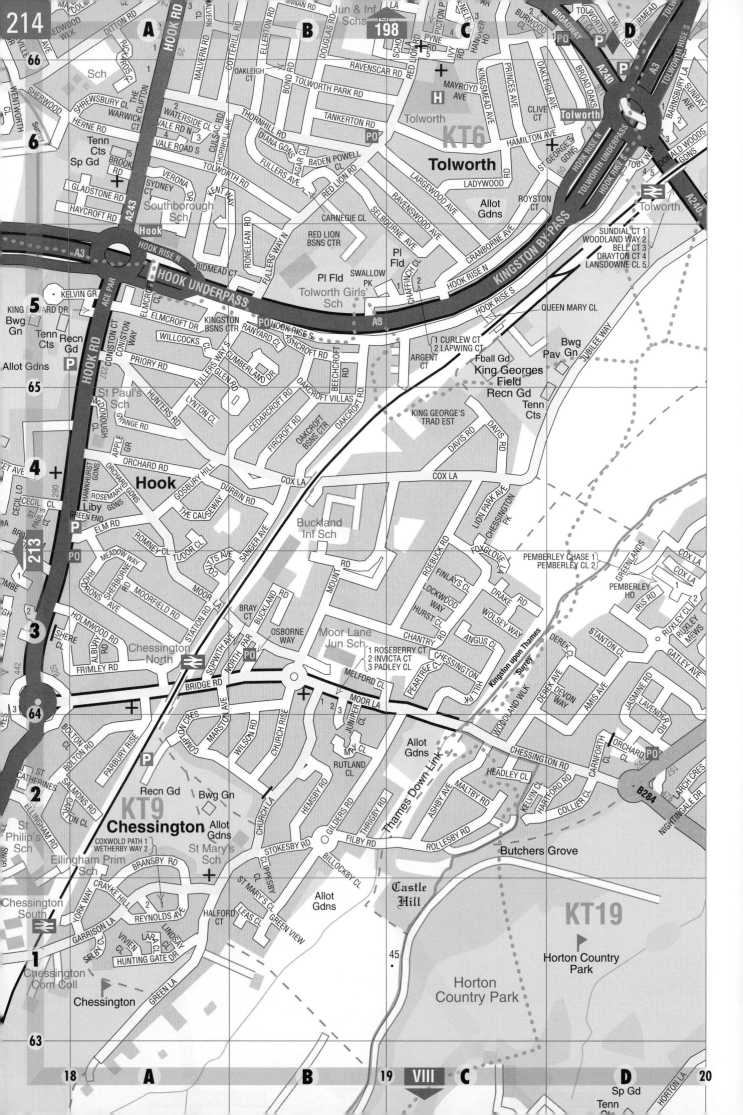

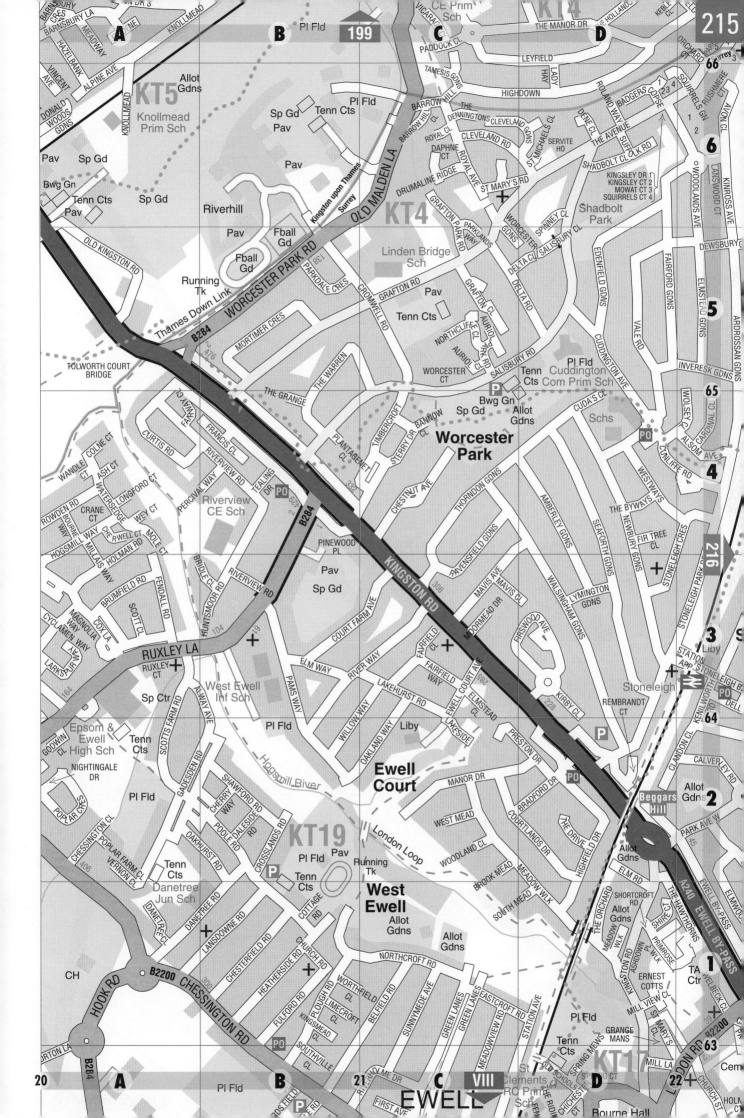

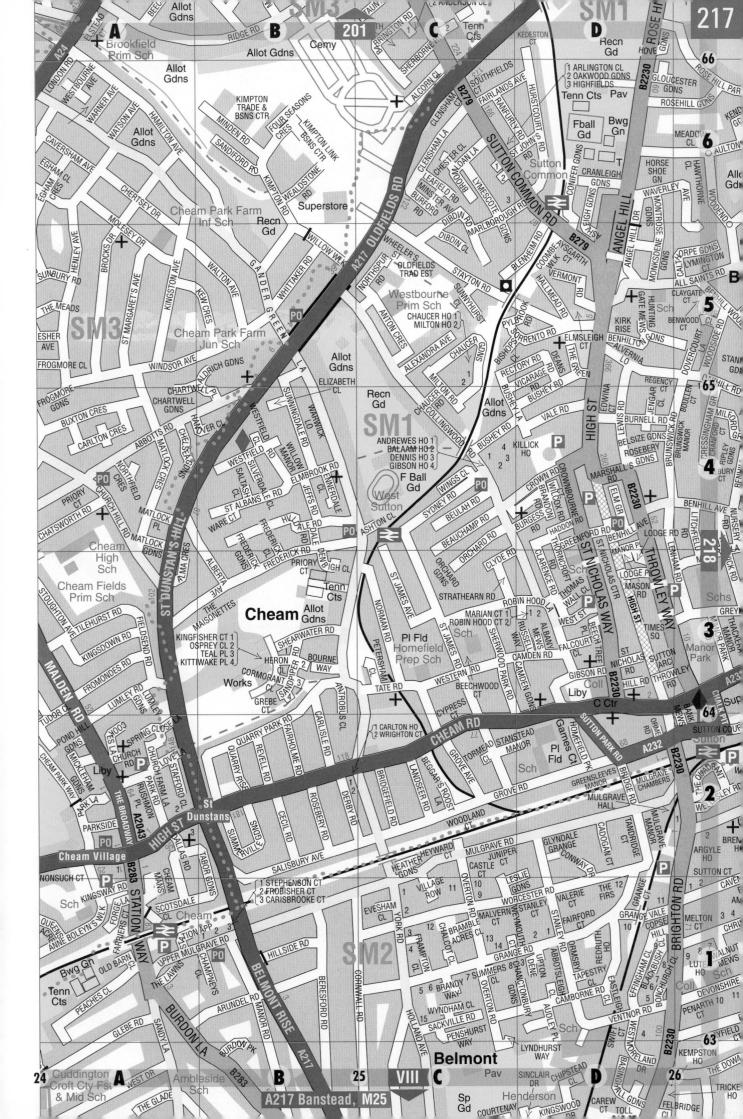

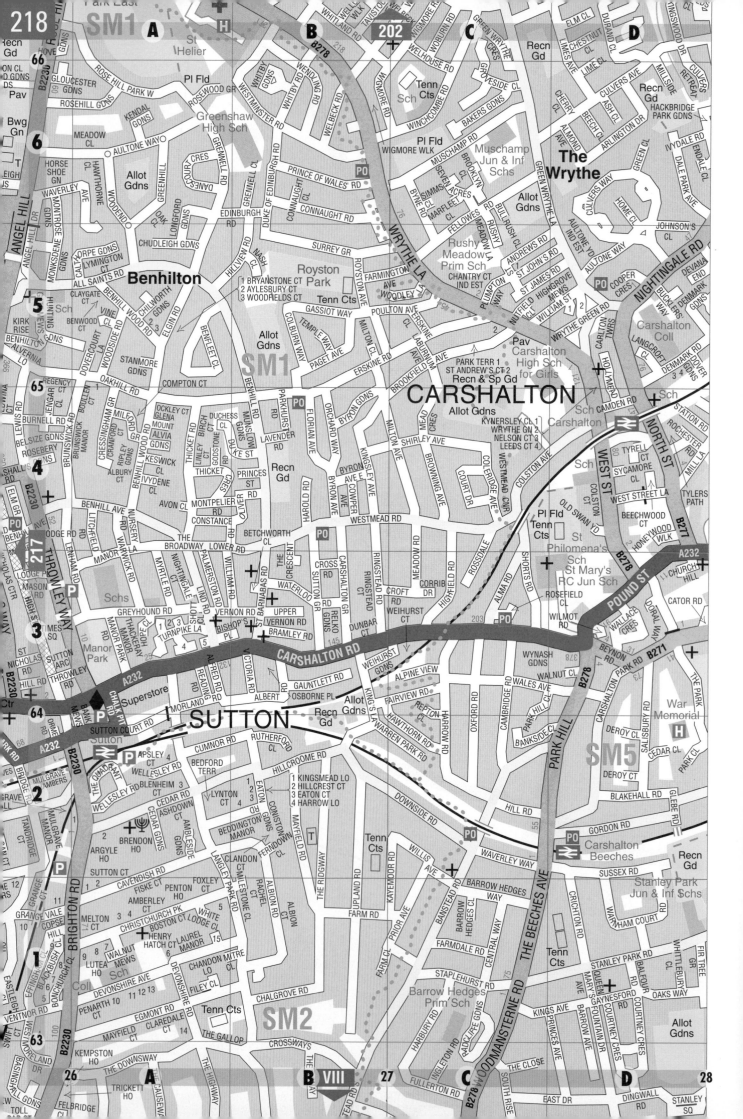

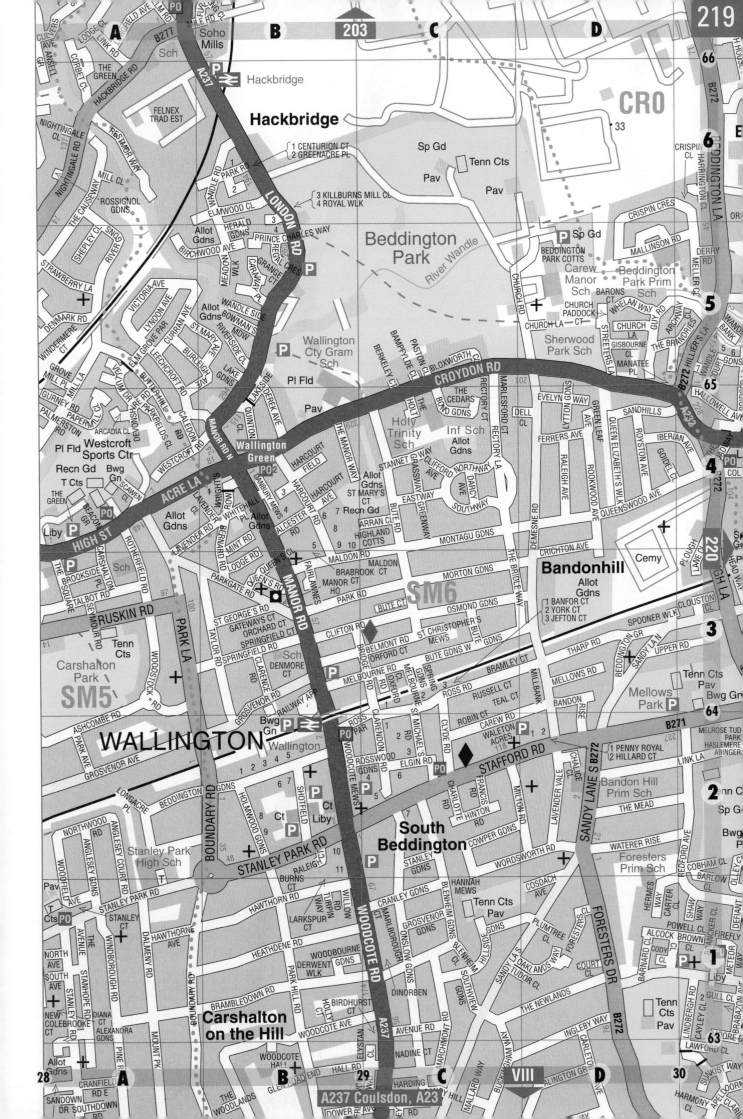

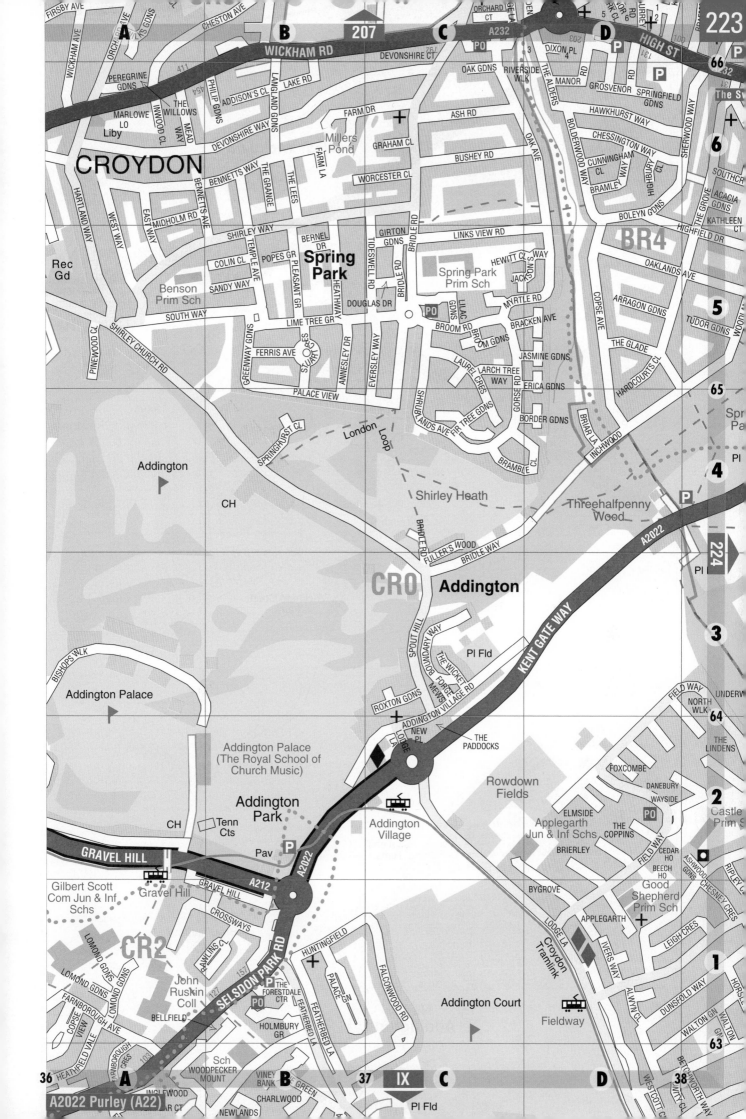

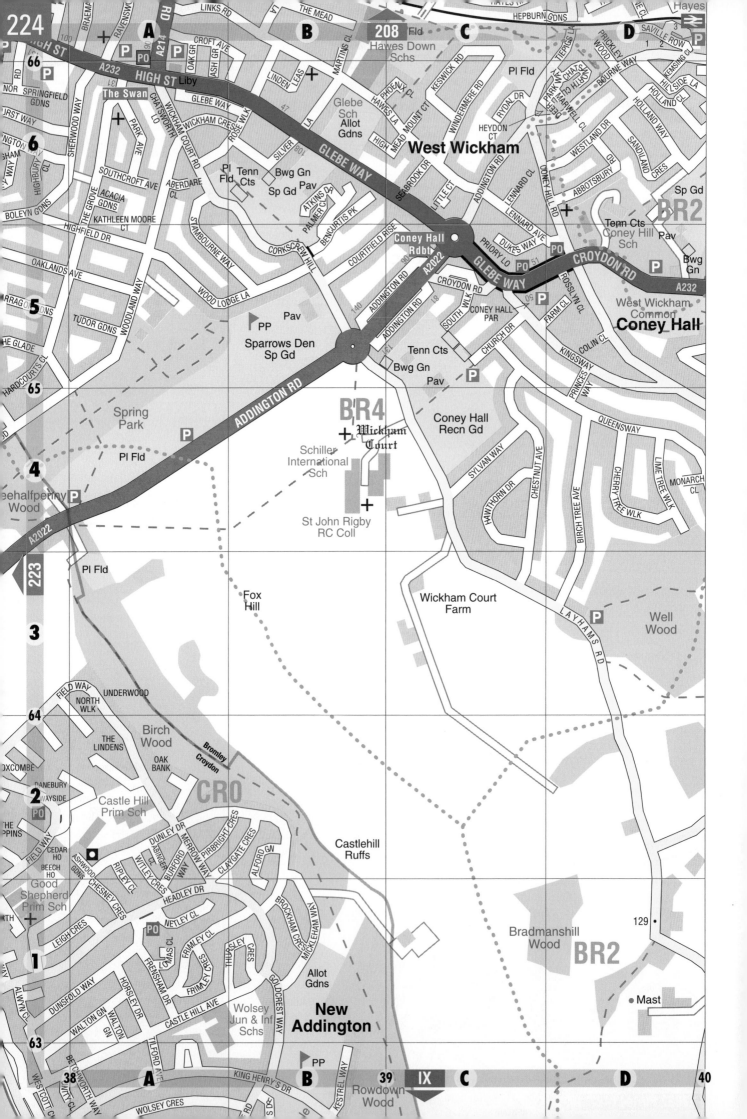

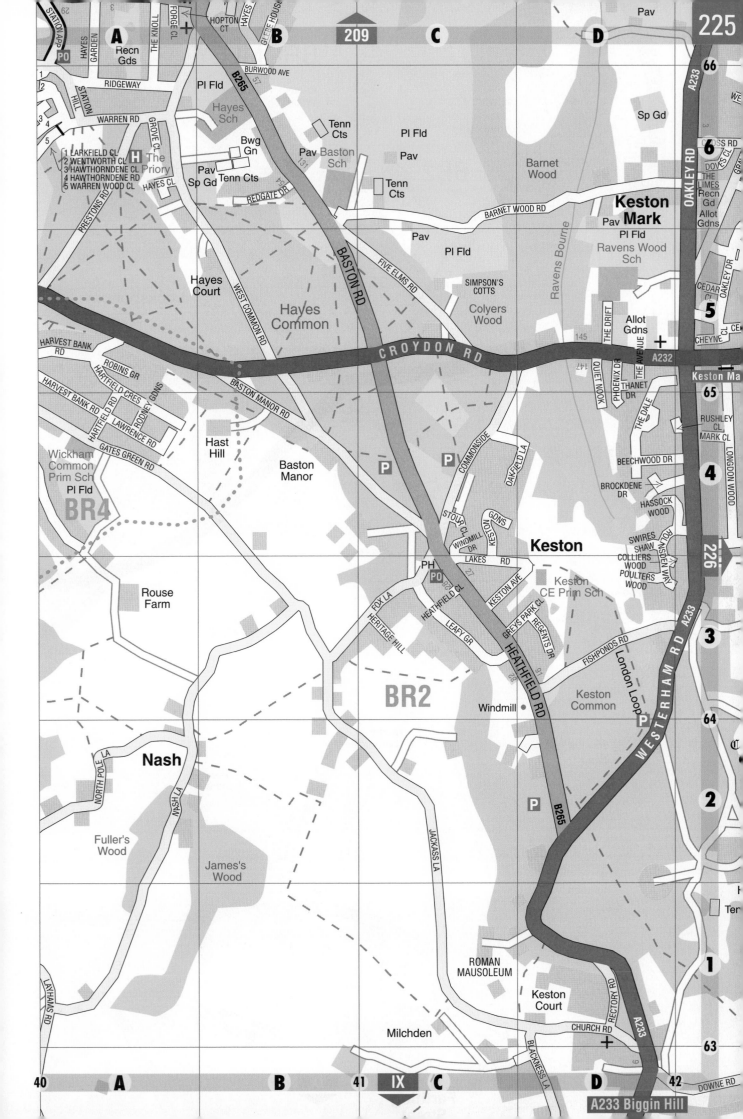

BROMLEY

Keston Mark

BR2

BR6

Locksbottom

Farnborough

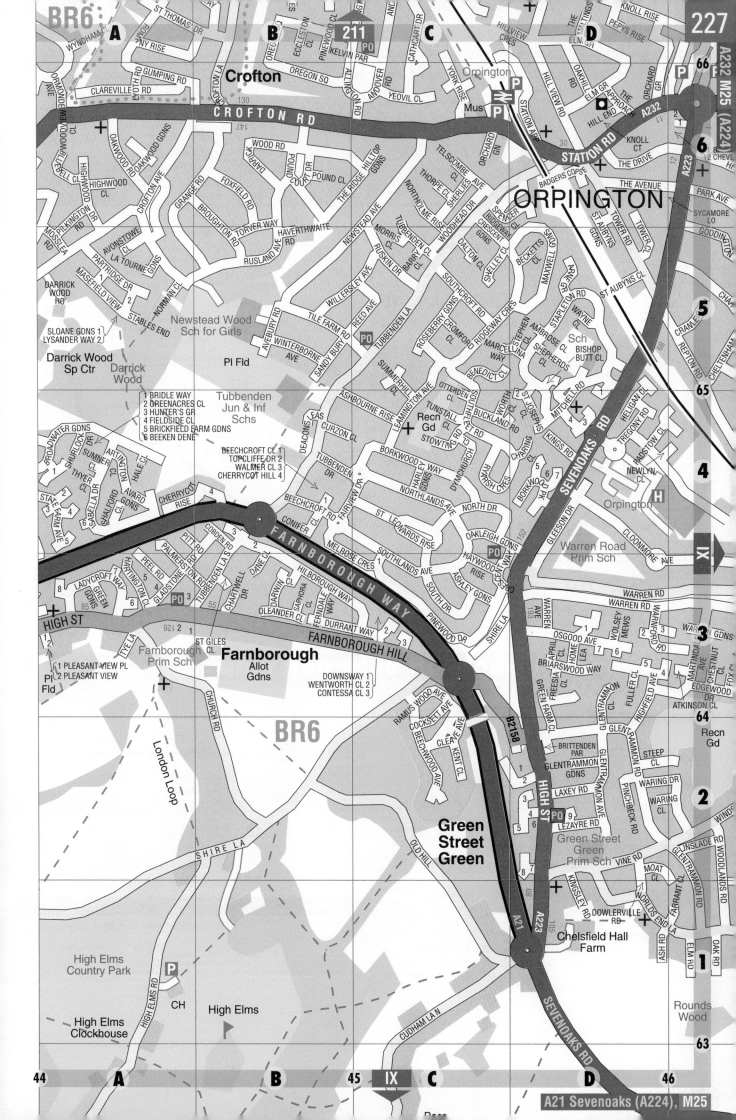

Key to enlarged map pages

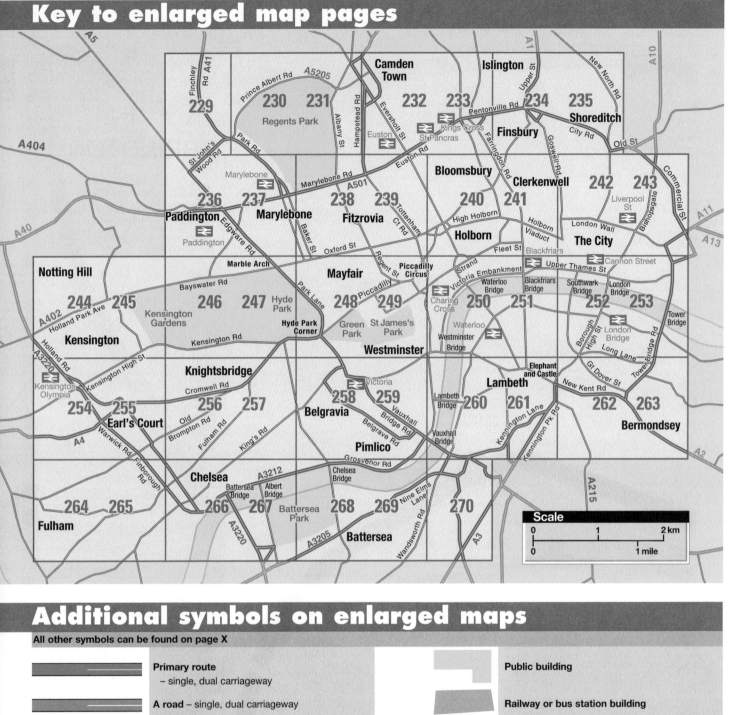

Additional symbols on enlarged maps

All other symbols can be found on page X

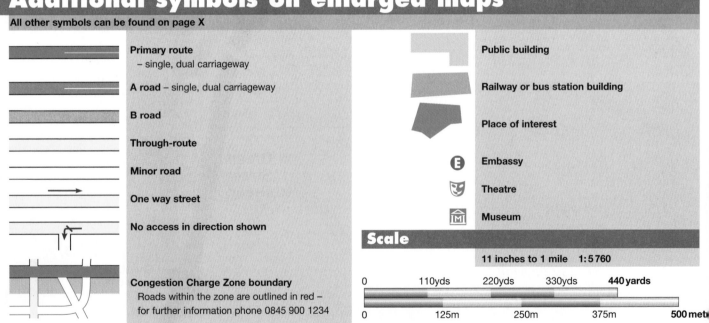

Primary route	– single, dual carriageway
A road	– single, dual carriageway
B road	
Through-route	
Minor road	
One way street	
No access in direction shown	
Public building	
Railway or bus station building	
Place of interest	
E	Embassy
	Theatre
M	Museum

Congestion Charge Zone boundary
Roads within the zone are outlined in red –
for further information phone 0845 900 1234

Scale

11 inches to 1 mile   1:5 760

0   110yds   220yds   330yds   440 yards

0   125m   250m   375m   500 metres

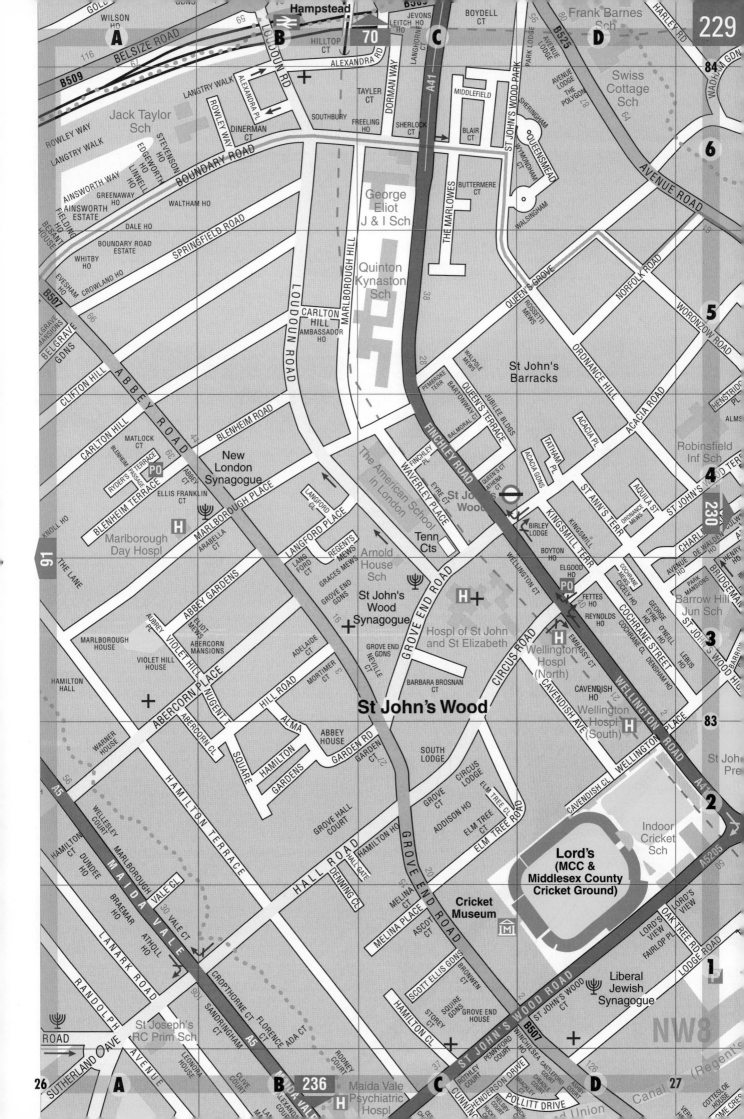

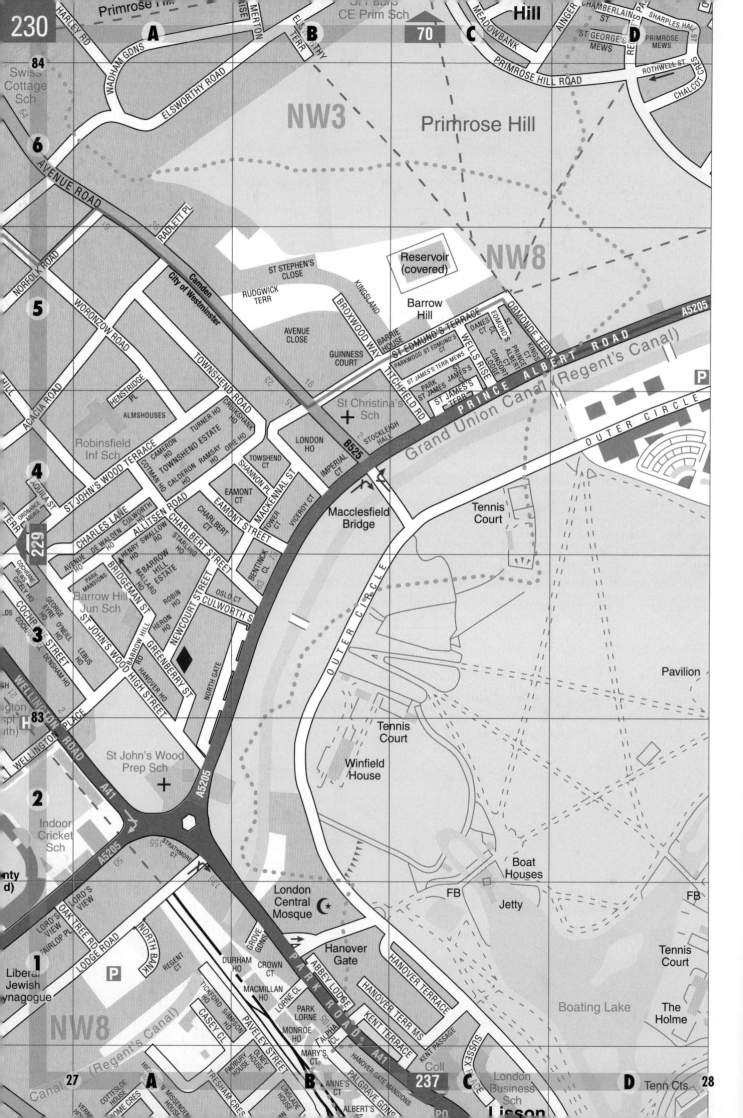

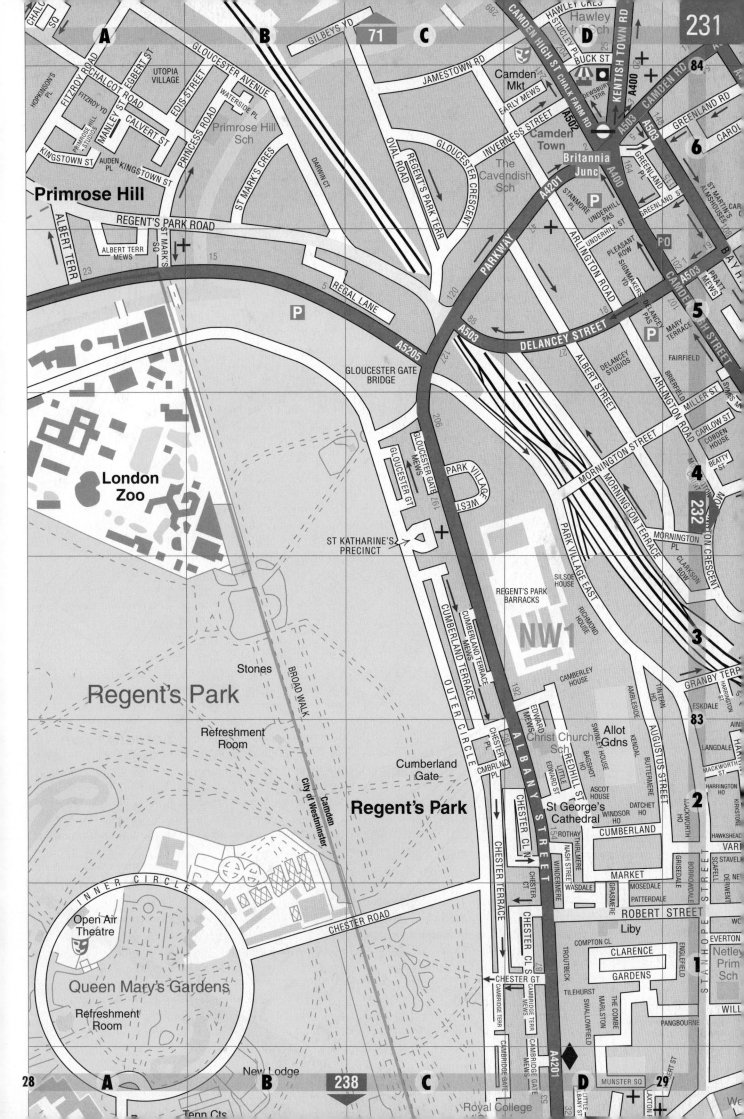

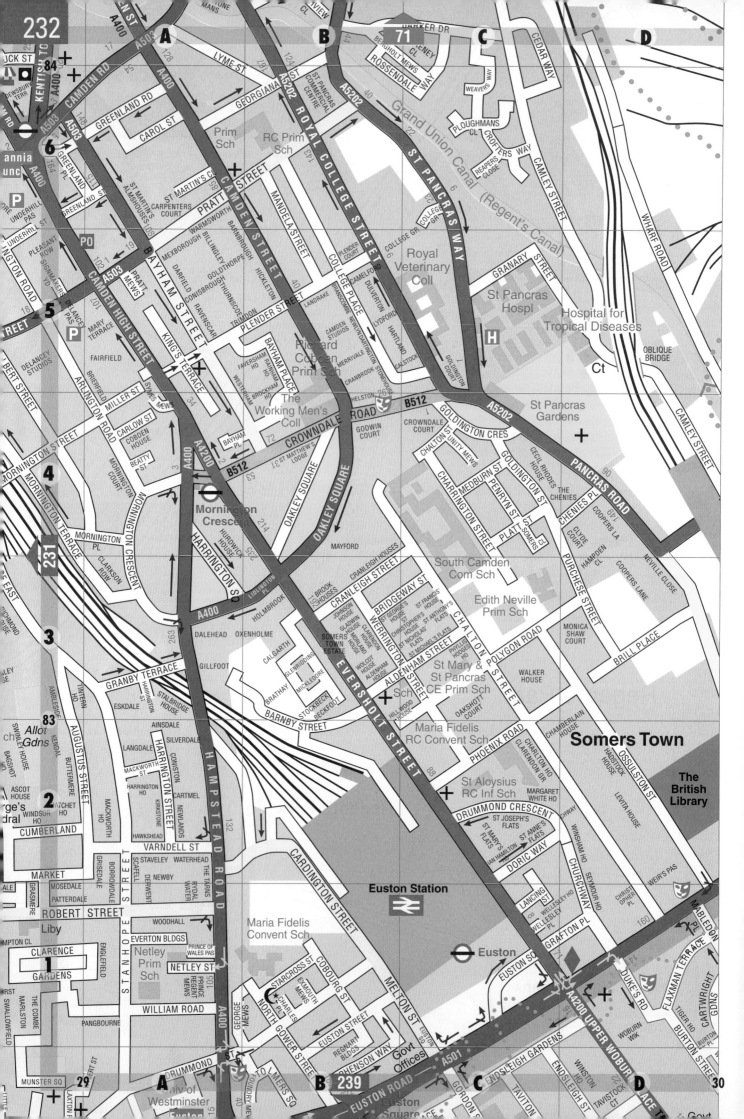

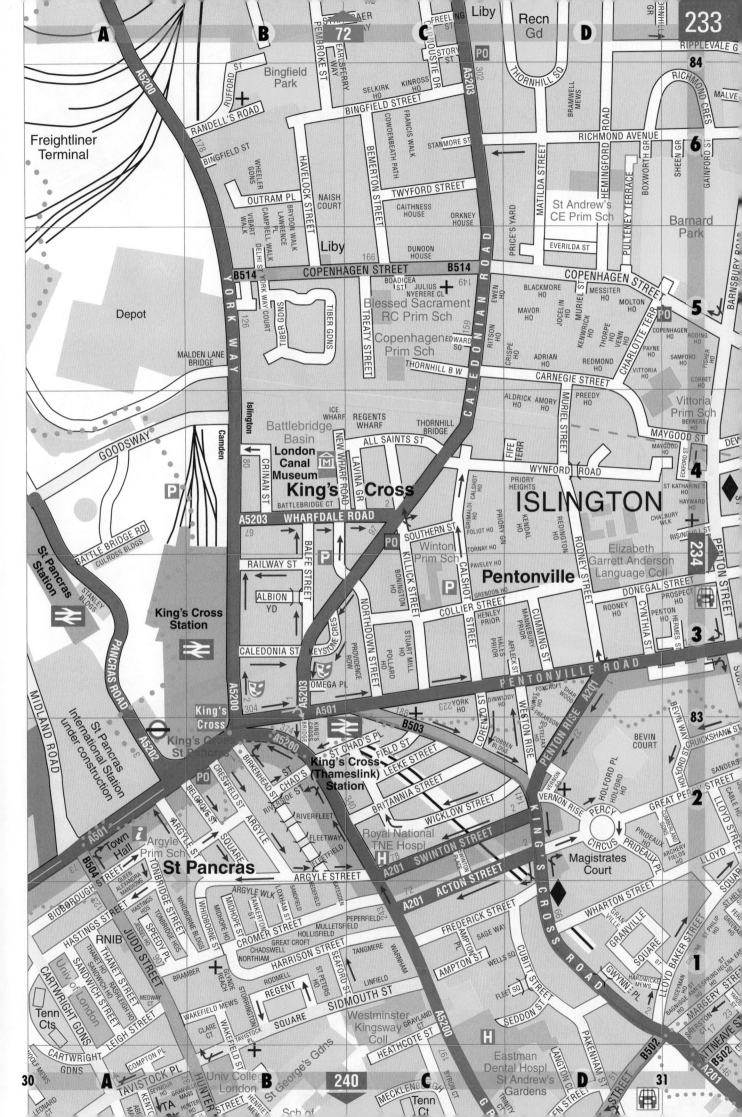

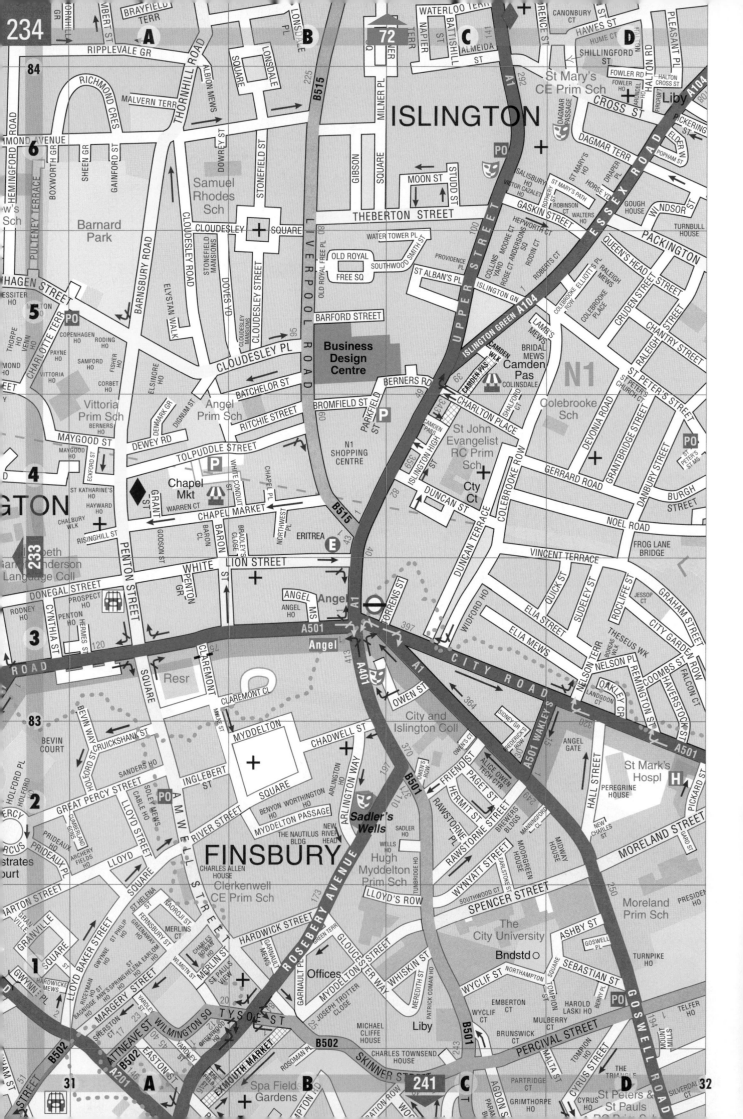

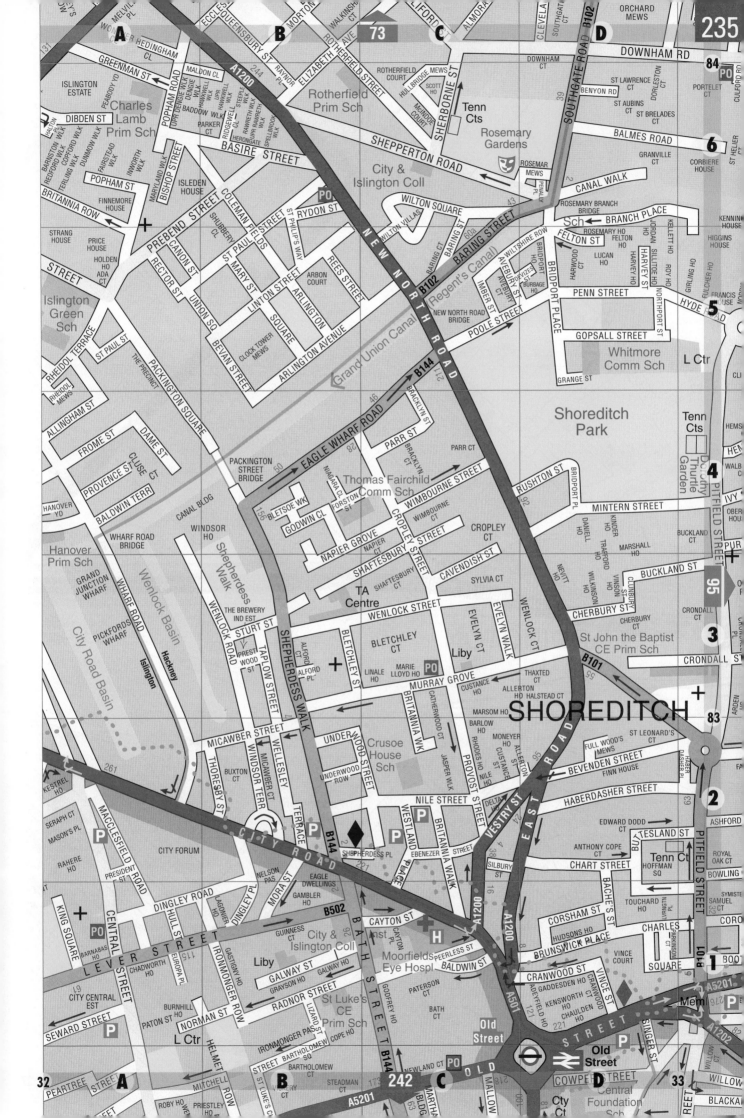

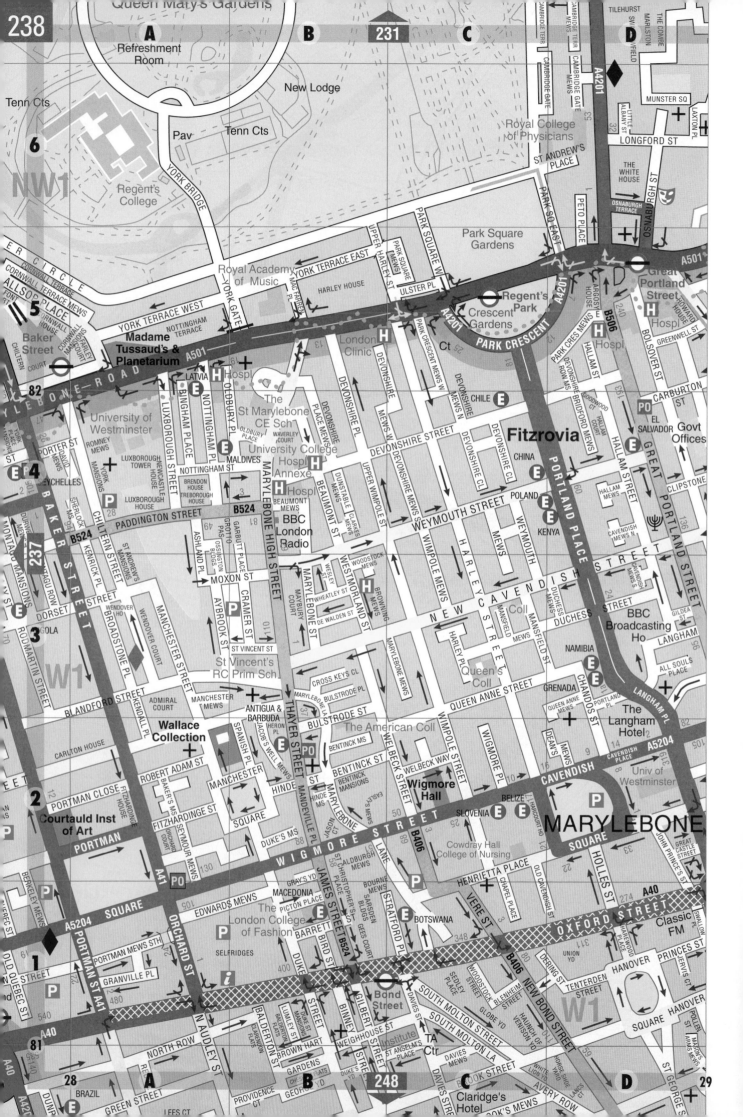

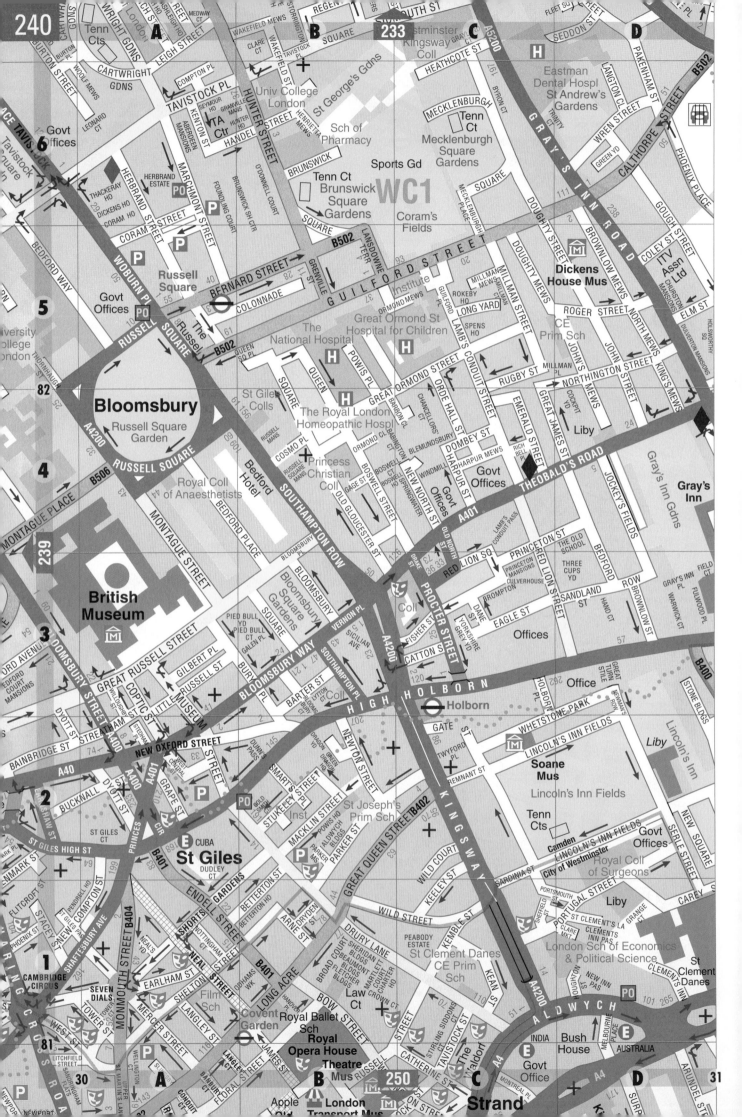

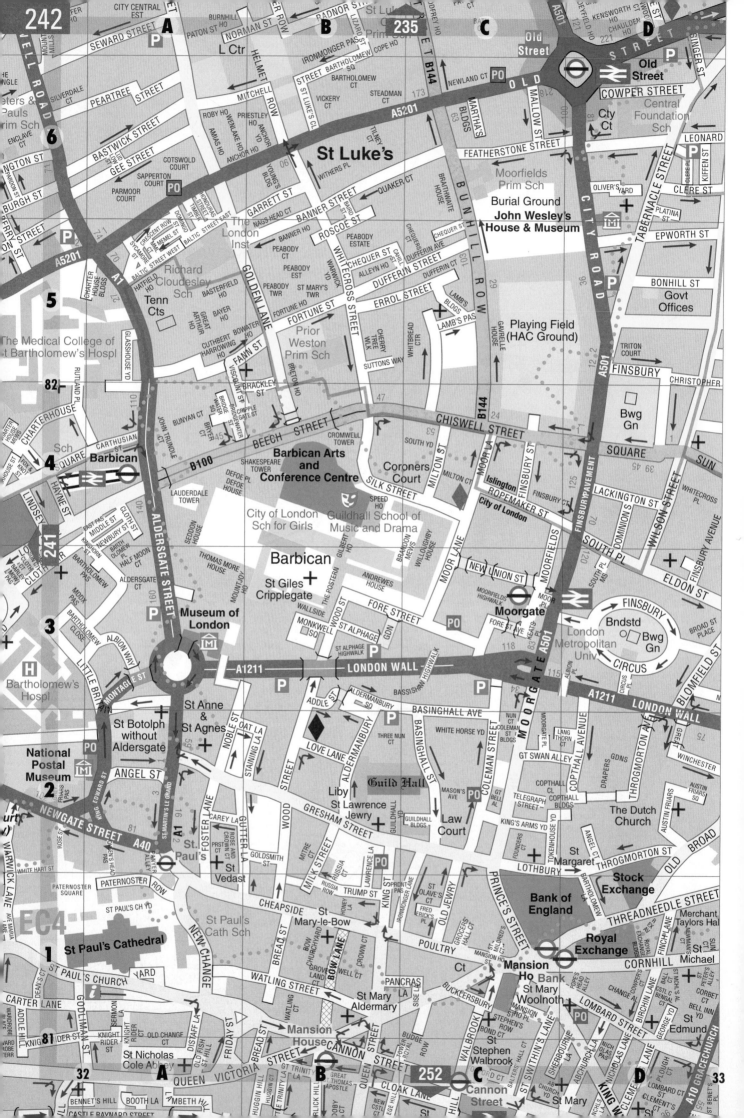

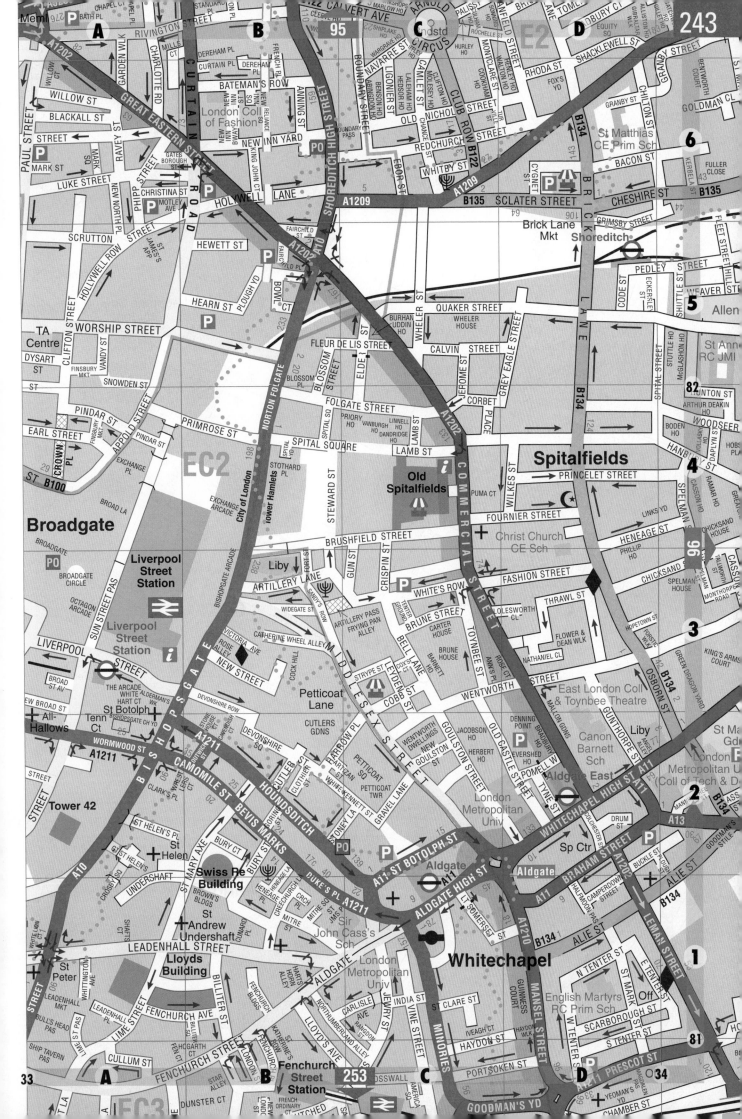

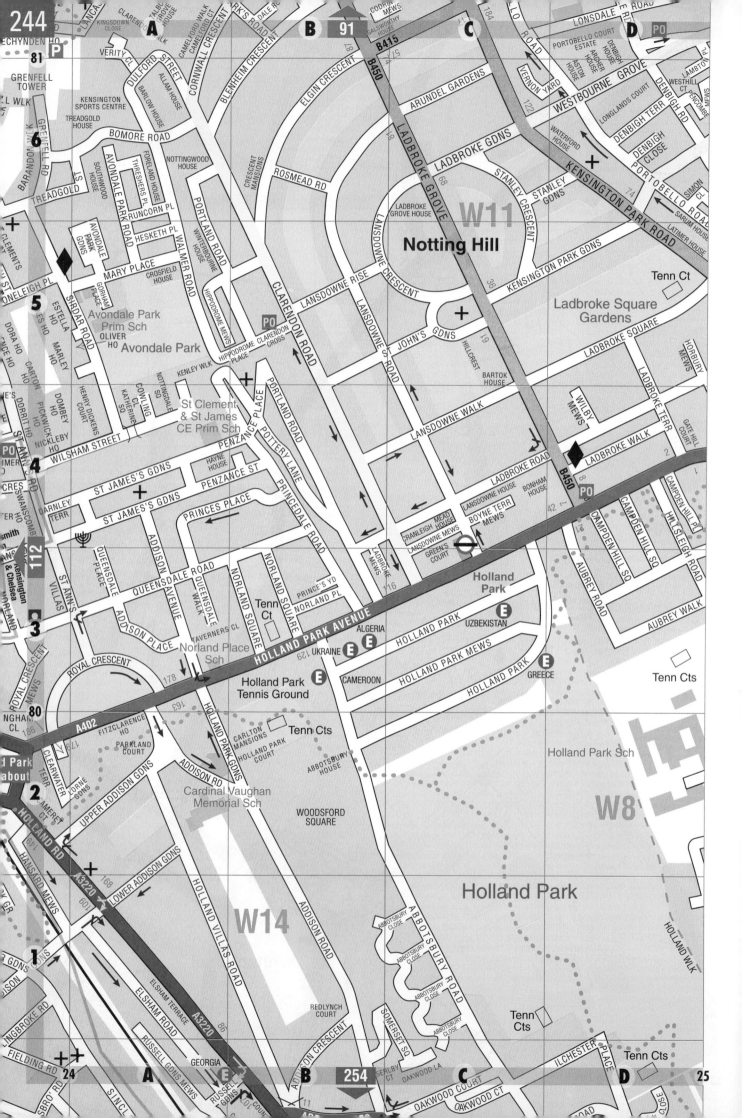

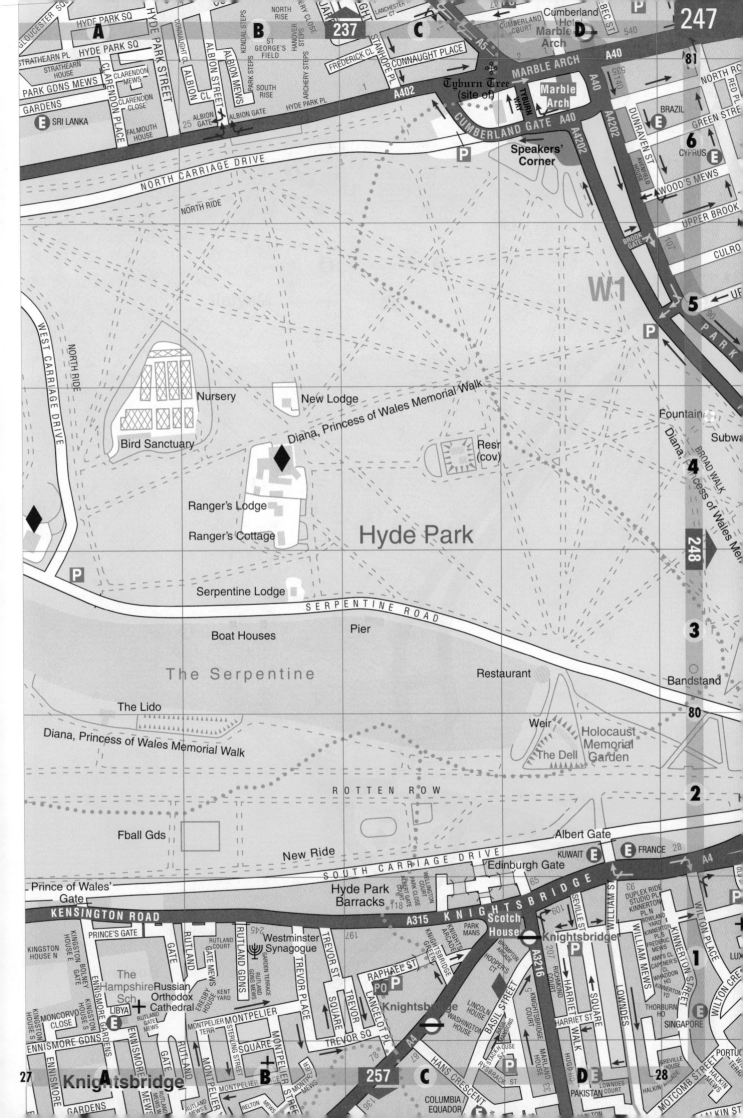

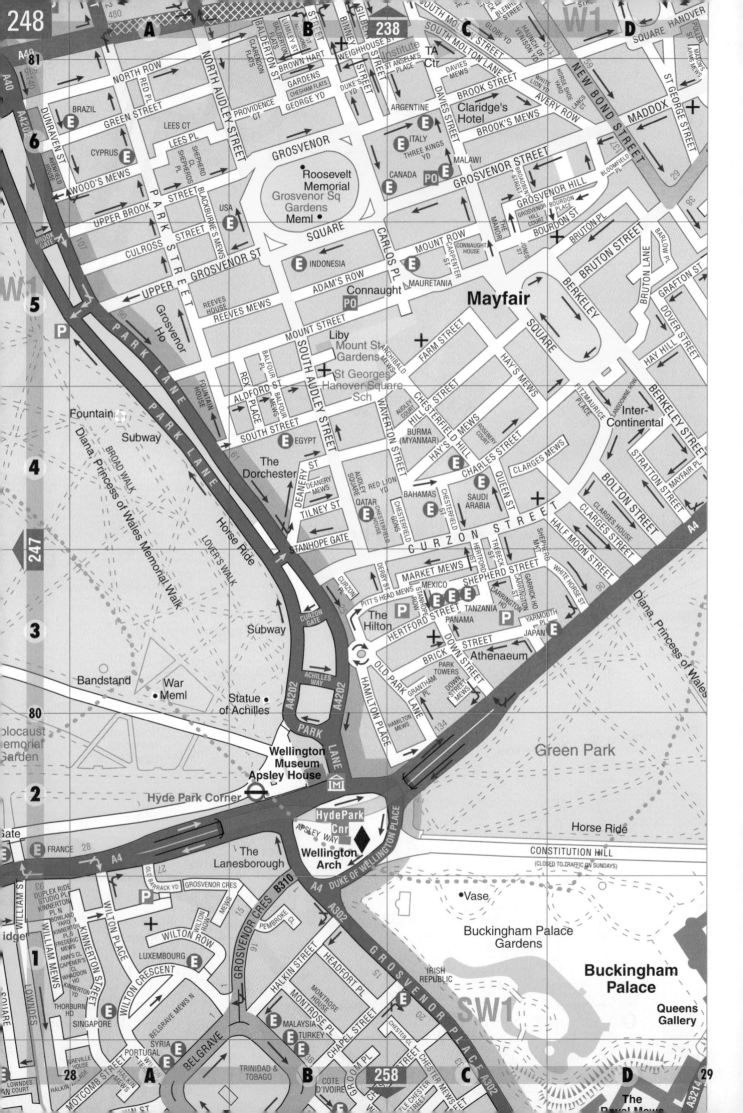

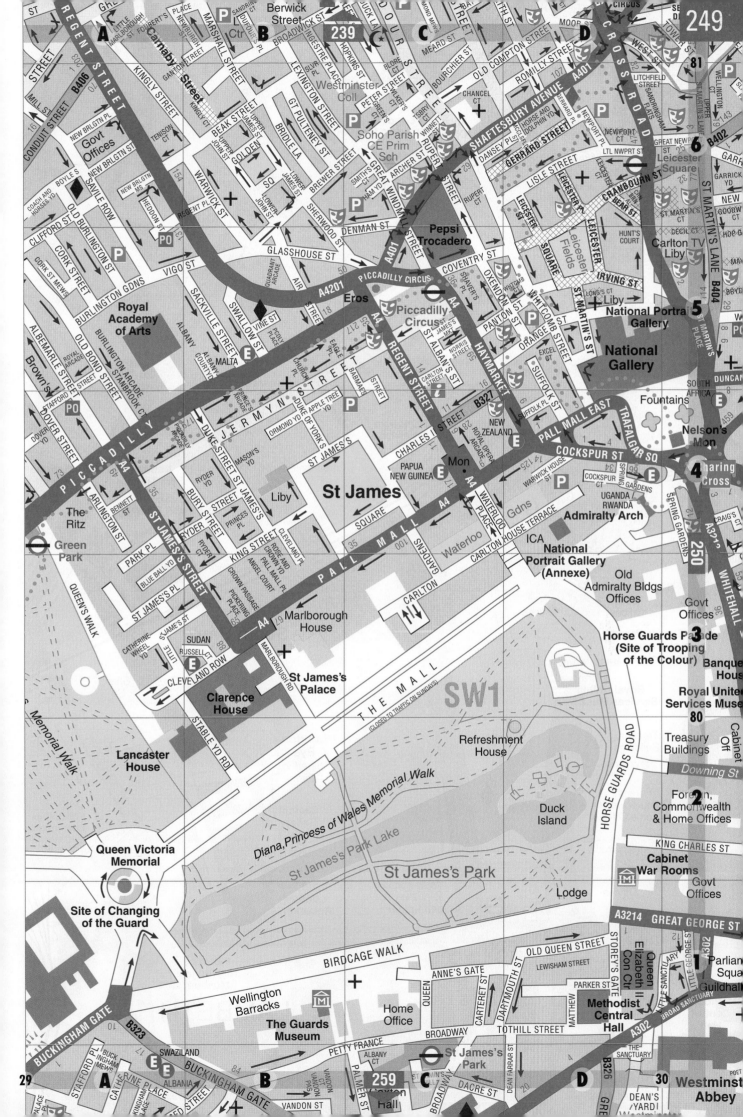

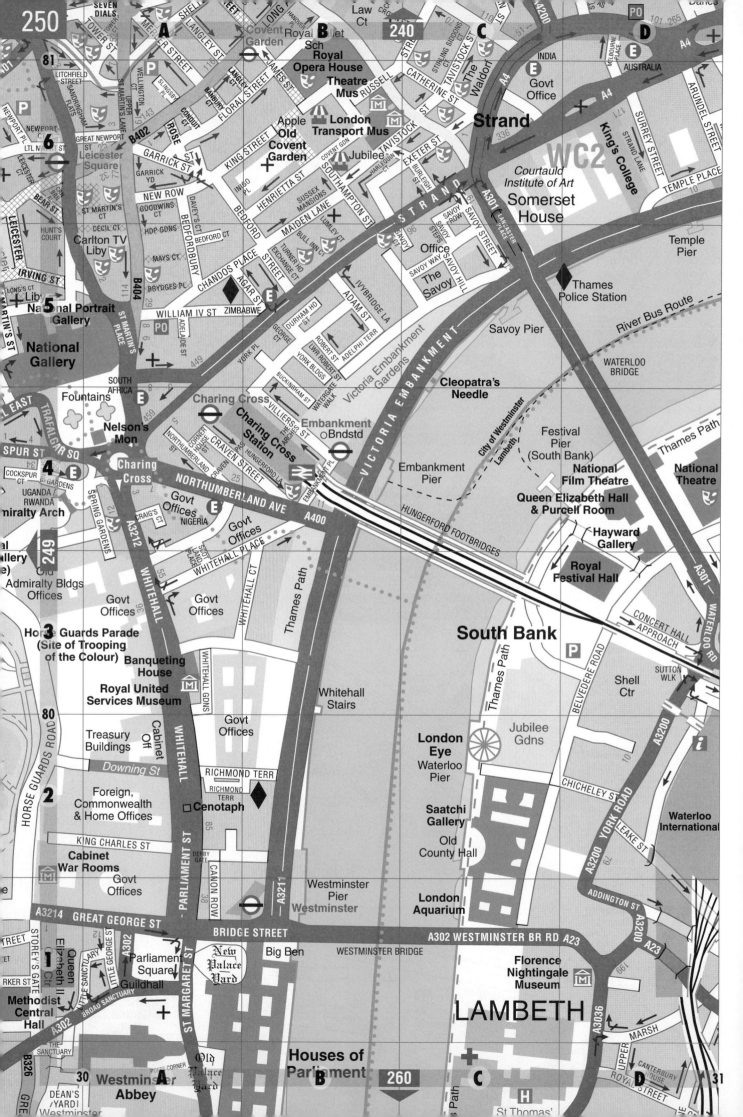

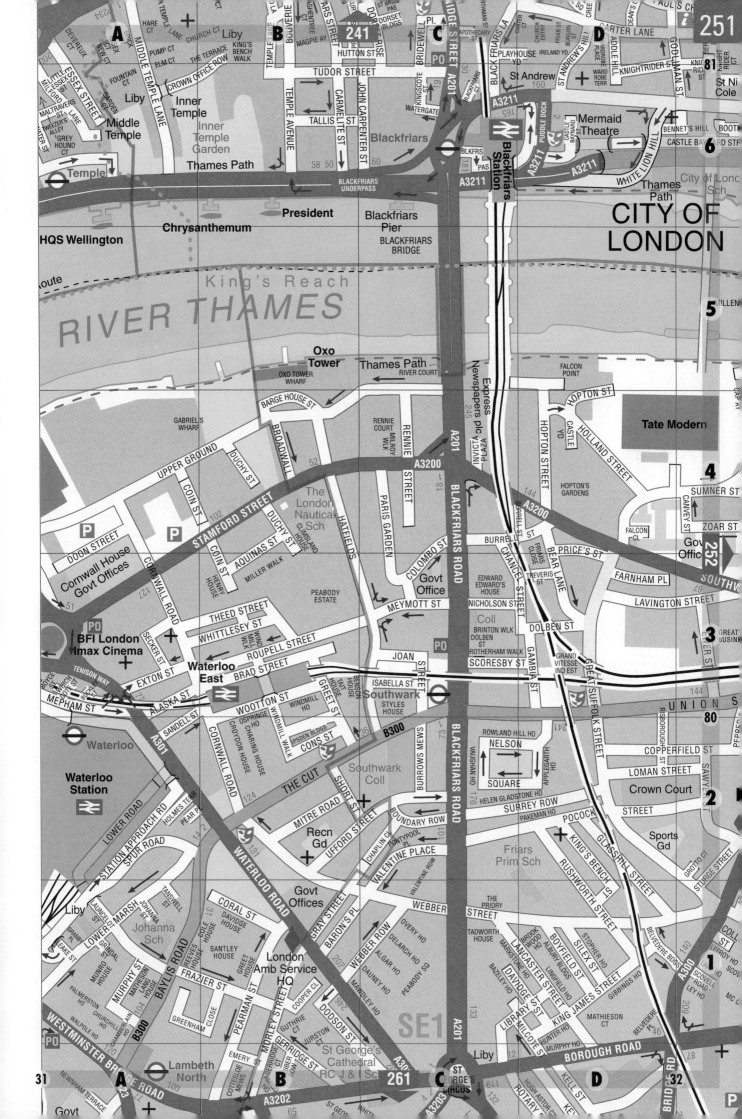

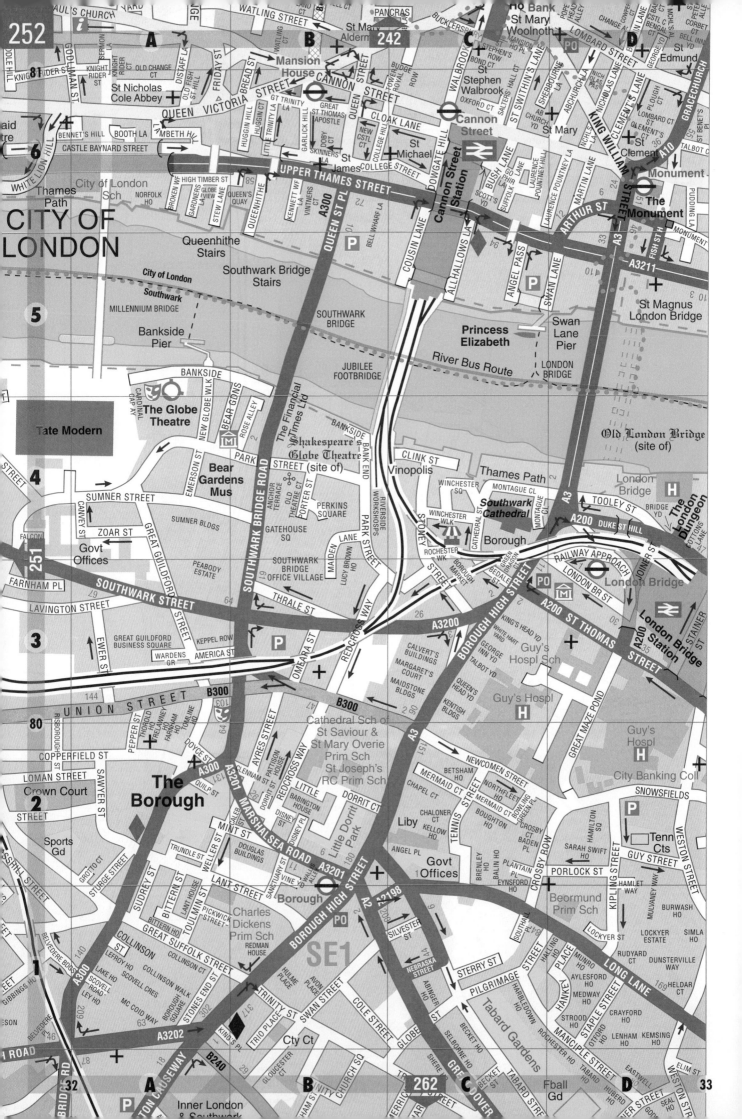

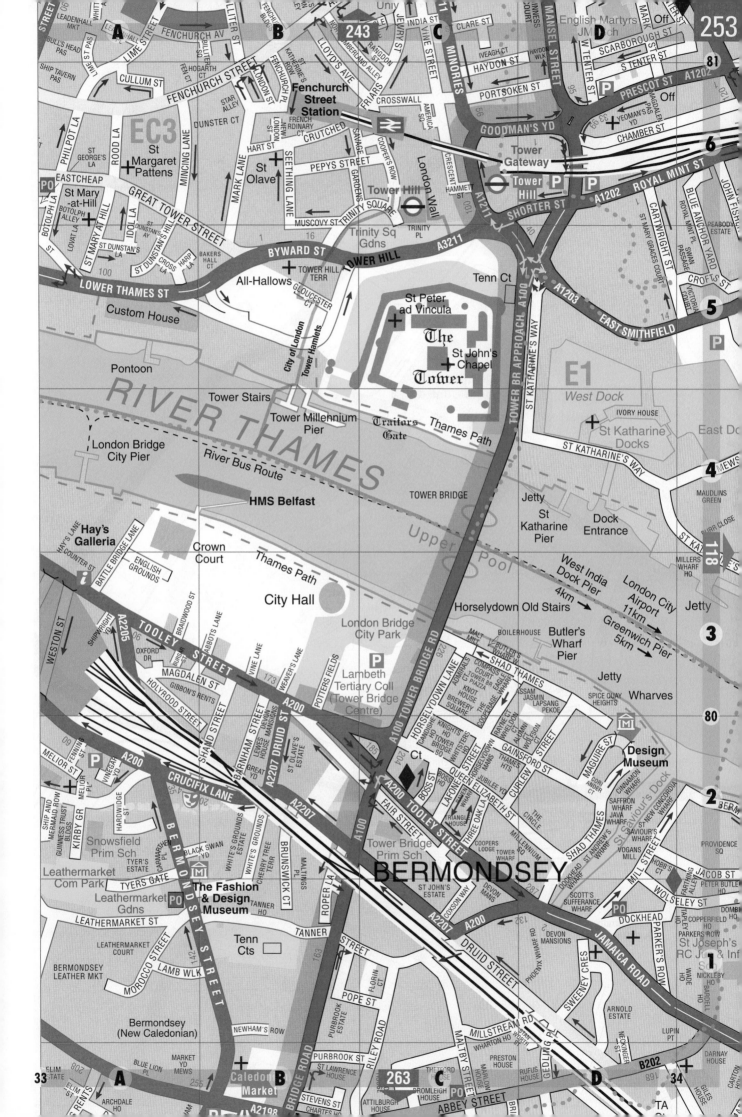

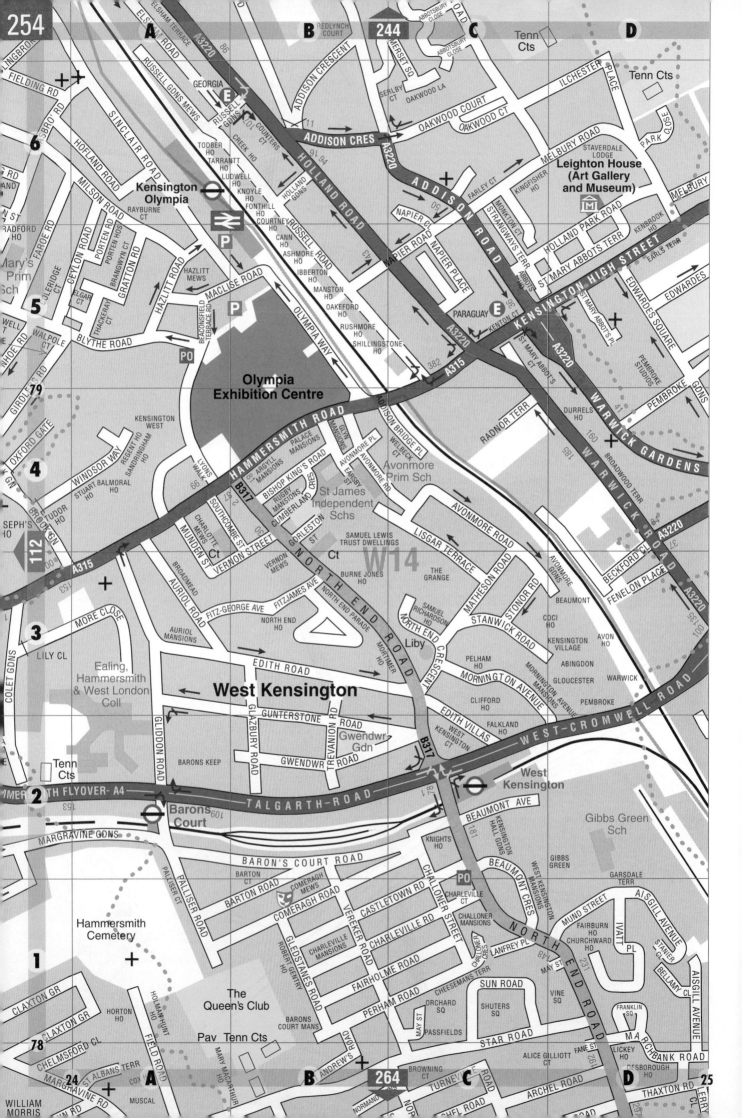

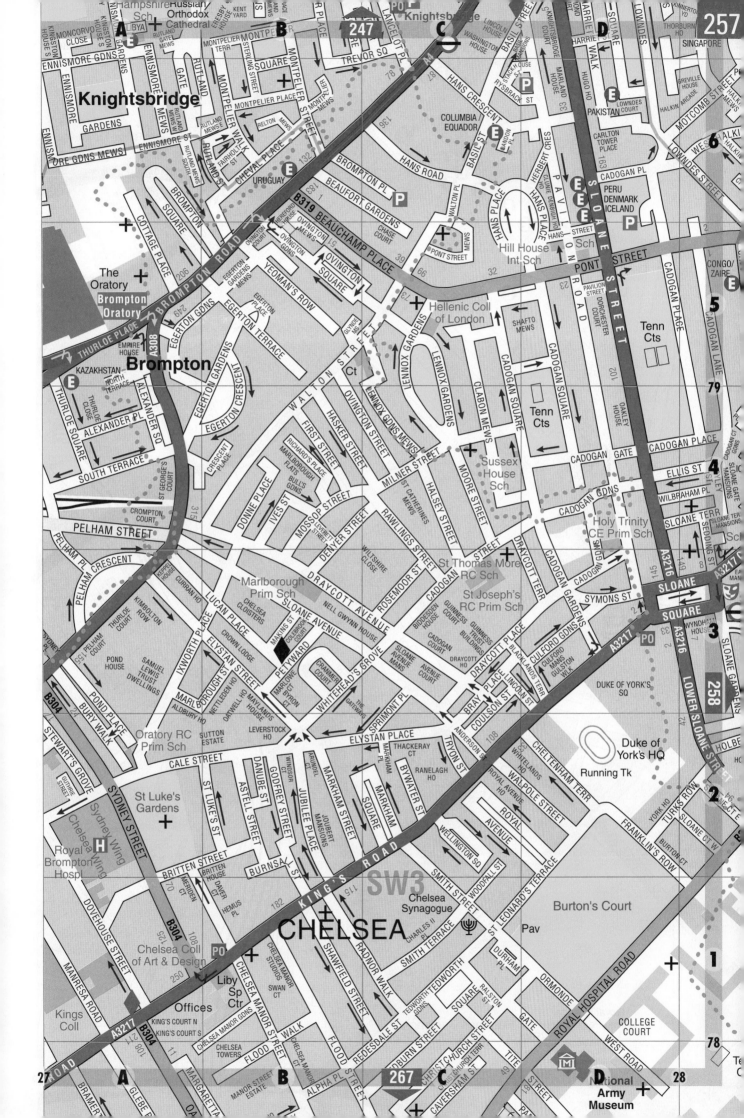

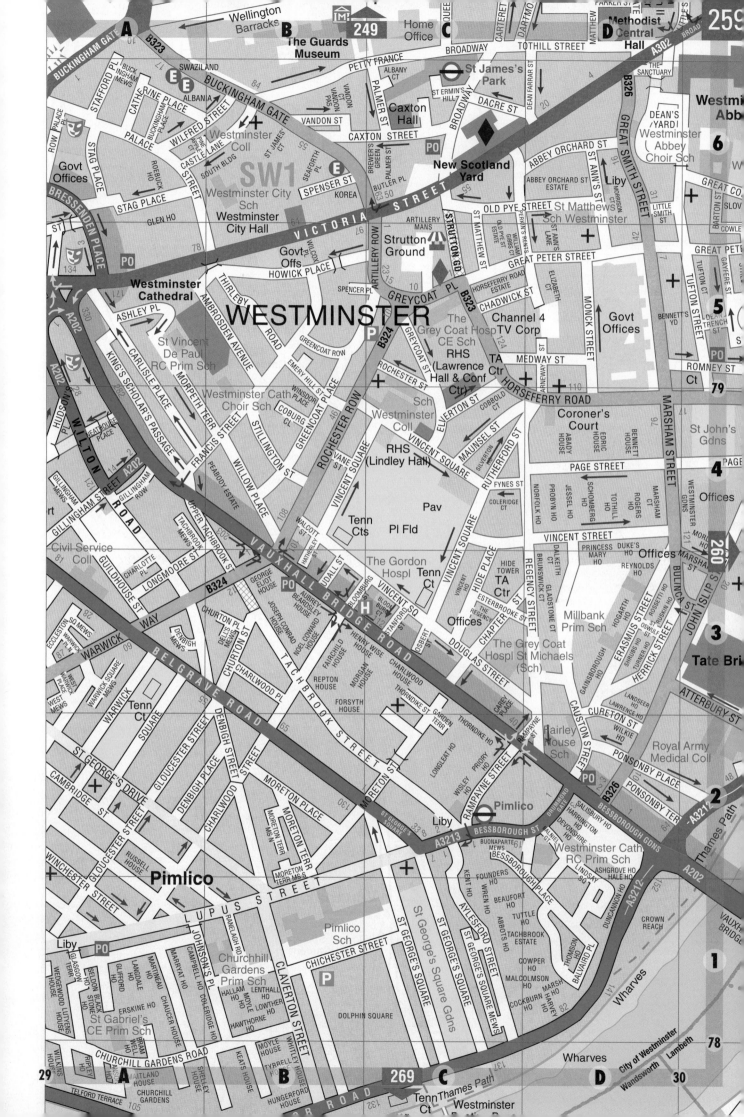

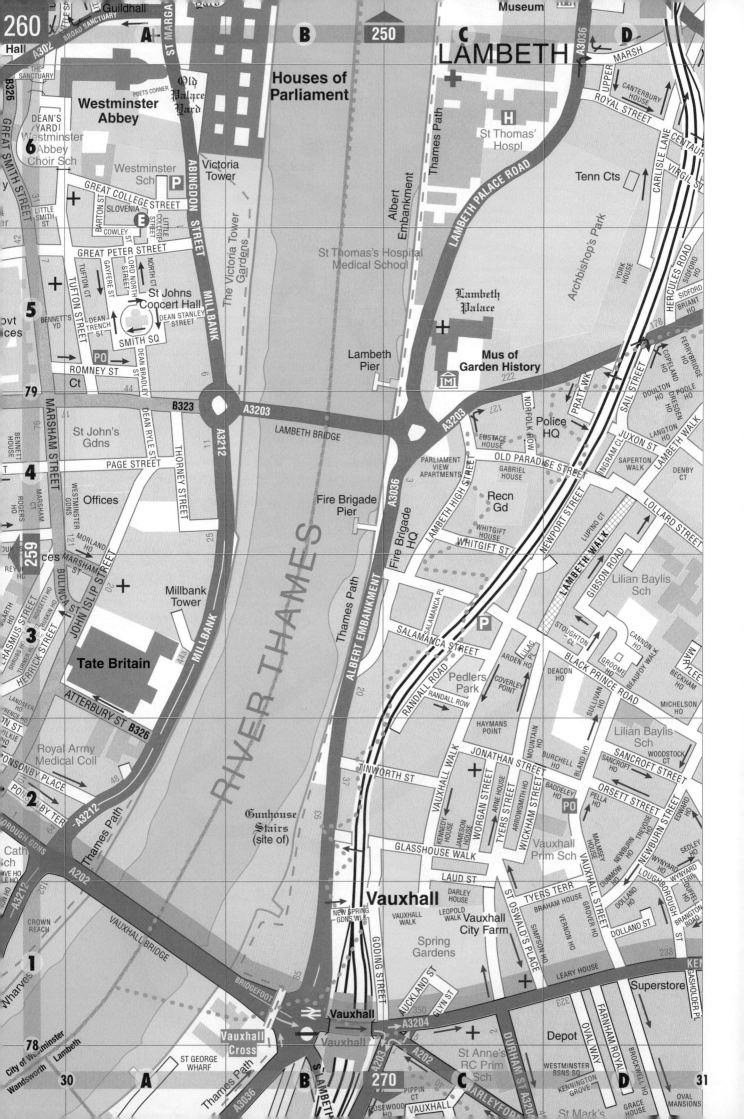

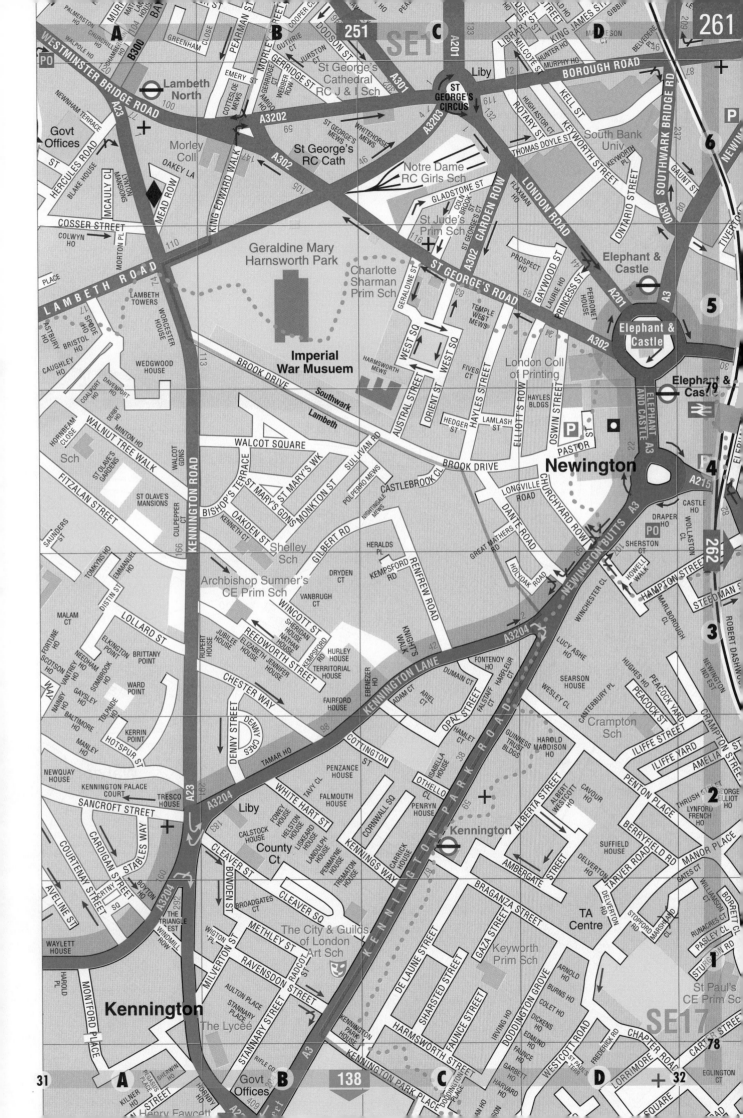

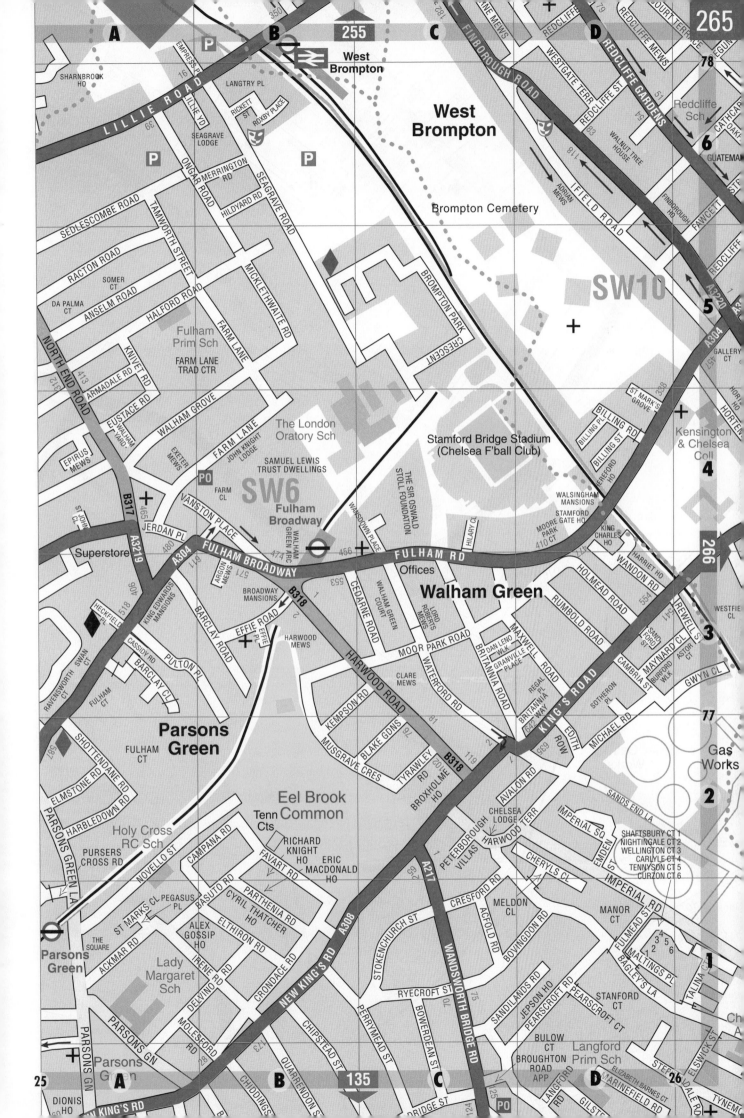

West Brompton

West Brompton

Brompton Cemetery

SW10

SHARNBROOK HO

LILLIE ROAD

LANGTRY PL

EMPRESS PL

ILLEYD

RICKETT ST

ROXBY PLACE

SEAGRAVE LODGE

SEDLESCOMBE ROAD

MERRINGTON RD

ONGAR ROAD

HILDYARD RD

SEAGRAVE ROAD

MICKLETHWAITE RD

RACTON ROAD

SOMER CT

DA PALMA CT

ANSELM ROAD

HALFORD ROAD

TAMWORTH STREET

Fulham Prim Sch

FARM LANE

FARM LANE TRAD CTR

NORTH END ROAD

ARMADALE RD

KNIVET RD

EUSTACE RD

WALHAM GROVE

WALHAM YARD

EPIRUS MEWS

EXETER MEWS

The London Oratory Sch

JOHN KNIGHT LODGE

SAMUEL LEWIS TRUST DWELLINGS

SW6

ST JOHN

B317

Brompton Park Crescent

Stamford Bridge Stadium (Chelsea F'ball Club)

THE SIR OSWALD STOLL FOUNDATION

BILLING RD

BILLING PL

BILLING ST

ST MARK'S GROVE

HEREFORD HO

WALSINGHAM MANSIONS

STAMFORD GATE HO

MOORE PARK CT

WALNUT TREE HOUSE

ADRIAN MEWS

FINBOROUGH RD

IFIELD ROAD

REDCLIFFE GARDENS

WESTGATE TERR

REDCLIFFE ST

Redcliffe Sch

Kensington & Chelsea Coll

GALLERY CT

PO

FARM CL

VANSTON PLACE

Fulham Broadway

WANSDOWN PLACE

Superstore

A3219

A304

JERDAN PL

FULHAM BROADWAY

WALHAM GREEN ARC

FULHAM RD

Offices

Walham Green

KING CHARLES HO

HARRIET HO

WANDON RD

HOLMEAD ROAD

RUMBOLD ROAD

A304

266

HECKFIELD PL

KING EDWARDS MANSIONS

ARGON MEWS

BROADWAY MANSIONS

B318

CEDARNE ROAD

WALHAM GREEN COURT

LORD ROBERTS MEWS

MAXWELL ROAD

SANDFORD ST

CAMBRIA ST

MAYNARD CL

BURFORD WLK

GWYN CL

ASTOR CT

WESTFIE CL

REWELL S

RAVENSWORTH

SWAN CT

CASSIDY RD

PULTON PL

BARCLAY ROAD

EFFIE ROAD

EFFIE PL

HARWOOD MEWS

MOOR PARK ROAD

WATERFORD RD

BRITANNIA ROAD

DAN LENO WLK

GRANVILLE PLACE

BRITANNIA PL

REGAL PL

SOTHERON PL

MICHAEL RD

EDITH ROW

CLARE MEWS

FULHAM CT

BARCLAY CL

Parsons Green

FULHAM CT

SHOTTENDANE RD

ELMSTONE RD

HARBLEDOWN RD

KEMPSON RD

BLAKE GDNS

MUSGRAVE CRES

TYRAWLEY RD

HARWOOD ROAD

BROXHOLME HO

B318

KING'S ROAD

77

Gas Works

AVALON RD

SANDS END LA

IMPERIAL SQ

SHAFTSBURY CT 1
NIGHTINGALE CT 2
WELLINGTON CT 3
CARLYLE CT 4
TENNYSON CT 5
CURZON CT 6

PARSONS GREEN LA

Holy Cross RC Sch

PURSERS CROSS RD

NOVELLO ST

CAMPANA RD

Tenn Cts

RICHARD KNIGHT HO

ERIC MACDONALD HO

FAVART RD

Eel Brook Common

CHELSEA LODGE

PETERBOROUGH VILLAS

HARWOOD TERR

CHERYLS CL

IMPERIAL RD

EMDEN ST

MANOR CT

Parsons Green

THE SQUARE

ST MARKS CL

PEGASUS PL

BASUTO RD

CYRIL THATCHER HO

PARTHENIA RD

ALEX GOSSIP HO

ELTHIRON RD

Lady Margaret Sch

ACKMAR RD

IRENE RD

DELVINO RD

CRONDACE RD

NEW KING'S RD

STOKENCHURCH ST

A308

WANDSWORTH BRIDGE RD

A217

CRESFORD RD

ACFOLD RD

MELDON CL

BOVINGDON RD

FULMEAD ST

MALTINGS PL

BAGLEY'S LA

STANFORD CT

TALINA C

PARSONS GREEN

DIONIS HO

KING'S RD

PARSONS GN

MOLESFORD RD

CHIPSTEAD ST

QUARRENDON S

RYECROFT ST

PERRYMEAD ST

BOWERDEAN ST

SANDILANDS RD

JEPSON HO

PEARSCROFT RD

PEARSCROFT CT

BULOW CT

BROUGHTON ROAD APP

Langford Prim Sch

LANGFORD RD

MARINEFIELD RD

ELIZABETH BARNES CT

STEPHENDALE

ELSWICK R

TYNEMO

GILSTE

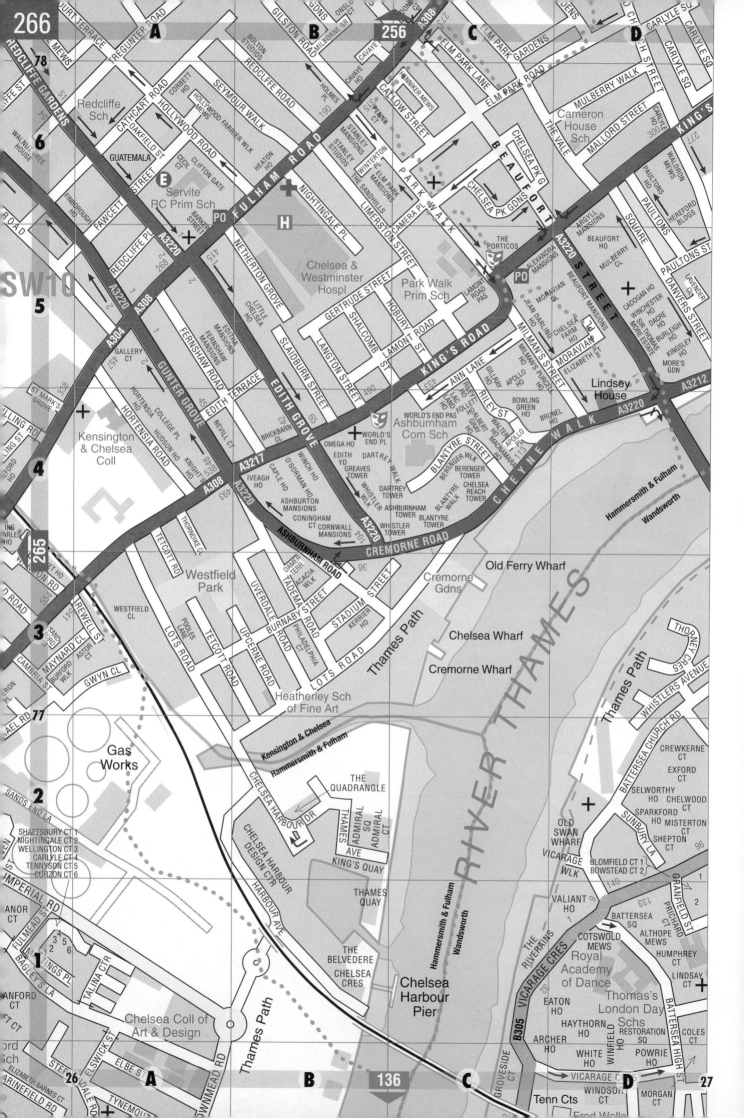

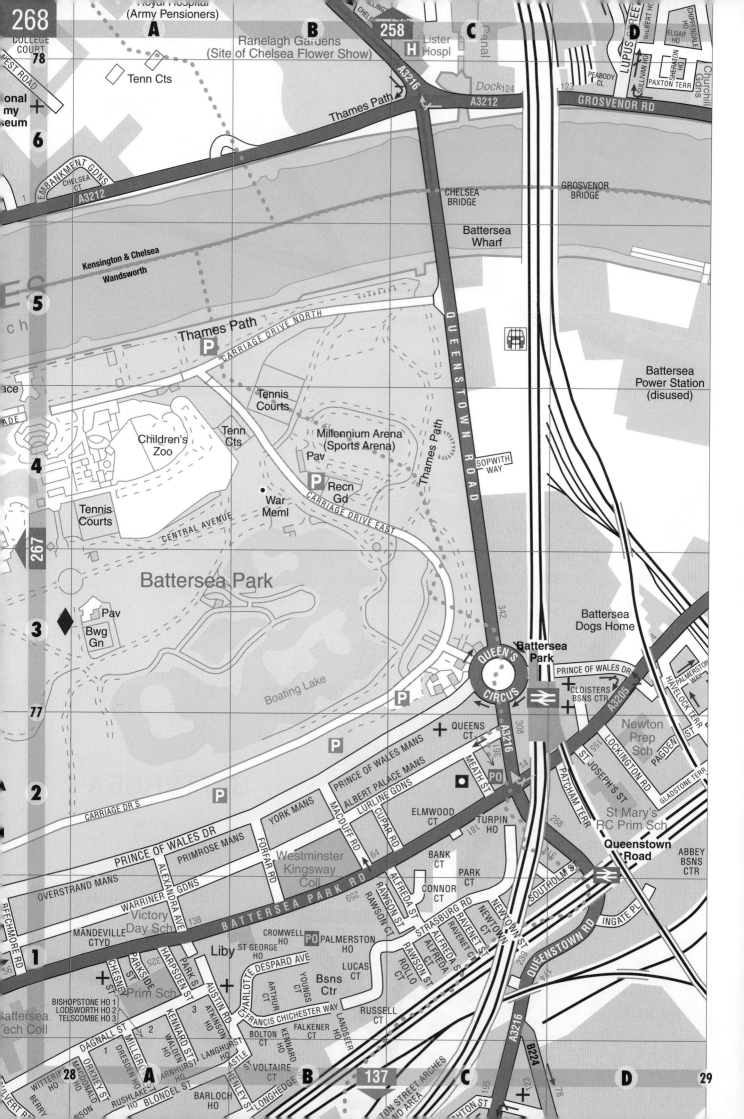

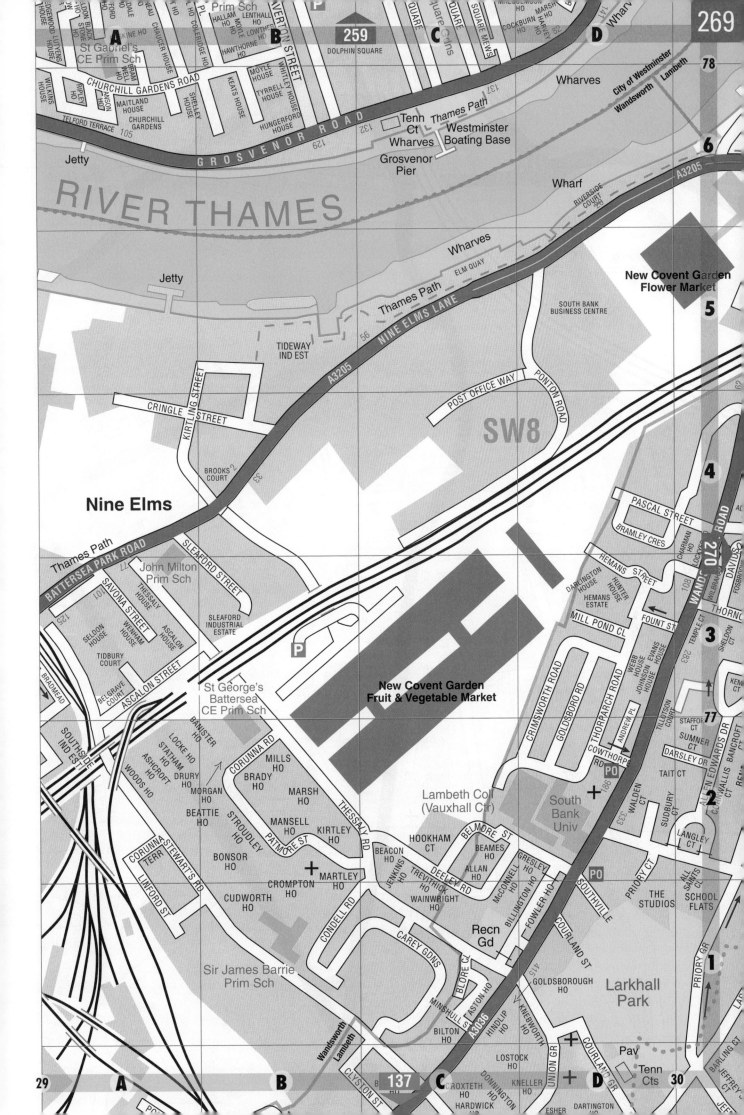

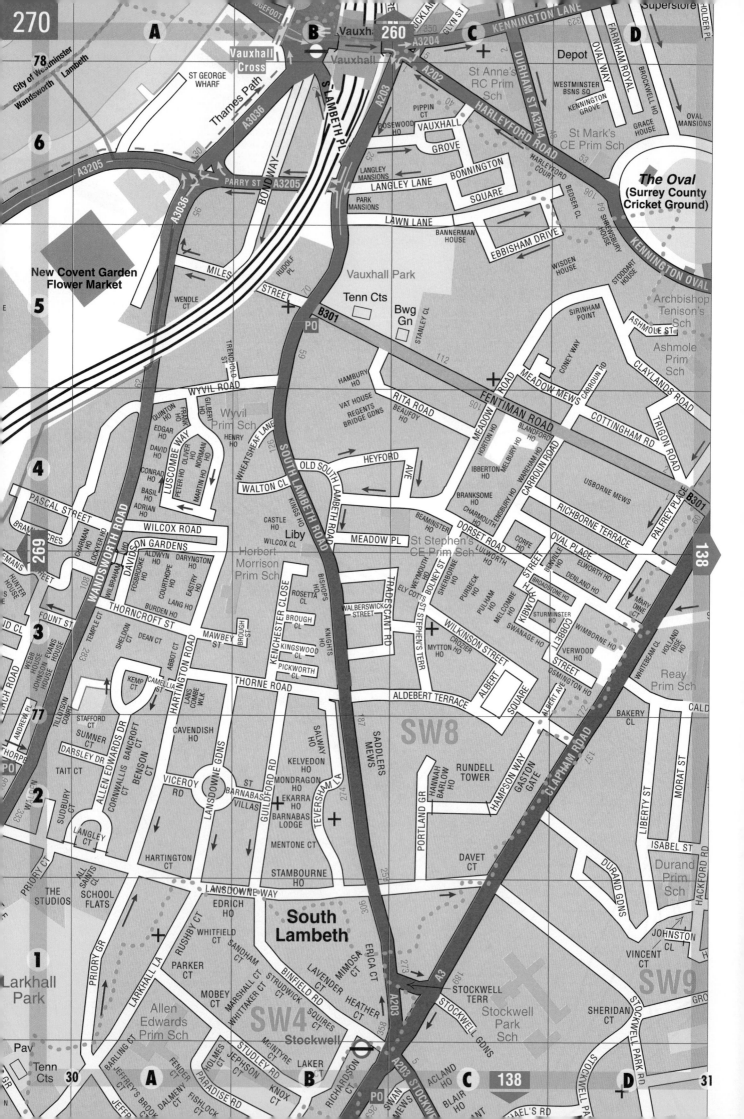

Church Rd **6** Beckenham BR2..........**53** C6 **228** C6

Place name	Location number	Locality, town or village	Postcode district	Standard scale reference	Enlarged scale reference
May be abbreviated on the map	Present when a number indicates the place's position in a crowded area of mapping	Shown when more than one place (outside London postal districts) has the same name	District for the indexed place	Page number and grid reference for the standard mapping	Page number and grid reference for the central London enlarged mapping, underlined in red

Public and commercial buildings are highlighted in magenta

Places of interest are highlighted in blue with a star★

Index of Localities, towns and villages

A

Abbey Wood 124 B3
Acton 111 B5
Acton Green 111 A2
Addington 223 C3
Addiscombe 206 A1
Aldborough Hatch ..57 C5
Aldersbrook 77 C6
Alperton 88 A4
Anerley 184 B2
Arkley 12 A6
Ashford 170 B4
Ashford Common ...171 B4
Avery Hill 167 B5

B

Balham 159 A3
Bandonhill 219 D3
Barbican 95 A2
Barking 79 B1
Barkingside 57 A6
Barnes 133 D4
Barnet 13 B6
Barnet Gate 11 D5
Barnsbury 72 A1
Battersea 136 D4
Bayswater 114 A6
Beckenham 185 C1
Beckton 100 D2
Becontree 81 A4
Beddington 220 A6
Beddington Corner .203 A2
Bedford Park 111 C3
Belgravia 115 B2
Bell Green 163 B1
Bellingham 185 C5
Belmont 25 B2
Belsize Park 70 C3
Belvedere 125 D2
Benhilton 218 A5
Bermondsey 118 A4
Berrylands 198 C3
Bethnal Green 96 B4
Bexley 146 B1
Bexleyheath 147 B2
Bickley 188 B1
Blackfen 168 A5
Blackheath 142 C2
Blackheath Park ..143 A1
Blackheath Vale ..142 D3
Blackwall 120 B6
Bloomsbury 93 D2
Borehamwood 11 C5
Borough The 117 A4
Bow 97 B5
Bow Common 97 D2
Bowes Park 32 A4
Brent Cross 46 D2
Brentford 131 B6

Brentford End 131 C4
Brimsdown 7 B3
Brixton 138 C2
Broad Green 204 D3
Broadgate 95 C2
Brockley 141 B1
Bromley 186 C2
Bromley
  (Tower Hamlets) ...97 D4
Bromley Common ...210 A3
Bromley Park 186 D2
Brompton 114 B3
Brondesbury 69 A2
Brondesbury Park ..90 D6
Brook Green 112 D2
Broom Hill 211 D2
Brunswick Park ...15 A1
Buckhurst Hill ...21 C2
Burnt Oak 27 B3
Bush Hill Park ...17 C5
Bushey 8 A2
Bushey Heath 8 C4
Bushey Mead 200 D6

C

Camberwell 139 A4
Camden Town 71 B1
Canary Wharf 119 D5
Canning Town 99 B1
Canonbury 73 A2
Canons Park 26 A3
Carshalton 218 C4
Carshalton Beeches .218 D1
Carshalton
  on the Hill 219 B1
Castle Green 102 C6
Catford 163 C3
Chadwell Heath ...58 D4
Charlton
  (Greenwich) 143 D6
Charlton (Surrey) .171 B1
Chattern Hill 170 D6
Cheam 217 B3
Chelsea 114 C1
Chertsey Meads ...192 A1
Chessington 214 A2
Child's Hill 69 C6
Chingford 20 C3
Chingford Green ..20 A4
Chingford Hatch ..36 B6
Chipping Barnet ..1 B1
Chislehurst 189 C3
Chislehurst West ..188 C4
Chiswick 111 D1
Church End
  (Barnet) 29 C1
Church End (Brent) .67 D2
City of London ...117 A6
Clapham 137 B2
Clapham Common ...137 B1

Clapham Junction ..136 C1
Clapham Park 159 D6
Clapton Park 74 D4
Clay Hill 5 A6
Claygate 212 D1
Clayhall 56 B6
Clerkenwell 94 D3
Cockfosters 2 D1
Colham Green 82 C2
Colindale 45 C6
College Park 90 B4
Collier's Wood ...180 C4
Colney Hatch 30 C4
Coney Hall 224 D5
Coombe 177 B3
Copse Hill 178 B3
Cottenham Park ...178 B2
Covent Garden 116 A6
Cowley Peachy 82 A2
Cranbrook 56 C1
Cranford 128 C4
Cranley Gardens ..49 B5
Creekmouth 101 D2
Cricklewood 68 D4
Crofton 227 B6
Crooked Billet ...178 C4
Crouch End 49 D3
Croydon 221 B5
Crystal Palace ...184 A5
Cubitt Town 120 A2
Custom House 121 C6
Cyprus 122 C6

D

Dagenham 81 D1
Dalston 74 A2
Dartmouth Park ...71 B5
De Beauvoir
  Town 73 C1
Deacons Hill 10 C5
Deptford 140 D6
Dollis Hill 68 B5
Dormer's Wells ...107 C6
Downham 186 C5
Ducks Island 12 D5
Dudden Hill 68 A3
Dulwich 161 C1
Dulwich Village ..161 C4

E

Ealing 109 D6
Earl's Court 113 C1
Earlsfield 158 A3
East Acton 111 C5
East Barnet 14 D4
East Bedfont 149 C3
East Dulwich 162 A6
East Finchley 48 B5
East Ham 100 A5

East Molesey 196 A4
East Sheen 133 B1
East Wickham 146 A5
Eastbury 22 A5
Eastcote 40 C3
Eastcote Village ..40 B4
Eden Park 207 C5
Edgware 26 C6
Edgware Bury 10 B3
Edmonton 33 D6
Elmers End 206 D6
Elmstead 188 A5
Elstree 10 A5
Eltham 166 B6
Enfield 6 B2
Enfield Highway ..6 C3
Enfield Lock 7 B6
Enfield Town 5 B1
Enfield Wash 6 D5
Erith 147 D6
Esher 212 A4
Euston 93 C4
Ewell 215 C1

F

Fair Cross 79 D3
Falconwood 145 C1
Farnborough 227 B3
Farthing Street ..226 B1
Feltham 150 A3
Felthamhill 171 D5
Finchley 29 D3
Finsbury 94 C4
Finsbury Park 50 D1
Fitzrovia 93 C1
Foots Cray 190 B4
Forest Gate 77 A3
Forest Hill 163 A3
Fortis Green 48 D5
Forty Hill 5 D4
Friday Hill 20 C1
Friern Barnet 31 A6
Fulham 134 D4
Furzedown 181 B6

G

Gants Hill 56 C3
Globe Town 96 D4
Golders Green 47 B4
Goodmayes 58 B1
Gospel Oak 70 D2
Grahame Park 27 C2
Grange Park 16 C6
Green Street Green .227 C2
Greenford 86 A4
Greenhill 42 D4
Greenwich 142 C6
Grove Park
  (Hounslow) 133 A4

Grove Park
  (Lewisham) 165 B1
Gunnersbury 110 D2

H

Hackbridge 219 B6
Hackney 74 B2
Hackney Wick 75 C2
Hadley 1 B2
Hadley Wood 2 B5
Haggerston 95 D5
Hale End 36 C4
Harlington 127 A6
Harmondsworth ...126 A6
Harringay 50 D4
Harrow 42 B3
Harrow on the Hill ..42 C1
Harrow Weald 24 B2
Hatch End 23 A3
Hatton 127 D1
Hayes (Bromley) ..209 A2
Hayes (Hillingdon) ..83 C1
Hayes End 83 B3
Hayes Town 106 B5
Headstone 41 D5
Hendon 46 C3
Herne Hill 161 A6
Heston 129 B5
High Barnet 1 A4
Higham Hill 35 A2
Highams Park 36 A3
Highbury 72 D4
Highgate 49 A2
Hillingdon 82 D5
Hillingdon Heath ..82 D2
Hinchley Wood 212 D6
Hither Green 164 C5
Holborn 94 C2
Homerton 74 D1
Honor Oak 162 C6
Hook 214 A4
Hornsey 50 A5
Hornsey Vale 50 B4
Hounslow 129 C3
Hounslow West 128 D2
Hoxton 95 C5
Hurst Park 174 A1
Hyde Park 114 D5

Hyde The 45 D4

I

Ickenham 60 C4
Ilford 78 D6
Isle of Dogs 120 A2
Isleworth 131 B2
Islington 72 D2

K

Kennington 116 C1
Kensal Green 90 C4
Kensal Rise 91 A5
Kensal Town 91 A3
Kensington 113 C4
Kentish Town 71 C3
Kenton 43 C3
Keston 225 D4
Keston Mark 225 D6
Kew 132 C6
Kidbrooke 143 C3
Kilburn 91 B6
King's Cross 94 A5
Kingsbury 45 B3
Kingsland 73 C2
Kingston upon
  Thames 197 C6
Kingston Vale 177 B6
Kitts End 1 C1
Knightsbridge 114 C4

L

Ladywell 163 C6
Lambeth 116 B4
Lampton 129 C4
Lea Bridge 74 D5
Lee 74 D5
Lessness Heath ...125 D1
Lewisham 142 A1
Leyton 76 B5
Leytonstone 54 D1
Limehouse 119 A6
Lisson Green 92 C3
Lisson Grove 92 B2
Little Heath 58 B5
Little Ilford 78 C3
Little Stanmore ..26 B2
Littleton 192 C6
Littleton Common ..171 B3
Locksbottom 226 D5
London City Airport .122 B5
Long Ditton 197 C1
Longlands 167 B1
Loughton 21 D1
Lower Clapton 74 C4
Lower Edmonton ...18 B1
Lower Feltham 149 D1
Lower Green 195 D1

Lower Halliford 193 C3
Lower Holloway 72 A3
Lower Morden 201 A2
Lower Place 89 A5
Lower Sydenham 185 A6
Loxford 79 A3

M

Maida Vale 91 D4
Maitland Park 71 A2
Manor Park 78 A4
Marylebone 93 B1
Mayfair 115 B6
Merton 179 C2
Merton Park 179 C1
Mile End 97 A3
Mill Hill 28 B3
Mill Meads 98 B5
Millwall 119 C3
Mitcham 202 D5
Monken Hadley 1 A3
Monks Orchard 207 A3
Morden 201 D3
Morden Park 201 A3
Mortlake 133 A2
Motspur Park 200 A3
Mottingham 165 D2
Muswell Hill 49 A6

N

Nash 225 A2
Neasden 67 B4
New Addington 224 B1
New Barnet 14 A6
New Beckenham ...185 A6
New Charlton 121 C2
New Cross 141 B4
New Cross Gate ...140 D4
New Eltham 167 A2
New Malden 199 D5
New Southgate 31 C6
Newbury Park 57 B3
Newham 98 D4
Newington 116 D2
Newyears Green 38 B3
Nine Elms 137 C5
Noel Park 32 D1
Norbiton 176 C1
Norbury 182 C2
North Acton 89 B4
North Cheam 216 C6
North Cray 169 B1
North End 70 A6
North Feltham 150 B6
North Finchley 30 A6

North Harrow 41 D2
North Hillingdon ...61 A2
North Hyde 107 A1
North Kensington ...90 D2
North Sheen 132 C3
North Wembley 65 C6
North Woolwich ...122 D4
Northolt 63 C1
Northwood 22 A3
Northwood Hills 22 A1
Norwood Green ...107 C2
Norwood New Town .183 A4
Notting Hill 113 B6
Nower Hill 41 B6
Nunhead 140 C1

O

Oakleigh Park 14 B3
Oakwood 15 D6
Old Bexley 169 D4
Old Ford 97 B6
Old Malden 199 C1
Old Oak Common ...89 D3
Orpington 227 D6
Osidge 15 C3
Osterley 130 B5

P

Paddington 92 A2
Palmers Green 16 A1
Park Langley 208 B4
Park Royal 88 D4
Parsons Green 135 C4
Peckham 140 A4
Penge 184 D4
Pentonville 94 B5
Perivale 87 B5
Petersham 153 D3
Petts Wood 211 B5
Pimlico 115 C1
Pinner 41 A6
Pinner Green 22 C1
Pinnerwood Park ...22 C3
Plaistow (Bromley) .187 A4
Plaistow (Newham) ..99 B4
Plashet 78 A2
Plumstead 123 C2
Plumstead Common .145 D6
Ponders End 18 D6
Poplar 97 C1
Preston 44 A1
Primrose Hill 70 D1
Putney 156 C6
Putney Heath 156 C6
Putney Vale 156 A1

Q

Queensbury 44 B6

R

Ratcliff 118 D6
Rayners Lane 41 B1
Raynes Park 200 C6
Redbridge 55 D3
Regent's Park 93 B4
Richmond 154 A6
Richmond Hill 154 A5
Richmond Park 155 A3
Roehampton 155 C4
Romford 59 C5
Rosehill 202 A1
Rotherhithe 118 D3
Roundshaw 220 B1
Roxeth 64 A6
Ruislip 39 B2
Ruislip Common 39 B4
Ruislip Gardens 61 D5
Ruislip Manor 40 A1
Ruxley 191 A3

S

Sands End 136 A2
Seething Wells 197 D3
Selhurst 205 B4
Selsdon 223 A1
Seven Kings 57 D2
Sewardstonebury 20 C6
Shacklewell 73 D4
Shadwell 118 C6
Shepherd's Bush ...112 B5
Shepperton 193 A3
Shepperton Green .192 D5
Shirley 206 C1
Shooters Hill 145 A4
Shoreditch 95 B5
Shortlands 208 C6
Sidcup 190 A5
Silvertown 121 C4
Sipson 126 C6
Snaresbrook 54 D6
Soho 93 D1
Somers Town 93 D4
South Acton 110 D3
South Bank 116 B4
South Beddington .219 C2
South Bromley 98 B2
South Croydon 221 B1
South Hackney 96 C6
South Hampstead ...70 A1
South Harrow 63 D5

South Kensington ...114 A1
South Lambeth 138 A4
South Norwood 205 C6
South Oxhey 22 B6
South Ruislip 62 D4
South Tottenham 51 D4
South Wimbledon ..179 D4
Southall 107 A5
Southborough
  (Bromley) 210 B3
Southborough (Kingston
  Upon Thames) ...197 D1
Southend 186 B6
Southfields 157 C3
Southgate 16 B4
Southwark 117 B5
Spitalfields 95 D2
Spring Grove 130 C3
Spring Park 223 B5
St George in
  the East 118 A6
St Giles 94 A1
St Helier 202 B2
St James 115 C5
St John's 141 C3
St John's Wood 92 B5
St Luke's 95 A3
St Margarets 153 A5
St Pancras 94 A4
St Paul's Cray 190 A1
Stamford Hill 51 C1
Stanmore 25 B2
Stanwell 148 A3
Stepney 96 D2
Stockwell 138 A2
Stoke Newington ...73 C6
Stonebridge 89 A6
Stoneleigh 216 A3
Strand 116 B6
Strand on the Green 132 C6
Stratford 76 A1
Stratford Marsh 97 D6
Stratford New Town ..76 A3
Strawberry Hill 152 D1
Streatham 182 A4
Streatham Hill 160 A3
Streatham Park 181 C6
Streatham Vale 181 D3
Stroud Green 50 C3
Sudbury 65 A4
Summerstown 158 A1
Sunbury 194 B6
Sunbury Common ..171 D3
Sundridge 187 C4
Surbiton 198 A2
Sutton 218 A1
Syon Park 131 B4

T

Teddington 175 C5
Temple Mills 75 D3
Thames Ditton 197 B2
Thamesmead 124 A5
Thornton Heath ...204 D3
Tokyngton 66 D2
Tolworth 214 C6
Tooting 180 D4
Tooting Graveney ..180 B5
Tottenham 33 D1
Tottenham Hale 52 A6
Totteridge 13 C3
Tower Hamlets 97 B2
Tufnell Park 71 D4
Tulse Hill 160 D4
Twickenham 152 D4

U

Underhill 13 C6
Upper Clapton 52 B1
Upper Edmonton ...34 B5
Upper Elmers End ..207 B4
Upper Halliford ...193 B5
Upper Holloway 71 D6
Upper Norwood ...183 C3
Upper Ruxley 191 C3
Upper Shirley 222 D4
Upper Sydenham ...184 A6
Upper Tooting 158 D1
Upper Walthamstow .54 C6
Upton 77 B1
Upton Park 99 D6
Uxbridge 82 A6

V

Vale of Health 70 B5
Vauxhall 116 A1

W

Waddon 220 D4
Walham Green 135 D5
Wallend 100 C6
Wallington 219 A2
Walthamstow 53 D6
Walton-on-Thames .194 C2
Walworth 117 B1
Wandsworth 157 C5
Wanstead 55 C3
Wapping 118 B5
Waterloo 116 C4
Wealdstone 42 D6
Welling 146 B2

Welsh Harp ....45 C
Wembley ....66 A
Wembley Park .....66 C
West Acton ....88 C
West Barnes ......200 C
West Bedfont .....148 C
West Brompton ...135 D
West Drayton 104 B4
West Dulwich 161 A2
West Ealing 109 B5
West Ewell 215 C1
West Green ....51 A
West Ham 99 B6
West Hampstead 69 C4
West Harrow ....42 A
West Heath 146 D6
West Hendon 45 D3
West Hill 157 B5
West Kensington ...113 A2
West Kilburn 91 A4
West Molesey 195 C5
West Norwood 161 A1
West Ruislip 61 B6
West Wickham 224 C6
Westbourne Green ..91 D3
Westminster 115 C4
Weston Green 196 D1
Whetstone 14 A2
Whitechapel 95 D1
Whitton 152 A4
Widmore 188 A1
Willesden 68 A4
Willesden Green 90 B6
Wimbledon 179 B4
Wimbledon Park ...157 B2
Winchmore Hill 16 D4
Wood End 83 D1
Wood End Green 83 C2
Wood Green 32 B2
Woodford 37 D5
Woodford Green 37 B3
Woodford Wells 21 B1
Woodlands 130 C2
Woodside 206 A4
Woodside Park 29 C6
Woolwich 122 D3
Worcester Park 215 C4
World's End 4 C1
Wrythe The 218 D6

Y

Yeading 84 D3
Yiewsley 104 A6

Abbreviations used in the index

Acad	Academy	Ct	Court	Int	International	Prom	Promenade
App	Approach	Ctr	Centre	Intc	Interchange	RC	Roman Catholic
Arc	Arcade	Crkt	Cricket	Jun	Junior	Rd	Road
Art Gall	Art Gallery	Ctry Pk	Country Park	Junc	Junction	Rdbt	Roundabout
Ave	Avenue	Cty	County	La	Lane	Ret Pk	Retail Park
Bglws	Bungalows	Ctyd	Courtyard	L Ctr	Leisure Centre	Sch	School
Bldgs	Buildings	Dr	Drive	Liby	Library	Sec	Secondary
Bsns Ctr	Business Centre	Ent Ctr	Enterprise Centre	Mans	Mansions	Sh Ctr	Shopping Centre
Bsns Pk	Business Park	Ent Pk	Enterprise Park	Mdw/s	Meadow/s	Sp	Sports
Bvd	Boulevard	Est	Estate	Meml	Memorial	Specl	Special
Cath	Cathedral, Catholic	Ex Ctr	Exhibition Centre	Mid	Middle	Sports Ctr	Sports Centre
CE	Church of England	Ex Hall	Exhibition Hall	Mix	Mixed	Sq	Square
Cemy	Cemetery	Fst	First	Mkt	Market	St	Street, Saint
Cir	Circus	Gdn	Garden	Mon	Monument	Sta	Station
Circ	Circle	Gdns	Gardens	Mus	Museum	Stad	Stadium
Cl	Close	Gn	Green	Obsy	Observatory	Tech	Technical/Technology
Coll	College	Gr	Grove	Orch	Orchard	Terr	Terrace
Com	Community	Gram	Grammar	Par	Parade	Trad Est	Trading Estate
Comm	Common	Her Ctr	Heritage Centre	Pas	Passage	Twr/s	Tower/s
Comp	Comprehensive	Ho	House	Pav	Pavilion	Univ	University
Con Ctr	Conference Centre	Hospl	Hospital	Pk	Park	Wlk	Walk
Cotts	Cottages	Hts	Heights	Pl	Place	Yd	Yard
Cres	Crescent	Ind Est	Industrial Estate	Prec	Precinct		
Cswy	Causeway	Inf	Infant	Prep	Preparatory		
		Inst	Institute	Prim	Primary		

Aaron Ct BR3 ....207 D6
Aaron Hill Rd E6 ....100 C2
Abady Ho SW1 ......259 D4
Abberley Mews 9
SW8 ....137 B2
Abberton IG8 ....37 C5
Abbess Cl 11 E6 .....100 A2
Streatham SW2 ......160 D3
Abbeville Mews 3
SW4 ....137 D1
Abbeville Rd N8 ......49 D5
SW4 ....159 C6
Abbey Ave HA0 ....88 A5
Abbey Bsns Ctr
SW8 ....137 B4 268 D2
Abbey Cl Hayes UB3 ..106 B5
Northolt UB5 ....85 B4
Pinner HA5 ....40 C6
Abbey Cres DA17 ....125 C2
Abbey Ct N3 ....47 C6
NW8 ....229 A4
SE17 ....262 B1
6 W12 ....111 C3
Abbeydale Ct 6 UB1 .85 D1
Abbeydale Rd HA0 ....88 C6
Abbey Dr SW17 ......181 A5
Abbeyfield UB4 ....83 D2
Abbeyfield Rd SE16 ..118 C2
Abbeyfields Cl NW10 ..88 C5
Abbey Gdns
NW8 ....92 A5 229 B3
9 SE16 ....118 A2
W6 ....135 A6 264 A5
Chislehurst BR7 ......188 C2
Abbey Gr SE2 ....124 B2
Abbeyhill Rd DA15 ..168 C2
Abbey Ho E15 ....98 C5
NW8 ....229 B2
Abbey Ind Est CR4 ..202 D4
Abbey La E15 ....98 B5
Beckenham BR3 ......185 C3
Abbey Lane Commercial
Est E15 ....98 C5
Abbey Lo NW8 ......230 B1
1 Ealing W5 ....109 C6
Abbey Manufacturing Est
HA0 ....88 B6
Abbey Mews E17 .....53 C4
Abbey Mount DA17 ..125 B1
Abbey Orchard St
SW1 ....115 D3 259 D6
Abbey Orchard Street Est
SW1 ....259 D6
Abbey Par Ealing NW10 88 B4
Merton SW19 ....180 A3
Abbey Park Ind Est
IG11 ....101 A6
Abbey Pk BR3 ....185 C3
Abbey Prim Sch SE2 124 C3
Abbey Rd E15 ....98 C5
NW8 ....92 A5 229 A4
Barking IG11 ....100 D6
Bexley DA6,DA7 ......147 A1
Croydon CR0 ....220 D5
Enfield EN1 ....17 C6
Erith DA17 ....125 A3
Ilford IG2 ....57 B4
Lower Halliford TW17 .192 C1
Merton SW19 ....180 A2
Wembley NW10 ....88 D5
Abbey St E13 ....99 A3
SE1 ....117 D3 263 C6
Abbey Terr SE2 ......124 C2
Abbey Tutorial Coll
W2 ....91 C1
Abbey View NW7 .....11 D1
Abbey Wlk KT8 ....195 D5
Abbey Wood Rd SE2 .124 C2
Abbey Wood Sch
SE2 ....124 A3
Abbey Wood Sta SE2 124 C3
Abbot Cl HA4 ....62 D5
Abbot Ct SW8 ....270 A3
Abbot Ho 13 E14 .....119 D6
Abbotsbury Cl E15 ....98 A5
W14 ....113 B4 244 C1
Abbotsbury Fst Sch
SM4 ....201 D4
Abbotsbury Gdns HA5 40 C3
Abbotsbury Ho W14 .244 B2
Abbotsbury Mews
SE15 ....140 C2
Abbotsbury Rd
W14 ....113 B4 244 C1
Coney Hall BR2,BR4 ..224 D6
Morden SM4 ....201 D5
Abbots Cl BR5 ....211 A1
Abbots Ct SE25 ......205 C6
Abbots Dr HA2 ....63 C6
Abbotsfield Sch UB10 82 D5
Abbotsford Ave N15 ..51 A5
Abbotsford Gdns IG8 .37 A3
Abbotsford Rd IG3 ....80 B6
Abbots Gdns N2 ....48 B5
Abbots Gn CR0,CR2 ..222 D2
Abbotshade Rd 15
SE16 ....118 D5
Abbotshall Ave N14 ..15 C1
Abbotshall Rd SE6 ...164 B2
Abbots Ho E17 ....35 B1
SW1 ....259 C1
W14 ....254 C5
Abbots La
SE1 ....117 C5 253 B3
Abbotsleigh Cl SM2 .217 D1
Abbotsleigh Rd
SW16 ....181 C5
Abbotsmede Cl TW1 .152 D2
Abbots Pk SW2 ......160 C3
Abbot's Pl NW6 ....91 D6
Abbots Rd E6 ....99 D6
HA8 ....27 A3
Abbot St E8 ....73 D2
Abbots Terr N8 ....50 A3
Abbotstone Ho 4 E5 .74 A6
Abbotstone Rd SW15 134 C2
Abbots Way BR3 .....207 A4
Abbotswell Rd SE4 ..163 B6
Abbotswood Cl 7
DA17 ....125 A3
Abbotswood Gdns IG5 56 B6
Abbotswood Rd SE22 139 C1
Streatham SW16 .....159 D1
Abbotswood Way
UB3 ....106 B5
Abbott Ave SW20 ....178 D2
Abbott Cl
Hampton TW12 ....173 A4
Northolt UB5 ....63 B2
Abbott Ho SW12 .....158 D4
Abbott Rd E14 ....98 B1
Abbotts Cl N1 ....73 A2
Romford RM7 ....59 D6
Woolwich SE28 ......124 C6
Abbotts Cres
Chingford E4 ....36 B6
Enfield EN2 ....4 D3
Abbotts Ct HA2 ....64 B6
Abbotts Dr HA0 ....65 B6
Abbotts Park Rd E10 ..54 A2
Abbotts Rd Barnet EN5 ..1 D1
Cheam SM3 ....217 A4
Mitcham CR4 ....203 C5
Southall UB1 ....107 A5
Abbott's Wlk DA7 ....146 D5
Abbyfield Cl CR4 ....180 C1
Abchurch La
EC2,EC4 .....117 B6 252 D6
Abchurch Yd EC4 ...252 C6
Abdale Rd W12 ......112 B5
Abel Ho 7 SE11 .....138 C6
Abenglen Ind Est
UB3 ....105 B4
Aberavon Rd E3 ......97 A4
Abercairn Rd SW16 ..181 C3
Aberconway Rd SM4 201 D5
Abercorn Cl NW7 .....29 A3
NW8 ....92 A4 229 A2
Abercorn Cres HA2 ...41 D1
Abercorn Gdns
Harrow HA3 ....43 D2
Ilford RM6 ....58 B3
Abercorn Gr HA4 .....39 B5
Abercorn Ho SE10 ...141 D5
Abercorn Mans NW8 229 B3
Abercorn Mews 10
TW10 ....132 B1
Abercorn Pl
NW8 ....92 A5 229 A3
Abercorn Rd NW7 ....29 A3
Stanmore HA7 ....25 C3
Abercorn Trad Est
HA0 ....87 D6
Abercorn Way SE1 ..118 A1
Abercrombie Dr EN1 ...6 A4
Abercrombie Ho 1
W12 ....112 B6
Abercrombie St
SW11 ....136 C3
Aberdale Ct 22 SE16 .118 D4
Aberdare Cl BR4 ....224 A6
Aberdare Gdns NW6 ..69 D1
NW7 ....28 D3
Aberdare Rd EN3 ....6 C1
Aberdeen Ct N5 ....73 A3
W2 ....236 C5
Aberdeen La N5 ......73 A3
Aberdeen Mans WC1 240 A6
Aberdeen Par N18 ....34 B5
Aberdeen Pk N5 ......73 A3
Aberdeen Pl
NW8 ....92 B3 236 C6
Aberdeen Rd N5 ......73 A4
NW10 ....67 D3
Croydon CR0 ....221 B4
Edmonton N18 ....34 B5
Harrow HA3 ....24 D1
Aberdeen Terr SE3 ..142 B3
Aberdour Rd IG3 .....80 B6
Aberdour St
SE1 ....117 C3 263 A4
Aberfeldy Ho SE5 ...138 D5
Aberfeldy St E14 ......98 A1
Aberford Gdns SE18 .144 A4
Aberfoyle Rd SW16 ..181 D4
Abergeldie Rd SE12 .165 B5
Abernethy Rd SE13 ..142 C1
Abersham Rd E8 ......73 D3
Abery St SE18 ......123 C2
Abingdon W14 ......254 D3
Abingdon Cl NW1 ....71 D2
SE1 ....263 D2
Hillingdon UB10 ....82 B6
Wimbledon SW19 ....180 A4
Abingdon Ct W8 .....255 B5
Edgware HA8 ....26 A6
Abingdon Gdns W8 ..255 B5
Abingdon Ho E2 .....243 C6
Abingdon Lo BR2 ....186 D1
Abingdon Mans W8 .255 A6
Abingdon Rd N3 ......30 A1
W8 ....113 C3 255 B5
Thornton Heath SW16 .182 A2
Abingdon St
SW1 ....116 A3 260 A6
Abingdon Villas
W8 ....113 C3 255 B5
Abinger Cl BR1 ......210 A6
Barking IG11 ....80 A4
New Addington CR0 ..224 A2
Wallington SM6 ......220 A3
Abinger Ct
3 Ealing W5 ....109 C6
Wallington SM6 ......220 A3
Abinger Gdns TW7 ..130 C2
Abinger Gr SE8 ......141 B6
Abinger Ho SE1 .....252 C1
2 Kingston KT2 .....176 D3
Abinger Mews W9 ....91 C3
Abinger Rd W4 ......111 C3
Abington Ho NW11 ....48 A3
Ablett St SE16 ......118 C1
Abney Gdns 5 N16 ...73 D6
Abney Park Cemetery*
N16 ....73 C6
Abney Park Ct N16 ...73 D6
Aborfield 6 NW5 ......71 C3
Aboyne Dr SW20 ....178 A1
Aboyne Rd NW10 .....67 C5
Wandsworth SW17 ...158 B1
Abraham Cl WD19 ....22 B6
Abridge Way IG11 ...102 B5
Abyssinia Cl SW11 ..136 C1
Abyssinia Rd SW11 ..136 C1
Acacia Ave N2 ....47 D6
Brentford TW8 ....131 B5
Hayes UB3 ....83 D1
Littleton TW17 ......192 C4
Ruislip HA4 ....40 B2
Tottenham N17 ....33 B3
Wembley HA9 ....66 A3
Yiewsley UB7 ....104 B6
Acacia Bsns Ctr 1
E11 ....76 C5
Acacia Cl BR5 ....211 B4
SE8 ....119 A2
Penge SE20 ....184 A1
Stanmore HA7 ....24 C4
Acacia Ct Harrow HA1 .41 D3
5 West Norwood
SW16 ....182 C5
Acacia Dr SM3 ....201 C1
Acacia Gdns NW8 ...229 D4
West Wickham BR4 ..224 A6
Acacia Gr
Dulwich SE21 ....161 B2
Kingston KT3 ....199 C6
Acacia Ho N16 ....73 B6
1 New Malden KT3 ..199 C5
Wood Green N22 ......32 C2
Acacia Pl NW8 92 B5 229 D4
Acacia Rd E11 ....76 C6
E17 ....53 A3
NW8 ....92 B5 229 D4
W3 ....111 A6
Beckenham BR3 ......207 B6
Enfield EN2 ....5 B4
Hampton TW12 ....173 C4
Acacia Rd *continued*
Mitcham CR4 ....181 B1
Thornton Heath SW16 .182 A2
Wood Green N22 ......32 C2
Acacias Lo EN4 ....14 B6
Acacias The EN4 ......14 B6
Acacia Way DA15 ....167 D3
Acacia Wlk SW10 ...266 B3
Academy Ct 13 E2 ....96 C4
Academy Gdns
Croydon CR0 ....205 D1
Northolt UB5 ....84 D5
Academy Pl SE18 ....144 C4
Academy Rd SE18 ...144 C4
Academy The 2 N19 ..49 C1
Acanthus Dr SE1 ....118 A1
Acanthus Rd SW11 ..137 A2
Accadia Ct NW9 ......67 A6
Accommodation Rd
NW11 ....47 B1
Ace Par KT9 ....214 A5
Acer Ave UB4 ....85 A2
Acer Ct NW2 ....68 D4
Acfold Rd SW6 ......265 C1
Achilles Cl SE1 .....118 A1
Achilles Ho 16 E2 ....96 B5
Achilles Rd NW6 ......69 C3
Achilles St SE14 .....141 A5
Achilles Way W1 ....248 B3
Acklam Rd W10 ....91 B2
Acklington Dr NW9 ...27 C2
Ackmar Rd
SW6 ....135 C4 265 A1
Ackroyd Dr E3 ....97 C2
Ackroyd Rd SE23 ....163 A4
Acland Burghley Sch
NW5 ....71 B4
Acland Cl SE18 ......145 B5
Acland Cres SE5 .....139 B2
Acland Ho SW9 ......138 B3
Acock Gr UB5 ....64 A4
Acol Cres HA4 ....62 B3
Acol Ct 3 NW6 ....69 C1
Acol Rd NW6 ....69 D1
Aconbury Rd RM9 ...102 B6
Acorn Cl Chingford E4 .35 D5
Chislehurst BR7 .....189 A5
Enfield EN2 ....4 D4
1 Hampton TW12 ....173 D4
Stanmore HA7 ....25 B3
Acorn Ct E6 ....78 A1
Ilford IG2 ....57 C4
Acorn Gdns W3 ....89 B2
South Norwood SE19 .183 D2
Acorn Gr
Harlington UB3 ......127 D5
Ruislip HA4 ....61 D4
Acorn Par 7 SE15 ...140 B5
Acorn Production Ctr
N7 ....72 A1
Acorns The 21 SW19 .156 D3
Acorns Way KT10 ....212 A3
Acorn Way
Beckenham BR3 ......208 A4
Forest Hill SE23 ......162 D1
Orpington BR6 ....226 D4
Acorn Wharf SE1 ....140 A6
Acorn Wlk SE16 .....119 A5
Acre Dr SE22 ....140 A1
Acrefield Ho 4 NW4 .46 D5
Acre La SW2 ....138 B1
Wallington SM5 ......219 A4
Acre Path UB5 ....63 A2
Acre Rd
Dagenham RM10 ......81 D1
Kingston KT2 ....176 B2
Mitcham SW19 ....180 B4
Acre Way HA6 ....22 A2
Acris St SW18 ....158 A6
Action Ct TW15 .....171 A2
Acton Bsns Ctr NW10 .89 B3
Acton Central Ind Est 4
W3 ....110 D5
Acton Central Sta
W3 ....111 B5
Acton Cl N9 ....18 A2
Acton High Sch W3 .110 C4
Acton Hill Mews W3 110 D5
Acton Ho 16 E8 ....95 D6
5 W3 ....89 A1
Acton Hospl W3 .....110 C4
Acton La Acton NW10 ..89 B5
Acton W3 ....111 A4
Acton W4 ....111 A2
Acton Main Line Sta
W3 ....89 A1
Acton Mews E8 ....95 D6
Acton Park Est W3 ..111 B4
Acton St WC1 .94 B4 233 C1
Acton Town Sta W3 .110 C4
Acton Vale Ind Pk
W3 ....111 D5
Acuba Ho SW18 .....157 D3
Acuba Rd SW18 .....157 D2
Acworth Cl N9 ....18 C4
Acworth Ho 1 SE18 .144 D6
Ada Ct N1 ....235 A5
W9 ....92 A4 229 B1
Ada Gdns E15 ....98 D6
South Bromley E14 ....98 B1
Ada Ho 23 E2 ....96 A6
Adair Cl SE25 ....206 B6
Adair Ho SW3 ....267 B6
Adair Rd W10 ....91 A3
Adair Twr 7 W10 .....91 A3
Ada Kennedy Ct 6
SE10 ....142 A5
Ada Lewis Ho HA9 ....66 B4
Adam Cl SE6 ....185 C6
Adam Ct SE11 ......261 C3
Adam & Eve Ct W1 ..239 B2
Adam & Eve Mews
W8 ....113 C3 255 B6
Adamfields NW3 ......70 B1
Adam Lo N21 ....16 B6
Adam Rd E4 ....35 B4
Adams Cl N3 ....29 C3
NW9 ....66 D6
Surbiton KT5 ....198 B3
Adams Ct E17 ....53 A3
Adams Gardens Est 5
SE16 ....118 C4
Adams Ho
3 South Bromley E14 ..98 B1
3 Streatham SW16 ..181 C5
Adams Mews N22 .....32 B3
Adamson Ct N2 ......48 C6
Adamson Rd E16 .....99 A1
NW3 ....70 B1
Adams Pl N7 ....72 B3
Adams Rd
Beckenham BR3 ......207 A4
Tottenham N17 ....33 B1
Adamsrill Cl EN1 ......17 B5
Adamsrill Prim Sch
SE26 ....163 A1
Adamsrill Rd SE26 ..185 A6
Adam's Row
W1 ....115 A6 248 B5
Adams Sq DA6 ......147 A2
Adam St WC2 116 A6 250 B5
Adams Way CR0 .....206 A3
Adams Wlk 11 KT1 ...176 A1
Adam Wlk SW6 ......134 C5
Ada Pl E2 ....96 A6
Ada Rd SE5 ....139 C5
Wembley HA0,HA9 ....65 D5
Adare Wlk SW16,SW2 160 B2
Ada St E8 ....96 B6
Adcot Wlk 6 BR6 ...227 D4
Adderley Gdns SE9 ..188 C6
Adderley Gr SW11 ..159 A6
Adderley Rd HA3 .....24 D2
Adderley St E14 ......98 A1
Addey Ho SE8 ....141 B5
Addey & Stanhope Sch
SE14 ....141 C4
Addington Ct 7
SW14 ....133 B2
Addington Dr N12 ....30 B4
Addington Gr SE26 ..185 A6
Addington Ho 13
SW9 ....138 B3
Addington Palace (The
Royal Sch of Church
Music) CR9 ....223 B2
Addington Rd E16 ....98 C3
E3 ....97 C4
N4 ....50 C3
Thornton Heath CR0 ..204 C1
West Wickham BR4 ..224 C6
West Wickham BR4,
CR0 ....224 B4
Addington Sq SE5 ...139 B5
Addington St
SE1 ....116 B4 250 D1
Addington Village Rd
CR0 ....223 C3
Addington Village Sta
CR0 ....223 C2
Addis Cl EN3 ....6 D4
Addiscombe Ave CR0 206 A2
Addiscombe Cl HA3 ..43 C4
Addiscombe Court Rd
CR0 ....221 C6
Addiscombe Ct UB10 .83 A3
Addiscombe Rd CR0 .222 B6
Addiscombe Sta CR0 206 A1
Addison Ave
W11 ....113 A5 244 A3
Addison Ave *continued*
Hounslow TW3 ....130 A4
Southgate N14 ....15 C5
Addison Bridge Pl
W14 ....113 B2 254 C4
Addison Cl
Northwood HA6 ....22 A2
Orpington BR5 ....211 A3
Addison Cres
W14 ....113 A3 254 B6
Addison Ct W5 ......110 C6
Addison Dr SE12 ....165 B6
Addison Gdns W14 ..112 D3
Kingston KT5 ....198 B5
Addison Gr W4 ......111 C3
Addison Ho
NW8 ....92 B4 229 C2
Addison Park Mans 12
W14 ....112 D4
Addison Pl
W11 ....113 A5 244 A3
Southall UB1 ....107 C6
Addison Prim Sch
W14 ....112 D3
Addison Rd BR2 .....209 D4
E17 ....54 A4
W14 ....113 B3 254 C6
Croydon SE25 ....206 A5
Enfield EN3 ....6 D4
Teddington TW11 ....175 B4
Wanstead E11 ....55 A3
Addison's Cl CR0 ...223 B6
Addison Way NW11 ...47 C5
Hayes UB3 ....84 A1
Northwood HA6 ....22 A2
Addle Hill EC4 ......241 D1
Addle St EC2 ....242 B3
Addlestone Ho W10 ..90 C2
Addy Ho SE16 ....118 C2
Adecroft Way KT8 ...196 A6
Adela Ave KT3 ......200 B5
Adela Ho 9 W6 ......112 C1
Adelaide Ave SE4 ....141 C1
Adelaide Cl SW9 ....138 C1
Enfield EN1 ....5 C5
Stanmore HA7 ....25 A6
Adelaide Ct NW8 ....229 B3
W7 ....108 D4
15 Beckenham BR3 ..185 C3
Adelaide Gdns RM6 ..59 A4
Adelaide Gr W12 ....112 A5
Adelaide Ho E17 .....53 B6
Adelaide Rd E10 .....76 A5
NW3 ....70 C1
2 SW18 ....157 C6
Ashford TW15 ....170 A6
Chislehurst BR7 .....188 D5
Ealing W13 ....109 A4
Heston TW5 ....129 A4
Ilford IG1 ....78 D6
Kingston KT6 ....198 A4
Richmond TW9 ......132 B1
Southall UB2 ....107 A2
Teddington TW11 ....174 D4
Adelaide St WC2 ...250 A5
Adelaide Terr TW8 ..109 D1
Adela St W10 ....91 A3
Adelina Gr E1 ....96 C2
Adelina Mews SW12 .159 D3
Adeline Pl
WC1 ....93 D2 239 D3
Adeliza Cl IG11 ....79 A1
Adelphi Cres UB4 ....83 D4
Adelphi Ct 20 SE16 ..118 D4
Adelphi Terr WC2 ...250 B5
Adelphi Way UB4 .....83 D4
Adeney Cl W6 ....134 D6
Aden Gr N16 ....73 B4
Aden Ho 12 E1 ....96 D2
Aden Lo N16 ....73 B4
Adenmore Rd SE6 ...163 C4
Aden Rd Enfield EN3 ...7 A1
Ilford IG1 ....57 A2
Adeyfield Ho EC1 ...235 D1
Adhara Rd HA6 ....22 A5
Adie Rd W6 ....112 C3
Adine Rd E13 ....99 B3
Adisham Ho 4 E5 ....74 B3
Adler Ind Est UB3 ...105 B4
Adler St E1 ....96 A1
Adley St E5 ....75 A3
Adlington Cl N18 .....33 C5
Admaston Rd SE18 ..145 A6
Admiral Ct NW4 ......46 A4
SW10 ....136 A4 266 B2
W1 ....238 A3
Barking IG11 ....102 C5

Admiral Ct *continued*
Carshalton SM5 ......202 C1
Admiral Ho TW11 ...175 A6
Admiral Hyson Ind Est
SE16 ....118 B1
Admiral Mews W10 ...90 D3
Admiral Pl SE16 .....119 A5
Admirals Cl E18 ......55 B5
Admirals Ct 3 E6 ...100 D1
SE1 ....253 C3
32 Putney SW19 .....156 D3
Admiral Seymour Rd
SE9 ....144 B1
Admirals Gate SE10 .141 D4
Admiral Sq
SW10 ....136 A4 266 B2
Admiral St SE8 ......141 C4
Admirals Way E14 ...119 C4
Admiral's Wlk NW3 ...70 A5
Admiralty Arch*
SW1 ....249 D4
Admiralty Cl 1 SE8 .141 C4
Admiralty Rd TW11 ..174 D4
Admiralty Way TW11 174 D4
Admiral Wlk W9 ......91 C2
Adolf St SE6 ....185 D6
Adolphus Rd N4 ......50 D1
Adolphus St SE8 .....141 B5
Adomar Rd RM8 ......81 A5
Adpar St W2 ..92 B2 236 C4
Adrian Ave NW2 ......46 B1
Adrian Bolt Ho 2 E2 .96 B4
Adrian Ho N1 ....233 D5
SW8 ....270 A4
Adrian Mews SW10 ..265 D6
Adriatic Bldg 18 E14 ....
Adriatic Ho 18 E1 ....96 D3
Adrienne Ave UB1 ....85 B4
Adron Ho 9 SE16 ...118 C2
Adstock Ho 5 N1 ....72 D1
ADT Coll SW15 ......157 B6
Advance Rd SE27 ...183 A6
Adventurers Ct 4
E14 ....120 B6
Advent Way N18 ......34 D5
Adys Lawn NW2 ......68 B2
Adys Rd SE15 ....139 D2
Aerodrome Rd NW4,
NW9 ....45 D6
Aerodrome Way
TW5 ....128 C6
Aeroville NW9 ....27 C1
Affleck St N1 ....233 D3
Afghan Rd SW11 ....136 C3
Agamemnon Rd NW6 .69 B3
Agar Cl KT6 ....214 B6
Agar Gr NW1 ....71 D1
Agar Ho 6 KT1 .....198 A6
Agar Pl NW1 ....71 C1
Agar St WC2 ....250 B5
Agate Cl E16 ....99 D1
Agate Ho
New Malden KT4 .....199 C1
12 Penge SE26 ......184 B5
Agate Rd W6 ....112 C3
Agatha Cl E1 ....118 C5
Agaton Rd BR7,SE9 ..167 A2
Agave Rd NW2 ....68 C4
Agdon St EC1 .94 D3 241 C6
Agincourt E11 ....54 D3
Agincourt Rd NW3 ....70 D4
Agnes Ave IG1 ....78 D4
Agnes Cl E6 ....122 C6
Agnes Ct 11 SW18 ...136 B1
Agnesfield Cl N12 ....30 C4
Agnes Gdns RM8 .....80 D4
Agnes Ho 13 W11 ...112 D6
Agnes Rd W3 ....111 D4
Agnes St E14 ....97 B1
Agnew Rd SE23 .....162 D4
Agricola Pl EN1 ......17 D6
Aidan Cl RM8 ....81 A4
Aidans Ct N12 ....30 C5
Aigburth Mans 5
SW9 ....138 C5
Ailantus Ct HA8 ......26 B5
Aileen Wlk E15 ....76 D1
Ailsa Ave TW1 ......153 B6
Ailsa Rd TW1 ....153 B6
Ailsa St E14 ....98 A2
Ainger Rd NW3 ....70 D1
Ainsdale NW1 ....232 A2
Ainsdale Cl BR6 .....211 B1
Ainsdale Cres HA5 ...41 C6
Ainsdale Dr SE1 .....118 A1
Ainsdale Rd W5 ......87 D3
Ainsley Ave RM7 .....59 D3
Ainsley Cl N9 ....17 C3
Ainsley St E2 ....96 B4
Ainsley Wood Prim Sch
E4 ....35 D5
Ainslie Ct 2 HA0 .....88 A5
Ainslie Wood Cres E4 .35 D5
Ainslie Wood Gdns E4 35 D5
Ainslie Wood Rd E4 ..35 D5
Ainsty St 14 SE16 ...118 C4
Ainsworth Cl NW2 ....68 A5
SE5 ....139 C3
Ainsworth Est
NW8 ....92 A6 229 A6
Ainsworth Ho NW8 ...91 D6
Ainsworth Rd E9 .....74 C1
Croydon CR0 ....220 D6
Ainsworth Way
NW8 ....92 A6 229 A6
Aintree Ave E6 ......100 A6
Aintree Cl UB8 ....82 D2
Aintree Ho SE26 ....184 B4
Aintree Rd UB6 ......87 B5
Aintree St
SW6 ....135 A5 264 B4
Airborne Ho 10 SM6 .219 B4
Air Call Bsns Ctr NW9 45 C6
Aird Ho SE1 ....262 A5
Airdrie Cl N1 ....72 B1
Hayes UB4 ....85 A2
Airedale Ave W4 ....111 D1
Airedale Ave S W4 ..111 D1
Airedale Rd W5 .....109 D3
Balham SW12 ....158 D4
Airlie Gdns
W8 ....113 C5 245 A3
Ilford IG1 ....56 D1
Airlinks Ind Est TW5 106 C1
Air Park Way TW13 ..150 B2
Airport Gate Bsns Ctr
UB7 ....126 B5
Airport Rdbt E16 ....121 D5
Air St W1 ....249 B5
Airthrie Rd IG3 ....80 B6
Aisgill Ave
SW5 ....113 B1 254 D1
Aisher Rd SE28 .....124 C6
Aislibie Rd SE12 ....142 C1
Aislobie Ho N21 .....17 B5
Aiten Pl W6 ....112 A2
Aithan Ho 9 E14 .....97 B1
Aitken Cl E8 ....96 A6
Carshalton CR4 ......202 D2
Aitken Rd Barnet EN5 ..12 C6
Catford SE6 ....163 D2
Ajax Ave NW9 ....45 C6
Ajax Ho 15 E2 ....96 B5
Ajax Rd NW6 ....69 C3
Akabusi Cl SE25 ....206 A3
Akbar Ho 7 E14 .....119 D2
Akehurst St SW15 ...156 A4
Akenside Ct 3 NW3 ...70 B3
Akenside Rd NW3 ....70 B3
Akerman Rd SW9 ...138 D4
Kingston KT6 ....197 C3
Akintaro Ho 7 SE8 ..141 B6
Akiva Sch N3 ....29 D1
Alabama St SE18 ....145 C5
Alacross Rd W5 .....109 D4
Alamaro Lo SE10 ...120 D3
Alandale Dr HA5 .....22 B2
Aland Ct SE16 ....119 A3
Alander Mews E17 ....54 A5
Alan Dr EN5 ....13 A5
Alan Gdns RM7 ....59 C2
Alan Hocken Way E15 .98 C5
Alan Lo N3 ....29 C2
Alan Preece Ct NW6 ..68 D1
Alan Rd SW19 ....179 A5
Alanthus Cl SE12 ....165 A5
Alaska St SE1 ....251 A3
Alba Cl UB4 ....84 D3
Albacore Cres SE13 .163 D5
Alba Gdns NW11 ......47 A3
Albain Cres TW15 ...148 A2
Alba Mews SW18,
SW19 ....157 C2
Alban Ho NW3 ....70 A2
Albans Cl SW16 .....160 A1
Albany N12 ....29 D4
W1 ....249 A5
Albany Cl N15 ....50 D5
Bushey WD23 ....8 B5
Ickenham UB10 ....60 C3
Mortlake SW14 .....132 D1
Sidcup DA5 ....168 D4
Albany Coll The NW4 .46 C4
Albany Cres
Claygate KT10 ....212 C2
Edgware HA8 ....26 C3
Albany Ct E10 ....53 C2
Albany Ct *continued*
HA8 ....27 B2
NW10 ....90 B4
SW1 ....259 C6
Kingston KT2 ....176 A4
Richmond TW10 .....153 B1
Chingford E4 ....19 D5
Albany Ctyd W1 ....249 B5
Albany Ho E5 ....74 C6
6 Brentford TW8 ....132 A6
Albany Mans SW11 .267 B3
Albany Mews BR1 ...187 A4
N1 ....72 C1
SE5 ....139 A6
Kingston KT2 ....175 D4
Sutton SM1 ....217 D3
Albany Par 4 TW8 ..132 A6
Albany Park Ave EN3 ...6 D4
Albany Park Rd KT2 .176 A4
Albany Park Sta
DA14 ....168 D2
Albany Pas 12 TW10 .154 A6
Albany Pl N7 ....72 C4
Brentford TW8 ....131 D6
Albany Rd E10 ....53 C2
E12 ....77 D4
E17 ....53 A3
N18 ....34 C5
N4 ....50 C3
SE5 ....139 C6
Brentford TW8 ......131 D6
Chislehurst BR7 .....188 D5
Dagenham RM6 ....59 B3
Ealing W13 ....109 B6
Enfield EN3 ....6 D5
Erith DA17 ....147 B6
New Malden KT3 .....199 B5
Richmond TW10 .....154 A6
Sidcup DA5 ....168 C4
Wimbledon SW19 ....179 D5
Albany Reach KT7 ...196 D4
Albany Sch EN3 ....6 D5
Albany St NW1 93 B4 231 D2
Albany Terr 6 TW10 .154 B6
Albany The
Kingston KT2 ....175 D4
Woodford IG8 ....36 D6
Albany View IG9 ......21 A3
Albany Wlk N15 ......50 D5
Alba Pl W11 ....91 B1
Albatross 31 NW9 ....27 D1
Albatross St SE18 ...145 C5
Albemarle SW19 ....156 D2
Albemarle App IG2 ...56 D3
Albemarle Ave TW2 .151 B3
Albemarle Gdns
Ilford IG2 ....56 D3
New Malden KT3 .....199 B5
Albemarle Ho SE8 ...119 B2
Albemarle Lo SE26 ..185 A5
Albemarle Mans NW3 .69 D4
Albemarle Pk
Beckenham BR3 ......185 D2
Stanmore HA7 ....25 C5
Albemarle Prim Sch
SW19 ....157 A2
Albemarle Rd
Beckenham BR2,BR3 ..186 A2
East Barnet EN4 ......14 C4
Albemarle St
W1 ....115 C6 249 A5
Albemarle Way EC1 .241 C5
Albermarle Ho 3
SW9 ....138 C2
Alberon Gdns NW11 ..47 B5
Alberta Ave SM1 ....217 B3
Alberta Ct 1 TW10 ..154 B6
Alberta Ho E14 .....120 A5
Hayes UB4 ....84 B4
Alberta Rd
Bexley DA7 ....147 D4
Enfield EN1 ....18 A5
Alberta St
SE17 ....116 D1 261 D2
Albert Ave SW8 .....270 C3
Chingford E4 ....35 C6
Albert Barnes Ho
SE1 ....262 A5
Albert Bigg Point E15 .98 A6
Albert Bridge Rd
SW11 ......136 D5 267 C3
Albert Carr Gdns
SW16 ....182 A5
Albert Cl 11 E9 ......96 B6
N22 ....31 D2
Albert Cotts 2 E1 ....96 A2
Albert Cres E4 ....35 C6
Albert Ct SW7 ......246 C1
9 Putney SW19 .....157 A3
Albert Dr SW19 .....157 A3
Albert Emb
SE1 ....116 A2 260 B3
Albert Gate Ct SW1 ..247 C1
Albert Gdns E1 ....96 D1
Albert Gr SW20 .....178 D2
Albert Gray Ho SW10 266 C4
Albert Hall Mans
SW7 ....114 B4 246 C1
Albert Ho 5 E18 .....55 B6
Albert Mans N8 ......50 A2
SW11 ....267 C2
Albert Memorial*
SW7 ....114 B4 246 C1
Albert Mews W8 ....256 A6
Albert Palace Mans
SW11 ....268 B2
Albert Pl N3 ....29 C2
W8 ....113 D4 245 D1
Albert Rd BR2 ......209 D4
E10 ....54 A1
E17 ....53 C4
N15 ....51 C3
N4 ....50 B2
NW4 ....46 D5
NW6 ....91 B5
NW7 ....27 D5
Ashford TW15 ....170 B5
Buckhurst Hill IG9 ....21 D2
Chislehurst SE9 .....166 A1
Croydon SE25 ....206 B5
Dagenham RM8 ....59 C1
Ealing W5 ....87 B3
East Barnet EN4 ....2 A1
Erith DA17 ....125 B1
Hampton TW12 ......174 A5
Harrow HA2 ....42 A6
Hayes UB3 ....105 C3
Hounslow TW3 ......129 C1
Ilford IG1 ....79 A5
Kingston KT1 ....176 B1
Mitcham CR4 ....202 D6
Newham E16 ....122 B4
New Malden KT3 .....199 D5
Penge SE20 ....184 D4
Richmond TW10 .....154 B6
Sidcup DA5 ....169 D4
Southall UB2 ....106 D3
Sutton SM1 ....218 B3
Teddington TW11 ....174 D4
Twickenham TW1 ....152 D3
4 Wanstead E18 ......55 B6
Wood Green N22 ......31 C2
Yiewsley UB7 ....104 A5
Albert's Ct NW1 ....237 B6
Albert Sq E15 ....76 C3
SW8 ....138 B5 270 C3
Albert St N12 ....30 A5
NW1 ....93 B6 231 D5
Albert Starr Ho 7
SE8 ....118 D2
Albert Studios SW11 .267 C2
Albert Terr NW10 .....89 A6
NW1 ....93 A6 231 A5
Buckhurst Hill IG9 ....21 D2
Albert Terr Mews
NW1 ....231 A5
Albert Victoria Ho
N22 ....32 C2
Albert Way SE15 ....140 B5
Albert Westcott Ho
SE17 ....261 D2
Albert Whicher Ho 3
E17 ....54 A5
Albert Wlk E16 .....122 D4
Albion Ave N10 ....31 A2
SW8 ....137 D3
Albion Cl W2 ....247 B6
Albion Ct 2 SE7 ....122 A2
7 W6 ....112 B2
Sutton SM2 ....218 B1
Albion Dr E8 ....74 A1
Albion Est SE16 .....118 C4
Albion Gate W2 .....247 B6
Albion Gdns 1 W6 ..112 B2
Albion Gr N16 ....73 C4
Albion Hill IG10 ......21 D6
Albion Ho E16 ......122 D5
Albion Mews N1 ....234 A6
W2 ....114 C6 247 B6
6 W6 ....112 B2
Albion Pk IG10 ....21 D6
Albion Pl EC1 ....241 C4
EC2 ....242 D3
W6 ....112 B2
South Norwood SE25 .206 A6
Albion Prim Sch
SE16 ....118 C4
Albion Rd E17 ....54 A6
N16 ....73 B4
Bexley DA6 ....147 C1
Albion Rd *continued*
Dagenham RM10 ......81 B3
Hayes UB3 ....83 C1
Hounslow TW3 ......129 C1
Kingston KT2 ....177 A2
Sutton SM2 ....218 B1
Tottenham N17 ....34 A1
Twickenham TW2 ....152 C3
Albion Sq E8 ....73 D1
Albion St SE16 .....118 C4
W2 ....114 C6 247 B6
Thornton Heath CR0 ..204 D1
Albion Terr E8 ....73 D1
Sewardstone E4 ....7 D1
Albion Villas Rd
SE23,SE26 ....162 C1
Albion Way EC1 ....242 A3
SE13 ....142 A1
Wembley HA9 ....66 C5
Albion Wharf SW11 ..267 A4
Albion Yd N1 ....233 B3
Albon Ho SE14 .....141 B4
Wandsworth SW18 ..157 D5
Albrighton Rd SE5,
SE22 ....139 C2
Albuhera Cl EN2 ......4 C4
Albury Ave DA7 .....147 A3
Hounslow TW7 ......130 D5
Albury Bldgs SE1 ...251 D1
Albury Cl TW12 .....173 D4
Albury Ct
4 Croydon CR0 .....221 A4
Mitcham CR4 ....180 B1
6 Northolt UB5 ......84 C4
Sutton SM1 ....218 A4
Albury Dr HA5 ....22 D3
Albury Lo 7 SW2 ...160 B4
Albury Mews E12 .....77 C6
Albury Rd KT9 ......214 A3
Albury St SE8 ......141 C6
Albyfield BR1 ......210 B6
Albyn Rd SE8 ....141 C4
Alcester Cres E5 .....74 B6
Alcester Ct 4 SM6 ..219 B4
Alcester Rd SM6 ....219 B4
Alcock Cl SM6 ......219 D1
Alcock Rd TW5 .....128 D5
Alconbury DA6 .....169 D6
Alconbury Rd E5 ....74 A6
Alcorn Cl SM3 ......217 C6
Alcott Cl W7 ....86 D2
Aldborough Ct
Chingford E4 ....19 D1
Ilford IG2 ....57 D4
Aldborough Rd IG2 ...57 D6
Aldborough Rd N IG2 .57 D4
Aldborough Rd S IG3 .57 C2
Aldbourne Rd W12 ..112 A5
Aldbridge St
SE17 ....117 C1 263 B2
Aldburgh Mews W1 .238 B2
Aldbury Ave HA9 ....66 D1
Aldbury Ho SW3 ....257 A3
Aldbury Mews N9 ....17 B4
Aldebert Terr
SW8 ....138 B5 270 C3
Aldeburgh Cl 16 E5 ..74 B6
Aldeburgh Pl IG8 ....37 A6
Aldeburgh St SE10 ..121 A1
Alden Ave E15 ....98 D4
Alden Ct
South Croydon CR0 ..221 C5
Wimbledon SW19 ....179 C4
Aldenham Ctry Pk WD6 9 B6
Aldenham Dr UB8 ....82 D3
Aldenham Ho NW1 ..232 B3
Aldenham Rd WD6 .....9 C6
Aldenham St
NW1 ....93 D5 232 C3
Alden Ho E8 ....96 B6
Aldensley Rd W6 ...112 B3
Alderbrook Prim Sch
SW12 ....159 B4
Alderbrook Rd SW12 159 B5
Alderbury Rd SW13 .134 A6
Alder Ct N2 ....48 B6
3 West Norwood
SW16 ....182 C5
Alder Gr NW2 ....68 B6
Aldergrove Gdns
TW4 ....129 A3
Aldergrove Ho 3 E5 ..74 A6
Alder Ho 1 NW3 ....70 D2
SE15 ....139 D6
SE4 ....141 C2
Alderley Ho 36 SW8 .137 D3
Alder Lo SW6 ......134 D4
Alderman Ave IG11 ..102 A4
Aldermanbury
EC2 ....95 A1 242 B2
Aldermanbury Sq
EC2 ....242 B3
Alderman Judge Mall 6
KT1 ....176 A1
Alderman's Hill N13 ..32 B6
Alderman's Wlk EC2 .243 A3
Aldermary Rd BR1 ..187 A2
Aldermead 2 TW3 ..129 D1
Alder Mews 9 N19 ...71 C6
Aldermoor Rd SE6 ..163 B1
Alderney Ave TW5 ..129 D5
Alderney Gdns UB5 ...63 B1
Alderney Ho 16 N1 ...73 A2
Enfield EN3 ....6 D5
Alderney Mews SE1 .262 C6
Alderney Rd E1 ....96 D3
Alderney St
SW1 ....115 B1 258 D2
Alder Rd DA14 ......167 D1
Mortlake SW14 ......133 B2
Alders Ave IG8 ....36 C4
Aldersbrook Ave EN1 ..5 C3
Aldersbrook Dr KT2 .176 B4
Aldersbrook House Coll of
Railway Tech E12 ...78 C5
Aldersbrook La E12 ...78 B5
Aldersbrook Prim Sch
E12 ....77 C6
Aldersbrook Rd E11,
E12 ....77 C6
Alders Cl HA8 ....27 A5
W5 ....109 D3
Wanstead E11 ....77 B6
Alders Ct N17 ....52 B5
Aldersey Gdns IG11 ...79 B2
Aldersford Cl SE4 ..140 D1
Aldersgate Ct EC1 ..242 A3
Aldersgate St
EC1 ....95 A2 242 A3
Alders Gr KT8 ......196 B4
Aldersgrove Ave SE9,
SE12 ....165 D1
Aldershot Rd NW6 ....91 B6
Aldersmead Ave CR0 206 D3
Aldersmead Rd BR3 .185 A3
Alderson Pl UB2 ....108 A5
Alderson St W10 .....91 A3
Alders Rd HA8 ....27 A5
Alders The
Feltham TW13 ....173 A6
Heston TW5 ....129 B6
Southgate N21 ....16 C5
Streatham SW16 .....181 C6
West Wickham BR4 ..223 D6
Alderton 9 KT2 ....176 D2
Alderton Cl NW10 ....67 B5
Alderton Cres NW4 ...46 B4
Alderton Ct KT8 ....195 B5
Alderton Rd SE24 ...139 A2
Croydon CR0 ....206 A2
Alderton Way NW4 ...46 B4
Alderville Rd SW6 ..135 B3
Alderwick Ct N7 ......72 B2
Alderwick Dr TW3 ..130 B2
Alderwood Prim Sch
SE9 ....167 C5
Alderwood Rd SE9 ..167 B5
Aldford St
W1 ....115 A5 248 B4
Aldgate EC3 ...95 C1 243 B1
Aldgate East Sta
E1 ....95 D1 243 D2
Aldgate High St
EC3 ....95 D1 243 C1
Aldgate Sta
EC3 ....95 D1 243 C1
Aldham Hall 1 E11 ..55 A3
Aldham Ho SE4 .....141 B4
Aldine Ct W12 ......112 C5
Aldine St W12 ......112 C4
Aldington Cl RM8 ....58 C1
Aldington Ct 1 E8 ...74 A1
Aldington Rd SE18 ..121 D3
Aldis Mews
Holdbrook EN3 ....7 C6
Upper Tooting SW17 ..180 C5
Aldis St SW17 ......180 C5
Aldred Rd NW6 ....69 C3
Aldren Rd SW17 ....158 A1
Aldriche Way E4 .....36 A4
Aldrich Gdns SM3 ..217 B5
Aldrich Terr SW18 ..158 A2
Aldrick Ho N1 ......233 D4
Aldridge Ave
Edgware HA8 ....10 D1
Holdbrook EN3 ....7 C5
Ruislip HA4 ....62 D6
Stanmore HA7 ....26 A2
Aldridge Ct W11 .....91 B2

Aldridge Rd Villas W11 ...91 B2
Aldridge Rise KT3 ...199 C3
Aldridge Wlk N14 ...16 A4
Aldrington Rd SW16 .181 C6
Aldsworth Cl W9 ...91 D3
Aldwick Cl BR7 ...167 B1
Aldwick Ct N12 ...30 A6
Aldwick Rd CR0 ...220 B4
Aldworth Gr SE13 ...164 A5
Aldworth Rd E15 ...76 C1
Aldwych WC2 .94 B1 240 D1
Aldwych Ave IG6 ...57 A5
Aldwych Bldgs WC2 .240 B2
Aldwyn Ho SW8 ...270 A3
Alers Rd DA6 ...168 D6
Alesia Cl N22 ...32 A3
Alestan Beck Rd E16 .99 D1
Alexander Ave NW10 ..68 B1
Alexander Cl Barnet EN4 2 B1
Hayes BR2 ...209 A1
Sidcup DA15 ...167 C5
Southall UB2 ...108 A5
Twickenham TW2 ...152 D2
Alexander Ct SW18 ..158 A6
Beckenham BR3 ...186 B2
Greenwich SE3 ...143 B3
Stanmore HA7 ...44 B6
14 Surbiton KT6 ...197 D2
Alexander Evans Mews SE23 ...162 D2
Alexander Ho 9 E14 119 C3
Alexander McLeod Jun Sch SE2 ...124 B1
Alexander McLeod Prim Sch SE2 ...124 B1
Alexander Mews 2 W2 ...91 D1
Alexander Pl SW7 ..257 A4
Alexander Rd N19 ...72 A6
Bexley DA16 ...146 D3
Chislehurst BR7 ...188 D5
Alexander Sq SW3 ...114 C2 257 A4
Alexander St W2 ...91 C1
Alexander Terr SE2 ..124 B1
Alexandra Ave N22 ...31 D2
SW11 ...268 A1
Harrow HA2 ...63 C5
Southall UB1 ...107 B6
Sutton SM1 ...217 C5
Alexandra Bsns Ctr EN3 ...6 D1
Alexandra Cl SE8 ...141 B6
Ashford TW15 ...171 B3
Harrow HA2 ...63 D5
Alexandra Cotts SE14 141 B4
Penge SE20 ...184 D4
Alexandra Cres BR1 .186 D4
Alexandra Ct 4 N16 ..73 D4
5 W12 ...112 A4
W9 ...236 B6
Ashford TW15 ...171 B4
Ealing W5 ...87 C2
Greenford UB6 ...85 D5
Hounslow TW3 ...129 D3
Southgate N14 ...15 C6
Wembley HA9 ...66 B4
Alexandra Dr
Surbiton KT5 ...198 C2
West Norwood SE19 ..183 C5
Alexandra Gdns N10 ..49 B5
Chiswick W4 ...133 C5
Hounslow TW3 ...129 D3
Wallington SM5 ...219 A1
Alexandra Gr N12 ...29 D4
N4 ...50 D1
Alexandra Ho 13 W6 .112 C1
Alexandra Inf Sch
Kingston KT2 ...176 C3
Penge BR3 ...184 D3
Alexandra Jun & Inf Sch TW3 ...129 D3
Alexandra Jun Sch SE26 ...184 D4
Alexandra Mans 6 NW6 ...69 C3
SW3 ...266 C5
Alexandra Mews N2 ..48 D6
Alexandra National Ho N4 ...72 D6
Alexandra Palace* N22 ...31 D1
Alexandra Palace Sta N22 ...32 A1
Alexandra Palace Way N10 ...49 C6
Alexandra Park Rd N10,N22 ...31 D2
Alexandra Park Sch N22 ...31 C2
Alexandra Pl NW8 ...92 A6 229 B6
Croydon CR0 ...205 C1
South Norwood SE25 ..205 B4
Alexandra Prim Sch N22 ...32 B1
Alexandra Rd E10 ...76 A5
E17 ...53 B2
N10 ...31 B3
N15 ...51 B4
N8,N22 ...50 C6
NW4 ...46 D5
NW8 ...70 B1
W4 ...111 B4
Ashford TW15 ...171 C4
10 Brentford TW8 ...131 D6
Croydon CR0 ...205 C2
Dagenham RM6 ...59 A3
Edmonton N9 ...18 B4
Enfield EN3 ...6 D1
Hounslow TW3 ...129 D3
Kingston KT2 ...176 C3
Mitcham SW19 ...180 C3
Mortlake SW14 ...133 B2
Penge SE26 ...184 D4
Richmond TW9 ...132 B3
Thames Ditton KT7 ...196 D4
Twickenham TW1 ...153 C5
Wallend E6 ...100 C4
Wanstead E18 ...55 B6
Wimbledon SW19 ...179 C5
Alexandra Sch HA2 ..63 C6
Alexandra Sq SM4 ..201 C4
Alexandra St E16 ...99 A2
5 SE14 ...141 A5
Alexandra Wlk 8 SE19 ...183 C5
Alexandria Rd W13 ..109 B6
Alex Gossip Ho SW6 .265 A1
Alexis St SE16 ...118 A2
Alfearn Rd E5 ...74 C4
Alford Ct N1 ...235 B3
5 Belmont SM2 ...217 D1
Alford Gn CR0 ...224 B2
Alford Ho N6 ...49 C3
6 SE18 ...144 D6
Alford Pl N1 ...235 B3
Alfoxton Ave N8,N15 ..50 D5
Alfreda Ct SW11 ...268 C1
Alfreda St SW11 ...137 B4 268 C1
Alfred Butt Ho SW17 158 D1
Alfred Cl W4 ...111 B2
Alfred Findley Ho N22 32 D1
Alfred Gdns UB1 ...107 A6
Alfred Ho E9 ...75 A3
Alfred Hurley Ho SW17 ...180 A6
Alfred Mews W1,WC1 239 C4
Alfred Mizen Prim Sch The CR4 ...203 D6
Alfred Nunn Ho NW10 89 D6
Alfred Pl WC1 .93 D2 239 C4
Alfred Prior Ho 6 E12 ...78 C4
Alfred Rd E15 ...76 D3
W2 ...91 C2
W3 ...111 A5
Buckhurst Hill IG9 ...21 D2
Croydon SE25 ...206 A4
Erith DA17 ...125 B1
Feltham TW13 ...150 C2
Kingston KT1 ...198 B6
Sutton SM1 ...218 A3
Alfred Salter Ho SE1 263 D3
Alfred Salter Prim Sch SE16 ...118 D4
Alfred's Gdns IG11 ..101 C5
Alfred St E3 ...97 B4
Alfred's Way (East Ham & Barking By-Pass) IG11 ...101 B5
Alfred's Way Ind Est IG11 ...102 A6
Alfred Villas 9 E17 ...54 A5
Alfreton Cl SW19 ...156 D1
Alfriston KT5 ...198 B3
Alfriston Ave
Harrow HA2 ...41 C2
Thornton Heath CR0 ..204 A2
Alfriston Cl KT5 ...198 B3
Alfriston Rd SW11 ...158 D6
Algar Cl
Isleworth TW7 ...131 A2
Stanmore HA7 ...24 D5
Algar Ho SE1 ...251 C1
Algar Rd TW7 ...131 A2
Algarve Rd SW18 ...157 D3
Algernon Rd NW4 ...46 A3
NW6 ...91 C6
SE13 ...141 D1
Algers Cl IG10 ...21 D6
Algers Rd IG10 ...21 D6
Alghers Mead IG10 ...21 D6
Algiers Rd SE13 ...141 C1
Alguin Ct HA7 ...25 C3
Alibon Gdns RM10 ...81 C3
Alibon Rd RM10 ...81 C3
Alice Ct SW15 ...135 B1
Alice Gilliott Ct W14 .264 D6
Alice La E3 ...97 B6
Alice Mews 8 TW11 174 D5
Alice Owen Tech Ctr EC1 ...234 C2
Alice Shepherd Ho 7 E14 ...120 A4
Alice St SE1 .117 C3 263 A5
Alice Thompson Cl SE12 ...165 C2
Alice Walker Cl 8 SE24 ...138 D1
Alice Way TW3 ...129 D1
Alicia Ave HA3 ...43 C5
Alicia Cl HA3 ...43 C5
Alicia Gdns HA3 ...43 C5
Alicia Ho DA16 ...146 B4
Alie St E1 ...95 D1 243 D1
Alington Cres NW9 ...45 A1
Alison Cl E6 ...100 C1
Croydon CR0 ...206 D1
Alison Ct 1 SE1 ...118 A1
Aliwal Rd SW11 ...136 C1
Alkerden Rd W4 ...111 C1
Alkham Rd N16 ...73 D6
Allam Ho W11 ...244 A6
Allan Barclay Cl N15 ..51 D3
Allanbridge N16 ...51 C2
Allan Cl KT3 ...199 B4
Allandale Ave N3 ...47 B6
Allan Ho SW8 ...269 C2
Allanson Ct E10 ...75 C6
Allan Way W3 ...89 A2
Allard Cres WD23 ...8 A2
Allard Gdns SW4 ...159 D6
Allardyce St SW4, SW9 ...138 B1
Allbrook Cl TW11 ...174 C5
Allbrook Ho 4 SW15 156 A4
Allcot Cl TW14 ...149 D3
Allcott Ho TW7 ...130 D2
Allcroft Rd NW5 ...71 A2
Allder Way CR2 ...220 D1
Allenby Cl UB6 ...85 C4
Allenby Inf Sch UB1 ..85 D1
Allenby Rd
Forest Hill SE23 ...163 A1
Southall UB1 ...85 C3
Allen Cl
Streatham CR4 ...181 C2
Sunbury TW16 ...172 B2
Allen Ct E17 ...53 C3
Allendale Ave UB1 ...85 C1
Allendale Cl SE5 ...139 B4
Forest Hill SE26 ...184 D5
Allendale Rd UB6 ...65 B2
Allendale Sch W8 ...113 C3 255 B6
Allen Edwards Dr SW8 ...138 A4 270 A2
Allen Edwards Prim Sch SW4 ...138 A4 270 A1
Allenford Ho 1 SW15 ...155 D5
All England Lawn Tennis & Croquet Club The SW19 ...157 A1
Allen Ho W8 ...255 B6
Allen Mans W8 ...255 B6
Allen Rd E3 ...97 B5
N16 ...73 C4
Penge BR3 ...184 D1
Sunbury TW16 ...172 B1
Thornton Heath CR0 ..204 C1
Allensbury Pl NW1 ...72 A1
7 NW1 ...71 D1
Allens Rd EN3 ...18 C6
Allen St W8 ..113 C3 255 B5
Allenswood 12 SW19 157 A3
Allenswood Rd SE9 ..144 B3
Allerdale Ho 7 N4 ...51 B2
Allerford Ct
Catford SE6 ...163 D1
Harrow HA2 ...42 A4
Allerford Rd SE6 ...185 D6
Allerton Ct 5 NW4 ...28 D1
North Cheam SM3 ...216 D6
Allerton Ho N1 ...235 D3
4 Merton SW19 ...180 A3
Allerton Rd N16 ...73 A6
Allerton St N1 ...235 D2
Allerton Wlk 11 N7 ..72 B6
Allestree Rd SW6 ...135 A5 264 A3
Alleyn Cres SE21 ...161 B2
Alleyndale Rd RM8 ...80 C6
Alleyn Ho EC1 ...242 B5
SE1 ...262 C5
Alleyn Pk
Dulwich SE21 ...161 C1
Southall UB2 ...107 C1
Alleyn Rd SE21 ...161 C1
Alleyn's Sch SE22 ..161 C6
Allfarthing La SW18 .158 A5
Allfarthing Prim Sch SW18 ...158 A5
Allgood Cl SM4 ...200 D3
Allgood St 10 E2 ...95 D5
Allhallows La EC4 ...252 C5
Allhallows Rd E6 ...100 A1
All Hallows Rd N17 ...33 C2
Alliance Cl HA0 ...65 D4
Alliance Ct Acton W3 ..88 D2
Ashford TW15 ...171 A6
Alliance Rd Acton W3 ..88 D3
Newham E16 ...99 C2
Woolwich SE18 ...146 A5
Allied Ind Est W3 ...111 C5
Allied Way W3 ...111 C4
Allingham Cl W7 ...108 D6
Allingham Ct NW3 ...70 C3
Allingham St N1 ...95 A5 235 A4
Allington Ave
Tottenham N17 ...33 C4
Upper Halliford TW17 .193 C6
Allington Cl
Greenford UB6 ...64 A1
3 Wimbledon SW19 ..178 D5
Allington Ct 6 SW8 .137 C3
Croydon CR0 ...206 C3
Allington Rd NW4 ...46 B3
W10 ...91 A5
Harrow HA2 ...42 A4
Orpington BR6 ...211 C1
Allington St SW1 ...258 D5
Allison Cl SE10 ...142 A4
Allison Gr SE21 ...161 C3
Allison Rd N8 ...50 D4
W3 ...111 A6
Alliston Ho 27 E2 ...95 D4
Allitsen Rd NW8 ...92 C5 230 A4
Allnutt Way SW4 ...159 D6
Alloa Ct N14 ...15 C2
Alloa Rd SE8 ...119 A1
Ilford IG3 ...80 A6
Allom Ct 11 SW4 ...138 A3
Allonby Dr HA4 ...38 D2
Allonby Gdns HA9 ...43 C1
Allonby Ho E14 ...97 A2
Alloway Rd E3 ...97 A4
Allport Ho SE5 ...139 B2
Allport Mews 38 E1 ...96 C3
All Saints' Benhilton CE Prim Sch SM1 ...217 D5
All Saints CE First Sch SW19 ...180 A3
All Saint's CE Jun Sch SE19 ...183 C3
All Saints' CE Prim Sch N20 ...14 B2
NW2 ...69 B5
SE3 ...142 C3
All Saints CE Prim Sch SW15 ...134 C2
All Saints' CE Prim Sch SM5 ...219 A3
All Saints' Cl N9 ...18 A2
All Saints Ct 9 E1 ...118 C6
E5 ...74 C4
Heston TW5 ...128 D4
All Saints Dr SE3 ...142 D3
All Saint's Inf Sch SE19 ...
All Saints Mews HA3 ..24 C4
All Saints Pas SW18 .157 C6
All Saints RC Sch RM8 59 C1
All Saints Rd W11 ...91 B1
All Saints' Rd W3 ...111 A3
All Saints Rd
Merton SW19 ...180 A3
Sutton SM1 ...218 A5
All Saints St N1 ...94 B5 233 C4
All Saints Sta E14 ...119 D6
All Saints Twr 18 E10 .53 D2
Allsop Pl NW1 92 D3 237 D5
All Souls' Ave NW10 ..90 B6
All Souls CE Prim Sch W1 ...93 C2 239 A4
All Souls Pl W1 ...238 D3
Allum La WD6 ...10 A6
Allum Way N20 ...14 A3
Allwood Cl SE26 ...184 D6
Alma Ave E4 ...36 A3
Alma Birk Ho 1 NW6 .69 B1
Almack Rd E5 ...74 C4
Alma Cl N10 ...31 B2
Alma Cres SM1 ...217 A3
Alma Gr SE1 .117 D2 263 D3
Alma Ho E5 ...74 B5
7 Brentford TW8 ...132 A6
2 Edmonton N9 ...34 A6
Alma Pl NW10 ...90 B4
Penge SE19 ...183 D3
Thornton Heath CR7 ..204 C4
Alma Prim Sch SE16 118 A2
Enfield EN3 ...18 D6
Alma Rd N10 ...31 B3
SW18 ...158 A6
Carshalton SM5 ...218 C3
Enfield EN3 ...7 A1
Sidcup DA14 ...168 A1
Southall UB1 ...107 A6
Thames Ditton KT10, KT7 ...196 C1
Alma Row HA3 ...24 B2
Alma Sq NW8 .92 A4 229 B2
Alma St E15 ...76 B2
NW5 ...71 B2
Alma Terr W8 ...255 B5
Wandsworth SW18 ...158 B4
Almeida St 10 N1 ...72 D1
Almeric Rd SW11 ...136 D1
Almer Rd SW20 ...178 A3
Almington St N4 ...50 B1
Almond Ave W5 ...110 A3
Carshalton SM5 ...218 D6
Uxbridge UB10 ...60 D5
West Drayton UB7 ...104 C3
Almond Cl BR2 ...210 C2
SE15 ...140 A3
Charlton TW17 ...171 A1
Hayes UB3 ...105 C6
Ruislip HA4 ...61 D5
Feltham TW14 ...150 A3
Almond Gr TW8 ...131 B5
Almond Ho SE4 ...141 B3
Almond Rd SE16 ...118 B2
Tottenham N17 ...34 A3
Almonds Ave IG9 ...21 A2
Almond Way BR2 ...210 C2
Harrow HA2 ...24 A1
Mitcham CR4 ...203 D5
Almorah Rd N1 ...73 B1
Heston TW5 ...128 D4
Almshouse La EN1 ...6 B6
Almshouses E10 ...75 D6
Sunbury TW16 ...171 D2
Almshouses The IG11 .79 A2
Al-Muntada Islamic Sch SW6 ...135 B4 264 D2
Alnmouth Ct 10 UB1 ..86 A1
Alnwick 8 N17 ...34 B3
Alnwick Gr SM4 ...201 D5
Alnwick Rd
Eltham SE12 ...165 B4
Newham E16 ...99 C1
Alonso Ct 4 DA17 ...125 C1
Alperton Com Lower Sch HA0 ...87 D6
Alperton Com Sch HA0 ...66 B1
Alperton La UB6 ...87 D5
Alperton St W10 ...91 B3
Alperton Sta HA0 ...88 A6
Alphabet Gdns SM5 ..202 B3
Alphabet Sq E3 ...97 C2
Alpha Bsns Ctr E17 ...53 B4
Alpha Cl NW8 .92 C4 230 B1
Alpha Ct 6 NW5 ...71 B2
Alpha Est The UB3 ..105 C4
Alpha Gr E14 ...119 C4
Alpha Ho NW6 ...91 C5
NW8 ...237 B5
19 SW4 ...138 B1
Alpha Pl NW6 ...91 C5
SW3 ...136 C6 267 B6
Alpha Rd SE14 ...141 B4
Chingford E4 ...19 D1
Croydon CR0 ...205 C1
Edmonton N18 ...34 A4
Enfield EN3 ...7 A1
Hillingdon UB10 ...82 D3
Surbiton KT5 ...198 B3
Teddington TW12 ...174 B5
Alpha St SE15 ...140 A3
Alphea Cl SW19 ...180 C3
Alpine Ave KT5 ...215 A6
Alpine Bsns Ctr E6 ..100 C2
Alpine Cl CR0 ...221 C5
Alpine Copse 2 BR1 188 C1
Alpine Gr 36 E9 ...74 C1
Alpine Rd SE16 ...118 D1
Walton-on-T KT12 ...194 A2
Alpine View SM1 ...218 C3
Alpine Way E6 ...100 C2
Alpine Wlk HA7 ...8 C2
Alric Ave NW10 ...67 B1
Kingston KT3 ...199 D6
Alroy Rd N4 ...50 C2
Alsace Rd SE17 ...117 C1 263 A2
Al Sadiq & Al Zahra Schs NW6 ...91 A6
Alscot Rd SE1 ...117 D3 263 D5
Alscot Road Ind Est SE1 ...263 D5
Alscot Way SE1 ...263 C4
Alsike Rd DA18 ...125 A3
Alsom Ave KT19,KT4 .216 A4
Alston Cl KT7 ...197 B2
Alston Ct EN5 ...1 A2
Alston Rd Barnet EN5 ...1 A2
Edmonton N18 ...34 B5
Upper Tooting SW17 ..180 B6
Altair Cl N17 ...33 D4
Altash Way SE9 ...166 C2
Altenburg Ave W13 ..109 B3
Altenburg Gdns SW11 ...136 D1
Alt Gr SW19 ...179 A3
Altham Rd HA5 ...23 A3
Althea St SW6 ...135 D2
Althope Mews SW11 .266 D1
Althorne Gdns E18 ...54 D5
Althorne Way RM10 ...81 C6
Althorp Cl EN5 ...12 A4
Althorpe Rd HA1 ...42 A4
Althorp Rd SW17 ...158 D3
Altior Ct N6 ...49 C3
Altmore Ave E6 ...100 B6
Altmore Inf Sch E6 ..100 B6
Alton Ave HA7 ...24 D3
Alton Cl DA5 ...169 A3
Isleworth TW7 ...130 D3
Alton Ct 18 BR3 ...185 C3
Alton Gdns
Beckenham BR3 ...185 C3
Twickenham TW2 ...152 B4
Alton Ho 3 E3 ...97 D4
Alton Rd N17 ...51 B6
Croydon CR0 ...220 C5
Richmond TW10,TW9 ..132 A1
Roehampton SW15 ...156 A3
Alton St E14 ...97 D2
Altyre Cl BR3 ...207 B4
Altyre Rd CR0 ...221 B6
Altyre Way BR3 ...207 B4
Alum Ct KT5 ...198 B3
Alumni Ct SE1 ...253 D2
Alvanley Ct NW3 ...69 D3
Alvanley Gdns NW6 ..69 D3
Alvanley Ho 14 SW9 .138 C4
Alverstone Ave
East Barnet EN4 ...14 C4
Wimbledon SW18, SW19 ...157 C2
Alverstone Gdns SE9 167 A3
Alverstone Ho 11 SE11 ...138 C6
Alverstone Rd NW2 ..68 C1
Little Ilford E12 ...78 C4
New Malden KT3 ...199 D5
Wembley HA9 ...44 B1
Alverston Gdns SE25 205 C4
Alverton St SE8 ...141 B6
Alveston Ave HA3 ...43 B6
Alvey St SE17 ...263 A2
Alvia Gdns SM1 ...218 A4
Alvington Cres E8 ...73 D3
Alway Ave KT19 ...215 B3
Alwen Cotts CR0 ...
Alwold Cres SE12 ...165 C5
Alwyn Ave W4 ...111 B1
Alwyn Cl
Borehamwood WD6 ...10 B5
New Addington CR0 ..223 D1
Alwyne La N1 ...72 D1
Alwyne Pl N1 ...73 A1
Alwyne Rd N1 ...73 A1
Ealing W7 ...108 C6
Wimbledon SW19 ...179 B4
Alwyne Sq N1 ...73 A2
Alwyne Villas N1 ...72 D1
Alwyn Gdns NW9 ...46 A5

Alwyn Gdns continued
Acton W3 ....88 D1
Alyn Ct N8 ....49 D3
Alyth Gdns NW11 .....47 C3
Alzette Ho **11** E2 ......96 D5
Amalgamated Dr
TW8 ....131 B6
Amanda Ct TW15 ...148 B2
Amar Ct SE18 ....123 D2
Amardeep Ct SE18 ..123 D1
Amazon St E1 ....96 B1
Ambassador Cl TW3 .129 A3
Ambassador Ct NW4 ..46 D4
9 NW6 ....69 C3
Ambassador Gdns
E6 ....100 B2
Ambassador Ho NW8 **229** B5
Ambassador Sq E14 .119 C2
Amber Ave E17 ......35 A2
Amber Ct N7 ....72 C2
NW9 ....45 C6
Mitcham CR4 ....202 C5
Amberden Ave N3 ....47 C6
Ambergate St
SE17 ....**116** D1 **261** D2
Amber Gr NW2 ....46 D1
Amberley Cl
2 Orpington BR6 ...227 D3
Pinner HA5 ....41 B6
Amberley Ct **2** SW9 .138 C2
Sidcup DA14 ....190 C5
Sutton SM2 ....218 A1
Amberley Gdns
Enfield EN1 ....17 C4
Worcester Park KT19 .215 C4
Amberley Gr
Croydon CR0 ....205 D2
Penge SE26 ....184 B5
Amberley Ho EN5 .....1 D1
Amberley Rd E10 .....53 D2
SE2 ....146 D6
W9 ....91 C2
Buckhurst Hill IG9 ....21 C3
Enfield EN1 ....17 D5
Palmers Green N13 ...16 B2
Amberley Way
Heston TW4 ....150 C6
Morden SM4 ....201 B2
Romford RM7 ....59 D5
Uxbridge UB10 ......82 A5
Amberside Cl TW2 ...152 B5
Amber Wharf **29** E2 ...95 D6
Amberwood Cl SM6 .220 A3
Amberwood Rise
KT3 ....199 C3
Amblecote Cl SE12 ..165 B1
Amblecote Mdw
SE12 ....165 B1
Amblecote Rd SE12 .165 B1
Ambler Prim Sch N4 .72 D6
Ambler Rd N4 ....72 D5
Ambleside NW1 .....**231** D3
Catford BR1 ....186 B4
13 Putney SW19 ...157 A3
Ambleside Ave
Beckenham BR3 .....207 A4
Streatham SW16 ....181 D6
Walton-on-T KT12 ...194 C1
Ambleside Cl E10 ....53 D2
E9 ....74 C3
Ambleside Cres EN3 ..6 D2
Ambleside Dr TW14 .149 D3
Ambleside Gdns
Redbridge IG4 ....56 A4
Streatham SW16 ....181 D6
Sutton SM2 ....218 A2
Wembley HA9 ....43 D1
Ambleside Jun Sch
KT12 ....194 C1
Ambleside Point **11**
SE15 ....140 C5
Ambleside Rd DA7 ..147 C3
NW10 ....67 A4
Ambrook Rd DA17 ..125 C3
Ambrosden Ave
SW1 ....**115** C3 **259** B5
Ambrose Ave NW11 ..47 B3
Ambrose Ct **6** E6 ....100 B2
Orpington BR6 ......227 D5
Ambrose Ho **9** E14 ..97 C2
Ambrose Mews **2**
SW11 ....136 D3
Ambrose St SE16 ...118 B2
Ambrose Wlk E3 .....97 C5
AMC Bsns Ctr NW10 .88 D4
Amelia Cl W3 ....110 D4
Amelia Ho **5** W6 ...112 C1

Amelia St
SE17 ....**117** A1 **262** A2
Amen Cnr EC4 ....**241** D1
Streatham SW17 ....181 A4
Amen Ct EC4 ..94 D1 **241** A4
Amenity Way SM4 ..200 C2
American Coll The
W1 ....93 A1 **238** B2
American Com Schs
UB10 ....82 B6
American Sch in London
The NW8 ..92 B5 **229** C4
America Sq EC3 .....**253** C6
America St SE1 ......**252** A3
Amerland Rd SW18 .157 A5
Amersham Ave N18 ..33 B4
Amersham Gr SE14 .141 B5
Amersham Rd SE14 .141 B4
Thornton Heath CR0 .205 B3
Amersham Vale SE14,
SE8 ....141 B4
Amery Gdns NW10 ..90 B6
Amery Ho SE17 .....**263** C1
Amery Rd HA1 ....65 A6
Amesbury Ave SW2 .160 B2
Amesbury Cl KT4 ...200 C1
Amesbury Ct EN2 ....4 C3
Amesbury Dr E4 .....19 C5
Amesbury Rd BR1 ..209 D6
Dagenham RM9 ......80 D1
Feltham TW13 ......150 D2
Amesbury Twr **4**
SW8 ....137 C3
Ames Cotts **14** E3 ...97 A2
Ames Ho **10** E2 .....96 D5
Amethyst Cl N11 .....31 D3
Amethyst Rd E15 .....76 B4
Amherst Ave W13 ...87 C1
Amherst Dr BR5 .....211 D5
Amherst Gdns **2** W13 .87 C1
Amherst Prim Sch E8 74 A3
Amherst Rd W13 .....87 C1
Amhurst Ct N4 ......51 B2
Amhurst Gdns TW7 .131 A3
Amhurst Par N16 .....51 D2
Amhurst Pk N4,N16 ..51 C2
Amhurst Rd E8,N16 ..74 A4
Amhurst Terr E8 .....74 A4
Amhurst Wlk SE28 ..124 A5
Amias Ho EC1 ......**242** A6
Amidas Gdns RM8 ..80 B4
Amiel St **17** E1 .....96 C3
Amies St SW11 ......136 D2
Amigo Ho SE1 ......**261** B6
Amina Way SE16 ...118 A3
Amis Ave KT19 ......214 D3
Amity Gr SW20 ......178 C2
Amity Rd E15 ....76 D1
Ammanford Gn NW9 .45 C3
Amner Rd SW11 .....159 A5
Amor Rd W6 ....112 C2
Amory Ho N1 ....**233** D4
Amott Rd SE15 .....140 A2
Amoy Pl E14 ....119 C6
Ampleforth Rd SE2 .124 C4
Ampton Pl WC1 .....**233** C1
Ampton St
WC1 ....94 B4 **233** C1
Amroth Cl SE23 ....162 B3
Amroth Gn NW9 .....45 C3
Amstel Ct **11** SE15 .139 C4
Amsterdam Rd E14 .120 A3
Amundsen Ho **5**
NW10 ....67 A4
Amwell Cl EN2 ......17 B6
Amwell St EC1 94 C4 **234** A2
Amyand Cotts **12**
TW1 ....153 B5
Amyand Park Gdns **2**
TW1 ....153 B4
Amyand Park Rd
TW1 ....153 B4
Amy Cl SM6 ....220 A1
Amy Johnson Ho HA8 .26 D1
Amy Johnson Prim Sch
SM6 ....220 A1
Amyruth Rd SE4 ....163 C6
Amy Warne Cl E6 ...100 A3
Anarth Ct KT13 .....193 C1
Anatola Rd N19 .....71 C6
Ancaster Cres KT3 ..200 A3
Ancaster Rd BR3 ...206 D6
Ancaster St SE18 ...145 C5
Anchorage Cl SW19 .179 C5
Anchorage Point E14 .119 C3
Anchorage Point Ind Est
SE7 ....121 C3
Anchor Bsns Pk CR0,
SM6 ....220 A5
Anchor Cl IG11 .....102 A4

Anchor Ct **5** EN1 .....17 C6
Anchor Ho EC1 .....**242** A6
Ilford IG3 ....80 A5
Newham E16 ....99 C1
Anchor & Hope La
SE7 ....121 C2
Anchor Mews SW12 .159 B5
Anchor Ret Pk E1 ...96 C3
Anchor St SE16 .....118 B2
Anchor Terr SE1 ....**252** B4
Anchor Yd EC1 .....**242** B6
Ancill Cl W6 .135 A6 **264** A5
SE18 ....123 B1
Ancona Rd NW10 ....90 A5
SE18 ....123 B1
Andace Pk BR1 .....187 C2
Andalus Rd SW9 ....138 A2
Andaman Ho **3** E1 ..97 A2
Ander Cl HA0 ....65 D4
Anderson Cl W3 .....89 B1
Morden SM3 ....201 C1
Southgate N21 ......16 B6
Anderson Ct NW2 ...46 C2
Anderson Dr TW15 .171 A6
Anderson Ho **10** E14 .120 A6
Barking IG11 ....101 A3
Upper Tooting SW17 .180 B5
Anderson Rd E9 .....74 D2
Redbridge IG8 ......55 D6
Anderson's Pl TW3 .129 C1
Anderson Sq N1 ....**234** C5
Anderson St SW3 ...**257** C2
Anderson Way
Erith DA17 ....125 D4
Erith DA17 ....125 D4
Anderton Cl SE5 ...139 B2
Anderton Ct N22 ....31 D1
Andhurst Ct KT2 ...176 D2
Andon Ct BR3 .....207 A6
Andorra Ct BR1 ....187 C2
Andover Ave E16 ....99 D1
Andover Cl
East Bedfont TW14 ..149 D3
Greenford UB6 ......85 D3
Andover Ho **5** N7 ...72 B6
Andover Pl NW6 .....91 D5
Andover Rd N7 .....72 B6
Orpington BR6 .....211 C1
Twickenham TW2 ...152 B3
Andoversford Ct **7**
SE15 ....139 C6
Andreck Ct BR3 ....186 A1
Andre St E8 ....74 A3
Andrew Borde St
WC2 ....**239** D2
Andrew Ct
Beckenham BR3 .....207 D6
Forest Hill SE23 ....162 D2
Andrewes Gdns E6 .100 A1
Andrewes Ho EC2 ..**242** B3
Sutton SM1 ....217 C4
Andrew Ewing Jun & Inf
Sch TW5 ....129 B4
Andrew Ho SE4 ....141 B4
Putney SW15 ....156 A6
Andrew Marvell Ho **12**
N16 ....73 C4
Andrew Pl SW8 ....**269** D2
Andrew Reed Ho
SW18 ....157 A4
Andrews Cl BR5 ...190 D1
Buckhurst Hill IG9 ...21 C2
Harrow HA1 ....42 B2
North Cheam KT4 ..216 D6
Andrews Crosse
WC2 ....**241** A1
Andrews Ct **2** W7 .108 C5
Andrew's Rd E8 .....96 B6
Andrew St E14 ......98 A1
Andrews Wlk SE17 .138 C6
Andrew Wells Ho
BR1 ....187 B3
Andringham Lo **4**
BR1 ....187 B2
Andrula Ct N22 .....32 D2
Andwell Cl SE2 ....124 B4
Anerley Gr SE20 ...184 B3
Anerley Gr SE19 ...183 D3
Anerley Hill SE19 ..183 D4
Anerley Park Rd
SE20 ....184 B3
Anerley Pk SE20 ...184 B3
Anerley Prim Sch
SE20 ....184 A2
Anerley Rd SE20 ...184 B2
Anerley Sch for Boys
SE20 ....184 A4
Anerley Sta SE20 ..184 B2
Anerley Station Rd
SE20 ....184 B2
Anerley Vale SE19 ..184 A3

Aneurin Bevan Ct
NW2 ....68 B6
Aneurin Bevan Ho
N11 ....31 D3
Anfield Cl SW12 ...159 C4
Angel EC1 ....94 C5 **234** B3
Angela Ct **2** SE23 ..162 C2
SW9 ....138 C2
Angel Alley E1 .....**243** D2
Angel Cl N18 ....34 A6
Angel Corner Par **6**
N18 ....34 A6
Angel Ct EC2 ......**242** D2
SW1 ....**249** B3
Angel Edmonton N18 .34 A5
Angelfield TW3 ....151 D6
Angel Gate EC1 ....**234** D2
Angel Hill SM1 .....217 D5
Angel Hill Dr SM1 ..217 D5
Angel Ho N1 ......**234** B3
Angelica Cl UB7 ....82 B1
Angelica Dr E6 .....100 C2
Angelica Gdns CR0 .206 D1
Angelina Ho **2** SE15 140 A4
Angel La E15 ....76 B2
Hayes UB3 ....83 B2
Angell Park Gdns **5**
SW9 ....138 C2
Angell Rd SW9 .....138 D2
Angel Mews N1 ....**234** B3
Putney SW15 ......156 A4
Stepney E1 ....118 B6
Angel Pas
EC4 ....**117** B6 **252** C5
Angel Pl SE1 ......**252** C2
1 Edmonton N18 ...34 A5
Angel Prim Sch
N1 ....94 C5 **234** B4
Angel Rd Harrow HA1 .42 C3
Thames Ditton KT7 ..197 A1
**Angel Rd (North Circular
Rd)** N18 ....34 B5
Angel Rd Works N18 .34 C5
Angel Road Sta N18 .34 B5
Angel St EC1 ..95 A1 **242** A2
Angel Sta EC1 .94 C5 **234** B3
Angel Wlk W6 ......112 C2
Angerstein Bsns Pk
SE10 ....121 A2
Angerstein La SE3 .142 D4
Anglebury **5** W2 ....91 C1
Angle Cl UB10 ......82 C6
Angle Gn RM8 ......58 C1
Anglers Cl TW10 ..175 C6
Anglers La NW5 .....71 B2
Anglers Reach KT6 .197 D4
Anglesea Ave **4**
SE18 ....122 C2
Anglesea Ho KT1 ...197 D5
Anglesea Rd SE18 .122 C2
Kingston KT1 ....197 D5
Anglesey Cl TW15 .148 C5
Anglesey Court Rd
SM5 ....219 A2
Anglesey Ct W7 ....86 D3
Anglesey Gdns SM5 .219 A2
Anglesey Ho **9** E14 .97 C1
Anglesey Rd Enfield EN3 .6 B1
South Oxhey WD19 ..22 A7
Anglesmede Cres HA5 41 C6
Anglesmede Way HA5 41 C6
Angles Rd SW16 ...182 A6
Anglia Ct IG11 .....34 B3
Anglia Ho **15** E14 ..97 A1
Anglian Ind Est IG11 101 D2
Anglian Rd E11 .....76 B5
Anglo American Laundry
SW17 ....158 A4
Anglo Rd **24** E3 ....97 B5
Angrave Ct **4** E8 ..95 D6
Angrave Pas **5** E8 ..95 D6
Angus Ct KT9 .....214 C3
Angus Dr HA4 ......62 C2
Angus Gdns NW9 ...27 C6
Angus Ho **12** SW12 .159 D4
Angus Rd E13 ......99 C4
Angus St SE14 .....141 A5
Anhalt Rd
SW11 ....**136** C5 **267** C5
Ankerdine Cres SE18 144 C4
Anlaby Rd TW11 ...174 C1
Anley Rd W14 ......112 C5
Anmersh Gr HA7 ....25 D3
Annabel Cl E14 .....97 D1
Anna Cl E8 ....95 D6
Annandale Gr UB10 ..61 A5
Annandale Prim Sch
SE10 ....120 D1
Annandale Rd DA15 .167 D4

Annandale Rd continued
SE10 ....120 D1
W4 ....111 C1
Croydon CR0 ......222 A6
Anna Neagle Cl **2** E7 .77 A4
Anne Boleyn's Wlk
Belmont SM3 ....217 A1
Kingston KT2 ....176 A5
Anne Carver Lo HA0 .66 A1
Anne Compton Mews
SE12 ....164 D4
Anne Goodman Ho **3**
E1 ....96 C1
Anne Kerr Ct **18**
SW15 ....156 D5
Anne's Ct NW8 ....**237** B6
Annesley Ave NW9 ..45 B6
Annesley Cl NW10 ..67 C5
Annesley Ho **15** SW9 .138 C5
31 SW9 ....138 C4
Annesley Rd SE3 ..143 B4
Annesley Wlk N19 ..71 C6
Annette Cl HA3 .....24 C1
Annette Cres **9** N1 .73 A4
Annette Rd N7 .....72 B4
Annett Cl TW17 ....193 C5
Annett Rd KT12 ....194 A2
Anne Way KT8 .....195 B5
Annie Besant Cl E3 .97 B6
Annie Taylor Ho **1**
E12 ....78 C4
Anning St E2 ......**243** B6
Annington Rd N2 ...48 D6
Annis Rd E9 ....75 A2
Ann La SW10 .136 B6 **266** B5
Ann Moss Way SE16 .118 C3
Ann Parkes Ct TW5 .128 D3
Ann's Cl SW1 ......**248** A1
Ann's Pl E1 ....**243** C3
Ann St SE18 ....123 C4
Ann Stroud Ct SE12 .165 A6
Annsworthy Ave CR7 .205 B6
Annsworthy Cres
CR7 ....183 B1
Annunciation RC Inf Sch
The HA8 ....27 B2
Annunciation RC Jun Sch
The HA8 ....27 B2
Ansar Gdns E17 ....53 B4
Ansdell Rd SE15 ...140 C3
Ansdell St
W8 ....113 D3 **255** D6
Ansdell Terr
W8 ....113 D3 **255** D6
Ansell Gr SM5 .....203 A1
Ansell Ho E1 ....96 C2
Ansell Rd SW17 ...158 D1
Anselm Cl CR0 ....221 D5
Anselm Rd
SW6 ....**135** C6 **265** A5
Pinner HA5 ....23 D1
Ansford Rd BR1,SE6 .186 B6
Ansleigh Pl W11 ....112 C6
Anslie Wlk SW12 ..159 B4
Anson **30** NW9 .....27 C6
Anson Ho **6** E1 ....97 A3
SW1 ....**269** A6
Anson Pl SE28 .....146 C6
Anson Prim Sch NW2 .68 B3
Anson Rd N7 ....71 D4
NW2 ....68 C3
Anstey Ct **6** W3 ...110 D4
Anstey Ho **8** E9 ...96 C6
Anstey Rd SE15 ...140 A2
Anstice Cl W4 .....133 C4
Anstridge Rd SE9 ..167 B5
Antelope Rd SE18 .122 B3
Antenor Ho **11** E2 ...96 B5
Anthony Cope Ct N1 **235** D2
Anthony Ct TW7 ...130 D2
Anthony Ho NW8 ...**237** B5
Anthony Rd DA16 ..146 A4
Croydon SE25 ......206 A3
Greenford UB6 .....86 C4
Anthony St E1 .....96 B1
Antigua Wlk SE19 .183 B5
Antill Rd E3 ....97 A4
N15 ....52 A5
Antill Terr **5** E1 ...96 C1
Antlers Hill E4 .....19 D6
Anton Cres SM1 ...217 C5
Antoneys Cl HA5 ...22 D1
Anton Pl HA9 ......66 D1

Anton St E8 ....74 A3
Antony Ho **4** SE14 .140 D5
2 SE16 ....118 C2
Antrim Gr NW3 .....70 D2
Antrim Mans NW3 ..70 D2
Antrim Rd NW3 ....70 D2
Antrobus Cl SM1 ...217 B3
Antrobus Rd W4 ...111 A3
Anvil Cl SW16 .....181 C3
Anvil Ho **10** N9 .....18 A1
Anvil Rd TW16 ....194 A6
Anworth Cl IG8 .....37 C4
Apex Cl BR3 ....185 D2
Apex Cnr NW7 .....27 B6
Twickenham TW13 ..151 B1
Apex Ct W13 ....87 A1
Aphrodite Ct **2** E14 .119 C2
Aplin Way **7** NW7 .130 C4
Apollo Ave BR1 ....187 B2
Moor Park HA6 .....22 A5
Apollo Bldg **20** E14 .119 C2
Apollo Ho **31** E2 ...96 B5
N6 ....48 D2
SW10 ....**266** C5
Apollo Ind Bsns Ctr **29**
SE8 ....140 D6
Apollo Pl E11 ......76 C5
SW10 ....**266** C4
Apollo Studios **18**
NW5 ....71 D3
Apollo Way SE28 ..123 B3
Apostle Way CR7 ..182 D1
Apothecary St EC4 .**241** C1
Appach Rd SW2 ...160 C5
Appin Ct HA1 ......42 C2
Appleby Cl N15 .....51 B4
Chingford E4 ....36 A4
Twickenham TW2 ..152 B2
Appleby Gdns TW14 149 C3
Appleby Rd E16 ....99 A1
E8 ....74 A1
Appleby St E2 .....95 D5
Appledore Ave HA4 .62 C3
Appledore Cl BR2 .209 A4
Edgware HA8 ......26 C2
Upper Tooting SW12,
SW17 ....158 D6
Appledore Cres
DA14,DA15 ....167 D1
Appleford **8** NW5 ..71 C3
Appleford Ho **6** W10 .91 A3
Appleford Rd W10 ..91 A3
Applegarth
Claygate KT10 .....212 D3
New Addington CR0 .223 D1
Apple Garth **8** 109 D2
Applegarth Dr IG2 ..57 D5
Applegarth Ho SE1 **251** D2
8 SE15 ....140 A5
Applegarth Inf Sch
CR0 ....223 D2
Applegarth Jun Sch
CR0 ....223 D2
Applegarth Rd W14 .112 D3
Woolwich SE28 ....124 C6
Apple Gr
Chessington KT9 ...214 A4
Enfield EN1 ....5 C2
Apple Lo HA0 ......65 C5
Apple Mkt* WC2 ..**250** B6
Kingston KT1 ....175 D1
Apple Rd E11 ......76 C5
Appleshaw Ho **4**
SE5 ....139 C2
Appleton Gdns KT3 .200 A3
Appleton Rd SE9 ...144 A2
Appleton Sq CR4 ..180 C2
Apple Tree Ave UB7 .82 B1
Appletree Cl **5** SE20 184 B2
Appletree Ct SE13 .142 B1
Appletrees Gdns EN4 ..2 C1
Apple Tree Yd SW1 .**249** B4
Applewood Cl N20 ..14 C3
NW2 ....68 B5
Ickenham UB10 .....60 A4
Applewood Dr E13 .99 B3
Appold St EC2 .95 C2 **243** A4
Appollo Ct **7** SW9 .138 C4
Apprentice Way **6** E5 74 B4
Approach Cl N16 ...73 C4
Approach La NW7 ..29 A5
Approach Rd E2 ....96 C5
Ashford TW15 .....171 A4
East Molesey KT8 ..195 C4
Edgware HA8 ......26 C4
Merton SW20 .....178 C1
New Barnet EN4,EN5 ..2 B1
Approach The BR6 .227 D4

Approach The *continued*
NW4 ....46 D4
W3 ....89 B1
Enfield EN1 ....6 B3
Aprey Gdns NW4 .....46 C5
April Cl Ealing W7 ...108 C6
Feltham TW13 ....150 A1
Orpington BR6 ......227 D3
April Ct 20 E2 ......96 A5
April Glen SE23 .....162 C1
April St E8 ....73 D4
Apsley Cl HA2 ....42 A4
Apsley Ct SM2 ......218 A2
Apsley Ctr The NW2 ..68 A6
Apsley Ho E1 ....96 C2
Hounslow TW4 ......129 B1
Apsley Rd
Croydon SE25 ......206 B5
Kingston KT3 ....199 A6
Apsley Way NW2 .....68 A6
W1 ....248 B2
Aquarius TW1 ....153 B3
Aquarius Way HA6 ...22 A6
Aquila St NW8 92 B5 229 D4
Aquinas St
SE1 ....116 C5 251 B3
Arabella Ct 5 SW9 ..138 C4
Arabella Dr SW15 ..133 C1
Arabia Cl E4 ....20 B4
Arabian Ho 3 E1 ....97 A3
Arabin Rd SE4 ......141 B1
Aragon Ave KT7 ....196 C6
Aragon Cl BR2 ......210 B1
Ashford TW16 ......171 D3
Enfield EN2 ....4 B5
Aragon Ct
Beckenham BR3 ....186 A2
East Molesey KT8 ..196 A5
Aragon Dr HA4 ......40 D1
Aragon Rd
Kingston KT2 ....176 A5
West Barnes SM4 ..200 D3
West Barnes SM4 ..201 A4
Aragon Twr SE8 ....119 B2
Arakan Ho 4 N16 ...73 B4
Aral Ho 14 E1 ......96 D3
Arandora Cres RM6 ..58 B2
Aranya Ct E17 ......35 A1
Arapiles Ho 6 E14 ..98 B1
Arbery Rd E3 ....97 A5
Arbon Ct N1 ....235 B5
Arbor Cl BR3 ....185 D1
Arbor Ct N16 ....73 B6
Arborfield Ho 6 E14 119 C6
Arbor Rd E4 ....20 B4
Arbourfield Cl SW2 .160 B3
Arbour Ho 3 E1 .....96 D1
Arbour Rd EN3 ......6 D2
Arbour Sq E1 ....96 D1
Arbroath Rd SE9 ...144 A2
Arbrook Chase KT10 .212 A2
Arbrook Ct BR5 ....190 A2
Chessington KT9 ...213 D3
Arbrook Hall KT10 ..212 D2
Arbrook La KT10 ...212 B2
Arbury Terr 3 SE26 .162 B1
Arbuthnot La DA5 ..169 A5
Arbuthnot Rd SE14 .140 D3
Arbutus St E8 ....95 D6
Arcade Ho 7 NW11 .47 B4
Arcade The E17 .....53 C5
EC2 ....243 A3
1 N7 ....72 A4
2 SE9 ....166 C5
Barking IG11 ....79 A1
Arcadia Ave N3 .....29 C2
Arcadia Cl SM5 ....219 A4
Arcadian Ave DA5 ..169 A5
Arcadian Cl DA5 ...169 A5
Arcadian Gdns N22 ..32 C3
Arcadian Rd DA5 ...169 A5
Arcadia St E14 .....97 C1
Archangel St SE16 .118 D4
Archbishop Lanfranc Sch
The CR0 ....204 A3
Archbishop Michael
Ramsey Tech Coll
SE5 ....138 D5
Archbishop's Pl 1
SW2 ....160 B4
Archbishop Sumner's CE
Prim Sch
SE11 ....116 C2 261 B3
Archbishop Tenison's CE
High Sch CR0 ......221 D5
Archbishop Tenison's Sch
SE11 ....138 B6 270 D5
Archdale Ct W12 ...112 B5
Archdale Ho SE1 ...263 A6
Archdale Pl KT3 ....198 D6

Archdale Rd SE22 ..139 D1
Archdeacon Cambridge's
CE Prim Sch TW2 ..152 C2
Archel Rd
W14 ....135 B6 264 C6
Archer Ho 25 N1 ....95 C6
1 SW11 ....136 B3
W11 ....244 D6
Ealing W13 ....87 A3
Archer Mews TW12 .174 A4
Archer Rd SE25 ....206 B5
Archers Dr EN3 .....6 C3
Archers Lo 14 SE16 .118 A1
Archer Sq SE14 ....141 A6
Archer St W1 ......249 C6
Archer Terr UB7 ...104 A6
Archery Cl W2 .....237 B1
Harrow HA3 ....42 D6
Archery Fields Ho
WC1 ....234 A2
Archery Rd SE9 ....166 B6
Archery Steps W2 ..247 B6
Arches Bsns Ctr The
UB2 ....107 B4
Arches The WC2 ....250 B4
Harrow HA1 ....63 D6
Archibald Mews W1 .248 C5
Archibald Rd N7 ...71 D4
Archibald St E3 ....97 C4
Archie Cl UB7 .....104 C4
Arch St SE1 ..117 A3 262 A5
Archway N19 ......71 C6
Archway Bsns Ctr 5
N19 ....71 D5
Archway Cl W10 ...90 D2
Wallington SM6 ...220 A5
Wimbledon SW19 ..179 D6
Archway Hts 5 N19 .49 C1
Archway Mews SW15 135 A1
Archway Rd N6 ....49 B6
Archway St SW13,
SW14 ....133 C2
Archway Sta N19 ..71 C6
Arcola St E8 ....73 D3
Arctic St NW5 .....71 B3
Arcus Rd BR1 .....186 C4
Ardbeg Rd SE24 ...161 B6
Arden 17 SW19 ....156 C6
Arden Cl Bushey WD23 ..8 D4
Erith SE28 ....102 D1
Harrow HA1 ....64 B5
Arden Court Gdns N2 .48 B3
Arden Cres E14 ...119 C2
Dagenham RM9 ....80 D1
Arden Gr BR6 .....226 D4
Arden Grange N12 ..30 A6
Arden Ho 21 N1 ...95 C5
SE11 ....260 C3
29 SW2 ....138 A3
Arden Mhor HA5 ..40 B4
Arden Rd N3 ......47 B6
Ealing W13 ....109 C6
Ardent Cl SE25 ...205 C6
Ardent Ho 28 E3 ..97 A5
Ardfern Ave SW16 .204 A6
Ardfillan Rd SE6 ..164 B2
Ardgowan Rd SE6 .164 C3
Ardilaun Rd N5 ....73 A4
Ardingly Cl CR0 ..222 D5
Ardleigh Gdns SM3 .201 C2
Ardleigh Ho 1
N1 ....73 C2
Ardleigh Rd E17 ..35 B2
N1 ....73 C2
Ardleigh Terr E17 .35 A1
Ardley Cl NW10 ...67 C5
Forest Hill SE6 ....163 A1
Ruislip HA4 ....39 A2
Ardlui Rd SE27 ...161 A2
Ardmay Gdns KT6 .198 A4
Ardmere Rd SE13 .164 B5
Ardmore La IG9 ...21 B4
Ardmore Pl IG9 ...21 B4
Ardoch Rd SE6 ....164 B2
Ardra Rd N9 ......18 D1
Ardrossan Gdns KT4 .216 A5
Ardshiel Cl SW15 ..134 D2
Ardwell Ave IG6 ..57 A4
Ardwell Rd SW2 ..160 A2
Ardwick Rd NW2 ..69 C4
Arena Bsns Ctr N4 .51 A3
Arena Est N4 ......50 D2
Arena Sta SE25 ...206 C4
Arena The EN3 ....7 B5
Ares Ct 8 E14 .....119 C2
Arethusa Ho 8 E14 119 D2
Argall Ave E10 ....52 D1
Argall Ho 3 DA18 .125 A3
Argall Way E10 ...53 A1
Argenta Way NW10 .66 D2
Argent Ct KT6 ....214 C5

Argent Ctr The UB3 .106 A4
Argon Mews SW6 ..265 B3
Argon Rd N18 .....34 D5
Argos Ct 5 SW9 ..138 C4
Argos Ho 8 E2 ....96 B5
Argosy Ho SE8 ....119 A2
W1 ....238 D5
Argus Way UB5 ...85 A4
Argyle Cl W13 ....87 A3
Argyle Ho E14 ....120 A3
Sutton SM2 ....218 A2
Argyle Pl W6 .....112 B2
Argyle Prim Sch
WC1 ....233 A2
Argyle Rd E1 .....96 D3
E15 ....76 C4
N12 ....29 C5
Ealing W13 ....87 A2
Edmonton N18 ....34 A6
Harrow HA2 ....41 D3
Hounslow TW3 ....151 D6
Ilford IG1 ....78 C6
Newham E16 ......99 B1
Tottenham N17 ...34 A2
Argyle Sq WC1 94 A4 233 A2
Argyle St WC1 94 A4 233 A2
Argyle Way SE16 ..118 A1
Argyle Wlk WC1 ...233 B1
Argyll Ave UB1 ...107 D5
Argyll Cl SW9 ....138 B2
Argyll Ct 15 SW2 .160 A4
Argyll Gdns HA8 ..26 D2
Argyll Mans SW3 ..266 D6
W14 ....254 B4
Argyll Rd SE18 ...123 A3
W8 ....113 C4 245 B1
Argyll St W1 ..93 C1 239 A1
Arica Ho SE16 ....118 C3
Arica Rd SE4 .....141 A2
Ariel Ct SE11 .....261 C3
W12 ....112 A3
5 Belvedere DA17 .125 C1
Ariel Rd NW6 .....69 C2
Ariel Way W12 ...112 C5
Hounslow TW4 ...128 B2
Aristotle Rd SW4 .137 D2
Arkansas Ho 21 N19 .49 D2
Arkell Gr SW16 ...182 C3
Arkindale Rd SE6 .164 A1
Arkle Rd NW6 ....91 B5
Arkley Cres E17 ..53 B4
Arkley Dr EN5 ....12 B6
Arkley Pk EN5 ....11 B5
Arkley Rd E17 ....53 B4
Arklow Ho SE17 ..139 B6
Arklow Mews 4 KT6 214 A6
Arklow Rd SE14 ..141 B6
Arklow Road Trad Est
SE14 ....141 B6
Arkwright Ho 23
SW2 ....160 A4
Arkwright Mans NW3 .70 A3
Arkwright Rd NW3 .70 A3
Arlesey Cl SW15 ..157 A6
Arlesford Rd SW9 .138 A2
Arless Ho 8 HA1 ..42 D4
Arlingford Rd SW2 .160 C5
Arlington N12 .....13 C1
Arlington Ave
N1 ....95 A6 235 B5
Arlington Cl DA15 .167 C4
Sutton SM1 ....217 C6
Twickenham TW1 .153 C5
Arlington Ct N6 ...49 A3
4 Twickenham TW1 .153 C5
Arlington Dr
Carshalton SM5 ..218 A6
Ruislip HA4 ....39 B3
Arlington Gdns W4 .111 A1
Ilford IG1 ....56 C1
Arlington Ho EC1 ..234 B2
3 SE8 ....141 B6
W12 ....112 B6
Arlington Lo SW2 .138 B1
Arlington Park Mans 1
W4 ....111 A1
Arlington Pl 7 SE10 .142 A5
Arlington Rd N14 ..15 C3
NW1 ....93 B6 231 D5
Ashford TW15 ....170 B5
Ealing W13 ....87 B1
Richmond TW10 ..153 D2
Surbiton KT6 .....197 D3
Teddington TW11 .174 D6
Twickenham TW1 .153 C5
Woodford IG8 ....37 B3
Arlington Sq
N1 ....95 A5 235 B5
Arlington St
SW1 ....115 C5 249 A4

Arlington Way
EC1 ....94 C4 234 B2
Arliss Way UB5 ...84 C6
Arlow Rd N21 ....16 C3
Armada Ct SE8 ...141 C6
Armada St 10 SE8 .141 C6
Armadale Cl N17 ..52 B5
Armadale Rd SW6 .265 A5
Feltham TW14 ....150 A6
Armada Way E6 ..101 A1
Armagh Rd E3 ....97 B6
Armeston KT3 ....199 B2
Armfield Cl KT8 ..195 B4
Armfield Cotts 3
SW19 ....180 D1
Armfield Cres CR4 .180 D1
Armfield Rd EN2 ..5 B4
Arminger Rd W12 .112 B5
Armitage Ho
NW1 ....92 C2 237 B4
SE10 ....120 C1
Armitage Rd NW11 .47 B5
SE10 ....120 C1
Armitice Gdns SE25 206 A6
Armour Cl N7 ....72 B2
Armoury Rd SE8 ..141 D3
Armoury Way SW18 157 C6
Armsby Ho 15 E1 ..96 C3
Armstead Wlk RM10 .81 C1
Armstrong Ave IG8 .36 C4
Armstrong Cl BR1 .210 A6
Dagenham RM8 ...58 D2
Newham E6 ....100 B1
Pinner HA5 ....40 A3
Walton-on-T KT12 .194 A3
Armstrong Cres EN4 .2 B2
Armstrong Ho 8
SW15 ....156 D5
Armstrong Rd SW7 .256 C5
W3 ....111 D5
Feltham TW13 ....173 A5
Armstrong Way UB2 107 D4
Armytage Rd TW5 .128 C5
Arnal Cres SW18 ..157 A4
Arncliffe NW6 ....91 B5
Arncliffe Cl N11 ...31 A4
Arncroft Ct IG11 ..102 B4
Arne Gr BR6 .....227 D5
Arne Ho SE11 ....260 C2
Arne St WC2 ..94 A1 240 B1
Arnett Sq E4 .....35 A4
Arneways Ave RM6 .58 D6
Arneway St SW1 ..259 B5
Arnewood Cl SW15 .156 A3
Arney's La CR4 ...203 A3
Arngask Rd SE6 ..164 B4
Arnhem Pl E14 ...119 C3
Arnhem Way 3 SE22 161 C6
Arnhem Wharf E14 .119 C3
Arnhem Wharf Prim Sch
E14 ....119 C3
Arnison Rd KT8 ...196 B5
Arnold Ave E EN3 ..7 C5
Arnold Ave W EN3 .7 C5
Arnold Cir E2 .....95 D4
Arnold Cl HA3 ....44 B2
Arnold Cres TW7 .152 B6
Arnold Ct E18 ....36 D2
Arnold Dr KT9 ...213 D2
Arnold Est SE1 ...253 D1
Arnold Gdns N13 ..32 D5
Arnold Ho 9 N16 ..73 C5
SE17 ....261 D1
Arnold House Sch
NW8 ....92 B5 229 C3
Arnold Rd E3 .....97 C4
N15 ....51 B6
Dagenham RM10 ..81 C1
Mitcham SW17 ...180 D3
Northolt UB5 .....63 A2
Arnos Gr N14 ....15 D1
Arnos Grove Ct 4
N11 ....31 C5
Arnos Grove Sta N11 .31 C6
Arnos Rd N11 ....31 C6
Arnot Ho 27 SE5 ..139 A5
Arnott Cl SE28 ...124 C5
W4 ....111 B2
Arnould Ave SE5 ..139 C1
Arnsberg Way DA7 .147 C1
Arnside Gdns HA9 .43 D1
Arnside Ho 2 SE17 139 B6
Arnside Rd DA7 ..147 C4
Arnside St SE17 ..139 A6
Arnulf St SE6 .....185 D6
Arnull's Rd SW16 .182 D4
Arodene Rd SW2 ..160 B5
Arosa Rd 4 TW1 ..153 D5
Arragon Gdns
Streatham SW16 ..182 A3

Arragon Gdns *continued*
West Wickham BR4 .223 D5
Arragon Rd E6 ...99 D6
Wandsworth SW18 .157 C3
Arran Cl SM6 ....219 C4
Arran Ct NW10 ...67 B5
32 NW9 ....27 D1
Arran Dr Stanmore HA7 25 C6
Wanstead E12 ....77 D6
Arran Ho N16 ....51 D1
Arran Mews W5 ..110 B5
Arran Rd SE6 ....164 A2
Arran Wlk N1 ....73 A1
Arras Ave SM4 ...202 A4
Arras Ho SE2 ....146 D6
Arrol Ho SE1 ....262 B5
Arrol Rd BR3 ....206 D6
Arrowe Ct 7 E5 ..74 B2
Arrowhead Ct E11 .54 B3
Arrow Rd E3 .....97 D4
Arrow Ho 24 N1 ..95 C6
Arrow Scout Wlk UB5 .85 A4
Arrowsmith Ho SE11 260 C2
Arsenal Rd SE9 ..144 B2
Arsenal Sta N5 ...72 C5
Artemis Ct 6 E14 .119 C2
Arterberry Rd SW20,
SW19 ....178 D3
Artesian Cl NW10 .67 B1
Artesian Gr EN5 ..2 A1
Artesian Rd W2 ..91 C1
Arthingworth St E15 .98 C6
Arthur Ct SW11 ..268 B1
10 W10 ....90 D1
W2 ....91 D1
South Croydon CR0 221 B5
Arthur Deakin Ho 1
E1 ....96 A2
Arthurdon Rd SE4 .163 C6
Arthur Gr SE18 ..123 A2
Arthur Henderson Ho
9 N19 ....49 D2
9 Fulham SW6 ..135 B3
Arthur Newton Ho 20
SW11 ....136 B2
Arthur Rd E6 .....100 B5
N7 ....72 B4
Dagenham RM6 ...58 D3
Edmonton N9 ....17 D2
6 Kingston KT2 ..176 C3
West Barnes KT3 .200 B4
Wimbledon SW19 .179 C6
Arthur Ruxley Est
DA14 ....190 D4
Arthur St EC4 117 B6 252 D6
Arthur Wade Ho 7 E2 95 D4
Arthur Walls Ho 3
E12 ....78 C5
Artichoke Hill 8 E1 .118 B6
Artichoke Mews 5
SE5 ....139 B4
Artichoke Pl SE5 ..139 B4
Artillery Cl IG2 ...57 A3
Artillery Ho SE18 .122 C1
Artillery La E1 .95 C2 243 B3
W12 ....90 A1
Artillery Pass E1 ..243 B3
Artillery Pl SE18 ..122 C2
Harrow HA3 ....24 A3
Artillery Row SW1 .259 C5
Artington Cl BR6 ..227 A4
Artisan Cl E16 ...122 D6
Artizan St E1 .....243 B2
Arton Wilson Ho 12
SW15 ....156 A6
Arts Educational Sch The
W4 ....111 C2
Arundel Ave SM4 .201 B5
Arundel Bldgs SE1 .263 B5
Arundel Cl E15 ...76 C4
SW11 ....158 C6
Croydon CR0 .....220 D5
Hampton TW12 ...173 D5
Sidcup DA5 ....169 B5
Arundel Ct 2 DA6 .147 A1
N12 ....30 C4
SW3 ....257 B2
Barnes SW13 .....134 B6
4 Beckenham BR2 .186 C1
Harrow HA2 ......63 C4
Putney SW15 ....156 D6
Tottenham N17 ...34 A1

Arundel Gdns *continued*
Southgate N21 ....16 C3
Arundel Gr N16 ...73 C3
Arundel Ho
N1 ....94 D6 234 D6
3 W3 ....110 B3
Croydon CR0 .....221 B3
Arundel Lo N3 ....29 B1
Arundel Mans SW6 264 D2
Barnes SW13 .....134 B6
Arundel Pl N1,N7 ..72 C2
Arundel Rd
Belmont SM2 .....217 B1
Cockfosters EN4 ..2 C1
Hounslow TW4 ...128 C2
Kingston KT1 .....177 A1
Thornton Heath CR0 205 B3
Arundel Sq N7 ...72 C2
Arundel St
WC2 ....116 B6 250 D6
Arundel Terr SW13 134 B6
Arun Ho 5 KT2 ...175 C2
Arvon Rd N5 .....72 C3
Asa Ct UB3 ....105 D3
Asaph Ho SE14 ..141 B4
Asbaston Terr IG11 .79 A2
Ascalon Ct 16 SW2 160 B4
Ascalon Ho SW8 ..269 A3
Ascalon St
SW8 ....137 C5 269 A3
Ascham Dr E4 ....35 C3
Ascham End E17 ..35 A2
Ascham St NW5 ..71 C3
Aschurch Rd CR0 .205 D4
Ascot Cl
Borehamwood WD6 .10 C6
Northolt UB5 .....63 C3
Ascot Ct DA5 .....169 B4
NW8 ....229 C1
8 SW4 ....138 A1
Ascot Gdns Enfield EN3 .6 C6
Southall UB1 .....85 C2
Ascot Ho NW1 ....231 D2
6 W4 ....111 A1
1 W9 ....91 C2
Penge SE26 ......184 B4
Ascot Lo NW6 ....91 D5
Ascot Par 9 SW4 .138 A1
Ascot Rd E6 ......100 B4
N15 ....51 A6
East Bedfont TW14 148 D3
Edmonton N18 ...34 A6
Orpington BR5 ...211 D5
Streatham SW17 .181 A4
Ascott Ave W5 ...110 A4
Ascott Ct HA5 ....40 A5
Asfil Ho EC1 .....241 B3
Ashbourne Ave DA7 147 A5
N20 ....14 D3
NW11 ....47 B4
Harrow HA2 ......64 D6
Wanstead E18 ....55 B5
Ashbourne Cl N12 .29 A5
Ealing W5 ....88 C2
Ashbourne Ct E5 ..75 A4
11 N12 ....29 D6
Beckenham BR3 ..186 A6
Ashbourne Gr NW7 .27 A5
SE22 ....139 D1
W4 ....111 C1
Ashbourne Par
2 NW11 ....47 B5
Ealing W5 ....88 B3
Ashbourne Rd
Ealing W5 ....88 B3
Mitcham CR4 .....181 A3
Ashbourne Rise BR6 227 C4
Ashbourne Terr 1
SW19 ....179 C3
Ashbourne Way NW11 47 B5
Ashbridge Rd E11 .54 C2
Ashbridge St
NW8 ....92 C3 237 A5
Ashbrook HA8 ....26 B4
Ashbrook Rd N19 ..71 D6
Dagenham RM10 ..81 D6
Ashburn Ct BR1 ..187 A3
Ashburn Gdns SW7 256 A4
Ashburnham Ave HA1 42 D3
Ashburnham Cl N2 .48 B5
Ashburnham Com Sch
SW10 ....266 C4
Ashburnham Gdns
HA1 ....42 D3
Ashburnham Gr SE10 141 D5
Ashburnham Pk
KT10 ....212 A4

Ashburnham Pl SE10 141 D5
Ashburnham Rd NW10 90 C5
SW10 .....136 A5 266 B3
Richmond TW10 .....153 B1
Ashburnham Retreat 6
SE10 .....141 D5
Ashburnham Twr
SW10 .....266 C4
Ashburn Pl
SW7 .....114 A2 256 A3
Ashburton Ave
Croydon CR0 .....206 B1
Ilford IG3 .....79 D4
Ashburton Cl CR0 .....206 A1
Ashburton Com Sch
CR9 .....206 B2
Ashburton Gdns CR0 222 A6
Ashburton Gr N7 .....72 C4
Ashburton Ho EN3 .....6 D2
Ashburton Jun & Inf Sch
CR0 .....206 B3
Ashburton Mans
SW10 .....266 B4
Ashburton Rd E16 .....99 A1
Croydon CR0 .....222 A6
Ruislip HA4 .....62 A6
Ashburton Terr 2
E13 .....99 A5
Ashbury Ct N21 .....16 A6
Ashbury Dr UB10 .....60 D5
Ashbury Gdns RM6 .....58 D4
Ashby Ave KT19,KT9 .214 C2
Ashby Ct NW8 .....236 D6
Ashby Gr N1 .....73 A1
Ashby Grange 7
SM6 .....219 C2
Ashby Ho 8 N1 .....73 A1
6 SW9 .....138 D3
Ashby Mews SE4 .....141 B3
Ashby Rd N15 .....52 A4
SE4 .....141 B3
Ashby St EC1 .....94 D4 234 D1
Ashby Way UB7 .....126 C5
Ashby Wlk CR0 .....205 A3
Ashchurch Ct W12 .....112 A3
Ashchurch Gr W12 .....112 A3
Ashchurch Park Villas
W12 .....112 A3
Ashchurch Terr W12 .112 A3
Ash Cl BR5 .....211 B4
HA8 .....27 A6
Carshalton SM5 .....218 D6
Kingston KT3 .....177 B1
Penge SE20 .....184 C1
Sidcup DA14 .....168 B1
Stanmore HA7 .....25 A4
Ashcombe Ave KT6 .197 D2
Ashcombe Ct 4
SW15 .....157 A6
Ashcombe Gdns HA8 .26 C6
Ashcombe Ho 39 E3 .....97 D4
Ashcombe Pk NW2 .....67 C5
Ashcombe Rd
Wallington SM5 .....219 A2
Wimbledon SW19 .....179 C5
Ashcombe Sq KT3 .199 A6
Ashcombe St SW6 .135 D3
Ashcroft N14 .....15 D2
Pinner HA5 .....23 C4
Ashcroft Ave DA15 .168 A5
Ashcroft Cres DA15 .168 A5
Ashcroft Ct N20 .....14 B2
5 SE9 .....166 C5
Ashcroft Ho SW8 .....269 C2
Ashcroft Rd E3 .....97 A4
Chessington KT9 .....214 B5
Ashcroft Sq W6 .....112 C2
Ash Ct N19 .....71 C6
SE12 .....165 A4
SW11 .....159 A6
W1 .....237 C2
Chingford E4 .....20 B4
Romford RM7 .....59 D3
West Ewell KT19 .....215 A4
2 West Norwood
SW16 .....182 C6
Woodford E18 .....37 C2
Ashdale Cl
Stanwell TW19 .....148 A2
Twickenham TW2 .....152 A4
Ashdale Gr HA7 .....24 D4
Ashdale Ho N4 .....51 B2
Ashdale Rd SE12 .....165 B3
Ashdale Way TW2 .....151 B4
Ashdene 8 SE15 .....140 B5
Pinner HA5 .....40 C6
Ashdene Cl TW15 .....171 A3

Ashdon Cl IG8 .....37 B4
Ashdown Ealing W13 .....87 B2
Putney SW15 .....156 D6
Ashdown Cl 18 BR3 .185 D1
Ashdown Ct
New Malden KT4 .....199 D2
Sutton SM2 .....218 A2
Ashdowne Ct N17 .....34 A2
Ashdown Ho 7 E5 .....74 A6
Ashdown Pl
Ewell KT17 .....215 D1
Thames Ditton KT7 .197 A2
Ashdown Rd NW10 .....89 C6
Enfield EN3 .....6 C1
Hillingdon UB10 .....82 C5
Kingston KT1 .....176 A1
Ashdown Way SW17 .159 A2
Ashdown Wlk 15 E14 119 C2
Ashe Ho 8 TW1 .....153 B1
Ashen E6 .....100 C1
Ashenden SE17 .....262 B4
Ashenden Rd E5 .....75 A3
Ashen Gr SW19 .....157 C2
Ashentree Ct EC4 .....241 B1
Asher Loftus Way N11 30 D4
Asher Way E1 .....118 A6
Ashfield Ave
Bushey WD23 .....8 A4
Feltham TW13 .....150 B3
Ashfield Cl
Beckenham BR3 .....185 D1
Richmond TW10 .....154 A1
Ashfield Ho 5 N5 .....73 A3
Ashfield La HA5 .....189 A3
Ashfield Par N14 .....15 D3
Ashfield Pl BR7 .....189 A3
Ashfield Rd N14 .....15 C1
N4 .....51 A3
W3 .....111 D5
Ashfield St E1 .....96 C2
Ashford Ave N8 .....50 A5
Ashford TW15 .....170 D4
Hayes UB4 .....84 D1
Ashford CE Prim Sch
TW15 .....170 D4
Ashford Cl E17 .....53 B3
Ashford TW15 .....170 A6
Ashford Cres
Ashford TW15 .....148 A1
Enfield EN3 .....6 C3
Ashford Ct NW2 .....68 C4
Edgware HA8 .....10 C1
Ashford Gn WD19 .....22 D5
Ashford High Sch The
TW15 .....148 A1
Ashford Ho 11 SE8 .141 B6
14 SW9 .....138 D1
Ashford Hospl TW15 148 A2
Ashford Ind Est
TW15 .....171 B4
Ashford Rd NW2 .....68 D4
Feltham TW13,TW15 .171 B6
Littleton TW15,TW17 .171 A3
Staines TW18 .....170 A4
Wallend E6 .....78 C1
Woodford E18 .....37 B1
Ashford St N1 .....95 C4
Ash Gr E8 .....96 B6
NW2 .....69 A4
W5 .....110 A3
East Bedfont TW14 .149 C3
Edmonton N13 .....17 A1
Enfield EN1 .....17 C4
Hayes UB3 .....105 B6
Heston TW5 .....128 D5
Penge SE20 .....184 C1
Southall UB1 .....85 C2
Wembley HA0 .....65 A4
West Wickham BR4 .208 A1
Yiewsley UB7 .....104 B6
Ashgrove SE12 .....165 A5
Ashgrove Ct 2 W9 .....91 C2
Ashgrove Ho SW1 .....259 D2
Ashgrove Rd
Ashford TW15 .....171 B5
Catford BR1 .....186 B4
Ilford IG3 .....58 A1
Ashgrove Sch BR1 .187 B1
Ash Hill Dr HA5 .....40 C6
Ash Ho 3 E14 .....120 A4
SE1 .....263 D3
Ashingdon Cl E4 .....20 A1
Ashington 1 NW5 .....71 B2
Ashington Ho 16 E1 .....96 B1
Ashington Rd SW6 .135 A3
Ashlake Rd SW16 .....182 A6
Ashland Pl W1 .....238 A4
Ashlar Ct N2 .....48 C1
Ashlar Pl SE18 .....122 D2

Ashleigh Commercial Est
SE7 .....121 D3
Ashleigh Ct N14 .....15 C4
W5 .....109 A5
Penge SE26 .....184 B4
Ashleigh Gdns SM1 .217 D6
Ashleigh Ho SW14 .133 C2
Ashleigh Point 8
SE26 .....162 D1
Ashleigh Rd
Mortlake SW14 .....133 C2
Penge SE20 .....206 B6
Ashley Ave SM4 .....201 C4
Ashley CE Prim Sch
KT12 .....194 A1
Ashley Cl NW4 .....28 C1
Oatlands Park KT12,
KT13 .....193 D1
Pinner HA5 .....22 B1
Ashley Cres SW11 .137 A2
Wood Green N22 .....32 C1
Ashley Ct 19 N16 .....73 C3
NW3 .....69 D3
NW4 .....28 C1
New Barnet EN5 .....14 A6
Northolt UB5 .....85 A6
Yiewsley UB7 .....104 A5
Ashley Dr
Borehamwood WD6 .....11 B6
Hounslow TW7 .....130 C6
Twickenham TW2 .....151 D3
Ashley Gdns
Edmonton N13 .....33 A6
Orpington BR6 .....227 C3
Richmond TW10 .....153 D2
Wembley HA9 .....66 A6
Ashley Ho BR5 .....190 A1
Ashley La NW4 .....28 C1
NW7 .....28 D3
Croydon CR0 .....220 D4
Ashley Park Ave
KT12 .....193 D1
Ashley Park Cres
KT12 .....194 A1
Ashley Pl
SW1 .....115 C3 259 A5
Ashley Rd E7 .....77 C1
N17 .....52 A6
N19 .....50 A2
Chingford E4 .....35 C4
Enfield EN3 .....6 C3
Hampton TW12 .....173 C2
Richmond TW9 .....132 A2
Thames Ditton KT7 .196 D3
Thornton Heath CR7 .204 B5
Walton-on-T KT12 .....194 A1
Wimbledon SW19 .....179 D4
Ashley Wlk NW7 .....28 D3
Ashling Rd CR0 .....206 A1
Ashlin Rd E15 .....76 B4
Ash Lo
2 Ashford TW16 .....171 D3
Fulham SW6 .....134 D4
Ashlone Rd SW15 .....134 D2
Ashlyns Way KT9 .....213 D2
Ashmead 4 N14 .....15 C6
Ashmead Bsns Ctr E16 98 B3
Ashmead Gate BR1 .187 C2
Ashmead Ho E9 .....75 A3
Ashmead Prim Sch
SE8 .....141 C3
Ashmead Rd SE8 .....141 C3
East Bedfont TW14 .150 A3
Ashmere Ave BR3 .186 B1
Ashmere Cl SM3 .....216 D3
Ashmere Gr 11 SW2,
SW4 .....138 A1
Ashmere Ho 10 SW2 .138 A1
Ashmill Ct CR0 .....205 A3
Ashmill St
NW8 .....92 C2 237 A4
Ashmole Prim Sch
SW8 .....138 B6 270 D5
Ashmole Sch N14 .....15 C3
Ashmole St SW8 .....270 D5
Ashmoor Lo NW7 .....27 B4
Ashmore NW1 .....71 D1
Ashmore Cl SE15 .....139 D5
Ashmore Ct N11 .....30 D4
Heston TW5 .....129 C6
Ashmore Gr DA16 .145 C2
Ashmore Ho W14 .....254 B5
Ashmore Rd W9 .....91 B4
Ashmount Prim Sch
N6 .....49 C2
Ashmount Rd N15 .....51 D4
N19 .....49 D2
Ashmount Terr W5 .109 D2
Ashness Gdns UB6 .65 B2

Ashness Rd SW11 .....158 D6
Ashpark Ho 4 E14 .....97 B1
Ash Rd E15 .....76 D3
Cheam SM3 .....201 B6
Croydon CR0 .....223 C6
Littleton TW17 .....192 C5
Orpington BR6 .....227 D1
Ashridge Cl HA3 .....43 C3
Ashridge Cres SE18 .145 A5
Ashridge Ct
Southall UB1 .....108 A6
Southgate N14 .....15 C6
Ashridge Dr WD19 .....22 C5
Ashridge Gdns
Bowes Park N13 .....32 A5
Pinner HA5 .....41 A5
Ashridge Ho DA14 .189 D6
Ashridge Way
Ashford TW16 .....172 A6
Merton SM4 .....201 B5
Ash Row BR2 .....210 C3
Ashtead Ct 15 SW19 .156 D3
Ashtead Rd E5 .....52 A2
Ashton Cl SM1 .....217 C4
Ashton Ct
1 Beckenham BR3 .185 B2
Harrow HA1 .....64 D5
Ashton Gdns
Dagenham RM6 .....59 A3
Hounslow TW4 .....129 B1
Ashton Ho 13 SW9 .138 C5
Roehampton SW15 .....156 A6
Ashton Rd E15 .....76 B3
Ashton St E14 .....120 A6
Ashtree Ave CR4 .....180 A1
Ashtree Cl BR6 .....226 D4
Ash Tree Cl
Croydon CR0 .....207 A3
1 Surbiton KT6 .....198 A1
Ashtree Ct W15 .....170 D5
Ash Tree Dell NW9 .....45 A4
Ash Tree Way CR0 .207 A3
Ashurst Cl SE20 .....184 B2
Ashurst Dr
Ilford IG2,IG6 .....57 A4
Littleton TW17 .....192 A4
Ashurst Lo N5 .....72 D3
Ashurst Rd N12 .....30 C5
Cockfosters EN4 .....14 D6
Ashurst Wlk CR0 .....222 B6
Ashvale Rd SW17 .....180 D5
Ashview Cl TW15 .....170 A5
Ashview Gdns TW15 .170 A5
Ashville Rd E11 .....76 B6
Ashwater Rd SE12 .165 A3
Ashway Ctr 5 KT2 .....176 A2
Ashwell Cl 8 E6 .....100 A1
Ashwell Ct TW15 .....148 A2
Ashwin St E8 .....73 D2
Ash Wlk HA0 .....65 C4
Ashwood Ave UB8 .....82 C1
Ashwood Gdns
Hayes UB3 .....105 D2
New Addington CR0 .224 A2
Ashwood Ho 5 NW4 .46 C5
Ashwood Lo N21 .....16 B5
Ashwood Pk 6 SM2 .217 C1
Ashwood Rd E4 .....20 B1
Ashworth Cl SE5 .....139 B3
Ashworth Mans W9 .91 A4
Ashworth Rd W9 .....91 A4
Aske Ho 2 N1 .....95 C4
Asker Ho N7 .....72 A4
Askern Cl DA6 .....146 D1
Aske St N1 .....95 C4
Askew Cres W12 .....112 A4
Askew Mans 14 W12 .112 A4
Askew Rd W12 .....112 A4
Askham Ct W12 .....112 A5
Askham Lo 5 SE12 .165 A4
Askham Rd W12 .....112 A5
Askill Dr SW15 .....157 A6
Asland Rd E15 .....98 B6
Aslett St SW18 .....158 A4
Asmara Rd NW2 .....69 A3
Asmuns Hill NW11 .....47 C4
Asmuns Pl NW11 .....47 C4
Asolando Dr SE17 .....262 B3
Aspen Cl 10 N19 .....71 C6
W5 .....110 B4
Yiewsley UB7 .....104 B5
Aspen Copse BR1 .....188 B1
Aspen Ct E8 .....73 C2
Hayes UB3 .....105 C2
Richmond TW9 .....132 C4
Aspen Dr HA0 .....65 A5
Aspen Gdns W6 .....112 B3
Ashford TW15 .....171 A5
Mitcham CR4 .....203 A4
Aspen Gn DA18 .....125 D3

Aspen Ho 2 DA15 .....168 A1
4 NW3 .....70 D2
8 SE15 .....140 C6
Southgate N21 .....16 B6
Aspen La UB5 .....85 A4
Aspenlea Rd W6 .....134 D6
Aspen Way E14 .....120 A6
Feltham TW13 .....150 B1
Aspern Gr NW3 .....70 C3
Aspinall Ho SW12 .160 A3
Aspinall Rd SE4 .....140 C2
Aspinden Rd SE16 .118 C3
Aspire Bld SW15 .....157 B6
Aspley Rd SW18 .....157 D5
Asplins Rd N17 .....34 B2
Asquith Cl RM8 .....58 C4
Asquith Court Sch
HA3 .....43 C3
Assam SE1 .....253 D3
Assam St E1 .....96 A1
Assata Mews N1 .....72 D2
Assembly Pas E1 .....96 C2
Assembly Wlk SM5 .202 C2
Assheton-Bennett Ho 15
KT6 .....198 A4
Ass House La HA3 .....23 D6
Assisi Ct
Upper Tooting SW12 .158 C5
Wembley HA0 .....64 D5
Astall Cl HA3 .....24 C2
Astbury Ho SE11 .....261 A5
Astbury Rd SE15 .....140 C4
Astell St SW3 114 C1 257 B2
Aste St E14 .....120 A4
Astey's Row 3 N1 .....73 A1
Asthall Gdns IG6 .....57 A5
Astins Ho 4 E17 .....53 D5
Astleham Rd TW17 .192 A6
Astleham Way TW17 .192 A6
Astle St SW11 .....137 A3
Astley Ave NW2 .....68 C3
Astley Ho SE1 .....263 D2
39 W2 .....91 C2
8 West Norwood
SE27 .....183 A6
Aston Ave HA3 .....43 C2
Aston Cl Bushey WD23 .8 A5
Sidcup DA14 .....168 A1
Aston Gn TW5 .....128 C3
Aston Ho SW8 .....269 C1
W11 .....244 D6
Aston House Sch W5 .87 C1
Aston Mews RM6 .....58 C2
Aston Pl SW16 .....182 C2
Aston Rd
Claygate KT10 .....212 C3
Ealing W5 .....87 D1
Merton SW20 .....178 C1
Aston St E14 .....97 A2
Astonville St SW18 .157 C3
Astor Ave RM7 .....59 D3
Astor Cl KT2 .....176 D4
Astor Ct SW6 .....266 A3
Newham E16 .....99 C1
Astoria Mans 18
SW16 .....160 A1
Astoria Par SW16 .160 A1
Astoria Wlk SW9 .....138 C2
Astra Ct W13 .....109 A5
Astra Ho 4 E3 .....97 B4
N4 .....50 B2
Astrid Ho TW13 .....150 C2
Astrop Mews W6 .....112 C3
Astrop Terr W6 .....112 C4
Astwood Mews SW7 .256 A4
Asylum Rd SE15 .....140 B5
Atalanta St
SW6 .....134 D5 264 A3
Atbara Ct TW11 .....175 D4
Atbara Rd TW11 .....175 B4
Atcham Rd TW3 .....130 A1
Atcost Rd IG11 .....102 A2
Atheldene Rd SW18 .158 A3
Athelney Prim Sch
SE6 .....163 C1
Athelney St SE6 .....163 C1
Athelstan Ct E6 .....100 C5
Athelstan Gdns 6
NW6 .....69 A1
Athelstan Ho E9 .....75 B3
N16 .....73 C4
Kingston KT1 .....198 B5
Athelstan House Sch
TW12 .....173 C2
Athelstan Rd KT1 .....198 B5
Athelstan Way BR5 .190 A2
Athelstone Rd HA3 .....24 B1
Athena Cl Harrow HA2 .64 C6

Athena Cl continued
Kingston KT1 .....198 B6
Athena Cl 5 NW8 .....229 C4
Athenaeum Pl 3 N10 .49 B6
Athenaeum Rd N20 .....14 B3
Athenia Ho 7 E14 .....98 B1
Athenlay Rd SE15 .....162 A6
Athenoeum Ct N5 .....73 A4
Athens Gdns W9 .....91 C3
Atherden Rd E5 .....74 C4
Atherfield Ct SE18 .157 D5
Atherfold Rd SW9 .....138 A2
Atherley Way TW4 .151 B4
Atherstone Ct W2 .....91 D2
Atherstone Mews
SW7 .....114 A2 256 B4
Atherton Dr SW19 .178 D6
Atherton Ho CR2 .....221 C2
Atherton Hts HA0 .....65 C2
Atherton Mews E7 .....77 C4
Atherton Pl
Harrow HA2 .....42 B6
Southall UB1 .....107 C6
Atherton Rd E7 .....76 D2
Barnes SW13 .....134 A5
Atherton St SW11 .136 C3
Athlone KT10 .....212 C2
Athlone Cl 24 E5 .....74 B3
Athlone Ct E17 .....54 B6
Athlone Ho 9 E1 .....96 C1
16 NW5 .....71 A2
Athlone House (The
Middlesex Hospl) N6 48 C1
Athlone Rd SW2 .....160 C4
Athlone St NW5 .....71 A2
Athlon Rd HA0 .....87 D1
Athol Cl HA5 .....22 B2
Athole Gdns EN1 .....17 C6
Athole Terr CR7 .....183 A1
Athol Gdns HA5 .....22 B2
Atholl Ho W9 .....229 A1
Atholl Rd IG3 .....58 A2
Athol Sq E14 .....98 A1
Athol Way UB10 .....82 C4
Atkins Ct 8 E3 .....97 B6
Atkins Dr BR4 .....224 B6
Atkinson Ct 3 E10 .....53 D2
Atkinson Ho E13 .....98 D3
13 E2 .....96 A5
SE17 .....262 D3
SW11 .....268 A1
Atkinson Morley Hospl
SW20 .....178 B3
Atkinson Rd E16 .....99 C2
Atkins Rd E10 .....53 D3
Streatham SW4,SW12 .159 D4
Atlanta Ct CR7 .....205 A6
Atlantic 6 E14 .....120 B6
Atlantic Ho 4 E1 .....97 A2
4 Putney SW15 .....157 D6
Atlantic Rd SW2,SW9,
SE24 .....138 C1
Atlantis Cl IG11 .....102 B4
Atlas Bsns Ctr NW2 .68 B6
Atlas Gdns SE7 .....121 C2
Atlas Mews E8 .....73 D2
Atlas Rd E13 .....99 A5
N11 .....31 A5
NW10 .....89 C4
Wembley HA9 .....67 A4
Atley Rd E3 .....97 C6
Atlip Rd HA0 .....88 A6
Atney Rd SW15 .....135 A1
Atria Rd HA6 .....22 A5
Atterbury Rd N4 .....50 D3
Atterbury St
SW1 .....116 A2 260 A3
Attewood Ave NW10 .67 C5
Attewood Rd UB5 .....63 A2
Attfield Cl N20 .....14 B2
Attilburgh Ho SE1 .....263 C6
Attleborough Ct 4
SE21 .....162 B2
Attle Cl UB10 .....82 C5
Attlee Cl Hayes UB4 .84 B4
Thornton Heath CR7 .205 A4
Attlee Ct UB4 .....84 B4
Attlee Rd SE28 .....124 B6
Hayes UB4 .....84 B4
Attlee Terr 3 E17 .....53 D5
Attneave St WC1 .....234 A1
Atwater Cl SW2 .....160 C3
Atwell Cl E10 .....53 D3
Atwell Pl KT7 .....197 A1
Atwell Rd 4 SE15 .....140 A3
Atwood Ave TW9 .....132 C3
Atwood Ho SE21 .....161 C2
Atwood Rd W6 .....112 B2
Aubert Ct N5 .....72 C1
Aubert Pk N5 .....72 D4

Aubert Rd N5 ....72 D4
Aubrey Beardsley Ho
  SW1 ....259 B3
Aubrey Mans NW1 .237 A4
Aubrey Moore Point
  E15 ....98 A5
Aubrey Pl NW8 .....229 A3
Aubrey Rd E17 .....53 D6
  N8 ....50 A4
  W14 ..113 B5 244 D3
Aubrey Wlk
  W14 ..113 B5 244 D3
Auburn Cl SE14 ...141 A5
Aubyn Hill SE27 ....183 B6
Aubyn Sq SW15 ...156 A6
Auckland Cl SE15 .183 D1
  South Norwood SE19 .183 D2
Auckland Ct UB4 ...84 C3
Auckland Gdns SE19 .183 D2
Auckland Hill SE27 .183 A6
Auckland Ho 11 W12 112 B6
Auckland Rd E10 ..75 D5
  SW11 ....136 C1
  Ilford IG1 ....57 A2
  Kingston KT1 ...198 C1
  South Norwood SE19 .183 D2
Auckland Rise SE19 .183 C2
Auckland St SE11 ..260 C1
Audax 29 NW9 .....27 D1
Auden Pl NW1 .....231 A6
Audley Cl N10 ....31 B3
Audley Ct E11,E18 ..54 D5
  W1 ....248 C4
  Ealing W5 ....88 C2
  Northolt UB5 ......84 C4
  Pinner HA5 ....22 C1
  Surbiton KT5 ....198 B3
  Twickenham TW2 ..152 B1
Audley Dr 3 E16 ...121 B5
Audley Gdns IG3 ...79 D6
Audley Ho 11 E5 ...74 C6
  N8 ....50 A5
Audley Pl SM2 ....217 D1
Audley Rd NW4 ....46 B3
  Ealing W5 ....88 B2
  Enfield EN2 ....4 D4
  Richmond TW10 ..154 B6
Audley Sq W1 .....248 B4
Audrey Cl BR3 ....207 D3
Audrey Gdns HA0 ...65 B6
Audrey Rd IG1 .....78 D5
Audrey St E2 ......96 A5
Audric Cl KT2 .....176 C2
Augurs La 3 E13 ...99 B4
Augusta Cl KT8 ...195 B6
Augusta Rd TW2 ..152 A2
Augustas Cl W12 ..112 B3
Augustine Rd W14 .112 D3
  Harrow HA3 ......24 A2
Augustines Ct E9 ..74 C3
Augustus Cl TW8 ..131 D5
Augustus Ct
  Isleworth TW3 ...130 A1
  8 Putney SW19 ..157 A3
  South Norwood SE19 .183 C4
  Streatham SW16 .159 D2
Augustus Rd SW19 .157 A3
Augustus St
  NW1 ....93 B4 231 D2
Aultone Way
  Carshalton SM5 ..218 D5
  Sutton SM1 ......218 A6
Aultone Yd Ind Est
  SM5 ....218 D5
Aulton Pl SE11 ....261 B1
Aurelia Gdns CR0 .204 B3
Aurelia Rd CR0 ...204 B3
Auriga Mews N1 ...73 B3
Auriol Cl KT4 .....215 C5
Auriol Dr
  Greenford UB6 ....64 B1
  Hillingdon UB10 ..60 D2
Auriol Jun Sch KT19 215 D4
Auriol Mans W14 ..254 A3
Auriol Park Rd KT4 .215 C5
Auriol Rd
  W14 ..113 A2 254 A3
Aurora Ct IG8 ......36 D6
Austell Gdns NW7 ..11 C1
Austell Hts NW7 ....11 C1
Austen Cl SE28 ....124 B5
Austen Ho 2 NW6 ..91 C4
  Harrow HA2 ......63 D6
Austin Ave BR1,BR2 .210 A4
Austin Cl
  Forest Hill SE23 ..163 B4
  Twickenham TW1 .153 C6
Austin Ct 10 E6 ...99 C6
  9 Enfield EN1 ....17 C1

Austin Friars EC2 ..242 D2
Austin Friars Sq EC2 242 D2
Austin Ho 1 SE14 .141 B5
  6 SW2 ....160 B6
  19 Kingston KT6 .198 A4
Austin Rd
  SW11 ....137 A4 268 A1
  Hayes UB3 ......105 D4
Austins Ct SE15 ...140 A2
Austin St E2 ......95 D4
Avenue The BR1 ...209 D6
  BR6 ....227 D6
  N10 ....31 C1
  N11 ....31 B5
  N8 ....50 C6
  NW6 ....91 A6
  SE10 ....142 B5
  SW4 ....159 A6
  W4 ....111 C3
  Barnet EN5 ....1 A2
  Beckenham BR3 ..186 A2
  8 Buckhurst Hill IG9 .21 C2
  Chingford E4 ......36 B5
  Claygate KT10 ...212 C3
  Cranford TW5 ....128 A4
  Ealing W13 ....87 B1
  Finchley N3 ....29 C1
  Hampton TW12 ...173 B4
  Hounslow TW3 ...151 D6
  Isleworth TW1 ...153 B6
  Keston Mark BR2 .225 D5
  Loughton IG10 ...21 D5
  4 New Malden KT4 .200 A1
  Pinner HA5 ....23 B4
  Pinner HA5 ....41 B3
  Richmond TW9 ...132 B3
  Sidcup DA5 ......168 D4
  South Croydon CR0 .221 C5
  Stoneleigh KT17,SM3 .216 C1
  St Paul's Cray BR5 .190 B3
  Sunbury TW16 ...172 B1
  Surbiton KT5 ....198 B3
  Tottenham N17 ...33 C1
  Uxbridge UB10 ...60 D5
  Wallington SM5 ..219 A1
  Wandsworth SW18,
  SW12 ....158 C4
  Wanstead E11 ....55 B4
  Wembley HA9 .....44 B1
  West Wickham BR4 .208 C2
  Worcester Park KT4 .215 D6
Averil Gr SW16 ...182 D4
Averill St W6 .....134 D6
Avern Gdns KT8 ..195 D5
Avernons Rd E13 ..99 A3
Avern Rd KT8 ....195 D5
Avery Ct SE20 ....184 B3
Avery Farm Row
  SW1 ....258 C3
Avery Gdns IG2 ...56 B4
Avery Hill Coll (Mile End
  Annexe) E3 ......97 B3
Avery Hill Rd SE9 .167 B3
Avery Row
  W1 ....115 B6 248 D6
Aviary Cl E16 .....98 C2
Aviemore Cl BR3 ..207 B4
Aviemore Way BR3 .207 A4
Avignon Rd SE4 ..140 D2
Avington Ct SE1 ..263 B3
Avington Gr SE20 .184 C3
Avion Cres NW7,NW9 .28 A3
Avis Sq E1 ....96 D1
Avoca Rd SW17 ...181 A6
Avocet Cl SE1 ....118 A1
Avocet Mews SE28 .123 B3
Avon Cl Hayes UB4 .84 C3
  Sutton SM1 .....218 A4
  Worcester Park KT4 .216 A6
Avon Ct N12 ......29 D5
  1 W3 ....89 A1
  Greenford UB6 ...85 D3
  11 Putney SW15 ..157 A6
  Wembley HA0 ....66 C2
Avondale Ave N12 .29 D5
  NW2 ....67 C6
  Barnet, London EN4 .14 D3
  Hinchley Wood KT10 .213 A5
  New Malden KT4 .199 A5
Avondale Cres
  Enfield EN3 ....7 A2
  Redbridge IG4 ....55 D4
Avondale Ct E11 ...54 C1
  E16 ....98 C2
  9 Sutton SM2 ...218 A1
  Woodford E18 ....37 B2
Avondale Dr UB3 .106 B5
Avondale Gdns TW4 .151 B6

Avenue Rd continued
  Teddington TW11 ..175 A4
  Wallington SM6 ..219 C1
  Wimbledon SW20 .178 B1
  Woodford IG8 ....37 C4
Avenue Rd Sta BR3 .184 D1
Avenue S KT5 .....198 C2
Avenue Sch The NW6 .69 A1
Avenue Terr Ilford IG2 .57 C3
  Kingston KT3 ....199 A6
Avenue The BR1 ...209 D6
Avenue Cl
  NW8 ....92 C6 230 B5
  Cranford TW5 ....128 B4
  Southgate N14 ...15 C5
Avenue Cres W3 ..110 D4
  Cranford TW5 ....128 B5
Avenue Ct NW2 ...69 A5
  SW3 ....257 C3
  Ealing W5 ....87 D2
  Penge SE20 .....184 C2
  Redbridge IG5 ....56 A6
Avenue Elmers KT6 .198 A4
Avenue Gate IG10 .21 C5
Avenue Gdns W3 ..110 D4
  Cranford TW5 ....128 B5
  Mortlake SW14 ..133 C2
  South Norwood SE25 .184 A1
  Teddington TW11 .174 A1
Avenue Hall N6 ...49 D3
Avenue Ho N16 ...74 A6
  NW10 ....90 B5
  NW10 ....230 A3
Avenue Ind Est E4 .35 B4
Avenue Lo 12 NW8 .70 B1
Avenue Mans N10 .31 C1
  NW3 ....69 D3
Avenue Mews N10 .49 B6
Avenue Par
  Southgate N21 ...17 B4
  Sunbury TW16 ...194 B6
Avenue Park Rd
  SE21,SE27 ......160 D2
Avenue Prim Sch E12 .78 A3
Avenue Rd E7 .....77 B4
  N12 ....30 A6
  N15 ....51 B4
  N6 ....49 D2
  NW10 ....89 D1
  NW8 ....92 C6 230 A6
  W3 ....110 D4
  Bexley DA6,DA7 ..147 A2
  Brentford TW8 ...109 C1
  Feltham TW13 ...149 D1
  Hampton TW12 ..173 D2
  Hounslow TW7 ...130 D4
  Ilford RM6 ....58 C2
  Kingston KT1 ....198 A4
  Mitcham SW16 ..181 D1
  New Malden KT3 .199 C5
  Pinner HA5 ....41 A6
  Southall UB1 ....107 A5
  Southgate N14 ...15 C5
  South Norwood SE25 .184 A1
  South Norwood, Elmers End
  BR3,SE20 ....184 D2

Avondale Ho 10 SE1 .118 A1
  6 Mortlake SW14 .133 B2
Avondale Mans SW6 .264 C2
Avondale Park Gdns
  W11 ......113 A6 244 A5
Avondale Park Prim Sch
  W11 ......113 A6 244 A5
Avondale Park Rd
  W11 ......113 A6 244 A6
Avondale Rd E16 ..98 C2
  E17 ....53 C2
  N15 ....50 B4
  N3 ....30 A4
  Bexley DA16 .....146 C3
  Bromley BR1 .....186 A6
  Chislehurst SE9 ..166 A2
  Harrow HA3 ......42 A6
  Mortlake SW14 ..133 B2
  South Croydon CR2 .221 A2
  Southgate N13 ...16 C2
  Wimbledon SW19 .179 D5
Avondale Rise SE15 .139 D2
Avondale Sq SE1 ..118 A1
Avonfield Ct E17 ...54 B6
Avonley Rd SE14 ..140 C5
Avon Mews HA5 ...23 B2
Avonmore Gdns W14 254 D3
Avonmore Pl W14 ..254 B4
Avonmore Prim Sch
  W14 ......113 A2 254 B4
Avonmore Rd
  W14 ......113 B2 254 C4
Avonmouth St SE1 .262 A6
Avon Pl SE1 ....252 B1
Avon Rd E17 ......54 B6
  SE4 ....141 C2
  Ashford TW16 ...171 D3
  Greenford UB6 ...85 D3
Avonstowe Cl BR6 .227 A4
Avon Way E18 .....55 A6
Avonwick Rd TW3 .129 D3
Avril Way E4 ......36 A5
Avriol Ho W12 ....112 B5
Avro Ct E9 ....75 A4
Avro Way SM6 ....220 A1
Awlfield Ave N17 ..33 B2
Awliscombe Rd
  DA16 ....145 D3
Axe St IG11 ....101 A4
Axford Ho SW2 ...160 D3
Axholm Ave HA8 ..26 D2
Axis Bsns Ctr E15 .97 C6
Axminster Cres DA16 146 C4
Axminster Rd N7 ..72 B5
Aybrook St
  W1 ....93 A2 238 A3
Aycliffe Cl BR1 ...210 A5
Aycliffe Ct KT1 ...176 C1
Aycliffe Rd W12 ..112 A5
Ayerst Ct 1 E10 ..54 A2
Aylands Cl HA9 ....66 A6
Aylesbury Cl E7 ...76 C2
Aylesbury Ct SM1 .218 A5
Aylesbury Ho 13
  SE15 ....140 A4
Aylesbury Rd BR2 .209 A6
  SE17 ....117 B1 262 D1
Aylesbury St
  EC1 ....94 D3 241 A5
  NW10 ....67 B5
Ayles Ct UB4 .....84 A6
Aylesford Ave BR3 .207 A4
Aylesford Ho SE1 .252 D1
Aylesford St
  SW1 ....115 D1 259 C1
Aylesham Cl NW7 .28 A3
Aylesham Ctr The
  SE15 ....140 A4
Aylesham Rd BR6 .211 D2
Ayles Rd UB4 .....84 B4
Aylestone Ave NW6 .90 C4
Aylett Rd
  Croydon SE25 ...206 B1
  Isleworth TW7 ...130 C3
Ayley Croft EN1 ...18 A6
Aylmer Cl HA7 ....25 A6
Aylmer Ct N2 .....48 B4
Aylmer Dr HA7 ....25 A6
Aylmer Ho SE10 ..120 B1
Aylmer Rd E11 ....54 C1
  N2 ....48 C4
  W12 ....111 D4
Aylmer Rd IG1 ....111 D4

Avondale Cres continued
Avondale Gdns TW4 .151 B6

Avondale Ho 10 SE1 .118 A1

Aylsham Dr UB10 .61 A6
Aylton Est 22 SE16 .118 C4
Aylward Fst & Mid Sch
  HA7 ....25 D5
Aylward Rd
  Forest Hill SE23 ..162 D2
  Merton SW20 ....201 B6
Aylward Sch N18 ..33 B6
Aylwards Rise HA7 .25 A6
Aylward St E1 .....96 D1
Aylwin Est SE1 ....263 B6
Aylwin Girls Sch
  SE1 ....117 D2 263 D4
Aynhoe Mans W14 .112 D2
Aynhoe Rd W14 ..112 D2
Ayr Ct W3 ....88 C2
Ayres Cl E13 ......99 A4
Ayres Cres NW10 ..67 B1
Ayres St SE1 ..117 A4 252 B2
Ayrsome Rd N16 ..73 C5
Ayrton Gould Ho 9
  E2 ....96 D4
Ayrton Ho HA9 ....65 D6
Ayrton Rd
  SW7 ....114 B3 256 C6
Aysgarth Ct SM1 ..217 D5
Aysgarth Rd SE21 .161 C4
Ayston Ho 19 SE8 .118 D2
Ayton Ho SE5 ....139 B5
Aytoun Ct 17 SW9 .138 C1
Aytoun Pl SW9 ...138 B1
Aytoun Rd SW9 ..138 B3
Azalea Cl Ealing W7 .108 D5
  Ilford IG1 ....78 D2
Azalea Ct W7 .....108 D5
Azalea Ho SE14 ..141 B5
Azalea Wlk HA5 ...40 B3
Azelea Ct IG8 .....36 C3
Azenby Rd SE15 ..139 D4
Azof St SE10 .....120 C2
Azov Ho 9 E1 ....97 A3

B

Baalbec Rd N5 ....72 D3
Babbacombe Cl KT9 .213 D3
Babbacombe Gdns
  IG4 ....56 A5
Babbacombe Rd BR1 187 A2
Baber Bridge Par
  TW14 ....150 C5
Baber Dr TW14 ...150 C5
Babington Ct WC1 .240 B1
  Streatham SW16 .181 D5
Babington Ho SE1 .252 B2
Babington House Sch
  BR7 ....188 B4
Babington Rd NW4 .46 B5
  Dagenham RM8 ..80 C4
  Streatham SW16 .181 D5
Babington Rise HA9 .66 C2
Babmaes St SW1 .249 C5
Bacchus Wlk 12 N1 .95 C5
Bache's St N1 .95 B4 235 D1
Back Church La E1 ..96 A1
Back Hill EC1 .....241 B5
Backhouse Pl SE1 .263 B3
Back La HA8 ......27 A2
  N8 ....50 A4
  NW3 ....70 A4
  Brentford TW8 ...131 D6
  Dagenham RM6 ..59 A2
  Richmond TW10 ..153 C2
  Sidcup DA5 .....169 C4
Backley Gdns SE25 .206 A3
Back Rd Sidcup DA14 .190 A6
  Teddington TW11 .174 C3
Bacon Gr SE1 117 C2 263 C5
Bacon La NW9 ....44 D5
  Edgware HA8 .....26 C2
Bacon's Coll SE16 .119 C4
Bacon's La N6 ....49 A1
Bacon St E2 .95 D3 243 D6
Bacon Terr RM8 ...80 B3
Bacton NW5 ......71 A3
Bacton St 2 E2 ...96 C4
Baddeley Cl EN3 ..7 C6
Baddeley Ho SE11 .260 D2
Baddow Cl
  Dagenham RM10 ..103 C6
  Woodford IG8 ....37 D4
Baddow Wlk N1 ..235 A6
Baden Ct N11 .....31 D3
Baden Ho 2 E3 ...252 D2
Baden Pl SE1 .....252 B2
Baden Powell Cl
  Dagenham RM9 ..103 A6
  Surbiton KT6 ....214 B6
Baden Powell Ho 11
  DA17 ....125 C3
Baden Powell Sch E5 .74 B5

Baden Rd N8 .....49 D5
  Ilford IG1 ....78 D3
Badger Cl
  Feltham TW13 ...150 B1
  Hounslow TW4 ...128 C2
  Ilford IG2 ....57 A2
Badger Ct NW2 ...68 C5
Badgers Cl
  Ashford TW15 ...170 B5
  Enfield EN2 ....4 D2
  Harrow HA1 ......42 B3
  Hayes UB3 ......105 C6
Badgers Copse BR6 .227 D6
  Worcester Park KT4 .215 D5
Badgers Croft SE9 .166 C1
  Barnet N20 ....13 A3
Badgers Hole CR0 .222 D5
Badgers Wlk KT3 .177 C1
Badlis Rd E17 ....53 C6
Badma Cl N9 ......18 C1
Badminton Cl KT2 .176 D2
Badminton Cl
  Harrow HA1 ......42 C5
  Northolt UB5 .....63 C2
Badminton Ct 9 N4 .51 A2
Badminton Ho SE22 .139 C1
Badminton Mews 10
  E16 ....121 A5
Badminton Rd SW12 159 A5
Badric Ct SW11 ...136 B3
Badsworth Rd 3
  SE5 ....139 A4
Bagley Cl UB7 ....104 A4
Bagley's La
  SW6 ....135 D4 265 D1
Bagleys Spring RM6 .59 A5
Bagnigge Ho WC1 .234 A1
Bagshot Ho NW1 .231 D2
Bagshot Rd EN1 ..17 D5
Bagshot St
  SE17 ....117 C1 263 B1
Baildon 28 E2 .....96 C5
Baildon St SE8 ...141 B5
Bailey Cl N11 .....31 D3
  Chingford E4 .....36 A4
Bailey Cres KT9 ..213 D1
Bailey Ct 9 W12 .112 A3
  4 Chingford E4 ..36 B5
Bailey Ho 11 SE26 .184 B4
Bailey Mews W4 ..132 C6
Bailey Pl SE26 ....184 D4
Bainbridge cl KT2 .176 A5
Bainbridge Rd RM9 .81 B4
Bainbridge St WC1 .239 D2
Baines Cl CR2 ....221 B3
Bain Ho 23 SW9 ..138 A1
Baird Ave UB1 ....108 A6
Baird Cl E10 ......53 C1
  NW9 ....45 A3
Baird Gdns SE19 .183 C6
Baird Ho 29 W12 .112 B6
  12 Belvedere DA17 .125 C3
Baird Rd EN1 ......6 B1
Baird St EC1 .....242 B6
Baizdon Rd SE3 ..142 C3
Baker Beall Ct DA7 .147 D2
Baker Ct E11 .....76 B1
Baker Ho 12 E3 ...97 D4
  Ealing W7 ....108 D5
Baker La CR4 ....203 A6
Baker Rd NW10 ...89 C6
  SE18 ....144 A4
Bakers' Almshouses
  E10 ....53 D3
Bakers Ave SE17 ..53 D3
Bakers Ct SE25 ..205 C6
Bakers End SW20 .179 A1
Bakers Field N7 ..72 A4
Bakers Gdns SM5 .218 C6
Bakers Hall Ct EC3 .253 B5
Bakers Hill E5 ....52 C1
  Barnet EN5 ....1 D3
Bakers Ho N5 .....109 D5
Baker's La N6 ....48 D3
Bakers Mews 9 BR6 227 D2
Baker's Mews W1 .238 A2
Bakers Rents 13 E2 .95 D4
Bakers Row E15 ..98 C5
Baker's Row
  EC1 ....94 C3 241 A5
Baker St W1 ..92 D2 237 D4
  Enfield EN1 ....5 A4
Baker Street
  W1 ....92 D2 237 D4
Baker Street Sta
  NW1 ....92 D3 237 D5
Baker's Yd EC1 ...241 A5

Bakery Cl SW9 ......**270** D3
Bakery Mews KT6 ...**198** C1
Balaam Ho SM1 ...**217** C4
Balaams La N14 ....**15** D2
Balaam St E13 ......**99** B4
Balaclava Rd
 SE1 ....**117** D2 **263** D3
 Kingston KT6 ......**197** C2
Balcaskie Rd SE9 ...**166** B6
Balchen Rd SE3 .....**143** D3
Balchier Rd SE22 ...**162** B5
Balcombe Cl DA6 ...**146** D1
Balcombe Ho NW1 ..**237** C6
 3 Streatham SW2 ....**160** B3
Balcombe St
 NW1 ....**92** D3 **237** C5
Balcon Ct W5 ......**88** B1
Balcorne St E9 .....**74** C1
Balder Rise SE12 ...**165** B2
Balderton Flats W1 .**238** B1
Balderton St
 W1 ....**93** A1 **238** B1
Baldewyne Ct N17 ...**34** A2
Baldock Ho **32** SE5 ..**139** A3
Baldock St E3 ......**97** D5
Baldrey Ho **1** SE10 ..**120** D1
Baldry Gdns SW16 ..**182** B4
Baldwin Cres SE5 ...**139** A4
Baldwin Gdns TW3 ..**130** A4
Baldwin Ho **15** SW2 ..**160** C3
Baldwin's Gdns
 EC1 ......**94** C2 **241** A4
Baldwin St EC1 .....**235** C1
Baldwin Terr
 N1 ......**95** A5 **235** A4
Baldwyn Gdns W3 ..**111** B6
Bale Rd E1 ....**97** A2
Bales Coll W10 .....**90** D4
Balfern Gr W4 .....**111** C1
Balfern St SW11 ....**136** C3
Balfe St N1 ..**94** A4 **233** B3
Balfour Ave W7 ....**108** D5
Balfour Bsns Ctr UB2 **106** D3
Balfour Gr N20 .....**14** D1
Balfour Ho W10 ....**90** D2
Balfour Mews W1 ...**248** B4
 Edmonton N9 ......**18** A1
Balfour Pl W1 ......**248** B5
 Putney SW15 .....**134** B1
Balfour Rd BR2 ....**209** D4
 N5 ....**73** A4
 W13 ....**109** B4
 W3 ....**89** A2
 Croydon SE25 .....**206** A5
 Harrow HA1 ......**42** B4
 Hounslow TW3 ....**129** D2
 Ilford IG1 ....**57** A1
 Merton SW19 .....**179** D3
 Southall UB2 ......**106** D4
 Wallington SM5 ....**218** D1
Balfour St
 SE17 ......**117** B2 **262** C4
Balfron Twr **2** E14 ...**98** A1
Balgonie Rd E4 .....**20** B3
Balgowan Cl KT3 ...**199** C5
Balgowan Prim Sch
 BR3 ....**185** A1
Balgowan Rd BR3 ...**185** B1
Balgowan St SE18 ...**123** D2
Balham Gr SW12 ...**159** A4
Balham High Rd
 SW12,SW17 ......**159** A3
Balham Hill SW12 ...**159** B5
Balham New Rd
 SW12 ....**159** B4
Balham Park Mans
 SW12 ....**158** D3
Balham Park Rd
 SW12,SW17 ......**159** A3
Balham Rd N9 ......**18** A2
Balham Sta SW12 ...**159** B3
Balham Station Rd
 SW12 ....**159** B3
Balin Ho SE1 ......**252** C2
Balkan Wlk E1 .....**118** B6
Balladier Wlk E14 ...**97** D2
Ballamore Rd BR1 ..**165** A1
Ballance Rd E9 .....**75** A2
Ballantine St SW18 ..**136** A1
Ballantrae Ho NW2 ..**69** B4
Ballard Cl KT2 .....**177** D3
Ballard Ho SE10 ....**141** D6
Ballards Cl RM10 ...**103** D6
Ballards Farm Rd
 CR0,CR2 ....**222** A2
Ballards La N3 .....**29** D3

Ballards Mews HA8 ..**26** C4
Ballards Rd NW2 ....**68** A4
 Dagenham RM10 ...**103** D6
Ballards Rise CR2 ...**222** A2
Ballards Way CR0,
 CR2 ....**222** B2
Ballast Quay SE10 ..**120** B1
Ballater Cl WD19 ...**22** C4
Ballater Rd SW2,SW4 **138** A1
 South Croydon CR2 .**221** D3
Ball Ct EC3 ....**242** D1
Ballina St SE23 ....**162** D4
Ballin Ct **9** E14 ....**120** A4
Ballingdon Rd SW11 .**159** A5
Ballinger Point **18** E3 .**97** D4
Balliol Ave E4 .....**36** C6
Balliol Ho **11** SW15 ..**156** D3
Balliol Rd DA16 ....**146** B3
 W10 ....**90** D1
 Tottenham N17 ....**33** D1
Balloch Rd SE6 ....**164** B2
Ballogie Ave NW10 ..**67** C4
Ballow Cl **23** SE5 ....**139** C5
Ball's Pond Pl **3** N1 .**73** B2
Ball's Pond Rd N1 ...**73** C2
Balmain Cl W5 .....**109** D5
Balmain Ct TW3 ....**129** D4
Balman Ho **3** SE16 ..**118** D2
Balmer Rd E3 ......**97** B5
Balmes Rd N1 .**95** B6 **235** D6
Balmoral Ave N11 ...**31** A5
 Beckenham BR3 ....**207** A5
Balmoral Cl **1** SW15 .**156** D5
Balmoral Cres KT8 ..**195** C6
Balmoral Ct NW8 ...**229** C4
 SE12 ....**187** B6
 21 SE16 ....**118** D6
 11 Belmont SM2 ...**217** C1
 Ealing W5 ....**87** D1
 Edgware HA8 .....**26** D6
 North Cheam KT4 ..**216** B6
 Wembley HA9 .....**66** B5
Balmoral Dr
 Borehamwood WD6 ..**11** B4
 Hayes UB4 ....**83** D3
 Southall UB1 ......**85** B3
Balmoral Gdns DA5 .**169** B4
 W13 ....**109** A3
 Ilford IG3 ....**57** D1
Balmoral Gr N7 ....**72** B2
Balmoral Ho E17 ...**35** B1
 N4 ....**51** A1
 W14 ....**254** A4
Balmoral Mews W12 **111** D3
Balmoral Rd E10 ...**75** D6
 E7 ....**77** C3
 NW2 ....**68** B2
 Harrow HA2 ......**63** C4
 Kingston KT1 .....**198** B5
 North Cheam KT4 ..**216** B6
Balmoral Trad Est
 IG11 ....**101** D2
Balmore Cres EN4 ...**15** A6
Balmore St N19 .....**71** B6
Balmuir Gdns SW15 .**134** C1
Balnacraig Ave NW10 .**67** C4
Balniel Gate SW1 ...**259** D2
Balsam Ho **8** E14 ...**119** D6
Baltic Cl SW19 .....**180** B3
Baltic Ho **7** SE5 ....**139** A3
Baltic St E EC1 **95** A3 **242** A5
Baltic St W
 EC1 ....**95** A3 **242** A5
Baltimore Ho SE11 ..**261** A2
Baltimore Pl DA16 ..**145** D3
Balvaird Pl SW1 ....**259** D1
Balvernie Gr SW18 ..**157** C4
Bamber Ho **5** IG11 ..**101** A6
Bamborough Gdns **12**
 W12 ....**112** C4
Bamburgh **9** N17 ...**34** B3
Bamford Ave HA0 ...**88** B5
Bamford Ct E15 ....**75** D3
Bamford Rd
 Barking IG11 ......**79** A2
 Catford BR1 ......**186** A6
Bampfylde Cl SM6 ..**219** C5
Bampton Ct W5 ....**87** D1
Bampton Dr NW7 ...**28** A3
Bampton Rd SE23 ..**162** D4
Banavie Gdns BR3 ..**186** A2
Banbury Cl EN2 ....**4** D4
Banbury Ct W13 ...**109** A3
 WC2 ....**250** A6
 8 Belmont SM2 ...**217** C1
Banbury Ho **5** E9 ..**74** D1
Banbury Rd E17 ....**35** A3
 E9 ....**74** D1
Banbury St **3** SW11 .**136** C3

Banbury Wlk UB5 ...**85** C5
Banchory Rd SE3 ...**143** B5
Bancroft Ave N2 ....**48** C4
 Woodford IG9 .....**21** A2
Bancroft Cl
 Ashford TW15 ....**170** C5
 Hillingdon UB8 ....**82** D2
Bancroft Ct SW8 ...**270** A2
 Northolt UB5 .....**84** C6
Bancroft Gdns BR6 .**211** D1
 Harrow HA3 ......**24** A1
Bancroft Ho **10** E1 ..**96** C3
Bancroft Rd E1 ....**96** C3
 Harrow HA3 ......**24** A1
Bancrofts Sch IG8 ...**21** A1
Bandon Cl UB10 ...**82** B5
Bandon Hill Prim Sch
 SM6 ....**219** D2
Bandon Rise SM6 ..**219** D3
Banff Ho **1** NW3 ...**70** C2
Banfield Rd SE15 ...**140** B2
Banfor Ct SM6 .....**219** C3
Bangabandhu Prim Sch
 E2 ....**96** C4
Bangalore St SW15 .**134** D2
Bangor Cl UB5 .....**63** D3
Banim St W6 ......**112** B2
Banister Ho E9 ....**74** D3
 SW8 ....**269** B2
 15 W10 ....**91** A4
Banister Rd W10 ...**90** D4
Bank Ave CR4 .....**180** B1
Bank Ct SW11 .....**268** C2
Bank End SE1 .....**252** B4
Bankfoot Rd BR1 ..**186** C6
Bankhurst Rd SE6 ..**163** B4
Bank La Kingston KT2 **176** A3
 Roehampton SW15 ..**155** C6
Bank Mews SM1 ...**218** A2
Bank of England★
 EC2 ....**242** C1
Bank Par N11 .....**31** B5
Banks Ho SE1 .....**262** A5
 Isleworth TW7 ....**130** C3
Banksia Rd N18 ....**34** D5
Bankside SE1 **117** A6 **252** A5
 SE1 ....**252** B4
 Enfield EN2 ....**4** D4
 Southall UB1 ......**106** D5
 South Croydon CR2 .**221** D2
Bankside Ave UB5 ..**84** A5
Bankside Cl
 Carshalton SM5 ...**218** C2
 Isleworth TW7 ....**130** D1
Bankside Dr KT7 ...**213** B6
Bankside Pier
 SE1 ....**117** A6 **252** A5
Bankside Pk IG11 ..**102** A4
Bankside Rd IG1 ...**79** B3
Bankside Way **6**
 SE19 ....**183** C4
Banks La DA6 .....**147** B1
Bank Sta EC3 .**95** B1 **242** D1
Banks Way E12 ....**78** C4
Bank The N6 ......**49** B1
Bankton Rd SW2 ..**138** C1
Bankwell Rd SE13 ..**142** C1
Banner Ho EC1 ....**242** B5
Bannerman Ho SW8 .**270** C3
Banner St EC1 **95** A3 **242** B6
Banning Ho **4** SW19 **156** D3
Banning St SE10 ...**120** C1
Bannister Cl
 Greenford UB6 ....**64** B3
 Streatham SW2 ...**160** C3
Bannister Ho **28**
 SE14 ....**140** D6
Bannister Sports Ctr The
 HA3 ....**24** A1
Bannockburn Prim Sch
 SE18 ....**123** D2
Bannockburn Rd
 SE18 ....**123** D2
Bannow Cl KT19 ...**215** C4
Banqueting House★
 SW1 ....**250** A3
Banstead Ct N4 ....**51** A1
Banstead Gdns N9 ..**17** C1
Banstead Rd SM2,
 SM5 ....**218** C1
Banstead St SE15 ..**140** C2
Banstead Way SM6 ..**220** A3
Banstock Rd HA8 ..**26** D4
Banting Dr N21 ....**16** B6
Banting Ho **6** NW2 ..**68** A4
Bantock Ho **14** W10 .**91** A4
Banton Cl EN1 ....**6** B3
Bantry Ho **13** E1 ...**96** D4
Bantry St SE5 .....**139** B5
Banwell Rd DA5 ...**168** D5

Banyan Ho **8** NW3 ..**69** D2
Banyard Rd SE16 ...**118** B3
Baptist Gdns NW5 ..**71** A2
Barandon Wlk **6**
 W11 ....**112** D6
Barbanel Ho **19** E1 ..**96** C3
Barbara Brosnan Ct
 NW8 ....**229** B3
Barbara Cl TW17 ...**192** D4
Barbara Hucklesbury Cl
 N22 ....**32** D1
Barbara Martin Ho **1**
 N11 ....**31** C5
Barbara Ward Ct **3**
 E11 ....**76** C6
Barbauld Rd N16 ...**73** C5
Barber Beaumont Ho **21**
 E1 ....**96** D4
Barber Cl N21 .....**16** C4
Barbers Alley **1** E13 .**99** B4
Barbers Rd E15 ....**97** D5
Barbican★
 EC2 ....**95** A2 **242** B3
Barbican Arts & Con Ctr★
 EC2 ....**95** A2 **242** B3
Barbican Rd UB1 ...**85** D1
Barbican Sta
 EC1 ....**95** A2 **242** A4
Barb Mews W6 ....**112** C3
Barbon Cl WC1 ....**240** C4
Barbrook Ho E9 ...**74** C2
Barchard St SW18 ..**157** D6
Barchester Cl W7 ..**108** D5
Barchester Rd HA3 ..**24** B1
Barchester St E14 ..**97** D2
Barclay Cl
 SW6 ......**135** C5 **265** A3
Barclay Cl N12 ....**30** A5
Barclay Ho **21** E9 ..**74** C1
Barclay Jun & Inf Schs
 E10 ....**54** D1
Barclay Oval IG8 ...**37** A6
Barclay Rd E11 ....**54** D1
 E13 ....**99** C3
 E17 ....**54** A4
 SW6 ......**135** C5 **265** B3
 Edmonton N18 ....**33** B4
 South Croydon CR0 .**221** B5
Barcombe Ave SW2 .**160** B2
Bardell Ho **14** SE1 ..**118** A4
Barden St SE18 ...**145** C6
Bardney Rd SM4 ..**201** D5
Bardolph Rd N7 ...**72** A4
 Richmond TW9 ....**132** B2
Bard Rd W10 .....**112** D6
Bardsey Pl **35** E1 ...**96** C3
Bardsey Wlk **2** N1 ..**73** A2
Bardsley Cl CR0 ...**221** D5
Bardsley Ho **5** SE10 .**142** A6
Bardsley La SE10 ..**142** A6
Barents Ho **10** E1 ..**96** D4
Barfett St W10 ....**91** B3
Barfield Ave N20 ...**14** D2
Barfield Rd BR1,BR7 .**210** C6
 E11 ....**54** D1
Barfleur La SE8 ....**119** B2
Barford Cl NW4 ...**28** A4
Barford Ho **19** E3 ..**97** B5
Barford St N1 .**94** C6 **234** B5
Barforth Rd SE15 ..**140** B2
Barfreston Way SE20 .**184** B2
Bargate Cl SE18 ...**123** D1
 New Malden KT3 ...**200** A2
Bargehouse Rd SE16 .**122** D4
Bargery Rd SE6 ...**163** D3
Barge House St SE1 .**251** B4
Barge Wlk KT1,KT6,
 KT7 ....**197** C3
Bargrove Cl **8** SE20 .**184** A3
Bargrove Cres SE6 ..**163** B2
Barham Cl
 Chislehurst BR7 ...**188** D5
 Keston Mark BR2 ..**210** A1
 Wembley HA0 .....**65** C2
Barham Ct N12 ....**29** B5
 8 Croydon CR2 ...**221** A3
 Keston Mark BR2 ..**210** A1
 Wembley HA0 .....**65** C2
Barham Ho SE17 ...**263** B2
Barham Prim Sch HA0 **65** C2
Barham Rd
 Chislehurst BR7 ...**188** D5
 Croydon CR2 .....**221** A3
 Wimbledon SW20 ..**178** A3
Baring Cl SE12 ....**165** A2
Baring Ct N1 ......**235** C5
Baring Ho **11** E14 ..**97** C1

Baring Prim Sch
 SE12 ....**165** A4
Baring Rd SE12 ...**165** A2
 Barnet EN4 ....**2** C1
 Croydon CR0 .....**206** A1
Baring St N1 .**95** B6 **235** C5
Barker Cl KT3 .....**198** D5
Barker Dr NW1 ....**71** D1
Barker Ho N15 ....**50** D5
 SE17 ....**263** A3
 Dulwich SE21 ....**161** C1
Barker Mews SW4 ..**137** B1
Barker St SW10 ...**266** A6
Barker Wlk SW16 ..**159** D1
Barkham Rd N17 ...**33** C2
Barking Abbey Comp Sch
 IG11 ....**79** D2
Barking Abbey Comp Sch
 (Lower Sch) IG11 ..**79** C3
Barking Bsns Ctr
 IG11 ....**102** A4
Barking Flyover IG11 .**78** D1
Barking Hospl IG11 ..**79** D1
Barking Ind Pk IG11 .**102** A6
Barking Rd E13 ...**99** B4
 E6 ....**100** B6
Barkingside Sta IG6 ..**57** B6
Barking Sta IG11 ...**79** A1
Bark Pl W2 ..**113** D6 **245** C6
Barkston Gdns
 SW5 ......**113** D2 **255** C3
Barkway Ct N4 ....**73** A6
Barkwith Ho **27** SE14 **140** D6
Barkworth Rd SE16 .**118** C1
Barlborough St SE14 **140** D5
Barlby Gdns W10 ..**90** D3
Barlby Prim Sch W10 **90** D3
Barlby Rd W10 ....**90** D2
Barley Cl WD23 ...**8** A6
Barleycorn Way E14 .**119** B6
Barleyfields Cl RM6 ..**58** C2
Barley La IG3 .....**58** B3
Barley Lane Prim Sch
 RM6 ....**58** B2
Barley Mow Pas EC1 **241** D3
 W4 ....**111** B1
Barley Mow Way
 TW17 ....**192** C5
Barling **6** NW1 ....**71** B1
Barling Ct **1** SW4 ..**138** A3
Barlings Ho **2** SE4 ..**140** D1
Barloch Ho **13** SW11 **137** A3
Barlow Cl SM6 ....**220** A1
Barlow Dr SE18 ...**144** A4
Barlow Ho N1 .....**235** C2
 14 SE16 ....**118** B2
 W11 ....**244** A6
Barlow Pl W1 .....**248** D5
Barlow Rd NW6 ...**69** B2
 Acton W3 ....**110** D5
 Hampton TW12 ...**173** C5
Barlow St
 SE17 ....**117** B2 **262** D3
Barmeston Rd SE6 ..**163** D2
Barmor Cl HA2 ....**23** D1
Barmouth Ave UB6 ..**86** D5
Barmouth Ho **6** N7 ..**72** B6
Barmouth Rd SW18 .**158** A5
 Croydon CR0 .....**222** D6
Barnabas Ct N21 ...**16** C6
Barnabas Ho EC1 ..**235** A1
Barnabas Lo SW8 ..**270** B2
Barnabas Rd E9 ...**74** D3
Barnaby Cl HA2 ...**64** A6
Barnaby Ct NW9 ...**45** C6
Barnaby Pl SW7 ...**256** C3
Barnard Cl
 Chislehurst BR7 ...**189** B2
 Sunbury TW16 ....**172** B3
 Wallington SM6 ...**219** D1
 Woolwich SE18 ...**122** C3
Barnard Gdns
 Hayes UB4 ....**84** B3
 West Barnes KT3 ..**200** A5
Barnard Gr E15 ...**76** D1
Barnard Hill N10 ..**31** B2
Barnard Ho **17** E2 ..**96** B4
Barnard Lo **10** W9 ..**91** C2
 New Barnet EN5 ...**2** A1
Barnard Mews SW11 **136** C1
Barnardo Dr IG6 ...**57** A5
Barnardo Gdns **1**
 E1 ....**118** D6
Barnardo St E1 ....**96** D1
Barnard Rd SW11 ..**136** C1
 Enfield EN1 ......**6** B3
 Mitcham CR4 .....**181** A1
Barnard's Inn EC4 ..**241** B2
Barnbrough NW1 ...**232** A5

Barnby Sq **1** E15 ..**98** C6
Barnby St **2** E15 ...**98** C6
 NW1 ......**93** C4 **232** B2
Barn Cl **19** NW5 ...**71** D3
 Ashford TW15 ....**170** D5
 Northolt UB5 .....**84** C5
Barn Cres HA7 ....**25** C4
Barn Croft Sch E17 ..**53** A3
Barneby Cl TW2 ...**152** C3
Barnehurst Rd DA7 .**147** D5
Barnersbury Ho N7 ..**72** A4
Barnes Ave
 Barnes SW13 .....**134** A5
 Southall UB2 .....**107** B2
Barnes Bridge Sta
 SW13 ....**133** C3
Barnes Cl E12 ....**77** D4
Barnes Common★
 SW13 ....**134** A2
Barnes Ct N1 .....**72** C1
 Barnet EN5 ....**1** D1
 Newham E16 .....**99** C2
 South Norwood CR7 .**205** A6
 Woodford IG8 ....**37** D5
Barnes End KT3 ...**200** A4
Barnes High St SW13 **133** D3
Barnes Ho **14** E2 ..**96** C5
 N19 ....**50** A2
 26 SE14 ....**140** D6
 8 Barking IG11 ...**101** B6
Barnes Hospl SW14 .**133** C2
Barnes Rd N18 ....**34** C6
 Ilford IG1 ....**79** A3
Barnes St E14 .....**97** A1
Barnes Sta SW13 ..**134** A2
Barnes Terr SE8 ...**119** B1
Barnes Wallis Ct HA9 **67** A5
Barnet Coll EN4 ...**15** A4
Barnet Coll of F Ed EN5 **1** B1
Barnet Dr BR2 ....**226** A4
Barnet Gate La EN5 .**11** D4
Barnet Gr E2 .....**96** A4
Barnet Hill EN5 ...**1** C1
Barnet Hill JMI Prim Sch
 EN5 ....**13** B6
Barnet Ho **36** SE5 ..**139** A3
Barnet La
 Barnet EN5,N20 ...**13** B4
 Borehamwood WD6 ..**10** B5
Barnet Mus★ EN5 ..**1** A1
Barnet Rd Barnet EN5 .**1** B5
 Edgware HA8 .....**11** C5
Barnett Ho E1 .....**243** C3
Barnett Homestead
 NW11 ....**47** C5
Barnet Trad Est EN5 .**1** B2
Barnetts Ct HA2 ...**63** D5
Barnett St **8** E1 ...**96** B1
Barnet Way (Barnet
 By-Pass) EN5,NW7,
 WD6 ....**11** B3
Barnet Wood Rd BR2 **225** C6
Barney Cl SE7 ....**121** C1
Barn Field NW3 ...**70** D3
Barnfield KT3 .....**199** C3
Barnfield Ave
 Croydon CR0 .....**222** A2
 Kingston KT2 .....**176** A5
 Mitcham CR4 .....**203** B6
Barnfield Cl N4 ...**50** A2
 Wandsworth SW17 .**158** A5
Barnfield Gdns SE18 .**144** D6
 Kingston KT2 .....**176** A5
Barnfield Pl E14 ...**119** C2
Barnfield Prim Sch
 HA8 ....**27** A2
Barnfield Rd HA8 ..**27** A2
 SE18 ....**144** D6
 Ealing W5 ....**87** C3
 Erith DA17 ......**147** C5
Barnfield Wood Cl
 BR3 ....**208** B3
Barnfield Wood Rd
 BR3 ....**208** B3
Barnham Dr SE28 ..**123** D5
Barnham Rd UB6 ..**86** A4
Barnham St SE1 ...**253** B2
Barnhill HA5 ......**40** C4
Barn Hill HA9 .....**44** D1
Barnhill Ave BR2 ..**208** D4
Barnhill Com High Sch
 UB4 ....**84** B5
Barnhill Cl UB4 ...**84** B4
Barnhill La UB4 ...**84** B3
Barnhill Rd Hayes UB4 **84** C3
 Wembley HA9 .....**67** A5
Barnhurst Path WD19 **22** C3
Barningham Way NW9 **45** B3
Barnlea Cl TW13 ...**151** A2

Barnmead Gdns RM9 .81 B3
Barnmead Rd
Dagenham RM9 ....81 B3
Penge BR3 ....185 A2
Barn Rise HA9 ....66 C6
Barnsbury Cl KT3 ....199 A5
Barnsbury Cres KT5 .199 A1
Barnsbury Gr N7 .....72 B1
Barnsbury Ho 12
SW4 ....159 D5
Barnsbury La KT5 ...199 A1
Barnsbury Pk N1 .....72 C1
Barnsbury Rd
N1 ....94 C6 234 A5
Barnsbury Sq N1 .....72 C1
Barnsbury St N1 .....72 C1
Barnsbury Terr N1 ....72 B1
Barnscroft SW20 ....200 B6
Barnsdale Ave E14 ..119 C2
Barnsdale Rd W9 .....91 B3
Barnsley St E1 ....96 B3
Barn St N16 ....73 C6
Barnstaple Ho SE12 .164 D6
Barnstaple La SE13 ..142 A1
Barnstaple Rd HA4 ...62 C5
Barnston Wlk N1 ....235 A6
Barnview Lo HA3 .....24 C2
Barn Way HA9 ....66 C6
Barnwell Ho 1 SE5 .139 C4
Barnwell Rd SW2 ....160 C6
Barnwood Cl W9 .....91 D3
Barnet N20 ....13 B3
Ruislip HA4 ....61 B6
Baron Cl N1 ....234 A4
N11 ....31 B5
Baron Ct CR4 ....202 C5
Baroness Rd 5 E2 ...95 D4
Baronet Gr N17 ....34 A2
Baronet Rd N17 ....34 A2
Baron Gdns IG6 ....57 A6
Baron Gr CR4 ....202 C5
Baron Rd RM8 ....58 D1
Barons Court Mans
W14 ....254 B1
Baron's Court Rd
W14 ....113 A1 254 B2
Barons Court Sta
W14 ....113 A1 254 A2
Barons Ct NW9 ....45 B3
Ilford IG1 ....79 B6
Wallington SM6 .....219 D5
Baronsfield Rd TW1 .153 B5
Barons Gate 13 W4 ..111 A3
East Barnet EN4 ....14 C5
Barons Keep
W14 ....113 A1 254 A2
Barons Lo 8 E14 ....120 A2
Barons Mead HA1 ....42 C5
Baronsmead Rd
SW13 ....134 A4
Baronsmede W5 .....110 B4
Baronsmere Ct 7 EN5 .1 A1
Baronsmere Rd N2 ...48 C5
Baron's Pl
SE1 ....116 C4 251 B1
Baron St N1 ...94 C5 234 A4
Barons The TW1 .....153 B5
Baron's Wlk CR0 .....207 A3
Baron Wlk E16 ....98 D2
Barque Mews SE8 ...141 C6
Barrack Rd TW4 .....129 A1
Barra Hall Cir UB3 ....83 C1
Barra Hall Rd UB3 ...105 C6
Barras Cl EN3 ....7 C6
Barratt Ave N22 ....32 B1
Barratt Ho 15 N1 .....72 D1
Barratt Ind Pk E3 ....98 A3
Southall UB1 ....107 C5
Barratt Way HA3 ......42 B6
Barr Beacon SE23 ...162 C4
Barrenger Rd N10 .....30 D1
Barret Ho NW6 ....91 C6
Barrett Rd E17 ....54 A5
Barrett's Gr N16 ......73 C3
Barrett's Green Rd
NW10 ....89 B5
Barrett St W1 .93 A1 238 B1
Barrhill Rd SW2 .....160 A2
Barrie Ct EN5 ....14 A6
Barriedale SE14 .....141 A3
Barrie Ho 8 N16 .....73 C5
NW8 ....230 B5
W2 ....246 B5
Acton W3 ....111 A4
Edmonton N9 ....18 B4
Barrier Gdns Pier
E16 ....121 D3
Barringer Sq SW17 ..181 A6
Barrington Cl NW5 ...71 A3
Barrington Ct 4 N10 .31 B1
Barrington Ct *continued*
NW5 ....71 A3
31 SW9 ....138 A3
Barrington Prim Sch
DA16 ....146 D3
Barrington Rd N8 ....49 D4
SW9 ....138 D2
Bexley DA16 ....146 D3
Cheam SM3 ....201 C1
Little Ilford E12 ....78 C2
Barrington Villas
SE18 ....144 C4
Barrington Wlk 9
SE19 ....183 C4
Barrow Ave SM5 ....218 D1
Barrow Cl N21 ....16 D2
Barrow Ct 6 SE6 ....164 D3
Barrowdene Cl HA5 ..23 A1
Barrowell Gn N21 ....17 A2
Barrowfield Cl N9 ....18 C1
Barrowgate Ho W4 ..111 B1
Barrowgate Rd W4 ..111 B1
Barrow Hedges Cl
SM5 ....218 C1
Barrow Hedges Prim Sch
SM5 ....218 C1
Barrow Hedges Way
SM5 ....218 C1
Barrow Hill KT4 .....215 C6
Barrow Hill Cl KT4 ..215 C6
Barrow Hill Est
NW8 ....92 C5 230 A3
Barrow Hill Jun Sch
NW8 ....92 C5 230 A3
Barrow Hill Rd NW8 .230 A3
Barrow Point Ave HA5 23 A1
Barrow Point La HA5 .23 A1
Barrow Rd
Croydon CR0 ....220 C3
Streatham SW16 .....181 D4
Barrow Wlk TW8 .....109 C1
Barrs Rd NW10 ....67 B1
Barry Ave DA7 ....147 A5
N15 ....51 D3
Barry Cl BR6 ....227 C5
Barry Ct SW4 ....159 C5
Barrydene N20 ....14 B2
Barrydene Ct EN2 ......4 D2
Barry Ho 4 SE16 ....118 B1
Barry Lo N4 ....50 B2
Barry Par SE22 ....140 A1
Barry Rd E6 ....100 A1
NW10 ....67 A1
SE22 ....162 A6
Barry Terr TW15 .....148 B2
Barset Rd SE15 ......140 C2
Barsons Cl SE20 .....184 C3
Barston Rd SE27 .....161 A1
Barstow Cres SW2 ..160 B3
Bartell Ho SW2 ....160 C5
Barter St WC1 .94 A2 240 B3
Bartholomew Cl EC1 242 A3
SW18 ....136 A1
Bartholomew Ct EC1 242 B6
Edgware HA8 ....25 D3
5 Poplar E14 ....120 B6
Bartholomew Ho
23 SE5 ....139 A3
Enfield EN3 ....7 A6
Enfield EN3 ....7 B6
Bartholomew La EC2 242 D1
Bartholomew Pas
EC1 ....241 D3
Bartholomew Pl EC1 242 A3
Bartholomew Rd NW5 71 C2
Bartholomew Sq 18
E1 ....96 B3
Bartholomew St
SE1 ....117 B3 262 D5
Bartholomew Villas
NW5 ....71 C2
Barth Rd SE18 ....123 C2
Bartle Ave E6 ....100 A5
Bartle Rd W11 ....91 A1
Bartlett Cl E14 ....97 C1
Bartlett Ct EC4 ....241 B2
Bartletts Ho 10 RM10 .81 D2
Bartlett St CR2 ......221 B3
Bartok Ho W11 ....244 C5
Bartolomew Sq EC1 .242 B6
Barton Ave RM7 ....59 D1
Barton Cl E9 ....74 C3
NW4 ....46 A5
SE15 ....140 B2
Bexley DA6 ....169 A6
8 Newham E6 ....100 B1
Shepperton TW17 ....192 D3
Barton Ct 10 SW4 ...138 A3
W14 ....254 B2
Beckenham BR2 ......208 B6
Barton Gn KT3 ......177 B1
Barton Ho 8 E3 ......97 D4
N1 ....72 D1
SW6 ....135 D2
Barton Mdws IG6 .....57 A5
Barton Rd
W14 ....113 A1 254 B1
Sidcup DA14 ....191 A4
Barton St SW1 ....260 A6
Bartons The WD6 ....9 D5
Bartonway NW8 .....229 C4
Bartram Cl UB8 ....82 D3
Bartram Rd SE4 ......163 A5
Bartrams La EN4 ....2 A5
Bartrip St E9 ....75 B2
Barts Cl BR3 ....207 C4
Barville Cl SE4 ....141 A1
Barwell Ho 6 E2 ......96 A3
Barwick Dr UB8 ....82 D2
Barwick Ho 7 W3 ....111 A4
Barwick Rd E7 ....77 B4
Barwood Ave BR4 ...207 D1
Bascome St 13 SW2 .160 C5
Basden Gr TW13 .....151 C2
Basedale Rd RM9 .....80 B1
Baseing Cl E6 ....122 C6
Basevi Way SE8 .....141 D6
Bashley Rd NW10 .....89 B3
Basil Ave E6 ....100 A4
Basildene Rd TW4,
TW5 ....128 D2
Basildon Rd SE2 .....124 A1
Basil Gdns
Croydon CR0 ....206 D1
West Norwood SE27 ..183 A5
Basil Ho 14 E1 ....96 A1
SW8 ....270 A4
Basil Mans SW1 .....247 C1
Basilon Rd DA7 ......147 A3
Basil Spence Ho N22 .32 B2
Basil St SW1 .114 D3 247 C1
SW1,SW3 ....114 D3 257 C6
Basin App 22 E14 .....97 A1
Basing Cl KT7 ....196 D2
Basing Ct 12 SE15 ..139 D4
Basingdon Way SE5 .139 B1
Basing Dr DA5 ....169 B5
Basingfield Rd KT7 ..196 D2
Basinghall Ave
EC2 ....95 B1 242 C2
Basinghall St
EC2 ....95 B1 242 C2
Basing Hill NW11 .....47 B1
Wembley HA9 ....44 C1
Basing Ho
7 Barking IG11 ......101 B6
Catford SE6 ....185 C6
Basing House Yd 23
E2 ....95 C4
Basing Pl E2 ....95 C4
Basing St W11 ....91 B1
Basing Way N3 ....47 D6
Thames Ditton KT7 ..196 D2
Basire St N1 ...95 A6 235 B6
Baskerville Gdns
NW10 ....67 C4
Baskerville Rd SW18 .158 C4
Basket Gdns SE9 ....166 A6
Baslow Cl HA3 ....24 B2
Baslow Wlk E5 ....74 D4
Basnett Rd 8 SW11 .137 A2
Basque Ct 21 SE16 ..118 D4
Bassano St SE22 ....161 D6
Bassant Rd SE18 ....145 D6
Bassein Park Rd
W12 ....111 D4
Bassett Gdns TW7 ...130 A5
Bassett Ho RM9 .....102 B6
Bassett Rd W10 ....90 D1
Bassetts Cl BR6 .....226 D4
Bassett St NW5 ....71 A2
Bassetts Way BR6 ...226 D4
Bassett Way UB1 .....85 D1
Bassingbourn Ho 3
N1 ....72 D1
Bassingham Rd
Wandsworth SW18 ...158 A4
Wembley HA0 ....65 D2
Bassishaw Highwalk
EC2 ....242 C3
Basswood Cl SE15 ..140 B2
Bastable Ave IG11 ...102 A5
Basterfield Ho EC1 ..242 A5
Bastion Rd SE18,SE2 .124 A1
Baston Manor Rd
BR2,BR4 ....225 B4
Baston Rd BR2 ....225 B5
Baston Sch BR2 .....225 B6
Bastwick St
EC1 ....95 A3 242 A6
Basuto Rd
SW6 ....135 C4 265 B1
Batavia Cl TW16 .....172 C2
Batavia Ho 1 SE14 ..141 A5
Batavia Mews 3
SE14 ....141 A5
Batavia Rd SE14 .....141 A5
Sunbury TW16 ....172 B2
Batchelor St
N1 ....94 C6 234 B5
Bateman Cl IG11 .....79 A2
Bateman Ho 8 SE17 138 D6
Bateman Rd E4 ....35 C4
Bateman's Bldgs W1 239 C1
Bateman's Row
EC2 ....95 C3 243 B6
Bateman St
W1 ....93 D1 239 C1
Bates Cres
Croydon CR0 ....220 C3
Streatham SW16 .....181 C3
Bateson St SE18 .....123 C2
Bates Point E13 ....99 A6
Bate St 10 E14 ......119 B6
Bath Cl SE15 ....140 B5
Bath Ct EC1 ....235 C1
EC1 ....241 A5
3 Forest Hill SE26 ...162 A1
Bathgate Ho 8 SW9 138 D4
Bathgate Rd SW19 ..156 D1
Bath Gr E2 ....96 A5
Bath Ho E2 ....96 A3
SE1 ....262 B6
Bath House Rd CR0 ..204 A1
Bath Pas KT1 ....175 D1
Bath Pl 11 EC2 ....95 C4
14 W6 ....112 C1
Barnet EN5 ....1 B2
Bath Rd E7 ....77 D2
N9 ....18 C2
W4 ....111 C2
Cranford TW3,TW4,
TW5 ....128 C4
Dagenham RM6 ....59 A3
Harlington TW6,UB7,
TW5 ....127 B4
Harmondsworth TW6,
UB7 ....126 B4
Baths App
SW6 ....135 B5 264 D4
Baths Rd BR1,BR2 ....209 D5
Bath St EC1 ...95 B4 235 C1
Bath Terr
SE1 ....117 A3 262 A6
Bathurst Ave SW19 ..179 D2
Bathurst Gdns NW10 ..90 B5
Bathurst Ho 2 W12 .112 B6
Bathurst Mews
W2 ....114 B6 246 D6
Bathurst Rd IG1 ....56 D1
Bathurst St W2 ......246 D6
Bathway 17 SE18 ....122 C2
Batley Cl CR4 ....202 D2
Batley Pl 3 N16 ......73 D5
Batley Rd N16 ....73 D5
Enfield EN2 ....5 B4
Batman Cl W12 ......112 B5
Batoum Gdns W6 ....112 C3
Batson Ho 21 E1 ......96 A1
Batson St W12 ....112 A4
Batsworth Rd CR4 ...202 B6
Battenberg Wlk 10
SE19 ....183 C5
Batten Cl E6 ....100 B1
Batten Ho 8 E17 ......53 D6
7 SW4 ....159 C6
13 W10 ....91 A4
Batten St SW11 ......136 C2
Battersby Rd SE6 ....164 B1
Battersea Bridge Rd
SW11 ....136 C5 267 A3
Battersea Church Rd
SW11 ....136 B4 266 D2
Battersea Dogs Home
SW8 ....137 B5 268 D3
Battersea Park★
SW11 ....137 A5 268 A3
Battersea Park Rd
SW11,SW8 ....267 D1
Battersea Park Sta
SW8 ....137 B5 268 C3
Battersea Power
Station(dis)★
SW8 ....137 B6 268 D6
Battersea Rise SW11 136 C1
Battersea Sq SW11 ..266 D1
Battersea Tech Coll
SW11 ....136 D4 267 D1
Battery Rd SE28 .....123 C4
Battishill St 9 N1 ....72 D1
Battlebridge Ct NW1 233 B4
Battle Bridge Ctr
NW1 ....233 A4
Battle Bridge La
SE1 ....117 C5 253 A3
Battle Bridge Rd
NW1 ....94 A5 233 A4
Battle Cl SW19 ....180 A4
Battledean Rd N5 ....72 D3
Battle Ho 8 SE15 ...140 A6
Battle of Britain Mus★
NW9 ....27 D1
Batty St E1 ....96 A1
Baty Ho SW2 ....160 B3
Baudwin Rd SE6 .....164 C2
Baugh Rd DA14 ......190 C5
Baulk The SW18 .....157 C4
Bavant Rd SW16 .....182 B1
Bavaria Rd N19 ....72 A6
Bavent Rd SE5 ....139 A3
Bawdale Rd SE22 ....161 D6
Bawdsey Ave IG2 .....57 D5
Bawtree Rd SE14 ....141 A5
Bawtry Rd N20 ....14 D1
Baxendale N20 ....14 A2
Baxendale St E2 ......96 A4
Baxter Cl
Hillingdon UB10 ....82 D4
Southall UB2 ....107 D3
Baxter Ho 11 E3 ......97 D4
Baxter Rd N1 ....73 B2
Edmonton N18 ....34 B6
Ilford IG1 ....78 D3
Newham E16 ....99 C1
Bayard Ct DA7 ....147 D1
Baycliffe Ho 8 E9 ....74 D2
Baycroft Cl HA5 ......40 C6
Bay Ct 7 E1 ....96 D3
W5 ....110 A3
Baydene Mews NW4 .46 B5
Baydon Ct BR2 ......208 D6
Bayer Ho EC1 ....242 A5
Bayes Ct NW3 ....70 D1
Bayeux Ho 10 SE7 ..143 C6
Bayfield Ho 3 SE4 ..140 D1
Bayfield Rd SE9 .....143 D1
Bayford Rd NW10 ....90 D4
Bayford St 5 E8 ......74 B1
Bayford St Ind Ctr 4
E8 ....74 B1
Bayham Pl
NW1 ....93 C6 232 B5
Bayham Rd W4 ......111 B3
Ealing W13 ....109 B5
Morden SM4 ....202 A5
Bayham St
NW1 ....93 C6 232 A5
Bayhurst Lo N4 ....51 A2
Bayhurst Wood
Countryside Park
UB9 ....38 B4
Bayleaf Cl TW12 .....174 B5
Bayley St WC1 ....239 C3
Bayley Wlk SE2 ......125 A1
Baylis Mews TW1 ....153 A4
Baylis Rd SE1 116 C4 251 A1
Bayliss Ave SE28 ....124 D6
Bayliss Cl N21 ....16 A6
Bayne Cl E6 ....100 B1
Baynes Cl EN1 ....6 A4
Baynes Mews 2 NW3 .70 B2
Baynes St NW1 ....71 C1
Baynham Cl DA5 ....169 B5
Bayon Ho 27 N19 .....49 D2
Bayonne Rd W6 .....264 A5
Bays Cl SE26 ....184 C5
Bays Ct HA8 ....26 D5
Bayshill Rise UB5 .....63 D2
Bayston Rd N16 ....73 D5
Bayswater Rd
W2 ....114 B6 246 C5
Bayswater Sta
W2 ....113 D6 245 D6
Baythorne St 5 E3 ...97 B2
Bayton Ct 2 E8 ......74 A1
Baytree Cl DA15 ....167 D3
Bromley BR1 ....187 D2
Baytree Ho E4 ....19 D4
Baytree Rd SW2 .....138 B1
Bazalgette Cl KT3 ...199 B4
Bazalgette Gdns KT3 199 B4
Bazalgette Ho NW8 .236 D6
Bazeley Ho SE1 .....251 C1
Bazely St E14 ....120 A6
Bazile Rd N21 ....16 C5
BBC Television Ctr
W12 ....112 C5
Beacham Cl SE7 .....143 D6
Beachborough Rd
BR1 ....186 A6
Beachcroft Ave UB1 .107 B5
Beachcroft Rd E11 ....76 C5
Beach Ct SE9 ....166 A5
Beach Gr TW13 ......151 C2
Beach Ho SW5 ....255 A2
Beachy Rd E3 ....75 C1
Beaconfield Terrace Rd
W14 ....254 A5
Beacon Gate SE14 ...140 D2
Beacon Gr SM5 ......219 A4
Beacon Hill N7 ....72 A3
Beacon Ho 19 SE5 ..139 C5
SW8 ....269 C2
10 Penge SE26 ......184 B5
Beacon House Sch
W5 ....110 B5
Beacon Pl CR0 ....220 A5
Beacon Rd SE13 .....164 B5
Harlington TW19,TW6 .148 C5
Beacon Rdbt TW6 ...148 C5
Beacons Cl 10 E6 ...100 A2
Beaconsfield Cl N11 ..31 A5
SE3 ....143 A6
W4 ....111 A1
Beaconsfield Ct N11 ..31 A5
Beaconsfield Gdns
KT10 ....212 C1
Beaconsfield Par 1
SE9 ....188 A6
Beaconsfield Prim Sch
UB2 ....107 A5
Beaconsfield Rd BR1 209 D6
E10 ....76 A5
E16 ....98 D3
E17 ....53 B3
N11 ....31 A6
N15 ....51 C5
NW10 ....67 D2
SE17 ....117 C1 263 A1
SE9 ....188 A6
W4 ....111 B3
W5 ....109 D4
Claygate KT10 ....212 C1
Edmonton N9 ....18 A1
Enfield EN3 ....6 D6
Greenwich SE3 ....143 A5
Hayes UB4 ....106 C5
Kingston KT3 ....177 B1
Southall UB1 ....107 A5
Surbiton KT5 ....198 B2
Thornton Heath CR0 .205 B3
Twickenham TW1 ....153 B5
Beaconsfield Wlk
SW6 ....135 B4 264 D1
Beaconshaw BR1 ....186 C3
Beacontree Ave E17 ..36 B1
Beacontree Rd E11 ...54 D2
Beadle Ct CR4 ....202 C6
Beadlow Cl SM4 .....202 B3
Beadman Pl SE27 ....182 D6
Beadman St SE27 ....182 D6
Beadnell Rd SE23 ...162 D3
Beadon Rd BR2 ......209 A4
W6 ....112 C2
Beaford Gr SW20 ....201 B6
Beagle Cl TW13 .....172 B6
Beak St W1 ...115 C6 249 B6
Beal Cl DA16 ....146 A4
Beale Cl N13 ....32 D5
Beale Ho 7 SW9 ....138 B3
Beale Pl E3 ....97 B5
Beale Rd E3 ....97 B6
Beal High Sch IG5 ....56 A5
Beal Rd IG1 ....78 C6
Beam Ave RM10 .....103 D6
Beames Ho SW8 .....269 C2
Beaminster Ct N15 ...51 B4
Beaminster Gdns IG6 .56 D6
Beaminster Ho SW8 .270 C4
Beamish Dr WD23 .....8 A3
Beamish Ho 5 SE16 .118 C2
Beamish Rd N9 ....18 A3
Beanacre Cl E9 ....75 B2
Bean Rd DA6 ....146 D1
Beanshaw SE9 ....188 C6
Beansland Gr RM6 ...59 A6
Bear Alley EC4 ......241 C2
Bear Cl RM7 ....59 D3
Bear Croft Ho 6
SW6 ....135 B3
Beardell St SE19 ....183 D4
Beardow Gr N14 ....15 C5
Beard Rd TW10 .....176 B5
Beardsfield E13 ....99 A5
Beard's Hill TW12 ...173 C2
Beards Hill Cl TW12 .173 C2
Beardsley Terr RM8 ..80 B3

Beardsley Way W3 . . .**111** B4
Beard's Rd TW15,
TW16 . . . .**171** C4
Bearfield Rd KT2 . . .**176** B3
Bear Gardens Mus★
SE1 . . . .**117** A5 **252** A4
Bear Gdns
SE1 . . . .**117** A5 **252** A4
Bear La SE1 .**116** D5 **251** D3
Bear Rd TW13 . . . . . .**172** D6
Bear St WC2 . . . . . .**249** D6
Bearstead Rise SE4 . .**163** B6
Bearsted Terr ☒
BR3 . . . .**185** C2
Beasley's Ait TW17 . .**193** D3
Beasley's Ait La
TW16,TW17 . . . . .**193** D3
Beaton Cl SE15 . . . . .**139** D4
Beatrice Ave
Thornton Heath SW16 .**182** B1
Wembley HA9 . . . .**66** A3
Beatrice Cl E13 . . . . .**99** A3
Pinner HA5 . . . .**40** A5
Beatrice Ct NW4 . . . .**46** C4
Buckhurst Hill IG9 . . . .**21** D2
Beatrice Ho ☒ SW2 .**160** B6
☒ W6 . . . .**112** C1
Beatrice Pl W8 . . . . .**255** C5
Beatrice Rd E17 . . . . .**53** C4
N4 . . . .**50** C2
N9 . . . .**18** C4
SE1 . . . .**118** A2
☒ Richmond TW10 . . .**154** B6
Southall UB1 . . . . . .**107** B5
Beatrice Tate Sch E2 . .**96** B4
Beatrice Webb Ho ☒
E3 . . . .**97** A5
Beatrix Ho SW5 . . .**255** D2
Beatrix Potter Prim Sch
SW18 . . . .**158** A3
Beattie Cl TW14 . . . .**149** D3
Beattie Ho SW8 . . .**269** D2
Beattock Rise N10 . . .**49** B5
Beatty Rd N16 . . . . . .**73** C4
Stanmore HA7 . . . . . .**25** C4
Beatty St NW1 . . . .**232** A4
Beattyville Gdns IG6 . .**56** D5
Beauchamp Cl ☒
W4 . . . .**111** A3
Beauchamp Ct HA7 . .**25** C5
Beauchamp Pl
SW3 . . . .**114** C3 **257** B5
Beauchamp Rd E7 . . .**77** B1
SW11 . . . .**136** D1
East Molesey KT8 . . .**196** A4
South Norwood SE19 . .**183** B2
Sutton SM1 . . . .**217** C4
Twickenham TW1 . . .**153** A4
Beauchamp St EC1 . .**241** A3
Beauchamp Terr
SW15 . . . .**134** B2
Beauclerc Cty Inf Sch
TW16 . . . .**194** C6
Beauclerc Rd W6 . . .**112** B3
Beauclere Ho ☒
SM2 . . . .**218** A1
Beauclerk Cl TW13 . .**150** B3
Beauclerk Ho ☒
SW16 . . . .**160** A1
Beaudesert Mews
UB7 . . . .**104** A4
Beaufort E6 . . . .**100** C2
Beaufort Ave HA3 . . .**43** B6
Beaufort Cl
Chingford E4 . . . .**35** D4
Ealing W5 . . . .**88** B2
Putney SW19 . . . . . .**156** B4
Beaufort Ct N11 . . . .**31** B5
New Barnet EN5 . . . . .**14** A6
Richmond TW10 . . . .**175** C6
Beaufort Dr NW11 . . .**47** C5
Beaufort Gdns NW4 . .**46** C3
SW3 . . . .**114** C3 **257** B6
Heston TW5 . . . .**129** A4
Ilford IG1 . . . .**56** C1
South Norwood SW16 .**182** B3
Beaufort Ho ☒ N15 . .**51** D5
NW11 . . . .**48** A3
SW1 . . . .**259** C1
SW11 . . . .**136** C3
SW3 . . . .**266** D5
☒ Wimbledon SW20 . .**178** D2
Beaufort Mans SW3 .**266** D5
Beaufort Mews SW6 .**264** D6
Beaufort Pk NW11 . . .**47** C5
Beaufort Rd Ealing W5 .**88** B2
Kingston KT1,KT5,KT6 .**198** A5

Beaufort Rd continued
Richmond TW10 . . . .**175** C6
Ruislip HA4 . . . .**61** B6
Twickenham TW1 . . .**153** C6
Beaufort St
SW3 . . . .**136** B6 **266** C6
Beaufort Way KT17 . .**216** A1
Beaufoy Ho SW8 . . .**270** C4
☒ West Norwood
SE27 . . . .**160** D1
Beaufoy Rd ☒ SW8 . .**137** B2
Tottenham N17 . . . . . .**33** C3
Beaufoy Wlk
SE11 . . . .**116** B2 **260** D3
Beaulieu Ave ☒ E16 .**121** B5
Forest Hill SE26 . . . .**184** B6
Beaulieu Cl NW9 . . . .**45** C5
SE5 . . . .**139** B2
Hounslow TW4 . . . . .**151** B6
Mitcham CR4 . . . . . .**181** A2
☒ Twickenham TW1 . .**153** D5
Beaulieu Ct W5 . . . . .**88** A2
Beaulieu Ho ☒ HA5 . .**40** D2
Beaulieu Gdns N21 . . .**17** A4
Beaulieu Ho NW4 . . . .**28** D1
Beaulieu Pl W4 . . . . .**111** A3
Beaumanor Gdns
SE9 . . . .**188** C6
Beaumanor Mans
W2 . . . .**245** D6
Beaumaris ☒ N11 . . .**32** A4
Beaumaris Dr IG8 . . . .**37** D3
Beaumaris Gn NW9 . . .**45** C5
Beaumaris Twr ☒
W3 . . . .**110** D4
Beaumont W14 . . . .**254** D3
Putney SW15 . . . . . .**157** A6
Beaumont Ave
W14 . . . .**113** B1 **254** C2
Harrow HA2 . . . .**41** D3
Richmond TW9 . . . . .**132** B2
Wembley HA0 . . . . . .**65** C4
Beaumont Bldgs
WC2 . . . .**240** B1
Beaumont Cl KT2 . . .**176** C3
Beaumont Cres
W14 . . . .**113** B1 **254** C1
Beaumont Ct E5 . . . . .**74** B5
☒ NW9 . . . .**27** D1
☒ W4 . . . .**111** A1
☒ Mitcham CR4 . . . . .**181** A1
Wembley HA0 . . . . . .**65** C3
☒ Wimbledon SW19 . .**178** D6
Beaumont Dr TW15 . .**171** B5
Beaumont Gdns NW3 . .**69** C5
Beaumont Gr E1 . . . . .**96** D3
Beaumont Ho ☒ E10 . .**53** D2
☒ Streatham SW2 . .**160** A3
Wimbledon SW19 . . .**157** C1
Beaumont Pl
NW1,WC1,W1 . .**93** C3 **239** B6
Barnet EN5 . . . .**1** B4
Isleworth TW7 . . . . .**152** D6
Beaumont Rd E10 . . . .**53** D2
E13 . . . .**99** B4
W4 . . . .**111** A4
Orpington BR5,BR6 . .**211** B5
Putney SW15,SW19 . .**157** A4
South Norwood SE19 . .**183** A4
Beaumont Rise N19 . . .**49** D1
Beaumont Sch The
E10 . . . .**53** D1
Beaumont Sq E1 . . . . .**96** D2
Beaumont St W1 . . .**238** B4
Beaumont Terr ☒
SE13 . . . .**164** C4
Beaumont Wlk NW3 . . .**70** D1
Beauvais Terr UB5 . . .**84** D4
Beauvale ☒ NW1 . . . .**71** A1
Beauval Rd SE22 . . . .**161** D5
Beaverbank Rd DA15,
SE9 . . . .**167** D5
Beaver Cl
Hampton TW12 . . . . .**173** D2
☒ Penge SE20 . . . . .**184** A3
Beaver Gr UB5 . . . . . .**85** A4
Beavers Comm Prim Sch
TW4 . . . .**128** A2
Beavers Cres TW4 . . .**128** A3
Beavers La TW4 . . . . .**128** C2
Beavers Lo DA14 . . . .**189** D4
Beaverwood Rd BR7 .**189** C4
Beaverwood Sch for Girls
BR7 . . . .**189** C4
Beavis Ho N16 . . . . . .**73** C5
Beavor La W6 . . . . . .**112** A1
Bebbington Rd SE18 .**123** C2
Beblets Cl ☒ BR6 . . .**227** D5
Bec Cl HA4 . . . .**62** D1
Beccles Dr IG11 . . . . .**79** D2

Beccles St E14 . . . . . .**119** B6
Bechervaise Ct ☒ E10 **53** D1
Beck Cl SE13 . . . . . .**141** D4
Beck Ct BR3 . . . .**206** D6
Beckenham Bsns Ctr
BR3 . . . .**185** A4
Beckenham Ct BR3 . .**185** C2
Beckenham Gdns N9 . .**17** C1
Beckenham Gr BR2 . .**186** B1
Beckenham Hill Rd
BR3,SE6 . . . .**186** A5
Beckenham Hill Sta
SE6 . . . .**186** A5
Beckenham Hospl
BR3 . . . .**185** B1
Beckenham Junction Sta
BR3 . . . .**185** C2
Beckenham La BR1,
BR2 . . . .**186** D1
Beckenham Place Pk
BR3 . . . .**185** D3
Beckenham Rd
Penge BR3 . . . .**185** A2
West Wickham BR3,
BR4 . . . .**208** A2
Beckenham Rd Sta
BR3 . . . .**185** A2
Beckers The N16 . . . . .**74** A4
Becket Ave E6 . . . . . .**100** C4
Becket Cl
Croydon SE25 . . . . .**206** A3
☒ Merton SW19 . . . .**179** D2
Becket Fold HA1 . . . . .**42** D4
Becket Ho SE1 . . . . .**252** C1
Becket Rd N18 . . . . . .**34** C6
Becket St SE1 . . . . .**262** C6
Beckett Cl DA17 . . . .**125** B3
NW10 . . . .**67** C2
Streatham SW16 . . . .**159** D2
Beckett Ho ☒ E1 . . . .**96** C2
☒ SW9 . . . .**138** A3
Becketts Cl
Feltham TW14 . . . . .**150** B5
Orpington BR6 . . . . .**227** D5
Becketts Pl KT1 . . . .**175** D2
Beckett Wlk BR3 . . . .**185** A4
Beckfoot NW1 . . . . .**232** B3
Beckford Cl W14 . . . .**254** D3
Beckford Dr BR5,BR6 .**211** B2
Beckford Ho ☒ N16 . .**73** C3
Beckford Prim Sch
NW6 . . . .**69** B3
Beckford Rd CR0 . . . .**205** D3
Beckham Ho SE11 . .**260** D3
Beckington ☒ NW5 . . .**71** A2
Beck La BR3 . . . .**206** D6
Beckley Ho E3 . . . . . .**97** B3
Becklow Mews ☒
W12 . . . .**112** A4
Becklow Rd W12 . . . .**112** A4
Beckmead Sch BR3 . .**207** C1
Beck Rd E8 . . . .**96** B6
Beck River Pk ☒
BR3 . . . .**185** C2
Becks Rd DA14 . . . . .**168** A1
Beckton Alps E6 . . . .**100** C3
Beckton Alps Ski Ctr
E6 . . . .**100** C3
Beckton Park Sta
E16 . . . .**122** B6
Beckton Rd E16 . . . . .**98** D2
Beckton Sta E6 . . . . .**100** C4
Beckton Triangle Ret Pk
E6 . . . .**100** D3
Beck Way BR3 . . . . .**207** B6
Beckway Rd SW16 . .**181** D1
Beckway St
SE17 . . . .**117** C2 **263** A3
Beckwith Ho ☒ E2 . . .**96** B5
Beckwith Rd SE24 . . .**161** B6
Beclands Rd SW17 . .**181** A4
Becmead Ave
Harrow HA3 . . . .**43** B4
Streatham SW16 . . . .**181** D6
Becondale Rd SE19 . .**183** C5
Becontree Ave RM8 . .**80** C5
Becontree Day RM8 . .**81** A6
Becontree Prim Sch
RM8 . . . .**80** B5
Becontree Sta RM9 . .**80** D2
Bective Pl SW15 . . . .**135** B1
Bective Rd E7 . . . . . .**77** A4
Putney SW15 . . . . . .**135** B1
Becton Pl
Erith DA7,DA8 . . . . .**147** D5
Erith DA8 . . . .**147** D5
Bedale Rd EN2 . . . .**5** A5
Bedale St SE1 . . . . .**252** C3

Beddington Cross
CR0 . . . .**204** A2
Beddington Farm Rd
CR0 . . . .**204** A1
Beddington Gdns
SM5,SM6 . . . .**219** A2
Beddington Gn BR5 . .**189** D2
Beddington Gr SM6 . .**219** D2
Beddington Inf Sch
SM6 . . . .**219** C4
Beddington La
Wallington CR0 . . . . .**220** A6
Wallington CR0 . . . . .**203** D2
Beddington Lane Sta
CR0 . . . .**203** C3
Beddington Manor
SM2 . . . .**218** B3
Beddington Park Cotts
SM6 . . . .**219** D5
Beddington Park Prim Sch
CR0 . . . .**219** C4
Beddington Rd BR5 . .**189** D2
Ilford IG3 . . . .**57** D2
Beddington Terr CR0 .**204** B2
Bede Cl HA5 . . . .**22** C2
Bede Ho SE14 . . . . . .**141** B4
☒ Putney SW15 . . . .**156** D5
Bedens Rd DA14 . . . .**191** A5
Bede Rd RM6 . . . .**58** C3
Bedfield WC1 . . . . . .**233** B1
Bedfont Cl
East Bedfont TW14 . .**149** C6
Mitcham CR4 . . . . . .**181** A1
Bedfont Green Cl
TW14 . . . .**149** C6
Bedfont Ind Pk N
TW15 . . . .**149** A1
Bedfont Jun Sch
TW14 . . . .**149** C5
Bedfont La TW14,
TW13 . . . .**149** D4
Bedfont Lakes Ctry Pk
TW14 . . . .**149** C2
Bedfont Rd
East Bedfont TW13,
TW14 . . . .**149** B2
Stanwell TW19 . . . . .**148** C5
Bedford Ave
WC1 . . . .**93** D2 **239** D3
Barnet EN5 . . . .**13** B6
Hayes UB4 . . . .**84** B1
Bedfordbury
WC2 . . . .**116** A6 **250** A5
Bedford Cl N10 . . . . . .**31** A3
Chiswick W4 . . . . . .**133** D6
Bedford Cnr ☒ W4 . .**111** C2
Bedford Court Mans
WC1 . . . .**239** D3
Bedford Ct WC2 . . . .**250** A5
☒ Richmond TW9 . . .**132** B1
South Norwood SE19 . .**183** D2
Wembley HA0 . . . . . .**65** D4
Bedford Gardens Ho
W8 . . . .**245** B3
Bedford Gdns
W8 . . . .**113** C5 **245** B3
Bedford Hill SW12 . . .**159** B2
Bedford Ho ☒ SW4 . .**138** A1
☒ W4 . . . .**111** C2
Bedford Park Cnr ☒
W4 . . . .**111** C2
Bedford Park Mans
W4 . . . .**111** B2
Bedford Pas SW6 . . .**264** B4
Bedford Pk CR0 . . . .**205** A1
Bedford Pl
WC1 . . . .**94** A2 **240** A4
Croydon CR0 . . . . . .**205** A1
Bedford Rd E17 . . . . . .**53** C6
N15 . . . .**51** C4
N2 . . . .**48** C6
N8 . . . .**49** B3
NW7 . . . .**11** C1
SW2,SW4 . . . .**138** A1
W4 . . . .**111** C3
Barking E6 . . . .**100** C4
Ealing W13 . . . .**109** B6
Edmonton N9 . . . . . .**18** B4
Harrow HA1 . . . .**42** A3
Ilford IG1 . . . .**78** D5
North Cheam KT4 . . .**216** C6
Ruislip HA4 . . . .**61** D4
Sidcup DA15 . . . . . .**167** C1
Twickenham TW2 . . .**152** B1
Woodford E18 . . . . . .**37** C4
Wood Green N22 . . . .**32** A4
Bedford Row
WC1 . . . .**94** B2 **240** D3

Bedford Sq
WC1 . . . .**93** D2 **239** D3
Bedford St
WC2 . . . .**116** A6 **250** B5
Bedford Terr SM2 . . .**218** A2
Bedford Way
WC1 . . . .**93** D2 **239** D5
Bedgebury Gdns
SW19 . . . .**157** A2
Bedgebury Rd SE9 . .**143** D1
Bedivere Rd BR1 . . . .**165** A1
Bedlow Cl NW8 . . . . .**236** D4
Bedlow Way CR0 . . . .**220** B4
Bedonwell Inf Sch
SE2 . . . .**147** A6
Bedonwell Jun Sch
DA17 . . . .**147** A6
Bedonwell Rd
Bexley DA7,DA17 . . .**147** A6
Erith DA7 . . . .**147** C5
Bedser Cl SE11 . . . .**270** D6
South Norwood CR7 . .**205** A6
Bedser Ct ☒ SW4 . . .**138** A3
Bedser Gdns KT8 . . .**195** D6
Bedster Gdns KT8 . . .**195** C6
Bedwardine Rd SE19 **183** C3
Bedwell Ct ☒ RM6 . . .**58** D2
Bedwell Gdns UB3 . . .**105** C2
Bedwell Ho ☒ SW9 . .**138** C3
Bedwell Rd
Belvedere DA17 . . . .**125** C1
Tottenham N17 . . . . . .**33** C2
Beeby Rd E16 . . . .**99** B2
Beech Ave N20 . . . . . .**14** C3
W3 . . . .**111** C5
Brentford TW8 . . . . .**131** B5
Chigwell IG9 . . . .**21** B2
Ruislip HA4 . . . .**40** B1
Sidcup DA15 . . . . . .**168** A4
Beech Cl SE8 . . . . . .**141** B6
Ashford TW15 . . . . .**171** B5
Carshalton SM5 . . . .**218** D6
Enfield N9 . . . .**18** B5
Putney SW15 . . . . . .**156** A4
Sunbury TW16 . . . . .**172** D1
West Drayton UB7 . . .**104** C3
Wimbledon SW19 . . .**178** C3
Beech Copse BR1 . . .**188** B6
South Croydon CR2 . .**221** C3
Beechcroft BR7 . . . . .**188** C3
☒ Kingston KT2 . . . .**176** D2
Beechcroft Ave NW11 .**47** B2
Harrow HA2 . . . .**41** C2
Kingston KT1,KT3 . . .**177** A1
Heston TW5 . . . .**129** A5
Streatham SW16 . . . .**182** B5
Beechcroft Cl BR6 . . .**227** B4
Heston TW5 . . . .**129** A5
Streatham SW16 . . . .**182** B5
Beechcroft Ct ☒ N12 . .**29** D6
☒ NW11 . . . .**47** B2
Beechcroft Gdns HA9 .**66** B5
Beechcroft Ho W5 . . . .**88** C4
Beechcroft Lo ☒
SM2 . . . .**218** A1
Beechcroft Mans
SW16 . . . .**182** B5
Beechcroft Rd BR6 . .**227** B4
Chessington KT9 . . .**214** B5
Mortlake SW14 . . . .**133** A2
Upper Tooting SW17 . .**158** C2
Woodford E18 . . . . . .**37** B1
Beechcroft Way N19 . .**49** D1
Beech Ct E17 . . . .**54** B6
NW2 . . . .**69** B6
W1 . . . .**237** C2
☒ W2 . . . .**91** C2
Beckenham BR3 . . . .**185** B3
☒ Buckhurst Hill IG9 . .**21** D2
Hayes UB3 . . . .**105** D5
☒ Ilford E12 . . . .**78** C5
Northolt UB5 . . . .**85** A6
Subiton KT6 . . . . . .**198** A2
Teddington TW11 . . .**175** C4
☒ West Norwood
SW16 . . . .**182** C5
Beechdale N21 . . . . . .**16** B2
Beechdale Rd SW2 . .**160** B5
Beech Dell BR2,BR6 . .**226** B4
Beechdene ☒ SE15 . .**140** B4
Beech Dr N2 . . . .**48** C6
Beechen Cliff Way
TW7 . . . .**130** D3
Beechen Gr HA5 . . . . .**41** B6
Beechen Pl SE23 . . . .**162** C2
Beeches Ave The
SM5 . . . .**218** C1
Beeches Cl SE20 . . . .**184** C2
Beeches Ct BR1 . . . . .**187** A4
Beeches Rd
Cheam SM3 . . . .**201** A1

Beeches Rd continued
Upper Tooting SW17 . .**158** D1
Beeches The E12 . . . . .**78** B1
☒ N19 . . . .**50** A1
N20 . . . .**14** C2
Hounslow TW3 . . . . .**129** D4
Mitcham CR4 . . . . . .**202** C4
Beechey Ho ☒ E1 . . .**118** B5
Beech Farm Cotts IG8 .**36** B3
Beechfield Cotts ☒
BR1 . . . .**187** C1
Beechfield Ct ☒ CR2 .**221** A4
Beechfield Rd BR1 . . .**187** D5
N4 . . . .**51** A3
Forest Hill SE6 . . . . .**163** B3
Beech Gdns W5 . . . . .**110** A3
Dagenham RM10 . . . .**81** D1
Beech Gr
Kingston KT3 . . . . . .**199** B6
Mitcham CR4 . . . . . .**203** C4
Beech Hall Cres E4 . . .**36** D3
Beech Hall Rd E4 . . . . .**36** B3
Beech Hill EN4 . . . .**2** C5
Beech Hill Ave EN4 . . . .**2** B4
Beechhill Rd SE9 . . . .**166** C6
Beech Ho ☒ DA15 . . .**168** A1
☒ N16 . . . .**73** B6
☒ NW3 . . . .**70** D2
☒ SE16 . . . .**118** C4
Hayes UB4 . . . .**84** D2
Heston TW5 . . . .**129** A5
New Addington CR0 . .**223** D2
Beech House Rd CR0 **221** B5
Beech La IG9 . . . .**21** D2
Beech Lawns N12 . . . .**30** B5
Beechmont Cl BR1 . . .**186** C5
Beechmore Gdns
SM3 . . . .**216** D6
Beechmore Rd
SW11 . . . .**136** D4 **267** D1
Beechmount Ave W7 . .**86** C2
Beecholme ☒ N12 . . . .**29** D6
Beecholme Ave CR4 . .**181** B2
Beecholme Est E5 . . . .**74** B4
Beecholme Prim Sch
CR4 . . . .**181** B2
Beech Rd
Bowes Park N11 . . . . .**32** A4
East Bedfont TW14 . .**149** C6
Thornton Heath SW16 .**204** B6
Beechrow KT2 . . . . . .**176** A6
Beech St EC2 . . .**95** A2 **242** B4
Stanmore HA7 . . . . . .**25** C4
Beech Tree Cl N1 . . . . .**72** C1
Stanmore HA7 . . . . . .**25** C5
Beech Tree Glade E4 . .**20** D3
Beech Tree Pl SM1 . .**217** D2
Beechvale Cl N12 . . . . .**30** C5
Beechway DA5 . . . . . .**168** D5
Beech Way NW10 . . . .**67** B1
Twickenham TW2 . . .**151** D4
Beech Wlk NW7 . . . . .**27** C4
Beechwood Ave N3 . . .**47** C6
Ashford TW16 . . . . . .**172** A4
Greenford UB6 . . . . . .**85** D4
Harrow HA2 . . . .**63** D5
Hayes UB3 . . . .**105** B6
Hillingdon UB8 . . . . . .**82** C5
Orpington BR6 . . . . .**227** C4
Richmond TW9 . . . . .**132** C4
Ruislip HA4 . . . .**61** D6
Thornton Heath CR7 . .**204** C5
Beechwood Circ HA2 . .**63** D5
Beechwood Cl N2 . . . . .**48** D5
NW7 . . . .**27** C5
Surbiton KT6 . . . . . .**197** D2
Beechwood Cres
DA7 . . . .**147** A2
Beechwood Ct N16 . . .**51** C2
Carshalton SM5 . . . .**218** D4
Chiswick W4 . . . . . .**133** C6
Sutton SM1 . . . .**217** C3
Beechwood Dr
Keston BR2 . . . .**225** D2
Woodford IG8 . . . . . .**36** D5
Beechwood Gdns
Ealing NW10 . . . .**88** B4
Harrow HA2 . . . .**63** D5
Ilford IG5 . . . .**56** C5
Beechwood Gr W3 . . .**111** C5
Beechwood Hall N3 . . .**47** B6
Beechwood Ho ☒ E2 . .**96** A5
Beechwood Mews ☒
N9 . . . .**18** A2
Beechwood Pk E18 . . .**55** A6
Beechwood Rd E8 . . . .**73** D2
N8 . . . .**50** A4
South Croydon CR2 . .**221** C4
Beechwood Rise
BR7 . . . .**188** D6
Beechwoods Ct SE19 **183** D5

Beechworth Cl NW3 ..69 C6
Beecroft Rd SE4 ..163 A6
Beehive Cl E8 ..73 D1
Elstree WD6 ..9 D5
Hillingdon UB10 ..60 B1
Beehive Ct IG1 ..56 B3
Beehive La IG1 ..56 B3
Beehive Pl SW9 ..138 C2
Beehive Prep Sch IG4 56 B4
Beeken Dene BR6 ..227 A4
Beeleigh Rd SM4 ..201 D5
Beeston Cl 5 E8 ..74 A3
South Oxhey WD19 ..22 D6
Beeston Pl SW1 ..258 D6
Beeston Rd EN4 ..14 B5
Beeston's Ho SE15 ..140 B2
Beeston Way TW14 ..150 C5
Beethoven Rd WD6 ..9 D5
Beethoven St W10 ..91 A4
Beeton Cl HA5 ..23 C3
Begbie Ho SW9 ..138 B3
Begbie Rd SE3 ..143 C4
Beggars Hill KT17 ..215 D2
Beggar's Roost La
SM1,SM2 ..217 C2
Begonia Cl E6 ..100 B3
Begonia Pl 1 TW12 .173 C4
Begonia Wlk W12 ..89 D1
Beira St SW12 ..159 B4
Beis Rachel D'Satmar Girls
Sch N16 ..51 C2
Beis Yaakov Prim Sch
NW9 ..45 B6
Bekesbourne St 19
E14 ..97 A1
Belcroft Cl BR1 ..186 D3
Beldanes Lo NW10 ..68 A1
Beldham Gdns KT8 ..195 D6
Belenoyd Ct SW16 ..160 B1
Belfairs Dr RM6 ..58 C2
Belfairs Gn WD19 ..22 D5
Belfast Rd N16 ..73 D6
Croydon SE25 ..206 B5
Belfield Rd KT19 ..215 C1
Belfont Wlk N7 ..72 A4
Belford Gr SE18 ..122 C2
Belford Ho 7 E8 ..95 D6
Belfort Rd SE15 ..140 C3
Belfry Cl 33 SE16 ..118 B1
Belgrade Ho N16 ..73 C4
Belgrade Rd N16 ..73 C4
Hampton TW12 ..173 D2
Belgrave Cl NW7 ..27 B5
1 Acton W3 ..111 A4
Southgate N14 ..15 C6
Belgrave Cres TW16 .172 B2
Belgrave Ct E13 ..99 C3
SE3 ..143 C5
SW8 ..269 A3
8 W4 ..111 A1
Belgrave Gdns NW8 ..91 D6
Southgate N14 ..3 D1
1 Stanmore HA7 ..25 C5
Belgrave Mans NW8 .229 A5
Belgrave Mews N
SW1 ..248 A1
Belgrave Mews S
SW1 ..115 A3 258 B6
Belgrave Mews W
SW1 ..258 A6
Belgrave Pl
SW1 ..115 A3 258 B5
Belgrave Rd E10 ..54 A1
E13 ..99 C3
E17 ..53 C3
SW1 ..115 C2 259 A3
Barnes SW13 ..133 D5
Hounslow TW4 ..129 B2
Mitcham CR4 ..202 B6
Redbridge IG1 ..56 B1
South Norwood SE25 ..205 D5
Sunbury TW16 ..172 B2
Wanstead E11 ..55 A1
Belgrave Sq
SW1 ..115 A3 258 A6
Belgrave St E1 ..96 D1
Belgrave Terr IG8 ..21 A1
Belgrave Wlk CR4 ..202 B6
Belgrave Wlk Sta
CR4 ..202 B5
Belgrave Yd SW1 ..258 C5
Belgravia Cl EN5 ..1 B2
Belgravia Ct SW1 ..258 C5
Belgravia Gdns BR1 .186 C4
Belgravia Ho 11 SW4 159 D5
Teddington TW11 ..175 C3
Belgravia Mews KT1 .197 D5
Belgrove St WC1 ..233 B2
Belham Wlk 13 SE5 ..139 B4
Belinda Rd 8 SW9 ..138 D2
Belitha Villas N1 ..72 C1
Bel La TW13 ..151 B1
Bellamy Cl 7 E14 ..119 C4
HA8 ..11 A1
SW5 ..254 D1
Uxbridge UB10 ..60 C5
Bellamy Ct HA7 ..25 B2
Bellamy Dr HA7 ..25 B2
Bellamy Ho
Harrow HA3 ..44 A2
Heston TW5 ..129 C6
Upper Tooting SW17 ..180 B6
Bellamy Rd
Chingford E4 ..35 D4
Enfield EN2 ..5 B3
Bellamy's Ct 16 SE16 118 D5
Bellamy St SW12 ..159 B4
Bellasis Ave SW2 ..160 A2
Bell Ave UB7 ..104 B3
Bell Cl Pinner HA5 ..40 C6
Ruislip HA4 ..61 D5
Bellclose Rd UB7 ..104 A4
Bell Ct NW4 ..46 C5
Tolworth KT5 ..214 D6
Bell Dr SW18 ..157 A4
Bellefields Rd SW9 ..138 B2
Bellegrove Cl DA16 ..145 D3
Bellegrove Par DA16 145 D2
Bellegrove Rd DA16 .145 D3
Bellenden Rd SE15 ..139 D3
Bellenden Rd Ret Pk
SE15 ..140 A4
Bellenden Sch SE15 .140 A3
Bellendon Road Bsns Ctr
SE15 ..139 D3
Bellerbys Coll SW15 .156 A5
Bellermine Cl SE28 ..123 D4
Belle Staines Pleasaunce
E4 ..19 C2
Belleville Prim Sch
SW11 ..158 D6
Belleville Rd SW11 ..158 D6
Belle Vue UB6 ..86 B6
Belle Vue Gdns SW9 .138 A3
Belle Vue La WD23 ..8 B3
Bellevue Pk CR7 ..205 A5
Bellevue Pl E1 ..96 C3
Bellevue Rd DA6 ..169 B6
N11 ..31 A5
Barnes SW13 ..134 A3
Ealing W13 ..87 B3
Kingston KT1 ..198 A6
Upper Tooting SW17 ..158 D3
Belle Vue Rd E17 ..36 B1
Bellew St SW17 ..158 A1
Bellfield CR0 ..223 B1
Bellfield Ave HA3 ..24 B4
Bellflower Cl 2 E6 ..100 A2
Bellgate Mews NW5 ..71 B5
Bell Gn SE26 ..185 B6
Bell Green La SE26 ..185 B6
Bellhill 6 CR0 ..221 A6
Bell Ho SE10 ..142 A6
SE2 ..124 D1
6 Dagenham RM10 ..81 D2
15 Streatham SW2 ..160 C4
Bellina Mews NW5 ..71 C4
Bell Ind Est 2 W4 ..111 A2
Bellingham 10 N17 ..34 B3
Bellingham Ct IG11 ..102 B4
Bellingham Gn SE6 ..163 C1
Bellingham Rd SE6 ..164 A1
Bellingham Sta SE6 .163 D1
Bellingham Trad Est
SE6 ..163 D2
Bell Inn Yd EC3 ..242 D1
Bell La E1 ..95 D2 243 C3
E16 ..121 A5
NW4 ..46 D5
Enfield EN3 ..6 D5
Twickenham TW1 ..153 A3
Wembley HA9 ..65 D6
Bell Lane Prim Sch
NW4 ..46 D5
Bellmaker Ct 19 E3 ..97 C2
Bell Mdw SE19 ..183 C6
Bell Moor NW3 ..70 A5
Bellmore Ct 5 CR0 ..205 D1
Bello Cl SE24,SW2 ..160 D3
Bellot Gdns 1 SE10 .120 C1
Bellot St SE10 ..120 C1
Bell Rd
East Molesey KT8 ..196 B4
Enfield EN1 ..5 B4
Hounslow TW3 ..129 D1
Bellring Cl DA17 ..147 C6
Bells Hill EN5 ..12 D6
Bell St NW1 ..92 C2 237 A4
SE18 ..144 A4
Bell The E17 ..53 C6
Belltrees Gr 1 SW16 182 C5
Bell View BR3 ..185 B3
Bell View Manor HA4 .39 C2
Bellview Mews N11 ..31 A5
Bell Water Gate
SE18 ..122 C3
Bell Wharf La EC4 ..252 B6
Bellwood Rd SE15 ..140 D1
Bell Yd WC2 ..94 C1 241 A1
Belmont Ave DA16 ..145 C2
N17 ..51 A6
Bowes Park N13 ..32 B5
Cockfosters EN4 ..14 D6
Edmonton N9 ..18 A3
Southall UB2 ..107 A3
Wembley HA0 ..88 B6
West Barnes KT3 ..200 A5
Belmont Circ HA3 ..25 B2
Belmont Cl N20 ..13 D3
SW4 ..137 C2
Chingford E4 ..36 B5
Cockfosters EN4 ..2 D1
Uxbridge UB8 ..60 A2
Woodford IG8 ..37 B6
Belmont Ct 6 N16 ..51 C1
N5 ..73 A4
NW11 ..47 B4
Belmont Gr SE13 ..142 B2
W4 ..111 B2
Belmont Hall Ct SE13 142 B2
Belmont Hill SE13 ..142 B2
Belmont Jun & Inf Schs
N22 ..51 A6
Belmont La
Chislehurst BR7 ..189 A5
Stanmore HA7 ..25 C3
Belmont Lo
Harrow HA3 ..24 B3
Stanmore HA7 ..25 C6
Belmont Mews SW19 156 D2
Belmont Mid Sch HA3 24 D1
Belmont Mill Hill Jun Sch
NW7 ..12 A1
Belmont Par 2 NW11 .47 B4
Chislehurst BR7 ..189 A5
Belmont Park Cl
SE13 ..142 C1
Belmont Park Rd E10 .53 D3
Belmont Pk SE13 ..142 C1
Belmont Prim Sch
W4 ..111 B2
Erith DA7 ..147 C5
Belmont Rd N15,N17 ..51 A5
SW4 ..137 C2
W4 ..111 B2
Beckenham BR3 ..185 B1
Chislehurst BR7 ..188 D5
Croydon SE25 ..206 B4
Erith DA8 ..147 D4
Harrow HA3 ..43 A6
Ilford IG1 ..79 A5
Twickenham TW2 ..152 B2
Uxbridge UB8 ..60 A2
Wallington SM6 ..219 C3
Belmont Rise SM1,
SM2 ..217 B1
Belmont St NW1 ..71 A1
Belmont Terr W4 ..111 B2
Belmor WD6 ..10 C5
Belmore Ave UB4 ..84 A1
Belmore Ho N7 ..71 D3
Belmore Prim Sch
UB4 ..84 B4
Belmore St
SW8 ..137 D4 269 C2
Beloe Cl SW15 ..134 A1
Belsham St E9 ..74 C2
Belsize Ave NW3 ..70 C3
W13 ..109 B3
Bowes Park N13 ..32 B4
Belsize Court Garages 1
NW3 ..70 B3
Belsize Cres NW3 ..70 B2
Belsize Ct NW3 ..70 B3
Belsize Gdns SM1 ..217 D4
Belsize Gr NW3 ..70 C2
Belsize La NW3 ..70 B3
Belsize Mews NW3 ..70 B2
Belsize Park Gdns
NW3 ..70 C2
Belsize Park Mews 1
NW3 ..70 B2
Belsize Park Sta NW3 70 C3
Belsize Pk NW3 ..70 B2
Belsize Pl NW3 ..70 B3
Belsize Rd NW6 ..91 D6
NW8 ..229 A6
Harrow HA3 ..24 B3
Belsize Sq NW3 ..70 B2
Belsize Terr NW3 ..70 B2
Belson Rd SE18 ..122 B2
Beltane Dr SW19 ..156 D1
Belthorn Cres SW12 .159 C4
Belton Rd E11 ..76 C4
E7 ..77 B1
N17 ..51 C6
NW2 ..68 A2
Sidcup DA14 ..190 A6
Belton Way E3 ..97 C2
Beltran Rd SW6 ..135 D3
Belvedere Ave SW19 .179 A5
Belvedere Bldgs SE1 251 D1
Belvedere Cl TW11 ..174 C5
Belvedere Ct DA17 ..125 B3
N2 ..48 B4
NW2 ..68 D2
7 SW4 ..159 D5
8 Kingston KT2 ..176 C3
Putney SW15 ..134 C1
Belvedere Dr SW19 ..179 A5
Belvedere Gdns KT8 .195 C4
Belvedere Gr SW19 ..179 A5
Belvedere Heights
NW8 ..237 A6
Belvedere Ho TW14 .150 A3
Belvedere Jun & Inf Sch
DA17 ..125 D3
Belvedere Mews
SE15 ..140 C2
SE3 ..143 B5
Belvedere Pl SE1 ..251 D1
18 SW2 ..138 B1
Belvedere Rd
SE1 ..116 B4 250 D3
W7 ..108 D3
Bexley DA7 ..147 B3
Erith SE28 ..124 D5
Penge SE19 ..183 D3
Walthamstow E10 ..53 A1
Belvedere Sq SW19 ..179 A5
Belvedere Sta DA17 .125 D3
Belvedere Strand
NW9 ..27 D1
Belvedere The SW10 .266 B1
Belvedere Way HA3 ..44 A3
Belvoir Cl SE9 ..166 A1
Belvoir Lo SE22 ..162 A4
Belvoir Rd SE22 ..162 A4
Belvue Bsns Ctr UB5 .63 D1
Belvue Cl UB5 ..63 C1
Belvue Rd UB5 ..63 C1
Belvue Sch UB5 ..85 C6
Bembridge Cl NW6 ..69 A1
Bembridge Gdns HA4 .61 B6
Bembridge Ho
8 SE8 ..119 B2
Wandsworth SW18 ..157 D5
Bemersyde Point 6
E13 ..99 B4
Bemerton St
N1 ..94 B6 233 C6
Bemish Rd SW15 ..134 D2
Bempton Dr HA4 ..62 B5
Bemsted Rd E17 ..53 B6
Benabo Ct 6 E8 ..74 A3
Benares Rd SE18,SE2 .123 D2
Benbow Ct W6 ..112 B3
Benbow Ho 12 SE8 ..141 C6
Benbow Rd W6 ..112 B3
Benbow St SE8 ..141 C6
Benbury Cl BR1 ..186 A5
Bence Ho 13 SE8 ..119 A2
Bench Field CR2 ..221 D3
Bencroft Rd SW16 ..181 C3
Bencurtis Pk BR4 ..224 B6
Bendall Mews NW1 ..237 B4
Bendemeer Rd SW15 134 D2
Benden Ho SE13 ..164 A6
Bendish Rd E6 ..78 A1
Bendmore Ave SE2 ..124 A2
Bendon Valley SW18 .157 D4
Benedict Cl BR6 ..227 C5
9 Erith DA17 ..125 A3
Benedict Ct RM9 ..59 B3
Benedict Dr TW14 ..149 B4
Benedict Fst Sch
CR4 ..202 B6
Benedict Prim Sch
CR4 ..202 B6
Benedict Rd SW9 ..138 B2
Mitcham CR4 ..202 B6
Benedict Way N2 ..48 A6
Benedict Wharf CR4 .202 C6
Benenden Gn BR2 ..209 A4
Benenden Ho SE17 ..263 B2
Benett Gdns SW16 ..182 A1
Ben Ezra Ct SE17 ..262 B3
Benfleet Cl SM1 ..218 A5
Benfleet Ct 6 E8 ..95 D6
Benfleet Way N11 ..15 A2
Bengal Ct EC3 ..242 D1
Bengal Ho E1 ..96 D2
Bengal Rd IG1 ..78 D5
Bengarth Dr HA3 ..24 B1
Bengarth Rd UB5 ..85 A6
Bengeo Gdns RM6 ..58 C3
Bengeworth Rd SE5 .139 A2
Harrow HA1 ..65 A5
Ben Hale Cl HA7 ..25 B5
Benham Cl 1 SW11 .136 B2
Chessington KT9 ..213 C2
Benham Gdns TW3,
TW4 ..151 B6
Benham Rd W7 ..86 C2
Benham's Pl 8 NW3 ..70 A4
Benhill Ave SM1 ..218 A4
Benhill Rd SE5 ..139 B4
Sutton SM1 ..218 B4
Benhill Wood Rd
SM1 ..218 A4
Benhilton Gdns SM1 .217 D5
Benhurst Ct
Ealing W5 ..110 A6
12 Penge SE20 ..184 B2
West Norwood SW16 ..182 C5
Benhurst La SW16 ..182 C5
Benin St SE13 ..164 B4
Benjafield Cl N18 ..34 B6
Benjamin Cl E8 ..96 A6
Benjamin Ct
4 Ealing W7 ..108 C5
4 Erith DA17 ..147 B6
Littleton TW15 ..171 A3
Benjamin St EC1 ..241 C4
Ben Jonson Ct 30 N1 .95 C5
Ben Jonson Prim Sch
E1 ..97 A3
Ben Jonson Rd E1 ..97 A2
Benledi St E14 ..98 B1
Bennelong Cl W12 ..90 B1
Bennerley Rd SW11 .158 D6
Bennetsfield Rd
UB11 ..104 D5
Bennet's Hill EC4 ..251 D6
Bennets Lo EN2 ..5 A2
Bennett Cl DA16 ..146 A3
Teddington KT1 ..175 C2
Bennett Ct N7 ..72 B5
NW6 ..69 D2
7 W3 ..110 D4
Bennett Gr SE13 ..141 D4
Bennett Ho SW1 ..259 D4
2 Streatham SW4 ..159 D4
Bennett Pk SE3 ..142 D2
Bennett Rd E13 ..99 C3
Dagenham RM6 ..59 A2
Bennetts Ave
Croydon CR0 ..223 A6
Greenford UB6 ..86 C6
Bennett's Castle La
RM8 ..80 D5
Bennetts Cl
Mitcham CR4,SW16 ..181 B2
Tottenham N17 ..33 D4
Bennetts Copse BR7 .188 A4
Bennett St SW1 ..249 A4
W4 ..111 C1
Bennetts Way CR0 ..223 B6
Bennett's Yd SW1 ..259 D5
Benn Ho 7 SE7 ..121 C1
Benningholme Rd
HA8 ..27 C4
Bennington Rd
Chingford IG8 ..36 C3
Tottenham N17 ..33 C2
Benn St E9 ..75 A2
Benns Wlk 8 TW9 ..132 A1
Bensbury Cl SW15 ..156 C4
Bensham Cl CR7 ..205 A5
Bensham Gr CR7 ..183 A1
Bensham La CR0,CR7 204 D3
Bensham Manor Rd
CR7 ..205 A5
Bensham Manor Sch
CR7 ..205 A4
Bensington Ct TW14 .149 B5
Bensley Cl 7 N11 ..30 D5
Ben Smith Way 21
SE16 ..118 A3
Benson Ave E13,E6 ..99 D5
Benson Cl
Hillingdon UB8 ..82 A2
Hounslow TW3 ..129 C1
Benson Ct 1 N19 ..71 C4
SW8 ..270 A2
Holdbrook EN3 ..7 C5
Benson Ho E2 ..243 C6
SE1 ..251 B3
Benson Prim sch
CR0 ..223 A5
Benson Quay E1 ..118 C6
Benson Rd
Croydon CR0 ..220 C5
Forest Hill SE23 ..162 C3
Bentall Sh Ctr The 10
KT2 ..176 A1
Bentfield Gdns SE9 ..165 D1
Benthal Ct N16 ..74 A5
Benthal Prim Sch N16 74 A5
Benthal Rd N16 ..74 A5
Bentham Ct 10 N1 ..73 A1
Bentham Ho SE1 ..262 C6
Bentham Rd E9 ..74 D2
Woolwich SE28 ..124 B5
Bentham Wlk NW10 ..67 A3
Ben Tillet Cl
Barking IG11 ..80 A1
Newham E16 ..122 B5
Ben Tillet Ho N15 ..50 D6
Bentinck Cl NW8 ..230 B3
Bentinck Ho 4 W12 .112 B6
Bentinck Mans W1 ..238 B2
Bentinck Mews W1 ..238 B2
Bentinck Rd UB7 ..104 A5
Bentinck St
W1 ..93 A1 238 B2
Bentley Cl SW19 ..157 C1
Bentley Dr IG2 ..57 A3
Bentley Ho 4 SE5 ..139 C4
6 Bow E3 ..97 C3
Bentley Lo WD23 ..8 C2
Bentley Mews EN1 ..17 B5
Bentley Rd N1 ..73 C2
Bentley Way
Stanmore HA7 ..25 A5
Woodford IG8 ..21 A1
Bentley Wood High Sch
HA7 ..24 D5
Benton Rd
Ilford IG1,IG2 ..57 B1
South Oxhey WD19 ..22 D5
Benton's La SE27 ..183 A6
Benton's Rise SE27 ..183 B5
Bentry Cl RM8 ..81 A6
Bentry Rd RM8 ..81 B6
Bentworth Ct 1 E2 ..96 A3
Bentworth Prim Sch
W12 ..90 B1
Bentworth Rd W12 ..90 B1
Benville Ho SW8 ..270 D3
Benwell Ct TW16 ..172 A2
Benwell Rd N7 ..72 C3
Benwick Cl SE16 ..118 B2
Benwick Ct SE20 ..184 C2
Benwood Ct SM1 ..218 A5
Benworth St E3 ..97 B4
Benyon Ho EC1 ..234 B2
Benyon Rd N1 .95 B6 235 D6
Beormund Prim Sch
SE1 ..117 B4 252 D1
Bequerel Ct SE10 ..120 D3
Berberis Ct IG1 ..78 D2
Berberis Ho 15 E3 ..97 C2
Berberis Wlk UB7 ..104 A2
Berber Pl 15 E14 ..119 C6
Berber Rd SW11 ..158 D6
Berberry Cl HA8 ..27 A6
Bercta Rd SE9 ..167 A2
Berebinder Ho 17 E3 ..97 B5
Berenger Twr SW10 .266 C4
Berenger Wlk SW10 .266 C4
Berens Ct DA14 ..189 D6
Berens Rd NW10 ..90 D4
Berens Way BR5,BR7 .211 D6
Beresford Ave N20 ..14 D2
Ealing W7 ..86 C2
Tolworth KT5 ..199 A2
Twickenham TW1 ..153 C5
Wembley HA0 ..88 C6
Beresford Ct E9 ..75 A3
11 Twickenham TW1 .153 C5
Beresford Dr BR1 ..210 A6
Woodford IG8 ..37 C6
Beresford Gdns
Dagenham RM6 ..59 A4
Enfield EN1 ..5 C1
Hounslow TW4 ..151 B6
Beresford Ho
14 SW4 ..138 A1
Dulwich SE21 ..161 C1
Beresford Lo N4 ..73 B3
Beresford Rd N2 ..48 C6
N5 ..73 B3
N8 ..50 D4
Belmont SM2 ..217 B1
Chingford, Chingford Green
E4 ..20 C3

Beresford Rd continued
Chingford, Highams Park
E17 ....35 D2
Harrow HA1 ....42 B4
Kingston KT2 ...176 B2
New Malden KT3 ...199 A5
Southall UB1 ...106 D5
Beresford Sq 1
SE18 ....122 D2
Beresford St SE18 ...122 D3
Beresford Terr 3 N5 ..73 A3
Bere St E1 ....118 D6
Berestede Rd 4 W6 .111 D1
Bergen Ho 1 SE5 ...139 A3
Bergen Sq SE16 ...119 A3
Berger Cl BR5 ......211 D3
Berger Prim Sch E9 .74 D1
Berger Rd E9 ....74 D2
Berghem Mews W14 112 D3
Bergholt Ave IG4 ...56 A4
Bergholt Cres N16 ...51 C2
Bergholt Mews 4
NW1 ....71 D1
Berglen Ct E14 .....119 C1
Bering Sq E14 ......119 C1
Bering Wlk E16 .....99 D1
Berisford Mews
SW18 ....158 A5
Berkeley Ave DA16 .146 D4
Cranford TW4 ......128 A3
Northolt UB6 ......64 C2
Berkeley Cl
Borehamwood WD6 ..10 C6
Kingston KT2 ......176 A3
Orpington BR5,BR6 .211 C2
Ruislip HA4 ....62 A5
Berkeley Cres EN4 ..14 B6
Berkeley Ct N3 .....29 D2
NW1 ....237 D5
1 NW1 ....47 B2
Ealing W5 ....109 C4
Edgware HA8 ....26 D5
16 Streatham SW2 .160 C3
Wallington SM6 ....219 C4
Berkeley Dr KT8 ....195 C6
Berkeley Gdns W8 ..245 B3
Claygate KT10 .....213 A2
Southgate N21 .....17 B4
Walton-on-T KT12 ..193 D2
Berkeley Ho 17 E3 ..97 C4
8 SE8 ....119 B1
11 Brentford TW8 ..131 D6
Berkeley Lo Enfield EN2 .4 C2
New Malden KT3 ...199 C5
Berkeley Mews W1 .237 D1
Sunbury TW16 .....194 C6
Berkeley Pl SW19 ..178 D4
Berkeley Prim Sch
TW5 ....128 D5
Berkeley Rd E12 ...78 A3
N15 ....51 B3
N8 ....49 D3
NW9 ....44 C4
Barnes SW13 ......134 A4
Hillingdon UB10 ...61 A1
Berkeley Sq
W1 ....115 B6 248 D5
Berkeley St
W1 ....115 B5 248 D4
Berkeleys The SE25 .206 A5
Berkeley The NW11 .47 D2
Berkeley Waye TW5 .128 D5
Berkeley Wlk 1 N7 ..72 B6
Berkerley Ct SW16 .156 A6
Berkhampstead Rd
DA17 ....125 C1
Berkhamsted Ave HA9 66 C2
Berkley Cl TW2 .....152 C1
Berkley Ct 6 TW1 .153 A4
Berkley Gr NW1 ....71 A1
Berkley Rd NW1 ....70 D1
Berkshire Ct 1 W7 ..86 D3
Berkshire Gdns
Edmonton N13 .....32 C4
Edmonton N18 .....34 B5
Berkshire Ho SE6 ...185 C6
Berkshire Rd E9 ....75 B2
Berkshire Sq CR4 ..204 A5
Berkshire Way CR4 .204 A5
Berleley Ct NW10 ..67 D4
Bermans Way NW10 .67 D4
Bermondsey Leather Mkt
SE1 ....253 A1
Bermondsey Mkt*
SE1 ....117 C3 263 B8
Bermondsey Sq SE1 .263 B6

Bermondsey St
SE1 ....117 C4 253 A1
Bermondsey Sta
SE16 ....118 A3
Bermondsey Trad Est
SE16 ....118 C1
Bermondsey Wall E
SE16 ....118 B4
Bermondsey Wall W
SE1,SE16 ....118 A4
Bermuda Ho HA1 ...64 B5
Bernal Cl SE28 .....124 D6
Bernard Angell Ho 4
SE10 ....142 B6
Bernard Ashley Dr
SE7 ....121 B1
Bernard Ave W13 ...109 B3
Bernard Cassidy St 4
E16 ....98 C2
Bernard Gdns SW19 .179 B5
Bernard Rd N15 ....51 D4
Wallington SM5,SM6 .219 B4
Bernard Shaw Ct 3
NW1 ....71 C1
Bernard Shaw Ho 2
NW10 ....89 B6
Bernard St
WC1 ....94 A3 240 B5
Bernays Cl HA7 .....25 C4
Bernay's Gr SW9 ...138 B1
Bernel Dr CR0 .....223 B6
Berne Rd CR7 .....205 A4
Berners Dr W13 ....109 A6
Berners Ho N1 .....234 A4
Bernersmede SE3 ...143 A2
Berners Mews
W1 ....93 C2 239 B3
Berners Pl W1 .....239 B2
Berners Rd N1 .....234 C5
Wood Green N22 ....32 C2
Berners St W1 .93 C1 239 B2
Berner Terr 30 E1 ..96 A1
Berney Ho BR3 .....207 A4
Berney Rd CR0 .....205 B2
Bernhart Cl HA8 ...27 A3
Bernwell Rd E4 ....20 C1
Bernwood Ho 6 N4 .51 B2
Berridge Gn HA8 ...26 C3
Berridge Mews NW6 .69 C3
Berridge Rd SE19 ..183 C5
Berriman Rd N7 ....72 B5
Berrite Works UB7 .104 C1
Berrybank Cl 4 E4 .20 C1
Berry Cl NW10 .....67 C1
Dagenham RM10 ....81 C3
Southgate N21 .....16 D3
Berry Ct TW4 ......151 B6
Berrydale Rd UB4 ..85 A3
Berryfield Cl BR1 ..188 A1
8 E17 ....53 D6
Berryfield Rd
SE17 ....116 D1 261 D2
Berryhill SE9 ......144 D1
Berry Hill HA7 .....25 D6
Berryhill Gdns SE9 .144 D1
Berry Ho 25 E1 ....96 B3
10 SW11 ....136 D3
Berry La SE21 .....183 B6
Berrylands
Surbiton KT5 ......198 C3
West Barnes SW20 ..200 C5
Berrylands Ct 7
SM2 ....217 D1
Berrylands Rd KT5 .198 B3
Berrylands Sta KT5 .198 D6
Berryman Cl RM8 ...80 C5
Berryman's La SE26 .184 D6
Berrymead Gdns W3 111 A4
Berrymede Inf Sch
W3 ....110 D1
Berrymede Jun Sch
W3 ....110 D1
Berrymede Rd W4 ..111 B3
Berry Pl EC1 ......234 D1
Berry St EC1 ......241 D5
Berry Way W5 .....110 A3
Bertal Rd SW17 ....180 B6
Bertha Hollamby Ct
DA14 ....190 C4
Bertha Neubergh Ho 1
SE5 ....139 A4
Berthan Gdns E17 ..54 B4
Berthon St SE8 ....141 C5
Bertie Rd NW10 ....68 C2
Penge SE26 ....184 D4
Bertram Cotts SW19 .179 C3
Bertram Rd NW4 ...46 A3
Enfield EN1 ....6 A1
Kingston KT2 ......176 C3

Bertram St N19 .....71 B6
Bertrand Ho 11
SW16 ....160 A1
Bertrand St SE13 ..141 D2
Bertrand Way SE28 .124 C6
Bert Rd CR7 ......205 A4
Bert Reilly Ho 1
SE18 ....123 B1
Bertrum House Sch
SW17 ....159 A2
Bert Way EN1 .....5 D1
Berwick Ave UB4 ...106 D6
Berwick Cl HA7 ....24 D4
Berwick Cres DA15 .167 C5
Berwick Ho 10 N2 ..30 B1
Newham E16 ....99 C1
Tottenham N22 .....32 D2
Berwick St W1 93 C1 239 B1
Berwyn Ave TW3 ...129 D4
Berwyn Ho 3 N16 ..51 D1
Berwyn Rd
Mortlake SW14,TW10 .132 D1
Streatham SE24 ....160 D1
Beryl Ave E6 ......100 A2
Beryl Harding Ho 3
SW19 ....178 D3
Beryl Ho SE18 .....123 B1
Beryl Rd W6 ......112 D1
Berystede KT2 .....176 D3
Besant Cl NW2 ....69 A5
Besant Ct N1 ......73 B1
15 SE28 ....124 B6
Besant Ho NW8 ....229 A5
Besant Rd NW2 ....69 A4
Besant Way NW10 ..67 A3
Besant Wlk N7 ....72 B6
Besford Ho 25 E2 ..96 A5
Besley St SW16 ....181 C4
Bessant Dr TW9 ...132 D4
Bessborough Gdns
SW1 ....115 D1 259 D2
Bessborough Pl
SW1 ....115 D1 259 D2
Bessborough Rd
Harrow HA1 ....42 B1
Roehampton SW15 ..156 A3
Bessborough St
SW1 ....115 D1 259 C2
Bessborough Wks
KT8 ....195 B4
Bessemer Ct 5 NW1 .71 C1
Bessemer Grange Prim
Sch SE5 ....139 C1
Bessemer Park Ind Est 3
SE24 ....138 D1
Bessemer Rd SE5 ..139 A3
Bessie Lansbury Cl
E6 ....100 C1
Bessingby Rd HA4 ..62 B6
Bessingham Wlk SE4 162 D6
Besson St SE14 ....140 D4
Bessy St E2 ....96 C4
Bestwood St SE8 ...118 D2
Beswick Mews 1
NW6 ....69 D2
Betam Rd UB3 .....105 B4
Beta Pl 20 SW4 ...138 B1
Betchworth Cl SM1 .218 B3
Betchworth Ho 8 N7 .71 D3
Betchworth Rd IG3 .79 C5
Betham Rd UB6 ....86 B4
Bethany Waye TW14 .149 C4
Bethecar Rd HA1 ...42 C4
Bethell Ave E13,E16 .98 D3
Ilford IG1 ....56 C2
Bethel Rd DA16 ....146 C2
Bethersden Cl BR3 .185 B3
Bethersden Ho SE17 .263 B2
Bethesda Ct 8 SE20 .184 C3
Beth Jacob Gram Sch
NW4 ....46 D5
Bethlehem Ho 13
E14 ....119 B6
Bethlem Royal Hospl
BR3 ....207 C2
Bethnal Green Mus of
Childhood* E2 .....96 C4
Bethnal Green Rd
E1,E2 ......96 A4 243 D6
Bethnal Green Sta E1 96 B3
E2 ....96 C4
Bethnal Green Tech Coll
E2 ....95 D4
Beths Gram Sch DA5 169 D5
Bethune Ave N11 ...30 D6
Bethune Rd N16 ....51 C2
NW10 ....89 B3
Bethwin Rd SE5 ....139 A5
Betjeman Cl HA5 ...41 C5

Betony Cl CR0 .....206 D1
Betoyne Ave E4 ....36 C5
Betsham Ho SE1 ...252 C2
Betspath Ho 6 N11 .31 C5
Betstyle Ho 2 N10 .31 A3
Betstyle Rd N11 ...31 B6
Betterton Dr DA14 .169 A2
Betterton Ho WC2 .240 B1
Betterton St
WC2 ....94 A1 240 B1
Bettons Pk E15 ....98 C6
Bettridge Rd SW6 ..135 B3
Betts Cl BR3 ......185 A1
Betts Ho E1 ......118 B6
Betts Mews E17 ....53 B2
Betts Rd E16 ......121 B6
Betts St E1 ......118 B6
Betts Way
Long Ditton KT6 ...197 B1
Penge SE20 ....184 B2
Bettswood Ct 15
SE20 ....184 B2
Betty Layward Prim Sch
N16 ....73 B5
Betty May Gray Ho 1
E14 ....120 A2
Beulah Ave CR7 ...183 A1
Beulah Cl HA8 .....10 D1
Beulah Cres CR7 ..183 A1
Beulah Gr CR0 ....205 A3
Beulah Hill SE19 ..183 A3
Beulah Inf Sch CR7 .205 A6
Beulah Rd E17 ....53 D4
Merton SW19 .....179 B3
South Norwood CR7 .205 A6
Sutton SM1 ....217 C4
Beulah Jun Sch CR7 205 A6
Beuleigh Ct E17 ...54 B4
Bevan Ave IG11 ...80 A1
Bevan Ct
9 Twickenham TW1 .153 D5
Cockfosters EN4 ...2 C1
Bevan Rd SE2 .....124 B1
Cockfosters EN4 ...2 C1
Bevan St N1 .95 A6 235 B5
Bev Callender Cl 4
SW8 ....137 B2
Bevenden St
N1 ....95 B4 235 D2
Bevercote Wlk 1
DA17 ....147 B6
Beveridge Ct 1 SE28 124 B6
Southgate N16 .....16 A6
Beveridge Rd 1
NW10 ....67 C1
Beverley Ave DA15 .167 D4
Hounslow TW4 ....129 B3
Wimbledon SW20 ...177 D2
Beverley Cl 6 SW11 .136 B1
Barnes SW13 ......134 A3
Chessington KT9 ...213 C4
Edmonton N21 .....17 A3
Enfield EN1 ....5 C1
Beverley Cotts SW15 155 C1
Beverley Cres IG8 ..37 B2
Beverley Ct N14 ...15 C4
N2 ....48 C4
N5 ....72 C4
SE4 ....141 B2
5 W12 ....111 C1
9 W4 ....111 A1
Harrow HA2 ....42 B6
Hounslow TW4 ....129 B1
Northolt UB5 .....84 C5
Wimbledon SW20 ...177 D2
Beverley Dr HA8 ...44 C6
Beverley Gdns NW11 .47 A2
Barnes SW13 ......133 D2
2 New Malden KT4 .200 A1
Stanmore HA7 .....25 A2
Wembley HA9 .....44 C1
Beverley Ho 5 BR1 .186 B5
Beverley Hyrst 10
CR0 ....221 D6
Beverley La KT2 ...177 C2
Beverley Lo 6 TW10 154 A6
Beverley Mans TW4 .129 B1
Beverley Path 9
SW13 ....133 D3
Beverley Rd BR2 ...226 A6
E6 ....99 C4
W4 ....111 D1
Barnes SW13 ......133 D1
Chingford E4 ....36 B4
Dagenham RM9 ....81 A4
Mitcham CR4 ......203 D5
North Cheam KT4 ..216 C6
Penge SE20 ....184 B1
Ruislip HA4 ....62 B6
Southall UB2 ......107 A3
Sunbury TW16 .....171 D2

Beverley Rd continued
Teddington KT1 ....175 C2
West Barnes KT3 ..200 A5
Beverley Sch KT3 ..200 A4
Beverley Trad Est
SM4 ....200 D2
Beverley Way KT3,
SW20,KT2 ....177 D2
**Beverley Way (Kingston By
Pass)** KT3,SW20 ..200 A6
Beverly Ct HA3 ....43 C5
Beversbrook Rd N19 .71 D5
Beverstone Rd SW2 .160 B6
Thornton Heath CR7 .204 D5
Beverston Mews
NW1 ....237 C3
Bevill Allen Cl SW17 180 D5
Bevill Cl SE25 .....206 A6
Bevin Cl SE16 .....119 A5
Bevin Ct WC1 .....233 D1
Bevington Rd W10 ..91 A2
Beckenham BR3 ....185 D1
Bevington St SE16 .118 A4
Bevin Ho 35 E2 ....96 C4
7 E3 ....97 C4
Bevin Rd UB4 .....84 B4
Bevin Sq SW17 ....158 A2
Bevin Way WC1 ...234 A2
Bevis Marks
EC3 ....95 C1 243 B2
Bewcastle Gdns EN2 .4 A1
Bew Ct SE21 ......162 A4
Bewdley Ho N4 ....51 A2
Bewdley St N1 .....72 C1
Bewick Mews SE15 .140 B5
Bewick St SW8 ....137 B3
Bewley Ct SW2 ....160 B5
Bewley Ho 7 E1 ...118 B6
Bewley St Stepney E1 .118 B6
Wimbledon SW19 ...180 A4
Bewlys Rd SE27 ...182 D5
Bexhill Cl TW13 ...151 A2
Bexhill Rd N11 ....31 D5
SE4 ....163 B5
Mortlake SW14 ....133 A2
Bexhill Wlk 6 E15 .98 C6
Bexley Coll SE2 ...146 D6
Bexley Coll (Erith Rd
Campus) DA17 ....125 D1
Bexley Gdns
Edmonton N9 ......17 B1
Ilford RM6 ....58 B4
Bexley Gram Sch
DA16 ....146 B3
Bexleyheath Sch
DA6 ....147 C2
Bexleyheath Sta DA7 147 A3
Bexley High St DA5 .169 D3
Bexley Ho SE4 .....141 A1
Bexley La DA14 ....168 C1
Bexley Rd SE9 .....167 A6
Bexley Sta DA5 ....169 C3
Beynon Rd SM5 ....218 D3
BFI London Imax Cinema
SE1 ....116 C5 251 A3
Bianca Rd SE1,SE15 .140 A6
Bibsworth Lo N3 ....29 B1
Bibsworth Rd N3 ..29 B1
Bicester Rd TW9 ..132 D2
Bickenhall Mans W1 237 D4
Bickenhall St
W1 ....92 D2 237 D4
Bickersteth Rd SW17 180 D4
Bickerton Rd N19 ..71 C6
Bickley Cres BR1 ..210 A5
Bickley Ct 1 HA7 ..25 C4
Bickley Park Rd BR1,
BR7 ....210 B6
Bickley Park Sch
BR1 ....210 A6
Bickley Prim Sch
BR1 ....209 C6
Bickley Rd BR1 ....187 D1
E10 ....53 D2
Bickley Sta BR1 ...210 A6
Bickley St SW17 ..180 D5
Bicknell Ho 23 E1 .96 A1
Bicknell Rd SE5 ...139 A2
Bicknoller Rd EN1 .5 D4
Bicknor Ho 2 E5 ...74 B3
Bicknor Rd BR6 ...211 C2
Bidborough Cl 3
BR2 ....208 D2
Bidborough St
N1,WC1 ......94 A4 233 A1
Biddenden Way SE9 .188 C6
Biddenham Ho 18
SE16 ....118 D2

Bidder St E16 ......98 C2
Biddesden Ho SW3 .257 C2
Biddestone Rd N7 ..72 B4
Biddulph Ho 23 SE18 122 B2
Biddulph Mans W9 .91 C4
Biddulph Rd W9 ...91 C4
Bideford Ave UB6 ..87 B5
Bideford Cl
Edgware HA8 ......26 C2
Twickenham TW13 ..151 B3
Bideford Gdns EN1 .17 C4
Bideford Rd DA16 ..146 B5
Catford BR1 ....164 D1
Enfield EN3 ....7 B5
Ruislip HA4 ....62 B5
Bidmead Ct KT6 ...214 A6
Bidwell Gdns N11 ..31 C3
Bidwell St SE15 ...140 B4
Big Ben* SW1 ......250 B1
Biggerstaff Rd E15 .98 A6
Biggerstaff St N4 ..72 C6
Biggin Ave CR4 ...180 D2
Biggin Hill SE19 ...182 D3
Biggin Hill Cl KT2 .175 C5
Biggin Way SE19 ..183 A3
Bigginwood Rd
SW16 ....182 D2
Bigg's Row SW15 ...134 D2
Big Hill E5 ....52 B1
Bigland Green Prim Sch
E1 ....96 B1
Bigland St E1 .....96 B1
Bignell Rd SE18 ...122 D1
Bignold Rd E7 ....77 A4
Bigwood Ct NW11 ..47 D4
Bigwood Rd NW11 ..47 D3
Bilberry Ho 13 E3 ..97 C2
Billet Rd E17 ......35 B2
Ilford RM6 ....58 C6
Billets Hart Cl W7 .108 C4
Bill Hamling Cl SE9 .166 B2
Billingford Cl SE4 .140 D1
Billing Ho 6 E1 ...96 D1
Billingley NW1 ....232 A5
Billing Pl
SW10 ....135 D5 265 D4
Billing Rd
SW10 ....135 D5 265 D4
Billings Cl RM9 ....80 C1
Billingsgate Mkt E14 119 D5
Billing St
SW10 ....135 D5 265 D4
Billington Ho SW8 ..269 D1
Billington Rd SE14 .140 D5
Billiter Sq EC3 ....243 B1
Billiter St EC3 .95 C1 243 B1
Bill Nicholson Way
N17 ....33 D3
Billockby Cl KT9 ..214 B2
Billsley Ct SE25 ...205 C5
Billson St E14 .....120 A2
Bilsby Gr SE9 .....187 D6
Bilton Ho SW8 ....269 C1
Bilton Rd UB6 .....87 B6
Bilton Twrs W1 ...237 D1
Bilton Way Enfield EN3 .7 B5
Hayes UB3 ....106 B4
Bina Gdns
SW5 ....114 A2 256 A3
Binbrook Ho W10 ..90 C2
Bincote Rd EN2 ...4 B2
Binden Rd W12 ...111 D3
Bindon Gn SM4 ...201 D5
Binfield Ct SE5 ...139 A3
Binfield Rd
SW4 ....138 A4 270 B1
South Croydon CR2 .221 D3
Bingfield St
N1 ....94 B6 233 C6
Bingham Cnr CR0 ..206 B1
Bingham Pl
W1 ....93 A2 238 A4
Bingham Point 11
SE18 ....122 D2
Bingham Rd CR0 ..206 B1
Bingham St N1 ....73 B2
Bingley Rd
Ashford TW16 ......172 A3
Newham E16 ....99 C1
Southall UB6 ......86 A2
Binley Ho SW15 ...155 D5
Binney St W1 .93 A1 238 B1
Binnie Ho SE1 ....262 A5
Binns Rd W4 ......111 C1
Binns Terr 3 W4 ..111 C1
Binsey Wlk 1 SE2 .124 C4
Binstead Cl UB4 ...85 A2
Binstead Ho SW18 .157 D5
Binyon Cres HA7 ..24 C6

Binyon Ho 8 N16 73 C4
Birbetts Rd SE9 166 B2
Bircham Path SE4 140 D1
Birchanger Rd SE25 206 A4
Birch Ave
Edmonton N13 17 A1
Hillingdon UB7 82 B1
Birch Cl E16 98 C2
N19 71 C6
SE15 140 A3
Brentford TW8 131 B5
Buckhurst Hill IG9 21 D1
Hounslow TW3 130 B3
Romford RM7 59 D6
Teddington TW11 175 A5
Birch Cres UB10 82 B6
Birch Ct E7 76 D4
Chingford E4 35 D4
Sutton SM1 218 A4
9 Wallington SM6 219 B4
Birchdale Gdns RM6 58 D2
Birchdale Rd E7 77 C3
Birchdene Dr SE28 124 A5
Birchdown Ho 32 E3 97 D4
Birchen Cl NW9 67 B6
Birchend Cl CR2 221 B2
Birchen Gr NW9 67 B6
Birches Cl
Mitcham CR4 202 D6
Pinner HA5 41 A4
Birches The E12 78 A4
SE5 139 C3
2 Beckenham BR2 208 D5
Bushey WD23 8 A6
Greenwich SE7 143 B6
Orpington BR6 226 C4
Southgate N21 16 B5
South Norwood SE25 183 D1
Twickenham TW4 151 B4
Birchfield Ho 2 E14 119 C6
Birchfield St E14 119 C6
Birch Gn NW9 27 C3
Birch Gr E11 76 C5
Acton W3 110 C6
Bexley DA16 146 A1
Lewisham SE12 164 D4
Upper Halliford TW17 171 C1
Birch Hill CR0 222 D3
Birch Ho SE14 141 B4
8 SW2 160 C5
Birchington Cl DA7 147 D4
Birchington Ct N8 49 D3
2 NW6 91 D6
Birchington Ho 1 E5 74 B3
Birchington Rd N8 49 D3
NW6 91 C6
Surbiton KT5 198 B2
Birchin La EC3 242 D1
Birchlands Ave SW12 158 D4
Birch Mead BR2,BR6 226 C6
Birchmead Ave HA5 40 C5
Birchmere Lo 18
SE16 118 B1
Birchmere Row SE3 142 D3
Birchmore Wlk N5 73 A5
Birch Pk HA3 24 A3
Birch Rd
Feltham TW13 172 D5
Romford RM7 59 D6
Birch Row BR2 210 C3
Birch Tree Ave BR4 224 D4
Birch Tree Ho 16 SE7 143 C6
Birch Tree Way CR0 222 B6
Birch Vale Ct NW8 236 D6
Birchway UB3 106 A5
Birch Wlk CR4 181 B2
Birchwood Ave N10 49 A6
Beckenham BR3 207 B5
Hackbridge SM5,SM6 219 B5
Sidcup DA14 168 C1
Birchwood Cl SM4 201 D5
Birchwood Ct HA8 27 A1
Edmonton N13 32 D5
Birchwood Dr NW3 69 D5
Birchwood Gr TW12 173 C4
Birchwood Rd
Orpington BR5 211 C5
Streatham SW17 181 B5
Birdbrook Rd SE3,
SE9 143 C2
Birdcage Wlk
SW1 115 D4 249 C1
Birdham Cl BR1 210 A4
Birdhurst Ave CR2 221 B4
Birdhurst Ct SM6 219 C1
Birdhurst Gdns CR2 221 B4
Birdhurst Rd SW18 158 A6
Mitcham SW19 180 C4
South Croydon CR2 221 C3
Birdhurst Rise CR2 221 C3
Bird In Bush Rd SE15 140 A5
Bird-in-Hand La
BR1 187 D1
Bird-in-Hand Pas
SE23 162 C2
Bird In Hand Yd 14
NW3 70 A4
Birdsall Ho 5 SE5 139 C2
Birdsfield La E3 97 B6
Bird St W1 238 B1
Bird Wlk TW2 151 B3
Birdwood Cl TW11 174 C6
Birkbeck Ave W3 111 A6
Greenford UB6 86 A6
Birkbeck Coll
W1 93 D1 239 C2
Birkbeck Ct W3 111 B5
Birkbeck Gdns IG8 21 A2
Birkbeck Gr W3 111 B4
Birkbeck Hill SE21 160 D3
Birkbeck Mews 5 E8 73 D3
Birkbeck Pl SE21 161 A2
Birkbeck Prim Sch
DA14 168 B1
Birkbeck Rd E8 73 D3
N12 30 A5
N8 50 A5
NW7 27 D5
W3 111 B5
W5 109 C2
Enfield EN2 5 B5
Ilford IG2 57 B4
Penge BR3 184 D1
Sidcup DA14 168 A1
Tottenham N17 33 D2
Wimbledon SW19 179 D4
Birkbeck St E2 96 B4
Birkbeck Sta SE20 206 C6
Birkbeck Way UB6 86 B6
Birkdale Ave HA5 41 C6
Birkdale Cl BR6 211 B2
30 SE16 118 B1
Erith SE28 102 D1
Birkdale Ct 3 UB1 86 A1
Birkdale Gdns CR0 222 D4
Birkdale Rd SE2 124 A2
Ealing W5 88 A3
Birkenhead Ave KT2 176 B2
Birkenhead Ho 11 N7 72 C3
Birkenhead St
WC1 94 A4 233 B2
Birkhall Rd SE6 164 B2
Birkwood Cl SW12 159 D4
Birley Lo NW8 229 D4
Birley Rd N20 14 A2
Birley St SW11 137 A3
Birnam Rd N4 72 B6
Birnbeck Ct NW11 47 B4
Birrell Ho 9 SW9 138 B3
Birse Cres NW10 67 C4
Birstal Gn WD19 22 D6
Birstall Rd N15 51 C4
Birtwhistle Ho 5 E3 97 B6
Biscay Ho 11 E1 96 D3
Biscay Rd W6 112 D1
Biscoe Cl TW5 129 C6
Biscoe Ho UB2 107 D2
Biscoe Way SE13 142 B2
Biscott Ho 3 E3 97 D3
Bisenden Rd CR0 221 C6
Bisham Cl CR4 202 D1
Bisham Gdns N6 49 A1
Bishop Butt Cl BR6 227 D5
Bishop Challoner
Collegiate Sch
E1 118 A6
E1 96 C1
Bishop Challoner Sch
BR2 186 B1
Bishop Ct 20 SW2 160 C5
Bishop Douglass RC High
Sch N2 48 A6
Bishop Duppa's
Almshouses 7
TW10 154 A6
Bishop Duppas Pk
TW17 193 C2
Bishop Fox Way KT8 195 B5
Bishopgate 32 N1 95 C6
Bishop Gilpins Prim Sch
SW19 179 B5
Bishop John Robinson CE
Prim Sch SE28 124 C6
Bishop Ken Rd HA3 24 D2
Bishop King's Rd
W14 113 A2 254 B4
Bishop Perrin CE Prim Sch
TW2 151 D3
Bishop Ramsey CE Sch
HA4 40 A2
Bishop Ramsey CE Sch
(Annexe) HA4 39 D2
Bishop Rd N14 15 B4
Bishops Ave BR1 209 C6
E13 99 B6
Borehamwood WD6 10 B6
Ilford RM6 58 C3
Bishop's Ave SW6 135 A3
Bishops Ave The N2 48 B3
Bishopsbourne Ho
BR1 187 B3
Bishop's Bridge Rd
W2 92 A1 236 A2
Bishops Cl SE9 167 A2
W4 111 A1
Bishop's Cl E17 53 D5
N19 71 C5
Bishops Cl Barnet EN5 12 D5
Enfield EN1 6 B3
Richmond TW10 153 D1
Sutton SM1 217 C5
Bishop's Cl UB10 82 C5
Bishopscourt 8 CR0 221 D6
Bishops Ct N2 48 C5
12 W2 91 D1
Bishop's Ct EC4 241 C2
WC2 241 A2
Bishops Ct
1 Ashford TW16 171 D3
Romford RM7 59 D5
Bishopsdale Ho 8
NW6 91 C6
Bishops Dr
East Bedfont TW14 149 B5
Northolt UB5 85 A6
Bishopsford Rd SM4 202 B3
Bishopsgate
EC2 95 C1 243 A2
Bishopsgate Arcade
E1 243 B3
Bishopsgate Church Yd
EC2 243 A2
Bishops Gn BR1 187 C2
Bishops Gr N2 48 C3
Feltham TW12 173 B6
Bishop's Hall KT1 175 D1
Bishopshalt Sch UB8 82 B4
Bishops Hill KT12 194 A2
Bishops Ho SW8 270 B3
Bishop's Mans SW6 134 D3
Bishops Mead SE5 139 A5
Bishops Park Rd
SW16 182 A2
Bishop's Park Rd
SW6 134 D3
Bishop's Pl SM1 218 A3
Bishops Rd N6 49 A3
Bishop's Rd W7 108 C4
Bishops Rd SW6 135 264 C2
Bishop's Rd Hayes UB3 83 A1
Thornton Heath CR0 204 D2
Bishop St N1 95 A6 235 A6
Bishop's Terr
SE11 116 C2 261 B4
Bishopsthorpe Rd
SE26 184 D6
Bishopstone Ho 4
SW11 137 A3
Bishop Stopford's Sch
EN1 6 B3
Bishop's Way E2 96 C5
Bishops Wlk
Chislehurst BR7 189 A2
South Croydon CR0,CR9 223 A3
Bishopswood Rd N6 48 D2
Bishop Thomas Grant RC
Sec Sch SW16 182 B5
Bishop Wand CE Sec Sch
TW16 171 D1
Bishop Way NW10 67 C1
Bishop Wilfred Wood Cl
SE15 140 A3
Bishop Wilfred Wood Ct 2
E13 99 C5
Bishop
Winnington-Ingram CE
Sch HA4 39 B2
Bisley Cl KT4 200 C1
Bisley Ho SW19 156 D2
Bispham Rd NW10 88 B4
Bissextile Ho SE13 141 D3
Bisson Rd E15 98 A5
Bistern Ave E17 54 B6
Bittacy Bsns Ctr NW7 29 A3
Bittacy Cl NW7 28 D4
Bittacy Ct NW7 29 A3
Bittacy Hill NW7 28 D4
Bittacy Park Ave NW7 28 D5
Bittacy Rd NW7 28 D4
Bittacy Rise NW7 28 D4
Bittern Cl UB4 84 D2
Bittern Ct NW9 27 C1
8 SE8 141 C6
Chingford E4 20 B4
Bittern Ho SE1 252 A1
Bittern St SE1 252 A1
Bittoms The KT1 197 D6
Bixley Cl UB2 107 B2
Blackall St EC2 243 A6
Blackberry Cl TW17 193 C5
Blackberry Farm Cl
TW5 129 A5
Blackberry Field BR5 190 A2
Blackbird Ct NW9 67 B5
Blackbird Hill NW9 67 B5
Blackborne Rd RM10 81 D2
Black Boy La N15 51 A4
Blackbrook La BR1,
BR2 210 C5
Blackburn 28 NW9 27 D1
Blackburn Ct 21 SW2 160 C5
Blackburne's Mews
W1 248 A5
Blackburn Rd NW6 69 D2
Blackburn Trad Est
TW19 148 B5
Blackbush Ave RM6 58 D4
Blackbush Cl SM2 217 D1
Blackcap Ct NW9 27 C1
Blackdown Cl N2 30 A1
Blackdown Ho E8 74 A4
Blackenham Rd
SW17 180 D6
Blackett St SW15 134 D2
Black Fan Cl EN2 5 A4
Blackfen Par DA15 168 A5
Blackfen Rd DA15 168 B5
Blackfen Sch for Girls
DA15 168 B5
Blackford Rd WD19 22 D5
Blackfriars Bridge
EC4 251 C5
Blackfriars Ct EC4 251 C6
Black Friars La
EC4 94 D1 241 C1
Blackfriars Pas EC4 251 C6
Blackfriars Pier EC4 251 C6
Blackfriars Rd
SE1 116 D4 251 C3
Blackfriars Sta
EC4 116 D6 251 C6
Blackfriars Underpass
EC4 116 C6 251 B6
Blackham Ho SW19 179 A4
Blackheath* SE3 142 C4
Blackheath Ave SE3 142 C5
Blackheath Bluecoat CE
Sch SE3 143 B5
Blackheath Bsns Est
SE10 142 A4
Blackheath Gr SE3 142 D3
Blackheath High Sch
SE3 143 A5
Blackheath High Sch
(Girls) SE3 142 D3
Blackheath High Sch
GPDST (Jun Dept)
SE3 143 A3
Blackheath Hill SE10 142 A4
Blackheath Hospl
SE3 142 C2
Blackheath Pk SE3 143 A2
Blackheath Rd SE10 141 D4
Blackheath Rise
SE13 142 A3
Blackheath Sta SE3 142 D2
Blackheath Vale SE3 142 C3
Blackheath Village
SE3 142 D3
Black Horse Ct SE1 262 D6
Blackhorse La E17 34 D1
Croydon CR0 206 A2
Blackhorse La Sta
CR0 206 A2
Blackhorse Mews E17 52 D6
Black Horse Par HA5 40 B4
Blackhorse Rd E17 53 A5
SE8 141 A6
Black Horse Rd DA14 190 A6
Blackhorse Road E17 52 D5
Blackhorse Road Sta
E17 52 D5
Blacklands Dr UB4 83 A3
Blacklands Rd SE6 186 A6
Blacklands Terr SW3 257 D3
Black Lion La W6 112 A2
Black Lion Mews 4
W6 112 A2
Blackmore Ave UB1 108 B5
Blackmore Ho N1 233 D5
Blackmore Ho *continued*
2 SW18 157 D6
Forest Hill SE23 163 B3
Blackmore's Gr
TW11 175 A4
Blackmore Twr 1
W3 111 A3
Blackness La BR2 225 D1
Blackpool Gdns UB4 83 C3
Blackpool Rd SE15 140 B3
Black Prince Intc
DA5 169 D5
Black Prince Rd
SE1,SE11 116 B2 260 D3
Black Rod Cl UB3 105 D3
Black Roof Ho 9
SE5 138 D4
Blackshaw Rd SW17 180 B5
Blacksmith Cl RM6 58 C3
Blacksmiths Ho 7
E17 53 C5
Black's Rd W6 112 C2
Blackstock Ho N5 72 D5
Blackstock Mews N4 72 D5
Blackstock Rd N4,N5 72 D6
Blackstone Ho SW1 259 A1
Dulwich SE21 161 C1
Blackstone Rd NW2 68 C4
Black Swan Yd SE1 253 A2
Blackthorn Ave UB7 104 C3
Blackthorn Ct 4 E15 76 B4
19 SE15 139 D5
Heston TW5 129 A5
6 West Norwood
SW16 182 C5
Blackthorne Ave CR0 206 C1
Blackthorne Dr E4 36 B6
Blackthorn Gr DA7 147 A2
Blackthorn St E3 97 C3
Blacktree Mews 12
SW9 138 C2
Blackwall Sta E14 120 A6
Blackwall Trad Est
E14 98 B2
Blackwall Tunnel
E14,SE10 120 B5
Blackwall Tunnel App
SE10 120 C4
Blackwall Tunnel Northern
Approach E14,E3 98 A3
Blackwall Way E14 120 A6
Blackwater Cl E7 76 D4
Blackwater Ho NW8 236 D4
Blackwater St SE22 161 D6
Blackwell Cl 10 E5 74 D4
Harrow HA3 24 B3
Blackwell Gdns HA8 10 C1
Blackwell Ho 3 SW4 159 D5
Blackwood Ho 11 E1 96 B3
Blackwood St
SE17 117 B1 262 C2
Blade Mews SW15 135 B1
Bladen Ho 4 E1 96 D1
Blades Ct SW15 135 B1
Blades Ho 12 SE11 138 C6
Blades Lo 16 SW2 160 C5
Bladindon Dr DA5 168 D4
Bladon Ct
Beckenham BR2 208 C6
Streatham SW16 182 A4
Bladon Gdns HA2 41 D3
Blagden's Cl N14 15 D2
Blagden's La N14 15 D2
Blagdon Ct W7 108 C6
Blagdon Rd SE13 163 D5
New Malden KT3 199 D5
Blagdon Wlk TW11 175 C4
Blagrove Rd 1 W10 91 B2
Blair Ave NW9 45 C2
Thames Ditton KT10 212 A6
Blair Cl DA15 167 C6
N1 73 A2
Hayes UB3 106 A2
Blair Ct NW8 229 C6
Beckenham BR3 185 D2
7 Catford SE6 164 D3
Blairderry Rd SW2 160 A2
Blair Ho SW9 138 B3
Blair Peach Prim Sch
UB1 106 D5
Blair St E14 98 B1
Blake Ave IG11 101 D6
Blake Cl DA16 145 C4
Carshalton SM5 202 C1
Blake Ct NW6 91 C4
8 SE16 118 B1
Blakeden Dr KT10 212 D2
Blake Gdns
SW6 135 D4 265 C2
Blake Hall Cres E11 55 A1
Blakehall Rd SM5 218 D2
Blake Hall Rd E11 55 A2
Blake Ho 14 N16 73 C4
1 N19 71 D3
SE1 261 A6
2 SE8 141 C6
6 Beckenham BR3 185 D4
Blake Lo N3 29 B1
Blake Mews 14 TW9 132 C4
Blakemore Rd
Streatham SW16 160 A1
Thornton Heath CR7 204 B4
Blakemore Way
DA17 125 A3
Blakeney Ave BR3 185 B2
Blakeney Cl 4 E8 74 A3
N20 14 A3
5 NW1 71 D1
Blakeney Ct EN2 17 B6
Blakeney Rd BR3 185 B2
Blakenham Ct W12 112 A5
Blakenham Rd SW17 180 D6
Blaker Ct SE7 143 C5
Blake Rd E16 98 D3
N11 31 C3
Croydon CR0 221 C6
Mitcham CR4 202 C6
Blaker Rd E15 98 A6
Blakes Ave KT3 199 D3
Blakes Cl W10 90 C2
Blake's Gn BR4 208 A1
Blakes La KT3 199 D4
Blakesley Ave W5 87 C1
Blakesley Ct W5 87 C1
Blakesley Ho 4 E12 78 C5
Blake's Rd SE15 139 C5
Blakes Terr KT3 200 A4
Blakesware Gdns N9 17 B4
Blakewood Cl TW13 172 C6
Blakewood Ct SE20 184 B3
Blanca Ho 16 N1 95 C5
Blanchard Cl SE9 166 A1
Blanchard Gr EN3 7 D5
Blanchard Ho 7
TW1 153 D5
Blanchard Way E8 74 A2
Blanch Cl SE15 140 C5
Blanchedowne SE5 139 B1
Blanche Ho NW8 237 A5
Blanche Nevile Sch The
N15 51 D6
Blanche St E16 98 D3
Blanchland Rd SM4 201 D4
Blandfield Rd SW12 159 A4
Blandford Ave
2 Beckenham BR3 185 A1
Twickenham TW2 151 D3
Blandford Cl N2 48 A5
Romford RM7 59 D5
Wallington CR0 220 A5
Blandford Cres E4 20 A4
Blandford Ct 6 N1 73 C1
NW6 69 A1
Blandford Ho SW8 270 C4
Blandford Rd W4 111 C3
W5 109 D4
Penge BR3 184 D1
Southall UB2 107 C2
Teddington TW11 174 C5
Blandford Sq NW1 237 B5
Blandford St
W1 93 A2 238 A3
Blandford Waye UB4 84 C1
Bland Ho SE11 260 D2
Bland St SE9 143 D1
Blaney Cres E6 100 D4
Blanmerle Rd SE9 166 D3
Blann Cl SE9 165 D5
Blantyre St
SW10 136 B5 266 C4
Blantyre Twr SW10 266 C4
Blantyre Wlk
SW10 136 B5 266 C4
Blashford NW3 70 D1
Blashford St SE13 164 B4
Blasker Wlk E14 119 D1
Blatchford Ct KT12 194 A1
Blatchford Ho 8
RM10 81 C5
Blawith Rd HA1 42 D5
Blaxland Ho 12 W12 112 B6
Blaydon Cl HA4 39 C2
Blaydon Ct 4 UB5 63 C2
Blaydon Wlk N17 34 B3
Bleak Hill La SE18 145 D6
Blean Gr SE20 184 C3
Bleasdale Ave UB6 87 A5

Blechynden Ho 17 W10 ...90 D1
Blechynden St W10 112 D6
Bleddyn Cl DA15 168 C5
Bledlow Cl SE28 124 C6
Bledlow Rise UB6 86 A5
Bleeding Heart Yd EC1 241 B3
Blegborough Rd SW16 181 C4
Blemundsbury WC1 240 C4
Blendon Dr DA5 168 D5
Blendon Path 7 BR1 186 D5
Blendon Rd DA5 168 D5
Blendon Terr SE18 145 A6
Blendworth Point 4 SW15 156 B3
Blenheim 26 SW19 156 D3
Blenheim Ave IG2 56 C3
Blenheim Bsns Ctr CR4 180 D1
Blenheim Cl
Edmonton N21 17 A3
Greenford UB6 86 B5
Wallington SM6 219 C1
West Barnes SW20 200 C6
Blenheim Cres
W11 113 A6 244 B6
W11 91 A1
Ruislip HA4 61 B6
South Croydon CR2 221 A1
Blenheim Ct DA15 167 B1
N19 72 A6
N7 72 A2
17 SE16 118 D5
Harrow HA3 43 A3
Richmond TW9 132 B2
South Norwood SE19 183 C2
Sutton SM2 218 A2
Blenheim Dr DA16 145 D4
Blenheim Gdns NW2 68 C3
SW2 160 B5
Kingston KT2 176 D3
Wallington SM6 219 C1
Wembley HA9 66 A5
Blenheim Gr SE15 140 A3
Blenheim Ho
6 Edmonton N9 18 A1
Hounslow TW3 2 129 C2
Blenheim Par 2 UB10 82 D3
Blenheim Park Rd CR2 221 A1
Blenheim Pas NW8 229 A4
Blenheim Pl TW11 174 D5
Blenheim Rd E15 76 C4
E17 53 A6
E6 99 D4
NW8 92 A5 229 B4
W4 111 C3
Bromley BR1,BR2 210 A5
Harrow HA2 41 D3
Northolt UB5 63 D2
Penge SE20 184 C3
Sidcup DA15 168 C3
Sutton SM1 217 D5
West Barnes SW20 200 C6
Blenheim Rise N15 51 D5
Blenheim St W1 238 C1
Blenheim Terr
NW8 92 A5 229 A4
Blenheim Way TW7 131 A4
Blenkarne Rd SW11 158 D5
Bleriot 27 NW9 27 D1
Bleriot Rd TW5 128 C5
Blessbury Rd HA8 27 A2
Blessed Dominic RC Prim Sch NW9 27 D1
Blessed John Roche RC Sch The E14 97 C1
Blessed Sacrament RC Prim Sch N1 94 B6 233 C5
Blessington Cl SE13 142 C1
Blessington Rd SE13 142 C1
Blessing Way IG11 102 C5
Bletchingley Cl CR7 204 D5
Bletchington Ct DA17 125 C2
Bletchley Ct N1 235 C3
Bletchley St N1 95 A5 235 B3
Bletchmore Cl
Hayes UB3 105 B1
Hayes UB3 127 B6
Bletsoe Wlk N1 235 B4
Blewbury Ho 3 SE2 124 C4
Blick Ho 1 SE16 118 C3
Bligh Ho 4 SE27 183 A6

Blincoe Cl SW19 156 D2
Blind Cnr SE25 206 C6
Blissett St SE10 142 A4
Blissland Ct N12 30 A4
Bliss Mews 17 W10 91 A4
Blisworth Cl UB4 85 A3
Blisworth Ho 12 E2 96 A6
Blithbury Rd RM9 80 B2
Blithdale Rd SE2 124 A2
Blithfield St W8 255 C5
Blockley Rd HA0 65 B6
Bloemfontein Ave W12 112 B5
Bloemfontein Rd W12 112 B6
Blomfield Ct SW11 266 D2
W9 236 B6
Blomfield Mans W12 112 C5
Blomfield Rd W9 92 A2 236 A4
Blomfield St EC2 95 B2 242 D3
Blomfield Villas W2 91 D2
W9 236 A4
Blomville Rd RM8 81 A5
Blondel St SW11 137 A3
Blondin Ave W5 109 C3
Blondin St E3 97 C5
Bloomburg St SW1 259 B3
Bloomfield Cres IG2 56 C3
Bloomfield Ct N6 49 A3
Bloomfield Ho 17 E1 96 A2
Bloomfield Pl W1 248 D6
Bloomfield Rd BR2 209 D4
N6 49 A3
SE18 122 D1
Kingston KT1 198 A6
Bloomfields The IG11 79 A2
Bloomfield Terr SW1 115 A1 258 B2
Bloom Gr SE27 160 C1
Bloomhall Rd SE19 183 B5
Bloom Park Rd SW6 264 C3
Bloomsbury Cl NW7 28 A3
Ealing W5 110 B6
Bloomsbury Ct E11 54 B1
WC1 240 B3
Bloomsbury Ho 10 SW4 159 D5
Bloomsbury Pl SW18 158 A6
WC1 240 B3
Bloomsbury Sq WC1 94 A2 240 B3
Bloomsbury St WC1 93 D2 239 D3
Bloomsbury Way WC1 94 A2 240 B3
Blore Cl SW8 269 C1
Blore Ct W1 249 C6
Blossom Cl W5 110 A4
Dagenham RM9 103 B6
South Croydon CR2 221 D3
Blossom La EN2 5 A4
Blossom Pl E1 243 B5
Blossom St E1 95 C3 243 B5
Blossom Way
Hillingdon UB10 60 B1
West Drayton UB7 104 C2
Blossom Waye TW5 129 A5
Blount St E14 97 A1
Bloxam Gdns SE9 166 A6
Bloxhall Rd E10 53 B1
Bloxham Cres TW12 173 B2
Bloxworth Cl SM6 219 C5
Blucher Rd SE5 139 A5
Blue Anchor Alley 4 TW9 132 A4
Blue Anchor La SE16 118 B2
Blue Anchor Yd E1 118 A6
Blue Ball Yd SW1 249 A3
Bluebell Ave E12 78 A3
Bluebell Cl 16 E9 96 C6
Forest Hill SE26 183 D6
Hackbridge SM6 203 B1
Orpington BR6 227 A6
Bluebell Way IG1 78 D2
Blueberry Cl IG8 37 A4
Bluebird La RM10 81 C1
Bluebird Way Cl SE28
Bluefield Cl TW12 173 C5
Blue Gate Fields Jun & Inf Schs E1 118 C6
Bluegate Mews E1 118 B6
Bluegates
Stoneleigh KT17 216 A1
Wimbledon SW19 179 A5
Bluehouse Rd E4 20 C1
Blue Lion Pl SE1 263 A6

Blue Point Ct 2 HA1 42 D4
Blue Sch The TW7 131 A2
Blundell Rd HA8 27 C3
Blundell St N7 72 A2
Blunden Cl RM8 58 C1
Blunt Rd CR0 221 B3
Blunts Ave UB7 126 C5
Blunts Rd SE9 166 C6
Blurton Rd E5 74 D4
Blyddon Ct N21 16 B6
Blyth Cl 4 E14 120 B2
Twickenham TW1 152 D5
Blythe Cl SE23 163 B4
Blythe Hill BR5 190 A2
Forest Hill SE6 163 B4
Blythe Hill La SE6 163 B3
Blythe Ho 8 SE11 138 C6
Blythe Mews 2 W14 112 D3
Blythendale Ho 31 E2 96 A5
Blythe Rd W14 112 D3 254 A5
Blythe St E2 96 B4
Blythe Vale SE6 163 B3
Blyth Rd E17 53 B2
Bromley BR1 186 D2
Hayes UB3 105 C4
Woolwich SE18 124 C6
Blyth's Wharf E14 119 A6
Blythswood Rd IG3 58 A2
Blythwood Pk 10 BR1 186 D2
Blythwood Rd N4 50 A2
Pinner HA5 22 D2
Boadicea St N1 233 C5
Boadoak Ho 18 NW6 91 D6
Boardman Ave E4 19 D6
Boardman Cl EN5 13 A6
Boardwalk Pl E14 120 A5
Boarhound 25 NW9 27 D1
Boarley Ho SE17 263 A3
Boathouse Ctr The W10 90 D3
Boat Lifter Way 19 SE16 119 A2
Bob Anker Cl 1 E13 99 A4
Bobbin Cl SW4 137 C2
Bobby Moore Bridge The HA9 66 C5
Bobington Ct WC1 94 A2 240 B4
Bob Marley Way 11 SE24 138 C1
Bockhampton Rd KT2 176 B3
Bocking St E8 96 B6
Boddicott Cl SW19 157 A2
Boddington Ho 14 SE14 140 C4
Bodeney Ho 10 SE5 139 C4
Boden Ho 4 E1 96 A2
Bodiam Cl EN1 5 C3
Bodiam Ct BR2 208 D5
Bodiam Rd SW16 181 D5
Bodicea Mews TW4 151 C5
Bodington Ct 2 W12 112 A2
Bodley Cl KT3 199 C4
Bodley Manor Way SE24 160 C4
Bodley Rd KT3 199 C4
Bodmin 26 NW9 27 D1
Bodmin Cl HA2 63 B5
Bodmin Gr SM4 201 D4
Bodmin St SW18 157 C3
Bodnant Gdns SW20 200 B6
Bodney Mans 14 E8 74 B3
Bodney Rd E5,E8 74 B3
Boeing Way UB2 106 B3
Boelyn Dr HA4 62 D6
Boevey Path
Erith DA17 125 B1
2 Erith DA17 147 B6
Bognor Gdns WD19 22 C5
Bognor Rd DA16 146 D4
Bohemia Pl 1 E8 74 B2
Bohn Rd E1 97 A2
Bohun Gr EN4 14 D5
Boileau Par 3 W5 88 B1
Boileau Rd
Barnes SW13 134 B6
Ealing W5 88 B1
Boilerhouse SE1 253 C3
Boisseau Ho 27 E1 96 C2
Bolden St SE8 141 D3
Boldero Pl NW8 237 A5
Bolderwood Way BR4 223 D6
Boldmere Rd HA5 40 C2
Boleyn Ave EN1 6 B4
Boleyn Cl E17 53 C5
Beckenham BR3 186 A2

Boleyn Ct continued
Buckhurst Hill IG9 21 B3
East Molesey KT8 196 B5
Boleyn Dr KT8 195 B6
Boleyn Gdns BR4 223 D6
Boleyn Ground(Upton Park) (West Ham United FC) E13,E6 99 D5
Boleyn Rd E6 99 D5
E7 77 B1
N16 73 C3
Boleyn Way EN5 2 A2
Bolina Rd SE16 118 C3
Bolingbroke Gr SW11 158 C5
Bolingbroke Ho
Beckenham BR3 207 A4
Catford BR3 185 D5
Bolingbroke Hospl The SW11 158 C4
Bolingbroke Rd W14 112 B1
Bolingbroke Way UB3,UB11 105 B5
Bolingbroke Wlk SW11 136 C4 267 A2
Bollo Bridge Rd W3 111 A4
Bollo Ct 2 W3 111 A3
Bollo La W3 110 D3
Bolney Ct KT6 197 D4
Bolney Gate SW7 247 A1
Bolney St SW8 138 B5 270 C3
Bolsover St W1 93 B3 238 D5
Bolstead Rd CR4 181 B2
Bolster Gr N22 31 D2
Bolt Ct EC4 241 B1
Boltmore Cl NW4 46 D6
Bolton Cl
Chessington KT9 214 A2
Penge SE20 184 A1
Bolton Cres SE5 138 D5
Bolton Ct SW11 268 B1
Bolton Gdns NW10 90 D5
SW5 113 D1 255 D2
Bromley BR1 186 D4
Teddington TW11 175 A4
Bolton Gdns Mews SW10 256 A2
Bolton Ho 4 SE10 120 C1
Bolton Rd E15 76 D2
NW10 89 C6
NW8 91 B6
Chessington KT9 214 A2
Chiswick W4 133 A5
Edmonton N18 33 D5
Harrow HA1 42 B5
Boltons Ct SW5 255 D2
Bolton's La TW6,UB7 127 A5
Bolton St W1 115 B5 248 D4
Boltons The
SW10 114 A1 256 A2
Wembley HA0 64 D4
Woodford IG8 37 A6
Bolton Studios SW10 256 B1
Bolton Wlk N7 72 B6
Bombay St SE16 118 B2
Bomer Cl UB7 126 C5
Bomore Rd W11 113 A6 244 A6
Bonar Pl BR7 188 A3
Bonar Rd SE15 140 A5
Bonchester Cl BR7 188 C3
Bonchurch Cl SM2 217 D1
Bonchurch Rd W10 91 A2
Ealing W13 109 B5
Bond Cl UB7 82 B1
Bond Ct EC4 242 C1
Bondfield Ave UB4 84 A4
Bondfield Rd 4 E6 100 B2
Bond Fst Sch CR4 180 C1
Bond Gdns SM6 219 C4
Bond Ho 4 NW6 91 B5
Bond Rd Mitcham CR4 180 D1
Surbiton KT6 214 B6
Bond St E15 76 C4
Ealing W5 109 D6
Bond Street Sta W1 93 B1 238 B1
Bondway SW8 138 A6 270 B6
Boneta Rd SE18 122 B3
Bonfield Rd SE13 142 A1
Bonham Gdns RM8 80 D6
Bonham Ho W11 244 C6
Bonham Rd SW2 160 B6
Dagenham RM8 80 D6
Bonheur Rd W4 111 B4

Bonhill St EC2 95 B3 242 D5
Boniface Gdns HA3 23 A3
Boniface Rd UB10 60 D5
Boniface Wlk HA3 23 A3
Bonington Ho N1 233 C3
Enfield EN1 18 A6
Bonita Mews SE15 140 D2
Bonne Marche Terr Mews 18 SE27 183 C6
Bonner Hill Rd KT1 198 C6
Bonner Ho 3 SW15 156 A6
Bonner Prim Sch E2 96 C4
Bonner Rd E2 96 C5
Bonner St E2 96 C5
Bonnersfield Cl HA1 43 A3
Bonnersfield La
Harrow HA1 42 D3
Harrow HA1,HA3 43 A3
Bonneville Gdns SW4 159 C5
Bonneville Prim Sch SW4 159 C5
Bonnington Ct 15 UB5 84 D5
Bonnington Sq SW8 138 B6 270 C6
Bonnington Twr BR2 210 A3
Bonny St NW1 71 C1
Bonser Rd TW1 152 D2
Bonsor Ho SW8 269 B2
Bonsor St SE5 139 C5
Bonthron Ho SW15 134 C3
Bonville Gdns 17 NW4 46 A5
Bonville Rd BR1 186 D5
Bookbinder Cotts N20 14 D1
Booker Cl 15 E3 97 B2
Booker Rd 5 N18 34 A5
Bookham Ct CR4 202 B6
Boone Ct N9 18 C1
Boones Rd SE13 142 C1
Boone St SE13 142 C1
Boord St SE10 120 C3
Boothby Ct E4 20 A1
Boothby Ho 2 SW16 181 C1
Boothby Rd N19 71 D6
Booth Cl 10 E9 96 B6
SE28 124 B6
Booth Ho 2 SW2 160 C4
Booth La EC4 252 A6
Boothman Ho HA3 43 D6
Booth Rd NW9 27 C1
Croydon CR0 220 D6
Boothroyd Ho TW7 130 D2
Booth's Pl W1 239 B3
Boot Par HA8 26 C4
Boot St N1 95 C4
Bordars Rd W7 86 D2
Bordars Wlk W7 86 C2
Borden Ave EN1 17 B5
Border Cres SE26 184 B5
Border Gate CR4 180 D2
Border Gdns CR0 223 D4
Border Rd SE26 184 B5
Bordesley Rd SM4 201 D5
Bordon Ct TW8 131 C2
Bordon Wlk 5 SW15 156 A4
Boreas Wlk N1 234 D3
Boreham Ave E16 99 A1
Boreham Cl E11 54 A1
Boreham Rd N22 33 A1
Boreman Ho 10 SE10 142 A6
Borgard Ho 3 SE18 144 A4
Borgard Rd SE18 122 B2
Borkwood Pk BR6 227 D4
Borkwood Way BR6 227 C4
Borland Rd SE15 140 C1
Teddington TW11 175 B3
Borneo St SW15 134 C3
Borough High St SE1 117 B5 252 C2
Borough Hill CR0 220 D5
Borough Mkt* SE1 252 C2
Borough Rd
SE1 116 D3 261 D6
Hounslow TW7 130 D4
7 Kingston KT2 176 C3
Mitcham CR4 180 C1
Borough Sq SE1 252 A1
Borough Sta The SE1 117 A4 252 B1
Borrett Cl SE17 117 A1 262 A1
Borrodaile Rd SW18 157 D5
Borrowdale NW1 232 A1
Borrowdale Ave HA3 25 A1
Borrowdale Cl IG4 56 A5
Borrowdale Ct EN2 5 A4
Borthwick Mews E15 76 C4
Borthwick Rd E15 76 C4

Borthwick Rd continued
NW9 45 D3
Borthwick St SE8 119 C1
Borwick Ave E17 53 B6
Bosbury Rd SE6 164 A1
Boscastle Rd NW5 71 B5
Boscobel Ho 4 E8 74 B2
Boscobel Pl SW1 258 B4
Boscobel St NW8 92 B3 236 D5
Boscombe Ave E10 54 B2
Boscombe Cl E5 75 C4
Boscombe Gdns SW16 182 A4
Boscombe Ho CR0 205 B1
Boscombe Rd W12 112 A4
Merton SW19 179 D6
North Cheam KT4 200 A6
Streatham SW17 181 A4
Bose Cl N3 29 A2
Bosgrove E4 20 A2
Boss Ho SE1 253 C2
Boss St SE1 253 C2
Bostall Hill SE2 124 B1
Bostall La SE2 124 B1
Bostall Manor Way SE2 124 B2
Bostall Park Ave DA7 147 A5
Bostall Rd BR5 190 B3
Bostock Ho TW5 129 C6
Boston Bsns Pk W7 108 C3
Boston Ct
South Norwood SE25 205 D5
Sutton SM2 218 A1
Boston Gdns
Brentford TW8 109 B2
Chiswick W4 133 C6
Boston Gr HA4 39 A3
Boston Ho NW1 237 C6
25 SE5 139 A3
SW5 255 D3
Boston Manor Ho TW8 109 B1
Boston Manor Rd TW8 109 B1
Boston Manor Sta TW8 109 A2
Boston Par W7 109 A2
Boston Pk Rd TW8 109 C1
Boston Pl NW1 92 D3 237 C5
Boston Rd E6 100 A4
HA8 27 A3
Ealing W7 109 A3
Thornton Heath CR0 204 A3
Bostonthorpe Rd W7 108 C3
Boston Vale W7 109 A2
Bosun Cl 8 E14 119 C4
Boswell Ct 9 W14 112 D3
WC1 240 C2
Kingston KT2 176 C2
Boswell Ho BR2 209 D4
WC1 240 C2
5 Streatham SW16 181 C3
Boswell Rd CR7 205 C4
Boswell St WC1 94 A2 240 B4
Boswood Ct TW4 129 C3
Bosworth Cl E17 35 B2
Bosworth Ho 4 W10 91 A3
Bosworth Rd N11 31 D4
W10 91 A3
Barnet EN5 1 C2
Dagenham RM10 81 C5
Botany Bay La BR7 189 A1
Botany Cl EN4 2 C1
Boteley Cl E4 20 B2
Botham Cl 6 HA8 27 A3
Botha Rd E13 99 C2
Bothwell Cl E16 98 D2
Bothwell St 4 W6 134 D6
Botolph Alley EC3 253 A6
Botolph La EC3 253 A6
Botsford Rd SW20 179 A1
Bott's Mews W2 91 C6
Botwell Common Rd UB3 105 C6
Botwell Cres UB3 83 C1
Botwell House RC Prim Sch UB3 105 D4
Botwell La UB3 105 C5
Boucher Cl TW11 174 D5
Bouchier Ho 6 N2 30 B1
Bough Beech Ct EN3 6 D6
Boughton Ave BR2 208 D2
Boughton Ho SE1 252 C2
Boughton Rd SE28 123 C2
Boulcott St E1 96 D1
Boulevard The 4 SW17 159 A2

Boullen Ct SM1 218 A4
Boulogne Ho SE1 263 C6
Boulogne Rd CR0 205 A3
Boulter Ho SE14 140 C4
Boulton Ho TW8 110 A1
Boulton Rd RM8 81 B6
Boultwood Rd E6 100 B1
Bounces La N9 18 B2
Bounces Rd N9 18 C2
Boundaries Mans 3 SW12 159 A3
Boundaries Rd
Feltham TW13 150 C3
Upper Tooting SW12 159 A3
Boundary Ave E17 53 B2
Boundary Bsns Ct CR4 202 B6
Boundary Cl Barnet EN5 1 B4
Ilford IG3 79 C4
Kingston KT1 198 D6
Penge SE20 184 A1
Southall UB2 107 C1
Boundary Ct 3 N18 33 D4
Boundary Ho 1 SE5 139 A5
Balham SW12 159 B3
Isleworth TW1 153 B6
Boundary La E13,E6 99 D3
SE17 139 A6
Boundary Pas E2 243 C6
Boundary Rd DA15 167 C6
E13 99 D4
E17 53 C3
N9 18 C5
NW8 92 A6 229 B6
Boundary Rd N2 30 B2
Boundary Rd
Mitcham SW19 180 B4
Pinner HA5 40 D2
Tottenham N22 33 A1
Wallington SM5,SM6 219 A1
Boundary Road Est NW8 92 A6 229 A5
Boundary Row SE1 251 C2
Boundary St E2 95 D3 243 C6
Boundary Way CR0 223 C3
Boundfield Rd SE6 164 C2
Bounds Green Ct N11 31 D4
Bounds Green Ind Est N11 31 C4
Bounds Green Jun & Inf Schs N11 32 A3
Bounds Green Rd N11 31 D4
Wood Green N22 32 A2
Bounds Green Sta N11 31 D3
Bourbon Ho 9 SE6 186 A6
Bourchier St W1 249 C6
Bourdillon Ct 2 SE9 166 A2
Bourdon Pl W1 248 D6
Bourdon Rd SE20 184 C1
Bourdon St W1 115 B6 248 D5
Bourke Cl NW10 67 C2
SW4 160 A5
Bourlet Cl W1 239 A3
Bourn Ave N15 51 B5
Hillingdon UB8 82 C3
New Barnet EN4 14 B6
Bournbrook Rd SE3, SE9 143 D2
Bourne Ave
Hayes UB3 105 B3
Palmers Green N14 16 A2
Ruislip HA4 62 C3
Bourne Cir UB3 105 A3
Bourne Cl KT7 212 D6
Bourne Ct
Chiswick W4 133 A6
Ruislip HA4 62 B3
Wanstead E11 55 A4
Woodford IG8 37 D1
Bourne Dr CR4 180 B1
Bourne Gdns E4 35 D6
Bourne Hill N13 16 B2
Bourne Ho 1 NW2 68 A5
5 SW4 137 C1
Ashford TW15 170 C5
Buckhurst Hill IG9 21 D1
Bournemead Ave UB5 84 A5
Bournemead Cl UB5 84 A4
Bournemead Way UB5 84 B5
Bourne Mews W1 238 B1
Bournemouth Cl SE15 140 A3
Bournemouth Rd SE15 140 A3
Merton SW19 179 C2
Bourne Par DA5 169 D4
Bourne Pl W4 111 B1
Bourne Prim Sch HA4 62 C2
Bourne Rd DA5 169 D5
E7,E11 76 D5
N8 50 A3
Bromley BR2 209 D5
Bournes Ho 4 N15 51 C3
Bourneside 5 N14 15 D3
Bourneside Cres 6 N14 15 D3
Bourneside Gdns SE6 186 A5
Bourne St SW1 115 A2 258 A3
Croydon CR0 220 D6
Bourne Terr W2 91 D2
Bourne The N14 16 A2
Bourne Vale BR2 208 D1
Bournevale Rd SW16 182 A6
Bourne View UB6 64 D3
Bourne Way
Cheam SM1 217 B3
Coney Hall BR2,BR4 224 D6
West Ewell KT19 215 A4
Bournewood Rd SE18,SE2 146 A5
Bournville Rd SE6 163 C4
Bournwell Cl EN4 2 D3
Bourton Cl UB3 106 A5
Bousfield Prim Sch SW10 114 A1 256 A2
Bousfield Rd SE14 140 D3
Boutcher CE Prim Sch SE1 117 D2 263 C4
Boutflower Rd SW11 136 C1
Bouverie Gdns HA3 43 D3
Bouverie Mews N16 73 C6
Bouverie Pl W2 236 D2
Bouverie Rd N16 73 C6
Harrow HA1 42 A3
Bouverie St EC4 94 C1 241 B1
Bouvier Rd EN3 6 C5
Boveney Rd SE23 162 D4
Bovill Rd SE23 162 D4
Bovingdon Ave HA9 66 C2
Bovingdon Cl 3 N19 71 C6
Bovingdon La NW9 27 C2
Bovingdon Rd SW6 135 D4 265 D1
Bovril Ho EN1 5 C2
Bowater Cl NW9 45 B4
SW2 160 A5
Bowater Gdns TW16 172 B2
Bowater Ho EC1 242 B5
Bowater Pl SE3 143 B5
Bowater Rd SE18 121 D3
Bow Brook The 20 E2 96 D5
Bow Church Sta E3 97 C4
Bow Churchyard EC2, EC4 242 B1
Bow Common La E3 97 B3
Bowden Cl TW14 149 C3
Bowden Ho 29 E3 97 D4
Bowden House Hospl (Private) HA1 64 C6
Bowden St SE11 116 C1 261 B1
Bowditch SE8 119 B1
Bowdon Rd E17 53 C2
Bowen Ct 2 N5 72 D4
Bowen Dr SE21 161 C1
Bowen Rd HA1 42 A2
Bowen St E14 97 D1
Bower Ave SE3 142 C5
Bower Cl UB5 84 C5
Bowerdean St SW6 135 D3
Bower Ho SE14 140 D4
Bowerman Ave SE14 141 A6
Bowerman Ct 1 N19 71 D6
Bowers Ho 5 IG11 78 D1
Bower St E1 96 D1
Bowers Wlk 1 E6 100 B1
Bowes Cl DA15 168 B5
Bowes Park Sta N22 32 A3
Bowes Prim Sch N11 31 D5
Bowes Rd N11 31 C5
W3 111 C6
Dagenham RM8 80 C4
Walton-on-T KT12 194 B1
Bowes Rd (North Circular Rd) N13 32 A5
Bowfell Rd W6 134 C6
Bowford Ave DA7 147 A4
Bowhill Cl SW9 138 C5
Bowie Cl SW4 159 D4
Bow Ind Pk E15 75 C1
Bow La EC2,EC4 95 A1 242 B1
N12 30 A3
Bowland Ho N4 51 A2
Bowland Rd SW4 137 D1
Woodford IG8 37 C4
Bowland Yd SW1 247 D1
Bowl Ct EC2 243 B5
Bowles Ct N12 30 C3
Bowles Rd 1 SE1 140 A6
Bowley Cl SE19 183 D4
Bowley Ho 6 SE16 118 A3
Bowley La SE19 183 D5
Bowling Cl UB10 82 B6
Bowling Green Cl SW19 156 B4
Bowling Green Ct HA9 66 B6
Bowling Green Ho SW10 266 C4
Bowling Green La EC1 94 C3 241 B6
Bowling Green Pl SE1 252 C2
Bowling Green Row 1 SE18 122 B2
Bowling Green St SE11 138 C6
Bowling Green Wlk N1 95 C4
Bowls Cl HA7 25 B5
Bowman Ave E16 120 D6
Bowman Mews E1 118 A6
Wandsworth SW18 157 B3
Bowmans Cl W13 109 B5
Bowmans Lea SE23 162 C4
Bowman's Meadow SM6 219 B5
Bowman's Mews N7 72 A5
Bowman's Pl N7 72 A5
Bowmead SE9 166 B2
Bowmore Wlk NW1 71 D1
Bowness Cl 5 E8 73 D2
Bowness Cres KT2, SW15 177 C5
Bowness Dr TW4 129 A1
Bowness Ho SE15 140 C5
Bowness Rd DA7 147 D3
Catford SE6 163 D4
Bowood Rd SW11 159 A6
Enfield EN3 6 D3
Bow Rd E3 97 C4
Bowring Gn WD19 22 C5
Bow Road Sta E3 97 C4
Bowrons Ave HA0 65 D1
Bowry Ho 14 E14 97 B2
Bow Sch E3 97 C4
Bowsley Ct TW13 150 A2
Bowsprit Point 5 E14 119 C3
Bow St E15 76 C3
WC2 94 A1 240 B1
Bowstead Ct SW11 266 D1
Bow Triangle Bsns Ctr E3 97 C3
Bowyer Cl E6 100 B2
Bowyer Ct 4 E4 20 A3
Bowyer Ho 28 N1 95 C6
Wandsworth SW18 157 D5
Bowyer Pl SE5 139 A5
Bowyer St 15 SE5 139 A5
Boxall Rd SE21 161 C5
Boxgrove Prim Sch SE2 124 C3
Boxgrove Rd SE2 124 C3
Box La IG11 102 C5
Boxley Ho 3 E5 74 B3
Boxley Rd SM4 202 A5
Boxley St E16 121 B5
Boxmoor Ho 16 E2 96 A6
9 W11 112 D5
Boxmoor Rd HA3 43 B5
Boxoll Rd RM9 81 B5
Boxshall Ho 7 SE18 144 D6
Box Tree Ho SE8 119 A1
Boxtree La HA3 24 B3
Boxtree Rd HA3 24 B3
Boxwood Cl UB7 104 B4
Boxworth Cl N12 30 B5
Boxworth Gr N1 94 B6 233 D6
Boyard Rd SE18 122 D1
Boyce Ho 1 W10 91 B4
Streatham SW16 181 C5
Boyce St SE1 251 A3
Boyce Way E13 99 A3
Boycroft Ave NW9 45 A3
Boyd Ave UB1 107 B5
Boyd Cl KT2 176 C3
Boyd Ct SW15 156 C5
Boydell Ct NW8 70 B1
Boyden Ho 8 E17 54 A6
Boyd Rd SW19 180 B4
Boyd St E1 96 A1
Boyfield St SE1 116 D4 251 D1
Boyland Rd BR1 186 D5
Boyle Ave HA7 25 A4
Boyle Cl UB10 82 B5
Boyle Farm Rd KT7 197 A3
Boyle Ho 13 DA17 125 C3
Boyle St W1 249 A6
Boyne Ave NW4 46 D5
Boyne Ct NW10 68 A1
Boyne Ho 10 E5 74 B6
Boyne Rd SE13 142 B2
Dagenham RM10 81 C5
Boyne Terr Mews W11 113 B5 244 C4
Boyson Rd 10 SE17 139 B6
Boyton Cl E1 96 D3
N8 50 A6
Boyton Ho NW8 229 D4
SE11 261 A1
Boyton Rd N8 50 A6
Brabant Rd N22 32 B1
Brabazon Ave SM6 220 A1
Brabazon Rd
Heston TW5 128 D5
Northolt UB5 85 C5
Brabazon St E14 97 D2
Brabner Ho 2 E2 96 A4
Brabourne Cl 7 SE19 183 C5
Brabourne Cres DA7 147 B6
Brabourne Hts NW7 11 C1
Brabourne Rise BR3 208 B4
Brabourn Gr SE15 140 C3
Brabrook Ct SM6 219 B3
Brabstone Ho 2 UB6 86 D5
Bracer Ho 1 N1 95 C5
Bracewell Ave UB6 65 A2
Bracewell Rd W10 90 C2
Bracewood Gdns CR0 221 D5
Bracey St N4 72 A6
Bracken Ave
Balham SW12 159 A4
Croydon CR0 223 C5
Brackenbridge Dr HA4 62 D5
Brackenbury N4 50 B1
Brackenbury Gdns W6 112 B3
Brackenbury Prim Sch W6 112 B3
Brackenbury Rd N2 48 A6
W6 112 B3
Bracken Cl E6 100 B2
Ashford TW16 171 D4
Twickenham TW4 151 C4
Brackendale
Kingston KT1 176 D1
Southgate N21 16 B2
Brackendale Cl TW5 129 D4
Brackendale Ct 2 BR3 185 C3
Bracken End TW7 152 B6
Brackenfield Cl E5 74 B5
Bracken Gdns SW13 134 A3
Brackenhill HA4 63 A4
Bracken Hill Cl 5 BR1 186 D2
Bracken Hill La BR1 186 D2
Bracken Ho 14 E3 97 C2
Bracken Mews
Chingford E4 20 A3
Romford RM7 59 D3
Brackens BR3 185 C3
Brackens The EN1 17 C4
Bracken The E4 20 A2
Brackenwood TW16 172 A2
Brackenwood Lo EN5 1 C1
Brackley Cl SM6 220 A1
Brackley Ct NW8 236 D6
Brackley Rd W4 111 C1
Beckenham BR3 185 C3
Brackley Sq IG8 37 D3
Brackley St EC1 242 B4
Brackley Terr 6 W4 111 C1
Bracklyn Ct N1 235 C4
Bracklyn St N1 235 C4
Bracknell Cl N22 32 C2
Bracknell Gate NW3 69 D3
Bracknell Gdns NW3 69 D4
Bracknell Way NW3 69 D4
Bracondale KT10 212 A3
Bracondale Rd SE2 124 A2
Bradbeer Ho 24 E2 96 C4
Bradbourne Rd DA5 169 C4
Bradbourne St SW6 135 C3
Bradbury Cl UB2 107 B2
Bradbury Ct 2 SE3 143 A5
Bradbury Ho E1 243 D2
Bradbury St 28 N16 73 C3
Bradby Ho NW8 91 D5
Braddock Cl TW7 130 D3
Braddock Ho 9 NW6 91 D6
Braddon Rd TW9 132 B2
Braddyll St SE10 120 C1
Bradenham 11 SE17 139 B6
Bradenham Ave DA16 146 A1
Bradenham Cl SE17 139 B6
Bradenham Rd
Harrow HA3 43 B5
Hayes UB4 83 C4
Braden St W9 91 D3
Bradfield Ct 14 NW1 71 B1
Bradfield Dr IG11 80 A3
Bradfield Ho 15 SW8 137 D3
Bradfield Rd E16 121 B4
Ruislip HA4 63 A3
Bradford Cl BR2 210 B1
Forest Hill SE26 184 B6
Tottenham N17 33 D4
Bradford Dr KT19 215 D2
Bradford Ho 4 W14 112 D3
Bradford Rd W3 111 C4
Ilford IG1 57 C1
Bradgate Rd SE6 163 D5
Brading Cres E11 77 B6
Brading Rd
Streatham SW2 160 B4
Thornton Heath CR0 204 B3
Brading Terr W12 112 A3
Bradiston Rd W9 91 B4
Bradley Cl N7 72 B2
Bradley Ct CR0 220 C4
Bradley Gdns W13 87 B1
Bradley Ho 4 E2 96 B5
1 E3 97 D4
SE16 118 B2
Twickenham TW1 152 D3
Bradley Mews SW12 158 D3
Bradley Rd Enfield EN3 7 A6
South Norwood SE19 183 A4
Wood Green N22 32 B1
Bradley's Cl N1 234 B4
Bradley Stone Rd E6 100 B2
Bradlord Ho SE21 161 C1
Bradman Row 7 HA8 27 A3
Bradmead SW8 137 C5 269 A3
Bradmore Park Rd W6 112 B2
Bradon 24 NW9 27 D1
Bradshaw Cl SW19 179 C4
Bradshawe Waye UB8 82 B2
Bradshaws Cl SE25 206 A6
Bradsole Ho 13 BR3 185 C3
Brad St SE1 116 C5 251 B3
Bradstock Ho E9 75 A1
Bradstock Rd E9 74 D2
Stoneleigh KT17 216 B3
Bradwell Ave RM10 81 C6
Bradwell Cl E18 54 D5
Bradwell Ho 9 E17 53 D6
6 NW6 91 D6
Bradwell Mews 5 N18 34 A6
Brady Ct RM8 58 D1
Brady Ho SW4 159 D6
SW8 269 B2
Bradymead E6 100 D1
Brady St E1 96 B3
Braeburn Ct 1 EN4 2 C1
Brae Ct
2 Kingston KT2 176 C2
South Norwood SE25 183 C2
Braefoot Ct SW15 156 D6
Braemar SW15 156 D5
Braemar Ave NW10 67 B6
Thornton Heath CR7 204 D6
Wembley HA0 66 A1
Wimbledon SW18, SW19 157 C2
Wood Green N22 32 A2
Braemar Ct
4 Brentford TW8 131 D6
5 Catford SE6 164 D3
Braemar Gdns DA15 167 B1
NW9 27 B2
West Wickham BR4 208 A1
Braemar Ho W9 229 A1
Richmond TW11 175 B5
Braemar Mans W8 255 D5
Braemar Rd E13 98 D3
N15 51 C4
Brentford TW8 131 D6
North Cheam KT4 216 B5
Braemore Ct EN4 3 A1
Braemore Ho 21 SE15 140 A5
Braeside BR3 185 D5
Braeside Ave SW19 179 A2
Braeside Cl HA5 23 C3
Braeside Rd SW16 181 C3
Braeside Sch
Buckhurst Hill IG9 21 B3
Buckhurst Hill IG9 21 C2
Braes St N1 72 D1
Braesyde Cl DA17 125 B2
Brafferton Rd CR0 221 A4
Braganza St SE17 116 D1 261 C1
Bragg Cl RM8 80 B2
Bragg Rd TW11 174 D4
Braham Ho SE11 260 D1
Braham St E1 243 D2
Brahma Kumaris World Spiritual Univ NW10 68 A1
Braid Ave W3 89 C1
Braid Cl TW13 151 B2
Braid Ho SE10 142 A4
Braidwood Rd SE6 164 B3
Braidwood St SE1 117 C5 253 A3
Braikenridge Ho N21 17 B5
Brailsford Cl SW19 180 C3
Brailsford Rd SW2 160 C5
Braintcroft Prim Sch NW2 67 D5
Brainton Ave TW14 150 C4
Braintree Ave IG4 56 A5
Braintree Ho 5 E1 96 C3
Braintree Rd
Dagenham RM10 81 C5
Ruislip HA4 62 B4
Braintree St E2 96 C4
Braithwaite Ave RM7 59 C2
Braithwaite Gdns HA7 25 C2
Braithwaite Ho EC1 242 C6
14 South Bromley E14 98 B1
Braithwaite Rd EN3 7 B2
Braithwaite Twr W2 236 C4
Bramah Gn SW9 138 C4
Bramall Cl E15 76 D3
Bramall Ct N7 72 B2
Bramber WC1 233 A1
Bramber Ct TW8 110 A2
Bramber Rd N12 30 C5
W14 135 B6 264 C6
Bramble Acres Cl SM2 217 C1
Bramblebury Rd SE18 123 A1
Bramble Cl N15 52 A5
Beckenham BR3 208 A4
Croydon CR0 223 D4
Hillingdon UB8 82 B1
Stanmore HA7 25 D3
Upper Halliford TW17 193 B6
Brambledown 4 N4 50 A2
Brambledown Cl BR2, BR4 208 C4
Brambledown Rd
South Croydon CR2 221 C1
Wallington SM5,SM6 219 B1
Bramble Gdns W12 111 D6
Bramble Ho 12 E3 97 C2
Bramble La TW12 173 B4
Brambles Cl TW7, TW8 131 B5
Brambles Farm Dr UB10 82 C4
Brambles The
West Drayton UB7 104 A2
8 Wimbledon SW19 179 B5
Bramblewood Cl SM5 202 C1
Brambling Ct 25 SE8 141 B6
Bramblings The E4 36 B6
Bramcote Ave CR4 202 D5
Bramcote Ct CR4 202 D5
Bramcote Gr SE16 118 C1
Bramcote Rd SW15 134 B1
Bramdean Cres SE12 165 A3
Bramdean Gdns SE12 165 A3
Bramerton NW6 68 D1
Bramerton Rd BR3 207 B6
Bramerton St SW3 136 C6 267 A6
Bramfield Ct N4 73 A6
Bramfield Rd SW11 158 D6
Bramford Ct N14 15 D2
Bramford Rd SW18 136 A1
Bramham Gdns SW5 113 D1 255 D2
Chessington KT9 213 D4

Bramham Ho SE22 ...**139** C1
Bramhope La SE7 ...**143** B6
Bramlands Cl SW11 .**136** C2
Bramlea Cl N6 ....**49** A3
Bramley Ave TW17 .**193** C6
Bramley Cl E17 ....**35** A1
Croydon CR2 ....**221** A3
East Barnet N14 .....**15** B6
Hayes UB3 ....**106** A6
Orpington BR6 ....**210** D1
Pinner HA5 ....**39** D6
Twickenham TW2 ...**152** A5
Woodford IG8 ....**37** C3
Bramley Cres
SW8 ....**137** D5 **269** D4
Ilford IG2 ....**56** C3
Bramley Ct DA16 ..**146** B4
NW2 ....**68** B5
2 Barnet EN4 ....**2** C1
9 Chingford E4 ....**20** A3
Feltham TW14 ......**149** C5
Mitcham CR4 ......**180** A1
Southall UB1 ....**108** A6
Wallington SM6 ....**219** C3
Bramley Gdns SW19 ..**22** C5
Bramley Hill CR2 ..**221** A4
Bramley Ho **19** W10 ..**90** D1
Hounslow TW3 ......**129** B1
Ilford IG2 ....**56** C3
1 Kingston KT2 ...**176** D3
5 Roehampton SW15 ..**155** D5
Bramley House Ct EN2 ..**5** B6
Bramleyhyrst CR2 ..**221** A3
Bramley Lo HA0 .....**65** D4
Bramley Rd W10 .....**90** D1
W5 ....**109** C3
Southgate N14 ....**15** C6
Sutton SM1 ....**218** B3
Bramley Way
Hounslow TW4 ......**151** B6
West Wickham BR4 ..**223** D6
Brampton Cl **14** E5 ..**74** B6
Brampton Ct NW4 ...**46** B5
Harrow HA3 ....**43** B5
Wembley HA9 ....**44** C1
Brampton La **4** NW4 .**46** C5
Brampton Manor Sch
E6 ....**99** D3
Brampton Park Rd
N22 ....**50** C6
Brampton Prim Sch
E6 ....**100** A4
Bexley DA16 ....**146** D3
Brampton Rd DA7 ...**147** A4
E6 ....**99** D4
N15 ....**51** A4
NW9 ....**44** C5
Croydon CR0 ....**205** D4
Hillingdon UB10 .....**82** D5
Bramshaw Gdns
WD3 ....**22** D5
Bramshaw Rd E9 .....**74** D2
Bramshaw Rise KT3 .**199** C3
Bramshill Gdns NW5 .**71** B5
Bramshill Rd NW10 ..**89** D5
Bramshot Ave SE7 ..**143** B6
Bramshott Ct **3** KT6 ..**198** A3
Bramshurst NW8 .....**91** D6
Bramston Rd NW10 ..**90** A5
Wandsworth SW17 ..**158** A1
Bramwell Cl TW16 ..**172** D1
Bramwell Ho SE1 ...**262** B5
SW1 ....**269** A6
Bramwell Mews N1 .**233** D6
Brancaster Dr NW7 ..**28** A3
Brancaster Ho **22** E1 ..**96** D4
N5 ....**72** D3
Brancaster Rd
Ilford E12 ....**78** B4
Ilford IG2 ....**57** C3
Streatham SW16 ....**160** A1
Brancepeth Gdns IG9 .**21** A2
Branch Hill NW3 .....**70** A5
Branch Pl N1 ..**95** B6 **235** D6
Branch Rd E14 .....**119** A6
Branch St SE15 ....**139** C5
Brancker Cl SM6 ...**220** A1
Brancker Rd HA3 ....**43** D6
Brancroft Way EN3 ....**7** B4
Brand Cl N4 ....**50** D1
Brandlehow Rd
SW15 ....**135** B1
Brandon Ho BR3 ...**185** D5
Brandon Mews EC2 .**242** C4
Brandon Rd E17 .....**54** A6
N7 ....**72** A1

Brandon Rd continued
Southall UB2 ....**107** B1
Sutton SM1 ....**217** D4
Brandon St
SE17 ......**117** A2 **262** B3
Brandram Rd SE13 .**142** C1
Brandrams Wharf
SE16 ....**118** D4
Brandreth Ct HA1 ...**42** D3
Brandreth Rd
Newham E6 ....**100** B1
Upper Tooting SW17 .**159** B2
Brandries The SM6 .**219** D5
Brand St SE10 .....**142** A5
Brandville Gdns IG6 .**56** D5
Brandville Rd UB7 .**104** A4
Brandy Way SM2 ...**217** C1
Brangbourne Rd BR1 .**186** A5
Brangton Rd **1** SE11 .**260** D1
Brangwyn Cres SW19 **180** B1
Brangwyn Ct W14 ..**254** A5
Branham Ho **1** SE18 .**122** D1
Branksea St
SW6 ....**135** A3 **264** A3
Branksome Ave N18 ..**33** D5
Branksome Cl KT12 .**194** D1
Branksome Ct **6** N2 ..**48** A6
Branksome Ho SW8 .**270** C4
Branksome Rd SW2 .**160** A6
Merton SW19 ......**179** C2
Branksome Way
Harrow HA3 ....**44** B3
Kingston KT3 ......**177** B2
Bransby Ct **4** N16 ....**73** C4
Bransby Rd KT9 ....**214** A2
Branscombe NW1 ..**232** B5
Branscombe St SE13 **141** D2
Branscombe Gdns
N21 ....**16** C4
Bransdale Cl NW6 ...**91** C6
Bransgrove Rd HA8 ..**26** B3
Branston Cres BR5 ..**211** B1
Branstone St **9** TW9 **132** B4
Branstone Rd TW9 ..**132** B4
Branston Ho N7 ......**72** C4
Brants Wlk W7 ....**86** C3
Brantwood Ave DA8 .**147** D5
Isleworth TW7 ......**131** A1
Brantwood Cl E17 ....**53** D6
Brantwood Gdns
Enfield EN2 ....**16** A6
Redbridge IG4 ......**56** A5
Brantwood Ho **9**
SE5 ....**139** A5
Brantwood Rd DA7 .**147** D2
SE24 ....**161** A6
Tottenham N17 ......**34** A4
Brasenose Dr SW13 .**134** C6
Brasher Cl UB6 ......**64** B3
Brassett Point **3** E15 ..**98** C6
Brassey Cl TW14 ...**150** A3
Brassey Ho **1** E14 ..**119** D2
Walton-on-T KT12 ..**194** A1
Brassey Rd NW6 ....**69** B2
Brassey Sq SW11 ..**137** A2
Brassie Ave W3 ......**89** C1
Brass Talley Alley **31**
SE16 ....**118** D4
Brasted Cl DA6 ....**168** D6
Forest Hill SE26 ....**184** C6
Brasted Lo **11** BR3 ..**185** C3
Brathay NW1 ....**232** B3
Brathway Rd SW18 .**157** C4
Bratley St **12** E1 .....**96** A3
Bratten Ct CR0 ....**205** B3
Braund Ave UB6 ......**85** D3
Braundton Ave DA15 **167** D3
Braunston Dr UB4 ...**85** A3
Bravington Cl TW17 .**192** B4
Bravington Pl W9 ...**91** B3
Bravington Rd W9 ...**91** B4
Brawne Ho **12** SE17 .**138** D6
Braxfield Rd SE4 ...**141** B1
Braxted Pk SW16 ..**182** B4
Bray NW3 ....**70** C1
Brayard's Rd SE15 .**140** B3
Braybourne Dr TW7 .**130** D5
Braybrooke Gdns
SE19 ....**183** C1
Braybrook St W12 ...**89** D1
Brayburne Ave SW4 .**137** C3
Braycourt Ave KT12 .**194** C2
Bray Cres SE16 ....**118** D4
Bray Ct
Chessington KT9 ..**214** B3
Streatham SW16 ...**182** A6
Braydon Rd N16 .....**52** A1
Bray Dr E16 ....**120** D6
Brayfield Terr N1 ....**72** A1

Brayford Sq **12** E1 ...**96** C1
Bray Pl SW3 ..**114** D2 **257** C3
Bray Rd NW7 ....**28** D4
Brayton Gdns EN2 ....**3** D1
Braywick Ct **9** KT2 .**176** C3
Braywood Rd SE9 ..**145** B1
Brazil Cl CR0 ......**204** A2
Breach La RM9 ....**103** C4
Bread St EC2,EC4 ..**242** B1
Breakspeare SE21 .**161** D1
Breakspear Jun & Inf Schs
UB10 ....**60** C6
Breakspear Rd HA4,
UB9 ....**38** D3
Breakspear Rd N UB9 .**38** B5
Breakspear Rd S UB9,
UB10 ....**38** C1
Breakspears Dr BR5 .**190** A2
Breakspears Mews
SE4 ....**141** C3
Breakspears Rd SE4 .**141** C2
Breakwell Ct **16** W10 .**91** A3
Bream Cl N17 ....**52** B5
Bream Gdns E6 ....**100** C4
Breamore Cl SW15 .**156** A4
Breamore Ct IG3 .....**80** A6
Breamore Rd IG3 ....**79** D6
Bream's Bldgs
EC4 ....**94** C1 **241** A2
Bream St E3 ....**75** C1
Breamwater Gdns
TW10 ....**153** B1
Brearley Cl HA8 ......**27** A3
Uxbridge UB8 ....**60** A2
Breaside Prep Sch
BR1 ....**187** D2
Breasley Cl SW15 ..**134** B1
Brechin Pl
SW7 ....**114** A2 **256** B3
Brecknock Prim Sch
NW1 ....**71** D2
Brecknock Rd N19 ..**71** D3
Breckonmead BR1 ..**187** C1
Breco Ho IG11 .....**102** B4
Brecon Cl
Mitcham CR4 ......**204** A6
North Cheam KT4 ..**216** C6
Brecon Ct N12 ......**14** A1
7 SE9 ....**166** C5
Brecon Gn NW9 .....**45** C3
Brecon Ho N16 ......**51** D1
W2 ....**236** A2
Wandsworth SW18 .**157** C4
Brecon Rd
W6 ....**135** A6 **264** B5
Enfield EN3 ....**6** C1
Brede Cl E6 ....**100** C4
Bredel Ho **1** E14 ....**97** C2
Bredgar SE13 ......**163** D6
Bredgar Rd N19 .....**71** C6
Bredhurst Cl SE20 .**184** C4
Bredinghurst SE22 .**162** A4
Bredinghurst Sch
SE15 ....**140** D1
Bredon Ct HA8 ......**26** B6
Bredon Rd CR0 ....**205** D2
Breer St SW6 ......**135** D2
Breezer's Ct **15** E1 .**118** A6
Breezer's Hill E1 ..**118** A6
Bremans Row SW18 .**158** A2
Brember Rd HA2 .....**64** A6
Bremer Mews E17 ....**53** D5
Bremner Rd SW7 ..**256** B6
Brenchley Cl
Chislehurst BR7 ...**188** C2
Hayes BR2 ....**208** D3
Brenchley Gdns SE15,
SE22,SE23 ....**162** D5
Brenchley Rd BR5 .**189** D1
Brenda Rd SW17 ..**158** D2
Brende Gdns KT8 ..**195** D5
Brendon Ave NW10 ..**67** C4
Brendon Cl
Esher KT10 ....**212** A2
Harlington UB7 ....**127** A5
Brendon Ct UB2 ...**107** D2
Brendon Dr KT10 ..**212** A2
Brendon Gdns
Harrow HA2 ....**63** D4
Ilford IG2 ....**57** C4
Brendon Gr N2 ....**30** A1
Brendon H SM2 ....**218** A4
Brendon Ho W1 ....**238** A4
Brendon Rd BR7 ...**167** B2
Dagenham RM8 .....**59** C1
Brendon St
W1 ......**92** C1 **237** B2
Brendon Villas N21 ..**17** A3
Brendon Way EN1 ...**17** C4
Brenley Cl CR4 ....**203** A6

Brenley Gdns SE9 .**143** D1
Brenley Ho SE1 ....**252** C2
Brent Cl DA5 ......**169** A3
Brentcot Cl W13 .....**87** B3
Brent Cres NW10 ....**88** B5
Brent Cross Flyover
NW2,NW4 ....**46** D2
Brent Cross Gdns
NW4 ....**46** D2
Brent Cross Interchange
NW2,NW4 ....**46** D2
Brent Cross Sh Ctr
NW4 ....**46** C2
Brent Cross Sta NW11 **46** D2
Brent Ct NW11 ....**46** D2
5 W12 ....**111** C3
Ealing W7 ....**108** B6
Brentfield NW10 .....**66** D1
Brentfield Cl NW10 ..**67** B2
Brentfield Gdns NW2 .**46** D2
Brentfield Ho **6**
NW10 ....**67** B1
Brentfield Prim Sch
NW10 ....**67** B2
Brentfield Rd NW10 ..**67** B2
Brentford Bsns Ctr
TW8 ....**131** C5
Brentford Ct UB4 ....**84** D3
Brentford Fountain Leisure
Centre W4 ....**110** C1
Brentford Ho **6** TW1 **153** B4
Brentford Sch for Girls
TW8 ....**131** D6
Brentford Sta TW8 .**131** C6
Brent Gn NW4 ....**46** D4
Brentham Way W5 ...**87** D3
Brent Ho **15** E9 ....**74** C2
3 Catford BR1 ......**186** B5
Brenthouse Rd E9 ...**74** C2
Brenthurst Rd NW10 ..**67** B2
Brent Knoll Sch SE26 **162** D1
Brent Lea TW8 .....**131** C5
Brent Mans NW4 ....**46** C4
Brentmead Cl W7 ..**108** C4
Brentmead Gdns
NW10 ....**88** B5
Brentmead Pl NW11 .**46** D3
Brent New Ent Ctr
NW10 ....**67** B2
Brenton Ct E9 ....**75** A3
Brenton St E14 ......**97** A1
Brent Park Ind Est
UB2 ....**106** C3
Brent Park Rd NW4 ..**46** B2
Brent Pl EN5 ....**13** B6
Brent Rd E16 ....**99** A2
Brentford TW8 .....**131** C6
Southall UB2 ......**106** C3
Woolwich SE18 ...**144** D5
Brent Side TW8 ...**131** C5
Brentside Cl W13 ....**87** A3
Brentside Executive Ctr
TW8 ....**131** B6
Brentside High Sch
W7 ....**86** C6
Brentside Prim Sch
W7 ....**86** C3
Brent St NW4 ....**46** C4
Brent Trad Est NW10 .**67** C3
Brentvale Ave
Southall UB1 ......**108** B5
Wembley HA0 ....**88** B6
Brent View Rd NW9 ..**46** A2
Brentwaters Bsns Pk
TW8 ....**131** C5
Brent Way N3 ....**29** C4
Brentford TW8 .....**131** D6
Wembley HA9 ....**66** D2
Brentwick Gdns TW8 **110** A2
Brentwood Cl SE9 .**167** A3
Brentwood Ho **2**
SE18 ....**143** D5
Brentwood Lo NW4 ..**46** D4
Brereton Ho **4** SW2 .**160** C4
Brereton Rd N17 .....**33** D3
Bressenden Pl
SW1 ......**115** C3 **259** A6
Bressey Ave EN1 ......**6** A4
Bressey Gr E18 ......**36** C1
Bretherton Ct CR2 .**221** C2
Breton EC2 ....**242** B5
SE1 ....**263** C6
Brett Cl N16 ....**73** C6
15 Northolt UB5 ......**84** D4
Brett Cres NW10 ....**89** B6
Brett Ct N9 ....**18** C2
Brettell St SE17 ...**262** D1
Brettenham Ave E17 ..**35** C2
Brettenham Prim Sch
N18 ....**34** A6

Brettenham Rd
Chingford E17 ....**35** C2
Edmonton N18 ....**34** A6
Brett Gdns RM9 .....**81** A1
Brett Ho **1** SW15 ...**156** A4
Brett House Cl **2**
SW15 ....**156** A4
Brettinghurst **7** SE1 .**118** A1
Brett Manor E8 ......**74** B1
Bretton Ho N19 ......**50** A1
Brett Pas **28** E8 ......**74** B3
Brett Rd E8 ....**74** B3
Barnet EN5 ....**12** C1
Brewers Bldgs EC1 .**234** C2
Brewers Ct W2 .....**236** A2
Brewer's Gn SW1 ..**259** C6
Brewers La **11** TW9 .**153** D6
Brewer St
W1 ......**115** C6 **249** B6
Brewery Cl HA0 ......**65** A4
Brewery Ind Est The
N1 ....**235** B3
Brewery Mews Bsns Ctr **1**
TW7 ....**131** A2
Brewery Rd N7 ....**72** A1
SE18 ....**123** B1
Keston Mark BR2 ..**210** A1
Brewery Sq **5** SE1 ..**253** C3
Brewhouse La E1 ..**118** B5
SE18 ....**122** B2
Brewhouse Rd **3**
SE18 ....**122** B2
Brewhouse St SW15 **135** A2
Brewhouse Wlk SE16 **119** A3
Brewhouse Yd EC1 .**241** C6
Brewood Rd RM8 ....**80** B2
Brewster Gdns W10 ..**90** C2
Brewster Ho E14 ....**119** B6
SE1 ....**263** D4
Brewster Rd E10 ....**53** D1
Brian Ct N10 ....**31** B2
Brian Rd RM6 ....**58** C4
Briant Ho SE1 .....**260** D5
Briants Cl HA5 ....**23** B1
Briant St SE14 .....**140** D5
Briar Ave SW16 ....**182** A3
Briar Cl N2 ....**30** A1
Buckhurst Hill IG9 ...**21** D2
Edmonton N13 ....**17** A1
Hampton TW12 .....**173** B5
Isleworth TW7 ......**152** D6
Briar Cres UB5 ......**63** D2
Briar Ct E8 ....**73** B2
E8 ....**73** D1
Cheam SM3 ....**216** C4
Hampton TW12 ....**173** D5
Briardale HA8 ....**27** B6
Wandsworth SW19 .**157** B3
Briardale Gdns NW3 ..**69** C5
Briardale Ho N16 ....**51** C1
Briarfield Ave N3 ....**29** D1
Briar Gdns BR2 ....**208** A1
Briaris Cl **11** N17 ....**34** B3
Briar La CR0 ....**223** D4
Briar Lo E18 ....**37** C2
Briar Rd NW2 ....**68** C4
Harrow HA3 ....**43** C4
Littleton TW17 .....**192** C4
Thornton Heath SW16 **204** B6
Twickenham TW2 ..**152** C3
Briars The WD23 ......**8** C4
Briarswood Way BR6 **227** D3
Briarview Ct **4** E4 ....**36** B4
Briar Way UB7 .....**104** C4
Briar Wlk HA8 ....**27** A3
W10 ....**91** A3
Briarwood Cl NW9 ...**45** A3
Feltham TW13 .....**149** C5
Briarwood Ct **5** KT4 .**200** A1
Briarwood Dr HA6 ...**22** A1
Briarwood Rd SW4 .**159** D6
Stoneleigh KT17 ..**216** A4
Briary Cl NW3 ....**70** C1
Briary Ct DA14 ....**190** B5
Barnet EN5 ....**187** B5
Briary Gdns BR1 ...**187** B5
Briary Gr HA8 ....**26** D1
Briary La N9 ....**17** C1
Brick Ct EC4 ....**241** A1
Brickett Cl HA4 ......**39** A4
Brick Farm Cl TW9 .**132** D4
Brickfield Cl TW8 ..**131** C5
Brickfield Cotts SE18 **145** D6
Brickfield Farm Gdns
BR6 ....**227** A4
Brickfield La
Edgware EN5 ....**11** D5
Harlington UB3 ....**127** B6

Brickfield Rd
South Norwood CR7,
SW16 ....**182** D2
Wimbledon SW19 .**179** D6
Brickfields HA2 ......**64** B6
Brickfields Way UB7 **104** B3
Brick La E1 ..**95** D3 **243** D5
E2 ....**95** D4
Enfield EN1 ....**6** B3
Stanmore HA7 ....**25** D3
Bricklayers Arms
SE1 ....**262** D5
Brick St W1 ..**115** B5 **248** C3
Brickwall La HA4 ....**39** D1
Brickwood Cl SE26 .**162** B1
Brickwood Rd CR0 .**221** C6
Brickworth Ho **26**
SW9 ....**138** C4
Bridal Mews N1 ....**234** C5
Brideale Cl SE15 ..**139** D2
Bride Ct EC4 ....**241** C1
Bride La EC4 ..**94** D1 **241** C1
Bride St N7 ....**72** B2
Bridewain St SE1 ..**263** C6
Bridewell Pl **20** E1 ..**118** B5
EC4 ....**241** C1
Bridford Mews W1 .**238** D4
Bridge App NW3 .....**71** A1
Bridge Ave W6 ....**112** C1
Ealing W7 ....**86** B2
Bridge Avenue Mans **1**
W6 ....**112** C1
Bridge Cl **13** W10 ....**90** D1
Enfield EN1 ....**6** B3
Teddington TW11 ..**174** D6
Walton-on-T KT12 .**193** D1
Bridge Ct E10 ....**53** B2
Bridge Dr N13 ....**32** B6
Bridge End E17 ......**36** A2
Bridge Field Ho **7**
W2 ....**91** D1
Bridge Gate N21 .....**17** A4
Bridge Gdns
East Molesey KT8 .**196** B5
Littleton TW15 ....**171** A3
Bridge Ho E9 ....**74** D3
1 NW1 ....**71** A1
SE4 ....**141** B1
TW8 ....**109** A2
Bridge Ho S TW8 ..**109** A2
Bridge House Quay
E14 ....**120** A5
Bridge La NW11 .....**47** B4
SW11 ......**136** C4 **267** B1
Bridgeland Rd E16 .**121** A6
Bridgeman Ho **19** E9 ..**74** C1
Bridgeman Rd N1 ....**72** B1
Teddington TW11 ..**175** A4
Bridgeman St
NW8 ....**92** C5 **230** A3
Bridge Meadows
SE14 ....**140** D6
Bridgend Rd SW18 .**136** A1
Bridgenhall Rd EN1 ...**5** D4
Bridgen Ho **15** E1 ....**96** B1
Bridgen Rd DA5 ....**169** A4
Bridge Par N21 ......**17** A4
Bridge Pk **7** SW18 .**157** C6
Wembley NW10 ......**66** D1
Bridge Pl
SW1 ......**115** B2 **258** D4
Croydon CR0 ......**205** B1
Bridgeport Pl **4** E1 .**118** A5
Bridge Rd DA7 .....**147** A3
E15 ....**98** B6
E17 ....**53** B2
E6 ....**78** B1
NW10 ....**67** C2
Beckenham BR3 ...**185** B3
Chessington KT9 ..**214** A3
East Molesey KT8 .**196** C4
Edmonton N9 ....**18** A1
Hounslow TW3 ....**130** A2
Isleworth TW3,TW7 **130** A2
Southall UB2 ......**107** C4
Sutton SM2 ....**217** D2
Twickenham TW1 ..**153** B5
Wallington SM6 ...**219** C3
Wembley HA9 ....**66** C5
Wood Green N22 ....**32** A2
Bridge Row CR0 ...**205** B1
Bridges Ct SW11 ..**136** B3
Bridges Ho **15** SE5 .**139** B5
Bridges La CR0 ....**220** A6
Bridges Rd
Stanmore HA7 ......**24** D5

Bridges Rd *continued*
Wimbledon SW19 ... 179 D4
Bridges Road Mews
SW19 ... 179 D4
Bridge St
SW1 ... 116 A4 250 B1
W4 ... 111 B2
Pinner HA5 ... 41 A6
Richmond TW10 ... 153 D6
Walton-on-T KT12 ... 193 D2
Bridge Terr E15 ... 76 B1
Bridge The HA3 ... 42 D5
Bridgetown Cl 5
SE19 ... 183 C5
Bridgeview 2 W6 ... 112 C1
Bridgewater Cl BR5,
BR7 ... 211 C6
Bridgewater Ct HA0 ... 65 C2
Bridgewater Gdns
HA8 ... 26 B1
Bridgewater Rd E15 ... 98 A6
Ruislip HA4 ... 62 B4
Wembley HA0 ... 65 C1
Bridgewater Sq EC2 ... 242 A4
Bridgewater St EC2 ... 242 A4
Bridge Way NW11 ... 47 B4
Bridgeway
Barking IG11 ... 79 D1
Wembley HA0 ... 66 B1
Bridge Way
Twickenham TW2 ... 152 A4
Uxbridge UB10 ... 60 D3
Bridgeway St
NW1 ... 93 C5 232 B3
Bridge Wharf 18 E2 ... 96 D5
Bridge Wharf Rd
TW7 ... 131 B2
Bridgewood Cl SE20 ... 184 B3
Bridgewood Rd
North Cheam KT17,KT4 216 A4
Streatham SW16 ... 181 D3
Bridge Yd SE1 ... 252 D4
Bridgford St SW17,
SW18 ... 158 A1
Bridgman Rd W4 ... 111 A3
Bridgnorth Ho 10
SE15 ... 140 A6
Bridgwater Ho W2 ... 236 A2
Bridle Cl Enfield EN3 ... 7 B6
Kingston KT1 ... 197 D5
Sunbury TW16 ... 194 A6
West Ewell KT19 ... 215 B3
Bridle La W1 .115 C6 249 B6
Twickenham TW1 ... 153 B5
Bridle Path CR0 ... 220 A5
Bridle Path The IG8 ... 36 C3
Bridlepath Way
TW14 ... 149 C3
Bridle Rd
Addington CR0 ... 223 C4
Claygate KT10 ... 213 B2
Croydon CR0 ... 223 C5
Pinner HA5 ... 40 C4
Bridle Way BR6 ... 227 A4
Addington CR0 ... 223 C3
Bridle Way The SM6 ... 219 C3
Bridlington Ho SW18 136 A1
Bridlington Rd N9 ... 18 B4
Bridport SE17 ... 262 B1
Bridport Ave RM7 ... 59 D3
Bridport Ho N1 ... 235 D5
6 Edmonton N18 ... 34 A5
Bridport Pl N1 95 B6 235 D5
Bridport Rd
Edmonton N18 ... 33 D5
Greenford UB6 ... 85 D6
Thornton Heath CR7 ... 204 D6
Bridstow Pl W2 ... 91 C1
Brief St SE5 ... 138 D4
Brierfield NW1 ... 232 A5
Brierley CR0 ... 223 D2
Brierley Ave N9 ... 18 C3
Brierley Cl SE25 ... 206 A5
Brierley Ct W7 ... 108 C6
Brierley Rd E11 ... 76 B4
Upper Tooting SW12 ... 159 C2
Brierly Gdns E2 ... 96 C5
Brigade Cl HA2 ... 64 B6
Brigade St SE3 ... 142 D3
Brigadier Ave EN2 ... 5 A4
Brigadier Hill EN2 ... 5 A5
Briggeford Cl 5 E5 ... 74 A6
Briggs Cl CR4 ... 181 B2
Briggs Ho 20 E2 ... 95 D4
Bright Cl DA17 ... 124 D2
Bright Ct 8 SE28 ... 124 C5
Brightfield Rd SE12 ... 164 D6
Brightling Rd SE4 ... 163 B5
Brightlingsea Pl 5
E14 ... 119 B6
Brightman Rd SW18 ... 158 B3
Brighton Ave E17 ... 53 B4
Brighton Bldgs SE1 ... 263 A5
Brighton Cl UB10 ... 60 D1
Brighton Ct SW15 ... 157 B5
Brighton Dr 3 UB5 ... 63 C2
Brighton Gr SE14 ... 141 A4
Brighton Ho 7 SE5 ... 139 B4
Brighton Rd N16 ... 73 C4
N2 ... 30 A1
Belmont SM2 ... 217 D1
South Croydon CR2 ... 221 B2
Surbiton KT6 ... 197 D3
Sutton SM2 ... 218 A1
Wallend E6 ... 100 C4
Brighton Terr SW9 ... 138 B1
Brightside Rd SE13 ... 164 B5
Brightside The EN3 ... 7 A4
Bright St E14 ... 97 D2
Brightwell Cl CR0 ... 204 C1
Brightwell Cres
SW17 ... 180 D5
Brightwell Ct N7 ... 72 B3
Brightwells 1 SW6 ... 135 D3
Brig Mews SE8 ... 141 C6
Brigstock Ho SE5 ... 139 A3
Brigstock Rd
Belvedere DA17 ... 125 D2
Thornton Heath CR7 ... 204 D4
Brill Ho NW10 ... 67 B5
Brill Pl NW1 ... 93 D5 232 D3
Brim Hill N2 ... 48 B5
Brimpsfield Cl SE2 ... 124 B3
Brimsdown Ave EN3 ... 7 A4
Brimsdown Ho E3 ... 98 A3
Brimsdown Jun & Inf Sch
EN3 ... 6 D2
Brimsdown Sta EN3 ... 7 A3
Brimstone Ho 3 E15 ... 76 C1
Brindishe Prim Sch
SE12 ... 164 D6
Brindle Gate DA15 ... 167 C3
Brindley Cl DA7 ... 147 C2
Wembley HA0 ... 87 D6
Brindley Ho 37 W2 ... 91 C2
22 Streatham SW12 ... 160 A4
Brindley St SE14 ... 141 B4
Brindley Way BR1 ... 187 B5
Southall UB1 ... 107 D6
Brindwood Rd E4 ... 19 C1
Brine Ct KT6 ... 197 D4
Brine Ho 10 E3 ... 97 A5
Brinkburn Cl SE2 ... 124 A2
Edgware HA8 ... 44 D6
Brinkburn Gdns HA8 ... 44 C6
Brinkley 18 KT1 ... 176 C1
Brinkley Rd KT4 ... 216 B6
Brinklow Cres SE18 ... 144 D5
Brinklow Ho W2 ... 91 D2
Brinkworth Rd IG5 ... 56 A6
Brinkworth Way E9 ... 75 B2
Brinsdale Rd NW4 ... 46 D6
Brinsley Ho 17 E1 ... 96 C1
Brinsley Rd HA3 ... 24 B1
Brinsley St 29 E1 ... 96 B1
Brinsworth Cl TW2 ... 152 B2
Brinton Wlk SE1 ... 251 C3
Brion Pl E14 ... 98 A2
Brisbane Ave SW19 ... 179 D2
Brisbane Ct N10 ... 31 B3
Brisbane Ho 3 W12 ... 112 B6
Brisbane Rd E10 ... 75 D6
Ealing W13 ... 109 A4
Ilford IG1 ... 57 A1
Brisbane St SE5 ... 139 B5
Briscoe Cl E11 ... 76 D6
Briscoe Rd SW19 ... 180 B4
Briset Rd SE9 ... 143 D1
Briset St EC1 ... 94 D3 241 C5
Briset Way N7 ... 72 B6
Bristol Cl
Stanwell TW19 ... 148 A5
Wallington SM6 ... 220 A1
Bristol Ct 11 TW19 ... 148 A5
Bristol Gdns W9 ... 91 D3
Bristol Ho SE11 ... 261 A5
1 Barking IG11 ... 80 A1
Bristol Mews W9 ... 91 D3
Bristol Park Rd 1 E17 53 A5
Bristol Rd E7 ... 77 D2
Greenford UB6 ... 85 D6
Morden SM4 ... 202 A4
Briston Gr N8 ... 50 A3
Briston Mews NW7 ... 28 A3
Bristow Rd DA7 ... 147 A4
Hounslow TW3 ... 130 A2
Wallington CR0 ... 220 A4
West Norwood SE19 ... 183 C5
Britannia Cl SW4 ... 137 D1
Northolt UB5 ... 84 D4
Britannia Gate 12
E16 ... 121 A5
Britannia Junc NW1 ... 231 D6
Britannia La TW2 ... 152 A4
Britannia Rd 11 E14 ... 119 C2
N12 ... 14 A1
SW6 ... 135 D5 265 C3
Ilford IG1 ... 78 D5
Surbiton KT5 ... 198 B2
Britannia Row
N1 ... 95 A6 235 A6
Britannia St
WC1 ... 94 B4 233 C2
Britannia Way
Acton NW10 ... 88 D3
Stanwell TW19 ... 148 A4
Britannia Wlk N1 ... 235 C2
British Gr W4 ... 111 D1
British Grove Pas 2
W4 ... 111 D1
British Grove S 3
W4 ... 111 D1
British Home & Hospl for
Incurables SE27 ... 182 D5
British Legion Rd E4 ... 20 D2
British Library (Newspaper
Library) NW9 ... 45 C6
British Library The★
WC1 ... 93 D4 232 D2
British Mus★
WC1 ... 94 A2 240 A3
British St E3 ... 97 B4
British Wharf Ind Est
SE14 ... 140 D6
Britley Ho 10 E14 ... 97 B1
Brittain Ct SE9 ... 166 A3
Brittain Ho SE9 ... 166 A3
Brittain Rd RM8 ... 81 B5
Brittany Ho SW15 ... 134 C1
Brittany Point SE11 ... 261 A3
Britten Cl NW11 ... 47 D1
Elstree WD6 ... 9 D5
Brittenden Cl 1 BR6 227 D2
Brittenden Par BR6 ... 227 D2
Britten Dr UB1 ... 85 C1
Britten Ho SW3 ... 257 B2
Britten St
SW3 ... 114 C1 257 A2
Britton Cl SE6 ... 164 B4
Britton St EC1 .94 D2 241 C5
Brixham Cres HA4 ... 40 A1
Brixham Gdns IG3 ... 79 C3
Brixham Rd DA16 ... 146 D4
Brixham St E16 ... 122 C5
Brixton Day Coll
SW9 ... 138 A2
Brixton Hill SW2 ... 160 B5
Brixton Hill Ct 5
SW2 ... 160 B6
Brixton Hill Pl SW2 ... 160 A4
Brixton Mkt★ SW9 ... 138 C1
Brixton Oval 7 SW2 ... 138 C1
Brixton Rd SW9 ... 138 C4
Brixton Sta SW9 ... 138 C1
Brixton Station Rd
SW9 ... 138 C2
Brixton Water La
SW2 ... 160 B6
Broadacre Cl UB10 ... 60 D5
Broadbent Cl N6 ... 49 B1
Broadbent St W1 ... 248 C6
Broad Berry Ct N18 ... 34 B5
Broad Bridge Cl SE3 ... 143 A5
Broad Common Est
N16 ... 52 A1
Broadcoombe CR2 ... 222 D1
Broadcroft Ave HA7 ... 25 D1
Broadcroft Rd BR5 ... 211 B2
Broad Ct WC2 ... 240 B1
Broadfield NW6 ... 69 D2
Broadfield Cl NW2 ... 68 C5
Croydon CR0 ... 220 B6
Broadfield Ct WD23 ... 8 C2
Broadfield La NW1 ... 72 A1
Broadfield Rd SE6 ... 164 C3
Broadfields
Harrow HA2 ... 23 D1
Thames Ditton KT8 ... 196 C3
Broadfields Ave
Edgware HA8 ... 10 D1
Southgate N21 ... 16 C4
Broadfields Hts HA8 ... 26 D6
Broadfields Inf Sch
HA8 ... 10 C2
Broadfields Jun Sch
HA8 ... 10 D2
Broadfield Sq EN1 ... 6 B3
Broadfields Way
NW10 ... 67 D3
Broadfield Way IG9 ... 21 C1
Broadford Ho 11 E1 ... 97 A3
Broadgate EC2 95 C2 243 A4
Broadgate Circ
EC2 ... 95 C2 243 A3
Broadgate Rd E16 ... 99 D1
Broadgates Ave EN4 ... 1 D4
Broadgates Ct SE11 ... 261 B1
Broadgates Rd SW18 158 B3
Broad Green Ave
CR0 ... 204 D2
Broadhead Strand
NW9 ... 27 D2
Broadheath Dr BR7 ... 188 B5
Broadhinton Rd SW4 137 C2
Broadhurst Ave
Edgware HA8 ... 26 D6
Ilford IG3 ... 79 D4
Broadhurst Cl NW6 ... 70 A2
9 Richmond TW10 ... 154 B6
Broadhurst Gdns NW6 69 D2
Ruislip HA4 ... 62 C6
Broadhurst Mans
NW6 ... 69 D2
Broad La EC2 ... 243 A4
N15 ... 51 D5
N15 ... 52 A5
N8 ... 50 B4
Hampton TW12 ... 173 C4
Broadlands N6 ... 49 A2
Feltham TW13 ... 151 C1
Broadlands Ave
Enfield EN3 ... 6 B2
Shepperton TW17 ... 193 A3
Streatham SW16 ... 160 A2
Broadlands Cl N6 ... 49 A2
Enfield EN3 ... 6 C2
Streatham SW16 ... 160 A2
Broadlands Ct TW9 ... 132 C5
Broadlands Lo N6 ... 48 D2
Broadlands Mans 2
SW16 ... 160 A2
Broadlands Rd BR1 ... 187 B6
N6 ... 48 D2
Broadlands Way KT3 199 D3
Broad Lawn SE9 ... 166 C3
Broadlawns Ct HA3 ... 24 D2
Broadley St
NW8 ... 92 C2 237 A4
Broadley Terr
NW1 ... 92 C3 237 B5
Broadmayne SE17 ... 262 C2
Broadmead W14 ... 254 A3
Catford SE6 ... 163 C1
Broadmead Ave KT4 ... 200 A2
Broadmead Cl
Hampton TW12 ... 173 C4
Pinner HA5 ... 23 A3
Broadmead Ct 6 IG8 ... 37 A4
Broadmead Inf Sch
CR0 ... 205 B2
Broadmead Jun Sch
CR0 ... 205 B3
Broadmead Rd
Northolt UB5 ... 85 A3
Woodford IG8 ... 37 B3
Broad Oak
Ashford TW16 ... 171 D4
Woodford IG8 ... 37 B5
Broad Oak Cl BR5 ... 190 A1
Chingford E4 ... 35 C5
Broadoak Ct 9 SW9 ... 138 C2
Broadoak Ho 18 NW6 ... 91 D6
Broad Oaks KT6 ... 214 D6
Broadoaks Way BR2 ... 208 D4
Broad Sanctuary
SW1 ... 250 A1
Broad St
Dagenham RM10 ... 81 C1
Teddington TW11 ... 174 D4
Broad St Ave EC2 ... 243 A3
Broadstone Ho SW8 ... 270 C3
Broadstone Pl W1 ... 238 A3
Broad St Pl EC2 ... 242 D3
Broadview NW9 ... 44 C3
Broadview Est TW19 148 C4
Broadview Ho RM8 ... 58 D1
Broadview Rd SW16 ... 181 D3
Broadwalk E18 ... 54 D6
Harrow HA2 ... 41 D4
Broadwalk Ho SW7 ... 246 A1
Broadwalk La NW11 ... 47 B2
Broadwalk Sh Ctr The
HA8 ... 26 D4
Broadwall
SE1 ... 116 C5 251 B4
Broadwater Farm Prim
Sch N17 ... 33 B1
Broadwater Gdns
BR6 ... 227 A4
Broadwater Prim Sch
SW17 ... 180 C6
Broadwater Rd SE18 ... 123 B3
Tottenham N17 ... 33 C1
Upper Tooting SW17 ... 180 C6
Broadway DA6 ... 147 B1
E15 ... 76 B1
SW1 ... 115 D3 259 C6
Barking IG11 ... 101 A6
Bexley DA6,DA7 ... 147 C1
Ealing W13 ... 109 A5
Ealing W7 ... 108 C5
Tolworth KT6 ... 198 D1
Broadway Arc 3 W6 112 C2
Broadway Ave
Thornton Heath CR0 ... 205 B4
Twickenham TW1 ... 153 B5
Broadway Bldgs 5
W7 ... 108 C5
Broadway Cl IG8 ... 37 B4
Broadway Ct
Beckenham BR3 ... 208 A6
Wimbledon SW19 ... 179 C4
Broadway Ctr Adult Coll
SW17 ... 180 C6
Broadway Gdns
Mitcham CR4 ... 202 C5
Woodford IG8 ... 37 B4
Broadway Ho 2 E8 ... 96 B6
Broadway Mans SW6 265 B3
Broadway Market E8 ... 96 B6
Broadway Market Mews 21
E8 ... 96 A6
Broadway Mews E5 ... 51 D2
Southgate N21 ... 16 D3
Bowes Park N13 ... 32 B5
Broadway Par N8 ... 50 A3
Chingford E4 ... 36 A4
Hayes UB3 ... 106 A5
West Drayton UB7 ... 104 A4
Broadway Pl SW19 ... 179 B4
Broadway Sh Ctr 5
DA6 ... 147 C1
Broadway The E13 ... 99 B5
N11 ... 31 A5
2 N14 ... 15 D3
N8 ... 50 A3
NW7 ... 27 D5
W3 ... 110 C4
Barnes SW13 ... 133 C3
Cheam SM3 ... 217 A2
Chingford E4 ... 36 B4
Dagenham RM8 ... 81 C6
Ealing W5 ... 109 D6
Edmonton N9 ... 18 A1
Greenford UB6 ... 86 A3
Harrow HA3 ... 24 D1
Merton SW19 ... 179 C3
Pinner HA5 ... 23 B3
Southall UB1 ... 107 A6
Stanmore HA7 ... 25 C5
Sutton SM1 ... 218 A4
Thames Ditton KT10 ... 196 C1
Tolworth KT6 ... 198 C1
Wallington SM6 ... 220 A4
Wembley HA9 ... 66 A5
Woodford IG8 ... 37 B4
Wood Green N22 ... 32 C1
Broadwell Ct TW5 ... 128 D4
Broadwick St
W1 ... 93 C1 239 B1
Broad Wlk
NW1 ... 93 A5 231 B3
W1 ... 115 A5 248 A4
Eltham SE3,SE18 ... 144 A3
Heston TW5 ... 129 A4
Richmond TW9 ... 132 B5
Southgate N21 ... 16 B3
Broad Wlk The
W8 ... 113 D5 245 D3
Broadwood Ave HA4 ... 39 C3
Broadwood Terr
W14 ... 254 D4
Broad Yd EC1 ... 241 C5
Brocas Cl NW3 ... 70 C1
Brockbridge Ho 11
SW15 ... 155 D5
Brockdene Dr BR2 ... 225 D4
Brockdish Ave IG11 ... 79 D3
Brockelbank Lo RM8 ... 80 D6
Brockenhurst KT8 ... 195 B3
Brockenhurst Ave
KT4 ... 199 C1
Brockenhurst Gdns
NW7 ... 27 C5
Ilford IG1 ... 79 A3
Brockenhurst Mews 9
N18 ... 34 A6
Brockenhurst Rd
CR0 ... 206 B2
Brockenhurst Way
SW16 ... 181 D1
Brocket Ho 16 SW8 ... 137 D3
Brockham Cl SW19 ... 179 B5
Brockham Cres CR0 ... 224 B1
Brockham Ct 6 SM2 217 D1
Brockham Dr
Ilford IG2 ... 57 A4
Streatham SW2 ... 160 B4
Brockham Ho NW1 ... 232 B5
11 Streatham SW2 ... 160 B4
Brockham St SE1 ... 262 B6
Brock Ho WC1 ... 239 C4
Brockhurst Cl HA7 ... 24 D4
Brockhurst Ho N4 ... 51 B2
Brockill Cres SE4 ... 141 A1
Brocklebank Ho 7
E16 ... 122 C5
Brocklebank Rd SE7 ... 121 B2
Wandsworth SW18 ... 158 A4
Brocklebank Road Ind Est
SE7 ... 121 A2
Brocklehurst St SE14 140 D5
Brocklesby Rd SE25 ... 206 B5
Brockley Ave HA7 ... 10 A1
Brockley Cl HA7 ... 26 A6
Brockley Cross SE4 ... 141 B2
Brockley Cross Bsns Ctr
SE4 ... 141 A2
Brockley Gdns SE4 ... 141 B3
Brockley Gr SE4 ... 163 B6
Brockley Hall Rd SE4 163 A6
Brockley Hill HA7,HA8 ... 9 D2
Brockley Hill Ho HA7 ... 9 C3
Brockley Ho SE17 ... 263 A2
Brockley Mews SE4 ... 163 A6
Brockley Pk SE23 ... 163 A4
Brockley Prim Sch
SE4 ... 163 B6
Brockley Rd SE4 ... 163 B6
Brockley Rise SE23 ... 163 A4
Brockleyside HA7 ... 26 A6
Brockley Sta SE4 ... 141 A2
Brockley View SE23 ... 163 A4
Brockley Way SE4 ... 163 A6
Brockman Rise BR1 ... 186 B6
Brockmer Ho 5 E1 ... 118 B6
Brock Pl E3 ... 97 D3
Brock Rd E13 ... 99 B2
Brocks Dr SM3 ... 217 A5
Brockshot Cl 1 TW8 131 D6
Brock St SE15 ... 140 C2
Brockway Cl E11 ... 76 C6
Brockweir 29 E2 ... 96 C5
Brockwell Cl BR5 ... 211 D4
Brockwell Ct 2 SW2 160 C6
Brockwell Ho SE11 ... 270 D6
Brockwell Park★
SE24 ... 160 D5
Brockwell Park Gdns
SE24 ... 160 D4
Brockworth 8 KT2 ... 176 D2
Broderick Ho SE21 ... 161 C1
Brodia Rd N16 ... 73 C5
Brodick Ho 11 E3 ... 97 B5
Brodie Ho SE1 ... 263 D2
7 Wallington SM6 ... 219 B4
Brodie Rd Chingford E4 20 A2
Enfield EN2 ... 5 A5
Brodie St
SE1 ... 117 D1 263 D2
Brodlove La E1 ... 118 D6
Brodrick Gr SE2 ... 124 B2
Brodrick Rd SW17 ... 158 C2
Brograve Gdns BR3 ... 185 D1
Broken Wharf EC4 ... 252 A6
Brokesley St E3 ... 97 B4
Broke Wlk E8 ... 95 D6
1 E8 ... 96 A6
Bromar Rd SE5 ... 139 C2
Bromborough Gn
WD19 ... 22 C5
Bromefield HA7 ... 25 C2
Bromehead St 8 E1 ... 96 C1
Brome Ho 5 SE18 ... 144 A4
Bromell's Rd SW4 ... 137 C1
Brome Rd SE9 ... 144 B2
Bromfelde Rd SW4 ... 137 D3
Bromfield Ct 20 SE16 118 A3
Bromfield St N1 ... 234 B4
Bromhall Rd RM8 ... 80 B2
Bromhedge SE9 ... 166 B1
Bromholm Rd SE2 ... 124 B3
Bromleigh Ct 1
SE21,SE22 ... 162 B2
Bromleigh Ho SE1 ... 263 C6
Bromley Ave BR1 ... 186 C3

Bromley-by-Bow Sta
E3 . . . . .97 D4
Bromley Coll of F & H Ed
BR2 . . . . .209 D3
Bromley Comm BR2 .209 D4
Bromley Cres
Beckenham BR2 . . . . .208 D6
Ruislip HA4 . . . . .61 D4
Bromley Ct SE13 . . . .164 B6
Bromley BR1 . . . . . . .186 D3
Bromley Gdns BR2 . .208 D6
Bromley Gr BR2 . . . . .186 B1
Bromley Hall Rd E14 . .98 D2
Bromley High Sch for Girls
BR1 . . . . .210 C5
Bromley High St E3 . .97 C4
Bromley Hill BR1 . . . .186 C4
Bromley Hospl BR1 . .209 B5
Bromley Ind Est BR1 209 D6
Bromley La BR7 . . . . .189 B3
Bromley Lo 2 W3 . . . .89 A1
Bromley Manor Mans 3
BR1 . . . . .209 A6
Bromley North Sta
BR1 . . . . .187 A2
Bromley Pk 11 BR1 . .186 D2
Bromley Pl W1 . . . . . .239 A4
Bromley Rd BR7 . . . .188 D2
E10 . . . . .53 D3
E17 . . . . .53 C6
Beckenham BR2,BR3 . .186 B1
Beckenham BR3 . . . .185 D2
Catford SE6 . . . . .163 D1
Edmonton N18 . . . . . .17 B1
Tottenham N17 . . . . . .34 A2
Bromley Rd Ret Pk
SE6 . . . . .163 D2
Bromley Road Inf Sch
BR3 . . . . .185 D2
Bromley South Sta
BR2 . . . . .209 A6
Bromley St E1 . . . . . . .96 D1
Brompton WC1 . . . . . .240 C3
Brompton Arc SW1 . .247 D1
Brompton Cl
Hounslow TW4 . . . . . .151 B6
Penge SE20 . . . . .184 A1
Brompton Ct 4 HA7 . .25 C6
Brompton Gr N2 . . . . .48 C5
Brompton Ho 3 N9 . . .34 A6
Brompton Oratory★
SW3 . . . . .114 C3 257 A5
Brompton Park Cres
SW6 . . . . . . .135 D6 265 C5
Brompton Pl
SW3 . . . . .114 C3 257 B6
Brompton Rd
SW3 . . . . .114 C3 257 A5
Brompton Sq
SW3 . . . . . . .114 C3 257 A6
Bromstone Ho 19
SW9 . . . . .138 C4
Bromwich Ave N6 . . . .71 A6
Bromwich Ho 3
TW10 . . . . .154 A5
Bromyard Ave W3 . . . .111 C6
Bromyard Ho 3
SE15 . . . . .140 B5
Bron Ct NW6 . . . . .91 C6
Brondesbury Coll for Boys
NW6 . . . . .69 A1
Brondesbury Ct NW2 .68 D2
Brondesbury Mews 11
NW6 . . . . .69 C1
Brondesbury Park Sta
NW6 . . . . .91 A6
Brondesbury Pk NW2 .68 D1
Brondesbury Rd NW6 .91 C5
Brondesbury Sta NW6 69 B1
Brondesbury Villas
NW6 . . . . .91 C5
Bronhill Terr N17 . . . .34 A2
Bronsart Rd
SW6 . . . . . . .135 A5 264 A3
Bronson Rd SW20 . . .179 A1
Bronte Cl DA8 . . . . . .147 D5
1 E7 . . . . .77 A4
Ilford IG2 . . . . .56 C5
Bronte Ct 8 W14 . . . .112 D3
Bronte Ho 6 N16 . . . .73 C3
NW6 . . . . .91 C4
Bronti Cl
SE17 . . . . . . .117 A1 262 B2
Bronwen Ct NW8 . . . .229 C1
Bronze Age Way
DA17 . . . . .125 D4
Bronze St SE8 . . . . . .141 C5

Brook Ave
Dagenham RM10 . . . . .81 D1
Edgware HA8 . . . . . . .26 D4
Wembley HA9 . . . . . . .66 C5
Brook Bank EN1 . . . . . . .6 B6
Brookbank Ave W7 . . .86 B2
Brookbank Rd SE13 . .141 D2
Brook Cl Acton W3 . . .110 C5
Finchley N12 . . . . .29 A3
Ruislip HA4 . . . . .39 C2
Stanwell TW19 . . . . . .148 B4
Upper Tooting SW17 . .159 A2
West Barnes SW20 . . .200 B6
Brook Cres
Chingford E4 . . . . .35 C6
Edmonton N9 . . . . . . .34 B6
Brook Ct 2 E11 . . . . . .76 C5
E15 . . . . .76 A3
E17 . . . . .53 A6
Beckenham BR3 . . . . .185 B2
5 Brentford TW8 . . . .131 D6
Cheam SM3 . . . . .216 C4
Edgware HA8 . . . . . . .26 D5
Mortlake SW14 . . . . . .133 C2
Brookdale N11 . . . . . . .31 C6
Brookdale Rd DA5 . . .169 A5
E17 . . . . .53 C6
SE6 . . . . .163 D5
Catford SE6 . . . . .163 D6
Brookdales The NW4 .47 A6
Brookdene N12 . . . . . .29 D6
Brookdene Rd SE18,
SE2 . . . . .123 D2
Brook Dr
SE11 . . . . . .116 D2 261 C4
Harrow HA1 . . . . .42 A5
Ruislip HA4 . . . . .39 C2
Brooke Ave HA2 . . . . .64 A5
Brooke Cl WD23 . . . . . .8 A4
Brooke Ct 7 KT2 . . . .175 D6
Brookehowse Rd
SE6 . . . . .163 D1
Brookend Rd DA15 . .167 C3
Brooke Rd E17 . . . . . . .54 A5
E5,N16 . . . . .74 A5
Brookes Ct EC1 . . . . .241 A4
Brookes Mkt EC1 . . . .241 A4
Brooke's Mkt EC1 . . . .241 B4
Brooke St EC1 .94 C2 241 A3
Brooke Way WD23 . . . . .8 A4
Brook Meadow Cl IG8 36 C4
Brookfield 1 N4 . . . . . .72 C6
N6 . . . . .71 B6
Brookfield Ave E17 . . .54 A5
NW7 . . . . .28 B4
Carshalton SM1,SM5 . .218 C5
Ealing W5 . . . . .87 D3
Brookfield Cl NW7 . . .28 B4
Brookfield Cres NW7 .28 B4
Harrow HA3 . . . . .44 A4
Brookfield Ct 1 N12 .29 D6
Greenford UB6 . . . . . .86 A4
Brookfield Gdns
KT10 . . . . .212 D2
Brookfield House Sch
IG8 . . . . .36 C4
Brookfield Path IG8 . .36 C4
Brookfield Pk NW5 . . .71 B5
Brookfield Prim Sch
N19 . . . . .71 B6
Cheam SM3 . . . . .201 A1
Brookfield Rd E9 . . . . .75 A2
W4 . . . . .111 B4
Edmonton N9 . . . . . . .18 B1
Brookfields EN3 . . . . . .6 D1
Brookfields Ave CR4 .202 C4
Brookgate N16 . . . . . .73 B6
Brook Gate
W1 . . . . .114 D6 247 D5
Brook Gdns
Barnes SW13 . . . . . . .133 D2
Chingford E4 . . . . .35 D6
Kingston KT2 . . . . . . .177 A2
Brook Gn W6 . . . . . . .112 D2
Brook Green Flats 11
W14 . . . . .112 D3
Brookhill Cl SE18 . . . .122 D1
East Barnet EN4 . . . . .14 C4
Brookhill Ct 2 EN4 . . .14 C5
Brookhill Rd SE18 . . .122 D1
East Barnet EN4 . . . . .14 C6
Brook Ho 3 SW4 . . . .159 C4
W3 . . . . .110 C4
4 W6 . . . . .112 C2
3 Edmonton N9 . . . . .18 A1
3 Twickenham TW1 . .153 D4
Brook Hos NW1 . . . . .232 B3
Brookhouse Gdns E4 .36 C6
Brook House Sixth Form
Coll The E5 . . . . .74 B5
Brook Ind Est UB4 . . .106 C5

Brooking Cl RM8 . . . . .80 C5
Brooking Rd E7 . . . . . .77 A3
Brook La BR1 . . . . . . .187 A4
DA5 . . . . .168 D5
Greenwich SE3 . . . . . .143 B3
Brookland Cl NW11 . . .47 C5
Brookland Garth
NW11 . . . . .47 D5
Brookland Hill NW11 .47 D5
Brookland Jun & Inf Schs
NW11 . . . . .47 D5
Brookland Rise NW11 .47 C5
Brooklands Ave
DA15 . . . . .167 B2
Wandsworth SW18 . . .157 D2
Brooklands Cl TW16 .171 C2
Brooklands Court
Apartments 3 NW6 .69 B1
Brooklands Ct 2 NW6 69 B1
Enfield N21 . . . . .17 B6
Kingston KT1 . . . . . . .197 D5
5 Mitcham CR4 . . . . .180 C1
Brooklands Dr UB6 . . .87 D6
Brooklands Pk SE3 . .143 A2
Brooklands Prim Sch
SE3 . . . . .143 A2
Brooklands Rd KT7 . .197 A1
Brooklands The TW7 .130 B4
Brook Lane Bns Ctr
TW8 . . . . .109 D1
Brooklea Cl NW9 . . . . .27 C2
Brook Lo N8 . . . . .49 D3
NW4 . . . . .46 D4
Brooklyn SE20 . . . . . .184 A3
Brooklyn Ave SE25 . .206 B5
Brooklyn Cl SM5 . . . .218 C6
Brooklyn Ct W12 . . . .112 C5
Brooklyn Gr SE25 . . .206 B5
Brooklyn Rd BR2 . . . .210 A4
Croydon SE25 . . . . . .206 B5
Brookmarsh Ind Est
SE10 . . . . .141 D5
Brook Mdw N12 . . . . . .13 D1
Brook Mead KT19 . . .215 C2
Brookmead Ave BR1,
BR2 . . . . .210 B4
Brookmead Ct N20 . . .14 A2
Brookmead Ind Est
CR4 . . . . .203 C3
Brookmead Rd CR0 . .203 C3
Brook Mews N
W2 . . . . .114 B6 246 B6
Brookmill Rd SE8 . . . .141 C4
Brook Park Cl N21 . . .16 D6
Brook Pl EN5 . . . . .13 C6
Brook Rd N12 . . . . . . .30 C3
N22 . . . . .50 B6
N8 . . . . .50 A5
NW2 . . . . .68 A6
Buckhurst Hill IG9 . . . .21 A3
Ilford IG2 . . . . .57 C3
South Norwood CR7 . .205 A5
Surbiton KT6 . . . . .214 A6
Twickenham TW1 . . . .153 A5
Brook Rd S TW8 . . . . .131 D6
Brooks Ave E6 . . . . . .100 B3
Brooksbank Ho 7 E9 .74 C2
Brooksbank St 9 E9 .74 C2
Brooksby Mews N1 . . .72 C1
Brooksby St N1 . . . . . .72 C1
Brooksby's Wlk E9 . . .74 D3
Brooks Cl SE9 . . . . . .166 C4
Brookscroft E17 . . . . . .35 D2
Brooks Ct 3 SW4 . . . .138 A3
SW8 . . . . .269 B4
Brookshill HA3 . . . . . . .24 B5
Brookshill Ave HA3 . . .24 C5
Brookshill Dr HA3 . . . .24 B5
Brooks Ho 6 SW2 . . .160 C3
Brookside BR6 . . . . . .211 D2
East Barnet EN4 . . . . .14 C5
Southgate N21 . . . . . .16 B5
Wallington SM5 . . . . . .219 A3
Brookside Cl
Barnet EN5 . . . . .13 A5
Feltham TW13 . . . . . .150 A1
Harrow HA3 . . . . .43 D4
South Harrow HA2,HA4 .63 A4
Brookside Cres 1
KT4 . . . . .200 A1
Brookside Ct SW16 . .181 C3
Brookside Gdns EN1 . . .6 C6
Brookside Ho N17 . . . .33 C1
Brookside Prim Sch
UB4 . . . . .84 C4
Brookside Rd N19 . . . .71 C6
NW11 . . . . .47 B3
Edmonton N9 . . . . . . .34 B6
Hayes UB4 . . . . .106 C6

Brookside S EN4 . . . . . .15 A4
Brookside Way
Croydon CR0 . . . . . . .206 D3
Hillingdon UB10 . . . . . .60 B1
Brooks La W4 . . . . . . .132 C6
Brook's Mans 5 IG3 . .58 B1
Brook's Mews
W1 . . . . .115 B6 248 C6
Brook's Par 6 IG3 . . .58 B1
Brook's Rd E13 . . . . . .99 A6
Brook St DA8 . . . . . . .147 D5
W1 . . . . .115 B6 248 C6
W2 . . . . .114 B6 246 D6
Kingston KT1 . . . . . . .176 A1
5 Tottenham N17 . . . .33 D1
Brookstone Ct SE15 . .140 B1
Brooksville Ave NW6 . .91 A6
Brook Vale DA7,DA8 . .147 D4
Brookview Ct 11 EN1 .17 C6
Brookview Rd SW16 . .181 C5
Brookville Rd
SW6 . . . . . . .135 B5 264 C3
Brookway SE3 . . . . . .143 A2
Brook Wlk HA8 . . . . . . .27 B4
N2 . . . . .30 B2
Brookwood Ave
SW13 . . . . .133 D3
Brookwood Cl BR2 . . .208 D5
Brookwood Ho SE1 . .251 D1
Brookwood Rd
Hounslow TW3 . . . . . .129 D4
Wandsworth SW18 . . .157 C3
Broom Ave BR5 . . . . .190 B1
Broom Cl BR2 . . . . . . .210 A3
Teddington KT1,TW11 .175 C4
Broomcroft Ave UB5 . .84 C4
Broome Ct 3 TW9 . . . .132 C4
Broome Ho 7 E5 . . . . .74 B3
Broome Rd TW12 . . . .173 B2
Broome Way SE5 . . . .139 B5
Broomfield E17 . . . . . . .53 B2
7 NW1 . . . . .71 A1
Sunbury TW16 . . . . . .172 A2
Broomfield Ave N13 . . .32 B5
Broomfield Cotts N13 .32 A5
Broomfield Ct N13 . . . .32 A5
Broomfield Ho
4 BR5 . . . . .190 B1
SE17 . . . . .263 A3
Stanmore HA7 . . . . .9 A1
Broomfield House Sch
TW9 . . . . .132 B4
Broomfield La N13 . . . .32 B6
Broomfield Pl W13 . . .109 B5
Broomfield Rd DA6 . .169 C6
Beckenham BR3 . . . . .207 B6
Bowes Park N13 . . . . .32 A5
Dagenham RM6 . . . . .58 D2
Ealing W13 . . . . .109 B5
Richmond TW9 . . . . . .132 B4
Surbiton KT5 . . . . .198 B1
Teddington TW11 . . . .175 C4
Broomfields KT10 . . .212 A3
Broomfield Sch N14 . .31 D5
Broomfield St E14 . . . .97 D4
Broom Gdns CR0 . . . .223 C5
Broomgrove Gdns
HA8 . . . . .26 C2
Broomgrove Rd SW9 138 B3
Broomhill Ct 2 IG8 . . .37 A4
Broomhill Rd BR6 . . .211 D2
SW18 . . . . .157 C6
Ilford IG3 . . . . .80 A6
Woodford IG8 . . . . . . .37 A4
Broomhill Rise DA6 . .169 C6
Broomhill Wlk IG8 . . . .36 D3
Broomhouse La SW6 135 C2
Broomhouse Rd SW6 135 C3
Broomleigh BR1 . . . . .187 A2
Broomleigh Bsns Pk
SE26 . . . . .185 B5
Broomloan La SM1 . .217 C6
Broom Lock TW11 . . .175 C4
Broom Mead DA6 . . .169 C6
Broom Pk KT1 . . . . . . .175 D3
Broom Rd
Croydon CR0 . . . . . . .223 C5
Richmond TW11 . . . . .175 D4
Teddington KT1,TW11 .175 C4
Broomsleigh St NW6 . .69 B3
Broom Water TW11 . .175 D5
Broom Water W
TW11 . . . . .175 C5
Broomwood Cl CR0 . .206 D4
Broomwood Hall Sch
SW12 . . . . .159 A4
Broomwood Rd BR5 . .190 B1
SW11 . . . . .159 A6
Broseley Gr SE26 . . . .185 A1

Broster Gdns SE25 . .205 D6
Brougham Rd E8 . . . . .96 A6
W3 . . . . .89 A1
Brougham St SW11 . .136 D3
Brough Cl SW8 . . . . . .270 B3
Kingston KT2 . . . . . . .175 D5
Brough St SW8 . . . . . .270 B3
Broughton Ave N3 . . . .47 A6
Richmond TW10 . . . . .175 C4
Broughton Ct W13 . . .109 B6
Broughton Dr 20
SW9 . . . . .138 C2
Broughton Gdns N6 . .49 C3
Broughton Rd SW6 . .135 C2
Ealing W13 . . . . .109 B6
Orpington BR6 . . . . . .227 B6
Thornton Heath CR7 . .204 C3
Broughton Road App 2
SW6 . . . . .135 C2
Broughton St SW8 . . .137 B3
Broughton Street Arches
Ind Area SW11 . . . . .137 A3
Brouncker Rd W3 . . . .111 A4
Browells La W13 . . . . .150 B2
Brown Bear Ct TW13 .172 D6
Brown Cl SM6 . . . . . . .220 A1
Browne Ho 13 SE8 . . .141 C5
9 Penge SE26 . . . . . .184 B5
Brownfield St E14 . . . .98 A1
Brownflete Ho SE4 . .141 A1
Browngraves Rd UB7 127 A5
Brown Hart Gdns W1 248 B6
Brownhill Rd SE6 . . . .164 A4
Browning Ave
Carshalton SM1 . . . . .218 C4
Ealing W7 . . . . .86 C1
North Cheam KT4 . . . .200 B1
Browning Cl DA16 . . .145 C4
E17 . . . . .54 A5
W9 . . . . .236 B5
Feltham TW12 . . . . . .173 B6
Browning Ct W14 . . . .264 C6
Browning Ho 10 N16 . .73 C4
W12 . . . . .90 C1
Browning Mews W1 . .238 B3
Browning Rd E11 . . . . .54 D2
E12 . . . . .78 B2
Enfield EN2 . . . . .5 B5
Browning St
SE17 . . . . . . .117 A2 262 B3
Browning Way TW5 . .128 D4
Brownlea Gdns IG3 . . .80 A6
Brownlow Cl EN4 . . . .14 B6
Brownlow Ct N2 . . . . . .48 A4
1 Bowes Park N11 . .32 A4
Brownlow Ho 7
SE16 . . . . .118 A4
Brownlow Mews
WC1 . . . . .94 B3 240 D5
Brownlow Rd 3 E7 . . .77 A4
E8 . . . . .96 A6
N3 . . . . .29 D3
NW10 . . . . .67 C1
Bowes Park N11 . . . . .32 A4
6 Ealing W13 . . . . . .109 A5
South Croydon CR0 . .221 D4
Brownlow St
WC1 . . . . .94 B2 240 D3
Brownrigg Rd TW15 . .170 C6
Brown's Bldgs EC3 . .243 B1
Brownspring Dr SE9 .166 D1
Brown's Rd E17 . . . . . .53 C6
Surbiton KT5,KT6 . . . .198 B2
Brown St W1 . .92 D1 237 C2
Brownswell Rd N2 . . . .30 B1
Brownswood Rd N4 . .73 A6
Broxash Rd SW11 . . . .159 A5
Broxbourne Ave E18 . .55 B5
Broxbourne Ho 1 E3 . .97 D3
Broxbourne Rd BR6 . .211 D2
Wanstead E7 . . . . .77 A5
Broxholme Ho SW6 . .265 C2
Broxholm Rd SE27,
SW16 . . . . .160 C6
Broxted Rd SE6 . . . . .163 B4
Broxwood Way
NW8 . . . . .92 C6 230 B5
Bruce Ave TW17 . . . . .193 A3
Bruce Castle Ct N17 . .33 C2
Bruce Castle Mus★
N17 . . . . .33 C2
Bruce Castle Rd N17 . .33 D2
Bruce Cl DA16 . . . . . .146 B4
W10 . . . . .90 D2
Bruce Ct DA15 . . . . . .189 D6
Bruce Gdns N20 . . . . .14 D1
Bruce Glasier Ho 13
N19 . . . . .49 D2
Bruce Gr N17 . . . . .33 D1
Bruce Grove N17 . . . . .33 D1

Bruce Grove Prim Sch
N17 . . . . .33 D1
Bruce Grove Sta N17 . .33 D1
Bruce Hall Mews
SW17 . . . . .181 A4
Bruce Ho 4 SW4 . . . .159 C4
W10 . . . . .90 D2
5 Harrow HA1 . . . . . .42 D4
Harrow HA3 . . . . .44 A4
Putney SW15 . . . . . . .156 B4
Bruce Lawns SW17 . .181 A4
Bruce Rd E3 . . . . .97 D2
NW10 . . . . .67 B3
Barnet EN5 . . . . .1 C4
Harrow HA3 . . . . .24 C1
Mitcham CR4 . . . . . . .181 A3
South Norwood SE25 . .205 B5
Bruckner St W10 . . . . .91 B4
Brudenell Rd SW17 . .181 A6
Bruffs Meadow UB5 . .63 A2
Bruges Pl 13 NW1 . . . .71 C1
Brumfield Rd KT19 . . .215 A3
Brune Ho E1 . . . . .243 C2
Brunel Cl
Cranford TW5 . . . . . . .128 B5
Northolt UB5 . . . . .85 B4
Penge SE19 . . . . .183 D4
Brunel Ct NW10 . . . . . .90 A4
Brunel Est W2 . . . . . . .91 C2
Brunel Ho E14 . . . . . .119 D1
4 NW5 . . . . .71 C2
SW10 . . . . .266 C4
Hayes UB3 . . . . .105 D3
25 Streatham SW2 . .160 A4
Brunel Pl 8 UB1 . . . . .85 D1
Brunel Rd E17 . . . . . . .53 A3
SE16 . . . . .118 C5
W3 . . . . .89 C2
Brunel St E16 . . . . .98 D1
Brunel Univ UB8 . . . . .82 A4
Brunel Univ Coll Osterley
Campus TW7 . . . . . . .130 C6
Brunel Univ Coll
(Twickenham Campus)
TW1 . . . . .131 B1
Brunlees Ho SE1 . . . . .262 B5
Brunner Cl NW11 . . . . .48 A4
Brunner Ho 6 SE6 . . .186 A6
Brunner Rd E17 . . . . . .53 B4
Ealing W5 . . . . .87 D3
Bruno Pl NW9 . . . . . . .67 A6
Brunswick Ave N11 . . .15 A1
Brunswick Cl DA6 . . .146 D1
Thames Ditton KT7 . . .196 D1
Twickenham TW2 . . . .152 B1
Brunswick Cres N11 . .15 A1
Brunswick Ct EC1 . . .234 C1
SE1 . . . . .117 C4 253 B2
SW1 . . . . .259 D3
Kingston KT2 . . . . . . .175 D4
New Barnet EN4 . . . . .14 B4
2 Penge SE19 . . . . . .184 A3
2 Wimbledon SW19 . .179 A3
Brunswick Gdns
W8 . . . . .113 C5 245 B5
Ealing W5 . . . . .88 A3
Brunswick Gr N11 . . . .15 A1
Brunswick Ho 4 E2 . . .95 D5
N3 . . . . .29 B2
NW1 . . . . .237 C6
Brunswick Lo 6 E4 . . .20 A1
Brunswick Manor
SM1 . . . . .218 A4
Brunswick Mews W1 237 D2
Streatham SW16 . . . .181 D4
Brunswick Park Gdns
N11 . . . . .15 A3
Brunswick Park Prim Sch
N14 . . . . .15 A2
SE5 . . . . .139 B5
Brunswick Park Rd
N11 . . . . .15 A1
Brunswick Pk SE5 . . .139 C4
Brunswick Pl
N1 . . . . .95 B4 235 D1
Penge SE19 . . . . .184 A3
Brunswick Quay
SE16 . . . . .118 D3
Brunswick Rd DA6 . . .147 A1
E10 . . . . .54 A1
E14 . . . . .98 A1
N15 . . . . .51 C5
Ealing W5 . . . . .88 A4
Holdbrook EN3 . . . . . . .7 C5
Kingston KT2 . . . . . . .176 C2
Sutton SM1 . . . . .217 D2

Brunswick Sh Ctr WC1 94 A3 240 B6
Brunswick Sq WC1 94 A3 240 B6
Tottenham N17 33 D4
Brunswick St E17 54 A4
Brunswick Villas 2 SE5 139 C4
Brunswick Way N11 31 B6
Brunton Pl E14 97 A1
Brushfield St E1 95 D2 243 C4
Brushwood Ho 4 E14 97 D2
Brushwood Lo DA17 125 C2
Brussels Rd SW11 136 B1
Bruton Cl BR7 188 B3
Bruton La W1 115 B6 248 D5
Bruton Pl W1 115 B6 248 D5
Bruton Rd SM4 202 A5
Bruton St W1 115 B6 248 D5
Bruton Way W13 87 A2
Bryan Ave NW10 68 B1
Bryan Cl TW16 172 A3
Bryan Ct W1 237 C2
Bryan Ho SE16 119 B4
Bryan Rd SE16 119 B4
Bryanston Ave TW2 151 D3
Bryanston Cl UB2 107 B2
Bryanston Ct W1 237 C2
Bryanstone Ct SM1 218 A5
Bryanstone Rd N8 49 D4
Bryanston Ho 11 SE15 139 D4
Bryanston Mans W1 237 C4
Bryanston Mews E W1 237 C3
Bryanston Mews W W1 92 D1 237 C2
Bryanston Pl W1 92 D2 237 C3
Bryanston Sq W1 92 D1 237 C2
Bryanston St W1 92 D1 237 D1
Bryant Cl EN5 13 B6
Bryant Ct E2 95 D5
Bryant Rd UB5 84 C4
Bryant St E15 76 C1
Bryantwood Rd N5,N7 72 C3
Brycedale Cres N14 15 D1
Bryce Ho 25 SE14 140 D6
Bryce Rd RM8 80 C4
Brydale Ho 2 SE16 118 D2
Bryden Cl SE26 185 A5
Brydges Pl WC2 250 A5
Brydges Rd E15 76 B3
Brydon Wlk N1 233 B6
Bryer Ct EC2 242 A4
Bryett Rd N7 72 A5
Bryher Ho W4 111 A1
Brymay Cl E3 97 C5
Brymon Ct W1 237 D3
Brynmaer Ho SW11 267 D1
Brynmaer Rd SW11 136 D4 267 D1
Bryn-y-Mawr Rd EN1 5 D1
Bryony Cl UB8 82 B2
Bryony Rd W12 112 A6
Bryony Way TW16 172 A4
B Sky B Hq TW7 131 A6
BT Telecom Twr★ W1 93 C2 239 A4
Buccleuch Ho E5 52 A2
Buchanan Cl N21 16 B6
Buchanan Ct 16 SE16 118 D2
Buchanan Gdns NW10 90 B5
Buchanan Ho
Dulwich SE21 161 C1
Wandsworth SW18 157 C4
Buchan Ho W3 110 D4
Buchan Rd SE15 140 C2
Bucharest Rd SW18 158 A4
Buckden Cl N2 48 D5
SE12 165 A5
Buckfast Ct W13 109 A6
Buckfast Ho N14 15 C6
Buckfast Rd SM4 201 D5
Buckfast St E2 96 A4
Buck Hill Wlk W2 114 B6 246 D5
Buckhold Rd SW18 157 C5
Buckhurst Ave CR4, SM5 202 D1
Buckhurst Hill Ho IG9 21 B2
Buckhurst Hill Sta IG9 21 D2
Buckhurst Ho 15 N7 71 D3
Buckhurst St E1 96 B3
Buckhurst Way IG9 21 D1
Buckingham Ave DA16 145 C1
N20 14 B4
East Molesey KT8 173 D1
Feltham TW14 150 B5
South Norwood CR7 182 C2
Wembley UB6 87 A6
Buckingham Cl BR5 211 C2
Ealing W5 87 C2
Enfield EN1 5 C3
Hampton TW12 173 B5
Buckingham College Sch HA1 42 C4
Buckingham Ct NW4 46 A6
2 Ealing W7 86 D3
Mitcham CR4 204 A4
Northolt UB5 85 A6
Wembley HA0 65 C2
Buckingham Dr BR7 189 A5
Buckingham Gate SW1 115 C3 259 B6
Buckingham Gdns
East Molesey KT8 173 D1
Edgware HA8 26 B3
South Norwood CR7 182 C1
Buckingham Gr UB10 82 C5
Buckingham Ho N4 51 A1
1 Acton W3 88 C1
Richmond TW10 154 C6
Buckingham La SE23 163 A4
Buckingham Lo N10 49 C5
Buckingham Mans NW6 69 D3
Buckingham Mews 7 N1 73 C2
NW10 89 D5
SW1 259 A6
Buckingham Palace★ SW1 115 C4 249 A1
Buckingham Palace Rd SW1 115 B2 258 D4
Buckingham Pl SW1 259 A6
Buckingham Prim Sch TW12 173 B5
Buckingham Rd E10 75 D5
E15 76 D3
N1 73 C2
NW10 89 D5
Edgware HA8 26 B3
Hampton TW12,TW13 173 B5
Harrow HA1 42 B4
Ilford IG1 79 B6
Kingston KT1 198 B5
Mitcham CR4 204 A4
Richmond TW10 153 D2
Wanstead E11 55 C4
Woodford E18 36 D2
Wood Green N22 32 A2
Buckingham St WC2 250 B5
Buckingham Way SM6 219 C1
Buckingham Yd NW10 89 D5
Buck La NW9 45 B4
Buckland Cres NW3 70 B2
Buckland Ct 6 N1 95 C5
Uxbridge UB10 61 A6
Buckland Inf Sch KT9 214 B4
Buckland Rd BR6 227 C4
E10 76 A6
Chessington KT9 214 B3
Buckland Rise HA5 22 D2
Bucklands Rd TW11 175 C4
Buckland St N1 95 B5 235 D3
Buckland Way KT4 200 C1
Buckland Wlk
2 Acton W3 111 A4
Morden SM4 202 A5
Buckleigh Ave SW20 201 B6
Buckleigh Ho SW17 180 B5
Buckleigh Rd SW16 182 A3
Buckleigh Way SE19 183 D3
Buckler Gdns SE9 166 B1
Buckler's Alley SW6 264 D4
Bucklersbury EC2, EC4 242 C1
Bucklers' Way SM5 218 D5
Buckles Ct DA17 124 D2
Buckle St E1 243 D2
9 E1 96 A1
Buckley Cl SE23 162 B4
Buckley Ct 5 NW6 69 B1
Buckley Rd NW6 69 B1
Buckley St SE1 251 A3
Buckmaster Cl SE17 262 B1
1 SW9 138 C2
Buckmaster Ho 1 N7 72 B4
Buckmaster Rd SW11 136 C1
Bucknall St WC1 240 A2
Bucknall Way BR3 208 A5
Bucknell Cl SW2 138 B1
Buckner Rd SW2 138 B1
Buckrell Rd E4 20 B2
Buckridge Bldg EC1 241 A4
Buckshead Ho 19 W2 91 C2
Buck St NW1 71 B1
Buckstone Cl SE23 162 C5
Buckstone Rd N18 34 A5
Buckters Rents SE16 119 A5
Buckthorne Rd SE4 163 A6
Buckthorn Ho DA15 167 D1
Buckwheat Ct DA18 124 D3
Budd Cl N12 29 D6
Buddings Circ HA9 67 A5
Bude Cl E17 53 B4
Budge La CR4 202 D2
Budge Row EC4 242 C1
Budge's Wlk W2 114 A5 246 B4
Budleigh Cres DA16 146 C4
Budleigh Ho 19 SE15 140 A5
Budoch Ct IG3 80 A6
Budoch Dr IG3 80 A6
Buer Rd SW6 135 A3
Bugsbys Way SE10 120 D2
Bugsby's Way SE7, SE10 121 B2
Buick Ho 4 E3 97 C3
Bulbarrow NW8 91 D6
Bulganak Rd CR7 205 A5
Bulinca St SW1 115 D2 259 D3
Bullace Row SE5 139 B4
Bull Alley DA16 146 B2
Bullard Rd TW11 174 D4
Bullards Pl 13 E2 96 D4
Bull Dog The (Juct) TW15 148 A2
Bulleid Way SW1 115 B2 258 D3
Bullen Ho 13 E1 96 B3
Bullen St SW11 136 C3
Buller Cl SE15 140 A5
Buller Rd NW10 90 D4
Barking IG11 79 C1
South Norwood CR7 205 B6
Tottenham N17 34 A1
Wood Green N22 32 C1
Bullers Cl DA14 191 A5
Bullers Wood Dr BR7 188 B3
Bullers Wood Sch BR7 188 B2
Bullescroft Rd HA8 10 D1
Bullfinch Ct 3 SE21 161 B2
Bullingham Mans W8 245 B2
Bull Inn Ct WC2 250 B5
Bullivant St 9 E14 120 A6
Bull La BR7 189 B3
Dagenham RM10 81 D5
Edmonton N18 33 C5
Bull Rd E15 98 D5
Bullrush Cl
Carshalton SM5 218 D6
Thornton Heath CR0 205 C3
Bulls Alley SW14 133 B3
Bulls Bridge Ind Est UB2 106 B2
Bulls Bridge Rd UB2 106 B2
Bullsbrook Rd UB4 106 C5
Bull's Cross EN1,EN2 6 A6
Bull's Gdns SW3 257 B4
Bulls Head Pas EC3 243 A1
Bull Yd SE15 140 A4
Bulmer Gdns HA3 43 D2
Bulmer Mews W11 113 C5 245 A4
Bulow Ct 3 SW6 135 D3
Bulstrode Ave TW3 129 C2
Bulstrode Gdns TW3 129 C2
Bulstrode Pl W1 238 B3
Bulstrode Rd TW3 129 C2
Bulstrode St W1 93 A1 238 B2
Bulwer Court Rd E11 54 B1
Bulwer Ct E11 54 B1
Bulwer Gdns EN5 2 A1
Bulwer Rd E11 54 B1
Edmonton N18 33 C6
New Barnet EN5 2 A1
Bulwer St W12 112 C5
Bunbury Ho SE15 140 A5
Bunces La IG8 36 D3
Bungalow Rd SE25 205 C5
Bungalows The E10 54 A3
Mitcham SW16 181 B3
Bunhill Row EC1 95 B3 242 C5
Bunhouse Pl SW1 258 B2
Bunkers Hill DA14 169 B1
NW11 48 A2
Bunker's Hill DA17 125 C2
Bunning Ho N7 72 A4
Bunning Way N7 72 B1
Bunn's La NW7 27 D4
Bunsen Ho 1 E3 97 A5
Bunsen St 2 E3 97 A5
Buntingbridge Rd IG2 57 B4
Bunting Cl N9 18 D3
Mitcham CR4 202 D4
Bunting Ct NW9 27 C1
Bunton St SE18 122 C3
Bunyan Ct EC2 242 A4
Bunyan Rd E17 53 A6
Buonaparte Mews SW1 259 C2
BUPA Bushey Hospl WD23 8 D3
Burbage Cl SE1 117 B3 262 C5
Hayes UB3 83 B1
Burbage Ho N1 235 D5
16 SE14 140 D6
Burbage Rd SE21, SE24 161 B4
Burbage Sch N1 95 C5
Burbank KT3 199 D6
Burberry Cl KT3 177 C1
Burbidge Rd TW17 192 C5
Burbridge Way N17 34 A1
Burcham St E14 98 A1
Burcharbro Rd SE2 146 D6
Burchell Ct WD23 8 A4
Burchell Ho SE11 260 D2
Burchell Rd E10 53 D1
SE15 140 B4
Burchetts Way TW17 192 D3
Burchett Way RM6 59 B3
Burcote Rd SW18 158 B4
Burden Cl TW8 109 C1
Burden Ho SW8 270 A3
Burdenshott Ave TW10 132 D1
Burden Way E11 77 B6
Burder Cl N1 73 C2
Burder Rd N1 73 C2
Burdett Ave SW20 178 A2
Burdett Cl DA14 191 A5
2 Ealing W7 108 D5
Burdett Coutts & Townshend CE Prim Sch SW1 115 D2 259 D3
Burdett Mews 4 W2 91 D1
Burdett Rd E3 97 B2
Richmond TW9 132 B2
Thornton Heath CR0 205 B3
Burdetts Rd RM9 103 B6
Burdock Cl CR0 206 D1
Burdock Rd N17 52 A6
Burdon La SM2 217 A1
Burdon Pk SM2 217 B1
Bure Ct 10 EN5 13 D6
Burfield Cl SW17 180 B6
Burford Cl
Dagenham RM8 80 C5
Ickenham UB10 60 A4
Ilford IG6 57 A5
Burford Gdns N13 16 B1
Burford Ho 11 SW9 138 B3
1 Brentford TW8 110 A1
Burford Rd BR1 210 A5
E15 98 B6
E6 100 A4
Brentford TW8 110 A1
Forest Hill SE6 163 B2
New Malden KT4 200 A2
Sutton SM1 217 C6
Burford Way CR0 224 A2
Burford Wlk SW6 265 D3
Burgate Ct 10 SW9 138 C2
Burges Gr SW13 134 B5
Burges Rd E6 78 B1
Burgess Ave NW9 45 B3
Burgess Cl 4 TW13 173 A6
Burgess Ct
3 Southall UB1 85 D1
Wallend E12 78 C1
Burgess Hill NW2 69 C4
Burgess Ho 3 SE5 139 A5
Burgess Ind Pk SE5 139 B5
Burgess Mews SW19 179 D4
Burgess Park Mans NW6 69 C4
Burgess Rd E15 76 C4
Sutton SM1 217 D4
Burgess St E14 97 C2
Burge St SE1 262 D5
Burghill Rd SE26 185 A6
Burghley Ave
Borehamwood WD6 11 A6
Kingston KT3 177 B2
Burghley Hall Cl SW19 157 A3
Burghley Ho SW19 157 A1
Burghley Pl CR4 202 D5
Burghley Rd E11 54 C1
N8 50 C6
NW5 71 B4
Wimbledon SW19 179 A6
Burghley Twr W3 111 D6
Burgh St N1 94 D5 234 D4
Burgon St EC4 241 D1
Burgos Cl CR0 220 C2
Burgos Gr SE10 141 D4
Burgoyne Rd N4 50 D3
SW9 138 B2
Ashford TW16 171 D4
South Norwood SE25 205 D5
Burham Cl SE20 184 C3
Burhan Uddin Ho E1 243 C5
Burhill Gr HA5 23 A1
Buriton Ho 9 SW15 156 B3
Burke Cl SW15 133 C1
Burke Ho 1 SW11 136 B1
Burke Lo E13 99 B4
Burke St E16 98 D2
Burket Cl UB2 107 B2
Burland Rd SW11 158 D6
Burleigh Ave DA15 167 D6
Hackbridge SM6 219 B5
Burleigh Ct N17 34 A4
Burleigh Gdns N14 15 C3
Ashford TW15 171 A5
Burleigh Ho SW3 266 D5
W10 90 D2
Enfield EN1 18 A6
Burleigh Par N14 15 D3
Burleigh Pl SW15 156 D6
Burleigh Rd
Cheam SM3 201 A1
Enfield EN1 5 C1
Hillingdon UB10 82 D6
Burleigh St WC2 250 C6
Burleigh Way EN2 5 B2
Burleigh Wlk SE6 164 A3
Burley Cl Chingford E4 35 C5
Mitcham SW16 181 D1
Burley Ho E1 96 D1
Burley Rd E16 99 C2
Burlington Arc W1 249 A5
Burlington Ave
Richmond TW9 132 C4
Romford RM7 59 D3
Burlington Cl 5 E6 100 A1
W9 91 C3
East Bedfont TW14 149 B4
Orpington BR6 226 D6
Pinner HA5 40 B6
Burlington Ct W4 133 A5
Burlington Danes Sch W12 90 B1
Burlington Gate SW20 179 A1
Burlington Gdns W1 115 C6 249 A5
W3 111 A5
W4 111 A1
Dagenham RM6 59 A2
Fulham SW6 135 A3
Burlington Ho NW3 70 B3
Burlington Jun Sch KT3 199 D5
Burlington La W4 133 B5
Burlington Lo BR7 188 B3
Burlington Mews W3 111 A5
1 Putney SW15 157 B6
Burlington Pl
Fulham SW6 135 A3
Woodford IG8 21 A1
Burlington Rd N10 49 A6
W4 111 A1
Enfield EN2 5 B4
Fulham SW6 135 A3
Hounslow TW7 130 B4
New Malden KT3 199 D5
South Norwood CR7 183 B1
Tottenham N17 34 A2
Burlington Rise EN4 14 D4
Burma Rd N16 73 B4
Burmarsh 6 NW5 71 A2
Burmarsh Ct SE20 184 C2
Burma Terr 11 SE19 183 C5
Burmester Ho SW17 158 A1
Burmester Rd SW17 158 A1
Burnaby Cres W4 133 A6
Burnaby Ct 27 SE16 118 A4
Burnaby Gdns W4 132 D6
Burnaby St SW10 136 A5 266 B3
Burnand Ho 3 W14 112 D3
Burnaston Ho 5 E5 74 A5
Burnbrae Cl N12 29 D4
Burnbury Rd SW12 159 C3
Burncroft Ave EN3 6 C3
Burndell Way UB4 84 D2
Burne Jones Ho W14 254 B3
Burnell Ave DA16 146 A3
Richmond TW10 175 C5
Burnell Gdns HA7 25 D1
Burnell Ho 19 SW2 160 C3
Burnell Rd SM1 217 D4
Burnell Wlk SE1 263 D2
Burnels Ave E6 100 C4
Burness Cl N7 72 B2
Burne St NW1 237 A4
Burnett Cl E9 74 C3
Burnett Ct SW11 267 A1
Burnett Ho 5 SE13 142 A3
Burney Ave KT5 198 B4
Burney Ho 4 SW16 181 C5
Burney St SE10 142 A5
Burnfoot Ave SW6 135 A4 264 B1
Burnham NW3 70 C1
Burnham Ave UB10 61 A4
Burnham Cl NW7 28 A3
SE1 263 D3
Enfield EN1 5 C5
Harrow HA3 43 A5
Burnham Cres E11 55 C5
Burnham Ct NW4 46 C5
W2 245 D6
Burnham Dr KT4 216 D6
Burnham Est 8 E2 96 C4
Burnham Gdns
Cranford TW4 128 B4
Croydon CR0 205 D2
Hayes UB3 105 B3
Burnham Rd DA14 169 A2
E4 35 B5
Dagenham RM9 102 B6
Morden SM4 201 D5
Burnham St E2 96 C4
Kingston KT2 176 C2
Burnham Way W13 109 B3
Penge SE26 185 B5
Burnhill Ho EC1 235 A1
Burnhill Rd BR3 185 C1
Burnley Cl WD19 22 C5
Burnley Rd NW10 68 A3
SW9 138 B3
Burnsall St SW3 114 C1 257 B2
Burns Ave DA15 168 B5
Feltham TW14 150 A5
Ilford RM6 58 C2
Southall UB1 107 C6
Burns Cl DA16 145 D4
Hayes UB4 84 A2
Mitcham SW17 180 B4
Burns Ct SM6 219 B1
Burns Ho 18 E2 96 C4
11 N16 73 C4
N7 72 B2
SE17 261 D1
Burn's Ho NW10 89 C6
Burnside RM8 58 C1
Burnside Ave E4 35 B4
Burnside Cl SE16 118 D5
Barnet EN5 1 C2
Twickenham TW1 153 A5
Burnside Cres HA0 87 D6
Burns Rd SW11 136 D3
W13 109 B4
Burn's Rd NW10 89 D6
Burns Rd HA0 88 A5
Burns Way TW5 128 D4
Burnt Ash Hill SE12 164 D5
Lewisham SE12 165 A3
Burnt Ash Hts BR1 187 B5
Burnt Ash La BR1, SE12 187 B5
Burnt Ash Prim Sch BR1 187 A5
Burnt Ash Rd SE12 164 D6
Burnthwaite Rd SW6 135 B5 264 D3
Burnt Oak Broadway HA8 26 D2
Burnt Oak Fields HA8 27 A2
Burnt Oak Jun Sch DA15 168 A3
Burnt Oak La DA15 168 B3
Burnt Oak Sta HA8 27 A2

Burntwood Cl SW18 .158 C3
Burntwood Ct SW17 .158 A1
Burntwood Grange Rd
SW18 . . . . .158 C3
Burntwood La SW17 .158 B2
Burntwood Sch
SW17 . . . . .158 B2
Burntwood View
SE19 . . . . .183 D5
Buross St E1 . . . . . . .96 B1
Burpham Cl UB4 . . . . .84 D2
Burrage Ct 17 SE16 . .118 D2
Burrage Gr SE18 . . . .123 A2
Burrage Pl SE18 . . . .122 D1
Burrage Rd SE18 . . . .123 A1
Burrard Ho 11 E2 . . . .96 C5
Burrard Rd NW6 . . . . .69 C4
Newham E16 . . . . . .99 C4
Burr Cl DA7 . . . . . . .147 B2
E1 . . . . .118 A5
Burrel Ct HA1 . . . . . .42 B2
Burrell Cl
Croydon CR0 . . . . .207 A3
Edgware HA8 . . . . . .10 D2
Burrell Ho 4 TW1 . . .153 B4
Burrell Row BR3 . . . .185 C1
Burrells 9 BR3 . . . .185 D1
Burrell St
SE1 . . . . . .116 D5 251 C4
Burrell's Wharf Sq
E14 . . . . .119 D1
Burrell Twrs E10 . . . .53 C2
Burrhill Ct SE16 . . . .118 D3
Burritt Rd KT1 . . . . .176 C1
Burrmead Ct NW2 . . . .67 D5
Burroughs Gdns NW4 .46 B5
Burroughs The NW4 . .46 B5
Burrow Ho 19 SW9 . .138 C4
Burrow Rd SE22 . . . .139 C1
Burrows Mews SE1 . .251 C2
Burrows Rd NW10 . . . .90 C4
Burrow Wlk SE21 . . . .161 A4
Burr Rd SW18 . . . . . .157 C4
Bursar St SE1 . . . . . .253 A3
Bursdon Cl DA15 . . . .167 D2
Bursland Rd EN3 . . . . .6 A1
Burslem St E1 . . . . . .96 A1
Bursted Wood Prim Sch
DA7 . . . . .147 D3
Burstock Rd SW15 . . .135 A1
Burston Rd SW15 . . . .156 D6
Burstow Rd SW20 . . .179 A2
Burtenshaw Rd KT7 . .197 A3
Burtley Cl N4 . . . . . . .51 A1
Burton Bank N1 . . . . .73 B1
Burton Cl
Chessington KT9 . . .213 D1
South Norwood 205 B6
Burton Ct SW3 . . . . .257 C2
Thames Ditton KT7 . .197 A3
Burton Dr EN3 . . . . . . .7 C6
Burton Gdns TW5 . . .129 B4
Burton Gr SE17 . . . . .262 C1
Burton Ho 6 SE16 . .118 B4
SE5 . . . . .138 D4
Penge SE26 . . . . . .184 B5
Burtonhole Cl NW7 . . .28 C6
Burtonhole La NW7 . . .28 D6
Burton Lo 5 SW15 . .157 B6
Burton Mews SW1 . . .258 B3
Burton Pl WC1 . . . . .232 D1
Burton Rd NW6 . . . . . .69 B1
SW9 . . . . .138 D3
8 SW9 . . . . .138 C3
Kingston KT2 . . . . .176 A3
Wanstead E18 . . . . .55 B6
Burtons Ct E15 . . . . . .76 B1
Burtons Rd TW12 . . .174 A6
Burton St WC1 93 D3 239 D6
Burtonwood Ho N4 . . .51 B2
Burt Rd E16 . . . . . . .121 C5
Burtt Ho 6 N1 . . . . . .95 C4
Burtwell La SE27, . . .183 B6
Burwash Ho SE1 . . . .252 D1
Burwash Rd SE18 . . .123 B1
Burwell 2 KT1 . . . . .176 C1
Burwell Ave UB6 . . . . .64 C2
Burwell Cl 25 E1 . . . . .96 B1
Burwell Rd E10 . . . . . .53 A1
Burwell Wlk 3 E3 . . . .97 C3
Burwood Ave BR2 . . .225 D4
Pinner HA5 . . . . . . .40 C4
Burwood Cl KT6 . . . .198 C1
Burwood Ct SE23 . . .162 C4
Burwood Ho 11 SW9 138 D1
Burwood Pl W2 . . . . .237 B2

Bury Ave Hayes UB4 . .83 C5
Ruislip HA4 . . . . .39 A3
Bury Ct EC3 . . . . . . .118 D5
Bury Ct EC3 . . . . . . .243 B2
Bury Gr SM4 . . . . . . .201 D4
Bury Hall Villas N9 . . .17 D4
Bury Pl WC1 . . .94 A2 240 B3
Bury Rd N22 . . . . . . .50 C6
Chingford E4 . . . . . .20 C6
Dagenham RM10 . . . .81 D3
Buryside IG2 . . . . . . .57 D6
Bury St EC3 . . .95 C1 243 B2
SW1 . . . . . .115 C5 249 B4
Edmonton N9 . . . . . .18 A3
Ruislip HA4 . . . . .39 B3
Bury St W N9 . . . . . . .17 C4
Bury Wlk
SW3 . . . . . .114 C1 257 A2
Burywood Ct EN3 . . . . .6 C3
Busbridge Ho 16 E14 .97 C2
Busby Ho SW16 . . . .181 C6
Busby Pl NW5 . . . . . .71 D2
Busch Cl TW7 . . . . . .131 B4
Busch Cnr TW7 . . . . .131 B4
Bushbaby Cl SE1 . . . .263 A5
Bushberry Rd E9 . . . . .75 A2
Bush Cl IG2 . . . . .57 C4
Bush Cotts 12 SW18 .157 C6
Bush Ct N14 . . . . .15 C3
7 W12 . . . . .112 D4
Bushell Cl SW2 . . . . .160 B2
Bushell Gn WD23 . . . . .8 B2
Bushell Ho 3 SE27 . .183 A6
Bushell St E1 . . . . . .118 A5
Bushell Way BR7 . . . .188 C5
Bushey Ave BR5 . . . .211 B2
E18 . . . . .54 D6
Bushey Cl Chingford E4 .20 A1
Ickenham UB10 . . . . .60 C6
Bushey Ct SW20 . . . .178 B1
Bushey Down SW12 . .159 B2
Bushey Fst Sch KT3 . .200 B6
Bushey Hall SE5 . . . .139 D4
Bushey Heath Prim Sch
WD23 . . . . .8 A4
Bushey Hill Rd SE5 . .139 D4
Bushey Ho SE12 . . . .165 C1
Bushey La SM1 . . . . .217 C4
Bushey Lees SE15 . . .167 D5
Bushey Meads Sch
WD23 . . . . .8 A6
Bushey Mid Sch
SW20 . . . . .200 B6
Bushey Rd E13 . . . . . .99 C5
N15 . . . . .51 C3
Croydon CR0 . . . . .223 C6
Hayes UB3 . . . . . . .105 C2
Ickenham UB10 . . . . .60 C6
Sutton SM1 . . . . . .217 C4
West Barnes SW20 . .178 D1
Bushey Way BR3 . . . .208 B4
Bush Fair Ct N14 . . . .15 B5
Bushfield Cl HA8 . . . . .10 D2
Bushfield Cres HA8 . . .10 D2
Bushfield Ho N5 . . . . .73 A3
Bush Gr NW9 . . . . . . .45 A2
Stanmore HA7 . . . . .25 D2
Bushgrove Rd RM8 . . .80 D5
Bush Hill N21 . . . . . . .17 A5
Bush Hill Par EN1 . . . .17 B4
Bush Hill Park Prim Sch
EN1 . . . . .18 A6
Bush Hill Park Sta
EN1 . . . . .17 D1
Bush Hill Rd
Enfield N21 . . . . . . .17 B5
Harrow HA3 . . . . . . .44 B3
Bush Ind Est NW10 . . .89 D3
Bush La EC4 . .117 B6 252 C6
Bushmead Cl 6 N15 . .51 D5
Bushmoor Cres SE18 144 D5
Bushnell Rd SW17 . . .159 B1
Bush Rd E8 . . . . .96 B6
SE8 . . . . .118 D2
Littleton TW17 . . . . .192 B4
Richmond TW9 . . . . .132 B6
Wanstead E11 . . . . . .55 A2
Woodford IG9 . . . . . .37 D6
Bushway RM8 . . . . . . .80 D5
Bushwood E11 . . . . . .55 A1
Bushwood Dr
SE1 . . . . . .117 D2 263 D3
Bushwood Rd TW9 . .132 C6
Bushy Ct KT1 . . . . . .175 C2
Bushy Park Gdns
TW12 . . . . .174 B5
Bushy Park Rd TW11 175 B3
Bushy Rd TW11 . . . . .174 D2
Business Acad The
DA18 . . . . .125 A4

Business Design Ctr ★
N1 . . . . .94 C6 234 B5
Buspace Studios 3
W10 . . . . .91 A3
Butcher Row E1 . . . . . .96 D1
Butchers Rd E16 . . . . .99 A1
Bute Ave TW10 . . . . .154 A2
Bute Ct SM6 . . . . . . .219 C3
Bute Gdns W6 . . . . . .112 D2
Wallington SM6 . . . .219 C3
Bute Gdns W SM6 . . .219 C3
Bute House Prep Sch
W6 . . . . .112 D2
Bute Rd Ilford IG6 . . . .56 D4
Thornton Heath CR0 .204 C1
Wallington SM6 . . . .219 C4
Bute St SW7 . .114 B2 256 C4
Butfield Ho 6 E9 . . . . .74 C2
Butler Ave HA1 . . . . . .42 B2
Butler Ct
Dagenham RM8 . . . . .81 C6
Wembley HA0 . . . . . .65 A4
Butler Ho 13 E14 . . . . .97 B1
32 E2 . . . . .96 C4
5 SW9 . . . . .138 D4
Butler Pl SW1 . . . . . .259 C6
Butler Rd NW10 . . . . .67 D1
Dagenham RM8 . . . . .80 B4
Harrow HA1 . . . . . . .42 A2
Butler's Cotts DA7 . .147 C3
Butler St 33 E2 . . . . . .96 C4
Hillingdon UB10 . . . . .82 D3
Butler's Wharf W
SE1 . . . . .253 C3
Butley Ct 7 E3 . . . . . .97 A5
Butterfield Cl
1 SE16 . . . . .118 B4
Tottenham N17 . . . . .33 A4
Twickenham TW1 . . .152 D5
Butterfield Row EN2 . . .5 A2
Butterfields E17 . . . . . .54 A4
Butterfield Sq 10 E6 .100 B1
Butterfly La SE9 . . . .166 D5
Butterfly Wlk 2 SE5 .139 B4
Butter Hill SM5,SM6 . .219 A4
Butteridges Cl RM9 . .103 B6
Buttermere NW1 . . . .231 D2
Buttermere Cl E11 . . . .76 B4
SE1 . . . . .263 C3
East Bedfont TW14 . .149 C2
West Barnes SM4 . . .200 D3
Buttermere Ct NW8 . .229 C6
Buttermere Dr SW15 .157 A6
Buttermere Ho 11 E3 .97 B4
N12 . . . . .30 C5
Buttermere Wlk 9 E8 73 D2
Butterwick W6 . . . . . .112 C2
Butterworth Ct SW16 160 A1
Butterworth Gdns IG8 37 A5
Buttesland St
N1 . . . . .95 B4 235 D2
Buttfield Cl RM10 . . . . .81 D2
Buttmarsh Cl SE18 . .122 D1
Buttsbury Rd IG1 . . . .79 A3
Butts Cotts TW13 . . .151 B1
Butts Cres TW13 . . . .151 C1
Butts Ho TW13 . . . . .151 C1
Butts Piece UB5 . . . . .84 B5
Butts Rd BR1 . . . . . .186 C5
Butts The TW8 . . . . . .131 D6
Buxhall Cres E9 . . . . . .75 B2
Buxlow Prep Sch HA9 66 A5
Buxted Rd E8 . . . . . . .73 D1
N12 . . . . .30 C5
SE22 . . . . .139 C1
Buxton Cl N9 . . . . .18 C2
Woodford IG8 . . . . . .37 D4
Buxton Cres SM3 . . . .217 A4
Buxton Ct N1 . . . . . . .235 B2
Buxton Dr E11 . . . . . . .54 C5
Kingston KT3 . . . . .177 B1
Buxton Gdns W3 . . . .110 D6
Buxton Ho E11 . . . . . .54 C5
3 SW11 . . . . .136 B1
Buxton Lo E11 . . . . . .77 B6
Buxton Rd E15 . . . . . .76 C3
E17 . . . . .53 A5
E6 . . . . .100 A4
N19 . . . . .49 D1
NW2 . . . . .68 B2
Chingford E4 . . . . . .20 B4
Ilford IG2 . . . . .57 C3
Mortlake SW14 . . . .133 C2
Thornton Heath CR7 .204 D4
Buxton St E1 . .96 A3 243 D5
Buzzard Creek Ind Est
IG11 . . . . .102 A2
Byam Shaw Sch of Art
N19 . . . . .71 D6
Byam St SW6 . . . . . .136 A3

Byards Croft SW16 . .181 D2
Byards Ct SE16 . . . . .118 D3
Byas Ho 6 E3 . . . . . . .97 B4
Byatt Wlk TW12 . . . .173 B4
Bychurch End 9
TW11 . . . . .174 D1
Bycroft Rd UB1 . . . . . .85 C3
Bycroft St SE20 . . . . .184 D3
Bycullah Ave EN2 . . . . .4 D3
Bycullah Rd EN2 . . . . . .4 D3
Byefield Cl SE16 . . . . .119 A4
Byelands Cl 12 SE16 .118 D5
Bye The W3 . . . . .89 C1
Byeways TW2 . . . . . .151 A5
Byeways The SW15 . .198 D4
Byeway The SW14 . . .133 A2
Bye Way The HA3 . . . . .24 D2
Byfeld Gdns SW13 . . .134 A4
Byfield Ct KT3 . . . . . .200 A5
Byfield Rd TW7 . . . . .131 A2
Byford Cl E15 . . . . . . .76 C1
Bygrove CR0 . . . . . . .223 D1
Bygrove Ct SW19 . . . .180 B4
Bygrove Prim Sch E14 97 D1
Bygrove Rd SW19 . . .180 B4
Bygrove St E14 . . . . . .97 D1
Byland Cl N21 . . . . . . .16 B3
Bylands Cl SE2 . . . . .124 B3
Byne Rd
Carshalton SM5 . . . .218 C6
Forest Hill SE26 . . .184 C5
Bynes Rd CR2 . . . . . .221 B1
Byng Pl WC1 . .93 D3 239 C5
Byng St E14 . . . . . . .119 C4
Bynon Ave DA7 . . . . .147 B2
Byre Rd N14 . . . . .15 B5
Byrne Ho 11 SW2 . . .160 B6
Byrne Rd SW12 . . . . .159 B2
Byron Ave E12 . . . . . .78 A2
NW9 . . . . .44 D6
Borehamwood WD6 . .10 C1
Cranford TW4 . . . . .128 B3
Sutton SM1 . . . . . .218 B4
West Barnes KT3 . . .200 A4
Woodford E18 . . . . . .36 D1
Byron Ave E SM1 . . . .218 B4
Byron Cl E8 . . . . .96 A6
SE28 . . . . .124 C5
Feltham TW12 . . . . .173 B6
Forest Hill SE26 . . .185 A6
Streatham SW16 . . .182 A4
Walton-on-T KT12 . .195 A1
Byron Court Prim Sch
HA0 . . . . .65 C6
Byron Ct 3 NW6 . . . . .70 A1
SW3 . . . . .257 B3
W7 . . . . .109 A2
W9 . . . . .91 C3
WC1 . . . . .240 C6
Dulwich SE21 . . . . .162 A2
Enfield EN2 . . . . .4 D3
Harrow HA1 . . . . . . .42 C3
Byron Dr DA8 . . . . . .147 D5
N2 . . . . .48 B3
Byron Gdns SM1 . . . .218 B4
Byron Hill Rd HA1,HA2 64 C6
Byron Ho 5 BR3 . . . .185 B4
Byron Mews NW3 . . . .70 C4
NW6 . . . . .70 A1
Byron Par UB10 . . . . . .83 A3
Byron Rd E10 . . . . . . .53 D1
E17 . . . . .53 C6
NW2 . . . . .68 B6
NW7 . . . . .28 A5
Ealing W5 . . . . .110 B5
Harrow HA1 . . . . . . .42 C3
Harrow HA3 . . . . . . .24 D1
Wembley HA0 . . . . . .65 C5
Byron St E14 . . . . .98 A1
Byron Way Hayes UB4 .83 D3
Northolt UB5 . . . . . .85 A4
West Drayton UB7 . .104 B2
Bysouth Cl N15 . . . . . .51 B5
Bythorn St SW9 . . . . .138 B1
Byton Rd SW17 . . . . .180 D4
Byward Ave TW14 . . .150 C2
Byward St
EC3 . . . . . .117 C6 253 B5
Bywater Ho SE18 . . . .122 A3
Bywater Pl SE16 . . . .119 A5
Bywater St
SW3 . . . . . .114 D1 257 C2
Byways The KT19 . . . .215 D4
Bywell Pl W1 . . . . . . .239 A3
Bywood Ave CR0 . . . .206 D3
Bywood Terr CR0 . . . .206 D3
Byworth Wlk N19 . . . . .50 A4

C

Cabbell St
NW1 . . . . . . .92 C2 237 A3
Cabinet Off SW1 . . . .250 A2
Cabinet War Rooms ★
SW1 . . . . . .115 D4 249 D2
Cabinet Way E4 . . . . . .35 D2
Cable Ho WC1 . . . . . .234 A1
Cable Pl SE10 . . . . . .142 A4
Cable St E1 . . . . .118 B6
Cabot Ct SE16 . . . . . .118 D3
Cabot Sq E14 . . . . . .119 C5
Cabot Way 3 E6 . . . . . .99 D6
Cabul Rd SW11 . . . . .136 C3
Cactus Cl SE5 . . . . . .139 C3
Cactus Wlk W12 . . . . .89 D1
Caddington Cl EN4 . . .14 C6
Caddington Rd NW2 . .69 A5
Caddis Cl HA7 . . . . . . .24 D3
Cadbury Cl
Ashford TW16 . . . . .171 C3
Isleworth TW7 . . . . .131 A4
Cadbury Rd TW16 . . .171 C4
Cadbury Way 1
SE16 . . . . .118 A2
Caddell Cl E2 . . . . . . .95 D5
Cadell Ho 12 E2 . . . . .95 D5
Cader Rd SW18 . . . . .158 A5
Cadet Dr SE1 117 D1 263 D2
Cadet Tyler Ho 10
SE10 . . . . .142 A4
Cadiz St SE17 117 A1 262 B1
Cadley Terr SE23 . . . .162 C2
Cadman Cl SW9 . . . . .138 D5
Cadmer Cl KT3 . . . . .199 C5
Cadmore Ho 4 N1 . . .72 D1
Cadmus Cl 9 SW4 . . .137 D2
Cadmus Ct 6 SW9 . . .138 C4
Cadnam Lo E14 . . . . .120 B3
Cadnam Point 15
SW15 . . . . .156 B3
Cadogan Cl E9 . . . . . .75 B1
Beckenham BR3 . . . .186 B1
Harrow HA2 . . . . . . .63 D4
Teddington TW11 . . .174 C5
Cadogan Ct SW3 . . . .257 C3
Sutton SM2 . . . . . . .217 D2
New Malden KT3 . . .199 C5
Cadogan Ct Gdns
SW1 . . . . .258 A4
Cadogan Gate
SW1 . . . . . .114 D2 257 D3
Cadogan Gdns N3 . . . .29 C2
SW3 . . . . . .114 D2 257 D3
Southgate N21 . . . . .16 C6
Wanstead E18 . . . . . .55 B6
Cadogan Ho SW3 . . .266 D5
Cadogan La
SW1 . . . . . .115 A3 258 A5
Cadogan Pl
SW1 . . . . . .114 D3 257 D5
1 Richmond TW10 . .175 D6
South Norwood CR7 .183 A1
11 Wanstead E11 . . .55 A5
Woodford E18 . . . . . .37 B2
Cadogan Rd SE18 . . .123 A3
Kingston KT6 . . . . .197 D4
Cadogan Sq
SW1 . . . . . .114 D3 257 D5
Cadogan St
SW3 . . . . . .114 D2 257 C3
Cadogan Terr E9 . . . . .75 D2
Cadoxton Ave 3 N15 .51 D3
Cadwallon Rd SE9 . . .167 A2
Caedmon Rd N7 . . . . .72 B4
Caerleon Cl
Claygate KT10 . . . . .213 B1
Sidcup DA14 . . . . . .190 C5
Caerleon Terr SE2 . . .124 B2
Caernarvon Cl CR4 . .204 A6
Caernarvon Ct 3
KT5 . . . . .198 B4
Caernarvon Ho W2 . .236 A2
Caesar Ct 25 E2 . . . . .96 D5
Caesar's Way TW17 . .193 D2
Caesars Wlk CR4 . . . .202 A2
Cahill St EC1 . . . . . . .242 B5
Cahir St E14 . . . . . . .119 D2
Cain Ct 2 W5 . . . . . . .87 C2
Caine Ho W3 . . . . . . .110 A4
Cain's La TW14 . . . . .149 C6
Caird St W10 . . . . .91 A4
Cairn Ave W5 . . . . . . .109 C5
Cairndale Cl BR1 . . . .186 C5
Cairnfield Ave NW2 . . .67 C2
Cairnfield Ct N7 . . . . . .72 C5
Cairns Ho 3 N7 . . . . .72 C4
Cairns Mews SE18 . . .144 C4
Cairns Rd SW11 . . . .158 C6
Cairn Way HA7 . . . . . .24 D4
Cairo New Rd CR0 . . .220 D6
Cairo Rd E17 . . . . .53 C5

Caister Ho N7 . . . . . . .72 B2
10 Balham SW12 . . .159 B4
Caister Ho 5 E15 . . . .98 D6
Caistor Mews SW12 .159 B4
Caistor Park Rd E15 . .98 D6
Caistor Rd SW12 . . . .159 B4
Caithness Gdns DA15 167 C5
Caithness Ho N1 . . . .233 C6
Caithness Rd W14 . . .112 D3
Mitcham CR4 . . . . . .181 B3
Calabria Rd N5 . . . . . .72 D3
Calais Gate SE5 . . . . .138 C4
Calais St SE5 . . . . . . .138 D4
Calbourne Rd SW12 .159 A4
Calcott Wlk SE9 . . . .187 D6
Calcraft Ho 10 E2 . . . .96 C5
Caldbeck Ave KT4 . . .200 B1
Caldecot Ct SE5 . . . .139 A3
Caldecote 3 KT1 . . . .176 C1
Caldecote Gdns WD23 .8 C4
Caldecote La WD23 . . .8 D5
Caldecot Rd SE5 . . . .139 A3
Caldecott Way E5 . . . .74 D5
Calder Ave UB6 . . . . . .86 D5
Calder Cl EN1 . . . . .5 C2
Calder Ct SE16 . . . . .119 B5
Calder Gdns HA8 . . . . .44 C6
Calderon Ho NW8 . . .230 A4
Calderon Pl W10 . . . . .90 C2
Calderon Rd E11 . . . . .76 B5
Calder Rd SM4 . . . . .202 A4
Caldervale Rd SW4 . .159 D5
Calderwood St SE18 .122 C2
Caldew Ct NW7 . . . . . .28 A3
Caldew St SE5 . . . . . .139 B5
Caldicote Gn NW9 . . . .45 C3
Caldwell Rd WD19 . . . .22 D6
Caldwell St
SW9 . . . . .138 B5 270 D3
Caldy Rd DA17 . . . . . .125 D3
Caldy Wlk 16 N1 . . . . .73 A2
Caleb St SE1 . . . . . . .252 B2
Caledonia Ct IG11 . . .102 C5
Caledonia Ho 17 E14 .97 A1
Caledonian Cl 1 IG3 .58 D1
Caledonian Market
SE1 . . . . . . .117 C3 263 B6
Caledonian Rd
N1 . . . . .94 B6 233 C5
N7 . . . . .72 B2
Caledonian Road &
Barnsbury Sta N7 . . .72 B1
Caledonian Road Sta
N7 . . . . .72 B2
Caledonian Wharf Rd
E14 . . . . .120 B2
Caledonia Rd TW19 . .148 A3
Caledonia St N1 . . . .233 B3
Caledon Rd E6 . . . . . .78 B1
Hackbridge SM5,SM6 .219 A4
Cale St SW3 . .114 C1 257 A2
Caletock Way SE10 . .120 D1
Calgarth NW1 . . . . . .232 B3
Calgary Ct 24 SE16 . .118 C4
Caliban Twr 9 N1 . . . .95 C5
Calico Ho 4 SW11 . . .136 A2
Calico Row 5 SW11 . .136 A2
Calidore Cl SW2 . . . .160 B5
California La WD23 . . . .8 B3
California Rd KT3 . . . .199 A5
Callaby Terr 11 N1 . . .73 B2
Callaghan Cl SE13 . . .142 C1
Callahan Cotts 8 E1 . .96 C2
Callander Rd SE6 . . . .164 A2
Callanders The WD23 . .8 C3
Callard Ave N13 . . . . .32 D6
Callcott Ct NW6 . . . . .69 B1
Callcott Rd NW6 . . . . .69 B1
Callcott St W8 . . . . . .245 A4
Callendar Rd SW7 . . .256 C6
Callingham Cl 17 E14 .97 B2
Callingham Ho 1
SW4 . . . . .138 A2
Callis Farm Cl TW19 .148 A5
Callis Rd E17 . . . . .53 B3
Callonfield 3 E17 . . . .53 A5
Callow St
SW3 . . . . . .136 B6 266 C6
Calmington Rd SE5 . .139 C6
Calmont Rd BR1 . . . .186 C6
Calonne Rd SW19 . . .178 D6
Calshot Ho N1 . . . . . .233 C4
Calshot Rd TW6 . . . . .126 D3
Calshot St N1 . .94 B5 233 C3
Calshot Way Enfield EN2 4 D2
Harlington TW6 . . . .126 D3
Calstock NW1 . . . . . .232 C5
Calstock Ho SE11 . . .261 B2
Calthorpe Gdns
Edgware HA8 . . . . . .26 B5

Calthorpe Gdns *continued*
Sutton SM1 218 A5
Calthorpe St
WC1 94 B3 240 D6
Calton Ave SE21 161 C5
Calton Rd EN5 14 B5
Calver 13 NW5 71 B4
Calver Ct E17 54 B6
Calverley Cl BR3 185 D4
Calverley Cres RM10 81 C6
Calverley Gr N19 49 D1
Calverley Rd KT17 216 A2
Calvert Ave E2 95 D4
Calvert Cl
Belvedere DA17 125 D2
Sidcup DA14 191 A4
Calvert Ct 1 N19 49 C1
5 Richmond TW9 132 B1
Calvert Ho 9 W12 112 B6
Calverton SE5 139 C6
Calverton Prim Sch
E16 99 D1
Calverton Rd E6 100 C6
Calvert Rd SE10 120 D1
Calvert's Bldgs SE1 252 C3
Calvert St
NW1 93 A6 231 A6
Calvin St E1 95 D3 243 C5
Calydon Rd SE7 121 B1
Calypso Cres 5
SE15 139 D5
Calypso Way SE8,
SE16 119 B2
Camac Rd TW2 152 B3
Camarthen Gn NW9 45 C3
Cambalt Ho 3 SW15 156 D6
Cambalt Rd SW15 156 D6
Cambell Inf Sch RM9 80 D1
Cambell Jun Sch RM9 80 D1
Cambell Wlk N1 233 B6
Camber Ho 4 SE15 140 C6
Camberley Ave
Enfield EN1 5 C1
Wimbledon SW20 178 B1
Camberley Cl SM3 216 D5
Camberley Ct 8
SM2 217 D1
Camberley Ho NW1 231 D3
Camberley Rd TW6 126 C2
Cambert Way SE9 143 B1
Camberwell Church St
SE5 139 B4
Camberwell Coll of Arts
SE15 139 D5
SE5 139 C4
Camberwell Glebe
SE5 139 C4
Camberwell Gn SE5 139 B4
Camberwell Gr SE5 139 C3
Camberwell Green
SE5 139 A4
Camberwell New Rd
SW9 138 D5
Camberwell Rd SE5 139 A5
Camberwell Station Rd
SE5 139 A4
Camberwell Trad Est
SE5 139 A4
Cambeys Rd RM10 81 D3
Cambisgate SW19 179 A5
Camborne Ave W13 109 C4
Camborne Cl TW6 126 C2
Camborne Cres TW6 126 C2
Camborne Rd DA16 145 D3
Belmont SM2 217 D1
Croydon CR0 206 A2
Sidcup DA14 168 C1
Wandsworth SW18 157 C4
West Barnes SM4 200 D4
Harmondsworth TW6 126 C2
Camborne Way
Harlington TW6 126 C2
Heston TW5 129 C4
Cambourne Ave N9 18 D4
Cambourne Mews 6
W11 91 A1
Cambray Rd BR6 211 D2
Streatham SW12 159 C3
Cambria 6 BR3 185 D1
Cambria Cl DA15 167 C3
Hounslow TW3 129 C1
Cambria Ct TW14 150 B4
Cambria Gdns TW19 148 A4
Cambria Ho 16 E14 97 A1
Forest Hill SE26 184 A6
Cambrian Ave IG2 57 C4
Cambrian Cl SE27 160 D1
Cambrian Ct UB2 107 D2
Cambrian Gn NW9 45 C4
Cambrian Rd E10 53 C1
Cambrian Rd *continued*
Richmond TW10 154 B5
Cambria Rd SE5 139 A2
Cambria St
SW6 135 D5 265 D3
Cambridge Ave DA16 145 D1
NW6 91 C5
Greenford UB6 64 D3
Kingston KT3,SW20 177 D1
Cambridge Barracks Rd 12
SE18 122 B2
Cambridge Cir
WC2 93 D1 239 D1
Cambridge Cl E17 53 B3
NW10 67 A5
Hounslow TW4 129 A1
Wimbledon SW20 178 B2
Wood Green N22 32 C2
Cambridge Cotts
TW9 132 C6
Cambridge Cres 20 E2 96 B5
Teddington TW11 175 A5
Cambridge Ct 25 E2 96 B5
N16 51 C2
2 NW6 91 C5
Wimbledon SW20 178 B2
Cambridge Dr SE12 165 A6
Ruislip HA4 62 D6
Cambridge Gate
NW1 238 C6
Cambridge Gate Mews
NW1 238 D6
Cambridge Gdns N10 31 B2
NW6 91 C5
W10 91 A1
Enfield EN1 6 A3
Kingston KT1 176 C1
Southgate N21 17 B4
Tottenham N17 33 B3
Cambridge Gn SE9 166 D3
Cambridge Gr W6 112 B2
Penge SE20 184 B2
Cambridge Grove Rd
Kingston KT1 198 C6
13 Kingston KT1 176 C1
Cambridge Heath Rd
E1,E2 96 B4
Cambridge Heath Sta
E2 96 B5
Cambridge Ho
Ealing W13 87 A1
Fulham SW6 135 A2
2 Teddington TW11 175 A5
7 Woolwich SE18 122 B2
Cambridge Mans
SW11 267 C1
Cambridge Par EN1 6 A4
Cambridge Park Ct
TW1 153 D4
Cambridge Park Rd
E11 55 A2
Cambridge Pas 9 E9 74 C1
Cambridge Pk
Twickenham TW1 153 D5
Wanstead E11 55 A3
Cambridge Pl W8 245 D1
Cambridge Rd BR1 187 A3
E11 54 D3
NW6 91 C4
NW6 91 C5
SW11 136 D4 267 C1
W7 108 D4
Barking IG11 79 A1
Barnes SW13 133 D3
Carshalton SM5 218 C3
3 Chingford E4 20 B3
East Molesey KT8 195 B5
Hampton TW12 173 B3
Harrow HA2 41 C4
Hounslow TW4 129 A1
Ilford IG3 57 C1
Kingston KT1 176 C1
Littleton TW15 171 A3
Mitcham CR4 203 C6
New Malden KT3 199 C5
Penge SE20 206 B6
Richmond TW9 132 C5
Sidcup DA14 189 C6
Southall UB1 107 B5
Teddington TW11 175 A5
Twickenham TW1 153 D5
Walton-on-T KT12 194 B3
Wimbledon SW20 178 B2
Cambridge Rd N W4 110 D1
Cambridge Rd S 3
W4 110 D1
Cambridge Row
SE18 122 D1
Cambridge Sch W6 112 B2
Cambridge Sq
W2 92 C1 237 A2
Cambridge St
SW1 115 C1 259 A2
Cambridge Terr
NW1 231 C1
Edmonton N9 17 D4
Cambridge Terr Mews
NW1 231 D1
Cambstone Cl N11 15 A2
Cambus Cl UB4 85 A2
Cambus Rd E16 99 A2
Cam Ct 2 SE15 139 D6
Camdale Rd SE18 145 D5
Camden Ave
Feltham TW13 150 C3
Hayes UB4 106 D6
Camden Cl BR7 189 A2
Camden Ct 9 DA17 125 C1
Camden Gdns NW1 71 B1
Sutton SM1 217 D3
Thornton Heath CR7 204 D6
Camden Gr BR7 188 D4
Camden High St
NW1 93 C6 232 A5
Camden Hill Rd SE19 183 C4
Camden Ho 6 SE8 119 B1
Camdenhurst St E14 97 A1
Camden Jun Sch
SM5 218 D4
Camden Lock Pl NW1 71 B1
Camden Mews NW1 71 D2
Camden Mkt*
NW1 93 B6 231 D6
Camden Park Rd
BR7 188 C3
NW1 71 D2
Camden Pas
N1 94 D6 234 C5
Camden Rd DA5 169 B4
E17 53 B3
NW1 71 D2 231 D6
Carshalton SM5 218 D4
Sutton SM1 217 D3
Wanstead E11 55 B3
Camden Road Sta
NW1 71 C1
Camden Row SE3 142 C3
Camden Sch for Girls The
NW5 71 C2
Camden Sq NW1 71 D2
Camden St
NW1 93 C6 232 B5
Camden Studios
NW1 232 B5
Camden Town Sta
NW1 93 B6 231 D6
Camden Way BR7 188 C3
Thornton Heath CR7 204 D6
Camden Wlk N1 234 C5
Cameford Ct 20
SW12 160 A4
Camel Ct HA9 66 D6
Camelford NW1 232 B5
Camelford Ct 7 W11 91 A1
Camelford Wlk 8
W11 91 A1
Camel Gr KT2 175 D5
Camelia Ct IG8 36 C4
Camellia Ct 20 BR3 185 C3
Camellia Ho SE8 141 B5
Camellia Pl TW2 151 D4
Camellia St SW8 270 A3
Camelot Cl SE18 123 B4
Wimbledon SW19 179 C6
Camelot Ho 6 NW1 71 D2
Camelot Prim Sch
SE15 140 B6
Camel Rd E16 121 D5
Camera Pl SW10 266 C6
Cameret Ct 6 W11 112 D4
Cameron Cl N20 14 C2
Edmonton N18 34 B5
Cameron Ct 3 SW19 157 A3
Cameron Ho NW8 230 A4
SE5 139 A5
8 Bromley BR1 186 D2
Cameron House Sch
SW10 266 D5
Cameron Lo TW3 130 A1
Cameron Rd BR2 209 A4
Forest Hill SE6 163 B2
Ilford IG3 57 C1
Thornton Heath CR0 204 D3
Cameron Sq CR4 180 C2
Camerton Cl 8 E8 73 D2
Camfrey Ct N8 50 A5
Camgate Ctr The
TW19 148 B4
Camilla Cl TW16 171 D4
Camilla Ct 14 SM2 217 C1
Camilla Rd SE16 118 B2
Camille Cl SE25 206 A6
Camlan Rd BR1 186 D6
Camlet St E2 243 C6
Camlet Way EN4 1 D4
Camley St
NW1 93 D5 232 D4
Camm 23 NW9 27 D1
Camm Gdns
5 Kingston KT1 176 B1
Thames Ditton KT7 196 D2
Camomile Ave CR4 180 D2
Camomile St
EC3 95 C1 243 B2
Camomile Way UB7 82 A1
Campaign Ct W9 91 B3
Campana Rd
SW6 135 C4 265 B2
Campasps Bsns Pk
TW16 193 D4
Campbell Ave IG6 57 A5
Campbell Cl SE18 144 C4
Ruislip HA4 40 A3
Streatham SW16 181 D6
Twickenham TW2 152 B3
Campbell Croft HA8 26 C5
Campbell Ct NW9 45 A3
SW7 256 A5
Dulwich SE21 162 A3
Ealing W7 108 C6
Tottenham N17 33 D2
Campbell Gordon Way
NW2 68 B4
Campbell Ho SW1 259 A1
30 W12 112 B6
W2 236 C5
6 Wallington SM6 219 B4
Campbell Rd E15 76 D4
E17 53 B5
E3 97 C4
E6 100 A6
Ealing W7 108 C6
Thornton Heath CR0 204 D3
Tottenham N17 34 A2
Twickenham TW2 152 B2
Campdale Rd N7 71 D5
Campden Cres
Dagenham RM8 80 C4
Wembley HA0 65 B5
Campden Gr
W8 113 C4 245 B2
Campden Hill
W8 113 C4 245 A2
Campden Hill Ct W8 245 B2
Campden Hill Gate
W8 245 A2
Campden Hill Gdns
W8 245 A4
Campden Hill Mans
W8 245 B4
Campden Hill Pl
W14 244 D4
Campden Hill Rd
W8 113 C4 245 A2
Campden Hill Sq
W14 113 B5 244 D4
Campden Ho 4 NW6 70 B1
W8 245 B3
Campden Hos W8 245 A3
Campden House Cl
W8 245 B2
Campden Rd
Ickenham UB10 60 B4
South Croydon CR2 221 C3
Campden St
W8 113 C5 245 A3
Campe Ho 1 N10 31 A3
Campen Cl SW19 157 A2
Camperdown St E1 243 D1
Campfield Rd SE9 165 D4
Campion Cl
Harrow HA3 44 B3
Hillingdon UB8 82 B2
Newham E6 122 B6
South Croydon CR2 221 C4
Campion Ct 10 HA0 88 A5
Campion Gdns IG8 37 A5
Campion Ho 15 N16 73 C3
Campion House
(Seminary) TW7 130 B4
Campion Pl SE28 124 B5
Campion Rd
Hounslow TW7 130 D4
Putney SW15 156 C6
Campion Terr NW2 68 D5
Campion Way HA8 27 A6
Camplin Rd HA3 44 A4
Camplin St SE14 140 D5
Camp Rd SW19 178 C5
Campsbourne Ho 3
N8 50 A5
Campsbourne Jun & Inf
Schs N8 50 A6
Campsbourne The N8 50 A5
Campsey Gdns RM9 80 B1
Campsey Rd RM9 80 B1
Campsfield Ho N8 50 A6
Campsfield Rd N8 50 A6
Campshill Pl SE13 164 A6
Campshill Rd SE13 164 A6
Camp Site The BR8 191 C3
Campton Hill Twrs
W8 245 A4
Campus Rd E17 53 B3
Camp View SW19 178 B5
Cam Rd E15 98 B6
Camrose Ave DA8 147 D6
Edgware HA8 26 B2
Feltham TW13 172 C6
Camrose Cl
Croydon CR0 207 A2
Morden SM4 201 C5
Camrose St SE2 124 A2
Camsey Ho 8 SW2 160 B6
Canada Ave N18 33 A4
Canada Cres W3 89 A3
Canada Gdns SE13 164 A6
Canada Rd W3 89 A2
Canada Sq E14 119 D5
Canada St SE16 118 D4
Canada Way W12 112 B6
Canadian Ave SE6 163 D3
Canal App SE8 141 A6
Canal Bldg N1 235 A4
Canal Bridge SE15 140 A6
Canal Cl E1 97 A3
W10 90 D3
Canal Gr SE15 140 B6
Canal Head Public Sq
SE15 140 A4
Canal Path 22 E2 95 D6
Canalside Studios 31
N1 95 C6
Canal St SE5 139 B6
Canal Way W10 90 D3
Canal Wlk N1 95 B6 235 D6
Croydon CR0 205 D3
Forest Hill SE26 184 C5
Canary Wharf* E14 119 D5
Canary Wharf Pier River
Bus) E14 119 B5
Canary Wharf Sta
E14 119 C5
Canberra Cl NW4 46 A6
Canberra Dr UB4 84 C4
Canberra Prim Sch
W12 112 B6
Canberra Rd E6 100 B6
SE7 143 D6
Erith DA7 146 D6
Harlington TW6 126 C2
Canbury 2000 Bsns Pk 3
KT2 176 A2
Canbury Ave KT2 176 B2
Canbury Ct KT2 176 A3
Canbury Mews SE26 162 A1
Canbury Park Rd KT2 176 B2
Canbury Sch KT2 176 D4
Cancell Rd SW9 138 C4
Candahar Rd SW11 136 C3
Candida Ct 9 NW1 71 B1
Candishe Ho SE1 253 C2
Candler Mews TW1 153 A4
Candler St N15 51 B3
Candover St W1 239 A3
Candy St E3 97 B6
Caney Mews NW2 68 D6
Canfield Dr HA4 62 B3
Canfield Gdns NW6 69 D1
Canfield Ho N15 51 C3
Canfield Pl NW6 70 A2
Canford Ave UB5 85 A6
Canford Cl EN2 4 C3
Canford Gdns KT3 199 C3
Canford Pl TW11 175 C4
Canford Rd SW11 159 A6
Canham Rd W3 111 C4
South Norwood SE25 205 C6
Canmore Gdns SW16 181 C3
Cann Hall Prim Sch
E11 76 D5
Cann Hall Rd E11 76 D4
Cann Ho W14 254 B5
Canning Cres N22 32 B2
Canning Cross SE5 139 C3
Canning Ct N22 32 B2
Canning Ho 23 W12 112 B6
Canning Pas
W8 114 A3 256 A6
Canning Pl
W8 114 A3 256 A6
Canning Pl Mews
W8 256 A6
Canning Rd E15 98 C5
E17 53 A6
N5 72 D5
Croydon CR0 221 D6
Harrow HA3 42 D6
Cannington 14 NW5 71 A2
Cannington Rd RM9 80 C2
Canning Town E16 98 C2
Canning Town Sta
E16 98 C2
Cannizaro Rd SW19 178 D5
Cannock Ho N4 51 B2
Cannock Lo EN1 17 C5
Cannonbury Ave HA5 40 D3
Cannon Cl
Hampton TW12 173 D4
West Barnes SW20 200 C6
Cannon Dr E14 119 C6
Cannon Hill NW6 69 C3
Palmers Green N14 16 A1
Cannon Hill La SM4,
SW20 201 A5
Cannon Hill Mews
N14 16 A1
Cannon Ho SE11 260 D3
Penge SE26 184 B4
Cannon La NW3 70 B5
Pinner HA5 41 A3
Cannon Pl NW3 70 B5
SE7 122 A1
Cannon Rd DA7 147 B4
Palmers Green N14 16 A1
Cannon St
EC4 117 B6 252 B6
Cannon Street Rd E1 96 B1
Cannon Street Sta
EC4 117 B6 252 C6
Cannon Trad Est HA9 66 D4
Cannon Way KT8 195 D5
Cannon Wharf Bsns Ctr 12
SE8 119 A2
Canon Ave RM6 58 C4
Canon Barnett CE Prim
Sch E1 95 D1 243 D2
Canon Beck Rd SE16 118 C4
Canonbie Rd SE23 162 C4
Canonbury Cres N1 73 A1
Canonbury Ct 21 N1 72 D1
Canonbury Gr N1 73 A1
Canonbury La N1 72 D1
Canonbury Pk N N1 73 A2
Canonbury Pk S N1 73 A2
Canonbury Pl N1 72 D2
Canonbury Prim Sch
N1 72 D2
Canonbury Rd N1 72 D1
Enfield EN1 5 C4
Canonbury Sq N1 72 D1
Canonbury St N1 73 A1
Canonbury Sta N1,N5 73 A3
Canonbury Villas N1 72 D1
Canon Lane Fst & Mid
Schs HA5 40 D3
Canon Mohan Cl N14 15 B5
Canon Murnane Rd
SE1 263 C5
Canon Palmer RC Sch
IG3 57 C1
Canon Rd BR1 209 D6
Canon Row
SW1 116 A4 250 A1
Canons Cl N2 48 B2
Edgware HA8 26 B4
Canons Cnr HA8 26 A6
Canons Ct HA8 26 B4
Canons Dr HA8 26 B4
Canons High Sch HA8 26 B1
Canons L Ctr The
CR4 202 D5
Canonsleigh Rd RM9 80 B1
Canons Park Cl HA8 26 A3
Canons Park Sta HA8 26 A3
Canon St N1 95 A6 235 A5
Canon's Wlk CR0 222 D5
Canopus Way
Moor Park HA6 22 A6
Stanwell TW19 148 A4
Canrobert St E2 96 B4
Cantelowes Ho EN5 12 D6
Cantelowes Rd NW1 71 D2
Canterbury SE13 164 A6
Canterbury Ave
DA14,DA15 168 C2

Canterbury Ave continued
Redbridge IG1 ....**56** A2
Canterbury Cl 16 SE5 **139** A3
Beckenham BR3 .....**185** D2
7 Newham E6 ....**100** B1
Southall UB6 ....**85** D2
Canterbury Cres
SW9 ....**138** C2
Canterbury Ct NW11 ..**47** A3
NW6 ....**91** C5
15 NW9 ....**27** D1
W3 ....**111** C5
Ashford TW15 ....**170** B6
South Croydon CR2 ..**221** C4
Canterbury Gr SE27,
SW16 ....**160** C1
Canterbury Ho 6 E3 ..**97** D4
SE1 ....**260** D6
2 Barking IG11 ......**80** A1
Canterbury Ind Pk 15
SE15 ....**140** C6
Canterbury Mans
NW6 ....**69** D2
Canterbury Pl SE17 ..**261** D3
Canterbury Rd E10 ...**54** A3
NW6 ....**91** C5
Feltham TW13 ....**151** A2
Harrow HA1,HA2 .....**42** A4
Morden SM4 ....**202** A3
Thornton Heath CR0 ..**204** C2
Canterbury Terr NW6 ..**91** C5
Cantium Ret Pk SE1 ..**140** A6
Cantley Gdns
Ilford IG2 ....**57** A3
South Norwood SE19 .**183** D2
Cantley Rd W7 ......**109** A3
Canton St E14 ....**97** C1
Cantrell Rd E3 ......**97** C3
Cantwell Ho SE18 ...**144** D5
Cantwell Rd SE18 ...**144** D5
Canute Ct SW16 .....**160** C1
Canute Gdns SE16 ...**118** D2
Canvey St SE1 ......**252** A4
Cape Cl IG11 ....**78** D1
Cape Henry Ct 7
E14 ....**120** B6
Capel KT5 ....**198** B2
Capel Ave SM6 ......**220** B3
Capel Cl N20 ....**14** A1
Keston Mark BR2 ....**210** A1
Capel Ct SE20 ......**184** C2
Capel Gdns Ilford IG3 ..**79** D4
Pinner HA5 ....**41** B5
Capel Ho 17 E9 .....**74** C1
South Oxhey WD19 ...**22** D6
Capella Ho SE7 .....**143** B6
Capel Lo
5 Richmond TW9 ...**132** B4
12 Streatham SW2 ..**160** B4
Capel Point E7 ......**77** B4
Capel Rd E7,E12 .....**77** C4
East Barnet EN4 .....**14** C5
Capener's Cl SW1 ...**248** A1
Cape Rd N17 ....**52** A6
Capern Rd SW18 ...**158** A3
Capital Bsns Ctr HA0 ..**87** D5
Capital Ind Est
Belvedere DA17 .....**125** D3
Mitcham CR4 ....**202** D4
Capital Interchange Way
TW8 ....**110** C1
Capital Wharf 15 E1 ..**118** A5
Capitol Way NW9 ....**45** A6
Capland Ho NW8 ...**236** D6
Capland St
NW8 ....**92** B3 **236** D6
Caplan Est CR4 .....**181** C2
Caple Ho SW10 .....**266** B4
Caple Rd NW10 ......**89** D5
Capper St WC1 **93** C3 **239** B5
Caprea Cl UB4 ....**84** D2
Capricorn Ctr RM8 ...**59** B2
Capri Ho E17 ....**35** B1
Capri Rd CR0 ....**205** D2
Capstan Cl RM6 .....**58** B3
Capstan Ho 5 E14 ..**120** A2
Capstan Rd SE8 ....**119** B2
Capstan Ride EN2 .....**4** C3
Capstan Sq E14 ....**120** A4
Capstan Way SE16 ..**119** A5
Capstone Rd BR1 ...**186** D6
Capthorne Ave HA2 ..**41** B1
Capuchin Cl HA7 ....**25** B4
Capulet Mews 1
E16 ....**121** A5
Capworth St E10 ....**53** D2
Caradoc Cl W2 ......**91** C1

Caradoc Evans Cl 1
N11 ....**31** B5
Caradoc St SE10 ...**120** C1
Caradon Ct E11 .....**54** C1
7 Twickenham TW1 .**153** C5
Caradon Way N15 ...**51** B5
Caranday Villas 5
W11 ....**112** D5
Caravel Cl E14 .....**119** C3
Caravelle Gdns 1
UB5 ....**84** D4
Caravel Mews 14 SE8 **141** C6
Caraway Cl E13 .....**99** B2
Caraway Hts E14 ...**120** A6
Caraway Pl SM6 ....**219** B2
Carberry Rd 12 SE19 **183** C4
Carbery Ave W3 ....**110** B4
Carbis Cl E4 ....**20** B3
Carbis Rd E14 ......**97** B1
Carbrooke Ho 10 E9 ..**96** C6
Carburton St
W1 ....**93** B3 **238** D5
Cardale St 1 E14 ...**120** A3
Cardamom Ct 7 E12 ..**78** C4
Carden Rd SE15 ....**140** B2
Cardiff Ho 9 SE15 ..**140** A6
Cardiff Rd Ealing W7 **109** A3
Enfield EN3 ....**6** B1
Cardiff St SE18 ....**145** C5
Cardigan Ct 3 W7 ..**86** D3
Cardigan Gdns IG3 ..**80** A6
Cardigan Rd E3 .....**97** B5
Barnes SW13 ....**134** A3
Richmond TW10 ....**154** A5
Wimbledon SW19 ...**180** A4
Cardigan St
SE11 ....**116** C1 **261** A2
Cardigan Wlk 12 N1 ..**73** A1
Cardinal Ave
Kingston KT2 ....**176** A4
West Barnes SM4 ...**201** A3
Cardinal Bourne St
SE1 ....**262** D5
Cardinal Cap Alley
SE1 ....**252** A4
Cardinal Cl HA8 .....**27** B3
Chislehurst BR7 .....**189** B2
West Barnes SM4 ...**201** A3
Worcester Park KT19,
KT4 ....**216** A4
Cardinal Cres KT3 ..**177** A1
Cardinal Dr KT12 ...**194** D1
Cardinal Hinsey Cl
NW10 ....**90** A6
**Cardinal Hinsley RC High
Sch (Boys)** NW10 ..**90** A6
Cardinal Pl SW15 ...**134** C1
Cardinal Pole RC Sch
E9 ....**75** A3
E9 ....**74** D1
Cardinal Rd
Feltham TW13 ......**150** B3
Ruislip HA4 ....**40** D1
Cardinal Road Inf Sch
TW13 ....**150** B3
Cardinals Way N19 ..**49** D2
**Cardinal Vaughan
Memorial Sch** W14 **244** A2
Cardinal Way HA3 ...**42** C6
**Cardinal Wiseman RC High
Sch** UB6 ....**86** A3
**Cardinal Wiseman RC Sch
The** UB6 ....**86** A2
Cardine Mews SE15 .**140** B5
Cardington Sq TW4 .**128** C2
Cardington St
NW1 ....**93** C4 **232** B1
Cardozo Rd N7 ......**72** A3
Cardrew Ave N12 ....**30** B5
Cardrew Cl N12 .....**30** B5
Cardrew Ct N12 .....**30** B5
Cardross St W6 ....**112** B3
Cardwell Prim Sch
SE18 ....**122** B2
Cardwell Rd N7 .....**72** A4
Career Ct 11 SE16 ..**118** D4
Carew Cl N7 ....**72** B6
Carew Ct 15 SE14 ..**140** D6
Carew Ho 24 SE18 ..**122** B2
West Norwood SW16 **160** C1
Carew Manor Sch
SM6 ....**219** D2
Carew Rd W13 ......**109** C4
Ashford TW15 ......**171** A4
Mitcham CR4 ....**181** A1
Thornton Heath CR7 .**204** D5
Tottenham N17 .....**34** A1

Carew Rd continued
Wallington SM6 .....**219** C2
Carew St SE5 ......**139** A3
Carey Ct DA6 ......**169** D6
20 SE5 ....**139** A5
Carey Gdns
SW8 ....**137** D4 **269** C1
Carey Ho E5 ....**74** B5
Carey Pl SW1 ......**259** C3
Carey Rd RM9 ......**81** A4
Carey St WC2 .**94** B1 **240** D1
Carey Way HA9 .....**66** D2
Carfax Pl SW4 .....**137** D1
Carfax Rd UB3 .....**106** A2
Carfree Cl 3 N1 ....**72** C1
Cargill Rd SW18 ...**158** A3
Cargreen Pl SE25 ..**205** D5
Cargreen Rd SE25 ..**205** D5
Cargrey Ho 9 HA7 ..**25** C5
Carholme Rd SE23 .**163** B3
Carillon Ct W5 .....**109** D6
Carinthia Ct 5 SE8 .**119** A2
Carisbrook Cl EN1 ...**5** D4
Carisbrook Ct 1
SW16 ....**160** B1
Carisbrooke Ave
DA5 ....**168** D3
Carisbrooke Cl HA7 ..**25** D1
Carisbrooke Ct
Acton W3 ....**111** A4
Belmont SM2 ......**217** B1
Northolt UB5 ....**85** B6
Carisbrooke Gdns
SE15 ....**139** D5
Carisbrooke Ho
TW10 ....**154** C6
Carisbrooke Rd E17 ..**53** A4
Bromley BR2 ......**209** C5
Mitcham CR4 ......**204** A5
Carleton Ave SM6 ..**219** D1
Carleton Cl KT10 ...**196** B1
Carleton Gdns N19 ..**71** C3
Carleton Rd N7 .....**71** D4
Carlile Cl E3 ....**97** B5
Carlile Ho SE1 .....**262** D5
Carlina Gdns IG8 ....**37** B5
Carlingford Gdns
CR4 ....**181** A3
Carlingford Rd N15 ..**50** D6
NW3 ....**70** B4
West Barnes SM4 ...**200** D3
Carlisle Ave EC3 ...**243** C1
W3 ....**89** C1
Carlisle Cl KT2 .....**176** C2
Carlisle Gdns
Harrow HA3 ....**43** D2
Redbridge IG1 ......**56** A3
Carlisle Ho IG1 .....**56** A3
Carlisle La
SE1 ....**116** B3 **260** D6
Carlisle Pl N11 .....**31** B6
SW1 ....**115** C3 **259** A5
Carlisle Prim Sch
TW12 ....**173** D4
Carlisle Rd E10 .....**53** C1
N4 ....**50** C2
NW6 ....**91** A6
NW9 ....**45** A6
Cheam SM1 ....**217** B2
Hampton TW12 ....**173** D3
Carlisle St W1 **93** D1 **239** C1
Carlisle Way SW17 .**181** A5
Carlisle Wlk 6 E8 ...**73** D2
Carlos Pl W1 .**115** B6 **248** C5
Carlow St NW1 ....**232** A4
Carlton Ave
Feltham TW14 .....**150** C5
Harrow HA3 ....**43** B4
Hayes UB3 ....**105** C2
South Croydon CR2 .**221** C1
Southgate N14 ......**15** D6
Carlton Ave E HA9 ..**44** A1
Carlton Ave W HA0 ..**65** B6
Carlton Cl NW3 .....**69** C6
Chessington KT9 ...**213** D2
Edgware HA8 ....**26** C5
Northolt UB5 ....**64** A3
Carlton Cres SM3 ..**217** A4
Carlton Ct NW2 .....**68** C2
NW6 ....**91** D5
SW9 ....**138** D4
Ilford IG6 ....**57** B6
11 Penge SE20 .....**184** B2
South Norwood SE19 **183** D2
Carlton Dr Ilford IG6 ..**57** B6
Putney SW15 ......**157** A6
Carlton Gdns
SW1 ....**115** D5 **249** C3

Carlton Gdns continued
Ealing W5 ....**109** C6
Carlton Gn DA14 ...**189** D6
Carlton Gr SE15 ....**140** B4
8 SE15 ....**140** B5
Carlton Hill
NW8 ....**92** A5 **229** A4
Carlton Ho NW6 ....**91** A4
8 NW6 ....**91** B5
W1 ....**237** D2
Cheam SM1 ....**217** B2
Hounslow TW4 .....**151** A2
Carlton House Terr
SW1 ....**115** D5 **249** D4
Carlton Lo N4 ....**50** C2
Carlton Mans N16 ...**51** D1
7 NW6 ....**69** C1
SW9 ....**138** C1
W14 ....**244** B2
W9 ....**91** B4
Barnet EN5 ....**1** A2
Woodford E18 ......**36** D2
Carnation St SE2 ...**124** B1
Carnbrook Rd SE3 ..**143** D2
Carnecke Gdns SE9 .**166** A6
Carnegie Cl
Holdbrook EN3 ......**7** D5
Surbiton KT6 ....**214** B6
Carnegie Ho NW3 ...**70** B5
Carnegie Pl SW19 ..**156** D1
Carnegie St
N1 ....**94** B6 **233** D5
Carnforth Cl KT19 ..**214** A2
Carnforth Rd SW16 .**181** D3
Carnicot Ho 9 SE15 **140** B4
Carnoustie Cl SE28 .**102** C1
Carnoustie Dr N1 ...**72** B1
Carnwath Ho SW6 ..**135** D2
Carnwath Rd SW6 ..**135** D2
Caroe Ct N9 ....**18** B3
Carole Ho 13 SE20 .**184** B2
Carolina Cl E15 .....**76** C3
Carolina Rd CR7 ...**183** A2
Caroline Cl N10 .....**31** B1
W2 ....**245** D1
Hounslow TW7 .....**130** C5
South Croydon CR0 .**221** C4
Streatham SW16 ...**160** B1
Caroline Ct NW11 ...**47** A3
Ashford TW15 .....**170** D4
Catford SE6 ....**186** B6
Stanmore HA7 .....**25** A4
17 Surbiton KT6 ....**197** C2
Caroline Gdns E2 ...**95** C4
Caroline Ho W2 ....**245** D5
20 W6 ....**112** C1
Caroline Martyn Ho 8
N19 ....**49** D2
Caroline Pl SW11 ...**137** A3
W2 ....**245** D5
Harlington UB3 .....**127** C5
Caroline Pl Mews
W2 ....**245** D5
Caroline Rd SW19 ..**179** B3
Caroline St E1 ......**96** D3
Caroline Terr
SW1 ....**115** A2 **258** A3
Caroline Wlk W6 ...**264** C5
Carol St NW1 .**93** C6 **232** A6
Caronia Ct 4 SE16 .**119** A2
Carpenter Gdns N21 ..**16** D2
Carpenter Ho 10 E14 ..**97** C2
6 N19 ....**71** D4
NW11 ....**48** A3
Carpenters Bsns Pk
E15 ....**75** D1
Carpenters Cl EN5 ...**13** D5
Carpenters Ct NW1 .**232** A6
5 Dagenham RM10 ..**81** D2
Twickenham TW2 ...**152** C2
Carpenter's Pl SW4 .**137** D1
Carpenters Prim Sch
E15 ....**98** A6
Carpenter's Rd E15 ..**75** D1
Carpenter St W1 ...**248** C5
Carrara Wharf SW6 .**135** A2
Carrara Wlk 19 SW9 **138** D1
Carr Gr SE18 ....**122** A2
Carriage Dr E SW11 .**137** A5 **268** B4
Carriage Drive E
SW11 ....**137** A5 **268** B4
Carriage Drive N
SW11,SW8 ...**136** D5 **267** C4
Carriage Dr N
SW8,SW11 ..**136** D5 **267** C4
SW8,SW11 ...**137** A6 **268** B5
Carriage Dr S
SW11 ....**137** A4 **268** A2
Carriage Dr W
SW11 ....**136** D5 **267** C3
Carriage Mews IG1 ..**79** A6
Carrick Cl TW7 .....**131** A2

Carrick Gate KT10 ..**212** A5
Carrick Gdns N17 ...**33** C3
Carrick Ho N7 ....**72** B2
SE11 ....**261** C2
Carrick Mews SE8 ..**141** C6
Carrill Way DA17 ...**124** D3
Carrington Ave
Borehamwood WD6 ..**10** A1
Hounslow TW3 .....**151** D6
Carrington Cl
Barnet EN5 ....**12** A6
Borehamwood WD6 ..**11** A6
Croydon CR0 ......**207** A2
Carrington Ct SW11 **136** C1
Carrington Gdns 4
E7 ....**77** A4
Carrington Ho W1 ..**248** C3
Wimbledon SW19 ..**179** C3
Carrington Lo 3
TW10 ....**154** A6
Carrington Pl KT10 .**212** A4
Carrington Rd TW10 **132** C1
Carrington Sq HA3 ..**24** A3
Carrington St W1 ..**248** C2
Carrol Cl NW5 ....**71** B4
Carroll Cl E15 ....**76** D3
Carroll Ho W2 ......**246** C6
Carronade Pl SE18 .**123** B3
Carron Cl E14 ......**97** D2
Carroun Rd
SW8 ....**138** B5 **270** C4
Carroway La UB6 ....**86** B4
Carrow Rd RM9 .....**80** B1
Northolt UB5 ....**64** A1
Carrs La N21 ....**17** B6
Carr St E14 ....**97** A2
**Carshalton, Beddington &
Wallington War Memorial
Hospl** SM5 ....**218** D2
Carshalton Beeches Sta
SM5 ....**218** D5
Carshalton Coll SM5 **218** D5
Carshalton Gr SM1 .**218** B3
**Carshalton High Sch for
Boys** SM5 ....**218** C4
**Carshalton High Sch for
Girls** SM5 ....**218** C5
Carshalton Park Rd
SM5 ....**218** D3
Carshalton Pl SM5 ..**219** A3
Carshalton Rd
Mitcham CR4 ......**203** A4
Sutton SM1,SM5 ...**218** B3
Carshalton Sta SM5 **218** D4
Carslake Rd SW15 .**156** C5
Carson Rd E16 ......**99** A2
Cockfosters EN4 ......**2** D1
Dulwich SE21 ......**161** B2
Carstairs Rd SE6 ..**164** A1
Carswell Cl IG4 .....**55** D5
Carswell Rd SE6 ...**164** A4
Carter Cl SM6 ......**219** D1
Carter Ct EC4 ......**241** D1
Carteret Ho 8 W12 .**112** B6
Carteret St SW1 ...**249** C1
Carteret Way SE8 ..**119** A2
Carterhatch Jun & Inf Schs
EN1 ....**6** B4
Carterhatch La EN1 ...**6** A4
Carterhatch Rd EN3 ..**6** D4
Carter Ho E1 ....**243** C3
11 SW2 ....**160** C6
Carter La EC4 .**94** D1 **241** D1
Carter Pl
SE17 ....**117** A1 **262** B1
Carter Rd E13 ....**99** B6
Mitcham SW19 ....**180** B4
Carters Cl 2 NW5 ...**71** D2
North Cheam KT4 ..**200** D1
Carters Hill Cl SE9 .**165** C3
Carters Rd N2 ......**30** C3
Carter St
SE17 ....**117** A1 **262** A1
Carter's Yd SW18 ..**157** C6
Carthew Rd W6 ....**112** B3
Carthew Villas W6 .**112** B3
Carthusian St EC1 ..**242** A4
Cartier Circ E14 ....**120** A5
Carting La
WC2 ....**116** A6 **250** B5
Cart La E4 ....**20** C3
Cartmel NW1 ......**232** A2
Cartmel Cl N17 .....**34** B3
Cartmel Ct
Beckenham BR2 ...**186** C1
Northolt UB5 ....**63** A2
Cartmel Gdns SM4 .**202** A4
Cartmel Rd DA7 ....**147** C4
Carton Ho 2 NW2 ...**68** A5

Carton Ho *continued*
4 SE16 .....118 A3
12 W11 .....112 D6
Cartwright Gdns
WC1 .....94 A4 233 A1
Cartwright Ho SE1 ...262 B5
Cartwright Rd RM9 ...81 B1
Cartwright St
E1 .....117 D6 253 D5
Cartwright Way
SW13 .....134 B5
Carvel Ho E14 .....120 A1
Carver Cl 15 W4 .....111 A3
Carver Rd SE24 .....161 A5
Carville Cres TW8 ...110 A2
Caryl Ho 6 SW19 ...156 D3
Cary Rd E11 .....76 C5
Carysfort Rd N16 .....73 B4
N8 .....49 D4
Casby Ho 7 SE16 ...118 A3
Cascade Ave N10 .....49 C5
Cascade Cl IG9 .....21 D2
Cascade Rd IG9 .....21 D2
Casella Rd SE14 .....140 D5
Casewick Rd SE27 ...182 D6
Casey Cl NW8 .92 C4 230 B1
Casimir Rd E5 .....74 C5
Casino Ave SE24 .....161 B6
Caspian Ho 7 E1 .....96 D2
Caspian St SE5 .....139 B5
Caspian Wlk E16 .....99 D1
Cassandra Cl UB5 .....64 B4
Cassanora Ct NW2 ...68 C2
Casselden Rd NW10 ...67 B1
Cassel Hospl TW10 ..175 D6
Cassell Ho 21 SW9 ..138 A3
Casserley Ho W4 .....111 B3
Cass Ho 23 E9 .....74 D2
Cassidy Rd SW6 .....265 A3
Cassilda Rd SE2 .....124 A2
Cassilis Rd TW1 .....153 B5
Cassinghurst SE24 ...161 B6
Cassiobury Ave
TW14 .....149 D4
Cassiobury Rd E17 ....53 A4
Cassland Rd E9 .....74 D2
South Norwood CR7 ..205 B5
Casslee Rd SE6 .....163 B4
Cassocks Sq TW17 ...193 B2
Casson Ho 10 E1 .....96 A2
Casson St E1 .....96 A2
Castalia Sq 6 E14 ...120 A4
Castellain Mans W9 ..91 D3
Castellain Rd W9 .....91 D3
Castellane Cl HA7 ....24 D3
Castell Ho 11 SE8 ...141 C5
Castello Ave SW15 ...156 C6
Castelnau SW13 .....134 B5
Casterbridge NW6 .....91 D6
3 W11 .....91 C1
Casterbridge Rd SE3 143 A2
Casterton St E8 .....74 B2
Castile Rd SE18 .....122 C2
Castilion Prim Sch
SE28 .....102 C1
Castillon Rd SE6 ....164 C2
Castlands Rd SE6 ....163 B2
Castleacre W2 .....237 A1
Castle Ave Chingford E4 36 B5
Yiewsley UB7 .....104 B6
Castlebar Ct 5 W5 ....87 C2
Castlebar Hill W5 ....87 C2
Castlebar Mews W5 ...87 C2
Castle Bar Park Sta
W7 .....86 D2
Castlebar Pk W5 .....87 B2
Castlebar Rd W5 .....87 C1
Castlebar Sch W13 ...87 A2
Castle Baynard St
EC4 .....117 A6 252 A6
Castlebrook Cl
SE11 .....116 D2 261 C4
Castle Cl E9 .....75 A3
W3 .....110 D4
Ashford TW16 .....171 C3
Beckenham BR2 .....208 C6
Wimbledon SW19 .....156 D1
Castlecombe Dr
SW19 .....156 D4
Castlecombe Prim Sch
SE9 .....188 A5
Castlecombe Rd SE9 188 A6
Castle Ct EC3 .....242 D1
Belmont SM2 .....217 C2
Forest Hill SE26 .....185 A6
Morden SM4 .....202 B4
Castleden Ho NW6 ....70 B1
Castledine Rd SE20 ..184 B3
Castle Dr IG4 .....56 A3
Castleford Ave SE9 ..166 D3
Castleford Cl N17 .....33 D4
Castleford Ct NW8 ..236 D6
Castlefrank Ho 21 N1 .95 C4
Castlegate TW9 .....132 B2
Castlehaven Rd NW1 ..71 B1
Castle Hill Ave CR0 ..224 A1
Castle Hill Prim Sch
CR0 .....224 A2
Castle Ho SE1 .....262 A4
SW8 .....270 B4
10 Belmont SM2 .....217 C1
3 Chingford E4 .....36 B5
Castleigh Ct EN2 .....17 B6
Castle Ind Est SE17 ..262 A4
Castle La
SW1 .....115 C3 259 A6
Castlemaine 8
SW11 .....136 D3
Castlemaine Ave
CR2 .....221 D3
Castle Mead SE5 ....139 A5
Castle Mews N12 .....30 A5
NW1 .....71 B2
Castlenau Gdns
SW13 .....134 B6
Castlenau Mans
SW13 .....134 B6
Castlenau Row SW13 134 B6
Castle Par KT17 .....216 A1
Castle Pl 8 W4 .....111 C2
Castle Point 3 E13 ...99 C5
Castle Rd N12 .....30 B5
NW1 .....71 B2
Dagenham RM9 .....102 B6
Enfield EN3 .....7 A5
Isleworth TW7 .....130 D3
Northolt UB5 .....63 D1
Southall UB2 .....107 B3
Castlereagh St W1 ..237 C2
Castle St E6 .....99 C5
Kingston KT2 .....176 A1
Castleton Ave HA9 ....66 A4
Castleton Cl CR0 .....207 A3
Castleton Ct KT5 .....198 B4
Castleton Gdns HA9 ..66 A5
Castleton Ho 2 E14 .120 A2
Castleton Rd
SE12,SE9 .....187 D6
Chingford E17 .....36 B1
Ilford IG3 .....58 B1
Mitcham CR4 .....203 D5
Ruislip HA4 .....40 D1
Castletown Rd
W14 .....113 A1 254 B1
Castleview Cl N4 .....73 A6
Castle View Gdns IG1 .56 B3
Castle Way
Feltham TW13 .....172 C6
Wimbledon SW19 .....156 D1
Castle Wlk TW16 .....194 C6
Castlewood Day Hospl
SE18 .....144 C4
Castlewood Dr SE9 ..144 B3
Castlewood Rd N16 ....52 A3
Barnet EN4 .....2 B2
Castle Yd N6 .....49 A2
SE1 .....251 D4
17 Richmond TW10 .....153 D6
Castor La E14 .....119 D6
Catalina Rd TW6 .....126 C2
Caterham Rd SE13 ...142 B2
Catesby Ho 25 E9 .....74 C1
Catesby St
SE17 .....117 B2 262 D3
Catford Br SE6 .....163 C4
Catford Bridge Sta
SE6 .....163 C4
Catford Broadway
SE6 .....163 D4
Catford Girls' Sch
SE6 .....164 A1
Catford Gyratory SE6 163 D4
Catford Hill SE6 .....163 C3
Catford Rd SE6 .....163 C4
Catford Sta SE6 .....163 C4
Cathall Rd E11 .....76 B5
Cathay Ho SE16 .....118 B4
Cathay St 9 SE16 ...118 B4
Cathay Wlk UB5 .....85 C5
Cathcart Dr BR6 .....211 C1
Cathcart Hill N19 .....71 C5
Cathcart Rd
SW10 .....136 A6 266 A6
Cathcart St NW5 .....71 B2
Cathedral Ct EC4 ....241 D1
Cathedral Sch of St
Saviour & St Mary Overie
Prim Sch
SE1 .....117 A4 252 B2
Cathedral St
SE1 .....117 B5 252 C4
Catherall Rd N5,N16 ..73 A5
Catherine Baird Ct 12
SW12 .....159 B4
Catherine Ct
1 Ilford IG2 .....57 A3
2 Southgate N14 .....15 C6
3 Wimbledon SW19 ..179 B5
Catherine Dr
Ashford TW16 .....171 D4
Richmond TW9 .....132 A1
Catherine Gdns TW3 .130 B1
Catherine Godfrey Ho
RM9 .....103 B6
Catherine Gr SE10 ...141 D4
Catherine Griffiths Ct
EC1 .....241 B6
Catherine Ho 16 N1 ...95 C6
Isleworth TW7 .....131 B4
Catherine Pl
SW1 .....115 C3 259 A6
Harrow HA1 .....42 D4
Catherine Rd
Enfield EN3 .....7 A6
Kingston KT6 .....197 D4
Catherine St
WC2 .....116 B6 250 C6
Catherine Wheel Alley
E1 .....243 B3
Catherine Wheel Rd
TW8 .....131 D5
Catherine Wheel Yd
SW1 .....249 A3
Catherwood Ct N1 ..235 C3
Cat Hill EN4 .....14 D6
Cathles Rd SW12 ....159 B5
Cathnor Rd W12 .....112 B4
Catisfield Rd EN3 .....7 A6
Catlin Cres TW17 ....193 B4
Catling Cl SE23 .....162 D1
Catlin's La HA5 .....40 B5
Catlin St SE16 .....118 B1
Catman Ho N4 .....50 B1
Caton Ct BR2 .....186 C1
Cato Rd SW4 .....137 D1
Cator La BR3 .....185 B2
Cator Park Sch for Girls
BR3 .....185 A3
Cator Rd
Penge SE20,SE26 .....184 D5
Wallington SM5 .....218 D3
Cator St SE15 .....139 D5
SE15 .....139 D6
Cato St W1 ....92 C1 237 B2
Catsey La WD23 .....8 A4
Catsey Wood WD23 ....8 A4
Catterick Cl N11 .....31 A4
Cattistock Rd SE9 ...188 B5
Cattley Cl EN5 .....1 A1
Catton St WC1 .....240 C3
Caughley Ho SE11 ..261 A5
Caulfield Ct 12 NW1 ..71 C1
Caulfield Rd E6 .....78 B1
SE15 .....140 B3
Causeway TW14,TW4 .128 B1
Causeway The N2 .....48 C5
SW18 .....157 D6
Carshalton SM5 .....219 A6
Chessington KT9 .....214 A4
Claygate KT10 .....212 D1
Teddington TW11 .....174 D4
Wimbledon SW19 .....178 C5
Causeyware Rd N9 ....18 C4
Causton Cotts 3 E14 .97 A1
Causton Ho SE5 .....139 A5
Causton Rd N6 .....49 B2
Causton Sq RM10 .....81 C1
Causton St
SW1 .....115 D1 259 D2
Cautley Ave SW4 ....159 C6
Cavalier Cl RM6 .....58 D5
Cavalier Gdns UB3 ....83 B1
Cavalry Cres TW4 ....128 D1
Cavalry Gdns SW15 ..157 B6
Cavan Pl HA5 .....23 B2
Cavaye Ho SW10 .....266 B6
Cavaye Pl SW10 .....256 B1
Cavell Dr EN2 .....4 C3
Cavell Ho 8 N1 .....95 C6
Cavell Rd N17 .....33 B3
Cavell St E1 .....96 B2
Cavendish Ave DA16 .145 D2
N3 .....29 C1
NW8 .....92 B5 229 D3
Ealing W13 .....87 A1
Harrow HA1 .....64 C4
Ruislip HA4 .....62 B3
Sidcup DA15 .....168 A4
West Barnes KT3 .....200 B5
Cavendish Ave *continued*
Woodford IG8 .....37 B3
Cavendish Cl NW6 ....69 B2
NW8 .....92 B4 229 D2
Ashford TW16 .....171 D4
Edmonton N18 .....34 B5
Hayes UB4 .....83 C2
3 Putney SW15 .....157 A6
Cavendish Cres
Borehamwood WD6 ....10 C6
Borehamwood WD6 ....10 C6
Cavendish Ct EC2 ...243 B2
Ashford TW16 .....171 D4
5 Chingford E4 .....20 C4
Cavendish Dr E11 .....54 B1
Claygate KT10 .....212 C3
Edgware HA8 .....26 B4
Cavendish Gdns SW4 159 C5
Barking IG11 .....79 D3
Dagenham RM6 .....59 A4
Ilford IG1 .....56 C1
Cavendish Ho N12 ....30 A6
NW8 .....229 D3
SW8 .....270 A2
Twickenham TW1 .....153 A5
Cavendish Mans E5 ...74 C3
EC1 .....241 A5
8 NW6 .....69 C3
2 SW12 .....159 C5
Cavendish Mews N
W1 .....238 D4
Cavendish Mews S
W1 .....238 D3
Cavendish Par
Balham SW12 .....159 B5
Hounslow TW4 .....129 A3
Cavendish Pl W1 ....238 D2
Cavendish Prim Sch
W4 .....133 C5
Cavendish Rd N4 .....50 D3
NW6 .....69 B1
SW12 .....159 C5
Ashford TW16 .....171 D4
Chingford E4 .....36 A4
Chiswick W4 .....133 A4
Edmonton N18 .....34 B5
Mitcham SW19 .....180 C3
New Malden KT3 .....199 D5
Sutton SM2 .....218 A1
Thornton Heath CR0 ..204 D1
Cavendish Sch The
NW1 .....93 B6 231 D6
Cavendish Sq
W1 .....93 B1 238 D2
Cavendish St
N1 .....95 B5 235 C3
Cavendish Terr 10 E3 .97 B4
Feltham TW13 .....150 A2
Cavendish The NW11 ..47 D2
Cavendish Way BR4 .207 D1
Cavenham Gdns IG1 ..79 B5
Cave Rd E13 .....99 B4
Richmond TW10 .....175 C6
Caverleigh Way KT4 .200 B2
Caverley Gdns HA3 ...43 D2
Caversham Ave
Cheam SM3 .....217 A6
Palmers Green N13 .....16 C1
Caversham Ct N11 ....15 A1
Caversham Ho N15 ...51 A5
7 SE15 .....140 A6
8 Kingston KT1 .....176 A1
Caversham Rd N15 ....51 A5
NW5 .....71 C2
Kingston KT1 .....176 B1
Caversham St
SW3 .....136 D6 267 C6
Caverswall St W12 ....90 C1
Caveside Cl BR7 .....188 C2
Cavour Ho SE17 .....261 D2
Cawdor Cres W7 .....109 A2
Cawnpore St SE19 ...183 C5
Cawston Ct 6 BR1 ...186 D3
Caxton Gr E3 .....97 C4
Caxton Hall SW1 ....259 C6
Caxton Rd W12 .....112 D4
Southall UB2 .....106 D3
Wimbledon SW19 .....180 A5
Wood Green N22 .....32 B1
Caxton St
SW1 .....115 D3 259 C6
Caxton St N E16 .....98 D1
Caxton Trad Est UB3 .105 C5
Cayford Ho 1 NW3 ....70 D3
Caygill Cl BR2 .....208 D5
Cayley Cl SM6 .....220 A1
Cayley Prim Sch E14 .97 A1
Cayley Rd UB2 .....107 D3
Cayton Pl EC1 .....235 C1
Cayton Rd UB6 .....86 C5
Cayton St EC1 .....235 C1
Cazenove Mans 1
N16 .....74 A6
Cazenove Rd N16 .....74 A6
Chingford E17 .....35 C2
Cearns Ho E6 .....99 D6
Cecil Ave Barking IG11 .79 B1
Enfield EN1 .....5 D1
Wembley HA9 .....66 B3
Cecil Cl
Chessington KT9 .....213 D4
Ealing W5 .....87 D2
Littleton TW15 .....171 A3
Cecil Ct NW6 .....69 D1
SW10 .....266 A6
WC2 .....250 A5
12 Croydon CR0 .....221 D6
Ealing W5 .....87 D2
Cecile Pk N8 .....50 A3
Cecil Ho 6 E5 .....74 C6
Chingford E17 .....35 C2
Cecilia Cl N2 .....48 A6
Cecilia Rd E8 .....74 A3
Cecil Lo KT9 .....213 D4
Cecil Mans 2 SW17 .159 A2
Cecil Pk HA5 .....41 A5
Cecil Pl CR4 .....202 D4
Cecil Rd E11 .....76 C5
E13 .....99 A6
N10 .....31 B1
N14 .....15 C3
NW10 .....89 C6
NW9 .....45 C6
W3 .....89 A2
Ashford TW15 .....171 A4
Cheam SM1,SM2 .....217 B2
Chingford E17 .....35 C2
Dagenham RM6 .....58 D2
Enfield EN2 .....5 B1
Harrow HA3 .....42 C6
Hounslow TW3 .....130 A3
Ilford IG1 .....78 D4
Merton SW19 .....179 D3
Thornton Heath CR0 ..204 B3
Cecil Rhodes Ho
NW1 .....232 C4
Cecil Rosen Ct HA0 ...65 B5
Cecil Way BR2 .....209 A1
Cedar Ave
Dagenham RM6 .....59 A4
East Barnet EN4 .....14 C4
Enfield EN3 .....6 C3
Hayes UB3 .....84 A1
Ruislip HA4 .....62 C3
Sidcup DA15 .....168 A4
Twickenham TW2 .....152 A5
Yiewsley UB7 .....104 B6
Cedar Cl Bow E3 .....97 B6
Buckhurst Hill IG9 .....21 D2
East Molesey KT8 .....196 C5
Keston Mark BR2 .....226 A5
Kingston KT2 .....177 B6
Wallington SM5 .....218 D2
West Norwood SE21 ..161 A2
Cedar Copse BR1 .....188 B1
Cedar Cres BR2 .....226 A5
Cedarcroft Rd KT9 ...214 B4
Cedar Ct HA8 .....11 A1
1 N10 .....31 B1
N1 .....73 A1
5 N11 .....31 C5
N20 .....14 B3
N3 .....29 C3
19 SE7 .....143 C6
W1 .....237 B2
7 Brentford TW8 .....131 D6
Eltham SE9 .....166 A5
Mortlake SW14 .....133 A1
Stoneleigh KT17 .....216 A1
3 Sutton SM2 .....218 A2
6 Wanstead E11 .....55 B4
Wimbledon SW19 .....156 D1
5 Woodford E18 .....37 A2
Cedar Dr N2 .....48 C5
Pinner HA5 .....23 C4
Cedar Gdns SM2 .....218 A2
Cedar Gr DA5 .....168 D5
W5 .....110 A3
Southall UB1 .....85 C2
Cedar Grange 10 EN1 .17 C6
Cedar Ho 5 E14 .....120 A4
SE14 .....140 D4
16 SE16 .....118 D4
W8 .....255 C6
Ashford TW16 .....171 D3
Hayes UB4 .....84 C3
New Addington CR0 ..223 D2
Wood Green N22 .....32 C2
Cedar Hts NW2 .....69 B2
Richmond TW10 .....154 A3
Cedarhurst Dr SE9 ..165 C6
Cedar Lawn Ave EN5 ..13 A6
Cedar Lo SW6 .....134 D4
Cedarmore Ct BR7 ..189 A2
Cedar Mount SE9 ...165 D3
Cedarne Rd
SW6 .....135 D5 265 C3
Cedar Park Gdns RM6 58 D2
Cedar Park Rd EN2 .....5 A5
Cedar Pl 3 SE7 .....121 C1
Cedar Rd BR1 .....187 C1
NW2 .....68 C4
Cranford TW5 .....128 C3
Croydon CR0 .....221 C6
East Bedfont TW14 ....149 B3
East Molesey KT8 .....196 C5
Enfield EN2 .....5 A5
Sutton SM2 .....218 A2
Tottenham N17 .....33 D2
Cedar Rise N14 .....15 A4
Cedars Ave E17 .....53 C4
Mitcham CR4 .....203 A6
Cedars Cl NW4 .....46 D6
SE13 .....142 B2
Cedars Ct Edmonton N9 17 D2
Putney SW15 .....156 A5
Cedars Dr UB10 .....82 C5
Cedars Fst & Mid Schs
HA3 .....24 A2
Cedars Ho 15 E17 ....53 D6
21 SW2 .....138 B1
5 West Norwood
SW27 .....182 D5
Cedars Mews SW4 ...137 B1
Cedars Prim Sch The
TW5 .....128 A5
Cedars Rd E15 .....76 C2
SW4 .....137 B1
W4 .....111 C1
Barnes SW13 .....134 A3
Beckenham BR3 .....185 B1
Edmonton N21 .....16 D2
4 Edmonton N9 .....18 A2
Morden SM4 .....201 C5
Teddington KT8 .....175 C2
Wallington CR0 .....220 A4
Cedars The E9 .....74 D1
Buckhurst Hill IG9 .....21 A3
Ealing W13 .....87 C1
4 Kingston KT2 .....176 D2
Teddington TW11 .....174 D4
Wallington SM6 .....219 C4
Cedar Terr
9 Dagenham RM8 .....58 D2
Richmond TW9 .....132 A1
Cedar Tree Ct SE5 ...139 A4
Cedar Tree Gr SE27 .182 D5
Cedarville Gdns
SW16 .....182 B4
Cedar Way
NW1 .....71 D1 232 C6
Ashford TW16 .....171 C3
Cedar Wlk KT10 .....212 D2
Cedarwood BR3 .....185 B3
Cedarwood Ho EN2 .....4 D3
Cedra Ct N16 .....52 A1
Cedric Chambers
NW8 .....236 C6
Cedric Rd SE9 .....167 A1
Celadon Cl EN3 .....7 A2
Celandine Cl E3,E14 ...97 C2
Celandine Dr E8 .....73 D1
Woolwich SE28 .....124 B5
Celandine Way E15 ....98 C4
Celbridge Mews W2 ..91 D1
Celendine Ct E4 .....19 D1
Celestial Gdns SE13 .142 B1
Celia Ct 7 TW9 .....132 B4
Celia Ho 10 N1 .....95 C5
Celia Rd N19 .....71 C4
Celtic Ave BR2 .....208 C6
Celtic St E14 .....97 D2
Cemetery La
Lower Halliford TW17 .192 D2
Woolwich SE7 .....144 A6
Cemetery Rd E7 .....76 D4
Tottenham N17 .....33 C3
Woolwich SE2 .....146 B5
Cenacle Cl NW3 .....69 C5
Cenotaph* SW1 .....250 A2
Centaur Ct 3 TW8 ...110 A1
Centaurs Bsns Pk
TW7 .....131 A6
Centaur St
SE1 .....116 B3 260 D6
Centenary Rd EN3 .....7 B1
Centennial Ave WD6 ...9 C4

Centennial Ct WD6 ....9 A4
Centennial Pk HA7,WD6 9 C4
Central Ave DA16 ....146 A3
E11 ....76 B6
N2 ....30 B1
N2 ....47 D6
SW11 ....136 D5 267 D3
East Molesey KT8 ...195 B4
Edmonton N9 ....17 D1
Enfield EN1 ....6 B3
Hayes UB3 ....106 A6
Isleworth TW3,TW7 130 A1
Pinner HA5 ....41 B2
Wallington SM6 ....220 A3
Central Bsns Ctr
NW10 ....67 C3
Central Cir NW4 ....46 B4
Central Criminal Court
(Old Bailey)*
EC4 ....94 D1 241 D2
Central Ct SE18 ....122 D2
Centrale Ctr CR0 ...221 A6
Central Foundation Lower
Sch E3 ....97 A4
Central Foundation Sch
EC2 ....95 B3 242 D6
Central Foundation Upper
Sch E3 ....97 B4
Central Gdns SM4 ...201 D4
Central Hill SE19 ...183 B4
Central Mans 8 NW4 .46 B4
Central Middlesex Hospl
NW10 ....89 A4
Central Par 8 E17 ...53 C5
W3 ....110 D4
Ealing UB6 ....87 A4
Enfield EN3 ....6 C3
Feltham TW14 ......150 C4
Harrow HA1 ....42 D4
Heston TW5 ....129 C5
Ilford IG2 ....57 B3
Penge SE20 ....184 D3
Surbiton KT6 ......198 A3
Central Park Ave
RM10 ....81 D5
Central Park Prim Sch
E6 ....99 D5
Central Park Rd E6 ..99 D5
Central Par Villas
BR5 ....190 C1
Central Pk Est TW4 .128 D1
Central Public Health
Laboratories NW9 ...45 C6
Central Rd
Morden SM4 ....201 D4
Wembley HA0 ....65 B3
Worcester Park KT4 .216 A6
Central Sch of Speech &
Drama The NW3 ....70 B1
Central School of Ballet
EC1 ....94 C3 241 B5
Central Sq NW11 ....47 D3
East Molesey KT8 ...195 B5
4 Wembley HA9 ....66 A3
Central St EC1 95 A4 235 A1
Central St Martins Coll of
Art & Design (The London
Inst) WC1 ....94 B2 240 C4
Central St Martin's Sch of
Art & Design
W1 ....93 D1 239 D1
Central Terr BR3 ....206 D6
Central Way NW10 ...89 A4
SE28 ....124 B6
Feltham TW14 ......150 B6
Sutton SM5 ....218 C4
Centre Ave N2 ......30 C1
NW10 ....90 C4
W3 ....111 B5
Centre Bldg SE17 ...262 B4
Centre Common Rd
BR7 ....189 A3
Centre Ct N20 ......14 B2
Centre Dr E7 ....77 C4
Centre Hts 5 NW3 ...70 B1
Centre Point 3 SE1 .118 A1
Centre Rd
Dagenham RM10 ...103 D5
Wanstead E7,E11 ....77 A6
Centre St E2 ....96 B5
Centre The
Feltham TW13 ......150 B2
Walton-on-T KT12 ...193 D1
Centre Way N9 .....18 D2
Centreway IG1 ......79 A6
Centurian Way DA18 .125 C3
Centurion Cl N7 .....72 B1

Centurion Ct SM6 ...219 B6
Centurion Ho 2 RM10 81 D2
Centurion La E3 .....97 B5
Century Cl NW4 .....46 C4
Century Ho SE13 ....141 D3
Wembley HA9 ....66 B6
Century Rd E17 .....53 A6
Century Yd SE23 ...162 C2
Cephas Ave E1 .....96 C3
Cephas Ho 8 E1 ....96 C3
Cephas St E1 ....96 C3
Ceres Rd SE18 .....123 D2
Cerise Rd SE15 ....140 A4
Cerne Cl UB4 ......106 C6
Cerne Rd SM4 .....202 A4
Cerney Mews W2 ...246 C6
Cervantes Ct 11 W2 .91 D1
Ceylon Rd W14 ....254 A5
6 W14 ....112 D3
Chace Com Sch EN1 ...5 C4
Chadacre Ave IG5 ...56 B6
Chadacre Ho 10 SW9 138 D1
Chadacre Rd KT17 ...216 D2
Chadbourn St E14 ...97 D2
Chadbury Ct NW7 ...28 A2
Chad Cres N9 ......18 C1
Chadd Dr BR1 ......210 A6
Chadd Gn E13 .....99 A6
Chadston Ho 17 N1 ..72 D1
Chadswell WC1 ....233 B1
Chadview Ct 2 RM6 .58 D2
Chadville Gdns RM6 ..58 D4
Chadway RM8 ......58 C1
Chadwell Ave RM6 ...58 B2
Chadwell Heath
Foundation Sch The
RM6 ....58 B4
Chadwell Heath Hospl
RM6 ....58 B4
Chadwell Heath Ind Pk
RM8 ....58 D1
Chadwell Heath La
RM6 ....58 C3
Chadwell Heath Sta
RM6 ....58 D2
Chadwell Prim Sch
RM6 ....58 C2
Chadwell St
EC1 ....94 C4 234 B2
Chadwick Ave
Chingford E4 ....36 B6
Wimbledon SW19 ...179 C4
Chadwick Cl
12 Ealing W7 ......86 D2
Roehampton SW15 ...
Teddington TW11 ...175 A4
Chadwick Ct 4 SE28 124 B5
Chadwick Pl KT6 ...197 C3
Chadwick Rd E11 ...54 D3
NW10 ....89 D6
SE15 ....139 D3
Ilford IG1 ....78 D1
Chadwick St
SW1 ....115 D3 259 C5
Chadwick Way SE28 .124 C6
Chadwin Rd E13 ....99 B2
Chadworth Ho EC1 .235 A1
N4 ....51 A1
Chadworth Way KT10 212 B3
Chaffey Ho 6 SE7 ..121 C1
Chaffinch Ave CR0 ..206 D3
Chaffinch Cl N9 .....18 D3
Croydon CR0 ....206 D3
Tolworth KT6 ......214 C5
Chaffinch Rd BR3 ...185 A2
Chafford Way RM6 ...58 C5
Chagford Ct SW19 ...180 C3
Chagford Ho 38 E3 ..97 D4
NW1 ....237 C5
Chagford St
NW1 ....92 D3 237 D5
Chailey Ave EN1 ....5 D4
Chailey Cl TW5 ....128 D4
Chailey Ind Est UB3 .106 A4
Chailey St E5 ......74 C1
Chalbury Ho 3 SW9 138 B1
Chalbury Wlk N1 ...234 A4
Chalcombe Rd SE2 ..124 B3
Chalcot Cl SM2 ....217 C1
Chalcot Cres
NW1 ....92 D6 230 D6
Chalcot Gdns NW3 ...70 D2
Chalcot Mews SW16 .160 A1
Chalcot Rd
NW1 ....93 A6 231 A6
Chalcot Sch NW1 ...71 B1
Chalcot Sq NW1 ...71 A1
Chalcott Gdns KT6 ..197 B2
Chalcroft Rd SE13 ..164 C6

Chaldon Rd
SW6 ....135 A5 264 B4
Chale Rd SW2 .....160 A5
Chalet Ct CR7 ......204 D4
Chalfont Ave HA9 ...66 D2
Chalfont Ct NW1 ....237 D5
NW9 ....45 D6
3 Belvedere DA17 ...125 C1
12 Harrow HA1 .....42 D3
Chalfont Ho NW10 ...67 B5
2 SE16 ....118 B3
Chalfont Rd
Edmonton N9 ......17 D1
Hayes UB3 ....106 A4
South Norwood SE25 .205 D6
Chalfont Way W13 ...109 B3
Chalfont Wlk 3 HA5 .22 C1
Chalford 7 NW3 .....70 A2
Chalford Cl KT8 ....195 C5
Chalford Ct Ilford IG2 .56 D4
15 Putney SW15 ...156 D5
Surbiton KT6 ......198 B2
Chalford Rd SE21 ...183 B6
Chalford Wlk IG8 ...37 D3
Chalgrove Ave SM4 .201 C4
Chalgrove Gdns N3 ..47 A6
Chalgrove Prim Sch
N3 ....47 A6
Chalgrove Rd
Sutton SM2 ....218 B1
Tottenham N17 .....34 A2
Chalice Cl SM6 ....219 D2
Chalice Ct N2 ......48 C5
Chalkenden Cl SE20 .184 B3
Chalkers Cnr TW9 ...132 D2
Chalk Farm Rd
NW1 ....71 A1 231 D6
Chalk Farm Sta NW3 .71 A1
Chalkhill Prim Sch
HA9 ....66 D5
Chalk Hill Rd W6 ...112 D2
Chalkhill Rd HA9 ...67 A5
Chalk La EN4 ......2 D1
Chalklands HA9 ....67 A5
Chalkley Cl CR4 ...181 A1
Chalkmill Dr EN1 ...6 B2
Chalk Pit Ave BR5 ..190 C1
Chalk Pit Rd SM1 ...218 A3
Chalk Rd E13 ......99 C2
Chalkstone Cl DA16 .146 A4
Chalkwell Ho 9 E1 ..96 D1
Chalkwell Park Ave
EN1 ....5 C1
Challenge Cl NW10 ..89 C6
Challenge Rd TW15 .149 B1
Challenger Ho 7
E14 ....119 A6
Challice Way SW2 ..160 B3
Challin St SE20 ....184 C2
Challis Rd TW8 ....109 D1
Challoner Cl N2 ....30 B1
Challoner Cres W14 .254 C1
Challoner Ct BR2 ..186 B1
Challoner Mans W14 254 C1
Challoners Cl KT8 ..196 B5
Challoner St
W14 ....113 B1 254 C1
Chalmers Ho E17 ...53 D4
13 SW11 ....136 A2
Chalmers Rd TW15 .170 D5
Chalmers Rd E TW15 171 A5
Chalmers Way TW14 .150 B6
Chalmer's Wlk 14
SE17 ....138 D6
Chalner Ho SW2 ...160 C3
Chaloner Ct SE1 ...252 C2
Chalsey Rd SE4 ....141 B1
Chalton Dr N2 .....48 B3
Chalton St
NW1 ....93 D5 232 C3
Chamberlain Cl SE18 123 B3
Chamberlain Cotts
SE5 ....139 B4
Chamberlain Cres
BR4 ....207 C2
Chamberlain Gdns
TW3 ....130 A4
Chamberlain Ho 5
E1 ....118 C6
Chamberlain La HA5 .40 A5
Chamberlain Pl E17 .53 A6
Chamberlain Rd N2 ..30 A1
Ealing W13 ....109 A4
Edmonton N9 ......18 A2
Chamberlain St 7
NW1 ....70 D1
Chamberlain Way
Pinner HA5 ....40 B6

Chamberlain Way continued
Surbiton KT6 ......198 A2
Chamberlain Wlk 5
TW13 ....173 A6
Chamberlayne Mans 3
NW10 ....90 D4
Chamberlayne Rd
NW10 ....90 C6
Chambers Gdns N2 ..30 B2
Chambers Ho 2
SW16 ....181 C6
Chambers La NW10 ..68 C1
Chambers Pl CR2 ...221 B1
Chambers Rd N7 ...72 A4
Chambers St SE16 ..118 A4
Chamber St
E1 ....117 D6 253 D6
Chambon Pl 7 W6 ..112 A2
Chambord Ho 24 E2 .95 D4
Chambord St E2 ....95 D4
Chamomile Ct E17 ...53 C3
Champion Cres SE26 185 A6
Champion Gr SE5 ...139 B2
Champion Hill SE5 ...139 B2
Champion Pk SE5 ...139 B3
Champion Rd SE26 ..185 A6
Champlain Ho 26
W12 ....112 B6
Champness Cl 9
SE27 ....183 B6
Champness Rd IG11 .79 D1
Champneys Cl SM2 .217 B1
Chancel Ct W1 ....249 C6
Chancellor Gr SE21 .161 A1
Chancellor Ho 29 E1 .118 B5
SW7 ....256 B6
Chancellor Pas E14 .119 C5
Chancellor Pl NW9 ..27 D1
Chancellors' Ct WC1 240 C4
Chancellor's Rd W6 .112 C1
Chancellors St W6 ..112 C1
Chancellors Wharf 21
W6 ....112 C1
Chancelot Rd SE2 ...124 B2
Chancel St
SE1 ....116 D5 251 C3
Chancery Bldgs 13
E1 ....118 C6
Chancery La
EC4 ....94 C1 241 A2
Beckenham BR3 ...185 D1
Chancery Lane Sta
WC1 ....94 C2 241 A3
Chance St E2 ......243 C6
Chanctonbury Cl SE9 166 D1
Chanctonbury Gdns
SM2 ....217 D1
Chanctonbury Way
N12 ....29 C6
Chandler Ave E16 ...99 A2
Chandler Cl TW12 ...173 C2
Chandler Ct
Feltham TW14 .....150 A5
2 Tolworth KT5 ....198 D1
8 Wallington SM6 ..219 B2
Chandler Cl TW14 ..149 D4
Chandlers Field Prim Sch
KT8 ....195 C4
Chandlers Mews E14 119 C4
Chandler St E1 ....118 B5
Chandlers Way 11
SE24 ....160 C4
Chandler Way SE15 .139 D5
Chandon Lo SM2 ...218 A1
Chandos Ave N14 ...15 C1
N20 ....14 B3
W5 ....109 D2
Chingford E17 .....35 C1
Chandos Cl IG9 ....21 B2
Chandos Cres HA8 ..26 C3
Chandos Ct N14 ...15 D2
Chandos Pl
WC2 ....116 A6 250 A5
Chandos Rd E15 ...76 B3
N2 ....30 C1
NW10 ....89 C3
NW2 ....68 C3
Harrow HA1 ....42 A4
Pinner HA5 ....40 D2
Tottenham N17 ....33 C1
Chandos St
W1 ....93 B2 238 D3
Chandos Way NW11 .47 D1
Change Alley EC3 ...242 D1
Channel Cl TW5 ...129 C4
Channel Ho E14 ...97 A2
Channelsea Bsns Ctr
E15 ....98 B5
Channing Sch N6 ...49 B1
Channon Ct 3 KT6 ..198 A4

Chantrey Cl DA14 ...191 A5
Chantrey Rd SW9 ...138 B2
Chantries The HA7 ..25 A5
Chantry Cl W9 .....91 B3
Edgware NW7 .....11 D4
Enfield EN2 ....5 A5
Harrow HA3 ......44 B4
Sunbury TW16 ....172 A3
Chantry Cres NW10 ..67 D2
Chantry Ct SW6 ...135 A2
Chantry Ct Ind Est
SM5 ....218 C5
Chantry La BR2 ....209 D4
Chantry Pl HA3 ....23 D2
Chantry Rd
Chessington KT9 ...214 C5
Harrow HA3 ......23 D2
Chantry Sch UB7 ...104 A6
Chantry Sq
W8 ....113 D3 255 C5
Chantry St N1 .94 D6 234 D5
Chantry The
3 Chingford E4 ....20 A3
Hillingdon UB8 .....82 B4
Chantry Way CR4 ..202 B6
Chant Sq E15 .....76 B1
Chant St E15 .....76 B1
Chapel Cl NW10 ...67 D2
Chapel Ct 12 EC2 ..95 C4
N2 ....48 C6
SE1 ....252 C2
Hayes UB3 ....105 D6
Chapel End Ho E17 ..35 D2
Chapel End Inf Sch
E17 ....35 D2
Chapel End Jun Sch
E17 ....35 D2
Chapel Farm Rd SE9 .166 D1
Chapel Hill N2 ....30 C1
Chapel House St E14 119 D2
Chapel La
5 Dagenham RM6 ..58 D2
Hillingdon UB8 .....82 C1
Pinner HA5 ....40 D6
Chapel Market
N1 ....94 C5 234 A4
Chapel Pl 13 EC2 ..95 C4
N1 ....234 B4
W1 ....238 C2
Tottenham N17 ....33 D3
Chapel Rd DA7 ...147 C1
Ealing W13 ....109 B5
Hounslow TW3 ....129 D2
Ilford IG1 ....78 C5
Twickenham TW1 ..153 B4
West Norwood SE27 .182 D6
Chapel Side
W2 ....113 D6 245 C5
Chapel St NW1 92 C2 237 A3
SW1 ....115 A4 248 B1
Enfield EN2 ....5 B2
Chapel View CR2 ...222 C1
Chapel Wlk NW4 ...46 C5
Chapleton Ho SW2 .160 C6
Chaplin Cl SE1 ....251 C2
Chaplin Cl TW14 ...149 D4
Chaplin Cres TW16 .171 C4
Chaplin Ho 6 SW9 .138 C1
Chaplin Rd E15 ....98 D6
2 N17 ....51 D6
NW2 ....68 A2
Dagenham RM9 ....81 A1
Wembley HA0 .....65 D2
Chapman Cl UB7 ...104 B3
Chapman Cres HA3 ..44 B4
Chapman Gn N22 ...32 C2
Chapman Ho 26 E1 ..96 B1
2 West Norwood
SE27 ....160 D1
Chapman Rd E9 ...75 B2
Belvedere DA17 ...125 D1
Thornton Heath CR0 .204 C1
Chapmans End BR5 ..191 A1
Chapman's La BR5 ..190 D1
Chapmans Park Ind Est
NW10 ....67 D2
Chapman Sq SW19 .156 C2
Chapman St E1 ....118 B6
Chapone Pl W1 ....239 C1
Chapter Cl 15 W4 ..111 A3
Hillingdon UB10 ...60 B1
Chapter Rd NW2 ...68 A3
SE17 ....116 D1 261 D2
Chapter St SW1 ...259 C3
Chapter Way TW12 .173 C6
Chara Pl W4 ......133 B6
Charcot Ho 9 SW15 .155 D5
Charcroft Ct 11 W14 .112 D4
Charcroft Gdns EN3 ..6 D1
Chard Ho 7 N7 ....72 B6

Chardin Ho 30 SW9 .138 C4
Chardin Rd 11 W4 ..111 C2
Chardmore Rd N16 ..52 A1
Chardwell Cl E6 ...100 B1
Charecroft Way W12 112 D4
Charfield Ct W9 ....91 D3
Charford Rd E16 ...99 A4
Chargeable La E13 ..99 A3
Chargeable St E16 ..98 D3
Chargrove Cl 24
SE16 ....118 D4
Charing Cl BR6 ....227 D4
Charing Cross
SW1 ....116 A5 250 A4
Charing Cross Hospl
W6 ....112 C1
Charing Cross Rd
WC2 ....93 D1 239 D1
Charing Cross Sta
WC2 ....116 A5 250 B4
Charing Ct BR2 ....186 C1
Charing Ho SE1 ...251 B2
Charlbert Ct NW8 ..230 A4
Charlbert St
NW8 ....92 C5 230 A4
Charlbury Ave HA7 ..25 D5
Charlbury Gdns IG3 .79 D6
Charlbury Gr W5 ...87 C1
Charlbury Ho 1 E12 .78 C5
Charlbury Rd UB10 ..60 B5
Charldane Rd SE9 ..166 D1
Charlecote Gr SE26 .162 B1
Charlecote Rd RM8 ..81 A5
Charlemont Rd E6 ..100 C4
Charles Allen Ho
EC1 ....234 A2
Charles Auffray Ho 26
E1 ....96 C2
Charles Babbage Cl
KT9 ....213 C1
Charles Barry Cl
SW4 ....137 C2
Charles Bradlaugh Ho 2
N17 ....34 B3
Charles Burton Ct E5 .75 A4
Charles Cl DA14 ...190 B6
Charles Cobb Gdns
CR0 ....220 C3
Charles Coveney Rd 4
SE15 ....139 C4
Charles Cres HA1 ...42 B2
Charles Ct N3 .....29 D1
Charles Darwin Ho
8 E2 ....96 B4
Bromley BR1 ....187 B3
Charles Dickens Ct
SE25 ....206 A5
Charles Dickens Ho 1
E2 ....96 B4
Charles Dickens Prim Sch
SE1 ....117 A4 252 A1
Charles Edward Brooke
Sch SW9 ....138 D4
Charlesfield SE12 ...165 C1
Charles Grinling Wlk
SE18 ....122 C2
Charles Haller St 25
SW2 ....160 C4
Charles Harrod Ct
SW13 ....134 C6
Charles Ho 1 N17 ..33 D3
Charles Hobson Ho
NW10 ....67 C1
Charles Hocking Ho 8
W3 ....111 A4
Charles II Pl
SW3 ....114 D1 257 C1
Charles II St
SW1 ....115 D5 249 C4
Charles La
NW8 ....92 C5 230 A4
Charles Lamb Prim Sch
N1 ....95 A5 235 A6
Charles Lesser KT9 .213 D3
Charles Mackenzie Ho 7
SE16 ....118 C4
Charles Mills Ct
SW16 ....182 A4
Charles Pl NW1 ....232 B1
Charles Rd E7 .....77 C1
Dagenham RM6 ....58 D3
Ealing W13 ....87 A1
Merton SW19 .....179 C2
Charles Rowan Ho
WC1 ....234 A4
Charles Sevright Dr
NW7 ....28 D5
Charles Sq N1 95 B4 235 D1
Charles St E16 ....121 C5
W1 ....115 B5 248 C5

Charles St *continued*
Barnes SW13 ....**133** C3
Croydon CR0 ....**221** A5
Enfield EN1 ....**17** D6
Hillingdon UB10 ......**82** D3
Hounslow TW3 ....**129** B3
Charles Staunton Ho 3
SE27 ....**183** B6
Charleston Cl TW13 .**150** A1
Charleston St SE17 ..**262** B3
Charles Townsend Ho
EC1 ....**241** C6
Charles Winchup Rd 2
E16 ....**121** B5
Charlesworth Ho 2
E14 ....**97** C1
Charleville Cir SE26 .**184** A5
Charleville Ct SW5 ..**254** C1
Charleville Mans
W14 ....**254** C1
Charleville Rd
W14 ....**113** A1 **254** C1
E18 ....**37** C1
Charlie Browns Rdbt
E18 ....**37** C1
Charlmont Rd SW17 .**180** D4
Charlotte Cl DA6 ...**169** A6
Charlotte Ct N8 ....**49** D3
Ilford IG2 ....**56** C3
5 Wembley HA0 ....**66** A2
Charlotte Ho 12 W6 .**112** C1
Charlotte Mews W10 .**90** D1
W1 ....**239** B4
W14 ....**254** A4
Charlotte Park Ave
BR1 ....**210** A6
Charlotte Pl SW1 ...**259** A3
W1 ....**239** B3
Charlotte Rd
EC2 ....**95** C3 **243** A6
Barnes SW13 ....**133** C4
Dagenham RM10 ....**81** D2
Wallington SM6 .....**219** C2
Charlotte Row SW4 .**137** C2
Charlotte Sharman Prim
Sch SE11 ...**116** D3 **261** C5
Charlotte Sq 5
TW10 ....**154** B5
Charlotte St
W1 ....**93** C2 **239** B4
Charlotte Terr
N1 ....**94** B6 **233** D5
Charlow SW6 ......**136** A3
Charlton Church La
SE7 ....**121** C1
Charlton Cl UB10 ...**60** D6
Charlton Cres IG11 ..**101** D5
Charlton Ct 25 E2 ...**95** D6
E6 ....**100** B4
17 N7 ....**71** D3
Charlton Dene SE7 .**143** D5
Charlton Ho NW1 ...**232** C2
5 Brentford TW8 ...**132** A6
Charlton King's Rd
NW5 ....**71** D3
Charlton La SE7 ....**121** D1
Upper Halliford TW17 .**193** B5
Upper Halliford TW17 .**193** C5
Charlton Lo 1 NW11 .**47** B3
Charlton Manor Prim Sch
SE7 ....**143** D5
Charlton Park La
SE7 ....**144** A6
Charlton Park Rd
SE7 ....**143** D6
Charlton Park Sch
SE7 ....**144** A6
Charlton Pl N1 **94** D5 **234** C4
Charlton Rd N9 .....**18** D4
NW10 ....**89** C6
SE3,SE7 ....**143** B6
Charlton TW17 .....**171** A1
Harrow HA3 ....**43** D5
Wembley HA9 ......**44** B1
Charlton Way SE10,
SE3 ....**142** C4
Charlwood Cl HA3 ..**24** C4
Charlwood Ho SW1 .**259** C3
1 Streatham SW2 ...**160** B3
Charlwood Pl
SW1 ....**115** C2 **259** B3
Charlwood Rd SW15 .**134** C1
Charlwood Sq CR4 .**202** B6
Charlwood St
SW1 ....**115** C1 **259** B2
Charlwood Terr 5
SW15 ....**134** D1
Charman Ho 18 SW2 **160** C5
SW8 ....**270** A4
Charmian Ave HA7 ..**25** C1
Charmian Ho 19 N1 ..**95** C5

Charminster Ave
SW19 ....**179** D1
Charminster Ct 3
KT6 ....**197** D2
Charminster Rd
SE12,SE9 ....**187** D6
North Cheam KT4 ...**200** D1
Charmouth Ct TW10 .**154** B6
Charmouth Ho SW8 .**270** C4
Charmouth Rd DA16 .**146** C4
Charnock Ho 22 W12 **112** B6
Charnock Rd E5 ....**74** B5
Charnwood Ave
SW19 ....**179** D1
Charnwood Cl KT3 ..**199** C5
Charnwood Dr E18 ..**55** B5
Charnwood Gdns
E14 ....**119** C2
Charnwood Ho 9 E5 .**74** B6
Charnwood Pl N20 ..**14** A1
Charnwood Rd
Hillingdon UB10 ....**82** C5
South Norwood SE25 .**205** B5
Charnwood St E5 ...**74** B6
Charrington Rd 2
CR0 ....**221** A6
Charrington St
NW1 ......**93** D5 **232** C4
Charsley Rd SE6 ...**163** D2
Chart Cl Bromley BR2 .**186** C2
Croydon CR0 ....**206** C3
Mitcham CR4 ....**202** D5
Charter Ave IG2 ...**57** B2
Charter Cres TW4 ..**129** A1
Charter Ct N4 ......**50** C1
1 W1 ....**237** A3
Kingston KT3 ....**199** C6
Southall UB1 ....**107** C5
Charter Dr DA5 ....**169** A4
Charter Ho WC2 ....**240** B1
Charterhouse Ave
HA0 ....**65** C3
Charterhouse Bldgs
EC1 ....**242** A5
Charterhouse Mews
EC1 ....**241** D4
Charterhouse Rd E8 .**74** A3
Charterhouse Sq
EC1 ....**94** D2 **241** D4
Charterhouse Square Prim
Sch The EC1 .**94** D2 **241** D3
Charterhouse St EC1 **242** A5
Charteris Rd N4 ....**50** C1
NW6 ....**91** B6
Woodford IG8 ......**37** B4
Charter Nightingale Hospl
The NW1 ...**92** C2 **237** B4
Charter Rd KT1 ....**198** D6
Charter Rd The IG8 .**36** D4
Charter Sch The
SE24 ....**161** B6
Charters Cl SE19 ...**183** C5
Charter Sq KT1 ....**176** D1
Charter Way NW3 ..**47** B5
Southgate N14 .....**15** D5
Chartes Ho SE1 ....**263** B6
Chartfield Ave SW15 .**156** C6
Chartfield Sch SW15 **156** B6
Chartfield Sq SW15 .**156** B6
Chartham Ct 13 SW9 **138** C2
Chartham Gr SE27 ..**160** D1
Chartham Ho SE1 ...**262** D6
Chart Hills Cl SE28 ..**103** A1
Chartley Ave NW2 ..**67** C5
Harrow HA7 ....**24** D4
Charton Cl 5 DA17 .**147** B6
Chartres Ct UB6 ....**86** B5
Chartridge SE17 ....**139** B6
Chartridge Cl
Barnet EN5 ....**12** A6
Bushey WD23 ......**8** A5
Chartridge Ct 6 HA7 **25** C5
Chart St N1 ..**95** B4 **235** D2
Chartwell 28 SW19 .**156** D3
Chartwell Bsns Ctr
BR1 ....**209** D6
Chartwell Cl
2 Croydon CR0 ....**205** B1
Greenford UB6 .....**85** D6
Sidcup BR7,DA15 ...**167** B2
Chartwell Ct
8 Barnet EN5 ......**1** A1
2 Woodford IG8 ...**37** A3
Chartwell Dr BR6 ..**227** B3
Chartwell Gdns SM3 **217** A4
Chartwell Lo 5 BR3 .**185** C3
Chartwell Pl
Cheam SM3 ....**217** B2
Harrow HA2 ....**64** B6

Chartwell Way 3
SE20 ....**184** B2
Charville Ct 8 HA1 ..**42** D3
Charville La UB4 ....**83** C5
Charville La W UB10 .**82** D4
Charville Prim Sch
UB4 ....**83** C5
Charwood SW16 ...**182** C6
Chase Bridge Prim Sch
TW2 ....**152** C1
Chase Court Gdns EN2 .**5** A2
Chase Ct SW3 .....**257** C5
Isleworth TW7 ......**131** A3
Merton SW20 ......**179** A1
Southgate N14 .....**15** C5
Wembley HA0 ......**65** D2
Chase Gdns
Chingford E4 ....**35** C6
Twickenham TW2 ...**152** B4
Chase Gn EN2 .....**5** A2
Chase Green Ave EN2 .**5** A3
Chase Hill EN2 .....**5** A2
Chase La IG6 ......**57** B4
Chase Lane Inf Sch E4 **35** B6
Chase Lane Jun Sch
E4 ....**35** B6
Chaseley Ct W4 ....**110** D1
Oatlands Park KT13 .**193** C1
Chaseley St E14 ....**97** A1
Chasemore Cl CR4 .**202** D2
Chasemore Gdns
CR0 ....**220** C3
Chasemore Ho SW6 .**264** B4
Chase Rd NW10 ....**89** B3
Southgate N14 .....**15** D5
Chase Ridings EN2 ..**4** C3
Chase Road Trad Est
NW10 ....**89** B3
Chase Side N14 ....**15** B4
Enfield EN2 ....**5** A3
Chaseside Ave SW20 **179** A1
Chase Side Ave EN2 ..**5** A4
Chase Side Cres EN2 ..**5** A4
Chase Side Pl EN2 ...**5** A4
Chase Side Prim Sch
EN2 ....**5** A3
Chase The DA7 ....**147** D2
E12 ....**77** D4
SW4 ....**137** B2
Bromley BR1 ....**209** B6
Edgware HA8 ......**26** D2
Ickenham UB10 ....**60** C3
Loughton IG10 .....**21** D4
Pinner HA5 ....**40** C3
Pinner HA5 ....**41** B5
South Norwood SW16 .**182** C3
Stanmore HA7 .....**25** A4
Sunbury TW16 .....**172** B2
Wallington CR0,SM6 .**220** B3
Dagenham RM6 ....**59** A3
Wanstead E11 .....**55** A3
Chaseville Par N21 ..**16** B6
Chaseville Park Rd
N21 ....**16** B6
Chase Way N14 ....**15** C3
Chasewood Ave EN2 ..**4** D3
Chasewood Ct NW7 .**27** B5
Chasewood Pk HA1 .**64** C5
Chater Ho 6 E2 ....**96** D4
Chatfield Rd SW11 .**136** A2
Thornton Heath CR0 .**204** D1
Chatham Ave BR2 ..**209** A4
Chatham Cl NW11 ..**47** C4
Cheam SM3 ....**201** B2
Chatham Ct SW1 ....**15** B2
Chatham Ho 22 SE18 **122** B2
7 SE5 ....**139** C3
Chatham Pl E9 .....**74** C2
Chatham Rd E17 ....**53** A6
SW11 ....**158** A6
Kingston KT1,KT2 ...**176** C1
1 Woodford E18 ...**36** D1
Chatham St
SE17 ....**117** B2 **262** D4
Chatsfield Pl W5 ....**88** A1
Chatsworth Ave BR1 **187** B6
DA15 ....**168** A3
NW4 ....**28** C1
Merton SW20 ......**179** A1
Wembley HA9 ......**66** B3
Chatsworth Cl NW4 ..**28** C1
Coney Hall BR2,BR4 .**224** D6
Chatsworth Cres
TW3,TW7 ....**130** B2
Chatsworth Ct E5 ...**74** D4
W8 ....**255** A4
5 Stanmore HA7 ...**25** C5
Chatsworth Dr EN1 ..**18** A5

Chatsworth Est E5 ...**74** D4
Chatsworth Gdns
Acton W3 ....**110** D5
Harrow HA2 ....**41** D1
New Malden KT3 ....**199** D4
Chatsworth Ho
2 BR2 ....**209** A5
Kingston KT6 ....**197** D4
Chatsworth Inf Sch
DA15 ....**168** A3
Isleworth TW3 ......**130** A1
Chatsworth Jun Sch
TW3 ....**130** A1
Chatsworth Lo
1 W4 ....**111** B1
West Wickham BR4 .**224** A6
Chatsworth Par BR5 .**211** A4
Chatsworth Pl
Mitcham CR4 ....**202** D6
Teddington TW11 ...**175** A4
Chatsworth Rd E15 ..**76** D3
E5 ....**74** D4
NW2 ....**68** D2
Cheam SM3 ....**217** A4
Chiswick W4 ....**133** A6
Ealing W5 ....**88** B3
Hayes UB4 ....**84** B3
South Croydon CR0 .**221** B5
Chatsworth Rise W5 .**88** B3
Chatsworth Way
SE27 ....**161** A1
Chattenden Ho 8 N4 **51** B2
Chattern Hill TW15 .**170** D6
Chattern Rd TW15 ..**171** A6
Chatterton Ct TW9 ..**132** B3
Chatterton Rd BR2 .**209** D4
N4 ....**72** C1
Chatto Rd SW11 ...**158** D6
Chatton Ct 5 NW9 ..**46** A5
Chaucer Ave
Cranford TW4 ......**128** B3
Hayes UB4 ....**84** A2
Richmond TW9 .....**132** C3
Chaucer Cl N11 ....**31** D5
Chaucer Ct 17 N16 .**73** C4
12 New Barnet EN5 .**13** D6
Chaucer Dr
SE1 ....**117** D2 **263** D3
Chaucer Gdns SM1 .**217** C5
Chaucer Gn CR0 ...**206** C2
Chaucer Ho SW1 ...**259** A1
Harrow HA2 ....**41** D4
Sutton SM1 ....**217** C5
2 West Norwood
SE27 ....**183** A6
Chaucer Rd DA16 ..**145** D4
E7 ....**77** A2
SE24 ....**160** D4
W3 ....**111** A5
Ashford TW15 .....**170** B6
Chingford E17 .....**36** A1
Sidcup DA15 ....**168** C3
Sutton SM1 ....**217** C4
Wanstead E11 .....**55** A3
Chaucer Way SW17 .**180** B5
Chaulden Ho EC1 ..**235** D1
Chauncey Cl N9 ....**18** A1
Chaundrye Cl SE9 ..**166** B5
Chauntler Cl E16 ...**121** B6
Chaville Ct N11 ....**31** A6
Cheadle Ct NW8 ...**236** D6
Cheadle Ho 11 E14 .**97** B1
Cheam Common Inf Sch
KT4 ....**216** A6
Cheam Common Jun Sch
KT4 ....**216** B6
Cheam Common Rd
KT4 ....**216** B6
Cheam Court Flats 1
SM3 ....**217** A2
Cheam Fields Prim Sch
SM3 ....**217** A4
Cheam High Sch
SM3 ....**217** A4
Cheam Mans SM3 ..**217** A2
Cheam Park Farm Inf Sch
SM3 ....**217** A4
Cheam Park Farm Jun Sch
SM3 ....**217** A5
Cheam Park Way
SM3 ....**217** A4
Cheam Rd
Belmont SM2,SM3 ..**216** D1
Cheam SM1 ....**217** C2
Cheam St 4 SE15 ..**140** B2
Cheam Sta SM2 ....**217** A1
Cheam Village SM3 .**217** A2
Cheapside EC2 **95** A1 **242** B1
Edmonton N13 .....**33** A4
Chearsley SE17 ....**262** B4

Cheddar Cl N11 ....**31** A4
Cheddar Rd TW6 ...**126** C3
Cheddar Waye UB4 .**84** B1
Cheddington Ho 9 E2 **96** A6
Cheddington Rd N18 .**33** C6
Chedworth Cl E16 ..**98** D1
Chedworth Ho 2 E5 .**74** A6
N15 ....**51** B5
Cheeseman Cl TW12 **173** A4
Cheesemans Terr
W14 ....**254** C1
Chelford Rd BR1 ...**186** B5
Chelmer Cres IG11 .**102** B5
Chelmer Rd E9 ....**74** D3
Chelmsford Cl W6 ..**134** D2
Newham E6 ....**100** B1
Chelmsford Ct N14 .**15** D4
Chelmsford Ho 5 N7 **72** B4
Chelmsford Rd E11 .**54** B1
E17 ....**53** C3
N14 ....**15** C4
Woodford E18 .....**36** D2
Chelmsford Sq NW10 **90** D4
Chelsea Barracks★
SW1 ....**115** A1 **258** B1
Chelsea Bridge
SW1 ....**137** B6 **268** C6
Chelsea Bridge Rd
SW1 ....**115** A1 **258** B1
Chelsea Cl NW10 ..**89** B6
Edgware HA8 ......**26** C1
Hampton TW12 .....**174** A5
New Malden KT4 ...**200** A2
Chelsea Cloisters
SW3 ....**257** B3
Chelsea Coll of Art &
Design
SW3 ....**114** C1 **257** A1
W12 ....**112** C4
Chelsea Cres SW10 .**266** B1
8 Chingford E4 ....**20** A3
Chelsea Ct SW3 ....**268** A6
Chelsea Emb
SW3 ....**136** D6 **267** C5
Chelsea Est SW3 ...**267** A5
Chelsea Farm Ho
SW10 ....**266** D5
Chelsea Fields SW19 **180** B2
Chelsea Gate SW1 ..**258** B1
Chelsea Gdns SW1 ..**258** B1
Cheam SM3 ....**217** A4
Ealing W13 ....**86** D2
Chelsea Harbour Design
Ctr SW10 ....**266** B2
Chelsea Harbour Dr
SW10 ....**136** A4 **266** B2
Chelsea Harbour Pier
SW10 ....**266** C1
Chelsea Lo SW3 ...**267** D6
SW6 ....**265** C2
Chelsea Manor Ct
SW3 ....**267** B6
Chelsea Manor Gdns
SW3 ....**257** A1
Chelsea Manor St
SW3 ....**114** C1 **257** B1
Chelsea Manor Studios
SW3 ....**257** B1
Chelsea Park Gdns
SW3 ....**136** B6 **266** C6
Chelsea Physic Gdn★
SW1 ....**267** C6
Chelsea Reach Twr
SW10 ....**266** C4
Chelsea Sq
SW3 ....**114** B1 **256** D1
Chelsea Twrs SW3 ..**267** B6
Chelsea & Westminster
Hospl SW10 .**136** A6 **266** B5
Chelsfield Ave N9 ..**18** D4
Chelsfield Gdns SE26 **162** C4
Chelsfield Gn N9 ...**18** D4
Chelsfield Ho SE17 .**263** A3
Chelsfield Point 3 E9 **74** D1
Chelsham Ho 1
SW4 ....**137** D2
Chelsham Rd SW4 ..**137** D2
South Croydon CR2 .**221** B2
Chelsiter Ct DA14 ..**189** D6
Chelston Ct 2 E11 ..**55** B4
Chelston Rd HA4 ...**40** A1
Cheltenham Ave 8
TW1 ....**153** A4
Cheltenham Cl
Kingston KT3 ....**199** A6
Northolt UB5 ....**63** D2
Cheltenham Ct 8 HA7 **25** C5
Cheltenham Gdns E6 **100** A5

Cheltenham Ho UB3 .**105** A3
Cheltenham Pl
1 W3 ....**110** D4
Harrow HA3 ....**44** A5
Cheltenham Rd E10 .**54** D4
SE15 ....**162** C6
Cheltenham Terr
SW3 ....**114** D1 **257** D2
Cheltenham Villas
CR7 ....**204** C3
Chelverton Ct SW15 .**134** C3
Chelverton Rd SW15 .**134** C1
Chelwood N20 .....**14** B2
NW5 ....**71** A3
Chelwood Cl E4 ....**19** D5
Chelwood Ct SW11 .**266** D2
Chelwood Gdns TW9 **132** C3
Chelwood Ho W2 ...**236** D1
Chenappa Cl E13 ..**99** A4
Chenduit Way HA7 .**24** C1
Chene Colline Ct
KT6 ....**198** A3
Cheney Ct SE23 ...**162** D3
Cheney Row E17 ...**35** B2
Cheneys Rd E11 ...**76** C5
Cheney St HA5 ....**40** C4
Chenies Ho W2 ....**245** C6
Chenies Mews WC1 .**239** C5
Chenies Pl NW1 ...**232** D4
Chenies St
WC1 ....**93** D2 **239** C4
Chenies The NW1 ..**232** D4
Orpington BR5,BR6 .**211** C3
Cheniston Gdns W8 .**255** C6
Chennestone Cty Prim Sch
TW16 ....**172** B1
Chepstow Cl SW15 .**157** A6
Chepstow Cres
W11 ....**113** C6 **245** A6
Ilford IG3 ....**57** C2
Chepstow Ct SW11 .**245** A6
Chepstow Gdns UB1 **85** B1
Chepstow Pl
W2 ....**113** C6 **245** B6
Chepstow Rd W2 ...**91** C1
Croydon CR0 ....**221** D5
Ealing W7 ....**109** A3
Chepstow Rise CR0 .**221** C5
Chepstow Villas
W11 ....**113** C6 **245** A6
Chequers IG9 ......**21** B3
Chequers Cl NW9 ..**45** C6
Orpington BR5 .....**211** D5
Chequers Ct EC1 ..**242** C5
7 Croydon CR0 ....**205** D1
Chequers Ho NW8 ..**237** A6
Chequers La RM9 ..**103** C5
Chequers Par
Dagenham RM9 ....**103** C5
Edmonton N13 .....**33** A5
Chequer St
EC1 ....**95** A3 **242** B5
Chequers The HA5 ..**40** D6
Chequers Way N13 .**32** D5
Cherbury Ct SE28 ..**102** D5
Cherbury Ct N1 ....**235** D2
Cherbury St
N1 ....**95** B5 **235** D3
Cherchefells Mews
HA7 ....**25** B5
Cherimoya Gdns KT8 **195** D6
Cherington Rd W7 ..**108** D5
Cheriton Ave BR2 ..**209** A4
Cheriton Cl
Cockfosters EN4 ....**2** D1
10 Ealing W5 ......**87** C2
South Norwood SE25 .**205** C4
Walton-on-T KT12 ..**194** C1
Cheriton Ct 4 SE12 .**165** C4
Cheriton Dr SE18 ..**145** C2
Cheriton Ho 9 E5 ..**74** A6
Cheriton Sq SW17 .**159** A2
Cherry Ave UB1 ...**106** C2
Cherry Blossom Cl
N13 ....**32** D5
Cherry Cl E17 .....**53** D4
W5 ....**109** D3
Carshalton SM5 ....**218** D6
Merton SM4 ....**201** A4
Ruislip HA4 ....**61** C5
7 Streatham SW2 ..**160** C4
Cherry Cres TW8 ..**131** B5
Cherry Croft Gdns 2
HA5 ....**23** B4
Cherry Ct W3 .....**111** C5

Cherry Ct continued
Ilford IG6 ....**56** D6
Pinner HA5 ....**22** D2
Sidcup DA14 ....**168** B1
Cherrydeal Ct E11 ....**54** B2
Cherrydown Ave E4 ...**19** C1
Cherrydown Cl E4 .....**19** C1
Cherrydown Rd
DA14 ....**168** D2
Cherry Garden Ho 🖪
SE16 ....**118** B4
Cherry Garden Sch
SE16 ....**118** A2
Cherry Garden St
SE16 ....**118** B4
Cherry Garth TW8 ....**109** D1
Cherry Gdns
Dagenham RM9 ....**81** B3
Northolt UB5 ....**63** D1
Cherry Gr Hayes UB3 .**106** B5
Hillingdon UB8 ....**83** A2
Cherry Hill
New Barnet EN5 ......**13** D5
Stanmore HA3 ....**24** C4
Cherry Hill Gdns CR0 **220** B4
Cherry Hills WD19 ...**23** A5
Cherry La UB7 ....**104** C2
Cherrylands Cl NW9 ..**67** A6
Cherry Lane Jun & Inf
Schs UB7 ....**104** B2
Cherry Laurel Wlk
SW2 ....**160** B5
Cherry Orch SE7 .....**143** C6
West Drayton UB7 ....**104** A4
Cherry Orchard Gdns
🗷 Croydon CR0 ....**205** B1
East Molesey KT8 ...**195** B4
🖪 South Croydon CR0 **221** B6
Cherry Orchard Prim Sch
SE7 ....**143** C5
Cherry Orchard Rd
BR2 ....**226** A6
Croydon CR0 ....**205** C1
East Molesey KT8 ...**195** C6
Cherry Rd EN3 ....**6** C5
Cherry Tree Ave UB7 ..**82** B1
Cherry Tree Cl 🗷 E9 ..**96** C6
Wembley HA0 ....**65** A4
Cherrytree Ct NW9 ...**45** A5
Cherry Tree Ct
🗷 SE7 ....**143** C6
🗷 Woodford E18 ....**36** D1
Cherry Tree Dr SW16 .**160** A1
Cherrytree Ho 🗷 W10 **90** D4
Cherry Tree Ho SE14 .**141** B3
Cherry Tree Rd E15 ...**76** C3
N2 ....**48** D5
Cherry Tree Rise IG9 ..**37** D6
Cherry Trees Sch The
E3 ....**97** C4
Cherry Tree Terr SE1 ..**253** B2
Cherry Tree Way HA7 ..**25** B4
Cherry Tree Wlk EC1 ..**242** B5
Beckenham BR3 .....**207** B5
Coney Hall BR4 .....**224** D4
Cherry Way
Upper Halliford TW17 .**193** C5
West Ewell KT19 ....**215** B2
Cherry Wlk BR2 ......**209** A4
Cherrywood Cl E3 ....**97** A4
Kingston KT2 ....**176** C2
Cherrywood Ct 🗖
TW11 ....**175** A5
Cherrywood Dr
SW15 ....**156** D6
Cherrywood La SM4,
SW20 ....**201** A5
Cherry Wood Way W5 **88** C2
Chertsey Ct SW14 ....**132** D2
Chertsey Dr SM3 ...**217** A6
Chertsey Ho 🗗 E2 ...**95** D4
Feltham TW13 ....**151** C1
Chertsey Rd E11 ......**76** B6
Ashford TW15,TW16 ..**171** C4
Feltham TW13,TW16 ..**171** C6
Ilford IG1 ....**79** B4
Lower Halliford TW17 .**192** C4
Shepperton TW17 ....**192** A4
Twickenham TW2 ....**152** B4
Chertsey St SW17 ....**181** A5
Chervil Cl TW13 ......**150** A1
Chervil Mews SE28 ..**124** B5
Cherwell Ct
Teddington TW11 ....**175** D3
West Ewell KT19 ....**215** A4
Cherwell Ho NW8 ...**236** D5
Cherwell Way HA4 ...**39** A3

Cheryls Cl
SW6 ....**135** D4 **265** D2
Cheseman St SE26 ...**162** B1
Chesfield Rd KT2 ....**176** A3
Chesham Ave BR2,
BR5 ....**210** B1
Chesham Cl SW1 .....**258** A5
Chesham Cres SE20 ..**184** C2
Chesham Ct SW18 ...**158** B4
Chesham Flats W1 ...**248** B6
Chesham Mews SW1 **258** A6
Chesham Pl
SW1 ....**115** A3 **258** A5
Chesham Rd
Kingston KT1,KT2 ...**176** C1
Penge SE20 ....**184** C2
Chesham St NW10 ...**67** B5
SW1 ....**115** A3 **258** A5
Chesham Terr W13 ...**109** A1
Cheshire Cl
Chingford, Highams Park
E17 ....**35** D2
Mitcham CR4,SW16 ..**204** A6
Cheshire Gdns KT9 ..**213** D2
Cheshire Ho SM4 ....**201** D2
Cheshire Rd N22 .....**32** B4
Cheshire St
E2 ....**95** D3 **243** D6
Cheshir Ho NW4 .....**46** C5
Chesholm Rd N16 ...**73** C5
Cheshunt Ho 🗗 NW6 .**91** D6
Cheshunt Rd E7 ......**77** B2
Belvedere DA17 .....**125** C1
Chesil Ct 🗖 E2 ....**96** C5
SW3 ....**267** B6
Chesilton Rd
SW6 ....**135** B4 **264** C2
Chesil Way UB4 .....**83** D4
Chesley Gdns E6 ....**100** A4
Chesney Cres CR0 ..**224** A1
Chesney Ct W9 ......**91** C3
Chesney Ho SE13 ...**142** B1
Chesney St SW11 ...**268** A1
Chesnut Gr N17 .....**51** D6
Chesnut Rd N17 .....**51** D6
Chessell Cl CR7 .....**204** D5
Chessholme Ct TW16 **171** C3
Chessholme Rd
TW15 ....**171** A4
Chessing Ct N2 .....**48** D6
Chessington Ave
DA7 ....**147** A5
N3 ....**47** B6
Chessington Cl KT19 **215** A2
Chessington Com Coll
KT9 ....**213** D1
Chessington Ct N3 ...**47** B6
Pinner HA5 ....**41** B5
Chessington Hall Gdns
KT9 ....**213** D1
Chessington Hill Pk
KT9 ....**214** C3
Chessington Ho 🖭
SW8 ....**137** D3
Chessington Lo N3 ...**47** B6
Chessington Mans
E10 ....**53** C2
E11 ....**54** C2
Chessington North Sta
KT9 ....**214** A3
Chessington Par KT9 **213** D3
Chessington Park
KT9 ....**214** C4
Chessington Pk KT9 **214** C4
Chessington Rd KT19 **215** B1
Chessington South Sta
KT9 ....**213** D1
Chessington Way
BR4 ....**223** D6
Chesson Rd
W14 ....**135** B6 **264** D6
Chesswood Way HA5 **22** D1
Chestbrook Ct 🗗 EN1 **17** C6
Chester Ave
Richmond TW10 ....**154** B5
Twickenham TW2 ...**151** B3
Chester Cl SW1 .....**248** C1
Ashford TW15 ......**171** B5
Barnes SW13 ......**134** B2
Hayes UB8 ....**82** D1
🗖 Richmond TW10 ..**154** B5
Sutton SM1 ....**217** C6
Chester Close N
NW1 ....**231** D2
Chester Close S
NW1 ....**231** D1
Chester Cres E8 .....**73** D3
Chester Ct SW1 .....**231** D1
NW5 ....**71** A4
🗗 SE5 ....**139** B5

Chester Ct continued
SE8 ....**118** D1
🗷 Acton W3 ....**88** C1
Chester Dr HA2 ......**41** C3
Chesterfield Ct KT6 ..**198** A4
Chesterfield Dr KT10 **213** A6
Chesterfield Flats EN5 **12** C1
Chesterfield Gdns N4 .**50** D4
SE10 ....**142** B5
W1 ....**248** C4
Chesterfield Gr SE22 **161** D6
Chesterfield Hill
W1 ....**115** B5 **248** C4
Chesterfield Ho W1 ..**248** B4
🗖 Streatham SW16 ..**181** C6
Chesterfield Jun & Inf Sch
EN3 ....**7** A6
Chesterfield Lo N21 ..**16** B3
Chesterfield Mews N4 **50** D4
Ashford TW15 ......**170** A4
Chesterfield Rd E10 ..**54** A3
N3 ....**29** C4
Ashford TW15 ......**170** A5
Barnet EN5 ....**12** C1
Chiswick W4 ....**133** A4
Enfield EN3 ....**7** A6
West Ewell KT19 ....**215** B1
Chesterfield St W1 ..**248** C4
Chesterfield Way
SE15 ....**140** C5
Hayes UB3 ....**106** A4
Chesterford Gdns
NW3 ....**69** D4
Chesterford Ho 🗖
SE18 ....**143** D5
Chesterford Rd E12 ...**78** B3
Chester Gate NW1 ..**231** D1
Chester Gdns
Ealing W13 ....**87** B1
Enfield EN3 ....**18** B5
Morden SM4 ....**202** A3
Chester Ho N19 .....**71** B6
🗖 SE8 ....**141** B6
Kingston KT1 ....**176** D1
Chesterman Ct W4 ..**133** C5
Chester Mews SW1 .**258** C6
Chester Pl NW1 .....**231** C2
Chester Rd DA15 ....**167** C6
E16 ....**98** C3
E17 ....**52** D4
E7 ....**77** D1
N17 ....**51** C6
N19 ....**71** B6
NW1 ......**93** B4 **231** C2
Edmonton N9 ....**18** B3
Harlington TW6 .....**126** C2
Hounslow TW4 .....**128** B2
Ilford IG3 ....**57** D2
Wanstead E11 .....**55** B3
Wimbledon SW19,
SW20 ....**178** C4
Chester Row
SW1 ....**115** A2 **258** B4
Chester Sq
SW1 ....**115** B2 **258** C4
Chester Sq Mews
SW1 ....**258** C5
Chester St E2 ....**96** A3
E2 ....**95** D3 **243** D6
SW1 ....**115** A3 **258** B6
Chesters The KT3 ...**177** C2
Chester Terr
NW1 ......**93** B4 **231** C2
Chesterton Cl SW18 .**157** C6
Greenford UB6 .....**85** D5
Chesterton Dr TW19 .**148** B3
Chesterton Ho
🗷 SW11 ....**136** B2
🗗 W10 ....**91** A2
Chesterton Prim Sch
SW11 ....**137** A4 **268** A1
Chesterton Rd E13 ...**99** A4
W10 ....**91** A4
Chesterton Sq W8 ..**255** A3
Chesterton Terr E13 ..**99** A4
🗖 Kingston KT1 .....**176** C1
Chester Way
SE11 ....**116** C2 **261** B3
Chesthunte Rd N17 ...**33** A2
Chestnut Alley SW6 ..**264** D5
Chestnut Ave E7 .....**77** B4
N8 ....**50** A4
Brentford TW8 .....**109** D2
Buckhurst Hill IG9 ...**21** D1
Coney Hall BR4 ....**224** C4
Edgware HA8 ......**26** B4
Hampton TW12 ....**173** C3
Hampton, Hampton Court
KT8,KT11 ....**174** D2
🖪 Mortlake SW14 ..**133** B2

Chestnut Ave continued
Thames Ditton KT10 ..**196** B1
Wembley HA0 ......**65** B3
Worcester Park KT19 .**215** C4
Yiewsley UB7 ......**104** B6
Chestnut Ave N E17 ..**54** B5
Chestnut Ave S E17 ..**54** B5
Chestnut Cl DA15 ...**168** A2
🖪 N16 ....**73** B6
SE14 ....**141** B4
Ashford TW15 ......**170** D6
Ashford TW16 ......**171** D4
Buckhurst Hill IG9 ...**21** D2
Carshalton SM5 ....**202** D1
Catford SE6 ....**186** A6
Harlington UB7 ....**126** D5
Hayes UB3 ....**105** C6
Southgate N14 .....**15** D6
West Norwood SW16 **182** C6
Chestnut Ct N8 ......**49** D3
N8 ....**50** A4
SW6 ....**264** D6
Beckenham BR3 ...**185** C3
🖪 Croydon CR0 ....**221** A4
Feltham TW13 .....**172** D5
Hounslow TW3 .....**129** C2
Kingston KT3 ......**199** C6
Surbiton KT6 ......**198** A2
Wembley HA0 .....**65** B3
Chestnut Dr DA7 ....**147** A2
Harrow HA3 ....**24** D2
Pinner HA5 ....**41** A3
Wanstead E11 .....**55** A3
Chestnut Gr W5 .....**109** D3
Cockfosters EN4 ...**14** D6
Isleworth TW7 .....**131** A4
Kingston KT3 ......**199** B6
Mitcham CR4 ......**203** D5
Penge SE20 ....**184** C3
South Croydon CR2 **222** B1
Upper Tooting SW12 **159** A3
Wembley HA0 ......**65** B3
Chestnut Grove Sch
SW12 ....**159** A3
Chestnut Ho 🗗 NW3 .**70** D2
SE4 ....**141** B2
🖪 W4 ....**111** C2
West Norwood SE27 **161** A1
Chestnut La N20 ....**13** A3
Chestnut Pl SE19 ...**183** D6
Chestnut Rd
Ashford TW15 .....**170** A4
Kingston KT2 ......**176** A3
Twickenham TW2 ...**152** C2
West Barnes SW20 .**178** D1
West Norwood SE21,
SE27 ....**161** A1
Chestnut Rise SE18 .**123** C1
Chestnut Row N3 ...**29** C3
Chestnuts Ct 🗗 E17 ..**54** A6
Chestnuts The N2 ...**48** B4
🖪 N5 ....**72** D4
NW9 ....**45** C6
SE18 ....**144** D4
🗖 Erith DA17 ......**125** B1
Penge BR3 ....**206** D6
Uxbridge UB10 ....**60** A1
Walton-on-T KT12 ..**194** B1
Chestnut Way TW13 .**150** B1
Chestnut Wlk
Upper Halliford TW17 .**193** C5
Woodford IG8 .....**37** A5
Cheston Ave CR0 ...**207** B1
Chestwood Gr UB10 .**60** B1
Chettle Cl SE1 ......**262** C6
Chettle Ct N8 ....**50** C3
Chetwode Ho NW8 ..**237** A6
Chetwode Rd SW17 .**158** D1
Chetwood Wlk 🗗 E6 **100** A2
Chetwynd Ave EN4 ..**14** D3
Chetwynd Dr UB10 ..**82** B5
Chetwynd Rd NW5 ..**71** B4
Cheval Ct SW15 ....**134** B1
Chevalier Cl HA7 ...**26** A6
Cheval Pl
SW7 ....**114** C3 **257** B6
Cheval St E14 ......**119** C3
Cheveney Wlk 🗷
BR2 ....**209** A6
Chevening Ho BR5 ..**190** A2
Chevening Rd NW6 ..**91** A6
SE10 ....**120** D1
South Norwood SE19 **183** B4
Chevenings The
DA14 ....**168** C1
Cheverell Ho 🗗 E2 ..**96** A5
Cheverton Rd N19 ...**49** C6
Chevet St E9 ....**75** A3
Chevington NW2 ....**69** B2
Cheviot 🗗 N17 ......**34** B3

Cheviot Cl Bushey WD23 .**8** A5
Enfield EN1 ....**5** B3
Harlington UB3 ....**127** B5
Cheviot Ct 🗖 SE14 ..**140** C5
Enfield EN2 ....**5** B3
Southall UB2 ......**107** D2
Cheviot Gate NW2 ..**69** A6
West Norwood SE27 **182** D6
Cheviot Ho N16 .....**51** C1
Cheviot Rd SE27 ...**182** D5
Cheviots Hostel EN1 ..**5** B3
Cheviot Way IG2 ....**57** C5
Chevron Cl E16 .....**99** A1
Chevy Rd UB2 ......**108** A4
Chewton Rd E17 ....**53** A6
Cheylesmore Ho
SW1 ....**258** C2
Cheyne Ave E18 ....**54** D6
Twickenham TW2 ...**151** B3
Cheyne Cl 🗖 NW4 ..**46** B4
Keston Mark BR2 ..**226** A5
Cheyne Ct SW3 .....**267** C6
🖪 Croydon CR0 ...**221** D6
🗗 Wallington SM6 .**219** B2
Cheyne Gdns
SW3 ....**136** C6 **267** B5
Cheyne Hill KT5 ....**198** B5
Cheyne Mews
SW3 ....**136** C6 **267** B5
Cheyne Path W7 ....**86** D1
Cheyne Pl TW15 ....**171** B4
Cheyne Row
SW3 ....**136** C6 **267** A5
Cheyne Wlk NW4 ...**46** C3
SW10 ......**136** B5 **266** C4
Croydon CR0 ......**222** A6
Southgate N21 ....**16** D6
Cheyney Ho 🗷 E9 ...**74** D2
Cheyneys Ave HA8 ..**25** C4
Chichele Gdns CR0 .**221** C4
Chichele Rd NW2 ...**68** D3
Chicheley Gdns HA3 .**24** A3
Chicheley Rd HA3 ...**24** A3
Chicheley St SE1 ...**250** A2
Chichelle Ho HA8 ...**26** B6
Chichester Ave HA4 .**61** B6
Chichester Cl E6 ...**100** A1
SE3 ....**143** C4
Hampton TW12 ....**173** B4
Chichester Ct
Edgware HA8 ......**26** C4
Harrow HA2 ....**41** B4
Northolt UB5 ......**85** A6
🗗 Sidcup DA5 ....**169** C4
Stanmore HA7 ....**44** A6
Stanwell TW19 ....**148** A3
Chichester Gdns IG1 .**56** B2
Chichester Ho NW6 ..**91** C5
🗷 Kingston KT2 ....**176** D2
Chichester Mews
SE27 ....**182** C6
Chichester Rd E11 ..**76** C5
NW6 ....**91** C5
W2 ....**91** D2
Edmonton N9 .....**18** A3
South Croydon CR0 **221** C5
Chichester Rents
WC2 ....**241** A2
Chichester St
SW1 ....**115** C1 **259** B1
Chichester Way E14 .**120** B2
Feltham TW14 ....**150** C4
Chicksand Ho 🗗 E1 .**96** A1
Chicksand St
E1 ....**95** D2 **243** D3
Chiddingfold N12 ...**13** C1
Chiddingstone SE13 .**164** A6
Chiddingstone Ave
DA7 ....**147** B5
Chiddingstone St
SW6 ....**135** C3
Chieveley Par DA7 ..**147** D2
Chieveley Rd DA7 ..**147** D1
Chignell Pl W13 ...**109** A5
Chigwell Hill E1 ....**118** B6
Chigwell Hurst Ct HA5 **40** D6
Chigwell Rd
Wanstead E18 .....**55** B6
Woodford IG8 .....**37** D3
Chilam Ho 🗖 SE15 ..**140** C5
Chilchester Ct 🗖
BR3 ....**207** D6
Chilcombe Ho 🗖
SW15 ....**156** A4
Chilcot Cl 🗖 E14 ....**97** C6
Chilcott Cl HA0 ....**65** C4
Child Ct E11 ....**54** B2
Childebert Rd SW17 **159** B2

Childeric Prim Sch
SE14 ....**141** A5
Childeric Rd SE14 ..**141** A5
Childerley St
SW6 ....**135** A4 **264** A2
Childerly KT1 ......**198** C6
Childers St SE8 ...**141** B6
Chlld La SE10 ......**120** D3
Childs Ct UB3 .....**106** A6
Child's Hill Prim Sch
NW2 ....**69** A5
Childs La 🗖 SE19 ..**183** D5
Child's Pl SW5 .....**255** B3
Child's St SW5 .....**255** B3
Childs Way NW11 ..**47** B4
Child's Wlk SW5 ...**255** B3
Wembley UB6 ......**87** A5
Chilham Cl 🖾 SW9 ..**138** C2
Chilham Ho SE1 ....**262** D4
Chilham Rd SE9 ...**188** A6
Chilham Way BR2 ..**209** A2
Chillerton Rd SW17 .**181** B5
Chillingford Ho
SW17 ....**180** A6
Chillingworth Gdns
TW1 ....**152** D1
Chillingworth Rd N7 .**72** C1
Chilmark Gdns KT3 .**200** A3
Chilmark Rd SW16 ..**181** D2
Chiltern Ave
Bushey WD23 ......**8** A1
Twickenham TW2 ...**151** C3
Chiltern Cl
Ickenham UB10 ....**60** C6
North Cheam KT4 ..**216** C6
South Croydon CR0 **221** C5
Bushey WD23 ......**8** A5
Chiltern Ct N10 ....**31** A1
NW1 ....**237** D5
🖫 SE14 ....**140** C5
🖪 SE9 ....**166** C5
Harrow HA1 ....**42** B4
Hillingdon UB8 ....**82** D3
New Barnet EN5 ...**14** A6
Chiltern Dene EN2 ...**4** B1
Chiltern Dr KT5 ....**198** D4
Chiltern Gdns NW2 ..**68** D5
Beckenham BR2 ...**208** D5
Chiltern Ho 🖪 N16 ..**51** D1
SE17 ....**139** B6
🗗 W10 ....**91** A2
Ealing W5 ....**88** A2
🖪 Edmonton N9 ...**18** A1
Chiltern Rd Bow E3 ..**97** C3
Ilford IG2 ....**57** C4
Pinner HA5 ....**40** C4
Chiltern St W1 93 A2 **238** A4
Chiltern Way IG8 ...**21** A1
Chilthorne Cl SE6 ..**163** B4
Chilton Ave W5 ....**109** D2
Chilton Gr SE8 .....**119** A2
Chiltonian Ind Est
SE12 ....**164** D5
Chilton Rd
Edgware HA8 ......**26** C4
Richmond TW9 ....**132** C2
Chilton St E2 ....**95** D3 **243** D6
Chiltons The E18 ....**37** A1
Chilvers Cl 🗖 TW2 ..**152** C2
Chilver St SE10 ....**120** D1
Chilwell Gdns WD19 .**22** C6
Chilworth Ct 🗖
SW19 ....**156** D3
Chilworth Gdns SM1 **218** A5
Chilworth Mews
W2 ....**92** B1 **236** C1
Chilworth St
W2 ....**92** A1 **236** B1
Chimes Ave N13 ....**32** D6
Chimney Ct 🗷 E1 ...**118** B6
Chimneys Ct 🗷
SW19 ....**178** C3
China Ct 🖬 E1 .....**118** B5
China Mews 🖪 SW2 .**160** B5
Chinbrook Cres SE12 **165** B1
Chinbrook Rd SE12 .**165** B1
Chinchilla Dr TW4 ..**128** C3
Chindit Ho 🖬 N16 ..**73** B4
Chine The N10 .....**49** C5
Southgate N21 ....**16** D6
Wembley HA0 .....**65** B3
Ching Ct E4 ....**20** C1
Chingdale Rd E4 ....**20** C1
Chingford Ave E4 ...**19** D2
Chingford CE Inf Sch
E4 ....**20** B3
Chingford CE Jun Sch
E4 ....**20** B3

Chingford Foundation Sch
E4 ....19 D3
Chingford Hall Com Prim
Sch E4 ....35 B4
Chingford Hospl E4 ..20 A1
Chingford Ind Ctr E4 ..35 A5
Chingford La IG8 ....36 D3
Chingford Mount Rd
E4 ....35 C5
Chingford Rd
Chingford E17 ....35 D1
Chingford E4 ....35 C5
Chingford Sch E4 ....19 D3
Chingford Sta E4 ....20 C4
Chingley Cl BR1 .....186 C4
Ching Way E4 ....35 C4
Chinnery Cl EN1 ......5 D4
Chinnocks Wharf
E14 ....119 A6
Chinnor Cres UB6 ...86 A5
Chipka St E14 ......120 A4
Chipley St SE14 ....141 A6
Chipmunk Gr UB5 ...85 A4
Chippendale Ho
SW1 ....258 D1
Chippendale St E5 ..74 D5
Chippenham 4 KT1 176 B1
Chippenham Ave HA9 .66 D3
Chippenham Cl HA5 ..39 C4
Chippenham Gdns
NW6 ....91 C4
Chippenham Mews
W9 ....91 C3
Chippenham Rd W9 ..91 C3
Chipperfield Rd BR5 .190 A1
Chipping Cl EN5 ......1 A2
Chip St SW4 ....137 D1
Chipstead Ave CR7 .204 D5
Chipstead Cl SE19 ..183 D3
Chipstead Gdns NW2 .68 B6
Chipstead Ho 4
SW2 ....160 A3
Chipstead St SW6 ..135 C3
Chirk Cl UB4 ....85 A4
Chisenhale Prim Sch
E3 ....97 A5
Chisenhale Rd E3 ...97 A5
Chisholm Ct W6 ....112 A1
Chisholm Rd
Croydon CR0 ......221 C6
13 Richmond TW10 ..154 B5
Chislehurst Ave N12 ..30 A1
Chislehurst High St
BR7 ....188 D4
Chislehurst Rd BR6 .211 D2
Bromley BR1,BR7 ....188 A2
Orpington,Petts Wood
BR5,BR6,BR7 ....211 C4
Richmond TW10 ....154 A6
Sidcup DA14 ....190 A6
Chislehurst & Sidcup Gram
Sch DA15 ....168 B2
Chislehurst Sta BR7 .188 C1
Chislehurst St Nicholas CE
Prim Sch BR7 ......189 A1
Chislet 5 NW5 .....71 A2
Chislet Cl BR3 .....185 C3
Chisley Rd 5 N15 ...51 C3
Chiswell Sq SE3 ....143 B3
Chiswell St
EC1 ....95 B2 242 C4
Chiswick & Bedford Park
Prep Sch W4 ......111 C3
Chiswick Cl CR0 ...220 B5
Chiswick Common Rd
W4 ....111 A3
Chiswick Com Sch
W4 ....133 B5
Chiswick Ct HA5 ....41 B6
Chiswick Green Studios 1
W4 ....111 A2
Chiswick High Rd
W4 ....111 C2
Chiswick High Road (North
Circular Rd) W4 ....110 C1
Chiswick Ho* W4 ...133 B6
Chiswick La W4 ....111 C1
Chiswick La S W4 ..133 D6
Chiswick Mall W4 ..111 D1
Chiswick Maternity Hospl
W4 ....111 D1
Chiswick Park Sta
W4 ....111 A1
Chiswick Pier W4 ..133 D5
Chiswick Pk W4 ....110 D2
Chiswick Plaza W4 .133 A6
Chiswick Quay W4 .133 A4
Chiswick Rd
Acton W4 ....111 A3

Chiswick Rd continued
Edmonton N9 ....18 A2
Chiswick Rdbt W4 ..110 C1
Chiswick Sq W4 ....133 C6
Chiswick Sta W4 ...133 A5
Chiswick Staithe W4 133 A4
Chiswick Terr 6 W4 111 A3
Chiswick Village W4 .132 D6
Chiswick Wharf W4 .133 D6
Chitterfield Gate
UB7 ....126 C5
Chitty's La RM8 .....80 D6
Chitty St W1 ...93 C2 239 B4
Chivalry Rd SW11 ..158 C6
Chivelston 27 SW19 .156 D3
Chivenor Gr KT2 ...175 D5
Chivers Rd E4 ......35 D6
Choats Rd IG11 ....102 D4
Chobham Gdns
SW19 ....156 D2
Chobham Rd E15 ...76 B3
Cholmeley Cres N6 ..49 B2
Cholmeley Ct N12 ...30 A6
Cholmeley Lo N6 ....49 A1
Cholmeley Pk N6 ...49 B1
Cholmley Gdns NW6 .69 C3
Cholmley Rd KT7 ...197 B3
Cholmondeley Ave
NW10 ....90 A5
Cholmondeley Wlk
TW9 ....153 C6
Chopin's Ct 13 E1 ..118 B5
Chopwell Cl E15 ....76 B1
Chorleywood Cres
BR5 ....190 A1
Choumert Gr SE15 ..140 A3
Choumert Mews
SE15 ....140 A3
Choumert Rd SE15 ..139 D3
Choumert Sq 2
SE15 ....140 A3
Chow Sq 2 E8 ......73 D3
Chrisp Ho SE10 ....142 C6
Chrisp St E14 ....97 D1
Christabel Cl TW7 ..130 C2
Christchurch Ave N12 .30 A1
NW6 ....69 A1
Harrow HA3 ....42 D5
Harrow HA3 ....43 A5
4 Teddington TW11 ..175 A5
Wembley HA0 ....66 A2
Christ Church Bentinck CE
Prim Sch
NW1 ....92 C2 237 B4
Christ Church CE Mid Sch
W5 ....109 D6
Christchurch CE Prim Sch
SW3 ....136 D6 267 C6
Christ Church CE Prim Sch
NW6 ....69 B1
SE10 ....120 C1
SE18 ....144 C4
SW11 ....136 C2
Forest Hill SE23 ....162 D2
Kingston KT3 ......199 C6
Christ Church CE Sch
E1 ....95 D2 243 D3
Christ Church CE Sec Sch
N12 ....30 B5
Christchurch Cl N12 ..30 B5
Enfield EN2 ....5 A3
Mitcham SW19 .....180 B3
Christ Church Ct
NW10 ....89 C6
NW6 ....69 A1
Christchurch Ct UB4 ..84 C3
Christchurch Gdns
HA3 ....43 A5
Christchurch Gn HA0 .66 A2
Christchurch Hill NW3 70 B4
Christchurch Ho 2
SW2 ....160 A3
Christ Church La EN5 ..1 A1
Christchurch Lo EN4 ..2 D1
Christchurch Pas
NW3 ....70 A5
Christchurch Pk SM2 218 A4
Christ Church Prim Sch,
Hampstead NW3 ...70 B5
Christchurch Rdbt
DA15 ....167 D1
Christ Church Rd N8 ..50 A3
Christchurch Rd
Harlington TW6 ....126 C2
Ilford IG1 ....57 A1
Mitcham SW19 ....180 B3
Mortlake SW14 ....155 A6
Surbiton KT5 ......198 B3
Christ Church Rd 1
BR3 ....185 C1

Christ Church Sch
NW1 ....93 B4 231 D2
Christ Church Sq 4
E9 ....96 C6
Christchurch St
SW3 ....136 D6 267 C6
Christ Church Streatham
CE Prim Sch SW2 ..160 B3
Christchurch Terr
SW3 ....267 C6
Christchurch Way
SE10 ....120 C1
Christian Ct SE16 ...119 B5
Christian Fields
SW16 ....182 C3
Christian St E1 ......96 A1
Christie Dr SE25 ...206 A4
Christie Gdns RM6 ..58 B2
Christie Ho DA6 ....169 D6
2 SE10 ....120 D1
4 West Wickham BR4 207 D1
Christie Rd E9 ......75 A2
Christina Sq N4 .....50 D1
Christina St EC2 ...243 A6
Christine Worsley Cl
N21 ....16 A1
Christopher Ave W7 .109 A3
Christopher Boone's
Almshouses SE13 ...142 A1
Christopher Cl DA15 .167 D6
SE16 ....118 A4
Christopher Ct
Ashford TW15 .....170 A5
Barnet EN5 ....1 D1
6 Croydon CR0 ...206 A4
Christopher Gdns
RM9 ....80 D3
Christopher Hatton Prim
Sch EC1 .....94 C3 241 A5
Christopher Lo 2 N6 .49 D2
Christopher Pl NW1 .232 D1
Christopher Rd UB2 .106 B2
Christopher St
EC2 ....95 B3 242 D5
SE3 ....143 A4
Christ's Coll NW11 ..47 D6
Christ's Coll Upper Sch
N3 ....29 B1
Christ's Sch (East Side)
TW10 ....154 C6
Christ's Sch (West Side)
TW10 ....154 B6
Christ the King RC Fst Sch
TW19 ....148 A5
Christ the King RC Prim
Sch N4 ....72 B6
Christ the King RC Sixth
Form Coll SE13 ....142 B2
Chryssell Rd SW9 ..138 C5
Chubworthy St SE14 .141 A6
Chudleigh 1 DA14 ..190 B6
Chudleigh Cres IG3 ..79 C4
Chudleigh Gdns SM1 218 A5
Chudleigh Rd NW6 ..68 D1
SE4 ....163 C6
Twickenham TW1,TW2 .152 D4
Chudleigh St E1 ....96 D1
Chudleigh Way HA4 ..40 A1
Chulsa Rd SE26 ....184 B5
Chumleigh Gdns SE5 139 C6
Chumleigh St SE5 ..139 C6
Chumleigh Wlk KT5 .198 B5
Church App SE21 ...161 B1
Church Ave DA14 ...190 B5
N2 ....30 B2
NW1 ....71 B2
Beckenham BR3 ....185 C2
Chingford E4 ....36 B4
Mortlake SW14 ....133 B2
Northolt UB5 ....63 B1
Pinner HA5 ....41 B3
Ruislip HA4 ....39 B1
Southall UB2 ....107 A3
Churchbank E17 ....53 C5
Churchbury Cl EN1 ...5 C3
Churchbury La EN1 ...5 C3
Churchbury Rd SE9 .165 D4
Enfield EN1 ....5 C3
Church Cl HA8 ....27 A5
N20 ....14 C1
W8 ....245 C2
Hayes UB4 ....83 B2
Hounslow TW4 ....129 B3
West Drayton UB7 .104 A3
Church Cres E9 .....74 D1
N10 ....49 B5
N20 ....14 C1
N3 ....29 B2

Churchcroft Cl SW12 159 A4
Church Ct EC4 .....241 B1
N2 ....48 B6
Forest Hill SE26 ...185 A6
27 Richmond TW10 .153 D6
Churchdale Ct 1
W4 ....110 D1
Churchdown BR1 ...186 C6
Church Dr NW9 .....45 B1
Coney Hall BR4 ....224 C5
Harrow HA2 ....41 C3
Church Elm La RM10 .81 C2
Church End E17 .....53 D5
Hendon NW4 ....46 B6
Church Entry EC4 ..241 D1
Church Estate Almshouses
8 TW9 ....132 B1
Church Farm House Mus★
NW4 ....46 B6
Church Farm La SM3 217 D3
Churchfield Ave N12 .30 B4
Churchfield Cl
Harrow HA2 ....42 A5
Hayes UB3 ....105 D6
Churchfield Ho W2 .236 C5
Churchfield Mans 5
SW6 ....135 B3
Churchfield Pl TW17 192 D2
Churchfield Prim Sch
N9 ....17 D3
W3 ....111 A5
W7 ....108 C4
Ealing W13 ....109 C5
Walton-on-T KT12 ..194 A1
Churchfields SE10 ..142 A6
East Molesey KT8 ..195 C6
Woodford E18 ......37 A2
Churchfields Ave
TW13 ....151 C1
Churchfield Sch SE2 124 A2
Churchfields Inf Sch
E18 ....37 A2
Churchfields Prim Sch
BR3 ....206 D6
Churchfields Rd BR3 185 A1
Churchfield Way N12 .30 A4
Church Garth 3 N19 .71 D6
Church Gate N20 ....14 C2
Fulham SW6 ....135 A4
Church Gdns W5 ...109 D4
Wembley HA0 ......65 A4
Church Gn 4 SW9 ..138 C3
Hayes UB3 ....83 D1
Church Gr SE13 ....163 D6
Teddington KT1 ....175 C1
Church Hill E17 .....53 D5
SE18 ....122 B3
Harrow HA1 ....42 C1
Southgate N21 .....16 C4
Wallington SM5 ....218 D3
Wimbledon SW19 ..179 B5
Church Hill Prim Sch
EN4 ....14 D4
Church Hill Rd E17 ..53 D5
Cheam SM1,SM3 ...217 D4
East Barnet EN4 ....14 C4
Kingston KT6 ......198 A4
Church Hill Wood
BR5 ....211 D6
Church Hyde SE18 .145 C6
Churchill Ave
Harrow HA3 ....43 B3
Hillingdon UB10 ....82 C4
Churchill Cl
East Bedfont TW14 .149 D3
Hillingdon UB10 ....82 D4
Churchill Ct 4 BR6 .227 A3
N4 ....50 C2
NW2 ....68 B3
Edmonton N9 ....17 B3
Harrow HA2 ....41 C4
7 Ilford IG1 ....78 D5
Northolt UB5 ....63 C3
Churchill Gardens Prim
Sch SW1 ....115 C1 259 B1
Churchill Gdns
SW1 ....137 C6 269 A6
Acton W3 ....88 C1
Churchill Gdns Rd
SW1 ....137 C6 269 A6
Churchill Ho TW8 ..109 A4
Churchill Lo IG8 .....36 D4
Churchill Mews IG8 ..36 D4
Churchill Pl E14 ...119 C6
Harrow HA1 ....42 C5
Churchill Rd NW2 ..68 B2
NW5 ....71 B4
Edgware HA8 ....26 C4
Newham E16 ....99 C1

Churchill Rd continued
South Croydon CR2 .221 A1
Churchill Terr E4 ....19 C1
Churchill Way BR1 .187 A1
Ashford TW16 .....172 A4
Churchill Wlk E9 ....74 C3
Church La E11 ....54 C1
E17 ....53 D5
N2 ....48 B6
N8 ....50 B5
NW9 ....45 B2
W5 ....109 D4
Chessington KT9 ..214 B2
Chislehurst BR7 ...189 A2
Dagenham RM10 ...81 D1
Edmonton N9 ....18 A2
Enfield EN1 ....5 B2
Harrow HA3 ....24 D2
Keston Mark BR2 ..210 A1
Pinner HA5 ....41 B6
Teddington TW11 ..174 D5
Thames Ditton KT7 .197 A3
Tottenham N17 .....33 C2
Twickenham TW1 ..153 A3
Upper Tooting SW17 181 A5
Wallington SM6 ....219 D5
Merton SW19 ......179 C2
Churchley Rd SE26 .184 B6
Churchley Villas
SE26 ....184 B6
Church Lo UB5 .....63 B1
Church Manor Way
SE18,SE2 ....124 A2
Church Mdw KT6 ...213 C6
Church Mead SE5 ..139 A5
Churchmead Cl 14 ..14 C5
EN4 ....14 C5
Church Mead Inf Sch
E10 ....53 C1
Church Mead Jun Sch
E10 ....53 C1
Churchmead Rd NW10 68 A2
Churchmore Rd
SW16 ....181 D2
Church Mount N2 ...48 B4
Church Paddock Ct
SM6 ....219 D5
Church Par TW15 ..170 B6
Church Path E17 ....53 D5
W4 ....111 A3
Merton SW19 ......179 C1
Mitcham CR4 ......202 C6
Wanstead E11 ......55 A4
Church Pl SW1 ....249 B5
W5 ....109 D4
Mitcham CR4 ......202 C6
Uxbridge UB10 .....61 A5
Church Rd BR1,BR2 187 A1
BR6 ....227 B3
DA16 ....146 B3
E10 ....75 C6
E12 ....78 A3
E17 ....35 A1
21 N1 ....73 A2
N6 ....49 A3
NW10 ....67 C1
NW4 ....46 C5
Acton W3 ....111 A4
Ashford TW15 .....170 B6
Barking IG11 ....79 A2
Barnes SW13 ......134 A4
Beckenham BR2 ...208 C6
Bexley DA6,DA7 ...147 B2
Buckhurst Hill IG9 ..21 B3
Cheam SM3 ....217 A2
Claygate KT10 ....212 D1
Croydon CR0 ......221 A5
Ealing W7 ....108 C6
East Molesey KT8 .196 B6
Enfield EN3 ....18 C6
Feltham TW13 .....172 D5
Hayes UB3 ....105 D6
Heston TW5 ....128 B6
Heston TW5 ....129 C5
Hillingdon UB8 .....82 A3
Hounslow TW7 ....130 C5
Ilford IG2 ....57 C3
Keston BR2 ....225 D1
Kingston KT1 ......176 B1
Long Ditton KT6 ...197 C1
Lower Halliford TW17 192 D2
Mitcham CR4,SW19 180 D2
New Malden KT4 ..199 C1
Northolt UB5 ....85 A6
Richmond TW10,TW9 154 A6
Richmond, Ham Common
TW10 ....176 A6
Sidcup DA14 ....190 A6
Southall UB2 ......107 B3
South Norwood SE19 183 C3
Stanmore HA7 .....25 B5

Church Rd continued
Teddington TW11 ..174 D5
Tottenham N17 .....33 D3
Wallington SM6 ...219 D5
West Drayton UB7 .104 A3
West Ewell KT19 ..215 B1
Wimbledon SW19 ..179 A6
Mitcham CR4 ......202 C6
Church Rd N N2 ....30 B2
Church Rd S N2 ....30 B2
Church Rise
Chessington KT9 ..214 A4
Forest Hill SE23 ...162 D2
Church Row NW3 ...70 A4
Chislehurst BR7 ...189 A2
Church Row Mews
BR7 ....189 A3
Church Sq TW17 ..192 A2
Church St E15 ....98 D6
E16 ....122 D6
NW8 ....92 C3 237 A5
Chiswick W4 ....133 D6
Croydon CR0 ......221 A6
Dagenham RM10 ...81 D2
Edmonton N9 ....17 C2
Enfield EN2 ....5 B2
Hampton TW12 ....174 A2
Isleworth TW7 .....131 B3
Kingston KT1 ......175 D1
Sunbury TW16 .....194 B6
Twickenham TW1 ..153 A3
Walton-on-T KT12 .194 A2
Church St N E15 ....98 C6
Church Stretton Rd
TW3 ....152 A6
Church St Sta CR0 .221 A6
Church Terr SE13 ..142 C2
Hendon NW4 ....46 B6
20 Richmond TW10 153 D6
Church Vale N2 .....48 C3
Forest Hill SE23 ...162 D2
Churchview Rd TW2 152 B2
Church Villa TW16 .194 B6
Churchward Ho SE17 138 D1
SW5 ....254 D1
Churchway NW1 ...232 D1
Churchway N20 ....14 C1
Churchway EN4 .....2 D1
Church Wlk N16 ....73 B4
NW2 ....69 B5
NW9 ....67 B1
Barnes SW13 ......134 A4
Brentford TW8 ....131 C6
Hayes UB3 ....83 D1
Mitcham SW16 ....181 C1
Thames Ditton KT7 196 C3
Walton-on-T KT12 .194 A1
West Barnes SW20 200 C6
Churchwood Gdns
IG8 ....37 A6
Churchyard Row
SE11 ....116 D2 261 D4
Churnfield 2 N4 ....72 C6
Churston Ave E13 ..99 B6
Churston Cl 17 SW2 160 C3
Churston Dr SM4 ..201 A4
Churston Gdns N11 .31 C4
Churston Mans WC1 240 D5
Churton Pl SW1 ...259 B3
Brentford W4 ......132 D6
Churton St
SW1 ....115 C2 259 B3
Chute Ho 18 SW9 ..138 C3
Chuter Ede Ho SW6 264 D5
Chyngton Cl DA15 .167 D1
Chyngton Ct HA1 ...64 C6
Cibber Rd SE23 ....162 D2
Cicada Rd SW18 ...158 A6
Cicely Ho NW8 ....229 D3
Cicely Rd SE15 ....140 A4
Cinderford Way BR1 186 C6
Cinema Par RM8 ....81 B6
Cinnabar Wharf Central 17
E1 ....118 A5
Cinnabar Wharf East 16
E1 ....118 A5
Cinnabar Wharf West 18
E1 ....118 A5
Cinnamon Cl 8 SE15 139 D5
Thornton Heath CR0 204 A2
Cinnamon Row 3
SW11 ....136 A2
Cinnamon St E1 ...118 B5
Cinnamon Wharf
SE1 ....253 D2
Cinque Cotts SW19 178 C4

Cintra Ct SE19 183 D4
Cintra Pk SE19 183 D3
Circle Ct HA0 65 D4
Circle Gdns SW19 179 C1
Circle Ho 12 E14 98 B1
Circle The NW2 67 C5
NW7 27 B4
SE1 253 D2
Circuit Rd SE28 124 A4
Circuits The HA5 40 C5
Circular Rd N17 51 D6
N2 30 B2
Circular Way SE18 144 C6
Circus Lo NW8 229 C2
Circus Mews W1 237 C4
Circus Pl EC2 242 D3
Circus Rd NW8 92 B5 229 C3
Circus St SE10 142 A5
Cirencester St W2 91 D2
Cirrus 17 NW9 27 D1
Cissbury Ho 6 SE26 162 A1
Cissbury Rd N15 51 B4
Cissbury Ring N N12 29 C5
Cissbury Ring S N12 29 B5
Citizen Ho N7 72 C4
Citizen Rd N7 72 C4
Citron Terr 3 SE15 140 B2
Citrus Ho 14 SE8 119 B1
City Airport Pier E16 120 D5
City and Islington Coll EC1 94 D4 234 C1
City Banking Coll SE1 117 B4 252 D2
City Bsns Ctr 26 SE16 118 C4
City Central Est EC1 235 A1
City Forum EC1 95 A4 235 A2
City Garden Row N1 94 D5 234 D3
City Gate E1 96 C3
City & Guilds of London Art Sch The SE11 116 C1 261 B1
City Harbour E14 119 D3
City & Islington Coll N1 95 B6 235 C6
N4 72 D6
City Literature Inst The WC2 94 A1 240 B2
City of London Sch EC4 117 A6 252 A6
City of London Sch for Girls EC2 95 A2 242 B4
City of Westminster Coll NW1 92 C2 237 B4
W2 92 B2 236 C4
City of Westminster Coll, Maida Vale Ctr W9 91 D4
City of Westminster Coll, Queens Park Ctr W9 91 C4
City Prospect 5 SE19 183 C4
City Rd EC1 95 A4 235 B2
City Thameslink Sta EC4 94 D1 241 C1
City Wharf Ho KT7 197 B3
Civic Way Ilford IG6 57 A5
Ruislip HA4 62 D3
Civil Service Coll SW1 115 C2 259 A3
Clabon Mews SW1 114 D2 257 C4
Clack St SE16 118 C4
Clacton Rd E17 53 A3
E6 99 D4
Tottenham N17 33 D1
Claigmar Gdns N3 29 D2
Claire Ct N12 14 A1
NW2 69 A2
Bushey WD23 8 B3
Claire Gdns HA7 25 C5
Claire Pl E14 119 C3
Clairvale Rd TW5 129 A4
Clairview Rd SW16 181 B5
Clairville Gdns W7 108 C5
Clairville Point 12 SE23 162 D1
Clamp Hill HA7 24 C5
Clancarty Rd SW6 135 C3
Clandon Cl W3 110 D4
Stoneleigh KT17 216 A2
Clandon Ct BR1 187 A4
Sutton SM2 218 B2
Clandon Gdns N3 47 C6
Clandon Ho N3 47 C6
12 Kingston KT2 176 D4
Clandon Rd IG3 79 C6
Clandon St SE8 141 C3
Clanfield Ho 12 SW15 156 A3
Clanricarde Gdns W2 113 C6 245 B5
Clapham Common* SW4 137 C1
Clapham Common North Side SW4 137 A1
Clapham Common South Side SW4 159 C6
Clapham Common Sta SW4 137 C1
Clapham Common West Side SW11 159 A6
SW4,SW11 136 D1
Clapham Court Terr 2 SW4 160 A6
Clapham Cres SW4 137 D1
Clapham Ct 3 SW4 160 A6
Clapham High St SW4 137 D1
Clapham High Street Sta SW4 137 D2
Clapham Junction Est SW11 136 C1
Clapham Junction Sta SW11 136 C1
Clapham Manor Ct 1 SW4 137 C2
Clapham Manor Prim Sch SW4 137 C2
Clapham Manor St SW4 137 D2
Clapham Mans SW4 159 B5
Clapham North Sta SW4 138 A2
Clapham Park Rd SW4 137 D1
Clapham Park Terr 4 SW2 160 A6
Clapham Rd SW9 138 B4 270 D2
Clapham South Sta SW4 159 B5
Claps Gate La E6 100 D3
Clapton Comm E5 52 A2
Clapton Girls Tec Coll E5 74 C4
Clapton Ho 7 E5 74 C6
Clapton Pas E5 74 C3
Clapton Sq E5 74 C3
Clapton Sta E5 74 B6
Clapton Terr E5 52 A1
Clapton Way E5 74 A5
Clara Grant Prim Sch The E3 97 C3
Clara Pl SE18 122 C2
Clare Cl N2 48 A6
Borehamwood WD6 10 B5
Clare Cnr SE9 166 D4
Clare Ct BR7 188 B2
WC1 233 B1
Wimbledon SW19 179 A4
Claredale Ct SM2 218 A1
Claredale Ho 3 E2 96 B5
Claredale St E2 96 A5
Clare Gdns E7 77 A4
W11 91 A1
Barking IG11 80 A1
Clare Grant Ho 3 E14 119 C3
Clare Ho 6 E3 97 B6
4 HA8 27 A1
SE1 263 D2
Clare House Prim Sch BR3 186 A1
Clare La N1 73 A1
Clare Lawn Ave SW14 155 B6
Clare Mews SW6 265 C3
Clare Mkt WC2 240 D1
Claremont
1 Putney SW15 157 A6
Shepperton TW17 192 D3
Claremont Ave
Harrow HA3 44 A4
Sunbury TW16 172 B2
West Barnes KT3 200 B4
Claremont Cl E16 122 C5
N1 94 C5 234 B3
Orpington BR6 226 C4
4 Streatham SW2 160 B3
Claremont Ct 1 W9 91 B5
Claremont Dr TW17 192 D3
Claremont Gdns
Ilford IG3 79 C6
Kingston KT6 198 A4
Claremont Gr
Chiswick W4 133 C5
Woodford IG8 37 C4
Claremont High Sch HA3 44 A4
Claremont Hts EN2 4 D1
Claremont La KT10 212 A3
Claremont Pk N3 29 A2
Claremont Rd BR1 210 B5
E17 35 A1
E7 76 B5
E7 77 C3
N6 49 C2
W9 91 B5
Claygate KT10 212 C1
Croydon CR0 206 A1
Ealing W13 87 A2
Hadley Wood EN4 2 B6
Harrow HA3 24 C1
Hendon NW2 68 D6
Kingston KT6 198 A4
Teddington TW11 174 D6
Twickenham TW1 153 C5
Claremont Sq N1 94 C5 234 A3
Claremont St E16 122 C4
SE10 141 D6
Edmonton N18 34 A4
Claremont Terr KT7 197 B2
Claremont Way NW2 46 C1
Claremont Way Ind Est NW2 46 C1
Clarence Ave SW4 159 D5
Bromley BR1,BR2 210 A5
Ilford IG2 56 C3
Kingston KT3 177 B1
Clarence Cl
Bushey WD23 8 D4
New Barnet EN4 14 B6
Clarence Cres DA14 168 B1
Clarence Ct NW7 27 D5
10 W6 112 B2
Clarence Gate Gdns NW1 237 D5
Clarence Gdns NW1 93 B4 231 D1
Clarence Ho SE17 139 A6
Clarence Ho* SW1 115 C5 249 B3
Clarence La SW15 155 D5
Clarence Mews E5 74 B3
1 SE16 118 D5
Balham SW12 159 B4
Clarence Pl 25 E5 74 B3
Clarence Rd DA6 147 A1
E12 77 D3
E16 98 C3
E17 34 D1
E5 74 B4
N15 51 A4
NW6 69 B1
W4 110 C1
Bromley BR1,BR2 210 A6
Chislehurst SE9 166 A2
Enfield EN3 18 C6
Richmond TW9 132 C4
Sidcup DA14 168 B1
Sutton SM1 217 D3
Teddington TW11 175 A4
Thornton Heath CR0 205 B2
Wallington SM6 219 B3
Wimbledon SW19 179 D4
Wood Green N22 32 A3
Clarence St
Kingston KT1,KT2 176 A1
5 Richmond TW9 132 A1
Southall UB2 106 D3
Clarence Terr NW1 237 D6
Hounslow TW3 129 D1
Clarence Way NW1 71 B1
Clarence Wlk 9 SW4 138 A3
Clarendon CE Infants Sch TW15 170 B6
Clarendon Cl W2 247 A6
37 Hackney E9 74 C1
Clarendon Cres TW2 152 B1
Clarendon Cross W11 244 B5
Clarendon Ct NW11 47 B5
NW2 68 C1
W9 236 B6
1 Richmond TW9 132 C4
Clarendon Dr SW15 134 C1
Clarendon Flats W1 238 B1
Clarendon Gdns
W9 92 A3 236 B5
Hendon NW4 46 B6
Redbridge IG1 56 B2
Wembley HA9 66 A4
Clarendon Gr NW1 232 C2
Mitcham CR4 202 D6
Clarendon Ho N12 30 A5
NW1 232 B3
Clarendon Mews DA5 169 D3
W2 247 A6
Clarendon Pl W2 114 C6 247 A6
Clarendon Rd E11 54 B1
E17 53 D3
N15 51 A5
N8 50 B6
W11 113 A6 244 B5
Ashford TW15 170 B6
Croydon CR0 220 D6
Ealing W5 88 A3
Edmonton N18 34 A5
Harrow HA1 42 C3
Hayes UB3 105 D4
Mitcham SW19 180 C3
Wallington SM6 219 C2
Wanstead E18 55 A6
Wood Green N22 32 B1
Clarendon Rise SE13 142 A1
Clarendon Sch TW12 173 D4
Clarendon St SW1 115 B1 258 D2
Clarendon Terr W9 236 B6
Clarendon Way BR5,BR7 211 D6
Enfield N21 17 A5
Clarendon Wlk 10 W11 91 A1
Clarens St SE6 163 B2
Clare Pl SW15
Clare Point NW2 46 D1
Clare Rd E11 54 B3
NW10 68 A1
SE14 141 B4
Hounslow TW4 129 B2
Northolt UB6 64 B2
Stanwell TW19 148 A4
Clare St E2 96 B5
Claret Gdns SE25 205 C5
Clareville Ct SW7 256 B3
Clareville Gr SW7 114 A2 256 B3
Clareville Grove Mews SW7 256 B3
Clareville Rd BR5,BR6 227 A6
Clareville St SW7 114 A2 256 B3
Clare Way DA7 147 A4
Clarewood Ct W1 237 C3
Clarewood Wlk SW9 138 C1
Clarges Ho W1 248 D4
Clarges Mews W1 115 B5 248 C4
Clarges St W1 115 B5 248 D4
Claribel Rd SW9 138 D3
Clarice Ct NW4 46 B6
Claridge Ct SW6 264 C1
Claridge Rd RM8 58 D1
Clarissa Ho 7 E14 97 D1
Clarissa Rd RM6 58 D2
Clarissa St E8 95 D6
Clark Ct NW10 67 A1
Clarke Ho 2 SW4 137 C2
Clarke Mans 8 IG11 79 D1
Clarke Mews N9 18 B1
Clarke Path N16 52 A1
Clarke's Ave KT4,SM3 216 D6
Clarkes Dr UB8 82 A2
Clarkes Mews W1 238 B4
Clark Lawrence Ct 11 SW11 136 B2
Clarks Mead WD23 8 B4
Clarkson Ho SW11 136 B1
Clarkson Rd E16 98 D1
Clarkson Row NW1 232 A3
Clarkson St E2 96 B4
Clarksons The IG11 101 A5
Clark's Pl EC2 243 A2
Clark's Rd IG1 79 B6
Clark St E1 96 C2
Clark Way TW5 128 D5
Classic Mans 33 E9 74 C1
Classinghall Ho 14 SW15 156 D5
Classon Cl UB7 104 A4
Claude Rd E10 54 A1
E13 99 B6
SE15 140 B3
Claude St E14 119 C2
Claudia Jones Way SW2 160 A5
Claudia Pl SW19 157 A3
Claughton Rd E13 99 C5
Clauson Ave UB5 64 A3
Clavell St 7 SE10 142 A6
Claverdale Rd SW2 160 C4
Clavering Ave SW13 134 B6
Clavering Cl TW1 175 A6
Clavering Ho SE13 142 B1
Clavering Rd E12 77 D6
Claverings Ind Est N9 18 C2
Claverley Gr N3 29 D2
Claverley Villas N3 29 D3
Claverton St SW1 115 C1 259 B1
Clave St E1 118 C5
Claxton Gr W6 112 D1 254 A1
Clay Ave CR4 181 B1
Claybank Gr SE13 141 D2
Claybourne Mews 2 SE19 183 D3
Claybridge Rd SE12 187 C6
Claybrook Cl N2 48 B6
Claybrook Rd W6 134 D6
Claybury Broadway IG5 56 A6
Clay Ct E17 54 B6
Claydon SE17 262 A4
Claydon Dr CR0 220 A4
Claydon Ho NW4 28 D1
Claydown Mews SE18 122 C1
Clayfarm Rd SE9 167 A2
Claygate Cres CR0 224 B2
Claygate La
Hinchley Wood KT10 213 A6
Thames Ditton KT7 197 A1
Claygate Lodge Cl KT10 212 C1
Claygate Prim Sch KT10 212 C1
Claygate Rd W13 109 B3
Claygate Sta KT10 212 C2
Clayhall Ct 16 E3 97 B5
Clay Hill EN2 5 B6
Clay Hill Cres SE12, SE9 187 D6
Clay La WD23 8 C4
Claylands Ct SE19 183 B5
Claylands Pl SW8 138 C5
Claylands Rd SW8 138 B6 270 D5
Claymill Ho 2 SE18 123 A1
Claymore Cl SM3,SM4 201 C2
Claypole Ct E17 53 C4
Claypole Dr TW5 129 A4
Claypole Rd E15 98 A5
Clayponds Ave TW8 110 A2
Clayponds Gdns W5 109 D2
Clayponds Hospl & Day Treatment Ctr TW8 110 A2
Clayponds La TW8 110 A1
Clays Ct N16 51 D1
Clays La E15 75 D3
Clays Lane Cl E15 75 D3
Clay St W1 92 D2 237 D3
Clayton 22 NW9 27 D1
Clayton Ave HA0 66 A1
Clayton Bsns Ctr UB3 105 C4
Clayton Cl 3 E6 100 B1
Clayton Cres TW8 109 D1
Clayton Ct E17 35 A1
N16 52 A2
Clayton Field NW9 27 C2
Clayton Ho 22 E9 74 C1
Long Ditton KT7 197 B1
Clayton Mews SE10 142 B4
Clayton Rd SE15 140 A4
Chessington KT10,KT9 213 D4
Hayes UB3 105 C4
Isleworth TW7 130 C2
Clayton St SE11 138 C6
Clayton Terr UB4 84 D2
Claytonville Terr DA17 125 D4
Clay Wood Cl BR6 211 C2
Clayworth Cl DA15 168 B5
Cleanthus Cl SE18 144 D4
Cleanthus Rd SE18 144 D4
Clearbrook Way 13 E1 96 C1
Clearmont Ho UB2 107 C3
Clearwater Ho 9 TW10 154 A6
Clearwater Pl KT6 197 C3
Clearwater Terr 4 W11 112 D4
Clearwell Dr W9 91 D3
Cleave Ave
Hayes UB3 105 C2
Orpington BR6 227 C2
Cleaveland Rd KT6 197 D4
Cleaver Ho 6 NW3 70 D1
Cleaverholme Cl SE25 206 B3
Cleaver Sq SE11 116 C1 261 B1
Cleaver St SE11 116 C1 261 B2
Cleave's Almshos 1 KT2 176 A1
Cleeve Ct N10 31 B3
East Bedfont TW14 149 C3
Cleeve Hill SE23 162 B3
Cleeve Ho 16 E2 95 C4
Cleeve Park Gdns DA14 168 B2
Cleeve Park Sch DA14 168 C1
Cleeve Way SW15
Clegg Ho SE3 143 B1
Clegg St 16 E1 118 B5
E13 99 A5
Cleland Ho 20 E2 96 C5
Clematis Gdns IG8 37 A5
Clematis St W12 112 A6
Clem Attlee Ct SW6 135 B6 264 D5
Clemence St E14 97 B2
Clement Attlee Ho NW10 67 D1
Clement Ave SW4 137 D1
Clement Cl NW6 68 C1
W4 111 B2
Clement Gdns UB3 105 C2
Clement Ho 14 SE8 119 A2
W10 90 C2
Clementhorpe Rd RM9 80 C2
Clementina Rd E10 53 B1
Clementine Churchill Hospl The HA1 64 D5
Clementine Cl W13 109 B4
Clement Rd
Penge BR3 184 D1
Wimbledon SW19 179 A5
Clements Ave 1 E16 121 A6
Clements Ct
Hounslow TW4 128 D1
5 Ilford IG1 78 D5
Clements Inn WC2 94 B1 240 D1
Clements Inn Pas WC2 240 D1
Clement's La EC2,EC4 117 B6 252 D6
Clements La IG1 78 D5
Clements Pl TW8 109 D1
Clements Rd E6 78 B1
Clement's Rd SE16 118 B3
Clements Rd IG1 78 D5
Clemson Ho 9 E8 95 D6
Clendon Way SE18 123 B2
Clenham St SE1 252 B2
Clensham Ct SM3 217 C6
Clensham La SM1 217 C6
Clenston Mews W1 237 C2
Clent Ho 4 N16 51 D1
Cleopatra's Needle* WC2 116 B5 250 C5
Clephane Rd 6 N1 73 A2
Clephane Rd N N1 73 A2
Clephane Rd S N1 73 B2
Clere Pl EC2 242 D6
Clere St EC2 95 B3 242 D6
Clerics Wlk TW17 193 B3
Clerkenwell Cl EC1 94 C3 241 B5
Clerkenwell Gn EC1 94 D3 241 C5
Clerkenwell Parochial CE Prim Sch EC1 94 C4 234 A2
Clerkenwell Rd EC1 94 D3 241 C5
Clermont Rd E9 96 C6
Cleveden Ct CR2 221 C3
Clevedon Ct SW11 267 A2
Dulwich SE21 161 B1
Clevedon Gdns
Cranford TW5 128 B4
Hayes UB3 105 B3
Clevedon Mans NW5 71 A4
Clevedon Rd
Kingston KT1 176 C1
Penge SE20 184 D2
Twickenham TW1 153 D5
Cleve Ho NW6 69 D1
Cleveland Ave W4 111 D2
Hampton TW12 173 B3
Merton SW20 179 B1
Cleveland Cres WD6 11 A6

Cleveland Ct
Ealing W13 . . . . .87 B2
Southall UB2 . . . . .107 D2
Cleveland Gdns
N4,N15 . . . . .51 A4
W2 . . . . .92 A1 236 A1
Barnes SW13 . . . . . . .133 D3
Hendon NW2 . . . . .68 C6
Worcester Park KT4 . . .215 D6
Cleveland Gr 33 E1 . .96 C3
Cleveland Ho 7 N2 . .30 B1
Cleveland Inf Sch IG1 78 D5
Cleveland Jun Sch
IG1 . . . . .78 D5
Cleveland Mans
4 NW6 . . . . .69 B1
8 SW9 . . . . .138 C5
W9 . . . . .91 C3
Cleveland Mews W1 .239 A4
Cleveland Park Ave
E17 . . . . .53 C5
Cleveland Park Cres
E17 . . . . .53 C5
Cleveland Pk TW19 . .148 A5
Cleveland Pl SW1 . . .249 B4
Cleveland Rd DA16 . .145 D3
N1 . . . . .73 B1
14 W4 . . . . .111 A3
Barnes SW13 . . . . . . .133 D3
Ealing W13 . . . . .87 B2
Edmonton N9 . . . . .18 B4
Ilford IG1 . . . . .78 D5
Isleworth TW7 . . . . . . .131 A1
New Malden KT3 . . . . .199 C5
Wanstead E18 . . . . .55 A6
Worcester Park KT4 . . .215 C6
Cleveland Rise SM4 .200 D2
Cleveland Row
SW1 . . . . . . .115 C5 249 B3
Cleveland Sq
W2 . . . . .92 A1 236 A1
Cleveland St
W1 . . . . .93 C3 239 A5
Clevelands The IG11 . .79 A4
Cleveland Terr
W2 . . . . .92 A1 236 A1
Cleveland Way E1 . . .96 C3
Cleveley Cres W5 . . . .88 B5
Cleveleys Rd E5 . . . . .74 B5
Clevely Cl SE7 . . . . .121 D2
Clevedon Cl N16 . . . . .73 D5
Cleve Rd DA14 . . . . .168 D1
NW6 . . . . .69 C1
Cleverly Cotts W12 . .111 D5
Cleverly Est W12 . . . .112 A6
Cleves Ct KT6 . . . . . .198 A3
Cleves Prim Sch E6 . .99 D6
Cleves Rd E6 . . . . . . .99 C5
Richmond TW10 . . . . .153 C1
Cleves Way
Ashford TW16 . . . . . .171 D4
Hampton TW12 . . . . . .173 B3
Ruislip HA4 . . . . .40 D1
Clewer Cres HA3 . . . .24 B2
Clewer Ct 2 E10 . . . .53 C1
Clewer Ho 8 SE2 . . .124 D1
Cley Ho SE4 . . . . . . .140 D1
Clichy Ho 22 E1 . . . . .96 C2
Clifden Centre (Richmond
Adult & Com Coll)
TW1 . . . . .152 D3
Clifden Ho 6 TW8 . .131 D6
Clifden Rd E5 . . . . . . .74 D3
Brentford TW8 . . . . . .131 D6
Twickenham TW1 . . . . .152 D3
Cliff Ct 5 NW1 . . . . . .71 D2
Cliffe Ho 4 SE10 . . .120 C1
Cliffe Rd CR2 . . . . . . .221 B3
Cliffe Wlk 2 SM1 . . .218 A3
Clifford Ave BR7 . . . .188 B4
Mortlake SW14 . . . . . .133 A3
Wallington SM6 . . . . . .219 C4
Clifford Cl UB5 . . . . . .85 A6
Clifford Ct NW10 . . . .67 C4
W2 . . . . .91 B2
Wandsworth SW18 . . . .158 B4
Clifford Dr SW9 . . . . .138 D1
Clifford Gdns NW10 . .90 C5
Hayes UB3 . . . . .105 B2
Clifford Gr TW15 . . . .170 C2
Clifford Haigh Ho
SW6 . . . . .134 D5
Clifford Ho W14 . . . . .254 C3
2 Beckenham BR3 . . .185 D4
Clifford Rd E16 . . . . . .98 D3
N9 . . . . .18 C4
Barnet EN5 . . . . .1 D2
Chingford E17 . . . . . . .36 A1
Croydon SE25 . . . . . . .206 A6
Hounslow TW4 . . . . . .128 C2

Clifford Rd continued
Richmond TW10 . . . . .153 D2
Wembley HA0 . . . . .87 D6
Clifford's Inn Pas
EC4 . . . . .241 A1
Clifford St
W1 . . . . .115 C6 249 A5
Clifford Way NW10 . . .67 C4
Cliffsend Ho 23 SW9 .138 C4
Cliff Terr SE8 . . . . . .141 C3
Cliffview Rd SE13 . . .141 C2
Cliff Villas NW1 . . . . .71 D2
Cliff Wlk E16 . . . . .98 C2
Clifton Ave E17 . . . . . .52 D6
N3 . . . . .29 B2
Feltham TW13 . . . . . . .150 C1
Shepherd's Bush W12 . .111 D5
Stanmore HA7 . . . . . . .25 B1
Wembley HA9 . . . . .66 B2
Clifton Cl 8 BR6 . . . .227 B2
Clifton Cres SE15 . . .140 B5
Clifton Ct N4 . . . . . . .72 C6
NW8 . . . . .236 C6
SE15 . . . . .140 B5
2 Beckenham BR3 . . .185 D4
Putney SW15 . . . . . . .156 D6
South Norwood SE25 . .205 C4
9 Stanwell TW19 . . .148 A5
Surbiton KT5 . . . . . . .198 A5
3 Woodford IG8 . . . . .37 A4
Clifton Gate SW10 . .266 A6
Clifton Gdns N15 . . . .51 A4
2 NW11 . . . . .47 B3
W4 . . . . .111 B2
W9 . . . . .92 A3 236 A5
Enfield EN2 . . . . .16 A4
Hillingdon UB10 . . . . . .82 D5
Clifton Gr E8 . . . . .74 B1
Clifton Hill
NW8 . . . . .92 A6 229 B1
E2 . . . . .243 C6
Clifton Lodge (Brunel Univ
Coll Twickenham
Campus) TW1 . . . . . .153 B6
Clifton Mans 4 SW9 138 C1
Clifton Mews SE25 . .205 C5
Clifton Par TW13 . . . .172 C6
Clifton Park Ave
SW20 . . . . .178 C1
Clifton Pl SE16 . . . . .118 C4
W2 . . . . .236 D1
Clifton Prim Sch
UB2 . . . . .107 A2
Clifton Rd E16 . . . . . . .98 C2
E7 . . . . .77 D2
N3 . . . . .30 A2
N8 . . . . .49 D3
NW10 . . . . .90 A5
W9 . . . . .92 A3 236 B6
Bexley DA16 . . . . .146 C2
Greenford UB6 . . . . . . .86 B5
Harlington TW6 . . . . . .126 D2
Harrow HA3 . . . . .44 B4
Ilford IG2 . . . . .57 B3
Isleworth TW7 . . . . . . .130 A1
Kingston KT2 . . . . . . .176 B3
Sidcup DA14 . . . . .189 C6
Southall UB2 . . . . .107 A2
South Norwood SE25 . .205 C4
Teddington TW11 . . . . .174 D4
Wallington SM6 . . . . . .219 B3
Wimbledon SW19 . . . .178 D4
Wood Green N22 . . . . .31 C2
Clifton Rise SE14 . . .141 A4
Cliftons Roundabout
SE9,SE12 . . . . .165 C5
Clifton St EC2 .95 C3 243 A5
Clifton Terr N4 . . . . . .72 C6
Clifton The KT6 . . . . .214 A6
Clifton Villas
W9 . . . . .92 A2 236 A4
Cliftonville Ct SE12 . .165 A4
Clifton Way SE15 . . .140 C5
Wembley HA0 . . . . .86 A4
Climsland Ho SE1 . . .251 B4
Clinch Ct 11 E16 . . . . .99 A2
Cline Ho SW15 . . . . .156 A6
Cline Rd N11 . . . . .31 C4
Clinger Ct N1 . . . . .95 C6
Clink St SE1 .117 B5 252 C6
Clinton Ave
Bexley DA16 . . . . .146 A1
East Molesey KT8 . . . .196 A5
Clinton Ho
New Malden KT3 . . . . .199 B1
6 Surbiton KT6 . . . . .197 D2
Clinton Rd E3 . . . . .97 A4
E7 . . . . .77 A4

Clinton Rd continued
N15 . . . . .51 B5
Clipper Cl 3 SE16 . . .118 D4
Clipper Ho E14 . . . . .120 A1
Clipper Way SE13 . . .142 A1
Clippesby Cl KT9 . . . .214 B2
Clipstone Ho 10
SW15 . . . . .156 A6
Clipstone Mews W1 . .239 A4
Clipstone Rd TW3 . . .129 C2
Clipstone St
W1 . . . . .93 C2 239 A4
Clissold Cl N2 . . . . . . .48 D6
Clissold Cres N16 . . . .73 B4
Clissold Ct N4 . . . . . . .73 A6
Clissold Ho 4 N16 . . . .73 B6
Clissold Rd N16 . . . . . .73 B5
Clitheroe Ave HA2 . . . .41 C1
Clitheroe Gdns WD19 .22 D6
Clitheroe Rd SW9 . . .138 A3
Clitherow Ave W7 . . .109 A3
Clitherow Rd TW8 . . .109 C1
Clitterhouse Cres
NW2 . . . . .46 C1
Clitterhouse Jun & Inf
Schs NW2 . . . . .68 D6
Clitterhouse Rd NW2 .46 C1
Clive Ave N18 . . . . . . .34 A4
Clive Ct W9 . . . . .236 B6
Streatham SW16 . . . . .181 D5
Tolworth KT6 . . . . . . .214 C6
Cliveden Cl N12 . . . . . .30 A6
Cliveden Pl
SW1 . . . . . . .115 A2 258 A4
Shepperton TW17 . . . .193 A3
Cliveden Rd SW19 . . .179 B2
Clivedon Ct W13 . . . . .87 B2
Clivedon Rd E4 . . . . . .36 C5
Clive Ho SE10 . . . . . .142 A6
18 SW8 . . . . .137 D3
3 Croydon CR0 . . . . .205 D1
Clive Lloyd Ho N15 . . .51 A4
Clive Lo NW4 . . . . .46 D3
Clive Rd
Belvedere DA17 . . . . . .125 C2
Enfield EN1 . . . . .6 A1
Feltham TW14 . . . . . . .150 A5
Mitcham SW19 . . . . . .180 C4
Teddington TW1 . . . . .175 A4
West Norwood SE21,
SE27 . . . . .161 B1
Clivesdale Dr UB3 . . .106 B5
Clive Way EN1 . . . . . . .6 A1
Cloak La EC4 .117 B6 252 C6
Clochar Ct NW10 . . . .89 D6
Clock Ct E11 . . . . .55 B5
Clock Ho E17 . . . . .54 B5
N16 . . . . .51 D2
Clock Ho The EN2 . . . .5 D6
Clockhouse Ave
IG11 . . . . .101 A6
Clockhouse Cl SW19 .156 C2
Clock House Ct 1
BR3 . . . . .185 A1
Clockhouse Junc N13 .32 C5
Clockhouse La TW14,
TW15 . . . . .148 D2
Clockhouse Par N13 . .32 C5
Clockhouse Par E11 . .55 B3
Clockhouse Pl SW15 .157 A6
Clock House Par BR3 .185 A1
Clockhouse Rdbt
TW14 . . . . .149 A3
Clock House Sta BR3 185 A2
Clockhouse The
SW19 . . . . .156 C1
Clock Tower Mews
N1 . . . . .235 B5
Thamesmead SE28 . . .124 B6
Clock Tower Pl N7 . . . .72 A2
Clock Tower Rd TW7 130 D2
Cloister Cl TW11 . . . . .175 B5
Cloister Gdns HA8 . . . .27 A5
Croydon SE25 . . . . . . .206 B3
Cloister Rd NW2 . . . . .69 B6
W3 . . . . .89 A4
Cloisters Ave BR1,
BR2 . . . . .210 B4
Cloisters Ct DA7 . . . . .147 D2
N6 . . . . .49 B1
Cloisters The 22 SW9 138 C4
Clonard Way HA5 . . . .23 C4
Clonbrock Rd N16 . . . .73 C4
Cloncurry St SW6 . . .134 D3
Clone Ct 4 W12 . . . . .111 C3
Clone The 5 KT2 . . . .176 D3
Clonmel Cl HA2 . . . . . .42 B1
Clonmell Rd N17 . . . . .51 B6
Clonmel Rd TW11 . . . .174 B6
Fulham SW6 . .135 B4 264 D2

Clonmore St SW18 . .157 B3
Cloonmore Ave BR6 .227 D4
Clorane Gdns NW3 . . .69 C5
Close The BR5 . . . . . .211 C3
DA14 . . . . .190 B5
N10 . . . . .31 B1
N14 . . . . .15 D2
N20 . . . . .13 B2
Beckenham BR3 . . . . . .207 A5
Cheam SM3 . . . . .201 B2
Chingford E4 . . . . .36 A3
Cockfosters EN4 . . . . . .14 C6
Croydon SE25 . . . . . . .206 A4
Dagenham RM6 . . . . . .59 A4
Hillingdon UB10 . . . . . .82 C6
Hounslow TW7 . . . . . .130 B3
Ilford IG2 . . . . .57 C3
Kingston KT3 . . . . . . .177 A1
Mitcham CR4 . . . . . . .202 D5
Mortlake TW9 . . . . . . .132 D2
Pinner HA5 . . . . .40 C3
Pinner HA5 . . . . .41 B2
1 Sidcup DA5 . . . . . .169 C4
Surbiton KT6 . . . . .198 A3
Wembley HA0 . . . . .66 A2
Wembley HA9 . . . . .67 A5
Cloth Ct EC1 . . . . . . .241 D3
Cloth Fair EC1 .94 D2 241 D3
Clothier Ho SE7 . . . . .122 A1
Clothier St EC3 . . . . .243 C3
Cloth St EC1 .95 A2 242 A4
Clothworkers Rd
SE18 . . . . .145 B5
Cloudesdale Rd
SW17 . . . . .159 B2
Cloudesley Mans N1 .234 B5
Cloudesley Pl
N1 . . . . .94 C6 234 B6
Cloudesley Rd DA7 . .147 B4
N1 . . . . .94 C6 234 A5
Cloudesley Sq
N1 . . . . .94 C6 234 B6
Cloudesley St
N1 . . . . .94 C6 234 B5
Clouston Cl SM6 . . . .220 A3
Clova Rd E7 . . . . .77 A3
Clove Cres E14 . . . . . .120 B6
Clovelly Ave NW9 . . . .45 D5
Uxbridge UB10 . . . . . . .61 A4
Clovelly Cl Pinner HA5 .40 C6
Uxbridge UB10 . . . . . . .61 A4
Clovelly Ct NW2 . . . . .68 C3
Clovelly Gdns EN1 . . . .17 C4
Clovelly Ho W2 . . . . . .236 A2
Clovelly Rd DA7 . . . . .147 A6
N8 . . . . .49 D5
W4 . . . . .111 B4
W5 . . . . .109 C4
Hounslow TW3 . . . . . .129 C4
Clovelly Way BR6 . . . .211 D3
E1 . . . . .96 C1
Harrow HA2 . . . . .63 B6
Cloverdale Gdns
DA15 . . . . .167 D5
Clover Ho SW3 . . . . .130 A4
Cloverleys IG10 . . . . . .21 C6
Clover Mews SW3 . . .267 D6
Clover Way SM6 . . . . .203 A1
Clove St 9 E13 . . . . . . .99 A3
Clowders Rd SE6 . . . .163 B1
Clowes Ho 3 SW4 . . .138 A1
Clowser Cl 4 SM1 . . .218 A3
Cloysters Gn E1 . . . . .118 A5
Cloyster Wood HA8 . . .25 D4
Club Gardens Rd
BR2 . . . . .209 A2
Club Row E2 .95 D3 243 C6
Bromley BR2 . . . . .210 A2
Edgware HA8 . . . . .26 D1
Enfield EN1 . . . . .6 A2
Wallington SM6 . . . . . .220 A2
Clumps The TW15 . . . .171 B6
Clunbury Ave UB2 . . .107 B1
Clunbury St N1 . . . . . .235 D3
Clunie Ho SW1 . . . . . .257 D6
Cluny Mews SW5 . . . .255 A3
Cluny Pl SE1 .117 C3 263 A6
Cluse Ct N1 . . . . .235 A4
Clutton St E14 . . . . . . .97 C2
Clydach Rd EN1 . . . . . .5 C1
Clyde Cir N15 . . . . . . .51 C5
Clyde Ct NW1 . . . . . . .232 D4
Clyde Flats SW6 . . . . .264 C4
Clyde Ho 9 KT2 . . . . .175 D2
Clyde Pl E10 . . . . .53 D2
Clyde Rd N15 . . . . .51 C5
N22 . . . . .31 D1
Croydon CR0 . . . . . . .221 D6
Stanwell TW19 . . . . . .148 A3
Sutton SM1 . . . . .217 D3
Wallington SM6 . . . . . .219 C2
Clydesdale EN3 . . . . . . .6 D1
Clydesdale Ave HA7 . .43 D6

Clydesdale Cl
Borehamwood WD6 . . . .11 B6
Isleworth TW7 . . . . . . .130 D2
Clydesdale Ct N20 . . . .14 B3
Clydesdale Gdns
TW10 . . . . .132 D1
Clydesdale Ho DA18 . .125 A4
4 W11 . . . . .91 B1
Clydesdale Path WD6 .11 B6
Clydesdale Rd W11 . . .91 B1
Clyde St SE8 . . . . . . .141 B6
Clyde Terr SE23 . . . . .162 C2
Clyde Vale SE23 . . . . .162 C2
Clyfford Rd HA4 . . . . . .61 D4
Clymping Dene
TW14 . . . . .150 B4
Clynes Ho 3 E2 . . . . . .96 D4
6 Dagenham RM10 . .81 C5
Hayes UB4 . . . . .84 A4
Clyro Ct N4 . . . . .50 B1
Clyston St SW8 . . . . .137 C3
Clytha Ct SE27 . . . . . .183 A6
Coach & Horses Yd
W1 . . . . .249 A6
Coach House La N5 . .72 D4
Coach House Mews
SE23 . . . . .162 D5
Coach House Yd NW3 .70 B4
Coachmaker Mews 5
SW9 . . . . .138 A2
Coachman Lo N12 . . . .30 A5
Coalbrook Mans 3
SW12 . . . . .159 B3
Coaldale Wlk SE21 . . .161 A4
Coalecroft Rd SW15 . .156 C2
Coalport Ho SE11 . . . .261 A4
Coal Wharf Rd W12 . . .112 D2
Coates Ave SW18 . . . .158 C5
Coates Ct NW3 . . . . . .70 C3
Coates Hill Rd BR1 . . .188 C1
Coates Rd WD6 . . . . . .9 A4
Coate St E2 . . . . .96 A5
Coates Wlk TW8 . . . . .110 A1
Cobbett Rd SE9 . . . . .144 A2
Twickenham TW2 . . . . .151 C3
Cobbett St
SW8 . . . . .138 B5 270 D3
Cobbetts Ave IG4 . . . . .55 D4
Cobbetts Ave IG4 . . . . .55 D4
Cobble La N1 . . . . .72 D1
Cobble Mews N4,N5 . .73 A5
Cobbler's Wlk
Teddington KT1,TW11 .175 A2
Teddington TW11 . . . .174 D3
Cobblestone Pl CR0 . .205 A1
Cobbold Ct SW1 . . . . .259 C4
Cobbold Ind Est NW10 67 D2
Cobbold Mews W12 . .111 D4
Cobbold Rd E11 . . . . . .76 D5
NW10 . . . . .67 D2
W12 . . . . .111 D4
Cobb's Hall 1 SW6 . .134 D6
Cobbs Rd TW4 . . . . . .129 B1
Cobb St E1 . . . . .243 C3
Cob Cl WD6 . . . . .11 A6
Cobden Bldgs WC1 . .233 C2
Cobden Ct 9 SE28 . . .124 C5
Cobden Ho 7 E2 . . . . .96 A4
NW1 . . . . .232 A4
Cobden Mews SE26 . .184 B5
Cobden Rd BR6 . . . . .227 B4
E11 . . . . .76 C6
Croydon SE25 . . . . . . .206 A4
Cobham 21 NW9 . . . . .27 D1
Cobham Ave KT3 . . . .200 A4
Cobham Cl 2 DA15 . .168 B5
SW11 . . . . .158 C5
Bromley BR2 . . . . .210 A2
Edgware HA8 . . . . .26 D1
Enfield EN1 . . . . .6 A2
Wallington SM6 . . . . . .220 A2
Cobham Ct CR4 . . . . .180 B1
Cobham Ho IG11 . . . .101 A2
Cobham Mews 3
NW1 . . . . .71 D1
Cobham Pl DA6 . . . . .168 D6
Cobham Rd N22 . . . . . .50 D6
Chingford E17 . . . . . . .36 A2
Heston TW5 . . . . .128 C5
Ilford IG3 . . . . .79 C5
Kingston KT1,KT2 . . . .176 C1
Cobland Rd SE12 . . . .187 D6
Coborn Mews 9 E3 . . .97 B4
Coborn Rd E3 . . . . .97 B4
Coborn St E3 . . . . .97 B4
Cobourg Prim Sch
SE5 . . . . .139 D6
Cobourg Rd SE5 . . . . .139 D6
Cobourg St
NW1 . . . . .93 C4 232 B1

Coburg Cl SW1 . . . . .259 B4
Coburg Cres SW2 . . .160 C3
Coburg Dwellings 10
E1 . . . . .118 C6
Coburg Gdns IG5 . . . . .37 C1
Coburg Rd N22 . . . . . .32 B1
Cochrane Cl NW8 . . . .229 D3
Cochrane Ct 3 E10 . . .53 C1
Cochrane Mews
NW8 . . . . .92 B5 229 D3
Cochrane Rd SW19 . .179 B3
Cochrane St
NW8 . . . . .92 B5 229 D3
Coci Ho W14 . . . . . . .254 D3
Cockburn Ho SW1 . . .259 D1
Cockerell Rd E17 . . . . .53 A3
Cockfosters Par EN4 . .3 C1
Cockfosters Rd EN4 . . .2 D3
Cockfosters Sta EN4 . .3 A1
Cock Hill E1 . . . . .243 B3
Cock La EC1 . . .94 C2 241 D3
Cockpit Yd WC1 . . . . .240 D4
Cocks Cres KT3 . . . . .199 D5
Cocksett Ave BR6 . . .227 C2
Cockspur Ct SW1 . . . .249 C4
Cockspur St
SW1 . . . . . . .115 D5 249 C4
Coda Ctr The
SW6 . . . . .135 A4 264 B2
Code St E1 . . .95 D3 243 D5
Codicote Ho 22 SE8 . .118 D2
Codicote Terr N4 . . . . .73 A6
Codling Cl 13 E1 . . . .118 A5
Codling Way HA0 . . . . .65 D4
Codrington Ct SE16 . .119 A5
Codrington Hill SE23 163 A4
Codrington Ho 7 E1 . .96 B3
Codrington Mews
W11 . . . . .91 A1
Cody Cl Harrow HA3 . . .43 D6
Wallington SM6 . . . . . .219 D1
Cody Rd E16 . . . . .98 B3
Coe Ave SE25 . . . . . . .206 A3
Coerdale Ct EN3 . . . . . .7 A6
Coe's Alley EN5 . . . . . .1 A1
Coffey St SE8 . . . . . . .141 C5
Cogan Ave E17 . . . . . . .35 A2
Cohen Ho NW7 . . . . . .28 A6
Cohen Lo E5 . . . . .75 A3
Coin St SE1 . .116 C5 251 A4
Coity Rd NW5 . . . . . . .71 A2
Cokers La SE21 . . . . .161 B3
Coke St E1 . . . . .96 A1
Colab Ct N22 . . . . .32 C2
Colas Mews 7 NW6 . .91 C6
Colbeck Mews
SW5 . . . . .113 D2 255 D3
Colbeck Rd HA1 . . . . . .42 A2
Colberg Pl N16 . . . . . .51 D2
Colbert 1 SE5 . . . . . . .139 D4
Colborne Ho 7 E14 . .119 C6
Colborne Way KT4 . . .216 C6
Colbrook Ave UB3 . . .105 B3
Colbrook Cl UB3 . . . .105 B3
Colburn Ave HA5 . . . . .23 A4
Colburn Way SM1 . . .218 B5
Colby Rd
Walton-on-T KT12 . . . .194 A1
West Norwood SE19 . . .183 C5
Colchester Ave E12 . . .78 B5
Colchester Dr HA5 . . . .40 D4
Colchester Ho 17
SW8 . . . . .137 D4
Colchester Rd E10 . . . .54 A2
E17 . . . . .53 C3
HA8 . . . . .27 A3
Pinner HA6 . . . . .22 A1
Colchester St E1 . . . . .243 D2
Colchester Villas
CR7 . . . . .204 C3
Coldbath Sq EC1 . . . .241 A6
Coldbath St SE13 . . . .141 D3
Coldblow La SE14 . . . .140 D6
Coldershaw Rd W13 .109 A4
Coldfall Ave N10 . . . . .31 A1
Coldfall Prim Sch N10 30 D1
Coldham Ct N22 . . . . . .32 D2
Coldham Gr EN3 . . . . . .7 A6
Coldharbour E14 . . . .120 A5
Coldharbour Crest
SE9 . . . . .166 C1
Coldharbour Ind Est
SE5 . . . . .139 A3
Coldharbour La SW9 138 D2
Bushey WD23 . . . . .8 A6

Coldharbour La continued
Hayes UB3 ....**106** A5
Coldharbour Lane Ho
UB3 ....**106** A5
Coldharbour Pl .**139** B3
Coldharbour Rd CR0 .**220** C3
Coldharbour Sports Ctr
SE9 ....**166** C2
Coldharbour Way
CR0 ....**220** C3
Coldstream Gdns
SW18 ....**157** B5
Colebeck Mews N1 ..**72** D2
Colebert Ave E1 ...**96** C3
Colebert Ho 20 E1 ...**96** C3
Colebrook Cl SW19 .**156** D4
Colebrook Ct SE3 ..**257** B3
Colebrooke Ave W13 .**87** B1
Colebrooke Ct DA14 .**190** B6
Colebrooke Dr E11 ..**55** C2
Colebrooke Pl N1 ..**234** D5
Colebrooke Row
N1 ....**94** D5 **234** C4
N1 ....**234** C5
Colebrooke Sch
N1 ....**94** D5 **234** A4
Colebrook Ho 1 E14 ..**97** D1
Colebrook Rd SW16 .**182** A2
Colebrook Rise BR2 .**186** C1
Colebrook Way N11 ..**31** B5
Coleby Path 21 SE5 .**139** B5
Colechurch Ho 8
SE1 ....**118** A1
Cole Cl SE28 ....**124** B5
Cole Court Lo 7
TW1 ....**153** A4
Coledale Dr HA7 ...**25** C2
Coleford Rd SW18 ..**158** A6
Cole Gdns TW5 ...**128** A5
Colegrave Prim Sch
E15 ....**76** B3
Colegrave Rd E15 ...**76** B3
Colegrove Rd SE15 .**139** D6
Coleherne Ct
SW10 ......**113** D1 **255** D1
Coleherne Mans
SW5 ....**255** D2
Coleherne Mews
SW10 ......**113** D1 **255** C1
Coleherne Rd
SW10 ......**113** D1 **255** C1
Colehill Gdns SW6 .**264** A1
Colehill La
SW6 ....**135** A4 **264** D1
Cole Ho SE1 ....**251** B1
Coleman Cl SE25 ...**184** A1
Coleman Ct SW18 ..**157** C4
Coleman Fields
N1 ....**95** A6 **235** B6
Coleman Mans N19 ..**50** A2
Coleman Rd SE5 ...**139** C5
Belvedere DA17 .....**125** C2
Dagenham RM9 ....**81** A2
Colemans Heath SE9 **166** D1
Coleman St
EC2 ....**95** B1 **242** C2
Coleman St Bldgs
EC2 ....**242** C2
Colenso Dr NW7 ....**28** A3
Colenso Rd E5 .....**74** C4
Ilford IG2 ....**57** C2
Cole Park Gdns TW1 **153** A5
Cole Park Rd TW1 ..**153** A5
Cole Park View 2
TW1 ....**153** A5
Colepits Wood Rd
SE9 ....**167** B6
Coleraine Park Prim Sch
N17 ....**34** A3
Coleraine Rd N8,N22 .**50** C6
SE3 ....**142** D6
Cole Rd TW1 ....**153** A5
Coleridge Ave E12 ..**72** B3
Carshalton SM1 .....**218** C4
Coleridge Cl SW8 ..**137** B3
Coleridge Ct W14 ..**112** D3
11 New Barnet EN5 ..**13** D6
2 Richmond TW10 ..**175** D6
Coleridge Gdns NW6 .**70** A1
SW1 ....**259** B1
Coleridge Prim Sch
N8 ....**49** D2
Coleridge Rd E17 ...**53** B5
N12 ....**30** A5
N4,N7 ....**72** C6
N8 ....**49** D3

Coleridge Rd continued
Ashford TW15 ....**170** B6
Croydon CR0 ....**206** C2
Coleridge Sq W13 ...**87** A1
Coleridge Way
Hayes UB4 ....**84** A1
West Drayton UB7 ..**104** B2
Coleridge Wlk NW11 .**47** C5
Colerne Ct NW4 ....**29** A1
Colesburg Rd BR3 ..**185** B1
Coles Cres HA2 ....**63** D6
Coles Ct SW11 ....**266** C1
Coles Gn WD23 .....**8** A3
Coles Green Ct NW2 .**68** A6
Coles Green Rd NW2 .**68** B6
Coleshill Flats SW1 .**258** B3
Coleshill Rd TW11 ..**174** C4
Coleswood N20 .....**14** C3
Colesworth Ho 1 HA8 **27** A1
Colet Cl N13 ....**32** D4
Colet Gdns W14 ....**112** D2
Colet Ho SE17 ......**261** D1
Colette Ct 5 SE16 ..**118** D4
Coley St WC1 ..**94** B3 **240** D5
Colfe & Hatchcliffe's Glebe
SE13 ....**163** D2
Colfe Rd SE23 ......**163** A3
Colfe's Prep Sch
SE12 ....**165** A5
Colfe's Sch SE12 ...**165** B5
Colgate Ct EN5 .....**13** A6
Colgate Ho SE13 ...**141** D3
Colgate Pl EN3 .....**7** C6
Colham Ave UB7 ...**104** A3
Colham Green Rd UB8 **82** C2
Colham Manor Jun & Inf
Schs UB8 ....**82** C1
Colham Rd UB8 .....**82** B3
Colina Mews N8,N15 .**50** D5
Colina Rd N8,N15 ..**50** D4
Colin Blanchard Ho
SE4 ....**141** C3
Colin Cl NW9 ......**45** C5
Coney Hall BR4 ......**224** D5
Croydon CR0 ....**223** B5
Colin Cres NW9 ....**45** D5
Colin Ct SW16 .....**159** D4
Colindale Ave NW9 ..**45** C6
Colindale Hospl NW9 .**45** C6
Colindale Prim Sch
NW9 ....**45** D5
Colindale Sta NW9 ..**45** C6
Colindeep Gdns NW4 .**46** A5
Colindeep La NW9,
NW4 ....**45** D5
Colin Dr NW9 ......**45** D5
Colinette Rd SW15 ..**134** C1
Colin Gdns NW9 ....**45** D5
Colin Par NW9 .....**45** D5
Colin Park Rd NW9 ..**45** C5
Colin Rd NW10 .....**68** A2
Colinsdale N1 ....**234** C5
Colinton Rd IG3 ....**80** B6
Colin Winter Ho 37 E1 **96** C3
Coliston Pass SW18 .**157** C4
Coliston Rd SW18 ..**157** C4
Collamore Ave SW18 **158** C3
Collapit Cl HA1 ....**41** D3
Collard Pl NW1 .....**71** B1
College App SE10 ..**142** A6
College Ave HA3 ...**24** C2
College Cl E5 ......**74** C3
Edmonton N18 ....**33** D5
Harrow HA3 ....**24** C3
Twickenham TW2 ...**152** B3
College Cres NW3 ...**70** B2
College Cross N1 ...**72** C1
College Ct NW3 ....**70** B2
SW3 ....**114** D1 **257** D1
3 W6 ....**112** C1
Croydon CR0 ....**222** A6
Ealing W5 ....**110** A6
Enfield EN3 ....**5** A2
College Dr Ruislip HA4 **40** A2
Thames Ditton KT7 ..**196** C2
College Fields Bsns Ctr
SW19 ....**180** C2
College Gdns
Chingford E4 ....**20** A3
Dulwich SE21 ....**161** A4
Edmonton N18 ....**34** A5
New Malden KT3 ...**199** D4
Redbridge IG4 ....**56** C4
Upper Tooting SW17 **158** C3
College Gn BR1 ....**187** A2
South Norwood SE19 **183** C4

College Gr NW1 ....**232** C6
College Hill EC4 ...**252** B6
College Hill Rd HA3 ..**24** C3
College La NW5 ....**71** B4
College Park Cl SE13 **142** B1
College Park Rd N17 .**33** D4
College Park Sch W2 .**91** D1
College Pl E17 .....**54** C5
NW1 ....**93** C6 **232** B5
SW10 ....**266** A4
College Pt E15 .....**76** D2
College Rd BR1 ....**187** A3
E17 ....**54** A4
NW10 ....**90** C5
Dulwich SE19,SE21 .**161** C2
Ealing W13 ....**87** B1
Enfield EN2 ....**5** B3
Harrow HA1 ....**42** C3
Harrow HA3 ....**24** C2
Hounslow TW7 .....**130** D4
Mitcham SW19 .....**180** C2
South Croydon CR0 .**221** B6
Southgate N21 ......**16** C2
Tottenham N17 .....**33** D4
Wembley HA9 ....**43** D1
College Rdbt 1 KT1 .**198** A6
College St
EC4 ....**117** A6 **252** B6
College Terr E3 ....**97** B4
N3 ....**29** B1
College View SE9 ..**165** D3
College Way
Ashford TW15 ......**170** A6
Hayes UB3 ....**106** A6
College Wlk 10 KT1 .**198** A6
Collent Ho 12 E9 ...**74** C2
Collent St E9 ......**74** C2
Colless Rd N15 ....**51** D4
Collett Rd SE16 ...**118** A3
Collett Way UB2 ..**107** A3
Colley Ho 12 N7 ....**71** D3
Collier Cl E16 ......**122** D6
West Ewell KT19 ...**214** D2
Collier Dr HA8 .....**26** C1
Collier St N1 ..**94** B5 **233** C3
Colliers Water La
CR7 ....**204** C4
Colliers Wood BR2 .**225** D3
Mitcham SW19 .....**180** B4
Collier's Wood Sta
SW19 ....**180** B3
Collindale Ave DA15 .**168** A3
DA8 ....**147** D6
Collingbourne Rd
W12 ....**112** B5
Collingham Gdns
SW5 ....**113** D2 **255** D3
Collingham Pl
SW5 ....**113** D2 **255** D4
Collingham Rd
SW5 ....**113** D2 **255** D3
Collings Cl N22 ....**32** B4
Collington Ho SE7 .**143** B6
Collington St SE10 .**120** B1
Collingtree Rd SE26 .**184** C6
Collingwood Ave N10 .**49** A5
Tolworth KT5 ......**199** A1
Collingwood Cl
2 Penge SE20 ......**184** B2
Twickenham TW2,TW4 **151** C4
Collingwood Ct 4 NW4 .**46** C4
New Barnet EN5 ....**13** D6
Collingwood Ho 27 E1 **96** B3
Collingwood Rd N15 .**51** C5
Hillingdon UB8 .....**82** D3
Mitcham CR4 ......**202** C6
Sutton SM1 ....**217** C4
Collingwood Sch
SM6 ....**219** B3
Collingwood St E1 ..**96** B3
Collins Ave HA7 ...**26** A1
Collins Ct E8 ......**74** A2
Collins Dr HA4 ....**62** C6
Collins Ho 4 E14 ..**120** A6
6 SE10 ....**120** D1
8 Barking IG11 ....**78** D1
Collinson Ct SE1 ...**252** A1
Edgware HA8 ....**26** B6
Collinson Ho 13 SE15 **140** A5
Collinson St SE1 ...**252** A1
Collinson Wlk SE1 ..**252** A1
Collins Rd N5,N16 ..**73** A4
Collins Sq SE3 .....**142** D3
Collins St SE3 .....**142** D3
Collins Yd N1 ......**234** C5
Collinwood Ave EN3 ..**6** C2
Collinwood Gdns IG5 .**56** C5

Collis Prim Sch
TW11 ....**175** B4
Coll of Liberal Arts
SM1 ....**217** D3
Coll of North East London
The
N11 ....**31** D3
N15 ....**51** D5
Coll of NW London
(Willesden Centre) The
NW10 ....**67** D3
Coll Sharp Ct 42 E2 ..**95** D4
Coll's Rd SE15 .....**140** C4
Collyer Ave CR0 ...**220** A4
Collyer Pl SE15 ....**140** A4
Collyer Rd CR0 ....**220** A4
Colman Ct N12 .....**30** A4
Stanmore HA7 ......**25** B4
Colman Rd E16 .....**99** C2
Colmans Wharf 6
E14 ....**97** D2
Colmar Cl 3 E1 ....**96** D3
Colmer Pl HA3 .....**24** B3
Colmer Rd SW16 ...**182** A3
Colmore Mews SE15 **140** B4
Colmore Rd EN3 ....**6** C1
Colnbrook Cl SW17 .**180** B6
Colnbrook St SE1 ..**261** C6
Colne Ct Ealing W7 .**86** B1
West Ewell KT19 ...**215** A4
Colne Ho NW8 .....**236** D5
Barking IG11 ....**78** D2
Colne Rd E5 ....**75** A4
Southgate N21 ......**17** B4
Twickenham TW1,TW2 **152** C3
Colne St E13 ......**99** A4
Colney Hatch N10 ..**31** A3
Colney Hatch La N10 .**31** A3
Cologne Rd SW11 ..**136** B1
Coloma Convent Girls Sch
CR0 ....**222** D5
Colombo Rd IG1 ....**57** A2
Colombo St SE1 ....**251** C3
Colomb St SE10 ...**120** C1
Colonades The 4
SE5 ....**139** B4
Colonels Wlk EN2 ..**4** D2
Colonial Ave TW2 ..**152** A5
Colonial Dr W4 ....**111** A2
Colonial Rd TW14 ..**149** D4
Colonnade WC1 ....**240** B5
Colonnades The 6 E8 **74** B2
Colonnade The 11
SE8 ....**119** B2
Colosseum Ct N3 ...**29** A1
Colroy Ct NW4 .....**47** A4
Colson Rd CR0 .....**221** C6
Colson Way SW16 ..**181** C6
Colstead Ho 28 E1 ..**96** B1
Colsterworth Rd N15 .**51** D5
Colston Ave SM1,SM5 **218** C4
Colston Ct SM5 ....**218** C4
Colston Rd E7 .....**77** D2
Mortlake SW14 .....**133** A1
Colthurst Cres N4 ..**73** A6
Colthurst Dr N9 ....**18** A1
Coltman Ho 1 E14 ..**97** A1
SE10 ....**142** A6
Colt Mews EN3 .....**7** C6
Coltness Cres SE2 .**124** A3
Colton Gdns N17 ...**51** A6
Colton Rd HA1 .....**42** C4
Coltsfoot Dr UB7 ...**82** A1
Columba Ho SE14 ..**141** B4
Columbas Dr NW3 ..**48** B1
Columbia Ave
Edgware HA8 ....**26** D2
New Malden KT4 ...**199** D2
Ruislip HA4 ....**40** B1
Columbia Ct KT3 ..**199** D2
Columbia Ho 16 E3 ..**97** C4
Columbia Point 7
SE16 ....**118** C3
Columbia Prim Sch
E2 ....**95** D4
Columbia Rd E13 ..**98** D3
E2 ....**95** D4
Columbine Ave E6 ..**100** A2
Croydon CR2 ....**220** D1
Columbus Gdns HA6 .**22** A2
Colveiw Ct SE9 ....**165** D3
Colville Gdns W11 ..**91** B1
Colville Ho 33 E2 ...**96** C4
Colville Mews W11 ..**91** B1
Colville Pl W1 ......**239** B3

Colville Prim Sch W11 **91** B1
Colville Rd E11 ....**76** A5
E17 ....**35** A1
W11 ....**91** B1
W3 ....**110** D3
Edmonton N9 ....**18** B3
Colville Sq W11 ....**91** B1
Colville Sq Mews 6
W11 ....**91** B1
Colville Terr W11 ..**91** B1
Colvin Cl SE26 .....**184** C5
Colvin Gdns
Chingford E4 ....**20** A1
Wanstead E11 ......**55** B5
Colvin Rd E6 ......**78** A1
Thornton Heath CR7 .**204** C4
Colwall Gdns IG8 ..**37** A5
Colwall Ho 18 SW9 .**138** B3
Colwell Rd SE22 ...**161** D6
Colwick Cl N6 .....**49** D2
Colwith Rd W6 ....**134** C6
Colwood Gdns SW19 **180** B3
Colworth Gr 1 SE17 .**262** B3
Colworth Rd E11 ...**54** C2
Croydon CR0 ....**206** A1
Colwyn Ave UB6 ...**86** D5
Colwyn Cl SW16 ...**181** C5
Colwyn Cres TW3 ..**130** A4
Colwyn Gn NW9 ....**45** C3
Colwyn Ho SE1 .....**261** A5
NW2 ....**68** B5
Colyer Cl SE9 ......**166** D2
Colyer Ho SE2 .....**124** D1
Colyton Cl DA16 ...**146** D4
Wembley HA0 ....**65** C2
Colyton Rd SE22 ...**162** B6
Colyton Way N18 ...**34** A5
Combe Ave SE3 ....**142** D5
Combedale Rd SE10 .**121** A1
Combe Ho 20 W2 ...**91** C2
Mortlake SW14 .....**133** A3
Combe Hurst KT2 ..**177** A5
Combe Lane Sta CR0 **222** C3
Combemartin Rd
SW18 ....**157** A3
Combe Mews 4 SE3 **142** D5
Comber Cl NW2 ....**68** B6
Comber Gr SE5 ....**139** B5
Comber Grove Prim Sch
SE5 ....**139** A5
Comber Ho SE5 ....**139** A5
Combermere Rd
SW9 ....**138** B2
Morden SM4 ....**201** D4
Comberton 10 KT1 ..**176** C1
Comberton Rd E5 ..**74** B6
Combeside SE18 ...**145** D5
Combes Rd RM9 ....**81** B1
Combe The NW1 ...**231** D1
Combwell Cres SE2 .**124** A3
Comely Bank Rd E17 .**54** A4
Comeragh Mews
W14 ....**254** B1
Comeragh Rd
W14 ....**113** A1 **254** B1
Comer Cres UB2 ...**108** A4
Comerford Rd SE4 .**141** B1
Comet Cl E12 ......**77** D4
Comet Pl SE8 ......**141** C5
Comet St SE8 ......**141** C5
Comins Ho SW4 ...**159** C6
Commerce Est E18 .**37** C1
Commerce Rd
Brentford TW8 .....**131** C5
Wood Green N22 ...**32** B2
Commerce Way CR0 **220** B6
Commercial Rd E1 ..**96** C1
Edmonton N18 ....**33** C4
Commercial St
E1 ....**95** D2 **243** C4
Commercial Way
SE15 ....**140** A5
Wembley NW10 .....**88** D5
Commerell Pl SE10 .**120** D1
Commerell St SE10 .**120** C1
Commodore Ct SE8 .**141** C4
Commodore Ho 7
E14 ....**120** A6
Commodore St E1 ..**97** A3
Commondale SW15 .**134** C2
Common La KT10 ..**213** A1
Common Rd
Barnes SW13 ....**134** A2
Claygate KT10 .....**213** A1
Stanmore HA7 ......**8** D1
Commonside BR2 ..**225** C4
Commonside Ct
SW16 ....**182** A4
Commonside E CR4 .**203** B6

Common The
Ealing W5 ....**110** A5
Southall UB2 ....**106** D2
Stanmore HA7 ......**8** D2
Common View SW15 .**134** C2
Commonwealth Ave
21 W12 ....**112** B6
Hayes UB3 ....**83** B1
Commonwealth Rd
N17 ....**34** A3
Commonwealth Way
SE2 ....**124** C2
Community Cl
Cranford TW5 ......**128** B4
Uxbridge UB10 .....**61** A3
Community Coll The
E9 ....**74** D2
E9 ....**96** D6
Community Rd E15 ..**76** B3
Greenford UB6 .....**86** A6
Como Rd SE23 .....**163** A2
Compania Bldg 12
E1 ....**118** D6
Compass Ct SE1 ...**253** C3
Compass Hill TW10 .**153** D5
Compass Ho SE8 ...**141** D6
W2 ....**91** D1
Compass Point 9
E14 ....**119** C6
Compayne Gdns NW6 .**69** D1
Compton Ave E6 ...**99** D5
N1 ....**72** D2
N6 ....**48** C2
Wembley HA0 ......**65** C4
Compton Cl 5 HA8 ..**27** A3
NW1 ....**231** D1
NW11 ....**68** D5
SE15 ....**139** D6
Ealing W13 ....**87** A1
Esher KT10 ....**212** B3
Compton Cres
Chessington KT9 ...**214** A2
Chiswick W4 ....**133** A6
Northolt UB5 ....**84** D6
Tottenham N17 .....**33** A3
Compton Ct
Sutton SM1 ....**218** A4
9 West Norwood
SE19 ....**183** C4
Compton High Sch &
Sports Coll UB5 ..**85** A6
Compton Ho SW11 .**267** A2
Compton Lo N21 ...**16** D3
Compton Pas EC1 ..**241** D6
South Oxhey WD19 .**23** A6
Compton Pl WC1 ..**240** A6
NW10 ....**90** D4
Croydon CR0 ....**206** D3
Southgate N21 .....**16** D3
Wimbledon SW19 ..**179** A1
Compton Rise HA5 .**41** B6
Compton Sch The N12 **30** D4
Compton St
EC1 ....**94** D3 **241** D6
Compton Terr N1 ...**72** D2
Southgate N21 .....**16** C3
Comreddy Cl EN2 ...**4** D4
Comus Ho SE17 ...**263** A3
Comus Pl
SE17 ....**117** C2 **263** A3
Comyn Rd SW11 ...**136** C1
Comyns Cl E16 ....**98** D2
Comyns Rd RM9 ...**81** C1
Comyns The WD23 ..**8** A3
Conal Ct SW16 ....**181** D5
Conant Ho SE11 ...**138** D6
Conant Mews 1 E1 .**118** A6
Concanon Rd SW2,
SW4 ....**138** D1
Concert Hall App
SE1 ....**116** B5 **250** D3
Concord Bsns Ctr W3 **88** D2
Concord Cl UB5 ....**85** A4
Concord Ct KT1 ...**198** B6
Concord Ctr W12 ..**112** D4
Concorde Cl
Hounslow TW3 .....**129** D3
Uxbridge UB10 .....**82** A5
Concorde Dr E6 ...**100** B2
Concord Ho
Kingston KT3 ......**199** C6
5 Tottenham N17 ..**33** D4
Concordia Wharf
E14 ....**120** A5
Concord Rd Acton W3 .**88** D3
Enfield EN3 ....**18** C6
Concourse The 7 N9 .**18** A2

Condell Rd
SW8 ....137 C4 269 B1
Conder St E14 ....97 A1
Condor Path UB5 ....85 C5
Condover Cres SE18 .144 D5
Condray Pl SW11 ...267 A3
Conduit Ct WC2 .....250 A6
Conduit Ho SE10 ...142 B4
Conduit La N18 .....34 C5
South Croydon CR0 ..222 A3
Conduit Mews
W2 ....92 B1 236 C1
Conduit Pas W2 ....236 C1
Conduit Pl W2 .....236 C1
Conduit Rd SE18 ...122 D1
Conduit St
W1 ....115 C6 249 A6
Conduit Way NW10 ..67 A1
Conewood St N5 ....72 D5
Coney Acre SE21 ...161 A3
Coney Burrows E4 ...20 C2
Coney Gr UB8 ....82 C4
Coneygrove Path UB5 .63 D2
Coney Hall Par BR4 .224 C5
Coney Hall Rdbt BR4 224 C5
Coney Hill Rd BR4 ..224 D6
Coney Hill Sch BR2 .224 C5
Coney Way SW8 ....270 D5
Conference Cl 3 E4 ..20 A2
Conference Ho UB8 ..83 A1
Conference Rd SE2 .124 C2
Congers Ho SE8 ....141 C5
Congo Rd SE18 .....123 B1
Congress Rd SE2 ...124 C2
Congreve Ho 10 N16 .73 C3
Congreve Rd SE9 ...144 B2
Congreve St
SE17 .....117 C2 263 A3
Congreve Wlk 6 E16 .99 D2
Conical Cnr EN2 .....5 A3
Conifer Ct BR6 .....227 B4
Conifer Ct Ilford IG1 .78 C2
23 Putney SW19 ...156 D3
Conifer Gdns
Enfield EN1 ....17 C5
Streatham SW16 ...160 B1
Sutton SM1 ....217 D6
Conifer Ho SE4 .....141 B1
Conifers Cl TW11 ..175 C3
Conifer Way
Hayes UB3 ....106 A6
Wembley HA0 ....65 C5
Coniger Rd SW6 ....135 C3
Coningham Ct SW10 266 B4
Coningham Mews
W12 ....112 A5
Coningham Rd W12 .112 B4
Coningsby Cotts W5 109 D4
Coningsby Ct 4 CR4 181 B1
Coningsby Gdns E4 ..35 D4
Coningsby Rd N4 ....50 D2
W5 ....109 C4
Conington Rd SE13 .142 A3
Conisbee Ct 3 N14 ..15 C6
Conisborough Cres
SE6 ....164 A1
Conisbrough NW1 ..232 A5
Coniscliffe Cl BR7 ..188 C2
Coniscliffe Rd N13 ..17 A1
Coniston NW1 .....232 A4
Coniston Ave DA16 .145 C2
Barking IG11 ....79 C1
Ealing UB6 ....87 B4
Coniston Cl N20 .....14 A1
Barking IG11 ....79 C1
Barnes SW13 ......133 D5
Chiswick W4 ....133 A5
West Barnes SM4 ..200 D3
Coniston Ct 6 SE16 .118 D4
W2 ....237 B1
Beckenham BR3 ....186 A2
Chessington KT9 ...214 A5
Edgware HA8 ....26 B5
Penge SE26 ....184 B4
3 Wallington SM6 .219 B4
Conistone Way N7 ...72 A1
Coniston Gdns N9 ...18 C3
NW9 ....45 B4
Pinner HA5 ....40 A5
Redbridge IG4 ......56 A5
Sutton SM2 ....218 B2
Wembley HA9 ....43 C1
Coniston Ho 13 E3 ...97 B4
18 SE5 ....139 A5
Coniston Rd N10 ....31 B1
Catford BR1 ....186 C4
Croydon CR0 ......206 A2
Tottenham N17 .....34 A4
Twickenham TW2 ..151 D5

Coniston Way KT9 ..214 A5
Coniston Wlk E9 ....74 C3
Conlan St W10 .....91 A3
Conley Rd NW10 ....67 C2
Conley St SE10 ....120 C1
Connaught Ave
Ashford TW15 ......170 A6
Barnet, London EN4 ..14 D3
Chingford E4 ....20 B4
Enfield EN1 ....5 C3
Hounslow TW4 .....129 A1
Mortlake SW14 ....133 A1
Connaught Bsns Ctr
NW9 ....45 D4
Mitcham CR4 ......202 D4
Wallington CR0 ....220 B2
Connaught Cl E10 ...75 A6
W2 ....237 B1
Carshalton SM1 ....218 B6
Enfield EN1 ....5 C3
Hillingdon UB8 .....83 A3
Connaught Ct 10 E17 .53 D5
1 Chingford E4 .....20 C4
Connaught Day Hospl
E11 ....54 C3
Connaught Dr NW11 .47 C4
Connaught Gdns N10 .49 B4
Edmonton N13 ......32 D6
Morden SM4 ....202 A5
Connaught Grange
N13 ....32 D6
Connaught Ho N10 ..49 B4
NW10 ....90 B4
W1 ....248 C5
Connaught La IG1 ...79 B6
Connaught Lo N4 ...50 C2
Connaught Mans
15 N16 ....73 B4
SW11 ....267 B1
SW6 ....264 A2
3 SW9 ....138 C1
Connaught Mews
SE18 ....122 C1
Ilford IG1 ....79 B6
Connaught Pl W2 ..237 C1
Connaught Rd E11 ..54 B1
E16 ....121 D5
E17 ....53 C4
N4 ....50 C2
NW10 ....89 C4
SE18 ....122 C1
Barnet EN5 ....12 C4
Chingford, Chingford Green
E4 ....20 C3
Ealing W13 ....109 B6
Harrow HA3 ....24 D2
Ilford IG1 ....79 B6
New Malden KT3 ...199 C5
5 Richmond TW10 .154 B6
Teddington TW11,
TW12 ....174 B5
Connaught Sch for Girls
E11 ....54 C1
Connaught Sch for Girls
(Annexe) E11 ....76 C6
Connaught Sq
W2 ....92 D1 237 C1
Connaught St
W2 ....92 C1 237 B1
Connaught Way N13 .32 D6
Connell Cres W5 ....88 B3
Connell Ct 6 SE14 .140 D6
Connell Ho 6 SM6 .219 C2
Connemara Cl WD6 ..11 B5
Connett Ho 5 E2 ....96 B5
Connington 5 KT1 .176 C1
Connington Cres E4 .20 B1
Connolly Ct NW2 ....68 B5
Connop Rd EN3 .....6 D5
Connor Cl E11 ......54 C2
Connor Ct SW11 ...268 C1
Connor Rd RM9 .....81 B4
Connor St E9 ....96 D6
Conolly Rd W7 .....108 C5
Conrad Dr KT4 .....200 D1
Conrad Ho 12 N16 ..73 C3
8 SE16 ....119 A4
SW8 ....270 A4
Consfield Ave KT3 ..200 A4
Consolata Missionary Coll
N20 ....13 C1
Consort Ho NW7 ....27 D5
W2 ....245 D5
Consort Lo NW8 ...230 C5
Consort Mews TW7 .152 B6
Consort Rd SE15 ...140 B3
Cons St SE1 ......251 B2
Constable Ave E16 .121 B5
Constable Cl NW11 ..47 D3

Constable Cl continued
Hayes UB4 ....83 A5
Constable Cres N15 ..52 A4
Constable Ct 11 SE16 118 B1
Constable Gdns
Edgware HA8 ....26 C1
Isleworth TW7 .....152 B6
Constable Ho NW3 ..70 D1
Enfield EN1 ....18 A4
14 Northolt UB5 ....84 D5
Constable Mews RM8 .80 B4
Constable Wlk SE21 .161 C1
Constance Cres BR2 .208 D1
Constance Rd
Enfield EN1 ....17 C5
Sutton SM1 ....218 A4
Thornton Heath CR0 .204 D2
Twickenham TW2 ..151 D4
Constance St E16 ..122 A5
Constant Ho 23 E14 .119 D6
Constantine Ho SW2 160 D3
Constantine Pl UB10 .82 B6
Constantine Rd NW3 .70 C4
Constitution Hill
SW1,W1 ....115 B4 248 D2
Constitution Rise
SE18 ....144 C4
Consul Ho 5 E3 ....97 C3
Content St
SE17 .....117 B2 262 C3
Contessa Cl BR6 ...227 C3
Control Tower Rd
TW6 ....126 D2
Convair Wlk 11 UB5 ..84 D4
Convent Cl BR3 ....186 A3
Convent Gdns W11 ..91 B1
W5 ....109 C2
Convent Hill SE19 ..183 A4
Convent Lo 4 ......170 C2
Convent Rd TW15 ..170 D5
Convent Way UB2 ..106 C2
Conway Cl HA7 ......25 A4
Conway Cres
Dagenham RM6 .....58 C4
Greenford UB6 ......86 C5
Conway Dr
Ashford TW15 ......171 A4
Hayes UB3 ....105 A3
Sutton SM2 ....217 D2
Conway Gdns
Enfield EN2 ....5 C5
Mitcham CR4 ......204 A4
Wembley HA9 ....43 C2
Conway Gr W3 ......89 B2
Conway Ho 5 E14 ..119 D2
6 Streatham SW2 ..160 A3
Conway Mews W1 ..239 A5
Conway Prim Sch
SE18 ....123 C2
Conway Rd N15 .....51 A4
NW2 ....68 C6
SE18 ....123 C2
Feltham TW13 .....172 D5
Harlington TW6 ....126 D2
Palmers Green N14 ..16 A1
Twickenham TW4 ..151 C4
Wimbledon SW20 ..178 C2
Conway St E3 ....97 B5
W1 ......93 C3 239 A5
Conway Wlk TW12 .173 B4
Conybeare NW3 .....70 C1
Conyers Cl IG8 .....36 C4
Conyer's Rd SW16 .181 D5
Conyer St 19 E3 ....97 A5
Cooden Cl BR1 ....187 B3
Cookes Cl E11 ......76 D6
Cookes La SM3 ....217 A2
Cookham Cl UB2 ...107 D4
Cookham Cres SE16 .118 D4
Cookham Dene Cl
BR7 ....189 B2
Cookham Ho E2 ...243 C6
Cookham Rd BR8 ..191 C2
Cookhill Rd SE2 ...124 B3
Cooks Ferry N18 ....34 D5
Cook's Hole Rd EN2 ..5 A5
Cookson Gr DA8 ...147 D5
Coolfin Rd E16 ......99 B1
Coolgardie Ave E4 ...36 B5
Coolgardie Rd TW15 171 A5
Coolhurst Rd N8 ....49 D3
Cool Oak La NW9 ....45 D2
Coomassie Rd W9 ...91 B3
Coombe Ave CR0 ...221 C4

Coombe Bank KT2,
KT3 ....177 C2
Coombe Cl
Edgware HA8 ....26 B1
Hounslow TW3 .....129 C1
Coombe Cnr N21 ...16 D3
Coombe Cres TW12 .173 A3
Coombe Ct
2 Beckenham BR3 .185 B2
3 Croydon CR0 ....221 B4
Coombe Dr HA4 .....40 C3
Coombe End KT2 ...177 B3
Coombefield Cl KT3 .199 C4
Coombe Gdns
New Malden KT3 ...199 D5
Wimbledon SW20 ..178 A2
Coombe Girls Sch
KT3 ....177 B1
Coombe Hill Glade
KT2 ....177 C3
Coombe Hill Inf Sch
KT3 ....177 B2
Coombe Hill Jun Sch
KT3 ....177 B2
Coombe Hill Rd KT2 .177 C3
Coombe Ho 13 N7 ...71 D3
Coombe House Chase
KT3 ....177 B2
Coombehurst Cl EN4 ..2 D3
Coombe La CR0 ....222 B3
Coombe Lane Flyover
SW20 ....177 D2
Coombe La W KT2 .177 B2
Coombe Lea BR1 ..210 A6
Coombe Lo SE7 ....143 C6
Coombe Neville KT2 .177 B3
Coombe Pk KT2 ...177 B5
Coombe Pl KT2 ....177 A5
Coombe Rd NW10 ...67 B5
W13 ....109 B3
W4 ....111 C1
Bushey WD23 ....8 B4
Croydon CR0 ......221 C1
Hampton TW12 ....173 B4
Kingston KT2 ......176 C2
Kingston KT3 ......199 C6
South Croydon CR0,CR2 .221 C4
Wood Green N22 ....32 C2
Coomber Ho SW6 ..135 D2
Coombe Ridings KT2 177 A5
Coombe Rise KT2 ..177 A2
Coombes Rd RM9 ..103 B6
Coombe Wlk SM1 ..217 D5
Coombewood Dr RM6 .59 B3
Coombe Wood Rd
KT2 ....177 A5
Coombs St N1 ....234 D3
Coomer Mews SW6 264 D5
Coomer Pl
SW6 ....135 B6 264 D5
Cooms Wlk HA8 .....27 A2
Cooperage Cl 5 N17 .33 D4
Cooperage The SE1 .253 C3
Cooper Ave E17 ....35 A2
Cooper Cl SE1 .....251 B1
Cooper Cres SM5 ..218 D5
Cooper Ct E15 ......76 A4
SE18 ....144 D6
Cooper Ho NW8 ...236 C5
Hounslow TW4 .....129 B2
7 West Norwood
SW27 ....182 D5
Cooper Rd NW10 ...68 A3
NW4 ....46 D3
Croydon CR0,CR9 ..220 D4
Coopersale Cl 3 IG8 .37 C3
Coopersale Rd E9 ...74 D3
Coopers Cl E1 ......96 C3
Dagenham RM10 ....81 D2
Coopers Ct E3 ......97 B3
9 W3 ....111 A5
Isleworth TW7 .....130 D3
Coopers La NW1 ..232 D3
SE12 ....165 B2
Cooper's La E10 .....54 A1
Coopers' Lane Prim Sch
SE12 ....165 B2
Coopers Lodge SE1 .253 C2
Cooper's Rd
SE1 ....117 D1 263 D2
Cooper's Row
EC3 ....117 D6 253 C6
Coopers Sch BR7 ..189 A2
Cooper St 10 E16 ...98 D2
Cooper's Yd SE19 ..183 C4
Coote Gdns RM8 ....81 B5
Coote Rd DA7 .....147 B4
Dagenham RM8 ....81 B5
Cope Ho EC1 ......235 B1
Copeland Dr E14 ...119 C2

Copeland Ho SE11 .260 D5
Upper Tooting SW17 ..180 B6
Copeland Rd E17 ....53 D3
SE15 ....140 D5
Copelands BR3 ....185 B3
Copeman Cl SE26 ..184 C5
Copenhagen Gdns
W4 ....111 B4
Copenhagen Ho N1 234 A5
Copenhagen Pl E14 ..97 B1
Copenhagen Prim Sch
N1 ....94 B6 233 C5
Copenhagen St
N1 ....94 B6 233 C5
Cope Pl W8 ..113 C3 255 A5
Cope St SE16 ......118 C4
Copeswood Ct UB7 .126 C5
Cope Yd 6 E1 .....118 A5
Copford Wlk N1 ...235 A6
Copinger Wlk HA8 ..26 D2
Copland Ave HA0 ...65 D3
Copland Cl HA0 .....65 D4
Copland Com Sch & Tech
Ctr HA9 ....66 B3
Copland Mews 3 HA0 66 A2
Copland Rd HA0 .....66 A2
Copleston Rd SE15 .139 D2
Copley Cl 15 SE17 .138 D6
Ealing W7 ....86 D2
Copley Dene BR1 ..187 D2
Copley Pk SW16 ...182 B4
Copley Rd HA7 ......25 C5
Coppard Gdns KT9 213 C2
Coppedhall 1 SE21 .161 B2
Coppelia Rd SE3 ...142 D1
Coppen Rd RM8 .....59 B2
Copperas St SE8 ...141 D6
Copper Beech N6 ...49 A2
Copperbeech Cl NW3 .70 B3
Copper Beech Ct N20 .14 A1
Copper Beeches
TW7 ....130 B4
Copper Cl SE19 ...183 D3
Copperdale Rd UB3 106 A4
Copperfield Ave UB8 .82 C3
Copperfield Dr N15 ..51 D5
Copperfield Ho 10
SE1 ....118 A4
Copperfield Mews
N18 ....33 C5
Copperfield Rd SE28 102 C1
Stepney E3 ....97 A4
Copperfields
5 Beckenham BR3 .186 A2
Harrow HA1 ....42 C2
Copperfields Ct W3 110 C4
Copperfield St
SE1 ....117 A4 252 A2
Copperfield Way
BR7 ....189 A4
Pinner HA5 ....41 B5
Coppergate Cl BR1 187 B2
Coppermead Rd NW2 .68 C5
Copper Mill Dr TW7 130 D3
Copper Mill La SW17 180 A6
Coppermill Prim Sch
E17 ....52 D4
Coppermill La E17 ..52 D4
Coppetts Cl N12 ....30 D3
Coppetts Ctr* N12 ..30 D3
Coppetts Rd N10 ....30 D2
Coppetts Wood Prim Sch
N10 ....31 A2
Coppice Cl
Beckenham BR3 ....207 D6
Harrow HA7 ....24 D4
Ruislip HA4 ....39 B3
West Barnes SW20 .200 C6
Coppice Dr SW15 ..156 B5
Coppice The
Ashford TW15 .....170 D4
Enfield EN2 ....4 D1
Hillingdon UB8 .....82 A1
New Barnet EN5 ....13 D5
Coppice Way E18 ...54 D6
Coppice Wlk N20 ....13 C1
Coppies Gr N11 .....31 B6
Copping Cl CR0 ....221 C4
Coppinger Ct UB7 ..104 A4
Coppins Ho SW2 ..160 D3
Coppins The
New Addington CR0 .223 D2
Stanmore HA3 ......24 C4
2 Ilford RM6 ....58 B2
Coppock Cl SW11 .136 C3
Coppsfield KT8 ....195 C6
Copse Ave BR4 ....223 D5
Copse Cl SE7 ......143 B6

Con – Cor 303

Copse Ct SW15 ....157 A6
Copse Glade KT6 ..197 D1
Copse Hill
Belmont SM2 ......217 D1
Wimbledon SW20 ..178 B3
Copsem Dr KT10 ...212 A2
Copsem La KT10 ...212 A1
Copsem Way KT10 .212 A2
Copse The N2 ....48 D6
Chingford E4 ....20 D4
Copse View CR2 ...223 A1
Copthall Ave
EC2 ....95 B1 242 D2
Copthall Bldgs EC2 242 D2
Copthall Cl EC2 ...242 C2
Copthall Dr NW7 ...28 A4
Copthall Gdns NW7 .28 A3
Twickenham TW1 ..152 D3
Copthall Rd E UB10 .60 C5
Copthall Rd W UB10 .60 C5
Copthall Sch NW7 ..28 B3
Copthall Sports Ctr
NW4 ....28 B2
Copthorne Ave BR2 226 B6
Streatham SW12 ...159 D4
Copthorne Chase
TW15 ....170 B6
Copthorne Cl TW17 193 A3
Copthorne Mews
UB3 ....105 C2
Coptic St WC1 94 A2 240 A3
Copton Cl E3 ....97 C2
Copwood Cl N12 ....30 B6
Coral Cl RM6 ....58 C6
Coral Ho 5 E1 ......97 A3
Coral Row 14 SW11 .136 A2
Coral St SE1 .116 C4 251 B1
Coraline Cl UB1 ....85 B4
Coralline Wlk 4 SE2 124 C4
Coram Ho 9 W4 ...111 C1
WC1 ....240 A6
Coram St WC1 94 A3 240 A5
Coran Cl N9 ....18 D4
Corban Rd TW3 ...129 C2
Corbar Cl EN4 ....2 B4
Corbden Cl SE15 ...139 D4
Corbet Cl CR4,SM6 .219 A6
Corbet Ct EC3 ....242 D1
Corbet Ho N1 .....234 A5
Corbet Pl E1 ..95 D2 243 C4
Corbett Ct SE26 ...185 B6
Corbett Gr N22 .....32 A3
Corbett Ho SW10 .266 A6
Wanstead E11 ......55 C3
Corbett's La SE16 .118 C2
Corbett Rd E17 .....54 A6
Wanstead E11 ......55 C3
Corbett's Villas RM8 .58 C1
Corbicum E11 ......54 C2
Corbidge Ct SE8 ...141 D6
Corbiere Ct SW19 .178 D4
Corbiere Ho 5 N1 ...95 C6
Corbin Ho 7 E3 .....97 D4
Corbin's La HA2 ....63 D5
Corbridge 5 N17 ....34 B3
Corbridge Cres E2 ..96 B5
Corby Cres EN2 .....4 A1
Corbyland Rd DA15 .167 C3
Corbylands Rd DA15 167 C4
Corbyn St N4,N19 ..50 A1
Corby Rd NW10 .....89 B5
Corby Way E3 ....97 C3
Cordelia Cl SE24 ..138 C1
Cordelia Gdns TW19 148 A4
Cordelia Ho 26 N1 ..95 C5
Cordelia Rd TW19 .148 A4
Cordelia St E14 .....97 D2
Cordell Ho N15 .....51 D4
Cordingley Rd HA4 ..61 B6
Cording St E14 .....97 D2
Cordwainers Coll E8 .74 B1
Cordwainers Ct 18 E9 74 C1
Cordwainers Wlk 9
E13 ....99 A5
Cordwain Ho 7 N18 .34 A5
Cord Way 7 E14 ...119 C3
Cordwell Rd SE13 .164 C6
Corefield Cl N11 ....15 A2
Corelli Rd SE3 .....144 A4
Corfe Ave HA2 ......63 C4
Corfe Cl UB4 ....84 C1
Corfe Ho SW8 ....270 C4
Corfe Lo SE21 .....161 C2
Corfe Twr 6 W3 ...111 A4
Corfield Rd N21 ....16 B6
Corfield St E2 ......96 B4
Corfton Lo W5 ......88 A2

Corfton Rd W5 .....88 A2
Coriander Ave E14 ...98 B1
Coriander Ct SE1 ....253 D2
Cories Cl RM8 ....80 D6
Corigan Ct **5** E11 ...76 C6
Corinium Cl HA9 .66 B4
Corinne Rd N19 .....71 C4
Corkscrew Hill BR4 ..224 B5
Cork Sq E1 ....118 B5
Cork St W1 ...115 C6 249 A5
Cork St Mews W1 ....249 A5
Cork Tree Ho **3**
SW27 ....182 D5
Cork Tree Ret Pk N18 .35 A4
Cork Tree Way E4 ....35 A5
Corlett St NW1 ......237 A4
Cormont Rd SE5 .....138 D4
Cormorant Cl E17 ....35 A3
Cheam SM1 ....217 B3
Cormorant Ct **34** SE8 141 B6
12 Dulwich SE21 ...161 B2
Cormorant Ho EN3 ..18 D6
Cormorant Rd E7 ....76 D3
Cornbury Ho **5** SE8 .141 B6
Cornbury Rd HA8 ...25 D3
Cornel Ho **4** DA15 .168 A1
Cornelia St N7 ......72 B2
Cornell Cl DA14 .....191 A4
Cornell Ho HA2 ......63 B5
Corner Fielde SW2 ..160 B3
Corner Gn SE3 ......143 A2
Corner House St
WC2 ....250 A4
Corner Mead NW9 ...27 D2
Cornerside TW15 ....171 A5
Cornerways
Harrow HA1 ....65 A5
Putney SW15 ....134 A1
Corney Rd W4 .....133 C6
Corney Reach Way
W4 ....133 C5
Cornflower La CR0 .206 D1
Cornflower Terr
SE22 ....162 B5
Cornford Cl BR2 ....209 A4
Cornford Gr SW12 ..159 B2
Cornhill EC3 ...95 B1 242 D1
Cornhill Dr EN3 .....7 A6
Cornick Ho **7** SE16 .118 B3
Cornish Ct N9 ....18 B4
Cornish Gr SE20 ....184 B2
Cornish Ho **7** SE17 .138 D6
Brentford TW8 .....110 B1
Cornmill La SW13 ..142 A2
Cornmow Dr NW10 ..68 A3
Cornshaw Rd RM8 ...58 D1
Cornthwaite Rd E5 ..74 C5
Cornwall Ave DA16 .145 D2
E2 ....96 C4
N3 ....29 C3
Claygate KT10 .....212 D6
Southall UB1 ....85 C2
Wood Green N22 ....32 A4
Cornwall Cl
Barking IG11 ....79 D2
3 Pinner HA5 .....23 B3
Cornwall Cres W11 ..91 A1
Cornwall Ct **5** W7 .86 D3
Cornwall Dr BR5 ...190 C3
Cornwall Gdns NW10 .68 B2
SW7 ....113 D3 255 D5
Cornwall Gdns Wlk
SW7 ....255 D5
Cornwall Gr W4 .....111 C1
Cornwall Ho NW1 ...237 D5
3 Putney SW15 ...156 C4
Cornwallis Ave DA15 .167 B2
N9 ....18 C2
Cornwallis Ct SW8 ..270 A2
Cornwallis Gr N9 ....18 C2
Cornwallis Ho **24**
W12 ....112 B6
Cornwallis Rd N19 ..72 A6
SE18 ....122 D3
Dagenham RM9 ....81 A4
Edmonton N9 ......18 B2
Walthamstow E17 ...52 D5
Cornwallis Sq N19 ..72 A6
Cornwallis Wlk SE9 .144 B2
Cornwall Mans NW1 .237 D5
SW10 ....266 B4
Cornwall Mews S
SW7 ....256 A5
Cornwall Mews W
SW7 ....255 D5
Cornwall Rd N15 ....51 B4
N4 ....50 C2

Cornwall Rd continued
SE1 ....116 C5 251 B2
Belmont SM2 ....217 B1
Croydon CR0 ....220 D6
Edmonton N18 .....34 A5
Harrow HA1 ....42 A3
Pinner HA5 ....23 B3
Ruislip HA4 ....61 D6
Twickenham TW1 ..153 A3
Cornwall Sq SE11 ...261 D2
Cornwall St **4** E1 ..118 B6
Cornwall Terr NW1 ..237 D5
Cornwall Terr Mews
NW1 ....237 D5
Corn Way E11 ......76 C5
Cornwall Ct **21** E10 .53 D2
Cornwood Cl N2 ....48 B5
Cornwood Dr E1 ....96 C1
Cornworthy Rd RM8 .80 C3
Corona Rd SE12 ....165 A3
Coronation Ave **1**
N16 ....73 D4
Coronation Cl DA5 .168 D5
Ilford IG6 ....57 A5
Coronation Ct E15 ..76 D2
W10 ....90 C2
Coronation Rd E13 ..99 C4
Acton NW10 ....88 C3
Hayes UB3 ....105 D2
Coronet Par **4** HA0 .66 A2
Coronet St N1 ......95 C4
Corporation Ave
TW4 ....129 A1
Corporation Row
EC1 ....241 B6
Corporation St E15 .98 D5
N7 ....72 A3
Corpus Christi RC Prim
Sch
SW2 ....160 B6
Kingston KT3 ....199 A6
Corrance Rd SW2,
SW4 ....138 A1
Corri Ave N14 ......31 D6
Corrib Ct N13 ......16 B1
Corrib Dr SM1 ......218 C3
Corrib Hts N8 ......49 D3
Corrigan Cl NW4 ...46 C6
Corringham Ct NW11 .47 C2
Corringham Ho **10** E1 .96 D1
Corringham Rd NW11 .47 C2
Wembley HA9 ......66 C6
Corringway NW11 ...47 D2
Ealing W5 ....88 C2
Corris Gn NW9 .....45 C3
Corry Dr SW9 ......138 D1
Corry Ho **2** E14 ...119 D1
Corscombe Cl KT2 ..177 A5
Corsehill St SW16 ..181 C4
Corseley Way E9 ...75 B2
Corsham Ho HA9 ...66 C2
Corsham St
N1 ....95 B4 235 D1
Corsica St N5 ......72 D2
Cortayne Rd SW6 ..135 B3
Cortis Rd SW15 ....156 B5
Cortis Terr SW15 ...156 B5
Corunna Rd
SW8 ....137 C4 269 B2
Corunna Terr SW8 ..269 A2
Corvette Sq **5** SE10 .142 B6
Corwell Gdns UB8 ..83 A1
Corwell La UB8 .....83 A1
Coryton Path W9 ...91 B3
Cosbycote Ave SE24 .161 A6
Cosdach Ave SM6 ..219 D1
Cosedge Cres CR0,
CR9 ....220 D3
Cosgrove Cl
Edmonton N21 .....17 A2
Hayes UB4 ....84 D3
Cosgrove Ho **11** E2 .96 A6
Cosmo Pl WC1 .....240 B4
Cosmur Cl W12 ....111 D3
Cossall Wlk SE15 ..140 B4
Cossar Mews **10** SW2 160 C6
Cosser St
SE1 ....116 C3 261 A6
Costa St SE15 .....140 A4
Coston Prim Sch UB6 86 A4
Costons Ave UB6 ...86 B4
Costons La UB6 ....86 B4
Coston Wlk **4** SE4 .140 D1
Cosway Ho NW11 ..48 A3
Cosway Mans NW1 ..237 B4
Cosway St
NW1 ....92 C2 237 B3
Cotall St E14 ....97 C1

Coteford Cl HA5 ....40 A4
Coteford Inf Sch HA5 .40 A3
Coteford Jun Sch HA5 39 D4
Coteford St SW17 ..181 A6
Cotelands CR0 .....221 C5
Cotesbach Rd E5 ...74 C5
Cotes Ho NW8 .....237 A5
Cotford Rd CR7 ....205 A5
Cotham St SE17 ....262 B3
Cotherstone Rd SW2 160 B3
Cotleigh Ave DA5 ..168 D2
Cotleigh Rd NW6 ...69 C1
Cotman Cl NW11 ...48 A3
Putney SW15 ......156 D6
Cotman Ct BR3 ....185 B2
Cotmandene Cres
BR5 ....190 A1
Cotman Gdns HA8 ..26 C1
Cotman Ho NW8 ...230 A4
6 Northolt UB5 ....84 D5
Cotmans Cl UB3 ...106 A5
Coton Rd DA16 ....146 A2
Cotsford Ave KT3 ..199 B4
Cotswold Ave WD23 .8 A5
Cotswold Cl
Hinchley Wood KT10 .212 D6
Kingston KT2 ......177 A4
Cotswold Ct EC1 ...242 A6
N11 ....31 A6
3 Wembley UB6 ...86 D5
Cotswold Gate NW2 .47 A1
Cotswold Gdns E6 ..99 D5
Hendon NW2 ......68 D6
Ilford IG2 ....57 B2
Cotswold Gn EN2 ...4 B1
Cotswold Ho N16 ...51 D1
Cotswold Mews
SW11 ....266 C6
Cotswold Rd TW12 .173 C4
Cotswold Rise BR6 .211 C6
Cotswold St SE27 ..182 D6
Cotswold Way
Enfield EN2 ....4 B2
North Cheam KT4 ..216 C6
Cottage Ave BR2 ...210 A1
Cottage Cl HA4 ....39 B1
Cottage Field Cl DA5,
DA15 ....168 C3
Cottage Gn SE5 ....139 B5
Cottage Gr SW9 ...138 A2
Cottage Pl
SW3 ....114 C3 257 A5
Cottage Rd KT19 ...215 A5
Cottage St E14 ....119 D6
Cottages The UB10 .60 D5
Cottage Wlk **2** N16 .73 D5
Cottenham Dr NW9 .45 D6
Wimbledon SW20 ..178 B3
Cottenham Ho **4** N19 72 A6
Cottenham Par SW20 178 B1
Cottenham Park Rd
SW20 ....178 C3
Cottenham Pl SW20 178 B3
Cottenham Rd E17 .53 B5
Cotterill Rd KT6 ....198 B1
Cottesbrook St **9**
SE14 ....141 A5
Cottesloe Ho NW8 ..237 A6
Cottesloe Mews SE1 .261 B6
Cottesmore Ct W8 ..255 D6
Cottesmore Gdns
W8 ....113 D3 255 D6
Cottimore Ave KT12 194 B1
Cottimore Cres KT12 194 B2
Cottimore Terr KT12 194 B2
Cottingham Chase
HA4 ....62 A5
Cottingham Rd
SW8 ....138 B5 270 D4
Penge SE20 ....184 D3
Cottington Rd TW13 172 D6
Cottington St SE11 .261 C2
Cotton Ave W3 .....89 B1
Cotton Cl RM9 .....80 C1
Cottongrass Cl **1**
CR0 ....206 D1
Cotton Hill BR1 ....186 B6
Cotton Ho W12 ....111 D4
18 Streatham SW12 .160 A4
Cotton Row SW11 ..136 B2
Cotton's Gdns E2 ..95 C4
Cottons La SE1 ....252 D4
Cotton St E14 .....120 A6
Cottrell Ct SE10 ...120 D3
Cotts Cl **13** W7 ...86 D2
Couchman Ho **8**
SW4 ....159 C5

Couchmore Ave
KT10 ....212 C6
Coulgate St SE4 ...141 A2
Coulsdon Ct **3** N8 ..49 D4
Coulsdon Ho **5** SW2 160 A3
Coulson Cl RM8 ....58 C1
Coulson St
SW3 ....114 D1 257 C2
Coulter Cl UB4 .....85 A3
Coulter Rd W6 .....78 B6
Coulthurst Ct SW16 .182 A3
Coults Cres NW5 ...71 A5
Councillor St SE5 ..139 A5
Counters Ct W14 ...254 B6
Counter St SE1 ....253 A2
Countess Rd NW5 ..71 C3
Countisbury Ave EN1 .17 D4
Countisbury Ho SE26 162 A1
Country Way TW13,
TW16 ....172 C5
County Gate BR7 ..167 A1
New Barnet EN5 ...13 D5
County Gr SE5 .....139 A4
County Ho **9** SW9 .138 C4
County Par TW8 ...131 D5
County Rd
Newham E6 ....100 D2
South Norwood CR7 .182 D1
County St
SE1 ....117 A3 262 B5
Coupland Pl SE18 ..123 A1
Courcy Rd N8,N22 ..50 C6
Courier Ho **17** SW2 .160 A1
Courland Gr SW8 ..137 D3
Courland St
SW8 ....137 D4 269 D1
Course The SE9 ....166 C1
Courtauld Galleries*
WC2 ....250 C6
Courtauld Ho **11** E2 .96 A5
Courtauld Inst of Art
W1 ....237 D2
Courtauld Rd N19 ..50 A1
Courtaulds Cl SE28 .124 A5
Court Ave DA17 ....125 B1
Court Cl Harrow HA3 .44 A6
Twickenham TW13,
TW2 ....151 D1
Wallington SM6 ...219 D1
Court Close Ave
TW13,TW2 ....151 D1
Court Cres KT9 ....213 D2
Court Downs Rd BR3 185 D1
Court Dr
Carshalton SM1 ...218 C4
Hillingdon UB10 ...82 C6
Stanmore HA7 ....26 A6
Wallington CR0 ...220 B4
Courtenay Ave N6 ..48 C2
Harrow HA3 ......24 A2
Courtenay Dr BR3 ..186 B1
Courtenay Gdns HA3 .24 A1
Courtenay Mews E17 .53 A4
Courtenay Pl E17 ..53 A4
Courtenay Rd E11 ..76 D5
North Cheam KT4,SM3 .216 C5
Penge BR3,SE20 ...184 D4
Walthamstow E17 ..52 D5
Wembley HA9 .....65 D5
Courtenay Sq SE11 .261 A1
Courtenay St
SE11 ....116 C1 261 A2
Courtens Mews HA7 .25 C4
Court Farm Ave KT19 215 B4
Court Farm Ind Est
TW19 ....148 B5
Court Farm Rd
Chislehurst SE9 ...166 A1
Northolt UB5 ......63 C1
Courtfield W13 .....87 C2
Courtfield Ave HA1 ..42 D4
Courtfield Cres HA1 .42 D4
Courtfield Gdns
SW5 ....113 D2 255 D3
Ealing W13 ....87 A1
Ruislip HA4 ....61 D6
Courtfield Ho EC1 ..241 A4
Courtfield Mews
SW7 ....255 D3
Courtfield Rd
SW7 ....114 A2 256 A3
Ashford TW15 .....170 D4
Courtfield Rise BR4 .224 B5
Court Gdns N7 .....72 C2
Courthill Rd SE13 ..142 A1
Courthope Ho
14 SE16 ....118 C3
SW8 ....270 A4
Courthope Rd NW3 .70 C4
Greenford UB6 ....86 B5

Courthope Rd continued
Wimbledon SW19 ..179 A5
Courthope Villas
SW19 ....179 A3
Court House Gdns N3 29 C4
Court House Rd N12 .29 C4
Court La SE21 .....161 D4
Courtland Ave NW7 .11 C1
Chingford E4 ......20 D2
Redbridge IG1 .....78 B6
South Norwood SW16 .182 B3
Courtland Gr SE28 .124 D6
Courtland JMI Sch
NW7 ....11 C2
Courtland Rd E6 ...100 A6
Courtlands **5** E5 ...52 B1
11 Beckenham BR3 .185 D1
10 Belmont SM2 ...217 D1
Ealing W5 ....87 C2
Richmond TW10 ...154 C6
Walton-on-T KT12 .194 A2
Courtlands Ave SE12 165 B6
Hampton TW12 ...173 B4
Hayes BR2 ....208 D1
Richmond TW9 ....132 C6
Courtlands Cl HA4 ..39 D2
Courtlands Dr KT19 .215 D2
Courtlands Rd KT5 .198 C2
Court Lane Gdns
SE21 ....161 C4
Courtleet Dr DA7 ..147 D4
Courtleigh **6** NW11 .47 B4
Courtleigh Ave EN4 .2 B5
Courtleigh Gdns
NW11 ....47 A5
Court Lo **11** DA17 ..125 C1
Courtman Rd N17 ..33 A3
Court Mans **8** W6 .112 A2
Court Mead UB5 ...85 B4
Courtmead Cl SE24 .161 B1
Courtnell St W2 ...91 C1
Courtney Cl SE19 ..183 C4
Courtney Cres SM5 .218 C1
Courtney Ct N7 ....72 C3
Courtney Ho **1** NW4 .46 C5
W14 ....254 B6
Courtney Pl CR0 ...220 C5
Courtney Rd N7 ...72 C3
Croydon CR0 ......220 C5
Harlington TW6 ...126 C1
Mitcham SW19 ....180 C3
Courtney Way TW6 .126 C2
Court Par HA0 .....65 B5
Court Rd Eltham SE9 166 B4
Southall UB2 ......107 B1
South Norwood SE25 205 D6
Uxbridge UB10 ....60 D4
Court Royal SW15 ..157 A6
Courtside N8 ......49 D3
Forest Hill SE23 ...162 C1
Court St BR1 ......187 A1
E1 ....96 B2
Courts The SW16 ..182 A3
Court The N10 .....49 C5
Ruislip HA4 ....63 A4
Courtville Ho **11** W10 .91 A4
Court Way NW9 ....45 C5
W3 ....89 A2
Courtway IG8 ......37 C5
Court Way Ilford IG6 .57 A6
Twickenham TW1,TW2 .152 D4
Courtyard The N1 ..72 B1
13 SW18 ....136 B1
Fulham SW6 ..135 A4 264 A1
Court Yd SE9 ......166 B4
Cousin La
EC4 ....117 B6 252 C5
Cousins Cl **2** UB7 .104 A6
Cousins Ct **2** NW9 .46 A5
Couthurst Rd SE3 ..143 B5
Coutts Ave KT9 ....214 A3
Coutts Ho SE7 .....143 C6
Couzens Ho **9** E3 ..97 B2
Coval Gdns SW14 ..132 D1
Coval La SW14 ....132 D1
Coval Rd SW14 ....133 A1
Covelees Wall E6 ..100 C1
Covell Ct **15** SE8 ...141 C4
Covent Garden Sta
WC2 ....94 A1 240 B1
Covent Gdn*
WC2 ....116 A6 250 B6
Coventry Cl NW6 ...91 C6
9 Newham E6 .....100 B1
Coventry Rd E1 ....96 B3
Croydon SE25 .....206 A5
Ilford IG1 ....56 D1
Coventry St W1 ....249 C5

Coverack Cl
Croydon CR0 ......207 A2
Southgate N14 ....15 C5
Coverdale Cl HA7 ..25 B5
Coverdale Gdns CR0 221 D5
Coverdale Pl NW6 ..68 D1
Coverdale Rd N11 ..31 A4
NW2 ....69 A2
W12 ....112 B4
Coverdales The IG11 101 B5
Coverham Ho **5** SE4 140 D1
Coverley Cl E1 .....96 A2
Coverley Point SE11 260 D1
Coverton Rd SW17 .180 C5
Coverts Rd KT10 ...212 D1
Covert The BR5,BR6 211 B5
Covert Way EN4 ...2 A3
Covet Wood Cl BR5 .211 D3
Covey Cl SW19 ....179 D1
Covington Gdns
SW16 ....182 D3
Covington Way
South Norwood SW16 .182 D3
South Norwood SW16 .182 D2
Cowan Cl E6 ......100 A2
Cowan Ct NW10 ...67 B1
Cowbridge La IG11 .78 D1
Cowbridge Rd HA3 .44 B5
Cowcross St
EC1 ....94 D2 241 C4
Cowdenbeath Path
N1 ....233 C6
Cowden Rd BR6 ...211 C3
Cowden St SE6 ....185 C6
Cowdray Hall Coll of
Nursing W1 ..93 B1 238 C2
Cowdray Ho **23** SE22 139 C2
Cowdrey Ho UB10 ..83 A6
Cowdrey Cl EN1 ....5 C3
Cowdrey Rd SW19 .180 A3
Cowdry Rd E9 .....75 B2
Cowell Lo E4 ......36 C5
Cowen Ave HA2 ...64 B6
Cowen Ho **4** SE18 .144 D6
Cowgate Rd UB6 ..86 B4
Cowick Rd SW17 ..180 D6
Cowings Mead UB5 .63 A2
Cowland Ave EN3 ..6 C1
Cow Leaze E6 .....100 C1
Cowleaze Rd KT2 ..176 A2
Cowley La E11 .....76 C5
Cowley Pl NW4 ....46 C4
Cowley Rd SW9 ...138 C4
16 SW9 ....138 C4
W3 ....111 D5
Mortlake SW14 ....133 C2
Redbridge IG1 .....56 B2
Wanstead E11 ....55 B4
Cowley St SW1 ....260 A5
Cowling Cl W11 ...244 A4
Cowper Ave E6 ....78 A4
Sutton SM1 ....218 B4
Cowper Cl
Bexley DA16 ......168 A4
Bromley BR2 ......209 D5
Cowper Gdns
Southgate N14 ....15 C5
Wallington SM6 ...219 C2
Cowper Ho SE17 ..262 B2
SW1 ....259 D1
Cowper Rd N14 ....15 B3
N16 ....73 C4
W3 ....111 B5
Belvedere DA17 ..125 C2
Bromley BR2 ......209 D5
Ealing W7 ....108 D2
Edmonton N18 ....34 A5
Richmond TW10 ..176 B5
Wimbledon SW19 .180 A3
Cowper's Ct EC3 ..242 D1
Cowper St EC1,
EC2 ....95 B3 242 D6
Cowper Terr W10 ..90 C2
Cowslip Cl UB10 ...60 A1
Cowslip Rd E18 ...37 B1
Cowthorpe Rd SW8 269 D2
Cox Ct **3** EN4 .....2 C1
Coxe Pl HA3 ......43 A5
Cox Ho W6 ....264 A6
Cox La
Chessington KT9 ..214 B4
West Ewell KT19 ..215 A3
Coxmount Rd SE7 ..121 D1
Coxs Ave TW17 ...193 C6
Cox's Ct E1 ....243 C7
Coxson Way SE1 ..253 C2
Coxwell Rd SE18 ..123 B1
South Norwood SE19 .183 C3
Coxwold Path KT9 .214 A1
Coysh Ct **8** SW15 .157 A6

Crabbs Croft Cl **7**
BR6 . . . . .227 A3
Crab Hill BR3 . . . . . . .186 B3
Crabtree Ave
Dagenham RM6 . . . . . .58 D5
Wembley HA0 . . . . . . .88 B5
Crabtree Cl E2 . . . . . . .95 D5
Crabtree Ct E15 . . . . . .75 D3
Crabtree Hall SW6 . .134 C5
Crabtree La SW6 . . . .134 D5
Craddock Rd EN1 . . . . .5 D2
Craddock St NW5 . . . .71 A2
Cradley Rd DA15,SE9 .167 B3
Craig Dr UB8 . . . . .82 D1
Craigen Ave CR0 . . . .206 B1
Craigerne Rd SE3 . . .143 B5
Craig Gdns E18 . . . . . .36 C1
Craigholm SE18 . . . .144 C4
Craigie Ho SE1 . . . . .263 D3
Craigleith SW15 . . . .156 D5
Craigmuir Pk HA0 . . . .88 B6
Craignair Rd SW2 . . .160 C4
Craig Park Rd N18 . . . .34 B6
Craignish Ave SW16 .182 B1
Craig Rd TW10 . . . . .175 C6
Craig's Ct SW1 . . . . .250 A4
Craigside KT2 . . . . . .176 D2
Craigton Rd SE9 . . . .144 B1
Craigweil Cl HA7 . . . . .25 D5
Craigweil Dr HA7 . . . . .25 D5
Craigwell Ave TW13 .150 A1
Craik Ct NW6 . . . . . . .91 B5
Crail Row
SE17 . . . . .117 B2 262 D3
Crales Ct SE18 . . . . .122 A3
Cramer Ct KT3 . . . . . .199 A6
Cramer St W1 . .93 A2 238 B3
Crammond Cl W6 . . . .264 A5
Cramond Ct TW14 . . .149 C3
Crampton Rd SE20 . . .184 C4
Crampton Sch
SE17 . . . . . . .116 D1 261 D2
Crampton St
SE17 . . . . . . .117 A1 262 A2
Cranberry Cl **2** UB5 . .84 D5
Cranberry La E16 . . . . .98 C2
Cranborne Ave
Southall UB2 . . . . . . .107 C2
Tolworth KT6,KT9 . . . .214 C5
Cranborne Rd IG11 . .101 B6
Cranborne Waye
Hayes UB4 . . . . .106 C6
Hayes UB4 . . . . .84 B1
Cranbourn Alley
WC2 . . . . .249 D6
Cranbourne Cl SW16 204 A6
Cranbourne Ct N2 . . . .47 D6
SW11 . . . . .267 B4
Wanstead E18 . . . . . . .55 B5
Cranbourne Dr HA5 . . .40 D4
Cranbourne Gdns
NW11 . . . . .47 B4
Ilford IG6 . . . . .57 A6
Cranbourne Rd E12 . .78 A3
E15 . . . . .76 A4
N10 . . . . .31 B1
Northwood HA6 . . . . . .39 D6
Cranbourn Ho **4**
SE16 . . . . .118 B4
Cranbourn St
WC2 . . . . . .115 D6 249 D6
Cranbrook NW1 . . . .232 B5
Cranbrook Cl BR2 . .209 A3
Cranbrook Coll (Boys)
IG1 . . . . .78 C4
Cranbrook Ct **8**
TW8 . . . . .131 D6
Cranbrook Dr
Thames Ditton KT10 . .196 A1
Twickenham TW2 . . . .151 D3
Cranbrook Ho **5** E5 . .74 B3
Cranbrook La N11 . . . .31 B6
Cranbrook Mews E17 .53 B4
Cranbrook Pk N22 . . .32 C2
Cranbrook Rd DA7 . .147 B4
SE8 . . . . .141 C4
W4 . . . . .111 C1
Hounslow TW4 . . . . .129 B1
Ilford IG1,IG2 . . . . . . .56 C3
New Barnet EN4 . . . . .14 B5
South Norwood CR7 . .183 A1
Wimbledon SW19 . . .179 A3
Cranbrook Rise IG1 . .56 B2
Cranbrook St E2 . . . . .96 D5
Cranbury Rd SW6 . . .135 D3
Crandale Ho **8** E5 . . .74 B3
Crandley Ct SE8 . . . .119 A2
Crane Ave W3 . . . . . .111 A6
Isleworth TW7 . . . . . .153 A6

Cranebrook TW2 . . . .152 A2
Crane Cl
Dagenham RM10 . . . . .81 C2
Harrow HA2 . . . . .64 A5
Crane Ct EC4 . . . . . .241 B1
7 W12 . . . . .111 C4
West Ewell KT19 . . . .215 A4
Craneford Way TW2 .152 D4
Crane Gdns UB3 . . . .105 D2
Crane Gr N7 . . . . .72 C4
Crane Ho **22** E3 . . . . .97 A5
9 SE15 . . . . .139 D4
9 Catford BR1 . . . . .186 B5
Feltham TW13 . . . . . .151 C1
Crane Lodge Rd TW5 128 B6
Crane Mead SE16 . . .118 D2
Crane Mead Ct TW1 .152 D4
Crane Park Prim Sch
TW3 . . . . .151 B2
Crane Park Rd TW2 .151 D2
Crane Rd
Stanwell TW19 . . . . .148 C5
Twickenham TW2 . . . .152 C3
Cranes Dr KT5 . . . . .198 B5
Cranes Park Ave KT5,
KT6 . . . . .198 B5
Cranes Park Cres
KT5 . . . . .198 B5
Cranes Pk KT5,KT6 .198 A4
Crane St SE10 . . . . . .120 B1
5 SE15 . . . . .139 C4
Craneswater TW6 . . .127 D5
Craneswater Pk UB2 .107 B1
Cranes Way WD6 . . . .11 A6
Crane Way TW2 . . . .152 A4
Cranfield Cl **1** 237 B3
2 Woodford IG8 . . . .37 A6
Cranfield Dr NW9 . . . .27 C3
Cranfield Rd SE4 . . .141 B2
Cranford Ave
Bowes Park N13 . . . . .32 A5
Stanwell TW19 . . . . .148 B4
Cranford Cl
Stanwell TW19 . . . . .148 A4
Wimbledon SW20 . . .178 A3
Cranford Comm Coll
TW5 . . . . .128 B6
Cranford Cotts **8** E1 118 D6
Cranford Ct SM1 . . . .218 A4
Cranford Dr UB3 . . . .105 D2
Cranford Jun Sch
TW4 . . . . .128 B6
Cranford La
Harlington UB3 . . . . .127 C5
Hatton TW6 . . . . . . .127 D4
Hatton, Hatton Cross
TW6 . . . . .127 D2
Heston TW5 . . . . . . .128 C5
Cranford Lo SW19 . . .156 D2
Cranford Park Prim Sch
UB3 . . . . .105 D2
Cranford Park Rd
UB3 . . . . .105 D2
Cranford Rise KT10 .212 A3
Cranford St E1 . . . . .118 D6
Cranford Way N8 . . . .50 D4
Cranhurst Rd NW2 . . .68 C3
Cranleigh W11 . . . . .244 C4
Cranleigh Cl DA5 . . .169 D5
Penge SE20 . . . . . . .184 B1
Cranleigh Ct **4** N16 . .51 C1
Mitcham CR4 . . . . . .202 B6
Richmond TW9 . . . . .132 C2
Southall UB1 . . . . . . .85 B1
Cranleigh Gardens Ind Est
UB1 . . . . .85 B2
Cranleigh Gdns
Barking IG11 . . . . . . .79 B2
Harrow HA3 . . . . .44 A4
Kingston KT2 . . . . . .176 B4
Southall UB1 . . . . . . .85 B1
Southgate N21 . . . . . .16 C3
South Norwood SE25 .205 C6
Sutton SM1 . . . . . . .217 D6
Cranleigh Ho SW20 .178 B1
Cranleigh Hos NW1 .232 B3
Cranleigh Mews
SW11 . . . . .136 D3
Cranleigh Rd N15 . . . .51 A4
Feltham TW13 . . . . . .171 D6
Merton SW19 . . . . . .201 C4
Thames Ditton KT10 . .196 A1
Cranleigh St
NW1 . . . . .93 C5 232 B3
Cranley Dene Ct N10 .49 B5
Cranley Dr Ilford IG2 .57 A2
Ruislip HA4 . . . . .61 D6
Cranley Gdns N10 . . .49 B5
SW7 . . . . .114 B1 256 C2

Cranley Gdns *continued*
Palmers Green N13 . . . .16 B1
Wallington SM6 . . . . .219 C1
Cranley Mews
SW7 . . . . .114 A1 256 B2
Cranley Par **2** SE9 . .188 A6
Cranley Pl
SW7 . . . . .114 B2 256 C3
Cranley Rd E13 . . . . .99 B2
Ilford IG2 . . . . .57 A2
Cranmer Ave W13 . . .109 B3
Cranmer Cl Ruislip HA4 40 D1
Stanmore HA7 . . . . . .25 C3
West Barnes SM4 . . .200 D3
Cranmer Ct N3 . . . . . .29 A1
SW3 . . . . .257 B3
Hampton TW12 . . . . .173 D5
Kingston KT2 . . . . . .175 D6
Cranmer Farm Cl
CR4 . . . . .202 D5
Cranmer Ho SW11 . .267 A2
Cranmer Mid Sch
CR4 . . . . .202 D5
Cranmer Rd E7 . . . . . .77 B4
SW9 . . . . .138 C5
Croydon CR0 . . . . . .221 A5
Edgware HA8 . . . . . . .10 D1
Hampton TW12 . . . . .173 D5
Hayes UB3 . . . . .83 B1
Kingston KT2 . . . . . .176 A5
Mitcham CR4 . . . . . .202 D5
Cranmer Terr SW17 .180 B5
Cranmore Ave TW7 . .130 A5
Cranmore Rd BR7 . . .188 B5
Catford BR1 . . . . . . .164 C5
Cranmore Way N10 . .49 C5
Cranston Cl
Hounslow TW3,TW4 . .129 A3
Uxbridge UB10 . . . . . .61 B6
Cranston Gdns E4 . . . .35 D4
Cranston Rd SE23 . .163 A2
Cranswick Rd SE16 .118 B1
Crantock Rd SE6 . . . .164 A2
Cranwell Cl E3 . . . . . .97 D3
Cranwell Gr **6** NW9 . .27 D3
Croydon CR0 . . . . . .222 D6
Cranwell Gr TW17 . .192 B5
Cranwell Rd TW6 . . .126 D4
Cranwich Ave N21 . . .17 B4
Cranwich Rd N16 . . . .51 C2
Cranwood Ct EC1 . . .235 D1
Cranwood St
EC1 . . . . .95 B4 235 D1
Cranworth Cres **7** E4 20 B3
Cranworth Gdns
SW9 . . . . .138 C4
Cranworth Ho **6** N7 . .72 B4
Craster Rd SW2 . . . .160 B4
Craston Ho **2** SE5 . .139 C3
Crathie Rd SE12 . . . .165 B5
Crathorne Ho **7** N7 . .72 B4
Cravan Ave TW13 . . .150 A2
Craven Ave Ealing W5 109 C6
Southall UB1 . . . . . . .85 B2
Craven Cl N16 . . . . . .52 A2
Hayes UB4 . . . . .84 A1
Craven Cottage (Fulham
FC) SW6 . . . . .134 D4
Craven Ct NW10 . . . .89 C6
Dagenham RM6 . . . . .59 A3
Edgware HA8 . . . . . . .26 B6
Craven Gdns
Barking IG11 . . . . . . .101 C5
Ilford IG6 . . . . .57 B6
Wimbledon SW19 . . .179 D5
Craven Hill
W2 . . . . .114 A6 246 B6
Craven Hill Gdns
W2 . . . . .114 A6 246 A6
Craven Hill Mews
W2 . . . . .246 B6
Craven Ho **18** N2 . . . .30 B1
2 Mortlake SW14 . . .133 B2
Craven Lo W2 . . . . . .246 B6
Fulham SW6 . . . . . . .134 D4
Craven Mews **6**
SW11 . . . . .137 A2
Craven Park Mews
NW10 . . . . .89 C6
Craven Park Rd N15 . .52 A3
NW10 . . . . .89 C6
Craven Park Sch N16 .52 A3
Craven Pas WC2 . . . .250 A4
Craven Pk NW10 . . . .89 C6
Craven Rd NW10 . . . .89 B6
W2 . . . . .92 A1 236 B1
Croydon CR0 . . . . . .206 B1
Ealing W5 . . . . .109 C6
Kingston KT2 . . . . . .176 B2

Craven St
WC2 . . . . .116 A5 250 A4
Craven Terr
W2 . . . . .114 A6 246 B6
Crawford Ave HA0 . . .65 D3
Crawford Bldgs NW1 .237 B3
Crawford Cl TW7 . . . .130 C2
Crawford Gdns
Edmonton N13 . . . . . .16 D1
Northolt UB5 . . . . . . .85 B4
Crawford Mews W1 . .237 C3
Crawford Pas EC1 . . .241 B5
Crawford Pl
W1 . . . . .92 C2 237 B3
Crawford Place Dwellings
NW1 . . . . .237 B3
Crawford Point **4**
E16 . . . . .98 D1
Crawford Prim Sch
SE5 . . . . .139 A4
Crawford Rd SE5 . . .139 A3
Crawford St
W1 . . . . .92 D2 237 C3
Crawley Rd E10 . . . . .53 D1
Enfield EN1 . . . . .17 D1
Tottenham N22 . . . . . .33 A1
Crawshay Ct SW9 . . .138 C4
Crawshay Ho **13** N16 .73 B4
Crawthew Gr SE22 . .139 D1
Craybrooke Rd DA14 .190 B6
Craybury End SE9 . .167 A2
Crayfields Bsns Pk
BR5 . . . . .190 C2
Crayfields Ind Pk
BR5 . . . . .190 C1
Crayford Cl E6 . . . . .100 A1
SE1 . . . . .252 D1
Crayford Ho N7 . . . . .72 A4
Crayke Hill KT9 . . . .214 D2
Crayle Ho EC1 . . . . .241 D6
Crayonne Cl TW16 . .171 C2
Cray Rd DA17 . . . . . .147 C6
Sidcup DA14 . . . . . . .190 C4
Crays Par The BR5 . .190 C1
Crealock Gr IG8 . . . . .36 D5
Crealock St SW18 . .157 D5
Creasy Est SE1 . . . .263 A5
Crebor St SE22 . . . .162 A5
Credenhall Dr BR2 . .210 B1
Credenhill Ho **2**
SE15 . . . . .140 B5
Credenhill St SW16 .181 C5
Crediton Hill NW6 . . .69 D3
Crediton Ho EN3 . . . . .6 D2
Crediton Rd E16 . . . . .99 A1
NW10 . . . . .90 D6
Crediton Way KT10 . .213 A3
Credon Rd E13 . . . . . .99 C5
SE16 . . . . .118 B1
Creechurch La EC3 . .243 B1
Creechurch Pl EC3 . .243 B1
Creed Ho SE15 . . . . .140 B5
Creed La EC4 . . . . . .241 D1
Creek Ho W14 . . . . . .254 B6
Creekmouth Ind Pk
IG11 . . . . .101 D3
Creek Rd SE10,SE8 . .141 D6
Barking IG11 . . . . . . .101 D4
East Molesey KT8 . . .196 A4
Creekside SE8 . . . . .141 D5
Creek The TW16 . . . .194 A4
Creeland Gr SE6 . . . .163 B3
Crefeld Cl
W6 . . . . .135 A6 264 A5
Creffield Rd W3,W5 . .110 C6
Creighton Ave E6 . . . .99 D5
N2,N10 . . . . .30 C1
Creighton Cl W12 . . .112 B6
Creighton Ho N2 . . . . .48 C6
Creighton Rd NW6 . . .90 D5
W5 . . . . .109 D4
Tottenham N17 . . . . . .33 C3
Cremer Bsns Ctr 8
E2 . . . . .95 D5
Cremer Ho **9** SE8 . . .141 D4
Cremer St E2 . . . . . . .95 D5
Cremorne Rd
SW10 . . . . . . .136 B5 266 C4
Creon Ct **3** SW9 . . . .138 C4
Crescent EC3 . . . . . .253 C6
Crescent Court Bsns Ctr
E16 . . . . .98 C3
Crescent Ct **14** DA15 .168 A1
SW4 . . . . .159 D6
Kingston KT6 . . . . . .197 C3
Crescent Dr BR5 . . . .211 A3
Crescent E EN4 . . . . . .2 A5

Crescent Gdns
Ruislip HA4 . . . . .40 B2
Wimbledon SW19 . . .157 C1
Crescent Gr SW4 . . .137 C1
Mitcham CR4 . . . . . .202 C5
Crescent Ho SE13 . .141 D3
5 Wimbledon SW20 .178 D2
Crescent La SW4 . . .159 D6
Crescent Mans N5 . . .72 C3
W11 . . . . .244 B6
Crescent Par UB10 . .82 C4
Crescent Pl SW3 . . .257 B4
Crescent Rd BR1 . . .187 A3
DA15 . . . . .167 B4
E10 . . . . .75 D6
E13 . . . . .99 A6
E6 . . . . .99 C6
N11 . . . . .30 D6
N15 . . . . .50 D6
N22 . . . . .31 D2
N3 . . . . .29 B2
N8 . . . . .49 D3
SE18 . . . . .122 D2
Beckenham BR3 . . . .185 D1
Chingford E4 . . . . . . .20 C4
Dagenham RM10 . . . .81 D5
East Barnet EN4 . . . . .14 C6
Enfield EN2 . . . . .4 D1
Kingston KT2 . . . . . .176 D4
Shepperton TW17 . . .193 A3
Wimbledon SW20 . . .178 D2
Woodford E18 . . . . . .37 C2
Crescent Rise N22 . . .31 D2
N3 . . . . .29 B2
3 N3 . . . . .29 C2
East Barnet EN4 . . . . .14 C6
Crescent Row EC1 . .242 A5
Crescent St N1 . . . . . .72 B1
Crescent Stables
SW15 . . . . .157 A6
Crescent The DA14 . .189 D6
E17 . . . . .53 A4
N11 . . . . .31 A6
N2 . . . . .47 D6
NW2 . . . . .68 B5
W3 . . . . .89 C1
Ashford TW15 . . . . . .170 B3
Barnes SW13 . . . . . .134 A3
Barnet EN5 . . . . .1 D3
Beckenham BR3 . . . .185 C2
East Molesey KT8 . . .195 C5
Harlington UB7 . . . . .127 B5
Harrow HA2 . . . . .42 A1
Ilford IG2 . . . . .56 C3
Kingston KT3 . . . . . .177 A1
Kingston KT6 . . . . . .198 A4
Loughton IG10 . . . . . .21 D5
Lower Halliford TW17 .193 D2
Sidcup DA5 . . . . .168 C4
Southall UB1 . . . . . . .107 A4
Sutton SM1 . . . . . . .218 B3
Thornton Heath CR0 . .205 B3
Wembley HA0 . . . . . . .65 B6
West Wickham BR4 . .208 C3
Wimbledon SW19 . . .157 C1
Crescent View IG10 . .21 D6
Crescent W EN4 . . . . .2 A5
Crescent Way N12 . . .30 C4
SE4 . . . . .141 C2
Orpington BR6 . . . . .227 C3
South Norwood SW16 .182 C3
Crescent Wood Rd
SE21,SE26 . . . . .162 A1
Cresford Rd
SW6 . . . . .135 D4 265 C1
Crespigny Rd NW4 . . .46 B3
Cressage Cl UB1 . . . .85 B1
Cressage Ho **9** TW8 132 A6
Cressall Ho **8** E14 . .119 C3
Cresset Ho **8** E9 . . . .74 C2
Cresset Rd E9 . . . . . .74 C2
Cresset St SW4 . . . .137 D2
Cressfield Cl NW5 . . .71 A3
Cressida Rd N19 . . . .49 D1
Cressingham Ct **1**
DA17 . . . . .125 C3
Cressingham Gr SM1 218 A4
Cressingham Rd HA8 .27 B3
SE13 . . . . .142 A2
Cressington Cl **4** N16 73 C2
Cress Mews BR1 . . . .186 B5
Cresswell Gdns SW5 .256 A2
Cresswell Pk SE3 . . .142 C2
Cresswell Pl
SW10 . . . . . . .114 A1 256 B2
Cresswell Rd
Croydon SE25 . . . . . .206 A5
Feltham TW13 . . . . . .173 A6
Twickenham TW1 . . .153 D5

Cresswell Way N21 . .16 C4
Cressy Ct **6** E1 . . . . .96 C2
W6 . . . . .112 B3
Cressy Ho SW13 . . . .134 B2
Cressy Hos **7** E1 . . . .96 C2
Cressy Pl E1 . . . . .96 C2
Cressy Rd NW3 . . . . .70 D4
Cresta Ct W5 . . . . . . .88 B3
Cresta Ho NW6 . . . . .70 B1
7 Bow E3 . . . . .97 C3
Crestbrook Ave N13 . .16 D1
Crestbrook Pl N13 . . .16 D1
Crest Ct NW4 . . . . . . .46 C4
Crest Dr EN3 . . . . .6 C4
Crestfield St N1,WC1 .233 B2
Crest Gdns HA4 . . . . .62 C5
Creston Way KT4 . . .200 D1
Crest Rd NW2 . . . . . .68 A6
Hayes BR2 . . . . .208 D2
South Croydon CR2 . .222 B1
Crest The NW4 . . . . . .46 C4
Edmonton N13 . . . . . .32 C6
Surbiton KT5 . . . . . .198 C4
10 West Norwood
SW27 . . . . .182 D5
Crestview NW5 . . . . .71 B5
Crest View HA5 . . . . .40 D5
Crest View Dr BR5 . .211 A4
Crestway SW15 . . . . .156 B5
Crestwood Way TW4 151 A6
Creswick Ct W3 . . . .110 D6
Creswick Rd W3 . . . .110 D6
Creswick Wlk **6** E3 . .97 C4
NW11 . . . . .47 B5
Creton St SE18 . . . . .122 C3
Crewdson Rd SW9 . .138 C5
Crewe Pl NW10 . . . . .89 D4
Crewkerne Ct SW11 .266 D2
Crews St E14 . . . . . .119 C2
Crewys Rd NW2 . . . . .69 B6
SE15 . . . . .140 B3
Crichton Ave SM6 . . .219 D4
Crichton Rd SM5 . . . .218 D1
Crichton St SW8 . . . .137 C3
Cricketers Arms Rd
EN2 . . . . .5 A3
Cricketers Cl N14 . . . .15 C4
Chessington KT9 . . . .213 D4
Cricketers Mews **4**
SW18 . . . . .157 D6
Cricketers Wlk SE26 .184 C5
Cricketfield Rd E5 . . .74 B4
Cricket Gn CR4 . . . . .202 D5
Cricket Green Sch
CR4 . . . . .202 C6
Cricket Ground Rd
BR7 . . . . .188 D2
Cricket La BR3 . . . . .185 A4
Cricket Row N2 . . . . .48 B6
Cricklade Ave SW2 . .160 B2
Cricklewood Broadway
NW2 . . . . .68 D4
Cricklewood La NW2 .69 B5
Cricklewood Sta NW2 68 D4
Cridland St E15 . . . . .98 C6
Crieff Ct TW11,KT8 . .175 C3
Crieff Rd SW18 . . . . .158 A5
Criffel Ave SW2 . . . .159 D3
Crimscott St
SE1 . . . . .117 C3 263 C5
Crimsworth Rd
SW8 . . . . .137 D5 269 D3
Crinan St N1 . .94 A5 233 B4
Cringle St
SW8 . . . . .137 C5 269 A4
Cripplegate St EC1 . .242 B4
Cripps Gn UB4 . . . . . .84 B3
Crispe Ho N1 . . . . . .233 B1
Barking IG11 . . . . . . .101 B5
Crispen Rd TW13 . . .173 A6
Crispian Cl NW10 . . .67 C4
Crispin Cl SM6 . . . . .220 A5
Crispin Cres SM6 . . .219 D6
Crispin Ct SE17 . . . .263 A3
Crispin Rd HA8 . . . . .27 A4
Crispin St E1 . .95 D2 243 C3
Crisp Rd W6 . . . . . . .112 C1
Cristowe Rd SW6 . . .135 B3
Criterion Mews N19 . .71 D6
Crittall's Cnr DA14 . .190 C3
Crittenden Lo BR4 . .207 C1
Crockerton Rd SW17 158 D2
Crockham Way SE9 . .188 C6
Crocus Cl CR0 . . . . . .206 D1
Crocus Field EN5 . . . .13 B5
Croft Ave BR4 . . . . . .208 A1
Croft Cl BR7 . . . . . . .188 B5

Croft Cl *continued*
NW7 .....11 C1
Erith DA17 .....125 B1
Harlington UB7 .....127 A5
Hillingdon UB10 .....60 C1
Croft Ct HA4 .....39 D1
Croftdown Rd NW5 .....71 B5
Crofters Cl TW7 .....152 B6
Crofters Ct 9 SE8 .....119 A2
Crofters Way
NW1 .....93 D6 232 C6
Croft Gdns W7 .....109 A4
Ruislip HA4 .....39 D1
Croft Ho 12 W10 .....91 A4
Putney SW15 .....157 A5
Croft Lodge Cl IG8 .....37 B4
Croft Mews N12 .....14 A1
Crofton Ave
Chiswick W4 .....133 B5
Orpington BR6 .....227 A6
Sidcup DA5 .....168 D4
Crofton Gate Way
SE4 .....163 A6
Crofton Gr E4 .....36 B6
Crofton Inf Sch BR5 .211 B2
Crofton Jun Sch BR5 211 B2
Crofton La BR5,BR6 .211 B2
Crofton L Ctr SE4 .....163 C5
Crofton Park Rd SE4 .163 B5
Crofton Park Sta SE4 163 B6
Crofton Rd BR6 .....226 C5
BR6 .....226 D5
E13 .....99 B3
SE5 .....139 C3
Crofton Sch SE4 .....163 C5
Crofton Terr E5 .....75 A3
Richmond TW9 .....132 B1
Crofton Way Enfield EN2 4 C3
New Barnet EN5 .....13 D5
Croft Rd BR1 .....187 A4
Carshalton SM1 .....218 C3
Enfield EN3 .....7 A4
Merton SW19 .....180 A3
South Norwood SW16 .182 C3
Crofts Ho 19 E2 .....96 A5
Croftside The SE25 .206 A6
Crofts La N22 .....32 C3
Crofts Rd HA1 .....43 A4
Crofts St E1 .....118 A6
Croft St SE8 .....119 A2
Crofts The TW17 .....193 C5
Croft The NW10 .....89 D5
Barnet EN5 .....1 A1
Chingford E4 .....20 C2
Ealing W5 .....88 A2
Edgware HA8 .....26 D3
Heston TW5 .....129 A5
New Malden KT3 .....199 C4
Pinner HA5 .....41 B2
Ruislip HA4 .....62 C4
Wembley HA0 .....65 C3
Croft Villas HA1 .....43 A3
Croft Way
Richmond TW10 .....153 B1
Sidcup DA15 .....167 C1
Crogsland Rd NW1 .....71 A1
Croham Cl CR2 .....221 C1
Croham Hurst Sch
CR2 .....221 D3
Croham Manor Rd
CR2 .....221 C2
Croham Mount CR2 .221 C1
Croham Park Ave
CR2 .....221 D3
Croham Rd CR2 .....221 C3
Croham Valley Rd
CR2 .....222 B1
Croindene Rd SW16 .182 A2
Crokesley Ho 2 HA8 ..27 A1
Cromartie Rd N19 .....49 D2
Cromarty Ct 5 BR1 .187 C1
Cromarty Ho 8 E1 .....97 A2
Cromarty Rd HA8 .....10 D2
Cromberdale Ct N17 ..34 A2
Crombie Cl IG4 .....56 B4
Crombie Mews 5
SW11 .....136 C3
Crombie Rd DA15 .....167 B3
Cromdale Ct N16 .....51 D2
Crome Ho UB5 .....85 A5
Cromer Cl UB8 .....83 A1
Cromer Ct
7 Southall UB1 .....85 D1
Streatham SW16 .....160 A1
Wandsworth SW18 .....157 B5
Cromer Pl 5 BR6 .....211 B1
Cromer Rd E10 .....54 B2
Cromer Rd *continued*
Barnet EN5 .....2 A2
Croydon SE25 .....206 B6
Dagenham RM6 .....59 A3
Harlington TW6 .....126 C3
Streatham SW17 .....181 A4
Tottenham N17 .....34 A1
Woodford IG8 .....37 A6
Cromer Road Prim Sch
EN5 .....2 A2
Cromer St
WC1 .....94 A4 233 B1
Cromer Terr E8 .....74 A3
Cromer Villas Rd
SW18 .....157 B5
Cromford Cl BR6 .....227 C5
Cromford Path 1 E5 .74 D4
Cromford Rd SW18 .157 C6
Cromford Way KT3 .177 B2
Cromlix Cl BR7 .....188 D1
Crompton Ct SW3 .257 A4
Crompton Ho SE1 .262 B5
SW8 .....269 B1
W2 .....236 C5
Crompton Pl EN3 .....7 C5
Crompton St
W2 .....92 B3 236 C5
Cromwell Ave BR2 .209 B5
N6 .....49 B1
W6 .....112 B2
New Malden KT3 .....199 D4
Cromwell Bsns Ctr
IG11 .....101 C4
Cromwell Cl N2 .....48 B5
W3 .....111 A5
2 W4 .....110 D1
Bromley BR2 .....209 B5
Walton-on-T KT12 .....194 B1
Cromwell Cres
SW5 .....113 C2 255 A4
Cromwell Ct
Enfield EN3 .....18 D6
15 Kingston KT2 .....176 C3
Wembley HA0 .....88 A5
Cromwell Ctr NW10 .89 B4
Barking IG11 .....102 A4
Cromwell Ctr The
RM8 .....59 B2
Cromwell Est E10 .....53 A1
Cromwell Gdns
SW7 .....114 B3 256 D5
Cromwell Gr W6 .....112 C3
Cromwell Ho SW11 .268 B1
Croydon CR0 .....220 D5
Putney SW15 .....134 A1
Cromwell Hospl
SW5 .....113 D2 255 C4
Cromwell Lo 36 E1 .....96 C3
Barking IG11 .....79 C3
Cromwell Mans SW5 255 B4
Cromwell Mews
SW7 .....256 D4
Cromwell Pl N6 .....49 B1
SW7 .....114 B2 256 D4
5 W3 .....111 A5
Mortlake SW14 .....133 A2
Cromwell Rd E17 .....54 A4
E7 .....77 C1
N10 .....31 A3
N3 .....30 A2
SW7 .....256 B4
SW9 .....138 D4
Beckenham BR3 .....207 A6
Feltham TW13 .....150 B3
Hayes UB3 .....83 B1
Hounslow TW3 .....129 C1
Kingston KT2 .....176 A2
Teddington TW11 .....175 A4
Thornton Heath CR0 .....205 B2
Walton-on-T KT12 .....194 B1
Wembley HA0 .....88 A5
Wimbledon SW19 .....179 D5
Worcester Park KT4 .....215 C5
Cromwell St TW3 .....129 C1
Cromwell Twr EC2 .....242 B4
Crondace Rd
SW6 .....135 C4 265 B1
Crondall Ct 7 N1 .....95 C5
Crondall Ho SW15 .....156 A3
Crondall Pl 15 N1 .....95 C5
Crondall St N1 .....95 C5
Crone Ct 5 NW6 .....91 B5
Cronin St SE15 .....139 D5
Crooked Billet E4 .....35 C3
Crooked Billet Yd 19
E2 .....95 C4
Crooked Usage N3 .....47 A6
Crooke Rd SE8 .....119 A1
Crookham Rd
SW6 .....135 B4 264 C1
Crook Log DA6 .....146 D1
Crook Log Prim Sch
DA6 .....146 D1
Crook Log Sports Ctr
DA16 .....146 D2
Crookston Rd SE9 .....144 C2
Croombs Rd E16 .....99 C2
Croom's Hill SE10 .....142 B5
Croom's Hill Gr SE10 142 A5
Cropley Ct N1 .....235 C4
Cropley St N1 .95 B5 235 C4
Croppath Rd RM10 .....81 C4
Cropthorne Ct W9 .....229 B1
Crosbie 10 NW9 .....27 D1
Crosbie Ho 20 E17 .....53 D6
Crosby Cl TW13 .....173 A6
Crosby Ct N2 .....48 A5
SE1 .....252 C2
Crosby Rd E7 .....77 A2
Dagenham RM10 .....103 D6
Crosby Row
SE1 .....117 B4 252 C2
Crosby Sq EC3 .....243 A2
Crosby Wlk 3 E8 .....73 D2
Streatham SE24 .....160 C4
Crosfield Ct 3 W10 .....90 D1
Crosfield Ho W11 .....244 A5
Crosier Cl SE3 .....144 A3
Crosier Rd UB10 .....61 A4
Crosier Way HA4 .....61 C5
Crosland Pl 5 SW11 137 A2
Crossbow Ho 15 N1 .....95 C6
Ealing W13 .....109 B5
Crossbrook Rd SE3 .....144 A2
Cross Cl SE15 .....140 B3
Cross Ct 11 SE28 .....124 B6
SE5 .....139 B2
Cross Deep TW1 .....153 A2
Cross Deep Gdns
TW1 .....152 D2
Crossfield Rd N17 .....51 A6
NW3 .....70 B2
Crossfield St SE8 .....141 C5
Crossford St SW9 .....138 B3
Crossgate Edgware HA8 10 C1
Wembley UB6 .....65 B2
Crossharbour & London
Arena Sta E14 .....119 D3
Cross Keys Cl W1 .....238 B3
5 Edmonton N9 .....18 A2
Cross La DA5 .....169 B4
EC3 .....253 A5
N8 .....50 B5
Cross Lances Rd
TW3 .....129 D1
Crossland Rd CR7 .....204 D3
Crosslands Ave
Ealing W5 .....110 B5
Southall UB2 .....107 B1
Crosslands Rd KT19 .215 B2
Crossleigh Ct 3
SE14 .....141 B5
Crosslet St SE17 .....262 D4
Crosslet Vale SE10 .....141 D4
Crossley St N7 .....72 C2
Crossman Hos 19
SW12 .....160 A4
Crossmead SE9 .....166 B3
Crossmead Ave UB6 .....85 C4
Crossmount Ho 13
SE5 .....139 A5
Crossness Rd IG11 .....101 D4
Cross Rd BR2 .....226 A6
N11 .....31 B5
N2 .....30 C1
SE5 .....139 C3
Chingford, Chingford Green
E4 .....20 C3
Croydon CR0 .....205 B1
Enfield EN1 .....5 C1
Feltham TW13 .....173 A6
Harrow HA1 .....42 B4
Harrow HA2 .....63 D5
Harrow HA3 .....25 A1
Ilford RM6 .....58 C2
Kingston KT2 .....176 B3
Merton SW19 .....179 C3
Romford RM7 .....59 C6
Sidcup DA14 .....190 B6
Sutton SM1 .....218 B3
Wood Green N22 .....32 C3
Cross St N1 .....94 D6 234 D6
2 Edmonton N18 .....34 A5
Hampton TW12 .....174 A5
Mortlake SW13 .....133 C2
Crossthwaite Ave
SE5,SE24 .....139 B1
Crosswall
EC3 .....117 D6 253 C6
Crossway BR5 .....211 B4
Crossway *continued*
E8,N16 .....73 C3
N12 .....30 B4
NW9 .....45 D5
SE28 .....102 D1
Dagenham RM8 .....80 C5
Ealing W13 .....87 A3
Enfield EN1 .....17 C4
Hayes UB3 .....106 A5
Pinner HA5 .....22 B1
Ruislip HA4 .....62 C4
West Barnes KT3,
SW20 .....200 C5
Woodford IG8 .....37 C6
Crossway Ct SE4 .....141 A3
Crossway Par N22 .....32 D3
Crossways
Ashford TW16 .....171 D3
South Croydon CR2 .....223 B1
Sutton SM2 .....218 B1
Crossways Rd
Beckenham BR3 .....207 C5
Mitcham CR4 .....203 B6
Crossways The
Heston TW5 .....129 B5
Wembley HA9 .....66 C6
Crossway The
Chislehurst SE9 .....165 D2
Hillingdon UB10 .....82 B5
Tottenham N22 .....32 D3
Cross Way The HA3 .....24 C1
Crosswell Cl TW17 .....171 A1
Croston St E8 .....96 A6
Crothall Cl N13 .....16 B1
Crouch Ave IG11 .....102 B5
Crouch Cl BR3 .....185 C4
Crouch Croft SE9 .....166 C1
Crouch End Hill N8 .....49 D2
Crouch Hall Ct N19 .....50 A1
Crouch Hall Rd N8 .....49 D3
Crouch Hill N4,N8,N19 .50 A2
Crouchmans Cl SE21,
SE26 .....162 A1
Crouch Rd NW10 .....67 B1
Crowborough Ct
W13 .....109 C6
Crowborough Path
WD19 .....22 D6
Crowborough Rd
SW17 .....181 A5
Crowden Way SE28 .....124 C6
Crowder St E1 .....118 B6
Crowfield Ho N5 .....73 A4
Crowfoot Cl E9 .....75 B3
Crowhurst SE25 .....206 A6
Crowhurst Cl SW9 .....138 C3
Crowhurst Ct N17 .....34 B2
Crowhurst Ho 21
SW9 .....138 B3
Crow La RM7,RM8 .....59 D2
Crowland Ave UB3 .....105 D2
Crowland Gdns N14 .....16 A4
Crowland Ho NW8 .....229 A5
Crowland Prim Sch
N15 .....52 A4
Crowland Rd N15 .....51 D4
South Norwood CR7 .....205 B5
Crowlands Ave RM7 .....59 D3
Crowland Terr N1 .....73 B1
Crowland Wlk SM4 .....202 A3
Crowley Cres CR0 .....220 C3
Crowline Wlk 1 N1 .....73 A2
Crowmarsh Gdns
SE23 .....162 C4
Crown Arc KT1 .....175 D1
Crown Bldgs 4 E4 .....20 B3
Crownbourne Ct
SM1 .....217 D4
Crown Cl E3 .....97 C6
NW6 .....69 D2
NW7 .....11 D2
Hayes UB3 .....105 D4
Walton-on-T KT12 .....194 C2
Crown Close Bsns Ctr
E3 .....97 C6
Crown Ct EC4 .....242 B1
6 N10 .....31 A3
NW8 .....230 B1
SE12 .....165 B5
WC2 .....240 B1
Bromley BR1 .....209 D4
4 Putney SW15 .....134 D1
3 Twickenham TW1 .....153 B4
Crown Dale SE19 .....183 A5
Crowndale Ct NW1 .....232 C4
Crowndale Rd
NW1 .....93 C5 232 B4
Crownfield Ave IG2 .....57 C4
Crownfield Rd E15 .....76 B4
Crown Hill CR0 .....221 A5
Crownhill Rd NW10 .....89 D6
Crown Ho HA4 .....40 A1
Crown La BR2 .....209 D4
N14 .....15 C3
Chislehurst BR7 .....189 A2
Merton SM4 .....201 C6
South Norwood SE19,
SW16 .....182 C5
Crown Lane Gdns
SE27 .....182 C5
Crown Lane Prim Sch
SE27 .....182 D5
Crown Lane Spur
BR2 .....209 D3
Crownleigh Ct SW2 .....160 C6
Crown Lo SW3 .....257 B3
Crownmead Way RM7 59 D5
Crown Mews 3 E13 .....99 C6
Crown Office Row
EC4 .....251 A6
Crown Par N14 .....15 C3
Morden SM4 .....201 D5
South Norwood SE19 .....182 D4
Crown Pas SW1 .....249 B3
Kingston KT1 .....175 D1
Crown Pl EC2 .....243 A4
NW5 .....71 B2
Crown Point SE19 .....182 D4
Crown Rd N10 .....31 A3
Enfield EN1 .....6 B2
Ilford IG6 .....57 B5
Kingston KT3 .....177 A2
Morden SM4 .....201 D5
Ruislip HA4 .....62 D3
Sutton SM1 .....217 D4
Twickenham TW1 .....153 B5
Crown Reach SW1 .....259 D1
Crown St SE5 .....139 A5
Acton W3 .....110 D5
Dagenham RM10 .....81 D2
Harrow HA2 .....42 C1
Crownstone Ct 1
SW2 .....160 C6
Crownstone Rd SW2 .160 C6
Crown Terr TW9 .....132 B1
Crown Trad Ctr UB3 .105 C4
Crowntree Cl TW7 .....130 D6
Crown Way UB7 .....104 B5
Crown Wlk HA9 .....66 B5
Crown Woods Sch
SE9 .....167 A6
Crown Woods Way
SE9 .....167 B6
Crown Yard TW3 .....130 A2
Crowshott Ave HA7 .....25 D2
Crows Rd E15 .....98 B4
Barking IG11 .....78 D2
Crowther Ave TW8 .....110 A2
Crowther Cl
SW6 .....135 B6 264 D5
Crowther Rd SE25 .....206 A5
Crowthorne Cl SW18 157 B3
Crowthorne Rd W10 .....90 D1
Croxall Ho KT12 .....194 C3
Croxden Cl HA8 .....44 C6
Croxden Wlk SM4 .....202 A3
Croxford Gdns N22 .....32 D3
Croxley Cl BR5 .....190 B1
Croxley Gn BR5 .....190 B2
Croxley Rd W9 .....91 B4
Croxted Cl SE21 .....161 A4
Croxted Mews SE24 .161 A5
Croxted Rd SE21,SE24 161 B3
Croxteth Ho 11 SW8 .....137 D3
Croxton 17 KT1 .....176 C1
Croyde Ave
Greenford UB6 .....86 A4
Hayes UB3 .....105 C2
Croyde Cl SE9 .....167 B4
Croydon N17 .....33 B1
Croydon Airport Ind Est
CR0 .....220 B2
Croydon Central Sta
CR0 .....221 A6
Croydon Coll CR0 .....221 B6
Croydon Coll Annexe
CR0 .....205 B1
Croydon Coll (Selhurst
Tertiary Ctr) SE25 .....205 B4
Croydon Flyover The
CR0 .....221 A5
Croydon Gr CR0 .....204 D1
Croydon Ho SE1 .....251 B2
Croydon Rd E13 .....98 D3
Beckenham BR3 .....207 A6
Coney Hall BR2,BR4 .....224 D5
Harlington TW6 .....126 D2
Keston Mark BR2,BR4,
BR6 .....225 C5
Mitcham CR0,CR4 .....203 C4
Croydon Rd *continued*
Penge SE20 .....184 C2
Wallington CR0 .....220 B4
Wallington CR0,SM5,
SM6 .....219 C5
Croydon Rd Ind Est
BR3 .....206 D5
Croyland Rd N9 .....18 A3
Croylands Dr KT6 .....198 A6
Croysdale Ave TW16 .194 A6
Crozier Ho SE3 .....143 B2
SW8 .....270 C3
Crozier Terr E9 .....74 D3
Crucible Cl RM6 .....58 B3
Crucifix La
SE1 .....117 C4 253 A2
Cruden Ho 23 E3 .....97 B5
11 SE17 .....138 D6
Cruden St N1 .94 D6 234 D5
Cruickshank St WC1 .234 A2
Cruikshank Ho NW8 .230 B4
Cruikshank Rd E15 .....76 C3
Crummock Gdns NW9 45 C4
Crumpsall St SE2 .....124 C2
Crundale Ave NW9 .....44 C4
Crunden Rd CR2 .....221 B1
Crusader Gdns CR0 .....221 C5
Crusader Ind Est N4 .....51 A3
Crusoe House Sch
N1 .....95 B4 235 C2
Crusoe Mews N16 .....73 B6
Crusoe Rd CR4 .....180 D3
Crutched Friars
EC3 .....117 C6 253 B6
Crutchfield La KT12 .194 B1
Crutchley Rd SE6 .....164 C2
Crystal Ct SE19 .....183 D5
Crystal Ctr The 1
HA1 .....42 D4
Crystal Ho SE18 .....123 D1
Crystal Palace Mus★
SE19 .....183 D4
Crystal Palace National
Sports Ctr SE20 .....184 A4
Crystal Palace Par
SE19 .....183 D5
Crystal Palace Park Rd
SE26 .....184 B5
Crystal Palace Rd
SE22 .....162 A6
Crystal Palace Sta
SE19 .....184 A4
Crystal Palace Station Rd
SE19 .....184 A4
Crystal Terr SE19 .....183 B4
Crystal View Ct BR1 .186 B6
Crystal Way
Dagenham RM8 .....58 C1
Harrow HA1 .....42 D4
Cuba Dr EN3 .....6 C3
Cuba St E14 .....119 C4
Cubitt Ho 4 SW4 .....159 C5
Cubitt Sq UB2 .....108 A5
Cubitt St WC1 .94 B4 233 D1
Cubitt Terr SW4 .....137 C2
Cubitt Town Jun & Inf Sch
E14 .....120 A3
Cuckoo Ave W7 .....86 C3
Cuckoo Dene W7 .....86 B2
Cuckoo Hall La N9 .....18 D4
Cuckoo Hall Prim Sch
N9 .....18 C4
Cuckoo Hill HA5 .....40 C6
Cuckoo Hill Dr HA5 .....40 C6
Cuckoo Hill Rd HA5 .....40 D5
Cuckoo La W7 .....108 C6
Cuda's Cl KT19 .....215 D4
Cuddington SE17 .....262 B4
Cuddington Ave
KT19,KT4 .....215 D5
Cuddington Com Prim Sch
KT4 .....215 D5
Cudham La N BR6 .....227 C1
Cudham St SE6 .....164 A4
Cudworth Ho SW8 .....269 B1
Cudworth St E1 .....96 B3
Cuff Cres SE9 .....165 D5
Cuffley Ho W10 .....90 C2
Cuff Point 12 E2 .....95 D4
Culand Ho SE17 .....263 A3
Culford Gdns
SW3 .....114 D2 257 D3
Culford Gr N1 .....73 C2
Culford Mans SW3 .....257 D3
Culford Mews N1 .....73 C2
Culford Rd N1 .....73 C2
N1 .....95 C6
Culgaith Gdns EN2 .....4 A1
Culham Ho 33 E2 .....95 D4
21 W2 .....91 C2

Cullen Ho W9 ....91 B5
Cullen Way NW10 ....89 A3
Culling Rd SE16 ....118 C3
Cullington Cl HA3 ....43 A5
Cullingworth Rd
NW10 .....15 SE16 ..68 B3
Culloden Cl 15 SE16 .118 A1
Culloden Prim Sch
E14 ....98 A1
Culloden Rd EN2 .....4 D3
Cullum St EC3 .....253 A6
Culmington Mans
W13 ....109 C6
Culmington Par W13 109 C6
Culmington Rd
Ealing W13,W5 .....109 C6
South Croydon CR2 ..221 A1
Culmore Rd SE15 ...140 C5
Culmstock Rd SW11 .159 A6
Culpepper Cl SE11 .261 A4
Culross Bldgs NW1 .233 A4
Culross Cl N15 ......51 A5
Culross St
W1 ....115 A6 248 A5
Culsac Rd KT6 .....214 A6
Culver Ct SW18 ....157 D5
Culverden Rd SW12 .159 C2
Culver Gr HA7 .....25 C1
Culverhouse WC1 ...240 C3
Culverhouse Gdns
SW16 ....160 B1
Culverlands Cl HA7 ..25 B6
Culverley Rd SE6 ...164 A3
Culvers Ave SM5,CR4 218 D6
Culvers House Prim Sch
CR4 ....203 A1
Culvers Retreat SM5 218 D6
Culverstone Cl BR2 .208 D4
Culvers Way SM5 ...218 D6
Culvert Ct SW11 ...137 A3
Culverton Ct 5 DA14 190 A6
Culvert Pl SW11 ...137 A3
Culvert Rd N15 .....51 C4
SW11 ....136 C1
Culworth Ho NW8 ..230 A4
Culworth St NW8 ..230 A4
Cumber Ho SW18 ...157 C3
Cumberland Ave
DA16 ....145 D1
Wembley NW10 ......88 D4
Cumberland Bsns Pk
NW10 ....88 D4
Cumberland Cl E8 ...73 D2
2 Twickenham TW1 .153 B5
8 Wimbledon SW20 ..178 D3
Cumberland Cres
W14 ....254 B4
Cumberland Ct W1 .237 D1
4 Croydon CR0 ....205 B1
Woodford IG8 ....37 B5
Cumberland Dr DA7 .147 A5
Chessington KT9 ....214 A6
Hinchley Wood KT10 .213 A6
Cumberland Gate
W1 ....114 D6 247 D6
Cumberland Gdns
NW4 ....29 A1
WC1 ....234 A2
Cumberland Ho N9 ..18 C3
Kingston KT2 ......176 D3
1 Putney SW15 ....156 C4
Cumberland Mans
7 NW6 ....69 C3
W1 ....237 C2
Cumberland Market
NW1 ......93 B4 231 D2
Cumberland Mills Sq
E14 ....120 B1
Cumberland Park Ind Est
NW10 ....90 A4
Cumberland Pk W3 .111 A6
Cumberland Pl NW1 .231 C2
Catford SE6 ....164 A4
Sunbury TW16 .....194 A4
Cumberland Rd E12 .77 D4
E13 ....99 B3
E17 ....35 A1
N9 ....18 C3
W3 ....111 A6
W7 ....108 D4
Ashford TW15 .....148 A1
Barnes SW13 ......134 A4
Beckenham BR2 ....208 D6
Croydon SE25 ......206 A4
Harrow HA1 ....41 D4
Richmond TW9 .....132 C5
Stanmore HA7,HA8 ..44 B6
Wood Green N22 ....32 B1
Cumberland Sch E16 .98 D2

Cumberland St
SW1 ....115 B1 258 D2
Cumberland Terr
NW1 ....231 C3
Cumberland Terrace Mews
NW1 ....231 C3
Cumberland Villas
W3 ....111 A6
Cumberlow Ave SE25 206 A6
Cumbernauld Gdns
TW16 ....171 D5
Cumberton Rd N17 ..33 B2
Cumbrae Gdns KT6 .213 D6
Cumbria Ho 2 SW15 157 B6
Cumbrian Gdns NW2 .69 A6
Cumming St N1 ....233 D3
Cumnor Cl 23 SW9 .138 B3
Cumnor Gdns KT17 .216 A2
Cumnor Rd SM2 ...218 A2
Cunard Cres N21 ....17 B5
Cunard Pl EC3 .....243 B1
Cunard Rd NW10 ...89 B4
Cunard Wlk 3 SE16 119 A2
Cundy Rd E16 ......99 C1
Cundy St
SW1 ....115 A2 258 B3
Cunliffe Rd KT19 ...215 D4
Cunliffe St SW16 ...181 C4
Cunningham Cl
Dagenham RM6 ......58 C4
West Wickham BR4 ..223 D6
Cunningham Ct W2 .236 C5
Cunningham Ho 16
SE5 ....139 B5
Cunningham Pk HA1 .42 B4
Cunningham Pl
NW8 ....92 B3 236 C6
Cunningham Rd N15 .52 A5
Cunnington St W4 ..111 A2
Cupar Rd SW11 ....268 B2
Cupola Cl BR1 .....187 B5
Cureton St
SW1 ....115 D2 259 D3
Curie Gdns NW9 ....27 C1
Curie Ho 1 HA7 ....67 A5
Curlew Cl SE28 ....124 D6
Curlew Ct KT6 .....214 C5
Curlew Ho 6 SE15 .139 D4
SE4 ....141 A1
Enfield EN3 ....18 C1
Curlew St
SE1 ....117 D4 253 D2
Curlew Way BR4 ....84 D2
Curnick's La SE27 .183 A6
Curnock Est
Hackbridge SM6 ....219 A5
Curran Ho 5 SW3 .257 A3
Currey Rd UB6 .....64 B2
Curricle St W3 ....111 C5
Currie Hill Cl SW19 .179 B6
Currie Ho 13 SW12 .159 D4
Curry Rise NW7 ....28 C5
Cursitor St
EC4 ....94 C1 241 A2
Curtain Pl EC2 ....243 B6
Curtain Rd EC2 95 C3 243 B6
Curthwaite Gdns EN2 .15 D6
Curtis Dr W3 ......89 B1
Curtis Field Rd SW16 182 C6
Curtis Ho 7 N11 ...31 C5
SE17 ....262 C2
Curtis La HA0 .....66 A3
Curtis Rd
Twickenham TW4 ...151 B4
West Ewell KT19 ...215 A4
Curtis St SE1 117 D2 263 C4
Curtis Way SE1 ....263 C4
7 SE28 ....124 B6
Curtlington Ho 3 HA8 27 A1
Curve The W12 ....112 A6
Curwen Ave E7 .....77 B4
Curwen Rd W12 ....112 A4
Curwen Sch E13 ....99 A5
Curzon Ave Enfield EN3 18 D6
Stanmore HA7 ......25 A2
Curzon Cl BR6 ....227 B4
Barking IG11 ......101 D4
Curzon Cres NW10 ..67 C1
SW6 ....265 D1
Curzon Ct SE9 ....167 A1
SW6 ....265 D1
Curzon Gate W1 ...248 B3
Curzon Ho W5 .....87 B3
Pinner HA5 ....40 C4
Curzon Pl W1 .....248 B3
Curzon Rd N10 ....31 B1
W5 ....87 B3
Ealing W5 ....87 B3
Thornton Heath CR7 .204 C3
Cusack Cl TW1 ....174 D6
Custance Ho N1 ...235 C3

Custance St N1 ....235 C2
Custom House★
EC3 ....117 C6 253 A5
Custom House for ExCeL
Sta E16 ....121 B6
Custom House Reach
SE16 ....119 B3
Cutbush Ho N7 .....71 D3
Cutcombe Mans 22
SE5 ....139 A3
Cutcombe Rd SE5 ..139 A3
Cuthberga Cl IG11 ..79 A1
Cuthbert Gdns SE25 205 C6
Cuthbert Harrowing Ho
EC1 ....242 A5
Cuthbert Ho W2 ...236 C4
Cuthbert Rd E17 ....54 A6
Croydon CR0 ......220 D6
8 Edmonton N18 ...34 A6
Cuthbert St W2 ...236 C4
Cuthill Wlk 3 SE5 .139 B4
Cutlers Gdns EC2 .243 B2
Cutlers Sq E14 ....119 C2
Cutler St EC2 .....243 B2
Cut The SE1 .116 C4 251 B1
Cutty Sark★ SE10 .142 A6
Cutty Sark Sta SE10 142 A6
Cuxton BR5 ....211 A4
Cuxton Cl DA6 ....169 A6
Cuxton Ho SE17 ...263 B2
Cyclamen Cl 4
TW12 ....173 C4
Cyclamen Way KT19 215 A3
Cyclops Mews 9
E14 ....119 C2
Cygnet Ave TW14 ..150 D4
Cygnet Cl NW10 ...67 B3
Cygnet St E1 ......243 D6
Cygnets The TW13 .173 A6
Cygnet Way UB4 ...84 D2
Cygnus Bsns Ctr
NW10 ....67 D2
Cymbeline Ct 6 HA1 .42 D3
Cyns 5 E11 ....55 A3
Cynthia St N1 ....233 D3
Cypress Ave N2 ....47 D6
Twickenham TW2 ...152 A4
Cypress Ct 5 E11 ..76 B4
Cheam SM1 ....217 C2
7 West Norwood
SW16 ....182 C5
Cypress Gdns SE4 .163 A6
Cypress Ho SE14 ..140 D4
Cypress Inf Sch SE25 183 C1
Cypress Jun Sch
SE25 ....183 C1
Cypress Lo SE25 ..183 C1
Cypress Pl W1 ....239 B5
Cypress Rd Harrow HA3 24 B1
South Norwood SE25 .183 C1
Cypress Tree Cl
DA15 ....167 D3
Cyprus Ave N3 ....29 A1
Cyprus Cl N4 .....50 C3
Cyprus Gdns N3 ...29 A1
Cyprus Pl 24 E2 ...96 C5
E6 ....122 C4
Cyprus Rd N3 .....29 A1
Edmonton N9 ......17 D2
Cyprus St E2 ......96 C5
Cyprus Sta E6 ....122 C4
Cyrena Rd SE22 ...161 D3
Cyril Jackson Prim Sch
(North Bldg) E14 ..119 B6
Cyril Jackson Prim Sch
(South Bldg) E14 ..119 B6
Cyril Lo 2 DA14 ...190 A6
Cyril Mans SW11 ..267 D1
Cyril Rd DA7 ......147 A3
Cyril Smith Ho N13 .32 B5
Cyril Thatcher Ho
SW6 ....265 B1
Cyrus Ho EC1 .....241 D6
Cyrus St EC1 .94 D3 241 D6
Czar St SE8 ....141 C6

D

Dabbs Hill La UB5 ..63 C3
Dabb's La EC1 ....241 B5
Dabin Cres SE10 ..142 A4
Dacca St SE8 .....141 B6
Dace Rd E3 ....97 C6
Dacre Cl UB6 ......85 D5
Dacre Gdns SE13 .142 C1
Borehamwood WD6 ..11 B6
Dacre Ho SW3 ....266 D5
Dacre Pk SE13 ....142 C1
Dacre Pl SE13 ....142 C1
Dacre Rd E11 .....54 D1

Dacre Rd continued
E13 ....99 B6
Thornton Heath CR0 .204 A2
Dacres Rd SE23 ...162 D1
Dacre St
SW1 ....115 D3 259 C6
Dade Way UB2 ....107 B1
Daerwood Cl BR2 ..210 B1
Daffodil Cl CR0 ...206 D1
Daffodil Gdns IG1 ..78 D3
Daffodil Pl 7 TW12 173 C4
Daffodil St W12 ...111 D6
Dafforne Rd SW17 .159 A1
Dagenham Ave RM9 103 A6
Dagenham Dock Sta
RM9 ....103 B5
Dagenham East Sta
RM10 ....81 D3
Dagenham Heathway Sta
RM9 ....81 B2
Dagenham Priory Comp
Sch RM10 ....103 D6
Dagenham Rd E10 ..53 B1
Dagenham RM10 .....81 D4
Dagger La WD23,WD6 .9 A4
Dagmar Ave HA9 ...66 B4
Dagmar Ct E14 ....120 A3
Dagmar Gdns NW10 .90 D5
Dagmar Mews UB2 .107 A3
Dagmar Pas N1 ...234 D6
Dagmar Rd N15 ....51 B5
N22 ....31 D2
N4 ....50 D2
SE5 ....139 C4
4 Kingston KT2 ...176 C3
Southall UB2 ......107 A3
South Norwood SE25 .205 C4
Dagmar Terr
N1 ....94 D6 234 D6
Dagnall Pk SE25 ..205 C4
Dagnall Rd SE25 ..205 C4
Dagnall St
SW11 .....137 A4 268 A1
Dagnan Rd SW12 ..159 C4
Dagobert Ho 25 E1 .96 C2
Dagonet Gdns BR1 .165 A1
Dagonet Rd BR1 ...165 A1
Dahlia Gdns Ilford IG1 78 D2
Mitcham CR4 ......203 D5
Dahlia Rd SE2 .....124 B2
Dahomey Rd SW16 .181 C4
Daiglen Sch The IG9 .21 C2
Daimler Ho 8 E3 ...97 C3
Daimler Way SM6 ..220 A1
Daines Cl E12 .....78 B5
Dainford Cl BR1 ...186 B5
Dainton Cl 2 BR1 .187 B2
Dainton Ho 22 W2 .91 C2
Daintry Cl HA3 ....43 A5
Daintry Way E9 ....75 B2
Dairsie Ct 2 BR1 ..187 C1
Dairsie Rd SE9 ....144 C2
Dairy Cl BR1 ......187 C2
South Norwood CR7 .183 A1
Dairy La SE18 .....122 B2
Dairyman Cl NW2 ..69 A5
Dairy Meadow Prim Sch
UB2 ....107 B3
Daisy Cl CR0 ......206 D1
Daisy Dormer Ct 11
SW9 ....138 B1
Daisy La SW6 .....135 C2
Daisy Rd E16 ......98 C3
Woodford E18 ......37 B1
Dakota Cl SM6 ....220 A3
Dakota Gdns
Newham E6 ....100 A3
Northolt UB5 ......85 A4
Dalberg Rd SW2 ..160 C6
Dalberg Way SE2 ..124 D3
Dalbury Ho 6 SW9 138 B1
Dalby Rd SW18 ...136 A1
Dalby St NW5 .....71 B2
Dalbys Cres N17 ...33 C4
Dalcross Rd TW4,
TW5 ....129 A3
Dale Ave Edgware HA8 .26 B1
Hounslow TW4 ....129 A2
Dalebury Rd SW17 .158 D2
Dale Cl SE3 ....143 A4
New Barnet EN5 ....13 D5
Pinner HA5 ....22 B2
Dale Croft N4 .....73 A5
Dale Ct N8 ....49 C6
3 Kingston KT2 ...176 B3
Woodford E18 ......37 A1
Dale Dr UB4 ....83 D4
Dalefield IG9 ......21 D3
Dale Gdns IG8 ....37 B6
Dale Gr N12 ......30 A5

Dale Green Rd N11 .15 B1
Dalehaed NW1 ....232 A3
Daleham Dr UB8 ...82 C1
Daleham Gdns NW3 .70 B2
Daleham Mews NW3 .70 B2
Dale Ho NW8 .....229 A6
SE4 ....141 A1
Dale Lo N6 ....49 C3
Dalemain Ho 5 SW8 137 D3
Dalemain Mews 13
E16 ....121 A5
Dale Park Ave SM5 .218 D6
Dale Park Rd SE19 .183 C3
Dale Rd NW5 ......71 A3
SE17 ....138 D6
Ashford TW16 .....171 B3
Cheam SM1 ....217 B4
Southall UB6 ......85 D2
Walton-on-T KT12 .193 D2
Dale Row W11 .....91 A1
Daleside Rd
Streatham SW17 ...181 B5
West Ewell KT19 ...215 B6
Dales Path WD6 ...11 B6
Dales Rd WD6 .....11 B6
Dale St W4 ....111 C1
Dale The BR2 .....225 D4
Dale View Ave E4 ..20 A2
Dale View Cres E4 ..20 A1
Dale View Gdns E4 ..20 A1
Daleview Rd N15 ...51 C3
Dalewood Gdns KT4 216 B6
Dale Wood Rd BR6 .211 C1
Daley Ho W12 .....90 B1
Daley St E9 ....74 D2
Daley Thompson Way 7
SW8 ....137 B2
Dalgarno Gdns W10 .90 C2
Dalgarno Way W10 .90 C2
Daling Way E3 ....97 A5
Dalkeith Ct SW1 ..259 D3
Dalkeith Gr HA7 ...26 A5
Dalkeith Ho 6 SW9 138 D4
Dalkeith Rd Ilford IG1 79 A5
West Norwood SE21 .161 A4
Dallas Rd NW4 ....46 A2
Cheam SM3 ....217 B2
Ealing W5 ....88 B2
Forest Hill SE26 ...162 B1
Dallas Terr UB3 ...105 D3
Dallega Cl UB3 ....105 B6
Dallinger Rd SE12 .164 C5
Dalling Rd W6 ....112 B2
Dallington Sch
EC1 ....94 D3 241 D6
Dallington St
EC1 ....94 D3 241 D6
Dallin Rd DA6 .....146 D1
Woolwich SE18 ....144 D5
Dalmain Prim Sch
SE23 ....163 A3
Dalmain Rd SE23 ..162 D3
Dalmally Rd CR0 ..206 A2
Dalmeny Ave N7 ...71 D4
Thornton Heath SW16 182 C1
Dalmeny Cl HA0 ...65 C2
Dalmeny Cres TW3 .130 B1
Dalmeny Ct 4 SW4 138 A3
Dalmeny Rd DA7,DA8 147 D4
N7 ....71 D4
New Barnet EN5 ...14 A5
North Cheam KT4 ..216 B5
Wallington SM5 ...219 A1
Dalmeyer Rd NW10 .67 D2
Dalmore Ave KT10 .212 D2
Dalmore Rd SE21 ..161 A2
Dalrymple Cl N14 ..15 C3
Dalrymple Rd SE4 .141 A1
Dalston Gdns HA7 ..26 A1
Dalston Jct E8 ....73 C2
Dalston Kingsland Sta
E8 ....73 C3
Dalston La E8 .....74 A3
Dalton Ave CR4 ...180 C1
Dalton Cl BR6 ....227 C3
Hayes UB4 ....83 B3
Dalton Ho 9 E3 ...97 A5
19 SE14 ....140 D6
Dalton St SE27 ...160 D1
Dalwood St SE5 ...139 C4
Daly Ct E15 ....76 A3
Dalyell Rd SW9 ...138 C1
Damascene Wlk
SE21 ....161 A3
Damask Cres E16 ..98 C3
Damer Ho 9 TW10 .154 B6
Damer Terr SW10 .266 B3
Dames Rd E7 ......77 A4
Dame St N1 ..95 A5 235 A4
Damien Ct 20 E1 ...96 B1

Damien St E1 ......96 B1
Damon Cl DA14 ...168 A4
Damon Ct DA14 ...168 A4
Damory Ho 1 SE16 118 C2
Damson Dr UB3 ...106 A6
Damsonwood Rd
UB2 ....107 C3
Danbrook Rd SW16 182 A3
Dan Bryant Ho 5
SW12 ....159 C4
Danbury Cl RM6 ...58 D6
Danbury Mans 3
IG11 ....78 D1
Danbury Mews SM5,
SM6 ....219 B4
Danbury St N1 94 D5 234 D4
Danbury Way IG8 ..37 C2
Danby Ct EN2 .....5 A2
Danby Ho 23 E9 ...74 C1
3 W10 ....91 B4
Danby St SE15 ....139 D2
Dancer Rd
Fulham SW6 ..135 B4 264 C1
Richmond TW9 ....132 C2
Dando Cres SE3 ...143 B2
Dandridge Cl SE10 120 C1
Dandridge Ho E1 ..243 C4
Danebury W10 ....90 C2
New Addington CR0 .223 C2
Danebury Ave SW15 155 D5
Daneby Rd SE6 ...164 A2
Dane Cl BR6 ......227 B3
Sidcup DA5 ....169 C4
Danecourt Gdns CR0 221 B1
Danecroft Rd SE24 .161 B6
Danegrove Prim Sch
EN4 ....14 C5
Danegrove Sch EN4 .14 D5
Dane Ho 15 SE5 ...139 A3
Danehurst TW8 ...131 C1
Danehurst Gdns IG4 .56 B4
Danehurst St
SW6 ....135 A4 264 A2
Daneland EN4 .....14 C4
Danemead Gr UB5 ..63 D3
Danemere St SW15 134 C2
Dane Pl E3 ....97 B5
Dane Rd N18 ......18 C1
Ashford TW15 .....171 B4
Ealing W13 ....109 C5
Ilford IG1 ....79 A3
Merton SW19 ......180 A2
Southall UB1 ......107 A6
Danesbury Rd TW13 150 B3
Danescombe SE12 .165 A3
Danescourt Cres
SM1 ....218 A6
Danescroft NW4 ...46 D4
Danescroft Ave NW4 46 D4
Danescroft Gdns NW4 46 D4
Danes Ct NW8 ....230 C5
Wembley HA9 .....66 B5
Danesdale Rd E9 ..75 B2
Danesfield SE5 ....139 C6
Danes Gate HA1 ..42 C6
Danes Ho W10 ....90 C2
Dane St WC1 .....240 C3
Daneswood Ave SE6 164 A1
Danethorpe Rd HA0 .65 D2
Danetree Cl KT19 .215 A1
Danetree Jun Sch
KT19 ....215 A1
Danetree Rd KT19 .215 A1
Danette Gdns RM8 ..81 B6
Daneville Rd SE5 ..139 B4
Danford Ho 9 N11 .31 C2
Dangan Rd E11 ....55 A3
Daniel Bolt Cl E14 ..97 C2
Daniel Cl N18 .....34 C4
Twickenham TW4 ...151 A4
Upper Tooting SW17 .180 C4
Daniel Ct 8 NW9 ...27 C2
W3 ....111 C4
3 Beckenham BR3 .185 C3
Daniel Gdns SE15 .139 D5
Daniell Ho 1 ....235 D4
Daniell Way CR0 ..204 D2
Daniel Pl NW4 .....46 B2
Daniel Rd W5 .....110 B6
Daniel's Rd SE15 .140 C2
Dan Leno Wlk SW6 .265 C3
Dansey Pl W1 ....249 C6
Dansington Rd DA16 146 A1
Danson Cres DA16 .146 B2
Danson Intc DA5,DA6 168 C5
Danson La DA16 ...146 B1

Danson Mead DA16 ..146 C2
Danson Prim Sch
  DA16 ....146 A1
Danson Rd DA5,DA6,
  DA15 ....168 D6
Danson Underpass
  DA15 ....168 C5
Dante Rd
  SE11 ....116 D2 261 C4
Danube Ct 12 SE15 .139 D5
Danube St
  SW3 ....114 C1 257 B2
Danvers Ho 22 E1 ....96 A1
Danvers Rd N8 ......49 D5
Danvers St
  SW3 ....136 B6 266 D5
Da Palma Ct SW6 ..265 A5
Daphne Ct Ealing W5 .87 C1
  Worcester Park KT4 ...215 C6
Daphne Gdns E4 ....20 A1
Daphne Ho N22 ......32 C2
Daphne St SW18 ....158 A5
Daplyn St 6 E1 ......96 A2
D'arblay St W1 93 C1 239 B1
Darby Cres TW16 ...172 C1
Darby Gdns TW16 ...172 C1
Darcy Ave SM6 ......219 C4
Darcy Cl N20 ....14 B2
D'arcy Dr HA3 ......43 D5
D'arcy Gdns
  Dagenham RM9 ....103 B6
  Harrow HA3 ....44 A5
Darcy Ho E8 ....96 B6
D'arcy Pl BR2 ....209 A6
Darcy Rd
  Isleworth TW7 ......131 A4
  Thornton Heath SW16 .182 A1
D'arcy Rd SM3 ......216 D4
Dare Ct 2 E10 ......54 A2
Dare Gdns RM8 .....81 A5
Darell Prim Sch TW9 132 C2
Darell Rd TW9 ......132 C2
Daren Ct N7 ....72 A4
Darent Ho NW8 .....236 D4
  4 Catford BR1 .....186 B5
Darenth Rd DA16 ...146 A4
  N16 ....51 D1
Darfield NW1 ....232 A5
Darfield Rd SE4 ....163 B6
Darfield Way W10 ...90 D1
Darfur St SW15 ....134 D2
Dargate Cl SE19 ....183 D3
Darien Ho 8 E1 .....96 D2
  17 SW11 ....136 B2
Darien Rd SW11 ....136 B2
Daring Ho 21 E3 .....97 A5
Darland Ct SW15 ...157 B5
Darlands Dr EN5 ....12 D6
Darlan Rd
  SW6 ....135 B5 264 D3
Darlaston Rd SW19 .179 A3
Darley Cl CR0 ....207 A3
Darley Dr KT3 ......177 B1
Darley Gdns SM4 ...201 D3
Darley Ho SE11 .....260 C1
Darley Rd SW11 ....158 D5
  Edmonton N9 ....17 D3
Darling Ho 5 TW1 ..153 D5
Darling Rd SE4 .....141 C2
Darling Row E1 .....96 B3
Darlington Ct 8 SE6 164 D4
Darlington Ho SW8 .269 D3
  2 Surbiton KT6 ....197 D2
Darlington Rd SE27 .182 D5
Darmaine Cl CR2 ...221 A1
Darnay Ho 3 SE16 ..118 A3
Darndale Cl E17 ....35 B1
Darnell Ho 4 SE10 ..142 A4
  9 SE10 ....142 A5
Darnley Ho 9 E14 ...97 A1
Darnley Rd E9 ......74 C2
  Woodford IG8 ....37 B2
Darnley Terr 12 W11 .112 D5
Darrell Ct BR2 ......208 C6
Darrell Rd SE22 ....162 A6
Darren Cl N4 ....50 B2
Darrick Wood Ho
  BR6 ....227 A5
Darrick Wood Inf Sch
  BR6 ....226 D5
Darrick Wood Jun Sch
  BR6 ....226 D4
Darrick Wood Rd
  BR6 ....227 B6
Darrick Wood Sec Sch
  BR6 ....226 D4

Darrick Wood Sports Ctr
  BR6 ....227 C6
Darris Cl UB4 ....85 A3
Darsley Dr
  SW8 ....138 A4 270 A2
Dartford Ave N9 ....18 D5
Dartford Gdns RM6 .58 B4
Dartford Ho SE1 ...263 D4
Dartford St SE17 ...139 A6
Dartington NW1 ...232 B5
Dartington Ho
  7 SW8 ....137 D3
  W2 ....91 D2
Dartle Ct 26 SE16 ..118 A4
Dartmoor Wlk 17
  E14 ....119 C2
Dartmouth Cl W11 ...91 C1
Dartmouth Ct SE10 142 A4
Dartmouth Gr SE10 142 A4
Dartmouth Hill SE10 142 A4
Dartmouth Ho N19 ..71 B6
  Lewisham SE10 .....142 A3
  Thornton Heath CR0 ..204 D2
Dartmouth Park Ave
  NW5 ....71 B5
Dartmouth Park Hill
  N19 ....71 B6
Dartmouth Park Rd
  NW5 ....71 B5
Dartmouth Pl
  Chiswick W4 ....133 C6
  Forest Hill SE23 ...162 A2
Dartmouth Rd NW2 ..68 C2
  NW4 ....46 A3
  Forest Hill SE23,SE26 ..162 A1
  Hayes BR2 ....209 A2
  Ruislip HA4 ....62 A5
Dartmouth Row SE10 142 A4
Dartmouth St
  SW1 ....115 D4 249 D1
Dartmouth Terr SE10 142 A4
Dartnell Rd CR0 ....205 D2
Darton Ct W3 ....111 A5
Dartrey Twr SW10 ..266 C4
Dartrey Wlk
  SW10 ....136 A5 266 B4
Dart St W10 ....91 B4
Darville Rd N16 .....73 D5
Darwell Cl E6 ......100 C5
Darwen Pl E2 ....96 B6
Darwin Cl BR6 .....227 B3
  N11 ....15 B1
Darwin Ct E13 ......99 B4
  NW1 ....231 B6
  SE9 ....166 C5
Darwin Dr UB1 .....85 D1
Darwin Gdns WD19 ..22 C5
Darwin Ho 2 HA9 ...67 A5
  SW1 ....260 A3
  W5 ....109 C2
  Tottenham N22 .....32 C1
Darwin St
  SE17 ....117 B2 262 D4
Daryngton Dr UB6 ..86 C5
Daryngton Ho SW8 .270 A3
Dashwood Cl DA6 ..169 C6
Dashwood Ct TW3 ..130 A1
Dashwood Ho SE21 .161 D1
Dashwood Rd N8 ....50 B3
Dassett Rd SE27 ...182 D5
Data Point Bsns Ctr
  E16 ....98 B3
Datchelor Pl 14 SE5 .139 B4
Datchet Ho NW1 ...231 D2
Datchet Rd SE6 ....163 B4
Datchett Ho 40 E2 ..95 D4
Datchwood Ct N4 ...73 A5
Datchworth Ct 7 EN1 17 C6
Datchworth Ho 8 N1 .72 D1
Date St SE17 .117 B1 262 C1
Daubeney Gdns N17 .33 A3
Daubeney Pl 7 TW9 173 D1
Daubeney Prim Sch
  E5 ....75 A4
Daubeney Rd E5 ....75 A4
  Tottenham N17 .....33 A3
Daubeney Twr 2
  SE8 ....119 B1
Dault Rd SW18 .....158 A5
Dauney Ho SE1 ....251 C1
Dave Adams Ho 7 E3 97 B5
Davenant Ho 18 E1 ..96 A2
Davenant Rd N19 ...71 D6
  Croydon CR0,CR9 ...220 D4
Davenant St E1 .....96 A2
Davenport Cl TW11 .175 A4
Davenport Ctr IG11 .102 B5
Davenport Ho SE11 .261 A1
Davenport Lo TW5 ..129 A3
Davenport Rd DA14 .169 A2

Davenport Rd continued
  SE6 ....164 A5
Daventer Dr HA7 ....24 D3
Daventry Ave E17 ...53 C3
Daventry St
  NW1 ....92 C2 237 A4
Dave Porter Hts
  SW19 ....157 A4
Daver Ct SW3 ......257 B1
Davern Cl SE10 ....120 D2
Davet Ct SW8 ......270 C2
Davey Cl N7 ....72 B2
  Bowes Park N13 ....32 B5
Davey Lo 2 N1 .....72 C1
Davey Rd E9 ....75 C1
Davey's Ct WC2 ...250 A6
Davey St SE15 .....139 D6
David Ave UB6 .....86 C5
David Cl UB3 ....127 C5
David Coffer Ct DA17 125 D2
David Devine Ho 7
  E8 ....74 A3
Davidge Ho SE1 ...251 B1
Davidge St
  SE1 ....116 D4 251 D1
David Ho 3 E14 ....97 D2
  SW8 ....270 A4
  8 Putney SW15 ....156 A6
  South Norwood SE25 ..206 A6
David Lee Point 4
  E15 ....98 C6
David Livingstone Prim
  Sch CR7 ....183 A2
David Mews W1 ....237 D4
David Rd RM8 ......81 A6
Davidson Gdns
  SW8 ....138 A5 270 A4
Davidson Ho 7 N19 .71 C4
Davidson Inf Sch
  CR0 ....205 D2
Davidson Jun Sch
  CR0 ....205 D2
Davidson Lo CR0 ..205 C2
Davidson Rd CR0 ..205 D3
Davidson Terrs E7 ..77 B3
Davidson Twr BR1 .187 B5
David's Rd SE23 ...162 C3
David St E15 ....76 B3
David Twigg Cl KT2 176 A2
Davies Cl CR0 .....206 A3
Davies La E11 ......76 C6
Davies Lane Jun & Inf Sch
  E11 ....76 D6
Davies Mews W1 ..248 C6
Davies St W1 115 B6 248 C6
Davies Walk TW7 ..130 B4
Da Vinci Ct 12 SE16 118 B1
Davington Gdns RM8 80 B3
Davington Rd RM8 .80 A3
Davis Ho W12 ......112 B6
Davis Rd W3 ....111 D4
  Chessington KT9 ...214 C4
Davis St E13 ....99 B5
Davisville Rd W12 ..112 A4
Davmor Ct TW8 ....109 C1
Davy Ho HA9 ....67 A6
Dawes Ave TW7 ...131 A1
Dawe's Ct 2 SE15 .139 B4
Dawes Ho SE17 ...262 C3
Dawes Rd
  SW6 ....135 B5 264 C4
Dawe's Rd UB10 ...82 A5
Dawes St
  SE17 ....117 B1 262 D2
Dawley Ave UB8 ...83 A1
Dawley Par 1 ......105 A6
Dawley Rd Hayes UB3 105 B6
  Hayes UB3 ....105 C2
Dawlish Ave
  Bowes Park N13 ....32 A5
  Wandsworth SW18 ..157 D2
  Wembley UB6 ....87 A5
Dawlish Dr Ilford IG3 79 D4
  Pinner HA5 ....41 A3
  Ruislip HA4 ....62 B6
Dawlish Prim Sch E10 54 A1
Dawlish Rd E10 ....76 A6
  N17 ....54 A6
  NW2 ....68 D2
Dawnay Gdns SW18 158 B2
Dawnay Rd SW17,
  SW18 ....158 B2
Dawn Cl TW4 ....129 A2
Dawn Cres E15 .....98 B6
Dawn Wlk BR2 .....186 B1
Dawpool Rd NW2 ..67 D6
Daws Ho 35 W12 ...112 B6
Daws La NW7 ......28 A5
Dawson Ave BR5 ...190 B1

Dawson Ave continued
  Barking IG11 ....79 D1
Dawson Cl SE18 ...123 A2
  Hayes UB3 ....83 B2
Dawson Gdns 9 IG11 79 D1
Dawson Ho 23 E2 ...96 C4
  5 SE5 ....139 C4
Dawson Pl
  W2 ....113 C6 245 B6
Dawson Rd NW2 ...68 C2
  Kingston KT1 ....198 B6
Dawson St E2 ......95 D3
Dawson Terr N9 ....18 C4
Dax Ct TW16 ......194 C6
Daybrook Rd SW19 201 D6
Day Ho SE5 ....138 D5
  2 SE5 ....139 C4
Daylesford Ave SW15 134 A1
Daymer Gdns HA5 ..40 C5
Daynor Ho 4 NW6 ..91 C6
Daysbrook Rd SW2 .160 B3
Days La DA15 ......167 C4
Days Lane Prim Sch
  DA15 ....167 B5
Daytone Ho SW20 .178 D2
Dayton Gr SE15 ...140 C4
Deaconess Ct 4 N15 .51 D5
Deacon Ho SE11 ..260 D3
Deacon Mews N1 ..73 B1
Deacon Rd NW2 ...68 A2
  Kingston KT2 ....176 B2
Deacons Cl HA5 ...22 B1
Deacons Hts WD6 ..10 C5
Deacons Leas BR6 227 B4
Deacons Rise N2 ..48 B4
Deacons Wlk TW12 173 C6
Deacon Way
  SE17 ....117 A2 262 B4
Deal Ct 13 NW9 ....27 C1
  7 Southall UB1 ....86 A1
Deal Ho SE15 ......140 D6
  SE17 ....263 B2
Deal Porters Way
  SE16 ....118 D3
Deal Rd SW17 .....181 A4
Deal St E1 ....96 A3
Dealtry Rd SW15 ...134 C1
Deal Wlk 3 SW9 ...138 C5
Dean Bradley St
  SW1 ....260 A5
Dean Cl E9 ....74 C3
  SE16 ....118 C5
  Hillingdon UB10 ....60 B1
Deancross St E1 ...96 C1
Dean Ct SW8 ......270 A3
  Edgware HA8 ....26 D4
  10 Kingston KT2 ...176 C2
  Wembley HA0 ......65 B5
Dean Dr HA7 ......26 A1
Deane Ave HA4 ....62 C3
Deane Croft Rd HA5 40 C3
Deanery Cl N2 .....48 C5
Deanery Mews W1 .248 B4
Deanery Rd E15 ...76 C2
Deanery St
  W1 ....115 A5 248 B4
Deane Way HA4 ...40 B3
Dean Farrar St SW1 259 D6
Deanfield Gdns CR0 221 B4
Dean Gdns E17 ....54 B5
Deanhill Ct 2 SW14 132 D1
Deanhill Rd SW14 .132 D1
Dean Ho 18 E1 .....96 C1
  N16 ....51 D1
  N4 ....51 A1
  SE14 ....141 B5
  Ruislip HA4 ....39 B1
Dean Rd NW2 ......68 C2
  Croydon CR0 ....221 B4
  Hampton TW12 .....173 C5
  Hounslow TW3 .....151 B4
  Thamesmead SE28 ..124 A6
Dean Ryle St SW1 .260 A4
Dean's Bldgs
  SE17 ....117 B2 262 D3
Deansbrook Cl HA8 .27 A3
Deansbrook Jun & Inf
  Schs HA8,NW7 ....27 A4
Deansbrook Rd HA8 27 B4
  Edgware HA8 ....26 D3
Deans Cl HA8 ......27 A4
  Chiswick W4 ....132 C6
  South Croydon CR0 .221 D5
Deanscroft Ave NW9 45 A1
Dean's Ct EC4 .....241 D1
Dean's Dr HA8 .....27 B5
Deans Dr N13 ......32 D4
Deansfield Prim HA4 62 D4

Deansfield Prim Sch
  SE9 ....144 C2
Deans Gate Cl SE23 162 D1
Deanshanger Ho 21
  SE8 ....118 D2
Dean's La HA8 .....27 A4
Dean's Mews W1 ...238 C2
Deans Rd SM1 .....217 D5
Dean St E7 ....77 A3
  W1 ....93 D1 239 C1
Dean Stanley St SW1 260 A5
Deansway N2 ......48 B5
Deansway N9 ......17 C1
Deanswood N11 ...31 D4
Dean's Yd SW1 ....259 D6
Dean Trench St SW1 260 A5
Dean Way UB2 .....107 D4
Dean Wlk HA8 .....27 B4
Dearmer Ho 6 SW2 160 C4
Dearne Cl HA7 .....25 A5
De'arn Gdns CR4 ..202 C6
Dearsley Rd EN1 ...6 A2
Deason St E15 .....98 A6
Deauville Ct 4 SE16 118 D4
  14 SW4 ....159 C5
Deauville Mans 13
  SW4 ....159 C5
De Barowe Mews N5 72 D3
Debdale Ho 20 E2 ..96 A6
Debden N17 ....33 B1
Debden Cl
  Kingston KT2 ....175 D5
  Woodford IG8 ....37 D3
De Beauvoir Cres N1 .95 C6
De Beauvoir Ct N1 .73 B1
De Beauvoir Pl 5 N1 .73 C2
De Beauvoir Prim Sch
  N1 ....73 C2
De Beauvoir Rd N1 .73 C1
De Beauvoir Sq N1 .73 C1
Debenham Ct E8 ...96 A6
  Barnet EN5 ....12 C6
Debham Ct NW2 ...68 C5
Debnams Rd SE16 .118 C2
De Bohun Ave N14 .15 B5
De Bohun Prim Sch
  N14 ....15 B6
Deborah Cl TW7 ...130 C4
Deborah Cres HA4 .39 B2
Deborah Ho 7 E18 .55 B6
De Broome Rd TW13 150 C3
De Burgh Ho 10
  SW19 ....180 A3
Deburgh Rd SW19 .180 A3
Debussy 9 NW9 ....27 C1
  10 Kingston KT2 ...176 C2
Decimal Ctr UB2 ...107 C4
Decima St
  SE1 ....117 C3 263 A6
Decimus Cl CR7 ...205 B6
Deck Cl SE16 ......118 D5
Decoy Ave NW11 ...47 A5
De Crespigny Pk SE5 139 B3
Dedham St E6 .....186 A6
Dee Ct W7 ....86 B1
Deena Cl W3 ....88 B1
Deepdale N4 ....72 C5
  Wimbledon SW19 ...178 A6
Deepdale Ave BR2 .208 D5
Deepdale Cl N11 ...31 A4
Deepdale Ct 4 CR0 221 B4
Deepdene N12 .....30 C6
Deepdene Ave CR0 221 D5
Deepdene Cl E11 ..55 A5
Deepdene Ct
  Beckenham BR2 ....208 C6
  Southgate N21 .....16 D5
Deepdene Gdns SW2 160 B4
Deepdene Ho N16 ..51 B1
Deepdene Lo 5 SW2 160 B1
Deepdene Mans
  SW6 ....264 C2
Deepdene Point 9
  SE26 ....162 D1
Deepdene Rd DA16 146 A2
  SE5,SE24 ....139 B1
Deepwell Cl TW7 ..131 A4
Deepwood La UB6 ..86 B4
Deerbrook Rd SE24,
  SW2 ....160 D3
Dee Rd TW9 ....132 B1
Deerdale Rd SE24 .139 A1
Deerhurst 7 KT2 ..176 D2
Deerhurst Cl TW13 172 B6
Deerhurst Cres
  TW12 ....174 A6

Deerhurst Ho 6
  SE15 ....140 A6
Deerhurst Rd NW2 .68 D2
  Streatham SW16 ...182 B5
Deerings Dr HA5 ...40 A4
Deerleap Gr E4 ....19 D6
Deer Lo SW6 ......135 A2
Deer Park Cl KT2 ..176 D3
Deer Park Gdns CR4 202 B5
Deer Park Rd SW19 180 A1
Deer Park Way BR2 224 D6
Deeside Rd SW17 .158 B1
Dee St E14 ....98 A1
Defiance Wlk SE18 122 B3
Defiant 18 NW9 ....27 D1
Defiant Way SM6 ..220 B1
Defoe Ave TW9 ....132 C5
Defoe Cl SW17 ....180 C4
Defoe Ho EC2 .....242 A4
  5 N16 ....73 C5
Defoe Pl EC2 ......242 A4
  Upper Tooting SW17 .180 D6
Defoe Rd N16 .....73 C5
  SE16 ....119 B4
De Frene Rd SE26 .163 A1
De Gama Pl E14 ...119 C1
Degema Rd BR7 ...188 D5
Dehar Cres NW9 ...46 A2
De Havilland Cl UB5 84 D4
De Havilland Rd
  Edgware HA8 ....26 D1
  Heston TW5 ....128 C5
De Havilland Way
  TW19 ....148 A5
Dekker Ho 19 SE5 .139 B5
Dekker Rd SE21 ...161 C5
Delacourt Rd SE3 .143 B5
Delafield Ho 18 E1 ..96 A1
Delafield Rd SE7 ...121 C1
Delaford Rd SE16 ..118 B1
Delaford St
  SW6 ....135 B6 264 B5
Delamare Cres CR0 206 C3
Delamere Gdns NW7 27 D4
Delamere Ho 4 N4 ..51 B2
Delamere Rd W5 ..110 A4
  Hayes UB4 ....106 D6
  Wimbledon SW20 ..178 D2
Delamere St W2 ...236 A3
Delamere Terr W2 ..91 D2
Delancey Pas NW1 231 D5
Delancey St
  NW1 ....93 B6 231 D5
Delancey Studios
  NW1 ....231 D5
Delany Ho SE10 ...142 A6
Delarch Ho SE1 ...251 C1
De Laune St
  SE17 ....116 D1 261 C1
Delaware Rd W9 ...91 D3
Delawyk Cres SE24 161 B5
Delcombe Ave KT4 200 C1
Delft Ho 8 KT2 ....176 B3
Delft Way 2 SE22 .161 C6
Delhi Rd EN1 ......17 D4
Delhi St N1 ..94 A6 233 B5
Delia St SW18 .....157 D4
Delisle Rd SE28 ...123 C5
Delius Cl WD6 .....9 C5
Delius Gr E15 ......98 A5
Dellafield N4 ......72 C6
Della Path E5 .....74 B5
Dellbow Rd TW14 .150 B6
Dell Cl E15 ....98 B6
  Wallington SM6 ....219 D4
  Woodford IG8 ......21 D1
Dellfield Cl BR3 ...186 A2
Dell La KT17 ......216 A3
Dellors Cl EN5 ....12 D6
Dellow Cl IG2 ......57 B2
Dellow Ho 6 E1 ...118 B6
Dellow St E1 ......118 B6
Dell Rd Enfield EN3 ..6 C5
  Stoneleigh KT17 ...216 A2
  West Drayton UB7 .104 B3
Dells Cl Chingford E4 .19 D4
  Teddington TW11 ..174 D4
Dell's Mews SW1 ..259 B3
Dell The SE2 ......124 A1
  Brentford TW8 .....131 C6
  Feltham TW14 .....150 B4
  Pinner HA5 ....22 D1
  South Norwood SE19 .183 D2
  Wembley HA0 ......65 B3
  Woodford IG8 ......21 B1
Dell Way W13 .....87 C1
Dell Wlk KT3 ......177 C1
Dellwood Gdns IG5 .56 C6
Delme Cres SE3 ...143 B3
Delmey Cl CR0 ....221 D5

Deloraine Ho SE8 ......141 C4
Deloraine St SE8 ......141 C4
Delorme St W6 ....134 D6
Delphian Ct 5 SW16 182 C6
Delroy Ct N20 ....14 A4
Delta Bldg 4 E14 ...98 A1
Delta Cl KT4 ....215 D5
Delta Ct NW2 ....68 A4
Delta Gr UB5 ....84 D4
Delta Ho N1 ....235 D2
Delta Pk SW18 ....135 D1
Delta Rd KT4 ....215 C6
Delta St 3 E2 ....96 A4
De Lucy Prim Sch
  SE2 ....124 B4
De Lucy St SE2 ......124 B2
Delvan Cl SE18 ......144 C5
Delverton Ho SE17 .261 D2
Delverton Rd SE17 .261 D1
Delvino Rd
  SW6 ....135 C4 265 B3
De Mandeville Ct E4 ..35 A6
De Mandeville Gate
  EN1 ....6 B1
Demesne Rd SM6 ..219 D4
Demeta Cl HA9 ....67 A5
De Montfort Par 1
  SW16 ....160 A1
De Montfort Rd
  SW16 ....160 A2
De Morgan Rd SW6 .135 D2
Dempster Cl KT6 ....197 C1
Dempster Rd SW18 .158 A6
Denberry Dr DA14 ...168 B1
Denbigh Cl BR7 ......188 B4
  NW10 ....67 C1
  W11 ....113 B6 244 D6
  Cheam SM1 ....217 B3
  Ruislip HA4 ....61 D6
  Southall UB1 ....85 B1
Denbigh Ct E6 ....99 D4
  1 Ealing W7 ....86 D2
Denbigh Dr UB3 ....105 A4
Denbigh Gdns TW10 154 B6
Denbigh Ho SW1 ...257 D6
  W11 ....244 D6
  7 W11 ....91 B1
Denbigh Mews SW1 .259 A3
Denbigh Pl
  SW1 ....115 C1 259 A2
Denbigh Rd E6 ....99 D4
  W11 ....113 B6 244 D6
  Ealing W13 ....87 B1
  Hounslow TW3 ....129 D3
  Southall UB1 ....85 B1
Denbigh St
  SW1 ....115 C1 259 B2
Denbigh Terr
  W11 ....113 B6 244 D6
Denbridge Rd BR1,
  BR7 ....188 B1
Denbury Ho 48 E3 ...97 C4
Denby Ct SE11 ......260 D4
Dence Ho 20 E2 .....96 A4
Denchworth Ho 15
  SW9 ....138 C3
Den Cl BR2,BR3 ....208 B6
Dencliffe TW15 .....170 C5
Dendridge Cl EN1 ....6 B6
Dendy St SW12 .....159 A3
Dene Ave DA15 .....168 B4
  Hounslow TW3 ....129 B2
Dene Cl SE4 ....141 A1
  Hayes BR2 ....208 D1
  Worcester Park KT4 .215 D6
Denecroft Cres UB10 .82 D6
Dene Ct W7 ....108 D4
  Ealing W5 ....87 C2
Dene Gdns
  Hinchley Wood KT7 ..213 A6
  Stanmore HA7 .....25 C5
Dene Ho N14 ....15 D4
Denehurst Gdns NW4 .46 C3
  Acton W3 ....110 D5
  Richmond TW10 ..132 C1
  Twickenham TW2 .152 B4
  Woodford IG8 ....37 B6
Dene Mans 1 NW6 ..69 C2
Dene Rd N11 ....14 D2
  Buckhurst Hill IG9 ...21 D3
Denesmead SE24 ..161 A6
Dene The Ealing W13 .87 B2
  East Molesey KT12,KT8 195 B4
  South Croydon CR0 .222 D4
  Wembley HA9 ......66 A4
Dengie Wlk N1 .....235 A6
Denham Cl
Denham Cres CR4 ..202 D5

Denham Ct
  Forest Hill SE26 ....162 B1
  Southall UB1 ......108 A6
Denham Dr IG2 ....57 A3
Denham Ho 32 W12 .112 B6
Denham Lo W5 ....88 A1
Denham Rd N20 ......14 D1
  Feltham TW14 .....150 C4
Denham St SE10 ....121 A1
Denham Way IG11 .101 D6
Denholme Rd W9 ....91 B4
Denise Ct HA0 ....65 C4
Denison Cl N2 ....48 A6
Denison Ho 8 E14 ...97 C1
Denison Rd Ealing W5 .87 C3
  Feltham TW13 .....171 D6
  Mitcham SW19 ....180 B4
Deniston Ave DA5 ..169 A3
Denland Ho SW8 ....270 D3
Denleigh Gdns
  Southgate N21 ......16 C4
  Thames Ditton KT7 .196 C3
Denman Dr NW11 ....47 C4
  Ashford TW15 .....170 D4
  Claygate KT10 .....213 A3
Denman Dr N NW11 ..47 C4
Denman Dr S NW11 ..47 C4
Denman Ho N16 ......73 C6
Denman Rd SE15 ...139 D3
Denman St W1 ......249 C5
Denmark Ave SW19 .179 A3
Denmark Ct SM4 ....201 C4
Denmark Gdns SM5 .218 D5
Denmark Gr N1 .....234 A4
Denmark Hill SE5 ..139 B3
Denmark Hill Dr NW9 .46 A6
Denmark Hill Sta
  SE5 ....139 B3
Denmark Ho 9 SE7 .122 A2
Denmark Mans 14
  SE5 ....139 A3
Denmark Pl WC2 ...239 D2
Denmark Rd BR1 ...187 B2
  N8 ....50 C5
  NW6 ....91 B5
  SE5 ....139 A3
  Carshalton SM5 ...218 D5
  Croydon SE25 .....206 B4
  Ealing W13 ....109 B6
  Kingston KT1 ......198 A6
  Twickenham TW2 .152 B1
  Wimbledon SW19 .178 D4
Denmark St 6 E11 ..76 C5
  E13 ....99 B2
  WC2 ....239 D2
  Tottenham N17 .....34 B3
Denmark Terr NW2 ..48 C6
Denmead Ho 8
  SW15 ....155 D5
Denmead Rd CR0 ...204 D1
Denmead Sch TW12 .173 D3
Denmead Upper Sch
  TW12 ....173 D3
Denmore Ct SM6 ...219 B3
Dennan Rd KT6 .....198 B1
Dennard Way BR6 ..226 C4
Denner Rd E4 ....19 C2
Denne Terr E8 ....95 D6
Dennett Rd CR0 ....204 C2
Dennett's Gr SE14 .140 D3
Dennett's Rd SE14 .140 C4
Denning Ave CR0 ..220 C3
Denning Cl
  NW8 ....92 A4 229 B1
  Hampton TW12 ...173 B5
Denning Point E1 ..243 D2
Denning Rd NW3 ....70 B4
Dennington Cl 17 E5 .74 B6
Dennington Park Rd
  NW6 ....69 C2
Denningtons The
  KT4 ....215 C6
Dennis Ave HA9 .....66 B3
Dennis Cl TW15 ....171 B3
Dennis Ct SE14 ......51 B1
Dennis Gdns HA7 ...25 C5
Dennis Ho 4 E3 .....97 B5
  Sutton SM1 ....217 C4
Dennis La HA7 ....25 B6
Dennison Point E15 .76 A1
Dennis Par 1 N14 ...15 D3
Dennis Park Cres
  SW20 ....179 A2
Dennis Rd KT8 .....196 A5
Dennis Reeve Cl CR4 180 C1
Dennis Way SW4 ..137 D2
Denny Cl 15 E6 .....100 A2
Denny Cres SE11 ...261 B2
Denny Gdns RM9 ....80 B2

Denny Rd N9 ....18 B3
Denny St
  SE11 ....116 C1 261 B2
Den Rd BR2 ....208 B6
Densham Ho NW8 ..229 D3
Densham Rd E15 .....98 C6
Densole Cl BR3 ....185 A3
Denstone Ho 5 SE15 140 A6
Densworth Gr N9 ...18 C2
Dent Ho SE17 ......263 A3
Denton NW1 ....71 A2
Denton Cl EN5 ....12 C6
Denton Ho N1 ....72 D1
Denton Rd N8 ....50 B3
  Bexley DA16 ......146 C5
  Edmonton N18 .....33 C6
  Twickenham TW1 .153 D5
Denton St SW18 ...157 D5
Denton Way E5 ......74 D5
Dents Rd SW11 ....158 D1
Denvale Trade Pk
  CR4 ....202 B5
Denver Cl BR6 .....211 C3
Denver Rd N16 ....51 C2
Denwood SE23 .....162 D1
Denyer Ho 1 NW5 ..71 B4
Denyer St
  SW3 ....114 C2 257 B4
Denys Bldg EC1 ....241 A4
Denziloe Ave UB10 ..82 D4
Denzil Rd NW10 .....67 D3
Deodar Rd SW15 ...135 A1
Deodora Cl N20 ......14 C2
Depot App NW2 ......68 C4
Depot Rd W12 ......112 C6
  Isleworth TW3,TW7 .130 B2
Depot St SE5 ....139 B6
Deptford Bridge SE8 141 C4
Deptford Bridge Sta
  SE8 ....141 C4
Deptford Broadway
  SE8,SE14 ....141 C4
Deptford Church St
  SE8 ....141 C5
Deptford Ferry Rd 12
  E14 ....119 C2
Deptford Gn SE8 ...141 C6
Deptford Green Sch
  SE14 ....141 B6
Deptford Green Sch
(Annexe) SE14 ....141 A5
Deptford High St
  SE8 ....141 C5
Deptford Park Prim Sch
  SE8 ....119 A1
Deptford Sta SE8 ..141 C5
Deptford Trad Est
  SE8 ....141 A6
Deptford Wharf SE8 .119 B2
Dept of Transport &
Environment SE1 ..259 D5
De Quincey Mews 3
  E16 ....121 A5
De Quincey Rd N17 .33 B2
Derby Ave N12 ....30 A5
  Harrow HA3 ....24 B2
  Romford RM7 ......59 D3
Derby Ct 8 E5 ....74 D4
  Woodford IG8 ......36 D2
Derby Gate SW1 ...250 A2
Derby Hill SE23 ....162 C2
Derby Hill Cres SE23 162 C2
Derby Ho NW4 ....46 C6
  SE11 ....261 A4
  Pinner HA5 ....22 D1
Derby Lo N3 ....29 B1
Derby Rd E7 ....77 D1
  E9 ....96 C6
  N18 ....34 C5
  Cheam SM1,SM2 ..217 B2
  Enfield EN3 ....18 C6
  Greenford UB6 .....85 D6
  Hounslow TW3 ....129 D1
  Merton SW19 .....179 C3
  Mortlake SW14 ...132 C1
  Surbiton KT5,KT6 .198 C1
  Thornton Heath CR0 .204 D1
  Woodford IG8 ......36 D2
Derby Rd Ind Est
  TW3 ....129 C1
Derbyshire St E2 ....96 A4
Derby St W1 ....248 B3
Dereham Ho 7 SE4 .140 D1
Dereham Pl EC2 ...243 B6
Dereham Rd IG11 ...79 D3
Derek Ave
  Chessington KT19 .214 D3
  Wallington SM6 ...219 B4
  Wembley HA9 ......66 D1
Derek Cl KT19 .....214 D3

Derek Walcott Cl
  SE24 ....160 D6
Dericote St E8 ....96 B6
Deri Dene Cl 2
  TW19 ....148 A5
Derifall Cl E6 ....100 B2
Dering Cl CR0 ......221 A4
Dering Rd CR0 .....221 A4
Dering St W1 ......238 D1
Derinton Rd SW17 .181 A6
Derley Rd UB2 .....106 D3
Dermody Gdns SE13 164 B6
Dermody Rd SE13 .164 B6
Deronda Rd SE24,
  SW2 ....160 D3
Deroy Cl SM5 ......218 D2
Deroy Ct SM5 ......218 D2
Derrick Gdns SE7 .121 C2
Derrick Ho 13 SW2 .160 C3
Derrick Rd BR3 ....207 B5
Derrick Rd SW11 ...158 D5
Derrycombe Ho W11 .91 B2
  18 W2 ....91 C2
Derry Rd CR0,SM6 .220 A5
Derry St W8 ..113 D4 245 C1
Dersingham Ave E12 .78 C3
Dersingham Inf Sch
  E12 ....78 C3
Dersingham Rd NW2 .69 A5
Derwent NW1 ......232 A1
Derwent Ave NW7 ..27 B4
  NW9 ....45 C4
  Barnet, London EN4 ..14 D3
  Edmonton N18 .....33 B5
  Kingston SW15 ...177 C6
  Pinner HA5 ....23 A4
  Uxbridge UB10 .....60 C5
Derwent Cl
  Claygate KT10 .....212 D2
  East Bedfont TW14 .149 D3
Derwent Cres DA7 .147 C3
  N20 ....14 A1
  Stanmore HA7 ......25 C1
Derwent Ct N8 ......50 A3
  8 SE16 ....118 C4
  2 W6 ....112 A2
Derwent Dr BR5 ...211 D2
  Hayes UB4 ....83 C2
Derwent Gdns
  Redbridge IG4 ......56 A5
  Wembley HA9 ......43 C2
Derwent Gr SE22 ..139 D1
Derwent Ho E3 ......97 B3
  SW7 ....256 B
  Penge SE20 ....184 B1
Derwent Lo
  Hounslow TW7 ....130 D1
  North Cheam KT4 .216 B6
Derwent Rd W5 ....109 C3
  Palmers Green N13 .16 B1
  Penge SE20 ....184 B1
  Southall UB1 ....85 B1
  Twickenham TW2 .151 D1
  West Barnes SM4 ..200 A3
Derwent Rise NW9 ..45 C3
Derwent St SE10 ..120 C1
Derwentwater Mans 2
  W3 ....111 A1
Derwentwater Prim Sch
  W3 ....111 A1
Derwentwater Rd
  W3 ....111 A1
Derwent Wlk SM6 .219 B1
Derwent Yd W5 ....109 C3
De Salis Rd UB10 ...83 A3
Desborough Cl W2 ..91 D2
  Lower Halliford TW17 .192 C2
Desborough Ct SE25 206 B5
Desborough Ho W14 264 D6
Desenfans Rd SE21 .161 C5
Desford Rd E16 ......98 D3
Desford Way TW15 .148 B2
Design Mus★
  SE1 ....117 D4 253 D2
Desmond Ho 4 EN4 .14 D1
Desmond St SE14 ..141 A6
Despard Ho SW2 ..160 C2
Despard Rd N19 ......49 C1
Dessouter 19 NW9 ..27 C1
Detherick Ct TW3 ..130 A1
Dethick Ct E3 ....97 A6
Detling Ho SE17 ...263 A3
Detling Rd BR1 ....187 A5
Detmold Rd E5 ....74 C6
Deutsche Schule
  TW10 ....153 D3
Devalls Cl E6 ......122 D4
Devana End SM5 ..218 D2
Devas Rd SW20 ...178 C2
Devas St E3 ....97 D3
Devema Cl BR7 ....188 C2

Devenay Rd E15 .....76 D1
Devenish Rd SE2 ..124 A4
Deventer Cres 8
  SE22 ....161 C6
De Vere Cotts W8 ..256 A6
De Vere Gdns
  W8 ....114 A4 246 A1
  Redbridge IG1 ......56 B1
Devereux Ct WC2 .241 A1
De Vere Mews W8 .256 A6
Devereux Ho 7
  SW15 ....156 A6
Devereux La SW13 .134 B5
Devereux Rd SW11 .158 D5
Deverill Ct SE20 ...184 C2
Devey Cl KT2 ......177 B5
Devitt Ho 4 E14 ...119 C6
Devizes St N1 ......235 D5
Devon Ave TW2 ....152 A3
Devon Cl N17 ....51 D6
  Chigwell IG9 ....21 B2
  Wembley UB6 ......87 C6
Devon Ct 3 Acton W3 .88 C1
  2 Ealing W7 ....86 D2
Devon Gdns N4 .....50 D3
Devon Ho E17 ....35 B1
  Penge SE20 ....184 B6
Devoncroft Gdns
  TW1 ....153 A4
Devonhurst Pl 4 W4 111 B1
Devonia Gdns N18 ..33 A4
Devonia Rd
  N1 ....94 D5 234 D4
Devon Mans SE1 ..253 B2
Devon Par HA3 ......43 C4
Devonport W2 ......237 A2
Devonport Gdns IG1 .56 B3
Devonport Ho 23 W2 .91 C2
Devonport Rd W12 .112 B4
Devonport St E1 .....96 C1
Devon Rd IG11 ....101 C6
Devon Rise N2 ......48 B5
Devonshire Ave SM2 218 A1
Devonshire Cl E15 ..76 C4
  W1 ....238 C4
  Edmonton N13 ......32 C6
Devonshire Cres NW7 28 D3
Devonshire Ct
  Croydon CR0 ....207 C1
  Feltham TW13 .....150 B2
  6 Richmond TW9 .132 B4
  Tottenham N17 .....33 A4
Devonshire Dr SE10 141 D4
  Long Ditton KT6 ...213 D6
Devonshire Gdns
  Chiswick W4 ......133 A5
  Edmonton N21 ......17 A4
  Tottenham N17 .....33 A4
Devonshire Gr SE15 140 B6
Devonshire Hall 14 E9 74 C2
Devonshire Hill La
  N17 ....33 A4
Devonshire Hill Prim Sch
  N17 ....33 B4
Devonshire Ho N12 .14 A1
  NW6 ....69 B2
  SE1 ....262 A6
  SW1 ....259 D2
  W2 ....236 D4
  14 Balham SW12 .159 B4
  Hounslow TW3 ....130 A2
  2 Putney SW15 ...156 C4
  10 Sutton SM2 ....218 A1
Devonshire Hospl
  W1 ....93 A2 238 B4
Devonshire House Prep
  Sch NW3 ....70 B3
Devonshire House Sch
  NW3 ....70 A3
Devonshire Mews 2
  W4 ....111 C1
Devonshire Mews N
  W1 ....238 C4
Devonshire Mews S
  W1 ....238 C4
Devonshire Mews W
  W1 ....238 C4
Devonshire Pl NW2 ..69 C5
  W1 ....93 A2 238 B4
  W8 ....255 C5
Devonshire Place Mews
  W1 ....238 B4
Devonshire Prim Sch
  SM2 ....218 A1
Devonshire Rd DA6 147 A1
  E16 ....99 A3
  E17 ....53 C3
  N9 ....18 C3

Devonshire Rd continued
  NW7 ....28 D3
  W4 ....111 C1
  W5 ....109 C3
  Chislehurst SE9 ...166 A2
  Edmonton N13 ......32 C6
  Feltham TW13 .....173 A6
  Forest Hill SE23 ...162 C4
  Hackbridge SM5,SM6 219 A4
  Harrow HA1 ....42 B3
  Ilford IG2 ....57 C2
  Mitcham SW17,SW19 .180 C3
  Newham E16 ....99 B1
  Pinner HA5 ....23 B2
  Pinner HA5 ....40 C2
  Southall UB1 ....85 C2
  Sutton SM2 ....218 A1
  Thornton Heath CR0 .205 B2
  Tottenham N17 .....33 A4
Devonshire Row EC2 243 B3
Devonshire Row Mews
  W1 ....238 D5
Devonshire Sq BR2 .209 B5
  EC2 ....95 C1 243 B3
Devonshire St
  W1 ....93 B2 238 C4
  W4 ....111 C1
Devonshire Terr
  W2 ....92 A1 236 B1
Devonshire Way
  Croydon CR0,CR9 .223 B6
  Hayes UB4 ....84 B1
Devons Rd E3 ....97 D3
Devons Road Sta E3 97 D3
Devon St SE15 .....140 B6
Devon Way
  Chessington KT19 .214 D3
  Chessington KT9 ..213 C3
  Hillingdon UB10 ....82 B5
Devon Waye TW5 ..129 B3
De Walden Ho NW8 230 A4
De Walden St W1 ..238 C3
Dewar Ho 2 SW17 .180 C5
Dewar St SE15 .....140 A4
Dewberry Gdns E6 .100 A2
Dewberry St E14 ....98 A2
Dewey Rd N1 .94 C5 234 D4
  Dagenham RM10 ...81 D2
Dewey St SW17 ...180 C5
Dewhurst Rd W14 .112 D3
Dewlands Ct NW4 ..28 D1
Dewsbury Cl 5 HA5 .41 A4
Dewsbury Ct 5 W4 .111 A2
Dewsbury Gdns KT4 216 A3
Dewsbury Rd NW10 .68 A3
Dewsbury Terr NW1 231 D6
Dexter Ho 2 DA18 .125 A3
Dexter Rd EN5 ......12 C5
Deyncourt Rd N17 ..33 A2
Deyncourt Gdns E11 55 C5
D'eynsford Rd SE5 .139 B4
Dhonau Ho SE16 ...263 D4
Diadem Ct W1 .....239 C2
Dial Wlk The
  W8 ....113 D4 245 D2
Diameter Rd BR5 ..211 A3
Diamond Cl RM8 ....58 C4
Diamond Est SW17 .158 C1
Diamond Ho 20 E3 ..97 A5
Diamond Rd HA4 ....63 A4
Diamond St SE15 ..139 C5
  13 NW10 ....67 B1
Diamond Terr SE10 142 A4
Diana Cl 45 SE8 ....141 B6
  Woodford E18 ......37 B2
Diana Ct SM5 ......219 A1
Diana Gdns KT6 ...214 C6
Diana Ho 4 SW2 ..160 C4
Diana, Princess of Wales
Mml Wlk
  W2 ....114 A5 246 A3
Diana Rd E17 ....53 B6
Dianne Ct SE12 ....165 A3
Dianne Way EN4 .....2 C1
Dianthus Cl SE2 ...124 B1
Dibden Ho 16 SE5 .139 C5
Dibdin Cl N1 ..95 A6 235 A6
Dibdin Cl SM1 .....217 C6
Dibdin Ho W9 ....91 D5
Dibdin Rd SM1 ....217 C6
Dicey Ave NW2 .....68 C4
Dickens Ave N3 .....30 A2
  Hayes UB8 ....82 D1
Dickens Cl DA8 ....147 D5
  Hayes UB3 ....105 C4
  Richmond TW10 ..154 A2

Dickens Ct
10 Wanstead E11 ...55 A5
Wembley HA0 ...65 C5
Dickens Dr BR7 ...189 A4
Dickens Ho NW6 ...91 C4
NW8 ...236 D6
SE17 ...261 D1
WC1 ...240 A6
3 Erith DA17 ...125 B1
Hayes UB3 ...105 C2
Dickens House Mus★
WC1 ...94 B3 240 D5
Dickens La N18 ...33 C5
Dickenson Cl N9 ...18 A3
Dickenson Ho N8 ...50 B3
Dickenson Rd N8 ...50 A2
Dickenson's La SE25 .206 A3
Dickenson's Pl SE25 .206 A3
Dickens Rd E6 ...99 D5
Dickens Sq
SE1 ...117 A3 262 B6
Dickens St SW8 ...137 B3
Dickens Wood Cl
SE19 ...182 D3
Dickerage Hill
Kingston KT3 ...199 A6
Kingston KT3 ...177 A1
Dickerage La KT3 ...199 A6
Dickerage Rd KT1,
KT2,KT3 ...177 A1
Dickinson Ho 21 E2 ...96 A4
Dickinson Rd TW13 ..172 D5
Dicksee Ho NW8 ...236 C5
Dick Shepherd Ct 17
SW2 ...160 C5
Dickson Fold HA5 ...40 D5
Dickson Ho 13 E1 ...96 B1
9 SE18 ...144 A4
Dickson Rd SE9 ...144 A2
Dick Turpin Way
TW14 ...127 D1
Didbin Ho N7 ...72 B6
Didsbury Cl E6 ...100 B6
Digby Bsns Ctr E9 ...74 D2
Digby Cres N4 ...73 A6
Digby Gdns RM10 ...103 C6
Digby Mans W6 ...112 C1
Digby Pl CR0 ...221 D5
Digby Rd E9 ...74 D2
Barking IG11 ...79 D1
Digby St E2 ...96 C4
Digby Stuart Coll
SW15 ...156 A6
Diggon St 16 E1 ...96 D2
Dighton Ct SE17 ...139 A6
Dighton Rd SW18 ...136 A1
Dignum St N1 ...234 A4
Digswell St N7 ...72 C2
Dilhorne Cl SE12 ...165 B1
Dilke St SW3 136 D6 267 D6
Dilloway Yd UB2 ...107 A4
Dillwyn Cl SE26 ...185 A6
Dilston Cl 1 UB5 ...84 C4
Dilston Gr SE16 ...118 C2
Dilton Gdns SW15 ...156 B3
Dilwyn Ct E17 ...35 A1
Dimes Pl 9 W6 ...112 B2
Dimmock Dr UB6 ...64 B3
Dimond Cl E7 ...77 A4
Dimsdale Dr NW9 ...45 A1
Enfield EN1 ...18 A5
Dimsdale Wlk 4 E13 .99 A5
Dimson Cres E3 ...97 C4
Dinerman Ct NW8 ...229 B6
Dingle Cl EN5 ...11 D5
Dingle Gdns E14 ...119 C6
Dingle Rd TW15 ...170 D5
Dingle The UB10 ...82 D4
Dingley La SW16 ...159 D2
Dingley Pl EC1 95 A4 235 B1
Dingley Rd
EC1 ...95 A4 235 A1
Dingwall Ave CR0 ...221 A6
Dingwall Gdns NW11 .47 C3
Dingwall Rd
South Croydon CR0 ...221 B6
Wandsworth SW18 ...158 A4
Dinmont Ho 26 E2 ...96 A5
Dinmont St 1 E2 ...96 B5
Dinmore Ho 7 E9 ...96 C6
Dinnington Ho 17 E1 ..96 B3
Dinorben SM6 ...219 C1
Dinsdale Ct EN5 ...13 D6
Dinsdale Gdns
New Barnet EN5 ...13 D6
South Norwood SE25 ..205 C4
Dinsdale Rd SE3 ...142 D6
Dinsmore Rd SW12 ..159 B4
Dinton Ho NW8 ...237 A6
Dinton Rd
Kingston KT2 ...176 B3
Mitcham SW19 ...180 B4
Dinwiddy Ho N1 ...233 C3
Diploma Ave N2 ...48 C5
Diploma Ct N2 ...48 C5
Dirleton Rd E15 ...98 D6
Disbrowe Rd
W6 ...135 A6 264 B5
Discovery Bsns Pk 13
SE16 ...118 A3
Discovery Ho 1 E14 .120 A6
Dishforth La NW9 ...27 C2
Disley Ct 2 UB1 ...85 D1
Disney Pl SE1 ...252 B2
Disney St SE1 ...252 B2
Dison Cl EN3 ...6 D4
Disraeli Cl SE28 ...124 C5
W4 ...111 B2
Disraeli Gdns SW15 ..135 B1
Disraeli Rd E7 ...77 A2
Acton NW10 ...89 B5
Ealing W5 ...109 D5
Putney SW15 ...135 A1
Diss St E2 ...95 D4
Distaff La EC4 ...252 A6
Distillery La W6 ...112 C1
Distillery Rd W6 ...112 C1
Distillery Wlk 14
TW8 ...132 A6
Distin St
SE11 ...116 C2 261 A3
District Rd HA0 ...65 B3
Ditchburn St E14 ...120 A6
Ditchfield Rd UB4 ...85 A3
Dittisham Rd SE9 ...188 A6
Ditton Cl KT7 ...197 A2
Dittoncroft Cl CR0 ...221 C4
Ditton Grange Cl
KT6 ...197 D1
Ditton Grange Dr
KT6 ...197 D1
Ditton Hill KT6 ...213 D6
Ditton Hill Rd KT6 ...197 C1
Ditton Ho 10 E5 ...74 B3
Ditton Lawn KT7 ...197 A1
Ditton Pl 6 SE20 ...184 B2
Ditton Rd Bexley DA6 .169 A6
Southall UB2 ...107 B1
Surbiton KT6 ...198 B1
Ditton Reach KT7 ...197 B3
Divis Way SW15 ...156 B5
Dixon Cl 4 E6 ...100 B1
Dixon Clark Ct N1 ...72 D2
Dixon Ct N4 ...50 C3
Dixon Ho SE2 ...124 C1
Dixon Pl BR4 ...207 D1
Dixon Rd SE14 ...141 A4
South Norwood SE25 ..205 D6
Dobbin Cl HA3 ...25 A1
Dobell Rd SE9 ...166 B6
Dobree Ave NW10 ...68 B1
Dobson Cl NW6 ...70 B1
Dobson Ho 18 SE14 ..140 D6
SE5 ...139 B5
Doby Ct EC4 ...252 B6
Dockers Tanner Rd 19
E14 ...119 C2
Dockett Eddy La
KT16,TW17 ...192 B1
Dockett Moorings
KT16 ...192 B1
Dockhead
SE1 ...117 D4 253 D1
Dockhead Wharf
SE1 ...253 D2
Dock Hill Ave SE16 ..118 D4
Docklands Heritage Mus★
SE16 ...119 B5
Docklands Mus (Museum
in Docklands)★ E14 119 C6
Dockland St E16 ...122 C5
Dockley Rd SE16 ...118 A3
Dockley Road Ind Est 11
SE16 ...118 A3
Dock Offices 12 SE16 118 C3
Dock Rd E16 ...120 D6
Brentford TW8 ...131 D5
Dockside Rd E16 ...121 D6
Dock St E1 ...118 A6
Dockwell Cl TW14 ...128 A1
Dockwell's Ind Est
TW14 ...150 C6
Doctors Cl SE26 ...184 C5
Doctor Spurstowe
Almshos 9 E8 ...74 B2
Docura Ho N7 ...72 B6
Docwra's Bldgs N1 ...73 C2
Dodbrooke Rd SE27 .160 D1
Dodd Ho 18 SE16 ...118 B2
Doddington Gr
SE17 ...116 D1 261 D1
Doddington Pl 4
SE17 ...138 D6
Dodsley Pl N9 ...18 C1
Dodson St
SE1 ...116 C4 251 B1
Dod St E14 ...97 C1
Doebury Wlk SE18 ...146 A6
Doel Cl SW19 ...180 A3
Doggett Rd SE6 ...163 C4
Doggetts Ct EN4 ...14 C6
Doghurst Ave UB3 ...126 D5
Doghurst Dr UB7 ...126 D5
Dog Kennel Hill SE22 139 C2
Dog Kennel Hill Sch
SE22 ...139 C2
Dog La NW10 ...67 C4
Dogrose Ct 14 NW9 ...46 A5
Doherty Rd E13 ...99 A3
Dokal Ind Est UB2 ...107 A4
Doland Ct SW17 ...180 D4
Dolben Ct SE8 ...119 B2
Dolben St
SE1 ...116 D5 251 D3
Dolby Rd SW6 ...135 B3
Dolland Ho SE11 ...260 D1
Dolland St SE11 ...260 D1
Dollar Bay E14 ...120 A4
Dollary Ct KT3 ...198 D6
Dollis Ave N3 ...29 B2
Dollis Brook Wlk EN5 .13 A5
Dollis Cres HA4 ...40 C1
Dolliscroft NW7 ...29 A3
Dollis Ct N3 ...29 B2
Dollis Hill Ave NW2 ...68 B5
Dollis Hill Est NW2 ...68 A5
Dollis Hill La NW2 ...68 A5
Dollis Hill Sta NW2 ...68 A3
Dollis Hts NW2 ...68 B5
Dollis Jun & Inf Schs
NW7 ...28 C3
Dollis Mews N3 ...29 C2
Dollis Pk N3 ...29 B2
Dollis Rd N3,NW7 ...29 B3
Dollis Valley Way EN5 .13 B5
Dolman Cl N3 ...30 A1
Dolman Rd W4 ...111 B2
Dolman St SW4 ...138 B1
Dolphin Cl 2 SE16 ...118 D4
SE28 ...102 D1
Kingston KT6 ...197 D4
Dolphin Ct N7 ...71 D4
NW11 ...47 A3
Harrow HA3 ...24 C1
Merton SW19 ...179 C3
2 Wallington SM6 ...219 B2
Dolphin Est The
TW16 ...171 B2
Dolphin La E14 ...119 D6
Dolphin Rd
Charlton TW16 ...171 C2
Northolt UB5 ...85 B5
Dolphin Rd N TW16 ..171 C2
Dolphin Rd S TW16 ..171 C2
Dolphin Rd W TW16 ..171 C2
Dolphin Sch SW11 ...158 D6
Dolphin Sq SW1 ...259 B1
Dolphin St KT2 ...176 A2
Dolphin Twr 21 SE8 ..141 B6
Dombey Ho 9 SE1 ...118 A4
4 W11 ...112 D5
Dombey St WC1 ...240 C4
Dome Hill Pk SE26 ..183 D6
Domelton Ho SW18 ..157 D5
Domett Cl SE5 ...139 B1
Domfe Pl E5 ...74 C4
Domingo St EC1 ...242 A5
Dominica Cl 6 E6 ...99 D5
Dominion Bsns Pk N9 18 D2
Dominion Ind Est
UB2 ...107 A4
Dominion Par HA1 ...42 D4
Dominion Rd
Croydon CR0 ...205 D2
Southall UB2 ...107 A3
Dominion St
EC2 ...95 B2 242 D4
Dominion Wks RM8 ...59 A1
Domonic Dr SE9 ...166 D1
Domville Cl N20 ...14 B2
Donaghue Cotts 13
E14 ...97 A2
Donald Dr RM6 ...58 C4
Donald Lynch Ho
CR4 ...180 D1
Donald Rd E13 ...99 B6
Thornton Heath CR0 ..204 B2
Donaldson Rd NW6 ...91 B6
SE18 ...144 C4
Donald Woods Gdns
KT5 ...215 A6
Doncaster Dr UB5 ...63 B3
Doncaster Gdns N4 ...51 A3
Northolt UB5 ...63 B3
Doncaster Gn WD19 ..22 C5
Doncaster Rd N9 ...18 B4
Doncel Ct E4 ...20 B4
Donegal Ho 2 E1 ...96 C3
Donegal St N1 94 B5 233 D3
Doneraile Ho SW1 ..258 C1
Doneraile St SW6 ...134 D4
Dongola Rd E1 ...97 A2
E13 ...99 B4
N17 ...51 C6
Dongola Rd W 5 E13 .99 B4
Donington Ave IG6 ...57 A4
Donkey Alley SE22 ..162 A5
Donkey La EN1 ...6 A3
Donkin Ho 15 SE16 ..118 B2
Donne Ct SE24 ...161 A5
Donnefield Ave HA8 ..26 A3
Donne Ho 7 E14 ...97 C1
18 N16 ...73 B4
14 SE14 ...140 D6
Donnelly Ct SW6 ...264 B4
Donne Pl
SW3 ...114 C2 257 B4
Mitcham CR4 ...203 B5
Donne Rd RM8 ...80 C6
Donnington Ct NW10 .68 B1
11 NW1 ...71 B1
Donnington Ho 12
SW8 ...137 D3
Donnington Prim Sch
NW10 ...90 B6
Donnington Rd NW10 .90 B6
Harrow HA3 ...43 D3
Worcester Park KT4 ..216 A6
Donnybrook Rd
SW16 ...181 D3
Donovan Ave N10 ...31 C1
Donovan Ct SW7 ...256 C1
Donovan Ho 3 E1 ...118 C6
Donovan Pl N21 ...16 B6
Don Phelan Cl SE5 ..139 B4
Doone Cl TW11 ...175 A4
Doon St SE1 .116 C5 251 A4
Doradus Ct 20 SW19 .156 D3
Dora Ho 1 E14 ...97 B1
11 W11 ...112 D6
Doral Way SM5 ...218 D3
Doran Ct E6 ...100 B5
Dorando Cl W12 ...112 B6
Doran Gr SE18 ...145 C5
Doran Manor N2 ...48 D4
Doran Wlk E15 ...76 A1
Dora Rd SW19 ...179 C6
Dora St E14 ...97 B1
Dorcas Ct 9 SW18 ..136 B1
Dorchester Ave
Edmonton N13 ...33 A6
Harrow HA2 ...42 A3
Sidcup DA5 ...168 D4
Dorchester Cl
Northolt UB5 ...63 D3
St Paul's Cray BR5 ...190 B3
Dorchester Ct 1 N10 .49 B6
1 N1 ...73 C1
N14 ...15 B4
NW2 ...68 D5
SE24 ...161 A6
SW1 ...257 D5
5 Streatham SW16 ..160 A2
2 Woodford E18 ...36 D2
Dorchester Dr SE24 .161 A6
Feltham TW14 ...149 C5
Dorchester Gdns
NW11 ...47 C5
Chingford E4 ...35 C6
Dorchester Gr W4 ...111 D1
Dorchester Mews
New Malden KT3 ...199 B5
Twickenham TW1 ...153 C5
Dorchester Prim Sch
KT4 ...200 C1
Dorchester Rd
Cheam SM4 ...202 A2
North Cheam KT4 ...200 C1
Northolt UB5 ...63 D3
Dorchester Way HA3 ..44 B3
Dorchester Waye
Hayes UB4 ...84 B1
Hayes UB4 ...84 C1
Dorcis Ave DA7 ...147 A3
Dordrecht Rd W3 ...111 C5
Dore Ave E12 ...78 C3
Doreen Ave NW9 ...45 B1
Doreen Capstan Ho 3
E11 ...76 C5
Dore Gdns SM4 ...201 D2
Dorell Cl UB1 ...85 B2
Doria Rd SW6 ...135 B3
Doric Ho 7 E2 ...96 D5
Doric Way
NW1 ...93 D4 232 C2
Dorien Rd SW20 ...178 D1
Doris Emmerton Ct
SW18 ...136 A1
Doris Rd E7 ...77 A1
Ashford TW15 ...171 B4
Dorking Cl SE8 ...141 B6
North Cheam KT4 ...216 D6
Dorking Ct N17 ...34 A2
Dorking Ho SE1 ...262 D6
Dorland Ho SE9 ...167 B5
Dorlcote Rd SW18 ...158 C4
Dorleston Ct N1 ...235 D6
Dorly Cl TW17 ...193 C4
Dorman Pl 6 N9 ...18 A2
Dorman Way
NW8 ...92 B6 229 C6
Dorman Wlk NW10 ...67 B2
Dorma Trad Pk E10 ...52 D1
Dormay St SW18 ...157 D6
Dormer Cl E15 ...76 D2
Barnet EN5 ...12 D6
Dormer's Ave UB1 ...85 C1
Dormers Lo EN4 ...2 D3
Dormers Rise UB1 ...85 D1
Dormer's Wells High Sch
UB1 ...85 C1
Dormers Wells Ho
UB4 ...84 C2
Dormer's Wells Inf Sch
UB1 ...107 D6
Dormer's Wells Jun Sch
UB1 ...107 D6
Dormer's Wells La
UB1 ...107 C5
Dormstone Ho SE17 .263 A3
Dormywood HA4 ...39 D4
Dornan Wlk E15 ...98 A6
Dornberg Cl SE3 ...143 A5
Dornberg Rd SE3 ...143 B5
Dorncliffe Rd SW6 ..135 A3
Dorney NW3 ...70 C1
Dorney Ct SW6 ...135 A2
Dorney Rise BR5 ...211 D5
Dorney Way TW4 ...151 A6
Dornfell St NW6 ...69 B3
Dornoch Ho 25 E3 ...97 B5
Dornton Rd
South Croydon CR2 ..221 C3
Upper Tooting SW12,
SW17 ...159 C2
Dorothy Ave HA0 ...66 A1
Dorothy Barley Inf Sch
RM8 ...80 B3
Dorothy Barley Jun Sch
RM8 ...80 B3
Dorothy Charrington Ho 1
SE22 ...162 A6
Dorothy Evans Cl
DA7 ...147 D1
Dorothy Gdns RM8 ...80 B4
Dorothy Rd SW11 ...136 D2
Dorrien Wlk SW16 ...159 D2
Dorrington Ct SE25 ..183 C1
Dorrington Point 20
E3 ...97 D4
Dorrington St EC1 ...241 A4
Dorrit Ho 2 W11 ...112 D5
Dorrit Mews N18 ...33 C5
Dorrit St SE1 ...252 B2
Dorrit Way BR7 ...189 A4
Dorryn Ct SE26 ...184 D5
Dors Cl NW9 ...45 B1
Dorset Ave DA16 ...145 D1
Hayes UB4 ...83 C4
Southall UB2 ...107 C2
Dorset Bldgs EC4 ...241 C1
Dorset Cl NW1 ...237 C4
Hayes UB4 ...83 C4
Dorset Ct 3 N1 ...73 C1
3 Ealing W7 ...86 D2
Dorset Dr HA8 ...26 B4
Dorset Gdns SW16 ..204 B5
Dorset Ho 1 SE20 ...184 B2
Dorset Mans 2 W6 ..134 D6
Dorset Mews N3 ...29 C2
SW1 ...258 C6
Dorset Pl E15 ...76 B2
Dorset Rd E7 ...77 C1
N15 ...51 B5
SW8 ...138 B5 270 C4
W5 ...109 D3
Ashford TW15 ...148 A1
Dorset Rd *continued*
Chislehurst SE9 ...166 A2
Harrow HA1 ...42 A3
Merton SW19 ...179 C1
Mitcham CR4 ...180 C1
Penge BR3 ...206 D6
Wood Green N22 ...32 A2
Dorset Rise
EC4 ...94 D1 241 C1
Dorset Road Inf Sch
SE9 ...166 A2
Dorset Sq
NW1 ...92 D3 237 C5
Dorset St W1 .92 D2 237 D3
Dorset Way
Hillingdon UB10 ...82 B5
Twickenham TW2 ...152 B3
Dorset Waye TW5 ...129 B5
Dorton Cl 6 SE15 ...139 C5
Dorville Cres W6 ...112 B3
Dorville Rd SE12 ...165 A6
Dothill Rd SE18 ...145 A5
Douai Gr TW12 ...174 A2
Douay Martyrs RC Sch
(Annexe) The UB10 ..60 D3
Doughty Ct 11 E1 ...118 B5
Doughty Mews
WC1 ...94 B3 240 C5
Doughty St
WC1 ...94 B3 240 C5
Douglas 20 NW9 ...27 D1
Douglas Ave
Chingford E17 ...35 C2
Wembley HA0 ...66 A1
West Barnes KT3 ...200 B5
Douglas Bader Ho N3 29 D4
Douglas Bldgs SE1 ..252 B2
Douglas Cl
Stanmore HA7 ...25 A5
Wallington SM6 ...220 A2
Douglas Cres UB4 ...84 D3
Douglas Ct N3 ...29 D1
5 NW6 ...69 C1
Douglas Dr CR0 ...223 C5
Douglas Gracey Ho
SW18 ...157 A4
Douglas Ho
Isleworth TW1 ...153 B6
Putney SW15 ...156 A5
Douglas Johnstone Ho
SW6 ...264 C5
Douglas Mews NW2 ..69 A5
Douglas Rd DA16 ...146 B4
5 E16 ...99 A2
N1 ...73 A1
NW6 ...91 B6
Chingford, Chingford Green
E4 ...20 C3
Hounslow TW3 ...129 D2
Ilford IG3 ...58 A3
Kingston KT1 ...176 D1
Stanwell TW19 ...148 A5
Surbiton KT6 ...198 B1
Thames Ditton KT10 ..212 A6
Wood Green N22 ...32 C2
Douglas Rd N N1 ...73 A2
Douglas Rd S N1 ...73 A2
Douglas Robinson Ct
SW16 ...182 A3
Douglas Sq SM4 ...201 C3
Douglas St
SW1 ...115 D2 259 C3
Douglas Terr E17 ...35 B2
Douglas Waite Ho
NW6 ...69 D1
Douglas Way SE8 ...141 B5
Doulton Ho SE11 ...260 D4
Doulton Mews 4
NW6 ...69 D2
Dounesforth Gdns
SW18 ...157 D3
Douro Pl W8 113 D3 255 D6
Douro St E3 ...97 C5
Douthwaite Sq 12 E1 118 A5
Dove App E6 ...100 A2
Dove Cl NW7 ...27 D3
Northolt UB5 ...84 D3
Wallington SM6 ...
Dovecot Cl HA5 ...40 C4
Dovecote Gdns 8
SW14 ...133 B2
Dove Ct Enfield EN3 ...18 B6
Stanwell TW19 ...148 A4
Dovedale Ave HA3 ...43 C3
Dovedale Cl DA16 ...146 A3
Dovedale Cotts 6
SW11 ...136 D3
Dovedale Ho N16 ...51 B2
Dovedale Rd SE22 ...162 B5
Dovedale Rise CR4 ..180 C3

Dovedon Cl N14 16 A2
Dove House Gdns E4 19 C2
Dovehouse Mead IG11 101 B5
Dovehouse St SW3 114 C1 257 A1
Dove Mews SW7 114 A2 256 B2
Dove Pk HA5 23 C3
Dover Cl NW2 68 D6
Dovercourt Ave CR7 204 C5
Dovercourt Gdns HA7 26 A5
Dovercourt La SM1 218 A5
Dovercourt Rd SE22 161 D5
Dover Ct EC1 241 C5
SE10 141 D4
Dove Rd N1 73 B2
Doverfield Rd SW2 160 A4
Dover Flats SE1 263 B3
Dover Gdns SM5 218 D5
Dover Ho 11 SE15 140 C6
SE5 138 D4
7 Beckenham BR3 185 C3
14 Penge SE20 184 B2
Dover House Rd SW15 156 B6
Doveridge Gdns N13 32 D6
Dover Mans 17 SW9 138 C2
Dove Row E2 96 A6
Dover Park Dr SW15 156 B5
Dover Patrol SE3 143 C3
Dover Rd N9 18 C2
Dagenham RM6 59 A3
South Norwood SE19 183 B4
Wanstead E12 77 C6
Woolwich SE18 145 A3
Dover St W1 115 C5 249 A4
Dover Terr TW9 132 C3
Dover Yd W1 249 A4
Doves Cl BR2 226 A6
Doves Yd N1 94 C6 234 A5
Doveton Ho 6 E1 96 C3
Doveton Rd CR2 221 B3
Doveton St 7 E1 96 C3
Dove Wlk SW1 258 A2
Dowanhill Rd SE6 164 B3
Dowdeswell Cl SW15 133 C1
Dowding Ho N6 49 A2
Dowding Pl HA7 25 A4
Dowding Rd UB10 60 B1
Dowe Ho SE3 142 C2
Dowell Ho SE21 161 D1
Dowes Ho 13 SW16 160 A1
Dowgate Hill EC4 252 C6
Dowland Ho EN1 5 D5
Dowland St W10 91 A4
Dowlas St SE5 139 C5
Dowler Ct 2 KT2 176 B2
Dowlerville Rd BR6 227 D2
Dowling Ho DA17 125 B3
Dowman Cl 2 SW19 179 D3
Downage NW4 46 C6
Downalong WD23 8 B3
Down Barns Rd HA4 62 D5
Downbarton Ho 11 SW9 138 C4
Downbury Mews 13 SW18 157 C6
Down Cl UB5 84 B5
Downderry Prim Sch BR1 186 C6
Downderry Rd BR1 186 C6
Downe Cl DA16 146 C5
Downe Ho 9 SE7 143 C6
Downe Manor Prim Sch UB5 84 B4
Downend SE18 144 D5
Downend Ct 8 SE15 139 C6
Downe Rd CR4 180 D1
Downer's Cotts SW4 137 C1
Downes Cl TW1 153 B5
Downes Ct N21 16 C3
Downey Ho 6 E1 96 D3
Downfield KT4 200 A1
Downfield Cl W9 91 D3
Downfield Ho KT3 199 B1
Down Hall Rd KT2 175 D2
Downham Ct N1 73 B1
Downham Ent Ctr SE6 164 D2
Downham La BR1 186 B5
Downham Rd N1 73 B1
Downham Way BR1 186 C6
Downhills Ave N17 51 B6
Downhills Jun & Inf Schs N15 51 B5
Downhills Park Rd N17 51 A6
Downhills Way N17 33 A1
Downhurst Ave NW7 27 B5
Downhurst Ct NW4 46 C6
Downing Cl HA2 42 A6
Downing Ct N12 29 D5
Downing Dr UB6 86 C6
Downing Ho 2 W10 90 D1
3 Merton SW19 179 C3
4 Putney SW15 156 A6
Downing Rd RM9 81 B1
Downings E6 100 C1
Downing St* SW1 116 A4 250 A2
Downland Cl N20 14 A3
Downland Ct E11 76 C6
Downleys Cl SE9 166 B2
Downman Rd SE9 144 A2
Down Pl W6 112 B1
Down Rd TW11 175 B4
Downs Ave BR7 188 B5
Pinner HA5 41 B2
Downs Bridge Rd BR3 186 B2
Downs Ct 16 E8 74 B3
12 Wimbledon SW19 178 D3
Downsell Jun & Inf Schs E15 76 B4
Downsell Rd E15 76 B4
Downsfield Rd E17 53 A3
Downshall Ave IG3 57 C3
Downshall Ct IG3 57 C3
Downs Hill BR2,BR3 186 B2
Downshire Hill NW3 70 B4
Downside
2 Putney SW15 157 A6
Sunbury TW16 172 A2
Twickenham TW1 152 D1
Downside Cl SW19 180 A4
Downside Cres NW3 70 C3
Ealing W13 87 A3
Downside Rd SM2 218 C2
Downside Wlk UB5 85 B4
Downs La 3 E5 74 B4
Downs Park Rd E5,E8 74 A3
Downs Rd E5,N16 74 A4
Beckenham BR3 185 D1
Enfield EN1 5 C1
South Norwood CR7 183 A2
Downs Side JMI Sch E5 74 A4
Down St W1 115 B5 248 C3
East Molesey KT8 195 C4
Downs The SW19, SW20 178 D3
Down St Mews W1 248 C3
Downs View TW7 131 A4
Downsview Gdns SE19 183 A3
Downs View Lo 9 KT6 198 A3
Downsview Prim Sch SE19 183 A3
Downsview Rd SE19 183 A3
Downsview Sch E5 74 B4
Downsway BR6 227 C3
Downsway The SM2 218 A1
Downton Ave SW2 160 B2
Downtown Rd SE16 119 A4
Downway N12 30 C3
Down Way UB5 84 B4
Dowrey St N1 234 A6
Dowsett Rd N17 34 A1
Dowson Cl SE5 139 B1
Dowson Ct SE13 142 B2
Dowson Ho 7 E1 96 D1
Doyce St SE1 252 A2
Doyle Gdns NW10 90 B6
Doyle Ho W3 110 D4
Doyle Rd SE25 206 A5
D'Oyley St SW1 258 A4
Doynton St N19 71 B6
Draco St SE17 139 A6
Dragonfly Cl E13 99 B4
Dragon Rd SE15 139 C6
Dragon Yd WC1 240 B2
Dragoon Rd SE8 119 B1
Dragor Rd NW10 89 A3
Drake Cl 30 SE16 118 D4
Drake Cres SE28 102 C1
Drake Croft N16 73 B6
Drake Ct 5 W12 112 B4
Dulwich SE19 183 D5
Kingston KT5 198 B5
Drakefell Rd SE4, SE14 140 D2
Drakefield Rd SW17 159 A1
Drake Ho 17 E1 96 C2
2 E14 119 A6
Drakeley Ct N5 72 D4
Drake Rd SE4 141 C2
Chessington KT9 214 C3
Harrow HA2 63 B6
Drake Rd *continued*
Mitcham CR4 203 A3
Thornton Heath CR0 204 B2
Drakes Ct SE23 162 C3
Drakes Ctyd NW6 69 B1
Drake St WC1 240 C3
Enfield EN2 5 B4
Drakes Wlk E6 100 B6
Drakewood Rd SW16 181 D3
Draldo Ho 6 SW15 157 A6
Draper Cl DA17 125 B2
Hounslow TW7 130 B3
Draper Ct BR1 210 A5
Draper Ho SE1 261 D4
Draper Pl N1 234 D6
Drapers Almshouses 4 E3 97 C4
Draper's Cottage Homes NW7 28 A6
Drapers Gdns EC2 242 D2
Drapers Rd E15 76 B4
N17 51 D6
Enfield EN2 4 D4
Drappers Way 8 SE16 118 A2
Draven Cl BR2 208 D2
Drawell Cl SE18 123 C1
Drax Ave SW20 178 A3
Draxmont SW19 179 A4
Draycot Rd
Tolworth KT6 198 C1
Wanstead E11 55 B2
Draycott Ave SW3 114 C2 257 B3
Harrow HA3 43 C3
Draycott Cl NW2 68 D5
Harrow HA3 43 B3
Draycott Ct SW11 267 A2
Draycott Ho SW3 257 C3
Draycott Pl SW3 114 D2 257 C3
Draycott Terr SW3 114 D2 257 D3
Drayford Cl W9 91 B3
Dray Gdns SW2 160 B6
Draymans Ct 4 SW9 138 B2
Draymans Way TW7 130 D2
Drayside Mews UB2 107 B4
Drayson Mews W8 113 C4 245 B1
Drayton Ave
Ealing W13 109 A6
Orpington BR6 210 D1
Drayton Bridge Rd
Ealing W13 87 A1
Ealing W7,W13 108 D6
Drayton Cl
Hounslow TW4 151 B6
Ilford IG1 57 B1
Drayton Ct SW10 256 B1
Tolworth KT5 214 D6
West Drayton UB7 104 B2
Drayton Gdns SW10 114 A1 256 B1
Ealing W13 109 A6
Southgate N21 16 D4
West Drayton UB7 104 A4
Drayton Gn W13 109 A6
Drayton Gr W13 109 A6
Drayton Green Prim Sch W13 109 A6
Drayton Green Rd W13 109 B6
Drayton Green Sta W7 86 D1
Drayton Ho E11 54 B1
14 SE5 139 B5
Drayton Manor High Sch W7 86 D1
Drayton Park Prim Sch N5 72 C3
Drayton Park Sta N5 72 C3
Drayton Pk N5,N7 72 C4
Drayton Rd E11 54 B1
NW10 89 D6
Croydon CR0 220 D6
Ealing W13 109 B6
Tottenham N17 33 C1
Drayton Sch The N15 52 A3
Drayton Waye HA3 43 B3
Dreadnought St SE10 120 C3
Drenon Sq UB3 105 D6
Dresden Cl NW6 69 D2
Dresden Ho SE11 260 D4
5 SW11 137 A3
Dresden Rd N19 49 D1
Dressington Ave SE4 163 C5
Drew Ave NW7 29 A4
Drewery Ct SE3 142 C2
Drewett Ho 19 E1 96 A1
Drew Gdns UB6 64 D2
Drew Ho 12 SW16 160 A1
Drew Prim Sch E16 122 A5
Drew Rd E16 122 A5
Drewstead Rd SW16 159 D2
Driffield Ct 4 NW9 27 C2
Driffield Rd E3 97 A5
Drift The BR2 225 D5
Driftway Ho 15 E3 97 B5
Driftway The CR4 181 A2
Drinkwater Ho 11 SE5 139 B5
Drinkwater Rd HA2 63 D6
Drive Mans SW6 135 A3
Drive The BR6 227 D6
BR7 189 D2
DA8 147 D6
E17 53 D6
HA9 67 A6
N11 31 D4
N3 29 C3
N6 48 D4
N7 72 B2
NW10 89 D6
NW11 47 A2
W3 89 A1
Ashford TW15 171 B3
Barking IG11 79 D1
Barnet EN5 1 A2
Beckenham BR3 185 C2
Buckhurst Hill IG9 21 C4
Chingford E4 20 B4
Edgware HA8 26 C5
Enfield EN2 5 B4
Feltham TW14 150 C4
Harrow HA2 41 C2
Hounslow TW3,TW7 130 B3
Ickenham UB10 60 A5
Kingston KT2 177 A3
Morden SM4 202 B4
New Barnet EN5 14 A5
Redbridge IG1 56 B2
Sidcup DA14 190 B6
Sidcup DA5 168 D4
South Norwood CR7 205 B5
St Paul's Cray BR7 211 D6
Surbiton KT6 198 A2
Thames Ditton KT10 196 A1
Wanstead E18 55 A6
West Ewell KT19 215 D2
West Wickham BR4 208 B2
Wimbledon SW19, SW20 178 C3
Barking IG11 80 A2
Dr Johnson Ave SW17 159 B1
Dr Johnson's House* EC4 241 B1
Droitwich Cl SE26 162 A1
Dromey Gdns HA3 24 D3
Dromore Rd SW15 157 A5
Dronfield Gdns RM8 80 C3
Dron Ho E1 96 C2
Droop St W10 91 A3
Drovers Ct SE13 142 A2
3 Kingston KT1 176 A1
Drovers Pl SE15 140 B5
Drovers Rd CR2 221 B3
Dr Triplett's CE Prim Sch UB3 83 D1
Druce Rd SE21 161 C5
Druid St SE1 117 D4 253 C1
Druids Way BR2 208 B5
Drumaline Ridge KT4 215 C6
Drummer Lo N7 72 B5
Drummond Castle Ct E7 76 D4
Drummond Cres NW1 93 D4 232 C2
Drummond Ct N12 30 C3
Drummond Ctr CR0 221 A6
Drummond Dr HA7 24 D3
Drummond Gate SW1 259 D2
Drummond Ho 12 E2 96 A5
N2 30 A1
Drummond Rd SE16 118 B3
Croydon CR0 221 A6
Wanstead E11 55 C3
Drummonds Pl TW9 132 A1
Drummond St NW1 93 C3 239 A6
Drummonds The IG9 21 B2
Drum St E1 243 D2
Drury Cres CR0 220 C6
Drury Ho SW8 269 A2
Drury La WC2 94 A1 240 B1
Drury Rd HA1 42 A2
Drury Way NW10 67 B3
Dryad St SW15 134 D2
Dryburgh Gdns NW9 44 C6
Dryburgh Ho SW1 258 D2
Dryburgh Mans SW15 134 C2
Dryburgh Rd SW15 134 C2
Dryden Ave W7 86 D1
Dryden Ct SE11 261 B3
11 Richmond TW10 175 D6
Dryden Ho BR2 209 D4
16 N16 73 C5
6 SE5 139 C4
Dryden Rd DA16,SE18 145 D4
Enfield EN1 17 D5
Harrow HA3 24 D2
Wimbledon SW19 180 A4
Dryden St WC2 240 B1
Dryer's Bldgs EC1 241 A3
Dryfield Cl NW10 67 A2
Dryfield Rd HA8 27 A4
Dryfield Wlk 1 SE8 141 C6
Dryhill Rd DA17 147 B6
Dryland Ave 5 BR6 227 D4
Drylands Rd N8 50 A3
Drysdale Ave E4 19 D5
Drysdale Flats 3 E8 73 D3
Drysdale Ho 20 E2 95 C4
Drysdale Pl N1 95 C4
Drysdale St N1 95 C4
Dublin Ave E8 96 A6
Du Burstow Terr W7 108 C4
Ducal St 25 E2 95 D4
Ducane Cl W12 90 C1
Du Cane Ct SW12 159 A3
Du Cane Rd W12 90 A1
Ducavel Ho SW2 160 B3
Duchess Cl N11 31 B5
Sutton SM1 218 A4
Duchess Gr IG9 21 B2
Duchess Mews W1 238 D3
Duchess of Bedford Ho W8 245 A2
Duchess of Bedford's Wlk W8 113 C4 245 A1
Duchess St W1 93 B2 238 D3
Duchy Rd EN4 2 B5
Duchy St SE1 116 C5 251 B4
Ducie Ho 8 SE7 143 C6
2 Putney SW15 156 C6
Ducie St SW4 138 B1
Duckett Mews N4 50 D3
Duckett Rd N4 50 D3
Duckett St E1 97 A2
Duck La W1 239 C1
Duck Lees La EN3 7 A1
Ducks Hill Rd HA4,HA6 39 A5
Duck's Wlk TW1 153 C6
Du Cros Dr HA7 25 D4
Du Cros Rd W3 111 C5
Dudden Hill La NW10 67 D3
Duddington Cl SE9 187 D6
Dudley Ave HA3,HA7 43 C6
Dudley Ct NW11 47 B5
W1 237 C1
WC2 240 A2
9 Wanstead E11 55 A4
Wembley HA0 65 D3
Dudley Dr Ruislip HA4 62 B3
West Barnes SM4 201 A2
Dudley Gdns W13 109 B4
Harrow HA2 42 B1
Dudley Ho 14 SW9 138 C3
W2 236 C3
Dudley Mews 14 SW2 160 C5
Dudley Rd N3 29 D1
NW6 91 B5
Ashford TW15 170 B6
Chingford E17 35 C1
East Bedfont TW14 149 B3
Harrow HA2 64 A6
Ilford IG1 78 D4
Kingston KT1 198 B6
Richmond TW9 132 B3
Southall UB2 106 D3
Walton-on-T KT12 194 A2
Wimbledon SW19 179 C4
Dudley St W2 236 C3
Dudlington Rd E5 74 C6
Dudmaston Mews SW3 256 D2
Dudsbury Rd DA14 190 B4
Dudset La TW5 128 A4
Duffell Ho SE11 260 D1
Dufferin Ave EC1 242 C5
Dufferin Ct EC1 242 C5
Dufferin St EC1 95 A3 242 B5
Duffield Cl HA1 42 D4
Duffield Dr N15 51 D5
Duffield Ho N4 51 A2
Duff St E14 97 D1
Dufour's Pl W1 239 B1
Dugdale Ho 10 N7 71 D3
Duke Gdns IG6 57 B5
Duke Humphrey Rd SE3 142 C3
Duke Of Cambridge Cl TW2 152 B5
Duke Of Edinburgh Rd SM1 218 B6
Duke of Wellington Pl SW1,W1 248 B2
Duke Of York's Sq SW3 114 D2 258 A4
Duke of York St SW1 249 B4
Duke Rd W4 111 B1
Ilford IG6 57 B5
Dukes Ave N10 49 C6
N3 29 D2
Duke's Ave W4 111 B1
Dukes Ave
Edgware HA8 26 B5
Harrow HA1 42 C5
Harrow HA2,HA5 41 B3
Hounslow TW4 129 A1
Kingston KT3 199 D6
Northolt UB5 63 A1
Richmond KT2,TW10 175 D6
Dukes Cl
Ashford TW15 171 A6
Hampton TW12 173 B5
Dukes Ct SE13 142 A3
SE22 162 A3
SE22 162 B6
Barking E6 100 C6
Beckenham BR3 207 A6
Ealing W13 87 B2
Dukes Gate 4 W4 111 A2
Dukes Green Ave TW14 150 A6
Dukes Head Yd N6 49 B1
Duke's Ho SW1 259 D4
Duke Shore Wharf E14 119 B6
Dukes La W8 113 D4 245 C2
Dukes Mews N10 49 B6
Duke's Mews W1 238 B2
Duke's Pl EC3 95 C1 243 B1
Dukes Point N6 49 B1
Duke's Rd WC1 93 D4 232 D1
Dukes Rd Acton W3 88 C3
Barking E6 100 C6
Dukes Ride UB10 60 A4
Duke St W1 93 A1 238 B1
Richmond TW10,TW9 153 D6
Sutton SM1 218 B4
Duke St Hill SE1 252 D4
Dukesthorpe Rd SE26 184 D6
Duke St Mans W1 238 B1
Duke St St James's SW1 115 C5 249 B4
Dukes Way BR4 224 C5
Duke's Yd W1 248 B6
Dulas St N4 50 B1
Dulford St W11 113 A6 244 A6
Dulka Rd SW11 158 D6
Dulverton NW1 232 B5
Dulverton Ct 12 KT6 198 A4
Dulverton Mans WC1 240 D5
Dulverton Prim Sch DA15 167 B2
Dulverton Rd DA15,DA15 167 B2
Ruislip HA4 62 A6
Dulwich Bsns Ctr SE23 162 D3
Dulwich Coll (Endowed) SE21 161 C2
Dulwich Coll Picture Gall* SE21 161 C4
Dulwich Coll Prep Sch SE21 161 C1
Dulwich Comm SE21 161 C3
Dulwich Ct SE22 162 B3
Dulwich Hamlet Jun Sch SE21 161 B5
Dulwich High Sch for Boys SE24 161 B6
Dulwich Hospl SE22 139 C1
Dulwich Mead SE24 161 A5

Dulwich Mews 1
SE22 ....139 D1
Dulwich Oaks The
SE21 ....161 D1
Dulwich Rd SE24 ....160 D5
Dulwich Village SE21 161 C5
Dulwich Village CE Inf Sch
SE21 ....161 C5
Dulwich Wood Ave
SE19 ....183 C5
Dulwich Wood Pk
SE19 ....183 C6
Dumain Ct SE11 ...261 C3
Du Maurier Ho 2
NW3 ....70 D3
Dumbarton Ct 16
SW2 ....160 A4
Dumbarton Rd SW2 .160 A5
Dumbleton Cl KT2 ..176 D2
Dumbreck Rd SE9 ..144 C2
Dumont Rd N16 ....73 C5
Dumphreys Ho 5
SW4 ....159 D4
Dumpton Pl NW1 ...71 A1
Dunally Pk TW17 ..193 B2
Dunbar Ave
Beckenham BR3 .....207 A5
Dagenham RM10 .....81 C5
Thornton Heath SW16 .182 C1
Dunbar Cl UB4 .....84 A2
Dunbar Ct 3 N12 ..29 D6
Sutton SM1 ....218 B3
Walton-on-T KT12 ....194 C1
Dunbar Gdns RM10 .81 D3
New Malden KT3 .....199 A5
Tottenham N22 ......32 D2
Dunbar Rd E7 .....77 A2
Dunbar St SE27 ...161 A1
Dunbar Wharf 20
E14 ....119 B6
Dunblane Rd SE9 ..144 A3
Dunboe Pl TW17 ...193 A2
Dunboyne Rd NW3 ..70 D3
Dunbridge Ho 7
SW15 ....155 D5
Dunbridge St E2 ...96 B3
Duncan Cl EN5 .....2 A1
Duncan Ct 3 E14 ..98 A2
Southgate N21 ......16 D3
Duncan Gr W3 .....89 C1
Duncan Ho 3 NW3 ..70 D1
Duncannon Ho SW1 259 D1
Duncannon St WC2 250 A5
Duncan Rd E8 .....96 B6
Richmond TW9 ....132 A1
Duncan St N1 .94 D5 234 C4
Duncan Terr
N1 ....94 D5 234 C4
Dunch St 30 E1 ...96 B1
Dunchurch Ho RM10 .81 C1
Duncombe Hill SE23 163 A4
Duncombe Ho 7
SW19 ....156 D3
Duncombe Prim Sch
N19 ....50 A1
Duncombe Rd N19 ..49 D1
Duncrievie Rd SE13 .164 B5
Duncroft SE18 .....145 C5
Dundalk Ho 2 E1 ..96 C1
Dundalk Rd SE4 ...141 A2
Dundas Gdns KT8 ..195 D6
Dundas Ho 12 E2 ..96 C5
Dundas Rd SE15 ...140 C3
Dundee Ct 36 E1 ..118 B5
Dundee Ho W9 .....229 A2
Dundee Mews EN3 ..7 C6
Dundee Rd E13 ....99 B5
Croydon SE25 ....206 B4
Dundee St E1 .....118 B5
Dundee Way EN3 ...7 A2
Dundee Wharf E14 ..119 B6
Dundela Gdns KT17,
KT4 ....216 B4
Dundonald Cl 6 E6 .100 A1
Dundonald Prim Sch
SW19 ....179 B3
Dundonald Rd NW10 .90 D6
Merton SW19 ....179 B3
Dundonald Road Sta
SW19 ....179 B3
Dundry Ho 8 SE26 .162 A1
Duneaves HA1 .....64 C5
Dunedin Rd E10 ...75 D5
Ilford IG1 ....57 A1
Dunedin Way UB4 ..84 C3
Dunelm Gr SE27 ...161 A1
Dunelm St E1 .....96 D1

Dunfield Gdns SE6 ..185 D5
Dunfield Rd SE6 ...185 D5
Dunford Rd N7 .....72 B4
Dungarvan Ave
SW15 ....134 A1
Dungeness Ho SW18 136 A1
Dunheved Cl CR7 ...204 C3
Dunheved Rd N CR7 .204 C3
Dunheved Rd S CR7 .204 C3
Dunheved Rd W CR7 204 C3
Dunhill Point 12
SW15 ....156 B3
Dunholme Gn N9 ...17 D1
Dunholme La N9 ...17 D1
Dunholme Rd N9 ...17 D1
Dunkeld Ho 13 E14 .98 D1
Dunkeld Rd
Dagenham RM8 ......80 C6
South Norwood SE25 .205 B5
Dunkery Rd SE9 ...166 A1
Dunkirk St 12 SE27 183 A6
Dunlace Rd E5 .....74 D4
Dunleary Cl TW4 ...151 B4
Dunley Dr CR0 .....224 A2
Dunlin Ct 11 SE21 .161 B2
Dunlin Ho 13 SE16 .118 D2
Dunloe Ave N17 ...51 B6
Dunloe Ct 7 E2 ...95 D5
Dunloe St E2 .....95 D5
Dunlop Pl
SE16 ....117 D3 263 D5
Dunlop Point 10 E16 118 D1
Dunmore Point 15 E2 95 D4
Dunmore Rd NW6 ...91 A6
Wimbledon SW20 ....178 D2
Dunmow Cl
Dagenham RM6 ......58 C4
3 Feltham TW13 ....173 A6
Dunmow Ho SE11 ..260 D2
Dagenham RM9 ......102 B6
Dunmow Rd E15 ...76 B4
Dunmow Wlk N1 ...235 A6
Dunnage Cres SE16 .119 A2
Dunnet Ho 26 E3 ..97 B5
Dunnico Ho 51 SE17 263 A2
Dunn Mead NW9 ...27 D3
Dunnock Cl N9 .....18 D3
Dunnock Ct 10 SE21 161 B2
Dunnock Rd E6 ....100 A1
Dunn's Pas WC1 ...240 B2
Dunn St E8 ....73 D3
Dunollie Pl NW5 ...71 C3
Dunollie Rd NW5 ...71 C3
Dunoon Gdns SE23 .162 D4
Dunoon Ho N1 .....233 C5
Dunoon Rd SE23 ...162 C4
Dunraven Dr EN2 ...4 C3
Dunraven Ho 12 TW9 132 B4
Dunraven Rd W12 ..112 A5
Dunraven St
W1 ....114 D6 247 D6
Dunraven Upper Sch
SW16 ....160 B1
Dunrobin Ct NW3 ..69 D3
Dunsany Rd W14 ...112 D3
Dunsfold Ct 9 SM2 217 D1
Dunsfold Ho
10 Kingston KT2 ....176 D4
4 Streatham SW2 ...160 B4
Dunsfold Way CR0 ..223 D1
Dunsford Ct 4 HA5 .23 D1
Dunsford Way SW15 156 B5
Dunsmore Cl
Bushey WD23 ....8 D5
Hayes UB4 ....85 A3
Dunsmore Rd KT12 .194 B3
Dunsmore Way WD23 .8 B5
Dunsmure Rd N16 ..51 C1
Dunstable Ct 3 SE3 143 A5
Dunstable Mews W1 238 B4
Dunstable Rd
East Molesey KT8 ...195 B5
Richmond TW10,TW9 .132 A1
Dunstall Ho 9 SE15 140 A4
Dunstall Rd SW19,
SW20 ....178 C4
Dunstall Way KT8 ..195 D6
Dunstall Welling Est
DA16 ....146 B3
Dunstan Cl 2 N2 ..48 A6
Dunstan Glade BR5 .211 B3
Dunstan Hos 5 E1 ..96 C2
Dunstan Rd NW11 ..47 C4
Dunstan's Gr SE22 .162 B5
Dunstan's Rd SE22 .162 A5
Dunster Ave SM4 ..200 D1
Dunster Ct EC3 ....253 B6
Dunster Dr NW9 ...45 A1
Dunster Gdns NW6 ..69 B1

Dunster Ho SE6 ...163 D1
Dunsterville Way
SE1 ....252 D1
Dunster Way
Carshalton CR4 .....203 A1
Harrow HA2 ....63 A5
Dunston Rd E8 ....95 D6
SW11 ....137 A3
Dunston St E8 ....95 D6
Dunton Cl KT6 ....198 A1
Dunton Ct 5 SE26 .162 B2
Dunton Ho 14 SW16 160 A1
Dunton Rd E10 ....53 D2
SE1 ....117 D2 263 C3
Duntshill Rd SW18 .157 D3
Dunvegan Cl KT8 ..195 D5
Dunvegan Rd SE9 ..144 B1
Dunwich Rd DA7 ...147 B4
Dunworth Mews W11 91 B1
Duplex Ride SW1 ..247 D5
Dupont Rd SW20 ...178 D1
Duppas Ave CR0 ...220 D4
Duppas Cl TW17 ...193 B4
Duppas Ct CR0 ....220 D5
Duppas Hill La CR0 .220 D4
Duppas Hill Rd CR0 .220 D4
Duppas Hill Terr CR0 220 D5
Duppas Jun Sch CR0 220 D3
Duppas Rd CR0 ....220 D5
Dupree Rd SE7 ....121 D1
Dura Den Cl BR3 ...185 D3
Durand Cl SM5 ....202 D1
Durand Gdns
SW9 ....138 B4 270 D1
Durand Prim Sch
SW9 ....138 B4 270 D1
Durand Way NW10 ..67 A1
Durants Lo EN3 ....6 D2
Durants Park Ave EN3 6 D1
Durants Rd EN3 ....6 D1
Durants Sch EN3 ..6 C4
Durant St E2 .....96 A4
Durban Ct E7 .....77 D1
Durban Ho 28 W12 .112 B6
Durban Rd E15 ....98 C4
E17 ....35 D2
Beckenham BR3 .....185 B1
Ilford IG2 ....57 C1
Tottenham N17 .....33 D4
West Norwood SE27 .183 B6
Durbin Ho 13 N9 ..18 A1
Durbin Rd KT9 ....214 B4
Durdans Ho 1 NW1 .71 C1
Durdans Park Prim Sch
UB1 ....85 B2
Durdans Rd UB1 ...85 B1
Durell Gdns RM9 ..80 D3
Durell Rd RM9 ....80 D3
Durfey Ho SE5 ....139 B5
Durford Cres SW15 .156 B3
Durham Ave
Beckenham BR2 .....208 D6
Hounslow TW5 ......107 B1
Woodford IG8 ......37 D5
Durham Cl SW20 ...178 B1
Durham Ct 3 NW6 ..91 C2
Teddington TW11 ....174 C6
Durham Hill BR1 ...186 D6
Durham Ho NW8 ...230 B1
3 Barking IG11 ....80 A1
Durham House St
WC2 ....250 B5
Durham Pl SW3 ....257 C1
Ilford IG1 ....79 A4
Durham Rd DA14 ...190 B5
E12 ....77 D4
E16 ....98 C3
N2 ....48 D6
N4,N7 ....72 B6
N9 ....18 A2
W5 ....109 D3
Beckenham BR2 .....208 D6
Edmonton N9 ......18 A2
Feltham TW14 ......150 C4
Wimbledon SW20 ....178 B2
Durham Rise SE18 ..123 B1
Durham Row E1 ....97 A2
Durham St
SE11 ....138 B6 270 C6
Durham Terr W2 ...91 D1
Durley Ave HA5 ...41 A3
Durley Rd N16 ....51 C2
Durlock Ho 16 SW9 138 C4
Durlston Rd E5 ....74 A6
Kingston KT2 ....176 A4
Durnford Ho SE6 ...163 D1
Durnford St N15 ...51 C4
3 SE10 ....142 A6
Durning Rd SE19 ...183 B5

Durnsford Ave SW18,
SW19 ....157 C2
Durnsford Rd N11 ..31 D3
Wimbledon SW18,
SW19 ....157 C1
Durrant Ct HA3 ....24 C2
Durrant Way BR6 ..227 B3
Durrell Rd SW6 ....264 C1
Durrell Way TW17 ..193 B3
Durrels Ho W14 ...254 D4
Durrington Ave
SW20 ....178 C2
Durrington Park Rd
SW20 ....178 C2
Durrington Rd E5 ..75 A4
Durrington Twr 3
SW8 ....137 C3
Durrisdeer Ho NW2 .69 B4
Dursley Cl SE3 ....143 C3
Dursley Gdns SE3 ..143 D4
Dursley Rd SE3 ...143 C3
Durston NW5 ......71 A3
Durston House Middleton's
Sch W5 ....87 D1
Durston House Prep Sch
W5 ....87 D1
Durward St E1 .....96 B2
Durweston Mews
W1 ....237 D4
Durweston St W1 ..237 D3
Dury Rd EN5 ......1 B3
Dutch Gdns KT2 ...176 D4
Dutch Yd SW18 ....157 C6
Dutton Ho SW2 ....160 D3
Dutton St SE10 ....142 A4
Duxberry Cl BR2 ...210 A4
Duxford 21 KT1 ...176 C1
Duxford Ho 12 SE2 124 D4
Dwight Ct SW6 ....135 A3
Dycer Ho 19 E9 ...74 D2
Dye House La E3 ..97 C6
Dyer Ho TW12 .....173 D1
Dyers Hall Rd E11 ..54 C1
E11 ....76 B6
Dyer's La SW15 ...134 B1
Dykes Ct 11 SW2 ..160 B3
Dykes Way BR2 ....208 D6
Dylan Cl WD6 .....9 D4
Dylan Ct 2 SE24 ..138 D1
Belvedere DA17 .....125 C3
Dylan Thomas Ho N8 50 B5
Dylways SE5 ......139 B1
Dymchurch Cl BR6 227 C4
Ilford IG5 ....56 C6
Dymchurch Ho 12 E5 74 B3
Dymes Path SW19 156 D2
Dymock St SW6 ...135 D2
Dyneley Rd SE12 ..165 C1
Dyne Rd NW6 .....69 B1
Dynevor Rd N16 ...73 D5
Richmond TW10 .....154 A6
Dynham Rd NW6 ...69 C1
Dyott St WC1 .....239 D2
WC1,WC2 ....94 A1 240 A2
Dysart Ave KT2,TW10 175 C6
Dysart Sch
Kingston KT2 ....175 D6
Surbiton KT6 ....198 B2
Dysart St EC2 .95 C3 243 A5
Dyson Ct NW2 ....46 C2
Wembley HA0 ......65 A4
Dyson Ho 3 SE10 ..120 D1
Dyson Rd E11 .....54 C1
E15 ....76 D2
Dyson's Rd N18 ...34 B4

E

Eade Rd N4 ....51 A2
Eagans Cl N2 .....48 B6
Eagle Ave RM6 ....59 A3
Eagle Cl SE16 .....118 C1
Enfield EN3 ....6 C1
Wallington SM6 .....220 A2
Eagle Ct EC1,
9 Dulwich SE21 ....161 B2
Edmonton N18 .....33 D4
6 Wanstead E11 ...55 A5
Eagle Dr NW9 .....27 C1
Eagle Dwellings EC1 235 B2
Eagle Hill SE19 ....183 B4
Eagle Ho 22 E1 ...96 B3
Eagle Hts 10 SW11 136 C4
Eagle La E11 .....55 A5
Eagle Lo E11 .....54 D5
NW11 ....47 B4
Eagle Mans N16 ...73 D3
Eagle Mews N1 ....73 C2
Eagle Pl SW1 .....249 B5
SW7 ....114 A1 256 B3

Eagle Rd Hatton TW6 127 D2
Wembley HA0 ......65 D1
Eaglesfield Rd SE18 144 D4
Eaglesfield Sch SE18 144 C4
Eagle St WC1 .94 B2 240 C3
Eagle Terr IG8 ....37 B3
Eagle Trad Est CR4 202 D3
Eagle Wharf E1 ...253 C3
Eagle Wharf Rd
N1 ....95 A5 235 B4
Ealcom Ct W5 .....110 B5
Ealdham Prim Sch
SE9 ....143 C1
Ealdham Sq SE9 ..143 C1
Ealing Almshouses
W5 ....109 D4
Ealing Broadway Ctr
W5 ....109 D6
Ealing Broadway Sta
W5 ....109 D6
Ealing Coll W13 ...87 B1
Ealing Common W5 110 B6
Ealing Common Sta
W5 ....110 B6
Ealing Gn W5 .....109 D5
Ealing,Hammersmith &
West London Coll
W14 ....113 A1 254 B1
Ealing Hospl UB1,UB2 108 B4
Ealing Park Gdns
W5 ....109 C2
Ealing Park Mans
W5 ....109 D3
Ealing Rd
Brentford TW8 ......109 D6
Northolt UB5 ....63 C1
Wembley HA0 ......66 A1
Ealing Road Trad Est
TW8 ....109 D1
Ealing Tertiary Coll
Acton W3 ....110 D5
Ealing W5 ....109 D5
Ealing Village W5 ..88 A1
Eamann Casey Ho 34
SW9 ....138 C4
Eamont Cl HA4 ....38 D2
Eamont Ct NW8 ...230 B4
Eamont St
NW8 ....92 C5 230 B4
Eardley Cres
SW5 ....113 C1 255 B6
Eardley Point 9
SE18 ....122 D2
Eardley Prim Sch
SW16 ....181 C4
Eardley Rd
Belvedere DA17 .....125 C1
Streatham SW16 ....181 C4
Earl Cl N11 ....31 B5
Earldom Rd SW15 ..134 C1
Earle Gdns KT2 ...176 A3
Earlham Gr E7 ....77 A3
Wood Green N22 ....32 B3
Earlham Prim Sch E7 76 D3
Earlham Prim Schs
N22 ....32 C3
Earlham St
WC2 ....94 A1 240 A1
Earl Ho NW1 ......237 B5
Earlom Ho WC1 ...234 A1
Earl Rd SW14 .....133 A1
Earl Rise SE18 ....123 A1
Earl's Court Ex Ctr
SW5 ....255 A1
Earl's Court Gdns
SW5 ....113 D2 255 C3
Earl's Court Rd
SW5,W8 ....113 C2 255 B4
Earl's Court Sq
SW5 ....113 D1 255 C2
Earl's Court Sta
SW5 ....113 C2 255 B3
Earls Cres HA1 ....42 C5
Earlsdown Ho IG11 101 B5
Earlsferry Way N1 ..72 A1
Earlsfield Prim Sch
SW18 ....158 A2
Earlsfield Rd SW18 .158 A4
Earlsfield Sta SW18 158 A3
Earlshall Rd SE9 ...144 C1
Earlsmead HA2 ....63 B4
Earlsmead Fst & Mid Sch
HA2 ....63 B4
Earlsmead Prim Sch
N15 ....51 D5
Earlsmead Rd N15 ..51 D4
NW10 ....90 C4
Earl St EC2 ...95 C2 243 A4
Earls Terr W8 .....254 D5

Earlsthorpe Mews 3
SW12 ....159 A5
Earlsthorpe Rd SE26 184 D6
Earlstoke St EC1 ..234 C2
Earlston Gr E9 ....96 B6
Earls Wlk W8 113 C3 255 A5
Dagenham RM8 ......80 B4
Earlswood Ave CR7 204 C4
Earlswood Cl 10
SE10 ....120 C1
Earlswood Gdns IG5 56 C6
Earlswood Ho 2
SW2 ....160 B3
Earlswood St SE10 .120 C1
Early Mews NW1 ..231 D6
Earnshaw St WC1,
WC2 ....239 D3
Earsby St W14 ....254 D4
Easby Cres SM4 ...201 D3
Easebourne Rd RM8 .80 C3
Easedale Ho TW7 ..152 D6
Eashing Point 5
SW15 ....156 B3
Easleys Mews W1 ..238 B2
East Acton Arc W3 ..89 D1
East Acton Ct W3 ..111 C6
East Acton La W3 ..111 C6
East Acton Prim Sch
W3 ....111 C6
East Acton Sta W12 .89 D1
East Arbour St E1 ..96 D1
East Ave E12 .....78 A1
E17 ....53 D5
NW2 ....48 A6
Croydon CR0 ....220 B3
Hayes UB3 ....106 A5
Southall UB1 ....107 B6
East Bank N16 ....51 C2
Eastbank Rd TW12 174 A5
East Barnet Main Sch
Barnet EN4 ....2 B2
East Barnet EN4 ....14 D5
East Barnet Rd EN4 .2 B1
East Beckton District Ctr
E6 ....100 B2
East Block 5 E1 ...118 D6
Eastbourne Ave W3 .89 B1
Eastbourne Gdns
SW14 ....133 A2
Eastbourne Mews
W2 ....92 A1 236 B2
Eastbourne Rd E15 ..98 C6
N15 ....51 C3
Brentford TW8 ......109 D1
Chiswick W4 ....133 A6
Feltham TW13 ......150 D2
Streatham SW17 ....181 A4
Wallend E6 ....100 C4
Eastbourne Terr
W2 ....92 A1 236 B2
Eastbournia Ave N9 .18 B1
Eastbrook Ave N9 ..18 C4
Eastbrook Rd SE3 ..143 D3
Eastbury Ave
Barking IG11 ....101 C6
Enfield EN1 ....5 D4
Moor Park HA6 .....22 A5
Eastbury Ct
Barking IG11 ....101 C6
New Barnet EN5 ....14 A6
Eastbury Gr W4 ...111 C1
Eastbury Inf Sch IG11 79 D1
Eastbury Rd E6 ...100 C3
Kingston KT2 ....176 A3
Eastbury Sq IG11 ..101 D6
Eastbury Terr E1 ..96 D3
Eastcastle St
W1 ....93 C1 239 B2
Eastcheap
EC3 ....117 C6 253 A6
East Churchfield Rd
W3 ....111 B5
Eastchurch Rd TW6 127 C2
Eastchurch Road Rdbt
TW6 ....127 C3
East Cl W5 ....88 C3
Cockfosters EN4 ....14 A5
Greenford UB6 .....86 A5
Eastcombe Ave SE7 143 B6
Eastcote BR6 .....211 D1
Eastcote Ave
East Molesey KT8 ...195 C4
Greenford UB6 .....65 A3
Harrow HA2 ....64 A6
Eastcote Ind Est HA4 40 C7
Eastcote La
Harrow HA2 ....63 C5
Northolt UB5 ....63 C2
Eastcote La N UB5 ..63 C2
Eastcote Pl HA5 ...40 B3

Eastcote Prim Sch
DA16 ....145 B2
Eastcote Rd DA16 ...145 B3
Harrow HA2 ....64 A5
Pinner HA5 ....40 D4
Ruislip HA4 ....40 A3
Eastcote St SW9 ....138 B3
Eastcote Sta HA5 ....40 C2
Eastcote View HA5 ....40 D4
Eastcourt Ind Sch IG3 58 A1
East Cres N11 ....30 D6
Enfield EN1 ....17 D6
Eastcroft Rd KT19 ...215 C1
East Cross Ctr E15 ...75 C2
East Cross Route E3 ..97 C6
E9 ....75 B3
East Croydon Sta
CR0 ....221 B6
East Ct HA0 ....65 C6
Eastdown Ho E8 ....74 A4
Eastdown Pk SE13 ...142 B1
East Duck Lees La EN3 .7 B1
East Dulwich Gr
SE22 ....161 C6
East Dulwich Rd
SE15,SE22 ....140 A1
East Dulwich Sta
SE22 ....139 C1
East End Rd N2 ....48 A6
N2,N3 ....47 D6
N3 ....29 C1
East End Way HA5 ....41 A6
East Entrance RM10 .103 D5
Eastern Ave
Ilford IG1,IG2,IG4, ...56 B3
Ilford IG1,IG2,IG4 ....56 C3
Ilford IG2 ....57 B3
Pinner HA5 ....40 D2
Wanstead E11 ....55 C3
Eastern Ave W RM7 ...59 C5
Eastern Bsns Pk
TW16 ....127 D3
Eastern Perimeter Rd
TW14 ....127 D3
Eastern Rd E13 ....99 B5
E17 ....54 A4
N2 ....48 D5
SE4 ....141 C1
Wood Green N22 ....32 A2
Easternville Gdns IG2 .57 A3
Eastern Way SE28 ...124 B4
East Ferry Rd E14 ...119 D2
Eastfield Gdns RM10 ..81 C4
Eastfield Prim Sch EN3 6 D5
Eastfield Rd E17 ....53 C5
N8 ....50 A6
Dagenham RM10 ....81 C4
Dagenham RM9 ....81 B4
Enfield EN3 ....6 D5
Eastfields HA5 ....40 C4
Eastfields Rd W3 ....89 A2
Mitcham CR4 ....181 A1
Eastfield St E14 ....97 A2
East Finchley Sta N2 .48 C5
Eastgate Cl SE28 ...102 D1
East Gdns SW17 ....180 C4
Eastglade HA5 ....41 B6
Eastham Cl EN5 ....13 B6
East Ham Ind Est E6 100 A2
East Ham Manor Way
E6 ....100 C1
East Ham Meml Hospl
E7 ....77 D1
East Ham Sta E6 ....78 A1
East Harding St EC4 .241 B2
East Heath Rd NW3 ..70 B5
East Hill SW18 ....158 A6
Wembley HA9 ....44 C1
Eastholm NW11 ....47 D5
Eastholme UB3 ....106 A5
East India Bldgs 8
E14 ....119 C6
East India Dock Basin
E14 ....120 C6
East India Dock Rd
E14 ....119 D6
East India Dock Road
Tunnel 17 E14 ....98 B1
East India Dock Wall Rd
E14 ....120 B6
East India Sta E14 ...120 B6
East La SE16 ....118 A4
Kingston KT1 ....197 D6
Wembley HA0,HA9 ....65 D5
Eastlake Ho NW8 ....236 D5
Eastlake Rd SE5 ....139 A3
Eastlands Cres SE21 .161 D5
Eastlea Com Sch E16 .98 C3
Eastlea Mews E16 ....98 C3
Eastleigh Ave HA2 ....63 D6
Eastleigh Cl NW2 ....67 C5
Belmont SM2 ....217 D1
Eastleigh Rd E17 ....35 B1
Eastleigh Way TW14 .150 A3
Eastleigh Wlk 9
SW15 ....156 A4
East London Coll &
Toynbee Theatre
E1 ....95 D2 243 D3
East London Stadium
E3 ....97 B2
Eastman Dental Hospl
WC1 ....94 B4 240 C6
Eastman Ho 7 SW4 .159 C5
Eastman Rd W3 ....111 B4
East Mascalls 15 SE7 143 C6
Eastmead IG3 ....58 A2
East Mead HA4 ....62 D5
Eastmead Ave UB6 ....85 D4
Eastmead Cl BR1 ....188 A1
Eastmearn Rd SE21,
SE27 ....161 A2
East Molesey Inf sch
KT8 ....196 B5
Eastmont Rd KT10 ..212 D6
Eastmoor Pl SE7 ....121 D3
Eastmoor St SE7 ....121 D3
East Mount St E1 ....96 B2
Eastney Rd CR0 ....204 D1
Eastney St SE10 ....120 B1
Eastnor Rd SE9 ....167 A3
Easton Ho 4 SE27 ..160 D1
Easton St WC1 ....241 A6
East Park Cl RM6 ....59 A4
East Parkside SE10 ..120 D4
East Pas EC1 ....242 A4
East Pl SE27 ....183 A6
East Point 4 SE1 ...118 A1
Eastpole Cotts N14 ....3 D1
East Poultry Ave EC1 241 C3
East Putney Sta
SW15 ....157 A6
East Ramp TW6 ....126 D4
East Rd DA16 ....146 B3
E15 ....99 A6
HA8 ....27 A2
N1 ....95 B4 235 D2
N2 ....30 C2
Dagenham RM6 ....59 A4
East Barnet EN4 ....15 A3
East Bedfont TW14 ....149 B4
Enfield EN3 ....6 C5
Kingston KT2 ....176 A2
West Drayton UB7 ....104 C2
Wimbledon SW19 ....180 A4
East Rochester Way
DA5,DA15,DA16,SE9 ..168 C5
East Row W10 ....91 A3
Wanstead E11 ....55 A3
Eastry Ave BR2 ....208 D3
Eastry Ho SW8 ....270 A3
Eastry Rd DA8 ....147 C5
East Sheen Ave
SW14 ....133 B1
East Sheen Prim Sch
SW14 ....133 C1
Eastside Rd NW11 ....47 B5
East Smithfield
E1 ....117 D6 253 D5
East St BR1 ....187 A1
DA7 ....147 C1
SE17 ....117 B1 262 C2
Barking IG11 ....79 A1
Brentford TW8 ....131 C5
East Surrey Gr SE15 .139 D5
East Tenter St
E1 ....95 D1 243 D1
East Terr DA15 ....167 C3
East Thamesmead Bsns Pk
DA18 ....125 B4
East Towers HA5 ....40 D3
Eastvale W3 ....111 D5
East View NW3 ....70 B6
Barnet EN5 ....1 B2
Chingford E4 ....36 A5
Eastview Ave SE18 ..145 C5
Eastville Ave NW11 ...47 B3
Eastway E3,E9 ....97 A6
E9,E10 ....75 C4
Hayes BR2 ....209 A2
Merton SM4,SW20 ..201 A5
Wallington SM6 ....219 C4
Wanstead E11 ....55 B4
East Way Croydon CR0 223 A5
Hayes UB3 ....106 A5
Ruislip HA4 ....40 A1
Eastwell Cl BR3 ....185 A2
Eastwell Ho SE1 ....262 D6
Eastwick Ct 2 SW19 156 D3
East Wickham Inf Sch
DA16 ....145 D4
East Wickham Jun Sch
DA16 ....146 A4
East Wlk
East Barnet EN4 ....15 A3
Hayes UB3 ....106 A5
Eastwood Cl
7 Tottenham N17 ....34 B3
Woodford E18 ....37 A1
Eastwood Rd N10 ....31 A1
Ilford IG3 ....58 A2
West Drayton UB7 ....104 C4
Woodford E18 ....37 A1
East Woodside DA5 ..169 A3
Eastwood St SW16 ..181 C4
Eatington Rd E10 ....54 B4
Eaton Cl SW1 ....258 A3
Stanmore HA7 ....25 B6
Eaton Ct BR7 ....189 A4
Ealing W5 ....87 D1
Edgware HA8 ....26 C6
Southall UB1 ....107 B6
Sutton SM2 ....218 B2
Eaton Dr SW9 ....138 D1
Kingston KT2 ....176 C3
Eaton Gate
SW1 ....115 A2 258 A4
Eaton Gdns RM9 ....81 A1
Eaton Ho SW11 ....266 D1
Ealing W5 ....87 D1
Eaton House The Manor
Sch SW4 ....137 B1
Eaton La SW1 115 B3 258 D5
Eaton Mans SW1 ....258 A3
Eaton Mews N
SW1 ....115 A3 258 B5
Eaton Mews S
SW1 ....115 B3 258 C5
Eaton Mews W SW1 ..258 B4
Eaton Park Rd N13 ...16 D2
Eaton Pl SW1 115 A3 258 B5
Eaton Rd DA14 ....168 D2
NW4 ....46 C4
Enfield EN1 ....5 C1
Isleworth TW3,TW7 ..130 B1
Sutton SM2 ....218 B2
Eaton Rise Ealing W5 ..87 D1
Wanstead E11 ....55 C4
Eaton Row
SW1 ....115 B3 258 C5
Eatons Mead E4 ....19 C2
Eaton Sq
SW1 ....115 A3 258 B5
Eaton Square Sch
SW1 ....115 B2 258 C4
Eaton Terr E3 ....97 A4
SW1 ....115 A2 258 B4
Eaton Terr Mews
SW1 ....258 A4
Eatonville Rd SW17 ..158 D2
Eatonville Villas
SW17 ....158 D2
Ebbisham Dr
SW8 ....138 B6 270 C5
Ebbisham Rd KT4 ....216 C6
Ebbsfleet Rd NW2 ....69 A4
Ebdon Way SE3 ....143 B2
Ebenezer Ho SE11 ....261 C3
Ebenezer Mussel Ho 5
E2 ....96 C5
Ebenezer St N1 ....235 C2
Ebenezer Wlk CR4 ...181 C2
Ebley Cl SE15 ....139 D6
Ebner St SW18 ....157 D6
Ebony Ho 10 NW3 ....69 D2
Ebor Cotts SW15 ....155 C1
Ebor St E1,E2 ....243 C6
Ebrington Rd HA3 ....43 D3
Ebsworth St SE23 ....162 D4
Eburne Rd N7 ....72 A5
Ebury Bridge Rd
SW1 ....115 A1 258 B1
Ebury Cl BR2 ....226 A5
Ebury Mews
SW1 ....115 B2 258 C4
Ebury Mews E SW1 ..258 C5
Ebury Sq SW1 ....258 B3
Ebury St SW1 115 B2 258 C4
Ecclesbourne Cl N13 .32 C5
Ecclesbourne Gdns
N13 ....32 C5
Ecclesbourne Inf Sch
CR7 ....205 A4
Ecclesbourne Jun Sch
CR7 ....205 A4
Ecclesbourne Prim Sch
N1 ....73 B1
Ecclesbourne Rd N1 ..73 A1
Thornton Heath CR7 ..205 A4
Eccleshill 3 BR2 ....208 D5
Eccles Rd SW11 ....136 D1
Eccleston Cl BR6 ....211 B1
Cockfosters EN4 ....2 D1
Eccleston Cres RM6 ..58 B2
Ecclestone Ct HA9 ....66 A3
Ecclestone Mews HA9 66 A3
Ecclestone Pl HA9 ....66 B3
Eccleston Ho 1 SW2 160 C5
Eccleston Mews
SW1 ....115 A3 258 B5
Eccleston Pl
SW1 ....115 B2 258 C4
Eccleston Rd W13 ...109 A5
Eccleston Sq
SW1 ....115 B2 258 D3
Eccleston Sq Mews
SW1 ....259 A3
Eccleston St
SW1 ....115 B2 258 C4
Echelford Cty Prim Sch
TW15 ....170 D5
Echelforde Dr TW15 .170 C6
Echo Hts E4 ....19 D3
Eckersley St E1 ....243 D5
8 E2 ....96 A3
Eckford St N1 ....234 A4
Eckington Ho N15 ....51 B3
Eckstein Rd SW11 ...136 C1
Eclipse Rd E13 ....99 B2
Ector Rd SE6 ....164 C2
Edam Ct 11 DA14 ....168 A1
Edans Ct W12 ....111 D4
Edbrooke Rd W9 ....91 C3
Eddisbury Ho 7
SE26 ....162 A1
Eddiscombe Rd SW6 135 B3
Eddy Cl RM7 ....59 D3
Eddystone Rd SE4 ...163 A6
Eddystone Twr SE8 ..119 A1
Eddystone Wlk TW19 148 A4
Ede Cl TW4 ....129 B2
Edenbridge Cl 29
SE16 ....118 B1
Edenbridge Rd E9 ....74 D1
Enfield EN1 ....17 C5
Eden Cl NW3 ....69 C6
W8 ....255 B6
Wembley HA0 ....87 D6
Edencourt W5 ....88 B1
Edencourt Rd SW16 .181 B4
Edendale W3 ....110 D6
Edenfield Gdns KT4 .215 D5
Eden Gr E17 ....53 D4
N7 ....72 B3
Edenham High Sch
CR0 ....207 B2
Edenham Way W10 ....91 B2
Eden Ho NW8 ....237 A5
15 SW11 ....136 C2
Edenhurst Ave SW6 ..135 B2
Eden Lodge NW6 ....68 D1
Eden Mews SW17 ....158 A1
Eden Park Ave BR3 ..207 C4
Eden Park Sta BR3 ..207 C4
Eden Rd E17 ....53 D4
Croydon CR0 ....221 B4
Penge BR3 ....185 A2
West Norwood SE27 ..182 D5
Edensmuir Ct SE3 ...143 A5
Edensor Gdns W4 ...133 C5
Edensor Rd W4 ....133 C5
Eden St KT1,KT2 ....176 A1
Edenvale Cl CR4 ....181 A3
Edenvale Rd CR4 ....181 A3
Edenvale St SW6 ....136 A3
Eden Way BR3 ....207 C3
Eden Wlk 5 KT1 ....176 A1
Ederline Ave SW16 ..182 C1
Edgar Ct KT3 ....199 C6
Edgar Ho E9 ....75 A3
SW8 ....270 A4
Wanstead E11 ....55 A2
Edgar Kail Way SE22 139 C1
Edgarley Terr SW6 ...264 A1
Edgar Rd E3 ....97 D4
Dagenham RM6 ....58 D2
Twickenham TW4 ....151 B4
Yiewsley UB7 ....104 A5
Edgcott Ho W10 ....90 C2
Edgeborough Way
BR1 ....187 D2
Edge Bsns Ctr The
NW2 ....68 B6
Edgebury BR7,SE9 ...188 D6
Edgebury Prim Sch
BR7 ....189 A6
Edgebury Wlk BR7 ...167 A1
Edgecombe Cl KT2 ...177 B3
Edgecombe Ho
4 SE5 ....139 C3
Putney SW19 ....157 A4
Edgecoombe CR2 ...222 C1
Edgecote Cl 7 W3 ...111 A5
Edgecot Gr N15 ....51 C4
Edgecumbe Ct 2
CR0 ....206 A1
Edgefield Ave IG11 ...79 D1
Edgefield Ct 2 IG11 ..79 D1
Edge Hill SE18 ....144 D6
Wimbledon SW19 ....178 D3
Edge Hill Ave N3 ....47 C5
Edge Hill Ct DA14 ...189 D6
Edgehill Ct KT12 ...194 C1
Edge Hill Ct SW19 ...178 D3
Edgehill Gdns RM10 ..81 C4
Edgehill Ho 4 SW9 .138 D3
Edgehill Rd BR7 ....189 A6
Ealing W13 ....87 C2
Mitcham CR4 ....181 B2
Edgeley La SW4 ....137 D2
Edgeley Rd SW4 ....137 D2
Edgel St SW18 ....135 D1
Edge Point Cl SE27 ..182 D5
Edge St W8 ..113 C5 245 B4
Edgewood Dr BR6 ...227 D3
Edgewood Gn CR0 ..206 D1
Edgeworth Ave NW4 ..46 A4
Edgeworth Cl NW4 ...46 A4
Edgeworth Cres NW4 .46 A4
Edgeworth Ct 10 EN4 ..2 C1
Edgeworth Ho NW8 .229 A6
Edgeworth Rd SE9 ..143 D1
Barnet EN4 ....2 C1
Edgington Rd SW16 .181 D4
Edgington Way DA14 190 D3
Edgson Ho SW1 ....258 C2
Edgwarebury Ct HA8 ..26 C5
Edgwarebury Gdns
HA8 ....26 C5
Edgwarebury La HA8 .10 C2
Edgware Community Hospl
HA8 ....26 D3
Edgware Ct HA8 ....26 C4
Edgware Jun & Inf Schs
HA8 ....26 C4
Edgware Rd NW2 ....68 C6
W1,W2,NW1,
NW8 ....92 C2 237 A3
Edgware Rd Burnt Oak
Broadway HA8 ....26 D3
Edgware Rd High St
HA8 ....26 C4
Edgware Road Sta
(Bakerloo)
NW1 ....92 C2 237 A3
Edgware Road Sta
(Met,Distr,Circle)
NW1 ....237 B3
Edgware Road The Hyde
NW9 ....45 C5
Edgware Road West
Hendon Broadway
NW9 ....46 A2
Edgware Sch The HA8 26 B6
Edgware Sta HA8 ....26 D4
Edgware Way (Watford
By-Pass) HA8 ....26 C6
Edinburgh Cl 7 E2 ..96 C5
Uxbridge UB10 ....60 D4
Edinburgh Ct E13 ....99 B5
10 SE16 ....118 D5
1 Catford SE6 ....164 D3
2 Kingston KT1 ....198 A6
West Barnes SM4 ....200 D4
Edinburgh Dr UB10 ..60 D4
Edinburgh Ho NW4 ...46 C6
3 W3 ....89 B1
W9 ....91 D4
Edinburgh Prim Sch
E17 ....53 B4
Edinburgh Rd E13 ....99 B5
E17 ....53 C4
W7 ....108 D4
Carshalton SM1 ....218 B6
Edmonton N18 ....34 A5
Edington 20 NW5 ....71 A2
Edington Rd SE2 ....124 B3
Enfield EN3 ....6 C3
Edison Bldg 11 E14 ..119 C4
Edison Cl E17 ....53 C4
Edison Ct SE10 ....120 D3
Edison Dr UB1 ....85 D1
Edison Gr SE18 ....145 D5
Edison Ho SE1 ....262 C4
10 Wembley HA9 ....67 A5
Edison Rd DA16 ....145 D4
N8 ....49 D3
Brimsdown EN3 ....7 B3
Edison Rd *continued*
Bromley BR2 ....187 A1
Edis St NW1 ..93 A6 231 B6
Editha Mans SW10 ..266 A5
Edith Cavell Cl 6 N19 50 A2
Edith Cavell Way
SE18 ....144 A4
Edith Gdns KT5 ....198 D2
Edith Gr
SW10 ....136 A5 266 B4
Edith Ho 6 W6 ....112 C1
Edithna St SW9 ....138 A2
Edith Neville Prim Sch
NW1 ....93 D5 232 C3
Edith Pond Ct SE9 ...166 D2
Edith Ramsay Ho 2
E1 ....97 A2
Edith Rd E15 ....76 B3
E6 ....77 D1
N11 ....31 D3
W14 ....113 A2 254 B3
Dagenham RM6 ....58 D2
South Norwood SE25 ..205 B4
Wimbledon SW19 ....179 D4
Edith Row SW6 ....265 D2
Edith St E2 ....96 A5
Edith Summerskill Ho
SW6 ....264 C4
Edith Terr
SW10 ....136 A5 266 A4
Edith Villas
W14 ....113 B2 254 C2
Edith Yd SW10 ....266 B4
Edmansons' Cl N17 ....33 D2
Edmeston Cl E9 ....75 A2
Edmond Ct SE14 ....140 C4
Edmonscote W13 ....87 A2
Edmonton Coll of F Ed
EN3 ....6 C4
Edmonton Ct 5
SE16 ....118 C3
Edmonton Cty Lower Sch
N9 ....17 C3
Edmonton Cty Upper Sch
EN1 ....17 D4
Edmonton Green Sh Ctr
N9 ....18 B2
Edmonton Green Sta
N9 ....18 A2
Edmonton Wharf N18 34 D4
Edmund Gr TW13 ....151 B2
Edmund Halley Way
SE10 ....120 C4
Edmund Ho SE14 ....141 B4
SE17 ....261 D1
Edmund Hurst Dr E6 100 D2
Edmund Rd DA16 ....146 A2
Mitcham CR4 ....202 C6
Edmundsbury Ct Est 16
SW9 ....138 B1
Edmunds Cl UB4 ....84 C2
Edmund St SE5 ....139 B5
Edmunds Wlk N2 ....48 C5
Edmund Waller Prim Sch
SE14 ....140 D3
Ednam Ho SE15 ....140 A6
Edna Rd SW20 ....178 D1
Edna St
SW11 ....136 C4 267 A1
Edred Ho E9 ....75 A4
Edrich Ho SW4 ....270 A1
Edric Ho SW1 ....259 D4
Edrick Rd HA8 ....27 A4
Edrick Wlk HA8 ....27 A4
Edric Rd SE14 ....140 D5
Edridge Cl WD23 ....8 A6
Edridge Ho 9 SE27 .160 D1
Edridge Rd CR0 ....221 B5
Edward Alleyn Ho
SE21 ....161 C4
Edward Ave
Chingford E4 ....35 D4
Morden SM4 ....202 B4
Edward Betham CE Prim
Sch UB6 ....86 A5
Edward Cl
Edmonton N9 ....17 D4
Hampton TW12 ....174 A5
Edward Ct 2 E16 ....99 A2
2 Ealing W5 ....87 B3
Harrow HA1 ....64 C6
Edward Dodd Ct N1 .235 D2
Edward Edward's Ho
SE1 ....251 C3
Edwardes Sq
W8 ....113 B3 254 D5

Edward Friend Ho **6**
  N16 . . . .**73** C5
Edward Gr EN4 . . . .**14** B6
Edward Harvey Ct
  DA17 . . . .**125** B1
Edward Ho SE11 . .**260** D2
  W2 . . . .**236** C5
Edward Kennedy **18**
  W10 . . . .**91** A3
Edward Mann Cl **12**
  E1 . . . .**96** D1
Edward Mans **7** IG11 **79** D1
Edward Mews NW1 . .**231** D3
Edward Pauling Ho
  TW14 . . . .**149** D4
Edward Pauling Prim Sch
  TW13 . . . .**149** C2
Edward Pinner Ct **5**
  KT6 . . . .**214** A6
Edward Pl SE8 . . . . . .**141** B6
Edward Rd E17 . . . .**52** C4
  Bromley BR1 . . . .**187** C3
  Chislehurst BR7 . . . . . .**188** D5
  Croydon CR0 . . . .**205** C2
  Dagenham RM6 . . . . . .**59** A3
  Hampton TW12 . . . . . .**174** A5
  Harrow HA2 . . . .**42** A6
  Hatton TW14 . . . .**149** C4
  New Barnet EN4 . . . . . .**14** B6
  Northolt UB5 . . . .**84** C5
  Penge SE20 . . . .**184** D4
Edward Redhead Jun & Inf
  Sch E17 . . . .**53** A6
Edward Robinson Ho **3**
  SE14 . . . .**140** D5
Edward's Ave HA4 . . . .**62** C2
Edwards Cl KT4 . . . . . .**216** D6
Edward's Cotts **11** N1 . .**72** D1
Edwards Dr N11 . . . . . .**31** D3
Edwards Language Sch
  W5 . . . .**110** A6
Edwards Mews N1 . . . .**72** C1
  W1 . . . .**93** A1 **238** A1
Edward Sq N1 . . . . . .**233** C5
  SE16 . . . .**119** A5
Edwards Rd DA17 . . . .**125** C2
Edward St **10** E16 . . . .**99** A3
  SE14 . . . .**141** B5
Edward Temme Ave
  E15 . . . .**76** D1
Edward Tyler Rd
  SE12 . . . .**165** C2
Edward VII Mans
  NW10 . . . .**90** D4
Edward Way TW15 . . . .**148** B2
Edward Wilson Prim Sch
  W2 . . . .**91** D2
Edwina Ct SM1 . . . . . .**217** D4
Edwina Gdns IG4 . . . . .**56** A4
Edwin Arnold Ct
  DA15 . . . .**189** D6
Edwin Ave E6 . . . .**100** C5
Edwin Cl DA7 . . . .**147** B6
Edwin Ho SE15 . . . . . .**140** A5
Edwin Rd HA8 . . . .**27** B4
  Twickenham TW1,TW2 . .**152** C4
Edwin's Mead E9 . . . . .**75** A4
Edwin St E1 . . . .**96** C3
  E16 . . . .**99** A2
Edwin Stray Ho
  TW13 . . . .**151** C1
Edwin Ware Ct **2** HA5 **22** C1
Edwy Ho E9 . . . .**75** B4
Edwyn Cl EN5 . . . .**12** D5
Edwyn Ho SW18 . . . . .**157** D5
Eel Pie Island* TW1 **153** A3
Effie Pl SW6 . . . .**265** B3
Effie Rd SW6 . .**135** C5 **265** B3
Effingham Cl SM2 . . . .**217** D1
Effingham Ct SW19 . . .**180** C3
Effingham Ho
  37 SW8 . . . .**137** D3
  9 Kingston KT2 . . . . .**176** D4
Effingham Lo **1** KT6 **198** A4
Effingham Rd N8 . . . . .**50** C5
  SE12 . . . .**164** D6
  Thames Ditton KT6,KT7 **197** C2
  Thornton Heath CR0 . . .**204** B2
Effort St SW17 . . . . . .**180** C5
Effra Ct SW2 . . . .**160** B6
  South Norwood SE19 . .**183** C4
Effra Mans SW2 . . . . .**160** C6
Effra Par SW2 . . . . . .**160** C6
Effra Rd SW2 . . . .**160** C6
  Wimbledon SW19 . . . .**179** D4

Effra Road Ret Pk
  SW2 . . . .**160** C6
Egan Way UB3 . . . . . .**105** C6
Egbert Ho E9 . . . .**75** A3
Egbert St NW1 **93** A6 **231** A6
Egbury Ho SW15 . . . . .**155** D5
Egerton Cl HA5 . . . . . .**40** A5
Egerton Cres
  SW3 . . . .**114** C2 **257** B4
Egerton Ct E11 . . . . . .**54** B2
  5 Richmond TW10 . . .**154** A6
Egerton Dr SE10 . . . . .**141** D4
Egerton Gdns NW4 . . . .**46** B5
  SW3 . . . .**114** C3 **257** A5
  Ealing W13 . . . .**87** B1
  Ilford IG3 . . . .**79** D5
  Willesden NW10 . . . . . .**90** C6
Egerton Gdns Mews
  SW3 . . . .**257** B5
Egerton Ho W4 . . . . . .**133** A6
Egerton Pl SW3 . . . . . .**257** B5
Egerton Rd N16 . . . . . .**51** D2
  New Malden KT3 . . . . .**199** D5
  South Norwood SE25 . .**205** C6
  Twickenham TW2 . . . . .**152** C4
  Wembley HA0 . . . .**66** B1
Egerton Terr
  SW3 . . . .**114** C3 **257** B5
Egerton Way UB3 . . . .**126** C5
Eggardon Ct UB5 . . . . .**64** A2
Egham Cl Cheam SM3 **217** A6
  Putney SW19 . . . .**157** A2
Egham Cres SM3 . . . . .**217** A6
Egham Ct KT6 . . . .**197** D4
Eglantine Rd SW18 . . .**158** A6
Egleston Rd SM4 . . . . .**201** D3
Eglington Ct SE17 . . . .**139** A6
Eglington Rd E4 . . . . . .**20** B4
Eglinton Hill SE18 . . . .**144** D5
Eglinton Prim Sch
  SE18 . . . .**144** C6
Eglinton Rd SE18 . . . . .**144** D6
Egliston Mews SW15 **134** C2
Egliston Rd SW15 . . . .**134** C2
Egmont Ave KT6 . . . . .**198** B1
Egmont Rd
  New Malden KT3 . . . . .**199** D5
  Sutton SM2 . . . .**218** A1
  Tolworth KT6 . . . .**198** C1
  Walton-on-T KT12 . . . .**194** B2
Egmont St SE14 . . . . .**140** D5
Egremont Ho SE13 . . . .**141** D3
Egremont Rd SE27 . . . .**160** C5
Egret Ho **11** SE16 . . . .**118** D2
Egret Way UB4 . . . . . .**84** D2
Eider Cl E7 . . . .**76** D3
  Hayes UB4 . . . .**84** D2
Eider Ct **39** SE8 . . . . .**141** B6
Eighteenth Rd CR4 . .**204** A5
Eighth Ave Hayes UB3 **106** A5
  Ilford E12 . . . .**78** B4
Eileen Ct BR7 . . . .**188** C5
Eileen Rd SE25 . . . . . .**205** B4
Eindhoven Cl SM5 . . .**203** A1
Einstein Ho HA9 . . . . . .**67** A5
Eisenhower Dr E6 . . . .**100** A2
Eisenhower Ho KT8 . .**175** C2
Ekarra Ho SW3 . . . . . .**270** B2
Elaine Ct **13** NW3 . . . .**70** D2
Elaine Gr NW5 . . . .**71** A3
Elaine Ho N4 . . . .**50** A1
Elam Cl SE5 . . . .**138** C3
Elam St SE5 . . . .**138** C3
Elan Ct E1 . . . .**96** B2
Eland Pl CR0 . . . .**220** D5
Eland Rd SW11 . . . . . .**136** D2
  Croydon CR0 . . . .**220** D5
Elba Pl SE17 **117** A2 **262** B4
Elberon Ave CR0 . . . .**203** C3
Elbe St SW6 . . . .**136** A3
Elborough Rd SE25 . .**206** A4
Elborough St SW18 . .**157** D3
Elbourne Trad Est
  DA17 . . . .**125** D3
Elbury Dr E16 . . . .**99** A1
Elcho St
  SW11 . . . .**136** C5 **267** B3
Elcot Ave SE15 . . . . . .**140** B5
Eldenwall Ind Est RM8 **59** B1
Elder Ave N8 . . . .**50** A4
Elderberry Gr **10**
  SE27 . . . .**183** A6
Elderberry Rd W5 . . . .**110** A4
Elder Cl DA15 . . . .**167** D3
  HA8 . . . .**27** A5
  Barnet N20 . . . .**13** D3
  Yiewsley UB7 . . . .**104** A6
Elder Ct WD23 . . . .**8** C3
Elderfield Ho **3** E14 . .**119** C6

Elderfield Pl SW17 . . .**181** B6
Elderfield Rd E5 . . . . . .**74** C4
Elderfield Wlk E11 . . . .**55** B4
Elderflower Way E15 . . .**76** C1
Elder Gdns **9** SE27 . .**183** A6
Elder Oak Cl SE20 . . .**184** B2
Elder St E1 . . .**95** D3 **243** C5
Elderslie Cl BR3 . . . . .**207** D3
Elderslie Rd SE9 . . . .**166** C6
Elderton Rd SE26 . . . .**185** A6
Eldertree Pl CR4 . . . . .**181** C2
Eldertree Way CR4 . . .**181** C2
Elder Wlk N1 . . . .**234** D6
Elderwood Pl SE27 . . .**183** A5
Eldon Ave
  Croydon CR0 . . . .**222** C6
  Heston TW5 . . . .**129** C5
Eldon Cl NW6 . . . .**91** C6
Eldon Gr NW3 . . . .**70** B3
Eldon Ho SW9 . . . . . .**138** D2
Eldon Jun & Inf Schs
  N9 . . . .**18** C3
Eldon Pk SE25 . . . . . .**206** B5
Eldon Rd E17 . . . .**53** B5
  N9 . . . .**18** C3
  W8 . . . .**113** D3 **255** D5
  Tottenham N22 . . . . . .**32** D2
Eldon St EC2 . .**95** B2 **242** D3
Eldon Way NW10 . . . . .**88** D5
Eldred Rd IG11 . . . . . .**101** C6
Eldrick Ct TW14 . . . . .**149** B3
Eldridge Cl TW14 . . . .**150** A3
Eldridge Ct SE16 . . . .**118** A3
Eleanor Cl N15 . . . . . .**51** D6
  SE16 . . . .**118** D4
Eleanor Cres NW7 . . . .**28** D6
Eleanor Ct **13** E2 . . . .**96** A6
Eleanor Gdns
  Barnet EN5 . . . .**12** D6
  Dagenham RM8 . . . . . .**81** B6
Eleanor Gr
  Mortlake SW13 . . . . . .**133** C2
  Uxbridge UB10 . . . . . .**60** D5
Eleanor Ho **1** NW5 . . .**71** C3
  18 W6 . . . .**112** C1
  6 Merton SW19 . . . .**179** D2
Eleanor Palmer Prim Sch
  NW5 . . . .**71** C4
Eleanor Rathbone Ho **1**
  N6 . . . .**49** D2
Eleanor Rd E15 . . . . . .**76** D2
  Bowes Park N11 . . . . . .**32** A4
Eleanor Smith Sch
  E13 . . . .**99** B5
Eleanor St E3 . . . .**97** C4
Eleanor Wlk **25** SE18 .**122** B2
Electra Ave TW6 . . . . .**127** D2
Electric Ave SW9 . . . .**138** C1
  Enfield EN3 . . . .**7** B6
Electric Ho **12** E3 . . . .**97** C4
Electric La **2** SW9 . . .**138** C1
Electric Mans **1**
  SW9 . . . .**138** C1
Electric Par Ilford IG3 . .**57** D1
  Surbiton KT6 . . . .**197** D3
Elephant & Castle
  SE1 . . . .**261** D4
  SE1 . . . .**117** A3 **261** D5
Elephant & Castle Sta
  SE1 . . . .**116** D3 **261** D5
  SE17 . . . .**117** A2 **262** A4
Elephant La SE16 . . . .**118** C4
Elephant Rd
  SE17 . . . .**117** A2 **262** A4
Elers Rd W13 . . . .**109** C4
  Hayes UB3 . . . .**105** B2
Eley Rd N18 . . . .**34** D5
Eley's Est N18 . . . .**34** D6
Elfindale Rd SE24 . . . .**161** A6
Elfin Gr TW11 . . . .**174** D5
Elford Cl SE9 . . . .**143** C1
Elfort Rd N5 . . . .**72** C4
Elfrida Cres SE6 . . . . .**185** C6
Elfrida Prim Sch SE6 **185** C6
Elf Row E1 . . . .**118** C6
Elfwine Rd W7 . . . .**86** C2
Elgal Cl BR6 . . . .**226** D3
Elgar Cl E13 . . . .**99** C5
  SE8 . . . .**141** C5
  Buckhurst Hill IG9 . . . . .**21** D2
  Elstree WD6 . . . .**9** D4
  Ickenham UB10 . . . . . .**60** C6
Elgar Ct W14 . . . .**254** A5

Elgar Ho NW6 . . . .**70** A1
  SW1 . . . .**258** D1
  Hayes UB4 . . . .**84** C2
  Isleworth TW2 . . . . . .**152** B5
Elgar St SE16 . . . .**119** A3
Elgin Ave W12 . . . . . .**112** B3
  W9 . . . .**91** B3
  Ashford TW15 . . . . . .**171** A4
  Harrow HA3 . . . .**25** B1
Elgin Cres
  W11 . . . .**113** A6 **244** B6
  Hatton TW6 . . . .**127** C3
Elgin Ct W9 . . . .**91** D3
Elgin Ho **8** E14 . . . . . .**97** D1
  Northolt UB5 . . . .**84** B5
Elgin Mans W9 . . . . . .**91** D4
Elgin Mews W11 . . . . . .**91** A1
Elgin Mews N W9 . . . . .**91** D4
Elgin Mews S W9 . . . . .**91** D4
Elgin Rd N22 . . . .**31** C1
  Croydon CR0 . . . .**221** D6
  Ilford IG3 . . . .**57** C2
  Sutton SM1 . . . .**218** A5
  Wallington SM6 . . . . .**219** C2
Elgood Ave HA6 . . . . . .**22** A3
Elgood Ho NW8 . . . . . .**229** D3
Elham Cl BR1 . . . .**187** D3
Elham Ho **13** E5 . . . . .**74** B3
Elia Mews N1 . .**94** D5 **234** C3
Elias Pl SW8 . . . .**138** C6
Elia St N1 . . . .**94** D5 **234** C3
Elibank Rd SE9 . . . . . .**144** C1
Elim Est SE1 . . . .**263** A6
Elim St SE1 . . . .**263** A6
Elim Way E13 . . . .**98** D4
Eliot Bank SE23,SE26 .**162** B2
Eliot Bank Prim Sch
  SE23 . . . .**162** B2
Eliot Ct SW18 . . . .**157** D5
Eliot Dr HA2 . . . .**63** D6
Eliot Gdns SW15 . . . .**134** A1
Eliot Hill SE13 . . . . . .**142** A3
Eliot Ho **10** TW10 . . .**154** B5
Eliot Mews NW8 . . . . .**229** A4
Eliot Pk SE13 . . . .**142** A3
Eliot Pl SE3 . . . .**142** C3
Eliot Rd RM9 . . . .**80** D4
Eliot Vale SE3 . . . .**142** B3
Elizabethan Ct N3 . . . .**47** A6
Elizabeth Ave
  N1 . . . .**73** B1 **235** B6
  Enfield EN2 . . . .**4** D2
  Ilford IG1 . . . .**79** B4
Elizabeth Barnes Ct **5**
  SW6 . . . .**135** D3
Elizabeth Blackwell Ho
  N22 . . . .**32** C2
Elizabeth Cl **12** E14 . . .**97** D1
  W9 . . . .**236** B5
  Cheam SM1 . . . .**217** B4
Elizabeth Clyde Cl
  N15 . . . .**51** C5
Elizabeth Cotts **5**
  TW9 . . . .**132** C4
Elizabeth Ct NW8 . . . .**237** B6
  SE22 . . . .**140** A1
  SW10 . . . .**266** D5
  SW1 . . . .**259** D5
  Buckhurst Hill IG9 . . . . .**21** B3
  Sunbury TW16 . . . . . .**194** C6
  3 Teddington TW11 . .**174** C5
  West Barnes SM4 . . . .**201** A2
  6 Woodford E18 . . . .**37** A2
  2 Woodford IG8 . . . .**37** C3
Elizabeth Finn Ho
  W12 . . . .**112** A4
Elizabeth Fry Ho
  UB3 . . . .**105** D4
Elizabeth Fry Pl SE18 **144** A4
Elizabeth Garrett
  Anderson Ho **9**
  DA17 . . . .**125** C2
Elizabeth Garrett
  Anderson Hospl
  NW1 . . . .**93** C3 **239** B6
Elizabeth Garrett
  Anderson Language Coll
  N1 . . . .**94** B5 **233** C3
Elizabeth Gdns W3 . . .**111** D5
  Stanmore HA7 . . . .**25** C5
  Sunbury TW16 . . . . . .**194** C6
Elizabeth Ho **46** E3 . . .**97** D4
  N20 . . . .**14** D1
  SE11 . . . .**261** B3
  15 W6 . . . .**112** C1
  Wembley HA9 . . . .**66** B3
Elizabeth Ind Est
  SE14 . . . .**140** D6

Elizabeth Kenny Ho
  N1 . . . .**73** A2
Elizabeth Mews NW3 . .**70** D2
Elizabeth Pl N15 . . . . .**51** B5
Elizabeth Rd E6 . . . . . .**99** D6
  N15 . . . .**51** C4
Elizabeth Ride N9 . . . . .**18** C4
Elizabeth Selby Inf Sch
  E2 . . . .**96** A4
Elizabeth Sq **13** SE16 **119** A6
Elizabeth St
  SW1 . . . .**115** A2 **258** B4
Elizabeth Terr SE9 . . .**166** B5
Elizabeth Way
  Feltham TW13 . . . . . .**172** C6
  South Norwood SE19 . .**183** B3
Elkanette Mews N20 . .**14** A2
Elkington Point SE11 **261** A3
Elkington Rd E13 . . . . .**99** B3
Elkstone Rd W10 . . . . .**91** B2
Ellacombe Ho **1**
  SW2 . . . .**160** C4
Ellaline Rd W6 . . . . . .**134** D6
Ella Mews NW3 . . . . . .**70** D4
Ellanby Cres N18 . . . . .**34** B5
Elland Ho **12** E14 . . . .**97** B1
Elland Rd SE15 . . . . . .**140** C1
Ella Rd N4,N8 . . . .**50** A2
Ellement Cl HA5 . . . . . .**40** D4
Ellena Ct N14 . . . .**16** A3
Ellenborough Ct N22 .**32** D2
Ellenborough Ho **5**
  W12 . . . .**112** B6
Ellenborough Pl
  SW15 . . . .**134** A1
Ellenborough Rd
  DA14 . . . .**191** B5
  Tottenham N22 . . . . . .**33** A2
Ellen Cl BR1 . . . .**209** D6
Ellen Ct N9 . . . .**18** C2
  6 Chingford E4 . . . . .**20** A3
Ellen Miller Ho **2** E17 **54** A4
Ellen St E1 . . . .**96** A1
Ellen Webb Dr HA3 . . .**42** C1
Ellen Wilkinson Ho
  7 E2 . . . .**96** B4
  SW6 . . . .**264** D5
  12 Dagenham RM10 . .**81** C5
Ellen Wilkinson Prim Sch
  E6 . . . .**100** A4
Ellen Wilkinson Sch for
  Girls W3 . . . .**88** B1
Elleray Rd TW11 . . . .**174** D4
Ellerby St SW6 . . . . . .**134** C4
Ellerdale Cl **22** NW3 . .**70** A4
Ellerdale Rd NW3 . . . .**70** A3
Ellerdale St SE13 . . . .**141** D2
Ellerdine Rd TW3 . . . .**130** B1
Ellerker Gdns TW10 . .**154** B5
Ellerman Ave TW2,
  TW4 . . . .**151** B3
Ellerslie Ct **6** SM6 . .**219** B2
Ellerslie Gdns NW10 . .**90** A6
Ellerslie Ind Est SW2 **160** A6
Ellerslie Rd W12 . . . .**112** B5
Ellerslie Sq SW2 . . . .**160** A6
Ellerton Ct W3 . . . . . .**110** D4
Ellerton Gdns RM9 . . .**80** C1
Ellerton Lo N3 . . . .**29** C1
Ellerton Rd
  Barnes SW13 . . . .**134** A4
  Dagenham RM9 . . . . . .**80** C1
  Surbiton KT6 . . . .**198** D1
  Wandsworth SW17,
  SW18 . . . .**158** B3
  Wimbledon SW20 . . . .**178** A3
Ellery Ho SE17 . . . . . .**262** D3
Ellery Rd SE19 . . . . . .**183** B3
Ellery St SE15 . . . . . .**140** B3
Ellesborough Cl WD19 **22** C5
Ellesmere Ave NW7 . . .**11** B1
  Beckenham BR3 . . . . .**185** D1
Ellesmere Cl E11 . . . . .**54** D4
  Ruislip HA4 . . . .**39** A2
Ellesmere Ct
  Chiswick W4 . . . .**133** B6
  Lewisham SE12 . . . . . .**165** A3
  Penge SE20 . . . .**184** B1
Ellesmere Gdns IG4 . .**56** A4
Ellesmere Gr EN5 . . . .**13** B6
Ellesmere Rd E3 . . . . .**97** A5
  NW10 . . . .**68** A3
  Chiswick W4 . . . .**133** B6
  Greenford UB6 . . . .**86** A3
  Twickenham TW1 . . . .**153** C6
Ellesmere St E14 . . . . .**97** C1
Ellies Mews TW15 . . . .**148** A2
Ellingfort Rd E8 . . . . . .**74** B1
Ellingham Prim Sch
  KT9 . . . .**213** D1
Ellingham Rd E15 . . . . .**76** B4

Ellingham Rd continued
  W12 . . . .**112** A4
  Chessington KT9 . . . .**213** D2
Ellington Ct N14 . . . . .**15** C2
Ellington Ho SE1 . . . .**262** B5
Ellington Rd N10 . . . . .**49** B5
  Feltham TW13 . . . . . .**171** D6
  Hounslow TW3 . . . . . .**129** D3
Ellington St N7 . . . . . .**72** C2
Elliot Cl E15 . . . .**76** C1
  Wembley HA9 . . . .**66** C5
Elliot Ct **5** N15 . . . . . .**51** D5
Elliot Rd NW4 . . . .**46** B3
  SW9 . . . .**138** D5
Elliott Ave HA4 . . . . . .**62** B6
Elliott Rd SW17 . . . . .**192** C5
Elliott Rd SW9 . . . . . .**138** D4
  W4 . . . .**111** C2
  Bromley BR2 . . . .**209** D5
  Stanmore HA7 . . . .**25** A4
  Thornton Heath CR7 . .**204** C5
Elliott Sch SW15 . . . .**156** C5
Elliott's Pl N1 . . . .**234** D5
Elliott Sq NW3 . . . . . .**70** C1
Elliott's Row
  SE11 . . . .**116** D2 **261** D4
Ellis Cl HA8 . . . .**27** C4
  NW10 . . . .**68** C2
  SE9 . . . .**167** A2
Elliscombe Mount **11**
  SE7 . . . .**143** C6
Elliscombe Rd SE7 . . .**143** C6
Ellis Ct W7 . . . .**86** C2
Ellisfield Dr SW15 . . .**156** A4
Ellis Franklin Ct
  NW8 . . . .**229** A4
Ellis Ho E17 . . . .**54** A4
  SE17 . . . .**262** C2
Ellison Gdns UB2 . . . .**107** B2
Ellison Ho **1** SE13 . . .**142** A3
Ellison Rd DA15 . . . . .**167** B3
  Barnes SW13 . . . .**133** D3
  Streatham SW16 . . . . .**182** A3
Ellis Rd Mitcham CR4 .**202** D3
  Southall UB1 . . . .**108** A5
Ellis St SW1 . . .**115** A2 **258** A4
Elliston Ho **14** SE18 . .**122** C2
Ellora Rd SW16 . . . . .**181** D5
Ellswood Ct **18** KT6 . .**197** D2
Ellsworth St E2 . . . . . .**96** B4
Ellwood Ct **1** W9 . . . .**91** D3
Elmar Rd N15 . . . .**51** B5
Elm Ave Ealing W5 . . .**110** B5
  Ruislip HA4 . . . .**40** B2
Elmbank N14 . . . .**16** A4
Elmbank Dr BR1 . . . .**187** D1
Elm Bank Gdns
  SW13 . . . .**133** C3
Elm Bank Mans
  SW13 . . . .**133** C3
Elmbank Way W7 . . . . .**86** B2
Elmbourne Dr DA17 . .**125** D2
Elmbourne Rd SW17 .**159** B1
Elmbridge Ave KT5 . .**199** A3
Elmbridge Cl HA4 . . . .**40** A3
Elmbridge Dr HA4 . . . .**40** A3
Elmbridge Wlk E8 . . . .**74** A1
Elmbrook **2** E18 . . . . .**55** A6
Elmbrook Cl TW16 . . .**172** B2
Elmbrook Gdns SE9 . .**144** A1
Elmbrook Rd SM1 . . .**217** B4
Elm Cl N19 . . . .**71** C6
  NW4 . . . .**46** D4
  Buckhurst Hill IG9 . . . .**21** D2
  Carshalton SM5 . . . . .**202** D1
  Harrow HA2 . . . .**41** D3
  Hayes UB3 . . . .**84** A1
  South Croydon CR2 . . .**221** C2
  Tolworth KT5 . . . .**199** A2
  Twickenham TW13,
  TW2 . . . .**151** D2
  Wanstead E11 . . . .**55** B3
  West Barnes SW20 . . .**200** C5
Elmcote HA5 . . . .**22** D1
Elmcourt Rd SE21,
  SE27 . . . .**160** D2
Elm Court Sch SE27 .**161** A2
Elm Cres W5 . . . .**110** A4
  Kingston KT2 . . . .**176** A2
Elmcroft N6 . . . .**49** C2
  N8 . . . .**50** B4
Elmcroft Ave DA15 . . .**168** A5
  NW11 . . . .**47** B2
  Enfield N9 . . . .**18** B5
  Wanstead E11 . . . .**55** B5
Elmcroft Cl
  Chessington KT9 . . . .**214** A5
  Ealing W5 . . . .**87** D1
  Feltham TW14 . . . . . .**149** D5
  Wanstead E11 . . . .**55** B5

Elmcroft Cres NW11 47 A2
Harrow HA2 41 C6
Elmcroft Dr
Ashford TW15 170 C5
Chessington KT9 214 A5
Elmcroft Gdns NW9 44 C4
Elmcroft St E5 74 C4
Elmcroft Terr UB8 82 C1
Elm Ct EC4 251 A6
4 N3 29 C2
SE13 142 B2
SW9 138 C4
42 W2 91 C2
5 Ashford TW16 171 D3
Catford SE6 163 D3
Chingford E4 36 A4
Mitcham CR4 180 D1
Elmdale Rd N13 32 B5
Elmdene KT5 199 A1
Elmdene Cl BR3 207 B4
Elmdene Rd SE18 122 D1
Elmdon Rd
Hatton, Hatton Cross
TW6 127 D2
Hounslow TW5 129 A3
Elm Dr Harrow HA2 41 D3
Sunbury TW16 172 C1
Elmer Cl EN2 4 B2
Elmer Ct SW6 135 A3
Elmer Gdns
Edgware HA8 26 D3
Isleworth TW7 130 B2
Elmer Ho NW1 237 A4
Elmer Rd SE6 164 A4
Elmer's Dr TW11 175 B4
Elmers End Rd BR3,
SE20 206 C6
Elmers End Sta BR3 206 D5
Elmerside Rd BR3 207 A5
Elmers Rd SE25 206 A2
Elmfield Ave N8 50 A4
Mitcham CR4 181 A2
Teddington TW11 174 D5
Elmfield Cl HA1 64 C6
Elmfield Ct DA16 146 B4
Elmfield Ho 17 N2 30 B1
6 N5 73 A3
W9 91 C3
Elmfield Mans 5
SW17 159 A2
Elmfield Pk BR1 209 A6
Elmfield Rd BR1 209 A6
E17 52 D3
N2 48 B6
Chingford E4 20 B2
Southall UB2 107 A3
Upper Tooting SW17 159 B2
Elmfield Way W9 91 C2
South Croydon CR2 221 D1
Elm Friars Wlk NW1 71 D1
Elmgate Ave TW13 150 C1
Elmgate Gdns HA8 27 B6
Elm Gdns N2 48 A6
Claygate KT10 212 D2
Enfield EN2 5 B5
Mitcham CR4 203 D5
Elm Gn W3 89 C1
Elm Gr BR6 211 D1
N8 50 A3
NW2 68 D4
SE15 140 A3
Harrow HA2 41 C2
Kingston KT2 176 A2
Sutton SM1 217 D4
Wimbledon SW19 179 A3
Woodford IG8 36 D5
Yiewsley UB7 104 B6
Elmgreen Cl 8 E15 98 C6
Elmgrove Cres HA1 43 A4
Elmgrove Fst & Mid Schs
HA3 43 A5
Elmgrove Gdns HA1 43 A4
Elm Grove Par SM6 219 A5
Elm Grove Rd W5 110 A4
Elmgrove Rd
Croydon CR0 206 B2
Harrow HA1 42 D4
Elm Grove Rd SW13 134 A3
Elm Hall Gdns E11 55 B3
Elm Hatch HA5 23 B3
Elm Ho 4 E14 120 A4
2 Kingston KT2 176 B3
Elmhurst DA17 147 A6
Elmhurst Ave N2 48 B6
Mitcham CR4 181 B3
Elmhurst Ct CR0 221 B3
Elmhurst Dr E18 37 A1
Elmhurst Lo 3 SM2 218 A1
Elmhurst Mans SW4 137 D2
Elmhurst Prim Sch E7 77 B1
Elmhurst Rd E7 77 B1
Chislehurst SE9 166 A1
Enfield EN3 6 C6
Tottenham N17 33 D1
Elmhurst Sch CR2 221 B3
Elmhurst St SW4 137 D2
Elmhurst Villas SE15 140 C1
Elmington Cl DA5 169 D5
Elmington Rd SE5 139 B5
Elmira St SE13 141 D2
Elm La SE6 163 B2
Elm Lawn Cl UB8 60 A1
Elmlea Dr UB3 83 D2
Elmlee Cl BR7 188 B4
Elmley Cl 12 E6 100 A2
Elmley St SE18 123 B2
Elm Lo SW6 134 D4
Elmore Cl HA0 88 A5
Elmore Ho SW9 138 D3
Elmore Rd E11 76 B5
Enfield EN3 6 D5
Elmore St N1 73 B1
Elm Park Ave N15 52 A3
Elm Park Ct HA5 40 C6
Elm Park Gdns NW4 46 D4
SW10 114 B1 256 C1
Elm Park Ho SW10 256 C1
Elm Park La
SW3 114 B1 256 C1
Elm Park Mans SW10 266 B6
Elm Park Rd N3 29 B3
SW3 136 B6 266 C6
Edmonton N21 17 A4
Pinner HA5 40 D6
South Norwood SE25 205 D6
Walthamstow E10 53 A1
Elm Pk Stanmore HA7 25 C5
Streatham SW2 160 B4
Elm Pl SW7 114 B1 256 C2
Elm Quay SW8 269 C5
Elm Rd E11 76 B6
E17 54 A4
E7 76 D2
Barnet EN5 1 B1
Beckenham BR3 185 B1
Chessington KT9 214 A4
Claygate KT10 212 D2
East Bedfont TW14 149 B4
Hackbridge SM6 203 A1
Kingston KT2 176 B2
Kingston KT3 199 B6
Mortlake SW14 133 A1
Sidcup DA14 190 A6
South Norwood CR7 205 B5
Stoneleigh KT17 215 D2
Tottenham N22 32 D2
Wembley HA9 66 A3
Elm Rd W SM4 201 B2
Elm Row NW3 70 A5
Elms Ave N10 49 B6
NW4 46 D4
Elmscott Gdns N21 17 A5
Elmscott Rd BR1 186 D5
Elms Cotts 1 CR4 180 D1
Elms Cres SW4 159 D5
Elms Ct Merton SW19 179 D3
Wembley HA0 65 A4
Elmsdale Rd E17 53 B5
Elms Gdns
Dagenham RM9 81 B4
Wembley HA0 65 A4
Elmshaw Rd SW15 156 A6
Elmshurst Cres N2 48 B5
Elmside CR0 223 D2
Elmside Rd HA9 66 C5
Elms La HA0 65 A5
Elmsleigh Ave HA3 43 C5
Elmsleigh Ct SM1 217 D5
Elmsleigh Ho TW2 152 B2
Elmsleigh Rd TW2 152 B2
Elmslie Ct SE9 166 C5
Elmslie Point 2 E3 97 B2
Elms Mews W2 246 C6
Elms Park Ave HA0 65 A4
Elms Rd SW4 159 C6
Harrow HA3 24 C3
Elm St WC1 94 B3 240 D5
Elmstead Ave BR7 188 B5
Wembley HA9 66 B6
Elmstead Cl N20 13 C2
West Ewell KT19 215 C3
Elmstead Gdns KT4 216 A5
Elmstead Glade BR7 188 B4
Elmstead La BR7 188 B5
Elmstead Rd IG3 79 D6
Elmstead Woods Sta
BR7 188 A4
Elmsted Cres DA16 146 C6
Elms The E12 78 A2
NW10 89 C5
Elms The *continued*
NW9 45 A3
Ashford TW15 170 C5
Barnes SW13 133 D2
Claygate KT10 212 D1
Croydon CR0 205 A1
Elmstone Rd SW6 265 A2
Elmsway TW15 170 C5
Elmsworth Ave TW3 129 D3
Elm Terr NW2 69 C5
3 SE9 166 C5
Harrow HA3 24 B2
Elmton Ct NW8 236 C6
Elmton Way E5 74 A5
Elm Tree Ave KT10 196 C2
Elm Tree Cl
NW8 92 B4 229 C2
Ashford TW15 170 D5
Northolt UB5 85 B5
Elm Tree Ct NW8 229 C2
5 SE5 139 A4
18 SE7 143 C6
Elm Tree Rd
NW8 92 B4 229 C2
Elmtree Rd TW11 174 C5
Elm View Ct UB2 107 C2
Elm Way N11 31 A4
NW10 67 C4
North Cheam KT4 216 C5
West Ewell KT19 215 B3
Elm Wlk NW3 69 C6
Orpington BR6 226 B5
West Barnes SW20 200 D5
Elmwood Ave
Bowes Park N13 32 A5
Feltham TW13 150 B1
Harrow HA3 43 B3
Elmwood Cl
Hackbridge SM6 219 B6
Stoneleigh KT17 216 A1
Elmwood Cres NW9 45 A5
Elmwood Ct SW11 268 C2
Wembley HA0 65 A5
Elmwood Dr DA5 169 A4
Stoneleigh KT17 216 A1
Elmwood Gdns W7 86 C1
Elmwood Inf Sch
CR0 204 D3
Elmwood Jun Sch
CR0 204 D2
Elm Wood Prim Sch
SE27 161 B1
Elmwood Rd SE24 161 B6
Chiswick W4 133 A6
Mitcham CR4 202 D6
Thornton Heath CR0 204 D2
Elmworth Gr SE21 161 B2
Elnathan Mews W9 91 D3
Elphinstone Ct SW16 182 A4
Elphinstone Rd E17 35 B1
Elphinstone St N5 72 D4
Elrington Rd E8 74 A2
Woodford IG8 37 A5
Elsa Ct BR3 185 B2
Elsa Rd DA16 146 C3
Elsa St E1 97 A2
Elsdale St E9 74 C2
Elsden Mews E2 96 C5
Elsden Rd N17 33 D2
Elsenham Rd E12 78 C3
Elsenham St SW18,
SW19 157 B2
Elsfield NW5 71 B3
Elsham Rd E11 76 C4
W14 113 A4 244 A1
Elsham Terr W14 244 A1
Elsiedene Rd N21 17 A4
Elsie Lane Ct W2 91 D2
Elsiemaud Rd SE4 163 B6
Elsie Rd SE22 139 D1
Elsinge Rd EN1 6 B6
Elsinore Ave TW19 148 A4
Elsinore Gdns NW2 69 A5
Elsinore Ho N1 234 A5
12 SE5 139 A3
7 SE7 122 A2
Elsinore Rd SE23 163 A3
Elsinore Way TW9 132 D2
Elsley Ct HA9 66 D2
Elsley Prim Sch HA9 66 B2
Elsley Rd SW11 137 A2
Elsley Sch SW11 137 A2
Elspeth Rd SW11 136 D1
Wembley HA0 66 A3
Elsrick Ave SM4 201 C4
Elstan Way CR0 207 A2
Elstead Ct SM4 201 A1
Elstead Ho 9 SW2 160 B4
Elsted St
SE17 117 B2 262 D3
Elstow Cl SE9 166 B6
Ruislip HA4 40 D2
Elstow Gdns RM9 103 A6
Elstow Grange NW6 68 D1
Elstow Rd RM9 103 A6
Elstree Gdns DA17 125 A2
Edmonton N9 18 B3
Ilford IG1 79 A3
Elstree Hill BR1 186 C3
Elstree Hill N WD6 9 D6
Elstree Hill S WD6 9 D4
Elstree Ho 3 HA7 25 C6
Elstree Pk WD6 11 B5
Elstree Rd Bushey WD23 8 C4
Elstree WD6 9 A5
Elswick Rd SE13 141 D3
Elswick St SW6 136 A3
Elsworth Cl TW14 149 C3
Elsworthy KT7 196 C3
Elsworthy Rd
NW3 92 C6 230 A6
Elsworthy Rise NW3 70 C1
Elsworthy Terr NW3 70 C1
Elsynge Rd SW18 158 B6
Elsynge Road Mans
SW18 158 B6
Eltham CE Prim Sch
SE9 166 B6
Eltham Coll SE9 165 D2
Eltham Green Rd
SE9 165 C6
Eltham Green Sch
SE9 165 D5
Eltham High St SE9 166 B5
Eltham Hill SE9 166 A6
Eltham Hill Sch SE9 166 A5
Eltham Hill Tech Coll for
Girls SE9 166 A5
Eltham Palace★ SE9 166 A4
Eltham Palace Rd
SE9 165 D5
Eltham Park Gdns
SE9 144 C1
Eltham Rd SE9,SE12 165 B6
Eltham Sta SE9 166 B6
Elthiron Rd
SW6 135 C4 265 B1
Elthorne Ave W7 109 A4
Elthorne Ct NW9 45 B3
Feltham TW13 150 C3
Elthorne Park High Sch
W7 108 D3
Elthorne Park Rd
W7 109 A4
Elthorne Rd N19 71 D6
NW9 45 B2
Elthorne Way NW9 45 B3
Elthruda Rd SE13 164 B5
Eltisley Rd IG1 78 D4
Elton Ave Barnet EN5 13 B6
Wembley HA0 65 B3
Wembley UB6 64 D2
Elton Cl KT1 175 C3
Elton Ho 3 E3 97 B6
Elton Lo 4 W5 110 A6
Elton Pl N16 73 C3
Elton Rd KT2 176 C2
Elton St 11 N16 73 C3
Eltringham St SW18 136 A1
Elvaston Ct EN5 12 C6
Elvaston Mews SW7 256 B6
Elvaston Pl
SW7 114 A3 256 B5
Elveden Ho 17 SW9 138 D1
Elveden Pl NW10 88 C5
Elveden Rd NW10 88 C5
Elvendon Rd N13 32 A4
Elver Gdns 6 E2 96 A4
Elverson Rd SE8 141 D3
Elverson Rd Sta SE8 141 D3
Elverton St
SW1 115 D2 259 C4
Elvin Ct NW9 45 A2
Elvington Gn BR2 208 D4
Elvington La NW9 27 C2
Elvin Ho 2 E9 74 C2
Elvino Rd SE26 185 A5
Elvis Rd NW2 68 C2
Elwill Way BR3 208 B5
Elwin St E2 96 A4
Elwood Ho N5 72 D5
Elwood St N4,N5 72 D5
Elworth Ho SW8 270 D3
Elwyn Gdns SE12 165 A4
Ely Cl SW20 177 D1
Ely Cottages SW8 270 C3
Ely Court Flats SW6 264 A1
Ely Ct KT1 198 C6
Ely Gdns
Borehamwood WD6 11 B6
Ely Gdns *continued*
Redbridge IG1 56 A2
Ely Ho 22 SE15 140 A5
Barnet EN4 2 C1
Elyne Rd N4 50 C3
Ely Pl EC1 94 C2 241 B3
Ely Rd E10 54 A2
Hatton TW6 127 D3
Hounslow TW4 128 C2
Thornton Heath CR0 205 B4
Elysian Ave BR5 211 D3
Elysium Gate 7 SW6 135 B3
Elysium Pl SW6 135 B3
Elysium St SW6 135 B3
Elystan Bsns Ctr UB4 106 C6
Elystan Pl
SW3 114 D1 257 C2
Elystan St
SW3 114 C2 257 B3
Elystan Wlk N1 234 A5
Elyston Ct SW15 156 B6
Emanuel Ave W3 89 A1
Emanuel Ct W3 89 B1
Emanuel Sch SW11 158 C6
Embankment SW15 134 D3
Embankment Gdns
SW3 136 D6 267 D6
Embankment Pier
WC2 116 B4 250 B4
Embankment Pl WC2 250 B4
Embankment Sta
WC2 116 A5 250 B4
Embankment The
TW1 153 A3
Embassey Ct DA14 168 B1
Embassy Ct DA16 146 B2
N11 31 D4
NW8 229 D3
Kingston KT6 197 D4
7 Wallington SM6 219 B2
7 Wanstead E18 55 A6
Ealing W5 110 B6
Embassy Gdns BR3 185 B2
Embassy Ho 2 NW6 69 C1
Embassy Lo N3 29 B1
Emba St SE16 118 A4
Ember Cl BR5 211 A2
Embercourt Rd KT10,
KT7,KT8 196 C3
Ember Ct 14 NW9 27 D1
2 W12 111 C3
Ember Farm Ave KT8 196 B3
Ember Farm Way
KT8 196 B4
Ember Gdns KT10,
KT8 196 C2
Ember Ho 8 BR1 186 B5
Ember La KT10,KT8 196 B2
Emberson Ho 7 E17 54 A5
Emberton SE5 139 C6
Emberton Ct EC1 234 C1
Embleton Rd SE13 141 D1
Embleton Wlk TW12 173 B5
Embley Point 2 E5 74 B4
Embry Cl HA7 25 A6
Embry Dr HA7 25 A4
Embry Way HA7 25 A6
Emden Cl UB7 104 C4
Emden St SW6 265 D2
Emerald Cl E16 100 A1
Emerald Ct N12 30 A6
Emerald Gdns RM8 59 C1
Emerald Sq UB2 106 D3
Emerald St
WC1 94 B2 240 C4
Emerson Gdns HA3 44 B3
Emerson Ho N16 73 C3
Emerson Rd IG1 56 C2
Emerson St
SE1 117 A5 252 A4
Emerton Cl DA6 147 A1
Emery Hill St SW1 259 B5
Emery St SE1 116 C3 261 B6
Emilia Cl EN3 18 B6
Emily Pl N7 72 C4
Emily St 7 E16 98 D1
Emlyn Gdns 3 W12 111 C3
Emlyn Rd W12 111 D3
Emmanuel CE Prim Sch
NW6 69 C3
Emmanuel Ct 9 E10 53 D2
Emmanuel Ho SE11 261 A3
Dulwich SE21 161 B1
Emmanuel Rd
Streatham SW12 159 D3
Northwood HA6 22 A3
Emma Rd E13 98 D5
Emma St E2 96 B5
Emmeline Ct KT12 194 C2
Emminster NW6 91 D6
Emmott Ave IG6 57 A4
Emmott Cl E1 97 A3
NW11 48 A3
Emperor's Gate
SW7 114 A2 256 A4
Empingham Ho 20
SE8 118 D2
Empire Ave N18 33 A4
Empire Ct HA9 66 D5
Empire Ho SW3 257 A5
Edmonton N18 33 B4
Empire Par
Edmonton N18 33 B4
Wembley HA9 66 C5
Empire Rd UB6 65 C1
Empire Sq N19 72 A5
Empire Way HA9 66 C4
Empire Wharf E3 97 A6
Empire Wharf Rd
E14 120 B2
Empress Ave
Chingford E4 35 D3
Ilford IG1 78 C6
Wanstead E12 77 D6
Woodford IG8 36 D3
Empress Dr BR7 188 D4
Empress Mews 37
SE5 139 A3
Empress Par E4 35 C3
Empress Pl
SW5 113 C1 255 A1
Empress St SE17 139 A6
Empson St E3 97 D3
Emsworth Cl N9 18 C3
Emsworth St SW2 160 B2
Emu Rd SW8 137 B3
Ena Rd SW16 204 A6
Enard Ho 27 E3 97 B5
Enbrook St W10 91 A4
Enclave Ct EC1 241 C6
Endale Cl SM5 218 D6
Endeavour Way
Barking IG11 102 A5
Thornton Heath CR0 204 A2
Wimbledon SW19 179 D6
Endell St WC2 94 A1 240 A1
Enderby St SE10 120 C1
Enderfield Ct BR7 188 C2
Enderley Cl HA3 24 C2
Enderley Ho SE19 183 D2
Enderley Rd HA3 24 C2
Endersby Rd EN5 12 C6
Endersleigh Gdns
NW4 46 A5
Endlebury Ct 3 E4 20 B2
Endlebury Rd E4 20 A2
Endlesham Ct 2
SW12 159 A4
Endlesham Rd SW12 159 A4
Endsleigh Gdns
WC1 93 D3 239 C6
Ilford IG1 56 D1
Kingston KT6 197 C3
Endsleigh Ind Est
UB2 107 B2
Endsleigh Mans 4
SW16 160 A1
Endsleigh Pl WC1 239 D6
Endsleigh Rd
Ealing W13 109 A6
Southall UB2 107 A2
Endsleigh St
WC1 93 D3 239 D6
Endway KT5 198 D2
Endwell Rd SE4 141 A3
Endymion Rd N4 50 D2
SW2 160 B5
Energen Cl NW10 67 C1
NW10 67 C2
Enfield Chase Sta EN2 5 A2
Enfield Cloisters 7
N1 95 C4
Enfield Coll EN3 6 C2
Enfield Gram Sch EN2 5 B2
Enfield Gram Sch Lower
EN1 5 B3
Enfield Ho 24 SW9 138 A3
Enfield Lock Sta EN3 7 A6
Enfield Rd E8,N1 73 C1
W3 110 D4
Brentford TW8 109 D1
Enfield EN2 4 A2
Hatton TW6 127 C3
Enfield Road Rdbt
TW6 127 C3
Enfield Town Sta EN1 5 B2
Enfield Wlk TW8 109 D1

Enford St W1 ....92 D2 237 C4
Engadine Cl CR0 ....221 D5
Engadine St SW18 ...157 C3
Engate St SE13 ....142 A1
Engel Pk NW7 ....28 C4
Engineer Cl SE18 ...144 C6
Engineers Way HA9 ...66 C4
England's La NW3 ....70 D2
England Way KT3 ....199 A5
Englefield NW1 ....232 A1
Englefield Cl Enfield EN2 4 C3
  Orpington BR5 ......211 D5
  Thornton Heath CR0 ...205 A3
Englefield Path BR5 ...211 D5
Englefield Rd N1 ....73 C1
Engleheart Dr TW14 ...149 D5
Engleheart Rd SE6 ...164 A4
Englewood Rd SW12 159 C5
English Gardening Sch The
  SW3 ....136 D6 267 C6
English Grounds SE1 ...118 B3
English Martyrs RC Prim
  Sch E1 .....95 D1 243 D1
English St E3 ....97 B3
Enid St SE16 ..117 D3 263 D6
Enid Stacy Ho 11 N19 .49 D2
Enmore Ave SE25 ...206 A4
Enmore Ct SW14 ....155 B6
Enmore Gdns SW14 .155 B6
Enmore Rd
  Croydon SE25 ......206 A4
  Putney SW15 ......156 C6
  Southall UB1 ....85 C3
Ennerdale Ave HA3,
  HA7 ....43 C6
Ennerdale Cl
  Cheam SM1 ....217 B4
  East Bedfont TW14 ...149 D3
Ennerdale Ct E11 ....55 A2
Ennerdale Dr NW9 ...45 C4
Ennerdale Gdns HA9 .43 C1
Ennerdale Ho 3 N4 ..51 B3
Ennerdale Rd DA7 ...147 C4
  Richmond TW9 ......132 B3
Ennersdale Prim Sch
  SE13 ....164 B6
Ennersdale Rd SE13 .164 B6
Ennis Ho 16 E14 ....97 D1
Ennismore Ave W4 ..111 D2
  Greenford UB6 ....64 C3
Ennismore Gdns
  SW7 ......114 C3 257 A6
  Thames Ditton KT7 ...196 C3
Ennismore Gdns Mews
  SW7 ......114 C3 257 A6
Ennismore Mews
  SW7 ......114 C3 257 A6
Ennismore St
  SW7 ......114 C3 257 A6
Ennis Rd N4 ....50 C1
  SE18 ....145 A6
Ennor Ct KT4 ....216 C4
Ensbury Ho SW8 ....270 C4
Ensign Cl TW19 ....148 A3
Ensign Ct 7 E1 ....118 A6
Ensign Dr N13 ....17 A1
Ensign St E1 ....118 A6
Ensign Way TW19 ...148 A3
Enslin Rd SE9 ......166 C4
Ensor Mews SW7 ...256 C2
Enstone Rd Enfield EN3 .7 A2
  Ickenham UB10 ......60 B5
Enterprise Cl CR0 ...204 C1
Enterprise Ho
  Barking IG11 ....101 D4
  Chingford E4 ....20 A4
  Walton-on-T KT12 ...194 B2
Enterprise Row N15 .51 D4
Enterprise Way NW10 .90 A4
  SW18 ....135 C1
  Teddington TW11 ...174 D4
Enterprize Way SE8 .119 B2
Enton Pl TW3 ....129 D1
Epirus Mews SW6 ...265 A4
Epirus Rd
  SW6 ......135 B5 264 D4
Epping Cl E14 ......119 C2
  Romford RM7 ....59 D6
Epping Forest* IG10 .21 B6
Epping Glade E4 ....20 A5
Epping Ho E5 ....74 A6
Epping New Rd IG9 .21 B5
Epping Pl N1 ....72 C2
Epping Way E4 ......19 D5
Epple Rd
  SW6 ......135 B4 264 D2
Epsom Cl DA7 ......147 D2

Epsom Cl continued
  Northolt UB5 ....63 B3
Epsom & Ewell High Sch
  KT19 ....215 A3
Epsom Rd E10 ......54 A3
  Croydon CR0 ......220 C4
  Ilford IG3 ....57 D3
  Morden SM4 ....201 B2
Epsom Sq TW6 .....127 C6
Epstein Rd SE28 ...124 B5
Epworth Rd TW7,TW8 131 B5
Epworth St
  EC2 ....95 B3 242 D5
Equity Sq 29 E2 ....95 D4
Erasmus St
  SW1 .....115 D2 259 D3
Erconwald St W12 ..89 D1
Erebus Dr SE28 ....123 B4
Eresby Dr BR3 .....207 C1
Eresby Ho SW7 ....247 B1
Eresby Pl NW6 .....69 C1
Erica Ct SW4 ......270 B1
Erica Gdns CR0 ...223 D5
Erica Ho SE4 ......141 B2
  Wood Green N22 ...32 C2
Erica St W12 ......112 A6
Eric Cl E7 ....77 A4
Eric Clarke La IG11 .101 A4
Ericcson Cl SW18 ...157 C6
Eric Fletcher Ct 7 N1 73 A1
Eric Macdonald Ho
  SW6 ....265 B1
Eric Rd E7 ....77 A4
  NW10 ....67 D2
  Dagenham RM6 .....58 D2
Eric Shipman Terr 2
  E13 ....99 A3
Ericson Ho N16 ...51 B4
  SE13 ....142 B1
Eric St E3 ....97 B3
Eric Wilkins Ho 13
  SE1 ....118 A1
Eridge Ho SE22 ...139 D2
Eridge Rd W4 .....111 B3
Erin Cl BR1 ....186 C3
Erindale SE18 .....145 B6
Erindale Ct 1 BR3 ..185 C2
Erindale Terr SE18 .145 B6
Erith Rd DA7 ......147 D2
  Belvedere DA17 ...125 C1
Erlanger Rd SE14 ..140 D3
Erlesmere Gdns W13 109 A3
Ermine Cl TW4 ....128 C3
Ermine Ho 3 N17 ..33 D1
Ermine Rd N15 ....51 D3
  SE13 ....141 D1
Ermine Side EN1 ...18 A6
Ermington Rd BR7,
  SE9 ....167 A2
Ernald Ave E6 .....100 A3
Erncroft Way TW1 ..152 D5
Ernest Ave SE27 ...182 C5
Ernest Bevin Coll
  SW17 ....158 C2
Ernest Cl BR3 .....207 C4
Ernest Cotts KT17 ..215 D1
Ernest Gdns W4 ...132 D6
Ernest Gr BR3 .....207 B4
Ernest Rd KT1 .....176 D1
Ernest Richards Twr
  E17 ....53 B6
Ernest Simmonds Ho
  SE14 ....140 C3
Ernest Sq KT1 .....176 D1
Ernest St E1 ......96 C3
Ernle Rd SW20 ....178 A3
Ernshaw Pl SW15 ..157 A6
Eros (Shaftesbury Meml)*
  W1 ....115 D2 249 C5
Erpingham Rd SW15 .134 C2
Erridge Rd SW19 ..179 C1
Errington Rd W9 ...91 B3
Errol Gdns Hayes UB4 .84 B3
  West Barnes KT3 ...200 A5
Errol St EC1 ..95 A3 242 B5
Erskine Cl SM1 ....218 C5
Erskine Cres N17 ..52 B5
Erskine Hill NW11 ...47 C4
Erskine Ho 7 SE7 ..143 C6
  SW1 ....259 A1
Erskine Rd E17 ....53 B5
  NW3 ....70 D1
  Carshalton SM1,SM5 .218 B5
Erwood Rd SE7 ....122 A1
Esam Way SW16 ...182 C5
Escot Rd TW16 ....171 D3
Escott Gdns SE9 ...188 A6
Escot Way EN5 ....12 C6
Escreet Gr SE18 ...122 C2
Escuan Lo N5 .....73 A2

Esher Ave Cheam SM3 216 D5
  Walton-on-T KT12 ...194 A1
Esher Church Sch
  KT10 ....212 A3
Esher Cl DA5 ......169 A3
Esher Coll KT7 ....196 C2
Esher Cres TW6 ...127 C6
Esher Gdns SW19 .156 D2
Esher Ho 8 SW8 ..137 D3
Esher Mews 4 CR4 202 D6
Esher Park Ave KT10 212 A3
Esher Rd
  East Molesey KT8 ...196 B4
  Ilford IG3 ....79 C5
Esher Sta KT10 ....212 B6
Eskdale NW1 ......232 A3
Eskdale Ave UB5 ...85 B6
Eskdale Cl HA9 ....65 D6
Eskdale Rd DA7 ...147 C4
Esk Ho E3 ....97 A4
Eskmont Ridge SE19 .183 C3
Esk Rd E13 ....99 B3
Esmar Cres NW9 ..46 A2
Esme Ho SW15 ....133 D1
Esmeralda Rd SE1 .118 A2
Esmond Ct W8 ....255 D6
Esmond Gdns W4 ..111 B2
Esmond Rd NW6 ...91 B6
  W4 ....111 B3
Esmond St SW15 ..135 A1
Esparto St SW18 ..157 D4
Essan Ho W13 .....87 B2
Essenden Rd
  Belvedere DA17 ...125 C1
  South Croydon CR2 .221 C1
Essendine Mans W9 .91 C4
Essendine Prim Sch
  W9 ....91 C4
Essendine Rd W9 ..91 C4
Essex Ave TW7 ....130 C2
Essex Cl E17 ....53 A5
  Romford RM7 ......59 D5
  Ruislip HA4 ....40 D1
  West Barnes SM4 ...200 D2
Essex Ct EC4 .....241 A1
  W6 ....112 C3
  Barnes SW13 .....133 D3
  South Norwood SE19 183 B4
Essex Gdns N4 ....50 D3
Essex Gr SE19 ....183 B4
Essex Ho 2 E14 ...97 D1
  4 Acton W3 ....88 C1
Essex Lo 5 N10 ...31 B1
Essex Mans E11 ...54 B2
Essex Park Mews
  W3 ....111 C5
Essex Pk N3 ......29 D4
Essex Pl W4 ......111 A2
Essex Place Sq W4 .111 B2
Essex Prim Sch E12 .78 A3
Essex Rd E10 ......54 A3
  E12 ....78 A2
  E17 ....53 A3
  N1 ....73 A1 234 D6
  NW10 ....67 C1
  W3 ....111 A6
  W4 ....111 B2
  Barking IG11 ......79 B1
  Chingford, Chingford Green
    E4 ....20 C3
  Enfield EN2 ....5 B1
  Ilford RM6 ....58 C2
  Romford RM7 .....59 D5
  Woodford IG8 .....37 B1
Essex Rd S E11 ...54 B2
Essex Sq E7 ......77 A3
Essex St E7 ....77 A3
  SE18 ....123 D3
  WC2 .....116 C6 251 A6
Essex Twr 4 SE20 .184 B2
Essex Villas
  W8 ....113 C4 245 A1
Essian St E1 ......97 A2
Essington SW15 ...157 A5
Essoldo Way HA8 ..44 B6
Estate Way E10 ...53 B1
Estcourt Rd
  SW6 ......135 B5 264 C4
  Croydon SE25 ....206 B3
Estella Ave KT3 ...200 B5
Estella Ho 11 W11 ..112 A6
Estelle Rd NW3 ...70 D4
Esterbrooke St SW1 259 C3
Este Rd SW11 ....136 C3
Esther Cl N21 .....16 C4
Esther Rd E11 ....54 C2
Estoria Cl 22 SW2 .160 C4
Estreham Rd SW16 .181 D4
Estridge Cl TW3 ...129 C1
Estuary Cl IG11 ...102 B4

Eswyn Rd SW17 ....180 D5
Etal Ho N1 ....72 D1
Etchingham Cl N12 ..30 A3
Etchingham Park Rd
  N3 ....29 D3
Etchingham Rd E15 .76 A4
Etfield Gr DA14 ....190 B5
Ethelbert Cl BR1 ...209 B4
Ethelbert Gdns IG2 .56 C4
Ethelbert Ho E9 ...75 A4
Ethelbert Rd
  Bromley BR1,BR2 ...209 B4
  Wimbledon SW20 ...178 D2
Ethelbert St SW12 .159 B3
Ethelburga St
  SW11 ......136 C4 267 B2
Ethelburga Twr
  SW11 ....267 B2
Ethel Cotts RM6 ...58 D6
Ethel Davis Sch RM6 .58 B4
Etheldene Ave N10 .49 C5
Ethelden Rd W12 ..112 B5
Ethel Rankin Ct 8
  SW6 ....135 B3
Ethel Rd
  Ashford TW15 .....170 A5
  Newham E16 ......99 B1
Ethel St SE17 .....262 B3
Ethelworth Ct 4
  SW2 ....160 C3
Etheridge Rd NW2 .46 C2
Etherley Rd N15 ..51 A4
Etherow St SE22 ..162 A4
Etherstone Gn SW16 182 C6
Etherstone Rd SW16 182 C6
Ethnard Rd SE15 ..140 B6
Etloe Ho E10 ......53 C1
Etloe Rd E10 ......75 C6
Eton Ave N12 .....30 A3
  NW3 ....70 D1
  East Barnet EN4 ...14 C1
  Heston TW5 ......129 C6
  New Malden KT3 ...199 B5
  Wembley HA0 .....65 C4
Eton Cl SW18 .....157 D4
Eton College Rd NW3 70 D2
Eton Ct NW3 ......70 B1
  Wembley HA0 .....65 C4
Eton Garages 11 NW3 70 C2
Eton Gr NW9 ......44 C5
  SE13 ....142 C2
Eton Hall NW3 ....70 D2
Eton Ho N5 ....72 C4
Eton Manor Ct E10 .75 C6
Eton Pl NW1 ......71 A1
Eton Rd NW3 .....70 D2
  Harlington UB3 ...127 D5
  Ilford IG1 ....79 B4
Eton Rise NW3 ....70 D2
Eton St TW10 .....154 A6
Eton Villas NW3 ...70 D2
Etta St SE8 ....141 A6
Ettrick Ho 8 E5 ...74 B4
Ettrick St E14 .....98 A1
Etwell Pl KT5 .....198 B3
Eugene Cotter Ho
  SE17 ....262 D3
Eugenia Rd SE16 ..118 C2
Eugenie Mews BR7 .188 D2
Eureka Rd 8 KT1 ..176 C1
Euro Bsns Ctr 3 E15 .98 D6
Euro Cl NW10 .....68 A2
Eurolink Bsns Ctr
  SW2 ....160 C6
Europa Pl EC1 ....235 A1
Europe Rd SE18 ..122 B3
Eusdon Cl N9 .....18 B1
Eustace Ho SE11 .260 C4
Eustace Pl SE18 ..122 B2
Eustace Rd E6 ....100 A4
  SW6 ......135 C5 265 A4
  Dagenham RM6 ...58 D2
Euston Rd
  NW1 ......93 D3 239 B6
  Thornton Heath CR0 204 B1
Euston Sq NW1 ...232 C1
Euston Square Sta
  WC1 .....93 C3 239 B6
Euston St NW1 93 C4 232 B1
Euston Sta
  NW1 ......93 D4 232 C1
Euston Underpass
  NW1 ....239 A6
Evandale Rd SW9 .138 C3
Evangelist Rd NW5 .71 B4
Evans Cl E8 ....73 D2
Evans Gr TW13 ...151 C2

Evans Ho SW8 ....269 D3
  34 W12 ....112 B6
Evans Rd SE6 .....164 C2
Evanston Ave E4 ..36 A3
Evanston Gdns IG4 .56 A3
Eveline Mans 8 SE5 139 B5
Eveline Rd SE14 ..140 C3
  Penge SE20 ......184 D3
Eveline Ct N10 ....49 B4
Eveline Lowe Prim Sch
  SE1 ....118 A2
Eveline Rd CR4 ...180 D2
  Ruislip HA4 ......39 D2
Evelyn Ave NW9 ...45 B5
Evelyn Cl TW2 ....151 D2
Evelyn Cres TW16 .171 D2
Evelyn Ct E8 ......74 A4
  N1 ....235 C3
  Croydon CR0 .....206 A2
Evelyn Denington Ct 2
  N1 ....72 D1
Evelyn Denington Rd
  E6 ....100 A3
Evelyn Dr HA5 ....22 D3
Evelyn Fox Ct W10 .90 C2
Evelyn Gdns
  SW7 ......114 B1 256 C1
  Richmond TW9 ...132 A1
Evelyn Gr Ealing W5 .110 B5
  Southall UB1 .....85 B1
Evelyn Ho 3 SW2 .160 B6
  W12 ....111 D4
Evelyn Rd E16 ....121 B5
  E17 ....54 A5
  W4 ....111 B3
  Cockfosters EN4 ...2 D1
  Richmond TW10 ..153 C1
  Richmond TW9 ...132 A2
  Wimbledon SW19 ..179 D4
Evelyns Cl UB8 ...82 C1
Evelyns Com Sch UB7 82 B1
Evelyn St SE8 .....119 A1
Evelyn Terr TW9 ..132 A2
Evelyn Way
  Sunbury TW16 ...171 D2
  Wallington SM6 ..219 D4
Evelyn Wlk N1 95 B5 235 C3
Evelyn Yd W1 ....239 C2
Evening Hill BR3 ..186 A3
Evenlode Ho 5 SE2 124 C4
Evenwood Cl SW15 156 A6
Everard Ave BR2 ..209 A1
Everard Ct N13 ...16 B1
Everard Ho 24 E1 ..96 A1
Everard Way HA9 ..66 A5
Everatt Cl SW18 ..157 B6
Everdale Ct N2 ...48 C5
Everdon Rd SW13 .134 A6
Everest Ct
  6 Chislehurst SE9 .166 A2
  South Norwood SE19 183 C2
Everest Pl E14 ....98 A2
  Stanwell TW19 ...148 A4
Everest Rd SE9 ...166 B6
  Stanwell TW19 ...148 A4
Everett Cl Bushey WD23 .8 C1
  Pinner HA5 ....39 D6
Everett Ho N7 ....72 C4
Everett Wlk DA17 .125 B1
Everglade Ho E17 .35 B1
Everglades
  Beckenham BR2 ..208 C6
  Hounslow TW3 ...130 A4
Everglade Strand
  NW9 ....27 D2
Evergreen Ct SE20 184 C3
Evergreen Sq 3 E8 .73 D1
Evergreen Way UB3 105 D6
Everilda St N1 ....233 D5
Evering Rd E5,N16 .74 A5
Everington Rd N10 .30 D1
Everington St W6 .134 D6
Everitt Rd NW10 ..89 B4
Everleigh St N4 ...50 B1
Eversfield Gdns HA8,
  NW7 ....27 C3
Eversfield Rd TW9 .132 B3
Evershed Ho E1 ...243 D2
Evershed Wlk W4 .111 B2
Eversholt Ct EN5 ..14 A6
Eversholt St
  NW1 ......93 C4 232 B3
Evershot Rd N4 ...50 B1

Eversleigh Ct N3 ....29 C3
Eversleigh Rd E6 ...99 D6
  N3 ....29 B3
  SW11 ....137 A3
  New Barnet EN5 ...14 A6
Eversley Ave HA9 ..66 C6
Eversley Cl N21 ...16 B5
Eversley Cres
  Hounslow TW7 ...130 B4
  Ruislip HA4 ......61 D6
  Southgate N21 ...16 C5
Eversley Ho 18 E2 .96 A4
Eversley Mount N21 16 B5
Eversley Park Rd N21 16 B5
Eversley Pk SW19 .178 B3
Eversley Prim Sch
  N21 ....16 B5
Eversley Rd
  Greenwich SE7 ...143 B6
  Kingston KT5 .....198 B4
  South Norwood SE19 183 B3
Eversley Way CR0 .223 C5
Everthorpe Rd SE15 139 D2
Everton Bldgs NW1 232 A1
Everton Ct HA0 ...65 D4
Everton Dr HA7 ...44 A6
Everton Rd CR0 ...206 A1
Evesham Ave E17 .35 C4
Evesham Cl
  Belmont SM2 .....217 C1
  Greenford UB6 ...85 D5
Evesham Ct
  2 Ealing W13 ....109 A5
  2 Richmond TW10 154 B5
Evesham Gn SM4 ..201 D3
Evesham Ho 1 E2 ..96 C5
  NW8 ....229 A3
  SW1 ....258 D2
Evesham Rd E15 ..76 D1
  N11 ....31 D5
  Morden SM4 .....201 D3
Evesham St W11 ..112 D6
Evesham Way SW11 137 A2
  Ilford IG5 ....56 C6
Evesham Wlk SE5 .139 B3
  SW9 ....138 C3
Evry Rd DA14 .....190 C4
Ewald Rd SW6 ....135 C4
Ewanrigg Terr IG8 .37 C5
Ewart Gr N22 .....32 C2
Ewart Pl 10 E3 ...97 B5
Ewart Rd SE23 ...162 C4
Ewe Cl N7 ....72 A2
Ewell By-Pass KT17 216 A1
Ewell Court Ave
  KT19 ....215 A3
Ewell Park Gdns
  KT17 ....216 A1
Ewell Park Way KT17 216 A1
Ewell Rd
  Cheam SM2,SM3 ...216 C2
  Surbiton KT5,KT6 ..198 B2
  Thames Ditton KT6,KT7 197 B2
  Tolworth KT6 ....198 D1
Ewelme Rd SE23 ..162 C3
Ewen Cres SW2 ...160 C4
Ewen Ho N1 ......233 C5
Ewer St SE1 .117 A5 252 A3
Ewhurst 19 SW15 .156 C5
Ewhurst Cl E1 ....96 C2
  CR4 ....202 B6
Ewhurst Ct CR4 ..202 B6
Ewhurst Rd SE4 ..163 B5
Exbury Ho E9 .....74 C1
  4 SW9 ....138 B2
Exbury Rd SE6 ....163 C2
Excel Ct WC2 .....249 D5
Excel Ex Ctr E16 ..121 D4
Excelsior Cl KT1 ..176 C1
Excelsior Gdns SE13 142 C4
Excelsior Ind Est
  SE16 ....140 C4
Exchange Arc EC2 243 B4
Exchange Cl N11 ...15 A2
Exchange Ct WC2 250 B5
Exchange Mans 2
  NW11 ....47 B2
Exchange Pl EC2 243 A4
Exchange The IG1 ..78 D6
Exeforde Ave TW15 170 C6
Exeter Cl E6 ......100 B1
Exeter Ct NW6 ....91 C5
  Kingston KT6 ....198 A4
  Mitcham SW19 ...180 C3
Exeter Gdns IG1 ..56 C5
Exeter Ho 11 SE15 140 A6
  W2 ....236 A2
  7 Barking IG11 ...80 A1
  Feltham TW13 ...151 C2
  Putney SW15 ....156 C5
Exeter Mans NW2 .69 A2

Exeter Mews SW6 ..265 A4
Exeter Rd DA16 ....145 D3
E16 ....99 A2
E17 ....53 C4
N14 ....15 B4
N9 ....18 C2
NW2 ....69 A2
Croydon CR0 ......205 D2
Dagenham RM10 ....81 D2
Enfield EN3 ....6 D2
Harrow HA2 ......63 A6
Hatton TW6 ......127 C2
Twickenham TW13 ..151 B1
Exeter St
WC2 ....116 B6 250 C6
Exeter Way 2 SE14 ..141 B5
Hatton TW6 ......127 C3
Exford Ct SW11 ...266 D2
Exford Gdns SE12 ..165 B3
Exford Rd SE12 ...165 B3
Exhibition Cl W12 ..112 C6
Exhibition Rd
SW7 ....114 B3 256 D6
Exmoor Ho 23 E3 ...97 A5
Exmoor St W10 .....90 D2
Exmouth Ho 6 E14 .119 D2
Exmouth Market
EC1 ....94 C3 241 B6
Exmouth Mews NW1 .232 B1
Exmouth Pl E8 .....74 B1
Exmouth Rd E17 ....53 B4
Bexley DA16 ......146 C5
Hayes UB4 ....83 C4
Ruislip HA4 ......62 C5
Exmouth St E1 .....96 C1
Exning Rd E16 .....98 D3
Exon St SE17 .117 C2 263 A3
Explorer Ave TW19 ..148 A3
Express Dr IG3 .....58 B1
Exton Cres NW10 ...67 A1
Exton Gdns RM8 ....80 C3
Exton St SE1 .116 C5 251 A3
Eyebright Cl 3 CR0 .206 D1
Eyhurst Cl NW2 ....68 A6
Eylewood Rd SE27 ..183 A5
Eynella Rd SE21 ...161 D4
Eynham Rd W12 ....90 C1
Eynsford Cl BR5 ...211 A3
Eynsford Cres DA5,
DA14 ....168 D3
Eynsford Ho SE1 ...252 C2
12 SE15 ....140 C6
SE17 ....263 A3
Eynsford Rd IG3 ....79 C6
Eynsford Terr UB7 ..82 B1
Eynsham Dr SE2 ...124 B3
Eynswood Dr DA14 .190 C5
Eyot Gdns W6 .....111 D3
Eyot Gn W4 ......111 D1
Eyre Ct NW8 ......229 C4
Eyre St Hill
EC1 ....94 C3 241 A5
Eysham Ct 8 EN5 ..13 D6
Eythorne Rd SW9 ..138 C2
Ezra St E2 ....95 D4

F

Faber Gdns NW4 ...46 A4
Fabian Rd
SW6 .....135 B5 264 D4
Fabian St E6 ......100 B3
Fabyc Ho TW9 .....132 C5
Factory La
Croydon CR0 .....220 D6
Tottenham N17 ....33 D1
Factory Rd E16 ....122 A4
Factory Yd W7 ....108 C5
Fagg's Rd TW14 ...150 A6
Faircare
Hounslow TW7 ....130 B4
Kingston KT3 .....199 C6
Pinner HA5 ......40 A5
Fair Acres BR2 ....209 A4
Fairacres
Putney SW15 .....134 A1
Ruislip HA4 ......39 D2
Fairbairn Gn 1 SW9 138 D4
Fairbank Ave BR6 ..226 B6
Fairbanks Rd N17 ..52 A6
Fairbourne Ho UB3 .105 A3
Fairbourne Rd N17 .51 C6
Fairbridge Rd N19 ..71 D6
Fairbrook Cl N13 ...32 C5
Fairbrook Rd N13 ..32 C4
Fairburn Ct SW15 ..157 A6
Fairburn Ho 9 N16 ..51 C1
SW5 ....254 D1
Fairby Ho SE1 .....263 D4

Fairby Rd SE12 ....165 B6
Faircharm Trad Est
SE8 ....141 D5
Fairchild Cl 6 SW11 136 B3
Fairchild Ho 13 E9 ..74 C1
5 N1 ....95 C4
SW1 ....259 B3
Fairchild Pl EC2 ...243 B5
Fairchild St EC2 ...243 B5
Fairclough St E1 ...96 A1
Faircourt 14 NW3 ...70 D2
Faircroft N16 ......51 B1
Forest Hill SE26 ...184 C6
Faircross Ave IG11 ..79 A2
Faircross Par IG11 ..79 A2
Fairdale Gdns
Hayes UB3 ....106 A4
Putney SW15 .....134 B1
Fairdene Ct N7 ....72 A3
Fairey Ave UB3 ....105 D3
Fairfax Cl KT12 ...194 B1
Fairfax Gdns SE3 ..143 C4
Fairfax Ho E1 .....96 A1
5 Ealing W5 ....88 A4
6 Putney SW15 .156 A6
Fairfax Mews E16 ..121 B5
N8 ....50 D5
Putney SW15 .....134 C1
Fairfax Pl NW6 ....70 A1
Fairfax Rd N8 .....50 C5
NW6 ....70 A1
W4 ....111 C3
Teddington TW11 ..175 B3
Fairfax Way N10 ...31 A3
Fairfield 4 E1 .....96 C2
N20 ....14 B4
NW1 ....232 A5
Pinner HA6 ......22 A1
Fairfield Ave NW4 ..46 B3
Edgware HA8 .....26 D3
Ruislip HA4 ......39 A2
Twickenham TW2 ..151 D3
Fairfield Cl DA15 ..167 D5
N12 ....30 A4
Enfield EN3 ......7 A1
Mitcham SW19 ....180 C3
West Ewell KT19 ..215 C4
Fairfield Cres HA8 ..26 D4
Fairfield Ct NW10 ..90 A4
1 SW18 ....157 D6
Ruislip HA4 ......39 B1
Harrow HA2 ......42 A6
Wembley UB6 ....87 C6
Fairfield E N1 .....176 A1
Fairfield Gdns N8 ..50 A4
Fairfield Gr SE7 ...143 D6
Fairfield Ind Est KT1 198 B6
Fairfield N KT1,KT2 .176 A1
Fairfield Path CR0 ..221 B5
Fairfield Pl KT1 ...198 A6
Fairfield Rd BR1 ...187 A3
BR5 ....211 B3
E17 ....35 A1
E3 ....97 C5
N8 ....50 A4
Beckenham BR3 ...185 C1
Bexley DA7 ......147 B3
Edmonton N18 ....34 A6
Ilford IG1 ....78 D2
Kingston KT1 .....176 A1
Southall UB1 .....85 B1
South Croydon CR0 .221 C5
Woodford IG8 ....37 A4
Yiewsley UB7 ....104 A6
Fairfields SE6 .....163 D4
Fairfields S KT1 ...176 B1
Fairfields Cl NW9 ..45 A4
Fairfields Cres NW9 .45 A4
Fairfields Rd TW3 ..130 A2
Fairfield St SW18 ..157 D6
Fairfield W KT1 ...176 A1
Fairfield Way
Barnet EN5 ......13 C6
West Ewell KT19 ..215 C4
Fairfoot Rd E3 ....97 C4
Fairford SE6 ......163 C3
Fairford Ave CR0 ..206 D4
Fairford Cl CR0 ...207 A5
Fairford Ct SM2 ...217 D1
Fairford Gdns KT4 .215 D5
Fairford Ho SE11 ..261 B3
Fairgreen EN4 .....2 D2
Fairgreen Ct EN4 ..2 D2
Fair Green Ct 1 CR4 202 D6
Fairgreen E EN4 ...2 D2
Fairgreen Rd CR7 ..204 D4
Fairhall Ct KT6 ...198 B4
Fairhaven Ave CR0 .206 D3

Fairhaven Ct CR2 ..221 A3
Fairhazel Gdns NW6 .70 A1
Fairheathe SW15 ..156 D5
Fairholme TW14 ...149 C4
Fairholme Cl N3 ...47 A5
Fairholme Cres UB4 .84 A3
Fairholme Gdns N3 .47 A5
Fairholme Ho 3 KT3 199 C5
Fairholme Jun & Inf Schs
TW14 ....149 B3
Fairholme Rd
W14 ....113 A1 254 B1
Ashford TW15 ....170 B5
Cheam SM1 ......217 B2
Harrow HA1 ......42 D4
Ilford IG1 ....56 C2
Thornton Heath CR0 .204 C2
Fairholt Cl N16 ....51 C1
Fairholt Rd N16 ...51 B1
Fairholt St SW7 ...257 B6
Fairhurst 4 NW6 ..70 A2
Fairland Ho BR2 ...209 B5
Fairland Rd E15 ...76 D1
Fairlands Ave
Sutton SM1 ......217 C6
Thornton Heath CR7 .204 C4
Woodford IG9 ....21 A2
Fairlands Ct 6 SE9 .166 C5
Fairlawn SE7 .....143 C6
Fairlawn Ave N2 ...48 C5
Acton W4 ....111 A2
Bexley DA16 .....146 D3
Fairlawn Cl
Claygate KT10 ....212 D2
Feltham TW13 ....173 B6
Kingston KT2 .....177 A4
Southgate N14 ....15 D5
Fairlawn Ct SE7 ...143 C5
3 Acton W4 ....111 A2
Fairlawn Dr IG8 ...37 A3
Fairlawnes SM6 ...219 B3
Fairlawn Gdns UB1 107 B6
Fairlawn Gr W4 ...111 A2
Fairlawn Mans SE14 140 D4
Fairlawn Pk SE26 ..185 A5
Fairlawn Prim Sch
Forest Hill SE23 ..162 C4
Forest Hill SE23 ..162 C3
Fairlawn Rd SW19 .179 B3
Fairlawns
3 Bowes Park N11 ..32 A4
10 Chingford E4 ..20 A2
Pinner WD19 .....22 D1
Putney SW15 .....156 D6
Sunbury TW16 ....194 A6
Twickenham TW1 ..153 C5
Fairlea Pl W5 .....87 D3
Fair Lea Pl W5 ....87 C2
Fairleas 12 BR3 ...185 D1
Fairley House Sch
SW1 ....259 D2
Fairlie Ct 22 E3 ...97 D4
1 N7 ....71 D4
Fairlie Gdns SE23 ..162 C4
Fairlight TW12 ....173 D5
Fairlight Ave NW10 .89 C5
Chingford E4 .....20 B2
Woodford IG8 ....37 A4
Fairlight Cl
Cheam KT4 ......216 C4
Chingford E4 .....20 B2
Fairlight Ct NW10 ..89 C5
Greenford UB6 ...86 B5
Fairlight Rd SW17 ..180 B6
Fairline Ct BR3 ...186 A1
Fairlop Ct E11 ....54 C1
Fairlop Pl NW8 ....229 D1
Fairlop Rd E11 ....54 B2
Fairmark Dr UB10 ..60 C2
Fairmead BR1 .....210 B6
Tolworth KT5,KT6 ..198 D1
Fairmead Cl BR1 ..210 B5
Heston TW5 .....128 D5
Kingston KT3 .....199 B6
Fairmead Cres HA8 .11 A1
Fairmead Ct 8 E4 ..20 C4
Fairmead Gdns IG4 .56 A4
Fairmead Ho E9 ...75 A4
Fairmead Rd N7,N19 72 A1
Thornton Heath CR0 .204 C2
Fairmeadside IG10 ..21 C6
Fairmile Ave SW16 .181 D5
Fairmile Ho BR5 ...190 A1
Teddington TW11 ..175 A6
Fairmont Cl DA17 ..125 B1
Fairmont Ho 1 E3 ..97 C3
Fairmount Ho SW2 .160 B5
Fairmount Rd SW2 .160 B5
Fairoak Cl BR5 ...210 D2
Fairoak Dr SE9 ...167 B6
Fairoaks Gr EN3 ...6 D6

Fairseat Cl WD23 ..8 C2
Fair St SE1 .117 D4 253 C2
Hounslow TW3 ....130 A2
Fairstead Lo 4 IG8 .37 A4
Fairstead Wlk N1 ..235 A6
Fairthorn Rd SE7,
SE10 ....121 A1
Fairview Ave HA0 ..65 D2
Hampton TW12 ...173 B3
Fair View Cl E17 ...35 A2
Fairview Cl SE26 ...185 A5
Fairview Cres HA2 ..41 C1
Fairview Ct NW4 ...28 D1
Ashford TW15 ....170 C5
Kingston KT2 .....176 D2
Fairview Dr BR6 ...227 B4
Littleton TW17 ....192 B4
Fairview Gdns IG8 .37 B2
Fairview Ho 9 SW2 .160 B4
Fairview Pl SW2 ...160 B4
Fairview Rd N15 ...51 D3
Carshalton SM1,SM5 218 C5
Enfield EN2 ......4 C4
Thornton Heath SW16 182 B2
Fairview Villas E4 ..35 D3
Fairview Way HA8 ..26 C4
Fairwall Ho 9 SE5 ..139 C4
Fairwater Ave DA16 .146 A1
Fairwater Ho TW11 .175 A6
Fairway BR5 ......211 A3
Bexley DA6 ......169 A6
West Barnes SW20 .200 A5
Woodford IG8 ....37 C5
Fairway Ave NW9 ..44 D6
Fairway Cl NW11 ..48 A2
Croydon CR0 .....207 A4
Hounslow TW4 ....150 A4
West Ewell KT19 ..215 A4
Fairway Ct NW7 ...11 B1
13 SE16 ....118 D4
12 SE9 ....166 C5
New Barnet EN5 ..13 D5
Fairway Dr Erith SE28 103 A1
Greenford UB6 ...63 D1
Fairway Est TW4 ..150 A4
Fairway Gdns
Ilford IG1 ....79 A3
West Wickham BR3 .208 B3
Fairway Prim Sch
NW7 ....11 B2
Fairways E17 .....54 A5
Ashford TW15 ....170 D4
4 Hounslow TW7 .130 C4
Stanmore HA7 ....26 A1
Teddington TW11 ..175 D3
Fairways Bsns Pk E10 75 A4
Fairway The BR1,BR2 210 B4
NW7 ....11 B1
W3 ....89 C1
East Molesey KT8 .195 D6
Edmonton N13 ....17 B1
Hillingdon UB10 ..82 B5
Kingston KT3 .....177 B2
New Barnet EN5 ..13 D5
Northolt UB5 .....64 A2
Ruislip HA4 ......62 D5
Southgate N14 ....15 D5
Wembley HA0 ....65 B6
Fairweather Cl N15 .51 C5
Fairweather Ct N13 .32 B6
Fairweather Ho N7 .72 A4
Fairweather Rd N16 .52 A3
Fairwood Ct E11 ...54 B2
Fairwyn Rd SE26 ..185 B4
Faith Ct NW2 .....68 C2
Faithfull Ho N5 ....73 A3
Fakenham Cl NW7 ..28 A3
5 Northolt UB5 ..63 C2
Fakruddin St E1 ...96 A1
Falaize Ave IG1 ...78 D4
Falcon Ave BR1 ...210 A5
Falconberg Ct W1 ..239 D2
Falconberg Mews
W1 ....239 D2
Falconbrook Inf Sch
SW11 ....136 B2
Falcon Cl SE1 .....251 D4
Chiswick W4 .....133 A6
Falcon Cres EN3 ..18 D6
Falcon Ct EC4 ....241 A1
N1 ....234 D3
8 Dulwich SE21 ..161 B2
New Barnet EN5 ..2 A1
6 Wanstead E18 ..55 B6
Falcon Dr TW19 ...148 A5
Falconer Ct N17 ...33 A3
Falconer Wlk 12 N7 .72 B6
Falcon Gr SW11 ...136 C2
Falcon Ho 10 SE15 .139 D4
Falconhurst 4 KT6 .198 A4

Falcon La SW11 ...136 C2
Falcon Lo NW3 ....69 D4
11 W9 ....91 C2
Falcon Pk Ind Est
NW10 ....67 C3
Falcon Point SE1 ..251 D5
Falcon Rd SW11 ...136 C2
Enfield EN3 ......18 D6
Hampton TW12 ...173 B3
Falconry Ct KT1 ...198 A6
Falcon St E13 .....99 A3
Falcon Terr SW11 ..136 C2
Falcon Way E14 ...119 D2
NW9 ....27 C1
Feltham TW14 ....150 B6
Harrow HA3 ......44 A4
Sunbury TW16 ...171 C1
Wanstead E11 ....55 A5
Falconwood Ave
DA16 ....145 C3
Falconwood Ct SE3 142 D3
Falconwood Par
DA16 ....145 D1
Falconwood Rd CR0 223 C5
Falconwood Sta SE9 145 B1
Falcourt Cl SM1 ...217 D3
Falkener Ct SW11 ..268 B1
Falkirk Ct 11 SE16 ..118 D5
Falkirk Gdns WD19 .22 D5
Falkirk Ho W9 ....91 D4
Falkirk St N1 .....95 C5
Falkland Ave N11 ..31 B6
N3 ....29 C3
Falkland Ho W14 ..254 C2
W8 ....255 C5
Catford SE6 ......186 A6
Falkland Park Ave
SE25 ....183 C1
Falkland Pl 2 NW5 .71 C3
Falkland Rd N8 ...50 C5
NW5 ....71 C3
Barnet EN5 ......1 A3
Falladon Ho W11 ..91 B2
Fallaize Ho SE11 ..261 B2
Fallodon Way NW11 47 C5
Fallodon Ho 6 SW8 137 D3
Fallow Court Ave N12 30 A4
Fallow Ct 18 SE16 ..118 A1
Fallowfield N4 ....72 B6
Stanmore HA7 ....9 A1
Fallowfield Ct HA7 ..9 A1
Fallowfields Dr N12 .30 C4
Fallows Cl N2 .....30 B1
Fallsbrook Rd SW16 181 C4
Falman Cl N9 .....18 A3
Falmer Rd E17 ....53 D6
N15 ....51 B4
Enfield EN1 ......5 C1
Falmouth Ave E4 ..36 C5
Falmouth Cl SE12 ..164 D6
Wood Green N22 ..32 B3
Falmouth Gdns IG4 .55 D5
Falmouth Ho SE11 .261 B2
W2 ....247 A6
Falmouth Rd
SE1 ....117 A3 262 B5
Falmouth St E15 ..76 B3
Falmouth Way E17 .53 B4
Falstaff Ct SE11 ...261 C3
Falstaff Ho 18 N1 ..95 C5
Fambridge Cl SE26 .185 B6
Fambridge Rd RM8 .81 C6
Fane St W14 ......264 D6
Fann St EC1 ..95 A3 242 B5
Fanshawe Ave IG11 .79 A2
Fanshawe Cres RM9 81 C3
Fanshawe Rd TW10 175 C6
Fanshaw Ho 6 E17 .53 D6
Fanshaw St N1 ...95 C4
Fantail Ct BR6 ....226 B5
Fanthorpe St SW15 .134 C2
Faraday Ave DA14 ..168 B2
Faraday Cl N7 ....72 B2
Faraday Ho 6 E14 .119 B6
5 NW5 ....71 B4
W10 ....91 A2
2 Balham SW12 ..159 B4
4 Belvedere DA17 125 C3
5 Hampton TW12 173 D4
Wembley HA9 ....67 A5
Faraday Lo SE10 ..120 D1
Faraday Rd DA16 ..146 A2
E15 ....76 D2
W10 ....91 A2
W3 ....111 A6
East Molesey KT8 .195 C5
Southall UB1 .....107 D6
Wimbledon SW19 .179 D4
Faraday Way SE18 .121 D3
Thornton Heath CR0 204 B1

Fareham Ho 13
SW15 ....156 A3
Fareham Rd TW14 ..150 C4
Fareham St W1 ...239 C2
Farewell Pl CR4 ...180 C2
Faringdon Ave BR2 210 C3
Faringford Rd E15 ..76 C1
Farjeon Ho NW6 ...70 B1
Farjeon Rd SE3 ...143 D4
Farleigh Ave BR2 ..209 A2
Farleigh Ct CR2 ...221 A3
Farleigh Ho 7 KT2 .176 D4
Farleigh Pl N16 ...73 D4
Farleigh Rd N16 ..73 D4
Farleycroft 1 CR0 .206 A1
Farley Croft BR2 ..186 C1
Farley Ct NW1 ....238 A5
W14 ....254 C6
Farley Dr IG3 .....57 C1
Farley Ho SE26 ...162 B1
Farley Pl SE25 ....206 A5
Farley Rd Catford SE6 164 A4
South Croydon CR2 .222 B1
Farlington Pl SW15 .156 B4
Farlow Rd SW15 ..134 D2
Farlton Rd SW18 ..157 D4
Farman Terr HA3 ..43 D5
Farm Ave SW16 ...69 B5
Harrow HA2,HA5 ..41 C3
Streatham SW16 ..182 A5
Wembley HA0 ....65 C2
Farm Avenue Ho HA0 65 C2
Farmborough Cl HA1 42 B2
Farm Cl SW6 .....265 B4
Barnet EN5 ......12 C6
Buckhurst Hill IG9 ..21 C1
Coney Hall BR4 ...224 D5
Lower Halliford TW17 192 C2
Southall UB2 .....107 D6
Sutton SM2 ......218 B1
Uxbridge UB10 ...60 D6
Farmcote Rd SE12 .165 A3
Farm Cotts E17 ...53 A4
Farm Ct NW4 .....46 A4
Farmdale Rd SE10 .121 A1
Sutton SM5 ......218 A5
Farm Dr CR0 .....223 B6
Farm End E4 .....20 C6
Farmer Ho 4 SE16 .118 B3
Farmer Rd E10 ...53 D1
Farmers Rd SE5 ..138 C4
Farmer St W8 .....245 A4
Farmfield Rd BR1 ..186 C5
Farm House Ct NW7 28 A3
Farmhouse Rd SW16 181 C3
Farmilo Rd E17 ...53 C2
Farmington Ave SM1 218 B5
Farm La SW6 .135 C5 265 B4
Croydon CR0 .....223 B6
East Barnet N14 ..15 B5
Farmlands Enfield EN2 4 C4
Pinner HA5 ......40 A5
Farmlands The UB5 .63 C2
Farmland Wlk BR7 .188 D5
Farm Lane Trad Ctr
SW6 .....135 C5 265 B5
Farmleigh N14 ....15 C4
Farmleigh Ho SW9 .160 B5
Farm Pl W8 ......245 A4
Farm Rd NW10 ...89 B6
Edmonton N21 ...17 A3
Morden SM4 .....201 D4
Sutton SM2 ......218 B1
Twickenham TW4 ..151 A3
Thames Ditton KT10 195 C1
Farm St W1 ..115 B6 248 C5
Farmstead Rd
Catford SE6 ......185 D6
Harrow HA3 ......24 B1
Farm Vale DA5 ...169 D5
Farm View N3 ....47 B6
Farmway RM8 ....80 C2
Farm Way
Buckhurst Hill IG9 ..37 C6
North Cheam KT4 .216 C5
Farm Wlk NW11 ..47 C4
Farnaby Ho 2 W10 .91 B4
Farnaby Rd SE9 ..143 C1
Bromley BR1,BR2 ..186 C3
Farnan Ave E17 ...53 C6
Farnan Rd SW16 ..182 A5
Farnborough Ave E17 53 A6
South Croydon CR2 .223 A1
Farnborough Cl HA9 66 D2
Farnborough Comm
Keston Mark BR2,BR6 226 B5
Orpington BR6 ...226 C4

Farnborough Cres
3 Hayes BR2 ....208 D1
South Croydon CR2 ...223 A1
Farnborough Ct **2**
BR6 ....227 A3
Farnborough Hill
BR6 ....227 C3
Farnborough Ho **1**
SW15 ....156 A3
Farnborough Hospl
BR6 ....226 C4
Farnborough Prim Sch
BR6 ....227 A3
Farnborough Way
BR6 ....227 B3
10 SE15 ....139 C5
Farncombe St SE16 ..118 A4
Farndale Ave N13 ....17 A1
Farndale Cres UB6 ...86 A4
Farndale Ho **3** NW6 ..91 D6
Farnell Mews SW5 ...255 C2
Farnell Pl W3 ....110 D6
Farnell Rd TW7 .....130 B2
Farnell's Almshouses
TW7 ....130 D3
Farnfield Ho **12** SW2 .160 B6
Farnham Cl N20 ......14 A4
Farnham Ct **2** N16 ...51 C1
2 Cheam SM3 .....217 A2
1 Southall UB1 .....86 A1
Farnham Gdns SW20 178 B1
Farnham Green Prim Sch
IG3 ....58 A3
Farnham Ho NW1 ...237 B5
SE1 ....252 A3
Farnham Pl SE1 ....251 D3
Farnham Rd
Bexley DA16 ......146 C3
Ilford IG3 ....57 D2
Farnham Royal
SE11 ....116 B1 260 D1
Farnhurst Ho **7**
SW11 ....137 A3
Farningham Ct SW16 181 D3
Farningham Ho **9** N4 .51 B2
Farningham Rd N17 ...34 A4
Farnley Ho **13** SW8 ..137 D3
Farnley Rd
Chingford E4 ....20 C4
South Norwood SE25 .205 B5
Farnsworth Ho **8**
SW27 ....182 D5
Farnworth Ho **5** E14 120 B2
Faro Cl BR1 ....188 C1
Faroe Rd W14 ......112 D3
Farorna Wlk EN2 .....4 C4
Farquhar Rd
Dulwich SE19 ......183 D5
Wimbledon SW19 ...157 C1
Farquharson Rd CR0 205 A1
Farrance Rd RM6 ....59 C4
Farrance St E14 .....97 C1
Farrans Ct HA3 ......43 B2
Farrant Ave N22 .....32 D1
Farrant Cl BR6 .....227 C1
Farrant Ho **15** SW11 .136 B2
Farr Ave IG11 ......102 A5
Farrell Ho E1 ......96 C1
Farren Rd SE23 ....163 A2
Farrer Ho SE8 .....141 C5
Farrer Mews N8 .....49 C5
Farrer Rd N8 ....49 D5
Harrow HA3 ....44 A4
Farrer's Pl CR0 ....222 D4
Farrier Cl BR1 .....209 D6
Hillingdon UB8 ......82 C1
Sunbury TW16 .....194 A5
Farrier Mews SE15 .140 C2
Farrier Rd UB5 .....85 C5
Farriers Ct
Belmont SM2 ......217 A1
Wimbledon SW19 ...179 A3
Farrier St NW1 ......71 C1
Farriers Way WD6 ...11 B6
Farrier Wlk
SW10 .....136 A6 266 A6
Farringdon La
EC1 ....94 C3 241 B5
Farringdon Rd
EC1 ....94 C3 241 B5
Farringdon St
EC4 ....94 D1 241 C2
Farringdon Sta
EC1 ....94 D2 241 C4
Farrington Pl BR7 ..189 B3
Farrington & Stratford
House Sch BR7 ...189 B3

Farrins Rents SE16 ..119 A5
Farrow La SE14 ....140 C5
Farrow Pl SE16 ....119 A5
Farr Rd EN2 ....5 B4
Farthingale Wlk E15 ..76 B1
Farthing Alley **5**
SE1 ....118 A4
Farthing Fields **8**
E1 ....118 B5
Farthings Cl
Chingford E4 ....20 C1
Pinner HA5 ....40 B3
Farthing St BR6 ....226 B1
Farthings The **1** KT2 176 C2
Farwell Rd DA14 ...190 C6
Farwig La BR1 .....187 A2
Fashion & Design Museum
The★ SE1 ....253 A2
Fashion St E1 .95 D2 243 D3
Fashoda Rd BR2 ...209 D5
Fassett Rd E8 ......74 A4
Kingston KT1 ......198 A5
Fassett Sq E8 ....74 A2
Fauconberg Ct W4 ..133 A6
Fauconberg Rd W4 ..133 A6
Faulkner Cl **6** RM8 ..58 D2
Faulkner Ho SW15 ..134 C3
Faulkner St SE14 ...140 C4
Faulkner's Alley EC1 .241 C4
Fauna Cl RM6 ....58 C3
Faunce Ho **1** SE17 .138 D6
Faunce St
SE17 ....116 D1 261 C1
Favart Rd
SW6 ....135 C4 265 B2
Favart Rd SE18 ....122 D3
F Ave SE18 ....122 D3
Faversham Ave
Chingford E4 ....20 D3
Enfield EN1 ....17 B5
Faversham Ho NW1 .232 B5
SE17 ....263 A1
Faversham Rd
Beckenham BR3 ...185 B1
Forest Hill SE6 ....163 B3
Morden SM4 ......201 B3
Fawcett Cl SW11 ...136 B3
West Norwood SW16 .182 C6
Fawcett Est E5 ......52 A1
Fawcett Ho **25** SW9 .138 A3
Fawcett Rd NW10 ...67 D1
Croydon CR0 ......221 A5
Fawcett St
SW10 .....136 A6 266 A6
Fawcus Cl KT10 ....212 C2
Fawe Park Rd SW15 .135 B1
Fawe St E14 ....97 C2
Fawkham Ho SE1 ...263 D3
Fawley Ct SE27 ....160 C2
Fawley Lo **2** E14 ..120 B2
Fawley Rd NW6 .....69 D3
Fawnbrake Ave SE24 161 A6
Fawn Rd E13 ....99 C5
Fawns Manor Cl
TW14 ....149 A3
Fawns Manor Rd
TW14 ....149 B3
Fawood Ave NW10 ...67 B1
Fayetville Ho **26** N19 ..49 D2
Faygate Cres DA6 ..169 C6
Faygate Rd SW2 ...160 B2
Fayland Ave SW16 ..181 C5
Fazal Laf IG1 ....79 A6
Fazerley Ct **49** W2 ...91 C2
Fearnley Cres TW12 173 B4
Fearnley Ho SE5 ...139 C3
Fearon St SE10 ....121 A1
Featherbed La CR0 .223 B1
Feathers Pl SE10 ..142 B6
Featherstone Ave **4**
SE23 ....162 C2
Featherstone Ho UB4 .84 C2
Featherstone Ind Est
UB2 ....107 A3
Featherstone Prim Sch
UB2 ....107 A3
Featherstone Rd NW7 28 B4
Southall UB2 ......107 A3
Featherstone St
EC1 ....95 B3 242 C6
Featherstone Terr
UB2 ....107 A3
Featley Rd SW9 ....138 C2
Federal Rd UB6 .....87 C5
Federation Rd SE2 .124 C2
Fee Farm Rd KT10 .212 D1
Felbridge Ave HA7 ..25 B2
Felbridge Cl SW16 .182 C6
Felbridge Ct
Croydon CR2 .....221 A1

Felbridge Ct continued
East Bedfont TW14 ...150 B3
Feltham TW14 ......150 A3
Harlington UB3 ....127 B6
Felbridge Ho **22**
SE22 ....139 C2
Felbrigge Rd IG3 ...57 D1
Felday Rd SE13 ...163 D5
Felden Cl HA5 ......23 A3
Felden St
SW6 ....135 B4 264 C1
Feldman Cl N16 .....52 A1
Felgate Mews **4** W6 112 B2
Felhampton Rd SE9 .166 D1
Felhurst Cres RM10 ..81 D4
Feline Ct **1** EN4 ....14 C5
Felix Ave N8 ....50 A3
Felix Ct E17 ....53 D4
Felix Dr E19 ......193 D3
Felix Manor BR7 ...189 C4
Felix Neubergh Ct EN1 .5 C1
Felix Rd Ealing W13 109 A6
Walton-on-T KT12 ..194 A3
Felix St **19** E2 ....96 B5
Felixstowe Ct E16 ..122 D5
Felixstowe Rd N17 ..51 D6
NW10 ....90 B4
SE2 ....124 B3
Edmonton N9 ......34 A6
Fellbrigg Rd SE22 .161 D6
Fellbrigg St **21** E1 ...96 B3
Fellbrook TW10 ....153 B1
Fellmongers Yd **3**
CR0 ....221 A5
Fellowes Cl UB4 ....84 D3
Fellowes Ct **1** UB3 .127 B6
Fellowes Rd SM1,SM5 218 C6
Fellows Ct E2 ....95 D5
Fellows Rd NW3 .....70 C1
Fell Rd CR0 ....221 A5
Fells Haugh **6** W3 ..89 A1
Felltram Way SE7 ..121 A1
Fell Wlk HA8 ....26 D2
Felmersham Cl **2**
SW4 ....137 D1
Felmingham Rd SE20 184 C1
Felsberg Rd SW2 ..160 A4
Fels Cl RM10 ....81 D5
Felsham Ho SW15 ..134 D2
Felsham Rd SW15 ..134 D2
Felspar Cl SE18 ...123 D1
Felstead Rd E11 ....55 A2
Felstead St E9 ......75 B2
Felstead Wharf E14 120 A1
Felsted Rd E16 .....99 D1
Feltham Ave KT8 ..196 C5
Felthambrook Ind Est
TW13 ....150 B1
Felthambrook Way
TW13 ....172 B6
Feltham Bsns Complex
TW13 ....150 B2
Feltham Comm Sch
TW13 ....150 C2
Feltham Corporate Ctr
TW13 ....150 B1
Feltham Hill Jun Sch
TW13 ....149 C1
Feltham Hill Rd
Ashford TW15 ......171 A4
Feltham TW13 .....172 B6
Feltham Rd
Ashford TW15 ......171 A6
Mitcham CR4 ......181 A1
Feltham Sta TW13 .150 B3
Felton Cl BR5 .....210 D3
Felton Gdns IG11 ...101 C5
Felton Ho N1 ......235 D5
SE9 ....143 C1
Felton Lea DA14 ...189 D5
Felton Rd W13 ....109 C4
Barking IG11 ......101 C5
Felton St N1 .95 B6 235 D5
Fenchurch **34** N1 ....95 C6
Fenchurch Ave
EC3 ....95 C1 243 A1
Fenchurch Bldgs
EC3 ....243 B1
Fenchurch Pl EC3 ..253 B6
Fenchurch St
EC3 ....117 C6 253 B6
Fenchurch Street Sta
EC3 ....117 C6 253 B6
Fen Ct EC3 ....253 A6
Fendall Rd KT19 ...215 A3
Fendall St
SE1 ....117 C3 263 B5
Fender Ct **5** SW4 ..138 A3
Fendt Cl **8** E16 .....98 D1

Fendyke Rd SE2,DA17 124 D3
Fenelon Pl
W14 ....113 B2 254 D3
Fen Gr DA15 ......167 D5
Fenham Rd SE15 ...140 B5
Fenman Ct N17 .....34 B2
Fenman Gdns IG3 ...58 B1
Fenn Cl BR1 ......187 A4
Fenn Ct HA1 ....43 A4
Fennel Cl E16 ......98 C3
Fennel St SE18 ....144 C6
Fenner Cl SE16 ....118 B2
Fenner Ho **25** E1 ...118 C1
Fenner Sq **10** SW11 .136 B2
Fenning Ct CR4 ....202 C5
Fenning St SE1 ....253 A2
Fenn St E9 ....74 C3
Fen St E16 ....120 D6
Fenstanton Ave N12 ..30 B5
Fenstanton Prim Sch
SW2 ....160 C3
Fentiman Rd
SW8 ....138 B5 270 C4
Fenton Cl BR7 .....188 B5
E8 ....73 D2
SW9 ....138 B3
Fenton Ho SE14 ...141 A5
Heston TW5 ......129 C6
Fenton Rd N17 .....33 A3
Fentons SE3 ......142 D5
Fenton's Ave E13 ...99 B5
Fenton St E1 ....96 B1
Fenwick Cl **16** SE18 144 C6
Fenwick Gr SE15 ...140 A5
Fenwick Pl SW9 ...138 A2
Croydon CR2 ......220 D1
Fenwick Rd SE15 ..140 A5
Ferby Ct DA15 ....189 D6
Ferdinand Ho **1** NW1 71 B1
Ferdinand Pl NW1 ..71 A1
Ferdinand St NW1 ..71 A1
Ferguson Ave KT5 .198 B4
Ferguson Cl BR2,BR2 208 B6
Ferguson Dr W3 ....89 B1
Ferguson Ho SE10 .142 A4
Ferguson's Cl E14 .119 C2
Fergus Rd N5 ....72 D3
Fermain Ct E N1 ....95 C6
Fermain Ct N N1 ....95 C6
Fermain Ct W N1 ...95 C6
Ferme Park Rd N4,N8 .50 B3
Fermor Rd SE23 ...163 A3
Fermoy Rd W9 .....91 B3
Greenford UB6 .....85 D3
Fern Ave CR4 .....203 D5
Fernbank IG9 ......21 B3
Fernbank Ave
Walton-on-T KT12 ..195 A2
Wembley HA0 ......64 C3
Fernbank Mews
SW12 ....159 B4
Fernbrook Dr HA2 ..41 D2
Fernbrook Rd SE13 .164 C5
Fern Cl **3** N1 ....95 C5
Ferncliff Rd E8 .....74 A4
Ferncroft Ave N12 ..30 D4
NW3 ....69 C4
Ruislip HA4 ....62 C6
Fern Ct DA7 ......147 C1
SE14 ....140 D3
Chingford E4 ....36 A4
Ferndale BR1 .....187 C1
Ferndale Ave E17 ...54 B4
Hounslow TW4 ....129 A2
Ferndale Cl DA7 ...147 A4
Ferndale Ct **3** SE3 142 D5
Ferndale Ho N16 ...51 B4
Ferndale Rd E11 ....76 D6
E7 ....77 B1
N15 ....51 D4
SW4,SW9 ....138 A1
Ashford TW15 ......170 A5
Croydon SE25 .....206 B4
Enfield EN3 ....7 A6
Ferndale St E6 ....100 D1
Ferndale Way BR6 .227 B3
Ferndene NW9 .....45 A4
Fern Dene W13 .....87 B2
Ferndene Rd SE24 .139 A1
Fernden Way RM7 ..59 D3
Ferndown
5 Kingston KT6 ...198 A4
Pinner HA6 ....22 A1
6 Wanstead E18 ...55 A6
Ferndown Ave BR6 211 B1
Ferndown Cl
Pinner HA5 ....23 A2
Sutton SM2 ....218 B2
Ferndown Ct **6** UB1 .86 A2

Ferndown Lo E14 ...120 A3
Ferndown Rd SE9 ..165 D4
South Oxhey WD19 ..22 C6
Ferndown Meade Way
TW7 ....131 A3
Ferney Rd EN4 .....15 A3
Fern Gr TW14 .....150 B4
Fernhall Dr IG4 .....55 D5
Fernham Rd CR7 ...205 A6
Fernhead Rd W9 ....91 B4
Fernhill Ct
Chingford E17 .....36 B1
Kingston KT2 .....175 D5
Fernhill Gdns KT2 ..176 A5
Fernhill Ho E5 ......74 A6
Fern Hill Pl **3** BR6 .227 A3
Fern Hill Prim Sch
KT2 ....176 A4
Fernhill St E16 ....122 B5
Fernholme Rd SE15 162 D6
Fernhurst Gdns HA8 .26 C4
Fernhurst Rd
Ashford TW15 ......171 A4
Croydon CR0 ......206 B1
Fulham SW6 ..135 A4 264 C1
Fernie Ho SE22 ...139 C2
Fern La TW5 ......107 A5
Fernlea Ho NW10 ..88 B4
Fernlea Rd
Balham SW12 .....159 B3
Mitcham CR4 ......181 A2
Fernleigh Cl W9 ....91 B4
Croydon CR0 ......220 C1
Fernleigh Ct
Harrow HA2 ....23 D1
Wembley HA9 ......44 A1
Fernleigh Rd N21 ..16 D2
Fernley Cl HA5 .....40 C5
Fern Lo **13** SW16 ...182 C5
Fernsbury St WC1 ..234 A1
Fernshaw Mans
SW10 ....266 A5
Fernshaw Rd
SW10 .....136 A6 266 A5
Fernside IG9 ......21 B3
Fernside Ave NW7 .11 B1
Feltham TW13 .....172 B6
Fernside Ct NW4 ..28 D1
Fernside Rd SW12 .159 A4
Ferns Rd E15 ....76 D2
Fern St E3 ....97 C3
Fernthorpe Rd SW16 181 C4
Ferntower Rd N5 ...73 B3
Fernways IG1 ......78 D4
Greenford UB6 .....85 D3
Fern Wlk **17** SE16 ..118 A1
Fernwood
Wandsworth SW19 ..157 B3
Wood Green N22 ...32 A3
Fernwood Ave
Streatham SW16 ...181 D6
Wembley HA0 ......65 C2
Fernwood Cl BR1 ..187 C6
Fernwood Cres N20 .14 D1
Ferny Hill EN4 ......3 A5
Ferranti Cl SE18 ..121 D3
Ferraro Cl TW5 ...129 C6
Ferrers Ave
Wallington SM6 ....219 D4
West Drayton UB7 .104 A4
Ferrers Rd SW16 ..181 D5
Ferrestone Rd N8 ..50 B5
Ferrey Mews **20** SW9 138 C3
Ferriby Cl N1 ......72 D5
Ferrier Ind Est SE18 135 D1
Ferrier Point **6** E16 .99 A2
Ferrier St SW18 ...135 D1
Ferring Cl HA2 .....42 A1
Ferrings SE21 .....161 C1
Ferris Ave CR0 ....223 A1
Ferris Rd SE22 ....140 A1
Ferron Rd E5 ....74 B5
Ferrour Ct N2 ......48 B6
Ferry Ho E5 ....52 B1
Ferry La N17 ......52 B5
Barnes SW13 .....133 D6
Brentford TW8 ....132 A6
Lower Halliford TW17 192 C1
Richmond TW9 ...132 B6
Ferry Lane Prim Sch
N17 ....52 B5
Ferrymead Ave UB6 .85 C5
Ferrymead Dr UB6 ..85 C5
Ferrymead Gdns UB6 86 A5
Ferrymoor TW10 ..153 B5
Ferry Rd Barnes SW13 134 A4
East Molesey KT8 ..195 C6
Richmond TW11 ...175 B5
Thames Ditton KT7 .197 B3

Ferry Sq **1** TW8 ...132 A6
Ferry St E14 ......120 A1
Ferry Wks TW17 ...192 C1
Festing Rd SW15 ..134 C3
Festival Cl DA5 ...168 D3
Hillingdon UB10 ...82 D6
Festival Pier
SE1 ....116 B5 250 C4
Festival Pleasure Gdns
SW11 .....136 D5 267 C3
Fetter La EC4 .94 C1 241 B2
Fettes Ho NW8 ....229 D3
Fews Lo RM6 ......58 D5
Ffinch St SE8 ......141 C5
Field Cl BR1 ......187 C1
Buckhurst Hill IG9 .21 C1
Chessington KT9 ..213 C6
Chingford E4 ....35 D4
Cranford TW4 ....128 B4
East Molesey KT8 ..195 C4
Harlington UB7 ....127 A5
Ruislip HA4 ....39 A1
Uxbridge UB10 .....60 D6
Fieldcommon La
KT12 ....195 B1
Field Ct N7 ....72 A3
NW3 ....70 A3
WC1 ....240 C3
Wimbledon SW19 ..157 C1
Field End Ruislip HA4 .62 C2
Twickenham TW11 ..174 D6
Field End Jun & Inf Schs
HA4 ....62 C2
Fieldend Rd SW16 .181 C2
Field End Rd HA5,HA4 .40 C1
Fielders Cl
2 Enfield EN1 ......5 C1
Harrow HA2 ....42 A1
Fieldfare Rd SE28 .124 C6
Fieldgate Mans **23** E1 .96 A2
Fieldgate St E1 .....96 A2
Field Ho **4** N9 .....34 A6
Fieldhouse Cl E18 .37 B2
Fieldhouse Rd SW12 159 C3
Fielding Ave TW2 .152 A1
Fielding Ho **3** NW6 .91 C4
NW8 ....229 A6
Chiswick W4 ......133 C6
Fielding Mews SW13 134 B5
Fielding Prim Sch
W13 ....109 B3
Fielding Rd W14 ...112 D3
W4 ....111 C3
Fielding St SE17 ..139 A6
Fieldings The SE23 162 C3
Fielding Terr W5 ...110 B6
Field La
Brentford TW8 ....131 C5
Teddington TW11 ..175 A5
Field Mead NW9,NW7 27 D3
Field Pl KT3 ......199 D3
Field Point E7 ......77 A4
Field Rd E7 ....77 A4
N17 ....51 C6
W6 ....135 A4 264 A6
Feltham TW14 .....150 B5
Fieldsend Rd SM3 .217 A3
Fields Est E8 ....74 A1
Fieldside Cl BR6 ..227 A4
Fieldside Rd BR1 ..186 B5
Fields Park Cres RM6 .58 D4
Field St WC1 ......233 C2
Fieldsway Ho N5 ...72 C3
Field View TW13 ..171 B6
Field View Ct N5 ...72 D3
NW9 ....44 C3
Fieldway BR5 .....211 B3
Field Way NW10 ...67 A1
Fieldway RM8 .....80 C4
Field Way
Greenford UB6 .....85 D6
New Addington CR0 .223 D2
Ruislip HA4 ....39 A1
Fieldway Cres N5,N7 .72 C3
Fieldwick Ho **14** E9 ..74 D2
Fiennes Cl RM8 ....58 C1
Fife Ct **5** W3 ....88 C1
Fifehead Cl TW15 ..170 A4
Fife Rd E16 ....99 A2
Kingston KT2 .....176 A1
Mortlake SW14 ...155 A6
Tottenham N22 ...32 D3
Fife Terr N1 ......233 D4
Fifield Path SE23 .162 D1
Fifteenpenny Fields
SE9 ....166 C6
Fifth Ave W10 ......91 A4
Hayes UB3 ....105 D5

Fifth Ave continued
Ilford E12 ....78 B4
Fifth Cross Rd TW2 ..152 B2
Fifth Way HA9 ....66 D4
Figge's Rd CR4 ......181 A3
Fig Tree Cl NW10 ....89 C6
Filanco Ct W7 ....108 D5
Filby Rd KT9 ....214 B2
Filey Ave N16 ....52 A1
Filey Cl SM2 ....218 A1
Filey Ho SW18 ....136 A1
Filey Waye HA4 ......62 B6
Filigree Ct SE16 ....119 B5
Fillebrook Ave EN1 ...5 D2
Fillebrook Hall E11 ..54 C2
Fillebrook Rd E11 ....54 C1
Filmer Ho SW6 ......264 B2
Filmer Rd
SW6 ....135 B5 264 C3
Filmer Road Studios
SW6 ....264 B2
Filston Rd DA8 ......125 D1
Filton Ct [14] SE14 ...140 C5
Finborough Ho SW10 266 A6
Finborough Rd
SW10 ......135 D6 265 D6
Upper Tooting SW17 ...180 C4
Finchale Rd SE2 .....124 A3
Fincham Cl UB10 .....61 A5
Finch Ave SE27 ......183 B6
Finch Cl NW10 ....67 B2
Barnet EN5 ....13 C6
Finch Dr TW14 ....150 A3
Finch Gdns E4 ....35 C5
Finch Ho [1] SE8 .....141 D6
Finchingfield Ave IG8 .37 C3
Finch La EC2,EC3 ....242 D1
Finchley Cath High Sch
N12 ....13 D1
Finchley Central Sta
N3 ....29 C2
Finchley Ct N3 ....29 C4
Finchley La NW4 .....46 C5
Finchley Lo N12 ......29 D5
Finchley Memorial Hospl
N12 ....30 A3
Finchley Pk N12 ......30 B6
Finchley Pl NW8 .....229 C4
NW3 ....70 A2
NW8 ....70 A2
Finchley Rd NW11 ....47 B3
Finchley Road & Frognal
Sta NW3 ....70 A3
Finchley Road Sta
NW3 ....70 A2
Finchley Way N3 .....29 C3
Finch Lo [15] W9 ......91 C2
Finch Mews [3] SE15 .139 D4
Finch's Ct [9] E14 ....119 C6
Finden Rd E7 ....77 C3
Findhorn Ave UB4 ....84 B2
Findhorn St E14 ......98 A1
Findon Cl SW18 ......157 C5
Harrow HA2 ....63 D5
Findon Rd W12 ....112 A4
Edmonton N9 ....18 B3
Fine Bush La HA4 .....38 D3
Fineran Ct [16] SW11 .136 B1
Fingal St SE10 ....120 D1
Fingest Ho NW8 .....237 A6
Finians Cl UB10 ......60 B1
Finland Rd SE4 ......141 A2
Finland St SE16 ......119 A3
Finlays Cl KT9 ....214 C3
Finlay St SW6 ....134 D4
Finley Ct [21] SE5 ....139 A5
Finmere Ho [1] N4 ....51 A2
Finnemore Ho N1 ....235 A6
Finney La TW7 ....131 A2
Finn Ho N1 ....235 D2
Finnis St E2 ....96 B3
Finnymore Rd RM9 ...81 A1
Finsbury Ave EC2 ....242 D3
Finsbury Cir
EC2 ....95 B2 242 D3
Finsbury Cotts N22 ..32 A3
Finsbury Ct EC2 .....242 C4
Finsbury Ho N22 .....32 A3
Finsbury Market EC2 243 A4
Finsbury Mkt EC2 ....243 A5
Finsbury Park Ave N4 .51 A3
Finsbury Park Rd N4,
N5 ....72 A6
Finsbury Park Sta N4 .72 C6
Finsbury Pavement
EC2 ....95 B2 242 D4
Finsbury Sq
EC2 ....95 B2 242 D4

Finsbury St EC2 .....242 C4
Finsbury Yd DA5 .....169 B5
Finsen Rd SE5 ....139 C1
Finstock Rd W10 .....90 D1
Finton House Sch
SW17 ....158 D2
Finucane Ct TW9 ....132 B2
Finucane Rise WD23 ..8 A1
Finwhale Ho E14 .....119 D3
Fiona Ct [9] NW6 .....91 B5
Enfield EN2 ....4 D2
Firbank Cl E16 ....99 D2
Enfield EN2 ....5 A1
Fir Tree Gr SM5 ......218 D1
Fircroft N1 ..94 D6 234 D6
Fircroft Prim Sch
SW17 ....158 D1
Fircroft Rd
Chessington KT9 .....214 B4
Upper Tooting SW17 ..158 D1
Fir Dene BR6 ....226 C5
Firdene KT5 ....199 A1
Fire Bell Alley KT6 ...198 A3
Firebell Mews KT6 ...198 A3
Fire Brigade Pier
SE1 ....260 B4
Firecrest Dr NW3 .....69 D5
Firefly [7] NW9 ....27 D1
Firefly Cl SM6 ....220 A1
Firefly Gdns E6 ......100 A3
Firemans Cotts N10 .49 A6
Fireman's Flats N22 ..32 A2
Firepower (The Royal
Artillery Mus) ★
SE18 ....122 D3
Fire Station Alley EN5 .1 A3
Fire Station Mews [3]
BR3 ....185 D2
Firethorn Cl HA8 .....27 A6
Fir Gr KT3 ....199 D3
Firhill Rd SE6 ....163 C1
Firle Ho W10 ....90 C2
Firmston Ho [9]
SW14 ....133 B2
Fir Rd Cheam SM3 ...201 B1
Feltham TW13 ....172 A6
Firs Ave N10 ....49 A5
N11 ....31 A4
Mortlake SW14 ......133 A1
Firs Cl N10 ....49 A6
Claygate KT10 ....212 C2
Forest Hill SE23 .....163 A4
Mitcham CR4 ....181 A4
Firscroft N13 ....17 A1
Firs Dr TW5 ....128 B5
Firs Farm Prim Sch
N13 ....17 B1
Firs Ho N22 ....32 C2
Firside Gr DA15 .....167 D3
Firs La N21,N13 .....17 A2
Firs Park Ave N21 ....17 B3
Firs Park Gdns N21 ...17 B3
First Ave E12 ....78 A3
E13 ....99 A4
E17 ....53 D4
N18 ....34 C6
NW4 ....46 C5
W10 ....91 B3
W3 ....111 D5
Bexley DA7 ....146 C5
Dagenham RM10 ....103 D5
Dagenham RM6 .....58 C4
East Molesey KT8 ...195 C5
Enfield EN1 ....17 D6
Hayes UB3 ....105 D5
Mortlake SW14 ......133 C2
Walton-on-T KT12 ...194 B3
Wembley HA9 ....65 D6
First Cl KT8 ....196 A6
First Cross Rd TW2 ..152 C2
First Dr NW10 ....67 A1
Firs The DA15 ....167 D1
E6 ....78 A1
N20 ....14 B3
Belmont SM2 ....217 D1
Claygate KT10 ....212 C2
Ealing W5 ....87 D2
Forest Hill SE23 .....184 C5
[2] Penge SE26 .....184 B5
Wimbledon SW20 ...178 A3
Woodford IG8 ....37 C3
First Way HA9 ....66 D4
Firstway SW20 ......178 C1
Firs Wlk IG8 ....37 A5

Firswood Ave KT19 ..215 D3
Firth Gdns
SW6 ....135 A4 264 A1
Fir Tree Ave UB7 .....104 C3
Fir Tree Cl Ealing W5 ..88 A1
Esher KT10 ....212 A3
[5] Orpington BR6 ...227 D3
Streatham SW16 ....181 C5
Worcester Park KT19 ..215 D4
Firtree Ct BR2 ....208 D6
Fir Tree Gdns CR0 ...223 D6
Fir Tree Ho [14] SE14 .140 B5
Fir Tree Rd TW4 .....129 A1
Fir Trees Cl SE16 ....119 A5
Fir Wlk KT17,SM3 ...216 D2
Fisher Cl Croydon CR0 205 D1
Southall UB6 ....85 C4
Holdbrook EN3 ......7 C6
Fisher Ho [8] E1 .....118 C6
N1 ....234 A5
[2] N19 ....71 C6
Fisherman Cl TW10 ..175 C6
Fishermans Dr SE16 .118 D4
Fishermans Wlk
SE28 ....123 C4
Fisherman's Wlk E14 119 C5
Fisher Rd HA3 ....24 D1
Fishers Cl SW16 .....159 D1
Fishers Ct SE14 .....140 D4
[4] Teddington TW11 .174 D5
Fisher's La W4 ......111 B2
Fisher St E16 ....99 A2
WC1 ....240 C3
Fisherton St
NW8 ....92 B3 236 D6
Fisherton Street Est
NW8 ....92 B3 236 D5
Fishguard Way E16 ..122 D5
Fishlock Ct [6] SW4 .138 A3
Fishponds Rd BR2 ...225 D3
Upper Tooting SW17 ..180 C6
Fish St Hill EC3 .....252 D5
Fiske Ct Barking IG11 .101 B5
[1] Merton SW19 ....180 A3
Sutton SM2 ....218 A1
Tottenham N17 .....34 A2
Fitch Ct SW2 ....160 C6
[8] Mitcham CR4 ....181 A1
Fitzalan Rd N3 ....47 B6
Claygate KT10 ....212 C1
Fitzalan St
SE11 ....116 C2 261 A4
Fitzclarence Ho W11 244 A4
Fitz-George Ave
W14 ....254 A3
Fitzgeorge Ave KT3,
KT3 ....177 B2
Fitzgerald Ave SW14 .133 C2
Fitzgerald Ct [1] E10 ..53 D1
Fitzgerald Ho [14] E14 .97 D1
[16] SW9 ....138 C3
Hayes UB3 ....106 B5
Fitzgerald Rd
Mortlake SW14 ......133 B2
Thames Ditton KT7 ..197 A3
Wanstead E11 ......55 A4
Fitzhardinge Ho W1 .238 A2
Fitzhardinge St W1 .238 A2
Fitzherbert Ho [11]
TW10 ....154 B5
Fitzhugh Gr SW18 ...158 A5
Fitzjames Ave W14 ..254 B3
Croydon CR0 ....222 A6
Fitzjohn Ave EN5 .....1 B1
Fitzjohn's Ave NW3 ..70 A3
Fitzjohns Mans NW3 .70 A2
Fitzjohns Prim Sch
NW3 ....70 B3
Fitzmaurice Ho [17]
SE16 ....118 B2
Fitzmaurice Pl W1 ...248 D4
Fitzneal St W12 ......89 D1
Fitzroy Cl N6 ....48 D1
Fitzroy Cres W4 .....133 B5
Fitzroy Ct N6 ....49 C3
W1 ....239 B5
Fitzroy Gdns SE19 ...183 C3
Fitzroy Ho [14] E14 ....97 B1
SE1 ....263 D2
Fitzroy Lo N21 ......16 D6
Fitzroy Mews W1 ...239 A5
Fitzroy Pk N6 ....48 D1
Fitzroy Rd
NW1 ....93 A6 231 A6
Fitzroy Sq W1 ....239 A5

Fitzroy St W1 .93 C3 239 A5
Fitzroy Yd NW1 .....231 A6
Fitzsimmons Ct [1]
NW10 ....89 B6
Fitzstephen Rd RM8 ..80 C3
Fitzwarren Gdns N19 .49 C1
Fitzwilliam Ave TW9 .132 B3
Fitzwilliam Ho TW9 ..131 D1
Fitzwilliam Hts [1]
SE23 ....162 C2
Fitzwilliam Mews
E16 ....121 A5
Fitzwilliam Rd SW4 .137 C2
Fitzwygram Cl TW12 .174 A5
Five Acre NW9 ....27 D1
Fiveacre Cl CR7 .....204 C3
Five Elms Prim Sch
RM8 ....81 B5
Five Elms Rd BR2 ...225 C5
Dagenham RM9 .....81 B5
Fives Ct SE11 ....261 C5
Fiveways SE9 ....166 D2
Croydon CR0 ....220 C4
Isleworth TW7 ......130 D3
Fiveways Cnr NW4 ...28 A2
Fiveways Rd SW9 ...138 C3
Five Ways Cnr NW4 ..28 A2
Five Ways Retail Pk
NW7 ....27 D3
Flack Ct [14] E10 .....53 D2
Fladbury Rd N15 .....51 B3
Fladgate Rd E11 .....54 C3
Flag Cl CR0 ....206 D1
Flag Wlk HA5 ....40 A3
Flambard Rd HA1,HA3 .43 D4
Flamborough Ho [11]
SE15 ....140 A4
Flamborough Rd HA4 .62 A5
Flamborough St E14 ..97 A1
Flamingo Ct [2] SE8 .141 C5
Flamingo Gdns UB5 ..85 A4
Flamstead Gdns RM9 .80 C5
Flamstead Rd RM9 ...80 C5
Flamsted Ave HA9 ...66 C2
Flamsteed Ho ★ SE10 142 B5
Flamsteed Rd SE7 ...122 A1
Flanchford Rd W12 ..111 A3
Flanders Cres SW17 .180 D4
Flanders Ct E17 .....53 A3
Flanders Mans [1]
W4 ....111 A2
Flanders Rd W4 .....111 A3
Walland E6 ....100 C5
Flanders Way E9 ....74 C2
Flank St [6] E1 ......118 A6
Flansham Ho [2] E14 ..97 B1
Flash La EN2 ....5 A6
Flask Wlk NW3 ......70 B4
Flatford Ho [2] SE6 ..186 A6
Flavell Mews SE10 ..120 C1
Flaxen Cl E4 ....19 D1
Flaxen Rd E4 ....19 D1
Flaxley Rd SM4 .....201 B2
Flaxman Ct W1 .....239 C1
[12] Belvedere DA17 ..125 C1
Flaxman Ho SE1 ....261 D6
[10] W4 ....111 C1
Flaxman Rd SE5 ....138 C3
Flaxman Terr
WC1 ....93 D4 232 D3
Flaxman Villas N2 ...48 A6
Flaxmore Ct DA7 ...147 D2
South Norwood CR7 .183 B1
Flaxton Rd SE18 ....145 C5
Flecker Cl HA7 ......24 D5
Flecker Ho [6] SE5 ..139 B5
Fleece Dr N9 ....34 A6
Fleecefield Prim Sch
N18 ....34 A6
Fleece Rd KT6 ....197 C3
Fleece Wlk N7 ......72 A2
Fleeming Cl E17 .....35 B1
Fleeming Rd E17 ....35 B1
Fleet Cl
East Molesey KT8 ...195 B4
Ruislip HA4 ....39 A3
Fleet Ct [1] W12 ....111 C3
Fleetfield WC1 ......233 B2
Fleet Ho [4] E14 .....119 A6
[6] SW2 ....160 C6
Fleet Pl EC4 ....241 C2
Fleet Prim Sch NW3 ..70 D3
Fleet Rd NW3 ....70 D3
Fleetside KT8 ......195 C4
Fleet Sq WC1 ....233 D2
Fleet St EC4 ..94 C1 241 B1
Fleet Street Hill [11] E1 96 A3
Fleet Terr SE6 ......164 C4
Fleetway WC1 ......233 B2
Fleetway West Bsns Pk
UB6 ....87 B5
Fleet Wood [6] N16 ..73 D6

Fleetwood Cl E16 ...99 D2
Chessington KT9 ....213 D1
South Croydon CR0 ..221 D5
Fleetwood Ct [1] E6 ..100 B2
Orpington BR6 .....226 C4
[8] Stanwell TW19 ..148 A5
Fleetwood Rd NW10 ..68 A3
Kingston KT3 ....198 D6
Fleetwood Sq KT3 ...198 D6
Fleetwood St N16 ....73 C6
Fleetwood Way WD19 .22 C6
Fleming Cl [3] W9 ...91 C3
Fleming Ct W2 ......236 C4
Croydon CR0 ....220 C3
Fleming Ho N4 ......51 A1
[8] SE16 ....118 A4
[8] Wembley HA9 ...67 A5
Fleming Mead CR4 ..180 D3
Fleming Rd SE17 ....138 D6
Southall UB1 ....86 A1
Fleming Way SE28 ..124 D6
Isleworth TW7 ......130 D3
Fleming Wlk NW9 ....27 C1
Flemming Ave HA4 ..62 B6
Flempton Rd E10 ....53 A1
Fletcher Bldgs ★ 240 B1
Fletcher Cl E16 .....122 D6
Fletcher Ct [9] NW5 ..71 B4
Fletcher Ho [22] N1 ..95 C6
[16] N16 ....73 C4
Fletcher La E10 .....54 A2
Fletcher Path [7] SE8 141 C5
Fletcher Rd W4 .....111 A3
Fletchers Cl BR2 ....209 B5
Fletcher St [10] E1 ..118 A6
Fletching Rd E5 .....74 C5
SE7 ....143 D6
Fletton Rd N11 ......32 A3
Fleur Gates [7] SW19 .156 D4
Flexmere Rd N17 ....33 C2
Flimwell Cl BR1 .....186 C5
Flinders Ho [28] E1 ..118 B5
Flint Cl [8] BR6 ......227 D2
Flint Down Cl BR5 ..190 B4
Flintmill Cres SE3,
SE9 ....144 A3
Flinton St
SE17 ....117 C1 263 B2
Flint St SE17 ..117 B2 262 D3
Flitton Ho [7] N1 ....95 C6
Floathaven Cl SE28 .124 A5
Flock Mill Pl SW18 ..157 D3
Flodden Rd SE5 .....139 A4
Flood St SW3 .136 C6 267 B6
Flood Wlk
SW3 ....136 C6 267 B6
Flora Cl E14 ....97 C1
Flint St SE17 ...117 B1 263 B2
Flora Gardens Prim Sch
W6 ....112 B2
Flora Gdns [2] W6 ..112 B2
Dagenham RM6 .....58 C2
Floral St WC2 116 A6 250 A6
Flora St DA17 ......125 B1
Florence Ave
Enfield EN2 ....5 A2
Morden SM4 ....202 A4
Florence Cl KT12 ...194 B2
Florence Ct [4] E5 ..74 A5
W9 ....229 B1
Wanstead E11 .....55 C5
[5] Wimbledon SW19 .179 A4
Florence Dr EN2 .....5 A2
Florence Elson Cl E12 78 C4
Florence Gdns
Chiswick W4 ....133 A6
Ilford RM6 ....58 C2
Florence Ho [20] SE16 118 B1
[2] SE18 ....144 B4
[7] SW18 ....136 B1
[2] SW2 ....160 B6
[10] W11 ....112 D6
[5] Kingston KT2 ...176 B2
Florence Mans
[4] NW4 ....46 B4
SW6 ....264 C2
Florence Nightingale Ho
[11] N1 ....73 A4
Florence Nightingale
Mus ★ SE1 ....250 D1
Florence Rd BR1 ....187 A2
E13 ....99 A5
[8] E6 ....99 C6
N4 ....50 C2
SE2 ....124 C2
W4 ....111 B3
[5] Beckenham BR3 .185 A1

Florence Rd continued
Ealing W5 ....110 A6
Feltham TW13 .....150 B3
[6] Kingston KT2 ...176 B3
Southall UB2 ....106 D3
Walton-on-T KT12 ..194 B2
Wimbledon SW19 ..179 D4
Florence Root Ho IG4 .56 B4
Florence St E16 .....98 D3
N1 ....72 D1
NW4 ....46 C5
Florence Terr SE14 ..141 B4
Kingston SW15 .....155 C1
Florence Way SW12 .158 D3
Florentine Ho [3] IG1 .78 D6
Flores Ho [10] E1 ....96 C2
Florfield Rd E8 ......74 B2
Florian SE5 ....139 C4
Florian Ave SM1 ....218 B4
Florian Rd SW15 ....135 A1
Florida Cl WD23 .....8 B2
Florida Ct BR2 ......208 D5
Florida Rd CR7 .....182 D2
Florida St E2 ....96 A4
Florin Ct SE1 ....253 C1
Edmonton N18 .....33 C6
Floris Pl [7] SW4 ....137 C2
Floriston Ave UB10 ..61 A1
Floriston Cl HA7 ....25 B2
Floriston Ct UB5 ....63 D3
Floriston Gdns HA7 ..25 B2
Florys Ct [7] SW19 ..157 A3
Floss St SW15 ......134 C3
Flower & Dean Wlk
E1 ....243 D3
Flower La NW7 ......27 D4
Flower Pot Cl N15 ...51 D3
Flowers Cl NW2 .....68 A5
Flowersmead SW17 .159 A2
Flowers Mews [1] N19 71 C6
Flower Wlk The
SW7 ....114 A4 246 B2
Floyd Rd SE7 ....121 C1
Fludyer St SE13 ....142 C1
Fluer De Lis St E1 ...243 C5
Flynn Ct [12] E14 ....119 C6
Fogerty Cl EN3 ......7 C6
Foley Cotts KT10 ....212 D2
Foley Ho [19] E1 .....96 C1
Foley Mews KT10 ...212 C2
Foley Rd KT10 ......212 D2
Foley St W1 ..93 C2 239 A3
Folgate St E1 ..95 D2 243 C4
Foliot Ho N1 ....233 C4
Foliot St W12 ......89 D1
Folkestone Ct UB5 ..63 D3
Folkestone Rd E17 ..53 D5
Edmonton N18 .....34 A4
Wallend E6 ....100 C4
Folkingham La [6]
NW9 ....27 C2
Folkington Cnr N12 ..29 B5
Folland [6] NW9 .....27 C2
Follett Ho SW10 ....266 C4
Follett St E14 ....98 A1
Folly La E17 ....35 A2
E4 ....35 A2
Folly Wall E14 ......120 A4
Fontaine Ct [3] BR3 .185 B2
Fontaine Rd SW16 ..182 B3
Fontarabia Rd SW11 .137 A1
Fontenelle SE5 .....139 C4
Fontenoy Ho SE11 ..261 C3
Fontenoy Rd SW12,
SW17 ....159 C2
Fonteyne Gdns IG8 ..37 D1
Fonthill Cl SE20 ....184 A1
Fonthill Ct SE23 ....162 C4
Fonthill Ho SW1 ....258 D2
W14 ....254 B6
Fonthill Mews N4 ...72 B6
Fonthill Rd N4 ......72 C6
Font Hills N2 ....30 A1
Fontley Way SW15 ..156 A4
Fontmell Cl TW15 ...170 C5
Fontmell Pk TW15 ..170 C5
Fontwell Cl
Harrow HA3 ....24 C3
Northolt UB5 ....63 C2
Fontwell Dr BR2 ....210 C4
Football La HA1 .....42 C1
Footpath The SW15 .156 A6
Foots Cray High St
DA14 ....190 D4
Foots Cray La DA5,
DA14 ....168 C3
Footscray Rd SE9 ...166 D3

Forber Ho 25 E2 96 C4
Forbes Cl NW2 68 A5
Forbes Ct SE19 183 C5
Forbes Ho 2 W4 110 C1
Forbes St E1 96 A1
Forbes Way HA4 62 B6
Forburg Rd N16 52 A1
Fordbridge Ct TW15 170 A4
Fordbridge Rd
Ashford TW15 170 B5
Lower Halliford TW16, TW17 193 D3
Sunbury TW16 194 A5
Fordbridge Rdbt
TW15 170 A4
Ford Cl 11 E3 97 A5
Ashford TW15 170 A4
Harrow HA1 42 B2
Littleton TW17 192 C4
Thornton Heath CR7 204 D4
Fordcombe 13 NW5 71 A2
Forde Ave BR1 209 C6
Fordel Rd SE6 164 B3
Ford End IG8 37 B4
Fordham 4 KT1 176 C1
Fordham Cl EN4 2 C2
Fordham Rd EN4 2 C2
Fordham St 7 E1 96 A1
Ford Ho 2 SE18 122 D1
2 New Barnet EN5 13 D6
Fordhook Ave W5 110 C6
Fordingley Rd W9 91 B4
Fordington Ho 2
SE26 162 B1
Fordington Rd N6 48 D5
Fordmill Rd SE6 163 C2
Ford Rd E3 97 B5
Ashford TW15 170 B6
Dagenham RM10 81 C1
Ford's Gr N21 17 A3
Fords Park Rd E16 99 A1
Ford Sq E1 96 B2
Ford St E16 98 D1
E3 97 A5
Fordwich Cl BR6 211 D2
Fordwych Ct NW2 69 A2
Fordwych Rd NW2 69 A3
Fordyce Ho 3 SW16 181 C6
Fordyce Rd SE13 164 A6
Fordyke Rd RM8 81 B6
Foreign, Commonwealth & Home Offices SW1 250 A2
Foreland Ct NW4 29 A2
Foreland Ho W11 244 A6
Foreland St SE18 123 B2
Foreshore SE8 119 B2
Fore St EC2 95 A2 242 B3
Edmonton N18 34 A6
Pinner HA5 40 A4
Forest App
Chingford E4 20 C4
Woodford IG8 37 A3
Fore St Ave EC2 242 C3
Forest Ave E4 20 C4
Forest Bsns Pk E17 52 D2
Forest Cl
Chislehurst BR7 188 C2
Wanstead E11 55 A4
Woodford IG8 37 B6
Forest Croft SE23 162 B2
Forest Ct E11 54 C5
12 N12 29 D6
Chingford E4 20 D3
Forestdale N14 31 D6
Forestdale Ctr The
CR0 223 B1
Forest Dene Ct 2
SM2 218 A2
Forest Dr
Ashford TW16 171 D3
Chingford IG8 36 C3
Keston Mark BR2 226 A4
Wanstead E12 77 D5
Forest Dr E E11 54 B3
Forest Dr W E11 54 B2
Forest Edge IG9 21 D1
Forester Rd SE15 140 B2
Foresters Cl SM6 219 D1
Foresters Cres DA7 147 D1
Foresters Dr E17 54 B5
Wallington SM6 219 D1
Foresters Prim Sch
SM6 219 D2
Forest Gate NW9 45 C4
Forest Gate Com Sch
E7 77 A3
Forest Gate Sta E7 77 A3
Forest Gdns N17 33 D1
Forest Glade E11 54 C3
Chingford E4 36 C5
Forest Gr E8 73 D2
Forest Hill SE23 162 C3
Forest Hill Bsns Ctr
SE23 162 C2
Forest Hill Ct 6
SE26 162 B1
Forest Hill Ind Est
SE23 162 C2
Forest Hill Rd SE22 162 B5
Forest Hill Sec Sch
SE23 162 D1
Forest Hill Sta SE23 162 C2
Forest Ho 9 E4 20 C4
Forestholme Cl SE23 162 C2
Forest Hts IG9 21 A2
Forest La E7,E15 76 D3
Forest Lawns BR1 187 C2
Forest Lea E11 54 D2
Forest Lo 1 SE23 162 C1
Forest Mount Rd IG8 36 B3
Forest Point E7 77 B3
Forest Rd E11 54 B2
E17 53 C6
E7 77 A4
E8 73 D2
Edmonton N9 18 B3
Feltham TW13 150 C2
Morden SM3,SM4 201 C2
Richmond TW9 132 C5
Romford RM7 59 D6
Woodford IG8 21 A1
Forest Ridge BR2 226 B4
Beckenham BR3 207 C6
Forest Rise E17 54 B5
Forest Sch E17 54 C5
Forest Side E7 77 B4
Buckhurst Hill IG9 21 C3
Chingford E4 20 D3
New Malden KT4 199 D1
Forest St E7 77 A3
Forest The E11 54 C5
Forest Trad Est E17 52 D6
Forest View E11 54 D2
Chingford E4 20 B4
Forest View Ave E10 54 B4
Forest View Rd E12 78 A4
Chingford E17 36 A2
Forest Way BR5 211 D4
6 N19 71 C6
Sidcup DA15 167 B4
Woodford IG8 37 B6
Forfar Rd
SW11 137 A4 268 B2
Tottenham N22 32 D2
Forge Cl BR2 209 A1
Forge Cotts W5 109 D5
Forge Dr KT10 213 A1
Forge La Belmont SM3 217 A1
Feltham TW13 173 A5
Sunbury TW16 194 A6
Forge Lane Inf Sch
TW13 173 A5
Forge Lane Jun Sch
TW13 173 A5
Forge Mews
Addington CR0 223 C3
Sunbury TW16 194 A6
Forge Pl NW1 71 A2
Forge The UB3 127 B6
Forlong Path UB5 63 A2
Forman Ct TW1 152 D3
Forman Gr 2 UB5 84 D4
Forman Ho SE4 140 D1
Forman Pl N16 73 D4
Formby Ave HA3,HA7 43 C6
Formby Ct 9 N7 72 C3
Formosa Ho 1 E1 97 A3
Formosa St W9 91 D3
Formunt Cl E16 98 D2
Forres Gdns NW11 47 C3
Forrest Ct N7 72 C2
Forrester Path SE26 184 C6
Forresters The HA5 40 B3
Forrest Gdns SW16 204 B6
Forrest Ho SW15 134 C3
Forris Ave UB3 105 D5
Forset Ct W1 237 B2
Forset St W1 92 C1 237 B2
Forstal Cl BR2 209 A6
Forster Ho SE6 164 B1
Forster Park Prim Sch
SE6 164 C1
Forster Rd E17 53 A3
N17 51 D6
Beckenham BR3 207 A6
Streatham SW2 160 A4
Thornton Heath CR0 205 A2
Forsters Cl RM6 59 B3
Forsters Way UB4 84 B1
Forstic Wlk E1 243 D3
Forston St N1 95 A5 235 B4
Forsyte Cres SE19 183 C2
Forsyte Ct KT2 176 D2
Forsyth Ct KT3 177 C1
Forsythe Shades BR3 186 A2
Forsyth Gdns SE17 138 D6
Forsyth Ho 14 E9 74 C1
SW1 259 B3
Forsythia Cl IG1 78 D3
Forsythia Ho SE4 141 A2
Forsyth Pl EN1 17 C6
Forterie Gdns IG3 80 A4
Fortescue Ave 1 E8 74 B1
Twickenham TW2 152 A1
Fortescue Rd HA8 27 B3
Mitcham SW19 180 B3
Fortess Gr NW5 71 C3
Fortess Rd NW5 71 C4
Fortess Wlk NW5 71 B3
Forthbridge Rd
SW11 137 A1
Forth Ho 28 E3 97 B5
Forties The 9 NW5 71 C3
Fortior Ct N6 49 C2
Fortis Cl E16 99 C1
Fortis Ct N10 49 A6
Fortis Gn N2,N10 48 D6
Fortis Green Ave N2 48 D5
Fortis Green Cotts N2 48 D6
Fortismere Ave N10 49 A6
Fortismere Sch N10 30 D1
Fortismere Sch (South Wing) N10 49 A6
Fortnam Rd N19 71 D6
Fortnums Acre HA7 24 D4
Fort Rd SE1 117 D2 263 D3
Northolt UB5 63 C1
Fortrose Gdns SW12,
SW2 160 A3
Fort St E1 243 B3
E16 121 B5
Fortuna Cl N7 72 B2
Fortune Ct IG11 102 B5
Fortune Gate Rd
NW10 89 C6
Fortune Green Rd
NW6 69 C4
Fortune Ho EC1 242 B5
SE11 261 A3
Fortune La WD6 9 D5
Fortunes Mead UB5 63 A2
Fortune St EC1 95 A3 242 B5
Fortune Way NW10 90 A4
Fortune Wlk SE28 123 B3
Forty Acre La E16 99 A2
Forty Ave HA9 66 B6
Forty Cl HA9 66 B5
Forty Hall* EN2 5 D6
Forty Hill EN2 5 D5
Forty Hill CE Prim Sch
EN2 6 A6
Forty Hill Ho EN1 5 D5
Forty La HA9 66 D6
Forumside HA8 26 C4
Forum The KT8 195 D5
Forum Way HA8 26 C4
Forval Cl CR4 202 D4
Forward Bsns Ctr The
E16 98 B3
Forward Dr HA3 42 D5
Fosbroke Ho SW8 270 A3
Fosbury Ho 7 SW9 138 B1
Fosbury Mews W2 245 D5
Foscote Mews W9 91 C2
Foscote Rd NW4 46 B3
Foskett Ho 16 N2 30 B1
Foskett Rd SW6 135 B3
Foss Ave CR0,CR9 220 C3
Fossdene Prim Sch
SE7 121 B1
Fossdene Rd SE7 121 B1
Fossdyke Cl UB4 85 A2
Fosse Way W13 87 A2
Fossil Rd SE13 141 C2
Fossington Rd DA17 124 D2
Foss Rd SW17 180 B6
Fossway RM8 80 C6
Foster Ct E16 120 D6
4 NW1 71 C1
NW4 46 C5
Foster Ho SE14 141 B4
Foster La EC2 95 A1 242 A2
Foster Rd E13 99 A3
W3 111 C6
W4 111 B1
Fosters Cl BR7 188 B5
Woodford E18 37 B2
Fosters Old Sch
DA16 146 B3
Foster's Prim Sch
DA16 146 C2
Foster St NW4 46 C5
Foster Wlk NW4 46 C5
Fothergill Cl E13 99 A5
Fothergill Dr N21 16 A6
Fotheringham Ct EN1 5 D1
Fotheringham Rd EN1 5 D1
Foubert's Pl W1 239 A1
Foulden Rd N16 73 D4
Foulden Terr N16 73 D4
Foulis Terr
SW7 114 B1 256 D2
Foulser Rd SW17 159 A1
Foulsham Rd CR7 205 B6
Foundary Ho 7 E14 97 D2
Founder Cl 2 E6 100 D1
Founders Ct EC2 242 C2
Founders Gdns SE19 183 A3
Founders Ho SW1 259 C2
Foundling Ct WC1 240 A6
Foundry Cl SE16 119 A5
Foundry Mews NW1 239 B6
Foundry Pl E1 96 C2
Fountain Cl UB8 83 A2
Fountain Ct DA15 168 B5
EC4 251 A6
SW1 258 C3
New Malden KT3 199 A5
Penge SE26 184 C4
Fountain Dr
Dulwich SE19 183 D6
Wallington SM5 218 D1
Fountain Green Sq 31
SE16 118 A4
Fountain Ho 1 NW6 69 A1
30 SE16 118 A4
W1 248 A4
Fountain Mews 1 N5 73 A4
NW3 70 D2
Fountain Pl SW9 138 C4
Fountain Rd
South Norwood CR7 183 A1
Upper Tooting SW17 180 B6
Fountains Ave TW13 151 B1
Fountains Cl TW13 151 B1
Fountains Cres N14 16 A4
Fountains The N3 29 D3
Loughton IG10 21 D4
Fountayne Bsns Ctr
N15 52 A5
Fountayne Rd N15 52 A5
N16 74 A6
Fount St
SW8 137 D5 269 D3
Four Acres N12 29 D6
Fouracres EN3 7 A4
Fourland Wlk HA8 27 A4
Fournier St E1 95 D2 243 D4
Four Seasons Cl E3 97 C5
Four Seasons Cres
SM3 217 B6
Four Square Ct TW4 151 C5
Fourth Ave W10 91 A4
Hayes UB3 105 D5
Ilford E12 78 B4
Fourth Cross Rd TW2 152 B2
Fourth Way
Wembley HA9 66 D4
Wembley HA9 67 A4
Four Tubs The WD23 8 B4
Fourways 2 CR0 221 D6
Four Wents The E4 20 B2
Fovant Ct 5 SW8 137 C3
Fowey Ave IG4 55 D4
Fowey Cl E1 118 B5
Fowey Ho SE11 261 B2
Fowler Cl DA14 191 A5
SW11 136 B2
Fowler Ho N1 94 D6 234 D6
N15 51 B4
5 SE5 139 C3
SW8 269 D1
Fowler Rd E7 77 A4
N1 94 D6 234 D6
Mitcham CR4 181 A1
Fowler's Wlk W5 87 D3
Fownes St SW11 136 C2
Foxberry Ct SE4 141 B1
Foxberry Rd SE4 141 A2
Foxborough Gdns
SE4 163 C6
Foxbourne Rd SW17 159 A2
Foxbury Ave BR7 189 B4
Foxbury Cl BR1 187 B4
Foxbury Rd BR1 187 B4
Fox Cl E1 96 C3
E16 99 A2
Fox Cl *continued*
Elstree WD6 9 D5
Foxcombe CR0 223 D2
Foxcombe Cl 1 E6 99 D5
Foxcombe Rd 6
SW15 156 A3
Foxcote SE5 263 B1
Foxcroft N1 233 D3
Foxcroft Rd SE18 144 D4
Foxes Dale SE3 143 A2
Beckenham BR2 208 B6
Foxfield Prim Sch
SE18 123 A2
Foxfield Rd BR6 227 B6
Foxglove Ave BR3 185 D3
Foxglove Cl UB1 107 A6
Foxglove Ct 11 HA0 88 A5
Foxglove Gdns E11 55 C5
Foxglove La KT9 214 C4
Foxglove St W12 111 D6
Foxglove Way SM6 203 B1
Fox Gr KT12 194 B2
Foxgrove N14 16 A1
Foxgrove Path WD19 22 D5
Foxgrove Rd BR3 186 A3
Foxham Rd N19 71 D5
Fox Hill SE19 183 D3
Fox Hill Gdns SE19 183 D3
Fox Ho 2 SW11 136 B1
Foxhole Rd 2 SE9 166 A6
Fox Hollow Cl 1
SE18 123 C1
Fox Hollow Dr DA16 146 D2
Foxholt Gdns NW10 67 A1
Foxhome Cl BR7 188 C4
Fox House Rd DA17 125 D1
Fox & Knot St EC1 241 D4
Fox La BR2 225 C3
Ealing W5 88 A3
Palmers Green N13 16 B1
Foxlands Rd RM10 81 D3
Foxlees HA0 65 A4
Foxley Cl E8 74 A3
Foxley Ct SM2 218 A1
Foxley Ho 4 E3 97 D4
Foxley Rd SW9 138 D5
Thornton Heath CR7 204 D5
Foxley Sq 3 SW9 138 D4
Foxmead Cl EN2 4 B2
Foxmore St SW11 267 C1
Fox Prim Sch
W8 113 C5 245 A3
Fox Rd E16 98 D2
Foxs Path CR4 180 C1
Fox's Yd E2 243 D6
Foxtail Ho TW3 130 A4
Foxton KT1 198 C6
Foxton Gr CR4 180 B1
Foxton Ho E16 122 C4
Foxwarren KT10 212 D1
Foxwell Mews SE4 141 A2
Foxwell St SE4 141 A2
Foxwood Cl NW7 27 C6
Feltham TW13 150 B1
Foxwood Green Cl
EN1 17 C5
Foxwood Rd SE3 142 D1
Foyle Rd SE3 142 D6
Tottenham N17 34 A2
Fradel Lo N16 51 B1
Framfield Cl N12 13 C1
Framfield Ct EN1 17 C5
Framfield Rd N5 72 D3
Ealing W7 86 D1
Mitcham CR4 181 A3
Framlingham Cl 2 E5 74 C6
Framlingham Cres
SE9 188 B6
Frampton NW1 71 D1
Frampton Cl SM2 217 C1
Frampton Ct 3 W3 111 A4
Frampton Ho NW8 236 D5
Frampton Park Rd E9 74 C1
Frampton Rd TW4 151 A6
Frampton St
NW8 92 B3 236 D5
Francemary Rd SE4 163 C6
Frances Ct E17 53 C3
South Norwood SE25 183 D1
Frances Grey Ho 13
E1 96 D2
Frances Rd E4 35 C4
Frances St SE18 122 B2
Franche Court Rd
SW17 158 A1
Francis Ave DA7 147 C3
Feltham TW13 150 A1
Ilford IG1 79 B6
Francis Barber Cl
SW16 182 B6
Franciscan Prim Sch
SW17 181 A5
Franciscan Rd SW17 181 A6
Francis Chichester Way
SW11 137 A4 268 B1
Francis Cl 6 E14 120 B2
Littleton TW17 192 C5
West Ewell KT19 215 B4
Francis Ct NW7 27 D5
12 SE14 140 D6
Ealing W5 110 B6
Kingston KT5 198 A5
Francis Gr SW19 179 B4
Francis Ho 11 N1 95 C6
NW10 89 D6
Francis Holland Sch
NW1 92 D3 237 D5
SW1 115 A2 258 B3
Francis Rd E10 76 A6
N2 48 D5
Harrow HA1 43 A6
Hounslow TW4 128 D3
Ilford IG1 79 B6
Pinner HA5 40 C4
Thornton Heath CR0 204 D2
Wallington SM6 219 C2
Wembley UB6 87 C6
Francis Snary Lo 11
SW18 157 C6
Francis St E15 76 C3
SW1 115 C2 259 B4
Ilford IG1 79 B6
Francis Terr N19 71 C5
Francis Wlk N1 233 C6
Francklyn Gdns HA8 10 C1
Franconia Rd SW4 159 D6
Frank Bailey Wlk E12 78 C2
Frank Barnes Prim Sch for Deaf Children NW3 70 B1
Frank Beswick Ho
SW6 264 D5
Frank Burton Cl 4
SE7 121 B1
Frank Dixon Cl SE21 161 C3
Frank Dixon Way
SE21 161 C3
Frank Douglas Ct
W6 112 A2
Frankfurt Rd SE24 161 A6
Frankham Ho 8 SE8 141 C5
Frankham St SE8 141 C5
Frank Ho SW8 270 A4
Frankland Cl SE16 118 B2
Woodford IG8 37 C5
Frankland Ho 4
SW12 159 B4
Frankland Rd
SW7 114 B3 256 C5
Chingford E4 35 C5
Franklin Bldg 6 E14 119 C4
Franklin Cl N20 14 A4
SE13 141 D4
Kingston KT1 198 C6
West Norwood SE27 160 D1
Franklin Cres CR4 203 C5
Franklin Ho 26 E1 118 B5
NW9 45 D2
Beckenham BR2 208 C6
Franklin Ind Est SE20 184 C2
Franklin Pas SE9 144 A2
Franklin Rd DA7 147 A4
Penge SE20 184 C3
Walton-on-T KT12 194 A3
Franklins Mews HA2 64 A6
Franklin Sq SW5 254 D1
Franklin's Row
SW3 114 D1 257 D2
Franklin St 43 E3 97 D4
N15 51 C3
Franklin Way CR0 204 A2
Franklyn Rd NW10 67 D2
Walton-on-T KT12 194 B3
Franks Ave KT3 199 A5
Franks Ho TW7 131 B1
Frank Slater Ho 4
IG3 58 B1
Frank Soskice Ho
SW6 264 D5
Frank St 5 E13 99 A3
Franks Wood Ave
BR2,BR5 211 A4
Frankswood Ave UB7 82 B1
Frank Towell Ct
TW14 150 A3
Frank Whymark Ho 4
SE16 118 C4
Franlaw Cres N13 33 A6
Fransfield Gr SE26 162 B1
Frans Hals Ct E14 120 B3
Franshams WD23 8 C2

Frant Cl SE20 ....184 C3
Franthorne Way SE6 163 D1
Frant Rd CR7 ......204 D4
Fraserburgh Ho 28 E3 97 B5
Fraser Cl 3 E6 ....100 A1
Fraser Ct SW11 ......267 A2
Fraser Ho 3 SE18 ...122 C2
40 SW8 ....137 D3
Brentford TW8 ......110 B1
Fraser Rd E17 ....53 D3
Edmonton N18 ....18 B1
Wembley UB6 ....87 C6
Fraser Regnart Ct 12
NW5 ....70 D3
Fraser St W4 ....111 C1
Frating Cres IG8 .....37 B4
Frazer Ave HA4 ......62 C3
Frazier St
SE1 ....116 C4 251 A1
Freame Ho N21 ......17 B5
Frean St SE16 ......118 C4
Frearson Ho WC1 ..233 D2
Freda Corbett Cl 9
SE15 ....140 A5
Frederica Rd E4 .....20 B4
Frederica St 4 N7 ...72 B1
Frederic Ho SE7 ....122 A3
Frederick Cl
W2 ....114 D6 247 C6
Cheam SM1 ....217 B3
Enfield EN3 ....6 C3
Frederick Ct SW6 ..135 A2
Frederick Cres SW9 .138 D5
Enfield EN3 ....6 C3
Frederick Gdns
Cheam SM1 ....217 B3
Thornton Heath CR0 ..204 D3
Frederick Ho UB1 ...107 B6
Frederick Pl SE18 ...122 C1
Frederick Rd SM1 ...217 B3
Frederick's Pl EC2 .242 C1
N12 ....30 A6
Frederick Sq 11 SE16 119 A6
Frederick's Row EC1 234 C2
Frederick St
WC1 ......94 B4 233 C1
Frederick Terr E8 ....73 C3
Frederic Mews SW1 248 A1
Frederic St E17 .....53 A4
Fredora Ave
UB4 ......83 D3
Fred Wigg Twr E11 ..76 D6
Freedom Cl E17 .....53 A5
Freedom St SW11 ..136 D3
Freegrove Rd N7 ....72 A3
Freehold Ind Ctr
TW4 ....150 C6
Freeland Ct W5 ....110 B6
Freeland Pk N3 ......29 A1
Freeland Rd W5 ....110 B6
Freelands Ave CR2 .222 D1
Freelands Gr BR1 ...187 B2
Freelands Rd BR1 ...187 B2
Freeling Ho NW8 ...229 C6
Freeling St 7 N1 ...72 B1
Freeman Cl
Northolt UB5 ....63 A1
Upper Halliford TW17 .193 C5
Freeman Dr KT8 ...195 B5
Freeman Ho 13 SW2 160 A4
Freemans La UB3 ...105 C6
Freemantle Ave EN3 .18 D6
Freemantle St
SE17 ....117 C1 263 A2
Freemasons Rd E16 .99 B1
Freemason's Rd CR0 205 C1
Freemens Hos 1
SW9 ....138 B1
Freesia Cl BR6 .....227 D3
Freethorpe Cl SE19 .183 C2
Freezeland Way UB10 .60 D2
Freke Rd SW11 ......137 A2
Fremantle Ho 14 E1 .96 B3
Fremantle Rd
Belvedere DA17 .....125 C2
Ilford IG6 ....57 A6
Fremont St E9 ......96 C6
French Ordinary Ct
EC3 ....253 B6
French Pl E1 ....243 B6
French St TW16 ....172 C1
Frendsbury Rd SE4 .141 A1
Frensham Cl UB1 ....85 B4
Frensham Ct N5 .....73 A3
4 NW9 ....46 A5
Mitcham CR4 ....202 B6
Frensham Dr
New Addington CR0 ..224 A1

Frensham Dr continued
Roehampton SW15 ....156 A2
Frensham Ho 7 KT6 198 A4
Frensham Rd DA15 ...167 B2
Frensham St SE15 ...140 A6
Fresham Ho 2 BR2 ..208 D6
Freshfield Ave E8 ....73 C1
Freshfield Cl SE13 ..142 B1
Freshfield Dr N14 ....15 B4
Freshfields CR0 ....207 B1
Freshford St SW17,
SW18 ....158 A1
Freshwater Cl SW17 .181 A4
Freshwater Ct UB1 ...85 C4
Freshwater Rd
Dagenham RM8 .....59 A1
Streatham SW17 .....181 A4
Freshwell Ave RM6 ..58 C5
Fresh Wharf Est
IG11 ....100 D6
Fresh Wharf Rd IG11 100 D5
Freshwood Cl BR3 ...185 D2
Freston Gdns EN4 ...15 A6
Freston Pk N3 ....29 B1
Freston Rd W10,W11 .112 D6
Freswick Ho 6 SE8 .119 A2
Freta Rd DA6 ....169 B6
Freud Mus The★ NW3 70 A2
Frewell Bldg EC1 ...241 A4
Frewing Cl BR7 .....188 C5
Frewin Rd SW18 ....158 B3
Friar Mews SE27 ...160 D1
Friar Rd UB4 ....84 D3
Friars Ave N20 ......30 C6
Roehampton SW15 ...155 D1
Friars Cl SE1 ......251 D3
Chingford E4 ....20 A1
Ilford IG1 ....57 B1
16 Northolt UB5 ...84 D4
Friars Ct 5 SM6 ...219 B4
Friars Gate Cl IG8 ...37 A6
Friars Gdns W3 .....89 B1
Friars La TW9 ......153 D6
Friars Mead E14 ...120 A3
Friars Mews SE9 ...166 C6
Friars Place La W3 ..111 B6
Friars Prim Sch
SE1 ....116 D4 251 D1
Friar's Rd E6 ....99 D6
Friars Stile Pl 9
TW10 ....154 A5
Friars Stile Rd TW10 .154 A5
Friar St EC4 ....241 D1
Friars Way W3 ......89 B1
Friars Wlk N14 ......15 B4
SE2 ....124 D1
Friary Cl N12 ....30 C5
Friary La IG8 ....37 A6
Friary Park Ct W3 ...89 A1
Friary Rd N12 ....30 C6
SE15 ....140 A5
W3 ....89 B1
Friary Way N12 .....30 C6
Friday Hill E4 ....20 C1
Friday Hill E E4 .....20 C1
Friday Hill W E4 .....20 C2
Friday Rd CR4 .....180 D3
Friday St EC4 117 A6 252 A6
Frideswide Pl NW5 ..71 C3
Friendly Pl SE13 ...141 D4
Friendly St SE8 ....141 C4
Friendly Street Mews
SE8 ....141 C3
Friendship Wlk UB5 .84 D4
Friends' Rd CR0 ...221 B5
Friend St EC1 .94 D4 234 C2
Friern Barnet La N20 .30 C6
Friern Barnet Rd N11 .31 A5
Friern Barnet Sch
N11 ....30 D5
Friern Bridge Ret Pk
N11 ....31 B4
Friern Ct N20 ....14 B1
Friern Mount Dr N20 .14 A4
Friern Pk N12 ....30 B5
Friern Rd SE22 ....162 A6
Friern Watch Ave N12 .30 B6
Frigate Ho 6 E14 ..120 A2
Frigate Mews SE8 ..141 C6
Frimley Ave SM6 ...220 B3
Frimley Cl
New Addington CR0 ..224 A1
Putney SW19 ......157 A2
Frimley Cres CR0 ..224 A1
Frimley Ct DA14 ...190 C5
Frimley Gdns CR4 ..202 C6
Frimley Ho CR4 ....202 C6
Frimley Rd
Chessington KT9 ...214 A2

Frimley Rd continued
Ilford IG3 ....79 C5
Frimley Way E1 .....96 D3
Frinstead Ho 1 W10 112 D6
Frinton Ct W13 ......87 B2
Frinton Dr IG8 ....36 B3
Frinton Mews IG2 ...56 C3
Frinton Rd DA14 ...169 A2
E6 ....99 D4
N15 ....51 C3
Streatham SW17 ....181 A4
Friston St SW6 ....135 D3
Friswell Pl 1 DA7 ..147 C1
Fritham Cl KT3 ....199 C3
Frith Ct NW7 ....29 A3
Frith Ho E2 ....96 A4
NW8 ....236 D5
Frith La NW7 ....29 A4
Frith Manor Sch N12 .29 B5
Frith Rd E11 ....76 B4
Croydon CR0 ......221 A6
Frith St W1 ..93 D1 239 C1
Frithville Ct W12 ...112 C5
Frithville Gdns W12 .112 C5
Frizlands La RM10 ...81 D5
Frobisher Cl HA5 ....40 D2
Frobisher Cres TW19 148 A4
Frobisher Ct NW9 ...27 C1
1 SE10 ....142 B6
3 W12 ....112 C4
Belmont SM2 ....217 B1
6 Forest Hill SE23 ..162 B2
Frobisher Gdns
TW19 ....148 A4
Frobisher Ho 27 E1 .118 B5
3 Ealing W5 ......88 A4
Frobisher Mews EN2 ..5 B1
Frobisher Pas E14 ..119 C5
Frobisher Pl SE14 ..140 C4
Frobisher Rd E6 ....100 B1
N8 ....50 C5
Frobisher St SE10 ..142 C6
Froebel Coll SW15 ..155 D5
Frogley Rd SE22 ...139 D1
Frogmore SW18 ....157 C6
Frogmore Ave UB4 ..83 C3
Frogmore Cl SM3 ..217 A5
Frogmore Ct UB2 ..107 B2
Frogmore Est NW10 .89 A2
Frogmore Gdns
Cheam SM3 ....217 A4
Hayes UB4 ....83 C3
Frogmore Ind Est N5 .73 A4
Frognal NW3 ....70 A3
Frognal Ave DA14 ..190 A4
Harrow HA1 ....42 D5
Frognal Cl NW3 .....70 A3
Frognal Cnr BR7 ...189 D4
Frognal Ct NW3 .....70 A2
Frognal Gdns NW3 ..70 A4
Frognal La NW3 .....69 D3
Frognal Par NW3 ....70 A2
Frognal Pl DA14 ...190 A5
Frognal Rise NW3 ...70 A4
Frognal Way NW3 ...70 A4
Froissart Rd SE9 ...166 A6
Frome Ho SE15 ....140 C1
Frome Rd N22 ......50 D6
Frome St N1 ..95 A5 235 A4
Fromondes Rd SM3 .217 A3
Frontenac NW10 .....68 B1
Frontier Works N17 ..33 C4
Froude St SW8 ....137 B3
Fruen Rd TW14 ....149 D4
Fryatt Rd N17 ......33 B3
Frye Ct E3 ....97 B4
Fryent Cl NW9 ......44 C3
Fryent Cres NW9 ...45 C3
Fryent Fields NW9 ..45 C3
Fryent Gr NW9 .....45 C3
Fryent Prim Sch NW9 45 A2
Fryent Way HA9,NW9 .44 D2
Fry Ho E6 ....77 C1
Frying Pan Alley E1 .243 C3
Fry Rd E6 ....77 C1
NW10 ....89 D6
Fryston Ave CR0 ...222 A6
Fuchsia St SE2 ....124 B1
Fulbeck Dr NW9 .....27 C2
Fulbeck Ho N7 ......72 B2
Fulbeck Way HA2 ...24 A1
Fulbourn 9 KT1 ...176 C1
Fulbourne Rd E17 ...36 A1
Fulbourne St E1 .....96 B2
Fulbrook Rd N19 ....71 C4
Fulcher Ho 10 N1 ...95 C6
13 SE8 ....119 B1
Fulford Mans N19 ...72 A5

Fulford Rd KT19 ....215 B1
Fulford St SE16 ....118 B4
Fulham Broadway
SW6 ....135 C5 265 B3
Fulham Broadway Sta
SW6 ....135 C5 265 B4
Fulham Cross Sec Sch
SW6 ....135 A5 264 B2
Fulham Ct
SW6 ....135 C4 265 A2
Fulham High St SW6 135 A3
Fulham Palace★
SW6 ....135 A3
Fulham Palace Rd
W6 ....134 D6
Fulham SW6 .135 A4 264 A1
Fulham Park Gdns
SW6 ....135 B3
Fulham Park Rd SW6 135 B3
Fulham Prep Sch
SW6 ....135 A3
Fulham Prim Sch
SW6 ....135 C6 265 A5
Fulham Rd
SW10 ....136 A6 266 B6
Fulham SW6 .135 B4 264 D2
Fulham Rd
Enfield EN1 ....5 C2
Woodford IG8 ......37 C3
Fullbrooks Ave KT4 .199 B1
Fuller Cl 3 E2 ......96 A3
Orpington BR6 ....227 D3
Fuller Rd RM8 ......80 C4
Fullers Ave KT6 ....214 B6
Fuller's Ave IG8 .....36 D3
Fullers Cotts N22 ...32 B3
Fullers Ho 6 SW18 .157 C6
Fuller's Rd E18 ......36 D3
Fuller St NW4 ....46 C5
Fullers Way N KT6 ..214 B5
Fullers Way S KT9 ..214 A5
Fuller's Wood CR0 ..223 C3
Fuller Terr IG1 ......79 B3
Fullerton Ct TW11 ..175 A4
Fullerton Rd SW18 .158 A6
Croydon CR0 .....205 D2
Fuller Way UB3 ....105 D1
Fullwood Prim Sch
IG6 ....57 A5
Fullwood's Mews N1 235 D2
Fulmar Ct
5 Dulwich SE21 ...161 B2
Surbiton KT5 ....198 B3
Fulmar Ho NW8 ....237 B5
12 SE16 ....118 D2
Fulmead St SW6 ...265 D1
Fulmer Cl TW12 ...173 A5
Fulmer Rd E16 ......99 D2
Fulmer Way W13 ...109 A5
Fulneck 1 E1 ....96 C3
Fulready Rd E10 .....54 B4
Fulstone Cl TW4 ...129 B1
Fulthorp Rd SE3 ...143 A3
Fulton Ct EN3 ....7 C5
Fulton Mews W2 ...246 A6
Fulton Rd HA9 ......66 C5
Fulwell Ct UB1 ....108 A4
Fulwell Park Ave
TW2 ....152 A2
Fulwell Rd TW11,
TW12 ....174 B6
Fulwell Sta TW11 ..174 B6
Fulwood Ave HA0 ...88 B5
Fulwood Cl UB3 .....83 D1
Fulwood Gdns TW1 .153 A5
Fulwood Pl WC1 ...240 D3
Fulwood Wlk SW19 .157 A3
Furber St W6 ....112 B3
Furham Field HA5 ...23 C3
Furley Ho 7 SE15 ..140 A4
Furley Rd SE15 ....140 A4
Furlong Cl SM6 ....203 B1
Furlong Rd N7 ......72 C2
Furmage St SW18 .157 D4
Furneaux Ave SE27 .182 D5
Furness Ho SW1 ...258 C2
Furness Lo 4 SW14 .132 D1
Furness Rd NW10 ...90 A5
SW6 ....135 D3
Harrow HA2 ....41 D1
Morden SM4 ......201 D3
Furnival St
EC4 ....94 C1 241 A2
Furrow La E9 ....74 C2
Furrows The KT12 ..194 C1
Fursby Ave N3 ......29 C4
Fursecroft W1 .....237 C2
Further Acre NW9 ...27 D1
Furtherfield Cl CR0 .204 C3
Further Green Rd
SE6 ....164 C1

Furze Cl WD19 ......22 C5
Furze Ct CR0 ......222 A6
Furzedown Dr SW17 .181 B5
Furzedown Prim Sch
SW17 ....181 A4
Furzedown Rd SW17 .181 A4
Furzefield Cl BR7 ...188 D4
Furzefield Rd SE3 ..143 B5
Furzeground Way
UB11 ....105 A5
Furzeham Rd UB7 ..104 A4
Furzehill Rd WD6 ....11 A6
Furze Inf Sch RM6 ..59 A3
Furzeland Ho 2 KT3 199 C2
Furze St E3 ....97 C2
Furzewood TW16 ...172 A2
Fuschia Ct IG8 ......36 C4
Fyfe Way BR1 ......187 A1
Fyfield N4 ....72 C6
Fyfield Cl BR2,BR3 .208 B5
Fyfield Ct E7 ....77 A2
Fyfield Ho RM9 .....80 B1
Fyfield Rd E17 ......54 B6
6 SW9 ....138 C2
Enfield EN1 ....5 C2
Woodford IG8 ......37 C3
Fynes St SW1 .....259 C4

G

Gable Cl HA5 ....23 C3
Gable Ct SE26 .....184 B6
Gable Ho 12 W4 ...111 C2
Gable Lo
Hadley Wood EN4 .....2 A5
West Wickham BR4 ..208 A1
Gables Ave TW15 ..170 B5
Gables Cl SE5 .....139 C4
Lewisham SE12 .....165 A3
Gables The BR1 ....187 B3
N10 ....49 A6
N12 ....29 D5
NW3 ....70 B6
3 SW4 ....137 C2
Barking IG11 ....79 A2
Gabriel Cl 1 TW13 .173 A6
Gabriel Ho SE11 ...260 C4
Gabrielle Cl HA9 ....66 B5
Gabrielle Ct 3 NW3 .70 B2
Gabriel St SE23 ...163 A4
Gabriel's Wharf★
SE1 ....251 A4
Gad Cl E13 ....99 B4
Gaddesden Ave HA9 .66 B5
Gaddesden Ho EC1 .235 D1
Gade Cl UB3 ......106 B5
Gadesbury Cl NW9 ..45 D3
Gadsden Ho 6 E9 ..74 D2
8 W10 ....91 A3
Gadwall Cl E16 .....99 B1
Gadwall Way SE28 .123 B4
Gagarin Ho SW11 ..136 C2
Gage Rd E16 ....98 C2
Gage St WC1 .....240 B4
Gainford Ho 18 E2 ..96 B4
Gainford St N1 94 C6 234 A6
Gainsboro Gdns UB6 .64 C3
Gainsborough Ave
E12 ....78 C3
Gainsborough Cl
Beckenham BR3 ...185 C3
Thames Ditton KT10 ..196 C1
6 SE16 ....118 B1
W12 ....112 C4
Barnet EN5 ....1 D1
Gainsborough Ct N12 .29 D5
6 SE16 ....118 B1
W12 ....112 C4
Dulwich SE21 ......161 C2
Gainsborough Gdns
NW11 ....47 B2
NW3 ....70 B5
Edgware HA8 ....26 C1
Isleworth TW7 .....152 B6
Gainsborough Ho
5 E14 ....119 A6
N4 ....50 B1
3 NW3 ....70 A4
SW1 ....259 D3
Dagenham RM8 .....80 B4
Enfield EN1 ....7 D5
Gainsborough Lo HA1 42 C4
Gainsborough Mews 5
SE26 ....162 B1
Gainsborough Prim Sch
E15 ....98 C4
E9 ....75 C2

Gainsborough Rd E11 .54 C2
E15 ....98 C4
N12 ....29 D5
W4 ....111 D2
Dagenham RM8 .....80 B5
Hayes UB4 ....83 B5
New Malden KT3 ..199 B2
Richmond TW9 ....132 B2
Gainsborough Sq
DA7 ....146 D2
Gainsborough Twr 8
UB5 ....84 C6
Gainsford Rd E17 ...53 B5
Gainsford St
SE1 ....117 D4 253 D2
Gairloch Ho 2 NW1 .71 D1
Gairloch Rd SE5 ...139 C3
Gaisford St NW5 ....71 C2
Gaitskell Ct SW11 ..136 C3
Gaitskell Ho 3 E17 .53 D6
2 E6 ....99 D6
SE17 ....139 B6
Gaitskell Rd SE9 ...167 A3
Galahad Rd BR1 ...187 A6
Galata Rd SW13 ...134 A5
Galatea Sq SE15 ..140 B2
Galba Ct 1 TW8 ...131 D5
Galbraith St E14 ...120 A3
Galdana Ave EN5 .....2 A2
Galeborough Ave IG8 .36 B3
Gale Cl
Hampton TW12 ....173 A4
Mitcham CR4 ......202 B6
Gale Ho 10 SW2 ...160 B6
Galena Ho SE18 ...123 D1
5 W6 ....112 B2
Galena Rd W6 .....112 B2
Galen Pl WC1 .....240 B3
Galesbury Rd SW18 .158 A5
Gales Gdns E2 ......96 B3
Gale St E3 ....97 C2
Dagenham RM9 ....80 D1
Galgate Cl 4 SW19 .157 A3
Gallants Farm Rd EN4 14 C3
Galleon Cl SE16 ...118 C4
Galleon Ho 7 E14 ..120 A2
Galleons Dr IG11 ..102 A4
Gallery Ct SW10 ..266 A5
Gallery Gdns UB5 ..84 D5
Gallery Rd SE21 ...161 B3
Galleywall Prim Sch
SE16 ....118 B2
Galleywall Rd SE16 118 B2
Galleywall Road Trad Est
12 SE16 ....118 B2
Galleywood Ho W10 .90 C2
Gallia Rd N5 ....72 C2
Galliard Cl N9 ......18 C5
Galliard Ct N9 ......18 A5
Galliard Rd N9 .....18 A5
Gallions Cl IG11 ...102 A4
Gallions Mount Prim Sch
SE18 ....123 D1
Gallions Rd
Greenwich SE7 ....121 A2
Newham E16 ......123 A4
Gallions Reach Sta
E16 ....122 D6
Gallions View Rd
SE28 ....123 C4
Gallon Cl SE7 .....121 C2
Gallop The
South Croydon CR2 .222 B1
Sutton SM2 ....218 A1
Gallosson Rd SE18 .123 C2
Galloway Path 5
CR0 ....221 B4
Galloway Rd W12 ..112 A5
Gallus Cl N21 ....16 B5
Gallus Sq SE3 ....143 B2
Galpin's Rd CR4,CR7 .204 B2
Galsworthy Ave E14 .97 A2
Ilford RM6 ....58 B2
Galsworthy Cl SE28 .124 B5
Galsworthy Cres SE3 143 C4
Galsworthy Ho 4
W11 ....91 A1
Galsworthy Rd NW2 .69 A4
Kingston KT2 ......176 D2
Galton Ho 1 SE18 .144 B4
Galton St W10 ......91 A4
Galva Cl EN4 ....3 A1
Galvani Way CR0 ..204 D4
Galveston Ho 2 E1 ..97 A3
Galveston Rd SW15 157 B6
Galway Cl 28 SE16 .118 B1
Galway Ho 6 E1 ....96 D2

Galway Ho *continued*
EC1 ... 235 B1
Galway St EC1 .95 A4 235 B1
Galy 5 NW9 ... 27 D1
Gambetta St 3 SW8 .137 B3
Gambia St
SE1 ... 116 D5 251 D3
Gambler Ho EC1 ... 235 B1
Gambole Rd SW17 .. 180 C6
Games Ho 6 SE7 ... 143 C6
Games Rd EN4 ... 2 D2
Gamlen Rd SW15 ... 134 D1
Gamuel Cl E17 ... 53 C3
Gander Green Cres
TW12 ... 173 C2
Gander Green La
KT4,SM1,SM3 ... 217 B5
Gandhi Cl E17 ... 53 C3
Gandolfi st 5 SE15 .. 139 C6
Ganley Ct 19 SW11 .. 136 B2
Gannet Ct 4 SE21 .. 161 B2
Gannet Ho SE15 ... 139 D4
Ganton St W1 ... 239 B1
Ganton Wlk WD19 ... 22 D6
Gants Hill IG2 ... 56 C3
Gants Hill Cres IG2 .. 56 C4
Gants Hill Sta IG2 ... 56 C3
Gap Rd SW19 ... 179 D5
Garage Rd W3 ... 88 C1
Garbett Ho 2 SE17 .. 138 D6
Garbutt Pl W1 ... 238 B3
Garden Ave DA7 ... 147 C2
Mitcham CR4 ... 181 B3
Garden City HA8 ... 26 C4
Garden Cl SE12 ... 165 B1
Ashford TW15 ... 171 A4
Chingford E4 ... 35 C5
Hampton TW12 ... 173 B5
Northolt UB5 ... 85 A6
Roehampton SW15 ... 156 B4
Ruislip HA4 ... 61 D6
Wallington SM6 ... 220 A3
Garden Cotts BR5 .. 190 C1
Garden Ct EC4 ... 251 A6
N12 ... 29 D5
NW8 ... 229 C2
10 SE9 ... 166 C5
12 W4 ... 111 A3
5 Belmont SM2 ... 217 C1
4 Richmond TW9 ... 132 B4
South Croydon CR0 .. 221 D5
4 Stanmore HA7 ... 25 C5
Wembley HA0 ... 65 C5
Gardeners Rd CR0 .. 204 D1
Garden Flats SW16 .. 160 A1
Garden Ho 2 N2 ... 30 B1
12 SW9 ... 138 A3
Garden Hospl The
NW4 ... 46 C6
Gardenia Ct 1 BR3 .. 185 C3
Gardenia Rd EN1 ... 17 C5
Gardenia Way IG8 ... 37 A5
Garden La
Bromley BR1 ... 187 B4
Streatham SW2 ... 160 B3
Garden Lodge Ct N2 .. 48 B6
Garden Mews W2 .. 245 B5
Garden Pl 28 E2 ... 95 D6
Garden Rd
NW8 ... 92 A4 229 B2
Bromley BR1 ... 187 B4
Penge SE20 ... 184 C2
Richmond TW9 ... 132 C2
Walton-on-T KT12 ... 194 B2
Garden Row
SE1 ... 116 D3 261 C6
Garden Royal 16
SW15 ... 156 D5
Garden St E1 ... 96 D2
Gardens The N16 ... 51 D2
SE22 ... 140 A1
Beckenham BR3 ... 186 A2
East Bedfont TW14 ... 149 B5
Harrow HA1,HA2 ... 42 A3
Pinner HA5 ... 41 B3
Garden Suburb Jun & Inf
Schs NW11 ... 47 B4
Garden Terr SW1 ... 259 C2
SW7 ... 247 B1
Garden Way NW10 ... 67 A2
Garden Wlk
EC2 ... 95 C3 243 A6
Beckenham BR3 ... 185 B2
Gardiner Ave NW2 ... 68 C3
Gardiner Cl BR5 ... 190 C1
Dagenham RM8 ... 80 D4
Enfield EN3 ... 18 D5
Gardiner Ct NW10 ... 89 B6
Gardiner Ho 3 SE18 .144 A5
SW11 ... 267 A2
Gardner Cl E11 ... 55 B3
Gardner Ct N5 ... 73 A4
Hounslow TW3 ... 129 C2
Tottenham N22 ... 32 D1
Gardner Ho
Feltham TW13 ... 151 B2
Southall UB1 ... 106 D6
Gardner Ind Est SE26 185 B5
Gardner Pl TW14 ... 150 B5
Gardner Rd E13 ... 99 B3
Gardners Cl N11 ... 15 A2
Gardners La EC4 ... 252 A6
Gardnor Mans 10 NW3 70 A4
Gardnor Rd NW3 ... 70 B4
Gard St EC1 ... 234 D2
Garendon Gdns SM4 .201 D2
Garendon Rd SM4 .. 201 D2
Garenne Ct 10 E4 ... 20 A3
Gareth Cl KT4 ... 216 D6
Gareth Ct SW16 ... 159 D1
Gareth Gr BR1 ... 187 A6
Garfield Edmonton N9 .. 18 B3
Enfield EN2 ... 17 B6
Garfield First Sch
SW19 ... 180 A4
Garfield Prim Sch N11 31 C5
Garfield Rd E13 ... 98 D3
SW11 ... 137 A2
Chingford E4 ... 20 B3
Enfield EN3 ... 6 C1
2 Twickenham TW1 .. 153 A3
Wimbledon SW19 ... 180 A4
Garford St E14 ... 119 C6
Garganey Ct NW10 ... 67 B2
Garganey Wlk SE28 .. 124 C6
Garibaldi St SE18 .. 123 C2
Garland Dr TW3 ... 130 A3
Garland Ho N16 ... 73 B5
Garland Rd SE18 ... 145 B5
Stanmore HA7 ... 26 A2
Garlands Ct 2 CR0 .. 221 B4
Garlands The HA1 ... 42 D2
Garlick Hill
EC4 ... 117 A6 252 B6
Garlies Rd SE23 ... 163 A1
Garlinge Ho 12 SW9 .138 C4
Garlinge Rd NW2 ... 69 B2
Garman Cl N18 ... 33 B5
Garman Rd N17 ... 34 C3
Garnault Mews EC1 .. 234 B1
Garnault Pl EC1 ... 234 B1
Garnault Rd EN1 ... 5 D5
Garner Cl RM8 ... 58 D1
Garner Rd E17 ... 36 A2
Garner St E2 ... 96 A5
Garnet Ho KT4 ... 199 B1
Garnet Rd NW10 ... 67 C2
South Norwood CR7 .. 205 B5
Garnet St E1 ... 118 C6
Garnett Cl SE9 ... 144 B2
Garnett Ho 5 NW3 ... 70 D3
Garnett Rd NW3 ... 70 D3
Garnett Way E17 ... 35 A2
Garnet Wlk 8 E6 .. 100 A2
Garnham Cl 2 N16 ... 73 D6
Garnham St 1 N16 ... 73 D6
Garnies Cl SE15 ... 139 D5
Garrad's Rd SW16 .. 159 D1
Garrard Cl DA7 ... 147 C2
Chislehurst BR7 ... 188 D5
Garrard Wlk NW10 ... 67 C2
Garratt Cl CR0 ... 220 A4
Garratt Ho 8 N16 ... 51 C1
Garratt La
Upper Tooting SW17,
SW18 ... 180 C6
Wandsworth SW18 ... 157 D3
Garratt Park Sch
SW18 ... 158 A1
Garratt Rd HA8 ... 26 C3
Garratts Rd WD23 ... 8 A4
Garratt Terr SW17 .. 180 C6
Garraway Ct SW13 .. 134 C5
Garraway Ho SE21 .. 161 D1
Garrett Cl W3 ... 89 B2
Garrett Ho W12 ... 90 B1
Teddington TW11 ... 175 B4
Garrett St EC1 .95 A3 242 B6
Garrick Ave NW11 ... 47 A3
Garrick Cl SW18 ... 136 A1
Ealing W5 ... 88 A3
1 Richmond TW9 ... 153 D6
Garrick Cres CR0 ... 221 C6
Garrick Ct HA8 ... 26 B6
Garrick Dr NW4 ... 28 C1
SE18 ... 123 B3
Garrick Gdns KT8 .. 195 C6
Garrick Ho W1 ... 248 C3
Chiswick W4 ... 133 C6
2 Kingston KT1 ... 198 A5
7 Streatham SW16 .. 181 C5
Garrick Ind Est NW9 .. 45 D4
Garrick Pk NW4 ... 28 D1
Garrick Rd NW9 ... 45 D3
Greenford UB6 ... 85 D3
Richmond TW9 ... 132 C3
Garrick's Ait KT8 ... 174 A1
Garricks Ho KT1 ... 175 D1
Garrick St
WC2 ... 116 A6 250 A6
Garrick Way NW4 ... 46 D5
Garrick Yd WC2 ... 250 A6
Garrison Cl SE18 ... 144 C5
Hounslow TW4 ... 151 B6
Garrison La KT9 ... 214 A1
Garrowsfield EN5 ... 13 B6
Garsdale Cl N11 ... 31 A4
Garsdale Terr SW5 ... 254 D2
Garside Cl SE28 ... 123 B3
Hampton TW12 ... 173 D4
Garsington Mews
SE4 ... 141 B2
Garson Ho W2 ... 246 C6
Garston Ho 6 N1 ... 72 D1
Garter Way SE16 ... 118 D4
Garth Cl Kingston KT2 .176 B5
Ruislip HA4 ... 40 D1
West Barnes SM4 ... 200 D2
Garth Ct Chiswick W4 .133 B6
Harrow HA1 ... 42 D3
Garth Ho NW2 ... 69 B6
Garthland Dr EN5 ... 12 C6
Garth Mews W5 ... 88 A3
Garthorne Rd SE23 .. 162 D4
Garth Rd NW2 ... 69 B6
8 W4 ... 111 B1
Kingston KT2 ... 176 B5
West Barnes SM4 ... 200 D2
Garthside TW10 ... 176 A5
Garth The N12 ... 29 D5
Hampton TW12 ... 173 D4
Harrow HA3 ... 44 B3
Garthway N12 ... 30 C4
Gartmoor Gdns
SW19 ... 157 B3
Gartmore Rd IG3 ... 79 D6
Garton Ho 6 N6 ... 49 D2
Garton Pl SW18 ... 158 A5
Gartons Cl EN3 ... 6 C1
Gartons Way SW11 .. 136 A2
Garvary Rd E16 ... 99 B1
Garvens SE19 ... 183 C5
Garway Rd W2 ... 91 D1
Gascoigne Gdns IG8 .. 36 C3
Gascoigne Pl 17 E2 ... 95 D4
Gascoigne Prim Sch
IG11 ... 101 A6
Gascoigne Rd IG11 .. 101 A5
Gascony Ave NW6 ... 69 C1
Gascoyne Ho 2 E9 ... 74 D1
Gascoyne Rd E9 ... 74 D1
Gaselee St E14 ... 120 A6
Gasholder Pl
SE11 ... 116 B1 260 D1
Gaskarth Rd HA8 ... 27 A1
Balham SW12 ... 159 B5
Gaskell Rd N6 ... 48 D3
Gaskell St SW4 ... 138 A3
Gaskin Ho N16 ... 73 B5
Gaskin St N1 .94 D6 234 C6
Gaspar Cl SW7 ... 255 D4
Gaspar Mews SW5 .. 255 D4
Gassiot Rd SW17 .. 180 D6
Gassiot Way SM1 ... 218 B5
Gasson Ho 24 SE14 .. 140 D6
Gastein Rd W6 ... 134 D6
Gastigny Ho EC1 ... 235 B1
Gaston Bell Cl TW9 .. 132 B2
Gaston Bridge Rd
TW17 ... 193 B3
Gaston Gate SW8 ... 270 C2
Gaston Rd CR4 ... 203 A6
Gaston Way TW17 .. 193 B4
Gataker Ho 5 SE16 .. 118 B3
Gataker St 6 SE16 .. 118 B3
Gatcliff Cl SW1 ... 258 B1
Gatcombe Ct BR3 ... 185 C3
Gatcombe Ho 20
SE22 ... 139 C2
Gatcombe Mews W5 110 B6
Gatcombe Rd 9 E16 121 A5
N19 ... 71 D5
Gatcombe Way EN4 ... 2 D2
Gateacre Ct DA14 .. 190 B6
Gatebeck Ho 21 SE22 139 C2
Gate End HA6 ... 22 A3
Gatefield Ct SE15 .. 140 A2
Gateforth St NW8 ... 237 A5
Gate Hill Ct W11 ... 244 D4
Gatehill Rd HA6 ... 22 A3
Gate Ho 4 KT6 ... 198 A1
Gatehouse Cl KT2 .. 177 A3
Gatehouse Sch E2 ... 96 D5
Gatehouse Sq SE1 .. 252 B4
Gateley Ho 6 SE4 ... 140 D1
Gateley Rd SW9 ... 138 B2
Gate Mews
SW7 ... 114 C4 247 B1
Gater Dr EN2 ... 5 B4
Gates 4 NW9 ... 27 D1
Gatesborough St
EC2 ... 243 A6
Gates Ct SE17 ... 262 A2
Gatesden WC1 ... 233 B1
Gates Green Rd
BR2,BR4 ... 225 A4
Coney Hall BR4 ... 224 D5
Gateside Rd SW17 .. 158 D1
Gate St WC2 .. 94 B1 240 C2
Gatestone Ct 10 SE19 183 C4
Gatestone Rd SE19 .. 183 C4
Gateway SE17 ... 139 A6
Gateway Mews 4 E8 .73 D3
Gateway Prim Sch
NW8 ... 92 B3 236 D6
Gateway Rd E10 ... 75 D5
Gateway Ret Pk E6 .. 100 D3
Gateways KT6 ... 198 A4
Gateways Ct SM6 ... 219 B3
Gateways The SW3 .. 257 B3
Richmond TW9 ... 131 D1
Gateway Trad Est
NW10 ... 89 D4
Gatfield Gr TW13 ... 151 C2
Gatfield Ho TW13 ... 151 C2
Gathorne Rd N22 ... 32 C2
Gathorne St 19 E2 ... 96 D5
Gatley Ave KT19 ... 214 D3
Gatliff Rd
SW1 ... 115 B1 258 C1
Gatling Rd SE18,SE2 .124 A1
Gatonby St SE15 ... 139 D4
Gatting Cl HA8 ... 27 A3
Gatting Way UB8 ... 60 A2
Gatton Rd SW17 ... 180 C6
Gattons Way DA14 .. 191 B6
Gatward Cl N21 ... 16 D5
Gatward Gn N9 ... 17 D2
Gatwick Ho 3 E14 ... 97 B1
Gatwick Rd SW18 ... 157 B4
Gauden Cl SW4 ... 137 D2
Gauden Rd SW4 ... 137 D2
Gaugin Ct 13 SE16 .. 118 B1
Gauntlet 1 NW9 ... 27 D1
Gauntlet Cl UB5 ... 63 A1
Gauntlett Ct HA0 ... 65 B3
Gauntlett Rd SM1 .. 218 B3
Gaunt St SE1 ... 262 A6
Gautrey Rd SE15 ... 140 C3
Gautrey Sq 5 E6 ... 100 B1
Gavel St SE17 ... 262 D4
Gaven Ho N17 ... 33 C1
Gavestone Cres SE12 165 B4
Gavestone Rd SE12 .. 165 B4
Gaviller Pl 4 E5 ... 74 B4
Gavina Cl SM4 ... 202 C4
Gavin Ho SE18 ... 123 C2
Gavrelle Ho EC1 ... 242 C5
Gawber St E2 ... 96 C4
Gawsworth Cl E15 ... 76 D3
Gawthorne Ave NW7 .. 29 A5
Gawthorne Ct E3 ... 97 C5
Gay Cl NW2 ... 68 B3
Gaydon Ho W2 ... 91 D2
Gaydon La NW9 ... 27 C2
Gayfere Rd
Redbridge IG5 ... 56 B6
Stoneleigh KT17 ... 216 A3
Gayfere St
SW1 ... 116 A3 260 A5
Gayford Rd W12 ... 111 D4
Gay Ho N16 ... 73 C3
Gayhurst SE17 ... 139 B6
Gayhurst Ct 9 UB5 .. 84 C4
Gayhurst Ho NW8 ... 237 B6
Gayhurst Rd E8 ... 74 A1
Gayhurst Sch E8 ... 74 A1
Gaylor Rd UB5 ... 63 B3
Gaymead NW8 ... 91 D6
Gaynesford Rd
Forest Hill SE23 ... 162 D2
Wallington SM5 ... 218 D1
Gay Rd E15 ... 98 B5
Gaysham Ave IG2 ... 56 D4
Gaysham Hall IG5 ... 56 D6
Gaysley Ho SE11 ... 261 A3
Gay St SW15 ... 134 D2
Gayton Cres NW3 ... 70 B4
Gayton Ct
3 Harrow HA1 ... 42 D3
New Malden KT3 ... 199 D4
Gayton Ho E3 ... 97 C3
Gayton Rd NW3 ... 70 B4
SE2 ... 124 C3
Harrow HA1 ... 43 A3
Gayville Rd SW11 ... 158 D5
Gaywood Cl SW2 ... 160 C3
Gaywood Rd E17 ... 53 C6
Gaywood St SE1 ... 261 D5
Gaza St SE17 .116 D1 261 C1
Gaze Ho 10 E14 ... 98 B1
Gean Ct 3 E11 ... 76 B4
Gearies Inf Sch IG2 .. 56 D4
Gearies Jun Sch IG2 .56 D4
Geariesville Gdns IG6 56 D5
Geary Ho N7 ... 72 B3
Geary Rd NW10 ... 68 A3
Geary St N7 ... 72 B3
GEC Est HA9 ... 65 D6
Geddes Pl 3 DA7 ... 147 C1
Gedeney Rd N17 ... 33 A2
Gedge Ct CR4 ... 202 C5
Gedling Ho SE22 ... 139 D2
Gedling Pl SE1 ... 263 D6
Geere Rd E15 ... 98 D6
Gees Ct W1 ... 238 B1
Gee St EC1 ... 95 A3 242 A6
Geffrey's Ct SE9 ... 166 A1
Geffrye Ct N1 ... 95 C5
Geffrye Mus* E2 ... 95 D5
Geffrye St E2 ... 95 D5
Geldart Rd SE15 ... 140 B5
Geldeston Rd E5 ... 74 A6
Gellatly Rd SE14 ... 140 D3
Gell Cl UB10 ... 60 B5
Gemini Bsns Ctr E16 .. 98 B3
Gemini Gr UB5 ... 85 A4
Gemini Ho SW15 ... 134 D1
Gemma Ct BR3 ... 185 B1
General Gordon Pl
SE18 ... 122 D2
Generals Wlk The EN3 .7 A6
General Wolfe Rd
SE10 ... 142 B4
Genesis Cl TW19 ... 148 B3
Genesta Rd SE18 ... 145 A6
Geneva Cl TW17 ... 171 C1
Geneva Ct N16 ... 51 B1
1 Putney SW15 ... 156 D6
Geneva Dr SW9 ... 138 C1
Geneva Gdns RM6 ... 59 A4
Geneva Rd
Kingston KT1 ... 198 A5
Thornton Heath CR7 .. 205 A4
Genever Cl E4 ... 35 C5
Genista Rd N18 ... 34 B5
Genoa Ave SW15 ... 156 C6
Genoa Ho 19 E1 ... 96 D3
Genoa Rd SE20 ... 184 C2
Genotin Rd EN1 ... 5 B2
Genotin Terr EN1 ... 5 B2
Gentleman's Row EN2 .. 5 A2
Gentry Gdns E13 ... 99 A4
Geoffrey Chaucer Tech
Coll SE1 ... 117 B3 262 B5
Geoffrey Cl SE5 ... 139 A3
Geoffrey Ct SE4 ... 141 B2
Geoffrey Gdns E6 ... 100 A5
Geoffrey Ho SE1 ... 262 D6
Geoffrey Jones Ct
NW10 ... 90 A6
Geoffrey Rd SE4 ... 141 B2
Geological Mus*
SW7 ... 114 B3 256 D5
George Akass Ho 3
SE18 ... 123 A1
George Beard Rd 10
SE8 ... 119 B2
George Beare Lo 9
SW4 ... 159 C6
George Belt Ho 8 E2 .96 D4
George Comberton Wlk 3
E12 ... 78 C3
George Cres N10 ... 31 A3
George Ct WC2 ... 250 B5
Buckhurst Hill IG9 ... 21 D2
George Downing Est
N16 ... 73 D6
George Eliot Ho SW1 259 B3
George Eliot Jun & Inf Sch
NW8 ... 92 B6 229 C6
George Elliot Ho
SE17 ... 262 A2
George Elliston Ho 12
SE1 ... 118 A1
George Eyre Ho
NW8 ... 229 D3
George Gange Way
HA3 ... 42 D6
George Green's Sec Sch
E14 ... 120 A1
George Groves Rd
SE20 ... 184 A2
George Ho 8 SE26 .. 184 B5
George Inn Yd SE1 .. 252 C3
George La SE13 ... 164 A5
Hayes BR2 ... 209 B1
Wanstead E18 ... 55 B6
Woodford E18 ... 37 A1
George Lansbury Ho
7 E3 ... 97 B4
NW10 ... 67 C1
Wood Green N22 ... 32 C2
George Lashwood Ct 12
SW9 ... 138 B1
George Leybourne Ho 9
E1 ... 118 A6
George Lindgren Ho
SW6 ... 264 D4
George Loveless Ho 4
E2 ... 95 D4
George Lovell Dr EN3 .. 7 C6
George Mews NW1 .. 232 A1
George Mitchell Com Sch
E10 ... 53 D1
George Orwell Sch N4 50 B1
George Parr Ho N21 .. 16 D4
George Peabody Ct
NW1 ... 237 A4
George Rd
Chingford E4 ... 35 C4
Kingston KT2 ... 177 A3
New Malden KT3 ... 199 D4
George Row SE16 ... 118 A4
Georges Mead WD6 ... 10 A5
George Spicer Prim Sch
EN1 ... 5 D2
George Sq SW19 ... 201 C6
George's Rd N7 ... 72 B3
George's Sq SW6 ... 264 D6
George St 6 E16 ... 98 D1
W1 ... 92 D1 237 D2
Barking IG11 ... 79 A1
Ealing W7 ... 108 C5
Hounslow TW3,TW5 .. 129 B3
Richmond TW10 ... 153 D6
Southall UB2 ... 107 A2
South Croydon CR0 ... 221 B6
George Tingle Ho
SE1 ... 263 D6
George Tomlinson Prim
Sch E11 ... 54 C1
Georgetown Cl 4
SE19 ... 183 C5
Georgette Pl SE10 ... 142 A5
George Vale Ho 32 E2 .96 A5
George V Ave HA2,HA5 41 C6
Georgeville Gdns IG6 .56 D5
George V Way UB6 ... 87 B6
George Walter Ho 7
SE16 ... 118 C2
George Wyver Cl
SW18 ... 157 A4
George Yd EC3 ... 242 D1
W1 ... 115 A6 248 B6
Georgiana St
NW1 ... 93 C6 232 B6
Georgian Cl
Hayes BR2 ... 209 B1
Ickenham UB10 ... 60 A4
Stanmore HA7 ... 25 A3
Georgian Ct 19 E9 ... 96 C6
3 NW4 ... 46 B4
Croydon CR0 ... 205 B1
Wembley HA9 ... 66 D2
Georgian Lo HA5 ... 40 B4
Georgian Way HA1 ... 64 B6
Georgia Rd
New Malden KT3 ... 199 A5
South Norwood CR7 .. 182 D2
Georgina Ct 5 TW1 .153 C5
Georgina Gdns 10 E2 .95 D4
Geraint Rd BR1 ... 187 A6
Geraldine Ct 6 NW9 .46 A5
Geraldine Rd SW18 .. 158 A6
Brentford W4 ... 132 C6
Geraldine St SE11 .. 261 C5
Gerald Mews SW1 ... 258 B4
Gerald Rd E16 ... 98 D3
SW1 ... 115 A2 258 B4
Dagenham RM8 ... 59 B1
Gerard Ave TW4 ... 151 C4
Gerard Ct NW2 ... 68 D3
Gerard Rd
Barnes SW13 ... 133 D4
Harrow HA1 ... 43 A3
Gerards Cl SE16 ... 118 C1

Gerboa Ct 6 E4 . . . . . . .36 B5
Gerda Rd SE9 . . . . . . .167 A2
Germander Way E15 . .98 C4
Gernigan Ho SW18 . .158 B5
Gernon Rd E3 . . . . .97 A5
Geron Way NW2 . . . . . .68 C6
Gerrard Gdns HA5 . . . . .40 A4
Gerrard Ho 5 SE14 . .140 D5
Gerrard Pl W1 . . . . . .249 D6
Gerrard Rd N1 94 D5 234 D4
Gerrards Cl N14 . . . . . .15 C6
Gerrard's Ct W5 . . . . . .109 D3
Gerrard St
 W1 . . . . .115 D6 249 D6
Gerridge Ct SE1 . . . . .261 B6
Gerridge St
 SE1 . . . . . .116 C3 261 B6
Gerry Raffles Sq E15 . .76 B2
Gertrude Rd DA17 . . . .125 C2
Gertrude St
 SW10 . . . .136 A6 266 B5
Gervase Cl HA9 . . . . . . .67 A5
Gervase Rd HA8 . . . . . .27 B2
Gervase St SE15 . . . . .140 B5
Ghent St SE6 . . . . . . .163 C2
Ghent Way E8 . . . . . . .73 D2
Giant Arches Rd
 SE24 . . . . .161 A5
Giant Tree Hill WD23 . . .8 B3
Gibbards Cott 1 IG11 79 D1
Gibbfield St RM6 . . . . . .59 A6
Gibbings Ho SE1 . . . . .251 D1
Gibbins Rd E15 . . . . . . .76 A1
Gibbon Ho NW8 . . . . .236 D5
Gibbon Rd SE15 . . . . .140 C3
 W3 . . . . .111 C6
 Kingston KT2 . . . . . . .176 A3
Gibbons Rd NW10 . . . .67 C2
Gibbon's Rents SE1 . .253 A3
Gibbon Wlk SW15 . . . .134 A1
Gibbs Ave SE19 . . . . . .183 B5
Gibbs Cl SE19 . . . . . . .183 B5
Gibbs Gn HA8 . . . . .27 A6
 W14 . . . . . . .113 B1 254 D2
Gibbs Green Sch
 W14 . . . . . . .113 B1 254 D2
Gibbs Ho
 6 Balham SW12 . . . .159 B4
 2 Bromley BR1 . . . . .186 D2
Gibbs Rd N18 . . . . .34 C6
Gibbs Sq SE19 . . . . . .183 B5
Gibraltar Ho NW10 . . .89 C5
Gibraltar Wlk 28 E2 . . .95 D4
Gibson Bsns Ctr N17 . .33 D3
Gibson Cl E1 . . . . .96 C3
 Chessington KT9 . . . .213 C3
 Isleworth TW7 . . . . . .130 B2
 Southgate N21 . . . . . . .16 C5
Gibson Ct KT10 . . . . . .212 D5
Gibson Gdns N16 . . . . .73 D6
Gibson Ho
 South Croydon CR2 . . .221 A2
 Sutton SM1 . . . . .217 C4
Gibson Rd SE11 . . . . .260 D3
 Dagenham RM8 . . . . . .58 C1
 Ickenham UB10 . . . . . .60 B4
 Sutton SM1 . . . . .217 D3
Gibson's Hill
 South Norwood SW16 .182 C3
 South Norwood SW16 .182 A6
Gibson Sq N1 .94 C6 234 B6
Gibson St SE10 . . . . . .120 C1
Gideon Cl DA17 . . . . . .125 D2
Gideon Mews W5 . . . .109 D4
Gideon Rd SW11 . . . . .137 A2
Giesbach Rd N19 . . . . .71 D6
Giffard Rd N18 . . . . . . .33 C4
Giffen Square Mkt
 SE8 . . . . .141 C5
Giffin St SE8 . . . . .141 C5
Gifford Gdns W7 . . . . .86 C2
Gifford Ho SE10 . . . . .120 B1
 5 SW4 . . . . .137 D1
Gifford Prim Sch UB5 .85 B5
Gifford St N1 . . . . .72 A1
Gift La E15 . . . . .98 D6
Giggs Hill BR5 . . . . . . .190 A4
Giggs Hill Gdns KT7 .197 A1
Giggs Hill Rd KT7 . . . .197 A2
Gilbert Cl SE18 . . . . . .144 B4
 1 Merton SW19 . . . . .179 D2
Gilbert Gr HA8 . . . . . . .27 B4
Gilbert Ho 5 E17 . . . . .54 A4
 5 E2 . . . . .96 D4
 EC2 . . . . .242 B3
 SE8 . . . . .141 C6
 SW1 . . . . .258 D1
 SW8 . . . . .270 A4
Gilbert Pl WC1 94 A2 240 A3

Gilbert Rd BR1 . . . . . .187 A3
 SE11 . . . . . . .116 C2 261 B4
 Belvedere DA17 . . . . .125 C5
 Merton SW19 . . . . . .180 A3
 Pinner HA5 . . . . .40 D5
Gilbert Scott Com Inf Sch
 CR2 . . . . .223 A1
Gilbert Scott Com Jun Sch
 CR2 . . . . .223 A1
Gilbert Sheldon Ho
 W2 . . . . .236 D4
Gilbertson Ho 4 E14 119 C3
Gilbert St E15 . . . . .76 C4
 W1 . . . . .93 A1 238 B1
 Enfield EN3 . . . . .6 C1
 Hounslow TW3 . . . . . .130 A2
Gilbey Cl UB10 . . . . . . .60 D4
Gilbey Rd SW17 . . . . .180 C5
Gilbeys Yd NW1 . . . . . .71 A1
Gilbourne Rd SE18 . . .145 D6
Gilby Ho 5 E9 . . . . .74 D2
Gilda Ave EN3 . . . . .19 A6
Gilda Cres N16 . . . . . . .52 A1
Gilda Ct NW7 . . . . .28 A2
Gildea Cl HA5 . . . . .23 C3
Gildea St W1 . . . . .238 D3
Gilden Cres NW5 . . . . .71 A3
Gildersome St SE18 . .144 C6
Gilders Rd KT9 . . . . . .214 B2
Giles Ho 5 SE16 . . . . .118 A3
 W11 . . . . .91 C1
Gilesmead SE5 . . . . . .139 B4
Gilfrid Cl UB8 . . . . .82 D1
Gilkes Cres SE21 . . . . .161 C5
Gilkes Pl SE21 . . . . . . .161 C5
Gillam Ho 6 SE16 . . . .118 C2
Gillan Ct SE12 . . . . . . .165 B1
Gillan Gn WD23 . . . . . . .8 A2
Gillards Mews 6 E17 .53 C5
Gillards Way E17 . . . . .53 C5
Gill Ave E16 . . . . .99 A1
Gill Ct SE18 . . . . .123 A2
Gillender St E3 . . . . . . .98 A4
Gillespie Prim Sch N5 72 D5
Gillespie Rd N4,N5 . . . .72 D5
Gillett Ave E6 . . . . . . .100 A5
Gillette Cnr TW7 . . . . .131 A4
Gillett Ho N8 . . . . .50 A6
Gillett Pl 27 E8 . . . . . . .73 C3
Gillett Rd CR7 . . . . . . .205 B5
Gillett St E8,N16 . . . . .73 C3
Gillfoot NW1 . . . . .232 A3
Gillham Terr N17 . . . . . .34 A3
Gillian Ho HA3 . . . . . . .24 C4
Gillian Park Rd SM3 . .201 B1
Gillian St SE13 . . . . . .163 D6
Gillies Ct DA14 . . . . . .189 C6
Gillies Ho NW6 . . . . . . .70 B1
Gilling Ct 5 NW3 . . . . .70 C2
Gillingham Mews
 SW1 . . . . .259 A4
Gillingham Rd NW2 . . .69 A5
Gillingham Row SW1 .259 A4
Gillingham St
 SW1 . . . . . . .115 C2 259 A4
Gillings Ct EN5 . . . . .1 A1
Gillison Wlk 19 SE16 .118 A3
Gillman Dr E15 . . . . . . .98 D6
Gillman Ho 23 E2 . . . . .96 A1
Gillray Ho SW10 . . . . .266 C5
Gill St E14 . . . . .119 B6
Gillum Cl EN4 . . . . .14 D3
Gilmore Cl UB10 . . . . . .60 C5
Gilmore Cres TW15 . . .170 C4
Gilmore Ct N11 . . . . . . .30 D5
Gilmore Ho SW4 . . . . .136 D1
Gilmore Rd SE13 . . . . .142 B1
Gilpin Ave SW14 . . . . .133 B1
Gilpin Cl
 Mitcham CR4 . . . . . . .180 C1
 W1 . . . . .236 B3
Gilpin Cres
 Edmonton N18 . . . . . . .33 D5
 Twickenham TW2 . . . .151 D4
Gilpin Ho
 9 Edmonton N9 . . . . . .18 A1
 New Malden KT3 . . . .199 C4
Gilpin Rd E5 . . . . .75 A4
Gilpin Way UB3 . . . . . .127 B5
Gilray Ho W2 . . . . .246 C6
Gilsland Rd CR7 . . . . .205 B5
Gilstead Ho IG11 . . . . .102 B5
Gilston Rd
 SW10 . . . . . . .114 A1 256 B1
Gilton Rd SE6 . . . . . . .164 C1
Giltspur St EC1 94 D1 241 D2
Gilwell Cl E4 . . . . .7 D1
Gilwell Ct 8 E5 . . . . . . .74 B4

Gippeswyck Cl HA5 . . .22 D2
Gipsy Cnr W3 . . . . .89 B2
Gipsy Hill SE19 . . . . . .183 C5
Gipsy Hill Sta SE19 . .183 C5
Gipsy La SW15 . . . . . .134 B2
Gipsy Moth IV★ SE10 142 A6
Gipsy Rd Bexley DA16 .146 D3
 West Norwood SE27 . .183 B6
Gipsy Road Gdns
 SE27 . . . . .183 A6
Giralda Cl E16 . . . . .99 D2
Giraud St E14 . . . . .97 D1
Girdlers Rd W14 . . . . .112 C5
Girdlestone Wlk N19 . .71 C6
Girdwood Rd SW18,
 SW19 . . . . .157 A4
Girling Ho 9 N1 . . . . . . .95 C6
Girling Way TW14 . . . .128 A2
Gironde Rd
 SW6 . . . . .135 B5 264 D3
Girton Ave NW9 . . . . . .44 C6
Girton Cl UB5 . . . . .64 A2
Girton Gdns CR0 . . . . .223 C5
Girton Ho SW15 . . . . . .156 C5
Girton Rd
 Forest Hill SE26 . . . . .184 C5
 Northolt UB5 . . . . .64 A2
Girton Villas 6 W10 . . .90 D1
Gisbourne Cl SM6 . . . .219 D5
Gisburn Mans N8 . . . . .50 A5
Gisburn Rd N8 . . . . . . .50 B5
Gissing Wlk N1 . . . . . .72 C1
Gistelword Ho 9
 TW7 . . . . .131 A2
Gittens Cl BR1 . . . . . . .186 C6
Given-Wilson Wlk
 E13 . . . . .98 D5
Glacier Way W3 . . . . . .89 B2
Gladbeck Way EN2 . . . .4 D1
Gladding Rd E12 . . . . . .77 D4
Glade Cl KT6 . . . . .213 D6
Glade Gdns CR0 . . . . .207 A2
Glade La UB2 . . . . .107 C4
Gladeside
 Croydon CR0 . . . . . . .206 D3
 Southgate N21 . . . . . . .16 B4
Gladeside Cl KT9 . . . . .213 D1
Gladesmore Com Sch
 N15 . . . . .52 A4
Gladesmore Rd N15 . .51 D3
Glades Sh Ctr The
 BR1 . . . . .187 A1
Gladeswood Rd
 DA17 . . . . .125 D2
Glade The BR1 . . . . . . .187 D1
 SE7 . . . . .143 C5
 Croydon CR0 . . . . . . .206 D3
 Enfield EN2 . . . . .4 C3
 Southgate N21 . . . . . . .16 B4
 Stoneleigh KT17 . . . . .216 A2
 West Wickham BR4 . . .223 D5
 Woodford IG8 . . . . . . .21 B1
Gladiator St SE23 . . . .163 A4
Glading Terr N16 . . . . .73 D5
Gladioli Cl 6 TW12 . . .173 C4
Gladsdale Dr HA5 . . . . .40 B5
Gladsmuir Rd N19 . . . . .49 C1
 Barnet EN5 . . . . .1 A4
Gladstone Ave E12 . . . .78 A1
 Feltham TW14 . . . . . .150 B5
 Tottenham N22 . . . . . . .32 D1
 Twickenham TW2 . . . .152 B4
Gladstone Ct NW2 . . . .68 B3
 SW1 . . . . .259 D3
 5 Merton SW19 . . . . .179 C3
Gladstone Gdns TW3 .130 A4
Gladstone Ho 14 E14 . .97 C1
Gladstone Mews
 3 Penge SE20 . . . . . .184 C3
 Wood Green N22 . . . . .32 C1
Gladstone Par NW2 . . .68 C4
Gladstone Park Gdns
 NW2 . . . . .68 B5
Gladstone Park Sch
 NW10 . . . . .68 B3
Gladstone Pl KT8 . . . .196 A5
Gladstone Rd BR6 . . .227 A3
 W4 . . . . .111 B3
 Buckhurst Hill IG9 . . . .21 C3
 Kingston KT1 . . . . . . .198 C1
 Merton SW19 . . . . . .179 D3
 Southall UB2 . . . . .107 A3
 Surbiton KT6 . . . . . . .214 A6
 Thornton Heath CR0 . .205 B2
Gladstone St SE1 . . . .261 C6
Gladstone Terr
 SW8 . . . . . . .137 B4 268 D2
 Woodford IG8 . . . . . . .37 A1
Gladstone Way HA3 . . .42 D2
Gladwell Rd BR1 . . . . .187 A4

Gladwell Rd continued
 N8 . . . . .50 B3
Gladwin Ho NW1 . . . . .232 B3
Gladwyn Rd SW15 . . . .134 D2
Gladys Dimson Ho E7 .76 D3
Gladys Rd NW6 . . . . . . .69 C1
Glaisher St 2 SE10 . . .142 A5
 SE8 . . . . .141 D6
Glamis Cres UB3 . . . . .105 A3
Glamis Ct W3 . . . . . . .110 D4
Glamis Est 3 E1 . . . . .118 D6
Glamis Pl E1 . . . . .118 C6
Glamis Rd E1 . . . . .118 C6
Glamis Way UB5 . . . . .64 A2
Glamorgan Cl CR4,
 SW16 . . . . .204 A6
Glamorgan Ct 4 W7 . . .86 D2
Glamorgan Rd KT1 . . .175 C3
Glanfield Rd BR3 . . . . .207 B5
Glanleam Rd HA7 . . . . .25 C6
Glanville Ho 4 SW12 159 C4
Glanville Rd SW2 . . . . .160 A6
 Bromley BR2 . . . . . . .209 B6
Glasbrook Ave TW2 . .151 B4
Glasbrook Rd SE9 . . . .165 D4
Glasbury Ho 5 SW9 . .138 B1
Glaserton Rd N16 . . . . .51 C2
Glasford St SW17 . . . .180 D4
Glasfryn Ct HA2 . . . . . .64 B6
Glasgow Ho W9 . . . . . .91 D5
Glasgow Rd E13 . . . . . .99 B5
 Edmonton N18 . . . . . . .34 D1
Glasgow Terr
 SW1 . . . . . . .115 C1 259 A1
Glasse Cl W13 . . . . . . .109 A6
Glasshill St
 SE1 . . . . .116 D4 251 D2
Glasshouse Fields
 E1 . . . . .118 D6
Glasshouse St
 W1 . . . . .115 C6 249 B5
Glasshouse Wlk
 SE11 . . . . . . .116 B1 260 C2
Glasshouse Yd EC1 . .242 A5
Glasslyn Rd N8 . . . . . . .49 D4
Glassmill La BR2 . . . . .186 D1
Glass St 4 E2 . . . . .96 B3
Glass Yd 1 SE18 . . . . .122 C3
Glastonbury Ave IG8 . .37 D4
Glastonbury Ct
 12 SE14 . . . . .140 C5
 1 Ealing W13 . . . . . . .109 A5
Glastonbury Ho SW1 258 C2
Glastonbury Pl 25 E1 . .96 C2
Glastonbury Rd
 Edmonton N9 . . . . .18 A3
 Morden SM4 . . . . .201 C2
Glastonbury St NW6 . .69 B3
Glaston Ct W5 . . . . . . .109 D5
Glaucus St E3 . . . . .97 D2
Glazbury Rd
 W14 . . . . . . .113 A1 254 B2
Glazebrook Cl SE21 . .161 B2
Glazebrook Rd TW11 174 D3
Glebe Ave Enfield EN2 . .4 D2
 Harrow HA3 . . . . .44 A4
 Mitcham CR4 . . . . . . .180 C1
 Ruislip HA4 . . . . .62 B2
 Uxbridge UB10 . . . . . .61 A4
 Woodford IG8 . . . . . . .37 A4
Glebe Cl 1 W4 . . . . . . .111 C1
 Uxbridge UB10 . . . . . .61 A4
Glebe Cotts NW13 . . . .151 C1
Glebe Cres NW4 . . . . . .46 C5
 Harrow HA3 . . . . .44 A6
Glebe Ct SE3 . . . . .142 C2
 Ealing W5 . . . . .109 C6
 Ealing W7 . . . . .108 B4
 Mitcham CR4 . . . . . . .202 D6
 Palmers Green N13 . . .16 C1
 Stanmore HA7 . . . . . . .25 C5
Glebe Fst & Mid Sch
 HA3 . . . . .44 A5
Glebe Gdns KT3 . . . . .199 C2
Glebe Ho 8 SE16 . . . .118 B3
 7 SE18 . . . . .122 C2
 Feltham TW13 . . . . . .151 C1
Glebe House Dr BR2 .209 B1
Glebehyrst SE19 . . . . .183 C6
Glebe La Barnet EN5 . .12 A5
 Harrow HA3 . . . . .44 A4
Glebeland Gdns
 TW17 . . . . .193 A3
Glebelands E10 . . . . . . .75 D6
 East Molesey KT8 . . . .195 D4
Glebelands Ave
 Ilford IG2 . . . . .57 B2
Glebelands Cl SE5 . . .139 C2
Glebelands Rd TW14 150 A4

Glebe Path CR4 . . . . . .202 D6
Glebe Pl SW3 136 C6 267 A6
Glebe Prim Sch UB10 .61 B4
Glebe Rd BR1 . . . . . . .187 A2
 E8 . . . . .73 D1
 N3 . . . . .30 A2
 N8 . . . . .50 B5
 NW10 . . . . .68 A2
 Barnes SW13 . . . . . . .134 A3
 Belmont SM2 . . . . . . .217 A1
 Dagenham RM10 . . . . .81 D2
 Hayes UB3 . . . . .105 D5
 Stanmore HA7 . . . . . . .25 C5
 Wallington SM5 . . . . .218 D3
Glebe Sch BR4 . . . . . .224 B6
Glebe Side TW1 . . . . . .152 C5
Glebe Sq CR4 . . . . . . .202 D6
Glebe St W4 . . . . .111 C1
Glebe Terr 15 E3 . . . . .97 C4
 New Malden KT4 . . . .199 D1
Glebe The SE3 . . . . . . .142 B2
 Chislehurst BR7 . . . . .189 A2
 New Malden KT4 . . . .199 D1
 Streatham SW16 . . . . .181 D6
 West Drayton UB7 . . . .104 C3
Glebeway IG8 . . . . .37 C5
Glebe Way
 Feltham TW13 . . . . . .151 C1
 West Wickham BR4 . . .224 B6
Gledhow Gdns SW5 . .256 A3
Gledstanes Rd
 W14 . . . . . . .113 A1 254 B1
Gledwood Ave UB4 . . .84 A2
Gledwood Cres UB4 . .83 D2
Gledwood Ct UB4 . . . . .83 D2
Gledwood Dr UB4 . . . . .83 D2
Gledwood Gdns UB4 . .84 A2
Gleed Ave WD23 . . . . . .8 B2
Gleeson Dr BR6 . . . . . .227 D4
Glegg Pl 3 SW15 . . . . .134 D1
Glenaffric Ave E14 . . . .120 B2
Glen Albyn Rd SW19 . .156 C2
Glenalla Rd HA4 . . . . . .39 D2
Glenalmond Ho
 Ashford TW15 . . . . . . .148 A1
 2 Putney SW15 . . . . .156 D5
Glenalmond Rd HA3 . .44 A5
Glenalvon Way 5
 SE7 . . . . .122 A2
Glena Mount SM1 . . . .218 A4
Glenarm Coll IG1 . . . . .78 D6
Glenarm Rd E5 . . . . . . .74 C4
Glen Ave TW15 . . . . . .170 C6
Glenavon Cl KT10 . . . .213 A1
Glenavon Ct KT4 . . . . .216 B6
Glenavon Lo 4 E18 . . .55 A6
Glenavon Rd E15 . . . . .76 C1
Glenbarr Cl SE9 . . . . .144 D2
Glenbow Rd BR1 . . . . .186 C5
Glenbrook Inf Sch
 SW4 . . . . .159 D5
Glenbrook Jun Sch
 SW4 . . . . .159 D5
Glenbrook N EN2 . . . . . .4 B1
Glenbrook Rd NW6 . . .69 C3
Glenbrook S EN2 . . . . . .4 B1
Glenbuck Ct 6 KT6 . . .198 A3
Glenbuck Rd KT6 . . . .198 A3
Glenburnie Rd SW17 158 C1
Glencairn Dr W5 . . . . . .87 C3
Glencairne Cl E16 . . . . .99 D2
Glencairn Rd SW16 . .182 A3
Glen Cl TW17 . . . . .192 C5
Glencoe Ave IG2 . . . . . .57 C2
Glencoe Dr RM10 . . . . .81 C2
Glencoe Mans 6
 SW9 . . . . .138 C5
Glencoe Rd UB4 . . . . . .84 D3
Glencorse Gn WD19 . . .22 C2
Glen Cres IG8 . . . . .37 B4
Glen Ct
 5 Bromley BR1 . . . . .186 D3
 9 Penge SE20 . . . . . .184 B3
 Sidcup DA14 . . . . . . .190 A6
Glendale Ave
 Edgware HA8 . . . . .26 A6
 Ilford RM6 . . . . .58 C2
 Wood Green N22 . . . . .32 C3
Glendale Cl SE9 . . . . .144 C4
Glendale Dr SW19 . . . .179 B5
Glendale Gdns HA9 . . .44 A1
Glendale Mews BR3 . .185 C2
Glendale Way SE28 . . .124 C2
Glendall St SW9 . . . . .138 B2
Glendarvon St SW15 . .134 D2
Glendevon Cl HA8 . . . .10 D1
Glendish Rd N17 . . . . . .34 C2
Glendor Gdns NW7 . . .27 B6
Glendower Gdns 10
 SW14 . . . . .133 B2
Glendower Pl SW7 . . .256 C4

Glendower Prep Sch
 SW7 . . . . . . .114 B2 256 D4
Glendower Rd
 Chingford E4 . . . . .20 B3
 Mortlake SW14 . . . . . .133 B2
Glendown Ho 2 E8 . . .74 A1
Glendown Rd SE2 . . . .124 A1
Glendun Ct W3 . . . . . .111 C6
Glendun Rd W3 . . . . . .111 C6
Gleneagle Lo BR3 . . . .185 C2
Gleneagle Mews
 SW16 . . . . .181 D5
Gleneagle Rd SW16 . .181 D5
Gleneagles Ealing W13 .87 B5
 Stanmore HA7 . . . . . . .25 B4
Gleneagles Cl BR6 . . .211 B1
 21 SE16 . . . . .118 C3
 South Oxhey WD19 . . . .22 C1
Gleneagles Ct 3
 TW11 . . . . .175 A5
Gleneagles Gn 1
 BR6 . . . . .211 B1
Gleneagles Twr 2
 UB1 . . . . .86 A1
Gleneldon Mews
 SW16 . . . . .182 A6
Gleneldon Rd SW16 . .182 A6
Glenelg Rd SW2 . . . . .160 A6
Glenesk Rd SE9 . . . . .144 D1
Glenfarg Rd SE6 . . . . .164 B3
Glenfield Cres HA4 . . . .39 C4
Glenfield Rd W13 . . . .109 B4
 Ashford TW15 . . . . . . .171 A4
 Streatham SW12 . . . . .159 C3
Glenfield Terr W13 . . .109 B5
Glenfinlas Way SE5 . .138 D5
Glenforth St SE10 . . . .120 D1
Glengall Gr E14 . . . . . .120 C3
Glengall Pass 2 NW6 91 C6
Glengall Rd DA7 . . . . .147 A2
 NW6 . . . . .91 B6
 SE15 . . . . .139 D6
 Edgware HA8 . . . . .10 D1
 Woodford IG8 . . . . . . .37 B4
Glengall Terr SE15 . . .139 D6
Glengarnock Ave
 E14 . . . . .120 A2
Glengarry Rd SE22 . . .161 D6
Glen Gdns CR0 . . . . . .220 C4
Glenham Dr IG2 . . . . . .56 D2
Glenhead Cl SE9 . . . . .144 D2
Glenhill Cl N3 . . . . .29 C1
Glen Ho 6 E16 . . . . . . .122 C5
 SW1 . . . . .259 A6
Glenhouse Rd SE9 . . .166 C4
Glenhurst 4 BR3 . . . . .186 A2
Glenhurst Ave DA5 . . .169 B3
 NW5 . . . . .71 A4
 Ruislip HA4 . . . . .39 A4
Glenhurst Ct SE19 . . .183 D5
Glenhurst Rd N12 . . . . .30 B5
 Brentford TW8 . . . . . .109 C1
Glenhurst Rise SE19 .183 A3
Glenilla Rd NW3 . . . . . .70 C2
Glenister Ho UB3 . . . .106 B5
Glenister Park Rd
 SW16 . . . . .181 D5
Glenister Rd SE10 . . . .120 D1
Glenister St E16 . . . . .122 C5
Glenlea Rd SE9 . . . . . .166 C6
Glenloch Ct 2 NW3 . . .70 C2
Glenloch Rd NW3 . . . . .70 C2
 Enfield EN3 . . . . .6 C3
Glenluce Rd SE3 . . . . .143 A6
Glenlyon Rd SE9 . . . . .166 C6
Glenmead IG9 . . . . .21 C3
Glenmere Ave NW7 . . .28 A4
Glen Mews E17 . . . . . . .53 B4
Glenmill TW12 . . . . . . .173 B5
Glenmore SW15 . . . . .156 D5
Glenmore Ho 6
 TW10 . . . . .154 A5
Glenmore Rd DA16 . . .145 D4
 NW3 . . . . .70 C2
Glenmore Way IG11 . .102 A5
Glenmount Path 1
 SE18 . . . . .123 A1
Glennie Ct SE21 . . . . .162 A3
Glennie Ho SE10 . . . . .142 A4
Glennie Rd SE27,
 SW16 . . . . .160 C1
Glenny Rd IG11 . . . . . . .79 C2
Glenorchy Cl UB4 . . . . .85 A2
Glenparke Rd E7 . . . . . .77 B2
Glen Rd E13 . . . . .99 C3
 E17 . . . . .53 B4

Glen Rd continued
Chessington KT9 .....**214** A5
Glenridding NW1 ....**232** B3
Glen Rise IG8 ....**37** B4
Glenrosa St SW6 ...**136** A5
Glenrose Ct DA14 ...**190** B5
Glenroy St W12 ....**90** C1
Glensdale Rd SE4 ...**141** B2
Glenshaw Mans 7
SW9 ....**138** C5
Glenshiel Rd SE9 ....**166** C6
Glentanner Way
SW17 ....**158** B1
Glen Terr E14 ....**120** A4
Glentham Gdns
SW13 ....**134** B6
Glentham Rd SW13 ..**134** B6
Glen The BR6 ....**226** C5
Beckenham BR2 .....**186** C1
Enfield EN2 ....**4** D1
Pinner HA5 ....**40** B4
Pinner HA5 ....**41** A2
Southall UB2 ....**107** B1
South Croydon CR0 ..**222** D5
Wembley HA9 ....**65** D4
Glenthorne Ave CR0 **206** C6
Glenthorne Cl SM3 ..**201** C1
Glenthorne Gdns
Cheam SM3 ....**201** C1
Ilford IG6 ....**56** D5
Glenthorne High Sch
SM3 ....**201** C1
Glenthorne Mews
W6 ....**112** B2
Glenthorne Rd E17 ...**53** A4
N11 ....**31** A5
W6 ....**112** B2
Kingston KT1 ....**198** B5
Glenthorpe SW15 ....**134** A1
Glenthorpe Rd SM4 ..**200** D4
Glenton St SE13 .....**142** C1
Glentrammon Ave
BR6 ....**227** D2
Glentrammon Cl BR6 **227** D3
Glentrammon Gdns
BR6 ....**227** D2
Glentrammon Rd
BR6 ....**227** D2
Glentworth St
NW1 ....**92** D3 **237** D5
Glenure Rd SE9 .....**166** C6
Glenview SE2 ....**146** D6
Glen View Rd BR1 ...**187** D1
Glenville Ave EN2 .....**5** A5
Glenville Gr SE8 .....**141** B5
Glenville Mews
SW18 ....**157** C4
Glenville Rd KT2 ....**176** C2
Glen Wlk TW7 ....**152** B6
Glenwood Ave NW9 ...**45** C1
Glenwood Cl HA1 .....**42** D4
Glenwood Ct
4 Sidcup DA14 ....**190** A6
5 Wanstead E18 .....**55** A6
Glenwood Gdns IG2 ..**56** C4
Glenwood Gr NW9 ....**45** A1
Glenwood Ho 3 EN5 ..**13** D1
Glenwood Rd N15 ....**50** D4
NW7 ....**11** C1
Forest Hill SE6 ......**163** C3
Hounslow TW3 ......**130** C3
Stoneleigh KT17 .....**216** A2
Glenwood Way CR0 ..**206** D3
Glenworth Ave E14 ..**120** B2
Gliddon Rd
W14 ....**113** A1 **254** A2
Glifford Ho SW1 ....**259** A1
Glimpsing Gn DA18 ..**143** A4
Glisson Rd UB10 .....**82** C5
Globe Pond Rd SE16 **119** A5
Globe Prim Sch E2 ..**96** C4
Globe Rd E15 ....**76** D3
E1,E2 ....**96** C3
Woodford IG8 ....**37** C4
Globe St SE1 .**117** B4 **252** C1
Globe Terr 9 E2 ....**96** C4
Globe Theatre The*
SE1 ....**252** A5
Globe View EC4 .....**252** A6
Globe Yd W1 ....**238** C1
Gloster Rd KT3 .....**199** C5
Gloucester
W14 ....**113** B2 **254** D3
Gloucester Ave DA16 **145** D1
NW1 ....**93** A6 **231** B6
Sidcup DA15 ....**167** C2
Gloucester Cir SE10 .**142** A5

Gloucester Cl NW10 ..**67** B1
Thames Ditton KT7 ..**197** A1
Gloucester Cres
NW1 ....**93** B6 **231** C6
Staines TW18 ....**170** A4
Gloucester Ct EC3 ..**253** B5
NW1 ....**47** B2
SE1 ....**262** B6
SE22 ....**162** A3
6 Acton W3 ....**88** C1
5 Ealing W7 ....**86** D2
Harrow HA1 ....**42** C6
Redbridge IG1 ....**56** B2
Richmond TW9 ......**132** C5
8 Surbiton KT6 .....**197** D2
Gloucester Dr N4 ....**72** D6
NW11 ....**47** C5
Gloucester Gate
NW1 ....**231** C4
Gloucester Gate Mews
NW1 ....**231** C4
Gloucester Gdns
NW11 ....**47** B2
W2 ....**236** A2
Cockfosters EN4 .....**15** A6
Redbridge IG1 ....**56** A2
Sutton SM1 ....**217** D6
Gloucester Gr HA8 ...**27** B2
Gloucester Ho NW6 ..**91** C5
Richmond TW10 .....**154** C6
Gloucester Lo 9
CR0 ....**221** C6
Gloucester Mews
W2 ....**236** B1
Gloucester Mews W
W2 ....**236** B1
Gloucester Par DA15 **168** A6
Hayes UB3 ....**105** A3
Gloucester Pk SW7 .**256** A4
Gloucester Pl
W1 ....**92** D2 **237** D4
Gloucester Pl Mews
W1 ....**92** D2 **237** D3
Gloucester Prim Sch
SE15 ....**139** C5
Gloucester Rd E10 ...**53** C2
E17 ....**34** D1
N17 ....**51** B6
SW7 ....**114** A3 **256** A4
W5 ....**109** C4
Acton W3 ....**111** A4
Croydon CR0 ....**205** C2
Edmonton N18 ......**33** D5
Enfield EN2 ....**5** A5
Erith DA17 ....**125** B1
Feltham TW13 ......**150** C3
Hampton TW12 .....**173** D3
Harrow HA1 ....**41** D4
Hounslow TW4 ......**129** A1
Ilford E12 ....**78** B4
Kingston KT1,KT2 ...**176** D1
New Barnet EN5 .....**14** A6
Richmond TW9 ......**132** C5
Teddington TW11 ....**174** D5
Twickenham TW2 ....**152** A3
Wanstead E11 ....**55** C4
Gloucester Road Sta
SW7 ....**114** A2 **256** A4
Gloucester Sq 6 E2 ..**96** A6
W2 ....**92** C1 **237** A1
Gloucester St
SW1 ....**115** C1 **259** A2
Gloucester Terr
W2 ....**92** A1 **236** B1
Gloucester Wlk
W8 ....**113** C4 **245** B2
Glover Cl SE2 ....**124** C2
Glover Dr N18 ....**34** C4
Glover Ho 2 NW6 ...**70** A1
SE15 ....**140** B1
Glovers Gr HA4 ....**38** D2
Gloxinia Wlk TW12 ..**173** D4
Glycena Rd SW11 ...**136** D2
Glyn Ave EN4 ....**2** C1
Glyn Cl SE25 ....**183** C2
Glyn Ct SE27 ....**160** C1
Glyndale Grange
SM2 ....**217** D2
Glyndebourne Ct 5
UB5 ....**84** C4
Glyndebourne Pk
BR6 ....**226** D6
Glynde Mews SW3 ..**257** B5
Glynde Rd DA7 .....**147** A2
Glynde Reach WC1 ..**233** B1
Glynde St SE4 ......**163** B5
Glyndon Rd SE18 ...**123** C2
Glyn Dr DA14 ......**190** B6

Glynfield Rd NW10 ...**67** C1
Glyn Mans W14 .....**254** B4
Glynne Rd N22 ....**32** C1
Glyn Rd E5 ....**74** D4
Enfield EN3 ....**6** C1
North Cheam KT4,SM3 **216** D6
Glyn St SE11 ....**260** C1
Glynwood Ct SE23 ..**162** C2
Goater's Alley SW6 .**264** D3
Goat La EN1 ....**5** D5
Goat Rd CR4 ....**202** D2
Goat Wharf TW8 ...**132** A6
Godalming Ave SM6 **220** B3
Godalming Rd E14 ...**97** D2
Godbold Rd E15 .....**98** C4
Goddard Cl TW17 ...**192** B6
Goddard Ho SW19 ..**156** D2
Goddard Pl N19 ......**71** C5
Goddard Rd BR3 ....**207** A5
Goddards Way IG1 ...**57** B1
Goddarts Ho E17 .....**53** C6
Godfrey Ave
Northolt UB5 ....**85** A6
Twickenham TW2 ....**152** B4
Godfrey Hill SE18 ...**122** A2
Godfrey Ho EC1 ....**235** C1
Godfrey Rd SE18 ...**122** B2
Godfrey St E15 ......**98** A5
SW3 ....**114** C1 **257** B2
Godfrey Way TW4 ..**151** B4
Goding St
SE11 ....**116** A1 **260** B1
Godley Rd SW18 ....**158** B3
Godliman St EC4 ...**252** A6
Godman Rd SE15 ...**140** B3
Godolphin Cl N13 ....**32** C4
Godolphin Ho NW3 ..**70** C1
7 Streatham SW2 ..**160** C3
Godolphin & Latymer Sch
W6 ....**112** B2
Godolphin Pl W3 ....**111** B6
Godolphin Rd W12 ..**112** B4
Godson Rd CR0 .....**220** C5
Godson St N1 ......**234** A4
Godstone Ct 1 N16 ..**51** C1
Godstone Ho SE1 ...**262** D6
1 Kingston KT2 ....**176** D4
Godstone Rd
Sutton SM1 ....**218** A4
Twickenham TW1 ....**153** B5
Godstow Rd SE2 ....**124** C4
Godwin Cl N1 ......**235** B4
West Ewell KT19 ....**215** A2
Godwin Ct NW1 ....**232** B4
Godwin Ho 2 E2 ....**95** D5
NW6 ....**91** D5
6 SE18 ....**144** B4
Godwin Jun Sch E7 ..**77** B4
Godwin Prim Sch RM9 **81** A1
Godwin Rd BR1,BR2 **209** C6
E7 ....**77** B4
Goffers Ho SE3 .....**142** C3
Goffers Rd SE3,SE13 **142** C3
Goffs Rd TW15 .....**171** B4
Goffton Ho 14 SW9 .**138** B3
Goidel Cl SM6 ......**219** D4
Golborne Gdns W10 ..**91** B3
Golborne Mews 9
W10 ....**91** A2
Golborne Rd W10 ....**91** A2
Golda Cl EN5 ....**12** D5
Goldbeaters Gr HA8 ..**27** C3
Goldbeaters Prim Sch
HA8 ....**27** B2
Goldcliff Cl SM4 ....**201** C2
Goldcrest Cl E16 .....**99** D2
Woolwich SE28 .....**124** C6
Goldcrest Mews W5 ..**87** D2
Goldcrest Way
Bushey WD23 ....**8** A3
New Addington CR0 .**224** B1
Golden Cres UB3 ...**105** D5
Golden Cross Mews 8
W11 ....**91** B1
Golden Ct 4 Barnet EN4 **2** C1
Ealing W7 ....**108** C2
10 Richmond TW9 ...**153** D6
Golden Hind Pl 4
SE8 ....**119** B2
Golden La EC1 **95** A3 **242** B5
Golden Manor W7 ..**108** C6
Golden Mews SE20 ..**184** C2
Golden Par 2 E17 ....**54** A6
Golden Plover Cl E16 **99** A1
Golden Sq
W1 ....**115** C6 **249** B6
Golders Cl HA8 ....**26** D5
Golders Ct NW11 ....**47** B2
Golders Gdns NW11 ..**47** A2

Golders Green Coll
NW11 ....**47** B1
Golders Green Cres
NW11 ....**47** C2
Golders Green Rd
NW11 ....**47** A2
Golders Green Sta
NW11 ....**47** C1
Golders Hill Sch
NW11 ....**47** C1
Golderslea NW11 .....**47** C1
Golders Manor Dr
NW11 ....**47** A3
Golders Park Cl NW11 **47** C1
Golders Rise NW4 ....**46** D4
Golders Way NW11 ...**47** B2
Golderton 2 NW4 ....**46** C5
Goldfinch Rd SE28 ..**123** B3
Goldhawk Ind Est The
W6 ....**112** B4
Goldhawk Mews 2
W12 ....**112** B4
Goldhawk Rd W12 ..**112** A3
Goldhawk Road Sta
W12 ....**112** C4
Goldhaze Cl IG8 ......**37** D3
Gold Hill HA8 ....**27** B4
Goldhurst Terr NW6 ..**70** A1
Goldie Ho N19 ....**49** D2
Goldie Leigh Hospl
SE2 ....**146** C6
Golding Cl KT9 .....**213** C2
Golding Ct 7 IG1 .....**78** C5
Golding St E1 ....**96** A1
Golding Terr 17 E1 ....**96** A1
Goldington Cres
NW1 ....**232** C4
Goldington Ct NW1 .**232** C5
Goldington St
NW1 ....**93** D5 **232** C4
Gold La HA8 ....**27** B4
Goldman Cl E2 ....**96** A3
Goldmark Ho SE3 ...**143** B2
Goldney Rd W9 ....**91** C3
Goldrill Dr N11 ....**15** A3
Goldsboro Rd
SW8 ....**137** D5 **269** D3
Goldsborough Cres
E4 ....**20** A2
Goldsborough Ho
SW8 ....**269** D1
Goldsdown Cl EN3 .....**7** A3
Goldsdown Rd EN3 ....**7** A3
Goldsmid St 2 SE18 **123** C1
Goldsmith Ave E12 ...**78** A2
NW9 ....**45** C3
W3 ....**111** B6
Dagenham RM7 ......**59** C2
Goldsmith Cl HA2 ....**41** D1
Goldsmith Ct WC1 ..**240** A2
Goldsmith Ho W3 ...**111** B6
Goldsmith La NW9 ...**45** A5
Goldsmith Rd E10 ....**53** D1
E17 ....**34** D1
N11 ....**30** C5
SE15 ....**140** A4
W3 ....**111** B5
Goldsmiths Bldgs
W3 ....**111** B5
Goldsmiths Cl W3 ...**111** B5
Goldsmiths Coll, Univ of
London SE14 ....**141** A4
Goldsmith's Ct N6 ....**49** B3
NW6 ....**91** D6
Goldsmith's Row E2 ..**96** A4
Goldsmith's Sq 16 E2 **96** A5
Goldsmith St EC2 ...**242** B2
Goldsworthy Gdns
SE16 ....**118** C5
Goldthorpe NW1 ....**232** A5
Goldwell Ho SE22 ...**139** C1
Goldwell Rd CR7 ....**204** B5
Goldwin Cl SE14 ....**140** C4
Goldwing Cl E16 .....**99** A1
Golf Cl
South Norwood SW16 **182** C2
Stanmore HA7 ....**25** C3
Golf Club Dr KT2 ...**177** B3
Golfe Rd IG1 ....**79** B5
Golf Rd BR1 ....**210** C6
Ealing W5 ....**88** C4
Golf Side TW2 ......**152** B1
Golfside Cl N20 ......**14** C1
Kingston KT3 ......**177** C1
Goliath Cl SM6 .....**220** A1
Gollogly Terr 9 SE7 .**121** C1
Gomer Gdns TW11 ..**175** A4
Gomer Pl TW11 .....**175** A4

Gomm Rd SE16 .....**118** C3
Gomshall Ave SM6 ..**220** A3
Gondar Gdns NW6 ....**69** B3
Gondar Mans NW6 ...**69** B3
Gonson St SE8 .....**141** D6
Gonston Ct SW19 ..**157** A2
Gonville Cres UB5 ....**63** D2
Gonville Ho 6 SW15 **156** D5
Gonville Prim Sch
CR7 ....**204** B4
Gonville Rd CR7 ....**204** B4
Gonville St SW6 ....**135** A2
Gooch Ho E5 ....**74** B5
EC1 ....**241** A4
Goodall Ho 10 SE4 .**140** D1
Goodall Rd E11 ......**76** A5
Goodbehere Ho 7
SE27 ....**183** A6
Gooden Ct HA1 ......**64** C5
Goodenough Rd
SW19 ....**179** B3
Goodey Rd IG11 .....**79** D1
Goodfaith Ho 16 E14 **119** D6
Goodge Pl W1 ......**239** B3
Goodge St W1 **93** C2 **239** B3
Goodge Street Sta
W1 ....**93** D2 **239** C4
Goodhall St NW10 ...**89** D4
Good Hart Pl E14 ...**119** A6
Goodhart Way BR4 .**208** C3
Goodhew Rd CR0 ...**206** A3
Goodhope Ho 15 E14 **119** D6
Gooding Cl KT3 ....**199** A4
Goodinge Cl N7 ......**72** A2
Goodinge Rd N7 .....**72** A2
Gooding Ho 4 SE7 ..**121** C1
Goodison Cl WD23 .....**8** A6
Goodland Ho 1 KT3 **199** C2
Goodman Cres SW2 **159** D2
Goodman Rd E10 ....**54** A2
Goodmans Ct HA0 ...**65** D4
Goodman's Stile 12 E1 **96** A1
Goodman's Yd
E1,EC3 .....**117** D6 **253** C6
Goodmayes Ave IG3 ..**58** A1
Goodmayes Hospl IG3 **58** A4
Goodmayes La IG3 ...**80** A5
Goodmayes Prim Sch
IG3 ....**58** B1
Goodmayes Rd IG3 ..**58** A1
Goodmayes Ret Pk
RM6 ....**58** B2
Goodmayes Sta IG3 ..**58** A1
Goodrich Com Sch
SE22 ....**162** A5
Goodrich Ct 9 W10 ...**90** D1
Goodrich Ho 21 E2 ...**96** C5
N16 ....**51** C2
Goodrich Rd SE22 ..**162** A5
Goodridge Ho E17 ...**36** A3
Good Shepherd RC Prim
Sch
Catford BR1 ....**186** D6
New Addington CR0 .**223** D1
Good Shepherd RC Prim
Sch The W12 ......**111** B6
Goodson Ho SM4 ...**202** A2
Goodson Rd NW10 ...**67** C1
Goodsway
NW1 ....**94** A5 **233** A4
Goodway Gdns E14 ...**98** B1
Goodwill Ho 19 E14 .**119** D6
Goodwin Cl
SE16 ....**117** D3 **263** D5
Mitcham CR4 ......**202** B6
Goodwin Ct N8 ......**50** A6
East Barnet EN4 .....**14** C5
Goodwin Dr DA14 ..**168** D2
Goodwin Gdns CR0,
CR2 ....**220** D2
Goodwin Ho N9 ......**18** C3
2 SE15 ....**140** B2
Goodwin Rd N9 ......**18** D3
W12 ....**112** A4
Croydon CR0 ....**220** D3
Goodwins Ct WC2 ...**250** A6
Goodwin St N4 ....**72** C6
Goodwood Ave EN3 ....**6** C6
Goodwood Cl
Morden SM4 ....**201** C6
11 Stanmore HA7 ....**25** C5
Goodwood Ct W1 ...**238** C4
Goodwood Dr UB5 ...**63** C2
Goodwood Ho 3 W4 **111** A1
Penge SE26 ....**184** B4
Goodwood Mans 4
SW9 ....**138** C2
Goodwood Par BR3 .**207** A5
Goodwood Rd SE14 .**141** B5
Goodwyn Ave NW7 ...**27** C5

Goodwyn Sch NW7 ...**28** A5
Goodwyn's Vale N10 ..**31** B2
Goodyear Ho 8 N2 ...**30** B1
Goodyers Gdns NW4 .**46** D4
Goosander Ct 34 NW9 **27** D1
Goosander Way SE18,
SE28 ....**123** B3
Gooseacre La HA3 ....**43** D4
Goose Green Cl BR5 .**190** A1
Goose Green Trad Est
SE22 ....**140** A1
Gooseley La E6 .....**100** C4
Goose Sq 8 E6 .....**100** C1
Goossens Cl 1 SM1 .**218** A3
Gophir La EC4 ......**252** C6
Gopsall St N1 .**95** B6 **235** D5
Gordon Ave
Chingford E4 ....**36** C4
Isleworth TW1 ......**153** B6
Mortlake SW14 .....**133** C1
Stanmore HA7 ....**25** A4
Gordonbrock Prim Sch
SE4 ....**163** C6
Gordonbrock Rd SE4 **163** C6
Gordon Cl E17 ....**53** C3
Gordon Cres
Croydon CR0 ....**205** D1
Hayes UB3 ....**106** A2
Gordon Ct W12 ....**90** C1
17 Wimbledon SW20 **178** D3
Gordondale Rd SW18,
SW19 ....**157** C2
Gordon Dr TW17 ...**193** B2
Gordon Gdns HA8 ....**26** D1
Gordon Gr SE5 .....**138** C3
Gordon Hill EN2 ....**5** A4
Gordon Hill Sta EN2 ...**4** D4
Gordon Ho 16 E1 ...**118** C6
3 SE10 ....**141** D5
SE12 ....**165** A4
2 Ealing W5 ....**88** A4
Gordon Hospl The
SW1 ....**115** D2 **259** C3
Gordon House Rd
NW5 ....**71** A4
Gordon Inf Sch IG1 ...**79** B5
Gordon Lo N16 ....**51** B1
Gordon Pl
W8 ....**113** C4 **245** B2
Gordon Prim Sch
SE9 ....**144** B2
Gordon Rd DA15 ...**167** C6
E15 ....**76** A4
N11 ....**31** D3
N3 ....**29** B3
SE15 ....**140** B3
Ashford TW15 .....**148** A1
Barking IG11 ....**101** C6
Beckenham BR3 ....**207** B6
Chingford E4 ....**20** C4
Chiswick W4 ....**132** D6
Claygate KT10 .....**212** C1
Dagenham RM6 ......**59** B3
Ealing W13 ....**109** C6
Edmonton N9 ....**18** B2
Enfield EN2 ....**5** B3
Harrow HA3 ....**42** C4
Ilford IG1 ....**79** B5
Isleworth TW3 ......**130** A1
Kingston KT2 ......**176** B2
Richmond TW9 .....**132** B3
Shepperton TW17 ..**193** B2
Southall UB2 ......**107** A2
Surbiton KT5 ......**198** B2
Wallington SM5 ....**218** C4
Wanstead E11 ....**55** A4
Woodford IG8 ....**37** B2
Yiewsley UB7 ......**104** A6
Gordon Sq
WC1 ....**93** D3 **239** D6
Gordon St E13 ....**99** A4
WC1 ....**93** D3 **239** C6
Gordon Way BR1 ...**187** B2
Barnet EN5 ....**1** B1
Gore Ct NW9 ....**44** C4
Gorefield Ho NW6 ....**91** C5
Gorefield Pl NW6 ....**91** C5
Gore Rd E9 ....**96** C6
Merton SW20 ......**178** C1
Goresbrook Rd RM9 **102** D6
Gore St SW7 .**114** A3 **256** B6
Gorham Ho 12 SW4 .**159** C4
Gorham Pl W11 .....**244** A5
Goring Gdns RM8 ....**80** C4
Goring Rd N11 ....**32** A4
Goring St EC3 ......**243** B2
Goring Way UB6 .....**86** A5
Gorleston Rd N15 ....**51** B4
Gorleston St
W14 ....**113** A2 **254** B4

Gorman Rd SE18 ....122 B2
Gorringe Park Ave
CR4 ....181 A3
Gorringe Park Prim Sch
CR4 ....181 A2
Gorse Cl E16 ....99 A1
Gorsefield Ho 5 E14 119 C6
Gorse Rd CR0 ....223 C5
Gorse Rise SW17 ...181 A5
Gorse Wlk UB7 ....82 A1
Gorst Rd NW10 ....89 B3
SW11 ....158 D5
Gorsuch Pl 1 E2 ....95 D4
Gorsuch St E2 ....95 D4
Gosberton Rd SW12 .159 A3
Gosbury Hill KT9 ....214 A4
Gosfield Rd RM8 ....59 C1
Gosfield St
W1 ....93 C2 239 A3
Gosford Gdns IG4 ....56 B4
Gosford Ho 21 E3 ....97 B5
Goshawk Gdns UB4 ...83 C5
Goslett Yd WC2 ....239 D2
Gosling Cl UB6 ....85 C4
Gosling Ho 1 E1 ....118 C6
Gosling Way SW9 ...138 C4
Gospatrick Rd N17 ...33 A2
Gospel Oak Prim Sch
NW5 ....71 A4
Gospel Oak Sta NW5 .71 A4
Gosport Ho 9 SW15 .156 A3
Gosport Rd E17 ....53 B4
Gosport Wlk N17 ....52 B5
Gossage Rd SE18 ....123 B1
Hillingdon UB10 ....60 B1
Gosset St E2 ....96 A4
Gosshill Rd BR7 ....188 C1
Gossington Cl BR7 ..188 D6
Gosterwood St SE8 ..141 A6
Gostling Rd TW2 ....151 C3
Goston Gdns CR7 ....204 C6
Goswell Pl EC1 ....234 D1
Goswell Rd
EC1 ....94 D4 234 D2
Gothic Ct 17 SE5 ....139 A5
Harlington UB3 ....127 B6
Gothic Rd TW2 ....152 B2
Gottfried Mews NW5 .71 C4
Goudhurst Ho 10
SE20 ....184 C3
Goudhurst Rd BR1 ..186 D5
Gough Ho N1 ....234 D6
4 Kingston KT1 ....176 A1
Gough Rd E15 ....76 D4
Enfield EN1 ....6 B3
Gough Sq EC4 .94 C1 241 B2
Gough St WC1 94 B3 240 D5
Gough Wlk 10 E14 ....97 C1
Gould Ct SE19 ....183 C5
Goulden Ho SW11 ...136 C3
Goulding Ct N8 ....50 B5
Goulding Gdns CR7 ..183 A1
Gouldman Ho 30 E1 ..96 C3
Gould Rd
East Bedfont TW14 ....149 C4
Twickenham TW2 ....152 C3
Gould's Gn UB8 ....104 D6
Gould Terr 26 E8 ....74 B3
Goulston St
E1 ....95 D1 243 C2
Goulton Rd E5 ....74 B4
Gourley Pl N15 ....51 C4
Gourley St N15 ....51 C4
Gourock Rd SE9 ....166 C6
Govan St E2 ....96 A6
Gover Ct 8 SW4 ....138 A3
Government Row EN3 ..7 C6
Govett Ave TW17 ....193 A4
Govier Cl E15 ....76 C1
Gowan Ave
SW6 ....135 A4 264 A2
Gowan Ho 22 E2 ....95 D4
Gowan Lea 4 E18 ....55 A5
Gowan Rd NW10 ....68 B2
Gower Cl SW4 ....159 C5
Gower Ct WC1 ....239 C6
Gower Ho 12 E17 ....53 D6
SE17 ....262 B2
Barking IG11 ....79 A1
Hayes UB3 ....105 C6
Upper Tooting SW17 ....180 B4
Gower House Sch
NW9 ....67 A6
Gower Mews WC1 ..239 D4
Gower Pl NW1,
WC1 ....93 D3 239 C6
Gower Rd E7 ....77 A2
Hounslow TW7 ....130 D6
Gower St WC1 93 D3 239 C5
Gower's Wlk E1 ....96 A1
Gowland Pl BR3 ....185 B1
Gowlett Rd SE15 ....140 A2
Gowrie Rd SW11 ....137 A2
Graburn Way KT8 ....196 B6
Grace Ave DA7 ....147 B3
Grace Bsns Ctr CR4 .202 D3
Gracechurch St EC2,
EC4 ....252 D6
Grace Cl HA8 ....27 A3
SE9 ....165 D1
Gracedale Rd SW16 .181 B5
Gracefield Gdns
SW16 ....160 A1
Gracehill 2 E1 ....96 C2
Grace Ho SE11 ....270 D6
Penge SE26 ....184 B5
Grace Jones Cl E8 ....74 A2
Grace Path SE26 ....184 C6
Grace Pl E3 ....97 D4
Grace Rd CR0 ....205 A3
Graces Mews NW8 ..229 B3
Grace's Mews SE5 ...139 C3
Grace's Rd SE5 ....139 C3
Grace St E3 ....97 D4
Gradient The SE26 ...184 A6
Graeme Rd EN1 ....5 C3
Graemesdyke Ave
SW14 ....132 D1
Grafton Cl Ealing W13 .87 A1
Twickenham TW4 ....151 B3
Worcester Park KT4 ..215 C5
Grafton Cres NW1 ....71 B2
Grafton Ct 10 E8 ....74 A3
East Bedfont TW14 ....149 B3
Grafton Gdns N4 ....51 A3
Dagenham RM8 ....81 A6
Grafton Ho 15 E3 ....97 C4
12 SE8 ....119 B1
Grafton Inf Sch RM8 ..81 B6
Grafton Jun Sch RM8 .81 B6
Grafton Mews W1 ..239 A5
Grafton Park Rd KT4 215 C6
Grafton Pl
NW1 ....93 D3 232 D1
Grafton Prim Sch N7 .72 A5
Grafton Rd NW5 ....71 A3
W3 ....111 A6
Dagenham RM8 ....81 A6
Enfield EN2 ....4 B2
Harrow HA1 ....42 A4
Kingston KT3 ....199 C6
Thornton Heath CR0 ...204 C1
Worcester Park KT4 ..215 C5
Grafton Sq SW4 ....137 C2
Grafton St
W1 ....115 B6 248 D5
Grafton Terr NW5 ....71 A3
Grafton Way W1 ....239 B5
East Molesey KT8 ....195 B5
Grafton Yd NW5 ....71 B2
Graham Ave W13 ....109 B4
Mitcham CR4 ....181 A2
Graham Cl CR0 ....223 C6
Graham Ct BR1 ....187 B3
5 SE14 ....140 D6
Northolt UB5 ....63 B3
Grahame Park Way
NW7,NW9 ....27 D2
Grahame White Ho
HA3 ....43 D6
Graham Gdns KT6 ...198 A1
Graham Ho 7 N19 ...71 D4
N9 ....18 C3
5 Balham SW12 ....159 B4
Woolwich SE18 ....144 D5
Graham Lo NW4 ....46 B3
Graham Mans 2 E8 ..74 B2
11 Barking IG11 ....80 A1
Graham Rd DA7 ....147 C1
E13 ....99 A3
E8 ....74 A2
N15 ....50 D6
NW4 ....46 B3
W4 ....111 B3
Hampton TW12 ....173 C6
Harrow HA3 ....42 C6
Merton SW19 ....179 B3
Mitcham CR4 ....181 A2
Graham St N1 94 D5 234 D3
Graham Terr
SW1 ....115 A2 258 B3
Grainger Cl UB5 ....64 A3
Grainger Ct 22 SE5 ....139 A5
Grainger Rd
Isleworth TW7 ....130 D3
Tottenham N22 ....33 A2
Gramer Cl E11 ....76 B6
Grampian Cl BR6 ...211 D3
Harlington UB3 ....127 B5
15 Sutton SM2 ....218 A1
Grampian Gdns NW2 .47 A1
Grampians The 10
W14 ....112 D4
Granada St SW17 ...180 D5
Granard Ave SW15 ...156 B6
Granard Bsns Ctr
NW7 ....27 C4
Granard Ho 20 E9 ....74 D2
Granard Prim Sch
SW15 ....156 B5
Granard Rd SW11,
SW12 ....158 D4
Granary Cl N9 ....18 C4
Granary Ct 3 RM6 ....58 D2
Granary Rd E1 ....96 B3
Granary St
NW1 ....93 D6 232 C5
Granby Ho 14 SE18 ..122 B2
Granby Pl SE1 ....251 A1
Granby Rd SE18 ....122 D3
SE9 ....144 B2
Granby St E2 ..96 A3 243 D6
Granby Terr
NW1 ....93 C5 232 A3
Grand Arc N12 ....30 A5
Grand Ave EC1 ....241 D4
N10 ....49 A5
Tolworth KT5 ....198 D3
Wembley HA9 ....66 C3
Grand Ave E HA9 ....66 D3
Grand Avenue Prim Sch
KT5 ....199 A3
Grand Ct RM8 ....81 A5
Grand Depot Rd
SE18 ....122 C1
Grand Dr Southall UB2 108 A4
West Barnes SM4,
SW20 ....200 C5
Granden Rd SW16 ...182 A1
Grandfield Ct W4 ...133 B6
Grandison Rd SW11 .158 D6
North Cheam KT4 ....216 C5
Grand Junction Wharf
N1 ....235 A3
Grand Par N4 ....50 D3
Mortlake SW14 ....133 A1
Tolworth KT6 ....198 C1
Wembley HA9 ....66 C6
Grand Union Cl W9 ...91 B2
Grand Union Cres E8 .96 A6
Grand Union Ind Est
NW10 ....88 D5
Grand Union Way
UB2 ....107 C4
Grand Vitesse Ind Est
SE1 ....251 D3
Granfield St SW11 ...266 D1
Grange Ave N12 ....30 A5
Barnet N20 ....13 A4
Barnet, London EN4 ....14 D3
South Norwood SE25 ..183 C1
Stanmore HA7 ....25 C1
Twickenham TW2 ....152 C2
Woodford IG8 ....37 A3
Grange Cl DA15 ....168 A1
HA8 ....27 A5
East Molesey KT8 ....195 D5
Hayes UB3 ....83 C2
Heston TW5 ....129 B6
Woodford IG8 ....37 A3
Grangecliffe Gdns
SE25 ....183 C1
Grangecourt Rd N16 ..51 C1
Grange Cres SE28 ...102 C1
Grange Ct SE15 ....139 D3
WC2 ....240 D1
Belmont SM2 ....217 D1
Hackbridge SM6 ....219 B5
Littleton TW17 ....192 C5
Loughton IG10 ....21 D6
Northolt UB5 ....84 C5
Pinner HA5 ....41 A6
Harrow HA1 ....64 D5
Grange Dr BR7 ....188 B4
Grange Farm Cl HA2 ..64 A6
Grange Farm Cvn Pk
TW17 ....193 C6
Grangefield NW1 ....72 A1
Grange Fst & Mid Schs
HA2 ....41 D1
Grange Gdns N14 ....15 D3
NW3 ....69 D5
Pinner HA5 ....41 A5
South Norwood SE25 ..183 C1
Grange Gr N1 ....73 A2
Grange Hill HA8 ....27 A5
South Norwood SE25 ..183 C1
Grangehill Pl SE9 ...144 B2
Grangehill Rd SE9 ...144 B1
Grange Ho NW10 ....68 B1
Grange Ho *continued*
SE1 ....263 C5
6 Barking IG11 ....101 B6
Grange Inf Sch E13 ...98 D4
Grange La SE21 ....161 D2
Grange Lo SW19 ....178 D4
Grange Mans KT17 ..215 D1
Grangemill 11 NW5 ...71 B4
Grangemill Rd SE6 ..163 C2
Grange Mills SW12 ..159 C3
Grangemill Way SE6 .163 C2
Grange Mus of Community
History The★ NW10 ..67 C4
Grange Park Ave N21 .17 A5
Grange Park Jun & Inf
Schs UB4 ....83 D3
Grange Park Pl
SW20 ....178 B3
Grange Park Prep Sch
N21 ....16 D5
Grange Park Rd E10 ..53 D1
South Norwood CR7 ...205 B6
Grange Park Sta N21 .16 D5
Grange Pk W5 ....110 A5
Grange Pl NW6 ....69 C1
Grange Prim Sch
SE1 ....117 C3 263 A5
W5 ....109 D4
Grange Rd E10 ....53 C1
E13 ....98 D4
E17 ....53 A4
HA8 ....27 B4
N6 ....49 A3
NW10 ....68 B2
SE1 ....117 D3 263 C5
W4 ....110 D1
Barnes SW13 ....134 A4
Belmont SM2 ....217 C1
Borehamwood WD6 ....10 B6
Chessington KT9 ....214 A4
Ealing W5 ....110 A5
East Molesey KT8 ....195 D5
Harrow HA1 ....43 A4
Harrow HA2 ....64 B6
Hayes UB3 ....83 C1
Ilford IG1 ....79 A4
Kingston KT1 ....198 A6
Orpington BR6 ....227 A6
Southall UB1 ....107 A4
South Norwood SE19,
SE25 ....183 B1
Tottenham N17 ....34 A4
Grange St N1 ....235 D5
Grange The 3 E17 ....53 A4
19 NW3 ....70 D2
SE1 ....117 D3 263 C5
W12 ....112 B3
W14 ....113 B2 254 C3
W3 ....110 D4
7 W4 ....110 D1
Cockfosters EN4 ....2 D2
Croydon CR0 ....223 B6
Ealing W13 ....87 C2
3 Wanstead E18 ....55 A6
Wembley HA0 ....66 C1
West Barnes KT3 ....200 A4
West Ewell KT19 ....215 B4
Wimbledon SW19 ....178 D4
Grange The(Eltham Coll
Jun Sch) SE9 ....165 D3
Grange Vale SM2 ...217 D1
Grangeview Rd N20 ..14 A3
Grangeway N12 ....29 D6
NW6 ....69 C1
Woodford IG8 ....37 C6
Grangeway Gdns IG4 .56 A4
Grangeway The N21 ..16 D5
Grange Wlk
SE1 ....117 D3 263 C5
Grangewood DA5 ...169 B3
Grangewood Cl HA5 ..40 A4
Grangewood Ind Sch
E7 ....77 D1
Grangewood La BR3 .185 B4
Grangewood Sch HA5 39 D4
Grangewood St E6 ...99 D6
Grange Yd
SE1 ....117 D3 263 C5
Granham Gdns N9 ....17 D2
Granite St SE18 ....123 D1
Granleigh Rd E11 ....76 C6
Gransden Ave E8 ....74 B1
Gransden Ho 1 SE8 .119 B1
Gransden Rd W12 ...111 D4
Grantbridge St
N1 ....94 D5 234 D4
Grantchester 12 KT1 .176 C1
Grantchester Cl HA1 ..64 D5
Grant Cl N14 ....15 C4
Shepperton TW17 ....192 D3
Grant Ct 11 NW9 ....27 D1
2 Chingford E4 ....20 A3
Grantham Cl HA8 ....10 A1
Grantham Ct 9 SE16 118 D4
Dagenham RM6 ....59 B2
Grantham Gdns RM6 ..59 B2
Grantham Gn WD6 ....11 A6
Grantham Ho
12 SE15 ....140 A6
Ashford TW16 ....171 C3
Grantham Pl W1 ....248 C3
Grantham Rd SW9 ...138 A3
Chiswick W4 ....133 C5
Little Ilford E12 ....78 C4
Grant Ho 38 SW8 ....137 D3
Grantley Ho 2 SE14 .140 D6
5 Putney SW19 ....156 D3
Grantley Pl KT10 ....212 A3
Grantley Rd TW4,TW5 128 C3
Grantley St E1 ....96 D3
Grantock Rd E17 ....36 B2
Granton Prim Sch
SW16 ....181 C3
Granton Rd Ilford IG3 .58 A1
Sidcup DA14 ....190 C4
Streatham SW16 ....181 C2
Grant Pl 2 CR0 ....205 D1
Grant Rd SW11 ....136 C2
Croydon CR0 ....205 D1
Harrow HA3 ....42 D6
Grants Cl NW7 ....28 D3
Grants Cotts KT10 ...212 B6
Grant St E13 ....99 A4
N1 ....234 A4
Grantully Rd W9 ....91 D4
Grant Way TW7 ....131 A6
Granville Ave N9 ....18 C1
Feltham TW13 ....150 A2
Hounslow TW3,TW4 ....151 C6
Granville Cl CR0 ....221 C6
Granville Ct N1 ....235 D6
N4 ....50 B3
8 SE14 ....141 A5
Granville Gdns
Ealing W5 ....110 B5
South Norwood SW16 .182 B3
Granville Gr SE13 ....142 A2
Granville Ho 13 E14 ...97 C1
Granville Mans
8 W12 ....112 C4
WC1 ....240 A6
Granville Mews
Sidcup DA14 ....190 A6
Stanmore HA7 ....25 A5
Granville Pk SE13 ...142 B2
Granville Pl N12 ....30 A3
SW6 ....265 C3
W1 ....93 A1 238 A1
Pinner HA5 ....40 D6
Granville Point NW2 ..69 B6
Granville Rd E17 ....53 D3
N12 ....30 A3
N4,N8 ....50 B3
NW2 ....69 B6
NW6 ....91 C5
Bexley DA16 ....146 C2
Bowes Park N13 ....32 B4
Hayes UB3 ....105 D2
Hillingdon UB10 ....60 D2
Ilford IG1 ....78 D6
Merton SW19 ....179 C3
Sidcup DA14 ....190 B6
Tottenham N22 ....32 D2
Wandsworth SW18 ....157 B4
Woodford E18 ....37 B1
Granville Sq 8 SE15 .139 C5
WC1 ....94 B4 233 D1
Granville St WC1 ....233 D1
Granwood Ct 5 TW7 130 C4
Grape St WC2 ....240 A2
Grapsome Cl KT9 ....213 C1
Grasdene Rd SE18,
SE2 ....146 A5
Grasmere NW1 ....231 D1
Grasmere Ave BR6 ...226 D5
W3 ....111 B6
Kingston SW15 ....177 C6
Merton SW19 ....201 C6
Ruislip HA4 ....39 A2
Twickenham TW3 ....151 D5
Wembley HA9 ....43 D1
Grasmere Cl TW14 ...149 D3
Grasmere Ct
Barnes SW13 ....134 A6
Bowes Park N22 ....32 B4
Forest Hill SE26 ....184 A5
Grasmere Gdns BR6 .226 D5
Harrow HA3 ....25 A1
Redbridge IG4 ....56 B4
Grasmere Ho 19 N16 ..73 B4
Grasmere JMI Sch
N16 ....73 B4
Grasmere Point 2
SE15 ....140 C5
Grasmere Rd BR6 ...226 D5
3 E13 ....99 A5
N10 ....31 B2
Bromley BR1 ....186 D3
Croydon SE25 ....206 B4
Streatham SW16 ....182 B5
Tottenham N17 ....34 A4
Grasshaven Way
SE28 ....123 D5
Grassington Cl N11 ...31 A4
Grassington Rd DA14 190 A6
Grassmere Ct 6 EN1 .17 C6
Grassmount SE23 ....162 B2
Grass Pk N3 ....29 B2
Grassway SM6 ....219 C4
Grasvenor Ave EN5 ...13 C5
Grasvenor Avenue Inf Sch
EN5 ....13 C5
Grately Ho 10 SW15 .156 B3
Gratton Rd
W14 ....113 A3 254 A5
Gratton Terr NW2 ....68 D5
Graveley 16 KT1 ....176 C1
Graveley Ave WD6 ...11 A6
Graveley Ho 7 SE8 ..119 A2
Gravel Hill DA6 ....169 D6
N3 ....29 B1
South Croydon CR0,CR2 223 B1
Gravel Hill Cl DA5,
DA6 ....169 D5
Gravel Hill Prim Sch
DA6 ....169 D6
Gravel Hill Sta CR0 ..223 A2
Gravel La E1 ..95 D1 243 C2
Gravel Rd BR2 ....226 A6
Twickenham TW2 ....152 C3
Gravelwood Cl BR7 ..167 A1
Gravenel Gdns 5
SW17 ....180 C5
Graveney Gr SE20 ...184 C3
Graveney Rd SW17 ..180 C6
Graveney Sch SW17 ..181 B5
Gravesend Rd W12 ..112 A6
Graves Est DA16 ....146 B3
Gray Ave RM8 ....59 B1
Gray Ct 8 KT2 ....175 D6
Grayfriars Pas EC1 ..241 D2
Grayham Cres KT3 ...199 B5
Grayham Rd KT3 ....199 B5
Gray Ho SE17 ....262 B2
Grayland Cl BR1 ....187 D2
Grayland Ct WC1 ...233 C1
Grayling Cl E16 ....98 C3
Grayling Ct N17 ....52 B5
Ealing W5 ....109 D5
Grayling Rd N16 ....73 B6
Grayling Sq E2 ....96 A4
Grays Cotts UB9 ....38 C1
Grayscroft Rd SW16 .181 D3
Grays Farm Prim Sch
BR5 ....190 B2
Grays Farm Production
Village BR5 ....190 B2
Grays Farm Rd BR5 ..190 B2
Grayshott Rd SW11 ..137 A2
Gray's Inn★
WC1 ....94 B2 240 D4
Gray's Inn Pl WC1 ...240 D3
Gray's Inn Rd
WC1 ....94 B3 240 D6
Gray's Inn Sq
WC1 ....94 C2 241 A4
Grays La TW15 ....170 D6
Grayson Ho EC1 ....235 B1
Gray's Rd UB10 ....60 A1
Gray St SE1 ..116 C4 251 B1
Grayswood Gdns
SW20 ....178 B1
Grayswood Point 14
SW15 ....156 A3
Gray's Yd W1 ....238 B2
Graywood Ct N12 ....30 A3
Grazebrook Prim Sch
N16 ....73 C6
Grazebrook Rd N16 ..73 B6
Grazeley Ct SE19 ...183 C5
Great Arthur Ho EC1 .242 A5
Great Bell Alley EC2 .242 C2
Great Benty UB7 ....104 A2
Great Brownings
SE21 ....183 D6
Great Bushey Dr N20 .13 D3

Great Cambridge Ind Est
EN1 ....18 B6
Great Cambridge Junction
N13,N18 ....33 B6
Great Cambridge Rd
Edmonton N9,N18 ...17 C3
Enfield EN1 ....6 A3
Great Castle St W1 .**239** A2
Great Central Ave
HA4 ....62 C3
Great Central St
NW1 ....**92** D2 **237** C4
Great Central Way
NW10 ....67 B4
Great Chapel St
W1 ....**93** D1 **239** C2
Great Chertsey Rd
Chiswick SW14,W4 ..133 B4
Feltham TW13,TW2 ...151 C1
Great Church La W6 .112 D1
Great College St
SW1 ....**116** A3 **260** A6
Great Croft WC1 ....**233** B1
Great Cumberland Mews
W1 ....**237** C1
Great Cumberland Pl
W1 ....**92** D1 **237** D1
Great Dover St
SE1 ....**117** B3 **262** C6
Greatdown Rd W7 ....86 D2
Great Eastern Bldgs 🔟
E8 ....74 B2
Great Eastern Ent Ctr
E14 ....119 D4
Great Eastern Pier
E14 ....119 C1
Great Eastern Rd E15 .76 B2
Great Eastern St
EC2 ....**95** C3 **243** A6
Great Eastern Wharf
SW11 ....**267** B3
Great Elms Rd BR2 ..**209** C5
Great Field 🔽 NW5 ...71 C3
NW9 ....27 D2
Greatfield Ave E6 ..100 B3
Greatfield Cl 🔽 N19 ..71 A4
SE4 ....141 C1
Greatfields Dr UB8 ...82 C2
Greatfields Rd IG11 .101 B5
Great Fleete Way
IG11 ....102 C5
Great Galley Cl IG11 .102 C4
Great Gatton Cl CR0 .**207** A2
Great George St
SW1 ....**116** A4 **250** A1
Great Guildford St
SE1 ....**117** A5 **252** A3
Great Guilford Bsns Sq
SE1 ....**252** A3
Greatham Wlk 🔽
SW15 ....156 A3
Great Harry Dr SE9 .166 C1
Great James St WC1 .**240** C4
Great Marlborough St
W1 ....**93** C1 **239** A1
Great Mathers Rd
SE11 ....**261** C4
Great Maze Pond
SE1 ....**117** B4 **252** D2
Great Newport St
WC2 ....**250** A6
Great New St
EC4 ....**94** C1 **241** B2
Great North Rd N2 ..48 C5
Barnet EN5 ....1 A2
New Barnet EN5 .....13 A4
**Great North Way (Barnet
By-Pass)** NW4 ....46 D6
Greatorex Ho 🔽 E1 ..96 A2
Greatorex St E1 .....96 A2
Great Ormond St
WC1 ....**94** B3 **240** C5
Great Ormond St Hospl for
Children WC1 94 B3 **240** C5
Great Percy St
WC1 ....**94** C4 **234** A2
Great Peter St
SW1 ....**115** D3 **259** D5
Great Portland St
W1 ....**93** B2 **238** D4
Great Portland Street Sta
W1 ....**93** B3 **238** D5
Great Pulteney St
W1 ....**249** B6
Great Queen St
WC2 ....**94** A1 **240** B2

Great Russell St
WC1 ....**94** A2 **240** A3
Great Scotland Yd
SW1,WC2 ....**116** A5 **250** A4
Great Smith St
SW1 ....**115** D3 **259** D6
Great South West Rd
TW6,TW14,TW4 ....126 B4
Great South-West Rd
TW5 ....128 B2
Great Spilmans SE22 161 C6
Great St Helen's EC3 .**243** A2
Greatstone Ho 🔽
SE20 ....184 C3
Great Strand NW9 ....27 D1
Great St Thomas Apostle
EC4 ....**252** B6
Great Suffolk St
SE1 ....**116** D4 **251** D8
Great Sutton St
EC1 ....**94** D3 **241** D5
Great Swan Alley
EC2 ....**242** C2
Great Thrift BR5 ....**211** A5
Great Titchfield St
W1 ....**93** C2 **239** A3
Great Tower St
EC3 ....**117** C6 **253** A6
Great Trinity La EC4 .**252** B6
Great Turnstile WC2 .**240** D3
Great Western Ind Pk
UB2 ....108 A4
Great Western Rd W2,
W9 ....91 B2
Great West Rd
Brentford TW7,TW8 ..131 A5
Chiswick W4,W6 ....133 B6
Heston TW5,TW7 ....129 A5
Hounslow TW5 .....129 A5
Hounslow TW5,TW7 ..130 B5
**Great West Road Cedars
Rd** W4 ....133 A6
**Great West Road Hogarth
La** W4 ....133 C6
Great West Trad Est
TW8 ....131 B6
Great Winchester St
EC2 ....**95** B1 **242** D2
Great Windmill St
W1 ....**115** D6 **249** C6
Greatwood BR7 .....188 C3
Great Yd SE1 ....**253** B2
Greaves Cl IG11 .....**79** C1
Greaves Cotts 🔽 E14 .97 A2
Greaves Pl SW17 ...180 C6
Greaves Twr SW10 ..**266** B4
Grebe 🔽 NW9 ......27 D1
Grebe Ave UB4 ......84 D1
Grebe Cl E17 ....35 A3
E7 ....76 D3
Barking IG11 ......102 A3
Cheam SM1 ....217 B3
Grebe Ct 🔽 E14 ....120 A4
Cheam SM1 ....217 B3
Grebe Terr 🔽 KT1 ..198 A6
Grecian Cres SE19 ..182 D4
Greek Ct W1 ....**239** D1
Greek St W1 .93 D1 **239** D1
Greenacre Cl Barnet EN5 1 B5
Northolt UB5 ....63 B3
Greenacre Ct E8 .....74 A3
Greenacre Gdns E17 .54 A5
Greenacre Pl SM6 ...219 B6
Greenacres N3 ......29 A1
SE9 ....166 C6
Green Acres DA14 ..189 D6
Greenacres WD23 ....8 B2
Green Acres CR0 ...221 D5
Greenacres Ave UB10 .60 C5
Greenacres Cl BR6 ..227 A4
Greenacres Dr HA7 ..25 B3
Greenacres Prim Sch
SE9 ....166 C6
Greenacre Sq 🔽
SE16 ....118 D4
Greenacre Wlk N14 ..15 D2
Green Arbour Ct EC1 **241** C2
Green Ave NW7 ......27 C6
W13 ....109 B3
Greenaway Gdns NW3 69 D4
Greenaway Ho NW8 .**229** A6
WC1 ....**234** A1
Greenaway Terr
TW19 ....148 A3
Green Bank E1 ......118 B5
N12 ....29 D5
Greenbank Ave HA0 ..65 A4
Greenbank Cl E4 .....20 C2
Greenbank Cres NW4 .47 A5
Greenbank Lo 🔽
BR7 ....188 C2

Greenbanks HA1 .....64 C4
Greenbay Rd SE7 ...143 D5
Greenberry St NW8 .**230** A3
Greenbrook Ave EN4 ..2 A4
Green CE Prim Sch The
N17 ....51 D6
Green CE Sch Holy Trinity
(Infants' Annexe) The
N15 ....51 D5
Green Cl NW11 ......48 A2
NW9 ....45 A3
Beckenham BR2 ....208 C6
Carshalton SM5 ....218 D6
Feltham TW13 .....173 A5
Greencoat Ho 🔽 KT1 176 A1
SE20 ....184 C3
Greencoat Pl
SW1 ....**115** C2 **259** B4
Greencoat Row SW1 .**259** B5
Greencourt Ave CR0 ..26 D2
Green Court Ave CR0 222 B6
Green Court Gdns
CR0 ....222 B6
Greencourt Ho E1 ....96 D3
Greencourt Rd BR5 ..211 C4
Greencroft HA8 ......27 A5
Greencroft Ave HA4 ..62 C6
Greencroft Cl E16 ....99 D2
Greencroft Gdns NW6 .70 A1
Enfield EN1 ....5 C2
Greencroft Rd TW5 ..129 B4
Greendale NW7 ......27 C6
Green Dale SE22 ....161 C6
Greendale Cl SE22 ..161 C6
Greendale Ct CR2 ...221 A2
Green Dr UB1 ......107 C5
Green Dragon Ct
SE1 ....**252** C3
Green Dragon Ho
WC1 ....**240** B2
Green Dragon Jun & Inf
Sch TW8 ....132 A6
Green Dragon La
Brentford TW8 .....110 B1
Southgate N21 .....16 D5
Green Dragon Yd 🔽
E1 ....96 A2
Greene Ct 🔽 SE14 ..140 D6
Greene Ho SE1 ......**262** C5
Green Elms IG6 ......57 A6
Green End
Chessington KT9 ....214 A4
Edmonton N21 ......16 D2
Greenend Rd W4 ....111 C4
Greener Ho 🔽 SW4 .137 D2
Green Farm Cl BR6 ..227 D3
Greenfell Mans SE8 .141 D6
Greenfield Ave KT5 ..198 D3
Greenfield Dr BR1 ...187 C1
N2 ....48 D5
Greenfield Gdns BR5 211 A3
NW2 ....69 A5
Dagenham RM9 .....102 D6
Greenfield Ho 🔽
SW19 ....156 D3
Greenfield Rd E1 .....96 A1
N15 ....51 D4
Dagenham RM9 .....102 C6
Greenfields UB1 .....85 C1
Greenfields JMI Sch
WD19 ....22 C5
Greenfields Sch N10 ..30 D2
Greenfield Way HA2 ..41 D6
Greenford Ave
Ealing W7 ....86 C1
Southall UB1 ......107 B6
Greenford High Sch
UB6 ....85 C4
Greenford Ind Est
UB6 ....85 D6
Greenford Rdbt UB6 ..86 B5
Greenford Sta UB6 ....86 B6
Greengate UB6 ......65 B2
Greengate St E13 ....99 B4
Green Gdns BR6 ....227 A4
Greenhalgh Wlk N2 ..48 A5
Greenham Cl SE1 ...**251** A1
Greenham Cres E4 ...35 B4
Greenham Ho 🔽 E9 ..96 C6
Isleworth TW7 .....130 B4
Greenham Rd N10 ...31 A1
Greenhaven Dr SE28 .102 B1
Greenheath Bsns Ctr 🔽
E2 ....96 B3

Green Hedges 🔽
TW1 ....153 C5
Greenheys Dr E18 ....54 D6
Greenhill HA9 ....66 D6
NW3 ....70 B4
Buckhurst Hill IG9 ...21 C3
Sutton SM1 ....218 A6
Green Hill SE18 .....122 B1
Greenhill Cts SE7 ...122 B1
Greenhill Gdns UB5 ..85 B5
Greenhill Gr E12 .....78 A4
Greenhill Par EN5 ...13 D6
New Barnet EN5 ....13 D6
Greenhill Pk NW10 ..89 C6
Greenhill Rd NW10 ..89 C6
Harrow HA1 ....42 C3
Greenhill's Rents
EC1 ....**241** C4
Greenhills Terr 🔽 N1 .73 B2
Greenhill Terr
Northolt UB5 ....85 B5
Woolwich SE18 .....122 B1
Greenhill Way HA9 ..66 D6
Harrow HA1 ....42 C3
Greenhithe Cl SE9 ..167 C4
Greenholm Rd SE9 ..166 D6
Green Ho The 🔽
SW19 ....157 A3
Green Hundred Rd
SE15 ....140 A6
Greenhurst Rd SE27 .182 C5
Greening St SE2 ....124 C2
Green La NW4 ....46 D4
SE9 ....166 D1
W7 ....108 C4
Ashford TW16 .....171 D4
Chessington KT9 ...214 A1
Dagenham RM8 .....81 B6
East Molesey KT8 ..195 D4
Edgware HA8 ......26 C5
Feltham TW13 .....173 A5
Hillingdon UB8 .....83 A2
Hounslow TW4 .....128 C1
Ilford IG1 ....79 C6
Ilford IG3 ....79 C6
Morden SM4 ......201 D3
New Malden KT3 ...199 A4
New Malden KT4 ...200 A1
Penge SE20 ......184 D3
Shepperton TW17 ..193 A4
South Norwood CR7,
SW16 ....182 C2
Stanmore HA7 .....25 B5
Greenland Cres UB2 .106 D3
Greenland Ho 🔽 E1 ..97 A3
SE8 ....118 D1
Greenland Mews
SE8 ....118 D1
Greenland Pl NW1 ..**231** D6
Greenland Quay
SE16 ....118 D2
Greenland Rd
NW1 ....**93** C6 **232** A6
Barnet EN5 ....12 C5
Greenland St NW1 ..**231** D6
Green Lane Bsns Pk
SE9 ....166 C2
Green Lane Cotts HA7 25 B6
Green Lane Gdns
CR7 ....183 A1
Green Lane Mews
SM4 ....201 D3
Green Lane Prim Sch
KT4 ....200 B2
Green Lanes
N4,N8,N15 ....50 D2
Palmers Green N13 ..16 C1
West Ewell KT19 ...215 C1
Greenlaw Ct W5 .....87 D1
Greenlaw Gdns KT3 .199 D2
Greenlawns N12 .....29 D4
Green Lawns
🔽 HA4 ....122 C2
Ruislip HA4 ....40 C1
Greenlaw St SE18 ..122 C3
Green Leaf Ave SM6 .219 D4
Greenleaf Cl 🔽 SW2 .160 C4
Greenleafe Dr IG6 ...56 C6
Greenleaf Prim Sch
E17 ....53 B6
Greenleaf Rd E17 ....53 B6
🔽 E6 ....99 C6
Greenlea Pk SW19 ..180 C2
Green Leas
Ashford TW16 .....171 D4
Kingston KT1 ......198 A6
Green Leas Cl TW16 .171 D4

Greenleaves Ct
TW15 ....170 D4
Green Man Gdns
W13 ....109 A6
Green Man Intc E11 ..54 D2
Green Man La
Ealing W13 ....109 A5
Hatton TW14 ......128 A1
Greenman St
N1 ....**95** A6 **235** A6
Greenmead Cl SE25 .**206** A4
Greenmead Sch
SW15 ....156 B6
Green Moor Link N21 .16 D4
Greenmoor Rd EN3 ...6 C3
Greenoak Pl EN4 .....2 D3
Green Oaks UB2 ....106 D2
Greenoak Way SW19 178 C6
Greenock Rd 🔽 W3 .111 A3
Mitcham SW16 .....181 D2
Greeno Cres TW17 ..192 C4
Green Park★
SW1,W1 .....**115** B4 **248** D2
Green Park Sta
W1 ....**115** C5 **249** A4
Green Pond Cl E17 ...53 B6
Green Pond Rd E17 ..53 B6
Green Pt E15 ....76 C2
Green Rd N20 ....14 A1
East Barnet N14 ....15 B5
Green Ride IG10,E4 ..21 A1
Green Sch for Girls The
TW7 ....131 A4
Greens Cl W1 ......**249** C6
Green's Ct W11 ....**244** C3
Greens Ct HA9 .....65 D5
Greens End SE18 ...122 C1
Greenshank Cl E17 ..35 A3
Greenshields Ind Est
E16 ....121 B5
Greenside DA5 .....169 A3
Greenside Cl N20 ....14 B2
Catford SE6 ....164 C1
Greenside Prim Sch
W12 ....112 A4
Greenside Rd W12 ..112 A4
Thornton Heath CR0 .204 C3
Greenslade Prim Sch
SE18 ....145 B6
Greenslade Rd IG11 .79 B1
Greensleeves Ho
UB2 ....107 D2
Greensleeves Manor
SM2 ....217 D2
Green St E13 ....99 C6
E7 ....77 C1
W1 ....**115** A6 **248** A6
Enfield EN3 ....6 D3
Sunbury TW16 .....172 A1
Greenstead Ave IG8 ..37 C4
Greenstead Cl IG8 ...37 C4
Greenstead Gdns
Putney SW15 ......156 C6
Woodford IG8 ......37 C4
Greenstone Mews E11 55 A3
Green Street Green Prim
Sch BR6 ....227 D2
Greenstreet Hill SE4 .140 D2
Green Terr EC1 .....**234** B1
Green The BR1 .....165 A1
DA16 ....145 C1
DA7 ....147 A4
E15 ....76 D2
N14 ....15 D1
W3 ....89 C1
Chingford E4 ....20 B3
Claygate KT10 .....212 C4
Ealing W5 ....109 D6
Edmonton N9 ......18 A2
Feltham TW13 .....150 B2
Hackbridge SM6 ...219 A4
Hayes BR2 ....209 A2
Heston TW5 ....129 C6
Kingston KT3 ......177 A1
Merton SM4 ......201 A5
🔽 Richmond TW9 ...153 D6
Sidcup DA14 ......190 A5
Southall UB2 ......107 B4
Southgate N21 .....16 C4
St Paul's Cray BR5 .190 B3
Sutton SM1 ....217 D1
Tottenham N17 .....33 A4
Twickenham TW2 ..152 D2
Uxbridge UB10 .....61 D1
Wallington SM5 ...219 A4
Wanstead E11 .....55 B3
Wembley HA0 ......65 A6

Green The continued
Wimbledon SW19 ...178 D5
Woodford IG8 ......37 A5
Buckhurst Hill IG9 ...21 B3
Green Vale DA6 .....168 D6
Ealing W5 ....88 B1
Greenvale Rd SE9 ...144 C1
Greenvale Specl Sch
SE23 ....163 A1
Green Verges HA7 ...25 D3
Green View KT9 ....214 A1
Greenview Ave CR0 .207 A3
Greenview Cl W3 ...111 A5
Greenview Ct TW15 .170 B6
Greenway N20 ......13 C2
Green Way BR2 ....210 A3
Greenway
Chislehurst BR7 ....188 D5
Dagenham RM8 .....58 C1
Harrow HA3 ....44 A4
Hayes UB4 ....84 B3
Palmers Green N14 ..16 A2
Pinner HA5 ....22 B1
Wallington SM6 ...219 C4
West Barnes SW20 .200 C5
Woodford IG8 ......37 C5
Green Way
Eltham SE9 ....165 D6
Sunbury TW16 .....194 A5
Greenway Ave E17 ...54 B5
Greenway Cl N11 ....31 A4
🔟 N15 ....51 D5
N20 ....13 C2
N4 ....73 A6
NW9 ....27 B1
Greenway Ct
Hayes UB4 ....84 B3
Ilford IG1 ....56 D1
Greenway Gdns NW9 .27 B1
Croydon CR0 ......223 B5
Greenford UB6 .....85 D4
Green Way Gdns HA3 .24 C1
Greenways
Beckenham BR3 ...185 C1
Forest Hill SE26 ...184 C6
Hinchley Wood KT10 .212 C4
Greenways The 🔟
TW1 ....153 A5
Greenway The NW9 ..27 B1
Hounslow TW4 ....129 B1
Pinner HA5 ....41 B3
Uxbridge UB10 .....61 A6
Uxbridge UB8 ......82 A5
Green Way The HA3 ..24 C2
Greenwell St W1 ...**238** D5
Greenwich Academy
SE10 ....141 B6
Greenwich Bsns Ctr
SE10 ....141 D5
Greenwich Bsns Pk
SE10 ....141 D5
Greenwich Church St
SE10 ....142 A6
Greenwich Com Coll
(Charlton Ctr) SE7 .121 D2
Greenwich Cres E6 ..100 A2
Greenwich Ct 🔽 E1 ..96 B1
Greenwich District Hospl
SE10 ....120 D1
Greenwich High Rd
SE10 ....141 D5
Greenwich Hts 🔽
SE18 ....144 A5
Greenwich Ind Est
SE10 ....141 D5
SE7 ....121 B2
Greenwich Mkt 🔟
SE10 ....142 A6
Greenwich Park
SE10 ....142 A5
Greenwich Park Sch
SE10 ....142 A6
Greenwich Park St
SE10 ....142 A5
Greenwich South St
SE10 ....142 A4
Greenwich Sta SE10 .141 D5
Greenwich View E14 .119 D3
Green Wlk NW4 ......46 D4
SE1 ....**263** A5
Hampton TW12 ....173 B4
Ruislip HA4 ....39 D1
Southall UB2 ......107 C4
Green Wlk The E4 ...20 B3
Green Wood NW5 ....71 D2
Greenwood
🔽 Putney SW19 ...156 D4
🔽 Woodford IG8 ...37 A4
Greenwood Ave
Dagenham RM10 ...81 D4

Greenwood Ave continued
Enfield EN3 ....7 A4
Greenwood Cl DA15 .168 A2
Bushey WD23 ....8 C3
Merton SM4 ....201 A5
Orpington BR5,BR6 ..211 C3
Thames Ditton KT7 ..197 A1
Greenwood Dr E4 ....36 B5
Greenwood Gdns N13 16 D1
Greenwood Ho
8 SE4 ....140 D1
WC1 ....234 A1
Wood Green N22 .....32 C2
Greenwood La TW12 173 D5
Greenwood Mans 9
IG11 ....80 A1
Greenwood Pk KT2 ..177 C3
Greenwood Pl NW5 ..71 B3
Greenwood Prim Sch
Mitcham CR4 ....203 D6
Northolt UB5 ....64 A3
Greenwood Rd E13 ..98 D5
E8 ....74 A2
Hinchley Wood KT7 ..213 A6
Isleworth TW7 ....130 D2
Mitcham CR4 ....203 D6
Thornton Heath CR0 .205 A2
Greenwoods The HA2 .64 A5
Greenwood Terr
NW10 ....89 B5
Green Wrythe Cres
SM5 ....202 C1
Green Wrythe La
SM5 ....202 C2
Green Wrythe Prim Sch
SM5 ....202 B3
Green Yd WC1 ....240 D6
Greer Rd HA3 ....24 A2
Greet Ho SE1 ....251 B1
Greet St SE1 ...116 C5 251 B1
Greg Cl E10 ....54 A3
Gregor Mews SE3 ...143 A5
Gregory Cres SE9 ...165 D4
Gregory Ho SE3 ....143 B3
Gregory Pl W8 ......245 C2
Gregory Rd
Dagenham RM6 ......58 D5
Southall UB2 ....107 C3
Greig Cl N8 ....50 A4
Greig Terr SE17 .....138 D6
Grenaby Ave CR0 ...205 B2
Grenaby Rd CR0 ....205 B2
Grenada Ho 18 E14 .119 B6
Grenada Rd SE7 ....143 C5
Grenade St E14 .....119 B6
Grenadier St E16 ...122 C5
Grena Gdns TW9 ...132 B1
Grena Rd TW10,TW9 .132 B1
Grenard Cl SE15 ....140 A4
Grendon Gdns HA9 ..66 C6
Grendon Ho 29 E9 ..74 C1
N1 ....233 C3
Grendon Lo HA8 .....11 A2
Grendon St
NW8 ....92 C3 237 A6
Grenfell Ct NW7 .....28 B4
Grenfell Gdns
Harrow HA3 ....44 A2
Ilford IG2 ....57 D4
Grenfell Ho SE5 ....139 A4
Grenfell Rd W11 ....112 D6
Mitcham CR4,SW17 ..180 D4
Grenfell Twr 5 W11 .112 D6
Grenfell Wlk 4 W11 112 D6
Grengate Lo 2 E13 ..99 B4
Grenell Cl SM1 .....218 B6
Grenell Rd SM1 .....218 A6
Grenoble Gdns N13 ..32 C4
Grenville Cl N3 ......29 B2
Tolworth KT5 ....199 A1
Grenville Ct
Dulwich SE19 ....183 D5
Ealing W13 ....87 B2
Edgware HA8 ....26 D6
Harrow HA1 ....64 C4
Grenville Gdns IG8 ..37 C3
Grenville Ho 24 E3 ..97 A5
4 SE8 ....141 C6
Grenville Lo N6 .....49 C2
Grenville Mews SW7 256 A3
Hampton TW12 ......173 D5
Grenville Pl NW7 ....27 B5
SW7 ....114 A2 256 A4
Grenville Rd N19 ....50 A1
Grenville St WC1 ...240 D1
Gresham Almshouses 3
SW9 ....138 C1
Gresham Ave N20 ...30 D6
Gresham Cl Enfield EN2 .5 A1
Sidcup DA5 ....169 B5

Gresham Coll
EC1 ....94 C2 241 B3
Gresham Ct TW3 ....130 A4
Gresham Dr RM6 .....58 B3
Gresham Gdns NW11 .47 A1
Gresham Ho
2 Teddington TW11 .174 D1
3 Thames Ditton KT7 .197 A2
West Barnes KT3 ....200 B5
Gresham Rd E6 .....100 B5
NW10 ....67 B3
SW9 ....138 C2
Beckenham BR3 .....185 A1
Croydon SE25 ....206 A5
Edgware HA8 ....26 B4
Hampton TW12 ......173 C4
Hillingdon UB10 ......82 C5
Hounslow TW3,TW5 ..130 A4
Newham E16 ....99 B1
Gresham St
EC2 ....95 A1 242 B2
Gresham Way SW19 .157 C1
Gresham Way Est
SW19 ....157 D1
Gresley Cl E17 ......53 A3
N15 ....51 B5
Gresley Ho SW8 ....269 C2
Gresley Rd N19 .....49 C2
Gressenhall Rd SW18 157 A4
Gresse St W1 .93 D1 239 C2
Gresswell Cl DA14 ..168 A1
Greswell St SW6 ...134 D4
Gretton Ho 2 E2 ....96 C4
Gretton Rd N17 .....33 D3
Greville Cl TW1 .....153 B4
Greville Hall NW6 ...91 D5
Greville Ho SW1 ...258 A6
Putney SW15 ....134 D2
Harrow HA2 ....42 B1
Greville Lo 14 N12 ..29 D6
5 W2 ....91 D1
Greville Mews 3 NW6 91 D6
Greville Pl W9 .....91 D5
Greville Rd E17 ....54 A5
NW6 ....91 D5
Richmond TW10 .....154 B5
Greville St EC1 94 C2 241 B4
Grey Coat Hospital CE Sch
The SW1 ...115 D3 259 C5
Grey Coat Hospital St
Michaels The
SW1 ....115 D2 259 C3
Greycoat Pl
SW1 ....115 D3 259 C5
Greycoat St
SW1 ....115 D3 259 C5
Greycot Rd BR3 ....185 C5
Grey Court Sch
TW10 ....153 C1
Grey Eagle St
E1 ....95 D3 243 D5
Greyfell Cl HA7 .....25 B5
Greyfriars 16 SE26 .162 A1
Greyfriars Ho SE3 ..142 C6
Grey Ho 27 W12 ....112 B6
Greyhound Ct WC2 .251 A6
Greyhound Hill NW4 .46 B6
Greyhound La SW16 181 D4
Greyhound Rd N17 ..51 C6
NW10 ....90 B4
W6 ....135 A6 264 A6
Sutton SM1 ....218 A3
Greyhound Terr
SW16 ....181 C2
Greyladies Gdns
SE10 ....142 A3
Greys Park Cl BR2 ..225 D3
Greystead Rd SE23 .162 C4
Greystoke Ave HA5 ..41 C6
Greystoke Ct W5 ....88 B3
Greystoke Dr HA4 ...38 D3
Greystoke Gdns
Ealing W5 ....88 B3
Enfield EN2 ....3 D1
Greystoke Ho SE15 140 A6
Greystoke Lo W5 ....88 B3
Greystoke Park Terr
W5 ....88 A4
Greystoke Pl EC4 ...241 B2
Greystone Gdns HA3 .43 C3
Greyswood St SW16 181 B4
Grey Turner Ho W12 .90 A1
Grice Ct N1 ....73 A2
Grierson Ho SW16 .181 C6
Grierson Rd SE23 ..162 D4
Griffin Cl NW10 ....68 B3
Griffin Ct W12 .....112 B5
8 Brentford TW8 ...132 A6

Griffin Ctr The
Feltham TW14 ......150 B5
Kingston KT1 ....175 D1
Griffin Gate SW15 .134 D2
Griffin Lo N12 ......30 A6
Griffin Manor Way
SE28 ....123 B3
Griffin Park (Brentford FC)
TW8 ....131 D6
Griffin Rd SE18 ....123 B1
Tottenham N17 .....33 C1
Griffin Way
Sunbury TW16 .....172 A1
Woolwich SE28 .....123 C3
Griffith Cl RM8 .....58 C1
Griffiths Cl KT4 ....216 B6
Griffiths Ho 2 SE18 .144 D6
Griffiths Rd SW19 ..179 D3
Grifton Ho 3 SW11 .136 C2
Griggs App IG1 .....79 A6
Grigg's Pl SE1 .....263 B5
Griggs Rd E10 .....54 A3
Grilse Cl N9 ....34 B6
Grimaldi Ho N1 ....233 C4
Grimsby Gr E16 ...122 D5
Grimsby St E2 .....243 D6
7 E2 ....96 A3
Grimsdyke Fst & Mid Sch
HA5 ....23 A4
Grimsdyke Rd HA5 ..23 A3
Grimsel Path SE5 ..138 D5
Grimshaw Cl N6 ....49 A2
Grimston Rd SW6 ..135 B3
Grimthorpe Ho EC1 .241 C6
Grimwade Ave CR0 .222 A5
Grimwade Cl SE15 .140 C2
Grimwood Rd TW1 ..152 D4
Grindall Cl CR0 ....220 D4
Grindall Ho 26 E1 ..96 C4
Grindal St SE1 .....251 B1
Grindleford Ave N11 .15 A2
Grindley Gdns CR0 .205 D3
Grindley Ho 3 E3 ..97 B2
Grinling Gibbons Prim Sch
SE8 ....141 B6
Grinling Ho 6 SE18 .122 C2
Grinling Pl SE8 ....141 C6
Grinstead Rd SE8 ..119 A1
Grisedale NW1 .....232 A2
Grittleton Ave HA9 ..66 D2
Grittleton Rd W9 ...91 C3
Grizedale Terr 8
SE23 ....162 B2
Grocers' Hall Ct EC2 .242 C1
Groombridge Cl
DA16 ....168 A6
Groombridge Ho 1
SE20 ....184 D3
Groombridge Rd E9 .74 D1
Groom Cl BR2 ......209 B6
Groom Cres SW18 .158 B4
Groome Ho SE11 ...260 B4
Groomfield Cl SW17 181 A6
Groom Pl
SW1 ....115 A3 258 B6
Grooms Dr HA5 ....40 A4
Grosmont Rd SE18 .123 D1
Grosse Way SW15 .156 A5
Grosslea SM4 ......202 B4
Grosvenor Ave N5 ..73 A3
Harrow HA2 ....41 D3
Hayes UB4 ....83 D5
Mortlake SW14 .....133 C2
Richmond TW10 .....154 A4
Wallington SM5,SM6 .219 A2
Grosvenor Bridge
SW1 ....137 B6 268 D6
Grosvenor Cotts
SW1 ....258 A5
Grosvenor Cres NW9 .44 C5
SW1 ....115 A4 248 B1
Hillingdon UB10 .....82 D6
Grosvenor Cres Mews
SW1 ....248 A1
Grosvenor Ct E10 ..53 C4
N14 ....15 C4
NW6 ....90 D1
NW7 ....27 B5
W4 ....110 D1
4 Acton W3 ....110 C5
1 Ealing W5 ....110 A6
Morden SM4 ....201 C5
Penge SE19 ....183 D4
Putney SW15 ......157 A6
1 Sutton SM2 .....218 A2
Teddington TW11 ...175 A4
3 Wanstead E11 ..55 B5
2 Wimbledon SW19 .179 A4
Grosvenor Ct Mans
W2 ....237 C1

Grosvenor Gdns E6 ..99 D4
N10 ....49 C6
NW11 ....47 B4
NW2 ....68 C3
SW1 ....115 B3 258 D5
Kingston KT2 ....175 D4
Mortlake SW14 .....133 C2
Southgate N14 .....15 C4
Wallington SM6 .....219 C1
Woodford IG8 ....37 B4
Grosvenor Gdns Mews E
SW1 ....258 D6
Grosvenor Gdns Mews N
SW1 ....258 C5
Grosvenor Gdns Mews S
SW1 ....258 D5
Grosvenor Hill
W1 ....115 B6 248 C6
Wimbledon SW19 ..179 A4
Grosvenor Hill Ct
W1 ....248 C6
Grosvenor Ho E5 ...52 A1
Grosvenor Lo 4 E18 .36 C1
Grosvenor Par 1
W5 ....110 C5
Grosvenor Park SE5 .139 A5
Grosvenor Park Rd
E17 ....53 D4
Grosvenor Pier SW1 .269 C6
Grosvenor Pk SE5 .139 A6
Grosvenor Pl
SW1 ....115 B4 248 C1
Grosvenor Rd DA17 .147 C4
E10 ....54 A1
E6 ....99 D6
E7 ....77 B2
N10 ....31 B2
N3 ....29 C3
SW1 ....137 C6 269 B6
W4 ....111 A1
Bexley DA6 ....169 A6
Brentford TW8 .....131 B6
Croydon SE25 ......206 A5
Dagenham RM8 ....59 B1
Ealing W7 ....109 A6
Edmonton N9 ......18 B3
Hounslow TW3,TW4 .129 C2
Ilford IG1 ....79 A5
Orpington BR5,BR6 ..211 C3
Richmond TW10 .....154 A6
Southall UB2 ....107 B3
Twickenham TW1 ...153 A3
Wallington SM6 ....219 B3
Wanstead E11 .....55 B4
West Wickham BR4 .223 D6
Grosvenor Residences 1
W14 ....112 D3
Grosvenor Rise E E17 .53 D4
Grosvenor Sq
W1 ....115 A6 248 B6
Grosvenor St
W1 ....115 B6 248 C6
Grosvenor Terr SE5 .139 A6
Grosvenor The NW11 .47 D2
Grosvenor Vale HA4 .61 D6
Grosvenor Way E5 ..74 C6
Grosvernor Wharf Rd
E14 ....120 B2
Grote's Bldgs SE3 ..142 C3
Grote's Pl SE3 ....142 C3
Groton Rd SW18 ...157 D2
Grotto Ct SE1 .....252 A2
Grotto Pas W1 ....238 A4
Grotto Rd TW1 ....152 D2
Grove Ave N10 .....31 C1
Cheam SM1,SM2 ..217 C2
Ealing W7 ....86 C1
Finchley N3 ....29 C3
Pinner HA5 ....41 A5
Twickenham TW1 ...152 D3
Grovebury Ct DA6 ..169 D6
Grovebury Rd SE2 .124 D4
Grove Cl BR2 ......225 A4
N14 ....15 B4
Forest Hill SE23 ...163 A3
Ickenham UB10 ....60 C3
Kingston KT1 ......198 B5
Grove Cres NW9 ...45 B5
Feltham TW13 ......173 A6
Kingston KT1 ......198 A6
Walton-on-T KT12 ..194 B2
Woodford IG8 ......36 D1
Grove Crescent Rd
E15 ....76 B2
Grove Ct NW8 .....229 C2
SE5 ....139 C3
SW10 ....256 B1
SW4 ....137 C2

Grove Ct continued
Ealing W5 ....110 A5
East Molesey KT8 ..196 B4
3 Forest Hill SE26 .185 A6
Hounslow TW3 .....129 C1
8 Kingston KT1 ....198 A6
Kingston KT3 ......199 C6
Kingston KT6 ......197 D6
Penge SE20 ....184 B3
Grovedale Rd N19 ..71 D6
Grove Dwellings E1 ..96 C2
Grove End NW5 ....71 B4
Woodford E18 ......36 D1
Grove End Gdns
NW8 ....229 B3
Grove End Ho NW8 229 C1
Grove End La KT10 .196 C1
Grove End Rd
NW8 ....92 B4 229 C1
Grove Farm Ct CR4 .202 D4
Grovefield 1 N11 ..31 B6
Grove Footpath KT5 198 A5
Grove Gdns NW4 ..46 A5
NW8 ....92 C4 230 B1
Enfield EN3 ....6 D5
Teddington TW11 ..175 A6
Grove Green Rd E11 .76 B6
Grove Hall Ct E3 ...97 C5
NW8 ....92 A4 229 B3
Grove Hill Harrow HA1 .42 C2
Woodford E18 ......36 D1
Grove Hill Rd SE5 .139 C2
Harrow HA1 ....42 D2
Grove Ho N3 ....46 D6
SE3 ....142 D3
SW3 ....267 B6
Walton-on-T KT12 ..194 B2
Grove House Rd N8 .50 A5
Grove La SE5 ......139 C2
Hillingdon UB8 .....82 B3
Kingston KT1 ......198 A5
Groveland Ave SW16 .182 B3
Groveland Ct EC4 ..242 B1
Groveland Rd BR3 ..207 B6
Grovelands
East Molesey KT8 ..195 C5
Kingston KT1 ......197 D5
Grovelands Cl SE5 .139 C3
Harrow HA2 ....63 D5
Grovelands Ct N14 ..15 D4
Grovelands Priory (Private
Hospl) N14 ....16 A3
Grovelands Rd BR5 .190 A3
N15 ....52 A3
Palmers Green N13 .16 B1
Grovelands Sch KT12 183 B3
Groveland Way KT3 .199 B4
Grove Lane Terr SE5 .139 B3
Groveley Ho 7 N4 ..51 A2
Groveley Rd TW13,
TW16 ....171 D5
Grove Lo SW4 .....137 C1
Grove Mans 3 N16 ..52 A1
SW4 ....136 D1
2 W6 ....112 C4
Grove Market Pl SE9 .166 B5
Grove Mews W6 ...112 C3
Grove Mill Pl SM5 .219 A6
Grove Park Ave E4 ..35 D4
Grove Park Bridge
W4 ....133 A5
Grove Park Gdns W4 133 A5
Grove Park Mews
W4 ....133 A5
Grove Park Prim Sch
W4 ....133 A5
Grove Park Rd N15 .51 C5
SE9,SE12 ....165 D2
Chiswick W4 ....132 D5
Grove Park Sch NW9 .45 A5
Grove Park Sta SE12 165 B1
Grove Park Terr W4 .132 D6
Grove Pk NW9 .....45 B5
SE5 ....139 C3
Wanstead E11 .....55 B4
Grove Pl NW3 .....70 B2
W3 ....111 A5
Balham SW12 .....159 A5
Grove Prim Sch RM6 .58 C4
Grover Ct SE13 ....141 D3
Grove Rd E11 .....54 C2
E17 ....53 D3
E3 ....97 A5
N11 ....31 B5
N12 ....30 B5
N15 ....51 C4
NW2 ....68 C2
W3 ....111 A5
Barnes SW13 .....133 D3

Grove Rd continued
Belmont SM2 ....217 C2
Brentford TW8 .....109 C1
Chingford E4 ....20 A1
Cockfosters EN4 ....2 C3
Dagenham RM6 ....58 C3
Ealing W5 ....109 D6
East Molesey KT8 ..196 B4
Edgware HA8 ....26 C4
8 Erith DA17 ......147 B6
Hounslow TW3 .....129 C1
Hounslow TW7 .....130 C4
Kingston KT6 ......197 D4
Merton SW19 ......180 A3
Mitcham CR4 ......181 B1
Pinner HA5 ....41 B4
Richmond TW10 ...154 B5
Shepperton TW17 ..193 A3
Thornton Heath CR7 .204 C5
Twickenham TW2 ..152 A3
Uxbridge UB8 ......60 A1
Woodford E18 ......36 D1
Grove Rd Prim Sch
TW3 ....129 C1
Grove Rd W EN3 ...6 C6
Grover Ho SE11 ...260 D1
4 SW4 ....159 C6
Groves Ho UB4 ....84 B4
Groveside Cl Acton W3 88 C1
Carshalton SM5 ...218 C6
Groveside Ct SW11 .136 B3
Groveside Rd E4 ...20 C1
Grove St SE8 ......119 B1
Edmonton N18 .....33 D4
Grovestile Waye
TW14 ....149 B4
Grove Terr NW5 ...71 B4
Southall UB1 ......107 C6
Teddington TW11 ..175 A6
Grove The DA6 ....146 D1
E15 ....76 C2
N3 ....29 C3
N4 ....50 B2
N6 ....49 A1
N8 ....49 D4
N11 ....47 A2
NW9 ....45 B4
Dulwich SE21 ......162 A3
Ealing W5 ....110 A5
Edgware HA8 ......26 D6
Edmonton N13 ....32 C4
Enfield EN2 ....4 C3
Hounslow TW7 .....130 C4
Ickenham UB10 ....60 C1
Sidcup DA14 ......191 A6
Southall UB6 ......86 A1
Teddington TW11 ..175 A6
1 Twickenham TW1 .153 B5
Walton-on-T KT12 ..194 B2
West Wickham BR4 .224 A6
Grove Vale BR7 ....188 C4
SE22 ....139 D1
Grove Vale Prim Sch
SE22 ....139 D1
Groveway
SW9 ....138 B4 270 D1
Dagenham RM8 ...80 D4
Grove Way
Thames Ditton KT10 .196 A1
Wembley HA9 ......67 D2
Grovewood 9 TW9 .132 C4
Grovewood Ct 6
TW7 ....130 C4
Grovewood Ho NW2 .69 B6
Grummant Rd SE15 .139 D4
Grundy St E14 .....97 C1
Gruneisen Rd N3 ...29 C4
Guardian Angels RC Prim
Sch E3 ....97 A4
Guardian Ct SE12 .164 C6
Guards Mus The*
SW1 ....115 C4 249 B1
Gubyon Ave SE24 .160 D6
Guerin Sq E3 ......97 B4
Guernsey Cl TW5 ..129 C5
Guernsey Gr SE24 .161 A4
Guernsey Ho 9 N1 .73 A2
Enfield EN3 ....6 D1
8 N1 ....73 A2
Guibal Rd SE12 ...165 B3
Guildersfield Rd
SW16 ....182 A3
Guildford Ave TW13 .150 A2
Guildford Gr SE10 .141 D4
Guildford Ho 24 SE5 .139 A3

Guildford Rd
SW8 ....138 A4 270 B2
Chingford E17 ....36 A2
Ilford IG3 ....79 C6
Newham E6 ....100 B1
Thornton Heath CR0 ..205 B3
Guildford Way SM6 ..220 A3
Guild Hall★
EC2 ....95 A1 242 B2
Guildhall Bldgs EC2 .242 C2
Guildhall Sch Music &
Drama EC2 ..95 A2 242 B4
Guildhall Yd EC2 ...242 B2
Guildhouse St
SW1 ....115 C2 259 A3
Guildown Ave N12 ....29 D6
Guild Rd SE7 ....143 C6
Guildsway E17 ......35 B2
Guilford Ave KT5 ...198 B4
Guilford Pl WC1 .....240 C5
Guilford St
WC1 ......94 A3 240 B5
Guilfoyle 2 NW9 ....27 D1
Guillemot Ct 28 SE8 .141 B6
Guilsborough Cl
NW10 ....67 C1
Guinness Cl E9 .....75 A1
Hayes UB3 ....105 B3
Guinness Ct E1 .....243 D1
EC1 ....235 B1
NW8 ....230 B5
SW3 ....257 C3
6 Croydon CR0 ....221 D6
Guinness Sq SE1 ...263 A4
Guinness Trust Bldgs
7 E2 ....96 A5
SE1 ....253 A2
SE11 ....261 C2
SW3 ....257 C3
W6 ....112 C1
Guion Rd SW6 .....135 B3
Gujarat Ho 1 N16 ...73 C5
Gulland Cl WD23 .....8 A6
Gulland Wlk 20 N1 ..73 A2
Gullane Ho 22 E3 ...97 B5
Gull Cl SM6 ....220 A1
Gulliver Cl UB5 .....85 B6
Gulliver Ct CR2 ....220 D1
Gulliver Rd DA15 ...167 C2
Gulliver St SE16 ...119 B3
Gulston Wlk SW3 ...257 D3
Gumleigh Rd W5 ...109 C2
Gumley Gdns TW7 ..131 A2
Gumley House Convent
Sch for Girls TW7 .131 A4
Gumping Rd BR5 ...227 A6
Gundulph Rd BR2 ..209 C6
Gunmakers La E3 ....97 A6
Gunnell Cl SE25 ....206 A3
Gunnell Ct 3 CR4 ..180 C2
Gunnels Ct & Hastingwood
Ct 6 IG9 ....21 C2
Gunner Dr EN3 ......7 C6
Gunner La SE18 ....122 C1
Gunnersbury Avenue
(North Circular Rd)
W3 ....110 C3
Gunnersbury Cl 8
W4 ....110 D1
Gunnersbury Cres
W3 ....110 C4
Gunnersbury Ct 8
W3 ....110 D4
Gunnersbury Dr W5 .110 B4
Gunnersbury Gdns
W3 ....110 C4
Gunnersbury La W3 .110 C4
Gunnersbury Manor
W5 ....110 B5
Gunnersbury Mews 6
W4 ....110 D1
Gunnersbury Park
W3 ....110 C3
Gunnersbury Park Mus★
W3 ....110 C3
Gunnersbury RC Sch
TW8 ....109 C1
Gunnersbury Sta W4 110 D1
Gunners Gr E4 ......20 A1
Gunners Rd SW18 ..158 B2
Gunning St SE18 ...123 C2
Gunpowder Sq EC4 .241 B2
Gunstor Rd N16 .....73 C4
Gunter Gr HA8 ......27 B2
SW6 ....136 A5 266 A4

Gunterstone Rd
W14 ....113 A1 254 B2
Gunthorpe St
E1 ....95 D1 243 D2
Gunton Rd E5 ......74 B6
Streatham SW17 ....181 A4
Gunwhale Cl SE16 ..118 D5
Gun Wharf E1 ......118 C5
E3 ....97 A6
Gurdon Ho 3 E14 ...97 C1
Gurdon Rd SE7 ....121 A1
Gurnell Gr W13 .....86 D3
Gurney Cl E15 ......76 A3
E17 ....34 D2
Barking IG11 ....78 D2
Gurney Cres CR0 ...204 B1
Gurney Dr N2 ....48 A5
Gurney Ho 14 E2 ....96 A5
3 W2 ....91 D1
Hayes UB3 ....105 C2
Gurney Rd E15 ......76 C3
SW6 ....136 A2
Northolt UB5 ....84 C4
Wallington SM5 ....219 A4
Guru Nanak Sikh Coll
UB4 ....106 C5
Guthrie Ct SE1 ....251 B1
Guthrie St SW3 ....257 A2
Gutter La EC2 .95 A1 242 A2
Guyatt Gdns CR4 ...181 A1
Guy Barnett Gr SE3 .143 A2
Guy Rd CR0,SM6 ...219 D5
Guyscliff Rd SE13 ..164 A6
Guy's Hospl
SE1 ....117 B5 252 D2
Guy's Hospl Sch
SE1 ....117 B5 252 D3
Guy's Retreat IG9 ...21 C4
Guy St SE1 ..117 B4 252 D3
Gwalior Ho N16 .....15 C5
Gwalior Rd SW15 ..134 D2
Gwendolen Ave
SW15 ....156 D6
Gwendolen Cl SW15 .156 D6
Gwendoline Ave E13 .99 B6
Gwendwr Rd
W14 ....113 A1 254 B2
Gwent Ct 18 SE16 ..118 D5
Gwillim Cl DA15 ...168 A6
Gwilym Maries Ho 11
E2 ....96 B4
Gwydor Rd BR3 ....206 D6
Gwydyr Rd BR2 ....208 D6
Gwyn Cl SW6 .136 A5 266 A3
Gwyn Jones Prim Sch
E11 ....54 B2
Gwynne Ave CR0 ...206 D2
Gwynne Cl W4 .....133 D6
Gwynne Ho WC1 ....234 A1
6 Streatham SW2 ..160 A6
3 Wanstead E11 ....55 A4
Gwynne Pl WC1 ....233 D1
Gwynne Rd SW11 ..136 B3
Gye Ho 2 SW4 .....138 A1
Gylcote Cl SE5 ....139 B1
Gyles Pk HA7 ....25 C4
Gyllyngdune Gdns
IG3 ....79 D5

H

Haarlem Rd 12 W14 .112 D3
Haberdasher Pl 4 N1 95 C4
Haberdasher St
N1 ....95 B4 235 D2
Habington Ho 9 SE5 139 B5
Haccombe Rd 1 SW6 .180 A4
Hackbridge Park Gdns
SM5 ....218 D6
Hackbridge Prim Sch
SM5 ....203 A1
Hackbridge Rd SM5,
SM6 ....219 A6
Hackbridge Sta SM6 .219 B6
Hackett Cl SE8 ....119 B2
Hackford Rd
SW9 ....138 C4 270 D2
Hackford Wlk SW9 .138 C4
Hackforth Cl EN5 ...12 B6
Hackington Cres
BR3 ....185 C4
Hackney Central Sta
E8 ....74 B2
Hackney Cl NW6 ....71 D6
Hackney Coll (Poplar Ctr)
E3 ....97 D3
Hackney Com Coll N1 95 C4
Hackney Downs Sch
E5,E8 ....74 B2

Hackney Downs Sta
E8 ....74 B3
Hackney Free & Parochial
CE Sch (Secondary)
E9 ....74 C2
Hackney Gr E8 ......74 B2
Hackney Hospl E9 ...75 A3
Hackney Rd E2 .....96 A5
Hackney Wick E9 ...75 B2
Hackney Wick Sta E9 .75 C2
Hackworth Point 24
E3 ....97 D4
Haddenham Ct SW17 180 B6
Hadden Rd SE28 ...123 C3
Hadden Way UB6 ....64 B2
Haddington Ct 4
SE10 ....141 D5
Haddington Rd BR1 .186 B6
Haddo Ho NW5 .....71 B4
SE10 ....141 D6
Haddon Cl Enfield EN1 18 A5
New Malden KT3 ....199 D4
Haddon Ct NW4 ....46 C6
W3 ....111 D6
Haddon Gr DA15 ...168 A4
Haddon Rd SM1 ...217 D4
Haddo St SE10 ....142 A6
Haden Ct N4 ....72 C6
Hadfield Cl UB1 ....85 B4
Hadfield Ho 26 E1 ..96 A1
Hadleigh Cl 16 E1 ..96 C3
Merton SW20 ......179 B1
Hadleigh Ct 8 E4 ...20 A1
Hadleigh Ho 15 E1 ..96 C3
Hadleigh Lo 5 IG8 ..37 A4
Hadleigh St E2 .....96 C4
Hadleigh Wlk 1 E6 .100 A1
Hadley Cl
Borehamwood WD6 ..10 B5
Southgate N21 ......16 C5
Hadley Ct N16 ......52 A1
Hadley Gdns W4 ...111 B1
Southall UB1 ....107 B1
Hadley Gn EN5 ......1 B3
Hadley Gn W EN5 ....1 B3
Hadley Gr EN5 ......1 A3
Hadley Green Rd EN5 .1 B3
Hadley Hall N21 .....16 C3
Hadley Highstone EN5 .1 B4
Hadley Ho BR5 ....189 D1
Hadley Rd DA17 ...125 B2
Barnet EN5 ....1 D2
Enfield EN2 ....4 A5
Mitcham CR4 ....203 D5
Hadley Ridge EN5 ....1 B2
Hadley St NW1 ......71 B2
Hadleyvale Ct EN5 ...1 D2
Hadley Way N21 .....16 C5
Hadley Wood Prim Sch
EN4 ....2 A5
Hadley Wood Rd
Barnet EN4 ....2 A3
Barnet EN5 ....1 C3
Hadley Wood Sta EN4 .2 A5
Hadlow Coll (Mottingham
Ctr) SE12 ....165 C3
Hadlow Ho SE17 ...263 B2
Hadlow Pl SE19 ...184 A3
Hadlow Rd
Bexley DA16 ....146 C5
Sidcup DA14 ....190 A6
Hadrian Cl TW19 ..148 A4
Hadrian Ct SE4 ....141 C2
Barnet EN5 ....1 D1
1 Belmont SM2 ....217 D1
Hadrian Est 30 E2 ..96 A5
Hadrian's Ride EN1 ..17 D6
Hadrian St SE10 ...120 C1
Hadrian Way TW19 .148 A4
Hadstock Ho NW1 .232 D2
Hadyn Park Ct 13
W12 ....112 A4
Hadyn Park Rd W12 .112 A4
Hafer Rd SW11 ....136 D1
Hafton Rd SE6 ....164 C2
Haggard Rd TW1 ..153 B4
Hagger Ct E17 ......54 B6
Haggerston Rd E8 ...95 D6
Haggerston Sch E2 ..95 D5
Hague Prim Sch E2 ..96 B3
Hague St 12 E2 .....96 A4
Ha-Ha Rd SE7,SE18 .144 B6
Haig Ct BR7 ....188 D5
Haig Ho 4 E2 ......96 A5
Haig Pl SM4 ......201 C3
Haig Rd Hillingdon UB8 .83 A2
Stanmore HA7 ......25 C5
Haig Rd E E13 .....99 C5
Haig Rd W E13 .....99 C5

Haigville Gdns IG6 ...56 D5
Hailes Cl SW19 ....180 A4
Haileybury Ave EN1 ..17 D5
Hailey Rd DA18 ...125 C4
Hailey Rd Bsns Pk
DA18 ....125 C5
Hailsham Ave SW2 .160 B2
Hailsham Cl KT6 ...197 D2
Hailsham Dr HA1 ....42 B6
Hailsham Ho NW8 ..237 A5
Hailsham Rd SW17 .181 A4
Hailsham Terr N18 ..33 B5
Haimo Prim Sch SE9 165 D6
Haimo Rd SE9 ....165 D6
Hainault Ave IG6 ....78 D6
Hainault Bridge Par 4
IG1 ....78 D6
Hainault Ct E17 .....54 B5
Hainault Gore RM6 ..59 A4
Hainault Rd E11 .....54 B2
Dagenham RM6 .....59 B3
Ilford RM6 ....58 A4
Hainault St SE9 ...166 D3
Ilford IG1 ....78 D6
Haines Wlk SM4 ...201 D2
Hainford Cl SE4 ...140 D1
Haining Cl 3 W4 ...110 C1
Hainthorpe Rd SE27 182 D6
Hainton Cl E1 ......96 B1
Halberd Mews E5 ...74 B6
Halbutt Gdns RM9 ..81 B5
Halcomb St N1 .....95 C6
Halcot Ave DA6 ...169 C6
Halcrow St E1 ......96 B1
Halcyon 1 EN1 .....17 C6
Halcyon Wharf 19 E1 118 A5
Haldane Cl N10 .....31 B3
Haldane Pl SW18 ..157 D3
Haldane Rd E6 ....100 A4
SE28 ....124 D3
SW6 ....135 B6 264 D5
Southall UB1 ....86 A1
Haldan Rd E4 ....36 A4
Haldon Rd SW18 ..157 B5
Hale Cl BR6 ....227 A4
HA8 ....27 A5
Chingford E4 ....20 A1
Hale Ct HA8 ....27 A5
Hale Dr NW7 ....27 B4
Hale End Cl HA4 ....40 A3
Hale End Rd E17 ....36 B2
Halefield Rd N17 ....34 B2
Hale Gdns N17 .....52 A6
Acton W3 ....110 C5
Hale Grove Gdns NW7 27 C5
Hale Ho SW1 ......259 D2
Enfield EN3 ....6 D6
Hale La NW7,HA8 ...27 B5
Hale Lo HA1 ....42 C2
Hale Rd N17 ....52 A6
Newham E6 ....100 A3
Hales Ct 5 TW11 ..175 A5
Hales Ho 3 SW12 ..159 B4
Halesowen Rd SM4 .201 D2
Hales Prior N1 .....233 C3
Hales St SE8 ......141 C5
Halesworth Cl 3 E5 .74 C6
Halesworth Rd SE13 141 D2
Hale The N17 ....52 A6
Chingford E4 ....36 B3
Hale Wlk W7 ....86 C2
Haley Rd NW4 ......46 C3
Half Acre TW8 ....131 D6
Half Acre Mews TW8 131 D6
Half Acre Rd W7 ...108 C5
Half Moon Ct EC1 ..242 A3
Half Moon La SE24 .161 A5
Halfmoon Pas E1 ..243 D1
Half Moon St
W1 ....115 B5 248 D3
Halford Cl HA8 .....26 C1
Halford Ct KT9 ....214 A1
Halford Ho 9 SW15 .156 C6
Halford Rd E10 .....54 B4
SW6 ....135 C6 265 A5
Ickenham UB10 .....60 C3
Richmond TW10 ...154 A6
Halfway St DA15 ...167 C3
Haliburton Rd TW1,
TW7 ....131 A1
Haliday Ho N1 ......73 B4
Haliday Wlk 4 N1 ...73 B2
Halidon Cl E9 ......74 C3
Halifax 8 NW9 .....27 D1
Halifax Cl TW11 ...174 D4
Halifax Rd Enfield EN2 ..5 B3
Greenford UB6 ......85 D6
Halifax St SE26 ...162 B1

Halifield Dr DA17 ..125 A3
Haling Gr CR2 ....221 A1
Haling Manor High Sch
CR2 ....220 D1
Haling Park Gdns
CR2 ....220 D2
Haling Park Rd CR2 221 A2
Haling Rd CR2 ....221 B2
Haliwell Ho 8 NW6 ..91 D6
Halkett Ho 1 E2 ....96 C6
Halkin Arc
SW1 ....114 D3 257 D6
Halkin Mews SW1 ..258 A6
Halkin Pl SW1 .....258 A6
Halkin St
SW1 ....115 A4 248 B1
Hallam Cl BR7 ....188 B5
Hallam Ct W1 .....238 D4
Hallam Gdns HA5 ...23 A3
Hallam Ho SW1 ....259 B1
17 SW9 ....138 C4
Hallam Mews W1 ..238 D4
Hallam Rd N15 .....50 D5
Barnes SW13 ......134 B3
Hallam St W1 .93 B2 238 D4
Hallane Ho SE27 ...183 A5
Hall Cl W5 ....88 A2
Hall Ct TW11 ......174 D5
Hall Dr Ealing W7 ...86 C3
Forest Hill SE26 ...184 C5
Halley Gdns SE13 ..142 B1
Halley Ho 15 E2 ....96 A5
8 SE10 ....120 D1
Halley Prim Sch E14 97 A2
Halley Rd E7,E12 ...77 D2
Halley St E14 ......97 A2
Hall Farm Cl HA7 ...25 B6
Hall Farm Dr TW2 .152 B2
Hallfield W2 ....236 A1
Hallfield Jun & Inf Schs
W2 ....91 D1
Hallgate SE3 ......143 A2
Hall Gate NW8 92 A4 229 B2
Hall Gdns E4 ....35 B6
Halliards The KT12 .194 A3
Halliday Ho 29 E1 ...96 A1
Halliday Sq UB2 ...108 B5
Halliford Cl TW17 ..193 C6
Halliford Rd
Sunbury TW16 .....194 A5
Upper Halliford TW16,
TW17 ....193 D5
Halliford Sch TW17 193 A2
Halliford St N1 ......73 B1
Halling Ho SE1 ....252 D1
Halliwell Ct 4 SE22 162 A6
Halliwell Rd SW2 ..160 B5
Halliwick Court Par 2
N12 ....30 D5
Halliwick Ct 1 N12 ..30 D5
Halliwick Ho N21 ...17 B5
Halliwick Rd N10 ...31 A2
Hall La E4 ....35 B5
NW4 ....28 A1
Harlington UB3 ....127 B5
Hall Lane E4 ....35 A5
Hallmark Trad Ctr
HA9 ....67 A4
Hallmead Rd SM1 .217 D5
Hall Oak Wlk NW6 ..69 B2
Hallowell Ave CR0 .220 A4
Hallowell Cl CR4 ...203 A6
Hallowfield Way CR4 202 C6
Hall Pl W2 ..92 B3 236 B5
Hall Rd E15 ....76 B4
E6 ....100 B6
NW8 ....92 A4 229 B2
Dagenham RM6 .....58 D2
Isleworth TW7 .....152 B6
Hall Sch SW20 ....178 D2
Hall Sch The NW3 ...70 D2
Hall Sch Wimbledon
SW15 ....156 A1
Hallside Rd EN1 .....5 D5
Hall St EC1 ..94 D4 234 D2
N12 ....30 A5
Halls Terr UB10 .....82 D1
Hallsville Prim Sch
E16 ....99 A1
Hallsville Rd E16 ...98 D1
Hallswelle Par 1
NW11 ....47 B4
Hallswelle Rd NW11 .47 B4
Hall The SE3 ......143 A2
Hall Twr W2 ....236 D4
Hall View SE9 ....165 D6
Hallywell Cres E6 ..100 B2
Halons Rd SE9 ....166 C4
Halpin Pl
SE17 ....117 B2 262 D3

Halsbrook Rd SE3 ..143 D2
Halsbury Cl HA7 ....25 B6
Halsbury Ho HA7 ...25 B6
Halsbury Ho 4 N7 ...72 B4
Halsbury Rd W12 ..112 B5
Halsbury Rd E UB5 ..64 A4
Halsbury Rd W UB5 ..63 D3
Halsend UB3 ......106 B5
Halsey St
SW3 ....114 D2 257 C4
Halsham Cres IG11 ..79 D3
Halsmere Rd SE5 ..138 C4
Halstead Cl 2 CR0 .221 A1
Halstead Ct N1 ....235 D2
Halstead Gdns N21 ..17 B3
Halstead Rd
Edmonton N21 .....17 B3
Enfield EN1 ....5 C1
Wanstead E11 ......55 B4
Halston Cl SW11 ..158 D5
Halstow 12 NW5 ....71 A2
Halstow Prim Sch
SE10 ....121 A1
Halstow Rd NW10 ...90 D4
SE3,SE10 ....121 A1
Halsway UB3 ......106 A5
Halter Cl WD6 ......11 B6
Halton Cl N11 ......30 C4
Halton Cross St
N1 ....94 D6 234 D6
Haltone Ho 1 SW4 .137 D3
Halton Ho 23 N1 ....72 C1
Halton Mans N1 ....72 C1
Halton Pl N1 ......235 A6
Halton Rd N1 .72 D1 234 D6
Halt Robin La DA17 125 C2
Halt Robin Rd DA17 125 C2
Halyard Ho E14 ...120 A1
Hamara Ghar 5 E13 .99 C6
Hambalt Rd SW4 ...159 C6
Hamble Cl HA4 ......61 C6
Hamble Ct KT1 ....175 D3
Hamble SE17 ......139 B6
Hambledon Chase N4 50 A2
Hambledon Cl UB8 ..82 D3
Hambledon Ct
5 Ealing W5 ....110 A6
9 Wallington SM6 .219 B2
Hambledon Gdns
SE25 ....205 D6
Hambledon Ho E5 ..74 B4
2 Kingston KT2 ....176 D4
Hambledon Pl SE21 161 D3
Hambledon Rd SW18 157 B4
Hambledown Rd SE9 167 C4
Hamble St SW6 ...135 D2
Hambleton Cl KT4 .216 C6
Hamble Wlk UB5 ....85 C5
Hambley Ho 5 SE16 118 B2
Hamblin Ho UB1 ...107 A6
Hamblyn Ct N16 ....51 D2
Hambridge Way SW2 160 C4
Hambro Ave BR2 ..209 A1
Hambrook Ct 13 NW5 71 B4
Hambrook Rd SE25 206 B6
Hambro Rd SW16 ..181 D5
Hambrough Ho UB4 ..84 C4
Hambrough Prim Sch
UB1 ....107 B5
Hambrough Rd UB1 107 A5
Hambury Ho SW8 ..270 B5
Ham Cl TW10 ......153 C1
Ham Comm TW10 ..153 D1
Ham Ct 12 NW9 .....27 D1
Hamden Cres RM10 ..81 D6
Hamel Cl HA3 ......43 D6
Hamelton Terr RM9 ..80 C1
Hamers Ho 16 SW2 160 C4
Hameway E6 ......100 C4
Ham Farm Rd KT2,
TW10 ....176 A6
Hamfrith Rd E15 ....76 D2
Ham Gate Ave TW10 176 A6
Ham Ho★ TW10 ...153 C2
Hamilton Ave
Cheam SM3 ....217 A6
Edmonton N9 ....18 A4
Ilford IG6 ....57 A4
Tolworth KT6,SM3 ..214 C6
Hamilton Cl N17 ....51 D6
NW8 ....92 B4 229 C1
SE16 ....119 A4
Ashford TW15 .....171 D5
Cockfosters EN4 .....2 D1
Teddington TW11 ..175 B4
Hamilton Cres
Edmonton N13 ......32 C6
Harrow HA2 ....63 D5
Hounslow TW3 ....151 D2
Hamilton Ct W9 ...229 A4

Hamilton Ct continued
9 Catford SE6 ......164 D3
Croydon CR0 ......206 A1
Ealing W5 ......110 B6
Hamilton Gdns
NW8 ......92 A4 229 B2
Hamilton Hall
NW8 ......92 A5 229 A3
Hamilton Ho 1 E14 .119 D2
19 E3 ......97 B4
NW8 ......229 C2
W8 ......245 C2
Chiswick W4 ......133 C6
Putney SW15 ......156 A6
10 Richmond TW9 ......132 C4
Hamilton La N5 ......72 C4
Hamilton Lo 32 E1 ..96 C3
Hamilton Mews W1 .248 C2
Hamilton Par TW13 .172 A6
Hamilton Pk N5 ......72 C4
Hamilton Pk W N5 ..72 C4
Hamilton Pl
W1 ......115 A5 248 B3
Sunbury TW16 ......172 B3
Tottenham N17 ......33 D1
Hamilton Rd DA7 .147 A3
E15 ......98 C4
E17 ......35 A1
N2 ......48 A6
NW10 ......68 C4
NW11 ......47 A2
W4 ......111 C4
Barnet EN4 ......2 C1
Brentford TW8 ......131 D6
Ealing W5 ......110 A6
Edmonton N9 ......18 A4
Feltham TW13 ......171 D6
Harrow HA1 ......42 C4
Hayes UB3 ......106 B6
Ilford IG1 ......78 D4
Merton SW19 ......179 D3
Sidcup DA15 ......190 A6
Southall UB1 ......107 B5
South Norwood CR7 ..205 B6
Twickenham TW2 ......152 C3
West Norwood SE27 ..183 B6
Hamilton Road Ctr
E15 ......98 C4
Hamilton Road Ind Est
SE27 ......183 B6
Hamilton Road Mews 1
SW19 ......179 D3
Hamilton Sq N12 ....30 A4
SE1 ......252 D2
Hamilton St SE8 ....141 C6
Hamilton Terr
NW8 ......92 A4 229 B2
Hamilton Way N3 ...29 C4
Edmonton N13 ......32 D6
Hamlea Cl SE12 ....165 A6
Hamlet Cl SE13 ....142 C4
Hamlet Ct SE11 ...261 C2
1 W6 ......112 A2
14 Enfield EN1 ......17 C6
Hamlet (Day) Hospl The
TW9 ......132 A4
Hamlet Gdns W6 ...112 A2
Hamlet Ho SE9 ....166 C6
Hamlet Ind Est E9 ..75 C1
Hamlet Rd SE19 ....184 A3
Hamlet Sq NW2 ......69 A5
Hamlet The SE5 ....139 B2
Hamlet Way SE1 ...252 D2
Hamlin Cres HA5 ...40 C4
Hamlyn Cl HA8 ......10 A1
Hamlyn Gdns SE19 .183 C3
Hammelton Ct 4
BR1 ......186 D2
Hammelton Gn 2
SW9 ......138 D4
Hammelton Rd BR1 .187 A2
Hammers La NW7 ...28 C4
Hammersley Ho 8
SE14 ......140 C5
Hammersmith Bridge Rd
W6,SW13 ......112 C1
Hammersmith Broadway
5 W6 ......112 C2
Hammersmith Flyover
W6 ......112 C1
Hammersmith Gr
W6 ......112 C2
Hammersmith Hospl
W12 ......90 B1
Hammersmith Rd
W14 ......254 B4
W6 ......112 D2
Hammersmith Sta
W6 ......112 A1

Hammersmith Terr
W6 ......112 A1
Hammet Cl UB4 ......84 D2
Hammett St EC3 ...253 C6
Hammond Ave CR4 .181 B1
Hammond Cl
Barnet EN5 ......13 B6
Greenford UB6 ......64 B3
Hampton TW12 ......173 C2
Hammond Ct 1 E10 ..75 D6
1 E17 ......53 A4
Hammond Ho E14 ...119 D3
10 SE14 ......140 C4
Hammond Lo 6 W9 ..91 C2
Hammond Rd
Enfield EN1 ......6 B3
Southall UB2 ......107 A3
Hammonds Cl RM8 ...80 C5
Hammond St NW5 ...71 C2
Hammond Way 2
SE28 ......124 C6
Hamonde Cl HA8 ......10 D2
Hamond Sq N1 ......95 C5
Ham Park Rd E15 ....76 D1
Hampden Ave BR3 ..185 A4
Hampden Cl NW1 ...232 D4
Hampden Ct 5 N10 ..31 A3
Hampden Gurney CE Prim
Sch W1 ......92 C1 237 B2
Hampden Gurney St
W1 ......237 C1
Hampden Ho SW9 ...138 C3
Hampden La N17 ....34 A2
Hampden Rd N10 ....31 A3
N19 ......71 D6
N8 ......50 C5
Beckenham BR3 ......185 A1
Harrow HA3 ......24 A1
Kingston KT1 ......198 C6
Tottenham N17 ......34 A2
Hampden Sq N14 ....15 B3
Hampden Way N14 ..15 B3
Hampshire Cl N18 ...34 B5
Hampshire Ct 6
SW13 ......133 D3
Hampshire Hog La 11
W6 ......112 B2
Hampshire Rd N22 ...32 B3
Hampshire Sch The
SW7 ......114 C4 247 B1
Hampshire St NW5 ...71 D2
Hampson Way
SW8 ......138 B4 270 C2
Hampstead Cl SE28 .124 B5
Hampstead Garden Suburb
Inst NW11 ......47 D4
Hampstead Gate NW3 70 A3
Hampstead Gdns
NW11 ......47 C3
Hampstead Gn NW3 ..70 C3
Hampstead Gr NW3 ..70 A5
Hampstead Heath★
NW3 ......70 B6
Hampstead Heath Sta
NW3 ......70 C4
Hampstead High St
NW3 ......70 B4
Hampstead Hill Gdns
NW3 ......70 C4
Hampstead Hill Sch
NW3 ......70 D4
Hampstead Hts N2 ...48 A6
Hampstead La N6 ....48 C2
Hampstead Parochial CE
Prim Sch NW3 ......70 A4
Hampstead Rd
NW1 ......93 C4 232 A2
Hampstead Sch NW2 .69 A4
Hampstead Sq NW3 ..70 A5
Hampstead Sta NW3 .70 A4
Hampstead Way
NW11 ......47 C3
Hampstead West 4
NW6 ......69 C2
Hampstead Wlk 1 E3 97 B6
Hampton Cl N11 ......31 B5
NW6 ......91 C4
Wimbledon SW20 ......178 C3
Hampton Com Coll
TW12 ......173 C5
Hampton Court KT8 .196 C6
Hampton Court Ave
KT8 ......196 B6
Hampton Court Cres
KT8 ......196 C6
Hampton Court Landing
Stage KT8 ......196 C6
Hampton Court Palace★
KT8 ......196 D6

Hampton Court Par
KT8 ......196 C5
Hampton Court Rd
KT1,KT8 ......197 B6
Hampton Court Sta
KT8 ......196 C5
Hampton Court Way
KT10,KT7,KT8 ......196 C3
Hampton Ct N1 ......72 D2
19 SE16 ......118 D5
Hampton Farm Ind Est
TW13 ......151 A1
Hampton Hill Bsns Pk
TW12 ......174 A5
Hampton Hill Jun Mix Sch
TW12 ......174 A5
Hampton Inf Sch
TW12 ......173 C3
Hampton Jun Sch
TW12 ......173 C2
Hampton La TW13 ...173 A6
Hampton Rd E11 ......54 B1
E4 ......35 B3
E7 ......77 C3
Ilford IG1 ......79 A4
North Cheam KT4 ......216 B6
Teddington TW11,
TW12 ......174 A5
Thornton Heath CR0 ...205 A3
Twickenham TW2 ......152 B1
Hampton Rd E TW13 .151 B1
Hampton Rd W TW13 151 A1
Hampton Rise HA3 ...44 A3
Hampton Road Ind Pk
CR0 ......205 A3
Hampton Sch TW12 .173 C5
Hampton St
SE1 ......116 D2 261 D3
Hampton Sta TW12 ..173 C2
Hampton Wick Inf Sch
KT1 ......175 D3
Hampton Wick Sta
KT1 ......175 C2
Ham Ridings TW10 ..176 B5
Ham Shades Cl 1
DA15 ......168 A1
Ham St TW10 ......153 C1
Ham The TW8 ......131 C4
Ham View CR0 ......207 A3
Ham Yd W1 ......249 C6
Hanameel St 6 E16 .121 A5
7 E16 ......121 B5
10 E16 ......121 B5
Hana Mews E5 ......74 B4
Hanbury Cl NW4 ......46 C6
Hanbury Ct HA1 ......42 D3
Hanbury Dr N21 ......16 B6
Hanbury Ho 8 E1 ....96 A2
Tottenham N17 ......34 A2
Hanbury Rd W3 ......110 A4
Tottenham N17 ......34 A2
Hanbury St E1 96 A2 243 D4
Hancocke Ho 4 E17 ..53 D6
Hancock Nunn Ho 1
NW3 ......70 D1
Hancock Rd E3 ......98 A4
South Norwood SE19 ..183 B4
Handcroft Rd CR0 ...204 D1
Hand Ct WC1 ......240 D3
Handel Cl HA8 ......26 B4
Handel Ho TW2 ......152 B5
Handel Mans SW13 .134 C5
Handel Pl NW10 ......67 B2
Handel St WC1 94 A3 240 B6
Handel Way HA8 ......26 C3
Handen Rd SE12 ....164 D6
Handforth Rd SW9 ..138 C5
6 Ilford IG1 ......78 D5
Handley Gr NW2 ......68 D5
Handley Page Rd SM6 ......
Handley Rd E9 ......96 C6
Handowe Cl NW4 ....46 A5
Handside Cl KT4 ....200 D1
Hands Wlk E16 ......99 A1
Handsworth Ave E4 ..36 B4
Handsworth Prim Sch
E4 ......36 B4
Handsworth Rd N17 .51 B6
Handtrough Way
IG11 ......100 D5
Hanford Cl SW18 ...157 C3
Hanger Ct W5 ......88 C3
Hanger Gn W5 ......88 B4
Hanger Lane Sta W5 .88 A4
Hanger La (North Circular
Rd) W5 ......88 B2
Hanger Vale La W5 ..88 B1
Hanger View Way W3 .88 C2

Hangmans Cnr BR7 ..188 D2
Hankey Pl
SE1 ......117 B4 252 D1
Hankins La NW7 ......11 C1
Hanley Gdns N4 ......50 B1
Hanley Pl BR3 ......185 C3
Hanley Rd N4,N19 ...50 A1
Hanmer Wlk N7 ......72 B6
Hannah Ct BR3 ......208 A4
Hannah Ct SW19 ....178 D3
Hannah Mary Way 15
SE1 ......118 A2
Hannah Mews SM6 ..219 C1
Hannan Cl NW10 ......67 A4
Hannay La N8 ......49 D2
Hannay Wlk SW16 ...159 D2
Hannell Rd
SW6 ......135 A5 264 B4
Hannen Ho SE5 ......139 B2
Hannen Rd SE27 ....160 D1
Hannibal Rd E1 ......96 C2
Stanwell TW19 ......148 A4
Hannibal Way CR0 ..220 D2
Hanning Lo TW3 ....130 A1
Hannington Rd SW4 .137 B2
Feltham TW13 ......150 A4
Hanover Ave E16 ....121 A5
Hanover Circ UB3 ...83 A2
Hanover Cl
Cheam SM3 ......217 B4
Richmond TW9 ......132 C5
Hanover Ct N16 ......51 D2
NW9 ......45 C6
W12 ......112 A5
1 Penge SE19 ......184 A3
Hanover Dr BR7 ....189 A6
Hanover Gate Mans
NW1 ......237 B6
Hanover Gdns SE11 .138 C6
New Barnet EN5 ......2 A1
Tolworth KT6 ......198 C1
Hanover Ho NW8 ...230 A3
Hanover Mans 5
SW2 ......160 C6
Hanover Mead NW11 .47 A3
Hanover Pk SE15 ...140 A4
Hanover Pl 12 E3 ...97 B4
WC2 ......240 B1
Hanover Prim Sch
N1 ......235 B4
Hanover Rd N15 ......51 D5
Merton SW19 ......180 A3
Willesden NW10 ......90 C6
Hanover Sq
W1 ......93 B1 238 D1
Hanover St
W1 ......93 B1 238 D1
Croydon CR0 ......220 D5
Hanover Steps W2 ..237 B1
Hanover Terr
NW1 ......92 D4 230 C1
Isleworth TW7 ......131 A4
Hanover Terr Mews
NW1 ......92 C4 230 B1
Hanover Way DA7 ...146 D2
Hanover Yd N1 ......235 A4
Hanover West Ind Est
NW10 ......89 B4
Hanover Yd N1 ......235 A4
Hansard Mews W14 .112 D4
Hansart Way EN2 ....4 C4
Hanscomb Mews 3
SW4 ......137 C1
Hans Cres
SW1 ......114 D3 257 C6
Hanselin Cl HA7 ......24 D5
Hansen Dr N21 ......16 B6
Hanshaw Dr HA8 ......27 B2
Hansler Gr KT8 ....196 B6
Hansler Rd SE22 ...161 D6
Hansol Rd DA6 ......169 A6
Hanson Cl
Balham SW12 ......159 B4
Beckenham BR3 ......185 D4
Mortlake SW14 ......133 A2
West Drayton UB7 ....104 B3
Hanson Ct E17 ......53 D3
Hanson Gdns UB1 ...107 A4
Hanson Ho 2 E1 ....118 A6
Hanson St W1 93 C2 239 A4
Hans Pl SW1 114 D3 257 C6
Hans Rd SW3 114 D3 257 C6
Hans St SW1 114 D3 257 C6
Hanway Ho 25 SW9 .138 C4
Hanway Pl W1 ......239 C2
Hanway Rd W7 ......86 C5
Hanway St W1 ......239 C2
Hanwell Ho 24 W2 ..91 C2
Hanwell Sta W7 ....108 C6
Hanworth Ho SE5 ...138 D5

Hanworth Rd
Ashford TW16 ......172 A3
Feltham TW13 ......150 B3
Hampton TW12 ......173 C5
Hounslow TW3,TW4 ..129 C4
Twickenham TW4 ......151 B4
Hanworth Terr TW3 .129 D1
Hanworth Trad Est
TW13 ......151 A1
Hapgood Cl UB6 ....64 B3
Harben Rd NW6 ......70 A1
Harberson Rd E15 ...98 D6
Balham SW12 ......159 B3
Harberton Rd N19 ...49 C1
Harbet Rd N18 ......35 A4
W2 ......92 B2 236 D3
Harbex Cl DA5 ......169 D4
Harbinger Prim Sch
E14 ......119 D2
Harbinger Rd E14 ...119 D2
Harbin Ho 5 SW2 ...160 C3
Harbledown Ho SE1 .252 C1
Harbledown Rd SW6 265 A2
Harbord Cl SE5 ......139 B3
Harbord Ho 5 SE16 .118 D2
Harbord St SW6 ....134 D4
Harborne Cl WD19 ...22 C5
Harborough Ave
DA15 ......167 D4
Harborough Rd
SW16 ......182 B6
Harborough Sch N19 .71 D6
Harbour Ave
SW10 ......136 A4 266 B1
Harbour Exchange Sq
E14 ......119 D4
Harbour Rd SE5 ....139 C2
Harbridge Ave SW15 .156 A4
Harbury Rd SM5 ....218 C1
Harbut Rd SW11 ....136 B1
Harcastle Cl UB4 ...85 A3
Harcombe Rd N16 ...73 C5
Harcourt Ave
DA5,DA15 ......168 C4
E12 ......78 B3
HA8 ......11 A1
Wallington SM6 ......219 B4
Harcourt Cl TW7 ...131 A2
Harcourt Field SM6 .219 B4
Harcourt Ho 27 SW8 137 D3
W1 ......238 C2
5 Chingford E4 ......36 B5
Harcourt Lo 2 SM6 .219 B4
Harcourt Rd E15 ....98 D5
N22 ......31 C2
SE4 ......141 B2
Bexley DA6,DA7 ......147 A1
Bushey WD23 ......8 A6
Merton SW19 ......179 C3
Thornton Heath CR7 ..204 C3
Wallington SM6 ......219 B4
Harcourt St
W1 ......92 C2 237 B3
Harcourt Terr
SW10 ......113 D1 255 D1
Hardcastle Ho SE25 .206 A3
Hardcastle Ho 8
SE15 ......140 A4
Hardcourts Cl BR4 ..223 D5
Hard Ct SE7 ......37 C4
Hardel Rise SW2 ....160 C3
Hardel Wlk SE24,SW2 160 C4
Harden Ct 1 SE7 ....122 A2
Harders Rd SE15 ...139 C3
Hardess St SE24 ...139 A2
Hardham Ho 5 SW2 160 C5
Hardie Cl NW10 ......67 A4
Hardie Rd SE17 ....139 A6
South Croydon CR0 ...221 D5
Harding Ct SE25 ....183 D1
Hardinge Cl UB8 ....82 D1
Hardinge Rd
Edmonton N18 ......33 C4
Willesden NW10 ......90 C6
Hardinge St E1 ......96 C1
SE18 ......122 B3
Harding Ho 16 SE18 .122 B2
Barnes SW13 ......134 B6
Hayes UB3 ......84 C1
Harding Pl SE23 ....163 A4
Harding Rd DA7 ....147 B3
Hardings Cl KT2 ....176 B2
Hardings La SE20 ...184 C4

Hardwicke Ho 14 E3 ..97 D4
Hardwicke Mews
WC1 ......233 D1
Hardwicke Rd W4 ...111 B2
Bowes Park N13 ......32 A4
Richmond TW10 ......175 C6
Hardwicke St IG11 .101 A6
Hardwick Gn W13 ...87 B2
Hardwick Ho NW8 ..237 B6
14 SW8 ......137 D4
Hardwick St
EC1 ......94 C4 234 B1
Hardwick's Way
SW18 ......157 C6
Hardwidge St SE1 ..253 A2
Hardy Ave 4 E16 ...121 A5
Ruislip HA4 ......62 B3
Hardy Cl SE16 ......118 C4
Barnet EN5 ......13 A6
Pinner HA5 ......40 D2
Hardy Cotts 2 SE10 .142 A4
Hardy Ct SE3 ......142 D6
9 Wanstead E11 ......55 A5
Hardyng Ho 4 E17 ..53 A5
Hardy Pas N22 ......32 C1
Hardy Rd E4 ......35 B4
SE3 ......142 D6
Merton SW19 ......179 D3
Hardys Cl KT8 ......196 C5
Hardy Way EN2 ......4 C4
Harebell Dr E6 ......100 C2
Hare & Billet Rd SE3 .142 B3
Harecourt Rd N1 ....73 A2
Hare Ct EC4 ......241 A1
Haredale Ho 22 SE16 118 A4
Haredale Rd SE24 ..139 A1
Haredon Cl SE23 ....162 D4
Harefield KT10 ....212 C6
Harefield Cl EN2 ....4 C4
Harefield Ct 6 SW19 179 C3
Harefield Mews SE4 .141 B2
Harefield Rd DA14 ..168 D1
N8 ......49 D4
SE4 ......141 B2
South Norwood SW16 .182 A6
Uxbridge UB8 ......60 A3
Hare La KT10 ......212 C2
Hare Marsh E2 ......96 A3
Harenc Sch Trust
DA14 ......190 C5
Hare Pl EC4 ......241 B1
Hare Row E2 ......96 B5
Haresfield Rd RM10 .81 C2
Hare St SE18 ......122 C3
Hare Wlk N1 ......95 C5
Harewood Ave
NW1 ......92 C3 237 B5
Northolt UB5 ......63 B1
Harewood Cl UB5 ...63 B1
Harewood Ct HA3 ...24 C2
Harewood Pl W1 ...238 D1
Harewood Rd
Hounslow TW7 ......130 D4
Mitcham SW19 ......180 C4
South Croydon CR2 ..221 C2
Harewood Row NW1 237 B3
Harewood Terr UB2 .107 B2
Harfield Gdns 1 SE5 139 C2
Harfield Rd TW16 ..172 D1
Harfleur Ct SE11 ...261 C3
Harford Cl E4 ......19 C4
Harford Ho SE5 ......139 A6
W11 ......91 B3
Harford Rd E4 ......19 C4
Harford St E1 ......97 A3
Harford Wlk N2 ......48 B5
Hargood Cl HA3 ......44 C3
Hargood Rd SE3 ....143 C4
Hargrave Mans 2
N19 ......71 C6
Hargrave Park Prim Sch
N19 ......71 C6
Hargrave Pk N19 ....71 C6
Hargrave Pl N7 ......71 D3
Hargrave Rd N19 ....71 C6
Hargraves Ho 14
W12 ......112 B6
Hargwyne St SW9 ..138 B2
Haringey Pk N8 ......50 A4
Haringey Rd N8 ......50 A5
Harington Terr N18 .17 D1
Harkett Cl HA3 ......24 D1
Harkness Ho 20 E1 ..96 A1
Harland Ave
Sidcup DA15 ......167 C2
South Croydon CR0 ..222 A5
Harland Cl SW19 ....201 D6

Harland Fst Sch CR4 180 B1
Harland Rd SE12 165 A3
Harlands Gr BR6 226 D4
Harlech Ct 1 SE23 162 C3
Harlech Gdns TW5 128 C5
Harlech Rd N14 16 A1
Harlech Twr 5 W3 111 A4
Harlequin Ave TW8 131 A6
Harlequin Cl
Hayes UB4 84 D2
Isleworth TW7 152 C6
Harlequin Ct NW10 67 B2
Croydon CR2 221 A1
Ealing W5 109 C6
Harlequin Ho 1
DA18 125 A3
Harlequin Rd TW11 175 B3
Harlescott Rd SE15 140 D1
Harlesden Gdns NW10 89 D6
Harlesden Plaza 2
NW10 89 D5
Harlesden Prim Sch
NW10 89 C5
Harlesden Rd NW10 90 A6
Harlesden Sta NW10 89 B5
Harleston Cl 4 E5 74 C6
Harley Cl HA0 65 D2
Harley Cres HA1 42 B5
Harley Ct N20 14 A1
Wanstead E11 55 A2
Harleyford BR1 187 C2
Harleyford Ct SW8 270 C6
Harleyford Manor 8
W3 111 A5
Harleyford Rd
SE11 138 B6 270 C6
Harleyford St SE11 138 C6
Harley Gdns BR6 227 C4
SW10 114 A1 256 B1
Harley Gr E3 97 B4
Harley Ho E11 54 B2
NW1 238 B5
Harley Pl W1 93 B2 238 C3
Harley Rd NW10 89 C5
NW3 70 B1
Harrow HA1 42 B5
Harley St W1 93 B2 238 C3
Harley Villas NW10 89 C5
Harling Ct 3 SW11 136 D3
Harlinger St SE18 122 A3
Harlington Bridge
UB3 105 C1
Harlington Cl UB7 127 A5
Harlington Cnr UB3 127 B4
Harlington Com Sch
UB3 105 B2
Harlington Rd DA7 147 A2
Hillingdon UB8 82 C3
Harlington Rd E
TW13,TW14 150 C3
Harlington Rd W
TW14 150 B5
Harlowe Ho 13 E8 95 D6
Harlow Mans 2 IG11 78 D1
Harlow Rd N13 17 B1
Harlyn Dr HA5 40 B6
Harlyn Prim Sch HA5 40 B6
Harlynwood 19 SE5 139 A5
Harman Ave IG8 36 D4
Harman Cl NW2 69 A5
9 SE1 118 A1
Chingford E4 36 B6
Harman Dr DA15 167 D5
NW2 69 A4
Harman Rd EN1 17 D6
Harmondsworth La
UB7 126 B6
Harmondsworth Rd
UB7 104 A2
Harmon Ho 6 SE8 119 B2
Harmony Cl NW11 47 A4
Harmony Way BR1 187 A1
NW4 46 C5
Harmood Gr NW1 71 B1
Harmood Ho 2 NW1 71 B1
Harmood St NW1 71 B1
Harmsworth St
SE17 116 D1 261 C1
Harmsworth Way N20 13 C3
Harness Rd SE28 124 A4
Harold Ave Erith DA17 125 B1
Hayes UB3 105 D3
Harold Ct 14 SE16 118 D4
Harold Est SE1 263 B5
Harold Gibbons Ct 12
SE7 143 C6
Harold Ho 16 E2 96 D5
Harold Laski Ho EC1 234 D1
Harold Maddison Ho
SE17 261 D2
Harold Pl SE11 261 A1
Harold Rd E11 54 C1
E13 99 B6
N15 51 D4
N8 50 B5
NW10 89 B4
Chingford E4 20 A1
South Norwood SE19 183 B3
Sutton SM1 218 B4
Woodford IG8 37 A2
Haroldstone Rd E17 53 A4
Harold Wilson Ho
SW6 264 D5
Harp Alley EC4 241 C2
Harp Bsns Ctr The
NW2 68 A6
Harpenden Rd
Wanstead E12 77 C6
West Norwood SE27,
SW16 160 D2
Harpenmead Point
NW2 69 B6
Harper Cl N14 15 C6
Harper Ho 3 SW9 138 D2
Harper Mews SW17 158 A1
Harper Rd
SE1 117 A3 262 B6
Newham E6 100 B1
Harper's Yd N17 33 D2
Harp Island Cl NW10 67 B6
Harp La EC3 253 A5
Harpley Sq E1 96 D3
Harpour Rd IG11 79 A2
Harp Rd W7 86 D3
Harpsden St SW11 268 A1
Harpur Mews WC1 240 C4
Harpur St WC1 94 B2 240 C4
Harraden Rd SE3 143 C4
Harrier Ave E11 55 B3
Harrier Ct TW4 129 A3
Harrier Ho 9 SW11 136 C2
Harrier Mews SE28 123 B4
Harrier Rd NW9 27 C1
Harriers Cl W5 110 A6
Harrier Way E6 100 B2
Harries Rd UB4 84 C3
Harriet Cl E8 96 A6
Harriet Gdns CR0 222 A6
Harriet Ho SW6 265 D3
Harriet St
SW1 114 D4 247 D1
Harriet Tubman Cl 21
SW2 160 C4
Harriet Way WD23 8 B4
Harriet Wlk
SW1 114 D4 247 D1
Harringay Gdns N8 50 D5
Harringay Green Lanes Sta
N4 50 D3
Harringay Rd N15 50 D5
Harringay Sta N4 50 C3
Harrington Cl NW10 67 B5
Wallington CR0 220 A6
Harrington Ct SW7 256 D4
9 W9 91 B4
6 South Croydon CR0 221 B6
Harrington Gdns
SW7 114 A2 256 A3
Harrington Hill E5 52 B1
Harrington Hill Prim Sch
E5 52 B1
Harrington Ho E5 52 C1
NW1 232 A2
SW1 259 D2
Harrington Rd E11 54 C1
SW7 114 B2 256 C4
Croydon SE25 206 B5
Harrington Rd Sta
SE25 206 C6
Harrington Sq
NW1 93 C5 232 A3
Harrington St
NW1 93 C4 232 A2
Harrington Way
SE18 121 D3
Harriott Cl SE10 120 D2
Harriott Ho 11 E1 96 C1
Harris City Tech Coll
SE19 183 D2
Harris Cl Enfield EN2 4 D4
Heston TW5 129 C4
Harris Cotts 1 E15 98 D6
Harris Ho 10 E3 97 C4
8 SW9 138 C2
Harris Lo SE6 164 A3
Harrison Cl N20 14 C3
Harrison Ho SE17 262 C2
Harrison Rd RM10 81 D2
Harrisons Ct 1 SE14 140 D6
Harrison's Rise CR0 220 D5
Harrison St
WC1 94 A4 233 B1
Harrison Way TW17 192 D4
Harris Rd DA7 147 B4
Dagenham RM9 81 B3
Harris St E17 53 B2
SE5 139 B5
Harris Way TW16 171 C2
Harrodian Sch The
SW13 133 D5
Harrogate Ct 2 SE26 162 A1
Harrold Ho 1 NW3 70 A1
Harrold Rd RM8 80 B3
Harrow Ave EN1 17 D5
Harroway Rd SW11 136 B3
Harrowby St
W1 92 C1 237 B2
Harrow Cl KT9 213 D1
Harrow Coll HA1 42 C2
Harrow Coll (Harrow
Weald Campus) HA3 24 C4
Harrowdene Cl HA0 65 D4
Harrowdene Ct
SW19 179 A5
Harrowdene Gdns
TW11 175 A3
Harrowdene Rd HA0 65 D4
Harrow Dr N9 17 D3
Harrowes Meade HA8 10 C1
Harrow Fields Gdns
HA1 64 C5
Harrowgate Ho 22 E9 74 D2
Harrowgate Rd E9 75 A1
Harrow Gn E11 76 C5
Harrow High Sch HA1 43 A3
Harrow Hospl HA2 64 C6
Harrow La E14 120 A6
Harrow Lo SM2 218 B2
Harrow Manor Way
SE2 124 C3
Harrow Mus & Her Ctr*
HA2 42 A6
Harrow-on-the-Hill Sta
HA1 42 C3
Harrow Pk HA1 64 C6
Harrow Pl E1 95 C1 243 B2
Harrow Rd E11 76 D5
2 E6 100 A6
W2 92 A2 236 B3
W2,W9 91 C3
Ashford TW15 148 C2
Barking IG11 101 C6
Carshalton SM1,SM2,
SM5 218 C2
Ilford IG1 79 A4
Wembley HA0 65 A4
Wembley HA0 65 D3
Wembley HA9 66 C2
Harrow Sch HA1 42 C1
Harrow St NW1 237 A4
Harrow View
Harrow HA1,HA2 42 B5
Hayes UB3 84 A1
Hillingdon UB10 83 A4
Harrow View Rd W5 87 B3
Harrow Way
Charlton TW17 171 A1
South Oxhey WD19 23 A6
Harrow Weald Pk HA3 24 B4
Harrow & Wealdstone Sta
HA1 42 C5
Harry Ct 15 NW9 46 A5
Harry Gosling Prim Sch
E1 96 A1
Harry Hinkins Ho
SE17 262 B1
Harry Lambourn Ho 10
SE15 140 B5
Harston 15 KT1 176 C1
Harston Dr EN3 7 C5
Hart Ct E12 78 C1
Harte Rd TW3 129 B3
Hartfield Ave
Borehamwood WD6 10 C6
Northolt UB5 84 B5
Hartfield Cl WD6 10 C6
Hartfield Cres BR4 225 A5
Merton SW19 179 B3
Hartfield Gr SE20 184 C2
Hartfield Ho UB5 84 B5
Hartfield Rd
Chessington KT9 213 D3
Hayes BR4 225 A4
Merton SW19 179 C3
Hartfield Terr E3 97 C5
Hartford Ave HA3 43 B6
Hartford Rd DA5 169 C5
Hartford Rd *continued*
West Ewell KT19 214 D2
Hart Gr Ealing W5 110 C5
Southall UB1 85 C2
Hart Grove Ct 3 W5 110 C5
Hartham Cl N7 72 A3
Isleworth TW7 131 A4
Hartham Rd N7 72 A3
Isleworth TW7 131 A4
Tottenham N17 33 D1
Hart Ho SW2 160 C3
Harting Rd SE9 166 A1
Hartington Cl BR6 227 A3
Harrow HA1 64 C4
Hartington Ct SW8 270 A2
Chiswick W4 132 D5
Hartington Rd E17 53 A3
SW8 138 A5 270 A3
Chiswick W4 133 A4
Ealing W13 109 B6
Newham E16 99 B1
Southall UB2 107 A3
Twickenham TW1 153 B5
Hartismere Rd
SW6 135 B5 264 D4
Hartlake Rd E9 75 A2
Hartland NW1 232 B5
Hartland Cl
Edgware HA8 10 C2
Enfield N21 17 A5
Hartland Ct 5 N11 30 D5
Hartland Dr
Edgware HA8 10 C2
Ruislip HA4 62 B4
Hartland Rd E15 76 D1
N11 30 D5
NW1 71 B1
NW6 91 B6
Cheam SM4 201 D2
Hampton TW12 173 D6
Isleworth TW7 131 A2
Hartlands Cl DA5 169 B5
Hartlands Cvn Pk The
TW5 128 B6
Hartland Way
Croydon CR0 223 A6
Morden SM4 201 B2
Hartlepool Ct E16 122 D5
Hartley Ave E6 100 A6
NW7 27 D5
Hartley Cl BR1 188 B1
NW7 27 D5
Hartley Ct W5 110 C5
Hartley Ho N3 29 D4
SE1 263 D4
Putney SW15 156 A6
Hartley Prim Sch E6 100 A6
Hartley Rd E11 54 D1
Bexley DA16 146 C5
Thornton Heath CR0 205 A2
Hartley St E2 96 C4
Hart Lo EN5 1 A2
Hartmann Rd E16 122 A5
Hartmoor Mews EN3 6 D6
Hartnoll Ho 4 N7 72 C3
Hartnoll St N7 72 B3
Harton Cl BR1 187 D2
Harton Lo 2 SE8 141 C4
Harton Rd N9 18 B2
Harton St SE8 141 C4
Hartopp Ct N16 73 C5
Hartopp Point SW6 264 B4
Hartsbourne Ave WD23 8 B2
Hartsbourne Cl WD23 8 B2
Hartsbourne Ct 5
UB1 86 A1
Hartsbourne Pk WD23 8 C2
Hartsbourne Prim Sch
WD23 8 B2
Hartsbourne Rd WD23 8 B2
Harts Gr IG8 37 A5
Hartshill Cl UB10 60 D2
Hartshorn Alley EC3 243 B1
Hartshorn Gdns E6 100 C3
Hart's La SE14 141 A4
Harts La IG11 78 D2
Hartslock Dr SE2 124 D4
Hartsmead Rd SE9 166 B2
Hart Sq SM4 201 C3
Hart St EC3 253 B6
Hartsway EN3 6 C1
Hartswood Gn WD23 8 B2
Hartswood Ho 10
SW2 160 A3
Hartswood Rd W12 111 D3
Hartsworth Cl E13 98 D5
Hartville Rd SE18 123 C2
Hartwell Dr E4 36 A4
Hartwell Ho 2 SE7 121 B1
Hartwell St E8 73 D2
Harvard Ct NW6 69 D3
9 SE9 166 C5
Harvard Hill W4 132 D6
Harvard Ho 3 SE17 138 D6
Putney SW15 156 D5
Harvard Mans 18
SW11 136 B1
Harvard Rd SE13 164 A6
W4 110 D1
11 W4 111 A1
Hounslow TW7 130 C4
Harvel Cres SE2 124 D1
Harvest Bank Rd BR4 225 A5
Harvest Ct
Beckenham BR3 185 C3
Littleton TW17 192 C5
Harvesters Cl TW7 152 B6
Harvest La
Loughton IG10 21 D4
Thames Ditton KT7 197 A3
Harvest Rd TW13 150 A1
Harvey Ct E17 53 C4
SW11 267 B2
Harvey Dr TW12 173 C2
Harvey Gdns E11 54 D1
SE7 121 C1
Harvey Ho 10 E1 96 B3
N1 235 D5
N8 50 A6
SW1 259 D1
Barking IG11 79 A1
Brentford TW8 110 A1
Dagenham RM6 58 D5
Harvey Lo 8 W9 91 C2
Harvey Mews N8 50 B4
Harvey Point 7 E16 99 A2
Harvey Rd E11 54 D1
N8 50 B4
15 SE5 139 B4
Hillingdon UB10 82 C5
Ilford IG1 78 D3
Ruislip UB5 62 C1
Twickenham TW4 151 B4
Walton-on-T KT12 194 A2
Harvey St N1 235 D5
Harvill Rd DA14 191 A5
UB9 38 A2
Harvil Rd UB9,UB10 38 A2
Harvington Sch W5 87 D1
Harvington Wlk E8 74 A1
Harvist Rd NW6 91 A5
Harwell Cl HA4 39 B1
Harwick Mans SE18 122 A3
Harwood Ave BR1 187 B1
Mitcham CR4 202 C6
Harwood Cl N12 30 C4
Wembley HA0 65 D4
Harwood Ct N1 235 D5
Putney SW15 134 C1
Harwood Dr UB10 82 B6
Harwood Point SE16 119 B4
Harwood Rd
SW6 135 D5 265 C3
Harwoods Yd N21 16 C4
Harwood Terr
SW6 135 D4 265 C2
Hascombe Ho 11
SW15 156 B3
Hascombe Terr 2
SE5 139 B3
Haselbury Rd N9 17 C1
Haseley End SE23 162 C4
Haselrigge Rd SW4 137 D1
Haseltine Prim Sch
SE26 185 B6
Haseltine Rd SE26 185 B6
Haselwood Dr EN2 4 D1
Haskard Rd RM9 80 D4
Hasker St
SW3 114 C2 257 B4
Haslam Ave SM3 201 A1
Haslam Cl N1 72 C1
Uxbridge UB10 61 A6
Haslam Ct N11 31 B6
Haslam Ho 1 N1 73 A1
Haslam St SE15 139 D4
Haslemere Ave NW4 46 D3
W13 109 A3
Barnet, London EN4 14 D3
Cranford TW5 128 C3
Mitcham CR4,SW19 180 B1
Wandsworth SW18 157 D2
Haslemere Cl
Hampton TW12 173 B5
Wallington SM6 220 A3
Haslemere Ct 5 N16 51 C1
Haslemere Fst Sch
CR4 180 B1
Haslemere Gdns N3 47 B5
Haslemere & Heathrow Est
The TW4 128 B2
Haslemere Ind Est
Feltham TW14 150 A6
Wandsworth SW18 157 D2
Haslemere Rd DA7 147 C3
N8 50 A2
Ilford IG3 79 D6
Southgate N21 16 D3
Thornton Heath CR7 204 D4
Hasler Cl SE28 124 C6
Hasler Ct E12 78 A4
Haslett Rd TW17 171 C1
Hasluck Gdns EN5 14 A5
Hasmonean High Sch
(Boys) NW4 28 D1
Hasmonean High Sch
(Girls) NW7 28 A2
Hasmonean Prim Sch
NW4 46 D4
Hassard St E2 95 D5
Hassendean Rd SE3 143 B5
Hassett Rd E9 75 A2
Hassocks Cl SE23,
SE26 162 B1
Hassocks Rd SW16 181 D2
Hassop Rd NW2 68 D4
Hassop Wlk SE9 188 A6
Hasted Rd SE7 121 D1
Hastings Ave IG6 57 A5
Hastings Cl 16 SE15 140 A5
New Barnet EN5 2 A1
Wembley HA0 65 C4
Hastings Dr KT6 197 C3
Hastings Ho 11 SE18 122 B2
18 W12 112 B6
Ealing W13 109 B6
Enfield EN3 6 C3
Tottenham N17 34 A2
Hastings Hos WC1 233 A1
Hastings Pl 1 CR0 205 D1
Hastings Rd BR2 226 A6
N11 31 D5
N17 51 B6
Croydon CR0 205 D1
Ealing W13 109 B6
Hastings St
WC1 94 A4 233 A1
Hastingwood Ct E17 53 D4
Hastingwood Trad Est
N18 34 D4
N18 35 A4
Hastoe Cl UB4 85 A3
Hatcham Mews Bsns Ctr
SE14 140 D4
Hatcham Park Mews
SE14 140 D4
Hatcham Park Rd
SE14 140 D4
Hatcham Rd SE15 140 C6
Hatchard Rd N19 72 A6
Hatchcroft NW4 46 B6
Hatch End High Sch
HA3 23 D2
Hatch End Sta HA5 23 C3
Hatchett Rd TW14 149 A3
Hatchfield Ho 8 N15 51 C3
Hatch Gr RM6 59 A5
Hatch La E4 20 C1
Hatch Pl TW10 176 B5
Hatch Rd SW16 182 A1
Hatch The EN3 6 D4
Hatchwoods IG8 36 D6
Hatcliffe Almshouses 8
SE10 120 C1
Hatcliffe Cl SE3 142 D2
Hatcliffe St SE10 120 D1
Hatfield Cl SE14 140 D5
Ilford IG6 56 D6
Mitcham CR4 202 B5
Hatfield Ct
Greenwich SE3 143 A5
8 Northolt UB5 84 C4
Hatfield First Sch
SM4 201 A3
Hatfield Ho E11 54 D2
EC1 242 A5
16 Kingston KT6 198 A4
Hatfield Mead SM4 201 C4
Hatfield Rd E15 76 C3
W4 111 B4
Dagenham RM9 81 A1
10 Ealing W13,W7 109 A5
Hatfields SE1 116 C5 251 B4
Hathaway Cl BR2 210 B1
Ruislip HA4 61 D4
Stanmore HA7 25 A5
Hathaway Cres E12 78 C2
Hathaway Gdns
Ealing W13 87 A2

Hat – Hea 331

Hathaway Gdns *continued*
Ilford RM6 ...58 D4
Hathaway Ho 3 N1 ...95 C4
Hathaway Prim Sch
W13 ...86 D2
Hathaway Rd CR0 ...204 D2
Hatherleigh Cl
Chessington KT9 ...213 D3
Morden SM4 ...201 C5
Hatherleigh Ho SM4 .201 C5
Hatherleigh Rd HA4 ..62 A6
Hatherley Cres DA14 .168 A2
Hatherley Ct 6 W2 ..91 D1
Hatherley Gdns E6 ..99 D4
N8 ...50 A3
Hatherley Gr W2 ...91 D1
Hatherley Ho 2 E17 ..53 C5
Hatherley Mews E17 ..53 C5
Hatherley Rd E17 ...53 C5
Richmond TW9 ...132 B4
Sidcup DA14 ...168 A1
Hatherley St SW1 ...259 B3
Hathern Gdns SE9 ...188 C6
Hatherop Rd TW12 ...173 B3
Hathersage Ct N1 ...73 B3
Hathersley Ho 3
SW2 ...160 C4
Hathorne Cl 3 SE15 .140 B3
Hathway Ho 3 SE15 .140 C3
Hathway St 4 SE15 .140 C3
Hatley Ave IG6 ...57 A5
Hatley Cl N11 ...30 D5
Hatley Rd N4,N7 ...72 B6
Hat & Mitre Ct EC1 ..241 D5
Hatteraick St 6
SE16 ...118 C4
Hattersfield Cl DA17 .125 B2
Hatton Cl SE18 ...145 B5
Hatton Cross Rdbt
TW6 ...127 D2
Hatton Cross Sta
TW6 ...127 D1
Hatton Ct BR7 ...188 B3
Hatton Gdn
EC1 ...94 C2 241 B4
Hatton Gdns CR4 ...202 D4
Hatton Gn TW14 ...128 A1
Hatton Ho 13 E1 ...118 A6
Hatton Pl EC1 ...241 B4
Hatton Rd
Hatton TW14,TW6 ...149 C6
Thornton Heath CR0 ..204 C1
Hatton Rd N TW6 ...127 B4
Hatton Row NW8 ...236 D5
Hatton Sch IG8 ...55 D6
Hatton St NW8 ...236 D5
Hatton Wall
EC1 ...94 C2 241 B4
Haughmond 4 N12 ..29 D6
Haunch of Venison Yd
W1 ...238 C1
Hauteville Court Gdns 2
W6 ...111 D3
Havana Rd SW18,
SW19 ...157 C2
Havannah St E14 ...119 C4
Havant Rd E17 ...54 A6
Havelock Cl 13 W12 .112 B6
Havelock Ct UB2 ...107 B3
Havelock Hall 8
CR0 ...205 D1
Havelock Ho
4 Croydon CR0 ...205 D1
Forest Hill SE23 ...162 C3
Havelock Pl HA1 ...42 C3
Havelock Prim Sch
UB2 ...107 B3
Havelock Rd DA17 ...125 B2
Bromley BR2 ...209 C5
Croydon CR0 ...221 D6
Harrow HA3 ...42 C6
Southall UB2 ...107 C3
Tottenham N17 ...34 A1
Wimbledon SW19 ...180 A5
Havelock St
N1 ...94 A6 233 B6
Ilford IG1 ...78 D6
Havelock Terr
SW8 ...137 B5 268 D3
Havelock Wlk SE23 ..162 C2
Haven Cl SE9 ...166 B1
Hayes UB4 ...83 C3
Sidcup DA14 ...190 C4
Wimbledon SW19 ...156 D1
Haven Ct BR3 ...186 A1
Haven Gn W5 ...87 D1
Haven Green Ct W5 ..87 D1
Havenhurst Rise EN2 ...4 C3
Haven La W5 ...88 A1
Haven Lo NW11 ...47 B4

Haven Lo *continued*
7 SE18 ...122 D2
15 Enfield EN1 ...17 C6
Haven Pl W5 ...109 D6
Havenpool NW8 ...91 D6
Haven Rd TW15 ...148 D1
Haven St 17 NW1 ...71 B1
Haven The
Ashford TW16 ...172 A3
East Barnet N14 ...15 B5
Richmond TW9 ...132 C2
Havenwood HA9 ...66 D5
Havercourt 3 NW3 ..70 C2
Haverfield Gdns TW9 132 C5
Haverfield Rd E3 ...97 A4
Haverford Way HA8 ..26 B2
Havergal Villas N15 ..50 D6
Haverhill Rd
Chingford E4 ...20 A3
Streatham SW12 ...159 C3
Havering 8 NW1 ...71 B1
Havering Gdns RM6 ..58 D4
Havering Ho N4 ...51 A2
Havering St E1 ...96 D1
Havering Way IG11 ..102 B4
Haverley 14 SW20 ..178 D3
Haversham Cl TW1 ..153 D5
Haversham Ct UB6 ..64 D2
Haversham Lo NW2 ..68 D3
Haversham Pl N6 ...70 D6
Haverstock Ct 2
BR5 ...190 B1
Haverstock Hill NW3 ..70 D2
Haverstock Rd NW5 ..71 A3
Haverstock Sch NW1 .71 A2
Haverstock St
N1 ...94 D5 234 D3
Haverthwaite Rd BR6 227 B5
Havilland Ct HA8 ...26 B6
Havil St SE5 ...139 C4
Havisham Ho 23
SE16 ...118 A4
Havisham Pl SW16 ..182 D3
Hawarden Gr SE24 ..161 A4
Hawarden Hill NW2 ..68 A5
Hawarden Rd E17 ...52 D5
Hawberry Ho N7 ...72 A2
Hawbridge Rd E11 ...54 B1
Hawes Down Inf Sch BR4 ..
Hawes Down Jun Sch
BR4 ...208 B1
Hawes La BR4 ...224 C6
Hawes Rd BR1 ...187 B2
Edmonton N18 ...34 B4
Hawes St N1 ...72 D1
Haweswater Ho TW1 152 D6
Hawfinch 29 NW9 ...27 D2
Hawgood St E3 ...97 C2
Hawkdene E4 ...20 A5
Hawke Ct UB4 ...84 C3
Hawkedale Fst Sch
TW16 ...193 D6
Hawke Ho 20 E1 ...96 D3
Hawke Park Rd N22 ..50 D6
Hawke Pl 29 SE16 ..118 D4
Hawker 28 NW9 ...27 D2
Hawker Ct 14 KT2 ..176 C3
Hawke Rd SE19 ...183 C4
Hawkesbury Rd
SW15 ...156 B6
Hawkesfield Rd SE23 163 B2
Hawkesley Cl TW1 ..175 A6
Hawkes Rd
Feltham TW14 ...150 A4
Mitcham CR4 ...180 D2
Hawkesworth Ho 5
SW4 ...159 C5
Hawke Twr 4 SE14 ..141 A6
Hawkewood Rd
TW16 ...194 A6
Hawkfield Ct TW7 ..130 C3
Hawk Ho 7 SW11 ..136 C2
Hawkhurst Gdns KT9 214 A4
Hawkhurst Rd SW16 .181 D2
Hawkhurst Way
New Malden KT3 ...199 B4
West Wickham BR4 ..223 D6
Hawkinge N17 ...33 B1
Hawkins Cl NW7 ...27 B5
Harrow HA1 ...42 B2
Hawkins Ho 3 SE8 ..141 C6
Hawkins Rd TW11 ..175 B4
Hawkins Way SE6 ..185 C5
Hawkley Gdns SE27 ..160 D2
Hawkridge 19 NW5 ..71 A2
Hawkridge Cl RM6 ..58 C3
Hawksbrook La BR3 .208 A3
Hawkshead NW1 ...232 A2
Hawkshead Cl BR1 ..186 C3
Hawkshead Rd NW10 .67 D1

Hawkshead Rd *continued*
W4 ...111 C4
Hawkslade Rd SE15 .162 D6
Hawksley Rd N16 ...73 C5
Hawks Mews 10 SE10 142 A5
Hawksmoor Cl 2 E6 100 A1
SE18 ...123 C1
Hawksmoor Mews
E1 ...118 B6
Hawksmoor Sch
SE28 ...124 B6
Hawksmoor St 5
W6 ...134 D6
Hawksmouth E4 ...20 A4
Hawks Rd KT1 ...176 B1
Hawkstone Rd SE16 .118 C2
Hawkswood Sch E4 ..20 A6
Hawkwell Ct E4 ...20 A1
Hawkwell Ho RM8 ...81 C6
Hawkwell Wlk N1 ..235 B6
Hawkwood Cres E4 ..19 D5
Hawkwood La BR7 ..189 A2
Hawkwood Mount 1
E5 ...52 B1
Hawlands Dr HA5 ...41 A2
Hawley Cl TW12 ...173 B4
Hawley Cres NW1 ...71 B1
Hawley Inf Sch NW1 ..71 B1
Hawley Mews 4 NW1 71 B1
Hawley Rd N18 ...34 D5
3 NW1 ...71 B1
Hawley St NW1 ...71 B1
Hawley Way TW15 ..170 D5
Haworth Ct E15 ...76 A3
Haworth Ho 7 SW2 .160 C5
Hawstead Rd SE6 ..163 D5
Hawsted IG9 ...21 B4
Hawthorn Ave Bow E3 .97 B6
Bowes Park N13 ...32 A5
South Norwood CR7 ..182 D2
Hawthorn Cl BR5 ..211 B3
Cranford TW5 ...128 B5
Hampton TW12 ...173 C5
Hawthorn Cres SW17 181 A5
Hawthorn Ct
Putney SW15 ...134 B2
Richmond TW9 ...132 D4
8 West Norwood
SW16 ...182 C5
Hawthorn Ctr HA1 ...43 A4
Hawthornden Cl N12 .30 C4
Hawthorndene Cl
BR2 ...225 A6
Hawthorndene Rd
BR2 ...225 A6
Hawthorn Dr
Coney Hall BR4 ...224 C4
Harrow HA2 ...41 C3
Hawthorne Ave
Harrow HA3 ...43 A3
Mitcham CR4 ...180 B1
Ruislip HA4 ...40 B2
Wallington SM5 ...219 A1
Hawthorne Cl BR1 ..210 B6
N1 ...73 C2
Sutton SM1 ...218 A6
Hawthorne Cres UB7 104 B4
Hawthorne Ct
Chingford E4 ...35 D4
Ealing W5 ...110 A5
Pinner HA6 ...22 A1
Hawthorne Gr NW9 ..45 A2
Hawthorne Ho SW1 ..259 B1
Hawthorne Mews UB6 86 A1
Hawthorne Rd BR1 ..210 B6
E17 ...53 C6
Edmonton N18 ...33 D5
Feltham TW14 ...150 A3
Hawthorne Way N9 ..17 D2
Hawthorn Farm Ave
UB5 ...85 A6
Hawthorn Gdns W5 .109 D3
Hawthorn Gr
Edgware EN5 ...11 D5
Enfield EN2 ...5 B5
Penge SE20 ...184 B2
Hawthorn Hatch
TW8 ...131 B5
Hawthorn Mews NW7 .29 A2
Hawthorn Pl UB3 ...105 D6
Hawthorn Rd DA6 ...147 B1
N8 ...50 A6
NW10 ...68 A1
Brentford TW8 ...131 B5
Carshalton SM1,SM2,
SM5 ...218 C2
Wallington SM5,SM6 ..219 B1
Woodford IG9 ...37 D6
Hawthorns IG8 ...21 A1
Hawthorns The KT17 .216 A1

Hawthorn Terr DA15 .167 D6
Hawthorn Way TW17 193 B5
Hawthorn Wlk W10 ...91 A3
Hawtrey Ave UB5 ...84 D5
Hawtrey Dr HA4 ...40 A2
Hawtrey Rd NW3 ...70 C1
Haxted Rd BR1 ...187 B2
Haybridge Ho 1 E5 ..74 C6
Hay Cl E15 ...76 D1
Haycroft Gdns NW10 ..90 B6
Haycroft Mans NW10 .90 A6
Haycroft Rd SW2 ...160 A6
Surbiton KT6 ...214 A6
Hay Currie St E14 ...97 D1
Hayday Rd E16 ...99 A2
Hayden's Pl W11 ...91 B1
Haydock Ave UB5 ...63 C2
Haydock Gn UB5 ...63 C2
Haydock Green Flats 2
UB5 ...63 C2
Haydon Cl NW9 ...45 A5
Enfield EN1 ...17 C6
Haydon Ct NW9 ...45 A5
Haydon Dr HA5 ...40 A5
Haydon Ho Ealing W7 108 D5
Teddington TW11 ...175 C3
Haydon Park Rd
SW19 ...179 D5
Haydon Rd RM8 ...80 C6
Haydon Sch HA5 ...39 D6
Haydon's Rd SW19 ...180 A4
Haydons Road Sta
SW19 ...180 A5
Haydon St E1,
EC3 ...117 D6 253 C6
Haydon Way SW11 ...136 B1
Haydon Wlk E1 ...243 D1
Hayes Bridge Ret Pk
UB4 ...106 D6
Hayes Chase BR4 ...208 C3
Hayes Cl BR2 ...225 A6
Hayes Cres NW11 ...47 B4
Cheam SM3 ...216 D4
Hayes Ct 23 SE5 ...139 A5
Streatham SW12 ...160 A3
Wimbledon SW19 ...179 A4
Hayes End Cl UB4 ...83 B2
Hayes End Dr UB4 ...83 B3
Hayesend Ho SW17 ..180 A6
Hayes End Rd UB4 ...83 B3
Hayesford Park Dr
BR2 ...208 D4
Hayes Garden BR2 ..209 A1
Hayes & Harlington Sta
UB3 ...105 D3
Hayes Hill BR2 ...208 C1
Hayes Hill Rd BR2 ..208 C1
Hayes La BR2 ...209 A4
Beckenham BR2,BR3 ..208 B5
Hayes Manor Sch UB3 83 C1
Hayes Mead Rd BR2 .208 C1
Hayes Park Sch UB4 ..83 D3
Hayes Pl NW1 ...237 B5
Hayes Prim Sch BR2 209 B1
Hayes Rd BR2 ...209 A5
Southall UB2 ...106 B2
Hayes Sch BR2 ...225 B6
Hayes St BR2 ...209 B1
Hayes Sta BR2 ...208 D1
Hayes Way BR3 ...208 B5
Hayes Wood Ave BR2 209 B1
Hayfield Pas E1 ...96 C3
Hayford Ct NW2 ...68 D5
Haygarth Pl 2 SW19 178 D5
Haygreen Cl KT2 ...176 D4
Hay Hill W1 ..115 B6 248 D5
Hay La NW9 ...45 B5
Hayland Cl NW9 ...45 B5
Hay Lane Sch NW9 ...45 A5
Hayles Bldgs SE11 ..261 D4
Hayles St
SE11 ...116 D3 261 C4
Haylett Gdns KT1 ..197 D5
Hayling Ave TW13 ..150 A1
Hayling Cl 20 N16 ...73 C3
Hayling Ct SM3 ...216 C4
Haymaker Cl UB10 ...60 B1
Hayman Cres UB4 ...83 B5
Haymans Point SE11 .260 C2
Haymarket
SW1 ...115 D6 249 C5
Haymeads Dr KT10 ..212 A2
Haymer Gdns KT4 ..216 A5
Haymerle Ho 6 SE15 140 A5
Haymerle Rd SE15 ..140 A6
Haymerle Sch SE15 .140 A6
Haymill Cl UB6 ...86 D4
Hayne Ho W11 ...244 A4
Hayne Rd BR3 ...185 B2
Haynes Cl N11 ...15 A1

Haynes Cl *continued*
SE3 ...142 C2
Tottenham N17 ...34 B3
Haynes Dr N9 ...18 B1
Haynes Ho 3 E9 ...74 D2
Haynes La SE19 ...183 C4
Haynes Rd HA0 ...66 A1
Hayne St EC1 .94 D2 241 D4
Haynt Wlk SW20 ...201 A6
Hay's Galleria SE1 ..253 A4
Hay's La SE1 ...253 A4
Haysleigh Gdns SE20 184 A1
Haysleigh Ho SE20 ..184 B1
Hay's Mews
W1 ...115 B6 248 C4
Hay St E2 ...96 A6
Haystall Cl UB4 ...83 C5
Haystocks E18 ...55 C6
Hayter Ho W12 ...112 A6
Hayter Rd SW2 ...160 B6
Haythorn Ho
SW11 ...136 B4 266 D1
Hayton Cl 11 E8 ...73 D2
Hayward Cl SW19 ..179 D2
Hayward Ct 14 SW4 .138 A3
Mitcham CR4 ...180 B1
Hayward Gallery*
SE1 ...116 B5 250 D4
Hayward Gdns SW15 156 C5
Hayward Ho E5 ...74 B5
N1 ...234 A4
Hayward Rd N20 ...14 A2
Thames Ditton KT7 ..196 D1
Haywards Cl RM6 ...58 C4
Haywards Pl EC1 ...241 C6
Haywood Cl HA5 ...22 D1
Haywood Lo N11 ...31 D4
23 N7 ...71 D3
Haywood Rd BR2 ...209 D5
Haywood Rise BR6 ..227 C3
Hazel Ave UB7 ...104 C3
Hazelbank KT5 ...199 A1
Hazel Bank SE25 ...183 C1
Hazelbank Rd SE6 ..164 C2
Hazelbourne Rd
SW12 ...159 B5
Hazelbury Cl SW19 ..179 C1
Hazelbury Gn N9 ...17 C1
Hazelbury Inf Sch N9 .17 C1
Hazelbury Jun Sch N9 17 C1
Hazelbury La N9 ...17 C1
Hazel Cl N19 ...71 C6
NW9 ...27 D1
SE15 ...140 A3
Brentford TW8 ...131 B5
Croydon CR0 ...206 D1
Edmonton N13 ...17 B1
Mitcham CR4 ...203 D5
Twickenham TW2 ...152 A4
Hazelcroft HA5 ...23 D4
Hazelcroft Cl UB10 ...60 B1
Hazel Ct Ealing W5 ..110 A6
9 West Norwood
SW16 ...182 C5
Hazeldean Rd NW10 ..67 B1
Hazeldene Dr HA5 ...40 C6
Hazeldene Gdns UB10 83 A6
Hazeldene Rd
Bexley DA16 ...146 C3
Ilford IG3 ...80 B6
Hazeldon Rd SE4 ..163 A6
Hazel Gdns HA8 ...26 D6
Hazel Gr
Dagenham RM6 ...59 A6
Enfield EN1 ...18 A5
Feltham TW14 ...150 A3
Forest Hill SE26 ...184 D6
Orpington BR6 ...226 D6
Wembley HA0 ...88 A6
Hazelgreen Cl N21 ...16 D3
Hazel Ho 12 NW3 ...70 D2
SE4 ...141 B2
Hazelhurst BR3 ...186 B2
Hazelhurst Ct SE6 ..186 A5
Hazelhurst Rd SW17 .180 B6
Hazellville Rd N19 ...49 D1
Hazel Mead EN5 ...12 B6
Hazelmere Cl
Feltham TW14 ...149 C5
Northolt UB5 ...85 B5
Hazelmere Ct 10
SW2 ...160 B3
Hazelmere Dr UB5 ...85 B5
Hazelmere Rd BR5 ..211 B5
NW6 ...91 B6
Northolt UB5 ...85 B5
Hazelmere Way BR2 .209 A3
Hazelmere Wlk UB5 ..85 B5
Hazel Rd E15 ...76 C3
NW10 ...90 C4

Hazeltree La UB5 ...85 A4
Hazel Way E4 ...35 B4
SE1 ...263 C4
Hazel Wlk BR2 ...210 C3
Hazelwood IG10 ...21 D6
Hazelwood Ave SM4 .201 D5
Hazelwood Cl E5 ...75 A5
W5 ...110 A4
Harrow HA2 ...41 D5
Hazelwood Cres N13 ..32 C6
Hazelwood Ct
1 NW10 ...67 C5
Surbiton KT6 ...198 A3
Hazelwood Dr HA5 ...22 B1
Hazelwood Ho
11 SE8 ...119 A2
Beckenham BR2 ...208 C6
Edmonton N13 ...32 D6
Hazelwood Jun & Inf Schs
N13 ...32 C6
Hazelwood La N13 ...32 C6
Hazelwood Lo BR4 ..208 A2
Hazelwood Mans
SW6 ...264 C2
Hazelwood Rd E17 ...53 A4
Enfield EN1 ...17 D5
Hazlebury Rd SW6 ..135 D3
Hazledean Rd CR0 ..221 B6
Hazledene Rd W4 ..133 A6
Hazlemere Bsns Ctr
EN1 ...18 B6
Hazlemere Gdns KT4 200 A1
Hazlewell Rd SW15 ..156 C6
Hazlewood Cres W10 .91 A3
Hazlewood Twr W10 ..91 B3
Hazlitt Cl TW13 ...173 A6
Hazlitt Ct 4 SE28 ..124 C5
Hazlitt Mews W14 ..254 A5
Hazlitt Rd
W14 ...113 A3 254 A5
Heacham Ave UB10 ...61 A5
Headbourne Ho SE1 .262 D6
Headcorn 10 NW5 ...71 A2
Headcorn Pl CR7 ..204 B5
Headcorn Rd BR1 ..187 A5
Thornton Heath CR7 ..204 B5
Tottenham N17 ...33 D3
Headfort Pl
SW1 ...115 A4 248 B1
Headington Rd SW18 158 A2
Headlam Rd SW4 ..159 D4
Headlam St E1 ...96 B3
Headley App IG2 ...56 D4
Headley Ave CR0,SM6 220 B3
Headley Cl KT19 ...214 C2
Headley Ct SE26 ...184 C5
Headley Dr Ilford IG2 ..56 D3
New Addington CR0 ..224 A1
Headley Ho 5 BR5 ..190 B1
Heads Mews W11 ...91 C1
Head St E1 ...96 D1
Headstone Dr HA1,HA3 42 C6
Headstone Gdns HA2 .42 A5
Headstone La
Harrow HA2 ...41 D5
Harrow HA2,HA3 ...23 D2
Headstone Lane Sta
HA3 ...23 D2
Headstone Rd HA1 ...42 C3
Headway Cl TW10 ..175 C6
Heald St SE8,SE14 ..141 C4
Healey St NW1 ...71 B2
Healy Ct EN5 ...12 D5
Healy Dr 1 BR6 ...227 D4
Healy Ho 2 E3 ...97 C3
12 SW9 ...138 C5
Heanor Ct 4 E5 ...74 D4
Hearne Rd W4 ...132 C6
Hearn Rise UB5 ...84 D6
Hearn's Bldgs SE17 ..262 D3
Hearn St EC2 ..95 C3 243 B5
Hearnville Rd SW12 .159 A3
Heart Hospl The
W1 ...93 A2 238 B4
Heatham Pk TW2 ...152 D4
Heath Ave DA7 ...146 D6
Heathbourne Rd WD23,
HA7 ...8 D3
Heathbrook Prim Sch
SW4 ...137 C3
Heath Brow NW3 ...70 A5
Heath Bsns Ctr The
TW3 ...130 A1
Heath Cl NW11 ...47 D2
Croydon CR2 ...220 D2
Ealing W5 ...88 B3
Harlington UB3 ...127 B5

Heathcote Gr E4 20 A2
Heathcote Rd TW1 153 B6
Heathcote Sch E4 20 C2
Heathcote St
WC1 94 B4 233 C1
Heathcroft NW11 47 D1
Ealing W5 88 B3
Heathcroft Ave
TW16 171 D3
Heathcroft Gdns E4 36 B2
Heath Ct E11 54 D3
N16 51 B1
2 NW3 70 A2
Uxbridge UB8 60 A1
Heathdale Ave TW4 129 A2
Heathdene N14 15 C4
Heathdene Dr DA17 125 D2
Heathdene Rd
South Norwood SW16 182 B3
Wallington SM5,SM6 219 B1
Heath Dr SW20 200 C5
Heathedge SE23,SE26 162 B2
Heatherbank BR7 188 C1
SE9 144 B3
Heather Cl E6 100 C1
SW8 137 B2
Hampton TW12 173 B2
Hillingdon UB8 82 B2
Isleworth TW7 152 B6
Heather Ct SW4 270 B1
Heatherdale Cl KT2 176 D3
Heatherdene Cl N12 30 A2
Mitcham CR4 202 C5
Heatherdene Mans 2
TW1 153 D5
Heather Dr EN2 4 D3
Heatherfold Way HA5,
HA6 39 D6
Heather Gdns NW11 47 A3
Belmont SM2 217 C2
Heather Ho 7 E14 98 A1
Heather La UB7 82 A1
Heatherlands TW16 172 A4
Heatherley Ct N16 74 A5
Heatherley Dr IG5 56 B6
Heatherley Sch of Fine Art
SW10 266 B3
Heather Lo N16 51 C1
Heather Park Dr HA0 66 C1
Heather Park Par HA0 66 B1
Heather Rd E4 35 B4
NW2 67 D6
Lewisham SE12 165 A3
Heatherset Cl KT10 212 A3
Heatherset Gdns
SW16 182 B3
Heatherside Rd
Sidcup DA14 168 C1
West Ewell KT19 215 B1
Heathers The TW19 148 B4
Heather Way HA7 24 D4
Heather Wlk W10 91 A3
Edgware HA8 26 D5
Twickenham TW4 151 C4
Heatherwood Cl E12 77 C6
Heatherwood Dr UB4 83 B5
Heathfield BR7 189 A4
Chingford E4 20 A1
Heathfield Ave SW18 158 B4
Heathfield Cl BR2 225 C3
E16 99 D2
Heathfield Ct DA14 190 B5
5 W4 111 B1
Ashford TW15 148 A1
Penge SE20 184 C3
Wandsworth SW18 158 B4
Heathfield Dr CR4 180 C2
Heathfielde N2 48 A4
Heathfield Gdns
NW11 46 D3
SW18 158 B5
W4 111 A1
Croydon CR0 221 B4
Heathfield Ho SE3 142 C3
Heathfield Inf Sch
TW2 151 C3
Heathfield Jun Sch
TW2 151 C3
Heathfield La BR7 189 A4
Heathfield N TW1,
TW2 152 D4
Heathfield Park Dr
RM6 58 B4
Heathfield Pk NW2 68 C2
Heathfield Rd BR2 225 D3
DA6 147 B1
SW18 158 B5
Heathfield Rd continued
W3 110 D4
Bromley BR1 186 D3
Croydon CR0 221 B4
Heathfield Rise HA4 39 A2
Heathfield S TW1,
TW2 152 D4
Heathfield Sch HA5 40 D2
Heathfield Sq SW18 158 B4
Heathfield Terr SE18 145 D6
W4 111 B1
Heathfield Vale CR2 223 A1
Heathgate NW11 47 D3
Heathgate Pl NW3 70 D4
Heath Gdns TW1 152 D2
Heath Gr
Ashford TW16 171 D3
Penge SE20 184 C3
Heath Ho DA15 189 D6
Thornton Heath CR7 204 C4
Uxbridge UB10 60 D4
Heath Hurst Rd NW3 70 C4
Heath La SE3 142 B3
Heathland Rd N16 51 C1
Heathland Sch SW19 156 D1
Heathland Sch The
TW4 151 B5
Heathlands Cl
Sunbury TW16 172 A1
Twickenham TW1 152 D3
Heathlands Ct
Hounslow TW4 151 A6
Mitcham CR4 203 A6
Heathlands Way
TW4 151 A6
Heathlee Rd SE3 142 D1
Heathley End BR7 189 A4
Heath Lo WD23 8 B3
Heath Mans 4 NW3 70 A4
Putney SW15 156 D5
Heathman's Rd
SW6 135 B4 264 D1
Heath Mead SW19 156 D1
Heathmere Prim Sch
SW15 156 A3
Heath Park Dr BR1 210 A6
Heath Park Gdns NW3 69 D5
Heathpool Ct 8 E1 96 B3
Heath Rd SW8 137 B3
Dagenham RM6 59 A2
Harrow HA1 42 A2
Hillingdon UB10 83 A3
Isleworth TW3,TW7 130 A1
South Norwood CR7 205 A6
Twickenham TW1 152 D3
Heath Rise Hayes BR2 209 A3
Putney SW15 156 D5
Heathrow Airport London
TW6 126 D3
Heathrow Bvd UB7 126 B5
Heathrow Causeway Est
TW4 128 B2
Heathrow International
Trad Est TW4 128 B2
Heathrow Sch UB7 126 B6
Heathrow Terminal 4 Sta
TW6 149 A5
Heathrow Terminals 1,2,3
TW6 126 D2
Heath Royal SW15 156 D5
Heath's Cl EN1 5 C3
Heathshot 8 TW10 154 A5
Heathside NW3 70 B4
Heath Side BR5 211 A2
Heathside
Hinchley Wood KT10 212 C5
Twickenham TW4 151 B4
Heathside Ave DA7 147 A3
Heathside Cl
Hinchley Wood KT10 212 C5
Ilford IG2 57 B4
Heathside Prep Sch
NW3 70 A4
Heath St NW3 70 A5
Heathstan Rd W12 90 A1
Heath Terr RM6 58 D2
Heath The W7 108 C5
Heath View N2 48 A5
NW5 71 A4
Heath View Cl N2 48 A5
Heathview Ct SW19 156 D2
Heath View Dr SE2 146 D6
Heathview Gdns
SW15 156 C4
Heathview Rd CR7 204 C5
Heath Villas SE18 123 D1
Heathville Rd N4,N19 50 A2
Heathwall St SW11 136 D2
Heathway 6 SE3 142 D5
Croydon CR0 223 B5
Heathway continued
Greenwich SE3 143 A5
Woodford IG8 37 C5
Heathway Ct NW3 69 C6
Heathwood Ct
1 Hounslow TW3 129 D1
Streatham SW12 159 C3
Heathwood Gdns
SE7 122 A1
Heathwood Point 7
SE26 162 D1
Heaton Cl E4 20 A1
Heaton Ho 6 SE15 140 B3
SW10 266 B6
Heaton Rd SE15 140 B3
Mitcham CR4 181 A3
Heaver Rd 24 SW11 136 B2
Heavers Farm Prim Sch
SE25 205 D4
Heavitree Cl SE18 123 B1
Heavitree Rd SE18 123 B1
Hebden Ct 24 E2 95 D6
Hebden Terr N17 33 C4
Hebdon Rd SW17 158 C1
Heber Prim Sch
SE22 161 D5
Heber Rd NW2 68 D4
SE22 161 D5
Hebron Rd W6 112 B3
Hecham Cl E17 35 A2
Heckfield Pl
SW6 135 C5 265 A3
Heckford St E1 118 D6
Hector 31 NW9 27 D2
Hector Ct 1 SW9 138 C4
Putney SW15 156 D6
Hector Ho 14 E2 96 B5
Hector St SE18 123 C2
Heddington Gr N7 72 B3
Heddon Cl TW7 131 A1
Heddon Court Ave
EN4 14 D6
Heddon Court Par
EN4 15 A6
Heddon Ct EN4 15 A6
Heddon Rd EN4 14 D6
Heddon St W1 249 A6
Hedge Hill EN2 4 D4
Hedge La N13 17 A1
Hedgeley IG4 56 B5
Hedgemans Rd RM9 81 A1
Hedgemans Way RM9 81 A2
Hedgemoor Ct 1 E4 36 B5
Hedgerley Gdns UB6 86 A5
Hedgerow La EN5 12 B6
Hedger's Gr E9 75 A2
Hedger St SE11 261 C4
Hedge Wlk SE6 185 D6
Hedgewood Gdns IG5 56 C4
Hedgewood Specl Sch
UB4 83 C4
Hedgley Mews SE12 164 D6
Hedgley St SE12 164 D6
Hedingham Cl 6 N1 73 A1
Hedingham Rd RM8 80 B3
Hedley Ct SW15 156 D5
Hedley Ho E14 120 A3
Hedley Rd TW4 151 C4
Hedley Row N5,N16 73 B3
Hedsor Ho E2 243 C6
Heenan Cl IG11 79 A2
Heene Rd EN2 5 B4
Heidegger Cres
SW13 134 B5
Heigham Rd E6 78 A1
Heighton Gdns CR0 220 D3
Heights Cl SW20 178 B3
Heights The N4 50 C3
NW3 70 A4
SE7 121 C1
Beckenham BR3 186 A3
Northolt UB5 63 C3
Heiron St SE17 138 D6
Helby Rd SW4 159 D5
Heldar Ct SE1 252 D1
Helder Gr SE12 164 D4
Helder St CR2 221 B2
Heldmann Cl TW7 130 B1
Helena Cl EN4 2 B5
Helena Ct W5 87 D2
Helena Rd E13 99 A5
E17 53 C4
NW10 68 B3
Ealing W5 87 D2
Helena Sq 12 SE16 119 A6
Helen Ave TW14 150 B4
Helen Cl N2 48 A6
East Molesey KT8 195 D5
Helen Ct N3 47 A6
Helen Gladstone Ho
SE1 251 C2
Helen Ho 9 E2 96 B5
Helen Mackay Ho 9
E14 98 B1
Helen Peele Cotts 10
SE16 118 C3
Helenslea Ave NW11 47 C1
Helen's Pl E2 96 C4
Helen St SE18 122 D2
Helen Taylor Ho 5
SE16 118 A2
Helford Cl HA4 61 C6
Helgiford Gdns
TW16 171 C3
Heligan Cl BR6 227 D4
Helios Rd CR4 203 A1
Heliport Est The
SW11 136 B3
Helix Gdns SW2 160 B5
Helix Ho TW7 131 B3
Helix Rd SW2 160 B5
Hellenic Coll of London
SW1 114 D3 257 C5
Hellings St E1 118 A5
Helme Cl SW19 179 B5
Helmet Row EC1 242 B6
Helmore Rd IG11 79 D1
Helmsdale Cl UB4 85 A3
Helmsdale Ho NW6 91 D5
Helmsdale Rd SW16 181 D2
Helmsley 10 E18 55 A6
Helmsley Pl E8 74 B1
Helmsley St 7 E8 74 B1
Helperby Rd NW10 67 C1
Helsby Ct NW8 236 C6
Helsinki Sq SE16 119 A3
Helston NW1 232 B4
Helston Cl HA5 23 B3
Helston Ct N15 51 C4
Helston Ho SE11 261 B2
Helvetia St SE6 163 B2
Helwys Ct E4 36 A4
Hemans Est
SW8 137 D5 269 D3
Hemans St
SW8 137 D5 269 D3
Hemberton Rd SW9 138 A2
Hemery Rd UB6 64 B3
Hemingford Cl N12 30 B5
Hemingford Rd
N1 72 B1 233 D6
Cheam SM3 216 C4
Heming Rd HA8 26 D3
Hemington Ave N11 30 D5
Hemlock Rd W12 111 D6
Hemmen La UB3 83 D1
Hemming Cl 5
TW12 173 C2
Hemmings Cl DA14 168 B2
Hemmings Ct HA8 27 A3
Hemming St E1 96 A3
Hempstead Cl IG9 21 A2
Hempstead Rd E17 36 B1
Hemp Wlk SE17 262 D4
Hemsby Rd KT9 214 B2
Hemstal Rd NW6 69 C1
Hemswell Dr NW9 27 C2
Hemsworth Ct N1 95 C5
Hemsworth St N1 95 C5
Hemus Pl SW3 257 B1
Henchman St W12 89 D1
Hendale Ave NW4 46 B6
Hendale Ho 13 E5 74 B6
Henderson Cl NW10 67 A2
Henderson Ct NW3 70 B3
8 SE14 140 D6
Henderson Dr
NW8 92 B3 236 C6
Henderson Ho 7
RM10 81 C5
Henderson Rd E7 77 C2
Edmonton N9 18 B3
Hayes UB4 84 A4
Thornton Heath CR0 205 B3
Wandsworth SW18 158 C4
Hendfield Ct 5 SM6 219 B2
Hendham Rd SW17 158 D2
Hendon Ave N3 29 A2
Hendon Central NW4 46 B4
Hendon Central Sta
NW4 46 B4
Hendon Coll NW9 27 D2
Hendon Coll of F Ed
NW4 46 A3
Hendon Hall Ct NW4 46 D6
Hendon Ho NW4 46 D4
Hendon La N3 29 B1
Hendon Lo NW4 46 B6
Hendon Park Mans
NW4 46 C4
Hendon Park Row
NW11 47 B3
Hendon Prep Sch
NW4 46 D6
Hendon Rd N9 18 A2
Hendon Sch NW4 46 D4
Hendon Sta NW4 46 A3
Hendon Terr TW15 171 B4
Hendon Way NW2 46 C3
NW2,NW4 46 C3
Hendon Wood La
NW7 12 A3
Hendre Ho SE1 263 B3
Hendren Cl UB6 64 B3
Hendre Rd
SE1 117 C2 263 B3
Hendrick Ave SW12 158 D4
Heneage La EC3 243 B1
Heneage Pl EC3 243 B1
Heneage St E1 95 D2 243 D4
Henfield Cl DA5 169 C5
N19 49 C1
Henfield Rd SW19,
SW20 179 B2
Hengelo Gdns CR4 202 B5
Hengist Rd DA8 147 D5
Eltham SE12 165 B4
Hengist Way BR2,BR3 208 C5
Hengrave Rd SE23 162 D4
Hengrove Ct DA5 169 A3
Henley Ave SM3 217 A5
Henley Cl SE16 118 C4
Greenford UB6 86 A5
Hounslow TW7 130 D4
Henley Ct N14 15 C4
NW2 68 D2
NW4 46 A6
SE15 140 A2
Mitcham CR4 203 A6
Henley Dr
SE1 117 D2 263 D4
Kingston KT2 177 D3
Henley Gdns
Dagenham RM6 59 A4
Pinner HA5 40 B6
Henley Ho E2 243 D6
N12 30 B5
Henley Lo E17 53 B4
South Norwood SE25 205 D5
Henley Prior N1 233 C3
Henley Rd
Edmonton N18 33 C6
Ilford IG1 79 B4
Newham E16 122 B4
Willesden NW10 90 C6
Henleys Cnr NW11 47 B5
Henley St SW11 137 A3
Henley Way TW13 172 D5
Henlow Pl TW10 153 D2
Henlys Rdbt TW5 128 C3
Hennel Cl SE23 162 C1
Hennessy Rd N9 18 C2
Henniker Gdns E6 100 A4
Henniker Mews SW3 266 C6
Henniker Point E15 76 C3
Henniker Rd E15 76 B3
Henningham Rd N17 33 B2
Henning St
SW11 136 C4 267 A1
Henrietta Barnett Sch
NW11 47 D3
Henrietta Cl SE8 141 C6
Henrietta Ho 3 N15 51 C3
11 W6 112 C1
Henrietta Mews WC1 240 B6
Henrietta Pl
W1 93 B1 238 C2
Henrietta St E15 76 A3
WC2 116 A6 250 B6
Henriques St E1 96 A1
Henry Addlington Cl
E6 100 D2
Henry Cavendish Prim Sch
SW12 159 C3
Henry Cl EN2 5 C5
Henry Compton Sec Sch
SW6 135 A4 264 A2
Henry Cooper Way
SE12 187 D6
Henry Darlot Dr NW7 29 A5
Henry Dent Cl SE5 139 B2
Henry Dickens Ct
W11 244 A4
Henry Doulton Dr
SW17 181 B6
Henry Fawcett Prim Sch
SE11 138 C6
Henry Green Prim Sch
RM8 80 D6
Henry Hatch Ct SM2 218 A1
Henry Ho NW8 230 A4
SE1 251 B3
SW8 270 A4
Henry Jackson Ho
SW15 134 D2
Henry Jackson Rd
SW15 134 D2
Henry Maynard Inf Sch
E17 54 A4
Henry Maynard Jun Sch
E17 54 A4
Henry Peters Dr
TW11 174 C5
Henry Rd E6 100 A5
N4 51 A1
New Barnet EN4 14 B6
Henry's Ave IG8 36 D5
Henryson Rd SE4 163 C6
Henry St BR1 187 B2
Henry Tate Mews
SW16 182 C5
Henry Wise Ho SW1 259 B3
Hensford Gdns SE26 184 B6
Henshall Point 19 E3 97 D4
Henshall St N1 73 B2
Henshawe Rd RM8 80 D5
Henshaw St
SE17 117 B2 262 C4
Henslowe Rd SE22 162 A6
Henslow Ho 11 SE15 140 A5
Henson Ave NW2 68 C3
Henson Cl BR6 226 D6
Henson Ct 3 N5 73 A4
Henson Path HA3 43 D6
Henson Pl UB5 84 C6
Henty Cl
SW11 136 C4 267 B2
Henty Wlk SW15 156 B6
Henville Rd BR1 187 B2
Henwick Prim Sch
SE9 144 A2
Henwick Rd SE9 144 A2
Hepburn Gdns BR2 208 D1
Hepburn Mews
SW11 158 D6
Hepple Cl TW7 131 B3
Hepplestone Cl
SW15 156 B5
Hepscott Rd E9 75 C1
Hepworth Ct N1 234 D6
Barking IG11 80 A3
Cheam SM3 201 C1
Hepworth Gdns IG11 80 A3
Hepworth Ho IG8 21 A1
Hepworth Rd SW16 182 A3
Hepworth Way KT12 193 D1
Heracles 30 NW9 27 D2
Heracles Cl SM6 220 A1
Hera Ct 7 E14 119 C2
Herald Gdns SM6 219 B5
Heralds Pl SE11 261 C4
Herald St 5 E2 96 B3
Herbal Hill EC1 241 B5
Herbert Chapman Ct
N5 72 D4
Herbert Cres SW1 257 D6
Herbert Gdns NW10 90 B5
Chiswick W4 132 D6
Dagenham RM6 58 D2
Herbert Ho E1 243 C2
Herbert Mews 15
SW2 160 C5
Herbert Morrison Ho
SW6 264 C5
Herbert Morrison Prim
Sch SW8 138 A5 270 B3
Herbert Pl SE18 144 D6
Herbert Rd BR2 210 A4
DA7 147 A3
E12 78 A4
E17 53 B2
N15 51 D4
NW9 46 A3
SE18 144 D6
Ilford IG3 79 C6
Kingston KT1 198 B6
Merton SW19 179 B3
Southall UB1 107 B5
Wood Green N11 32 A3
Herbert St E13 99 A5
NW5 71 A2
Herbrand Est
WC1 94 A3 240 A6
Herbrand St
WC1 94 A3 240 A6
Hercies Rd UB10 60 C2
Hercules Pl N7 72 A5

Hercules Rd
SE1 ....116 B3 260 D5
Hercules St N7 ....72 A5
Hereford Ave EN4 ....14 D3
Hereford Bldgs SW3 .266 D6
Hereford Ct
12 Belmont SM2 ....217 C1
6 Croydon CR0 ....205 D1
6 Ealing W7 ....86 D2
Harrow HA1 ....42 C6
Hereford Gdns SE13 .164 C6
Pinner HA5 ....41 A4
Redbridge IG1 ....56 A2
Twickenham TW2 ....152 A3
Hereford Ho 28 SE5 .139 A3
5 SW2 ....138 C1
SW3 ....257 B6
7 Acton W3 ....257 B6
Hereford Mans 10 W2 91 C1
Hereford Mews 11 W2 91 C1
Hereford Pl SE14 ....141 B5
Hereford Rd
W2 ....91 C1 245 B6
W3 ....111 A6
W5 ....109 C3
Feltham TW13 ....150 C3
Wanstead E11 ....55 B4
Hereford Retreat 5
SE15 ....140 A5
Hereford Sq
SW7 ....114 A2 256 B3
Herent Dr IG5 ....56 B6
Hereward Gdns N13 ...32 C5
Hereward House Sch
NW3 ....70 B2
Hereward Rd SW17 ...180 D6
Herga Ct HA1 ....64 C6
Herga Rd HA3 ....42 D5
Heriot Ave E4 ....19 C2
Heriot Rd NW4 ....46 C4
Heriots Cl HA7 ....25 A6
Heritage Cl SW9 .....138 C2
Heritage Ct SE8 .....118 D1
Heritage Hill BR2 ....225 C3
Heritage Ho 22 SW19 156 D3
Heritage View HA1 ....64 C6
Herlwyn Ave HA4 ....61 C5
Herlwyn Gdns SW17 .180 D6
Herm Cl 4 W9 ......130 A5
Hermes Cl 4 W9 ......91 C1
Hermes Ct 4 SW9 ...138 C4
Hermes Ho BR3 .....185 A2
Hermes St N1 ....234 A3
Hermes Way SM6 ....219 D1
Hermes Wlk UB5 ....85 C5
Herm Ho 10 N1 .....73 A2
Enfield EN3 ....6 D5
Hermiston Ave N8 ....50 A4
Hermitage Cl E18 ....54 D5
Claygate KT10 ......213 A2
Enfield EN2 ....4 D3
Littleton TW17 ......192 C5
Hermitage Ct 14 E1 .118 A5
2 NW2 ....69 C5
3 Wanstead E18 ....55 A5
Hermitage Gdns NW2 .69 C5
South Norwood SE19 .183 A3
Hermitage La NW2 ...69 C5
Croydon CR0 ....206 A3
South Norwood SW16 .182 B3
Hermitage Prim Sch
E1 ....118 A5
Hermitage Rd N4,N15 .51 A3
South Norwood SE19 .183 A3
Hermitage Row 9 E8 .74 A3
Hermitage St W2 ...236 C3
Hermitage The
Barnes SW13 ......133 D4
Feltham TW13 ......149 D1
Forest Hill SE23 .....162 C3
Kingston KT1 ....197 D5
Richmond TW10 ....154 A6
Uxbridge UB8 ....60 A2
Hermitage Wall E1 ..118 A5
Hermitage Way HA7 ..25 A2
Hermitage Wlk E18 ...54 D5
Hermit Pl NW6 ......91 D6
Hermit Rd E16 ......98 D3
Hermit St EC1 ....234 C2
Hermon Gr UB3 ....106 A5
Hermon Hill E11 .....55 A5
Herndon Rd SW18 ...158 A6
Herne Cl NW10 .....67 B3
Herne Ct WD23 ......8 A4
Herne Hill SE24 ....139 A1
Herne Hill Ho SE24 .160 D5

Herne Hill Mans
SE24 ....161 A5
Herne Hill Rd SE24 .139 A1
Herne Hill Sta SE24 .160 D5
Herne Hill Stad SE24 161 B5
Herne Mews N18 ....34 A6
Herne Pl SE24 ......160 D6
Herne Rd KT6 ......214 A6
Heron Cl E17 ....35 B1
NW10 ....67 C2
Buckhurst Hill IG9 ....21 A3
Cheam SM1 ....217 B3
Heron Cres DA14 ...189 C6
Heron Ct 14 E14 ....120 A3
Bromley BR2 ....209 C5
6 Dulwich SE21 ....161 B2
9 Forest Hill SE23 ..162 C3
Ilford IG1 ....78 D6
5 Kingston KT1 ....198 A6
Ruislip HA4 ....61 B6
Stanwell TW19 ....148 A3
SE15 ....139 D4
SW11 ....267 B2
Ealing W13 ....87 A3
Teddington KT1 ....175 C2
Heron Ind Est E15 ....97 D5
Heron Mead EN3 ......7 C5
Heron Mews IG1 .....78 D6
Heron Pl SE16 ......119 A5
W1 ....238 B2
Heron Quays E14 ...119 C5
Heron Quays Sta E14 119 C5
Heron Rd SE24 .....139 A1
Croydon CR0 ....221 C6
Isleworth TW1 .....131 B1
Herondale Ave SW18 158 C3
Heron Dr N4 ....73 A6
Herongate N1 ......235 B6
Herongate Rd E12 ...77 C6
Heron Hill DA17 ...125 B2
Heron Ho NW8 .....230 A3
SE15 ....139 D4
SW11 ....267 B2
Ealing W13 ....87 A3
Teddington KT1 ....175 C2
Heron Ind Est E15 ....97 D5
Heronsforde W13 ....87 C1
Heron's Lea N6 ......48 D3
Heronslea Dr HA7 ...26 A5
Herons Pl TW7 ......131 B2
Heron Sq 25 TW10 .153 D6
Herons Rise EN4 ......2 C1
Herons The E11 .....54 D3
Heron Trad Est W3 ...88 D2
Heronway IG8 ....37 C6
Heron Way TW14 ...128 A1
Herrick Ct 4 TW10 .175 D6
Herrick Ho 17 N16 ...73 B4
18 SE5 ....139 B5
Herrick Rd N5 ......73 A5
Herrick St
SW1 ....115 D2 259 D3
Herries St W10 ......91 A5
Herringham Rd SE7 .121 C3
Herrongate Cl EN1 ...5 D3
Hersant Cl NW10 ...90 A6
Herschell Rd SE23 ..163 A4
Herschell's Mews
SE5 ....139 A2
Hersham Cl SW15 ..156 A4
Hersham Rd KT12 ..194 A1
Hershell Ct SW14 ..132 D1
Hershell Ct 1 SW14 .132 D1
Hertford Ave SW14 .133 C1
Hertford Cl EN4 ......2 B2
Hertford Ct E6 ......100 B4
16 SW11 ....136 C2
Palmers Green N13 ..16 C1
Hertford Lo 10 SW19 157 A3
Hertford Pl W1 .....239 B5
Hertford Rd N1 ......95 C6
N2 ....48 C6
Barking IG11 ....78 D1
Barnet EN4 ....2 A3
Edmonton N9 ....18 B3
Enfield EN3 ....6 C5
Ilford IG2 ....57 C3
Hertford Rd High St
EN3 ....18 C6
Hertford Sq CR4 ...204 A5
Hertford St
W1 ....115 B5 248 C3
Hertford Way CR4 ..204 A5
Hertford Wlk 13
DA17 ....125 C1
Hertmitage The 4
SE13 ....142 A4
Hertslet Rd N7 ......72 B5
Hertsmere Rd E14 ..119 C6
Hertswood Ct 1 EN5 ..1 A1
Hervey Cl N3 ....29 C2
Hervey Park Rd E17 ..53 A5
Hervey Rd SE3 .....143 B4

Hesa Rd UB3 ....106 A6
Hesewall Cl SW4 ...137 C3
Hesketh Pl W11 ....244 A5
Hesketh Rd E7 ......77 A5
Heslop Ct 1 SW12 .159 A3
Heslop Rd SW12 ...158 D3
Hesper Mews
SW5 ....113 D2 255 C3
Hesperus Cres E14 .119 D2
Hessel Rd W13 ....109 B4
Hessel St E1 ....96 B1
Hestercombe Ave
SW6 ....135 B4 264 B1
Hesterman Way CR0 .204 B1
Hester Rd
SW11 ....136 C5 267 A3
Edmonton N18 ......34 A5
Hester Terr TW9 ...132 C2
Heston Ave TW5 ...129 A5
Heston Com Sch
TW5 ....129 C5
Heston Ctr The TW5 .106 C2
Heston Grange TW5 129 B6
Heston Grange La
TW5 ....129 B6
Heston Ho 5 SE8 ..141 C4
W4 ....110 D1
Heston Ind Mall TW5 129 B5
Heston Inf Sch TW5 .129 C5
Heston Jun Sch TW5 129 C5
Heston Phoenix
Distribution Pk
TW5 ....128 C6
Heston Rd TW5 ....129 C5
Heston St SE14 ....141 C4
Hetherington Rd
SW2,SW4 ....138 A1
Charlton TW17 .....171 A1
Hetherington Way
UB10 ....60 A4
Hethpool Ho W2 ...236 C5
Hetley Gdns 1 SE19 183 D3
Hetley Rd W12 .....112 B4
Heton Gdns NW4 ...46 A5
Hevelius Cl SE10 ..120 D1
Hever Croft SE9 ...188 C6
Heverfield Ct CR4 ..180 D3
Hever Gdns BR1 ....188 C1
Heverham Rd SE18 .123 C2
Hever Ho SE15 ....140 D6
Heversham Ho SE15 .140 C6
Heversham Rd DA7 .147 C4
Hewens Rd UB4 .....83 A3
Hewer Ho 6 SW4 ..159 C6
Hewer St W10 ......90 D2
Hewes Ho 11 E1 .....52 D5
Hewett Cl HA7 ......25 B6
Hewett Ho 7 SE18 .122 D1
Hewett Rd RM8 .....80 D4
Hewett St EC2 ..95 C3 243 B5
Hewish Rd N18 .....33 C6
Hewison St E3 ......97 B5
Hewitt Ave N22 .....32 D1
Hewitt Cl CR0 .....223 C6
Hewitt Ho 2 E4 .....36 B5
Hewitt Rd N8 ......50 D4
Hewlett Rd E3 ......97 A5
Hewling Ho 1 N16 ..73 C3
Hewtt Ho SW15 ...134 C3
Hexagon The N6 ....48 B1
Hexal Rd SE6 ......164 C6
Hexham Gdns TW7 .131 A5
Hexham Rd Barnet EN5 .1 D1
Cheam SM4 ....201 D1
West Norwood SE27 .161 A2
Heybourne Ho N17 .34 B3
Hey Bridge 9 NW1 ..71 B2
Heybridge Ave SW16 .182 B4
Heybridge Dr IG6 ...57 B6
Heybridge Way E10 ..53 B1
Heydon Ct BR4 ....224 C6
Heydon Ho SE14 ..140 D4
Heyford Ave
SW8 ....138 A5 270 B4
Merton SW20 ......201 B6
Heyford Rd CR4 ....180 C1
Heygate St
SE17 ....117 A2 262 B4
Heylyn Sq E3 ....97 B4
Heynes Rd RM8 .....80 C4
Heysham Dr WD19 ..22 D5
Heysham La NW3 ...69 D5
Heysham Rd N15 ...51 B3
Heythorp St SW18 .157 B2
Heythrop Dr UB10 ...60 B4
Heyward Ct SM2 ...217 C2
Heywood Ave NW9 ..27 C2
Heywood Ho 11 SE14 140 D6
6 SW2 ....160 C5

Heyworth Rd E15 ...76 D4
E5 ....74 B4
Hibbert Rd E17 .....53 B2
Hibbert St SW11 ..136 B2
Hibernia Gdns TW3 .151 C6
Hibernia Point 11
SE2 ....124 D4
Hibernia Rd TW3 ..129 C1
Hibiscus Cl HA8 .....27 A6
Hibiscus Lo E15 ....76 C1
Hichisson Rd SE15 .162 C6
Hickes Ho 6 NW6 ...70 B1
Hickey's Almshouses 7
TW9 ....132 B1
Hickin Cl SE7 ......121 C2
Hickin St 2 E14 ...120 A3
Hickleton Ho 11 ...232 B5
Hickling Ho 10 SE16 118 B3
Hickling Rd IG1 ......78 D3
Hickman Ave E4 ....36 A4
Hickman Cl E16 .....99 D2
Hickman Rd RM6 ...58 C2
Hickmore Wlk SW4 .137 C2
Hickory Cl N9 ......18 A4
Hicks Ave UB6 .....86 C4
Hicks Cl SW11 ....136 C2
Hicks Ct RM10 .....81 D5
Hicks St SE8 ......119 A1
Hidaburn Ct 7 SW16 181 C6
Hidcote Gdns SW20 200 B6
Hidcote Ho 11 SM2 .218 A1
Hide E6 ....100 C1
Hide Pl SW1 .115 D2 259 C3
Hide Rd HA1 ....42 B5
Hide Twr SW1 .....259 C3
Hieover SE21 ......161 A2
Higgins Ho 7 N1 ...95 C6
Higginson Ho 2 NW3 70 D1
Higgins Wlk TW12 .173 A4
Higgs Ind Est 9
SE24 ....138 D2
High Acre EN2 ....4 D2
Higham Ct 9 IG8 ...37 A4
Higham Hill Ho E17 .34 D2
Higham Hill Rd E17 .35 A1
Higham Ho E4 ......35 C4
Higham Pl E17 .....53 A6
Higham Rd N17 ....51 B6
Woodford IG8 ......37 A4
Highams Lodge Bsns Ctr
E17 ....52 D6
Highams Park Sch E4 36 B4
Highams Park Sta E4 36 B4
Higham St E17 .....53 A6
Higham Station Ave
E4 ....35 D4
Highams The E17 ...36 A4
High Ashton 11 KT2 .176 D3
Highbanks Cl DA16 .146 B5
Highbanks Rd HA5 ..23 D4
Highbank Way N8 ..50 C3
High Barnet Sta EN5 ..1 C1
Highbarrow Rd CR0 .206 A1
High Beech
South Croydon CR2 .221 C1
Southgate N21 ......16 B5
High Beeches DA14 .191 A5
High Birch Ct 7 EN4 ..2 C1
Highbridge Ct 13
SE14 ....140 C5
Highbridge Rd IG11 .100 D6
High Bridge Wharf
SE10 ....120 B1
Highbrook Rd SE3 .143 D2
High Broom Cres
BR4 ....207 D2
Highbury (Arsenal FC)
N5 ....72 D5
Highbury Ave CR7 .182 D1
Highbury Cl
New Malden KT3 ...199 A4
West Wickham BR4 .223 D6
Highbury Cnr N5 ....72 D2
Highbury Corner N5 .72 D2
Highbury Cres N5 ...72 C2
Highbury Fields Sch
N5 ....72 D3
Highbury Gdns IG3 ..79 C6
Highbury Gr N5 .....72 D2
Highbury Grange N5 .73 A3
Highbury Grove Sch
N5 ....73 A3
Highbury Hill N5 ....72 C1
Highbury & Islington Sta
N1 ....72 D2
Highbury New Pk N5 .73 A4
Highbury Pk N5 ....72 D2
Highbury Pl N5 .....72 D1

Highbury Quadrant
N5 ....73 A5
Highbury Quadrant Prim
Sch N5 ....73 A4
Highbury Rd SW19 .179 A5
Highbury Station Rd
N1 ....72 C2
Highbury Terr N5 ...72 D3
Highbury Terrace Mews
N5 ....72 D3
High Cedar Dr SW20 .178 B3
Highclere Rd KT3 ...199 B6
Highclere St SE26 ..185 A6
Highcliffe
Beckenham BR3 ...185 D2
Ealing W13 ....87 D2
Highcliffe Dr SW15 .155 D5
Highcliffe Gdns IG4 ..56 A4
Highcombe SE7 ....143 B6
Highcombe Cl SE9 .166 A3
High Coombe Pl KT2 177 B3
Highcroft N6 ....49 A3
NW9 ....45 C4
2 Kingston KT5 ...198 B4
Highcroft Ave HA0 ..88 C6
Highcroft Gdns NW11 47 B3
Highcroft Rd N19 ...50 C2
High Cross Ctr The
N15 ....52 A5
High Cross Rd N17 ..52 A6
Highcross Way 4
SW15 ....156 A3
Highdaun Dr SW16 .204 B5
High Dene EN2 ......4 D2
Highdown KT4 ....215 D6
Highdown Rd SW15 .156 B5
High Dr KT2,KT3 ...177 A1
High Elms IG8 ......37 A5
High Elms Rd BR6 .227 A1
Highenden Ho NW8 .237 A6
Highfield WD23 ......8 C2
Highfield Ave DA8 .147 D6
NW11 ....47 A2
NW9 ....45 A4
Greenford UB6 .....64 D3
Orpington BR6 .....227 D3
Pinner HA5 ....41 B4
Wembley HA9 ......66 B5
Highfield Cl NW9 ...45 A4
SE13 ....164 B5
Long Ditton KT6 ....197 C1
Wood Green N22 ...32 C2
Highfield Ct NW11 ..47 A3
Mitcham CR4 ......202 C5
Southgate N14 .....15 C3
Wanstead E11 ......77 C6
Highfield Dr
Beckenham BR2 ...208 D5
Ickenham UB10 .....60 A5
West Ewell KT19 ...215 D2
West Wickham BR4 .224 A5
Highfield Gdns NW11 47 A3
Highfield Gr N6 .....48 D3
Highfield Hill SE19 .183 C3
Highfield Ho N21 ...16 D3
Highfield Inf Sch
BR2 ....208 D5
Highfield Jun Sch
BR2 ....208 D5
Highfield Prim Sch
Edmonton N21 .....17 A3
Hillingdon UB10 .....82 D4
Highfield Rd BR1 ..210 B5
BR5,BR7 ....211 D6
DA6 ....169 B6
NW11 ....47 A3
W3 ....89 A2
Carshalton SM1 ...218 C3
Edmonton N21 .....16 D2
Feltham TW13 .....150 A2
Hounslow TW7 ....130 D4
Tolworth KT5 ......199 A3
Upper Halliford TW16 193 D4
Walton-on-T KT12 ..194 A1
Highfields SM7 ....217 C6
Highfield Sch SW18 .158 C4
High Foleys KT10 ..213 C4
High Gables
Beckenham BR2 ...186 C5
Loughton IG10 ......21 D6
High Garth KT10 ..212 A3
Highgate Archway N6 49 C1
Highgate Ave N6 ...49 B2
Highgate Ballet Sch
NW11 ....47 D5
Highgate Cemetery*
N19 ....71 B6
Highgate Cl N6 .....49 A2
High Gate Edge N2 ..48 C4
Highgate High St N6 49 B1

Highgate Hill N19 ...49 C1
Highgate Ho 11 SE26 162 A1
Highgate Hts N6 ....49 C4
Highgate Jun Sch N6 48 D2
Highgate Prim Sch
N6 ....48 D3
Highgate Private Hospl
N6 ....48 D3
Highgate Rd NW5 ..71 B4
Highgate Sch N6 ...49 A2
Highgate Spinney N8 49 C3
Highgate Sta N6 ...49 B3
Highgate West Hill N6 71 A6
Highgate Wlk SE23 .162 C2
Highgate Wood Sch
N8 ....49 C4
High Gr Bromley BR1 .187 D2
Woolwich SE18 .....145 B4
Highgrove Cl BR7 ..188 A2
N11 ....31 A5
Highgrove Ct BR3 .185 C3
Highgrove Ho HA4 ..40 A3
Highgrove Mews
SM5 ....218 D5
Highgrove Point 2
NW3 ....70 A4
Highgrove Rd RM8 ..80 C4
Highgrove Way HA4 ..40 A2
High Hill Ferry 3 E5 .52 B1
High Holborn
WC1 ....94 B2 240 C3
High La W7 ....86 B1
Highland Ave W7 ...86 C6
Highland Cotts SM6 .219 C4
Highland Croft BR3 .185 C4
Highland Ct E18 ....37 B2
Highland Dr WD23 ...8 A4
Highland Lo 3 SE19 .183 D3
Highland Pk TW13 .171 A3
Highland Rd
Bexley DA6 ....147 C1
Bromley BR1 ....186 D2
Pinner HA6 ....22 A1
West Norwood SE19 .183 C4
Highlands N20 ......14 B2
Highlands Ave W3 ..111 A6
Southgate N21 ......16 B6
Highlands Cl N4 ....50 A2
Hounslow TW3 ....129 D4
Highlands Ct SE19 .183 C4
Highlands Gdns IG1 .56 B1
Highlands Heath
SW15 ....156 A4
Highlands Prim Sch
IG1 ....56 B1
Highlands Rd EN5 ..13 C6
Highlands Sch N21 ..6 C1
Highlands The
Barnet EN5 ....1 D1
Edgware HA8 ....26 D1
Highlawn Hall HA1 ..64 C6
Highlea Cl NW9 .....27 C2
High Level Dr SE26 .184 A6
Highlever Rd W10 ..90 C2
High Limes 2 SE19 .183 C4
High London 5 N6 ..49 D2
Highmead SE18 ...145 B4
9 Edmonton N18 ...34 B4
High Mead Harrow HA1 42 D4
West Wickham BR4 .224 C6
Highmead Cres HA0 .66 B1
High Meadow Cl HA5 .40 C5
High Meadow Cres
NW9 ....45 B4
High Meads Rd E16 ..99 D1
Highmore Rd SE3 ..142 C5
High Mount NW4 ...46 A4
High Oaks EN2 ......4 B5
High Park Ave TW9 .132 A4
High Park Rd TW9 .132 A4
High Par The SW16 .160 A4
High Path SW19 ...180 A2
High Point N6 ......49 A4
SE9 ....166 D1
Highpoint EN5 ......14 A6
High Range SW20 .178 C3
High Rd E10 ....53 C6
N11 ....31 B5
N15,N17 ....51 D5
N20 ....14 A4
N2 ....48 C6
N2,N12 ....30 A3
NW10 ....68 A2
Buckhurst Hill IG9,IG10 21 C6
Bushey WD23 ....8 B3
Harrow HA3 ....24 C3
Ilford IG1 ....78 D6

High Rd continued
Ilford IG1,IG3 ....79 C6
Ilford IG3 ....57 D1
Ilford RM6 ....58 B2
Tottenham N17 ....33 D2
Wembley HA0,HA9 ..66 A3
Woodford E18 ....37 A2
Wood Green N22 ..32 B3
High Ridge N10 ....31 B2
High Road Eastcote
HA5 ....40 B4
High Road, Ickenham
UB10 ....61 A6
High Road Leyton E10 75 D6
High Road Leytonstone
E11 ....76 C6
High Road Woodford Gn
IG8 ....37 A6
High Sheldon N6 ....48 D3
Highshore Rd SE15 .139 D3
Highshore Sch SE15 .139 D4
High Silver IG10 ....21 D6
High St BR1 ....187 A1
BR6 ....227 A3
BR6 ....227 D2
E13 ....99 A5
E15 ....98 A6
E17 ....53 B5
N14 ....15 D2
N8 ....50 B5
NW7 ....28 B5
Acton W3 ....110 D5
Barnet EN5 ....1 B1
Beckenham BR3 ....185 C1
Brentford TW8 ....132 A6
Cheam SM1,KT17 ..217 A2
Cranford TW5 ....128 B5
Croydon CR0 ....221 A5
Croydon SE25 ....206 A5
Ealing W5 ....109 D6
East Molesey KT8 ..195 C5
Elstree WD6 ....9 D5
Feltham TW13 ....150 A2
Hampton TW12 ....174 A4
Harlington UB3 ....127 B6
Harrow HA1 ....42 C1
Harrow HA3 ....42 C6
Hounslow TW3 ....129 D2
Ilford IG6 ....57 A6
Kingston KT1 ....197 D6
New Malden KT3 ..199 C5
Penge SE20 ....184 D3
Pinner HA5 ....41 A6
Ruislip HA4 ....39 C1
Shepperton TW17 ..193 A3
Sidcup DA14 ....190 A6
Southall UB1 ....107 B5
South Norwood CR7 ..205 B5
Sutton SM1 ....217 D4
Sutton SM1,SM2 ..217 D3
Teddington KT1 ....175 D2
Teddington KT1 ....175 A5
Thames Ditton KT7 ..197 A3
Twickenham TW2 ..152 A4
Wallington SM5 ....219 A4
Walton-on-T KT12 ..194 A1
Wanstead E11 ....55 A4
Wembley HA9 ....66 B4
West Wickham BR4 ..207 D1
Wimbledon SW19 ..178 D5
Yiewsley UB7 ....104 A6
High St Mews SW19 .179 A5
High St N E12 ....78 A2
E6 ....100 A6
Highstone Ave E11 ..55 A3
Highstone Ct E11 ....54 D3
High Street Collier's Wood
SW17,SW19 ....180 B4
High Street Harlesden
NW10 ....89 D5
High Street Harlington
TW6 ....127 B5
High Street Kensington
Sta W8 ....113 D3 245 C1
High St S E6 ....100 B4
High The SW16 ....160 A1
High Timber St EC4 .252 A6
High Tor Cl BR1 ....187 B3
High Tor View SE28 .123 C5
High Trees N20 ....14 A1
Croydon CR0 ....207 A1
East Barnet EN4 ....14 C6
Streatham SW2 ....160 C3
Uxbridge UB10 ....61 A6
Hightrees Ct W7 ..108 C6
Hightrees Ho SW12 .159 A5

Highview N8 ....50 A2
Northolt UB5 ....85 A4
Woolwich SE18 ....144 D5
High View
[6] Penge SE19 ....183 D3
Pinner HA5 ....40 C6
Highview Ave HA8 ..27 A6
High View Ave CR0,
SM6 ....220 B3
High View Cl
Loughton IG10 ....21 C6
South Norwood SE19 .183 D1
Highview Ct [2] SW19 157 A3
High View Ct HA3 ..24 C3
Highview Gdns HA8 ..27 A6
N11 ....31 C5
N3 ....47 A6
High View Par [1] IG4 .56 B4
High View Prim Sch
SW11 ....136 B1
Wallington SM6 ....220 A3
High View Rd E18 ..54 D6
N10 ....30 D2
Highview Rd
Ealing W13 ....87 A1
Sidcup DA14 ....190 B6
High View Rd SE19 .183 B4
Highway Bsns Pk The [7]
E1 ....118 D6
Highway The E1 ..118 C6
Stanmore HA7 ....25 A3
Highway Trad Ctr The [6]
E1 ....118 D6
High Wigsell TW11 .175 A5
Highwood Ave N12 ..30 A6
Highwood Cl BR6 ..227 A6
Highwood Ct N12 ..14 A1
Barnet EN5 ....13 C6
Highwood Dr BR6 ..227 A6
Highwood Gdns IG5 ..56 B5
Highwood Gr NW7 ..27 B5
Highwood Hill NW7 ..11 D2
Highwood Rd N19 ..72 A5
High Worple HA2 ..41 B1
Highworth Rd N11 ..31 D5
Highworth St NW1 .237 B4
Hilary Ave CR4 ....203 A6
Hilary Cl SW6 ....265 C4
Bexley DA7 ....147 C4
Hilary Ct N9 ....18 D3
Hilary Rd W12 ....111 D6
Hilbert Rd SM3 ....216 D6
Hilborough Cl SW19 .180 A3
Hilborough Ct [1] E8 ..95 D6
Hilborough Ct [1] E8 ..73 D1
Hilborough Way BR6 227 B3
Hilda Rd E16 ....98 C3
E6 ....77 D1
Hilda Terr [2] SW9 .138 C3
Hilda Vale Cl BR6 ..226 A3
Hilda Vale Rd BR6 ..226 A3
Hildenborough Gdns
BR1 ....186 D4
Hildenbrough Ho
BR3 ....185 B3
Hildenlea Pl BR2 ..186 C1
Hilditch Ho [7] TW10 .154 B1
Hildred Ho SW1 ..258 C4
Hildreth St SW12 ..159 B3
Hildreth Street Mews [2]
SW12 ....159 B3
Hildyard Rd SW6 ..265 B6
Hiley Rd NW10 ....90 C4
Hilfield La WD23 ..8 C5
Hilfield La S WD23 ..8 D5
Hilgrove Rd NW6 ..70 A1
Hiliary Gdns HA7 ..25 C1
Hillard Ct SM6 ....219 D1
Hillary Cres KT12 ..194 C1
Hillary Ct
[3] Chislehurst SE9 .166 A2
Stanwell TW19 ....148 A3
Hillary Dr TW7 ....152 D6
Hillary Rd UB2 ....107 C3
Hillary Rise EN5 ....1 C1
Hillbeck Cl SE15 ..140 C5
SE15 ....140 C6
Hillbeck Way UB6 ..86 B6
Hillborne Cl UB3 ..106 A1
Hillboro Ct E11 ....54 B2
[1] Woodford E18 ..36 D2
Hillbrook Rd SW17 .181 A6
Hillbrook Sch SW17 .181 B6
Hillbrow Kingston KT3 199 D6
[7] Richmond TW10 .154 A6
Hill Brow BR1 ....187 D2
Hillbrow Ct KT10 ..212 A4
Hillbrow Rd
Catford BR1 ....186 C4

Hillbrow Rd continued
Esher KT10 ....212 A4
Hill Bunker's DA17 .125 C2
Hillbury Ave HA3 ..43 B4
Hillbury Rd SW17 ..159 B1
Hill Cl NW11 ....47 C3
NW2 ....68 B5
Barnet EN5 ....12 C6
Chislehurst BR7 ....188 D5
Harrow HA1 ....64 C5
Stanmore HA7 ....25 B6
Hillcote Ave SW16 .182 C3
Hillcourt Ave N12 ..29 D4
Hillcourt Rd SE22 ..162 B5
Hill Cres N20 ....13 D2
Harrow HA1 ....43 A4
Kingston KT5 ....198 B4
North Cheam KT4 ..216 C6
Hill Crest DA15 ....168 B4
Hillcrest N21 ....16 C4
Hillcrest Ave NW11 ..47 B4
Edgware HA8 ....26 D6
Pinner HA5 ....40 D5
Hillcrest Cl
Beckenham BR3 ....207 B3
Forest Hill SE26 ....184 A6
Hillcrest Ct NW2 ..69 A3
Sutton SM2 ....218 B2
Hillcrest Gdns N3 ..47 A5
NW2 ....68 A5
Hinchley Wood KT10 .212 D5
Hillcrest Hts W5 ..88 A3
Hillcrest Rd BR1 ..187 A6
Acton W3 ....110 D5
Chingford E17 ....36 B1
Ealing W5 ....88 A2
Loughton IG10 ....21 D5
Woodford E18 ....37 A1
Hillcrest View BR3 .207 B3
Hillcroft Ave HA5 ..41 B3
Hillcroft Coll KT6 ..198 A3
Hillcroft Cres
Ealing W5 ....87 D1
Ruislip HA4 ....62 D5
Wembley HA9 ....66 B4
Hillcroft Rd E6 ....100 D2
Hillcroome Rd SM2 .218 B2
Hillcross Ave SM4 .201 A4
Hillcross Prim Sch
SM4 ....201 B5
Hill Ct NW3 ....70 C4
Barnet EN4 ....2 C1
Ealing W5 ....88 B3
[8] Kingston KT2 ..176 D3
[14] Kingston KT6 ..198 A4
Northolt UB5 ....63 C3
Putney SW15 ....156 D6
Hilldale Rd SM1 ..217 B4
Hilldown Ct SW16 ..182 A4
Hilldown Rd
Hayes BR2 ....208 D1
South Norwood SW16 .182 B3
Hill Dr NW9 ....45 A1
Thornton Heath SW16 .204 B6
Hilldrop Cres N7 ..71 D3
Hilldrop Est [4] N7 ..71 D4
Hilldrop La N7 ....71 D3
Hilldrop Rd N7 ....71 D3
Bromley BR1 ....187 B4
Hill End BR6 ....227 D6
SE18 ....144 C4
Hillersdon Ave
Barnes SW13 ....134 A3
Edgware HA8 ....26 B5
Hillersdon Ho SW1 .258 C2
Hillery Cl SE17 ....262 D3
Hill Farm Rd W10 ..90 D2
Hillfield Ave N8 ....50 A5
NW9 ....45 C5
Mitcham SM4 ....202 C4
Wembley HA0 ....66 B1
Hillfield Cl HA2 ....42 A5
Hillfield Ct NW3 ..70 C3
Hillfield Ho N5 ....73 A3
Hillfield Mans NW3 ..70 C3
Hillfield Par SM4 ..202 B3
Hillfield Park Mews
N10 ....49 B6
Hillfield Pk N10 ..49 B6
Southgate N21 ....16 C4
Hillfield Rd NW6 ..69 C3
Hampton TW12 ....173 B2
Hillgate Pl
W8 ....113 C5 245 A4
Balham SW12 ....159 B4
Hillgate St W8 ....245 A4
Hill Gr TW13 ....151 B2

Hill Ho E5 ....52 B1
Stanmore HA7 ....9 A1
Hill House Ave HA7 ..24 D3
Hill House Cl N21 ..16 C4
Hill House Dr TW12 .173 C2
Hill House Rd SW16 .182 B5
Hill House Sch
SW1 ....114 D3 257 D5
Hilliard Ho [15] E1 ..118 B5
Hilliard's Ct E1 ....118 C5
Hillier Cl EN5 ....13 D5
Hillier Gdns CR0 ..220 C3
Hillier Ho [1] NW1 ..71 D1
Hillier Lo [1] W1 ..174 D3
Hillier Pl KT9 ....213 D2
Hillier Rd SW11 ....158 D5
Hilliers Ave UB8 ..82 C4
Hillier's La CR0,SM6 .220 A5
Hillingdon Ave TW19 148 A3
Hillingdon Circus
UB10 ....60 D2
Hillingdon Hill UB10 .82 B4
Hillingdon Hospl UB8 .82 B2
Hillingdon Par [6]
UB10 ....82 D3
Hillingdon Prim Sch
UB10 ....82 D4
Hillingdon Rd UB10 .82 A5
Hillingdon Sta UB10 .60 D6
Hillington Gdns IG8 ..37 D1
Hill La HA4 ....39 A1
Hill Lo SW11 ....136 B1
Hillman Cl UB8 ....60 A3
Hillman St E8 ....74 B2
Hillmarton Rd N7 ..72 A3
Hillmead Dr SW9 ..138 D1
Hill Mead Prim Sch
SW9 ....138 D1
Hillmont Rd KT10 ..212 C5
Hillmore Ct SE13 ..142 B2
Hillmore Gr SE26 ..185 B5
Hill Rd N10 ....30 D2
NW8 ....92 A5 229 B3
Carshalton SM5 ....218 C2
Harrow HA1 ....43 A4
Mitcham CR4 ....181 B3
Pinner HA5 ....41 A3
Sutton SM1 ....217 D3
Wembley HA0 ....65 B5
Hillreach SE7,SE18 .122 B1
Hill Rise NW11 ....47 D5
Hillrise KT12 ....193 D2
Hill Rise Enfield N9 ..18 B5
Forest Hill SE23 ....162 B3
Greenford UB6 ....86 A6
Hinchley Wood KT10 .213 B6
Richmond TW10 ....153 D6
Ruislip HA4 ....39 B1
Hillrise Mans N19 ..50 A2
Hillrise Rd N19 ....50 A2
Hillsboro Rd SE22 ..161 C6
Hillsborough Ct [11]
NW6 ....91 D6
Hillsgrove Cl DA16 .146 C5
Hillsgrove Prim Sch
DA16 ....146 C5
Hillside N8 ....49 D3
NW10 ....89 B6
NW9 ....45 B5
Barnet EN5 ....14 A6
Wimbledon SW19 ..178 D4
Hill Side EN5 ....14 A6
Hillside Ave N11 ..30 D4
Wembley HA9 ....66 B4
Woodford IG8 ....37 C5
Hillside Cl NW8 ..91 D5
Merton SM4 ....201 A6
Woodford IG8 ....37 C5
Hillside Cres Enfield EN2 5 B5
Harrow HA2 ....42 A1
Northwood HA6 ....22 A2
Hillside Ct NW3 ..69 D3
[7] Kingston KT2 ..176 D3
Hillside Dr HA8 ....26 C5
Hillside Gdns E17 ..54 B6
N6 ....49 B3
Barnet EN5 ....1 A1
Barnet N11 ....31 C4
Edgware HA8 ....26 B6
Harrow HA3 ....44 A2
Northwood HA6 ....22 B2
Streatham SW2 ....160 C2
Wallington SM6 ....219 C1
Hillside Gr N14 ....15 D4
NW7 ....28 A5
Hillside Jun Inf Schs
HA6 ....22 A3
Hillside La BR2 ....224 D6
Hillside Mans EN5 ..1 B1

Hillside Rd N15 ....51 C3
Beckenham BR2 ..208 D6
Belmont SM2 ....217 B1
Croydon CR0 ....220 D4
Ealing W5 ....88 A2
Northwood HA6,HA5 ..22 A4
Southall UB1 ....85 C3
Streatham SW2 ....160 C2
Surbiton KT5 ....198 C4
Hillside Rise HA6 ..22 A4
Hillsleigh Rd
W14 ....113 B5 244 D4
Hills Mews [2] W5 .110 A5
Hills Pl W1 ....239 A1
Hill's Rd IG9 ....21 B3
Hill St W1 ....115 B6 248 C4
Richmond TW10 ....153 D6
Hillstone Ct [5] E3 ..97 D3
Hillstowe St E5 ....74 C5
Hilltop N17 ....53 D6
Cheam SM3 ....201 B2
Hilltop Ct NW8 ....70 A1
[12] SW18 ....136 B1
South Norwood SE19 .183 B2
Hilltop Gdns BR6 ..227 C6
Hilltop Ho [7] N6 ..49 D2
Hilltop Rd NW6 ....69 C1
Hilltop Way HA7 ..9 A1
Hillview SW20 ....178 B3
Hill View CR4 ....204 A5
Hillview Ave HA3 ..44 A4
Hillview Cl Pinner HA5 .23 B4
Wembley HA9 ....66 B6
Hill View Cres IG1 ..56 B3
Hillview Ct SE19 ..183 C6
Hill View Dr DA16 .145 C3
Woolwich SE28 ....123 C3
Hillview Gdns NW4 ..46 D5
Hill View Gdns NW9 ..45 A4
Hillview Gdns HA2 ..41 C5
Hillview Rd BR7 ..188 D6
NW7 ....28 D6
Hill View Rd BR6 ..227 D6
Hillview Rd
Carshalton SM1 ....218 B5
Pinner HA5 ....23 B4
Hill View Rd
Claygate KT10 ....213 A4
Twickenham TW1 ..153 A5
Hillway N6 ....71 A6
NW9 ....45 C1
Hill Wood Ho NW1 .232 C3
Hillworth [7] BR3 ..185 D1
Hillworth Rd SW2 .160 C4
Hillyard Rd W7 ....86 C2
Hillyard St SW9 ..138 C4
Hillyfield E17 ....35 A1
Hillyfield Cl E9 ....75 A3
Hilly Fields Cres SE4 141 C2
Hilly Mead SW19 ..179 A3
Hilsea Point [7] SW15 156 B3
Hilsea St E5 ....74 C4
Hilton Ave N12 ....30 B5
Hilton Ho N7 ....72 A4
[9] SE4 ....140 C1
[4] Ealing W13 ....87 C1
Hilversum Cres [10]
SE22 ....161 C6
Himley Rd SW17 ..180 D4
Hinchley Cl KT10 ..212 D5
Hinchley Dr KT10 ..212 D5
Hinchley Way KT10 .213 A6
Hinchley Wood Prim Sch
KT10 ....213 A6
Hinchley Wood Sch
KT10 ....213 A6
Hinchley Wood Sta
KT10 ....212 D5
Hinckley Rd SE15 ..140 A1
Hind Ct EC4 ....241 B1
Hinde Mews W1 ..238 B2
Hindes Rd HA1 ....42 C4
Hinde St W1 ..93 A1 238 B2
Hind Gr E14 ....97 C1
Hindhead Cl UB8 ..82 D2
Hindhead Gdns UB5 ..85 A6
Hindhead Gn WD19 ..22 C1
Hindhead Point [6]
SW15 ....156 C6
Hindhead Way SM6 .220 A3
Hind Ho N7 ....72 A4
[13] SE14 ....140 D6
Hindhurst Ct NW9 ..45 A5
Hindle Ho E8 ....73 D2
Hindley Ho N7 ....72 B5
Hindlip Ho SW8 ..269 C1
Hindmans Rd SE22 .162 A6
Hindmans Way RM9 .103 B3

Hindmarsh Cl E1 ..118 A6
Hindrey Rd E5 ....74 B3
Hindsley's Pl SE23 .162 C2
Hines Ct HA1 ....43 A4
Hinkler Rd HA3 ....43 D6
Hinksey Path SE2 .124 D3
Hinstock NW6 ....91 D6
Hinstock Rd SE18 .145 A5
Hinton Ave TW4 ..128 D1
Hinton Cl SE9 ....166 A3
Hinton Ct [3] E10 ..75 D6
Hinton Rd SE24 ....138 D2
Edmonton N18 ....33 C6
Wallington SM6 ....219 C2
Hippodrome Mews
W11 ....244 A5
Hippodrome Pl W11 .244 B5
Hiscocks Ho NW10 ..67 A1
Hitcham Rd E17 ....53 B2
Hitchcock Cl TW17 .192 B6
Hitchin Sq E3 ....97 A5
Hitherbroom Rd UB3 106 A6
Hither Farm Rd SE3 .143 C2
Hitherfield Prim Sch
SW2 ....160 C2
Hitherfield Rd
Dagenham RM8 ....81 A6
Streatham SW16,SW27 160 C1
Hither Green La SE13 164 B5
Hither Green Prim Sch
SE13 ....164 B5
Hither Green Sta
SE13 ....164 C5
Hitherlands SW12 ..159 B2
Hitherwell Dr HA3 ..24 B2
Hitherwood Ct SE21 .183 D6
Hitherwood Dr SE19 .183 D6
Hive Cl WD23 ....8 B2
Hive Rd WD23 ....8 C2
HM Prison Wormwood
Scrubs W12 ....90 A1
HMS Belfast* SE1 .253 B4
Hoadly Rd SW16 ..159 D2
Hobart Cl N20 ......14 C2
Hayes UB4 ....84 D3
Hobart Ct Harrow HA1 .42 C2
Woodford IG8 ....36 D6
Hobart Dr UB4 ....84 D3
Hobart Gdns CR7 ..205 B6
Hobart La UB4 ....84 D3
Hobart Pl
SW1 ....115 B3 258 C6
Richmond TW10 ....154 B4
Hobart Rd
Dagenham RM9 ....80 D4
Hayes UB4 ....84 D3
North Cheam KT4 ..216 B5
Hobbayne Prim Sch
W7 ....86 D1
Hobbayne Rd W7 ..86 B1
Hobbes Wlk SW15 .156 A6
Hobb's Ct SE1 ....253 D2
Hobbs Gn N2 ....48 A6
Hobbs Mews IG3 ..79 D6
Hobbs' Pl N1 ....95 C6
Hobbs Rd [5] SE27 .183 A6
Hobday St E14 ....97 D1
Hobill Wlk KT5 ....198 B3
Hoblands End BR7 .189 C4
Hobsons Pl [7] E1 ..96 C4
Hobury St
SW10 ....136 B6 266 C5
Hockenden La BR5,
BR8 ....191 D1
Hocker St [41] E2 ..95 D4
Hockington Ct [7] EN5 13 D6
Hockley Ave E6 ....100 A5
Hockley Ct [2] E18 ..37 A2
Hockley Ho [4] E9 ..74 C2
Hockley Mews IG11 .101 C5
Hockliffe Ho W10 ..90 C2
Hockney Ct [1] SE16 .118 B1
Hockworth Ho [7] N16 51 C1
Hocroft Ave NW2 ..69 C4
Hocroft Ct NW2 ....69 B5
Hocroft Rd NW2 ....69 B5
Hocroft Wlk NW2 ..69 B5
Hodder Dr UB6 ....86 D5
Hoddesdon Rd DA17 .125 C1
Hodford Rd NW11 ..47 B1
Hodgkins Cl SE28 ..124 D6
Hodister Cl [26] SE5 .139 A5
Hodnet Gr SE16 ..118 D2
Hodson Cl HA2 ....63 D6
Hodson Pl EN3 ....7 C5
Hoecroft Ct EN3 ..6 C5
Hoe La EN1 ....6 B5
Hoe St E17 ....53 C4
Hoffman Sq N1 ..235 B2

Hofland Rd
W14 ....113 A3 **254** A6
Hogan Mews W2 ...**236** C4
Hogan Way E5 ......74 A6
Hogarth Ave TW15 ..171 A4
Hogarth Bsns Pk W4 133 C6
Hogarth Cl E16 ......99 D2
Ealing W5 ....88 A4
Hogarth Cres
Mitcham SW19 .....180 B2
Thornton Heath CR0 ..205 A4
Hogarth Ct 15 E1 ...96 A1
EC3 ....**253** B6
6 NW1 ....71 C1
Dulwich SE19 ......183 D6
Heston TW5 ....129 A5
Hogarth Gdns TW5 .129 C5
Hogarth Hill NW11 ..47 B5
Hogarth Ho SW1 .**259** D3
Enfield EN1 ....18 A6
13 Northolt UB5 .....84 D5
6 West Norwood
SE27 ....183 A6
Hogarth Ind Est NW10 90 A3
Hogarth La W4 .....133 C6
Hogarth Pl SW5 ...**255** C3
Hogarth Prim Sch
W4 ....111 C1
Hogarth Rd
SW5 ....113 D2 **255** C3
Barking RM8 ....80 B3
Edgware HA8 ......26 C1
Hogarth Roundabout
W4 ....133 C6
Hogarth Way TW12 .174 A2
Hogsmill Wlk KT19 .215 A4
Holbeach Gdns DA15 167 D5
Holbeach Mews 1
SW12 ....159 B3
Holbeach Prim Sch
SE6 ....163 C4
Holbeach Rd SE6 ...163 D4
Holbeck Row SE15 .140 A5
Holbein Ho SW1 ..**258** A2
10 Stanmore HA7 ....25 C5
Holbein Mews
SW1 ....115 A1 **258** A2
Holbein Pl
SW1 ....115 A2 **258** A2
Holberry Ho 5 SE21 .183 C6
Holberton Gdns NW10 90 B4
Holborn EC1 ..94 C2 **241** B3
Holborn Cir
EC1 ....94 C2 **241** B3
Holborn Pl WC1 ....**240** C3
Holborn Rd E13 .....99 B3
Holborn Sta
WC1 ....94 B2 **240** D3
Holborn Way CR4 ...180 D1
Holbrook Cl N19 .....49 B1
Enfield EN1 ....6 A5
Holbrooke Ct N7 ....72 A4
Holbrooke Pl 23
TW10 ....153 D6
Holbrook Ho W3 ....89 B2
Chislehurst BR7 ....189 B2
5 Streatham SW2 ...160 A4
Holbrook La BR7 ...189 B3
Holbrook Rd E15 ....98 D5
Holbrook Way BR2 .210 D4
Holburn 33 N1 ......95 C6
Holburne Cl SE3 ...143 C4
Holburne Gdns SE3 .143 D4
Holburne Rd SE3 ...143 D4
Holburn Viaduct
EC1 ....94 D2 **241** C3
Holcombe Hill NW7 ..12 A1
Holcombe Ho SW9 ..138 A2
Holcombe Rd N17 ...52 A6
1 N17 ....51 D6
Ilford IG1 ....56 C2
Holcombe St W6 ...112 B2
Holcote Cl DA17 ....125 A3
Holcroft Ct W1 ....**239** A4
Holcroft Ho SE10 ..142 A4
SW11 ....136 B2
Holcroft Rd E9 .....74 C1
Holden Ave N12 ....29 D5
NW9 ....45 A1
Holdenby Rd SE4 ...163 A6
Holden Cl RM8 .....80 B5
Holden Ho N1 ....**235** A5
12 SE8 ....141 C5
Holden Hts N12 .....13 D1
Holdenhurst Ave N12 .30 A3
Holden Lo N11 .....31 C3
Holden Rd N12 .....29 D6
Holden St SW11 ....137 A3
Holdernesse Rd
Isleworth TW7 .....131 A4

Holdernesse Rd continued
6 Upper Tooting
SW17 ....159 A2
Holderness Ho SE5 .139 C2
Holderness Way
SE27 ....182 D5
Holders Hill Ave NW4 .46 D6
Holders Hill Cres NW4 28 D1
Holders Hill Dr NW4 .28 D1
Holders Hill Gdns
NW4 ....29 A1
Holders Hill Par NW7 .29 A1
Holders Hill Rd NW4 .28 D1
NW4,NW7 ....29 A2
Holdsworth Ho 5
SW2 ....160 C4
Holford Ho 6 SE16 .118 B2
WC1 ....**233** D2
Holford Pl WC1 ....**233** D2
Holford Rd NW3 ....70 A5
Holford St WC1 ....**234** A2
Holgate Ave SW11 .136 B2
Holgate Ct HA8 .....26 B6
Holgate Gdns RM10 ..81 C3
Holgate Rd RM10 ...81 C3
Holgate St SE7 ....121 D3
Hollam Ho N8 ......50 B5
Holland Ave
Belmont SM2 ......217 C1
Wimbledon SW20 ...177 D2
Holland Cl
Coney Hall BR2 ....224 D6
New Barnet EN5 ....14 B4
Stanmore HA7 .....25 B5
Holland Ct 6 E17 ...54 A5
NW7 ....28 A4
Holland Dr SE23 ...163 A1
Holland Gdns W14 .**254** B6
Holland Gr SW9 ...138 C5
Holland Ho E4 .....36 A6
Holland House Sch
HA8 ....26 D6
Holland Park
W11 ....113 B5 **244** C3
Holland Park Ave
W11 ....113 A5 **244** B3
Ilford IG3 ....57 D4
Holland Park Ct W14 244 B2
Holland Park Gdns
W14 ....113 A4 **244** A2
Holland Park Mews
W11 ....113 B5 **244** C3
Holland Park Rd
W14 ....113 A4 **254** D5
Holland Park Rdbt
W12 ....112 D4
Holland Park Sch
W8 ....113 A4 **244** D2
Holland Park Sta
W11 ....113 B5 **244** C3
Holland Pl W8 .....**245** C2
Holland Rd E15 .....98 C4
NW10 ....90 B5
W14 ....113 A3 **254** B6
Croydon SE25 ......206 A4
Wallend E6 ....78 C1
Wembley HA0 ......65 D2
Holland Rise Ho
SW9 ....**270** D3
Holland St
SE1 ....116 D5 **251** D4
W8 ....113 C4 **245** B2
Hollands The
Feltham TW13 .....172 D6
New Malden KT4 ...199 D1
Holland Villas Rd
W14 ....113 A4 **244** A1
Holland Way BR2 ..224 D6
Holland Wlk N19 ...49 D3
W14 ....113 B4 **244** D1
Stanmore HA7 .....25 A5
Hollar Rd N16 ......73 D5
Hollen St W1 .....**239** C2
Holles Cl TW12 ....173 C5
Holles Ho 9 SW9 ..138 C3
Holles St W1 ..93 B1 **238** B3
Holley Rd W3 .....111 C4
Hollickwood Ave N12 .30 D4
Hollickwood Prim Sch
N10 ....31 B3
Holliday Sq 7 SW11 .136 B2
Hollidge Way RM10 .81 D1
Hollies Ave DA15 ..167 D3
Hollies Cl
South Norwood SW16 .182 C4
Twickenham TW1 ...152 D2
Hollies End NW7 ....28 B5
Hollies Rd W5 .....109 C2
Hollies The N20 ....14 B3
Harrow HA3 ....43 A5

Hollies The continued
7 Wanstead E11 ....55 A4
Hollies Way 1 SW12 159 A4
Holligrave Rd BR1 .187 A2
Hollingbourne Ave
DA7 ....147 B4
Hollingbourne Gdns
W13 ....87 B2
Hollingbourne Rd
SE24 ....161 A6
Hollingbury Ct 1 E17 53 D6
Hollingsworth Rd
CR0 ....222 B2
Hollington Cres KT3 .199 D3
Hollington Ct BR7 ..188 D4
Hollington Rd E6 ...100 B4
Tottenham N17 .....34 A1
Hollingworth Cl KT8 .195 D3
Hollingworth Ct 7
KT6 ....197 D3
Hollingworth Rd BR2,
BR5 ....210 D2
Hollins Ho N7 ......72 A4
Hollisfield WC1 ....**233** B1
Hollman Gdns SW16 .182 A4
Holloway Cl UB7 ...104 A1
Holloway La UB7 ...104 B1
E6 ....100 B4
Holloway Rd E11 ...76 B5
N19 ....71 D6
N7 ....72 A4
Holloway Road Sta N7 72 B3
Holloway Sch N7 ...71 B3
Holloway St TW3 ..129 D2
Hollowfield Wlk UB5 .63 A2
Hollow The IG8 .....36 D6
Holly Ave N2 ......47 D6
Stanmore HA7 .....26 A1
Walton-on-T KT12 ..194 D1
Hollybank Ct TW12 .173 C5
Holly Berry La 6 NW3 70 A4
Hollybrake Cl BR7 .189 B3
Hollybush Cl
Harrow HA3 ....24 C2
Wanstead E11 .....55 A4
Hollybush Gdns E2 .96 B4
Hollybush Hill E11 ..54 D3
Holly Bush Hill 23
NW3 ....70 A4
Hollybush Ho 23 E2 .96 B4
Holly Bush La TW12 .173 C3
Hollybush Pl E2 ....96 B4
Hollybush Rd KT2 ..176 A4
Hollybush St E13 ...99 B4
Holly Bush Vale 9
NW3 ....70 A4
Holly Cl NW10 .....67 C1
Beckenham BR3 ...208 A5
Buckhurst Hill IG9 ..21 D1
Feltham TW13 .....173 A5
Holly Cott KT7 ....197 A1
Holly Cottage Mews
UB8 ....82 C2
Holly Cres
Beckenham BR3 ...207 B4
Chingford IG8 .....36 B3
Hollycroft Ave NW3 .69 C5
Wembley HA9 ......66 B5
Hollycroft Cl
Harmondsworth UB7 .126 C6
South Croydon CR2 .221 C1
Hollycroft Gdns UB7 .126 C6
Holly Ct N15 ......51 C5
9 Belmont SM2 ....217 C1
4 Sidcup DA14 ....190 B6
Wallington SM6 ...219 B1
Hollydale Cl UB5 ...63 D4
Hollydale Dr BR2 ..226 B5
Holly Dale Prim Sch
SE15 ....140 C4
Hollydale Rd SE15 .140 C4
Hollydene SE13 ...164 B5
5 SE15 ....140 B4
Hollydown Way E11 .76 B5
Holly Dr E4 ....19 D4
Holly Farm Rd UB2 .107 A1
Hollyfield Ave N11 ..30 D5
Hollyfield Rd KT5 ..198 B2
Hollyfield Sch KT6 .198 A4
Holly Gdns UB7 ...104 B4
Holly Gr NW9 .....45 A2
SE15 ....140 A4
Pinner HA5 ....23 A2
Hollygrove WD23 ....8 A1
Hollygrove Cl TW3 .129 B1
Holly Hedge Terr
SE13 ....164 B6
Holly Hill NW3 .....70 A4
Southgate N21 .....16 A4

Holly Hill Rd DA8,
DA17 ....125 D1
Holly Ho TW8 .....131 C6
Holly House Hospl
IG9 ....21 B2
Holly Lo SE13 .....142 B1
Harrow HA1 ....42 B4
Southgate N21 .....16 C3
4 Wimbledon SW19 .179 A4
Wimbledon SW20 ..178 B1
Holly Lodge Gdns N6 .49 A1
Holly Lodge Mans N6 .71 A6
Hollymead SM5 ...218 D5
Holly Mews SW10 .**256** B1
Holly Mount NW3 ..70 A4
Hollymount Cl 9
SE10 ....142 A4
Hollymount Prim Sch
SW20 ....178 C2
Holly Park Est N4 ...50 B2
Holly Park Gdns N3 .47 C6
Holly Park Prim Sch
N11 ....31 A5
Ealing W7 ....108 D5
Holly Park Rd N11 ..31 A5
Ealing W7 ....108 D5
Holly Pk N3 ....47 C6
N4 ....50 B2
Holly Pl NW3 ......70 A4
Holly Rd E11 ......54 D2
W4 ....111 B2
Hampton TW12 ....174 A4
Hounslow TW3 ....129 D1
Twickenham TW1 ..153 A3
Holly St E8 ....73 D1
Holly Terr N6 ......49 A1
Hollytree Cl SW19 .156 D3
Holly Tree Ho SE4 .141 B4
Holly Tree Lo EN2 ...4 D3
Hollyview Cl NW4 ..46 A3
Holly Village N6 ....71 B6
Holly Way CR4 ....203 B1
Hollywell Row
EC2 ....95 C3 **243** A5
Enfield EN2 ....5 B2
Hollywood Ct W5 ..110 B6
Hollywood Gdns UB4 .84 B1
Hollywood Mews
SW10 ....**266** A6
Hollywood Rd E4 ...35 A5
SW10 ....136 A6 **266** A6
Hollywood Way IG8 .36 B4
Holman Ho 2 E2 ...96 D4
Holman Hunt Ho
W14 ....**254** A1
Holman Rd SW11 ..136 B3
West Ewell KT19 ...215 A3
Holmbank Dr TW17 .193 C5
Holmbridge Gdns EN3 .6 D1
Holmbrook NW1 ..**232** B3
Holmbrook Dr NW4 .46 D4
Holmbush Cl WD23 ..8 C2
Holmbury Ct
Mitcham SW19 ....180 C3
Upper Tooting SW17 .158 B3
Holmbury Gdns UB3 .105 D5
Holmbury Gr CR0 ..223 B1
Holmbury Ho SW9 .160 D6
Holmbury Manor 6
DA14 ....190 A6
Holmbury Pk BR7 .188 A3
Holmbury View 2 E5 .52 B1
Holmbush Rd SW15 .157 A5
Holmcote Gdns N5 .73 A3
Holmcroft Ho 9 E17 .53 D5
Holmcroft Way BR2 210 B4
Holm Ct SE12 ......165 B1
Holmdale Gdns NW4 .46 D4
Holmdale Rd NW6 ..69 C3
Chislehurst BR7 ...189 A5
Holmdale Terr N15 ..51 C3
Holmdene N12 ......29 C5
Holmdene Ave NW7 .28 A4
SE24 ....161 A6
Harrow HA2 ....24 A4
Holmdene Cl BR3 ..186 A1
Holmdene Ct BR1 ..210 A6
Holmead Rd
SW6 ....135 D5 **265** D3
Holmefield Ho W10 ..91 A1
Holme Lacey Rd
SE12 ....164 D5
Holmeleigh Ct EN3 ...6 C1
Holme Rd E6 ......100 A4
Holmes Ave E17 ...53 B6
NW7 ....29 A5
Holmes Ct 18 SW4 .138 A3
17 W4 ....111 A3
5 Chingford E4 ....20 B2

Holmesdale Ave
SW14 ....132 A6
Holmesdale Cl SE25 .205 B6
Holmesdale Ho 12
NW6 ....91 C6
Holmesdale Rd N6 ..49 B2
Bexley DA16 ......146 D3
Richmond TW9 ....132 B4
South Norwood SE25 .205 C5
Teddington TW11 ..175 C4
Thornton Heath CR0 .205 B4
Holmesley Rd SE23 .163 A5
Holmes Pl SW10 ..**266** B6
Holmes Rd NW5 ...71 B3
Merton SW19 .....180 A3
Twickenham TW1 ..152 B2
Holmes Terr SE1 ..**251** A2
Holmeswood Ct 3
N22 ....32 C1
Holme Way HA7 ....24 C4
Holmewood Gdns
SW2 ....160 B4
Holmewood Rd
South Norwood SE25 .205 C6
Streatham SW2 ...160 A4
Holmfield Ave NW4 .46 D4
Holmfield Ct 4 NW3 .70 C2
Holmfield Ho E17 ...54 B5
Holm Gr UB10 .....60 C1
Holmhurst SE13 ...164 B5
Holmhurst Rd DA17 .125 D1
Holmlea 1 CR0 ....221 B4
Holmleigh Prim Sch
N16 ....51 C1
Holmleigh Rd N16 ..51 C1
Holm Oak Cl SW15 .157 B5
Holmoaks Ho BR3 .186 A1
Holmsbury Ho 6 N7 .71 D3
Holmsdale Ho
21 E14 ....119 C6
6 N11 ....31 B6
Holmshaw Cl SE26 .185 A6
Holmside Ct SW12 .159 A5
Holmside Rd SW12 .159 A5
Holmsley Cl KT3 ...199 D2
Holmsley Ho SW15 .155 C5
Holmstall Ave HA8 ..27 A1
Holmstall Par HA8 ..27 A1
Holm Wlk SE3 .....143 A3
Holmwood 2 KT5 ..198 B3
3 N16 ....51 D2
Kingston KT3 ......199 B6
Holmwood Cl
Cheam SM2 ......216 D1
Harrow HA2 ....42 A6
Northolt UB5 ....63 D2
Holmwood Ct DA14 .189 D5
Holmwood Gdns N3 .29 C1
Wallington SM6 ...219 B2
Holmwood Gr NW7 .27 B5
Holmwood Mans W3 110 C5
Holmwood Rd
Chessington KT9 ..214 A3
Ilford IG3 ....79 C6
Holne Chase N2 ....48 A3
Morden SM4 ......201 C3
Holness Rd E15 ....76 D2
Holocaust Meml Gdn★
W2 ....114 D4 **247** D2
Holroyd Rd SW15 .156 C6
Holsgrove Ct W3 ..111 C5
Holstein Way 6
DA18 ....125 A3
Holst Mans SW13 .134 C5
Holstock Rd IG1 ...79 A6
Holsworth Cl HA2 ..42 A4
Holsworthy Ho 49 E3 .97 C4
Holsworthy Way KT9 213 C3
Holt Cl N10 ......49 A6
Woolwich SE28 ...124 C6
Holt Ct E15 ....76 A4
Holt Ho SW2 ......160 C5
Holtoake Ct 1 W5 ..87 B2
Holtoake Ho 3 W5 ..87 B2
Holton St E1 ......96 D3
Holt Rd E16 ....122 A5
Wembley HA0 ......65 C2
Holt The Morden SM4 201 C5
Wallington SM6 ...219 C4
Holtwhite Ave EN2 ...5 A3
Holtwhite's Hill EN2 ..5 A4
Holwell Pl HA5 .....41 A5
Holwood Park Ave
BR2,BR6 ....226 B4
Holwood Pl 7 SW4 .137 D2
Holybourne Ave
SW15 ....156 A4
Holy Cross RC Sch
SW6 ....135 C4 **265** A2

Holy Cross Sch The
KT3 ....199 C4
Holy Family RC Prim Sch
E14 ....119 C6
SE9 ....143 C1
Holy Ghost RC Prim Sch
SW12 ....159 A4
Holyhead Cl E3 .....97 C4
3 E6 ....100 B1
Holyhead Ct KT1 ..197 D5
Holy Innocents RC Prim
Sch BR2 ....227 D5
Holyoake Ct SE16 .119 B4
Holyoake Wlk N2 ..48 A5
Ealing W5 ....87 C3
Holyoak Rd
SE11 ....116 D2 **261** D3
Holyport Rd SW6 .134 D5
Holyrood Ave HA2 ..63 B4
Holyrood Gdns HA8 .26 C3
Holyrood Ho N4 ...50 D1
Holyrood Mews 11
E16 ....121 A5
Holyrood Rd EN5 ...14 B5
Holyrood St
SE1 ....117 C5 **253** A3
Holy Trinity CE First Sch
SW19 ....179 D4
Holy Trinity CE Inf Sch
SW17 ....158 D2
Holy Trinity CE JMI Sch
E8 ....73 D2
Holy Trinity CE Jun Sch
Richmond TW10 ...132 C1
Wallington SM6 ...219 C3
Holy Trinity CE Prim Sch
DA15 ....168 A3
N2 ....48 B6
NW3 ....70 A2
SW1 ....114 D2 **257** D4
SW1 ....115 A2 **258** A4
Forest Hill SE23 ...162 C2
Streatham SW2 ...160 A4
Holy Trinity Coll BR1 187 C2
Holy Trinity & St Silas CE
Prim Sch NW1 ...71 B1
Holywell Cl 35 SE16 .118 B1
2 SE3 ....143 A6
Stanwell TW19 ....148 A3
Holywell La EC2 ..**243** B6
Holywell Way TW19 .148 B3
Homan Ct N12 .....30 A6
Homan Ho 6 SW4 .159 D4
Homebush Ho E4 ...19 D4
Home Cl
Carshalton SM5 ...218 D6
Northolt UB5 ......85 B4
Homecoppice Ho 1
BR1 ....186 D3
Homecroft Rd
Forest Hill SE26 ...184 C5
Tottenham N22 .....33 A2
Home Ct KT6 ......197 C6
Home Farm Cl
Thames Ditton KT7 .196 D2
Upper Halliford TW17 193 C5
Home Farm Cotts
BR5 ....190 D2
Homefarm Rd W7 ..86 D1
Homefield SM4 ....201 C5
Home Field EN5 ....13 B4
Homefield Ave IG2 ..57 C4
Homefield Cl NW10 .67 A2
Hayes UB4 ....84 D3
Homefield Ct NW4 ..46 C5
Homefield Gdns N2 .48 B6
Mitcham CR4,SW19 .180 B1
Homefield Ho SE23 .162 D1
Homefield Pk SM1,
SM2 ....217 C3
Homefield Pl 4
SW19 ....178 D5
Homefield Prep Sch
SM1 ....217 C3
Homefield Rd BR1 .187 C2
HA8 ....27 B4
W4 ....111 A2
Walton-on-T KT12 ..195 A1
Wembley HA0 ......65 B4
Wimbledon SW19 ..179 A4
Homefield St 14 N1 ..95 C5
Homefirs Ho 7 .....66 B5
Homelands Dr SE19 .183 C3
Home Lea BR6 ....227 D3
Homeleigh Ct 8
SW16 ....160 A1
Homeleigh Rd SE15 .162 D6

Homemead SW12 ...159 B2
Home Mead HA7 .....25 C2
Homemead Rd BR2 .210 B4
  Wallington CR0 .....203 C3
Home Office SW1 ...249 C1
Home Park Rd SW19 .157 B1
Home Park Terr KT1 .175 D1
Home Park Wlk KT1 .197 D5
Home Rd SW11 ....136 C3
Homer Dr E14 ....119 C2
Homer Rd E9 ....75 A2
  Croydon CR0 ......206 D3
Homer Row W1 .....237 B3
Homersham Rd KT1 .176 D1
Homer St W1 ..92 C2 237 B3
Homerton Coll of
  Technology E9 ....74 C3
Homerton Gr E9 .....74 D3
Homerton High St E9 .74 D3
Homerton Hospl E9 ..74 D3
Homerton Rd E9 .....75 B3
Homerton Row E9 ....74 C3
Homerton Sta E9 ....74 D2
Homerton Terr E9 ....74 C2
Homesdale Cl E11 ...55 A4
Homesdale Rd
  BR1,BR2 ....209 C6
  Orpington BR5,BR6 .211 C2
Homesfield NW11 ....47 C4
Homes Of Rest (CE
  Temperance Society)
  IG1 ....79 B5
Homestall Rd SE22 .162 C6
Homestead Ct EN5 ...13 C6
Homestead Gdns
  KT10 ....212 C3
Homestead Paddock
  N14 ....15 B6
Homestead Pk NW2 ..67 D5
Homestead Rd
  SW6 .....135 B5 264 D3
  Dagenham RM8 .....81 B6
Homesteads The
  BR3 ....185 D4
Homestead The N11 ..31 B6
Homewalk Ho SE26 .184 C6
Homewaters Ave
  TW16 ....171 D2
Homewillow Cl N21 ..16 D5
Homewood Cl TW12 .173 B4
Homewood Cres BR7 189 C4
Homewood Gdns
  SE25 ....205 C4
Homewoods 2
  SW12 ....159 C4
Homildon Ho 10
  SE26 ....162 A1
Homington Ct KT2 ..176 A3
Honduras St EC1 ....242 A6
Honeybourne Rd NW6 69 D3
Honeybourne Way
  BR5 ....211 B1
Honeybrook Rd
  SW12,SW4 ....159 C4
Honey Cl RM10 ......81 D2
Honeycroft Hill UB10 .60 A1
Honeyden Rd DA14 .191 A4
Honeyfield N4 ....72 C6
Honey Hill UB10 .....60 B1
Honey La EC2 ....242 B1
Honeyman Cl NW6 ...68 D1
Honeypot Bsns Ctr
  HA7 ....26 A2
Honeypot Cl NW9 ...44 B5
Honeypot La HA3,HA7,
  NW9 ....44 B6
Honeysett Rd 1 N17 .33 D1
Honeysuckle Cl UB1 .107 A6
Honeysuckle Ct
  2 SE12 ....165 A4
  Ilford IG1 ....78 D2
Honeysuckle Gdns
  CR0 ....206 D1
Honeywell Jun & Inf Schs
  SW11 ....158 D5
Honeywell Rd SW11 .158 D5
Honeywood Ho 5
  SE15 ....140 A4
Honeywood Rd NW10 .89 D5
  Isleworth TW7 .....131 A1
Honeywood Wlk
  SM5 ....218 D4
Honister Cl HA7 .....25 B2
Honister Gdns HA7 ..25 B2
Honister Pl HA7 .....25 B2
Honiton Gdns 1
  SE15 ....140 C3

Honiton Ho 30 SE5 ..139 A3
Honiton Rd DA16 ...145 D3
  NW6 ....91 B5
Honley Rd SE6 .....163 D4
Honnor Gdns TW7 ..130 B3
Honor Oak Park Sta
  SE23 ....162 D5
Honor Oak Pk SE23 .162 D5
Honor Oak Rd SE23 .162 C4
Honor Oak Rise SE23 162 C5
Honwell Ho W2 .....91 C2
Hood Ave
  East Barnet N14 ....15 B5
  Mortlake SW14 ....155 A6
Hood Cl CR0 ....204 D1
Hoodcote Gdns N21 .16 D4
Hood Ct N7 ....72 B5
Hood Ho 17 SE5 ...139 B5
Hood La 1 ....77 B6
Hood Rd SW20 ....177 D3
Hooke Ct SE10 .....142 A4
Hooke Ho 30 E3 ....97 A5
Hooker's Rd E17 ....52 D6
Hookham Ct SW8 ..269 C2
Hook Ho 9 SW27 ..182 D5
Hooking Gn HA2 ....41 D4
Hook La DA16 ......146 A1
Hook Lane Prim Sch
  DA16 ....146 A2
Hook Rd KT19,KT17 .215 A1
Hook Rise N
  Surbiton KT6 ......214 A5
  Tolworth KT6,KT9 ..214 D6
Hook Rise S KT6,KT9 .214 A6
Hook Rise South KT6 214 A5
Hooks Cl SE15 .....140 B4
Hookstone Way IG8 ..37 D3
Hook The N5 ....14 B5
Hook Underpass KT4 214 A6
Hook Wlk HA8 ......27 A4
Hooper Ho 8 SW18 .157 B6
Hooper Rd E16 .....99 A1
Hooper's Ct SW1 ...247 C1
Hooper's Mews 4
  W3 ....111 A5
Hooper St E1 ....96 A1
Hoop La NW11 ......47 C2
Hoover Ho 5 SE6 ..186 A6
Hope Cl N1 ....73 A2
  SE12 ....165 B1
  2 Brentford TW8 ..110 A1
  Dagenham RM6 ....58 D5
  Sutton SM1 ....218 A3
  1 Woodford IG8 ...37 C4
Hopedale Rd SE7 ..143 B6
Hopefield 3 W7 ....108 D5
Hopefield Ave NW6 ..91 A5
Hope Pk BR1 ......186 D4
Hopes Cl TW5 .....129 C6
Hope St SW11 .....136 B2
Hopetown St E1 ....243 D3
Hopewell St SE5 ...139 B5
Hop Gdns WC2 .....250 A5
Hopgood St W12 ..112 C5
Hopkins Cl N10 .....31 A3
Hopkins Ho 12 E14 .97 C1
Hopkins Mews E15 ..98 D6
Hopkinson Ho 1
  SW11 ....137 A3
Hopkinson's Pl NW1 .231 A6
Hopkins St W1 93 D1 239 C1
Hoppers Rd N21 ....16 C2
Hoppett Rd E4 .....20 C2
Hopping La N1 ......72 D2
Hoppingwood Ave
  KT3 ....199 C6
Hoppner Rd UB4 ....83 B5
Hop St SE10 ....120 D3
Hopton Ct BR2 .....209 A1
Hopton Gdns KT3 ..200 A3
Hopton Ho 5 SW9 .138 D3
Hopton Rd SW16 ..182 A5
Hopton's Gdns SE1 .251 D4
Hopton St
  SE1 .....116 D5 251 D4
Hoptree Cl N12 .....29 D6
Hopwood Cl SW17 .158 A1
Hopwood Rd SE17 .139 B6
Hopwood Wlk E8 ....74 A1
Horace Rd E7 ......77 B4
  Ilford IG6 ....57 A6
  Kingston KT1 ......198 B6
Horatio Ho 13 E2 ...95 D5
Horatio Pl E14 .....120 A5
Horatio St 11 E2 ...95 D5
Horatius Way CR0 ..220 B2
Horbury Cres
  W11 ....113 C6 245 A5

Horbury Mews
  W11 ....113 B6 244 D5
Horder Rd
  SW6 ....135 A4 264 B1
Hordle Prom E 14
  SE15 ....139 D5
Hordle Prom N 3
  SE15 ....139 D5
Hordle Prom S 7
  SE15 ....139 D5
Hordle Prom W 13
  SE15 ....139 C5
Horizon Bldg 14 E14 .119 C6
Horizon Sch N16 ....73 C4
Horle Wlk SE5 .....138 D3
Horley Cl DA6 .....169 C6
Horley Rd SE9 .....188 A6
Hormead Rd W9 ....91 B3
Hornbeam Cl NW7 .11 D1
  SE11 ....261 A4
  Barking IG11 ......102 B3
  Buckhurst Hill IG9 ..21 D1
  Northolt UB5 ....63 B3
Hornbeam Cres TW8 131 B5
Hornbeam Gr E4 ....20 D1
Hornbeam Ho
  6 DA15 ....168 A1
  2 NW3 ....70 D2
  Buckhurst Hill IG9 ..21 D1
Hornbeam La E4 ....20 C6
Hornbeam Rd
  Buckhurst Hill IG9 ..21 D1
  Hayes UB4 ....84 C2
Hornbeams Rise N11 .31 A4
Hornbeam Terr SM5 202 C1
Hornbeam Twr E11 ..76 B5
Hornbeam Way BR2 210 C3
Hornblower Cl 2
  SE16 ....119 A2
Hornbuckle Cl HA2 ..64 B6
Hornby Cl NW3 .....70 B1
Hornby Ho 6 SE11 .138 C6
Horncastle Cl SE12 .165 A4
Horncastle Rd SE12 .165 A4
Hornchurch N17 .....33 B1
Hornchurch Cl KT2 .175 D6
Horndean Cl 3
  SW15 ....156 A3
Horne Ho 7 SE18 ..144 A4
Horner Ct E11 ......76 B5
Horne Rd TW17 ....192 C5
Horner Hos 18 N1 ..95 C6
Horner La 1 CR4 ...180 B1
Horne Way SW15 ..134 C3
Hornfair Rd SE7 ....143 D5
Horniman Dr SE23 .162 C4
Horniman Grange 7
  SE23 ....162 C3
Horniman Mus & Gdns★
  SE23 ....162 B3
Horniman Sch SE23 .162 B3
Horning Cl SE9 ....188 A6
Horn La SE10 ......121 A2
  W3 ....89 A1
  Woodford IG8 ......37 A3
Horn Link Way SE10 .121 A2
Horn Park Cl SE12 .165 B6
Horn Park La SE12 .165 B5
Horn Park Prim Sch
  SE12 ....165 B4
Hornsby House Sch
  SW12 ....159 A3
Horns End Pl HA5 ...40 C4
Hornsey Central Hospl
  N8 ....49 D4
Hornsey La N6 .....49 C2
Hornsey Lane Gdns
  N6 ....49 C2
Hornsey Park Rd N8 .50 B6
Hornsey Rd N7,N19 .72 B6
Hornsey Rise Gdns
  N19 ....50 A2
Hornsey Sch for Girls
  N8 ....50 B4
Hornsey St N7 .....72 B3
Hornsey Sta N8 .....50 B4
Hornshay St SE15 .140 C6
Horns Rd IG2,IG6 ...57 A4
Hornton Ct W8 .....245 B1
Hornton Pl W8 .....245 B1
Hornton St
  W8 ....113 C4 245 B2
Horrocks Ho SW15 .156 B6
Horsa Rd DA8 .....147 D5
  Eltham SE12 ......165 C4
Horsebridge Cl RM9 .103 A6
Horse & Dolphin Yd
  W1 ....249 D6

Horseferry Pl SE10 .142 A6
Horseferry Rd E14 ..119 A6
  SW1 .....115 D2 259 D4
Horseferry Rd Est
  SW1 ....259 C5
Horseguards Ave
  SW1 .....116 A5 250 A3
Horse Guards Par★
  SW1 .....115 D5 249 D3
Horse Guards Rd
  SW1 .....115 D4 249 D2
Horse Leaze E6 ....100 C1
Horsell Rd BR5 ....190 B2
  N5 ....72 C3
Horselydown La
  SE1 .....117 D5 253 C3
Horselydown Mans
  SE1 ....253 C2
Horsenden Ave UB6 ..64 D3
Horsenden Cres UB6 .64 D3
Horsenden La N UB6 .64 D1
Horsenden La S UB6 .87 A6
Horsenden Prim Sch
  UB6 ....64 C2
Horsendon Ho 11 N7 .71 D3
Horseshoe Cl E14 ..120 A1
  NW2 ....68 B6
Horse Shoe Cres UB5 .85 C5
Horseshoe Dr UB8 ..82 C1
Horse Shoe Gn SM1 .217 D6
Horseshoe La
  Barnet N20 ....12 D3
  Enfield EN2 ....5 A2
Horse Shoe Yd W1 .248 D6
Horse Yd N1 ......234 D6
Horsfeld Gdns 1
  SE9 ....166 A6
Horsfeld Rd SE9 ...165 D6
Horsfield Ho 2 N1 ..73 A1
Horsford Rd SW2 ..160 B6
Horsham Ave N12 ..30 C5
Horsham Ct N17 ....34 A4
Horsham Rd DA6 ...169 C4
  East Bedfont TW14 .149 A5
Horsley Dr
  Kingston KT2 ......175 D5
  New Addington CR0 .224 A1
Horsley Ho 11 SE4 .140 D1
Horsley Rd BR1 ....187 B2
  Chingford E4 ....20 A2
Horsley St 3 SE17 .139 B6
Horsman Ho SE5 ...139 A6
Horsman St SE5 ...139 A6
Horsmonden Cl BR6 .211 D2
Horsmonden Rd SE4 .163 B5
Horston Ho N4 .....51 A4
Hortensia Ho SW10 .266 A4
Hortensia Rd
  SW10 .....136 A5 266 A4
Horticultural Pl 6
  W4 ....111 A1
Horton Ave NW2 ...69 A4
Horton Bridge Rd
  UB7 ....104 B5
Horton Cl UB7 .....104 B5
Horton Ctry Pk KT19 214 C1
Horton Ho 13 SE15 .140 C6
  SW8 ....270 C4
  W14 ....254 A1
Horton Ind Pk UB7 .104 B5
Horton La KT19 ....215 A1
Horton Par UB7 ....104 A5
Horton Rd E8 ......74 B2
  Yiewsley UB7 ......104 B5
Horton Road Ind Est
  UB7 ....104 B5
Horton St SE13 ....141 D4
Horton Way CR0 ...206 D4
Hortus Rd Chingford E4 20 A2
  Southall UB2 ......107 B4
Horwood Ho 24 E2 .96 B4
  NW8 ....237 B6
Hosack Rd SW12,
  SW17 ....159 A2
Hoser Ave SE12 ....165 A2
Hosier La EC1 .94 D2 241 D3
Hoskins Cl UB3 ....105 D1
Hoskin's Cl E16 ....99 C1
Hoskins St SE10 ...120 B1
Hospital Bridge Rd
  TW2 ....151 D2
Hospital Bridge Rdbt
  TW2 ....151 D2
Hospital of the Holy Trinity
  (Almshouses) 5
  CR0 ....221 A6
Hospital Rd TW3 ...129 C2
Hospl for Tropical
  Diseases NW1 ....232 C5

Hospl of St John & St
  Elizabeth
  NW8 .....92 B5 229 C3
Hotham Cl KT8 ....195 C6
Hotham Prim Sch
  SW15 ....134 D1
Hotham Rd
  Merton SW19 .....180 A3
  Putney SW15 ......134 C4
Hotham Road Mews 12
  SW19 ....180 A3
Hotham St E15 .....98 C6
Hothfield Pl SE16 .118 C3
Hotspur Ind Est N17 .34 B4
Hotspur Rd UB5 ....85 C5
Hotspur St
  SE11 .....116 C1 261 A2
Houblon Rd TW10 .154 A6
Houghton Cl 10 E8 .73 D2
  Hampton TW12 ....173 A4
Houghton Rd N15 ..51 D5
Houghton St WC2 .240 D1
Houlder Cres CR0 ..220 D2
Houndsden Rd N21 ..16 C5
Houndsditch
  EC3 .....95 C1 243 B2
Houndsfield Prim Sch
  N9 ....18 B4
Houndsfield Rd N9 ..18 B4
Hounslow Ave TW3 .151 D6
Hounslow Bsns Pk
  TW3 ....129 D1
Hounslow Central Sta
  TW3 ....129 D2
Hounslow Ctr The
  TW3 ....129 D2
Hounslow East Sta
  TW3 ....130 A3
Hounslow Ed Ctr (Specl
  Sch) The TW4 ....129 A2
Hounslow Gdns TW3 151 D6
Hounslow Heath Jun & Inf
  Schs TW4 ....129 A2
Hounslow Heath Nature
  Reserve TW4 .....151 A4
Hounslow Manor Sch
  TW3 ....130 A2
Hounslow Rd
  Feltham TW13 .....151 A2
  Twickenham TW2,TW3 152 A5
  Feltham TW14 ....150 B4
Hounslow Sta TW3 .151 D6
Hounslow Town Prim Sch
  TW3 ....130 A2
Hounslow West Sta
  TW3 ....129 A3
Houseman Way 20
  SE5 ....139 B5
Houses of Parliament★
  SW1 .....116 A3 260 B6
Houston Ct 3 CR0 .205 C1
Houston Rd
  Forest Hill SE23 ...163 A1
  Thames Ditton KT6 .197 B3
Houstoun Ct TW5 ..129 B5
Hove Ave E17 ......53 C4
Hove Gdns SM1 ...201 D1
Hoveden Rd NW2 ..69 A4
Hoveton Rd SE28 .102 C1
Hovenden Ho 6
  SE21 ....183 C6
Howard Ave DA5 ..168 C4
Howard Cl N11 .....15 A2
  NW2 ....69 A4
  Acton W3 ....88 D1
  Ashford TW16 ....171 D4
  Bushey WD23 .....8 C4
  Hampton TW12 ...174 A4
Howard Ct SE15 ...140 A2
  12 Barking IG11 ..101 B6
  Beckenham BR3 ...186 A1
Howard Ho 8 E5 ...74 C6
  14 SE8 ....141 B6
  7 SW9 ....138 C2
  W1 ....238 D5
Howard Mans E17 ..53 D6
Howard Prim Sch
  CR0 ....221 A4
Howard Rd BR1 ....187 A3
  E11 ....76 C5
  E17 ....53 D6
  E6 ....100 B5
  N15 ....51 C3
  N16 ....73 B4
  NW2 ....68 D4
  Barking IG11 ......101 B6
  Croydon SE25 ....206 A3
  Ilford IG1 ....78 D4
  Isleworth TW7 ....130 D2

Howard Rd continued
  New Malden KT3 ..199 D5
  Penge SE20 ......184 C2
  Southall UB1 ......85 D1
  Surbiton KT5 ......198 B3
Howards Cl HA5 ....22 B1
Howards Crest Cl
  BR3 ....186 A1
Howard's La SW15 .134 C1
Howard's Rd E13 ...99 A4
Howard Way EN5 ..12 D6
Howard Wlk N2 .....48 B5
Howarth Rd SE2 ...124 A2
Howberry Cl HA8 ...25 C4
Howberry Rd
  South Norwood CR7 .183 B1
  Stanmore HA7,H8 ..25 D4
Howbury Rd SE15 .140 C2
Howcroft Cres N3 ...29 C3
Howcroft Ho 3 E3 ..97 B4
Howcroft La UB6 ...86 B4
Howden Cl SE28 ...124 D6
Howden Ct SE25 ...183 D1
Howden Rd SE25 ..183 D1
Howden St SE15 ..140 A2
Howell Cl RM6 .....58 D4
Howell Ct 2 E10 ...53 D2
Howell Ho 5 N7 ....71 D3
Howell Wlk SE1 ...261 D3
Howerd Way SE18 .144 A4
Howes Cl N3 ....47 C6
Howfield Pl N17 ....51 D6
Howgate Rd SW14 .133 B2
Howick Pl
  SW1 .....115 C3 259 B5
Howie St
  SW11 ....136 C5 267 A3
Howitt Cl 6 NW3 ...70 C2
Howitt Rd NW3 ....70 C2
Howland Ho 9 SW16 160 A1
Howland Mews E W1 239 B4
Howland St
  W1 ....93 C2 239 B4
Howland Way SE16 .119 A4
Howletts La HA4 ....39 A3
Howletts Rd SE24 ..161 A5
Howley Pl W2 ..92 A2 236 B4
Howley Rd CR0 ....221 A5
Howmic Ct 1 TW1 .153 C5
Howsman Rd SW13 .134 A6
Howson Rd SE4 ...141 A1
Howson Terr TW10 .154 A5
How's St E2 ....95 D5
Howton Pl WD23 ...8 B3
Hoxton Mkt 10 N1 .95 C4
Hoxton Point EC1 ..95 C4
Hoxton Sq N1 .....95 C4
Hoxton St N1 ......95 C5
Hoylake Cres UB10 .60 D6
Hoylake Gdns
  Mitcham CR4 .....203 C6
  Ruislip HA4 ....40 B1
  South Oxhey WD19 .22 D6
Hoylake Rd W3 ....89 C1
Hoyland Cl 4 SE15 .140 B5
Hoyle Rd SW17 ...180 C5
Hoy St E16 ....98 D1
Huan Ct N20 ......14 C2
Hubbard Dr KT9 ...213 D2
Hubbard Rd SE27 .183 A6
Hubbards Cl UB8 ...82 D1
Hubbard St E15 ...98 C6
Hub Buildings The 4
  SW12 ....159 B3
Huberd Ho SE1 ...262 D6
Hubert Gr SW9 ....138 A2
Hubert Ho NW8 ...237 A5
Hubert Rd E6 ......99 D4
Hucknall Ct NW8 ..236 C6
Huddart St E3 .....97 B2
Huddleston Cl E2 ...96 C5
Huddlestone Rd E7 ..76 D4
  NW2 ....68 B2
Huddleston Rd N7 ..71 C4
Hudson 27 NW9 ...27 D2
Hudson 15 W12 ...112 B6
Hudson Ct
  Croydon SE25 ....206 A5
  4 Merton SW19 ..179 D2
  3 Millwall E14 ....119 C1
Hudson Ho SW10 .266 A4
  5 W11 ....91 A1
Hudson Pl SE18 ...123 A1
Hudson Rd DA7 ...147 B4
  Harlington UB7 ....127 B6
Hudsons Ho N1 ...235 D1
Hudson's Pl
  SW1 .....115 C2 259 A4
Hudson Way N9 ....18 C2

Huggin Ct EC4 ......**252** B6
Huggin Hill EC4 .....**252** B6
Huggins Ho **8** E3 .....**97** C4
Huggins Pl SW2 ....**160** B3
Hughan Rd E15 ....76 B3
Hugh Astor Ct SE1 ..**261** D6
Hugh Clark Ho W13 ..109 A5
Hughenden Ave HA3 ..43 B4
Hughenden Gdns UB5 84 C4
Hughenden Rd KT4 ..200 A2
Hughendon EN5 ....1 D1
Hughendon Terr E15 ..76 A4
Hughes Cl N12 ....30 A5
Hughes Ho **26** E2 ....96 C4
SE17 ....**261** D3
SE5 ....139 A4
15 SE8 ....141 C6
Hughes Mans E1 ...96 A3
Hughes Rd
Ashford TW15 ....171 A4
Hayes UB3 ......106 B6
Hughes Terr **6** E16 ..98 D2
Hughes Wlk CR0 ...205 A2
Hugh Gaitskell Cl
SW6 ....**264** C5
Hugh Gaitskell Ho
N16 ....73 D6
NW10 ....67 D1
Hugh Herland KT1 ..198 A6
Hugh Mews SW1 ....**258** D3
Hugh Morgan Ho **5**
SW4 ....137 D2
Hugh Myddelton Prim Sch
EC1 ....94 C4 **234** B1
Hugh Platt Ho **29** E2 ..96 B5
Hugh St SW1 ...115 B2 **258** D3
Hugo Ho SW1 ....**257** D6
Hugon Rd SW6 ....135 D2
Hugo Rd N19 ....71 C4
Huguenot Pl SW18 ..158 A6
Huguenot Sq SE15 ..140 B2
Hullbridge Mews N1 **235** C6
Hull Cl SE16 ....118 D5
Hull Ct SE5 ....139 B3
Hull Pl E16 ....123 A5
Hull St EC1 ....**235** A1
Hulme Pl SE1 ....**252** B1
Hulse Ave IG11 ....79 C2
Humber Ct W7 ......86 B1
Humber Dr W10 ....90 D3
Humber Rd NW2 ....68 B6
SE3 ....142 D6
Humberstone Rd E13 .99 C4
Humberton Cl E9 ....75 A3
Humbolt Rd
W6 ....135 A6 **264** A5
Hume Ct N1 ....72 C1
Hume Ho **14** W11 ...112 D5
Humes Ave W7 .....108 D4
Hume Terr E16 .....99 B1
Hume Way HA4 .....40 A3
Humphrey Ct SW11 .**266** D1
Humphrey St
SE1 ....117 D1 **263** C2
Humphries Cl RM9 ..81 B4
Humphry Ho **10**
SW15 ....156 D6
Hundred Acre NW9 ..27 D1
Hungerdown E4 ....20 A3
Hungerford Bridge
WC2 ....**250** C4
Hungerford Ho SW1 **269** B6
Hungerford Inf Sch
N7 ....72 A2
Hungerford Jun & Inf Schs
N7 ....71 D2
Hungerford La WC2 **250** B4
Hungerford Prim Sch
N7 ....72 A2
Hungerford Rd N7 ..72 A3
4 N7 ....72 A2
Hungerford St **24** E1 ..96 B1
Hunsdon Cl RM9 ...81 A2
Hunsdon Ho E5 ....74 B5
Hunsdon Rd SE14 .140 D5
Hunslett St **27** E2 ..96 C5
Hunstanton Ho NW1 **237** B4
Hunston Rd SM4 ...201 D1
Hunt Ct N14 ....15 B4
11 Northolt UB5 ....84 D5
Hunter Cl SE1 ....**262** D5
Borehamwood WD6 ..11 A6
Upper Tooting SW12 .159 A3
Huntercrombe Gdns
WD19 ....22 C5
Hunter Ct **8** SE5 ..139 B1
27 Streatham SW2 ..160 C4
Hunter Ho **1** N19 ..71 C5
SE1 ....**251** D1
SW5 ....**255** B1

Hunter Ho continued
SW8 ....**269** D3
WC1 ....**240** B1
Feltham TW14 ....150 A3
Hunter Lo **9** W9 ...91 C2
Hunter Rd
South Norwood CR7 .205 B6
Wimbledon SW20 ..178 C2
Hunters Ct **5** TW9 .153 D6
Hunter's Gr BR6 ...227 A4
Hunters Gr Harrow HA3 43 C5
Hayes UB3 ....106 A1
Hunters Hall Prim Sch
RM10 ....81 D3
Hunters Hall Rd RM10 81 C2
Hunters Hill HA4 ..62 D5
Hunters Mdw SE19 .183 C6
Hunters Rd
Chessington KT9 ..214 A4
Ilford IG1 ....78 D3
Hunters Sq RM10 ..81 C4
Hunter St WC1 ..94 A3 **240** B6
Hunters The **2** BR3 .186 A2
Hunters Way Enfield EN2 4 C4
South Croydon CR0 .221 C4
Hunter Wlk E13 ....99 A5
Borehamwood WD6 ..11 B6
Huntingdon Cl CR4,
SW16 ....204 A5
Huntingdon Ct SW14 133 A2
Huntingdon Gdns
Chiswick W4 .....133 A5
North Cheam KT4 ..216 C5
Huntingdon Ho SW5 **255** B4
N9 ....18 C3
Huntingdon Rd N2 ..18 C3
Huntingdon St E16 ..98 D1
N1 ....72 B1
Huntingfield CR0 ..223 B1
Huntingfield Rd
SW15 ....156 A6
Huntingford Ho
SW15 ....134 C3
Hunting Gate Cl EN2 ..4 C4
Hunting Gate Dr KT9 214 A4
Hunting Gate Mews
Sutton SM1 ......217 D5
Twickenham TW2 ..152 C3
Huntings Farm IG1 .79 C6
Huntings Rd RM10 ..81 C2
Huntley Ho **7** SE21 .183 C6
Huntley St
WC1 ....93 D3 **239** C5
Huntley Way SW20 .178 A1
Huntly Dr N3 ......29 C4
Huntly Rd SE25 ...205 C5
Hunton St E1 ......96 A4
Hunt Rd UB2 ......107 C3
Hunts Cl SE3 .....143 A3
Hunt's Ct WC2 ....**249** D5
Huntshaw Ho **37** E3 ..97 C4
Hunt's La E15 .....98 A5
Huntsman Cl TW13 .172 B6
Huntsman St SE17 .**263** A3
Hunts Mead EN3 ....6 D2
Hunts Mead Cl BR7 .188 B3
Huntsmoor Rd KT19 215 B3
Huntspill St SW17 .158 A1
Hunts Slip Rd SE21 .161 C2
Huntsworth Ct SE6 .163 C3
Huntsworth Mews
NW1 ....92 D3 **237** C5
Hurdwick Ho NW1 ..**232** A1
Hurleston Ho **11** SE8 .119 B1
Hurley Cres SE16 ..118 D4
Hurley Ct **1** W5 ...87 C1
Hurley Ho **34** E2 ...95 D4
SE11 ....**261** B3
Hurley Lo SE22 ...162 C5
Hurley Rd UB6 ....85 D2
Hurlingham Bsns Pk
SW6 ....135 C2
Hurlingham & Chelsea Sec
Sch SW6 ....135 C2
Hurlingham Court Mans
SW6 ....135 C2
Hurlingham Ct SW6 .135 B2
Hurlingham Gdns
SW6 ....135 B2
Hurlingham Rd DA7 .147 B5
Fulham SW6 .....135 B5
Hurlingham Sq SW6 .135 D2
Hurlock Ho N5 ....72 D5
Hurlock St N5 .....72 D5
Hurlstone Rd SE25 .205 D5
Hurn Court Rd TW5 .128 D3
Hurn Ct TW5 ......128 D3
Huron Cl BR6 .....227 D3
Huron Rd SW17 ...159 A1

Hurren Cl SE3 ....142 C2
Hurricane Rd SM6 ..220 B1
Hurry Cl E15 ......76 C1
Hursley Ct **11** KT6 ..197 D2
Hurst Ave N6 ......49 C3
Chingford E4 .....19 C1
Hurstbourne KT10 ..212 D2
Hurstbourne Cotts
DA5 ....169 D4
Hurstbourne Gdns
IG11 ....79 C2
Hurstbourne Ho **12**
SW15 ....155 D5
Hurstbourne Priors
CR2 ....221 C1
Hurstbourne Rd
SE23 ....163 A3
Hurst Cl NW11 ....47 D3
Chessington KT9 ..214 C3
Chingford E4 .....19 C1
Hayes BR2 ......208 D1
Northolt UB5 .....63 B3
Hurstcombe IG9 ...21 A2
Hurstcourt Rd SM1 .217 D6
Hurst Ct
Beckenham BR3 ..185 C3
South Norwood SE25 205 D5
Woodford IG8 ....37 B4
Hurstdene Ave BR2 .208 D1
Hurstdene Gdns N15 .51 C2
Hurstfield BR2 ....209 A4
Hurstfield Cres UB4 .83 C2
Hurstfield Rd KT8 .195 C6
Hurst Gr KT12 ....193 D1
Hurst Ho N1 ......**233** D3
SE2 ....124 D1
7 Penge SE26 ....184 B5
Hurst La SE2 .....124 D1
East Molesey KT8 .196 A6
Hurst Lo **18** W9 ...91 C3
Hurstmead Ct HA8 ..26 D6
Hurst Park Prim Sch
KT8 ....195 C6
Hurst Pl SE2 .....146 D6
Hurst Prim Sch DA5 168 C3
Hurst Rd DA5,DA15 .168 C3
E17 ....53 D6
Buckhurst Hill IG9 ..21 D3
Croydon CR0 ....221 B3
East Molesey KT8,KT12 195 C6
Southgate N21 ...16 C3
Walton-on-T KT8&KT12 194 D5
Hurst Rise EN5 ....1 C2
Hurst Springs DA5 .169 A3
Hurst St SE24 ....160 B1
Hurstview Grange
CR2 ....220 D1
Hurst View Rd CR2 .221 C1
Hurst Way CR2 ...221 C2
Hurstway Wlk **2**
W11 ....112 D6
Hurstwood Ave DA5 .169 A3
Wanstead E18 ....55 B5
Hurstwood Ct N12 ..30 C4
NW11 ....47 B5
Hurstwood Dr BR1 .210 B6
Hurstwood Rd NW11 .47 B5
Hurtwood Rd KT12 .195 B2
Husborne Ho **8**
SE8 ....119 A2
Huson Cl NW3 ....70 C1
Hussain Cl HA1 ....64 D4
Hussars Cl TW4 ...129 A2
Husseywell Cres BR2 209 A1
Hutching's St E14 .119 C4
Hutchins Cl E15 ...76 A1
Hutchins Ho **8** SW4 159 D4
Hutchinson Ct RM6 .58 D5
Hutchinson Ho **9**
SE14 ....140 C5
Hutchinson Terr HA9 .65 D5
Hutchins Rd SE28 .124 A6
Thamesmead SE28 .124 A6
Hutton Cl
Greenford UB6 ...64 B3
Woodford IG8 ....37 B4
Hutton Ct **3** N4 ...50 B1
N9 ....18 C4
1 Ealing W5 ....87 C2
Hutton Gdns HA3 ..24 A3
Hutton Gr N12 ....29 D5
Hutton Ho **22** E2 ...96 A4
Hutton La HA3 ....24 A3
Hutton Row **4** HA8 .27 A4
Hutton St EC4 ....**241** B1
Hutton Wlk HA3 ...24 A3
Huxbear St SE4 ...163 B6

Huxley Cl UB5 .....85 A6
Huxley Dr RM6 .....58 B2
Huxley Gdns NW10 ..88 B5
Huxley Ho NW8 ...**236** D5
SE2 ....124 D1
4 SW9 ....138 B3
Huxley Par N18 ....33 B5
Huxley Pl N13 .....16 D1
Huxley Rd DA16 ...145 C2
E10 ....76 A6
Edmonton N18 ....33 C6
Huxley Sayze N18 ..33 B5
Huxley South N18 ..33 B5
Huxley St W10 ....91 A4
Hyacinth Cl
3 Hampton TW12 .173 C4
Ilford IG1 ....78 D2
Hyacinth Dr UB10 ..60 A1
Hyacinth Rd SW15 .156 A3
Hyde Cl E13 ......99 A5
Ashford TW16 ....171 A5
Barnet EN5 ......1 B2
Hyde Cres NW9 ...45 C4
Hyde Ct N20 .....14 B1
NW9 ....45 B2
Hounslow TW4 ...151 B6
Hyde Estate Rd NW9 .45 C4
Hyde Farm Mews
SW12 ....159 D3
Hydefield Cl N21 ..17 C2
Hydefield Ct N9 ...17 C2
Hyde Ho TW3 .....130 A2
Hyde La
SW11 ......136 C4 **267** A2
Hyde Park★
W2 ....114 D5 **247** C3
Hyde Park Ave N21 .17 B5
Hyde Park Cnr SW1 .**248** B2
Hyde Park Corner Sta
SW1 ....115 A4 **248** B2
Hyde Park Cres
W2 ....92 C1 **237** A1
Hyde Park Gate Mews
SW7 ....**246** B1
Hyde Park Gdns
W2 ....114 C6 **246** D6
Edmonton N21 ....17 A3
Hyde Park Gdns Mews
W2 ....114 C6 **247** A6
Hyde Park Mans
NW1 ....**237** A3
Hyde Park Pl W2 ..**247** B6
Hyde Park Sq
W2 ....92 C1 **237** A1
Hyde Park Square Mews
W2 ....**237** A1
Hyde Park St
W2 ....92 C1 **237** A1
Hyde Park Twrs W2 .**246** A5
Hyderabad Way E15 .76 C1
Hyde Rd N1 ......95 C6
Bexley DA7 .....147 B3
Richmond TW10 ..154 B6
Hyde Sch The NW9 .45 D3
Hydeside Gdns N9 ..17 D2
Hyde's Pl **12** N1 ...72 D1
Hyde St SE8 .....141 C6
Hyde Terr TW15,
TW16 ....171 C4
Hyde Vale SE10 ...142 A5
Hyde Way Edmonton N9 17 D2
Hayes UB3 ......105 D2
Hyde Wlk SM4 ....201 C2
Hydon Ct N11 ....30 D5
Hyh Ho E17 ......35 B2
Hyland House Sch E17 36 B1
Hylands Rd E17 ...36 B1
Hylda Ct NW5 ....71 A5
Hyleford Sch IG3 ..79 C4
Hylton St SE18 ...123 D2
Hyndewood **14** SE23 162 C2
Hyndman Ho **5** N19 .71 D4
5 Dagenham RM10 ..81 C5
Hyndman St SE15 .140 B6
Hynton Rd RM8 ...80 C5
Hyperion Ho **25** E3 ..97 A4
Streatham SW2 ..160 B4
Hyrstdene CR0 ...220 D4
Hyson Rd SE16 ...118 B1
Hythe Ave DA7 ...147 B5
Hythe Cl N18 .....34 A6
Hythe Ho **7** SE16 ..118 C4
Hythe Rd NW10 ...90 A3
South Norwood CR7 .183 B1
Hythe Road Ind Est
NW10 ....90 A3
Hyver Hill NW7 ....11 B4

I

Ian Ct SE23 ....162 C2
Ian Hamilton Ho
NW1 ....**232** C2
Ian Sq EN3 ....6 D4
Ibberton Ho SW8 ..**270** C4
W14 ....**254** B6
Ibbotson Ave E16 ..98 D1
Ibbott St **22** E1 ...96 C3
Iberia Ho **17** N19 ..49 D2
Iberian Ave CR0,SM6 220 A4
Ibis Ct **16** SE8 ...141 B6
Ibis La W4 ....133 A4
Ibis Way UB4 ....84 C1
Ibrox Ct **3** IG9 ...21 A2
Ibsley Gdns SW15 .156 A3
Ibsley Way EN4 ...2 C1
Ibstock Place Sch
SW15 ....155 C5
Icarus Ho **16** E3 ..97 B4
Iceland Rd E3 ....97 C6
Iceland Wharf SE16 .119 A2
Ice Wharf NW1 ...**233** B4
Ickburgh Est E5 ..74 B6
Ickburgh Rd E5 ...74 B5
Ickburgh Sch E5 ..74 B5
Ickenham Cl HA4 ..61 B6
Ickenham Rd HA4 ..39 B1
Ickenham Sta UB10 .61 A4
Ickleton Rd SE9 ..188 A6
Icknield Dr IG2 ...56 D4
Ickworth Park Rd E17 .53 A5
Icough Ct SE3 ...143 B5
Ida Rd N15 ....51 B5
Ida St E14 ....98 A1
Iden Cl BR2 ......208 C6
Idlecombe Rd SW17 .181 A4
Idmiston Rd E15 ..76 D3
New Malden KT4 ..199 D2
West Norwood SE21,
SE27 ....161 A2
Idmiston Sq KT4 ..199 D2
Idol La EC3 ...117 C6 **253** A5
Idonia St SE8 ....141 C5
Iffley Ho **47** E2 ..95 D4
Iffley Rd W6 ......112 B3
Ifield Ho SE17 ...**263** B2
Ifield Rd
SW10 ......135 D6 **265** D6
Ifor Evans Pl E1 ..96 D3
Ightham Ho SE17 .**263** A3
Beckenham BR3 ..185 B3
Ightham Rd DA8 ..147 C5
Ilbert St W10 ....91 A4
Ilchester Gdns W2 **245** C6
Ilchester Mans W8 **255** A6
Ilchester Pl
W14 ....113 B3 **254** D6
Ilchester Rd RM8 ..80 C3
Ildersly Gr SE21 ..161 B2
Ilderton Prim Sch
SE16 ....118 C1
Ilderton Rd SE15,
SE16 ....140 C6
Ilex Cl TW16 ....172 C1
Ilex Rd NW10 ....67 D2
Ilex Way SW16 ...182 C5
Ilford Hill IG1 ....78 C5
Ilford Ho **14** N1 ..73 B2
Ilford Interchange
IG1 ....78 D6
Ilford Jewish Prim Sch
IG6 ....57 B6
Ilford La IG1 .....78 D4
Ilford Prep Sch IG3 .58 A1
Ilford Ret Pk IG1 ..79 A6
Ilford Sta IG1 ....78 D6
Ilford Ursuline High Sch
IG1 ....78 D6
Ilfracombe Gdns RM6 58 B2
Ilfracombe Rd BR1 .164 D1
Iliffe St SE17 .116 D1 **261** D2
Iliffe Yd SE17 116 D1 **261** D2
Ilkeston Ct **7** E5 ..74 D4
Ilkley Ct N11 .....31 A4
Ilkley Rd Newham E16 .99 C5
South Oxhey WD19 ..22 D5
Ilkley Ct N11 .....31 A4
Illingworth Cl CR4 .202 B6
Illingworth Way EN1 .17 C6
Ilminster Gdns SW11 136 C1
Ilsley Ct **3** SW8 ..137 C3
Imber Cl N14 .....15 C4
Thames Ditton KT7 .196 B1
Imber Court Trad Est
KT8 ....196 B3
Imber Cross KT7 ..196 D3
Imber Ct **4** SE9 ..166 C5

Imber Gr KT10 ....196 B2
Imber Park Rd KT10 .196 B1
Imber St N1 ......**235** C5
Immanuel Coll WD23 .8 C4
Immanuel & St Andrew CE
Prim Sch SW16 ..182 A4
Impact Ct SE20 ...184 B1
Imperial Ave **5** N16 .73 C4
Imperial Cl HA2 ...41 C3
Imperial College Rd
SW7 ....114 B3 **256** C6
Imperial Coll of Science,
Technology & Medicine
SW7 ....114 B3 **256** C6
Imperial Ct N20 ...14 A1
NW8 ....**230** B4
Wembley HA9 ....66 C5
Harrow HA2 .....41 C2
Imperial Dr HA2 ..41 C3
Imperial Gdns CR4 .203 B6
Imperial Ho **2** E14 .119 B6
E3 ....97 A4
Imperial Mews **5** E6 .99 D5
Imperial Pl BR7 ...188 C2
Imperial Rd SW6 .**265** D1
East Bedfont TW14 .149 C4
Wood Green N22 ..32 A2
Imperial Sq SW6 .**265** D2
Imperial St E3 ....98 A4
Imperial Twrs **3** NW3 .70 A2
Imperial War Mus★
SE1,SE11 ...116 C3 **261** B5
Imperial Way
BR7,SE9 ....167 A1
Croydon CR0,CR9 .220 C2
Harrow HA3 .....44 A3
Impington **19** KT1 .176 C1
Imre Cl W12 ......112 B5
Inca Dr SE9 ......166 D4
Inchmery Rd SE6 .164 C2
Inchwood BR4,CR0 .223 D4
Independant Jewish Day
Sch NW4 ....46 D4
Independant Pl E8 .73 D3
Independents Rd
SE3 ....142 D2
Inderwick Rd N8 ..50 A4
Indescon Ct E14 ..119 C4
India St EC3 .....**243** C1
India Way W12 ...112 B6
Indigo Mews N16 ..73 B5
Indus Ct **15** SE15 .139 D5
Indus Rd SE7 ....143 C5
Ingal Rd E13 .....99 A3
Ingate Pl
SW8 ....137 B4 **268** D1
Ingatestone Rd
Croydon SE25 ...206 B5
Wanstead E12 ...55 C1
Woodford IG8 ....37 B3
Ingelow Ho W8 ...**245** C2
Ingelow St SW8 ..137 B3
Ingersoll Rd W12 .112 B5
Enfield EN3 .....6 C5
Ingestre Pl W1 ...**239** B1
Ingestre Rd E7 ...77 A4
NW5 ....71 B4
Ingham Rd NW6 ..69 C4
Inglebert St
EC1 ....94 C4 **234** A2
Ingleborough Ct N17 .51 D6
Ingleborough St
SW9 ....138 C3
Ingleby Dr HA1 ...64 B5
Ingleby Rd N7 ....72 A5
Dagenham RM10 ..81 D2
Ilford IG1 ....56 D1
Ingleby Way BR7 ..188 C3
Wallington SM6 ..219 D1
Ingle Cl HA5 .....41 B6
Ingledew Rd SE18 .123 D4
Inglefield Sq **12** E1 .118 C4
Ingle Ho **3** SW12 .159 D3
Inglehurst Gdns IG4 .56 B4
Inglemere Ct CR4,
SW17 ....180 D3
Inglemere Rd
Forest Hill SE23 ..162 D3
Mitcham CR4,SW17 .180 D3
Ingleshaw Wlk E9 .75 B2
Ingleside Cl BR3 ..185 C3
Ingleside Gr SE3 .142 D6
Inglethorpe Ho **6** E5 .74 A4
Inglethorpe St SW6 .134 D4
Ingleton Ave DA16 .168 A6
Ingleton Rd N18 ..34 A4
Ingleton St SW9 ..138 C3

Ingle Way N12 ....30 C4
Inglewood BR7 ....189 B4
Inglewood Cl E14 ....119 C2
Inglewood Copse
  BR1 ....188 B1
Inglewood Ct **3** BR1 186 D3
Inglewood Mans **11**
  NW6 ....69 C3
Inglewood Rd NW6 ...69 C3
Inglis Ct W5 ....110 B6
Inglis Ho **1** SW15 ...156 C6
Inglis Rd Croydon CR0 205 D1
  Ealing W5 ....110 B6
Inglis St SE5 ....138 D4
Ingram Ave NW11 ...48 A2
Ingram Cl SE11 .....260 D4
  Stanmore HA7 ......25 C5
Ingram Ct EN1 ......17 D5
Ingram Ho E3 ....97 A6
  7 Harrow HA1 .....42 D4
  Teddington KT8 ....175 C2
Ingram Lo **8** SW4 ...159 D5
Ingram Rd N2 ....48 C5
  South Norwood CR7 .183 A2
Ingram Way UB6 ....86 B6
Ingrave Ho RM9 .....102 B6
Ingrave St SW11 ....136 C2
Ingrebourne Ct E4 ..19 D2
Ingrebourne Ho
  NW8 ....236 D4
  2 Catford BR1 ....186 B5
Ingress St **4** W4 ....111 C1
Inigo Jones Rd SE7 ..144 A5
Inigo Pl WC2 ....250 A6
Inkerman Rd NW5 ...71 B2
Inkerman Terr W8 ...255 B1
Inks Gn E4 ....36 A5
Inkster Ho **8** SW11 ..136 C2
Inkwell Cl N12 ....14 A1
Inman Rd NW10 .....89 C6
  Wandsworth SW18 ..158 A4
Inmans Row IG8 .....37 A6
Inner Circ
  NW1 ....93 A4 **231 A2**
Inner Park Rd SW19 156 D2
Inner Ring E TW6 ...126 D2
Inner Ring W TW6 ...126 C2
Inner Temple* EC4 ..**251 A6**
Inner Temple La EC4 **241 A1**
Innes Cl SW20 ......179 A1
Innes Gdns SW15 ...156 B5
Innes Lo SE23 ....162 D1
Innes Yd CR0 ....221 A5
Innis Ho SE17 ....**263 A2**
Inniskilling Rd E13 ..99 C5
Innovation Cl HA0 ...88 A6
Inskip Cl E10 ....75 D6
Inskip Rd RM8 ......58 D1
Insley Ho **13** E3 .....97 D4
Inst for Child Health
  WC1 ....94 B3 **240 C5**
Institute Pl E8 ......74 B3
Instituto Espanol Vicente
  Canada Blanch W10 .91 A2
Inst of Ophthalmology
  EC1 ....**235 D2**
Integer Gdns E11 ...54 B2
Interchange The NW5 71 B3
International Ave
  TW5 ....106 C1
International Sch of
  London W3 ....110 C2
International Trad Est
  UB2 ....106 B3
Inveagh Cl E9 ....96 D6
Inverary Pl SE18 ...145 B6
Inver Cl E5 ....74 C6
Inverclyde Gdns RM6 58 D5
Inver Ct W2 ....91 D1
Inveresk Gdns KT4 ..216 A5
Inverforth Cl NW3 ...70 A6
Inverforth Ho NW3 ..70 A6
Inverforth Rd N11 ..31 B5
Invergarry Ho NW6 ..91 D5
Inverine Rd SE7 ....121 B1
Invermore Pl SE18 ..123 A2
Inverness Ave EN1 ..5 C4
Inverness Ct
  8 Acton W3 ......88 C1
  10 Catford SE6 ...164 D3
Inverness Gdns W8 .**245 C3**
Inverness Mews E16 122 D5
  W2 ....**245 D6**
  North Woolwich E16 123 A5
Inverness Pl W2 ....**245 D6**
Inverness Rd
  Edmonton N18 ....34 B5

Inverness Rd continued
  Hounslow TW3 ....129 C1
  North Cheam KT4 ..200 D1
  Southall UB2 .....107 A2
Inverness St NW1 ...231 D6
Inverness Terr
  W2 ....113 D6 **245 D6**
Inverton Rd SE15 ...140 D1
Invicta Cl BR7 ......188 C5
  18 E3 ....97 C2
  East Bedfont TW14 149 D3
Invicta Ct KT9 ......214 B3
Invicta Gr UB5 .....85 B4
Invicta Plaza SE1 ...**251 C4**
Invicta Prim Sch SE3 143 A5
Invicta Rd SE3,SE7 ..143 A5
Inville Rd
  SE17 ......117 B1 **262 D1**
Inwen Ct SE8 ....119 A1
Inwood Ave TW3 ....130 A1
Inwood Bsns Pk TW3 129 D1
Inwood Cl CR0 .....223 A6
Inwood Ct **10** NW1 ..71 C1
Inwood Ho **19** SE22 .139 C2
Inwood Rd TW3 ....130 A1
Inworth St SW11 ...136 C3
Inworth Wlk N1 .....**235 A6**
Iona Cl Catford SE6 .163 C4
  Morden SM4 ......201 D2
Ion Ct **8** E2 ....96 A5
Ionian Bldg **19** E14 .119 A6
Ionian Ho **22** E1 ....96 C1
Ipsden Bldgs SE1 ...**251 B2**
Ipswich Ho SE4 ....162 B6
Irby Ho SW2 ....160 C1
Ireland Cl E6 ....100 B2
Ireland Pl N22 .....32 A3
Ireland Yd EC4 .....**241 D1**
Irene Rd BR6 ....211 D2
  SW6 ....135 C4 **265 B1**
Ireton Cl N10 ....31 A3
Ireton Ho **9** SW9 ...138 C3
Ireton St **12** E3 .....97 C3
Iris Ave DA5 ....169 A5
Iris Cl Croydon CR0 206 D1
  Newham E6 ....100 A3
  Surbiton KT6 .....198 B2
Iris Cres DA7 ....147 B6
Iris Rd KT19 ....214 D3
Iris Way E4 ....35 B4
Iris Wlk **1** HA8 .....27 A6
Irkdale Ave EN1 ....5 D4
Iroko Ho **7** NW3 ...69 D2
Iron Bridge Cl NW10 67 C3
  Southall UB2 .....108 A5
Iron Bridge Ho NW3 70 D3
Iron Bridge Rd N
  UB11 ....104 C5
Iron Bridge Rd S
  UB7 ....104 C4
Iron Mill Pl SW18 ..157 D5
Iron Mill Rd SW18 ..157 D5
Ironmonger La
  EC2 ....95 B1 **242 C1**
Ironmonger Pas EC1 **235 B1**
Ironmonger Row
  EC1 ....95 A4 **235 B1**
Ironmonger's Pl **13**
  E14 ....119 C2
Ironside Cl SE16 ...118 D4
Ironside Ho E9 .....75 A4
Irvine Ave HA3 .....43 B6
Irvine Cl N20 ....14 C2
Irvine Ct W1 ....**239 B5**
  Thornton Heath CR7 204 C3
Irvine Ho **2** E14 ....97 C2
  N7 ....72 B2
Irvine Way BR6 .....211 D2
Irving Ave UB5 .....84 D6
Irving Gr SW9 ......138 B3
Irving Ho SE17 .....**261 C1**
Irving Mews N1 ....73 A2
Irving Rd W14 .....112 D3
Irving St WC2 ......**249 D1**
Irwell Ct W7 ....86 B1
Irwell Est **25** SE16 ..118 C4
Irwin Ave SE18 ....145 C5
Irwin Cl UB10 ......60 C1
Irwin Gdns NW10 ..90 B6
Isabella Cl N14 .....15 C4
Isabella Ct **8** TW10 154 B5
Isabella Dr BR6 ....227 A4
Isabella Ho SE11 ...**261 C1**
  19 W6 ....112 C1
Isabella Rd E9 .....74 C3
Isabella St SE1 .....**251 C3**

Isabel St SW9 ......**270 D2**
Isambard Mews E14 120 A3
Isambard Pl SE16 ..118 C5
Iseldon Ct N7 ......72 A4
Isel Way **4** SE22 ...161 C6
Isham Ho SW16 ....182 A1
Isis Cl Putney SW15 134 C1
  Ruislip HA4 ....39 A3
Isis Ct W4 ....132 D5
Isis Ho NW8 ....**236 D5**
  2 Edmonton N18 ..33 D4
Isis St SW18 ....158 A2
Island Centre Way EN3 .7 C6
Island Farm Ave KT8 195 B4
Island Farm Rd KT8 195 B4
Island Gardens Sta
  E14 ....120 A1
Island Ho SW19 ....202 A5
Island Rd CR4 .....180 D3
Island Row E14 ....97 B1
Isla Rd SE18 ....145 A6
Islay Gdns TW4 ....150 D6
Isleden Ho N1 .....**235 A6**
Isledon Rd N4,N7 ..72 C5
Islehurst Cl BR7 ...188 C2
Isleworth Bsns Complex
  TW7 ....130 D3
Isleworth Sta TW7 .130 D3
Isleworth & Syon Sch for
  Boys TW7 ....130 D3
Isleworth Town Sch
  TW7 ....131 A3
Islington Est
  N1 ....95 A6 **235 A6**
Islington Gn
  N1 ....94 D6 **234 C5**
Islington Green Sch
  N1 ....95 A6 **235 A5**
Islington High St
  N1 ....94 D6 **234 C4**
Islington Park Mews **1**
  N1 ....72 D1
Islington Park St N1 .72 D1
Islington Sixth Form Ctr
  N7 ....72 C4
Islip Gdns HA8 .....27 B3
  Northolt UB5 .....63 A1
Islip Manor Rd UB5 63 A1
Islip St NW5 ....71 C3
Ismailia Rd E7 .....77 B1
Isobel Ho
  10 Ashford TW16 171 D4
  Harrow HA1 ......42 D4
Isokon Flats **3** NW3 70 D3
Isom Cl E13 ....99 B4
Ivanhoe Dr HA3 ...25 B1
Ivanhoe Ho **32** E3 ..97 A5
  11 Balham SW12 ..159 B4
Ivanhoe Rd SE5 ....139 D2
  Hounslow TW4 ....128 D2
Ivatt Pl W14 ...113 B1 **254 D1**
Ivatt Way N17 .....50 D6
Iveagh Ave NW10 ..88 C5
Iveagh Cl NW10 ...88 C5
  E9 ....96 D6
Iveagh Ct EC3 .....**243 C1**
  4 Beckenham BR3 207 D6
Iveagh Ho SW10 ...**266 B4**
  2 SW9 ....138 D3
Ivebury Ct W10 ....90 C1
Ivedon Rd DA16 ...146 C3
Iveley Rd SW4 .....137 C3
Ivere Dr EN5 ....13 D5
Iverhurst Cl DA6 ...168 D6
Iver Ct N1 ....73 A2
Iverna Ct W8 ......**255 B6**
Iverna Gdns
  W8 ....113 C3 **255 B6**
  Hatton TW14 .....149 B6
Iverson Rd NW6 ...69 C2
Ivers Way CR0 .....223 D1
Ives Rd E16 ....98 C2
Ives St SW3 ...114 C2 **257 B4**
Ivestor Terr SE23 ..162 C4
Ivimey St E2 ....96 A4
Ivinghoe Cl EN1 ...5 C4
Ivinghoe Ho **14** N7 71 D3
Ivinghoe Rd
  Barking RM8 ......80 B3
  Bushey WD23 .....8 B4
Ivor Ct N8 ....50 A3
  NW1 ....**237 C6**
Ivor Gr SE9 ....166 D3
Ivories The N1 .....73 A1

Ivor Pl NW1 ...92 D3 **237 C5**
Ivor St NW1 ....71 C1
Ivory Ct TW13 .....150 A3
Ivorydown BR1 ....187 A6
Ivory Ho E1 ....**253 D4**
  9 SW11 ....136 A2
Ivybridge Cl
  2 Twickenham TW1 153 A4
  Uxbridge UB8 .....82 A4
Ivybridge Ho **18** SE22 139 C2
Ivybridge La WC2 ..**250 B5**
Ivybridge Prim Sch
  TW1 ....152 D5
Ivybridge Ret Pk
  TW7 ....152 D6
Ivychurch Cl SE20 .184 C3
Ivy Church La SE1,
  SE17 ....**263 C2**
Ivy Cl Harrow HA2 ..63 C1
  Pinner HA5 ....40 C2
  Sunbury TW16 ....172 C1
Ivy Cotts UB10 ....82 C4
Ivy Cres W4 ....111 A2
Ivy Ct SE13 ....163 C2
  18 SE16 ....118 A1
  SE3 ....142 D1
Ivydale Prim Sch
  SE15 ....140 D1
Ivydale Rd SE15 ...140 D1
  Carshalton SM5 ..218 D6
Ivyday Gr SW16 ...160 B1
Ivydene KT12,KT8 ..195 B4
Ivydene Cl SM1 ....218 A4
Ivy Gdns N8 ....50 A3
  Mitcham CR4 .....203 D6
Ivy Ho **6** E5 ....52 B1
  Croydon CR0 .....206 D1
Ivyhouse Rd
  Dagenham RM9 ..81 A2
  Uxbridge UB10 ...60 D5
Ivy La TW4 ....129 B1
Ivy Lo W8 ....**245 A4**
Ivymount Rd SE27 .160 C1
Ivy Rd E16 ....99 A1
  E17 ....53 C3
  N14 ....15 D4
  NW2 ....68 C4
  SE4 ....141 C1
  Hounslow TW3 ....129 C1
  Tolworth KT6 .....198 C1
  Upper Tooting SW17 .180 C5
Ivy St N1 ....95 C5
Ivy Terr **3** IG2 ....57 A3
Ivy Wlk RM9 ......81 A2
Ixworth Pl
  SW3 ......114 C2 **257 A3**
Izane Rd DA6 ......147 B1

J

Jacaranda Cl KT3 ..199 C6
Jacaranda Gr E8 ...73 D1
Jack Ashley Ct **5**
  NW9 ....27 C2
Jackass La BR2 ....225 C2
Jack Barnett Way N22 32 B1
Jack Clow Rd E15 ..98 C5
Jack Cook Ho **9** IG11 78 D1
Jack Cornwell St E12 78 C4
Jack Goodchild Way
  KT3 ....198 D6
Jacklin Gn IG8 .....37 A6
Jackman Ho **24** E1 .118 B5
Jackman Mews NW2 67 C5
Jackman St E8 ....96 B6
Jackson Cl E9 .....74 D1
  Uxbridge UB10 ...60 A1
Jackson Ct E7 .....77 B2
  Wanstead E11 ....55 C5
Jackson Ho **16** SW11 136 B2
Jackson Rd BR2 ...226 B6
  N7 ....72 B4
  Barking IG11 .....101 A1
  East Barnet EN4 ..14 C5
  Uxbridge UB10 ...60 A1
Jackson's La N6 ...49 B2
Jackson's Pl CR0 ..205 C1
Jackson St SE18 ...144 C6
Jackson's Way CR0 223 C5
Jackson Way UB2 ..107 D4
Jack Taylor Sch
  NW8 ......92 A6 **229 A6**
Jack Tizard Sch SW6 134 D4
Jack Walker Ct N5 .72 C4
Jacob Ho **5** DA18 ..124 D4
Jacob Mans **1** E1 ..96 B1
Jacobin Lo N7 .....72 A3
Jacob St SE1 ......118 A4
Jacobs Cl RM10 ...81 D4
Jacobs Ho E13 ....99 C4

Jacobson Ct SW11 ..**267 B1**
Jacobson Ho E1 ...**243 C2**
Jacob St SE1 ......118 A4
Jacob's Well Mews
  W1 ....**238 B2**
Jacotts Ho W10 ...90 D2
Jacqueline Cl UB5 .85 A6
Jade Cl E16 ....99 D1
  NW2 ....46 D2
  Dagenham RM8 ..58 C1
Jaffe Rd IG1 ......57 B1
Jaffray Rd BR2 ....209 D5
Jaggard Way SW12 158 D4
Jagger Ho SW11 ..**267 C2**
Jago Cl SE18 ......145 A6
Jago Wlk **22** SE5 ..139 B5
Jamahirya Sch
  SW3 ......136 C6 **267 A6**
Jamaica Rd SE1 ...**253 D1**
  SE16 ....118 B3
  Thornton Heath CR7 204 D3
Jamaica St E1 .....96 C2
James Allen's Girls'
  Sch SE22 ....161 C6
James Anderson Ct **29**
  E2 ....95 C5
James Ave NW2 ...68 C3
  Dagenham RM8 ..59 B1
James Bedford Cl
  HA5 ....22 C1
James Boswell Cl **1**
  SW16 ....182 C6
James Brine Ho **6** E2 95 D4
James Campbell Ho **2**
  E2 ....96 C5
James Cl **8** E13 ...99 A5
  NW11 ....47 A3
James Collins Cl W9 91 B3
James Ct N12 .....30 C3
  NW9 ....27 C1
  4 Chingford E4 ..20 B2
  3 Woodford E18 ..37 B1
James Dixon Prim Sch
  SE20 ....184 B3
James Docherty Ho **4**
  E2 ....96 C5
James Dudson Ct
  NW10 ....67 A1
James Est CR4 ....180 D1
James Gdns N22 ..32 D3
James Hammett Ho **9**
  E2 ....95 D5
James Ho E1 ......97 A3
  33 SE16 ....118 D4
James Joyes Wlk **7**
  SE24 ....138 D1
James La E10,E11 ..54 B3
James Lee Sq EN3 7 C5
James Leicester Hall of
  Residence N7 ....72 A2
James Lind Ho **5**
  SE8 ....119 B2
James Middleton Ho **20**
  E2 ....96 B4
James Newman Ct
  SE9 ....166 C1
Jameson Ct **6** E2 ..96 C5
Jameson Ho SE11 .**260 C2**
Jameson Lo N6 ...49 C3
Jameson Pl **11** W3 .111 A4
Jameson St W8 ...**245 B4**
James Pl N17 .....33 D2
James St W1 ..93 A1 **238 B1**
  WC2 ....116 A6 **250 B6**
  Barking IG11 .....79 A1
  Enfield EN1 ......17 D6
  Hounslow TW3 ...130 B2
James Stewart Ho
  NW6 ....69 B1
James Stroud Ho
  SE17 ....**262 B1**
Jamestown Rd
  NW1 ......93 B6 **231 C6**
Jamestown Way E14 120 B6
James Wolfe Prim Sch
  SE10 ....142 A5
Jamieson Ho TW4 .151 B5
Jamuna Cl E14 ....97 A2
Jane Sabina Colard's
  Almshouses **1** E17 .54 A4
Jane St E1 ....96 B1
Janet Ct **4** DA7 ...147 C1
Janet St E14 ......119 C3
Janeway Pl **2** SE16 118 B4
Janeway St SE16 ..118 A4
Janice Mews **3** IG1 78 D5
Jansen Wlk SW11 .136 B1
Janson Cl E15 .....76 C3
  NW10 ....67 C5

Janson Rd E15 .....76 C3
Jansons Rd N15 ...51 C6
Japan Cres N4 ....50 A2
Japanese Sch The
  W3 ....110 C6
Japan Rd RM6 ....58 D3
Jaquets Ct DA5 ...169 C2
Jardine Rd E1 .....118 D6
Jarman Ho **13** E1 ..96 C2
  SE16 ....118 D2
Jarret Ho **1** E3 ....97 C4
Jarrett Cl SW2 ....160 D3
Jarrow Cl SM4 ....201 A4
Jarrow Rd N17 ....52 B5
  SE16 ....118 C1
  Dagenham RM6 ..58 C4
Jarrow Way E9 ....75 D4
Jarvis Cl
  1 Barking IG11 ...101 B6
  Barnet EN5 ......12 D6
Jarvis Ct **2** SE10 ..142 A4
Jarvis Ho **3** SE15 ..140 A4
Jarvis Rd SE22 ....139 C1
  South Croydon CR2 221 B2
Jashada Ho SE18 ..122 C1
Jasmin SE1 ....**253 D3**
Jasmine Cl Ilford IG1 78 D5
  Orpington BR6 ...226 D6
  Southall UB1 .....107 A6
Jasmine Ct SE12 ..165 A5
  11 Wallington SM6 219 B2
Jasmine Gdns
  Harrow HA2 .....63 C6
  West Wickham CR0 223 D5
Jasmine Gr SE20 ..184 B2
Jasmine Rd KT19 ..214 D3
Jasmine Terr UB7 .104 C4
Jasmine Way KT7 .196 C5
Jasmin Ho SE4 ....141 B2
Jasmin Lo **17** SE16 118 B1
Jason Ct **2** SW9 ...138 C4
  W1 ....**238 B2**
Jason Ho UB5 .....84 B4
Jason Wlk SE9 ....188 C4
Jasper Cl EN3 .....6 C5
Jasper Ho KT4 ....199 B1
Jasper Rd E16 ....99 D1
  Penge SE19 ......183 D4
Jasper Wlk N1 ....**235 C2**
Java Wharf SE1 ...**253 D2**
Javelin Way UB5 ..84 D4
Jawahar Bagh SW16 182 D4
Jaycroft EN2 ......4 C4
Jay Gdns BR7 .....188 B6
Jay Ho SW15 .....134 C2
Jay Mews
  SW7 .....114 A4 **246 B1**
Jayson Ct **7** CR0 ..206 A1
Jean Batten Cl SM6 220 B1
Jean Darling Ho
  SW10 ....**266 C5**
Jean Ho **3** SW17 ..180 C5
Jean Humbert Ho **2**
  SE27 ....183 B4
Jean Pardies Ho **21**
  E1 ....96 C2
Jebb Ave SW2 ....160 A5
Jebb St E3 ....97 C5
Jedburgh Rd E13 ..99 C4
Jedburgh St SW11 137 A1
Jeddo Mews W12 .111 D4
Jeddo Rd W12 ....111 D4
Jefferies Ho **12** NW10 67 B1
Jefferson Bldg **3**
  E14 ....119 C4
Jefferson Cl W13 ..109 B3
  Ilford IG2 ....56 D4
Jefferson Wlk **13**
  SE18 ....144 C6
Jeffrey Row SE12 ..165 B6
Jeffrey's Ct **2** SW4 138 A3
Jeffrey's Pl NW1 ..71 C1
Jeffrey's Rd SW4 ..138 A3
Jeffreys Rd EN3 ...7 B1
Jeffrey's St NW1 ..71 C1
Jeffs Cl TW12 .....173 D4
Jeffs Rd SM1 .....217 B4
Jefton Ct SM6 ....219 C1
Jeger Ave E2 .....95 D6
Jeken Rd SE9 .....143 C1
Jelf Rd SW2 ......160 C6
Jellicoe Ct E4 .....36 B4
Jellicoe Gdns HA7 25 A4
Jellicoe Ho E2 ....96 A5
  11 Putney SW15 156 D6
Jellicoe Rd **4** E13 ..99 A3
  Tottenham N17 ...33 B3
Jemmett Cl KT2 ...176 D2
Jemotts Ct **9** SE14 140 D4
Jem Paterson Ct HA1 64 C4

Jengar Cl SM1 .....217 D4
Jenkins Ho SW8 ....269 C2
Jenkins La IG11 .....101 A4
Jenkinson Ho 12 E2 ..96 D4
Jenkins Rd E13 .....99 B3
Jenner Ave W3 ......89 B2
Jenner Ct N21 ....16 A6
Jenner Ho SE3 .....142 C6
  5 Belvedere DA17 ..125 C3
Jenner Pl SW13 .....134 B6
Jenner Rd N16 ......73 D5
Jennett Rd CR0 ....220 C5
Jennifer Ho SE11 ...261 B3
Jennifer Rd E17 ....164 D1
Jennings Cl KT6 ....197 C2
Jennings Ho SE10 ..120 B1
Jennings Rd SE22 ..161 D5
Jenny Hammond Cl
  E11 ....76 D5
Jenny Hammond Sch
  E11 ....76 C4
Jensen Ho 10 E3 ....97 C3
Jenson Way SE19 ...183 D3
Jenton Ave DA7 ....147 A3
Jephson Ct 17 SW4 .138 A3
Jephson Ho 6 SE17 .138 D6
Jephson Rd E7 ......77 C1
Jephson St SE5 .....139 B4
Jephtha Rd SW18 ...157 C5
Jeppo's La CR4 .....202 D5
Jerdan Pl SW6 .....265 A4
Jeremiah St 11 E14 ..97 D1
Jeremy Bentham Ho 9
  E2 ....96 A4
Jeremy's Gn N18 ....34 C6
Jermyn St
  SW1 ....115 C5 249 B4
Jerningham Ct SE14 .141 A4
Jerningham Rd SE14 141 A4
Jerome Cres
  NW8 ......92 C3 237 A6
Jerome Ct 2 N11 ...31 C5
Jerome Ho NW1 ....237 B4
  Kingston KT1 .....175 D1
Jerome Pl KT1 .....175 D1
Jerome St E1 .95 D3 243 C5
Jerome Twr 5 W3 ..110 D4
Jerrard St SE13 ....141 D2
Jerrold Lo SW15 ...134 C2
Jerrold St 24 N1 ....95 C5
Jersey Ave HA7 ....25 C1
Jersey Ct UB2 ......107 B3
Jersey Dr BR5 .....211 B3
Jersey Ho 12 N1 .....73 A2
  Enfield EN3 ....6 D5
Jersey Rd E11 ......54 B1
  N1 ....73 A2
  W7 ....109 A4
  Hounslow TW5,TW7 .130 B5
  Ilford IG1 ....78 D4
  Mitcham SW17 ....181 B4
  Newham E16 ....99 C1
Jersey St E2 ....96 B4
Jerusalem Pas EC1 .241 C5
Jervis Bay Ho 8 E14 .98 B1
Jervis Ct W1 ....238 D1
  9 Dagenham RM10 ..81 D2
Jerviston Gdns SW16 182 C4
Jesmond Ave HA9 ..66 B2
Jesmond Cl CR4 ...203 B6
Jesmond Rd CR0 ...205 D2
Jesmond Way HA7 ..26 A5
Jessam Ave E5 .....52 B1
Jessamine Rd W7 ..108 D5
Jessel Ho SW1 .....259 D4
  WC1 ....233 A1
Jesse Rd E10 ....54 A1
Jessica Rd SW18 ...158 A6
Jessie Blythe La 2
  N19 ....50 A2
Jessie Duffett Ho 11
  SE5 ....139 A5
Jessie's Cotts E17 ..53 A3
Jessiman Terr TW17 .192 C4
Jesson Ho SE17 ....262 C6
Jessop Ave UB2 ....107 B2
Jessop Ct N1 ......234 D3
Jessop Prim Sch
  SE24 ....139 A1
Jessop Sq E14 .....119 C5
Jessops Way CR0 ...203 C3
Jessup Cl SE18 ....123 A2
Jeston Ho 10 SE27 ..160 D1
Jethou Ho 13 N1 ....73 A4
Jetstar Way UB5 ...85 A4
Jevington Way SE12 165 B3
Jevons Ho 9 NW6 ..70 B1
Jewell Ho SW12 ...159 C4
Jewel Rd E17 ....53 C6

Jewish Prep Sch The
  NW6 ....91 D5
Jewry St EC3 .95 D1 243 C1
Jews Coll NW4 .....46 D5
Jews Free Sch NW1 .71 D2
Jews Row SW18 ....136 A1
Jews Wlk SE26 .....184 B6
Jeymer Ave NW2 ...68 C3
Jeymer Dr UB6 .....86 A6
Jeypore Rd SW18 ..158 A5
JFS Sch NW9 ....44 C3
Jillian Cl TW12 ....173 C3
Jim Bradley Cl 16
  SE18 ....122 C4
Jim Griffiths Ho
  SW6 ....264 D5
Joan Cres SE9 .....165 D4
Joan Gdns RM8 .....81 A6
Joanna Ho 7 W6 ...112 C1
Joan Player Ho EN3 ..6 D6
Joan Rd RM8 ....81 A6
Joan St SE1 ..116 D5 251 C3
Jocelin Ho N1 ......233 D5
Jocelyn Rd TW9 ....132 A2
Jocelyn St SE15 ....140 A4
Jockey's Fields
  WC1 ....94 B2 240 D4
Jodane Rd SE8 .....119 B2
Jodrell Cl TW7 .....131 A4
Jodrell Rd E3 ....75 B1
Joe Hunte Ct 2
  SW27 ....182 D5
Joel St HA5,HA6 ....40 A5
Johanna Prim Sch
  SE1 ....116 C4 251 A1
Johanna St SE1 ....251 A1
John Adam St
  WC2 ....116 A6 250 B5
John Aird Ct
  W2 ....92 A2 236 A4
John Archer Way
  SW18 ....158 B5
John Ashby Cl SW2 .160 A5
John Austin Cl KT2 .176 B2
John Baird Ct SE26 .184 D6
John Baird Ho 14
  SE20 ....184 C3
John Ball Prim Sch
  SE3 ....142 C3
John Barker Ct NW6 .69 A1
John Barker Ho IG1 ..79 B6
John Barnes Wlk E15 76 C2
John Barter Ho TW3 129 B3
John Betts' Ho W12 112 A3
John Betts Prim Sch
  W6 ....112 B3
John Bond Ho 2 E3 .97 B1
John Bradshaw Rd
  N14 ....15 D3
John Brent Ho 8
  SE8 ....118 D2
John Buck Ho NW10 .89 D6
John Burns Dr IG11 .79 C1
John Burns Prim Sch
  SW11 ....137 A3
John Busch Sch TW7 131 B4
Johnby Cl EN3 ....7 A6
John Campbell Rd 26
  N16 ....73 C3
John Carpenter St
  EC4 ....251 C6
John Cartwright Ho 7
  E2 ....96 B4
John Chilton Sch UB5 63 A1
John Clifford Ho N8 .50 A3
John Conwey Ho 23
  SW2 ....160 C6
John Cornwell VC Ho 5
  E12 ....78 C4
John Dee Ho 3
  SW14 ....133 B2
John Donne Prim Sch
  SE15 ....140 B4
John Drinkwater Cl
  E11 ....54 D2
John Dwight Ho
  SW6 ....135 D2
John Felton Rd 16
  SE16 ....118 A4
John Fielden Ho 10
  E2 ....96 B4
John Fisher St E1 ..118 A6
John F. Kennedy Specl
  Sch E15 ....98 B6
John Glynes Ct SW15 134 B1
John Gooch Dr EN2 ..4 D4
John Harris Ho SE15 140 A4
John Harrison Way
  SE10 ....120 D3
John Hunt Ct 5 SE9 166 A2

John Islip St
  SW1 ......116 A2 260 A3
John Kaye Ct TW17 .192 C4
John Keall Ho SW15 .134 D2
John Keats Lo EN2 ...5 B4
John Keble CE Prim Sch
  NW10 ....89 D6
John Kelly Tech Colls
  NW2 ....67 D5
John Kennedy Ct 1
  N1 ....73 B2
John Kennedy Ho 1
  SE16 ....118 D2
John Kennedy Lo 2
  N1 ....73 B2
John King Ct 4 N19 .71 D6
John Kirk Ho
  22 SW11 ....136 B2
  Beckenham BR3 ...207 A5
  5 Streatham SW16 .160 A1
John Knight Lo SW6 265 B4
John Lamb Ct HA3 ..24 C2
John Loughborough Sch
  The N17 ....33 D1
John Lyon Sch The
  HA2 ....42 B1
John Masefield Ho
  N15 ....51 B3
John Maurice Cl
  SE17 ....117 B2 262 C4
John McDonald Ho 3
  E14 ....120 A3
John McKenna Wlk 17
  SE16 ....118 A3
John Milton Prim Sch
  SW8 ....137 C5 269 A3
John Nettleford Ho 14
  E2 ....96 B4
John Newton Ct
  DA16 ....146 B2
John Nightingale Sch
  KT8 ....195 B6
John Orwell Sports Ctr
  E1 ....118 B5
John Parker Cl RM10 .81 D1
John Parker Sq 8
  SW11 ....136 B2
John Parry Ct 28 N1 .95 C5
John Paul II Sch
  SW19 ....156 D4
John Penn St SE13 .141 D4
John Perrin Pl HA3 ..44 A2
John Perryn Prim Sch
  W3 ....89 C1
John Prince's St W1 238 D2
John Pritchard Ho 14
  E1 ....96 A3
John Ratcliffe Ho 5
  NW6 ....91 C4
John Rennie Wlk 1
  E1 ....118 C5
John Roan Sch The
  SE3 ....142 C5
John Roll Way SE16 118 A3
John Ruskin Coll
  CR2 ....223 A1
John Ruskin Prim Sch
  SE5 ....139 A6
John Ruskin St SE5 .139 A6
John's Ave NW4 ....46 C5
John Scurr Ho 20 E14 97 A1
John Scurr Prim Sch
  E1 ....96 C3
John Silkin La SE8 .118 D1
Johns Cl TW15 ....171 A6
John's Cl SM4 .....202 A4
John's Mews
  WC1 ......94 B3 240 D5
John Smith Ave
  SW6 ......135 B5 264 C4
Johnson Cl E8 ......96 A6
Johnson Ct 10 SW18 136 B1
Johnson Ho 14 E2 ..96 A4
  NW1 ....232 B3
  SW1 ....258 B3
  SW8 ....269 D3
Johnson Lo 12 W9 ..91 C2
Johnson Rd BR2 ...209 D4
  NW10 ....89 B6
  Heston TW5 ......128 C5
  Thornton Heath CR0 .205 B2
Johnson's Cl SM5 ..218 D5
Johnsons Ct SE14 .241 B1
Johnsons Dr TW12 .174 A2
Johnson's Ind Est
  UB3 ....106 A3
Johnson's Pl
  SW1 ....115 C1 259 A1
Johnson St E1 ......96 C1
  Southall UB2 .....106 D3

Johnsons Way NW10 .88 D3
John Spencer Sq N1 .72 D2
John's Pl E1 ....96 B1
John St E15 ....98 D6
  WC1 ......94 B3 240 D5
  Croydon SE25 ....206 A5
  Enfield EN1 ....17 D1
  Hounslow TW3,TW5 .129 A3
John Stainer Com Prim
  Sch SE4 ....141 A2
John's Terr CR0 ....205 C1
Johnston Cl SW9 ...270 D1
Johnstone Ho SE13 .142 B2
Johnstone Rd E6 ...100 B4
Johnston Rd IG8 ....37 A5
Johnston Terr NW2 ..68 D5
John Strachey Ho
  SW6 ....264 D5
John Strype Ct E10 .53 D1
John Trundle Ct EC2 242 A4
John Tucker Ho 2
  E14 ....119 C3
John Walsh Twr E11 .76 D1
John Wesley Ct 5
  TW1 ....153 A3
John Wesley's House &
  Mus* EC1 ....242 D6
John Wheatley Ho
  14 N19 ....49 D2
  SW6 ....264 D5
John Williams Cl
  SE14 ....140 D6
  12 Kingston KT2 ..175 D2
John Wilson St SE18 122 C2
John Wooley Cl SE13 142 C1
Johsen Ho 5 SW15 156 A6
Joiners Arms Yd 1
  SE5 ....139 B4
Joiner St SE1 ......252 D3
Joint Rd N10 ....30 C2
Jolles Ho 9 E3 ......97 D4
Jollys La Harrow HA2 42 B1
  Hayes UB4 ....84 D2
Jonathan Ct 9 W4 .111 C2
Jonathan St
  SE11 ......116 B1 260 C2
Jones Ho N16 ....51 C1
  4 South Bromley E14 98 B1
Jones Rd E13 ....99 B3
Jones St W1 ....248 C5
Jones Wlk 6 TW10 .154 B5
Jonquil Gdns 5
  TW12 ....173 C4
Jonson Cl Hayes UB4 84 A2
  Mitcham CR4 .....203 B6
Jonson Ho 16 N16 ..73 B4
  SE1 ....262 D5
Jordan Cl HA2 ......63 B5
Jordan Ct SW15 ...134 D1
Jordan Hill N10 .....30 C2
Jordan ho N1 ......235 D5
  12 SE4 ....140 C2
Jordan Rd UB6 .....87 C6
Jordans Cl RM10 ...81 D4
Jordans Ho NW8 ..237 A5
Jordans Mews TW11 152 C2
Jo Richardson Com Sch
  RM9 ....80 C2
Joscoyne Ho 14 E1 ..96 B1
Josef Perrin Ho 1
  SE27 ....183 B6
Joseph Ave W3 .....89 B1
Joseph Clarke Sch E4 36 B4
Joseph Conrad Ho
  SW1 ....259 B3
Joseph Ct N16 ......51 B4
Joseph Hood Fst Sch
  SW20 ....201 A6
Josephine Ave SW2 .160 B6
Joseph Irwin Ho 11
  E14 ....119 B6
Joseph Lancaster Prim
  Sch SE1 ...117 B3 262 C5
Joseph Lister Ct E7 .77 A1
Joseph Lister Lo 11 .55 B1
Joseph Powell Cl 1
  SW12 ....159 C5
Joseph Priestley Ho 12
  E2 ....96 B4
Joseph Ray Rd E11 ..76 C6
Joseph St E3 ....97 B3
Joseph Trotter Cl
  EC1 ....234 B1
Joshua Cl N10 ......31 B3
  Croydon CR0 .....220 D1
Joshua St E14 ....98 A1
Joslings Cl W12 ....112 A6
Joslyn Cl EN3 ....7 C5
Josseline Ct 8 E3 ...97 A5
Joubert Mans SW3 257 B2

Joubert St SW11 ...136 D3
Jowett St 37 SW9 ..138 A3
Jowett St SE15 ....139 D5
Joyce Ave N18 ......33 C5
Joyce Butler Ho N22 32 B2
Joyce Dawson Way
  SE28 ....124 A6
  12 Ealing W5 ....87 C2
Joyce Page Cl SE7 .143 D6
Joy Ct NW2 ....68 D5
Joydon Dr RM6 ....58 B3
Joyners Cl RM9 .....81 B4
Joystone Ct 8 EN4 ...2 C1
Jubb Powell Ho N15 .51 C3
Jubet Ho 9 N16 ....73 B4
Jubilee Ave
  Chingford E4 ......36 A4
  Romford RM7 ......59 D4
  Twickenham TW2 ..152 A3
Jubilee Bldgs NW8 229 C4
Jubilee Cl NW9 ....45 B3
  Pinner HA5 ....22 C1
  Romford RM7 ......59 D4
  Teddington KT1 ..175 C2
Jubilee Cres E14 ...120 A3
  Edmonton N9 ......18 A3
Jubilee Ct Harrow HA3 44 A2
  Hounslow TW3 ....129 D2
  Thornton Heath CR7 204 C5
Jubilee Dr HA4 .....63 A4
Jubilee Gdns UB1 ..85 C1
Jubilee Ho SE11 ...261 B3
  3 Hampton TW12 .173 C2
Jubilee Mans 10 E1 .96 C1
Jubilee Mkt WC2 ..250 B6
Jubilee Par IG8 .....37 C4
Jubilee Pl
  SW3 ......114 C1 257 B2
Jubilee Prim Sch N16 52 A1
  SW2 ....160 C5
  Woolwich SE28 ...124 C5
Jubilee Rd
  Cheam SM3 ......216 D1
  Wembley UB6 ......87 B6
Jubilee St E1 ....96 C2
Jubilee The 2 SE10 141 D5
Jubilee Villas KT10 196 C1
Jubilee Way DA14 ..168 A2
  East Bedfont TW14 150 A3
  Merton SW19 .....179 D2
  Tolworth KT4,KT9 .214 D5
Jubilee Wks SW19 .180 A1
Jubilee Yd SE1 ....253 C2
Judd St WC1 .94 A4 233 A1
Jude St E16 ....98 D1
Judge Heath La UB3 .83 B1
Judges' Wlk NW3 ..70 A5
Judge Wlk KT10 ...212 C2
Juer St SW11 136 C5 267 B3
Jules Thorn Ave EN1 ..6 A1
Julia Ct E17 ....53 D4
Julia Garfield Mews 4
  E16 ....121 B5
Juliana Cl N2 ....48 A6
Julian Ave W3 .....110 D6
Julian Cl EN5 ....1 D2
Julian Ho HA1 ......64 C6
Julian Pl E14 ......119 D1
Julian Rd W5 ......109 C3
Julian St NW5 ....71 A3
Julian Taylor Path 7
  SE23 ....162 B2
Julia St NW5 ....71 A3
Julie Garfield Mews 4
  E16 ....121 B5
Julius Ct TW8 ......132 A5
Julius Nyerere Cl N1 233 C5
Junction App SE13 .142 A2
  SW11 ....136 C2
Junction Mews W2 237 A2
Junction Pl W2 ....236 D2
Junction Rd E13 ....99 B5
  N17 ....52 A6
  N19 ....71 C5
  Ashford TW15 ....171 B5
  Brentford TW8 ...109 D2
  Croydon CR2 .....221 B3
  Edmonton N9 ......18 A3
  Harrow HA1 ....42 C3
Junction Rd E RM6 .59 D2
Junction Rd W RM6 .59 A2
Juniper Cl Barnet EN5 .12 D6
  Chessington KT9 ..214 B3
  Wembley HA9 ......66 C3
Juniper Cres NW1 ..71 A1

Juniper Ct N16 .....73 B6
  Belmont SM2 .....217 C2
  Dagenham RM6 ...58 C3
  12 Ealing W5 ......87 C2
  Harrow HA3 ....24 D2
  Hounslow TW3 ...129 D1
Juniper Gdns
  Ashford TW16 ....171 C4
  Streatham CR4 ...181 C2
Juniper La E6 ......100 A2
Juniper Rd IG1 .....78 D4
Juniper St 15 E1 ...118 C2
Juniper Way UB3 ..105 C6
Juno Ct 11 SW9 ...138 C5
Juno Way SE14 ....140 D6
Juno Way Ind Est
  SE14 ....140 D6
Jupiter Ct 10 SW9 .138 C5
  8 Northolt UB5 ....84 D4
Jupiter Hts UB10 ...82 B6
Jupiter Way N7 .....72 B2
Jupp Rd E15 ....76 B1
Jupp Rd W E15 .....98 B6
Jura Ho SE16 ......119 A2
Jurston Ct SE1 .....251 B1
Justice Wlk SW3 ..267 A5
Justin Cl TW8 ......131 D5
Justin Rd E4 ....35 B4
Jute La EN3 ....7 A2
Jutland Cl N19 ......50 A1
Jutland Ho 4 SE5 ..139 A3
  10 SE7 ....122 A2
Jutland Rd E13 ......99 A3
  Catford SE6 ......164 A4
Jutsums Ave RM7 ..59 D3
Jutsums Ct RM7 ...59 D3
Jutsums La RM7 ...59 D3
Juxon Cl HA3 ....23 D2
Juxon St
  SE11 ......116 B2 260 D4
JVC Bsns Pk NW2 ..46 A1

K

Kaduna Cl HA5 .....40 B4
Kale Rd DA18 ......125 A4
Kangley Bridge Ctr
  SE26 ....185 B6
Kangley Bridge Rd
  SE26 ....185 B5
Kaplan Dr N21 ......16 B6
Kara Way NW2 .....68 D4
Karen Ct 2 SE5 ....139 C2
  Bromley BR1 .....186 D2
Karen Ho 7 N16 ...73 B4
Karens Ct EN3 ......6 D6
Karen Terr E11 .....76 D6
  Ilford IG2 ....57 B4
Karenza Ct HA9 ....43 C2
Kariba Cl N9 ....18 C1
Karoline Gdns UB6 .86 B5
Kashgar Rd SE18 ..123 D2
Kashmir Rd SE7 ...143 D5
Kasmin Ct NW10 ..68 A1
Kassala Rd
  SW11 ......136 D4 267 D1
Katella Trad Est
  IG11 ....101 C4
Kates Cl EN5 ....12 A6
Katharine Rd 1 TW1 153 A3
Katharine St CR0 ..221 A5
Katherine Cl 3 SE16 118 C4
Katherine Ct
  10 Forest Hill SE23 162 C3
  Penge SE20 ......184 C2
Katherine Gdns SE9 143 C1
Katherine Ho 15 W10 91 A3
Katherine Rd E6,E7 .77 C1
Katherine Sq W11 .244 A4
Kathleen Ave W3 ..89 C3
  Wembley HA0 ......66 A1
Kathleen Ferrier Ct 4
  N17 ....33 D3
Kathleen Moore Ct
  BR4 ....224 A6
Kathleen Rd SW11 .136 D2
Katrine Ct NW2 ....68 C5
Kayemoor Rd SM2 218 C2
Kay Rd SW9 ....138 B3
Kays Ct EN3 ....6 C1
Kay St DA16 ......146 B4
  E2 ....96 A5
Kean Ho 5 SE17 ...138 C6
Kean St WC2 .94 B1 240 C1
Keates Est N16 .....73 C6
Keatley Gn E4 ......35 B4

Keats Ave E16 ....121 B5
Keats Cl NW3 ....70 C4
  SE1 ....263 C3
  Enfield EN3 ....18 D6
  Hayes UB4 ....84 A4
  Mitcham SW19 .....180 B4
  Wanstead E11 ....55 B4
Keats Ct RM6 ....65 C5
Keats Gr NW3 ....70 C4
Keats Ho **22** E2 ......96 C4
  30 SE5 ....139 A5
  SW1 ....269 B6
  7 Beckenham BR3 ..185 D4
Keats House Mus★
  NW3 ....70 C4
Keats Par **3** N9 .....18 A2
Keats Pl EC2 ....242 C3
Keats Rd DA16 ....145 D4
Keats Way
  Croydon CR0 ....206 C3
  Southall UB6 ....85 D2
  West Drayton UB7 ...104 B2
Kebbell Terr E7 ....77 B3
Keble Cl
  New Malden KT4 ....199 D1
  Northolt UB5 ....64 A3
Keble Ho **4** SW15 ...156 D5
Keble Pl SW13 ....134 B6
Keble Prep Sch N21 ...16 C4
Keble St SW17 ....180 A6
Kechill Gdns BR2 ....209 A2
Kedeston Cl SM3 ....201 D1
Kedge Ho **10** E14 ....119 C3
Kedleston Ct E5 ....75 A4
Kedleston Dr BR5 ....211 D4
Kedleston Wlk **21** E2 ..96 B4
Kedyngton Ho **5** HA8 .27 A1
Keeble Cl SE18 ......144 D6
Keedonwood Rd BR1 .186 D5
Keel Cl SE16 ....118 D5
  Barking IG11 ....102 C5
Keeley St WC2 94 B1 240 C1
Keeling Ho **2** TW11 ..174 C5
Keeling Rd SE9 ......165 D6
Keely Cl EN4 ....14 C6
Keemor Cl SE18 .....144 C5
Keens Cl SW16 ......181 D5
Keen's Rd CR0 ....221 A4
Keen's Yd N1 ....72 D2
Keepers Mews TW11 175 C4
Keeper Wharf E1 ....118 D6
Keepier Wharf **15** E1 118 D6
Keep The SE3 ....143 A3
  Forest Hill SE6 .....163 C3
  Kingston KT2 ....176 B3
Keeton's Rd SE16 ...118 B3
Keevil Dr SW19 ......157 A4
Keighley Cl N7 ....72 A4
Keightley Dr SE9 ....167 A3
Keilder Cl UB10 ......82 C5
Keildon Rd SW11 ....136 D1
Keir Hardie Est E5 ....74 D2
Keir Hardie Ho **15** N19 49 D2
  NW10 ....67 D1
  W6 ....134 D6
Keir Hardie Way
  Barking IG11 ....80 A1
  Hayes UB4 ....84 A4
Keir Hardy Ho **6**
  DA17 ....125 C3
Keir The SW19 ......178 C5
Keith Connor Cl **5**
  SW8 ....137 B2
Keith Gr W12 ....112 A5
Keith Ho NW6 ....91 D5
Keith Park Rd UB10 ...60 B1
Keith Rd E17 ....35 B2
  Barking IG11 ....101 B3
  Hayes UB3 ....105 C3
Keith Sutton Ho **3**
  SE9 ....167 A2
Kelbrook Rd SE3 ....144 A2
Kelby Ho N7 ....72 B2
Kelceda Cl NW2 ......68 A6
Kelf Gr UB3 ....83 D1
Kelfield Ct **1** W10 ...90 D1
Kelfield Gdns W10 ....90 D1
Kelfield Mews W10 ...90 D1
Kelham Ho **10** SE18 ..144 D6
Kelland Cl **1** N8 .....49 D4
Kelland Rd E13 ....99 A3
Kellaway Rd SE3 ....143 D3
Keller Cres E12 ....77 D4
Kellerton Rd SE13 ...164 C6
Kellett Ho N1 ....235 D5
Kellett Rd SW2 .....138 C1
Kelling Gdns CR0 ...204 D2

Kellino St SW17 .....180 D6
Kellner Rd SE28 .....123 D3
Kellow Ho SE1 ......252 C2
Kell St SE1 .116 D3 261 D6
Kelly Ave SE15 ......139 D4
Kelly Cl NW10 ....67 B5
  Upper Halliford TW17 .171 C1
Kelly Ct **11** E14 ....119 C6
Kelly Rd NW7 ....29 A4
Kelly St NW1 ....71 B2
Kelly Way RM6 ....59 A3
Kelman Cl SW4 .....137 D3
Kelmore Gr SE22 ...140 A1
Kelmscott **5** SE23 ..162 D1
Kelmscott Cl E17 .....35 B2
Kelmscott Ct **2** HA7 .25 C6
Kelmscott Gdns W12 112 A3
Kelmscott Rd SW11 .158 D6
Kelmscott Sch E17 ...53 B3
Kelross Rd N5 ....73 A4
Kelsall Cl SE3 ....143 B3
Kelsey Gate **8** BR3 .185 D1
Kelsey La BR3 ....207 C6
Kelsey Park Ave BR3 .185 D1
Kelsey Park Rd BR3 .185 C1
Kelsey Park Sch BR3 207 C6
Kelsey Rd BR5 ......190 B1
Kelsey Sq BR3 ......185 C1
Kelsey Way BR3 ....207 C6
Kelshall Ct N4 ....73 A6
Kelso Ct SE20 ......184 B3
Kelso Lo E18 ....37 B1
Kelson Ho E14 ......120 A3
Kelso Pl W8 .113 D3 255 D6
Kelso Rd SM5 ......202 A2
Kelvedon Cl KT2 ....176 C4
Kelvedon Ho SW8 ...270 B2
Kelvedon Rd
  SW6 ....135 B5 264 C6
Kelvin Ave N13 ....32 B4
  Barking IG11 ....101 C6
  Edmonton N18 ....33 B6
Kelvin Cl KT19 ......214 C2
Kelvin Cres HA3 ......24 C1
Kelvin Ct W11 ......245 A5
  Chiswick W4 ....133 A5
  Isleworth TW7 ......130 C3
  7 Penge SE20 .....184 B2
  8 Twickenham TW1 .153 B5
Kelvin Dr TW1 ......153 B5
Kelvin Gdns
  Southall UB1 ....85 C1
  Thornton Heath CR0 ..204 A2
Kelvin Gr
  Forest Hill SE26 ....162 B1
  Surbiton KT6 ....214 A5
Kelvin Grove Prim Sch
  SE26 ....162 B1
Kelvington Cl CR0 ...207 A2
Kelvington Rd SE15 .162 D6
Kelvin Ho **3** DA17 ..125 C3
Kelvin Par BR6 ......211 C1
Kelvin Rd DA16 .....146 A2
  N5 ....73 A4
Kelyway Ho **20** SW2 .160 C4
Kember St N1 ....72 B1
Kemble Dr BR2 .....226 A5
Kemble Ho SW9 ....138 D2
Kemble Rd
  Croydon CR0 ....220 D5
  Forest Hill SE23 ....162 D3
  Tottenham N17 ......34 A2
Kemble St
  WC2 ....94 B1 240 C1
Kemerton Rd SE5 ...139 A2
  Beckenham BR3 ....185 D1
  Croydon CR0 ....205 D2
Kemey's St E9 ....75 A3
Kemnal Rd BR7 .....189 B5
Kemnal Tech Coll
  BR5 ....190 B3
Kemnal Warren BR7 .189 B4
Kemp **24** NW9 ......27 D2
Kemp Ct SW8 ......270 A2
Kempe Ho SE1 .....262 D5
Kempe Rd NW6 ......90 D5
  Wallend E6 ....78 C2
Kempis Way **5** SE22 .161 C6
Kemplay Rd NW3 .....70 B4
Kemp Rd RM8 ....58 D1
Kemps Ct NW2 ....68 D5
Kemp's Ct W1 ......239 C1
Kemps Dr E14 ....119 C6
Kempsford Gdns
  SW5 ....113 C1 255 B1
Kempsford Rd SE11 .261 B3
Kemps Gdns SE13 ..164 A6

Kempshott Rd SW16 .182 A3
Kempson Rd
  SW6 ....135 C5 265 B3
Kempthorne Rd SE8 .119 B2
Kempton Ave
  Northolt UB5 ....63 C3
  Sunbury TW16 ......172 B2
Kempton Cl UB10 .....61 A4
Kempton Ct E1 ....96 B2
  Sunbury TW16 ......172 B2
Kempton Ho **13** N1 ...95 C6
Kempton Park Race
  Course TW16 ......172 C3
Kempton Park Sta
  TW16 ....172 B3
Kempton Rd E6 ......100 B6
Kempton Wlk CR0 ...207 A3
Kemsing Cl DA5 .....169 A4
  Coney Hall BR2 .....224 D6
  South Norwood CR7 ..205 A5
Kemsing Ho **1** SE1 .252 D1
Kemsing Rd SE10 ...121 A1
Kemsley SE13 ......163 D6
Kemsley Ct W13 ....109 C5
Kemsway Ct BR5 ....190 B1
Kenbrook Ho **5** NW5 .71 C4
  W14 ....254 D5
Kenbury Cl UB10 .....60 C5
Kenbury Gdns **10**
  SE5 ....139 A3
Kenbury Mans **18**
  SE5 ....139 A3
Kenbury St SE5 .....139 A3
Kenchester Cl
  SW8 ....138 A5 270 B3
Kencot Cl DA18 .....125 B4
  Erith DA18 ....125 B4
Kendal NW1 ....231 D2
Kendal Ave Acton W3 .88 C3
  Barking IG11 ....101 C6
  Edmonton N18 ....33 B6
Kendal Cl SE5 ......138 D5
  East Bedfont TW14 ..149 D3
  Hayes UB4 ....83 C5
  Woodford IG8 ....20 D2
Kendal Ct NW2 ....69 A3
  Acton W3 ....88 C2
  11 Chingford E4 ...20 A3
  7 Croydon CR0 ....205 C1
Kendale Rd BR1 .....186 C5
Kendal Gdns
  Edmonton N18 ....33 B6
  Sutton SM1 ....218 A6
Kendal Ho **32** E9 ....74 C1
  N1 ....233 D4
  5 Croydon CR0 ....205 C1
  Penge SE20 ....184 B1
Kendall Ave BR3 ....185 A1
Kendall Ct DA15 ....168 A1
  3 SE22 ....162 A6
  Mitcham SW19 .....180 B4
  5 Penge SE19 ....183 D3
Kendall Ho **5** SE12 .164 D4
Kendall Lo **5** BR1 ..187 B2
Kendall Pl W1 ......238 A3
Kendall Rd SE18 ....144 A4
  Beckenham BR3 ....185 A1
  Isleworth TW7 ......131 A3
Kendalmere Cl N10 ...31 B2
Kendal Par N18 ......33 B6
Kendal Pl SW15 ....157 B6
Kendal Rd NW10 .....68 A4
Kendal St W2 .92 C1 237 B1
Kendal Steps W2 ...237 B1
Kender Prim Sch
  SE14 ....140 C4
Kender St SE14 .....140 C4
Kendoa Rd **1** SW4 ..137 D1
Kendon Cl E11 ....55 B4
Kendra Hall Rd CR2 .220 D1
Kendrey Gdns TW2 ..152 C4
Kendrick Ct **11** SE15 .140 B4
Kendrick Mews SW7 256 C3
Kendrick Pl SW7 ....256 C3
Kenelm Cl HA1 ....65 A5
Kenerne Dr EN5 ......13 A6
Kenilford Rd SW12 .159 B4
Kenilworth Ave E17 ..53 C6
  Harrow HA2 ....63 D4
  Wimbledon SW19 ...179 C6
Kenilworth Cres EN1 ..5 C4
Kenilworth Ct
  7 Chingford E4 ...20 A2
  Fulham SW6 ....135 A2
  Twickenham TW2 ...152 C2
Kenilworth Gdns
  Hayes UB4 ....83 D2
  Ilford IG3 ....79 D6

Kenilworth Gdns continued
  Southall UB1 ....85 B4
  South Oxhey WD19 ...22 C1
  Woolwich SE18 .....144 D3
Kenilworth Rd E3 .....97 A5
  HA8 ....11 A1
  NW6 ....91 B6
  Ashford TW15,TW19 .148 A5
  Ealing W5 ....110 A5
  Orpington BR5 .....211 A3
  Penge SE20 ....184 D2
  Stoneleigh KT17 ....216 A3
Kenilworth Terr **3**
  SM2 ....217 C1
Kenley N17 ....33 B1
Kenley Ave NW9 .....27 C1
Kenley Cl Barnet EN4 ..2 C1
  Sidcup DA5 ....169 C4
  St Paul's Cray BR7 ..211 C6
Kenley Gdns CR7 ...204 D5
Kenley Ho **6** BR5 ...190 B1
  5 Croydon CR0 ....206 A1
Kenley Rd
  Kingston KT1,KT3 ...176 D1
  Merton SW19 ......201 C6
  Twickenham TW1 ...153 B5
Kenley Wlk W11 ....244 A5
  Cheam SM3 ....216 D4
Kenlor Rd SW17 ....180 A5
Kenmare Ct **5** HA7 ..25 C6
Kenmare Dr CR4 ....180 D3
Kenmare Gdns N13 ...33 A6
Kenmare Mans NW6 ..69 B3
Kenmare Rd CR7 ....204 C3
Kenmere Gdns HA0 ...88 C6
Kenmere Mans W5 ...87 C3
Kenmere Rd DA16 ..146 C3
Kenmont Gdns NW10 .90 B4
Kenmont Prim Sch
  NW10 ....90 B4
Kenmore Ave HA3 ....43 A6
Kenmore Cl TW9 ....132 C5
Kenmore Cres UB4 ...83 C4
Kenmore Ct NW6 .....69 C1
Kenmore Gdns HA8 ..26 D1
Kenmore Park Fst & Mid
  Schs HA3 ....44 A6
Kenmore Rd HA3 .....43 D5
Kenmure Rd E8 ....74 B3
Kenmure Yd E8 ....74 B3
Kennacraig Cl **7**
  E16 ....121 A5
Kennard Ho **11** SW11 137 A3
Kennard Mans **6** N11 30 D5
  N11 ....30 D5
Kennard Rd E15 ......76 B1
  N11 ....30 D5
Kennard St **9** SW11 .137 A3
  Newham E16 ....122 B5
Kennedy Ave EN3 ....18 C5
Kennedy Cl BR5 ....211 B1
  E13 ....99 A5
  1 Mitcham CR4 ...181 A1
  Pinner HA5 ....23 B4
Kennedy Cox Ho **9**
  E16 ....98 D2
Kennedy Ct TW15 ...171 A4
Kennedy Ho SE11 ...260 C2
Kennedy Path W7 ...86 D3
Kennedy Rd
  Barking IG11 ....101 C6
  Ealing W7 ....86 C2
Kennedy Wlk SE17 ..262 C2
Kennet Cl SW11 ....136 B1
Kennet Ct **47** W2 ....91 C2
Kennet Dr UB4 ....85 A2
Kenneth Ave IG1 .....78 D4
Kenneth Campbell Ho
  NW8 ....236 D6
Kenneth Cres NW2 ...68 B3
Kenneth Ct SE11 ...261 B4
Kenneth Gdns HA7 ...25 A4
Kenneth Moor Rd **4**
  IG1 ....78 D5
Kenneth Rd RM6 .....59 C4
Kenneth Robbins Ho **1**
  N17 ....34 B3
Kenneth Younger Ho
  SW6 ....264 D5
Kennet Rd W9 ....91 B3
  Isleworth TW7 ......130 D2
Kennet Sq CR4 ......180 C2
Kennet St E1 ....118 A5
Kennet Wharf La EC4 252 B6
Kenninghall N18 .....34 C5
Kenninghall Rd E5 ...74 B5
  N18 ....34 C5
Kenning Ho **6** N1 ....95 C6
Kenning St **12** SE16 .118 C4

Kennings Way
  SE11 ....116 C1 261 B2
Kennington Gdns
  KT1 ....197 C2
Kennington Gr SE11 .270 D6
Kennington La
  SE11 ....116 C1 260 D1
Kennington Oval
  SE11 ....138 C6 270 D5
Kennington Palace Ct
  SE11 ....261 A2
Kennington Park Gdns
  SE17 ....138 D6
Kennington Park Ho
  SE11 ....261 B1
Kennington Park Pl
  SE11 ....138 D6
Kennington Park Rd
  SE11 ....116 D1 261 C2
Kennington Rd
  SE11 ....116 C2 261 A3
Kennington Sta
  SE11 ....116 D1 261 C2
Kennoldes SE21 ....161 B2
Kennyland Lo NW4 ...46 B3
Kenny Rd NW7 ....29 A5
Kenrick Pl W1 ......238 A3
Kensal Green Cemy (All
  Souls)★ NW10 ......90 C4
Kensal Green Sta
  NW10 ....90 C4
Kensal Ho W10 ......90 D3
Kensal Rd W10 ......91 A3
Kensal Rise Prim Sch
  NW6 ....90 D5
Kensal Rise Sta NW10 90 D5
Kensington Ave E12 ..78 B2
  South Norwood CR7 ..182 C2
Kensington Avenue Inf Sch
  CR7 ....182 C2
Kensington Avenue Jun
  Sch CR7 ....182 C2
Kensington & Chelsea Coll
  SW10 ....136 A5 266 A4
  W10 ....91 A4
Kensington Church Ct
  W8 ....245 C1
Kensington Church St
  W8 ....113 C5 245 B3
Kensington Church Wlk
  W8 ....245 C1
Kensington Cl N11 ...31 A4
Kensington Court Mans
  W8 ....245 D1
Kensington Court Mews
  W8 ....255 D6
Kensington Court Pl
  W8 ....113 D3 255 D6
Kensington Ct **2** NW7 27 B5
  W8 ....113 D4 245 D1
  Enfield EN2 ....5 C5
Kensington Ct Gdns
  W8 ....255 D6
Kensington Dr IG8 ...37 D1
Kensington Gardens★
  W2 ....114 C3 246 B3
Kensington Gate
  W8 ....114 A3 256 A6
Kensington Gdns IG1 .56 B1
Kensington Gdns Sq
  W2 ....91 D1
Kensington Gore
  SW7 ....114 B4 246 C1
Kensington Hall Gdns
  W14 ....254 C2
Kensington Hgts HA1 .42 D3
Kensington High St
  W8 ....113 C3 255 B6
Kensington Ho **3**
  NW5 ....71 C3
Kensington Hts W8 ..245 A3
Kensington Mall W8 .245 B4
Kensington Mans
  SW5 ....255 B2
Kensington Olympia Sta
  W14 ....113 A3 254 A6
Kensington Palace★
  W8 ....113 D5 245 D3
Kensington Palace Gdns
  W8 ....113 D5 245 C4
Kensington Park Gdns
  W11 ....113 B6 244 D5
Kensington Park Mews
  W11 ....91 B1
Kensington Park Rd
  W11 ....113 B6 244 D6
Kensington Pl
  W8 ....113 C5 245 A4
Kensington Prep Sch
  SW6 ....135 B4 264 D2

Kensington Prim Sch
  E12 ....78 B2
Kensington Rd
  SW7 ....114 C4 246 B1
  Northolt UB5 ....85 C5
Kensington Sports Ctr
  W11 ....244 A6
Kensington Sq
  W8 ....113 D4 245 C1
Kensington Terr CR2 .221 B1
Kensington Village
  W14 ....113 B2 254 D3
Kensington W W14 ..254 A4
Kensworth Ho EC1 ..235 D1
Kent Ave Bexley DA16 .167 D6
  Dagenham RM9 .....103 C3
  Ealing W13 ....87 B2
Kent Cl
  Mitcham CR4,SW16 .204 A5
  Orpington BR6 .....227 C2
Kent Ct **3** E2 ....95 D5
  NW9 ....27 C1
  Acton W3 ....88 B1
Kent Dr
  Cockfosters EN4 .....15 A6
  Teddington TW11 ...174 C5
Kentford Way UB5 ...85 A6
Kent Gate Way CR0 .223 D6
Kent Gdns Ealing W13 .87 B2
  Ruislip HA4 ....40 B3
Kent Ho SE1 ....263 D1
  SW1 ....259 C1
  13 W4 ....111 C1
  Richmond TW10 ....154 C6
Kent House La BR3 ..185 A5
Kent House Rd BR3 .185 A5
Kent House Sta BR3 .185 A2
Kent House Station App
  BR3 ....184 D2
Kentish Bldgs SE1 ..252 C2
Kentish Rd DA17 ....125 C2
Kentish Town CE Prim Sch
  NW5 ....71 C3
Kentish Town Rd NW1 .71 B2
Kentish Town Sta
  NW5 ....71 C3
Kentish Town West Sta
  NW5 ....71 B2
Kentish Way BR1,BR2 209 B6
Kentlea Rd SE28 ....123 C4
Kent Lo **9** SW19 ...156 D3
Kentmere Ho SE15 ..140 C6
Kentmere Rd SE18 ..123 C2
Kenton Ave
  Harrow HA1 ....42 D2
  Southall UB1 ....107 C6
  Sunbury TW16 .....173 A1
Kenton Ct W14 .....254 C5
  2 Forest Hill SE26 .185 A6
  Harrow HA3 ....43 B3
  3 Richmond TW10 .153 D5
Kenton Gdns HA3 ....43 C4
Kenton Ho **21** E1 ....96 C3
  N5 ....72 C3
Kenton La Harrow HA3 .24 D3
  Harrow HA3 ....43 C6
Kenton Park Ave HA3 .43 D5
Kenton Park Cl HA3 ..43 C5
Kenton Park Cres HA3 .43 D5
Kenton Park Par HA3 .43 D4
Kenton Park Rd HA3 ..43 D5
Kenton Rd E9 ....74 D2
  Harrow HA3 ....43 C4
Kenton St WC1 .....240 A6
Kenton Sta HA3 .....43 B3
Kenton Way UB4 .....83 C2
Kent Pas NW1 ......237 C6
Kent Rd W4 ....111 A3
  Dagenham RM10 ....81 D3
  East Molesey KT8 ...196 A5
  Kingston KT1 ....197 D6
  Richmond TW9 .....132 C5
  Southgate N21 ......17 B4
  West Wickham BR4 ..207 D1
Kent St E13 ....99 B4
  E2 ....95 D5
Kent Terr NW1 .92 C4 230 B1
Kent Twr SE20 ......184 B3
Kent View Gdns IG3 ..79 C6
Kent Way KT6 ......214 B6
Kentwell Cl SE4 ....141 A1
Kentwode Gn SW13 .134 C3
Kent Yard SW7 .....247 B1
Kenver Ave N12 ......30 B4
Kenward Rd SE9 ....165 D6
Ken Way HA9 ....67 A5
Kenway Rd
  SW5 ....113 D2 255 C3
Ken Wilson Ho **17** E2 .96 A5
Kenwood EN1 ....17 C5

Kenwood Ave N14 . . . .15 D6
Kenwood CI NW3 . . . .48 B1
Harmondsworth UB7 . .126 C6
Kenwood Ct NW9 . . . .45 A5
Kenwood Dr BR3 . . . .208 A6
Kenwood Gdns
Ilford IG2 . . . . .56 C4
2 Wanstead E18 . . . .55 B6
Kenwood Ho* NW3 . . .48 C1
15 SW9 . . . . .138 D1
Kenwood Rd N6 . . . . .48 D3
Edmonton N9 . . . . . .18 A3
Kenworthy Rd E9 . . . .75 D3
Kenwrick Ho N1 . . . . .233 D5
Kenwyn Dr NW2 . . . . .67 B3
Kenwyn Rd SW4 . . . .137 D1
Wimbledon SW20 . . . .178 C2
Kenya Rd SE7 . . . . . .143 D5
Kenyngton Dr TW16 . .172 A5
Kenyngton Manor Prim
Sch TW16 . . . . . . .172 A4
Kenyngton Pl HA3 . . .43 C4
Kenyon Ho 31 SE5 . . .139 C1
Kenyon St SW6 . . . . .134 D4
Keogh Rd E15 . . . . . .76 D2
Kepler Ho 9 SE10 . . .120 D1
Kepler Rd SW2,SW4 . .138 A1
Keppel Ho 5 SE8 . . . .119 B1
SW3 . . . . .257 A3
Keppel Rd E6 . . . . . .100 B6
Dagenham RM9 . . . . .81 A4
Keppel Row SE1 . . . .252 A3
Keppel St WC1 . . . . .239 D4
Kerala St N17 . . . . . .33 D2
Kerbela St 2 E2 . . . . .96 A3
Kerbey St E14 . . . . . .97 D1
Kerem Sch N2 . . . . . .48 B4
Kerfield Cres SE5 . . . .139 B4
Kerfield Pl SE5 . . . . .139 B4
Kerridge Ct N1 . . . . .73 C2
Kerrier Ho SW10 . . . .266 B3
Kerrington Ct 7
W12 . . . . .112 C4
Kerrin Point SE11 . . .261 A2
Kerrison Pl W5 . . . . .109 D5
Kerrison Rd E15 . . . . .98 B6
SW11 . . . . .136 C2
Ealing W5 . . . . .109 D5
Kerrison Villas W5 . . .109 D5
Kerry N7 . . . . .72 A2
Kerry Ave HA7 . . . . . .25 D6
Kerry CI Newham E16 .99 B1
Palmers Green N13 . . .16 B2
Kerry Ct HA7 . . . . . . .25 D6
Kerry Ho 5 E1 . . . . . .96 C1
Kerry Path SE8 . . . . .141 B6
Kerry Rd SE8 . . . . . . .141 B6
Kerscott Ho 30 E3 . . .97 D4
Kersey Gdns SE9 . . . .188 A6
Kersfield Ho SW15 . . .156 D5
Kersfield Rd SW15 . . .156 D5
Kershaw CI SW18 . . . .158 B5
Kershaw Ho 7 SE27 . .160 D1
Kershaw Rd RM10 . . . .81 C5
Kersley Mews SW11 . .267 C1
Kersley Rd N16 . . . . .73 C5
Kersley St SW11 . . . .136 C2
Kerstin CI UB3 . . . . . .105 C6
Kerswell CI N15 . . . . .51 C4
Kerwick CI 1 N7 . . . . .72 B1
Keslake Mans NW10 . .90 D5
Keslake Rd NW6 . . . . .90 D5
Kessock CI N17 . . . . .52 B4
Kestlake Rd DA5 . . . .168 C5
Keston Ave BR2 . . . . .225 C3
Keston CE Prim Sch
BR2 . . . . .225 D3
Keston CI
Bexley DA16 . . . . . . .146 C5
Edmonton N18 . . . . . .17 B1
Keston Ct DA5 . . . . .169 B4
Keston Gdns BR2 . . . .225 C4
Keston Ho SE17 . . . . .263 B2
Keston Mark BR2 . . . .226 A5
Keston Park CI BR2 . .226 B5
Keston Rd N17 . . . . . .51 A4
SE15 . . . . .140 A2
Thornton Heath CR7 . .204 C3
Kestral Ho EC1 . . . . .235 A2
Kestrel Ave E6 . . . . . .100 C4
SE24 . . . . .161 A6
Kestrel CI NW10 . . . . .67 B3
NW9 . . . . .27 C1
Kingston KT2 . . . . . .175 D6
Kestrel Ct E17 . . . . . .34 D1
Ruislip HA4 . . . . .61 B6
South Croydon CR2 . .221 A2
Kestrel Ho 4 SW11 . .136 C1
Enfield EN3 . . . . .19 A6
Kestrel Pl SE14 . . . . .141 A6

Kestrel Way UB3 . . . .105 B4
Keswick Ave
Kingston KT2,SW15 . .177 C5
Merton SW19 . . . . . .179 C4
Upper Halliford TW17 .193 C6
Keswick CI SM1 . . . . .218 A4
Keswick Ct 2 SE22 . .162 A6
13 Catford SE6 . . . . .164 D3
Keswick Dr EN3 . . . . .6 C6
Keswick Gdns
Redbridge IG4 . . . . . .56 C5
Ruislip HA4 . . . . .39 B3
Wembley HA9 . . . . . . .66 A4
Keswick Ho 8 SE5 . . .139 A4
Keswick Hts 9 SW15 . 157 A6
Keswick Lo E8 . . . . . .73 D2
Keswick Mews W5 . . .110 A5
Keswick Rd BR6 . . . . .211 D1
DA7 . . . . .147 C4
Putney SW15 . . . . . .157 A6
Twickenham TW2 . . . .152 A5
West Wickham BR4 . . .224 C6
Kettering Ct CR7 . . . .205 A5
Kettering Rd EN3 . . . . .6 D6
Kettering St SW16 . . .181 C4
Kett Gdns SW2 . . . . .160 B6
Kettlebaston Rd E10 . .53 B4
Kettleby Ho SW9 . . . .138 D2
Kettlewell CI N11 . . . .31 A4
Ketton Ho W10 . . . . . .90 C3
Kevan Ct 6 E17 . . . . .53 D5
Kevan Ho SE5 . . . . . .139 A4
Kevelioc Rd N17 . . . . .33 A2
Kevin CI TW4 . . . . . . .128 D3
Kevington CI BR5 . . . .211 D5
Kevington Dr BR5,
BR7 . . . . .211 D5
Kew Bridge TW8 . . . .110 B1
Kew Bridge Ct 8
W4 . . . . .110 C1
Kew Bridge Distribution
Ctr TW8 . . . . .110 B1
Kew Bridge Rd TW8 . .110 B1
Kew Bridge Sta TW8 . 110 B1
Kew Bridge Steam Mus★
TW8 . . . . .110 B1
Kew Cres SM3 . . . . . .217 B5
Kew Foot Rd TW9 . . . .132 C4
Kew Gardens Rd
TW9 . . . . .132 C4
Kew Gardens(Royal
Botanic)★ TW9 . . . .132 A4
Kew Gardens Sta
TW9 . . . . .132 C4
Kew Gn TW9 . . . . . . .132 B6
Kew Green TW9 . . . . .132 C6
Kew Lo 11 TW9 . . . . .132 B4
Kew Obsy★ TW9 . . . .131 C2
Kew Palace★ TW9 . . .132 A5
Kew Pier TW9 . . . . . .132 C6
Kew Ret Pk TW9 . . . . .132 D4
Key CI E1 . . . . .96 B3
Keyes Ct SE22 . . . . . .162 A6
Keyes Rd NW2 . . . . . .68 D3
Keyham Ho 31 W2 . . .91 C2
Key Ho 9 SE11 . . . . .138 C6
Keymer Rd SW2 . . . . .160 B2
Keynes CI N2 . . . . . . .48 D6
Keynes Ct 9 SE28 . . .124 B6
Keynsham Ave IG8 . . . .36 C6
Keynsham Gdns SE9 . .166 A6
Keynsham Ho 2 N4 . .51 B4
Keynsham Rd SE9 . . . .166 A6
Cheam SM4 . . . . . . .201 D3
Keynsham Wlk SM4 . .201 D3
Keyse Rd SE1 117 D3 263 C5
Keysham Ave TW5 . . .128 A4
Keystone Cres N1 . . . .233 B3
Keywood Dr TW16 . . .172 A4
Keyworth CI E5 . . . . . .75 D4
Keyworth Pl SE1 . . . .261 D6
Keyworth Prim Sch
SE17 . . . . . .116 D1 261 C2
Keyworth St
SE1 . . . . . . .116 D3 261 D6
Kezia St SE8 . . . . . . .119 A4
Khalsa St N22 . . . . . . .32 D2
Khama Rd SW17 . . . . .180 C5
Khartoum Rd E13 . . . .99 B4
Ilford IG1 . . . . .78 D3
Upper Tooting SW17 . .180 B6
Khyber Rd SW11 . . . .136 C3
Kibworth St
SW8 . . . . . . .138 B5 270 C3
Kidbrooke Gr SE3 . . . .143 B4
Kidbrooke Interchange
SE3 . . . . .143 C2

Kidbrooke La SE9 . . . .144 A1
Kidbrooke Park CI
SE3 . . . . .143 B4
Kidbrooke Park Prim Sch
SE3 . . . . .143 C4
Kidbrooke Park Rd
SE12,SE3 . . . . .143 B2
Kidbrooke Sch SE3 . . .143 D3
Kidbrooke Sta SE3 . . .143 B2
Kidbrooke Way SE3 . .143 B3
Kiddens BR8 . . . . . . .191 D1
Kidderminster Pl
CR0 . . . . .204 D1
Kidderminster Rd
CR0 . . . . .205 A2
Kidderpore Ave NW3 . .69 C4
Kidderpore Gdns NW3 69 C4
Kidd Ho RM9 . . . . . . .81 B4
Kidd Pl SE7 . . . . .122 A1
Kidlington Way NW9 . . .27 C2
Kierbeck Bsns Complex
E16 . . . . .121 B4
Kiffen St EC2 . . . . . . .242 D6
Kilberry CI TW7 . . . . .130 A4
Kilbrennan Ho 5 E14 .98 A1
Kilburn Bridge 14
NW6 . . . . .91 C6
Kilburn Gate NW6 . . . .91 D5
Kilburn High Rd NW6 .91 C6
Kilburn High Road Sta
NW6 . . . . .91 C6
Kilburn Ho 13 W9 . . . .91 B4
Kilburn La W10 . . . . . .91 A5
Kilburn Park Jun Sch
NW6 . . . . .91 B5
Kilburn Park Rd NW6 .91 C4
Kilburn Park Sta NW6 91 C5
Kilburn Pl NW6 . . . . . .91 C6
Kilburn Priory NW6 . . .91 D6
Kilburn Sq NW6 . . . . .91 C6
Kilburn Sta NW2 . . . . .69 B2
Kilburn Vale NW6 . . . .91 D6
Kilburn Vale Est 13
NW6 . . . . .91 C6
Kildare CI HA4 . . . . . .40 C1
Kildare Ct W2 . . . . . . .91 C1
Kildare Gdns W2 . . . . .91 C1
Kildare Rd E16 . . . . . .99 A2
Kildare Terr W2 . . . . . .91 C1
Kildare Wlk E14 . . . . .97 C1
Kildoran Rd SW2 . . . .160 A6
Kildowan Rd IG3 . . . . .58 A1
Kilgour Rd SE23 . . . . .163 A5
Kilkie St SW6 . . . . . . .136 A3
Killarney Rd SW18 . . .158 A5
Killburns Mill CI SM6 219 B6
Killearn Rd SE6 . . . . .164 B3
Killester Gdns KT17,
KT4 . . . . .216 A4
Killick Ho SM1 . . . . . .217 D4
Killick St N1 . .94 B5 233 C3
Killieser Ave SW2 . . . .160 A2
Killigrew Ho TW16 . . .171 C3
Killip CI E16 . . . . .98 D1
Killowen Ave UB5 . . . .64 C5
Killowen Rd E9 . . . . . .74 D2
Killross Rd TW14 . . . .149 B3
Killyon Rd SW8 . . . . .137 C1
Kilmaine Rd
SW6 . . . . . . .135 A5 264 B3
Kilmarnock Gdns RM8 80 C5
Kilmarnock Rd WD19 . .22 D6
Kilmarsh Rd W6 . . . . .112 C2
Kilmartin Ave SW16 . .204 C6
Kilmartin Rd IG3 . . . . .80 A6
Kilmington Rd SW13 . .134 A6
Kilmiston Ave TW17 . .193 A3
Kilmiston Ho TW17 . . .193 A3
Kilmore Ho 17 E14 . . .97 D1
Kilmorey Gdns TW1 . .131 B1
Kilmorey Rd TW1 . . . .131 B1
Kilmorie Prim Sch
SE23 . . . . .163 A2
Kilmorie Rd SE23 . . . .163 A2
Kilmuir Ho SW1 . . . . .258 A3
Kiln CI UB3 . . . . .127 B6
Kiln Ct E14 . . . . .119 B6
Kilner Ho 3 SE11 . . . .138 C6
Kilner St E14 . . . . . . .97 C2
Kiln Mews SW17 . . . .180 B5
Kiln Pl NW5 . . . . .71 A3
Kilnside KT10 . . . . . . .213 A1
Kiloh CI 1 SW11 . . . .136 C2
Kilpatrick Ct N16 . . . . .51 D1
Kilpatrick Way UB4 . . .85 A2
Kilpeck Ho 3 N4 . . . . .51 B4
Kilravock Ho SE25 . . .205 C6
Kilravock St W10 . . . . .91 A4
Kilronan 5 W3 . . . . . .89 B1
Kilross Rd TW14 . . . . .149 C3

Kilsby Wlk RM9 . . . . .80 B2
Kilsha Rd KT12 . . . . . .194 C3
Kilvinton Dr EN2 . . . . .5 B1
Kimbell Gdns
SW6 . . . . . . .135 A4 264 A1
Kimbell Pl SE9 . . . . . .143 C1
Kimber Ctr The
SW18 . . . . .157 C4
Kimber Ho 11 SE18 . .144 D6
Kimberley Ave E6 . . . .100 A5
SE15 . . . . .140 C2
Ilford IG2 . . . . .57 C2
Kimberley Dr DA14 . .168 B2
Kimberley Gate 2
BR1 . . . . .186 D3
Kimberley Gdns N4 . . .50 D4
Enfield EN1 . . . . .5 D2
Kimberley Ho 7 E14 . .120 A4
Kimberley Ind Est E17 35 B2
Kimberley Rd E11 . . . .76 B6
E16 . . . . .98 D3
E17 . . . . .35 B2
NW6 . . . . .91 A6
SW9 . . . . .138 D1
Chingford, Chingford Green
E4 . . . . .20 C3
Edmonton N18 . . . . . .34 B4
Penge BR3 . . . . .184 D1
Thornton Heath CR0 . .204 D3
Tottenham N17 . . . . . .34 A1
Kimberley Way E4 . . . .20 C3
Kimberley Wlk KT12 . .194 B2
Kimber Rd SW18 . . . .157 D4
Kimble Cres WD23 . . . .8 A4
Kimble Ho 1 N7 . . . . .72 A3
NW8 . . . . .237 B6
Kimble Rd
Mitcham SW17 . . . . .180 D1
Upper Tooting SW17 . .180 B5
Kimbolton CI SE12 . . .164 D5
Kimbolton Row SW3 . .257 A3
Kimmeridge Gdns 3
SE9 . . . . .188 A6
Kimmeridge Rd SE9 . .188 A6
Kimm Ho 16 E17 . . . . .53 D6
Kimpton Ct 12 SE5 . .139 B4
Kimpton Ho SW15 . . .156 A4
Kimpton Link Bsns Ctr
SM3 . . . . .217 B6
Kimpton Rd SE5 . . . . .139 B4
Cheam SM3 . . . . . . .217 B6
Kimpton Trade & Bsns Ctr
SM3 . . . . .217 B6
Kinburn St SE16 . . . .118 D4
Kincaid Rd SE15 . . . .140 B5
Kincardine Gdns W9 . .91 C3
Kinch Gr HA3,HA9 . . . .44 B2
Kincraig BR7 . . . . . . .188 C2
Kindell Ho 4 SW14 . .133 D4
Kinder Ho N1 . . . . . . .235 D4
Kinder CI SE28 . . . . . .124 D6
Kinder Ho N1 . . . . . . .235 D4
Kindersley Ho 27 E1 . .96 A1
Kinder St 9 E1 . . . . . .96 B1
Kinefold Ho N7 . . . . . .72 A2
Kinetic Cres EN3 . . . . .7 B6
King Alfred Ave SE6 . .185 C2
King Alfred Sch NW11 47 D1
King Arthur CI SE15 . .140 C5
King Athelstan Prim Sch
KT1 . . . . .198 B6
King Charles Cres
KT5 . . . . .198 B2
King Charles Ho
SW6 . . . . .265 D4
King Charles' Rd KT5,
KT6 . . . . .198 B2
King Charles St
SW1 . . . . . . .116 A4 250 A2
King Charles Wlk 6
SW19 . . . . .157 A4
King Ct 15 E10 . . . . . .53 D2
Kingcup CI CR0 . . . . .206 D4
King David La E1 . . . . .118 C6
Kingdon Ho 8 E14 . . .120 A3
Kingdon Rd NW6 . . . . .69 C2
King Edward Dr KT6 . .214 A5
King Edward Mans 12
E8 . . . . .96 B6
King Edward Mews
SW13 . . . . .134 A4
King Edward Rd E10 . .54 A1
E17 . . . . .53 A6
Barnet EN5 . . . . .1 D1
King Edward's Gdns
W3 . . . . .110 C5
King Edward's Gr
TW11 . . . . .175 D4

Kilsby Wlk RM9 . . . . .80 B2
King Edwards Mans
SW6 . . . . .265 A3
King Edward's Rd E9 . .96 C6
Barking IG11 . . . . . . .101 B5
Edmonton N9 . . . . . . .18 B4
Enfield EN3 . . . . .6 D1
Ruislip HA4 . . . . .39 B1
King Edward St EC1 . .242 A2
King Edward The Third
Mews 8 SE16 . . . . .118 B4
King Edward Wlk
SE1 . . . . . . .116 C3 261 B6
King Fahd Acad The
W5 . . . . .109 C2
King Fahed Acad W3 111 D6
Kingfield Rd W5 . . . . .87 D3
Kingfield St E14 . . . . .120 A2
Kingfisher Ave E11 . . .55 B3
Kingfisher CI
Harrow HA3 . . . . .24 D3
Woolwich SE28 . . . . .124 C6
Kingfisher Ct 12 E14 . .120 A4
11 SW11 . . . . .136 C2
Cheam SM1 . . . . . . .217 B3
East Molesey KT8 . . . .196 C5
Enfield EN2 . . . . .4 B5
Hounslow TW3 . . . . . .151 D6
Merton SW19 . . . . . .179 B3
Putney SW19 . . . . . .157 A2
Kingfisher Dr TW10 . .175 B6
Kingfisher Ho SE15 . .139 D4
W14 . . . . .254 C4
Kingfisher Lo TW11 . .175 A6
Kingfisher Mews
SE13 . . . . .163 D6
Kingfisher Sports Ctr The
12 KT1 . . . . .176 A1
Kingfisher Sq 19 SE8 141 B6
Kingfisher St E6 . . . . .100 A2
Kingfisher Way NW10 .67 B3
Croydon CR0 . . . . . . .206 D4
Kingfisher Wlk NW9 . . .27 C1
King Frederick IX Ct
SE16 . . . . .119 B3
King Garth Mews
SE23 . . . . .162 C2
King Gdns CR0 . . . . . .220 D3
King George Ave E16 . .99 D1
Ilford IG2 . . . . .57 B3
Walton-on-T KT12 . . .194 D1
King George CI
TW16 . . . . .171 C5
King George Hospl
IG3 . . . . .58 A4
King George Sq
TW10 . . . . .154 B5
King George St SE10 142 A5
King George's Trad Est
KT9 . . . . .214 C4
King George VI Ave
CR4 . . . . .202 D5
Kingham CI 3 W11 . .112 D4
Wandsworth SW18 . . .158 A4
King Harolds Way
DA7 . . . . .147 A5
King Henry Mews 7
BR6 . . . . .227 D3
King Henry's Mews EN3 7 C6
King Henry's Rd NW3 .70 C1
Kingston KT1,KT3 . . .198 D6
King Henry's Reach
W6 . . . . .134 C6
King Henry St N16 . . . .73 C3
King Henry's Wlk N1 . .73 C2
King Henry's Yd 5
N16 . . . . .73 C3
King Ho W12 . . . . . . .90 B1
Kinghorn St EC1 . . . . .242 A3
King James St
SE1 . . . . . . .116 D4 251 D1
King John Ct EC2 . . . .243 B6
King John St E1 . . . . . .96 D2
King John's Wlk SE9 . .166 A5
Kinglake St
SE17 . . . . . .117 C1 263 B2
Kingly Ct W1 . . . . . . .249 B6
Kingly St W1 .115 C6 249 A6
King & Queen CI 4
SE9 . . . . .188 A4
King & Queen St
SE17 . . . . . .117 A1 262 B2
Kingsand Rd SE12 . . .165 A2
Kings Arbour UB2 . . . .107 A1
King's Arms Ct 22 E1 . .96 A2
King's Arms Yd EC2 . .242 C2
Kingsash Dr UB4 . . . . .85 A3
Kings Ave N10 . . . . . . .49 A6
SW4 . . . . .160 A5
Bromley BR1 . . . . . . .186 D4
Dagenham RM6 . . . . .59 B3

Kings Ave continued
Ealing W5 . . . . .87 D1
New Malden KT3 . . . .199 D5
Wallington SM5 . . . . .218 D1
King's Ave
Ashford TW16 . . . . . .171 D4
Buckhurst Hill IG9 . . . .21 D2
Hounslow TW3,TW5 . .129 D4
Southall UB1 . . . . . . .85 D1
Southgate N21 . . . . . .16 D3
Woodford IG8 . . . . . . .37 C5
Kings Avenue Sch
SW4 . . . . .160 A6
King's Bench St
SE1 . . . . . . .116 D4 251 D2
King's Bench Wlk
EC4 . . . . .241 B1
Kingsbridge N16 . . . . .51 B1
Kingsbridge Ave W3 . .110 B4
Kingsbridge Cres UB1 .85 B3
Kingsbridge Ct E14 . .119 C2
Edmonton N21 . . . . . .16 D2
Kingsbridge Ho 10
SE20 . . . . .184 D2
Kingsbridge Ind Est
IG11 . . . . .101 C4
Kingsbridge Rd W10 . .90 C1
Barking IG11 . . . . . . .101 B5
Southall UB2 . . . . . . .107 A2
Walton-on-T KT12 . . .194 B2
West Barnes SM4 . . . .200 D2
Kingsbridge Way UB4 .83 C4
Kingsbury Green Prim Sch
NW9 . . . . .44 A5
Kingsbury High Sch
Annexe NW9 . . . . . .44 D5
Kingsbury Rd N1 . . . . .73 C2
NW9 . . . . .44 D4
Kingsbury Sta NW9 . . .44 C4
Kingsbury Terr N1 . . . .73 C2
Kingsbury Trad Est
NW9 . . . . .45 B3
Kings Chace View EN2 .4 C3
Kings Chase KT8 . . . .196 A6
Kings CI NW4 . . . . . . .46 D5
King's CI E10 . . . . .53 D2
Kings CI KT12 . . . . . . .194 B1
King's CI KT7 . . . . . . .197 A2
Kingsclere CI SW15 . .156 A4
Kingsclere Ct N12 . . . .30 C5
New Barnet EN5 . . . . .14 A6
Kingsclere Pl EN2 . . . .5 A3
Kingscliffe Gdns
SW19 . . . . .157 B3
King's Coll SE24 . . . . .161 B5
WC2 . . . . . . .116 B6 250 D6
Kings College Ct NW3 70 C1
King's College Hospl
SE5 . . . . .139 B3
King's College London
NW3 . . . . .69 C4
Kings College Rd NW3 70 B1
Ruislip HA4 . . . . .39 D3
Kings Coll London
W8 . . . . .245 A2
Kings Coll London
(Chelsea Campus)
SW3 . . . . . . .114 C1 257 A1
King's Coll Sch SW19 178 D4
Kingscote NW11 . . . . .47 B1
Kingscote Rd W4 . . . .111 B3
Croydon CR0 . . . . . . .206 B2
Kingston KT3 . . . . . . .199 B3
Kingscote St EC4 . . . .251 C6
King's Court N SW3 . .257 A1
Kingscourt Rd SW16 . .160 A1
King's Court S SW3 . .257 A1
King's Cres N4,N5 . . . .73 A5
Kingscroft SW4 . . . . .160 A5
Kingscroft Rd NW2 . . .69 B2
King's Cross
WC1 . . . . . . .94 A4 233 B2
King's Cross Bridge
WC1 . . . . .233 B2
King's Cross Rd
WC1 . . . . . . .94 B4 233 D1
King's Cross Sta
N1 . . . . .94 A5 233 B3
King's Cross, St Pancras
N1 . . . . .233 A2
King's Cross (Thames Link)
Sta WC1 . . . . .233 B3
Kings Ct E13 . . . . .99 C6
HA9 . . . . .66 D6
6 N7 . . . . .72 B1
NW8 . . . . .230 D1
SE22 . . . . .140 A1

Kings Ct *continued*
W6 ... 112 A2
2 Buckhurst Hill IG9 ... 21 D2
16 Kingston KT2 ... 176 C3
10 Putney SW15 ... 156 A4
3 Wallington SM6 ... 219 B2
King's Ct
Beckenham BR3 ... 207 D6
9 Ealing W5 ... 87 C2
Wimbledon SW19 ... 179 C4
Kingsdale Gdns W11 112 D5
Kingsdale Rd SE18 ... 145 D6
Penge SE20 ... 184 D3
Kingsdale Sec Sch
SE21 ... 161 C1
Kingsdown 1 SW19 ... 178 D3
Kingsdown Ave W13 ... 109 B4
W3 ... 111 C6
Kingsdown Cl
26 SE16 ... 118 B1
W10 ... 90 D1
11 W11 ... 91 A1
Kingsdown Ct SW11 ... 158 C5
Kingsdowne Rd KT6 ... 198 B2
Kingsdown Ho 1 E8 ... 74 A3
Kingsdown Rd E11 ... 76 C5
3 N19 ... 72 A6
Cheam SM3 ... 217 A3
Kingsdown Way BR2 ... 209 A3
Kings Dr HA9 ... 66 D6
Edgware HA8 ... 26 B6
Surbiton KT5 ... 198 C3
King's Dr KT7 ... 197 B2
Kingsend HA4 ... 39 C1
Kings Farm E17 ... 35 D2
Kings Farm Ave
TW10 ... 132 C1
Kingsfield Ave HA1,
HA2 ... 42 A4
Kingsfield Ho 18 N16 ... 73 C5
SE9 ... 165 D1
Kingsfield Rd HA1 ... 42 B2
Kingsford Com Sch
E13 ... 99 C3
Newham E6 ... 100 B1
Kingsford St NW5 ... 70 D3
Kingsford Way E6 ... 100 B2
Kingsgate HA9 ... 67 A5
Kingsgate Ave N3 ... 47 C6
Kingsgate Bsns Ctr
KT2 ... 176 A2
Kingsgate Cl BR5 ... 190 C1
DA7 ... 147 A4
Kingsgate Est N1 ... 73 C2
Kingsgate Ho 29
SW9 ... 138 C4
Kingsgate Pl NW6 ... 69 C1
Kingsgate Prim Sch
NW6 ... 69 C1
Kingsgate Rd NW6 ... 69 C1
Kingston KT2 ... 176 A2
King's Gdns 6 NW6 ... 69 C1
Kings Gdns IG1 ... 57 B1
King's Gr SE15 ... 140 B4
SE15 ... 140 B5
Kings Grange HA4 ... 39 D1
Kingsground SE9 ... 166 A5
Kings Hall Mews
SE13 ... 142 A2
Kings Hall Rd BR3 ... 185 A2
Kings Head Hill E4 ... 19 D4
King's Head Yd SE1 ... 252 C3
King's Highway SE18,
SE2 ... 145 D6
Kingshill SE17 ... 262 B4
Kingshill Ave
Harrow HA3 ... 43 B5
Hayes UB4 ... 83 D4
New Malden KT4 ... 200 B2
Northolt UB5 ... 84 B4
Kingshill Ct 6 EN5 ... 1 A1
Kingshill Dr HA3 ... 43 B6
Kings Ho 19 E14 ... 119 B6
SW8 ... 270 B4
Kingshold Rd E9 ... 74 C1
Kingsholm Gdns SE9 144 A1
King's House Jun Sch
TW10 ... 154 B6
King's House Prep Sch
TW10 ... 154 B6
Kingshurst Rd SE12 ... 165 A4
Kings Keep KT6 ... 198 A5
King's Keep 6 SW15 156 D6
King's La SM1,SM2 ... 218 B3
Kingsland
NW8 ... 92 C6 230 B5
Kingsland Gn 1 E8,N1 73 C2
Kingsland High St E8 ... 73 D3
Kingsland Pas 2 E8 ... 73 C2
Kingsland Rd E13 ... 99 C4
E2 ... 95 C5
Kingsland Sch E8 ... 73 D3
Kingsland Sh Ctr E8 ... 73 D2
Kingslawn Cl SW15 ... 156 B6
Kingslee Ct 12 SM2 ... 217 D1
Kingsleigh Pl CR4 ... 202 D6
Kingsleigh Wlk BR2 ... 208 D5
Kingsley Ave
Ealing W13 ... 87 A1
Hounslow TW3 ... 130 A3
Southall UB1 ... 107 C6
Sutton SM1 ... 218 B4
Kingsley Cl N2 ... 48 A4
Dagenham RM10 ... 81 D4
Kingsley Ct E11 ... 54 D3
NW2 ... 68 B2
1 SE28 ... 124 C5
Bexley DA6 ... 147 C1
Edgware HA8 ... 10 D2
Wood Green N22 ... 32 B3
2 Worcester Park
KT4 ... 215 D6
Kingsley Dr 1 KT4 ... 215 D6
Kingsley Flats SE1 ... 263 B3
Kingsley Gdns E4 ... 35 C5
Kingsley Grange 1
E11 ... 55 A4
Kingsley Ho NW11 ... 48 A3
SW3 ... 266 D5
3 SW4 ... 137 D3
8 Kingston KT6 ... 198 A4
Kingsley Mews BR7 ... 188 D4
W8 ... 255 D5
Dagenham RM9 ... 80 D4
Kingsley Pl N6 ... 49 A2
Kingsley Prim Sch
CR9 ... 204 C1
Kingsley Rd E7 ... 77 A1
NW6 ... 91 B6
Chingford E17 ... 36 A1
Edmonton N13 ... 32 D6
Harrow HA2 ... 64 A5
Hounslow TW3 ... 130 A3
Orpington BR6 ... 227 D1
Pinner HA5 ... 41 B5
Thornton Heath CR0 ... 204 C1
Wimbledon SW19 ... 179 D5
Kingsley St SW11 ... 136 D2
Kingsley Way N2 ... 48 A4
Kingsley Wood Dr
SE9 ... 166 B1
Kings Lo HA4 ... 39 C1
Kingslyn Cres SE19 ... 183 C2
Kings Mall W6 ... 112 C2
Kingsman Par SE18 ... 122 B3
King's Mans SW3 ... 267 A5
Kingsman St SE18 ... 122 B2
Kingsmead Barnet EN5 ... 1 C1
Richmond TW10 ... 154 B5
Kingsmead Ave NW9 ... 45 B2
Edmonton N9 ... 18 B3
Mitcham CR4 ... 203 C6
North Cheam KT4 ... 216 B5
Sunbury TW16 ... 172 C1
Tolworth KT6 ... 214 C6
Kingsmead Cl DA15 ... 168 A2
Teddington TW11 ... 175 B4
West Ewell KT19 ... 215 B1
Kingsmead Ct N6 ... 49 D2
Bromley BR1 ... 186 D3
Kingsmead Dr UB5 ... 63 B1
Kingsmead Ho E9 ... 75 A4
Kingsmead Lo
9 Chingford E4 ... 20 A2
Sutton SM2 ... 218 B2
Kings Mead Pk KT10 ... 212 C1
Kingsmead Prim Sch
E9 ... 75 A4
Kingsmead Rd SW2 ... 160 C2
Kingsmead Sch EN1 ... 6 A2
Kingsmead Way E5,E9 75 A4
Kingsmere BR7 ... 188 A2
Catford SE6 ... 163 D3
Kingsmere Cl SW15 ... 134 D2
Kingsmere Ct NW9 ... 44 D1
Kingsmere Pk NW9 ... 45 A1
Kingsmere Pl N16 ... 51 B1
Kingsmere Rd SW19 ... 156 D2
King's Mews 1 SW4 ... 160 A6
WC1 ... 94 B3 240 D5
Kingsmill NW8 92 B5 229 D4
Kingsmill Bsns Pk
KT1 ... 198 B6
Kingsmill Gdns RM9 ... 81 B3
Kingsmill Rd RM9 ... 81 B3
Kingsmill Terr
NW8 ... 92 B5 229 D4
Kingsnorth Ho 12
W10 ... 90 D1
Kingsnympton Pk
KT2 ... 176 D4
Kings Oak RM7 ... 59 C6
Kings Oak Hospl (Private)
The EN2 ... 4 C5
King's Orch SE9 ... 166 A5
King's Paddock
TW12 ... 174 A2
King's Par W12 ... 112 A3
Willesden NW10 ... 90 C6
Kingspark Ct E18 ... 55 A6
King's Pas KT2 ... 175 D2
King's Pl SE1 ... 252 A1
Kings Pl Acton W4 ... 111 A2
Buckhurst Hill IG9 ... 21 D2
Loughton IG10 ... 21 D4
King Sq EC1 ... 95 A4 235 A1
King's Quay SW10 ... 266 B2
Kings Rd BR6 ... 227 D4
NW10 ... 68 B1
King's Rd E11 ... 54 C2
E6 ... 99 C6
SW10 ... 136 B6 266 C5
SW3 ... 257 B1
Kings Rd Ealing W5 ... 87 D2
Feltham TW13 ... 150 C3
Harrow HA2 ... 63 B6
Mitcham CR4 ... 203 A6
Richmond TW10,TW9 ... 154 B6
Walton-on-T KT12 ... 194 B1
West Drayton UB7 ... 104 B4
Wood Green N22 ... 32 B2
King's Rd Barking IG11 ... 79 A1
Chingford E4 ... 20 B3
Edmonton N18 ... 34 A6
Kingston KT2 ... 176 B3
Long Ditton KT6 ... 197 C1
Mortlake SW14 ... 133 B2
South Norwood SE25 ... 206 A6
Teddington TW11,
TW12 ... 174 B5
Tottenham N17 ... 33 D2
Twickenham TW1 ... 153 B5
Wimbledon SW19 ... 179 C4
Kings Ride Gate
TW10 ... 132 C1
Kingsridge SW19 ... 157 A2
Kings Road Bglws
HA2 ... 63 B5
King's Scholars' Pas
SW1 ... 259 A4
King St E13 ... 98 D3
E13 ... 99 A3
EC2 ... 95 A1 242 B1
N2 ... 48 B6
SW1 ... 115 C5 249 B4
W3 ... 111 A5
W6 ... 112 A2
WC2 ... 250 A6
Richmond TW9 ... 153 D6
Southall UB2 ... 107 A3
Tottenham N17 ... 33 D2
Twickenham TW1 ... 153 A3
King Stairs Cl SE16 ... 118 B4
King's Terr
NW1 ... 93 C6 232 A5
8 Isleworth TW7 ... 131 A2
Kingsthorpe Rd SE26 184 D6
Kingston Ave
Cheam SM3 ... 217 A5
Feltham TW14 ... 149 D5
Yiewsley UB7 ... 104 B6
Kingston Bsns Ctr
KT9 ... 214 B5
Kingston By-Pass
KT6,KT7,KT9 ... 213 C5
Kingston By - Pass
KT6 ... 214 C5
Kingston Cl
Dagenham RM6 ... 59 A6
Northolt UB5 ... 85 B6
Teddington TW11 ... 175 B4
Kingston Coll of F Ed
KT1 ... 197 D6
Kingston Coll of F Ed (M V
Annex) KT2 ... 176 A2
Kingston Cres BR3 ... 185 B2
Kingston Gdns CR0 ... 220 A5
Kingston Gram Sch
KT2 ... 176 B1
Kingston Hall Rd
KT1 ... 197 D6
Kingston Hill KT2 ... 177 A5
Kingston Hill Ave RM6 59 A6
Kingston Hill Pl KT2,
TW10 ... 177 A6
Kingston Ho 2 NW6 ... 69 A1
Kingston Ho E SW7 ... 247 A1
Kingston Ho N SW7 ... 247 A1
Kingston Ho S SW7 ... 247 A1
Kingston Hospl KT2 ... 176 D2
Kingston House Estate
KT6 ... 197 B3
Kingston La
Teddington TW11 ... 175 B4
Uxbridge UB8 ... 82 A4
West Drayton UB7 ... 104 B4
Kingston Lo 2 KT3 ... 199 C5
Kingston Mus KT1 ... 176 A1
Kingston Pl HA3 ... 24 D3
Kingston Rd
SW15,SW19 ... 156 B3
Ashford TW15 ... 170 A4
Ashford TW15,TW17 ... 170 B4
Edmonton N9 ... 18 A2
Ilford IG1 ... 79 A4
Kingston KT1,KT3 ... 199 A5
Merton SW19,SW20 ... 179 B1
New Barnet EN4 ... 14 B6
Southall UB2 ... 107 B4
Teddington TW11 ... 175 B4
Ewell KT17 ... 215 D1
Kingston Sq SE19 ... 183 B5
Kingston Sta KT2 ... 176 A2
Kingston Univ
Kingston KT1 ... 198 A6
Kingston KT2 ... 177 B5
Kingston Univ Annex
KT1 ... 176 B1
Kingston Univ
Roehampton Vale Ctr
SW15 ... 155 D1
Kingston Vale SW15 ... 155 C1
Kingstown St
NW1 ... 93 A6 231 A6
King Street Cloisters 8
W6 ... 112 B2
King Street Coll W12 112 C4
W6 ... 112 C2
King Street Par 6
TW1 ... 153 A3
Kings View Ct 1
SW20 ... 178 D3
Kingswater Pl SW11 ... 267 A3
Kingsway BR5 ... 211 B4
N12 ... 30 A4
WC2 ... 94 B1 240 C2
Coney Hall BR4 ... 224 D5
Enfield EN3 ... 18 B6
Hayes UB3 ... 83 A2
Mortlake SW14,TW9 ... 132 D2
Stanwell TW19 ... 148 A3
Wembley HA9 ... 66 A4
West Barnes KT3 ... 200 C4
Woodford IG8 ... 37 C5
Kings Way
Croydon CR0 ... 220 B3
Harrow HA1 ... 42 C5
Kingsway Bsns Pk
TW12 ... 173 B2
Kingsway Coll NW5 ... 71 B2
Kingsway Cres HA2 ... 42 A5
Kingsway Est N18 ... 34 D4
Kingsway Pl EC1 ... 241 C6
Kingsway Rd SM3 ... 217 A1
Kingswear Ho 5
SE23 ... 162 C2
Kingswear Rd NW5 ... 71 B5
Ruislip HA4 ... 62 A6
Kingswood 32 E2 ... 96 C5
Kingswood Ave DA17 125 B2
NW6 ... 91 A5
Beckenham BR2,BR3 ... 208 C5
Hampton TW12 ... 173 D4
Hounslow TW3,TW5 ... 129 B3
Thornton Heath CR7 ... 204 C4
Kingswood Cl BR6 ... 211 B2
N20 ... 14 A4
SW8 ... 270 B3
Enfield EN1 ... 17 D6
New Malden KT3 ... 199 D3
Surbiton KT6 ... 198 A2
Kings Wood Ct 4
NW6 ... 69 C1
Kingswood Ct
Chingford E4 ... 35 C5
7 Richmond TW10 ... 154 B6
Kingswood Dr
Carshalton SM5 ... 202 D1
Dulwich SE19,SE21 ... 183 D6
Kingswood Ho 3
KT2 ... 176 D4
Kingswood Pk N3 ... 29 B1
Kingswood Pl SE13 ... 142 C1
Kingswood Prim Sch
SE27 ... 183 B5
Kingswood Rd E11 ... 54 C2
W4 ... 111 A3
Kingswood Rd *continued*
Beckenham BR2 ... 208 C6
Ilford IG3 ... 58 A2
Merton SW19 ... 179 B2
Penge SE20 ... 184 C4
Streatham SW2 ... 160 A4
Kingswood Terr W4 ... 111 A3
Kingswood Way SM6 220 A3
Kingsworth Cl BR3 ... 207 A4
Kingsworthy Cl KT1 ... 198 B6
Kings Yd E15 ... 75 C2
Kingthorpe Rd NW10 ... 67 B1
Kingthorpe Terr 1
NW10 ... 67 B1
Kington Ho 16 NW6 ... 91 D6
Kingward Ho E1 ... 96 A2
Kingwell Rd EN4 ... 2 B5
King William IV Gdns
SE20 ... 184 C4
King William La 3
SE10 ... 120 C1
King William St
EC4 ... 117 B6 252 D6
King William Wlk
SE10 ... 142 A6
Kingwood Rd
SW6 ... 135 A5 264 A3
Kinlet Rd SE18 ... 145 A4
Kinloch Dr NW9 ... 45 C2
Kinloch St N7 ... 72 B5
Kinloss Ct NW3 ... 47 B5
Kinloss Gdns NW3 ... 47 B5
Kinloss Rd SM5 ... 202 A2
Kinnaird Ave
Bromley BR1 ... 186 D4
Chiswick W4 ... 133 A5
Kinnaird Cl BR1 ... 186 D4
Kinnear Ct 2 SW20 ... 178 D2
Kinnear Rd W12 ... 111 D4
Kinnerton Pl N SW1 ... 247 D1
Kinnerton Pl S SW1 ... 247 D1
Kinnerton St
SW1 ... 115 A4 248 A1
Kinnerton Yd SW1 ... 248 A1
Kinnoull Mans 10 E5 ... 74 B4
Kinnoul Rd
W6 ... 135 A6 264 A6
Kinross Ave KT4 ... 216 A6
Kinross Cl
Ashford TW16 ... 171 D5
Harrow HA3 ... 44 B4
Kinross Ct 1 SE6 ... 164 D2
Kinross Dr TW16 ... 171 D5
Kinross Ho N1 ... 233 C6
Kinross Terr E17 ... 35 B1
Kinsale Rd SE15 ... 140 A2
Kinsella Gdns SW19 ... 178 B5
Kinsey Ho SE21 ... 183 C6
Kinsham Ho 4 E2 ... 96 A3
Kintore Way SE1 ... 263 C4
Kintyre Cl SW16 ... 204 B6
Kintyre Ct 17 SW2 ... 160 A4
Kinveachy Gdns SE7 ... 122 A1
Kinver Ho N4 ... 51 B2
Kinver Rd SE26 ... 184 C6
Kipling Ct W7 ... 108 D6
Kipling Dr SW17 ... 180 B4
Kipling Ho 29 SE5 ... 139 A5
Kipling Pl HA7 ... 24 D4
Kipling Rd DA7 ... 147 A4
Kipling St
SE1 ... 117 B4 252 D2
Kipling Terr N9 ... 17 B2
Kipling Twr 3 W3 ... 111 A3
Kippington Dr SE9 ... 165 D3
Kirby Cl KT19 ... 215 D3
Kirby Est SE16 ... 118 B3
Kirby Gr SE1 ... 117 C4 253 A2
Kirby St EC1 ... 94 C2 241 B4
Kirby Way KT12 ... 194 C3
Kirchen Rd W13 ... 109 B6
Kirkby Cl N11 ... 31 A4
Kirkdale SE26 ... 162 B1
Kirkdale Rd E11 ... 54 C2
Kirkeby Bldg EC1 ... 241 A4
Kirkfield Cl W13 ... 109 B5
Kirkham Rd E6 ... 100 A1
Kirkham St SE18 ... 145 C6
Kirk La SE18 ... 145 A6
Kirkland Cl DA15 ... 167 C5
Kirkland Dr EN2 ... 5 A4
Kirkland Wlk 4 E8 ... 73 D2
Kirkleas Rd KT6 ... 198 A1
Kirklees Rd
Dagenham RM8 ... 80 C3
Thornton Heath CR7 ... 204 C4
Kirkley Ho N16 ... 51 C1
Kirkley Rd SW19 ... 179 C2
Kirkman Pl W1 ... 239 C3
Kirkmichael Rd E14 ... 98 A1
Kirk Rd E17 ... 53 B3
Kirk Rise SM1 ... 217 D5
Kirkside Rd SE3 ... 143 A6
Kirk's Pl E3 ... 97 B2
Kirkstall Ave N17 ... 51 B5
Kirkstall Gdns SW2 ... 160 A3
Kirkstall Ho SW1 ... 258 C2
Kirkstall Rd SW2 ... 160 A3
Kirkstead Ct E5 ... 75 A4
Kirksted Rd SM4 ... 201 D1
Kirkstone NW1 ... 232 A2
Kirkstone Way BR1 ... 186 C3
Kirkton Lo SW18 ... 157 D5
Kirkton Rd N15 ... 51 C5
Kirkwall Pl E2 ... 96 C4
Kirkwood Rd SE15 ... 140 B3
Kirn Rd W13 ... 109 B6
Kirrane Cl KT3 ... 199 D4
Kirtley Ho SW8 ... 269 B2
Kirtley Rd SE26 ... 185 A6
Kirtling St
SW8 ... 137 C5 269 A4
Kirton Cl W4 ... 111 B2
Kirton Rd E13 ... 99 C5
Kirton Wlk HA8 ... 27 A3
Kirwin Way SE5 ... 138 D5
Kisharon Day Sch
NW11 ... 47 B3
Kitcat Terr E3 ... 97 C4
Kitchener Rd E7 ... 77 B2
N17 ... 51 C6
N2 ... 48 C6
Chingford, Highams Park
E17 ... 35 D2
Dagenham RM10 ... 81 D2
South Norwood CR7 ... 205 B6
Kite Ho 5 SW11 ... 136 C2
Kitley Gdns SE19 ... 183 D2
Kitson Rd SE5 ... 139 A5
Barnes SW13 ... 134 A4
Kittiwake Ct 26 SE8 ... 141 B6
Kittiwake Pl SM1 ... 217 B3
Kittiwake Rd UB5 ... 84 D4
Kittiwake Way UB4 ... 84 D2
Kitto Rd SE14 ... 140 D3
Kitt's End Rd EN5 ... 1 A6
Kiver Rd N19 ... 72 A6
Klea Ave SW4 ... 159 C5
Kleffens Ct 2 SE3 ... 142 D5
Knaggs Ho 1 TW11 ... 174 C5
Knapdale Cl SE23 ... 162 B2
Knapmill Rd SE6 ... 163 D2
Knapmill Way SE6 ... 163 D2
Knapp Cl NW10 ... 67 C2
Knapp Rd
Ashford TW15 ... 170 B6
Bow E3 ... 97 C3
Knapton Mews SW17 181 A4
Knaresborough Dr
SW18 ... 157 D3
Knaresborough Ho 4
N4 ... 51 A2
Knaresborough Pl
SW5 ... 113 D2 255 C4
Knatchbull Rd NW10 ... 89 B6
SE5 ... 138 D4
Knebworth Ave E17 ... 35 C2
Knebworth Ho 2 N16 73 C4
SW8 ... 269 D1
Chingford E17 ... 35 C2
Knebworth Rd 3 N16 73 C4
Knee Hill SE2 ... 124 C1
Knee Hill Cres SE2 ... 124 C2
Kneller Gdns TW7 ... 152 B5
Kneller Ho 9 SW8 ... 137 D3
4 Northolt UB5 ... 84 D5
Kneller Rd SE4 ... 141 A1
Isleworth TW2 ... 152 B5
New Malden KT3 ... 199 C2
Knight Cl RM8 ... 80 C6
Knight Ct N15 ... 51 C4
1 Chingford E4 ... 20 A3
Knighten St E1 ... 118 B5
Knighthead Point
E14 ... 119 C4
Knight Ho SE17 ... 263 A3
Knightland Ho E5 ... 74 B6
Knightland Rd E5 ... 74 B6
Knightleas Ct NW2 ... 68 C2
Knighton Cl
Croydon CR2 ... 220 D1
Woodford IG8 ... 37 B6
Knighton Dr IG8 ... 37 B6
Knighton Gn IG9 ... 21 B2
Knighton La IG9 ... 21 B2
Knighton Park Rd
SE26 ... 184 D5
Knighton Rd E7 ... 77 A4
Knightrider Ct EC4 ... 252 A6
Knightrider St EC4 ... 251 D6

Knights Arc SW1 ....247 C1
Knight's Ave W5 .....110 A4
Knightsbridge
SW1,SW7 ....114 D4 247 C1
Knightsbridge Ct
SW1 ....247 D1
Knightsbridge Gn
SW1 ....247 C1
Knightsbridge Mews
BR7 ....188 B3
Knights Cl E9 ....74 C3
Knights Ct Bushey WD23 .8 B3
Kingston KT1 ....198 A6
Penge BR3 ....185 A2
Knightshayes Ho NW4 28 D1
Knight's Hill SE19,
SE27 ....182 D6
Knight's Hill Sq SE27 182 D6
Knights Ho SE1 .....253 C2
SW5 ....254 C2
SW8 ....270 B3
Knight's Ho SW10 ...266 A4
Knight's La N9 ....18 A1
Knight's Pk KT1 .....198 A6
Knight's Pl TW2 .....152 C3
Knights Rd
Newham E16 ....121 A4
Stanmore HA7 ....25 C6
Knight's Wlk SE11 ..261 C3
Knightswood Cl HA8 ..11 A2
Knightswood Ct N6 ...49 D2
Knightswood Ho N12 .30 A4
Knightwood Cres
KT3 ....199 C3
Knivet Rd SW6 ......265 A5
Knobs Hill Rd E15 ....97 D6
Knockholt Rd SE9 ..165 D6
Knole Cl CR0 ....206 C3
Knole Ct UB5 ....84 C4
Knole Gate DA15 ....167 C1
Knole The SE9 ....188 C6
Knoll Ct BR6 ....227 D6
Dulwich SE19 ....183 D5
Knoll Dr N14 ....15 A4
Knoll Ho NW8 ....229 A4
Knollmead KT4,KT5 ..199 A1
Knollmead Prim Sch
KT5 ....215 A6
Knoll Rd DA5 ....169 C5
SW18 ....158 A6
Sidcup DA14 ....190 B6
Knoll Rise BR6 ......211 D1
Knolls Cl KT4 ....216 B5
Knoll The
Beckenham BR3 ......185 D2
Ealing W13 ....87 C2
Hayes BR2 ....209 A1
Knolly's Cl SE27,SW16 160 C1
Knolly's Rd SE27,
SW16 ....160 C1
Knot Ho SE1 ....253 C3
Knottisford St E2 .....96 C4
Knotts Green Mews
E10 ....54 A3
Knotts Green Rd E10 .54 A3
Knowlden Ho 4 E1 ..118 C6
Knowle Ave DA7 .....147 B5
Knowle Cl SW9 ......138 C2
Knowle Lo BR7 ....188 B4
Knowle Rd BR2 ......226 A6
Twickenham TW2 .....152 C3
Knowles Cl UB7 .....104 A5
Knowles Ct 7 HA1 ...42 D3
Knowles Hill Cres
SE13 ....164 B6
Knowles Ho NW10 ....90 A6
Wandsworth SW18 ...157 D5
Knowles Wlk SW4 ...137 C2
Knowl Pk WD6 ....10 A6
Knowlton Gn 1 BR2 208 D4
Knowlton Ho 32 SW9 138 C4
Knowl Way WD6 ......10 B6
Knowsley Ave UB1 ...107 D5
Knowsley Rd SW11 ..136 D3
Knox Ct 16 SW4 .....138 A3
Knox Ho SW15 ....134 C3
Knox Rd E7 ....77 A2
Knox St W1 ...92 D2 237 C4
Knoyle Ho W14 .....254 B5
Knoyle St SE14 .....141 A6
Kobi Nazrul Prim Sch
E1 ....96 A1
Koblenz Ho N8 ....50 A6
Kohat Rd SW19 ......179 D5
Korda Cl TW17 ......192 B6
Kossuth St SE10 ....120 C1
Kotree Way 16 SE1 ..118 A2
Kramer Mews SW5 ..255 C1
Kreedman Wlk 8 E8 .74 A3
Kreisel Wlk TW9 ....132 B6
Kuala Gdns SW16 ....182 B2
Kubrick Bsns Est E7 ..77 B4
Kuhn Way E7 ....77 A3
Kwesi Johnson Ct 4
N22 ....32 C1
Kydbrook Cl BR5 ....211 A2
Kylemore Cl 3 E6 ....99 D5
Kylemore Ct 4 W12 .112 A4
Kylemore Rd NW6 ....69 C1
Kylestrome Ho SW1 .258 B3
Kymberley Rd HA1 ....42 C3
Kynance Gdns HA7 ...25 C2
Kynance Mews
SW7 ....113 D3 255 D5
Kynance Pl SW7 .....256 A5
Kynaston Ave CR7 ...205 A4
Kynaston Cl HA3 ......24 B3
Kynaston Cres CR7 ..205 A4
Kynaston Ho 7 SW2 160 B3
Kynaston Rd BR1 ....187 A5
N16 ....73 C5
Enfield EN2 ....5 B4
Thornton Heath CR7 ..205 A4
Kynaston Wood HA3 ..24 B3
Kynersley Cl SM5 ....218 D5
Kynoch Rd N18 ....34 D6
Kyrle Rd SW11 ......159 A5
Kyverdale Rd N16 ....51 D1

L

Laburnam Ct 12
SW16 ....182 C5
Laburnam Cl 5
SE15 ....140 C5
Laburnham Ct NW2 ...69 B6
Laburnham Ho SE4 ..141 B3
Laburnham Pl SE9 ...166 C6
Laburnum Ave
Carshalton SM1 ......218 C5
Edmonton N9 ....17 D2
Tottenham N17 ....33 B3
Yiewsley UB7 ....104 B6
Laburnum Cl E4 ......35 B4
N11 ....31 A4
Laburnum Cres
TW16 ....172 B2
Laburnum Ct 26 E2 ....95 D6
Harrow HA1 ....41 D3
5 Mitcham CR4 ......181 A1
Stanmore HA7 ....25 C6
Laburnum Gdns
Croydon CR0 ....206 D1
Edmonton N21 ....17 A2
Laburnum Gr NW9 ....45 A2
Edmonton N21 ....17 A2
Hounslow TW3 ....129 B1
Kingston KT3 ....177 B1
Ruislip HA4 ....39 B3
Southall UB1 ....85 B3
Laburnum Ho 6 N16 .73 B6
Dagenham RM10 ......81 C6
Laburnum JMI Sch E2 95 D6
Laburnum Lo N3 ......29 B1
Laburnum Rd
Hayes UB3 ....105 D2
Merton SW19 ....180 A3
Mitcham CR4 ....181 A1
Laburnum St E2 ......95 D6
Laburnums The E6 ..100 A3
Laburnum Way BR2 .210 D2
Stanwell TW19 ....148 B3
Lacebark Cl DA15 ...167 D4
Lacey Cl N9 ....18 A2
Lacey Dr
Dagenham RM8 ....80 C5
Edgware HA8 ....26 B6
Hampton TW12 ......173 B2
Lacey Ho 6 SE13 ...142 A3
Lacey Wlk E3 ....97 C5
Lacine Ct 12 SE16 ...118 D4
Lackington St EC2 ...242 D4
Lackland Ho SE1 ....263 D2
Lacland Ho SW10 ...266 C4
Lacock Cl SW19 .....180 A4
Lacock Ct 3 W13 ...109 A5
Lacon Rd SE22 ......140 A1
Lacrosse Way SW16 .181 D2
Lacy Rd SW15 ....134 D1
Ladas Rd SE27 ......183 A5
Ladbroke Cres W11 ...91 A1
Ladbroke Gdns
W11 ....113 B6 244 C6
Ladbroke Gr W10 .....91 A2
W11 ....113 B6 244 C6
Ladbroke Grove Ho
W11 ....244 C6
Ladbroke Grove Sta
W10 ....91 A1
Ladbroke Mews W11 244 B3
Ladbroke Rd
W11 ....113 B5 244 C4
Enfield EN1 ....17 D5
Ladbroke Sq
W11 ....113 B6 244 D5
Ladbroke Terr
W11 ....113 B5 244 D4
Ladbroke Wlk
W11 ....113 B5 244 D4
Ladbrook Cl HA5 .....41 B4
Ladbrooke Cres
DA14 ....168 D1
Ladbrook Rd SE25 ..205 B5
Ladderstile Ride KT2,
TW10 ....176 D5
Ladderswood Way
N11 ....31 C5
Ladlands SE22 ......162 A4
Lady Aylesford Ave
HA7 ....25 B5
Lady Bankes Jun & Inf
Schs HA4 ....62 A6
Lady Booth Rd 7
KT1 ....176 A1
Ladybower Ct 6 E5 ..74 D4
Ladycroft Gdns 6
BR6 ....227 A3
Ladycroft Rd SE13 ..141 D2
Ladycroft Way BR6 ..227 A3
Ladycroft Wlk HA7 ...25 D1
Lady Eleanor Holles Sch
The (Jun Girls)
TW12 ....173 D5
Lady Eleanor Holles Sch
The (Senior Girls)
TW12 ....173 D5
Lady Elizabeth Ho
SW14 ....133 A2
Lady Florence Ctyd 14
SE8 ....141 C5
Ladygate La HA4 .....39 A3
Lady Hay KT4 ....215 D6
Lady Margaret Prim Sch
UB1 ....85 B2
Lady Margaret Rd
NW5 ....71 C3
Southall UB1 ....85 B2
Lady Margaret Sch
SW6 ....135 C4 265 A1
Lady Shaw Ct N13 ....16 B1
Ladysmith Ave E6 ...100 A5
Ilford IG2 ....57 C2
Ladysmith Cl NW7 ....28 A3
Ladysmith Rd E16 ....98 D4
SE9 ....166 C5
Edmonton N18 ....34 B5
Enfield EN1 ....5 D3
Harrow HA3 ....24 C1
Tottenham N17 ....34 A1
Lady Somerset Rd
NW5 ....71 B4
Ladywell Cl SE4 .....141 C1
Ladywell Ho 7 BR5 .190 B1
Ladywell Hts SE4 ...163 B5
Ladywell Rd SE13 ...163 D6
Ladywell St 4 E15 ...98 D6
Ladywell Sta SE13 ..163 D6
Ladywell Water Twr
SE4 ....163 C6
Ladywood Ave BR5 ..211 C4
Ladywood Rd KT6 ...214 C6
Lafitte Ho 22 N19 ....49 D2
Lafone Ave TW13 ....150 C2
Lafone Ho 11 SW2 ...160 A4
Lafone St
SE1 ....117 D4 253 C2
Lagado Mews SE16 ..118 D5
Lagonda Ho 11 E3 ....97 C3
Lagonier Ho EC1 ....235 B1
Laidlaw Dr N21 ....16 B6
Laindon Ho 6 N16 ....51 D1
Laing Dean UB5 ......84 C6
Laing Ho SE5 ....139 A5
Laings Ave CR4 .....180 D1
Laings Cnr CR4 .....180 D2
Lainlock Pl TW3 .....129 D4
Lainson St SW18 ....157 C4
Lairdale Cl SE21 ....161 A4
Laird Ho SE5 ....139 A5
Lairs Cl N7 ....72 A2
Laitwood Rd SW12 ..159 B3
Lakanal 14 SE5 .....139 C4
Lake Ave BR1 ....187 A4
Lake Bsns Ctr N17 ...34 A3
Lake Cl Dagenham RM8 .80 D5
6 Wimbledon SW19 ..179 B5
Lakedale Rd SE18 ...123 C1
Lake Dr WD23 ....8 B2
Lakefield Cl SE20 ...184 B3
Lakefield Rd N22 .....32 D1
Lake Gdns
Dagenham RM10 ......81 C3
Hackbridge SM6 .....219 B5
Richmond TW10 .....153 B2
Lakehall Gdns CR7 ..204 D4
Lakehall Rd CR7 ....204 D4
Lake Ho SE1 ....252 A1
4 West Norwood
SW27 ....182 D5
Lake House Rd E11 ..77 A6
Lakehurst Rd KT19 ..215 C3
Lakeland Cl HA3 ......24 B4
Lakeman Ct CR7 ....183 A1
Lakenheath N14 ......15 D6
Laker Ct SW4 ....138 A3
Lake Rd Croydon CR0 .223 B6
Dagenham RM6 ....58 D5
Dagenham RM9 ......103 D4
Wimbledon SW19 ....179 B5
Laker Pl SW15 ......157 A5
Lakeside
Beckenham BR3 .....207 D6
Borehamwood WD6 ...10 C6
Ealing W13 ....87 C1
Enfield EN2 ....3 D1
10 Kingston KT2 .....176 D3
Wallington SM6 .....219 B4
West Ewell KT19 ....215 C2
Lakeside Ave SE28 ..124 A5
Redbridge IG4 ....55 D5
Lakeside Cl Ruislip HA4 39 B5
Sidcup DA15 ....168 C6
South Norwood SE25 ..184 A1
Lakeside Complex The
SE2 ....124 D5
Lakeside Cres EN4 ....14 D6
Lakeside Ct N4 ....51 A1
Lakeside Dr
Esher KT10 ....212 A2
Keston Mark BR2 ....226 A5
Lakeside Lo NW4 .....47 A5
Lakeside Rd W14 ....112 D3
Palmers Green N13 ....16 B1
Lakeside Way HA9 ....66 C4
Lakes Rd BR2 ....225 C3
Lakeswood Rd BR5 ..211 A3
Lake The WD23 ....8 B3
Lakeview 23 E3 ....96 D5
Lake View HA8 ....26 B5
Lake View Ct SW1 ..258 D6
Lakeview Ct E4 ....36 B4
Lakeview Rd DA16 ..146 B1
West Norwood SE27 ..182 D5
Lake View Terr N18 ...33 D6
Lakis Cl NW3 ....70 A4
Laleham Ave NW7 .....11 B1
Laleham Ho E2 ......243 C6
Laleham Rd
Catford SE6 ....164 A4
Littleton TW17 ....192 C4
Lambarde Ave SE9 ..188 C6
Lamb Ct 16 E14 .....119 A6
Lamberhurst Ho 14
SE15 ....140 C6
Lamberhurst Rd
Dagenham RM8 ....59 B1
West Norwood SE27 ..182 C5
Lambert Ave TW9 ....132 D2
Lambert Ho 19 N19 ...49 D2
17 SW9 ....138 C3
Lambert Lo TW8 .....109 D1
Lambert Rd N12 ....30 B5
SW2 ....160 B6
Newham E16 ....99 B1
Lambert's Pl CR0 ...205 B1
Lambert's Rd KT6 ...198 B4
Lambert St N1 ....72 C1
Lambert Way N12 ....30 A5
Lambert Wlk HA9 .....65 D5
Lambeth Coll (Brixton Ctr)
SW2 ....160 B6
Lambeth Coll (Clapham
Ctr) SW4 ....159 C6
Lambeth Coll (Tower
Bridge Ctr)
SE1 ....117 C5 253 B3
Lambeth Coll (Vauxhall
Ctr) SW8 ...137 D4 269 C2
Lambeth Ct 8 SW18 157 C6
Lambeth High St
SE1 ....116 B2 260 C4
Lambeth Hill EC4 ...252 A6
Lambeth Hospl SW9 .138 B2
Lambeth Inst Strand Ctr
SW2 ....160 B4
Lambeth North Sta
SE1 ....116 C3 261 A6
Lambeth Palace*
SE1 ....116 B3 260 C5
Lambeth Palace Rd
SE1 ....116 B3 260 C6
Lambeth Pier SE1 ...260 B5
Lambeth Prospect
SE19 ....183 B4
Lambeth Rd
SE1 ....116 C3 261 B5
Thornton Heath CR0 ..204 D1
Lambeth Twrs SE11 ..261 A5
Lambeth Wlk
SE11 ....116 B2 260 D4
Lambfold Ho N7 ......72 A2
Lamb Ho SE10 ....142 A6
11 SE5 ....139 B4
28 SE5 ....139 A5
Lamb La E8 ....74 B1
Lamble St NW5 ....71 A4
Lambley Rd RM9 ......80 B2
Lambolle Pl NW3 .....70 C2
Lambolle Rd NW3 .....70 C2
Lambourn Cl 9 NW5 .71 C4
W7 ....108 D4
Lambourne Ave
SW19 ....179 B6
Lambourne Ct 5 IG8 .37 C3
Lambourne Gdns
4 Barking IG11 ....79 D1
Chingford E4 ....19 C2
Enfield EN1 ....5 D3
Lambourne Gr KT1 ..176 D1
Lambourne Ho NW8 .236 D4
SE16 ....118 D2
Lambourne Pl SE3 ...143 B4
Lambourne Rd E11 ...54 A2
Barking IG11 ....79 D1
Ilford IG3 ....79 C6
Lambourn Rd SW4 ...137 B2
Lambrook Ho 12
SE15 ....140 A4
Lambrook Terr
SW6 ....135 A4 264 A2
Lamb's Bldgs EC1 ...242 C5
Lamb's Cl N9 ....18 A2
Lamb's Conduit Pas
WC1 ....240 C4
Lamb's Conduit St
WC1 ....94 B3 240 C5
Lambscroft Ave SE9,
SE12 ....165 D1
Lambs Mdw IG8 ......37 D1
Lamb's Mews N1 ....234 C5
Lamb's Pas
EC1 ....95 B3 242 C5
Lamb St E1 ...95 D2 243 C4
Lamb's Terr N9 ....17 B2
Lambs Wlk EN2 ....5 A3
Lambton Ct 2 N19 ....50 A1
Lambton Pl W11 ....244 D6
Lambton Rd N19 ......50 A1
Wimbledon SW20 ....178 C2
Lamb Wlk SE1 ......253 A1
Lamerock Rd BR1 ...186 D6
Lamerton Lo 10 TW9 132 B4
Lamerton St 9 SE8 .141 C6
Lamford Cl N17 ....33 B3
Lamington St 3 W6 .112 B2
Lamlash St SE11 ....261 C4
Lamley Ho SE10 .....141 D5
Lammas Ave CR4 ....181 A1
Lammas Gn SE26 ....162 B1
Lammas Park Gdns
W5 ....109 C5
Lammas Park Rd W5 109 D4
Lammas Rd E9 ....74 D1
Richmond TW10 .....175 C6
Walthamstow E10 .....53 A1
Lammas Sch The E10 .53 B1
Lammermoor Rd
SW12 ....159 B4
Lamont Rd
SW10 ......136 B6 266 C5
Lamont Rd Pas SW10 266 C5
Lamorbey Cl DA15 ..167 D2
Lamorna Cl E17 ......36 A2
Lamorna Gr HA7 ......25 D1
Lampard Gr N16 ......51 D1
Lampern Sq 8 E2 ....96 A4
Lampeter Cl NW9 .....45 C3
Lampeter Sq W6 ....264 A5
Lamplighter Cl 31 E1 .96 C3
Lampmead Rd SE12 .142 D1
Lamport Cl SE18 ....122 B2
Lampson Ho 6 N19 ..71 C4
Lampton Ave TW5 ...129 D4
Lampton Ct TW5 ....129 D4
Lampton House Cl
SW19 ....178 D6
Lampton Park Rd
TW3 ....129 D3
Lampton Rd TW3,
TW5 ....129 D3
Lampton Sch TW5 ..129 C4
Lanacre Ave NW9 .....27 C2
Lanain Ct SE12 .....164 D4
Lanark Cl W5 ....87 C2
Lanark Ct UB5 ....63 C3
Lanark Ho 11 SE1 ...118 A1
Lanark Mans 6 W12 112 C4
W9 ....236 B6
Lanark Pl W9 .92 A3 236 B6
Lanark Rd W9 .92 A4 229 A1
Lanark Sq E14 ......119 D3
Lanata Wlk UB4 ......84 D3
Lanbury Rd SE15 ....140 D1
Lancashire Ct W1 ..248 D6
Lancaster Ave
Barking IG11 ....101 C6
Hadley Wood EN4 ....2 B5
Wanstead E18 ....55 B5
West Norwood SE21,
SE27 ....161 A2
Wimbledon SW19 ....178 D5
Lancaster Cl 9 N1 ...73 C1
NW9 ....27 D3
W2 ....245 C5
Beckenham BR2 .....208 D5
Kingston KT2 ....175 D5
Stanwell TW19 ....148 A5
Tottenham N17 ....34 A3
Lancaster Cotts 1
TW10 ....154 A5
Lancaster Ct SW6 ...264 D3
W2 ....246 B6
1 Belmont SM2 .....217 C1
Stanwell TW19 ......148 A3
Walton-on-T KT12 ...194 B2
West Norwood SE27 ..160 D2
Lancaster Dr E14 ...120 A5
NW3 ....70 C2
Lancaster Gate
W2 ....114 A6 246 B6
Lancaster Gate Sta
W2 ....114 B6 246 C6
Lancaster Gdns W13 .109 B4
Kingston KT2 ....175 D5
Wimbledon SW19 ....179 A5
Lancaster Gr NW3 ....70 B2
Lancaster Ho
Enfield EN2 ....5 B4
Putney SW15 ....134 C3
Wandsworth SW18 ...157 D4
Lancaster House
SW1 ....249 A2
Lancasterian Inf Sch
N17 ....33 D2
Lancaster Lo 2 W11 .91 A1
Lancaster Mews
3 SW18 ....157 D6
W2 ....114 A6 246 B6
2 Richmond TW10 ...154 A5
Lancaster Pk TW10 ..154 A6
Lancaster Pl
WC2 ....116 B6 250 C5
Hounslow TW5 ....128 D3
Ilford IG1 ....79 A4
Twickenham TW1 ....153 A4
1 Wimbledon SW19 ..178 D5
Lancaster Rd E11 .....76 C6
E17 ....34 D1
E7 ....77 A1
N11 ....31 D4
N4 ....50 C2
NW10 ....68 A3
W11 ....91 A1
Edmonton N18 ....33 D5
Enfield EN2 ....5 B4
Harrow HA2 ....41 C4
New Barnet EN4 ....14 B6
Northolt UB5 ....64 A2
Southall UB1 ....107 A6
South Norwood SE25 ..206 A6
Wimbledon SW19 ....178 D5
Lancaster Road Ind Est 2
EN4 ....14 B6
Lancaster St
SE1 ....116 D4 251 D1
Lancaster Stables 10
NW3 ....70 C2
Lancaster Terr
W2 ....114 B6 246 C6
Lancaster Wlk
W2 ....114 A5 246 B4
Hayes UB3 ....83 A1
Lancastrian Rd SM6 .220 B1
Lancefield Ct 1 NW6 .91 A5
Lancefield Ho SE15 ..140 B2

Lancefield St W10 91 B4
Lancell St N16 73 C6
Lancelot Ave HA0 65 D4
Lancelot Cres HA0 65 D4
Lancelot Gdns EN4 15 A4
Lancelot Par 4 HA0 65 D3
Lancelot Pl SW7 114 D4 247 C1
Lancelot Rd DA16 146 A2
  Wembley HA0 65 D3
Lance Rd HA1 42 A2
Lancer Sq W8 245 C2
Lancey Cl SE7 122 A2
Lanchester Ct W2 237 C1
Lanchester Rd N6 48 D4
Lancing Gdns N9 17 D3
Lancing Rd
  Ealing W13 109 B6
  Feltham TW13 149 D2
  Ilford IG2 57 B2
  Thornton Heath CR0 204 B2
Lancing St NW1 232 C1
Lancresse Ct N1 95 C6
Landale Ho 13 SE16 118 C3
Landcroft Rd SE22 161 D5
Landells Rd SE22 162 A5
Lander Ct EN5 14 A6
Landford Rd SW15 134 C2
Landgrove Rd SW19 179 C5
Landin Ho 1 E14 97 C1
Landleys Field 21 N7 71 D3
Landmann Ho 16 SE16 118 B2
Landmann Way SE14 118 D1
Landmark Commercial Ctr N18 33 C4
Landon Pl SW1 257 C6
Landons Cl E14 120 A5
Landon Way TW15 170 D4
Landon Wlk 14 E14 119 D6
Landor Ct N16 73 C3
Landor Ho 7 SE5 139 B5
Landor Rd SW9 138 A2
Landor Wlk 11 W12 112 A4
Landra Gdns N21 16 D5
Landrake NW1 232 B5
Landridge Dr EN1 6 B5
Landridge Rd SW6 135 B3
Landrock Rd N8 50 B3
Landscape Rd IG8 37 B3
Landseer Ave E12 78 C3
Landseer Cl
  Edgware HA8 26 C1
  Mitcham SW19 180 B2
Landseer Ct UB4 83 B5
Landseer Ho NW8 236 D6
  SW1 259 D3
  SW11 268 B1
  17 Northolt UB5 84 D5
Landseer Rd N19 72 A6
  Cheam SM1,SM2 217 C2
  Enfield EN1 18 A6
  New Malden KT3 199 B2
Lands' End WD6 9 D5
Landstead Rd SE18 145 B5
Landulph Ho SE11 261 B2
Landward Ct W1 237 B2
Lane Cl NW2 68 B5
Lane Ct SW11 158 D4
Lane End DA7 147 D2
Lane Gdns Bushey WD23 8 C4
  Claygate KT10 212 D1
Lane Mews E12 78 B5
Lanercost Cl SW2 160 C2
Lanercost Gdns N14 16 A4
Lanercost Rd SW2 160 C2
Laneside HA8 27 A5
  Chislehurst BR7 189 A5
Laneside Ave RM8 59 B2
Lane The NW8 92 A5 229 A3
  SE3 143 A2
Laneway SW15 156 B6
Laney Bldg EC1 241 A4
Lanfranc Ct HA1 64 D5
Lanfranc Rd E3 97 A5
Lanfrey Pl W14 254 C1
Langbourne Ave N6 71 A6
Langbourne Ct E17 53 A3
Langbourne Ho 7 SW2 160 C6
Langbourne Mans N6 71 A6
Langbourne Pl E14 119 D1
Langbourne Prim Sch SE21 161 C1
Langbourne Way KT10 213 A2
Langbrook Rd SE3 143 D3
Langcroft Cl SM5 218 D5
Langdale NW1 232 A2
Langdale Ave CR4 202 D6
Langdale Cl BR6 226 D5
  SE17 139 A6
  Dagenham RM8 58 C1
  Mortlake SW14 132 D1
Langdale Cres DA7 147 C4
Langdale Ct
  3 Ealing W5 87 C2
  9 Ilford IG1 78 D5
Langdale Dr UB4 83 C5
Langdale Gdns UB6 87 B4
Langdale Ho SW1 259 A1
Langdale Rd SE10 142 A5
  Thornton Heath CR7 204 C5
Langdale St 3 E1 96 B1
Langdon Cres E6 100 C5
Langdon Ct EC1 234 D3
  NW10 89 C6
Langdon Dr NW9 45 A1
Langdon Ho 1 E14 98 A1
Langdon Park Rd N6 49 C2
Langdon Park Sec Sch E14 98 A1
Langdon Pl SW14 133 A2
Langdon Rd
  Barking E6 100 C6
  Bromley BR2 209 B6
  Morden SM4 202 A4
Langdon Sch E6 100 D6
Langdons Ct UB2 107 C3
Langdon Shaw DA14 189 D5
Langdon Way 14 SE1 118 A2
Langdon Wlk SM4 202 A4
Langford Cl E8 74 A3
  7 N15 51 C3
  NW8 229 B4
Langford Cres EN4 2 D1
Langford Ct NW8 229 B3
Langford Gn SE5 139 C2
Langford Ho 5 SE8 141 C6
Langford Pl
  NW8 92 A5 229 B4
  Sidcup DA14 168 A1
Langford Prim Sch SW6 135 D3
Langford Rd 4 SW6 135 D3
  Cockfosters EN4 2 D1
  Woodford IG8 37 C4
Langfords IG9 21 D2
Langham Cl N15 50 D6
Langham Ct NW4 46 D4
  Merton SW20 178 C1
  4 Putney SW15 156 D6
  Ruislip HA4 62 B3
  12 Twickenham TW1 153 C5
Langham Dr RM6 58 B3
Langham Gdns HA8 27 A3
  Ealing W13 109 B6
  Richmond TW10 175 C6
  Southgate N21 16 D6
  Wembley HA0 65 C6
Langham Ho SW4 159 C6
Langham House Cl TW10 175 D6
Langham Mans SW5 255 C1
Langham Park Pl BR2 208 D5
Langham Pl N15 50 D6
  W1 93 B2 238 D3
  Chiswick W4 133 C6
Langham Rd HA8 27 A4
  N15 51 A6
  Teddington TW11 175 B4
  Wimbledon SW20 178 C2
Langham Sch The N15 51 A5
Langham St W1 93 B2 238 D3
Langhedge Cl N18 33 D4
Langhedge La N18 33 D4
Langhedge Lane Ind Est N18 33 D4
Lang Ho 3 N19 71 C5
  SW8 270 A3
Langholm Cl SW12 159 D4
Langholme WD23 8 A3
Langhorn Dr TW2 152 C4
Langhorne Ct 10 NW8 70 B1
Langhorne Ho 5 SE7 143 C6
Langhorne Rd RM10 81 C1
Langhurst Ho 10 SW11 137 A3
Langland Cres HA7 25 D1
Langland Dr HA5 23 A3
Langland Gdns NW3 69 D3
  Croydon CR0 223 B6
Langland Ho 10 SE5 139 B5
Langland Ho *continued*
  Upper Tooting SW17 180 B5
Langler Rd NW10 90 C5
Langley Ave
  North Cheam KT4,SM3 216 D6
  Ruislip HA4 62 B6
  Surbiton KT6 198 A1
Langley Cres HA8 11 A1
  Dagenham RM9 80 D1
  Harlington UB3 127 D5
  Wanstead E11 55 C2
Langley Ct SW8 270 A2
  WC2 250 A6
Langley Dr W3 110 D4
  Wanstead E11 55 B2
Langley Gdns BR5 210 D3
  Bromley BR2 209 C5
  Dagenham RM9 80 D1
Langley Gr KT3 177 C1
Langley Ho BR1 187 B3
  11 E5 74 B3
  36 W2 91 C2
Langley La
  SW8 138 A6 270 B6
Langley Manor BR3 208 A4
Langley Mans SW8 270 B6
Langley Park Rd
  SM1,SM2 218 A1
Langley Park Sch for Boys
  BR3 207 D3
Langley Park Sch for Girls
  BR3 208 A3
Langley Pk NW7 27 C4
Langley Rd DA16 146 C4
  Beckenham BR3 207 A5
  Isleworth TW7 130 D3
  Merton SW19 179 C2
  Surbiton KT6 198 A2
Langley Row EN5 1 B4
Langley St
  WC2 94 A1 240 A1
Langley Way BR4 208 C2
Langmead Dr WD23 8 B3
Langmead Ho 34 E3 97 D4
Langmead St SE27 183 A6
Langmore Ct DA7 146 D2
Langmore Ho 28 E1 96 A1
Langport Ct KT12 194 C1
Langport Ho 1 SW9 138 D3
Langridge 15 NW5 71 A2
Langridge Mews
  TW12 173 B4
Langroyd Rd SW17 158 D2
Langside Ave SW15 134 A1
Langside Cres N14 15 D1
Lang St E1 96 C3
Langston Hughes Cl 5
  SE24 138 D1
Langthorn Ct EC2 242 D2
Langthorne Ct 4
  SE6 186 A6
Langthorne Ho UB3 105 C2
Langthorne Lo 30
  SW2 160 C4
Langthorne Rd E11 76 B5
Langthorne St SW6 134 D5
Langton Ave N20 14 B4
  Wallend E6 100 C4
Langton Cl
  WC1 94 B3 240 D6
Langton Ct SW15 157 B5
Langton Ho SE11 260 D4
  5 Streatham SW16 181 C6
Langton Pl SW18 157 C3
Langton Rd NW2 68 C5
  SW9 138 D5
  East Molesey KT8 196 A5
  Harrow HA3 24 A3
Langton Rise SE22,
  SE23 162 B4
Langton St
  SW10 136 A6 266 B5
Langton Way
  Greenwich SE3 143 A5
  South Croydon CR0 221 C4
Langtry Pl SW6 265 B6
Langtry Rd NW8 91 D6
  Northolt UB5 84 D5
Langtry Wlk
  NW8 92 A6 229 A6
  NW8 91 D6
Langwood Chase
  TW11 175 C4
Langworth Dr UB4 84 B1
Langworthy HA5 23 C4
Lanherne Ho 7
  SW19 178 D3
Lanhill Rd W9 91 C3
Lanier Rd SE13 164 B5
Lanigan Dr TW3 151 D6
Lankaster Gdns N2 30 B2
Lankers Dr HA2 41 B3
Lankton Cl BR3 186 A2
Lanner Ho 2 SW11 136 C2
Lannock Rd UB3 105 D5
Lannoy Point SW6 264 B4
Lannoy Rd SE9 167 A3
Lanrick Rd E14 98 C1
Lanridge Rd SE2 124 D3
Lansbury Ave
  Barking IG11 80 A1
  Dagenham RM6 59 A4
  Edmonton N18 33 C5
  Feltham TW14 150 B5
Lansbury Cl NW10 67 A3
Lansbury Ct 4 SE28 124 B6
Lansbury Dr UB4 83 D3
Lansbury Gdns 1 E14 98 B1
Lansbury Ho 5 DA17 125 B1
Lansbury Rd EN3 6 D4
Lansbury Way N18 33 C5
Lanscombe Wlk SW8 270 A3
Lansdell Rd CR4 181 A1
Lansdown Cl KT12 194 C1
Lansdowne Ave DA7 146 D5
  Orpington BR6 210 D1
Lansdowne Cl
  Tolworth KT5 214 D6
  Twickenham TW1 152 D3
  Wimbledon SW20 178 D3
Lansdowne Copse 1
  KT4 216 A6
Lansdowne Cres
  W11 113 A6 244 B5
Lansdowne Ct 2
  KT4 216 A6
Lansdowne Dr E8 74 A1
Lansdowne Gdns
  SW8 138 A4 270 A2
Lansdowne Gr NW10 67 C4
Lansdowne Hill SE27 160 D1
Lansdowne Ho W11 244 C4
  Enfield EN2 4 C3
Lansdowne La SE7 121 D1
Lansdowne Mews
  SE7 121 D1
  W11 244 C4
Lansdowne Pl SE1 262 D6
  Penge SE19 183 D3
Lansdowne Rd BR1 187 B3
  E11 76 D6
  E17 53 C3
  E8 74 A2
  N10 31 C1
  N3 29 C3
  W11 113 A6 244 B5
  Chingford E4 19 C2
  Croydon CR0 205 B1
  Harrow HA1 42 C2
  Hayes UB8 83 A1
  Hounslow TW3 129 D2
  Ilford IG3 57 D2
  Stanmore HA7 25 C4
  Tottenham N17 34 A2
  Wanstead E18 55 A6
  West Ewell KT19 215 B1
  Wimbledon SW19,
  SW20 178 C3
Lansdowne Rise
  W11 113 A6 244 B5
Lansdowne Row W1 248 D4
Lansdowne Sch SW9 138 B2
Lansdowne Terr
  WC1 240 B5
Lansdowne Way
  SW4,SW8 138 A4 270 B1
Lansdowne Wlk
  W11 113 B5 244 C4
Lansdowne Wood Cl 11
  SE27 160 D1
Lansdown Ho 29 SE5 139 A3
Lansdown Rd E7 77 C1
  Sidcup DA14 168 B1
Lansfield Ave N18 34 A6
Lanson Ct E11 76 D6
Lanson Ho HA8 26 C4
Lanswood Ct KT4 216 A6
Lantern Cl
  Putney SW15 134 A1
  Wembley HA0 65 D3
Lantern Ct 4 SW20 178 D2
Lantern Ho E14 119 C4
Lanterns Ct E14 119 C3
Lanterns The N12 29 D4
Lantern Way UB7 104 B4
Lant Ho SE1 252 A1
Lantry Ct 1 W3 110 D5
Lant St SE1 117 A4 252 B1
Lanvanor Rd SE15 140 C3
Lanyard Ho 3 SE8 119 B2
Lapford Cl W9 91 B3
Lapponum Wlk UB4 84 D2
Lapsang SE1 253 D3
Lapse Wood Wlk
  SE22 162 B3
Lapstone Gdns HA3 43 C3
Lapwing Ct NW9 27 C1
  Tolworth KT6 214 C5
Lapwing Twr 31 SE8 141 B6
Lapwing Way UB4 84 D1
Lapworth 2 N11 31 B6
Lapworth Ct W2 91 D2
Lara Cl SE13 164 A5
  Chessington KT9 214 A1
Larbert Rd SW16 181 C3
Larch Ave W3 111 C5
Larch Cl E13 99 C3
  N11 31 A3
  7 N19 71 C6
  15 SE8 141 B6
  Balham SW12 159 B2
Larch Cres Hayes UB4 84 D2
  West Ewell KT19 214 D2
Larch Ct 41 W2 91 C2
Larch Dene BR6 226 C6
Larches Ave SW14 133 B1
Larches The
  Edmonton N13 17 A1
  Hillingdon UB10 82 D5
Larchfield Ho 2 N5 73 A3
Larch Gn NW9 27 C2
Larch Gr DA15 167 D3
Larch Ho 17 SE16 118 C4
  Hayes UB4 84 C2
Larchmore Ct N19 72 A6
Larch Rd E10 75 C6
  NW2 68 C4
Larch Tree Way CR0 223 C5
Larchvale Ct 4 SM2 217 D1
Larch Way BR2 210 C2
Larchwood Rd SE9 166 D2
Larcombe Cl CR0 221 D4
Larcom St
  SE17 117 A2 262 B3
Larden Rd W3 111 C4
La Retraite RC Girls Sch
  SW12 159 C4
Largewood Ave KT6 214 C6
Larissa St SE17 262 D3
Larix Ct NW10 90 A6
Larkbere Rd SE26 185 A6
Larken Cl WD23 8 A3
Larken Dr WD23 8 A3
Larkfield Ave HA3 43 B6
Larkfield Cl BR2 225 A6
Larkfield Rd DA14 167 D1
  Richmond TW9 132 A1
Lark Hall Inf Sch
  SW4 137 D3
Lark Hall Jun Sch
  SW4 138 A3
Larkhall La
  SW4 138 A4 270 A1
Larkhall Rise SW4 137 D3
Larkham Cl TW13 149 C1
Lark Row E2 96 C6
Larksfield Gr EN1 6 B4
Larks Gr IG11 79 C1
Larkshall Bsns Ctr 2
  E4 20 B2
Larkshall Cres E4 36 A6
Larkshall Ct E4 36 A5
Larkshall Rd E4 36 B6
Larkspur Cl 4 E6 100 A2
  NW9 44 D4
  Ruislip HA4 39 A2
  Tottenham N17 33 B3
Larkspur Ct SM6 219 B1
Larkspur Gr HA8 27 A6
Larkspur Way KT19 215 A3
Larkswood Ct E4 36 B5
Larkswood Jun & Inf Sch
  E4 35 D6
Larkswood Rd E4 35 D6
Larkswood Rise HA5 40 C5
Lark Way SM5 202 C2
Larkway Cl NW9 45 B5
Larmenier & Sacred Heart
  RC Prim Sch W6 112 D2
Larnaca Ho SE1 263 C6
Larnach Rd W6 134 D6
Larne Rd HA4 39 D2
Larpent Ave SW15 156 C6
Larwood Cl UB6 64 B3
La Saint Union Rc Sec Sch
  NW5 71 A5
Lascelles Ave HA1 42 B2
Lascelles Cl E11 76 B6
Lascelles Ho NW1 237 B5
Lascott's Rd N22 32 B4
Lashford Ho HA8 27 A4
Lassa Rd SE9 166 B6
Lassell St SE10 120 B1
Lasseter Pl SE3 142 D6
Latchett Rd E18 37 B2
Latchingdon Ct E17 52 D5
Latchmere Cl KT2,
  TW10 176 A5
Latchmere Jun & Inf Schs
  KT2 176 B4
Latchmere La KT2,
  TW10 176 B5
Latchmere Rd SW11 136 D3
  Kingston KT2 176 B4
Latchmere St 5
  SW11 136 D3
Lateward Rd TW8 131 D6
Latham Cl E6 100 A1
  4 Twickenham TW1 153 A4
Latham Ct
  2 Bowes Park N11 32 A4
  7 Northolt UB5 84 D4
Latham Ho E1 96 D1
  18 E17 53 D6
Latham Rd DA6 169 C6
  Twickenham TW1 152 D4
Latham's Way CR0 220 B6
Lathkill Cl EN1 18 A4
Lathkill Ct BR3 185 B2
Lathom Jun Sch E6 78 A1
Lathom Rd E6 78 B1
Lathwood Ho 6
  SE26 184 B5
Latimer SE17 263 A1
Latimer Ave E6 100 B6
Latimer Cl
  North Cheam KT4 216 B4
  Pinner HA5 22 C2
Latimer Gdns HA5 22 C2
Latimer Ho 11 E9 74 D2
  W11 244 D5
Latimer Pl W10 90 C1
Latimer Rd E7 77 B4
  N15 51 C3
  W10 90 C1
  Barnet EN5 1 D2
  Croydon CR0 220 D5
  Teddington TW11 174 D5
  Wimbledon SW19 179 D4
Latimer Road Sta
  W10 112 D6
Latona Rd SE15 140 A6
La Tourne Gdns BR6 227 A5
Lattimer Pl W4 133 C6
Latton Cl KT12 195 A2
Latymer All Saints CE Prim
  Sch N9 17 D2
Latymer Ct W6 112 D2
Latymer Rd N9 17 D3
Latymer Sch The N9 17 C2
Latymer Upper Sch
  W6 112 A1
Latymer Way N9 17 C2
Lauder Cl UB5 84 D5
Lauder Ct N14 16 A4
Lauderdale Dr TW10 153 D1
Lauderdale Mans W9 91 D4
Lauderdale Rd W9 91 D4
Lauderdale Twr EC2 242 A4
Laud St SE11 116 B1 260 C2
  Croydon CR0 221 A5
Laughton Ho 11 SW2 160 C5
Laughton Rd UB5 84 D6
Launcelot Prim Sch
  BR1 187 A6
Launcelot Rd BR1,
  SE12 187 A6
Launcelot St SE1 251 A1
Launceston Ct CR7 204 C3
Launceston Gdns UB6 65 C1
Launceston Pl
  W8 114 A3 256 A5
Launceston Rd UB6 87 C6
Launch St E14 120 A3
Laundress La N16 74 A5
Laundry La 15 N1 73 A1
Laundry Mews SE23 162 D4
Laundry Rd
  W6 135 A6 264 A5
Laura Cl Enfield EN1 17 C6
  Wanstead E11 55 C4
Lauradale Rd N2 48 D5
Laura Pl E5 74 C4
Laurel Ave TW1 152 D3
Laurel Bank Gdns 3
  SW6 135 B3
Laurel Bank Rd EN2 5 B4
Laurel Cl 5 N19 71 C6
  Sidcup DA14 168 A1
  Upper Tooting SW17 180 C5

Laurel Cres CR0 .....223 C5
Laurel Ct E8 ....73 D2
2 Putney SW15 ....156 D6
South Norwood SE25 ..205 A4
8 Wembley HA0 ....88 A5
Laurel Dr N21 ....16 C4
Laurel Gdns NW7 ....11 B1
Chingford E4 ....19 D4
Ealing W7 ....108 C5
Hounslow TW4 ......129 A1
Laurel Gr
Forest Hill SE26 .....185 A6
Penge SE20 ....184 C3
Laurel Ho **5** NW3 ...69 D2
9 SE8 ....141 B6
Morden SM4 ....201 D4
Laurel La UB7 ....104 A2
Laurel Manor SM2 ..218 A1
Laurel Mead Ct **8** E18 37 A2
Laurel Pk HA3 ....24 D3
Laurel Rd
Barnes SW13 ....134 A3
Teddington TW12 ...174 B5
Wimbledon SW20 ..178 B2
Laurel St E8 ....73 D2
Laurels The **8** BR1 .187 B2
BR2 ....209 A5
N3 ....29 D4
Bushey WD23 ....8 C2
8 Belvedere DA17 ..125 C1
Buckhurst Hill IG9 ...21 C3
Laurel View N12 .....13 D1
Laurel Way E18 .....54 D5
N20 ....13 C1
Laurence Ct E10 ....53 D2
Laurence Mews **12**
W12 ....112 A4
Laurence Pountney Hill
EC4 ....252 C6
Laurence Pountney La
EC4 ....252 D6
Laurie Gr SE14 ......141 A4
Laurie Ho SE1 ......261 D5
W8 ....113 C5 245 A3
Laurier Rd W7 ....86 C2
Laurier Rd NW5 .....71 C4
Croydon CR0 ....205 D2
Laurimel Cl HA7 .....25 B4
Laurino Pl W23 ....8 A2
Lauriston Lo NW6 ...69 B2
Lauriston Rd E9 .....74 D1
Wimbledon SW19 ...178 D4
Lauriston Sch E9 ....96 D6
Lausanne Rd N8 .....50 C4
SE15 ....140 C4
Lavehham Ho E17 ...35 D2
Lavell St N16 ....73 B4
Lavender Ave NW9 ..45 A1
Mitcham CR4 ....180 D2
North Cheam KT4,SM3 .216 C5
Lavender Cl BR2 ....210 A3
SW3 ....266 D5
Wallington SM5 ....219 B4
Enfield EN2 ....4 D4
Stanmore HA3 ......24 C4
Lavender Ct SW4 ...270 B1
East Molesey KT8 ..195 D6
Lavender Gdns SW11 136 C1
Enfield EN2 ....4 D4
Lavender Gr E8 ......74 A1
Mitcham CR4 ....180 C2
Lavender Hill SW11 .137 C4
Enfield EN2 ....4 D4
Lavender Ho **14** SE16 118 D5
Lavender Pk IG1 .....78 D3
Lavender Prim Sch EN2 5 C1
Lavender Rd SE16 ..119 A5
SW11 ....136 B2
Enfield EN2 ....5 B4
Hillingdon UB8 ......82 B2
Sutton SM1 ....218 B4
Thornton Heath CR0 .204 B3
Wallington SM5 .....219 A4
West Ewell KT19 ...214 D2
Lavender Rise UB7 .104 C4
Lavender St E15 .....76 C2
Lavender Sweep
SW11 ....136 D1
Lavender Terr **12**
SW11 ....136 C2
Lavender Vale SM6 .219 D2
Lavender Way CR0 .206 D3
Lavender Wlk SW11 .136 C2
Lavendon Ho NW8 ..237 B6
Lavengro Rd SE27 ..161 A2
Lavenham Ho E17 ...35 D2
Lavenham Rd SW18 .157 C4
Lavernock Rd DA7 .147 C3
Lavers Rd N16 ....73 C5
Laverstoke Gdns
SW15 ....156 A4

Laverton Mews SW5 .255 D3
Laverton Pl SW5 ....255 D3
Lavidge Rd SE9 .....166 B2
Lavina Gr N1 ....233 C4
Lavington Cl E9 .....75 B2
Lavington Rd
Ealing W13 ....109 B5
Wallington CR0 .....220 B4
Lavington St
SE1 ....116 D5 251 D3
Lavinia Ct BR1 ......186 C3
Lavisham Ho BR1 ...187 B5
Lawdale Jun Sch E2 ..96 A4
Lawdon Gdns CR0 ..220 D4
Lawford Cl SM6 .....220 A1
Lawford Rd N1 ......73 C1
NW5 ....71 C2
Chiswick W4 ....133 A5
Lawfords Wharf **15**
NW1 ....71 C1
Lawless Ho **5** E14 .120 A6
Lawless St **11** E14 ...119 D6
Lawley Ho **10** TW1 ..153 B4
Lawley Rd N14 ....15 B4
Lawley St E5 ....74 C4
Lawman Ct **2** TW9 .132 B4
Lawn Cl BR1 ....187 B3
Edmonton N9 ....17 D4
Kingston KT3 ....177 C1
Ruislip HA4 ....61 D5
Lawn Cres TW9 .....132 C3
Lawn Farm Gr RM6 ...59 B4
Lawnfield NW6 ......68 D1
Lawn Gdns W7 .....108 C5
Lawn House Cl E14 .120 A4
Lawn La SW8 ...138 B6 270 C6
Lawn Rd NW3 ....70 D3
Beckenham BR3 ....185 B3
Lawns Ct HA9 ....66 C6
Lawns The N16 ....73 C3
SE3 ....142 D2
Belmont SM2 ......217 A1
Chingford E4 ....35 C5
Harrow HA3 ....23 D3
Sidcup DA14 ....190 B6
South Norwood SE19 .183 B2
Lawn Terr SE3 ......142 C2
Lawn The UB2 ......107 C1
Lawn Vale HA5 ....23 A1
Lawrence Ave E17 ..34 D2
NW7 ....27 D6
Edmonton N13 ......32 D6
Little Ilford E12 ......78 C4
New Malden KT3 ...199 C2
Lawrence Camp Ct
N20 ....14 B1
Lawrence Cl E3 .....97 C5
N15 ....51 C5
6 W12 ....112 B6
Lawrence Cres
Dagenham RM10 ....81 D5
Edgware HA8 ....26 C1
Lawrence Ct N10 ....49 C6
N16 ....73 D5
NW7 ....27 C5
4 W3 ....111 A3
Lawrence Dr UB10 ...61 A4
Lawrence Est TW4 .128 C2
Lawrence Gdns NW7 .11 D1
Lawrence Hill E4 ....19 C2
Lawrence Ho SW1 ..259 D3
Bowes Park N22 .....32 B4
Lawrence La EC2 ...242 B2
Lawrence Mans SW3 267 A5
Lawrence Pl N1 .....233 B6
Lawrence Rd DA8 ..147 D5
E6 ....100 A6
E13 ....99 B6
N15 ....51 C5
W5 ....109 D2
Edmonton N18 ......34 B6
Hampton TW12 .....173 B3
Hayes BR4 ....225 A4
Hayes UB4 ....83 A5
Hounslow TW4 .....128 C1
Pinner HA5 ....40 D4
Richmond TW10 ...175 C6
South Norwood SE25 .205 D5
Lawrence's Bldgs **1**
N16 ....73 D5
Lawrence St E16 ....98 D2
NW7 ....27 D6
SW3 ....136 C6 267 A5
Lawrence Trad Est
SE10 ....120 C2
Lawrence Way NW10 .67 B5
Lawrence Weaver Cl
SM4 ....201 C3

Lawrence Yd N15 ...51 C5
Lawrie Ct HA3 ....24 D3
Lawrie Park Ave
SE26 ....184 B5
Lawrie Park Cres
SE26 ....184 B5
Lawrie Park Gdns
SE26 ....184 B5
Lawrie Park Rd SE26 184 C5
Lawson Cl Newham E16 99 C2
Wimbledon SW19 ..156 D1
Lawson Gdns HA5 ...40 B6
Lawson Ho **1** SE18 .144 C6
17 W12 ....112 B6
Lawson Rd Enfield EN3 ..6 C4
Southall UB1 ....85 C3
Law St SE1 ....117 B3 262 D6
Lawton Rd E10 ......54 A1
E3 ....97 A4
Barnet EN4 ....2 B2
Laxcon Cl NW10 ....67 B3
Laxey Rd BR6 ....227 C2
Laxfield Ct E8 ....96 A6
Laxley Cl SE5 ....138 D5
Laxton Ct CR7 ......205 A4
Laxton Path **1** SE4 .140 D1
Laxton Pl NW1 .....238 D6
Layard Rd SE16 ....118 B2
Enfield EN1 ....5 D4
South Norwood CR7 .183 B1
Layard Sq SE16 ....118 B2
Laycock Prim Sch N1 72 D2
Laycock St N1 ......72 C2
Layer Gdns W3 ....110 C6
Layfield Cl NW4 .....46 B2
Layfield Cres NW4 ..46 B2
Layfield Ho **1** SE10 .121 A1
Layfield Rd NW4 ....46 B2
Laymarsh Cl DA17 .125 B3
Laymead Cl UB5 .....63 A2
Laystall Ct EC1 .....241 A5
Laystall St EC1 .....241 A5
Layton Cres CR0 ...220 B4
Layton Ct TW8 ......109 D1
Layton Pl TW9 .....132 C4
Layton Rd
Brentford TW8 .....109 D1
Hounslow TW3 .....129 D1
Layton's La TW16 ..171 D1
Layzell Wlk SE9 ....165 D3
Lazar Wlk **2** N7 .....72 B6
Leabank Cl HA1 .....64 C5
Leabank Sq E9 ......75 C2
Leabank View N15 ...52 A3
Leabourne Rd N16 ..52 A2
Lea Bridge Rd E10 ..53 C2
Lea Cl TW2 ....151 B4
Lea Cres HA4 ....61 C4
Leacroft Ave SW12 .158 C4
Leacroft Cl
Southgate N21 ......16 D2
3 Yiewsley UB7 ...104 A6
Lea Ct **2** E13 ......99 A4
3 W12 ....111 C4
1 Chingford E4 ....20 A2
3 Hillingdon UB10 ..82 D3
Leadale Ave E4 ......19 C2
Leadale Rd N16 .....52 A3
Leadbeaters Cl N11 .30 D5
Leadbetter Ct **10**
NW10 ....67 B1
Leadenhall Mkt EC3 243 A1
Leadenhall Pl EC3 .243 A1
Leadenhall St
EC3 ....95 C1 243 A1
Leadenham Ct **15** E3 .97 C3
Leader Ave E12 ......78 C4
Leadings The HA9 ...67 A5
Leaf Cl KT7,KT8 ....196 C4
Leaf Gr SE27 ....182 C5
Leaf Ho **9** HA1 ......42 C4
Leafield Cl SW16 ...182 A5
Leafield La DA14 ...169 B2
Leafield Rd
Merton SW19,SW20 .201 B6
Sutton SM1 ....217 C6
Leafy Gr BR2 ....225 B3
Leafy Oak Rd SE12 .165 C1
Leafy Way CR0 .....221 D6
Lea Gdns HA9 ......66 B4
Leagrave St E5 ......74 C5
Lea Hall Gdns E10 ..53 C1
Lea Hall Rd E10 ....53 C1
Lea Ho E5 ....52 C1
NW8 ....237 A5
2 Edmonton N9 ...18 A1
Leaholme Waye HA4 .39 A3
Leahurst Rd SE13 ..164 C6

Lea Int E9 ....75 C3
Leake St SE1 ..116 B4 250 D2
SE1 ....251 A1
Lealand Rd N15 .....51 D3
Leamington Ave BR6 227 C4
E17 ....53 C4
Bromley BR1 ....187 C5
Merton SM4 ....201 B5
Leamington Cl E12 .78 A3
Bromley BR1 ....187 C5
Hounslow TW3 .....152 A6
Leamington Cres HA2 .63 B6
Leamington Ct W3 ..89 B2
4 Forest Hill SE26 .162 A1
Leamington Gdns IG3 79 D6
Leamington Ho
3 W11 ....91 B2
Edgware HA8 ....26 B5
Leamington Pk W3 ..89 B2
Leamington Pl UB4 .83 D3
Leamington Rd UB2 .106 D2
Leamington Rd Villas
W11 ....91 B2
Leamington Villas
SE13 ....164 C6
Leamore St W6 .....112 C2
Leamouth Rd E6 ...100 A2
South Bromley E14 ..98 B1
Leander Ct **27** E9 ...74 C1
7 NW9 ....27 C2
SE8 ....141 C4
5 Surbiton KT6 ...197 D2
Leander Rd SW2 ...160 C5
Northolt UB5 ....85 C5
Thornton Heath CR7 .204 B5
Lea Rd
2 Beckenham BR3 .185 C3
Enfield EN2 ....5 B4
Southall UB2 ....107 A2
Learner Dr HA2 .....63 C6
Learoyd Gdns E6 ..122 C6
Leary Ho SE11 .....260 D1
Leas Cl KT9 ....214 B1
Leas Dale SE9 .....166 C1
Leas Gn BR7 ....189 D4
Leaside Ave N10 ....49 A5
Leaside Bsns Ctr EN3 ..7 B3
Leaside Ct UB10 ....82 D4
Leaside Ho **4** E5 ....52 B1
Leaside Mans N10 ..49 A6
Leaside Rd E5 ....52 C1
Leasowes Rd E10 ...53 C1
Leas The SE18 .....144 C4
Leatherbottle Gn
DA18 ....125 B3
Leather Cl CR4 .....181 A1
Leatherdale St **29** E1 .96 C3
Leather Gdns E15 ...98 C6
Leatherhead Cl N16 .51 D1
Leatherhead Rd KT9 213 D1
Leather La EC1 ..94 C2 241 B4
Leathermarket Ct
SE1 ....253 A1
Leathermarket St
SE1 ....117 C4 253 A1
Leathersellers Cl EN5 ..1 A2
Leathsale Rd HA2 ...63 C6
Leathwaite Rd SW11 158 D6
Leathwell Rd SE8 ..141 D3
Lea Valley Prim Sch
N17 ....34 A3
Lea Valley Rd EN3 ..19 B5
Lea Valley Riding Sch
E10 ....52 D1
Lea Valley Technopark
N17 ....52 A6
Lea Valley Trad Est
N18 ....34 D1
Leaveland Cl BR3 ..207 D5
Leaver Gdns UB6 ...86 C5
Leavesden Rd HA7 ..25 A4
Leaview E4 ....20 A3
Lea View Ho E5 ......52 B1
Lebanon Ave TW13 .172 D5
Lebanon Ct **10** TW1 .153 B4
Lebanon Gdns SW18 .157 C5
Lebanon Pk TW1 ...153 B4
Lebanon Rd SW18 ..157 C5
Croydon CR0 ....205 C1
Lebanon Road Sta
CR0 ....221 D6
Lebrun Sq SE3 .....143 C6
Lebus Ho NW8 .....230 A3
Le Chateau CR0 ....221 B5
Lechmere App IG8 ..37 C1
Lechmere Ave IG8 ..37 D1
Lechmere Rd NW2 ..68 C4
Leckford Rd SW18 .158 A3
Leckhampton Pl **23**
SW2 ....160 C2

Leckwith Ave DA17 .147 A6
Lecky St SW7 114 B1 256 C2
Leclair Ho SE3 .....143 B4
L'Ecole des Petits
SW6 ....135 D3
Leconfield Ave SW13,
SW15 ....133 D2
Leconfield Ho SE5 .139 C2
Leconfield Rd N5 ...73 B4
Leda Ave EN3 ....6 D5
Leda Ct SW9 ....138 C5
Ledalle Ho NW2 ....68 B2
Ledam Bldg EC1 ...241 A4
Leda Rd SE18 ......122 C4
Ledbury Mews N W11 91 C1
Ledbury Mews W
W11 ....245 A6
Ledbury Pl **10** CR0 ..221 A4
Ledbury Rd W11 ....91 C1
Croydon CR0 ....221 D6
Ledbury St SE15 ...140 A5
Ledo Ho **1** N16 .....73 B4
Ledrington Rd SE19 .184 A4
Ledway Dr HA9 ......44 B2
Lee Ave RM6 ....59 A3
Leechcroft Ave SW13 167 D6
Leechcroft Rd SM6 .219 A6
Lee Church St SE13 .142 C1
Lee Cl E17 ....34 D2
New Barnet EN5 .....2 A1
Lee Conservancy Rd
E9 ....75 B3
Leecroft Rd EN5 .....1 A1
Leeds Ct EC1 ....241 C5
Carshalton SM5 ...218 D5
Catford SE6 ....163 D1
Leeds Rd IG1 ....57 B1
Leeds St N18 ....34 A5
Leegate SE12 ......164 D6
Lee Green SE12 ....142 D1
Lee High Rd SE12,
SE13 ....142 C1
Lee Ho **3** N19 ......71 D3
7 NW9 ....27 A2
Leeke St WC1 .94 B4 233 C2
Leeland Mans W13 .109 A5
Leeland Rd W13 ...109 A5
Leeland Terr W13 ..109 A5
Leeland Way NW10 ..67 D4
Lee Manor Sch SE13 164 C5
Leemount Cl NW4 ..46 D5
Lee Park Way N9,N18 .19 A1
Lee Pk SE3 ....142 D2
Lee Rd NW7 ....28 D3
SE3 ....142 D2
Enfield EN1 ....18 A5
Merton SW19 ......179 D2
Wembley UB6 ....87 C6
Leerdam Dr E14 ...120 A3
Lees Ct W1 ....248 A6
Lees Ho SE1 ....262 D1
Leeside EN5 ....13 C4
Leeside Cres NW11 .47 B5
Leeside Rd N17 ....34 B3
Leeside Ind Est N17 34 B3
Leeside Trad Est N17 34 C3
Leeside Works N17 .34 C3
Leeson Ho **7** TW1 ..153 B4
Leeson Rd **6** SE24 .139 C2
Leesons Hill BR5,BR7 211 D6
Leesons Way BR5 .189 D1
Lees Par UB10 ......82 D3
Lees Pl W1 ....115 A6 248 A6
Lees Rd UB8 ....82 D3
Lee St E8 ....95 D6
Lees The CR0 ......223 B6
Leet Ct N16 ....73 B4
Lee Terr SE3 ....142 C2
Lee Valley L Ctr N9 ..19 A3
Lee Valley Sp Ctr E15 .75 D4
Leeve Ho **7** W9 ......91 B4
Lee View EN2 ....4 D1
Leeward Ct **3** E1 ...118 A5
Leeward Gdns SW19 179 B5
Leeway SE8 ....119 B1
Leeway Cl HA5 ......23 B3
Leewood Cl SE12 ..165 A5
Lefevre Wlk E3 .....97 B6
Leffern Rd W12 ....112 A4
Leff Ho **7** NW6 .....69 A1
Legard Rd N5 ....72 D5
Legat Ct N4 ....51 A4
Legatt Rd SE9 .....165 D6
Legge St SE13 ....164 A6
Leghorn Rd NW10 ..67 D3
SE18 ....123 B1

Lau – Lei 345

Legion Cl N1 ....72 C1
Legion Ct SM4 .....201 C3
Legion Rd UB6 ......86 A5
Legion Terr E3 ......97 C6
Legion Way N12 ....30 C1
Legrace Ave TW4,
TW5 ....128 D3
Leicester Ave CR4 .204 A5
Leicester Cl KT4 ...216 C4
Leicester Ct **46** W2 ..91 C4
WC2 ....249 D6
11 Twickenham TW1 .153 D5
Leicester Gdns IG3 .57 C2
Leicester Ho **4** SW9 138 C1
5 Putney SW15 ...156 C4
2 Thames Ditton KT7 .197 A2
Leicester Mews N2 ..48 C6
Leicester Pl WC2 ..249 D6
Leicester Rd N2 .....48 C6
NW10 ....67 B1
Barnet EN5 ....1 C1
Croydon CR0 ....205 C2
Wanstead E11 ....55 B4
Leicester Sq*
WC2 ....115 D6 249 D5
Leicester Square Sta
WC2 ....115 D6 249 D5
Leicester St WC2 .249 D6
Leigham Ave SW16 .160 A1
Leigham Cl SW16 ..182 C6
Leigham Court Rd
SW16 ....182 C6
Leigham Dr TW7 ...130 C2
Leigham Hall **3**
SW16 ....160 A1
Leigham Hall Par **2**
SW16 ....160 A1
Leigham Vale SE27,
SW16,SW2 ....160 C2
Leigh Ave IG4 ....55 D5
Leigh Cl KT3 ....199 B5
Leigh Cres CR0 ....223 C1
Leigh Ct **22** SW2 ...160 C1
Harrow HA2 ....42 C1
3 Woodford E18 ...37 A1
Leighfield Ho **5** N4 ..51 A2
Leigh Gdns NW10 ..90 C1
Leigh Ho
4 Kingston KT2 ....176 D3
9 Putney SW15 ...156 A6
Leigh Hunt Dr N14 ..15 D3
Leigh Orchard Cl
SW16 ....160 B1
Leigh Pl DA16 .....146 A3
EC1 ....241 A4
Leigh Rd E10 ....54 A2
N5 ....72 D4
Isleworth TW3 ......130 B1
Wallend E6 ....78 C2
Leigh St WC1 ..94 A4 233 A1
Leigh The KT2 ......177 C3
Leighton Ave
Little Ilford E12 ......78 C4
Pinner HA5 ....41 A6
Leighton Cl HA8 ....26 C1
Leighton Cres NW5 .71 C3
Leighton Gdns NW10 90 C6
Thornton Heath CR0 .204 D1
Leighton Gr NW5 ...71 C3
Leighton Ho **3** KT6 ..198 A3
Leighton House (Art Gall &
Mus)* W14 ....254 D6
Leighton Pl NW5 ...71 C3
Leighton Rd NW5 ...71 C3
Ealing W13 ....109 A4
Enfield EN1 ....18 A6
Harrow HA3 ....24 B1
Leighton St CR0 ...204 D1
Leila Parnell Pl **14**
SE7 ....143 C6
Leinster Ave SW14 .133 A1
Leinster Ct NW6 .....91 C4
Leinster Gdns
W2 ....114 A6 246 A6
Leinster Mews W2 .246 A6
Leinster Pl W2 ......236 A1
Leinster Rd N10 .....49 B5
Leinster Sq W2 ......91 C1
Leinster Terr W2 ...246 D6
Leisure Way N12 ....30 B3
Leitch Ho NW8 ......70 B1
Leith Cl NW9 ....45 A1
Leithcote Gdns SW16 182 A6
Leithcote Path SW16 160 B1
Leith Hill BR5 ....190 A4
Leith Hill Gn BR5 ..190 A4
Leith Ho **7** N7 ......71 C4

Leith Ho continued
🔞 Streatham SW2 ....160 B4
Leith Mans W9 ......91 D4
Leith Rd N22 ....32 D2
Leith Towers 🔟 SM2 .217 D1
Leith Yd 🔞 NW6 .....91 C6
Lela Ave TW4,TW5 ..128 C3
Lelitia Cl E8 ....96 A6
Lelland Ho 🔞 SE7 ..122 A4
Lely Ho 🔞 UB5 ......84 D5
Leman St E1 ....96 A1
Lemark Cl HA7 ......25 C4
Le May Ave SE12 ...165 B1
Lemmon Rd SE10 ..142 C6
Lemna Ct E11 ....54 C2
Lemna Rd E11 ......54 C2
Le Moal Ho 🔞 E1 ...96 C2
Lemon Gr TW14 .....150 A3
Lemonwell Ct SE9 .167 A6
Lemonwell Dr SE9 .167 A6
Lemsford Cl N15 ....52 A4
Lemsford Ct N4 .....73 A6
Lena Cres N9 ....18 C2
Lena Gardens Prim Sch
W6 ....112 C3
Lena Gdns W6 .....112 C3
Lena Kennedy Cl E4 ..36 A4
Len Clifton Ho 🔞
SE18 ....122 B2
Lendal Terr 🔞 SW4 .137 D2
Lenelby Rd KT6 ....198 C1
Lenham 🔟 NW5 ....71 A2
Lenham Ho SE1 ....252 D1
Lenham Rd DA7 ...147 B6
SE12 ....142 D1
South Norwood CR7 ..183 B1
Sutton SM1 ....218 A3
Lennard Ave BR4 ..224 C6
Lennard Cl BR4 ....224 C6
Lennard Rd BR2 ...210 B1
Croydon CR0 ......205 A1
Penge BR3 ....185 A4
Lennon Rd NW2 ....68 C2
Lennox Gdns NW10 ..67 D4
SW1 ....114 D3 257 C5
Croydon CR0 ......220 D4
Redbridge IG1 ......56 B1
Lennox Gdns Mews
SW1 ....257 C4
Lennox Ho 🔟 E9 ...74 C2
🔞 Belvedere DA17 ..125 C3
Lennox Rd E17 ......53 C3
N4,N7 ....72 C6
Lenor Cl DA6 ....147 A1
Lensbury Way SE2 .124 D3
Lens Rd E7 ....77 C1
Lenthall Ho SW1 ...259 B1
Lenthall Rd E8 ......74 A1
Lenthorp Rd SE10 .120 D2
Lentmead Rd BR1 .164 D1
Lenton Rise TW9 ...132 A2
Lenton St SE18 ....123 B2
Len Williams Ct NW6 .91 C5
Leo Ct 🔞 TW8 ......131 D5
Leof Cres SE6 ....185 D5
Leominster Rd SM4 .202 A3
Leominster Wlk SM4 .202 A3
Leonard Ave SM4 ...202 A4
Leonard Ct W8 .....255 A6
WC1 ....240 A6
Leonard Day Ho 🔞
NW5 ....71 B2
Leonard Pl 🔞 N16 ..73 C4
Leonard Rd E7 ......77 A4
Chingford E4 ......35 C4
Edmonton N9 ......18 A1
Mitcham CR4,SW16 ..181 C2
Southall UB2 ......106 D2
Leonard Robbins Path 🔞
SE28 ....124 B6
Leonard St E16 ....122 A5
EC2 ....95 B3 242 D6
Leonora Ho W9 ....236 A6
Leontine Cl SE15 ..140 A5
Leopards Ct EC1 ...241 A4
Leopold Ave SW19 .179 B5
Leopold Bldgs 🔞 E2 .95 D4
Leopold Mews E9 ..96 C6
Leopold Prim Sch
NW10 ....67 D1
Leopold Rd E17 .....53 C4
N2 ....48 B6
NW10 ....67 C1
Ealing W5 ....110 B5
Edmonton N18 ....34 B5
Wimbledon SW19 ..179 B5

Leopold St E3 ....97 B2
Leopold Terr SW19 .179 C5
Leopold Wlk SE11 .260 C1
Leo St SE15 ....140 B5
Leo Yd EC1 ....241 D5
Leppoc Rd SW4 ...159 D6
Leroy St SE1 ..117 C2 263 A4
Lerry Cl W14 ......264 D6
Lerwick Ct 🔞 EN1 ..17 C6
Lerwick Ho SW18 .136 A1
Lescombe Cl SE23 .163 A1
Lescombe Rd SE23,
SE6 ....163 A1
Lesley Cl DA5 .....169 D4
Lesley Ct 🔞 SM6 ..219 B4
Leslie Gdns SM2 ..217 C1
Leslie Gr CR0 .....205 C1
Leslie Grove Pl CR0 .205 C1
Leslie Park Rd CR0 .205 C1
Leslie Rd E11 ......76 B4
N2 ....48 B6
Newham E16 ......99 B1
Leslie Smith Sq 🔞
SE18 ....144 C6
Lessar Ave SW4 ...159 C5
Lessar Ct SW4 ....159 C5
Lessingham Ave
Ilford IG5 ....56 C6
Upper Tooting SW17 .181 A6
Lessing St SE23 ...163 A4
Lessness Ave DA7 .146 D5
Lessness Heath Prim Sch
DA17 ....125 C1
Lessness Pk DA17 .125 C1
Lessness Rd
Belvedere DA17 ..125 C1
Morden SM4 ......202 A4
Lester Ave E16 .....98 C3
Lester Ct 🔞 E3 .....97 D4
Lester Ho IG8 ......36 B3
Lestock Ho SE3 ...143 D4
Lestor Ct TW7 .....130 D2
Leswin Pl N16 ......73 D5
Leswin Rd N16 ....73 D5
Letchford Gdns NW10 .90 A4
Letchford Mews
NW10 ....90 A4
Letchmore Ho W10 ..90 A4
Letchworth Ave
TW14 ....149 C4
Letchworth Cl BR2 .209 A4
South Oxhey WD19 ..22 A1
Letchworth Dr BR2 .209 A4
Letchworth St SW17 .180 D6
Lethaby Ho 🔞 SW4 .138 B1
Lethbridge Cl SE13 .142 A3
Letterstone Rd SW6 .264 C3
Lettice St
SW6 ....135 B4 264 D1
Lettsom St SE5 ....139 C3
Lettsom Wlk 🔞 E13 .99 A5
Leucha Rd E17 ....53 A4
Levana Cl SW19 ...157 A3
Levant Ho 🔞 E1 ....96 D3
Levehurst Ho SE27 .183 A6
Levehurst Way SW4,
SW9 ....138 A3
Leven Cl WD19 ...22 C5
Levendale Rd SE23 .163 B2
Leven Rd E14 ......98 B1
Leven Way UB3 ...83 C1
Lever Ct 🔞 E9 .....74 C2
Leverett St SW3 ...257 B4
Leverholme Gdns
SE9 ....188 C6
Leverington Pl N1 .235 D1
Leverson St SW16 .181 C4
Lever St EC1 ..95 A4 235 A1
Leverstock Ho SW3 .257 B2
Leverton Pl NW5 ..71 C3
Leverton St NW5 ..71 C3
Levett Gdns IG3 ..80 A5
Levett Ho 🔞 SW16 .181 D6
Levett Rd IG11 ....79 C2
Levine Gdns IG11 .102 D5
Levison Way 🔞 N19 .49 D1
Levita Ho NW1 ...232 D2
Levyne Ct EC1 ....241 A6
Lewes Cl UB5 ......63 C2
Lewes Ct 🔞 CR4 ..202 A6
Lewesdon Cl 🔞
SW19 ....156 D3
Lewes Ho SE1 ....253 B2
SE15 ....140 A6
Lewes Rd BR1 ....187 A3
N12 ....30 C5
Leweston Pl N16 ..51 D2
Lewey Ho E3 ......97 B3
Lewgars Ave NW9 .45 A3

Lewin Ct SW16 ....182 A4
Lewing Cl BR6 ....211 C1
Lewin Rd DA6 .....147 A1
Mortlake SW14 ....133 B2
Streatham SW16 ..181 D4
Lewis Ave E17 .....35 C2
Lewis Cl N14 ......15 C4
Lewis Cres NW10 .67 B3
Lewis Ct 🔞 SE16 ..118 B3
Lewis Gdns N2 ....30 B1
Lewis Gr SE13 ....142 A2
Lewisham Bridge Prim Sch
SE13 ....141 D1
Lewisham Bsns Ctr
SE14 ....140 D6
Lewisham Coll SE4 .141 D4
Lewisham Ctr SE13 .142 A2
Lewisham High St
SE13 ....163 D6
Lewisham Hill SE13 .142 A2
Lewisham Hospl
SE13 ....163 D6
Lewisham Pk SE13 .164 A5
Lewisham Rd SE13 .142 A3
Lewisham St SW1 .249 D1
Lewisham Sta SE13 .142 A2
Lewisham Way SE4,
SE14 ....141 B4
Lewis King Ho BR1 .187 B3
Lewis Pl E8 ....74 A3
Lewis Rd Bexley DA16 146 C2
Mitcham CR4 ......180 C1
🔞 Richmond TW10 .153 D6
Sidcup DA14 .....168 C2
Southall UB1 .....107 A4
Sutton SM1 ......217 D4
Lewis Silkin Ho 🔞
SE15 ....140 C6
Lewis Sports & L Ctr
SE19 ....183 D2
Lewis St NW1 .....71 B2
Lewis Way RM10 .81 D2
Lexden Dr RM6 ..58 B3
Lexden Rd Acton W3 .110 D5
Mitcham CR4 .....203 D5
Lexfield Ho N5 ....73 A4
Lexham Gardens Mews
W8 ....255 D5
Lexham Gdns
W8 ....113 D2 255 C4
Lexham Ho 🔞 IG11 .101 B6
Lexham Mews
W8 ....113 C2 255 B4
Lexham Wlk W8 ..255 D5
Lexington St
W1 ....115 C6 249 B6
Lexton Gdns SW12 .159 D3
Leyborne Ave W13 .109 C4
Leyborne Pk TW9 .132 C4
Leybourne Cl BR2 .209 A3
Leybourne Ho 🔞 E14 .97 B1
🔞 SE15 ....140 C6
Leybourne Rd E11 .54 D1
🔞 NW1 ....71 B1
NW9 ....44 C4
Hillingdon UB10 ..83 A6
Leybourne St 🔞 NW1 .71 B1
Leybridge Ct SE12 .165 A6
Leyburn Cl 🔞 E17 .53 D5
Leyburn Gdns CR0 .221 C6
Leyburn Gr N18 ...34 A4
Leyburn Ho 🔞 SE18 .144 A5
Leyburn Rd N18 ..34 B4
Leyden Mans 🔞 N19 .50 A2
Leyden St E1 ..95 D2 243 C3
Leydon Cl SE16 ...118 D5
Leyes Rd E16 ......99 D1
Leyfield KT4 ......199 D1
Ley Ho SE1 ......252 A1
Leyland Ave EN3 .7 A3
Leyland Gdns IG8 .37 C5
Leyland Ho 🔞 E14 .119 D6
Leyland Rd SE12 .165 A6
Leylands SW18 ...157 B5
Leylang Rd SE14 .140 D5
Leys Ct 🔞 SW9 ..138 C3
Leysdown 🔞 NW5 .71 A2
Leysdown Ho SE17 .263 B2
Leysdown Rd SE9 .166 B2
Leysfield Rd W12 .112 A4
Leys Gdns EN4 ...15 A6
Leyspring Rd E11 .54 D1
Leys Rd E N3 ......7 A4
Leys Rd W N3 .....7 A4
Leys The N2 ......48 A5
Harrow HA3 ....44 B3
Leyswood Dr IG2 .57 C4

Leythe Rd W3 .....111 A4
Leyton Bsns Ctr E10 .75 C6
Leyton Ct SE23 ....162 C3
Leyton Grange E10 .53 C1
Leyton Green Rd E10 .54 A3
Leyton Ind Village
E10 ....52 D2
Leyton Midland Road Sta
E10 ....54 A2
Leyton Park Rd E10 .76 A5
Leyton Rd E15 ....76 B2
Merton SW19 .....180 A3
Leyton Sixth Form Coll
E10 ....54 B3
Leyton Sta E11 ...76 C6
Leyton Stadium (Leyton
Orient FC) E10 ..75 D5
Leytonstone High Road Sta
E11 ....76 C6
Leytonstone Rd E15 .76 C3
Leytonstone Sch E11 .54 C3
Leytonstone Sta E11 .54 C1
Leyton Town Ctr E10 .76 A5
Lezayre Rd BR6 ..227 D2
Liardet St SE14 ...141 A6
Liberia Rd N5 .....72 D2
Liberty Ave SW19 .180 B2
Liberty Ct IG11 ...102 C5
Liberty Mews SW12 .159 B5
Liberty Mid Sch CR4 180 C1
Liberty Pl 🔞 E1 ...118 C4
Liberty St
SW9 ....138 B4 270 D2
Libra Ct E4 ....35 C6
Libra Rd E13 .....99 A5
🔞 E3 ....97 B5
Library Ct N17 ....51 D6
Library Mans 🔞 W12 112 C4
Library Par NW10 .89 C6
Library Pl E1 .....118 B6
Library St
SE1 ....116 D4 251 D1
Lichen Cl IG6 .....56 D6
Lichfield Cl EN4 ..2 C1
Lichfield Ct
Kingston KT6 .....198 A4
Richmond TW9 ...132 A1
Lichfield Gdns TW9,
TW9 ....154 A6
Lichfield Gr N3 ...29 C1
Lichfield Ho 🔞 SE5 .139 A3
Lichfield Rd E3 ...97 A4
E6 ....99 D4
NW2 ....69 A4
Dagenham RM8 ...80 C5
Edmonton N9 .....18 A2
Hounslow TW4 ...128 C2
Richmond TW9 ...132 B4
Woodford IG8 .....36 C6
Lichfield Terr 🔞
TW9 ....154 A6
Lichlade Cl 🔞 BR6 .227 D4
Lichport Ct N4 ....50 D1
Lickey Ho W14 ...264 D6
Lidbury Rd NW7 ..29 A4
Lidcote Gdns 🔞 SW9 138 B3
Liddall Way UB7 .104 B5
Liddell Cl HA3 ....43 D6
Liddell Gdns NW10 .90 C5
Liddell Rd NW6 ..69 C2
Lidding Rd HA3 ...43 D4
Liddington Rd E15 .98 D6
Liddlesdale Ho E 🔞
KT2 ....176 D2
Liddlesdale Ho W 🔞
KT2 ....176 D2
Liddon Rd BR1 ...209 D6
E13 ....99 B4
Liden Cl E10,E17 .53 B1
Lidfield Rd N16 ...73 B4
Lidgate Rd 🔞 SE15 139 D5
Lidiard Rd SW18 .158 A2
Lidlington Pl NW1 .232 B3
Lido Sq N17 ......33 B1
Lidyard Rd N19 ...49 C1
Liffey Ct NW10 ...68 A1
Liffler Rd SE18 ...123 C1
Liffords Pl SW13 .133 D3
Lifford St SW15 ..134 D1
Lightcliffe Rd N13 .16 C1
Lighter Cl 🔞 SE16 .119 C4
Lighterman Mews 🔞
E1 ....96 C1
Lighterman's Rd E14 119 D4
Lighterman's Wlk
SW18 ....135 C1
Lightfoot Rd N8 ..50 A4

Lightley Cl HA0 ....88 B6
Ligonier St E2 ....243 C6
Lilac Cl E4 ....35 B4
Lilac Ct 🔞 E13 ....99 C6
Croydon CR0 .....223 C5
Hayes UB3 ....83 C1
Lilac Ho SE4 ......141 B2
Lilac Gdns W5 ...109 B3
Croydon CR0 .....223 C5
Hayes UB3 ....83 C1
Lilac Ho SE4 ......141 B2
Lilac Pl SE11 ..116 B2 260 C3
Yiewsley UB7 .....104 B6
Lilac St W12 ......112 A6
Lilburn Ct SW15 .134 D2
Lilburne Gdns SE9 .166 A6
Lilburne Rd SE9 ..166 A6
Lilburne Wlk NW10 .67 A2
Lile Cres W7 ......86 C2
Lilestone Est NW8 .236 D5
Lilestone Ho NW8 .236 D6
Lilestone St
NW8 ....92 C3 237 A6
Lilford Ho 🔞 SE5 .139 A3
Lilford Rd SE5 ...138 D3
Lilian Barker Cl SE12 165 A6
Lilian Baylis Ho N1 .73 A2
Lilian Baylis Sch
SE11 ....116 B1 260 C2
Lilian Board Way UB6 .64 B3
Lilian Gdns IG8 ..37 B2
Lilian Rd SW16 ...181 C2
Lilian Rolfe Ho 🔞
SE27 ....183 B6
Lillechurch Rd RM8 .80 C2
Lilleshall Rd SM4 .202 B3
Lilley Cl E1 ....118 A5
Lillian Ave W3 ...110 C4
Lillian Cl 🔞 N16 ..73 C5
Lillian Rd SW13 ..134 B6
Lillie Ho N5 ......72 C4
Lillie Rd SW6 ..135 B6 264 C5
Lilleshall Rd SW4 .137 C2
Lillie Yd SW6 ..135 C6 265 A6
Lillingston Ho N7 .72 C4
Lilliput Ave UB5 ..85 B6
Lillywhite 🔞 NW9 .27 D2
Lily Cl W14 ......112 D2
Lily Gdns HA0 ....87 C5
Lily Pl EC1 ......241 B4
Lily Rd E17 ....53 C3
Lilyville Rd
SW6 ....135 B4 264 C2
Limavady Ho 🔞 SE18 122 C2
Limberg Ho SE8 .119 B2
Limborough Ho 🔞
E14 ....97 C2
Limbourne Ave RM8 .59 B2
Limburg Rd SW11 .136 C1
Lime Ave UB7 ....104 B6
Limeburner La
EC4 ....94 D1 241 C2
Lime Cl BR1 ......210 A5
E1 ....118 A5
Buckhurst Hill IG9 .21 D2
Carshalton SM5 ..218 D6
Harrow HA3 ......25 A1
Pinner HA5 ......39 D6
Lime Cres TW16 .172 C1
Limecroft Cl KT19 .215 D2
Lime Ct 🔞 E11 ....76 C6
🔞 Harrow HA1 ...42 D3
Kingston KT3 .....198 D6
Mitcham CR4 .....180 B1
Limedene Cl HA5 .22 D2
Lime Gr DA15 ...167 D5
W12 ....112 C4
Barnet N20 ......13 A3
Hayes UB3 ....105 B6
Kingston KT3 .....199 C6
Orpington BR6 ...226 C6
Ruislip HA4 ......40 A2
Twickenham TW1 .153 A5
Limeharbour E14 .119 D4
Limehouse Cswy E14 119 B6
Limehouse Cut 🔞 E14 97 D2
Limehouse Fields Est
E14 ....97 A2
Limehouse Link (Tunnel)
E14 ....119 B6
Limehouse Sta E14 .97 A1
Lime Kiln Dr SE7 .143 B6
Limekiln Pl SE19 .183 D3
Limekiln Wharf 🔞
E14 ....119 B6
Lime Lo 🔞 TW16 .171 D3
Limerick Cl 🔞 SW12 159 C4
Limerick Ct 🔞 SW12 159 C4
Lime Row DA18 ..125 B3
Limerston St
SW10 ....136 A6 266 B5
Limes Ave N12 ...30 A6

Limes Ave continued
NW11 ....47 A2
NW7 ....27 C4
Barnes SW13 ....133 D4
Carshalton SM5 ..202 D1
Croydon CR0 .....220 C6
Penge SE20 ......184 B5
Wanstead E11 ....55 B1
Limes Ave The N11 .31 C1
Limes Cl 🔞 N11 ..31 C1
Ashford TW15 ....170 C1
Limes Ct NW6 ....68 D2
Beckenham BR3 ..185 B1
Limes Field Rd SW14 133 C1
Limesdale Gdns HA8 .27 A1
Limes Gdns SW18 .157 C5
Limes Gr SE13 ...142 A1
Limes Rd
Beckenham BR3 ..185 B1
Thornton Heath CR0 205 B2
Limes Row BR6 ..226 D1
Lime St E17 ......53 A5
EC3 ....95 C1 243 B1
Limes The BR2 ..226 A4
SE5 ....139 C2
W2 ....245 B6
East Molesey KT8 .195 D5
Lime St Pas EC3 .253 A6
Limes Wlk SE15 .140 C1
W5 ....109 D4
Lime Terr W7 .....108 C6
Lime Tree Ave KT10,
KT7 ....196 C6
Limetree Cl SW2 .160 B3
Lime Tree Ct N2 ..47 D6
Limetree Ct HA5 ..23 C3
Lime Tree Ct CR2 .221 A2
Lime Tree Gr CR0 .223 C5
Lime Tree Pl CR4 .181 B2
Lime Tree Rd TW5 .129 C3
Limetree Wlk 🔞
SW17 ....181 D4
Lime Tree Wlk
Bushey WD23 ....8 C2
Coney Hall BR4 ..224 D4
Enfield EN2 ......5 A5
Lime Wlk 🔟 E15 .98 C6
Limewood Cl E17 .53 B5
Beckenham BR3 ..208 A4
Ealing W13 ......87 B2
Limewood Ct IG4 .56 B4
Limpsfield Ave
Putney SW19 .....156 C2
Thornton Heath CR7 204 B4
Limscott Ho 🔞 E3 .97 D4
Linacre Ct SE15 ..140 B2
Linacre Ct W6 ....112 C1
Linacre Rd NW2 .68 B2
Linale Ho N1 .....235 C2
Linberry Wlk 🔞 SE8 119 B2
Linchmere Rd SE12 164 D4
Lincoln Ave N14 ..15 C2
Twickenham TW2 .152 A2
Wimbledon SW19 .156 D1
Lincoln Cl
Croydon SE25 ....206 B3
Greenford UB6 ...86 A6
Harrow HA2 ......41 B4
Lincoln Cres EN1 .17 C6
Lincoln Ct N16 ...51 B2
NW4 ....46 B4
SE12 ....165 C1
Borehamwood WD6 .11 B6
Enfield EN2 ......5 B1
Hampton TW12 ..173 B5
🔞 Ilford IG2 .....57 A3
Mitcham CR4 .....204 A4
Redbridge IG1 ...56 B2
Lincoln Gdns IG1 .56 B2
Lincoln Green Rd
BR5 ....211 D4
Lincoln Ho SW1 .247 C1
🔟 Putney SW15 .157 A2
Lincoln Lo 🔟 BR3 .185 D1
Lincoln Mews NW6 .91 B6
Lincoln Rd DA14 .190 B5
E13 ....99 B3
E7 ....77 D2
N2 ....48 C6
Croydon SE25 ....206 B6
Enfield EN1,EN3 ..18 A6
Harrow HA2,HA5 .41 B4
Kingston KT3 .....199 A6
Mitcham CR4 .....204 A4
North Cheam KT4 .200 B1
Northwood HA6 ..39 C6
Twickenham TW13 151 B1
Wembley HA0 ....65 D2
Woodford E18 ....37 A2

Lincoln's Inn★ WC2 ....94 B1 **240** D2
Lincoln's Inn Fields WC2 ....94 B1 **240** D2
Lincoln St E11 ......76 C6
SW3 ....**257** C3
Lincolns The NW7 ......11 D1
Lincoln Terr **4** SM2 ..217 C1
Lincoln Way
  Charlton TW16 ....171 C2
  Enfield EN3 ....18 B6
Lincombe Rd BR1 ...164 D1
Linda Ct KT9 ....213 D4
Lindal Cres EN2 ....4 B1
Lindal Ct **1** E18 .....37 A2
Lindale SW19 ......157 A2
Lindales The N17 ....33 A6
Lindal Rd SE4 ....163 B6
Lindbergh Rd SM6 ..220 A1
Linden Ave NW10 ....90 D5
  Enfield EN1 ....6 A4
  Hounslow TW3 ......151 D6
  Ruislip HA4 ....40 A1
  Thornton Cr7 ......204 D5
  Wembley HA9 ....66 B3
Linden Bridge Sch KT4 ......215 C5
Linden Cl Ruislip HA4 ..40 A1
  Southgate N14 ......15 C5
  Stanmore HA7 ......25 B5
  Thames Ditton KT7 ..197 A2
Linden Cotts **6**
  SW19 ....179 A3
Linden Cres
  Kingston KT1 ....176 B1
  Wembley UB6 ....64 D2
  Woodford IG8 ......37 B4
Linden Ct NW7 ....27 B5
  8 SW18 ....136 B1
  W12 ....112 C5
  1 Beckenham BR3 ..207 D6
  Penge SE20 ....184 B3
  Sidcup DA14 ......189 C6
Lindenfield BR7 .....188 D1
Linden Gdns
  W2 ....113 C6 **245** B5
  W4 ....111 B1
  Enfield EN1 ....6 A4
Linden Gr SE15 ....140 C2
  Kingston KT3 ......199 C6
  Penge SE20 ....184 C4
  Teddington TW11 ..174 D5
Linden Ho **10** SE8 ..141 B6
Linden Lawns HA9 ..66 B4
Linden Lea N2 ......48 A4
Lindenlea Ct E17 ....53 B5
Linden Leas BR4 ..224 B4
Linden Lodge Sch
  SW19 ....157 A3
Linden Mans N6 ....49 B1
Linden Mews N1 ....73 B3
  W2 ....**245** B5
Linden Pl CR4 ......202 C5
Linden Rd N10 ......49 B5
  N11 ....15 A2
  N15 ....51 A5
  Hampton TW12 .....173 C2
Lindens The **5** E17 ..53 D5
  N12 ....30 B5
  Chiswick W4 ....133 A4
  New Addington CR0 ..224 A2
Linden Way
  Shepperton TW17 ..193 A4
  Southgate N14 ......15 C5
Lindeth Cl HA7 .....25 B4
Lindfield Gdns NW3 ..70 A3
Lindfield Hts NW3 ....70 A3
Lindfield Rd
  Croydon CR0 ....205 D3
  Ealing W5 ....87 C3
Lindfield St E14 ....97 C1
Lindhill Cl EN3 ......6 D3
Lindholme Ct **3** NW9 ..27 C2
Lindisfarne Rd
  Dagenham RM8 ....80 C5
  Wimbledon SW20 ..178 A3
Lindisfarne Way E9 ..75 A4
Lindley Ct KT1 .....175 C2
Lindley Ho **12** SE15 ..140 A5
Lindley Pl TW9 ....132 C4
Lindley Rd E10 .....76 A6
Lindley St E1 ....96 C2
Lindon Bennett Sch
  TW13 ....172 D5
Lindop Ho **7** E3 ....97 A1
Lindore Rd SW11 ..136 D1
Lindores Rd SM5 ..202 A1
Lindo St SE15 .....140 C3
Lind Rd SM1 ......218 A3
Lindrop St SW6 ....136 A4

Lindsay Cl KT9 .....214 A1
Lindsay Ct SW11 ...**266** D1
Lindsay Dr Harrow HA3 ..44 B4
  Shepperton TW17 ..193 B3
Lindsay Ho **2** SE18 ..122 C2
Lindsay Rd
  Hampton TW12 .....173 D6
  North Cheam KT4 ..216 B6
Lindsay Sq
  SW1 ....115 D1 **259** D2
Lindsell St **3** SE10 ..142 A4
Lindsey Cl BR1 ....210 A6
  Mitcham CR4,SW16 ..204 A5
Lindsey Ct N13 ......16 C1
Lindsey Gdns TW14 ..149 B4
Lindsey Ho★ SW10 ..**266** D4
  W5 ....109 D2
Lindsey Mews **13** N1 ..73 A1
Lindsey Rd RM8 ....80 C5
Lindsey St EC1 94 D2 **241** D4
Lind St SE8 ....141 D3
Lindum Rd TW11 ...175 C3
Lindums The BR3 ..185 B4
Lindway SE27 .....182 D5
Lindwood Cl **8** E6 ..100 B2
Linfield WC1 ....**233** C1
Linfield Cl NW4 ....46 C5
Linford Ct **1** CR4 ..180 C2
Linford Ho **17** E2 ..96 A6
Linford Rd E17 .....54 A6
Linford St
  SW8 ....137 C4 **269** A1
Lingard Ho **9** E14 ..120 A3
Lingards Rd SE13 ..142 A1
Lingey Cl DA15 ....167 D2
  Bushey WD23 ....8 A3
Lingfield Ave KT1,KT5 198 B5
Lingfield Cl EN1 .....17 C5
Lingfield Cres SE9,
  DA16 ....145 B1
Lingfield Ct
  Northolt UB5 ....85 C5
  Wimbledon SW19 ..178 D4
Lingfield Gdns N9 ..18 B4
Lingfield Ho SE1 ..**251** D1
  5 W4 ....111 A1
  Penge SE26 ....184 B4
Lingfield Rd
  North Cheam KT4 ..216 C5
  Wimbledon SW19 ..178 D4
Lingham St SW9 ..138 B3
Lingholm Way EN5 ..12 D6
Ling Rd E16 ....99 A2
Lingrove Gdns IG9 ..21 B2
Ling's Coppice SE21 ..161 B2
Lingwell Rd SW17 ..158 C1
Lingwood DA7 ....147 D3
Lingwood Gdns TW7 130 C5
Lingwood Rd E5 ....52 A2
Linhope St
  NW1 ....92 D3 **237** C5
Linkenholt Mans **3**
  W6 ....111 A2
Linkfield KT8 ......195 D6
Link Field BR2 .....209 A3
Linkfield Rd TW7 ..130 D3
Link La SM6 ....220 A2
Linklea Cl NW9 .....27 C3
Link Prim Sch CR0 ..220 A4
Link Rd N11 ....31 A6
  Dagenham RM9 ....103 D5
  East Bedfont TW14 ..149 D4
  Hackbridge SM6 ....203 A1
Links Ave SM4 ....201 C5
Linkscroft Ave TW15 ..170 D4
Links Ct N20 ......14 B1
Links Dr N20 ......13 D3
Link Sec Sch CR0 ..220 B4
Links Gdns SW16 ..182 C5
Linkside N12 ......29 C4
  Kingston KT3 ....177 C1
Linkside Cl EN2 .....4 C2
Linkside Gdns EN2 ..4 B2
Links Ind Est TW13 ..151 A2
Links Prim Sch SW17 181 A4
Links Rd NW2 ......67 D6
  Acton W3 ....88 C1
  Ashford TW15 .....170 A4
  Mitcham SW16,SW17 ..181 A4
  West Wickham BR4 ..208 A1
  Woodford IG8 ......37 A5
Links Side EN2 ......4 C2
Link St E9 ....74 C1
Links The E17 ......53 A5
Linksview N2 ......48 D4
Links View N3 ......29 B3
  SE18 ....144 A4
Links View Cl HA7 ..25 A4
Links View Rd
  Croydon CR0 ....223 C2
  Hampton TW12 .....174 A4

Linksway NW4 ....28 D1
Links Way
  Beckenham BR3 ....207 C3
  Streatham SW17 ..181 A4
Links Yd E1 ....**243** D4
  9 E1 ....96 A2
Link The NW2 ....46 A1
  SE9 ....166 C1
  Acton W3 ....88 D1
  Enfield EN3 ....7 A4
  Northolt UB5 ......63 B3
  Pinner HA5 ....40 C2
  Teddington TW11 ..174 D4
  Wembley HA0 ....43 C5
Linkway N4 ....51 A2
  Dagenham RM8 ....80 C4
  Pinner HA5 ....22 D2
  West Barnes SW20 ..200 B6
Link Way Bromley BR2 210 A2
  Richmond TW10 ....153 B2
Linkway The EN5 ....13 D5
Linkwood Wlk NW1 ..71 D1
Linley Cres RM7 ....59 D6
Linley Ct
  1 Dulwich SE21 ..183 C6
  Sutton SM1 ....218 A4
Linley Rd N17 ......33 C1
Linnell Cl NW11 ....47 D3
Linnell Dr NW11 ...47 D3
Linnell Ho E1 .....**243** C4
  NW8 ....**229** A6
Linnell Rd SE5 ....139 C3
  Edmonton N18 ......34 A6
Linnet Cl N9 ....18 D3
  Bushey WD23 ....8 A3
  Woolwich SE28 ....124 C6
Linnet Mews SW12 ..159 A4
Linnett Cl E4 ......36 A6
Linom Rd SW4 ....138 A1
Linscott Rd E5 .....74 C4
Linsdell Rd IG11 ..101 A6
Linsey St SE16 ....118 A2
  SE16 ....118 A2
Linslade Cl
  Hounslow TW4 ....151 A6
  Pinner HA5 ....40 B6
Linslade Ho **10** E2 ..96 A6
  NW8 ....**237** B6
Linstead St **1** NW6 ..69 C1
Linstead Way SW18,
  SW19 ....157 A4
Linsted Ct SE9,DA15 ..167 C5
Linster Gr WD6 .....11 A6
Linthorpe Ave HA0 ..65 C2
Linthorpe Rd N16 ..51 C2
  Cockfosters EN4 .....2 C2
Linton Cl DA16 ....146 B4
  2 SE7 ....121 C1
  Carshalton CR4 ....202 D2
Linton Gdns E6 ....100 A1
Linton Gr SE27 ....183 A5
Linton Ho **2** E3 ....97 C2
Linton Mead Prim Sch
  SE28 ....124 B6
Linton Rd IG11 .....79 A1
Lintons The IG11 ....79 A1
Linver Rd SW6 ....135 C3
Linwood Cl SE5 ....139 D3
Linwood Cres EN1 ....6 A4
Linzee Rd N8 ......50 A5
Lion Ave TW1 .....152 D3
Lion Cl SE4 ....163 C5
  Littleton TW17 ....192 A6
Lion Ct **12** NW9 ....46 A5
Lion Ctr The TW13 ..151 A1
Lionel Gdns SE9 ..165 D6
Lionel Ho **5** W10 ..91 A2
  Bowes Park N22 ....32 B4
Lionel Mans **14** W14 ..112 D3
Lionel Mews W10 ..91 A2
Lionel Rd SE9 ....165 D6
Lionel Road Jun & Inf Sch
  TW8 ....110 A2
Lionel Road N TW8 ..110 A2
Lionel Road S TW8 ..110 B1
Lion Gate Gdns TW9 ..132 B2
Lion Gate Mews
  SW18 ....157 C4
Lion Mills **33** E2 ..96 A5
Lion Park Ave KT9 ..214 C4
Lion Rd DA6 ......147 B1
  E6 ....100 B2
  Edmonton N9 ......18 A2
  Thornton Heath CR0 ..205 A4
  Twickenham TW1,TW2 ..152 D3
Lions Cl SE12 .....165 D1
Lion Way TW8 ....131 D5
Lion Wharf Rd TW7 ..131 B2

Lion Yd SW4 ......137 D1
Liphook Cres SE23 ..162 C4
Liphook Rd WD19 ..22 D6
Lipton Cl SE28 ....124 C4
Lipton Rd **8** E1 ....96 D1
Lisa Lo **5** EN5 ....13 D6
Lisbon Ave TW2 ..152 A4
Lisbon Cl E17 ......35 A1
Lisburne Rd NW3 ..70 D4
Lisford St SE15 ...139 D4
Lisgar Terr
  W14 ....113 B2 **254** C4
Liskeard Cl BR7 ..189 A4
Liskeard Gdns SE3 ..143 A4
Liskeard Ho **2** SE11 ..**261** B2
Lisle Cl SW17 ....181 B6
Lisle Ct NW2 ......69 A5
Lisle St WC2 ..115 D6 **249** D6
Lismirrane Ind Pk WD6 ..9 B5
Lismore **9** SW19 ..179 B5
Lismore Cl TW7 ..131 A3
Lismore Rd N17 ....51 B6
  South Croydon CR2 ..221 C2
Lismore Wlk **4** N1 ..73 A2
Lissant Cl KT6 ....197 D2
Lisselton Ho **3** NW4 ..46 D5
Lissenden Gdns NW5 ..71 A4
Lissenden Mans NW5 ..71 A4
Lisson Cotts NW1 ..**237** B4
Lisson Gr NW1,
  NW8 ....92 C3 **237** A4
Lisson Ho NW1 ....**237** A4
Lisson St NW1 92 C2 **237** A4
Lister Cl W3 ......89 B2
  Mitcham SW19 ....180 C2
Lister Com Sch E13 ..99 B5
Lister Ct N16 ......73 C6
  NW9 ....27 C1
Lister Gdns N18 ....33 A5
Lister Ho E1 ......96 A2
  SE2 ....124 D1
  SE3 ....142 C6
  Hayes UB3 ....105 C2
  9 Wembley HA9 ..67 A5
Lister Hospl
  SW1 ....115 B1 **258** C1
Lister Mews N7 ....72 B4
Lister Rd E11 ......54 D1
Lister Wlk SE28 ..124 C6
Liston Ho N21 ......16 B6
Liston Rd SW4 ....137 C2
  Tottenham N17 ......34 A2
Liston Way **1** IG8 ..37 C3
Listowel Cl **2** SW9 ..138 C5
Listowel Rd RM10 ..81 C5
Listria La N16 ......73 C6
Listria Pk N16 ......73 C6
Litcham Ho **23** E1 ..96 D4
Litchfield Ave E15 ..76 C4
  Morden SM4 ......201 B2
Litchfield Ct E17 ....53 C2
Litchfield Gdns NW10 ..68 A2
Litchfield Rd SM1 ..218 A4
Litchfield St WC2 ..249 D6
Litchfield Way NW11 ..48 A4
Lithgow's Rd TW14,
  TW6 ....127 D1
Lithos Rd NW3 ....70 A2
Little Acre BR3 ....207 C6
Little Albany St NW1 ..238 D2
Little Argyll St W1 ..**239** A1
Little Birches DA15 ..167 A2
Little Boltons The
  SW10 ....**255** C6
Little Bornes SE21 ..183 C6
Littlebourne **2** SE13 164 C4
Little Britain EC1 ..**242** A3
Littlebrook Cl CR0 ..206 D3
Little Brownings
  SE23 ....162 B2
Littleburg Ave E4 ..20 D3
Little Bury St N9 ....17 C4
Little Bushey La WD23 ..8 B5
Little Cedars N12 ..30 A6
Little Chelsea Ho
  SW10 ....**266** D3
Little Chester St
  SW1 ....**258** C6
Little College St
  SW1 ....**260** A6
Littlecombe SE7 ..143 B6
Little Combe Cl **18**
  SW15 ....156 C5
Little Common HA7 ..9 A4
Littlecote Cl SW19 ..157 A4
Littlecote Pl HA5 ..23 B4
Littlecroft SE9 ....144 C2
Little Ct BR4 ......224 C6
Littledale SE2 ....146 A6
Little Dimocks SW12 ..159 B2

Little Dorrit Ct SE1 ..**252** B2
Little Ealing La W5 ..109 C2
Little Ealing Prim Sch
  W5 ....109 C3
Little Edward St
  NW1 ....**231** D2
Little Elms UB3 ....127 B5
Little Essex St WC2 ..**251** A6
Little Ferry Rd TW1 ..153 B3
Littlefield Cl N19 ....71 C4
  9 Kingston KT1 ..176 A1
Littlefield Ct UB7 ..126 A5
Littlefield Ho KT1 ..176 A1
Littlefield Rd HA8 ..27 A3
Little Friday Rd E4 ..20 C2
Little Gearies IG6 ..56 D5
Little George St SW1 ..**250** A1
Little Gn NW9 .....131 D1
Little Grange UB6 ..87 A4
Little Green St NW5 ..71 B4
Littlegrove EN4 ....14 C5
Littlegrove Ct **3** EN4 ..14 C5
Little Halliards KT12 ..194 A3
Little Heath SE7 ..122 A1
  Ilford RM6 ....58 B5
Little Heath Rd DA7 ..147 B5
Littleheath Rd CR2 ..222 B1
Little Heath Sch RM6 ..58 B5
Little Holt **8** E11 ..55 A4
Little Ilford La E12 ..78 B4
Little Ilford Sch E12 ..78 B3
Littlejohn Rd W7 ..86 D1
Little Larkins EN5 ..13 A5
Little Marlborough St
  W1 ....**239** A1
Littlemead KT10 ..212 B4
Littlemede SE9 ....166 B1
Littlemoor Rd IG1 ..79 B5
Littlemore Rd SE2 ..124 A4
Little Moss La HA5 ..23 A4
Little Newport St
  WC2 ....**249** D6
Little New St EC4 ..**241** B2
Little Orchard HA7 ..23 A6
Little Oxhey La WD19 ..23 A6
Little Park Dr TW13 ..151 A2
Little Park Gdns EN2 ..5 B2
Little Pluckett's Way
  IG9 ....21 D3
Little Portland St
  W1 ....**239** A2
Little Potters WD23 ..8 C4
Little Queens Rd
  TW11 ....174 D4
Little Rd UB3 .....105 D4
Little Redlands BR1 ..188 A1
Little Road Mans
  SW6 ....**264** B5
Littlers Cl SW19 ..180 B2
Little Russell St WC1 ..**240** B3
Little Sanctuary SW1 ..**250** A1
Little Smith St SW1 ..**259** D6
Little Somerset St
  E1 ....**243** C1
Little Stanmore Fst & Mid
  Sch HA8 ....26 B2
Little St James's St
  SW1 ....**249** A3
Little St Leonards
  SW14 ....133 A2
Littlestone Cl BR3 ..185 C4
Little Strand NW9 ..27 D1
Little Thrift BR5 ..211 A3
Little Titchfield St
  W1 ....**239** A3
Littleton Ave E4 ....20 D3
Littleton CE Inf Sch
  TW17 ....192 C6
Littleton Cres HA1 ..64 D6
Littleton La TW17,
  TW18 ....192 A4
Littleton Rd
  Harrow HA1 ....64 D6
  Littleton TW15,TW17 ..171 A3
Littleton St SW18 ..158 B2
Little Trinity La EC4 ..**252** B6
Little Venice★
  W9 ....92 A2 **236** A4
Littlewood SE13 ..164 A5
Littlewood Cl W13 ..109 B3
Littlewood SE13 ....164 A5
Little Wood Cl BR5 ..190 A6
Littleworth Ave KT10 212 B3
Littleworth Common Rd
  KT10 ....212 B6
Littleworth La KT10 ..212 B4
Littleworth Pl KT10 ..212 B4
Littleworth Rd KT10 ..212 C4
Livermere Ct **3** E8 ..95 D6
Livermere Rd E8 ....95 D6

Liverpool Gr
  SE17 ....117 B1 **262** C1
Liverpool Ho N7 ....72 C2
Liverpool Rd E10 ..54 A3
  E16 ....98 C2
  N1 ....**234** B5
  N1,N7 ....72 C1
  W5 ....109 D4
  Kingston KT2 .....176 C3
  South Norwood CR7 ..205 A6
Liverpool St
  EC2 ....95 C2 **243** A3
Liverpool Street Sta
  EC2 ....95 C2 **243** A3
Livesey Cl KT1 ....198 B6
Livesey Mus★ SE15 ..140 A6
Livesey Pl SE15 ..140 A6
Livingstone Ct E10 ..54 A3
  Barnet EN5 ....1 A3
  Stanwell TW19 ....148 A3
Livingstone Ho **16**
  SE5 ....139 A5
Livingstone Lo **13** W9 ..91 C2
Livingstone Pl E14 ..120 C1
Livingstone Prim Sch
  EN4 ....2 B2
Livingstone Rd E15 ..98 A4
  E17 ....53 D3
  14 SW11 ....136 B2
  Bowes Park N13 ....32 A5
  Isleworth TW3 ....130 A1
  Southall UB1 .....106 D6
  South Norwood CR7 ..183 B3
Livity Sch The SW2 ..160 A6
Livonia St W1 ....**239** B1
Lizard St EC1 ..95 A4 **235** B1
Lizban St SE3 ....143 B5
Llandovery Ho **1**
  E14 ....120 A4
Llanelly Rd NW2 ..69 B6
Llanover Ct HA9 ..65 D4
Llanover Rd SE18 ..144 C5
  Wembley HA9 ....65 D5
Llanthony Rd SM4 ..202 B4
Llanvanor Rd NW2 ..69 B6
Llewellyn Ct SE20 ..184 C2
Llewellyn St SE16 ..118 A4
Lloyd Ave SW16 ..182 A2
Lloyd Baker St
  WC1 ....94 C4 **234** A1
Lloyd Ct SE13 .....163 D6
  Pinner HA5 ....40 D4
  6 West Norwood
  SE27 ....160 D1
Lloyd Ho N16 ......73 B5
  3 Beckenham BR3 ..185 D4
  Bromley BR1 ......187 B5
Lloyd Mews EN3 ....7 C5
Lloyd Park Ave CR0 ..221 D4
Lloyd Park Ho E17 ..53 C6
Lloyd Park Sta CR0 ..221 D4
Lloyd Rd E6 ......100 B6
  Dagenham RM9 ....81 B1
  North Cheam KT4,SM3 216 D5
  Walthamstow E17 ..52 D5
Lloyd's Ave EC3 ..**243** B1
Lloyd's Bldg★
  EC3 ....95 C1 **243** A1
Lloyd's Pl SE3 ....142 C3
Lloyd Sq WC1 ..94 C4 **234** A2
Lloyd's Row
  EC1 ....94 D4 **234** C1
Lloyd St WC1 ..94 C4 **234** A2
Lloyds Way BR3 ..207 B4
Lloyd Villas SE4 ..141 C4
Loampit Hill SE13 ..141 D3
Loampit Vale SE13 ..142 A2
Loanda Cl **1** E8 ....95 D6
Loanda Ho SE15 ..140 C2
Loats Rd SW2 ....160 A5
Lobelia Cl **5** E6 ..100 A4
Locarno Rd **6** W3 ..111 A5
  Greenford UB6 .....86 B3
Lochaber Rd SE13 ..142 C1
Lochaline St W6 ..134 C6
Lochan Cl UB4 .....85 A3
Lochbie **5** N4 .....50 A2
Lochinvar St SW12 ..159 A4
Lochleven Ho **9** N2 ..30 B1
Lochmere Cl DA8 ..147 D6
Lochmore Ho SW1 ..**258** B3
Lochnagar St E14 ..98 A2
Lockbridge Ct **3** W9 ..91 C2
Lock Chase SE3 ..142 C2
Lock Cl UB2 ....108 A4
Locke Ho SW8 ....**269** A2
Lockesfield Pl E14 ..119 D1

Lockesley Dr BR5 . . 211 D3
Lockesley Sq KT6 . . 197 D3
Locket Rd HA3 . . 24 D1
Lockfield Ave EN3 . . 7 B4
Lockgate Cl E9 . . 75 B3
Lockhart Cl N7 . . 72 B2
Enfield EN3 . . 18 B6
Lockhart Lo 4 E4 . . 20 C4
Lockhart St E3 . . 97 B3
Lock Ho N16 . . 51 D1
Lockhurst St E5 . . 74 D4
Lockier Wlk HA9 . . 65 D5
Lockington Rd
SW8 . . 137 B4 268 D2
Lockmead Rd N15 . . 52 A3
SE13 . . 142 A2
Lock Rd TW10 . . 175 C6
Lockside 17 E14 . . 119 A6
Lock's La CR4 . . 181 A1
Locksley St E14 . . 97 B2
Locksmeade Rd
TW10 . . 175 C6
Lock View Ct 9 E14 . . 119 A6
Lockwood Cl SE26 . . 184 D6
Lockwood Ct KT3 . . 199 A5
Lockwood Ho 10
SE11 . . 138 C6
Lockwood Ind Pk N17 52 B6
Lockwood Sq SE16 . . 118 B3
Lockwood Way E17 . . 34 D1
Chessington KT9 . . 214 C3
Lockyer Est SE1 . . 252 D1
Lockyer Ho 7 SE10 . . 120 D1
SW8 . . 270 A4
Putney SW15 . . 134 D2
Lockyer St SE1 . . 252 D1
Locomotive Dr TW14 150 A3
Locton Gn 4 E3 . . 97 B6
Lodden Lo 13 SM2 . . 218 A1
Loddiges Ho 5 E9 . . 74 C1
Loddiges Rd E9 . . 74 C1
Loddon Ho NW8 . . 236 D5
Loder St SE15 . . 140 C5
Lodge Ave
Borehamwood WD6 . . 10 B6
Croydon CR0 . . 220 C5
Dagenham RM8,RM9,
IG11 . . 80 B3
Harrow HA3 . . 44 A5
Lodge Cl Edgware HA8 26 C4
Edmonton N18 . . 33 A5
Hackbridge SM6 . . 203 A1
Isleworth TW7 . . 131 B4
Lodge Ct 3 HA0 . . 66 A3
Lodge Dr N13 . . 32 C6
Lodge Gdns BR3 . . 207 B4
Lodge Hill DA16 . . 146 B5
Redbridge IG4 . . 56 A5
Lodgehill Park Cl HA2 63 D6
Lodge La DA5 . . 168 D5
N12 . . 30 A5
New Addington CR0 . . 223 D1
Lodge Pl SM1 . . 217 D3
Lodge Rd NW4 . . 46 C5
NW8 . . 92 C4 230 A1
Bromley BR1 . . 187 C3
Sutton SM1 . . 217 D3
Thornton Heath CR0 . . 204 D2
Wallington SM6 . . 219 B3
Lodge Villas IG8 . . 36 D4
Lodge Way
Charlton TW17 . . 171 A1
Stanwell TW15 . . 148 A2
Lodore Gdns NW9 . . 45 C4
Lodore Gn UB10 . . 60 A5
Lodore St E14 . . 98 A1
Lodsworth Ho SW11 . 268 A1
Lofthouse Pl KT9 . . 213 C2
Loftie St SE16 . . 118 A4
Lofting Rd N1 . . 72 C1
Lofts on the Park 24
E9 . . 74 D2
Loftus Rd W12 . . 112 B5
Loftus Rd (Queens Park
Rangers FC) W12 . 112 B5
Logan Cl Enfield EN3 . . 6 D4
Hounslow TW4 . . 129 B2
Logan Mews W8 . . 255 A4
Logan Pl W8 . 113 C2 255 A4
Logan Rd Edmonton N9 . 18 B2
Wembley HA9 . . 66 A6
Loggetts SE21 . . 161 C2
Logs Hill BR1,BR7 . . 188 A2
Logs Hill Cl BR7 . . 188 A2
Lohmann Ho 5 SE11 138 C6
Lois Dr TW17 . . 192 D4
Lolesworth Cl E1 . . 243 D3
Lollard St
SE11 . . 116 C2 261 A3
Loman St
SE1 . . 116 D4 251 D2
Lomas Cl CR0 . . 224 A1
Lomas St E1 . . 96 A2
Lombard Ave
Enfield EN3 . . 6 C4
Ilford IG3 . . 57 C1
Lombard Bsns Pk
Merton SW19 . . 179 D1
Thornton Heath CR0 . . 204 B2
Lombard Ct EC3 . . 252 D6
Lombard Ho 4 SE10 142 A5
Lombard La EC4 . . 241 B1
Lombard Rd N11 . . 31 B5
SW11 . . 136 B3
Merton SW19 . . 179 D1
Lombard Rdbt CR0 . . 204 B2
Lombard St
EC3 . . 95 B1 242 D1
Lombard Trad Est
SE7 . . 121 B2
Lombard Wall SE7 . . 121 B2
Lombardy Pl W2 . . 245 D5
Lombardy Ret Pk
UB3 . . 106 B6
Lomley Ho 10 SW2 . . 160 C5
Lomond Cl N15 . . 51 C4
Wembley HA0 . . 66 B1
Lomond Ct HA3 . . 42 D6
Lomond Gdns CR2 . . 223 A1
Lomond Gr SE5 . . 139 B5
Lomond Ho 10 SE5 . . 139 B4
Loncroft Rd SE5 . . 139 C6
Londale Ct SE10 . . 142 A4
Londesborough Ho 1
N16 . . 73 C4
Londesborough Rd
N16 . . 73 C4
London Aquarium*
SE1 . . 250 C1
London Bridge
EC4,SE1 . . 117 B6 252 D5
London Bridge City Pier
SE1 . . 117 C5 253 A4
London Bridge Hospl
SE1 . . 117 B5 252 D4
London Bridge St
SE1 . . 117 B5 252 D3
London Bridge Sta
SE1 . . 117 B5 252 D3
London Business Sch
NW1 . . 92 D3 237 C6
London Butterfly Ho*
TW8 . . 131 B4
London Canal Mus*
N1 . . 94 A5 233 B4
London Central Mosque*
NW8 . . 92 C4 230 B1
London Chest Hospl
E2 . . 96 C5
London City Airport
E16 . . 122 B5
London Clinic
NW1 . . 93 A3 238 B5
London Coll of Fashion
EC2 . . 95 C3 243 B6
London Coll of Fashion
The W1 . . 238 B1
London Coll of
International Business
Studies WC1 . . 240 B3
London Coll of Printing
SE11 . . 116 D3 261 D5
London Ct 3 SW18 . . 157 C6
London Docklands Visitor
Ctr E14 . . 120 A4
London Dungeon The*
SE1 . . 117 B5 252 D4
London Eye (Millennium
Wheel)*
SE1 . . 116 B4 250 C2
London Fields East Side
E8 . . 74 B1
London Fields Prim Sch
E8 . . 96 B6
London Fields Sta E8 . 74 B1
London Fields West Side
E8 . . 74 A1
London Foot Hospl
W1 . . 93 C3 239 A5
London Gas Mus The*
E3,E16 . . 98 B3
London Group Bsns Pk
NW2 . . 46 A1
London Ho NW8 . . 230 B4
Edgware HA8 . . 26 A6
London Hospital Dental
Inst E1 . . 96 B2
London Independent Hospl
The E1 . . 96 D2
London Ind Pk The
E6 . . 100 C2
London Inst The W1 . 238 C1
Streatham SW17 . . 181 B5
London International Film
Sch WC2 . . 94 A1 240 B1
London La E8 . . 74 B1
Bromley BR1 . . 186 D3
London Metropolitan Univ
E1 . . 95 D1 243 D2
London Metropolitan Univ
(Carleton Grange Hall) 2
N7 . . 71 D4
London Metropolitan Univ
(Central Ho) E1 . . 96 A1
London Metropolitan Univ
(Coll of Tech & Design)
E1 . . 96 A1
London Metropolitan Univ
(Commercial Rd) E1 . 96 A1
London Metropolitan Univ
(Ladbrook Ho) N5 . . 72 D3
London Metropolitan Univ
(Moorgate)
EC2 . . 95 B2 242 C3
London Metropolitan Univ
(North London Campus)
N7 . . 72 C3
London Metropolitan Univ
(Tufnel Park Hall)
N7 . . 71 C5
London Metropolitan Univ
(Spring Ho) N7 . . 72 C2
London Mews W2 . . 236 D2
London Nautical Sch The
SE1 . . 116 C5 251 B4
London Oratory Sch The
SW6 . . 135 C5 265 B4
London Peace Pagoda*
SW3 . . 267 D4
London Rd E13 . . 99 A5
SE1 . . 116 D3 261 D6
Ashford TW15,TW18,
TW19,TW14 . . 148 B2
Brentford TW7,TW8 . . 131 B4
Bromley BR1 . . 186 D3
Enfield EN2 . . 5 B1
Forest Hill SE22,SE23 . . 162 C3
Hackbridge SM6,CR4 . . 219 B6
Harrow HA1 . . 64 C6
Hounslow TW3,TW7,
TW1,TW8 . . 130 B3
Kingston KT1,KT2 . . 176 B1
Morden SM4 . . 201 C5
Romford RM7,RM8 . . 59 C3
Stanmore HA7 . . 25 D6
Stoneleigh KT17 . . 216 B3
Stoneleigh KT17,KT4,
SM3 . . 216 B3
Thornton Heath CR0,
CR7,SW16 . . 204 C3
Twickenham TW1 . . 153 A4
Wembley HA9 . . 66 A2
Carshalton CR4 . . 203 A2
London Road Rdbt
TW1 . . 153 A5
London Sch of Economics
& Political Science
WC2 . . 94 B1 240 D1
London St EC3 . . 253 B6
W2 . . 92 B1 236 C1
London Stile 5 W4 . 110 C1
London Terr 1 E2 . . 96 A5
London Theological
Seminary at Kensit
Memorial Coll N3 . . 29 A1
London Toy & Model
Mus* W2 . . 114 A6 246 A6
London Transport Mus*
WC2 . . 250 B6
London Wall
EC2 . . 95 B2 242 D3
London Wharf 4 E2 . . 96 B6
London Zoo*
NW1 . . 93 A5 231 A4
Lonesome Prim Sch
CR4 . . 181 B1
Lonesome Way CR4 . 181 C2
Long Acre
WC2 . . 94 A1 240 B1
Long Acre Ct W13 . . 87 A2
Longacre Pl SM5 . . 219 A2
Longacre Rd E17 . . 36 B2
Longbeach Rd SW11 136 D2
Longberrys NW2 . . 69 B5
Longboat Row UB1 . . 85 B1
Longbow Ho 29 N1 . . 95 C6
Longbridge Ho RM8 . . 80 B4
Longbridge Rd
Barking IG11 . . 79 C3
Dagenham RM8 . . 80 B4
Longbridge Way
SE13 . . 164 A6
Longbury Dr BR5 . . 190 B1
Longcliffe Ho SW18 . 157 D6
Longcroft SE9 . . 166 C1
Longcrofte Rd HA8 . . 25 D3
Longdale Sq N1 . . 234 B6
Long Deacon Rd E4 . . 20 C3
Long Ditton Cty Inf Sch
KT6 . . 197 C1
Longdon Wood BR2 . 226 A4
Longdown Rd SE6 . . 185 C6
Long Dr W3 . . 89 C1
Greenford UB6 . . 85 D6
Ruislip HA4 . . 62 D4
Long Elmes HA3 . . 24 A2
Longfellow Rd E17 . . 53 B3
North Cheam KT4 . . 200 B1
Longfellow Way SE1 . 263 D3
Long Field NW9 . . 27 D3
Longfield
3 Bromley BR1 . . 186 D2
Loughton IG10 . . 21 C6
Longfield Ave E17 . . 53 A5
NW7 . . 28 A3
Ealing W5 . . 109 C6
Enfield EN3 . . 6 C5
Hackbridge SM6 . . 203 A1
Wembley HA9 . . 44 A1
Longfield Cres SE23,
SE26 . . 162 C1
Longfield Ct 4 N2 . . 48 A6
Longfield Dr
Mitcham SW19 . . 180 C2
Mortlake SW14 . . 154 D6
Longfield Est SE1 . . 263 D3
Longfield Fst & Mid Schs
HA2 . . 41 C3
Longfield Ho E17 . . 53 B4
Ealing W5 . . 109 C6
Longfield Rd W5 . . 87 C1
Longfield St SW18 . . 157 C4
Longford Ave
Feltham TW14 . . 149 D5
Southall UB1 . . 107 D6
Stanwell TW19 . . 148 A3
Longford Cl
Feltham TW13 . . 151 A1
Hampton TW12 . . 173 C6
Hayes UB4 . . 106 D6
Longford Ct 2 E5 . . 74 D4
6 NW4 . . 46 C5
1 W12 . . 111 C4
Southall UB1 . . 107 C5
West Ewell KT19 . . 215 A4
Longford Gdns
Hayes UB4 . . 106 D6
Sutton SM1 . . 218 A6
Longford Ho 7 E1 . . 96 C1
1 Catford BR1 . . 186 B5
Hampton TW12 . . 173 C6
Longford Ind Est
TW12 . . 173 D4
Longford Rd TW2 . . 151 D3
Longford Sch TW14 . 149 D4
Longford St
NW1 . . 93 B3 238 D6
Longford Way TW19 . 148 A3
Longford Wlk 9
SW2 . . 160 C4
Longhayes Ave RM6 . . 58 D5
Longhayes Ct RM6 . . 58 D5
Longheath Gdns CR0 206 C4
Longhedge Ho SE26 . 184 A6
Longhill Rd SE6 . . 164 B1
Longhook Gdns UB5 . . 84 B4
Longhope Cl SE15 . . 139 D6
Longhurst Ho 8 W9 . . 91 B4
Longhurst Rd SE13 . 164 C6
Croydon CR0 . . 206 B3
Long La DA7 . . 147 B4
EC1 . . 94 D2 241 D4
N2 . . 48 B6
N3 . . 29 D2
SE1 . . 117 B4 252 D1
Croydon CR0 . . 206 C3
Hillingdon UB10 . . 60 D1
Stanwell TW15,TW19 . 148 B3
Longland Ct E9 . . 75 A3
SE1 . . 118 A1
Longland Dr N20 . . 13 D2
Longlands Ct DA15 . 167 D1
E17 . . 35 A2
W11 . . 244 D6
Mitcham CR4 . . 181 A2
Longlands Park Cres
DA15 . . 167 C2
Longlands Prim Sch
DA15 . . 167 C1
Longlands Rd DA15 . 167 D1
Longleat Ho SW1 . . 259 C2
Longleat Rd EN1 . . 17 C6
Longleat Villas 3
DA6 . . 147 A1
Longleat Way TW14 . 149 B4
Longleigh Ho 8 SE5 139 C4
Longleigh La SE2 . . 146 C6
Longlents Ho 3 NW10 89 B6
Longley Ave HA0 . . 88 B6
Longley Ho 5 N19 . . 71 C4
Longley Rd Harrow HA1 42 B5
Thornton Heath CR0 . 204 D2
Upper Tooting SW17 . 180 D4
Long Leys E4 . . 36 A4
Longley St SE1 . . 118 A2
Longley Way NW2 . . 68 C5
Longman Ho 9 E2 . . 96 D5
10 E8 . . 95 D6
Long Mark Rd 5 E16 . 99 D2
Longmead BR7 . . 188 C1
Long Mead NW9 . . 27 D2
Longmead Dr DA14 . 168 D2
Longmead Ho SE27 . 183 A5
Long Meadow 20 N7 . . 71 D3
Long Meadow Cl
BR3,BR4 . . 208 A2
Longmeadow Rd
DA15 . . 167 C3
Longmead Prim Sch
UB7 . . 104 A2
Longmead Rd
Hayes UB3 . . 105 D6
Thames Ditton KT7 . . 196 D2
Upper Tooting SW17 . 180 D5
Longmoor Point 14
SW15 . . 156 B3
Longmore Ave EN4,
EN5 . . 14 B5
Longmore St
SW1 . . 115 C2 259 A3
Longnor Rd E1 . . 96 D4
Long Pond Rd SE3 . . 142 C4
Long Rd SW4 . . 137 C1
Longreach Ct IG11 . . 101 B5
Long Reach Rd IG11 . 101 D3
Longridge Ho SE1 . . 262 B5
Longridge La UB1 . . 85 D1
Longridge Rd
SW5 . . 113 C2 255 B3
Long Ridges N2 . . 49 A6
Long's Ct W1 . . 249 D5
Longs Ct 2 TW9 . . 132 B1
Longshaw Prim Sch
E4 . . 20 B1
Longshaw Rd E4 . . 20 B1
Longshore SE8 . . 119 B2
Long St E2 . . 95 D4
Longstaff Cres SW18 157 C4
Longstaff Rd SW18 . 157 C5
Longstone Ave NW10 . 89 D6
Longstone Rd SW17 . 181 B5
Longthorne Ho 20 E3 . 97 B4
Longthornton Rd
SW16 . . 181 D1
Longton Ave SE26 . . 184 A6
Longton Gr SE26 . . 184 B6
Longville Rd SE11 . . 261 D4
Longwalk Rd UB11 . . 104 D5
Long Wlk SE1 . . 263 B6
SE18 . . 144 D6
Kingston KT3 . . 199 A6
Longwood Bsns Pk
TW16 . . 193 D4
Longwood Dr SW15 . 156 A5
Longwood Gdns IG2,
IG6,IG5 . . 56 C6
Longwood Par IG6 . . 56 D6
Longworth Cl SE28 . 102 D1
Long Yd WC1 . . 94 B3 240 C5
Loning The NW9 . . 45 D5
Enfield EN3 . . 6 C5
Lonsdale Ave
Newham E6 . . 100 A3
Wembley HA9 . . 66 A3
Lonsdale Cl SE12 . . 165 D1
Edgware HA8 . . 26 B5
Hillingdon UB8 . . 83 A2
Newham E6 . . 100 A3
Pinner HA5 . . 23 A2
Lonsdale Cres IG2 . . 56 D3
Lonsdale Dr EN2 . . 16 A6
Lonsdale Dr N EN2 . . 4 A1
Lonsdale Gdns CR7,
SW16 . . 204 B5
Lonsdale Ho 6 N4 . . 51 A2
SW6 . . 135 C2
Lonsdale Mews W11 . 91 B1
Lonsdale Mews *continued*
4 Richmond TW9 . . 132 C4
Lonsdale Pl N1 . . 72 C1
Lonsdale Rd E11 . . 54 D2
NW6 . . 91 B6
W11 . . 91 B1
W4 . . 111 D2
Barnes SW13 . . 133 D5
Bexley DA7 . . 147 B3
Croydon SE25 . . 206 B5
Southall UB2 . . 106 D3
Lonsdell Ho 9 SW2 . 160 C5
Loobert Rd N15 . . 51 C6
Looe Gdns IG6 . . 56 D6
Loop Rd BR7 . . 189 A4
Lopen Rd N18 . . 33 C6
Lopen Works N18 . . 33 C6
Lopez Ho 4 SW9 . . 138 A2
Lorac Ct 18 SM2 . . 217 C1
Loraine Cl EN3 . . 18 C6
Loraine Ct BR7 . . 188 D5
Loraine Ho 1 SM5 . . 219 B4
Loraine Rd N7 . . 72 B4
Chiswick W4 . . 132 D6
Lord Ave IG5 . . 56 B6
Lord Chancellor Wlk
KT2 . . 177 A2
Lord David Pitt Ho 8
SE24 . . 138 C1
Lordell Pl SW19 . . 178 C4
Lorden Wlk 25 E2 . . 96 A4
Lord Gdns IG5 . . 56 B5
Lord Hills Rd W2 . . 91 D2
Lord Holland La 5
SW9 . . 138 C3
Lord Knyvetts Ct 3
TW19 . . 148 A5
Lord Napier Pl W6 . . 112 A1
Lord North St SW1 . . 260 A5
Lord Roberts Mews
SW6 . . 265 C3
Lord Roberts Terr
SE18 . . 122 C1
Lords Cl
Feltham TW13 . . 151 A2
West Norwood SE21 . . 161 A2
Lord's Cricket Mus*
NW8 . . 92 B4 229 D1
Lords Ct 3 HA8 . . 27 A3
Lordship Gr N16 . . 73 B6
Lordship Ho 3 N16 . . 73 B6
Lordship La SE22 . . 161 D5
Tottenham N22 . . 33 B2
Lordship Lane Prim Sch
N22 . . 33 A2
Lordship Park Mews
N16 . . 73 A6
Lordship Pk N16 . . 73 B6
Lordship Pl SW3 . . 267 A5
Lordship Rd N16 . . 73 B6
Northolt UB5 . . 63 A1
Lordship Terr N16 . . 73 B6
Lord's Indoor Cricket Sch
NW8 . . 229 D2
NW8 . . 230 A2
Lord's (MCC & Middlesex
Cty Cricket Ground)*
NW8 . . 92 B4 229 D2
Lordsmead Rd N17 . . 33 C1
Lord St E16 . . 122 A5
Lord's View NW8 . . 229 D1
Lord Warwick St
SE18 . . 122 B3
Loreburn Ho 2 N7 . . 72 B4
Lorenzo St N1,WC1 . 233 C2
Loretto Gdns HA3 . . 44 A5
Lorian Cl N12 . . 29 D6
Loring Rd N20 . . 14 C2
Isleworth TW7 . . 130 D3
Loris Rd W6 . . 112 C3
Lorn Ct SW9 . . 138 C3
Lorne Ave CR0 . . 206 D2
Lorne Cl NW8 . 92 C4 230 B1
Lorne Ct SW15 . . 156 D5
Lorne Gdns 5 W11 . 112 D4
Croydon CR0 . . 206 D2
Wanstead E11 . . 55 C5
Lorne Ho 7 E1 . . 97 A2
3 N11 . . 31 B5
Lorne Rd E17 . . 53 C4
E7 . . 77 C4
N4 . . 50 B1
Harrow HA3 . . 24 D1
3 Richmond TW10 . . 154 B6
Lorn Rd SW9 . . 138 C3
Lorraine Ct 10 NW1 . . 71 B1
Beckenham BR3 . . 186 A2
Lorraine Pk HA3 . . 24 C3
Lorrimore Rd SE17 . 138 D6
Lorrimore Sq SE17 . 138 D6

Lorton Ho **9** NW6 ....**91** C6
Loseberry Rd KT10 .**212** B3
Lostock Ho **10** SW8 .**137** D3
Lothair Rd N W5 ......**109** D4
Lothair Rd N N4 .....**50** D3
Lothair Rd S N4 .....**50** D2
Lothbury EC2 ..**95** B1 **242** C2
Lothian Cl UB4 .....**84** B2
Lothian Cl HA0 ......**65** A5
Lothian Rd SW9 ......**138** D4
Lothrop St W10 .....**91** A4
Lots Rd SW10 136 A5 **266** B3
Loubet St SW17 ....**180** D4
Loudoun Ave IG6 ....**56** D4
Loudoun Rd
NW8 ....**92** A6 **229** B5
Loudwater Cl TW16 .**194** A5
Loudwater Rd TW16 .**194** A5
Loughborough Ct **7**
SW9 ....**138** D2
Loughborough Junction
Sta SW9 ....**138** D2
Loughborough Pk
SW9 ....**138** D1
Loughborough Prim Sch
SW9 ....**138** D3
Loughborough Rd
SE5,SW9 ....**138** D3
Loughborough St
SE11 ......**116** B1 **260** D1
Lough Rd N7 ....**72** B2
Loughton Way IG9 ..**21** D3
Louisa Cl E9 ....**96** D6
Louisa Ct TW2 ....**152** C3
Louisa Gdns E1 ....**96** D3
Louisa Ho SW15 ...**133** D1
Louisa St E1 ....**96** D3
Louis Ct **3** RM10 ...**81** D2
Louise Bennett Cl **9**
SE24 ....**138** D1
Louise Ct
4 Wanstead E11 ...**55** B4
Wood Green N22 ...**32** C2
Louise De Marillac Ho **18**
E1 ....**96** C2
Louise Graham Ho **5**
IG11 ....**101** B6
Louise Rd E15 ......**76** C2
Louise White Ho **1**
N19 ....**49** D1
Louis Gdns BR7 ...**188** B6
Louis Mews N10 ...**31** B2
Louisville Rd SW17 .**159** A1
Lousada Lo N14 ....**15** C5
Louvaine Rd SW11 .**136** B1
Lovage App E6 ....**100** A2
Lovat Cl NW2 ......**67** D5
Lovat La EC3 ....**253** A1
Lovatt Cl HA8 ......**26** D4
Lovatt Ct SW12 ...**159** B3
Lovatt Dr HA4 .....**39** C4
Lovat Wlk TW5 ...**129** A5
Loveday Ho **2** SW2 .**160** A4
Loveday Rd W13 ...**109** B5
Lovegrove St SE1 .**140** A6
Lovegrove Wlk E14 .**120** A5
Lovekyn Cl KT2 ...**176** B1
Love La DA5 ......**169** C5
EC2 ....**95** A1 **242** B2
SE18 ....**122** D2
Cheam SM3 ....**217** A2
Cheam SM4 ....**201** D2
Croydon SE25 .....**206** B6
Long Ditton KT6 ..**213** D6
Mitcham CR4 .....**202** C6
Pinner HA5 ....**41** A6
Tottenham N17 ....**33** D3
Lovelace Ave BR2 ..**210** C3
Lovelace Gdns
Barking IG11 ....**80** A4
Surbiton KT6 .....**197** D2
Lovelace Gn SE9 ..**144** B2
Lovelace Ho **12** E8 ..**95** D6
Lovelace Prim Sch
KT9 ....**213** C3
Lovelace Rd
East Barnet EN4 ...**14** C4
Surbiton KT6 .....**197** D2
West Norwood SE21 .**161** A3
Loveland Mans **6**
IG11 ....**79** D1
Lovel Ave DA16 ....**146** A4
Lovelinch Cl SE15 .**140** C6
Lovell Ho E8 ....**96** A6
4 Merton SW19 ...**180** A2
Lovell Pl SE16 ....**119** A3
Lovell Rd
Richmond TW10 ...**153** C1
Southall UB1 ....**85** D1
Loveridge Mews NW6 .**69** B2

Loveridge Rd NW6 ...**69** B2
Lover's Wlk
W1 ....**115** A5 **248** A3
Lovett Dr SM5 ....**202** B2
Lovette Ho **3** E3 ...**97** C4
Lovett Way NW10 ..**67** A3
Love Wlk SE5 .....**139** B3
Lovibonds Ave BR6 .**226** D5
Hillingdon UB7 .....**82** B1
Low Brook Rd IG1 ..**78** D4
Low Cross Wood La
SE21 ....**161** D1
Lowdell Cl UB7 .....**82** A1
Lowden Rd SE24 ...**139** A1
Edmonton N9 ......**18** B3
Loweswater Cl HA9 .**65** D6
Loweswater Ho E3 ..**97** B3
Lowfield Rd NW6 ...**69** C1
W3 ....**89** A1
Low Hall Cl E4 .....**19** D4
Low Hall La E17 ....**53** C3
Low Ho IG1 ....**102** A5
Lowick Rd HA1 ....**42** C4
Lowland Gdns RM7 .**59** D3
Lowlands Rd
Harrow HA1 ....**42** C2
Pinner HA5 ....**40** C3
Lowman Rd N7 ....**72** B4
Lowndes Cl SW1 ...**258** B5
Lowndes Ct SW1 ...**257** D6
Lowndes Lo EN5 ...**1** D2
Lowndes Pl
SW1 ......**115** A3 **258** A5
Lowndes Sq
SW1 ......**114** D4 **247** D1
Lowndes St
SW1 ......**115** A3 **258** A6
Lownds Ct BR1 ...**187** A1
Lowood Ct SE19 ...**183** D5
Lowood Ho **11** E1 ..**118** C6
Lowood St E1 .....**118** B6
Lowry Cres CR4 ...**180** C5
Lowry Ct **3** SE16 ..**118** B1
Lowry Ho N17 .....**33** D2
Lowry Lo **2** HA0 ...**65** D3
Lowry Rd RM8 .....**80** B3
Lowther Cl WD6 ...**10** B6
Lowther Dr EN2 ....**4** A1
Lowther Hill SE23 .**163** A4
Lowther Ho **11** E8 ..**95** D6
SW1 ....**259** B1
Lowther Prim Sch
SW13 ....**134** A6
Lowther Rd E17 ....**35** A1
N7 ....**72** C3
Barnes SW13 ......**133** D4
Kingston KT2 .....**176** B2
Stanmore HA7 .....**44** B6
Lowth Rd SE5 ......**139** A4
Loxdon Ct RM6 ....**58** B3
Loxford Ave E6 .....**99** D5
Loxford Ho **1** N1 ...**258** B3
Loxford La IG1 .....**79** B3
Loxford Rd IG11 ...**78** D2
Loxford Sch of Science &
Tech IG1 ....**79** B3
Loxham Rd E4 ......**35** D3
Loxham St WC1 ....**233** B1
Loxley Cl SE26 ....**184** D5
Loxley Rd
Feltham TW12 .....**173** B6
Wandsworth SW18 .**158** B3
Loxton Rd SE23 ...**163** A3
Loxwood Cl TW14 .**149** C3
Loxwood Rd N17 ...**51** C6
Loyola Prep Sch IG9 .**21** D3
Lubavitch House Gram Sch
N2 ....**48** A4
Lubbock Ct BR7 ...**125** C2
Lubbock Ho **18** E14 .**119** D6
Lubbock Rd BR7 ...**188** B3
Lubbock St SE14 ..**140** C5
Lucan Ho N1 ......**235** D5
Lucan Pl SW3 114 C1 **257** B3
Lucan Rd EN5 .....**1** A2
Lucas Ave E13 .....**99** B6
Lucas Gdns N2 ....**30** A1
Lucas Ho **2** SW8 ..**137** C3
Lucas Rd SE20 ...**184** C4
Lucas Sq NW11 ...**47** C3
Lucas St SE4,SE8 ..**141** C4
Lucas Vale Prim Sch
SE8 ....**141** C4
Lucerne Cl N14 ....**16** A1
Lucerne Ct **5** DA18 .**125** A3
8 Beckenham BR3 .**185** C3
Lucerne Gr E17 ....**54** B5
Lucerne Mews W8 ..**245** B4

Lower Sydenham Sta
SE26 ....**185** B5
Lower Teddington Rd
KT1 ....**175** D2
Lower Terr NW3 ....**70** A5
Lower Thames St
EC3 ....**117** C6 **253** A5
Lower Tub WD23 ....**8** B4
Lowerwood Ct W11 .**91** A1
Lower Wood Rd
KT10 ....**213** B2
Lowestoft Cl **5** E5 ..**74** C6
Lowestoft Mews E16 .**122** D4
Lowfield Rd NW6 ...**69** C1
Lower Addiscombe Rd
CR0 ....**205** C1
Lower Addison Gdns
W14 .....**113** A4 **244** A1
Lower Belgrave St
SW1 ......**115** B3 **258** C5
Lower Boston Rd W7 .**108** C4
Lower Broad St
RM10 ....**103** C6
Lower Camden BR7 .**188** B2
Lower Church St
CR0 ....**220** D6
Lower Clapton Rd E5 .**74** C4
Lower Clarendon Wlk **12**
W11 ....**91** A1
Lower Comm S SW15 **134** B2
Lower Coombe St
CR0 ....**221** A4
Lower Downs Rd
SW20 ....**178** D2
Lower Fosters NW4 ..**46** C4
Lower George St
TW10 ....**153** D6
Lower Gn W CR4 ..**202** C6
Lower Gravel Rd BR2 **210** B1
Lower Green Gdns
KT4 ....**200** A1
Lower Green Rd
KT10 ....**212** A6
Lower Grosvenor Pl
SW1 ......**115** B3 **258** D6
Lower Grove Rd
TW10 ....**154** B6
Lower Hall La E4 ...**35** A6
Lower Hampton Rd
TW12,TW16 ......**172** D1
Lower Ham Rd KT2 .**175** D4
Lower James St W1 .**249** B6
Lower John St W1 ..**249** B6
Lower Kenwood Ave
EN2 ....**16** A6
Lower Lea Crossing
E14,E16 ....**120** C6
Lower Maidstone Rd
N11 ....**31** C4
Lower Mall W6 ....**112** B1
Lower Marsh
SE1 ......**116** C4 **251** A1
Lower Marsh La KT1,
KT5 ....**198** C5
Lower Merton Rise
NW3 ....**70** C1
Lower Morden La
SM4 ....**201** A3
Lower Mortlake Rd
TW9 ....**132** B2
Lower Park Rd N11 ..**31** C5
Belvedere DA17 ...**125** C2
Loughton IG10 .....**21** D4
Lower Pk **5** SW15 ..**156** D6
Lower Place Bsns Ctr
NW10 ....**89** A5
Lower Queen's Rd IG9 **21** D2
Lower Rd N2 ......**30** D4
SE16 ....**118** C4
Belvedere DA17 ...**125** D3
Harrow HA2 ....**42** B1
Sutton SM1 ......**218** A4
Lower Richmond Rd
Mortlake SW14,TW9 .**132** D2
Putney SW15 .....**134** C2
Lower Robert St
WC2 ....**250** B5
Lower Sand Hills
KT6 ....**197** C2
Lower Sloane St
SW1 ......**115** A1 **258** A2
Lower Strand NW9 ..**27** D1
Lower Sunbury Rd
TW12 ....**173** C1

Lucerne Rd BR6 ...**211** D1
N5 ....**72** D4
South Norwood CR7 .**205** A5
Lucey Rd SE16 ....**118** A3
Lucey Way SE16 ..**118** A2
Lucie Ave TW15 ...**170** D4
Lucien Rd
Upper Tooting SW17 .**181** A6
Wandsworth SW18 .**157** D2
Lucille Ho SE26 ...**184** B4
Lucknow St SE18 ..**145** C5
Lucorn Cl SE12 ...**164** D5
Lucraft Ho **12** SW2 .**160** A4
Luctons Ave IG9 ...**21** C3
Lucy Ashe Ho SE17 .**261** D3
Lucy Brown Ho SE1 .**252** B3
Lucy Cres W3 ......**89** A2
Lucy Gdns RM8 ....**81** A5
Luddesdon Rd DA8 .**147** C5
Ludford Cl NW9 ....**27** C1
Croydon CR0 .....**220** D1
Ludgate Broadway
EC4 ....**241** D1
Ludgate Cir
EC4 ....**94** D1 **241** C1
Ludgate Hill
EC4 ....**94** D1 **241** D1
Ludgate Sq EC4 ...**241** D1
Ludham NW5 ......**70** D3
Ludham Cl SE28 ..**102** C1
Ludlow Cl BR2 ....**209** A6
Harrow HA2 ....**63** B4
Ludlow Ct W3 ....**111** A4
Ludlow Rd Ealing W5 .**87** C3
Feltham TW13 .....**172** A6
Ludlow St EC1 ....**242** A6
Ludlow Way N2 ....**48** A5
Ludovick Wlk SW15 .**133** C1
Ludwell Ho W14 ...**254** B6
Ludwick Mews SE14 .**141** A5
Luffield Rd SE2 ...**124** B3
Luffman Rd SE12 .**165** D1
Lugard Ho W12 ...**112** A6
Lugard Rd SE15 ..**140** B4
Lugg App E12 .....**78** C5
Luke Ho **31** E1 ....**96** B1
Luke St EC2 ..**95** C3 **243** B4
Lukin Cres E4 .....**20** B1
Lukin St E1 ....**96** C1
Lullingstone Cl BR5 .**190** B5
Lullingstone Cres
BR5 ....**190** B3
Lullingstone Ho **20**
SE15 ....**140** C6
Lullingstone La SE13 **164** B5
Lullingstone Rd **3**
DA17 ....**147** B6
Lullington Garth N12 .**29** B5
Borehamwood WD6 .**10** D6
Bromley BR1 .....**186** C3
Lullington Rd
Dagenham RM9 ....**81** A1
Penge SE20 ......**184** A3
Lulot Gdns N19 ....**71** B6
Lulworth NW1 ......**71** D1
SE17 ....**262** C2
Lulworth Ave
Hounslow TW5,TW7 .**130** A5
Wembley HA9 .....**43** C2
Lulworth Cl HA2 ...**63** B5
Lulworth Cres CR4 .**180** C1
Lulworth Ct N14 ...**16** A1
Lulworth Dr HA5 ...**41** A2
Lulworth Gdns HA2 .**63** B6
Lulworth Ho SW8 ..**270** C3
Lulworth Rd DA16 .**145** D3
SE15 ....**140** B3
Chislehurst SE9 ..**166** A2
Lulworth Waye UB4 .**84** B1
Lumen Rd HA9 ....**65** D6
Lumiere Bldg The E7 .**77** D3
Lumiere Ct SW17 ..**159** A2
Lumley Cl DA17 ...**125** C1
Lumley Ct WC2 ...**250** B5
Lumley Flats SW1 .**258** A2
Lumley Gdns SM3 .**217** A3
Lumley Ho KT3 ...**199** B1
Lumley Rd SM1,SM3 .**217** A3
Lumley St W1 .....**238** B1
Lumsdon NW8 .....**91** D6
Lunan Ho **12** E3 ...**97** B5
Luna Rd CR7 .....**205** A6
Lundin Wlk WD19 ..**22** D6
Lund Point E15 ....**98** A6
Lundy Dr UB3 ....**105** C2
Lunham Rd SE19 ..**183** C4
Lupin Cl Croydon CR0 **206** D1
Streatham SW2 ...**160** C2
Lupin Cres IG11 ...**78** C2

Lupino Ct SE11 ....**260** C4
Lupin Point SE1 ...**253** D1
Lupton Cl SE12 ...**187** B6
Lupton St NW5 ....**71** C4
Lupus St SW1 115 C1 **259** B1
Luralda Gdns E14 .**120** B1
Lurgan Ave W6 ...**134** D6
Lurline Gdns
SW11 .....**137** A4 **268** B2
Luscombe Ct BR2 .**186** C1
Luscombe Ho SW18 .**157** B6
Luscombe Way
SW8 ....**138** A5 **270** A4
Lusher Ho **11** SW15 .**156** D5
Lushington Ho KT12 .**194** C3
Lushington Rd NW10 .**90** B5
Catford SE6 .....**185** D5
Lushington Terr **11** E8 **74** A3
Lutea Ho SM2 ....**218** A3
Luther Cl HA8 .....**11** A2
Luther King Cl E17 .**53** A3
Luther Rd TW11 ..**174** D5
Luton Pl SE10 ....**142** A5
Luton Rd E13 .....**99** A3
E17 ....**53** B6
Sidcup DA14 .....**168** C1
Luton St NW8 ..92 B3 **236** D5
Luttrell Ave SW15 .**156** B6
Lutwyche Rd SE6 .**163** B2
Lutyens Ho SW1 ..**259** A1
Luxborough Ho **1** W1 **238** A4
Luxborough St
W1 ....**93** A2 **238** A4
Luxborough Twr W1 .**238** A4
Luxemburg Gdns W6 .**112** D2
Luxfield Rd SE9 ...**166** A3
Luxford St SE16 ..**118** D2
Luxmore St SE4 ..**141** B4
Luxor St SE5 .....**139** A2
Lyall Ave SE21 ...**183** D6
Lyall Mews
SW1 ......**115** A3 **258** A5
Lyall Mews W SW1 .**258** A5
Lyall St SW1 .115 A3 **258** A5
Lyal Rd E3 ....**97** A5
Lycée Francais Charles de
Gaulle (French Univ Coll)
SW7 ......**114** B2 **256** C4
Lycée The
SE11 ......**116** C1 **261** B1
Lycett Ho **10** SW2 ..**160** A4
Lycett Pl **3** W12 ...**112** A4
Lychgate Manor HA1 .**42** C2
Lych Gate Wlk UB3 .**105** D6
Lyconby Gdns CR0 .**207** A2
Lydd Cl DA15 .....**167** C1
Lydden Ct SE9 ...**167** C5
Lydden Gr SW18 ..**157** D4
Lydden Rd SW18 ..**157** D4
Lydd Rd DA7 .....**147** B5
Lydeard Rd E6 .....**78** B1
Lydford NW1 .....**232** B5
Lydford Cl **22** N16 ..**73** C3
Lydford Rd N15 ...**51** B4
NW2 ....**68** D2
W9 ....**91** B3
Lydgate Ho **8** N16 ..**73** C3
Lydhurst Ave SW2 .**160** B2
Lydia Lo HA1 ......**64** C4
Lydney Cl SE15 ...**139** C5
Putney SW19 .....**157** A2
Lydon Rd SW4 ....**137** C2
Lydstep Rd BR7 ..**188** C6
Lydwell Ho **29** SW8 .**137** D3
Lyford Rd SW18 ..**158** C3
Lyford St SE7 ....**122** A2
Lygoe Ho **18** N6 ...**49** D2
Lygon Ho N2 ......**30** B2
Lygon Ho **1** E2 ...**96** A4
Lygon Pl SW1 ....**258** C5
Lyham Cl SW2 ...**160** A5
Lyham Rd SW2 ...**160** A5
Lyle Cl CR4 ......**203** A2
Lyly Ho SE1 ......**262** D5
Lyme Farm Rd SE12 .**143** B1
Lyme Gr E9 ....**74** C1
Lyme Grove Ho **2** E9 .**74** C1
Lymer Ave SE19 ..**183** D5
Lyme Rd DA16 ...**146** B4
Lymescote Gdns
SM1 ....**217** C6
Lyme St NW1 .71 C1 **232** A6
Lyminge Cl DA14 .**189** D1
Lyminge Gdns SW17,
SW18 ....**158** C3
Lymington Ave N22 .**32** D1
Lymington Cl **2** E6 .**100** B2
Mitcham SW16 ...**181** D1
Lymington Ct SM1 .**218** A5

Lymington Dr HA4 ...**61** B6
Lymington Gdns
KT19 ....**215** D3
Lymington Mans NW6 .**69** D2
Lymington Rd NW6 .**69** D2
Dagenham RM8 ....**58** D1
Lyminster Cl UB4 ..**85** A2
Lympne N17 ......**33** B1
Lympstone Gdns
SE15 ....**140** A5
Lynbridge Gdns N13 .**32** D6
Lynch Cl SE3 ....**142** D3
Lynchen Cl TW5 ..**128** B4
Lynch Wlk **2** SE8 .**141** B6
Lyncott Cres SW4 .**137** B1
Lyncourt SE3 ....**142** B3
Lyncroft Ave HA5 ..**41** A4
Lyncroft Gdns NW6 .**69** C3
Ealing W13 ....**109** C5
Hounslow TW3 ...**152** A6
Lyncroft Mans **4** NW6 **69** C3
Lyndale NW2 .....**69** B5
Lyndale Ave NW2 ..**69** B5
Lyndale Cl SE3 ...**142** D4
Lyndean Ind Est SE2 .**124** C3
Lynde Ho **2** SW4 .**137** D2
Walton-on-T KT12 .**194** C3
Lynden Gate SW15 .**156** B4
Lynden Hyrst CR0 .**221** D6
Lyndhurst BR7 ...**188** D4
Lyndhurst Ave N12 .**30** D4
NW7 ....**27** C4
Mitcham SW16 ...**181** D1
Pinner HA5 ....**22** B2
Southall UB1 .....**107** D5
Sunbury TW16 ...**194** A6
Tolworth KT5 ....**198** D1
Twickenham TW2,TW4 .**151** C3
Lyndhurst Cl DA7 .**147** D2
NW10 ....**67** B5
Orpington BR6 ...**226** D4
South Croydon CR0 .**221** D6
Lyndhurst Ct
7 Belmont SM2 ...**217** C1
11 Woodford E18 ...**37** A2
Lyndhurst Dr E10 ..**54** A2
New Malden KT3 ..**199** D3
Lyndhurst Gdns N3 .**29** A2
NW3 ....**70** B3
Barking IG11 ......**79** C2
Enfield EN1 ....**5** C1
Ilford IG2 ....**57** C3
Pinner HA5 ....**22** B2
Lyndhurst Gr SE5,
SE15 ....**139** D3
Lyndhurst Ho **2**
SW15 ....**156** A4
Lyndhurst House Prep Sch
NW3 ....**70** B3
Lyndhurst Lo **3** E14 .**120** B2
Lyndhurst Rd DA7 .**147** D2
NW3 ....**70** B3
Chingford E4 ......**36** A3
Edmonton N18 ....**34** A6
Greenford UB6 ....**85** A3
Thornton Heath CR7 .**204** C5
Tottenham N22 ...**32** C4
Lyndhurst Sch SE5 .**139** B3
Lyndhurst Sq SE15 .**139** D4
Lyndhurst Terr NW3 .**70** B3
Lyndhurst Way SE15 .**139** D3
Belmont SM2 ....**217** C1
Lyndon Ave DA15 .**167** D6
Hackbridge SM6 .**219** A5
Pinner HA5 ....**23** A4
Lyndon Rd DA17 ..**125** C2
Lyndon Yd SW17 .**179** D6
Lyndum Ct N22 ...**32** C2
Lyne Cres E17 ....**35** B2
Lyne Ct NW9 .....**45** B2
Lynegrove Ave TW15 **171** A5
Lyneham Wlk E5 ..**75** D2
Pinner HA5 ....**39** C6
Lynette Ave SW4 .**159** C5
Lynfield Ct SE23 .**162** D4
Lynford Cl HA8 ...**27** A2
Edgware EN5 ......**11** D2
Lynford French Ho
SE17 ....**262** A2
Lynford Gdns
Edgware HA8 ......**10** D1
Ilford IG3 ....**79** D6
Lynford Terr N9 ...**17** D3
Lynhurst Cres UB10 .**61** B1
Lynhurst Rd UB10 .**61** A1
Lynmere Rd DA16 .**146** B3

Lynmouth Ave
  Enfield EN1 ....17 D5
  West Barnes SM4 .....200 D2
Lynmouth Dr HA4 ....62 B5
Lynmouth Gdns
  Heston TW5 ....128 D4
  Wembley UB6 ....65 B1
Lynmouth Rd E17 ....53 A4
  N16 ....51 D1
  N2 ....48 D5
  Wembley UB6 ....87 B6
Lynn Cl Ashford TW15 .171 B5
  Harrow HA3 ....24 B1
Lynn Ct SW16 ....181 D5
Lynne Cl 7 BR6 ....227 D2
Lynne Ct NW6 ....69 D1
  Forest Hill SE23 ...163 B4
  South Croydon CR2 ..221 C4
  Wimbledon SW20 ....178 B2
Lynnett Ct E9 ....75 A2
Lynnett Rd M8 ....58 D1
Lynne Way NW10 ......67 C2
  Northolt UB5 ....84 D5
Lynne Wlk KT10 .....212 A3
Lynn Ho SE15 ....140 A6
Lynn Mews E11 ....76 C6
Lynn Rd E11 ....76 C5
  Balham SW12 ....159 B4
  Ilford IG2 ....57 B2
Lynn St EN2 ....5 B4
Lynstead Cl BR1 ....187 C1
Lynsted Cl DA6 .....169 D6
Lynsted Ct 4 BR3 ..185 A1
Lynsted Gdns SE9 ...143 D2
Lynton KT7 ....197 A2
Lynton Ave N12 ......30 B6
  NW9 ....45 D5
  Ealing W13 ....87 A1
Lynton Cl NW10 ......67 D3
  Chessington KT9 ...214 A4
  Isleworth TW7 .....130 D1
Lynton Cres IG2 .....56 D3
Lynton Ct 9 W3 .....89 A1
  Bowes Park N13 .....32 A5
  Penge SE20 ....184 B2
  Sutton SM2 ....218 A4
Lynton Est SE1 .....118 A2
Lynton Gdns N11 ....31 D4
  Enfield EN1 ....17 C4
Lynton Grange N2 ....48 D6
Lynton Ho 15 W2 ....91 B1
Lynton Lo N5 ....72 D3
Lynton Mans SE1 ....261 A6
Lynton Mead N20 ....14 A2
Lynton Rd N8 ....50 A4
  NW6 ....91 B5
  SE1 ....118 D3263
  Acton W3 ....110 D6
  Chingford E4 ....35 C5
  Harrow HA2 ....63 A6
  New Malden KT3 ....199 B4
  Thornton Heath CR0 .204 C3
Lynton Terr 4 W3 ...89 A1
Lynton Wlk UB4 .....83 C4
Lynwood Cl
  Harrow HA2 ....63 A5
  Woodford E18 ....37 C2
Lynwood Dr KT4 ....216 A6
Lynwood Gdns
  Southall UB1 ....85 B1
  Wallington CR0 ....220 B4
Lynwood Gr
  Orpington BR6 .....211 C1
  Southgate N21 ......16 C3
Lynwood Rd Ealing W5 .88 A3
  Thames Ditton KT7 .196 D1
  Upper Tooting SW17 .180 D6
Lyon Bsns Pk IG11 .101 C5
Lyon Cl HA4 ....39 D1
Lyon Ho NW8 ....237 A5
Lyon Meade HA7 .....25 C2
Lyon Park Ave HA0 ..66 B2
Lyon Park Jun & Inf Schs
  HA0 ....66 B1
Lyon Rd Harrow HA1 ..42 D3
  Merton SW19 ....180 A2
Lyonsdown Ave EN5 ..14 A5
Lyonsdown Ct EN5 ...14 A6
Lyonsdown Rd EN5 ...14 A6
Lyonsdown Sch EN5 ..14 A6
Lyons Pl NW8 .92 B3 236 C5
Lyon St N1 ....72 B1
Lyons Wlk W14 .....254 A4
Lyon Way UB6 ....86 C6
Lyoth Rd BR5 ....227 A6
Lyric Dr UB6 ....85 D3
Lyric Mews SE26 ...184 C6

Lyric Rd SW13 .....133 D4
Lysander 20 NW9 ....27 D2
Lysander Gdns KT5 .198 B3
Lysander Gr N19 ....49 D1
Lysander Ho 10 E2 ..96 B5
Lysander Rd
  Ruislip HA4 ....61 B6
  Wallington CR0 ....220 B2
Lysander Way BR6 ..227 A5
Lysia Ct SW6 ....134 D5
Lysias Rd SW12 ....159 B5
Lysia St SW6 ....134 D5
Lysons Wlk SW15 ...156 A6
Lytchet Rd BR1 ....187 B3
Lytchet Way EN3 .....6 C4
Lytchgate Cl CR2 ..221 C1
Lytcott Dr KT8 ....195 B6
Lytcott Gr SE22 ...161 D6
Lytham Ave WD19 ....22 D5
Lytham Cl SE28 ....103 A1
Lytham Ct 5 UB1 ...85 D1
Lytham Gr W5 ....88 B4
Lytham St
  SE17 ....117 B1 262 C1
Lyttelton Cl NW3 ...70 C1
Lyttelton Ct N2 ....48 A4
Lyttelton Rd E10 ...76 A5
  N2 ....48 A4
Lytten Ct 6 W12 ...112 A4
Lyttleton Ct UB4 ...84 C3
Lyttleton Ho 10 E9 .74 C1
Lyttleton Rd N8 ....50 C6
Lytton Ave Enfield EN3 .7 A5
  Southgate N13 ......16 C2
Lytton Cl N2 ....48 A4
  Northolt UB5 ....63 B1
Lytton Ct WC1 .....240 B3
Lytton Gdns SM6 ...219 D4
Lytton Gr SW15 ....157 A5
Lytton Ho 3 TW12 .173 D4
Lytton Rd E11 ......54 C2
  New Barnet EN5 .....2 A1
  Pinner HA5 ....23 A3
Lytton Strachy Path 8
  SE28 ....124 B6
Lyveden Rd SE3 ....143 B5
  Mitcham SW17,SW19 .180 D4

M

Mabbett Ho 2 SE18 .144 C6
Mabel Evetts Ct UB3 .106 B6
Mabel Thornton Ho 12
  N16 ....73 B4
Maberley Cres SE19 .184 A3
Maberley Ct SE19 ..184 A3
Maberley Rd SE19 ..184 B3
  Beckenham BR3 ....208 D1
Mabledon Pl NW1,
  WC1 ....232 D1
Mablethorpe Rd
  SW6 ....264 A3
Mabley St E9 ....75 A3
Mcadam Dr EN2 ......4 D3
Macallister Ho 8
  SE18 ....144 D6
Macaret Cl N20 .....14 A4
Macarthur Cl E7 ....77 A2
MacArthur Ho 4
  SW2 ....160 A4
Macaulay Ave KT10 .212 A3
Macaulay CE Prim Sch
  SW4 ....137 B1
Macaulay Ct SW4 ..137 B1
Macaulay Ho 10 N16 .73 C5
  2 W10 ....91 A2
Macaulay Rd E6 .....99 D5
  SW4 ....137 B2
Macaulay Sq SW4 ..137 B1
Macaulay Way 2
  SE28 ....124 B5
McAuley Cl
  SE1 ....116 C3 261 A6
  SE9 ....166 C6
Macbean St SE18 ...122 D3
Macbeth Ho 4 N1 ...95 C5
Macbeth St W6 .....112 B1
McBride Ho 5 E3 ....97 B5
McCall Cl SW4 .....138 A2
McCall Cres SE7 ...122 A1
McCall Ho N7 ....72 A4
Mccarthy Ct SW11 .267 B1
McCarthy Rd TW13 .172 D5
Macclesfield Rd
  EC1 ....95 A4 235 A2
  Croydon SE25 .....206 C4
Macclesfield St W1 .249 D6
McClintock Pl EN3 ...7 C4
McCoid Way SE1 ...252 A1
Mcconnell Ho SW8 .269 C1

McCormick Ho 9
  SW2 ....160 C3
McCrone Mews 3
  NW3 ....70 B2
McCullum Rd E3 ....97 B6
McDermott Cl SW11 .136 C2
McDermott Rd SE15 .140 A2
Macdonald Ave RM10 .81 D5
Macdonald Ct TW3 .130 A1
Macdonald Ho 2
  SW11 ....137 A3
McDonald Ho 1 KT2 176 B3
Macdonald Rd E7 ....77 A4
  N11 ....30 D5
  N19 ....71 C6
  Chingford E17 ......36 A1
McDonough Cl KT9 .214 A4
McDougall Ct TW9 .132 C3
McDowall Cl E16 ....98 D2
McDowall Rd SE5 ...139 A4
Macduff Rd
  SW11 ....137 A4 268 B2
Mace Cl E1 ....118 B5
Mace Gateway E16 ..121 B2
Mace Ho 2 E17 ......53 D6
McEntee Ave E17 ...35 A2
Mace St E2 ....96 D5
McEwan Way E15 ....98 B6
Macey Ho 9 SE10 ..142 A6
  SW11 ....267 A1
Macfarlane La TW7 .131 A6
Macfarlane Rd W12 .112 A4
Macfarren Ho 9 W10 91 A4
MacFarren Pl NW1 ..238 B5
McGlashon Ho 10 E1 .96 A3
McGrath Rd E15 .....76 D2
McGregor Ct 8 N1 ..95 C4
MacGregor Ho 2
  SW12 ....159 D3
McGregor Rd W11 ..31 B2
Macgregor Rd E16 ..99 C2
Mcguffie Ct E17 ....53 B6
Machell Rd SE15 ...140 C2
McIndoe Ct N1 .....235 C6
McIntosh Cl SM6 ..220 A1
McIntosh Ho 11 SE16 118 C2
McIntyre Ct 19 SW4 .138 A3
Mackay Ho 33 W12 .112 B6
Mackay Rd SW4 ....137 B2
McKay Rd SW20 ....178 C4
McKellar Cl WD23 ...8 A2
McKenna Ho 3 E3 ..97 B5
Mackennal St
  NW8 ....92 C5 230 B4
Mackenzie Cl 7 W12 112 B6
Mackenzie Ct 1 N8 .50 A5
Mackenzie Ho 5 NW2 68 A5
Mackenzie Rd N7 ...72 B2
  Penge BR3 ....184 D1
Mackenzie Wlk E14 .119 C5
McKerrell Rd SE15 .140 A4
Mackeson Rd NW3 ..70 D4
Mackie Ho SW2 ....160 C4
Mackie Rd 18 SW2 .160 C4
McKiernan Ct 2
  SW11 ....136 C3
Mc Killop Way DA14 .190 C3
McKinlay Ct BR3 ..185 B1
McKinnon Wood Ho 23
  E2 ....96 A4
Mackintosh La E9 ...74 D3
Macklin Ho SE23 ...162 B2
Macklin St
  WC2 ....94 A1 240 B2
Mackonochie Ho
  EC1 ....241 A4
Mackrow Wlk 11 E14 120 A6
Macks Rd SE16 ....118 A2
Mackworth Ho NW1 .232 A2
Mackworth St NW1 .232 A2
Maclean Rd SE23 ..163 A5
Mcleod Ct SE21 ....164 B2
McLeod Ho 4 SE18 .144 A4
Mcleod Ho 3 SE23 .162 C2
McLeod Rd SE2 ....124 D2
Mcleod Rd N21 .....16 A4
McLeod's Mews
  SW7 ....113 D2 255 D4
Macleod St
  SE17 ....117 A1 262 B1
Maclise Rd
  W14 ....113 A3 254 A5
McManus Ho 3
  SW11 ....136 B2
McMillan Ct 2 SE6 .164 D3
Macmillan Ho HA2 ..41 C1
Mcmillan Ho SE4 ..141 A2
Macmillan Ho NW4 ..68 B4
McMillan St SE8 ...141 C6

Macmillan Way
  SW17 ....181 B6
Mcmorran Ho N7 ....72 A4
McNair Rd UB2 ....107 D3
Macnamara Ho
  SW10 ....266 C4
Mcneil Rd SE5 .....139 C3
McNicol Dr NW10 ..89 A5
Macoma Rd SE18 ..145 B6
Macoma Terr SE18 .145 B6
Maconochies Rd E14 119 D1
Macquarie Way E14 .119 D2
McRae La CR4 .....202 D2
Macready Ho W1 ...237 B3
Macready Pl 2 N7 ..72 A4
Macroom Ho W9 ....91 B4
Macroom Rd W9 ....91 B4
Mac's Pl EC4 ......241 B2
Madame Tussaud's*
  NW1 ....93 A3 238 A5
Mada Rd BR6 ......226 D5
Maddams St E3 .....97 D3
Maddison Cl TW11 .174 A3
Maddocks Cl DA14 .191 A3
Maddocks Ho 3 E1 .118 B6
Maddock Way SE17 .138 D6
Maddox Ct 1 E4 ....20 D3
Maddox St W1 .....248 C6
Madeira Ave BR1 ..186 C3
Madeira Gr IG8 .....37 C4
Madeira Rd E11 ....54 C1
  Edmonton N13 .....16 D1
  Mitcham CR4 ......202 D5
  Streatham SW16 ..182 A5
Madeley Ct W5 .....88 A1
Madeley Rd W5 .....88 A1
Madeline Gr IG1 ....79 B3
Madeline Rd SE20 .184 B3
Madge Gill Way 4
  E6 ....100 A6
Madge Hill W7 .....108 C6
Madinah Rd E8 .....74 A3
Madingley 11 KT1 .176 C1
Madingley Ct TW1 .153 D6
Madison Cres DA7 .146 C5
Madison Gdns
  Beckenham BR2 ....208 D6
  Bexley DA7 ....146 C5
Madison Ho E3 ......98 A4
Madras Ho IG1 .....78 C6
Madras Pl N7 ....72 C2
Madras Rd IG1 .....78 C6
Madrid Rd SW13 ...134 C3
Madron St
  SE17 ....117 C1 263 B2
Mafeking Ave E6 ..100 A5
  Brentford TW8 ....132 A6
  Ilford IG2 ....57 B2
Mafeking Rd E16 ...98 D3
  Enfield EN1 ....5 D2
  Tottenham N17 .....34 A1
Magdala Ave N19 ...71 C6
Magdala Rd
  Isleworth TW7 .....131 A2
  South Croydon CR2 .221 B1
Magdalen Ct SE25 .206 A4
Magdalene Cl 25
  SE15 ....140 B3
Magdalene Gdns E6 .100 C3
Magdalene Ho 7
  SW15 ....156 D5
Magdalene Rd TW17 .192 B6
Magdalen Pas E1 ..253 D6
Magdalen Rd SW18 .158 B3
Magdalen St SE1 ..253 A3
Magee St SE11 ....138 C6
Magellan Ct 9 NW10 .67 B1
Magellan Ho 16 E1 .96 B3
Magellan Pl 10 E14 .119 C2
Magnaville Rd WD23 ..8 D4
Magnet Rd HA9 .....65 D6
Magnin Cl 5 E8 .....96 A6
Magnolia Cl E10 ....75 C6
  Kingston KT2 .....176 D1
Magnolia Ct 2 N12 .29 D5
  SW11 ....158 D5
  3 Belmont SM2 ....217 D1
  Feltham TW14 .....150 A3
  Forest Hill SE26 ..184 C5
  Harrow HA3 ....44 B2
  Hillingdon UB10 ...60 D2
  Northolt UB5 ....85 A3
  Richmond TW9 .....132 D4
Magnolia Ho 13 SE8 .141 B6
Magnolia Lo E4 .....19 C1
Magnolia Pl SW4 ..160 A6
  Ealing W5 ....87 D2
Magnolia Rd W4 ...132 C6
Magnolia Way KT19 .215 A6
Magnolia Wharf W4 .132 C6

Magpie Cl E7 ....76 D3
  NW9 ....27 C1
  Enfield EN1 ....6 A4
Magpie Hall Cl BR2 .210 A3
Magpie Hall La BR2 .210 B3
Magpie Hall Rd WD23 .8 C2
Magpie Ho 7 E3 .....97 B6
Magpie Pl SE14 ....141 A6
Maguire Dr TW10 ..175 D6
Maguire St
  SE1 ....117 D4 253 D2
Mahatma Gandhi Ind Est
  1 SE24 ....138 D1
Mahlon Ave HA4 ....62 D2
Mahogany Cl SE16 .119 C6
Mahon Cl EN1 ......5 D4
Mahoney Ho SE14 .141 B4
Maida Ave W2 .92 A3 236 B5
  Chingford E4 ....19 D4
Maida Rd DA17 ....125 C3
Maida Vale
  W9 ....92 A4 229 A1
Maida Vale Psychiatric
  Hospl W9 ...92 A3 236 B6
Maida Vale Sta W9 .91 D4
Maida Way E4 ......19 D4
Maiden Erlegh Ave
  DA5 ....169 A3
Maiden La NW1 .....71 D1
  SE1 ....117 A5 252 B1
  WC2 ....116 A6 250 B6
Maidenstone Hill
  SE10 ....142 A2
Maids of Honour Row 4
  TW9 ....153 D6
Maidstone Bldgs SE1 252 C3
Maidstone Ho 4 E14 .97 D1
Maidstone Rd N11 ..31 D4
  Ruxley DA14 ......191 C3
Mail Coach Yd 24 E2 .95 C4
Main Ave EN1 ....17 D6
Main Dr HA9 ....65 D5
Main Rd BR5 ......190 C1
  Sidcup DA14,DA15 .167 C1
Mainridge Rd BR7,
  SE9 ....188 C6
Main St TW13 .....172 D5
Mainwaring Ct 3
  CR4 ....181 A1
Main Yd E9 ....75 C2
Mais Ho SE26 .....162 B2
Maismore St SE15 .140 A6
Maison Alfort HA3 ..24 C2
Maisonettes The
  SM1 ....217 B3
Maitland Cl 5 SE10 .141 D5
  Hounslow TW4 .....129 B2
Maitland Ct W2 ....246 C6
Maitland Ho 17 E2 ..96 C5
  SW1 ....269 A6
Maitland Park Rd
  NW3 ....70 D2
Maitland Park Villas
  NW3 ....70 D2
Maitland Pl E5 ......74 C4
Maitland Rd E15 ....76 D2
  Penge SE26 ....184 D4
Majendie Rd SE18 .123 B1
Majestic Ct N4 .....50 D1
Majestic Way CR4 .180 D1
Major Rd E15 ....76 B3
  22 SE16 ....118 A3
Makepeace Ave N6 .71 A6
Makepeace Mans N6 .71 A5
Makepeace Rd
  Northolt UB5 ....85 A6
  Wanstead E11 ......55 A5
Makinen Ho IG9 ....21 C2
Makins St SW3 ....257 B3
Malabar Ct 20 W12 .112 B6
Malabar St E14 ....119 C4
Malam Ct SE11 ....261 A3
Malam Gdns 3 E14 .119 D6
Malay Ho 2 E1 .....118 C5
Malbrook Rd SW15 .134 B1
Malcolm Cl SE20 ..184 C3
Malcolm Cres NW4 .46 A3
Malcolm Ct E7 .....76 D2
  NW4 ....46 A4
  Ealing W5 ....88 B4
  Stanmore HA7 .....25 C5
Malcolm Dr KT6 ...198 A1
Malcolm Gavin Cl
  SW17 ....158 C2
Malcolm Ho 13 N1 ..95 C5
Malcolm Pl E2 ......96 C3
Malcolm Prim Sch
  SE20 ....184 C3

Malcolm Rd E1 .....96 C3
  Croydon SE25 .....206 A3
  Ickenham UB10 ....60 B4
  Penge SE20 ....184 C3
  Wimbledon SW19 ..179 A4
Malcolmson Ho SW1 259 D1
Malcolms Way N14 ..15 C6
Malcolm Pl E11 .....55 A5
Malden Ave
  Croydon SE25 .....206 B6
  Northolt UB6 ....64 C2
Malden CE Prim Sch
  KT4 ....199 C1
Malden Cres NW1 ..71 A2
Malden Ct N4 ....51 A3
  West Barnes KT3 ..200 B4
Malden Green Ave
  KT4 ....200 A1
Malden Hill KT3 ...199 D6
Malden Hill Gdns
  KT3 ....199 D6
Malden Junc KT3 ..199 D4
Malden Manor Prim Sch
  KT3 ....199 C2
Malden Manor Sta
  KT3 ....199 C2
Malden Pk KT3 ....199 D3
Malden Pl NW5 .....71 A3
Malden Rd NW5 ....71 A2
  Cheam KT4,SM3 ..216 D4
  New Malden KT3,KT4 .199 D2
Malden Way KT3 ..200 A5
Malden Way (Kingston By
  Pass) KT3,KT5 ....199 D2
Maldon Cl E15 ......76 B3
  N1 ....235 B6
  SE5 ....139 A2
Maldon Ct Barking E6 .100 C6
  Wallington SM6 ...219 C3
Maldon Rd W3 .....111 A6
  Edmonton N9 ....17 C1
  Wallington SM6 ...219 B3
Maldon Wlk IG8 ....37 C4
Malet Pl WC1 ......239 C5
Malet St WC1 .93 D2 239 D4
Maley Ave SE27 ...160 D2
Malford Ct E18 .....37 A1
Malford Gr E18 .....54 D6
Malfort Rd SE5 ....139 C2
Malham Cl N11 .....31 A4
Malham Rd SE23 ..162 D3
Malham Road Ind Est
  SE23 ....162 D3
Malins Cl EN5 .....12 C6
Mallams Mews 1
  SW9 ....138 D2
Mallard Cl E9 ....75 B2
  NW6 ....91 C6
  W7 ....108 C4
  New Barnet EN5 ...14 B5
  Twickenham TW4 ..151 A4
Mallard Ct E12 .....78 B3
  E17 ....54 B6
  NW9 ....45 A2
  Chingford E4 ......20 A4
  Ilford IG2 ....79 A6
  15 Richmond TW10 .153 D5
Mallard Ho NW8 ...230 A3
  7 SE15 ....139 D2
Mallard Path SE28 .123 B3
Mallard Pl TW1 ...153 A1
Mallard Point 5 E3 .97 C4
Mallards E11 ....55 A2
Mallards Rd
  Barking IG11 ......102 A3
  Woodford IG8 ......37 B3
Mallard Way NW9 ..45 A2
Mallard Wlk
  Beckenham BR3 ...206 D4
  Sidcup DA14 ......190 C4
Mall Ct W5 ....110 A6
Mallet Dr UB5 .....63 B3
Mallet Ho 11 SW15 .156 A6
Mallet Rd SE13 ...164 B5
Malling SE13 ......163 D6
Malling Cl CR0 ....206 C3
Malling Gdns SM4 .202 A3
Malling Ho 9 BR3 .185 C3
Malling Way BR2 ..208 D2
Mallinson Ct 2 E11 .76 C4
Mallinson Rd SW11 .158 D2
  Wallington SM6 ...219 D5
Mallon Gdns E1 ...243 D3
Mallord St
  SW3 ....136 B6 266 D6
Mallory Bldgs EC1 .241 C5
Mallory Cl SE4 ....141 A1
Mallory Gdns EN4 .15 A4
Mallory Ho E14 .....98 A4

Mal – Mar 351

Mallory St
NW8 92 C3 237 B6
Mallow Cl CR0 206 D1
Mallow Mead NW7 29 A3
Mallow St EC1 242 C6
Mallows The UB10 60 D5
Mall Rd W6 112 B1
Mall Studios 9 NW3 70 D3
Mall The 4 BR1 209 A6
SW1 115 D5 249 C3
6 Bexley DA6 147 C1
Brentford TW8 131 D6
Ealing W5 110 A6
Harrow HA3 44 B3
Kingston KT6 197 D4
Mortlake SW14 155 A6
Palmers Green N14 16 A1
Mall The (Prep Sch)
TW2 152 B1
Malmains Cl BR3 208 B5
Malmains Way BR3 208 B5
Malmesbury 31 E2 96 C5
Malmesbury Cl HA5 40 A5
Malmesbury Fst Sch
SM4 202 A2
Malmesbury Mid Sch
SM4 202 A3
Malmesbury Prim Sch
E3 97 B4
Malmesbury Rd E16 98 C2
E3 97 B5
Morden SM4 202 A3
Woodford E18 36 D2
Malmesbury Terr E16 98 D2
Malmsey Ho SE11 260 D2
Malmsmead Ho E9 75 A3
Malorees Jun & Inf Schs
NW6 68 D1
Malory Sch BR1 187 A6
Malpas Dr HA5 40 D4
Malpas Rd E8 74 B2
SE4 141 B3
Dagenham RM9 80 D2
Malta Rd E10 53 C2
Malta St EC1 241 D6
Maltby Dr EN1 6 B5
Maltby Rd KT9 214 C2
Maltby St
SE1 117 D3 263 C6
Maltham Terr N18 34 B4
Malthouse Dr
Chiswick W4 133 D6
Feltham TW13 172 D5
Malthouse Pas SW13 133 C3
Malthus Path 7
SE28 124 C5
Malting Ho E14 119 B6
Maltings W4 110 C1
Maltings Cl SW13 133 C3
Maltings Lo W4 133 C5
Maltings Pl SE1 253 B2
SW6 265 D1
Maltings The BR6 211 D1
Malting Way TW7 130 D2
Malt Mill SE1 253 C3
Malton Ho SE25 205 C5
Malton Mews SE18 145 C6
1 W10 91 A1
Malton Rd W10 91 A1
Malton St SE18 145 C6
Maltravers St WC2 251 A6
Malt St SE1 140 A6
Malva Cl SW18 157 D6
Malvern Ave DA7 147 A5
Chingford E4 36 B3
Harrow HA2 63 B5
Malvern Cl W10 91 B2
Ickenham UB10 60 C6
Mitcham CR4 203 C6
Penge SE20 184 A1
Surbiton KT6 198 A1
Malvern Court SW7 256 D4
Malvern Ct
Belmont SM2 217 C1
3 Surbiton KT6 198 A1
Malvern Dr
Feltham TW13 172 D5
Ilford IG3 79 D4
Woodford IG8 37 C6
Malvern Gdns NW2 69 A6
Harrow HA3 44 A5
Malvern Ho N16 51 D1
Malvern Lo N12 30 B6
Malvern Mews NW6 91 C4
Malvern Pl NW6 91 B4
Malvern Rd E11 76 D6
E6 100 A6
E8 74 A1
N17 52 A6
N19 49 D1
Malvern Rd *continued*
N8 50 C6
NW6 91 C4
Enfield EN3 7 A6
Hampton TW12 173 C3
Harlington UB3 127 C5
Surbiton KT6 198 A1
Thornton Heath CR7 204 C5
Malvern Terr N1 234 A6
Edmonton N9 17 D3
Malvern Way W13 87 B2
Malwood Rd SW12 159 B5
Malyons Rd SE13 163 D6
Malyons Terr SE13 163 D6
Malyons The TW17 193 B3
Managers St E14 120 A5
Manatee Pl SM6 219 D5
Manaton Cl SE15 140 B2
Manaton Cres UB1 85 C1
Manbey Gr E15 76 C2
Manbey Park Rd E15 76 C2
Manbey Rd E15 76 C2
Manbey St E15 76 C2
Manbre Rd W6 134 C6
Manbrough Ave E6 100 C4
Manchester Ct E16 99 B1
Manchester Dr W10 91 A3
Manchester Gr E14 120 A1
Manchester Ho SE17 262 B2
Manchester Mans
N19 49 D2
Manchester Mews
W1 238 A3
Manchester Rd E14 120 A3
N15 51 B3
South Norwood CR7 205 A6
Manchester Sq
W1 93 A1 238 B2
Manchester St
W1 93 A2 238 A3
Manchester Way
RM10 81 D4
Manchuria Rd SW11 159 A5
Manciple St
SE1 117 B3 262 D6
Mandalay Ho 6 N16 73 B4
Mandalay Rd SW4 159 C6
Mandarin Ct NW10 67 B2
6 SE8 141 C6
Mandarin Way UB4 84 D1
Mandela Cl NW10 67 A1
36 W12 112 B6
Mandela Ho 18 E2 95 D4
Mandela Rd E16 99 A1
Mandela St
NW1 93 C6 232 B6
SW9 138 C5
Mandela Way
SE1 117 C2 263 B4
Manderville Ho SE1 263 D2
Mandeville Cl 5 SE3 142 D5
Merton SW19 179 A2
Mandeville Ct NW3 69 D3
Mandeville Ctyd
SW11 268 A1
Mandeville Dr KT6 197 D1
Mandeville Ho 8
SW4 159 C6
Mandeville Pl W1 238 B2
Mandeville Prim Sch
E5 74 D5
Mandeville Rd N14 15 C2
Enfield EN3 7 A6
Isleworth TW7 131 A3
Littleton TW17 192 C4
Northolt UB5 63 C1
Mandeville Sch UB5 63 B2
Mandeville St E5 75 A5
Mandrake Rd SW17 158 D1
Mandrake Way 2 E15 76 C1
Mandrell Rd SW2 160 A6
Manesty Ct N14 15 D4
Manette St W1 239 D1
Manfred Ct 6 SW15 157 B6
Manfred Rd SW15 157 B6
Manger Rd N7 72 A2
Mangold Way 4
DA18 125 A3
Manilla St E14 119 C4
Manister Rd SE2 124 A3
Manitoba Ct 23 SE16 118 C4
Manitoba Gdns 6
BR6 227 D2
Manley Ct N16 73 D5
Manley Ho SE11 261 A2
Manley St NW1 231 A6
Manly Dixon Dr EN3 7 A6
Mann Cl 1 CR0 221 A5
Mannebury Prior N1 233 D3
Mannering Ho 16
SW2 160 B6
Manning Ct 3 SE28 124 B5
Manningford Cl EC1 234 C2
Manning Gdns HA3 43 D2
Manning Ho 6 E17 54 A6
3 W11 91 A1
Manning Pl TW10 154 B5
Manning Rd E17 53 A4
Dagenham RM10 81 C1
Manningtree Cl
SW19 157 A3
Manningtree Rd HA4 62 B4
Manningtree St 1 E1 96 A1
Mannin Rd RM6 58 B2
Mannock Rd N22 50 D6
Mann's Cl TW7 152 D6
Manns Rd HA8 26 C4
Manny Shinwell Ho
SW6 264 D5
Manoel Rd TW2 152 A2
Manor Ave SE4 141 B3
Hounslow TW4 128 D3
Northolt UB5 63 B1
Manorbrook SE12,
SE3 143 A1
Manor Circus TW9 132 C2
Manor Cl E17 35 A1
NW7 27 B5
NW9 44 D4
SE28 102 C1
Barnet EN5 1 A1
New Malden KT4 199 C1
Ruislip HA4 39 D1
Manor Cottages App
N2 30 A1
Manor Cotts N2 30 A1
Manor Court Rd W7 108 C6
Manor Cres KT5 198 C3
Manor Ct E10 53 D1
N14 15 D2
N20 14 D1
N2 48 D4
SE15 139 D4
7 SW2 160 B6
SW6 265 D1
W3 110 C2
3 Barking IG11 79 D1
Chingford, Chingford Green
E4 20 C3
Harrow HA1 42 D3
Kingston KT2 176 C2
Streatham SW16 160 A1
Surbiton KT5 198 C3
Twickenham TW2 152 A2
5 Wembley HA9 66 A3
Manordene Cl KT7 197 A1
Manordene Rd SE28 102 D1
Manor Dr N14 15 B3
N20 14 D1
NW7 27 B5
Feltham TW13 172 D5
Hinchley Wood KT10 213 A5
Sunbury TW16 172 A1
Surbiton KT5 198 C3
Wembley HA9 66 B4
West Ewell KT19 215 C2
Manor Dr N KT3,KT4 199 B2
Manor Dr The KT4 199 D1
Manor Farm Ave
TW17 192 D3
Manor Farm Cl KT4 199 C1
Manor Farm Ct E6 100 B4
Manor Farm Dr E4 20 C1
Manor Farm Rd
Thornton Heath CR7,
SW16 182 C1
Wembley HA0 87 D5
Manorfield Cl 3 N19 71 C4
Manorfield Prim Sch
E14 97 D2
Manorfields Cl BR7 211 D6
Manor Gate UB5 63 A1
Manorgate Rd KT2 176 C2
Manor Gdns N7 72 A5
SW4 137 C3
W3 110 C2
8 W4 111 C1
Hampton TW12 174 A3
Merton SW20 179 B1
Richmond TW10,TW9 132 B1
Ruislip HA4 62 C3
South Croydon CR2 221 D2
Sunbury TW16 172 A1
Manor Gr SE15 140 C6
Beckenham BR3 185 D1
Richmond TW9 132 C2
Manor Gt SW15 157 A6
Manor Hall Ave NW4 28 D1
Manor Hall Dr NW4 28 D1
Manor Hall Gdns E10 53 C1
Manor Ho E12 77 D4
N14 15 D3
NW1 237 B4
Brentford TW8 109 C1
Wallington SM6 219 B3
Manor House Ct W9 236 A5
Manor House Dr NW6 68 D1
Manor House Est HA7 25 B5
Manor House Sch
W7 108 C6
Manor House Way
TW7 131 B2
Manor Inf Sch IG11 79 D2
Manor Jun Sch IG11 79 D2
Manor La SE12 164 C5
Feltham TW13 150 A2
Harlington UB3 127 B6
Sunbury TW16 172 B1
Sutton SM1 218 A3
Manor Lane Terr
SE13 164 C6
Manor Lodge NW2 68 D2
Manor Mans N7 72 A5
7 NW3 70 C2
Manor Mead Sch
TW17 192 D4
Manor Mews NW6 91 C5
SE4 141 B3
Manor Mount SE23 162 C3
Manor Oak Mans
SE22 162 B5
Manor Par N16 73 D6
Harrow HA1 42 D2
Manor Park Cl BR4 207 D1
Manor Park Cres HA8 26 C4
Manor Park Dr HA2 41 D6
Manor Park Gdns HA8 26 C4
Manor Park Prim Sch
SM1 218 A3
Manor Park Rd E12 77 D4
N2 48 B6
NW10 89 D6
Chislehurst BR7 189 B2
Sutton SM1 218 A3
West Wickham BR4 207 D1
Manor Park Sta E12 77 D4
Manor Pk SE13 164 C6
Chislehurst BR7 189 B2
Richmond TW9 132 B1
Manor Pl BR7 189 B1
SE17 117 A1 262 A2
East Bedfont TW14 150 A3
Mitcham CR4 203 C6
Sutton SM1 217 D4
Walton-on-T KT12 194 A2
Manor Prim Sch E15 98 C5
Manor Rd DA15 168 A1
DA5 169 D3
E10 53 C2
E15,E16 98 C4
E17 35 A1
N16 51 C1
Ashford TW15 170 C5
Barking IG11 79 D2
Barnet EN5 1 A1
Beckenham BR3 185 D1
Belmont SM2 217 B1
Bowes Park N22 32 A4
Dagenham RM6 58 D3
Ealing W13 109 A6
East Molesey KT8 196 B5
Enfield EN2 5 B3
Harrow HA1 43 A3
Hayes UB3 84 A1
Loughton IG10 21 B5
Merton SW20 179 B1
Mitcham CR4 203 C6
Richmond TW10,TW9 132 B1
Richmond TW11 175 B5
Ruislip HA4 39 B1
South Norwood SE25 206 A6
Tottenham N17 34 B2
Twickenham TW2 152 B2
Wallington SM5,SM6 219 B3
Walton-on-T KT12 193 D2
West Wickham BR4 223 D6
Manor Rd N
Hinchley Wood KT7 213 A6
Wallington SM5,SM6 219 B4
Manor Rd S KT10 212 C4
Manor Sch NW10 90 C6
Manorside EN5 1 A1
Manorside Cl SE2 124 D2
Manorside Prim Sch
N3 30 A2
Manor Sq RM8 80 C6
Manor Street Est
SW3 267 B6
Manor The W1 248 C5
Manor Vale TW8 109 C1
Manor View N3 29 D1
Manor Way BR2 210 A3
BR5 211 A5
DA5 169 C3
NW9 45 C5
W3 110 C2
Manorway Enfield EN1 17 C4
Woodford IG8 37 C5
Manor Way
Beckenham BR3 207 C6
Chingford E4 36 B6
Greenwich SE3 143 A1
Harrow HA2 41 D5
Mitcham CR4 203 C6
New Malden KT4 199 D1
Ruislip HA4 39 D1
Southall UB2 106 D2
South Croydon CR2 221 D2
Manor Waye UB8 82 A6
Manor Way The SM6 219 B4
Manpreet Ct E12 78 B3
Manresa Rd
SW3 114 C1 257 A1
Mansard Beeches
SW17 181 A5
Mansard Cl HA5 40 D6
Mansard Manor 4
SM2 218 A1
Manse Cl UB3 127 B6
Manse Ct DA14 190 C5
Mansel Ct SW11 267 B1
Mansel Gr E17 35 C2
Mansell Ho SW8 269 B2
Mansell Rd W3 111 B4
Southall UB6 85 D2
Mansell St E1 95 D1 243 D1
Mansel Rd SW19 179 B4
Manse Rd N16 73 D5
Mansergh Cl SE18 144 A5
Mansfield Ave N15 51 B5
East Barnet EN4 15 A5
Ruislip HA4 40 B1
Mansfield Cl N9 18 A5
Mansfield Ct 27 E2 95 D6
Mansfield Dr UB4 83 C3
Mansfield Hill E4 19 D3
Mansfield Ho SW15 156 D5
Mansfield Hts N2 48 D4
Mansfield Mews W1 238 C3
Mansfield Pl 11 NW3 70 A4
Mansfield Rd E17 53 B5
NW3 70 D4
Acton W3 88 D3
Chessington KT9 213 D3
Ilford IG1 78 C6
South Croydon CR2 221 B2
Wanstead E11 55 B3
Mansfield St
W1 93 B2 238 C3
Mansford St E2 96 A5
Manship Rd CR4 181 A2
Mansion Cl SW9 138 C4
Mansion Gdns NW3 69 D5
Mansion House★
EC4 242 C1
Mansion House Pl
EC3,EC4 242 C1
Mansion House St
EC2 242 C1
Mansion House Sta
EC4 117 A6 252 B6
Mansions The NW6 69 B3
Manson Mews
SW7 114 B2 256 C3
Manson Pl
SW7 114 B2 256 C3
Manstead Gdns RM6 58 C2
Manston NW1 71 C1
Tottenham N17 33 B1
Manston Ave UB2 107 C2
Manston Cl SE20 184 C2
Manstone Rd NW2 69 A3
Manston Gr KT2 175 D5
Manston Ho W14 254 B5
Mantell Ho SW4 159 C6
Manthorpe Rd SE18 123 A1
Mantilla Rd SW17 181 A6
Mantle Rd SE4 141 A2
Mantlet Cl SW16 181 C3
Mantle Way E15 76 C1
Manton Ave W7 109 A4
Manton Cl UB3 105 C6
Manton Ho N16 73 B5
Manton Rd SE2 124 A2
Holdbrook EN3 7 C5
Mantua St 23 SW11 136 B2
Mantus Cl E1 96 C3
Mantus Rd E1 96 C3
Manus Way N20 14 A3
Manville Gdns SW17 159 B1
Manville Rd SW17 159 B1
Manwood Rd SE4 163 B5
Manwood St E16 122 B5
Manygate La TW17 193 A3
Many Gates SW12 159 B2
Mapesbury Ct NW2 69 A3
Mapesbury Rd NW2 69 A2
Mapeshill Pl NW2 68 C2
Mapes Ho 5 NW6 69 A1
Mape St E2 96 B3
Maple Ave E4 35 B4
W3 111 C5
Harrow HA2 63 D6
Yiewsley UB7 104 B6
Maple Cl BR5 211 B4
N16 52 A3
N3 29 C4
SW4 159 D5
Buckhurst Hill IG9 21 D1
Hampton TW12 173 B4
Hayes UB4 84 D4
Mitcham CR4 181 B2
Ruislip HA4 40 B3
Maple Cres DA15 168 A5
Maplecroft Cl E6 100 A1
Maple Ct E6 100 C2
NW2 68 D4
Catford SE6 163 D3
2 Croydon CR0 221 A4
7 Dagenham RM8 58 D2
Kingston KT3 199 B6
4 Pinner HA5 22 C1
Sidcup DA14 190 B5
11 West Norwood
SW16 182 C5
Mapledale Ave CR0 222 A5
Mapledene BR7 189 A5
Mapledene Est E8 74 A1
Mapledene Rd E8 74 A1
Mapledown Sch NW2 46 C2
Maple Gdns HA8 27 C3
Stanwell TW19 148 A2
Maple Gr NW9 45 A2
W5 109 D3
Brentford TW8 131 B5
Southall UB1 85 B2
Maple Gr Bsns Ctr
TW4 128 C1
Maple Ho 13 E17 53 D6
11 NW3 70 D2
5 SE8 141 B5
2 Kingston KT6 198 A4
Maplehurst 2 BR2 186 C1
Maplehurst Cl KT1 198 A5
Maple Ind Est TW13 150 A1
Maple Inf Sch KT6 197 D4
Maple Leaf Dr DA15 167 D3
Mapleleafe Gdns IG6 56 D6
Maple Leaf Sq 27
SE16 118 D4
Maple Lo NW9 67 B6
Putney SW15 157 A5
Maple Mews NW6 91 D5
Streatham SW16 182 B5
Maple Pl W1 239 B5
Tottenham N17 34 A3
Yiewsley UB7 104 B6
Maple Rd E11 54 C3
Hayes UB4 84 D4
Kingston KT6 197 D4
Penge SE20 184 C2
Maples Pl E1 96 B2
Maple St W1 93 C3 239 B5
Maplestead Rd
Dagenham RM9 102 B6
Streatham SW2 160 B4
Maples The KT8 175 C3
Maplethorpe Rd CR7 204 D5
Mapleton Cl BR2 209 A3
Mapleton Cres
Enfield EN3 6 C5
Wandsworth SW18 157 D5
Mapleton Rd
Chingford E4 20 A1
Enfield EN1 6 B3
Wandsworth SW18 157 D5
Maple Way TW13 150 B1
Maple Wlk W10 90 D3
Maplin Cl N21 16 B5
Maplin Ho 9 SE2 124 D4
Maplin Rd E16 99 B1
Maplin St E3 97 B4
Mapperley Cl 3 E11 55 A3
Mapperley Dr IG8 36 C3
Marada Ho NW6 69 A1
Marais W4 133 A5

Maran Way DA18 ....**124** D3
Marathon Way SE28 ..**123** D4
Marban Rd W9 ....**91** B4
Marble Arch★
  W1 ....**114** D6 **247** D6
Marble Arch Sta
  W1 ......**92** D1 **237** D1
Marble Cl W3 ......**110** D5
Marble Dr NW2 ......**46** B2
Marbleford Ct **4** N6 ..**49** D2
Marble Hill★ TW1 ...**153** C4
Marble Hill Cl TW1 ..**153** B4
Marble Hill Gdns
  TW1 ....**153** B4
  W9 ....**91** B3
Marbrook Ct SE12 ...**165** C1
Marcella Rd SW9 ....**138** C3
Marcellina Way BR6 .**227** D5
March **23** NW9 .....**27** D2
Marchant Ct SE1 ....**263** D2
Marchant Ho **13** SW2 **160** B6
Marchant Rd E11 ....**76** B6
Marchant St SE14 ...**141** A6
Marchbank Rd
  W14 .....**135** B6 **264** D6
March Ct SW15 .....**134** B1
Marchmont Ho **10**
  SW16 ....**181** C5
Marchmont Rd
  Richmond TW10 .....**154** B6
  Wallington SM6 .....**219** C1
Marchmont St
  WC1 .....**94** A3 **240** A6
March Rd **5** TW1 ...**153** C4
Marchside Cl TW5 ..**128** D4
Marchwood Cl **17**
  SE5 ....**139** C5
Marchwood Cres W5 .**87** D1
Marcia Rd
  SE1 .....**117** C2 **263** B3
Marcilly Rd SW18 ...**158** B6
Marcon Ct **29** E8 ....**74** B3
Marconi Pl N11 ......**31** B6
Marconi Rd E10 .....**53** C1
Marconi Way UB1 ...**85** D1
Marcon Pl E8 ....**74** B3
Marco Rd W6 ......**112** C3
Marcourt Lawns W5 ..**88** A3
Marcus Ct E15 ......**98** C6
  Brentford TW8 .....**132** C4
Marcus Garvey Mews
  SE22 ....**162** B6
Marcus Garvey Way **9**
  SE24 ....**138** C1
Marcus Ho **13** SE15 .**139** D4
Marcus St E15 ......**98** D6
  Wandsworth SW18 ...**157** D5
Marcus Terr SW18 ...**157** D5
Mardale Ct NW7 ....**28** A3
Mardale Dr NW9 ....**45** B4
Mardell Rd CR0 .....**206** D4
Marden Ave BR2 ....**209** A3
Marden Cres CR0 ....**204** B3
Marden Ho **6** E8 ....**74** B3
Marden Rd
  Thornton Heath CR0 .**204** B3
  Tottenham N17 .....**33** C1
Marden Sq SE16 ....**118** B3
Marder Rd W13 .....**109** A4
Mardyke Ho SE17 ...**262** D4
Marechal Niel Ave
  DA15 ....**167** B1
Marechal Niel Par
  DA15 ....**167** B1
Maresby Ho E4 ......**19** D2
Maresfield CR0 .....**221** C5
Maresfield Gdns NW3 .**70** A2
Mare St E8 ....**74** B2
  E8,E2 ....**96** B6
Marfleet Cl SM5 ....**218** C6
Margaret Ave E4 ....**19** D5
Margaret Bondfield Ave
  IG11 ....**80** A1
Margaret Bondfield Ho
  4 E3 ....**97** A5
  22 N7 ....**71** D3
Margaret Ct W1 ....**239** A2
  Barnet EN4 ....**2** B1
Margaret Gardner Dr
  SE9 ....**166** B2
Margaret Herbison Ho
  SW6 ....**264** D5
Margaret Hill Ho N8 ..**50** A4
Margaret Ho **16** W6 .**112** C1
Margaret Ingram Cl
  SW6 ....**264** C5

Margaret Lockwood Cl
  KT5 ....**198** B5
Margaret Mcmillan Ho **10**
  N19 ....**49** D2
Margaret Rd DA5 ....**168** D5
  N16 ....**51** D1
  Barnet EN4 ....**2** B1
Margaret's Ct E11 ....**54** B2
  SE1 ....**252** C3
Margarets Ct HA8 ...**26** D5
Margaret St
  W1 ....**93** C1 **239** A2
Margaretta Terr
  SW3 ......**136** C6 **267** B6
Margaretting Rd E12 .**55** C1
Margaret Way IG4 ...**56** A3
Margaret White Ho
  NW1 ....**232** C2
Margate Rd SW2 ....**160** A6
Margery Fry Ct N7 ...**72** A5
Margery Park Rd E7 ..**77** A2
Margery Rd RM8 ....**80** D5
Margery St
  WC1 ......**94** C4 **234** A1
Margetson Ho N16 ...**51** D3
Margin Dr SW19 .....**178** D6
Margravine Gdns
  W14 ....**254** A2
  W6 ....**112** D1
Margravine Rd
  W6 ......**112** D1 **264** A6
Marham Gdns
  Morden SM4 ......**202** A3
  Wandsworth SW17,
  SW18 ....**158** C3
Mar Ho **4** SE7 .....**143** C6
Maria Cl **10** SE1 ....**118** C2
Maria Fidelis RC Convent
  Sch NW1 .....**93** D4 **232** C2
Maria Ho **15** SW9 ...**138** C4
Marian Cl UB4 ......**84** D3
Marian Ct E9 ....**74** C2
  Sutton SM1 ....**217** D3
Marian Lo **5** SW20 .**178** D3
Marian Pl E2 ....**96** B5
Marian Rd SW16 ....**181** C2
Marian Sq E2 ......**96** B5
Marian St **2** E2 ....**96** B5
Marian Vian Prim Sch
  BR3 ....**207** A4
Marian Way NW10 ...**67** D1
Maria Terr E1 ......**96** D3
Maria Theresa Cl
  KT3 ....**199** B4
Maribor **13** SE10 ...**142** A5
Maricas Ave HA3 ....**24** B2
Marie Curie SE5 ....**139** C4
Marie Lloyd Ct **13**
  SW9 ....**138** B1
Marie Lloyd Gdns **1**
  N19 ....**50** A2
Marie Lloyd Ho N1 ..**235** C3
Marien Ct E4 ....**36** B5
Marigold Cl UB1 ....**107** A6
Marigold Rd N17 ....**34** C3
Marigold St SE16 ...**118** B4
Marigold Way CR0 ..**206** D1
Marilea Ct W5 ......**109** A4
Marina App UB4 ....**85** A2
Marina Ave KT3 ....**200** B4
Marina Cl **1** BR2 ...**209** A6
Marina Ct **11** E3 ....**97** C4
Marina Dr DA16 ....**145** C2
Marina Gdns RM7 ...**59** D4
Marina Way TW1 ....**175** D3
Marine Dr **5** SE18 ..**122** B2
  Barking IG11 ......**102** A4
Marinefield Rd SW6 .**135** D3
Marinel Ho **25** SE5 ..**139** A5
Mariner Gdns TW10 .**153** C1
Mariner Rd E12 .....**78** C4
Mariners Mews E14 ..**120** B2
Marine St SE16 .....**118** A3
Marine Twr **29** SE8 ..**141** B6
Marion Ave TW17 ...**192** D4
Marion Ct **4** SW17 ..**180** C5
  N14 ....**15** C1
Marion Gr IG8 ......**36** C3
Marion Rd NW7 ....**28** A5
  Thornton Heath CR0 .**205** B4
Marion Richardson Prim
  Sch E1 ....**96** D1
Marischal Rd SE13 ..**142** B2
Maritime Ho **5** SW4 .**137** C2
Maritime Ind Est SE7 **121** B2
Maritime Quay **6**
  E14 ....**119** C1
Maritime St E3 .....**97** B3
Marius Mans **3**
  SW17 ....**159** A2
Marius Rd SW17 ....**159** A2

Marjorie Gr SW11 ...**136** D1
Marjorie McClure Sch
  BR7 ....**189** A2
Marjory Kinnon Sch
  TW14 ....**149** C6
Markab Rd HA6 .....**22** A5
Mark Ave E4 ....**19** D5
Mark Cl BR2 ....**226** A4
  DA7 ....**147** A4
  Southall UB1 ......**107** D5
Markeston Gn WD19 .**22** D6
Market Ctr The UB2 .**106** B2
Market La HA8 .....**27** D2
Market Mews
  W1 ....**115** B5 **248** C3
  E17 ....**53** B6
  Croydon SE25 ......**206** A5
  1 Edmonton N9 .....**18** A2
  Feltham TW13 ......**151** A4
Market Pl **2** DA7 ...**147** C1
  N2 ....**48** C6
  1 SE16 ....**118** B2
  W1 ....**239** A2
  3 W3 ....**111** A5
  Brentford TW8 .....**131** C5
  Enfield EN2 ....**5** B2
  Kingston KT1 ......**175** D1
Market Pl The NW11 .**47** D5
Market Rd N7 ......**72** A2
  Richmond TW9 .....**132** C2
Market Sq BR1 .....**187** A1
  E14 ....**97** D1
Market Sq The N9 ...**18** B2
Market St SE18 .....**122** C2
  Wallend E6 ....**100** C5
Market The SM1,SM5 .**202** A1
Market Way E14 ....**97** D1
  1 Wembley HA0 .....**66** A3
Market Yd Mews SE1 **263** A6
Markfield Gdns E4 ...**19** D4
Markfield Ho N15 ...**52** A5
Markfield Rd N15 ...**52** A4
Markham Ct NW4 ...**46** C6
Markham Ho
  1 Dagenham RM10 ..**81** C5
  9 Dulwich SE21 ....**183** C6
Markham Pl SW3 ...**257** C2
Markham Sq
  SW3 ....**114** D1 **257** C2
Markham St
  SW3 ....**114** C1 **257** B2
Mark Ho **3** E2 .....**96** B5
Markhole Cl TW12 ..**173** B3
Markhouse Ave E17 ..**53** A3
Markhouse Pas E17 ..**53** B3
Markhouse Rd E17 ...**53** B3
Mark La EC3 ...**117** C6 **253** B6
Markland Ho W10 ...**112** D6
Mark Lo **9** EN4 .....**2** C1
Markmanor Ave E17 ..**53** B2
Mark Mans W12 ....**112** A4
Mark Rd N22 ......**32** D1
Marksbury Ave TW9 .**132** C2
Marks Gate Inf Sch
  RM6 ....**59** A6
Marks Gate Jun Sch
  RM6 ....**59** A6
Mark Sq EC2 ......**243** A6
Mark St E15 ....**76** C4
  EC2 ....**243** A6
Markstone Ho SE1 ..**251** C1
Mark Wade Cl E12 ...**55** D1
Markway The TW16 ..**172** C1
Markwell Cl SE26 ...**184** B6
Markyate Ho W10 ...**90** C3
Markyate Rd RM8 ...**80** B3
Marland Ho SW1 ...**257** D6
Marlands Rd IG5 ....**56** B6
Marlang Ct BR3 ....**186** B2
Marlborough
  11 Putney SW19 ....**156** D3
Marlborough Ave
  3 E8 ....**96** A6
  N14 ....**15** C1
  Edgware HA8 ....**10** D1
  Ruislip HA4 ....**39** B3
Marlborough Cl BR6 .**211** D3
  N20 ....**14** D1
  SE17 ....**261** D3
  Mitcham SW19 .....**180** C4
Marlborough Cres
  W4 ....**111** C3
  Harlington UB3 .....**127** B5
Marlborough Ct W8 .**255** A4
  7 Buckhurst Hill IG9 .**21** C2
  Harrow HA1 ....**42** B5
  Wallington SM6 ....**219** C1

Marlborough Day Hospl
  NW8 ......**92** A5 **229** A4
Marlborough Dr IG5 .**56** A6
Marlborough Flats
  SW3 ....**257** B4
Marlborough Fst & Mid
  Sch HA1 ....**42** C5
Marlborough Gdns
  N20 ....**14** D1
  Surbiton KT6 ......**197** D2
Marlborough Gr SE1 .**118** A1
Marlborough Hill
  NW8 ......**92** A6 **229** B5
  Harrow HA1 ....**42** C5
Marlborough Ho N4 .**51** A1
  NW8 ....**229** A3
  Richmond TW10 ....**154** C6
  Wimbledon SW19 ...**156** D1
Marlborough House
  SW1 ....**249** B3
  1 Edmonton N9 .....**18** A2
  Feltham TW13 ......**151** A2
Marlborough La SE7 .**143** C5
Marlborough Mans **5**
  NW6 ....**69** C3
Marlborough Mews
  SW2 ....**138** B1
Marlborough Par **1**
  UB10 ....**82** D3
Marlborough Park Ave
  DA15 ....**168** A3
Marlborough Pl
  NW8 ......**92** A5 **229** B4
Marlborough Prim Sch
  SW3 ......**114** C2 **257** B3
Marlborough Rd
  DA16 ....**146** D2
  E15 ....**76** C4
  E7 ....**77** C1
  N19 ....**72** A6
  SE18 ....**123** A3
  SW1 ....**115** C5 **249** B3
  W4 ....**111** A1
  W5 ....**109** D4
  Ashford TW15 ......**170** A5
  Bowes Park N22 ....**32** B4
  Brentford TW7 .....**131** B5
  Bromley BR2 ......**209** C5
  Chingford E4 ......**35** D4
  Dagenham RM8 .....**80** C4
  Edmonton N9 ......**18** A3
  Feltham TW13 .....**150** D2
  Hampton TW12 .....**173** C4
  Hillingdon UB10 ...**82** D4
  Mitcham SW19 .....**180** C4
  Richmond TW10 ....**154** B5
  Romford RM7 .....**59** D5
  Southall UB2 ......**106** C3
  South Croydon CR2 .**221** A1
  Sutton SM1 ....**217** C6
  Wanstead E18 .....**55** A6
Marlborough Sch
  Isleworth TW7 .....**131** A4
  Sidcup DA15 ......**168** A4
Marlborough St
  SW3 ....**114** C2 **257** B3
Marlborough Trad Est
  TW9 ....**132** D4
Marlborough Yd N19 .**71** D6
Marlbury NW8 .....**91** D6
Marler Rd SE23 ....**163** B3
Marlesford Ct SM6 ..**219** C4
Marley Ave DA7 ....**146** C6
Marley Cl N15 .....**50** D5
  Southall UB6 ......**85** C4
Marley Ho **4** W11 ...**112** D6
Marley Wlk NW2 ...**68** C3
Marlfield Cl KT4 ....**200** A1
Marlfield Ct KT3 ....**199** D2
Marlin Cl TW16 ....**171** C4
Marling Ct TW12 ...**173** B4
Marlingdene Cl
  TW12 ....**173** C4
Marlings Cl BR7 ....**211** C6
Marlings Park Ave
  BR7 ....**211** C6
Marlin Ho SW15 ....**157** A6
Marlins Cl **3** SM1 ...**218** A3
Marloes Cl HA0 .....**65** C4
Marloes Rd
  W8 ......**113** D3 **255** C5
Marlow Cl SE20 ....**206** B6
Marlow Cres TW1 ...**152** D5
Marlow Ct N14 .....**15** C4
  NW6 ....**68** D1
  NW9 ....**45** D6
  1 Ealing W7 ......**108** C5
Marlow Dr SM3 ....**216** D3
Marlowe Bsns Ctr **2**
  SE14 ....**141** A5
Marlowe Cl BR7 ....**189** B4
Marlowe Ct SW3 ...**257** B3

Marlowe Ct continued
  Dulwich SE19 ......**183** D5
  6 Kingston KT2 .....**175** D6
Marlowe Gdns SE9 ..**166** C5
Marlowe Ho **15** N16 .**73** C4
  SE8 ....**119** B1
  Kingston KT1 ......**197** D5
Marlowe Lo CR0 ....**223** A6
Marlowe Rd E17 ....**54** C5
Marlowe Sq CR4 ...**203** C5
Marlowes The
  NW8 ......**92** B6 **229** C6
Marlowe Way CR0 ..**220** A6
Marlow Gdns UB3 ..**105** B3
Marlow Ho **44** E2 ...**95** D4
  SE1 ....**263** C6
  14 W2 ....**91** D1
  Teddington TW11 ...**175** A6
Marlow Rd E6 .....**100** B4
  Penge SE20 ......**184** B1
  Southall UB2 ......**107** B3
Marlow Studio Workshops
  43 E2 ....**95** D4
Marlow Way SE16 ...**118** C4
Marl Rd SW18 .....**136** A1
Marlston NW1 .....**231** D1
Marlton St SE10 ...**120** D1
Marlwood Cl DA15 ..**167** C2
Marmadon Rd SE18, **123** D4
Marmion App E4 ....**35** C6
Marmion Ave E4 ....**35** B6
Marmion Cl E4 .....**35** B6
Marmion Ho **13**
  SW12 ....**159** B4
Marmion Mews **4**
  SW11 ....**137** A2
Marmion Rd SW11 ..**137** A1
Marmont Rd SE15 ..**140** A5
Marmora Ho E1 ....**97** A2
Marmora Rd SE22 ..**162** C5
Marmot Rd TW4 ...**128** D2
Marne Ave DA16 ...**146** A2
  N11 ....**31** B6
Marnell Way TW4 ..**128** D2
Marne St W10 .....**91** A4
Marner Prim Sch E3 .**97** D3
Marney Rd SW11 ...**137** A1
Marnfield Cres SW2 .**160** B3
Marnham Ave NW2 ..**69** A4
Marnham Cres UB6 .**85** D5
Marnham Ct HA0 ...**65** C3
Marnock Ho SE17 ..**262** C2
Marnock Rd SE4 ...**163** B6
Maroon St E14 .....**97** A2
Maroons Way SE6 ..**185** C5
Marqueen Twrs
  SW16 ....**182** B3
Marquess Rd N1 ...**73** B4
Marquess Rd N **1** N1 .**73** B4
Marquess Rd S **17** N1 .**73** A2
Marquis Cl HA0 ....**66** B1
Marquis Ct N4 .....**50** B1
  Barking IG11 ......**79** C3
  1 Kingston KT1 ....**198** A5
Marquis Rd N4 .....**50** C1
  NW1 ....**71** D2
  Bowes Park N22 ....**32** B4
Marrabon Cl DA15 ..**168** A3
Marrayat Sq SW6 ..**264** A3
Marrick Cl SW15 ...**134** A1
Marrick Ho **17** NW6 .**91** D6
Marrilyne Ave EN3 ..**7** B5
Marriner Ct UB3 ...**105** C6
Marriott Cl TW14 ..**149** B5
Marriott Ho **8** SE6 ..**186** A6
Marriott Rd E15 ...**98** C6
  N10 ....**30** D2
  N4 ....**50** B1
Marriotts Cl NW9 ...**45** D3
Marryat Ct **12** W6 ..**112** B2
Marryat Ho SW1 ...**259** A1
Marryat Pl SW19 ...**179** A6
Marryat Rd SW19 ..**179** A6
Marryatt Ct W5 ....**88** B1
Marsala Rd SE13 ...**141** D1
Marsalis Ho **2** E3 ...**97** C4
Marsden Rd SE15 ..**139** C2
  Edmonton N9 ......**18** B2
Marsden St NW5 ...**71** A2
Marsden Way BR6 ..**227** D4
Marshall Cl N11 ....**15** B1
  SW18 ....**158** A5
  Harrow HA1 ....**42** B2
  Hounslow TW4 ....**151** B6
Marshall Dr UB4 ...**83** D2
Marshall Ho N1 ....**235** D4
  NW6 ....**91** B5
  SE17 ....**262** C2

Marshall Ho continued
  4 New Malden KT3 ..**199** C
Marshall Path **10**
  SE28 ....**124** D
Marshall Rd Leyton E10 **75** D
  Tottenham N17 ....**33** B
Marshalls Gr SE18 ..**122** A
Marshall's Pl SE16 ..**263** D
Marshall's Rd SM1 ..**217** D
Marshall St
  W1 ....**93** C1 **239** B
Marshalsea Rd
  SE1 ......**117** A4 **252** B
Marsham Cl BR7 ...**188** D
Marsham Ct SW1 ...**259** D
  19 Putney SW19 ....**156** D
Marsham St
  SW1 ......**115** D2 **259** D
Marsh Ave CR4 ....**181** A
Marshbrook Cl SE3 .**143** D
Marsh Cl NW7 .....**11** D
Marsh Ct E8 ....**74** A
  3 Merton SW19 ....**180** A
Marsh Dr NW9 .....**45** D
Marsh Farm Rd TW2 **152** D
Marshfield St E14 ..**120** A
Marshgate Bsns Ctr
  E15 ....**98** A
Marshgate Ctr The
  E15 ....**97** D
Marshgate La E15 ..**75** D
Marsh Green Prim Sch
  RM10 ....**103** C
Marsh Green Rd
  RM10 ....**103** C
Marsh Hall HA9 ....**66** B
Marsh Hill E9 .....**75** A
Marsh Ho SW1 .....**259** D
  SW8 ....**269** B
Marsh La E10 .....**75** C
  NW7 ....**11** C
  Stanmore HA7 .....**25** C
  Tottenham N17 ....**34** B
Marsh Rd Pinner HA5 .**41** A
  Wembley HA0 ......**87** D
Marshside Cl N9 ...**18** C
Marsh St E14 ......**119** D
Marsh Wall E14 ....**119** D
Marshwood Ho **10**
  NW6 ....**91** C
Marsland Cl SE17 ..**261** D
Marsom Ho N1 ....**235** C
Marston SE17 .....**262** B
Marston Ave
  Chessington KT9 ...**214** A
  Dagenham RM10 ...**81** C
Marston Cl NW6 ...**70** A
  Dagenham RM10 ...**81** C
Marston Ct DA14 ..**189** D
  Walton-on-T KT12 ..**194** C
Marston Ho SW9 ...**138** C
Marston Rd TW11 ..**175** B
Marston Way SE19 .**183** A
Marsworth Ave HA5 .**22** D
Marsworth Cl UB4 ..**85** A
Marsworth Ho **8** E2 .**96** B
Martaban Rd N16 ..**73** D
Martello St E8 .....**74** B
Martello Terr E8 ...**74** B
Martell Rd SE21 ...**161** B
Martel Pl E8 ......**73** D
Marten Rd E17 ....**35** C
Martens Ave DA7 ..**147** D
Martham Cl SE28 ..**124** D
Martha Rd E15 ....**76** C
Martha's Bldgs EC1 .**242** C
Martha St E1 .....**96** C
Marthorne Cres HA3 .**24** B
Martin Bowes Rd
  SE9 ....**144** D
Martinbridge Trad Est
  EN1 ....**18** B
Martin Cl N9 .....**18** D
  Uxbridge UB10 ....**82** A
Martin Cres CR0 ...**204** C
Martin Ct **10** E14 ..**120** A
  Merton SW19 .....**179** C
  Southall UB2 ......**107** B
Martindale SW14 ..**155** A
Martindale Ave **2**
  E16 ....**121** A
Martindale Ho **20**
  E14 ....**119** D
Martindale Rd
  Balham SW12 .....**159** B
  Hounslow TW4 ....**129** A
Martin Dene DA6 ..**169** B
Martin Dr UB5 ....**63** D
Martineau Cl KT10 .**212** B
Martineau Ho SW1 .**259** A

Martineau Mews N5 ..72 D4
Martineau Rd N5 ...72 D4
Martingale Cl TW16 .194 A5
Martingales Cl TW10 153 D1
Martin Gdns RM8 ...80 D4
Martin Gr SM4 ......201 C6
Martin Ho SE1 .....262 B5
SW8 ....270 A4
6 New Malden KT3 ..199 C5
Martini Dr EN3 ......7 C6
Martin La EC4 .....252 D6
Martin Prim Sch N2 ..30 C1
Martin Rd RM8 .....80 D4
Martin Rise DA6 ...169 B6
Martins Cl BR4 ....224 B6
Martins Mount EN5 ...1 C1
Martin's Rd BR2 ...186 A1
Martin St SE28 ....123 C5
Martins The
  Penge SE26 ......184 B5
  Wembley HA9 .....66 B5
  Woolwich SE28 ...123 C5
Martin Way SW19,
  SW20,SM4 ......201 B6
Martlesham N17 ...33 C1
Martlet Gr 5 UB5 ..84 D4
Martlett Ct WC2 ...240 B1
Martlett Lo NW3 ..69 D4
Martley Dr IG2 ....56 D4
Martley Ho SW8 ..269 B2
Martock Cl HA3 ....43 A5
Martock Ct 10 SE15 140 B4
Martock Gdns N11 ..31 A5
Marton Cl SE6 .....163 C1
Marton Rd 2 N16 ...73 C5
Martyn Ct HA8 ....26 B6
Martyn Ho SE2 ....146 D6
Martynside 22 NW9 ..27 D2
Marvel Ho 5 SE15 .139 B5
Marvell Ave UB4 ...84 A2
Marvels Cl SE12 ..165 B2
Marvels La SE12 ..165 C1
Marvels Lane Prim Sch
  SE12 ....187 D6
Marville Ho SW18 .158 B5
Marville Rd
  SW6 ....135 B5 264 C3
Marvin St 9 E8 ...74 B2
Marwell Cl BR4 ....224 D6
Marwick Rd UB7 ...104 B4
Marwood Cl DA16 ..146 B2
Mary Adelaide Cl
  Kingston SW15 ...155 C1
  Kingston SW15 ...177 C6
Mary Adelaide Ho
  W2 ....236 D4
Mary Ann Bldgs SE8 .141 C6
Maryatt Ave HA2 ...63 D6
Marybank SE18 ...122 B2
Mary Batchelor Sch (Girls)
  SE5 ....139 B4
Mary Cl HA7 ....44 B5
Mary Datchelor Cl
  SE5 ....139 B4
Mary Dine Ct SW8 .270 D3
Mary Gn NW8 .....91 D6
Marygold Ho TW3 .130 A4
Mary Ho 6 SW9 ..138 C1
8 W6 ....112 C1
Mary James Ho 29 E2 96 A5
Mary Jones Ho 13
  E14 ....119 C6
Maryland Ct KT1 ..176 D1
Maryland Pk E15 ..76 C3
Maryland Point E15 .76 C2
Maryland Prim Sch
  E15 ....76 C3
Maryland Rd E15 ...76 B3
  W9 ....91 C3
  South Norwood CR7 .182 D2
  Tottenham N22 ...32 C4
Marylands Ind Est E15 76 C3
Maryland Sq E15 ..76 C3
Marylands Rd W9 ..91 D3
Maryland St E15 ...76 C3
Maryland Sta E15 ..76 C2
Maryland Way TW16 .172 A1
Maryland Wlk N1 ..235 A6
Mary Lawrenson Pl 1
  SE3 ....143 A5
Marylebone Flyover
  NW1 ....92 C3 237 A3
Marylebone High St
  W1 ....93 A2 238 B4
Marylebone La
  W1 ....93 A1 238 B2
Marylebone Mews
  W1 ....238 C3

Marylebone Pas W1 .239 B2
Marylebone Rd
  NW1 ....92 D2 237 D4
Marylebone St
  W1 ....93 A2 238 B3
Marylebone Sta
  NW1 ....92 D3 237 C5
Marylee Way
  SE11 ....116 B2 260 D3
Mary Macarthur Ho
  15 E2 ....96 D4
  W14 ....264 A6
  8 Belvedere DA17 .125 C3
  11 Dagenham RM10 ..81 C5
Mary McArthur Ho 12
  N19 ....49 D2
Marymount International
  Sch KT2 ....177 A3
Maryon Gr SE7 ....122 A2
Maryon Mews NW3 ..70 C4
Maryon Rd SE7 ....122 A2
Mary Peters Dr UB6 ..64 B3
Mary Pl W11 ..113 A4 244 A5
Mary Rose Cl TW12 .173 C2
Mary Rose Mall E6 .100 B2
Maryrose Way N20 ..14 B3
Mary's Ct WC2 .....237 B6
Mary Secole Cl 21 E8 .95 D6
Mary St 5 E16 ....98 C2
  N1 ....95 A6 235 B5
Mary's Terr TW1 ..153 A4
Mary Terr NW1 ....232 A5
Maryville DA16 ....145 D3
Mary Wharrie Ho 4
  NW3 ....70 D1
Masbro' Rd W14 ..112 D3
Mascalls Ct 13 SE7 .143 C6
Mascalls Rd SE7 ..143 C6
Mascotte Rd 2
  SW15 ....134 D1
Mascotts Cl NW2 ..68 A3
Masefield Ave
  Borehamwood WD6 ..10 D6
  Southall UB1 ....107 C6
  Stanmore HA7 ...24 D5
Masefield Cres N14 ..15 C5
  New Barnet EN5 ....2 A1
  19 Surbiton KT6 ..197 D2
Masefield Gdns E6 .100 C3
Masefield Ho 1 NW6 .91 C4
Masefield La UB4 ..84 C3
Masefield Rd TW13 .173 B6
Masefield View BR6 .227 A5
Masefield Way TW19 148 B3
Masham Ho 6 DA18 124 D4
Mashie Rd W3 .....89 C1
Maskall Cl SW2 ...160 C1
Maskani Wlk SW16 .181 C3
Maskell Rd SW17 .158 A1
Maskelyne Cl
  SW11 ....136 C4 267 B2
Mason Cl DA7 ....147 D2
  E16 ....121 A6
  SE16 ....118 A1
  Hampton TW12 ..173 B4
  Wimbledon SW20 .178 D2
Mason Ct
  4 Penge SE19 ...183 D3
  Wembley HA9 ....66 C6
Mason Ho 16 E9 ..74 C1
  8 N11 ....31 C5
  13 SE1 ....118 A2
Mason Rd Sutton SM1 217 D3
  Woodford IG8 ....36 C4
Mason's Arms Mews
  W1 ....248 D6
Mason's Ave EC2 ..242 C2
Masons Ave HA3 ...42 C6
Mason's Ave CR0 ..221 A5
Masons Hill BR2 ..209 B5
  SE18 ....122 D2
Mason's Pl EC1 ...235 A2
  Mitcham CR4 ....180 D2
Mason St
  SE17 ....117 B2 262 D4
Mason's Yd SW1 ..249 B4
  Wimbledon SW19 ..178 D5
Massey Cl N11 ....31 B5
Massey Ct 7 E6 ...99 C6
Massie Rd E8 .....74 B2
Massingberd Way
  SW17 ....181 B6
Massinger St SE1, ..263 A3
Massingham St E1 ..96 D3
Masson Ave HA4 ..62 C2
Mast Ct 17 SE16 ..119 A2
Master Gunner's Pl 1
  SE18 ....144 A4

Masterman Ho 1
  SE5 ....139 B5
Masterman Rd E6 ..100 A4
Masters Cl SW16 ..181 C4
Masters Ct HA4 ...61 C6
Masters Dr SE16 ..118 B1
Masters Lo 22 E1 ..96 C1
Master's St 14 E1 ..96 D2
Mast House Terr E14 119 C2
Mastin Ho SW18 ..157 C3
Mastmaker Rd E14 .119 C4
Maswell Park Cres
  TW3 ....152 A6
Maswell Park Rd
  TW3 ....130 A1
Matcham Rd E11 ...76 D5
Matching Ct 13 E3 ..97 C4
Matchless Dr SE18 .144 C5
Matfield Cl BR2 ...209 A4
Matfield Rd DA17 .147 C6
Matham Gr SE22 ..139 D1
Matham Rd KT8 ...196 B4
Mathart Ct E4 .....36 A4
Matheson Lang Ho
  SE1 ....251 A1
Matheson Rd
  W14 ....113 B2 254 C3
Mathews Ave E6 ..100 C5
Mathews Park Ave
  E15 ....76 D2
Mathieson Ct SE1 .251 D1
Mathieson Ho 10 E4 ..20 C4
Matilda Cl SE19 ...183 B3
Matilda Ho E1 ....118 A5
Matilda Marks-Kennedy
  Jewish Prim Sch
  NW7 ....27 B5
Matilda St N1 ..94 B6 233 D6
Matlock Cl SE24 ..139 A1
  Barnet EN5 ......12 D6
Matlock Cres SM3 .217 A4
Matlock Ct NW8 ...229 A4
  7 SE5 ....139 B1
Matlock Gdns SM1,
  SM3 ....217 A4
Matlock Pl SM1,SM3 .217 A4
Matlock Rd E10 ...54 A3
Matlock St E14 ....97 A1
Matlock Way KT3 ..177 B2
Maton Ho SW6 ....264 C4
Matson Ct IG8 ....36 C3
Matson Ho 16 E9 ..74 D2
  9 SE16 ....118 B3
Matthew Cl W10 ..90 D3
Matthew Ct 4 E17 ..54 A6
  Mitcham CR4 .....203 D4
Matthew Parker St
  SW1 ....249 D1
Matthews Ct N5 ...73 A4
Matthews Ho 3 E14 .97 C2
Matthews Rd UB6 ..64 B3
Matthews St SW11 .136 D3
Matthias Ct 12 TW10 154 A5
Matthias Ho 2 N16 .73 C3
Matthias Rd N16 ..73 C3
Mattingly Way 4
  SE15 ....139 D5
Mattison Rd N4 ...50 D3
Mattock La W5,W13 .109 C5
Maud Cashmore Way
  SE18 ....122 B3
Maude Ho 3 E2 ...96 A5
Maude Rd E17 ....53 A4
  SE5 ....139 C4
Maudesville Cotts
  W7 ....108 C5
Maude Terr E17 ...53 A4
Maud Gdns E13 ...98 D5
  Barking IG11 ....101 D5
Maudlins Gn E1 ...118 A5
Maud Rd E10 .....76 A5
  E13 ....98 D5
Maudslay Rd SE9 .144 B2
Maudsley Ho TW8 .110 A1
Maudsley Hospl The
  SE5 ....139 B3
Maud St E16 ......98 D2
Maugham Ct 5 W3 .111 A3
Mauleverer Rd SW2 .160 A6
Maundeby Wlk NW10 .67 C1
Maunder Rd 4 W7 .108 D5
Maunsel St
  SW1 ....115 D2 259 C4
Mauretania Bldg 11
  E1 ....118 D6
Maurice Ave N22 ..32 D1
Maurice Browne Cl
  NW7 ....28 A4
Maurice Ct 3 TW8 .131 D5
Maurice Ho 1 SW9 .138 B3

Maurice St W12 ...90 B1
Maurice Wlk NW11 .48 A5
Maurier Cl UB5 ...84 C6
Mauritius Rd SE10 .120 C2
Maury Rd N16 ....74 A5
Mauveine Gdns TW3 .129 C1
Mavelstone Cl BR1 .188 C3
Mavelstone Rd BR1 .188 C3
Maverton Rd E3 ...97 C6
Mavery Ct 4 BR1 ..186 D3
Mavis Ave KT19 ...215 C3
Mavis Cl KT19 ....215 C3
Mavis Ct 33 NW9 ..27 D1
Mavis Wlk 9 E6 ..100 A2
Mavor Ho N1 .....233 D5
Mawbey Ho SE1 ..263 A1
Mawbey Pl
  SE1 ....117 D1 263 D1
Mawbey Rd SE1 ..263 D1
Mawbey St SW8 ..270 A3
Mawdley Ho SE1 ..251 B1
Mawney Cl RM7 ...59 D3
Mawney Rd RM7 ..59 D6
Mawson Cl SW20 .179 A1
Mawson Ho EC1 ..241 A4
Mawson La W4 ...133 D6
Maxden Ct SE15 ..140 A2
Maxey Gdns RM9 ..81 A4
Maxey Rd SE18 ...123 A4
  Dagenham RM9 ...81 A4
Maxfield Cl N20 ...14 A4
Maxim Rd N21 ....16 C5
Maxted Pk HA1 ...42 C2
Maxted Rd SE15 ..139 D2
Maxwell Cl
  Croydon CR0 .....204 A1
  Hayes UB3 ......106 A6
Maxwell Ct SE21 ..162 A3
Maxwell Gdns BR6 .227 D5
Maxwell Ho 12 SE18 .144 D6
  N16 ....51 C2
Maxwell Rd DA16 .146 A4
  SW6 ....135 D5 265 D3
  Ashford TW15 ...171 A4
  West Drayton UB7 .104 A3
Maxwelton Ave NW7 .27 B5
Maxwelton Cl NW7 ..27 B5
Maya Cl SE15 ....140 B3
Mayall Cl EN3 ....7 C5
Mayall Rd SE24 ..160 D6
Maya Pl N11 .....31 D3
Maya Rd N2 ......48 A5
Maybank Ave
  Wembley HA0 ....65 A3
  Woodford E18 ...37 B1
Maybank Gdns HA5 .40 A4
Maybank Rd E18 ..37 C5
May Bate Ave KT2 .175 D2
Maybells Commercial Est
  IG11 ....102 D5
Mayberry Pl KT5 ..198 B2
Maybourne Cl SE26 .184 B4
Maybourne Grange
  CR0 ....221 C6
Maybury Cl BR5 ..210 D4
  Enfield EN1 ......6 B5
Maybury Ct W1 ...238 B3
  Beckenham BR3 ..185 B3
  Harrow HA1 .....42 B3
Maybury Gdns NW10 .68 B2
Maybury Mews N6 ..49 C2
Maybury Rd E13 ..99 C3
  Barking IG11 ....102 A5
Maybury St SW17 .180 C5
Maychurch Cl HA7 ..25 D3
May Cl KT9 ......214 B2
Maycroft HA5 ....22 B1
  2 Hayes BR2 ....208 D1
  Pinner HA5 .....22 B1
Maycross Ave SM4 .201 C5
May Ct 2 SW19 ..180 A2
Mayday Gdns SE3 .144 A2
Mayday Rd CR0,CR7 .204 D2
Mayday University Hospl
  CR7 ....204 D3
Maydeb Ct RM6 ..59 B3
Maydew Ho SE16 .118 C2
Maydwell Ho 6 E14 .97 C2
Maye Angelou Ct E4 .36 A6
Mayefield Rd CR7 .204 B4
Mayerne Rd SE9 ..165 A6
Mayers Ct E8 .....74 A4
Mayesbrook Rd
  Barking IG11 ....101 D4
  Dagenham RM8,IG3 .80 B5
Mayesford Rd RM6 .58 C2
Mayespark Prim Sch
  IG3 ....80 A6
Mayeswood Rd SE12 .187 D6

Mayfair Ave DA16 .146 C1
  Dagenham RM6 ...58 D3
  Ilford IG1 ....56 C1
  New Malden KT4 .200 A1
  Twickenham TW2 .152 A4
Mayfair Cl
  Beckenham BR3 ..185 D2
  Surbiton KT6 ....198 A1
Mayfair Ct
  1 Beckenham BR3 .185 D2
  7 Croydon CR0 ..221 D6
  1 Wimbledon SW19 .179 A3
Mayfair Gdns
  Tottenham N17 ...33 B4
  Woodford IG8 ....37 A3
Mayfair Pl W1 ....248 D4
Mayfair Terr N14 ..15 D4
Mayfield DA7 .....147 B2
Mayfield Ave BR6 .211 D2
  N12 ....30 B6
  N14 ....15 D2
  W13 ....109 B3
  W4 ....111 C2
  Harrow HA3 .....43 B4
  Woodford IG8 ....37 A3
Mayfield Cl E8 ....73 D2
  SW4 ....159 D6
  Ashford TW15 ...170 A4
  Hillingdon UB10 ..82 D4
  Long Ditton KT7 ..197 B1
  Penge SE20 .....184 B2
Mayfield Cres
  Enfield N9 ......18 B5
  Thornton Heath CR7 .204 B4
Mayfield Ct SM2 ..218 A1
Mayfield Dr HA5 ..41 B5
Mayfield Gdns NW4 .46 D3
  Ealing W7 ......86 C2
Mayfield Ho 30 E2 ..96 B5
  N16 ....51 C2
Mayfield Mans SW15 157 B6
Mayfield Prim Sch W7 86 B1
Mayfield Rd BR1 ..210 A4
  E13 ....98 D3
  E17 ....35 A1
  E8 ....73 D1
  N8 ....50 B2
  W12 ....111 C4
  Acton W3 ....110 D6
  Chingford E4 ....20 B2
  Dagenham RM8 ...58 D1
  Enfield N9 ......6 D3
  Merton SW19 ....179 B2
  South Croydon CR2 .221 B1
  Sutton SM2 .....218 A2
  Wembley HA9 ....66 C6
Mayfields HA9 ....66 C6
Mayfield Sch & Coll
  RM8 ....58 C1
Mayfields Cl HA9 ..66 C6
Mayfield Villas DA14 .190 C4
Mayflower Cl SE16 .118 C2
  Ruislip HA4 .....39 A3
Mayflower Ho 2
  IG11 ....101 B6
Mayflower Lo N10 ..31 A2
  N3 ....47 B6
Mayflower Prim Sch
  E14 ....97 D1
Mayflower Rd SW9 .138 A2
Mayflower St 1
  SE16 ....118 C4
Mayfly Cl HA5 ....40 C2
Mayfly Gdns 12 UB5 ..84 D4
Mayford NW1 .....232 B4
Mayford Cl
  Balham SW12 ...158 C1
  Penge BR3 ......206 D6
Mayford Rd SW12 .159 A4
Maygood Ho N1 ..234 A4
Maygood St
  N1 ....94 C5 234 A4
Maygrove Rd NW6 .69 B2
Mayhew Cl E4 ....19 C1
Mayhew Ct 2 SE5 .139 B1
Mayhill Rd Barnet EN5 .13 A5
  Greenwich SE7 ...143 B6
Mayland Mans 4
  IG11 ....78 D1
Maylands Dr DA14 .168 D1
Maylands Ho SW3 .257 B3
Maylands Rd WD19 ..22 C6
Maynard Cl N15 ...51 D1
  SW6 ....135 D5 265 D3
Maynard Ct EN3 ..7 C5
Maynard Ho E1 ...97 A4
  SE18 ....123 A4
Maynard Rd E17 ..54 A4
Maynards Quay E1 .118 C6

Maynooth Gdns CR4 .202 D2
Mayo Ct W13 .....109 B3
Mayola Rd E5 ....74 C4
Mayo Rd NW10 ...67 C2
  Thornton Heath CR0 .205 B4
  Walton-on-T KT12 .194 A2
Mayow Rd SE23,SE26 .184 D6
Mayplace Cl DA7 ..147 D2
Mayplace La SE18 .144 A4
Mayplace Rd W DA7 .147 C1
Maypole Ct UB2 ..107 A4
May Rd E13 ......99 A5
  Chingford E4 ....35 C4
  Twickenham TW2 .152 C3
Mayroyd Ave KT6 .214 C6
May's Buildings Mews
  SE10 ....142 B5
Mays Ct WC2 .....250 A5
May's Ct SE10 ....142 B5
May's Hill Rd BR2 .208 C6
Mays La EN5 .....12 C5
Maysoule Rd SW11 .136 B1
Mays Rd TW11,TW12 .174 C2
Mayston Mews 3
  SE10 ....121 A1
May Terr IG1 .....78 D4
Maythorne Cotts
  SE13 ....164 B5
Maytime Prep Sch
  IG1 ....78 B6
Mayton St N7 ....72 B6
Maytree Cl HA8 ...11 A1
Maytree Ct
  Mitcham CR4 ....203 B6
  Northolt UB5 ....85 A4
May Tree Ho SE4 .141 B2
Maytree La HA7 ..24 D3
Maytree Wlk SW2 .160 C2
Mayville Prim Sch E11 76 C6
Mayville Rd E11 ..76 C6
  Ilford IG1 ....78 D3
Mayward Ho 7 SE5 .139 C4
May Wlk E13 .....99 B5
Maywood Cl BR3 ..185 D3
May Wynne Ho E16 .99 B1
Maze Hill SE10,SE3 .142 C4
Maze Hill Lo 8 SE10 142 B4
Maze Hill Specl Sch
  SE10 ....142 A5
Maze Hill Sta SE10 .142 C6
Mazenod Ave NW6 .69 C1
Maze Rd TW9 ....132 C5
Mead Cl 3 NW1 ..71 A1
  Harrow HA3 .....24 B4
Mead Cres
  Carshalton SM1 ..218 C4
  Chingford E4 ....36 A6
Meadcroft Ho 4 KT3 199 C2
Meadcroft Rd SE17 .138 D6
Mead Ct NW9 ....45 A4
Meade Cl W4 .....132 C6
Meader Ct SE14 ..140 D5
Mead Field HA2 ...63 B4
Meadfield HA8 ...10 D2
Mead Field HA2 ...63 B4
Meadfield Gn HA8 .10 D2
Meadfoot Rd SW16 .181 C2
Mead Gr RM6 ....58 C6
Mead Ho W11 ....244 C4
Mead House La UB4 .83 D4
Meadhurst Pk TW16 .171 C4
Mead Inf Sch The
  KT19 ....215 D4
Meadlands Dr TW10 .153 D2
Meadlands Prim Sch
  TW10 ....175 C6
Mead Lo W4 .....111 B4
Meadow Ave CR0 .206 D4
Meadowbank NW3 .70 D1
  SE3 ....142 D6
  Southgate N21 ...16 B5
  Surbiton KT5 ....198 B3
Meadow Bank 7
  SW15 ....157 B6
Meadowbank Cl SW6 134 C5
Meadowbank Gdns
  TW5 ....128 B4
Meadowbank Rd NW9 45 B2
Meadowbanks EN5 .12 A6
Meadowbrook Ct
  TW7 ....130 C2
Meadow Cl DA6 ..169 B6
  E9 ....75 B3
  Barnet EN5 ......13 B3
  Catford SE6 .....185 C5
  Chingford E4 ....19 D3
  Chislehurst BR7 ..188 D5
  Enfield EN3 ......7 A5

Meadow Cl continued
Hinchley Wood KT10 ..212 D5
Northolt UB5 ....85 C5
Richmond TW10 ....154 A3
Ruislip HA4 ....39 C5
Sutton SM1 ....218 A6
West Barnes SW20 ..200 C5
Hounslow TW4 ......151 C5
Meadowcourt Rd
SE3 ....142 D1
Meadowcroft 9 W4 .110 C1
Meadow Croft BR1 .210 B6
Meadowcroft Rd N13 .16 C2
Meadow Dr N10 .....49 B6
NW4 ....28 C1
Meadowford Cl SE28 124 D4
Meadow Garth NW10 .67 B2
Meadowgate Sch
SE4 ....141 A2
Meadow Gdns HA8 ...27 A4
Meadow High Sch
UB8 ....82 A2
Meadow Hill KT3 ...199 C3
Meadow La SE12 ...165 B1
Meadow Mews SW8 .270 C5
Meadow Pl
SW8 ....138 A5 270 B4
Chiswick W4 ......133 C5
Meadow Rd
SW8 ....138 B5 270 C4
Ashford TW15 ......171 B5
Barking IG11 ....80 A1
Beckenham BR2 ....186 C1
Carshalton SM1 ....218 C4
Claygate KT10 .....212 C2
Dagenham RM9 .....81 B2
Feltham TW13 .....151 A2
Loughton IG10 ......21 D6
Merton SW19 ......180 A3
Pinner HA5 ....41 A5
Southall UB1 ......107 B6
Meadow Row SE1 ..262 A5
Meadows Cl E10 ....75 C6
Meadows Ct DA14 ..190 B4
Meadows End TW16 .172 A2
Meadowside SE9 ...143 C5
Twickenham TW1 ...153 D4
Meadow Stile CR0 ..221 A5
Meadowsweet Cl
3 E16 ....99 D2
West Barnes KT3 ...200 C5
Meadow The BR7 ...189 A4
Meadow View DA15 .168 B4
Meadowview TW17 .193 A2
Meadow View HA1 ...42 C1
Meadowview Rd
Catford SE6 ....185 C5
Sidcup DA5 ....169 B5
West Ewell KT19 ...215 C1
Meadow View Rd
Hayes UB4 ....83 B3
Thornton Heath CR7 .204 D4
Meadow Way BR6 ..226 C5
NW9 ....45 B4
Chessington KT9 ...214 A3
Ruislip HA4 ....40 B3
Wembley HA9 ....65 D4
Meadow Waye TW5 .129 A5
Meadow Way The HA3 24 C2
Meadow Wlk
Dagenham RM9 .....81 B2
Ewell KT17 ....215 D1
Hackbridge SM6 ....219 B5
Wanstead E18 ......55 A5
West Ewell KT17,KT19 .215 D1
Meadow Wood Sch
WD23 ....8 A6
Mead Pl E9 ....74 C2
Croydon CR0 ....205 A1
Mead Plat NW10 ....67 A2
Mead Rd BR7 ......189 A4
Edgware HA8 ....26 C4
Richmond TW10 ....153 C1
Mead Road Inf Sch
BR7 ....189 A4
Mead Row
SE1 ....116 C3 261 A6
Meads Ct E15 ......76 D2
Meadside Cl BR3 ...185 A2
Meads La IG3 ....57 D2
Meads Rd Enfield EN3 ..7 A4
Tottenham N22 .....32 C1
Meads The HA8 .....27 B4
Cheam SM3 ....217 A5
Hillingdon UB8 .....82 A3
Mead The N2 ....30 A1
Beckenham BR3 ....186 A2

Mead The continued
Ealing W13 ....87 B2
Ickenham UB10 .....60 C6
Wallington SM6 ....219 D2
West Wickham BR4 ..208 B1
Meadvale Rd
Croydon CR0 ....206 A3
Ealing W5 ....87 C3
Meadway NW11 .....47 D3
Ashford TW15 ......170 C6
Barnet EN5 ....1 C1
Beckenham BR3 ....186 B2
Enfield EN3 ....6 D6
Palmers Green N14 ..16 A2
Tolworth KT5 ....199 A1
Twickenham TW2 ...152 B3
West Barnes SW20 ..200 C5
Woodford IG8 ....37 C5
Mead Way CR0 .....223 A6
Meadway KT10 .....212 A1
Hayes BR2 ....209 D3
Hayes BR2,BR4 ....208 D3
Ilford IG3 ....79 C4
Ruislip HA4 ....39 B3
Meadway Cl NW11 ..47 D3
Barnet EN5 ....1 C1
Pinner HA5 ....23 D4
Meadway Ct NW11 ..47 D3
Dagenham RM8 .....81 B6
Ealing W5 ....88 B2
Meadway Gate NW11 .47 C3
Meadway Gdns HA4 ..39 B3
Meadway The SE3 ..142 B3
Buckhurst Hill IG9 ...21 D3
Meaford Way SE20 ..184 B4
Meakin Est SE1 ....263 A6
Meakin Ho N7 ....72 B3
Meard St W1 ....239 C1
Meath Ho SE24 ....160 D5
Meath Rd E15 ......98 D5
Ilford IG1 ....79 A4
Meath St
SW11 ....137 B4 268 C2
Mecklenburgh Pl
WC1 ....240 C6
Mecklenburgh Sq
WC1 ....94 B3 240 C6
Medburn St NW1 ...232 C4
Medcalf Rd EN3 .....7 B6
Medcroft Gdns SW14 133 A1
Medebourne Cl SE3 .143 A2
Mede Ho BR1 ......187 B5
Medesenge Way N13 .32 C6
Medfield St SW15 ...156 A4
Medhurst Cl 17 E3 ..97 A5
Median Rd E5 ....74 C2
Medical Coll of St
Bartholomew's Hospl The
EC1 ....94 D3 241 D5
Medina Ave KT10 ..212 C5
Medina Ct N7 ......72 C5
Medina Gr N7 ......72 C5
Medina Ho SE15 ...140 C1
Medina Rd N7 ......72 C5
Medland Cl CR4 ...203 A1
Medlar Cl 1 UB5 ...84 D5
Medlar Ho 3 DA15 .168 A1
Medlar St SE5 ......139 A4
Medley Rd NW6 .....69 C2
Medora Rd SW2 ...160 B4
Medresco Ho NW3 ...70 B3
Medusa SE6,SE13 .163 D5
Medway Bldgs E3 ...97 A5
Medway Cl
Croydon CR0 ....206 C3
Ilford IG1 ....79 A4
Medway Ct WC1 ...233 A1
South Norwood SE25 .205 C4
Medway Dr UB6 ....86 D5
Medway Gdns HA0 ..65 A4
Medway Ho N16 .....73 B4
NW8 ....237 A4
SE1 ....252 D1
6 Kingston KT2 ...175 D2
Medway Mews 33 E3 .97 A5
Medway Par 1 UB6 ..86 D5
Medway Rd E3 ....97 A5
Medway St
SW1 ....115 D3 259 D5
Medwin St SW4 ....138 D1
Meecham Ct 1
SW11 ....136 C3
Meerbrook Rd SE3,
SE9 ....143 C2
Meeson Rd E15 .....76 D1
Meeson St E5 ....75 A4
Meeting House Alley 7
E1 ....118 B3

Mead The continued
SE15 ....140 B5
Mehetabel Rd E9 ...74 C3
Meister Cl IG1 ......57 B1
Melanda Cl BR7 ...188 B5
Melanie Cl DA7 ....147 A4
Melba Ct E8 ....73 D1
Melbourne Ave
Bowes Park N13 ....32 B4
Ealing W13 ....109 A5
Pinner HA2,HA5 ....41 D6
Melbourne Cl BR6 .211 C3
Ickenham UB10 .....60 C4
Wallington SM6 ....219 C3
Melbourne Ct E5 ...75 A4
N10 ....31 B3
W9 ....236 B6
Penge SE20 ....184 A3
Twickenham TW2 ...152 B3
Melbourne Gdns RM6 .59 A4
Melbourne Gr SE22 .139 C1
Melbourne Ho W8 .245 A3
Hayes UB4 ....84 C3
Melbourne Mews
SW9 ....138 C4
Catford SE6 ....164 A4
Melbourne Pl WC2 .240 D1
Melbourne Rd E10 ..53 D2
E17 ....53 A5
E6 ....100 B5
Ilford IG1 ....56 D1
Merton SW19 ......179 C2
Teddington TW11 ..175 C4
Wallington SM6 ....219 C4
Melbourne Sq 21
SW9 ....138 C4
Melbourne Way EN1 .17 D5
Melbrook Ho 11
SE22 ....139 C2
Melbury Ave UB2 ..107 D3
Melbury Cl BR7 ...188 B4
Claygate KT10 .....213 B2
Melbury Ct
W8 ....113 B3 254 D6
Melbury Dr SE5 ....139 C5
Melbury Gdns SW20 .178 B2
Melbury Ho SW8 ...270 C4
Twickenham TW2 ...152 B2
Melbury Rd
W14 ....113 B3 254 D6
Harrow HA3 ....44 B4
Melchester 3 W11 ..91 B1
Melchester Ho N19 .71 D5
Melcombe Ct NW1 .237 C4
Melcombe Gdns HA3 .44 B3
Melcombe Ho SW8 .270 C3
Melcombe Pl NW1 .237 C4
Melcombe Prim Sch
W6 ....134 D6
Melcombe St
NW1 ....92 D3 237 D5
Meldex Cl NW7 .....28 C4
Meldon Cl SW6 ...265 D2
Meldone KT3 ......199 B1
Meldone Cl BR3 ...198 D3
Meldrum Rd IG3 ....80 A6
Melfield Gdns SE6 .186 A5
Melfont Ave CR7 ..204 D6
Melford Ave IG11 ...79 D2
Melford Cl KT9 ....214 B3
Melford Ct E5 ......74 B5
Dulwich SE22 .....162 A4
2 Sutton SM2 ....218 A1
Melford Rd E11 ....76 C6
E17 ....53 B5
E6 ....100 B4
Dulwich SE21,SE22 .162 A3
Ilford IG1 ....79 B6
Melfort Rd CR7 ....204 D6
Melgund Rd N5 .....72 C3
Melina Cl UB3 ......83 B2
Melina Ct NW8 ....229 C1
Putney SW15 ......134 A4
Melina Pl NW8 92 B4 229 C1
Melina Rd W12 ....112 B4
Melior Ct N6 ....49 C3
Melior Pl SE1 .....253 A2
Melior St SE1 117 C4 253 A2
Meliot Rd SE6 ....164 B2
Melisa Ct N6 ....49 C2
Mellan Cl SM6 ....220 A5
Melling Dr EN1 ......6 A4
Melling St SE18 ...145 C6
Mellington Ct 2 N16 .74 A5
Mellis Ave TW9 ...132 D4
Mellish Cl IG11 ...101 D6
Mellish Flats E10 ...53 C2
Mellish Gdns IG8 ..37 A5
Mellish Ho 12 E1 ...96 B1

Mellish Ind Est E16 .121 D3
Mellish St E14 .....119 C3
Mellison Rd SW17 .180 C5
Mellitus St W12 .....89 D1
Mellor Cl KT12 ....195 B2
Mellor Ct 2 SW19 .180 A3
Mellor Ho 5 SE21 .183 C6
Mellow La E HA3 ...83 A3
Mellow Lane Sch UB4 83 A3
Mellows Rd
Redbridge IG5 ......56 B6
Wallington SM6 ....219 D3
Mells Cres SE9 ....188 B6
Mell St 6 SE10 ....120 C1
Melody Rd SW18 ..158 A6
Melon Pl W8 ......245 B2
Melon Rd E11 ......76 C5
SE15 ....140 A4
Melrose Ave NW2 ..68 C3
Borehamwood WD6 ..10 D6
Greenford UB6 .....85 D5
Mitcham CR4 .....181 B3
Thornton Heath SW16 .204 C6
Tottenham N22 .....32 D2
Twickenham TW2 ...151 D4
Wimbledon SW19 ..157 C1
Melrose Cl SE12 ..165 B3
Greenford UB6 .....85 D5
Hayes UB4 ....84 A2
Melrose Cres BR6 .227 B3
Melrose Ct
5 Ealing W13 .....109 A5
Wandsworth SW18 .157 B5
Melrose Dr UB1 ...107 C5
Melrose Gdns W6 ..112 C3
Edgware HA8 ....26 C1
Kingston KT3 ......199 B6
Melrose Ho NW6 ...91 C4
SW1 ....258 D2
Melrose Rd
1 Barnes SW13 ..133 D3
Merton SW19 ......179 C2
Pinner HA5 ....41 B5
Wandsworth SW18 .157 B5
Melrose Sch CR4 .202 C6
Melrose Terr W6 ..112 C3
Melrose Tudor SM6 .220 A3
Melsa Rd SM4 ....202 A3
Melthorne Dr HA4 ..62 C5
Melthorpe Gdns SE3 .144 A4
Melton Cl HA4 .....40 C1
Melton Ct SW7 ....256 D3
11 Croydon CR0 ..221 D6
Sutton SM2 ....218 A1
1 Twickenham TW1 .153 B4
Melton Ho E5 ......74 A6
Melton St
NW1 ....93 D4 232 C1
Melville Ave
Greenford UB6 .....64 D3
South Croydon CR2 .221 D3
Wimbledon SW20 ..178 A3
Melville Cl UB10 ...61 B5
Melville Court Flats
W12 ....112 B4
Melville Ct SE8 ...119 A2
4 W4 ....110 C1
Melville Gdns N13 ..32 D5
Melville Ho SE10 ..142 A4
New Barnet EN5 ...14 B3
Melville Pl 4 N1 ...73 A1
Melville Rd E17 ....53 B6
NW10 ....67 B1
Barnes SW13 .....134 A4
Sidcup DA14 ......168 C2
Melville Villas Rd
W3 ....111 B5
Melvin Ct 11 TW9 .132 C4
Melvin Rd SE20 ...184 C2
Melwood Ho 22 E1 .96 B1
Melyn Cl N7 ....71 C4
Memel Ct EC1 .....242 A5
Memel St EC1 .....242 A5
Memess Path 4
SE18 ....144 C6
Memorial Ave E15 ..98 C4
Memorial Cl TW5 ..129 B6
Memorial Hospl
SE18 ....144 C6
Mendham Ho SE1 .263 A6
Mendip Cl
Forest Hill SE26 ...184 C6
Harlington UB3 ....127 D6
North Cheam KT4 .216 C6
Mendip Ct SE14 ..140 C6
12 SW11 ....136 A2
Mendip Dr NW2,NW11 .69 A6
Mendip Ho 2 N4 ...51 B2
Mendip Hos 12 E2 ..96 C1

Mendip Rd SW11 ..136 A2
Bushey WD23 ....8 A5
Ilford IG2 ....57 C4
Mendora Rd
SW6 ....135 B5 264 C4
Menelik Rd NW2 ...69 B4
Menlo Gdns SE19 .183 B3
Mennie Ho SE18 ..144 B4
Menon Dr N9 ....18 B1
Menora Foundation Sch
HA8 ....27 A3
Menorah Gram Sch
NW11 ....47 A2
Menorah Prim Sch
NW11 ....47 A2
Menotti St 5 E2 ....96 A3
Menteath Ho 5 E14 .97 C1
Mentmore Cl HA3 ..43 C3
Mentmore Terr E8 ..74 B1
Mentone Ct SW8 ..270 B2
Meon Ct TW7 ......130 C3
Meon Rd W3 ......111 A4
Meopham Rd CR4,
SW16 ....181 C2
Mepham Cres HA3 ..24 A3
Mepham Gdns HA3 ..24 A3
Mepham St
SE1 ....116 C5 251 A3
Mera Dr DA7 ......147 D1
Merantun Way SW19 180 A2
Merbury Cl SE13 ..164 B6
Merbury Rd SE28 ..123 C4
Merbury St SE18 ..122 D3
Mercator Pl E14 ..119 C1
Mercator Rd SE13 .142 B1
Mercer Cl KT7 ....196 D2
Merceron Ho 3 E2 ..96 C4
Merceron St E1 .....96 B3
Mercer Pl HA5 .....22 C1
Mercers Cl SE10 ..120 C2
Mercer's Cotts 10 E3 .97 A1
Mercers Pl W6 ....112 C2
Mercers Rd N19 ....71 D5
Mercer St
WC2 ....94 A1 240 A1
Merchant Ct E1 ...118 C5
Merchants Cl SE25 .206 A6
Merchants Lo 5 E17 .53 C5
Merchant St E3 ....97 B4
Merchant Taylors'
Almshouses SE13 .142 C1
Merchant Taylors Hall★
EC3 ....242 D1
Merchiston Rd SE6 .164 B2
Merchland Rd SE9 .167 A3
Merchon Ho N7 ....71 C4
Mercia Gr SE13 ...142 A1
Mercia Ho 9 SE5 .139 A3
Mercier Rd SW15 .157 A6
Mercury 25 NW9 ...27 D2
Mercury Ct 3 E14 .119 C2
8 SW9 ....138 C4
Mercury Ctr TW14 .150 B6
Mercury Ho TW8 ..109 D1
Mercury Rd TW8 ..109 C1
Mercury Way SE14 .140 D6
Mercy Terr SE13 ..163 D6
Merebank La CR0,
SM6 ....220 B3
Mere Cl
Orpington BR6 ....226 D6
Putney SW15,SW19 .156 A4
Mere End CR0 .....206 D2
Mere Rd TW17 ....192 D3
Mereside BR6 .....226 C6
Meretone Cl SE4 ..141 A1
Meretune Ct SM4 .201 B6
Merevale Cres SM4 .202 A3
Mereway Industry
TW2 ....152 C3
Mereway Rd TW2 ..152 C3
Merewood Cl 1 BR1 188 C1
Mereworth Cl BR2 .208 D4
Mereworth Dr SE18 .145 A5
Mereworth Ho 3
SE15 ....140 C6

Meriden Ho continued
3 Barnet EN5 ......1 A1
Meridian Building
SE10 ....142 B5
Meridian Ct
4 Catford SE6 ...164 D3
Croydon CR0 .....220 C4
Meridian Ho SE10 .120 C2
Meridian Pl E14 ...120 A4
Meridian Prim Sch
SE10 ....142 B6
Meridian Rd SE7 ..143 D5
Meridian Sq E15 ...76 B2
Meridian Trad Est
SE7 ....121 D2
Meridian Wlk N9,N18 .18 A5
Merifield Rd SE9 ..143 C1
Merino Cl E11 ......55 C5
Merino Pl DA15 ...168 A6
Merioneth Ct 7 W7 .86 D2
Merivale Rd
Harrow HA1 ....42 A2
Putney SW15 .....135 A1
Merlewood Dr BR7 .188 B2
Merley Ct NW9 .....45 A1
Merlin 26 NW9 .....27 D2
Merlin Cl
Mitcham CR4 .....202 C6
4 Northolt UB5 ....84 C4
South Croydon CR0 .221 C4
Wallington SM6 ...220 B2
Merlin Cres HA8 ...26 B2
Merlin Ct
Beckenham BR2 ..208 D5
6 Ealing W7 ....86 D3
Ruislip HA4 ....61 B6
Wood Green N22 ...32 C2
Merling Cl KT9 ...213 D3
Merlin Gdns BR1 ..165 A1
Merlin Gr BR3 ....207 C4
Merlin Ho NW3 ....69 D4
7 W4 ....111 B1
Enfield EN3 ....18 D6
Merlin Prim Sch BR1 165 A1
Merlin Rd
Bexley DA16 ......146 A1
Wanstead E12 .....77 D6
Merlin Rd N DA16 .146 A1
Merlins Ave HA2 ...63 B5
Merlins Ct WC1 ...234 A1
Merlin St EC1 .94 C4 234 A1
Mermaid Ct N4 .....50 C3
SE1 ....117 B4 252 C2
SE16 ....119 B5
Mermaid Ho 8 E14 .120 A6
Mermaid Twr 22 SE8 .141 B6
Meroe Ct N16 ......73 C6
Merredene St SW2 .160 B5
Merriam Ave 3 E9 ..75 B2
Merrick Ct E4 ......36 A5
Merrick Rd UB2 ...107 B3
Merricks Ct 5 SW14 132 D1
Merrick Sq
SE1 ....117 B3 262 C6
Merridale SE12 ...164 D6
Merridene N21 .....16 D5
Merrielands Cres
RM9 ....103 B3
Merrielands Ret Pk
RM9 ....103 B5
Merrilands Rd KT4 .200 C1
Merrilees Rd DA15 .167 C4
Merrilyn Cl KT10 ..213 A2
Merriman Rd SE3 .143 C4
Merrington Rd SW6 .265 B6
Merrion Ave HA7 ...25 D5
Merritt Gdns KT9 .213 C2
Merritt Rd SE4 ....163 B6
Merrivale NW1 ....232 B5
Southgate N14 .....15 D6
Merrivale Ave IG4 ..55 D5
Merrow CR4 ....180 B1
Merrow St
SE17 ....117 B1 262 C1
Merrow Way CR0 .224 A2
Merrow Wlk SE17 .262 D2
Merrydown Way BR7 188 B2
Merry Fiddlers RM8 .81 B6
Merryfield SE3 ....142 D3
Merryfield Gdns HA7 .25 C5
Merryfield Ho SE12 .165 C1
Merryhill Cl E4 .....19 C4
Merry Hill Rd WD23 .8 A3
Merry Hill Sch WD23 .8 A4
Merryhills Ct N14 ..15 C6
Merryhills Dr EN2 ...4 A1
Merryhills Prim Sch
EN2 ....4 B1

Merryweather Ct **1**
KT3 ....199 C4
Mersea Ho IG11 .....78 D2
Mersey Ct **10** KT2 ..175 D2
Mersey Ho **10** N7 ....72 C3
Mersey Rd E17 ......53 B6
Mersey Wlk UB5 .....85 C5
Mersham Dr NW9 ....44 D4
Mersham Pl
  Penge SE20 ......184 B2
  South Norwood CR7 ...183 B1
Mersham Rd CR7 ...183 B1
Merstone Ho SW18 .157 D5
Merten Rd RM6 ......59 A2
Merthyr Terr SW13 .134 B6
Merton Abbey Mills
  Merton SW19 ......180 A2
  Wandsworth SW18 ...157 D3
Merton Abbey Prim Sch
  SW19 ....179 D2
Merton Ave W4 .....111 D2
  Hillingdon UB10 ....60 D1
  Northolt UB5 ....64 A3
Merton Coll SM4 ...201 B4
Merton Court Sch
  DA14 ....190 C6
Merton Ct DA16 ...146 B3
Merton Gdns BR5 ..210 C4
Merton Hall Gdns
  SW20 ....179 A2
Merton Hall Rd
  SW19 ....179 A2
Merton High St
  SW19 ....180 A3
Merton Ho SW18 ...157 C3
Merton Ind Pk SW19 180 A2
Merton La N6 ....70 D6
Merton Lo EN5 ......14 A6
Merton Mans SW20 .178 D1
Merton Park Fst Sch
  SW19 ....179 C1
Merton Park Par
  SW19 ....179 B2
Merton Park Sta
  SW19 ....179 C2
Merton Pl **9** SW19 .180 A3
Merton Rd E17 ......54 A3
  Barking IG11 ....79 D1
  Croydon SE25 .....206 A4
  Enfield EN2 ....5 B5
  Harrow HA2 ....42 A1
  Ilford IG3 ....57 D2
  Merton SW19 ......179 D3
  Wandsworth SW18 .157 C4
Merton Rise NW3 ....70 C1
Merton Road Ind Est
  SW18 ....157 C4
Merton Way
  East Molesey KT8 ..196 A6
  Hillingdon UB10 ....60 D1
Merttins Rd SE15 ..162 D6
Meru Cl NW5 ....71 A3
Mervan Rd SW2 ....138 C1
Mervyn Ave BR7,SE9 .167 A2
Mervyn Rd W13 ....109 A3
  Shepperton TW17 ...193 A2
Mervyn Stockwood Ho **1**
  SE9 ....167 A2
Messaline Ave W3 ...89 A1
Messent Rd SE9 ...165 D6
Messeter Pl SE9 ...166 C5
Messina Ave NW6 ...69 C1
Messiter Ho N1 ....233 D5
Metcalfe Ho **28** SW8 .137 D3
Metcalfe Wlk **2**
  TW13 ....173 A6
Metcalf Rd TW15 ..170 D5
Meteor St SW11 ...137 A1
Meteor Way SM6 ..220 A1
Metford Cres EN3 ....7 C5
Metherell Ho N21 ...17 B5
Metheringham Way
  NW9 ....27 C2
Methley Ho **8** N7 ...72 B6
Methley St
  SE11 ....116 C1 261 B1
Methodist Central Hall★
  SW1 ....115 D4 249 D1
Methuen Cl HA8 ....26 C3
Methuen Pk N10 ....49 B6
Methuen Rd DA6 ...147 B1
  Belvedere DA17 ...125 D2
  Edgware HA8 ......26 C3
Methwold Rd W10 ...90 D2
Metro Bsns Ctr The
  SE26 ....185 B5
Metro Ctr Hayes UB4 .106 C6
  West Barnes SM4 ..200 D2
Metro Ind Ctr TW7 .130 C2

Metropolitan Benefit
Societies Almshs **3**
  N1 ....73 C2
Metropolitan Cl **17**
  E14 ....97 C2
Metropoliton Police Cadet
  Training Sch NW9 ..45 C6
Metro Trad Ctr HA9 .66 D4
Meudon Ct KT6 ....197 D4
Mews Pl IG8 ....37 A6
Mews St E1 ....118 A5
Mews The N8 ....50 C5
  Beckenham BR3 ...185 C2
  Redbridge IG4 ......55 D4
  Thornton Heath SW16 .182 B2
Mexborough NW1 ..232 A5
Mexfield Rd SW15 .157 B6
Meyer Gn EN1 ....6 A5
Meyer Ho **1** SW12 .159 D4
Meymott St
  SE1 ....116 D5 251 C3
Meynell Cres E9 ....74 D1
Meynell Gdns E9 ...74 D1
Meynell Rd E9 .....74 D1
  SW11 ....136 C2
Meyrick Ho **8** E14 ..97 C2
Meyrick Rd NW10 ...68 A2
  SW11 ....136 C2
Miah Terr **10** E1 ...118 A5
Miall Wlk SE26 ....185 A6
Micawber Ave UB8 ..82 C3
Micawber Ct **1** N1 .235 B2
Micawber Ho **24**
  SE16 ....118 A4
Micawber St
  N1 ....95 A4 235 A2
Michael Cliffe Ho
  EC1 ....234 B1
Michael Faraday Ho
  SE17 ....262 D1
Michael Faraday Sch
  SE17 ....117 B1 262 D1
Michael Gaynor Cl
  W7 ....108 D5
Michael Marshall Ho **2**
  SE9 ....167 A2
Michaelmas Cl SW20 200 C6
Michael Rd E11 .....54 D1
  SW6 ....135 D4 265 D2
  South Norwood SE25 .205 C6
Michaels Cl SE13 ..142 C1
Michael Sobell Sinai Sch
  HA3 ....44 C3
Michaelson Ho **4**
  SE21 ....183 C6
Michelangelo Ct **14**
  SE16 ....118 B1
Micheldever Rd SE12 164 D5
Michelham Gdns
  TW1 ....152 D1
Michelle Ct N12 .....30 A5
  W3 ....111 B6
Michell Ho TW1 ...152 D3
Michels Almshouses **11**
  TW10 ....154 A4
Michelsdale Dr **3**
  TW9 ....132 A1
Michelson Ho SE11 .260 D3
Michel's Row **1** TW9 132 A1
Michigan Ave E12 ...78 B4
Michigan Ho E14 ...119 C3
Micklehan Down N12 29 B6
Mickledore NW1 ...232 B3
Micklefield Way BR5 .190 B2
Micklethwaite Rd
  SW6 ....135 C6 265 B5
Mickleton Ho **30** W2 .91 C2
Midas Bsns Ctr RM10 .81 D4
Midcroft HA4 ....39 C1
Middle Dene NW7 ...11 B1
Middlefield
  NW8 ....92 B6 229 C6
Middlefielde W13 ...87 B2
Middlefield Gdns IG2 .56 D3
Middle Green Cl **3**
  KT5 ....198 B3
Middleham Gdns N18 .34 A4
Middleham Rd N18 ..34 A4
Middle La N8 ....50 A4
  Teddington TW11 ...174 D4
Middle Lane Mews N8 50 A4
Middle Mill KT5 ....198 B6
Middle Park Ave SE9 165 D4
Middle Park Prim Sch
  SE9 ....165 D4
Middle Rd **12** E13 ..99 A5
  N10 ....30 C2

Middle Rd continued
  East Barnet EN4 ....14 C5
  Harrow HA2 ....42 B1
  Mitcham SW16 ....181 D1
Middle Row W10 ....91 A3
Middle Row Prim Sch
  W10 ....91 A3
Middlesborough Rd
  N18 ....34 A4
Middlesex Bsns Ctr
  UB2 ....107 B4
Middlesex Coll of
Computing & Tech
  HA9 ....66 A3
Middlesex Ct **5** W4 .111 D2
  Harrow HA1 ....42 D4
Middlesex Ho **6**
  SE20 ....184 C3
Middlesex Hospl
  W1 ....93 C2 239 B3
Middlesex Hospl Annexe
  W1 ....239 B4
Middlesex Pas EC1 .241 D3
Middlesex Pl **13** E9 ..74 C2
Middlesex Rd CR4 ..204 A4
Middlesex St
  E1 ....95 D2 243 C2
Middlesex Univ N17 ..33 D4
Middlesex Univ (Bounds
  Green) N11 ....31 C4
Middlesex Univ (Cat Hill)
  EN4 ....15 A6
Middlesex Univ (Enfield
  Campus) EN3 ......18 C6
Middlesex Univ (Hendon
  Campus) NW4 .....46 B5
Middlesex Univ Trent Park
  EN4 ....3 C3
Middle St EC1 .....242 A4
  Croydon CR0 .....221 A5
Middle Temple★
  EC4 ....116 C6 251 A6
Middle Temple La
  EC4 ....116 C6 251 A6
Middleton Ave E4 ...19 B1
  Greenford UB5 .....86 B5
  Sidcup DA14 ......190 C5
Middleton Bldgs W1 239 A3
Middleton Cl E4 ....19 B1
Middleton Ct BR1 ..187 B3
Middleton Dr SE16 .118 D4
  Pinner HA5 ....40 A6
Middleton Gdns IG2 .56 D3
Middleton Gr N7 ....72 A3
Middleton Ho E8 ....73 D1
  SE1 ....262 C5
Middleton Mews N7 .72 A3
Middleton Rd E8 ....73 D1
  NW11 ....47 C2
  Carshalton CR4,SM5 .202 B2
  Hayes UB3 ....83 B2
Middleton St E2 .....96 B4
Middleton Way SE13 142 B1
Middleway NW11 ....47 D4
Middle Way Hayes UB4 84 C3
  Mitcham SW16 ....181 D1
Middle Way The HA3 .24 D1
Midfield Prim Sch
  BR5 ....190 A3
Midfield Way BR5 ..190 B2
Midford Ho **1** NW4 .46 D5
Midford Pl W1 .....239 B5
Midholm NW11 .....47 D5
  Wembley HA9 ......44 C1
Midholm Cl NW11 ..47 D5
Midhope Ho WC1 ..233 B1
Midhope St WC1 ...233 B1
Midhurst SE26 ....184 C4
Midhurst Ave N10 ..49 A6
  Thornton Heath CR0 .204 C2
Midhurst Ct N8 .....50 A2
Midhurst Gdns UB10 .61 A1
Midhurst Hill DA6 .169 C6
Midhurst Ho **6** E14 .97 B1
Midhurst Par N10 ...49 A6
Midhurst Rd W13 ..109 A3
Midhurst Way E5 ...74 A4
Midland Pl E14 ....120 A1
Midland Rd E10 .....54 A2
  NW1 ....94 A3 233 A3
Midland Terr NW10 ..89 C3
  NW2 ....68 D5
Midleton Rd KT3 ...177 A1
Midlothian Rd E3 ...97 B3
Midmoor Rd
  Merton SW19 .....179 A1
  Streatham SW12 ..159 C3

Middleship Cl SE16 ...118 D5
Midship Point E14 ..119 C4
Midstrath Rd NW10 .67 C4
Midsummer Apmts **15**
  SM2 ....217 C1
Midsummer Ave TW4 129 B1
Midsummer Ct SE12 143 A1
Midway SM3 ....201 B2
Midway Ho EC1 ....234 D2
Midwinter Cl **3**
  DA16 ....146 A2
Midwood Cl NW2 ...68 B5
Mighell Ave IG4 .....55 A1
Milan Cl N11 ....31 D2
Milan Rd UB1 .....107 A2
Milborne Gr SW10 .256 B1
Milborne Ho **11** E9 ..74 C2
Milborne St E9 .....74 C2
Milborough Cres
  SE12 ....164 C5
Milbourne La KT10 .212 A3
Milbourne Lodge Jun Sch
  KT10 ....212 B2
Milbourne Lodge Sen Sch
  KT10 ....212 B2
Milbrook KT10 ....212 A2
Milburn Dr **1** UB7 .104 A6
Milburn Ho SW20 ..178 B1
Milcote St SE1 ....251 D1
Milday Gr N N1 .....73 B3
Mildenhall Rd E5 ...74 C5
Mildmay Ave N1 ....73 B2
Mildmay Ct N1 .....73 B3
Mildmay Gr N N1 ...73 B3
Mildmay Gr S N1 ...73 B3
Mildmay Ho **6** SW15 156 C6
Mildmay Mission Hospl
  E2 ....95 D4
Mildmay Pk N1 .....73 B3
Mildmay Rd N1 .....73 C3
  Ilford IG1 ....78 C3
Mildmay St N1 .....73 B2
Mildon Ho EN3 ......6 C3
Mildred Ave
  Hayes UB3 ....105 A3
  Northolt UB5 ....63 D3
Mile End Pl E1 ......96 D3
Mile End Rd E1,E3 ..96 D3
Mile End Sta E3 ....97 B4
Mile End The E17 ...34 D2
Mile Rd
  Hackbridge SM6 ..203 A1
  Wallington CR0, CR4,
    CR9 ....203 D1
Miles Bldgs NW1 ..237 A4
Miles Coverdale Prim Sch
  W12 ....112 C4
Miles Ct E1 ....96 B1
  Croydon CR0 .....220 D6
Miles Dr SE28 .....123 C5
Miles Ho **5** SE10 ..120 C1
Miles Lo E15 ....76 B3
  Harrow HA1 ....42 B4
Milespit Hill NW7 ...28 C5
Miles Pl NW1 ......236 D4
Miles Rd N8 ....50 A6
  Mitcham CR4 .....202 C6
Miles St SW8 ..138 A6 270 B5
Milestone Cl
  Edmonton N9 .....18 A2
  Sutton SM2 ....218 A1
Milestone Ct TW7 .131 A4
Milestone Green
  SW14 ....133 B1
Milestone Ho KT1 .197 D5
Milestone Rd SE19 .183 D4
Miles Way N20 .....14 C2
Milfoil St W12 .....112 A6
Milford Cl SE2 ....147 A6
Milford Ct **3** N16 ...51 C1
  Southall UB1 .....107 C6
Milford Gdns
  Croydon CR0 .....206 D4
  Edgware HA8 ......26 C3
  Wembley HA0 ......65 D3
Milford Gr SM1 ....218 A4
Milford La
  WC2 ....116 C6 251 A6
Milford Mews SW16 160 B1
Milford Rd Ealing W13 109 B5
  Southall UB1 .....107 C6
Milk St E16 ....122 D5
  EC2 ....95 A1 242 B2
  Bromley BR1 ......187 B4
Milkwell Gdns IG8 ..37 B3
Milkwell Yd SE5 ...139 C4
Milkwood Rd SE24 .138 D1
Milk Yd E1 ....118 C6
Millais Ave E12 .....78 C4
Millais Ct **10** UB5 ..84 D1

Millais Gdns HA8 ...26 C1
Millais Rd E11 .....76 B1
  Enfield EN1 ....17 D6
  New Malden KT3 ..199 C2
Millais Way KT19 ..215 A4
Milland Ho **11** SW15 .156 A3
Millard Cl **21** N16 ..73 C3
Millard Ho SE8 ....119 B1
Millard Terr RM10 ..81 D2
Millbank
  SW1 ....116 A2 260 A3
  Wallington SM6 ...219 D3
Millbank Ho KT6 ..198 D1
Millbank Prim Sch
  SW1 ....115 D2 259 D3
Millbank Way SE12 165 A6
Millbourne Rd TW13 173 A6
Mill Bridge EN5 ....13 B5
Millbrook **1** E18 ...55 A6
Millbrook Ave DA16 145 B1
Millbrooke Ct **7**
  SW15 ....157 A6
Millbrook Gdns RM6 .59 A3
Millbrook Ho **4**
  SE15 ....140 A6
Millbrook Rd SW9 .138 D2
  Edmonton N9 ....18 B3
Millbrook Ho **4**
  SE15 ....140 A6
Millcroft Ho SE6 ..185 D6
Mill Ct E10 ....76 A5
  NW7 ....29 A2
Millender Wlk SE16 .118 C2
Millennium Bsns Ctr
  NW2 ....68 B6
Millennium Bridge★
  SE1,EC4 ....252 A5
Millennium Dome★
  SE10 ....120 C5
Millennium Dr E14 .120 B2
Millennium Harbour
  E14 ....119 C4
Millennium Pl **27** E2 ..96 B5
Millennium Prim Sch
  SE10 ....120 D3
Millennium Sq SE1 .253 D2
Millennium Way
  SE10 ....120 C3
Miller Ave EN3 ......7 C5
Miller Cl
  Carshalton CR4 ...202 D2
  Pinner HA5 ....22 C1
Miller Ct DA7 .....147 D2
  8 NW9 ....46 A5
Miller Ho N15 ......50 D5
  9 Streatham SW2 .160 A4
Miller Rd SW19 ...180 B4
  Mitcham SW19 ...180 B4
  Croydon CR0 .....220 D6
  Thornton Heath CR0 .204 C1
Miller's Ave E8,N16 .73 D3
Millers Cl NW7 .....28 A6
Miller's Ct **1** W4 ..111 D1
  SE3 HA0 ....88 A5
Millers Green Cl EN2 ..4 D2
Millers Mead Ct
  SW19 ....180 B4
Miller St NW1 .....232 A4
Miller's Terr **1** E8 ..73 D3
Miller's Way W6 ...112 C4
Millers Yd N3 ....29 D3
Millers Wharf Ho E1 .118 A5
Miller Wlk SE1 ....251 B3
Millet Rd UB6 ....85 D5
Millfarm Bsns Pk
  TW4 ....151 A4
Mill Farm Cl HA5 ...22 C1
Mill Farm Cres TW4 151 A3
Millfield N4 ....72 C6
  Charlton TW16 ...171 B2
  Kingston KT1 .....198 B6
Millfield Ave E17 ...35 B2
Millfield La N6 .....70 D6
Millfield Pl N6 .....71 A6
Millfield Rd HA8 ...27 A1
  Twickenham TW4 ..151 B3
Millfields Com Sch E5 74 C4
Millfields Rd E5 ....74 C5
Mill Gdns SE26 ...162 B1
Mill Gn CR4 ....203 A2
Mill Green Bsns Pk
  CR4 ....203 A2
Mill Green Rd CR4 .203 A2
Millgrove St **6** SW11 137 A3
Millhaven Cl RM6 ...58 B3
Mill Hill SW13 ....134 A2
Mill Hill Broadway Sta
  NW7 ....27 C4

Mill Hill Circus NW7 .27 D5
Mill Hill Cty High Sch
  NW7 ....11 C2
Mill Hill East Sta NW7 29 A3
Mill Hill Gr **11** W3 ..110 D5
Mill Hill Ind Est NW7 .27 D4
Mill Hill Rd W3 ....110 D4
  Barnes SW13 .....134 A3
Mill Hill Sch NW7 ...28 B6
Mill Hill Terr **9** W3 .110 D5
Mill Ho IG8 ....36 D5
Millhouse Pl SE27 .182 D6
Millicent Fawcett Ct
  N17 ....33 D2
Millicent Preston Ho **4**
  IG11 ....101 B6
Millicent Rd E10 ...53 B1
Milligan St E14 ....119 C6
Milling Rd HA8 .....27 B3
Millington Rd N16 ..73 B5
Millington Rd UB3 .105 C3
Mill La NW6 ....69 B3
  SE18 ....122 C1
  Carshalton SM5 ...219 A5
  Croydon CR0 .....220 C5
  Dagenham RM6 ...59 A4
  Sewardstone E4 ....7 D2
  Woodford IG8 ......36 C5
Mill Lane Trad Est
  CR0 ....220 B5
Millman Ct SE3 ...143 B5
  WC1 ....240 C5
Millman Mews WC1 .240 C5
Millman Pl WC1 ...240 D5
Millman St
  WC1 ....94 B3 240 C5
Millmark Gr SE14 ..141 A3
Millmarsh La EN3 ...7 B3
Millmead Bsns Ctr
  N17 ....52 B6
Millmead Ind Ctr N17 .52 B6
Mill Mead Rd N17 ..52 B6
Millner Ct SE4 ....141 B3
Mill Pl BR7 ....188 D2
  E14 ....97 A1
  Kingston KT1 .....198 B6
Mill Plat TW7 .....131 A3
Mill Plat Ave TW7 .131 A3
Mill Pond Cl
  SW8 ....137 D5 269 D3
Millpond Est SE16 .118 B4
Mill Rd E16 ....121 B5
  Ilford IG1 ....78 C5
  Merton SW19 .....180 A3
  Twickenham TW2 ..152 A2
Mill Ridge HA8 .....26 C5
Mill River Trad Est EN3 .7 A1
Mill Row N1 ....95 C6
Mills Cl UB10 ....82 C5
Mills Ct **7** E11 .....76 C5
Mills Gr **1** E14 ....98 A2
  NW4 ....46 D6
Mills Ho E17 ....54 B6
  SW8 ....269 B2
Millshot Cl SW6 ...134 C4
Millside SM5 ......218 D6
Millside Pl TW7 ...131 B3
Millson Cl N20 .....14 B2
Mills Row W4 .....111 B2
Mill St SE1 ..117 D4 253 D2
  W1 ....249 A6
  Kingston KT1 .....198 A6
Millstream Cl N13 ..32 C1
Millstream Rd
  SE1 ....117 D4 253 C1
Mill Trad Est The
  NW10 ....89 A4
Mill Vale BR2 .....186 D1
Mill View Cl KT17 .215 D1
Mill View Gdns CR0 222 D1
Millwall Dock Rd
  E14 ....119 C3
Millward Wlk **14**
  SE18 ....144 C6
Mill Way NW7 .....27 C5
  Feltham TW14 ....150 B6
Millway Gdns UB5 ..63 B2
Millwood Rd TW3,
  TW7 ....152 A6
Millwood St **10** W10 .91 A2
Mill Yd E1 ....118 A6
Milman Cl HA5 .....40 D6
Milman Rd NW6 ....91 A4
Milman's Ho SW10 266 C5
Milman's St
  SW10 .....136 B6 266 C5
Milne Ct **4** E18 ...37 A2

Milne Field HA5 ....23 C3
Milne Gdns SE9 .....166 A6
Milne Ho SE18 .....122 B2
Milner Dr TW2 ....152 B4
Milner Ho 2 SW11 .136 B2
  Hayes UB4 ....84 B4
Milner Pl N1 ..94 C6 234 B6
Milner Rd E15 ....98 C4
  Dagenham RM8 ......80 C6
  Kingston KT1 ......197 D6
  Merton SW19 ....179 D2
  Morden SM4 ....202 B4
  South Norwood CR7 .205 B6
Milner Sq N1 ....72 D1
Milner St
  SW3 ......114 D2 257 C4
Milner Wlk DA15 ....167 B3
Milnthorpe Rd W4 ...133 B6
Milo Rd SE22 ....161 C5
Milrood Ho 4 E1 ....96 D2
Milroy Wlk SE1 .....251 C4
Milson Rd
  W14 ....112 D3 254 A6
Milsted Ho 23 E5 ....74 B3
Milton Ave E6 ....78 A1
  N6 ....49 C2
  NW10 ....89 B6
  NW9 ....45 A6
  Barnet EN5 ....13 B6
  Carshalton SM1 ....218 C4
  Thornton Heath CR0 .205 B2
Milton Cl N2 ....48 A3
  SE1 ......117 D2 263 C3
  Carshalton SM1 ....218 B5
  Hayes UB4 ....84 A1
Milton Court Rd
  SE14 ....141 A6
Milton Cres IG2 ......57 A3
Milton Ct EC2 ....242 C4
  NW11 ....47 A3
  SE14 ....141 A6
  9 SW18 ....157 C6
  Fulham SW6 ....135 A2
  Ilford RM6 ....58 C2
  Kingston KT2 ......176 A6
  Twickenham TW2 ....152 C1
  Uxbridge UB10 .....60 D5
Milton Dr
  Borehamwood WD6 ..10 D6
  Littleton TW17 ....192 A5
Milton Gdns TW19 ..148 B3
Milton Gr N11 ....31 D5
  N16 ....73 C4
Milton Ho 19 E2 .....96 C4
  2 SE5 ....139 B5
  12 Beckenham BR3 .185 C3
  5 Kingston KT2 ...176 D4
  Sutton SM1 ....217 C5
Milton House Mans
  E8 ....73 D4
Milton Lo
  3 Sidcup DA14 ....190 A6
  Southgate N21 .....16 D3
  Twickenham TW1 ...152 D4
Milton Pk N6 ....49 C2
Milton Pl 3 N7 ......72 C4
Milton Rd DA16 .....145 D4
  E17 ....53 C5
  N15 ....50 D6
  N6 ....49 C2
  NW7 ....28 A5
  1 NW9 ....46 A2
  SE24 ....160 D6
  W3 ....111 B5
  Belvedere DA17 ....125 C4
  Ealing W7 ....108 D6
  Harrow HA1 ....42 C5
  Mitcham CR4 ....181 A3
  Mortlake SW14 .....133 B2
  Sutton SM1 ....217 C4
  Thornton Heath CR0 .205 B2
  Uxbridge UB10 .....60 D4
  Wallington SM6 ....219 D4
  Wimbledon SW19 ...180 A4
  Hampton TW12 .....173 C3
Milton St EC1,
  EC2 ......95 B2 242 C4
Milton Way UB7 .....104 B2
Milverton NW5 ....71 A3
Milverton Dr UB10 ..61 A4
Milverton Gdns IG3 .79 D6
Milverton Ho SE23 .163 A1
Milverton St
  SE11 ....116 C1 261 B1
Milverton Way SE9 .188 C6
Milward St E1 ....96 B2

Mimosa N15 ....51 B4
Mimosa Ct SW4 ....270 B1
Mimosa Ho UB4 .....84 C2
Mimosa Rd UB4 .....84 C2
Mimosa St
  SW6 ......135 B4 264 D1
Mina Rd SE17 117 C1 263 B2
  Merton SW19 ....179 C1
Minard Rd SE6 ......164 C3
Minchenden Cres N14 15 C1
Minchenden Ct N14 ..15 D1
Minchin Ho 6 E14 ..97 C1
Mincing La
  EC3 ......117 C6 253 A6
Minden Rd
  Cheam SM3 ....217 B6
  Penge SE20 ....184 B2
Minehead Ct HA2 ....63 C4
Minehead Rd
  Harrow HA2 ....63 C5
  Streatham SW16 ...182 B5
Mineral St SE18 ....123 C2
Minera Mews SW1 ..258 B4
  Sidcup DA14 ....189 C6
Minerva Cl SW9 ....138 C5
  Sidcup DA14 ....189 C6
Minerva Rd NW10 ..89 A4
  Chingford E4 ....35 D3
  Kingston KT1 ......176 B1
Minerva St E2 ......96 B5
Minerva Wlk EC1 ..241 D2
Minet Ave NW10 ....89 C5
Minet Dr UB3 ......106 A5
Minet Gdns NW10 ..89 C5
  Hayes UB3 ....106 B5
Minet Jun & Inf Schs
  UB3 ....106 B5
Minet Rd SE5,SW9 .138 D3
Minford Gdns W14 .112 D4
Mingard Wlk N7 ....72 B5
Ming St E14 ....119 C6
Minimax Cl TW14 ..150 A5
Ministry Way SE9 ..166 B3
Mink Ct TW4 ....128 C3
Minniedale KT5 ....198 B4
Minnow Wlk SE17 ..263 B3
Minories EC3 117 D6 253 C6
Minshaw Ct DA14 ..189 D6
  1 Sidcup DA14 ....190 A6
Minshull Pl 28 BR3 .185 C3
Minshull St SW8 ...269 C1
Minson Rd E9 ......96 D6
Minstead Gdns SW15 155 D4
Minstead Way KT3 .199 C3
Minster Ave SM1 ...217 C6
Minster Dr CR0 ....221 C4
Minster Gdns KT8 .195 B5
Minster Rd BR1 ....187 B3
  NW2 ....69 A3
Minster Wlk N8 ....50 A5
Minsterley Ave TW16,
  TW17 ....193 C5
Minstrel Ct HA3 ....24 C1
Minstrel Gdns KT5 .198 B5
Mint Bsns Pk 12 E16 .99 A2
Mint Cl UB10 ....82 D4
Mintern Cl N13 .....16 D1
Minterne Ave UB2 .107 C2
Minterne Rd HA3 ....44 B4
Minterne Waye UB4 .84 C1
Mintern St N1 .95 B5 235 D4
Minton Ho SE11 ....261 A4
Minton Mews 1 NW6 69 D2
Mint Rd SM5,SM6 ..219 B4
Mint St SE1 ....252 B2
Mint Wlk CR0 ......221 C5
Mirabel Rd
  SW6 ......135 B5 264 D4
Mirage Ctr The HA9 .66 D4
Miranda Cl 16 E1 ...96 C4
Miranda Ct W3 .....88 B1
Miranda Ho 17 N1 ..95 C5
  6 Belvedere DA17 .125 C1
Miranda Rd N19 ....49 C1
Mirfield Ct SE20 ...184 A1
Mirfield St SE7 ....121 D3
Miriam Ct DA14 ....190 B6
Miriam Rd SE18 ....123 C1
Mirravale Trad Est
  RM6 ....59 A2
Mirren Cl HA2 ......63 B5
Mirror Path SE12 ..165 C1
Misbourne Rd UB10 .82 C6
Missenden SE17 ....262 D1
Missenden Cl TW14 149 A3
Missenden Gdns
  SM4 ....202 A3
Missenden Ho NW8 237 A6
Mission Gr E17 ....53 C5
Mission Grove Prim Sch
  E17 ....53 B5

Mission Pl SE15 ....140 A4
Mission Sq 13 TW8 .132 A6
Misterton Ct SW11 266 D2
Mistletoe Cl CR0 ..206 D1
Mistley Thorn IG1 ..56 C2
Mistral SE5 ....139 C4
Mistral Ct E4 ......19 D1
Mistys Field KT12 .194 D4
Mitali Pas 13 E1 ...96 A1
Mitcham Garden Village
  CR4 ....203 A4
Mitcham Ho 9 SE5 .139 A4
Mitcham Ind Est CR4 181 A2
Mitcham Junction Sta
  CR4 ....203 A4
Mitcham La SW16 ..181 C5
Mitcham Pk CR4 ...202 D5
Mitcham Rd E6 ....100 A4
  Ilford IG3 ....57 D2
  Upper Tooting SW17 180 D5
Mitcham Sta CR4 ..202 C5
Mitcham Vale High Sch
  CR4 ....181 B1
Mitchell 19 NW9 ...27 D4
Mitchell Brook Prim Sch
  NW10 ....67 C2
Mitchellbrook Way
  NW10 ....67 B2
Mitchell Cl SE2 ....124 C2
  Belvedere DA17 ...125 D3
Mitchell Ct 20 IG6 .53 D2
  W4 ....110 D1
Mitchell Ho 31 W12 112 B6
Mitchell Rd BR6 ...227 D4
  Edmonton N13 .....33 A5
Mitchell's Pl SE21 161 C4
Mitchell St
  EC1 ......95 A3 242 B6
Mitchell Way NW10 .67 A2
  Bromley BR1 ......187 A2
Mitchell Wlk E6 ...100 B2
Mitchison Rd N1 ...73 B2
Mitchley Rd N17 ...52 A6
Mitford Cl KT9 ....213 C2
Mitford Rd N19 ....72 A6
Mitre Bridge Ind Pk
  W10 ....90 B3
Mitre Cl
  Shepperton TW17 .193 B3
  Sutton SM2 ....218 B1
Mitre Ct EC2 ....242 B2
  Belvedere DA17 ...125 C1
  1 Ilford RM6 .....58 C2
  9 Woodford E18 ..37 A2
Mitre Ho RM7 ......59 D5
Mitre Rd E15 ....98 C5
  SE1 ......116 C4 251 B4
Mitre Sq EC3 ......243 B1
Mitre St EC3 ..95 C1 243 B1
Mitre The 9 E14 ...119 B6
Mitre Way W10 ....90 B3
Moatbridge Sch SE9 165 D5
Moat Cl BR6 ....227 D2
Moat Cres N3 ......47 D6
Moat Croft DA16 ..146 C2
Moat Ct DA15 .....167 D1
  9 DA15 ....168 A1
  SE9 ....166 B5
Moat Dr 4 E13 ....99 C5
  Harrow HA1 ....42 B5
  Ruislip HA4 ....39 C2
Moat Farm Rd UB5 .63 B1
Moatfield NW6 .....69 A1
Moat Lo The HA1 ..64 C6
Moat Pl SW9 ......138 B2
  Acton W3 ....88 D1
Moat Side Enfield EN3 ..6 D1
  Feltham TW13 .....172 C6
Moat The KT3 .....177 C2
Moberly Rd SW4 ..159 D4
Mobey Ct SW4 ....270 A1
Moblin Lo IG9 .....21 C3
Moby Dick RM6 ....59 B5
Mocatta Ho 9 E1 ..96 B3
Modbury Gdns NW5 71 A2
Modder Pl SW15 ...134 D1
Model Cotts SW14 .133 A2
Model Farm Cl SE9 166 A1
Modling Ho 8 E2 ..96 D5
Moelwyn Hughes Ct
  N7 ....71 D3
Moelyn Mews HA1 .43 A4
Moffat Ct
  Upper Tooting SW17 180 C6
  Wimbledon SW19 ..179 C5
Moffat Ho 24 SE5 .139 A5
Moffat Rd
  Bowes Park N13 ...32 A4
  South Norwood CR7 183 B1
  Upper Tooting SW17 180 D6

Mogden La TW7 ....152 D6
Mohawk Ho 31 E3 ..97 A5
Mohmmad Khan Rd
  E11 ....54 D1
Mohr Ct N22 ....32 B3
Moineau 18 NW9 ...27 D2
Moira Cl N17 ......33 C1
Moira Ct SW17 ....159 A2
Moira Rd SE9 .....144 B1
Moland Mead SE16 118 D1
Molasses Ho 1
  SW11 ....136 A2
Molasses Row 2
  SW11 ....136 A2
Mole Abbey Gdns
  KT8 ....195 D6
Mole Ct 2 W12 ....111 C4
  West Ewell KT19 ..215 A4
Mole Ho NW8 .....236 D5
Molember Ct KT7 ..196 C5
Molember Rd KT8 .196 C4
Molescroft SE9 ....167 A1
Molesey Ave KT12,
  KT8 ....195 B4
Molesey Dr SM3 ...217 A5
Molesey Ho E2 ....243 C6
Molesey Hospl KT8 195 C4
Molesey Park Ave
  KT8 ....195 D4
Molesey Park Cl KT8 196 A4
Molesey Park Rd
  KT8 ....196 A4
Molesey Rd KT12 ..195 A2
Molesford Rd SW6 265 A1
Molesham Cl KT8 .195 D6
Molesham Way KT8 195 D6
Molesworth Ho 9
  SE17 ....138 D6
Molesworth St SE13 142 A2
Moliner Ct 4 BR3 .185 C3
Mollie Davis Ct SE19 183 D4
Mollison Ave EN3 ..7 B5
Mollison Dr SM6 ..220 A1
Mollison Way HA8 .26 C1
Molly Huggins Cl
  SW12 ....159 C4
Molton Ho N1 .....233 D5
Molyneux Dr SW17 181 B6
Molyneux St
  W1 ......92 C2 237 B3
Monarch Cl
  Coney Hall BR4 ...224 D4
  East Bedfont TW14 149 C4
Monarch Ct N2 ....48 A4
  Ealing W5 ....87 C2
Monarch Dr E16 ...99 D2
Monarch Mews E17 53 D3
  West Norwood SW16 182 C5
Monarch Par CR4 ..180 D1
Monarch Pl IG9 ....21 C2
Monarch Rd DA17 .125 C3
Monarchs Ct 1 NW7 27 C5
Monarch's Way HA4 39 C1
Mona Rd SE15 ....140 C3
Mona St E16 ......98 D2
Monastery Gdns EN2 .5 B3
Monaveen Gdns KT8 195 D6
Monck's Row SW18 157 B5
Monck St
  SW1 ......115 D3 259 D5
Monclar Rd SE5 ...139 B1
Moncorvo Cl
  SW7 ......114 C4 247 A1
Moncrieff Cl 4 E6 .100 A1
Moncrieff St SE15 .140 A3
Mondial Way UB7 .127 A5
Mondragon Ho 5 .270 B2
Monega Prim Sch E12 77 D2
Monega Rd E7,E12 .77 D2
Monet Ct 15 SE16 .118 D2
Moneyer Ho N1 ...235 C2
Monica James Ho 12
  DA14 ....168 A1
Monica Shaw Ct
  NW1 ....232 D3
Monier Rd E3 .....75 C1
Monivea Rd BR3 ..185 B3
Monk Ct W12 .....112 A5
Monk Dr E16 ......121 A4
Monken Hadley CE Prim
  Sch EN4 ....1 C4
Monkfrith Ave N14 15 B5
Monkfrith Cl N14 ..15 B5
Monkfrith Prim Sch
  N14 ....15 A5
Monkfrith Way N14 15 A5
Monkham's Ave IG8 37 B5
Monkham's Dr IG8 .37 B5
Monkham's La IG8 .37 B5

Monkleigh Rd SM4,
  SW20 ....201 A5
Monkridge 3 N8 ...49 D2
Monks Ave
  East Molesey KT8 .195 B4
  New Barnet EN5 ...14 A5
Monks Cl SE2 .....124 D2
  Enfield EN2 ....5 A3
  Harrow HA2 ....63 D6
  Ruislip HA4 ....62 D4
Monks Cres KT12 ..194 B1
Monksdene Gdns
  SM1 ....217 D5
Monks Dr W3 .....88 C1
Monksfield N4 .....72 C6
Monks Orchard Rd
  BR3,CR0 ....207 C2
Monks Orchard Sch
  CR0 ....206 D4
Monks Park Gdns HA9 66 D1
Monks Pk HA9 ....67 A2
Monks Rd EN2 ....5 A3
Monk St SE18 .....122 C2
Monks Way BR5 ..211 B1
  NW11 ....47 B5
  Beckenham BR3 ..207 C3
  Harmondsworth UB7 126 A6
Monkswell Ct N10 .31 A2
Monkswood Gdns
  Borehamwood WD6 .11 B6
  Ilford IG5 ....56 C6
Monkton Ct W14 ..254 C6
Monkton Ho 22 E5 .74 B3
  32 SE16 ....118 D4
Monkton Rd DA16 145 D3
Monkton St
  SE11 ....116 C2 261 B4
Monkville Ave NW11 47 B5
Monkville Par 1
  NW11 ....47 B5
Monkwell Sq EC2 .242 B3
Monmouth Ave
  Teddington KT1 ...175 C3
  Wanstead E18 .....55 B6
Monmouth Cl W4 .111 B3
  Bexley DA16 ......146 A1
  Mitcham CR4,SW16 204 A5
Monmouth Gr TW8 110 A2
Monmouth Ho 5 NW5 71 B2
  SW18 ....157 C5
Monmouth Pl W2 .91 C1
Monmouth Rd E6 .100 B4
  N9 ....18 C2
  W2 ....91 C1
  Dagenham RM9 ...81 B3
  Hayes UB3 ....105 D2
Monmouth St
  WC2 ......94 A1 240 A1
Monnery Rd N19 ..71 C5
Monnow Rd SE1 ..118 A2
Mono La TW13 ....150 B2
Monoux Almshouses
  E17 ....53 D5
Monoux Gr E17 ...35 C2
Monro Dr N11 ....31 C4
Monroe Cres EN1 .6 B4
Monroe Dr SW14 .154 D6
Monroe Ho 16 N19 49 D2
  NW8 ....230 A1
Monro Gdns HA3 ..24 C3
Monro Ho 21 NW3 70 A4
  Putney SW15 .....156 B6
Monro way E5 .....74 A4
Monsal Ct E5 .....75 A4
Monsell Rd N4,N5 .72 D5
Monson Prim Sch
  SE14 ....140 D5
Monson Rd NW10 .90 B5
  SE14 ....140 D5
Mons Way BR2 ....210 A3
Montacute Rd
  Bushey WD23 .....8 C4
  Carshalton SM4 ..202 B3
  Forest Hill SE6 ...163 B4
Montagu Cres N18 .34 B6
Montagu Ct W1 ...237 D3
Montague Ave SE4 141 C1
  Ealing W7 ....108 D5
Montague Cl SE1 .252 C4
  Walton-on-T KT12 .194 A2
Montague Fell HA0 65 A4
Montague Gdns W3 110 C6
Montague Pl
  WC1 ......93 D2 239 D4

Montague Rd continued
  Ealing W13 ....87 B1
  Hounslow TW3 ....129 D2
  Merton SW19 ......179 D3
  Richmond TW10 ..154 A5
  Southall UB2 ......107 A2
  Thornton Heath CR0 204 D1
  Uxbridge UB8 .....60 A1
Montague Sq SE15 140 C5
Montague St
  WC1 ......94 A2 240 A4
Montague Street
  EC1 ....242 A3
Montague Terr 1
  BR2 ....209 A5
Montague Way UB2 107 A2
Montagu Gdns
  Edmonton N18 ....34 B6
  Wallington SM6 ...219 C4
Montagu Ind Est N18 34 C4
Montagu Mans
  W1 ......92 D2 237 D3
Montagu Mews N
  W1 ....237 D3
Montagu Mews S
  W1 ....237 D2
Montagu Mews W
  W1 ....237 D2
Montagu Pl
  W1 ......92 D2 237 D3
Montagu Rd N9,N18 18 C1
  NW4 ....46 A3
Montagu Row W1 .237 D3
Montagu Sq
  W1 ......92 D1 237 D2
Montagu St
  W1 ......92 D1 237 D2
Montalt Ho IG8 ...36 D6
Montalt Rd IG8 ...36 D5
Montana Gdns
  Penge SE26 ....185 B5
  5 Sutton SM1 ....218 A3
Montana Rd
  Upper Tooting SW17 159 A1
  Wimbledon SW20 ..178 C2
Montbelle Prim Sch
  SE9 ....166 D1
Montbelle Rd SE9 .166 D1
Montcalm Cl
  Hayes BR2 ....209 A3
  Hayes UB4 ....84 B4
Montcalm Ho E14 .119 C3
Montcalm Rd SE7 .143 D2
Montclare St
  E2 ......95 D3 243 C6
Monteagle Ave IG11 79 A2
Monteagle Ct 27 N1 95 C5
Monteagle Prim Sch
  RM9 ....102 B6
Monteagle Way E5 74 A5
  SE15 ....140 B2
Montefiore Ct 2 N16 51 D1
Montefiore St 2
  SW8 ....137 B2
Montem Prim Sch N7 72 B5
Montem Rd
  Forest Hill SE23 ..163 B4
  New Malden KT3 ..199 C3
Montem St N4 .....50 B1
Montenotte Rd N8 .49 C4
Montesole Ct 5 HA5 22 C1
Montesquieu Terr 3
  E16 ....98 C4
Montessori Coll
  SW19 ....179 C4
Montford Pl
  SE11 ....116 C1 261 A1
Montford Rd TW16 194 A5
Montfort Ho E14 ..120 A3
  4 E2 ....96 C4
Montfort Pl SW19 .156 B3
Montgo Cl 10 SW2 138 C1
Montgolfier Wlk UB5 85 A4
Montgomery Ave
  KT10 ....212 A4
Montgomery Cl
  DA15 ....167 D5
  Mitcham CR4 .....204 A5
Montgomery Ct W4 133 C4
Montgomery Ho 5
  SW14 ....133 B2
Montgomery Lo 34 E1 96 C3
Montgomery Rd
  Acton W4 ....111 A2
  Edgware HA8 .....26 B4
Montholme Rd SW11 158 D5
Monthorpe Rd 16 E1 96 A2
Montolieu Gdns
  SW15 ....156 B6

Montpelier Ave
Ealing W5 ....87 C2
Sidcup DA5 ....168 D4
Montpelier Cl UB10 ..82 C6
Montpelier Ct
5 Beckenham BR2 ..208 D5
Ealing W5 ....87 D2
Montpelier Gdns E6 ..99 D4
Ilford RM6 ....58 C2
Montpelier Gr NW5 ..71 C3
Montpelier Mews
SW7 ....257 B6
Montpelier Pl 21 E1 ..96 C1
SW7 ....257 B6
Montpelier Prim Sch
W5 ....87 D2
Montpelier Rd N3 ....30 A2
SE15 ....140 B4
Ealing W5 ....87 D2
Sutton SM1 ....218 A4
Montpelier Rise NW11 47 A2
Wembley HA9 ....43 D1
Montpelier Row SE3 .142 D3
Twickenham TW1 ....153 C4
Montpelier Sq
SW7 ....114 C4 247 B1
Montpelier St
SW7 ....114 C3 257 B6
Montpelier Terr SW7 .247 B1
Montpelier Vale SE3 .142 D3
Montpelier Way NW11 47 A2
Montpelier Wlk
SW7 ....114 C3 257 B6
Montrave Rd SE20 ..184 C3
Montreal Ho UB4 ....84 B4
Montreal Pl WC2 ...250 C6
Montreal Rd IG1 ....57 A2
Montrell Rd SW2 ...160 A3
Montrose Ave DA16 ..145 C2
HA8 ....27 B2
NW6 ....91 A5
Sidcup DA15 ....168 A4
Twickenham TW2 ....151 D4
Montrose Cl DA16 ..145 D2
Ashford TW15 ....171 A5
Woodford IG8 ....37 A6
Montrose Cres N12 ...30 A4
1 Wembley HA0 ....66 A2
Montrose Ct NW11 ...47 B5
NW9 ....27 A1
SW7 ....114 B4 246 D1
2 Catford SE6 ....164 D2
Montrose Gdns
Mitcham CR4 ....180 D1
Sutton SM1 ....217 D6
Montrose Ho E14 ...119 C3
SW1 ....248 B1
Montrose Pl
SW1 ....115 A4 248 B1
Montrose Rd
East Bedfont TW14 ...149 B5
Harrow HA3 ....24 D1
Montrose Villas W6 ..112 A1
Montrose Way SE23 .162 D3
Montserrat Ave IG8 ...36 B3
Montserrat Cl SE19 ..183 B5
Montserrat Rd SW15 135 A1
Montway Hts SW19 ..179 D3
Monument Gdns
SE13 ....164 A6
Monument St
EC3 ....117 B6 252 D6
Monument Sta
EC3 ....117 B6 252 D6
Monument The★
EC3 ....252 D6
Monument Way N17 ..51 D6
Monza St E1 ....118 C6
Moodkee St SE16 ...118 C3
Moody Rd SE15 ....139 D4
Moody St E1 ....96 D4
Moon Ct SE12 ....143 A1
Moon La EN5 ....1 B2
Moon St N1 ...94 D6 234 C6
Moorcroft HA8 ....26 D2
Moorcroft Gdns BR1 .210 A4
Moorcroft La UB8 ....82 C2
Moorcroft Rd SW16 .160 A1
Moorcroft Sch UB8 ...82 D2
Moorcroft Way HA5 ..41 A4
Moordown SE18 ....144 D4
Moore Cl
Mitcham CR4 ....181 B1
Mortlake SW14 ....133 A2
Wallington SM6 ....220 A1
Moore Cres RM9 ....102 B6
Moore Ct N1 ....234 C5
Moorefield Rd N17 ....33 D1
Moore Ho 6 E1 ....118 C6
16 E2 ....96 C4
Moore Ho *continued*
N8 ....50 A5
5 SE10 ....120 D1
Wandsworth SW17 ...158 B1
1 West Norwood
SE27 ....183 A6
Mooreland Rd BR1 ..187 A2
Moore Park Ct SW6 .265 D4
Moore Park Rd
SW6 ....135 D5 265 C3
Moore Rd SE19 ....183 A4
Moore St
SW3 ....114 D2 257 C4
Moore Wlk E7 ....77 A4
Moorey Cl 2 E15 ....98 D6
Moorfield Ave W5 ...87 D3
Moorfield Rd
Chessington KT9 ....214 A3
Enfield EN3 ....6 C4
Moorfields
EC2 ....95 B2 242 C3
Moorfields Ct 6
SW16 ....181 C6
Moorfields Eye Hospl
EC1 ....95 B4 235 C1
Moorfields Highwalk
EC2 ....242 C3
Moorfields Prim Sch
EC1 ....95 B3 242 C6
Moorgate EC2 .95 B2 242 C3
Moorgate Pl EC2 ...242 C2
Moorgate Sta
EC2 ....95 B2 242 C3
Moorgreen Ho EC1 ..234 C2
Moorhead Way SE3 ..143 B2
Moorhouse 17 NW9 ...27 D2
Moorhouse Rd W2 ....91 C1
Harrow HA3 ....43 D6
Moorings The E16 ....99 C2
Moor La EC2 ..95 B2 242 C3
Chessington KT9 ....214 A3
Moorland Cl TW4 ...151 C4
Moorland Rd SW9 ...138 D1
Moorlands UB5 ....85 A6
Moorlands Ave NW7 ..28 B4
Moor Lane Jun Sch
KT9 ....214 B3
Moormead Dr KT19 .215 C3
Moor Mead Rd TW1 .153 A5
Moor Park Gdns KT2 177 C3
Moor Pl EC2 ....242 C3
Moorside Rd BR1 ...186 D6
Moor St W1 ....239 D1
Moortown Rd WD19 ..22 C6
Moot Ct NW9 ....44 C4
Morant Ho SW9 ....138 B3
Morant Pl N22 ....32 B2
Morant St E14 ....119 C6
Mora Prim Sch NW2 ..68 C4
Mora Rd NW2 ....68 C4
Mora St EC1 ...95 A4 235 B1
Morat St SW9 138 B4 270 D2
Moravian Cl SW3 ...266 D5
Moravian Pl
SW10 ....136 B6 266 D5
Moravian St 10 E2 ....96 C4
Moray Ave UB3 ....105 D5
Moray Cl HA8 ....10 D2
Moray Ho 8 E1 ....97 A3
11 Kingston KT6 ....198 A4
Moray Mews N4,N7 ...72 B6
Moray Rd N4,N7 ....72 B6
Mordaunt Gdns RM9 ..81 A1
Mordaunt Ho 4 NW10 89 B6
34 SW8 ....137 D3
Mordaunt Rd NW10 ...89 B6
Mordaunt St SW9 ...138 B2
Morden Court Par
SM4 ....201 D5
Morden Ct SM4 ....201 D5
Morden Gdns
Greenford UB6 ....64 D3
Mitcham CR4 ....202 B5
Morden Hall SW19 ..201 D6
Morden Hall Rd SM4 202 A5
Morden Hill SE13 ...142 A3
Morden Ho 19 SW2 ..160 C5
Morden SM4 ....201 C5
Morden La SE13 ...142 A4
Morden Lo BR2 ....186 B1
Morden Mount Prim Sch
SE13 ....141 D3
Morden Park Sch Sports
Ctr SM4 ....201 B4
Morden Prim Sch
SM4 ....201 C4
Morden Rd SE3 ....143 A3
Dagenham RM6 ....59 A2
Merton SW19 ....179 D1
Mitcham CR4,SM4 ...202 B5
Morden Road Mews
SE3 ....143 A3
Morden Road Sta
SW19 ....179 D1
Morden South Sta
SM4 ....201 C4
Morden St SE13 ....141 D4
Morden Sta SW19 ..201 D6
Morden Way SM3 ...201 C2
Morden Wharf Rd
SE10 ....120 C3
Mordern Ho NW1 ...237 B5
Mordon Rd IG3 ....57 D2
Mordred Rd SE6 ...164 C2
Morecambe Cl 2 E1 .96 D2
Morecambe Gdns HA7 25 D6
Morecambe St
SE17 ....117 B2 262 B2
Morecambe Terr N18 .33 B6
More Cl E16 ....98 D1
W14 ....113 A2 254 A3
Morecoombe Cl KT2 .176 D3
Moredown Ho 3 E8 ..74 A3
Moree Way N18 ....34 A6
More House Sch
SW1 ....114 D3 257 D5
Moreland Ct 3 NW2 ..69 C5
Moreland Prim Sch
EC1 ....94 D4 234 D1
Moreland St
EC1 ....94 D4 234 D2
Moreland Way E4 ....20 A1
Morella Rd SW11,
SW12 ....158 D4
Morell Ho 5 SW9 ...138 B3
Morello Ave UB8 ....82 D2
Morello Ct HA9 ....66 B5
Moremead Rd SE6 ..185 C6
Morena St SE6 ....163 D4
Moresby Ave KT5 ...198 D2
Moresby Rd E5 ....52 B1
Moresby Wlk 6 SW8 137 B3
More's Gdn SW3 ...266 D5
Moreton Ave TW7 ...130 C4
Moreton Cl E5 ....52 C1
N15 ....51 B3
NW7 ....28 C4
Moreton Green Fst Sch
SM4 ....202 B4
Moreton Ho SE16 ...118 B3
Upper Tooting SW17 ...180 B6
Moreton Pl
SW1 ....115 C1 259 B2
Moreton Rd N15 ....51 B3
Croydon CR2 ....221 B3
North Cheam KT4 ....216 B6
Moreton St
SW1 ....115 D1 259 C2
Moreton Terr
SW1 ....115 C1 259 B2
Moreton Terr Mews N
SW1 ....259 B2
Moreton Terr Mews S
SW1 ....259 B2
Moreton Twr 3 W3 .110 D5
Morford Cl HA4 ....40 B2
Morford Way HA4 ....40 B2
Morgan Ave E17 ....54 B5
Morgan Cl RM10 ....81 C1
Morgan Ct 5 SW11 ..136 B3
Ashford TW15 ....170 D5
Morgan Ho SW1 ...259 B3
SW8 ....269 B2
Morgan Rd BR1 ....187 A3
N7 ....72 C3
W10 ....91 B2
Teddington TW11 ....174 C4
Morgan's La UB3 ....83 B2
Morgan St E16 ....98 D2
E3 ....96 D4
Morgan's Wlk SW11 .267 A3
Morgan Terr RM6 ....58 C4
Moriah Jewish Day Sch
The HA5 ....41 A1
Moriatry Cl N7 ....72 A4
Morie St SW18 ....157 D6
Morieux Rd E10 ....53 B1
Moring Rd SW17 ....181 A6
Moriss Ho 5 E5 ....74 B6
Morkyns Wlk SE21 ...161 C1
Morland Ave CR0 ...205 C1
Morland Cl NW11 ....47 D1
Hampton TW12 ....173 B5
Mitcham CR4 ....202 C6
Morland Ct W12 ....112 B4
Morland Est E8 ....74 A1
Morland Gdns NW10 ..67 B1
Southall UB1 ....107 D5
Morland Ho NW1 ...232 B3
NW6 ....91 C6
Morland Ho *continued*
SW1 ....260 A4
W11 ....91 A1
Morland Mews N1 ...72 C1
Morland Rd E17 ....52 D4
Croydon CR0 ....205 D2
Dagenham RM10 ....81 C1
Harrow HA3 ....44 A5
Ilford IG1 ....78 D6
Penge SE20 ....184 D4
Sutton SM1 ....218 A3
Morland Road Day Hospl
RM10 ....103 C6
Morley Ave
Chingford E4 ....36 B3
Edmonton N18 ....34 A6
Tottenham N22 ....32 D1
Morley Cl BR6 ....226 D6
Morley Coll
SE1 ....116 C3 261 B6
Morley Cres HA8 ....11 A2
Ruislip HA4 ....62 C6
Morley Cres E HA7 ...43 D6
Morley Cres W HA7 ..43 C6
Morley Ct E4 ....35 B5
Beckenham BR2 ....208 D5
Beckenham BR3 ....186 B2
Morley Hill EN2 ....5 B5
Morley Ho N16 ....74 A6
Streatham SW2 ....160 A4
Morley Rd E10 ....54 A1
E15 ....98 D5
SE13 ....142 A1
Barking IG11 ....101 B6
Cheam SM3 ....201 B1
Chislehurst BR7 ....189 A2
Dagenham RM6 ....59 A4
Twickenham TW1 ....153 D5
Morley St
SE1 ....116 C4 251 B1
Morna Rd SE5 ....139 A3
Morning La E9 ....74 C2
Morningside Prim Sch
E9 ....74 C2
Morningside Rd KT4 .216 C6
Mornington Ave BR1 209 D6
W14 ....113 B2 254 C3
Ilford IG1 ....56 C2
Mornington Avenue Mans
W14 ....254 C3
Mornington Cl IG8 ...37 A6
Mornington Cres
NW1 ....93 C5 232 A4
Cranford TW5 ....128 B4
Mornington Crescent Sta
NW1 ....93 C5 232 A4
Mornington Ct NW1 .232 A4
Mornington Gr E3 ....97 C4
Mornington Mews 2
SE5 ....139 A4
Mornington Pl NW1 .232 A4
4 SE8 ....141 B5
Mornington Rd E11 ...54 D1
SE14,SE8 ....141 B5
Ashford TW15 ....171 A5
Chingford E4 ....20 B4
Greenford UB6 ....85 D3
Woodford IG8 ....36 D6
Mornington St
NW1 ....93 B5 231 D4
Mornington Terr
NW1 ....93 B5 231 D4
Mornington Wlk
TW10 ....175 C6
Morocco St
SE1 ....117 C4 253 A1
Morpeth Gr E9 ....96 D6
Morpeth Rd E9 ....96 D6
Morpeth Sec Sch E2 .96 C4
Morpeth St E2 ....96 D4
Morpeth Terr
SW1 ....115 C3 259 A4
Morpeth Wlk N17 ....34 B3
Morrab Gdns IG3 ....79 D5
Morrel Cl EN5 ....2 A2
Morrel Ct 10 E2 ....96 A5
Morris Ave E12 ....78 B3
Morris Blitz Ct 2 N16 73 D4
Morris Cl BR6 ....227 C5
Croydon CR0 ....207 A4
Morris Ct 3 SE5 ....139 B1
Chingford E4 ....19 D1
Morris Gdns SW18 ..157 C4
Morris Ho 17 E2 ....96 C4
10 N19 ....71 C4
NW8 ....237 A5
1 SW4 ....138 A1
Morrish Rd SW2 ....160 A4
Morrison Ave N17 ....51 C6
Morrison Bldgs 3 E1 .96 A1
Morrison Ct N12 ....30 C3
5 Barnet EN5 ....1 A1
Morrison Ho SW2 ...160 C3
Morrison Rd
Barking IG11 ....103 A5
Hayes UB4 ....84 B4
Morrison St SW11 ...137 A2
Morrison Yd N17 ....33 D1
Morris Pl N4 ....72 C6
Morris Rd E15 ....76 C4
Dagenham RM8 ....81 B6
Isleworth TW7 ....130 D2
Morriss Ho 7 SE16 ...118 B4
Morris St E1 ....96 B1
E14 ....97 D2
Morriston Cl WD19 ...22 C5
Morritt Ho 3 HA0 ....65 D3
Morse Cl E13 ....99 A4
Morshead Mans W9 ..91 C4
Morshead Rd W9 ....91 C4
Morson Rd EN3 ....19 A5
Morston Gdns SE9 ...188 B6
Mortain Ho 9 SE16 ..118 B2
Morten Cl SW4 ....159 D5
Morteyne Rd N17 ....33 B2
Mortgramit Sq SE18 .122 C3
Mortham St E15 ....98 C6
Mortimer Cl 1 NW2 ..69 B5
Streatham SW16 ....159 D2
Mortimer Cres NW6 ..91 D6
Worcester Park KT4 ...215 B5
Mortimer Ct NW8 ...229 B3
Mortimer Dr EN1 ....17 C6
Mortimer Est NW6 ...91 D6
Mortimer Ho 6 W11 112 D5
W14 ....254 B3
Mortimer Lo 11
SW19 ....157 A3
Mortimer Market
WC1 ....239 B5
Mortimer Pl NW6 ....91 D6
Mortimer Rd E6 ....100 B4
N1 ....73 C1
NW10 ....90 C4
Ealing W13 ....87 C1
Mitcham CR4 ....180 D2
Mortimer Sq W11 ...112 D6
Mortimer St
W1 ....93 C2 239 B3
Mortimer Terr NW5 ..71 B4
Mortlake Cl CR0 ....220 A5
Mortlake Dr CR4 ....180 C2
Mortlake High St
SW14 ....133 B2
Mortlake Rd Ilford IG1 .79 B4
Newham E16 ....99 B1
Richmond SW14,TW9 ..132 C4
Mortlake Sta SW14 ..133 A2
Mortlock Cl SE15 ...140 B4
Mortlock Ct E12 ....77 D4
Morton Cl SM6 ....220 B1
Morton Cres N14 ....31 D6
Morton Ct UB5 ....64 A3
Morton Gdns SM6 ...219 C3
Morton Ho SE17 ....138 D6
West Norwood SE27 ...183 B5
Morton Mews SW5 ...255 C3
Morton Pl SE1 ....261 A5
Morton Rd E15 ....76 D1
N1 ....73 A1
Morden SM4 ....202 B4
Morton Way N14 ....31 D6
Morvale Cl DA17 ...125 B2
Morval Rd SW2 ....160 C6
Morven Rd SW17 ...158 D1
Morville St E3 ....97 C5
Morwell St WC1 ...239 D3
Moscow Pl W2 ....245 C6
Moscow Rd
W2 ....113 D6 245 C6
Mosedale NW1 ....231 D1
Moseley Way SE10 ..120 D3
Moselle Ave N22 ....32 C1
Moselle Cl N8 ....50 B6
Moselle Ho 2 N17 ....33 D3
Moselle Pl N17 ....33 D3
Moselle Sch N17 ....51 A6
Tottenham N17 ....33 C1
Moselle St N17 ....33 D3
Mosque Terr E1 ....96 A2
Mosque Tower 24 E1 ..96 A2
Mossborough Cl N12 .29 D4
Mossbury Rd SW11 ..136 C2
Moss Cl E1 ....96 A2
Pinner HA5 ....23 A1
Mossdown Cl DA17 ..125 C2
Mossford Ct IG6 ....56 D6
Mossford Gn IG6 ....57 A6
Mossford St E3 ....97 B3
Moss Gdns
Feltham TW13 ....150 A2
South Croydon CR2 ...222 D1
Moss Hall Cres N12 ..30 A4
Moss Hall Ct N12 ....29 D4
Moss Hall Gr N12 ....29 D4
Moss Hall Jun & Inf Schs
N12 ....29 D4
Mossington Gdns
SE16 ....118 C2
Moss La HA5 ....23 A1
Mosslea Rd BR2 ....209 D4
BR6 ....227 A5
Penge SE20 ....184 C4
Mossop St
SW3 ....114 C2 257 B4
Moss Rd RM10 ....81 C1
Mossville Gdns SM4 .201 B5
Mosswell Ho 4 N10 ..31 A3
Moston Cl UB3 ....105 D1
Mostyn Ave HA9 ....66 B3
Mostyn Gdns NW10 ..90 D5
Mostyn Gr E3 ....97 C5
Mostyn Lo N5 ....73 A4
Mostyn Rd HA8 ....27 C3
SW9 ....138 C4
Bushey WD23 ....8 A6
Merton SW19 ....179 B1
Mosul Way BR2 ....210 A3
Motcomb St
SW1 ....115 A3 258 A6
Moth Cl SM6 ....220 A1
Mothers Sq The 13 E5 .74 B4
Motley Ave EC2 ....243 A6
Motley St SW8 ....137 C3
Motspur Park Sta
KT3 ....200 B4
Motspur Pk KT3 ....200 A3
Mottingham Ct SE9 ..166 B3
Mottingham Gdns
SE9 ....165 D3
Mottingham Prim Sch
SE9 ....166 B1
Mottingham Rd N9 ...18 D4
SE9 ....166 B1
Mottingham Sta SE9 166 B3
Mottisfont Rd SE2 ..124 B2
Moules Ct SE5 ....139 A5
Moulins Rd E9 ....74 C1
Moulsford Ho 5 N7 ..72 A3
32 W2 ....91 C2
Moulton Ave TW3,
TW5 ....129 B3
Moundfield Rd N16 ..52 A3
Mound The SE9 ....166 C1
Mounsey Ho 10 W10 ..91 A4
Mountacre Cl SE26 ..183 D6
Mount Adon Pk SE21,
SE22 ....162 A4
Mountague Pl 2
E14 ....120 A6
Mountain Ho SE11 ..260 C2
Mountaire Ct NW9 ....45 B4
Mount Angelus Rd
SW15 ....155 D4
Mount Ararat Rd
TW10 ....154 A6
Mount Arlington 3
BR2 ....186 C1
Mount Ash Rd SE26 ..162 B1
Mount Ave
Chingford E4 ....19 D1
Ealing W5 ....87 D2
Southall UB1 ....85 C1
Mountbatten Cl SE18 145 C6
6 West Norwood
SE19 ....183 C5
Mountbatten Ct IG9 ..21 D2
Mountbatten Gdns
BR3 ....207 A5
Mountbatten Ho N6 ..49 A2
Mountbatten Mews
SW18 ....158 A3
Mountbel Rd HA7 ....25 A1
Mount Carmel RC Coll
N19 ....49 D1
Mount Carmel RC Sec Sch
N7 ....72 B3
Mount Cl BR1 ....188 A2
Cockfosters EN4 ....3 A1
Ealing W5 ....87 C2
Mountcombe Cl KT6 .198 A2
Mountcombe Ho
SW17 ....180 B5
Mount Ct
6 Kingston KT2 ....176 D3
West Wickham BR4 ...224 C6

Mount Culver Ave
DA14 ....190 D4
Mount Dr HA9 ....67 A6
Bexley DA6 ....169 A6
Harrow HA2,HA5 ...41 B4
Mountearl Gdns
SW16,SW2 ....160 B1
Mount Eaton Ct W5 .87 C2
Mount Echo Ave E4 .19 D3
Mount Echo Dr E4 ...19 D3
Mount Ephraim La
SW16 ....159 D1
Mount Ephraim Rd
SW16 ....159 D1
Mount Felix KT12 .193 D1
Mountfield NW2 ....69 B6
Mountfield Cl SE6 .164 B4
Mountfield Ct SE13 .164 B5
Mountfield Rd N3 ...47 C6
Ealing W5 ....88 A1
Wallend E6 ....100 C4
Mountford Ho EN2 ...4 D1
Mountford St 4 E1 .96 A1
Mountfort Cres N1 ..72 C1
Mountfort Terr 1 N1 .72 C1
Mount Gdns SE26 ..162 B1
Mountgrove Rd N5 ..73 A5
Mount House (St Martha's
Senior Sch) The EN4 ...1 C4
Mounthurst Rd BR2 .208 D2
Mountington Park Cl
HA3 ....43 D2
Mountjoy Cl SE2 ...124 B4
Mountjoy Ho EC2 ..242 A3
Mount Lo N6 ....49 C3
Mount Lodge N6 ....137 C1
Mount Mews TW12 .173 D2
Mount Mills EC1 ...234 D1
Mount Nod Rd SW16,
SW2 ....160 B1
Mount Olive Ct W7 .108 C4
Mount Park Ave HA1 .64 C6
Mount Park Cres W5 .87 D1
Mount Park Rd
Ealing W5 ....87 D1
Harrow HA1 ....64 B5
Pinner HA5 ....40 A4
Mount Pk SM5 .....219 A1
Mount Pl 7 W3 ....110 D5
Mount Pleasant N14 .15 D4
WC1 ....94 C3 241 A5
Cockfosters EN4 ....2 D1
Ilford IG1 ....79 A3
Ruislip HA4 ....62 D6
Wembley HA0 ....88 B6
West Norwood SE27 .183 A6
Mount Pleasant Cres
N4 ....50 B2
Mount Pleasant Hill
E5 ....74 C6
Mount Pleasant La E5 52 B1
Mount Pleasant Pl
SE18 ....123 B2
Mount Pleasant Rd
E17 ....35 A1
SE13 ....164 A5
Ealing W5 ....87 C3
Kingston KT3 ....199 A6
Tottenham N17 ......33 C1
Willesden NW10 .....90 C1
Mount Pleasant Villas
N4 ....50 B2
Mount Prim Sch The
KT3 ....199 A6
Mount Rd NW2 .....68 C5
NW4 ....46 A3
Bexley DA6 ....169 A6
Chessington KT9 ...214 B3
Dagenham RM8 .....59 B1
East Barnet EN4 ....14 C6
Feltham TW13 ......151 A1
Hayes UB3 ....106 A4
Kingston KT3 ....199 B6
Mitcham CR4 ....180 C1
South Norwood SE19 .183 B4
Wimbledon SW18,
SW19 ....157 D2
Mount Row
W1 ....115 B6 248 C5
Mount Sch The W3 .28 C5
Mountside HA7 .....25 A2
Mounts Pond Rd SE3,
SE13 ....142 B3
Mount Sq The NW3 .70 A5
Mount St W1 115 A6 248 B5

Mount Stewart Ave
HA3 ....43 D2
Mount Stewart Jun & Inf
Schs HA3 ....43 D2
Mount Terr E1 ......96 B2
Mount The DA6 ....169 D6
E5 ....74 B6
HA9 ....67 A6
N20 ....14 A2
N2 ....30 C1
NW3 ....70 A4
W8 ....245 A3
Croydon CR2 ....221 A3
Kingston KT3 ....199 D6
North Cheam KT4 ..216 B4
Northolt UB5 ....63 D1
Mount Tyndal NW3 .48 B1
Mount Vernon NW3 .70 A4
Mountview NW7 ....11 B1
5 Streatham SW16 .160 B1
Mount View Ealing W5 .87 D3
Enfield EN2 ....4 B5
Southall UB1 ....106 D2
Northwood HA6 .....22 A4
Mountview Cl NW11 .48 A1
Mountview Ct N8 ...50 D5
Mount View Rd N4 ..50 B3
NW9 ....45 B4
Chingford E4 ....20 A4
Claygate KT10 .....213 B1
Mountview Theatre Sch
N8 ....50 A3
Mount Villas SE27 .160 D1
Mountwood KT8 ...195 D6
Mountwood Ho W5 .87 D3
Mourne Ho NW3 ....70 A2
Movers La IG11 ....101 C6
Mowat Ct 3 KT4 ...215 D6
Mowatt Cl N19 .....49 D1
Mowbray Ct
South Norwood SE19 .183 D2
Wood Green N22 ...32 C2
Mowbray Gdns UB5 .85 C6
Mowbray Ho 5 N2 .30 B1
Mowbray Rd NW6 ..69 A1
Edgware HA8 ....26 C6
New Barnet EN5 ....14 A6
Richmond TW10 ...153 C1
South Norwood SE19 .183 D2
Mowlem Prim Sch E2 96 C5
Mowlem St E2 ......96 B5
Mowlem Trad Est N17 34 C3
Mowll St SW9 .....138 C5
Moxon Cl E13 ....98 D5
Moxon St W1 .93 A2 238 A3
Barnet EN5 ....1 B2
Moye Cl 9 E2 ....96 A5
Moyers Rd E10 .....54 A2
Moylan Rd
W6 ....135 A6 264 B6
Moyle Ho SW1 ....269 B6
Moyne Ho 16 SW9 .138 C4
Moyne Pl NW10 ....88 C5
Moynihan Dr N21 ..16 A6
Moys Cl CR0 ....204 A3
Moyser Rd SW16 ..181 B5
Mozart St W10 .....91 B4
Mt Carmel RC Prim Sch
W5 ....109 C3
Muchelney Rd SM4 .202 A3
Mudchute Sta E14 .119 C2
Mudie Ho 8 SW2 ..160 A4
Muggeridge Cl CR2 .221 B3
Muggeridge Rd RM10 .81 D4
Muir Cl SW18 ......158 C5
Muirdown Ave SW14 .133 B1
Muirfield W3 ....89 C1
South Oxhey WD19 .22 C6
Muirfield Cl 23 SE16 .118 B1
South Oxhey WD19 .22 C6
Muirfield Cres E14 .119 D3
Muirfield Gn WD19 .22 C6
Muirfield Rd WD19 .22 C6
Muirkirk Rd SE6 ...164 A3
Muir Rd E5 ....74 A5
Muir St E16 ....122 A5
Mulbarton Ct BR7 .189 B4
Mulberry Ave TW19 .148 B3
Mulberry Bsns Ctr
SE16 ....118 D3
Mulberry Cl N8 .....50 A4
NW3 ....70 B4
NW4 ....46 C6
SE22 ....162 A5
SE7 ....143 D6
SW3 ....266 A4
Barnet EN4 ....2 B1
Chingford E4 ....19 C2
Northolt UB5 ....85 A5
Streatham SW16 ..181 C6

Mulberry Cres
Brentford TW8 .....131 C5
West Drayton UB7 .104 C4
Mulberry Ct 1 E11 .76 B4
EC1 ....234 D1
N5 ....72 D3
NW10 ....67 B2
10 W9 ....91 B4
Barking IG11 ....79 D1
4 Surbiton KT6 ....197 D2
Twickenham TW1 ..152 D1
Mulberry Ho 1 E2 .96 C4
8 SE8 ....141 B6
Mulberry House Sch
NW2 ....69 A3
Mulberry La CR0 ..205 D1
Mulberry Mews SE14 141 B4
2 Wallington SM6 .219 C2
Mulberry Par UB7 .104 C4
Mulberry Pl W6 ....112 A1
Mulberry Rd E8 .....73 C1
Mulberry Sch for Girls
E1 ....96 B1
Stepney E1 ....118 B6
Mulberry St 5 E1 ..96 A1
Mulberry Trees
TW17 ....193 B2
Mulberry Way
Ilford IG6 ....57 A5
Woodford E18 ....37 B1
Mulberry Wlk
SW3 ....136 B6 266 D6
Mulgrave Chambers
SM2 ....217 D2
Mulgrave Hall SM2 .217 D2
Mulgrave Ho 20 SE18 122 B2
Mulgrave Manor
SM2 ....217 D2
Mulgrave Prim Sch
SE18 ....122 D3
Mulgrave Rd NW10 .67 D4
SE18 ....122 C2
W14 ....264 C6
Belmont SM2 ....217 C2
Ealing W5 ....87 D3
Harrow HA1 ....65 A6
South Croydon CR0 .221 B5
Mulholland Cl CR4 .181 B1
Mulkern Rd N19 ....49 D1
Mullard Ho WC1 ...239 C4
Mullards Cl CR4 ...202 D1
Mullens Ho 7 SW15 156 C6
Mullen Twr EC1 ...241 A5
Muller Ho SE18 ....122 C1
Mullet Gdns 5 E2 ..96 A4
Mulletsfield WC1 ..233 B1
Mull Ho 13 E3 ......97 B5
Mullins Path SW14 .133 B2
Mullion Cl HA3 .....23 D2
Mullion Wlk WD19 .22 C6
Mulready St NW8 ..237 A5
Multi Way W3 ......111 C4
Multon Ho E9 ....74 C1
Multon Rd SW18 ..158 B4
Mulvaney Way SE1 .252 D1
Mumford Ct EC2 ...242 D1
Mumford Rd SE24 .160 D6
Muncaster Cl TW15 .170 C6
Muncaster Rd SW11 .159 A6
Ashford TW15 ......170 D5
Muncies Mews SE6 .164 A2
Mundania Ct SE22 .162 B5
Mundania Rd SE22 .162 C5
Munday Ho SE1 ...262 C5
Munday Rd E16 ....121 A6
Munden Ho 5 E3 ...97 D4
Munden St
W14 ....113 A2 254 A4
Mundesley Cl WD19 .22 C6
Mundford Rd E5 ....74 C6
Mundon Gdns IG1 ..57 B1
Mund St W14 113 B1 254 D1
Mundy Ho 8 W10 ..91 A4
Mundy St N1 ....95 C4
Mungo-Park Cl WD23 .8 A2
Munnery Way BR6 ..226 D6
Munnings Gdns TW2 152 B6
Munro Ho SE1 .....251 A1
SE1 ....252 D1
Munro Mews W10 ..91 A2
Munro Rd WD23 ....8 A6
Munslow Gdns SM1 .218 B4
Munstead Ct 12 SM2 .218 A1
Munster Ave TW4 ..151 A6
Munster Ct
Fulham SW6 ....135 B3
Teddington TW11 ..175 C4
Munster Gdns N13 .33 A6
Munster Rd
SW6 ....135 A4 264 B2
Teddington TW11 ..175 C4

Munster Residences
SW6 ....264 B2
Munster Sq
NW1 ....93 B3 238 D6
Munton Rd
SE1,SE17 ...117 A2 262 B4
Murchison Ave DA5 .169 A3
Murchison Ho 1 W10 91 A2
Murchison Rd E10 ..76 A6
Murdoch Ho 4 SE16 118 C3
Murdock Cl E16 .....98 D1
Murdock St SE15 ..140 B6
Murfett Cl SW19 ..157 A2
Muriel Ct 17 E10 ...53 D2
Muriel St N1 .94 B6 233 D4
Murillo Rd SE13 ...142 C1
Murley Ct N21 ......17 A4
Murphy Ho SE1 ...261 D6
Murphy St
SE1 ....116 C4 251 A4
Murray Ave BR1 ...187 A1
Hounslow TW3 .....151 D6
Murray Cres HA5 ..22 D2
Murray Ct 5 HA1 ..42 D3
Murray Gr N1 .95 B5 235 C3
Murray Ho 21 SE18 .122 B2
Murray Mews NW1 .71 D1
Murray Rd W5 .....109 C2
Richmond TW10 ...153 C2
Wimbledon SW19 ..178 D4
Murray Sq E16 ....121 B6
Murray St NW1 .....71 D1
Murray Terr NW3 ..70 B4
Musard Rd
W6 ....135 A6 264 B6
Musbury St E1 .....96 C1
Muscal W6 ....264 A6
Muscatel Pl SE5 ..139 C4
Muschamp Inf Sch
SM5 ....218 B6
Muschamp Jun Sch
SM5 ....218 C6
Muschamp Rd SE15 .139 D2
Carshalton SM1,SM5 .218 C6
Muscott Ho 15 E2 ..96 A6
Muscovy Ho DA18 .125 A4
Muscovy St EC3 ...253 B6
Museum Ho 7 E2 ..96 C4
Museum in Docklands *
E14 ....119 C6
Museum St
WC1 ....94 A1 240 A2
Musgrave Cl EN4 ...2 A1
Musgrave Cres
SW6 ....135 C4 265 B2
Musgrave Ct 4 SW11 267 A2
Musgrave Rd TW7 .130 C4
Musgrove Ho 1 E9 .74 D2
Musgrove Rd SE14 .141 A4
Musical Mus The *
TW8 ....132 A4
Musjid Rd 7 SW11 .136 B3
Muslim Coll The W5 .110 C6
Mus of Garden History *
SE1 ....260 C5
Mus of London *
EC2 ....95 A2 242 A3
Mus of Richmond *
TW10 ....153 D4
Mus of the Great Eastern
Railway * E16 .....122 C4
Musquash Way TW4 .128 C3
Muston Rd E5 ......74 B6
Mustow Pl 2 SW6 .135 B3
Muswell Ave N10 ...31 B4
Muswell Hill N10 ...49 C6
Muswell Hill Bdwy
N10 ....49 B6
Muswell Hill Jun & Inf
Schs N10 ....49 B6
Muswell Hill Pl N10 .49 B5
Muswell Hill Rd N10 .49 A4
Muswell Mews N10 .49 B6
Muswell Rd N10 ...31 B4
Mutrix Rd NW6 ....91 C6
Mutton Pl NW1 ....71 A2
Muybridge Rd KT3 .177 A1
Myatt Ct SE4 ....141 B3
Myatt Garden Prim Sch
SE4 ....141 B3
Myatt Ho SE5 ......138 D3
Myatt Rd SW9 .....138 D3
Myatts Field Ct SE5 139 A4
Mycenae Rd SE3 ..143 A6
Mychell Ho 8 SW19 .180 A4
Myddelton Ave EN1 .5 C5
Myddelton Cl EN1 ..5 C5
Myddelton Gdns N21 .17 A4
Myddelton Ho N8 ..50 B4

Myddelton Pas
EC1 ....94 C4 234 B2
Myddelton Pk N20 ..14 B2
Myddelton Rd N8 ...50 A5
Myddelton Sq
EC1 ....94 C4 234 B2
Myddelton St
EC1 ....94 C4 234 B1
Myddleton Ave N4 ..73 A6
Myddleton Mews N22 .32 A3
Myddleton Rd N22 ..32 B3
Myers Ho 5 SE5 ...139 A5
Myers La SE14 ....140 D6
Mylis Cl SE26 ......184 B6
Mylius Cl SE14 ....140 C4
Mylne Cl W6 ....112 A1
Mylne Ho N21 ......17 B5
Mylne St EC1 ......234 A3
Mynterne Ct 16
SW19 ....156 D3
Myra St SE2 ....124 A2
Myrdle Ct 8 E1 .....96 A1
Myrdle St E1 ....96 A1
Myrna Cl SW19 ....180 C3
Myron Pl SE13 .....142 A2
Myrtle Alley SE18 .122 C3
Myrtle Ave
Hatton TW14 ....149 C6
Ruislip HA4 ....40 B2
Myrtle Cl
Barnet, London EN4 .14 D3
Hillingdon UB8 .....82 B2
West Drayton UB7 .104 B3
Myrtledene Rd SE2 .124 A1
Myrtle Gdns W7 ...108 C5
Myrtle Gr Enfield EN2 .5 B5
Kingston KT3 ....177 A1
Myrtle Ho SE14 ....140 D4
Myrtle Rd E17 ......53 A3
E6 ....100 A6
W3 ....111 A5
Croydon CR0 ....223 C5
Edmonton N13 .....17 B1
Hampton TW12 ....174 A4
Hounslow TW3 .....130 A3
Ilford IG1 ....78 D6
Sutton SM1 ....218 A3
Myrtle Wlk 20 N1 ..95 C5
Mysore Rd SW11 ..136 D1
Myton Rd SE21 ...161 B1
Mytton Ho SW8 ...270 C3

N

N1 Shopping Ctr
N1 ....94 C5 234 B4
Nadine St SE7 .....121 C1
Nadir Ct E11 ....55 A2
Naffenton Rise IG10 .21 D6
Nagle Cl E17 ....36 B1
Nags Head N7 ......72 B4
Nags Head Ct EC1 .242 B5
Nag's Head La DA16 .146 B2
Nags Head Rd EN3 ..6 D1
Nainby Ho SE11 ...261 A3
Nairn Ct
3 Wallington SM6 .219 C2
Wimbledon SW19 ..179 D4
Nairne Gr SE5,SE24 .139 B1
Nairn Rd HA4 ......62 C2
Nairn St E14 ....98 A2
Naish Ct N1 ....233 B6
Nallhead Rd TW13 .172 C5
Nalton Ho 4 NW6 ..70 A1
Namba Roy Cl SW16 .182 B6
Namton Dr CR7,SW16 204 B5
Nan Clark's La NW7 .11 D2
Nankin St E14 ......97 C1
Nansen Ct 1 E11 ..76 C6
Nansen Ho 7 NW10 .67 B1
Nansen Rd SW11 ..137 A2
Nansen Village 5
N12 ....29 D6
Naoroji St WC1 ....234 A1
Napier 15 NW9 .....27 D2
Napier Ave E14 ....119 C1
Fulham SW6 ....135 B2
Napier Cl SE14,SE8 .141 B5
W14 ....254 C6
West Drayton UB7 .104 B3
Napier Ct N1 ....235 C4
SE12 ....165 B1
13 Croydon CR0 ...221 D6
Fulham SW6 ....135 B2
Hayes UB4 ....84 C3
1 Surbiton KT6 ....197 D2

Napier Gr N1 ..95 A5 235 B4
Napier Lo TW15 ...171 A4
Napier Pl
W14 ....113 B3 254 C5
Napier Rd BR2 ....209 B5
DA17 ....125 B2
E11 ....76 C5
E15 ....98 C5
N17 ....51 C6
NW10 ....90 B4
W14 ....113 B3 254 C5
Ashford TW15 .....171 B3
Croydon SE25 .....206 B5
Enfield EN3 ....18 C4
Isleworth TW7 .....131 A1
South Croydon CR2 221 A1
Wembley HA0 ......65 D2
Napier Terr N1 .....72 C1
Napier Wlk TW15 .171 B3
Napoleon Rd E5 ...74 B5
Twickenham TW1 ..153 B4
Napton Cl UB4 .....85 A3
Narbonne Ave SW4 .159 C6
Narborough Cl UB10 .61 A6
Narborough St SW6 .135 C3
Narcissus Rd NW6 ..69 C3
Nardini 12 NW9 ...27 D2
Naresby Fold HA7 ..25 C4
Narford Rd E5 ......74 A5
Narrow Boat Cl SE28 123 B4
Narrow St E14 .....119 A6
6 Acton W3 ....110 D5
Narrow Way BR2 ..210 A3
Nascot St W12 .....90 C1
Naseby Cl NW6 ....70 A1
Hounslow TW7 ....130 A4
Naseby Ct DA14 ..189 D6
Naseby Rd
Dagenham RM10 ..81 C5
South Norwood SE19 183 B4
Nash Cl SM1 ....218 A3
Nash Ct HA3 ....43 B3
Nashe Ho SE1 .....262 C5
Nash Gn BR1 ......187 A4
Nash Ho 1 E17 ....53 D5
SW1 ....258 D1
Nash La BR2 ....225 A2
Nash Rd N9 ....18 C2
SE4 ....163 A4
Dagenham RM6 ....58 D5
Nash Street NW1 .231 D2
Nash Way HA3 .....43 B3
Nasmyth St W6 ...112 B3
Nassau Path 6 SE28 124 C3
Nassau Rd SW13 ..133 D4
Nassau St W1 .....239 A3
Nassington Rd NW3 .70 D4
Natalie Cl TW14 ..149 A3
Natalie Mews TW2 .152 B4
Natal Rd
Bowes Park N11 ...32 A4
Ilford IG1 ....78 D4
South Norwood CR7 205 B6
Streatham SW16 ..181 C4
Nathan Ct N9 ....18 C4
Nathan Ho SE11 ..261 B3
Nathaniel Cl E1 ...243 D3
Nathaniel Ct E17 ..53 A3
Nathans Rd HA0 ...65 C4
Nathan Way SE28,
SE18 ....123 D2
National Army Mus *
SW3 ....136 D6 267 D6
National Fan Mus *
SE10 ....142 A5
National Film Theatre *
SE1 ....250 D4
National Gallery *
W1 ....115 D6 249 D5
National Hospital for
Neurology &
Neurosurgery N2 ...48 C5
National Hospl The
WC1 ....94 A3 240 B5
National Maritime Mus *
SE10 ....142 B6
National Physical
Laboratory TW11 ..174 C4
National Portrait Gallery *
W1 ....115 D6 249 D5
National Portrait Gallery
(Annexe) *
SW1 ....115 D5 249 D4
National Postal Mus *
EC1 ....95 A1 242 A2
National Theatre *
SE1 ....116 B5 250 D4
National Wks TW4 .129 B2
Nation Way E4 .....20 A3

Natural History Mus★
SW7 ....114 B3 256 C5
Nat West Twr★ EC2 .243 A2
Nautilus Bldg The
EC1 ....234 B2
Naval Row E14 ......120 A6
Navarino Gr E8 ....74 A2
Navarino Mans E8 ...74 A2
Navarino Rd E8 ......74 A2
Navarre Rd E6 ....100 A5
Navarre St E2 ....243 C6
Navenby Wlk 13 E3 ..97 C3
Navestock Cl E4 ......20 A1
Navestock Ho IG11 .102 B5
Navigator Dr UB2 ...108 A4
Navy St SW4 ....137 D2
Nayland Ho SE6 .....186 A6
Naylor Gr EN3 ....18 D6
Naylor Ho SE17 .....262 D2
33 SW8 ....137 D4
5 W10 ....91 B4
Naylor Rd N20 ....14 A1
SE15 ....140 B5
Nazareth Cl SE15 ...140 B3
Nazrul St E2 ....95 C4
Neal Ave UB1 ....85 B3
Neal Cl HA6 ....22 A2
Nealden St SW9 .....138 B2
Neale Cl N2 ....48 A6
Neale Ct N10 ....31 B3
Neal St WC2 .94 A1 240 A1
Neal's Yd WC2 ......240 A1
Near Acre NW9 ....27 D2
Neasden Cl NW10 ....67 C3
Neasden Junc NW10 .67 C4
Neasden La NW10 ....67 B5
NW10 ....67 C3
Neasden La N NW10 .67 C5
Neasden Sta NW10 ..67 C3
Neasham Rd RM8 .....80 B3
Neate St SE5 ....139 C6
SE5 ....139 D6
Neath Gdns SM4 ....202 A3
Neathouse Pl SW1 ..259 A4
Neats Acre HA4 ....39 B2
Neatscourt Rd E16 ...99 D2
Nebraska St
SE1 ....117 B4 252 C1
Neckinger
SE16 ......117 D3 263 D6
Neckinger Est SE16 .263 D6
Neckinger St SE1 ...263 D6
Nectarine Way SE13 .141 D3
Nedahall Ct 4 NW11 .47 B2
Needham Ho SE11 ...261 A3
Needham Rd W11 .....91 C1
Needham Terr NW2 ...68 C5
Needleman St SE16 .118 C4
Needwood Ho N4 .....51 A1
Neela Cl UB10 ....60 D4
Neeld Cres NW4 ......46 B4
Wembley HA9 .....66 C3
Neeld Ct HA9 ....66 C3
Neeld Par HA9 ....66 B3
Neil Cl TW15 ....171 A5
Neilson-Terry Ct 9
SW9 ....138 B1
Neil Wates Cres 18
SW2 ....160 C5
Nelgarde Rd SE6 ....163 C4
Nelland Ct SE6 ......163 B2
Nella Rd W6 ....134 D6
Nelldale Rd SE16 ....118 C4
Nellgrove Rd UB10 ...82 D3
Nell Gwynne Ave
TW17 ....193 B3
Nell Gwynn Ho SW3 .257 B3
Nello James Gdns
SE27 ....183 B6
Nelson Cl 9 NW6 ....91 C4
East Bedfont TW14 .149 D3
Hillingdon UB8 ......82 D4
Thornton Heath CR0 .204 D1
Walton-on-T KT12 ...194 A1
Nelson Ct SE16 .....119 B5
Carshalton SM5 .....218 D5
Nelson Gdns E2 ......96 A4
Twickenham TW3,TW4 .151 C5
Nelson Grove Rd
SW19 ....180 A2
Nelson Ho 1 W5 .....88 A4
Nelson Hospl SW20 .179 B1
Nelson La UB10 ......82 D4
Nelson Mandela Cl
N10 ....31 A1
Nelson Mandela Rd
SE3 ....143 C2
Nelson Pas EC1 .....235 B2
Nelson Pl N1 ....234 D3
Sidcup DA14 ....190 A6

Nelson Prim Sch
Twickenham TW2 .....151 D5
Wallend E6 ....100 C5
Nelson Rd N15 ....51 C5
N8 ....50 B3
Ashford TW15 ......170 A5
Bromley BR2 ....209 C5
Chingford E4 ....35 D4
Edmonton N9 ....18 B2
Enfield EN3 ....18 B5
Erith DA17 ....125 B1
Harmondsworth TW6 .126 B4
Harrow HA1 ....42 C1
Hillingdon UB10 .....82 D4
Merton SW19 ....180 A3
New Malden KT3 ....199 B4
Sidcup DA14 ....190 A6
Stanmore HA7 ....25 C4
Twickenham TW2,TW4 .151 C5
Wanstead E11 ....55 B5
Nelson's Monument★
WC2 ....250 A4
Nelson Sq
SE1 ......116 D4 251 C2
Nelsons Row SW4 ...137 D1
Nelson St E1 ....96 B1
E16 ....120 D6
E6 ....100 B5
Barking E6 ....100 C6
Nelson Terr N1 .....234 D3
Nelson Trad Est
SW19 ....179 D2
Nemoure Rd W3 .....111 A6
Nene Gdns TW13 ....151 B2
Nene Rd TW6,UB7 ...126 D4
Nene Road Rdbt
TW6 ....126 D4
Nepaul Rd 17 SW11 .136 C2
Nepean St SW15 ....156 A4
Neptune Ct 5 E14 ..119 C2
Neptune Ho 14 N16 .73 C3
2 SE16 ....118 C3
Neptune Rd
Harlington TW6 .....127 A4
Harrow HA1 ....42 B3
Neptune St SE16 ....118 C3
Nero Ct 6 TW8 .....131 D5
Nesbit Cl SE3 ......142 C2
Nesbit Rd SE9 ......143 D1
Nesbitt Ho DA6 .....169 D6
Nesbitt Sq SE19 ....183 C3
Nesham Ho 14 N1 ....95 C6
Nesham St E1 ....118 A5
Ness St 9 SE16 ....118 A3
Nesta Rd IG8 ....36 D4
Nestle's Ave UB3 ...105 D3
Nestor Ave N21 ......16 D5
Nestor Ho 13 E2 .....96 B5
Netheravon Rd W4 ..111 D1
Ealing W7 ....108 D3
Netheravon Rd S W4 111 D1
Netherbury Rd W5 ..109 D3
Netherby Gdns EN2 ...4 A1
Netherby Ho 23 SW9 137 D3
Netherby Rd SE23 ..162 C4
Nether Cl N3 ....29 C3
Nethercombe Ho 1
SE3 ....143 A6
Nethercott Ho 27 E3 .97 B1
Nethercourt Ave N3 .29 C4
Netherfield Gdns IG11 79 B1
Netherfield Rd N12 ..29 D5
Upper Tooting SW17 .159 A1
Netherford Rd SW4 .137 C2
Netherhall Gdns NW3 70 A3
Netherhall Way NW3 .70 A3
Netherlands Rd EN5 .14 B5
Netherleigh Cl N6 ...49 B1
Nether St N12 ....30 A4
N3 ....29 D4
Netherton Gr
SW10 ....136 A6 266 B5
Netherton Rd N15 ...51 B4
Isleworth TW1 ......153 B6
Netherwood 19 N2 ...30 B1
Netherwood Rd W14 112 D4
Netherwood St NW6 .69 C2
Nethewode Ct DA17 .125 D3
Netley 13 SE5 ......139 C4
Netley Cl Cheam SM3 216 D3
New Addington CR0 .224 A1
Netley Ct IG2 ....57 B4
Netley Dr KT12 .....195 B2
Netley Gdns SM4 ...202 A2
Netley Prim Sch
NW1 ......93 C4 232 A1
Netley Rd E17 ....53 B4
Brentford TW8 .....132 A6
Cheam SM4 ....202 A2

Netley Rd continued
Ilford IG2 ....57 B4
Netley Rd (W) TW6 .127 B4
Netley St NW1 93 C4 232 A1
Nettlecombe NW1 ....71 D1
Nettleden Ave HA9 ..66 C2
Nettleden Ho 3 SW3 257 B3
Nettlefold Pl SE27 ..160 B1
Nettlestead Cl 16
BR3 ....185 C3
Nettleton Rd SE14 ..140 D4
Harlington TW6 .....126 D4
Ickenham UB10 .....60 B4
Nettlewood Rd SW16 181 D3
Neuchatel Rd SE6 ..163 B2
Nevada Cl KT3 .....199 A5
Nevada St SE10 ....142 A6
Nevena Ct 3 SW2 ..160 C6
Nevern Mans SW5 ..255 A2
Nevern Pl
SW5 ......113 C2 255 B3
Nevern Rd SW5 .....255 A3
Nevern Sq
SW5 ......113 C2 255 B3
Nevil Ho 7 SW9 ....138 D3
Nevill Ct SW10 .....266 A4
Neville Ave KT3 ....177 B2
Neville Cl DA15 ....189 D6
E11 ....76 D5
NW1 ....232 D3
NW6 ....91 B5
SE15 ....140 A4
17 SE15 ....140 A5
Acton W3 ....111 A4
Hounslow TW3 .....129 D3
Neville Ct 10 SW12 .159 C4
Neville Dr N2 ....48 A3
Neville Gdns RM8 ...80 D5
Neville Gill Cl SW18 157 D5
Neville Ho N11 ....31 A6
Neville Pl N22 ....32 B2
Neville Rd E7 ....77 B1
NW6 ....91 B5
Dagenham RM8 ......80 D5
Ealing W5 ....87 D3
Kingston KT1 ......176 C1
Richmond TW10 ....153 C2
Thornton Heath CR0 .205 B2
Neville's Ct NW2 .....68 A5
Neville St SW7 114 B1 256 C2
Neville Terr SW7 ....256 C2
Neville Wlk SM5 ....202 C4
Nevill Rd N16 ....73 C5
Nevin Dr E4 ....19 D3
Nevin Ho UB3 ......105 A3
Nevinson Cl SW18 ..158 B5
Nevis Rd SW17 .....159 A2
Nevitt Ho N1 ....235 D3
New Acres Rd SE28 .123 C5
Newall Ho SE1 .....262 B6
Newall Rd TW6 ....127 A4
Newark Cres NW10 ..89 B4
Newark Ct KT12 ....194 C1
Newark Ho 23 SW9 .138 D3
Newark Knok E6 ....100 C2
Newark Par NW4 ....46 A6
Newark St E1 ....96 B2
Newark Way NW4 ...46 A6
New Ash Cl N2 ....48 B6
New Barn Cl SM6 ..220 B2
New Barnet Sta EN5 .14 B8
New Barns Ave CR4 .203 D5
New Barn St E13 .....99 B3
New Beckenham Sta
BR3 ....185 C3
New Belmont Ho 4
SE23 ....162 C3
New Bentham Ct 11
N1 ....73 A1
Newberry Ho N1 .....73 A1
Newbiggin Path WD19 22 C6
Newbold Cotts 4 E1 .96 C1
Newbolt Ave SM3 ...216 D3
Newbolt Ho SE17 ...262 C2
Newbolt Rd HA7 .....24 D5
New Bond St
W1 ....115 B6 248 D6
Newborough Gn KT3 199 B5
Newborough Ho
SW19 ....180 A3
New Brent St NW4 ...46 C4
Newbridge Cl SW17 180 A6
Newbridge Point 3
SE23 ....162 A4
New Bridge St
EC4 ......94 D1 241 C1
New Broad St
EC2 ......95 C2 243 A3

New Broadway
Ealing W5 ....109 D6
7 Hillingdon UB10 ..82 D3
Teddington TW12 ...174 B3
New Bsns Ctr The
NW10 ....89 D5
Newburgh Rd W3 ...111 A5
Newburgh St W1 ...239 B1
New Burlington Mews
W1 ....249 A6
New Burlington Pl
W1 ....249 A6
New Burlington St
W1 ....249 A6
Newburn Ho SE11 ..260 D2
Newburn St
SE11 ......116 B1 260 D2
Newbury Ave EN3 ....7 B6
Newbury Cl UB5 .....63 D2
Newbury Cotts 4 IG2 57 A3
E5 ....75 A3
7 Wanstead E11 ....55 A5
Newbury Gdns KT19 215 D4
Newbury Ho SW9 ...138 D3
13 W2 ....91 D1
Wood Green N22 ....32 A2
Newbury Mews NW5 71 C2
Newbury Park Prim Sch
IG2 ....57 B3
Newbury Park Sta IG2 57 B3
Newbury Rd BR2 ...209 A6
Chingford E4 ....36 A4
Harmondsworth TW6 .126 B4
Ilford IG2 ....57 C3
Newbury St EC1 ....242 A4
Newbury Way UB5 ...63 D2
Newby NW1 ....232 A2
Newby Cl EN1 ....5 C3
Newby Pl E14 ......120 A4
Newby St SW8 .....137 A2
New Caledonian Wharf
SE16 ....119 B3
New Campden Ct 7
NW3 ....70 A4
Newcastle Cl EC4 ...241 C2
Newcastle Ct EC4 ..252 B6
Newcastle Ho W1 ..238 A4
Newcastle Pl
W2 ....92 B2 236 D4
Newcastle Row EC1 .241 B5
New Cavendish St
W1 ....93 B2 238 C3
New Change
EC4 ......95 A1 242 A1
New Chapel Sq TW13 150 B3
New Charles St EC1 .234 D1
New Church Ct 8
SE19 ....184 A3
New Church Rd SE5 139 B6
32 SE5 ....139 A6
New City Prim Sch
E13 ....99 C4
New City Rd E13 ....99 C4
New Cl Feltham TW13 173 A5
Morden SW19 .....202 A6
New Colebrooke Ct
SM5 ....219 A4
New College Ct 6
NW3 ....70 A4
New College Mews 4
N1 ....72 C1
New College Par 1
NW3 ....70 B1
Newcombe Ho N5 ...73 A3
Newcombe Pk NW7 .27 C5
Wembley HA0 ....88 B6
Newcombe Rise UB7 .82 A1
Newcombe St W8 ...245 B4
Newcome Gdns
SW16 ....182 A6
Newcome Ho E5 .....74 B5
Newcomen Ho 5
NW5 ....71 B4
Newcomen Rd E11 ...76 D5
SW11 ....136 C2
Newcomen St
SE1 ......117 B4 252 C2
New Compton St
WC2 ......94 A1 240 A1
New Concordia Wharf
SE1 ....253 D2
Newcourt Ho 26 E2 ..96 B4
Newcourt St
NW8 .....92 C5 230 A3
New Covent Garden
Flower Market
SW8 ....138 A6 270 A5

New Covent Garden Fruit
& Vegetable Mkt
SW8 ......137 D5 269 C3
New Crescent Yd 1
NW10 ....89 D5
Newcroft Cl UB8 .....82 B2
New Cross SE14 ....141 B5
New Cross Gate
SE14 ....140 D4
New Cross Gate Sta
SE14 ....141 A4
New Cross Hospl
SE14 ....140 C5
New Cross Rd SE14 141 A4
New Cross Sta SE14 141 B5
New Ct EC4 ....241 A1
N16 ....51 B1
13 NW3 ....70 A4
Northolt UB5 ....65 D3
Newdales Cl N9 ......18 A2
Newdene Ave UB5 ...84 D5
Newdigate Ho 5 E14 97 B1
6 Kingston KT2 ...176 D4
New Eltham Sta SE9 166 D3
New End NW3 ....70 A4
New End Prim Sch
NW3 ....70 A4
New End Sq NW3 ....70 B4
New England Est
IG11 ....101 A5
Newent Cl SE15 ....139 C5
Carshalton SM5 ....202 D1
New Farm Ave BR2 .209 A5
New Ferry App SE18 122 C3
New Fetter La
EC4 ......94 C1 241 B2
Newfield Cl TW12 ...173 C2
Newfield Prim Sch
NW10 ....67 D1
Newfield Rise NW2 ..68 B5
New Furness Prim Sch The
NW10 ....90 A6
Newgale Gdns HA8 ..26 B2
New Garden Dr UB7 104 A4
Newgate CR0 ......205 A1
Newgate Cl TW13 ...151 A1
Newgate St
EC1 ....94 D1 241 D2
Chingford E4 ....20 C1
New Globe Wlk SE1 252 A4
New Goulston St E1 243 C2
New Green Pl SE19 183 C4
Newham Acad of Music
E6 ....100 A6
Newham Coll of FE
E6 ....100 B5
Newham Coll of F Ed
(Royal Docks Campus)
E16 ....123 A5
Newham Ctr for Mental
Health E16 ....99 D3
Newham General Hospl
E13 ....99 C3
Newham Gn N22 .....32 C2
Newham Ho IG10 ....21 D5
Newham Sch of Nursing
E3 ....97 D3
Newham Sixth Form Coll
E13 ....99 B3
Newham's Row SE1 253 B1
Newham Way E13 ...99 B2
E6 ....100 B3
New Heston Rd TW5 129 B5
Newhaven Cl UB3 ..105 D2
Newhaven Cres
TW15 ....171 B5
Newhaven Gdns SE9 143 D1
Newhaven La 3 E16 99 A2
Newhaven Rd SE25 205 B4
Newhouse 5 KT3 ..199 C2
Newhouse Ave RM6 .58 D6
Newhouse Cl KT3 ..199 C2
Newhouse Wlk SM4 202 A2
Newick Cl DA5 .....169 D4
Newick Rd E5 ....74 C5
Newing Gn BR1 ....187 D3
Newington Barrow Way
N7 ....72 B5
Newington Butts
SE1,SE11 ....116 D2 261 D3
Newington Cswy
SE1 ......117 A3 262 A6
Newington Green Mans
N16 ....73 B3
Newington Green Prim
Sch N16 ....73 B3

Newington Green Rd
N1 ....73 B3
Newington Ind Est
SE17 ....262 A3
New Inn Broadway
EC2 ....243 B6
New Inn Pas WC2 ..240 D1
New Inn Sq EC2 ....243 B6
New Inn St EC2 ....243 B6
New Inn Yd
EC2 ......95 C3 243 B6
New James Ct SE15 140 B2
New Jubilee Ct 1 IG8 37 A3
New Kelvin Ave
TW11 ....174 C4
New Kent Rd
SE1 ......117 A2 262 B4
New King's Prim Sch
SW6 ....135 B3
New Kings Rd SW6 .135 B3
New King's Rd
SW6 ......135 C3 265 B1
New King St SE8 ...141 C6
Newland Cl HA5 .....23 B4
Newland Ct EC1 ....242 C6
Wembley HA9 ......66 C6
Newland Dr EN1 ......6 B4
Newland Gdns W13 109 A4
Newland Ho N8 ......50 A6
17 SE14 ....140 D6
Newland House Sch
TW1 ....174 D6
Newland House Sch Annex
TW1 ....174 D6
Newland Rd N8 ......50 A6
Newlands NW1 .....232 A2
Newlands Ave KT7 .196 C1
Newlands Cl
Edgware HA8 ....10 A1
Southall UB2 ....107 A1
Wembley HA0 ....65 C2
Newlands Croft SE20 184 D4
Newlands Ct 8 SE9 166 C5
Streatham SW16 ...182 A5
Newlands Pk SE26 .184 D5
Newlands Pl EN5 .....12 A4
Newlands Quay E1 .118 C2
Newlands Rd
Thornton Heath SW16 .182 A1
Woodford IG8 ....20 D2
Newland St E16 ....122 B5
Newlands The
Thames Ditton KT7 .196 C1
Wallington SM6 ...219 D1
Newlands Way KT9 213 C3
Newling Cl E6 ......100 B1
New London St EC3 253 B6
New Lydenburg
Commercial Est E16 121 C3
New Lydenburg St
SE7 ....121 C3
Newlyn NW1 ....232 B5
Newlyn Cl
Hillingdon UB8 ......82 C2
Orpington BR6 .....227 D1
Newlyn Gdns HA2 ...41 B2
Newlyn Rd DA16 ...145 D3
Barnet EN5 ....1 B1
Tottenham N17 ......33 D2
New Malden Sta KT3 199 C6
Newman Ct BR1 ....187 A2
Newman Pas W1 ...239 B3
Newman Rd BR1 ...187 A2
E13 ....99 B4
E17 ....52 A4
Hayes UB3 ....106 B6
Thornton Heath CR0 204 B5
Newman's Ct EC3 ..242 D1
Newman's Row WC2 240 D3
Newman St
W1 ....93 C2 239 B3
Newman's Way EN4 ..2 A4
Newmarket Ave UB5 63 B3
Newmarket Gn SE9 165 D4
Newmarsh Rd SE28 123 D5
Newmill Ho E3 ....98 A3
New Mill Rd BR5 ...190 C2
Newminster Rd SM4 202 A3
New Mount St E15 ...76 B1
Newnes Path SW15 134 B1
Newnham Ave HA4 ..40 C1
Newnham Cl
Loughton IG10 ......21 D5
Northolt UB5 ....64 A2
South Norwood CR7 183 A1
Newnham Gdns UB5 64 A2

Newnham Ho
Catford SE6 ....**164** A1
9 Putney SW15 ....**156** D5
Newnham Jun & Inf Schs
HA4 ....**40** C1
Newnham Lo 10
DA17 ....**125** C2
Newnham Rd N22 ....**32** C2
Newnhams CI BR1 ...**210** B6
Newnham Terr SE1 ..**261** A6
Newnham Way HA3 ..**44** A4
New North PI EC2 ...**243** A6
New North Rd
N1 ....**95** B6 **235** C5
New North Road Bridge
N1 ....**235** C5
New North St
WC1 ......**94** B2 **240** C4
Newnton CI N4 .....**51** B2
New Oak Rd N2 ....**30** A1
New Oxford St
WC1 ......**94** A1 **240** A2
New Palace Yd
SW1 ......**116** A4 **250** A1
New Par
Ashford TW15 ......**170** B6
Yiewsley UB7 ......**104** A5
New Park Ave N13 ...**17** B1
New Park CI UB5 ....**63** A2
New Park Ct 26 SW2 **160** A4
New Park Ho N13 ...**32** B6
New Park Par 14
SW2 ....**160** A4
New Park Est N18 ...**34** C5
New Park Rd
Ashford TW15 ......**171** A5
Streatham SW2 .....**160** A4
New PI CR0 ....**223** C2
New Place Sq SE16 ..**118** B3
New Plaistow Rd E15 .**98** C6
New Pond Par HA4 ..**62** A5
Newport Ave E13 ...**99** B3
E14 ....**120** B6
Newport CI EN3 ....**7** A6
Newport Ct WC2 ...**249** D6
Newport Ho 2 EN1 ..**17** C6
Newport Mead WD19 .**22** D6
Newport PI WC2 ....**249** D6
Newport Rd E10 ....**76** B6
E17 ....**53** A5
Barnes SW13 ......**134** A4
Harmondsworth TW6 ..**126** C4
Hayes UB4 ....**83** B2
Newport St
SE11 .....**116** B2 **260** D4
New Priory Ct 9 NW6 **69** C1
Newquay Cres HA2 ...**63** A6
Newquay Ho SE11 ...**261** A2
Newquay Rd SE6 ....**164** A2
New Quebec St W1 ..**237** D1
New Rd DA16 .....**146** B3
E1 ....**96** B2
N10 ....**30** C2
N8 ....**50** A4
NW7 ....**29** A3
SE2 ....**124** D1
Brentford TW8 .....**109** D1
Carshalton CR4 ....**203** A1
Chingford E4 ......**36** A6
Dagenham RM10 ....**103** D5
East Bedfont TW14 ..**149** B5
East Bedfont TW14 ..**150** B3
East Molesey KT8 ...**195** C6
Edmonton N9 ......**18** A2
Elstree WD6 ......**9** D5
Esher KT10 ....**212** A4
Feltham TW13 .....**173** A5
Harlington TW6,UB7 ..**127** A5
Harrow HA1 ......**64** D4
Hillingdon UB8 .....**83** A2
Hounslow TW3 .....**129** D1
Ilford IG3 ....**79** C6
Kingston KT2 .....**176** C3
Littleton TW17 ....**192** D6
Richmond TW10 ....**175** C6
Tottenham N22 .....**33** A2
New Rd Units TW3 ..**129** D1
New River Cres N13 ..**32** D6
New River Ct N5 ....**73** B4
New River Sports &
Recreation Ctr N22 ..**32** D3
New River Way N4 ...**51** B2
New Row
WC2 ......**116** A6 **250** A6

Newry Rd TW1 .....**153** A6
Newsam Ave N15 ....**51** B4
New Scotland Yard★
SW1 ......**115** D3 **259** C6
Newsholme Dr N21 ...**16** B6
New Southgate Ind Est **10**
N11 ....**31** C5
New Southgate Sta
N11 ....**31** B5
New Spring Gdns Wlk
SE11 ....**260** B1
New Sq WC2 ..**94** B1 **240** D2
East Bedfont TW14 ...**149** A3
New Sq Pas WC2 ....**241** A2
New St EC2 ...**95** C2 **243** B3
New Stanford Prim Sch
SW16 ....**181** D2
Newstead Ave BR6 ..**227** C6
Newstead CI N12 ....**30** C4
Newstead Ct UB5 ...**85** A4
Newstead Rd SE12 ..**164** D4
Newstead Way SW19 **178** D6
Newstead Wlk SM5 ..**202** A2
Newstead Wood Sch for
Girls BR6 ....**227** B5
New Street Hill BR1 .**187** C5
New St Sq EC4 **94** C1 **241** B2
Newton Ave N10 ....**31** B2
Acton W3 ....**111** A4
Newton CI E17 .....**53** A3
Harrow HA2 ......**63** B6
Newton Farm Fst & Mid
Sch HA2 ....**63** B6
Newton Gr W4 .....**111** C2
Newton Ho 10 E17 ..**54** A6
NW8 ....**91** D6
22 SW8 ....**137** D6
1 Stepney E1 .....**118** B6
Newton PI E14 .....**119** C2
Newton Point 1 E16 .**98** C1
Newton Prep Sch
SW8 .....**137** B4 **268** D2
Newton Rd DA16 ...**146** A2
E15 ....**76** B3
N15 ....**52** A4
NW2 ....**68** C5
W2 ....**91** D1
Harrow HA3 ......**24** C1
Isleworth TW7 .....**130** D1
Wembley HA0 ......**66** B1
Wimbledon SW19 ....**179** A3
Newton St
WC2 ......**94** A1 **240** A1
Newton's Yd 14
SW18 ....**157** C6
Newton Terr BR2 ...**209** D3
Newton Way N18 ...**33** A5
Newton Wlk HA8 ...**26** C1
New Tower Bldgs 21
E1 ....**118** B5
Newtown Ct SW11 ..**268** C1
SW4 ....**159** B6
New Trinity Rd 1 N2 .**30** B1
New Union CI E14 ..**120** A3
New Union St EC2 ..**242** C3
New Victoria Hospl
KT3 ....**177** C2
New Wanstead E11 ..**55** A3
New Way Rd NW9 ...**45** C5
New Wharf Rd
N1 ....**94** A5 **233** B4
New Woodlands Sch
BR1 ....**186** C6
Newyears Green La
UB9 ....**38** B3
New Zealand Ave
KT12 ....**193** D1
Niagara Ave W5 ....**109** C4
Niagara CI N1 .....**235** B4
Niagara Ct 6 SE16 ..**118** C3
Niagara Ho W5 ....**109** C2
Nibthwaite Rd HA1 ..**42** C4
Nicholas CI UB6 ....**85** D5
Nicholas Ct
Chiswick W4 ......**133** C4
Lewisham SE12 ....**165** A3
Nicholas Gdns W5 ..**109** D4
Nicholas Ho
Ealing W13 ......**87** C1
Penge SE26 ......**184** B4
2 Putney SW15 ....**156** A6
Nicholas La EC2,EC4 .**252** D6
Nicholas Pas EC3 ...**252** D6
Nicholas Rd E1 ....**96** C3
Borehamwood WD6 ...**10** B3
Dagenham RM8 ....**81** B5
Wallington CR0 ....**220** A4
Nicholas Stacey Ho 3
SE7 ....**121** B1
Nicholay Rd N19 ...**49** D1

Nichol CI N14 .....**15** D3
Nicholes Rd TW3 ...**129** C1
Nichol La BR1 .....**187** A1
Nicholl Ho N4 .....**51** A1
Nicholls Ave UB8 ...**82** C3
Nicholls Point E15 ..**99** A6
Nicholl St E2 .....**96** A6
Nichols CI N4 .....**50** C1
Chessington KT9 ...**213** C2
Nichols Ct E2 .....**95** D5
Nichols Gn W5 ....**88** A2
Nicholson Dr WD23 ..**8** A2
Nicholson Ho SE17 ..**262** C2
2 SE18 ....**144** A4
Nicholson Rd CR0 ..**205** D1
Nicholson St SE1 ...**251** C3
Nickelby CI SE28 ...**102** C1
Nickleby CI UB8 ...**82** D1
Nickleby Ho 16 SE1 .**118** A4
7 W11 ....**112** D5
Nicola CI Harrow HA3 .**24** B1
South Croydon CR2 ..**221** A2
Nicola Terr DA7 ...**147** A4
Nicol CI 6 TW1 ....**153** B5
Nicole Ho SE25 ....**206** A6
Nicoll Ct N10 .....**31** B3
NW10 ....**89** C6
Nicoll PI NW4 .....**46** B2
Nicoll Rd NW10 ....**89** C6
Nicoll Way WD6 ...**11** B6
Nicolson 14 NW9 ...**27** D2
Nicosia Rd SW18 ...**158** C4
Nield Rd UB3 .....**105** D4
Nigel Bldg EC1 ....**241** A4
Nigel CI UB5 .....**85** A6
Nigel Ct N3 ......**29** D3
Nigel Fisher Way
KT9 ....**213** D1
Nigel Mews IG1 ....**78** D4
Nigel Playfair Ave
W6 ....**112** B1
Nigel Rd E7 ......**77** C3
SE15 ....**140** A2
Nigeria Rd SE7 ....**143** D5
Nighthawk 16 NW9 ..**27** D2
Nightingale Ave
Chingford E4 ......**36** C5
Harrow HA1 ......**43** B1
Nightingale CI
Carshalton SM5 ....**219** A6
Chingford E4 ......**36** C6
Chiswick W4 ......**133** A4
Pinner HA5 ......**40** C4
Nightingale Ct
12 E14 ....**120** A3
N4 ....**72** B6
SW6 ....**265** D1
1 Harrow HA1 ....**42** D3
Penge SE19 ......**183** D4
Sutton SM1 ......**218** A3
1 Wanstead E11 ...**55** B4
Nightingale Dr KT19 .**214** D2
Nightingale Gr SE13 .**164** B6
Nightingale Ho
7 E1 ....**118** A5
21 E1 ....**95** C6
SE18 ....**122** C1
W12 ....**90** C1
Hayes UB3 ......**105** D2
Nightingale La BR1 .**187** D1
N8 ....**50** A6
Balham SW11,SW12 ..**159** A5
Richmond TW10 ....**154** A4
Wanstead E11 .....**55** B4
Nightingale Lo 5 W9 .**91** C2
Nightingale Mews
SE11 ....**261** D4
Nightingale PI SE18 ..**144** D6
SW10 ......**136** A6 **266** B6
Nightingale Prim Sch
SE18 ....**122** D1
Wanstead E18 .....**55** C5
Wood Green N22 ....**32** B2
Nightingale Rd E5 ..**74** B5
N9 ....**18** C4
NW10 ....**89** D5
Carshalton SM5 ....**219** A6
Ealing W7 ....**108** A4
East Molesey KT8 ...**195** D4
Hampton TW12 ....**173** C4
Orpington BR5 ....**211** A3
Walton-on-T KT12 ..**194** D3
Wood Green N22 ....**32** B3
Nightingale Sch
SW17 ....**158** C2
Nightingale Sq SW12 **159** A4
Nightingales The
TW19 ....**148** B3

Nightingale Vale
SE18 ....**144** C6
Nightingale Way E6 ..**100** A2
Nightingale Wlk
SW18,SW4 ....**159** B5
Nile CI N16 ......**73** D5
Nile Dr N9 ......**18** C2
Nile Ho N1 ......**235** C2
Nile Path 6 SE18 ...**144** C6
Nile Rd E13 ......**99** C5
Nile St N1 ...**95** B4 **235** C2
Nile Terr SE1,
SE15 ....**117** D1 **263** D1
Nimegen Way 9
SE22 ....**161** C6
Nimmo Dr WD23 ...**8** B4
Nimrod 9 NW9 ....**27** C2
Nimrod CI UB5 ....**84** D4
Nimrod Pas 8 N1 ...**73** C2
Nimrod Rd SW16 ...**181** B5
Nina Mackay CI 10
E15 ....**98** C6
Nine Acres CI E12 ..**78** A3
Nine Elms CI TW14 ..**149** C4
Nine Elms La
SW8 ....**137** D6 **269** C5
Nineteenth Rd CR4 ..**204** A5
Ninhams Wood BR6 ..**226** C4
Ninth Ave UB3 ....**106** A4
Nisbet 10 NW9 ....**27** C2
Nisbet Ho E9 .....**74** D3
Nita Ct SE12 .....**165** A3
Nithdale Rd SE18 ...**145** A5
Nithsdale Gr UB10 ..**61** A5
Niton CI EN5 .....**12** D5
Niton Rd TW9 ....**132** C2
Niton St SW6 .....**134** D5
No 1 St SE18 .....**122** D3
Noam Prim Sch N12 ..**29** D6
Nobel Dr TW6 ....**127** C5
Nobel Ho 8 SE5 ...**139** A3
Nobel Rd N18 ....**34** C4
Noble Cnr TW5 ....**129** C4
Noble Ct Mitcham CR4 **180** B1
Stepney E1 ......**118** B6
Noble Ho 12 E1 ...**118** A4
Noble St EC2 ..**95** A1 **242** A2
Noel 13 NW9 .....**27** D2
Noel Baker Ct 4 E11 .**76** C6
Noel Coward Ho
SW1 ....**259** B3
Noel Ct TW4 .....**129** B2
Noel Dene W5 ....**109** C1
Noel Ho 3 NW3 ...**70** B1
Noel Park Prim Schs
N22 ....**32** C1
Noel Park Rd N22 ...**32** C1
Noel Rd N1 ..**94** D5 **234** D4
Acton W3 ....**88** D1
Newham E6 ......**100** A3
Noel Sq RM8 .....**80** C4
Noel St W1 ..**93** C1 **239** B1
Noel Terr SE23 ....**162** C2
Nolan Way E5 ....**74** A4
Noll Ho N7 ......**72** B6
Nolton PI HA8 ....**26** B2
Nonsuch Ct SM3 ...**217** A2
Nonsuch High Sch for
Girls SM3 ....**216** D1
Nonsuch Prim Sch
KT17 ....**216** B3
Noor Ul Islam Prim Sch
E10 ....**76** A6
Nora Gdns NW4 ...**46** D5
Norbiton Ave KT1,
KT2 ....**176** C1
Norbiton Common Rd
KT1,KT3 ....**198** D6
Norbiton Hall KT2 ..**176** B1
Norbiton Rd E14 ...**97** B1
Norbiton Sta KT1 ...**176** C1
Norbreck Gdns NW10 **88** B4
Norbreck Par NW10 ..**88** B4
Norbroke St W12 ...**111** D6
Norburn St W10 ...**91** A2
Norbury Ave
Isleworth TW3 .....**130** B1
Thornton Heath CR7,
SW16 ....**182** C1
Norbury CI SW16 ...**182** D1
Norbury Court Rd
SW16 ....**182** A1
Norbury Cres SW16 ..**182** C1
Norbury Cross SW16 .**204** B6
Norbury Gdns RM6 ..**58** D4
Norbury Gr NW7 ...**11** C1
Norbury Hill SW16 ..**182** D3
Norbury Manor Girls High
Sch CR7 ....**182** C2

Norbury Manor Prim Sch
SW16 ....**182** A2
Norbury Rd
Chingford E4 ......**35** C5
South Norwood CR7 ..**205** A6
Norbury Rise SW16 ..**204** A6
Norbury Sch HA1 ...**42** C4
Norbury Sta SW16 ..**182** B2
Norbury Trad Est
SW16 ....**182** B1
Norcombe Gdns HA3 .**43** C4
Norcombe Ho 2 N19 .**71** D5
Norcott CI UB4 ....**84** C3
Norcott Rd N16 ...**74** A5
Norcroft Gdns SE22 ..**162** A4
Norcutt Rd TW2 ...**152** C3
Norden Ho 25 E2 ...**96** B4
Norden Point NW2 ..**46** C1
Nore Ct NW10 ....**68** A1
Norfolk Ave N15 ...**51** C3
Edmonton N13 .....**32** D4
Norfolk CI N2 .....**48** C6
Cockfosters EN4 ...**3** A1
Edmonton N13 .....**32** D4
5 Twickenham TW1 .**153** C4
Norfolk Cres DA15 ..**167** C4
W2 ....**92** C1 **237** B2
Norfolk Ct
4 Barnet EN5 ....**1** A1
Surbiton KT5 .....**198** B3
Wembley HA0 .....**65** C2
Norfolk Gdns DA7 ..**147** A4
Norfolk Ho E8 ....**73** D4
EC4 ....**252** A6
SE3 ....**142** C6
SE8 ....**141** C4
SW1 ....**259** D4
13 Acton W3 .....**88** C1
11 Merton SW19 ...**180** A3
Penge SE20 ......**184** C2
4 Putney SW15 ...**156** C4
Richmond TW10 ....**154** C6
2 South Croydon CR0 **221** B6
3 Stanmore HA7 ..**25** C5
Norfolk House Rd
SW16 ....**160** A1
Norfolk House Sch
N10 ....**31** B1
Norfolk Mans SW11 ..**267** D1
10 SW18 ....**157** C6
Norfolk Mews 12 W10 **91** A2
Norfolk PI DA16 ...**146** A3
W2 ....**92** B1 **236** D2
Norfolk Rd E17 ....**34** C1
E6 ....**100** B6
NW10 ....**67** C1
NW8 ......**92** B6 **229** D5
Barking IG11 .....**79** C1
Barnet EN5 ......**1** C2
Claygate KT10 ....**212** C3
Dagenham RM10 ...**81** D3
Enfield EN3 ......**18** B6
Feltham TW13 ....**150** C3
Harrow HA1 ......**41** D4
Ilford IG3 ....**57** C2
South Norwood CR7 ..**205** A6
Norfolk Row
SE1,SE11 ...**116** B2 **260** C4
Norfolk Sq W2 **92** B1 **236** D2
Norfolk Sq Mews
W2 ....**236** D1
Norfolk St E7 .....**77** A3
Norgrove St SW12 ..**159** A4
Norhyrst Ave SE25 ..**205** D6
Norland Ho 13 W11 ..**112** D5
Norland PI
W11 ......**113** A5 **244** B3
Norland Place Sch
W11 ......**113** A5 **244** A3
Norland Rd W11 ...**112** D5
Norlands Cres BR7 ..**188** D2
Norland Sq
W11 ......**113** A5 **244** B3
Norley Vale SW15 ...**156** A3
Norlington Rd E10,E11 **54** B1
Norlington Sch for Boys
E10 ....**54** B1
Norman Ave
Feltham TW13 ....**151** B2
Southall UB1 .....**107** A6
Tottenham N22 ....**33** A2
Twickenham TW1 ...**153** C4
Norman Butler Ho 10
W10 ....**91** A3
Normanby CI SW15 ..**157** B6
Normanby Rd NW10 ..**67** D4
Norman CI BR6 ....**227** A5
Tottenham N22 ....**33** A2

Norman Cres
Heston TW5 ......**128** D5
Pinner HA5 ......**22** C2
Norman Ct N4 ....**50** C2
NW10 ....**68** A1
Dulwich SE22 .....**162** A4
7 Hampton TW12 ..**173** C2
Ilford IG2 ....**57** B2
West Norwood SW16 .**182** C5
Woodford IG8 .....**37** B5
Normand Mews W14 ..**264** B6
Normand Park Prim Sch
W14 ......**135** B6 **264** D6
Normand Rd
W14 ......**135** B6 **264** D6
Normandy Ave EN5 ..**1** B1
Normandy CI SE26 ..**163** A4
Normandy Dr UB3 ..**83** A1
Normandy Ho 4 NW4 **28** D1
Normandy Rd SW9 ..**138** C2
Normandy Terr E16 ..**99** B1
Norman Gr E3 ....**97** A5
Norman Ho 6 E11 ..**76** C6
SW8 ....**270** A4
Feltham TW13 ....**151** B2
Lower Halliford TW17 .**192** C2
Normanhurst TW15 ..**170** C5
Normanhurst Ave
DA16 ....**146** D4
Normanhurst Dr
TW1 ....**153** B6
Normanhurst Rd BR5 .**190** B1
Streatham SW2 ....**160** B2
Walton-on-T KT12 ..**194** D1
Normanhurst Sch E4 .**20** B4
Norman Par DA14 ..**168** C2
Norman Rd E11 ...**76** C6
E6 ....**100** B3
N15 ....**51** D4
SE10 ....**141** D5
Ashford TW15 ....**171** B4
Ilford IG1 ....**78** D3
Merton SW19 .....**180** A3
Sutton SM1 ......**217** C3
Thornton Heath CR7 ..**204** D4
Normans CI NW10 ..**67** B2
Hillingdon UB8 ....**82** A2
Normansfield Ave
KT1,KT8 ....**175** C3
Normanshire Dr E4 ..**35** D6
Normans Mead NW10 **67** B2
Norman St EC1 **95** A4 **235** B1
Normanton Ave
SW18,SW19 ....**157** C2
Normanton Ct CR2 ..**221** C3
Normanton Ho 6
SW4 ....**159** C5
Normanton Pk E4 ...**20** C4
Normanton Rd CR2 ..**221** C2
Normanton St SE23 .**162** C2
Norman Way Acton W3 **88** D1
Palmers Green N14 ..**16** A2
Normington CI SW16 **182** C5
Norrice Lea N2 ....**48** B4
Norris 11 NW9 ....**27** D2
Norris Ho 22 E9 ...**96** C6
12 N1 ....**95** C6
Norris St SW1 .....**249** C5
Norroy Rd SW15 ...**134** D1
Norrys CI EN4 ....**2** D1
Norrys Rd EN4 ....**2** D1
Norse Ho 13 SE5 ...**139** A3
Norseman CI 3 IG3 ..**58** D1
Norseman Way UB6 ..**85** D6
Norstead PI SW15 ..**156** A2
North Access Rd E17 .**52** D3
North Acre NW9 ...**27** C6
North Acton Rd NW10 **89** B4
North Acton Sta W3 ..**89** B2
Northampton Gr N1 ..**73** B3
Northampton Pk N1 ..**73** B3
Northampton Rd
EC1 ....**94** C3 **241** B3
Croydon CR0 .....**222** A6
Enfield EN3 ......**7** D1
Northampton Sq
EC1 ....**94** D4 **234** C1
Northampton St N1 ..**73** A1
Northanger Rd SW16 **182** A4
North Audley St
W1 ....**115** A6 **248** A6
North Ave Ealing W13 .**87** B2
Edmonton N18 ....**34** A4
Harrow HA2 ......**41** D3
Hayes UB3 ......**106** A4
8 Richmond TW9 ..**132** C4
Southall UB1 .....**107** A6
Wallington SM5 ...**219** A1
Northaw Ho W10 ...**90** C3

North Bank
NW8 . . . . .92 C4 **230 A1**
Northbank Rd E17 . . .36 A1
North Beckton Prim Sch
E6 . . . . .100 B2
North Birkbeck Rd
E11 . . . . .76 B5
North Block **18** E1 . .118 C6
Northborough Rd
SW16 . . . . .182 A1
Northbourne BR2 . .209 A4
Northbourne Ho **21** E5 74 B5
N14 . . . . .15 D4
Northbourne Rd
SW4 . . . . .159 D6
North Branch Ave
NW10 . . . . .90 C4
Northbrook CE Sch
SE12 . . . . .164 D6
Northbrook Rd SE13 .164 C6
Barnet EN5 . . . . .13 A5
Ilford IG1 . . . . .78 C6
Thornton Heath CR0 . .205 B4
Wood Green N22 . . . .32 A3
Northburgh St
EC1 . . . . .94 D3 **241 D6**
Northbury Jun & Inf Sch
IG11 . . . . .79 A2
North Carriage Dr
W2 . . . . .114 C6 **247 B6**
Northchurch SE17 . .262 D2
North Church Ho **19**
E2 . . . . .96 A4
Northchurch Rd N1 . .73 B1
Wembley HA9 . . . . . .66 C2
Northchurch Terr N1 .73 C1
North Circular Rd N2 .30 B2
N3,NW2,NW4 . . . . . .47 A4
NW10 . . . . .67 C3
NW2 . . . . .67 C3
Chingford, Highams Park
E17 . . . . .35 D2
Edmonton N13 . . . . .32 C5
Ilford IG1,E12 . . . . . .78 C4
Woodford E18 . . . . . .37 C1
North Cl DA6 . . . . .146 D1
Barnet EN5 . . . . .12 C6
Dagenham RM10 . . .103 C6
East Bedfont TW14 . . .149 B5
Merton SM4 . . . . . . .201 A5
Northcliffe Cl KT4 . .215 C5
Northcliffe Dr N20 . .13 B3
North Colonnade
E14 . . . . .119 C5
North Common Rd
Ealing W5 . . . . .110 A6
Uxbridge UB10 . . . . .60 A3
Northcote **1** HA5 . .22 C1
Northcote Ave
Ealing W5 . . . . .110 A6
Isleworth TW7 . . . . .153 A6
Southall UB1 . . . . . .107 A6
Tolworth KT5 . . . . . .198 D2
Northcote Ho UB4 . . .84 D2
Northcote Lodge Sch
SW11 . . . . .158 B3
Northcote Rd E17 . . .53 A5
NW10 . . . . .67 C1
SW11 . . . . .158 D6
Isleworth TW7 . . . . .153 A6
Kingston KT3 . . . . . .199 B6
Sidcup DA14 . . . . . .189 C6
Thornton Heath CR0 . .205 B3
Northcott Ave N22 . .32 A2
North Countess Rd
E17 . . . . .35 B2
Northcourt W1 . . . . .239 B4
North Cray Prim Sch
DA14 . . . . .191 A4
North Cray Rd DA14 .191 A5
North Cres E16 . . . . .98 B3
N3 . . . . .29 B1
WC1 . . . . .239 C4
Northcroft Ct **8**
W12 . . . . .112 A4
Northcroft Rd W13 . .109 B3
West Ewell KT19 . . .215 C1
North Crofts SE21 . .162 B3
North Cross Rd SE22 162 A6
Ilford IG6 . . . . .57 A5
North Ct SW1 . . . . . .260 A6
North Dene NW7 . . . .11 B1
Hounslow TW5 . . . .129 D4
Northdene Gdns N15 .51 D3
Northdown Cl HA4 . . .61 C6
Northdown Gdns IG2 .57 C4
Northdown Rd DA16 .146 C3
Northdown St
N1 . . . . .94 B5 **233 C3**
North Dr BR6 . . . . . .227 C4

North Dr continued
Beckenham BR3 . . . .207 D5
Hounslow TW3,TW7 . .130 A3
Ruislip HA4 . . . . .39 C2
Streatham SW16 . . . .181 C6
North Dulwich Sta
SE21 . . . . .161 B6
North Ealing Prim Sch
W5 . . . . .87 B3
North Ealing Sta W3 .88 B1
North End NW3 . . . . .70 A6
Buckhurst Hill IG9 . . .21 C4
Croydon CR0 . . . . . .221 A6
North End Ave NW3 . .70 A6
North End Cres
W14 . . . . . . .113 B2 **254 C3**
North End Ho
W14 . . . . . . .113 A2 **254 B3**
North End La BR6 . . .226 D1
North End Par W14 . .254 B3
North End Rd NW11 . .47 D1
W14 . . . . . . .113 B1 **254 D1**
Wembley HA9 . . . . . .66 D5
North End Way NW3 . .70 A6
Northern Ave N9 . . . .17 D2
Northernhay Wlk
SM4 . . . . .201 A5
Northern Hts N8 . . . .49 D2
Northern Perimeter Rd
TW6 . . . . .127 C4
Northern Perimeter Road
(W) TW6 . . . . .126 B4
Northern Rd E13 . . . .99 B5
Northern Relief Rd
IG11 . . . . .79 A2
Northesk Ho **6** E1 . .96 B3
North Eyot Gdns **5**
W6 . . . . .111 D1
Northey St E14 . . . . .119 A6
North Farm IG10 . . . .21 C5
North Feltham Trad Est
TW14 . . . . .128 B1
Northfield IG10 . . . . .21 D6
Northfield Ave
W13,W5 . . . . .109 B4
Pinner HA5 . . . . .40 D5
Northfield Cl BR1 . . .188 A2
Hayes UB3 . . . . .105 D3
Northfield Cres SM3 .217 A4
Northfield Gdns RM9 .81 B4
Northfield Hall N6 . . .49 A2
Northfield Ho **3**
SE15 . . . . .140 A6
Northfield Ind Est HA0 88 C6
Northfield Par UB3 . .105 D3
Northfield Path RM9 . .81 B4
Northfield Pk UB3 . . .105 D3
Northfield Rd E6 . . . .78 B1
N16 . . . . .51 C2
W13 . . . . .109 B4
Cockfosters EN4 . . . . .2 C1
Dagenham RM9 . . . . .81 B4
Enfield EN3 . . . . .18 B6
Heston TW5 . . . . . . .128 D5
Northfields SW18 . . .135 C1
Northfields Prospect
SW18 . . . . .135 C1
Northfields Rd W3 . . .89 A2
Northfields Sta W3 . .109 C3
Northfleet Ho SE1 . . .252 C2
North Flower Wlk
W2 . . . . .114 **246 C5**
North Gate
NW8 . . . . .92 C5 **230 A3**
Northgate Bsns Ctr EN1 6 B1
Northgate Ct **15** SW9 138 C2
Northgate Dr NW9 . . .45 C3
North Gates N12 . . . .30 A2
North Gdns SW19 . . .180 B3
North Glade DA5 . . .169 B3
North Gn NW9 . . . . . .27 D6
North Gower St
NW1 . . . . .93 C4 **232 B1**
North Gr N15 . . . . . . .51 B4
N6 . . . . .49 A2
North Greenwich Sta
SE10 . . . . .120 C4
North Haringay Jun & Inf
Sch N8 . . . . .50 C5
North Harrow Sta HA2 41 D4
North Hill N6 . . . . . . .49 A3
North Hill Ave N6 . . .48 D3
North Hill Ct N6 . . . .49 A2
North Ho **8** SE8 . . . .119 B1
North Hyde Gdns
UB3 . . . . .106 A2
North Hyde La UB2 . .107 A1
North Hyde Rd UB3 . .105 D3
Northiam N12 . . . . . .29 C6
WC1 . . . . .233 B1

Northiam St E9 . . . . . .96 B6
Northington St
WC1 . . . . .94 B3 **240 D5**
North La TW11 . . . . .174 D4
Northlands Ave BR6 .227 C4
Northlands St SE5 . .139 A3
Northleigh Ho **36** E3 .97 D4
New Barnet EN5 . . . .14 A6
North Lo N22 . . . . . . .31 D1
North Lodge Cl
SW15 . . . . .156 D6
North London Boys Sch
N16 . . . . .52 A1
North London Collegiate
Sch HA7,HA8 . . . . . .26 A5
North London Collegiate
Sch The HA7,HA8 . . .26 A5
North London Nuffield
Hosp EN2 . . . . .4 C3
North Mall The N9 . . .18 B2
North Mews
WC1 . . . . .94 B3 **240 D5**
North Middlesex Hospl
N18 . . . . .33 C5
Northmoor **4** SE23 .162 D1
North Mount N20 . . . .14 A2
Northolm HA8 . . . . . .27 B6
Northolme Gdns HA8 .26 C2
Northolme Rd N5 . . . .73 A4
Northolme Rise BR6 .227 C6
Northolt N17 . . . . . . .33 C1
Northolt Ave HA4 . . . .62 B3
Northolt Gdns UB6 . . .64 D3
Northolt High Sch
UB5 . . . . .63 B2
Northolt Park Inf Sch
UB5 . . . . .63 D3
Northolt Park Sta HA2 63 D4
Northolt Prim Sch
UB5 . . . . .63 A1
Northolt Rd
Harmondsworth TW6 .126 A4
Harrow HA2 . . . . .64 A5
Northolt Sta UB5 . . . .63 C2
Northover BR1 . . . . .164 D1
North Par
Chessington KT9 . . . .214 B3
Edgware HA8 . . . . . .26 C1
Southall UB1 . . . . . . .85 C1
North Pas SW18 . . . .157 C6
North Pk SE9 . . . . . .166 C5
North Pl
Mitcham SW19 . . . . .180 D3
Teddington TW11 . . .174 D4
Northpoint BR1 . . . . .187 A2
North Point UB7 . . . .104 A5
North Pole La BR2 . .225 A2
North Pole Rd W10 . . .90 C2
Northport St N1 . . . . .235 D5
North Prim Sch UB1 .107 B6
North Rd BR1 . . . . . .187 B2
N2 . . . . .30 C2
N6 . . . . .49 A2
N7 . . . . .72 A4
SE18 . . . . .123 C2
W5 . . . . .109 D3
Brentford TW8 . . . . .132 A6
Dagenham RM6 . . . . .59 A4
East Bedfont TW14 . . .149 B5
Edgware HA8 . . . . . .26 D2
Edmonton N9 . . . . . .18 B3
Erith DA17 . . . . .125 D4
Hayes UB3 . . . . .83 B2
Heston TW5 . . . . . . .128 C6
Ilford IG3 . . . . .79 C6
Richmond TW9 . . . . .132 C3
Southall UB1 . . . . . .107 C6
Surbiton KT6 . . . . . .197 D3
West Drayton UB7 . . .104 B3
Wimbledon SW19 . . .180 A4
1 West Wickham BR4 207 D1
North Residence IG3 .58 B4
North Ride
W2 . . . . .114 C6 **247 A5**
North Rise W2 . . . . .237 B1
Northrop Rd TW6 . . .127 C4
North Row
W1 . . . . .115 A6 **248 A6**
North Sheen Sta
TW10 . . . . .132 C1
Northside Prim Sch
N12 . . . . .30 A5
Northside Rd BR1 . . .187 A2
North Side Wandsworth
Comm SW18 . . . . . .158 B6
Northspur Rd SM1 . .217 C5
North Sq NW11 . . . . .47 D4
Edmonton N9 . . . . . .18 B2
North St BR1 . . . . . .187 A2
DA7 . . . . .147 C1

North St continued
E13 . . . . .99 B5
E17 . . . . .46 C4
SW4 . . . . .137 C2
Barking IG11 . . . . . . .79 A1
Carshalton SM5 . . . .218 D4
Isleworth TW7 . . . . .131 A2
Northstead Rd SW2 .160 A2
North Tenter St E1 . .243 D1
North Terr SW3 . . . . .257 A5
Northumberland Alley
EC3 . . . . .243 B1
Northumberland Ave
DA16 . . . . .145 C2
WC2 . . . . .116 A5 **250 A4**
Enfield EN1 . . . . .6 B4
Hounslow TW7 . . . . .130 A4
Wanstead E12 . . . . . .55 C1
Northumberland Cl
TW19 . . . . .148 A5
Northumberland Cres
TW14 . . . . .149 C5
Northumberland Ct
3 Hounslow TW3 . . .129 D1
South Croydon CR2 . .221 C3
Northumberland Gdns
BR1 . . . . .210 C5
Brentford TW7 . . . . .131 A2
Edmonton N9 . . . . . .17 D1
Mitcham CR4 . . . . . .203 D4
Northumberland Gr
N17 . . . . .34 B3
Northumberland Heath
Prim Sch DA8 . . . . .147 D5
Northumberland Ho
NW5 . . . . .71 C2
Northumberland Mans
E5 . . . . .74 C4
Northumberland Park Com
Sch N17 . . . . .34 A3
Northumberland Park Ind
Est N17 . . . . .34 B3
Northumberland Park
Sports Ctr N17 . . . . .34 A3
Northumberland Park Sta
N17 . . . . .34 B3
Northumberland Pk
DA8 . . . . .147 D5
Tottenham N17 . . . . .34 A3
Northumberland Pl
W2 . . . . .91 C1
26 Richmond TW10 . . .153 D6
Northumberland Rd
E17 . . . . .53 C2
E6 . . . . .100 A1
Harrow HA2 . . . . .41 C4
New Barnet EN5 . . . .14 A4
Northumberland St
WC2 . . . . .250 A4
Northumbria St E14 . .97 C1
North Verbena Gdns
W6 . . . . .112 A1
Northview **1** N7 . . .72 A5
North View Ealing W5 .87 C3
Pinner HA5 . . . . .40 C2
Wimbledon SW19 . . .178 C5
Northview Cres NW10 67 D4
Northview Dr IG8 . . . .37 D1
Northview Prim Sch
NW10 . . . . .67 D3
North View Rd N8 . . .49 D6
North Villas NW1 . . . .71 D2
Northway NW11 . . . . .47 D4
North Way N11 . . . . . .31 C4
N9 . . . . .18 D2
NW9 . . . . .44 D6
Northway Merton SM4 201 A5
Wallington SM6 . . . .219 C4
North Way Pinner HA5 .40 D5
Uxbridge UB10 . . . . .60 A1
Northway Cir NW7 . . .27 B6
Northway Cres NW7 . .27 C6
Northway Ct NW11 . . .47 D4
NW7 . . . . .27 B6
Northway Rd SE5 . . .139 A2
Croydon CR0 . . . . . .205 D2
Northway Sch NW7 . .11 D1
Northways Par **2**
NW3 . . . . .70 B1
Northweald La KT2 . .175 D5
North Wembley Sta
HA0,HA9 . . . . .65 D5
North Western Ave
(Watford By-Pass)
WD6 . . . . .9 B5
North Westminster Com
Sch
W2 . . . . .92 B2 **236 D6**
W9 . . . . .91 C3
Northwest Pl N1 . . . .234 B4

North Wharf Rd
W2 . . . . .92 B2 **236 C3**
Northwick Ave HA3 . .43 B3
Northwick Circ HA3 . .43 C3
Northwick Cl
NW8 . . . . .92 B3 **236 C6**
Harrow HA1 . . . . .65 B6
Northwick Ho NW8 . .236 B6
Northwick Park Hospl
HA1 . . . . .43 A2
Northwick Park Rd
HA1 . . . . .42 D3
Northwick Park Sta
HA3 . . . . .43 B2
Northwick Rd
South Oxhey WD19 . . .22 C6
Wembley HA0 . . . . . .87 D6
Northwick Terr
NW8 . . . . .92 B3 **236 C6**
North Wlk
W2 . . . . .114 A6 **246 A5**
New Addington CR0 . .224 A3
Northwold Dr HA5 . . .40 C4
Northwold Prim Sch
E5 . . . . .74 A4
Northwold Rd E5,N16 .74 C5
Northwood Comp Sch
HA6 . . . . .22 B2
Northwood Gdns N12 .30 B5
Greenford UB6 . . . . . .64 D3
Ilford IG5 . . . . .56 C5
Northwood Hills Cir
HA6 . . . . .22 A2
Northwood Hills Sta
HA6 . . . . .22 A1
North Wood Lo NW3 . .69 D4
Northwood & Pinner Com
Hospl HA6 . . . . .22 A2
Northwood Pl DA18 . .125 B3
Northwood Prim Sch
DA18 . . . . .125 B3
Northwood Rd N6 . . .49 B2
Forest Hill SE23 . . . .163 D3
South Norwood CR7 .183 A1
Wallington SM5 . . . .219 A2
Northwood Twr **1**
E17 . . . . .54 A5
Northwood Way
Northwood HA6 . . . . .22 A3
1 West Norwood
SE19 . . . . .183 C4
North Woolwich Rd
E16 . . . . .121 B5
North Woolwich Rdbt
E16 . . . . .121 D5
North Woolwich Sta
E16 . . . . .122 C4
North Worple Way
SW14 . . . . .133 B2
Norton Ave KT5 . . . .198 D2
Norton Cl Chingford E4 .35 C5
Enfield EN1 . . . . .6 B3
Norton Ct
Beckenham BR3 . . . .185 B2
Ilford IG2 . . . . .57 B3
Norton Folgate E1 . . .243 B4
Norton Gdns SW16 . .182 A1
Norton Ho **33** E1 . . .96 B1
14 E2 . . . . .96 C5
16 SW9 . . . . .138 B3
5 New Malden KT3 . .199 C5
Norton Rd E10 . . . . . .53 B1
Wembley HA0 . . . . . .65 D2
Norval Gn **1** SW9 . .138 C3
Norval Rd HA0 . . . . . .43 B1
Norvic Ho **5** SE5 . . .139 A3
Norway Gate SE16 . .119 A3
Norway Pl E14 . . . . . .97 B1
Norway St SE10 . . . .141 D6
Norwegian Sch
SW19 . . . . .178 C3
Norwich Ho **6** E14 . .97 C1
Norwich Mews IG3 . . .58 A1
Norwich Pl **7** DA6 . .147 C1
Norwich Rd E7 . . . . . .77 C3
Greenford UB6 . . . . . .85 D6
Northwood HA6 . . . . .39 C6
South Norwood CR7 .205 A6
Norwich St
EC4 . . . . .94 C1 **241 A4**
Norwich Wlk HA8 . . . .27 A3
Norwood Ave HA0 . . .88 B5
Norwood Cl
Southall UB2 . . . . . .107 C2
Twickenham TW2 . . .152 B2
Norwood Dr HA2 . . . .41 C3
Norwood Gdns
Hayes UB4 . . . . .84 C1
Southall UB2 . . . . . .107 B2

Norwood Green Inf Sch
UB2 . . . . .107 B1
Norwood Green Jun Sch
UB2 . . . . .107 A1
Norwood Green Rd
UB2 . . . . .107 C2
Norwood Heights Sh Ctr **13**
SE19 . . . . .183 C4
Norwood High St
SE27 . . . . .183 A5
Norwood Ho **22** E14 .119 D6
Norwood Hospl SE19 183 B4
Norwood Junction Sta
SE25 . . . . .206 A5
Norwood Park Rd
SE27 . . . . .183 A5
Norwood Rd
Southall UB2 . . . . . .107 C2
West Norwood SE24,
SE27 . . . . .160 D3
Norwood Terr UB2 . .107 D2
Notley St SE5 . . . . . .139 B5
Notre Dame RC Girls Sch
SE1 . . . . .116 D3 **261 D5**
Notson Rd SE25 . . . .206 B5
Notting Barn Rd W10 .90 C1
Nottingdale Sq W11 .244 A4
Nottingham Ave E16 .99 C1
Nottingham Ct WC2 .240 A1
Nottingham Ho N4 . . .51 A2
34 SE5 . . . . .139 A3
Nottingham Pl
W1 . . . . .93 A2 **238 A4**
Nottingham Rd E10 . .54 A2
Croydon CR2 . . . . . .221 A3
Isleworth TW7 . . . . .130 D3
Upper Tooting SW17 .158 D3
Nottingham St W1 . . .238 A4
Nottingham Terr
NW1 . . . . .238 A5
Notting Hill & Ealing High
Sch W13 . . . . .87 B2
Notting Hill Gate
W11 . . . . .113 C5 **245 A4**
Notting Hill Gate Sta
W11 . . . . .113 C5 **245 A4**
Nottingwood Ho
W11 . . . . .244 A6
Nova Bldg **21** E14 . .119 C2
Nova Mews SM4 . . . .201 A2
Novar Cl BR6 . . . . . .211 D2
Nova Rd CR0 . . . . . .205 A2
Novar Rd SE9 . . . . . .167 A3
Novello St
SW6 . . . . .135 C4 **265 A2**
Nowell Rd SW13 . . . .134 A6
Nower Ct HA5 . . . . . .41 B5
Nower Hill HA5 . . . . .41 B5
Nower Hill High Sch
HA5 . . . . .41 C5
Noyna Rd SW17 . . . .158 D1
Nubia Way SE6 . . . . .164 C1
Nuding Cl SE13 . . . . .141 C2
Nuffield Ct TW5 . . . .129 B5
Nuffield Lo **14** W9 . . .91 C2
Nugent Ct SW16 . . . .181 C6
Nugent Rd N19 . . . . .50 A1
South Norwood SE25 .205 D6
Nugents Ct HA5 . . . . .23 A2
Nugent's Pk HA5 . . . .23 B2
Nugent Terr
NW8 . . . . .92 A5 **229 B3**
Numa Ct TW8 . . . . . .131 D5
Nun Ct EC2 . . . . .242 C2
Nuneaton Rd RM9 . . .81 A1
Nuneham SW16 . . . .181 C6
Nunhead Cres SE15 .140 B2
Nunhead Gr SE15 . . .140 C2
Nunhead La SE15 . . .140 B2
Nunhead Sta SE15 . .140 C3
Nunnington Cl SE9 . .166 A1
Nunn's Rd EN2 . . . . . .5 A3
Nupton Dr EN5 . . . . .12 C5
Nurse Cl HA8 . . . . . . .27 A2
Nursery Ave DA7 . . . .147 B2
N3 . . . . .30 A1
Croydon CR0 . . . . . .222 D6
Nursery Cl BR6 . . . . .211 D2
SE4 . . . . .141 B3
Croydon CR0 . . . . . .222 D6
Dagenham RM6 . . . . .58 D2
Enfield EN3 . . . . .6 D1
Feltham TW14 . . . . .150 B4
Putney SW15 . . . . . .134 D1
Woodford IG8 . . . . . .37 B5
Nursery Ct Ealing W13 .87 A2
7 Tottenham N17 . . .33 D3

Nursery Gdns BR7 ...**188** D4
 Enfield EN3 ....**6** D4
 Hampton TW13 ....**173** B6
 Hounslow TW4 ....**151** B6
 Sunbury TW16 .....**171** D1
Nursery La E2 ....**95** D6
 E7 ....**77** A2
 W10 ....**90** C2
Nurserymans Rd N11 .**15** A2
Nursery Rd E9 ....**74** C2
 N14 ....**15** C4
 N2 ....**30** B2
 SW9 ....**138** B1
 Loughton IG10 ......**21** C6
 Merton SW19 ......**179** D1
 Mitcham CR4 ......**202** C6
 Pinner HA5 ....**40** C6
 South Norwood CR7 ..**205** B5
 Sunbury TW16 .....**171** D1
 Sutton SM1 ....**218** A4
 Wimbledon SW19 ...**179** A3
Nursery Row SE17 ..**262** C3
Nursery St N17 ......**33** D3
Nursery Walk Ct NW4 .**46** B6
Nursery Wlk NW4 ....**46** B6
Nurstead Rd DA8 ...**147** C5
Nutborn Ho SW19 ..**178** D4
Nutbourne St W10 ...**91** A4
Nutbrook St SE15 ...**140** A4
Nutbrowne Rd RM9 ..**103** B6
Nutcroft Rd SE15 ..**140** B5
Nutfield Cl
 Carshalton SM5 ....**218** C5
 Edmonton N18 ......**34** A4
Nutfield Gdns
 Ilford IG3 ....**80** A6
 Northolt UB5 ....**84** C5
Nutfield Rd E15 .....**76** A4
 NW2 ....**68** A5
 SE22 ....**139** D1
 Thornton Heath CR7 ..**204** D5
Nutfield Way BR6 ...**226** D6
Nutford Pl W1 **92** D1 **237** C2
Nuthatch Cl TW19 ..**148** B3
Nuthatch Gdns SE28 .**123** B4
Nuthurst Ave SW2 ..**160** B2
Nutkin Wlk UB8 .....**60** A1
Nutley Terr NW3 .....**70** B2
Nutmeg Cl E16 ......**98** C3
Nutmeg La E14 ......**98** B1
Nuttall St N1 ....**95** C5
Nutter La E11 ....**55** C4
Nutt Gr HA8 ....**9** D2
Nutt St SE15 ....**139** D5
Nutty La TW17 ......**193** A6
Nutwell St SW17 ...**180** C5
Nuxley Rd DA17 ....**125** C1
NW London Jewish Day
 Sch NW6 ....**69** A1
Nyanza St SE18 .....**145** B6
Nye Bevan Est E5 ...**74** D5
Nye Bevan Ho NW6 .**264** C4
Nye's Wharf SE15 ...**140** A6
Nylands Ave TW9 ...**132** C3
Nymans Gdns SW20 .**200** B6
Nynehead St SE14 ..**141** A5
Nyon Gr SE6 ....**163** B2
Nyton Cl N19 ....**50** A1

O

Oak Apple Ct SE12 ..**165** A3
Oak Ave N10 ....**31** B3
 N8 ....**50** A5
 Croydon CR0 ....**223** D6
 Enfield EN2 ....**4** B5
 Hampton TW12,TW13 .**173** A4
 Heston TW5 ....**129** A5
 Tottenham N17 .....**33** C3
 Uxbridge UB10 .....**60** D6
 West Drayton UB7 ..**104** C3
Oak Bank CR0 ......**224** A2
Oakbank KT12 .....**195** B2
Oakbank Gr SE24 ..**139** A1
Oakbrook BR3 .....**185** D1
Oakbrook Cl BR1 ...**187** B6
Oakbury Rd SW6 ...**155** D3
Oak Cl N14 ....**15** B4
 Sutton SM1 ....**218** A6
Oakcombe Cl KT3 ..**177** C2
Oak Cottage Cl **164** D3
 SE6 ....**164** D3
Oak Cotts W7 ....**108** C4
Oakcourt SE15 .....**139** D5
Oak Cres E16 ....**98** C2
Oakcroft SE12 .....**165** B3

Oakcroft Bsns Ctr
 KT9 ....**214** B4
Oakcroft Cl HA5 .....**22** B1
Oakcroft Ho KT3 ...**199** C2
 Chessington KT9 ...**214** B4
Oakcroft Rd SE13 ..**142** B3
 Chessington KT9 ...**214** B4
Oakcroft Villas KT9 .**214** B4
Oak Ct BR1 ....**188** B1
 Chingford E4 ....**35** D4
Oakdale N14 ....**15** B3
 Beckenham BR3 ...**186** A1
Oakdale Ave
 Harrow HA3 ....**44** A4
 Pinner HA6 ....**22** A1
Oakdale Cl WD19 ....**22** C6
Oakdale Ct N19 .....**72** A6
Oakdale Gdns E4 ....**36** A5
Oakdale Inf Sch E18 .**37** B1
Oakdale Jun Sch E18 .**37** B1
Oakdale Lo NW4 .....**29** A2
Oakdale Rd E11 .....**76** B6
 E7 ....**77** B1
 N4 ....**51** B3
 SE15 ....**140** C2
 South Oxhey WD19 ..**22** C6
 Streatham SW16 ...**182** A5
 Woodford E18 ....**37** B1
Oakdale Way CR4 ..**203** A2
Oakden St SE11 **116** C2 **261** B4
Oak Dene W13 ....**87** B2
Oakdene SE15 .....**140** B4
 West Norwood
 SE19 ....**183** C5
Oakdene Ave BR7 ..**188** C5
 Thames Ditton KT7 .**197** A1
Oakdene Cl HA5 .....**23** B3
Oakdene Dr KT5 ...**199** A1
Oakdene Ho N16 ....**51** C1
 Enfield EN2 ....**4** D2
Oakdene Lo SE20 ..**184** B3
Oakdene Mews SM3 .**201** B1
Oakdene Pk N3 ......**29** B3
Oakdene Rd BR5 ...**211** D4
 Hillingdon UB10 .....**82** D5
Oaken St
 SE11 ....**116** C2 **261** B4
Oake Ct SW15 .....**157** A6
Oakeford Ho W14 ..**254** B5
Oakend Ho N4 ......**51** B2
Oaken Dr KT10 .....**212** D2
Oaken La KT10 .....**212** C3
Oakenholt Ho SE2 **124** D4
Oaken La KT10 .....**212** C3
Oakenshaw Cl KT6 .**198** A2
Oakes Cl E6 ....**100** B1
Oakeshott Ave N6 ..**71** A6
Oakey La SE1 ......**261** A6
Oak Farm WD6 ......**11** A6
Oak Farm Jun & Inf Schs
 UB10 ....**82** D6
Oakfield E4 ....**35** D5
Oakfield Ave HA3 ...**43** B6
Oakfield Cl
 New Malden KT3 ...**199** D4
 Ruislip HA4 ....**39** D3
Oakfield Ct N3 ......**29** D2
 N8 ....**50** A2
 NW2 ....**46** B2
 SW4 ....**160** A5
 South Croydon CR2 .**221** A2
Oakfield Gdns
 Beckenham BR3 ...**207** C4
 Carshalton SM5 ....**202** A1
 Edmonton N18 ......**33** C6
 Greenford UB6 ......**86** B4
 West Norwood
 SE19 ....**183** C5
Oakfield Ho IG1 .....**78** D5
Oakfield La BR2 ....**225** C4
Oakfield Lo IG1 .....**78** D5
Oakfield Prep Sch
 SE21 ....**161** B3
Oakfield Rd E17 .....**35** A1
 E6 ....**100** A6
 N3 ....**29** D2
 N4 ....**50** D2
 Ashford TW15 .....**170** D5
 Croydon CR0 ....**205** A1
 Ilford IG1 ....**78** D5
 Palmers Green N14 ..**16** A2
 Penge SE20 ....**184** B3
 Wimbledon SW19 ...**156** D1
Oakfield St
 SW10 ....**136** A6 **266** A6
Oakford Rd NW5 .....**71** C4
Oak Gdns HA8 ....**27** C4
 Croydon CR0 ....**223** C6
Oak Gr NW2 ....**69** A4
 Ruislip HA4 ....**40** B1

Oak Gr continued
 Sunbury TW16 .....**172** B3
 West Wickham BR4 .**208** A1
Oak Grove Rd SE20 .**184** C1
Oakhall Ct
 Ashford TW16 .....**171** D5
Oakhall Dr TW16 ...**171** D5
Oakham Cl SE6 ....**163** B2
Oakham Dr BR2 ....**208** D5
Oakham Ho W10 .....**90** C2
Oakhampton Rd NW7 .**28** D3
Oak Hill Chingford IG8 .**36** C3
 Surbiton KT6 ......**198** A2
Oakhill Ave NW3 .....**69** D4
 Pinner HA5 ....**23** A1
Oak Hill Cl IG8 ....**36** B3
Oak Hill Coll N14 .....**15** A5
Oak Hill Cres
 Chingford IG8 ....**36** C3
 Surbiton KT6 ......**198** A2
Oakhill Ct SE23 ....**162** C5
 Putney SW15 ......**157** B6
 Surbiton KT6 ....**198** A3
 Wimbledon SW19 ..**178** D3
Oak Hill Ct IG8 ......**36** C3
Oak Hill Gdns E4 ....**36** C2
Oakhill Ho BR5 .....**190** A2
Oak Hill Lo NW3 .....**69** D4
Oak Hill Park Mews
 NW3 ....**70** A4
Oak Hill Pk NW3 .....**69** D4
Oakhill Pl SW15 ....**157** C6
Oakhill Prim Sch IG8 .**36** C4
Oakhill Rd BR6 ....**227** D6
 Beckenham BR3 ...**186** A1
 Putney SW15 ......**157** B6
 Sutton SM1 ....**218** A4
 Thornton Heath SW16 .**182** B2
Oak Hill Rd KT6 ....**198** A3
Oak Hill Way NW3 ...**70** A4
Oak Ho DA15 ......**168** A1
 E14 ....**120** A4
 N16 ....**73** B6
 N2 ....**30** B1
 NW3 ....**70** D2
 Penge SE20 ....**184** B4
 Wood Green N22 ....**32** A3
Oakhouse Rd DA6 ..**169** C6
Oakhurst Ave DA7 ..**147** A5
 East Barnet EN4 ....**14** C4
Oakhurst Cl BR7 ...**188** B2
 E17 ....**54** C5
 Teddington TW11 .**174** C5
Oakhurst Ct E17 .....**54** C5
Oakhurst Gdns DA7 .**147** A5
 E11,E17 ....**54** C5
 Chingford E4 ....**20** D3
Oakhurst Gr SE22 ..**140** A1
Oakhurst Rd KT19 ..**215** B2
Oakington KT1 .....**176** C1
Oakington Ave
 Harrow HA2 ....**41** C2
 Hayes UB3 ....**105** B2
 Wembley HA9 ......**66** B5
Oakington Dr TW16 .**172** C1
Oakington Manor Dr
 HA9 ....**66** C3
Oakington Manor Prim
 Sch HA9 ....**66** D3
Oakington Rd W9 ....**91** C3
Oakington Way N8 ...**50** A2
Oak La E14 ....**119** B6
 N11 ....**31** D4
 N2 ....**30** B1
 Isleworth TW7 .....**130** C1
 Twickenham TW1 ..**153** A4
 Woodford IG8 ......**36** D6
Oakland Pl IG9 ......**21** A2
Oakland Rd E15 .....**76** C4
Oaklands BR7 .....**189** B4
 Croydon CR0 ....**220** D3
 Ealing W13 ....**87** A4
 Southgate N21 .....**16** B2
Oaklands Ave DA15 .**167** D4
 Enfield N9 ....**18** B5
 Hounslow TW7 ....**130** D6
 Thames Ditton KT10 .**196** B1
 Thornton Heath CR7 .**204** C5
 West Wickham BR4 .**223** D5
Oaklands Cl BR5 ...**211** C3
 Chessington KT9 ...**213** D4
 Wembley HA0 ......**65** D3
Oaklands Ct NW10 ..**89** C6
 Wembley HA0 ....**65** D3
Oaklands Dr TW2 ..**152** A4

Oaklands Gr W12 ..**112** A5
Oaklands Ho SE4 ..**141** B2
Oaklands Mews NW2 .**68** D4
Oaklands Park Ave
 IG1 ....**79** A6
Oaklands Pas NW2 ..**68** D4
Oaklands Pl SW4 ..**137** D1
Oaklands Prim Sch
 W7 ....**108** D4
Oaklands Rd DA6 ..**169** B6
 NW2 ....**68** D4
 W7,W13 ....**109** A4
 Barnet N20 ....**13** B4
 Bromley BR1 ......**186** C3
 Ealing W7 ....**108** D4
 Mortlake SW14 ...**133** B2
Oaklands Sch
 Hounslow TW3 ....**130** B2
 Loughton IG10 .....**21** C6
Oaklands Sec Sch E2 .**96** B4
Oaklands Way SM6 .**219** D1
Oakland Way KT19 .**215** C2
Oakleafe Gdns IG6 ..**56** D6
Oaklea Pas KT1 ....**197** D6
Oakleigh Ave N20 ...**14** C3
 Edgware HA8 ....**26** D2
 Tolworth KT6 ......**214** D6
Oakleigh Cl N20 .....**14** D1
Oakleigh Cres N20 ..**14** C1
Oakleigh Ct HA8 ....**27** A1
 East Barnet EN4 ....**14** C5
 Penge SE20 ....**184** B3
 Southall UB1 ......**107** B5
 Surbiton KT6 ......**214** B6
Oakleigh Gdns BR6 .**227** C4
 N20 ....**14** B3
 Edgware HA8 ....**26** B5
Oakleigh Lo IG3 .....**80** A5
Oakleigh Mews N20 .**14** A2
Oakleigh Park Ave
 BR7 ....**188** C2
Oakleigh Park Sta
 EN4 ....**14** C4
Oakleigh Pk N N20 ..**14** B3
Oakleigh Pk S N20 ..**14** C3
Oakleigh Rd
 Hillingdon UB10 .....**61** A1
 Pinner HA5 ....**23** B4
Oakleigh Rd N N20 ..**14** C2
Oakleigh Rd S N11 ..**31** A6
Oakleigh Sch N20 ...**14** D1
Oakleigh Way
 Mitcham CR4 ......**181** B2
 Tolworth KT6 ....**198** D1
Oakley Ave
 Barking IG11 ....**79** D1
 Ealing W5 ....**110** C6
 Wallington CR0 ....**220** A4
Oakley Cl E6 ....**100** A1
 Chingford E4 ....**20** C1
 Ealing W7 ....**108** C6
 Hounslow TW7 ....**130** B4
Oakley Cres EC1 ...**234** D3
Oakley Ct CR4 .....**203** A2
 SE13 ....**164** B5
 Keston Mark BR2 ..**226** A5
Oakley Dr DA15 ....**167** B3
 SE13 ....**164** B5
 Keston Mark BR2 ..**226** A6
Oakley Gdns N8 .....**50** B4
 SW3 ....**136** C6 **267** B6
Oakley Ho SW1 ....**257** D4
 Ealing W5 ....**110** C6
Oakley Pk DA5,DA15 .**168** C4
Oakley Pl
 SE1 ....**117** D1 **263** C1
Oakley Rd N1 ....**73** B1
 Croydon SE25 .....**206** A4
 Harrow HA1 ....**42** C3
 Keston Mark BR2 ..**226** A6
Oakley Sq
 NW1 ....**93** C5 **232** B4
Oakley St
 SW3 ....**136** C6 **267** A6
Oakley Wlk W6 ....**134** D6
Oak Lo
 Ashford TW16 .....**171** D3
 Southgate N21 .....**16** B5
 Wanstead E11 .....**55** A2
Oak Lodge Cl HA7 ...**25** C5
Oak Lodge Dr BR4 ..**207** B5
Oak Lodge Sch N2 ..**48** A5
 Balham SW12 .....**159** A4
Oaklodge Way NW7 ..**27** D4
Oakman Ho SW19 ..**156** D4
Oakmead Ave BR2 ..**209** A3
Oakmead Ct HA7 ....**25** C6
Oakmeade HA5 ......**23** C4
Oakmead Gdns HA8 ..**27** B6
Oakmead Pl CR4 ...**180** C2
Oakmead Rd
 Balham SW12 .....**159** B3

Oakmead Rd continued
 Wallington CR0 ....**203** D3
Oakmere Rd SE2 ...**146** A6
Oakmont Pl BR6 ...**211** B1
Oak Park Gdns SW19 .**156** D3
Oak Park Mews N16 .**73** D5
Oak Rd Ealing W5 ..**109** D6
 Kingston KT3 ......**177** B1
Oakridge Dr N2 .....**48** B6
Oakridge La BR1 ..**186** B5
Oakridge Rd BR1 ..**186** C6
Oak Rise IG9 ....**21** D1
Oak Row CR4 .....**181** C1
Oaks Ave
 Feltham TW13 .....**151** A2
 North Cheam KT4 ..**216** B4
 West Norwood SE19 .**183** C5
Oaksford Ave SE26 .**162** B5
Oaks Gr E4 ....**20** C2
Oakshade Rd BR1 ..**186** B6
Oakshaw Rd SW18 .**157** D4
Oakshott Ct NW1 ..**232** C3
Oaks La Ilford IG2 ...**57** C5
 South Croydon CR0 .**222** C6
Oaks Park High Sch
 IG2 ....**57** C4
Oaks Rd CR0 ......**222** C4
Oaks Sh Ctr The W3 .**111** A5
Oaks The BR2 .....**210** B3
 N12 ....**29** D6
 NW10 ....**68** B1
 NW6 ....**68** B1
 SE18 ....**123** A4
 Chingford IG8 ......**36** B1
 Enfield EN2 ....**4** D1
 Hayes UB4 ....**83** A5
 Long Ditton KT6 ...**213** C5
 Ruislip HA4 ....**39** C2
 Wimbledon SW19 ..**179** A3
Oaks Way
 Surbiton KT6 ......**197** D1
 Wallington SM5 ....**218** D1
Oakthorpe Ct N13 ...**33** A5
Oakthorpe Prim Sch
 N13 ....**33** A5
Oakthorpe Rd N13 ...**32** C5
Oaktree Ave N13 ....**16** C1
Oak Tree Cl Ealing W5 .**87** C1
 Stanmore HA7 .....**25** C3
Oak Tree Ct SW4 ...**160** A6
 Acton W3 ....**110** D6
 Elstree WD6 ....**9** D5
Oak Tree Dell NW9 ..**45** B4
Oak Tree Dr N20 ....**13** D3
Oak Tree Gdns BR1 .**187** B5
Oaktree Gr IG1 .....**79** B3
Oak Tree Ho W9 .....**91** D3
Oak Tree Rd
 NW8 ....**92** C4 **230** A1
Oaktree Sch EN4 ....**15** A5
Oakview Gdns N2 ....**48** B5
Oakview Gr CR0 ...**207** A1
Oakview Lo NW11 ...**47** B2
Oakview Rd SE6 ...**185** D5
Oak Village NW5 ....**71** A4
Oak Way N14 ....**15** B4
 W3 ....**111** C5
Oakway
 Beckenham BR2 ...**186** B4
 West Barnes SW20 .**200** C3
Oak Way Croydon CR0 .**206** D3
 East Bedfont TW14 .**149** C3
Oakway Cl DA5 .....**169** A5
Oakways SE9 ......**166** D5
Oakwell Ho SW8 ...**137** D3
Oak Wlk CR4 ......**203** A1
Oakwood Ave N14 ...**15** D4
 Beckenham BR2,BR3 .**186** A1
 Bromley BR2 ......**209** B6
 Mitcham CR4 ......**180** B1
 Southall UB1 ......**107** C6
Oakwood Cl BR7 ...**188** C6
 Southgate N14 .....**15** C5
Oakwood Cres
 Southgate N21 .....**16** B6
 Wembley UB6 ......**65** B2
Oakwood Ct E6 ....**100** A6
 W14 ....**113** B3 **254** C6
 Beckenham BR3 ...**186** A1
 Chingford E4 ....**20** C4
Oakwood Dr HA8 ....**27** A4
 West Norwood SE19 .**183** C6
Oakwood Gdns
 Ilford IG3 ....**79** D6
 Orpington BR6 ....**227** A6
 Sutton SM1 ....**217** C6
Oakwood La
 W14 ....**113** B3 **254** C6

Oakwood Park Rd
 N14 ....**16** A5
Oakwood Pl CR0 ...**204** C3
Oakwood Rd NW11 ..**47** D4
 Orpington BR6 ....**227** A6
 Pinner HA5 ....**22** B1
 Thornton Heath CR0 .**204** C3
 Wimbledon SW20 ..**178** A2
Oakwood Sta N14 ...**15** C6
Oakwood View N14 ..**15** D4
Oakworth Rd W10 ...**90** D2
Oarsman Pl KT8 ...**196** C5
Oasis The BR1 .....**187** C1
Oast Ct E14 ....**119** B6
Oast Lo W4 ....**133** C5
Oates Cl BR2 ......**208** B6
Oatfield Ho N15 .....**51** C3
Oatfield Rd BR6 ...**211** D1
Oat La EC2 ..**95** A1 **242** B2
Oatland Rise E17 ....**35** A1
Oatlands Ct SW19 **156** D3
Oatlands Dr KT13 ..**193** C1
Oatlands Rd EN3 .....**6** A4
Oatwell Ho SW3 ...**257** B3
Oban Cl E13 ....**99** C3
Oban Ho Barking IG11 **101** B5
 South Bromley E14 ..**98** B1
Oban Rd E13 ....**99** C4
 South Norwood SE25 .**205** B5
Oban St E14 ....**98** B1
Oberon Ho N1 ....**95** C5
Oberon Way TW17 ..**192** A6
Oberstein Rd
 SW11 ....**136** B2
Oborne Cl SE24 ...**160** D6
O'Brian Ho E1 ....**96** D4
Observatory Gdns
 W8 ....**245** B2
Observatory Mews
 E14 ....**120** B2
Observatory Rd
 SW14 ....**133** A1
Occupation La SE18 .**144** D4
 W5 ....**109** D2
Occupation Rd
 SE17 ....**117** A1 **262** A2
 W13 ....**109** B4
Ocean St E1 ....**96** D2
Ocean Wharf E14 ..**119** C4
Ockbrook E1 ....**96** C2
Ockendon Rd N1 ....**73** B2
Ockham Dr BR5 ...**190** A3
Ockley Ct SM1 ....**218** A4
Ockley Ho KT2 ....**176** D4
Ockley Rd
 Streatham SW16 ...**160** A1
 Thornton Heath CR0 .**204** B2
Octagon Arc EC2 ...**243** A3
Octagon The NW3 ...**69** C4
Octavia Cl CR4 ....**202** C4
Octavia Ho W10 .....**91** A3
Octavia Rd TW7 ...**130** D2
Octavia St
 SW11 ....**136** C4 **267** B1
Octavia Way SE28 **124** B6
Octavius St SE8 ...**141** C4
October Ct BR2 ...**208** B6
October Pl NW4 .....**46** D6
Odard Rd KT8 .....**195** C5
Odell Cl IG11 ....**79** D1
Odeon Ct E16 ....**99** A2
 NW10 ....**89** C6
Odeon Par SE9 ....**144** A1
 Wembley UB6 ......**65** B2
Odessa Inf Sch E7 ...**77** A3
Odessa Rd E7 ....**76** D4
 NW10 ....**90** A5
Odessa St SE16 ...**119** B3
Odette Ct N20 ....**14** A1
Odette Duval Ho
 E1 ....**96** C2
Odette Ho SE27 ...**183** B6
Odger St SW11 ....**136** D3
Odhams Wlk WC2 ..**240** C1
Odin Ho SE5 ....**139** A4
O'Donnell Ct WC1 ..**240** B6
O'Driscoll Ho W12 ..**90** B1
Odyssey Bsns Pk HA4 .**62** B3
Offa's Mead E9 ......**75** A4
Offenbach Ho E2 ...**96** D5
Offenham Rd BR7,SE9 **188** B6
Offers Ct KT1 ......**198** B6
Offerton Rd SW4 ..**137** C2
Offham Ho SE17 ...**263** A3
Offham Slope N12 ...**29** B5
Offley Ho E9 ....**74** D2
Offley Pl TW7 .....**130** B3
Offley Rd SW9 ....**138** C5
Offord Cl N17 ....**34** A4
Offord Rd N1 ....**72** B1

Off – Ord 363

Offord St N1 ... 72 B1
Ogden Ho TW13 ... 173 A6
Ogilby St SE18 ... 122 B2
Ogilvie Ho 11 E1 ... 96 D1
Oglander Rd SE15 ... 139 D2
Ogle St W1 ... 93 C2 239 A4
Oglethorpe Rd RM10 ... 81 C5
O'Gorman Ho SW10 ... 266 B4
O'Grady Ho 17 E17 ... 53 D6
Ohio Rd E13 ... 98 D3
Oil Mill La W6 ... 112 A1
Okeburn Rd SW17 ... 181 A5
Okehampton Cl N12 ... 30 B5
Okehampton Cres DA16 ... 146 C4
Okehampton Rd NW10 ... 90 D6
Okeover Manor SW4 ... 137 B1
Olaf Palme Ho TW13 ... 150 B1
Olaf St W11 ... 112 D6
Old Bailey EC4 94 D1 241 D1
Old Barn Cl SM2 ... 217 A1
Old Barrack Yd SW1 ... 248 A1
Old Bellgate Wharf E14 ... 119 C3
Oldberry Rd HA8 ... 27 B4
Old Bethnal Green Rd E2 ... 96 B4
Old Bexley Bsns Pk DA5 ... 169 D4
Old Bexley CE Prim Sch DA5 ... 169 B3
Old Bldgs WC2 ... 241 A2
Old Bond St W1 ... 115 C6 249 A5
Oldborough Rd HA0 ... 65 C5
Old Borrowfield 7 E15 ... 98 C6
Old Brewery Mews NW3 ... 70 B4
Old Bridge Cl UB5 ... 85 C5
Old Bridge St KT1 ... 175 D1
Old Broad St EC2 ... 95 B1 242 D2
Old Bromley Rd BR1 ... 186 B5
Old Brompton Rd SW5,SW7 ... 114 A1 256 B3
Old Burlington St W1 ... 115 C6 249 A5
Oldbury Ct E9 ... 75 A3
Oldbury Pl W1 93 A2 238 B4
Oldbury Rd EN1 ... 6 A3
Old Castle St E1 ... 95 D1 243 D2
Old Cavendish St W1 238 C1
Old Change Ct EC4 ... 242 A1
Old Chapel Pl 2 N10 ... 49 B6
Old Charlton Rd TW17 ... 193 A4
Old Chiswick Yd W4 ... 133 C6
Old Church Ct N11 ... 31 B5
Old Church La NW9 ... 67 B6
Ealing UB6 ... 87 A4
Stanmore HA7 ... 25 C4
Old Church Path KT10 ... 212 A4
Old Church Rd E1 ... 96 D1
Chingford E4 ... 19 C1
Old Church St SW3 ... 256 D1
Old Claygate La KT10 213 A3
Old Clem Sq 12 SE18 144 C6
Old Compton St W1 ... 93 D1 239 C1
Old Cote Dr TW5 ... 129 C6
Old County Hall SE1 ... 250 C2
Old Court Ho W8 ... 245 C1
Old Court (Mus & Liby) HA0 ... 65 C3
Old Court Pl W8 ... 113 D4 245 C1
Old Covent Garden WC2 ... 250 B6
Old Ctyd The BR1 ... 187 B2
Old Dairy Mews
4 NW5 ... 71 B2
5 Balham SW12 ... 159 A3
Old Deer Park Gdns TW9 ... 132 A2
Old Devonshire Rd SW12 ... 159 B4
Old Dock Cl TW9 ... 132 C6
Old Dover Rd SE3 ... 143 B5
Oldegate Ho 1 E6 ... 99 D6
Old Farm Ave N14 ... 15 C4
Sidcup DA15 ... 167 C2
Old Farm Cl TW4 ... 129 B1
Old Farm Ct UB2 ... 107 D2
Old Farm Rd N2 ... 30 B2
Hampton TW12 ... 173 C4
Old Farm Rd E DA15 ... 168 A2
Old Farm Rd W DA15 167 D2
Oldfield Cl BR1 ... 210 B5
Stanmore HA7 ... 25 A5
Oldfield Farm Gdns UB6 ... 86 B6
Oldfield Gr SE16 ... 118 D2
Oldfield Ho 14 W4 ... 111 C1
Streatham SW16 ... 181 B6
Oldfield House Sch TW12 ... 173 B2
Oldfield Mews N6 ... 49 C2
Oldfield Prim Sch UB6 86 B5
Oldfield Rd BR1 ... 210 B5
DA7 ... 147 A3
N16 ... 73 C5
NW10 ... 67 D1
W3,W12 ... 111 D4
Hampton TW12 ... 173 B2
Wimbledon SW19 ... 179 A4
Oldfields Cir UB5 ... 64 A2
Oldfields Rd SM1, SM3 ... 217 C6
Oldfields Trad Est SM1 ... 217 C5
Old Fish St Hill EC4 ... 252 A6
Old Fleet La EC4 ... 241 C2
Old Fold Cl EN5 ... 1 B4
Old Fold La EN5 ... 1 B4
Old Ford Ho CR0 ... 220 A5
Old Ford Prim Sch E3 97 B5
Old Ford Rd E2,E3 ... 96 D5
Old Ford Trad Ctr E3 ... 97 C6
Old Forge Cl HA7 ... 25 A6
Old Forge Cres TW17 ... 192 D3
Old Forge Mews W12 ... 112 B4
Old Forge Rd EN1 ... 5 D5
Old Forge Way DA14 ... 190 B6
Old Gloucester St WC1 ... 94 A2 240 B4
Old Hall Cl HA5 ... 23 A2
Old Hall Dr HA5 ... 23 A2
Oldham Ho 10 SE21 ... 183 C6
Oldham Terr W3 ... 111 A5
Old Hatch Manor HA4 40 A2
Old Hill
Chislehurst BR7 ... 188 C2
Orpington BR6 ... 227 C2
Oldhill St N16 ... 52 A1
Old Homesdale Rd BR2 ... 209 C5
Old Hospital Cl SW12,SW17 ... 158 D3
Old House Cl SW19 ... 179 A5
Old House Gdns 9 TW1 ... 153 C5
Old Howlett's La HA4 ... 39 B3
Olding Ho 6 SW12 ... 159 C4
Old Jamaica Bsns Est 23 SE16 ... 118 A3
Old Jamaica Rd SE16 118 A3
Old James St SE15 ... 140 B2
Old Jewry EC2 95 B1 242 C1
Old Kenton La NW9 ... 44 D4
Old Kent Rd
SE1 ... 117 C1 263 B2
SE1,SE15 ... 140 B6
Old Kingston Rd KT4 215 A5
Old Laundry The 14 SW18 ... 136 B1
Old Lodge Pl 7 TW1 153 B5
Old Lodge Way HA7 ... 25 A5
Old Maidstone Rd BR8,DA14 ... 191 B3
Old Malden La KT4 ... 215 C6
Oldman Ct SE12 ... 165 B2
Old Manor Dr TW7 ... 152 A5
Old Manor Rd UB2 ... 106 D2
Old Manor Way BR7, SE9 ... 188 B5
Old Manor Yd SW5 ... 255 C3
Old Market Sq 11 E2 ... 95 D4
Old Marylebone Rd NW1 ... 92 C2 237 B3
Oldmead Ho 8 RM10 ... 81 D2
Old Mill Ct E18 ... 55 C6
Old Mill Rd SE18 ... 145 B6
Old Mitre Ct EC4 ... 241 B1
Old Montague St E1 ... 96 A2
Old Nichol St E2 ... 95 D3 243 C6
Old North St WC1 ... 240 C4
Old Nursery Pl TW15 170 D5
Old Oak Common La NW10 ... 89 C3
Old Oak La NW10 ... 89 D4
Old Oak Prim Sch W12 ... 89 D1
Old Oak Rd W3 ... 111 D6
Old Orch TW16 ... 172 C1
Old Orchard Cl
Hadley Wood EN4 ... 2 B5
Hillingdon UB8 ... 82 C1
Old Orch The NW3 ... 70 D4
Old Palace La TW9 ... 153 C6
Old Palace Prim Sch E3 ... 97 D4
Old Palace Rd CR0 ... 221 A5
Old Palace Sch of John Whitgift CR9 ... 220 D5
Old Palace Terr 8 TW9 ... 153 D6
Old Palace Yd 2 TW9 ... 153 D6
Old Paradise St SE11 ... 116 B2 260 C4
Old Park Ave SW12 ... 159 A5
Enfield EN2 ... 5 A1
Old Park Gr EN2 ... 5 A1
Old Park Ho N13 ... 32 B6
Old Park La W1 ... 115 B5 248 C3
Old Park Mews TW5 ... 129 B5
Old Park Rd SE2 ... 124 A1
Enfield EN2 ... 4 D2
Palmers Green N13 ... 32 B6
Old Park Rd S EN2 ... 4 D1
Old Park Ridings N21 ... 17 A6
Old Park View EN2 ... 4 D2
Old Perry St BR7 ... 189 C3
Old Pound Cl TW7 ... 131 A4
Old Priory UB9 ... 38 D2
Old Pye St SW1 ... 259 C6
Old Pye Street Est SW1 ... 259 C5
Old Quebec St W1 ... 237 D1
Old Queen St SW1 ... 115 D4 249 D1
Old Rd SE13 ... 142 C1
Enfield EN3 ... 6 C4
Old Rectory Gdns HA8 26 C4
Old Redding HA3 ... 24 A6
Oldridge Rd SW12 ... 159 B4
Old Royal Free Pl N1 234 B5
Old Royal Free Sq N1 ... 94 C6 234 B5
Old Royal Observatory Greenwich (National Maritime Mus Annexe)★ SE10 ... 142 B5
Old Ruislip Rd UB5 ... 84 C5
Old School Cl
3 Beckenham BR3 ... 185 A1
Merton SW19 ... 179 C1
Old School Cres E7 ... 77 A2
Old School Ho The EN2 4 D2
Old School Pl CR0 ... 220 C4
Old School Rd UB8 ... 82 B3
Old School Sq 19 E14 ... 97 C1
Thames Ditton KT7 ... 196 D3
Old School The WC1 ... 240 C4
Old Seacoal La EC4 ... 241 C1
Old South Lambeth Rd SW8 ... 138 A5 270 B4
Old Spitalfields Mkt E1 ... 95 D2 243 D2
Old Sq WC2 ... 241 A2
Old St E13 ... 99 B5
EC1 ... 95 B3 242 B6
Old Stable Mews N5 ... 73 A5
Old St Andrews Mans NW9 ... 67 B6
Old Station Rd UB3 ... 105 D3
Oldstead Rd BR1 ... 186 B6
Old Street Sta EC1 ... 95 B3 242 D6
Old Sun Wharf E14 ... 119 A6
Old Swan Wharf SW11 ... 266 D2
Old Swan Yd SM5 ... 218 D4
Old Theatre Ct SE1 ... 252 B4
Old Town SW4 ... 137 C2
Croydon CR0 ... 220 D5
Old Tramyard SE18 ... 123 C2
Old Woolwich Rd SE10 ... 120 B1
Old York Rd SW18 ... 157 D6
Oleander Cl BR6 ... 227 B3
O'Leary Sq E1 ... 96 C2
Olga Prim Sch E3 ... 97 A5
Olga St 18 E3 ... 97 A5
Olinda Rd N16 ... 51 D3
Oliphant St W10 ... 91 A4
Olive Blythe Ho 14 W10 ... 91 A3
Oliver Ave SE25 ... 205 D6
Oliver Bsns Pk NW10 ... 89 A5
Oliver Cl W4 ... 132 D6
Oliver Ct SE18 ... 123 A2
Oliver Ct *continued*
Isleworth TW7 ... 130 D2
Olive Rd E13 ... 99 C4
NW2 ... 68 C4
W5 ... 109 D3
3 Merton SW19 ... 180 A3
Oliver Gdns E6 ... 100 A2
Oliver Goldsmith Prim Sch NW9 ... 45 B4
Oliver Goldsmith Prim Schs SE5 ... 139 D4
Oliver Gr SE25 ... 205 D5
Oliver Ho 19 SE16 ... 118 A4
SW8 ... 270 A4
W11 ... 244 B5
Oliver Mews SE15 ... 140 A3
Oliver Rd E10 ... 75 D5
E17 ... 54 A4
Kingston KT3 ... 177 A1
Sutton SM1 ... 218 B4
Oliver's Yd EC1 ... 242 D6
Olive Tree Ho N4 ... 50 C3
7 SE15 ... 140 C6
Olivette St 1 SW15 ... 134 D1
Olive Waite Ho NW6 ... 69 D1
Ollard's Gr IG10 ... 21 D6
Ollerton Gn E3 ... 97 B6
Ollerton Rd N11 ... 31 D5
Olley Cl SM6 ... 220 A2
Ollgar Cl W12 ... 111 D5
Olliffe St E14 ... 120 A3
Olmar St SE1 ... 140 A6
Olmar Wharf SE1 ... 140 A6
Olney Ho NW8 ... 237 B6
Olney Rd SE17 ... 139 A6
Olron Cres DA6 ... 169 A6
Olven Rd SE18 ... 145 A6
Olveston Wlk SM5 ... 202 B3
Olwen Mews HA5 ... 22 D1
Olyffe Ave DA16 ... 146 A3
Olyffe Dr BR3 ... 186 A2
Olympia Ex Ctr★ W14 ... 112 D3 254 A6
Olympian Ct 1 E14 ... 119 C2
Olympia Way W14 ... 113 A3 254 B5
Olympia Yd W2 ... 245 D5
Olympic Ho W10 ... 90 C1
Olympic Ret Pk HA9 ... 66 D4
Olympic Way
Greenford UB6 ... 85 D6
Wembley HA9 ... 66 C4
Olympus Sq E5 ... 74 A5
Oman Ave NW2 ... 68 C4
Oman Ct NW4 ... 68 B4
Ombersley Ho N4 ... 51 A2
Omeara St SE1 ... 252 B3
Omega Cl E14 ... 119 D3
Omega Ho SW10 ... 266 B4
Omega Pl N1 ... 233 B3
Omega St SE14 ... 141 C4
Ommaney Rd SE14 ... 141 A4
Omnibus Way E17 ... 35 C1
Ondine Rd SE15 ... 139 D1
Onedin Point 17 E1 ... 118 A6
Onega Gate SE16 ... 119 A3
O'Neill Ho NW8 ... 229 D3
O'Neill Path 11 SE18 ... 144 C6
One Tree Cl SE23 ... 162 C5
Ongar Cl RM6 ... 58 C4
Ongar Ho 15 N1 ... 73 B2
Ongar Rd SW6 ... 135 C6 265 B6
Onra Rd E17 ... 53 C2
Onslow Ave TW10 ... 154 A6
Onslow Avenue Mans 10 TW10 ... 154 A6
Onslow Cl Chingford E4 20 B2
Thames Ditton KT7 ... 196 C1
Onslow Cres BR7 ... 188 D2
Onslow Ct SW10 ... 256 B1
Onslow Dr DA14 ... 168 D2
Onslow Gdns N10 ... 49 B4
SW7 ... 114 B1 256 C2
Southgate N21 ... 16 C6
Thames Ditton KT7 ... 196 C1
Wallington SM6 ... 219 C1
Wanstead E18 ... 55 C6
Onslow Ho 1 KT2 ... 176 B2
Onslow Lo 28 SW2 ... 160 C4
Onslow Mews E SW7 256 C3
Onslow Mews W SW7 ... 256 C3
Onslow Par N14 ... 15 B3
Onslow Rd
Richmond TW10 ... 154 A5
Thornton Heath CR0 ... 204 C1
West Barnes KT3 ... 200 A5
Onslow Sq SW7 ... 114 B2 256 D3
Onslow St EC1 ... 241 B5
Onslow Way KT7 ... 196 C1
Ontario St SE1 ... 116 D3 261 D6
Ontario Way E14 ... 119 C6
Onyx Ho KT4 ... 199 B1
Opal Cl E16 ... 99 D1
Opal Ho KT4 ... 199 B1
Opal Mews 2 IG1 ... 78 D6
Opal St SE11 ... 116 D1 261 C2
Open Air Theatre, Regent's Park NW1 ... 231 A1
Openshaw Rd SE2 ... 124 B2
Openview SW17,SW18 158 B2
Operating Theatre Mus & Herb Garret★ SE1 ... 117 B5 252 D3
Ophelia Gdns NW2 ... 69 A5
Ophir Terr SE15 ... 140 A4
Opie Ho NW8 ... 230 B4
Opossum Way TW4 ... 128 C2
Oppenheim Rd SE13 ... 142 A3
Oppidans Rd NW3 ... 70 D1
Orange Hill Rd HA8 ... 27 A3
Orange Pl SE16 ... 118 C3
Orangery La SE9 ... 166 B6
Orangery The TW10 ... 153 C2
Orange St WC2 ... 115 D6 249 D5
Orange Yd WC2 ... 239 D1
Oratory La SW3 ... 256 D2
Oratory RC Prim Sch SW3 ... 114 C1 257 A2
Oratory The★ SW7 ... 114 C3 257 A5
Orbain Rd SW6 ... 135 A5 264 B3
Orbel St SW11 ... 136 C4 267 A1
Orb St SE17 ... 117 B2 262 C3
Orchard Ave N14 ... 15 C4
N20 ... 14 B2
N3 ... 47 C6
Ashford TW15 ... 171 A4
Carshalton CR4 ... 203 A1
Croydon CR0 ... 207 A1
Erith DA17 ... 147 B6
Hatton TW14 ... 149 B6
Heston TW5 ... 129 A5
Hinchley Wood KT7 ... 213 A6
Kingston KT3 ... 199 C6
Southall UB1 ... 107 B5
Orchard Bsns Ctr SE26 ... 185 B5
Orchard Cl DA7 ... 147 A4
N1 ... 73 A1
NW2 ... 68 A5
SE23 ... 162 C5
W10 ... 91 A2
Ashford TW15 ... 171 A4
Bushey WD23 ... 8 B3
Chingford E4 ... 35 C6
Edgware HA8 ... 26 A4
Northolt UB5 ... 64 A2
Ruislip HA4 ... 39 A2
Thames Ditton KT7 ... 197 B2
Walton-on-T KT12 ... 194 B2
Wanstead E11 ... 55 B5
Wembley HA0 ... 88 A6
West Barnes SW20 ... 200 C5
West Ewell KT19 ... 214 D2
Orchard Cotts UB3 ... 105 C4
Orchard Cres HA8 ... 27 A5
Enfield EN1 ... 5 D4
Orchard Ct E10 ... 53 D1
W1 ... 238 A2
Barnes SW13 ... 133 D2
Croydon BR3 ... 207 C1
Edgware HA8 ... 26 B5
Hounslow TW7 ... 130 B5
New Malden KT4 ... 200 A1
Southgate N14 ... 15 C5
Wallington SM6 ... 219 B3
Walton-on-T KT12 ... 193 D1
Wood Green N22 ... 32 A3
Orchard Dr SE3 ... 142 C3
Edgware HA8 ... 26 B5
Upper Halliford TW17 ... 193 C6
Orchard Gate NW9 ... 45 C5
Thames Ditton KT10 ... 196 B1
Wembley UB6 ... 65 B2
Orchard Gdns
Chessington KT9 ... 214 A4
Sutton SM1 ... 217 C3
Orchard Gn BR6 ... 227 C6
Orchard Gr BR6 ... 211 D1
BR6 ... 227 D6
Croydon CR0 ... 207 A2
Edgware HA8 ... 26 D2
Harrow HA3 ... 44 B4
Orchard Gr *continued*
Penge SE20 ... 184 A3
Orchard Hill SE13 ... 141 D4
Orchard Ho 11 SE16 ... 118 C3
SE5 ... 139 A4
W12 ... 112 A5
Orchard Jun & Inf Sch The TW3 ... 151 C6
Orchard La
Thames Ditton KT8 ... 196 B3
Wimbledon SW20 ... 178 B2
Woodford IG8 ... 37 C6
Orchardleigh Ave EN3 ... 6 C3
Orchard Lo N12 ... 14 A1
Orchard Mead Ho NW11 ... 69 C6
Orchardmede N21 ... 17 B5
Orchard Mews N1 ... 73 B1
Orchard Pl E14 ... 120 C6
Tottenham N17 ... 33 D3
Orchard Prim Sch E9 ... 74 C1
Orchard Rd BR1 ... 187 C2
BR6 ... 226 D3
DA16 ... 146 B2
N6 ... 49 B2
Barnet EN5 ... 1 B1
Belvedere DA17 ... 125 C2
Brentford TW8 ... 131 C6
Carshalton CR4 ... 203 A1
Chessington KT9 ... 214 A4
Dagenham RM10 ... 103 C6
Enfield EN3 ... 18 C6
Feltham TW14 ... 150 A3
Hampton TW12 ... 173 B3
Hayes UB3 ... 106 A6
Hounslow TW4 ... 151 C6
Isleworth TW1 ... 153 B6
Kingston KT1 ... 176 A1
Richmond TW9 ... 132 C2
Sidcup DA14 ... 189 C6
Sunbury TW16 ... 172 B3
Sutton SM1 ... 217 C4
Orchard Rise
Croydon CR0 ... 207 B1
Kingston KT2 ... 177 A2
Mortlake TW10 ... 132 D1
Pinner HA5 ... 39 D6
Orchard Rise E DA15 167 D6
Orchard Rise W DA15 ... 167 C6
Orchard School Sports Ctr SE20 ... 184 A2
Orchardson Ho NW8 ... 236 D5
Orchardson St NW8 ... 92 B3 236 D5
Orchard Sq W14 ... 254 C1
Orchard St E17 ... 53 A5
W1 ... 238 A1
Orchard Terr EN1 ... 18 A5
Orchard The N20 ... 13 D3
NW11 ... 47 C4
SE3 ... 142 B3
W4 ... 111 B2
Ealing W5 ... 87 D2
East Barnet N14 ... 15 B6
Enfield N21 ... 17 B5
Ewell KT17 ... 215 D1
Hounslow TW3 ... 130 A3
Orchard Way
Ashford TW15 ... 148 B2
Croydon BR3,CR0 ... 207 A3
Enfield EN1 ... 5 C2
Esher KT10 ... 212 A2
Sutton SM1 ... 218 B4
Orchard Way Prim Sch CR0 ... 207 A2
Orchid Cl 1 E6 ... 100 A2
Chessington KT9 ... 213 C1
Southall UB1 ... 85 A1
Orchid Ct HA9 ... 66 A6
Orchid Grange N14 ... 15 C4
Orchid Lo N14 ... 15 C4
Orchid Rd N14 ... 15 C4
Orchid St W12 ... 112 A6
Orde 6 NW9 ... 27 D2
Orde Hall St WC1 ... 94 B2 240 C4
Orde Ho 10 N16 ... 73 B4
Ordell Ct 30 E3 ... 97 B5
Ordell Rd E3 ... 97 B5
Ordnance Cl TW13 ... 150 A2
Ordnance Cres SE10 ... 120 C4
Ordnance Hill NW8 ... 92 B6 229 D5
Ordnance Mews NW8 ... 229 D4
Ordnance Rd E16 ... 98 D2

Ordnance Rd *continued*
SE18 ....144 C6
Enfield EN3 ....7 B6
Oregano Cl UB7 ....104 B6
Oregano Dr E14 ....98 B1
Oregon Ave E12 ....78 B4
Oregon Cl KT3 .....199 A5
Oregon Sq BR6 ....211 B1
Orestes Cl 8 E18 ...55 A6
Orestes Mews 1 NW6 69 C3
Orford Ct
Stanmore HA7 .....25 C4
Wallington SM6 ....219 C3
West Norwood SE27 ..160 D2
Orford Gdns TW1 ..152 D2
Orford Rd E17 .....53 D4
Catford SE6 ....163 D1
Wanstead E18 .....55 B6
Organ Crossroads
KT17 ....216 A1
Oriana Ho 3 E14 ..119 B6
Oriel Cl CR4 ......203 D6
Oriel Ct NW3 .....70 A4
6 Croydon CR0 ...205 B1
Oriel Dr SW13 ....134 C6
Oriel Gdns IG5 ....56 B6
Oriel Jun & Inf Sch
TW13 ....151 A1
Oriel Rd E9 ......74 D2
E9 ....75 A2
Oriel Way UB5 ....63 D1
Oriental City NW9 ..45 B6
Oriental Rd E16 ...121 D5
Orient Ind Pk E10 ..75 C6
Orient St
SE11 ....116 D2 261 C4
Orient Way E5 ....74 D5
Oriole Way SE28 ..124 B6
Orion Bsns Ctr SE14 118 D1
Orion Ctr The CR0 ..220 A6
Orion Ho 20 E1 ....96 B3
Orion Prim Sch The
NW9 ....27 D2
Orion Rd N11 .....31 A4
Orion Way HA6 ....22 A6
Orissa Rd SE18 ...123 C1
Orkney Ho N1 .....233 C6
Orkney St SW11 ...137 A3
Orlando Rd SW4 ...137 C2
Orleans Cl KT10 ...212 B6
Orleans Ct 9 TW1 ..153 B4
Orleans Inf Sch TW1 153 B4
Orleans Park Sec Sch
TW1 ....153 B4
Orleans Rd
South Norwood SE19 ..183 B4
Twickenham TW1 ...153 C4
Orleston Mews N7 ...72 C2
Orleston Rd N7 ....72 C2
Orley Farm Rd HA1 ..64 C5
Orley Farm Sch HA1 ..64 B5
Orlop St SE10 ....120 C1
Ormanton Rd SE26 ..184 A6
Orme Ct W2 .113 D6 245 C5
Orme Ct Mews W2 ..245 D5
Orme Ho 8 E8 .....95 D6
Orme La W2 .113 D6 245 C5
Ormeley Rd SW12 ...159 B3
Orme Rd
Kingston KT1,KT3 ...176 D1
Sutton SM1 ....217 D2
Ormerod Gdns CR4 ..181 A2
Ormesby Cl SE28 ...124 D6
Ormesby Way HA3 ..44 B4
Orme Sq W2 ......245 C5
Ormiston Gr W12 ..112 B5
Ormiston Rd SE10 ..121 A1
Ormond Ave
Hampton TW12 ....173 D2
22 Richmond TW10 ..153 D6
Ormond Cl WC1 ....240 B4
Ormond Cres TW12 ..173 D2
Ormond Dr TW12 ...173 D2
Ormonde Ave BR6 ..227 A6
Ormonde Ct SW15 ..134 C1
Ormonde Gate
SW3 ......114 D1 257 D1
Ormonde Pl SW1 ...258 B3
Ormonde Rd SW14 ..133 A2
Ormonde Rise IG9 ..21 C3
Ormonde Terr
NW8 ......92 D6 230 C5
Ormond Ho 7 N16 ..73 B4
Ormond Mews WC1 ..240 B5
Ormond Rd N4,N19 ..50 A1
Richmond TW10 ....153 D6
Ormond Yd SW1 ...249 B4

Ormrod Ct W11 ....91 B1
Ormsby SM2 ......217 D1
Ormsby Gdns UB6 ..86 A5
Ormsby Lo 7 W4 ..111 C3
Ormsby Pl N16 ....73 D5
Ormsby Point 6
SE18 ....122 D2
Ormsby St E2 .....95 D5
Ormside St SE15 ..140 C6
Ormskirk Rd WD19 ..22 D5
Ornan Rd NW3 ....70 C3
Oronsay Rd 18 N1 ..73 A2
Orpheus Ho 25 N19 ..49 D2
Orpheus St SE5 ...139 B4
Orpington Gdns N18 ..17 C1
Orpington Hospl BR6 227 D1
Orpington Mans N21 ..16 C3
Orpington Rd
Southgate N21 ....16 D3
St Paul's Cray BR7 ..211 C6
Orpington Sta BR6 ..227 C6
Orpwood Cl TW12 ..173 B4
Orsett Mews
W2 ....91 D1 236 A2
Orsett St
SE11 ......116 B1 260 D2
Orsett Terr
W2 ....92 A1 236 A2
Woodford IG8 .....37 C3
Orsman Rd N1 ....95 C6
Orton St E1 ......118 A5
Orville Rd SW11 ...136 B3
Orwell Cl UB3 ....105 C4
Orwell Ct E8 .....96 A6
N5 ....73 A4
Orwell Ho N1 .....112 A6
Orwell Lo 2 E18 ...55 A6
Orwell Rd E13 ....99 C6
Osbaldeston Rd N16 ..52 A1
Osberton Rd SE12 ..165 A6
Osbert St SW1 ....259 C3
Osborn Cl E8 .....96 A6
Osborne Ave TW19 .148 B3
Osborne Cl
Beckenham BR3 ...207 A5
Cockfosters EN4 ....2 D2
Feltham TW13 ....172 D5
Osborne Cl 16 E10 ..53 D2
Ealing W5 ....88 A2
10 Surbiton KT6 ...198 A3
Osborne Gdns CR7 ..183 A1
Osborne Gr E17 ...53 B5
Osborne Mews E17 ..53 B5
Osborne Pl SM1 ...218 B3
Osborne Rd E10 ...75 D6
E7 ....77 B3
E9 ....75 B2
N4 ....50 C1
NW2 ....68 B2
W3 ....110 A3
Buckhurst Hill IG9 ..21 B3
Dagenham RM9 ....81 B3
Enfield EN3 ....7 A3
Erith DA17 ....147 B6
Hounslow TW3,TW4 ..129 B2
Kingston KT2 .....176 A3
Palmers Green N13 ..16 C1
Southall UB1 ......86 A1
South Norwood SE19 ..183 A4
Walton-on-T KT12 ..194 A1
Osborne Sq RM9 ...81 B4
Osborne Way KT9 ..214 B3
Osborn Gdns NW7 ..28 D3
Osborn La SE23 ...163 A4
Osborn St E1 .95 D2 243 D2
Osborn Terr SE3 ...142 D1
Osbourne Ct HA2 ...41 C5
Osbourne Ho TW10 ..154 C6
Osbourne Terr 1
SW17 ....181 A5
Oscar Faber Pl 8 N1 .73 C1
Oscar St SE8 .....141 C4
Oseney Cres NW5 ..71 D2
Osgood Ave BR6 ...227 D3
Osgood Gdns 1 BR6 227 D3
O'Shea Gr E3 .....97 B4
Osidge JMI Sch N14 ..15 C3
Osidge La N14 ....15 B3
Osier Cres N10 ....30 D2
Osier Ct E1 ......96 C6
Osier Mews W4 ...133 C6
Osiers Ct 3 KT1 ...175 D2
Osiers Rd SW18 ...135 C4
Osier St E1 ......96 C6
Osier Way E10 ....75 D5
Mitcham CR4 .....202 D4
Oslac Rd SE6 ....185 A6
Oslo Ct NW8 .....230 A3
Oslo Ho 2 SE5 ...139 A3

Oslo Sq SE16 .....119 A3
Osman Cl N15 ....51 B3
Osmani Prim Sch E1 ..96 A2
Osman Rd W6 ....112 C3
Edmonton N9 .....18 A1
Osmington Ho SW8 270 D3
Osmond Cl HA2 ....64 A6
Osmond Gdns SM6 .219 C3
Osmund St W12 ...89 D1
Osnaburgh St
NW1 ....93 B3 238 D6
Osnaburgh Terr
NW1 ....238 D6
Osney Ho 4 SE2 ..124 D4
Osney Wlk SM5 ...202 B3
Osprey 7 NW9 ....27 D2
Osprey Cl E17 ....35 A3
E6 ....100 A2
Cheam SM1 ......217 B3
Wanstead E11 ....55 A5
West Drayton UB7 ..104 A4
Osprey Ct NW3 ....69 D3
7 Ealing W7 .....86 D3
Thornton Heath SW16 .182 B1
Osprey Ho 3 E14 ..119 A6
E4 ....35 B4
SE15 ....139 D4
Osprey Mews EN3 ...18 B6
Ospringe Cl 9 SE20 .184 C3
Ospringe Ct SE9 ..167 B5
Ospringe Ho SE1 ..251 B3
Ospringe Rd NW5 ..71 C4
Osram Ct W6 .....112 C3
Osram Rd HA9 ....65 D5
Osric Path 8 N1 ...95 C5
Ossian Rd N4 .....50 B2
Ossie Garvin Rdbt
UB4 ....106 C6
Ossington Bldgs W1 238 A3
Ossington Cl W2 ...245 B5
Ossington St
W2 ....113 D6 245 C5
Ossory Rd SE1 ....140 A6
Ossulston St
NW1 ....93 D4 232 D2
Ossultan Pl N2 ....48 A6
Ossulton Way N2 ..48 A5
Ostade Rd SW2 ...160 B4
Ostell Cres EN3 ....7 C5
Osten Mews
SW7 ....113 D3 255 D5
Osterley Ave TW7 ..130 B5
Osterley Cl BR5 ...190 A2
Osterley Cres TW7 .130 C4
Osterley Ct
Hounslow TW7 ....130 B4
7 Northolt UB5 ....84 C4
Osterley Gdns UB2 ..108 A4
Osterley Ho 5 E14 ..97 D1
Osterley La
Isleworth TW7 ....108 C1
Southall UB2,TW7 ..107 D1
Osterley Lo 1 TW7 .130 C4
Osterley Park★ TW7 108 B1
Osterley Park Rd
UB2 ....107 B3
Osterley Park View Rd
W7 ....108 C4
Osterley Rd N16 ...73 C4
Hounslow TW7 ....130 C4
Osterley Sta TW7 ..130 B4
Osterley Views UB2 108 B4
Osterly Gdns CR7 ..183 A1
Oster Terr E17 ....52 C4
Ostliffe Rd N13 ...33 C4
Oswald Rd UB1 ...107 A5
Oswald's Mead E9 ...75 A4
Oswald St E5 .....74 D5
Oswald Terr NW2 ..68 C2
Osward Pl N9 .....18 B2
Osward Rd SW12,
SW17 ....158 D2
Oswell Ho 9 E1 ...118 B5
Oswin St
SE11 ......116 D2 261 D4
Oswyth Rd SE5 ...139 C3
Otford Cl BR1 ....210 C6
DA5 ....169 D5
Penge SE20 ......184 C2
Otford Cres SE4 ...163 B5
Otford Ho SE1 ....252 D1
6 SE15 ....140 C6
Otha Ho 13 SW9 ..138 A3
Othello Cl SE11 ...261 C4
Otho Ct 5 TW8 ...131 D5
Otis St E3 ....98 A4
Otley App IG2 ....56 D3
Otley Ct N11 .....31 A4
Otley Dr IG2 .....56 D3
Otley Ho N5 ......72 D5

Otley Rd E16 .....99 C1
Otley Terr E5 .....74 D5
Ottawa Ho 4 HA4 ..40 C1
Ottaway Ct E5 ....74 A5
Ottaway St E5 ....74 A5
Otterbourne Rd
Chingford E4 .....20 B1
1 Croydon CR0 ...221 A6
Otterburn Gdns TW7 131 A5
Otterburn Ho 12 SE5 139 A5
Otterburn St SW17 .180 D4
Otterden Cl BR6 ...227 C4
Otterden St SE6 ..185 C6
Otterfield Rd UB7 ..104 A6
Otter Cl E5 ......74 A6
Ottershaw Ho BR5 .190 B2
Ottoman Ct W5 ...109 D2
Otto St SE17 .....138 D6
Otway Ct N4 .....50 B3
Otway Gdns WD23 ..8 C4
Oulton Cl E5 .....74 C6
Erith SE28 ......102 C1
Oulton Cres IG11 ...79 D3
Oulton Rd N15 ....51 B4
Oulton Way WD19 ..23 B6
Oundle Ave WD23 ..8 A5
Our Lady Immaculate
RC Prim Sch KT6 ..198 D1
Our Lady of Dolours RC
Prim Sch W2 .....91 D2
Our Lady of Grace RC Inf
Sch NW2 ....68 C6
Our Lady of Grace RC Jun
Sch NW2 ....68 B5
Our Lady of Grace Sch
SE7 ....143 B6
Our Lady of Lourdes RC
Prim Sch
N11 ....31 C5
N12 ....30 A2
SE13 ....142 B2
Our Lady of Lourdes
Sch NW10 ....89 A6
Our Lady of Lourds RC
Prim Sch E11 ....55 A3
Our Lady of Muswell Prim
Sch N10 ....49 A6
Our Lady of Muswell RC
Prim Sch N10 ....31 A1
Our Lady of the
Assumption RC Prim Sch
E2 ....96 C5
Our Lady of the Rosary RC
Prim Sch DA15 ...167 C4
Our Lady of the Sacred
Heart RC Prim Sch
(Annexe) N7 .....72 B2
Our Lady of the Sacred
Heart RC Sch N7 ..72 B3
Our Lady of the Visitation
RC Prim Sch UB6 ..86 A3
Our Lady of Victories RC
Prim Sch
SW7 ....114 A2 256 B3
Putney SW15 .....134 D1
Our Lady Queen of Heaven
RC Sch SW19 ....156 D1
Our Lady RC Prim Sch
E14 ....97 B1
NW1 ....93 C6 232 B5
Our Lady's Convent High
Sch N15,N16 .....51 C2
Our Lady & St John's RC
Jun & Inf Sch TW8 .109 C1
Our Lady & St Joseph RC
Prim Sch N1 .....73 C2
Our Lady & St Philip Neri
RC Prim Sch SE26 .185 A6
Our Lady & St Philip Neri
RC Sch SE26 .....185 A6
Ouseley Rd SW12 ..158 D3
Outer Circ
NW8 ......92 C4 230 B3
Outgate Rd NW10 ..67 D1
Outram Pl N1 .94 A6 233 B6
Outram Rd E6 ....100 A6
N22 ....31 D2
Croydon CR0 .....221 D6
Outwich St EC3 ...243 B2
Outwood Ho 2 SW2 160 B4
Outwood Ho 3 SW2 160 B4
Oval Ct HA8 ......27 A3
Oval Mans SE11 ...270 D6
Oval Pl SW8 .138 B5 270 D4
Oval Prim Sch CR0 205 B4
Oval Rd NW1 .93 B6 231 C6
Croydon CR0 .....205 C1
Oval Rd N RM10 ..103 D6
Oval Rd S RM10 ..103 D5
Oval Sta SE11 ....138 C6

Oval The E2 ......96 B5
Sidcup DA15 .....168 A4
Oval The (Surrey Cnty Crkt
Gd) SE11 ....138 C5
Oval Way
SE11 ......116 B1 260 D1
Overbrae BR3 .....185 C5
Overbrook Wlk HA8 ..26 C3
Overbury Ave BR3 .208 A6
Overbury Ct 1 BR3 .208 A6
Overbury Ho 3 E5 ..74 D4
Overbury Rd N4,N15 .51 B3
Overbury St E5 ...74 D4
Overcliff Rd SE13 ..141 C2
Overcourt Cl DA15 .168 B5
Overdale Ave KT3 ..177 B1
Overdale Rd W5 ...109 C5
Overdown Rd SE6 ..185 D6
Overhill Rd SE21,SE22 162 A4
Overhill Way BR3 ..208 B4
Overlea Rd E5 ....52 A2
Overmead SE9 ....167 B4
Oversley Ho 17 W2 ..91 C1
Overstand Cl BR3 ..207 C4
Overstone Gdns CR0 207 B2
Overstone Ho 17 E14 97 C1
Overstone Rd W6 ..112 C2
Overstrand Mans
SW11 ....268 A1
Overton Cl NW10 ..67 A2
Hounslow TW7 ....130 D4
Overton Ct E11 ...55 B2
Overton Dr Ilford RM6 58 C2
Wanstead E11 ....55 B2
Overton Grange Sch
SM2 ....217 D1
Overton Ho SW15 .155 C4
Overton Rd SE2 ...124 D3
SW9 ....138 C3
Belmont SM2 .....217 C1
Southgate N14 ....16 A6
Walthamstow E10 ..53 A1
Overton's Yd CR0 ..221 A5
Overy Ho SE1 ....251 C1
Ovesdon Ave HA2 ..41 B1
Ovett Cl SE19 ....183 C6
Ovex Cl E14 ......120 A4
Ovington Ct SW3 ..257 B5
Ovington Gdns SW3 257 B5
Ovington Mews SW3 257 B5
Ovington Sq
SW3 ....114 C3 257 B5
Ovington St
SW3 ....114 C2 257 B5
Owen Cl SE28 ....124 C5
Hayes UB4 ....84 B4
Thornton Heath CR0 205 B3
Owen Ct UB4 .....84 B4
Owen Ho 11 N19 ..71 C4
Feltham TW14 ....150 A4
5 Twickenham TW1 153 B4
Owenite St SE2 ...124 B2
Owen Rd Edmonton N13 33 A5
Hayes UB4 ....84 B4
Owen's Ct EC1 ....234 C2
Owen's Row EC1 ..234 C2
Owen St EC1 .....234 C2
Owens Way SE23 ..163 A4
Owen Way NW10 ..67 A3
Owen Wlk 7 SE20 .184 A3
Owgan Cl SE5 ....139 C4
Oxberry Ave SW6 ..135 A3
Oxbridge Ct 4 W4 .110 D1
Oxendon St
SW1,W1 ....115 D6 249 C5
Oxenford St SE15 .139 D4
Oxenham Ho 13 SE8 141 C6
Oxenholme NW1 ..232 B3
Oxenpark Ave HA9 ..44 A2
Oxestalls Rd SE8 ..119 A1
Oxford Ave NW10 ..90 C4
Harlington TW6 ...127 C5
Hounslow TW5 ....107 C1
Merton SW20 ....179 A1
Oxford & Cambridge Mans
NW1 ....237 B3
Oxford Cir W1 .93 C1 239 A1
Oxford Circus Ave
W1 ....239 A1
Oxford Circus Sta
W1 ....93 C1 239 A1
Oxford Cl Edmonton N9 18 B2
Littleton TW15,TW17 171 A3
Mitcham CR4 .....203 C6
Oxford Cres KT3 ..199 A5
Oxford Ct EC4 ....252 C2
48 W2 ....91 C1
W4 ....110 D1
16 Acton W3 .....88 C1
8 Ealing W7 .....86 D2

Oxford Ct *continued*
17 Kingston KT6 ..198 A4
Oxford Dr SE1 ....253 B1
Ruislip HA4 ......62 C1
Oxford Gardens Prim Sch
W10 ....90 D1
Oxford Gate W6 ..112 D2
Oxford Gdns N20 ..14 B3
W10 ....90 D1
Brentford W4 .....132 C6
Edmonton N21 ....17 A4
Oxford Mews DA5 .169 C4
Oxford Rd DA14 ..190 B5
E15 ....76 B2
N4 ....50 C1
NW6 ....91 C5
Carshalton SM2,SM5 218 C3
Ealing W5 ....109 D6
Edmonton N9 .....18 B2
Enfield EN3 ......18 B6
Harrow HA1 ......42 A3
Harrow HA3 ......42 D6
Ilford IG1 ....79 A3
Putney SW15 .....135 A1
South Norwood SE19 183 B4
Teddington TW11,
TW12 ....174 B5
Wallington SM6 ...219 C3
Woodford IG8 .....37 D5
Oxford Rd N W4 ..110 D1
Oxford Rd S W4 ..110 D1
Oxford Sq W2 .92 C1 237 B1
Oxford St W1 .93 B1 238 D1
Oxford Way TW13 .172 D6
Oxford Wlk UB1 ..107 B5
Oxgate Ct Par NW2 ..68 A6
Oxgate Ctr NW2 ...68 A6
Oxgate Gdns NW2 ..68 B6
Oxgate La NW2 ...68 B6
Oxhawth Cres BR2 210 D3
Oxhey Dr HA6,WD19 ..22 B6
Oxhey La HA5 ....23 C5
Oxhey Ridge Cl HA6 22 B5
Oxhey Wood JMI Schs
WD19 ....22 C6
Oxleas E6 ....100 D1
Oxleas Cl DA16 ...145 B3
Oxleay Rd HA2 ...41 C1
Oxleigh Cl KT3 ...199 C4
Oxley Cl SE1 .....118 A1
Oxleys Rd NW2 ...68 B5
Oxlip Cl 2 CR0 ...206 D1
Oxlow La RM10 ...81 C4
Oxonian St SE22 ..139 D1
Oxo Tower SE1 ...251 B5
Oxo Tower Wharf
SE1 ....251 B5
Oxted Cl CR4 ....202 B6
Oxted Ct N16 ....51 C1
Oxtoby Way SW16 .181 D2
Oyster Catchers Cl
E16 ....99 B1
Oyster Catcher Terr
IG5 ....56 C6
Oyster Row E1 ...96 C1
Ozolins Way E16 ..99 B1

P

Pablo Neruda Cl 4
SE24 ....138 D1
Pace Pl E1 ....96 B1
Pacific Cl TW14 ...149 D3
Pacific Ho 15 E1 ...96 D3
Pacific Hts BR3 ...185 C3
Pacific Rd E16 ....99 A1
Pacific Wharf SE16 118 D5
Packenham Ho 21 E2 95 D4
24 N19 ....49 D2
Packham Ct KT4 ..216 C5
Packington Ho 22
SW9 ....138 C4
Packington Sq
N1 ......95 A6 235 A6
Packington St
N1 ....94 D6 234 D5
Packmores Rd SE9 167 B6
Padbury SE17 ....263 B1
Padbury Cl TW14 ..149 B3
Padbury Ct E2 ....95 D4
Padbury Ho NW8 ..237 B6
Paddenswick Ct W6 112 B3
Paddenswick Rd W6 112 A3
Paddington Cl UB4 .84 D3
Paddington Com Hospl
W9 ....91 C2
Paddington Ct 10 W7 86 D2
Paddington Gn
W2 ....92 B2 236 C4

Paddington Green Prim Sch NW8 .....92 B3 236 C5
Paddington St W1 ...238 A4
Paddington Sta W2 ....92 B1 236 C2
Paddock Cl SE3 .....143 A3
Forest Hill SE26 ......184 D6
New Malden KT4 ......199 C1
Northolt UB5 ....85 C5
Orpington BR6 ....226 D4
Paddock Ct SW20 ...200 C5
Paddock Gdns SE19 .183 C4
Paddock Lo 13 EN1 ...17 C6
Paddock Rd DA6 ....147 A1
NW2 ....68 A6
Ruislip HA4 ....62 D5
Paddock Sch SW15 .133 D1
Paddocks Cl HA2 ....63 D4
Paddocks Gn NW9 ....44 D1
Paddocks The HA9 ....66 D6
Addington CR0 ....223 C2
Cockfosters EN4 ....2 D2
Paddock The UB10 ....60 D4
Paddock Way BR7 ...189 B3
Padfield Ct HA9 ......66 B5
Padfield Rd SE5 .....139 A2
Padley Cl KT9 ....214 B3
Padnall Ct RM6 ....58 D6
Padnall Rd RM6 ......58 D5
Padstow Cl BR6 .....227 D4
Padstow Ho 12 E14 ..119 B6
Padstow Rd EN2 ....4 D4
Padstow Wlk TW14 ..149 D3
Padua Rd SE20 ......184 C2
Pagden St SW8 ....268 D2
Pageant Ave NW9 ....27 C2
Pageant Cres SE16 ..119 B5
Pageantmaster Ct EC4 ....241 C1
Pageant Wlk CR0 ....221 C5
Page Cl Dagenham RM9 81 A3
Hampton TW12 ....173 A4
Harrow HA3 ....44 B3
Page Cres CR0 ......220 D3
Page Ct NW7 ....28 A3
Page Green Rd N15 ...52 A4
Page Green Terr N15 .51 D4
Page Heath La BR1 ..209 D6
Page Heath Villas BR1 ....209 D6
Page High N22 ....50 C6
Page Ho SE10 ....142 A6
Pagehurst Rd CR0 ...206 B2
Page Mdw NW7 ....28 A3
Page Rd TW14 ......149 B5
Page's Ct N10 ....31 A1
Page's Hill N10 ....31 A1
Page's La N10 ....31 A1
Page St NW7 ....28 A3
SW1 ......115 D2 259 D4
Page's Wlk SE1 ....117 C3 263 B5
Page's Yd W4 ....133 C6
Paget Ave SM1 ......218 B5
Paget Cl TW12 ....174 B6
Paget Ct UB7 ....104 A4
Paget Gdns BR7 .....188 D2
Paget Ho 15 E2 ....96 C5
Paget La TW7 ....130 C2
Paget Pl Kingston KT2 177 A4
Thames Ditton KT7 ....196 D1
Paget Rd N16 ....51 B1
Hillingdon UB10 ....83 A3
Ilford IG1 ....78 D4
Paget Rise SE18 .....144 C5
Paget St EC1 ....234 C2
Paget Terr SE18 .....144 D6
Pagham Ho W10 .....90 C3
Pagin Ho N15 ....51 C4
Pagitts Gr EN4 ....1 D4
Pagnell St SE14 .....141 B5
Pagoda Ave TW9 ...132 B2
Pagoda Gdns SE3 ...142 B3
Paignton Rd N15 .....51 C3
Ruislip HA4 ....62 A5
Paine Ct SE3 ....142 D6
Paines Cl HA5 ....41 A6
Paine's La HA5 ....23 A1
Pain's Cl CR4 ....181 B1
Painsthorpe Rd 3 N16 ....73 C5
Painswick Ct 1 SE15 ....139 D5
Painters Mews SE16 .118 A2
Painters Rd IG2,RM6 ..58 A6
Paisley Rd
Carshalton SM5 ......202 B1
Tottenham N22 ....32 D2
Pakeman Ho SE1 ....251 D2
Pakeman Prim Sch N7 ....72 B5
Pakeman St N7 ....72 B5
Pakenham Cl SW12 ..159 A3
Pakenham St WC1 ....94 B3 240 D6
Palace Ave W8 ....113 D4 245 D2
Palace Court Gdns N10 ....49 C6
Palace Ct NW3 ....69 D3
SE9 ....166 B5
W2 ....113 D6 245 C5
Harrow HA3 ....44 A3
South Norwood CR7 ...205 B5
Streatham SW2 ......160 C2
Palace Garden Mews W8 ....245 B4
Palace Gardens Terr W8 ....113 D5 245 C3
Palace Gate W8 ....114 A4 246 A1
Palace Gates Rd N22 .31 D2
Palace Gdns
Buckhurst Hill IG9 .....21 D3
Enfield EN2 ....5 B1
Palace Gdns Mews W8 ....113 D5 245 D3
Palace Gn W8 ....113 D5 245 C3
New Addington CR0 ...223 B1
Palace Gr BR1 ....187 B2
Penge SE19 ....183 D3
Palace Mans W14 ...254 B4
Palace Mews E17 .....53 B5
SW1 ....258 B3
SW6 ....264 D4
Palace of Ind HA9 ....66 C4
Palace Par E17 ....53 C5
Palace Pl SW1 ......259 A6
Palace Rd BR1 ......187 B2
N8 ....49 D4
East Molesey KT8 ......196 B6
Kingston KT1 ....197 D5
Penge SE19 ....183 D3
Ruislip HA4 ....63 A4
Streatham SE27,SW16, SW2 ....160 C2
Wood Green N11 ......32 A3
Palace Sq SE19 .....183 D3
Palace St SW1 ....115 C3 259 A6
Palace View SE12 ....165 A2
Bromley BR1 ....209 B6
Croydon CR0 ....223 B4
Palace View Rd E4 ....35 D5
Palamon Ct SE1 .....263 D2
Palamos Rd E10 .....53 C1
Palatine Ave N16 .....73 C4
Palatine Rd N16 .....73 C4
Palemead Cl SW6 ...134 D4
Palermo Rd NW10 ....90 A5
Palestine Gr SW19 ...180 B2
Palewell Cl BR5 .....190 B1
Palewell Common Dr SW14 ....155 B6
Palewell Pk SW14 ...133 B1
Palfrey Pl SW8 ....138 B5 270 D4
Palgrave Ave UB1 ...107 C6
Palgrave Gdns NW1 .237 A5
Palgrave Ho 4 NW3 ...70 D3
7 SE5 ....139 A5
Twickenham TW2 ......152 A4
Palgrave Rd W12 ....111 D3
Palissy St 35 E2 ......95 D4
Pallant Ho SE1 ......262 D5
Pallant Way BR6 .....226 C5
Pallet Way SE18 .....144 A4
Palliser Ct W14 ......254 A1
Palliser Ho 21 E1 ....96 D3
3 SE10 ....142 B6
Palliser Rd W14 ....113 A1 254 A1
Pallister Terr SW15 ..155 D2
Pall Mall SW1 ....115 D5 249 C3
Pall Mall E SW1 ....115 D5 249 D4
Pall Mall Pl SW1 ....249 B3
Palmar Cres DA7 .....147 C3
Palmar Rd DA7 ......147 C3
Palm Ave DA14 ......190 D4
Palm Cl E10 ....75 D5
Palm Ct N16 ....73 B6
17 SE15 ....139 D5
Beckenham BR3 ......207 B6
Wood Green N22 ......32 B3
Palmeira Rd DA16 ...146 D2
Palmer Ave KT4,SM3 .216 C4
Palmer Cl
Heston TW5 ....129 C4
West Wickham BR4 ...224 B6
Palmer Cres KT1 ....198 A6
Palmer Ct NW10 .....89 B6
Palmer Gdns EN5 .....12 D6
Palmer Ho 5 N19 ....71 C5
8 NW5 ....71 C4
6 SE14 ....140 D5
Palmer Pl N7 ....72 C3
Palmer Rd E13 ....99 B3
Dagenham RM8 ....58 D1
Palmer's Ct 11 N11 ...31 C5
Palmers Gr KT8 .....195 C5
Palmers Green High Sch N21 ....16 C2
Palmers Green Sta N13 ....32 B6
Palmers La EN3 ....6 C4
Palmers Rd E2 ....96 D5
Palmer's Rd N11 ......31 C5
Palmers Rd
Mortlake SW14 ......133 A2
Thornton Heath SW16 .182 B1
Palmer St SW1 ......259 C6
Palmerston Cres SE18 ....145 A6
Bowes Park N13 ......32 B5
Palmerston Ct E17 ....53 B5
22 E3 ....96 D5
2 Buckhurst Hill IG9 ...21 C2
9 Surbiton KT6 ......197 D2
Palmerston Ctr HA3 ..42 D6
Palmerston Gr 4 SW19 ....179 C3
Palmerston Ho SW11 268 B1
W8 ....245 A3
Palmerston Rd BR6 ..227 A3
E17 ....53 B5
E7 ....77 B2
NW6 ....69 B1
NW6 ....69 C1
W3 ....111 A3
Bowes Park N22 ....32 B4
Buckhurst Hill IG9 .....21 C3
Harrow HA3 ....42 D6
Hounslow TW3 ....130 A4
Merton SW19 ....179 C3
Mortlake SW14 ......133 A1
Sutton SM1 ....218 A3
Thornton Heath CR0 ...205 B4
Twickenham TW2 ......152 C5
Wallington SM5 ......219 A4
Palmerston Way SW8 ....268 D3
Palm Gr W5 ....110 A3
Palm Tree Ct 3 N17 ...33 D1
Palm Tree Ho 2 SE14 ....140 D5
Pamela Ct N12 ....29 D4
NW10 ....68 A1
Pamela Gdns HA5 ....40 B4
Pamela Ho 14 E8 ......95 D6
Pamlion Ct N4 ....50 A2
Pams Way KT19 ......215 B3
Panama Ho 5 E1 ....96 D2
Panbro Ho 7 SE18 ..144 B4
Pancras La EC2 .....242 C1
Pancras Rd NW1 ....93 D5 232 D4
Pandora Ct 4 KT6 ...198 A3
Pandora Rd NW6 .....69 C2
Panfield Mews IG2 ....56 C3
Panfield Rd SE2 ......124 A3
Pangbourne NW1 ....232 A1
Pangbourne Ave W10 .90 C2
Pangbourne Ct N20 ..14 A4
Upper Tooting SW17 ..180 A6
Pangbourne Dr HA7 ..26 A5
Pangbourne Ho 4 N7 72 A3
Panhard Pl UB1 .....107 D6
Pank Ave EN5 ....14 A6
Pankhurst Cl 7 SE14 140 D5
Isleworth TW7 ....130 D2
Pankhurst Rd KT12 ..194 C2
Panmuir Rd SW20 ...178 B2
Panmure Cl N5 ....72 D4
Panmure Ct 11 UB1 ...86 A1
Panmure Rd SE26 ...162 B1
Panorama Ct N6 ......49 C3
Pansy Gdns W12 .....112 A6
Panther Dr NW10 .....67 B3
Pantiles Cl N13 ....32 D5
Pantiles The BR1 ....210 A6
DA7 ....147 B5
NW11 ....47 B4
Bushey WD23 ....8 B3
Panton Cl CR0 ....204 D1
Panton St SW1 ......249 C5
Panyer Alley EC2 ....242 A2
Papermill Cl SM5 ....219 A4
Paper Mill Wharf E14 ....119 A6
Papillons Wlk SE3 ...143 A2
Papworth Gdns N7 ...72 B3
Papworth Way SW2 .160 C4
Parade Mans 2 NW4 .46 B4
19 SE5 ....139 A3
Parade Mews SE27, SW2 ....160 D2
Parade The SW11 ....136 D5 267 D4
Ashford TW16 ....171 D3
Claygate KT10 ....212 C2
Croydon CR0 ....220 B3
Greenford UB6 ....65 B3
2 Kingston KT2 .....176 A1
Paradise Pas N7 ......72 C3
Paradise Pl 15 SE7 ..122 A2
Paradise Rd SW4 ....138 A3
Richmond TW10 ......154 A6
Paradise Row E2 .....96 B4
Paradise St SE16 ....118 B4
Paradise Wlk SW3 ....136 D6 267 D6
Paragon Cl E16 ....99 A1
Paragon Ct NW4 ......29 A2
Paragon Gr KT5 .....198 B3
Paragon Mews SE1 ..262 D4
Paragon Pl SE3 .....142 D3
Surbiton KT5 ....198 B3
Paragon Rd E9 ....74 C2
Paragon The SE17 ...262 C4
SE3 ....143 A3
Paramount Bldg EC1 241 C6
Paramount Ct WC1 ..239 B5
Paramount Ho 8 E11 .76 C5
Parayhouse Sch W12 112 B5
Parbury Rd SE23 ....163 A5
Parbury Rise KT9 ...214 A2
Parchmore Rd CR7 ..205 A6
Parchmore Way CR7 .182 D1
Pardes House & Beis Yaakov Sch (Boys) N3 ....29 B1
Pardoner St SE1 ....117 B3 262 D6
Pardon St EC1 ....241 D6
Parfett St E1 ....96 A1
Parfew Ct 2 SE22 ..162 B2
Parfitt Cl NW3 ....48 A1
Parfrey St W6 ....134 C6
Pargraves Ct HA9 ....66 C6
Parham Dr IG2 ....56 D4
Paris Gdn SE1 ....116 D5 251 C4
Parish CE Prim Sch BR1 ....187 A3
Parish Church CE Inf & Jun Schs CR0 ......220 D5
Parish Ct KT6 ....198 A3
Parish Gate Dr DA15 .167 C5
Parish La SE20 ......184 D3
Paris Ho 12 E2 ....96 B5
Parish Wharf 6 SE7 .122 A2
Park App DA16 ....146 B1
Park Ave BR1 ....187 A4
BR6 ....226 C6
E15 ....76 C2
N3 ....29 D2
NW11 ....47 D1
NW2 ....68 C2
Barking IG11 ....79 A2
Edmonton N18 ....34 A6
Enfield EN1 ....17 C5
Ilford IG1 ....56 C1
Mitcham CR4 ....181 B3
Mortlake SW14 ......133 B1
Palmers Green N13 .....16 C1
Ruislip HA4 ....39 C3
Southall UB1 ....107 C5
Twickenham TW3 .....151 D5
Upper Halliford TW17 .193 C6
Wallend E6 ....100 C5
Wallington SM5 ......219 A2
West Wickham BR4 ...224 A6
Woodford IG8 ....37 B5
Wood Green N22 ....32 B2
Park Ave E KT17 .....216 A2
Park Ave N N8 ....49 D5
NW10 ....68 B3
Park Avenue Mews CR4 ....181 B3
Park Avenue Rd N17 ..34 B3
Park Ave S N8 ....49 D5
Park Ave W KT17 ....216 A2
Park Bsns Ctr 4 NW6 91 C4
Park Chase HA9 ......66 B4
Park Cl 20 E9 ....96 C6
N12 ....30 B6
Park Cl *continued*
NW2 ....68 B5
SW1 ....247 C1
W14 ....113 B3 254 D6
Ealing NW10 ....88 B4
Hampton TW12 ....174 A2
Harrow HA3 ....24 C2
Isleworth TW3,TW7 ...152 A6
Kingston KT2 ....176 C2
Wallington SM5 ......218 D2
Park Cotts 10 TW1 ...153 B5
Park Cres N3 ....30 A3
W1 ....93 B3 238 C5
Enfield EN2 ....5 B1
Harrow HA3 ....24 C2
Twickenham TW2 .....152 B3
Park Cres Mews E W1 ....238 D5
Park Cres Mews W W1 ....238 C5
Park Croft HA8 ....27 A2
Parkcroft Rd SE12 ...164 D4
Park Ct E17 ....53 D4
N11 ....31 D3
N12 ....30 B5
SW11 ....268 C2
SW4 ....159 D6
2 Beckenham BR3 ...207 D6
2 Chingford E4 ......20 A2
Dulwich SE21 ....161 B1
New Barnet EN5 ....14 B4
New Malden KT3 .....199 B5
Teddington KT1 ......175 C2
Upper Tooting SW12 ..159 A3
Wallington SM6 ......220 A3
Wembley HA9 ....66 A3
Parkdale N11 ....31 D4
Parkdale Cres KT4 ...215 B5
Parkdale Rd SE18 ...123 C1
Park Dr NW11 ....47 D1
Acton W3 ....110 C3
Enfield N21 ....17 A5
Harrow HA2 ....41 C2
Mortlake SW14 ......133 B1
Stanmore HA3 ....24 C4
Woolwich SE7 ....144 A6
Park Dwellings 7 NW3 ....70 D3
Park End NW3 ....70 C4
Bromley BR1 ....186 D2
Parker Cl E16 ....122 A5
Parker Ct N1 ....235 B6
SW4 ....270 A1
Wimbledon SW19 .....179 A3
Parke Rd
Barnes SW13 ....134 A4
Sunbury TW16 ....194 A5
Parker Ho 4 SE18 ...122 D1
Parker Mews WC2 ..240 B2
Parker Rd CR0 ....221 A4
Parkers Rd N10 ......30 C2
Parkers Row 12 SE16 118 A4
Parker's Row SE1 ...253 D1
Parker St E16 ....122 A5
WC2 ....94 A1 240 B2
Park Farm SE7 ......144 A6
Park Farm Cl N2 .....48 A6
Pinner HA5 ....40 B4
Park Farm Ct UB3 ...105 C6
Park Farm Rd
Bromley BR1 ....187 D2
Kingston KT2 ....176 A3
Parkfield 3 TW7 ....130 C4
Parkfield Ave
Feltham TW13 ....150 A1
Harrow HA2 ....24 A1
Hillingdon UB10 ......82 D4
Mortlake SW14 ......133 C1
Northolt UB5 ....84 D5
Parkfield Cl
Edgware HA8 ....26 D4
Northolt UB5 ....85 A5
Parkfield Cres
Feltham TW13 ....150 A1
Harrow HA2 ....24 A1
Ruislip HA4 ....63 A5
Parkfield Dr UB5 .....84 D5
Parkfield Gdns HA2 ...41 D6
Parkfield Ho HA2 ....23 D2
Parkfield Ind Est SW11 ....137 A3
Parkfield Par TW13 ..150 A1
Parkfield Prim Sch NW4 ....46 B2
Parkfield Rd NW10 ...68 B1
SE14 ....141 B4
Feltham TW13 ....150 A1
Harrow HA2 ....64 A5
Northolt UB5 ....85 A5
Uxbridge UB10 ....60 D6
Parkfields
Croydon CR0 ....207 B1
Putney SW15 ....134 C1
Parkfields Ave NW9 ...45 B1
Wimbledon SW20 ....178 B1
Parkfields Cl SM5 ...219 A4
Parkfields Rd TW10 ..176 B5
Parkfield St N1 ....94 C5 234 B4
Parkfield Way BR2 ..210 B4
Park Flats N6 ....48 C2
Parkgate SE3 ....142 D2
Park Gate N2 ....48 B6
Ealing W5 ....87 D2
Southgate N21 ....16 B4
Parkgate Ave EN4 ......2 A4
Parkgate Cl KT2 .....176 D4
Parkgate Cres EN4 .....2 A4
Park Gate Ct TW12 ..174 A5
Parkgate Gdns SW14 155 B6
Parkgate House Sch SW11 ....137 A1
Park Gate Mans N2 ...48 B6
Parkgate Mews N6 ...49 C2
Parkgate Rd SW11 ....136 C5 267 B3
Wallington SM5,SM6 ..219 B3
Park Gates HA2 ......63 C4
Park Gdns NW9 ......44 D6
Kingston KT2 ....176 B5
Park Gr BR1 ....187 B2
E15 ....99 A6
N11 ....31 D3
Edgware HA8 ....26 B5
Park Grove Rd E11 ...76 C6
Park Hall Rd N2 ......48 C5
Dulwich SE21 ....161 B1
Park Hall Road Trad Est SE21 ....161 B1
Parkham Ct BR2 .....186 C1
Parkham St SW11 ....136 C4 267 A1
Parkham Way N10 ....31 C1
Park High Sch HA7 ...25 D1
Park Hill BR1 ....210 B5
SW4 ....159 D6
Ealing W5 ....87 D2
Forest Hill SE23 ......162 C3
Loughton IG10 ....21 D6
Richmond TW10 ......154 B5
Wallington SM5 ......218 D2
Park Hill Cl SM5 .....218 C3
Park Hill Ct
Croydon CR0 ....221 C6
Ealing W5 ....87 D2
Upper Tooting SW17 ..158 D1
Parkhill Inf Sch IG5 ..56 C6
Park Hill Inf Sch CR0 221 C5
Parkhill Jun Sch IG5 .56 C6
Park Hill Jun Sch CR0 ....221 C5
Parkhill Rd DA5 .....169 B4
NW3 ....70 D3
Chingford E4 ....20 A4
Sidcup DA15 ....167 C1
Park Hill Rd
Beckenham BR2 ......186 C1
South Croydon CR0 ...221 C5
Wallington SM6 ......219 B1
Park Hill Rise CR0 ..221 D5
Park Hill Sch KT2 ..176 C3
Park Hill Wlk 10 NW3 .70 D3
Park Ho 35 E9 ....74 C1
N4 ....72 D6
8 SE5 ....139 B4
Forest Hill SE26 ....184 A5
Sidcup DA14 ....190 A5
Southgate N21 ....16 B4
Parkholme Rd E8 .....74 A2
Park House Gdns TW1 ....153 C6
Park House Mid Sch SW19 ....179 B6
Parkhouse St SE5 ...139 B5
Parkhurst Ct N7 ......72 A4
Parkhurst Gdns 2 DA5 ....169 C4
Parkhurst Rd E17 ....53 A5
N11 ....31 A5
N7 ....72 A4
Bowes Park N22 ....32 B4
Little Ilford E12 ....78 C4
Sidcup DA5 ....169 C4
Sutton SM1 ....218 B4
Tottenham N17 ....34 A1
Parkin Ho SE20 .....184 D3
Parkinson Ct EC1 ...235 D2

Parkinson Ct continued
N1 . . . 235 C1
Parkinson Ho 6 E9 . . .74 C1
Park La E15 . . .98 B6
W1 . . .115 A6 248 A5
Cheam SM3 . . .217 A2
Cranford TW5 . . .128 A5
Dagenham RM6 . . .58 D3
Edmonton N9 . . .17 D1
Harrow HA2 . . .63 D5
Hayes UB4 . . .83 C3
Richmond TW9 . . .131 D1
South Croydon CR0 . . .221 B5
Stanmore HA7 . . .9 A1
Teddington TW11 . . .174 D4
Tottenham N17 . . .34 A3
Wallington SM5,SM6 . .219 A3
Wembley HA9 . . .66 A4
Parkland Ct E15 . . .76 C3
W14 . . .244 A2
Parkland Gdns 12
SW19 . . .156 D3
Parkland Gr
Ashford TW15 . . .170 C6
Hounslow TW7 . . .130 D4
Parkland Rd
Ashford TW15 . . .170 C6
Woodford IG8 . . .37 B3
Wood Green N22 . . .32 B1
Parklands N6 . . .49 B2
SE22 . . .162 B6
Bushey WD23 . . .8 A5
Kingston KT5 . . .198 B4
Parklands Cl
Hadley Wood EN4 . . .2 B5
Ilford IG2 . . .57 A2
Mortlake SW14 . . .155 A6
Parklands Ct TW5 . . .128 D3
Parklands Dr N3 . . .47 A6
Parklands Par TW5 . . .128 D3
Parklands Rd SW16 . . .181 B5
Parklands Way KT4 . . .215 C6
Parkland Wlk N4,N8 . . .50 B2
Park Lane Cl N17 . . .34 A3
Park Lane Prim Sch
HA9 . . .66 A3
Park Lawn CR7 . . .183 A1
Parklea Cl NW9 . . .27 C2
Park Lea N16 . . .51 C2
Parkleigh Ct SW19 . . .179 D1
Parkleigh Rd SW19 . . .179 D1
Parkleys
Richmond KT2,TW10 . .175 D6
Richmond, Ham Common
TW10 . . .176 A6
Park Lo 10 E1 . . .118 B5
N12 . . .30 A5
NW2 . . .68 C4
11 NW8 . . .70 B1
3 Ealing W5 . . .87 B3
Park Lofts 7 SW4 . . .160 A6
Park Lorne NW8 . . .230 B1
Park Mans 5 NW4 . . .46 B4
NW8 . . .230 A3
SW1 . . .247 C1
SW11 . . .267 C1
SW6 . . .264 B1
SW8 . . .270 B6
W6 . . .111 D3
Forest Hill SE26 . . .162 C1
Park Mead DA15 . . .168 B5
Parkmead SW15 . . .156 B5
Park Mead HA2 . . .63 D5
Parkmead Gdns NW7 . . .28 D4
Park Mews BR7 . . .188 D4
W10 . . .91 A5
Stanwell TW19 . . .148 B4
Parkmore Cl IG8 . . .37 A6
Park Nook Gdns EN2 . . .5 B4
Park Par NW10 . . .89 D5
NW9 . . .45 B6
Acton W3 . . .110 C3
Hayes UB3 . . .83 C1
Park Pl E14 . . .119 C5
SW1 . . .115 C5 249 A4
W3 . . .110 C2
Ealing W5 . . .109 D5
Hampton TW12 . . .174 A4
Wembley HA9 . . .66 B4
Park Place Dr W3 . . .110 C3
Park Place Villas W2 . .236 B4
Park Prim Sch E15 . . .76 D1
Park Rd BR1 . . .187 B2
BR7 . . .188 D4
E10 . . .53 C1
E15 . . .99 A6
E17 . . .53 B4

Park Rd continued
E6 . . .99 C6
N11 . . .31 D3
N14 . . .15 D4
N2 . . .48 B6
N8 . . .49 D4
N8,N15 . . .50 D5
NW10 . . .89 D4
NW1,NW8 . .92 C3 237 B6
NW4 . . .46 B3
NW9 . . .45 B2
Ashford TW15 . . .170 D5
Barnet EN4 . . .2 C1
Barnet EN5 . . .1 B1
Beckenham BR3 . . .185 C3
Cheam SM3 . . .217 A2
Chiswick W4 . . .133 B6
Ealing W7 . . .108 D6
East Molesey KT8 . . .196 A5
Edmonton N18 . . .34 A6
Feltham TW13 . . .172 D6
Hackbridge SM6 . . .219 B6
Hampton TW12 . . .174 A5
Hayes UB4 . . .83 C2
Ilford IG1 . . .79 B5
Isleworth TW3,TW7 . . .152 A6
Isleworth TW7 . . .131 B3
Kingston KT2,TW10 . . .176 C3
Lower Halliford TW17 . .192 C1
Mitcham SW19 . . .180 C4
New Malden KT3 . . .199 B5
Richmond TW10 . . .154 B3
South Norwood SE25 . . .205 C5
Sunbury TW16 . . .172 B3
Teddington KT1 . . .175 C2
Teddington TW11 . . .174 D4
Twickenham TW1 . . .153 C5
Uxbridge UB8 . . .60 A2
Wallington SM6 . . .219 B3
Wanstead E12 . . .77 B6
Wembley HA0 . . .66 A2
Park Rd E Acton W3 . . .111 A4
Uxbridge UB10 . . .82 A5
Park Rd N W3 . . .110 D4
W4 . . .111 B1
Park Ridings N8 . . .50 C6
Park Rise
Forest Hill SE23 . . .163 A3
Harrow HA3 . . .24 C4
Park Rise Rd SE23 . . .163 A3
Park Road Ho 3 KT2 176 C3
Park Row SE10 . . .142 B6
Park Royal NW10 . . .88 D3
Park Royal Bsns Ctr
NW10 . . .89 A3
Park Royal Metro Ctr
NW10 . . .88 D2
Park Royal Rd NW10,
W3 . . .89 A3
Park Royal Sta W5 . . .88 C3
Park S SW11 . . .268 A1
Park Sch IG1 . . .56 D1
Park Sheen 3 SW14 132 D1
Parkshot TW9 . . .132 A1
Parkside DA14 . . .168 B2
N3 . . .29 D3
NW7 . . .28 A4
SE3 . . .142 D5
W3 . . .111 C5
Park Side NW2 . . .68 B4
Parkside
1 Beckenham BR3 . . .185 D1
Cheam SM3 . . .217 A2
Ealing W5 . . .110 A6
Hampton TW12 . . .174 A5
Hayes UB3 . . .105 C6
Wimbledon SW19 . . .178 D6
Park Side IG9 . . .21 B2
Parkside Ave BR1 . . .210 A5
Wimbledon SW19 . . .178 D5
Parkside Cl SE20 . . .184 C3
Parkside Cres N7 . . .72 C5
Tolworth KT5 . . .199 A3
Parkside Ct
Bowes Park N22 . . .32 B4
2 Wanstead E11 . . .55 A3
Parkside Dr HA8 . . .10 C1
Parkside Est E9 . . .96 D6
Parkside Gdns
East Barnet EN4 . . .15 A4
Wimbledon SW19 . . .178 D6
Parkside Lo DA17 . . .125 D2
Parkside Rd
Belvedere DA17 . . .125 D2
Hounslow TW3 . . .151 D4
Parkside St SW11 . . .268 A1
Parkside Terr N18 . . .33 B6
Parkside Way HA2 . . .42 A5
Park Sq E NW1 93 B3 238 D6
Park Sq Mews NW1 . 238 C5

Park Sq W
NW1 . . .93 B3 238 C5
Park St SE1 . . .117 A5 252 B4
W1 . . .115 A6 248 A5
Croydon CR0 . . .221 A6
Teddington TW11 . . .174 C4
Parkstead Rd SW15 . . .156 B6
Park Steps W2 . . .247 B6
Park St James NW8 . . .230 C5
Parkstone Ave N18 . . .33 C5
Parkstone Rd E17 . . .54 A6
3 SE15 . . .140 A3
Park Terr
Carshalton SM5 . . .218 C5
Enfield EN3 . . .7 A5
New Malden KT4 . . .200 A1
Park The N6 . . .49 A3
NW11 . . .47 D1
Ealing W5 . . .109 D5
Forest Hill SE23 . . .162 C5
Sidcup DA14 . . .190 A5
Wallington SM5 . . .218 C5
Parkthorne Cl HA2 . . .41 D3
Parkthorne Dr HA2 . . .41 C3
Parkthorne Rd SW12 159 D4
Park Twrs W1 . . .248 C3
Park View N5 . . .73 A4
NW2 . . .68 C4
W3 . . .89 A2
Parkview UB6 . . .87 A4
Park View
Kingston KT3 . . .199 D6
Morden SM4 . . .202 B4
Pinner HA5 . . .23 B2
Southgate N21 . . .16 B4
Wembley HA9 . . .66 D3
Yiewsley UB7 . . .104 A6
Park View Cres N11 . . .31 B6
Park View Ct N12 . . .30 C6
NW9 . . .45 A5
SW18 . . .157 C5
Parkview Ct
Fulham SW6 . . .135 A3
Penge SE20 . . .184 B2
Park View Dr CR4 . . .180 B1
Park View Gdns NW4 . .46 D4
Redbridge IG4 . . .56 B5
Wood Green N22 . . .32 C2
Park View Ho SE24 . . .160 D1
Parkview Lo BR3 . . .207 D6
Park View Mews 24
SW9 . . .138 B3
Park View Rd DA16 . . .146 D2
N3 . . .29 D2
NW10 . . .67 D4
SE9 . . .166 D2
Parkview Rd CR0 . . .206 A1
Park View Rd
Ealing W5 . . .88 A2
Hillingdon UB8 . . .82 C1
Pinner HA5 . . .22 B3
Southall UB1 . . .107 C5
Tottenham N17 . . .34 A1
Park Village E
NW1 . . .93 B5 231 D3
Park Village W
NW1 . . .93 B5 231 C4
Park Villas RM6 . . .58 D3
Parkville Rd
SW6 . . .135 B5 264 C3
Park Vista SE10 . . .142 B6
Park Walk Prim Sch
SW10 . . .136 B6 266 C5
Parkway DA18 . . .125 A3
NW1 . . .93 B6 231 C5
Park Way N20 . . .30 D6
NW11 . . .47 A4
W3 . . .110 C2
Parkway
Hillingdon UB10 . . .60 D1
Ilford IG3 . . .79 D5
Palmers Green N14 . . .16 A2
West Barnes SW20 . . .200 D5
Woodford IG8 . . .37 C5
Park Way
East Molesey KT8 . . .195 D6
Edgware HA8 . . .26 D2
Enfield EN2 . . .4 C3
Feltham TW14 . . .150 B4
Ruislip HA4 . . .40 A1
Park Way Ct HA4 . . .39 D1
Parkway Prim Sch
DA18 . . .125 A3
Parkway The
Cranford TW5 . . .128 B5
Hayes UB2,UB3,UB4,
TW5 . . .106 B3
Hayes UB4 . . .84 D2
Parkway Trad Est
TW5 . . .128 C6

Park West W2 . .92 C1 237 B1
Park West Pl
W1,W2 . . .92 C1 237 B2
Park Wlk
SW10 . . .136 B6 266 C6
Parkwood N20 . . .14 D2
NW8 . . .230 C5
Beckenham BR3 . . .185 C3
Parkwood Ave KT10 . . .196 A1
Parkwood Gr TW16 . . .194 A6
Parkwood Mews N6 . . .49 B3
Parkwood Prim Sch
N4 . . .72 D6
Parkwood Rd DA5 . . .169 B4
Hounslow TW7 . . .130 D4
Wimbledon SW19 . . .179 B5
Parliament Ct NW3 . . .70 C4
Parliament Hill NW3 . . .70 C4
Parliament Hill Mans
NW5 . . .71 A4
Parliament Hill Sch
NW5 . . .71 A4
Parliament Mews
SW14 . . .133 A3
Parliament Sq *
SW1 . . .116 A4 250 A1
Parliament St
SW1 . . .116 A4 250 A2
Parliament View
Apartments SE11 . . .260 B4
Parma Cres SW11 . . .136 D1
Parmiter Ind Est 23
E2 . . .96 B5
Parmiter St E2 . . .96 B5
Parmoor Ct EC1 . . .242 A6
Parnall Ho 11 SE19 . . .183 C6
Parnell Cl HA8 . . .27 A6
W12 . . .112 B3
Parnell Rd E3 . . .97 B6
Parnham St E14 . . .97 A1
Parolles Rd N19 . . .49 C1
Paroma Rd DA17 . . .125 C3
Parr Cl N9 . . .34 B6
Parr Ct N1 . . .235 C4
Feltham TW13 . . .172 C6
Parrington Ho 1
SW4 . . .159 D5
Parr Pl W4 . . .111 D2
Parr Rd E6 . . .99 D6
Stanmore HA7 . . .26 A2
Parr's Pl TW12 . . .173 C2
Parr St N1 . . .95 B5 235 C4
Parry Ave E6 . . .100 B3
Parry Cl KT17 . . .216 A1
Parry Ho 32 E1 . . .118 C3
Parry Pl SE18 . . .122 D2
Parry Rd W10 . . .91 A4
South Norwood SE25 . .205 C6
Parry St SW8 138 A6 270 B6
Parsifal Coll NW3 . . .69 C4
Parsifal Ho NW3 . . .69 C4
Parsifal Rd NW6 . . .69 C3
Parsley Gdns CR0 . . .206 D1
Parsloes Ave RM9 . . .81 A3
Parsloes Prim Sch
RM9 . . .81 B2
Parsonage Cl UB3 . . .83 D1
Parsonage Gdns EN2 . . .5 A3
Parsonage La DA14 . . .191 B6
Enfield EN2 . . .5 A3
Parsonage Manorway
DA8,DA17 . . .147 C6
Parsonage St E14 . . .120 A2
Parson Ct SE13 . . .141 D2
Parsons Gn
SW6 . . .135 C3 265 A1
Parsons Gr 2 E4 . . .10 C1
Parsons Green La
SW6 . . .135 C4 265 A2
Parsons Green Sta
SW6 . . .135 C4 265 A1
Parsons Hill SE18 . . .122 C3
Parsons Ho W2 . . .236 C5
21 Streatham SW12 . .160 A4
Parsons Lo NW6 . . .69 D1
Parsons Mead KT8 . . .196 A6
Parson's Mead CR0 . . .204 D1
Parsons Rd E13 . . .99 C5
Edgware HA8 . . .10 C1
Parson St NW4 . . .46 C5
Parthenia Rd
SW6 . . .135 C4 265 B1
Partingdale La NW7 . . .28 D5
Partington Cl N19 . . .49 D1
Partridge Cl 1 E16 . . .99 D2
Barnet EN5 . . .12 C5
Bushey WD23 . . .8 A1
Stanmore HA7 . . .26 A6
Partridge Ct EC1 . . .241 C6
Partridge Dr BR6 . . .227 A5

Partridge Gn SE9 . . .166 C1
Partridge Ho 20 E3 . . .97 B5
Partridge Rd
8 Hampton TW12 . . .173 C4
Sidcup DA14 . . .189 C6
Partridge Sq 3 E6 . . .100 A2
Partridge Way N22 . . .32 A2
Pasadena Cl UB3 . . .106 B4
Pascall Ho SE17 . . .139 A6
Pascal St
SW8 . . .137 D5 269 D2
Pascoe Rd SE13 . . .164 B6
Pasley Cl SE17 . . .262 A1
Pasquier Rd E17 . . .53 A6
Passey Pl SE9 . . .166 B5
Passfield Dr E14 . . .97 D2
Passfield Ho SE18 . . .123 A4
Passfield Path 13
SE28 . . .124 B6
Passfields W14 . . .254 C1
Catford SE6 . . .164 A1
Passing Alley EC1 . . .241 D5
Passingham Ho TW5 129 C6
Passmore Gdns N11 . . .31 D4
Passmore Ho 12 N9 . . .18 A1
Passmores Edwards Ho
N11 . . .31 D3
Passmore St
SW1 . . .115 A1 258 A2
Pasteur Cl NW9 . . .27 C1
Pasteur Gdns N18 . . .33 A5
Paston Cl SM6 . . .219 C5
Paston Cres SE12 . . .165 B4
Pastor Ct N6 . . .49 C3
Pastor St SE11,
SE11 . . .116 D2 261 D1
Pasture Cl Bushey WD23 . .8 A4
Wembley HA0 . . .65 B5
Pasture Rd
Catford SE6 . . .164 D3
Dagenham RM9 . . .81 B4
Wembley HA0 . . .65 B5
Pastures Mead UB10 . . .60 C2
Pastures The N20 . . .13 B3
Patcham Terr SW8 . . .268 D2
Patch Cl UB10 . . .82 B6
Patching Way UB4 . . .85 A2
Patent Ho E14 . . .97 D2
Paternoster Row
EC2,EC4 . . .95 A1 242 A1
Paternoster Sq
EC4 . . .94 D1 241 D2
Pater St W8 . . .113 C3 255 A5
Pates Manor Dr
TW14 . . .149 B4
Pathfield Rd SW16 . . .181 D4
Path The SW19 . . .179 D2
Patience Rd SW11 . . .136 C3
Patio Cl SW4 . . .159 D5
Patmore Ho 9 N16 . . .73 C3
Patmore St
SW8 . . .137 C4 269 B2
Paton Cl E3 . . .97 C4
Paton Ho 3 SW9 . . .138 B3
Paton St EC1 . . .235 A1
Patricia Ct
Chislehurst BR7 . . .189 B2
Woolwich SE2 . . .146 B5
Patricia Villas N17 . . .34 B2
Patrick Coman Ho
EC1 . . .234 C1
Patrick Connolly Gdns 41
E3 . . .97 D4
Patrick Rd E13 . . .99 C4
Patriot Sq E2 . . .96 B5
Patrol Pl SE6 . . .163 D5
Pat Shaw Ho 2 E1 . . .96 D3
Patshull Pl NW5 . . .71 C2
Patshull Rd NW5 . . .71 C2
Patson Cl E5 . . .74 D5
Pattenden Rd SE6 . . .163 B3
Patten Ho N4 . . .51 A1
Patten Rd SW18 . . .158 C4
Patterdale NW1 . . .231 D1
Patterdale Cl BR1 . . .186 C4
Patterdale Rd SE15 . . .140 C5
Patterson Ct SE19 . . .183 D4
Patterson Rd SE19 . . .183 D4
Pattina Wlk SE16 . . .119 A5
Pattinson Point 10
E16 . . .99 A2
Pattison Ho 1 E1 . . .96 D1
SE1 . . .252 B2
Pattison Rd NW2 . . .69 C5
Pattison Wlk SE18 . . .123 A1
Paul Byrne Ho 3 N2 . .48 A6
Paul Cl E15 . . .76 C1
Paul Ct N3 . . .29 A1
7 Edmonton N18 . . .34 A4
Paulet Rd SE5 . . .138 D4

Paul Gdns CR0 . . .221 D6
Paulhan Rd HA3 . . .43 D5
Paul Ho 13 W10 . . .91 A3
Paulin Dr N21 . . .16 C4
Pauline Cres TW2 . . .152 A3
Pauline Ho 19 E1 . . .96 A2
Paulinus Cl BR5 . . .190 C1
Paul Julius Cl E14 . . .120 A6
Paul Robeson Cl E6 . . .100 C4
Paul's Ho E3 . . .97 B4
Paulson Ho 7 IG11 . . .78 D1
Paul St E15 . . .98 C4
EC2 . . .95 C3 243 B4
Paultons Ho SW3 . . .266 C6
Paultons Sq
SW3 . . .136 B6 266 C6
Paultons St
SW3 . . .136 B6 266 D5
Pauntley Ho 6 N19 . . .49 C1
Pauntley St 4 N19 . . .49 C1
Pavan Ct 29 E2 . . .96 C4
Paved Ct 9 TW9 . . .153 C6
Paveley Dr
SW11 . . .136 C5 267 A3
Paveley Ho N1 . . .233 C2
Paveley St
NW8 . . .92 C3 237 B6
Pavement Mews 1
RM6 . . .58 D2
Pavement Sq CR0 . . .206 A4
Pavement The E11 . . .54 A1
SW4 . . .137 C1
W5 . . .110 A3
11 West Norwood
SE27 . . .183 A6
Pavet Cl RM10 . . .81 D2
Pavilion Ct NW3 . . .70 C4
5 NW3 . . .70 A4
8 NW6 . . .91 C4
3 Wimbledon SW19 . .179 A4
Pavilion L Ctr The
BR1 . . .187 A1
Pavilion Lo HA2 . . .42 B1
Pavilion Mans 10
SW9 . . .138 B1
Pavilion Mews N3 . . .29 C1
Pavilion Rd
SW1 . . .114 D3 257 D5
Redbridge IG1 . . .56 B2
Pavilion St SW1 . . .257 D5
Pavilion Terr W12 . . .90 C1
Hampton KT1 . . .197 A4
Pavilion Way HA8 . . .27 A3
Ruislip HA4 . . .62 C6
Pawleyne Cl SE20 . . .184 C3
Pawsey Cl E13 . . .99 A6
Pawson's Rd CR0 . . .205 A4
Paxford Rd HA0 . . .65 B6
Paxton Cl
Richmond TW9 . . .132 B3
Walton-on-T KT12 . . .194 C2
Paxton Ct SE9 . . .165 C1
1 Forest Hill SE26 . . .185 A6
Mitcham CR4 . . .180 D1
Paxton Ho SE17 . . .262 B2
Paxton Pl SE27 . . .183 C4
Paxton Prim Sch
SE19 . . .183 C6
Paxton Rd BR1 . . .187 A3
Forest Hill SE23 . . .163 A4
Tottenham N17 . . .34 A3
Chiswick W4 . . .133 C4
Paxton Terr SW1 . . .268 C2
Payens Wlk
W6 . . .135 A6 264 A5
Paymal Ho 28 E1 . . .96 C2
Payne Cl IG11 . . .79 D1
Payne Ho N1 . . .233 D5
Paynell Ct SE3 . . .142 C4
Payne Rd E3 . . .97 D5
Paynesfield Ave
SW14 . . .133 B2
Paynesfield Rd WD23 . .8 D4
Payne St SE8 . . .141 B5
Payzes Gdns IG8 . . .36 D6
Peabody Ave
SW1 . . .115 B1 258 D1
Peabody Bldgs SE17 . .262 C3
6 SE5 . . .139 B4
Peabody Cl SW1 . . .268 D6
Croydon CR0 . . .206 C1
Peabody Cotts N17 . . .33 C4
Peabody Ct EC1 . . .242 B5
9 SE5 . . .139 B4
Peabody Est E1 . . .118 A6
4 E1 . . .118 C6
18 E2 . . .96 B5
EC1 . . .241 B5
EC1 . . .242 B5
SE1 . . .251 B3

Peabody Est *continued*
SE1 . . . . **252** A3
SW1 . . . . **259** B4
SW6 . . . .**135** B6 **264** D6
W10 . . . .**90** C2
17 W6 . . . .**112** C1
WC2 . . . .**240** C1
Streatham SE24 . . . .161 A4
Peabody Hill SE21 . . .161 A3
Peabody Sq SE1 . . . .**251** C1
Peabody Twr EC1 . . .**242** B5
Peabody Yd N1 . . . .**235** A6
Peace Cl
East Barnet N14 . . . . . .15 B6
Greenford UB6 . . . . . .86 B6
South Norwood SE25 . .205 C5
Peace Ct 10 NW9 . . . .46 A5
Peace Gr HA9 . . . . . . .66 D6
Peace St SE18 . . . . .144 C6
Peaches Cl SM2 . . . .217 A1
Peach Rd W10 . . . . . .91 A4
Feltham TW14 . . . . . .150 A3
Peach Tree Ave UB7 . .82 B1
Peachum Rd SE3 . . . .142 D6
Peach Walk Mews 23
E3 . . . . .96 D5
Peacock Ave TW14 . .149 B3
Peacock Cl NW17 . . . .80 C6
Peacock Est N17 . . . .33 D3
Peacock St
SE17 . . . . . .116 D2 **261** D3
Peacock Wlk E16 . . . .99 B1
Peacock Yd SE17 . . .**261** D3
Peaketon Ave IG4 . . .55 D4
Peak Hill SE26 . . . . .184 C6
Peak Hill Ave SE26 . .184 C6
Peak Hill Gdns SE26 .184 C6
Peak Ho N4 . . . . .51 A1
Peak The SE26 . . . . .162 C1
Peal Gdns W13 . . . . . .87 A3
Peall Rd CR0 . . . . . .204 B3
Pearce Cl 2 CR4 . . . .181 A1
Pearcefield Ave 5
SE23 . . . . .162 C3
Pearce Ho N19 . . . . .71 C5
7 Streatham SW2 . . .160 A4
Pear Cl NW9 . . . . . . .45 B5
SE14 . . . . .141 A5
Pearcroft Rd E11 . . . .76 B6
Pear Ct 20 SE15 . . . .139 D5
Peardon St SW8 . . . .137 B3
Pearswood Gdns
HA7 . . . . .25 D2
Pearfield Ho 1 N5 . .73 A3
Pearfield Rd SE23 . . .163 A1
Pearl Cl E6 . . . . .100 C1
NW2 . . . . .46 D2
Pearl Ct 18 NW9 . . . .46 A5
Pearl Rd E17 . . . . . . .53 C6
Pearl St E1 . . . . .118 B5
Pearlstones Ct RM10 103 C4
Pearmain Cl TW17 . . .192 D4
Pearman St
SE1 . . . . . . .116 C4 **251** B1
Pear Pl SE1 . . . .**251** A2
Pear Rd E11 . . . . .76 C5
Pearscroft Ct
SW6 . . . . . .135 D4 **265** D1
Pearscroft Rd
SW6 . . . . . .135 D4 **265** D1
Pearse St 3 SE15 . . .139 C6
Pearson Ct SM4 . . . .201 D4
Pearson Ho N15 . . . .134 C3
Pearson's Ave SE8,
SE14 . . . . .141 C4
Pearson St E2 . . . . . .95 D5
Pears Rd TW3 . . . . . .130 A2
Peartree Ave SW17 . .158 A1
Pear Tree Ave UB7 . . .82 B1
Pear Tree Cl 23 E2 . . .95 D6
Peartree Cl KT9 . . . .214 C3
Pear Tree Cl CR4 . . .180 C1
Pear Tree Ct EC1 . . .**241** B5
Putney SW15 . . . . . .134 B1
Peartree Gdns RM8 . .80 B4
Pear Tree Ho SE4 . . .141 B1
Hayes UB8 . . . . .83 A1
Peartree La E1 . . . . .118 C6
Peartree Rd EN1 . . . . .5 C4
Pear Tree Rd TW15 . .171 A5
Peartree St
EC1 . . . . . . .95 A3 **242** A6
Peartree Way SE10 . .121 A2
Peary Ho 3 NW10 . . .67 B1
Peary Pl E2 . . . . .96 C4
Peas Mead Terr E4 . .36 A6
Peatfield Cl DA15 . . .167 C1
Pebworth Lo SE25 . . .205 D5
Pebworth Rd HA1 . . . .65 A6

Peckarmans Wood
SE21,SE26 . . . . . . .162 A1
Peckett Sq 3 N5 . . . .72 C4
Peckford Pl SW9 . . . .138 C3
Peckham Gr SE15 . . .139 C5
Peckham High St
SE15 . . . . .140 A4
Peckham Hill St
SE15 . . . . .140 A5
Peckham Park Prim Sch
SE15 . . . . .140 A5
Peckham Park Rd
SE15 . . . . .140 A5
Peckham Rd SE5 . . . .139 C4
Peckham Rye SE22 . .140 A1
Peckham SE15,SE22 . .140 B1
Peckham Rye Prim Sch
SE15 . . . . .140 B2
Peckham Rye Sta
SE15 . . . . .140 A3
Peckwater St NW5 . . .71 C3
Pedlars Wlk N7 . . . . .72 A3
Pedley Rd RM8 . . . . .58 C1
Pedley St E1 . .95 D3 **243** D5
Pedro St E5 . . . . .74 D4
Pedworth Gdns 4
SE16 . . . . .118 C2
Peebles Ct UB1 . . . . .86 A1
Peek Cres SW19 . . . .178 D5
Peel Centre (Metropoliton
Police Training
Establishment) NW9 45 D6
Peel Cl Chingford E4 . . .19 C1
Edmonton N9 . . . . . . .18 A1
Peel Ct UB6 . . . . .86 A4
Peel Dr NW9 . . . . . . .45 D6
Redbridge IG5 . . . . . . .56 A6
Peel Gr E2 . . . . .96 C5
Peel Pass W8 . . . . . .**245** A3
Peel Pl IG5 . . . . .37 C1
Peel Prec NW6 . . . . . .91 C1
Peel Rd BR6 . . . . . . .227 A3
NW6 . . . . .91 B4
Harrow HA3 . . . . .42 D6
Wembley HA0,HA9 . . .65 D5
Woodford E18 . . . . . . .36 D2
Peel St W8 . .113 C5 **245** A3
Peel Way UB8 . . . . . .82 A2
Peel Yates Ho 13
SE7 . . . . .122 A2
Peerglow Est EN3 . . .18 C6
Peerless St
EC1 . . . . . . .95 B4 **235** C1
Pegamoid Rd N18 . . .18 C1
Pegasus Ct NW10 . . . .90 B4
Brentford TW8 . . . . . .110 B1
Kingston KT1 . . . . . . .197 D6
Pegasus Ho 9 E1 . . .96 D3
Pegasus Rd CR0,CR9 .220 C2
Pegasus Way N11 . . .31 B4
Peggotty Way UB8 . . .82 D1
Pegg Rd TW5 . . . . . .128 D5
Peggy Quirke Ct 2
HA0 . . . . .66 A2
Pegley Gdns SE12 . . .165 A2
Pegwell Ho 19 E5 . . .74 B3
Pegwell St SE18 . . . .145 C5
Pekin St E14 . . . . . . .97 C1
Pekoe SE1 . . . .**253** D3
Peldon Ct TW10 . . . .154 B6
Pele Ct N17 . . . . .33 B3
Pelham Ave IG11 . . . .101 D6
Pelham Cl SE5 . . . . .139 C4
Pelham Cotts DA5 . . .169 D3
Pelham Cres SW7 . . .**257** A3
Pelham Ct SW3 . . . . .**257** A3
Pelham Ho W14 . . . .**254** C3
Pelham Pl SW7 . . . . .**257** A3
8 Ealing W7 . . . . . . .86 D3
Pelham Prim Sch
DA7 . . . . .147 C2
Pelham Rd DA7 . . . . .147 C2
N15 . . . . .51 D5
Ilford IG1 . . . . .79 B6
Merton SW19 . . . . . .179 C3
Penge BR3,SE20 . . . .184 C1
Wanstead E18 . . . . . . .55 B6
Wood Green N22 . . . . .32 C1
Pelham St
SW7 . . . . . .114 B2 **256** D4
Pelican Ho 7 SE8 . . .119 B2
Pelier St SE17 . . . . . .139 A6
Pelinore Rd SE6 . . . .164 C2
Pella Ho SE11 . . . . . .**260** D2
Pellant Rd
SW6 . . . . . . .135 A5 **264** B4
Pellatt Gr N22 . . . . . .32 C2
Pellatt Rd SE22 . . . . .161 D6
Wembley HA9 . . . . . . .66 A6
Pellerin Rd N16 . . . . .73 C3

Pellew Ho 15 E1 . . . . .96 B3
Pelling St E14 . . . . . . .97 C1
Pellipar Cl N13 . . . . . .16 C1
Pellipar Gdns SE18 . .122 B1
Pellipar Rd SE18 . . . .122 B1
Pelly Ct 4 E17 . . . . . .54 A5
Pelly Rd E13 . . . . .99 A5
Pelter St E2 . . . . .95 D4
Pelton Ct CR2 . . . . . .221 A2
Pelton Rd SE10 . . . . .120 C1
Pembar Ave E17 . . . . .53 A6
Pemberley Chase
KT19 . . . . .214 D3
Pemberley Cl KT19 . .214 D3
Pemberley Ho 7 KT19 214 D3
Pember Rd NW10 . . . .90 D4
Pemberton Ct 18 E1 . .96 D4
Pemberton Gdns N19 .71 C5
Dagenham RM6 . . . . . .59 A4
Pemberton Ho 26 SE4 .184 A6
Pemberton Pl 2 E8 . . .74 B1
Esher KT10 . . . . .212 A5
Pemberton Rd N4 . . . .50 D4
East Molesey KT8 . . . .196 A5
Pemberton Row EC4 .**241** B2
Pemberton Terr N19 . .71 C5
Pembridge Ave TW4 . .151 B3
Pembridge Cres
W11 . . . . . .113 C6 **245** A6
Pembridge Gdns
W2 . . . . . . .113 C6 **245** A5
Pembridge Mews
W11 . . . . . .113 C6 **245** A5
Pembridge Pl
1 SW15 . . . . .157 C6
W2 . . . . . . .113 C6 **245** B6
Pembridge Rd
W11 . . . . . .113 C6 **245** A5
Pembridge Sq
W2 . . . . . . .113 C6 **245** B5
Pembridge Villas
W11 . . . . . .113 C6 **245** A6
Pembroke W14 . . . . .**254** D3
Pembroke Ave
Enfield EN1 . . . . .6 B4
Harrow HA3 . . . . .43 B6
Surbiton KT5 . . . . . . .198 D4
Pembroke Bldgs
NW10 . . . . .90 A4
Pembroke Cl SW1 . . .**248** B1
Pembroke Ct 11 W7 . .86 D2
Pembroke Gdns
W8 . . . . . . .113 C3 **254** D4
Dagenham RM10 . . . . .81 D5
Pembroke Gdns Cl
W8 . . . .**255** A4
Pembroke Hall NW4 . .46 C6
Pembroke Ho 16 W2 . .91 C1
Acton W3 . . . . .111 A4
Putney SW15 . . . . . .156 A6
Upper Tooting SW17 . .180 B5
Pembroke Mews E3 . .31 A2
W8 . . . .**255** A5
Pembroke Pl W8 . . . .**255** A5
Edgware HA8 . . . . . . .26 C3
Isleworth TW7 . . . . . .130 C3
Pembroke Rd BR1 . . .187 D1
E17 . . . . .53 D4
E6 . . . . .100 B2
N10 . . . . .31 A3
N15 . . . . .51 D4
N8 . . . . .50 A5
W8 . . . . . . .113 C2 **255** A4
Edmonton N13 . . . . . .17 A1
Greenford UB6 . . . . . .85 D3
Ilford IG3 . . . . .57 D2
Mitcham CR4 . . . . . . .181 A1
Ruislip HA4 . . . . .39 C1
South Norwood SE25 . .205 C5
Wembley HA9 . . . . . . .65 D5
Pembroke Sq
W8 . . . . . . .113 C3 **255** A5
Pembroke St
N1 . . . . .72 A1 **233** B6
Pembroke Studios
W8 . . . .**254** D5
Pembroke Terr NW8 . .**229** C5
Pembroke Villas W8 . .**255** A4
Richmond TW9 . . . . . .131 D1
Pembroke Way UB3 . .105 A3
Pembroke Wlk W8 . . .**255** A4
Pembrook Lo 2
SW16 . . . . .160 B1
Pembry Ave KT4 . . . .200 A3
Pembury Cl E5 . . . . . .74 B3
Hayes BR2 . . . . .208 D2
Pembury Cres DA14 . .169 A2
Pembury Ct UB3 . . . .127 B6
Pembury Ho SE5 . . . .139 C3
Pembury Pl 15 E5,E8 . .74 B3

Pembury Rd DA7 . . . .147 A6
E5 . . . . .74 B3
Croydon SE25 . . . . . .206 A5
Tottenham N17 . . . . . .33 C1
Pemdevon Rd CR0 . . .204 C2
Pemell Cl 27 E1 . . . . .96 C3
Pemell Ho 28 E1 . . . .96 C3
Pemerich Ct UB3 . . . .105 D1
Pempath Pl HA9 . . . . .65 D6
Penally Pl N1 . . . .**235** D6
Penang St E1 . . . . . . .118 B5
Penard Rd UB2 . . . . .107 D3
Penarth Ct SM2 . . . . .218 A1
Penarth St SE15 . . . .140 C6
Penates KT10 . . . . . .212 B4
Penberth Rd SE6 . . . .164 A3
Penbury Rd UB2 . . . .107 D3
Penceat SE20 . . . . . .184 C1
Pencombe Mews
W11 . . . .**244** D6
Pencraig Way SE15 . .140 B6
Pendall Cl EN4 . . . . . .2 C1
Penda Rd DA8 . . . . . .147 D5
Pendarves Rd SW20 . .178 C2
Penda's Mead E9 . . . .75 A4
Pendell Ave UB3 . . . .127 D5
Pendennis Ho 15 SE8 119 A2
Pendennis Rd N17 . . .51 B6
Streatham SW16 . . . .182 A6
Penderel Rd TW3 . . . .151 C6
Penderry Rise SE6 . . .164 B2
Penderyn Way N7 . . . .71 D4
Pendlebury Gn 8
SE18 . . . . .144 A4
Pendle Ho 13 SE26 . .162 A1
Pendle Rd SW16 . . . .181 B5
Pendlestone Rd E17 . .53 D4
Pendley Ho 18 E2 . . .96 A6
Pendragon Rd BR1 . .165 A1
Pendragon Sec Sch
BR1 . . . . .165 A1
Pendrell Ho WC2 . . . .**239** D1
Pendrell Rd SE4 . . . .141 A3
Pendrell St SE18 . . . .145 B6
Pendula Dr UB4 . . . . .84 D3
Penelope Ho 20 SW9 138 C4
Penerley Rd SE6 . . . .163 D3
Penfield Lo 7 W9 . . . .91 C2
Penfields Ho N7 . . . . .72 A2
Penfold Cl CR0 . . . . .220 C5
Penfold Ct NW8 . . . . .**236** D5
7 Mitcham CR4 . . . . .181 A1
Penfold Ho 14 SE18 . .144 D6
Penfold La DA5 . . . . .168 D2
Penfold Pl
NW1 . . . . . . .92 C2 **237** A4
Penfold Rd N9 . . . . . .18 D3
Penfold St
NW8 . . . . . . .92 B3 **236** D5
Penford Gdns SE9 . . .143 D2
Penford St SE5 . . . . .138 D3
Pengarth Rd DA5 . . . .168 D5
Penge East Sta SE20 184 C4
Penge La SE20 . . . . .184 D3
Penge Rd E13 . . . . . . .99 C6
South Norwood SE25 . .206 A6
Penge West Sta SE20 184 B4
Penhall Rd SE7 . . . . .121 D2
Penhill Rd DA5 . . . . .168 C4
Penhurst Mans
SW6 . . . .**264** C2
Penifather La UB6 . . . .86 A4
Peninsula Ct E14 . . . .119 D3
Peninsular Cl TW14 . .149 C5
Peninsular Park Rd
SE7 . . . . .121 A2
Penistone Rd SW16 . .182 A3
Penketh Dr HA1 . . . . .64 B5
Penmayne Ho SE11 . .**261** B2
Penmon Rd SE2 . . . .124 A3
Penn Almshouse 1
SE10 . . . . .142 A4
Pennant Mews
W8 . . . . . . .113 D2 **255** C4
Pennant Terr E17 . . . .35 B1
Pennard Mans 5
W12 . . . . .112 C4
Pennard Rd W12 . . . .112 C4
Pennards The TW16 . .194 C6
Penn Cl Greenford UB6 .85 D5
Harrow HA3 . . . . .43 C5
Penn Ct NW9 . . . . . . .45 B6
Penner Cl SW19 . . . .157 A2
Penners Gdns KT6 . . .198 A2
Pennethorne Cl E9 . . .96 C6
Pennethorne Ho
SW11 . . . . .136 B2
Pennethorne Rd
SE15 . . . . .140 B5

Penn Ho NW8 . . . . . .**237** A5
7 Edmonton N9 . . . . .18 A1
Pennine Dr NW2 . . . . .68 D6
Pennine La NW2 . . . . .69 A6
Pennine Mans NW2 . .69 A6
Pennine Par NW2 . . . .69 A6
Pennine Way UB7 . . .127 B5
Pennington Cl 10
SE27 . . . . .183 B6
Pennington Ct 16 E1 118 A6
SE16 . . . . .119 A5
Pennington Dr N21 . . .16 A6
Pennington Lo 18
KT5 . . . . .198 A4
Pennington St E1 . . . .118 B6
Pennington Way
SE12 . . . . .165 B2
Penniston Cl N17 . . . .33 A1
Penn La DA5 . . . . . . .169 A5
Penn Rd N7 . . . . .72 A4
Penn St N1 . . .95 B6 **235** D5
Penny Ct SW10 . . . . .**266** B6
Pennyfields E14 . . . . .119 C6
Pennyford Ct NW8 . . .**236** C6
Penny La TW17 . . . . .193 C2
Penny Mews SW12 . .159 B4
Pennymore Wlk W9 . .91 B3
Penny Rd NW10 . . . . .88 D4
Penny Royal SM6 . . . .219 D2
Pennyroyal Ave E6 . . .100 C1
Penpoll Rd E8 . . . . . .74 B2
Penpool La DA16 . . . .146 B2
Penrhyn Ave E17 . . . .35 C2
Penrhyn Cres
Chingford E17 . . . . . . .35 C2
Mortlake SW14 . . . . . .133 A1
Penrhyn Gdns KT1 . . .197 D6
Penrhyn Gr E17 . . . . . .35 C2
Penrhyn Rd KT1 . . . . .198 A6
Penrith Cl
Beckenham BR3 . . . . .185 D2
Putney SW15 . . . . . .157 A6
Penrith Pl SE27 . . . . .160 D2
Penrith Rd N15 . . . . . .51 B4
New Malden KT3 . . . .199 B5
South Norwood CR7 . .183 A1
Penrith St SW16 . . . .181 C4
Penrose Gr
SE17 . . . . . .117 A1 **262** A1
Penrose Ho SE17 . . .**262** A1
Southgate N21 . . . . . .16 B6
Penrose St
SE17 . . . . . .117 A1 **262** A1
Penryn Ho SE11 . . . .**261** C2
Penryn St
NW1 . . . . . . .93 D5 **232** C4
Penry St SE1 . . . .**263** B3
Pensbury Pl SW8 . . . .137 C3
Pensbury St SW8 . . . .137 C3
Pensford Ave TW9 . . .132 C3
Penshurst 2 NW5 . . .71 A2
Penshurst Ave DA15 . .168 A5
Penshurst Gdns HA8 . .26 D5
Penshurst Gn BR2 . . .208 D4
Penshurst Ho 1
SE15 . . . . .140 C6
Penshurst Rd DA7 . . .147 B4
E9 . . . . .74 D1
Thornton Heath CR7 . .204 D4
Tottenham N17 . . . . . .33 D4
Penshurst Way SM2 . .217 C1
Penshurst Wlk 4
BR2 . . . . .208 D4
Pensilver Cl EN4 . . . . .2 C1
Penstemon Cl N3 . . . .29 C4
Pentelow Gdns TW14 150 A5
Pentire Rd E17 . . . . . .36 B2
Pentland Ave
Edgware HA8 . . . . . . .10 C3
Littleton TW17 . . . . . .192 C4
Pentland Cl N9 . . . . . .18 C2
NW11 . . . . .69 A6
Pentland Ho 7 N16 . .51 D4
17 NW5 . . . . .71 A2
Pentland Pl UB5 . . . . .85 A6
Pentland Rd WD23 . . .8 A5
Pentlands BR3 . . . . . .186 A2
Pentlands Cl CR4 . . . .203 B6
Pentland St SW18 . . .158 A1
Pentland Way UB10 . .61 A2
Pentlow St SW15 . . . .134 C2
Pentney Rd
5 Chingford E4 . . . . .20 B3
Merton SW19,SW20 . .179 A2
Streatham SW12 . . . .159 C3
Penton Gr N1 . . . .**234** A3
Penton Ho N1 . . . . . .**234** A3
3 SE2 . . . . .124 D4
Sutton SM2 . . . . .218 A1

Penton Pl
SE17 . . . . . .116 D1 **261** D2
Penton Rise
WC1 . . . . . . .94 B4 **233** D2
Penton St N1 .94 C5 **234** A3
Pentonville Rd
N1 . . . . .94 B5 **233** C3
Pentrich Ave EN1 . . . .6 A5
Pentridge St SE15 . . .139 D5
Pentyre Ave N18 . . . . .33 B5
Penwerris Ave TW5,
TW7 . . . . .130 A5
Penwerris Ct TW7 . . .130 A5
Penwith Rd SW18 . . .157 D2
Penwood Ho 4
SW15 . . . . .155 D5
Penwortham Ct 1
N22 . . . . .32 C1
Penwortham Prim Sch
SW17 . . . . .181 B4
Penwortham Rd
SW16 . . . . .181 C4
Penylan Pl HA8 . . . . .26 C3
Penywern Rd
SW5 . . . . . .113 C1 **255** B2
Penzance Ho SE11 . . .**261** B2
Penzance Pl
W11 . . . . . .113 A5 **244** B4
Penzance St
W11 . . . . . .113 A5 **244** A4
Peony Ct IG8 . . . . . . .36 C3
Peony Gdns W12 . . . .112 A6
Peperfield WC1 . . . . .**233** C1
Pepler Ho 17 W10 . . .91 A3
Pepler Mews SE1 . . . .**263** C1
Peploe Rd NW6 . . . . .90 D5
Pepper Cl E6 . . . . . . .100 B2
Peppermead Sq
SE13 . . . . .163 C6
Peppermint Cl CR0 . .204 A2
Peppermint Pl 5 E11 .76 C5
Pepper St E14 . . . . . .119 D3
SE1 . . . .**252** A2
Peppie Cl N16 . . . . . .73 C4
Pepsi Trocadero W1 .**249** C5
Pepys Cres 2 E16 . . .121 C4
Barnet EN5 . . . . .12 C6
Pepys Ct SW20 . . . . .178 C1
Pepys Ent Ctr 12 SE8 119 B2
Pepys Ho 14 E2 . . . . .96 C4
SW4 . . . . .159 D6
Pepys Rd SE14 . . . . .140 D3
Wimbledon SW20 . . . .178 C2
Pepys Rise BR6 . . . . .211 D1
Pepys St EC3 .117 C6 **253** B6
Perak Ct KT5 . . . . . . .199 A2
Perceval Ave NW3 . . .70 C3
Perceval Ct UB5 . . . . .63 C3
Percheron Cl TW7 . . .130 D2
Percheron Ct 3 SW9 138 B2
Percheron Rd WD6 . . .11 B5
Perch St E8 . . . . .73 D4
Percival Ct N17 . . . . .33 D3
Percival Gdns RM6 . . .58 C3
Percival Rd Enfield EN1 .5 D1
Feltham TW13 . . . . . .149 D2
Mortlake SW14 . . . . . .133 A1
Orpington BR6 . . . . . .226 D6
Percival St
EC1 . . . . . . .94 D4 **234** D1
Percival Way KT19 . . .215 B4
Percy Ave TW15 . . . . .170 C5
Percy Bilton Ct TW5 .129 D4
Percy Bryant Rd
TW16 . . . . .171 C3
Percy Bush Rd UB7 . .104 B3
Percy Cir WC1 .94 B4 **233** D2
Percy Ct 1 KT5 . . . . .198 B3
Percy Gdns Enfield EN3 18 D6
Hayes UB4 . . . . .83 D1
3 Isleworth TW7 . . . .131 A2
New Malden KT3 . . . .199 C1
Percy Ho 4 SW16 . . .181 C6
Percy Mews W1 . . . . .**239** C3
Percy Pas W1 . . . . . .**239** C3
Percy Rd DA7 . . . . . .147 A3
E11 . . . . .54 C2
E16 . . . . .98 C2
N12 . . . . .30 A5
W12 . . . . .112 A4
Carshalton CR4 . . . . .203 A2
Croydon SE25 . . . . . .206 A4
Edmonton N21 . . . . . .17 A4
Hampton TW12 . . . . .173 C3
Ilford IG3 . . . . .58 A2
Isleworth TW7 . . . . . .131 A1

Percy Rd continued
Penge SE20 ....184 D2
Romford RM7 ....59 D6
Twickenham TW2 ....152 A3
Percy St W1 .93 D2 **239** C3
Percy Way TW2 ......152 A3
Peregrine Cl NW10 ..67 B3
Peregrine Ct DA16 ..145 D4
Streatham SW16 .....182 B6
Peregrine Gdns CR0 .223 A6
Peregrine Ho EC1 ..**234** D2
6 SW11 ....136 C2
Peregrine Rd TW16 .171 D1
Peregrine Way SW19,
SW20 ....178 C3
Performing Arts & Tech
Sch SE25 ....205 B3
Perham Rd
W14 ....113 B1 **254** B1
Peridot St E6 ....100 A2
Perifield SE21 ......161 A3
Perimeade Rd UB6 ...87 C5
Periton Rd SE9 .....143 D1
Perivale UB6 ....86 D5
Perivale Fst & Mid Schs
UB6 ....87 C5
Perivale Gdns W13 ..87 B3
Perivale Grange UB6 .87 A4
Perivale Ind Pk UB6 .87 B5
Perivale La UB6 .....87 A4
Perivale Lo UB6 .....87 A4
Perivale New Bsns Ctr
UB6 ....87 C5
Perivale Sta UB6 ....87 A5
Perkin Cl
Hounslow TW3 ......129 D1
Wembley HA0 ....65 B3
Perkins Cl TW15 ....170 B5
Perkins Ho **13** E14 ....97 B2
Perkins Rd IG2 .....57 B4
Perkins Rents SW1 .**259** C5
Perkins Sq SE1 ....**252** B4
Perley Ho **10** E3 .....97 B2
Perotti Ho SW4 .....135 D2
Perpins Rd SE9 .....167 C5
Perran Rd SE24,SW2 .160 D2
Perren St NW5 ......71 B2
Perrers Rd W6 ......112 B2
Perrin Cl TW15 .....170 B5
Perrin Ct **17** NW3 ...70 A4
Perrin Grange HA9 ..66 B6
Perrin Rd HA0 ......65 B4
Perrin's Ct **5** NW3 ..70 A4
Perrin's La NW3 ....70 A4
Perrin's Wlk NW3 ...70 A4
Perronet Ho SE1 ...**261** D5
Perry Ave W3 ....89 B1
Perry Cl UB8 ....82 D1
Perry Ct **2** N15 .....51 C3
5 Millwall E14 .....119 C1
Perryfield Way NW9 ..45 D3
Richmond TW10 .....153 B2
Perry Garth UB5 ....84 C6
Perry Gdns N9 ......17 C1
Perry Hall Prim Sch
BR6 ....211 D3
Perry Hill SE6 ......163 B1
Perry Ho **24** SW2 ...160 A4
Perry How KT4 .....199 D1
Perryman Ho IG11 ..101 A6
Perrymans Farm Rd
IG2 ....57 B4
Perry Mead
Bushey WD23 ......8 A5
Enfield EN2 ....4 D3
Perrymead St
SW6 ....135 D3 **265** C1
Perrymount Prim Sch
SE23 ....162 D2
Perryn Ct **1** TW1 ..153 A4
Perryn Ho W3 ......111 C6
Perryn Rd SE16 ....118 B3
W3 ....111 B6
Perry Rise SE23 ....163 A1
Perry's Pl W1 .....**239** C2
Perry St BR7 ....189 C4
Perry Street Gdns
BR7 ....189 C4
Perry Vale SE23 ....162 D2
Perrywood Ho **17** E5 .74 B3
Persant Rd SE6 ....164 C2
Perseverance Pl
SW9 ....138 C5
Perseverance Works **18**
E2 ....95 C4
Pershore Cl IG2 ....56 D4

Pershore Gr SM5 ...**202** B3
Pert Cl N10 ....31 B4
Perth Ave NW9 .....45 B2
Hayes UB4 ....84 C3
Perth Cl SW20 .....178 A1
Perth Ct **5** SE5 ....139 B1
Perth Ho N1 ....72 B1
12 Acton W3 ....88 C1
Perth Rd E10 ......53 B1
E13 ....99 B5
N4 ....50 C1
Barking IG11 ....101 B6
Beckenham BR3 ....186 A1
Ilford IG2 ....56 D3
Tottenham N22 .....32 D2
Perth Terr IG2 .....57 A2
Perwell Ave HA2 ...41 B1
Perystreete SE23 ..162 C2
Petavel Rd TW11 ..174 C4
Peter Ave NW10 ...68 B3
Peter Best Ho **6** E1 .96 B1
Peterboat Cl SE10 .120 C2
Peterborough Ct EC4 **241** A2
Peterborough Gdns
IG1 ....56 A2
Peterborough Mews
SW6 ....135 C3
Peterborough Prim Sch
SW6 ....135 C3
Peterborough Rd E10 .54 B3
SW6 ....135 C2
Carshalton SM5 ....202 C3
Harrow HA1 ....42 D2
Peterborough Villas
SW6 ....**265** C2
Peter Bradley Ct RM9 .81 B1
Petergate SW11 ....136 A1
Peterhead Ct **12** UB1 .86 A1
Peter Hills Ho **6**
SE16 ....118 A2
Peter Hills with St Mary's
& St Paul's CE Prim Sch
SE16 ....118 D5
Peter Ho SW8 ......**270** A4
Peter James Bsns Ctr
UB3 ....106 A4
Peter Kennedy Ct
CR0 ....207 B3
Peterley Bsns Ctr **21**
E2 ....96 B5
Peters Cl DA16 ....145 D4
Dagenham RM8 ....58 D1
Stanmore HA7 .....25 D4
Peters Ct **9** W2 ...91 D1
Peter's Ct SW4 ....160 A5
Peter's Ct **9** W2 ...91 D1
Petersfield Cl N18 .33 A5
Petersfield Rd W3 ..111 A4
Petersfield Rise
SW15 ....156 B3
Petersham Cl
Richmond TW10 ....153 D2
Sutton SM1 ....217 C3
Petersham Dr BR5 ..190 A1
Petersham Gdns BR5 189 D1
Petersham Ho SW7 .**256** C4
Petersham La SW7 .**256** A6
Petersham Mews
SW7 ....114 A3 **256** B5
Petersham Pl
SW7 ....114 A3 **256** B6
Petersham Rd TW10 .154 A3
Petersham Terr CR0 .220 A5
Peter's La EC1 .....**241** D4
Peter's Lo **2** E6 ....26 A4
Peter's Path SE26 ..184 B6
Peter St W1 .115 D6 **249** C6
Peterstone Rd SE2 .124 B4
Peterstow Cl SW19 .157 A2
Peterwood Pk CR0 .220 B6
Peterwood Way CR0 .220 B6
Petherton Ct NW10 .90 D6
10 Harrow HA1 .....42 D3
Petherton Ho N4 ...51 A1
Petherton Rd N5 ...73 A3
Petiver Cl **28** E9 ....74 C1
Petley Rd W6 ......134 D5
Peto Pl NW1 ....**238** D6
Peto St N E16 ......98 D1
Petrel Ct **7** SE21 ...161 B2
Petrie Cl NW2 .....69 C2
Petrie Ho **8** SE18 ..144 C6
Petros Gdns **1** NW3 .70 A2
Petticoat Lane Mkt*
EC2 ......95 D2 **243** C3
Petticoat Sq E1 ...**243** C2
Petticoat Twr E1 ..**243** C2
Pettit's Pl RM10 ...81 C3

Pettit's Rd RM10 ....81 C3
Pettiward Cl SW15 ..134 C1
Pettman Cres SE18,
SE28 ....123 B3
Pettsgrove Ave HA0 .65 C3
Pett's Hill UB5 .....63 D3
Petts La TW17 .....192 C5
Pett St SE7 ....122 A2
Petty France
SW1 ....115 C3 **259** C6
Petworth Cl UB5 ....63 B1
Petworth Gdns
Hillingdon UB10 .....83 A6
West Barnes SW20 ..200 B6
Petworth Ho **16** SE22 139 C2
Petworth Rd DA6 ...169 C6
N12 ....30 C5
Petworth St
SW11 ....136 C4 **267** B2
Petyt Pl SW3 .136 C6 **267** A5
Petyward
SW3 ....114 C2 **257** B3
Pevensey Ave N11 ..31 D5
Enfield EN1 ....5 C3
Pevensey Cl TW7 ..130 A5
Pevensey Ct **4** W3 .110 D4
West Norwood SW16 .160 C1
10 Woodford E18 ...37 A2
Pevensey Ho **5** E1 ..97 A2
Pevensey Rd E7 ....77 A4
Feltham TW13 ......151 A3
Upper Tooting SW17 .180 B6
Peverel E6 ....100 C1
Peverel Ho RM10 ..81 C6
Peverett Cl N11 ....31 B5
Peveril Dr TW11 ...174 B5
Peveril Ho SE1 ....**262** D5
Pewsey Cl E4 ......35 C5
Pewsham Ho N4 ...51 A1
Pewterers Ct N3 ...29 B2
Peyton Ho N11 ....31 A6
Peyton Pl SE10 ....142 A5
Pharamond NW2 ...68 D2
Pharaoh Cl CR4 ...202 D2
Pheasant Cl E16 ...99 B1
Phelps Ho SW15 ...134 D2
Phelp St SE17 .....139 B6
Phelps Way UB3 ...105 D2
Phene St
SW3 ....136 C6 **267** B6
Philadelphia Ct
SW10 ....**266** B3
Philbeach Gdns
SW5 ....113 C1 **255** A2
Phil Brown Pl **3**
SW8 ....137 B2
Philchurch Pl **25** E1 .96 A1
Phildor Ct NW11 ...47 A3
Philia Ho **2** E1 ....71 C1
Philimore Cl SE18 .123 C1
Philip Ct W2 ......**236** C4
Enfield EN2 ....5 B4
Philip Gdns CR0 ...223 B6
Philip Ho N20 .....14 D2
10 NW6 ....91 D6
Philip La N15 ......51 C6
Philipot Almshouse
SE9 ....166 B5
Philipot Path SE9 ..166 B5
Philippa Gdns SE9 .165 D6
Philip Rd SE15 ....140 A2
Philips Cl CR4 ....203 A1
Philip St E13 ......99 A3
Philip Turner Est **28**
E9 ....74 C1
Philip Wlk SE15 ...140 B2
Phillimore Ct W8 ..**245** B1
Phillimore Gardens Cl
W8 ....113 C3 **255** A6
Phillimore Gdns
W8 ....113 C4 **245** A1
Willesden NW10 ....90 C6
Phillimore Pl
W8 ....113 C4 **245** A1
Phillimore Terr W8 .**255** B6
Phillimore Wlk
W8 ....113 C3 **255** B6
Phillip Ho E1 ......**243** D3
Phillipp St N1 .....95 C4
Phillips Ct
Edgware HA8 ......26 C4
Hayes UB4 ....84 B4
Philpot La EC3 ....**253** A6
Philpot Sq SW6 ...135 D2
Philpot St E1 ......96 B1
Phineas Pett Rd SE9 .144 A2
Phipp's Bridge Rd
CR4,SW19 ....202 B6

Phipps Bridge Sta
CR4 ....202 B6
Phipps Hatch La EN2 ..5 A5
Phipps Ho **1** SE7 ..121 B1
16 W12 ....112 B6
Phipp St EC2 .95 C3 **243** A6
Phoebeth Rd SE4 ..163 C6
Phoenix Bsns Ctr E3 .97 C2
Phoenix Cl E17 ....35 C1
18 E8 ....95 D6
West Wickham BR4 ..224 C6
Phoenix Coll SM4 .202 A4
Phoenix Ct E14 ....119 C2
2 SE14 ....141 A4
4 Brentford TW8 ..110 A1
Chingford E4 ......19 D1
Croydon SE25 .....206 A4
Enfield EN3 ....6 C5
Phoenix Dr BR2 ...225 D5
Phoenix High Sch
W12 ....112 A6
Phoenix Ind Est HA1 .42 D5
Phoenix Lodge Mans **1**
W6 ....112 C2
Phoenix Pk NW2 ...68 A6
Phoenix Pl
WC1 ......94 B3 **240** D6
Phoenix Rd
NW1 ......93 D4 **232** C2
Penge SE20 ....184 C4
Phoenix Sch E3 ...97 B4
Phoenix Sch The NW3 70 A2
Phoenix St WC2 ...**239** D1
Phoenix Trad Est UB6 .87 D6
Phoenix Trad Pk
TW8 ....109 D1
Phoenix Way TW5 .128 D6
Phoenix Wharf Rd
SE1 ....**253** D1
Phyllis Ave KT3 ...200 B4
Phyllis Ho CR0 ....220 A4
Phyllis Hodges Ho
NW1 ......93 D5 **232** C3
Physic Pl
SW3 ....136 D6 **267** C6
Picador Ho **1** RM10 .81 D2
Picardy Manorway
DA17 ....125 D4
Picardy Rd DA17 ..125 C2
Picardy St DA17 ..125 C3
Piccadilly
W1 ....115 C5 **249** A4
Piccadilly Arc SW1 .**249** A3
Piccadilly Cir*
W1 ....115 D6 **249** C5
Piccadilly Circus Sta
SW1 ....115 D6 **249** C5
Piccadilly Pl W1 ..**249** B5
Pickard St EC1 ....**234** D2
Pickering Ave E6 ..100 C4
Pickering Gdns N11 .31 A4
Croydon SE25 .....205 C6
Pickering Ho N4 ...51 B2
4 SE18 ....122 C4
17 W2 ....91 D1
W5 ....109 C2
Pickering Mews W2 .91 D1
Pickering Pl SW1 ..**249** B3
Pickering St N1 ...**234** D6
Pickets Cl WD23 ..8 C3
Pickets St SW12 ..159 B4
Pickett Croft HA7 .25 D2
Pickett's Lock La N9 .18 D2
Pickford Cl DA7 ...147 A3
Pickford La DA7 ..147 A3
Pickford Rd DA7 ..147 A3
Pickfords Wharf N1 .**235** A3
1 SE1 ....**252** A1
Pickhurst Gn BR2 .208 D2
Pickhurst Inf Sch
BR2 ....208 D3
Pickhurst Jun Sch
BR2 ....208 D3
Pickhurst La BR2,BR3,
BR4 ....208 D1
Pickhurst Mead BR2 .208 D2
Pickhurst Pk BR2 .208 D4
Pickhurst Rise BR4 .208 B1
Pickwick Cl TW4 ..151 A6
Pickwick Ct SE9 ..166 B3
Pickwick Ho **18** SE16 118 A4
3 W11 ....112 D5
Pickwick Mews N18 .33 C5
Pickwick Pl HA1 ..42 C1
Pickwick Rd SE21 .161 C4
Pickwick St SE1 ..**252** A1
Pickwick Way BR7 .189 A4
Pickworth Cl SW8 .**270** A4
Picton Ho **1** SW4 ..160 A4
Picton Pl W1 ......**238** B1
Picton St SE5 .....139 B5

Picton St SE5 .....139 B5
Pied Bull Ct WC1 .**240** B3
Pied Bull Yd WC1 .**240** B3
Piedmont Rd SE18 .123 B1
Pield Heath Ave UB8 .82 C3
Pield Heath Rd UB8 .82 B3
Pield Heath Sch UB8 .82 A3
Pierhead Wharf **37**
E1 ....118 B5
Pier Ho SW3 ......**267** B5
Piermont Pl BR1 ..188 A1
Piermont Rd SE22 .162 B6
Pier Par **3** E16 ...122 C5
2 SE14 ....141 A4
Pierpoint Bldg **5**
E14 ....119 C4
Pier Rd E16 ....122 C4
Feltham TW14 .....150 B2
Pierrepoint SE25 ..205 C6
Pierrepoint Rd W3 .110 B6
Pierson Ho **12** SE19 .183 C6
Pier St E14 ....120 A2
Pier Terr SW18 ...136 A1
Pier Way SE18 ....123 B3
Pigeon Ct E4 ......36 A4
Pigeon La TW12 ..173 C6
Piggott Ho **2** E2 ..96 D5
Pigott St E14 .....97 C1
Pike Cl BR1 ......187 B5
Hillingdon UB10 ....82 B6
Pike Rd NW7 .....27 B6
Pike's End HA5 ...40 B5
Pikestone Cl UB4 .85 A3
Pikethorne SE23 ..162 D2
Pilgrimage St
SE1 ....117 B4 **252** C1
Pilgrim Cl SW16 ..201 D2
Pilgrim Hill SE27 ..183 A6
Pilgrim Ho SE1 ...**262** D5
Pilgrims Cl
Northolt UB5 ......64 A3
Palmers Green N13 ..32 B6
Pilgrims Cloisters **18**
SE5 ....139 C5
Pilgrims Ct SE3 ...143 A4
Enfield EN1 ....5 B3
Pilgrim's La NW3 ..70 A4
Pilgrims Mews E14 .120 B6
Pilgrim's Rise EN4 .14 C6
Pilgrim St EC4 ....**241** C1
Pilgrims Way **5** E6 .100 A6
N19 ....49 D1
Wembley HA9 .....44 D1
Pilgrim's Way CR2 .221 D5
Pilgrims Way Prim Sch
SE15 ....140 C6
Pilkington Ct **1** NW9 .46 A5
Pilkington Rd
4 SE15 ....140 B3
Orpington BR6 .....227 A6
Pillar of Fire Society
Church & Bible Sch
NW4 ....46 D4
Pillions La UB4 ....83 B3
Pilot Ind Ctr NW10 .89 C3
Pilsden Cl **1** SW19 .156 D3
Piltdown Rd WD19 .22 C6
Pilton Est The CR0 .220 D6
Pilton Pl SE17 ....**262** B2
Pimento Ct W5 ...109 D2
Pimlico Sta
SW1 ....115 D1 **259** C2
Pimlico Rd
SW1 ....115 A1 **258** B2
Pimlico Sch
SW1 ....115 C1 **259** B1
Pimlico Wlk **1** N1 ..95 C4
Pinchbeck Rd BR6 .227 D2
Pinchin St E1 ......118 A6
Pincombe Ho SE17 .**262** D2
Pincott Pl SE4 ....140 D2
Pincott Rd
8 Bexley DA6 ....147 C1
Merton SW19 .....180 A2
Pindar St EC2 .95 C2 **243** A4
Pindock Mews W9 .91 D3
Pine Apple Ct SW1 .**259** A6
Pine Ave E15 ......76 B3
West Wickham BR4 .207 D1
Pine Cl N14 ......15 C4
8 N19 ....71 C6
E10 ....75 D6
3 Penge SE20 ...184 C2
Stanmore HA7 .....25 B6
Pine Coombe CR0 ..222 D4
Pinecroft DA16 ....146 A5
Harrow HA3 ......44 B4
Pinecroft Cres EN5 .1 A1
Pine Ct UB5 ......85 A4
Pinedene **2** SE15 ..140 B4

Pinefield Cl E14 ...119 C6
Pine Gdns Ruislip HA4 .62 B6
Surbiton KT5 ....198 C3
Pine Glade BR6 ...226 B4
Pine Gr N20 ....13 C3
N4,N19 ....72 B6
Wimbledon SW19 ..179 B5
Pine Ho **15** SE16 ..118 C4
Pinehurst BR7 ....188 D4
Pinehurst Ct **5** W11 .91 B1
Pinehurst Wlk **4**
BR6 ....211 B3
Pinelands Cl **7** SE3 .142 C5
Pine Lo SW15 .....157 C5
Pinemartin Cl NW2 .68 C5
Pine Pl UB4 ......83 D3
NW2 ....68 C5
Pine Ridge SM5 ...219 A1
Pines Ct **14** SW19 .156 D3
Pines Rd BR1 .....188 A1
Pine St EC1 ...94 C3 **241** A6
Pines The
Southgate N14 .....15 C6
South Norwood SE19 .182 D4
Sunbury TW16 .....194 B6
Woodford IG8 .....21 A1
Pine Tree Cl TW5 .128 B4
Pine Tree Ho SE14 .140 D5
Pine Tree Lo BR2 .208 D2
Pine Trees Dr UB10 .60 A4
Pineview Ct **5** E4 ..20 A3
Pine Wlk KT5 ....198 C3
Pinewood BR7 ....188 D4
Pine Wood TW16 ..172 A2
Pinewood Ave DA15 .167 C3
Hillingdon UB8 .....82 D1
Pinner HA5 ....23 D4
Pinewood Cl BR6 ..211 B4
Croydon CR0 ......223 A5
Pinner HA5 ....23 D4
Pinewood Ct SW4 ..159 D4
Enfield EN2 ....4 D1
Pinewood Dr BR6 .227 C3
Pinewood Gr W5 ..87 C1
Pinewood Pl KT19 .215 B5
Pinewood Rd BR2 .209 A3
SE2 ....146 D6
Feltham TW13 .....150 B1
Pinfold Rd SW16 ..182 A6
Pinglestone Cl UB7 .126 A5
Pinkcoat Cl TW13 .150 B1
Pinkerton Pl SW16 .181 D1
Pinkham Mans W4 .110 C4
Pinkham Way (North
Circular Rd)
N12 ....30 D3
N12 ....31 A3
Pinkwell Ave UB3 .105 A2
Pinkwell Jun & Inf Schs
UB3 ....105 A2
Pinkwell La UB3 ..105 A2
Pinley Gdns RM9 ..102 B3
Pinnacle Hill DA7 .147 D1
Pinnacle Hill N DA7 .147 D1
Pinnacle Ho E14 ..120 A3
Pinnell Rd SE9 ....143 D1
Pinner Ct HA5 ....41 C5
Pinner Gn HA5 ...22 B3
Pinner Gr HA5 ....41 A4
Pinner Hill HA5 ...22 B3
Pinner Hill Rd HA5 .22 C1
Pinner Ho **31** SE5 .139 A4
Pinner Park Ave HA2 .24 C1
Pinner Park Fst & Mid
Schs HA5 ....41 D6
Pinner Park Gdns HA2 24 A1
Pinner Rd
Harrow HA1,HA2 ...42 A1
Harrow, Pinner HA2,HA5 41 C5
Pinner HA6 ....22 A1
Pinner Sta HA5 ...41 B5
Pinner View HA1,HA2 .42 A4
Pinner Wood Fst & Mid
Schs HA5 ....22 C2
Pinn Way HA4 ....39 C2
Pintail Cl E6 ......100 A2
Pintail Rd **40** SE8 ..141 B6
Pintail Rd IG8 ....37 B3
Pintail Way UB4 ..84 D2
Pinter Ho **30** SW9 ..138 A2
Pinto Cl WD6 .....11 B5
Pinto Way SE3 ....143 B1
Pioneer Cl W12 ...90 B1
Pioneers Ind Pk CR0 204 A3
Pioneer St SE15 ..140 A4
Pioneer Way W12 .90 C1
Piper Cl N7 ....72 B2
Piper Rd KT1 .....198 C6

Pipers Gdns CR0 ....207 A2
Pipers Gn NW9 ....45 A4
Pipers Green La HA8 ...10 A1
Pipewell Rd SM5 .....202 C3
Pippenhall SE9 ......166 D5
Pippin Cl NW2 ....68 B5
Croydon CR0 ....207 B1
Pippin Ct 5 EN4 ....2 C1
Pippins Ct TW15 .....170 A4
Piquet Rd SE20 .....184 C1
Pirbright Cres CR0 ...224 A2
Pirbright Ho 11 KT2 .176 D4
Pirbright Rd SW18 ...157 C3
Pirie St 6 E16 ....121 B5
Pitcairn Cl RM7 ....59 C5
Pitcairn Ho 1 E9 ....74 C1
Pitcairn Rd CR4 .....180 C3
Pitchford St E15 ......76 C1
Pitfield Cres SE28 ...124 A5
Pitfield Ho N5 ......73 A3
Pitfield St N1 ....95 C5
Pitfield Way NW10 ...67 A2
Enfield EN3 ....6 C4
Pitfold Cl SE12 .....165 B5
Pitfold Rd SE12 .....165 A4
Pit Ho NW10 ....67 B5
Pitlake CR0 ....220 D6
Pitman Ho 4 SE8 ....141 C4
Southgate N21 ......16 B6
Pitmans Coll HA0 ....65 D2
Pitman St SE5 ......139 A5
Pitmaston Ho 2
SE13 ....142 A3
Pitsea Pl E1 ....96 D1
Pitsea St E1 ....96 D1
Pitshanger Ct 2 W5 .87 C3
Pitshanger La W5 ....87 C3
Pitshanger Manor Mus &
Art Gallery* W5 ...109 D5
Pitt Cres SW19 .....179 D6
Pitt Ho 4 SW11 ....136 B1
Pittman Gdns IG1 ....79 A3
Pitt Rd BR6 ....227 A4
Harrow HA2 ....64 A6
Thornton Heath CR0,
CR7 ....205 A4
Pitt's Head Mews W1 248 B3
Pittsmead Ave BR2 ..209 A2
Pitt St W8 ....113 C4 245 B2
Pittville Gdns SE25 ..206 A6
Pixfield Ct BR2 .....186 D1
Pixley St E14 ....97 B1
Pixton 11 NW9 ......27 C2
Pixton Way CR2 .....223 B1
Place Farm Ave BR5,
BR6 ....211 B1
Plains The 7 E4 .....20 C4
Plaistow Gr BR1 ....187 B3
E15 ....98 D6
Plaistow Hospl E13 ..99 C5
Plaistow La BR1 ....187 C2
Plaistow Park Rd E13 .99 B5
Plaistow Prim Sch
E13 ....99 B5
Plaistow Rd E13,E15 ..98 D5
Plaistow Sta E13 ....98 D5
Plane St SE26 ......162 B4
Planetarium The*
NW1 ....93 A3 238 A5
Plane Tree Cres
TW13 ....150 B1
Planetree Ct W6 ....112 D2
Plane Tree Ho SE7 ..121 D1
SE8 ....141 A6
Plane Tree Wlk 4
SE19 ....183 C4
Plantagenet Cl KT19 .215 B4
Plantagenet Gdns
RM6 ....58 C4
Plantagenet Ho SE18 122 B3
Plantagenet Pl RM6 .58 C4
Plantagenet Rd EN5 ..2 A1
Plantain Pl SE1 ....252 C2
Plantation The SE3 ..143 A3
Plasel Ct E13 ....99 B6
Plashet Gr E7 ....77 D1
Plashet Rd E13 ......77 B1
Plashet Sch E6 ......78 A1
Plassy Rd SE6 ......163 D4
Platina St EC2 .....242 D6
Plato Pl 1 SW6 ....135 B3
Plato Rd SW2 ......138 A1
Platt Halls (a) 35 NW9 27 D1
Platt Halls (b) 37 NW9 27 D1
Platt Halls (c) 38 NW9 27 D1
Platt's Eyot TW12 ..173 C3
Platt's La NW3 ......69 C5
Platts Rd EN3 ....6 C4
Platt St NW1 ......232 C4
Plaxdale Ho SE17 ..263 A3

Plaxtol Cl BR1 ......187 C2
Plaxtol Rd DA8 .....147 C5
Plaxton Ct E11 ......76 D5
Playfair St W6 ......112 C1
Playfield Cres SE22 .161 D6
Playfield Rd HA8 ....27 A1
Playford Rd N4 .....72 B6
N4 ....72 C6
Playgreen Way SE6 .185 C6
Playground Cl BR3 .184 D1
Playhouse Yd EC4 ..241 C1
Plaza Bsns Ctr EN3 ..7 B3
Pleasance Rd BR5 ..190 B1
Putney SW15 ......156 B6
Pleasance The SW15 134 B1
Pleasant Gr CR0 ....223 B5
Pleasant Pl N1 ......72 D1
Pleasant Row NW1 .231 D5
Pleasant View BR6 .227 A3
Pleasant View Pl
BR6 ....227 A3
Pleasant Way HA0 ..87 C5
Pleasaunce Ct SE9 .144 B1
Plender Ct NW1 ....232 B5
Plender St
NW1 ....93 C6 232 B5
Pleshey Rd N7 ......71 D4
Plevna Cres N15 ....51 C3
Plevna Ho 1 N9 .....18 A1
Plevna Rd Edmonton N9 18 B1
Hampton TW12 ....173 D2
Plevna St E14 .....120 A3
Pleydell Ave W6 ....111 D2
Penge SE19 ....183 D3
Pleydell Ct EC4 ....241 B1
Pleydell Gdns SE19 .183 D4
Pleydell St EC4 ....241 B1
Plimsoll Cl E14 ......97 D1
Plimsoll Rd N4 ......72 D5
Plough Ct EC3 .....252 D6
Plough Farm Cl HA4 .39 B3
Plough La SE22 ....161 D2
Wallington CR0,SM6 .220 A3
Wimbledon SW17,
SW19 ....180 A6
Plough Lane Cl CR0,
SM6 ....220 A3
Ploughmans Cl NW1 232 C6
Ploughmans End
TW7 ....152 B6
Plough Pl EC4 .....241 B2
Plough Rd SW11 ...136 B1
West Ewell KT19 ...215 B1
Plough St 10 E1 ....96 A1
Plough Terr SW11 ..136 B1
Plough Way SE16 ..119 A2
Plough Yd EC2 .....243 B5
Plover Ho 4 SW9 ..138 C5
Plover Way SE16 ...119 A3
Hayes UB4 ....84 D2
Plowman Cl N18 ....33 B5
Plowman Ho SW19 .156 D2
Plowman Way RM8 .58 C1
Plumbers Row E1 ...96 A1
Plumbridge St 7
SE10 ....142 A4
Plum Cl TW14 ......150 A3
Plumcroft Prim Sch
SE18 ....145 A6
Plume Ho SE10 ....141 D6
Plum Garth TW8 ...109 D2
Plum La SE18 ......145 A5
Plummer Ct SE13 ..163 D5
Plummer La CR4 ...180 D1
Plummer Rd SW4 ..159 D4
Plumpton Cl UB5 ....63 C2
Plumpton Way SM5 .218 C5
Plumstead Common Rd
SE18 ....145 A6
Plumstead High St
SE18,SE2 ....123 C2
Plumstead Manor Sch
SE18 ....145 B6
Plumstead Rd SE18,
SE28 ....123 A2
Plumstead Sta SE18 123 A2
Plumtree Cl
Dagenham RM10 ...81 D2
Wallington SM6 ....219 D1
Plumtree Ct EC4 ...241 C2
Plymouth Ho 10 IG11 80 A1
Plymouth Rd BR1 ..187 B2
E16 ....99 A2
Plymouth Wharf E14 120 B2
Plympton Ave NW6 ..69 B1
Plympton Cl 8 DA17 125 A3
Plympton Pl NW1 ..237 A5
Plympton Rd NW6 ..69 B1
Plympton St NW8 ..237 A5
Plymstock Rd DA16 146 C5

Pocklington Cl NW9 .27 C1
Pocklington Ct SW15 156 A3
Pocock Ave UB7 ...104 B3
Pocock St
SE1 ....116 D4 251 D2
Podmore Rd SW18 .136 A1
Poets Corner SW1 ..260 A6
Poet's Rd N5 ....73 B3
Poets Way HA1 .....42 C5
Pointalls Cl N3 ......30 A1
Point Cl SE10 ......142 A4
Pointer Cl SE28 ....102 D1
Pointer Sch The SE3 143 A5
Pointers Cl E14 ....119 D1
Point Hill SE10 ....142 A4
Point Ho HA9 ....66 D1
Point Pleasant SW18 135 C1
Point Terr E7 ....77 B3
Poland St W1 .93 C1 239 B1
Polebrook Rd SE3 ..143 C2
Polecroft La SE6 ...163 B2
Polehamptons The
TW12 ....174 A2
Pole Hill Rd
Chingford E4 ......20 A1
Hillingdon UB4 ....83 A4
Polesden Gdns SW20 178 B1
Polesworth Ho 16 W2 91 C2
Polesworth Rd RM9 .80 C1
Polish Univ Abroad
W6 ....112 A2
Polish War Meml HA4 62 C2
Pollard Cl E16 .....121 A6
N7 ....72 B4
Pollard Ho N1 ......233 C3
Cheam KT4 ....216 C4
Pollard Rd N20 .....14 C2
Morden SM4 ......202 B4
Pollard Row E2 .....96 A4
Pollards Cl IG10 ....21 C6
Pollards Cres SW16 204 A6
Pollards Hill E SW16 204 B6
Pollards Hill N SW16 204 B6
Pollards Hill S SW16 204 B6
Pollards Hill W SW16 204 B6
Pollard St E2 ....96 A4
Pollards Wood Rd
SW16 ....204 A6
Pollard Wlk DA14 ..190 C4
Pollen St W1 ......238 D1
Pollitt Dr NW8 92 B3 236 A6
Pollock Ho W10 .....91 A3
Polperro Cl BR6 ....211 D3
Polperro Mans 3
NW6 ....69 C3
Polperro Mews SE11 261 D4
Polsted Rd SE6 ....163 B4
Polsten Mews EN3 ..7 C6
Polthorne Gr SE18 .123 B2
Polworth Rd SW16 .182 A5
Polygon Rd
NW1 ....93 D5 232 C3
Polygon The NW8 ..229 D6
1 SW4 ....137 C1
Polytechnic St SE18 122 C2
Pomell Way E1 ....243 D2
Pomeroy Ct W11 ....91 A1
Pomeroy Ho 5 E2 ..96 D5
Pomeroy St SE14 ..140 C4
Pomfret Rd SE5 ....138 D2
Pomoja La N19 .....72 A6
Pomona Ho 10 SE8 .119 A2
Pond Cl N12 ....30 C4
SE3 ....143 A3
Pond Cottage La
BR3,BR4 ....207 C1
Pond Cotts SE21 ..161 C3
Ponders End Ind Est
EN3 ....19 A6
Ponders End Sta EN3 19 A6
Ponder St 5 N7 .....72 B1
Pond Farm Est E5 ..74 C5
Pondfield End IG10 .21 C4
Pondfield Ho 4 N5 .73 A3
West Norwood SE27 .183 A1
Pondfield Rd BR6 ..226 D5
Dagenham RM10 ...81 D3
West Wickham BR2 .208 C1
Pond Gn HA4 ......61 C6
Pond Hill Gdns SM3 217 A2
Pond Ho SW3 .....257 A3
Pond Mead SE21 ..161 B5
Pond Path BR7 ....188 A4
Pond Pl SW3 .114 C2 257 A3
Pond Rd E15 ....98 C5
SE3 ....142 D3
Pond Sq N6 ....49 A2
Pond St NW3 ....70 C2
Pond Way TW11 ...175 C4

Pondwood Rise BR6 .211 C2
Ponler St E1 ....96 B1
Ponsard Rd NW10 ..90 A4
Ponsford St E9 .....74 C2
Ponsonby Pl
SW1 ....115 D1 259 D2
Ponsonby Rd SW15 156 A4
Ponsonby Terr SW1 259 D2
Pontefract Ct UB5 ..63 D3
Pontefract Rd BR1 ..186 D5
Ponton Ho SW2 ...160 C3
Ponton Rd
SW8 ....137 D6 269 D5
Pont St SW1 .114 D3 257 D5
Pont St Mews SW1 .257 C5
Pontypool Pl SE1 ..251 C2
Pool Cl
Beckenham BR3 ...185 C5
East Molesey KT8 .195 B4
Pool Ct SE6 ....163 C2
Poole Cl HA4 ....61 C6
Poole Court Rd TW5 129 A3
Poole Ct N1 ....73 C1
Hounslow TW5 ....129 A3
Poole Ho SE11 ....260 D5
Poole Rd E9 ......74 D2
West Ewell KT19 ...215 B2
Pooles Bldgs EC1 ..241 A4
Pooles Ct IG3 .....80 A5
Pooles La SW10 ...266 A3
Pooles Park Prim Sch
N4 ....72 B6
Pooles Pk N4 ......72 C6
Poole St N1 .95 B6 235 C5
Poole Way UB4 ....83 C4
Pool Ho NW8 ......236 D4
Poolmans St SE16 .118 D4
Poonah St E1 ......96 C1
Pope Cl
East Bedfont TW14 .149 D3
Mitcham SW17,SW19 180 A6
Pope Ct 10 KT2 ....175 D6
Pope Ho 7 SE16 ...118 B2
3 SE5 ....139 A5
Pope John RC Prim Sch
W12 ....112 B6
Pope Rd BR2 ......209 D4
Pope's Ave TW2 ...152 C2
Popes Dr N3 ....29 C2
Pope's Gr CR0 ....223 B5
Pope's Gr TW1,TW2 152 D2
Pope's Head Alley
EC3 ....242 D1
Pope's La W5 .....110 A3
Pope's Rd SW9 ...138 C2
Pope St SE1 ......253 B1
Pope Street Ct SE9 166 B3
Popham Cl TW13 ..151 B1
Popham Ct N16 ....73 C5
Popham Gdns TW9 132 C2
Popham Rd
N1 ....95 A6 235 A6
Popham St N1 ....234 D6
N1 ....95 A6 235 A6
Poplar Ave
Mitcham CR4 ......180 C2
Orpington BR6 ....226 D6
Southall UB2 .....107 D3
Yiewsley UB7 .....104 B6
Poplar Bath St 10
E14 ....119 D6
Poplar Bsns Pk E14 120 A6
Poplar Cl E9 ....75 B3
Pinner HA5 ....22 D2
Poplar Cres KT19 .215 A2
Poplar Ct Chingford E4 .35 D4
Northolt UB5 ......84 C5
4 Streatham SW16 160 B1
13 Twickenham TW1 153 C5
Wimbledon SW19 ..179 C5
Poplar Farm Cl KT19 215 A2
Poplar Fst Sch SW19 201 C6
Poplar Gdns KT3 ..177 B1
Poplar Gr N11 .....31 A4
W6 ....112 C4
Kingston KT3 .....199 B6
Wembley HA9 .....67 A5
Poplar High St E14 119 D6
Poplar Ho 19 SE16 .118 D4
SE4 ....141 B1
Poplar Mews W12 .112 C4
Poplar Mount DA17 125 C2
Poplar Pl W2 113 D6 245 D6
Hayes UB3 ....106 A6
Poplar Rd SE24 ...139 A1
Ashford TW15 ....171 A5
Cheam SM3 ......201 B1
Merton SW19 ....179 C1

Poplar Rd S SW19 .201 C6
Poplars Cl HA4 ....39 C1
Poplars Ho 14 E17 .53 D6
Poplars Rd E17 ....53 D6
Poplars Sta E14 ...119 D6
East Barnet N14 ..15 B4
Poplar View HA9 ..65 D6
Poplar Way
Feltham TW13 ....150 B1
Ilford IG6 ....57 A5
Poplar Wlk SE24 ..139 A1
Croydon CR0 ....205 A6
Poppins Ct EC4 ...241 C1
Poppleton Rd E11 .54 C3
Poppy Cl
Belvedere DA17 ..125 D4
Hackbridge SM6 ..203 A1
Poppy La CR0 .....206 C2
Porchester Ct 10 W2 245 D6
Porchester Gate W2 246 A6
Porchester Gdn Mews
W2 ....91 D1
Porchester Gdns
W2 ....113 D6 245 D6
Porchester Mead
BR3 ....185 D4
Porchester Mews W2 91 D1
Porchester Pl W2 ..237 B1
Porchester Rd W2 ..91 D1
Kingston KT1 .....176 B1
Porchester Sq W2 ..91 D1
Porchester Terr
W2 ....114 A6 246 A6
Porchester Terr N W2 91 D1
Porch Way N20 ....14 D1
Porcupine Cl SE9 ..166 A2
Porden Rd SW2 ...138 B1
Porland Ct SE1 ...262 C6
Porlock Ave HA1,HA2 42 A4
Porlock Ho 5 SE26 162 A1
Porlock Rd EN1 ....17 D4
Porlock St
SE1 ....117 B4 252 D2
Porrington Cl BR7 .188 C2
Portal Cl
Hillingdon UB10 ..60 B1
Ruislip HA4 ......62 C4
West Norwood SE27 160 C1
Portbury Cl 16 SE15 140 A4
Portchester Cl SE24 139 C5
Portchester Ct W2 .91 D1
Port Cres E13 .....99 B3
Portcullis Lodge Rd
EN1 ....5 B2
Porte 10 NW9 .....27 C2
Portelet Ct 1 N1 ..95 C6
Portelet Rd E1 .....96 C3
Porten Hos W14 ..254 A5
Porten Rd W14 ...254 A5
Porter Rd E6 ......100 B1
Porters Ave RM8,RM9 80 C3
Porter Sq N19 .....50 A1
Porter St SE1 117 A5 252 B4
W1 ....237 D2
Porters & Walters
Almshouses N22 ..32 B3
Porters Way UB7 ..104 A4
Porteus Rd W2 ....236 A4
Portgate Cl W9 ....91 B3
Porthcawe Rd SE26 185 B6
Porthkerry Ave DA16 146 A1
Port Ho 6 SW11 ..136 A4
Portia Ct 2 IG11 ...80 A1
Portia Way E3 .....97 B3
Porticos The SW3 .266 C5
Portinscale Rd SW15 157 B6
Portishead Ho 29 W2 91 C2
Portland Ave DA15 168 A5
N16 ....51 D2
New Malden KT3 .199 D2
Portland Cl RM6 ...59 A4
Portland Commercial Est
IG11 ....102 C5
Portland Cotts CR0 203 B4
Portland Cres
1 Chislehurst SE9 166 A2
Feltham TW13 ....171 B6
Southall UB6 .....86 A6
Stanmore HA7 ....25 D1
Portland Cres W HA7 43 D6
Portland Ct 7 N1 ...73 C1
1 SE14 ....141 A1
Portland Dr EN2 ...5 D5
Portland Gdns N4 .50 D3
Ilford RM6 ....58 D4

Portland Gr
SW8 ....138 B4 270 C2
Portland Ho 20 SW2 160 C3
Portland Hospl for Women
& Children The W1 238 D5
Portland Mans SE25 206 B4
Portland Mews W1 239 B1
Portland Pl
W1 ....93 B2 238 D3
Croydon SE25 ....206 A5
Portland Rd N15 ...51 D1
W11 ....113 A6 244 A5
W11 ....113 A5 244 B4
Ashford TW15 ....148 A5
Bromley BR1 .....187 C5
Chislehurst SE9 ..166 A2
Croydon SE25 ....206 B4
Hayes UB4 ....83 C4
Kingston KT1 .....198 B6
Mitcham CR4 .....180 C1
Southall UB2 .....107 B3
Portland Rise N4 ..51 A3
Portland Sq 4 E1 .118 B5
Portland St
SE17 ....117 B1 262 D1
Portland Terr TW9 .131 D1
Portland Village W6 112 C3
Portman Ave SW14 133 B2
Portman Cl DA7 ...147 A2
W1 ....93 A1 238 A2
Portman Dr IG8 ...37 D1
Portman Gate NW1 237 B5
Portman Gdns NW9 27 B1
Hillingdon UB10 ..60 C1
Portman Hts 1 NW3 69 C5
Portman Lo N21 ...16 D6
Portman Mews S W1 238 A1
Portman Pl E2 .....96 C4
Portman Rd KT1 ...176 B1
Portman Sq
W1 ....93 A1 238 A2
Portman St
W1 ....93 A1 238 A1
Portman The NW11 47 C2
Portman Twrs W1 237 D2
Portmeadow Wlk
SE2 ....124 D4
Portmeers Cl E17 ..53 C3
Portnall Rd W9 ....91 B4
Portobello Ct Est W11 91 B1
Portobello Ho 6
SW27 ....182 D5
Portobello Mews
W11 ....245 A5
Portobello Rd W10 .91 A2
W11 ....113 B6 244 D6
Portobello Road Mkt*
W10 ....91 A2
Porton Ct KT6 ....197 C3
Portpool La
EC1 ....94 C2 241 A4
Portree Cl N22 ....32 B3
Portree St E14 ....98 B1
Port Royal Pl 3 N16 73 C3
Portrush Ct 9 UB1 .86 A1
Portsdown HA8 ....26 C5
Portsdown Ave NW11 47 B3
Portsdown Mews
NW11 ....47 B3
Portsea Hall W2 ...237 B1
Portsea Ho 3 SW15 156 B3
Portsea Mews W2 .237 B1
Portsea Pl W2 ....237 B1
Portslade Rd SW8 137 C3
Portsmouth Ave KT7 197 A2
Portsmouth Rd
Esher KT10 ......212 A5
Putney SW15 .....156 C4
Thames Ditton KT6,KT7 197 C3
Portsmouth St WC2 240 D1
Portsoken St E1,EC3 253 C6
Portswood Pl 10
SW15 ....155 C5
Portugal Gdns TW2 152 A2
Portugal St
WC2 ....94 B1 240 D1
Portway E15 ......98 C6
Portway Gdns SE18 143 D5
Portway Sch E13 ..98 D6
Poseidon Ct 4 E14 119 C2
Postern Gn EN2 ...4 C2
Postern The EC2 ..242 B3
Post La TW2 ......152 B2
Postmill Cl CR0 ...222 D5
Post Office App E7 .77 B3
Post Office Way
SW8 ....137 D5 269 C4

Post Rd UB2 . . . . .107 D3
Postway Mews **1** IG1 78 D5
Potier St SE1 . . . .**262** D5
Potter Cl CR4 . . . . .181 B1
Potterhill Ct TW11 .175 B3
Potteries The EN5 . . .13 C6
Potterne Cl **5** SW19 156 D4
Potters Cl CR0 . . . .207 A1
Pottersfield EN5 . . . . .5 C1
Potters Fields
  SE1 . . . . . . .117 C5 **253** B3
Potters Gr KT3 . . . .199 A5
Potters Heights Cl
  HA5 . . . . .22 B3
Potter's La Barnet EN5 . .1 C1
  Streatham SW16 . . . .181 D4
Potters Lo E14 . . . . .120 A1
Potters Mews **4** WD6 . .9 D5
Potters Rd SW6 . . . .136 A4
Potter's Rd EN5 . . . . . .1 D1
Potter St HA5 . . . . . .22 B3
Potter Street Hill HA5 .22 B3
Pottery La
  W11 . . . . . . .113 A5 **244** B4
Pottery Rd TW8 . . . .132 A6
Pottery St SE16 . . . .118 B4
Pott St E2 . . . . .96 B4
Poulett Gdns TW1 . .153 A3
Poulett Rd E6 . . . . .100 B5
Poullett Ho SW2 . . . .160 D3
Poulters Wood BR2 .225 D3
Poulton Ave SM1,SM5 218 B5
Poulton Cl E8 . . . . . .74 B2
Poultry EC2 . . .95 B1 **242** C1
Pound Cl
  Long Ditton KT6 . . . .197 C1
  Orpington BR6 . . . . .227 B6
Pound Court Dr BR6 .227 B6
Pound Green Ct **4**
  DA5 . . . . .169 C4
Pound La NW10 . . . . .68 A2
Pound Park Rd SE7 .121 C2
Pound Pl SE9 . . . . . .166 C5
Pound St SM5 . . . . .218 D3
Pountney Rd SW11 .137 A2
Poverest Rd BR5 . . .211 D4
Povey Ho SE17 . . . . .**263** A3
  SW2 . . . . .160 C5
Powder Mill La TW2,
  TW4 . . . . .151 C3
Powell Cl
  Chessington KT9 . . . .213 D3
  Edgware HA8 . . . . . .26 B4
  Wallington SM6 . . . .220 A1
Powell Ct **19** E17 . . . .53 D6
  Croydon CR2 . . . . . .221 A4
Powell Gdns RM10 . . .81 C4
Powell Rd E5 . . . . . . .74 B5
  Buckhurst Hill IG9 . . . .21 C4
Powell's Wlk W4 . . .133 D6
Powergate Bsns Pk
  NW10 . . . . .89 B4
Power Ho **12** TW9 . . .132 C4
Power Ho The W4 . . .111 D2
Power Rd W4 . . . . .110 C2
Powerscroft Rd E5 . . .74 C4
  Sidcup DA14 . . . . . .190 C4
Powers Ct TW1 . . . .153 D4
Powis Ct Bushey WD23 . .8 D1
  Edgware HA8 . . . . . .26 B6
Powis Gdns NW11 . . .47 B2
  W11 . . . . .91 B1
Powis Ho WC2 . . . . .**240** B2
Powis Mews W11 . . . .91 B1
Powis Pl WC1 . .94 A3 **240** B5
Powis Rd E3 . . . . . . .97 C4
Powis Sq W11 . . . . . .91 B1
Powis St SE18 . . . . .122 D2
Powis Terr W11 . . . . .91 B1
Powlesland Ct **23** E14 .97 A1
Powle Terr IG1 . . . . .79 B3
Powlett Ho NW1 . . . .71 B2
Powlett Pl NW1 . . . . .71 B1
Pownall Gdns TW3 .129 C1
Pownall Rd E8 . . . . . .96 A6
  Hounslow TW3 . . . . .129 D1
Pownsett Terr IG1 . . .79 A3
Powrie Ho **4** SW11 .136 B3
Powster Rd BR1 . . . .187 B5
Powys Cl DA7 . . . . .146 D6
Powys Ct N11 . . . . . .32 A5
Powys La
  Bowes Park N13 . . . .32 A5
  Palmers Green N14 . . .32 A6
Poynder Ct **3** N7 . . .72 A3
Poynder Lo TW7 . . .131 A4
Poynders Ct **9** SW4 .159 C5

Poynders Gdns SW12 159 C4
Poynders Rd SW12,
  SW4 . . . . .159 C4
Poynings Rd N19 . . . .71 C5
Poynings Way N12 . . .29 C5
Poyntell Cres BR7 . . .189 B2
Poynter Ct **12** UB5 . . .84 C5
Poynter Ho NW8 . . . .**236** C6
  10 W11 . . . . .112 D5
Poynter Rd EN1 . . . . .18 A6
Poynton Rd N17 . . . . .34 A1
Poyntz Rd SW11 . . . .136 D3
Poyser St E2 . . . . . . .96 B5
Praed Mews W2 . . . .**236** D2
Praed St W2 . .92 B1 **236** D2
Pragel St E13 . . . . . .99 C5
Pragnell Rd SE12 . . .165 B2
Prague Pl SW2 . . . . .160 A6
Prah Rd N4 . . . . .72 C6
Prairie St SW8 . . . . .137 B3
Pratt Mews NW1 . . . .**232** A5
Pratt St NW1 . .93 C6 **232** A6
Pratt Wlk
  SE1,SE11 . . .116 B2 **260** D4
Prayle Gr NW2 . . . . . .46 D1
Prebend Gdns W4,
  W6 . . . . .111 D2
Prebend Mans **4**
  W4 . . . . .111 D2
Prebend St N1 95 A6 **235** A6
Precinct Rd UB3 . . . .106 A6
Precincts The SM4 . .201 C3
Precinct The N1 . . . . .**235** A6
  N5 . . . . .72 D3
  East Molesey KT8 . . .195 D6
Preedy Ho N1 . . . . . .**233** D4
Premier Ct EN3 . . . . . .6 C5
Premier Lo N3 . . . . . .29 C2
Premier Park Rd
  NW10 . . . . .88 D5
Premier Pl E14 . . . . .119 C6
Prendergast Ho **7**
  SW4 . . . . .159 D4
Prendergast Rd SE3 .142 C2
Prendergast Sch SE4 141 C1
Prentice Ct **2** SW19 .179 B5
Prentis Rd SW16 . . . .181 D6
Prentiss Ct SE7 . . . .121 C2
Presburg Rd KT3 . . .199 C4
Prescelly Pl HA8 . . . .26 B2
Prescot St
  E1 . . . . . . .117 D6 **253** D6
Prescott Ho SE17 . . .210 D3
Prescott Ho **13** SE17 .138 D6
Prescott Pl SW4 . . . .137 D1
Presentation Mews
  SW2 . . . . .160 B3
President Dr E1 . . . . .118 B5
President Ho EC1 . . . .**234** D1
President St EC1 . . . .**235** A2
Prespa Ct N9 . . . . . .18 C2
Press Ho NW10 . . . . .67 B5
Press Rd NW10 . . . . .67 B5
Prestage Way E14 . . .120 A6
Prestbury Rd E7 . . . . .77 C1
Prestbury Sq SE9 . . .188 B6
Prested Rd SW11 . . . .136 C1
Preston Ave E4 . . . . . .36 B4
Preston Cl SE1 . . . . .**263** A4
  Twickenham TW2 . . . .152 C1
Preston Ct DA14 . . . .189 D6
  Walton-on-T KT12 . . .194 C1
Preston Dr DA16 . . . .146 A4
  Wanstead E11 . . . . .55 C4
  West Ewell KT19 . . . .215 D2
Preston Gdns NW10 . .67 C2
  Enfield EN3 . . . . .7 A6
  Redbridge IG1 . . . . . .56 A3
Preston Hill HA3 . . . .44 B3
Preston Ho SE1 . . . . .**263** A4
  SE1 . . . .**263** C6
  1 SE18 . . . . .122 C2
  3 Dagenham RM10 . .81 C4
Preston Manor High Sch
  HA9 . . . . .66 B6
Preston Park Prim Sch
  HA9 . . . . .43 D1
Preston Pl NW2 . . . . .68 A2
  Richmond TW10 . . . .154 A6
Preston Rd E11 . . . . . .54 C3
  Littleton TW17 . . . . .192 C4
  South Norwood SE19 .182 D4
  Wembley HA3,HA9 . . .66 A6
  Wimbledon SW20 . . . .177 D3
Preston Road Sta HA3 44 A1
Prestons Rd BR2 . . . .225 A6
Preston's Rd E14 . . . .120 A5
Preston Waye HA3 . . .44 A1
Prestwich Terr SW4 .159 D6
Prestwick Cl UB2 . . . .107 A1

Prestwick Ct UB1 . . . .108 A6
Prestwick Rd WD19 . . .22 D6
Prestwood Ave HA3 . . .43 B5
Prestwood Cl SE18 . .146 A6
  Harrow HA3 . . . . .43 A6
Prestwood Gdns CR0 205 A2
Prestwood Ho **3**
  SE16 . . . . .118 B3
Prestwood St N1 . . . .**235** B3
Pretoria Ave E17 . . . . .53 A5
Pretoria Cres E4 . . . . .20 A3
Pretoria Ho **3** HA4 . . .40 C1
Pretoria Rd E11 . . . . .54 B1
  E16 . . . . .98 D3
  Chingford E4 . . . . . .20 B3
  Ilford IG1 . . . . .78 D3
  Streatham SW16 . . . .181 C5
  Tottenham N17 . . . . .33 D4
Pretoria Rd N N18 . . . .33 D4
Pretty Cnr HA6 . . . . . .22 A5
Prevost Rd N11 . . . . . .15 A2
Priam Ho **17** E2 . . . . .96 B5
Price Cl NW7 . . . . . . .29 A4
  Upper Tooting SW17 . .158 D1
Price Ct HA1 . . . . . . .43 A4
Price Ho N1 . . . .**235** A5
Price Rd CR0 . . . . . .220 D3
Prices St SE1 . . . . . .**251** D4
Price's St SE1 . . . . . .**251** D4
Price's Yd N1 . . . . . .**233** D5
Price Way TW12 . . . .173 A4
Prichard Ct N7 . . . . . .72 B3
  SW11 . . . .**266** D2
Pricklers Hill EN5 . . . .13 D5
Prickley Wood BR2 . .208 D1
Priddy's Yd **4** CR0 . .221 A6
Prideaux Ho **4** WC1 .**233** D2
Prideaux Pl W3 . . . . .111 B6
  WC1 . . . . . . .94 B4 **233** D2
Prideaux Rd SW9 . . .138 A4
Pridham Rd CR7 . . . .205 B5
Priestfield Rd SE23 . .163 A1
Priestlands Park Rd
  DA15 . . . . .167 D1
Priestley Cl N16 . . . . .51 D2
Priestley Gdns RM6 . .58 B3
Priestley Ho EC1 . . . .**242** B6
  2 NW5 . . . . .71 B2
  6 Wembley HA9 . . .67 A5
Priestley Rd CR4 . . . .181 A1
Priestley Way E17 . . . .52 D6
  NW2 . . . . .46 A1
Priestman Point **25**
  E3 . . . . .97 D4
Priestmead Fst & Mid Schs
  HA3 . . . . .43 B6
Priest Park Ave HA2 . .63 C6
Priests Bridge SW14 .133 C2
Priest's Ct EC2 . . . . .**242** A2
Prima Rd SW9 . . . . .138 C5
Primrose Ave
  Enfield EN2 . . . . .5 C4
  Ilford RM6 . . . . .58 B2
Primrose Cl
  Catford SE6 . . . . . . .186 A5
  Hackbridge SM6 . . . .203 B1
  Harrow HA2 . . . . . . .63 B1
Primrose Ct
  New Malden KT4 . . . .200 A2
  11 Streatham SW16 .182 A6
Primrose Gdns NW3 . .70 C2
  Ruislip HA4 . . . . . . .62 C3
Primrose Hill EC4 . . . .**241** B1
Primrose Hill*
  NW1,NW3 . . . . . . .230 C6
Primrose Hill Ct NW3 .70 D1
Primrose Hill Rd
  NW1,NW3 . . .70 D1 **230** C6
Primrose Hill Sch
  NW1 . . . . . . .93 A6 **231** B6
Primrose Hill Studios
  NW1 . . . .**231** A6
Primrose Ho **7** SE15 140 A4
  1 Richmond TW9 . . .132 A4
Primrose La CR0 . . . .206 D1
Primrose Mans
  SW11 . . . .**268** A2
Primrose Mews **9**
  NW1 . . . . .70 D1
Primrose Rd E10 . . . . .53 D1
  Woodford E18 . . . . . .37 B1
Primrose Sq E9 . . . . .96 C6
Primrose St
  EC2 . . . . . . .95 C2 **243** B4
Primrose Way HA0 . . .87 D5
Primrose Wlk
  6 SE14 . . . . .141 A5
  Ewell KT17 . . . . . . .215 D1
Primula St W12 . . . . .90 A1

Prince Albert Ct
  NW8 . . . .**230** C5
  Sunbury TW16 . . . . .171 C3
Prince Albert Rd
  NW8 . . . . .92 D5 **230** C5
Prince Arthur Ct **19**
  NW3 . . . . .70 A4
Prince Arthur Mews **20**
  NW3 . . . . .70 A4
Prince Arthur Rd NW3 70 A3
Prince Charles Dr
  NW2 . . . . .46 C2
Prince Charles Rd
  SE3 . . . . .142 D4
Prince Charles Way
  SM6 . . . . .219 B5
Prince Consort Dr
  BR7 . . . . .189 B2
Prince Consort Rd
  SW7 . . . . . .114 B2 **256** C6
Princedale Rd
  W11 . . . . . . .113 A5 **244** B4
Prince Edward Mans
  W2 . . . .**245** B6
Prince Edward Rd E9 .75 B2
Prince George Ave
  N14 . . . . .15 D6
Prince George Rd N16 73 C4
Prince George's Ave
  SW20 . . . . .178 C1
Prince Georges Rd
  SW19 . . . . .180 B2
Prince Henry Rd SE7 143 D5
Prince Imperial Rd
  SE18 . . . . .144 B4
  Chislehurst BR7 . . . .188 D3
Prince John Rd SE9 .166 A6
Princelet St
  E1 . . . . .95 D2 **243** D4
Prince of Orange La **3**
  SE10 . . . . .142 A5
Prince Of Wales Cl
  NW4 . . . . .46 B5
Prince of Wales Dr
  SW11 . . . . .137 A4 **268** A4
Prince of Wales Mans
  SW11 . . . .**268** B2
  SW4 . . . . .159 B6
Prince of Wales Pas
  NW1 . . . .**232** A1
Prince of Wales Prim Sch
  EN3 . . . . .7 B6
Prince Of Wales Rd
  NW5 . . . . .71 A4
  SE3 . . . . .142 D4
  Newham E16 . . . . . .99 C1
Prince Of Wales' Rd
  SM1 . . . . .218 A6
Prince Of Wales Terr
  W4 . . . . .111 C1
  W8 . . . .**245** D1
Prince Rd SE25 . . . . .205 C4
Prince Regent E16 . . . .99 C2
Prince Regent Ct
  SE16 . . . . .119 C6
Prince Regent La E13 .99 C3
Prince Regent Mews
  NW1 . . . .**232** A1
Prince Regent Rd
  TW3 . . . . .130 C2
Prince Regent Sta
  E16 . . . . .121 C6
Prince Rupert Rd
  SE9 . . . . .144 A4
Princes Arc SW1 . . . .**249** B4
Princes Ave BR5 . . . .211 C4
  N10 . . . . .49 B6
  N22 . . . . .31 D2
  N3 . . . . .29 C2
  NW9 . . . . .44 D5
  Acton W3 . . . . .110 C3
  Edmonton N13 . . . . .32 C5
  Tolworth KT6 . . . . . .214 C6
  Wallington SM5 . . . .218 D1
  Woodford IG8 . . . . . .37 C6
Prince's Ave UB1 . . . . .85 D1
Princes Cir
  WC2 . . . . . .94 A1 **240** A2
Princes Cl DA14 . . . . .168 D1
  N4 . . . . .50 D1
  NW9 . . . . .44 C5
  Edgware HA8 . . . . . .26 C4
Prince's Cl TW11,
  TW12 . . . . .174 B6
Princes Ct NW2 . . . . .69 A3
  NW3 . . . . .70 B1
Prince's Ct SE16 . . . .119 B3
Princes Ct
  Kingston KT3 . . . . . .199 D6
  Stepney E1 . . . . . . .118 A6

Princes Ct continued
  Wembley HA9 . . . . . .66 A3
Princes Dr HA1 . . . . .42 C6
Princes Gate
  SW7 . . . . . .114 C4 **246** D1
Prince's Gate
  SW7 . . . . . .114 B4 **247** A1
Princes Gate Ct SW7 **246** D1
Princes Gate Mews
  SW7 . . . . . .114 B3 **256** D6
Princes Gdns
  SW7 . . . . . .114 B3 **256** D6
  Acton W3 . . . . .88 C2
  Ealing W5 . . . . .87 C3
Princes Ho W11 . . . . .**245** A5
Princes La N10 . . . . . .49 B6
Prince's Mews
  W2 . . . . . . .113 D6 **245** C6
  W6 . . . . .112 B1
Princes Mews TW3 . .129 C1
Princes Par NW11 . . .47 A3
Princes Park Ave
  NW11 . . . . .47 A3
  Hayes UB3 . . . . . . .105 B6
Princes Park Circ
  UB3 . . . . .105 B6
Princes Park Cl UB3 .105 B6
Princes Park La UB3 .105 B6
Princes Park Par
  UB3 . . . . .105 B6
Princes Pl SW1 . . . . .**249** B4
  W11 . . . . . . .113 A5 **244** A4
Prince's Plain BR2 . . .210 A1
Prince's Plain Prim Sch
  BR2 . . . . .210 A2
Princes Rd N18 . . . . . .34 C6
  Ashford TW15 . . . . .170 B5
  Buckhurst Hill IG9 . . .21 C4
  Ealing W13 . . . . . . .109 B5
  Feltham TW13 . . . . .149 D1
  Ilford IG6 . . . . .57 B5
  Kingston KT2 . . . . . .176 C3
  Richmond TW10 . . . .154 B6
  Richmond TW9 . . . . .132 B4
Prince's Rd
  Mortlake SW14 . . . . .133 B2
  Teddington TW11,
  TW12 . . . . .174 B6
  Wimbledon SW19 . . .179 C4
Princes Rise SE13 . . .142 A3
Princes Riverside Rd **7**
  SE16 . . . . .118 D5
Princessa Ct EN2 . . . .17 B6
Princess Alexandra School
  of Nursing The E1 . . .96 B2
Princess Alice Ho
  W10 . . . . .90 C3
Princess Alice Way
  SE28 . . . . .123 B4
Princess Ave HA9 . . . .66 A6
Princess Beatrice Ho
  SW10 . . . .**255** C1
Princess Christian Coll
  WC1 . . . . . .94 A2 **240** B4
Princess Cres N4 . . . .72 D6
Princess Ct NW6 . . . .69 D1
  W1 . . . .**237** C3
  W2 . . . .**245** D6
  Catford BR1 . . . . . . .186 C4
  3 Croydon CR0 . . .221 D4
  11 Wimbledon SW19 .178 D3
Princess Frederica CE
  Prim Sch NW10 . . . .90 C5
Princess Grace Hospl The
  W1 . . . . . . .93 A3 **238** A5
Princess La HA4 . . . . .39 C1
Princess Louise Cl
  W2 . . . .**236** D4
Princess Louise Hospl
  W10 . . . . .90 C2
Princess Mary Ho
  SW1 . . . .**259** D3
Princess May Prim Sch
  N16 . . . . .73 D4
Princess May Rd N16 .73 C4
Princess Mews NW3 . .70 B2
  Kingston KT1 . . . . . .198 B6
Princess Par BR6 . . . .226 C5
  Dagenham RM10 . . . .103 C5
Princess Park Manor
  N11 . . . . .31 A5
Prince's Sq
  W2 . . . . . . .113 D6 **245** C6
Princess Rd
  NW1 . . . . . .93 A6 **231** B6
  NW6 . . . . .91 C6
  Thornton Heath CR0 .205 A3
Princess St SE1 . . . . .**261** D5
Princes St DA7 . . . . .147 B2

Princes St continued
  W1 . . . .**238** D1
Prince's St EC2 95 B1 **242** C1
  W1 . . . .**238** D1
  Sutton SM1 . . . . . . .217 D3
  Tottenham N17 . . . . .33 C4
Prince's St TW10,TW9 154 A6
Prince St SE8 . . . . . .141 B6
Prince's Terr E13 . . . . .99 B6
Princes Way
  Acton W3 . . . . .110 C3
  Buckhurst Hill IG9 . . .21 C2
  Coney Hall BR4 . . . . .224 C5
  Croydon CR0 . . . . . .220 B3
  Putney SW15,SW19 .157 A3
  Ruislip HA4 . . . . . . .63 A4
Princes Yd **1** W11 . .113 A3
Princethorpe Ho W2 .91 C2
Princethorpe Rd
  SE26 . . . . .184 D6
Princeton Ct SW15 . . .134 D2
Princeton Mans WC1 .**240** C3
Princeton Mews **3**
  KT2 . . . . .176 C2
Princeton St
  WC1 . . . . . .94 B2 **240** C4
Prince William Ct
  TW15 . . . . .170 B5
Pringle Gdns SW16 . .181 C6
Printers Mews E3 . . . .97 A6
Printer St EC4 . . . . . .**241** B2
Printinghouse La
  UB3 . . . . .105 C4
Printing House Yd **17**
  E2 . . . . .95 C4
Printon Ho **12** E3 . . .97 B2
Print Village Ind Est
  SE15 . . . . .139 D3
Priolo Rd SE7 . . . . . .121 C1
Prior Ave SM2,SM5 . .218 C1
Prior Bolton St N1 . . . .72 D2
Prioress Ho **2** E3 . . . .97 D4
Prioress Rd SE27 . . . .160 D1
Prioress St SE1 . . . . .**262** D5
Prior Rd IG1 . . . . . . .78 C5
Priors Croft E17 . . . . . .35 B1
Priors Field UB5 . . . . .63 A2
Priors Gdns HA4 . . . . .62 C3
Priors Lo **4** TW10 . .154 A5
Priors Mead EN1 . . . . .5 C4
Prior St SE10 . . . . . .142 A5
Priorty Ct SE15 . . . . .140 C1
Prior Weston Prim Sch
  EC1 . . . . . . .95 A3 **242** B5
Priory Ave BR5 . . . . .211 B3
  E17 . . . . .53 C4
  N8 . . . . .49 D5
  W4 . . . . .111 C3
  Cheam SM3 . . . . . . .216 D4
  Chingford E4 . . . . . .19 C1
  Wembley HA0 . . . . . .64 D4
Priory CE Prim Sch
  SW19 . . . . .179 D5
Priory Cl BR7 . . . . . .188 B2
  E4 . . . . .19 B1
  N3 . . . . .29 B2
  Ashford TW16 . . . . . .172 A3
  Barnet N20 . . . . . . .13 B4
  Beckenham BR3 . . . .207 A6
  East Barnet N14 . . . .15 B4
  Hampton TW12 . . . . .173 B2
  Hayes UB3 . . . . . . .106 B6
  3 Merton SW19 . . .179 D2
  Ruislip HA4 . . . . . . .39 D1
  Stanmore HA7 . . . . . .8 D1
  Wembley HA0 . . . . . .64 D4
  Woodford E18 . . . . . .37 A2
Priory Cres
  Cheam SM3 . . . . . . .216 D4
  South Norwood SE19 .183 A3
  Wembley HA0 . . . . . .65 A5
Priory Ct E17 . . . . . . .35 B1
  E17 . . . . .53 B6
  E6 . . . . .99 D6
  E9 . . . . .74 D3
  EC4 . . . .**241** D1
  SW8 . . . . . . .137 D4 **269** D2
  Bushey WD23 . . . . . . .8 A3
  Cheam SM1 . . . . . . .217 B3
  Cheam SM3 . . . . . . .217 A4
  Hounslow TW3 . . . . .129 D2
  Ilford RM6 . . . . .58 B3
  Putney SW15 . . . . . .156 C5
  Roehampton SW15 . .133 D1
  4 Wembley HA0 . . .88 A5
Priory Dr SE2 . . . . . .124 D1
  Stanmore HA7 . . . . . .8 D1
Priory Field Dr HA8 . .26 D6
Priory Gdns N6 . . . . . .49 B5
  6 W4 . . . . .111 C2
  Ashford TW15 . . . . .171 B5

Priory Gdns *continued*
Barnes SW13 . . . . .133 D2
Ealing W5 . . . . .88 A4
Hampton TW12 . . . . . .173 B2
South Norwood SE25 . .205 D5
Wembley HA0 . . . . .65 A4
Priory Gn N1 . . . . . . .233 C4
Priory Gr
SW8 . . . . .138 A4 270 A1
Priory Grange N2 . . . .48 D6
Priory Heights N1 . .233 D4
Priory Hill HA0 . . . . . .65 A4
Priory Ho E1 . . . . . . .243 C6
EC1 . . . . .241 C6
3 SE7 . . . . .143 C6
SW1 . . . . .259 C2
Priory Hospl Hayes Grove
The BR2 . . . . .225 A6
Priory Hospl The
SW15 . . . . .133 D1
Priory House Ct SE6 .163 D3
Priory La
East Molesey KT8 . . . .195 D5
Roehampton SW15 . . .155 D6
Priory Leas SE9 . . . . .166 A3
Priory Lo 7 W4 . . . . .110 C1
Coney Hall BR4 . . . . . .224 C5
Ealing W5 . . . . .87 C1
Priory Mans 17 NW3 . . .70 D2
SW10 . . . . .256 B1
Priory Park Rd NW6 . .91 B6
Wembley HA0 . . . . .65 A4
Priory Pk SE3 . . . . . .142 D2
Priory Rd E6 . . . . .99 D5
N8 . . . . .49 D5
NW6 . . . . .69 D1
W4 . . . . .111 A3
Barking IG11 . . . . .79 B1
Cheam SM3 . . . . .216 D4
Chessington KT9 . . . . .214 A5
Hampton TW12 . . . . . .173 C3
Hounslow TW3 . . . . . .152 A6
Mitcham SW19 . . . . . .180 B3
Richmond TW9 . . . . . .132 C5
Thornton Heath CR0 . .204 C2
Priory Ret Pk SW19 . .180 B3
Priory Sch SE25 . . . .205 D5
Priory St 16 E3 . . . . . .97 D4
Priory Terr NW6 . . . . .91 D6
Priory The N8 . . . . . . .49 D5
SE1 . . . . .251 C1
SE3 . . . . .142 D1
Croydon CR0 . . . . . . .220 C5
21 Kingston KT6 . . . .198 A4
Priory View WD23 . . . . .8 C4
Priory Villas N11 . . . . .30 D5
Priory Way
Harmondsworth UB7 . .126 A6
Harrow HA2 . . . . .41 D5
Southall UB2 . . . . .106 D3
Priory Wlk
SW10 . . . . .114 A1 256 B1
Priscilla Ho 8 TW16 171 D3
Pritchard Ho 34 E2 . .96 A5
Pritchard's Rd E2 . . . .96 A5
Pritchett Cl EN3 . . . . . .7 C6
Priter Rd SE16 . . . . . .118 A3
Priter Road Hostel 14
SE16 . . . . .118 A3
Private Rd EN1 . . . . . .17 C6
Probert Rd SW2 . . . . .160 C6
Probyn Ho SW1 . . . . .259 D4
Probyn Rd SW2 . . . . .160 D6
Procter Ho 12 SE5 . . .139 B5
Procter St
WC1 . . . . .94 B2 240 C3
Proctor Cl CR4 . . . . . .181 A2
Proctor Ho 5 SE1 . . .118 A1
Proctors Cl TW14 . . .150 A3
Prodger 8 NW9 . . . . . .27 D2
Progress Bsns Pk
CR9 . . . . .220 B6
Progress Way
Croydon CR0 . . . . . . .220 B6
Enfield EN1 . . . . .18 A6
Wood Green N22 . . . . .32 C2
Prologis Pk TW4 . . . .128 C1
Prome Ho 3 N16 . . . . .73 B4
Promenade Approach Rd
W4 . . . . .133 C5
Promenade Mans HA8 26 C5
Promenade The W4 .133 C4
Pronto Trad Est UB4 .83 C2
Prospect Cl
Belvedere DA17 . . . . .125 C2
Forest Hill SE26 . . . . .184 B6
Hounslow TW5 . . . . . .129 B4
Ruislip HA4 . . . . .40 D2
Prospect Cotts SW18 135 C1
Prospect Cres TW2 . .152 A5

Prospect Hill E17 . . . . .53 D5
Prospect Ho 9 E17 . . .54 A6
1 E8 . . . . .73 D2
N1 . . . . .234 A3
SE1 . . . . .261 D5
14 W10 . . . . .90 D1
Prospect House Sch
SW15 . . . . .156 D4
Prospect Pl E1 . . . . . .118 C5
N2 . . . . .48 B5
4 NW2 . . . . .69 B5
24 NW3 . . . . .70 A4
6 SE8 . . . . .141 B6
2 W4 . . . . .111 B1
Bromley BR2 . . . . . . .209 B6
Tottenham N17 . . . . . .33 C3
Wimbledon SW20 . . . .178 B3
Prospect Quay SW18 135 C1
Prospect Rd NW2 . . . .69 C5
Barnet EN5 . . . . .1 D1
Kingston KT6 . . . . . . .197 C3
Woodford IG8 . . . . . . .37 C5
Prospect Ring N2 . . . .48 B6
Prospect St SE16 . . . .118 B4
Prospect Vale SE7,
SE18 . . . . .122 A2
Prospect Wharf E1 . .118 C6
Prospero Ho 7 DA17 125 C3
Prospero Rd N19 . . . . .49 D1
Protea Cl E16 . . . . . . .98 D3
Protheroe Ho 4 N17 . .51 D6
Prothero Gdns NW4 . .46 B4
Prothero Ho 10 NW10 .67 B1
Prothero Rd
SW6 . . . . .135 B5 264 C4
Prout Gr NW10 . . . . . .67 D4
Prout Rd E5 . . . . .74 B5
Provence St N1 . . . . .235 A4
Providence Ct W1 . . .248 B6
Providence Ho E9 . . . .96 D6
Providence La UB3 . .127 B5
Providence Pl N1 . . . .234 C5
Providence Rd UB7 . .104 B5
Providence Row N1 .233 C3
Providence Sq 4
SE1 . . . . .118 A4
Providence Twr 1
SE16 . . . . .118 A4
Provident Ind Est
UB3 . . . . .106 A4
Provincial Terr 2
SE20 . . . . .184 D3
Provost Rd NW3 . . . . .70 D2
Provost St N1 .95 B4 235 C2
Prowse Ave WD23 . . . .8 A2
Prowse Pl NW1 . . . . . .71 C1
Pruden Cl N14 . . . . . . .15 C2
Prudent Pas EC2 . . . .242 B1
Prusom's Island 8
E1 . . . . .118 C5
Prusom St E1 . . . . . . .118 B5
Pryors The NW3 . . . . .70 B5
Public Record Office
EC4,WC2 . . . .94 C1 241 A2
Richmond TW9 . . . . . .132 C5
Public Record Office
Mus★ EC4,WC2 . . . .241 A2
Pudding La EC3 . . . . .252 D6
Pudding Mill La E15 . .97 D6
Pudding Mill Lane Sta
E15 . . . . .97 D6
Puddle Dock
EC4 . . . . .116 D6 251 D6
Puffin Cl Barking IG11 102 B4
Beckenham BR3 . . . . .206 D4
Puffin Terr IG5 . . . . . . .56 C6
Pugin Ct N1 . . . . .72 C1
Pulborough Rd SW18 157 B4
Pulborough Way
TW4 . . . . .128 C1
Pulford Rd N15 . . . . . .51 B3
Pulham Ave N2 . . . . . .48 B5
Pulham Ho SW8 . . . . .270 C3
Puller Rd EN5 . . . . .1 A3
Pulleyns Ave E6 . . . . .100 A4
Pullman Ct SW2 . . . . .160 B3
Pullman Gdns SW15 .156 C5
Pullman Mews SE12 .165 B1
Pullman Pl SE9 . . . . . .166 A6
Pulross Rd SW9 . . . . .138 B2
Pulteney Cl 18 E3 . . . .97 B4
Pulteney Gdns 9 E18 .55 B2
Pulteney Rd E18 . . . . . .55 B2
Pulteney Terr
N1 . . . . .94 B6 233 D6
Pulton Ho SE4 . . . . . .141 A1
Pulton Pl
SW6 . . . . .135 C5 265 A3
Puma Ct E1 . . . . .243 C4

Pump Alley 8 TW8 . .131 D5
Pump Cl UB5 . . . . .85 C5
Pump Ct EC4 . . . . . . .241 A1
Pump House Cl SE16 118 C4
Bromley BR2 . . . . . . .186 D1
Pumping Station Rd
W4 . . . . .133 C6
Pump La SE14 . . . . . .140 C5
Hayes UB3 . . . . .106 A4
Pump Pail N CR0 . . . .221 A5
Pump Pail S CR0 . . . .221 A5
Punchard Cres EN3 . . .7 D5
Punderson's Gdns E2 .96 B4
Puran Ho E13 . . . . . . .99 C5
Purbeck Ave KT3 . . . .199 D3
Purbeck Dr NW2 . . . . .68 D6
Purbeck Ho SW8 . . . .270 C3
Purbrook Est SE1 . . . .253 B1
Purbrook Ho 2
SW15 . . . . .156 B4
Purbrook St SE1 . . . .263 B6
Purcell Cres
SW6 . . . . .135 A5 264 A4
Purcell Ho SW10 . . . .266 C5
Isleworth TW2 . . . . . .152 B5
Southall UB1 . . . . .85 C1
Purcell Mews NW10 . .67 C5
Purcell Rd UB6 . . . . . .86 B2
Purcell St N1 . . . . .95 C5
Purcells Ave HA8 . . . . .26 C5
Purchese St
NW1 . . . . .93 D5 232 D3
Purday Ho 4 W10 . . . .91 B4
Purdey Ct 3 KT4 . . . .200 A1
Purdon Ho 10 SE15 . .140 A4
Purdy St E3 . . . . .97 D3
Purland Cl RM8 . . . . . .59 B1
Purland Rd SE28,
SE18 . . . . .123 D4
Purley Ave NW2 . . . . . .69 A6
Purley Oaks Prim Sch
CR2 . . . . .221 B1
Purley Pl N1 . . . . .72 A4
Purley Rd Edmonton N9 17 C1
South Croydon CR2 . . .221 B1
Purley View Terr
CR2 . . . . .221 B1
Purley Way
Croydon CR0,CR9 . . . .220 C3
Thornton Heath CR0 . .204 B4
Purley Way Cres CR0 204 B2
Purneys Rd SE9 . . . . .143 D1
Purrett Rd SE18 . . . . .123 D1
Purser Ho 3 SW2 . . . .160 C2
Pursers Cross Rd
SW6 . . . . .135 B4 264 D2
Pursewardens Cl
W13 . . . . .109 C5
Pursley Rd NW7 . . . . .28 B3
Purves Rd NW10 . . . . .90 C5
Purvis Ho CR0 . . . . . .205 B2
Pusey Ho 16 E14 . . . .97 C1
Puteaux Ho 6 E2 . . . .96 D5
Putney Bridge App
SW6 . . . . .135 A2
Putney Bridge Rd
SW15 . . . . .135 B1
Putney Bridge Sta
SW6 . . . . .135 B2
Putney Comm SW15 .134 C2
Putney Gdns RM6 . . . .58 B4
Putney Heath SW15 .156 C5
Putney Heath La
SW15 . . . . .156 D5
Putney High Sch
SW15 . . . . .156 D6
Putney High St SW15 135 A1
Putney Hill SW15 . . . .156 D6
Putney Hospl SW15 .134 C2
Putney Park Ave
SW15 . . . . .134 A1
Putney Park La SW15 156 B6
Putney Pier SW15 . . . .135 A2
Putney School of Art &
Design SW15 . . . . . . .135 C1
Putney Sta SW15 . . . .135 A1
Putney Wharf Twr
SW15 . . . . .135 A2
Pycombe Cnr N12 . . . .29 B6
Pycroft Way N9 . . . . . .34 A6
Pylbrook Rd SM1 . . . .217 D5
Pylon Trad Est E16 . . .98 B2
Pylon Way CR0 . . . . . .204 A1
Pym Cl EN4 . . . . .14 B6
Pymers Mead SE21 . .161 A3
Pymmes Brook Ho 3
N10 . . . . .31 A3
Pymmes Cl
Bowes Park N13 . . . . .32 B5
Tottenham N17 . . . . . .34 B2

Pymmes Gdns N N9 . .17 D1
Pymmes Gdns S N9 . .17 D1
Pymmes Green Rd
N11 . . . . .15 C1
Pymmes Rd N13 . . . . . .32 A5
Pymms Brook Dr EN4 . .2 C1
Pynchester Cl UB10 . .60 C6
Pyne Rd KT6 . . . . .198 C1
Pynfolds SE16 . . . . . .118 B4
Pynham Cl SE2 . . . . . .124 B3
Pynnacles Cl HA7 . . . . .25 B5
Pynnersmead SE24 . .161 A6
Pyrford Ho 12 SW9 . .138 D1
Pyrland Rd N5 . . . . . . .73 B3
Richmond TW10 . . . . .154 B5
Pyrmont Gr SE27 . . . .160 D5
Pyrmont Rd W4 . . . . . .132 C6
Pytchley Cres SE19 . .183 A4
Pytchley Rd SE22 . . . .139 C4

Q

Quadrangle Cl SE1 . . .263 A4
Quadrangle Lo SW19 179 C4
Quadrangle The E17 . .35 B1
SE24 . . . . .161 A6
SW10 . . . . .266 B2
SW6 . . . . .264 A3
W12 . . . . .90 C1
W2 . . . . .237 A2
Quadrant Arc W1 . . . .249 C6
Quadrant Bsns Pk
NW6 . . . . .91 A6
Quadrant Cl NW4 . . . . .46 B4
Quadrant Gr NW5 . . . .70 D3
Quadrant Ho E15 . . . . .98 C4
Richmond TW9 . . . . . .131 D1
Thornton Heath CR7 . .204 D5
Quadrant Rd
Richmond TW9 . . . . . .131 D1
Thornton Heath CR7 . .204 D5
Quadrant The DA7 . . .146 D5
4 W10 . . . . .90 D4
Richmond TW9 . . . . . .132 A1
Sutton SM2 . . . . .218 A4
Wimbledon SW20 . . . .179 A2
Quad Rd HA9 . . . . .65 D5
Quaggy Wlk SE3 . . . . .143 A1
Quainton St NW10 . . . .67 B5
Quaker Ct EC1 . . . . . .242 B6
Quaker La UB2 . . . . . .107 C3
Quakers Course NW9 .27 D2
Quaker's Pl E7 . . . . . . .77 D3
Quaker St E1 . . .95 D3 243 C5
Quakers Wlk N21 . . . . .17 B5
Quality Ct WC2 . . . . . .241 A2
Quantock Cl UB3 . . . .127 B5
Quantock Ct UB6 . . . . .64 C3
Quantock Dr KT4 . . . .216 C6
Quantock Gdns NW2 . .68 D6
Quantock Ho N16 . . . . .51 D1
Quarrendon St SW6 . .135 C3
Quarr Rd SM5 . . . . . . .202 C3
Quarry Park Rd SM1 .217 B2
Quarry Rd SW18 . . . . .158 A5
Quarry Rise SM1 . . . . .217 B2
Quarterdeck The
E14 . . . . .119 C4
Quartermain Ho SM4 202 A4
Quartermile La E10,
E15 . . . . .75 D4
Quayside Ct 6 SE16 .118 C4
Quay West TW11 . . . . .175 B5
Quebec & Crown Wharves
E14 . . . . .97 B1
Quebeck Ind Est
SE16 . . . . .119 A3
Quebec Mews W1 . . . .237 D1
Quebec Rd Hayes UB4 .84 C1
Ilford IG1 . . . . .56 D2
Quebec Way SE16 . . .119 A4
Quedgeley Ct 3
SE15 . . . . .139 D6
Queen Adelaide Ct
SE20 . . . . .184 C4
Queen Adelaide Rd
SE20 . . . . .184 C3
Queen Alexandra Mans
WC1 . . . . .233 A1
Queen Alexandra's Ct 5
SW19 . . . . .179 B5
Queen Anne Ave BR2 208 D6
Queen Anne Dr KT10 212 C1
Queen Anne Gate
DA7 . . . . .146 C2
Queen Anne Mews
W1 . . . . .238 D3
Queen Anne Rd E9 . . .74 D2

Queen Annes Cl TW2 152 B1
Queen Anne's Gate
SW1 . . . . .115 D4 249 C1
Queen Anne's Gdns
W4 . . . . .111 C3
W5 . . . . .110 A4
Enfield EN1 . . . . .17 C5
Mitcham CR4 . . . . . . .202 D6
Queen Anne's Gr W4 111 C3
W5 . . . . .110 A4
Enfield EN1 . . . . .17 C5
Queen Anne's Pl EN1 .17 C5
Queen Anne St
W1 . . . . .93 B2 238 C3
Queen Borough Gdns
BR7 . . . . .189 D4
Queenborough Gdns
IG2 . . . . .56 C5
Queen Caroline St
W6 . . . . .112 C1
Queen Charlottes &
Chelsea Hospl W12 . .90 A1
Queen Elizabeth College
15 SE10 . . . . .142 A5
Queen Elizabeth Ct EN5 1 B1
Queen Elizabeth Gdns
SM4 . . . . .201 C5
Queen Elizabeth Hall &
Purcell Room SE1 . . .250 D4
Queen Elizabeth Hospital
for Children The E2 .96 A5
Queen Elizabeth Hospl
SE7 . . . . .144 A5
Queen Elizabeth II Con Ctr
SW1 . . . . .249 D1
Queen Elizabeth II Jubilee
Sch W9 . . . . .91 B3
Queen Elizabeth II Pier
SE10 . . . . .120 D5
Queen Elizabeth Rd
E17 . . . . .53 A6
Kingston KT2 . . . . . . .176 B1
Queen Elizabeth's Cl
N16 . . . . .73 B6
Queen Elizabeth's Dr
N14 . . . . .16 A3
Queen Elizabeth's Girls
Sch EN5 . . . . .1 B1
Queen Elizabeth's Hunting
Lodge Mus★ E4 . . . .20 D4
Queen Elizabeth St
SE1 . . . . .117 D4 253 C2
Queen Elizabeth's Wlk
N16 . . . . .73 B6
Wallington SM6 . . . . .219 D4
Queen Elizabeth Wlk
SW13 . . . . .134 B4
Queenhithe EC4 . . . . .252 B6
Queen Margaret Flats 22
E2 . . . . .96 B4
Queen Margarets Ct
N1 . . . . .73 C3
Queen Margaret's Gr
N1 . . . . .73 C3
Queen Mary Ave
SM4 . . . . .200 D4
Queen Mary Cl KT9 . .214 C5
Queen Mary Rd
Charlton TW17 . . . . . .171 A1
South Norwood SE19 .182 D4
Queen Mary's Ave
SM5 . . . . .218 D1
Queen Mary's Gdns★
NW1 . . . . .231 A1
Queen Mary's Hospl
DA14 . . . . .190 A4
NW3 . . . . .70 A6
Queen Mary's Univ Hospl
SW15 . . . . .156 A5
Queen Mary, Univ of
London E1 . . . . .97 A3
Queen of Denmark Ct
SE16 . . . . .119 B3
Queens Acre SM3 . . .217 A1
Queens Ave N10 . . . . .49 B6
N20 . . . . .14 B2
Queen's Ave N3 . . . . . .30 A2
Queens Ave
Feltham TW13 . . . . . . .172 C6
Stanmore HA7 . . . . . . .25 C1
Queen's Ave
Southall UB1 . . . . .86 A1
Southgate N21 . . . . . . .16 D3
Woodford IG8 . . . . . . .37 B5
Queensberry Ho 6
TW9 . . . . .153 D6
Queensberry Mews W
SW7 . . . . .256 C4
Queensberry Pl E12 . .78 A3
SW7 . . . . .114 B2 256 C4

Queensberry Way
SW7 . . . . .256 C4
Queensborough Ct N3 47 B5
Queensborough Mews
W2 . . . . .246 A6
Queensborough Pas
W2 . . . . .246 A6
Queensborough Terr
W2 . . . . .113 D6 245 D6
Queensbridge Ct 1
E2 . . . . .95 D5
Queensbridge Inf Sch
E8 . . . . .73 D1
Queensbridge Pk
TW7 . . . . .152 C6
Queensbridge Rd
E2,E8 . . . . .95 D6
E8 . . . . .73 D1
Queensbury IG9 . . . . . .21 B3
Queensbury Circ Par
HA3 . . . . .44 A4
Queensbury Ct CR7 . .183 A1
Queensbury Rd NW9 . .45 C2
Wembley HA0 . . . . .88 B5
Queensbury St N1 . . . .73 A1
Queensbury Sta HA7,
HA8 . . . . .44 B6
Queensbury Station Par
HA8 . . . . .44 B6
Queen's CE Prim Sch The
TW9 . . . . .132 C5
Queen's Cir
SW11 . . . . .137 B5 268 C3
Queen's Cl
Edgware HA8 . . . . .26 C5
Wallington SM6 . . . . .219 B3
Queen's Club Gdns
W14 . . . . .135 A6 264 B6
Queen's Club The★
W14 . . . . .113 A1 254 B1
Queen's Coll
W1 . . . . .93 B2 238 C3
Queenscourt HA9 . . . .66 A4
Queen's Cres NW5 . . .71 A4
Queens Cres TW10 . .154 B6
Queenscroft Rd SE9 . .165 D5
Queens Ct E10 . . . . . . .53 C6
4 E14 . . . . .119 B6
E17 . . . . .53 C4
8 NW11 . . . . .47 B4
SE5 . . . . .139 C4
SW11 . . . . .268 C2
Queen's Ct E11 . . . . . .54 C2
NW11 . . . . .47 C4
NW8 . . . . .229 C4
W2 . . . . .245 D5
Queens Ct
Beckenham BR3 . . . . .185 D4
5 Buckhurst Hill IG9 . .21 A3
Stanmore HA7 . . . . . . .25 C1
Queen's Ct
Barnes SW13 . . . . . . .134 B4
Beckenham BR3 . . . . .185 D4
Croydon CR2 . . . . . . .221 A3
8 Ealing W5 . . . . .87 C2
1 Kingston KT2 . . . . .176 C3
3 Richmond TW10 . . .154 B6
Thornton Heath CR7 . .204 D4
Queensdale Cres
W11 . . . . .112 C5
Queensdale Pl W11 . .244 A3
Queensdale Rd
W11 . . . . .113 A5 244 A3
Queensdale Wlk
W11 . . . . .244 A3
Queens Down Rd E5 . .74 B4
Queen's Dr E10 . . . . . .53 C2
Queen's Dr N4 . . . . . . .72 D6
Queens Dr KT5 . . . . . .198 C3
Queen's Dr Acton W3 . .88 C3
Thames Ditton KT7 . . .197 A3
Queen's Elm Sq SW3 256 D1
Queensferry Wlk N17 .52 B5
Queensfield Ct SM3 .216 C4
Queen's Gallery The★
SW1 . . . . .115 B4 248 D1
Queen's Gate
SW7 . . . . .114 A3 256 B5
Queens Gate IG4 . . . . .56 B5
Queensgate Ct N12 . . .29 C5
Queen's Gate Gdns
SW7 . . . . .114 A3 256 B5
Queensgate Gdns
SW15 . . . . .134 B1
Queens Gate Gdns
BR7 . . . . .189 B2

Queen's Gate Mews
SW7 . . . . . . .114 A3 256 B6
Queensgate Pl 10
NW6 . . . . .69 C1
Queen's Gate Pl
SW7 . . . . . . .114 A3 256 B5
Queen's Gate Pl Mews
SW7 . . . . . . .114 A3 256 B5
Queen's Gate Terr
SW7 . . . . . . .114 A3 256 B6
Queens Gate Villas E9 .75 A1
Queen's Gdns
W2 . . . . . . .114 A6 246 A6
Ealing W5 . . . . .87 C3
Heston TW5 . . . . . .129 A4
Queen's Gr
NW8 . . . . . . .92 B6 229 D5
Queen's Grove Rd E4 .20 B3
Queen's Head Pas
EC2 . . . . .242 A2
Queen's Head St
N1 . . . . .94 D6 234 D5
Queen's Head Yd
SE1 . . . . .252 C3
Queens Ho 1 SE17 .139 B6
Queen's Ho TW11 .174 D4
Queen's Hospl CR0 .205 A3
Queen's House The★
SE10 . . . . .142 B6
Queens Keep 10 TW1 153 C5
Queens La N10 . . . . .49 B6
Queensland Ave
Edmonton N18 . . . . .33 A4
Merton SW19 . . . . .179 D2
Queensland Cl E17 . . .35 B1
Queensland Ct N10 . .31 B3
Queensland Ho 2
E16 . . . . .122 C5
Queensland Pl N7 . . .72 C4
Queensland Rd N7 . . .72 C4
Queens Manor Prim Sch
SW6 . . . . .134 D5
Queens Mans NW4 . .46 B4
NW6 . . . . .69 D3
Queen's Mans W6 . . .112 D2
Queensmead
NW8 . . . . . . .92 B6 229 D6
Queen's Mead Rd
BR2 . . . . .186 D1
Queensmead Sch HA4 62 D4
Queensmere Cl
SW19 . . . . .156 D2
Queensmere Ct
SW13 . . . . .134 A6
Queensmere Rd
SW19 . . . . .156 D2
Queen's Mews
W2 . . . . . . .113 D6 245 C6
Queensmill Rd SW6 .134 D5
Queensmill Sch SW6 135 C3
Queen's Mkt 1 E13 . .99 C6
Queens Par NW2 . . .68 C2
7 NW4 . . . . .46 B4
Queen's Par 3 N11 . .30 D5
Queen's Par W5 . . . .88 B1
Queen's Par N11 . . . .32 A3
Queens Parade Cl
N11 . . . . .30 D5
Queens Park Com Sch
NW6 . . . . .90 D6
Queens Park Ct 5
W10 . . . . .90 D4
Queens Park Gdns
TW13 . . . . .149 D1
Queens Park Prim Sch
W10 . . . . .91 A3
Queen's Park Sta NW6 91 B5
Queen's Pas BR7 . . .188 D4
Queen Sq WC1 94 A2 240 B4
Queen Sq Pl WC1 . . .240 B5
Queen's Quay EC4 . .252 B6
Queen's Rd BR1 . . . .187 A4
BR7 . . . . .188 D4
DA16 . . . . .146 B3
E11 . . . . .54 C2
E13 . . . . .99 C6
E17 . . . . .53 C5
N3 . . . . .30 A2
NW4 . . . . .46 C4
SE14,SE15 . . . . . . .140 C4
Queens Rd Hayes UB3 .83 C1
Morden SM4 . . . . . .201 C5
Twickenham TW1 . . .153 A3
West Drayton UB7 . . .104 B4

Queen's Rd
Barking IG11 . . . . . . .79 A2
Beckenham BR3 . . . .185 A1
Bowes Park N11 . . . .32 A4
Buckhurst Hill IG9 . . .21 C2
Ealing W5 . . . . .88 A1
Edmonton N9 . . . . . .18 A2
Enfield EN1 . . . . .5 C1
Feltham TW13 . . . . .150 B3
Hampton TW12 . . . .173 D6
Hounslow TW3 . . . . .129 D2
Kingston KT2 . . . . . .176 C3
Mitcham CR4 . . . . . .202 B6
Mortlake SW14 . . . . .133 B2
New Malden KT3 . . . .199 D4
Richmond TW10 . . . .154 B5
Richmond, Richmond Park
 KT2,TW10 . . . . . .176 C5
Southall UB2 . . . . . .107 A4
Teddington TW11 . . .174 D4
Thames Ditton KT7 . .196 D4
Thornton Heath CR0 .205 A3
Wallington SM6 . . . . .219 B3
Wimbledon SW19 . . .179 C4
Queen's Rd W E13 . . .99 B5
Queens Reach KT8 .196 B5
Queen's Ride SW13 .134 B2
Queen's Rise TW10 .154 B5
Queen's Road Sta
SE15 . . . . .140 C4
Queen's Row SE17 .139 B6
Queen St DA7 . . . . . .147 B2
EC4 . . . . . . .117 A6 252 B6
W1 . . . . .115 B5 248 C4
Croydon CR0 . . . . . .221 A4
Tottenham N17 . . . . .33 C4
Queens Terr E13 . . . .99 B6
NW8 . . . . . . .92 B5 229 C4
Queen's Terr TW7 . .131 A1
Queensthorpe Rd
SE26 . . . . .184 D6
Queenstown Rd
SW8 . . . . . . .137 B5 268 C4
Queenstown Road Sta
SW8 . . . . . . .137 B4 268 D2
Queen St Pl EC4 . . .252 B6
Queensville Rd SW12,
SW4 . . . . .159 D4
Queens Walk Ho W5 .87 C2
Queensway
W2 . . . . . . .113 D6 245 D6
Queens Way NW4 . . .46 C4
Queensway
Coney Hall BR4 . . . .224 D5
Enfield EN3 . . . . .6 C1
Orpington BR5 . . . . .211 A3
Sunbury TW16 . . . . .172 B1
Queens Way
Croydon CR0 . . . . . .220 B3
Feltham TW13 . . . . .172 C6
Queensway Sta
W2 . . . . . . .113 D6 245 D5
Queenswell Jun & Inf Schs
N20 . . . . .14 B2
Queens Wlk NW9 . . .67 A6
Queen's Wlk
SW1 . . . . . . .115 C5 249 A3
Queens Wlk
Ashford TW15 . . . . .170 A6
Chingford E4 . . . . . . .20 B3
Harrow HA1 . . . . .42 C5
Ruislip HA4 . . . . .62 C5
Queen's Wlk W5 . . . .87 C2
Queenswood Ave
Chingford E17 . . . . . .36 A2
Hampton TW12 . . . .173 D4
Hounslow TW3,TW5 .129 B3
Thornton Heath CR7 .204 C4
Wallington CR0,SM6 .219 D4
Queenswood Ct
5 SW4 . . . . .160 A6
11 West Norwood
SE27 . . . . .183 B6
Queenswood Gdns
E11 . . . . .55 B1
Queenswood Pk N3 . .29 A2
Queenswood Rd
DA15 . . . . .167 D5
Queen's Wood Rd N6 .49 B3
Queenswood Rd
SE23 . . . . .163 A1
Queens Yd E9 . . . . . .75 C2
Queen's Yd W1 . . . .239 B5
Queen Terr Cotts
W7 . . . . .108 C4
Queen Victoria Ave
HA0 . . . . .65 D1
Queen Victoria Mon★
SW1 . . . . .249 A2

Queen Victoria St
EC4 . . . . . . .117 A6 252 A6
Quelch Ho 2 N19 . . .71 D3
Quemerford Rd N7 . .72 B3
Quendon Ho W10 . . .90 C3
Quenington Ct 5
SE15 . . . . .139 D6
Quennel Ho 7 SW12 159 C4
Quentington Mans
SW6 . . . . .264 C2
Quentin Pl SE13 . . . .142 C2
Quentin Rd SE13 . . .142 C2
Quernmore Cl BR1 .187 A4
Quernmore Rd BR1 .187 A4
N4 . . . . .50 C3
Querrin St SW6 . . . .136 A3
Quested Ct 27 E8 . . .74 B3
Quick Ho W4 . . . . . . .111 C1
Quicks Rd SW19 . . . .179 D3
Quick St N1 . .94 D5 234 D3
Quickswood NW3 . . .70 C1
Quiet Nook BR2 . . . .225 D5
Quill La SW15 . . . . . .134 D1
Quill St N4 . . . . .72 C5
Ealing W5 . . . . .88 A5
Quilp St SE1 . . . . . . .252 A2
Quilter Ho 11 W9 . . .91 B4
Quilter St E2 . . . . . . .96 A4
SE18 . . . . .123 D1
Quilting Ct 23 SE16 .118 D4
Quinta Dr EN5 . . . . .12 C6
Quintin Ave SW20 . .179 B2
Quintin Ct W4 . . . . . .133 A5
Quintock Ho 2 TW9 .132 C4
Quinton Cl
Beckenham BR3 . . . .208 A6
Cranford TW5 . . . . .128 B5
Wallington SM6 . . . . .219 B4
Quinton Ho 5 SW8 . .270 A4
Quinton Kynaston Sch
NW8 . . . . . . .92 B6 229 C5
Quinton Rd KT7 . . . .197 A1
Quinton St SW18 . . .158 A2
Quixley St E14 . . . . .120 B6
Quorn Rd SE22 . . . . .139 C2

R

Rabbit Row W8 . . . . .245 B4
Rabbits Rd E12 . . . . .78 A4
Rabbs Farm Prim Sch
UB7 . . . . .104 A6
Rabournmead Dr UB5 .63 A3
Raby Rd KT3 . . . . . . .199 B5
Raby St E14 . . . . .97 A1
Raccoon Way TW4 . .128 C3
Rachel Cl IG6 . . . . . . .57 B6
Rachel Ct SM2 . . . . .218 B1
Rachel Point E5 . . . . .74 A4
Racine 15 SE5 . . . . .139 C4
Rackham Cl DA16 . . .146 B3
Rackham Mews
SW16 . . . . .181 C4
Racton Rd
SW6 . . . . . . .135 C6 265 A5
Radbourne Ave W5 .109 C2
Radbourne Cl E5 . . . .74 D4
Radbourne Cres E17 . .36 B1
Radbourne Ct HA3 . . .43 B3
Radbourne Rd SW12 159 D3
Radcliff Bldg EC1 . . .241 A4
Radcliffe Ave NW10 . .90 A5
Enfield EN2 . . . . .5 A4
Radcliffe Gdns SM5 .218 C1
Radcliffe Ho 10 SE16 118 B2
Radcliffe Mews
TW12 . . . . .174 A5
Radcliffe Path 5
SW8 . . . . .137 B3
Radcliffe Rd SE1 . . . .263 B6
Harrow HA3 . . . . .25 A1
South Croydon CR0 . .221 D5
Southgate N21 . . . . . .16 D3
Radcliffe Sq SW15 . .156 B6
Radcliffe Way UB5 . . .84 D4
Radcot Point 2
SE23 . . . . .162 D1
Radcot St SE11 . . . . .261 B1
Raddington Rd W10 . .91 A2
Radfield Way SE9 . . .167 B4
Radford Ho 8 E14 . . .97 D2
N7 . . . . .72 B3
Radford Rd SE13 . . . .164 A5
Radford Way IG11 . . .101 D4
Radipole Rd
SW6 . . . . . . .135 B4 264 C2
Radius Pk TW6 . . . . .127 D1
Radland Rd E16 . . . . .99 A1

Radlet Ave SE23 . . . .162 B2
Radlett Cl E7 . . . . . . .76 D2
Radlett Pl
NW8 . . . . . . .92 C6 230 A6
Radley Ave IG3 . . . . .80 A4
Radley Cl TW14 . . . . .149 D3
Radley Ct 25 SE16 . .118 D4
3 Catford BR1 . . . . .186 A6
Radley Gdns HA3 . . . .44 A5
Radley Ho NW1 . . . . .237 C6
13 SE2 . . . . .124 C1
Radley Lo 30 SW19 . .156 D3
Radley Mews W8 . . .255 B5
Radley Rd N17 . . . . . .33 C1
Radley's La E18 . . . . .37 A1
Radleys Mead RM10 . .81 D2
Radley Sq E5 . . . . . . .74 C5
Radley Terr 1 E16 . . .98 D2
Radlix Rd E10 . . . . . . .53 C1
Radnor Ave DA16 . . .168 B6
Harrow HA1 . . . . .42 C4
Radnor Cl BR7 . . . . . .189 C4
Mitcham CR4 . . . . . .204 A5
Radnor Cres
Redbridge IG4 . . . . . .56 B4
Woolwich SE18 . . . . .146 A4
Radnor Ct Ealing W7 . .86 D1
6 Forest Hill SE23 . .162 D1
Harrow HA3 . . . . .24 D2
Radnor Gdns Enfield EN1 5 C4
Twickenham TW1 . . .152 D2
Radnor Gr UB10 . . . . .82 C5
Radnor Lo 2 W2 . . . .236 D1
Radnor Mews
W2 . . . . .92 B1 236 D1
Radnor Pl W2 .92 C1 237 A1
Radnor Rd NW6 . . . . .91 A6
SE15 . . . . .140 A5
Twickenham TW1 . . .152 D2
Radnor St EC1 .95 A4 235 B1
Radnor Terr
W14 . . . . . . .113 B2 254 C4
Radnor Way NW10 . . .88 D3
Radnor Wlk 14 E14 .119 C2
SW3 . . . . . . .114 D1 257 C1
Croydon CR0 . . . . . .207 A3
Radstock Ave HA3 . . .43 B6
Radstock Cl N11 . . . . .31 A4
Radstock St SW11 . .267 A3
Radway Ho 38 W2 . . .91 C2
Radwell Ho SW2 . . . .160 C6
Raebarn Ct 6 SW16 .160 A1
Raeburn Gdns EN5 . .12 B6
Raeburn Ave
Surbiton KT3 . . . . . .198 D3
Tolworth KT5,KT6 . . .198 D3
Raeburn Cl NW11 . . . .48 A3
Teddington KT1 . . . . .175 D3
Raeburn Ho 7 UB5 . .84 D1
Raeburn Rd
Edgware HA8 . . . . . .26 C2
Hayes UB4 . . . . .83 B5
Sidcup DA15 . . . . . .167 C5
Raeburn St SW2 . . . .138 A1
Raffles Ct HA8 . . . . . .26 B6
Raffles Ho NW4 . . . . .46 B5
Rafford Way BR1 . . . .209 B6
RAF Mus★ NW9 . . . .28 A1
Ragate Ho E5 . . . . . . .74 A5
Ragged School Mus The★
E3 . . . . .97 A2
Raggleswood BR7 . . .188 C2
Raglan Cl TW4 . . . . . .151 B6
Raglan Ct SE12 . . . . .165 A6
SW9 . . . . .138 C2
Croydon CR0,CR2 . . .220 D3
Wembley HA9 . . . . . .66 C5
Raglan Jun & Inf Schs
EN1 . . . . .17 C2
Raglan Prim Sch
BR2 . . . . .209 D5
Raglan Rd DA17 . . . . .125 B2
E17 . . . . .54 B4
SE18 . . . . .123 A1
Bromley BR2 . . . . . .209 C5
Enfield EN1 . . . . . . .17 C2
Raglan St NW5 . . . . . .71 B2
Raglan Terr HA2 . . . . .63 D4
Raglan Way UB5 . . . .64 A2
Ragley Cl W3 . . . . . . .111 A4
Ragwort Ct 1 SE26 .184 B5
Rahere Ho EC1 . . . . .235 A2
Railey Mews NW5 . . .71 C3
Railshead Rd TW1,
TW7 . . . . .131 B1
Railton Rd SE24 . . . .160 D6
Railway App N4 . . . . .50 C3
SE1 . . . . .252 D4
Harrow HA1,HA3 . . . .42 D5
9 Twickenham TW1 . .153 A4

Railway App continued
Wallington SM6 . . . . .219 B3
Railway Ave SE16 . . .118 C4
Railway Cotts W6 . . .112 C4
Railway Gr SE14 . . . .141 B5
Railway Pl DA17 . . . . .125 C3
Railway Rd TW11 . . . .174 D6
Railway Rise SE22 . . .139 C1
Railway Side SW13 . .133 C2
Railway St N1 . . . . . .233 B3
Ilford RM6 . . . . .58 C2
Railway Terr SE13 . . .163 D6
Chingford E17 . . . . . .36 A2
Feltham TW13,TW14 .150 A3
Rainborough Cl NW10 67 A2
Rainbow Ave E14 . . . .119 D1
Rainbow Ct 3 SE14 .141 A6
Rainbow Ind Est
SW20 . . . . .178 B1
Rainbow Quay SE16 .119 A3
Rainbow St SE5 . . . . .139 C5
Rainbow Works N15 .52 A4
Raine's Foundation Sch
E2 . . . . .96 B4
Raines Foundation Sec
Sch E2 . . . . .96 C5
Raine St E1 . . . . .118 B5
Rainford Ho 9 N7 . . .72 B6
Rainham Cl SE9 . . . . .167 C5
SW11 . . . . .158 C5
Rainham Ho NW1 . . .232 B5
Rainham Rd NW10 . . .90 C4
Rainham Rd N RM10 . .81 D6
Rainham Rd S RM10 . .81 D4
Rainhill Way E3 . . . . .97 C5
Rainsborough Ave
SE8 . . . . .119 A2
Rainsford Cl HA7 . . . .25 C5
Rainsford Ct NW10 . .88 D5
Rainsford Ho 14 SW2 160 B6
Rainsford Rd NW10 . .88 D5
Rainsford St W2 . . . .237 A2
Rainstar Est N18 . . . .34 C6
Rainton Rd SE7 . . . . .121 A1
Rainville Rd W6 . . . . .134 C6
Raisins Hill HA5 . . . . .40 C6
Raith Ave N14 . . . . . .15 D1
Raleigh Ave Hayes UB4 84 B2
Wallington SM6 . . . . .219 D4
Raleigh Cl NW4 . . . . .46 C4
Pinner HA5 . . . . .40 D2
Ruislip HA4 . . . . .61 D6
Raleigh Ct 2 SE16 . .118 C5
Beckenham BR3 . . . .185 D2
Dulwich SE19 . . . . . .183 D5
Ealing W13 . . . . .87 B2
Wallington SM6 . . . . .219 B2
Raleigh Dr N20 . . . . .14 C1
Esher KT10 . . . . . . .212 B3
Tolworth KT5 . . . . . .199 A1
Raleigh Gdns SW2 . .160 B5
Mitcham CR4 . . . . . .202 D6
Raleigh Ho 30 SW8 .137 D3
1 Thames Ditton KT7 .197 A2
Raleigh Mews N1 . . .234 D5
6 Orpington BR6 . . .227 D3
Raleigh Rd N10 . . . . .30 C2
N8 . . . . .50 C5
Enfield EN2 . . . . .5 B1
Feltham TW13 . . . . .149 D2
Penge SE20 . . . . . . .184 D3
Richmond TW9 . . . . .132 A2
Southall UB2 . . . . . .107 A1
Raleigh St N1 .94 D6 234 D5
Raleigh Way
Feltham TW13 . . . . .172 C5
Southgate N14 . . . . .16 A3
Ralph Ct 8 W2 . . . . . .91 D1
Ralph Perring Ct
BR3 . . . . .207 C5
Ralston St SW3 . . . . .257 C1
Ramac Ind Est SE7 . .121 B1
Rama Ct HA1 . . . . . . .64 C6
Ramac Way SE7 . . . .121 B1
Rama La SE19 . . . . . .183 D3
Ramar Ho 11 E1 . . . .96 A2
Rambler Cl SW16 . . . .181 C6
Rambler Ct 11 NW9 . .46 A5
Rame Cl SW17 . . . . . .181 A5
Ramilles Cl 1 SW2 . .160 A5
Ramillies Pl
W1 . . . . .93 C1 239 A1
Ramillies Rd DA15 . . .168 B5
NW7 . . . . .11 C2
W4 . . . . .111 B3
Ramillies St W1 . . . . .239 A1
Ramney Dr EN3 . . . . .7 A6
Rampart St E1 . . . . . .96 B1
Rampayne St SW1 . .259 C2

Rampton Cl E4 . . . . . .19 C1
Ramsay Ho NW8 . . . .230 A4
Ramsay Rd E7 . . . . . .76 D4
Acton W3 . . . . .111 A4
Ramscroft Cl N9 . . . . .17 C4
Ramsdale Rd SW17 . .181 A5
Ramsdean Ho 1
SW15 . . . . .156 B3
Ramsden Rd N11 . . . .30 D5
Balham SW12 . . . . .159 A4
Ramsey Cl NW9 . . . . .45 D3
Greenford UB6 . . . . . .64 B3
Ramsey Ct N8 . . . . . .49 D4
Croydon CR0 . . . . . .220 D6
Ramsey Ho 14 SW9 .138 C5
7 Merton SW19 . . . .179 D2
Ramsey Rd CR7 . . . . .204 B3
Ramsey St E2 . . . . . . .96 A3
Ramsey Way N14 . . . .15 C4
Ramsfort Ho 4 SE16 118 B2
Ramsgate Cl 8 E16 . .121 B5
11 E16 . . . . .121 B5
Ramsgate St E8 . . . . .73 D2
Ramsgill App IG2 . . . .57 D5
Ramsgill Dr IG2 . . . . .57 D5
Rams Gr RM6 . . . . . . .59 A5
Rams Pas KT1 . . . . . .175 D1
Ram St SW18 . . . . . . .157 D6
Ramulis Dr UB4 . . . . .84 D3
Ramus Wood Ave
BR6 . . . . .227 C3
Rance Ho 12 SE7 . . . .122 A2
Rancliffe Gdns SE9 . .144 A1
Rancliffe Rd E6 . . . . .100 A5
Randal Cremer JMI Sch
E2 . . . . .95 D5
Randall 9 NW9 . . . . .27 D2
Randall Ct NW2 . . . . .67 C5
Randall Cl
SW11 . . . . . . .136 C4 267 A2
Randall Ct NW7 . . . . .28 A3
Randall Pl SE10 . . . . .142 C4
Randall Rd
SE11 . . . . . . .116 B2 260 C3
Randall Row SE11 . . .260 C3
Randell's Rd
N1 . . . . .94 A6 233 B6
Randisbourne Gdns
SE6 . . . . .163 D1
Randle Rd TW10 . . . . .175 C6
Randlesdown Rd SE6 163 D1
Randmore Ct 6 BR3 185 C3
Randolph App E16 . . .99 C4
Randolph Ave
W9 . . . . .92 A4 229 A1
Randolph Cl KT2 . . . .177 A5
Randolph Cres
W9 . . . . .92 A3 236 A6
Randolph Ct HA5 . . . .23 C3
Randolph Gdns NW6 . .91 D5
Randolph Gr RM6 . . . .58 C4
Randolph Mews
W9 . . . . .92 A3 236 B5
Randolph Rd BR2 . . . .210 B1
E17 . . . . .53 C4
W9 . . . . .92 A3 236 B5
Southall UB1 . . . . . .107 B4
Randolph St NW1 . . . .71 C1
Randon Cl HA2 . . . . . .23 C1
Ranelagh Ave
Barnes SW13 . . . . . .134 A3
Fulham SW6 . . . . . . .135 A2
Ranelagh Cl HA8 . . . .26 C6
Ranelagh Dr
Edgware HA8 . . . . . .26 C6
Twickenham TW1 . . .153 C6
Ranelagh Gardens Mans
SW6 . . . . .135 A2
Ranelagh Gardens (site of
Chelsea Flower Show)★
SW1 . . . . . . .115 A1 258 B1
Ranelagh Gdns
3 W6 . . . . .111 D3
Chiswick W4 . . . . . .133 A5
Fulham SW6 . . . . . . .135 B2
Ilford IG1 . . . . .56 C1
Wanstead E11 . . . . . .55 C4
Ranelagh Gr
SW1 . . . . . . .115 A1 258 B2
Ranelagh Ho SW3 . . .257 C2
Ranelagh Mans 4
SW6 . . . . .135 B3
Ranelagh Pl KT3 . . . .199 C4
Ranelagh Prim Sch
E15 . . . . .98 C5
Ranelagh Rd E11 . . . .76 C4
E15 . . . . .98 C5
N17 . . . . .51 C6
NW10 . . . . .89 D5
SW1 . . . . . . .115 C1 259 B1

Ranelagh Rd continued
W5 ....109 D4
Southall UB1 ....106 D5
Wallend E6 ....100 C5
Wembley HA0 ....65 D2
Wood Green N22 ......32 B2
Ranfurly Rd SM1 .....217 C6
Rangdon St EC3 ......243 C1
Rangefield Prim Sch
BR1 ....186 C5
Rangefield Rd BR1 ..186 D5
Rangemoor Rd N15 ...51 D4
Ranger's Rd
Buckhurst Hill IG9,IG10 .21 A4
Chingford E4 ....20 D4
Rangers Sq SE10 ....142 B4
Range Villas TW17 ..192 A2
Range Way TW17 ....192 C2
Rangeworth Pl DA15 167 D1
Rangoon Ho 5 N16 ..73 B4
Rankin Cl NW9 ......45 C6
Rankine Ho 1 SE1 ..262 A5
Ranleigh Gdns DA7 .147 B5
Ranmere St SW12 ...159 B3
Ranmoor Cl HA1 .....42 B5
Ranmoor Gdns HA1 ..42 C5
Ranmore Ave CR0 ...221 D5
Ranmore Ct
Kingston KT6 ....197 D4
3 Wimbledon SW20 ..178 D2
Rann Ho 1 N14 .....133 B2
Rannoch Cl HA8 .....10 D2
Rannoch Ct 9 KT6 ..198 A4
Rannoch Rd W6 .....134 D6
Rannock Ave NW9 ...45 C2
Ransford Ho 16 SE21 183 C6
Ransom Rd 1 SE7 ..121 C1
Ranston St NW1 ....237 A4
Ranulf Rd NW2 ......69 B4
Ranwell Cl 11 E3 ...97 B6
Ranwell Ho 10 E3 ...97 B6
Ranworth Rd N9 .....18 C2
Ranyard Ct KT9 ....214 B5
Raphael Ct 9 SE16 118 B1
Raphael Dr KT7 ....196 D2
Raphael St SW7 ....247 C1
Rapide Rd NW9 ......27 C2
Rapley Ho 19 E2 ....96 A4
Rashleigh Ct 8 SW8 137 B2
Rashleigh Ho WC1 ..233 A1
Rasper Rd N20 ......14 A2
Rastell Ave SW12 ..159 D3
Ratcliffe Cl SE12 ..165 A4
Ratcliffe Cross St E1 .96 D1
Ratcliffe Ho 12 E14 ..97 A1
Ratcliffe La 18 E14 ..97 A1
Ratcliffe Orch 9 E1 .118 D6
Ratcliff Rd E7 ......77 C3
Rathbone Ho 5 E16 .98 D1
NW6 ....91 C6
10 Wimbledon SW19 .178 D3
Rathbone Mkt 2 E16 .98 D2
Rathbone Pl
W1 ....93 D1 239 C2
Rathbone Point E5 ..74 A4
Rathbone St E16 ....98 D1
W1 ....93 C2 239 B3
Rathcoole Ave N8 ...50 B4
Rathcoole Gdns N8 .50 B4
Rathfern Prim Sch
SE23 ....163 B3
Rathfern Rd SE6 ...163 B3
Rathgar Ave W13 ..109 C5
Rathgar Cl N3 ......29 B1
Rathgar Rd SW9 ...138 D2
Rathmell Dr SW4 ..159 D5
Rathmore Rd SE7 ..121 C5
Ratier 13 NW9 ......27 C2
Rattray Ct 3 SE6 ..164 D2
Rattray Rd SW2 ...160 C6
Raul Rd SE15 ......140 A4
Raveley St NW5 .....71 C4
Raven Cl NW9 ......27 C1
Ravendale Rd TW16 171 D1
Ravenet Ct SW11 ...268 C1
SW4 ....159 B6
Ravenet St
SW11 ....137 B4 268 C1
Ravenfield Rd SW17 158 D1
Ravenhill Rd E13 ...99 C5
Raven Ho 10 SE16 .118 D2
Ravenings Par IG3 ..58 A1
Ravenna Rd SW15 .156 D6
Ravenor Ct UB6 .....85 D3
Ravenor Park Rd UB6 .86 A4
Ravenor Prim Sch
UB6 ....85 C4
Raven Rd E18 ....37 C1
Raven Row E1 ......96 B2

Ravensbourne 3
TW1 ....153 C5
Ravensbourne Ave
Bromley BR2,BR3 ...186 C2
Catford BR2 ....186 B3
Stanwell TW19 ......148 A3
Ravensbourne Coll of
Design & Communication
BR7 ....188 B5
Ravensbourne Ct
SE6 ....163 C4
Ravensbourne Gdns
W13 ....87 B2
Ravensbourne Ho
NW8 ....237 A4
10 Catford BR1 ....186 B5
Ravensbourne Park Cres
SE6 ....163 B4
Ravensbourne Pk
SE6 ....163 C4
Ravensbourne Pl
SE13 ....141 D3
Ravensbourne Rd
Bromley BR1,BR2 ...209 A6
Forest Hill SE23 ...163 B3
Twickenham TW1 ...153 C5
Ravensbourne Sch The
BR2 ....209 B4
Ravensbourne Sta
BR3 ....186 B3
Ravensbury Ave SM4 202 A4
Ravensbury Ct CR4 .202 B5
Ravensbury Gr CR4 .202 B5
Ravensbury La CR4 .202 B5
Ravensbury Rd
Orpington BR5 .....211 D5
Wandsworth SW18 .157 D2
Ravensbury Terr
SW18 ....157 D2
Ravenscar NW1 ....232 A5
Ravenscar Lo 13
SW19 ....178 D3
Ravenscar Rd
Catford BR1 ....186 C6
Surbiton KT6 ....214 B6
Ravens Cl
Bromley BR2 ....186 D1
Enfield EN1 ....5 C3
Kingston KT6 ......197 D3
Ravenscourt 1 N16 .74 A5
Ravenscourt Cl HA4 .39 C4
Ravenscourt Gdns
W6 ....112 A2
Ravenscourt Park Mans
W6 ....112 B2
Ravenscourt Park Prep
Sch W6 ....112 A2
Ravenscourt Park Sta
W6 ....112 B2
Ravenscourt Pk W6 112 B2
Ravenscourt Pl W6 112 B2
Ravenscourt Rd BR5 190 B1
W6 ....112 B2
Ravenscourt Sq W6 112 A3
Ravenscourt Theatre Sch
W6 ....112 B2
Ravenscraig Rd N11 .31 C6
Ravenscroft Ave NW11 47 B2
Wembley HA9 ....44 B2
Ravenscroft Cl 4 E16 99 A2
Ravenscroft Cres
SE9 ....166 B1
Ravenscroft Ct NW11 47 B2
Ravenscroft Prim Sch
E16 ....99 A4
Ravenscroft Rd E16 .99 A4
Acton W4 ....111 A2
Penge BR3 ....184 D1
Ravenscroft Sch N20 .13 B4
Ravenscroft St E2 ..95 D4
Ravensdale Ave N12 .30 B6
Ravensdale Com Est
N16 ....52 A3
Ravensdale Gdns
Hounslow TW4 .....129 A2
South Norwood SE19 .183 B3
Ravensdale Mans N8 .50 A3
Ravensdale Rd N16 .51 D3
Hounslow TW4 .....129 A2
Ravensdon St
SE11 ....116 C1 261 B1
Ravensfield Cl RM9 ..80 D4
Ravensfield Gdns
KT19 ....215 C4
Ravenshaw St NW6 ..69 B3
Ravenshill BR7 .....188 D2
Ravens Ho KT1 .....175 D1
Ravenshurst Ave NW4 46 C5

Ravenside KT6 .....197 D4
Ravenside Rd N18 ...34 D5
Ravenslea Rd SW11,
SW12 ....158 D4
Ravensleigh Gdns
BR1 ....187 B5
Ravensmead Rd BR2 186 B3
Ravensmede Way
W4 ....111 D2
Ravensroost SE19 .183 B2
Ravenstone
SE17 ....117 C1 263 B1
Ravenstone Prim Sch
SW12 ....159 A2
Ravenstone Rd N8 ..50 C6
NW9 ....45 D3
Ravenstone St SW12 159 A3
Ravensview Cl KT6 .197 D4
Ravens Way SE3,SE12 165 A6
Ravenswood DA5 ...169 A3
Ravenswood Ave
Tolworth KT6 ......214 C6
West Wickham BR4 208 A1
Ravenswood Cres
Harrow HA2 ....63 B6
West Wickham BR4 208 A1
Ravenswood Gdns
TW7 ....130 C4
Ravenswood Pk HA6 .22 A4
Ravenswood Rd E17 .54 A5
Balham SW12 ......159 B4
Croydon CR0 ......220 D5
Ravenswood Road Ind Est
5 E17 ....54 A5
Ravens Wood Sch
BR2 ....225 D5
Ravensworth Ct SW6 265 A3
Ravensworth Rd
NW10 ....90 B4
SE9 ....188 B6
Raven Wharf SE1 ..253 C2
Ravey St EC2 ..95 C3 243 A6
Ravine Gr SE18 ....145 C6
Rav Pinter Cl N16 ..51 C2
Rawlings Cl 3 BR6 .227 D3
Rawlings Cres HA9 ..66 D5
Rawlings St
SW3 ....114 D2 257 C4
Rawlins Cl N3 ......47 A6
South Croydon CR2 .223 B1
Rawnsley Ct N14 ..146 C2
Rawlinson Ho SE13 .142 B1
Rawlinson Point 8
E16 ....98 D2
Rawnsley Ave CR4 .202 C4
Rawreth Wlk N1 ...235 B6
Rawson Ct SW11 ...268 B1
Rawson St
SW11 ....137 B4 268 C1
Rawsthorne Cl E16 .122 B5
Rawstone Wlk 5 E13 .99 A5
Rawstorne Pl EC1 .234 C2
Rawstorne St
EC1 ....94 D4 234 C2
Raybell Ct TW7 ....130 D3
Rayburne Ct W14 ..254 A6
Ray Cl KT9 ....213 C2
Ray Ct Ealing W13 .109 B5
Woodford IG8 ....37 D4
Raydean Rd EN5 ...13 D6
Raydons Gdns RM9 ..81 A3
Raydons Rd RM9 ...81 A3
Raydon St N19 .....71 B6
Rayfield Cl BR2 ...210 A3
Rayford Ave SE12 .164 D4
Ray Gdns
Barking IG11 ......102 A5
Stanmore HA7 ......25 B5
Ray Ho 7 W10 ......90 D1
Rayleas Cl SE18 ...144 D4
Rayleigh Ave TW11 174 C4
Rayleigh Cl N13 ....17 B1
Rayleigh Ct
2 Kingston KT1 ...176 B1
Tottenham N22 .....33 A2
Rayleigh Rd 5 E16 .121 B5
7 E16 ....121 B5
Edmonton N13 ......17 B1
Merton SW19 ......179 B2
Woodford IG8 ....37 C3
Rayleigh Rise CR2 .221 C2
Ray Lodge Prim Sch
IG8 ....37 D4
Ray Lodge Rd IG8 ..37 D4
Ray Massey Way 3
E6 ....100 A6
Raymead Ave CR7 .204 C4
Raymede Twr W10 ..90 D2
Raymere Gdns SE18 145 C5

Raymond Ave W13 .109 A3
Woodford E18 ....36 D1
Raymond Cl SE26 ..184 C5
Raymond Ct N10 ...31 A3
Raymond Postgate Ct 5
SE28 ....124 B6
Raymond Rd E13 ...99 C6
Beckenham BR3 ...207 A5
Ilford IG2 ....57 B2
Wimbledon SW19 ..179 A4
Raymond Way KT10 213 A4
Raymouth Rd SE16 118 B2
Raynald Ho 15 SW16 160 A1
Rayne Ct E18 ....54 D5
SE1 ....253 C2
Rayne Ho 1 SW12 .159 A4
W9 ....91 D3
Rayner Ct 10 W12 .112 C4
Rayner Gn HA0 .....65 D3
Rayners Cres UB5 ..84 B4
Rayners Gdns UB5 ..84 B4
Rayners La
Harrow HA2 ....63 D6
Pinner HA5 ....41 B3
Rayners Lane Sta HA5 41 B2
Rayner's Rd SW15 .157 A6
Rayner Twrs E10 ...53 C2
Raynes Ave E11 ....55 C3
Raynes Ct NW2 .....69 B4
Raynesfield SW20 .200 C6
Raynes Park High Sch
KT3 ....200 B6
Raynes Park Sta
SW20 ....178 C1
Raynham W2 ....237 A2
Raynham Ave N18 ..34 A2
Raynham Ho 1 E1 ..96 D3
Raynham Prim Sch
N18 ....34 A4
Raynham Rd W6 ...112 B2
Edmonton N18 ......34 A4
Raynham Terr N18 ..34 A4
Raynor Cl UB1 .....107 B5
Raynor Pl N1 ......235 B6
Raynton Cl Harrow HA2 41 A2
Hayes UB4 ....83 D3
Raynton Dr Hayes UB4 83 C5
Hayes UB4 ....83 D3
Raynton Rd EN3 .....6 D6
Ray Rd KT8 ....195 D4
Rays Ave N18 ......34 C6
Rays Rd N18 ....34 C6
West Wickham BR4 208 A2
Ray St EC1 ....241 B5
Ray Wlk N7 ....72 B6
Raywood Cl UB7 ...127 A5
Reachview Cl 14 NW1 71 C1
Read Cl KT9 ....197 A4
Read Ct E17 ....53 D3
Reade Ct 6 W3 ....111 A3
Reade Ho 7 SE10 .142 B6
Reade Wlk NW10 ...67 C1
Read Ho N11 ....30 C4
4 SE11 ....138 C6
Reading Ho SE15 .140 A4
W2 ....236 A1
Reading La E8 ......74 B2
Reading Rd
Northolt UB5 ....64 C3
Sutton SM1 ....218 A3
Reading Way NW7 ..29 A5
Readman Ct 8 SE20 184 B2
Reads Cl IG1 ....78 D5
Reapers Cl NW1 ...232 C6
Reapers Way TW7 .152 B2
Reardon Ho 5 E1 ..118 B5
Reardon Path 31 E1 118 B5
Reardon St E1 .....118 B5
Reaston St SE14 ..140 D5
Reay Prim Sch
SW9 ....138 B5 270 D3
Rebecca Ct
Beckenham BR3 ...185 C2
Sidcup DA14 ....190 B6
Rebecca Ho 10 N12 .29 D6
Reckitt Rd W4 .....111 C1
Record St SE16 ...140 C6
Recovery St SW17 180 C5
Recreation Rd
Bromley BR2 ....186 D1
Forest Hill SE26 ..184 D6
Southall UB2 ......107 A3
Recreation Way CR4,
SW16 ....204 A6
Rector St N1 ..95 A6 235 A5
Rectory Bsns Ctr 5
DA14 ....190 B6
Rectory Cl N3 ....29 B2
Chingford E4 ....19 C1
Littleton TW17 .....192 C6

Rectory Cl continued
Long Ditton KT6 ...197 C1
Sidcup DA14 ....190 B6
Stanmore HA7 ......25 B5
West Barnes SW20 200 C6
Rectory Cres E11 ...55 C3
Rectory Ct E11 .....76 D5
Cranford TW5 ......128 C3
Feltham TW13 .....172 C6
Wallington SM6 ...219 C4
Woodford E18 ....36 D2
Rectory Field Cres
SE7 ....143 C5
Rectory Gdns N8 ...50 A5
SW4 ....137 C2
Beckenham BR3 ...185 C2
Northolt UB5 ....85 B6
Rectory Gn BR3 ...185 B2
Rectory Gr SW4 ...137 C2
Croydon CR0 ......220 D6
Hampton TW12,TW13 173 B6
Rectory La DA14 ..190 C6
Edgware HA8 ....26 C4
Long Ditton KT6 ...197 C1
Stanmore HA7 ......25 B5
Upper Tooting SW17 181 A5
Wallington SM6 ...219 C4
Rectory Orch SW19 179 A6
Rectory Paddock Sch
BR5 ....190 C1
Rectory Park Ave UB5 85 B4
Rectory Pl SE18 ...122 C2
Rectory Rd E12 .....78 B3
E17 ....53 D5
N16 ....73 D5
1 W3 ....111 A5
Barnes SW13 ......134 A3
Beckenham BR3 ...185 C2
Cranford TW5 ......128 C3
Dagenham RM10 ...81 D1
Hayes UB3 ....84 A1
Keston BR2 ....225 D1
Southall UB1 ......107 B3
Sutton SM1 ....217 D5
Rectory Road Sta N16 73 D5
Rectory Sq E1 ......96 D2
Rectory Way UB10 ..60 D5
Reculver Ho 2 SE15 140 C6
Reculver Mews N18 .34 A6
Reculver Rd SE16 .118 D1
Red Anchor Cl SW3 267 A5
Redan Pl W2 ....91 D1
Redan St W14 .....112 A5
Redan Terr SE5 ....138 D3
Red Barracks Rd 4
SE18 ....122 B2
Redberry Gr SE23,
SE26 ....162 C1
Redbourne Ave N3 ..29 C2
Redbourne Dr SE28 102 D1
Redbourne Ho 7 E14 97 B1
N3 ....29 C2
Redbourn Ho W10 ..90 C3
Redbridge Coll RM6 .58 B4
Redbridge Ent Ctr IG1 79 A6
Redbridge Gdns SE5 139 C5
Redbridge Inf Sch IG4 56 A4
Redbridge Jun Sch
IG4 ....56 A4
Redbridge La E IG4 .56 A4
Redbridge La W E11 .55 C3
Redbridge Rdbt IG4 .55 D3
Redbridge Sta IG4 .55 D3
Redburn St
SW3 ....136 D6 267 C6
Redburn Trad Est EN3 18 D5
Redcar Ho SE26 ...184 B4
Redcar St SE5 ....139 A5
Redcastle Cl E1 ...118 C6
Red Cedars Rd BR6 211 C2
Redchurch St
E2 ....95 D3 243 C6
Redcliffe Cl SW5 ..255 C1
Redcliffe Gdns
SW10 ....135 D6 265 D6
Chiswick W4 ....132 D6
Ilford IG1 ....56 C1
Redcliffe Mews
SW10 ....255 D1
Redcliffe Pl SW10 266 A5
Redcliffe Rd
SW10 ....136 A6 266 B6
Redcliffe Sch
SW10 ....136 A6 266 B6
Redcliffe Sq
SW10 ....113 D1 255 D1
Redcliffe St SW10 265 D6
Redcliffe Wlk HA9 ..66 D5
Redclose Ave SM4 201 C4

Redclyffe Rd E6 ....99 C6
Redclyffe Terr 2
SM2 ....217 C1
Redclyf Ho 12 E1 ...96 C3
Redcroft 5 NW6 ....69 C2
Redcroft Rd UB1 ...86 A1
Redcross Way
SE1 ....117 A5 252 B3
Redding Ho SE18 ..122 A3
Reddings Ave WD23 ..8 A6
Reddings Cl NW7 ...27 D6
Reddings The NW7 ..11 D3
Reddins Rd SE15 ..140 A6
Reddons Rd BR3 ...185 A5
Rede Ho 2 E12 ....78 C3
Rede Pl W2 ...113 C6 245 B6
Redesdale Gdns TW7 131 A5
Redesdale St SW3 267 C6
Redfern Ave TW2,
TW4 ....151 C4
Redfern Ho 6 E13 ..98 D6
Redfern Rd NW10 ...67 C1
Catford SE6 ....164 A4
Redfield La
SW5 ....113 D2 255 C4
Redfield Mews SW5 255 B4
Redfiff Est SE16 ..119 B3
Redford Ave
Thornton Heath CR7 204 B5
Wallington SM6 ...220 A2
Redford Cl TW13 ..149 D2
Redford Wlk N1 ...235 A6
Redgate Dr BR2 ...225 B6
Red Gates Sch CR9 220 C3
Redgate Terr SW15 156 D5
Redgrave Cl SE25 .205 D3
Redgrave Rd SW15 134 D2
Red Hill BR7 ....188 D5
Redhill Ct SW2 ....160 C1
Redhill Dr HA8 .....27 A1
Red Hill Prim Sch
BR7 ....188 D5
Redhill St
NW1 ....93 B4 231 D2
Red House La DA6 147 A1
Red House Rd CR0 203 D3
Redif Ho RM10 .....81 D1
Redington Gdns NW3 69 D4
Redington Ho N1 ...233 D1
Redington Rd NW3 .69 D4
Redknap Ho TW10 153 C1
Red La KT10 ....213 A4
Redland Gdns KT8 195 B5
Redlands N15 ......51 B5
Teddington TW11 .175 A4
Redlands Ct BR1 ..186 B6
Redlands Prim Sch E1 96 C2
Redlands Rd EN3 ....7 A4
Redlands The 5 BR3 185 D1
Redlands Way SW2 160 B4
Redleaf Cl DA17 ...147 C6
Redleaves Ave TW15 170 D4
Redlees Cl TW7 ....131 A1
Red Leys UB8 ....60 A1
Red Lion Bsns Ctr
KT6 ....214 B5
Red Lion Cl 9 SE17 139 B6
Red Lion Ct EC4 ..241 B1
Red Lion Hill N2 ....30 B1
Red Lion La SE18 ..144 C4
Red Lion Pl SE18 ..144 C4
Red Lion Rd KT6 ..214 C6
Red Lion Row SE17 139 C6
Red Lion Sq
WC1 ....94 B2 240 C3
Red Lion St
WC1 ....94 B2 240 C3
Richmond TW10 ...153 D6
Red Lion Yd W1 ...248 B4
Red Lo BR4 ....208 A2
Red Lodge Rd BR3,
BR4 ....208 A2
Redlynch Ct
W14 ....113 A4 244 B1
Redlynch Ho 27 SW9 138 C4
Redman Bldg EC1 .241 A4
Redman Cl UB5 .....84 C5
Redman Ho SE1 ...252 B1
Redman's Rd E1 ....96 C2
Redmayne Ho 15
SW9 ....138 B3
Redmead La E1 ...118 A5
Redmead Rd UB3 .105 A2
Redmill Ho 24 E1 ...96 B3
Redmond Ho N1 ...233 D5
Redmore Rd W6 ...112 B2
Red Oak Cl BR6 ...226 D6

Red Pl W1 . . . . .248 A6
Redpoll Way DA18 . .124 D3
Red Post Hill SE21,
SE24 . . . . .161 B6
Red Post Ho E6 . . . . . .77 D1
Redriffe Rd E13 . . . . . .98 D6
Redriff Prim Sch
SE16 . . . . .119 A4
Redriff Rd SE16 . . . . .119 A3
Redroofs Cl BR3 . . . . .185 D2
Redrose Trad Ctr **1**
EN4 . . . . .14 B6
Red Rover SW13 . . . .134 A2
Redrup Ho **21** SE14 . .140 D6
Redruth Cl N22 . . . . . .32 B3
Redruth Ho SM2 . . . .217 D1
Redruth Rd E9 . . . . . .96 C6
Red Sq The N16 . . . . . .73 B5
Redstart Cl E6 . . . . . .100 A1
SE14 . . . . .141 A5
Redston Rd N8 . . . . . .49 D5
Redvers Rd N22 . . . . . .32 C1
Redvers St E2 . . . . . . .95 C4
Redway Dr TW2 . . . . .152 A4
Redwing Path SE28 . .124 B7
Redwood Cl DA15 . . .168 A3
N14 . . . . .15 D4
SE16 . . . . .119 A5
Chigwell IG9 . . . . .21 B2
Hillingdon UB10 . . . . . .82 D5
South Oxhey WD19 . . . . .22 D6
Redwood Ct N19 . . . . .49 D2
NW6 . . . . .69 A1
Northolt UB5 . . . . . . .85 A4
10 Surbiton KT6 . . .197 D2
Redwood Est TW5 . . .128 B6
Redwood Gdns E4 . . . .19 D5
Redwood Mews
2 SW4 . . . . .137 B2
Ashford TW15 . . . . . .171 B3
Redwoods SW15 . . . .156 A3
Redwood Twr E11 . . . .78 C2
Redwood Way EN5 . . .12 D6
Redwood Wlk KT6 . . .197 D1
Reece Mews SW7 . . . .256 C4
Reed Ave BR6 . . . . . .227 C5
Reed Cl E16 . . . . .99 A2
SE12 . . . . .165 A6
Reede Gdns RM10 . . . .81 D3
Reede Rd RM10 . . . . . .81 D2
Reede Way RM10 . . . . .81 D2
Reed Ho SW15 . . . . . .156 A5
Reedholm Villas N16 . .73 B4
Reed Mans **6** E11 . . . .55 A3
Reed Pl Bsns Pk
TW17 . . . . .192 B1
Reed Rd N17 . . . . .33 D1
Reedsfield Cl TW15 . .148 D1
Reedsfield Rd TW15 . .170 D6
Reed's Pl NW1 . . . . . . .71 C1
Reedworth St
SE11 . . . . .116 C2 261 B3
Reef Ho E14 . . . . .120 A3
Reenglass Rd HA7 . . . .25 D6
Rees Dr HA7 . . . . .26 A6
Rees Gdns CR0 . . . . . .205 D3
Rees Ho **6** N17 . . . . . . .33 D3
Reesland Cl E12 . . . . . .78 C2
Rees St N1 . . .95 A6 235 B5
Reets Farm Cl NW9 . . .45 C3
Reeves Ave NW9 . . . . .45 B2
Reeves Cnr CR0 . . . . .220 D6
Reeves Cnr Sta CR0 . .220 D6
Reeves Ho SE1 . . . . . .251 A1
W1 . . . . .248 A5
Reeves Mews
W1 . . . . .115 A6 248 B5
Reeves Rd E3 . . . . .97 D3
SE18 . . . . .144 D6
Reflection The E16 . .122 D4
Reform Row N17 . . . . .33 D1
Reform St SW11 . . . . .136 D3
Regal Cl E1 . . . . .96 A2
Ealing W5 . . . . .87 D2
Regal Cres SM6 . . . . .219 B5
Regal Ct Edmonton N18 .33 D5
2 Mitcham CR4 . . . .202 D6
Wembley HA0 . . . . . . .65 D4
Regal Dr N11 . . . . .31 B5
Regal La NW1 . . . . . . .231 B5
Regal Pl **8** E3 . . . . . . .97 B4
SW6 . . . . .265 D3
Regal Way HA3 . . . . . .44 A3
Regan Ho **1** N18 . . . . .33 D4
Regan Way N1 . . . . . . .95 C4

Regatta Ho TW11 . . . .175 A6
Regatta Point TW8 . .132 B6
Regency Cl Ealing W5 . .88 A1
Hampton TW12 . . . . . .173 B5
Regency Cres **3** NW4 28 D1
Regency Ct **21** E9 . . . .96 C6
Enfield EN1 . . . . .17 B6
4 Kingston KT5 . . . .198 B4
4 Penge SE19 . . . . .184 A3
Sutton SM1 . . . . .217 D4
Wimbledon SW19 . . . .179 B3
Regency Dr HA4 . . . . . .39 C1
Regency Gdns KT12 . .194 C1
Regency Ho N3 . . . . . . .29 C1
Regency Lo NW3 . . . . .70 B1
1 Buckhurst Hill IG9 . .21 D2
Regency Mews
1 NW10 . . . . .68 A2
Beckenham BR3 . . . . .186 A2
Isleworth TW7 . . . . . .152 C4
Regency St
SW1 . . . . .115 D2 259 D3
Regency Way DA7 . . .147 A2
Regency Wlk
Croydon CR0 . . . . . . .207 B2
8 Richmond TW10 . . .154 A6
Regent Ave UB10 . . . . .60 D1
Regent Bsns Ctr UB3 106 A4
Regent Cl N12 . . . . . . .30 A1
Cranford TW4 . . . . . .128 B4
Harrow HA3 . . . . .44 A3
Regent Ct **1** N16 . . . . .51 D2
N3 . . . . .29 D3
NW8 . . . . .230 A1
South Norwood SE19 . .182 D4
Regent Gdns IG3 . . . . .58 A2
Regent Ho W14 . . . . .254 A4
Regent Lo **9** SW2 . . . .160 B3
Regent Pl W1 . . . . . . .249 B6
Croydon CR0 . . . . . . .205 D1
Wimbledon SW19 . . . .180 A5
Regent Rd SE24 . . . . .160 D6
Surbiton KT5 . . . . . . .198 C4
Regents Ave N13 . . . . .32 C5
Regents Bridge Gdns
SW8 . . . . .270 B4
Regents Canal Ho **21**
E14 . . . . .97 A1
Regents Cl Hayes UB4 .83 C2
South Croydon CR2 . . .221 C2
Regent's Coll
NW1 . . . . .93 A3 238 A6
Regents Ct E8 . . . . . . .96 A6
22 Beckenham BR3 . .185 C3
Bromley BR1 . . . . . . .186 D3
Edgware HA8 . . . . . . .26 A6
1 Kingston KT2 . . . .176 A2
Regents Dr BR2 . . . . .225 D3
Regents Gate Ho **20**
E14 . . . . .119 A6
Regents Mews
NW8 . . . . .92 A5 229 B4
Regent's Park★
NW1 . . . . .93 A4 231 A3
Regent's Park Barracks
NW1 . . . . .231 D3
Regent's Park Rd N3 . .47 B6
NW1 . . . . .93 A6 231 A6
Regent's Park Sta
NW1 . . . . .93 B3 238 C5
Regent's Park Terr
NW1 . . . . .231 C6
Regent's Pl SE3 . . . . .143 A3
Regents Pl IG10 . . . . . .21 D4
Regents Plaza **2** NW6 91 D5
Regent Sq **23** E3 . . . . .97 D4
WC1 . . . . .94 A4 233 B1
Belvedere DA17 . . . . .125 D2
Regent's Row E8 . . . . .96 A6
Regent St
W1 . . . . .115 C6 249 A6
W4 . . . . .110 C1
Regents Wharf **3** E2 . .96 B6
N1 . . . . .233 C4
Regina Coeli RC Prim Sch
CR2 . . . . .220 D1
Reginald Ct BR3 . . . . .186 A2
Reginald Pl **6** SE8 . . .141 C5
Reginald Rd E7 . . . . . .77 A2
SE8 . . . . .141 C5
Reginald Sorenson Ct
E11 . . . . .54 B2
Reginald Sq SE8 . . . . .141 C5
Regina Point SE16 . . .118 C3
Regina Rd N4 . . . . .50 B1
Ealing W13 . . . . .109 A5
Southall UB2 . . . . . . .107 A2
South Norwood SE25 . .206 A6
Regina Terr W13 . . . . .109 B5
Regis Ct N8 . . . . .50 B5

Regis Ct continued
NW1 . . . . .237 C4
East Bedfont TW14 . . .149 B5
Mitcham SW19 . . . . . .180 C2
Regis Pl **17** SW2 . . . . .138 D1
Regis Rd NW5 . . . . . . .71 B3
Regnart Bldgs NW1 . .232 B1
Regnoruf Ct KT12 . . . .194 A2
Reid Cl HA5 . . . . .40 A5
Reid Ct SW14 . . . . . . .133 A3
Reidhaven Rd SE18 . . .123 C2
Reigate Ave SM3,SM4 201 D1
Reigate Rd BR1,SE12 .165 A2
Catford BR1 . . . . .164 D1
Ilford IG3 . . . . .79 D6
Reigate Way SM6 . . . .220 A3
Reighton Rd E5 . . . . . .74 A4
Reizel Cl N16 . . . . .51 C1
Relay Rd W12 . . . . . . .112 C5
Relf Rd SE15 . . . . .140 A2
Reliance Sq E2 . . . . . .243 A6
Relko Gdns SM1 . . . . .218 A3
Relton Mews SW7 . . .257 B6
Rembrandt Cl E14 . . . .120 B3
Rembrandt Ct
10 SE16 . . . . .118 B1
West Ewell KT19 . . . . .215 D2
Edgware HA8 . . . . . . .26 C1
Remembrance Ave N2 47 D6
Remington Rd E6 . . . .100 A1
N15 . . . . .51 B3
Remington St
N1 . . . . .94 D5 234 D3
Remnant St WC2 . . . .240 C2
Remsted Ho **5** NW6 . .91 D6
Remus Rd E3 . . . . .75 C1
Renbold Ho **5** SE10 . .142 A4
Rendle Cl CR0 . . . . . .206 A4
Rendlesham Ho **3** E5,
N16 . . . . .74 A5
Rendlesham Rd E5 . . . .74 A5
Enfield EN2 . . . . .4 D4
Renforth St SE16 . . . .118 C4
Renfree Way TW17 . . .192 C2
Renfrew Cl E6 . . . . . . .122 C6
Renfrew Ct TW5 . . . . .129 A3
Renfrew Ho E17 . . . . . .35 B1
NW6 . . . . .91 D5
Renfrew Rd
SE11 . . . . . . .116 D2 261 C3
Hounslow TW5 . . . . . .129 A3
Kingston KT2 . . . . . . .177 A3
Renmuir St SW17 . . . .180 D4
Rennell Ho **18** E9 . . . .74 D2
Rennell St SE13 . . . . .142 A2
Renness Rd E17 . . . . . .53 A6
Rennets Cl SE9 . . . . . .167 C6
Rennets Wood Rd
SE9 . . . . .167 B6
Rennie Cotts **24** E1 . . .96 C3
Rennie Ct SE1 . . . . . . .251 C4
Holbrook EN3 . . . . .7 C5
Rennie Ho SE1 . . . . . .262 A5
Rennie St
SE1 . . . . .116 D5 251 C4
Renoir Ct **7** SE16 . . .118 B1
Renovation The E16 . .122 D4
Renown Cl CR0 . . . . . .204 D1
Rensburg Rd E17 . . . . .52 D3
Rensburg Villas E17 . . .52 D4
Renshaw Cl **7** DA17 . .147 B6
Renshaw Dr SW19 . . .179 A6
Renshaw Ho **11**
SW27 . . . . .182 D5
Renters Ave NW4 . . . . .46 C3
Renton Cl SW2 . . . . . .160 B5
Renwick Rd IG11 . . . . .102 B4
Repens Way UB4 . . . . .84 D3
Rephidim St SE1 . . . . .263 A5
Replingham Rd
SW18 . . . . .157 C3
Reporton Rd
SW6 . . . . .135 A5 264 B3
Repository Rd SE7,
SE18 . . . . .122 B1
Repton Ave
Hayes UB3 . . . . .105 B2
Wembley HA0 . . . . . . .65 C4
Repton Cl SM1,SM5 . .218 C3
Repton Ct BR3 . . . . . .185 D2
Repton Ho **2** E14 . . . .97 A1
SW1 . . . . .259 B3
Repton Rd Harrow HA3 44 B5
Orpington BR6 . . . . . .227 D5
Repton St E14 . . . . . . .97 A1
Re Sassoon Ho SE15 . .140 C4
Reservoir Cl CR7 . . . .205 B5
Reservoir Rd SE4 . . . .141 A3

Ruislip HA4 . . . . .39 B5
Southgate N14 . . . . . . .15 C6
Resolution Wlk SE18 .122 B3
Restell Cl SE3 . . . . . . .142 C6
Restmor Way SM5,
SM6 . . . . .219 A6
Reston Pl SW7 . . . . . .246 A1
Restons Cres DA15,
SE9 . . . . .167 C5
Restoration Sq SW11 266 D1
Restormel Cl TW3 . . . .151 C6
Retcar Pl N19 . . . . .71 B6
Retford St E2 . . . . .95 C5
Retingham Way E4 . . . .19 D2
Retreat Cl HA3 . . . . . . .43 C4
Retreat Ho **5** E9 . . . . .74 C1
Retreat Pl E9 . . . . .74 C2
Retreat Rd TW9 . . . . .153 D6
Retreat The NW9 . . . . .45 B4
Harrow HA2 . . . . .41 C1
Mortlake SW14 . . . . . .133 C2
North Cheam KT4 . . . .216 B6
South Norwood CR7 . . .205 B5
Surbiton KT5 . . . . . . .198 B3
Reunion Row E1 . . . . .118 B6
Reveley Sq SE16 . . . . .119 A4
Revell Rd Cheam SM1 .217 B2
Kingston KT1 . . . . . . .176 D2
Revell Rise SE18 . . . . .145 D6
Revelon Rd SE4 . . . . . .141 A2
Revelstoke Rd SW18,
SW19 . . . . .157 C2
Reventlow Rd SE9 . . . .167 A3
Reverdy Rd SE1 . . . . . .118 A2
Reverend Cl HA2 . . . . .63 D5
Revesby Rd SM5 . . . . .202 C3
Review Rd NW2 . . . . . .67 D6
Dagenham RM10 . . . . .103 D6
Rewell St
SW6 . . . . . . .136 A5 266 A3
Rewley Rd SM4 . . . . . .202 B3
Rex Ave TW15 . . . . . . .170 C5
Rex Ho TW13 . . . . . . .151 A1
Rex Par **2** IG8 . . . . . .37 C4
Rex Pl W1 . . .115 A5 248 B4
Reydon Ave E11 . . . . . .55 C3
Reygate Ct N4 . . . . . . .51 A3
Reynard Cl BR1 . . . . .210 C6
SE4 . . . . .141 A2
Reynard Dr SE19 . . . .183 D3
Reynard Mills Trad Est
TW8 . . . . .109 C1
Reynard Pl SE14 . . . . .141 A6
Reynardson Rd N17 . . .33 A3
Reynardson's Ct **3**
N17 . . . . .51 B4
Reynolds Ave
Chessington KT9 . . . . .214 A1
Ilford RM6 . . . . .58 C2
Little Ilford E12 . . . . . .78 C3
Reynolds Cl NW11 . . . .47 D2
Carshalton SM5 . . . . .202 D1
Mitcham SW19 . . . . . .180 B2
Reynolds Ct E11 . . . . . .76 C5
Ilford RM6 . . . . .58 D6
Reynolds Dr HA8 . . . . .44 B6
Reynolds Ho **19** E2 . . .96 C5
N4 . . . . .50 A1
NW8 . . . . .229 D3
SW1 . . . . .259 D3
Enfield EN1 . . . . .18 A6
Reynolds Pl SE3 . . . . .143 B5
12 Richmond TW10 . .154 B5
Reynolds Rd SE15 . . . .140 C1
W4 . . . . .111 A3
Hayes UB4 . . . . .84 C3
New Malden KT3 . . . . .199 B2
Reynolds Way CR0 . . .221 C4
Rheidol Mews N1 . . . .235 A4
Rheidol Terr
N1 . . . . .95 A6 235 A5
Rhein Ho N8 . . . . .50 A6
Rheola Cl N17 . . . . . . .33 D2
Rhoda St E2 . .95 D3 243 D6
Rhodes Ave N22 . . . . . .31 C2
Rhodes Avenue Prim Sch
N22 . . . . .31 C2
Rhodes Ho N1 . . . . . . .235 C2
Rhodesia Rd E11 . . . . .76 B6
SW9 . . . . .138 A3
Rhodes-Moorhouse
SM4 . . . . .201 C3
Rhodes St N7 . . . . .72 B5
Rhodeswell Rd E14 . . . .97 A2
Rhodrons Ave KT9 . . .214 A4
Rhondda Gr E3 . . . . . . .97 B4
Rhyl Prim Sch NW5 . . .71 A2
Rhyl Rd UB6 . . . . .86 D5
Rhyl St NW5 . . . . .71 A2

Rhys Ave N11 . . . . .31 D3
Rialto Rd CR4 . . . . . . .181 A1
Ribble Cl IG8 . . . . .37 C4
Ribblesdale Ave N11 . .31 A4
Northolt UB5 . . . . .63 D2
Ribblesdale Ho **11**
NW6 . . . . .91 C6
Ribblesdale Rd N8 . . . .50 B5
Streatham SW16 . . . . .181 B5
Ribbon Dance Mews
SE5 . . . . .139 B4
Ribchester Ave UB6 . . .86 D4
Ribston Cl BR2 . . . . . .210 B1
Ribstone Ho **12** E9 . . .74 D2
Ricardo Path **5**
SE28 . . . . .124 C5
Ricardo St E14 . . . . . . .97 D1
Ricards Lodge High Sch
SW19 . . . . .179 B5
Ricards Rd SW19 . . . .179 B5
Riccal Ct **2** NW9 . . . .27 C2
Riceyman Ho WC1 . . .234 A1
Richard Alibon Prim Sch
RM10 . . . . .81 C3
Richard Anderson Ct **1**
SE14 . . . . .140 D5
Richard Atkins Prim Sch
SW2 . . . . .160 A4
Richard Burbidge Mans
SW13 . . . . .134 C6
Richard Burton Ct **4**
IG9 . . . . .21 C2
Richard Challoner Sch
KT3 . . . . .199 B2
Richard Cl SE18 . . . . .122 A1
Richard Cloudesley Sch
EC1 . . . . .95 A3 242 A5
Richard Cobden Prim Sch
NW1 . . . . .93 C6 232 B5
Richard Ct EN5 . . . . . . .1 A2
Richard Fell Ho **2**
E12 . . . . .78 C4
Richard Fox Ho N4 . . .73 B2
Richard Ho **8** SE16 . .118 C2
Richard House Dr E16 99 D1
E6 . . . . .100 A1
Richard Knight Ho
SW6 . . . . .265 B2
Richard Neale Ho **2**
E1 . . . . .118 B6
Richards Cl
Bushey WD23 . . . . .8 B4
Harlington UB3 . . . . . .127 B6
Harrow HA1 . . . . .43 A4
Hillingdon UB10 . . . . . .82 C6
Richards Ct BR3 . . . . .184 D2
Richardson Cl **19** E8 . .95 D6
Richardson Ct **20**
SW4 . . . . .138 A3
Richardson Gdns **12**
RM10 . . . . .81 D2
Richardson Ho TW7 . .130 D2
Richardson Rd E15 . . . .98 C5
Richardson's Mews
W1 . . . . .239 A5
Richards Pl E17 . . . . . .53 C6
Richard's Pl SW3 . . . .257 A4
Richard St **10** E1 . . . . .96 B1
Richard Thornton Ho
SW19 . . . . .179 C1
Richbell Pl WC1 . . . . .240 C1
Richborne Terr
SW8 . . . . .138 B5 270 D4
Richborough Ho **14** E5 74 B4
10 SE15 . . . . .140 C6
Richborough Rd NW2 .69 A4
Richens Cl TW3 . . . . . .130 B3
Riches Rd IG1 . . . . .79 A6
Richfield Ct **4** BR3 . .185 B2
Richfield Rd WD23 . . . .8 A4
Richford Gate W6 . . . .112 C3
Richford Rd E15 . . . . . .98 D6
Richford St W6 . . . . . .112 C3
Richings Ho BR5 . . . . .190 A2
Rich La SW5 . . . . .255 C2
Richland Ho **4** SE15 .140 A4
Richlands Ave KT17 . .216 A4
Richman Ho **10** SE8 . .119 B1
Richmond Adult & Com
Coll TW9 . . . . .131 D1
Richmond Ave
N1 . . . . .94 B6 233 D6
NW10 . . . . .68 C2
Chingford E4 . . . . .36 B5
Feltham TW14 . . . . . . .149 C5
Hillingdon UB10 . . . . . .60 D2
Wimbledon SW20 . . . .179 A2
Richmond Bldgs W1 . .239 C1
Richmond Bridge
TW1 . . . . .153 D5

Richmond Bridge Mans **1**
TW1 . . . . .153 D5
Richmond Circus
TW9 . . . . .132 A1
Richmond Cl E17 . . . . .53 C1
Borehamwood WD6 . . .11 A3
Richmond Coll
W8 . . . . .113 D3 255 D6
Richmond TW10 . . . . .154 A4
Richmond Cres
N1 . . . . .94 C6 234 A6
Chingford E4 . . . . .36 B5
Edmonton N9 . . . . .18 A3
Richmond Ct BR1 . . . .187 B3
SW1 . . . . .247 D1
12 Kingston KT2 . . . .176 C3
Mitcham CR4 . . . . . . .202 B6
Wembley HA9 . . . . . . .66 C6
Richmond Dr TW17 . .193 B3
Richmond Gdns NW4 .46 A4
Harrow HA3 . . . . .24 D3
Richmond Gn CR0 . . .220 A5
Richmond Gr N1 . . . . .72 D1
Surbiton KT5 . . . . . . .198 B3
Richmond Hill TW10 .154 A5
Richmond Hill Ct **5**
TW10 . . . . .154 A5
Richmond Ho NW1 . .231 D3
SE17 . . . . .262 C2
12 Forest Hill SE26 . .162 A1
Richmond Ho(Annexe of
Rectory Sch) TW12 .173 B5
Richmond International
Bsns Ctr **9** TW9 . . .132 B1
Richmond Mans
SW5 . . . . .255 C2
Putney SW15 . . . . . . .135 A2
14 Twickenham TW1 . .153 D5
Richmond Mews W1 .239 C1
Richmond Park★
TW10 . . . . .155 A3
Richmond Park Rd
Kingston KT2 . . . . . . .176 A3
Mortlake SW14 . . . . . .133 B1
Richmond Pk IG10 . . . .21 D4
Richmond Pl SE18 . . .123 A2
Richmond Rd E11 . . . . .76 B6
E7 . . . . .77 B3
E8 . . . . .74 A1
N15 . . . . .51 C3
N2 . . . . .30 A1
W5 . . . . .110 A4
Bowes Park N11 . . . . . .32 A4
Chingford E4 . . . . .20 B3
Ilford IG1 . . . . .79 A5
Isleworth TW7 . . . . . .131 A2
Kingston KT2 . . . . . . .176 A4
New Barnet EN5 . . . . .14 A6
Thornton Heath CR7 . . .204 D5
Twickenham TW1 . . . .153 C4
Wallington CR0 . . . . . .220 A5
Wimbledon SW20 . . . .178 B2
Richmond St E13 . . . . .99 A5
Richmond Sta TW9 . .132 A1
Richmond Terr
SW1 . . . . .116 A4 250 A2
Richmond upon Thames
Coll TW2 . . . . .152 A4
Richmond Way
W12,W14 . . . . .112 D4
Wanstead E11 . . . . . . .77 A6
Richmount Gdns SE3 143 A2
Rich St E14 . . . . .119 B6
Rickard Cl NW4 . . . . . .46 A5
Streatham SW2 . . . . . .160 C3
Rickards Cl KT6 . . . . .214 A6
Rickett St SW6 . . . . . .265 B6
Rickman Ho **26** E2 . . .96 C3
Rickman St **25** E1 . . . .96 C3
Rickmansworth Rd
HA5 . . . . .22 C1
Rick Roberts Way E15 98 B5
Rickthorne Rd **6** N19 72 A6
Rickyard Path SE9 . . .144 A1
Riddell Ct SE1 . . . . . . .263 C2
Riddons Rd SE12 . . . . .187 C6
Rideout St SE18 . . . . .122 B2
Rider Cl DA15 . . . . . . .167 C4
Ride The
Brentford TW8 . . . . . .109 C4
Enfield EN3 . . . . .6 D2
Ridgdale St E3 . . . . . . .97 C4
Ridge Ave N21 . . . . . . .17 A4
Ridgebrook Rd SE3,
SE9 . . . . .143 D2
Ridge Cl NW4 . . . . . . .28 C3
NW9 . . . . .45 B5
SE28 . . . . .123 B4

Ridge Crest EN2 ....4 B4
Ridge Hill NW11 ......47 A1
Ridge Ho 4 KT2 .....176 D3
Ridgemead Cl N13,N14 16 A2
Ridgemont Gdns HA8 .27 A6
Ridgemount Ave 222 D6
Ridgemount Cl SE20 .184 B3
Ridgemount Gdns EN2 .4 D3
Ridgeon Ct N22 ......32 B4
Ridge Rd N8 ....50 B3
NW2 ....69 B5
Cheam SM3 ....201 B1
Edmonton N21 ......17 B3
Mitcham SW4 ......181 B3
Ridges The E4 ....35 C6
Ridge Terr E21 ......17 A4
Ridge The DA5 .....169 B4
Barnet EN5 ....13 B6
Orpington BR6 .....227 B6
Surbiton KT5 ....198 C4
Twickenham TW2 ...152 B4
Ridgeview Cl EN5 ...12 C5
Ridgeview Rd N20 ...14 A1
Ridgeway BR2 .....225 A6
11 Richmond TW10 ..154 B3
Walton-on-T KT12 ..193 D1
Woodford IG8 ......37 C6
Ridge Way
  Feltham TW13 ......151 A1
  7 West Norwood
  SE19 ....183 A4
Ridgeway Ave EN4 ..14 D5
Ridgeway Cres BR6 ..227 C5
Ridgeway Crescent Gdns
  BR6 ....227 C5
Ridgeway Ct HA5 ...23 C3
Ridgeway Dr BR1 ..187 B6
Acton W3 ....110 C3
Ridgeway E HA5 ...167 D6
Ridgeway Gdns N6 ..49 C2
Redbridge IG4 ......56 A4
Ridgeway Rd TW7 ..130 C4
Ridgeway Rd N TW7 .130 C5
Ridgeway The N11 ..30 D6
N3 ....29 D3
NW11 ....47 B1
NW7 ....28 B6
NW9 ....45 B5
Acton W3 ....110 C3
Chingford E4 ......20 A3
Enfield EN2 ....4 B5
Harrow HA2 ....41 B4
Harrow HA2 ....41 D3
Harrow HA3 ....43 C3
Palmers Green N14 ..16 A2
Ruislip HA4 ....40 A2
Stanmore HA7 ......25 C4
Wallington CR0 ....220 B5
Ridgeway W DA15 ..167 C6
Ridgway Wlk NW1 ..63 A2
Ridgewell Cl N1 ...235 B6
Dagenham RM10 ....103 D6
Forest Hill SE26 ...185 B6
Ridgmount Gdns
  WC1 ....93 D2 239 C4
Ridgmount Pl WC1 .239 C4
Ridgmount Rd SW18 157 D6
Ridgmount St
  WC1 ....93 D2 239 C4
Ridgway SW19,SW20 178 D4
Ridgway Ct SW19 ..178 D4
Ridgway Gdns SW19 178 D3
Ridgway Pl SW19 ..179 A4
Ridgway Rd SW9 ..138 D2
Ridgway The SM2 ..218 B1
Ridgwell Rd E16 ...99 C2
Riding House St
  W1 ....93 C2 239 A3
Ridings Ave N21 ...17 A6
Ridings Cl N6 .....49 C2
Ridings The EN4 ...14 B4
Ealing W5 ....88 B3
Sunbury TW16 .....172 A2
Surbiton KT5 ......198 C4
Riding The NW11 ...47 B2
Ridler Rd EN1 .....5 C5
Ridley Ave W13 ...109 B3
Ridley Cl IG11 ....79 D1
Ridley Ct SW16 ...182 A4
Ridley Ho 14 SW11 .136 C2
Ridley Rd DA16 ..146 B4
E7 ....77 C4
E8 ....73 D3
NW10 ....90 A5
Beckenham BR2 ...208 D6
Merton SW19 .....179 D3
Ridley Road Mkt E8 .73 D3
Ridsdale Rd SE20 ..184 B2
Riefield Rd SE9 ...167 A6
Riesco Dr CR0 ....222 C2

Riffel Rd NW2 .....68 C3
Rifle Ct SE11 .....138 C6
Rifle Pl W11 ......112 D5
Rifle Range La HA1 ..42 D1
Rifle St E14 ......97 D2
Rigault Rd SW6 ...135 A3
Rigby Cl CR0 .....220 C5
Rigby La UB3 .....105 A4
Rigby Mews IG1 ...78 C6
Rigby Pl EN3 ......7 C6
Rigden St E14 ....97 D1
Rigeley Rd NW10 ..90 A4
Rigg App E10 .....53 A1
Rigg Ho 9 E1 .....96 D2
Rigg Ho 2 SW4 ...160 A4
Riggindale Rd SW16 181 D6
Rignold Ho 6 SE5 .139 C3
Rigo Ho 9 E1 .....96 D2
Riley Ho SW10 ...266 C5
  9 Bow E3 ......97 C3
  1 Streatham SW4 .159 D4
Riley Rd SE1 .117 D3 263 C6
Riley St SW10 136 B5 266 C4
Rill Ho 24 SE5 ...139 C5
Rimini Ct SW12 ...158 D3
Rinaldo Rd SW12 .159 B4
Ring Cl BR1 ......187 B3
Ringcroft St N7 ...72 C3
Ring Cross Prim Sch
  N7 ....72 B3
Ringer's Rd BR1 ..209 A6
Ringford Ho SW18 157 B6
Ringford Rd SW18 157 B6
Ring Ho 14 E1 ....118 C6
Ringlet Cl E16 ....99 B2
Ringlewell Cl EN1 ..6 B3
Ringmer Ave
  SW6 ....135 A4 264 B1
Ringmer Gdns 2 N19 72 A6
Ringmer Ho 15 SE22 139 C2
Ringmer Pl N21 ...17 B6
Ringmer Way IG1 ...72 A6
Ringmore Rise SE23 162 B4
Ringsfield Ho SE17 262 B1
Ringslade Rd N22 ..32 B1
Ringstead Ct SM1 .218 B3
Ringstead Rd
  Catford SE6 ....163 D4
  Sutton SM1 ....218 B3
Ring Way N11 .....31 C4
Ringway UB2 .....107 A1
Ringwold Cl BR3 ..185 A3
Ringwood Ave N2 ..48 D6
  Thornton Heath CR0 .204 A2
Ringwood Cl HA5 ..40 C6
Ringwood Gdns
  18 E14 ....119 C2
  Roehampton SW15 .156 A3
Ringwood Rd E17 ..53 B3
Ringwood Way
  Hampton TW12 ....173 C6
  Southgate N21 ....16 D4
Ripley Cl BR1 ....210 B4
  New Addington CR0 .224 A2
Ripley Ct 1 CR4 ..180 B1
Ripley Gdns
  Mortlake SW14 ...133 B2
  Sutton SM1 ......218 A4
Ripley Ho SW1 ...269 A6
  13 Kingston KT2 ...176 D4
  Mortlake SW14 ...133 C2
  5 Penge SE26 ...184 B4
Ripley Mews E11 ..54 C3
Ripley Rd
  Belvedere DA17 ...125 C2
  Enfield EN2 ....5 A4
  Hampton TW12 ...173 C4
  Ilford IG3 ....79 D6
  Newham E16 .....99 C1
Riplington Ct SW15 156 B4
Ripon Cl UB5 ......63 C2
Ripon Gdns
  Chessington KT9 ..213 D3
  Redbridge IG1 ....56 A4
Ripon Rd N17 .....51 B6
SE18 ....144 D6
  Edmonton N9 .....18 B4
Ripon Way WD6 ...11 B6
Rippersley Rd DA16 146 A4
Ripple Ct 10 IG11 .101 B6
Ripple Rd
  Barking IG11 .....101 C6
  Barking RM9 .....102 A4
Rippleside Commercial Est
  IG11 ....102 C5
Ripplevale Gr N1 ..72 B1
Rippolson Rd SE18 .123 D1
Ripston Rd TW15 .171 B5
Risborough SE17 .262 A4

Risborough Cl 4 N10 .49 B6
Risborough Dr KT4 .200 A2
Risborough Ho NW8 .237 B6
Risborough St SE1 .251 D2
Risdon Ho 20 SE16 .118 C4
Risdon St 21 SE16 .118 C4
Risedale Rd DA7 ..147 D2
Riseholme Ho 14
  SE22 ....139 C2
Riseldine Rd SE23 .163 A5
Rise The NW10 ....67 B5
NW7 ....27 D4
  Borehamwood WD6 ..10 B6
  Buckhurst Hill IG9 ..21 D4
  Chingford, Chingford Green
  E4 ....20 C3
  Edgware HA8 .....26 D5
  Edmonton N13 ....32 C6
  Greenford HA0,UB6 ..65 A3
  Hillingdon UB10 ...82 C4
  Sidcup DA5 ......168 C4
  Wanstead E11 ....55 A4
Risinghill St N1 ...234 A4
Risingholme Cl HA3 .24 C2
Risingholme Rd HA3 .24 C1
Risings The E17 ...54 B5
Rising Sun Ct EC1 .241 D3
Risley Ave N17 ...33 B2
Risley Avenue Prim Sch
  N17 ....33 C2
Risley Ho 7 E9 ...74 C2
Rita Rd SW8 .138 B5 270 C4
Ritches Rd N15 ...51 A4
Ritchie Ho N19 ...49 D2
  8 SE16 ....118 C3
  11 South Bromley E14 .98 B1
Ritchie Rd CR0 ...206 A3
Ritchie St N1 .94 C5 234 B4
Ritchings Ave E17 ..53 A5
Ritherdon Rd SW17 159 B2
Ritson Ho N1 .....233 C5
Ritson Rd E8 .....74 A2
Ritter St SE18 ....144 C6
Ritz Par W5 ......88 B3
Rivaz Pl E9 ......74 C2
Riven Ct 10 W2 ...91 D1
Rivenhall Gdns E11,
  E18 ....54 D5
Riverains The SW11 266 C1
River Ave
  Southgate N13 ....16 D2
  Thames Ditton KT7 .197 A2
Riverbank KT8 ....196 C5
River Bank
  Edmonton N21 ....17 A4
  Thames Ditton KT7 .196 D4
Riverbank Rd BR1 .165 A1
Riverbank Way TW8 131 C6
River Barge Cl E14 120 A4
River Brent Bsns Pk
  W7 ....108 C3
River Cl Ruislip HA4 .39 D3
  Southall UB2 .....108 A4
  Wanstead E11 ....55 C3
River Cotts BR5 ..190 C1
Rivercourt Rd W6 .112 B1
River Crane Way
  TW13 ....151 B2
River Ct SE1 .....251 A2
  Kingston KT6 .....197 D4
  Wanstead E11 ....55 C3
Riverdale Dr SW18 .157 D3
Riverdale Gdns TW1 .153 C6
Riverdale Rd SE18 .123 D1
  Erith DA8 ....125 D1
  Feltham TW13 ....173 B6
  Sidcup DA5 ......169 B5
  Twickenham TW1 .153 C6
Riverdene HA8 ....11 A1
Riverdene Rd IG1 ..78 D5
Riverfleet WC1 ...233 B2
Riverford Ho 28 W2 .91 C2
River Front EN1 ...5 C2
River Gdns
  Carshalton SM5 ..219 A5
  Feltham TW14 ....150 B4
River Gdns Bsns Ctr
  TW14 ....128 B1
River Grove Pk BR3 .185 B2
Riverhead Cl E17 ..34 C1
River Ho Barnes SW13 133 C3
  1 Forest Hill SE26 .162 B1
Riverholme KT8 ..196 C6
Riverhope Mans
  SE18 ....122 A3
Riverine Lo HA7 ..25 A5
River La TW10 ....153 D1
Rivermead
  East Molesey KT8 ..196 A6
  Kingston KT6 ....197 D4

Rivermead Cl TW11 ..175 B5
Rivermead Ct
  Ealing UB6 ....87 A4
  Fulham SW6 ......135 B2
Rivermead Ho E9 ..75 A3
  Sunbury TW16 ....194 C6
Rivermeads Ave
  TW13, TW2 ......151 D1
River Mount KT12 .193 D2
Rivernook Cl KT12 .194 C6
River Park Gdns BR2 186 B3
River Park Rd N22 ..32 B1
River Pl N1 ....73 A1
River Rd Barking IG11 101 D3
  Buckhurst Hill IG9 ..21 D3
River Reach TW11 .175 C5
River Road Bsns Pk
  IG11 ....101 D4
Riversdale Gdns N22 32 C2
Riversdale Prim Sch
  SW18 ....157 C3
Riversdale Rd N5 ..73 A5
  Thames Ditton KT7 .197 A3
Riversdene N5 ....73 A5
Riversfield Rd EN1 ..5 C2
Rivers Ho 11 TW8 .44 C2
Riverside NW4 ....46 B2
  SW11 ....267 B4
  WC1 ....233 B2
  Forest Hill SE6 ...185 B6
  Greenwich SE7 ..121 B3
  Oatlands Park TW17 193 C2
  Sunbury TW16 ...172 D1
  Twickenham TW1 .153 B3
Riverside Apartments
  N13 ....32 B5
Riverside Ave KT8 .196 B4
Riverside Bsns Ctr
  SW18 ....157 C3
Riverside Bsns Pk
  SW19 ....180 A2
Riverside Cl BR5 ..190 C1
  E5 ....74 C6
  Ealing W7 ....86 C3
  Hackbridge SM6 ..219 B5
  Kingston KT1 ....197 D5
Riverside Cotts IG11 101 B5
Riverside Ct SE12 .142 D1
  SW8 ....269 D6
  Chingford E4 .....19 D5
  Richmond TW11 ..175 C5
Riverside Dr NW11 ..47 A3
  Chiswick W4 .....133 C4
  Mitcham CR4 .....202 C4
  Richmond TW10 ..153 B1
Riverside Est EN3 ..19 A5
Riverside Gdns N3 .47 A6
  W6 ....112 B1
  Enfield EN2 ......5 A3
  Wembley HA0 .....88 A5
Riverside Ho N12 ..29 D6
  Morden SW19 ....202 A5
Riverside Ind Est
  IG11 ....102 A4
Riverside Mans 4
  E1 ....118 C5
Riverside Pl N11 ..15 C1
  Stanwell TW19 ...148 A5
Riverside Prim Sch
  SE16 ....118 A4
Riverside Rd DA14 .169 A2
  E15 ....98 A5
  N15 ....52 A3
  Stanwell TW19 ...148 A5
  Wandsworth SW17,
  SW19 ....158 A1
Riverside The KT8 .196 B6
Riverside West SW18 135 C1
Riverside Wlk
  Isleworth TW7 ...130 C2
  3 West Wickham BR4 207 D1
Riverside Works IG11 78 D1
Riverside Workshops
  SE1 ....252 B4
River St EC1 ..94 C4 234 A2
Riverstone Ct KT2 .176 B2
Riverton Sch SE12 .165 A6
River Terr W6 ....112 C1
Riverton Cl W9 ....91 B4
Riverview TW17 ..193 B2
River View EN2 ....5 A2
Riverview CE Sch
  KT19 ....215 B4
Riverview Ct 14 DA17 125 C1
Riverview Gdns
  Barnes SW13 .....134 B6
  Twickenham TW1 .152 D2
Riverview Gr W4 .132 C6
Riverview Hts SE18 .144 D5
Riverview Lo NW9 ..67 B6

Riverview Pk SE6 ..163 C2
Riverview Prim Sch
  KT19 ....215 B4
Riverview Rd
  Chiswick W4 .....132 D6
  West Ewell KT19 .215 B4
River Way SE10 ...120 D3
Riverway N13 .....32 C6
River Way
  Twickenham TW13,
  TW2 ....151 D2
  West Ewell KT19 .215 B4
River Wlk KT12 ..194 A3
Riverwood La BR7 .189 B2
Rivet Ho SE1 .....263 D2
Rivington Ave IG8 ..37 D1
Rivington Cres NW7 .27 D3
Rivington Ct NW10 ..90 A6
Rivington Pl EC2 ..95 C3
Rivington St EC2 ..95 C3
Rivington Wlk 4 E8 .96 A6
Rivulet Rd N17 ...33 A3
Rixon Ho SE18 ...144 D6
Rixon St N7 ......72 C5
Rixsen Rd E12 ...78 A3
Roach Rd E3 .....75 C1
Roach Works E3 ..75 C1
Roads Pl N19 .....72 A6
Roan Ind Est CR4 .180 D2
Roan St SE10 ....142 A6
Robarts Cl HA5 ...40 B4
Robbins Hall EN3 ..18 D5
Robb Rd HA7 .....25 A4
Robert Adam St W1 .238 A2
Roberta St E2 ....96 A4
Robert Bell Ho 2
  SE16 ....118 A2
Robert Blair Prim Sch
  N7 ....72 A2
Robert Browning Prim Sch
  SE17 ....117 B1 262 D2
Robert Burns Ho N17 34 B3
Robert Cl W9 .....236 B5
Robert Clack Lower Sch
  RM8 ....81 B6
Robert Clack Upper Sch
  RM8 ....59 C1
Robert Dashwood Way
  SE17 ....262 A3
Robert Gentry Ho
  W14 ....254 B1
Robert Gerard Ho 7
  SE27 ....183 B6
Robert Jones Ho 3
  SE16 ....118 A2
Robert Keen Cl 17
  SE15 ....140 A4
Robert Lowe Cl SE14 140 D5
Robert Owen Ho
  8 E2 ....95 D4
  Fulham SW6 .....134 D4
Robert Owen Lo 5 E5 74 B4
Robertsbridge Rd
  SM5 ....202 B2
Roberts Cl SE9 ...167 B3
  Cheam SM3 .....216 C1
  Yiewsley UB7 ....104 A5
Roberts Ct N1 ....234 D5
  Chessington KT9 ..213 D3
  Ealing W5 ....88 A1
  Penge SE20 .....184 C2
Roberts Ho 2 N11 ..31 B5
  10 SE18 ....144 A4
  5 West Norwood
  SE27 ....160 D1
Roberts Mews SW1 .258 A5
Robertson Ho
  11 SE10 ....142 A4
  4 SE18 ....144 B4
  1 Upper Tooting
  SW17 ....180 C5
Robertson Rd E15 ..98 A6
Robertson St SW8 .137 B3
Robert's Pl EC1 ...241 B6
Roberts Rd NW7 ..29 A4
  Belvedere DA17 ..125 C2
  Chingford, Highams Park
  E17 ....35 D2
Robert St E16 ....122 D5
  NW1 ....93 B4 231 D1
  SE18 ....123 B2
  WC2 ....250 B5
  Croydon CR0 ....221 A5
Robert Sutton Ho 20
  E1 ....96 C1
Robeson St 8 E3 ..97 B2
Robina Cl DA6 ...146 D1
  Northwood HA6 ...22 A4

Robin Cl NW7 .....11 C1
  Hampton TW12 ..173 A5
Robin Cres E6 ....99 D2
Robin Ct 13 E14 .120 A3
  Wallington SM6 ..219 C2
Robin Gr N6 .....71 A6
  Brentford TW8 ...131 C6
  Harrow HA3 .....44 B1
Robin Hill Dr BR7 .188 C3
Robin Ho NW8 ...230 A3
Robinhood Cl CR4 .203 C6
Robin Hood Ct SM1 217 D3
Robin Hood Dr HA3 .24 D3
Robin Hood Gdns 12
  E14 ....120 A6
Robin Hood Inf Sch
  SM1 ....217 C3
Robin Hood Jun Sch
  SM1 ....217 C3
Robin Hood La E14 120 A6
Robinhood La CR4 .203 C6
Robin Hood La
  Bexley DA6 ......169 A6
  Kingston SW15 ...177 C6
  Sutton SM1 .....217 D3
Robin Hood Prim Sch
  SW15 ....177 C5
Robin Hood Way UB6 .64 D2
Robin Hood Way (Kingston
  By Pass) KT2,SW15,
  SW20 ....177 C5
Robinia Cl SE20 ..184 A4
Robinia Cres E10 ..75 D6
Robinscroft Mews
  SE10 ....141 D4
Robins Ct SE12 ...165 C5
Robin's Ct SW4 ...160 A5
Robins Ct TW10 ..154 A5
Robin's Ct BR3 ...186 B1
Robinsfield Inf Sch
  NW8 ....92 C5 230 A4
Robins Gr BR4 ...225 A5
Robinson Cres WD23 ..8 A3
Robinson Ct N1 ...234 D6
  4 Richmond TW9 .132 A2
Robinson Ho 11 E14 ..97 C2
  4 W10 ....90 D1
Robinson Rd E2 ..96 C5
  Dagenham RM10 ..81 C4
  Mitcham SW19 ...180 C4
Robinson's Cl W13 .87 A2
Robinson St SW3 .267 C6
Robinwood Gr UB8 .82 B3
Robinwood Pl SW15 177 B6
Robsart St SW9 ..138 C3
Robson Ave NW10 ..68 A1
Robson Cl E6 ....100 A1
  Enfield EN2 ......4 D3
Robson Ct N12 ...30 A5
Robson Rd SE21,SE27 161 A1
Roby Ho EC1 ....242 A6
Roch Ave HA8 ....26 A4
Rochdale 8 SE19 .183 C4
Rochdale Rd E10 ..53 C2
  SE2 ....124 B2
Rochdale Way 4
  SE8 ....141 C5
Roche Ho 16 E14 .119 B6
Rochelle Ct SW11 .136 B1
Rochelle Ct 14 E1 ..96 C1
  Beckenham BR3 ..185 D3
Rochelle St 81 E2 .95 D4
Rochemont Wlk 2 E8 96 A6
Roche Rd SW16 ..182 B2
Rochester Ave BR1 .187 B1
  E13 ....99 C6
  Feltham TW13 ...149 D2
Rochester Cl
  1 DA15 ....168 B5
  SE3 ....143 C2
  Enfield EN1 ......5 C4
  Streatham SW16 .182 A3
Rochester Ct 1 E2 ..96 B3
  7 NW1 ....71 C1
  NW9 ....45 B4
  South Norwood SE25 184 A1
Rochester Dr DA5 .169 C6
  Pinner HA5 ......40 D4
Rochester Gdns
  Redbridge IG1 ....56 B2
  South Croydon CR0 221 C5
Rochester Ho SE1 .252 D1
  18 SE15 ....140 C6
Rochester Mews NW1 71 C1
Rochester Par TW13 .150 A1
Rochester Pl NW1 ..71 C1

Rochester Rd NW1 . .71 C2
Carshalton SM5 . . . . .218 D4
Northwood HA6 . . . . . .39 D6
Rochester Row
SW1 . . . . .115 C2 259 B4
Rochester Sq NW1 . . . .71 C1
Rochester St SW1 . . .259 C5
Rochester Terr NW1 . . .71 C2
Rochester Way
SE3,SE9 . . . . .143 D2
SE9 . . . . .144 C2
Rochester Wlk SE1 . .252 C4
Roche Wlk SM5 . . . . .202 B3
Rochford N17 . . . . . . .33 C1
Rochford Ave RM6 . . .58 C4
Rochford Cl **2** E6 . . . .99 D5
Rochford Way CR0 . .204 A3
Rochford Wlk **3** E8 . . .74 A1
Rock Ave **13** SW14 . .133 B2
Rockbourne Rd SE23 162 D3
Rock Cl CR4 . . . . . . .180 B1
Rockfield Ho **2** NW4 .46 D5
SE10 . . . . .142 A6
Rockford Ave UB6 . . .87 B5
Rock Gdns RM10 . . . .81 D3
Rock Grove Way
SE16 . . . . .118 A2
Rockhall Rd NW2 . . . .68 D4
Rockhampton Cl **4**
SE27 . . . . .182 C6
Rockhampton Rd
South Croydon CR2 . .221 C2
West Norwood SE27,
SW16 . . . . .182 C6
Rock Hill SE19 . . . . .183 D6
Rockingham Cl
SW15 . . . . .133 D1
Rockingham Ct **19**
BR3 . . . . .185 C3
Rockingham Gate
WD23 . . . . .8 A5
Rockingham St
SE1 . . . . .117 A3 262 A5
Rockland Rd SW15 . .135 A1
Rocklands N3 . . . . . . .29 B3
Rocklands Dr HA7 . . . .25 C1
Rockley Ct **9** W14 . .112 D4
Rockley Rd W14 . . . .112 D4
Rockliffe Manor Prim Sch
SE18 . . . . .145 D6
Rockmount Prim Sch
SE19 . . . . .183 B4
Rockmount Rd
SE18,SE2 . . . . .123 D1
South Norwood SE19 .183 B4
Rocks La SW13 . . . . .134 A2
Rock St N4 . . . . .72 C6
Rockstraw Ho **5** NW3 70 D1
Rockware Ave UB6 . . .86 C6
Rockways EN5 . . . . . . .11 D5
Rockwell Gdns SE19 .183 C6
Rockwell Rd RM10 . . .81 D3
Rockwood Ct N16 . . . .52 A2
Rocliffe St N1 . .94 D5 234 D3
Rocombe Cres SE23 .162 C4
Rocque Ho SW6 . . . .264 C4
Rocque La SE3 . . . . .142 D2
Rodborough Rd NW11 47 C1
Rodd Est TW17 . . . . .193 B4
Roden Gdns CR0 . . . .205 C3
Rodenhurst Ct SW4 .159 D6
Rodenhurst Rd SW4 .159 D5
Roden St N7 . . . . .72 B5
Ilford IG1 . . . . .78 C5
Roderick Ho **3** SE16 118 C2
Roderick Rd NW3 . . . .70 D4
Rodgers Cl WD6 . . . . . .9 D5
Rodgers Ho **4** SW4 159 D4
Rodin Ct N1 . . . . . . .234 C5
Roding Ct **6** W12 . . .111 C4
Roding Ho N1 . . . . . .234 A5
Roding Hospl IG4 . . . .55 D6
Roding La IG9 . . . . . .21 D3
Roding La N IG8 . . . . .37 D1
Roding La S IG4 . . . . .55 D5
Roding Lo IG1 . . . . . . .55 D3
Roding Mews E1 . . . .118 A5
Roding Prim Sch RM8 80 C3
Roding Rd E5 . . . . . . .75 A3
Newham E6 . . . . . . .100 D2
Rodings Ct E4 . . . . . . .36 B5
Rodings The Barnet EN5 .1 A1
4 Woodford IG8 . . . .37 C4
Roding Valley Sta IG9 37 D6
Roding View IG9 . . . . .21 D3

Rodmarton St
W1 . . . . .92 D2 237 D3
Rodmell WC1 . . . . . .233 B1
Rodmell Cl UB4 . . . . .85 A3
Rodmell Slope N12 . . .29 B5
Rodmere St SE10 . . .120 C1
Rodmill La SW2 . . . . .160 A4
Rodney Cl
New Malden KT3 . . . .199 C4
Pinner HA5 . . . . .41 A2
Thornton Heath CR0 . .204 D1
Walton-on-T KT12 . . .194 C1
Rodney Ct NW8 . . . .236 B6
Rodney Gdns
Hayes BR4 . . . . .225 A4
Pinner HA5 . . . . .40 C4
Rodney Ho **4** E14 . .119 D2
N1 . . . . .233 D3
W11 . . . . .245 A6
Rodney Pl E17 . . . . . .35 B1
SE17 . . . . . . .117 A2 262 B4
Merton SW19 . . . . . .180 A2
Rodney Rd
SE17 . . . . . . .117 B2 262 C3
Mitcham CR4 . . . . . .202 C6
New Malden KT3 . . . .199 C4
Twickenham TW4 . . . .151 C6
Walton-on-T KT12 . . .194 C1
Wanstead E11 . . . . . .55 B5
Rodney St N1 . .94 B5 233 D3
Rodway Rd BR1 . . . . .187 B2
Putney SW15 . . . . . .156 A4
Rodwell Cl **2** HA4 . . .40 C1
Rodwell Rd SE22 . . . .161 D5
Roe **5** NW9 . . . . . . .27 D2
Roebourne Way E16 .122 C4
Roebuck Cl
Feltham TW13 . . . . . .172 B6
Tottenham N17 . . . . . .33 D4
Roebuck Ct
Chingford E4 . . . . . . .36 A3
2 New Malden KT3 . .199 C4
Roebuck Ho SW1 . . .259 A6
Roebuck La IG9 . . . . .21 C3
Roebuck Rd KT9 . . . .214 C4
Roedean Ave EN3 . . . .6 C5
Roedean Cl EN3 . . . . . .6 C4
Roedean Cres SW15 .155 C6
Roe End NW9 . . . . . . .45 A5
Roe Gn NW9 . . . . . . .45 A4
Roe Green Jun & Inf Schs
NW9 . . . . .44 D5
Roehampton CE Prim Sch
SW15 . . . . .156 B4
Roehampton Cl
SW15 . . . . .134 A1
Roehampton Ct
SW13 . . . . .134 A2
Roehampton Dr BR7 .189 A4
Roehampton Gate
SW15 . . . . .155 C6
Roehampton High St
SW15 . . . . .156 A4
Roehampton La
Putney SW15 . . . . . .156 A5
Roehampton SW15 . .156 B3
Roehampton Vale
SW15 . . . . .155 D2
Roe La NW9 . . . . .45 A5
Roe Way SM6 . . . . . .220 A4
Roffey Ct **9** NW9 . . .46 A5
Roffey St E14 . . . . . .120 A4
Roger Ascham Prim Sch
E17 . . . . .35 B3
Roger Dowley Ct **8**
E2 . . . . .96 C5
Roger's Almshouses **2**
SW9 . . . . .138 B1
Rogers Est **28** E2 . . .96 C4
Rogers Gdns RM10 . .81 C3
Rogers Ho SW1 . . . .259 D4
9 Dagenham RM10 . .81 C5
Rogers Rd E16 . . . . . .98 D1
Dagenham RM10 . . . .81 C3
Upper Tooting SW17 . .180 C6
Roger St WC1 .94 B3 240 D5
Roger Stone Ct SE10 .67 B6
Rogers Wlk N12 . . . . .13 D1
Rojack Rd SE23 . . . . .162 D3
Rokeby Gdns IG8 . . . .37 A2
Rokeby Ho **2** SW12 .159 B4
9 Balham SW12 . . . .159 B4
Rokeby Pl SW20 . . . .178 B3
Rokeby Rd SE4 . . . . .141 B3
Rokeby Sch E15 . . . . .76 B1
Kingston KT2 . . . . . . .177 A3
Rokeby St E15 . . . . . .98 C6
Rokeland Ho SE4 . . . .141 A1
Rokell Ho BR3 . . . . . .185 D5
Roker Park Ave UB10 .60 A4

Rokesby Cl DA16 . . . .145 B3
Rokesby Pl HA0 . . . . .65 D3
Rokesly Ave N8 . . . . .50 A4
Rokesly Jun & Inf Schs
N8 . . . . .50 A4
Roland Ct SE19 . . . . .183 D2
Roland Gdns
SW7 . . . . .114 A1 256 B2
Roland Mews **1** E1 . . .96 D2
Roland Rd E17 . . . . . .54 B5
Roland Way SE17 . . .262 D1
SW7 . . . . .114 A1 256 B2
Worcester Park KT4 . .215 D6
Roles Gr RM6 . . . . . . .59 A5
Rolfe Cl EN4 . . . . .2 C1
Rolfe Ho N11 . . . . . . .30 D2
Rolinsden Way BR2 . .225 D4
Rolland Ho W7 . . . . . .86 C2
Rollesby Rd KT19,KT9 214 C2
Rollesby Way SE28 . .102 C1
Rolleston Ave BR5 . . .210 D3
Rolleston Cl BR5 . . . .210 D2
Rolleston Rd CR2 . . .221 B1
Roll Gdns IG2 . . . . . . .56 C4
Rollins St SE15 . . . . .140 C6
Rollit Cres TW3 . . . . .151 C6
Rollit Ho N7 . . . . .72 C3
Rollit St N7 . . . . .72 C3
Rollo Ct SW11 . . . . . .268 C1
Rolls Bldgs EC4 . . . .241 B2
Rollscourt Ave SE24 .161 A6
Rolls Park Ave E4 . . . .35 D5
Rolls Park Rd E4 . . . . .35 D5
Rolls Pas EC4 . . . . . .241 A2
Rolls Rd SE1 .118 A1 263 D2
Rolt St SE8 . . . . .141 A6
Rolvenden Gdns BR1 187 D3
Rolvenden Pl N17 . . . .34 A2
Roman Cl W3 . . . . . .110 D4
Romanfield Rd SW2 . .160 B4
Romanhurst Ave BR2 208 C5
Romanhurst Gdns
BR2,BR3 . . . . .208 C5
Roman Ind Est CR0 . .205 C2
Roman Rd E2,E3 . . . . .96 D5
E3 . . . . .97 B6
N10 . . . . .31 B3
N12 . . . . .30 C2
W4 . . . . .111 D2
Ilford IG1 . . . . .78 D2
Newham E6 . . . . . . .100 A3
Roman Rise SE19 . . .183 B4
Roman Road Prim Sch
E6 . . . . .99 D3
Roman Sq SE28 . . . .124 A5
Roman Square Mkt **1**
E3 . . . . .97 B5
Roman Way N7 . . . . . .72 B2
4 SE15 . . . . .140 C5
Croydon CR0 . . . . . .220 D6
Enfield EN1 . . . . .17 D6
Romany Gdns E17 . . .35 A2
Cheam SM3 . . . . . . .201 C2
Romany Ho **8** N9 . . . .18 A1
Romany Prospect
SE19 . . . . .183 B4
Romany Rise BR5 . . .211 A1
Roma Rd E17 . . . . . . .35 A2
Roma Read Cl SW15 .156 B4
Romayne Ho SW4 . . .137 D2
Romberg Rd SW17 . .159 A1
Romborough Gdns
SE13 . . . . .164 A6
Romborough Way
SE13 . . . . .164 A6
Romeland WD6 . . . . . . .9 D5
Romer Ho **9** SE20 . .160 B6
12 W10 . . . . .91 B4
Romero Cl SW9 . . . . .138 C2
Romero Sq SE9 . . . . .143 C1
Romey Mews W1 . . .238 A4
Romeyn Rd SW16 . . .160 B1
Romford Ho **17** N1 . . .73 B2
Romford Rd E15 . . . . .76 D2
E7,E12 . . . . .77 C3
Romford St E1 . . . . . .96 B2
Romilly Dr WD19 . . . .23 A6
Romilly Rd N4 . . . . . . .72 D6
Romilly St W1 . . . . . .249 D6
Romily Ct SW6 . . . . .135 A3
Rommany Ct SE27 . . .183 B6
Rommany Rd SE27 . .183 B6
Romney Cl NW11 . . . .48 A1
7 SE14 . . . . .140 C5
Ashford TW15 . . . . . .171 A5
Chessington KT9 . . . .214 A4
Harrow HA2 . . . . .41 C2
Tottenham N17 . . . . . .34 B2
Romney Ho **9** NW3 . .70 C2

Romney Ct continued
9 W12 . . . . .112 C4
16 Northolt UB5 . . . .84 D5
Romney Dr
Bromley BR1 . . . . . . .187 D3
Harrow HA2 . . . . .41 C2
Romney Gdns DA7 . .147 B4
Ashford TW15 . . . . . .170 D6
Romney Ho EN1 . . . . .18 A6
Romney Par UB4 . . . .83 B5
Romney Rd SE10 . . . .142 B6
Hayes UB4 . . . . .83 B5
New Malden KT3 . . . .199 B3
Romney Row NW2 . . .68 D6
Romney St
SW1 . . . . .116 A3 260 A5
Romola Rd SE24,SW2 160 D3
Romsey Cl BR6 . . . . .227 A4
Romsey Gdns RM9 . .102 D6
Romsey Ho **5** SW11 .136 B1
Romsey Rd
Dagenham RM9 . . . .102 D6
Ealing W13 . . . . .109 A6
Romulus Ct **7** TW8 .131 D5
Ronald Ave E15 . . . . .98 C4
Ronald Cl BR3 . . . . . .207 B4
Ronald Ho SE9 . . . . .143 C1
Ronaldshay N4 . . . . . .50 C1
Ronalds Rd BR1 . . . . .187 A2
N5 . . . . .72 C3
Ronald St E1 . . . . .96 C1
Ronaldstone Rd
DA15 . . . . .167 C5
Rona Rd NW3 . . . . . . .71 A4
Ronart St HA3 . . . . . . .42 D6
Rona Wlk **7** N1 . . . . .73 B2
Rondu Rd NW2 . . . . . .69 A3
Ronelean Rd KT6 . . . .214 B5
Ron Leighton Way
E6 . . . . .100 A6
Ronver Lo E4 . . . . . . .20 C1
Ronver Rd SE12 . . . . .164 D3
Rood La EC3 .117 C6 253 A6
Rookby Ct N21 . . . . . .16 D2
Rookby Ct N21 . . . . . .16 D2
Rook Cl HA9 . . . . .66 D5
Rookeries Cl TW13 . .150 C1
Rookery Cl NW9 . . . . .45 D4
Rookery Cotts EN4 . . . .3 B2
Rookery Cres RM10 . .81 D1
Rookery Dr BR7 . . . . .188 C2
Rookery La BR2 . . . . .209 C3
Rookery Rd SW4 . . . .137 C1
Rookery Way NW9 . . .45 D4
Rookes Heath High Sch
HA2 . . . . .63 C5
Rooke Way SE10 . . . .120 D1
Rookfield Ave N10 . . . .49 C5
Rookfield Cl N10 . . . . .49 C5
Rook Lo IG1 . . . . .55 D3
Rooksmead Rd TW16 172 A1
Rooks Terr UB7 . . . . .104 A4
Rookstone Rd SW17 .180 D5
Rook Wlk E6 . . . . . . .100 A1
Rookwood Ave
Wallington SM6 . . . . .219 D4
West Barnes KT3 . . . .200 A5
Rookwood Gdns E4 . .20 D2
Rookwood Ho IG11 . .101 B5
Rookwood Rd N16 . . .52 A4
Rootes Dr W10 . . . . . .90 D2
Ropemaker Rd SE16 .119 A3
Ropemaker's Fields **7**
E14 . . . . .119 B6
Ropemaker St
EC2 . . . . .95 B2 242 C4
Roper Ho **13** SE21 . .183 C6
Roper La SE1 .117 C4 253 B1
Ropers Ave E4 . . . . . .36 A5
Roper's Orchard
SW3 . . . . .267 A5
Roper St **1** SE9 . . . .166 C5
Ropers Wlk **13** SE24 .160 C4
Roper Way CR4 . . . . .181 A1
Ropery Bsns Est SE7 121 C2
Ropery St E3 . . . . .97 B3
Rope St SE16 . . . . . .119 A3
Ropewalk Gdns **16** E1 .96 A1
Rope Yard Rails
SE18 . . . . .122 D3
Ropley St **6** E2 . . . . . .96 A5
Rosa Alba Mews N5 . .73 A4
Rosa Ave TW15 . . . . .170 C6
Rosalind Ct **6** IG11 . .80 A1
Rosalind Ho **25** N1 . . .95 C4
Rosaline Rd
SW6 . . . . .135 A5 264 B3
Rosaline Terr SW6 . .264 B3
Rosamond St SE26 . .162 B1
Rosamund Cl CR2 . . .221 B4

Rosamun St UB2 . . . .107 A2
Rosa Parks Ho **8**
SW9 . . . . .138 B3
Rosary Cl TW3,TW5 . .129 A3
Rosary Gdns
SW7 . . . . .114 A2 256 B3
Ashford TW15 . . . . . .170 D6
Bushey WD23 . . . . . . .8 C4
Rosary RC Inf Sch
TW5 . . . . .129 C6
Rosary RC Jun Sch
TW5 . . . . .129 C6
Rosary RC Prim Sch
NW3 . . . . .70 C3
Rosaville Rd
SW6 . . . . .135 B5 264 C3
Rosbury SW15 . . . . . .157 A5
Roscoe St EC1 .95 A3 242 B5
Roscoff Cl HA8 . . . . . .27 A2
Roscommon Ho **2**
NW3 . . . . .70 B3
Roseacre Cl Ealing W13 87 B2
Littleton TW17 . . . . . .192 C4
Roseacre Lo **3** 6 C1
Roseacre Rd DA16 . .146 B2
Rosealeigh Rd
SW6 . . . . .134 C5
Morden SM4 . . . . . . .202 A4
Woodford E18 . . . . . .37 B1
Rosebank SW6 . . . . .134 C5
2 W3 . . . . .89 B1
Penge SE20 . . . . . . .184 B3
Rosebank Ave HA0 . . .64 D4
Rose Bank Cl N12 . . . .30 C5
Rosebank Cl TW11 . .175 A4
Rosebank Gdns E3 . . .97 B5
1 W3 . . . . .89 B1
Rosebank Gr E17 . . . .53 B6
Rosebank Rd E17 . . . .53 D3
W7 . . . . .108 C4
Rosebank Villas E17 . .53 C5
Rosebank Way W3 . . .89 B1
Rosebank Wlk NW1 . .71 D1
14 SE7 . . . . .122 A2
Rose Bates Dr NW9 . .44 C5
Roseberry Gdns BR6 .227 C5
N4 . . . . .50 D3
Roseberry Pl E8 . . . . .73 D2
Roseberry St SE16 . .118 B2
Rosebery Ave DA15 .167 C4
E12 . . . . .78 B2
EC1 . . . . .94 C4 234 B1
Harrow HA2 . . . . .63 B4
Kingston KT3 . . . . . . .199 D6
South Norwood CR7 . .183 A1
Tottenham N17 . . . . . .34 A1
Rosebery Cl SM4 . . . .200 D3
Rosebery Ct EC1 . . . .241 A6
W1 . . . . .248 C4
Chessington KT9 . . . .214 A1
Rosebery Gdns N8 . . .50 A4
Ealing W13 . . . . .87 A1
Sutton SM1 . . . . .217 D4
Rosebery Ho **22** E2 . .96 C5
Rosebery Ind Pk N17 .34 B1
Rosebery Mews N10 . .31 C1
Rosebery Rd N10 . . . .31 C1
SW2 . . . . .160 A5
Cheam SM1,SM2 . . . .217 B2
Edmonton N9 . . . . . . .18 A2
Isleworth TW3,TW7 . .152 A6
Kingston KT1 . . . . . . .176 D1
Rosebery Sq EC1 . . .241 A5
Kingston KT1 . . . . . . .176 D1
Rosebine Ave TW2 . .152 B4
Rosebriars KT10 . . . .212 A3
Rose Bruford Coll
SE8 . . . . .141 C6
Rose Bruford Coll of
Speech & Drama
DA15 . . . . .168 B3
Rosebury Rd SW6 . . .135 D3
Rosebury Vale HA4 . . .62 A6
Rose Bush Ct NW3 . . .70 D3
Rose Cotts KT10 . . . .212 B4
Rosecourt Rd CR0 . .204 B3
Rosecroft N22 . . . . . .32 B2
Rosecroft Ave NW3 . .69 D4
Rosecroft Gdns NW2 .68 A5
Twickenham TW2 . . . .152 B3
Rosecroft Rd UB1 . . . .85 C4
Rosecroft Wlk
Pinner HA5 . . . . .40 D4
Wembley HA0 . . . . . .65 D3
Rose & Crown Ct
EC2 . . . . .242 A2
Rose & Crown Yd
SW1 . . . . .249 B3

Rose Ct E1 . . . . .243 D3
N1 . . . . .234 D6
Harrow HA2 . . . . .64 A6
Ilford IG1 . . . . .78 C2
7 Wembley HA0 . . . .88 A5
10 Wimbledon SW19 .179 A5
Rose Dale BR6 . . . . .226 D6
Rosedale Ave UB3 . . .83 B2
Rosedale Cl SE2 . . . .124 D3
W7 . . . . .108 D4
Stanmore HA7 . . . . . .25 B4
Rosedale Ct N5 . . . . .72 C4
Rosedale Gdns RM9 . .80 B3
Rosedale Ho N16 . . . .51 B3
Rosedale Lo N14 . . . .15 B4
Rosedale Rd E7 . . . . .77 C3
Dagenham RM9 . . . . .80 B3
Richmond TW9 . . . . . .132 A1
Stoneleigh KT17 . . . .216 A3
Rosedale Terr W6 . . .112 B3
Rosedene NW6 . . . . . .90 D6
Rosedene Ave
Morden SM4 . . . . . . .201 C4
Southall UB6 . . . . . . .85 C4
Streatham SW16 . . . .160 B1
Thornton Heath CR0 . .204 A2
Rosedene Gdns IG2 . .56 C4
Rosedene Terr E10 . . .75 D6
Rosedew Rd W6 . . . .134 D6
Rose End KT4 . . . . . .200 D1
Rosefield Cl SM5 . . . .218 C4
Rosefield Ct EN4 . . . . .2 C1
Rosefield Gdns E14 . .119 C6
Rose Garden Cl HA8 . .26 A4
Rose Gdns W5 . . . . .109 D3
Feltham TW13 . . . . . .150 A2
Southall UB1 . . . . . . .85 C3
Rose Glen NW9 . . . . .45 B5
Rosehart Mews **8**
W11 . . . . .91 C1
Rose Hatch Ave RM6 .58 C6
Roseheath Rd TW4 . .151 B2
Rosehill Claygate KT10 213 C4
Hampton TW12 . . . . .173 C2
Rose Hill
Carshalton SM4,SM5 .202 A4
Cheam SM1 . . . . . . .201 D1
Rosehill Ave SM1,
SM5 . . . . .202 A4
Rosehill Ct SM4 . . . .202 A4
Rosehill Gdns
Greenford UB6 . . . . . .64 D3
Sutton SM1 . . . . .218 A4
Rose Hill Park W
SM1 . . . . .218 A6
Rosehill Rd SW18 . . .158 A6
Rose La RM6 . . . . . . .59 A5
Roseland Cl N17 . . . . .33 B4
Roseland Ho SW6 . . .135 A2
Rose Lawn WD23 . . . . .8 A3
Roseleigh Ave N5 . . . .72 D4
Roseleigh Cl **12** TW1 153 D5
Roselle Ct W5 . . . . . . .88 A1
Rosemary Ave N3 . . . .29 D1
NW2 . . . . .47 D5
East Molesey KT8 . . .195 C4
Edmonton N9 . . . . . . .18 B3
Enfield EN2 . . . . .5 C4
Hounslow TW4 . . . . .128 D3
Rosemary Branch Bridge
N1 . . . . .235 C6
Rosemary Cl
Hillingdon UB8 . . . . . .82 C2
Thornton Heath CR0 . .204 A3
Rosemary Cotts **3**
SW19 . . . . .178 C3
Rosemary Ct **43** SE8 .141 B6
Rosemary Dr
Redbridge IG4 . . . . . .55 D4
15 South Bromley E14 .98 D1
Rosemary Gdns
Chessington KT9 . . . .214 A4
Dagenham RM8 . . . . .59 B4
Mortlake SW14 . . . . .133 A2
Rosemary Ho N1 . . . .235 D5
Rosemary La SW14 . .133 A2
Rosemary Mews N1 .235 D5
Rosemary Rd DA16 . .145 D4
SE15 . . . . .139 D5
Wandsworth SW17 . .158 A1
Rosemary Works Sch
N1 . . . . .235 D5
Rosemead NW9 . . . . .46 A2
Rosemead Ave
Feltham TW13 . . . . . .149 D2
Mitcham CR4 . . . . . . .181 C1
Wembley HA9 . . . . . . .66 A3
Rosemead Prep Sch
SE27 . . . . .161 A2
Rose Mews N18 . . . . .34 C6

Rosemont Ave N12 ...30 A4
Rosemont Mans [11]
NW3 ....69 D2
Rosemont Rd NW3 ..70 A2
Acton W3 ....110 D6
Kingston KT3 .....199 A6
Richmond TW10 ...154 A5
Wembley HA0 ......88 A6
Rosemoor St
SW3 ......114 D2 257 C3
Rosemount Ct [2]
[2] Acton W3 ....110 D5
South Norwood SE25 .205 C6
Rosemount Dr BR1 .210 B5
Rosemount Lo W3 ..110 C6
Rosemount Point [10]
SE23 ....162 D1
Rosemount Rd W13 .87 A1
Rosemount Towers [5]
SM6 ....219 C2
Rosenau Cres SW11 .267 C1
Rosenau Rd
SW11 .....136 D4 267 C2
Rosendale Prim Sch
SE21 ....161 A4
Rosendale Rd SE21,
SE24 ....161 A3
Roseneath Ave N21 ..16 D3
Roseneath Rd SW11 .159 A5
Roseneath Wlk EN1 ...5 C1
Rosens Wlk HA8 .....10 C1
Rosenthal Rd SE6 ...164 C4
Rosenthorpe Rd
SE15 ....162 D6
Roserton St E14 ....120 A4
Rosery The CR0 ....206 D3
Rose Sq SW7 ....256 D2
Rose St EC4 ....241 D1
WC2 ....116 A6 250 A6
Roses The IG8 ......36 D3
Rosethorn Cl SW12 .159 D4
Rosetta Cl SW8 .....270 B3
Rosetta Ct SE19 ...183 C3
Rosetta Prim Sch E16 99 B2
Rosetti Terr RM8 ...80 B4
Roseveare Rd SE12 .187 C6
Roseville N21 ....16 C3
Roseville Ave TW3,
TW4 ....151 C6
Roseville Rd UB3 ..106 A2
Rosevine Rd SW20 .178 C2
Roseway SE21 .....161 B5
Rose Way HA8 ......27 A6
SE12 ....165 A6
Rosewell Cl SE20 ..184 B3
Rose Wlk
Surbiton KT5 ......198 D4
West Wickham BR4 ..224 B6
Rosewood Ave UB6 ..65 A2
Rosewood Cl DA14 .168 C1
Rosewood Ct [2] E11 ..76 B4
Bromley BR1 ......187 D2
Dagenham RM6 ....58 C4
Kingston KT2 .....176 C3
Rosewood Dr TW17 .192 B4
Rosewood Gr SM1 .218 A6
Rosewood Sq W12 ..90 A1
Rosher Cl E15 ......76 B1
Roshni Ho SW17 ...180 C4
Rosh Pinah Prim Sch
HA8 ....10 D1
Rosina Ct SW17 ....180 C5
Rosina St E9 ....74 D2
Roskeen Ct [1] SW19 .178 C3
Roskell Rd SW15 ..134 D2
Roskild Ct HA9 .....66 B4
Roslin Ho [2] E1 ...118 D6
Roslin Rd W3 ......110 D3
Roslin Way BR1 ...187 A5
Roslyn Cl CR4 .....180 C1
Roslyn Rd N15 .....51 C4
Rosmead Rd
W11 ....113 A6 244 B6
Rosoman Pl EC1 ...241 B6
Rossall Cl RM6 ....58 C4
Rossall Cres NW10 ..88 B4
NW9 ....45 A1
Rossdale SM1 .....218 C3
Rossdale Dr N9 .....18 C5
NW9 ....45 A1
Rossdale Rd SW15 .134 C1

Rosse Mews SE3 ...143 B4
Rossendale Cl EN2 ...4 D6
Rossendale Ho [7] E5 .74 B6
Rossendale St E5 ...74 B6
Rossendale Way
NW1 ....93 C6 232 B6
Rossendon Ct [1]
SM6 ....219 C2
Rossetti Ct WC1 ...239 C4
Rossetti Gdns Mans
SW3 ....267 C6
Rossetti Ho SW1 ...259 D3
Rossetti Mews NW8 .229 D5
Rossetti Rd SE16 ..118 B1
Ross Ho [18] E1 ...118 B5
[6] SE18 ....144 A4
Twickenham TW2 ...151 D2
Rossignol Gdns SM5 .219 A6
Rossindel Rd TW3 .151 C6
Rossington Cl EN1 ...6 B5
Rossington St E5 ...74 A6
Rossiter Fields EN5 .13 B5
Rossiter Rd SW12 .159 B3
Rossland Cl DA6 ...169 D6
Rosslyn Ave
Barnes SW13 ......133 D2
Chingford E4 ......20 D2
Dagenham RM8 ....59 C2
East Barnet EN4 ...14 C5
Feltham TW14 .....150 A5
Rosslyn Cl
Ashford TW16 .....171 C4
Coney Hall BR4 ...224 D5
Hayes UB3 ....83 B2
Rosslyn Cres
Harrow HA1 ....42 D5
Wembley HA9 .....66 A4
Rosslyn Ct NW3 ....70 C3
Rosslyn Hill NW3 ..70 B3
Rosslyn Ho [8] TW9 .132 M4
Rosslyn Mans NW6 .70 A2
Rosslyn Park Mews
NW3 ....70 B3
Rosslyn Rd E17 ....54 A5
Barking IG11 ......79 B1
Twickenham TW1 .153 C5
Rossmore Ct NW1 .237 C6
Rossmore Rd
NW1 ....92 C3 237 B6
Ross Par SM6 .....219 B2
Ross Rd
South Norwood SE25 .205 C6
Twickenham TW2 ..152 A3
Wallington SM6 ...219 C3
Ross Way SE9 .....144 A2
Rossway Dr WD23 ...8 B6
Rosswood Gdns SM6 219 C2
Rosswood Lo CR0 .222 D6
Rostella Rd SW17 .180 B6
Rostrevor Gdns UB3 .105 C5
Rostrevor Ave N15 .51 C3
Rostrevor Gdns UB2 .107 A1
Rostrevor Mans SW6 264 C2
Rostrevor Rd
Fulham SW6 ..135 B4 264 C2
Wimbledon SW19 .179 C5
Rotary St SE1 ....261 D6
Rothay NW1 ......231 D2
Rothbury Gdns TW7 .131 C5
Rothbury Rd E9 ....75 C1
Rothbury Wlk N17 ..34 A3
Rotherfield Ct
N1 ....73 B1 235 C6
Rotherfield Prim Sch
N1 ....95 A6 235 B6
Rotherfield Rd
Enfield EN3 ....6 D6
Wallington SM5 ..219 A3
Rotherfield St
N1 ....73 A1 235 B6
Rotherham Wlk SE1 .251 C3
Rotherhill Ave SW16 .181 D4
Rotherhithe SE16 ..119 B5
Rotherhithe Holiday Inn
Pier SE16 ....119 B5
Rotherhithe New Rd
SE16 ....118 B1
Rotherhithe Old Rd
SE16 ....118 D2
Rotherhithe Prim Sch
SE16 ....118 D2
[10] SE16 ....118 B4
Rotherhithe St SE16 .118 C4
Rotherhithe Sta SE16 118 C4
Rotherhithe Tunnel
SE16 ....118 D5
Rother Ho SE15 ...140 B1
Rotherwick Hill W5 .88 B3
Rotherwick Rd NW11 .47 C2
Rotherwood Cl SW20 179 A2

Rotherwood Rd
SW15 ....134 D2
Rothery St N1 .....234 D6
Rothesay Ave
Merton SW20 ......179 A1
Mortlake SW14,TW10 .132 D1
Northolt UB6 ......64 B2
Rothesay Ct [13] SE11 .138 C6
SE12 ....165 B1
[4] Catford SE6 ...164 D2
Rothesay Rd SE25 .205 C5
Rothley Ct NW8 ...236 C6
Rothsay Rd E7 .....77 C2
Rothsay St
SE1 ....117 C3 263 A5
Rothsay Wlk [16] E14 .119 C2
Rothschild Rd W4 ..111 A3
Rothschild St SE27 .182 D6
Rothwell Ct HA1 ....42 D4
Rothwell Gdns RM9 .102 C6
Rothwell Ho TW5 ..129 C6
Rothwell Rd RM9 ..102 C6
Rothwell St NW1 ..230 D6
[10] NW1 ....70 D1
Roth Wlk N7 ......72 B6
Rotten Row*
SW1 ....114 D4 247 C2
Rotterdam Dr E14 .120 A3
Rotunda Mus* SE18 .122 B1
Rouel Rd SE16 ....118 A2
SE16 ....118 A2
Rougemont Ave SM4 201 C3
Roundabout Ho HA6 ..22 A2
Roundacre SW19 ..156 D2
Roundel Cl SE4 ....141 B1
Roundell Ho [14] SE21 183 C6
Rounders Ct [7] RM10 .81 C2
Round Gr CR0 .....206 D2
Roundhay Ct SE23 .183 C6
Roundhedge Way EN2 ..4 B5
Round Hill SE23 ...162 C1
Roundhill Dr EN2 ....4 B1
Roundshaw Ctr SM6 220 A1
Roundtable Rd BR1 .164 D1
Roundtree Rd HA0 ..65 B3
Roundways HA4 ....61 D5
Roundway The
Claygate KT10 .....212 D2
Tottenham N17 ....33 B2
Roundwood BR7 ...188 D1
Roundwood Ave
UB11 ....105 A5
Roundwood Cl HA4 ..39 B2
Roundwood Rd NW10 .67 D1
Rounton Rd E3 .....97 C3
Roupell Ho [7] KT2 .176 B3
Roupell Rd SW2 ..160 B3
Roupell St
SE1 ....116 C5 251 B3
Rousden St NW1 ...71 C1
Rouse Gdns SE21 .183 C6
Routemaster Cl E13 .99 B4
Routh Ct TW14 ....149 B4
Routh Rd SW18 ...158 C4
Routh St E6 ....100 B2
Rover Ho [27] N1 ...95 C6
Rowallan Ct [3] SE6 .164 D3
Rowallan Rd
SW6 ....135 A5 264 A3
Rowallen Par RM8 .58 C1
Rowan N10 ....31 B1
Rowan Ave E4 .....35 B4
Rowan Cl W5 ......110 A4
Harrow HA7 ....24 D4
Kingston KT3 .....177 C1
Streatham SW16 ..181 C2
Wembley HA0 .....65 A5
Rowan Cres SW16 .181 C2
Rowan Ct [18] SE15 .139 D5
SW11 ....158 D5
Forest Hill SE26 ...184 C6
[11] Kingston KT2 .176 C3
Wimbledon SW20 .178 B1
Rowan Dr NW9 ....46 A6
Rowan Gdns CR0 .221 D5
Rowan High Sch
SW16 ....181 C1
Rowan Ho DA14 ...167 D1
NW10 ....89 C3
[5] NW3 ....70 D2
East Bedfont TW14 .149 B5
Ilford IG1 ....79 B3
Rowan Pl UB3 .....105 D6
Rowan Rd DA7 ....147 A2
W6 ....112 D2
Brentford TW8 ....131 B5
Mitcham SW16 ...181 C1
West Drayton UB7 .104 A2
Rowans The
Ashford TW16 .....171 D5

Rowans The continued
Edmonton N13 .....17 A1
Rowan Terr W6 ....112 D2
Rowantree Cl N21 ..17 B3
Rowantree Rd
Edmonton N21 .....17 B3
Enfield EN2 ....4 D3
Rowan Way RM6 ...58 C6
Rowan Wlk BR2 ...226 B5
N19 ....71 C6
N2 ....48 A4
W10 ....91 A3
[1] New Barnet EN5 .13 D6
Rowanwood Ave
DA15 ....168 A3
Rowanwood Mews EN2 4 D3
Rowben Cl N20 ....13 D3
Rowberry Cl SW6 .134 C5
Rowcross St
SE1 ....117 D1 263 D2
Rowdell Rd UB5 ....85 C6
Rowden Par E4 .....35 C4
Rowden Park Gdns E4 35 C4
Rowden Rd
Beckenham BR3 ...185 B2
Chingford E4 ......35 C4
West Ewell KT19 ..215 A4
Rowditch La SW11 .137 A3
Rowdon Ave NW10 ..68 B1
Rowdowns Rd RM9 ..81 B1
Rowe Gdns IG11 ..102 A5
Rowe La E9 ....74 C3
Rowena Cres SW11 .136 C3
Rowe Wlk HA2 .....63 C5
Rowfant Rd SW12,
SW17 ....159 A4
Rowhill Mans [11] E5 .74 B4
Rowhill Rd E5 .....74 B4
Rowington Cl W2 ...91 D2
Rowland Ave HA3 ..43 C6
Rowland Ct E16 ....98 D3
Rowland Gr SE26 .162 B1
Rowland Hill Almshouses
TW15 ....170 C5
Rowland Hill Ave N17 .33 B4
Rowland Hill Ho SE1 251 C2
Rowland Hill St NW3 .70 C3
Rowlands Ave HA5 ..23 D4
Rowlands Cl N6 ....49 A3
NW7 ....28 A3
Rowlands Rd RM8 ..81 C6
Rowland Way
Ashford TW15 .....171 B3
Merton SW19 .....179 D1
Rowley Ave DA15 .168 B4
Rowley Cl HA0 .....66 B1
Rowley Gdns N4 ...51 A2
Rowley Green Rd EN5 .12 A6
Rowley Ho SE8 ...141 C6
Rowley Ind Pk W3 .110 D3
Rowley La EN5 .....11 D6
Rowley Rd N15 ....51 A4
Rowlheys Pl UB7 ..104 A3
Rowlls Rd KT1 .....198 B6
Rowney Gdns RM9 .80 C2
Rowney Rd RM9 ...80 B2
Rowntree Cl NW6 ..69 C2
Rowntree Clifford Cl [7]
E13 ....99 B4
Rowntree Path [1]
SE28 ....124 B5
Rowntree Rd TW2 .152 C3
Rowse Cl E15 .....98 A6
Rowsham Ct HA1 ..64 C6
Rowsley Ave NW4 ..46 C6
Rowstock [1] NW5 ..71 D2
Rowstock Gdns N7 .71 D3
Rowton Rd SE18 ..145 A5
Roxborough Ave
Harrow HA1 ....42 C2
Hounslow TW7 ...130 D5
Roxborough Pk HA1 .42 C2
Roxborough Rd HA1 .42 C2
Roxbourne Cl UB5 ..62 D2
Roxbourne Fst & Mid Schs
HA2 ....63 A6
Roxburgh Rd SE27 .182 D5
Roxburn Way HA4 ..61 C5
Roxby Pl SW6 135 C6 265 B6
Roxeth Ct TW15 ...170 C5
Roxeth Fst & Mid Sch
HA2 ....64 B6
Roxeth Gr HA2 .....63 D4
Roxeth Green Ave
HA2 ....63 D6
Roxeth Hill HA2 ....64 C4
Roxeth Manor Fst & Mid
Schs HA2 ....63 C5
Roxeth Mead Sch HA2 64 B6
Roxford Cl TW17 ..193 C4

Roxford Ho [2] E3 ...97 D3
Roxley Rd SE13 ...163 D5
Roxton Gdns CR0 .223 C3
Roxwell [10] NW1 ..71 B2
Roxwell Rd W12 ...112 A4
Barking IG11 ......102 A5
Roxwell Trad Pk E10 .53 A2
Roxwell Way IG8 ...37 C3
Roxy Ave RM6 .....58 C6
Royal Academy of
Dramatic Art*
WC1 ....93 D2 239 C4
Royal Acad of Arts*
W1 ....115 C6 249 A5
Royal Acad of Dance
SW11 ....266 D1
Royal Acad of Music
NW1 ....238 B5
Royal Albert Hall*
SW7 ....114 B4 246 C1
Royal Albert Rd E16 .122 D6
Royal Albert Sta E16 122 A6
Royal Albert Way
E16 ....122 B6
Royal Arc W1 .....249 A5
Royal Army Medical Coll
SW1 ....116 A1 260 A2
Royal Ave
SW3 ....114 D1 257 C2
Worcester Park KT4 .215 C6
Royal Avenue Ho
SW3 ....257 C2
Royal Ballet Sch The
WC2 ....240 B1
Royal Brompton Hospl
SW3 ....114 B1 256 C2
SW3 ....114 C1 257 B1
Royal Cir SE27 ....160 D1
Royal Cl BR6 ......226 D4
N16 ....51 C1
SE8 ....141 B6
Hillingdon UB7 ....82 B1
Ilford IG3 ....58 A2
Putney SW19 .....156 D2
Worcester Park KT4 .215 C6
Royal College St
NW1 ....93 C6 232 B6
Royal Coll of Anaesthetists
WC1 ....94 A2 240 B4
Royal Coll of Art
SW7 ....114 B4 246 C1
Royal Coll of Art Sculpture
Sch SW11 ..136 C5 267 A3
Royal Coll of Midwives
W1 ....93 B2 238 C3
Royal Coll of Music
SW7 ....114 B3 256 C6
Royal Coll of Obstetricians
& Gynaecologists
NW1 ....92 D3 237 C6
Royal Coll of Physicians
NW1 ....93 B3 238 D6
Royal Coll of Science
SW7 ....114 B3 256 C6
Royal Coll of Surgeons
WC2 ....94 B1 240 D2
Royal Connaught Apps
E16 ....121 D5
Royal Courts of Justice
WC2 ....94 C1 241 A1
Royal Cres
W11 ....113 A5 244 A3
Ruislip HA4 ....63 A5
Royal Crescent Mews
W11 ....112 D5
Royal Ct SE16 ....119 B3
SE9 ....166 B3
Enfield EN1 ....17 C5
[9] Kingston KT2 .176 D3
Royal Docks Rd E6 .100 D2
Royal Duchess Mews
SW12 ....159 B4
Royal Exchange*
EC3 ....242 D1
Royal Exchange Ave
EC3 ....242 D1
Royal Exchange Bldgs
EC3 ....242 D1
Royal Festival Hall*
SE1 ....116 B3 250 D3
Royal Free Hospl NW3 70 C3
Royal Gdns W7 ...109 A3
Royal Geographical
Society SW7 114 B4 246 D1
Royal Hill SE10 ...142 A5
Royal Horticultural Society
(Lawrence Hall & Conf
Ctr) SW1 ....259 D5
Royal Horticultural Society
(Lindley Hall) SW1 .259 C4

Royal Hospital (Army
Pensioners)*
SW1 ....115 A1 258 A1
Royal Hospital Rd
SW3 ....114 D1 257 D1
Royal Hospl and Home
SW15 ....157 A5
Royal La Hillingdon UB7 .82 B1
Hillingdon UB8 .....82 B3
Royal Langford [3]
NW6 ....91 B5
Royal London Est N17 34 B4
Royal London Est The
.................89 D6
Royal London
Homeopathic Hospl The
WC1 ....94 A2 240 B4
Royal London Hospl (Mile
End) The E2 ....96 D4
Royal London Hospl (St
Clements) The E3 ..97 B4
Royal London Hospl
(Whitechapel) The
E1 ....96 B2
Royal Marsden Hospl
SW3 ....114 B1 256 D2
Royal Mews KT8 ..196 B3
Royal Mews The*
SW1 ....115 B3 258 D6
Royal Military Sch of
Music (Kneller Hall)
TW2 ....152 B5
Royal Mint Pl [5] E1 .118 A6
Royal Mint St
E1 ....117 D6 253 D6
Royal National
Orthopaedic Hospl
W1 ....93 B3 238 D5
Stanmore HA7 ......9 C2
Royal National TNE Hospl
The WC1 ..94 B4 233 C2
Royal Nat TN&E Hospl The
W5 ....87 C2
Royal Naval Pl SE14 .141 B5
Royal Oak Ct [9] N1 .95 C4
Dagenham RM8 ...80 C6
Royal Oak Pl SE22 .162 B5
Royal Oak Rd [5] E8 ..74 B2
Bexley DA6 ....147 C1
Royal Oak Sta W2 ..91 D2
Royal Opera Arc
SW1 ....249 C4
Royal Orchard Cl
SW18 ....157 A4
Royal Par BR7 ....189 A3
SE3 ....142 B2
SW6 ....264 A4
Ealing W5 ....88 A4
[11] Dagenham RM10 ..81 D2
Royal Parade Mews
BR7 ....189 A3
Royal Park Prim Sch
DA14 ....169 A1
Royal Pl [11] SE10 .142 A5
Royal Rd DA14 ...168 D1
E16 ....99 D1
SE17 ....138 D6
Teddington TW11 .174 B5
Royal Route HA9 ...66 B4
Royal Russell Sch
(Ballards) CR0 ....222 B3
Royal Sch Hampstead The
NW3 ....70 B3
Royal St SE1 116 B3 260 D6
Royalty Mews W1 .239 C1
Royalty Studios W11 .91 A1
Royal United Services
Mus* SW1 ....250 A3
Royal Veterinary Coll
NW1 ....93 D6 232 C5
Royal Victoria Pl E16 121 B5
Royal Victoria Sta
E16 ....121 A6
Royal Victor Pl E3 ..96 D5
Royal Wlk SM6 ...219 B5
Roycraft Ave IG11 .101 C5
Roycroft Cl
Streatham SW2 ...160 C3
Woodford E18 .....37 B2
Roydene Rd SE18 .123 C1
Roydon Cl [7] SW11 .136 D3
Roy Gdns IG2 .....57 D4
Roy Gr TW12 .....173 D4
Roy Ho N1 ....235 D3
Royle Cres W13 ...87 A3
Roymount Ct TW2 .152 C1

Roy Ridley Ho 6
SW4 . . . . .137 D2
Roy Sq E14 . . . . .119 A6
Royston Ave
Carshalton SM1 . . . . . .218 B5
Chingford E4 . . . . .35 D5
Wallington SM6 . . . . . .219 D4
Royston Cl
Cranford TW5 . . . . . . .128 B4
Walton-on-T KT12 . . .194 A1
Royston Ct 1 E13 . . . .99 A6
Hinchley Wood KT10 . .212 D6
Redbridge IG1 . . . . . . .55 D3
3 Richmond TW9 . . .132 B4
Tolworth KT6 . . . . . . .214 C6
Royston Gdns IG1 . . . .55 D3
Royston Gr HA5 . . . . . .23 C4
Royston Ho N11 . . . . . .31 A6
14 SE15 . . . . .140 A6
Royston Par IG1 . . . . . .55 D3
Royston Park Rd HA5 .23 C5
Royston Prim Sch
SE20 . . . . .184 D2
Royston Rd
Penge SE20 . . . . .184 D2
Richmond TW10 . . . . .154 A6
Royston St 25 E2 . . . . .96 C5
Roystons The N1 . . . .198 D4
Rozel Ct 3 N1 . . . . . . .95 C6
Rozel Rd SW4 . . . . . . .137 C2
Rubastic Rd UB2 . . . . .106 C3
Rubens Rd UB5 . . . . . .84 D5
Rubens St SE6 . . . . . .163 B5
Rubin Pl EN3 . . . . .7 C6
Ruby Rd E17 . . . . .53 C6
Ruby St NW10 . . . . . . .67 A1
SE15 . . . . .140 B6
Ruby Triangle SE15 . .140 B6
Ruckholt Cl E10 . . . . . .75 D5
Ruckholt Rd E10 . . . . .75 D5
Rucklidge Ave NW10 . .90 A5
Rudall Cres NW3 . . . .70 B4
Rudbeck Ho 10 SE15 .140 A5
Ruddington Cl E5 . . . . .75 A4
Ruddock Cl HA8 . . . . . .27 A3
Ruddstreet Cl SE18 . .123 A2
Rudge Ho 1 SE16 . . .118 A3
Rudgwick Terr
NW8 . . . . .92 C6 230 B5
Rudhall Ho 4 SW2 . .160 C5
Rudland Rd DA7 . . . . .147 D2
Rudloe Rd SW12 . . . . .159 C4
Rudolf Pl SW8 . . . . . . .270 B5
Rudolph Ct SE22 . . . .162 B4
Rudolph Rd E13 . . . . . .98 D5
NW6 . . . . .91 C5
Rudstone Ho 10 E3 . . .97 D4
Rudyard Ct SE1 . . . . . .252 D1
Rudyard Gr NW7 . . . . .27 A4
Ruegg Ho 5 SE18 . . .144 C6
Ruffetts Cl CR2 . . . . . .222 B1
Ruffetts The CR2 . . . .222 B1
Ruffle Cl UB7 . . . . . . .104 B4
Rufford Cl HA3 . . . . . . .43 A3
Rufford St N1 . .94 A6 233 B6
Rufford Street Mews
N1 . . . . .72 A1
Rufford Twr 5 W3 . .110 D5
Rufforth Ct 1 NW9 . . .27 C2
Rufus Bsns Ctr SW18 157 D2
Rufus Cl HA4 . . . . .63 A5
Rufus Ho SE1 . . . . . . .263 D6
Rufus St N1 . . . . .95 C4
Rugby Ave
Edmonton N9 . . . . . . .17 D3
Northolt UB6 . . . . .64 B2
Wembley HA0 . . . . . . .65 C4
Rugby Cl HA1 . . . . .42 C5
Rugby Gdns RM9 . . . . .80 C2
Rugby Mans W14 . . . .254 B4
Rugby Rd NW9 . . . . . . .44 D5
W4 . . . . .111 C4
Dagenham RM9 . . . . . .80 C2
Twickenham TW1,TW2,
TW7 . . . . .152 C5
Rugby St WC1 .94 B3 240 C6
Rugg St E14 . . . . .119 C6
Rugless Ho 2 E14 . . .120 A4
Rugmere 4 NW1 . . . . .71 A1
Ruislip Cl UB6 . . . . . . .85 D3
Ruislip Ct HA4 . . . . . . .61 D6
Ruislip Gardens Prim Sch
HA4 . . . . .61 D4
Ruislip Gardens Sta
HA4 . . . . .62 A4
Ruislip Lido★ HA4,HA5 39 B5

Ruislip Lido Railway★
HA4 . . . . .39 B5
Ruislip Manor Sta
HA4 . . . . .40 A1
Ruislip Rd UB6,UB5 . . .85 C4
Ruislip Rd E
Ealing UB6,W7 . . . . . .86 D3
Greenford UB6 . . . . . . .86 B3
Ruislip St SW17 . . . . .180 D6
Ruislip Sta HA4 . . . . . .39 D1
Rumball Ho 22 SE5 . .139 C5
Rum Cl E1 . . . . .118 C6
Rumbold Rd
SW6 . . . . .135 D5 265 D3
Rumford Ho SE1 . . . . .262 A5
Rumsey Cl TW12 . . . .173 B4
Rumsey Rd SW9 . . . . .138 B2
Runacres Ct SE17 . . . .262 A1
Runbury Circ NW9 . . . .67 B6
Runcorn Cl N17 . . . . . .52 B5
Runcorn Pl W11 . . . . .244 A6
Rundell Cres NW4 . . . .46 B4
Rundell Twr SW8 . . . .270 C2
Runes Cl CR4 . . . . . . .202 C2
Runnelfield HA1 . . . . . .64 C5
Running Horse Yd 12
TW8 . . . . .132 A6
Runnymede SW19 . . .180 B2
Runnymede Cl TW2 . .151 D4
Runnymede Cres
SW16 . . . . .182 A2
Runnymede Ct 1
SM6 . . . . .219 B2
Runnymede Gdns
Greenford UB6 . . . . . . .86 C5
Twickenham TW2 . . . .151 D4
Runnymede Ho E9 . . . .75 A4
Richmond TW10 . . . . .154 C6
Runnymede Rd TW2 .151 D6
Runway The HA4 . . . . .62 C3
Rupack St 3 SE16 . . .118 C4
Rupert Ave 6 HA9 . . .66 A3
Rupert Ct W1 . . . . . . .249 C6
Rupert Gdns SW9 . . . .138 D3
Rupert Ho SE11 . . . . .261 B3
NW6 . . . . .91 B5
W4 . . . . .111 C3
Rupert Rd N19 . . . . . .71 D6
NW6 . . . . .91 B5
W4 . . . . .111 C3
Rupert St W1 115 D6 249 C6
Rural Way SW16 . . . . .181 B3
Rusbridge Cl E8 . . . . . .74 C1
Ruscoe Ho 12 SW27 .182 D5
Ruscoe Rd E16 . . . . . . .98 D1
Ruscombe Way
TW14 . . . . .149 D4
Rusham Rd SW12 . . . .158 D4
Rushbrook Cres E17 . .35 B4
Rushbrook Ho 20
SW8 . . . . .137 D3
Rushbrook Rd SE9 . . .167 A2
Rushbury Ct 4 TW12 173 C2
Rushby Ct SW4 . . . . . .270 A1
Rush Common Mews 18
SW2 . . . . .160 B4
Rushcroft Rd
SW2,SW9 . . . . .138 C1
Chingford E4 . . . . .35 D3
Rush Croft Sch E4 . . .35 D3
Rushcutters Ct 18
SE16 . . . . .119 A2
Rushden Cl SE19 . . . .183 B3
Rushdene SE2 . . . . . . .124 D3
Rushdene Ave EN4 . . . .14 C4
Rushdene Cl UB5 . . . . .84 C5
Rushdene Cres UB5 . .84 C4
Rushdene Rd HA5 . . . .40 D3
Rushden Gdns NW7 . .28 C4
Ilford IG5 . . . . .56 C6
Rushen Wlk SM5 . . . .202 B1
Rushet Rd BR5 . . . . . .190 A1
Rushett Cl KT7 . . . . . .197 B1
Rushett Rd KT7 . . . . . .197 B2
Rushey Cl KT3 . . . . . . .199 B5
Rushey Gn SE6 . . . . . .163 D4
Rushey Green Prim Sch
SE6 . . . . .163 D3
Rushey Hill EN2 . . . . . .4 B1
Rushey Mead SE4 . . .163 C6
Rushford Rd SE4 . . . .163 B5
Rush Green Rd RM7,
RM8,RM10 . . . . .59 D1
Rushgrove Ave NW9 . .45 D5
Rushgrove Ct SW9 . . . .45 C4
Rushgrove St SE18 . .122 C4
Rush Hill Mews 3
SW11 . . . . .137 A2
Rush Hill Rd SW11 . . .137 A2
Rushlake Ho 3
SW11 . . . . .137 A4
Rushley Cl BR2 . . . . . .226 A4

Rushman Villas KT3 .199 D5
Rushmead 5 E2 . . . . .96 B4
Richmond TW10 . . . . .153 B5
Rushmead Cl CR0 . . . .221 D4
Rushmere Ct KT4 . . . .216 A6
Rushmere Ho 2
SW15 . . . . .156 A3
Rushmere Pl SW19 . .178 D5
Rushmon Pl SM3 . . . .217 A2
Rushmoor Cl HA5 . . . .40 B5
Rushmore Cl BR1 . . . .210 A6
Rushmore Cres 9 E5 .74 D4
Rushmore Ho 9 N7 . .71 D3
W14 . . . . .254 B5
Rushmore Prim Sch
E5 . . . . .74 D4
Rushmore Rd E5 . . . . .74 D4
E5 . . . . .75 A4
Rusholme Ave RM10 . .81 C5
Rusholme Gr SE19 . . .183 C5
Rusholme Rd SW15 . .157 A5
Rushout Ave HA3 . . . . .43 B3
Rush The SW20 . . . . . .179 B2
Rushton Ho 26 SW8 .137 D3
Rushton St N1 95 B5 235 D4
Rushworth St
SE1 . . . . .116 D4 251 D1
Rushy Meadow La
SM5 . . . . .218 C5
Rushy Meadow Prim Sch
SM5 . . . . .218 C5
Ruskin Ave DA16 . . . .146 A3
E12 . . . . .78 A2
Feltham TW14 . . . . . .149 D5
Richmond TW9 . . . . . .132 C5
Ruskin Cl NW11 . . . . . .47 D3
Ruskin Ct SE5 . . . . . . .139 B2
SE9 . . . . .166 B5
Southgate N21 . . . . . .16 B4
Ruskin Dr BR6 . . . . . .227 C5
DA16 . . . . .146 A2
North Cheam KT4 . . . .216 C6
Ruskin Gdns Ealing W5 87 D3
Harrow HA3 . . . . .44 B5
Ruskin Gr DA16 . . . . .146 A3
Ruskin Ho SW1 . . . . . .259 D3
Ruskin Par CR0 . . . . . .221 B3
Ruskin Park Ho SE5 .139 B2
Ruskin Rd
Belvedere DA17 . . . . .125 C2
Croydon CR0 . . . . .220 D6
Isleworth TW7 . . . . . .130 D2
Southall UB1 . . . . .107 A6
Tottenham N17 . . . . . .33 D2
Wallington SM5 . . . . .219 A3
Ruskin Wlk SW19 . . . .180 B2
Harrow HA3 . . . . .44 B5
SE24 . . . . .161 A6
Edmonton N9 . . . . . . .18 A2
Rusland Ave BR6 . . . .227 B5
Rusland Hts HA1 . . . . .42 C5
Rusland Park Rd HA1 .42 C5
Rusper Cl NW2 . . . . . .68 C5
Stanmore HA7 . . . . . . .25 C6
Rusper Ct SW9 . . . . . .138 A3
Rusper Rd N17,N22 . .51 A6
Dagenham RM9 . . . . . .80 C2
Russel Ct BR3 . . . . . . .208 A6
Russel Ct N14 . . . . . . .15 D6
Russell Ave N22 . . . . .32 D1
Russell Cl DA7 . . . . . . .147 C1
NW10 . . . . .67 A1
SE7 . . . . .143 C5
Chiswick W4 . . . . .133 D6
Ruislip HA4 . . . . .62 C6
Russell Ct 4 E10 . . . .53 D2
5 SE15 . . . . .140 B3
SW1 . . . . .249 B3
SW11 . . . . .268 B1
Bromley BR1 . . . . .186 D3
New Barnet EN5 . . . . . .2 A1
Streatham SW16 . . . .182 B5
Surbiton KT6 . . . . . . .198 A4
Wallington SM6 . . . . .219 C3
Wembley HA0 . . . . . . .66 A1
Russell Gdns N20 . . . .14 C2
NW11 . . . . .47 A3
W14 . . . . .113 A3 254 A6
Ilford IG2 . . . . .57 B2
Richmond TW10 . . . . .153 C2
West Drayton UB7 . . .104 C1
Russell Gdns Mews
W14 . . . . .113 A3 254 A6
Russell Gr NW7 . . . . . .27 C6
33 SW9 . . . . .138 C4
Russell Ho 15 E14 . . .97 C1
SW1 . . . . .259 D2
Russell Kerr Cl W4 . .133 A5
Russell La N20 . . . . . . .14 D2
Russell Lo 5 E4 . . . . .20 A2

Russell Lodge SE1 . . .262 C6
Russell Mans WC1 . . .240 B4
Russell Par NW11 . . . .47 A3
Russell Pickering Ho 2
SW4 . . . . .138 A2
Russell Pl NW3 . . . . . .70 C3
SE16 . . . . .119 A3
Russell Prim Sch The
TW10 . . . . .153 D3
Russell Rd E10 . . . . . .53 D3
E17 . . . . .53 B6
E4 . . . . .35 B6
N15 . . . . .51 C4
N20 . . . . .14 C2
N8 . . . . .49 D3
NW9 . . . . .45 D3
W14 . . . . .113 A3 254 B5
Bowes Park N13 . . . . .32 B4
Buckhurst Hill IG9 . . . .21 C3
Enfield EN1 . . . . .5 D5
Merton SW19 . . . . . . .179 C3
Mitcham CR4 . . . . . . .202 C6
Newham E16 . . . . .99 B1
Northolt UB5 . . . . .64 A3
Shepperton TW17 . . . .193 A2
Twickenham TW1,TW2 .152 D5
Walton-on-T KT12 . . .194 A3
Russell Sch The
TW10 . . . . .153 D2
Russell Sq
WC1 . . . . .94 A3 240 A5
Russell Square Mans
WC1 . . . . .240 B4
Russell Square Sta
WC1 . . . . .94 A3 240 A5
Russell St
WC2 . . . . .116 A6 250 B6
Russell's Wharf 2 W9 91 B3
Russell Way SM1 . . . .217 D3
Russell Wlk 4 TW10 154 B5
Russet Ave TW16,
TW17 . . . . .193 C6
Russet Cl UB10 . . . . . .83 A3
Russet Cres N7 . . . . . .72 B3
Russet Ct NW2 . . . . . .68 B5
6 Barnet EN4 . . . . . .2 C1
Russet Dr CR0 . . . . . . .207 A1
Russet Ho TW3 . . . . . .129 B1
Russet House Sch EN1 .6 B4
Russets Cl E4 . . . . .36 B6
Russett Way SE13 . . .141 D3
Russia Ct EC2 . . . . . . .242 B2
Russia Dock Rd SE16 119 A5
Russia La E2 . . . . .96 C5
Russian Submarine
SE18 . . . . .121 D3
Russia Row EC2 . . . . .242 B1
Russington Rd TW17 .193 B3
Rusthall Ave W4 . . . . .111 B3
Rusthall Cl CR0 . . . . . .206 C3
Rusthall Mans W4 . . .111 B2
Rustic Ave SW16 . . . .181 B3
Rustic Pl HA0 . . . . .65 D4
Rustic Wlk 6 E16 . . . .99 B1
Rustington Wlk SM4 .201 B2
Ruston Ave KT5 . . . . . .198 C2
Ruston Gdns N14 . . . .15 A5
Ruston Mews W11 . . . .91 A1
Ruston Rd SE18 . . . . .122 A3
Ruston St E3 . . . . .97 B6
Rust Sq SE5 . . . . .139 C5
Rutford Rd SW16 . . . .182 A5
Ruth Cl HA7 . . . . .44 B5
Ruth Ct 14 E3 . . . . . . .97 A5
Rutherford Cl
Hillingdon UB8 . . . . . .82 A3
Sutton SM2 . . . . .218 B2
Rutherford Ho 12 E1 .96 B3
Teddington TW11 . . . .174 D5
7 Wembley HA9 . . . .67 A5
Rutherford St
SW1 . . . . .115 D2 259 C6
Rutherford Twr 10
UB1 . . . . .85 D1
Rutherford Way
Bushey WD23 . . . . . . .8 C2
Wembley HA9 . . . . . . .66 C4
Rutherglen Rd SE2 . .146 A6
Rutherwyke Cl KT17 .216 A2
Ruth Ho W10 . . . . .91 A3
Ruthin Cl NW9 . . . . . . .45 C3
Ruthin Rd SE3 . . . . . . .143 A6
Ruthven St E9 . . . . . . .96 D6
Rutland Ave DA15 . . . .168 A4
Chessington KT9 . . . . .214 B2
Mitcham SW19 . . . . . .180 C3
Mortlake SW14 . . . . . .133 A2
Rutland Cl DA5 . . . . . .168 D3
SW7 . . . . .247 B1
Rutland Lo N17 . . . . . .34 A2

Rutland Ct continued
15 Acton W3 . . . . . . .88 C1
Chislehurst BR7 . . . . .188 C2
Enfield EN3 . . . . .18 B6
Sidcup BR7 . . . . .167 A2
Rutland Dr
Morden SM4 . . . . .201 C3
Richmond TW10 . . . . .154 A3
Rutland Gate
SW7 . . . . .114 C4 247 B1
Beckenham BR2 . . . . .208 D5
Belvedere DA17 . . . . .125 D1
Rutland Gate Mews
SW7 . . . . .247 A1
Rutland Gdns N4 . . . . .51 A3
SW7 . . . . .114 C4 247 B1
Dagenham RM8 . . . . . .80 C1
Ealing W13 . . . . .87 A2
South Croydon CR0 . . .221 C4
Rutland Gdns Mews
SW7 . . . . .247 B1
Rutland Gr W6 . . . . . .112 B1
Rutland Ho 18 SE18 .122 B2
W8 . . . . .255 C5
6 Northolt UB5 . . . . .63 C2
2 Penge SE20 . . . . .184 C2
10 Putney SW15 . . .156 C4
Tolworth KT6 . . . . . . .198 C1
Rutland Mews E SW7 257 B6
Rutland Mews S
SW7 . . . . .257 A6
Rutland Mews W
SW7 . . . . .257 A6
Rutland Park Gdns
NW2 . . . . .68 C2
Rutland Park Mans
NW2 . . . . .68 C2
Rutland Pk NW2 . . . . .68 C2
Forest Hill SE6 . . . . . .163 B2
Rutland Pl EC1 . . . . . .241 D4
Bushey WD23 . . . . . . .8 B3
Rutland Rd E17 . . . . . .53 C3
E7 . . . . .77 D1
E9 . . . . .96 C6
Harrow HA1 . . . . .42 A3
Hayes UB3 . . . . .105 B2
Ilford IG1 . . . . .78 D5
Mitcham SW19 . . . . . .180 C3
Southall UB1 . . . . .85 C2
Twickenham TW2 . . . .152 B2
Wanstead E11 . . . . . . .55 B4
Rutland St SW7 . . . . . .257 B6
Rutland Studios NW10 90 A4
Rutley Cl SE11 . . . . . . .138 C6
Rutlish Rd SW19 . . . .179 C2
Rutlish Sch (Boys)
SW20 . . . . .179 B1
Rutter Gdns CR4 . . . .202 B5
Rutters Cl UB7 . . . . . .104 C4
Rutt's Terr SE14 . . . . .140 D4
Rutts The WD23 . . . . .8 B3
Ruvigny Gdns SW15 .134 D2
Ruvigny Mans SW15 .134 D2
Ruxbury Ct TW15 . . . .148 A1
Ruxley Cl
Chessington KT19 . . . .214 D3
Sidcup DA14 . . . . .191 A4
Ruxley Cnr DA14 . . . . .191 A4
Ruxley Corner Ind Est
DA14 . . . . .190 D4
Ruxley Cres KT10 . . . .213 B5
Ruxley Ct KT19 . . . . . .215 A3
Ruxley Gdns TW17 . . .193 A4
Ruxley La KT19 . . . . . .215 B3
Ruxley Mews KT19 . . .214 D3
Ruxley Ridge KT10 . . .213 A1
Ryall's Ct N20 . . . . . . .14 D1
Ryan Cl SE9 . . . . .143 C1
Ruislip HA4 . . . . .40 B1
Ryan Ct SW16 . . . . . . .182 A3
Ryan Dr TW8 . . . . .131 A6
Ryan Ho 3 HA1 . . . . .42 D4
Ryarsh Cres BR6 . . . .227 C4
Rycott Path SE22 . . . .162 A4
Rycroft Way N17 . . . . .51 D6
Ryculff Sq SE3 . . . . . .142 D3
Rydal Cl NW4 . . . . . . .29 A2
Rydal Cres UB6 . . . . . .87 C5
Rydal Ct Edgware HA8 .26 B5
Wembley HA9 . . . . . . .44 A2
Rydal Dr DA7 . . . . .147 C4
West Wickham BR4 . . .224 C6
Rydal Gdns NW9 . . . . .45 C4
Kingston SW15 . . . . . .177 C5
Twickenham TW2,TW3 .151 D5
Wembley HA9 . . . . . . .43 C1
Rydal Ho 25 SW8 . . . .137 D3
Rydal Lo N17 . . . . .34 A2

Rydal Rd SW16 . . . . . .181 D6
Rydal Water NW1 . . . .232 A1
Chislehurst BR7 . . . . .188 C2
Ruislip HA4 . . . . .62 C4
Ryde Ho 1 NW6 . . . . .91 C6
Rydens Ho SE9 . . . . . .165 C1
Rydens Rd KT12 . . . . .194 D1
Ryde Pl TW1 . . . . .153 D5
Ryder Cl BR1 . . . . .187 B5
Ryder Ct E10 . . . . .75 D6
SW1 . . . . .249 B2
Ryder Dr SE16 . . . . . . .118 B3
Ryder Ho 14 E1 . . . . .96 C3
5 Merton SW19 . . . .179 D2
Ryder St SW1 . . . . . . .249 B2
Ryder's Terr
NW8 . . . . .92 A5 229 A4
Ryder Yd SW1 . . . . . . .249 B2
Ryde Vale Rd SW12 . .159 C2
Rydon Mews SW19 . .178 C3
Rydons Cl SE9 . . . . . .144 A2
Rydon St N1 . . . . .235 B6
Rydston Cl 2 N7 . . . . .72 B1
Rye Cl DA5 . . . . .169 D5
Ryecotes Mead SE21 161 C3
Ryecroft Ave TW2 . . .151 D3
Ryecroft Cres EN5 . . .12 B6
Ryecroft Rd BR5 . . . . .211 B3
SE13 . . . . .164 A6
South Norwood SW16 .182 C4
Ryecroft St
SW6 . . . . .135 D4 265 C1
Rye Ct BR3 . . . . .185 B2
Ryedale SE22 . . . . . . .162 B5
Ryedale Ct 6 TW12 .173 C2
Ryefield Ave UB10 . . . .60 D1
Ryefield Cres HA5,HA6 22 A1
Ryefield Ct HA6 . . . . . .22 A1
Ryefield Path 7
SW15 . . . . .156 A3
Ryefield Prim Sch
UB10 . . . . .83 B6
Ryefield Rd SE19 . . . .183 A4
Ryegates 2 SE15 . . . .140 B3
Ryehill Ct KT3 . . . . . . .199 D2
Rye Hill Pk SE15 . . . .140 C1
Rye La SE15 . . . . .140 A3
Ryeland Cl UB7 . . . . . .82 A1
Ryelands Cres SE12 .165 C5
Ryelands Prim Sch
SE25 . . . . .206 B4
Rye Rd SE15 . . . . .140 D1
Rye The N14 . . . . .15 C4
Rye Way HA8 . . . . .26 B4
Rye Wlk SW15 . . . . . .156 D6
Ryfold Rd SW19 . . . . .157 C1
Ryhope Rd N11 . . . . . .31 B6
Ryland Cl TW13 . . . . .171 D6
Ryland Ct EN2 . . . . . . .5 B1
Rylandes Rd NW2 . . . .68 A5
Ryland Ho 11 SW16 .181 C5
Ryland Rd NW5 . . . . . .71 B2
Rylett Cres W12 . . . . .111 D3
Rylett Rd W12 . . . . . . .111 D3
Rylston Rd
SW6 . . . . .135 B6 264 C5
Edmonton N13 . . . . . .17 B1
Rylton Ho KT12 . . . . . .194 D1
Rymer Rd CR0 . . . . . . .205 C2
Rymer St SE24 . . . . . .160 D5
Rymill St E16 . . . . .122 C5
Rysbrack St SW1 . . . .257 C6
Rythe Cl KT9 . . . . .213 C1
Rythe Ct KT7 . . . . .197 A2
Rythe Ho 7 BR1 . . . .186 B5
Rythe Rd KT10 . . . . . .212 C4

S

Saatchi Gallery★
SE1 . . . . .250 C2
Sabah Ct TW15 . . . . . .170 C6
Sabbarton St 9 E16 . .98 D1
Sabella Ct E3 . . . . .97 B5
Sabine Rd SW11 . . . . .137 A2
Sable Cl TW4 . . . . .128 C2
Sable Ct 3 KT3 . . . . .199 C4
Sable St N1 . . . . .72 D1
Sach Rd E5 . . . . .74 D4
Sacketts Ho 24 SW9 .138 C4
Sackville Ave BR2 . . . .209 A1
Sackville Cl HA2 . . . . .64 C5
Sackville Gdns IG1 . . .56 D3
Sackville Ho N8 . . . . . .50 A5
16 Streatham SW16 .160 A1
Sackville Rd SM2 . . . .217 C2
Sackville St
W1 . . . . .115 C6 249 B6
Sacred Heart High Sch
W6 . . . . .112 C2

Sacred Heart Jun Sch
W6 ....112 D2
Sacred Heart Prim Sch,
Battersea SW11 ...136 C3
Sacred Heart RC High Sch
The HA3 ....24 C1
Sacred Heart RC Prim Sch
N20 ....14 C2
Putney SW15 ......156 A6
Ruislip HA4 ....61 C6
Teddington TW11 ...175 B3
West Barnes KT3 ...200 A5
Sacred Heart RC Sch The
SE5 ....139 A4
Saddlebrook Pk
TW16 ....171 C3
Saddlers Cl Barnet EN5 12 B6
Borehamwood WD6 ....11 B5
Pinner HA5 ....23 C5
Saddlers Mews SW8 .270 B2
Teddington KT1 ....175 C2
Wembley HA0 ....64 D4
Saddlers Path WD6 ...11 B6
Saddlescombe Way
N12 ....29 C5
Sadler Cl CR4 ......180 D1
Sadler Ho 17 E3 ....97 D4
EC1 ....234 C2
Sadlers Ride KT8 ...174 A1
Saffron Ave E14 ...120 B6
Saffron Cl NW11 ....47 B3
Thornton Heath CR0 ..204 A3
Saffron Ct E15 ......76 C3
10 N1 ....73 B2
Saffron Hill
EC1 ....94 C2 241 B4
Saffron St EC1 .....241 B4
Saffron Way KT6 ...197 D1
Saffron Wharf SE1 ..253 D2
Sage Cl 7 E6 ....100 B2
Sage Mews SE22 ...161 D6
Sage St E1 ....118 C6
Sage Way WC1 .....233 C1
Sage Yd KT6 ....198 B1
Sahara Cl UB1 .....107 A6
Saigasso Cl E16 .....99 D1
Sailmakers Ct SW6 .136 A2
Sail St E1 ...116 C3 260 D4
Saimet 3 NW9 ....27 C2
Sainfoin Rd SW17 ..159 A2
Sainsbury Rd SE19 .183 C5
St Agatha's Dr KT2 .176 B4
St Agatha's Gr SM5 .202 D1
St Agatha's RC Prim Sch
KT2 ....176 B4
St Agatha's RC Sch
KT2 ....176 B4
St Agnes Cl E9 ......96 C6
St Agnes Pl SE11 ...138 D6
St Agnes RC Prim Sch
E3 ....97 D4
St Agnes RC Sch NW2 69 A5
St Aidans Ct IG11 ...102 B5
St Aidan's Prim Sch
N4 ....50 C2
St Aidan's RC Prim Sch
IG1 ....57 B1
St Aidan's Rd SE22 .162 B6
W13 ....109 B4
St Albans Ave W4 ..111 B3
Feltham TW13 .....172 D5
St Alban's Ave E6 ..100 C4
EC1 ....94 C2 241 A4
St Alban's CE Prim Sch
EC1 ....94 C2 241 A4
St Alban's Cl NW11 ..47 C1
St Albans Cres N22 ..32 C2
St Alban's Cres IG8 ..37 A2
St Alban's Gdns
TW11 ....175 A5
St Alban's Gr
W8 ....113 D3 255 D6
Carshalton SM5 ...202 C1
St Albans Ho 2
SW16 ....182 C6
St Albans La NW11 ..47 C1
St Albans Mans W8 .255 D6
St Alban's Pl
N1 ....94 D6 234 C5
St Alban's RC Prim Sch
KT8 ....196 A4
St Albans Rd NW10 ..89 C6
NW5 ....71 B5
St Albans Rd Barnet EN5 1 A3
Cheam SM1 ....217 B4
Ilford IG3 ....57 D2
Kingston KT2 .....176 A4
St Alban's Rd IG8 ....37 A3
St Alban's St SW1 ..249 C5
St Albans Studios
W8 ....255 D6

St Albans Terr W6 .264 A6
St Alban's Villas NW5 .71 A5
St Alfege Pas SE10 .142 A6
St Alfege Rd SE7 ...143 D6
St Alfege with St Peter's
CE Prim Sch SE10 .142 A6
St Aloysius RC Inf Sch
NW1 ....232 D1
St Aloysius' RC Jun & Inf
Sch NW1 ....232 C2
St Aloysius RC Jun Sch
NW1 ....93 D5 232 D3
St Alphage Ct NW9 ..45 B6
St Alphage Gdn EC2 .242 B3
St Alphage Highwalk
EC2 ....242 B3
St Alphage Wlk HA8 ..27 A1
St Alphege Rd N9 ....18 C4
St Alphonsus Rd
SW4 ....137 D1
St Amunds Cl SE6 ..185 C6
St Andrew's CE Prim Sch
N1 ....94 B6 233 D6
N14 ....15 D3
SW9 ....138 A3
Enfield EN1 ....5 C3
St Andrew's CE Sch
N20 ....13 B2
St Andrews Cl 25
SE16 ....118 B1
St Andrew's Cl N12 ..30 A4
NW2 ....68 B5
St Andrews Cl
Erith SE28 ....102 A3
Hinchley Wood KT7 .197 B1
Ruislip HA4 ....62 D6
Stanmore HA7 ....25 C1
St Andrew's Cl
2 Hounslow TW7 ...130 C4
Upper Halliford TW17 .193 A5
St Andrew's Ct E17 ..35 A1
St Andrews Ct W4 ..133 A4
St Andrew's Ct
Kingston KT3 ......199 D6
Wandsworth SW18 .158 A4
St Andrews Dr HA7 ..25 C2
St Andrew's Gr N16 ..51 B1
St Andrew's Greek Sch
NW1 ....71 C2
St Andrew's High Sch
CR0 ....220 D4
St Andrew's Hill
EC4 ....94 D1 241 D1
St Andrews Ho 11
SE16 ....118 B3
St Andrew's Hospl E3 97 D3
St Andrew's Mans
W1 ....238 A3
St Andrew's Mews
N16 ....51 C1
St Andrews Mews
Greenwich SE3 .....143 A5
4 Streatham SW12 .159 D3
St Andrew's Pl NW1 .238 D6
St Andrews RC Prim Sch
SW16 ....182 A5
St Andrews Rd DA14 .168 D1
E17 ....35 A1
E9 ....18 C4
NW9 ....45 B1
St Andrew's Rd E11 ..54 C3
E13 ....99 B4
N9 ....47 B3
NW2 ....68 A2
W14 ....264 B6
W3 ....89 C1
W7 ....108 C4
St Andrews Rd SM5 .218 C5
St Andrew's Rd
3 Croydon CR0 ....221 A4
Enfield EN1 ....5 B2
Hillingdon UB10 .....82 B6
Redbridge IG1 ....56 B2
Surbiton KT6 ......197 D3
St Andrew's Sq W11 ..91 A1
Surbiton KT6 ......197 D3
St Andrew's & St Mark's CE
Jun Sch KT6 ......197 D4
St Andrews Terr
WD19 ....22 C5
St Andrew & St Francis CE
Prim Sch NW2 ......68 A2
St Andrew's Twr UB1 .108 A6
St Andrews Way E3 ..97 D3
St Andrew's Wharf
SE1 ....253 D2
St Angela's Ursuline
Convent Sch E7 ....77 B2

St Anna Rd EN5 .....12 D6
St Anne RC Prim Sch
E1 ....96 A3
St Annes Catholic High
Sch for Girls (Upper)
N13 ....32 C6
St Anne's CE Prim Sch
SW18 ....157 D6
St Anne's Cl N6 .....71 A5
St Annes Cl WD19 ...22 C6
St Anne's Ct NW6 ....91 A6
W1 ....239 C1
St Annes Flats NW1 .232 C2
St Annes Gdns NW10 .88 B4
St Anne's Pas E14 ...97 B1
St Anne's Prim Sch
TW19 ....148 A4
St Anne's RC Prim Sch
SE11 ....138 B6 270 C6
St Anne's Rd E11 ....76 B6
Wembley HA0 ....65 D3
St Anne's Row E14 ..97 B1
St Anne St E14 ......97 B1
St Anne's Trad Est E14 97 B1
St Ann's IG11 ....101 A6
St Ann's CE Prim Sch
N15 ....51 B4
St Ann's Cres SW18 .158 A5
St Ann's Ct NW4 .....46 B6
St Ann's Ctr HA1 ....42 C3
St Ann's Gdns NW5 ..71 A2
St Ann's General Hospl
N4,N15 ....51 A4
St Ann's Hill SW18 .158 A5
St Ann's Ho WC1 ...234 A1
St Ann's La SW1 ...259 D5
St Ann's Park Rd
SW18 ....158 A5
St Ann's Rd N15 .....51 B4
W11 ....112 D6
St Anns Rd SW13 ...133 D4
St Ann's Rd
2 Barking IG11 .....101 A6
Edmonton N9 ....17 D3
Harrow HA1 ....42 C3
St Ann's Sch
Ealing W7 ....108 C5
Morden SM4 ....201 D4
St Ann's St
SW1 ....115 D3 259 D6
St Ann's Terr
NW8 ....92 B5 229 D4
St Ann's Villas
W11 ....112 D5 244 A3
St Ann's Way CR2 ..220 D2
St Anselm RC Prim Sch
UB2 ....107 B3
St Anselm's Ct SW16 .182 A5
St Anselm's Pl W1 .248 C6
St Anselm's RC Prim Sch
Harrow HA1 ....42 C2
Upper Tooting SW17 .159 A1
St Anselms Rd UB3 .105 D4
St Anthony's Ave IG8 .37 C3
St Anthony's Cl 8
E1 ....118 C4
St Anthonys Cl SW17 158 C2
St Anthony's Ct
2 SW12 ....159 A5
Orpington BR6 .....226 D6
Upper Tooting SW17 .159 A2
St Anthony's Flats
NW1 ....232 C2
St Anthony Hospl
KT4 ....200 D1
St Anthony's RC Prim Sch
E7 ....77 B1
SE22 ....162 A5
Penge SE20 ....184 B2
St Anthony's Way
TW14 ....127 D1
St Antony's RC Prim Sch
IG8 ....37 A6
St Antony's Rd E7 ...77 B1
St Arvans Cl CR0 ...221 C5
St Asaph Cl SE4 ....140 D2
St Asaph Rd SE4 ...140 D2
St Aubins Ct N1 ....235 D6
St Aubyns E18 ....54 D5
St Aubyns Ave
Hounslow TW3,TW4 .151 C6
Wimbledon SW19 ...179 B5
St Aubyns Cl BR6 ..227 D5
St Aubyn's Cl BR6 ..227 D6
St Aubyns Gdns BR6 .227 D6
St Aubyn's Prep Sch
IG8 ....36 D3
St Aubyn's Rd SE19 .183 D4
St Aubyn's Sch IG8 ..36 D3
St Audrey Ave DA7 .147 C3

St Augustine's Ave
BR1,BR2 ....210 A4
Ealing W5 ....88 A4
South Croydon CR2 .221 A1
Wembley HA9 ....66 A5
St Augustine's CE High Sch
NW6 ....91 C5
St Augustine's CE Prim
Sch NW6 ....91 D5
St Augustine's Ct E11 .54 D1
St Augustine's Ct BR3 185 A1
St Augustine's Prim Sch
DA17 ....125 B2
St Augustine's RC Prim
Sch
W6 ....135 A6 264 B5
Ilford IG2 ....56 D4
St Augustine's Rd
DA17 ....125 B2
NW1 ....71 C1
St Augustines's RC Prim
Sch SE6 ....186 A5
St Austell Cl HA8 ....26 B1
St Austell Rd SE13 .142 B3
St Awdry's Rd IG11 ..79 B1
St Barnabas CE Prim Sch
SW1 ....115 A4 258 B2
St Barnabas Cl
11 SE22 ....161 C6
Beckenham BR3 ...186 A1
St Barnabas Gdns
KT8 ....195 C4
St Barnabas Rd E17 .53 C3
Mitcham CR4 ......181 A4
Sutton SM1 ....218 B3
Woodford IG8 ....37 B3
St Barnabas St SW1 .258 B2
St Barnabas & St Philip's
CE Prim Sch
W8 ....113 C3 255 A5
St Barnabas Terr E9 .74 D3
St Barnabas Villas
SW8 ....138 A4 270 B2
St Bartholomews CE Prim
Sch SE26 ....162 C1
St Bartholomew's CE Prim
Sch SE26 ....184 C6
St Bartholomew's Cl
SE26 ....184 C6
St Bartholomew's Hospl
EC1 ....94 D2 241 D3
St Bartholomew's Rd
E6 ....100 B5
St Bede's RC Inf Sch
SW12 ....159 D3
St Bede's RC Prim Sch
RM6 ....58 C4
St Benedict's Cl
SW17 ....181 A4
St Benedict's Jun Sch
W5 ....87 C2
St Benedict's Sch W5 87 D2
St Benets Cl SW17 .158 C2
St Benet's Gr SM5 ..202 A4
St Benet's Pl EC3 ...252 D6
St Bernadette RC Jun Sch
SW12 ....159 C4
St Bernadette's RC Fst &
Mid Sch HA3 ....44 B5
St Bernadette's RC Prim
Sch UB10 ....82 D6
St Bernard Ho 6
E14 ....120 A3
St Bernards CR0 ...221 C5
St Bernards Cl 8
SE27 ....183 B6
St Bernards Ho 1
KT6 ....214 A6
St Bernard's Rd E6 ..99 D6
St Blaise Ave BR1 ..187 B1
St Bonaventure's RC Sec
Sch E7 ....77 A1
St Boniface Catholic Prim
Sch SW17 ....180 D5
St Botolph St
E1,EC3 .....95 D1 243 C2
St Brelades Ct N1 ..235 D6
St Bride's Ave EC4 .241 C1
St Brides Cl DA18 ..124 D4
Edgware HA8 ....26 B2
St Bride's Pas EC4 .241 C1
St Bride St
EC4 ....94 D1 241 C2
St Catherines Cl
Chessington KT9 ...213 C4
Upper Tooting SW17 .158 C2
St Catherine's Convent
Girls Prep & Senior Schs
TW1 ....153 A2

St Catherine's Ct 8
W4 ....111 C3
St Catherines Ct
TW13 ....150 A3
St Catherine's Dr
SE14 ....140 D5
St Catherines Farm Ct
HA4 ....39 A3
St Catherines Mews
SW3 ....257 C2
St Catherine's RC Mid Sch
SW20 ....200 C4
St Catherine's RC Prim Sch
EN5 ....1 C1
St Catherine's RC Sch for
Girls DA6 ....169 A4
St Catherines Rd
Chingford E4 ....19 C2
Ruislip HA4 ....39 B3
St Cecilia's Cl SM3 .201 A1
St Cecilia's RC Prim Sch
SM3 ....216 D6
St Chads Cl KT6 ....197 C2
St Chad's Gdns RM6 .59 A2
St Chad's Pl WC1 ..233 C2
St Chad's RC Prim Sch
SE25 ....205 C4
St Chad's Rd RM6 ...59 A2
St Chad's St WC1 ..233 B2
St Charles' Hospl W10 90 D2
St Charles Pl W10 ...91 A2
St Charles RC Prim Sch
W10 ....90 D2
St Charles RC Sixth Form
Coll W10 ....90 D2
St Charles Sq W10 ..90 D2
St Christina's Sch
NW8 ....92 C5 230 A3
St Christopher's Cl
TW7 ....130 C4
St Christophers Dr
UB3 ....106 B6
St Christophers Gdns
CR7 ....204 C6
St Christopher's Ho
NW1 ....232 C3
St Christopher's Hospice
SE26 ....184 C5
St Christopher's Mews
SM6 ....219 C3
St Christopher's Pl
W1 ....238 B2
St Christopher's Sch
NW3 ....70 B3
Beckenham BR3 ...186 A1
Wembley HA9 ....66 B5
St Clair Dr KT4 .....216 B4
St Clair Ho 14 E3 ....97 B4
St Clair Rd E13 ......99 B5
St Clair's Rd CR0 ...221 C4
St Clare Bsns Pk
TW12 ....174 A4
St Clare St EC3 ....243 C1
St Clement Danes CE Prim
Sch WC2 ....94 B1 240 C1
St Clements Ct N7 ...72 B2
7 SE14 ....140 D6
8 W11 ....112 D6
St Clements Ho KT12 194 A2
St Clement's Hts
SE26 ....184 A6
St Clement's La WC2 240 D1
St Clements Mans 3
SW6 ....134 D6
St Clements St N7 ...72 C1
St Clement & St James CE
Prim Sch
W11 ....112 D5 244 A3
St Cloud Rd SE27 ..183 B6
St Columba's Ct E15 .76 C4
St Columbas Ho 2
E17 ....53 D5
St Columba's RC Sch for
Boys DA6 ....169 A4
St Columb's Ho 11
W10 ....91 A2
St Crispins Cl NW3 ..70 C4
St Crispin's Cl UB1 ..85 B1
St Cross St
EC1 ....94 C2 241 B4
St Cuthberts Gdns 1
HA5 ....23 B3
St Cuthbert's Rd NW2 .69 B2
St Cuthberts Rd N13 .32 C4
St Cuthbert with St
Matthias Prim Sch
SW5 ....113 D1 255 C6

St Cyprian's Greek
Orthodox Prim Sch
CR7 ....183 A2
St Cyprian's St SW17 180 D6
St Davids Cl 27 SE16 .118 B1
Wembley HA9 ....67 A5
St David's Cl BR4 ..207 D2
St David's Coll BR4 .207 D2
St David's Ct 1 E17 ..54 A6
St Davids Ct 5 E11 ..55 B4
St David's Ct 8 UB1 ..86 A1
St David's Dr HA8 ...26 B2
St David's Pl NW4 ...46 B2
St David's Sch TW15 .148 B3
St David's Sq E14 ..119 D1
St Denis Rd SE27 ..183 B6
St Dionis Rd SW6 ..135 B3
St Domingo Ho SE18 122 B3
St Dominic RC Prim Sch
NW5 ....70 D3
St Dominics RC Prim Sch
E9 ....75 A2
St Dominic's Sixth Form
Coll (RC) HA1 ....64 C6
St Donatt's Rd SE14 .141 B4
St Dunstans SM1 ...217 B2
St Dunstan's Alley
EC3 ....253 A5
St Dunstan's Ave W3 111 B6
St Dunstan's CE Prim Sch
SM3 ....217 A1
St Dunstans Cl UB3 .105 D2
St Dunstan's Coll
SE6 ....163 C3
St Dunstan's Ct EC4 .241 B1
St Dunstans Gdns
W3 ....111 B6
St Dunstan's Hill EC3 253 A5
Cheam SM1,SM3 ...217 A3
St Dunstan's La EC3 253 A5
Beckenham BR3 ...208 A4
St Dunstans Rd E7 ...77 C2
W6 ....112 D1
W7 ....108 C4
Cranford TW5 .....128 B3
Feltham TW13 .....149 D1
South Norwood SE25 .205 B6
St Edmund RC Sch
E14 ....119 C2
St Edmunds Ave HA4 .39 B3
St Edmunds Cl DA18 .124 D4
St Edmund's Cl NW8 .230 C5
St Edmunds Cl SW17 158 C2
St Edmund's Cl NW8 .230 C5
St Edmund's Dr HA7 ..25 A2
St Edmund's La TW2 .151 D4
St Edmund's RC Prim Sch
Edmonton N9 ....18 B3
Twickenham TW2 .151 D4
St Edmund's Rd N9 ..18 A4
St Edmund's Rd IG1 ..56 B3
St Edmund's Sq
SW13 ....134 C6
St Edmund's Terr
NW8 ....92 D6 230 C5
RM7 ....59 C4
St Edward's CE Comp Sch
RM7 ....59 C4
St Edward's Cl NW11 .47 C3
St Edwards Ct 3 E10 .54 C4
St Edward's Cl NW11 .47 C3
St Edward's RC Prim Sch
E6 ....99 C6
NW1 ....92 C3 237 B5
St Egberts Way E4 ...20 A3
St Elizabeth Ct 8 E10 53 D2
N12 ....30 A6
St Elizabeth's RC Prim Sch
TW10 ....154 A4
St Elmo Rd W12 ....111 D4
St Elmos Rd SE16 ..119 A4
St Elphege's RC Inf Sch
SM6 ....220 A2
St Elphege's RC Jun Sch
SM6 ....220 A2
St Erkenwald Mews
IG11 ....101 A6
St Erkenwald Rd
IG11 ....101 B6
St Ermin's Hill SW1 .259 C6
St Ervan's Rd W10 ...91 B2
St Eugene de Mazenod RC
Prim Sch NW6 .....91 C6
St Faith's CE Prim Sch
SW18 ....158 A6
St Faith's Cl EN2 .....5 A4
St Faith's Rd SE24 .160 D3

St Fillans Rd SE6 ....164 A4
St Francesca Cabrini Prim
  Sch SE23 ....162 C5
St Francis Cl BR6 ...211 D3
St Francis de Sales RC Jun
  Sch N17 ....33 D3
St Francis' Ho NW1 .232 C3
St Francis Lo HA0 ....64 D5
St Francis of Assisi RC
  Prim Sch W11 .....112 D6
St Francis RC Prim Sch
  E15 ....76 C3
  SE15 ....140 A5
St Francis Rd SE22 ...139 C1
St Francis Way IG1 ...79 B4
St Francis Xavier Sixth
  Form Coll SW12 ...159 B5
St Gables Ct N11 ....31 D3
St Gabriel's CE Prim Sch
  SW1 ....115 C1 259 A1
St Gabriel's Cl E11 ...55 C1
St Gabriel's Rd NW2 ..68 D3
St George Ho SW11 ..268 B1
St George's Ave E7 ...77 B1
  N7 ....71 D4
  NW9 ....45 B5
  W5 ....109 D4
  Southall UB1 .....107 B6
St George's Battersea CE
  Prim Sch
  SW8 ......137 C5 269 B3
St George's Bickley CE
  Prim Sch BR1 ....187 D1
St George's Cath
  NW1 ....231 D2
St George's Cath RC Jun &
  Inf Sch SE1 .116 D3 261 C6
St George's CE Prim Sch
  SE5 ....139 C5
St George's Circ
  SE1 ....116 D3 261 C6
St George's Cl NW11 ..47 B3
St Georges Cl
  Erith SE28 ....102 D1
  Wembley HA0 ......65 A5
St Georges Ct E17 ....54 B4
  E6 ....100 B3
St George's Ct SE1 ..261 C5
  SW3 ....257 A4
  SW7 ....256 A5
St Georges Ct
  Harrow HA3 ....43 A3
  Penge SE20 ....184 B2
  Putney SW15 ......135 B1
St George's Dr
  SW1 ....115 C1 259 A2
  Ickenham UB10 .....60 B6
  South Oxhey WD19 ..23 A6
St George's Field
  W2 ....92 C1 237 B1
St George's Gdns
  KT6 ....214 D6
St Georges Hanover Sq
  Sch W1 ....115 A6 248 B5
St George's Ho NW1 .232 B3
St George's Hospl
  SW17 ....180 B5
St Georges Ind Est
  Kingston KT2 ......175 D5
  Tottenham N22 .....32 D3
St Georges La EC3 ...253 A6
St Georges Lo N10 ...49 C5
St Georges Mews 11
  NW1 ....70 D1
St George's Mews
  SE1 ....261 B6
St George's RC Cath
  SE1 ....116 D3 261 B6
St George's RC Prim Sch
  Enfield EN2 ....5 B3
  Harrow HA1 ....64 D5
St George's RC Sec Sch
  W9 ....91 D5
St Georges Rd BR1 ..210 B6
  BR5 ....211 B3
  W4 ....111 B4
St George's Rd DA14 .190 D4
  E10 ....76 A5
  E7 ....77 B2
  NW11 ....47 B3
  SE1 ....116 D3 261 C6
St Georges Rd RM9 ...81 A4
St George's Rd
  Beckenham BR3 ....185 D2
  Ealing W7 ....108 D5
  Edmonton N9 ......18 A1

St George's Rd continued
  Enfield EN1 ....5 D5
  Feltham TW13 .....172 D6
  Isleworth TW1 .....153 B6
  2 Kingston KT2 ...176 C3
  Mitcham CR4 ......203 B6
  Palmers Green N13 ..16 B2
  Redbridge IG1 .....56 B2
  Richmond TW9 .....132 B2
  Wallington SM6 ....219 B3
  Wimbledon SW19 ...179 B4
St Georges Rd W
  BR1 ....188 A1
St George's Residences 4
  SW2 ....160 C6
St Georges's Ct EC4 .241 C2
St Georges Sh & L Ctr
  HA1 ....42 C3
St Georges Sq 1
  E14 ....119 A6
St George's Sq E7 ...77 B1
  SE8 ....119 B2
  SW1 ....115 C1 259 C1
  Kingston KT3 .....199 C6
St George's Square Mews
  SW1 ....259 C1
St George St
  W1 ....115 B6 248 D6
St Georges Terr NW1 .70 D1
St George's Way
  SE15 ....139 C6
St George's Wlk CR0 .221 A5
St George the Martyr CE
  Prim Sch
  WC1 ......94 B3 240 D5
St Gerards Cl SW4 ...159 C6
St German's Pl SE3 ..143 A4
St German's Rd SE23 163 A3
St Gildas' RC Jun Sch
  N8 ....50 A3
St Giles Ave
  Dagenham RM10 ....81 D1
  Uxbridge UB10 .....61 A4
St Giles Cir
  WC1 ......93 D1 239 D2
St Giles Cl BR6 .....227 B3
  Dagenham RM10 ....81 D1
St Giles Coll
  WC1 ......94 A2 240 B4
St Giles Ct WC2 .....240 A2
  Ealing W13 ....109 C5
St Giles High St
  WC2 ......93 D1 239 D2
St Giles Hospl SE5 ..139 C4
St Giles Pas WC2 ....239 D1
St Giles Rd SE5 .....139 C4
St Giles' Sch CR2 ...220 D2
St Giles Twr 3 SE5 ..139 C4
St Gilles Ho 15 E2 ...96 D5
St Gothard Rd SE21,
  SE27 ....183 B6
St Gregory Cl HA4 ...62 C4
St Gregory RC High Sch
  HA3 ....43 D4
St Gregory's RC Prim Sch
  W5 ....87 D2
St Helena Ho WC1 ...234 A1
St Helena Pier TW9 ..153 D6
St Helena Rd SE16 ...118 D2
St Helena St WC1 ....234 A1
St Helena Terr 23
  TW9 ....153 D6
St Helens KT7 ....196 D2
Saint Helens Coll
  UB10 ....60 C1
St Helen's Cres SW16 182 B2
St Helen's Gdns W10 .90 D1
St Helen's Pl EC3 ...243 A2
St Helen's RC Inf Sch
  E17 ....54 A4
St Helen's RC Prim Sch
  E13 ....99 A3
  SW9 ....138 C2
St Helens Rd 7
  DA18 ....124 D4
St Helen's Rd
  Ealing W13 ....109 C5
  Redbridge IG1 .....56 B3
  Thornton Heath SW16 182 B2
St Helens Sch UB10 ..60 C1
St Helier Ave SM4 ...202 A3
St Helier Ct 4 N1 ...95 C6
St Helier Hospl SM5 .202 A1
St Heliers Ave TW3,
  TW4 ....151 C6
St Helier's Rd E10 ...54 A4
St Helier Sta SM4 ...201 D4
St Hilda's Ave N7 ....70 A5
St Hilda's Cl NW6 ....68 D1
St Hildas Cl SW17 ...158 C2

St Hilda's Rd SW13 ..134 B6
St Hildas Wharf E1 ..118 C5
St Hubert's Ho 1
  E14 ....119 C3
St Hughes Cl SW17 ..158 C2
St Hugh's Rd SE20 ...184 B3
St Ignatius Coll IG1 ..6 B6
St Ignatius' RC Prim Sch
  N15 ....51 D3
St Ignatius RC Prim Sch
  TW16 ....172 A2
St Ivian Ct 3 N10 ...31 B1
St James Apartments 2
  E17 ....53 A4
St James Ave N20 ....14 C1
  Sutton SM1 ....217 C3
St James' Ave W13 ..109 A5
St James CE Jun Sch
  E7 ....77 A3
St James CE Prim Sch
  EN3 ....6 C3
St James Cl N20 .....14 C1
  Barnet EN4 ....2 B1
St James' Cl
  New Malden KT3 ...199 D4
  Ruislip HA4 ....62 C6
St James Ct 11 E2 ...96 A4
  SE3 ....143 B4
  10 W4 ....110 C4
St James' Ct SW1 ...259
  W4 ....111 B3
St James Ct
  Thornton Heath CR4 204 D2
  Wanstead E12 .....77 C6
St James' Ct 7 KT1 ..198 A6
St James Gate W6 ...112 C1
St James Gdns IG6 ...58 B5
  HA0 ....66 A1
St James Hatcham CE
  Prim Sch SE14 ....141 A4
St James Independent
  Schs W14 ...113 A2 254 A4
St James Ind Mews
  SE1 ....118 A1
St James' Mans NW6 .69 C1
St James Mews E14 ..120 A3
St James RC Prim Sch
  BR5 ....210 D4
St James' Rd E15 ....76 D3
St James Rd
  Carshalton SM5 ....218 C5
  Kingston KT1 ......175 D1
  Sutton SM1,SM2 ...217 C3
St James' Rd
  Edmonton N9 ......18 B2
  Mitcham CR4 ......181 A3
  Surbiton KT6 ......197 D3
St James's SE14 ....141 A4
St James's App EC2 ..243 A5
St James's Ave E2 ...96 C5
  Beckenham BR3 ....207 A6
  Hampton TW12 ....174 A5
St James's CE Prim Sch
  N10 ....49 A5
  N20 ....14 A2
  Buckhurst Hill IG9 ..21 B3
  Fulham SW6 .135 A4 264 B1
  Kingston KT1 ......198 A6
  Penge SE20 ....184 C3
St John's Church Rd
  E9 ....74 C3
St John's Cl N20 .....14 A1
St John's Cl N14 .....15 C5
St John's Cl HA9 .....66 A3
St Johns Concert Hall
  SW1 ....260 A5
St John's Cotts 2
  SE20 ....184 C3
St John's Cres SW9 ..138 C2
St Johns Ct E11 .....118 B5
St John's Ct E11 .....54 D1
  N4 ....72 D6
  N5 ....72 D4
  5 NW3 ....70 A2
  SE13 ....142 A3
  W6 ....112 C1
  Buckhurst Hill IG9 ..21 B3
  2 Harrow HA1 .....42 D3
  Isleworth TW7 .....130 D4
  Kingston KT1 ......198 A5
St Johns Dr KT12 ....194 C1
St John's Dr SW18 ...157 D3
St John's Est SE1 ...253 C1
St John's Gdns
  W11 ....113 B6 244 C5
St John's Gr N19 .....71 C6
  3 Barnes SW13 ...133 D3
  1 Richmond TW9 ..132 A1

St James's RC Prim Sch
  TW2 ....152 C1
St James's Rd
  SE1,SE16 ....118 A2
  Hampton TW12 ....173 D5
  Thornton Heath CR0 205 B2
St James's Sq
  SW1 ....115 C5 249 B4
St James's St E17 ....53 A4
  SW1 ....115 C5 249 A4
St James's & St Michael's
  CE Prim Sch
  W2 ....114 A6 246 A6
St James St W6 .....112 C1
St James's Terr NW8 .230 C4
  2 Upper Tooting
  SW12 ....159 A3
St James's Terrace Mews
  NW8 ....230 C5
St James Street Sta
  E17 ....53 A4
St James's Wlk EC1 .241 C6
St James The Great RC
  Prim Sch
  SE15 ....139 D4
  South Norwood CR7 182 D1
St James Way IG3 ...114 A5
St Jerome's Gr UB3 ..83 A1
St Joachim's RC Prim Sch
  E16 ....99 C1
St Joan of Arc RC Prim
  Sch N5 ....73 A4
St Joan's Rd N9 .....17 D2
St John Baptist CE Prim
  Sch BR1 ....186 A6
St John CE Prim Sch
  SE17 ....117 A2 262 B3
St John Cl SW6 .....265 A4
St John Evangelist RC
  Prim Sch N1 .94 D5 234 C4
St John Fisher RC Fst &
  Mid Sch HA5 ......41 C5
St John Fisher RC Prim
  Sch
  DA18 ....125 A3
  Wembley UB6 ......87 C4
  West Barnes SW20 .200 D4
St John of Jerusalem CE
  Prim Sch E9 ......74 C2
St John Rigby RC Coll
  BR4 ....224 B4
St John's Angell Town CE
  Prim Sch SW9 .....138 C2
St John's Ave N11 ....30 D5
  NW10 ....89 D6
  Putney SW15 ......156 C6
St Johns CE Fst Sch
  HA7 ....25 B6
St John's CE Inf Sch
  NW4 ....46 B4
St John's CE JMI Sch
  N11 ....30 D6
St Johns CE Mid Sch
  HA7 ....25 A6
St John's CE Prim Sch
  E2 ....96 C6
  N20 ....14 A2
St John's Cl N20 .....14 A1
St John's Cl N14 .....15 C5
St John's Cl HA9 .....66 A3
St Johns Concert Hall
  SW1 ....260 A5
St John's Cotts 2
  SE20 ....184 C3
St John's Cres SW9 ..138 C2
St Johns Ct E11 .....118 B5
St John's Ct E11 .....54 D1
  N4 ....72 D6
  N5 ....72 D4
  5 NW3 ....70 A2
  SE13 ....142 A3
  W6 ....112 C1
  Buckhurst Hill IG9 ..21 B3
  2 Harrow HA1 .....42 D3
  Isleworth TW7 .....130 D4
  Kingston KT1 ......198 A5
St Johns Dr KT12 ....194 C1
St John's Dr SW18 ...157 D3
St John's Est SE1 ...253 C1
St John's Gdns
  W11 ....113 B6 244 C5
St John's Gr N19 .....71 C6
  3 Barnes SW13 ...133 D3
  1 Richmond TW9 ..132 A1

St John's (Highbury Vale)
  CE Prim Sch N5 ...72 D5
St John's Hill SW11 ..136 B1
St John's Hill Gr
  SW11 ....136 B1
St Johns Ho 5 SE17 .139 B6
St John's La
  EC1 ....94 D2 241 D4
St John's Mans E5 ...74 C3
St John's Par
  Ealing W13 ....109 B5
  3 Sidcup DA14 ....190 B6
St John's Park Mans
  N19 ....71 C5
St John's Path EC1 ..241 C5
St John's Pk SE3 ....143 A5
St John's Pl EC1 ....241 C5
St John's Prim Sch
  W13 ....109 A6
St John's RC Prim Sch
  SE16 ....119 A4
  E16 ....99 A1
  E6 ....100 A6
  N15 ....51 A3
  NW11 ....47 B3
  SW11 ....136 C1
St Johns Rd DA16 ...146 B2
  Kingston KT3 .....199 A6
St John's Rd
  Barking IG11 ......101 C6
  Carshalton SM5 ....218 C5
  Chingford E17 .....36 A1
  Chingford E4 ......35 D6
  Croydon CR0 ......220 D5
  East Molesey KT8 ..196 B5
  Feltham TW13 .....173 B6
  Harrow HA1 ....42 D3
  Isleworth TW7 .....130 D3
  Orpington BR5,BR6 .211 C3
  Penge SE20 ....184 C4
  Richmond TW9 .....132 A1
  Sidcup DA14 ......190 B6
  Southall UB2 ......107 A3
  Sutton SM1 ....217 D6
  Teddington KT1 ....175 C1
  Wembley HA9 ......66 A3
  Wimbledon SW19 ...179 A4
St John's (Shirley) CE Prim
  Sch CR0 ....222 D5
St John St EC1 94 D3 241 C6
St John's Terr E7 ....77 B2
  SE18 ....145 B6
  W10 ....90 D3
  Enfield EN2 ....5 B6
St John & St James CE
  Prim Sch
  E9 ....74 C3
  Edmonton N18 .....33 D5
St Johnstone Ho 15
  N12 ....29 D6
St John's (Upper
  Holloway) Prim Sch
  N19 ....71 D6
St John's Vale SE8 ...141 C4
St John's Village 4
  N11 ....30 D5
St John's Villas N19 ..71 D6
  W8 ....255 D6
St John's Way N19 ...49 D1
St John's Wood Ct
  NW8 ....229 D1
St John's Wood High St
  NW8 ....92 C5 230 A4
St John's Wood Park
  NW8 ....92 B6 229 C6
St John's Wood Prep Sch
  NW8 ....229 D1
St John's Wood Rd
  NW8 ....92 B4 229 D1
St John's Wood Sta
  NW8 ....92 B5 229 C4
St John's Wood Terr
  NW8 ....92 C5 230 A4
St John the Baptist CE Jun
  Sch KT1 ....175 D1
St John the Baptist CE
  Prim Sch N1 ......95 C5
St John the Divine CE Jun
  & Inf Sch SE5 .....138 D4
St John Vianney RC Prim
  Sch N8 ....50 D5
St Joseph RC Prim Sch
  W7 ....108 C5

St Joseph's Acad
  SE3 ....142 C2
St Joseph's Cl BR6 ..227 C4
St Joseph's Cl W10 ..91 A2
St Joseph's Coll Mill Hill
  Missionaries NW7 ..27 D6
St Joseph's Convent Prep
  Sch KT8 ....196 A4
St Joseph's Convent Prim
  Sch NW4 ....46 B5
St Joseph's Convent Sch
  E11 ....55 A3
St Josephs Ct 19 E10 53 D2
  3 NW10 ....89 D5
St Joseph's Dr UB1 ..107 B5
St Joseph's Flats
  NW1 ....232 C2
St Josephs Gr NW4 ..46 B5
St Joseph's Ho W6 ...112 C1
St Joseph's Hospice
  E9,E8 ....96 B6
St Joseph's RC Coll
  SW16 ....182 C6
St Josephs RC Fst & Mid
  Sch HA3 ....25 A1
St Joseph's RC Inf Sch
  E10 ....75 C6
  South Norwood SE19 183 A4
St Joseph's RC Jun & Inf
  Sch
  SE1 ....117 A4 252 B2
  SE16 ....118 A4
  SE16 ....118 C3
St Joseph's RC Jun & Inf
  Schs HA9 ....66 B3
St Joseph's RC Jun Sch
  E10 ....53 D1
  SE5 ....139 A5
  South Norwood SE19 183 A4
St Joseph's RC Prim Sch
  N19 ....49 B1
  NW10 ....67 C1
  SE16 ....120 C1
  SE8 ....141 C5
  SW18 ....157 C6
  SW3 ....114 D2 257 C3
  W9 ....92 A4 229 A1
  WC2 ....94 A1 240 B2
  Barking IG11 ......101 A6
  Dagenham RM9 ....81 B4
  Kingston KT1 ......176 B1
St Joseph's RC Sch
  BR1 ....187 B3
St Joseph's Rd N9 ...18 C3
St Joseph's St SW8 ..268 D2
St Joseph's Vale SE3 .142 B2
St Jude's CE Prim Sch
  SE24 ....160 D6
St Judes Ho 6 W10 ..91 B4
St Jude's Prim Sch
  SE1 ....116 D3 261 C5
St Jude's Rd E2 .....96 B5
St Jude's & St Paul's Prim
  Sch N1 ....73 C2
St Jude St N16 ......73 C3
St Julian's Cl SW16 ..182 C6
St Julian's Farm Rd
  SE27,SW16 ....182 C6
St Julian's Rd NW6 ..91 C6
St Katharine Docks *
  E1 ....117 D5 253 D4
St Katharine's Ho N1 234 A4
St Katharine's Pier
  E1 ....117 D5 253 D4
St Katharine's Way
  E1 ....117 D5 253 D4
St Katharine's Prec
  NW1 ....231 C4
St Katherines Rd
  DA18 ....124 D4
St Katherine's Row
  EC3 ....243 B1
St Katherine's Wlk 1
  W11 ....112 D5
St Keverne Rd SE9 ...188 A6
St Kilda Rd BR6 .....211 D1
  Ealing W13 ....109 A4
St Kilda's Rd N16 ....51 C1
  Harrow HA1 ....42 C3
St Kitts Terr SE19 ...183 C5
St Laurence's Cl NW6 90 D6
St Lawrence CE Jun & Mid
  Sch HA6 ....196 B5
St Lawrence Cl HA8 ..26 B3
St Lawrence Ct N1 ...235 D6
St Lawrence Dr HA5 ..40 B4
St Lawrence Ho SE1 .263 B6
St Lawrence RC Sch
  TW13 ....150 B2

St Lawrence St E14 ... 120 A5
St Lawrence Terr W10 ... 91 A2
St Lawrence Way SW9 ... 138 C3
St Leonards Ave HA3 ... 43 C4
St Leonard's Ave E4 ... 36 B4
St Leonards CE Prim Sch SW16 ... 181 D5
St Leonards Cl 4 DA16 ... 146 A2
St Leonard's Ct N1 ... 235 D2
St Leonards Ct SW14 ... 133 A2
St Leonards Gdns IG1 ... 79 A3
St Leonard's Gdns TW5 ... 129 A4
St Leonard's Hospl N1 ... 95 C5
St Leonard's Rd E14 ... 98 A2
NW10 ... 89 B3
St Leonards Rd SW14 ... 133 A2
St Leonard's Rd
Claygate KT10 ... 212 D2
Croydon CR0 ... 220 D5
Ealing W13 ... 109 C6
Kingston KT6 ... 197 D4
Thames Ditton KT7 ... 197 A2
St Leonards Rise BR6 ... 227 C4
St Leonard's Sq NW5 ... 71 A2
Kingston KT6 ... 197 D4
St Leonard's St E3 ... 97 D4
St Leonard's Terr SW3 ... 114 D1 257 D1
St Leonard's Wlk SW16 ... 182 B3
St Loo Ave SW3 ... 136 C6 267 B6
St Loo Ct SW3 ... 267 C6
St Louis Rd SE27 ... 183 B6
St Loy's Rd N17 ... 51 D6
St Lucia Dr E15 ... 98 D6
St Luke Ct 5 E10 ... 53 D2
St Luke's Ave SW4 ... 137 D1
Enfield EN2 ... 5 B5
Ilford IG1 ... 78 D3
St Luke's CE Prim Sch E14 ... 120 B2
St Luke's CE Prim Sch EC1 ... 235 A2
W9 ... 91 B4
Kingston KT2 ... 176 B2
Richmond TW9 ... 132 C4
West Norwood SE27 ... 183 A5
St Luke's Cl EC1 ... 95 A3 242 B6
Croydon SE25 ... 206 B3
St Luke's Ct W11 ... 91 B1
St Luke's Hospl W1 ... 93 C3 239 A5
St Luke's Mews W11 ... 91 B1
St Luke's Path 1 IG1 ... 78 D3
St Luke's Prim Sch E16 ... 98 D1
St Luke's Rd W11 ... 91 B2
Uxbridge UB10 ... 60 A1
St Luke's Sq E16 ... 98 D1
St Luke's St SW3 ... 257 B2
St Luke's Woodside Hospl N10 ... 49 A5
St Malo Ave N9 ... 18 C1
St Margaret Clitherow RC Prim Sch NW10 ... 67 A4
Woolwich SE28 ... 124 B5
St Margarets IG11 ... 101 B6
St Margarets Ave DA15 ... 167 B1
N20 ... 14 A3
St Margaret's Ave N8, N15 ... 50 D5
St Margarets Ave Ashford TW15 ... 170 D5
Hillingdon UB8 ... 82 C3
St Margaret's Ave Cheam SM3 ... 217 A5
Harrow HA2 ... 64 A5
St Margarets Bsns Ctr 11 TW1 ... 153 B5
St Margaret's CE Prim Sch SE18 ... 123 A1
Barking IG11 ... 79 A1
St Margaret's Cres SW15 ... 156 B6
St Margaret's Ct E15 ... 76 C4
Putney SW15 ... 134 B1
9 Twickenham TW1 ... 153 B5
St Margaret's Dr TW1 ... 153 B6
St Margaret's Gr E11 ... 76 D5
SE18 ... 145 A6
St Margaret's Gr *continued*
Twickenham TW1 ... 153 A5
St Margaret's La W8 ... 113 D3 255 C5
St Margaret's Lee CE Prim Sch SE13 ... 142 C1
St Margarets Lo W3 ... 110 D4
St Margaret's Rd N17 ... 51 C6
NW10 ... 90 C4
SE4 ... 141 B1
W7 ... 108 C4
St Margarets Rd
Edgware HA8 ... 26 D5
Ruislip HA4 ... 39 B3
St Margaret's Rd
Isleworth TW1 ... 153 B6
Wanstead E12 ... 77 C6
St Margarets Rdbt TW1 ... 153 B6
St Margaret's Sch NW3 ... 69 D4
St Margaret's Sta TW1 ... 153 B5
St Margaret St SW1 ... 250 A1
St Margaret's Terr SE18 ... 123 A1
St Mark's CE Prim Sch BR2 ... 209 A6
SE11 ... 138 B6 270 D6
Croydon SE25 ... 206 A5
St Marks Cl 5 SE10 ... 142 A5
St Mark's Cl Barnet EN5 ... 1 D2
Harrow HA1 ... 43 B1
St Mark's Cres NW1 ... 93 A6 231 B6
St Mark's Ct 7 E10 ... 53 D2
W7 ... 108 C4
St Mark's Fst Sch CR4 ... 180 D1
St Marks Gate E9 ... 75 B1
St Mark's Gr SW10 ... 135 D5 265 D4
St Mark's Hill KT6 ... 198 A3
St Marks Ho 6 SE17 ... 139 B6
St Mark's Ho 8 E17 ... 54 A5
St Mark's Hospl EC1 ... 94 D4 234 D2
St Marks Ind Est E16 ... 121 D5
St Mark's Pl W11 ... 91 A1
Wimbledon SW19 ... 179 B4
St Mark's Prim Sch N19 ... 72 A6
W7 ... 108 C4
St Mark's RC Sch TW3 ... 129 C2
St Mark's Rd W10 ... 90 D2
W11 ... 91 A1
W7 ... 108 C4
Bromley BR2 ... 209 B6
Croydon SE25 ... 206 A5
Ealing W5 ... 110 A5
Enfield EN1 ... 17 D6
Mitcham CR4 ... 181 A1
Teddington TW11 ... 175 B3
St Mark's Rise E8 ... 73 D3
St Mark's Sq NW1 ... 231 A5
St Mark St E1 ... 95 D1 243 D1
St Martha's Convent Jun Sch for Girls EN5 ... 1 A1
St Martin-in-the-Fields High Sch for Girls SW2 ... 160 C3
St Martin of Porres RC Prim Sch N11 ... 31 C4
St Martin's Almshos NW1 ... 232 A6
St Martin's App HA4 ... 39 C2
St Martin's Ave E6 ... 99 D5
St Martins Cl DA18 ... 124 D4
St Martin's Cl NW1 ... 232 A6
St Martins Cl WD19 ... 22 C6
St Martin's Cl EN1 ... 6 B4
St Martins Ct N1 ... 95 C6
St Martin's Ct WC2 ... 250 A6
West Norwood SE27 ... 160 D2
St Martin's La WC2 ... 116 A6 250 A5
St Martins La BR3 ... 207 D4
St Martin's Le Grand EC1 ... 242 A2
St Martin's Pl WC2 ... 250 A5
St Martin's Rd N2 ... 30 B2
SW9 ... 138 B3
Edmonton N9 ... 18 B2
St Martin's Sch NW7 ... 27 B5
St Martin's St WC2 ... 249 D5
St Martin's Way SW17 ... 158 A1
St Mary Abbots CE Prim Sch W8 ... 113 D4 245 C1
St Mary Abbot's Ct W14 ... 254 C5
St Mary Abbot's Pl W8 ... 254 D5
St Mary Abbots Terr W14 ... 254 D5
St Mary at Hill EC3 ... 117 C6 253 A5
St Mary Ave SM6 ... 219 B5
St Mary Axe EC3 ... 95 C1 243 B2
St Marychurch St SE16 ... 118 C4
St Mary Graces Ct E1 ... 253 D5
St Marylebone CE Sch The W1 ... 93 A2 238 A3
St Mary le Bow Church★ EC2 ... 242 B1
St Mary- le-Park Ct SW11 ... 267 B3
St Mary Magdalene CE Prim Sch
N7 ... 72 C2
SE15 ... 140 B3
W2 ... 91 D2
St Mary Magdalens RC Prim Sch SE4 ... 141 A1
St Mary Magdalen's RC Prim Sch SW14 ... 133 B2
St Mary Magdelen's RC Jun Sch NW2 ... 68 B2
St Mary Newington Cl SE17 ... 263 B2
St Mary of the Angels RC Prim Sch W2 ... 91 C1
St Mary RC Prim Sch W10 ... 91 A3
St Mary Rd E17 ... 53 D5
St Marys IG11 ... 101 B6
St Mary's App E12 ... 78 B3
St Mary's Ave N3 ... 29 B1
St Marys Ave UB2 ... 107 D2
St Mary's Ave
Beckenham BR2 ... 208 C6
Teddington TW11 ... 174 D4
Wanstead E11 ... 55 B2
St Mary's Bryanston Square CE Sch W1 ... 92 D2 237 C4
St Mary's CE High Sch (Lower & Upper) NW4 ... 46 C6
St Mary's CE High Sch (Middle) NW4 ... 46 C6
St Mary's CE Inf Sch N8 ... 50 B5
St Mary's CE Jun Sch N8 ... 50 A5
NW4 ... 46 B4
St Mary's CE Prim Sch E17 ... 53 D5
N1 ... 94 D6 234 D6
N3 ... 29 B3
NW10 ... 67 C2
SE18 ... 122 C2
Chessington KT9 ... 214 B2
East Barnet EN4 ... 14 C5
Long Ditton KT7 ... 197 B1
Putney SW15 ... 134 D2
St Mary's CE Sch TW19 ... 148 A4
St Mary's Church Sch TW1 ... 153 A4
St Mary's Cl BR5 ... 190 B1
Chessington KT9 ... 214 B1
Ewell KT17 ... 215 D1
Sunbury TW16 ... 194 A5
Tottenham N17 ... 34 A2
St Mary's Coll TW1 ... 152 D1
St Mary's Cottage Hospl TW12 ... 173 B2
St Mary's Cres
Hayes UB3 ... 105 D6
Hendon NW4 ... 46 B6
Hounslow TW7 ... 130 C5
St Marys Ct E6 ... 100 B3
SE7 ... 143 D5
St Mary's Ct E11 ... 54 D1
N12 ... 30 A3
W5 ... 109 D4
W6 ... 111 D3
Kingston KT3 ... 199 C6
Wallington SM6 ... 219 C4
St Mary's Dr TW14 ... 149 A4
St Mary's Est 2 SE16 ... 118 C4
St Mary's Flats NW1 ... 232 C2
St Mary's Gate W8 ... 255 C5
St Mary's Gdns SE11 ... 261 B4
St Mary's Gn 1 N2 ... 48 A6
St Mary's Gr N1 ... 72 D2
Barnes SW13 ... 134 B2
Chiswick W4 ... 132 D6
Richmond TW10,TW9 ... 132 B1
St Mary's Ho N1 ... 234 D6
W5 ... 109 D3
St Mary's Hospl W2 ... 92 B1 236 D2
St Mary's Inf Sch E17 ... 53 D5
St Mary's Kilburn CE Prim Sch NW6 ... 91 C6
St Mary's Lewisham CE Prim Sch SE13 ... 163 D6
St Mary's Lo E11 ... 55 B3
St Mary's Mans NW10 ... 89 C6
W2 ... 92 B2 236 C4
St Mary's Medical Sch W2 ... 92 B1 236 D2
St Mary's Mews NW6 ... 69 D1
St Mary's Path N1 ... 234 D6
St Mary's Pl SE9 ... 166 C5
W5 ... 109 D4
W8 ... 113 D3 255 C5
St Mary's RC High Sch CR0 ... 205 A1
St Mary's RC Inf Sch CR0 ... 205 B1
St Mary's RC Jun & Inf Schs N15 ... 51 B4
St Mary's RC Jun Sch E17 ... 54 A6
Croydon CR0 ... 205 B1
Wallington SM5 ... 218 D3
St Mary's RC Prim Sch NW6 ... 91 C5
SE9 ... 166 C6
SW4 ... 159 C6
SW8 ... 137 B4 268 D2
W14 ... 112 D3
Beckenham BR3 ... 186 A3
Chingford E4 ... 20 B3
Chiswick W4 ... 133 C6
Enfield EN3 ... 6 D1
Isleworth TW7 ... 131 A2
Merton SW19 ... 179 C3
St Mary's RC Sch TW7 ... 131 A2
St Mary's Rd E10 ... 76 A6
E13 ... 99 B5
N2 ... 30 B2
N8 ... 50 A5
N9 ... 18 C3
NW10 ... 89 C6
NW11 ... 47 A2
SE15 ... 140 C3
St Marys Rd IG1 ... 79 B6
St Mary's Rd
Ealing W5 ... 109 D5
East Barnet EN4 ... 14 D4
East Molesey KT8 ... 196 B4
Hayes UB3 ... 105 D6
Long Ditton KT6 ... 197 C1
South Norwood SE25 ... 205 C6
Surbiton KT6 ... 197 D3
Wimbledon SW19 ... 179 B5
Worcester Park KT4 ... 215 C6
St Mary's Roman Catholic Inf Sch SM5 ... 218 D4
St Mary's Sch Hampstead NW3 ... 70 B3
St Mary's Sq W2 ... 236 C4
W5 ... 109 D4
St Mary's Stoke Newington CE Prim Sch N16 ... 73 C6
St Mary's & St Peter's CE Prim Sch TW11 ... 174 D5
St Mary St SE18 ... 122 C2
St Mary's Terr W2 ... 236 C4
St Mary & St Joseph's Sch DA14 ... 190 A5
St Mary & St Michael Prim Sch E1 ... 96 C1
St Mary & St Pancras CE Prim Sch NW1 ... 93 D5 232 C3
St Mary's Twr EC1 ... 242 B5
St Marys View HA3 ... 43 C4
St Mary's Wlk SE11 ... 261 B4
Hayes UB3 ... 105 D6
St Matthew's Ave KT6 ... 198 B1
St Matthew's CE Fst Sch SW20 ... 178 A2
St Matthew's CE Prim Sch
Enfield EN3 ... 18 C6
Surbiton KT6 ... 198 A2
Yiewsley UB7 ... 104 A5
St Matthews Ct
6 E10 ... 53 D2
E15 ... 76 D1
St Matthews Ct *continued*
N10 ... 31 A1
SE1 ... 262 A5
St Matthew's Ct TW15 ... 170 C5
St Matthews Dr BR1 ... 210 B6
St Matthew's Ho 8 SE17 ... 139 B6
St Matthew's Lo NW1 ... 232 B4
St Matthew's Rd SW2 ... 160 B6
Ealing W5 ... 110 A5
St Matthew's Row E2 ... 96 A3
St Matthews Sch Westminster SW1 ... 115 D3 259 D6
St Matthew St SW1 ... 259 C5
St Matthias CE Prim Sch E2 ... 95 D3 243 D6
St Matthias Cl NW9 ... 45 D4
St Matthias's CE Prim Sch N16 ... 73 C4
St Maur Rd SW6 ... 135 B4 264 D1
St Mellion Cl SE28 ... 102 D1
St Merryn Cl SE18 ... 145 B5
St Merryn Ct BR3 ... 185 C3
St Michael-at-Bowes CE Jun Sch N13 ... 32 C4
St Michael's Alley EC3 ... 242 D1
St Michaels Ave N9 ... 18 C4
St Michael's Ave HA9 ... 66 C2
St Michael's CE Jun & Inf Sch N22 ... 32 B2
St Michael's CE Prim Sch
N6 ... 49 A2
NW1 ... 93 C6 232 A6
Enfield EN2 ... 5 A4
Forest Hill SE26 ... 185 A6
Wandsworth SW18 ... 157 B4
St Michaels Cl BR1 ... 210 A6
4 E16 ... 99 D2
St Michael's Cl DA18 ... 124 D4
N12 ... 30 C5
N3 ... 29 B1
St Michaels Cl KT4 ... 215 D6
St Michael's Cres HA5 ... 41 A3
St Michaels Ct E14 ... 98 A2
St Michael's Ct N11 ... 15 A1
NW11 ... 47 B2
St Michael's East Wickham CE Sch DA16 ... 146 C4
St Michael's Flats NW1 ... 232 C3
St Michael's Gdns W10 ... 91 A2
St Michael's Hospl EN2 ... 5 B4
St Michael's RC Gram Sch N12 ... 30 A5
St Michael's RC Prim Sch E6 ... 100 B5
Ashford TW15 ... 170 C5
St Michael's RC Sch SE16 ... 118 A4
St Michael's Rd DA16 ... 146 B2
NW2 ... 68 C4
SW9 ... 138 B3
St Michaels Rd TW15 ... 170 C5
St Michael's Rd
Croydon CR0 ... 205 A1
Wallington SM6 ... 219 C2
St Michael's Rise DA16 ... 146 B4
St Michael's St W2 ... 92 C1 237 A2
St Michael's Terr N22 ... 32 A2
St Michael & St Martin RC Prim Sch TW4 ... 129 B2
St Michael Twr E17 ... 53 B4
St Mildred's Ct EC2 ... 242 C1
St Mildreds Rd SE12, SE6 ... 164 D4
St Mirren Ct EN5 ... 14 A6
St Monica's RC Prim Sch N1 ... 95 C4
St Nicholas CE JMI Sch WD6 ... 9 D5
St Nicholas CE Prim Sch TW17 ... 192 D3
St Nicholas Cl WD6 ... 9 D5
St Nicholas Ct SE18 ... 123 D1
St Nicholas Ctr SM1 ... 217 D3
St Nicholas Dr TW17 ... 192 C2
St Nicholas Elstree CE Prim Sch WD6 ... 9 D5
St Nicholas' Flats NW1 ... 232 C3
St Nicholas Glebe SW17 ... 181 A4
St Nicholas Ho SE8 ... 141 C6
St Nicholas Rd SE18 ... 123 D2
Sutton SM1 ... 217 D3
Thames Ditton KT7 ... 196 D3
St Nicholas Sch NW9 ... 67 A6
St Nicholas St SE8 ... 141 C4
St Nicholas Way SM1 ... 217 D3
St Nicolas La BR7 ... 188 A2
St Ninian's Ct N20 ... 14 D1
St Norbert Gn SE4 ... 141 A1
St Norbert Rd SE4 ... 141 A1
St Olaf's Rd SW6 ... 135 A5 264 B3
St Olaves Ct W2 ... 245 C5
St Olave's Ct EC2 ... 242 C1
St Olave's Est SE1 ... 253 B2
St Olave's Gdns SE11 ... 261 A4
St Olave's Mans SE11 ... 261 A4
St Olaves Prep Sch SE9 ... 166 D2
St Olave's Rd E6 ... 100 C6
St Olave's Wlk SW16 ... 181 D1
St Olav's Sq 27 SE16 ... 118 C4
St Osmund's RC Prim Sch SW13 ... 133 D4
St Oswald's Pl SE11 ... 116 B1 260 C1
St Oswald's Rd SW16 ... 182 D2
St Oswulf St SW1 ... 259 D3
St Owen Ho SE1 ... 263 B6
St Pancras Almshouses 13 NW5 ... 70 D3
St Pancras Commercial Ctr NW1 ... 232 B6
St Pancras Ct N2 ... 30 B1
St Pancras Hospl NW1 ... 93 D6 232 C5
St Pancras Sta WC1 ... 94 A4 233 A2
St Pancras Way NW1 ... 93 C6 232 C6
St Patrick's RC Inf Sch E1 ... 118 B5
St Patrick's RC Prim Sch E17 ... 53 A5
NW5 ... 71 B3
SE18 ... 123 B2
St Paul's & All Hallows CE Jun & Inf Sch N17 ... 34 A3
St Paul's Ave NW2 ... 68 C2
SE16 ... 118 D5
Harrow HA3 ... 44 B5
St Paul's Cath★ EC4 ... 95 A1 242 A1
St Paul's Catholic Coll TW16 ... 172 A2
St Pauls Catholic Sch TW16 ... 172 A2
St Paul's Cath Sch EC4 ... 95 A1 242 A1
St Paul's CE Jun Sch KT2 ... 176 C3
St Paul's CE Prim Sch
N11 ... 31 B5
NW3 ... 70 D1
NW7 ... 28 B6
SE17 ... 262 B2
W6 ... 112 C1
St Pauls CE Prim Sch TW8 ... 131 D6
St Paul's CE Prim Sch
Chessington KT9 ... 214 A4
Southgate N21 ... 16 D4
St Paul's Church Yd EC4 ... 95 A1 242 A1
St Pauls Cl W5 ... 110 B4
St Paul's Cl SE7 ... 121 D1
St Pauls Cl UB3 ... 105 B1
St Paul's Cl
Ashford TW15 ... 171 A5
Carshalton SM5 ... 202 C1
Chessington KT9 ... 213 D4
Hounslow TW3,TW4 ... 129 A3
St Paul's Cray Rd BR7 ... 189 B2
St Pauls Cres NW1 ... 71 D1
St Paul's Ct 5 N19 ... 72 A6
SW4 ... 137 D1
Hounslow TW4 ... 129 A2
St Paul's Dr E15 ... 76 B3
St Paul's Girls' Sch W6 ... 112 D2
St Pauls Mews NW1 ... 71 D1
St Paul's Pl N1 ... 73 B2
St Paul's RC Prim Sch
Thames Ditton KT7 ... 196 C2
Wood Green N22 ... 32 B1

St Paul's RC Sec Sch
SE2 . . . .**146** A6
St Paul's Rd N1 . . . . .**73** A2
St Pauls Rd
Barking IG11 . . . .**101** A6
Richmond TW9 . . . . . .**132** B2
St Paul's Rd
Brentford TW8 . . . .**131** D6
South Norwood CR7 . .**205** A6
Tottenham N17 . . . .**34** A2
St Pauls Rise N13 . . . .**32** D4
St Paul's Sch SW13 . . .**112** A1
St Paul's Sq BR2 . . . . .**187** A1
St Paul's Sta
EC2 . . . .**95** A1 **242** A2
St Paul St N1 . . . .**235** B5
St Paul's Terr SE17 . . .**138** D6
St Paul's Twr [18] E10 . .**53** D2
St Pauls View WC1 . .**234** A1
St Paul's Way E3 . . . .**97** C2
N3 . . . .**29** D3
St Paul's Way Com Sch
E3 . . . .**97** C2
St Paul's Whitechapel CE
Prim Sch E1 . . . .**118** A6
St Paul's with St Michael's
Prim Sch E8 . . . .**96** A6
St Paul's Wood Hill
BR5,BR7 . . . .**189** D1
St Paul with St Luke CE
Prim Sch E3 . . . .**97** B2
St Peter Chanel RC Prim
Sch DA14 . . . .**190** C5
St Peter in Chains RC Inf
Sch N8 . . . .**50** A3
SS Peter & Paul RC Prim
Sch BR5 . . . .**189** C1
SS Peter & Paul's RC Prim
Sch
Ilford IG1 . . . .**79** B5
Mitcham CR4 . . . .**202** D5
St Peters Alley EC3 . .**242** D1
St Peters Ave N12 . . . .**30** C3
St Peter's Ave N18 . . .**34** A6
St Petersburgh Mews
W2 . . . .**245** C6
St Petersburgh Pl
W2 . . . .**113** D6 **245** C5
St Peter's CE Prim Sch
SE17 . . . .**262** D1
W9 . . . .**91** C3
St Peter's Church Ct
N1 . . . .**234** D5
St Peters Cl BR7 . . . . .**189** B3
St Peters Cl E2 . . . .**96** A5
St Peters Cl Ilford IG2 . .**57** D5
Upper Tooting SW17 . .**158** C2
St Peter's Cl
Barnet EN5 . . . .**12** B6
Bushey WD23 . . . .**8** B3
Ruislip HA4 . . . .**62** D6
St Peters Ct SE12 . . . .**164** D6
SE4 . . . .**141** B3
St Peter's Ct NW4 . . . .**46** C4
St Peters Ct KT8 . . . .**195** C5
St Peter's Eaton Square CE
Sch SW1 . . . . .**115** B3 **258** D5
St Peter's Gdns SE27 . .**160** C1
St Peter's Gr W6 . . . .**112** A2
St Peters Ho N15 . . . . .**52** A5
WC1 . . . .**233** B1
St Peter's Ho N16 . . . .**51** C2
[4] SE17 . . . .**139** B6
St Peters La BR5 . . . .**138** C5
St Peter's London Docks
CE Prim Sch E1 . . .**118** C5
St Peter's Path E17 . . .**54** C5
St Peter's Pl W9 . . . . .**91** D3
St Peter's Prim Sch
W6 . . . .**112** A1
South Croydon CR2 . .**221** C2
St Peter's RC Prim Sch
SE18 . . . .**122** D2
Dagenham RM9 . . . . .**103** B6
St Peter's Rd W6 . . . .**112** A1
St Peters Rd KT1 . . . .**176** C1
St Peter's Rd
Croydon CR0 . . . .**221** B4
East Molesey KT8 . . . .**195** C5
Edmonton N9 . . . .**18** B3
Isleworth TW1 . . . . . .**153** B6
Southall UB1 . . . .**85** C1
St Peter's Sq E2 . . . . . .**96** A5
W6 . . . .**111** D1
St Peter's St
N1 . . . .**94** D6 **234** D5
Croydon CR2 . . . .**221** B3

St Peters & St Pauls RC
Prim Sch EC1 **94** D3 **241** D6
St Peter's Street Mews
N1 . . . .**234** D4
St Peter's Terr SW6 . .**264** B3
St Peter's Villas [5]
W6 . . . .**112** A2
St Peters Way N1 . . . .**73** C1
St Peters Way UB3 . .**105** B1
St Peter's Way W5 . . . .**87** D2
St Philip Ho WC1 . . .**234** A1
St Philip's Ave KT4 . .**216** B6
St Philip Sq [1] SW8 . .**137** B3
St Philip's Rd E8 . . . . .**74** C1
Surbiton KT6 . . . .**197** D3
St Philip's Sch SW7 . .**256** B4
Chessington KT9 . . . .**213** D2
St Philip St SW8 . . . .**137** B3
St Philip's Way N1 . . .**235** B5
St Philomena's Sch
SM5 . . . .**218** C3
St Quentin Ho SW18 . .**158** A5
St Quentin Rd DA16 . .**145** D2
St Quintin Ave W10 . . .**90** C2
St Quintin Gdns W10 . .**90** C2
St Quintin Rd E13 . . . .**99** B5
St Raphael's RC Prim Sch
UB5 . . . .**84** C5
St Raphael's Way
NW10 . . . .**67** A3
St Regis Cl N10 . . . . . .**31** B1
St Regis Hts NW3 . . . .**69** D5
St Richard of Chichester
RC Sec Sch NW1 . . .**71** C1
St Richards Ct TW10 . .**153** B1
St Richard's with St
Andrew's CE Prim Sch
TW10 . . . .**153** B1
St Ronan's [2] N3 . . . . .**29** C2
St Ronans Ct EN4 . . . . .**2** B5
St Ronans Cres IG8 . . .**37** A3
St Rule St SW8 . . . . . .**137** C3
St Savior's CE Inf Sch
W5 . . . .**109** D6
St Saviours SW4 . . . .**137** A1
St Saviour's CE Prim Sch
E14 . . . .**97** D2
E17 . . . .**53** B2
SE24 . . . .**139** A2
W9 . . . .**91** D3
St Saviour's Coll
SE27 . . . .**183** B6
St Saviours Ct N22 . . . .**31** D1
Harrow HA1 . . . .**42** C4
St Saviours Ho [4]
SE1 . . . .**118** A4
St Saviour's RC Prim Sch
SE13 . . . .**142** A1
St Saviour's Rd SW2 . .**160** B6
Thornton Heath CR0 . .**205** A3
St Saviours & St Olaves CE
Sch SE1 . . . .**117** B3 **262** D5
St Saviour's Wharf
SE1 . . . .**253** D2
St Scholastica's RC Prim
Sch E5 . . . .**74** A5
Saints Cl SE27 . . . . . .**182** D6
Saints Dr E7 . . . .**77** D3
St Silas Pl NW5 . . . . . .**71** A2
St Simon's Ave SW15 . .**156** C6
St Stephen's Ave E17 . .**54** A4
W12 . . . .**112** B4
Ealing W13 . . . .**87** B1
St Stephen's CE Prim Sch
SE8 . . . .**141** C3
SW8 . . . .**138** B5 **270** C4
W12 . . . .**112** C4
W2 . . . .**91** C2
St Stephen's Cl E17 . . .**53** D4
NW5 . . . .**70** D3
NW8 . . . .**230** B5
Southall UB1 . . . .**85** C2
St Stephen's Cres W2 . .**91** C1
Thornton Heath CR7 . .**204** C6
St Stephens Ct N8 . . . . .**50** B3
Ealing W13 . . . .**87** B1
St Stephen's Gdns W2 . **91** C1
[3] Putney SW15 . . . . .**157** B6
Twickenham TW1 . . . .**153** C5
St Stephen's Gr SE13 . .**142** A2
St Stephens Ho [7]
SE17 . . . .**139** B6
St Stephen's Mews [34]
W2 . . . .**91** C2
St Stephens Par E6 . . .**77** C1
St Stephens Prim Sch
E6 . . . .**77** C1
St Stephen's RC Prim Sch
DA16 . . . .**146** A3
St Stephens Rd E6 . . . .**77** C1

St Stephen's Rd E17 . . .**53** D4
E3 . . . .**97** B5
St Stephens Rd EN5 . . .**12** D6
St Stephen's Rd
Ealing W13 . . . .**87** C1
Enfield EN3 . . . .**6** D6
Hounslow TW3,TW4 . .**151** C6
Yiewsley UB7 . . . .**104** A5
St Stephen's Row
EC4 . . . .**242** C1
St Stephen's Terr
SW8 . . . .**270** C3
St Swithin's La
EC4 . . . .**117** B6 **252** C6
St Swithun's Rd SE13 . .**164** B6
St Swithun Wells RC Prim
Sch HA4 . . . .**62** D5
St Teresa RC Prim Sch The
RM8 . . . .**80** C4
St Teresa's RC Fst & Mid
Sch HA3 . . . .**24** A2
St Teresa's RC Prim Sch
SM4 . . . .**202** B3
St Theresa Ct E4 . . . . .**20** B4
St Theresa's RC Sch
N3 . . . .**47** D6
St Theresa's Rd
TW14 . . . .**127** D1
St Thomas a Beckett RC
Prim Sch SE2 . . . . . .**124** A3
St Thomas Becket RC Prim
Sch SE25 . . . .**206** A4
St Thomas' CE Prim Sch
N16 . . . .**52** A1
W10 . . . .**91** A3
St Thomas' Cl KT6 . . . .**198** B1
St Thomas Ct [10] E10 . .**53** D2
Sidcup DA5 . . . .**169** C4
St Thomas' Dr BR5 . . .**211** A1
Pinner HA5 . . . .**23** A2
St Thomas' Gdns NW5 . .**71** A2
St Thomas Gdns IG1 . . .**79** A2
St Thomas Ho [2] E1 . . .**96** D1
St Thomas More RC Prim
Sch
SE9 . . . .**144** A2
Bexley DA7 . . . .**147** B3
St Thomas More RC Sch
SE9 . . . .**166** C5
SW3 . . . .**114** D2 **257** C3
East Molesey KT8 . . . .**196** A4
St Thomas More Sch
N22 . . . .**32** C5
St Thomas of Canterbury
RC Mid Sch CR4 . . . .**203** A6
St Thomas of Canterbury
RC Prim Sch
SW6 . . . .**135** B5 **264** C4
St Thomas Rd E16 . . . .**99** A1
N14 . . . .**15** D4
St Thomas' Rd W4 . . . .**133** A6
St Thomas's Hospl
SE1 . . . .**116** B3 **260** C6
St Thomas's Hospl Medical
Sch SE1 . . . .**116** B3 **260** C5
St Thomas's Pl [20] E9 . .**74** C1
St Thomas's Rd N4,N5 . .**72** C5
NW10 . . . .**89** C6
St Thomas's Sq E9 . . . .**74** C1
St Thomas St
SE1 . . . .**117** B5 **252** D3
St Thomas's Way
SW6 . . . .**135** B5 **264** D4
St Thomas the Apostle Coll
The SE15 . . . .**140** C4
St Timothy's Mews [3]
BR1 . . . .**187** B2
St Ursula Gr HA5 . . . . .**41** A4
St Ursula Rd UB1 . . . . .**85** C1
St Ursula's Convent Sch
SE10 . . . .**142** B5
St Vincent Cl SE27 . . .**182** D5
St Vincent De Paul Ho [20]
E1 . . . .**96** C2
St Vincent De Paul RC
Prim Sch
SW1 . . . .**115** C3 **259** B6
St Vincent Ho SE1 . . .**263** C6
St Vincent Rd TW2 . . .**152** A5
St Vincent's Hospl
HA5 . . . .**39** D6
St Vincents RC Prim Sch
SE9 . . . .**188** A6
St Vincent's RC Prim Sch
W1 . . . .**93** A2 **238** B3
Acton W3 . . . .**110** D6
Dagenham RM8 . . . . . .**80** C6
St Vincent's RC Sch
NW7 . . . .**28** C5
St Vincent St W1 . . . .**238** B3

St Wilfrid's Cl EN4 . . . .**14** C6
St Wilfrid's Rd EN4 . . . .**14** C6
St William of York RC Prim
Sch SE23 . . . .**163** A3
St William of York RC Sec
Boys Sch (Upper) N1 . **72** A1
St Winefride's Ave
E12 . . . .**78** B3
St Winefride's RC Prim Sch
E12 . . . .**78** B3
St Winifred's RC Inf Sch
SE12 . . . .**164** C6
St Winifred's RC Jun Sch
SE12 . . . .**164** D4
St Winifred's Rd
TW11 . . . .**175** B4
Sala Ho SE3 . . . .**143** B1
Salamanca Pl SE1 . . .**260** C3
Salamanca St
SE1,SE11 . . .**116** B2 **260** C3
Salamander Cl KT2 . . .**175** C5
Salamander Quay
KT1 . . . .**175** D2
Salcombe Dr
Dagenham RM6 . . . . . .**59** B3
North Cheam SM4 . . . .**200** D1
SW4 . . . .**137** B1
Salcombe Gdns NW7 . . .**28** C4
SW4 . . . .**137** B1
Salcombe Ho [6]
SE23 . . . .**162** C2
Salcombe Lo NW5 . . . .**71** A4
Salcombe Pk IG10 . . . .**21** D6
Salcombe Prep Sch
N14 . . . .**15** B4
Salcombe Rd E17 . . . . .**53** B2
[23] N16 . . . .**73** C3
Ashford TW15 . . . . . .**148** A1
Salcombe Villas [13]
TW10 . . . .**154** A6
Salcombe Way
Hayes UB4 . . . .**83** C4
Ruislip HA4 . . . .**62** A6
Salcot N4 . . . .**72** B6
Salcott Rd SW11 . . . . .**158** C6
Wallington CR0 . . . . . .**220** B4
Salehurst Cl HA3 . . . . .**44** A4
Salehurst Rd SE4 . . . .**163** B5
Salem Ho [13] E9 . . . . . .**74** D2
Salem Pl CR0 . . . .**221** A5
Salem Rd W2 **113** D6 **245** D6
Sale Pl W2 . . . .**92** C1 **237** A2
Salesian Coll
SW11 . . . .**136** C4 **267** A1
Sale St E2 . . . .**96** A3
Salford Ho [4] E14 . . . .**120** A2
Salford Rd SW2,SW12 .**159** D3
Salhouse Cl SE28 . . . .**102** C1
Salisbury Ave N3 . . . . .**47** B6
Barking IG11 . . . .**79** C1
Cheam SM1,SM2 . . . .**217** B2
Salisbury Ct E9 . . . . . .**75** A3
EC4 . . . .**241** C1
N9 . . . .**18** B1
[15] SE16 . . . .**118** A3
W4 . . . .**111** A2
Edgware HA8 . . . .**26** B6
Enfield EN2 . . . .**5** B1
Northolt UB5 . . . .**63** D3
Salisbury Gdns
Buckhurst Hill IG9 . . . .**21** D2
Wimbledon SW19 . . . .**179** A3
Salisbury Hall Gdns
E4 . . . .**35** C4
Salisbury Ho [3] E14 . . .**97** D1
N1 . . . .**234** C4
SW1 . . . .**259** D2
[1] Ruislip HA4 . . . .**40** C1
Stanmore HA7 . . . .**25** A4
Wimbledon SW19 . . . .**156** D1
Salisbury Lower Sch
N9 . . . .**18** C4
Salisbury Mans N4,
N15 . . . .**50** D4
Salisbury Mews BR2 . .**210** A4
SW6 . . . .**264** C3
Salisbury Pl SW9 . . . .**138** D5
W1 . . . .**237** C4
Salisbury Prim Sch
E12 . . . .**78** A3
Salisbury Rd BR2 . . . .**210** A4
DA5 . . . .**169** C3
E10 . . . .**76** A6
E12 . . . .**77** D3
E17 . . . .**54** C5
E7 . . . .**77** A2
N4 . . . .**50** D4
W13 . . . .**109** A4
Barnet EN5 . . . .**1** A1

Salisbury Rd continued
Chingford E4 . . . .**19** C1
Croydon SE25 . . . .**206** A3
Dagenham RM10 . . . . .**81** D2
East Bedfont TW6 . . . .**149** A5
Edmonton N9 . . . .**18** A1
Enfield EN3 . . . .**7** B6
Feltham TW13 . . . .**150** C1
Harrow HA1 . . . .**42** B4
Hounslow TW4 . . . . . .**128** C2
Ilford IG3 . . . .**79** C6
Kingston KT3 . . . .**199** B6
Pinner HA5 . . . .**40** A5
Richmond TW9 . . . . . .**132** A1
Southall UB2 . . . .**107** A2
Tottenham N22 . . . .**32** D1
Wallington SM5 . . . . . .**218** D2
Wimbledon SW19 . . . .**179** A3
Worcester Park KT4 . .**215** C5
Salisbury Sq EC4 . . . .**241** C1
Salisbury St NW8 . . . .**237** A5
[10] Acton W3 . . . .**111** A4
Salisbury Terr SE15 . .**140** C2
Salisbury Upper Sch
N9 . . . .**18** C4
Salisbury Wlk N19 . . . .**71** C6
Salix Cl TW16 . . . .**172** B3
Salix Ct N3 . . . .**29** C4
Salliesfield TW2 . . . . .**152** B5
Sally Murray Cl E12 . . .**78** C4
Salmen Rd E13 . . . .**98** D5
Salmon Cl SW17 . . . . .**180** C5
Salmond Cl HA7 . . . . . .**25** A4
Salmon La E14 . . . .**97** A1
Salmon Rd DA17 . . . . .**125** C1
Salmons Rd
Chessington KT9 . . . . .**214** A2
Edmonton N9 . . . .**18** A3
Salmon St [6] E14 . . . . .**97** B1
NW9 . . . .**45** A2
Salomons Rd E13 . . . . .**99** C2
Salop Rd E17 . . . .**52** D3
Saltash Cl SM1 . . . . . .**217** B4
Saltash Rd DA16 . . . . .**146** C4
Saltcoats Rd W4 . . . . .**111** C4
Saltcroft Cl HA9 . . . . . .**44** D1
Saltdene N4 . . . .**50** B1
Salter Cl HA2 . . . .**63** B4
Salterford Rd SW17 . . .**181** A4
Salter Ho [8] SW16 . . .**181** C6
Salter Rd SE16 . . . . . .**119** A5
Salters' Hall Ct EC4 . .**252** C6
Salter's Hill SE19 . . . .**183** B5
Salters Rd E17 . . . .**54** B5
W10 . . . .**90** D3
Salter St [10] E14 . . . . .**119** C6
NW10 . . . .**90** A4
Salterton Rd N7 . . . . . .**72** B5
Salt Hill Cl UB8 . . . . . .**60** A3
Saltley Cl E6 . . . .**100** A1
Saltoun Rd SW2,SW9 .**138** C1
Saltram Cl N15 . . . .**51** D5
Saltram Cres W9 . . . . .**91** C4
Saltwell St E14 . . . . . .**119** C6
Saltwood Gr SE17 . . . .**262** C1
Salusbury Prim Sch
NW6 . . . .**91** B6
Salusbury Rd NW6 . . . .**91** A6
Salutation Rd SE10 . . .**120** C2
Salvador SW17 . . . . . .**180** D5
Salvatorian RC Coll
HA3 . . . .**24** C1
Salvia Gdns UB6 . . . . .**87** A5
Salvin Rd SW15 . . . . . .**134** D2
Salway Cl IG8 . . . .**37** A3
Salway Ho E10 . . . .**75** D6
SW8 . . . .**270** B2
Salway Pl E15 . . . .**76** C2
Salway Rd E15 . . . .**76** B2
Salween Ho [2] N16 . . . .**73** B4
Samantha Cl E17 . . . . .**53** B2
Samantha Ct E11 . . . . .**54** C2
Samaritan Hospl for
Women NW1 . . . . . .**237** C4
Sam Bartram Cl SE7 . .**121** C1
Sambrooke Ct EN1 . . . .**17** C6
Sambrook Ho [19] E1 . . .**96** C2
Sambruck Mews SE6 . .**163** D3
Samels Ct W6 . . . .**112** A1
Samford Ho N1 . . . . . .**234** A5
Samford St
NW8 . . . .**92** C3 **237** A5
Samira Cl E17 . . . .**53** C3
Sam Manners Ho [7]
SE10 . . . .**120** C1
Sam March Ho [5] E14 . **98** B1
Samos Rd SE20 . . . . . .**184** B1
Sampson Ave EN5 . . . .**12** D6
Sampson Cl DA17 . . . .**125** A3
Sampson Ct TW17 . . . .**193** A4
Sampson St E1 . . . . . .**118** A2

Samson Ho SE18 . . . .**123** A2
Samson St E13 . . . .**99** C5
SE14 . . . .**140** D6
SE18 . . . .**122** A2
Samuel Cl E8 . . . .**95** D6
SE14 . . . .**140** D6
SE18 . . . .**122** A2
Samuel Ct BR3 . . . . . .**207** D6
Samuel Gray Gdns
KT2 . . . .**175** D2
Samuel Ho [15] E8 . . . .**95** D6
Samuel Johnson Cl
SW16 . . . .**182** B6
Samuel Jones Ind Est [15]
SE15 . . . .**139** C5
Samuel Lewis Bldgs
[6] N1 . . . .**72** C2
Samuel Lewis Trust
Dwellings
[6] SE5 . . . .**139** A4
SW3 . . . .**257** A3
SW6 . . . . . .**135** C5 **265** B4
W14 . . . .**254** B4
Samuel Lewis Trust Est
N15 . . . .**51** C3
Samuel Rhodes Sch
N1 . . . .**94** C6 **234** A6
Samuel's Cl [2] W6 . . .**112** C2
Samuel St [6] SE15 . . .**139** D5
SE18 . . . .**122** B2
Sancroft Cl NW2 . . . . . .**68** B5
Sancroft Ct SW11 . . . .**267** B2
Sancroft Rd HA3 . . . . . .**25** A1
Sancroft St
SE11 . . . .**116** C1 **260** D2
Sanctuary Rd TW19,
TW6 . . . .**148** C5
Sanctuary St SE1 . . . .**252** B2
Sanctuary The DA5 . .**168** D5
[35] E1 . . . .**118** B5
SW1 . . . .**115** D3 **259** D6
Morden SM4 . . . .**201** C3
Sandale Cl N16 . . . .**73** B5
Sandall Cl W5 . . . .**88** A3
Sandall Ho [6] E3 . . . . .**97** A5
Sandall Rd NW5 . . . . . .**71** C2
Ealing W5 . . . .**88** A3
Sandal Rd
Edmonton N18 . . . .**34** A5
New Malden KT3 . . . . .**199** C2
Sandal St E15 . . . .**98** C6
Sandalwood Cl [10] E1 . .**97** A3
Sandalwood Dr HA4 . . .**39** A2
Sandalwood Ho
DA15 . . . .**167** D1
[6] NW3 . . . .**69** D2
Sandalwood Rd
TW13 . . . .**150** B1
Sandbach Pl SE18 . . . .**123** A1
Sandbourne [12] NW8 . .**91** B6
[4] W11 . . . .**91** C1
Sandbourne Ave
SW19 . . . .**179** D1
Sandbourne Rd SE4 . .**141** A3
Sandbrook Cl NW7 . . . .**27** B4
Sandbrook Rd N16 . . . .**73** C5
Sandby Ct BR3 . . . . . .**185** B2
Sandby Gn SE9 . . . . . .**144** A3
Sandby Ho [6] NW6 . . . .**91** C6
[11] SE5 . . . .**139** C6
Sandcroft Cl N13 . . . . . .**32** D4
Sandcroft Ho SE11 . . .**260** D2
Sandells Ave
Ashford TW15 . . . . . .**171** A6
Ashford TW15 . . . .**171** A6
Sandell St SE1 . . . . . .**251** A1
Sanderling Ct [20] SE8 . **141** B6
Woolwich SE28 . . . . . .**124** C6
Sanders Cl TW12 . . . . .**174** A5
Sanders Ho WC1 . . . . .**234** A2
Streatham SW16 . . . . .**182** A4
Sanders La NW7 . . . . . .**28** C3
Sanderson Cl NW5 . . . .**71** B4
Sanderson Ho [7] SE8 **119** B1
Sanderstead Ave NW2 **69** A4
Sanderstead Cl
SW12 . . . .**159** C4
Sanderstead Rd
South Croydon CR2 . .**221** B1
Walthamstow E10 . . . . .**53** A1
Sanders Way [3] N19 . .**49** D1
Sandfield WC1 . . . . . .**233** B1
Sandfield Gdns CR7 . .**204** C6
Sandfield Pl CR7 . . . . .**205** A6
Sandfield Rd CR7 . . . .**204** D6
Sandford Ave N22 . . . .**33** A4
Sandford Cl E6 . . . . . .**100** B3
Sandford Ct N16 . . . . . .**51** C1
Barnet EN5 . . . .**1** D2
Sandford Rd BR2 . . . .**209** A4

Sandford Rd continued
E6 . . . .**100** B4
Bexley DA6,DA7 . . .**147** A2
Sandford Row SE17 . .**262** D2
Sandford St SW6 . .**265** D3
Sandford Wlk ▣ N16 .**73** D6
SE14 . . . .**141** A4
Sandgate Ho ▣ E5 . .**74** B4
▣ Beckenham BR3 . .**185** A3
Ealing W5 . . . .**87** C2
Sandgate La SW17,
SW18 . . . .**158** C3
Sandgate Rd DA16 . .**146** C5
Sandgate St SE15 . .**140** B6
Sandgate Trad Est
SE15 . . . .**140** B6
Sandham Ct SW4 . .**270** B1
Sandham Point ▣
SE18 . . . .**122** D2
Sandhills CR0,SM6 . .**219** D4
Sandhills Mdw TW17 **193** A2
Sandhills The SW10 .**266** B6
Sandhurst Ave
Harrow HA2 . . . . . .**41** D3
Tolworth KT5 . . . . .**198** D2
Sandhurst Cl NW9 . . .**44** C6
South Croydon CR2 .**221** C1
Sandhurst Ct SW2 . .**138** A1
Sandhurst Dr IG3 . . .**79** C4
Sandhurst Ho ▣ E1 . .**96** C2
Sandhurst Jun & Inf Sch
SE6 . . . .**164** C3
Sandhurst Mkt SE6 . .**164** A3
Sandhurst Rd DA15 . .**168** A1
HA8,NW9 . . . .**44** C6
N9 . . . .**18** D5
Bexley DA5 . . . . . .**168** D6
Catford SE6 . . . . . .**164** B3
Sandhurst Way CR2 .**221** C1
Sandifer Dr NW2,
NW11 . . . .**68** D5
Sandiford Rd SM3 . .**217** B6
Sandiland Cres BR2 .**224** D6
Sandilands CR0 . . . .**222** A5
Sandilands Rd
SW6 . . . .**135** D4 **265** C1
Sandilands Sta CR0 .**221** D6
Sandison St SE15 . .**140** A2
Sandland St WC1 . .**240** D3
Sandling Rise SE9 . .**166** C1
Sandlings Cl SE15 . .**140** B3
Sandlings The N22 . . .**50** D6
▣ Wood Green N22 . . .**32** C1
Sandmartin Way CR4 **203** A1
Sandmere Rd SW4 . .**138** A1
Sandon Cl KT10 . . . .**196** B1
Sandon Ct IG3 . . . . .**80** A5
Sandon Ho ▣ SW2 . .**160** A4
Sandow Cres UB3 . .**105** D3
Sandown Ave KT10 .**212** A3
Sandown Cl TW5 . . .**128** A4
Sandown Gate KT10 .**212** B5
Sandown Ho ▣ W4 . .**111** A1
Penge SE26 . . . . . .**184** B4
Sandown Park KT10 .**212** A6
Sandown Rd
Croydon SE25 . . . . .**206** B4
Esher KT10 . . . . . .**212** A4
Sandown Way UB5 . . .**63** B3
Sandpiper Cl E17 . . .**34** D3
SE16 . . . .**119** B4
Sandpiper Ct ▣ E14 .**120** A3
▣ SE8 . . . .**141** C4
Sandpiper Rd SM1 . .**217** B3
Sandpiper Terr IG5 . .**56** D6
Sandpit Pl SE7 . . . .**122** A1
Sandpit Rd BR1 . . .**186** C5
Sandpits Rd
Richmond TW10 . . .**153** D2
South Croydon CR0 .**222** D4
Sandra Cl
Hounslow TW3 . . . .**151** D6
Tottenham N17 . . . .**33** A2
Sandra Ho KT8 . . . .**196** B4
Sandridge Cl HA1 . . .**42** C5
Sandridge Ct N4 . . . .**73** A6
Sandridge St ▣ N19 . .**71** C6
Sandringham Ave
SW20 . . . .**179** A1
Sandringham Cl
Enfield EN1 . . . .**5** D3
Ilford IG6 . . . .**57** A6
▣ Putney SW19 . . .**156** D3
Sandringham Cres
HA2 . . . .**63** D6
Sandringham Ct
▣ SE16 . . . .**118** D5
W1 . . . .**239** B1
W9 . . . .**229** B1
▣ Beckenham BR3 . .**186** A2

Sandringham Ct continued
Edgware HA8 . . . . . .**26** D6
Hillingdon UB10 . . . . .**83** A3
Putney SW15 . . . . .**156** D5
Sandringham Dr
DA16 . . . .**145** C3
Ashford TW15 . . . .**170** A6
Sandringham Flats
WC2 . . . .**249** D6
Sandringham Gdns
N12 . . . .**30** B4
N8 . . . .**50** A3
Cranford TW5 . . . .**128** A4
East Molesey KT8 . .**195** C5
Ilford IG6 . . . .**57** A6
Sandringham Ho
W14 . . . .**254** A4
Richmond TW10 . . .**154** C6
Sandringham Prim Sch
E7 . . . .**77** C3
Sandringham Rd
BR1 . . . .**187** A5
E10 . . . .**54** B3
E7 . . . .**77** C3
E8 . . . .**73** D3
NW11 . . . .**47** A2
NW2 . . . .**68** B2
Barking IG11 . . . . . .**79** D2
Northolt UB5 . . . . . .**63** C1
Stanwell TW19,TW6 .**148** A6
Thornton Heath CR0 .**205** A4
Tottenham N22 . . . . .**32** D2
Worcester Park KT4 .**216** A5
Sandrock Pl CR0 . . .**222** D4
Sandrock Rd SE13 . .**141** C2
Sands End La
SW6 . . . .**135** D4 **265** D2
Sandstone TW9 . . . .**132** C5
Sandstone Pl N19 . . .**71** B6
Sandstone Rd SE12 .**165** B2
Sandtoft Rd SE7 . . .**143** B6
Sandways ▣ TW9 . . .**132** C4
Sandwell Cres ▣
NW6 . . . .**69** C2
Sandwell Mans ▣
NW6 . . . .**69** C2
Sandwich Ho
▣ SE16 . . . .**118** C4
WC1 . . . .**233** A1
Sandwich St
WC1 . . . .**94** A4 **233** A1
Sandwick Cl NW7 . . .**28** A3
Sandy Bury BR6 . . .**227** B5
Sandycombe Rd
East Bedfont TW14 . .**150** A3
Richmond TW9 . . . .**132** C3
Sandycoombe Rd
TW1 . . . .**153** C5
Sandycroft SE2 . . . .**146** A6
Sandy Dr TW14 . . . .**149** C3
Sandy Hill Ave SE18 .**122** D1
Sandy Hill La SE18 . .**122** D2
Sandy Hill Rd SE18 . .**122** D1
Sandyhill Rd IG1 . . . .**78** D4
Sandy La BR5 . . . . .**190** D2
Belmont SM2 . . . . .**217** A1
Harrow HA3 . . . .**44** C3
Mitcham CR4 . . . . .**181** A2
Moor Park HA6 . . . . .**22** A6
Richmond TW10 . . .**153** D2
Teddington KT8,TW11 **175** B3
Walton-on-T KT12 . .**194** C3
Sandy La N SM6 . . .**219** D3
Sandy La S SM6 . . .**219** C1
Sandy Lo N6 . . . . . .**49** C2
Sandy Ridge BR7 . .**188** C4
Sandy's Row E1 . . .**243** B3
Sandy Way
Croydon CR0 . . . . .**223** B5
Walton-on-T KT12 . .**193** D1

Sapcote Trad Ctr
NW10 . . . .**67** D2
Saperton Wlk SE11 . .**260** D4
Saphora Cl BR6 . . . .**227** B3
Sapperton Ct EC1 . .**242** A6
Sapphire Cl E6 . . . .**100** C1
Dagenham RM8 . . . . .**58** C1
Sapphire Ct ▣ E1 . .**118** A6
Sapphire Rd SE8 . . .**119** A2
Saracen Cl CR0 . . . .**205** B3
Saracen St E14 . . . .**97** C1
Sarah Bonnell Sch
E15 . . . .**76** C2
Sarah Ct UB5 . . . . . .**85** B6
Sarah Ho ▣ E1 . . . . .**96** B1
Roehampton SW15 . .**133** D1
Sarah Swift Ho SE1 .**252** D2
Sara Lane Ct ▣ N1 . . .**95** C5
Saratoga Rd E5 . . . .**74** C4
Sara Turnbull Ho ▣
SE18 . . . .**122** B2
Sardeson Ho ▣
SW27 . . . .**182** D5
Sardinia St WC2 . . .**240** C2
Sargents Hill N2 . . . .**30** C2
Sarjant Path SW19 . .**156** D2
Sark Cl TW5 . . . . . .**129** C5
Sark Ho ▣ N1 . . . . .**73** A2
Enfield EN3 . . . .**6** D5
Sark Wlk E16 . . . . . .**99** B1
Sarnersfield Ho SE15 **140** B6
Sarnes Ct ▣ N11 . . . .**31** B6
Sarnesfield Rd EN2 . . .**5** B2
Sarratt Ho W10 . . . . .**90** C2
Sarre Rd NW2 . . . . .**69** B3
Sarsden Bldgs W1 . .**238** B1
Sarsen Ave TW3 . . .**129** C3
Sarsfeld Rd SW12,
SW17 . . . .**158** A3
Sarsfield Rd UB6 . . . .**87** C5
Sartor Rd SE15 . . . .**140** D1
Sarum Hall Sch NW3 . .**70** C1
Sarum Ho W11 . . . .**244** D5
Sassoon ▣ NW9 . . . .**27** D2
Satanita Cl E16 . . . . .**99** D1
Satchell Mead NW9 . . .**27** D2
Satchwell Rd ▣ E2 . . .**96** A4
Saul Ct ▣ SE15 . . . .**139** C4
Sauls Gn E11 . . . . . .**76** C5
Saunders Cl ▣ E14 . .**119** B6
Saunders Ho ▣ SW2 .**160** C1
Saunders Ness Rd
E14 . . . .**120** B2
Saunders Rd SE18 . .**123** D1
Hillingdon UB10 . . . .**82** B6
Saunders St SE11 . .**261** A4
Saunders Way SE28 .**124** B4
Saunderton Rd HA0 . .**65** B3
Saunton Ave UB3 . .**127** D5
Saunton Ct UB1 . . .**108** A6
Savage Gdns EC3 . .**253** B6
Newham E6 . . . . . .**100** C1
Savana N16 . . . .**73** C6
Savannah Cl ▣ SE15 .**139** D5
Savernake Ct HA7 . . .**25** B4
Savernake Ho N4 . . . .**51** B2
Savernake Rd NW3 . .**70** C3
Enfield N9 . . . .**18** A5
Savery Dr KT6 . . . .**197** C3
Savile Cl
New Malden KT3 . . .**199** C4
Thames Ditton KT7 . .**197** A1
Savile Gdns CR0 . . .**221** D6
Saville Cres TW15 . .**171** B4
Saville Rd E16 . . . .**122** A5
W4 . . . .**111** B3
Dagenham RM6 . . . . .**59** B2
Twickenham TW1 . . .**152** B3
Saville Row
W1 . . . .**115** C6 **249** A6
Enfield EN3 . . . .**6** D3
Hayes BR2 . . . . . .**208** D1
Savill Gdns SW20 . .**200** A6
Savill Ho E16 . . . . .**122** A5
▣ SW4 . . . .**159** D5
Savill Row IG8 . . . . .**36** D2
Savin Lo ▣ SM2 . . .**218** A1
Savina Ho SE10 . . . .**144** D5
Savona Cl ▣ SW19 . .**178** D3
Savona Ct SW20 . . .**178** D2
Savona St
SW8 . . . .**137** C5 **269** A3
Savoy Ave UB3 . . . .**105** C4
Savoy Bldgs WC2 . .**111** D6
Savoy Circus W3 . . .**111** B6
Savoy Cl E15 . . . . . .**98** C6
Edgware HA8 . . . . . .**26** D6
Savoy Ct SW5 . . . . .**255** B4
WC2 . . . .**250** B5
Savoy Hill WC2 . . . .**250** C5

Savoy Par EN1 . . . .**5** C2
Savoy Pier WC2 . . . .**250** C5
Savoy Pl WC2 **116** B6 **250** C5
Savoy Row WC2 . . . .**250** C6
Savoy St WC2 **116** B6 **250** C5
Savoy Steps WC2 . .**250** C5
Savoy Way WC2 . . .**250** C5
Sawbill Cl UB4 . . . . .**84** D2
Sawkins Cl SW19 . .**157** A3
Sawley Rd W12 . . . .**112** A5
Sawmill Yd ▣ E3 . . . .**97** A6
Sawtry Cl SM5 . . . .**202** D2
Sawyer Cl N9 . . . . . .**18** A2
Sawyer Ho ▣ SE21 . .**183** C6
Sawyer's Hill TW10 . .**154** B4
Sawyers Lawn W13 . .**87** A1
Sawyer St
SE1 . . . .**117** A4 **252** A2
Saxby Rd SW2 . . . .**160** A4
Saxham Rd IG11 . . .**101** D5
Saxlingham Rd E4 . . .**20** D1
Saxon Ave TW13 . . .**151** B2
Saxon Bsns Ctr SW19 **180** A2
Saxonbury Ave TW16 **172** B5
Saxonbury Cl CR4 . .**202** B6
Saxonbury Ct ▣ N7 . .**72** A3
▣ N7 . . . .**71** D3
Saxonbury Gdns KT6 **197** C1
Hillingdon UB8 . . . . .**82** A2
Surbiton KT6 . . . . . .**197** D3
Saxoncroft Ho SW16 **159** D1
Saxon Cl E17 . . . . . .**53** C2
Saxon Ctr Jun Sch
TW17 . . . .**192** C4
Saxon Dr W3 . . . . . .**88** D2
Saxonfield Cl SW2 . .**160** B4
Saxon Gdns UB1 . . .**107** A5
Saxon Hall W2 . . . .**245** C5
Saxon Ho ▣ SW4 . . .**137** D1
Feltham TW13 . . . .**151** B2
Saxon Rd E3 . . . .**97** B5
E6 . . . .**100** A3
Ashford TW15 . . . .**171** B4
Bromley BR1 . . . . .**186** D3
Ilford IG1 . . . .**78** D3
Ilford E12 . . . .**78** B4
Hounslow TW3 . . . .**130** A2
Kingston KT2 . . . . .**176** A2
Southall UB1 . . . . .**107** A6
South Norwood SE25 .**205** B4
Tottenham N22 . . . . .**32** D2
Wembley HA9 . . . . . .**67** A5
Saxon Way N14 . . . .**15** D5
Saxon Wlk DA14 . . .**190** C4
Saxony Par UB3 . . . .**83** A2
Saxton Cl SE13 . . . .**142** B2
Saxville Rd BR5 . . . .**190** B1
Sayer Ho SE4 . . . . .**141** A1
Sayers Ho ▣ N2 . . . .**30** B1
Sayer's Wlk TW10 . .**154** B4
Sayesbury La N18 . . .**34** A5
Sayes Court St SE8 . .**141** B6
Sayes Ct SE8 . . . . .**141** B6
Scadbury Gdns BR5 .**190** A1
Scadbury Park Nature
Reserve ✦ BR7 . . . .**189** D4
Scads Hill Cl BR5,BR6 **211** D3
Scafell NW1 . . . . . .**232** A2
Scala St W1 . . . . . .**239** B4
Scales Rd N17 . . . . .**52** A6
Scampston Mews ▣
W10 . . . .**90** D1
Scandrett St ▣ E1 . .**118** B5
Scarba Wlk N1 . . . . .**73** D2
Scarborough Rd E11 .**54** B1
N4 . . . .**50** C1
N9 . . . .**18** C4
East Bedfont TW6 . .**149** A5
Scarborough St E1 . .**243** D1
Scarbrook Rd CR0 . .**221** A5
Scardale Ho ▣ E5 . . .**74** B6
Scarle Rd HA0 . . . . .**65** D2
Scarlet Rd SE6 . . . .**164** C1
Scarlette Manor Wlk ▣
SE24 . . . .**160** C4
Scarsbrook Ho ▣
SW2 . . . .**160** C5
Scarsbrook Rd SE3 . .**143** D2
Scarsdale Pl W8 . . .**255** C6
Scarsdale Rd HA2 . . .**64** C5
Scarsdale Villas
W8 . . . .**113** C3 **255** B5
Scarth Rd SW13 . . .**133** C2
Scawen Cl SM5 . . . .**219** A4
Scawen Rd SE8 . . . .**119** A1
Scawfell St ▣ E2 . . . .**95** C5
Scaynes Link N12 . . .**29** C6
Sceptre Ho ▣ E1 . . . .**96** C1
Sceptre Rd E2 . . . . .**96** C4
Schiller International Sch
SE1 . . . .**251** B1

Sch of Nursing
W1 . . . .**93** C2 **239** A4
Sch of Pharmacy
WC1 . . . .**94** A3 **240** B6
Sch of the Douay Martyrs
UB10 . . . .**60** D4
Scholars Ho ▣ E4 . . .**20** B3
Scholars Rd
Chingford E4 . . . . . .**20** B3
Streatham SW12 . . .**159** C3
Scholefield Rd N19 . .**71** D6
Scholey Ho SW11 . .**136** C1
Schomberg Ho SW1 .**259** D4
Schonfeld Sq N16 . . .**51** B1
School App ▣ E2 . . . .**95** C4
Schoolbank Rd SE10 **120** D3
School Bell Cloisters ▣
E3 . . . .**97** A5
Schoolbell Mews ▣
E3 . . . .**97** A5
School Cotts DA14 . .**190** C5
School Flats SW8 . . .**270** A1
School Ho SE1 . . . .**263** A4
Schoolhouse La E1 . .**118** D6
School House La
TW11 . . . .**175** C3
School La DA16 . . . .**146** B2
Lower Halliford TW17 .**192** D2
Pinner HA5 . . . .**41** A5
Surbiton KT6 . . . . .**198** B1
Teddington KT1 . . . .**175** C2
School of Finance &
Management N7 . . . .**72** B2
School of St David & St
Katharine The N8 . . .**50** A5
School Pas
▣ Kingston KT1 . . .**176** B1
Southall UB1 . . . . .**107** B6
School Rd BR7 . . . .**189** A3
E12 . . . .**78** B4
NW10 . . . .**89** B3
Ashford TW15 . . . .**170** D4
Dagenham RM10 . . .**103** D6
East Molesey KT8 . .**196** B5
Hampton TW12 . . . .**174** A4
Hounslow TW3 . . . .**130** A2
Ilford E12 . . . .**78** B4
Littleton TW15 . . . .**170** D3
Teddington KT1 . . . .**175** C2
School Road Ave
TW12 . . . .**174** A4
School Sq SE10 . . . .**120** D3
Schoolway N12 . . . . .**30** B4
School Way RM8 . . . .**80** C5
School Wlk TW16 . . .**193** D6
Schooner Cl E14 . . . .**120** B3
▣ SE16 . . . .**118** D4
Barking IG11 . . . . .**102** B4
Schubert Rd
Elstree WD6 . . . .**9** D5
Putney SW15 . . . . .**157** B6
Science Mus ✦
SW7 . . . . . .**114** B3 **256** C5
Scilly Isles KT10 . . .**212** C6
Sclater St E1 . . . . .**243** D6
Scoles Cres SW2 . . .**160** C3
Scope Way KT1 . . . .**198** A5
Scoresby St SE1 . . .**251** C3
Scoresdale SE19 . . .**183** C2
Scorton Ave UB6 . . . .**87** A5
Scorton Ho ▣ N1 . . . .**95** C5
Scotch Comm W13 . . .**87** B2
Scotch Ho
SW1 . . . . . .**114** D4 **247** C1
Scoter Cl IG8 . . . . . .**37** B3
Scoter Ct ▣ SE8 . . .**141** B6
Scot Gr HA5 . . . .**22** D3
Scotia Bldg ▣ E1 . . .**118** D6
Scotia Ct ▣ SE16 . . .**118** C3
Scotia Rd ▣ SW2 . . .**160** C4
Scotland Gn N17 . . . .**33** D1
Scotland Green Rd
EN3 . . . .**18** D6
Scotland Green Rd N
EN3 . . . .**7** A1
Scotland Pl SW1 . . .**250** A3
Scotland Rd IG9 . . . .**21** C3
Scotney Ho E9 . . . . .**74** C2
Scots Cl TW19 . . . . .**148** A3
Scotsdale Cl BR5,BR7 **211** C5
Belmont SM3 . . . . .**217** A1
Scotsdale Rd SE12 . .**165** B6
Scotson Ho SE11 . . .**261** A3
Scotswood St
EC1 . . . .**94** C3 **241** B6
Scotswood Wlk N17 . .**34** A1
Scott Cl
Thornton Heath SW16 **182** B2
West Drayton UB7 . .**104** B2
West Ewell KT19 . . .**215** A3
Scott Ct ▣ N16 . . . . .**73** C5

Scott Ct continued
▣ SW11 . . . .**137** B3
W4 . . . .**111** B4
Scott Ellis Gdns
NW8 . . . .**92** B4 **229** C1
Scottes La RM8 . . . . .**58** D1
Scott Farm Cl KT7 . .**197** B1
Scott Gdns TW5 . . .**128** C5
Scott Ho ▣ E13 . . . . .**99** A5
N1 . . . .**235** C6
N7 . . . .**72** B2
▣ NW10 . . . .**67** B1
NW8 . . . .**237** A5
▣ Edmonton N18 . . .**34** A5
▣ Erith DA17 . . . . .**125** B1
Richmond TW10 . . .**153** C2
Scott Lidgett Cres
SE16 . . . .**118** A4
Scott's Ave
Ashford TW16 . . . .**171** C3
Beckenham BR2 . . .**186** B1
Scotts Ct ▣ W12 . . .**112** B4
Scotts Dr TW12 . . . .**173** D3
Scotts Farm Rd KT19 **215** A2
Scott's La BR2,BR3 . .**186** B1
Scotts Park Prim Sch
BR1 . . . .**187** C2
Scotts Rd BR1 . . . .**187** A3
E10 . . . .**54** A1
W12 . . . .**112** B4
Scotts Rd UB2 . . . .**106** C3
Scott's Sufferance Wharf
SE1 . . . .**253** C2
Scott St E1 . . . .**96** B1
Scott's Way TW16 . .**171** C3
Scott's Yd EC4 . . . . .**252** C6
Scott Trimmer Way
TW3 . . . .**129** A3
Scottwell Dr NW9 . . .**45** D4
Scott Wilkie Prim Sch
E16 . . . .**99** C1
Scoulding Ho ▣ E14 **119** C3
Scoulding Rd E16 . . .**99** A1
Scouler St E14 . . . .**120** B6
Scout App NW10 . . . .**67** C4
Scout Way NW7 . . . .**27** D6
Scovell Cres SE1 . . .**252** A1
Scovell Rd SE1 . . . .**252** A1
Scrattons Terr IG11 . .**103** A5
Scriven Ct ▣ E8 . . . .**95** D6
Scriven St E8 . . . . . .**95** D6
Scrooby St SE6 . . . .**163** D5
Scrope Bldg EC1 . . .**241** A4
Scrubs La NW10,W10,
W12 . . . .**90** B3
Scrutton Cl SW12 . . .**159** D4
Scrutton St
EC2 . . . .**95** C3 **243** A5
Scudamore La NW9 . .**45** A5
Scutari Rd SE22 . . . .**162** C6
Scylla Cres
TW6&TW14 . . . . . .**148** D5
Scylla Rd SE15 . . . .**140** B2
East Bedfont TW14,
TW6 . . . .**148** D5
Seabright St ▣ E2 . . .**96** B4
Seabrook Dr BR4 . . .**224** C5
Seabrook Gdns RM7 . .**59** C2
Seabrook Rd RM8 . . .**80** D5
Seacole Cl W3 . . . . .**89** B2
Seacole Ct N15 . . . . .**51** B4
Seacole Lo N21 . . . . .**16** B6
Seacourt Rd SE2 . . .**124** D4
Seacroft Gdns WD19 .**22** D6
Seafield Rd N11 . . . . .**31** D6
Seaford Cl HA4 . . . . .**61** B6
Seaford Ho ▣ SE16 . .**118** C4
Seaford Rd E17 . . . . .**53** D6
N15 . . . .**51** C4
Ealing W13 . . . . . .**109** B3
Enfield EN1 . . . .**5** C1
Seaford St WC1 . . . .**233** B1
Seaforth Ave SW20 . .**200** B5
Seaforth Cres N5 . . .**73** A3
Seaforth Gdns
Southgate N21 . . . . .**16** C3
Woodford IG8 . . . . . .**37** C5
Worcester Park KT19 **215** D3
Seaforth Lo ▣ SW13 **133** D3
Seaforth Pl SW1 . . .**259** B6
Seager Pl E3 . . . . . .**97** B2
Seagrave Lo SW6 . . .**265** B6
Seagrave Rd
SW6 . . . .**135** C6 **265** B6
Seagrove Cl E1 . . . . .**96** D2
Seagry Rd E11 . . . . .**55** B2
Seagull Cl IG11 . . . .**102** A4

Sealand Rd TW6 ....148 C5
Sealand Wlk UB5 .....85 A4
Seal Ho SE1 ....262 D6
Seal St E8 ....73 D4
Searle Ct **2** CR4 ....180 C2
Searle Pl N4 ....50 B1
Searles Cl
SW11 ......136 C5 267 B3
Searles Dr E6 ....100 D2
Searles Rd SE1 ....262 D4
Searson Ho SE17 ....261 D3
Sears St SE5 ....139 B5
Seasalter Ho **10** SW9 138 C4
Seasprite Cl **10** UB5 ..84 D4
Seath Ho **4** SE26 ....184 B5
Seaton Ave IG3 ......79 D3
Seaton Cl **6** E13 ....99 A3
Isleworth TW2 ....152 B5
Roehampton SW15 ...156 B4
Seaton Dr TW15 .....148 A2
Seaton Gdns HA4 ....62 A6
Seaton Point E5 .....74 A4
Seaton Rd
Bexley DA16 ....146 C5
Hayes UB3 ....105 A3
Mitcham CR4 ....180 C1
Twickenham TW2 ....152 A5
Wembley HA0 ....88 A5
Seaton Sq NW7 ......28 D3
Seaton St N18 ....34 A4
Seavington Ho **3**
SE5 ....139 C2
Sebastian Ct **10** IG11 .79 D1
Sebastian Ho **22** N1 ..95 C5
Sebastion St
EC1 ....94 D4 234 D1
Sebastopol Rd N9 ....34 A6
Sebbon St N1 ....72 D1
Sebergham Gr NW7 ...28 A3
Sebert Rd E7 ....77 B4
Sebright Ho **21** E2 ...96 A5
Sebright Rd EN5 ......1 A2
Sebright Sch E2 .....96 A5
Secker Cres HA3 .....24 A2
Secker Ho SW9 .....138 D3
Secker St SE1 ......251 A3
Second Ave E12 ......78 A5
E13 ....99 A4
E17 ....53 C4
N18 ....34 C6
NW4 ....46 D5
W10 ....91 A3
W3 ....111 D5
Dagenham RM10 ....103 D5
Dagenham RM6 ......58 C4
Enfield EN1 ....17 D6
Hayes UB3 ....105 D5
Mortlake SW14 ......133 C2
Walton-on-T KT12 ...194 B3
Wembley HA9 ....65 D6
Second Cl KT8 ......196 A5
Second Cross Rd
TW2 ....152 C2
Second Way HA9 .....66 D4
Sedan Way
SE17 ....117 C1 263 A2
Sedcombe Cl DA14 ..190 C6
Sedcote Rd EN3 .....18 D6
Sedding St SW1 ....258 A4
Seddon Ho EC2 .....242 A4
Seddon Rd SM4 ....202 B4
Seddon St
WC1 ....94 B4 233 D1
Sedgebrook Rd SE3 .143 D2
Sedgecombe Ave HA3 43 C4
Sedgefield Ct UB5 ...63 D3
Sedgeford Rd W12 ..111 D5
Sedgehill Rd SE6 ...185 D5
Sedgehill Sch SE6 ..185 D5
Sedgemere Ave N2 ..48 A6
Sedgemere Rd SE2 .124 C3
Sedgemoor Dr RM10 .81 C4
Sedge Rd N17 ....34 C3
Sedgeway SE6 ......164 D3
Sedgewick Ho SW19 156 D2
Sedgewood Cl BR2 .208 D2
Sedgley Ho N4 ......72 B6
Sedgmoor Pl SE5 ...139 C5
Sedgwick Ave UB10 ..60 D1
Sedgwick Rd E10 ....76 A6
Sedgwick St E9 .....74 D3
Sedleigh Rd SW18 ..157 B5
Sedlescombe Rd
SW6 ....135 C6 265 A6
Sedley Cl EN1 ....6 B5
Sedley Ct SE26 .....162 B2
Sedley Ho SE11 ....260 D2

Sedley Pl W1 ....238 C1
Sedum Cl NW9 ....44 D4
Seeley Dr SE21 .....183 C6
Seelig Ave NW9 .....46 A2
Seely Rd SW17 .....181 A4
Seething La
EC3 ....117 C6 253 B6
Seething Wells Halls of
Residence KT6 .....197 C3
Seething Wells La
KT6 ....197 C3
Sefton Ave NW7 ......27 B5
Harrow HA3 ....24 B2
Sefton Cl BR5 ......211 D5
Sefton Ct TW5 ......129 C4
Sefton Lo **2** TW1 ...153 C1
Sefton Rd
Croydon CR0 ....206 A1
Orpington BR5 ......211 D5
Sefton St SW15 ....134 C2
Segal Cl SE23 ......163 A4
Sekforde St
EC1 ....94 D3 241 C6
Sekhon Terr TW13 ..151 C1
Selan Gdns UB4 .....84 B2
Selbie Ave NW10 ....67 D3
Selborne **2** SW11 ..137 A2
Selborne Ave DA5 ..169 A3
E17 ....53 B5
Little Ilford E12 .....78 C4
Selborne Gdns NW4 .46 A5
Wembley HA0 ....87 A5
Selborne Ho SE1 ...252 C1
Selborne Prim Sch
UB6 ....86 D5
Selborne Rd E17 ....53 C4
1 SE5 ....139 B3
Ilford IG1 ....78 C6
Kingston KT3 ....177 C1
Palmers Green N14 ..16 A1
Sidcup DA14 ....190 B6
South Croydon CR0 .221 D5
Wood Green N22 ....32 B2
Selborne Wlk E17 ...53 B5
Selbourne Ave KT6 .214 C5
Selby Chase HA4 ....62 B6
Selby Cl BR7 ....188 C4
14 E6 ....100 A2
Chessington KT9 ...214 A1
Selby Ct TW2 ......152 B2
Selby Gdns UB1 .....85 C3
Selby Gn SM5 ......202 C2
Selby Ho **10** SW4 ..159 C5
6 W10 ....91 A4
Selby Rd E11 ....76 C5
E13 ....99 B2
Ashford TW15 ......171 A4
Carshalton SM5 ....202 C2
Ealing W5 ....87 C3
Penge SE20 ....184 A1
Tottenham N17 ......33 C4
Selby St E1 ....96 A3
Selden Ho **2** SE15 .140 C3
Selden Rd SE15 ....140 C3
Selden Wlk N7 ....72 B6
Seldon Ho SW1 ....259 A1
SW8 ....269 A3
Selena Ct N20 ......14 D1
Selfridges W1 .....238 B1
Selhurst Cl SW19 ..156 D3
Selhurst New Ct
SE25 ....205 C3
Selhurst New Rd
SE25 ....205 C3
Selhurst Park (Crystal
Palace FC) SE25 ..205 C5
Selhurst Pl SE25 ...205 C3
Selhurst Rd
Edmonton N9 ....17 C1
South Norwood SE25 205 C4
Selhurst Sta SE25 .205 C4
Selina Ho NW8 .....236 D6
Selinas La RM8 .....59 B2
Selkirk Ct N17 ......33 C1
Selkirk Ho N1 ......233 C6
4 N16 ....73 C5
Selkirk Rd
Twickenham TW2 ...152 A3
Upper Tooting SW17 .180 C6
Sellers Hall Cl N3 ...29 C3
Sellincourt Inf Sch
SW17 ....180 C4
Sellincourt Jun Sch
SW17 ....180 C4
Sellincourt Rd SW17 180 C4
Sellindge Cl BR3 ..185 B3
Sellons Ave NW10 ..89 D6
Sellsby Ct N11 ......31 B5
Sellwood Dr EN5 ....12 C6
Selma Ho W12 ......90 B1

Selman Ho **3** E9 ....75 A2
Selsdon Ave CR2 ...221 B2
Selsdon Cl KT6 .....198 A4
Selsdon Ct **4** UB1 ..85 D1
Selsdon High Sch
CR2 ....222 D1
Selsdon Park Rd CR0,
CR2 ....223 B1
Selsdon Rd E13 .....99 C5
NW2 ....67 D6
South Croydon CR2 .221 B2
Wanstead E11 ....55 A2
West Norwood SE27 .182 D6
Selsdon Road Ind Est
CR2 ....221 B2
Selsdon Way E14 ...119 D3
Selsea Pl N16 ....73 C3
Selsey Cres DA16 ..146 D4
Selsey St E14 ....97 C3
Selvage La NW7 .....27 B6
Selway Cl HA5 ......40 B6
Selwood Ho **1** N4 ..51 B2
Selwood Pl
SW7 ....114 B1 256 C2
Selwood Rd
Cheam SM3 ....201 B1
Chessington KT9 ...213 D4
Croydon CR0 ....206 B1
Selwood Terr SW7 .256 C2
Selworthy Cl E11 ....55 A4
Selworthy Ho SW11 266 D2
Selworthy Rd SE6 ..163 B1
Selwyn Ave
Chingford E4 ....36 A4
Ilford IG3 ....57 D3
Richmond TW9 .....132 B2
Selwyn Cl TW4 .....129 A1
Selwyn Cres DA16 ..146 B1
Selwyn Ct E17 ......53 C4
SE3 ....142 D2
Edgware HA8 ....26 D3
8 Richmond TW10 .154 B6
Selwyn Ho **3** SW15 156 D5
Selwyn Inf Sch E4 ...36 A4
Selwyn Jun Sch E4 ..36 A4
Selwyn Prim Sch E13 99 A6
Selwyn Rd E13 ......99 B6
E3 ....97 B5
NW10 ....67 C1
New Malden KT3 ...199 B4
Semley Gate E9 .....75 B2
Semley Ho SW1 ....258 C3
Semley Pl
SW1 ....115 B2 258 C3
Semley Rd SW16 ...182 A1
Senate St SE15 ....140 C3
Senators Lo **29** E3 ..97 A5
Senator Wlk SE28 ..123 B3
Sencler Ho SE2 ....146 D6
Sendall Ct **13** SW11 .136 B2
Seneca Rd CR7 ....205 A5
Senga Rd SM6 .....203 A1
Senhouse Rd SM3 .216 D5
Senior St W2 ....91 D2
Senlac Rd SE12 ....165 B3
Sennen Rd EN1 .....17 D4
Sennen Wlk SE9 ...166 A1
Senrab St E1 ....96 D1
Sentinel Cl UB5 .....85 A3
Sentinel Ho NW4 ....46 C5
Sentinel Sq NW4 ....46 C5
September Ct UB1 ..107 D5
September Way HA7 .25 A4
Sequoia Cl WD23 ....8 B3
Sequoia Gdns BR6 .211 D2
Sequoia Pk HA5 ....23 D4
Seraph Ct EC1 95 A4 235 A2
Serbin Cl E10 ....54 A2
Serenaders Rd **21**
SW9 ....138 C3
Sergeant Ind Est The
SW18 ....157 D5
Serica Ct **14** SE10 ..142 A4
Serjeants' Inn EC4 .241 B1
Serlby Ct W14 .....254 C6
Serle St WC2 .94 B1 240 D2
Serle La E4 ....242 A1
Sermon La EC4 ....242 A1
Serpentine Ct **10**
SE16 ....118 D4
Serpentine Gallery★
W2 ....114 B4 246 D4
Serpentine Rd
W2 ....114 D5 247 C3
Serpentine The★
W2 ....114 C4 247 B3
Service Route No 1
E15 ....76 B1
Service Route No 2
E15 ....76 B1

Service Route No 3
E15 ....76 B1
Servden Dr BR1 ....187 D2
Servite Ho SE13 ....141 D4
Beckenham BR3 ....185 B2
East Barnet N14 .....15 B6
Penge SE26 ....184 C4
Worcester Park KT4 .215 D4
Servite RC Prim Sch
SW10 ......136 A6 266 A6
Servius Ct **2** TW8 ..131 D5
Setchell Rd
SE1 ....117 D2 263 C4
Setchell Way SE1 ..263 C4
Seth St SE16 ....118 C4
Seton Ct **3** NW9 ....46 A5
Seton Gdns RM9 ....80 C1
Settle Point **11** E13 .99 A5
Settlers Ct **2** E14 ..120 B6
Settles St E1 ....96 A1
Settrington Rd SW6 .135 D3
Seven Acres
Carshalton SM5 ....218 C6
Northwood HA6 .....22 A4
Seven Dials
WC2 ....94 A1 240 A1
Seven Kings High Sch
IG2 ....57 B2
Seven Kings Rd IG3 .79 D6
Seven Kings Sta IG3 .57 C1
Seven Kings Way
KT2 ....176 A2
Seven Mills Prim Sch
E14 ....119 C4
Sevenoaks Rd BR6 .227 D4
SE4 ....163 B5
Sevenoaks Way BR5 .190 C2
Seven Sisters N15 ..51 D4
Seven Sisters Inf Sch
N15 ....51 B4
Seven Sisters Rd N4,
N7,N15 ....51 A2
Seven Sisters Sta N15 51 C4
Seven Stars Cnr W12 112 A3
Seventh Ave
Hayes UB3 ....106 A5
Ilford E12 ....78 B4
Seven Ways Par IG2 .56 C4
Severnake Cl E14 ..119 C2
Severn Ct **11** KT2 ..175 D2
Severn Dr Enfield EN1 .6 A5
Hinchley Wood KT10 .213 A6
Severn Way NW10 ...67 D3
Severus Rd SW11 ..136 C1
Seville Ho **11** E1 ...118 A5
Seville Mews N1 ....73 C1
Seville St SW1 .....247 D1
Sevington Rd NW4 ..46 B2
Sevington St W9 ....91 D2
Seward Rd W7 .....109 A4
Penge BR3 ....184 B1
Seward St EC1 95 A4 235 A1
Sewardstone Gdns E4 19 D6
Sewardstone Rd E2 .96 C5
Chingford E4 ....19 D6
Sewdley St E5 ......74 D5
Sewell Ho **7** N16 ..73 C3
Sewell Rd SE28 ....124 B4
Sewell St E13 ....99 A4
Sextant Ave E14 ...120 B2
Sexton's Ho **4** SE13 .142 A4
Seychelle Ct BR3 ..185 D3
Seymour Ave
Tottenham N17 ......34 A1
West Barnes SM4 ..200 D2
Seymour Cl
East Molesey KT8 ..196 A4
Pinner HA5 ....23 B2
Seymour Ct N10 ....31 A4
N16 ....52 A1
NW2 ....68 B6
Chingford E4 ....20 D2
Putney SW15 ....134 B3
Southgate N21 ......16 B5
Seymour Dr BR2 ...210 D2
Seymour Gdns SE4 .141 A2
Feltham TW13 ......172 C6
Kingston KT5 ....198 B4
Redbridge IG1 ......56 B1
Ruislip HA4 ....40 D1
Twickenham TW1 ..153 B4
Seymour Ho NW1 ..232 D1
1 SW8 ....137 C3
WC1 ....240 A6
Seymour Mews W1 .238 A2
Seymour Pl
W1 ....92 D1 237 C2
Croydon SE25 ......206 B5
Seymour Rd E10 ....53 B1
E6 ....99 D6

Seymour Rd continued
N3 ....29 D3
N8 ....50 D4
Acton W4 ....111 A5
Carshalton CR4 ....203 A3
Chingford E4 ....19 D3
East Molesey KT8 ..196 A4
Edmonton N9 ....18 B2
Hampton TW12 .....174 A5
Teddington KT1 .....175 D2
Wallington SM5 ....219 A3
Wandsworth SW18 .157 B5
Wimbledon SW19 ..156 D1
Seymour St SE18 ..123 A3
W1 ....92 D1 237 D1
Seymour Terr SE20 .184 B2
Seymour Villas SE20 .184 B2
Seymour Way TW16 .171 C3
Seymour Wlk
SW10 ......136 A6 266 A6
Seyssel St E14 ....120 D2
Shaa Rd W3 ....111 B6
Shacklegate La
TW11 ....174 C6
Shackleton Cl SE23 .162 B2
Shackleton Ct
4 W12 ....112 B4
4 Dulwich SE21 ...161 B2
4 Millwall E14 ....119 C1
7 Stanwell TW19 ..148 B3
Shackleton Ho **5** E1 118 C5
4 Millwall E14 ....67 B1
Shackleton Rd UB1 .107 B6
Shacklewell Ho **3** E8 73 D4
Shacklewell La E8 ..73 D3
Shacklewell Prim Sch
E8 ....73 D4
Shacklewell Rd N16 .73 D3
Shacklewell Row E8 .73 D4
Shacklewell Sta **30** E2 .95 D4
Shadbolt Cl KT4 ...215 D3
Shad Thames
SE1 ....117 D4 253 D2
Shadwell Ct UB5 ....85 B5
Shadwell Dr UB5 ....85 B4
Shadwell Gdns E1 .118 C6
Shadwell Pierhead
E1 ....118 C6
Shadwell Sta E1 ...118 B6
Shady Bush Cl WD23 ..8 A4
Shaef Way TW11 ...175 A3
Shafter Rd RM10 ....81 D2
Shaftesbury Ave
W1 ....115 D6 249 D6
Enfield EN3 ....6 D3
Feltham TW14 ......150 A5
Harrow HA1,HA2 ....42 A1
Harrow HA3 ....44 A3
New Barnet EN5 .....2 A1
Southall UB2 ....107 C3
Shaftesbury Circ HA2 .42 A1
Shaftesbury Ct N1 .235 C3
SE1 ....262 C6
3 SE28 ....124 C5
1 SE5 ....139 B1
Ilford RM6 ....58 C2
Shaftesbury Gdns
NW10 ....89 C3
Shaftesbury Ho
13 N16 ....73 C5
W2 ....245 D6
Croydon SE25 ......206 A3
Shaftesbury Lo **9** E14 97 C1
Shaftesbury Mews
W8 ....255 B5
Shaftesbury Park
Chambers **1** SW11 .137 A2
Shaftesbury Prim Sch
E7 ....77 C1
Shaftesbury Rd E10 ...53 C1
E17 ....53 D3
Chingford E4 ....20 D2
N4,N19 ....50 A1
Beckenham BR3 ....185 A1
Carshalton SM5 ....202 C2
Chingford E4 ....20 B3
Edmonton N18 ....33 D4
Richmond TW9 .....132 A2
Shaftesbury Sch HA3 .23 D2
Shaftesbury St N1 .235 C3
Shaftesburys The
IG11 ....101 A4
Shaftesbury Way
TW2 ....152 B1
Shaftesbury Waye
UB4 ....84 C1
Shafteswood Ct
SW17 ....158 D1
Shafto Mews SW1 .257 D5
Shafton Rd E9 ......96 D6

Shaftsbury Ct E6 ...100 C1
SW6 ....265 D1
Shaftsbury Mews **2**
SW4 ....159 C6
Shaftsbury Park Prim Sch
SW11 ....137 A3
Shafts Ct EC3 ......243 A1
Shahjalal Ho **18** E2 .96 A5
Shakespeare Ave N11 .31 C5
NW10 ....89 B6
Feltham TW14 ......150 A5
Hayes UB4 ....84 B2
Shakespeare Cl HA3 .44 C2
Shakespeare Cres E12 78 B2
NW10 ....89 B6
Shakespeare Dr HA3 .44 B3
Shakespeare Gdns N2 48 D5
Shakespeare Ho **3** E9 74 C1
N14 ....15 C2
1 Erith DA17 ....125 B1
Shakespeare Rd DA7 147 A4
E17 ....34 D1
N3 ....29 C2
NW7 ....28 A6
SE24 ....138 D1
W3 ....111 A5
Ealing W7 ....108 D6
Shakespeare's Globe
Theatre (site of)★
SE1 ....252 B4
Shakespeare Twr
EC2 ....242 B4
Shakespeare Way
TW13 ....172 C6
Shakspeare Mews **7**
N16 ....73 C4
Shakspeare Wlk N16 .73 C4
Shalbourne Sq E9 ..75 B2
Shalcomb St
SW10 ......136 A6 266 B5
Shalden Ho **6** SW15 155 D5
West Barnes SM4 ..201 A4
Shaldon Rd HA8 ....26 B1
Shaldon Dr Ruislip HA4 62 C5
Shalfleet Dr W10 ...112 D6
Shalford NW10 .....90 A6
3 Woodford IG8 .....37 C4
Shalford Cl BR6 ....227 A4
Shalford Ct N1 ....234 C2
Shalford Ho SE1 ...262 D6
Shalimar Gdns W3 .111 A6
Shalimar Lo W3 ....111 A6
Shalimar Rd W3 ....111 A6
Shallons Rd SE9 ...188 D6
Shalstone Rd SW14,
TW9 ....132 D2
Shalston Villas KT5,
KT6 ....198 B3
Shamrock Ho SE26 .184 A6
Shamrock Rd CR0 ..204 B3
Shamrock St SW4 ..137 D2
Shamrock Way N14 .15 B3
Shandon Rd SW4 ..159 C5
Shand St SE1 117 C4 253 B2
Shandy St E1 ....96 D2
Shanklin Gdns WD19 .22 C6
Shanklin Ho E17 ....35 B1
Shanklin Rd N15 ....52 A5
N8 ....49 D4
Shannon Cl NW2 ....68 C5
Southall UB2 ....106 D1
Shannon Cnr KT3 ..200 A5
Shannon Cnr Ret Pk
KT3 ....200 A5
Shannon Commercial Ctr
KT3 ....200 A5
Shannon Ct N16 ....73 C5
NW10 ....68 A2
Croydon CR0 ....205 A1
Shannon Gr SW9 ..138 B1
Shannon Pl
NW8 ....92 C5 230 B4
Shannon Way BR3 .185 D4
Shanti Ct SW18 ....157 C3
Shap Cres SM5 ....202 D1
Shapland Way N13 .32 A5
Shapla Prim Sch E1 .118 A6
Shapwick Cl N11 ....30 D5
Shardcroft Ave SE24 160 D6
Shardeloes Rd SE14 141 B3
Shard's Sq SE15 ...140 A6
Sharebourne Ho
SW2 ....160 C6
Sharland Cl CR7 ...204 C3
Sharman Ct DA14 ..190 A6
Sharnbrooke Cl
DA16 ....146 C2
Sharnbrook Ho W6 .265 A6
Sharon Cl KT6 .....197 C1
Sharon Gdns E9 ....96 C5

Sharon Rd W4 ...111 B1
Enfield EN3 ...7 A3
Sharpe Cl W7 ...86 D2
Sharp Ho SW8 ...137 B2
Sharples Hall St 8 NW1 ...70 D1
Sharpness Cl UB4 ...85 A2
Sharpness Ct 2 SE15 ...139 D5
Sharps La HA4 ...39 B2
Sharratt St SE15 ...140 C6
Sharstead St SE17 ...116 D1 261 C1
Sharvel La UB5 ...84 B6
Sharwell Ho SW18 ...157 D5
Sharwood WC1 ...233 D3
Shaver's Pl SW1 ...249 C5
Shaw Ave IG11 ...103 A5
Shawbrooke Rd SE9 ...143 D1
Shawbury Ct SE22 ...161 D6
Shawbury Rd SE22 ...161 D6
Shaw Cl Bushey WD23 ...8 C2
Woolwich SE28 ...124 B5
Shaw Ct N19 ...72 A6
12 SW11 ...136 B2
8 W3 ...111 A3
Shaw Dr KT12 ...194 C2
Shawfield Ct UB7 ...104 A3
Shawfield Pk BR1 ...187 D1
Shawfield St SW3 ...114 C1 257 B1
Shawford Ct 8 SW15 ...156 A4
Shawford Rd KT19 ...215 B2
Shaw Gdns IG11 ...103 A5
Shaw Ho 5 E16 ...122 C5
6 Erith DA17 ...125 B1
Shaw Path BR1 ...164 D1
Shaw Rd SE22 ...139 C1
Catford BR1 ...164 D1
Enfield EN3 ...6 D4
Shaw Sq E17 ...35 A2
Shaws Wood Cotts EN4 3 C3
Shaw Way SM6 ...220 A1
Shearing Dr SM4 ...202 A2
Shearling Way N7 ...72 A2
Shearman Rd SE3 ...142 D2
Shears Ct TW16 ...171 C3
Shearsmith Ho 14 E1 118 A6
Shears The TW16 ...171 C3
Shearwater Cl IG11 ...102 A4
Shearwater Ct 24 SE8 ...141 B6
Shearwater Rd SM1 ...217 B3
Shearwater Way UB4 84 D1
Sheaveshill Ave NW9 ...45 C5
Sheaveshill Ct NW9 ...45 C5
Sheaveshill Par NW9 ...45 C5
Sheen Common Dr SW14,TW10 ...154 C6
Sheen Court Rd TW10 ...132 C1
Sheen Ct TW10 ...132 C1
Sheendale Rd TW9 ...132 B1
Sheenewood SE26 ...184 B6
Sheen Gate Gdns SW14 ...133 A1
Sheen Gr N1 ...94 C6 234 A6
Sheen La SW14 ...133 A1
Sheen Mount JMI Sch SW14 ...154 D6
Sheen Pk TW10,TW9 ...132 A1
Sheen Rd
Orpington BR5 ...211 D5
Richmond TW10,TW9 ...132 B1
Sheen Way SM6 ...220 B3
Sheen Wood SW14 ...155 A6
Sheepcote Cl TW5 ...128 A5
Sheepcote La SW11 ...136 D3
Sheepcote Rd HA1 ...42 D3
Sheepcotes Rd RM6 ...59 A5
Sheephouse Way KT3 ...199 C2
Sheep La E8 ...96 B6
Sheepwalk TW17 ...192 B3
Sheep Walk Mews 7 SW19 ...179 A4
Sheerness Mews E16 ...122 D4
Sheerwater Rd E16 ...99 D2
Sheffield Ho 14 SE15 139 D4
Sheffield Rd TW14, TW6 ...149 A6
Sheffield Sq 2 E3 ...97 B4
Sheffield St WC2 ...240 C1
Sheffield Terr W8 ...113 C5 245 B3
Sheffield Way TW14, TW6 ...149 B6
Shefton Rise HA6 ...22 A3
Shelbey Ct BR1 ...186 D2
Shelbourne Cl HA5 ...41 B6
Shelbourne Ho 20 N19 ...49 D2
Shelbourne Rd N17 ...34 B2
Shelburne Ct SW15 ...156 D6
Shelburne Dr TW4 ...151 C5
Shelburne Ho 9 SW16 ...181 C5
Shelburne Rd N7 ...72 B4
Shelbury Cl DA14 ...168 A1
Shelbury Rd SE22 ...162 B6
Sheldon Ave N6 ...48 D3
Sheldon Cl SE12 ...165 B6
Penge SE20 ...184 B2
Sheldon Ct SW8 ...270 A3
Barnet EN5 ...1 D1
Sheldon Ho 9 E9 ...74 D2
Chingford E4 ...36 C4
Teddington TW11 ...175 A4
Sheldon Rd DA7 ...147 B4
NW2 ...68 D4
Dagenham RM9 ...81 A1
Edmonton N18 ...33 C6
Sheldon St CR0 ...221 A5
Sheldrake Cl E16 ...122 B5
Sheldrake Ho 15 SE16 ...118 D2
Sheldrake Pl W8 ...113 C4 245 A2
Sheldrick Cl CR4 ...180 B1
Shelduck Cl E15 ...76 D3
Shelduck Ct 36 SE8 ...141 B6
Sheldwich Terr BR2 ...210 A3
Shelford 20 KT1 ...176 C1
Shelford Ct 7 E5 ...52 B1
Shelford Pl N16 ...73 B5
Shelford Rd EN5 ...12 C5
Shelford Rise SE19 ...183 D3
Shelgate Rd SW11 ...158 D6
Shell Cl BR2 ...210 A3
Shell Ctr SE1 ...250 D3
Shellduck Cl NW9 ...27 C1
Shelley N8 ...50 A6
Shelley Ave E12 ...78 A2
Greenford UB6 ...86 B4
Shelley Cl BR6 ...227 C5
SE15 ...140 B3
Edgware HA8 ...26 C6
Greenford UB6 ...86 B4
Hayes UB4 ...84 A2
Shelley Cres
Heston TW5 ...128 D4
Southall UB1 ...85 B1
Shelley Ct 12 E10 ...53 D2
N4 ...50 B1
SW3 ...267 D6
9 Kingston KT2 ...175 D6
8 Wanstead E11 ...55 A5
Wembley HA0 ...65 C4
West Barnes KT3 ...200 A4
Shelley Dr DA16 ...145 C4
Shelley Gdns HA0 ...65 C6
Shelley Ho 21 E2 ...96 C4
9 N16 ...73 C4
SE17 ...262 B2
SW1 ...269 A6
Shelley Rd NW10 ...89 B6
Shelley Sch SE11 ...116 C2 261 B3
Shelley Way SW17 ...180 B4
Shellgrove Rd N16 ...73 C3
Shellness Rd E5 ...74 B3
Shell Rd SE13 ...141 D2
Shellwood Rd SW11 ...136 D3
Shelly Lo EN2 ...5 B4
Shelmerdine Cl E3 ...97 C2
Shelson Ave TW13 ...171 D6
Shelton Rd SW19 ...179 C2
Shelton St WC2 ...94 A1 240 A1
Shene Bldg EC1 ...241 A4
Shene Int Sch SW14 ...133 C1
Shenfield Ho 3 SE18 ...143 D5
Shenfield Rd IG8 ...37 B3
Shenfield St N1 ...95 C5
Shenley Ave HA4 ...39 D1
Shenley Rd SE5 ...139 C4
Heston TW5 ...129 A4
Shenstone W13 ...109 C5
Shenstone Gdns IG2 ...57 D4
Shenstone Ho SW16 ...181 C5
Shepherd Cl W1 ...248 A6
Feltham TW13 ...173 A6
Shepherdess Pl N1 ...235 B2
Shepherdess Wlk N1 ...95 A5 235 B3
Shepherd Ho 10 E14 ...97 D1
N7 ...72 A2
Shepherd Mkt W1 ...248 C3
Shepherd's Bush (Central Line) Sta W12 ...112 D4
Shepherd's Bush Gn W12 ...112 C4
Shepherd's Bush (Hamm & City) Sta W12 ...112 C5
Shepherd's Bush Market W12 ...112 C4
Shepherd's Bush Pl W12 ...112 D4
Shepherd's Bush Rd W6 ...112 C3
Shepherd's Cl N6 ...49 B3
Shepherds Cl
Dagenham RM6 ...58 D5
Orpington BR6 ...227 D5
Shepperton TW17 ...192 D3
Shepherds Ct 8 W12 ...112 D4
Shepherds Gn BR7 ...189 B3
Shepherd's Hill N6 ...49 C3
Shepherd's La E9 ...74 D2
Shepherds Leas SE9 ...145 B1
Shepherds Path UB5 ...63 A2
Shepherds Pl W1 ...248 A6
Shepherd St W1 ...115 B5 248 C3
Shepherds Way CR2 ...222 D1
Shepherds Wlk NW2 ...68 A6
Shepherd's Wlk NW3 ...70 B4
Shepherds Wlk WD23 ...8 B2
Shepiston La UB3 ...105 A1
Shepley Cl SM5 ...219 A5
Shepley Ct SW16 ...181 C6
Shepley Mews EN3 ...7 C6
Sheppard Cl Enfield EN1 ...6 B5
Kingston KT6 ...198 A5
Sheppard Dr SE16 ...118 B1
Sheppard Ho 28 E2 ...96 A5
18 SW11 ...136 B2
8 Streatham SW2 ...160 C3
Sheppard's Ct
Harrow HA1 ...42 C2
Wembley UB6 ...64 D2
Sheppard St E16 ...98 D3
Shepperton Bsns Park TW17 ...193 A4
Shepperton Court Dr TW17 ...192 D4
Shepperton Ct TW17 192 D3
Shepperton Rd N1 ...95 B6 235 C6
Littleton TW17,TW18 ...192 A5
Orpington BR5 ...211 A3
Shepperton Sta TW17 ...193 A4
Shepperton Studios TW17 ...192 B6
Sheppey Gdns RM9 ...80 C1
Sheppey Ho 16 E5 ...74 B4
Sheppey Rd RM9 ...80 C1
Sheppey Wlk N1 ...73 A1
Shepton Ct SW11 ...266 D2
Shepton Hos 11 E2 ...96 C4
Sherard Ct N19 ...72 A5
Sherard Ho 24 E9 ...74 C1
Sherard Rd SE9 ...166 A6
Sheraton Bsns Ctr UB6 ...87 C5
Sheraton Cl WD6 ...10 B6
Sheraton Ho SW1 ...268 D6
Sheraton Lo HA3 ...42 C6
Sheraton St W1 ...239 C1
Sheraton The 22 KT6 198 A4
Sherborne Ave
Enfield EN3 ...6 C3
Southall UB2 ...107 C2
Sherborne Cl UB4 ...84 C1
Sherborne Cres SM5 202 C2
Sherborne Ct SE20 ...184 C1
Sherborne Gdns NW9 ...44 C6
Ealing W13 ...87 B2
Sherborne Ho SW1 ...258 D2
SW8 ...270 C3
Sherborne La EC4 ...252 D6
Sherborne Rd BR5 ...211 D4
Cheam SM3 ...201 C1
Chessington KT9 ...214 A3
East Bedfont TW14 ...149 B3
Sherborne St N1 ...95 B6 235 C6
Sherboro Rd 1 N15 ...51 D3
Sherbourne Ct 1 TW12 ...173 C2
Sherbourne Gdns TW17 ...193 C2
Sherbourne Pl HA7 ...25 A4
Sherbrooke Cl DA7 ...147 C1
Sherbrooke Ho 9 E2 ...96 C5
Sherbrooke Rd SW6 ...135 A5 264 B3
Sherbrooke Terr SW6 ...264 B3
Sherbrook Gdns N21 ...16 D4
Shere Cl KT9 ...213 D3
Sheredan Rd E4 ...36 C5
Shere Ho SE1 ...262 C6
Shere Rd IG2 ...56 C4
Sherfield Cl KT3 ...198 D5
Sherfield Gdns SW15 155 D5
Sheridan N8 ...50 C5
Sheridan Bldgs WC2 ...240 B1
Sheridan Cl UB10 ...83 A3
Sheridan Cres BR7 ...188 D1
Sheridan Ct NW6 ...70 A1
SW9 ...270 D1
Ealing W7 ...108 D6
Harrow HA1 ...42 B3
Hounslow TW4 ...151 A6
Sheridan Gdns HA3 ...43 D3
Sheridan Ho 16 E1 ...96 C1
7 N16 ...73 C5
SE11 ...261 B3
Sheridan Lo EN5 ...1 D1
Sheridan Mews E11 ...55 B3
Sheridan Pl
Barnes SW13 ...133 D2
Hampton TW12 ...174 A2
Harrow HA1 ...42 C2
Sheridan Rd DA7 ...147 A2
E12 ...78 B3
E7 ...76 D5
Belvedere DA17 ...125 C2
Merton SW19 ...179 B2
Richmond TW10 ...153 C1
Sheridan St 28 E1 ...96 B1
Sheridan Terr UB5 ...63 D3
Sheridan Way 5 BR3 185 B2
Sheridan Wlk NW11 ...47 C3
Sheridon Ct SW5 ...255 C3
Sheringdale Prim Sch SW18 ...157 B3
Sheringham NW8 ...229 D6
Sheringham Ave E12 ...78 B3
Southgate N14 ...15 D5
Twickenham TW2 ...151 C3
Sheringham Dr IG11 ...80 A3
Sheringham Ho NW1 237 B4
Sheringham Jun Sch E12 ...78 B4
Sheringham Rd N7 ...72 C2
Penge SE20 ...206 C6
Sheringham Twr UB1 ...107 D6
Sherington Ave HA5 ...23 C3
Sherington Prim Sch SE7 ...143 B6
Sherington Rd SE7 ...143 B6
Sherland Rd TW1 ...152 D3
Sherleys Ct HA4 ...61 C6
Sherlies Ave BR6 ...227 C6
Sherlock Ct NW8 ...229 C6
Sherlock Holmes Mus* NW1 ...92 D3 237 D5
Sherlock Mews W1 ...238 A4
Sherman Gdns RM6 ...58 C3
Sherman Rd BR1 ...187 A2
Shernwood Ho 1 E18 55 A5
Sherrard Rd E7,E12 ...77 D2
Sherrards Way EN5 ...13 D5
Sherrick Green Rd NW10 ...68 B3
Sherriff Ct NW6 ...69 C2
Sherriff Rd NW6 ...69 C2
Sherringham Ave
Feltham TW13 ...150 A1
Tottenham N17 ...34 A1
Sherringham Ct 1 N3 29 C2
Sherrin Rd E10 ...75 D4
Sherrock Gdns NW4 ...46 A5
Sherry Mews IG11 ...79 B1
Sherston Ct SE1 ...261 D4
WC1 ...234 A1
Sherwin Ho 1 SE11 ...138 C6
Sherwin Rd SE14 ...140 D4
Sherwood NW6 ...69 A1
Long Ditton KT6 ...213 D6
Sherwood Ave
Greenford UB6 ...64 C3
Hayes UB4 ...84 B3
Mitcham SW16 ...181 D2
Ruislip HA4 ...39 C3
Wanstead E18 ...55 B6
Sherwood Cl DA5 ...168 C5
E17 ...35 B1
Barnes SW13 ...134 B2
Ealing W13 ...109 B5
Sherwood Ct SE13 ...141 D3
11 SW11 ...136 A2
Sherwood Ct *continued*
W1 ...237 C3
5 West Wickham BR4 207 D1
Sherwood Gdns E14 ...119 C2
SE16 ...118 B1
Barking IG11 ...79 B1
Sherwood Hall 7 N2 ...48 A6
Sherwood Ho N4 ...51 A2
Sherwood Park Ave DA15 ...168 B5
Sherwood Park Prim Sch DA15 ...168 B5
Sherwood Park Rd
Mitcham CR4 ...203 D5
Sutton SM1 ...217 C3
Sherwood Park Sch SM6 ...219 D5
Sherwood Prim Sch CR4 ...203 C5
Sherwood Rd DA16 ...145 C2
NW4 ...46 C6
Croydon CR0 ...206 B1
Hampton TW12 ...174 A5
Harrow HA2 ...64 A6
Ilford IG6 ...57 B5
Merton SW19 ...179 B3
Sherwood St N20 ...14 B1
W1 ...249 B6
Sherwood Terr N20 ...14 B1
Sherwood Way BR4 ...224 A6
Shetland Cl WD6 ...11 B5
Shetland Rd E3 ...97 B5
East Bedfont TW6 ...149 A5
Shield Dr TW8 ...131 A6
Shieldhall St SE2 ...124 C2
Shield Rd TW15 ...171 B6
Shifford Path SE23 ...162 D1
Shillaker Ct W3 ...111 D5
Shillibeer Pl W1 ...237 B3
Shillingford Ho 40 E3 ...97 D4
Shillingford St 22 N1 ...72 D1
Shillingstone Ho W14 ...254 B5
Shinfield St W12 ...90 C1
Shinglewell Rd DA8 ...147 C5
Shinners Cl SE25 ...206 A4
Shipka Rd SW12 ...159 B3
Ship La SW14 ...133 A3
Shiplake Ct SW17 ...180 B6
Shiplake Ho 45 E2 ...95 D4
Shipley Ct SE20 ...184 A1
Shipley Ho 32 SW8 ...137 D3
Shipman Par SE23 ...163 A2
Shipman Rd
Forest Hill SE23 ...162 D2
Newham E16 ...99 C1
Ship & Mermaid Row SE1 ...253 A2
Ship St SE8 ...141 C4
Ship Tavern Pas EC3 ...253 A6
Shipton Cl RM8 ...80 D5
Shipton Ho 14 E2 ...95 D5
7 NW5 ...71 A2
Shipton Rd UB8 ...60 B4
Shipton St E2 ...95 D4
Shipwright Rd SE16 ...119 A4
Shipwright Yd SE1 ...253 A3
Shirburn Cl SE23 ...162 C4
Shirbutt St E14 ...119 D6
Shirebrook Rd SE3 ...143 D2
Shire Ct DA18 ...124 D3
Ewell KT17 ...215 D1
Shirehall Cl NW4 ...46 D3
Shirehall Gdns NW4 ...46 D3
Shirehall La NW4 ...46 D3
Shirehall Pk NW4 ...46 D3
Shire Ho E11 ...76 D5
Shire Horse Way TW7 ...130 D2
Shire La
Farthing Street BR6, BR2 ...227 B2
Orpington BR6 ...227 C3
Shiremeade WD6 ...10 B6
Shire Pl SW18 ...158 A4
Shires The TW10 ...176 A6
Shirland Mews W9 ...91 B4
Shirland Rd W9 ...91 C3
Shirley Ave DA5 ...168 D3
Carshalton SM1 ...218 C4
Croydon CR0 ...206 D1
Shirley Church Rd CR0 ...223 A5
Shirley Cl TW3 ...152 A6
Shirley Cres BR3 ...207 A5
Shirley Ct NW9 ...45 B4
8 Ealing W13 ...109 A5
Ilford IG2 ...57 B4
Thornton Heath SW16 ...204 B6
Shirley Dr TW3 ...152 A6
Shirley Gdns
Barking IG11 ...79 C2
Ealing W7 ...108 D5
Shirley Gr N9 ...18 D4
SW11 ...137 A2
Shirley High Sch CR0 ...222 D5
Shirley Hills Rd CR0 ...222 D3
Shirley Ho 13 SE5 ...139 B5
Shirley House Dr SE7 ...143 C5
Shirley Lo 4 SE26 ...185 A6
Shirley Oaks Hospl CR0 ...206 C2
Shirley Oaks Rd CR0 ...222 D6
Shirley Park Rd CR0 ...206 C1
Shirley Rd E15 ...76 C1
W4 ...111 B4
Croydon CR0 ...206 B1
Enfield EN2 ...5 A2
Sidcup DA15 ...167 C1
Shirleys Cl E17 ...53 D4
Shirley St E16 ...98 D1
Shirley Way CR0 ...223 B5
Shirlock Rd NW3 ...70 D4
Shobden Rd N17 ...33 B2
Shobroke Cl NW2 ...68 C5
Shoebury Rd E6 ...78 B1
Shoe La EC4 ...94 C1 241 B2
Shoelands Ct NW9 ...45 B6
Shooters Ave HA3 ...43 C5
Shooters Hill SE18 ...144 C4
Shooters Hill Rd SE18,SE3,SE7 ...143 D5
SE3,SE10 ...142 C4
Shooters Rd EN2 ...4 D4
Shoot-Up Hill NW2 ...69 A2
Shore Bsns Ctr 31 E9 ...74 C1
Shore Cl
Feltham TW14 ...150 A4
Hampton TW12 ...173 A5
Shorediche Cl UB10 ...60 B5
Shoreditch Ct 2 E8 ...73 D1
Shoreditch High St E2 ...95 C3 243 B6
Shoreditch Sta E1 ...95 D3 243 D5
Shore Gr TW13 ...151 C2
Shoreham Cl DA5 ...168 D3
SW18 ...157 D6
Croydon CR0 ...206 C3
Shoreham Rd BR5 ...190 B1
Shoreham Rd (E) TW6 ...148 A6
Shoreham Rd (W) TW6 ...148 A6
Shoreham Way BR2 ...209 A3
Shore Ho SW8 ...137 B2
Shore Mews 30 E9 ...74 C1
Shore Pl E9 ...74 C1
Shore Rd E9 ...74 C1
Shorncliffe Rd SE1 ...117 D1 263 C2
Shorndean St SE6 ...164 A3
Shorne Cl 3 DA15 ...168 B5
Shornefield Cl BR1 ...210 C6
Shornells Way SE2 ...124 C1
Shorrolds Rd SW6 ...135 B5 264 D4
Shortcroft Mead Ct NW10 ...68 A3
Shortcroft Rd KT17 ...215 D1
Shortcrofts Rd RM9 ...81 B2
Shorter St EC3 ...117 D6 253 D6
Shortgate N12 ...29 B6
Short La TW15,TW19 ...148 B3
Shortlands W6 ...112 D2
Harlington UB3 ...127 B6
Shortlands Cl DA17 ...125 B3
Edmonton N18 ...17 B1
Shortlands Gdns BR2 186 C1
Shortlands Gr BR2 ...208 B6
Shortlands Rd E10 ...53 D2
Beckenham BR2,BR3 ...208 C6
Kingston KT2 ...176 B3
Shortlands Sta BR2 ...186 C1
Short Path SE18 ...144 D6
Short Rd E11 ...76 C6
Chiswick W4 ...133 C6
Stanwell TW19 ...148 A5
Shorts Croft NW9 ...44 D5
Shorts Gdns WC2 ...94 A1 240 A1
Shorts Rd SM5 ...218 C3
Short St 7 NW4 ...46 C5
SE1 ...251 B2

Shortway SE9 ....144 A2
Short Way N12 ....30 C4
Twickenham TW2 ....152 A4
Shotfield SM6 ....219 B2
Shott Cl SM1 ....218 A3
Shottendane Rd
SW6 ....135 C4 265 A2
Shottery Cl SE9 ....166 A1
Shottfield Ave SW14 .133 C1
Shottsford [1] W11 ....91 C1
Shoulder of Mutton Alley
[10] E14 ....119 A6
Shouldham St
W1 ....92 C2 237 B3
Showers Way UB3 ....106 A5
Shrapnel Cl SE18 ....144 A5
Shrapnel Rd SE9 ....144 B2
Shreveport Ho [23] N19 49 D2
Shrewsbury Ave
Harrow HA3 ....44 A5
Mortlake SW14 ....133 B1
Shrewsbury Cl KT6 ....214 A6
Shrewsbury Cres
NW10 ....89 B6
Shrewsbury Ho SE11 270 D5
SW3 ....267 A5
Shrewsbury House Sch
KT6 ....214 A6
Shrewsbury La SE18 .144 D4
Shrewsbury Mews [33]
W2 ....91 C2
Shrewsbury Rd E7 ....77 D2
N11 ....31 D4
W2 ....91 C1
Beckenham BR3 ....207 A6
Carshalton SM5 ....202 C2
Harlington TW14,TW6 .149 B5
Shrewsbury St W10 ....90 C3
Shrewsbury Wlk [7]
TW7 ....131 A2
Shrewton Rd SW17 ..180 D3
Shroffold Rd BR1 ....164 D1
Shropshire Cl CR4 ....204 A5
Shropshire Ct W7 ....86 D1
Shropshire Pl WC1 ..239 B5
Shropshire Rd N22 ....32 B3
Shroton St
NW1 ....92 C2 237 B4
Shrubberies The
Ilford IG2 ....57 D4
Woodford E18 ....37 A1
Shrubbery Gdns N21 .16 D4
Shrubbery Rd
Edmonton N9 ....18 A1
Southall UB1 ....107 C5
Streatham SW16 ....182 A6
Shrubbery The
[2] Surbiton KT6 ....198 A1
[7] Wanstead E11 ....55 B4
Shrubland Gr KT4 ....216 C5
Shrubland Rd E10 ....53 C2
E8 ....96 A6
Walthamstow E10 ....53 C4
Shrublands Ave CR0 .223 C4
Shrublands Cl N20 ....14 B2
Forest Hill SE26 ....162 C1
Shrubsall Cl SE9 ....166 A3
Shrubs Ho SW1 ....259 D3
Shubbery Cl N1 ....235 B5
Shurland Ave EN4 ....14 B5
Shurland Gdns SE15 .138 D4
Shurlock Dr BR6 ....227 A4
Shuters Sq W14 ....254 C1
Shuttle Cl DA15 ....167 D4
Shuttlemead DA5 ....169 B4
Shuttle St E1 ....96 A4
Shuttleworth Rd
SW11 ....136 C3
Sibella Rd SW4 ....137 D3
Sibford Ct [5] CR4 ..202 D6
Sibley Cl DA6 ....169 A6
Sibley Ct UB8 ....83 A2
Sibley Gr E12 ....78 A1
Sibthorpe Rd SE12 ..165 C4
Sibthorp Rd [2] CR4 .180 D1
Sibton Rd SM5 ....202 C2
Sicilian Ave WC1 ....240 B3
Sidbury St
SW6 ....135 A4 264 A2
Sidcup By Pass Rd
Sidcup DA14 ....189 C6
St Paul's Cray BR5,BR7 .190 B3
Sidcup Hill DA14 ....190 B5
Sidcup Hill Gdns
DA14 ....190 C5
Sidcup Hill Prim Sch
DA14 ....190 B5

Sidcup Pl DA14 ....190 A5
Sidcup Rd SE9 ....166 A3
Sidcup Sta DA14,
DA15 ....168 A3
Sidcup Tech Ctr
DA14 ....190 D4
Siddeley Dr TW4 ....129 A3
Siddons Ct WC2 ....240 C1
Siddons Ho [8] NW3 ..70 D3
W2 ....236 D3
Siddons La
NW1 ....92 D3 237 D5
Siddons Rd
Croydon CR0 ....220 D5
Forest Hill SE23 ....163 A4
Tottenham N17 ....34 A2
Side Rd E17 ....53 B4
Sidewood Rd DA15,
SE9 ....167 D3
Sidford Ho SE1 ....260 D5
Sidford Pl
SE1 ....116 B3 260 D5
Sidgwick Ho [26] SW9 138 A3
Sidings Mews N7 ....72 C4
Sidings The E11 ....54 A1
Sidlaw Ho N16 ....51 D1
Sidmouth Ave TW7 ..130 C3
Sidmouth Dr HA4 ....62 A5
Sidmouth Ho
[18] SE15 ....140 A5
W1 ....237 B2
[26] Streatham SW2 ..160 C4
Sidmouth Par NW2 ....68 C1
Sidmouth Rd E10 ....76 A5
NW2 ....68 C1
Bexley DA16 ....146 C3
Sidmouth St
WC1 ....94 B4 233 C1
Sidney Ave N13 ....32 B5
Sidney Boyd Ct NW6 ..69 C1
Sidney Elson Way E6 100 C5
Sidney Gdns TW8 ...131 D6
Sidney Godley (VC) Ho [31]
E2 ....96 C4
Sidney Gr EC1 ....234 C2
Sidney Ho [4] E2 ....96 D5
[3] SE18 ....144 B4
Sidney Miller Ct [8]
W3 ....110 D5
Sidney Rd SW9 ....138 B3
Beckenham BR3 ....185 A1
Croydon SE25 ....206 A4
Harrow HA2 ....42 A6
Twickenham TW1 ...153 B4
Walton-on-T KT12 ...194 B1
Wanstead E7 ....77 A5
Wood Green N22 ....32 B3
Sidney Sq E1 ....96 C2
Sidney St E1 ....96 C2
Sidworth St [6] E8 ..74 B1
Siebert Rd SE3 ....143 A6
Siedle Ho [9] SE18 ..144 C6
Siege Ho [21] E1 ....96 B1
Siemens Rd SE18 ....121 D3
Sierra Dr RM9 ....103 D5
Sigdon Rd E8 ....74 A3
Sigers The HA5 ....40 B3
Signmakers Yd NW1 .231 D5
Sigrist Sq [4] KT2 ..176 A2
Silbury Ave CR4 ....180 C2
Silbury Ho [9] SE26 .162 A1
Silbury St N1 ....235 C2
Silchester Ct
Stanwell TW19 ....148 A2
Thornton Heath CR7 ..204 C4
Silchester Rd W10 ..90 D1
Silecroft Rd DA7 ....147 C4
Silesia Bldgs E8 ....74 B1
Silex St SE1 ....116 D4 251 D1
Silicone Bsns Ctr UB6 87 C5
Silk Cl SE12 ....165 A5
Silkfield Rd NW9 ....45 C4
Silk Ho NW9 ....45 B6
Silk Mills Path SE13 .142 A2
Silk Mills Sq E9 ....75 B2
Silks Ct E11 ....54 C1
Silk St EC2 ....95 A1 242 B4
Silkstream Par HA8 ..27 A2
Silkstream Rd HA8 ..27 A2
Sillitoe Ho N1 ....235 D5
Silsoe Ho NW1 ....231 B1
Silsoe Rd N22 ....50 B6
Silver Birch Ave E4 ..35 A2
Silver Birch Cl N11 ..31 A4
Forest Hill SE6 ....163 B1
Ickenham UB10 ....60 A4
Silver Birch Ct EN3 ..18 D6
Silver Birch Gdns E6 100 B3
Silver Birch Rd SE28 .124 C6

Silverbirch Wlk [1]
NW3 ....71 A2
Silverburn Ho [4]
SW9 ....138 D4
Silver Cl SE14 ....141 A5
Harrow HA3 ....24 B3
Silvercliffe Gdns EN4 ..2 C1
Silver Cres W4 ....110 D2
Silver Ct N19 ....71 C5
Silverdale NW1 ....232 A2
Enfield EN2 ....4 A1
Forest Hill SE26 ....184 C6
Silverdale Ave IG3 ....57 D4
Silverdale Cl
Cheam SM1 ....217 B4
[1] Ealing W7 ....108 D5
Northolt UB5 ....63 B4
Silverdale Ct EC1 ....241 D6
Silverdale Dr
Chislehurst SE9 ....166 A2
Sunbury TW16 ....172 B1
Silverdale Factory Ctr
UB3 ....106 A4
Silverdale Gdns UB3 .106 A4
Silverdale Par IG3 ....57 D4
Silverdale Rd BR5 ....211 A5
DA7 ....147 D3
Chingford E4 ....36 B4
Hayes UB3 ....106 A4
Silverhall St TW7 ....131 A2
Silverholme Cl HA3 ..44 A2
Silver Ind Est N17 ....33 D1
Silver Jubilee Way
TW4 ....128 B3
Silver La BR4 ....224 B6
Silverland St E16 ....122 B5
Silverleigh Rd CR7 ..204 B4
Silvermead [7] E18 ..37 A2
Silvermere Rd SE6 ..163 D5
Silver Pl W1 ....249 B6
Silver Rd W12 ....112 D6
Silvers IG9 ....21 C3
Silver Spring Cl DA8 .147 D6
Silver St Edmonton N18 .33 C6
Enfield EN1 ....5 B2
Silverstone Ct [6]
BR1 ....187 C1
Silverston Way HA7 ..25 C4
Silver Street Sta N18 .33 C6
Silverthorn [15] NW6 ..91 D6
Silverthorne Rd SW8 137 B3
Silverthorn Gdns E4 ..19 C2
Silverton Lo SE19 ....183 C3
Silverton Rd W6 ....134 D6
Silvertown Sta E16 ..122 A5
Silvertown Way E16 .121 A5
Silvertree La UB6 ....86 B4
Silver Way
Hillingdon UB10 ....82 D5
Romford RM7 ....59 D6
Silver Wlk SE16 ....119 B5
Silverwood Cl BR3 ..185 C3
Silvester Ho [17] E1 ..96 B1
[27] E2 ....96 C4
[2] W11 ....91 B1
Pinner HA5 ....40 A5
Silvester Rd SE22 ....161 D6
Silvester St SE1 ....252 C1
Silwood St SE16 ....118 C1
Simba Ct TW1 ....152 D3
Simla Ho SE1 ....252 D1
Simmil Rd KT10 ....212 C3
Simmons Cl N20 ....14 C3
Chessington KT9 ....213 C2
Simmons Gate KT10 .212 A3
Simmons Ho [16] E2 ..96 A4
N7 ....72 B6
Simmons La E4 ....20 B2
Simmons Rd SE18 ....122 C1
Simmons' Way N20 ..14 C2
Simms Cl SM5 ....218 C6
Simms Ct SW6 ....135 A2
Simms Gdns N2 ....30 A4
Simms Rd SE1 ....118 A2
Simnel Rd SE12 ....165 B4
Simon Cl
W11 ....113 B6 244 D6
Simon Ct W9 ....91 C4
[5] Woolwich SE28 ..124 B5
Simonds Rd E10 ....76 B5
Simone Cl BR1 ....187 D2
Simon Lo [31] SW19 ..156 D1
Simon Marks (Jewish)
Prim Sch N16 ....73 D6
Simon Peter Ct EN2 ..4 D3
Simons Wlk E15 ....76 B3
Simpson Cl N21 ....16 B6
Simpson Dr W3 ....89 B1
Simpson Ho NW8 ....230 A1
SE11 ....260 C1

Simpson Ho continued
Wembley HA9 ....65 D6
Simpson Rd
Hounslow TW4 ....151 B5
Richmond TW10 ....175 C6
Simpson's Cotts BR2 .225 C5
Simpson's Rd BR2 ..209 A6
E14 ....119 D6
Simpson St SW11 ....136 C3
Simpson Way KT6 ....197 C3
Sim's Cotts KT10 ....212 D2
Sims Wlk SE3 ....142 D1
Sinclair Ct N5 ....73 A2
[21] Beckenham BR3 ...185 C3
[5] Croydon CR0 ....221 D6
Sinclair Gdns W14 ..112 A4
Sinclair Gr NW11 ....46 D3
Sinclair Ho [1] SW12 .159 D3
Sinclair Mans [13]
W12 ....112 C4
Sinclair Rd E4 ....35 B5
W14 ....113 A3 254 A6
Sinclairs Ho [14] E3 ..97 B5
Sinclare Cl EN1 ....5 D4
Singapore Rd W13 ..109 A5
Singer St EC2 ....235 D1
Singlegate First Sch
SW19 ....180 B3
Singleton Cl
Mitcham SW17,SW19 ..180 D3
Thornton Heath CR0 ..205 A2
Singleton Rd RM9 ....81 B3
Singleton Scarp N12 .29 C5
Sinnott Rd E17 ....34 D2
Sion Ct TW1 ....153 B3
Sion-Manning RC Sch for
Girls
W10 ....90 D2
W10 ....91 A2
Sion Rd TW1 ....153 B3
Sippetts St IG1 ....57 B1
Sipson Cl UB7 ....126 C6
Sipson La UB3,UB7 ..126 D6
Sipson Rd
Harmondsworth UB7 .126 C6
West Drayton UB7 ....104 B2
West Drayton UB7 ....104 C1
Sipson Way UB7 ....126 C5
Sir Abraham Dawes Cotts
SW15 ....135 A4
Sir Alexander Cl W3 .111 D5
Sir Alexander Rd W3 111 D5
Sir Cyril Black Way [2]
SW19 ....179 C3
Sirdar Rd
W11 ....113 A6 244 A5
Mitcham CR4 ....181 A4
Tottenham N22 ....33 A4
Sir Francis Drake Prim Sch
SE8 ....119 A1
Sir George Monoux Sixth
Form Coll E17 ....35 D1
Sir Henry Floyd Ct HA7 .9 B2
Sirinham Point SW8 .270 D5
Sirius Bldg [13] E1 ..118 D6
Sir James Barrie Prim Sch
SW8 ....137 C4 269 B3
Sir John Cass Foundation
& Redcoat CE Sec Sch
E1 ....96 D2
Sir John Cass's Prim Sch
EC3 ....95 C1 243 A1
Sir John Heron Prim Sch
E12 ....78 B4
Sir John Kirk Cl [33]
SE5 ....139 A5
Sir John Lillie Prim Sch
SW6 ....135 A6 264 B5
Sir Martin Bowes Ho [15]
SE18 ....122 C2
Sir Oswald Stoll
Foundation The
SW6 ....265 C4
Sir Thomas Abney Sch
N16 ....51 B1
Sir Thomas More Est
SW3 ....136 B6 266 D5
Sirus Rd HA6 ....22 A5
Sir William Burrough Prim
Sch E14 ....97 A1
Sir William Powell's
Almshos SW6 ....135 A4
Sise La EC4 ....242 C1
Siskin Ho [14] SE16 ..118 C2
Sisley Rd IG11 ....101 D6
Sispara Gdns SW18 .157 B5
Sissinghurst Cl BR1 .186 C5
Sissinghurst Ho [17]
SE15 ....140 C6
Sissinghurst Rd CR0 .206 A4

Sissulu Ct [9] E6 ....99 C6
Sister Mabel's Way [14]
SE15 ....140 A5
Sisters Ave SW11 ....136 D1
Sistova Rd SW12 ....159 B3
Sisulu Pl SW9 ....138 C2
Site of Changing of the
Guard★ SW1 ....249 A1
Sittingbourne Ave
EN1 ....17 B5
Sitwell Gr HA7 ....24 C5
Siverst St UB5 ....63 D2
Sivill Ho [9] E2 ....95 D4
Siviter Way RM10 ....81 D1
Siward Rd
Bromley BR2 ....209 C6
Tottenham N17 ....33 B2
Wandsworth SW17 ..158 A1
Six Bridges Ind Est
SE1 ....118 A1
Sixth Ave W10 ....91 A4
Hayes UB3 ....105 D5
Ilford E12 ....78 B4
Sixth Cross Rd TW2 .152 A1
Skardu Rd NW2 ....69 A3
Skeena Hill SW18,
SW19 ....157 A4
Skeffington Rd E6 ..100 B6
Skeggs Ho [5] E14 ..120 A3
Skegness Ho [3] N7 ..72 B1
Skelbrook St SW18 ..158 A2
Skelgill Rd SW15 ....135 B1
Skelley Rd E15 ....76 D1
Skelton Cl [7] E8 ....73 D2
Skelton Ho N16 ....73 D6
Skelton Rd E7 ....77 A2
Skelton's La E10 ....53 D2
Skelwith Rd W6 ....134 C6
Skenfrith Ho SE15 ..140 B6
Skerne Rd KT2 ....175 D2
Sketchley Gdns SE16 118 D1
Sketty Rd EN1 ....5 D2
Skiers St E15 ....98 C6
Skiffington Cl SW2 ..160 C3
Skinner Ct E17 ....53 C4
Skinner Pl SW1 ....258 A4
Skinners Almshouses
N13 ....16 C1
Skinners Company Sch
(Upper) N16 ....51 D2
Skinner's Company's
Lower Sch E5 ....52 B1
Skinners La EC4 ....252 B6
Hounslow TW5 ....129 D4
Skinner St EC1 94 C3 241 B6
Skipsea Ho SW18 ....158 A5
Skipsey Ave E6 ....100 B4
Skipton Cl N11 ....31 A4
Skipton Dr UB3 ....105 A3
Skipton Ho SE4 ....141 A1
Skipwith Bldg EC1 ..241 A4
Skipworth Rd E9 ....96 C6
Skua Ct [42] SE8 ....141 B6
Skyline Ct SE1 ....263 C5
Skylines E14 ....120 A4
Sky Peals Rd IG8 ....36 B3
Sladebrook Rd SE3 ..143 D2
Slade Ct NW2 ....69 A3
Barnet EN5 ....1 D2
Sladedale Rd SE18 ..123 C1
Slade Ho TW4 ....151 B4
Sladen Pl [12] E5 ....74 B4
Slades Cl EN2 ....4 C2
Slades Dr BR7 ....189 A6
Slades Gdns EN2 ....4 C2
Slades Hill EN2 ....4 C2
Slades Rise EN2 ....4 C2
Slade The SE18 ....145 C6
Slade Twr E10 ....75 C6
Slade Wlk SE17 ....139 A6
Slagrove Pl SE13 ....163 D6
Slaidburn St
SW10 ....136 A6 266 B5
Slaithwaite Rd SE13 .142 A1
Slaney Ct NW10 ....68 C1
Slaney Pl [1] N7 ....72 C3
Slater Cl [13] SE18 ..122 C2
Slater Ho [4] N16 ....51 D1
Slatter [1] NW9 ....27 C2
Slattery Rd TW13 ....150 C3
Sleaford Ho [16] E3 ..97 C3
Sleaford Ind Est
SW8 ....137 C5 269 B3
Sleaford St
SW8 ....137 C5 269 B3
Sleat Ho [9] E3 ....97 C5
Sledmere Ct TW14 ..149 C3
Slievemore Cl [8]
SW4 ....137 D2
Sligo Ho [8] E1 ....96 D3

Slingsby Pl WC2 ....250 A6
Slippers Pl SE16 ....118 B3
Sloane Ave
SW3 ....114 C2 257 B3
Sloane Avenue Mans
SW3 ....257 C3
Sloane Ct E SW3 ....258 A2
Sloane Ct W SW3 ....258 A2
Sloane Gate Mans
SW1 ....258 A4
Sloane Gdns BR6 ....227 A5
SW1 ....115 A2 258 A3
Sloane Ho [7] E9 ....74 C1
Sloane Hospl BR3 ....186 B2
Sloane Sq SW1 ....257 D3
Sloane Square Sta
SW1 ....115 A2 258 A3
Sloane St
SW1 ....114 D3 257 D5
Sloane Terr SW1 ....258 A4
Sloane Terr Mans
SW1 ....258 A4
Sloane Wlk CR0 ....207 B3
Slocum Cl SE28 ....124 C6
Slomon Ho [2] W10 ..91 A4
Slough La NW9 ....45 A3
Sly St [7] E1 ....96 B1
Smaldon Cl UB7 ....104 C3
Smallberry Ave TW7 .130 C3
Smallberry Green Prim
Sch TW7 ....131 A4
Smallbrook Mews
W2 ....236 C1
Smalley Cl N16 ....73 D5
Smallwood Prim Sch
SW17 ....180 B6
Smallwood Rd SW17 .180 B6
Smarden Cl DA17 ....125 C3
Smarden Gr SE9 ....188 B6
Smart's Pl WC1,WC2 .240 B2
Edmonton N18 ....34 A5
Smart St E2 ....96 D4
Smeaton Cl KT9 ....213 D2
Smeaton Ct SE1 ....262 A5
Smeaton Rd
Holdbrook EN3 ....7 C6
Wandsworth SW18 ..157 C4
Smeaton St E1 ....118 B5
Smedley St SW4 ....137 D3
Smeed Rd E3 ....75 C1
Smiles Pl SE13 ....142 A3
Smith Cl SE16 ....118 D5
Smithers Ho [3] SE20 184 D3
Smithfield Mkt EC1 ..241 D3
Smithfield St
EC1 ....94 D2 241 C3
Smithies Ct E15 ....76 A3
Smithies Rd SE2 ....124 B2
Smith's Ct W1 ....249 C6
Smithson Rd N17 ....33 B2
Smiths Point E13 ....99 A6
Smith Sq
SW1 ....116 A3 260 A5
Smith St SW3 114 D1 257 C1
Surbiton KT5 ....198 B3
Smith's Yd SW18 ....158 A4
Smith Terr
SW3 ....114 D1 257 C1
Smithwood Cl SW19 .157 A2
Smithy St E1 ....96 C2
Smithy Street Sch E1 .96 C2
Smock Wlk CR0 ....205 A3
Smoothfield TW3 ....129 C1
Smugglers Way
SW18 ....135 D1
Smyrk's Rd
SE17 ....117 C1 263 B1
Smyrna Mans [8] NW6 69 C1
Smyrna Rd NW6 ....69 C1
Smythe St E14 ....119 D6
Snakes La EN4,N14 ..3 C1
Snakes La E IG8 ....37 C4
Snakes La W IG8 ....37 B4
Snaresbrook Dr HA7 ..26 A6
Snaresbrook Hall [11]
E18 ....55 A6
Snaresbrook Ho E18 ..54 D1
Snaresbrook Prim Sch
E18 ....55 A5
Snaresbrook Rd E11 .54 D5
Snaresbrook Sta E11 .55 A4
Snarsgate St W10 ....90 C2
Sneath Ave NW11 ....47 B2
Sneyd Rd NW2 ....68 C4
Snowberry Cl E11 ....76 B4
Snowbury Rd [6]
SW6 ....135 D3
Snow Ct [6] HA0 ....65 D2
Snowden Ave UB10 ..82 D5

Snowden St
EC2 ....95 C3 243 A5
Snowdon Cres UB3 ..105 A3
Snowdon Dr NW9 .....45 C3
Snowdon Rd TW6 ..149 C6
Snowdown Cl SE20 ..184 D2
Snowdrop Cl 2
TW12 ....173 C4
Snow Hill EC1 .94 D2 241 C3
Snow Ho SE27 ......160 D1
Snowman Ho NW6 ...91 D6
Snowsfield Prim Sch
SE1 ....117 C4 253 A2
Snowsfields
SE1 ....117 B4 252 D2
Snowshill Rd E12 .....78 A3
Snowy Fielder Waye
TW7 ....131 B3
Soames St SE15 ....139 D2
Soames Wlk KT3 ...177 C2
Soane Cl W5 ....109 D4
Soane Ct 8 NW1 ....71 C1
Soane Ho SE17 .....262 D1
Soane Mus★
WC2 ....94 B1 240 C1
Soaphouse La TW8 .132 A5
Soham Rd EN3 ....7 B6
Soho★ W1 ...93 D1 239 C2
Soho Mills SM6 ....203 B1
Soho Parish CE Prim Sch
W1 ....115 D6 249 C6
Soho Sq W1 ..93 D1 239 C2
Soho St W1 ....239 C2
Sojourner-Truth Cl 11
E8 ....74 B2
Solander Gdns 12 E1 118 C6
Stepney E1 ....118 B6
Solar Ct N3 ....29 D3
Soldene Ct N7 ......72 B2
Solebay St E1 ....97 A3
Solent Ct N12 ......182 B1
Solent Ho 6 E1 .....97 A2
Solent Rd NW6 ......69 C3
Solent Rise E13 .....99 A4
Soley Mews WC1 ...234 A2
Solna Ave SW15 ...156 C6
Solna Rd N21 ....17 B4
Solomon Ave N9 ....34 A6
Solomon's Pas SE15 .140 B1
Solon New Rd SW4 .138 A1
Solon Rd SW2 ......138 A1
Solway Cl TW4 .....129 A2
Solway Ho 12 E1 .....96 D3
Solway Lo 4 IG8 .....37 A3
Solway Rd SE22 ....140 A1
Tottenham N22 ....32 D2
Somaford Gr EN4 ....14 B5
Somali Rd NW2 ......69 B3
Somborne Ho SW15 .156 A4
Sombrook Ho SE11 .261 A3
Somerby Rd IG11 .....79 B1
Somercoates Cl EN4 ...2 C2
Somer Ct SW6 .....265 A5
Somerfield Ho SE16 .118 D1
Somerfield Rd N4 ....72 D6
Somerford Cl HA5 ....40 A5
Somerford Gr N16 ....73 D4
Tottenham N17 ....34 A3
Somerford Grove Est
N16 ....73 D4
Somerford St E1 .....96 B3
Somerford Way SE16 119 A4
Somerhill Ave DA15 .168 B4
Somerhill Rd DA16 ..146 B3
Somerleyton Rd SW9 138 C1
Somersby Est SE20 .184 D2
Somersby Gdns IG4 ..56 B4
Somers Cl NW1 ....232 C4
Somers Cres W2 ...237 A1
Somerset Ave DA16 .145 C2
Chessington KT9 ...213 D4
Wimbledon SW20 ...178 B1
Somerset Cl
New Malden KT3 ...199 C4
Tottenham N17 ....33 B1
Woodford IG8 ....37 A2
Somerset Ct Ealing W7 86 D1
2 Hampton TW12 ..173 C4
Somerset Gdns N6 ..49 A2
SE13 ....141 D3
Teddington TW11 ...174 C5
Thornton Heath SW16 204 B6
Tottenham N17 ....33 C3
Somerset Hall N17 ..33 C3
Somerset Ho★
WC2 ......116 B6 250 D6
Wimbledon SW19 ...157 A1
Somerset Lo
9 Brentford TW8 ..131 D6
Putney SW15 ....134 B1

Somerset Rd E17 .....53 C3
N17 ....51 D6
NW4 ....46 C5
W4 ....111 B3
Brentford TW8 .....131 C6
Ealing W13 ....109 C5
Edmonton N18 ......33 D5
Harrow HA1 ....42 A4
Holdbrook EN3 ....7 C5
Kingston KT1 ......176 B1
New Barnet EN5 .....14 A6
Southall UB1 ....85 C2
Teddington TW11 ...174 C5
Wimbledon SW19 ...157 A1
Somerset Sq
W14 ....113 B4 244 C1
Somerset Waye TW5 129 A5
Somersham Rd DA7 .147 A3
Somers Pl SW2 .....160 B4
Somers Rd E17 ......53 B5
SW2 ....160 B4
Somers Town Est
NW1 ....93 C5 232 B3
Somers Way E1 ....8 A4
Somerton Ave TW9 .132 C2
Somerton Rd NW2 ...69 A5
SE15 ....140 B1
Somertrees Ave SE12 165 B2
Somervell Rd HA2 ....63 C3
Somerville Ave SW13 134 C6
Somerville Ct SW16 .181 D4
Somerville Ho 10
SW15 ....156 D5
Somerville Point
SE16 ....119 B4
Somerville Rd
Dagenham RM6 ......58 C4
Penge SE20 ....184 D3
Sonderburg Rd 13 N7 .72 B6
Sondes St SE17 ....139 B6
Sonia Ct N12 ....30 A4
Edgware HA8 ....26 B3
Sonia Gdns N12 .....30 A6
NW10 ....67 D4
Heston TW5 ....129 C5
Sonning Ct CR0 ....222 A6
Sonning Gdns TW12 173 A4
Sonning Ho 32 E2 ...95 D4
Sonning Rd CR0 ....206 A3
Soper Cl E4 ....35 B5
4 Forest Hill SE23 162 D2
Soper Mews EN3 ......7 C5
Sophia Cl N7 ....72 B2
Sophia Ho N15 ......51 D5
10 W6 ....112 C1
Sophia Rd E10 ......53 D1
E13 ....99 B2
Sophia Sq 14 SE16 .119 A6
Sopwith 2 NW9 .....27 D2
Sopwith Ave KT9 ...214 A3
Sopwith Cl TW10 ...176 B5
Sopwith Rd TW5 ...128 C5
Sopwith Way SW11 268 C4
Kingston KT2 ......176 A2
Sorbus Ct EN2 ....4 D3
Sorensen Ct 2 E10 ..75 D6
Sorrel Cl SE28 .....124 A5
Sorrel Gdns E6 ....100 A2
Sorrel Ho TW3 .....130 A4
Sorrel La 16 E14 ....98 B1
Sorrell Cl SE14 ....141 A5
7 SW9 ....138 C3
Sorrento Rd SM1 ...217 D5
Sotheby Rd N5 ......73 A4
Sotheran Cl E8 ......96 A6
Sotheron Pl SW6 ..265 D3
Soudan Rd
SW11 ......136 D4 267 C1
Souldern Rd 10 W14 112 D3
South Access Rd E17 .53 A3
South Acre NW9 .....27 D1
Southacre Way HA5 .22 C2
South Acton Sta W3,
W4 ....111 A4
South Africa Rd W12 112 B6
South Carriage Dr
SW1,SW7 ...114 D4 247 C2
South Church Ct E6 100 B5
Southchurch Rd E6 100 B5
South Cl DA6 ......146 D1
N6 ....49 B3
Barnet EN5 ....1 B2
Dagenham RM10 ...103 C6
Morden SM4 ....201 A3
Pinner HA5 ....22 D2
Pinner HA5 ....41 B2
Twickenham TW2 ...151 C1
West Drayton UB7 ..104 C3
South Colonnade
E14 ....119 C5

Southampton Pl
WC1 ....240 B3
Southampton Rd NW5 70 D3
Stanwell TW19,TW6 ..148 B3
Southampton Row
WC1 ....94 A2 240 B4
Southampton St
WC2 ....250 B6
Southampton Way
SE5 ....139 C5
Southam St W10 ....91 A3
South Audley St
W1 ....115 A5 248 B4
South Ave NW11 .....47 D5
Chingford E4 ....20 A4
Richmond TW9 .....132 C3
Southall UB1 ....107 B6
Wallington SM5 ....219 A1
South Avenue Gdns
UB1 ....107 B6
South Bank KT6 ....198 A3
South Bank KT6 ....198 A3
South Bank Lo 2
KT6 ....198 A3
South Bank Terr KT6 198 A3
South Bank Univ
SW8 ......137 D4 269 D2
SE1 ......116 D3 261 D6
South Birkbeck Rd
E11 ....76 B5
South Black Lion La
W6 ....112 A1
South Bldg SW1 ...259 B5
South Block 19 E1 ..118 C4
South Bolton Gdns
SW10 ....255 D2
Southborough Cl
KT6 ....197 D1
Southborough Ho
SE17 ....263 B2
Southborough La
BR1,BR2 ....210 C4
Southborough Rd E9 96 D6
Bromley BR1,BR2 ..210 A5
Surbiton KT6 ......198 A1
Southborough Rd (The
Lane) KT6 ....198 A1
Southborough Sch
KT6 ....214 A5
Southbourne BR2 ..209 A2
Southbourne Ave
NW9 ....27 B1
Southbourne Cl HA5 .41 A2
Southbourne Cres
NW4 ....47 A5
Southbourne Ct NW9 .27 A1
Southbourne Gdns
SE12 ....165 B6
Ilford IG1 ....79 A3
Ruislip HA4 ....40 A3
Southbridge Pl CR0 221 A4
Southbridge Rd CR0 221 A4
Southbridge Way
UB2 ....107 A4
Southbrook Mews
SE12 ....164 D5
Southbrook Rd SE12 164 D5
Thornton Heath SW16 182 A2
South Building SE10 142 B5
Southbury NW8 ....229 B6
Southbury Ave EN1 ...6 A1
Southbury Prim Sch
EN3 ....6 C1
Southbury Rd
Enfield EN1 ....5 D1
Enfield EN1,EN3 .....6 B1
Southbury Sta EN3 ...6 B1
South Camden Com Sch
NW1 ....93 D5 232 C3
South Carriage Dr

South Church Ct E6 .100 B5

Southcombe St W14 254 A4
South Common Rd
UB8 ....60 A2
Southcote Ave
Feltham TW13 .....150 A2
Tolworth KT5 ......198 D2
Southcote Rd E17 ...53 A4
N19 ....71 C4
Croydon SE25 .....206 B3
Southcote Rise HA4 .39 B2
Southcott Ho 31 E3 ..97 C4
W9 ....236 B5
South Cres E16 ......98 B3
WC1 ....239 C3
Southcroft Ave DA16 145 C2
West Wickham BR4 .224 A6
Southcroft Rd BR6 .227 C4
Streatham SW17 ...181 A4
South Cross Rd IG6 ..57 A3
South Croxted Rd
SE21 ....183 B6
South Croydon Sta
CR2 ....221 B3
South Ct 17 SW15 ..156 D5
Southdean Gdns
SW19 ....157 A3
South Dene NW7 ....11 A3
Southdene Ct N11 ...15 C1
Southdown N7 ......72 A2
Southdown Ave W7 .109 A3
Southdown Cres
Harrow HA2 ....42 A1
Ilford IG2 ....57 C4
Southdown Dr SW20 178 D3
Southdown Rd SW20 178 D2
South Dr
Orpington BR6 ....227 C3
Ruislip HA4 ....39 C1
South Ealing Cemy
W5 ....109 D2
South Ealing Rd W5 109 D3
South Ealing Sta W5 109 D3
South Eastern Ave N9 17 D1
South Eaton Pl
SW1 ....115 A2 258 B4
South Eden Park Rd
BR3 ....207 D2
South Edwardes Sq
W8 ....255 A5
South End
W8 ....113 D3 255 D6
Croydon CR0 ......221 A4
Southend Cl SE9 ...166 D5
South End Cl NW3 ...70 C4
Southend Cres SE9 .166 C5
South End Gn NW3 ..70 C4
Southend La SE6 ...185 C6
Southend Rd E6 .....78 B1
South End Rd NW3 ..70 C4
Southend Rd
Beckenham BR3 ...185 C2
Woodford IG8 ....37 D1
Southend Road (North
Circular Rd) E17,E18 .36 C2
South End Row
W8 ....113 D3 255 D6
Southern Ave
East Bedfont TW14 ..150 A3
South Norwood SE25 205 D6
Southerngate Way
SE14 ....141 A5
Southern Gr E3 ......97 B3
Southernhay IG10 ...21 D6
Southern Perimeter Rd
Harlington TW14,TW6 149 B4
Harlington TW19,TW6 148 C5
Stanwell TW6 .....148 C5
Southern Rd E13 ....99 B5
N2 ....48 D5
Southern Road Inf Sch
E13 ....99 B5
Southern Road Prim Sch
E13 ....99 B5
Southern Row W10 ..91 A3
Southern St N1 ....233 C4
Southern Way SE10 120 D3
Romford RM7 ....59 C3
Southern Wd W6 ...112 C2
South Esk Rd E7 ....77 C2
Southey Ho SE17 ..262 B2
Southey Rd N15 .....51 C4
SW9 ....138 C4
Merton SW19 ......179 C3
Southey St SE20 ...184 D3
Southfield EN5 ......12 C5
Southfield Cl UB8 ...82 C4
Southfield Cotts W7 108 C4
Southfield Gdns
TW1,TW2 ....174 D6
Southfield Pk HA2 ...41 D5

Southfield Prim Sch
W4 ....111 C4
Southfield Rd W4 ..111 B4
Enfield EN3 ....18 C1
St Paul's Cray BR7 211 D6
Southfields
Hendon NW4 ....46 B6
Thames Ditton KT8 196 C3
Southfields Ave
TW15 ....170 D4
Southfields Com Coll
SW18 ....157 C3
Southfields Ct SM3 217 C6
Southfields Rd SW18 157 C5
Southfields Sta
SW18 ....157 B3
Southfleet Rd BR6 .227 C4
South Gate Ave
TW13 ....171 B6
Southgate Cir 3 N14 15 D2
Southgate Coll N14 .15 D2
Southgate Ct N1 ....73 B1
Southgate Gr N1 ....73 B1
Southgate Ho 7 E17 54 A6
Southgate Rd
N1 ....73 B1 235 D6
Southgate Sch EN4 ..15 B6
Southgate Sta N14 ..15 D3
Southgate Way N2 ..30 C2
South Gdns
Mitcham SW19 ....180 B3
Wembley HA9 ......66 C6
South Gipsy Rd DA16 146 D2
South Glade DA5 ..169 B3
South Gn NW9 ......27 C2
N15 ....51 B4
N6 ....49 A1
South Greenford Sta
UB6 ....86 C4
South Grove Ho N6 ..49 A1
South Grove Prim Sch
E17 ....53 B3
South Hampstead High
Sch NW3 ....70 B2
South Hampstead Jun Sch
NW3 ....70 A4
South Hampstead Sta
NW8 ....70 A1
South Harringay Jun & Inf
Schs N4 ....50 D4
South Harrow Sta
HA2 ....64 A5
South Hill BR7 .....188 B4
South Hill Ave HA1,
HA2 ....64 B5
South Hill Gr HA1 ...64 C4
South Hill Pk NW3 ...70 C4
South Hill Pk Gdns
NW3 ....70 C4
South Hill Rd BR2 ..208 C5
Southholme Cl SE19 183 C2
Southill La HA5 ......40 B5
Southill Rd BR7 ....188 B3
Southill St E14 ......97 D1
South Island Pl SW9 138 C5
South Kensington Sta
SW7 ......114 B2 256 D4
South Kenton Sta HA9 43 C1
South La KT6 ......197 D6
New Malden KT3 ...199 B3
Southlake Prim Sch
SE2 ....124 D4
South Lambeth Pl
SW8 ....270 B6
South Lambeth Rd
SW8 ......138 A5 270 B4
Southland Rd SE18 145 D5
Southlands Ave BR6 227 C3
Southlands Coll
SW15 ....156 A6
Southlands Dr SW19 156 D2
Southlands Gr BR1 .210 A6
Southlands Rd BR1,
BR2 ....209 D5
Southland Way TW7 152 B6
South La W KT3 ....199 B5
South Lo NW8 .....229 C2
6 New Barnet EN5 .13 D6
Twickenham TW2 ..152 A5
South Lodge Ave
CR4,CR7,SW16 ....204 A6
South Lodge Cres EN2 .3 D1
South Lodge Dr N14 .15 D3
South London Montessori
Sch SW11 ....267 A1
South London Tamil Sch
CR0 ....205 A2
South Mall The N9 ..18 A1
South Mead NW9 ....27 D2

South Mead continued
West Ewell KT19 ...215 D1
Southmead Prim Sch
SW19 ....157 A3
Southmead Rd SW19 157 A3
South Merton Sta
SW20 ....201 B6
South Molton La
W1 ....93 B1 238 C1
South Molton Rd E16 .99 A1
South Molton St
W1 ....93 B1 238 C1
Southmont Rd KT10 212 C6
Southmoor Way E9 .75 D2
South Mount N20 ...14 A2
South Norwood Ctry Pk★
SE25 ....206 C4
South Norwood Hill
SE19,SE25 ....183 D1
South Norwood Prim Sch
SE25 ....206 A6
South Oak Rd SW16 182 B6
Southold Rise SE9 .166 B1
Southolm St
SW11 ......137 B4 268 D1
South Ordnance Rd
EN3 ....7 C5
Southover BR1 .....187 A5
N12 ....29 C6
South Par W4 ......111 B2
Edgware HA8 ....26 C1
South Parade
SW3 ......114 B1 256 D2
South Park Cres
Catford SE6 ....164 D3
Ilford IG1 ....79 C5
South Park Ct 24
BR3 ....185 C3
South Park Dr
Barking IG11 ....79 C4
Ilford IG3 ....79 C5
South Park Gr KT3 .199 A5
South Park Hill Rd
CR2 ....221 B4
South Park Mews
SW6 ....135 D2
South Park Prim Sch
IG3 ....79 C5
South Park Rd
Ilford IG1 ....79 C5
Wimbledon SW19 ..179 D4
South Park Terr IG1 .79 C5
South Park Villas IG3 79 C4
South Park Way HA4 62 C3
South Pl EC2 .95 B2 242 D3
Enfield EN3 ....18 C6
Surbiton KT5 ......198 B2
South Pl Mews EC2 242 D3
Southport Rd SE18 .123 B2
South Quay Plaza
E14 ....119 D4
South Quay Sta E14 119 D4
South Rd W5 ....109 D2
Edgware HA8 ....26 D2
Edmonton N9 ....18 A3
Feltham TW13 .....172 D5
Forest Hill SE23 ...162 D2
Hampton TW12 ....173 B4
Mitcham SW19 ....180 B4
Southall UB1 ......107 B5
Twickenham TW2 ..152 B1
West Drayton UB7 104 C3
Heston TW5 ....128 C3
South Residence IG3 58 B4
Southridge Pl SW20 178 D3
South Rise W2 ....247 D3
South Rise Prim Sch
SE18 ....123 B1
South Rise Way SE18 123 B2
South Row SE3 ....142 D3
South Ruislip Sta HA4 62 C2
Southsea Rd KT1 ..198 A5
South Sea St SE16 119 B3
Southside N7 ....71 D4
South Side W6 .....111 D4
Southside Comm
SW19 ....178 D4
Southside Ind Est
SW8 ....269 A2
Southside Quarter 4
SW11 ....136 D3
Southspring SE9 ..167 B4
South Sq NW11 .....47 D3
WC1 ....241 A3
South St BR1 ......187 A1
W1 ....115 A5 248 B4
Enfield EN3 ....18 D6

South St continued
Isleworth TW7 ....**131** A2
South Tenter St
E1 ....**95** D1 **243** D1
South Terr N22 ....**31** D1
SW7 ....**114** C2 **257** A4
Surbiton KT6 ....**198** A3
South Thames Coll
SW18 ....**157** D6
Putney SW15 ....**156** D6
South Tottenham Sta
N15 ....**51** D4
South Vale Harrow HA1 **64** C4
West Norwood SE19 ..**183** A4
Southvale Rd SE3 ....**142** C3
Southview Ave NW10 ..**67** D3
Southview Cl SW17 ....**181** A5
South View Cl DA5 ...**169** B5
South View Cres IG2 ..**56** D3
South View Ct
2 Forest Hill SE23 ...**162** C3
South Norwood SE19 ..**183** A3
Southview Dr E18 ......**55** B6
Southview Gdns SM6 **219** C1
South View Rd N8 ....**50** A6
Southview Rd BR1 ....**186** B6
South View Rd HA5 ...**22** B4
South Villas NW1 .....**71** D2
Southville
SW8 ....**137** D4 **269** D1
Southville Cl
East Bedfont TW14 ...**149** C3
West Ewell KT19 .....**215** B1
Southville Cres
TW14 ....**149** C3
Southville Jun Sch
TW14 ....**149** D3
Southville Rd
East Bedfont TW14 ...**149** C4
Thames Ditton KT7 ...**197** B2
Southwark Bridge
SE1,EC4 ....**117** A6 **252** B5
Southwark Bridge Office
Village SE1 ....**252** B3
Southwark Bridge Rd
SE1 ....**117** A5 **252** B3
Southwark Cath★
SE1 ....**117** B5 **252** C4
Southwark Coll
SE1 ....**116** D4 **251** C2
SE15 ....**140** B5
Southwark Coll
(Blackfriars Ctr)
SE1 ....**251** C3
Southwark Coll
(Camberwell Ctr)
SE5 ....**139** C5
Southwark Coll (Grange
Ctr) SE1 ....**263** B5
Southwark Coll (Surrey
Docks Ctr) SE16 ....**118** B3
Southwark Park Est 11
SE16 ....**118** B2
Southwark Park Prim Sch
SE16 ....**118** B2
Southwark Park Rd
SE16 ....**118** A2 **263** D4
Southwark Pl BR1 .....**210** B6
Southwark St
SE1 ....**117** A5 **252** A3
Southwater Cl 8 E14 ..**97** B1
Beckenham BR3 ......**185** D3
Southway N20 ....**13** C2
NW11 ....**47** D4
South Way Hayes BR2 **209** A2
Wallington SM6 ......**219** C4
West Barnes SW20 ...**200** D5
South Way
Croydon CR0 ....**223** A5
Harrow HA2 ....**41** C5
Wembley HA9 ....**66** C3
Southwell Ave UB5 ...**63** C2
Southwell Gdns SW7 **256** A3
Southwell Grove Rd
E11 ....**76** C6
Southwell Ho 13 N16 .**73** C3
8 SE16 ....**118** B2
Southwell Rd SE5 ....**139** A2
Harrow HA3 ....**43** D1
Thornton Heath CR0 ..**204** C3
South Western Rd
TW1 ....**153** B5
Southwest Rd E11 ....**54** B1

South Wharf Rd
W2 ....**92** B1 **236** D2
Southwick Mews W2 **236** D2
Southwick Pl W2 ...**237** A1
W2 ....**92** C1 **237** A2
Southwick Yd W2 ...**237** A1
South Wimbledon Sta
SW19 ....**179** D3
South Wlk
Coney Hall BR4 ......**224** C5
Hayes UB3 ....**83** B2
Southwold Dr IG11 ...**80** A3
Southwold Mans W9 .**91** C4
Southwold Prim Sch
E5 ....**74** B6
Southwold Rd DA5 .**169** B5
E5 ....**74** C6
Southwood Ave N6 ..**49** B2
Kingston KT2,KT3 ....**177** A2
Southwood Cl BR1 ..**210** B5
North Cheam KT4 ....**200** D1
Southwood Ct EC1 ..**234** C1
NW11 ....**47** D4
Southwood Dr KT5 ..**199** A1
South Woodford Sta
E18 ....**37** B1
Southwood Gdns
Hinchley Wood KT10 .**213** A4
Ilford IG2 ....**56** D5
Southwood Hall N6 ..**49** B3
Southwood Ho SE9 .**166** D2
W11 ....**244** A6
Southwood Hospl
(Geriatric) N6 ....**49** A2
Southwood Hts N6 ..**49** B3
Southwood La N6 ...**49** A2
Southwood Lawn Rd
N6 ....**49** B2
Southwood Mans N6 .**49** B3
Southwood Park N6 ..**49** A2
Southwood Prim Sch
RM9 ....**81** A4
Southwood Rd SE9 .**166** D2
Woolwich SE28 ......**124** B5
Southwood Smith Ho 4
E2 ....**96** B4
Southwood Smith St
N1 ....**234** C5
South Worple Way
SW14 ....**133** B2
Southwyck Ho SW9 .**138** C1
South Yd EC1 ....**242** A4
Sovereign Bsns Ctr EN3 7 B2
Sovereign Cl Ealing W5 **87** C2
Ruislip HA4 ....**39** C1
Stepney E1 ....**118** B6
Sovereign Cres SE16 **119** A6
Sovereign Ct BR2 ...**210** B3
East Molesey KT8 ...**195** B5
Harlington UB7 ......**126** D3
3 Richmond TW9 ...**132** B1
Stepney E1 ....**118** B6
Sovereign Gr HA0 ...**65** D5
Sovereign Ho 23 E1 ..**96** B3
NW7 ....**27** B6
SE18 ....**122** B3
Ashford TW15 ......**170** A6
3 Wimbledon SW19 .**179** A4
Sovereign Mews
6 E2 ....**95** D5
Barnet EN4 ....**2** D2
Sovereign Pk NW10 .**88** D3
Sovereign Pl HA1 ...**42** D4
Sovereign Rd IG11 ..**102** C4
Sowerby Cl SE9 ....**166** B6
Space Waye TW14 ..**150** B6
Spa Cl SE19 ....**183** C2
Spa Ct 12 SE16 ......**118** A3
Spa Hill CR7,SE19 ..**183** B2
Spalding Cl HA8 .....**27** C3
Spalding Ct HA8 ....**26** B6
Spalding Ho SE4 ...**163** A6
Spalding Rd NW4 ...**46** C3
Streatham SW17 .....**181** B5
Spanby Rd E3 ....**97** C3
Spangate SE3 ......**142** D2
Spaniards Cl NW11 ..**48** B1
Spaniards End NW3 ..**48** B1
Spaniards Rd NW3 ...**70** A6
Spanish Pl W1 .....**238** B2
Spanish Rd SW18 ..**158** A6
Spa Rd SE16 .**117** D3 **263** D5
Sparkbridge Rd HA1 ..**42** C5
Sparke Terr 2 E16 ...**98** D2
Sparkford Gdns N11 ..**31** A5
Sparkford Ho SW11 .**266** D2
Sparks Cl W3 ....**89** B1
Dagenham RM8 ......**80** D1

Sparks Cl continued
Hampton TW12 ....**173** A4
Sparrow Cl TW12 ...**173** A4
Sparrow Dr BR5 ....**211** B5
Sparrow Farm Com Jun
Sch KT17 ....**216** B4
Sparrow Farm Dr
TW14 ....**150** D4
Sparrow Farm Inf Sch
TW14 ....**150** C4
Sparrow Farm Jun Sch
TW14 ....**150** C4
Sparrow Farm Rd
KT17,KT4 ....**216** B4
Sparrow Gn RM10 ...**81** D5
Sparrow's Farm L Ctr
SE9 ....**167** A4
Sparrows Herne WD23 .**8** A4
Sparrows La SE9 ...**167** A3
Sparrows Way WD23 ..**8** A4
Sparsholt Rd N19 ....**50** B1
Barking IG11 ....**101** C6
Sparta St SE10 ....**142** A4
Spa Sch SE1 ....**118** A2
Spa View 6 SW16 ..**160** B1
Speakers' Corner★
W1 ....**114** D6 **247** D6
Speaker's Ct 3 CR0 .**205** B1
Speakman Ho SE4 ..**141** A2
Spearman St 8 SE18 **144** C6
Spear Mews
SW5 ....**113** C2 **255** B3
Spearpoint Gdns IG2 .**57** D5
Spears Rd N19 ......**50** A1
Speart La TW5 .....**129** A5
Spectrum Ho NW5 ...**71** A4
Spedan Cl NW3 .....**70** A5
Speechly Mews E8 ..**73** B3
Speed Ho EC2 ......**242** B4
Speedwell Ct 7 N12 .**29** D6
Speedwell Ho 9 N12 .**29** D6
Speedwell St 8 SE8 **141** C5
Speedy Pl WC1 .....**233** A1
Speer Rd KT7 ....**196** D3
Speirs Cl KT3 ....**199** D3
Spekehill SE9 ....**166** B1
Speke Rd CR7 ......**183** B1
Speldhurst Cl 2 BR2 **208** D4
Speldhurst Rd E9 ....**74** D1
W4 ....**111** B3
Spellbrook Wlk N1 ..**235** B6
Spelman Ho 14 E1 ...**96** A2
Spelman St E1 ......**96** A2
Spelthorne Coll
TW15 ....**170** B6
Spelthorne Cty Inf Sch
TW15 ....**171** B4
Spelthorne Gr TW16 **171** D3
Spelthorne La TW15,
TW17 ....**171** A2
Spence Cl SE16 ....**119** B4
Spencer Ave
Bowes Park N13 .....**32** B4
Hayes UB4 ....**84** A2
Spencer Cl BR6 ....**227** D6
N3 ....**29** C1
Ealing NW10 ....**88** B4
Woodford IG8 ......**37** C5
Spencer Ct 5 BR6 ..**227** A3
Wimbledon SW20 ...**178** B2
Spencer Dr N2 ......**48** A3
Spencer Gdns SW14 **155** A6
Spencer Hill SW19 ..**179** A3
SW19 ....**179** A3
Spencer Hill Rd
SW19 ....**179** A3
Spencer Ho NW3 ...**70** B5
NW4 ....**46** B4
31 SW8 ....**137** D3
24 Putney SW19 ...**156** D1
Wimbledon SW19 ...**156** D1
Spencer Mews W6 ..**264** A6
Spencer Park Ct
SW18 ....**158** B6
Spencer Pk SW18 ..**158** B6
Spencer Pl 16 N1 ...**72** D1
SW1 ....**259** B5
Thornton Heath CR0 **205** B2
Spencer Rd E6 ......**99** D6
N11 ....**31** B6
N8 ....**50** B4
SW18 ....**158** B6
W3 ....**111** A5
Bromley BR1 ....**186** D3
Carshalton CR4 .....**203** A2
Chingford E17 ......**36** A1
Chiswick W4 ....**133** A5
East Molesey KT8 ...**196** A4
Harrow HA3 ....**24** C1
Hounslow TW3,TW5,
TW7 ....**130** A4

Spencer Rd continued
Ilford IG3 ....**57** D1
Mitcham CR4 ....**203** A6
South Croydon CR2 .**221** C5
Tottenham N17 .....**34** A3
Twickenham TW2 ...**152** C2
Wembley HA0 ....**65** C6
Wimbledon SW20 ..**178** B2
Spencer Rise NW5 ..**71** B5
Spencer St
EC1 ....**94** D4 **234** C1
Southall UB2 ......**106** D4
Spencer Wlk 15 NW3 .**70** D4
Putney SW15 ......**134** D1
Spenlow Ho 2 SE16 **118** A3
Spenser Ct 5 TW10 **175** D6
Spenser Gr N16 .....**73** C4
Spenser Mews SE21 **161** B3
Spenser Rd SE24 ...**160** D6
Spenser St SW1 ....**259** B6
Spens Ho WC1 .....**240** C5
Spensley Wlk N16 ...**73** B5
Speranza St SE18 ..**123** D1
Sperling Rd N17 ....**33** C1
Spert St E14 ....**119** A6
Speyside N14 ......**15** C5
Spey St E14 ....**98** A2
Spezia Rd NW10 ....**90** A5
Spice Ct 2 E1 .....**118** A5
10 SW11 ....**136** A2
Spice Quay Heights
SE1 ....**253** D3
Spicer Cl SE5,SW9 .**138** C3
Walton-on-T KT12 ...**194** C3
Spicer Ct EN1 ....**5** C2
Spices Yd CR0 .....**221** A4
Spigurnell Rd N17 ...**33** B2
Spikes Bridge Rd
UB1 ....**107** A6
Spilsby Cl NW9 .....**27** C1
Spindle Cl SE18 ...**122** A3
Spindle Ho 8 DA15 **168** A1
Spindlewood Gdns
CR0 ....**221** C4
Spindrift Ave E14 ..**119** D2
Spinel Cl SE18 .....**123** D1
Spinnaker Cl IG11 ..**102** B4
Spinnaker Ct 2 KT1 **175** D2
Spinnaker Ho E14 ..**119** C4
Spinnells Rd HA2 ...**41** B1
Spinney Cl
Beckenham BR3 .....**207** D5
New Malden KT3 ....**199** C4
Worcester Park KT4 .**215** D6
Yiewsley UB7 ......**104** A6
Spinney Dr TW14 ..**149** A4
Spinney Gdns
Dagenham RM9 .....**81** A3
Dulwich SE19 ......**183** D5
Spinney Oak BR1 ..**188** A1
Spinneys The BR1 ..**188** B1
Spinney The DA14 ..**191** A5
Barnes SW13 ......**134** B6
Barnet EN5 ....**1** D3
Cheam SM3 ....**216** C4
Southgate N21 .....**16** C4
Stanmore HA7 .....**26** A6
Streatham SW16 ...**159** D1
Sunbury TW16 .....**172** A1
Wembley HA0 .....**65** A5
Spire Ct 10 TW10 ..**154** A5
Spire Ho W2 ....**246** B6
Spires The EN5 ....**1** A2
Spirit Quay E1 .....**118** B5
Spital Sq E1 .**95** C2 **243** B4
Spital St E1 ....**96** A2
Spital Yd E1 ....**243** B4
Spitfire Est The TW5 **106** C1
Spitfire Rd SM6 ....**220** B1
Spitfire Way TW5 ..**106** C1
Splendour Wlk SE16 **118** C1
Spode Ho SE11 ....**261** A5
Spode Wlk NW3 ....**69** D3
Spondon Rd N15 ...**52** A5
Spoonbill Way UB4 ..**84** D2
Spooner 8 NW9 ....**27** D3
Spooner Ho TW5 ..**129** C6
Spooner Wlk SM6 ..**219** D3
Sporle Ct 6 SW11 .**136** B2
Sportsbank St SE6 **164** A4
Spottons Gr N17 ...**33** A2
Spout Hill CR0 .....**223** C3
Spratt Hall Rd E11 ..**55** A3
Spray St SE18 .....**122** C2
Spreighton Rd KT8 .**195** D5
Sprewell SW15 ....**157** A5
Spriggs Ho 14 N1 ..**72** D1
Sprimont Pl
SW3 ....**114** D2 **257** C2
Springall St 9 SE15 **140** B5

Springalls Wharf 2
SE16 ....**118** A4
Springbank N21 .....**16** B5
Springbank Rd SE13 **164** C5
Springbank Wlk NW1 .**71** D1
Springbourne Ct BR3 **186** A2
Spring Bridge Rd
W5 ....**109** D6
Spring Cl Barnet EN5 .**12** D6
Dagenham RM8 ....**58** D1
Springclose La SM3 **217** A2
Spring Cnr TW13 ...**149** D1
Spring Cott 10 W12 **112** A4
Spring Cotts KT6 ..**197** D4
Spring Court Rd EN2 .**4** C5
Springcroft Ave N2 ..**48** D5
Spring Ct Ealing W7 **108** B2
10 Wanstead E18 ..**55** B6
Springdale Rd N16 ..**73** B5
Spring Dr HA5 .....**40** A3
Springett Ho 15 SW2 **160** B6
Springfield E5 .....**52** B1
Bushey WD23 ......**8** B3
South Norwood SE25 **206** A6
Springfield Ave N10 .**49** C6
Hampton TW12 .....**173** D4
Merton SW20 ......**201** B6
Springfield Cl N12 ..**29** C5
Stanmore HA7 .....**9** A1
10 SW11 ....**136** A2
Springfield Ct E5 ...**52** B1
NW3 ....**70** C1
7 W3 ....**89** A1
8 Ilford IG1 ....**78** D3
9 Kingston KT1 ...**198** A6
Wallington SM6 ....**219** B3
Springfield Dr IG2 ..**57** A3
Springfield Gdns
BR1 ....**210** B5
E5 ....**52** B1
NW9 ....**45** D4
Ruislip HA4 ....**40** B1
West Wickham BR4 .**223** D6
Woodford IG8 .....**37** C3
Springfield Gr SE7 **143** C6
Sunbury TW16 .....**172** A2
Springfield Ho
1 SE5 ....**139** C3
W3 ....**111** A5
Springfield Hospl
SW17 ....**158** C1
Springfield La NW6 **91** D6
Springfield Mount
NW9 ....**45** C4
Springfield Pl KT3 ..**199** A5
Springfield Rd BR1 .**210** B5
DA16 ....**146** B2
DA7 ....**147** D1
E15 ....**98** C4
E17 ....**53** B3
E6 ....**78** B6
N11 ....**31** C5
N15 ....**52** A5
NW8 ....**92** A6 **229** B5
Ashford TW15 .....**170** B5
Chingford E4 ......**20** C4
Ealing W7 ....**108** C5
Harrow HA1 ....**42** C5
Hayes UB4 ....**106** C5
Kingston KT1 ......**198** A6
Penge SE26 ....**184** B5
South Norwood CR7 **183** A4
6 Teddington TW11 **175** A5
Twickenham TW2 ..**151** C3
Wallington SM6 ....**219** B3
Wimbledon SW19 ..**179** B5
Springfield Rise
SE26 ....**162** B1
Springfields 9 EN5 .**13** D6
Springfield Wlk
3 BR6 ....**211** B1
NW6 ....**91** D6
Spring Gdns N5 ....**73** A3
SW1 ....**116** A5 **250** A4
East Molesey KT8 ..**196** A4
Wallington SM6 ....**219** B3
Woodford IG8 .....**37** C3
Spring Gr
Brentford W4 ......**132** C4
Hampton TW12 .....**173** D2
Loughton IG10 .....**21** D5
Mitcham CR4 ......**181** A2
Spring Grove Cres
TW3,TW5 ....**130** A4
Spring Grove Prim Sch
TW7 ....**130** D3
Spring Grove Rd
Hounslow TW3,TW5,
TW7 ....**130** A4
Richmond TW10 ....**154** B6

Springhallow Sch
W13 ....**87** A1
Spring Hill E5 ......**52** A2
Forest Hill SE26 ....**184** C6
Springhill Cl SE5 ...**139** B2
Spring Ho WC1 ....**234** A1
Merton SW19 ......**179** B2
Springhurst Cl CR0 **223** B4
Spring La E5 ....**52** B1
N10 ....**49** A6
Croydon SE25 .....**206** B3
Spring Lake HA7 ...**25** B6
Spring Mews W1 ..**237** D4
Springpark Dr N4 ..**51** A1
Beckenham BR3 ...**208** A4
Spring Park Prim Sch
CR0 ....**223** C5
Spring Park Rd CR0 **222** D6
Spring Pl N3 ....**47** C6
NW5 ....**71** B3
Springpond Rd RM9 .**81** A3
Spring Rd TW13 ...**149** D1
Springrice Rd SE13 .**164** C5
Spring Shaw Rd BR5 **190** A2
Spring St W2 .**92** B1 **236** C1
Spring Terr TW10 ..**154** A6
Spring Vale DA7 ...**147** D2
Springvale Ave TW8 **110** A1
Springvale Ct SE12 **143** A1
Springvale Terr 5
W14 ....**112** D3
Spring Villa Rd HA8 **26** C3
Springwater WC1 ..**240** C4
Springwater Cl SE18 **144** C4
Springway HA1 .....**42** B2
Springwell Ave NW10 **89** D6
Springwell Cl SW16 **182** B6
Springwell Ct TW5 **128** D3
Springwell Jun & Inf Schs
TW5 ....**129** A5
Springwell Rd
Heston TW5 ....**128** D4
West Norwood SW16 **182** C5
Spring Wlk E1 ......**96** A2
Springwood Cres HA8 **11** A3
Springwood Ct CR2 **221** C4
Sprowston Mews E7 .**77** A3
Sprowston Rd E7 ...**77** A3
Spruce Ct W5 .....**110** A3
Sprucedale Gdns
CR0 ....**222** D4
Spruce Hills Rd E17 ..**36** A1
Spruce Ho 15 SE16 .**118** D4
Spruce Pk BR2 ....**208** D5
Sprules Rd SE4 ...**141** A3
Spurfield KT8 ......**195** D6
Spurgeon Ave SE19 **183** B2
Spurgeon Rd SE19 **183** B3
Spurgeon's Coll SE25 **183** C1
Spurgeon St
SE1 ....**117** B3 **262** C6
Spurling Rd SE22 ..**139** D1
Dagenham RM9 ....**81** B2
Spur Rd N15 ....**51** B5
SE1 ....**116** C4 **251** A2
Brentford TW7 .....**131** A5
Edgware HA8 ......**26** A6
Feltham TW14 .....**128** B4
Wallend IG11 ......**101** A4
Spurstowe Rd E8 ..**74** B2
Spurstowe Terr E8 ..**74** B3
Spurway Par 2 IG2 ..**56** B4
Square Rigger Row 7
SW11 ....**136** A2
Square The SW6 ..**265** A1
W6 ....**112** C1
Hayes UB11 ....**105** B5
Ilford IG1 ....**56** C2
12 Richmond TW10 **153** D6
Wallington SM5 ....**219** A3
Woodford IG8 .....**37** A5
Squarey St SW17 ..**158** A1
Squire Ct 2 CR0 ..**205** C1
Squire Gdns NW8 ..**229** C1
Squire's Almshouses 7
E17 ....**53** D6
Squires Bridge Rd
KT17 ....**192** B5
Squires Ct N3 ......**30** A2
SW4 ....**270** D1
Wimbledon SW19 ..**179** C6
Squires Ho 3 SE18 **144** D6
Squires La N3 .....**30** A2
Squire's Mount NW3 .**70** B5
Squires The RM7 ..**59** D3
Squires Wlk TW15 ..**171** B3
Squires Wood Dr
BR7 ....**188** B3

Squirrel Cl TW4 ...128 C2
Squirrel Mews W13 ...109 A6
Squirrels Cl N12 ...30 A6
Hillingdon UB10 ...60 C1
Orpington BR6 ...211 C1
Squirrels Ct 4 KT4 ...215 D6
Squirrels Gn KT4 ...216 A6
Squirrel's La IG9 ...21 D1
Squirrels The SE13 ...142 B2
Bushey WD23 ...8 B5
Pinner HA5 ...41 B6
Squirrels Trad Est UB3 ...105 D3
Squirries St E2 ...96 A4
Stable Cl UB5 ...85 C5
Stable Mews SE27 ...183 A5
Stables End BR6 ...227 A5
Stables The IG9 ...21 C4
Stables Way SE11 ...116 C1 261 A2
Stable Way W10 ...90 C1
Stable Wlk N2 ...30 B2
Stable Yd Rd SW1 ...115 C4 249 B2
Staburn Ct HA8 ...27 A1
Stacey Ave N18 ...34 C6
Stacey Cl E10 ...54 B4
Stacey St N7 ...72 C5
WC2 ...93 D1 239 D1
Stack Ho SW1 ...258 B3
Stackhouse St SW1 ...257 C6
Stacy Path 21 SE5 ...139 C5
Staddon Ct BR3 ...207 A5
Stadium Bsns Ctr HA9 66 D5
Stadium Rd SE7,SE18 ...144 B6
Stadium Ret Pk HA9 ...66 C5
Stadium St SW10 ...136 A5 266 B3
Stadium Way HA9 ...66 C4
Staffa Rd E10 ...53 A1
Stafford Cl E17 ...53 B3
NW6 ...91 C4
Cheam SM3 ...217 A2
Southgate N14 ...15 C6
Stafford Cripps Ho 30 E2 ...96 C4
SW6 ...264 D5
Stafford Cross CR0 ...220 B3
Stafford Ct SW8 ...270 A2
W8 ...255 B6
Ealing W7 ...86 D1
Stafford Gdns CR0 ...220 B3
Stafford Ho SE1 ...263 D2
Stafford Mans SW11 ...267 C3
13 SW4 ...138 A1
13 W14 ...112 D3
Stafford Morris Ho 9 E15 ...98 C6
Stafford Pl SW1 ...115 C3 259 A6
Richmond TW10 ...154 B4
Stafford Rd E3 ...97 B5
E7 ...77 D2
NW6 ...91 C4
Croydon CR0 ...220 C4
Harrow HA3 ...24 A3
Kingston KT3 ...199 A6
Ruislip HA4 ...61 D4
Sidcup DA14 ...189 C6
Wallington CR0,SM6 ...220 A3
Staffordshire St SE15 ...140 A4
SE15 ...140 B4
Stafford St W1 ...249 A4
Stafford Terr W8 ...113 C3 255 A6
Stag Cl HA8 ...27 A1
Stagg Hill EN4 ...2 C6
Stag La Chigwell IG9 ...21 B2
Edgware HA8,NW9 ...45 A6
Roehampton SW15 ...155 D2
Stag Lane Fst & Mid Schs HA8 ...26 C1
Stag Pl SW1 ...115 C3 259 A6
Stags Ct KT7 ...197 A2
Stagshaw Ho 17 SE22 ...139 C2
Stags Way TW7 ...130 D6
Stainbank Rd CR4 ...203 B6
Stainby Cl UB7 ...104 A3
Stainby Rd N15 ...51 D5
Stainer Ho SE9 ...143 C1
Stainer St SE1 ...252 D3
Staines Ave SM3 ...216 D6
Staines By-Pass TW15 ...170 A4
Staines Rd
East Bedfont TW14 ...149 B4
Feltham TW14,TW3 ...150 C6
Ilford IG1 ...79 B4
Staines Rd *continued*
Twickenham TW13, TW2 ...151 D1
Hounslow TW3 ...129 C1
Twickenham TW2 ...152 A1
Staines Rd E TW12, TW16 ...172 C2
Staines Rd W TW15 ...171 B3
Staines Wlk DA14 ...190 C4
Stainford Cl TW15 ...171 B5
Stainforth Rd E17 ...53 C5
Ilford IG2 ...57 B2
Staining La EC2 ...242 B2
Stainmore Cl BR7 ...189 B2
Stainsbury St 26 E2 ...96 C5
Stainsby Pl E14 ...97 C1
Stainsby Rd E14 ...97 C1
Stainton Rd Enfield EN3 ...6 C4
Lewisham SE13 ...164 B4
Stalbridge Ho NW1 ...232 A3
Stalbridge St NW1 ...237 B4
Stalham St SE16 ...118 B3
Stambourne Ho SW8 270 B2
Stambourne Way
Penge SE19 ...183 D3
West Wickham BR4 ...224 A5
Stamford Bridge Stadium (Chelsea FC) SW6 ...135 D5 265 C4
Stamford Brook Ave W6 ...111 D3
Stamford Brook Gdns 1 W6 ...111 D3
Stamford Brook Mans 2 W6 ...111 D2
Stamford Brook Rd W6 ...111 D3
Stamford Brook Sta W6 ...111 D2
Stamford Cl N15 ...52 A5
2 NW3 ...70 A5
Harrow HA3 ...24 C3
Southall UB1 ...107 C6
Stamford Ct W6 ...112 A2
Edgware HA8 ...26 B6
Stamford Dr BR2 ...208 D5
Stamford Gdns RM9 ...80 C1
Stamford Grove E 1 N16 ...52 A1
Stamford Grove W 4 N16 ...52 A1
Stamford Hill N16 ...51 D1
Stamford Hill Mans 1 N16 ...51 D1
Stamford Hill Prim Sch N15 ...51 B3
Stamford Hill Sta N16 51 C2
Stamford Ho N15 ...52 A5
Stamford Hospl W6 ...112 A2
Stamford Lo 2 N16 ...51 D2
Stamford Mans 2 N16 ...52 A1
Stamford Rd E6 ...100 A6
N1 ...73 C2
N15 ...52 A4
Dagenham RM9 ...80 C1
Stamford St SE1 ...116 C5 251 B4
Stamp Pl E2 ...95 D4
Stanard Cl N16 ...51 C2
Stanborough Cl TW12 ...173 B4
Stanborough Ho 4 E3 ...97 D3
Stanborough Pas E8 ...73 D2
Stanborough Rd TW3,TW7 ...130 B2
Stanbridge Mans SW15 ...134 C2
Stanbridge Pl N21 ...16 D2
Stanbridge Rd SW15 ...134 C2
Stanbrook Ct W1 ...249 A4
Stanbrook Rd SE2 ...124 B4
Stanburn Fst & Mid Schs HA7 ...25 C3
Stanbury Ct 16 NW3 ...70 D2
Stanbury Rd SE15 ...140 B3
SE15 ...140 C3
Stancroft NW9 ...45 C4
Standale Gr HA4 ...39 A4
Standard Ind Est E16 122 B4
Standard Pl 14 EC2 ...95 C4
Standard Rd DA6 ...147 A1
NW10 ...89 B3
Belvedere DA17 ...125 C1
Enfield EN3 ...7 A6
Hounslow TW4 ...129 A2
Standen Rd SW18 ...157 C4
Standfield Gdns RM10 81 C2
Standfield Rd RM10 ...81 C3
Standish Ho SE9 ...143 B1
6 W6 ...112 A2
Standish Rd W6 ...112 A2
Standlake Point 1 SE23 ...162 D1
Stane Cl SW19 ...179 D3
Stanedge Ct SW16 ...182 A5
Stanesgate Ho 20 SE15 ...140 A5
Stanetto Ct 3 RM6 ...58 B2
Stane Way SE18 ...144 A5
Stanfield Ho NW8 ...236 D6
9 Northolt UB5 ...84 D5
Stanfield Rd 13 E3 ...97 A5
Stanford Cl
Hampton TW12 ...173 B4
Romford RM7 ...59 D3
Ruislip HA4 ...39 A3
Stanford Ct N11 ...31 A5
SW6 ...265 D1
W8 ...255 D5
Stanford Ho IG11 ...102 B5
Stanford Pl SE1 ...117 C2 263 A3
Stanford Rd N11 ...30 D5
W8 ...113 D3 255 D6
Thornton Heath SW16 ...182 A1
Stanford St SW1 ...259 C3
Stanford Way SW16 ...181 D1
Stangate Cres WD6 ...11 C6
Stangate Gdns HA7 ...25 B6
Stangate Lo N21 ...16 B4
Stangate Mansi TW1 152 D1
Stanger Rd SE25 ...206 A5
Stanhope Ave N3 ...47 B6
Harrow HA3 ...24 B2
Hayes BR2 ...209 A1
Stanhope Cl 28 SE16 118 D4
Stanhope Ct N3 ...29 B1
Stanhope Gate W1 ...248 B4
Stanhope Gdns N4 ...51 A3
N6 ...49 C3
NW7 ...27 D5
SW7 ...114 A2 256 B4
Dagenham RM8 ...81 B5
Redbridge IG1 ...56 B1
Stanhope Gr BR3 ...207 B5
Stanhope Ho 5 N11 ...31 B6
N6 ...49 C3
SE8 ...141 B5
4 Putney SW15 ...156 C6
Stanhope Mews E SW7 ...114 A2 256 B4
Stanhope Mews S SW7 ...256 B3
Stanhope Mews W SW7 ...114 A2 256 B4
Stanhope Park Rd UB6 ...86 A3
Stanhope Pl W2 ...237 C1
Stanhope Prim Sch UB6 ...86 A3
Stanhope Rd DA7 ...147 A3
E17 ...53 D4
N12 ...30 A5
N6 ...49 C2
Barnet EN5 ...12 D5
Dagenham RM8 ...81 B5
Sidcup DA15 ...190 A6
Southall UB6 ...86 A2
South Croydon CR0 ...221 C5
Wallington SM5 ...219 A1
Stanhope Row W1 ...248 C3
Stanhope St NW1 ...93 C4 232 A1
Stanhope Terr W2 ...114 B6 246 D6
Stanier Cl SW5 ...254 D1
Stanlake Rd W12 ...112 C5
Stanlake Villas W12 ...112 C5
Stanley Ave
Barking IG11 ...101 D5
Beckenham BR2,BR3 ...208 A6
Dagenham RM8 ...59 B2
Greenford UB6 ...86 A6
Wembley HA0 ...66 A1
West Barnes KT3 ...200 A4
Stanley Bldgs NW1 ...233 A3
Stanley Cl SW8 ...270 C5
Wembley HA0 ...66 A1
Stanley Cres W11 ...113 B6 244 C6
Stanleycroft Cl TW7 ...130 C4
Stanley Ct
Belmont SM2 ...217 D1
11 Ealing W5 ...87 C2
Wallington SM5 ...219 A1
Wimbledon SW19 ...179 C4
Stanley Gardens Rd TW11 ...174 C5
Stanley Gdns NW2 ...68 C3
W11 ...244 C6
W3 ...111 C4
Mitcham CR4 ...181 A4
Wallington SM6 ...219 C2
Stanley Gr SW11 ...137 A3
Thornton Heath CR0 ...204 C3
Stanley Ho E11 ...54 C3
18 E14 ...97 C1
35 SW8 ...137 D3
Stanley Horstead Twr E10 ...75 D6
Stanley Inf Sch TW2 ...174 C6
Stanley Jun Sch TW2 174 C6
Stanley Mans SW10 ...266 B6
Upper Tooting SW17 ...158 D2
Stanley Park Dr HA0 ...88 B6
Stanley Park High Sch SM5 ...219 A2
Stanley Park Inf Sch SM5 ...218 D1
Stanley Park Jun Sch SM5 ...218 D1
Stanley Park Rd SM5, SM6 ...219 A1
Stanley Rd BR6 ...211 D1
E10 ...53 D3
E12 ...78 A3
E15 ...98 B6
N10 ...31 B3
N11 ...31 D5
N15 ...50 D5
N2 ...48 B6
2 NW9 ...46 A2
W3 ...111 A3
Ashford TW15 ...170 A5
Belmont SM2 ...217 D1
Bromley BR2 ...209 C5
Chingford E4 ...20 B3
Edmonton N9 ...17 D2
Enfield EN1 ...5 C2
Harrow HA2 ...64 A6
Ilford IG1 ...79 B6
Isleworth TW3 ...130 A1
Mitcham CR4 ...181 A3
Morden SM4 ...201 C5
Mortlake SW14 ...132 D1
Northwood HA6 ...22 A2
Sidcup DA14 ...168 A1
Southall UB1 ...107 A6
Teddington TW11,TW2 ...174 C5
Thornton Heath CR0 ...204 C3
Twickenham TW2 ...152 B1
Wallington SM5 ...219 A1
Wembley HA9 ...66 B2
Wimbledon SW19 ...179 C4
Woodford E18 ...36 D2
Stanley St SE14,SE8 ...141 B5
Stanley Studios SW10 ...266 B6
Stanley Tech High Sch for Boys SE25 ...205 D6
Stanley Terr 7 N19 ...72 A6
Stanmer St SW11 ...136 C3
Stanmore Coll HA7 ...25 C4
Stanmore Gdns
Richmond TW9 ...132 B2
Sutton SM1 ...218 A5
Stanmore Hill HA7 ...25 A6
Stanmore Ho 21 SW8 ...137 D3
Stanmore Lo HA7 ...25 B6
Stanmore Pl NW1 ...231 D6
Stanmore Rd E11 ...54 D1
N15 ...50 D5
Richmond TW9 ...132 B2
Stanmore St N1 ...94 B6 233 C6
Stanmore Sta HA7 ...25 D6
Stanmore Terr 3 BR3 ...185 C1
Stannard Cotts 23 E1 ...96 C3
Stannard Mews E8 ...74 A2
Stannard Rd E8 ...74 A2
Stannary Pl SE11 ...261 B1
Stannary St SE11 ...116 C1 261 B1
Stannet Way SM6 ...219 C4
Stansbury Ho 3 W10 ...91 A4
Stansfeld Ho SE1 ...263 D3
Stansfeld Rd E6 ...99 D1
Stansfield Rd SW9 ...138 B2
Cranford TW4,TW5 ...128 B3
Stansgate Rd RM10 ...81 C5
Stanstead Cl BR2 ...208 D3
Stanstead Gr SE23 ...163 B3
Stanstead Ho E3 ...98 A3
Stanstead Manor SM1 ...217 C2
Stanstead Rd
Forest Hill SE23,SE6 ...163 A3
Wanstead E11 ...55 B4
Stansted Cres DA5 ...168 D3
Stansted Rd TW6 ...148 B5
Stanswood Gdns SE5 139 C5
Stanthorpe Cl SW16 ...182 A5
Stanthorpe Rd SW16 182 A5
Stanton Ave TW11 ...174 C4
Stanton Cl
Chessington KT19 ...214 D3
North Cheam KT4 ...200 D1
Stanton Ct 5 DA15 ...168 A1
N16 ...51 B2
N3 ...29 C2
Stanton Ho 8 SE10 ...142 A6
Stanton Rd
Barnes SW13 ...133 D3
Thornton Heath CR0 ...205 A2
Wimbledon SW20 ...178 D2
Stanton Sq SE26 ...185 B6
Stanton Way SE26 ...185 B6
Stanway Ct 23 N1 ...95 C5
Stanway Gdns HA8 ...27 A5
Acton W3 ...110 C5
Stanway St N1 ...95 C5
Stanwell Rd
Ashford TW15 ...170 A6
East Bedfont TW14, TW19,TW6 ...148 D4
Stanwell TW15 ...148 A1
Ashford TW15 ...148 A1
Stanwick Rd W14 ...113 B2 254 C3
Stanworth Ct TW5 ...129 C5
Stanworth St SE1 ...253 D1
Stanyhurst SE23 ...163 A3
Stapelhurst Ho 18 E5 ...74 B3
Stapenhill Rd HA0 ...65 B5
Staplefield Cl
Pinner HA5 ...23 A3
3 Streatham SW2 ...160 A3
Stapleford N17 ...33 C1
Stapleford Ave IG2 ...57 C4
Stapleford Cl
Chingford E4 ...20 A1
Kingston KT1 ...198 C6
Putney SW19 ...157 A4
Stapleford Rd HA0 ...65 D1
Stapleford Way IG11 ...102 B4
Staplehurst Ct SW11 158 D5
Staplehurst Rd SE13 ...164 C6
Sutton SM5 ...218 C1
Staple Inn WC2 ...241 A3
Staple Inn Bldgs WC2 ...241 A3
Staples Cl SE16 ...119 A5
Staples Corner Bsns Pk NW2 ...46 B1
Staples Corner (East) NW2 ...46 B1
Staples Corner (West) NW2 ...46 B1
Staple St SE1 117 B4 252 D1
Stapleton Gdns CR0 ...220 C3
Stapleton Hall N4 ...50 B2
Stapleton Hall Rd N4 ...50 B2
Stapleton Ho 19 E2 ...96 B4
Stapleton Rd DA7 ...147 B6
Orpington BR6 ...227 D5
Upper Tooting SW17 ...159 A1
Stapley Rd DA17 ...125 C1
Staplyton Rd EN5 ...1 A2
Star Alley EC3 ...253 B6
Star and Garter Hill TW10 ...154 A4
Starboard Way E14 ...119 C3
Starcross St NW1 ...93 C4 232 B1
Star Ct UB10 ...83 A3
Starfield Rd W12 ...112 A4
Star & Garter Mans SW15 ...134 D2
Star La E16 ...98 C3
Starliner Ct N7 ...72 C2
Starling Cl
Buckhurst Hill IG9 ...21 A3
Pinner HA5 ...40 C6
Starling Ho NW8 ...230 A4
Starling Wlk TW12 ...173 A5
Starmans Cl RM9 ...103 A6
Star Path UB5 ...85 C5
Star Pl E1 ...118 A6
Star Prim Sch E16 ...98 C3
Star Rd W14 ...113 B1 254 C1
Hillingdon UB10 ...83 A3
Hounslow TW7 ...130 B3
Star St W2 ...92 C1 237 A2
Starts Cl BR6 ...226 C5
Starts Hill Ave BR6 ...226 D4
Starts Hill Rd BR6 ...226 D4
Starveall Cl UB7 ...104 B3
Star Works NW10 ...90 A4
Star Yd WC2 ...94 C1 241 A2
State Farm Ave BR6 ...227 A4
Staten Gdns TW1 ...152 D3
Statham Gr N16 ...73 B5
Edmonton N18 ...33 C5
Statham Ho SW8 ...269 A2
Stathard Ho 18 E1 ...96 C3
Station App BR6 ...227 D6
BR7 ...188 A4
BR7 ...188 C1
DA16 ...146 A3
DA7 ...147 A3
E17 ...53 C4
E7 ...77 B4
N11 ...31 B5
N12 ...29 D6
NW10 ...89 D4
SE3 ...143 B2
SE9 ...166 B3
Ashford TW15 ...170 B6
5 Beckenham BR3 ...185 C2
Belmont SM2 ...217 A1
Fulham SW6 ...135 A2
Greenford UB6 ...64 B1
Hampton TW12 ...173 C2
Hayes BR2 ...209 A1
Hayes UB3 ...105 D3
Hinchley Wood KT10 ...212 D5
4 Kingston KT1,KT2 ...176 C2
New Barnet EN5 ...2 A1
6 New Malden KT4 ...200 A1
Penge SE26 ...185 B5
Pinner HA5 ...41 A6
Richmond TW9 ...132 C4
Ruislip HA4 ...39 D1
Ruislip HA4 ...62 B3
Shepperton TW17 ...193 A4
3 South Croydon CR0 ...221 B6
Streatham SW16 ...181 D5
Sunbury TW16 ...172 A2
1 Surbiton KT6 ...198 A3
Wanstead E11 ...55 A4
Wembley HA0 ...65 B2
2 Woodford E18 ...37 B1
Woodford IG9 ...37 D6
Worcester Park KT19 ...216 A3
Yiewsley UB7 ...104 A5
Station App Rd SE1 ...116 C4 251 A2
Station Approach Rd W4 ...133 A5
Station Ave 5 SW9 ...138 D2
Kingston KT3 ...199 C6
13 Richmond TW9 ...132 C4
West Ewell KT19 ...215 D1
Station Bldgs SW20 ...178 C1
Station Blgs W5 ...110 B5
Station Cl N3 ...29 C2
Hampton TW12 ...173 D2
Station Cres N15 ...51 B5
SE3 ...121 A1
Ashford TW15 ...170 A6
Wembley HA0 ...65 B2
Station Ct 1 E10 ...53 D2
5 SE15 ...140 C3
Stationers Hall Ct EC4 ...241 D1
Station Est
Beckenham BR3 ...206 D5
1 Woodford E18 ...37 B1
Station Estate Rd TW14 ...150 B3
Station Gdns W4 ...133 A5
Station Hill BR2 ...225 A6
Station House Mews N9 ...34 A6
Station Par 4 N14 ...15 D3
NW2 ...68 C2
Acton W3 ...88 C1
Ashford TW15 ...170 B6
Barking IG11 ...79 A1
Cockfosters EN4 ...3 A1
Dagenham RM10 ...81 C2
Ealing W5 ...110 B5
Edgware HA8 ...26 A3
Feltham TW14 ...150 B4
Harrow HA2 ...63 D4
Harrow HA3 ...25 A1
Richmond TW9 ...132 C4
Ruislip HA4 ...61 B6
4 Upper Tooting SW12 ...159 A3
2 Wanstead E11 ...55 A4
Woodford IG9 ...37 D6

Station Pas SE15 ....140 C4
Woodford E18 ....37 B1
Station Pl N4 ....72 C6
Station Rd BR1 ......187 A2
BR6 ....227 D6
DA7 ....147 A2
E10 ....76 A5
E12 ....78 A4
E17 ....53 A4
E7 ....77 A4
N11 ....31 B5
N17 ....52 A6
N19 ....71 C5
N3 ....29 C1
NW10 ....89 D5
NW4 ....46 A4
NW7 ....27 C4
SE13 ....142 A2
Ashford TW15 ....170 B6
Ashford TW16 ....172 A3
Barnes SW13 ....133 D3
Beckenham BR2 ......186 C1
Belvedere DA17 .....125 C3
Carshalton SM5 .....218 D4
Chessington KT9 ....214 A3
Chingford E4 ....20 B3
Claygate KT10 ......212 C3
Croydon CR0 ....205 A1
Dagenham RM6 ....58 D2
Ealing W5 ....88 B1
Ealing W7 ....108 C5
Edgware HA8 ....26 C4
Esher KT10 ....212 B6
Hampton TW12 ....173 D2
Harrow HA1 ....42 D4
Harrow HA1,HA2 ......41 D4
Hayes UB3 ....105 C2
Hounslow TW3 ....129 D1
Ilford IG1 ....78 D5
Ilford IG6 ....57 B6
Kingston KT2 ....176 C2
Merton SW19 ....180 A2
New Barnet EN5 ......13 D6
Penge SE20 ....184 C4
Shepperton TW17 ....193 A4
Sidcup DA14,DA15 ...168 A1
Southgate N21 ....16 D3
South Norwood SE25 .205 D5
Teddington KT1 .....175 D2
Teddington TW11 ....175 A4
Thames Ditton KT7 ..196 D2
Twickenham TW1 .....152 D4
West Barnes KT3 ....200 B4
West Drayton UB7 ...104 A4
West Wickham BR4 ...208 A1
Wood Green N22 ......32 B1
Station Rd N DA17 ..125 D3
Station Rise SE27 ..160 D2
Station Sq BR5 .....211 A4
Station St E15 ......76 B1
E16 ....122 C4
Station Terr NW10 ...90 D5
SE5 ....139 A4
Station View UB6 ....86 B6
Station Way
Cheam SM2,SM3 ......217 A1
Woodford IG9 ....37 D6
Station Yd TW1 .....153 A4
Staunton Ho SE17 ...263 A4
Staunton Rd KT2 ....176 C2
Staunton St SE8 ....141 B6
Staveley NW1 ....232 A2
Staveley Cl E9 ......74 C3
N7 ....72 A4
SE15 ....140 C4
8 SE15 ....140 B4
Staveley Ct **4** E11 ...55 C4
Staveley Gdns W4 ...133 B4
Staveley Rd
Ashford TW15 ....171 B4
Chiswick W4 ....133 B4
Staverdale Lo W14 ..254 D6
Stavers Ho **18** E3 .....97 B5
Staverton Rd NW2 ....68 C1
Stavordale Rd N5 ....72 C4
Carshalton SM5 .....202 A2
Stayner's Rd E1 .....96 D3
Stayton Rd SM1 .....217 C5
Steadfast Rd KT1 ...175 D2
Steadman Ct EC1 ....242 B6
Steadman Ho **4** RM10 81 C4
Stead St SE17 117 B2 262 C3
Steam Farm La
TW14 ....127 D1
Stean St E8 ....95 D6
Stebbing Ho **8** W11 .112 D5

Stebbing Way IG11 ...102 A5
Stebondale St E14 ..120 A2
Stebon Prim Sch E14 .97 C2
Stedham Pl WC1 .....240 A2
Stedman Cl UB10 .....60 C5
Steedman St
SE17 ....117 A2 262 A3
Steeds Rd N10 ....30 D4
Steele App IG11 ....102 A5
Steele Rd E11 ....76 C4
N17 ....51 C6
NW10 ....89 A5
W4 ....111 A3
Isleworth TW7 ......131 A1
Steele's Mews N NW3 .70 D2
Steele's Mews S NW3 .70 D2
Steele's Rd NW3 .....70 D2
Steele Wlk DA8 .....147 D5
Steel's La **23** E1 .....96 C1
Steep Cl BR6 ....227 D4
Steep Hill
South Croydon CR0 ..221 C4
Streatham SW16 .....159 D1
Steeple Cl
Fulham SW6 ....135 A3
Wimbledon SW19 .....179 A6
Steeple Ct **19** E1 ......96 B3
Steeplestone Cl N18 ..8 A3
Steeple Wlk N1 .....235 B6
Steerforth St SW18 .158 A2
Steers Mead CR4 ....180 D2
Steers Way SE16 ....119 A4
Steetley Ct **14** SM2 ..218 A1
Steinman Ct TW7 ...130 D2
Stelfax Ho WC1 .....233 D2
Stella Rd SW17 .....180 D4
Stellar Ho **4** N17 ....33 D4
Stellman Cl E5 ......74 A5
Stembridge Rd SE20 .184 B1
Sten Cl EN3 ....7 C6
Stephan Cl E8 ....96 A6
Stephen Cl BR6 .....227 D5
Stephen Ct **18** SW19 ..156 D3
Stephendale Rd SW6 136 A3
Stephen Fox Ho **7**
W4 ....111 C1
Stephen Hawking Sch
E14 ....97 A1
Stephen Mews W1 ...239 C3
Stephen Pl SW4 .....137 C2
Stephen Saunders Ct
SW11 ....158 C6
Stephens Ct E16 .....98 D3
SE4 ....141 A2
Stephens Lo N12 .....14 A1
Stephenson Ct SM2 .217 B1
Stephenson Ho
6 NW3 ....70 D3
2 NW5 ....71 B4
SE1 ....262 A6
SE2 ....124 D1
Stephenson Rd E17 ..53 A4
Ealing W7 ....86 D1
Twickenham TW4 ....151 C4
Stephenson St E16 ...98 C2
NW10 ....89 D4
Stephenson Way
NW1 ....93 C3 239 B6
Stephen's Rd E15 ....98 C6
Stephen St W1 .....239 C3
Stepney Cswy E1 .....96 D1
Stepney Day Hospl E1 96 C1
Stepney Gn E1 ....96 D2
Stepney Greencoat CE
Prim Sch The E14 ....97 B1
Stepney Green Ct **3**
E1 ....96 D2
Stepney Green Sch
E1 ....96 D2
Stepney Green Sta E1 96 D3
Stepney High St E1 ..96 D2
Stepney Way E1 ......96 C2
Sterling Ave
Edgware HA8 ....26 B6
Upper Halliford TW17 193 C6
Sterling Gdns SE14 .141 A6
Sterling Ho SE9 ....143 B1
Sterling Ind Est RM10 81 D4
Sterling Pl W5 .....110 A2
Sterling Rd EN2 ......5 B5
Sterling St SW7 ....257 B6
Sterling Way (North
Circular Rd) N18 ...33 C5
Stern Cl IG11 ......102 C5
Sterndale Rd W14 ...112 D3
Sterne St W12 ......112 D4
Sternhall La SE15 ..140 A2

Sternhold Ave SW12,
SW2 ....159 D2
Sterry Cres RM10 ....81 C3
Sterry Dr
Thames Ditton KT7 ..196 C3
Worcester Park KT19 215 C4
Sterry Gdns RM10 ...81 C2
Sterry Rd
Barking IG11 ....101 D6
Dagenham RM10 ......81 C3
Sterry St SE1 ......252 C1
Steucers La SE23 ...163 A3
Stevanne Ct **1** DA17 125 C1
Steve Biko Ct W10 ...90 D3
Steve Biko La SE6 ..185 C6
Steve Biko Rd N7 ....72 C5
Steve Biko Way TW3 .129 C2
Stevedale Rd DA16 ..146 C3
Stevedore St **3** E1 .118 B5
Stevenage Rd
Fulham SW6 ....134 D4
Wallend E6 ....78 C2
Stevens Ave E9 ......74 C2
Stevens Cl
Beckenham BR3 .....185 C4
Hampton TW12 ......173 B4
Pinner HA5 ....40 C4
Stevens Ct BR3 .....185 C4
Stevens Gn WD23 .....8 A3
Stevens Ho KT1 .....175 D1
Stevens' La KT10 ...213 A2
Stevens Rd RM8 .....80 C5
Stevens St SE1 .....263 B6
Steventon Rd W12 ..111 D6
Stewards Holte Wlk **8**
N11 ....31 B6
Steward St E1 .95 C2 243 B4
Stewart Ave TW17 ..192 C5
Stewart Cl BR7 .....188 C6
NW9 ....45 A3
Hampton TW12 ......173 A4
Stewart Fleming Prim Sch
SE20 ....206 C6
Stewart Headlam Prim Sch
E1 ....96 B3
Stewart Ho SE1 .....263 A5
Stewart Quay UB3 ..105 C4
Stewart Rainbird Ho **1**
E12 ....78 C3
Stewart Rd E15 ......76 B4
Stewartsby Cl N18 ..33 A5
Stewart's Gr
SW3 ....114 C1 257 A2
Stewart's Rd
SW8 ....137 C4 269 A2
Stewart St E14 .....120 A4
Stew La EC4 ....252 A6
Steyne Rd W3 ......110 D5
Steyning Gr SE9 ...188 B6
Steynings Way N12 ..29 C5
Steyning Way TW4 ..128 C1
Steynton Ave DA5 ..168 D2
Stickland Rd DA17 .125 D2
Stickleton Cl UB6 ...85 D4
Stifford Ho E1 ......96 C2
Stilecroft Gdns HA0 .65 B5
Stile Hall Gdns W4 .110 C1
Stile Hall Par **6** W4 .110 C1
Stileman Ho **4** E3 ...97 B2
Stile Path TW16 ....194 A5
Stiles Cl BR2 ......210 B3
Erith DA8 ....125 D1
Stillingfleet Rd SW13 134 A6
Stillington St
SW1 ....115 C2 259 B4
Stillness Jun & Inf Schs
SE23 ....163 A5
Stillness Rd SE23 ..163 B5
Stilwell Dr UB8 .....82 B3
Stilwell Rdbt UB8 ..104 D6
Stipularis Dr UB4 ...84 D3
Stirling Ave Pinner HA5 41 A2
Wallington SM6 .....220 A1
Stirling Cl SW16 ...181 C2
Stirling Cnr EN5,WD6 .11 B5
Stirling Ct EC1 ....241 C6
WC2 ....240 C1
Ealing W13 ....109 B6
Stirling Gr TW3 ....130 A3
Stirling Ho **5** SE18 ..122 D1
Stirling Mans NW6 ..70 A2
Stirling Rd E13 .....99 B5
E17 ....53 A6
SW9 ....138 A3
W3 ....110 D3

Stirling Rd continued
Harrow HA3 ....42 D6
Hayes UB3 ....106 B6
Stanwell TW19,TW6 ..148 B5
Tottenham N17 ....34 A2
Tottenham N22 ....32 D2
Twickenham TW2 ....151 D4
Stirling Way
Borehamwood WD6 ....11 B6
Thornton Heath CR0 204 A2
Stiven Cres HA2 .....63 B5
Stoatley Ho **10** SW15 156 A3
Stockbeck NW1 .....232 B3
Stockbridge Ho EN2 ..4 D3
Stockbury Rd CR0 ..206 C3
Stockdale Rd RM8 ...81 B6
Stockdove Way UB6 ..86 C1
Stocker Gdns RM9 ...80 C1
Stock Exchange★
EC2 ....242 D1
Stockfield Rd
Claygate KT10 ......212 C3
Streatham SW16 .....160 B1
Stockholm Ho E1 ...118 A6
Stockholm Rd SE16 .118 C1
Stockholm Way **9**
E1 ....118 A5
Stockhurst Cl SW15 134 D3
Stockingswater La EN3 .7 B2
Stockleigh Hall NW8 230 B4
Stockley Cl UB7 ....104 D4
Stockley Ctry Pk UB7 104 C6
Stockley Farm Rd
UB7 ....104 D3
Stockley Park Bsns Pk
UB11 ....105 A5
Stockley Rd UB7,UB8,
UB11 ....104 D4
Stock Orchard Cres
N7 ....72 B3
Stock Orchard St N7 .72 B3
Stockport Rd SW16 .181 D2
Stocks Ct **5** E1 .....96 D3
Stocksfield Rd E17 ..54 A6
Stocks Pl **16** E14 ...119 B6
Stock St E13 ....99 A5
Stockton Cl EN5 .....2 A1
Stockton Gdns NW7 ..11 C1
Tottenham N17 ......33 A3
Stockton Ho **16** E2 ...96 B4
Harrow HA2 ....41 C1
Stockton Rd
Edmonton N18 ....34 B4
Tottenham N17 ......33 A3
Stockwell Ave SW9 .138 B2
Stockwell Cl BR1 ...187 B1
Stockwell Gdns
SW9 ....138 B4
Stockwell Gdns Est
SW9 ....138 B4 270 C1
Stockwell Gn SW9 ..138 B3
Stockwell La SW9 ..138 B3
Stockwell Park Cres
SW9 ....138 B3
Stockwell Park Rd
SW9 ....138 B4 270 D1
Stockwell Park Sch
SW9 ....138 B4 270 C1
Stockwell Park Wlk
SW9 ....138 C2
Stockwell Prim Sch
SW9 ....138 B2
Stockwell Rd SW9 ..138 B3
Stockwell St SE10 ..142 A6
Stockwell Sta SW4 .138 C4
Stockwell Terr SW9 270 C1
Stodart Rd SE20 ....184 C2
Stoddart Ho SW8 ...270 D5
Stodmarsh Ho **28**
SW9 ....138 C4
Stofield Gdns SE9 ..165 D1
Stoford Cl SW19 ....157 A4
Stokenchurch St
SW6 ....135 D4 265 C1
Stoke Newington Church
St N16 ....73 C5
Stoke Newington Comm
N16 ....73 D5
Stoke Newington High St
N16 ....73 D5
Stoke Newington Rd
N16 ....73 D4
Stoke Newington Sch
N16 ....73 B5
Stoke Newington Sta
N16 ....73 D6
Stoke Pl NW10 ......89 D4
Stoke Rd KT2 ....177 A3
Stokesby Rd KT9 ...214 B2
Stokes Ct N2 ....48 C5
Stokesley St W12 ....89 D1

Stokes Rd
Croydon CR0 ....206 D3
Newham E6 ....100 A3
Stokley Ct N8 ....50 A5
Stoll Cl NW2 ....68 C5
Stoms Path SE6 ....185 C5
Stonard Rd
Dagenham RM8 ......80 B4
Palmers Green N13 ..16 C1
Stondon Pk SE23 ...163 A5
Stondon Wlk E6 ....100 A1
4 E6 ....99 D5
Stonebanks KT12 ...194 A2
Stone Bldgs
WC2 ....94 B2 240 D3
Stonebridge Ct **8**
NW10 ....67 B1
Stonebridge Ctr The
N15 ....52 A4
Stonebridge Park HA9 66 D1
Stonebridge Park Sta
NW10 ....66 D1
Stonebridge Pk NW10 67 B1
Stonebridge Rd N15 .51 D4
Stonebridge Sch The
NW10 ....89 B6
Stonebridge Sh Ctr **6**
NW10 ....89 B6
Stonechat Sq **6** E6 .100 A2
Stone Cl SW4 ......137 C3
Dagenham RM8 ......81 B6
Yiewsley UB7 ......104 B5
Stonecot Cl SM3 ...201 A1
Stonecot Hill SM4 .201 A1
Stone Cres TW14 ..149 D4
Stonecroft Way CR0 204 A2
Stonecutter St EC4 241 C2
Stonefield N4 ....72 B6
Stonefield Cl DA7 ..147 C2
Ruislip HA4 ....63 A3
Stonefield Mans N1 234 A5
Stonefield St
N1 ....94 C6 234 B6
Stonefield Way SE7 143 D5
Ruislip HA4 ....63 A3
Stone Gate **8** NW5 ..71 A2
Stone Gr HA8 ....26 B5
Stone Grove Ct HA8 .26 B5
Stonegrove Gdns HA8 26 A5
Stonehall Ave IG1 ...56 A3
Stone Hall Rd N21 ..16 C4
Stoneham Rd N11 ...31 C5
Stonehaven BR3 ....185 D1
Stonehill Cl SW14 ..155 B6
Stonehill Ct E4 ......19 D4
Stonehill Rd W4 ....110 C1
Mortlake SW14 .....155 B6
Stonehills Ct SE21 .161 C1
Stonehill's Mans **3**
SW16 ....160 A2
Stonehill Woods Pk
DA14 ....169 D3
Stonehorse Rd EN3 ..18 C6
Stonehouse NW1 ...232 B5
Stonehouse Ct EC2 243 B2
Stonehouse **27** W2 91 C2
Stone Lake Ind Pk
SE7 ....121 C2
Stone Lake Ret Pk
SE7 ....121 C2
Stoneleigh Ave
Enfield EN1 ....6 B4
North Cheam KT17,KT4 216 A5
Stoneleigh Broadway
KT17 ....216 A4
Stoneleigh Cres
KT19 ....215 D3
Stoneleigh Ct
Redbridge IG5 ......56 A6
4 Tottenham N17 ....33 D1
Stoneleigh Fst Sch
KT17 ....216 B4
Stoneleigh Lo **13**
TW9 ....132 B4
Stoneleigh Park Ave
CR0 ....206 D3
Stoneleigh Park Rd
KT19,KT4 ....216 A3
Stoneleigh Pl W11 ..112 D6
Stoneleigh Rd
Carshalton SM5 .....202 C5
Redbridge IG5 ......56 A6
Tottenham N17 ......33 D1
Stoneleigh St W11 ..112 D6
Stoneleigh Sta KT19 216 A3
Stoneleigh Terr N19 .71 B6
Stonell's Rd SW11 .158 C6
Stonemasons Cl N15 .51 B6
Stonenest St N4 .....50 D1

Stone Park Ave BR3 .207 D5
Stone Pl KT4 ....216 A6
Stone Rd BR2 ......208 D4
Stones End St SE1 ..252 A1
Stonewall E6 ....100 C2
Stoneyard La E14 ..119 D6
Stoneycroft Cl SE12 164 C4
Stoney Deep TW11 .175 A6
Stoneydown E17 .....53 A5
Stoneydown Ave E17 .53 A5
Stoneydown Ho **2**
E17 ....53 A5
Stoneyfields Gdns
HA8 ....27 A6
Stoneyfields La HA8 .27 A6
Stoney La E1 ....243 B2
Penge SE19 ....183 D4
Stoney St
SE1 ....117 B5 252 C4
Stonhouse St SW4 .137 D1
Stonor Rd
W14 ....113 B2 254 C3
Stonycroft Cl EN3 ...7 C6
Stopes St SE15 ....139 D5
Stopford Rd E13 .....99 A6
SE17 ....261 D1
Stopher Ho SE1 ....251 D1
Storace Ho **6** SW4 .138 A1
Store Rd E16 ....122 C4
Storers Quay E14 ..120 B2
Store St E15 ....76 B3
WC1 ....93 D2 239 C4
Storey Ct NW8 .....229 C1
Storey Ho **12** E14 ..119 D6
Storey Prim Sch E16 122 D5
Storey Rd E17 ......53 B5
N6 ....48 D3
Storey's Gate
SW1 ....115 D4 249 D1
Storey St E16 ......122 C4
Stories Rd SE5 ....139 C2
Stork Rd E7 ....77 A2
Storksmead Rd HA8 .27 C3
Storks Rd SE16 ....118 A3
Stormont House Sch
E5 ....74 B5
Stormont Rd N6 .....48 D2
SW11 ....137 A1
Stormont Way KT9 .213 C3
Stormount Dr UB3 ..105 A4
Storrington WC1 ...233 B1
Storrington Rd CR0 205 D1
Story St N1 ....72 B1
Stothard Pl E1 .....243 B4
Stothard St **11** E1 ...96 C1
Stott Cl SW18 .....158 B5
Stoughton Ave SM3 217 A3
Stoughton Cl SE11 260 D3
Roehampton SW15 ..156 A3
Stour Ave UB2 .....107 C3
Stour Cl BR2 ......225 C4
Stourcliffe Cl W1 ..237 C2
Stourcliffe St W1 ..237 C1
Stourhead Cl **6**
SW19 ....156 D4
Stourhead Gdns
SW20 ....200 A6
Stour Rd E3 ....75 C1
Dagenham RM10 .....81 C6
Stourton Ave TW13 173 B6
Stowage SE8 ....141 D6
Stow Cres E17 ......35 A3
Stowe Cres HA4 .....39 A3
Stowe Gdns N9 ......17 D3
Stowe Ho **11** N16 ....73 C5
NW11 ....48 A3
Stowell Ho **2** N8 ....50 A5
Stowe Pl N15 ....51 C6
Stowe Rd W12 .....112 B4
Stowford Coll SM2 .218 A1
Stowting Rd BR6 ...227 C4
Stox Mead HA3 ......24 B2
Stracey Rd E7 ....77 A4
NW10 ....89 A5
Strachan Pl SW19,
SW20 ....178 C4
Stradbroke Gr
Buckhurst Hill IG9 ...21 D3
Redbridge IG5 ......56 B6
Stradbroke Rd N5 ...73 A4
Stradbrook Cl HA2 ..63 B5
Stradella Rd SE24 ..161 A5
Straffan Lo **8** NW3 .70 C2
Strafford Ho **9** SE8 .119 B1
Strafford Rd
Acton W3 ....111 A4

Strafford Rd *continued*
Barnet EN5 ....1 A2
Hounslow TW3 ....129 B2
Twickenham TW1 .....153 A4
Strafford St E14 ......119 C4
Strahan Rd E3 ....97 A4
Straightsmouth SE10 142 A5
Straight The UB2 .....107 A4
Strait Rd E6 ....122 B6
Straker's Rd SE15 .....140 B1
Strale Ho [17] N1 ....95 C6
Strand WC2 ..116 B6 250 C6
Strandfield Cl SE18 ..123 C1
Strand La WC2 ....250 D6
Strand-on-the-Green
W4 ....132 C6
Strand-on-the-Green Sch
W4 ....132 C6
Strand Pl N18 ....33 C6
Strang Ho N1 ....235 A5
Strangways Terr
W14 ....254 C5
Stranraer Way N1 ..72 A1
[1] Stanwell TW6 .....148 A5
Strasburg Rd
SW11 ......137 B4 268 C1
Stratfield Ho SE12 ..165 A2
Stratfield Park Cl N21 16 D4
Stratford Ave UB10 ..82 B5
Stratford Bus Sta E15 .76 B1
Stratford Cir E15 ....76 B2
Stratford Cl E11 .....80 A1
Stratford Ct KT3 ....199 B5
Stratford Ctr E15 ....76 B1
Stratford Gr SW15 ..134 D1
Stratford House Ave
BR1 ....210 A6
Stratford Office Village
The [1] E15 ....76 C1
Stratford Pl W1 ....238 C1
Stratford Rd E13 .....99 A6
W8 ....113 C3 255 B5
Harlington TW6 ....149 A6
Hayes UB4 ....84 B3
Southall UB2 ....107 A2
Thornton Heath CR7 ..204 D6
Stratford Sta E15 ....76 B1
Stratford Studios
W8 ....255 C5
Stratford Villas NW1 ..71 D1
Stratford Workshops
E15 ....98 B6
Strathan Cl SW18 ....157 A5
Strathaven Rd SE12 ..165 B5
Strathblaine Rd
SW11 ....136 B1
Strathbrook Rd
SW16 ....182 B3
Strathcona Rd HA9 ..65 D6
Strathdale SW16 ....182 B5
Strathdon Dr SW17 ..158 B1
Strathearn Ave
Harlington UB3 ....127 D5
Twickenham TW2 ...152 A3
Strathearn House
W2 ....247 A6
Strathearn Pl
W2 ....114 C6 247 A6
Strathearn Rd
Sutton SM1 ....217 C3
Wimbledon SW19 ...179 C1
Stratheden Par SE3 .143 A5
Stratheden Rd SE3 ..143 A5
Strathfield Gdns IG11 .79 B2
Strathleven Rd SW2 .160 A6
Strathmore Ct NW8 .230 A2
Strathmore Gdns N3 .29 D2
W8 ....245 B4
Edgware HA8 ....26 D1
Strathmore Rd
Teddington TW11,TW2 .174 C6
Thornton Heath CR0 .205 B2
Wimbledon SW19 ...157 C1
Strathmore Sch
TW10 ....153 D2
Strathnairn St SE1 ..118 A2
Strathray Gdns NW3 .70 C2
Strath Terr SW11 ....136 C1
Strathville Rd SW18 .157 D2
Strathyre Ave SW16 .204 C6
Stratton Ave EN2 .....5 B6
Stratton Cl DA7 .....147 A2
Edgware HA8 ....26 B4
Heston TW5 ....129 C4
Merton SW19 ......179 C1
Walton-on-T KT12 ..194 C1
Stratton Ct [4] N1 ....73 C1
[10] Kingston KT6 .....198 A4
Strattondale St E14 ..120 A3
Stratton Dr IG11 .....79 D2

Stratton Gdns UB1 ...85 C1
Stratton Ho HA8 .....26 B6
Stratton Rd DA7 .....147 A2
Merton SW19 ......179 C1
Sunbury TW16 .....171 D1
Stratton St
W1 ....115 B5 248 D4
Strauss Rd W4 ....111 B4
Strawberry Hill Cl
TW1 ....152 D1
Strawberry Hill Rd
TW1 ....152 D1
Strawberry Hill Sta
TW2 ....152 D1
Strawberry La SM5 ..219 A5
Strawberry Terr N10 .30 D2
Strawberry Vale N2 ..30 B2
Twickenham TW1 ...153 A1
Strayfield Rd EN2 .....4 D6
Streakes Field Rd
NW2 ....68 A6
Streamdale SE2 ....146 B6
Streamline Mews
SE22 ....162 A3
Streamside Cl BR2 ..209 A5
Edmonton N9 ....17 D3
Stream Way DA17 ...147 C6
Streatfield Ave E6 ..100 B6
Streatfield Rd HA3,
HA7 ....43 D6
Streatham Cl SW16 ..160 A2
Streatham & Clapham
High Sch SW16 ....159 D1
Streatham Comm N
SW16 ....182 B5
Streatham Common Sta
SW16 ....181 D3
Streatham Comm S
SW16 ....182 B4
Streatham Ct SW16 ..160 A1
Streatham High Rd
SW16,SW2 ....182 A5
Streatham Hill SW2 .160 A3
Streatham Hill & Clapham
High Sch SW2 .....160 B3
Streatham Hill Sta
SW2 ....160 A2
Streatham Pl SW2 ..160 A4
Streatham Rd CR4 ..181 A2
East Barnet EN4 .....14 D4
Harrow HA3 ....42 D6
Richmond TW10 ....153 B1
South Norwood CR7 .205 A5
Wimbledon SW19 ..157 C1
Streatham Sta SW16 .181 D5
Streatham & Tooting Adult
Inst SW16 ....160 B2
Streatham Vale
SW16 ....181 D3
Streathbourne Rd
SW17 ....159 A1
Streathem Wells Prim Sch
SW2 ....160 C2
Streatleigh Par [4]
SW16 ....160 A2
Streatley Pl NW3 .....70 B4
[12] NW3 ....70 A4
Streatley Rd NW6 .....69 B1
Streeters La SM6 ...219 D5
Streetfield Mews
SE3 ....143 A2
Streimer Rd E15 .....98 A5
Strelley Way W3 ....111 C6
Stretton Lo W13 ....109 B6
Stretton Mans [16]
SE8 ....141 C6
Stretton Rd
Croydon CR0 ......205 C2
Richmond TW10 ....153 C2
Strickland Ct SE15 ..140 A2
Strickland Ho [26] E2 ..95 D4
Strickland Row
SW18 ....158 B4
Strickland St SE8 ...141 C4
Strickland Way [4]
BR6 ....227 D4
Stride Rd E13 ....98 D5
Strimon Cl N9 ....18 C2
Stringer Hos [19] N1 ..95 C6
Strode Cl N10 ....31 A3
Strode Ho [3] SW2 ..160 C3
Strode Rd E7 ....77 A4
NW10 ....68 A2
SW6 ....135 A5 264 A4
Tottenham N17 .....33 C1
Strome Ho NW6 .....91 D5
Strone Rd E7,E12 ....77 D2
Strone Way UB4 .....85 A3
Strongbow Cres SE9 .166 B6
Strongbow Rd SE9 ..166 B6
Strongbridge Cl HA2 .41 C1
Stronsa Rd W12 ....111 D4
Strood Ho SE1 .....252 D1
[12] Penge SE20 ....184 C3

Stroud Cres SW15 ...156 A1
Stroudes Cl KT4 ....199 D2
Stroud Field UB5 .....63 A2
Stroud Gate HA2 .....63 D4
Stroud Green Gdns
CR0 ....206 C2
Stroud Green JMI Sch
N4 ....50 C1
Stroud Green Rd N4 .50 C1
Stroud Green Way
CR0 ....206 C2
Stroudley Ho SW8 ..269 B2
Stroudley Wlk E3 .....97 C4
Stroud Rd
Croydon SE25 .....206 A3
Wimbledon SW19 ..157 C1
Strouds Cl RM6 ......58 B4
Stroud Way TW15 ...171 A4
Strout's Pl [2] E2 ....95 D4
Struan Ho [11] E11 ...55 A4
Strudwick Ct SW8 ..270 B1
Strutton Ground
SW1 ....115 D3 259 C5
Strype St E1 ....243 C3
Stuart Ave NW9 .....46 A3
W5 ....110 B4
Harrow HA2 ....63 B5
Hayes BR2 ....209 A1
Walton-on-T KT12 ..194 B1
Stuart Cl UB10 ....60 C2
Stuart Cres
Croydon CR0 ......223 B5
Hayes UB3 ....83 A1
Wood Green N22 ...32 B2
Stuart Ct Chingford E4 .20 D2
[2] Elstree WD6 ....9 D5
Stuart Evans Cl DA16 146 C2
Stuart Gr TW11 ......174 C5
Stuart Ho [1] E9 ......74 D1
[5] SW4 ....138 A1
W14 ....254 A4
Stuart Lo SE25 ......183 C1
Stuart Mill Ho N1 ..233 C3
Stuart Pl CR4 ....180 C2
Stuart Rd DA16 .....146 B4
NW6 ....91 C4
SE15 ....140 C1
W3 ....111 A5
East Barnet EN4 ....14 C4
Harrow HA3 ....42 D6
Richmond TW10 ....153 B1
South Norwood CR7 .205 A5
Wimbledon SW19 ..157 C1
Stubbs Cl NW9 ....45 A4
Stubbs Dr SE16 .....118 A4
Stubbs Ho [1] E2 .....96 D4
N4 ....50 B1
Stubbs Mews RM8 ...80 B4
Stubbs Point E13 .....99 B3
Stubbs Way SW19 ..180 B2
Stucley Pl [18] NW1 ..71 B1
Stucley Rd TW5,TW7 .130 A5
Studdridge St SW6 ..135 C3
Studholme Ct NW3 ..69 C4
Studholme St SE15 ..140 B5
Studio Pl SW1 ......247 D1
Studios Rd TW17 ...192 B6
Studios The [4] SW4 .137 C1
SW8 ....269 D6
Studland SE17 .....262 C2
Studland Cl DA15 ...167 D1
Studland Ho E14 .....97 A1
Studland Rd Ealing W7 .86 D1
Forest Hill SE26 ...184 D1
Kingston KT2 ......176 A4
Studland St W6 .....112 B2
Studley Ave E4 ....36 B3
Studley Cl E5 ....75 A4
Studley Ct DA14 ....190 B5
[9] Poplar E14 .....120 B6
Redbridge IG4 ......55 D3
Studley Dr IG4 ....55 D3
Studley Grange Rd
W7 ....108 D4
Studley Rd E7 ....77 B2
SW4 ....138 A1
Dagenham RM9 .....80 D1
Study Prep Sch The
SW19 ....178 C5
Study Sch The KT3 ..199 C4
Stukeley Rd E7 ....77 B1
Stukeley St
WC2 ......94 A1 240 B2
Stumps Hill La BR3 .185 C4
Sugar House La E15 .98 A5
Sugar Loaf Wlk [6] E2 .96 C4
Sugden Rd SW11 ...137 A1
Long Ditton KT7 ...197 B1
Sugden Way IG11 ...101 D5
Sulby Ho SE4 ....141 A4
Sulgrave Gdns [11]
W6 ....112 C4
Sulgrave Rd W6 ....112 C3
Sulina Rd SW2 ......160 A4
Sulivan Ct SW6 .....135 C3
Sulivan Ent Ctr SW6 .135 C2
Sulivan Prim Sch
SW6 ....135 C3
Sulivan Rd SW6 ....135 C3
Sulkin Ho [11] E2 .....96 D4

Sturgeon Rd
SE17 ......117 A1 262 A1
Sturges Field BR7 ..189 B4
Sturgess Ave NW4 ...46 B2
Sturge St SE1 117 A4 252 A2
Sturmer Way N7 .....72 B3
Sturminster Cl UB4 ..84 C1
Sturminster Ho SW8 270 D2
Sturrock Cl N15 .....51 B5
Sturry St E14 ....97 D1
Sturt St N1 ....235 B3
Stutfield St E1 ....96 A1
Stuttle Ho [9] E1 .....96 A1
Styles Gdns SW9 ...138 D2
Styles Ho SE1 .....251 C3
Styles Way BR3 ....208 A5
Sudbourne Prim Sch
SW2 ....160 B6
Sudbourne Rd SW2 .160 B6
Sudbrooke Rd SW12 159 A5
Sudbrook Gdns
TW10 ....154 A1
Sudbrook La TW10 ..154 A2
Sudbury E6 ....100 C1
Sudbury Ave HA0 ....65 D4
Sudbury Court Dr HA1 65 A5
Sudbury Court Rd
HA1 ....65 A5
Wembley HA0 ....65 B3
Sudbury Cres BR1 ..187 A6
Wembley HA0 ....65 B3
Sudbury Croft HA0 ..64 D4
Sudbury Ct E5 ....75 A4
SW8 ....269 D2
Sudbury Gdns CR0 ..221 C4
Sudbury & Harrow Road
Sta HA0 ....65 B3
Sudbury Heights Ave
UB6 ....65 A3
Sudbury Hill HA1 ....64 C5
Sudbury Hill Cl HA0 .64 D5
Sudbury Hill Harrow Sta
HA1 ....64 C4
Sudbury Hill Sta HA1 .64 C4
Sudbury Ho SW18 ..157 D6
Sudbury Jun & Inf Schs
HA0 ....65 B4
Sudbury Rd IG11 ....79 D3
Sudbury Town Sta
UB6 ....65 B2
Sudeley St N1 94 D5 234 D3
Sudlow Rd SW18 ...157 C6
Sudrey St SE1 .....252 A1
Suez Ave UB6 ....86 D5
Suez Rd EN3 ....7 A2
Suffield Ho SE17 ...261 D2
Suffield Rd [2] N15 ..51 D4
Chingford E4 ....35 D6
Penge SE20 ....184 D1
Suffolk Cl WD6 ....11 B6
Suffolk Ct Ilford IG3 ..57 C3
[3] West Norwood
SW16 ....182 C6
Suffolk Ho
[11] Acton W3 ......88 C1
Penge SE20 ....184 C2
[4] South Croydon CR0 221 B6
Suffolk La EC4 .....252 C2
Suffolk Park Rd E17 .53 A5
Suffolk Pl SW1 .....249 D4
Suffolk Rd [4] E13 ..99 A4
N15 ....51 B3
NW10 ....67 C1
Barking IG11 ....79 B1
Barnes SW13 ......134 A5
Dagenham RM10 ...81 D3
Enfield EN3 ....18 B6
Harrow HA2 ....41 B4
Ilford IG3 ....57 C3
Sidcup DA14 ......190 C4
South Norwood SE25 205 A5
Worcester Park KT4 215 D6
Suffolks Prim Sch EN1 .6 B3
Suffolk St E7 ....77 A4
SW1 ....115 D5 249 D4
Sugar House La E15 .98 A5

Sullivan Ave E16 ......99 D2
Sullivan Cl SW11 ...136 C2
East Molesey KT8 ..195 D6
Northolt UB4 ....84 C2
Sullivan Ct N16 .....51 D1
SW5 ....255 B4
[4] Croydon CR0 ..206 A1
Sullivan Ho SE11 ..260 D3
SW1 ....268 D6
Isleworth TW2 ....152 B5
Sullivan Rd
SE11 ......116 C2 261 B3
Sullivans Reach
KT12 ....193 D2
Sullivan Way WD6 ....9 C5
Sultan Ho SE11 ......55 B5
Sultan St SE5 ....139 A5
Penge BR3 ....184 D1
Sumal Ct E9 ....76 B6
Sumatra Rd NW6 ....69 C2
Sumburgh Rd SW12 159 A5
Summer Ave KT8 ...196 C4
Summercourt Rd E1 .96 C1
Summerene Cl SW16 181 C3
Summerfield [6] BR1 187 B2
Summerfield Ave N12 30 C4
NW6 ....91 A5
Summerfield La KT6 213 D6
Summerfield Rd
Ealing W5 ....87 B3
Loughton IG10 ....21 D5
Summerfield St SE12 164 D4
Summer Gdns KT8 ..196 C4
Summer Gr WD6 .....9 D5
Summer Hill BR7 ...188 C1
Borehamwood WD6 10 C6
Summerhill Cl BR6 ..227 C5
Summerhill Gr EN1 ..17 C5
Summerhill Rd N15 ..51 B5
Summerhill Way CR4 181 A2
Summer Ho SE13 ...142 B1
Summerhouse Ave
TW5 ....129 A4
Summerhouse Rd N16 73 C6
Summerland Gdns
N10 ....49 B6
Summerland Grange
N10 ....49 B6
Summerlands Ave
W3 ....111 A6
Summerlands Lo
BR6 ....226 C4
Summerlee Ave N2 ..48 D5
Summerlee Gdns N2 .48 D5
Summerley St SW18 157 D2
Summer Rd
East Molesey KT8 ..196 B4
Thames Ditton KT7,KT8 196 D4
Summersby Rd N6 ...49 B3
Summers Cl
Belmont SM2 .....217 C1
Wembley HA9 ....44 D1
Summersell Ho SE27 183 B5
Summerside Prim Sch
N12 ....30 B4
Summerskille Cl N9 ..18 B2
Summers La N12 .....30 B3
Summers Row N12 ...30 C4
Summers St EC1 ...241 A5
Summerstown SW17 180 A6
Summerton Way
SE28 ....102 D1
Summer Trees TW16 172 B2
Summerville Gdns
SM1 ....217 B2
Summerwood Rd
TW1,TW7 ....152 D1
Summit Ave NW9 ....45 A4
Summit Bsns Pk The
TW16 ....172 A3
Summit Cl N14 ....15 C2
NW9 ....45 B5
Edgware HA8 ....26 C3
Summit Ct NW2 .....69 A3
Summit Dr IG8 ....37 D1
Summit Est N16 .....52 A2
Summit Rd E17 ......53 D5
Northolt UB5 ......63 C1
Summit The TW16 ..172 A3
Summit Way N14 ....15 B2
South Norwood SE19 183 C1
Sumner Ave SE15 ..139 D4
Sumner Bldgs SE1 .252 A4
Sumner Cl BR6 .....227 C4
Sumner Ct SW8 ....270 A2
Sumner Gdns CR0 ..204 C1
Sumner Ho [1] E3 ...97 D2
Sumner Pl
SW7 ....114 B2 256 D3

Sumner Place Mews
SW7 ....256 D3
Sumner Rd SE15 ...139 D5
Harrow HA1 ....42 A2
Thornton Heath CR0 204 C1
Sumner Rd S CR0 ..204 C1
Sumner St
SE1 ....117 A5 252 A4
Sumpter Cl NW3 .....70 A2
Sun Alley [6] TW9 ...132 A1
Sunbeam Cres W10 ..90 C3
Sunbeam Rd NW10 ..89 B3
Sunbury Ave NW7 ...27 B6
Mortlake SW14 ....133 B1
Sunbury Cl KT12 ...194 A3
Sunbury Court Island
TW16 ....194 D6
Sunbury Court Rd
TW16 ....172 C1
Sunbury Cres TW13 171 D6
Sunbury Cross TW16 172 A3
Sunbury Cross Ctr [9]
TW16 ....171 D3
Sunbury Ct [3] SE14 140 D6
[2] Barnet EN5 ....1 A1
Sunbury TW16 .....172 C1
Sunbury Ct (Con Ctr)
TW16 ....172 D1
Sunbury Gdns NW7 ..27 B5
Sunbury Ho [38] E2 ..95 D4
Sunbury Int Bsns Ctr
TW16 ....171 C2
Sunbury La
SW11 ......136 B4 266 D2
Walton-on-T KT12 ..194 A3
Sunbury Manor Sch
TW16 ....171 D2
Sunbury Rd
Cheam SM3 ....217 A5
Feltham TW13 .....171 D6
Sunbury St SE18 ...122 B3
Sunbury Sta TW16 .172 A2
Sunbury Way TW13 172 C5
Sunbury Workshops [39]
E2 ....95 D4
Suncroft Pl SE26 ..162 C1
Sun Ct EC3 ....242 D1
Sunderland Ct
Dulwich SE22 .....162 A4
[12] Stanwell TW19 148 A5
Sunderland Ho [26] W2 91 C2
Sunderland Mount
SE23 ....162 D2
Sunderland Pt E16 .123 A5
Sunderland Rd W5 .109 D3
Forest Hill SE23 ...162 D2
Sunderland Terr W2 .91 C1
Sunderland Way E12 77 C6
Sundew Ave W12 ...112 A6
Sundew Ct [9] HA0 ..88 A5
Sundial Ave SE25 ..205 D6
Sundial Ct KT5 .....214 D6
Sundorne Rd SE7 ...121 C1
Sundown Rd TW15 .171 A5
Sundridge Ave DA16 145 B2
Bromley BR1,BR7 ..188 A3
Sundridge Ho [4] E9 .74 D1
Sundridge Par BR1 .187 B3
Sundridge Park Sta
BR1 ....187 B3
Sundridge Rd CR0 ..206 A1
Sunfields Pl SE3 ...143 B5
Sun in the Sands SE3 143 B5
Sunken Rd CR0 .....222 C3
Sun La SE3 ....143 B5
Sunland Ave DA6 ...147 A1
Sunleigh Ct HA0 .....88 A6
Sunleigh Rd HA0 ....88 A6
Sunley Gdns UB6 ....87 A6
Sun Life Trad Est
TW14 ....128 A2
Sunlight Cl SW19 ..180 A4
Sunlight Sq [29] E2 ...96 B4
Sunmead Rd TW16 .194 A6
Sunna Gdns TW16 ..172 B1
Sunniholme Ct CR2 221 A3
Sunningdale N14 ....31 D5
Ealing W5 ....87 B2
Sunningdale Ave W3 111 C6
Barking IG11 ....79 B1
Feltham TW13 .....151 A2
Ruislip HA4 ....40 C1
Sunningdale Cl E6 ..100 B4
[22] SE16 ....118 C2
Erith SE28 ....103 A1
Stanmore HA7 ......25 A3
[3] Surbiton KT6 ...214 A6

Sunningdale Ct
🆂 Kingston KT2 .....**176** C3
🆂 Southall UB1 ....**86** A1
Sunningdale Gdns
NW9 ....**45** A4
W8 ....**255** B5
Sunningdale Rd
BR1,BR2 ....**210** A4
Cheam SM1 ....**217** B4
Sunningfields Cres
NW4 ....**28** B1
Sunningfields Rd NW4 46 B6
Sunninghill Ct 🆂 W3 **111** A4
Sunninghill Gdns IG2 .**57** C3
Sunninghill Rd SE13 .**141** D3
Sunny Bank SE25 .**206** A6
Sunny Cres NW10 ....**67** A1
Sunnycroft Rd
Hounslow TW3 .....**129** D3
Southall UB1 ....**85** C2
South Norwood SE25 ..**206** A6
Sunnydale BR6 ....**226** C6
Sunnydale Gdns NW7 .**27** C4
Sunnydale Rd SE12 .**165** B6
Sunnydene Ave
Chingford E4 ......**36** B5
Ruislip HA4 ....**62** A6
Sunnydene Gdns HA0 .**65** C2
Sunnydene St SE26 .**185** A6
Sunnyfield NW7 .....**27** D6
Sunnyfields Prim Sch
NW4 ....**46** B6
Sunny Gardens Par
NW4 ....**28** B1
Sunny Gardens Rd
NW4 ....**46** C6
Sunny Hill NW4 .....**46** B6
Sunnyhill Cl E5 .....**75** A4
Sunny Hill Ct NW4 ..**28** A1
Sunnyhill Prim Sch
SW16 ....**182** B6
Sunnyhill Rd SW16 .**182** A6
Sunnyhurst Cl SM1 .**217** C5
Sunnymead Ave CR4 203 D6
Sunnymead Ct W5 .**109** D6
Sunnymead Rd NW9 ..**45** B2
Putney SW15 ......**156** B6
Sunnymede Ave
KT19 ....**215** C1
Sunnymede Dr IG6 ..**56** D5
Sunny Nook Gdns
CR2 ....**221** B2
Sunny Pl NW4 ....**46** C5
Sunny Rd The EN3 ....**6** C4
Sunnyside 🆂 NW2 ...**69** B5
Walton-on-T KT12 ..**194** C4
Wimbledon SW19 ..**179** A4
Sunnyside Dr E4 .....**20** A4
Sunnyside Ho 🆂 NW2 69 B5
Sunnyside Pl SW19 .**179** A4
Sunnyside Rd E10 ...**53** C1
N19 ....**49** D2
Ealing W5 ....**109** D5
Ilford IG1 ....**79** B5
Teddington TW11 ...**174** B6
Sunnyside Rd E N9 ...**18** A1
Sunnyside Rd N N9 ...**18** A1
Sunnyside Rd S N9 ...**18** A1
Sunny View NW9 ....**45** B4
Sunny Way N12 .....**30** C3
Sun Pas 🆂 SE16 ...**118** A3
Sunray Ave BR2 ...**210** B3
SE5,SE24 ....**139** B1
Tolworth KT5 ......**214** D6
Sun Rd W14 .**113** B1 **254** C1
Sunrise Cl TW13 ....**151** B1
Sunrise View NW7 ...**27** D4
Sunset Ave
Chingford E4 ......**19** D3
Woodford IG8 ......**36** D6
Sunset Ct 🆂 IG8 ...**37** C3
Sunset Gdns SE25 .**183** D1
Sunset Rd SE28 ...**124** A5
SE5 ....**139** B1
Wimbledon SW19 ..**178** B5
Sunset View EN5 .....**1** A3
Sunshine Way CR4 .**180** D1
Sun St EC2 ..**95** B2 **242** D4
Sun St Pas
EC2 ..**95** C2 **243** A3
Sunwell Cl SE15 ...**140** B4
Superior Dr 🆂 BR6 .**227** D2
Surbiton Cres KT1,
KT6 ....**198** A5
Surbiton Ct KT6 ....**197** D3
Surbiton Hall Cl KT1 .**198** A5

Surbiton High Sch
KT1 ....**198** A5
Surbiton High Sch Jun Sch
for Girls KT1 ......**198** A5
Surbiton Hill Pk KT5 .**198** C4
Surbiton Hill Rd KT6 .**198** A4
Surbiton Hospl KT6 .**198** A3
Surbiton Prep Sch
KT6 ....**198** A4
Surbiton Rd KT1 ....**198** A5
Surbiton Sta KT6 ...**198** A3
Surcot Ho 🆂 SW4 ..**137** D3
Surlingham Cl SE28 .**124** D6
Surma Cl E1 ....**96** A3
Surmans Cl RM9 ...**102** C6
Surrendale Pl W9 ...**91** C3
Surrey Canal Rd
SE14,SE16,SE8 ....**140** D6
Surrey Cres 🆂 W4 .**110** C1
Surrey Ct N3 ....**47** A6
Surrey Gdns N4 .....**51** A3
Surrey Gr SE17 ....**263** A1
Carshalton SM1 ...**218** B5
Surrey Ho 🆂 SE16 .**118** D5
Surrey La
SW11 ....**136** C4 **267** B1
Surrey Lo SW20 ....**178** C1
Surrey Mews SE27 .**183** C6
Surrey Mount SE23 .**162** B3
Surrey Quays Rd
SE16 ....**118** D4
Surrey Quays Sh Ctr
SE16 ....**118** D4
Surrey Quays Sta
SE16 ....**118** D2
Surrey Rd SE15 ...**162** D6
Barking IG11 ......**79** C1
Dagenham RM10 ...**81** D3
Harrow HA1 ....**42** A4
West Wickham BR4 .**207** D1
Surrey Row
SE1 ....**116** D4 **251** D3
Surrey Sq
SE17 ....**117** C1 **263** B2
Surrey Square Inf Sch
SE17 ....**117** C1 **263** A2
Surrey Square Jun Sch
SE17 ....**117** C1 **263** A2
Surrey St 🆂 E13 ...**99** B4
WC2 ....**116** B6 **250** D6
Croydon CR0 ......**221** A5
Surrey Terr SE17 ..**263** B2
Surrey Water Rd
SE16 ....**118** D5
Surridge Ct 🆂 SW9 .**138** A3
Surridge Gdns SE19 .**183** B4
Surr St N7 ....**72** A3
Sury Basin KT2 ....**176** A2
Susan Constant Ct 🆂
E14 ....**120** B6
Susan Lawrence Ho 🆂
E12 ....**78** C4
Susan Lawrence Prim Schs
E14 ....**97** D1
Susannah St E14 ....**98** A1
Susan Rd SE3 .....**143** B3
Susan Wood BR7 ..**188** C2
Sussex Ave TW7 ...**130** C2
Sussex Cl IG1 ......**72** A6
New Malden KT3 ..**199** C5
Redbridge IG4 .....**56** B4
🆂 Twickenham TW1 .**153** B5
Sussex Cres UB5 ....**63** C2
Sussex Ct SE10 ....**142** A6
W2 ....**236** C1
🆂 Barnes SW13 ...**133** C4
Mitcham CR4 .....**204** A4
Sussex Gate N6 .....**48** C4
Sussex Gdns N4 .....**51** A4
N6 ....**48** D4
W2 ....**92** B1 **236** D1
Chessington KT9 ..**213** D2
Sussex Ho NW3 .....**70** C2
Richmond TW9 ....**132** B3
Sussex House Sch
SW3 ....**114** D2 **257** C3
Sussex Lo W2 .....**236** D1
Sussex Mans SW7 .**256** C3
WC2 ....**250** B6
Sussex Mews SE6 .**163** C3
Sussex Mews E W2 .**236** D1
Sussex Mews W W2 .**246** D1
Sussex Pl NW1 **92** D3 **237** C6
W2 ....**92** B1 **236** D1
🆂 W6 ....**112** C1
New Malden KT3 ..**199** C5
Sussex Rd DA14 ...**190** B5
DA8 ....**147** D5
Barking E6 ....**100** C4

Sussex Rd continued
Harrow HA1 ....**42** A4
Mitcham CR4 .....**204** A4
New Malden KT3 ..**199** C5
Southall UB2 ......**106** A3
South Croydon CR2 .**221** B2
Uxbridge UB10 ....**61** A3
Wallington SM5 ...**218** D2
🆂 West Wickham BR4 **207** D1
Sussex Ring N12 ....**29** C5
Sussex Sq
W2 ....**114** B6 **246** D6
Sussex St E13 ......**99** B4
SW1 ....**258** D2
Sussex Way N19 ....**49** D1
N7,N19 ....**72** A6
Cockfosters EN4 ...**15** A3
Sutcliffe Cl NW11 ...**47** A4
Sutcliffe Ho UB3 ....**84** A1
Sutcliffe Rd SE18 .**145** C6
Bexley DA16 .....**146** C1
Sutherland Ave BR5 .**211** D4
DA16 ....**145** C1
W9 ....**92** A3 **236** A6
Ealing W13 ....**87** B1
Hayes UB3 ....**106** A2
Sunbury TW16 ....**171** D1
Sutherland Ct EN5 ....**1** C1
🆂 W9 ....**91** C3
Sutherland Dr SW19 .**180** B2
Sutherland Gdns
Mortlake SW14 ...**133** C2
North Cheam KT4 .**200** B1
Sunbury TW16 ....**171** D1
Sutherland Gr
Putney SW18,SW19 .**157** B4
Teddington TW11 .**174** C5
Sutherland Ho
🆂 NW6 ....**70** A2
🆂 SE18 ....**144** B4
W8 ....**255** C5
Ealing W13 ....**109** A6
🆂 Putney SW15 ...**156** C4
Richmond TW10 ...**153** C2
Sutherland Pl W2 ...**91** C1
Sutherland Point 🆂
E5 ....**74** B4
Sutherland Rd E17 ...**53** A6
E3 ....**97** B5
Belvedere DA17 ...**125** C3
Chiswick W4 ......**133** C6
Ealing W13 ....**87** A1
Edmonton N9 .....**18** B3
Enfield EN3 ....**18** D6
Southall UB1 ......**85** B1
Thornton Heath CR0 .**204** C2
Tottenham N17 ...**34** A2
Sutherland Row
SW1 ....**258** D2
Sutherland Sq
SE17 ....**117** A1 **262** A1
Sutherland St
SW1 ....**115** B1 **258** D2
Sutherland Wlk SE17 **262** B1
Sutlej Rd SE7 ....**143** C5
Sutterton St N7 .....**72** B2
Sutton Arc SM1 ...**217** D3
Sutton Cl
Beckenham BR3 ..**185** D2
Pinner HA5 ....**40** A4
Sutton Common Rd
Cheam SM3 ......**201** C1
Sutton SM1,SM3 ..**217** D6
Sutton Common Sta
SM1 ....**217** D6
Sutton Courtenay Ho
SW17 ....**180** B6
Sutton Court Rd E13 .**99** C4
Chiswick W4 ......**133** A6
Hillingdon UB10 ...**82** D6
Sutton SM1,SM2 ..**218** A2
Sutton Cres EN5 ....**12** D6
Sutton Ct 🆂 E5 ....**74** B4
Chiswick W4 ......**133** A6
Ealing W5 ....**110** A5
East Molesey KT8 .**195** B4
Penge SE19 ......**183** D3
Sutton SM2 ......**218** A2
Sutton Dene TW3 ..**129** C4
Sutton Est
SW3 ....**114** C1 **257** B2
Sutton Est The W10 .**90** C2
Sutton Gdns
Barking IG11 ......**101** C5
Croydon CR0 ......**205** D4
Sutton Gn IG11 ...**101** C6
Sutton Gr SM1 ...**218** B3

Sutton Gram Sch For Boys
SM1 ....**218** A3
Sutton Hall Rd TW5 .**129** C5
Sutton High Sch
SM1 ....**217** D2
Sutton Ho N21 .....**16** B6
Sutton La TW3,TW4,
TW5 ....**129** B3
Sutton La N W4 ....**111** A1
Sutton La S W4 ....**133** A6
Sutton Par NW4 ....**46** C5
Sutton Park Rd SM1,
SM2 ....**217** D2
Sutton Pl E9 ....**74** C3
Sutton Rd E13 .....**98** D3
E17 ....**34** D2
N10 ....**31** A2
Barking IG11 ......**101** C6
Heston TW5 ......**129** C4
Sutton Row W1 ...**239** D2
Sutton Sq E9 ......**74** C3
Hounslow TW5 ...**129** B4
Sutton Sta SM2 ..**218** A2
Suttons Way EC1 ..**242** B5
Sutton Way W10 ..**90** C2
Hounslow TW5 ...**129** B4
Sutton Wlk
SE1 ....**116** B5 **250** D3
Swaby Rd SW17,
SW18 ....**158** A2
Swaffield Prim Sch
SW18 ....**158** A4
Swaffield Rd SW18 .**158** A4
Swain Cl SW16 ...**181** B4
Swain Rd CR7 ...**205** A4
Swains Cl UB7 ....**104** A4
Swain's La N6 .....**71** B6
Swainson Ho N7 ...**72** C4
Swainson Rd W3 ..**111** C4
Swains Rd CR4,SW17,
SW19 ....**180** D3
Swakeleys Dr UB10 ..**60** C3
Swakeleys Rd UB10 ..**60** C5
Swakeleys Rdbt UB8,
UB10 ....**60** A4
Swakeleys Sch UB10 .**82** D5
Swaledale Cl N11 ...**31** A4
Swallands Rd SE6 .**163** C1
Swallowbrook Bsns Ctr
UB4 ....**106** D5
Swallow Cl SE14 ..**140** D4
Bushey WD23 ......**8** A3
Swallow Ct 🆂 SE12 .**165** A4
🆂 W9 ....**91** C2
Chingford IG8 .....**36** B3
Ilford IG2 ....**56** D4
🆂 Ruislip HA4 .....**40** C1
Swallow Dr NW10 ...**67** B2
Northolt UB5 .....**85** C5
Swallowfield NW1 .**231** D1
Swallowfield Rd SE7 .**121** B1
Swallowfield Way
UB3 ....**105** B4
Swallow Gdns SW16 .**181** D5
Swallow Ho NW8 ...**50** B6
NW8 ....**230** A4
Swallow Pk KT6 ..**214** B6
Swallow Pl W1 ...**238** D1
Swallows Ct 🆂 SE20 **184** D3
Swallow St E6 ....**100** A4
W1 ....**115** C6 **249** B5
Swaminarayan Sch The
NW10 ....**67** B2
Swanage Ct 🆂 N1 ..**73** C1
Swanage Ho SW8 .**270** C3
Swanage Rd SW18 .**158** A5
Chingford E4 ......**36** A3
Swanage Waye UB4 ..**84** C1
Swan App E6 ......**100** A1
Swanbourne SE17 .**262** A3
Swanbourne Ho
NW8 ....**237** A6
Swanbridge Rd DA7 .**147** C4
Swan Cl E17 ......**35** C1
Croydon CR0 .....**205** C2
Feltham TW13 ....**173** A6
Swan Ct E14 ......**97** B1
N20 ....**14** A2
SW3 ....**257** B1
SW6 ....**265** A3
Swan Ctr SW17 ...**158** A2
Swandon Way SW18 .**135** C4
Swan Dr NW9 ......**27** C6
Swanfield St E2 ....**95** D4
Swan Ho N1 ......**73** B1
Enfield EN3 ......**18** C6
Swan La EC4 .**117** B6 **252** D5
N20 ....**14** A1
Loughton IG10 ....**21** C4

Swan Lane Pier
EC4 ....**117** B6 **252** C5
Swanlea Sec Sch E1 .**96** B3
Swanley Ho SE17 .**263** B2
Swanley Rd DA16 .**146** C4
Swan Mead
SE1 ....**117** C3 **263** A5
Swan Mews SW9 ..**138** B3
Swanmore Ct SW18 .**158** A5
Swann Ct 🆂 TW7 .**131** B2
Swanne Ho 🆂 SE10 .**142** A5
Swan Pas 🆂 E1 ...**118** A6
Swan Pl SW13 ....**133** C3
Swan Rd SE16 ....**118** C4
SE18 ....**121** D5
Feltham TW13 ....**173** A6
Southall UB1 ......**85** D1
West Drayton UB7 .**104** A4
Swanscombe Ho
🆂 BR5 ....**190** B1
🆂 W11 ....**112** C5
Swanscombe Point 🆂
E16 ....**98** D2
Swanscombe Rd
W11 ....**112** C5
🆂 W4 ....**111** C1
Swansea Ct E16 ..**122** D5
Swansea Rd Enfield EN3 .**6** D1
Harlington TW14,TW6 .**149** B5
Swansland Gdns E17 .**35** A2
Swansmere Sch
KT12 ....**194** C1
Swan St SE1 .**117** A4 **252** B1
Isleworth TW7 ....**131** C1
Swan The BR4 ....**224** A6
Swanton Gdns SW19 156 D3
Swanton Rd DA8 ..**147** D5
Swan Way EN3 .....**6** D1
Swan Wlk
SW3 ....**136** D6 **267** C6
Oatlands Park TW17 .**193** C2
Swan Yd N1 ......**72** D2
Swaton Rd E3 .....**97** C3
Swaylands Rd DA17 .**147** C6
Swaythling Cl N18 ..**34** B2
Swaythling Ho 🆂
SW15 ....**155** D5
Swedenborg Gdns
E1 ....**118** B6
Sweden Gate SE16 .**119** A2
Swedish Sch The
SW13 ....**133** D6
Sweeney Cres SE1 .**253** D1
Sweet Briar Gn N9 ..**17** D1
Sweet Briar Gr N9 ...**17** D1
Sweet Briar Wlk N18 .**33** D6
Sweetcroft La UB10 ..**60** C1
Sweetmans Ave HA5 .**40** D6
Sweets Way N20 ...**14** B2
Swell Ct E17 ......**53** D3
Swetenham Wlk
SE18 ....**123** A1
Swete St E13 .....**99** A5
Sweyn Pl SE3 ....**143** A3
Swift Cl E17 ......**35** A3
Harrow HA2 ......**63** D2
Hayes UB3 ....**83** D1
Swift Ct SM2 ....**217** D1
Swift Ctr CR0 ...**220** B1
Swift Ho 🆂 E1 ....**96** C1
🆂 N16 ....**73** C1
🆂 SW9 ....**138** C5
🆂 Wanstead E18 ..**55** B6
Swift Pl
Feltham TW13 ....**173** A6
Southall UB2 ......**107** B3
Swiftsden Way BR1 .**186** C4
Swift St SW6 .**135** B4 **264** C2
Swinbrook Rd W10 ..**91** A2
Swinburne Cres CR0 .**206** A4
Swinburne Ct 🆂 SE5 **139** B1
Swinburne Ho 🆂 E2 .**96** C4
Swinburne Rd SW15 .**134** C1
Swinderby Rd HA0 ..**66** C2
Swindon Cl IG3 ....**57** C1
Swindon Rd TW6 ..**149** A6
Swindon St W12 ..**112** C5
Swinfield Cl TW13 .**173** A4
Swinford Gdns SW9 .**138** D2
Swingate La SE18 .**145** C5
Swingfield Ho 🆂 E9 .**96** C6
Swinley Ho NW1 .**231** D2
Swinnerton St E9 ..**75** A3
Swinton Cl HA9 ...**44** D1
Swinton Ho 🆂 E2 ..**96** A4
Swinton Pl WC1 .**233** C2
Swinton St
WC1 ....**94** B4 **233** C2
Swires Shaw BR2 .**225** D4

Swiss Cottage NW3 ..**70** B1
Swiss Cottage Sch
NW8 ....**92** B6 **229** D6
Swiss Cottage Sta
NW3 ....**70** B1
Swiss Re Building*
EC2 ....**243** B2
Swiss Terr 🆂 NW3 ..**70** B1
Swithland Gdns SE9 .**188** D3
Swyncombe Ave W5 .**109** B2
Swynford Gdns 🆂
NW4 ....**46** A5
Sybil Elgar Sch UB2 .**107** B3
Sybil Mews N4 ....**50** D3
Sybil Phoenix Cl SE8 **118** D1
Sybil Thorndike Casson Ho
SW5 ....**255** B1
Sybil Thorndike Ho 🆂
N1 ....**73** A2
Sybourn Inf Sch Annexe
E10 ....**53** A4
Sybourn Jun & Inf Schs
E17 ....**53** B2
Sybourn St E17 ...**53** B2
Sycamore Ave DA15 .**167** C5
N3 ....**47** D6
W5 ....**109** D3
Bow E3 ....**97** B6
Hayes UB3 ....**105** C6
Sycamore Cl E16 ..**98** C3
W3 ....**111** C5
🆂 HA8 ....**27** A6
Carshalton SM5 ..**218** D4
Chislehurst SE9 .**166** A2
Edmonton N9 .....**34** A6
Feltham TW13 ....**150** A1
New Barnet EN4 ..**14** B5
Northolt UB5 .....**85** A6
South Croydon CR2 .**221** C3
Yiewsley UB7 ....**104** B6
Sycamore Ct E7 ...**77** A2
N19 ....**71** D5
NW6 ....**91** C6
SE12 ....**164** D5
🆂 SE5 ....**139** A4
Forest Hill SE26 .**184** C6
Hillingdon UB8 ...**82** C3
Hounslow TW4 ...**129** A1
Surbiton KT6 .....**198** A2
🆂 West Norwood
SW16 ....**182** C5
Sycamore Gdns N15 .**51** D5
W6,W12 ....**112** B3
Mitcham CR4 .....**180** B1
Sycamore Gr NW9 ..**45** A2
SE6 ....**164** A5
Kingston KT3 ....**199** C6
Penge SE20 ......**184** A2
Sycamore Hill N11 ..**31** A4
Sycamore Ho 🆂 N16 .**73** B6
🆂 N2 ....**30** B1
🆂 NW3 ....**70** D2
🆂 SE16 ....**118** D4
🆂 W6 ....**112** B4
🆂 Buckhurst Hill IG9 .**21** D2
Penge SE20 ......**184** D4
Sycamore Lo
🆂 Ashford TW16 ..**171** D3
Putney SW15 ....**134** B2
Sycamore Mews 🆂
SW4 ....**137** C2
Sycamore Rd SW19,
SW20 ....**178** C4
Sycamore St EC1 .**242** A5
Sycamore Way TW11 175 C4
Sycamore Wlk 🆂 W10 91 A3
Ilford IG6 ....**57** A5
Sydenham Ave
Penge SE26 ......**184** B5
Southgate N21 ...**16** B6
Sydenham High Sch For
Girls SE26 ....**184** B6
Sydenham Hill SE21,
SE22,SE23,SE26,SE19 .**162** A1
Sydenham Hill Sta
SE21 ....**161** D1
Sydenham Ho 🆂 KT6 **197** D2
Sydenham Ind Est
SE26 ....**185** B5
Sydenham Park Mans 🆂
SE26 ....**162** C1
Sydenham Park Rd
SE23,SE26 ....**162** C1
Sydenham Pk SE26 .**162** C1
Sydenham Rd
Forest Hill SE26 .**184** D5
Forest Hill SE26 .**185** A6
Thornton Heath CR0 .**205** D4
Sydenham Rise SE23 162 B2

Sydenham Sec Sch
SE26 ... 162 B1
Sydenham Sta SE26 ... 184 C6
Sydenham Station App
SE26 ... 184 C6
Sydmons Ct SE23 ... 162 C4
Sydner Mews N16 ... 73 D4
Sydner Rd N16 ... 73 D4
Sydney Cl SW3 ... 256 D3
Sydney Cotts KT10 ... 212 D2
Sydney Cres TW15 ... 170 D4
Sydney Ct Hayes UB4 ... 84 C3
Surbiton KT6 ... 214 A6
Sydney Gr NW4 ... 46 C4
Sydney Ho 4 W4 ... 111 C2
Sydney Mews SW3 ... 256 D3
Sydney Pl SW7 ... 257 A3
Sydney Rd DA6 ... 146 D1
N10 ... 31 B3
N8 ... 50 C5
SE2 ... 124 D3
Ealing W13 ... 109 A4
East Bedfont TW14 ... 150 A3
Enfield EN2 ... 5 B1
Richmond TW10,TW9 ... 132 A1
Sidcup DA14 ... 189 C6
Sutton SM1 ... 217 C4
Teddington TW11 ... 174 D5
Wanstead E11 ... 55 B3
West Barnes SW20 ... 178 D1
Woodford IG8 ... 37 A6
Sydney Russell Sch The
RM9 ... 80 D3
Sydney St
SW3 ... 114 C1 257 A2
Sydney Terr KT10 ... 212 D2
Sylva Ct 3 SW15 ... 156 D4
Sylvana Cl UB10 ... 82 B6
Sylvan Ave N3 ... 29 C1
NW7 ... 27 D4
Dagenham RM6 ... 59 B3
Wood Green N22 ... 32 C3
Sylvan Ct N12 ... 29 D6
South Croydon CR2 ... 221 A2
Sylvan Gdns KT6 ... 197 D2
Sylvan Gr NW2 ... 68 D4
SE15 ... 140 B6
Sylvan Hill SE19 ... 183 C2
Sylvan Ho N21 ... 16 B6
Sylvan Rd E17 ... 53 C4
E7 ... 77 B2
Ilford IG1 ... 79 A6
South Norwood SE19 ... 183 D2
Wanstead E11 ... 55 A4
Sylvan Way
Coney Hall BR4 ... 224 C4
Dagenham RM8 ... 80 B5
Sylvan Wlk BR1 ... 210 B6
Sylverdale Rd CR0 ... 220 D5
Sylvester Ave BR7 ... 188 B4
Sylvester Ho 7 E8 ... 74 B2
Sylvester Path 8 E8 ... 74 B2
Sylvester Rd E17 ... 53 B2
E8 ... 74 B2
N2 ... 30 B1
Wembley HA0 ... 65 C3
Sylvestrus Cl KT1 ... 176 C1
Sylvia Ave HA5 ... 23 B4
Sylvia Cotts 3 SE8 ... 141 C4
Sylvia Ct N1 ... 235 C3
Wembley HA9 ... 66 D1
Sylvia Gdns HA9 ... 66 D1
Sylvia Pankhurst Ho
14 E2 ... 96 D4
10 Dagenham RM10 ... 81 C5
Sylvia Young Theatre Sch
NW1 ... 237 B5
Symes Mews NW1 ... 232 A4
Symington Ho SE1 ... 262 C5
Symington Mews E9 ... 74 D3
Symister Mews N1 ... 95 C4
Symons St
SW3 ... 114 D2 257 D3
Symphony Mews 16
W10 ... 91 A4
Syon Gate Way
Brentford TW7,TW8 ... 131 A5
Brentford TW8 ... 131 B5
Syon Ho TW8 ... 131 C2
Syon La
Brentford TW7,TW8 ... 131 B5
Hounslow TW7 ... 130 D6
Syon Lane Sta TW7 ... 131 A5
Syon Lo 6 SE12 ... 165 A4
Syon Park Cotts TW8 131 C2
Syon Park Gdns TW7 130 D5
Syringa Ho SE4 ... 141 B2

T

Tabard Ct 3 E14 ... 98 A1
Tabard Ho SE1 ... 262 D6
Teddington KT1 ... 175 C2
Tabard St
SE1 ... 117 B3 262 C6
Tabernacle Ave 7
E13 ... 99 A3
Tabernacle St
EC2 ... 95 B3 242 D6
Tableer Ave SW4 ... 159 D6
Tabley Rd N7 ... 72 A4
Tabor Ct 3 SM3 ... 217 A2
Tabor Gdns SM2,SM3 ... 217 B1
Tabor Gr SW19 ... 179 B3
Tabor Rd W6 ... 112 B3
Tachbrook Est
SW1 ... 115 D1 259 D1
Tachbrook Mews
SW1 ... 259 A4
Tachbrook Rd
East Bedfont TW14 ... 149 D4
Southall UB2 ... 106 D2
Tachbrook St
SW1 ... 115 C2 259 B3
Tack Mews SE4 ... 141 C2
Tadbourne Ct 1 HA8 ... 27 A3
Tadema Ho NW8 ... 236 D5
Tadema Rd
SW10 ... 136 A5 266 B3
Tadlow KT1 ... 198 C6
Tadmor Cl TW16 ... 193 D5
Tadmor St W12 ... 112 D5
Tadworth Ave KT3 ... 199 D4
Tadworth Ho SE1 ... 251 C1
Tadworth Rd NW2 ... 68 A6
Taeping St E14 ... 119 D2
Taffy's How CR4 ... 202 C6
Taft Way 44 E3 ... 97 D4
Taggs Ho KT1 ... 175 D1
Tailworth St 15 E1 ... 96 A2
Tait 7 NW9 ... 27 D3
Tait Ct 9 E3 ... 97 B6
SW8 ... 269 D2
Tait Ho 2 N19 ... 71 C4
SE1 ... 251 B3
Tait Rd CR0 ... 205 C2
Tait Rd Ind Est CR0 ... 205 C2
Takhar Mews SW11 ... 136 C3
Talacre Rd NW5 ... 71 A2
Talbot Ave N2 ... 48 B6
Talbot Cl N15 ... 51 D5
Talbot Cres NW4 ... 46 A4
Talbot Ct EC3 ... 252 D6
NW9 ... 67 B5
Talbot Gdns IG3 ... 80 A6
Talbot Grove Ho 9
W11 ... 91 A1
Talbot Ho E14 ... 97 D1
N7 ... 72 C5
Talbot Pl SE3 ... 142 C3
Talbot Rd E7 ... 77 A4
N15 ... 51 D5
N6 ... 49 A3
SE22 ... 139 C1
W11 ... 91 B1
W2 ... 91 C1
Ashford TW15 ... 170 A5
Dagenham RM9 ... 81 B1
Ealing W13 ... 109 A5
Harrow HA3 ... 24 D1
Isleworth TW1,TW7 ... 131 A1
Southall UB2 ... 107 A2
South Norwood CR7 ... 205 B5
Twickenham TW2 ... 152 D3
Wallend E6 ... 100 C5
Wallington SM5 ... 219 A3
Wembley HA0 ... 65 D2
Wood Green N22 ... 31 C2
Talbot Sq W2 ... 92 B1 236 C1
Talbot Wlk NW10 ... 67 C2
W11 ... 91 A1
Talbot Yd SE1 ... 252 C3
Talcott Path 12 SW2 ... 160 C3
Talfourd Pl SE15 ... 139 D4
Talfourd Rd SE15 ... 139 D4
Talgarth Rd
W14 ... 113 A1 254 B2
W6 ... 112 D1
Talgarth Wlk NW9 ... 45 C4
Talia Ho E14 ... 120 A3
Talina Ctr SW6 ... 266 A1
Talisman Cl 2 IG3 ... 58 B1
Talisman Sq SE26 ... 184 A6
Talisman Way HA9 ... 66 B5
Tallack Cl HA3 ... 24 C3
Tallack Rd E10 ... 53 B1
Tall Elms Cl BR2 ... 208 D4
Talleyrand Ho SE5 ... 139 A3
Tallis Cl E16 ... 99 B1
Tallis Gr SE7 ... 143 B6
Tallis St EC4 ... 251 B6
Tallis View NW10 ... 67 B2
Tall Trees SW16 ... 204 B6
Talma Gdns TW2 ... 152 C4
Talmage Cl SE23 ... 162 C4
Talman Gr HA7 ... 25 D4
Talma Rd SW2 ... 138 C1
Talmudical Coll N16 ... 51 B2
Talmud Torah Sch
N16 ... 51 D2
Talwin St E3 ... 97 D4
Tamar Cl E3 ... 97 B6
Tamar Ho SE11 ... 261 B2
Tamarind Ct 8 W3 ... 89 A1
Tamarind Ho 4
SE15 ... 140 A5
Tamarind Yd 5 E1 ... 118 A5
Tamarisk Sq W12 ... 111 D6
Tamar Sq IG8 ... 37 B4
Tamar St SE7 ... 122 A2
Tamar Way N17 ... 52 A6
Tamesa Ho TW17 ... 192 C2
Tamesis Gdns KT4 ... 215 C6
Tamian Ind Est TW4 ... 128 C1
Tamian Way TW4 ... 128 C1
Tamworth N7 ... 72 A2
Tamworth Ave IG8 ... 36 C4
Tamworth La CR4 ... 203 B6
Tamworth Manor High Sch
CR4 ... 203 D6
Tamworth Pk CR4 ... 203 B6
Tamworth Pl 3 CR0 ... 221 A6
Tamworth Rd CR0 ... 221 A6
Tamworth St
SW6 ... 135 C6 265 A5
Tancred Rd N4 ... 50 D3
Tandem Ctr SW19 ... 180 B2
Tandridge Ct SM2 ... 217 D2
Tandridge Dr BR5,
BR6 ... 211 B1
Tandridge Pl 2 BR6 ... 211 B1
Tanfield Ave NW2 ... 67 D5
Tanfield Rd CR0 ... 221 A4
Tangier Rd TW10 ... 132 D2
Tangleberry Cl BR1 ... 210 B5
Tangle Tree Cl N3 ... 29 D1
Tanglewood Cl
Hillingdon UB10 ... 82 C3
South Croydon CR0 ... 222 C5
Stanmore HA7 ... 8 C2
Tanglewood Way
TW13 ... 150 B1
Tangley Gr SW15 ... 155 D4
Tangley Park Rd
TW12 ... 173 B4
Tanglyn Ave TW17 ... 192 D4
Tangmere WC1 ... 233 C1
Tottenham N17 ... 33 D1
Tangmere Gdns UB5 ... 84 C5
Tangmere Gr KT2 ... 175 D5
Tangmere Way NW9 ... 27 C1
Tanhurst Ho 27 SW2 ... 160 A4
Tankerton Rd KT6 ... 214 B6
Tankerton St WC1 ... 233 B1
Tankerton Terr CR0 ... 204 B3
Tankerville Rd SW16 ... 182 A3
Tankridge Rd NW2 ... 68 B6
Tanner Ho SE1 ... 253 B1
1 Merton SW19 ... 180 A2
Tanner Point E13 ... 99 A6
Tanners Cl KT12 ... 194 B3
Tanners End La N18 ... 33 C5
Tanner's Hill SE8 ... 141 C4
Tanners La IG6 ... 57 A6
Tanner St
SE1 ... 117 C4 253 B1
Barking IG11 ... 79 A2
Tanners Yd 32 E2 ... 96 B5
Tannery Cl
Beckenham BR3,CR0 ... 206 D4
Dagenham RM10 ... 81 D5
Tannery Ho 20 E1 ... 96 A2
Tannington Terr N5 ... 72 C5
Tannsfeld Rd SE26 ... 184 D5
Tansley Cl N7 ... 71 D3
Tanswell St SE1 ... 251 A1
Tansy Cl E6 ... 100 C1
Tantallon Rd SW12 ... 159 A3
Tant Ave E16 ... 98 D1
Tantony Gr RM6 ... 58 D6
Tanworth Gdns HA5 ... 22 C1
Tan Yard La DA5 ... 169 C4
Tanza Rd NW3 ... 70 D4
Tapestry Cl SM2 ... 217 D1
Tapley Ho 11 SE1 ... 118 A4
Taplow NW3 ... 70 B1
Taplow Ct CR4 ... 202 C5
Taplow Ho 36 E2 ... 95 D4
Taplow Rd N13 ... 33 A6
Taplow St N1 ... 95 A5 235 B3
Tappesfield Rd SE15 ... 140 C2
Tapping Cl 5 KT2 ... 176 C3
Tapp St E1 ... 96 B3
Tapster St EN5 ... 1 B2
Tara Ct
4 Beckenham BR3 ... 185 D1
9 Buckhurst Hill IG9 ... 21 C2
Taranto Ho 11 E1 ... 96 D2
Tarbert Rd SE22 ... 161 C6
Tarbert Wlk E1 ... 118 C6
Target Cl TW14 ... 149 C5
Target Ho W13 ... 109 B5
Target Rdbt UB5 ... 85 B6
Tariff Rd N17 ... 34 A4
Tarleton Ct 2 N22 ... 32 C1
Tarleton Gdns SE23 ... 162 B3
Tarling Cl DA14 ... 168 B1
Tarling Ho 27 E1 ... 96 B1
Tarling Rd E16 ... 98 D1
N2 ... 30 A1
Tarling St E1 ... 96 C1
Tarnbank EN2 ... 16 A6
Tarnbrook Ct SW1 ... 258 A3
Tarn St SE1 ... 117 A3 262 A5
Tarns The NW1 ... 232 A2
Tarnwood Pk SE9 ... 166 B3
Tarplett Ho 22 SE14 ... 140 D6
Tarquin Ho SE26 ... 184 A6
Tarragon Cl SE14 ... 141 A5
Tarragon Gr SE26 ... 184 D4
Tarranbrae NW6 ... 69 A1
Tarrant Ho E2 ... 96 C4
Tarrant Pl W1 ... 237 C3
Tarrantt Ho W14 ... 254 B5
Tarriff Cres SE8 ... 119 B2
Tarrington Cl SW16 ... 159 D1
Tartan Ho 8 E14 ... 98 A1
Tarver Rd
SE17 ... 116 D1 261 D2
Tarves Way SE10 ... 141 D5
Tash Pl N11 ... 31 B5
Tasker Cl UB7 ... 127 A5
Tasker Ho 18 E14 ... 97 B2
Barking IG11 ... 101 B5
Tasker Rd NW3 ... 70 D3
Tasman Ct 9 E14 ... 119 D2
Ashford TW16 ... 171 C3
Tasman Ho 17 E1 ... 118 B5
Tasmania Terr N18 ... 33 A4
Tasman Rd SW9 ... 138 A2
Tasman Wlk E16 ... 99 D1
Tasso Rd W6 ... 135 A6 264 A6
Tasso Yd W6 ... 264 A5
Tatchbury Ho 3
SW15 ... 155 D5
Tate Britain★
SW1 ... 116 A2 260 A3
Tate Gdns WD23 ... 8 C4
Tate Ho 13 E2 ... 96 D5
Tate Modern★
EC4 ... 116 D5 251 C3
Tate Rd Newham E16 ... 122 B5
Sutton SM1 ... 217 C3
Tatham Pl
NW8 ... 92 B5 229 D4
Tatnell Rd SE23 ... 163 A5
Tattersall Cl SE9 ... 166 A6
Tatton Cres E5,N16 ... 52 D2
Tatum Rd NW10 ... 67 B1
Tatum St
SE17 ... 117 C2 262 D3
Tauheed Cl N4 ... 73 A6
Taunton Ave
Hounslow TW3 ... 130 A3
Wimbledon SW20 ... 178 B1
Taunton Cl SM3 ... 201 C1
Taunton Dr N2 ... 30 A1
Enfield EN2 ... 4 C2
Taunton Ho W2 ... 236 A1
Taunton Mews NW1 ... 237 C5
Taunton Pl
NW1 ... 92 D3 237 C6
Taunton Rd SE12 ... 164 D6
Greenford UB6 ... 85 D6
Taunton Way HA7 ... 26 A1
Tavern Cl SM5 ... 202 C2
Taverner Ho N16 ... 73 B5
Taverners Cl W11 ... 244 A3
Taverners Ct HA9 ... 66 B6
Taverner Sq 4 N5 ... 73 A4
Taverners Way E4 ... 20 C3
Tavern La SW9 ... 138 C3
Tavistock Ave E17 ... 53 A6
NW7 ... 28 D3
Wembley UB6 ... 87 A5
Tavistock Cl N16 ... 73 C3
Tavistock Cres W11 ... 91 B2
Mitcham CR4 ... 204 A5
Tavistock Ct WC1 ... 239 D6
1 Croydon CR0 ... 205 B1
Tavistock Gdns IG3 ... 79 C4
Tavistock Gr CR0 ... 205 B2
Tavistock Ho 2 W11 ... 91 B2
Tavistock Mews 1
W11 ... 91 B1
Tavistock Pl
WC1 ... 94 A3 240 A6
East Barnet N14 ... 15 B5
Tavistock Rd DA16 ... 146 C4
E15 ... 76 D2
E7 ... 76 D4
N4,N15 ... 51 B3
NW10 ... 89 D5
W11 ... 91 B2
4 Beckenham BR2 ... 208 D5
Carshalton SM5 ... 202 B1
Croydon CR0 ... 205 B1
Edgware HA8 ... 26 C2
Uxbridge UB10 ... 61 A3
Wanstead E18 ... 55 A6
Tavistock Sq
WC1 ... 93 D3 239 D6
Tavistock St
WC2 ... 116 A6 250 B6
Tavistock Terr N19 ... 71 D5
Tavistock Twr SE16 ... 119 A3
Tavistock Wlk SM5 ... 202 B1
Taviton St
WC1 ... 93 D3 239 C6
Tavy Bridge SE2 ... 124 C4
Tavy Cl SE11 ... 261 B2
Tawney Rd SE28 ... 124 B6
Tawny Cl Ealing W13 ... 109 B5
Feltham TW13 ... 150 A1
Tawny Way SE16 ... 118 D2
Tayben Ave TW2 ... 152 C5
Taybridge Rd SW11 ... 137 A1
Tayburn Cl E14 ... 98 A1
Tayfield Cl UB10 ... 61 A5
Tay Ho 8 E3 ... 97 B5
Tayler Ct NW8 ... 229 C6
Taylor Ave TW9 ... 132 D3
Taylor Cl 3 BR6 ... 227 D4
Hampton TW12 ... 174 A5
Hounslow TW3 ... 130 A4
Tottenham N17 ... 34 A3
Taylor Ct E15 ... 76 A3
Ealing W13 ... 109 C5
Penge SE20 ... 184 C1
Taylor Ho 10 SW2 ... 160 C3
Taylor Rd
Mitcham CR4 ... 180 C3
Wallington SM6 ... 219 B3
Taylor's Bldgs SE18 ... 122 D2
Taylors Cl DA14 ... 167 D1
Taylors Ct TW13 ... 150 A2
Taylor's Gn W3 ... 89 C1
Taylor's La NW10 ... 67 C1
Barnet EN5 ... 1 B4
Forest Hill SE26 ... 184 B6
Taylorsmead NW7 ... 28 A5
Taymount Grange 2
SE23 ... 162 C2
Taymount Rise SE23 ... 162 C2
Tayport Cl N1 ... 72 A1
Tayside Ct 6 SE5 ... 139 B1
Tayside Dr HA8 ... 10 D2
Taywood Rd UB5 ... 85 B4
Teak Cl SE16 ... 119 A5
Tealby Ct N7 ... 72 B2
Teal Cl E16 ... 99 D2
Teal Ct NW10 ... 67 B2
30 SE8 ... 141 B6
Wallington SM6 ... 219 C3
Teale St E2 ... 96 A5
Tealing Dr KT19 ... 215 B4
Teal Pl SM1 ... 217 B3
Teasel Cl CR0 ... 206 D1
Teasel Way E15 ... 98 C4
Teather St 20 SE5 ... 139 C5
Tebbs Ho 14 SW2 ... 160 C4
Tebworth Rd N17 ... 33 D3
Teck Cl TW7 ... 131 A3
Tedder 5 NW9 ... 27 D3
Tedder Cl
Chessington KT9 ... 213 C3
Hillingdon UB10 ... 60 B1
Tedder Rd CR2 ... 222 D1
Teddington Memorial
Hospl TW11 ... 174 C4
Teddington Park Rd
TW11 ... 174 D6
Teddington Pk TW11 174 D5
Teddington Sch
TW11 ... 175 C4
Teddington Sta
TW11 ... 175 A4
Ted Hennem Ho RM10 81 D5
Ted Roberts Ho 24 E2 ... 96 B5
Tedworth Gdns SW3 ... 257 C1
Tedworth Sq
SW3 ... 114 D1 257 C1
Tees Ave UB6 ... 86 D5
Tees Ct W7 ... 86 B1
Teesdale Ave TW7 ... 131 A4
Teesdale Cl E2 ... 96 B5
Teesdale Gdns
Isleworth TW7 ... 131 A4
South Norwood SE25 ... 183 C1
Teesdale Rd E11 ... 54 D2
Teesdale St E2 ... 96 B5
Teesdale Yd 33 E2 ... 96 B5
Teeswater Ct DA18 ... 124 D3
Tee The W3 ... 89 C1
Teevan Cl CR0 ... 206 A2
Teevan Rd CR0 ... 206 A2
Teignmouth Cl
6 SW4 ... 137 D1
Edgware HA8 ... 26 B1
Teignmouth Gdns UB6 87 A4
Teignmouth Rd NW2 ... 68 D2
Bexley DA16 ... 146 C3
Telcote Way HA4 ... 40 C2
Telegraph Hill NW3 ... 69 D5
Telegraph La KT10 ... 212 D3
Telegraph Mews IG3 ... 58 A1
Telegraph Pl E14 ... 119 D2
Telegraph Rd SW15 ... 156 C4
Telegraph St EC2 ... 242 C2
Telemann Sq SE3 ... 143 B2
Telfer Cl 4 W3 ... 111 A4
Telfer Ho EC1 ... 234 D1
8 Dulwich SE21 ... 183 C6
Telferscot JMI Sch
SW12 ... 159 D3
Telferscot Prim Sch
SW12 ... 159 D3
Telferscot Rd SW12 ... 159 D3
Telford Ave SW12,
SW2 ... 160 A3
Telford Avenue Mans 7
SW2 ... 160 A3
Telford Cl E17 ... 53 A2
Penge SE19 ... 183 D4
Telford Dr KT12 ... 194 C2
Telford Ho SE1 ... 262 A6
8 W10 ... 91 A2
2 Belvedere DA17 ... 125 C3
Telford Parade Mans 8
SW2 ... 160 A3
Telford Rd 2 NW9 ... 46 A3
W10 ... 91 A2
Sidcup BR7,DA15 ... 167 B2
Southall UB1 ... 85 D1
Twickenham TW4 ... 151 C4
Telford Rd (North Circular
Rd) N11 ... 31 C5
Telford Terr SW1 ... 269 A6
Telford Way W3 ... 89 C2
Hayes UB4 ... 85 A2
Telham Rd E6 ... 100 C5
Tell Gr SE22 ... 139 D1
Tellson Ave SE18 ... 144 A4
Telscombe Cl BR6 ... 227 C6
Telscombe Ho SW11 ... 268 A1
Temair Ho 1 SE10 ... 142 A5
Temeraire St SE16 ... 118 C4
Temperley Rd SW12 ... 159 A4
Templar Ct RM7 ... 59 D5
Templar Dr SE28 ... 102 D1
Templar Ho 9 E5 ... 74 C6
NW2 ... 69 B2
Templar Pl TW12 ... 173 C3
Templars Ave NW11 ... 47 B3
Templars Cres N3 ... 29 C1
Templars Dr HA3 ... 24 B4
Templars Ho E15 ... 75 D3
Templar St SE5 ... 138 D3
Temple Ave
EC4 ... 116 C6 251 B6
N20 ... 14 B4
Croydon CR0 ... 223 B5
Dagenham RM8 ... 59 C1
Temple Cl E11 ... 54 C2
N3 ... 29 B1
SE18 ... 123 A3
Templecombe Rd E9 ... 96 C6
Templecombe Way
SM4 ... 201 A4
Templecroft TW15 ... 171 B4
Temple Ct SW8 ... 270 A3
Templedene BR2 ... 186 B1
Temple Dwellings 7
E2 ... 96 B5

Temple Fortune Ct 9
NW11 . . . . .47 B4
Temple Fortune Hill
NW11 . . . . .47 C4
Temple Fortune Ho 3
NW11 . . . . .47 B4
Temple Fortune La
NW11 . . . . .47 C3
Temple Fortune Par 5
NW11 . . . . .47 B4
Temple Gdns NW11 . . .47 B3
Dagenham RM8 . . . . . .80 D5
Edmonton N21 . . . . . . .16 D2
Temple Gr NW11 . . . . .47 C3
Enfield EN2 . . . . .4 D2
Temple Hall Ct 1 E4 . .20 B2
Temple Ho 11 E17 . . .53 D6
4 N7 . . . . .71 C5
13 SW11 . . . . .136 C2
Templehof Ave NW2 . .46 C2
Temple La EC4 94 C1 241 B1
Temple Lo EN5 . . . . . . .14 B4
Templeman Rd W7 . . . .86 D2
Templemead Cl W3 . . .89 C1
Temple Mead Cl HA7 . .25 A2
Templemead Ho E9 . . .75 A4
Temple Mills La E10,
E15 . . . . .76 A4
Temple Mills Rd E9 . . .75 C4
Templemore DA14 . . .190 B5
Temple Par EN5 . . . . . .14 B4
Temple Pk UB8 . . . . . .82 C4
Temple Pl
WC2 . . . . . .116 B6 250 D6
Temple Rd E6 . . . . . . .100 A6
N8 . . . . .50 B5
NW2 . . . . .68 C5
W4 . . . . .111 A3
W5 . . . . .109 D3
Croydon CR0 . . . . .221 B4
Isleworth TW3 . . . . . . .130 A1
Richmond TW9 . . . . . .132 B2
Temple Sheen SW14 .155 A6
Temple Sheen Rd
SW14 . . . . .133 A1
Temple St E2 . . . . .96 B5
Temple Sta
WC2 . . . . . .116 C6 251 A6
Temple Terr N22 . . . . .32 C1
Templeton Ave E4 . . . .35 D6
Templeton Cl 25 N16 . .73 C3
South Norwood SE19 .183 B2
Templeton Ct E10 . . . .53 D1
Templeton Pl
SW5 . . . . . . .113 C2 255 B3
Templeton Rd N4,N15 . .51 B3
Temple Way SM1 . . .218 B5
Temple West Mews
SE11 . . . . .261 C5
Templewood W13 . . . .87 B2
Templewood Ave
NW3 . . . . .69 D5
Templewood Gdns
NW3 . . . . .69 D5
Templewood Point
NW2 . . . . .69 B6
Tempsford Cl EN2 . . . . .5 A2
Tempsford Ct HA1 . . . .42 D3
Temsford Cl HA2 . . . . .24 A1
Tenbury Cl E7 . . . . .77 D3
Tenbury Ct SW12 . . . .159 D3
Tenby Ave HA3 . . . . . .25 B1
Tenby Cl N15 . . . . .51 D5
Dagenham RM6 . . . . . .59 A3
Tenby Ct E17 . . . . .53 A4
Tenby Gdns UB5 . . . . .63 C2
Tenby Ho N7 . . . . .72 C4
W2 . . . . .236 A1
Hayes UB3 . . . . .105 A3
Tenby Rd DA16 . . . . .146 D4
E17 . . . . .53 A4
Dagenham RM6 . . . . . .59 A3
Edgware HA8 . . . . .26 B1
Enfield EN3 . . . . .6 C1
Tench St E1 . . . . .118 B5
Tenda Rd SE16 . . . . . .118 B2
Tendring Ho SW2 . . . .160 C5
Tendring Way RM6 . . .58 C4
Tenham Ave SW2 . . . .159 D2
Tenison Ct W1 . . . . . .249 A6
Tenison Way SE1 . . . .251 A3
Tenniel Cl W2 . . . . . . .245 D6
Tennis St SE1 117 B4 252 C2
Tenniswood Rd EN1 . . .5 C4
Tennyson Ave E12 . . . .78 A1

Tennyson Ave *continued*
NW9 . . . . .45 A6
Twickenham TW1 . . . .152 D3
Wanstead E11 . . . . . . .55 A2
West Barnes KT3 . . . .200 B4
Tennyson Cl DA16 . . .145 D4
Enfield EN3 . . . . .18 D6
Feltham TW14 . . . . . . .150 A5
Tennyson Ct SW6 . . . .265 D1
3 Richmond TW10 . .175 D6
Tennyson Ho SE17 . . .262 B2
2 Erith DA17 . . . . . . .125 B1
Tennyson Rd E10 . . . . .75 D6
E15 . . . . .76 C1
E17 . . . . .53 B5
NW6 . . . . .91 B6
NW7 . . . . .28 A5
Ashford TW15 . . . . . . .170 A5
Ealing W7 . . . . .108 C6
Hounslow TW3 . . . . . .130 A3
Penge SE20 . . . . .184 D3
Wimbledon SW19 . . . .180 A4
Tennyson St SW8 . . . .137 B3
Tensing Ct TW19 . . . .148 A3
Tensing Ho N1 . . . . . . .72 D2
Tensing Rd UB2 . . . . .107 C3
Tentelow La UB2 . . . .107 C3
Tenterden Cl NW4 . . . .46 D6
SE9 . . . . .188 B6
Tenterden Dr NW4 . . . .46 D6
Tenterden Gdns NW4 .46 D6
Croydon CR0 . . . . .206 A2
Tenterden Gr NW4 . . . .46 D6
Tenterden Ho SE17 . . .263 B2
Tenterden Rd
Croydon CR0 . . . . .206 A2
Dagenham RM8 . . . . . .81 B6
Tottenham N17 . . . . . . .33 D3
Tenterden St W1 . . . .238 D1
Tenter Ground E1 . . . .243 C3
Tent Peg La BR5 . . . .211 A4
Tent St E1 . . . . .96 B3
Tenzing Ct 4 SE9 . . .166 A2
Terborah Way 6
SE22 . . . . .161 C6
Terence Ct 6 DA17 . .147 B6
Terence Messenger Twr
E10 . . . . .75 D6
Teresa Mews E17 . . . .53 C5
Teresa Wlk N10 . . . . . .49 B4
Terling Cl E11 . . . . . . .76 D5
Terling Ho W10 . . . . . .90 C2
Terling Rd RM8 . . . . . .81 C6
Terling Wlk N1 . . . . . .235 A6
Terminal Rdbt TW6 . .149 A5
Terminus Pl SW1 . . . .258 D5
Tern Ho 8 SE15 . . . . .139 D4
Terrace Ave NW10 . . . .90 C4
Terrace Gdns SW13 . .133 A3
Terrace La TW10 . . . .154 A5
Terrace Rd E13 . . . . . .99 B6
E9 . . . . .74 C1
Walton-on-T KT12 . . .194 B3
Terraces The 6
SW20 . . . . .178 D3
Terrace The EC4 . . . .241 B1
N2 . . . . .49 A5
NW6 . . . . .91 C6
9 SE8 . . . . .119 B2
SW13,SW14 . . . . .133 C3
Chingford E4 . . . . .20 C1
1 Woodford IG8 . . . . .37 A4
Terrace Wlk RM9 . . . . .81 A3
Terrapin Ct SW17 . . . .159 B1
Terrapin Rd SW17 . . .159 B1
Terrapins KT6 . . . . . .197 D2
Terrick Rd N22 . . . . . .32 A2
Terrick St W12 . . . . . .90 B1
Terrilands HA5 . . . . . .41 B6
Territorial Ho SE11 . .261 B3
Terront Rd N15 . . . . . .51 A5
Terry Ho SW2 . . . . . . .160 C5
Tersha St TW9 . . . . . .132 B1
Tessa Sanderson Pl 6
SW8 . . . . .137 A2
Tessa Sanderson Way
UB6 . . . . .64 B3
Testerton Wlk 3
W11 . . . . .112 D3
Testwood Rd TW7 . . .108 C6
Tetcott Rd
SW10 . . . . . .136 A5 266 A3
Tetherdown N10 . . . . .49 A6
Tetherdown Prim Sch
N10 . . . . .49 A6
Tetty Way BR1,BR2 . . .187 A1
Teversham La
SW8 . . . . . . .138 A4 270 B2
Teviot Cl DA16 . . . . . .146 B4
Teviot St E14 . . . . .98 A2

Tewkesbury Ave
Forest Hill SE23 . . . . .162 B4
Pinner HA5 . . . . .41 A4
Tewkesbury Cl N15 . . .51 B3
Tewkesbury Gdns
NW9 . . . . .44 D6
Tewkesbury Rd N15 . . .51 B3
Carshalton SM5 . . . . .202 B1
Ealing W13 . . . . .109 A6
Tewkesbury Terr N11 . .31 D4
Tewson Rd SE18 . . . .123 C1
Teyham Ct N11 . . . . . .158 D5
Teynham Ave EN1 . . . .17 B5
Teynham Gn BR2 . . . .209 A4
Teynham Ho SE9 . . . .167 B5
Teynton Terr N17 . . . . .33 A2
Thackeray Ave N17 . . .34 A1
Thackeray Cl
Harrow HA2 . . . . .41 C1
Hayes UB8 . . . . .82 D1
Isleworth TW7 . . . . . .131 A3
Wimbledon SW19 . . . .178 D3
Thackeray Ct SW3 . . .257 C2
W14 . . . . .254 A5
Ealing W5 . . . . .88 B1
Thackeray Dr RM6 . . . .58 B2
Thackeray Ho WC1 . . .240 A6
Thackeray Manor
SM1 . . . . .218 A3
Thackeray Mews E8 . .74 A2
Thackeray Rd E6 . . . . .99 D5
SW8 . . . . .137 B3
Thackeray St W8 . . . .255 D6
Thackery Lo TW14 . . .149 B5
Thackran Cl N2 . . . . . .30 A1
Thakeham Cl SE26 . . .184 B5
Thalia Cl SE10 . . . . . .142 B6
Thame Rd SE16 . . . . . .118 D4
Thames Ave
SW10 . . . . . .136 A4 266 B4
Dagenham RM9,RM13 .103 D3
Wembley UB6 . . . . . . .86 D5
Thames Bank SW14 . .133 A3
Thamesbank Pl SE28 .102 C1
Thames Barrier Visitor
Ctr* SE18 . . . . .121 D3
Thames Circ E14 . . . .119 C2
Thames Cl TW12 . . . .173 D1
Thames Cres W4 . . . .133 C5
Thames Ct 10 SE15 . .139 D5
West Molesey KT8 . . .173 D1
Thames Ditton Cty Fst Sch
KT7 . . . . .196 D3
Thames Ditton Island
KT7 . . . . .197 A4
Thames Ditton Jun Sch
KT7 . . . . .196 D2
Thames Ditton Sta
KT7 . . . . .196 D2
Thames Dr HA4 . . . . . .39 A3
Thames Eyot 7 TW1 .153 A3
Thamesfield Ct
TW17 . . . . .193 A2
Thamesgate Cl TW10 .175 B6
Thames Gateway Pk
RM9 . . . . .103 B4
Thames Haven KT6 . .197 D4
Thames Hts SE1 . . . . .253 C2
Thameside TW11 . . . .175 D3
Thameside Ctr TW8 . .132 B6
Thameside Ind Est
E16 . . . . .121 D4
Thames Link Ho 7
TW9 . . . . .132 A1
Thames Mead KT12 . .194 A2
Thames Meadow
East Molesey KT8 . . . .195 C6
Lower Halliford KT12,
TW17 . . . . .193 C1
Thamesmead Sec Sch
TW17 . . . . .193 B3
Thamesmead Sh Ctr
SE28 . . . . .124 A6
Thamesmere Dr
SE28 . . . . .124 A6
Thames Pl SW15 . . . .134 D2
Thamespoint TW11 . .175 D3
Thames Quay E14 . . .119 D4
SW10 . . . . .266 B1
Thames Rd E16 . . . . . .121 D5
Barking IG11 . . . . .102 A4
Chiswick W4 . . . . .132 D6
Thames Reach W6 . . .134 C6
Thames Road Ind Est
E16 . . . . .121 D4
Thames Side
Teddington KT1 . . . . . .175 D2
Thames Ditton KT7 . . .197 B3
Thames St SE10 . . . . .141 D6
Hampton TW12 . . . . . .173 D1

Thames St *continued*
Kingston KT1,KT2 . . . .175 D1
Sunbury TW16 . . . . . .194 B6
Walton-on-T KT12 . . .193 D2
Thamesvale Cl TW3 . .129 C3
Thames Valley Univ
W5 . . . . .109 D3
Thames View Ho
TW12 . . . . .194 A3
Thames View Inf Sch
IG11 . . . . .102 A5
Thames View Jun Sch
IG11 . . . . .101 D5
Thames View Lodge
IG11 . . . . .101 C4
Thames Village W4 . .133 A4
Thames Wlk
SW11 . . . . . .136 C5 267 A4
Thane Mans N7 . . . . . .72 B5
Thanescroft Gdns
CR0 . . . . .221 C5
Thanet Ct 14 W3 . . . . .88 C1
Thanet Dr BR2 . . . . . .225 D5
Thanet Ho WC1 . . . . . .233 A1
1 West Norwood
SE27 . . . . .160 D1
Thanet Lo NW2 . . . . . .69 A2
Thanet Pl CR0 . . . . . . .221 B4
Thanet Rd DA5 . . . . . .169 C4
Thanet St WC1 94 A4 233 A1
Thane Villas N7 . . . . . .72 B5
Thane Works N7 . . . . .72 B5
Thanington Ct DA15 . .167 C5
Thant Cl E10 . . . . .75 D5
Tharp Rd SM6 . . . . . . .219 D3
Thatcham Ct N20 . . . . .14 A4
Thatcham Gdns N20 . .14 A4
Thatcher Cl UB7 . . . . .104 A4
Thatchers Way TW7 . .152 B6
Thatches Gr RM6 . . . . .59 A5
Thavie's Inn EC4 . . . .241 B2
Thaxted Ct N1 . . . . . . .235 D3
Thaxted Ho SE16 . . . .118 C2
Dagenham RM10 . . . . .81 D1
Thaxted Lo 3 E18 . . . .55 B6
Thaxted Pl 9 SW20 . .178 D3
Thaxted Rd SE9 . . . . .167 A2
Buckhurst Hill IG9 . . . .21 D4
Thaxton Rd
W14 . . . . . . .135 B6 264 D6
Thayers Farm Rd
BR3 . . . . .185 A2
Thayer St W1 . .93 A2 238 B2
Theatre Mus* WC2 . .250 B6
Theatre Sq E15 . . . . . .76 B2
Theatre St SW11 . . . .136 C2
Theberton St
N1 . . . . .94 D6 234 C6
Theed St SE1 116 C5 251 B3
Thelbridge Ho 28 E3 . .97 D4
Thelma Gdns SE3 . . . .144 A4
Thelma Gr TW11 . . . .175 A4
Theobald Cres HA3 . . .24 A2
Theobald Rd E17 . . . . .53 C2
Croydon CR0 . . . . .220 D6
Theobalds Av N12 . . . .30 A4
Theobalds Ct N4 . . . . .73 A6
Theobalds Park Rd EN2 4 D6
Theobald's Rd
WC1 . . . . . . .94 B2 240 C4
Theobald St SE1 . . . . .262 C5
Theodora Way HA5 . . .39 D6
Theodore Ho 1
SW15 . . . . .156 A6
Theodore Rd SE13 . . .164 B5
Therapia La
Thornton Heath CR0 . .204 A3
Thornton Heath CR0 . .204 A3
Wallington CR0 . . . . . .203 D2
Therapia Lane Sta
CR0 . . . . .204 A2
Therapia Rd SE22 . . .162 C5
Theresa Rd W6 . . . . . .112 A2
Therfield Ct N4 . . . . . .73 A6
Thermopylae Gate
E14 . . . . .119 D2
Theseus Ho 2 E14 . . .98 B1
Theseus Wlk N1 . . . . .234 D3
Thesiger Rd SE20 . . . .184 D3
Thessaly Ho SW8 . . . .269 A3
Thessaly Rd
SW8 . . . . . . .137 C4 269 B2
Thesus Ho 2 E14 . . . .98 B1
Thetford Cl N13 . . . . . .32 C4
Thetford Ct
3 Dulwich SE21 . . . .162 B2
New Malden KT3 . . . .199 B4
Thetford Gdns RM9 . .103 A4
Thetford Ho SE1 . . . . .263 C6

Thetford Rd
Ashford TW15 . . . . . . .148 A1
Dagenham RM9 . . . . . .80 D1
New Malden KT3 . . . .199 C4
Thetis Terr TW9 . . . . .132 C6
Theydon Gr IG8 . . . . . .37 C4
Theydon Rd E5 . . . . . . .74 C6
Theydon St E17 . . . . . .53 B6
Thicket Cres SM1 . . . .218 A4
Thicket Gr
Dagenham RM9 . . . . . .80 C2
Penge SE20 . . . . .184 A3
Thicket Rd
Penge SE20 . . . . .184 B3
Sutton SM1 . . . . .218 A4
Thicket The UB7 . . . . .82 A1
Third Ave E12 . . . . .78 B3
3 E13 . . . . .99 A4
E17 . . . . .53 C4
W10 . . . . .91 A4
W3 . . . . .111 D5
Dagenham RM10 . . . . .103 D5
Dagenham RM6 . . . . . .58 C3
Enfield EN1 . . . . .17 D1
Hayes UB3 . . . . .105 D3
Wembley HA9 . . . . . . .65 D1
Third Cl SW16 . . . . . . .196 A5
Third Cross Rd TW2 . .152 B2
Third Way HA9 . . . . . . .66 D4
Thirleby Rd HA8 . . . . . .27 D2
SW1 . . . . . . .115 C3 259 B5
Thirlestone Ct N10 . . .31 A1
Thirlmere NW1 . . . . . .231 D2
Thirlmere Ave UB6 . . .87 C4
Thirlmere Gdns HA9 . .43 D1
Thirlmere Ho 20 N16 . .73 B4
Isleworth TW1 . . . . . .152 D6
Thirlmere Rd N10 . . . . .31 A1
Streatham SW16 . . . .181 D5
Thirlmere Rise BR1 . .186 D4
Thirsk Cl UB5 . . . . .63 C2
Thirsk Rd SW11 . . . . .137 A1
Mitcham CR4 . . . . . . .181 A3
South Norwood SE25 .205 B5
Thisilefield Cl DA5 . . .168 B3
Thistlebrook SE2 . . . .124 C4
Thistlecroft Gdns HA7 25 D1
Thistle Cl N17 . . . . .52 B5
Thistledene KT7 . . . . .196 A5
Thistledene Ave HA2 . .63 A5
Thistledown Ct SE25 .205 C6
Thistle Gr SW7 . . . . . .256 B1
Thistle Ho 6 E14 . . . . .98 A1
Thistlemead BR7 . . . .188 D1
Thistlewaite Rd E5 . . .74 B5
Thistlewood Cl 3 N7 .72 B6
Thistleworth Cl TW7 . .130 B5
Thistley Cl N12 . . . . . . .30 C4
Thistly Ct SE8 . . . . . . .141 D6
Thomas a' Beckett Cl
HA0 . . . . .64 D4
Thomas Arnold Prim Sch
RM9 . . . . .81 B1
Thomas Baines Rd
SW11 . . . . .136 B2
Thomas Burt Ho 9 E2 96 B4
Thomas Buxton Jun & Inf
Sch E1 . . . . .96 A3
Thomas Cribb Mews
E6 . . . . .100 B1
Thomas Ct E17 . . . . . . .53 D4
Dagenham RM8 . . . . . .80 C1
Ealing W7 . . . . .86 C1
Thomas Dean Rd
SE26 . . . . .185 B6
Thomas Dinwiddy Rd
SE12 . . . . .165 B2
Thomas Doyle St
SE1 . . . . .261 D6
Thomas Fairchild Comm
Sch N1 . . . . . .95 A5 235 B4
Thomas Gamuel Prim Sch
E17 . . . . .53 C3
Thomas Hardy Ho N22 32 B2
Thomas Hewlett Ho
HA1 . . . . .64 C4
Thomas Ho 3 E9 . . . . .74 C2
4 SW4 . . . . .138 A1
Thomas Hollywood Ho 3
E2 . . . . .96 C5
Thomas Jones Prim Sch
W11 . . . . .91 A1
Thomas's La SE6 . . . . .163 C4
Thomas More Ho
EC2 . . . . .242 A3
Thomas More Sq E1 .118 A6
Thomas More St E1 . .118 A5
Thomas More Way N2 48 A6
Thomas North Terr 3
E16 . . . . .98 D2

Thomas Pl W8 . . . . . .255 C5
Thomas Pooley Ct
KT6 . . . . .198 A2
Thomas Rd E14 . . . . . .97 C2
Thomas Road Ind Est
E14 . . . . .97 C1
Thomas's London Day Schs
SW11 . . . . . .136 B4 266 D2
Thomas's Prep Sch
Clapham SW11 . . . . .158 D6
Thomas St SE18 . . . . .122 D2
Thomas Tallis Sch
SE3 . . . . .143 B2
Thomas Wall Cl SM1 .217 D3
Thomas Watson Cottage
Homes The EN5 . . . . .13 A6
Thompson Ave TW9 . .132 C2
Thompson Cl
Ilford IG1 . . . . .79 A6
Morden SM3 . . . . .201 C1
Thompson Ho SE14 . .140 D6
11 W10 . . . . .91 A3
Thompson Rd SE22 . . .161 C5
Dagenham RM9 . . . . . .81 B5
Hounslow TW3 . . . . . .129 D1
Uxbridge UB10 . . . . . .60 A1
Thompson's Ave 6
SE5 . . . . .139 A5
Thomson Cres CR0 . . .204 C1
Thomson Ho SE17 . . .263 A3
SW1 . . . . .259 D1
Southall UB1 . . . . . . .107 A6
Thomson Rd HA3 . . . . .42 C6
Thorburn Ho SW1 . . . .248 A1
Thorburn Sq SE1 . . . .118 A2
Thorburn Way SW19 . .180 B2
Thoresby Ho N16 . . . . .73 B5
Thoresby St
N1 . . . . .95 A4 235 B2
Thorkhill Gdns KT7 . . .197 B1
Thorkhill Rd KT7 . . . . .197 B1
Thornaby Gdns N18 . . .34 B5
Thornaby Ho 15 E2 . . .96 B4
Thorn Ave WD23 . . . . . .8 A3
Thornbill Ho 1 SE15 140 A4
Thornbury 3 NW4 . . . .46 C5
Thornbury Ave TW7 . .130 B5
Thornbury Cl N16 . . . .73 C3
Thornbury Ct W11 . . . .245 A6
Croydon CR2 . . . . .221 B3
Hounslow TW7 . . . . . .130 C5
Thornbury Ho N6 . . . . .49 C1
Thornbury Rd SW2 . . .160 A5
Isleworth TW7 . . . . . .130 B4
Thornbury Sq N6 . . . . .49 C1
Thornby Rd E5 . . . . . . .74 C5
Thorn Cl BR2 . . . . .210 C3
Northolt UB5 . . . . .85 B4
Thorncliffe Ct SW2 . . .160 A5
Thorncliffe Rd SW2 . .160 A5
Southall UB2 . . . . . . .107 C1
Thorncombe Rd
SE22 . . . . .161 C6
Thorncroft Rd SM1 . .217 D4
Thorncroft St
SW8 . . . . . . .138 A5 270 A3
Thorndale Ho N16 . . . .51 C1
Thorndean St SE18 . .158 A2
Thorndene Ave N11 . . .15 A3
Thorndike Ave UB5 . . .84 C4
Thorndike Cl
SW10 . . . . . .136 A5 266 A4
Thorndike Ho SW1 . . .259 C2
Thorndike St
SW1 . . . . . . .115 D2 259 C3
Thorndon Cl BR5 . . . .189 D1
Thorndon Gdns KT19 215 C4
Thorndon Rd BR5 . . . .189 D1
Thorndyke Ct HA5 . . . .23 B3
Thorne Cl DA8 . . . . . . .147 D6
E11 . . . . .76 C4
E16 . . . . .99 A1
Littleton TW15 . . . . . .171 A3
Thorne Ho 4 E14 . . . .120 A3
34 E2 . . . . .96 C4
Thorneloe Gdns CR0,
CR9 . . . . .220 D3
Thorne Pas 7 SW13 133 D3
Thorne Rd
SW8 . . . . . . .138 A5 270 B3
Thorne's Cl BR3 . . . . .208 A6
Thorness Ct SW18 . . .158 A5
Thorne St SW13,
SW14 . . . . .133 C2
Thornet Wood Rd
BR1 . . . . .210 C6
Thornewill Ho 7 E1 . .118 C6
Thorney Cres
SW11 . . . . . .136 B5 266 D3
Thorneycroft Cl KT12 194 C3

Thorneycroft Dr EN3 ..7 C6
Thorneycroft Ho **11**
 W4 ....111 C1
Thorney Ct W8 ....246 A1
Thorney Hedge Rd
 W4 ....110 D2
Thorney St
 SW1 ......116 A2 260 A4
Thornfield Ave NW7 ..29 A2
Thornfield Ct NW7 ...29 A2
Thornfield Ho **4** E14 119 C6
Thornfield Par NW7 ..29 A3
Thornford Rd SE13 .164 A6
Thorngate Rd W9 ...91 C3
Thorngrove Rd E13 ..99 B6
Thornham Gr E15 ...76 B3
Thorn Ham Ho SE1 ..262 D6
Thornham St SE10 .141 D6
Thornhaugh St WC1 .239 D5
Thornhill Ave SE18 .145 C5
 Surbiton KT6 ......214 A6
Thornhill Bridge Wharf
 N1 ....233 C5
Thornhill Cres N1 ...72 B1
Thornhill Ct N8 ....49 D3
Thornhill Gdns E10 ..75 D6
 Barking IG11 ......79 C1
Thornhill Gr N1 ....72 C1
Thornhill Ho N1 ....72 C1
 12 W4 ....111 C1
Thornhill Prim Sch
 N1 ....72 C1
Thornhill Rd E10 ...75 D6
 N1 .....72 C1 234 A6
 Ickenham UB10 ....60 C4
 Surbiton KT6 ......214 B6
 Thornton Heath CR0 .205 A3
Thornhill Sq N1 ....72 B1
Thornhill Way TW17 .192 C4
Thornicroft Ho **12**
 SW9 ....138 C3
Thornlaw Rd SE27 .182 D6
Thornley Cl N17 ....34 A3
Thornley Dr HA2 ...63 D6
Thornley Pl **2** SE10 .120 C1
Thornsbeach Rd SE6 164 A2
Thornsett Pl SE20 ..184 B1
Thornsett Rd
 Penge SE20 ......184 B1
 Wandsworth SW18 .157 D3
Thornsett Terr SE20 .184 B1
Thornton Ave W4 ..111 C2
 Streatham SW2 ....159 D3
 Thornton Heath CR0 .204 B3
 West Drayton UB7 .104 B3
Thornton Cl UB7 ...104 B3
Thornton Ct N7 ....72 A3
 West Barnes SW20 .200 D4
Thornton Dene BR3 .185 C1
Thornton Gdns SW12 159 D3
Thornton Gr HA5 ...23 C4
Thornton Heath Pond
 CR7 ....204 C4
Thornton Heath Sta
 CR7 ....205 A5
Thornton Hill SW19 .179 A3
Thornton Ho SE17 ..263 A3
 7 Wanstead E11 ...55 A3
Thornton Lo CR7 ...205 A6
Thornton Pl W1 ....237 D4
Thornton Rd BR1 ...187 A5
 E11 ....76 B6
 N18 ....18 C1
 Barnet EN5 ....1 A2
 Belvedere DA17 ...125 D2
 Carshalton SM5 ...202 B1
 Ilford IG1 ....78 D4
 Mortlake SW14 ....133 B2
 Streatham SW12,SW2 159 D3
 Thornton Heath CR0,
 CR7 ....204 B3
 Wimbledon SW19 ..178 D3
Thornton Rd E SW19 178 D4
Thornton Row CR7 .204 C4
Thornton St SW9 ...138 C3
Thornton Way NW11 .47 D4
Thorntree Ct W5 ...88 A2
Thorntree Rd SE7 ..121 D1
Thorntree Sch SE7 .121 B1
Thornville Gr CR4 ..180 B1
Thornville St SE8 ..141 C4
Thornwell Ct W7 ...108 C4
Thornwood Cl E18 ..37 B1
Thornwood Rd SE13 .164 C6
Thornycroft Ct TW9 .132 B3
Thorogood Gdns E15 .76 C3
Thorold Ho SE1 ....252 A2
 6 Streatham SW2 ..160 A4
Thorold Rd Ilford IG1 ..57 A1

Thorold Rd continued
 Wood Green N22 .....32 A3
Thorparch Rd
 SW8 ....137 D5 269 D3
Thorpebank Rd W12 .112 A5
Thorpe Cl BR6 .....227 C6
 W10 ....91 A1
 Forest Hill SE26 ...184 D6
Thorpe Coombe Hospl
 E17 ....54 A6
Thorpe Cres E17 ...35 B1
Thorpe Ct EN2 .....4 D2
Thorpedale Gdns IG6 .56 D5
Thorpedale Rd N4 ..50 B1
Thorpe Hall W5 ....87 D2
Thorpe Hall Rd E17 .36 A2
Thorpe Ho N1 .....233 D5
Thorpe Rd E6 .....100 B6
 E7 ....76 D4
 N15 ....51 C3
 Barking IG11 ......79 B1
 Chingford E17 ....36 A1
 Kingston KT2 .....176 A3
Thorpewood Ave
 SE23,SE26 ....162 B2
Thorpland Ave UB10 .61 A5
Thorsden Way **2**
 SE19 ....183 C5
Thorverton Rd NW2 .69 A5
Thoydon Rd E3 ....97 A5
Thrale Almshouses
 SW16 ....182 A5
Thrale Rd SW16 ...181 C5
Thrale St SE1 .....252 B3
Thrasher Cl **20** E8 ..95 D6
Thrawl St E1 ..95 D2 243 D3
Thrayle Ho **2** SW9 .138 B2
Threadgold Ho **8** N1 .73 B2
Threadneedle St
 EC2,EC3 ....95 B1 242 D1
Three Bridges Bsns Ctr
 UB2 ....108 A4
Three Bridges Prim Sch
 UB2 ....107 D3
Three Colts La E2 ...96 B3
Three Colt St E14 ..119 B6
Three Corners DA7 .147 D3
Three Cups Yd WC1 .240 D3
Three Kings Yd W1 .248 C6
Three Meadows Mews
 HA7 ....24 D2
Three Mill La E3 ....98 A4
Three Nun Ct EC2 ..242 B2
Three Oak La SE1 ..253 C2
Three Oaks Cl UB10 .60 B5
Threshers Pl W11 ..244 A6
Thriffwood SE23,SE26 162 D1
Thrigby Rd KT9 ....213 A3
Thring Ho **2** SW9 .138 B3
Throckmorten Rd E16 99 B1
Throgmorton Ave
 EC2 ......95 B1 242 D2
Throgmorton St
 EC2 ......95 B1 242 D2
Throwley Cl SE2 ...124 C3
Throwley Rd SM1 ..217 D3
Throwley Way SM1 .217 D3
Thrupp Cl CR4 ....181 B1
Thrush Gn HA2 ....41 C5
Thrush St SE17 ....262 A2
Thunderer Rd RM9 .103 B3
Thunder Rd RM9 ...103 B3
Thurbarn Rd SE6 ..185 D5
Thurland Ho **3** SE16 118 B2
Thurland Rd SE16 ..118 A4
Thurlby Cl HA1 ....43 A3
Thurlby Croft NW4 ..46 C6
Thurlby Rd
 Wembley HA0 .....65 D2
 West Norwood SE27 .182 C6
Thurleigh Ave SW12 .159 A5
Thurleigh Ct SW12 .159 A5
Thurleigh Rd SW12 .159 A5
Thurleston Ave SM4 .201 A4
Thurlestone Ave N12 .30 D4
 Ilford IG3 ....79 D4
Thurlestone Ct **1**
 UB1 ....85 D1
Thurlestone Par
 TW17 ....193 A3
Thurlestone Rd SE27 182 C6
Thurloe Cl SW7 ...257 A4
Thurloe Ct SW3 ...257 A3
Thurloe Pl
 SW7 ......114 B2 256 D4
Thurloe Place Mews
 SW7 ....256 D4
Thurloe Sq
 SW7 ......114 C2 257 A4

Thurloe St
 SW7 ......114 B2 256 D4
Thurlow Cl E4 .....35 C4
Thurlow Ct **6** E11 ..55 A4
Thurlow Gdns HA0 ..65 D3
Thurlow Hill SE21 ..161 A2
Thurlow Ho **17** SW16 160 A1
Thurlow Park Rd
 SE21,SE24 ....161 A2
Thurlow Rd NW3 ...70 B3
 W7 ....109 A4
Thurlow St
 SE17 .....117 C1 263 A1
Thurlow Terr NW5 ..71 A3
Thurlow Twrs SE27 .160 C1
Thurlston Rd HA4 ...62 A5
Thurnby Ct TW2 ...152 C1
Thurnscoe NW1 ...232 A5
Thursland Rd DA14 .191 A5
Thursley Cres CR0 .224 B1
Thursley Gdns SW19 .156 D2
Thursley Ho
 3 Kingston KT2 ...176 D3
 10 Streatham SW2 ...160 A4
Thursley Rd SE9 ...166 B1
Thurso Ho NW6 ...91 D5
Thurso St SW17 ...180 B6
Thurstan Rd SW20 .178 B3
Thurston Ho **4** BR3 .185 D6
Thurston Ind Est
 SE13 ....141 D2
Thurston Rd
 SE8,SE13 ....141 D2
 Southall UB1 .....85 A4
Thurtle Rd E2 .....95 D5
Thurza Ct TW7 ....130 A3
Thyer Ct BR6 .....227 A4
Thyra Gr N12 .....29 A4
Tibbatt's Rd E3 ....97 D3
Tibbenham Pl SE6 .163 C2
Tibbenham Wlk E13 .98 D5
Tibbets Cl SW19 ..156 D3
Tibbet's Corner
 SW19 ....156 D4
Tibbet's Ride SW19 .156 D4
Tiber Gdns N1 ....233 B5
Ticehurst Cl BR5 ..190 A3
Ticehurst Rd SE23 .163 A3
Tickford Cl SE2 ...124 C4
Tickford Ho NW8 ..230 A1
Tidal Basin Rd E16 .120 D6
Tidbury Ct SW8 ...269 A3
Tidemill Prim Sch
 SE8 ....141 C5
Tidenham Gdns CR0 .221 C5
Tideside Ct SE18 ..122 A3
Tideswell **10** NW5 ...71 B4
Tideswell Rd
 Croydon CR0 .....223 C6
 Putney SW15 .....134 C1
Tideway Cl TW10 ..175 D2
Tideway Ct **9** SE16 .118 D5
Tideway Ho E14 ...119 C4
Tideway Ind Est
 SW8 ....137 C6 269 B5
Tideway Wharf SW13 133 C3
Tideway Yd SW13 ..133 C3
Tidey St E3 ....97 C2
Tidford Rd DA16 ...145 D3
Tidworth Ho **13** SE22 139 C2
Tidworth Rd E3 ....97 C3
Tiepigs La BR2,BR4 .208 D1
Tierney Ct **4** CR0 .221 D6
Tierney Rd SW2 ...160 A3
Tierney Terr SW2 ..160 A3
Tiffin Girls' Sch KT2 .176 A4
Tiffin Sch KT2 ....176 B1
Tiger Ho WC1 .....232 D1
Tiger La BR2 ......209 B5
Tiger Way E5 .....74 B4
Tigris Cl N9 ......18 C2
Tilbrook Rd SE3,SE9 .143 C2
Tilbury Cl BR5 ....190 B1
 13 SE15 ....139 D5
Tilbury Ho **4** SE14 .140 D6
Tilbury Rd E10 ....54 C2
 E6 ....100 B5
Tildesley Rd SW15 .156 C5
Tile Farm Rd BR6 ..227 B5
Tile Kiln La N6 ....49 C1
 Edmonton N13 ....33 A5
 Harefield UB9 .....38 D2
Tileyard Rd N7 ....72 C1

Tilford Ave CR0 ...224 A1
Tilford Gdns SW19 .156 D3
Tilford Ho **8** SW2 .160 B4
Tilia Rd E5 ....74 B4
Tilia Wlk **21** SW9 .138 D1
Tilleard Ho **4** W10 ..91 A4
Tiller Ho **30** N1 ...95 C6
Tiller Rd E14 .....119 C3
Tillet Sq SE16 ....119 A4
Tillett Cl NW10 ...67 A2
Tillett Way **4** E2 ..96 A4
Tilley Rd TW14 ...150 A3
Tillingbourne Gdns
 N3 ....47 B6
Tillingbourne Way N3 47 B5
Tillingham Way N12 .29 C6
Tilling Ho **1** SE15 .140 B2
Tilling Rd NW2 ...46 C2
Tilling Way HA9 ...65 D6
Tillman Ho **8** SW2 .160 B3
Tillman St E1 .....96 B1
Tillotson Ct SW8 ..269 D3
Tillotson Rd
 Edmonton N9 .....17 D2
 Harrow HA3 ......23 A3
 Ilford IG1 ....56 C2
Tilney Ct EC1 .....242 B6
 Kingston KT6 .....197 D4
 Woodford IG9 ....21 A2
Tilney Dr IG9 .....21 A2
Tilney Gdns **12** N1 ..73 B2
Tilney Rd Chigwell IG9 .21 B2
 Dagenham RM9 ...81 B2
 Southall UB2 .....106 A2
Tilney St W1 ......248 B4
Tilson Cl **2** SE15 .139 C5
Tilson Gdns SW2,
 SW4 ....160 A4
Tilson Ho SW2 ....160 A4
Tilson Rd N17 .....34 A2
Tilston Cl **11** E11 ..76 D5
Tilton St SW6 .....264 B5
Tiltwood The W3 ..111 A6
Tilt Yard App SE9 .166 B5
Timber Cl BR7 ....188 C1
Timbercroft KT19 ..215 C4
Timbercroft La SE18 .145 C4
Timbercroft Prim Sch
 SE18 ....145 C5
Timberdene NW4 ..28 D1
Timberland Cl **15**
 SE15 ....140 A5
Timberland Rd E1 ..96 B1
Timber Mill Way
 SW4 ....137 D2
Timber Pond Rd
 SE16 ....118 D4
Timber St EC1 ....242 A6
Timberwharf Rd N16 .52 A3
Time Sq E8 ......73 D3
Times Sq SM1 ....217 D3
Timothy Cl **1** SW4 .159 C6
 Bexley DA6 ......169 A6
Timothy Ho DA18 ..125 A4
Timothy Rd E3 ....97 B2
Timsbury Wlk **5**
 SW15 ....156 A3
Tina Ct SW16 ....160 C1
Tindal St SW9 ....138 D4
Tinniswood Cl N5 ..72 C3
Tinsley Rd E1 ....96 C2
Tintagel Cres SE22 .139 D1
Tintagel Ct EC1 ...241 C6
Tintagel Dr HA7 ...25 D6
Tintagel Gdns **2** SE22 .139 D1
Tintagel Ho SE20 .184 A3
Tintern Ave NW9 ..44 D6
Tintern Cl
 Putney SW15 .....157 A6
 Wimbledon SW19 .180 A4
Tintern Ct W13 ...109 A4
Tintern Gdns N14 ..16 A4
Tintern Ho NW1 ...231 D3
 SW1 ....258 C3
Tintern Path NW9 ..45 C3
Tintern Rd
 Carshalton SM5 ...202 B1
 Tottenham N22 ...33 A2
Tintern St SW4 ...138 A1
Tintern Way HA2 ..41 D1
Tinto Rd E16 .....99 A3
Tinwell Mews WD6 .11 B6
Tinworth St
 SE11 ......116 A1 260 B2
Tippett Ct E6 .....100 B5
Tippetts Cl EN2 ...5 A4
Tipthorpe Rd SW11 .137 A2
Tipton Dr CR0 ....221 D6
Tiptree **7** NW1 ...71 B1
Tiptree Cl E4 .....20 A1
Tiptree Cres IG5 ...56 C6

Tiptree Ct EN2 .....5 B1
Tiptree Dr EN2 .....5 B1
Tiptree Rd HA4 ....62 B4
Tirlemont Rd CR2 ..221 A1
Tirrell Rd CR0 ....205 A3
Tisbury Ct W1 ....249 C6
Tisbury Rd SW16 ..182 A1
Tisdall Pl
 SE17 ......117 B2 262 D3
Tissington Ct **4**
 SE16 ....118 D2
Titan Bsns Est **3**
 SE8 ....141 C5
Titan Ct TW8 .....110 B2
Titchborne Row W2 .237 B1
Titchfield Rd
 NW8 ....92 D6 230 C4
 Carshalton SM5 ...202 B2
 Enfield EN3 ......7 A6
Titchfield Wlk SM5 .202 B2
Titchwell Rd SW18 .158 B3
Tite St SW3 ..136 D6 267 C6
Tithe Barn Cl KT2 ..176 B2
Tithe Barn Way UB5 .84 B5
Tithe Cl NW7 .....28 A2
 Hayes UB4 ....83 D2
 Walton-on-T KT12 .194 B3
Tithe Ct NW7 .....28 A2
Tithe Farm Ave HA2 .63 C5
Tithe Farm Cl HA2 .63 C5
Tithe Wlk NW7 ...28 A2
Titian Ave WD23 ..8 C4
Titley Cl E4 ......35 C5
Titmus Cl UB8 ....83 A1
Titmuss Ave SE28 .124 B6
Titmuss St W12 ...112 C4
Tivendale HA1 ....50 A6
Tiverton Ave IG5 ...56 C6
Tiverton Dr SE9 ...167 A3
Tiverton Prim Sch
 N15 ....51 B3
Tiverton Rd N4,N15 .51 B3
 NW6,NW10 ......90 D6
 Edgware HA8 .....26 B1
 Edmonton N18 ....33 C5
 Hounslow TW3 ...130 A3
 Ruislip HA4 ......62 A5
 Wembley HA0 ....88 A5
Tiverton St
 SE1 ....117 A3 262 A6
Tiverton Way KT9 ..213 D3
Tivoli Ct SE16 ....119 B5
Tivoli Gdns **11** SE7 .122 A2
Tivoli Rd N8 .....49 D4
 Hounslow TW4 ...129 A1
 West Norwood SE27 .183 A5
Toad La TW4 .....129 B1
Tobago St E14 ....119 C4
Tobin Cl NW3 ....70 C1
Toby Ct N9 ......18 C4
Toby La E1 ......97 A3
Toby Way KT5,KT6 .214 D6
Todber Ho W14 ...254 B5
Todd Ho **3** N2 ...30 B1
Todds Wlk N7 ....72 C6
Tokenhouse Yd EC2 .242 C2
Tokyngton Ave HA9 .66 C2
Toland Sq SW15 ..156 A6
Tolcairn Ct **2** DA17 .125 C1
Tolcarne Dr HA5 ..40 B6
Tolchurch **2** W11 ..91 C1
Toley Ave HA3,HA9 .44 A2
Tollbridge Cl W10 ..91 A3
Tollesbury Gdns IG6 .57 B6
Tollet St E1 ......96 C3
Tollgate Dr
 Dulwich SE21 .....161 C2
 Hayes UB4 ....106 A6
Tollgate Ho **1** NW6 .91 D5
Tollgate Prim Sch E13 99 C3
 Croydon CR0 .....206 C3
Tollgate Rd E6 ....100 A2
Tollhouse Way N19 .71 C6
Tollington Ct N4 ...72 B5
Tollington Pk N4 ..72 B5
Tollington Pl N4 ...72 B5
Tollington Rd N7 ..72 B4
Tollington Way N7 .72 A5
Tolmers Sq
 NW1 ......93 C3 239 B6
Tolpaide Ho SE11 ..261 A3
Tolpuddle Ave **2** E13 .99 C6
Tolpuddle St N1 ...233 A1
Tolsford Rd E5 ...74 B2
Tolson Ho **2** TW7 .131 A2
Tolson Rd TW7 ...131 A2
Tolverne Rd SW20 .178 C2
Tolworth Cl KT6 ...198 D1
Tolworth Gdns RM6 .58 D4
Tolworth Girls' Sch
 KT6 ....214 B6

Tho – Tor   395

Tolworth Hospl KT6 .214 C6
Tolworth Inf Sch KT6 198 B1
Tolworth Junc KT6 .214 D6
Tolworth Jun Sch
 KT6 ....198 B1
Tolworth Par RM6 ..59 A4
Tolworth Park Rd
 KT6 ....214 B6
Tolworth Rd KT6 ..214 A6
Tolworth Rise N KT5 .198 D1
Tolworth Rise S KT5 .198 D1
Tolworth Sta KT5 ..214 D6
Tolworth Underpass
 KT5,KT6 ....214 D6
Tomahawk Gdns **4**
 UB5 ....84 D4
Tom Coombs Cl SE9 .144 A1
Tom Cribb Rd SE18,
 SE28 ....123 B3
Tom Groves Cl E15 .76 B3
Tom Hood Cl E15 ..76 B3
Tom Hood Sch E11 .76 D5
Tom Jenkinson Rd **5**
 E16 ....121 A5
Tomkyns Ho SE11 ..261 A3
Tomline Ho SE1 ...252 A3
Tomlin's Gr E3 ...97 C4
Tomlinson Cl E2 ...95 D4
 5 W4 ....110 D1
Tomlins Orch IG11 .101 A6
Tomlin's Terr E14 ..97 A1
Tomlins Wlk **4** N7 ..72 B6
Tom Mann Cl IG11 .101 C6
Tom Nolan Cl E15 ..98 C5
Tompion Ho EC1 ..241 D6
Tompion St EC1 ...234 D1
Tomson Ho SE1 ...263 C6
Tom Smith Cl SE10 .142 C6
Tom Smith Ho **8** E17 .54 A4
Tom Williams Ho
 SW6 ....264 C5
Tonbridge Cres HA3 .44 A3
Tonbridge Ho WC1 .233 A1
Tonbridge Rd KT12,
 KT8 ....195 B5
Tonbridge St
 WC1 ......94 A4 233 A1
Toneborough **14** NW8 .91 D6
Tonfield Rd SM3 ..201 B1
Tonge Cl BR3 .....207 C4
Tonsley Hill SW18 .157 D6
Tonsley Pl SW18 ..157 D6
Tonsley Rd SW18 ..157 D6
Tonsley St SW18 ..157 D6
Tonstall Rd CR4 ...181 A1
Tooke Cl HA5 .....23 A2
Tookey Cl HA3 ...44 B2
Took's Ct EC4 ....241 A2
Tooley St SE1 117 C5 253 A3
Toorack Rd HA3 ...24 B1
Tooting Bec SW17 .159 A1
Tooting Bec Gdns
 SW16 ....181 C6
Tooting Bec Rd
 Streatham SW16 ..181 C5
 Upper Tooting, Furzedown
 SW17 ....181 B6
Tooting Bec Sta
 SW17 ....159 A1
Tooting Broadway
 SW17 ....180 D5
Tooting Broadway Sta
 SW17 ....180 C5
Tooting Gr SW17 ..180 C5
Tooting High St
 SW17,SW19 .....180 C5
Tooting Sta SW17 .180 D4
Tootswood Rd BR2,
 BR3 ....208 C5
Topaz Ho NW2 ...199 B1
Topaz Wlk NW2 ...46 C2
Topcliffe Dr BR6 ..227 C4
Topham Ho **8** SE10 .142 A5
Topham Sq N17 ...33 A2
Topham St EC1 ...241 A6
Top House Rise E4 .20 A4
Topiary Sq TW9 ..132 B2
Topley St SE9 ....143 D1
Topmast Point E14 .119 C4
Top Pk BR3 ......208 C4
Topsfield Cl N8 ...49 D4
Topsfield Par N8 ..50 A3
Topsfield Rd N8 ..50 A4
Topsham Rd SW17 .181 A6
Torbay Ct **13** NW1 .71 B1
Torbay Mans NW6 ..91 B6
Torbay Rd NW6 ...69 B1

Torbay Rd continued
Harrow HA2 ....63 A6
Torbay St **15** NW1 ...71 B1
Torbitt Way IG2 .....57 D4
Torbridge Cl HA8 ....26 A3
Torbrook Cl DA5 ....169 A5
Torcross Dr SE23 ....162 C2
Torcross Rd HA4 .....62 C5
Tor Ct **8** 245 B2
Torfell **5** E18 ....36 D1
Tor Gdns W8 .113 C4 245 A2
Tor Ho N6 ....49 B3
Tormead Cl SM1 .....217 C2
Tormount Rd SE18 ...145 C6
Tornay Ho E9 ....74 C1
N1 ....233 C4
Toronto Ave E12 .....78 B4
Toronto Rd IG1 ......57 A1
Torquay Gdns IG4 ....55 D5
Torquay St W2 ....91 D2
Tor Rd HA6 ....146 C4
Torrens Ct SE5 ......139 B2
Torrens Rd E15 ......76 D2
SW2 ....160 B6
Torrens Sq E15 ......76 D2
Torrens St EC1 94 D5 234 C3
Torres Sq E14 ....119 C1
Torre Wlk SM5 ....202 C1
Torriano Ave NW5 ....71 D3
Torriano Cotts NW5 ..71 C3
Torriano Jun & Inf Schs
NW5 ....71 D3
Torridge Gdns SE15 .140 C1
Torridge Rd CR7 ....204 D4
Torridon Ho NW6 ....91 D5
Torridon Inf Sch SE6 164 B2
Torridon Jun Sch
SE6 ....164 B2
Torridon Rd SE13,SE6 164 B3
Torrington Ave N12 ..30 B5
Torrington Cl N12 ...30 B6
Claygate KT10 ......212 C2
Torrington Ct N12 ...30 B6
Forest Hill SE26 ...184 A5
Harrow HA2 ....63 D5
Torrington Dr HA2 ...63 D5
Torrington Gdns N11 .31 C4
Wembley UB6 ....65 C1
Torrington Gr N12 ...30 C5
Torrington Pk N12 ...30 B6
Torrington Pl E1 ....118 A5
WC1 ....93 D2 239 C4
Torrington Rd
Claygate KT10 ......212 C2
Dagenham RM8 ......59 B1
Ruislip HA4 ....62 A5
Wanstead E18 ....55 A6
Wembley UB6 ....87 C6
Torrington Sq
WC1 ....93 D3 239 D5
Thornton Heath CR0 .205 B2
Torr Rd SE20 ....184 D3
Tortington Ho **1**
SE15 ....140 B5
Torver Rd HA1 ......42 C5
Torver Way BR6 .....227 B5
Torwood Rd SW15 ...156 A6
Totham Lo SW20 ....178 B2
Tothill Ho SW1 .....259 D4
Tothill St
SW1 ....115 D4 249 D1
Totland Ho SW18 ...157 D5
Totnes Rd DA16 ....146 C5
Totnes Villas N11 ..31 C5
Totnes Wlk N2 .....48 B5
Tottan Terr E1 .....96 D1
Tottenhall **5** NW1 ..71 A1
Tottenhall Inf Sch
N13 ....32 C4
Tottenhall Rd N13 ..32 D4
Tottenham Court Rd
W1 ....93 C2 239 B4
Tottenham Court Road Sta
W1 ....93 D1 239 D2
Tottenham Gn E **2**
N15 ....51 D5
Tottenham Gn E South
Side **3** N15 ....51 D5
Tottenham Hale N15 .52 A5
Tottenham Hale Ret Pk
N15 ....52 A5
Tottenham Hale Sta
N17 ....52 B6
Tottenham La N8 ...50 B4
Tottenham Mews
W1 ....239 B4

Tottenham Rd N1 ....73 C2
Tottenham St
W1 ....93 C2 239 B4
Totterdown St SW17 .180 D5
Totteridge Comm N20 12 C3
Totteridge Ho SW11 .136 B3
Totteridge La N20 ...13 D3
Totteridge Rd EN3 ...6 D6
Totteridge Village
N20 ....13 B3
Totteridge & Whetstone
Sta N20 ....14 A2
Totternhoe Cl HA3 ..43 C4
Totton Rd CR7 ......204 C6
Touchard Ho N1 .....235 D1
Toulmin St
SE1 ....117 A4 252 A1
Toulon St SE5 ......139 A5
Toulouse Ct **2** SE16 .118 B1
Tournay Rd
SW6 ....135 B5 264 D4
Toussaint Wlk **18**
SE16 ....118 A3
Tovil Cl SE20 ......184 B1
Tovy Ho **6** SE1 .....118 A1
Towcester Rd E3 ....98 A3
Tower 42* EC2 ......243 A2
Tower Bldgs **22** E1 ..118 B5
Tower Br App E1,EC3 253 C5
Tower Bridge*
E1,EC3,SE1 ..117 D5 253 C4
Tower Bridge Bsns
Complex SE16 ......118 B3
Tower Bridge Bsns Sq
SE16 ....118 B2
Tower Bridge Piazza
SE1 ....253 C3
Tower Bridge Prim Sch
SE1 ....117 D4 253 C2
Tower Bridge Rd
SE1 ....117 C1 253 C3
Tower Bridge Sq SE1 253 C3
Tower Cl NW3 ....70 B3
Orpington BR6 ......227 D5
Penge SE20 ....184 B3
Tower Ct E5 ....51 D2
NW8 ....230 B4
WC2 ....240 A1
Tower Gardens Rd
N17 ....33 B2
Towergate SE1 ......263 A4
Towergate Cl UB8 ...60 A3
Tower Gateway Sta
EC3 ....117 D6 253 C6
Tower Gdns KT10 ...213 A1
Tower Gr KT13 .....193 C1
Tower Hamlets Coll
E1 ....96 C2
E1 ....96 D1
E14 ....119 D6
E14 ....97 D1
Tower Hamlets Rd
E17 ....53 C6
E7 ....76 D3
Tower Hill
EC3 ....117 D6 253 C5
Tower Hill Sta
EC3 ....117 D6 253 C6
Tower Hill Terr EC3 .253 B5
Tower La HA9 ......65 D5
Tower Mans SE1 ....263 C5
Tower Mews E17 ....53 C5
E5 ....75 A3
Tower Millennium Pier
EC3 ....117 D5 253 B4
Tower Mill Rd **1**
SE15 ....139 C5
Tower Pl DA7 ......147 D1
NW10 ....68 A3
Orpington BR6 ......227 D5
Twickenham TW1,TW2 152 D1
Tower Rise TW9 ....132 A2
Tower Royal EC4 ...252 C6
Towers Ave UB10 ...83 A4
Towers Ct UB10 ....83 A4
Towers Pl TW10 ....154 A6
Towers Rd Pinner HA5 23 A2
Southall UB1 ....85 C3
Tower St WC2 ......240 A1
Towers The NW5 ....71 B5
1 Richmond TW9 ...132 B1
Tower Terr SE4 ....141 A1
Wood Green N22 ....32 B1
Tower The*
EC3 ....117 D6 253 C6
Tower View CR0 ...207 A2
Tower Wharf SE1 ...253 C2
Tower Wlk SE1 .....263 A4
Towfield Ct TW13 ..151 B2
Towfield Rd TW13 ..151 B2

Towncourt Cres BR5 .211 B5
Towncourt La BR5 ...211 B2
Towncourt Path N4 ..51 A1
Townend Ct **6** BR1 ..186 D2
Townfield Rd UB3 ...105 A5
Townfield Sq UB3 ...105 A5
Town Field Way TW7 131 A3
Town Hall Approach Rd
N15 ....51 D5
Townhall Ave **3** W4 .111 B1
Town Hall Rd SW11 .136 D2
Townholm Cres W7 ..108 D3
Town La TW19 ......148 A2
Townley Gram Sch for
Girls DA5 ....169 B6
Townley Rd DA6 ....169 B6
SE22 ....161 C6
Townley St
SE17 ....117 B1 262 C2
Townmead Bsns Ctr
SW6 ....136 A2
Town Meadow TW8 .131 D5
Townmead Rd SW6 .136 A3
Richmond TW9 .....132 D3
Town Quay IG11 ....100 D6
Town Quay Wharf
IG11 ....100 D6
Town Rd N9 ....18 B2
Townsend Ave N14 ..31 D6
Townsend Ho **12** SE1 118 A2
Townsend Ind Est
NW10 ....89 A5
Townsend La NW9 ...45 B3
Townsend Prim Sch
SE17 ....117 C2 263 A4
Townsend Rd N15 ...51 D4
Ashford TW15 ......170 A5
Southall UB1 ....107 A5
Townsend St
SE1,SE17 ....117 C2 263 A4
Townsend Way HA6 .22 A3
Townsend Yd N6 ....49 B1
Townshend Cl DA14 .190 C4
Townshend Ct NW8 .230 B4
Townshend Est
NW8 ....92 C5 230 A4
Townshend Ho **19**
SE18 ....122 B2
Townshend Rd
NW8 ....92 C6 230 A5
Chislehurst BR7 ...188 D5
Richmond TW9 .....132 B1
Townshend Terr
TW9 ....132 B1
Towns Ho **4** SW4 ...137 D2
Townson Ave UB5 ..84 B5
Townson Way UB5 ..84 A5
Town The EN2 ......5 B2
Town Tree Rd TW15 .170 C5
Towpath TW17 .....192 B1
Towpath Way CR0 ..205 D4
Towton Rd SE27 ...161 A2
Toxteth Ho N4 .....51 A2
Toynbec Cl BR7 ....188 D6
Toynbee Rd SW19,
SW20 ....179 A2
Toynbee St E1 95 D2 243 C2
Toyne Way N6 .....48 D3
Tracey Ave NW2 ...68 C3
Tracy Ct HA7 ......25 C3
Tracy Ho **12** E3 .....97 B4
Trade Cl N13 ......32 C6
Trader Rd E6 ......100 D1
Tradescant Ho **15** E9 74 C1
Tradescant Rd
SW8 ....138 A5 270 B3
Trade Twr **8** SW11 .136 A2
Trade Winds Ct **1**
E1 ....118 A5
Trading Estate Rd
NW10 ....89 A3
Traemore Ct SW16 .160 C1
Trafalgar Ave SE15 .139 D6
North Cheam KT4,SM3,
SM4 ....200 D1
Tottenham N17 ....33 C4
Trafalgar Bsns Ctr
IG11 ....101 D3
Trafalgar Cl **1** SE16 119 A2
Trafalgar Ct
Barking E6 ....100 C6
Hounslow TW3 .....129 B2
West Barnes KT3 ...200 B6
Trafalgar Gdns E1 ...96 D2
W8 ....255 D6
Trafalgar Gr SE10 ..142 B6
Trafalgar Ho SE17 ..262 B2

Trafalgar Ho continued
Barking IG11 ....102 B4
Trafalgar Inf Sch
TW2 ....152 B2
Trafalgar Jun Sch
TW2 ....152 B2
Trafalgar Mews E9 ..75 B2
Trafalgar Pl
Edmonton N18 .....34 A5
Wanstead E11 ......55 A5
Trafalgar Rd SE10 ..120 C1
Merton SW19 ......180 A3
Twickenham TW2 ...152 B2
Trafalgar Sq*
SW1 ....115 D5 249 D4
Trafalgar St
SE17 ....117 B1 262 D2
Trafalgar Terr HA1 ..42 C1
Trafalgar Trad Est EN3 7 A1
Trafalgar Way E14 ..120 A5
Croydon CR0 ....220 C6
Trafford Cl E15 .....75 D3
Trafford Ho N1 .....235 D4
Trafford Rd CR7 ...204 B4
Tragail SW15 ......157 A6
Traherne Lo **3**
TW11 ....174 D5
Traitors Gate*
EC3 ....117 D5 253 C4
Tralee Ct **31** SE16 ..118 B1
Tramsheds The CR0,
CR4 ....203 D2
Tramway Ave E15 ..76 B1
N9 ....18 C4
Tramway Path CR4 .202 C5
Trance Way W3 ....110 C3
Tranmere Ct **5** SM2 218 A1
Tranmere Ho **7** N7 .72 C3
Tranmere Rd
Edmonton N9 ......17 C4
Twickenham TW2 ...151 D4
Wandsworth SW17,
SW18 ....158 A2
Tranquil Pass SE3 .142 D3
Tranquil Vale SE3 .142 C3
Transept St NW1 ...237 B3
Transmere Cl BR5 ..211 A3
Transmere Rd BR5 .211 A3
Transom Cl SE16 ..119 A2
Transom Sq E14 ...119 D1
Transport Ave TW8 .131 B6
Tranton Rd SE16 ...118 B3
Trappes Ho **2** SE16 .118 B2
Traps La KT2,KT3 ..177 C2
Travel Clinic, Hospl for
Tropical Diseases
WC1 ....93 C3 239 B5
Travellers Way TW5 128 C3
Travers Cl E17 .....34 D2
Travers Ho **6** SE10 .142 B6
Travers Rd N7 .....72 C5
Travis Ho SE10 ....142 A4
Treacy Cl WD23 ...8 A2
Treadgold Ho **7**
W11 ....112 D6
Treadgold St W11 ..112 D6
Treadway St E2 ....96 B5
Treasury Buildings
SW1 ....250 A2
Treaty Ctr TW3 ....129 C7
Treaty St N1 ..94 B6 233 C5
Trebeck St W1 .....248 C3
Treborough Ho W1 .238 A4
Trebovir Rd
SW5 ....113 C2 255 B3
Treby St E3 ....97 B3
Trecastle Way **3** N7 .71 D4
Tredegar Rd E3 ....97 B5
N11 ....31 D3
Tredegar Sq E3 ....97 B4
Tredegar Terr E3 ...97 B4
Trederwen Rd E8 ...96 A6
Tredown Rd SE26 ..184 A6
Tredwell Cl BR2 ...210 A5
Tredwell Rd SE27 ..182 C5
Tree Cl TW10 ......153 D3
Treen Ave SW13 ...133 C2
Tree Rd E16 ....99 C1
Trees The N16 .....51 B2
Tree Tops **1** IG8 ...37 A6
Treetops Cl SE2 ...125 A1
Treetops Ct CR7 ...205 A4
Treetops View IG10 .21 D4
Treewall Gdns BR1 .187 B6
Trefgarne Rd RM10 .81 C6
Trefil Wlk N7 ......72 A4
Trefoil Ho DA18 ...125 A4
Trefoil Rd SW18 ...158 A6
Trefusis Ct TW5 ...128 A3

Tregaron Ave N8 ....50 A3
Tregaron Gdns KT3 .199 C5
Tregarvon Rd SW11 137 A1
Tregenna Ave HA2 ..63 C4
Tregenna Cl **1** N14 ..15 C6
Tregenna Ct HA2 ...63 C4
Tregony Rd BR6 ...227 D4
Trego Rd E9 ....75 C1
Tregothnan Rd SW9 138 A2
Tregunter Rd
SW10 ....114 A1 256 A1
Treherne Ct SW9 ..138 D4
Upper Tooting SW17 181 A6
Trehern Rd **12** SW14 133 D2
Trehurst St E5 .....75 A3
Trelawney Est E9 ..74 C2
Trelawney Ho SE1 .252 A2
Trelawn Rd E10 ...76 A3
SW2 ....160 C6
Trelawny Cl E17 ...53 D5
Trellis Ho SW19 ...180 A3
Trellis Sq **1** E3 ....97 B4
Treloar Gdns SE19 183 B6
Tremadoc Rd SW4 137 D1
Tremaine Cl SE4 ...141 C4
Tremaine Rd SE20 .184 B1
Trematon Ho SE11 .261 B2
Trematon Pl TW11 .175 C3
Tremlett Gr N19 ...71 C5
Tremlett Mews N19 .71 C5
Trenance Gdns IG3 .80 A5
Trenchard Ave HA4 .62 B4
Trenchard Cl NW9 .27 C2
Stanmore HA7 .....25 B4
Trenchard Ct SM4 .201 C3
Trenchard St SE10 .120 B1
Trenchold St
SW8 ....138 A6 270 A5
Trend Ct W13 .....109 B5
Trendell Ho **4** E14 .97 C1
Trenholme Cl SE20 184 B3
Trenholme Rd SE20 184 B3
Trenholme Terr SE20 184 B3
Trenmar Gdns NW10 90 B4
Trenmar Lo NW10 ..90 B4
Trent Ave W5 .....109 C3
Trent CE Prim Sch EN4 2 D1
Trent Ct E11 ....55 A4
Trent Ctry Pk EN4 ..3 A3
Trent Gdns N14 ....15 C3
Trentham Lo **8** EN1 17 C6
Trentham St SW18 .157 C3
Trent Ho SE15 .....140 C1
4 Kingston KT2 ...175 D2
Trent Rd SW2 .....160 B6
Buckhurst Hill IG9 ..21 B3
Trent Way Hayes UB4 83 C4
North Cheam KT4 ..216 C5
Trentwood Side EN2 4 B2
Treport St SW18 ...157 D4
Tresco Cl BR1 .....186 C4
Trescoe Gdns HA2 ..41 A4
Tresco Gdns IG3 ...80 A6
Tresco Ho SE11 ...261 A2
Tresco Rd SE15 ...140 B1
Tresham Cres
NW8 ....92 C3 237 A6
Tresham Rd IG11 ..79 D1
Tresham Wlk E9 ...74 C3
Tresidder Ho **10** SW4 159 D4
Tresilian Ave N21 ..16 B6
Tressel Cl **20** N1 ...72 D1
Tressell Cl UB4 ....84 D2
Tressillian Cres SE4 141 C2
Tressillian Rd SE4 .141 C1
Trestis Cl UB4 .....84 D2
Treswell Rd RM9 ...103 B1
Tretawn Gdns NW7 11 C1
Tretawn Pk NW7 ...27 C6
Trevallyn Lo **1** KT2 176 D2
Trevanion Rd W14 .254 B2
Treve Ave HA1 .....42 B2
Trevelyan Ho SW17 180 D4
Trevelyan Ave E12 .78 B4
Trevelyan Cres HA3 43 D2
Trevelyan Ct KT3 ..199 D2
Trevelyan Gdns NW10 90 C6
Trevelyan Ho **16** E2 .96 C4
SE5 ....138 D5
6 Twickenham TW1 153 C5
Trevelyan Rd E15 ..76 D4
Trevenna Ho **13** SE23 162 D1
Treveris St SE1 ....251 D3
Treversh Ct **7** BR1 .186 D2
Treverton St W10 ..90 D3
Treverton Twr W10 .90 D2
Treves Cl N21 .....16 A6
Treves Ho E1 ......96 A3
Treville St SW15 ...156 B4
Treviso Rd SE23 ...163 A2
Trevithick Cl TW14 149 D3

Trevithick Ho **3** NW5 71 B4
13 SE16 ....118 B2
SW8 ....269 C2
Trevithick St SE8 ..141 C6
Trevone Gdns HA5 ..41 A3
Trevor Cl Harrow HA3 24 C1
Hayes BR2 ....209 A2
Isleworth TW7 .....152 B6
New Barnet EN4 ...14 B5
Northolt UB5 ....84 A6
Trevor Cres HA4 ...61 D4
Trevor Gdns HA8 ...27 B2
Northolt UB5 ....84 A6
Trevor Pl
SW7 ....114 C4 247 B1
Trevor Rd HA8 .....27 B2
Hayes UB3 ....105 C4
Wimbledon SW19 .179 A3
Woodford IG8 .....37 A3
Trevor Roberts Tutorial
Coll NW8 ....70 B1
Trevor Sq
SW7 ....114 C4 247 B1
Trevor St
SW7 ....114 C4 247 B1
Trevose Ho SE11 ..260 D2
Trevose Rd E17 ....36 B1
Trewenna Dr KT9 ..213 D3
Trewince Rd SW20 .178 C2
Trewint St SW18 ...158 A2
Trewsbury Ho **2**
SE2 ....124 D4
Trewsbury Rd SE26 184 D5
Triandra Way UB4 ..84 C2
Triangle Ct E16 ....99 C3
Triangle Ctr UB1 ..108 C2
Triangle Est The
SE11 ....261 A1
Triangle Ho SE1 ...253 C2
Triangle Pl SW4 ...137 D1
Triangle Rd **7** E8 ..96 B6
Triangle The E8 ...96 B6
EC1 ....241 D6
N19 ....49 D2
Barking IG11 ....79 A2
Kingston KT3 ......177 A1
Tribune Ct **16** NW9 .46 B2
Trident Gdns **6** UB5 84 D4
Trident Ho **9** E14 ..98 A1
Trident St SE16 ....118 D2
Trident Way UB2 ..106 B3
Trieste Ct SW12 ...158 D2
Trigon Rd
SW8 ....138 B5 270 D4
Trilby Rd SE23 ....162 D2
Trillo Ct IG1 ....57 D2
Trimdon NW1 ......232 B5
Trimmer Ct TW7 ...130 D2
Trimmer Wlk **11** TW8 132 A2
Trim St SE8 ....141 B6
Trinder Gdns N19 ..50 A1
Trinder Rd N4,N19 ..50 A1
Barnet EN5 ....12 C6
Tring Ave Ealing W5 110 A3
Southall UB1 ......85 B1
Wembley HA9 ......66 C2
Tring Cl IG2 ....57 B4
Tring Ct TW1 ......175 D1
Trinidad Ho **17** E14 119 C6
Trinidad St E14 ...119 B6
Trinity Ave N2 ....48 B6
Enfield EN1 ....17 D5
Trinity Church Rd
SW13 ....134 B6
Trinity Church Sq
SE1 ....117 A3 262 B6
Trinity Cl E11 .....76 C4
SE13 ....142 B1
3 SW4 ....137 C1
Hounslow TW4 ....129 A1
Keston Mark BR2 ..210 A1
Trinity Cotts TW9 ..132 B2
Trinity Cres SW17 .159 A2
Trinity Ct **2** N1 ...95 C6
SE16 ....119 A4
SE9 ....166 D5
WC1 ....240 C6
8 Chingford E4 ...20 A2
Edmonton N18 ....33 D4
Forest Hill SE23 ..162 C1
Southgate N21 ....16 D3
Thornton Heath SE25 205 C3
Twickenham TW2 ..152 C2
Trinity Gdns E16 ..98 C2
SW2,SW9 ....138 B3
11 Wanstead E18 ..55 B4
Trinity Gn E1 .....96 C4
Trinity Gr **8** SE10 .142 A4
Trinity Ho **5** E17 ..53 D6
SE1 ....262 B6

Trinity Homes 14
SW2 . . . . .138 B1
Trinity Mews SE9 . . .167 B5
Penge SE20 . . . . . . .184 B2
Wandsworth SW18 . . .157 C3
Trinity Par TW3 . . . . .129 C2
Trinity Pl DA6 . . . . . . .147 B1
EC3 . . . . .253 C5
Trinity RC High Sch
(Lower) IG8 . . . . . . .37 A6
Trinity RC High Sch (Upper
Sch) IG8 . . . . .36 D6
Trinity RC High Sch
(Upper) IG8 . . . . . . .37 A6
Trinity Rd N2 . . . . . . .48 B6
Ilford IG6 . . . . .57 A6
Richmond TW9 . . . . .132 B2
Southall UB1 . . . . . .107 A5
Wandsworth SW17,
SW18 . . . . .158 C4
Wimbledon SW19 . . .179 C4
Wood Green N22 . . . .32 A3
Wood Green N22 . . . .32 B2
Trinity Rise SE24,
SW2 . . . . .160 D4
Trinity Sch
Croydon CR0 . . . . . .222 C6
Dagenham RM10 . . . .81 C4
Trinity Sq
EC3 . . . . . . .117 C6 253 B6
Trinity St 9 E16 . . . . .99 A2
SE1 . . . . . .117 B3 262 C6
Enfield EN2 . . . . .5 A3
Trinity St Mary's CE Prim
Sch SW12 . . . . . . .159 A3
Trinity Terr IG9 . . . . . .21 B4
Trinity Way E4 . . . . . .35 B4
W3 . . . . .111 D6
Trio Pl SE1 . . . .117 A4 252 B1
Triscott Ho UB3 . . . . .106 A5
Tristan Ct 41 SE8 . . . .141 B6
Tristan Sq SE3 . . . . . .142 C2
Tristram Cl E17 . . . . . .54 B6
Tristram Rd BR1 . . . .186 D6
Triton Ct EC2 . . . . . .242 D5
Triton Ho 2 E14 . . . .119 D2
Triton Sq NW1 . . . . .239 A6
Tritton Ave CR0 . . . . .220 A4
Tritton Ho N21 . . . . . .17 B5
Tritton Rd SE21,SE27 .161 B1
Triumph Cl UB7 . . . . .127 A4
Triumph Ho IG11 . . . .102 A4
Triumph Rd E6 . . . . . .100 B1
Triumph Trad Est N17 . .34 A4
Trocette Mans SE1 . .263 B6
Trojan Ct NW6 . . . . . .69 A1
9 Ealing W7 . . . . . .109 A5
Trojan Ind Est NW10 . .67 D2
Trojan Way CR0 . . . . .220 B5
Troon Ct 34 SE16 . . . .118 B1
Erith SE28 . . . . .102 D1
Troon Ho 11 E14 . . . . .97 A1
Troon St E1 . . . . .97 A1
Tropical Ct 2 W10 . . . .90 D4
Trosley Rd DA17 . . . .147 C6
Trossachs Rd SE22 . .161 C6
Trothy Rd SE1 . . . . . .118 A2
Trotman Ho SE14 . . . .140 C4
Trott Rd N10 . . . . .31 A3
Trott St
SW11 . . . . .136 C4 267 A1
Trotwood Ho 3 SE16 118 B4
Troubridge Ct 12 W4 .111 A1
Troughton Rd SE7 . . .121 B1
Trouville Rd SW4 . . . .159 C5
Trowbridge Rd E9 . . . .75 B2
Trower Ho 5 E9 . . . . .75 A2
Trowlock Ave TW11 . .175 C4
Trowlock Island
TW11 . . . . .175 D4
Trowlock Way TW11 . .175 D4
Troy Ct 5 SE18 . . . . .122 D2
W8 . . . . .255 A6
Troyes Ho NW3 . . . . . .70 D3
Troy Rd SE19 . . . . . .183 B4
Troy Town SE15 . . . .140 A2
Troy Town Flats
SE15 . . . . .140 A2
Trubshaw Rd UB2 . . .107 A4
Truesdale Rd E6 . . . .100 B1
Trulock Ct N17 . . . . . .34 A3
Trulock Rd N17 . . . . . .34 A3
Truman Cl 2 HA8 . . . .27 C4
Truman's Rd 24 N16 . .73 C3
Trumpers Way W7 . . .108 D3
Trumpeters Inn TW9 .153 C6
Trumpington Rd E7 . . . .76 D3
Trump St EC2 . . . . . .242 B1

Trundlers Way WD23 . . .8 C3
Trundle St SE1 . . . . . .252 A2
Trundleys Rd SE8 . . . .118 D1
Trundley's Rd SE8 . . . .118 D1
Trundley's Terr SE8 . . .118 D2
Truro Gdns IG1 . . . . . .56 A2
Truro Ho 25 W2 . . . . . .91 C2
Wood Green N22 . . . .32 B3
Truro Rd E17 . . . . .53 B5
Wood Green N22 . . . .32 A3
Truro St NW5 . . . . . . .71 A2
Truro Way UB4 . . . . . .83 C4
Truslove Rd SE27 . . . .182 D5
Trussley Rd W6 . . . . .112 C3
Tryfan Cl IG4 . . . . .55 D4
Tryon Cres E9 . . . . . . .96 C6
Tryon St SW3 . . .114 D1 257 C2
Trystings Cl KT10 . . . .213 A2
Tuam Rd SE18 . . . . . .145 B6
Tubbenden Cl BR6 . . .227 C5
Tubbenden Dr BR6 . . .227 B4
Tubbenden Jun & Inf Schs
BR6 . . . . .227 B4
Tubbenden La BR6 . . .227 C5
Tubbenden La S BR6 227 B3
Tubbs Rd NW10 . . . . .89 D5
Tudor Ave
Hampton TW12 . . . .173 C3
North Cheam KT4 . . .216 B4
Tudor Cl BR7 . . . . . . .188 B2
N6 . . . . .49 C2
NW3 . . . . .70 C2
NW7 . . . . .28 A4
NW9 . . . . .67 A6
SW2 . . . . .160 B5
Ashford TW15 . . . . . .170 A6
Cheam SM3 . . . . . . .217 A2
Chessington KT9 . . . .214 A3
Hampton TW12 . . . . .174 A5
Pinner HA5 . . . . .40 A4
Wallington SM6 . . . . .219 C1
Woodford IG8 . . . . . . .37 B5
Tudor Cres EN2 . . . . . .5 A4
Tudor Ct E17 . . . . . . .53 B2
N1 . . . . .73 C2
5 SE16 . . . . .118 D5
W5 . . . . .110 C4
Feltham TW13 . . . . . .172 C6
Sidcup DA14 . . . . . .168 A1
4 Stanwell TW19 . . .148 A5
Teddington TW11 . . . .174 D4
3 Ealing W13 . . . . . .87 C1
Tudor Ct N HA9 . . . . . .66 C3
Tudor Ct S HA9 . . . . . .66 C3
Tudor Dr Kingston KT2 176 A5
Walton-on-T KT12 . . .194 D1
West Barnes SM4 . . .201 A3
Tudor Ent Pk HA3 . . . .42 B6
Tudor Est NW10 . . . . .88 D5
Tudor Gables NW7 . . .27 D6
Tudor Gdns NW9 . . . . .67 A6
Acton W3 . . . . .88 C1
Harrow HA3 . . . . .24 B1
Mortlake SW14 . . . . .133 C2
Twickenham TW1 . . . .152 D3
West Wickham BR4 . .224 A5
Tudor Gr E9 . . . . .74 C1
Tudor Ho 34 E9 . . . . . .74 C1
W14 . . . . .112 D2
Tolworth KT6 . . . . . . .198 C1
Tudor Mews 2 NW10 .68 A2
Tudor Par SE9 . . . . . .144 A1
Dagenham RM6 . . . . .58 D2
Tudor Pl SW19 . . . . . .180 C3
Tudor Prim Sch N3 . . .30 A2
Southall UB1 . . . . . .107 A6
West Barnes SM4 . . .200 D2
Tudor Rd E6 . . . . .99 C6
E9 . . . . .96 B6
N9 . . . . .18 C4
Ashford TW15 . . . . . .171 B4
Barking IG11 . . . . . .101 C6
Barnet EN5 . . . . .1 D2
Beckenham BR3 . . . .208 A6
Chingford E4 . . . . . . .35 D4
Croydon CR25 . . . . .206 B4
Hampton TW12 . . . . .173 C3
Harrow HA3 . . . . .24 B1
Hayes UB3 . . . . .83 B1
Isleworth TW3 . . . . . .130 B1
Kingston KT2 . . . . . .176 C3
Penge SE19 . . . . . .183 D3
Pinner HA5 . . . . .22 C1
Southall UB1 . . . . . .107 A6
Tudor Sq UB3 . . . . . . .83 B2
Tudor St EC4 . .116 C6 251 B6
Tudors The 2 BR3 . . .185 D1
Tudor Way BR5 . . . . .211 B3
N14 . . . . .15 D3
W3 . . . . .110 C4

Tudor Way continued
Hillingdon UB10 . . . . .60 C2
Tudor Well Cl HA7 . . . .25 B5
Tudor Wlk DA5 . . . . . .169 A5
Tudway Rd SE3,SE9 . .143 C1
Tufnell Ct 12 E3 . . . . . .97 B6
Tufnell Park Mans 2
N7 . . . . .72 A4
Tufnell Park Prim Sch
N7 . . . . .71 D4
Tufnell Park Rd N19,
N7 . . . . .71 D4
Tufnell Park Sta N19 . .71 C4
Tufton Ct SW1 . . . . . .260 A5
Tufton Gdns KT8 . . . .173 D1
Tufton Rd E4 . . . . .35 C2
Tufton St
SW1 . . . . . . .116 A3 260 A5
Tugboat St SE28 . . . .123 C4
Tugela Rd CR0 . . . . . .205 B3
Tugela St SE6 . . . . . .163 B2
Tugmutton Cl BR6 . . .226 D4
Tuke Sch SE15 . . . . . .140 B4
Tulip Cl 5 E6 . . . . . . .100 B4
Croydon CR0 . . . . . .206 D1
Hampton TW12 . . . . .173 B4
Southall UB2 . . . . . .108 A4
Tulip Gdns
Chingford E4 . . . . . . .20 B1
Ilford IG1 . . . . .78 D2
Tullis Ho 12 E9 . . . . . .74 C1
Tull St CR4 . . . . .202 D2
Tulse Cl BR3 . . . . . . .208 A6
Tulse Hill
Streatham SW2 . . . .160 B5
Streatham SW2,SE24 .160 C4
Tulse Hill Sta SE27 . .160 D2
Tulse Ho SW2 . . . . . .160 C5
Tulsemere Rd SE21,
SE27 . . . . .161 A2
Tumbling Bay KT12 . .194 A3
Tummons Gdns SE25 183 C1
Tunbridge Ct 1
SE26 . . . . .162 A1
Tunbridge Ho EC1 . . .234 C2
Tuncombe Rd N18 . . . .33 C6
Tunley Gn 16 E14 . . . .97 B2
Tunley Rd NW10 . . . . .89 C6
Upper Tooting SW12,
SW17 . . . . .159 A2
Tunmarsh La E13 . . . . .99 C4
Tunnan Leys E6 . . . . .100 C1
Tunnel Avenue Trad Est
SE10 . . . . .120 B4
Tunnel Gdns N11 . . . . .31 C3
Tunnel Link Rd TW6 . .148 C4
Tunnel Rd SE16 . . . . .118 C4
Tunnel Rd E TW6 . . . .126 D4
Tunnel Rd W TW6 . . . .126 D4
Tunstall Cl BR6 . . . . . .227 C4
Tunstall Ct 14 TW9 . . .132 B4
Tunstall Rd SW9 . . . .138 B1
Croydon CR0 . . . . . .205 C1
Tunstall Wlk 10 TW8 .132 A6
Tunstock Way DA17 . .125 A3
Tunworth Cl NW9 . . . . .45 A3
Tunworth Cres SW15 155 D5
Tupelo Rd E10 . . . . . . .75 D6
Tupman Ho 21 SE16 . .118 A4
Turberville Ho 1
SW9 . . . . .138 B2
Turene Cl SW18 . . . . .136 A1
Turin Rd N9 . . . . .18 C4
Turin St E2 . . . . .96 A4
Turkey Oak Cl SE19 . .183 C2
Turkey St Enfield EN1 . . .6 B6
Enfield EN3 . . . . .6 B6
Turkey Street Sta EN3 . .6 C6
Turks Cl UB8 . . . . .82 C4
Turk's Head Yd EC1 . .241 C4
Turks Row
SW3 . . . . . . .114 D1 257 D2
Turle Rd N4 . . . . .72 B6
Thornton Heath SW16 .182 A1
Turlewray Cl N4 . . . . . .72 B6
Turley Cl E15 . . . . .98 C6
Turnagain La EC4 . . . .241 C2
Turnage Rd RM8 . . . . .59 A1
Turnant Rd N17 . . . . . .33 A2
Turnberry Cl NW4 . . . .28 D1
24 SE16 . . . . .118 C1
Turnberry Way BR6 . .211 B3
Turnbull Ho N1 . . . . . .234 D6
Turnbury Cl SE28 . . . .102 D1
Turnchapel Mews 1
SW4 . . . . .137 A2
Turner Ave N15 . . . . . .51 C5
Mitcham CR4 . . . . . .180 D2
Twickenham TW2 . . . .152 A1

Turner Cl NW11 . . . . . .47 D3
7 SW9 . . . . .138 D4
Hillingdon UB4 . . . . . .83 A4
Wembley HA0 . . . . . . .65 D2
Turner Ct 19 SE16 . . .118 C2
9 SE5 . . . . .139 B1
Turner Dr NW11 . . . . . .47 D3
Turner Ho N4 . . . . .50 B1
NW8 . . . . .230 A4
SW1 . . . . .259 D3
WC2 . . . . .250 B5
6 Twickenham TW1 . .153 D5
Turner Lo 10 SW19 . .156 D3
Turner Pl SW11 . . . . .158 C6
Turner Rd E17 . . . . . . .54 A6
Edgware HA8 . . . . . . .26 B1
New Malden KT3 . . . .199 B2
Turners Meadow Way
BR3 . . . . .185 B2
Turner's Rd E3 . . . . . .97 B2
Turner St E1 . . . . .96 C1
E16 . . . . .98 D1
Turners Way CR0 . . . .220 C6
Turneville Rd
W14 . . . . . . .135 B6 264 C6
Turney Rd SE21 . . . . .161 B4
Turney Sch SE21 . . . .161 A4
Turnham Green Sta
W4 . . . . .111 C2
Turnham Green Terr
W4 . . . . .111 C2
Turnham Ho SE4 . . . .141 A1
Turnham Prim Sch
SE4 . . . . .141 A1
Turnham Rd SE4 . . . .141 A1
Turnmill Ho 8 SW2 . .160 C6
Turnmill St
EC1 . . . . .94 D2 241 C4
Turnour Ho 32 E1 . . . . .96 B1
Turnpike Cl SE8 . . . . .141 B5
Turnpike Ct DA6 . . . . .146 D1
Turnpike Ho EC1 . . . .234 D1
Turnpike La N8 . . . . . .50 C6
Sutton SM1 . . . . . . .218 A3
Uxbridge UB10 . . . . . .82 A5
Turnpike Lane Sta
N15 . . . . .50 D6
Turnpike Link CR0 . . .221 C6
Turnpike Way TW7 . . .131 A4
Turnpin La 2 SE10 . . .142 A6
Turnstone Cl E13 . . . . .99 A4
NW9 . . . . .27 C1
Uxbridge UB10 . . . . . .60 D3
Turpentine La
SW1 . . . . . . .115 B1 258 D1
Turpin Cl EN3 . . . . .7 C6
Turpington Cl BR2 . . .210 A3
Turpington La BR2 . . .210 A3
Turpin Ho SW11 . . . . .268 C2
Turpin Rd TW14 . . . . .149 D5
Turpin Way N19 . . . . . .49 D1
Wallington SM6 . . . . .219 B1
Turquand St SE17 . . .262 B3
Turret Gr SW4 . . . . . .137 C2
Turret Ho KT2 . . . . . . .176 A4
Turton Ho 5 SE18 . . .144 D6
Turton Rd HA0 . . . . . . .66 A3
Turville Ho NW8 . . . . .237 A6
Turville St E2 . . . . . . .243 C6
Tuscan Ho 36 E2 . . . . .96 C4
Tuscan Rd SE18 . . . . .123 B1
Tuskar St SE10 . . . . .120 C1

Twickenham Rd continued
Teddington TW11 . . . .175 A6
Twickenham TW13 . . .151 B1
Twickenham Rugby
Football Union Ground★
TW2 . . . . .152 C5
Twickenham Sta
TW1 . . . . .153 A4
Twickenham Trad Ctr
TW1 . . . . .152 D5
Twig Folly Cl E2 . . . . . .96 C5
Twilley St SW18 . . . . .157 D4
Twine Cl IG11 . . . . . .102 B4
Twine Ct E1 . . . . .118 C6
Twineham Gn N12 . . . .29 C6
Twining Ave TW2 . . . .152 B1
Twinn Rd NW7 . . . . . . .29 A4
Twisden Rd NW5 . . . . .71 B4
Twiss Ho 6 SE18 . . . .122 C1
Twybridge Way NW10 .67 A1
Twyford Abbey Rd
NW10 . . . . .88 B4
Twyford Ave N2 . . . . . .48 D6
Acton W3 . . . . .110 C6
Twyford CE High Sch
W3 . . . . .110 D5
Twyford Cres W3 . . . .110 C5
Twyford Ct N10 . . . . . .49 A6
Acton W3 . . . . .110 C6
6 Wembley HA0 . . . .88 A5
Twyford Ho 6 N15 . . . .51 C3
N5 . . . . .72 D5
Twyford Par KT6 . . . .198 C1
Twyford Pl WC2 . . . . .240 C2
Twyford Rd
Carshalton SM5 . . . .202 B1
Harrow HA2 . . . . .41 D2
Ilford IG1 . . . . .79 A3
Twyford St N1 . .94 B6 233 C6
Twynholm Mans
SW6 . . . . .264 A4
Tyas Rd E16 . . . . .98 D3
Tybenham Rd SW19 . .201 C6
Tyberry Rd EN3 . . . . . . .6 C6
Tyburn La HA1 . . . . . . .42 D2
Tyburn Tree (site of)★
W2 . . . . .247 C6
Tyburn Way W1 . . . . .247 C6
Tye La BR6 . . . . .227 A3
Tyer's Est SE1 . . . . . .253 A2
Tyers Gate
SE1 . . . . . . .117 C4 253 A1
Tyers Ho 1 SW16 . . .181 C5
Tyers St SE11 116 B1 260 C2
Tyers Terr
SE11 . . . . . .116 B1 260 D1
Tyeshurst Cl SE2 . . . .125 A1
Tylecroft Rd SW16 . . .182 A1
Tylehurst Gdns IG1 . . .79 A3
Tyler Cl E2 . . . . .95 C5
Tyler Ho UB2 . . . . . . .107 D3
Tylers Ct 4 E17 . . . . .53 C5
5 Wembley HA0 . . . .88 A5
Tylers Gate HA3 . . . . .44 A3
Tylers Path SM5 . . . .218 D4
Tyler St SE10 . . . . . . .120 C1
Tylers Way WD23 . . . . .8 C6
Tylney Ave SE19 . . . .183 C5
Tylney Ho 19 E1 . . . . .96 B1
Tylney Rd BR1 . . . . . .187 D1
E7 . . . . .77 C4
Tymperley Ct SW19 . .157 A3
Tynamara KT1 . . . . . .197 D5
Tyndale Ct SW19 . . . .150 A3
Tyndale La N1 . . . . . . .72 D1
Tyndale Mans N1 . . . .72 D1
Tyndale Terr 18 N1 . . .72 D1
Tyndall Gdns E10 . . . .76 A6
E10 . . . . .76 A6
Tyndall Rd DA16 . . . . .145 D2
E10 . . . . .76 A6
Tyne Ct W7 . . . . .86 C1
Tynedale Ct E14 . . . . .119 D1
Tyneham Cl 10 SW11 137 A2
Tyne Ho 8 KT2 . . . . .175 D2
Tynemouth Cl E6 . . . .100 D1
Tynemouth Dr EN1 . . . .6 A5
Tynemouth Rd N15 . . .51 D5
SE18 . . . . .123 C1
Mitcham CR4 . . . . . .181 A3
Tynemouth St SW6 . .136 A3
Tynemouth Terr 8
N15 . . . . .51 D5
Tyne St E1 . . . . .243 D2
Tynsdale Rd NW10 . . .67 C2
Tynte Ct E9 . . . . .75 A3
Tynwald Ho 14 SE26 .162 A1
Type St E2 . . . . .96 C5
Tyrawley Rd SW6 . . . .265 C2
Tyrell Cl HA1 . . . . .64 C2
Tyrell Ct SM5 . . . . . . .218 C4

Tyrols Rd SE23 . . . . . .162 D3
Tyrone Rd E6 . . . . . . .100 B4
Tyron Way DA14 . . . . .189 D5
Tyrrell Ave DA16 . . . . .168 B6
Tyrrell Ho SW1 . . . . . .269 B6
Catford BR3 . . . . . . .185 D5
Tyrrell Rd SE22 . . . . .140 A1
Tyrrell Sq CR4 . . . . . .180 C2
Tyrrel Way NW9 . . . . . .46 A3
Tyrwhitt Rd SE4 . . . . .141 C2
Tysoe Ave EN3 . . . . . . .7 B6
Tysoe St EC1 . . . . . . .234 B1
Tyson Rd SE23 . . . . . .162 C4
Tyssen Rd N16 . . . . . .73 D5
Tyssen Sch N16 . . . . . .52 A1
Tyssen St E8 . . . . .73 D2
N1 . . . . .95 C5
Tytherton 30 E2 . . . . . .96 C5
Tytherton Rd N19 . . . .71 D5

U

Uamvar St E14 . . . . . . .97 D2
Uckfield Gr CR4 . . . . .181 A2
Uckfield Rd EN3 . . . . . .6 C6
Udall St SW1 . . . . . . .259 B3
Udimore Ho W10 . . . . .90 C2
Udney Park Rd TW11 175 A4
Uffington Rd NW10 . . . .90 B6
West Norwood SE27 .182 C6
Ufford Cl HA3 . . . . . . .23 D3
Ufford Rd HA3 . . . . . . .23 D3
Ufford St SE1 116 C4 251 B2
Ufton Ct UB5 . . . . .84 C4
Ufton Gr N1 . . . . .73 B1
Ufton Rd N1 . . . . .73 C1
Uhura Sq 19 N16 . . . . .73 C5
Ujima Ct N19 . . . . .50 A1
Streatham SW16 . . . .182 A6
Ujima Ho SW16 . . . . .182 A6
Uk Cotts UB3 . . . . . . .105 B4
Ullathorne Rd SW16 . .181 C5
Ulleswater Rd N14 . . . .16 B1
Ullin St E14 . . . . .98 A2
Ullswater SW15 . . . . .156 D5
Ullswater Cl
Bromley BR1 . . . . . .186 C3
Hayes UB4 . . . . .83 C5
Kingston KT2,SW15 . .177 B6
Ullswater Cres SW15 177 B6
Ullswater Ct
2 Woodford E18 . . . .37 A1
Harrow HA2 . . . . .41 C2
Ullswater Ho SE15 . . .140 C6
Ullswater Rd
Barnes SW13 . . . . . .134 A5
West Norwood SE27,
SW16 . . . . .160 D2
Ulster Ct KT2 . . . . . . .175 D4
Ulster Gdns N13 . . . . .33 A6
Ulster Pl NW1 . . . . . .238 C5
Ulundi Rd SE3 . . . . . .142 C6
Ulva Rd SW15 . . . . . .134 D1
Ulverscroft Rd SE22 .162 A6
Ulverstone Rd SE27 . .160 D2
Ulverston Rd E17 . . . . .36 B1
Ulysses Rd NW6 . . . . .69 B4
Umberston St E1 . . . . .96 B1
Umbria St SW15 . . . . .156 A5
Umfreville Rd N4 . . . . .50 D3
Una Ho 7 NW5 . . . . . .71 B2
Under Cliff SE10 . . . . .142 A4
Undercliff Rd SE13 . . .141 D2
Underhill EN5 . . . . . . .13 C6
Underhill Ct EN5 . . . . .13 C6
Underhill Ho 7 E14 . . .97 C2
Underhill Jun & Inf Schs
EN5 . . . . .13 A6
Underhill Pas NW1 . . .231 D6
Underhill Rd SE21,
SE22 . . . . .162 B4
Underhill St NW1 . . . .231 D5
Underne Ave N14 . . . . .15 B2
Undershaft
EC3 . . . . .95 C1 243 A1
Undershaw Rd BR1 . .164 D1
Underwood CR0 . . . . . .20 A4
Underwood Ct 3 E10 .53 D1
Underwood Ho W6 . . .112 B3
Underwood Rd E1 . . . .96 A3
Chingford E4 . . . . . . .35 D5
Woodford IG8 . . . . . . .37 D3
Underwood Row N1 . .235 B2
Underwood St
N1 . . . . .95 A4 235 B2
Underwood The SE9 .166 B2
Undine Rd E14 . . . . . .119 D2

Undine St SW17 .....**180** D5
Uneeda Dr UB6 ....**86** B6
Unicorn Bldg **14** E1 ..**118** D6
Unicorn Sch TW9 ...**132** B4
Unicorn Works N17 ..**34** C3
Union Cl E11 ....**76** B4
Union Ct SW4 ....**138** A3
45 W2 ....**91** C2
2 Richmond TW10 ...**154** A6
Union Dr E1 ....**97** C3
Union Gr SW8 ....**137** D3
Union Mews SW9 ....**138** A3
Union Rd BR2 ....**209** D4
N11 ....**31** D4
SW8 ....**137** D3
Northolt UB5 ....**85** C5
Thornton Heath CR0 ..**205** A2
Wembley HA0 ....**66** A2
Union Sq N1 ..**95** A6 **235** B5
Union St E15 ......**98** B6
SE1 ....**117** A5 **252** A3
Barnet EN5 ....**1** A2
Kingston KT1 ....**175** D1
Union Wlk E2 ......**95** C4
Union Yd W1 ....**238** D1
Unity Cl NW10 ......**68** A2
West Norwood SE19 ..**183** A5
Unity Mews NW1 ..**232** C4
Unity Rd EN3 ....**6** C6
Unity Way SE18 ...**121** D3
Univ College Hospl
(Annexe) W1 .**93** A2 **238** B4
Univ Coll Jun Sch
NW3 ....**70** A4
Univ Coll London
W1 ....**93** C2 **239** B4
WC1 ....**93** D3 **239** C6
WC1 ....**94** A3 **240** B6
University Cl NW7 ...**27** D3
University Coll Hospl
WC1 ....**93** C3 **239** B5
University Coll Sch
NW3 ....**70** A3
University Gdns DA5 .**169** B4
University Mans
SW15 ....**134** D2
University of North London
(Tufnel Park Hall)
N7 ....**71** C5
University Pl DA8 ..**147** D5
University Rd SW19 ..**180** B4
University St
WC1 ....**93** C3 **239** B5
University Way E16 ..**122** D6
Univ of East London
E15 ....**76** C2
E15 ....**98** B6
E6 ....**122** C6
Barking RM8 ....**80** A4
Univ of East London
(Holbrook Ctr) E15 ..**98** D5
Univ of Greenwich Avery
Hill Campus Mansion Site
SE9 ....**167** A5
Univ of Greenwich Avery
Hill Campus Southwood
Site SE9 ....**167** B4
Univ of Greenwich Rachel
Mcmillan Campus
SE8 ....**141** C6
Univ of Greenwich
Riverside Ho Annexe
SE18 ....**122** C3
Univ of Greenwich The
SW15 ....**156** A4
Univ of London
WC1 ....**94** A4 **233** A1
Univ of London (King's
Coll Hall) SE5 .....**139** B2
Univ of London
Observatory NW7 ...**27** D4
Univ of London (Queen
Mary & Westfield Coll)
E1 ....**97** A3
Univ of Westminster
NW1 ....**93** C3 **239** A6
NW8 ....**92** C3 **237** A5
W1 ....**93** A2 **238** A4
W1 ....**93** B1 **238** D2
Univ of Westminster
(Harrow Campus)
HA1 ....**43** A2
Unwin Ave TW14 ...**149** B6
Unwin Cl SE15 ......**140** A6
Unwin Rd
SW7 ......**114** B3 **256** D6
Isleworth TW7 ....**130** C2

Upbrook Mews
W2 ....**92** A1 **236** B1
Upcerne Rd
SW10 .....**136** A5 **266** B3
Upchurch Cl SE20 ..**184** B3
Upcott Ho **33** E3 .....**97** D4
4 E1 ....**74** C1
Upcroft Ave HA8 .....**27** A6
Updale Rd DA14 ....**189** D6
Upfield CR0 ....**222** B5
Upfield Rd W7 ......**86** D2
Upgrove Manor Way **12**
SE24 ....**160** C4
Uphall Prim Sch IG1 .**78** D3
Uphall Rd IG1 ....**78** D3
Upham Park Rd W4 .**111** C2
Uphill Dr NW7 ......**27** C5
NW9 ....**45** A4
Uphill Gr NW7 ......**27** C5
Uphill Rd NW7 ......**27** C6
Upland Ct SE23 ....**162** B2
Upland Inf Sch DA7 .**147** B2
Upland Jun Sch DA7 **147** B2
Upland Rd DA7 ....**147** B2
8 E13 ....**99** A3
SE22 ....**162** A5
Croydon CR2 ....**221** B3
Sutton SM2 ....**218** B1
Uplands BR3 ....**185** C1
Uplands Ave E17 ....**34** D1
Uplands Bsns Pk E17 .**52** D6
Uplands Cl SW14 ...**154** D6
Uplands Ct N21 ......**16** C4
Uplands Park Rd EN2 ..**4** C3
Uplands Rd N8 ......**50** B4
East Barnet EN4 .....**15** A3
Ilford RM6 ....**58** D6
Woodford IG8 ....**37** D3
Uplands The HA4 ....**40** A1
Uplands Way N21 ...**16** C6
Upnall Ho **16** SE15 ..**140** C6
Upney La IG11 ....**79** D1
Upney Sta IG11 ......**79** D1
Upnor Way SE17 ...**263** B2
Uppark Dr IG2 ....**57** A3
Upper Abbey Rd
DA17 ....**125** C2
Upper Addison Gdns
W14 ....**113** A4 **244** A2
Upper Belgrave St
SW1 ....**115** A3 **258** B6
Upper Berkeley St
W1 ....**92** D1 **237** D1
Upper Beulah Hill
SE19 ....**183** C2
Upper Brighton Rd
KT6 ....**198** A2
Upper Brockley Rd
SE4 ....**141** B3
Upper Brook St
W1 ....**115** A6 **248** A6
Upper Butts TW8 ...**131** C4
Upper Caldy Wlk **14**
N1 ....**73** A2
Upper Cavendish Ave
N3 ....**47** C6
Upper Cheyne Row
SW3 ....**136** C6 **267** A6
Upper Clapton Rd E5 .**74** B6
Upper Clarendon Wlk **13**
W11 ....**91** A1
Upper Dengie Wlk
N1 ....**235** A6
Upper Elmers End Rd
BR3 ....**207** A4
Upper Farm Rd KT8 .**195** B5
Upper Fosters NW4 ..**46** C5
Upper Gn E CR4 ....**203** A6
Upper Gn W CR4 ...**180** D1
Upper Gr SE25 .....**205** D5
Upper Grosvenor St
W1 ....**115** A6 **248** A5
Upper Grotto Rd
TW1 ....**152** D2
Upper Ground
SE1 ....**116** C5 **251** A4
Upper Grove Rd
DA17 ....**147** B6
Upper Gulland Wlk **19**
N1 ....**73** A2
Upper Halliford Rd
TW17 ....**193** C6
Upper Halliford Sta
TW16 ....**171** C1
Upper Ham Rd KT2,
TW10 ....**175** D6
Upper Harley St NW1 **238** B5
Upper Hawkwell Wlk
N1 ....**235** B6

Upper Holloway Sta
N19 ....**71** D6
Upper Holly Hill Rd
DA17 ....**125** D1
Upper James St W1 .**249** B6
Upper John St W1 ..**249** B6
Upper Lodge Mews
TW12 ....**174** A4
Upper Mall W6 .....**112** B1
Upper Marsh
SE1 ....**116** B4 **260** D6
Upper Montague St
W1 ....**92** D2 **237** C3
Upper Mulgrave Rd
SM2 ....**217** A1
Upper North St E3,E14 **97** C2
Upper Park Rd BR1 .**187** C2
N11 ....**31** C5
NW3 ....**70** D3
Belvedere DA17 .....**125** D2
Kingston KT2 ....**176** C4
Upper Phillimore Gdns
W8 ....**113** C4 **245** A1
Upper Pk IG10 ......**21** D6
Upper Rawreth Wlk
N1 ....**235** B6
Upper Rd E13 ......**99** A4
N2 ....**30** C2
Wallington SM6 ....**219** D3
Upper Richmond Rd
SW15 ....**134** C1
Upper Richmond Rd W
TW10,SW14,SW15 ..**133** A1
Upper Selsdon Rd
CR2 ....**221** D1
Upper Sheridan Rd
DA17 ....**125** C2
Upper Shirley Rd
CR0 ....**222** D5
Upper Sq TW7 .....**131** A2
Upper St N1 ..**94** D6 **234** C5
Upper St Martin's La
WC2 ....**250** A6
Upper Sunbury Rd
TW12 ....**173** C2
Upper Sutton La
TW5 ....**129** C4
Upper Tachbrook St
SW1 ....**259** B4
Upper Teddington Rd
KT1,KT8 ....**175** C2
Upper Terr NW3 ....**70** A5
Upper Thames St
EC4 ....**117** A6 **252** B6
Upper Tollington Pk
N4 ....**50** C1
Upperton Rd DA14 .**189** D5
Upperton Rd E E13 ..**99** C4
Upperton Rd W E13 .**99** C4
Upper Tooting Park Mans
1 SW17 ....**159** A4
Upper Tooting Pk
SW17 ....**158** D2
Upper Tooting Rd
SW17 ....**158** D1
Upper Town Rd UB6 ..**85** D3
Upper Tulse Hill
SW2 ....**160** B3
Upper Vernon Rd
SM1 ....**218** B3
Upper Walthamstow Rd
E17 ....**54** B6
Upper Wickham La
DA16 ....**146** B4
Upper Wimpole St
W1 ....**93** A2 **238** B4
Upper Woburn Pl
NW1,WC1 ...**93** D4 **232** D1
Uppingham Ave HA7 .**25** C1
Upsdell Ave N13 .....**32** C4
Upshire Ho E17 ......**35** B1
Upstall St SE5 ......**138** D4
Upton Ave E7 ....**77** A1
Upton Cl NW2 ......**69** A5
Sidcup DA5 ....**169** B5
Upton Cross E13 ....**99** A6
Upton Cross Prim Sch
E13 ....**99** B6
Upton Ct Penge SE20 .**184** C3
Southall UB1 ....**107** D5
4 Wimbledon SW19 ..**178** D3
Upton Day Hospl
DA6 ....**147** A1
Upton Dene SM2 ...**217** D1
Upton Gdns HA3 .....**43** C3
Upton La E7 ....**77** A1
Upton Lodge Cl WD23 ..**8** A4
Upton Park Rd E7 ....**77** B1
Upton Park Sta E13 ..**99** C6
Upton Prim Sch DA5 **169** B6

Upton Rd SE18 ....**145** A6
Bexley DA6 ....**169** A6
Edmonton N18 ......**34** A5
Hounslow TW3 .....**129** C2
South Norwood CR7 .**183** B1
Upton Rd S DA5 ...**169** B5
Upton Villas **4** DA6 ..**147** A1
Upway N12 ....**30** C4
Upwood Rd SE12 ...**165** A5
Thornton Heath SW16 .**182** A2
Urlwin St SE5 ......**139** A6
Urlwin Wlk SW9 ...**138** D4
Urmston Dr SW19 ..**157** A3
Urmston Ho **3** E14 ..**120** A2
Urquhart Ct BR3 ...**185** B3
Ursula Lo DA14 ....**190** B5
Ursula Mews N4 ....**51** A1
Ursula St
SW11 ......**136** C4 **267** A1
Ursuline High Sch
SW20 ....**178** D2
Urswick Gdns RM9 ..**81** A1
Urswick Rd E5,E9 ...**74** C3
Dagenham RM9 ......**81** A1
Usborne Mews SW8 .**270** D4
Usher Rd E3 ....**97** B5
Usk Rd SW11 ......**136** A1
Usk St E2 ....**96** D4
Utopia Village
NW1 ......**71** A1 **231** A6
Uvedale Rd
Dagenham RM10 ....**81** C5
Enfield EN2 ....**17** B6
Uverdale Rd
SW10 .....**136** A5 **266** B3
Uxbridge Coll
Hayes UB3 ....**106** A3
Uxbridge UB8 ....**60** A2
Uxbridge High Sch
UB8 ....**82** A5
Uxbridge Rd W12 ..**112** B5
Acton W3,W5 ....**110** C5
Ealing W13 ....**109** C6
Feltham TW13 ......**150** D2
Hampton TW12,TW13 .**173** D5
Hayes UB4 ....**106** C6
Hillingdon UB10,UB4 ..**83** C2
Kingston KT1,KT6 ...**197** D4
Southall UB1,UB2,UB5, ...
Stanmore HA7 ....**25** A5
Uxbridge Road (Harrow
Weald) HA3 ....**24** D3
Uxbridge Road (Hatch
End) HA5 ....**23** B3
Uxbridge St
W8 ....**113** C5 **245** A4
Uxendon Cres HA3,
HA9 ....**44** A1
Uxendon Hill HA9 ...**44** B2
Uxendon Manor Prim Sch
HA3 ....**44** A4

V

Vaine Ho **4** E9 .....**75** A2
Valance Ave E4 .....**20** D3
Valan Leas BR2 ....**208** C6
Vale Ave WD6 ......**10** D6
Vale Cl N2 ....**48** D6
W9 ....**92** A4 **229** A1
Orpington BR6 ......**226** C4
Twickenham TW1 ...**153** A1
Vale Cres SW15 ...**177** C6
Vale Croft
Claygate KT10 ......**212** D1
Pinner HA5 ....**41** A4
Vale Ct W3 ....**111** D5
W9 ....**92** A4 **229** A1
Barnet EN5 ....**1** D1
Wembley HA0 ....**65** C5
Vale Dr EN5 ....**13** C6
Vale End SE22 .....**139** D1
Vale Est The W3 ...**111** C5
Vale Farm Sports Ctr
HA0 ....**65** B4
Vale Gr N4 ....**51** A2
W3 ....**111** B5
Vale La W3 ....**88** C2
Vale Lo SE23 ......**162** C2
Valence Ave RM8 ....**80** D6
Valence Cir RM8 ....**81** A5
Valence House Mus*
RM8 ....**81** A6
Valence Inf Sch RM8 .**80** D6
Valence Jun Sch RM8 **80** D6
Valence Wood Rd
RM8 ....**81** A6
Valencia Rd HA7 ...**25** C4
Valens Ho **1** SW2 ..**160** C4

Valentia Pl SW9 ....**138** C1
Valentine Ave DA5 ..**169** A3
Valentine Ct SE23 ..**162** D2
Valentine Ho **11** SW4 **159** C5
Valentine Pl
SE1 ....**116** D4 **251** C2
Valentine Rd E9 ....**74** D2
Harrow HA2 ....**64** A5
Valentine Row SE1 ..**251** C1
Valentines High Sch
IG2 ....**56** C3
Valentines Rd IG1 ...**56** D1
Vale of Health NW3 ..**70** B5
Vale Rd BR1 ....**188** C1
E7 ....**77** B2
N4 ....**51** A2
Claygate KT10 ......**212** D1
Mitcham CR4 ......**203** D5
Sutton SM1 ....**217** D4
Worcester Park KT19, ...
KT4 ....**215** D5
Vale Rd N KT6 .....**214** A6
Vale Rd S KT6 .....**214** A6
Valerian Way E15 ...**98** C4
Valerie Ct
Belmont SM2 ......**217** D1
Bushey WD23 ....**8** A4
Vale Rise NW11 .....**47** B1
Vale Row N5 ......**72** D5
Vale Royal N7 ......**72** A1
Valery Pl TW12 ....**173** C3
Valeswood Rd BR1 .**186** D5
Vale Terr N4 ....**51** B3
Vale The N10 ......**31** A2
NW11 ....**69** A6
SW3 ....**136** B6 **266** D6
W3 ....**111** C5
Ashford TW16 ......**172** A4
Croydon CR0 ....**222** D6
Feltham TW14 ......**150** B5
Heston TW5 ....**129** A6
Ruislip HA4 ....**62** C4
Southgate N14 ......**16** A4
Woodford IG8 ....**37** A3
Valetta Gr E13 .....**99** A5
Valetta Rd W3 .....**111** D4
Valette Ct N10 .....**49** B5
Valette Ho E9 ......**74** C2
Valette St E8 ......**74** B2
Valiant Cl **13** UB5 ...**84** D4
Valiant Ho **5** SE7 ..**121** C1
SW11 ....**266** D1
Valiant Way E6 ....**100** B2
Vallance Rd E1 .....**96** A3
N22 ....**31** C1
Vallentin Rd E17 ...**54** A5
Valley Ave N12 .....**30** B6
Valley (Charlton Athletic
FC) The SE7 .....**121** C1
Valley Cl HA5 ......**22** B1
Valley Ct IG8 ......**37** B3
Valley Dr NW9 .....**44** D3
Valleyfield Rd SW16 .**182** B5
Valley Fields Cres EN2 ..**4** C3
Valley Gdns
Mitcham SW19 ....**180** B3
Wembley HA0 ....**66** B1
Valley Gr SE7 .....**121** C1
Valley Ho E5 ......**52** C1
4 Edmonton N9 ....**18** A1
Valley L Ctr SE9 ...**167** A4
Valleylink Est EN3 ..**19** A5
Valley Mews TW1 ..**153** A2
Valley Pl KT6 .....**198** A3
Valley Prim Sch BR2 **186** D1
Valley Prospect **3**
SE19 ....**183** C4
Valley Rd BR5 .....**190** B2
Beckenham BR2 ....**186** C1
Streatham SW16 ...**182** B6
Uxbridge UB10 ......**82** A5
Valleyside SE7 .....**121** C1
Valley Side E4 .....**19** C3
Valley Side Par E4 ..**19** C2
Valley View EN5 ....**13** A5
Valley Wlk CR0 ....**222** C6
Valliere Rd NW10 ...**90** A4
Valliers Wood Rd
DA15 ....**167** C3
Vallis Way
Chessington KT9 ...**213** D4
Ealing W13 ....**87** A2
Valmar Rd SE5 ....**139** A4
Valmar Trad Est **7**
SE5 ....**139** A4
Valnay St SW17 ...**180** D5
Valognes Ave E17 ..**35** A2
Valois Ho SE1 .....**263** C6
Valonia Gdns SW18 .**157** B5

Vambery Rd SE18 ..**145** A6
Vanbern Ho NW5 ....**71** A2
Vanborough Ct **4**
SM2 ....**218** C2
Vanbrugh Cres UB5 ..**84** C6
Vanbrugh Cl **2** E16 ..**99** D2
Vanbrugh Ct SE11 ..**261** B3
Vanbrugh Dr KT12 .**194** C3
Vanbrugh Fields SE3 **142** D5
Vanbrugh Hill SE10,
SE3 ....**142** D6
Vanbrugh Ho **8** E9 ..**74** C1
Vanbrugh Mews
KT12 ....**194** C2
Vanbrugh Park Rd
SE3 ....**142** D5
Vanbrugh Park Rd W
SE3 ....**142** D5
Vanbrugh Pk SE3 ..**142** D5
Vanbrugh Rd W4 ..**111** B3
Vanbrugh Terr SE3 .**142** D4
Vanburgh Cl BR6 ...**211** C1
Vanburgh Ho E1 ...**243** C4
Vancouver Rd
Edgware HA8 ......**26** D2
Forest Hill SE23 ...**163** B2
Hayes UB4 ....**84** B3
Richmond TW10 ...**175** C6
Vancover Ho **33** E1 ..**118** B5
Vanderbilt Rd SW18 .**158** A3
Vanderbilt Villas **1**
W12 ....**112** D4
Vanderville Gdns N2 ..**30** B1
Vandome Cl E16 ....**99** B1
Vandon Ct SW1 ....**259** B6
Vandon Pas SW1 ..**259** B6
Vandon St SW1 ...**259** B6
Van Dyck Ave KT3 ..**199** B2
Vandyke Cl SW15 ..**156** D5
Vandyke Cross SE9 .**166** A6
Vandy St EC2 .....**243** A5
Vane Cl NW3 ......**70** B4
Harrow HA3 ....**44** B3
Vane Ho **15** N2 .....**30** B1
Vanessa Cl DA17 ..**125** C1
Vane St SW1 ......**259** B4
Vanfame Ct KT3 ...**199** D6
Vanguard Way TW6 .**127** C2
Vange Ho W10 .....**90** C2
Van Gogh Ct E14 ..**120** B3
Vanguard Bldg **12**
E14 ....**119** C4
Vanguard Cl E16 ...**99** B2
Thornton Heath CR0 .**204** D1
Vanguard Ho
7 Merton SW19 ...**180** A3
6 Stanwell TW19 ..**148** A5
Vanguard St SE8 ..**141** C4
Vanguard Trad Ctr
E15 ....**98** A6
Vanguard Way SM6 .**220** A1
Vanneck Sq SW15 ..**156** A6
Vanoc Gdns BR1 ..**187** A6
Vansittart Rd E7 ...**77** A4
Vansittart St **7** SE14 **141** A5
Vanston Pl
SW6 ....**135** C5 **265** B4
Vantage Mews E14 .**120** C4
Vant Rd SW17 ....**180** D5
Vantrey Ho SE11 ..**261** A3
Varcoe Rd SE16 ...**118** C1
Vardens Rd SW11 ..**136** B1
Varden St E1 ......**96** B1
Vardon Cl W3 .....**89** B1
Vardon Ho SE10 ...**142** A4
Varey Ho E1 ....**97** A4
Varley Ho **5** NW6 ...**91** C6
Varley Par NW9 ....**45** C5
Varley Rd E16 .....**99** B1
Varley Way CR4 ...**180** B1
Varna Rd
SW6 ....**135** B5 **264** C3
Hampton TW12 ....**173** D2
Varndell St
NW1 ......**93** C4 **232** A2
Varsity Dr TW1,TW7 .**152** D5
Varsity Row SW14 .**133** A3
Vartry Rd N15 .....**51** C3
Vassal Ho E3 ......**97** A4
Vassall Rd SW9 ...**138** C5
Vat Ho SW8 ....**270** B4
Vauban Est SE16 ..**263** D5
Vauban St
SE16 ......**117** D3 **263** D5
Vaudeville Ct N4 ...**72** C6
Vaughan Almshouses
TW15 ....**170** D5
Vaughan Ave NW4 ..**46** A4
W6 ....**111** D2
Vaughan Est **3** E2 ..**95** D4

Vaughan Fst & Mid Sch
HA1 42 A3
Vaughan Gdns IG1 56 B2
Vaughan Ho SE1 251 C2
Vaughan Rd DA16 145 D3
E15 76 D2
SE5 139 A2
Harrow HA1 42 B3
Thames Ditton KT7 197 B2
Vaughan St SE16 119 B4
Vaughan Way E1 118 A5
Vaughan Williams Cl
SE8 141 C5
Vauxhall Bridge Rd
SW1 115 C2 259 B3
Vauxhall Cross
SE1,SW8 116 A1 260 B1
Vauxhall Gdns CR2 221 A2
Vauxhall Gr
SW8 138 B6 270 C6
Vauxhall Prim Sch
SE11 116 B1 260 D2
Vauxhall St
SE11 116 B1 260 B2
Vauxhall Sta
SE11 116 A1 260 B1
Vauxhall Wlk SE11 260 C2
Vawdrey Cl E1 96 C3
Vaynor Ho N7 72 A4
Veals Mead CR4 180 C2
Vectis Ct SW18 157 D5
Vectis Gdns SW17 181 B4
Vectis Rd SW17 181 B4
Veda Rd SE13 141 C1
Vega Cres HA6 22 A5
Vega Rd WD23 8 A4
Veitch Cl TW14 149 D4
Veldene Way HA2 63 B5
Velde Way 1 SE22 161 C6
Vellacott Ho W12 90 B1
Velletri Ho 17 E2 96 D5
Vellum Dr SM5 219 A5
Venables Cl RM10 81 D4
Venables St
NW8 92 B2 236 D4
Vencourt Pl W6 112 A2
Venetian Rd SE5 139 A3
Venetia Rd N4 50 D3
W5 109 D4
Venice Ct 14 SE5 139 A5
Venita Manor SE27 182 C5
Venmead Ct DA17 125 C2
Venner Rd SE26 184 C5
Venn Ho N1 233 D5
Venn St SW4 137 C1
Ventnor Ave HA7 25 B1
Ventnor Dr N20 13 D2
Ventnor Gdns IG11 79 C2
Ventnor Mans IG11 79 C2
Ventnor Rd SE14 140 D5
Belmont SM2 217 D1
Ventnor Terr N15 52 A5
Venture Cl DA5 169 A4
Venture Ct 3 SE12 165 A4
Venue St E14 98 A2
Venus Rd SE18 122 B3
Vera Ave N21 16 C6
Vera Ct 1 W2 91 D1
Vera Lynn Cl 5 E7 77 A4
Vera Rd SW6 135 A4 264 B2
Verbena Cl E16 98 D3
Verbena Gdns W6 112 A1
Verdant Ct 3 SE6 164 C4
Verdant La SE6 164 C3
Verdayne Ave CR0 222 D6
Verdi Ho 2 NW6 91 A5
Verdun Rd SE18,SE2 146 A6
Barnes SW13 134 A5
Vere Bank SW19 157 B3
Vereker Dr TW16 194 A6
Vereker Rd W14 254 B1
Vere St W1 93 B1 238 C1
Verity Cl W11 91 A1
Verity Ct N9 18 D3
Verity Ho 15 E3 97 B4
Vermeer Ct E14 120 B3
Vermont Cl EN2 4 D1
Vermont Ho E17 35 B1
Vermont Rd
Sutton SM1 217 D5
Wandsworth SW18 157 D5
West Norwood SE19 183 C4
Verne Ct 9 W3 111 A3
Verney Gdns RM9 81 A4
Verney Ho NW8 237 A6
Isleworth TW3 130 A1
Verney Rd SE16 118 B1
Dagenham RM9 81 A4
Verney St NW10 67 B5
Verney Way SE16 118 B1
Vernham Rd SE18 145 A6
Vernon Ave Ilford E12 78 B4
West Barnes SW20 178 D1
Woodford IG8 37 B3
Vernon Cl KT19 215 A2
Vernon Cres EN4 15 A5
Vernon Ct NW2 69 B5
Ealing W5 109 C6
Stanmore HA7 25 B2
Vernon Dr HA7 25 A2
Vernon Ho NW9 45 D4
SE11 260 D1
Vernon House Sch
NW10 67 B3
Vernon Mews W14 254 B3
Vernon Pl WC1 240 B3
Vernon Rd E11 54 C1
E15 76 C1
E17 53 B4
E3 97 B5
N8 50 C6
Feltham TW13 149 D2
Ilford IG3 57 D1
Mortlake SW14 133 B2
Sutton SM1 218 B3
Vernon Rise WC1 233 D2
Greenford UB6 64 B3
Vernon Sq WC1 233 D2
Vernon St
W14 113 A2 254 B3
Vernon Yd
W11 113 B6 244 C6
Veroan Rd DA7 147 A3
Verona Ct 10 SE14 140 D6
W4 111 C1
Verona Dr KT6 214 A6
Verona Rd E7 77 A1
Veronica Gdns CR4,
SW16 181 C2
Veronica Ho SE4 141 B2
Veronica Rd SW17 159 B2
Veronique Gdns IG6 57 A4
Verran Rd SW12 159 B4
Versailles Rd SE20 184 A3
Verulam Ave E17 53 B2
Verulam Ct NW9 46 A2
4 Southall UB1 86 A1
Verulam Ho 1 W6 112 C4
Verulam Rd UB6 85 C3
Verulam St
EC1 94 C2 241 A4
Vervain Ho 2 SE15 140 A5
Verwood Dr EN4 2 D2
Verwood Ho SW8 270 D3
Verwood Lo 1 E14 120 B2
Verwood Rd HA2 24 A1
Veryan Ct 2 N8 49 D4
Vesage Ct EC1 241 B3
Vesey Path 15 E14 97 D1
Vespan Rd W12 112 A4
Vesta Rd SE4,SE14 141 A3
Vestris Rd SE23 162 D2
Vestry House (Mus)★
E17 53 D5
Vestry Mews 12 SE5 139 C4
Vestry Rd E17 53 D5
SE5 139 C4
Vestry St N1 95 B4 235 C2
Vevey St SE23,SE6 163 B2
Veysey Gdns RM10 81 C5
Viaduct Pl 28 E2 96 B4
Viaduct Rd N2 30 C1
Viaduct St E2 96 B4
Viaduct The
Harrow HA2 64 A5
Woodford E18 37 B1
Vian St SE13 141 D2
Viant Ho 11 NW10 67 B1
Vibart Gdns SW2 160 B4
Vibart Wlk N1 233 B6
Vicarage Ave SE3 143 A5
Vicarage Cl
New Malden KT4 199 C1
Northolt UB5 63 B1
Ruislip HA4 39 B2
Vicarage Cres
SW11 136 B4 266 C1
Vicarage Ct N12 29 D5
W8 245 C2
Beckenham BR3 207 A6
East Bedfont TW14 149 A4
7 Putney SW15 156 A4
Vicarage Dr
Barking IG11 79 A1
Beckenham BR3 185 C2
Mortlake SW14 155 B6
Vicarage Farm Ct
TW5 129 B5
Vicarage Farm Rd
TW3,TW4,TW5 129 A4
Vicarage Fields KT12 194 C3
Vicarage Fields Sh Ctr The
IG11 79 A1
Vicarage Gate
W8 113 D5 245 C3
Vicarage Gdns W8 245 B3
Mitcham CR4 202 C6
Mortlake SW14 155 B6
Vicarage Gr SE5 139 B4
Vicarage Ho 1 KT1 176 B1
Vicarage La E15 76 D1
Ilford IG1 57 B1
Wallend E6 100 C4
Vicarage Pk SE18 123 A1
Vicarage Prim Sch
E6 100 B4
Vicarage Rd DA5 169 D3
E10 53 D1
E15 76 D1
NW4 46 A3
SE18 123 A1
Ashford TW16 171 D4
Croydon CR0 220 C5
Dagenham RM10 81 D1
Kingston KT1,KT2 175 D1
Mortlake SW14 155 B6
Sutton SM1 217 D5
Teddington KT1,KT8 175 C2
Teddington TW11 175 A5
Tottenham N17 34 A2
Vicarage Way NW10 67 B5
Harrow HA2 41 C2
Vicarage Wlk
SW11 136 B4 266 D2
Vicars Bridge Cl HA0 88 A5
Vicar's Cl E15 99 A6
E9 96 C6
Enfield EN1 5 C3
Vicar's Green Prim Sch
HA0 87 C5
Vicars Hill SE13 141 D1
Vicar's Moor La N21 16 D4
Vicars Oak Rd SE19 183 C4
Vicar's Rd NW5 71 A3
Vicar's Wlk RM8 80 B5
Viceroy Cl N2 48 C6
Viceroy Ct NW8 230 B4
5 Croydon CR0 205 B1
Viceroy Lo 6 KT6 198 A4
Viceroy Par N2 48 C6
Viceroy Rd
SW8 138 A4 270 A2
Vic Johnson Ho 14 E3 97 B6
Vickers Cl SM6 220 B1
Vickers Ct 10 TW19 148 A5
Vickery Ct EC1 242 B6
Vickery Ho 12 SW4 138 A1
Victor Cazalet Ho N1 234 C6
Victor Gr HA0 66 A1
Victor Ho N20 14 D1
Victoria & Albert Mus★
SW7 114 B3 256 D5
Victoria Arc SW1 258 D5
Victoria Ave E6 99 D6
EC2 243 B3
N3 29 B2
Barnet EN4 2 B1
East Molesey KT8 195 D6
Hackbridge SM5,SM6 219 A5
Hillingdon UB10 60 D1
Hounslow TW3,TW4 151 C6
Surbiton KT6 197 D3
Wembley HA9 66 D2
Victoria Bglws DA14 191 B3
Victoria Bldgs 13 E8 96 B6
Victoria Bsns Ctr
DA16 146 B3
Victoria Cl Barnet EN4 2 B1
East Molesey KT8 195 C6
Harrow HA1 42 D3
Hayes UB3 83 B1
Victoria Coach Sta
SW1 115 B2 258 C3
Victoria Cotts N10 31 A1
3 E1 96 A2
Ilford IG6 57 A4
7 Richmond TW9 132 C4
Victoria Cres N15 51 C4
Merton SW19 179 B3
West Norwood SE19 183 C4
Victoria Ct 3 E1 118 A6
5 SW4 159 D5
W3 110 C4
Penge SE26 184 C4
1 Wanstead E18 55 B6
Wembley HA9 66 C2
Victoria Dock Rd E16 121 B6
Victoria Dr SW19 156 D3
Victoria Emb
WC2 116 C6 251 A5
Victoria Gdns
W11 113 C5 245 A4
Heston TW5 129 A4
Victoria Gr N12 30 B5
W8 114 A3 256 A6
Victoria Gr Mews
W2 245 C5
Victoria Ho SW1 258 C2
6 SW4 159 D5
2 W12 112 A4
Edgware HA8 26 D4
Victoria Ind Est W3 89 C2
Victoria Jun Sch The
TW13 150 B3
Victoria La Barnet EN5 1 B1
Hayes UB3 105 B1
Victoria Lo 4 SW19 178 C3
Victoria Mans 8 N7 72 C3
NW10 68 B1
Victoria Mews NW6 91 C6
Wandsworth SW18 158 A3
Victorian Gr N16 73 C5
Victorian Rd N16 73 D5
Victoria Park Ct 11 E9 74 C1
Victoria Park Ind Ctr
E3 75 B1
Victoria Park Lofts E9 96 D6
Victoria Park Rd E9 74 D1
Victoria Park Sq E2 96 C4
Victoria Pas NW8 236 C6
Victoria Pl 16 TW10 153 D6
Victoria Point 10 E13 99 A5
Victoria Rd BR2 209 D4
BR7 188 C5
DA15 168 A1
E11 76 C4
E13 99 A5
N15 52 A5
N22 31 D2
N4 50 B1
NW10 89 C3
NW4 46 D5
NW6 91 B6
NW7 27 D5
W8 114 A3 256 A6
Barking IG11 78 D2
Barnet EN4 2 B1
Bexley DA6 147 C1
Buckhurst Hill IG9 21 D2
Chingford E17 36 A1
Chingford, Chingford Green
E4 20 C3
Dagenham RM10 81 D3
Ealing W5 87 B2
Edmonton N18 33 D6
Edmonton N9 17 D1
Feltham TW13 150 B3
Kingston KT1 176 B1
Mitcham CR4 180 D3
Mortlake SW14 133 B2
Ruislip HA4 62 B4
Southall UB2 107 B3
Surbiton KT6 197 D3
Sutton SM1 218 B3
Teddington TW11 175 A4
Twickenham TW1 153 B4
Wanstead E18 55 B6
Victoria Ret Pk HA4 62 D3
Victoria Rise SW4 137 B2
Victoria Sq SW1 258 D6
Victoria St E15 76 C1
SW1 115 C3 259 B5
Erith DA17 125 B1
Victoria Sta
SW1 115 B2 258 D4
Victoria Terr N4 50 C1
NW10 89 C3
Harrow HA1 42 C1
Victoria Villas TW9 132 B1
Victoria Way SE7 143 C6
Victoria Yd 31 E1 96 A1
Victor Mills Cotts
BR8 191 C3
Victor Rd NW10 90 B4
Harrow HA2 42 A6
Penge SE20 184 D3
Teddington TW11 174 C6
Victors Dr TW12 173 A4
Victor Seymour Inf Sch
SM5 218 D4
Victors Way EN5 1 B2
Victor Villas N9 17 B1
Victory Ave SM4 202 A4
Victory Bsns Ctr The
TW7 130 D1
Victory Ct IG11 102 B4
Victory Day Sch
SW11 137 A4 268 A1
Victory Pl 6 E14 119 A6
SE17 117 B2 262 C4
Victory Pl *continued*
West Norwood SE19 183 C4
Victory Prim Sch
SE17 117 A2 262 B4
Victory Rd
Merton SW19 180 A3
Wanstead E11 55 B5
Victory Road Mews 5
SW19 180 A3
Victory Way SE16 119 A4
Hounslow TW5 106 C1
Victory Wharf E14 119 A6
Victory Wlk SE8 141 C4
Video Ct N4 50 A2
Vidler Cl KT9 213 C2
Vienna Cl IG5 37 D1
View Cl N6 48 D2
Harrow HA1 42 B5
View Cres N8 49 D4
Viewfield Cl HA3 44 A2
Viewfield Rd DA5 168 C3
Wandsworth SW18 157 B5
Viewland Rd SE18 123 D1
View Point SE3 142 D2
View Rd N6 48 D3
Viewside Lo N6 49 C3
View The SE2 125 A1
Viga Rd N21 16 C5
Vigilant Cl SE26 184 A6
Vignoles Rd RM7 59 C2
Vigo St W1 115 C6 249 A5
Vi & John Rubens Ho
IG2 56 C3
Viking Cl 12 E3 97 A5
Viking Ct TW12 173 D2
Viking Fst & Mid Sch
UB5 84 D4
Viking Gdns E6 100 A3
Viking Ho 3 SE5 139 A3
3 SE7 122 A2
Viking Pl E10 53 B1
Viking Rd UB1 107 A6
Villacourt Rd SE18,
SE2 146 A6
Village Arc The 2 E4 20 B3
Village Cl NW3 70 B3
Chingford E4 36 A5
Village Ct E17 53 D4
SE3 142 C2
Village Gate TW17 192 D4
Village Home The IG6 57 A6
Village Hts IG8 36 D5
Village Inf Sch RM10 81 C1
Village Mount 18 NW3 70 A4
Village Park Cl EN1 17 C5
Village Rd N3 29 A1
Enfield EN1 17 C6
Village Row SM2 217 C1
Village Sch The NW3 70 D2
Village The SE7 143 D6
SW11 136 D2
Village Way NW10 67 B4
SE21 161 B5
Ashford TW15 170 C6
Beckenham BR3 207 C6
Pinner HA5 41 B2
Village Way E HA2 41 C2
Villa Rd SW9 138 C2
Villas Rd SE18 123 A2
Villa St SE17 117 B1 262 D1
Villiers Ave
Kingston KT5 198 B5
Twickenham TW2 151 B3
Villiers Cl E10 75 C6
Kingston KT5 198 B5
Villiers Ct N20 14 A4
SW11 267 B2
Villiers High Sch
UB1 107 B5
Villiers Ho W5 109 D6
Villiers Rd NW2 68 A2
Isleworth TW7 130 C3
Kingston KT1 198 B6
Penge BR3 184 D1
Southall UB1 107 B5
Villiers St WC2 250 B4
Vincam Cl TW2 151 C4
Vince Ct N1 235 D1
Vincent Ave KT5 215 A6
Vincent Cl BR2 209 B5
DA15 167 C3
Barnet EN5 1 D2
Harmondsworth UB7 126 C6
Vincent Ct N4 50 A1
NW4 46 D5
SW9 270 D1
W1 237 C2
Vincent Dr
Hillingdon UB10 82 B6
Upper Halliford TW17 193 C6
Vincent Gdns NW2 67 D5
Vincent Ho KT3 199 D5
Vincent Rd N15 51 A5
SE18 122 D2
W3 111 A3
Chingford E4 36 B4
Croydon CR0 205 C2
Dagenham RM9 81 A1
Hounslow TW4 128 D2
Hounslow TW7 130 B4
Kingston KT1 198 C6
Wembley HA0 66 B1
Wood Green N22 32 C1
Vincent Row TW12 174 A5
Vincents Cl SE16 119 A4
Vincents Path UB5 63 A2
Vincent Sq
SW1 115 D2 259 C4
Wood Green N22 32 C1
Vincent St E16 98 D2
SW1 115 D2 259 D4
Vincent Terr
N1 94 D5 234 D4
Vince St EC1 95 B4 235 D1
Vine Cl Surbiton KT5 198 B3
Sutton SM1 218 A5
West Drayton UB7 104 C2
Vine Cotts
3 Ealing W7 108 C5
Southall UB2 107 D2
Vine Ct E1 96 A2
Harrow HA3 44 A3
Vinegar St E1 118 B5
Vinegar Yd SE1 253 A2
Vine Gdns IG1 79 A3
Vine Gr UB10 60 C1
Vine Hill EC1 241 A5
Vine La SE1 117 C5 253 B3
Hillingdon UB10 82 B6
Uxbridge UB10 60 B1
Vine Lo N12 30 A4
Vine Pl Ealing W5 110 A5
Hounslow TW3 129 D1
Vine Rd BR6 227 D2
E15 76 D1
Barnes SW13 133 D2
East Molesey KT8 196 A5
Vineries Bank NW7 28 B5
Vineries Cl
Dagenham RM9 81 B2
Harmondsworth UB7 126 C6
Vineries The Enfield EN1 5 C2
Southgate N14 15 C5
Viners Cl KT12 194 C3
Vines Ave N3 29 D2
Vine Sq W14 254 D1
Vines Sch The SW11 137 A1
Vine St EC3 95 D1 243 C1
W1 249 B5
Vine St Bridge EC1 241 B5
Vinewood Ct E17 54 B4
Vineyard Ave NW7 29 A3
Vineyard Cl
Forest Hill SE6 163 C3
Kingston KT1 198 B6
Vineyard Gr N3 29 D2
Vineyard Hill Rd
SW19 179 C6
Vineyard Path SW14 133 B2
Vineyard Rd TW13 150 A1
Vineyard Row KT1,
KT8 175 C2
Vineyard Sch The
TW10 154 A5
Vineyards The TW13 150 A1
Vineyard The TW10 154 A6
Vineyard Wlk EC1 241 A6
Viney Ct 9 SW4 159 D5
Vine Yd SE1 252 B2
Viney Rd SE13 141 D2
Vining St SW2,SW9 138 C1
Vinlake Ave UB10 60 C5
Vinson Ho N1 235 D3
Vinter Ct TW17 192 C4
Vintners Ct EC4 252 B6
Vintry Mews 3 E17 53 C5
Viola Ave SE2 124 B1
Feltham TW14 150 C5
Stanwell TW19 148 A3
Viola Sq W12 111 D6
Violet Ave Enfield EN2 5 B5
Hillingdon UB8 82 B2
Violet Cl E16 98 C3
44 SE8 141 B6
Hackbridge SM6 203 A1
Violet Gdns CR0 220 D3

Violet Hill
NW8 ....92 A5 **229** A3
Violet Hill Ho NW8 ..**229** A3
Violet La CR0 ....220 D3
Violet Rd E17 ....53 C3
E3 ....97 D3
Woodford E18 ......37 B1
Violet St E2 ....96 B3
Violet Terr UB8 ....82 C2
Violette Szabo Ho **4**
SE27 ....183 B6
VIP Trad Est SE7 ....121 C2
Virgil Pl W1 ....**237** C3
Virgil St SE1 .116 B3 **260** D6
Virginia Cl KT3 .....199 A5
Virginia Ct **7** SE16 ..118 D4
Virginia Ho **3** E14 ..120 A4
Teddington TW11 ....175 A5
Virginia Prim Sch E2 .95 D4
Virginia Rd E2 **19** 95 D4
South Norwood CR7 ..182 D2
Virginia St E1 ....118 A6
Virginia Wlk SW2 ....160 B5
Viscount Cl N11 .....31 B5
Viscount Ct **9** W11 ..91 C1
Viscount Dr E6 .....100 B2
Viscount Gr **3** UB5 ..84 D4
Viscount Point **7**
SW19 ....179 C3
Viscount Rd TW19 ..148 A3
Viscount St EC1 ...**242** A4
Viscount Way TW6 ..127 C1
Vista Ave EN3 ....6 D3
Vista Dr IG4 ....55 C4
Vista The SE9 ....165 D4
Vista Way HA3 ......44 A3
Vita Et Pax Sch N14 ..15 B6
Vittoria Ho N1 .....**233** D5
Vittoria Prim Sch
N1 ....94 C5 **234** A4
Viveash Cl UB3 ....105 D3
Vivian Ave NW4 ......46 B4
Wembley HA9 ......66 C2
Vivian Ct N12 ....29 D5
Vivian Gdns HA9 .....66 C3
Vivian Ho N4 ....51 B2
Vivian Mans **1** NW4 ..46 B4
Vivian Rd E3 ....97 A5
Vivian Sq SE15 .....140 B2
Vivian Way N2 ....48 B4
Vivien Cl KT9 ....214 A1
Vivienne Cl TW1 ....153 D5
Voce Rd SE18 ....145 B5
Voewood Cl KT3 ....199 D3
Vogans Mill SE1 ...**253** D2
Vogler Ho **2** E1 ....118 C6
Vollasky Ho **5** E1 ...96 A2
Volta Cl N9 ....18 C1
Voltaire **2** SE5 ....139 D4
15 Richmond TW9 ..132 B4
Voltaire Ct **12** SW11 .137 A3
Voltaire Rd SW4 ....137 D2
Voltaire Way UB3 ...105 C6
Volt Ave NW10 ......89 C4
Volta Way CR0 .....204 B1
Voluntary Pl E11 .....55 A3
Vorley Rd N19 ....71 C6
Voss Ct SW16 ......182 A4
Voss St E2 ....96 A4
Voyager Bsns Est **10**
SE16 ....118 A3
Voyagers Cl IG11 ...102 C1
Voysey Cl N3 ....47 A6
Vulcan Cl E6 ....100 C1
Vulcan Gate EN2 ......4 C3
Vulcan Rd SE4 .....141 B3
Vulcan Sq E14 .....119 C2
Vulcan Terr SE4 ....141 B3
Vulcan Way N7 ....72 C5
Vyner Ct E5 ....74 A6
Vyner Rd W3 ....111 B6
Vyners Sch UB10 ....60 B4
Vyner St E2 ....96 B6
Vyners Way UB10 ....60 B4
Vyne The DA7 ......147 D2
Vyvyan Ho SE18 ....144 C4

W

Wadbrook St KT1 ...175 D1
Wadding St
SE17 ....117 B2 **262** C3
Waddington Cl EN1 ...5 C1
Waddington Rd E15 ..76 B2
Waddington St E15 ..76 B2
Waddington Way
SE19 ....183 B2

Waddon Cl CR0 .....**220** C5
Waddon Court Rd
CR0 ....220 C5
Waddon Inf Sch CR9 220 C5
Waddon Marsh Sta
CR0 ....220 C6
Waddon Marsh Way
CR0 ....204 B1
Waddon New Rd
CR0 ....220 D6
Waddon Park Ave
CR0 ....220 C5
Waddon Rd CR0 ....220 D5
Waddon Sta CR0 ...220 C4
Waddon Way CR0,
CR2,CR9 ....220 D2
Wade Ct N10 ....31 B3
Wembley HA0 .....65 D5
Wade Ho **13** SE1 ...118 A4
1 Enfield EN1 .....17 C6
Wade's Gr N21 ......16 A4
Wade's Hill N21 .....16 C4
Wade's La TW11 ....175 A5
Wade's Pl E14 ......119 D6
Wadeson St E2 ......96 B5
Wadeville Ave RM6 ..59 B2
Wadeville Cl DA17 ..125 C1
Wadham Ave E17 ....35 D3
Wadham Cl TW17 ...193 A2
Wadham Gdns
NW3 ....70 C1 **230** A6
Wadham Rd
Chingford, Highams Park
E17 ....35 D2
Putney SW15 .....135 A1
Wadhurst Cl SE20 ..184 B1
Wadhurst Ct E6 ....100 B1
Wadhurst Rd W4 ...111 B3
Wadley Rd E11 ......54 C2
Wadsworth Bsns Ctr
UB6 ....87 C5
Wadsworth Cl
Enfield EN3 ....18 D6
Wembley UB6 .....87 C5
Wadsworth Rd UB6 ..87 C5
Wager St E3 ....97 B3
Waggoners Rdbt
TW5 ....128 B4
Waggon Mews N14 ..15 C3
Waghorn Rd E13 ....99 C6
Harrow HA3 ......43 D6
Waghorn St SE15 ..140 A2
Wagner St SE15 ...140 C4
Wagon Rd EN4,EN5 ...1 D6
Wagstaff Gdns RM9 ..80 C1
Wagtail Cl NW9 .....27 C1
Wagtail Wlk BR3 ...208 A4
Waights Ct KT2 ....176 A2
Wainford Cl SW19 ..156 D3
Wainwright Gr TW7 .130 B1
Wainwright Ho **3** E1 118 C4
Waite Davies Rd
SE12 ....164 D4
Waitelands Rd KT3 .199 B6
Waite St SE15 .....139 D6
Waithman St EC4 ..**241** C1
Wakefield Gdns
Redbridge IG1 .....56 A3
South Norwood SE19 ..183 C3
Wakefield Ho
6 SE15 ....140 A4
Dulwich SE22 ....162 B3
Wakefield Mews
WC1 ....**233** B1
Wakefield Rd N11 ...31 D5
N15 ....51 A4
19 Richmond TW10 ..153 D6
Wakefield St E6 ....100 A6
WC1 ....94 A4 **233** B1
Edmonton N18 ....34 A5
Wakeford Cl SW4 ..159 C6
Wakehams Hill HA5 .41 B6
Wakeham St **9** N1 ..73 B1
Wakehurst Rd SW11 158 D6
Wakeling Ho **8** SE27 160 D1
Wakeling Rd W7 .....86 D2
Wakeling St **13** E14 ..97 A1
Wakelin Ho **19** N1 ...72 D1
Forest Hill SE23 ....163 A4
Wakelin Rd E15 .....98 C5
Wakeman Ho HA8 ..26 A6
Wakeman Rd NW10 ..90 D4
Wakemans Hill Ave
NW9 ....45 B4
Wakering Rd IG11 ...79 A1
Wakerings The IG11 ..79 A1
Wakerly Cl **6** E6 ...100 B1
Wakley St EC1 .94 D4 **234** C2
Walberswick St SW8 .**270** B3

Walbrook EC4 ......**252** C6
9 Wanstead E18 .....55 A6
Walbrook Ct **32** N1 ..95 C5
Walburgh St E1 ......96 B1
Walcorde Ave SE17 .**262** B3
Walcot Cl BR7 ......222 A6
Walcot Gdns SE11 ..**261** A4
Walcot Ho **9** SE22 .139 C2
Walcot Rd EN3 ....7 B3
Walcot Sq
SE11 ....116 C2 **261** B4
Walcott St SW1 ....**259** B4
Waldair Ct E16 .....122 D4
Waldeck Gr SE27 ...160 D1
Waldeck Rd N15 .....50 D6
Brentford W4 .....132 C4
Ealing W13 ....87 B1
Mortlake SW14 ...133 A2
Waldeck Terr SW14 .133 A2
Waldegrave Ct
11 Barking IG11 ...101 B6
1 Teddington TW11 ..174 D5
Waldegrave Gdns
TW1 ....152 D1
Waldegrave Ho **5**
SW15 ....156 C6
Waldegrave Pk TW1 .174 D6
Waldegrave Rd BR1 .210 B5
N8 ....50 C6
Dagenham RM8 ....80 C6
Ealing W5 ....110 B6
Penge SE19 ......183 D2
Teddington TW11 ..174 D6
Waldegrave Sch TW2 152 B1
Waldegrove CR0 ...221 D5
Waldemar Ave
Ealing W13 ....109 C5
Fulham SW6 ......135 A3
Waldemar Avenue Mans
SW6 ....**264** A1
Waldemar Rd SW19 .179 C5
Walden Ave BR7 ....188 B6
Edmonton N13 ....33 A6
Walden Cl DA17 ....125 B1
Walden Ct SW8 ....**269** D2
Walden Gdns CR7,
SW16 ....204 B5
Walden Ho SW1 ...**258** B3
8 SW11 ....137 A3
Barnet EN4 ....2 C1
Walden Rd BR7 ....188 B4
Tottenham N17 ....33 B2
Waldenshaw Rd
SE23 ....162 C3
Walden St E1 ....96 B1
Walden Way NW7 ...28 D4
Waldo Cl SW4 ......159 C6
Waldo Ind Est BR1 .209 D6
Waldo Pl SW19 .....180 C3
Waldo Rd BR1 .....209 D6
NW10 ....90 B4
Waldorf Cl CR2 ....220 D1
Waldram Cres SE23 .162 C3
Waldram Park Rd
SE23 ....162 D3
Waldram Pl **6** SE23 .162 C3
Waldrist Way DA18 .125 B4
Waldron Gdns BR2 .208 B6
Waldron Ho **17** SW2 .160 B6
Waldronhyrst CR0,
CR2 ....220 D4
Waldron Mews SW3 .**266** D6
Waldron Rd
Harrow HA1,HA2 ...42 C1
Wandsworth SW18 ..158 A1
Waldrons The CR0 ..221 A4
Waldron's Yd HA2 ...64 B6
Waldstock Rd SE28 .124 A4
Waleran Cl HA7 .....24 C1
Walerand Rd SE13 ..142 A3
Waleran Flats SE1 ..**263** A4
Wales Ave SM5 .....218 C4
Wales Cl SE15 .....140 B6
Wales Farm Rd W3 ..89 B2
Waleton Acres SM6 .219 C2
Waley St **1** E1 .....97 A2
Walfield Ave N20 .....13 D4

Walkden Hall (Hall of
Residence) KT2 ....177 B6
Walkden Rd BR7 ...188 C5
Walker Cl N11 ....31 C6
SE18 ....123 A2
Ealing W7 ....108 C5
East Bedfont TW14 .149 C4
Hampton TW12 ...173 B4
Walker Ho NW1 ....**232** C3
Walker Mews SW2 .160 C6
Walker Prim Sch N14 .15 D2
Walkerscroft Mead
SE21 ....161 A3
Walker's Ct W1 ....**249** C6
Walkers Lo **7** E14 .120 A4
Walker's Pl SW15 ..135 A1
Walkinshaw Ct **14** N1 .73 A1
Walks The N2 ....48 B6
Walk The
Ashford TW16 .....171 D3
Palmers Green N13 .16 C1
Walkynscroft **1**
SE15 ....140 B3
Wallace Cl SE28 ...124 D6
Upper Halliford TW17 .193 B5
Uxbridge UB10 .....82 A5
Wallace Collection★
W1 ....**238** A2
Wallace Cres SM5 ..218 D3
Wallace Ho N7 ......72 B2
Wallace Rd N1,N5 ...73 A2
Wallasey Cres UB10 ..60 C5
Wallbrook Bsns Ctr
TW4 ....128 B2
Wallbrook Ho N9 ...18 C2
Wallbutton Rd SE4 ..141 A3
Wallcote Ave NW2 ..46 D1
Wall Ct N4 ....50 B1
Walled Garden Cl
BR3 ....207 D5
Walled Gdn The
TW16 ....194 B6
Wall End Ct E6 .....100 C4
Wall End Rd E6 ....78 C1
Waller Dr HA6 ......22 A2
Waller Rd SE14 .....140 D3
Wallers Cl RM9 ....103 B6
Wallett Ct **9** NW1 ...71 C1
Wallflower St W12 ..111 D6
Wallgrave Rd SW5 ..**255** C3
Wallingford Ave W10 .90 D1
Wallington Cl HA4 ...39 A3
Wallington Ct **10**
SM6 ....219 B2
Wallington Cty Gram Sch
SM6 ....219 B5
Wallington Green
SM6 ....219 B4
Wallington Rd IG3 ...57 D2
Wallington Sq **4**
SM6 ....219 C2
Wallington Sta SM6 .219 B2
Wallis Alley SE1 ...**252** B5
Wallis Cl SW11 ....136 B3
Wallis Rd E9 ....75 C2
Southall UB1 ......85 D1
Wallorton Gdns
SW14 ....133 B1
Wallside EC2 ......**242** B3
Wall St N1 ....73 B2
Wallwood Rd E11 ...54 B2
Wallwood St E14 ...97 B5
Walmar Cl EN4 ......2 B4
Walmer Cl BR6 ....227 B4
Chingford E4 ......19 D2
Walmer Gdns W13 .109 A4
Walmer Ho **8** W10 ..90 D1
11 Penge SE20 .....184 C3
Walmer Pl W1 .....**237** C4
Walmer Rd W10 ....90 C1
W11 ......113 A6 **244** A5
Walmer St NW1 ....**237** C4
Walmer Terr SE18 ..123 B2
Walmgate Rd UB6 ..87 B6
Walmington Fold N12 29 C4
Walm La NW2 ....68 C2
Walmsley Ho **1**
SW16 ....181 C6
Walnut Ave UB7 ...104 C3
Walnut Cl SE8 .....141 B6
Hayes UB3 ....105 C4
Ilford IG6 ....57 A5
Wallington SM5 ...218 C4
Walnut Ct **2** E17 ..54 A5
Walnut Gdns E15 ...76 C3
Walnut Gr EN1 .....17 B6
Walnut Mews SM2 .218 A1
Walnut Rd E10 .....75 D6
Walnut Tree Ave CR4 202 C6

Walnut Tree Cl
Barnes SW13 .....133 D4
Chislehurst BR7 ...189 A2
Walnut Tree Cotts
SW19 ....179 A5
Walnut Tree Ho
SW10 ....**265** D6
Walnut Tree Rd SE10 .120 C1
Brentford TW8 ....132 A6
Charlton TW17 ...171 A1
Dagenham RM8 ....81 A4
Heston TW5 ......129 B6
Walnut Tree Walk Prim
Sch SE11 ...116 C2 **261** A4
Walnut Tree Wlk
SE11 ....116 C2 **261** A4
Walnut Way
Buckhurst Hill IG9 ..21 D1
Ruislip HA4 ....62 C2
Walpole Ave TW9 ..132 C6
Walpole Cl W13 ...109 C4
Pinner HA5 ....23 C4
Walpole Cres **7**
TW11 ....174 D5
Walpole Ct NW6 ...70 A1
7 W14 ....112 D3
Ealing W5 ....109 D5
Twickenham TW2 ..152 C2
Walpole Gdns W4 ...111 A1
Twickenham TW2 ..152 C1
Walpole Lo **3** W13 .109 C5
Walpole Mews NW8 .**229** C6
Walpole Pl **3** SE18 .122 D2
6 Teddington TW11 ..174 D5
Walpole Rd BR2 ...209 D4
E17 ....53 A5
E6 ....77 C1
N17 ....51 A6
Mitcham SW19 ...180 B4
South Croydon CR0 .221 B6
Surbiton KT6 .....198 A3
Teddington TW11 ..174 D5
Tottenham N17 ...33 A1
Twickenham TW2 ..152 C2
Woodford E18 .....36 D2
Walpole St
SW3 ....114 D1 **257** D2
Walrond Ave HA9 ...66 A3
Walsham Cl N16 ....52 A1
SE28 ....124 D6
Walsham Ho SE14 ..140 D3
SE17 ....**262** C2
Walsham Rd SE14 ..140 D3
Feltham TW14 ....150 B4
Walsingham NW8 ..**229** D6
Walsingham Gdns
KT19 ....215 D3
Walsingham Ho E4 ..20 B4
Walsingham Lo
SW13 ....134 A4
Walsingham Mans
SW6 ....**265** D4
Walsingham Pk BR7 .189 B1
Walsingham Pl SW4,
SW11 ....159 A5
Walsingham Rd BR5 .190 B2
E5 ....74 A5
Ealing W13 ....109 A5
Enfield EN2 ....17 B6
Mitcham CR4 .....202 D4
Walsingham Wlk
DA17 ....147 C6
Walter Besant Ho **20**
E1 ....96 D6
Walter Ct **3** W3 ...89 A1
Walter Green Ho
SE15 ....140 C4
Walter Ho SW10 ..**266** C4
Walter Hurford Par **4**
E12 ....78 C4
Walter Northcott Ho **2**
NW6 ....69 C3
Walter Savill Twr E17 .53 C3
Walters Cl SE17 ...**262** B3
Hayes UB3 ....105 C4
Walters Ho N1 .....**234** D5
10 SE17 ....138 D6
3 SE5 ....139 C3
Walters Rd EN3 ......6 C1
Walter's Rd SE25 ..205 C5
Walter St E2 ....96 D4
2 Kingston KT2 ...176 A2
Walters Way SE23 ..162 D5
Walters Yd BR1 ...187 A1
Walter Terr E1 ......96 D1
Walter Wlk HA8 ....27 A4
Waltham Ave NW9 ..44 C3
Hayes UB3 ....105 A4
Waltham Ct E17 ....36 A3

Waltham Dr HA8 .....44 C6
Waltham Forest Coll
E17 ....35 D1
Waltham Gdns EN3 ..6 C6
Waltham Green Ct
SW6 ....**265** C3
Waltham Ho NW8 ..**229** A6
10 SW9 ....138 C3
Waltham Park Way
E17 ....35 C2
Waltham Pk E17 ....35 C2
Waltham Rd
Carshalton SM5 ..202 A4
Southall UB2 .....107 A4
Walthamstow Ave E4 .35 A4
Walthamstow Ave (North
Circular Rd) E4 ....35 B4
Walthamstow Bsns Ctr
E17 ....36 A1
Walthamstow Central Sta
E17 ....53 C4
Walthamstow Queens
Road Sta E17 .....53 C4
Walthamstow Sch for Girls
E17 ....53 C4
Waltham Way E4 ....19 C2
Waltheof Ave N17 ...33 B2
Waltheof Gdns N17 .33 B2
Walton Ave
Cheam SM3 ....217 B5
Harrow HA2 ......63 B4
New Malden KT3 ..199 C5
Wembley HA9 ....66 C2
Walton Bridge Rd
KT12,TW17 ......193 C2
Walton Cl E5 ....74 C5
NW2 ....68 B6
SW8 ....138 A5 **270** B4
Harrow HA1 ......42 A5
Walton Croft HA1 ...64 C4
Walton Ct EN5 ......14 C4
Walton Dr NW10 ....67 B2
Harrow HA1 ......42 A5
Walton Gdns Acton W3 .88 B2
Feltham TW13 ....171 A1
Wembley HA9 ....66 A4
Walton Gn CR0 ....224 A5
Walton Ho **10** E17 ..53 D6
E2 ....**243** D2
N7 ....72 B5
SW18 ....157 C5
1 Edmonton N9 ....34 A6
Kingston KT2 .....176 A3
Walton La
Oatlands Park KT13,
TW17 ....193 B1
Shepperton TW17 .193 B2
Walton Pl SW3 ....**257** C6
Walton Rd E13 .....99 C5
N15 ....51 D5
East Molesey KT8,KT12 195 C5
Harrow HA1 ......42 B5
Little Ilford E12 ....78 C4
Sidcup DA14 .....168 C1
Walton-on-T KT12&KT8 194 D1
Walton St
SW3 ....114 C3 **257** B6
Enfield EN2 ....5 A4
Walton Way Acton W3 ..88 D2
Mitcham CR4 .....203 D3
Walt Whitman Cl **6**
SE24 ....138 C4
Walworth Pl
SE17 ....117 A1 **262** B1
Walworth Rd
SE17 ....117 A1 **262** B2
Walworth Sch
SE17 ....117 C1 **263** B1
Walwyn Ave BR1 ...209 D6
Wanborough Dr
SW15 ....156 B3
Wanderer Dr IG11 ..102 C1
Wandle Bank
Mitcham SW19 ...180 D3
Wallington CR0 ...220 B5
Wandle Court Gdns
CR0 ....220 A5
Wandle Ct **4** W12 ..111 C4
Wallington CR0 ...220 A5
West Ewell KT19 ..215 A4
Wandle Ho NW8 ...**237** A4
6 Catford BR1 ....186 B5
Wandsworth SW18 ..157 D4
Wandle Lo CR0 ....220 A5
Wandle Pk Sta CR0 .220 D4
Wandle Prim Sch
SW18 ....157 D3
Wandle Rd
Croydon CR0 .....221 D4
Hackbridge SM6 ..219 B6

Wandle Rd *continued*
Morden SM4 .....202 B4
Upper Tooting SW17 ...158 C2
Wallington CR0 .....220 A5
Wandle Side
Hackbridge SM6 .....219 B5
Wallington CR0 .....220 B5
Wandle Tech Pk CR4 202 D2
Wandle Trad Est CR4 202 D2
Wandle Valley Sch
SM5 .....202 C2
Wandle Way
Mitcham CR4 .....202 D4
Wandsworth SW18 ...157 D3
Wandon Rd
SW6 .....135 D5 265 D3
Wandsworth Bridge Rd
SW6 .....135 D2 265 C1
Wandsworth Common Sta
SW12 .....158 D4
Wandsworth Common
West Side SW18 ....158 A6
Wandsworth Gyratory
SW18 .....157 D6
Wandsworth High St
SW18 .....157 D6
Wandsworth Plain
SW18 .....157 D6
Wandsworth Rd
SW8 .....138 A5 270 A3
Wandsworth Road Sta
SW4 .....137 C3
Wandsworth Town Sta
SW18 .....135 D1
Wangey Rd RM6 .....58 D2
Wangford Ho 13
SW9 .....138 D1
Wanless Rd SE24 ....139 A2
Wanley Rd SE5 .....139 B1
Wanlip Rd E13 .....99 B3
Wansbeck Ct EN2 .....4 D2
Wansbeck Rd E3,E9 ..75 B1
Wansdown Pl
SW6 .....135 D5 265 C4
Wansey St
SE17 .....117 A2 262 B3
Wansford Rd IG8 .....37 C2
Wanstead Church Sch
E11 .....55 A4
Wanstead Cl BR1 ....187 C1
Wanstead High Sch
E11 .....55 C3
Wanstead Hospl E11 ...55 B5
Wanstead La IG1 .....56 A3
Wanstead Park Ave
E12 .....77 D6
Wanstead Park Rd
IG1 .....56 A1
Wanstead Park Sta E7 77 B4
Wanstead Pl E11 .....55 A4
Wanstead Rd BR1 ...187 C1
Wanstead Sta E11 ....55 B3
Wantage Rd SE12 ....164 D6
Wantz Rd RM10 .....81 D3
Wapping Dock St 19
E1 .....118 B5
Wapping High St E1 .118 B5
Wapping La E1 .....118 B5
Wapping Sta E1 .....118 C5
Wapping Wall E1 ....118 C5
Warbank La KT2 .....177 D3
Warbeck Rd W12 ....112 B4
Warberry Rd N22 .....32 B1
Warboys App KT2 ...176 D4
Warboys Cres E4 .....36 A5
Warboys Rd KT2 .....176 D4
Warburton Cl 6 N1 ...73 C2
Stanmore HA3 .....24 B4
Warburton Ct SE15 ..140 A2
Ruislip HA4 .....62 A6
Warburton Ho 5 E8 ..96 B6
Warburton Rd 8 E8 ..96 B6
Twickenham TW2 .....151 D3
Warburton St 6 E8 ...96 B6
Warburton Terr E17 ...35 D1
Wardalls Ho 12 SE8 ..141 B6
Ward Cl CR2 .....221 C3
Ward Cotts TW19 ....148 B4
Wardell Cl NW7 .....27 C3
Wardell Ct N2 .....48 B6
Wardell Ho 6 SE10 ..142 A6
Warden Ave HA2 .....41 B1
Warden Rd NW5 .....71 A2
Wardens Field Cl 2
BR6 .....227 D2
Wardens Gr SE1 ....252 A3
Wardle St E9 .....74 D3
Wardley Lo E11 .....54 D3
Wardley St SW18 ...157 D4
Wardlow 8 NW5 .....71 B4
Wardo Ave
SW6 .....135 A4 264 A2
Wardour Mews W1 ..239 B1
Wardour St
W1 .....93 D1 239 C1
Ward Point SE11 ....261 A3
Ward Rd E15 .....98 B6
N19 .....71 C5
Wardrobe Pl EC4 ....241 D1
Wardrobe Terr EC4 ..251 D6
Wardrobe The 3
TW9 .....153 D6
Wards Rd IG2 .....57 B2
Ware Ct Cheam SM1 ..217 B4
Edgware HA8 .....26 A6
Wareham Cl TW3 ....129 D1
Wareham Ct 2 N1 ...73 C1
Wareham Ho SW8 ...270 C4
Waremead Rd IG2 ....56 D4
Ware Point Dr SE28 ..123 B4
Warfield Rd NW10 ....90 D4
East Bedfont TW14 ....149 C4
Hampton TW12 .....173 D2
Warfield Yd 6 NW10 .90 D4
Wargrave Ave N15 ....51 D3
Wargrave Ho 46 E2 ...95 D4
Wargrave Rd HA2 .....64 A5
Warham Rd N4 .....50 D4
Croydon CR2 .....221 A3
Harrow HA3 .....24 D1
Warham St SE5 .....138 D5
Waring Cl BR6 .....227 D2
Waring Dr BR6 .....227 D2
Waring Ho 10 E2 .....96 A4
Waring Rd DA14 ....190 C4
Waring St SE27 .....183 A6
Warkworth Gdns
TW7 .....131 A5
Warkworth Rd N17 ...33 B3
Warland Rd SE18 ...145 C5
Warley Ave
Dagenham RM8 .....59 B2
Hayes UB4 .....84 A1
Warley Cl E10 .....53 B1
Warley Ho N1 .....73 B2
Warley Rd N9 .....18 C2
Hayes UB4 .....84 A2
Woodford IG8 .....37 B3
Warley St E2 .....96 D4
Warlingham Rd CR7 .204 D5
Warlock Rd W9 .....91 C3
Warlow Cl EN3 .....7 C6
Warlters Cl N7 .....72 A4
Warlters Rd N7 .....72 A4
Warltersville Mans
N19 .....50 A2
Warltersville Rd N4,N8,
N19 .....50 A2
War Memorial Homes
W4 .....133 B5
Warming Cl E5 .....74 D5
Warmington Rd SE24 161 A5
Warmington St 3 E13 99 A3
Warminster Gdns
SE25 .....184 A1
Warminster Rd SE25 .184 A1
Warminster Sq SE25 .184 A1
Warminster Way CR4 181 B1
Warmsworth NW1 ...232 A6
Warncliffe Ho 3
SW15 .....156 C6
Warndon St SE16 ....118 C2
Warneford Rd HA3 ....44 A6
Warneford St E9 .....96 B6
Warne Pl 4 DA15 ...168 B5
Warner Ave SM3 ....217 A6
Warner Cl E15 .....76 C3
NW9 .....46 A2
Hampton TW12 .....173 B5
Harlington UB3 .....127 B5
Warner Ct SM3 .....217 A6
Warner Ho 4 E9 .....74 D2
NW8 .....229 A2
SE13 .....141 D3
1 Beckenham BR3 ...185 D4
Warner Pl E2 .....96 A4
Warner Rd E17 .....53 A5
N8 .....49 D5
SE5 .....139 A4
Bromley BR1 .....186 D3
Warners Cl IG8 .....37 A5
Warner St EC1 94 C3 241 A5
Warner Yd EC1 .....241 A5
Warnford Ho SW15 ..155 C5
Warnford Ind Est
UB3 .....105 C4
Warnford Rd BR6 ...227 D3
Warnham WC1 .....233 C1
Warnham Court Rd
SM5 .....218 D1
Warnham Ho 6 SW2 160 B4
Warnham Rd N12 .....30 C5
Warple Mews W3 ...111 C4
Warple Way W3,W12 .111 C4
Warren Ave E11 .....76 B5
Bromley BR1 .....186 C3
Mortlake SW14,TW10 .132 D1
Orpington BR6 .....227 D3
South Croydon CR2 ...222 D1
Warren Cl DA6 .....169 C6
N9 .....18 D4
Hayes UB4 .....84 C2
Wembley HA9 .....65 D6
West Norwood SE21 ..161 A4
Esher KT10 .....212 A4
Warren Comp Sch
RM6 .....59 B4
Warren Cres N9 .....17 D4
Warren Ct N1 .....234 A4
N17 .....52 A6
17 Beckenham BR3 ...185 C3
6 Croydon CR0 .....205 C1
6 Ealing W5 .....87 C2
Warren Cutting KT2 .177 B3
Warrender Prim Sch
HA4 .....39 D2
Warrender Rd N19 ....71 C4
Warrender Way HA4 ..40 A2
Warren Dr
Greenford UB6 .....86 A3
Ruislip HA4 .....40 D2
Warren Dr N KT5,KT6 198 D1
Warren Dr S KT5 ....199 A1
Warren Dr The E11 ...55 C2
Warren Fields HA7 ....25 C6
Warren Gdns E15 .....76 B3
Warren Hill IG10 .....21 C6
Warren Ho 21 E3 .....97 D4
Warren Jun Sch RM6 .59 B4
Warren La SE18 .....122 D3
Stanmore HA7 .....9 A2
Warren Mews W1 ..239 A5
Warren Park Rd SM1,
SM2 .....218 C2
Warren Pk KT2 .....177 A4
Warren Pond Rd E4 ..20 D4
Warren Rd BR2 .....225 A6
DA6 .....169 C6
E10 .....76 A5
NW2 .....67 D6
Ashford TW15 .....171 C3
Bushey WD23 .....8 B3
Chingford E4 .....20 A2
Croydon CR0 .....205 D1
Ickenham UB10 .....60 B4
Ilford IG6 .....57 B4
Isleworth TW2 .....152 B5
Kingston KT2 .....177 A4
Mitcham SW19 .....180 C4
Sidcup DA14 .....168 C1
Wanstead E11 .....55 C2
Warren Rise KT3 ....177 B2
Warren Road Prim Sch
BR6 .....227 D4
Warrens Shawe La
HA8 .....10 D2
Warren St W1 .93 C3 239 A5
Warren Street Sta
NW1 .....93 C3 239 B6
Warren Terr RM6 .....58 D5
Warren The E12 .....78 A4
Hayes UB4 .....84 A1
Heston TW5 .....129 B5
Worcester Park KT19 .215 B5
Warren Way NW7 .....29 A4
Warren Wlk 1 SE7 ..143 C6
Warren Wood Cl BR2 225 A6
Warriner Dr N9 .....18 A1
Warriner Gdns
SW11 .....137 A4 268 A1
Warrington Cres
W9 .....92 A3 236 A6
Warrington Gdns W9 236 A5
Warrington Pl E14 ...120 A5
Warrington Rd
Croydon CR0 .....220 D5
Dagenham RM8 .....81 A6
Harrow HA1 .....42 C4
21 Richmond TW10 ...153 D6
Warrington Sq RM8 ..80 D6
Warrior Sq E12 .....78 C4
Warsaw Cl HA4 .....62 B2
Warspite Ho 3 E14 ..119 D2
Warspite Rd SE18 ...122 A3
Warton Rd E15 .....98 A6
Warwall E6 .....100 D1
Warwick W14 113 B2 254 D3
Warwick Ave HA8 .....11 A1
W9 .....92 A3 236 A5
Harrow HA2 .....63 B4
Warwick Avenue Sta
W9 .....92 A3 236 A5
Warwick Chambers
W8 .....255 A6
Warwick Cl DA5 .....169 B4
Bushey WD23 .....8 C4
Hampton TW12 .....174 A3
New Barnet EN4 .....14 B6
Warwick Cres
W2 .....92 A2 236 A4
Hayes UB4 .....83 D3
Warwick Ct 3 E5 .....74 B6
N11 .....31 D4
5 N2 .....48 A6
NW2 .....69 A3
WC1 .....240 D3
1 Beckenham BR2 ...186 C1
Ealing W7 .....86 D1
Harrow HA1 .....42 C6
Merton SW19 .....179 C2
Northolt UB5 .....63 C3
Surbiton KT6 .....214 A6
Warwick Dene W5 ...110 A5
Warwick Dr SW15 ...134 B2
Warwick Gdns N4 ....51 A4
W14 .....113 B2 254 D4
Ilford IG1 .....56 D1
Thames Ditton KT7 ....196 D4
Thornton Heath CR7 ..204 C5
Warwick Gr E5 .....52 B1
Surbiton KT5 .....198 B2
Warwick Ho 10 E5 ....74 C6
N4 .....51 A1
11 SW9 .....138 C3
9 Acton W3 .....88 C1
6 Kingston KT2 .....176 A2
6 Putney SW15 .....156 C4
Warwick House St
SW1 .....249 D4
Warwick La
EC4 .....94 D1 241 D1
Warwick Lo
Cheam SM1 .....217 B4
Twickenham TW2 .....151 D1
Warwick Mans SW5 .255 A4
Warwick Park Sch
SE15 .....139 D4
Warwick Pas EC4 ...241 D2
Warwick Pl W5 .....109 D4
W9 .....92 A2 236 A4
Warwick Pl N SW1 ..259 A3
Warwick Rd DA14 ...190 B5
E12 .....78 A3
E15 .....76 D2
E17 .....35 B1
N11 .....31 D4
W14,SW5 ....113 B2 254 D4
Ashford TW15 .....170 A5
Barnet EN5 .....1 D1
Bexley DA16 .....146 C2
Chingford E4 .....35 C5
Ealing W5 .....110 A5
Edmonton N18 .....33 D6
Enfield EN3 .....7 B6
Hounslow TW4 .....128 B2
Kingston KT3 .....199 A6
Penge SE20 .....206 B6
Southall UB2 .....107 B3
Sutton SM1 .....218 A3
Teddington KT1 .....175 C2
Thames Ditton KT7 ....196 D4
Thornton Heath CR7 ..204 C6
Twickenham TW2 .....152 C3
Wanstead E11 .....55 B4
Yiewsley UB7 .....104 A5
Warwick Row
SW1 .....115 B3 258 D6
Warwick Sch for Boys
E17 .....54 A5
Warwickshire Path
SE8 .....141 B5
Warwickshire Rd N16 .73 C4
Warwick Sq EC4 ....241 D2
SW1 .....115 C1 259 A2
Warwick Sq Mews
SW1 .....259 A3
Warwick St
W1 .....115 C6 249 B6
Warwick Terr E17 ....54 B4
SE18 .....145 B6
Warwick Way
SW1 .....115 B2 258 D2
Warwick Yd EC1 ....242 B5
Wasdale NW1 .....231 D1
Washbrook Ho SW2 .160 C5
Washington Ave E12 ..78 B4
Washington Cl 45 E3 .97 D4
Washington Ct SW17 180 D4
Washington Ho E17 ...35 B1
SW1 .....247 C1
Washington Rd E6 ....77 C1
Barnes SW13 .....134 A5
Kingston KT1 .....176 C1
North Cheam KT4 .....200 B1
2 Woodford E18 .....36 D1
Wastdale Rd SE23 ...162 D3
Watchfield Ct 7 W4 111 A1
Watcombe Cotts
TW9 .....132 C6
Watcombe Rd SE25 ..206 B4
Waterbank Rd SE6 ..186 A6
Waterbeach Rd RM9 ..80 C2
Water Brook La NW4 .46 C4
Watercress Pl N1 ....73 C1
Waterdale Rd SE2 ...146 A6
Waterden Cres E9 ....75 C3
Waterden Rd E15 .....75 C2
Waterer Ho 7 SE6 ..186 A6
Waterer Rise SM6 ...219 D2
Waterfall Cl N14 .....15 C1
Waterfall Cotts SW19 180 B4
Waterfall Rd N11,N14 .15 C1
Mitcham SW19 .....180 B4
Waterfall Terr SW17 .180 C4
Waterfield Cl
Belvedere DA17 .....125 C3
Woolwich SE28 .....124 B5
Waterfield Gdns
SE25 .....205 C4
Waterford Rd
SW6 .....135 D5 265 C3
Watergardens The
KT2 .....177 A4
Watergate EC4 .....251 C6
Watergate Ho 5
SE18 .....122 C2
Watergate Sch SE13 .141 D1
Watergate St SE8 ...141 C6
Watergate Wlk WC2 .250 B4
Water Gdns HA7 .....25 B4
Water Gdns The
W2 .....92 C1 237 B2
Waterglade Ctr The
W5 .....109 D6
Waterhall Ave E4 .....36 C6
Waterhall Cl E17 .....34 D2
Waterhead NW1 .....232 A2
Waterhedge Mews
EN1 .....17 D6
Waterhouse Cl E16 ...99 D2
NW3 .....70 B3
W6 .....112 D1
Waterhouse Ct 5
TW11 .....174 D5
Wateridge Cl E14 ...119 C3
Wateringbury Cl BR5 190 B1
Water La E15 .....76 C2
SE14 .....140 C5
Edmonton N9 .....18 B4
Ilford IG3 .....79 D5
Richmond TW10,TW9 .153 D6
Sidcup DA14 .....169 B2
Teddington KT1 .....175 D2
Twickenham TW1 .....153 A3
Water Lily Cl UB2 ..108 A4
Waterloo Bridge
SE1,WC2 ....116 B6 250 D5
Waterloo Cl E9 .....74 C3
East Bedfont TW14 ....149 D3
Waterloo East Sta
SE1 .....116 C5 251 B3
Waterloo Gdns E2 ....96 C5
Waterloo Int Sta
SE1 .....116 B4 250 D2
Waterloo Pier SE1 ..250 C2
Waterloo Pl
SW1 .....115 D5 249 C4
Waterloo Rd E10 .....53 C2
E6 .....77 C1
E7 .....76 D3
NW2 .....68 A6
SE1 .....116 C4 251 B2
Sutton SM1 .....218 B3
Waterloo Sta
SE1 .....116 C4 251 A2
Waterloo Terr N1 ....72 D1
Waterlow Ct NW11 ...47 D2
Waterlow Rd N19 .....49 C1
Waterman Bldg 4
E14 .....119 C4
Watermans Mews 1
W5 .....110 A6
Waterman St SW15 ..134 D2
Waterman Way E1 ..118 B5
Watermead TW14 ...149 C3
Watermead Ho E9 ...75 B3
Watermead La CR4 ..202 D2
Watermeadow La
SW6 .....136 A3
Watermead Rd SE6 ..186 A6
Watermeads High Sch
SM4 .....202 B3
Watermead Way N17 .34 B1
Watermen's Sq 1
SE20 .....184 C3
Water Mews SE15 ..140 C1
Watermill Bsns Ctr EN3 7 B3
Watermill Cl TW10 ..153 C1
Watermill La N18 .....33 C5
Watermill Way
Feltham TW13 .....151 C2
Merton SW19 .....180 A2
Watermint Quay N16 .52 A2
Water Rd HA0 .....88 B6
Watersedge KT19 ...215 A4
Water's Edge SW6 ..134 C4
Watersfield Way HA8 .26 A3
Waters Gdns RM10 ....81 C3
Watership Down Ho
E11 .....54 D2
Waterside E17 .....52 C3
4 Beckenham BR3 ...185 C2
Waterside Cl E3 .....97 B6
28 SE16 .....118 A4
Barking IG11 .....80 A4
Northolt UB5 .....85 B4
Surbiton KT6 .....214 A6
Waterside Ct SE13 ..142 B1
Waterside Dr KT12 ..194 B4
Waterside Pl NW1 ..231 B6
Waterside Point
SW11 .....267 B4
Waterside Rd UB2 ..107 C3
Waterside Sch SE18 .123 B1
Waterside Trad Ctr
W7 .....108 C3
Waterside Way SW17 180 A5
Watersmeet Way
SE28 .....102 D1
Waterson St E2 .....95 D4
Waters Pl SW15 .....134 C3
Watersplash Cl KT1 ..198 A6
Watersplash La
Hayes UB3 .....106 A2
Southall TW5 .....106 B1
Watersplash Rd
TW17 .....192 C5
Waters Rd
Catford SE6 .....164 C1
Kingston KT1 .....176 D1
Waters Sq KT1 .....198 D6
Water St WC2 .....251 A6
Water Tower Cl UB8 ..60 A3
Water Tower Hill
CR0 .....221 B4
Water Tower Ho W8 .245 A3
Water Tower Pl N1 ..234 C5
Waterview Ho E14 ....97 A2
Waterworks Cnr E17 ..36 C1
Waterworks La E5 ....74 D6
Waterworks Rd SW2 .160 B5
Watery La DA14 .....190 B4
Hayes UB3 .....105 B1
Merton SW19,SW20 ...179 B1
Northolt UB5 .....84 C5
Wates Way CR4 .....202 D3
Wateville Rd N17 .....33 A2
Watford Cl SW11 ...267 B2
Watford Rd E16 .....99 A2
Elstree WD6 .....9 C5
Harrow HA0,HA1 .....65 A5
Harrow HA1 .....43 A1
Northwood HA6 .....22 A4
Watford Way NW4 ....46 A5
Watford Way (Barnet
By-Pass) NW9 .....27 D3
Watkin Ho N16 .....51 D2
Watkin Rd HA9 .....66 D5
Watkinson Rd N7 .....72 B2
Watling Ave HA8 .....27 B2
Watling Ct EC4 .....242 B1
1 Elstree WD6 .....9 D5
Watling Gate NW9 ....45 C5
Watling Gdns NW2 ....69 A2
Watling Ho 10 SE18 ..144 C6
Watlings Cl CR0 .....207 A3
Watling St DA6,DA7 ..147 D1
EC4 .....95 A1 242 B1
4 SE15 .....139 C6
Watlington Gr SE26 ..185 A5
Watney Cotts SW14 ..133 A2
Watney Mkt E1 .....96 B1
Watney Rd SW14 ....133 A2
Watneys Rd CR4 .....203 D4
Watney St E1 .....96 B1
Watson Ave
Cheam SM3 .....217 A6

Watson Ave *continued*
Wallend E6 ....78 C1
Watson Cl N16 ....73 B3
Mitcham SW19 ......180 C1
Watson Ho **3** SW2 ...160 A4
Watsons Lo **4** RM10 ...81 D2
Watson's Mews W1 ...**237** B3
Watsons Rd N22 ......32 B2
Watson's St SE8 ......141 C5
Watson St E13 ....99 B5
Wattisfield Rd E5 .....74 C5
Watts Cl N15 ....51 C4
Watts Gr E3 ....97 D2
Watts Ho **6** W10 .....91 A2
Watt's La
Chislehurst BR7 ......189 A2
Teddington TW11 ....175 A5
Watts Point E13 ....99 A6
Watts Rd KT7 ....197 A2
Watts St E1 ....118 B5
SE15 ....139 D4
Wat Tyler Ho N8 ....50 A6
Wat Tyler Rd SE10 ...142 B4
Wauthier Cl N13 ......32 D5
Wavel Ct **7** E1 ......118 C5
7 Streatham SW16 ...160 A1
Wavell Dr DA15 .....167 C5
Wavell Ho N6 ....49 A3
Wavel Mews N8 ......49 D5
NW6 ....69 D1
Wavel Pl SE26 ....183 D6
Wavendon Ave W4 ...111 B1
Waveney Ave SE15 ...140 B1
Waveney Cl E1 ......118 A5
Waveney Ho SE15 ...140 B1
Waverley Ave E17 ...54 B6
E4 ....35 B6
Sutton SM1 ....217 D6
Tolworth KT5 ....199 A3
Twickenham TW2,TW4 .151 C3
Wembley HA9 ....66 B3
Waverley Cl BR2 .....209 D4
East Molesey KT8 ....195 C4
Hayes UB3 ....105 B2
Woodford E18 ....37 C1
Waverley Cres SE18 ..123 B1
Waverley Ct **3** NW6 ..69 A1
W1 ....**238** B4
Enfield EN2 ....5 A2
Waverley Gdns E6 ..100 A2
Barking IG11 ....101 C5
Ealing NW10 ....88 B5
Ilford IG6 ....57 B6
Northwood HA6 ......22 A2
Waverley Gr N3 ....47 A6
Waverley Ind Pk HA1 .42 B6
Waverley Pl N4 ....50 D1
NW8 ....92 B5 **229** C4
Waverley Rd E17 .....54 A6
N8 ....50 A2
SE18 ....123 B1
Croydon SE25 ......206 B6
Enfield EN2 ....4 D2
Harrow HA2 ....41 A1
Southall UB1 ....107 C4
Stoneleigh KT17,KT4 .216 B3
Tottenham N17 ......34 B3
Woodford E18 ....37 C2
Waverley Sch EN3 .....6 C1
Waverley Sch (lower)
SE22 ....162 B6
Waverley Sch (Upper)
SE15 ....162 C6
Waverley Way SM2,
SM5 ....218 C2
Waverly Ct NW3 ......70 D2
Waverton Ho **2** E3 ...97 B6
Waverton Rd SW18 ..158 A4
Waverton St
W1 ....115 B5 **248** C4
Wavertree Ct **9** SW2 160 A3
Wavertree Rd
Streatham SW2 ......160 B3
Woodford E18 ....37 A1
Waxham NW5 ....70 D3
Waxlow Cres UB1 ....85 C1
Waxlow Ho UB4 .....84 C2
Waxlow Rd NW10 ....89 B5
Waxwell Cl HA5 ......22 D1
Waxwell La HA5 ......22 D1
Wayborne Gr HA4 ....39 A3
Waye Ave TW5 ......128 A4
Wayfarer Rd UB5 ....85 A4
Wayfield Link SE9 ...167 B5
Wayford St SW11 ...136 C3
Wayland Ave E8 .....74 A3
Wayland Ho **13** SW9 .138 C3

Waylands UB3 ....83 B2
Waylands Cl IG1 ......79 B4
Waylands Mead BR3 .185 D2
Waylett Ho SE11 ....**261** A1
Waylett Pl
Wembley HA0 ....65 D4
West Norwood SE27 ..160 D1
Wayman Ct E8 ....74 B2
Wayne Cl BR6 ......227 D5
Waynflete Ave CR0 ..220 B5
Waynflete Sq
16 W10 ....112 D6
18 W10 ....90 D1
Waynflete St SW18 ..158 A2
Wayside NW11 ......47 A1
Mortlake SW14 ......155 A6
New Addington CR0 ..223 D2
Wayside Ave WD23 ....8 B5
Wayside Cl N14 ......15 C5
Wayside Commercial Est
IG11 ....102 A5
Wayside Ct
Isleworth TW7 ....130 C3
Twickenham TW1 ....153 C5
Wembley HA9 ....66 C5
Wayside Gdns RM10 ..81 C3
Wayside Gr SW7,SE9 .188 B6
Wayside Mews IG2 ...56 C4
Weald Cl BR2 ......226 A6
16 SE16 ....118 B1
Weald Fst & Mid Schs
HA3 ....24 D3
Weald La HA3 ....24 B2
Weald Rd UB10 ......82 C5
Weald Rise HA3 ......24 D2
Weald Sq E5 ....74 B6
Wealdstone Rd SM3 .217 B6
Weald The BR7 ......188 B4
Weald Way Hayes UB4 .83 C4
Romford RM7 ....59 D3
Wealdwood Gdns HA5 23 D4
Weale Rd E4 ....20 B1
Weall Ct HA5 ....41 A5
Weardale Ct E5 ......12 C6
Weardale Gdns EN2 ...5 B4
Weardale Ho N4 ......51 A2
Weardale Rd SE13 ..142 B1
Wearmouth Ho **11** E3 .97 B2
Wear Pl **13** E2 ....96 B4
Wearside Rd SE13 ...141 D1
Weatherbury **6** W2 .91 C1
Weatherbury Ho **3**
N19 ....71 D5
Weatherill Ct SE25 ..206 B3
Weatherley Cl E3 .....97 B2
Weathersfield Ct SE9 166 B5
Weaver Cl E16 ......122 D6
South Croydon CR0 ..221 D4
Weaver Ct **2** E2 ......96 B3
Weaver Ho **13** E1 .....96 A3
Weavers Cl TW7 ....130 C1
Weavers Ho **4** E11 ...55 A3
Weaver's La
SE1 ....117 C5 **253** B3
Weaver St E1 ....96 A3
Weavers Way NW1 ...**232** C6
6 NW1 ....71 D1
Weaver Wlk SE27 ...182 D6
Webb Ct **6** SE28 ...124 B6
Webb Ho SW8 ......**269** D3
2 Dagenham RM10 ..81 C5
W3 ....110 D4
Webb Pl NW10 ......89 D4
Webb Rd SE3 ....142 D6
Webbscroft Rd RM10 .81 D4
Webb's Rd SW11 ...158 D6
Webbs Rd UB4 ......84 B4
Webb St SE1 .117 C3 **263** A5
Weddell Ho **23** E1 ....96 D3
Barking IG11 ....101 C6
Wedgewood Ho DA5 .169 B4
11 Beckenham BR2 ..208 D3
Wedgewood Mews
W1 ....**239** D1

Wedgewood Wlk NW3 69 D3
Wedgwood Ho **17** E2 ..96 D2
SE11 ....**261** A5
Wedgwood Way
SE19 ....183 A3
Wedlake St W10 ......91 A3
Wedmore Gdns N19 ..71 D6
Wedmore Rd UB6 ....86 B4
Wedmore St N19 ......71 D5
Weech Rd NW6 ......69 C4
Weedington Rd NW5 .71 A3
Weedon Ho W12 ......90 A1
Weekley Sq SW11 ...136 B2
Weeks Ho TW10 ....175 C6
Weigall Rd SE12,SE9 .143 A1
Weighhouse St W1 ..**238** B1
Weighton Rd
Harrow HA3 ....24 B2
Penge SE20 ....184 B1
Weihurst Ct SM1 ....218 C3
Weihurst Gdns SM1 .218 B3
Weimar St SW15 ....135 A2
Weirdale Ave N20 ....14 D2
Weir Hall Ave N18 ....33 B4
Weir Hall Gdns N18 ..33 B5
Weir Hall Rd N18 .....33 B4
Weir Ho **8** SW2 .....159 C4
Weir Rd Sidcup DA5 .169 D4
Streatham SW12 ....159 C4
Walton-on-T KT12 ..194 A3
Wimbledon SW18,
SW19 ....157 D1
Weir's Pas NW1 ....**232** D2
Weiss Rd SW15 .....134 D2
Welbeck Ave BR1 ...187 B6
DA15 ....168 A3
Hayes UB4 ....84 B3
Welbeck Cl N12 ......30 B5
New Malden KT3 ...199 D4
Stoneleigh KT17 ...216 A1
Welbeck Ct W14 ....**254** C4
Hayes UB4 ....84 B3
Welbeck Mans **10**
NW6 ....69 C3
Welbeck Rd E6 ......99 D4
Carshalton SM1,SM5 .218 B6
East Barnet EN4 .....14 C5
Harrow HA2 ....41 D1
Carshalton SM5 ....202 C1
Welbeck St
W1 ....93 B1 **238** C2
Welbeck Villas N21 ..17 A3
Welbeck Way W1 ...**238** C2
Welbeck Wlk SM5 ..202 B1
Welbourne Prim Sch
N17 ....52 A6
Welby Ho N19 ....49 D2
Welby St SE5 ....138 D4
Welch Pl HA5 ....22 C2
Welcome Ct E17 .....53 C2
Weldon Cl HA4 ......62 B2
Weldon Ct
Southgate N21 ......16 B6
Thornton Heath CR7 .204 D4
Weldon Dr KT8 .....195 B5
Weld Pl N11 ....31 B5
Welfare Rd E15 ......76 C1
Welford Cl E5 ....74 D5
Welford Ct **12** NW1 ..71 B1
7 SW8 ....137 C3
Welford Pl SW19 ...179 A6
Welham Rd SW16,
SW17 ....181 B4
Welhouse Rd SM5 ..202 C1
Wellacre Rd HA3 .....43 B3
Wellan Cl DA15,DA16 .168 B6
Welland Gdns UB6 ...86 D5
Welland Ho SE15 ...140 C1
Welland Mews E1 ..118 A5
Wellands Cl BR1 ....188 B1
Welland St SE10 ...142 A6
Well App EN5 ....12 C6
Wellby Ct **1** E13 ....99 C5
Well Cl Ruislip HA4 ..63 A5
Streatham SW16 ....182 A6

Wellesley Court Rd **1**
CR0 ....**221** B6
Wellesley Cres TW2 .152 C1
Wellesley Ct
W9 ....92 A4 **229** A2
Cheam SM3 ....201 A1
Twickenham TW2 ...152 C1
Wellesley Gr CR0 ...221 B6
Wellesley Ho NW1 ..**232** C1
Wellesley Park Mews
EN2 ....4 D3
Wellesley Pl NW1 ..**232** C1
NW5 ....71 A3
Wellesley Rd E17 ....53 C3
NW5 ....71 A3
W4 ....110 D1
Croydon CR0 ....205 A4
Harrow HA1 ....42 C4
Ilford IG1 ....57 A1
Sutton SM2 ....218 A2
Twickenham TW2 ...152 C1
Wanstead E11 ....55 A4
Wood Green N22 ....32 C1
Wellesley Road Sta
CR0 ....221 B6
Wellesley St E1 .....96 D2
Wellesley Terr
N1 ....95 A4 **235** B2
Wellfield Ave N10 ....49 B6
Wellfield Rd SW16 ..182 A6
Wellfit St **6** SE24 ..138 D2
Wellgarth UB6 ....65 B2
Wellgarth Rd NW11 ..47 D1
Well Gr N20 ....14 B3
Well Hall Par SE9 ...144 A2
Well Hall Pleasaunce★
SE9 ....144 A1
Well Hall Rd SE9 ...144 A1
Well Ho **11** N9 ......18 A1
Wellhouse Rd BR3 ..207 C5
Wellingfield Ct **1**
DA16 ....146 A2
Welling High St
DA16 ....146 B2
Welling Sch DA16 ..146 B4
Wellings Ho UB3 ...106 B5
Welling Sta DA16 ...146 A3
Wellington N8 ......50 A5
1 NW9 ....27 C1
Wellington Arch★
SW1 ....**248** B2
Wellington Ave DA15 168 A5
N15 ....52 A3
SE18 ....123 A3
Chingford E4 ....19 D2
Edmonton N9 ....18 B1
Hounslow TW3,TW4 .151 C6
North Cheam KT4 ..216 C5
Pinner HA5 ....23 D4
Wellington Bldgs
14 E3 ....97 C4
SW1 ....**258** B1
Wellington Cl SE14 .140 D4
W11 ....91 C1
Walton-on-T KT12 ..193 D1
Wellington Cres KT3 .199 A6
Wellington Ct NW8 ..**229** D3
SW1 ....**247** C1
SW3 ....158 C6
SW6 ....**265** D1
WC2 ....**250** A6
Ashford TW15 ....170 A6
Stanwell TW19 .....148 A4
5 Surbiton KT6 .....198 A3
Teddington TW12 ...174 B5
Wellington Gr SE10 .142 B5
Wellington Ho
18 NW3 ....70 D2
4 Ealing W5 ....88 A4
Northolt UB5 ....63 C1
Stanmore HA7 ....9 A1
Wellington Hospl (North)
NW8 ....92 B5 **229** D3
Wellington Hospl (South)
NW8 ....92 B5 **229** D3
Wellington Mans
1 E10 ....53 C4
N16 ....73 D4
Wellington Mews
SE22 ....140 A2
Streatham SW16 ...159 C1
Wellington Mus (Apsley
Ho)★ SW1 ..115 B5 **248** B2
Wellington Par DA15 168 A6
Wellington Park Est
NW2 ....68 A6
Wellington Pl N2 ....48 C4
NW8 ....92 B4 **229** D3

Wellington Prim Sch
E3 ....97 C4
Chingford E4 ....19 D2
Hounslow TW3 .....129 B3
Wellington Rd E17 ..53 A5
E6 ....100 B5
E7 ....76 D4
NW10 ....90 D4
NW8 ....92 B5 **229** D3
W5 ....109 C3
Ashford TW15 ......170 A5
Bexley DA5 ....168 B6
Bromley BR2 ....209 C5
Enfield EN1 ....17 C5
Erith DA17 ....125 B1
Harrow HA3 ....42 C6
Hatton TW14 ......149 C6
Pinner HA5 ....23 B2
Teddington TW12,TW2 .174 B6
Thornton Heath CR0 .204 D3
Walthamstow E10 ....53 A1
Wanstead E11 ....55 A4
Wimbledon SW19 ...157 C2
Wellington Rd N
TW4 ....129 B2
Wellington Rd S TW4 151 B6
Wellington Row E2 ..96 A4
Wellington Sq
SW3 ....114 D1 **257** C2
Wellington St SE18 .122 C2
WC2 ....116 B6 **250** C6
1 Barking IG11 .....101 A6
Wellington Terr
2 E1 ....118 B5
Harrow HA1 ....42 B1
Wellington Way E3 ..97 C4
Welling Way DA16 ..145 B2
Well La SW14 ....155 A6
Wellmead IG3 ....58 A2
Wellmeadow Rd W7 .109 A2
Catford SE13,SE6 ..164 C2
Wellow Wlk SM5 ...202 B1
Well Rd NW3 ....70 B5
Barnet EN5 ....12 C6
Wells Cl
2 Northolt UB5 .....84 C4
South Croydon CR2 ..221 C3
Wells Ct N1 ....73 C3
16 NW3 ....70 A4
1 NW6 ....91 C5
Wells Dr NW9 ......45 B1
Wells Gdns
Dagenham RM10 .....81 D4
Redbridge IG1 ....56 A2
Wells Ho BR1 ......187 B5
EC1 ....**234** C2
9 SE16 ....118 C3
12 W10 ....91 A3
4 Barking IG11 .....80 A1
Ealing W5 ....109 D6
Wells Ho The NW3 ..70 B4
Wells House Rd NW10 89 C2
Wellside Gdns SW14 .155 A6
Wells Mews W1 ....**239** B2
Wellsmoor Gdns BR1 210 C6
Wells Park Ct SE26 .184 B6
Wells Park Rd SE26 .184 B6
Wells Pl SW18 .....158 A4
Wells Prim Sch IG8 ..37 A6
Wells Rd BR1 ......188 B1
W12 ....112 C4
Wells Rise
NW8 ....92 D6 **230** C5
Wells Sq WC1 .....**233** D1
Wells St W1 ....93 C1 **239** B2
Well St E15 ....76 C2
E9 ....74 C1
Wellstead Ave N9 ....18 D4
Wellstead Rd E6 ...100 C5
Wells The N14 ......15 D4
Wells Way SE5 .....139 C6
SW7 ....114 B3 **256** C6
Wells Yd **2** N7 .....72 C3
Well Wlk NW3 ....70 B5
Wellwood Ct SW15 .134 C1
Wellwood Rd IG3 ....58 A2
Welsby Ct W5 ....87 C2
Welsford St SE1 ....118 A2
Welsh Cl E13 ....99 A4
Welsh Harp Field Centre
NW9 ....45 B1
Welsh Ho **14** E1 ...118 B5
Welshpool Ho **22** E8 .96 A5
Welshpool St **1** E8 .96 B6
Welshside NW9 ......45 C3
Welshside Wlk NW9 .45 C3
Welstead Ho **5** E1 ..96 B1
Welstead Way W4 ..111 D2
Weltje Rd W6 ......112 A1

Welton Ho E1 ....96 D2
SE5 ....139 C4
Welton Rd SE18 ....145 C1
Welwyn Ave TW14 ..149 D5
Welwyn St E2 ....96 C4
Welwyn Way UB4 ....83 C3
Wembley HA0 ....66 C4
Wembley Arena HA9 .66 C4
Wembley Bsns Ctr
HA9 ....66 D5
Wembley Central Sta
HA9 ....66 A3
Wembley Commercial Ctr
HA9 ....65 D6
Wembley Conference Ctr
HA9 ....66 C4
Wembley Exhibition Halls
HA9 ....66 C4
Wembley High Sch
HA0 ....65 C5
Wembley Hill Rd HA9 66 B4
Wembley Hospl HA0 .65 D2
Wembley Manor Jun & Inf
Schs HA9 ....66 A5
Wembley Park Dr HA9 66 B5
Wembley Park Sta
HA9 ....66 C5
Wembley Rd TW12 ..173 C2
Wembley Stadium
HA9 ....66 C3
Wembley Stadium Ind Est
Wembley HA9 ....66 C5
Wembley HA9 ....66 D4
Wembley Stadium Sta
HA9 ....66 C3
Wembley Way HA9 ..66 D2
Wemborough Rd HA7 .25 C3
Wembury Rd N6 .....49 B2
Wemyss Rd SE3 ...142 D3
Wendela Ct HA1 ....66 C3
Wendell Park Prim Sch
W12 ....111 D4
Wendell Rd W12 ...111 D4
Wenderholme CR2 ..221 B3
Wendle Ct SW8 ....**270** A5
Wendling NW5 ......70 D3
Wendling Rd SM1,
SM5 ....218 B6
Wendon St E3 ....97 B6
Wendover NW9 .....45 D3
SE17 ....117 C1 **263** A1
Wendover Cl UB4 ...84 D3
Wendover Ct **4** NW2 .69 C5
W1 ....**238** A3
W3 ....89 A3
Bromley BR2 ....209 B6
Wendover Dr KT3 ..199 D3
Wendover Ho W1 ..**238** A3
Wendover Rd
BR1,BR2 ....209 B6
NW10 ....89 D5
SE9 ....143 D2
Wendover Way
Bexley DA16 ....146 A1
Bushey WD23 ....8 A5
Wendy Cl EN1 ....17 D5
Wendy Ho N12 ......30 B5
Wendy Way HA0 ....88 A4
Wengham Ho N12 ..112 A6
Wenham Ho SW8 ..**269** A3
Wenlake Ho EC1 ...**242** A6
Wenlock Ct N1 ....**235** D3
Wenlock Gdns **13**
NW4 ....46 A5
Wenlock Rd HA8 ....27 A4
N1 ....95 A5 **235** B3
Wenlock St N1 95 B5 **235** C3
Wennington Rd E3 ...96 C5
Wensdale Ho E5 .....74 A6
Wensley Ave IG8 ....37 A3
Wensley Cl SE9 ....166 B5
Barnet N11 ....31 A5
Wensleydale Gdns
TW12 ....173 D3
Wensleydale Ho **8**
N4 ....51 A2
Wensleydale Rd
TW12 ....173 D3
Wensley Rd N18 .....34 B4
Wentland Cl SE6 ...164 B2
Wentland Rd SE6 ..164 B2
Wentway Ct W13 ....87 A3
Wentwood Ho **1** E5 .74 B6
Wentworth Ave N3 ...29 C3
Borehamwood WD6 ..10 B6
Wentworth Cl BR2 ..225 A6
N3 ....29 C3
SE28 ....102 D1
Ashford TW15 ......170 D6
Long Ditton KT6 ...213 D6

Wentworth Cl continued
Morden SM4 ....201 C2
Orpington BR6 ....227 C3
Wentworth Cres
SE15 ....140 A5
Hayes UB3 ....105 B3
Wentworth Ct W6 ...264 A5
Barnet EN5 ....1 A2
20 Kingston KT6 .....198 A4
Southall UB2 ....106 C2
2 Surbiton KT6 .....214 A6
Twickenham TW2 .....152 C1
Wandsworth SW18 ...157 D5
Wentworth Dr HA5 ..40 A4
Wentworth Dwellings
E1 ....243 C2
Wentworth Gdns N13 .16 D1
Wentworth Hall NW7 .28 C5
Wentworth Hill HA9 ..44 B1
Wentworth Lo N3 ....29 D3
Wentworth Mews E3 .97 B4
Wentworth Pk N3 ....29 D3
Wentworth Pl HA7 ...25 B4
Wentworth Rd E12 ...77 D4
NW11 ....47 B3
Southall UB2 ....106 D2
Thornton Heath CR0 .204 C2
Wentworth St
E1 ....95 D2 243 D3
Wentworth Way HA5 .41 A5
Wenvoe Ave DA7 ...147 D3
Wepham Cl UB4 ......84 D2
Wernbrook St SE18 .145 A6
Werndee Rd SE25 ...206 A5
Werneth Hall Rd IG5 .56 C6
Werrington St
NW1 ....93 C5 232 B3
Werter Rd SW15 ....135 A1
Wesleyan Pl NW5 ...71 B4
Wesley Ave E16 ....121 B5
NW10 ....89 B4
Hounslow TW3 ......129 B3
Wesley Cl N7 ....72 B6
SE17 ....261 D3
Harrow HA2 ....64 A6
Wesley Ho SE24 ....161 B5
Wesley Rd E10 ......54 A2
N10 ....30 C2
NW10 ....89 A6
Hayes UB3 ....84 A1
Wesley Sq W11 .....91 A1
Wesley St W1 ......238 B3
Wessex Ave SW19 ..201 C6
Wessex Cl
Hinchley Wood KT10,
 KT7 ....212 D6
Ilford IG3 ....57 C3
Kingston KT1,KT2 ..176 D2
Wessex Ct
Putney SW15 ....156 D6
5 Stanwell TW19 ...148 A5
Wessex Dr HA5 ......23 A3
Wessex Gardens Prim Sch
NW11 ....47 A1
Wessex Gdns NW11 .47 A1
Wessex Ho 4 N19 ..71 D5
SE1 ....263 D1
Wessex La UB6 ......86 B5
Wessex Rd TW6 ....126 A2
Wessex St E2 ....96 C4
Wessex Way NW11 ..47 A1
Wesson Ho 3 CR0 .206 A1
Westacott UB4 ......83 C2
Westacott Cl N19 ...49 D1
West Acton Prim Sch
W3 ....88 D1
West Acton Sta W3 .88 C1
West App BR5 ......211 A4
West Arbour St E1 ..96 D1
West Ave E17 ....53 D4
N2 ....47 D6
N3 ....29 C4
NW4 ....46 D4
Hayes UB3 ....105 D6
Pinner HA5 ....41 B2
Southall UB1 ....107 B6
Wallington SM6 ....220 A3
West Avenue Rd E17 .53 D5
West Bank N16 .....51 C2
Barking IG11 ....100 D6
Enfield EN2 ....5 A1
Westbank Rd TW12 .174 A4
West Barnes La KT3,
SW20 ....200 B5
Westbeech Rd N22 ..50 C6
Westbere Dr HA7 ...25 D5
Westbere Rd NW2 ...69 A3
West Block 17 E1 ..118 C6
Westbourne Ave W3 .89 B1
Cheam SM3 ....217 A6

Westbourne Cl UB4 ..84 C3
Westbourne Cres
W2 ....246 C6
Westbourne Ct W2 .236 A2
Westbourne Dr SE23 162 D2
Westbourne Gdns W2 91 D1
Westbourne Gr
W11 ....113 B1 244 D6
W2,W11 ....91 C1
Westbourne Gr Mews 7
W11 ....91 C1
Westbourne Gr Terr
W2 ....91 D1
Westbourne Ho SW1 258 C2
Heston TW5 ....129 C6
8 Twickenham TW1 .153 B4
Westbourne Par 4
UB10 ....82 D3
Westbourne Park Rd
W11 ....91 B1
W2 ....91 C1
Westbourne Park Sta
W11 ....91 B2
Westbourne Park Villas
W2 ....91 C2
Westbourne Pl N9 ...18 B1
Westbourne Prim Sch
SM1 ....217 C5
Westbourne Rd DA7 .147 A5
N7 ....72 B2
Croydon CR0 ....205 D3
Feltham TW13 ......149 D1
Hillingdon UB8 ......82 D3
Penge SE26 ....184 D4
Westbourne St
W2 ....114 B6 246 C6
Westbourne Terr
W2 ....92 A1 236 B2
Westbourne Terr Mews
W2 ....236 A2
Westbourne Terr Rd
W2 ....92 A1 236 A3
Westbridge Cl W12 .112 A5
Westbridge Prim Sch
SW11 ....267 B2
Westbridge Rd
SW11 ....136 C4 267 A2
West Brompton Sta
SW5 ....113 C1 255 B1
Westbrook Ave TW12 173 B3
Westbrook Cl EN4 ....2 B2
Westbrook Cres EN4 ..2 B2
Westbrook Ct SE3 ..143 A4
Westbrooke Cres
DA16 ....146 C2
Westbrooke Rd DA15 167 B2
Bexley DA16 ....146 C2
Westbrooke Sch
DA16 ....146 D2
Westbrook Ho 5 E2 .96 C4
5 SW4 ....159 C6
Westbrook Rd SE3 .143 A4
Heston TW5 ....129 B5
South Norwood CR7 .183 B1
Westbrook Sq EN4 ...2 B2
West Brow BR7 .....188 D3
Westbury Ave
Claygate KT10 .....212 D2
Southall UB1 ....85 C3
Tottenham N22 .....32 C1
Wembley HA0 ......66 A1
Westbury Cl
Ruislip HA4 ....40 A2
Shepperton TW17 ..192 D3
Westbury Ct SW4 ..159 B5
3 Barking IG11 ....101 B6
Beckenham BR3 ...185 D2
1 Buckhurst Hill IG9 21 C2
Tottenham N22 .....33 A1
Westbury Gr N12 ...29 C4
Westbury Ho 1 E17 .53 C5
Westbury House Sch The
KT3 ....199 B4
Westbury La IG9 ....21 C2
Westbury Lodge Cl
HA5 ....40 D6
Westbury Pl 2 TW8 131 D6
Westbury Rd E17 ...53 C5
E7 ....77 B2
N12 ....29 C5
Barking IG11 ....101 B6
Beckenham BR3 ...207 A6
Bowes Park N11 ...32 A4
Bromley BR1 ....187 D2
Buckhurst Hill IG9 ..21 C3
Ealing W5 ....88 A1
Feltham TW13 ......150 D3
Ilford IG1 ....78 C6
New Malden KT3 ..199 B4
Penge SE20 ....184 D4

Westbury Rd continued
Thornton Heath CR0 .205 B3
Wembley HA0 ......66 A1
Westbury Terr E7 ...77 B2
Westbush Ct 1 W12 .112 B4
West Carriage Dr
W2 ....114 C5 247 A4
West Central Ave
NW10 ....90 B4
West Central St WC1 240 A2
West Chantry HA3 ..23 D2
Westchester Ct NW4 .46 D6
Westchester Dr NW4 .46 D6
Westchester Ho W2 237 C1
West Cl Ashford TW15 .170 A6
Barnet EN5 ....12 B6
Cockfosters EN4 .....3 A1
Edmonton N9 ......17 D1
Greenford UB6 .....86 A5
Wembley HA9 ......44 B1
Westcliff Ho 13 N1 ..73 B2
Westcombe Ave CR0 204 B2
Westcombe Ct 1
SE3 ....142 D5
Westcombe Dr EN5 .13 C6
Westcombe Hill SE3,
SE10 ....143 A6
Westcombe Park Lo
UB4 ....83 B2
Westcombe Park Rd
SE3 ....142 D5
Westcombe Park Sta
SE3 ....121 A1
West Common Rd
BR2 ....225 B5
Westcoombe Ave
SW20 ....177 D2
Westcote Rd SW16 .181 C5
Westcote Rise HA4 ..39 A2
Westcott Cl BR1 ....210 A4
2 N15 ....51 D3
Westcott Cres W7 ..86 C2
Westcott Ho 1 E14 119 D6
Westcott Rd SE17 ..138 D6
West Cotts NW6 ....69 C3
Westcroft Cl NW2 ...69 A4
Enfield EN3 ....6 C5
Westcroft Ct NW9 ..44 D4
3 W6 ....112 A2
Westcroft Gdns SM4 201 B5
Westcroft Rd SM5,
SM6 ....219 A4
Westcroft Sq W6 ...112 A2
Westcroft Way NW2 .69 A4
West Cromwell Rd
W14 ....113 B1 254 D2
West Cross Ctr TW8 131 B6
West Cross Route
W10,W11 ....112 D6
West Cross Way TW8 131 B6
West Croydon Sta
CR9 ....205 A1
West Ct E17 ....53 D5
Hounslow TW7 .....130 A4
Wembley HA0 ......65 C6
Westdale Rd SE18 .144 B6
Westdean Ave SE12 165 C3
Westdean Cl SW18 157 D5
Westdown Rd E15 ..76 A4
Catford SE6 ....163 C4
West Dr Stanmore HA3 24 B4
Streatham SW16 ...181 C6
West Drayton Park Ave
UB7 ....104 A3
West Drayton Prim Sch
UB7 ....104 A4
West Drayton Rd UB8 82 D1
West Drayton Sta
UB7 ....104 A4
West Drive Gdns HA3 24 B4
West Dulwich Sta
SE21 ....161 B3
West Ealing Bsns Ctr
W13 ....109 A6
West Ealing Sta W13 109 B6
West Eaton Pl SW1 .258 A4
West Eaton Pl Mews
SW1 ....258 A4
West Ella Rd NW10 .67 C1
West End Ave E10 ..54 B4
Pinner HA5 ....40 D5
West End Cl NW10 ..67 A1
West End Ct NW6 ...69 D2
Pinner HA5 ....40 D5
West End Gdns UB5 .84 C5
West End La NW6 ...69 D2
Harlington UB7 ....127 A4
Pinner HA5 ....40 D5
West End Rd
Ruislip HA4,UB5 ....62 A4

West End Rd continued
Ruislip UB5 ....62 C1
Southall UB1 ....107 A5
Westerdale Ct N5 ...72 D4
Westerdale Rd 2
SE10 ....121 A1
Westerfield Rd 1 N15 51 D4
Westergate W5 .....88 A2
Westergate Rd SE2 147 A6
Westerham NW1 ...232 A5
13 Kingston KT6 ...198 A4
Westerham Ave N9 .17 C1
Westerham Dr DA15 168 B3
Westerham Ho SE1 262 D6
BR3 ....185 C3
Westerham Rd E10 .53 D2
Keston BR2 ....225 D2
Westerland BR7 ....189 A4
Westerley Cres SE26 185 B5
Western Ave NW11 .46 B5
W3 ....89 B1
Hillingdon HA4,UB4,UB5,
 UB10 ....61 C1
Northolt UB5 ....85 C6
Northolt UB5,UB6 ..85 B6
Ruislip UB8,UB9,UB10 60 B3
Wembley UB6 ......87 C4
Western Avenue Bsns Pk
W3 ....88 D3
Western Ct N3 .....29 C4
4 W3 ....89 B1
3 W9 ....91 B5
Southall UB2 ....107 A3
Western Dr TW17 ..193 B3
Western Eye Hospl The
NW1 ....92 D1 237 C4
Western Gdns W5 .110 C6
Western Ho 1 W9 ..91 B3
Western International
Market UB2 ....106 B2
Western La SW12 ..159 A4
Western Mews W9 ..91 B3
Western Par EN5 ...13 C6
Western Pl 13 SE16 118 C2
Western Rd E13 ....99 C5
E17 ....54 A4
N2 ....48 D5
NW10 ....89 A3
SW9 ....138 C2
Ealing W5 ....109 D6
Mitcham CR4,SW19 180 C1
Southall UB2 ....106 C2
Sutton SM1 ....217 C3
Wood Green N22 ...32 B1
Western Terr 1 W6 112 A1
Western View UB3 ..105 D4
Westernville Gdns
IG2 ....57 A2
Western Way SE28 123 C4
New Barnet EN5 ...13 D5
Western Wharf 2
SE15 ....140 A6
West Ewell Inf Sch
KT19 ....215 B3
Westferry Cir E14 ..119 C5
Westferry Rd E14 ..119 C5
Westferry Sta E14 ..119 C6
Westfield 1 BR6 ...227 A3
NW3 ....69 C4
Loughton IG10 .....21 C6
Westfield Cl NW9 ...45 A6
SW10 ....266 A3
Cheam SM1 ....217 B4
Enfield EN3 ....7 A2
Westfield Ct 1 W10 .90 D4
Kingston KT6 ......197 D4
Westfield Dr HA3 ...43 D5
Westfield Gdns HA3 .43 D5
Westfield Ho 6
SE16 ....118 D2
Westfield La HA3 ...43 D5
Westfield Pk HA5 ...23 B3
Westfield Rd NW7 ..11 C1
Beckenham BR3 ...185 B1
Cheam SM1 ....217 B4
Croydon CR0 ......220 D6
Dagenham RM9 ....81 B4
Ealing W13 ....109 A5
Kingston KT6 ......197 D4
Mitcham CR4 ......180 C1
Walton-on-T KT12 ..195 A4
Westfields SW13 ...133 D2
Westfields Ave SW13 133 C2
Westfields Gdns RM6 58 C3
Westfields Rd W3 ..88 D2
Westfields Sch SW13 133 D2
Westfield St SE18 ..121 D3
Westfield Way E1 ...97 A3
Ruislip HA4 ....61 D5

West Finchley Sta N3 29 D4
West Garden Pl W2 237 B1
West Gate W5 ......88 A4
Westgate Bsns Ctr
W10 ....90 D3
2 W10 ....91 A3
Westgate Ct 16 SW9 138 C2
6 Beckenham BR3 186 A4
Lewisham SE12 ....165 A3
Westgate Est TW14 148 A3
Westgate Rd
Beckenham BR3 ...186 A4
Croydon SE25 .....206 B5
Westgate St E8 .....96 B6
Westgate Terr
SW10 ....135 D6 265 D6
West Gdns
Mitcham SW19 ....180 C4
Stepney E1 ....118 B6
Westglade Ct HA3 ..43 D5
West Gr SE10 ......142 B4
Woodford IG8 ......37 C5
West Green Pl 6 ...86 B6
West Green Prim Sch
N15 ....51 A5
West Green Rd N15 51 B5
Westgrove La SE10 142 A4
West Grove Prim Sch
N14 ....15 D4
West Halkin St
SW1 ....115 A3 258 A6
West Hallowes SE9 166 A3
West Hall Rd TW9 .132 A4
West Ham Church Prim
Sch E15 ....98 D6
West Ham La E15 ...76 C1
West Ham Sta E15 ..98 C4
West Harding St EC4 241 B2
West Harrow Sta HA1 42 A4
West Hatch Manor
HA4 ....39 D2
Westhay Gdns SW14 154 D6
West Heath Ave NW11 47 C1
West Heath Cl NW3 69 C5
West Heath Ct NW11 47 C1
West Heath Dr NW11 47 C1
West Heath Gdns
NW3 ....69 C5
West Heath Rd NW3 69 D5
SE2 ....146 B6
West Hill N6 ....49 A1
Harrow HA2 ....64 C6
Putney SW15 ......157 A5
South Croydon CR2 221 C1
Wembley HA9 ......44 B1
West Hill Ct N6 .....71 A5
West Hill Hall HA2 ..64 C6
West Hill Pk N6 .....70 D6
N6 ....71 A6
West Hill Prim Sch
SW18 ....157 C6
West Hill Rd SW18 157 B5
West Hill Way N20 ..13 D3
West Ho Barking IG11 78 D2
4 Penge SE20 .....184 D4
9 Streatham SW12 159 C4
Westholm NW11 ....47 D5
Westholme BR6 ....211 D2
Westholme Gdns HA4 40 A1
Westhope Ho 13 E2 96 A4
Westhorne Ave SE9,
SE12 ....165 C5
Westhorpe Gdns NW4 46 C6
Westhorpe Rd SW15 134 C2
West House Cl SW19 157 A3
Westhurst Dr BR7 ..188 D5
West India Ave E14 119 C5
West India Dock Rd
E14 ....119 C6
West India Ho 1
E14 ....119 C6
West India Quay Sta
E14 ....119 C6
West Kensington Ct
W14 ....254 C2
West Kensington Mans
W14 ....254 C2
West Kensington Sta
W14 ....113 B1 254 C2
West La SE16 ......118 B4
Westlake 10 SE16 ..118 C4
Westlake Cl Hayes UB4 85 A3
Palmers Green N13 .16 C1

Westlake Rd HA9 ...65 D6
Westland Cl TW19 .148 A5
Westland Ct 9 UB5 ..84 D4
Westland Dr BR2,BR4 224 D6
Westland Ho 1 E16 .122 C5
Westland Lo 1 BR1 187 C1
Westland Pl N1 ....235 C2
Westlands Cl UB3 ...106 A2
Westlands Ct KT8 ..196 C5
Westlands Terr 3
SW12 ....159 C5
Westlea Rd W7 ....109 A3
West Lea Sch N9 ...17 C1
Westleigh Ave SW15 156 C1
Westleigh Ct N12 ...29 D4
12 Wanstead E11 ...55 A4
Westleigh Dr BR1 ..188 B2
Westleigh Gdns HA8 26 C1
West Links HA0 .....87 D4
Westlinton Cl NW7 .29 A4
West Lodge Ave W3 109 C5
West Lodge Ct W3 110 C5
West Lodge Fst & Mid
Schs HA5 ....40 D5
West Lodge Sch
DA15 ....168 A1
West London Shooting
Grounds UB5 ....84 B5
West London Stad The
W12 ....90 B2
Westly Ct NW2 .....68 D3
Westmacott Dr
TW14 ....149 D3
Westmacott Ho NW8 236 D5
West Mall W11 .....245 B4
Westmark Point 13
SW15 ....156 B3
Westmead SW15 ...156 B5
West Mead Ruislip HA4 62 C4
West Ewell KT19 ...215 C2
Westmead Cnr SM5 218 C4
Westmead Rd SM1 218 B4
Westmeath Ho NW2 68 A5
Westmere Dr NW7 ..11 B2
West Mersea Cl 9
E16 ....121 C5
West Mews SW1 ...259 A3
West Middlesex Univ Hosp
TW7 ....131 A3
Westmill Ct N4 .....73 A6
Westminster Abbey★
SW1 ....116 A3 260 A6
Westminster Abbey Choir
Sch SW1 ....115 B3 259 D6
Westminster Ave
CR7 ....182 D1
Westminster Boating Base
SW1 ....269 C6
Westminster Bridge
SE1,SW1 ...116 A4 250 B1
Westminster Bridge Rd
SE1 ....116 A4 250 C1
Westminster Cath★
SW1 ....115 C3 259 A5
Westminster Cath Choir
Sch SW1 ...115 C2 259 A4
Westminster Cath RC Prim
Sch SW1 ...115 D1 259 D2
Westminster City Hall
SW1 ....259 B6
Westminster City Sch
SW1 ....259 B6
Westminster Cl
East Bedfont TW14 150 A2
Teddington TW11 ..175 A5
Westminster Coll of Bsns
& Computing HA9 ..66 A1
Westminster Ct
22 SE16 ....118 C2
5 SW18 ....157 C6
South Norwood CR7 183 A1
Wanstead E11 .....55 B4
Westminster Dr N13 32 A4
Westminster Gdns
SW1 ....260 A4
Barking IG11 ....101 C2
Chingford, Chingford Green
E4 ....20 C3
Westminster Ind Est
E16 ....121 D3
Westminster Kingsway
Coll
SW11 ....137 A4 268 D3
WC1 ....94 B4 233 C1
Westminster Pier
SW1 ....250 B1

Westminster Rd
Carshalton SM1,SM5 .218 B6
Ealing W7 ....108 C5
Edmonton N9 ....18 B3
Westminster Sch
SW1 ....116 A3 260 A6
Westminster Sta
SW1 ....116 A3 250 B1
Westmoat Cl BR3 ...186 A3
Westmont Rd KT10 ..212 C6
Westmoor Gdns EN3 ...6 D3
Westmoor Rd EN3 .....6 D3
Westmoor St SE7 ...121 D3
Westmore Ct SW15 .157 A6
Westmoreland Ave
DA16 ....145 C1
Westmoreland Ho
NW10 ....90 A4
Westmoreland Pl
5 BR1 ....209 A6
SW1 ....258 D1
Ealing W5 ....87 D2
Westmoreland Rd
BR2 ....209 A5
HA3,NW9 ....44 B5
SE17 ....139 B6
Barnes SW13 ......134 A4
Beckenham BR2,BR3 .208 D5
Westmoreland St
W1 ....238 B3
Westmoreland Terr
SW1 ....115 B1 258 D1
Penge SE20 ....184 B3
Westmorland Cl
3 Twickenham TW1 .153 B5
Wanstead E12 ......77 D6
Westmorland Ct 12
KT6 ....197 D2
Westmorland Dr
SM2 ....217 D1
Westmorland Rd
BR2 ....209 A5
E17 ....53 C3
Harrow HA1 ....41 D4
Westmorland Sq CR4 204 A4
Westmorland Way
CR4 ....203 D4
Westmount Ct W5 ...88 B2
Westmount Rd SE9 .144 C1
West Norwood Sta
SE27 ....160 D1
West Oak BR3 ......186 B2
Westoe Rd N9 ....18 B2
Weston Ave
East Molesey KT8 ..195 B5
Thames Ditton KT10,
KT7 ....196 C2
Westonbirt Ct 6
SE15 ....139 D6
Weston Ct N20 .....14 A4
N4 ....73 A5
3 Kingston KT1 ...198 A6
Weston Dr HA7 .....25 B2
Weston Ed Ctr The
SE5 ....139 A3
West One Ho W1 ...239 A3
Westone Mans 5
IG11 ....79 D1
Weston Gdns TW7 .130 C4
Weston Gn
Dagenham RM9 ......81 B4
Thames Ditton KT7 .196 C1
Weston Gr 1 BR1 .186 D2
Weston Green Prep Sch
KT7 ....196 C1
Weston Green Rd
KT7 ....196 C2
Weston Ho 9 E9 ...96 C6
4 NW6 ....69 A1
Weston Park Cl KT7 .196 C1
Weston Park Prim Sch
N8 ....50 B4
Weston Pk N8 ......50 B3
Kingston KT1 ......176 A1
Thames Ditton KT10,
KT7 ....196 C1
Weston Rd W4 .....111 A1
Bromley BR1 ......186 D3
Dagenham RM9 ......81 A4
Enfield EN2 ....5 B3
Ruislip HA4 ....61 D1
Thames Ditton KT7 .196 C1
Weston Rise
N1,WC1 ......94 B4 233 D2
Weston St
SE1 ....117 B4 252 D2
Weston Wlk 3 E8,E9 .74 B1

Westover Hill NW3 ...69 C6
Westover Rd SW18 ..158 A5
Westow Hill SE19 ...183 D4
Westow St SE19 ....183 D4
Westpark W5 ....87 D1
West Park Ave TW9 .132 D4
West Park Cl
Heston TW5 ....129 B6
Ilford RM6 ....58 D4
West Park Rd
Richmond TW9 .....132 C4
Southall UB2 ......108 B5
West Parkside SE10 .121 A2
Greenwich SE10 ....120 D3
West Pk HA5 ......166 A3
West Pl SW19 .....178 C5
West Point 2 SE1 .118 A1
Westpoint
Beckenham BR2 ....208 B6
Putney SW15 ......156 D5
Westpoint Trad Est
W3 ....88 D2
Westpole Ave EN4 ....3 B1
Westport Ct UB4 ...84 C3
Westport Rd E13 ....99 B3
Westport St E1 .....96 D1
West Poultry Ave
EC1 ....241 C3
West Quarters W12 ..90 A1
West Quay Dr UB4 ..85 A2
West Ramp TW6 ...126 C4
West Rd E15 ....98 D6
N2 ....30 B2
SW3 ....136 D6 267 D6
SW4 ....159 D6
Dagenham RM6 ......59 A3
Ealing W5 ....88 A2
East Barnet EN4 ....15 A3
East Bedfont TW14 .149 B4
Kingston KT2,KT3 ..177 A2
Tottenham N17 .....34 B4
West Drayton UB7 .104 B3
West Ridge Gdns UB6 .86 A5
West Row W10 .....91 A3
Westrow SW15 .....156 C5
Westrow Dr IG11 ....80 A2
Westrow Gdns IG3 ..79 D5
West Ruislip Elementary
Sch UB10 ....61 A5
West Ruislip Sta HA4 .61 A6
West Sheen Vale
TW9 ....132 B1
Westside N2 ....48 D6
NW4 ....28 B1
West Side Comm
SW19 ....178 C5
Westside Ct 1 W9 ..91 C3
West Smithfield
EC1 ....94 D2 241 D3
West Sq SE11 116 D3 261 C5
West St BR1 ....187 A1
DA7 ....147 B2
E11 ....76 C5
E17 ....53 D4
26 E2 ....96 B5
WC2 ....93 D1 239 D1
Carshalton SM5 ....218 D4
Croydon CR0 ......221 A4
Harrow HA1 ....42 C1
Sutton SM1 ....217 D3
West Street La SM5 .218 D4
West Street Pl 1
CR0 ....221 A4
West Surrey Ests
TW15 ....171 A2
West Sutton Sta SM1 217 C4
West Temple Sheen
SW14 ....154 A4
West Tenter St
E1 ....95 D1 243 D1
West Terr DA15 ....167 C3
West Thames Coll
TW7 ....130 C4
West Thamesmead Bsns
Pk SE28 ....123 D3
West Thornton Prim Sch
CR0 ....204 B3
West Towers HA5 ...40 D3
West Twyford Prim Sch
NW10 ....88 C5
Westvale Mews W3 .111 C4
Westview W7 ....86 C1
West View
Dagenham RM6 .....58 C4
East Bedfont TW14 .149 A4
Westview Cl NW10 ..67 D3
W10 ....90 C1
Westview Cres N9 ...17 C4
Westview Ct 3 WD6 ..9 D5
Westview Dr IG8 .....37 D3

West View Gdns WD6 ..9 D5
Westville Rd W12 ...112 A4
Thames Ditton KT7 .197 A2
Westward Rd E4 .....35 B5
Westward Way HA3 ..44 A3
West Warwick Pl
SW1 ....259 A3
West Way
Croydon CR0 ......223 A5
Edmonton N18 ......33 B6
Hounslow TW5 .....129 B4
Pinner HA5 ....40 D5
Ruislip HA4 ....39 D1
Shepperton TW17 ..193 B3
West Wickham BR4 .208 C3
Westway Cl SW20 ..200 B6
Westway Ct UB5 ....85 C5
Westway (Elevated Rd)
W10 ....91 B2
West Way Gdns CR0 .222 D6
Westway Lo 35 W2 ..91 C2
Westways KT19 ....215 D4
West Ways HA6 .....22 A1
Westwell 4 NW5 ....71 A2
Westwell Rd SW16 .182 A4
Westwell Road App
SW16 ....182 A4
Westwick 7 KT1 ...176 C1
Westwick Gdns W14 .112 D4
Cranford TW4,TW5 .128 C3
West Wickham Sta
BR3 ....208 A2
West Wlk
East Barnet EN4 ....15 A3
Hayes UB3 ....106 A5
Westwood Ave
Harrow HA2 ....63 D4
South Norwood SE19 .183 A4
Westwood Cl BR1 ..209 D6
Esher KT10 ....212 A5
Ruislip HA4 ....38 D3
Westwood Ct
Enfield EN1 ....17 C5
3 Forest Hill SE23 .162 C3
7 Wimbledon SW19 .179 B5
Westwood Gdns
SW13 ....133 D2
Westwood Hill SE26 .184 B6
Westwood Ho 5 N4 ..51 B2
W12 ....112 C5
Westwood La DA16 .145 D1
Westwood Language
College for Girls
SE19 ....183 B3
Westwood Pk SE23 .162 B4
Westwood Pl SE26 .184 A6
Westwood Prim Sch
DA16 ....145 C1
Westwood Rd 12 E16 121 B5
Barnes SW13 ......133 D2
Ilford IG3 ....58 A2
Westwood Sch WD23 ..8 B2
West Woodside DA5 .169 A3
Westwood Tech Coll
DA16 ....145 C1
Wetheral Ct SW17 ..180 B6
Wetheral Dr HA7 ....25 C1
Wetherby Cl UB5 ...63 D2
Wetherby Ct SE25 .183 C1
Wetherby Gdns
SW5 ....114 A2 256 A3
Wetherby Mans SW5 255 C2
Wetherby Mews
SW5 ....255 D2
Wetherby Pl
SW7 ....114 A2 256 B3
Wetherby Rd EN2 ....5 A4
Wetherby Way KT9 .214 A1
Wetherden St E17 ...53 B2
Wetherell Rd E9 .....96 D6
Wetherill Rd N10 ....31 A2
Wetland Centre The*
SW13 ....133 D3
Wevco Wharf SE15 .140 B6
Wexford Ho 9 E1 ...96 C2
Wexford Rd SW12 .158 D4
Weybourne St SW18 .158 A4
Weybridge Ct 19
SE16 ....118 B1
Weybridge Ho N4 ...51 A2
Weybridge Point 11
SW11 ....136 D3
Weybridge Rd CR7 .204 C5

Wey Ct KT19 ....215 A4
Weydown Cl SW19 .157 A3
Weyhill Ho 27 SE5 ..139 A3
Weyhill Rd 6 E1 ....96 A1
Wey Ho NW8 ......236 D5
Weylands Cl KT12 ..195 B1
Weylond Rd RM8 ....81 B5
Weyman Rd SE3 ...143 C4
Weymarks The N17 ...33 B4
Weymouth Ave NW7 .27 C5
W5 ....109 C3
Weymouth Cl 1 E6 .100 A1
Weymouth Ct 5 E2 ..95 D5
Belmont SM2 ......217 C1
15 Streatham SW2 .160 B4
Weymouth Ho SW8 .270 C3
Bromley BR2 ......186 D1
Weymouth Mews
W1 ....93 B2 238 C4
Weymouth Rd UB4 ..83 C4
Weymouth St
W1 ....93 B2 238 C4
Weymouth Terr 2 ...95 D5
SE28 ....123 B3
Weymouth Wlk HA7 .25 A4
Whadcoat St N4 .....72 C6
Whadden Ho 10 SE5 .139 C2
Whaddon Ho SW1 .247 D1
Whalebone Ave RM6 .59 B3
Whalebone Gr RM6 ..59 B3
Whalebone La E15 ...76 C1
Whalebone La N RM6 .59 A6
Whalebone La S RM6,
RM8 ....59 B2
Whales Yd E15 .....76 C1
Wharfdale Cl N11 ...31 A4
Wharfdale Rd
N1 ....94 A5 233 B4
Wharfedale Ct 5 E5 .74 D4
Wharfedale Gdns
CR7,SW16 ....204 B6
Wharfedale St SW10 255 C1
Wharf La TW1 .....153 A3
Wharf Pl E2 ....96 B6
Wharf Rd E15 ....98 B6
N1 ....95 A5 235 A3
NW1 ......93 D6 232 D5
Enfield EN3 ....19 A5
Wharfside Rd E16 ...98 C2
Wharf St E16 ....98 C2
Wharncliffe Dr UB1 .108 B5
Wharncliffe Gdns
SE25 ....183 C1
Wharncliffe Rd SE25 .183 C1
Wharton Cl NW10 ...67 C2
Wharton Ho SE1 ...263 C6
Wharton Rd BR1 ...187 B2
Wharton St
WC1 ....94 B4 233 D1
Whateley Rd SE22 .161 D6
Penge SE20 ....184 D3
Whatley Ave SW20 .201 A6
Whatman Rd SE23 .162 D4
Wheatfields E6 .....100 D1
Enfield EN3 ....19 A5
Wheatfield Way KT1 .176 A1
Wheathill Ho SE20 .184 B1
Wheathill Rd SE20 .206 B6
Wheatland Ho 7
SE22 ....139 C2
Wheatlands TW5 ...129 C6
Wheatlands Rd
SW17 ....159 A1
Wheatley Cl NW4 ...28 A1
Wheatley Gdns N9 ..17 C2
Wheatley Ho NW5 ..71 B4
3 Putney SW15 ...156 A4
Wheatley Mans 8
IG11 ....80 A1
Wheatley Rd TW7 ..130 D2
Wheatley's Ait TW16 .194 A4
Wheatley St W1 ...238 B3
Wheatly Cres UB3 .106 A6
Wheat Sheaf Cl E14 .119 D2
Wheatsheaf Cl UB5 ..63 D4
Wheatsheaf La SW6 .134 C5
SW8 ....270 B4
Wheatsheaf Par 6
BR4 ....207 B1
Wheatsheaf Terr
SW6 ....264 D3
Wheatstone Cl SW19 180 C2
Wheatstone Ho 7
W10 ....91 A2
Wheatstone Rd W10 .91 A2
Wheeler 2 NW9 ....27 D3
Wheeler Ct 5 SW11 .136 C2
Wheeler Gdns N1 ..233 B6
Wheelers Cross IG11 101 B5
Wheelers Dr HA4 ....39 A1

Wheeler's St SM1 ...217 C5
Wheelock Cl DA8 ...147 D5
Wheelwright St N7 ..72 B1
Whelan Way SM6 ..219 D5
Wheldon Ct SE1 ...253 C2
Wheler Ho E1 .....243 C5
Wheler St E1 ..95 D3 243 C5
Whellock Rd W4 ...111 C3
Whernside Cl SE28 .124 C6
Whetstone Cl N20 ...14 B2
Whetstone Park
WC2 ......94 B1 240 C2
Whetstone Rd SE3 .143 D4
Whewell Rd N19 ....72 A6
Whichcote St SE1 .251 A3
Whidborne Bldgs
WC1 ....233 A1
Whidborne Cl SE8 .141 C3
Whidborne St WC1 .233 B1
Whimbrel Cl SE28 .124 C6
Whimbrel Way UB4 ..84 D2
Whinchat Rd SE18,
Whinfell Cl SW16 ..181 D5
Whinyates Rd SE9 .144 A2
Whippendell Cl BR5 .190 B1
Whippendell Way
BR5 ....190 B1
Whippingham Ho 17
E3 ....97 B4
Whipps Cross E17 ...54 B4
Whipps Cross Ho E17 .54 B4
Whipps Cross Hospl
E10,E11 ....54 C3
Whipps Cross Rd E11 .54 C3
Whiskin St
EC1 ....94 D4 234 C1
Whisperwood Cl HA3 .24 C1
Whistler Gdns HA8 ..26 B1
Whistler Mews
2 SE15 ....139 D5
Dagenham RM8 .....80 C1
Whistlers Ave
SW11 .....136 B5 266 D3
Whistler St N5 ......72 B3
Whistler Twr SW10 .266 A3
Whistler Wlk SW10 .266 B4
Whiston Ho 18 N1 ...72 C1
Whiston Rd E2 .....96 A6
Whitakers Lo EN2 ...5 B4
Whitbread Cl N17 ...34 A2
Whitbread Ctr EC1 .242 C5
Whitbread Rd SE4 .141 B1
Whitburn Rd SE13 .142 A1
Whitby Ave NW10 ...88 D4
Whitby Ct N7 ....72 A4
Whitby Gdns
Carshalton SM1,SM5 .218 B6
Whitby Ho NW8 ...229 A5
Whitby Rd SE18 ...122 B2
Carshalton SM1,SM5 .218 B6
Harrow HA2 ....64 A5
Ruislip HA4 ....62 C6
Whitby St E1 ......243 C6
Whitcher Cl SE14 ..141 A6
Whitcher Pl NW1 ....71 C2
Whitchurch Ave HA8 .26 B3
Whitchurch Cl HA8 ..26 B3
Whitchurch Ct HA8 ..26 B3
Whitchurch Fst & Mid
Schs HA7 ....25 D3
Whitchurch Gdns HA8 26 B4
Whitchurch Ho
16 W10 ....90 D3
Catford SE6 ....164 A1
Whitchurch La HA8 ..26 B3
Whitchurch La W11 .112 D6
Whitcomb Ct W1 ...249 D5
Whitcombe Mews
TW9 ....132 D4
Whitcomb St
WC2 ......115 D6 249 D5
Whiteadder Way E14 119 D2
Whitear Wlk E15 ....76 B2
Whitebarn La RM10 .103 C6
Whitebeam Ave BR2 .210 C3
Whitebeam Cl SW9 .270 D5
Whitebeam Ho 3
NW3 ....70 D2
White Bear Pl NW3 ..70 B4
White Bear Yd EC1 .241 A5
White Bridge Ave
CR4 ....202 B6
White Bridge Cl
TW14 ....149 C5
White Butts Rd HA4 .62 D5
Whitechapel High St
E1 ....95 D1 243 D2
Whitechapel Rd E1 ..96 B2
Whitechapel Sta E1 ..96 B2

Whitechurch La 2 E1 96 A1
White City W10 .....90 C1
White City Cl W12 ..112 C6
White City Est 21
W12 ....112 B6
White City Rd W12 .112 C6
White City Sta W12 .112 C6
Whitecliff Ho SW18 .157 D5
White Conduit St N1 234 B4
Whitecote Rd UB1 ...86 A1
White Craig Cl HA5 ..23 C5
Whitecroft Cl BR3 ..208 B5
Whitecroft Way BR3 .208 B5
Whitecross Pl EC2 .242 D4
Whitecross St
EC1 ....95 A3 242 B5
White Cube art gallery*
N1 ....95 C4
Whitefield Ave NW2 ..46 C1
Whitefield Cl SW15 .157 A5
Whitefield Sch NW11 .46 D1
Chingford E17 .....36 A1
Whitefoot La BR1 ..164 B1
Whitefoot Terr BR1 .164 D1
Whitefriars Ave HA3 .24 C1
Whitefriars Centre Coll
HA3 ....42 C6
Whitefriars Ct N12 ..30 B5
Whitefriars Dr HA3 ..24 C1
Whitefriars Fst & Mid Sch
HA3 ....24 C1
Whitefriars St
EC4 ....94 C1 241 B1
Whitefriars Trad Est
HA3 ....24 B1
White Gate Gdns HA3 24 D1
Whitegates 4 EN5 ...13 D6
White Gdns RM10 ...81 C2
Whitehall SW1 .....250 A2
Whitehall Cres KT9 .213 D3
Whitehall Ct
SW1 ....116 A5 250 B3
Whitehall Gdns SW1 250 A3
Acton W3 ....110 C5
Chingford, Chingford Green
E4 ....20 C3
Chiswick W4 ......132 D6
Whitehall La IG9 ....21 A2
Whitehall Lo N10 ....49 A6
Woodford IG8 ......21 A1
Whitehall Mans 3
N19 ....49 C1
Whitehall Park Rd
W4 ....132 D6
Whitehall Pk N19 ...49 C1
Whitehall Pl
WC2,SW1 ...116 A5 250 A3
Wallington SM5 ...219 B4
Whitehall Prim Sch
E4 ....20 C2
Whitehall Rd W7 ...109 A4
Bromley BR2 ......209 D5
Chingford E4 ......20 C2
Harrow HA1 ....42 C2
Thornton Heath CR7 .204 C4
Woodford IG8 ......21 A1
Whitehall St N17 ....33 D3
White Hart Ct EC2 .243 A3
White Hart La NW10 .67 D2
Mortlake SW13 ....133 C2
White Hart Lane Sch
N22 ....32 D3
White Hart Lane Sta
N17 ....33 D3
White Hart Lane
(Tottenham Hotspur FC)
N17 ....34 A3
White Hart Rd SE18 .123 C2
White Hart Rdbt UB5 .84 D5
White Hart St EC4 ..241 D2
SE11 .....116 C1 261 B2
White Hart Terr N17 .33 D3
White Hart Yd SE1 .252 C3
Whitehaven Cl BR2 .209 A5
Whitehaven St NW8 .237 A5
Whitehead Cl
Edmonton N18 .....33 B5
Wandsworth SW18 .158 A4
Whitehead Ct N10 ...31 A2
Whitehead Ho 8
SW15 ....156 D6
Whitehead's Gr
SW3 ....114 C2 257 B3
White Heart Ave UB8 .83 A2
Whiteheath Ave HA4 .39 A2
Whiteheath Inf Sch
HA4 ....39 A3
Whiteheath Jun Sch
HA4 ....39 A2

White Heron Mews
 TW11 ....174 D4
White Ho N9 ....18 C2
2 SW11 ....136 B3
3 Streatham SW4 ..159 D4
Whitehorn Ho **6** E1 .118 C5
White Horse Hill BR7,
 SE9 ....188 C6
White Horse La E1 ..96 D2
Whitehorse La SE25 .205 C5
Whitehorse Manor Inf Sch
 CR7 ....205 B5
Whitehorse Manor Jun
 Sch CR7 ....205 B5
Whitehorse Mews
 SE1 ....261 C6
Whitehorse Rd E1 ...97 A2
E6 ....100 B4
Whitehorse Rd CR0,
 CR7 ....205 B5
White Horse St
 W1 ....115 B5 248 D3
White Horse Yd W1 .242 C2
White Ho The N17 ...51 C6
 NW1 ....238 D6
White House Ct N14 .15 D2
1 Beckenham BR3 ..186 A2
White House Dr HA7 .25 C6
Whitehouse Est E10 .54 A3
White House La EN2 ..5 A4
Whitehouse Way N14 .15 B1
White Kennett St E1 .243 B2
Whitelands Coll,
 Roehampton, Univ of
 Surrey SW18 ....157 A4
Whitelands Ho SW3 .257 D2
Whiteledges W13 ....87 C1
Whitelegg Rd E13 ....98 D5
Whiteley Ho **9** SW4 .159 D4
Whiteley Rd SE19 ...183 B5
Whiteleys Ctr W2 ....91 C1
Whiteleys Ho TW13 .151 C1
Whiteleys Par **5**
 UB10 ....82 D3
Whiteleys Way TW13 151 C1
White Lion Ct EC3 ...243 A1
White Lion Hill
 EC4 ......116 D6 251 D6
White Lion St
 N1 ....94 C5 234 B3
White Lion Yd W1 ...248 C6
White Lo **7** Ealing W5 .87 C2
 South Norwood SE19 ..182 C3
Whitelock Ho **21** E9 ..74 D2
White Lodge Cl N2 ..48 B3
 Sutton SM2 ....218 A4
White Lodge The Royal
 Ballet Sch TW10 ...155 B3
Whitely Ct TW13 ....151 B1
Whiteness Ho **18**
 SW9 ....138 C4
White Oak Dr BR3 ..186 A1
White Oak Gdns
 DA15 ....167 D4
Whiteoak Ho SE19 ..183 A4
Whiteoaks La UB6 ...86 B5
White Orchards
 Barnet N20 ....13 B3
 Stanmore HA7 ....25 A5
White Post La E9 ...75 C2
White Post St SE14,
 SE15 ....140 C5
White Rd E15 ....76 C1
Whites Ave IG2 .....57 C3
Whites Dr BR2 .....208 D2
White's Grounds
 SE1 ......117 C4 253 B2
White's Grounds Est
 SE1 ....253 B2
White's Mdw BR1 ...210 C5
White's Row
 E1 ....95 D2 243 C3
White's Sq SW4 ....137 D1
White St UB2 ......106 D4
Whitestile Rd TW8 ..109 D1
Whitestone La TW3 ..70 A5
Whitestone Wlk NW3 .70 A5
Whitethorn Ave UB7 .104 B6
Whitethorn Gdns
 Croydon CR0 ......222 B6
 Enfield EN2 ....17 B6
Whitethorn Pl UB7 .104 B5
Whitethorn St E3 ....97 C2
Whiteways 46 D5
Whitewebbs Way
 BR5 ....189 D2
Whitfield Ct SW4 ...270 A1
3 Dulwich SE21 ....183 C6
 Redbridge IG1 ....56 B2

Whitfield Gdns W1 ..239 B4
Whitfield Ho NW8 ..237 A5
Whitfield Pl W1 ....239 B5
Whitfield Rd DA7 ..147 B5
E6 ....77 C1
SE10,SE13 ....142 B4
Whitfield St
 W1 ....93 C2 239 B4
Whitford Gdns CR4 ..202 D6
Whitgift Ave CR2 ...221 A3
Whitgift Ct CR2 ....221 A3
Whitgift Ctr CR0 ...221 A6
Whitgift Ho SE11 ...260 C4
 SW11 ....267 A2
 Croydon CR2 ......221 A3
Whitgift Sch CR2 ...221 A3
Whitgift St
 SE11 .....116 B2 260 C4
 Croydon CR0 ......221 A5
Whiting Ave IG11 ....78 D1
Whitings Hill Prim Sch
 EN5 ....12 C6
Whitings Rd EN5 ....12 C6
Whitings The IG2 ....57 C4
Whitings Way E6 ...100 C2
Whitland Rd SM5 ...202 B1
Whitley Cl TW19 ...148 A5
Whitley Ho SE19 ...269 B6
Whitley Rd N17 ....33 C1
Whitlock Dr SW19 ..157 A3
Whitman Ho **20** E2 ..96 C4
Whitman Rd E3 ....97 A3
Whitmead Cl CR2 ..221 C2
Whitmore Cl N11 ....31 B5
Whitmore Comm Sch
 N1 ....235 C6
Whitmore Gdns NW10 90 C5
Whitmore High Sch
 HA1,HA2 ....42 A1
Whitmore Ho **20** E1 ..95 C6
 N11 ....30 D6
Whitmore Rd N1 ....95 C6
 Beckenham BR3 ....207 B6
 Harrow HA1 ....42 A2
Whitnell Ct **7** SW15 .156 D6
Whitnell Way SW15 .156 D6
Whitney Ave IG4 ....55 D5
Whitney Ho **6** SE22 ..138 C1
Whitney Rd E10 ....53 D2
Whitney Wlk DA14 ..191 A4
Whitstable Cl
 Beckenham BR3 ....185 B2
 Ruislip HA4 ....61 C6
Whitstable Ho **11** W10 90 D1
Whitstable Pl **9** CR0 221 A4
Whitsters Ho SE1 ...253 C2
Whittaker **3** NW9 ....27 D3
Whittaker Ave TW10,
 TW9 ....153 D6
Whittaker Ct SW4 ..270 B1
Whittaker Pl **24**
 TW10 ....153 D6
Whittaker Rd E6 ....77 D1
 Cheam SM3 ....217 B5
Whittaker St SW1 ..258 A3
Whittaker Way **17**
 SE1 ....118 A2
Whittam Ho SE27 ..183 A5
Whitta Rd E12 ......77 D4
Whittell Gdns SE26 .162 C1
Whitten Lo N12 .....30 C6
Whittingham **6** N17 ..34 B3
Whittingham Ct W4 .133 C5
Whittingstall Mans
 SW6 ....264 D1
Whittingstall Rd
 SW6 ......135 B4 264 D1
Whittington Ave UB4 .83 D2
Whittington Ct N2 ...48 D4
 Penge SE20 ....184 B1
Whittington Hospl The
 N19 ....71 C6
Whittington Mews
 N12 ....30 A6
Whittington Rd N22 .32 A3
Whittington Way HA5 .41 A4
Whittle **4** NW9 .....27 D3
Whittle Cl E17 .....53 A2
 Southall UB1 ....85 D1
Whittle Rd
 Heston TW5 ....128 C5
 Southall UB2 ....107 D4
Whittlesea Cl HA3 ...24 A3
Whittlesea Path HA3 .24 A2
Whittlesea Rd HA3 ..24 A2
Whittlesea Sch HA3 .24 A3

Whittlesey St
 SE1 ......116 C5 251 B3
Whitton NW3 ....70 D1
Whitton Ave E UB6 ..65 A2
Whitton Ave W UB5,
 UB6 ....64 B3
Whitton Cl UB6 .....65 D1
Whitton Dene
 Isleworth TW3,TW7 ..152 B5
 Isleworth TW3,TW7 ..152 B6
Whitton Dr UB6 .....65 A2
Whitton Manor Rd
 TW7 ....152 A5
Whitton Rd
 Hounslow TW3 .....151 D6
 Twickenham TW1 ...153 A4
Whitton Road Rdbt
 TW1 ....152 D5
Whitton Sch TW2 ...151 D2
Whitton Sta TW2 ...152 A4
Whitton Waye TW2,
 TW3 ....151 C5
Whitton Wlk E3 .....97 C4
Whitwell Rd **11** E5 ...74 B6
Whitwell Rd E13 ....99 A4
Whitworth Cres EN3 ..7 C6
Whitworth Ho SE1 ..262 B5
Whitworth Rd SE18 .144 C5
 South Norwood SE25 .205 D5
Whitworth St SE10 .120 C1
Whorlton Rd SE15 ..140 B2
Whychcote Point NW2 46 C2
Whymark Ave N22 ...50 D4
Whytecroft TW5 ....128 D5
Whyteville Ho E7 ....77 B2
Whyteville Rd E7 ....77 B2
Whytlaw Ho **11** E3 ...97 B2
Wickers Oake SE19 ..183 D6
Wicker St **2** E1 .....96 B1
Wicket Rd UB6 ......87 A4
Wickets The TW15 ..170 A6
Wicket The CR0 ....223 C3
Wickfield Ho **29** SE16 118 A4
Wickford Ho **4** E1 ...96 C3
Wickford St E1 .....96 C3
Wickford Way E17 ...52 D1
Wickham Ave
 Cheam KT4,SM3 ...216 C3
 Croydon CR0 ......207 A1
Wickham Chase BR4 208 C2
Wickham Cl E1 .....96 C2
 Enfield EN3 ....6 C2
 New Malden KT3 ...199 D4
Wickham Common Prim
 Sch BR4 ....225 A4
Wickham Court Rd
 BR4 ....224 A6
Wickham Cres BR4 ..224 A6
Wickham Ct DA16 ..145 C3
Wickham Gdns SE4 ..141 B3
Wickham Ho SW15 ..156 D5
Wickham La SE2,
 SE18 ....146 A6
Wickham Mews SE4 .141 B3
Wickham Rd SE4 ...141 B2
 Beckenham BR3 ....207 D6
 Chingford E4 ....36 A3
 Croydon CR0 ....207 B1
 Harrow HA3 ....24 B1
Wickham St DA16 ..146 A4
 SE11 .....116 B1 260 C2
 Bexley DA16 ....145 C3
Wickham Way BR3 ..208 A4
Wick Ho **1** KT1 .....175 D2
Wick La E3 ....75 B1
E3 ....97 C6
Wickliffe Ave N3 ....29 A1
Wickliffe Gdns HA9 ..66 D6
Wicklow Ct SE26 ...184 C5
Wicklow Ho N16 ....51 D1
Wicklow St
 WC1 ......94 B4 233 C2
Wick Mews **1** E9 ....75 A2
Wick Rd E9 ....75 A2
 Hackney E9 ....74 D2
 Teddington TW11 ...175 C3
Wicks Cl SE12 .....187 D6
Wick Sq E9 ....75 B2
Wickstead Ho TW8 ..110 B1
Wicksteed Ho SE1 ..262 B5
Wickway Ct **7** SE15 .139 D6
Wickwood St SE5 ...138 D3
Widdenham Rd N7 ...72 B4
Widdicombe Ave HA2 .63 A6
Widdin St E15 ......76 C1
Widecombe Ct N2 ...48 B4
Widecombe Gdns IG4 56 A5
Widecombe Ho **33**
 SE5 ....139 A3
Widecombe Rd SE9 .166 A1

Widecombe Way N2 ..48 B5
Widegate St E1 ....243 B3
Widenham CI HA5 ...40 C4
Wide Way CR4 .....203 D6
Widewing CI TW11 ..175 B3
Widford **8** NW1 ....71 B2
Widford Ho N1 .....234 C3
Widgeon CI E16 .....99 B1
Widgeon Path SE28 .123 C5
Widley Rd W9 ......91 C3
Widmer Ct TW5 ....129 A3
Widmore Lodge Rd
 BR1 ....187 D1
Widmore Rd BR1 ...187 C1
 Hillingdon UB8 ......82 C3
Widnes Ho **6** N7 ...72 C3
Wieland Rd HA6 ....22 C3
Wigan Ho E5 ....52 B1
Wigeon Way UB4 ...84 D1
Wiggins La TW10 ...153 C2
Wiggins Mead NW9 ..27 D3
Wigginton Ave HA9 ..66 D2
Wightman Rd N4,N8 ..50 C4
Wighton Mews TW7 .130 C3
Wigley Rd TW13 ...150 B3
Wigmore Ct **4** W13 .109 A5
Wigmore Hall W1 ..238 C2
Wigmore Pl
 W1 ....93 B1 238 C2
Wigmore Rd SM5 ...202 C1
Wigmore St
 W1 ....93 A1 238 B2
Wigmore Wlk SM5 ..218 C6
Wigram Ct SW11 ...267 A2
Wigram Ho **6** E14 ..119 D6
Wigram Rd E11 ....55 C3
Wigram Sq E17 .....54 A6
Wigston CI N18 ....33 C5
Wigston Rd E13 ....99 B3
Wigton Pl SE11 ....261 B1
Wigton Rd E17 .....35 C2
Wilberforce Ct
 2 SE28 ....124 C5
 Edgware HA8 ....26 B6
Wilberforce Ho **4**
 SW11 ....136 B2
Wilberforce Prim Sch
 W10 ....91 A4
Wilberforce Rd N4 ..72 D6
 N4,N5 ....73 A5
 NW9 ....46 A3
Wilberforce Way
 SW19 ....178 A4
Wilbraham Ho SW8 .270 A3
Wilbraham Pl SW1 ..258 A4
Wilbury Prim Sch N18 33 B5
Wilbury Way N18 ...33 B5
Wilby Mews
 W11 ......113 B5 244 D4
Wilcox Cl SW8 ....270 A4
Wilcox Gdns TW17 .192 B6
Wilcox Ho **6** E3 ....97 B2
Wilcox Pl SW1 .....259 B5
Wilcox Rd
 SW8 ......138 A5 270 A4
 Sutton SM1 ....217 D4
 Teddington TW11 ...174 B6
Wildcroft Gdns HA8 ..25 D4
Wildcroft Manor
 SW15 ....156 C4
Wildcroft Rd SW15 .156 C4
Wild Ct WC2 ..94 B1 240 C2
Wilde Cl E8 ....96 A6
Wilde Pl Edmonton N13 32 D4
 Wandsworth SW18 ..158 B4
Wilder Cl HA4 ......40 B1
Wilde Rd DA8 .....147 D5
Wilderness Mews
 SW4 ....137 B1
Wilderness Rd BR7 .188 D3
Wilderness The
 East Molesey KT8 ..196 A6
 Hampton TW12 ....173 D6
Wilderton Rd N16 ...51 C2
Wildfell Rd SE6 ....163 D4
Wild Goose Dr SE14 .140 C4
Wild Hatch NW11 ...47 D3
Wilding Ho **17** E9 ...74 D2
Wild March Ct EN3 ...7 A4
Wild's Rents
 SE1 ......117 C3 263 A6
Wild St WC2 ..94 B1 240 C1
Wildwood Cl SE12 ..164 D4
Wildwood Gr NW3 ..48 A5
Wildwood Rd NW11 ..48 A3
Wildwood Rise NW11 .48 A3
Wildwood Terr NW3 ..48 A1
Wilford Cl EN2 ......5 B2
Wilford Ho **3** SE18 .122 D1

Wilford Rd CR0 ....205 A2
Wilfred Fienburgh Ho
 N7 ....71 D4
Wilfred Owen Cl
 SW19 ....180 A4
Wilfred St
 SW1 ......115 C3 259 A6
Wilfrid Gdns W3 ....89 A2
Wilkes Rd **3** TW8 ..132 A6
Wilkes St E1 .95 D2 243 D4
Wilkie Ho SW1 .....259 D2
Wilkins Cl Hayes UB3 .105 D1
 Mitcham CR4 ......180 C2
Wilkins Ho SW1 ...269 A6
Wilkinson Cl UB10 ..83 A6
Wilkinson Ho SW17 .180 B6
Wilkinson Ho N1 ...235 D3
 Isleworth TW7 .....130 D2
Wilkinson Rd E16 ...99 C1
Wilkinson St
 SW8 ......138 B5 270 C3
Wilkinson Way W4 ..111 B4
Wilkin St NW5 .....71 B2
Wilks Gdns CR0 ...207 A1
Wilks Pl N1 ....95 C5
Willan Rd N17 .....33 C1
Willan Wall E16 ...120 D6
Willard St SW8 ....137 B2
Willbury Ho **4** N7 ..71 D3
Willcocks Cl KT9 ..214 A5
Willcott Rd W3 ....110 D5
Will Crooks Gdns
 SE9 ....143 D1
Willenfield Rd NW10 .89 A5
Willenhall Ave EN5 ..14 A5
Willenhall Ct EN5 ...14 A5
Willenhall Dr UB3 ..105 C6
Willenhall Rd SE18 .122 D1
Willersley Ave BR6 ..227 B5
 DA15 ....167 D4
Willersley Cl DA15 ..167 D3
Willesden Community
 Hospl The NW10 ...68 A1
Willesden Green Sta
 NW2 ....68 C2
Willesden High Sch
 NW10 ....90 B6
Willesden Junction Sta
 NW10 ....89 D4
Willesden La NW2,
 NW6 ....68 D2
Willes Rd NW5 .....71 B2
Willet Cl **3** UB5 ....84 C4
Willett Cl BR5 .....211 C3
Willett Ho **7** E13 ...99 A5
 SW9 ....138 C2
Willett Pl CR7 .....204 C4
Willett Rd CR7 ....204 C4
Willett Way BR5,BR6 .211 C3
William Allen Ho HA8 .26 B3
William Atkinson Ho
 N17 ....33 C3
William Banfield Ho **10**
 SW6 ....135 B3
William Barefoot Dr
 SE9 ....166 C1
William Bellamy Inf Sch
 RM10 ....81 C6
William Bellamy Jun Sch
 RM10 ....81 C6
William Booth Meml
 Training Coll SE5 ..139 B3
William Booth Rd
 SE20 ....184 A2
William Brown Ct
 SE27 ....160 D2
William Byrd Sch
 UB3 ....127 A6
William Carey Way
 HA1 ....42 C3
William Caslon Ho **28**
 E2 ....96 B5
William Channing Ho **6**
 E2 ....96 B4
William C Harvey Sch
 N17 ....33 B1
William Cl SE13 ....142 A2
 Finchley N2 ....30 B1
 Southall UB2 ....108 A4
William Covell Cl EN2 ..4 B3
William Ct
 4 Ealing W5 ......87 C2
 Ilford IG6 ....57 B5
William Davies Prim Sch
 E7 ....77 D2
William Davis Prim Sch
 E2 ....96 A3
William Dromey Ct
 NW6 ....69 B1

William Dunbar Ho
 NW6 ....91 B5
William Dyce Mews **1**
 SW16 ....181 D6
William Ellis Sch NW5 71 A5
William Ellis Way **16**
 SE16 ....118 A3
William Evans Ho **9**
 SE8 ....118 D2
William Ford CE Jun Sch
 RM10 ....81 C1
William Gdns SW15 .156 A6
William Guy Gdns **47**
 E3 ....97 C4
William Harvey Ho **1**
 SW19 ....157 A3
William Ho NW2 ....68 C5
 Edmonton N13 ......32 D4
William Hunt Mans
 SW13 ....134 C6
William IV St
 WC2 ......116 A6 250 A5
William Margrie Cl **1**
 SE15 ....140 A3
William Mews
 SW1 ......114 D4 247 D1
William Morley Cl E6 .99 D6
William Morris Acad
 W6 ....112 D1
William Morris Cl E17 .53 B6
William Morris Ho
 W6 ....134 D6
William Morris Mid Sch
 CR4 ....203 D6
William Morris Sch
 E17 ....35 A2
William Morris Way
 SW6 ....136 A3
William Patten Prim Sch
 N16 ....73 B3
William Pl **31** E3 ....97 B5
William Rainbird Ho **8**
 N17 ....33 D3
William Rathbone Ho **3**
 E2 ....96 B4
William Rd
 NW1 ......93 C4 232 A1
 Sutton SM1 ....218 A3
 Wimbledon SW19 ...179 A3
William Rushbrooke Ho **4**
 SE16 ....118 A2
Williams Ave E17 ...35 B2
William Saville Ho **2**
 NW6 ....91 B5
William's Bldgs **1** E2 .96 C3
Williams Cl SW6 ...135 B3
Williams Dr TW3 ...129 C1
Williams Gr
 Kingston KT6 ......197 C3
 Wood Green N22 ...32 C2
Williams Ho **9** E3 ...97 C4
 9 E9 ....96 B6
 14 Streatham SW2 .160 C2
Williams La
 Morden SM4 ....202 A4
 Mortlake SW14 ....133 A3
William Smith Ho **10**
 DA17 ....125 C3
Williamson Cl SE10 .120 D1
Williamson Ct SE17 .262 A1
Williamson Rd N4 ...50 D2
Williamson St N7 ...72 A4
Williamson Way NW7 .29 A4
William Sq **15** SE16 .119 A6
Williams Rd W13 ...109 A5
William's Rd W13 ...109 A5
William St E10 .....53 D3
 SW1 ......114 D4 247 D1
 Barking IG11 ....79 A1
 Carshalton SM5 ....218 D5
 Tottenham N17 .....33 D3
Williams Terr CR0 ..220 C2
William Torbitt Prim Sch
 IG2 ....57 D4
William Tyndale Prim Sch
 N1 ....72 D1
William Winter Ct **29**
 SW2 ....160 C4
William Wood Ho **3**
 SE26 ....162 C1
Willifield Way NW11 .47 C4
Willingale Cl IG8 ....37 C4
Willingdon Rd N22 ..32 C4
Willingham Cl **4** NW5 71 C3
Willingham Terr NW5 .71 C3
Willingham Way KT1 176 C1
Willington Ct E5 ....75 A5

Willington Prep Sch
SW19 ....**179** B5
Willington Rd SW9 ....**138** A2
Willis Ave SM2 .....**218** C2
Willis Ho 7 E14 .....**119** D6
2 Ilford E12 ....**78** C1
Willis Rd E15 ....**98** D5
Thornton Heath CR0 ...**205** A2
Willis St E14 ....**97** D1
Willows The CR0 ....**223** A6
Will Miles Ct 6
SW19 ....**180** A3
Willmore End SW19 ..**179** D1
Willoughby Ave CR0 ..**220** B4
Willoughby Gr N17 ....**34** B3
Willoughby Hall Dyslexia
Ctr NW3 ....**70** B4
Willoughby Ho 34 E1 **118** B5
EC2 ....**242** C3
Willoughby La N17 ....**34** B3
Willoughby Mews N17 **34** B3
Willoughby Park Rd
N17 ....**34** B3
Willoughby Rd N8 ....**50** C5
NW3 ....**70** B4
Kingston KT2 ....**176** B2
Twickenham TW1 ....**153** D6
Willoughby St WC1 ..**240** A3
Willoughbys The
SW14 ....**133** C1
Willoughby Way SE7 .**121** B2
Willow Ave DA15 ....**168** A5
Barnes SW13 ......**133** D3
Yiewsley UB7 ......**104** B6
Willowbank SW6 .....**135** A2
Willow Bank TW10 ..**153** B1
Willowbank Rd SE15 .**139** D6
Willow Bridge Rd N1 ..**73** A2
Willowbrook Rd
Southall UB2 ......**107** C3
Stanwell TW19 .....**148** A2
Willow Bsns Pk SE26 **162** C1
Willow Cl BR2 ......**210** B4
Brentford TW8 .....**131** C6
Buckhurst Hill IG9 ...**21** D1
12 Catford SE6 ....**164** D3
Sidcup DA5 ....**169** B5
Willow Cotts
Carshalton CR4 ....**202** D2
Feltham TW13 .....**151** A1
Richmond TW9 ....**132** C6
Willowcourt Ave HA3 .**43** B4
Willow Ct EC2 ....**243** A6
N7 ....**72** B3
SW9 ....**138** C4
40 W2 ....**91** C2
7 E11 ....**76** C6
Ashford TW16 .....**171** C3
Beckenham BR3 ...**185** C2
Chiswick W4 ......**133** C5
8 Dagenham RM8 ..**58** D2
Edgware HA8 ......**26** A6
Harrow HA3 ....**24** D2
Ilford IG1 ....**79** A3
Kingston KT3 .....**198** D6
3 Streatham SW16 .**160** B1
Thornton Heath CR7 .**205** B4
Willow Ctr The CR4 .**202** D2
Willow Dean HA5 ....**22** D1
Willowdene N6 ......**48** D2
1 SE15 ....**140** B4
5 SE15 ....**140** B5
Willow Dene WD23 ...**8** C4
Willowdene Cl TW2 ..**152** A4
Willowdene Ct N20 ..**14** A4
Willow Dene Sch
SE18 ....**145** C4
Willow Dr EN5 ....**1** A1
Willow End N20 ....**13** C2
Northwood HA6 ....**22** A4
Surbiton KT6 ......**198** A1
Willow Farm La
SW15 ....**134** B2
Willowfields Cl SE18 .**123** C1
Willowfield Sec Sch
E17 ....**52** D6
Willow Gdns
Heston TW5 ....**129** C4
Ruislip HA4 ....**61** D6
Willow Gn NW9 .....**27** C2
Borehamwood WD6 ..**11** B6
Willow Gr BR7 ......**188** D4
E13 ....**99** A5
Ruislip HA4 ....**39** D1
Willow Hall NW3 ....**70** B4

Willowhayne Gdns
KT4 ....**216** C4
Willow Ho 14 N2 ......**30** B1
9 NW3 ....**70** D2
W10 ....**90** D3
Feltham TW14 .....**150** B6
Willow La SE18 ....**122** C2
Mitcham CR4 ......**202** D3
Willow Lo
6 Ashford TW16 ...**171** D3
Fulham SW6 ......**134** D4
New Barnet EN5 ...**14** A4
Putney SW15 .....**134** B4
Willow Lodge 10
SW8 ....**137** B2
Willow Manor SM1 ..**217** B4
Willowmead Cl W5 ...**87** D2
Willow Mount CR0 ..**221** C5
Willow Pl
SW1 ......**115** C2 **259** B4
Willow Rd NW3 .....**70** B4
W5 ....**110** A4
Dagenham RM6 ....**59** A3
Enfield EN1 ....**5** C3
New Malden KT3 ...**199** A4
Wallington SM6 ...**219** B1
Willows Ave SM4 ...**201** D4
Willows Cl HA5 ......**22** C1
Willows Sch The UB4 .**84** D3
Chingford E4 ....**20** B4
Willows Terr NW10 ..**89** D5
Willows The N20 ....**14** A1
Beckenham BR3 ...**185** C2
Claygate KT10 ....**212** A4
Wallend E12 ....**78** C1
Loughton IG10 .....**21** D6
Willow Tree Cl E3 ...**97** B6
Willowtree Cl UB10 ..**61** A5
Willow Tree Cl
Hayes UB4 ....**84** C3
Wandsworth SW18 .**157** D3
Willow Tree Ct DA14 .**189** D5
5 Wembley HA0 ...**65** D3
Willow Tree La UB4 ..**84** C3
Willow Tree Prim Sch
UB5 ....**63** A2
Willowtree Way
SW16 ....**182** C2
Willow Tree Wlk BR1 **187** B2
Willow Vale BR7 ....**188** D4
W12 ....**112** A5
Willow View SW19 ..**180** B2
Willow Way N3 ......**29** D3
9 W11 ....**112** D6
Forest Hill SE26 ...**162** C1
Sunbury TW16 ....**194** A5
Twickenham TW2 ..**151** D2
Wembley HA0 .....**65** A5
West Ewell KT19 ..**215** B2
Willow Wlk BR6 ....**226** D5
E17 ....**53** B4
N15 ....**50** D5
12 N2 ....**30** B1
SE1 ......**117** D2 **263** C4
Cheam SM1,SM3 ..**217** B5
Southgate N21 .....**16** B5
Willow Wood Cres
SE25 ....**205** C4
Willrose Cres SE2 ..**124** C1
Willsbridge Ct 1
SE15 ....**139** D6
Wills Cres TW3 ....**151** D5
Wills Gr NW7 ....**28** B5
Willshaw St SE14 ...**141** C4
Will Thorne Pav The
E16 ....**100** A1
Wilman Gr E8 ....**74** A1
Wilmar Cl UB4 ......**83** B3
Wilmar Gdns BR4 ..**207** D1
Wilmcote Ho W2 ....**91** D2
Wilmer Cl KT10 ....**176** B5
Wilmer Cres KT2,
TW10 ....**176** B5
Wilmer Gdns N1 .....**95** C6
Wilmer Ho 3 E3 .....**97** A5
Wilmer Lea Cl E15 ..**76** B1
Wilmer Pl N16 ......**73** D1
Wilmers Ct 5 NW10 .**89** B6
Wilmer Way N14 ....**31** D5
Wilmington Ave W4 .**133** B5
Wilmington Ct SW16 **182** A3
Wilmington Gdns
IG11 ....**79** C1
Wilmington Sq
WC1 ......**94** C4 **234** A1
Wilmington St WC1 .**234** A1
Wilmot Cl N2 ....**30** A1
SE15 ....**140** A5

Wilmot Pl NW1 ......**71** C1
Ealing W7 ....**108** C5
Wilmot Rd E10 ......**75** D6
N17 ....**51** B6
Wallington SM5 ...**218** D3
Wilmot St E2 ....**96** B3
Wilmount St SE18 ..**122** D2
Wilna Rd SW18 ....**158** A4
Wilnett Ct 4 RM6 ....**58** B2
Wilnett Villas 5 RM6 .**58** B2
Wilsham St
W11 ......**113** A5 **244** A4
Wilshaw Ho 10 SE8 ..**141** C5
Wilsmere Dr HA3 ....**24** C3
Wilson Ave CR4 ....**180** C2
Wilson Cl
Croydon CR2 .....**221** B3
Wembley HA9 .....**44** B2
Wilson Dr HA9 ......**44** B2
Wilson Gdns HA1 ....**42** A2
Wilson Gr SE16 ....**118** B4
Wilson Ho NW6 .....**70** A1
2 SE7 ....**143** C6
39 SW8 ....**137** D3
Wilson Rd E6 ....**99** D4
SE5 ....**139** C4
Chessington KT9 ..**214** B2
Redbridge IG1 .....**56** B2
Wilson's Ave 2 N17 ..**33** D1
Wilson's Pl E14 .....**97** B1
Wilson's Rd W6 ....**112** D1
Wilson's Sch SM6 ..**220** A2
Wilson St E17 ....**54** A4
EC2 ......**95** B2 **242** D4
Southgate N21 .....**16** C4
Wilstone Cl UB4 .....**85** A3
Wiltern Ct NW2 ......**69** A2
Wilthorne Gdns RM10 **81** D1
Wilton Ave W4 .....**111** C1
Wilton Cres
SW1 ......**115** A4 **248** A1
Merton SW19 .....**179** B2
Wilton Ct 16 E1 ......**96** B1
N10 ....**31** A1
4 Richmond TW10 **154** A6
7 Woodford IG8 ...**37** A4
Wilton Est E8 ....**74** A2
Wilton Gdns
East Molesey KT8 ..**195** C6
Walton-on-T KT12 .**194** D1
Wilton Gr
Merton SW19 .....**179** B2
New Malden KT3 ..**199** D3
Wilton Ho 8 SE22 ..**139** C2
Wilton Mews
SW1 ......**115** B3 **258** B6
Wilton Par TW13 ...**150** B2
Wilton Pl
SW1 ......**115** A4 **248** A1
2 Beckenham BR3 .**208** A6
4 Harrow HA1 ....**42** D3
Wilton Rd N10 ......**31** A1
SE2 ....**124** C2
SW1 ......**115** C2 **259** A4
Cockfosters EN4 .....**2** D1
Hounslow TW4 ....**128** D2
Mitcham SW19 ...**180** C3
Wilton Row SW1 ...**248** A1
Wilton Sq N1 ..**95** B6 **235** C6
Wilton St
SW1 ......**115** B3 **258** C6
Wilton Terr SW1 ....**258** A6
Wilton Villas N1 ....**235** C5
Wilton Way E8 ......**74** A2
Wilton Wlk TW13 ...**150** B3
Wiltshire Cl NW7 ....**27** D5
SW3 ....**257** C3
Wiltshire Ct 2 N4 ....**50** B1
Barking IG11 ....**79** A2
Wiltshire Gdns N4 ...**51** A3
Twickenham TW2 ..**152** A3
Wiltshire La HA5 ....**40** A5
Wiltshire Rd SW9 ..**138** C2
Thornton Heath CR7 .**204** C6
Wiltshire Row
N1 ....**95** B6 **235** D5
Wilverley Cres KT3 ..**199** B3
Wimbart Rd SW2 ...**160** B4
Wimbledon Bridge
SW19 ....**179** B4
Wimbledon Central
SW19 ....**179** B4
Wimbledon Chase Prim
Sch SW20 ....**179** A2
Wimbledon Chase Sta
SW20 ....**179** A1
Wimbledon Cl 2
SW20 ....**178** D3
Wimbledon Coll
SW19 ....**178** D1

Wimbledon Common*
SW19 ....**178** B6
Wimbledon Common Prep
Sch SW19 ....**178** D3
Wimbledon High Sch
SW19 ....**179** A4
Wimbledon Hill Rd
SW19 ....**179** B4
Wimbledon House Sch
SW19 ....**179** C2
Wimbledon Lawn Tennis
Mus* SW19 ......**157** A1
Wimbledon Park Ct
SW19 ....**157** B3
Wimbledon Park First Sch
SW19 ....**157** D2
Wimbledon Park Rd
SW18,SW19 ......**157** B3
Wimbledon Park Side
SW19 ....**156** D3
Wimbledon Park Sta
SW19 ....**157** C1
Wimbledon Rd SW17 **180** A6
Wimbledon Sch of Art
SW19 ....**179** A2
Wimbledon Sch of Art
Annexe SW19 ....**179** C3
Wimbledon Sta
SW19 ....**179** B4
Wimbledon Stadium
SW17 ....**180** A6
Wimbledon Stadium Bsns
Ctr SW17 ....**157** D1
Wimbledon Windmill
Mus* SW19 ......**156** C1
Wimbolt St E2 ......**96** A4
Wimborne 2 DA14 ..**190** B6
Wimborne Ave
Hayes UB4 ....**84** B1
Southall UB2 ......**107** C2
Wimborne Cl SE12 ..**164** D6
Buckhurst Hill IG9 ..**21** C2
North Cheam KT4 ..**200** C1
Wimborne Ct 1 UB5 ..**63** C2
Wimborne Dr
HA8,NW9 ....**44** D6
Pinner HA5 ....**41** A2
Wimborne Gdns W13 .**87** B2
Wimborne Ho E16 ..**120** D6
NW1 ....**237** B5
SW8 ....**270** D3
Croydon CR0 .....**206** C4
Upper Tooting SW12 **159** C1
Wimborne Rd
Edmonton N9 ....**18** A2
Tottenham N17 ....**33** C1
Wimborne Way BR3 .**207** A5
Wimbourne Ct N1 ..**235** C4
Mitcham SW19 ...**180** B3
South Croydon CR2 **221** C2
Wimbourne St
N1 ....**95** B5 **235** C4
Wimpole Cl
Bromley BR2 ......**209** C5
1 Kingston KT1 ...**176** C1
Wimpole Mews
W1 ....**93** B2 **238** C3
Wimpole St
W1 ....**93** B1 **238** C2
Wimshurst Cl CR0 ..**204** A1
Winans Wlk SW9 ...**138** C3
Winant Ho 17 E14 ..**119** D6
Wincanton Cres UB5 **63** C3
Wincanton Gdns IG6 **56** D6
Wincanton Rd SW18 **157** B4
Winchcombe Rd
SM5 ....**202** C1
Winchcomb Gdns
SE9 ....**143** D2
Winchelsea Ave DA7 **147** B5
Winchelsea Cl SW15 **156** D6
Winchelsea Ho 11
SE16 ....**118** C4
Winchelsea Rd E7 ...**77** A4
N17 ....**51** C6
NW10 ....**89** B6
Winchelsey Rise CR2 **221** D2
Winchendon Rd
Fulham SW6 ..**135** B4 **264** D2
Teddington TW11,
TW12 ....**174** B6
Winchester Ave NW6 .**69** A1
NW9 ....**44** C6
Heston TW5 ......**129** B6
Winchester Cl SE17 .**261** D3
Beckenham BR2 ..**208** D6
Enfield EN1 ....**17** C1
Kingston KT2 .....**176** D1
11 Newham E6 ...**100** B1
Winchester Ct W8 ..**245** C2

Winchester Ct continued
Belvedere DA17 ...**125** C1
Winchester Dr HA5 ..**40** D4
Winchester Ho 18 E3 .**97** B4
1 SE18 ....**143** D5
SW3 ....**266** D5
W2 ....**236** A1
5 Barking IG11 ...**80** A1
Winchester Pk BR2 ..**208** D6
Winchester Pl 6 E8 ..**73** D2
N6 ....**49** B1
Winchester Rd N6 ....**49** B1
NW3 ....**70** B1
Beckenham BR2 ...**208** D6
Bexley DA16 ......**146** D3
Chingford E4 ....**36** A3
Edmonton N9 ....**18** A3
Harlington UB3 ...**127** C5
Harrow HA3 ....**44** A5
Ilford IG1 ....**79** B5
Northwood HA6 ....**40** A6
Twickenham TW1 ..**153** B5
Twickenham TW13 **151** B1
Walton-on-T KT12 .**194** A1
Winchester Sq SE1 .**252** C4
Winchester St
SW1 ......**115** B1 **258** D2
Acton W3 ....**111** A4
Winchester Wlk SE1 **252** C4
Winchet Wlk CR0 ..**206** C3
Winchfield Cl HA3 ..**43** C3
Winchfield Ho SW15 **155** D5
Winchfield Rd SE26 .**185** A5
Winch Ho SW10 ....**266** B4
Winchilsea Cres KT8 **174** A1
Winchilsea Ho NW8 .**229** D1
Winchmore Hill Rd
N14,N21 ....**16** A4
Winchmore Hill Sta
N21 ....**16** D4
Winchmore Sch N21 .**17** A2
Winchmore Villas N21 **16** B4
Winchstone Cl TW17 **192** B3
Winckley Cl HA3 ....**44** B4
Wincott St
SE11 .....**116** C2 **261** B3
Wincrofts Dr SE9 ...**145** B1
Windall Cl SE20 ....**184** D6
Windborough Rd
SM5 ....**219** A1
Windcott Ct HA3 ....**43** C2
Windermere NW1 ..**231** D2
12 Putney SW15 ..**156** D5
Windermere Ave N3 ..**47** C6
NW6 ....**91** A6
Merton SW19 .....**201** D6
Ruislip HA4 ....**40** D2
Wembley HA9 .....**43** C1
Windermere Cl BR6 .**226** D5
East Bedfont TW14 **149** D3
Stanwell TW19 ...**148** A2
Windermere Ct
Barnes SW13 .....**133** D6
Barnet EN5 ....**1** D1
Carshalton SM5 ...**219** A5
Wembley HA9 .....**43** C2
Windermere Gdns IG4 **56** A4
Windermere Gr HA9 .**43** C1
Windermere Hall HA8 **26** B5
Windermere Ho E3 ..**97** B3
Isleworth TW1 ....**152** C6
Windermere Point 3
SE15 ....**140** C5
Windermere Rd N10 .**31** B2
N19 ....**71** C6
W5 ....**109** C2
Croydon CR0 .....**205** D1
Kingston SW15 ...**177** C5
Mitcham SW16 ...**181** D1
Southall UB1 ......**85** B2
West Wickham BR4 **224** C6
Windermere Way
UB7 ....**104** B5
Winders Rd SW11 ..**136** C5
Windfield Cl SE26 ..**184** D6
Windham Rd TW9 ..**132** B2
Winding Way RM8 ..**80** C5
Windlass Pl SE8 ...**119** A2
Windlesham Gr
SW19 ....**156** D3
Windley Cl SE23 ...**162** C2
Windmill WC1 ......**240** C4
Windmill Alley 7
W4 ....**111** C2
Windmill Ave UB2 ..**108** A4
Windmill Bridge Ho 1
CR0 ....**205** D2
Windmill Bsns Ctr
UB2 ....**108** A5

Windmill Bsns Village
TW16 ....**171** C2
Windmill Cl NW2 ....**69** A5
11 SE1 ....**118** A2
3 SE13 ....**142** A3
Ashford TW16 .....**171** C3
Kingston KT6 .....**197** C2
Windmill Ct NW2 ....**69** A2
W5 ....**109** C2
Windmill Dr BR2 ...**225** C4
SW4 ....**159** B6
Windmill Gdns EN2 ....**4** C2
Windmill Gr CR0 ...**205** A3
Windmill Hill NW3 ..**70** A5
1 NW3 ....**70** A4
Enfield EN2 ....**5** A2
Ruislip HA4 ....**39** C1
Windmill Ho SE1 ...**251** B3
Windmill La E15 ....**76** B2
Bushey WD23 ......**8** C3
Edgware HA5 ......**11** C3
Isleworth TW7,UB2,W7 **108** C2
Southall UB2 .....**108** A4
Southall UB6 ......**86** A2
Thames Ditton KT7 **197** B2
Windmill Lo TW16 ..**171** C2
Windmill Pas 10 W4 **111** C2
Windmill Rd SW18 ..**158** B5
W4 ....**111** C2
Brentford TW8,W5 **109** C1
Charlton TW16 ....**171** C2
Edmonton N18 .....**33** B6
Hampton TW12 ...**174** A5
Mitcham CR4 .....**203** C5
Roehampton SW19 **156** B1
Thornton Heath CR0 **205** A2
Windmill Rd W TW16 **171** C1
Windmill Rise KT2 ..**176** D3
Windmill Row SE11 .**261** A1
Windmill St
W1 ....**93** D2 **239** C3
Bushey WD23 ......**8** C3
Windmill Terr TW17 .**193** C2
Windmill Trad Est
TW16 ....**171** C2
Windmill Way HA4 ..**39** D1
Windmill Wlk SE1 ..**251** B2
Windmore Cl HA0 ...**65** A3
Windrose Cl SE16 ..**118** C4
Windrush KT3 ......**199** A5
Windrush Cl SW11 .**136** B1
Chiswick W4 ......**133** A5
Ickenham UB10 ....**60** B4
Windrush Ho NW8 ..**236** D4
Windrush La SE23 ..**162** D1
Windrush Prim Sch
SE28 ....**124** B5
Windrush Rd NW10 ..**20** B4
Windsock Cl 1 SE16 **119** B2
Windsor Ave E17 ....**35** A1
Cheam SM3 ....**217** A5
East Molesey KT8 .**195** C6
Edgware HA8 ......**10** D1
Hillingdon UB10 ...**60** D1
Merton SW19 ....**180** A2
New Malden KT3 ..**199** A4
Windsor Cl N3 ....**29** A1
Brentford TW8 ....**131** B6
Chislehurst BR7 ..**188** D5
Harrow HA2 ....**63** C2
Pinner HA6 ....**22** A1
West Norwood SE27 **183** A6
Windsor Cres
Harrow HA2 ....**63** C2
Wembley HA9 .....**66** D5
Windsor Ct BR1 ....**210** A6
E17 ....**53** B6
N11 ....**30** D5
N14 ....**15** C4
NW11 ....**47** A3
NW3 ....**69** C4
20 SE16 ....**118** C5
SW11 ....**136** B3
4 SW18 ....**157** C6
SW3 ....**257** B2
2 SW4 ....**137** C1
W2 ....**245** C6
Bushey WD23 ......**8** A4
Fulham SW6 .....**135** A2
South Norwood SE19 **183** C2
Sunbury TW16 ....**172** A3
Windsor Ctr The
SE27 ....**183** A6
Windsor Dr EN4 ....**14** D5
Windsor Gdns W9 ...**91** C3
Hayes UB3 ....**105** B3
Wallington CR0 ...**220** A5
Windsor Gr SE27 ..**183** A6
Windsor Ho 4 E2 ...**96** C4
N1 ....**235** B4

Windsor Ho *continued*
N4 51 A1
NW1 231 D2
NW2 69 A2
2 NW4 28 D1
4 W4 111 A1
7 Northolt UB5 63 C2
Windsor Mews
Catford SE6 164 A3
Forest Hill SE23 163 A3
Windsor Park Rd
UB3 127 D5
Windsor Pk SW19 180 A2
Windsor Pl SW1 259 B4
Windsor Rd DA6 147 A1
E10 75 D6
E7 77 C3
N3 29 A1
N7 72 A5
NW2 68 B2
Ashford TW16 172 A4
Barnet EN5 12 D5
Chingford E4 35 D6
Cranford TW4,TW5 128 C3
Dagenham RM8 81 A5
Ealing W5 110 A6
Harrow HA3 24 B2
Ilford IG1 79 A4
Kingston KT2 176 A3
Palmers Green N13 16 C1
Richmond TW9 132 B3
Southall UB2 107 B3
South Norwood CR7 182 D1
Teddington TW11 174 B5
Tottenham N17 34 A1
Wanstead E11 77 A6
Worcester Park KT4 216 A6
Windsor St N1 94 D6 234 D6
Windsor Terr
N1 95 A4 235 B2
Windsor Way
W14 113 A2 254 A4
Windsor Wharf E9 75 B3
Windsor Wlk SE5 139 B3
Walton-on-T KT12 194 D1
Windspoint Dr SE15 140 B6
Windus Rd N16 51 D1
Windus Wlk N16 51 D1
Windy Ridge BR1 188 A2
Windy Ridge Cl
SW19 178 D5
Wine Cl E1 118 C6
Wine Office Ct EC4 241 B2
Winery La KT1 198 B6
Winey Cl KT9 213 C1
Winfield Ho SW11 136 B3
Winford Ct 15 SE15 140 A4
Winford Ho E3 75 B1
Winford Par 9 UB1 85 D1
Winforton St SE10 142 A4
Winfrith Rd SW18 158 A3
Wingate Cres CR0 204 A3
Wingate Ho 26 E3 97 D4
8 N16 73 B4
Wingate Rd W6 112 B3
Ilford IG1 78 D3
Sidcup DA14 190 C4
Wingate Trad Est N17 33 D3
Wingfield Ct 10 E14 120 B6
Wingfield Ho 16 E2 95 D4
NW6 91 D5
Wingfield Mews
SE15 140 A2
Wingfield Prim Sch
SE3 143 B2
Wingfield Rd E15 76 C4
E17 53 D4
Kingston KT2 176 C4
Wingfield St SE15 140 A2
Wingfield Way HA4 62 B2
Wingford Rd SW2 160 A5
Wingham 3 NW5 71 A2
Wingham Ho 3 SE26 184 B5
Wingmore Rd SE24 139 A2
Wingrad Ho 14 E1 96 C2
Wingrave SE17 262 C3
Wingrave Rd W6 134 C6
Wingreen 13 NW8 91 D6
Wingrove Rd SE6 164 C2
Wings Cl SM1 217 C4
Winicotte Ho W2 236 D4
Winifred Cl EN5 11 D5
Winifrede Paul Ho 7
NW5 71 B4
Winifred Pl N12 30 A5
Winifred Rd
Dagenham RM8 59 A1
Hampton TW12 173 C6
Merton SW19 179 C2
Winifred St E16 122 B5
Winifred Terr EN1 17 D4
Winkfield Rd E13 99 B5
Wood Green N22 32 C2
Winkley Ct N10 49 B5
Harrow HA2 63 C5
Winkley St 6 E2 96 B5
Winkworth Cotts 13
E1 96 C3
Winlaton Rd BR1 186 B6
Winmill Rd RM8 81 B5
Winn Common Rd
SE18 145 C6
Winnett St W1 249 C6
Winningales Ct IG5 56 A6
Winnings Wlk UB5 63 A2
Winnington Cl N2 48 B3
Winnington Ho
8 SE5 139 A5
19 W10 91 A3
Winnington Rd N2 48 B3
Enfield EN3 6 C6
Winnipeg Dr 3 BR6 227 D2
Winnipeg Ho UB4 84 B3
Winn Rd SE12 165 B3
Winns Ave E17 53 B6
Winns Mews N15 51 C5
Winns Prim Sch E17 35 B1
Winns Terr E17 53 C6
Winsbeach E17 36 B1
Winscombe Cres W5 87 D3
Winscombe Ct W5 87 D3
Winscombe St N19 71 B6
Winscombe Way HA7 25 A5
Winsford Rd SE6 163 B1
Winsford Terr N18 33 B5
Winsham Gr SW11 159 A6
Winsham Ho NW1 232 D2
Winslade Ho 4 E5 74 B6
Winslade Rd SW2 160 A6
Winslade Way SE6 163 D4
Winsland Mews W2 236 C2
Winsland St
W2 92 B1 236 C2
Winsley St W1 239 B2
Winslow SE17 263 A1
Winslow Cl 2 NW10 67 C5
Pinner HA5 40 B3
Winslow Gr E4 20 C2
Winslow Rd W6 134 C6
Winslow Way TW13 151 A1
Winsmoor Ct EN2 4 D2
Winsor Prim Sch E6 100 C1
Winsor Terr E6 100 C2
Winstanley Rd SW11 136 B2
Winston Ave NW9 45 C2
Winston Cl Harrow HA3 24 D4
Romford RM7 59 D5
Winston Ct 7 BR1 187 B2
Harrow HA3 23 D3
Winston Ho WC1 239 D6
Winston Rd N16 73 B4
Winston Way IG1 79 A5
Winston Wlk W4 111 B2
Winter Ave E6 100 A6
Winterborne Ave
BR6 227 B5
Winterbourne Ho
W11 244 A5
Winterbourne Jun & Inf
Schs CR7 204 C5
Winterbourne Rd
Dagenham RM8 80 C6
Forest Hill SE6 163 B3
Thornton Heath CR7 204 C5
Winter Box Wlk
TW10 154 B6
Winterbrook Rd
SE24 161 A5
Winterburn Cl N11 31 A4
Winterfold Cl SW19 157 A2
Wintergreen Cl 7
E6 100 A2
Winterleys 7 NW6 91 B5
Winter Lo 19 SE16 118 A1
Winter's Ct E4 19 D1
Winterslow Ho 20
SE5 139 A3
Winters Rd KT7 197 B2
Winterstoke Gdns
NW7 28 A5
Winterstoke Rd SE6 163 B3
Winterton Ct KT1 175 D2
Winterton Ho 15 E1 96 C1
Winterton Pl SW10 266 B6
Winterwell Rd SW2 160 A6
Winthorpe Rd SW15 135 A1
Winthrop Ho 10 W12 112 B6
Winthrop St E1 96 B2
Winthrop Wlk HA9 66 A5
Winton Ave N11 31 C3
Winton Cl N9 18 D4
Winton Ct 15 KT6 197 D2
Winton Gdns HA8 26 B3
Winton Prim Sch
N1 94 B5 233 C3
Winton Rd BR6 226 D4
Winton Way SW16 182 C5
Wintour Ho HA9 65 D6
Wirrall Ho 15 SE26 162 A1
Wirral Wood Cl BR7 188 C4
Wisbeach Rd CR0 205 B4
Wisden Ho SW8 270 D5
Wisdom Ct 5 TW7 131 A2
Wisdons Cl RM7,RM9 59 D1
Wise La NW7 28 A4
Wiseman Ct 12 SE19 183 C5
Wiseman Rd E10 75 C6
Wise Rd E15 98 B6
Wiseton Rd SW17 158 D3
Wishart Rd SE3 143 D3
Wishaw Wlk N13 32 A4
Wisley Ho SW1 259 C2
Wisley Rd SW11 159 A6
St Paul's Cray BR5 190 B3
Wistaria Cl BR6 226 D6
Wisteria Cl NW7 27 D4
Ilford IG1 78 D3
Wisteria Rd SE13 142 B1
Wistow Ho 14 E2 96 A6
Witanhurst La N6 49 A1
Witan St E2 96 B4
Witchwood Ho 11
SW9 138 C2
Witcombe Point 13
SE15 140 A4
Witham Ct E10 75 D5
Upper Tooting SW17 158 D1
Witham Ho 35 SE5 139 A3
Witham Rd
Dagenham RM10 81 C3
Ealing W13 109 B5
Hounslow TW7 130 B4
Penge SE20 206 C6
Witherby Cl CR0 221 C4
Witherington Rd N5 72 C3
Withers Cl KT9 213 C2
Withers Mead NW9 27 D2
Withers Pl EC1 242 B6
Witherston Way SE9 166 C1
Withington Rd N2 30 C2
Withycombe Rd
SW19 156 D4
Withy Ho 4 E1 96 D3
Withy La HA4 39 A4
Withy Mead E4 20 B1
Witley Cres CR0 224 A2
Witley Ct UB2 107 B2
Witley Gdns UB2 107 B2
Witley Ho 2 SW2 160 B4
Witley Ind Est UB2 107 B2
Witley Point 8 SW15 156 B3
Witley Rd N19 71 C6
Witney Cl
Ickenham UB10 60 B4
Pinner HA5 23 B4
Witney Path SE23 162 D1
Wittenham Way E4 20 B1
Witten Ho KT3 199 B1
Wittering Cl KT2 175 D5
Wittering Ho 9
SW11 136 D3
Wittersham Rd BR1 186 D5
Wittingham Com Prim Sch
E17 35 A2
Witts Ho KT2 198 B6
Wivenhoe Cl SE15 140 B2
Wivenhoe Ct TW4 129 B1
Wivenhoe Rd IG11 102 B5
Wiverton Rd SE26 184 C5
Wixom Ho SE9 143 C1
Wix Prim Sch SW4 137 B1
Wix Rd RM9 102 D6
Wix's La SW4 137 B1
Woburn W13 87 B2
Woburn Cl SE28 102 D1
Bushey WD23 8 A5
Wimbledon SW19 180 A4
Woburn Ct 32 SE16 118 B1
1 DA6 147 A1
Croydon CR0 205 A1
Richmond TW9 132 B2
4 Woodford E18 37 A1
Woburn Pl
WC1 94 A3 240 A5
Woburn Rd
Carshalton SM5 202 C1
Croydon CR0 205 A1
Woburn Sq
WC1 93 D3 239 D5
Woburn Twr 14 UB5 84 D4
Woburn Wlk WC1 232 D1
Wodehouse Ave
SE15 139 D4
Wodehouse Ct 10
W3 111 A3
Woffington Cl KT1,
KT8 175 C2
Woking Cl SW15 133 D1
Wolcot Ho NW1 232 B3
Woldham Pl BR2 209 C5
Woldham Rd BR2 209 C5
Wolds Dr BR6 226 C4
Wolfe Cl Hayes BR2 209 A3
Hayes UB4 84 B4
Wolfe Cres 34 SE16 118 D4
SE7 121 D1
Wolfe Ho 19 W12 112 B6
Wolferton Rd E12 78 B4
Wolf Fields Prim Sch
UB2 107 B2
Wolfington Rd SE27 182 D6
Wolfram Cl SE13 164 C6
Wolfson Ct NW11 47 A2
SE1 253 D2
Wolfson Hillel Prim Sch
N14 15 D5
Wolftencroft Cl
SW11 136 B2
Wollaston Cl SE1 262 A4
Wolmer Cl HA8 26 D6
Wolmer Gdns HA8 10 C1
Wolmer Rd HA8 26 D6
Wolseley Ave SW18,
SW19 157 C2
Wolseley Gdns W4 132 D6
Wolseley Rd E7 77 B1
N8 49 D4
Acton W4 111 A2
Carshalton CR4 203 A2
Harrow HA3 42 C6
Wood Green N22 32 B2
Wolseley St
SE1 117 D4 253 D1
Wolsey Ave E17 53 B6
Wallend E6 100 C4
Wolsey Cl
Isleworth TW3 130 A1
Kingston KT2 176 D2
Southall UB2 108 A3
Wimbledon SW20 178 B3
Worcester Park KT19,
KT4 216 A4
Wolsey Cres SM4 201 B2
Wolsey Ct NW6 70 A1
SE9 166 B5
Bromley BR1 186 D3
Wolsey Dr
Kingston KT2 176 A4
Walton-on-T KT12 194 D1
Wolsey Gr HA8 27 B3
Wolsey Ho 2 TW12 173 D4
Wolsey Inf Sch CR0 224 A1
Wolsey Jun Sch CR0 224 A1
Wolsey Mews NW5 71 C2
Orpington BR6 227 D3
Wolsey Rd N1 73 B3
Ashford TW15 170 B6
Ashford TW16 171 D4
East Molesey KT8 196 B5
Enfield EN1 6 B3
Hampton TW12 174 A4
Wolsey St E1 96 C2
Wolsey Way KT9 214 C3
Wolstenholme HA7 25 B5
Wolstonbury N12 29 C5
Wolvercote Rd SE2 124 D4
Wolverley St E2 96 B4
Wolverton SE17 263 A2
Wolverton Ave KT2 176 C2
Wolverton Gdns W6 112 D2
Ealing W5 110 B6
Wolverton Mans W5 110 B5
Wolverton Rd HA7 25 B3
Wolverton Way N14 15 C6
Wolves La N22 32 C4
Womersley Rd N4,N8 50 B3
Wonford Cl KT2,KT3 177 C2
Wontner Cl 5 N1 73 A1
Wontner Rd SW12,
SW17 158 D2
Wooburn Cl UB8 82 D3
Woodall Cl 24 E14 119 D6
Chessington KT9 213 D2
Woodall Ho TW7 130 D2
Woodall Rd EN3 18 D5
Woodbank Rd BR1 164 D1
Woodbastwick Rd
SE26 185 A5
Woodberry Ave
Edmonton N21 16 D2
Woodberry Ave *continued*
Harrow HA2 42 A5
Woodberry Cl NW7 28 D3
Ashford TW16 172 A4
Woodberry Cres N10 49 B6
Woodberry Down N4 51 A2
Woodberry Down Com
Prim Sch N4 51 A2
Woodberry Gdns N12 30 A4
Woodberry Gr N12 30 A4
N4 51 A2
Woodberry Way N12 30 A4
Chingford E4 20 A4
Woodbine Cl TW2 152 B2
Woodbine Gr
Enfield EN2 5 B5
Penge SE20 184 B3
Woodbine La KT4 216 C5
Woodbine Pl E11 55 A3
Woodbine Rd DA15 167 C3
Woodbines Ave KT1 197 D6
Woodbine Terr E9 74 C2
Woodborough Rd
SW15 134 B1
Woodbourne Ave
SW16 159 D1
Woodbourne Cl
SW16 160 A1
Woodbourne Dr
KT10 212 D2
Woodbourne Gdns
SM6 219 B1
Woodbridge Cl 10 N7 72 B6
4 NW2 68 A5
Woodbridge Ct N16 73 B5
Woodbridge High Sch
IG8 37 B3
Woodbridge Ho E11 54 D1
Woodbridge Rd IG11 79 D3
Woodbridge St
EC1 94 D3 241 C6
Woodbrook Rd SE2 146 B6
Woodbrook Sch BR3 185 B2
Woodburn Cl NW4 46 D4
Woodbury Cl
Croydon CR0 221 D6
Wanstead E11 55 B5
Woodbury Ct 1 W13 87 B3
Woodbury Ho 4
SE26 162 B1
Woodbury Park Rd
W13 87 B3
Woodbury Rd E17 53 D5
Woodbury St SW17 180 C5
Woodchester Sq W2 91 D2
Woodchurch Cl DA14 167 B1
Woodchurch Dr BR1 187 D3
Woodchurch Ho 15
SW9 138 C4
Woodchurch Rd NW6 69 D1
Wood Cl E2 96 A3
NW9 45 B2
Harrow HA1 42 B2
Woodclyffe Dr BR7 188 C1
Woodcock Ct HA3 44 A2
Woodcock Dell Ave
HA3 43 D2
Woodcock Hill HA3 43 C3
Woodcock Ho 4 E14 97 C2
Woodcocks E16 99 D2
Woodcombe Cres
SE23 162 C3
Woodcote Ave NW7 28 C4
Thornton Heath CR7 204 D5
Wallington SM6 219 B1
Woodcote Cl
Enfield N9 18 C5
Kingston KT2 176 B5
Woodcote Dr BR6 211 B2
Woodcote Ho 4 SE8 141 B6
Woodcote Mews
Loughton IG10 21 D4
Wallington SM6 219 B2
Woodcote Pl 1 SE27 182 D5
Woodcote Rd
Wallington SM6 219 C1
Wanstead E11 55 A2
Woodcott Ho 1
SW15 156 A4
Woodcroft SE9 166 B1
South Croydon CR0 221 C5
Southgate N21 16 C3
Wembley UB6 65 A2
Woodcroft Ave NW7 27 C4
Stanmore HA7 25 A2
Woodcroft Cres UB10 82 D6
Woodcroft Jun & Inf Schs
HA8 27 C3
Woodcroft Mews
SE8 119 A2
Woodcroft Rd CR7 204 D3
Wood Dene 6 SE15 140 B4
Wood Dr BR7 188 A4
Woodedge Cl E4 20 D3
Woodend
South Norwood SE19 183 A4
Sutton SM1 218 A6
Thames Ditton KT10 212 A6
Wood End UB3 83 C1
Wood End Ave HA2 64 A4
Wood End Cl UB5 64 B3
Woodend Gdns EN2 4 A1
Wood End Gdns UB5 64 A3
Wood End Green Rd
UB3 83 C1
Wood End Inf Sch
UB5 64 B3
Wood End Jun Sch
UB6 64 B3
Wood End La UB5 63 D3
Wood End Park Jun & Inf
Sch UB3 105 A6
Woodend Rd E17 36 A1
Wood End Rd HA1,UB5 64 B4
Wood End Way UB5 64 A3
Wooder Gdns E7 77 A4
Wooderson Cl SE25 205 C5
Woodfall Ave EN5 13 B6
Woodfall Rd N4 72 C6
Woodfall St SW3 257 C1
Woodfarrs SE5 139 B1
Wood Field NW3 70 D3
Woodfield Ave NW9 45 C5
Ealing W5 87 C3
Streatham SW16 159 D1
Wallington SM5 219 A1
Wembley HA0 65 C5
Woodfield Cl
1 Enfield EN1 5 C1
South Norwood SE19 183 A3
Woodfield Cres W5 87 D3
Woodfield Ct SW16 159 D1
Woodfield Ctr The
SW16 159 D2
Woodfield Dr EN4 15 A3
Woodfield Gdns KT3 199 D4
Woodfield Gr SW16 159 D1
Woodfield Ho 6 E5 74 B6
11 Forest Hill SE23 162 D1
New Malden KT3 199 D4
Woodfield Pl W9 91 B3
Woodfield Rd W9 91 B2
Cranford TW4,TW5 128 B3
Ealing W5 87 C3
Hinchley Wood KT10,
KT7 212 D6
Woodfield Rise WD23 8 B4
Woodfield Sch NW9 45 C1
Woodfields Ct SM1 218 A5
Woodfield Way N11 31 D3
Woodford Ave IG2,IG4,
IG5,IG8 56 B5
Woodford Bridge Rd
IG4 56 A5
Woodford Cres HA5 22 B1
Woodford Cty High Sch
IG8 36 D4
Woodforde Ct UB3 105 B1
Woodford Green Prep Sch
IG8 37 A4
Woodford Ho
13 SE18 144 D6
5 Wanstead E18 55 A5
Woodford New Rd
E17 54 C6
Woodford E18 36 D3
Woodford Pl HA9 44 A1
Woodford Rd E7 77 B4
Wanstead E18 55 A6
Woodford Sta IG8 37 B4
Woodford Trad Est
IG8 37 D1
Woodgate Ave KT9 213 D3
Woodgate Cres HA6 22 A4
Woodgate Dr SW16 181 D3
Woodger Rd W12 112 C4
Woodget Cl E6 100 A1
Woodgrange Ave N12 30 B4
Ealing W5 110 C5
Enfield EN1 18 A5
Harrow HA3 43 D4
Woodgrange Cl HA3 43 D4
Woodgrange Ct 1
BR2 208 D1
Woodgrange Gdns
EN1 18 A5

Woodgrange Inf Sch
E7 ....**77** B4
Woodgrange Mans
HA3 ....**43** C4
Woodgrange Park Sta
E12 ....**77** D3
Woodgrange Rd E7 ...**77** A3
Woodgrange Terr EN1 **18** A5
Wood Green Sta N22 .**32** C1
Woodhall NW1 .....**232** A1
Woodhall Ave
Dulwich SE21 ....**161** D1
Pinner HA5 ....**23** A2
Woodhall Dr
Dulwich SE21 ....**161** D1
Pinner HA5 ....**23** A2
Woodhall Gate HA5 ..**22** D3
Woodhall Ho SW18 ..**158** B5
Woodhall La WD19 ...**23** A6
Woodhall Sch WD19 .**23** A6
Woodham Ct E11 ....**54** D5
Woodham Rd SE6 ...**164** A1
Woodhatch Cl 16 E6 ..**100** A2
Woodhaven Gdns IG6 .**57** A5
Woodhayes BR7 ....**188** D4
Woodhayes Rd SW19,
SW20 ....**178** C4
Woodhead Dr BR6 ..**227** C6
Woodheyes Rd NW10 .**67** C3
Woodhill SE7,SE18 ..**122** A6
Woodhill Cres HA3 ..**43** D3
Woodhill Prim Sch
SE18 ....**122** A2
Wood Ho 6 NW6 .....**91** B4
4 SW4 ....**137** D3
Woodhouse Ave UB6 .**86** D5
Woodhouse Cl
Hayes UB3 ....**105** C3
Wembley UB6 ....**86** D5
Woodhouse Eaves
HA6 ....**22** A5
Woodhouse Gr E12 ..**78** A4
Woodhouse Rd E11 ..**76** D5
N12 ....**30** C4
Woodhouse Sixth Form
Coll N12 ....**30** A2
Woodhurst Ave BR5 .**211** A3
Woodhurst Rd SE2 ..**124** A2
W3 ....**111** A6
Woodington Cl SE9 .**166** C5
Woodison St E3 .....**97** A3
Woodknoll Dr BR7 ..**188** B2
Wood La N6 ....**49** B3
NW9 ....**45** B2
W12 ....**112** C6
Dagenham RM10 ......**81** A5
Hounslow TW7 ....**130** D5
Ruislip HA4 ....**61** C6
Stanmore HA7 ....**9** B2
Woodford IG8 ....**36** D5
Woodland App UB6 ..**65** A2
Woodland Cl NW9 ...**45** A3
Uxbridge UB10 ....**60** D6
West Ewell KT19 ....**215** C2
West Norwood SE19 ..**183** C4
Woodford IG8 ....**37** B1
Woodland Cres SE10 **142** C6
18 SE16 ....**118** D4
Woodland Ct NW4 ...**47** A4
Cheam SM1 ....**217** C2
10 Wanstead E11 ....**55** A4
Woodland Gdns E17 .**54** C5
N10 ....**49** B4
Isleworth TW7 ....**130** C2
Woodland Gr SE10 ..**120** C1
Woodland Hill SE19 .**183** C4
Woodland Rd N11 ...**31** B5
Chingford E4 ....**20** A3
Penge SE19 ....**183** D4
Thornton Heath CR7 .**204** C5
Woodland Rise N10 ..**49** B5
Wembley UB6 ....**65** A2
Woodlands N12 .....**30** A4
NW11 ....**47** A4
SW4 ....**137** B1
Beckenham BR3 .....**185** D3
Harrow HA2 ....**41** C5
West Barnes SW20 ..**200** D5
Woodlands Ave DA15 **167** C3
N3 ....**30** A2
Acton W3 ....**110** D5
Dagenham RM6 ......**59** A2
Kingston KT3 ....**177** B2
Ruislip HA4 ....**40** D2
Wanstead E11 ....**55** B1
Worcester Park KT4 ..**216** A6
Woodlands Cl BR1 ..**188** B1

Woodlands Cl continued
NW11 ....**47** A4
Claygate KT10 ......**212** D1
Woodlands Ct NW10 ..**90** D6
9 Bromley BR1 .....**186** D2
Dulwich SE22 ....**162** B4
Southall UB1 ....**107** C6
Woodlands Dr
Harrow HA7 ....**24** D4
Sunbury TW16 ......**172** C1
Woodlands Gr TW7 .**130** C3
Woodlands Gt SW15 .**157** B6
Woodlands Inf Sch
IG1 ....**79** B3
Woodlands Jun Sch
IG1 ....**79** B3
Woodlands Par
TW15 ....**171** A4
Woodlands Park Jun & Inf
Schs N15 ....**51** A4
Woodlands Park Rd
N15 ....**51** A4
SE10 ....**142** C6
Woodlands Rd BR1 ..**188** B1
DA7 ....**147** A4
E11 ....**76** C6
E17 ....**54** A6
N9 ....**18** C3
Barnes SW13 ......**133** D2
Enfield EN2 ....**5** B4
Harrow HA1 ....**42** D4
Ilford IG1 ....**79** A5
Isleworth TW7 ......**130** C3
Southall UB1 ....**106** D5
Surbiton KT6 ....**197** D2
Woodlands St SE13 .**164** B4
Woodland St 2 E8 ..**73** D2
Woodlands The N14 ..**15** B3
N5 ....**73** A4
Isleworth TW7 ......**130** C3
Lewisham SE13 .....**164** B4
Mitcham CR4 ....**203** A6
South Norwood SE19 .**183** A3
Stanmore HA7 ......**25** B5
Thames Ditton KT10 .**212** A4
Woodlands Way
SW15 ....**157** B6
Woodland Terr SE7 .**122** A2
Woodland Way BR5 .**211** A4
NW7 ....**27** D4
SE2 ....**124** D2
Croydon CR0 ......**207** A1
Merton SM4 ....**201** B5
Mitcham CR4 ....**181** A4
Southgate N21 ......**16** C2
Tolworth KT5 ......**214** D6
West Wickham BR4 ..**224** A5
Woodford IG8 ....**21** B1
Woodland Wlk NW3 ..**70** C3
9 SE10 ....**120** C1
Chessington KT19 ..**214** C2
Woodlane High Sch
W12 ....**90** B1
Woodlawn Cl SW15 .**157** B6
Woodlawn Cres TW2 **151** D2
Woodlawn Dr TW13 .**150** D2
Woodlawn Rd SW6 .**134** D4
Woodlea Dr BR2 ....**208** C4
Woodlea Lo EN1 .....**17** C5
Woodlea Rd N16 ....**73** C5
Woodleigh
1 Kingston KT5 ....**198** B4
3 Woodford E18 .....**37** A2
Woodleigh Ave N12 ..**30** C4
Woodleigh Ct N22 ..**32** B2
Woodleigh Gdns
SW16 ....**160** A1
Woodley Cl SW17 ...**180** D3
Woodley La SM1,SM5 **218** C5
Woodlodge 4 SW19 .**179** B5
Wood Lodge Gdns
BR1 ....**188** A3
Wood Lodge La BR4 .**224** A5
Woodman La E4 .....**20** C6
Woodman Par 4
E16 ....**122** C5
Woodmans Gr NW10 ..**67** D3
Woodmans Mews
W12 ....**90** B2
Woodman St E16 ...**122** C5
E16 ....**122** C5
Woodmansterne Prim Sch
SW16 ....**181** D1
Woodmansterne Rd
Mitcham SW16 .....**181** D2
Sutton SM5 ....**218** C1
Wood Mead N17 ....**34** B5
Woodmere SE9 .....**166** B3
Woodmere Ave CR0 .**206** D2

Woodmere Cl
10 SW11 ....**137** A2
Croydon CR0 ......**206** D2
Woodmere Ct N14 ...**15** B4
Woodmere Gdns
CR0 ....**206** D2
Woodmere Way BR3 .**208** A4
Woodnook Rd SW16 .**181** B5
Woodpecker Cl
Bushey WD23 ....**8** A3
Enfield N9 ....**18** B5
Harrow HA3 ....**24** D2
Woodpecker Mews
SE13 ....**142** B1
Woodpecker Rd
6 SE14 ....**141** A6
Woolwich SE28 .....**124** C6
Wood Point 8 E16 ...**99** A6
Woodquest Ave SE24 **161** A6
Wood Rd TW17 .....**192** C6
Wood Ride Barnet EN4 ..**2** B4
Orpington BR5 .....**211** C5
Woodridge Cl EN2 ....**4** C4
Woodridge Prim Sch
N12 ....**13** C1
Woodridings Ave HA5 .**23** B2
Woodridings Cl HA5 ..**23** B3
Woodridings Ct N22 .**31** D2
Woodriffe Rd E11 ...**54** B2
Wood Rise HA5 .....**40** A4
Woodrow SE18 .....**122** B2
Woodrow Ave UB4 ...**83** D3
Woodrow Cl UB6 ....**65** B1
Woodrow Ct 3 N17 ..**34** B3
Woodruff Ho SW2 ..**160** C5
Woodrush Cl 4 SE14 **141** A5
Woodrush Way RM6 .**58** D5
Woodseer St
E1 ....**95** D2 **243** D4
Woodsford SE17 ...**262** C1
Woodsford Sq
W14 ....**113** A4 **244** B2
Woodshire Rd RM10 .**81** D5
Woods Ho SW8 ....**269** A2
Woodside N10 ......**49** A6
NW11 ....**47** A4
Buckhurst Hill IG9 ...**21** C2
Palmers Green N13 ..**16** C1
Walton-on-T KT12 ..**194** A1
Wimbledon SW19 ...**179** B5
Woodside Ave N12 ..**30** A6
N6 ....**48** D5
Chislehurst BR7 ....**189** A5
Croydon SE25 .....**206** B4
Thames Ditton KT10 .**196** C2
Wembley HA0 ....**88** A6
Woodside Cl
Ruislip HA4 ....**39** B3
Stanmore HA7 ......**25** B5
Tolworth KT5 ......**199** A2
Wembley HA0 ....**88** A6
Woodside Court Rd
CR0 ....**206** A2
Woodside Cres DA15 **167** C1
Woodside Ct 8 N12 ..**29** D6
Ealing W5 ....**110** A5
Enfield EN2 ....**4** D4
Woodside End HA0 ..**88** A6
Woodside Gdns
Chingford E4 ....**35** D4
Tottenham N17 .....**33** D1
Woodside Gn SE25 .**206** A3
Woodside Gr N12 ...**14** A1
Woodside Grange Rd
N12 ....**29** D6
Woodside Ho SW19 .**179** B4
Woodside Jun & Inf Sch
CR0 ....**206** A2
Woodside Jun & Inf Schs
E17 ....**54** A6
Woodside La DA5 ..**168** D5
N12 ....**14** A1
Woodside Park Ave
E17 ....**54** B5
Woodside Park Rd
N12 ....**30** A6
Woodside Pk SE25 .**206** B3
Woodside Pl HA0 ....**88** A6
Woodside Rd BR1 ..**210** A4
E13 ....**99** C3
Croydon SE25 .....**206** B3
Kingston KT2 ....**176** A3
Kingston KT3 ....**177** C1
Northwood HA6 .....**22** A3
Sidcup DA15 ......**167** C1
Sutton SM1 ....**218** A5
Woodford IG8 ....**37** A6
Wood Green N22 ....**32** C3
Woodside Sch DA17 .**125** D2
Woodside Sta SE25 .**206** B3

Woodside Way
Croydon CR0 ......**206** C3
Streatham CR4 .....**181** C2
Wood's Mews
W1 ....**115** A6 **248** A6
Woodsome Rd NW5 ..**71** B5
Wood's Pl SE1 .....**263** B5
Woodspring Rd
SW19 ....**157** A2
Wood's Rd SE15 ...**140** B4
Wood St E16 ......**121** B6
E17 ....**54** B5
EC2 ....**95** A1 **242** B2
W4 ....**111** C1
Barnet EN5 ....**1** A1
Carshalton CR4 ....**203** A3
Kingston KT1 ......**175** D1
Kingston KT2 ....**176** A2
Woodstar Ho 3
SE15 ....**140** A5
Woodstead Gr HA8 ..**26** A4
Woods The
Moor Park HA6 .....**22** A5
Uxbridge UB10 .....**60** D4
Woodstock Ave NW11 .**47** A2
W13 ....**109** A3
Cheam SM3 ....**201** B2
Isleworth TW7 .....**153** A6
Southall UB1 ....**85** B4
Woodstock Cl DA5 ..**169** B3
Stanmore HA7 ......**26** A1
Woodstock Cres N9 ...**18** A5
Woodstock Ct SE11 .**260** D2
SE12 ....**165** A5
Kingston KT2 ....**176** D1
Woodstock Dr UB10 .**60** B4
Woodstock Gdns
Beckenham BR3 ....**185** D3
Hayes UB4 ....**83** D2
Ilford IG3 ....**80** A6
Woodstock Gr W12 .**112** D4
Woodstock Ho 2 N5 .**73** A4
Hayes UB3 ....**83** B2
Woodstock La N KT6 **213** C6
Woodstock La S
KT10,KT6 ....**213** C4
Woodstock Mews
W1 ....**238** B3
Woodstock Rd E7 ...**77** C1
N4 ....**50** C1
NW11 ....**47** B1
W4 ....**111** C3
Bushey WD23 ....**8** D4
Chingford E17 ......**36** B1
South Croydon CR0 .**221** B5
Wallington SM5,SM6 .**219** A3
Wembley HA0 ....**88** A6
Woodstock Rise SM3 **201** B2
Woodstock St W1 ..**238** C1
Woodstock Terr E14 .**119** D6
Woodstock The SM3 .**200** B3
Woodstock Way CR4 .**181** C1
Woodstone Ave KT17,
KT4 ....**216** A3
Wood Street Sta E17 .**54** B5
Woodsyre SE26 ....**183** D4
Woodthorpe Rd
Ashford TW15 ......**170** A6
Putney SW15 ......**134** B1
Woodtree Cl NW4 ...**28** C1
Wood Vale N10 .....**49** C4
Dulwich SE22 ......**162** B4
Woodvale Ave SE25 .**183** D1
Woodvale Ct BR1 ..**187** B1
South Norwood SE25 .**205** D6
Woodvale Way NW11 .**68** D5
Woodvale Wlk SE27 .**183** A5
Woodview Ave E4 ...**36** A6
Woodview Cl N4 ....**50** D2
Kingston SW15 .....**177** B6
Orpington BR6 .....**227** A4
Woodville SE3 .....**143** B4
Woodville Cl SE12 ..**165** A6
Teddington TW11 ...**175** A6
Woodville Ct 3 SE10 **142** A4
Woodville Gdns NW11 **46** D2
Ealing W5 ....**88** A1
Ilford IG6 ....**56** D5
Ruislip HA4 ....**39** A2
Surbiton KT6 ......**197** D2
Woodville Gr 2
DA16 ....**146** A2
Woodville Ho SE1 ..**263** C6
Woodville Rd E11 ...**54** D1
E17 ....**53** B5
N16 ....**73** C3
NW11 ....**47** A4
NW6 ....**91** B5
Barnet EN5 ....**1** D2
Ealing W5 ....**87** D1

Woodville Rd continued
Morden SM4 ....**201** C5
Richmond TW10 ....**153** C1
South Norwood CR7 .**205** B6
Woodford E18 ....**37** B1
Woodville St 16 SE7 .**122** A2
Woodville The NW5 ..**87** D1
Woodward Ave NW4 .**46** A4
Woodward Cl KT10 .**212** D2
Woodwarde Rd SE22 **161** C5
Woodward Gdns
Dagenham RM9 .....**80** C1
Harrow HA7 ....**24** D3
Woodward Rd RM9 ..**80** C1
Wood Way BR6 ....**226** C6
Woodway Cres HA1 ..**43** A3
Woodwell St SW18 .**158** A6
Wood Wharf SE10 ..**142** A6
Woodyard Cl NW5 ...**71** A3
Woodyard La SE21 ..**161** C4
Woodyates Rd SE12 .**165** B4
Woolacombe Rd SE3 **143** C3
Woolacombe Way
UB3 ....**105** C2
Woolden Ho 2 E4 ...**20** C4
Wooler St
SE17 ......**117** B1 **262** D2
Woolf Cl SE28 ......**124** B5
Woolf Ct 7 W3 ....**111** A3
Woolf Mews WC1 ..**240** A6
Woollaston Rd N4 ...**50** D4
Woolley Ho SW9 ...**138** D2
Woollon Ho 1 E1 ...**96** C1
Woolmead Ave NW9 .**46** A2
Woolmer Gdns N18 ..**34** A5
Woolmer Ho 2 E5 ...**74** B6
Woolmer Rd N18 ....**34** A5
Woolmore Prim Sch
E14 ....**120** A6
Woolmore St E14 ..**120** A6
Woolneigh St SW6 .**135** D3
Woolpack Ho 1 E9 ..**74** C2
Wool Rd SW20 ....**178** A4
Woolridge Way E9 ..**74** C1
Woolstaplers Way
SE16 ....**118** A2
Woolston Cl E17 ....**34** D1
Woolstone Ho 7 E2 .**96** A6
Woolstone Rd SE23 .**163** A2
Woolven Ho SE3 ...**142** D6
Woolwich Arsenal Sta
SE18 ....**122** A6
Woolwich Church St
SE7,SE18 ....**122** A3
Woolwich SE18 ....**122** C3
Woolwich Comm
SE18 ....**144** C6
Woolwich Dockyard Ind
Est SE18 ....**122** B2
Woolwich Dockyard Sta
SE18 ....**122** B2
Woolwich & Greenwich
Com Coll SE18 ....**123** A2
Woolwich High St
SE18 ....**122** A6
Woolwich Manorway
E16 ....**122** C6
Woolwich Manor Way
E16 ....**122** C6
E6 ....**100** C1
Woolwich New Rd
SE18 ....**122** C6
Woolwich Poly Sch for
Boys SE28 ....**124** A5
Woolwich Rd DA7 ..**147** C2
Belvedere DA17 ....**125** C1
Erith SE2 ....**125** D1
Greenwich SE7,SE10 .**121** C2
Wooster Gdns E14 ..**98** B1
Wootton KT10 .....**212** A4
Wootton Gr N3 .....**29** C2
Wootton Ho SE9 ...**167** A5
Wootton St
SE1 ....**116** C5 **251** B3
Worbeck Rd SE20 ..**184** C1
Worcester Ave N17 .**34** A3
Worcester Cl NW2 ..**68** B5
Croydon CR0 ......**223** C6
Mitcham CR4 ......**181** A4
Worcester Cres NW7 ..**11** C1
Woodford IG8 ....**37** C6
Worcester Ct N12 ..**29** D5
44 W2 ....**91** C2
Ashford TW15 .....**170** D4
Ealing W7 ....**86** D1
Harrow HA1 ....**42** C6
Walton-on-T KT12 .**194** C1
Worcester Park KT4 .**215** C5

Worcester Dr W4 ...**111** C4
Ashford TW15 .....**170** D5
Worcester Gdns
SW11 ....**158** D6
Northolt UB6 ....**64** D1
Redbridge IG1 ......**56** A2
Worcester Park KT4 .**215** C5
Worcester Ho SE11 .**261** A4
W2 ....**236** A1
9 Putney SW15 ....**156** C4
Worcester Mews 2
NW6 ....**69** D2
Worcester Park Rd
KT4 ....**215** B5
Worcester Park Sta
KT4 ....**200** A1
Worcester Rd E17 ..**34** D1
Belmont SM2 ......**217** C1
Ilford E12 ....**78** B4
11 Wimbledon SW19 .**179** B5
Worcesters Ave EN1 ..**6** A5
Worcesters Prim Sch
EN1 ....**5** D5
Wordsworth N8 ....**50** C5
Wordsworth Ave E12 .**78** A4
E18 ....**54** D6
Greenford UB6 .....**86** B5
Wordsworth Cl HA1 .**42** B2
Wordsworth Dr KT4,
SM3 ....**216** C4
Wordsworth Ho NW6 .**91** C4
15 SE18 ....**144** C6
Wordsworth Par 1
N15 ....**50** D5
Wordsworth Pl 11
NW5 ....**70** D3
Wordsworth Rd
DA16 ....**145** C4
N16 ....**73** C4
SE1 ....**263** B2
Hampton TW12,TW13 .**173** B6
Penge SE20 ....**184** D3
Wallington SM6 ....**219** D2
Wordsworth Way
UB7 ....**104** D2
Wordsworth Wlk
NW11 ....**47** C5
Worfield St
SW11 ......**136** C5 **267** B3
Worgan St
SE11 ......**116** B1 **260** C2
SE16 ....**118** D2
Working Men's Coll The
NW1 ....**93** C3 **232** A4
Worland Rd E15 ....**76** C1
World Bsns Ctr TW6 .**127** A4
Worlds End La BR6 .**227** D1
World's End La EN2 ...**4** B1
World's End Pas
SW10 ....**266** C4
World's End Pl SW10 **266** B4
Worley Ct NW2 .....**68** D5
Worlidge St W6 ....**112** C1
Worlingham Rd SE22 **139** D1
Wormholt Park Prim Sch
W12 ....**112** A6
Wormholt Rd W12 ..**112** A5
Wormwood St EC2 .**243** A2
Wornington Rd W10 .**91** A2
Wornum Ho 3 NW6 .**91** A4
Woronzow Rd
NW8 ....**92** C6 **230** A5
Worple Ave
Isleworth TW7 .....**153** A6
Wimbledon SW19 ..**178** D3
Worple Cl HA2 .....**41** B1
Worple Ct SW19 ...**179** A4
Worple Prim Sch
TW7 ....**131** A1
Worple Rd
Isleworth TW7 .....**131** A1
Wimbledon SW19,
SW20 ....**178** D2
Worple Road Mews
SW19 ....**179** B4
Worple St SW14 ...**133** C2
Worple Way
Harrow HA2 ....**41** B1
Richmond TW10 ...**132** A1
Worship St
EC2 ....**95** C3 **243** A5
Worslade Rd SW17 .**180** B6
Worsley Bridge Jun Sch
BR3 ....**185** C3
Worsley Bridge Rd
BR3,SE6 ....**185** C5
Worsley Ct N3 .....**29** D4
Worsley Gr E5 .....**74** A4
Worsley Ho 9 SE23 .**162** B2
Worsley Rd E11 ....**76** C4

Worsopp Dr SW4 . . . . .159 C6
Worth Cl BR6 . . . . .227 C4
Worthfield Cl KT19 . . . .215 B1
Worth Gr SE17 . . . . . .262 C1
Worthing Cl **5** E15 . . .98 C6
Worthing Rd TW5 . . . . .129 B6
Worthington Cl CR4 . . .203 B6
Worthington Ho EC1 . .234 B2
16 Streatham SW2 . . .160 C4
Worthington Rd KT6 .198 B1
Wortley Rd E6 . . . . .77 D1
  Thornton Heath CR0 . . .204 C2
Worton Ct TW7 . . . . . . .130 C1
Worton Gdns TW7 . . . . .130 B3
Worton Hall Ind Est
  TW7 . . . . .130 C1
Worton Rd TW7 . . . . . .130 C2
Worton Way TW3,
  TW7 . . . . .130 B3
Wotton Ct **8** E14 . . . .120 B6
Wotton Rd NW2 . . . . . .68 C5
18 SE8 . . . . .141 B6
Wouldham Rd E16 . . .98 D1
Wragby Rd E11 . . . . . . .76 C5
Wrampling Pl N9 . . . .18 A3
Wrangthorne Wlk
  CR0 . . . . .220 C4
Wray Ave IG5 . . . . .56 C6
Wrayburn Ho **25**
  SE16 . . . . .118 A4
Wray Cres N4 . . . . .72 B6
Wray Ct N4 . . . . .72 B6
Wrayfield Rd SM3 . . . .216 D5
Wray Ho **11** SW2 . . . .160 A4
Wraysbury Cl TW4 . . . .151 A6
Wrays Way UB4 . . . . .83 C3
Wrekin Rd SE18 . . . . . .145 A5
Wren Ave NW2 . . . . . . .68 C4
  Southall UB2 . . . . .107 B2
Wren Cl E16 . . . . .98 D1
  N9 . . . . .18 D3
Wren Cres WD23 . . . . . .8 A3
Wren Ct CR0 . . . . .221 B4
Wren Gdns RM9 . . . . . .80 D3
Wren Ho **27** E3 . . . . . .97 A5
  SW1 . . . . .259 C1
  4 Hampton TW12 . . .173 D4
Wren Landing E14 . . . .119 C5
Wrenn Ho SW13 . . . . . .134 C6
Wren Path SE28 . . . . .123 B4
Wren Rd SE5 . . . . .139 B4
  Dagenham RM9 . . . . . .80 D3
  Sidcup DA14 . . . . .168 C1
Wrens Ave TW15 . . . . .171 A6
Wren's Park Ho E5 . . .74 B6
Wren St WC1 . .94 B3 240 D6
Wrentham Ave NW10 . .90 D5
Wrenthorpe Rd BR1 . .186 C6
Wren View N6 . . . . .49 C1
Wrenwood Way HA5 . .40 B5
Wrestlers Ct EC3 . . . . .243 A2
Wrexham Rd E3 . . . . . .97 C5
Wricklemarsh Rd
  SE3 . . . . .143 D4
Wrigglesworth St
  SE14 . . . . .140 D5
Wright Cl SE13 . . . . . .142 B1
Wright Gdns TW17 . . .192 C4
Wright Ho SW15 . . . . .156 B6
Wrighton Ct SM1 . . . .217 B2
Wright Rd TW5 . . . . . .128 C5
Wrights Cl RM10 . . . . .81 D4
Wright's Gn SW4 . . . . .137 D1
Wright's La
  W8 . . . . . .113 D3 255 C6
Wrights Pl NW10 . . . . .67 A2
Wright's Rd E3 . . . . . . .97 B5
Wrights Rd SE25 . . . . .205 C6
Wright's Row SM5 . . . .219 B4
Wrights Wlk SW14 . . . .133 B2
Writtle Ho **36** NW9 . . .27 D1
Wrotham Ho SE1 . . . . .262 D6
  Beckenham BR3 . . . . . .185 B3
Wrotham Rd DA16 . . .146 C4
  11 NW1 . . . . .71 C1
  Barnet EN5 . . . . .1 A3
  Ealing W13 . . . . .109 C5
Wrottesley Rd NW10 . .90 A5
  SE18 . . . . .145 A6

Wroughton Rd SW11 158 D5
Wroughton Terr NW4 . .46 B5
Wroxall Rd RM9 . . . . . .80 C2
Wroxham Gdns N11 . . .31 D3
Wroxham Rd SE28 . . . .124 D6
Wroxton Rd SE15 . . . .140 C3
Wrythe Gn SM5 . . . . . .218 D5
Wrythe Green Rd
  SM5 . . . . .218 D5
Wrythe La SM1,SM5,
  SM4 . . . . .218 C5
Wulfstan St W12 . . . . .89 D1
Wyatt Cl SE16 . . . . . . .119 B4
  Bushey WD23 . . . . .8 C4
  Feltham TW13 . . . . .150 D3
  Hayes UB4 . . . . .84 A2
Wyatt Ct HA0 . . . . .66 A1
Wyatt Dr SW13 . . . . . .134 B5
Wyatt Ho NW8 . . . . . . .236 D5
  SE3 . . . . .142 D3
Wyatt Park Mans **1**
  SW2 . . . . .160 A2
Wyatt Park Rd SW2 . .160 B2
Wyatt Rd E7 . . . . .77 A2
  N5 . . . . .73 A5
Wyatt's La E17 . . . . . . .54 A6
Wybert St NW1 . . . . . .239 A6
Wyborne Ho NW10 . . .67 A1
Wyborne Prim Sch
  SE9 . . . . .166 D3
Wyborne Way NW10 . .67 A1
Wyburn Ave EN5 . . . . . .1 B2
Wyche Gr CR2 . . . . . . .221 A1
Wycherley Cl SE3 . . . .142 D5
Wycherley Cres EN5 . .13 D5
Wychwood Ave
  Edgware HA8 . . . . .25 D4
  South Norwood CR7 . . .205 A6
Wychwood Cl
  Ashford TW16 . . . . .172 A4
  Edgware HA8 . . . . .25 D4
Wychwood End N6 . . .49 C2
Wychwood Gdns IG5 . .56 C5
Wychwood Ho N4 . . . .51 A2
Wychwood Way SE19 183 B4
Wyclif Ct EC1 . . . . . . .234 C1
Wycliffe Cl DA16 . . . . .145 D4
Wycliffe Ho **13** N16 . .73 C4
Wycliffe Rd SW19 . . . .179 D4
Wyclif St EC1 . . . . . . .234 C1
Wycombe Ct SE3 . . . .143 A5
Wycombe Gdns NW11 69 C6
Wycombe Ho NW8 . . .237 A6
Wycombe Pl SW18 . . .158 A5
Wycombe Rd
  Redbridge IG2 . . . . .56 B4
  Tottenham N17 . . . . . . .34 A2
  Wembley HA0 . . . . .88 C6
Wydell Cl SM4 . . . . . . .200 D3
Wydenhurst Rd CR0 . .206 B2
Wydeville Manor Rd
  SE12 . . . . .187 B6
Wye Cl BR6 . . . . .211 D2
  Ashford TW15 . . . . .170 D6
  Ruislip HA4 . . . . .39 A3
Wye Ct W13 . . . . .87 B2
Wyemead Cres E4 . . . .20 C2
Wyersdale Ho N4 . . . .51 A2
Wye St SW11 . . . . .136 B3
Wyevale Cl HA5 . . . . . .40 A6
Wyfold Ho **10** SE2 . . .124 D4
Wyfold Rd
  SW6 . . . . . . .135 A5 264 A3
Wyke Cl TW7 . . . . .130 D6
Wyke Gdns W7 . . . . . .109 A3
Wykeham Ave RM9 . . .80 C2
Wykeham Cl UB7 . . . .126 C6
Wykeham Ct NW4 . . . .46 C4
Wykeham Gn RM9 . . . .80 C2
Wykeham Hill HA9 . . .44 B1
Wykeham Ho SW19 . . .179 C2
Wykeham Prim Sch
  NW9 . . . . .67 C5
Wykeham Rd NW4 . . . .46 C4
  Harrow HA3 . . . . .43 B5
Wykeham Rise N20 . . .13 A3
Wykehurst Ho SW17 188 B2
Wyke Rd E3 . . . . .75 C1
  Merton SW20 . . . . .178 C1

Wylchin Cl HA5 . . . . . .39 D6
Wyldes Cl NW11 . . . . . .48 A1
Wyldfield Gdns N9 . . .17 D2
Wyld Way HA9 . . . . . . .66 D2
Wyleu St SE23 . . . . . . .163 A4
Wylie Rd UB2 . . . . .107 A3
Wyllen Cl E1 . . . . .96 C3
Wylo Dr EN5 . . . . .12 A5
Wymering Mans **6**
  W9 . . . . .91 C4
Wymering Rd W9 . . . . .91 C4
Wymondham Ct
  NW8 . . . . .229 D6
Wymond St SW15 . . . .134 C2
Wynan Rd E14 . . . . . . .119 D1
Wynard Terr SE11 . . . .260 D2
Wynash Gdns SM5 . . .218 C3
Wynaud Ct N22 . . . . . .32 B4
Wynbourne Ct SE20 . .184 B1
Wyncham Ave DA15 . .167 C3
Wynchgate
  Harrow HA3 . . . . .24 C3
  Southgate N14 . . . . . . .16 A4
Wyncroft Cl BR1 . . . . .210 B6
Wyndale Ave NW9 . . . .44 C3
Wyndcliff Rd SE7 . . . .143 B6
Wyndcroft Cl EN2 . . . . .4 D2
Wyndham Cl
  Belmont SM2 . . . . .217 C1
  Orpington BR6 . . . . . . .211 B1
Wyndham Cres N19 . .71 C5
  Hounslow TW4 . . . . . . .151 C5
Wyndham Ct W7 . . . . .109 A2
Wyndham Deedes Ho **27**
  E2 . . . . .96 A5
Wyndham Ho SW1 . . .258 A3
Wyndham Mews W1 . .237 C3
Wyndham Pl W1 . . . . .237 C3
Wyndham Rd E6 . . . . . .77 D1
  SE5 . . . . .139 A5
  W13 . . . . .109 B3
  Barnet, London EN4 . . . .14 D3
  Kingston KT2 . . . . .176 B3
Wyndham St
  W1 . . . . . . .92 D2 237 C4
Wyndham Yd W1 . . . . .237 C3
Wyneham Rd SE24 . . .161 B6
Wynell Rd SE23 . . . . . .162 D1
Wynford Pl DA17 . . . . .147 C6
Wynford Rd
  N1 . . . . .94 B5 233 D4
Wynford Way SE9 . . . .166 B1
Wynlie Gdns HA5 . . . .22 B1
Wynn Bridge Cl IG8 . .37 D2
Wynndale Rd E18 . . . .37 B2
Wynne Ct **4** TW7 . . . .131 A2
Wynne Ho SE14 . . . . . .140 D4
Wynne Rd SW9 . . . . . .138 C3
Wynn's Ave DA15 . . . .168 A6
Wynnstay Gdns
  W8 . . . . . . .113 C3 255 B6
Wynter Ho **20** SW9 . .138 B3
Wynter St SW11 . . . . .136 A1
Wynton Gdns SE25 . .205 D4
Wynton Pl W3 . . . . . . .88 D1
Wynyard Ho SE11 . . . .260 D2
Wynyatt St
  EC1 . . . . . . .94 D4 234 C2
Wyre Gr Edgware HA8 .10 D1
  Hayes UB3 . . . . .106 A2
Wyresdale Cres UB6 . .86 D4
Wytham Ho NW8 . . . .236 D5
Wythburn Ct W1 . . . . .237 C2
Wythburn Pl W1 . . . . .237 C2
Wythenshawe Rd
  RM10 . . . . .81 C5
Wythens Wlk SE9 . . . .166 D5
Wythes Cl BR1 . . . . . .188 B1
Wythes Rd E16 . . . . . .122 A5
Wythfield Rd SE9 . . . .166 B5
Wyvenhoe Rd HA2 . . . .64 D5
Wyvern Est The KT3 . .200 A5
Wyvil Prim Sch
  SW8 . . . . . . .138 A5 270 B4
Wyvil Rd
  SW8 . . . . . . .138 A5 270 A4
Wyvis St E14 . . . . .97 D2

X

Xavier Ho E17 . . . . . . .35 B1

Y

Yabsley St E14 . . . . . . .120 A5
Yaldam Ho SE1 . . . . . .263 A3
Yalding Ho **20** E5 . . . .74 B2
Yalding Rd SE16 . . . . .118 A2
Yale Cl TW4 . . . . .151 B6
Yale Ct NW6 . . . . .69 D3
Yarborough Rd
  SW19 . . . . .180 B2
Yardley Cl E4 . . . . .19 D6
Yardley Ct SM3 . . . . . .216 D4
Yardley La E4 . . . . .19 D6
Yardley Prim Sch E4 .20 A5
Yardley St WC1 . . . . . .234 A1
Yarmouth Cres N17 . .52 B4
Yarmouth Pl W1 . . . . .248 C3
Yarnfield Sq **14** SE15 .140 C4
Yarnton Way DA17,
  DA18 . . . . .125 B3
Yarrow Cres E6 . . . . . .100 A2
Yarrow Ho **10** E14 . . .120 A3
  W10 . . . . .90 C2
Yateley St SE18 . . . . . .121 D3
Yatesbury Ct E5 . . . . . .75 A3
Yates Ct NW2 . . . . .68 D2
Yates Ho **15** E2 . . . . . .96 A4
Yatton Ho W10 . . . . . .90 C2
Yeading Ave HA2 . . . . .41 A1
Yeading Ct UB4 . . . . . .84 A3
Yeading Fork UB4 . . . .84 C3
Yeading Gdns UB4 . . .84 B2
Yeading Jun & Inf Schs
  UB4 . . . . .84 C2
Yeading La Hayes UB4 .84 B2
  Hayes, Northolt UB4,UB5 84 C4
Yeadon Ho W10 . . . . . .90 C2
Yeames Cl W13 . . . . . .87 A1
Yearby Ho W10 . . . . . .90 C3
Yeate St N1 . . . . .73 B1
Yeatman Rd N6 . . . . . .48 D3
Yeats Cl NW10 . . . . . . .67 C2
Yeend Cl KT8 . . . . .195 C5
Yeldham Ho W6 . . . . . .112 D1
Yeldham Rd W6 . . . . . .112 D1
Yellowhammer Ct
  NW9 . . . . .27 C1
Yelverton Lo TW1 . . . .153 C4
Yelverton Rd SW11 . . .136 B3
Ye Market CR0 . . . . . . .221 B3
Yenston Cl SM4 . . . . . .201 C3
Yeoman Cl E16 . . . . . .122 D6
  West Norwood SE27 . . .160 D1
Yeoman Ct TW5 . . . . . .129 B5
Yeoman Ho SE1 . . . . . .263 D2
Yeoman Rd UB5 . . . . . .63 A1
Yeomans Acre HA4 . . .40 A3
Yeomans Mews TW7 .152 B6
Yeoman's Row
  SW3 . . . . . . .114 C3 257 B5
Yeoman St SE8 . . . . . .119 A2
Yeomans Way EN3 . . . .6 C3
Yeo St E3 . . . . .97 D2
Yeovil Cl BR6 . . . . .227 C6
Yeovil Ho N7 . . . . .72 B6
Yeovilton Pl KT2 . . . . .175 C5
Yerbury Prim Sch N19 71 D5
Yerbury Rd N19 . . . . . .71 D5
Yesodey Hatorah Sch
  N16 . . . . .51 D2
Yester Dr BR7 . . . . . . .188 A3
Yester Pk BR7 . . . . . . .188 B4
Yester Rd BR7 . . . . . . .188 B3
Yew Ave UB7 . . . . .104 A6
Yew Cl IG9 . . . . .21 D2
Yewdale Cl BR1 . . . . . .186 C4
Yewfield Rd NW10 . . . .67 D2
Yew Gr NW2 . . . . .68 D4
Yew Ho SE14 . . . . .141 B3
Yews The TW15 . . . . . .170 D6
Yew Tree Ave N2 . . . . .47 D6
Yew Tree Cl DA16 . . . .146 A4

Yewtree Cl
  Harrow HA2 . . . . .41 D5
  Wood Green N22 . . . . . .31 C2
Yew Tree Cl
  New Malden KT4 . . . . .199 C1
  Southgate N21 . . . . . . .16 C4
Yew Tree Cotts KT10 .212 B6
Yew Tree Ct **4** NW11 .47 M4
  Elstree WD6 . . . . .9 D5
  8 Sutton SM2 . . . . . .218 A1
Yew Tree Gdns RM6 . .59 A4
Yew Tree Grange **2**
  W5 . . . . .109 C6
Yew Tree Ho KT4 . . . .199 C1
Yew Tree Rd W12 . . . . .111 D6
Yewtree Rd BR3 . . . . . .207 B6
Yew Tree Rd UB10 . . . .82 B6
Yew Trees TW17 . . . . .192 B5
Yew Tree Wlk TW4 . . . .151 B6
Yew Wlk HA1 . . . . .42 C1
Yiewsley Ct UB7 . . . . .104 C3
Yoakley Rd N16 . . . . . .73 C5
Yoke Cl N7 . . . . .72 A2
Yolande Gdns SE9 . . .166 A6
Yonge Pk N4,N7 . . . . .72 C5
York Ave DA15 . . . . . . .167 D2
  SE17 . . . . .262 B2
  Ealing W7 . . . . .108 C5
  Hayes UB3 . . . . .83 A1
  Mortlake SW14 . . . . . . .155 A6
  Stanmore HA7 . . . . .25 B1
York Bldgs
  WC2 . . . . . . .116 A6 250 B5
York Bridge
  NW1 . . . . .93 A3 238 A6
York Cl **17** SE5 . . . . . .139 A3
  Ealing W7 . . . . .108 C5
  Morden SM4 . . . . .201 D5
  Newham E6 . . . . .100 B1
York Ct
  Beckenham BR3 . . . . . .186 B2
  Kingston KT2 . . . . .175 D4
  Wallington SM6 . . . . . . .219 C3
York Gate NW1 . . . . . .238 B5
  Southgate N14 . . . . . . .16 A4
York Gr SE15 . . . . .140 C4
York Hill SE27,SW16 .160 D1
York Ho N1 . . . . .233 C3
  N5 . . . . .72 C3
  3 N7 . . . . .71 D2
  1 NW4 . . . . .28 D1
  SE1 . . . . . . .116 B3 260 D5
  SW3 . . . . .257 C2
  W1 . . . . .237 C4
  W3 . . . . .111 A6
  W8 . . . . .245 C2
  10 Acton W3 . . . . . . .88 C1
  Chingford E4 . . . . .35 C6
  Enfield EN2 . . . . .5 A4
  Forest Hill SE26 . . . . . .184 C5
  1 Ilford IG1 . . . . .78 C6
  4 Kingston KT2 . . . . .176 B3
  Richmond TW10 . . . . . .154 C6
  Richmond TW9 . . . . . . .132 C2
  South Norwood SE25 . .205 C5
York House Pl
  W8 . . . . . . .113 D4 245 C2
Yorkland Ave DA16 . . .145 D1
Yorkley Ho W10 . . . . . .90 C3
York Mans **1** NW9 . . .46 A3
  SW11 . . . . .268 B2
  W1 . . . . .238 A4
York Mews NW5 . . . . .71 B3
  Ilford IG1 . . . . .78 C6
York Par
  Brentford TW8 . . . . . . .109 D1
York Pl SW11 . . . . . . .136 B2
  WC2 . . . . .250 B5
  Ilford IG1 . . . . .78 C6
York Place Mans
  NW1 . . . . .237 D4
York Rd E10 . . . . .76 A5
  E17 . . . . .52 D4
  E7 . . . . .77 A2
  N11 . . . . .31 D4
  SE1 . . . . . . .116 B4 250 D2
  SW11,SW18 . . . . .136 B2
  W3 . . . . .89 B1
  W5 . . . . .109 C3

Wor – Zof 409

York Rd continued
  Belmont SM1,SM2 . . .217 C1
  Brentford TW8 . . . . . . .109 D1
  Chingford E4 . . . . .35 C5
  Edmonton N18 . . . . . . .34 B5
  Hounslow TW3 . . . . . . .129 D2
  Ilford IG1 . . . . .78 C6
  Kingston KT2 . . . . .176 B3
  New Barnet EN5 . . . . . .14 B6
  Pinner HA6 . . . . .22 A1
  4 Richmond TW10 . .154 B4
  Southgate N21 . . . . . . .17 B4
  Teddington TW11 . . . . .174 C6
  Thornton Heath CR0 . .204 C2
  Wimbledon SW19 . . . .180 A4
York Rise BR6 . . . . . . .227 C6
  NW5 . . . . .71 B5
York Road Bsns Ctr
  SW11 . . . . .136 B3
Yorkshire Cl N16 . . . . .73 C5
Yorkshire Gdns N18 . .34 B5
Yorkshire Grey SE9 . .165 D6
Yorkshire Grey Yd
  WC1 . . . . .240 C3
Yorkshire Rd E14 . . . . .97 A1
  Mitcham CR4 . . . . .204 A5
York Sq **14** E14 . . . . . .97 A1
York St W1 . . .92 D2 237 D4
  Barking IG11 . . . . .101 A6
  Carshalton CR4 . . . . . .203 A2
  Twickenham TW1 . . . . .153 A3
York St Chambers
  W1 . . . . .237 C4
York Terr EN2 . . . . .5 A5
York Terr E
  NW1 . . . . .93 A3 238 B5
York Terr W
  NW1 . . . . .93 A3 238 A5
Yorkton St E2 . . . . .96 A5
York Way N1 . . . . .233 B5
  N1,N7,NW1 . . . . .72 A1
  N20 . . . . .14 D1
  Chessington KT9 . . . . .214 A1
  Twickenham TW13 . . . .151 B1
York Way Ct N1 . . . . . .233 B5
Youngmans Cl EN2 . . .5 A4
Young Rd E16 . . . . .99 C1
Young's Bldgs EC1 . . .242 B6
Youngs Ct SW11 . . . . .268 B1
Youngs Rd IG2 . . . . . . .57 B4
Young St W8 113 D4 245 C1
Yoxall Ho W10 . . . . . . .90 C3
Yoxley App IG2 . . . . . . .57 A3
Yoxley Dr IG2 . . . . .57 A3
Yukon Rd SW12 . . . . .159 B4
Yuletide Cl NW10 . . . .67 C6
Yunus Khan Cl E17 . . .53 C4

Z

Zampa Rd SE16 . . . . .118 C1
Zander Ct E2 . . . . .96 A4
Zangwill Ho NW6 . . . . .91 B5
Zangwill Rd SE18,SE3 143 D4
Zealand Ave UB7 . . . .126 A5
Zealand Ho **11** SE5 . .139 A3
  4 SE7 . . . . .122 A2
Zealand Rd E3 . . . . . . .97 A5
Zennor Rd SW12 . . . . .159 C3
Zenoria St SE22 . . . . .139 D1
Zermatt Rd CR7 . . . . . .205 A5
Zetland Ho W8 . . . . . .255 C6
Zetland St E14 . . . . . . .98 A2
Zion Ho **6** E1 . . . . . . .96 C1
Zion Pl CR7 . . . . .205 B5
Zion Rd CR7 . . . . .205 B5
Zoar St SE1 . .117 A5 252 A4
Zodiac Ct CR0 . . . . . . .204 D1
Zodiac Ho **3** E3 . . . . .97 C3
Zoffany St N19 . . . . . . .71 D6

List of numbered locations

This atlas shows thousands more place names than any other London street atlas. In some busy areas it is impossible to fit the name of every place.

Where not all names will fit, some smaller places are shown by a number. If you wish to find out the name associated with a number, use this listing.

The places in this list are also listed normally in the Index.

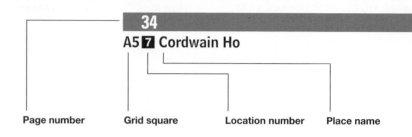

Page number   Grid square   Location number   Place name

1
A1 1 Hertswood Ct
2 Sunbury Ct
3 Meriden Ho
4 Norfolk Ct
5 Morrison Ct
6 Kingshill Ct
7 Baronsmere Ct
8 Chartwell Ct

2
C1 1 Braeburn Ct
2 Bramley Ct
3 Cox Ct
4 Golden Ct
5 Pippin Ct
6 Russet Ct
7 High Birch Ct
8 Joystone Ct
9 Mark Lo
10 Edgeworth Ct

5
1 Woodfield Cl
2 Fielders Cl

9
D5 1 Watling Ct
2 Stuart Ct
3 Westview Ct
4 Potters Mews

13
D6 1 Rowan Wlk
2 Ford Ho
3 Glenwood Ho
4 Whitegates
5 Lisa Lo
6 South Lo
7 Hockington Ct
8 Eysham Ct
9 Springfields
10 Bure Ct
11 Coleridge Ct
12 Chaucer Ct

14
B6 1 Redrose Trad Ctr
2 Lancaster Road Ind Est
C5 1 Feline Ct
2 Brookhill Ct
3 Littlegrove Ct
4 Desmond Ho

15
C6 1 Tregenna Cl
2 Catherine Ct
3 Conisbee Ct
4 Ashmead
D3 1 Dennis Par
2 Broadway The
3 Southgate Cir
4 Station Par
5 Bourneside
6 Bourneside Cres

17
C6 1 Wade Ho

2 Newport Lo
3 Halcyon
4 Lerwick Ct
5 Anchor Ct
6 Grassmere Ct
7 Datchworth Ct
8 Trentham Lo
9 Austin Ct
10 Cedar Grange
11 Brookview Ct
12 Chestbrook Ct
13 Paddock Lo
14 Hamlet Ct
15 Haven Lo

18
A1 1 Plevna Ho
2 Lea Ho
3 Brook Ho
4 Valley Ho
5 Chiltern Ho
6 Blenheim Ho
7 Penn Ho
8 Romany Ho
9 Gilpin Ho
10 Anvil Ho
11 Well Ho
12 Passmore Ho
13 Durbin Ho
A2 1 Market Par
2 Beechwood Mews
3 Keats Par
4 Cedars Rd
5 Cross Keys Cl
6 Dorman Pl
7 Concourse The

20
1 Lea Ct
2 Park Ct
3 Conference Cl
4 Berrybank Cl
5 Russell Ct
6 Brunswick Lo
7 Kenilworth Ct
8 Trinity Ct
9 Kingsmead Lo
10 Fairlawns
A3 1 Knight Ct
2 Grant Ct
3 Chantry The
4 Bowyer Ct
5 Pineview Ct
6 Ellen Ct
7 Leaview Ct
8 Chelsea Ct
9 Bramley Ct
10 Garenne Ct
11 Kendal Ct
B2 1 Temple Hall Ct
2 Larkshall Bsns Ctr
3 Endlebury Ct
4 James Ct
5 Holmes Ct
B3 1 Maddox Ct
2 Village Arc The
3 Cambridge Rd
4 Crown Bldgs
5 Pentney Rd
6 Scholars Ho
7 Cranworth Cres
C4 1 Connaught Ct
2 Woolden Ho

3 Fairmead Ct
4 Lockhart Lo
5 Cavendish Ct
6 Oakwood Ct
7 Plains The
8 Hadleigh Ct
9 Forest Ho
10 Mathieson Ho

21
C2 1 Westbury Ct
2 Palmerston Ct
3 Ibrox Ct
4 Richard Burton Ct
5 Queens Ct
6 Gunnels Ct & Hastingwood Ct
7 Marlborough Ct
8 Avenue The
9 Tara Ct
D2 1 Regency Lo
2 Kings Ct
3 Beech Ct
4 Sycamore Ho

22
C1 1 Northcote
2 Edwin Ware Ct
3 Chalfont Wlk
4 Maple Ct
5 Montesole Ct

23
B3 1 St Cuthberts Gdns
2 Cherry Croft Gdns
3 Cornwall Cl
4 Dunsford Ct

25
C5 1 Belgrave Gdns
2 Heywood Ct
3 Norfolk Ho
4 Garden Ct
5 Chatsworth Ct
6 Chartridge Ct
7 Hardwick Cl
8 Cheltenham Ct
9 Cargrey Ho
10 Holbein Ho
11 Goodwood Cl
C6 1 Bickley Ct
2 Kelmscott Ct
3 Elstree Ho
4 Brompton Ct
5 Kenmare Ct

27
A1 1 Colesworth Ho
2 Crokesley Ho
3 Curtlington Ho
4 Clare Ho
5 Kedyngton Ho
A3 1 Tadbourne Ct
2 Truman Cl
3 Lords Ct
4 Hutton Row
5 Compton Cl
6 Botham Cl
7 Bradman Row

A6 1 Iris Wlk
2 Sycamore Cl
B5 1 Monarchs Ct
2 Kensington Ct
C2 1 Rufforth Ct
2 Riccal Ct
3 Lindholme Ct
4 Driffield Ct
5 Jack Ashley Ct
6 Folkingham La
7 Leander Ct
8 Daniel Ct
9 Nimrod
10 Nisbet
11 Pixton
12 Rapide
13 Ratier
D1 1 Gauntlet
2 Guilfoyle
3 Grebe
4 Gates
5 Galy
6 Folland
7 Firefly
8 Halifax
9 Debussy
10 Crosbie
11 Grant Ct
12 Ham Ct
13 Deal Ct
14 Ember Ct
15 Canterbury Ct
16 Beaumont Ct
17 Cirrus
18 Defiant
19 Dessouter
20 Douglas
21 Clayton
22 Cobham
23 Camm
24 Bradon
25 Boarhound
26 Bodmin
27 Bleriot
28 Blackburn
29 Audax
30 Anson
31 Albatross
32 Arran Ct
33 Mavis Ct
34 Goosander Ct
35 Platt Halls (a)
36 Writtle Ho
37 Platt Halls (b)
38 Platt Halls (c)
D2 1 Slatter
2 Sopwith
3 Saimet
4 Sassoon
5 Roe
6 Orde
7 Osprey
8 Prodger
9 Randall
10 Porte
11 Norris
12 Nardini
13 Noel
14 Nicolson
15 Napier
16 Nighthawk
17 Moorhouse
18 Moineau
19 Mitchell
20 Lysander
21 Lillywhite
22 Martynside

23 March
24 Kemp
25 Mercury
26 Merlin
27 Hudson
28 Hawker
29 Hawfinch
30 Heracles
31 Hector
D3 1 Wellington
2 Wheeler
3 Whittaker
4 Whittle
5 Tedder
6 Cranwell Ct
7 Tait
8 Spooner

28
D1 1 York Ho
2 Windsor Ho
3 Regency Cres
4 Normandy Ho
5 Allerton Ct

29
C2 1 Sherringham Ct
2 St Ronan's
3 Crescent Rise
4 Elm Ct
D6 1 Brookfield Ct
2 Magnolia Ct
3 Dunbar Ct
4 Haughmond
5 Nansen Village
6 Beechcroft Ct
7 Speedwell Ct
8 Woodside Ct
9 Speedwell Ho
10 Rebecca Ho
11 Ashbourne Ct
12 Forest Ct
13 Beecholme
14 Greville Lo
15 St Johnstone Ho

30
B1 1 New Trinity Rd
2 Garden Ho
3 Todd Ho
4 Sayers Ho
5 Mowbray Ho
6 Bouchier Ho
7 Cleveland Ho
8 Goodyear Ho
9 Lochleven Ho
10 Berwick Ho
11 Oak Ho
12 Willow Wlk
13 Craven Ho
14 Willow Ho
15 Vane Ho
16 Foskett Ho
17 Elmfield Ho
18 Sycamore Ho
19 Netherwood
D5 1 Halliwick Ct
2 Halliwick Court Par
3 Queen's Par
4 St John's Village
5 Hartland Ct
6 Kennard Mans
7 Bensley Cl

31
A3 1 Campe Ho
2 Betstyle Ho
3 Pymmes Brook Ho
4 Mosswell Ho
5 Hampden Ct
6 Crown Ct
B1 1 Cedar Ct
2 Carisbrook
3 St Ivian Ct
4 Barrington Ct
5 Essex Lo
B5 1 Caradoc Evans Cl
2 Roberts Ho
3 Lorne Ho
B6 1 Grovefield
2 Lapworth
3 Stewards Holte Wlk
4 Sarnes Ct
5 Stanhope Ho
6 Holmsdale Ho
C5 1 Barbara Martin Ho
2 Jerome Ct
3 Limes Cl
4 Arnos Grove Ct
5 Cedar Ct
6 Betspath Ho
7 Curtis Ho
8 Mason Ho
9 Danford Ho
10 New Southgate Ind Est
11 Palmer's Ct

32
A4 1 Brownlow Ct
2 Latham Ct
3 Fairlawns
4 Beaumaris
C1 1 Penwortham Ct
2 Tarleton Ct
3 Holmeswood Ct
4 Kwesi Johnson Ct
5 Sandlings The

33
D1 1 Honeysett Rd
2 Wilson's Ave
3 Palm Tree Ct
4 Stoneleigh Ct
5 Brook St
D3 1 Charles Ho
2 Moselle Ho
3 Ermine Ho
4 Kathleen Ferrier Ct
5 Concord Ho
6 Rees Ho
7 Nursery Ct
8 William Rainbird Ho
D4 1 Regan Ho
2 Isis Ho
3 Boundary Ct
4 Stellar Ho
5 Cooperage Cl

34
A5 1 Angel Pl
2 Cross St
3 Scott Ho
4 Beck Ho
5 Booker Rd
6 Bridport Ho
7 Cordwain Ho
8 St James's Ct
9 Highmead
A6 1 Walton Ho
2 Alma Ho
3 Brompton Ho
4 Field Ho
5 Bradwell Mews
6 Angel Corner Par
7 Paul Ct
8 Cuthbert Rd
9 Brockenhurst Mews
B3 1 Kenneth Robbins Ho
2 Charles Bradlaugh Ho
3 Woodrow Ct
4 Cheviot
5 Corbridge
6 Whittingham
7 Eastwood Ct
8 Alnwick
9 Bamburgh
10 Bellingham
11 Briaris Cl

36
B5 1 Hedgemoor Ct
2 Hewitt Ho
3 Castle Ho
4 Bailey Ct
5 Harcourt Ho
6 Gerboa Ct
D1 1 Chatham Rd
2 Washington Rd
3 Cherry Tree Ct
4 Grosvenor Lo
5 Torfell
D2 1 Hillboro Ct
2 Dorchester Ct

37
A1 1 Chiltons The
2 Ullswater Ho
3 Leigh Ct
4 Woburn Ct
A2 1 Lindal Ct
2 Hockley Ct
3 Woodleigh
4 Milne Ct
5 Cedar Ct
6 Elizabeth Ct
7 Silvermead
8 Laurel Mead Ct
9 Mitre Ct
10 Pevensey Ct
11 Lyndhurst Ct
A3 1 New Jubilee Ct
2 Chartwell Ct
3 Greenwood
4 Solway Lo
A4 1 Terrace The
2 Broomhill Ct
3 Clifton Ct
4 Fairstead Lo

5 Hadleigh Lo
6 Broadmead Ct
7 Wilton Ct
8 Fairfield Ct
9 Higham Ct
A6 1 Tree Tops
2 Cranfield Ct
B1 1 Station Est
2 Station App
3 James Ct
C3 1 Liston Way
2 Elizabeth Ct
3 Coopersale Cl
4 Sunset Ct
5 Lambourne Ct
C4 1 Hope Cl
2 Rex Par
3 Shalford
4 Rodings The

40
C1 1 Salisbury Ho
2 Rodwell Cl
3 Pretoria Ho
4 Ottawa Ho
5 Swallow Ct

42
D3 1 Nightingale Ct
2 St John's Ct
3 Gayton Ct
4 Wilton Pl
5 Murray Ct
6 Cymbeline Ct
7 Knowles Ct
8 Charville Ct
9 Lime Ct
10 Petherton Ct
12 Chalfont Ct
D4 1 Crystal Ctr The
2 Blue Point Ct
3 Ryan Ho
4 Bruce Ho
5 Ingram Ho
6 Arless Ho
7 Leaf Ho

46
A2 1 Milton Rd
2 Stanley Rd
A3 1 York Mans
2 Telford Rd
A5 1 Pilkington Ct
2 Cousins Ct
3 Seton Ct
4 Frensham Ct
5 Chatton Ct
6 Geraldine Ct
7 Swynford Gdns
8 Miller Ct
9 Roffey Ct
10 Peace Ct
11 Rambler Ct
12 Lion Ct
13 Wenlock Gdns
14 Dogrose Ct
15 Harry Ct
16 Tribune Ct
17 Bonville Gdns
18 Pearl Ct
B4 1 Vivian Mans
2 Parade Mans
3 Georgian Ct
4 Florence Mans
5 Park Mans
6 Cheyne Cl
7 Queens Par
8 Central Mans
C5 1 Courtney Ho
2 Golderton
3 Thornbury
4 Brampton La
5 Ashwood Ho
6 Longford Ct
7 Short St
D5 1 Midford Ho
2 Rockfield Ho
3 Lisselton Ho
4 Acrefield Ho

47
B2 1 Berkeley Ct
2 Exchange Mans
3 Beechcroft Ct
4 Nedahall Ct
B3 1 Charlton Lo

2 Clifton Gdns
B4 1 Hallswelle Par
2 Belmont Par
3 Temple Fortune Ho
4 Yew Tree Ct
5 Temple Fortune Par
6 Courtleigh
7 Arcade Ho
8 Queens Ct
9 Temple Fortune Ct
B5 1 Monkville Par
2 Ashbourne Par

48
A6 1 St Mary's Gn
2 Dunstan Cl
3 Paul Byrne Ho
4 Longfield Ct
5 Warwick Ct
6 Branksome Ct
7 Sherwood Hall

49
B6 1 Dorchester Ct
2 Old Chapel Pl
3 Athenaeum Pl
4 Risborough Cl
C1 1 Calvert Ct
2 Academy The
3 Whitehall Mans
4 Pauntley St
5 Archway Hts
6 Pauntley Ho
D1 1 Louise White Ho
2 Levison Way
3 Sanders Way
D2 1 Eleanor Rathbone Ho
2 Christopher Lo
3 Monkridge
4 Marbleford Ct
5 High London
6 Garton Ho
7 Hilltop Ho
8 Caroline Martyn Ho
9 Arthur Henderson Ho
10 Margaret Mcmillan Ho
11 Enid Stacy Ho
12 Mary McArthur Ho
13 Bruce Glasier Ho
14 John Wheatley Ho
15 Keir Hardie Ho
16 Monroe Ho
17 Iberia Ho
18 Lygoe Ho
19 Lambert Ho
20 Shelbourne Ho
21 Arkansas Ho
22 Lafitte Ho
23 Shreveport Ho
24 Packenham Ho
25 Orpheus Ho
26 Fayetville Ho
27 Bayon Ho
D4 1 Kelland Cl
2 Veryan Ct
3 Coulsdon Ct

50
A1 1 Beeches The
2 Lambton Ct
A2 1 Marie Lloyd Gdns
2 Jessie Blythe La
3 Leyden Mans
4 Brambledown
5 Lochbie
6 Edith Cavell Cl
A5 1 Mackenzie Ct
2 Stowell Ho
3 Campsbourne Ho
B1 1 Lawson Ct
2 Wiltshire Ct
3 Hutton Ct
D5 1 Wordsworth Par

51
A2 1 Finmere Ho
2 Keynsham Ho
3 Kilpeck Ho
4 Knaresborough Ho
5 Leighfield Ho
6 Lonsdale Ho
7 Groveley Ho
8 Wensleydale Ho
9 Badminton Ct
B2 1 Selwood Ho
2 Mendip Ho
3 Ennerdale Ho
4 Delamere Ho
5 Westwood Ho
6 Bernwood Ho
7 Allerdale Ho
8 Chattenden Ho
9 Farningham Ho
10 Oakend Ho
C1 1 Godstone Ho
2 Farnham Ct
3 Milford Ct
4 Cranleigh Ct
5 Haslemere Ct
6 Belmont Ct
7 Hockworth Ho
8 Garratt Ho
9 Fairburn Ho
C3 1 Oatfield Ho
2 Perry Ct
3 Henrietta Ho
4 Bournes Ho
5 Chisley Rd
6 Twyford Ho
7 Langford Cl
8 Hatchfield Ho
D1 1 Stamford Hill Mans
2 Montefiore Ct
3 Berwyn Ho
4 Clent Ho
5 Chiltern Ho
6 Laindon Ho
7 Pentland Ho
D2 1 Regent Ct
2 Stamford Lo
3 Holmwood Ct
D3 1 Sherboro Rd
2 Westcott Cl
3 Cadoxton Ave
4 Slater Ho
D4 1 Westerfield Rd
2 Suffield Rd
D5 1 Greenway Cl
2 Tottenham Gn E
3 Tottenham Gn E South Side
4 Deaconess Ct
5 Elliot Ct
6 Bushmead Cl
7 Beaufort Ho
8 Tynemouth Terr
D6 1 Holcombe Rd
2 Chaplin Rd
3 Reynardson's Ct
4 Protheroe Ho

52
A1 1 Stamford Grove E
2 Stamford Mans
3 Grove Mans
4 Stamford Grove W
B1 1 Hawkwood Mount
2 Holmbury View
3 High Hill Ferry
4 Leaside Ho
5 Courtlands
6 Ivy Ho
7 Shelford Ct

53
A4 1 Hammond Ct
2 St James Apartments
3 Grange The
A5 1 Bristol Park Rd
2 Stoneydown Ho
3 Callonfield
4 Hardyng Ho
C1 1 Wellington Mans
2 Clewer Ct
3 Cochrane Ct

C5 1 Westbury Ho
2 Hatherley Ho
3 Vintry Mews
4 Tylers Ct
5 Merchants Lo
6 Gillards Mews
7 Blacksmiths Lo
8 Central Par
D1 1 Fitzgerald Ct
2 Bechervaise Ct
3 Underwood Ct
D2 1 Station Ct
2 Howell Ct
3 Atkinson Ct
4 Russell Ct
5 St Luke Ct
6 St Matthews Ct
7 St Mark's Ct
8 St Elizabeth Ct
9 Emmanuel Ct
10 St Thomas Ct
11 Beaumont Ho
12 Shelley Ct
13 St Paul's Twr
14 Flack Ct
15 King Ct
16 Osborne Ct
17 Muriel Ct
18 All Saints Twr
19 St Josephs Ct
20 Mitchell Ct
21 Cornwell Ct
D5 1 Nash Ho
2 St Columbas Ho
3 Attlee Terr
4 Astins Ho
5 Lindens The
6 Kevan Ct
7 Squire's Almshouses
8 Berry Field Cl
9 Holmcroft Ho
10 Connaught Ct
D6 1 Hollingbury Ct
2 Mace Ho
3 Gaitskell Ho
4 Hancocke Ho
5 Trinity Ho
6 Fanshaw Ho
7 Hilltop
8 Batten Ho
9 Bradwell Ho
10 Walton Ho
11 Temple Ho
12 Gower Ho
13 Maple Ho
14 Poplars Ho
15 Cedars Ho
16 Kimm Ho
17 O'Grady Ho
18 Latham Ho
19 Powell Ct
20 Crosbie Ho

54
A2 1 Ayerst Ct
2 Dare Ct
3 St Edwards Ct
A4 1 Jane Sabina Colard's Almshouses
2 Ellen Miller Ho
3 Tom Smith Ho
A5 1 Northwood Twr
2 Walnut Ct
3 Albert Whicher Ho
4 Pelly Ct
5 Ravenswood Road Ind Est
6 Holland Ct
7 Emberson Ho
8 St Mark's Ho
9 Alfred Villas
A6 1 St David's Ct
2 Golden Par
3 Chestnuts Ct
4 Matthew Ct
5 Gilbert Ho
6 Manning Ho
7 Southgate Ho
8 Boyden Ho
9 Prospect Ho
10 Newton Ho

55
A3 1 Aldham Hall
2 Parkside Ct

3 Mapperley Cl
4 Weavers Ho
5 Cyns Ct
6 Reed Mans
7 Thornton Ho
8 Hardwick Ct
A4 1 Kingsley Grange
2 Station Par
3 Gwynne Ho
4 Staveley Ct
5 Devon Ho
6 Thurlow Ho
7 Hollies The
8 Little Holt
9 Dudley Ct
10 Woodland Ct
11 Struan Ho
12 Westleigh Ct
A5 1 Shernwood Ho
2 Orwell Lo
3 Hermitage Ct
4 Gowan Lea
5 Woodford Ho
6 Eagle Ct
7 Newbury Ct
8 Shelley Ct
9 Hardy Ct
10 Dickens Ct
11 Byron Ct
A6 1 Millbrook
2 Elmbrook
3 Grange The
4 Glenavon Lo
5 Glenwood Ct
6 Ferndown
7 Embassy Ct
8 Orestes Ct
9 Walbrook
10 Helmsley
11 Snaresbrook Hall
B4 1 Nightingale Ct
2 Chelston Ct
3 Grosvenor Ct
4 Louise Ct
5 St Davids Ct
6 Cedar Ct
7 Shrubbery The
B6 1 Victoria Ct
2 Kenwood Gdns
3 Thaxted Lo
4 Albert Rd
5 Albert Ho
6 Falcon Ct
7 Deborah Ct
8 Swift Ho
9 Pulteney Gdns
10 Spring Ct
11 Trinity Gdns

56
B4 1 High View Par
2 Spurway Par

57
A3 1 Catherine Ct
2 Lincoln Ct
3 Ivy Terr
4 Newbury Cotts

58
B1 1 Caledonian Cl
2 Talisman Cl
3 Norseman Cl
4 Frank Slater Ho
5 Brook's Mans
6 Brook's Par
B2 1 Mitre Ct
2 Coppins The
3 Stanetto Ct
4 Wilnett Ct
5 Wilnett Villas
D2 1 Pavement Mews
2 Chadview Ct
3 Granary Ct
4 Bedwell Ct
5 Chapel La
6 Faulkner Cl
7 Maple Ct
8 Willow Ct
9 Cedar Terr

63
C2 1 Wimborne Ct
2 Haydock Green Flats

3 Brighton Dr
4 Blaydon Ct
5 Fakenham Cl
6 Rutland Ho
7 Windsor Ho

65
D3 1 Oaklands Ct
2 Lowry Lo
3 Morritt Ho
4 Lancelot Par
5 Willow Tree Ct
6 Snow Ct

66
A2 1 Montrose Cres
2 Peggy Quirke Ct
3 Copland Mews
4 Coronet Par
5 Charlotte Ct
A3 1 Market Way
2 Lodge Ct
3 Central Sq
4 Manor Ct
5 Rupert Ave

67
A5 1 Curie Ho
2 Darwin Ho
6 Priestley Ho
7 Rutherford Ho
8 Fleming Ho
9 Lister Ho
10 Edison Ho
B1 1 Kingthorpe Terr
2 Scott Ho
3 Peary Ho
4 Shackleton Ho
5 Amundsen Ho
6 Brentfield Ho
7 Nansen Ho
8 Stonebridge Ct
9 Magellan Ct
10 Leadbetter Ct
11 Viant Ho
12 Jefferies Ho
13 Diamond St
C1 1 Beveridge Rd
C5 1 Hazelwood Ct
2 Winslow Cl

68
A2 1 Regency Mews
2 Tudor Mews
A5 1 Bourne Ho
2 Carton Ho
4 Woodbridge Cl
5 Mackenzie Ho
6 Banting Ho

69
A1 1 Fountain Ho
2 Kingston Ho
3 Waverley Ct
4 Weston Ho
5 Mapes Ho
6 Athelstan Gdns
7 Leff Ho
B1 1 Alma Birk Ho
2 Brooklands Ct
3 Brooklands Court Apartments
4 Cleveland Mans
5 Buckley Ct
6 Webheath
B5 1 Mortimer Cl
2 Sunnyside Ho
3 Sunnyside
4 Prospect Pl
C1 1 Linstead St
2 Embassy Ct
3 Acol Ct
4 Kings Wood Ct
5 Douglas Ct
6 King's Gdns
7 Carlton Mans
8 Smyrna Mans
9 New Priory Ct
10 Queensgate Pl
11 Brondesbury Mews
C2 1 Dene Mans
2 Sandwell Cres
3 Sandwell Mans

4 Hampstead West
5 Redcroft
C3 1 Orestes Mews
2 Walter Northcott Ho
3 Polperro Mans
4 Lyncroft Mans
5 Marlborough Mans
6 Alexandra Mans
7 Cumberland Mans
8 Cavendish Mans
9 Ambassador Ct
10 Welbeck Mans
11 Inglewood Mans
C5 1 Portman Hts
2 Hermitage Ct
3 Moreland Ct
4 Wendover Ct
D2 1 Beswick Mews
2 Worcester Mews
3 Minton Mews
4 Doulton Mews
5 Laurel Ho
6 Sandalwood Ho
7 Iroko Ho
8 Banyan Ho
9 Ebony Ho
11 Rosemont Mans

70
A1 1 Harrold Ho
2 Glover Ho
3 Byron Ct
4 Nalton Ho
A2 1 Petros Gdns
2 Heath Ct
3 Imperial Twrs
4 Fairhurst
5 St John's Ct
6 New College Ct
7 Chalford
8 Sutherland Ho
A4 1 Windmill Hill
2 Highgrove Point
3 Gainsborough Ho
4 Heath Mans
5 Pavilion Ct
6 Holly Berry La
7 New Campden Ct
8 Benham's Pl
9 Holly Bush Vale
10 Gardnor Mans
11 Mansfield Pl
12 Streatley Pl
13 New Ct
14 Bird In Hand Yd
15 Spencer Wlk
16 Wells Ct
17 Perrin's Ct
18 Village Mount
19 Prince Arthur Ct
20 Prince Arthur Mews
21 Monro Ho
22 Ellerdale Cl
23 Holly Bush Hill
24 Prospect Pl
A5 2 Stamford Cl
B1 1 New College Par
2 Northways Par
3 Noel Ho
4 Campden Ho
5 Centre Hts
6 Hickes Ho
7 Swiss Terr
8 Leitch Ho
9 Jevons Ho
10 Langhorne Ct
11 Park Lo
12 Avenue Lo
B2 1 Belsize Park Mews
2 Baynes Mews
3 McCrone Mews
B3 1 Belsize Court Garages
2 Roscommon Ho
3 Akenside Ct
C2 1 Banff Ho
2 Glenloch Ct
3 Havercourt
4 Holmfield Ct

412 **70 C2**

5 Gilling Ct
6 Howitt Cl
7 Manor Mans
8 Straffan Lo
9 Romney Ct
10 Lancaster Stables
11 Eton Garages
D1 1 Hancock Nunn Ho
2 Higginson Ho
3 Duncan Ho
4 Mary Wharrie Ho
5 Rockstraw Ho
6 Cleaver Ho
7 Chamberlain St
8 Sharples Hall St
9 Primrose Mews
10 Rothwell St
11 St Georges Mews
D2 1 Alder Ho
2 Hornbeam Ho
3 Whitebeam Ho
4 Aspen Ho
5 Rowan Ho
6 Beech Ho
7 Chestnut Ho
8 Oak Ho
9 Willow Ho
10 Sycamore Ho
11 Maple Ho
12 Hazel Ho
13 Elaine Ct
14 Faircourt
15 Walham Ct
16 Stanbury Ct
17 Priory Mans
18 Wellington Ho
19 Grange The
D3 1 Cayford Ho
2 Du Maurier Ho
3 Isokon Flats
4 Palgrave Ho
5 Garnett Ho
6 Stephenson Ho
7 Park Dwellings
8 Siddons Ho
9 Mall Studios
10 Park Hill Wlk
11 Wordsworth Pl
12 Fraser Regnart Ct
13 St Pancras Almshouses

71

A1 1 Bridge Ho
2 Hardington
3 Mead Cl
4 Rugmere
5 Tottenhall
6 Beauvale
7 Broomfield
A2 1 Silverbirch Wlk
2 Penshurst
3 Wingham
4 Westwell
5 Chislet
6 Burmarsh
7 Shipton Ho
8 Stone Gate
9 Leysdown
10 Headcorn
11 Lenham
12 Halstow
13 Fordcombe
14 Cannington
15 Langridge
16 Athlone Ho
17 Pentland Ho
18 Beckington
19 Hawkridge
20 Edington
B1 1 Ferdinand Ho
2 Harmood Ho
3 Hawley Rd
4 Hawley Mews
5 Leybourne St
6 Barling
7 Tiptree
8 Havering
9 Candida Ct
10 Lorraine Ct
11 Donnington Ct

12 Welford Ct
13 Torbay Ct
14 Bradfield Ct
15 Torbay St
16 Leybourne Rd
17 Haven St
18 Stucley Pl
B2 1 Ashington
2 Priestley Ho
3 Leonard Day Ho
4 Old Dairy Mews
5 Monmouth Ho
6 Alpha Ct
7 Una Ho
8 Widford
9 Hey Bridge
10 Roxwell
B4 1 Denyer Ho
2 Stephenson Ho
3 Trevithick Ho
4 Brunel Ho
5 Newcomen Ho
6 Faraday Ho
7 Winifrede Paul Ho
8 Wardlow
9 Fletcher Ct
10 Tideswell
11 Grangemill
12 Hambrook Ct
13 Calver
C1 1 Durdans Ho
2 Philia Ho
3 Bernard Shaw Ct
4 Foster Ct
5 Bessemer Ct
6 Hogarth Ct
7 Rochester Ct
8 Soane Ct
9 Wallett Ct
10 Inwood Ct
11 Wrotham Rd
12 Caulfield Ct
13 Bruges Pl
14 Reachview Cl
15 Lawfords Wharf
C3 1 Eleanor Ho
2 Falkland Pl
3 Kensington Ho
4 Willingham Cl
5 Kenbrook Ho
6 Aborfield
7 Great Field
8 Appleford
9 Forties The
C4 1 Benson Ct
2 Tait Ho
3 Manorfield Cl
4 Greatfield Cl
5 Longley Ho
6 Lampson Ho
7 Davidson Ho
8 Palmer Ho
9 Lambourn Cl
10 Morris Ho
11 Owen Ho
C5 1 Hunter Ho
2 Fisher Ho
3 Lang Ho
4 Temple Ho
5 Palmer Ho
C6 1 Flowers Mews
2 Sandridge St
3 Bovingdon Cl
4 Laurel Cl
5 Forest Way
6 Larch Cl
7 Pine Cl
8 Alder Mews
9 Aspen Cl
D1 1 Hillier Ho
2 Gairloch Ho
3 Cobham Mews
4 Bergholt Mews
5 Blakeney Cl
6 Weavers Way
7 Allensbury Pl
D2 1 Rowstock
2 Carters Cl
3 York Ho
4 Hungerford Rd
5 Cliff Ct
6 Camelot Ho
D3 1 Blake Ho
2 Quelch Ho
3 Lee Ho
4 Willbury Ho
5 Howell Ho
6 Holmsbury Ho
7 Leith Ho

8 Betchworth Ho
9 Rushmore Ho
10 Dugdale Ho
11 Horsendon Ho
12 Colley Ho
13 Coombe Ho
14 Ivinghoe Ho
15 Buckhurst Ho
16 Saxonbury Ct
17 Charlton Ct
18 Apollo Studios
19 Barn Cl
20 Long Meadow
21 Landleys Field
22 Margaret Bondfield Ho
23 Haywood Lo
D4 1 Fairlie Ct
2 London Metropolitan Univ (Carleton Grange Hall)
3 Trecastle Way
4 Hilldrop Est
5 Hyndman Ho
6 Carpenter Ho
7 Graham Ho
D5 1 Melchester Ho
2 Norcombe Ho
3 Weatherbury Ho
4 Wessex Ho
5 Archway Bsns Ctr
D6 1 Bowerman Ct
2 Hargrave Mans
3 Church Garth
4 John King Ct

72

A3 1 Kimble Ho
2 Saxonbury Ct
3 Poynder Ct
4 Pangbourne Ho
5 Moulsford Ho
A4 1 Arcade The
2 Macready Pl
A5 1 Northview
2 Tufnell Park Mans
A6 1 Christie Ct
2 Ringmer Gdns
3 Kingsdown Rd
4 Cottenham Ho
5 St Paul's Ct
6 Rickthorne Rd
7 Stanley Terr
B1 1 Kerwick Cl
2 Rydston Cl
3 Skegness Ho
4 Frederica St
5 Ponder St
6 Kings Ct
7 Freeling St
B4 1 Buckmaster Ho
2 Loreburn Ho
3 Cairns Ho
4 Halsbury Ho
5 Chelmsford Ho
6 Cranworth Ho
B6 1 Berkeley Wlk
2 Lazar Wlk
3 Thistlewood Cl
4 Tomlins Wlk
5 Andover Ho
6 Barmouth Ho
7 Chard Ho
8 Methley Ho
9 Rainford Ho
10 Woodbridge Cl
11 Allerton Wlk
12 Falconer Wlk
13 Sonderburg Rd
C1 1 Mountfort Terr
2 Davey Lo
3 Carfree Cl
4 New College Mews
C3 1 Slaney Pl
2 Wells Yd
3 Milton Pl
4 Hartnoll Pl
5 St James School Flats
6 Widnes Ho
7 Tranmere Ho
8 Victoria Mans
9 Formby Ct
10 Mersey Ho
11 Birkenhead Ho

C6 1 Brookfield
2 Churnfield
D1 1 Islington Park Mews
2 Evelyn Denington Ct
3 Bassingbourn Ho
4 Cadmore Ho
5 Adstock Ho
6 Garston Ho
7 Flitton Ho
8 Datchworth Ho
9 Battishill St
10 Almeida St
11 Edward's Cotts
12 Hyde's Pl
13 Tyndale Terr
14 Spriggs Ho
15 Barratt Ho
16 Spencer Pl
17 Chadston Ho
18 Whiston Ho
19 Wakelin Ho
20 Tressel Cl
21 Canonbury Ct
22 Shillingford St
23 Halton Ho
D4 1 Chestnuts The
2 Bowen Ct
3 Peckett Sq

73

A1 1 Haslam Ho
2 Horsfield Ho
3 Astey's Row
4 Melville Pl
5 Wontner Cl
6 Hedingham Cl
7 Eric Fletcher Ct
8 Ashby Ho
9 Annette Cres
10 Bentham Ct
11 New Bentham Ct
12 Cardigan Wlk
13 Lindsey Mews
14 Walkinshaw Ct
15 Laundry La
A2 1 Crowline Wlk
2 Bardsey Wlk
3 Handa Wlk
4 Lismore Wlk
5 Sark Ho
6 Clephane Rd
7 Sybil Thorndike Ho
8 Guernsey Rd
9 Guernsey Ho
10 Herm Ho
11 Florence Nightingale Ho
12 Jersey Ho
13 Jethou Ho
14 Upper Caldy Wlk
15 Caldy Wlk
16 Alderney Ho
17 Marquess Rd S
18 Oronsay Rd
19 Upper Gulland Wlk
20 Gulland Wlk
21 Church Rd
A3 1 Pearfield Ho
2 Larchfield Ho
3 Beresford Terr
4 Pondfield Ho
5 Ashfield Ho
6 Elmfield Ho
A4 1 Fountain Mews
2 Woodstock Ho
3 Henson Ct
4 Taverner Sq
B2 1 John Kennedy Ct
2 John Kennedy Lo
3 Ball's Pond Pl
4 Haliday Wlk
5 Rona Wlk
6 Threadgold Ho
7 Wakeham St
8 Saffron Ct
9 Callaby Terr
10 Tilney Gdns
11 Westcliff Ho
12 Ilford Ho
13 Ongar Ho
14 Greenhills Terr
15 Romford Ho
B4 1 Ledo Ho

2 Salween Ho
3 Prome Ho
4 Arakan Ho
5 Rangoon Ho
6 Mandalay Ho
7 Karen Ho
8 Wingate Ho
9 Jubet Ho
10 Orde Ho
11 Chindit Ho
12 Mabel Thornton Ho
13 Crawshay Ho
14 Avon Ho
15 Connaught Mans
16 Jonson Ho
17 Herrick Ho
18 Donne Ho
19 Grasmere Ho
20 Thirlmere Ho
B6 1 Chestnut Cl
2 Sycamore Ho
3 Lordship Ho
4 Clissold Ho
5 Beech Ho
6 Laburnum Ho
7 Ormond Ho
C1 1 Dorchester Ct
2 Wareham Ho
3 Dorset Ct
4 Stratton Ct
5 Swanage Ct
6 Blandford Ct
7 Portland Ct
8 Oscar Faber Pl
9 Lancaster Cl
C2 1 Kingsland Gn
2 Kingsland Pas
3 Metropolitan Benefit Societies Almshs
4 Nimrod Pas
5 De Beauvoir Pl
6 Warburton Cl
7 Buckingham Mews
C3 1 Hewling Ho
2 Matthias Ho
3 Port Royal Pl
4 Cressington Cl
5 King Henry's Yd
6 Bronte Ho
7 Sewell Ho
8 Lydgate Ho
9 Patmore Ho
10 Congreve Ho
11 Elton St
12 Conrad Ho
13 Southwell Ho
14 Neptune Ho
15 Campion Ho
16 Webster Ho
17 Meredith Ho
18 Beckford Ho
19 Ashley Ct
20 Hayling Cl
21 Millard Cl
22 Lydford Cl
23 Salcombe Rd
24 Truman's Rd
25 Templeton Cl
26 John Campbell Rd
27 Gillett Pl
28 Bradbury St
C4 1 Londesborough Ho
2 Knebworth Ho
3 Knebworth Rd
4 Bransby Ct
5 Imperial Ave
6 Leonard Pl
7 Shakspeare Mews
8 Binyon Ho
9 Shelley Ho
10 Browning Ho
11 Burns Ho
12 Andrew Marvell Ho
13 Wycliffe Ho
14 Blake Ho
15 Marlowe Ho
16 Fletcher Ho
17 Chaucer Ct
C5 1 Gujarat Ho
2 Marton Rd
3 Painsthorpe Rd
4 Selkirk Ho
5 Defoe Ho

6 Edward Friend Ho
7 Sheridan Ho
8 Barrie Ho
9 Arnold Ho
10 Macaulay Ho
11 Stowe Ho
12 Carlyle Ho
13 Shaftesbury Ho
14 Lillian Cl
15 Swift Ho
16 Dryden Ho
17 Scott Ct
18 Kingsfield Ho
19 Uhura Sq
D1 1 Hilborough Rd
2 Shoreditch Ct
3 Evergreen Sq
D2 1 Prospect Ho
2 Woodland St
3 Crosby Wlk
4 Kirkland Wlk
5 Bowness Cl
6 Carlisle Wlk
7 Skelton Cl
8 Camerton Cl
9 Buttermere Wlk
10 Houghton Cl
11 Hayton Cl
D3 1 Miller's Terr
2 Chow Sq
3 Drysdale Flats
4 Gateway Mews
5 Birkbeck Mews
6 Winchester Pl
D4 1 Coronation Ave
2 Morris Blitz Ct
3 Shacklewell Ho
4 Alexandra Ct
D5 1 Lawrence's Bldgs
2 Cottage Wlk
3 Batley Pl
D6 1 Garnham St
2 Garnham St
3 Sanford La
4 Sandford Wlk
5 Abney Gdns
6 Fleet Wood

74

A1 1 Aldington Ct
2 Bayton Ct
3 Rochford Wlk
A3 1 Kingsdown Ho
2 Glendown Ho
3 Moredown Ho
4 Blakeney Cl
5 Beeston Cl
6 Benabo Ct
7 David Devine Ho
8 Kreedman Wlk
9 Hermitage Row
10 Grafton Ct
11 Lushington Terr
A5 1 Ravenscourt
2 Mellington Ct
3 Rendlesham Ho
4 Florence Ct
5 Burnaston Ho
A6 1 Cazenove Mans
2 Chedworth Ho
3 Aldergrove Ho
4 Abbotstone Ho
5 Briggeford Cl
6 Inglethorpe Ho
7 Ashdown Ho
B1 1 Fortescue Ave
2 Pemberton Pl
3 Weston Wlk
4 Bayford St Ind Ctr
5 Bayford St
6 Sidworth St
7 Helmsley St
B2 1 Bohemia Pl
2 Graham Mans
3 Marvin St
4 Boscobel Ho
5 Royal Oak Rd
6 Colonnades The
7 Sylvester Ho
8 Sylvester Path
9 Doctor Spurstowe Almshos
10 Great Eastern Bldgs

11 Sojourner-Truth Cl
B3 1 Birchington Ho
2 Bicknor Ho
3 Boxley Ho
4 Adisham Ho
5 Cranbrook Ho
6 Marden Ho
7 Broome Ho
8 Crandale Ho
9 Cheriton Ho
10 Ditton Ho
11 Langley Ho
12 Dymchurch Ho
13 Elham Ho
14 Bodney Mans
15 Pembury Ho
16 Downs Ct
17 Perrywood Ho
18 Stapelhurst Ho
19 Pegwell Ho
20 Yalding Ho
21 Northbourne Ho
22 Monkton Ho
23 Milsted Ho
24 Athlone Cl
25 Clarence Pl
26 Gould Terr
27 Quested Ct
28 Brett Pas
29 Marcon Ct
B4 1 Sutherland Point
2 Embley Point
3 Downs La
4 Gaviller Pl
5 Robert Owen Lo
6 Apprentice Way
7 Arrowe Ct
8 Gilwell Ct
9 Sutton Ct
10 Kinnoull Mans
11 Rowhill Mans
12 Sladen Pl
13 Mothers Sq The
14 Richborough Ho
15 Sandgate Ho
16 Sheppey Ho
B6 1 Wentwood Ho
2 Woolmer Ho
3 Warwick Ho
4 Winslade Ho
5 Moriss Ho
6 Woodfield Ho
7 Rossendale Ho
8 Ettrick Ho
9 Charnwood Ho
10 Boyne Ho
11 Whitwell Ho
12 Scardale Ho
13 Hendale Ho
14 Brampton Cl
15 Aveley Ct
16 Aldeburgh Cl
17 Dennington Cl
C1 1 Pitcairn Ho
2 Lyme Grove Ho
3 Shakespeare Ho
4 Upcott Ho
5 Loddiges Ho
6 Parkinson Ho
7 Sloane Ho
8 Vanbrugh Ho
9 Cambridge Pas
10 Lyttleton Ho
11 Victoria Park Ct
12 Tullis Ho
13 Fairchild Ho
14 Forsyth Ho
15 Tradescant Ho
16 Mason Ho
17 Capel Ho
18 Cordwainers Ct
19 Bridgeman Ho
20 St Thomas's Pl
21 Barclay Ho
22 Clayton Ho
23 Danby Ho
24 Sherard Ho
25 Catesby Ho
26 Petiver Cl
27 Leander Ct
28 Philip Turner Est
29 Grendon Ho
30 Shore Mews
31 Shore Bsns Ctr
32 Kendal Ho
33 Classic Mans
34 Tudor Ho
35 Park Ho
36 Alpine Gr

37 Clarendon Cl

C2 1 Woolpack Ho
2 Elvin Ho
3 Thomas Ho
4 Hockley Ho
5 Retreat Ho
6 Butfield Ho
7 Brooksbank Ho
8 Cresset Ho
9 Brooksbank St
10 Lennox Ho
11 Milborne Ho
12 Collent Ho
13 Middlesex Pl
14 Devonshire Hall
15 Brent Ho
C6 1 Haybridge Ho
2 Framlingham Cl
3 Halesworth Cl
4 Harleston Cl
5 Lowestoft Cl
6 Cecil Ho
7 Clapton Ho
8 Howard Ho
9 Templar Ho
10 Warwick Ho
11 Audley Ho
D1 1 Stuart Ho
2 Gascoyne Ho
3 Chelsfield Point
4 Sundridge Ho
5 Banbury Ho
D2 1 Musgrove Ho
2 Cheyney Ho
3 Haynes Ho
4 Warner Ho
5 Gilby Ho
6 Gadsden Ho
7 Risley Ho
8 Baycliffe Ho
9 Sheldon Ho
10 Offley Ho
11 Latimer Ho
12 Ribstone Ho
13 Salem Ho
14 Fieldwick Ho
15 Lever Ct
16 Matson Ho
17 Wilding Ho
18 Rennell Ho
19 Dycer Ho
20 Granard Ho
21 Whitelock Ho
22 Harrowgate Ho
23 Cass Ho
24 Lofts on the Park
D4 1 Cromford Path
2 Longford Ct
3 Overbury Ho
4 Heanor Ct
5 Wharfedale Ct
6 Ladybower Ct
7 Ilkeston Ct
8 Derby Ct
9 Rushmore Cres
10 Blackwell Cl

75
A2 1 Wick Mews
2 Wellday Ho
3 Selman Ho
4 Vaine Ho
5 Trower Ho
B2 3 Merriam Ave
D6 1 Hammond Ct
2 Sorenson Ct
3 Hinton Ct

76
B4 1 Mulberry Ct
2 Rosewood Ct
3 Gean Ct
4 Blackthorn Ct
5 Cypress Ct
C1 1 Stratford Office Village The
2 Mandrake Way
3 Brimstone Ho
C5 1 Acacia Bsns Ctr
2 Brook Ct
3 Doreen Capstan Ho
5 Peppermint Pl
6 Denmark St
7 Mills Ct
8 Paramount Ho
C6 1 Nansen Ct

2 Mallinson Ct
4 Barbara Ward Ct
4 Noel Baker Ct
5 Corigan Ct
6 Norman Ho
7 Willow Ct
8 Lime Ct

77
A4 1 Bronte Cl
2 Anna Neagle Cl
3 Brownlow Rd
4 Carrington Gdns
5 Vera Lynn Cl

78
C3 1 Stewart Rainbird Ho
2 Rede Ho
3 George Comberton Wlk
C4 1 Annie Taylor Ho
2 Richard Fell Ho
3 Susan Lawrence Ho
4 Walter Hurford Par
5 John Cornwell VC Ho
6 Alfred Prior Ho
7 Cardamom Ct
C5 1 Charlbury Ho
2 Willis Ho
3 Arthur Walls Ho
4 Blakesley Ho
5 Twelve Acre Ho
6 Beech Ct
7 Golding Ct
D1 1 Aveley Mans
2 Harlow Mans
3 Danbury Mans
4 Mayland Mans
5 Bowers Ho
6 Webber Ho
7 Paulson Ho
8 Collins Ho
9 Jack Cook Ho
D3 1 St Luke's Path
2 Springfield Ct
D5 1 Postway Mews
2 Oakfield Ct
3 Janice Mews
4 Kenneth Moor Rd
5 Clements Ct
6 Handforth Rd
7 Churchill Ct
8 Oakfield Lo
9 Langdale Ho
D6 1 York Ho
2 Opal Mews
3 Florentine Ho
4 Hainault Bridge Par

79
D1 1 Gibbards Cott
2 Edgefield Ct
3 Manor Ct
4 Lambourne Gdns
5 Westone Mans
6 Loveland Mans
7 Edward Mans
8 Clarke Mans
9 Dawson Gdns
10 Sebastian Ct

80
A1 1 Bristol Ho
2 Canterbury Ho
3 Durham Ho
4 Wells Ho
5 Winchester Ho
6 Rosalind Ct
7 Exeter Ho
8 Wheatley Mans
9 Greenwood Mans
10 Plymouth Ho
11 Graham Mans
12 Portia Ct

81
C5 1 Markham Ho
2 Webb Ho

3 Preston Ho
4 Steadman Ho
5 Hyndman Ho
6 Clynes Ho
7 Henderson Ho
8 Blatchford Ho
9 Rogers Ho
10 Sylvia Pankhurst Ho
11 Mary Macarthur Ho
12 Ellen Wilkinson Ho
D2 1 Picador Ho
2 Centurion Ho
3 Louis Ct
4 Watsons Lo
5 Carpenters Ct
6 Bell Ho
7 Rounders Ct
8 Oldmead Ho
9 Jervis Ct
10 Bartletts Ho
11 Royal Par
12 Richardson Gdns

82
D3 1 Marlborough Par
2 Blenheim Par
3 Lea Ct
4 Westbourne Par
5 Whiteleys Par
6 Hillingdon Par
7 New Broadway

84
C4 1 Dilston Cl
2 Wells Cl
3 Willet Cl
4 Merlin Cl
5 Glyndebourne Ct
6 Albury Ct
7 Osterley Ct
8 Hatfield Ct
9 Gayhurst Ct
D4 1 Caravelle Gdns
2 Forman Gr
3 Viscount Gr
4 Tomahawk Gdns
5 Martlet Gr
6 Trident Gdns
7 Latham Ct
8 Jupiter Ct
9 Westland Ct
10 Seasprite Cl
11 Convair Wlk
12 Mayfly Gdns
13 Valiant Cl
14 Woburn Twr
15 Brett Cl
16 Friars Cl
D5 1 Medlar Cl
2 Cranberry Cl
3 Lely Ho
4 Kneller Ho
5 Girtin Ho
6 Cotman Ho
7 Raeburn Ho
8 Gainsborough Twr
9 Stanfield Ho
10 Millais Ct
11 Hunt Ct
12 Poynter Ct
13 Hogarth Ho
14 Constable Ho
15 Bonnington Ct
16 Romney Ct
17 Landseer Ho

85
D1 1 Thurlestone Ct
2 Disley Ct
3 Burgess Ct
4 Seldson Ct
5 Lytham Ct
6 Abbeydale Ct
7 Cromer Ct
8 Brunel Pl
9 Winford Par
10 Rutherford Twr

86
A1 1 Farnham Ct
2 Gleneagles Twr

3 Birkdale Ct
4 Verulam Ho
5 Hartsbourne Ct
6 Ferndown Ct
7 Deal Ct
8 St David's Ct
9 Portrush Ct
10 Alnmouth Ct
11 Panmure Ct
12 Peterhead Ct
13 Sunningdale Ct
D2 1 Denbigh Ct
2 Devon Ct
3 Dorset Ct
4 Glamorgan Ct
5 Gloucester Ct
6 Hereford Ct
7 Merioneth Ct
8 Oxford Ct
9 Monmouth Ct
10 Paddington Ct
11 Pembroke Ct
12 Chadwick Cl
13 Cotts Cl
D3 1 Berkshire Ct
2 Buckingham Ct
3 Cardigan Ct
4 Carmarthen Ct
5 Cornwall Ct
6 Merlin Ct
7 Osprey Ct
8 Pelham Pl
D5 1 Medway Par
2 Brabstone Ho
3 Cotswold Ct

87
B3 1 Woodbury Ct
2 Edward Ct
3 Park Lo
C1 1 Hurley Ct
2 Amherst Gdns
3 Tudor Ct
4 Hilton Ho
C2 1 Hutton Ct
2 Cain Ct
3 Langdale Ct
4 William Ct
5 Castlebar Ct
6 Warren Ct
7 White Lo
8 Queen's Ct
9 King's Ct
10 Cheriton Cl
11 Stanley Ct
12 Juniper Ct
C3 1 Holtoake Ct
2 Pitshanger Ct
3 Holtoake Ho

88
A4 1 Nelson Ho
2 Gordon Ho
3 Frobisher Ho
4 Wellington Ho
5 Fairfax Ho
A5 1 Carlyon Mans
2 Ainslie Ct
3 Millers Ct
4 Priory Ct
5 Tylers Ct
6 Twyford Ct
7 Rose Ct
8 Laurel Ct
9 Sundew Ct
10 Campion Ct
11 Foxglove Ct
C1 1 Buckingham Ho
2 Chester Ct
3 Devon Ct
4 Essex Ho
5 Fife Ct
6 Gloucester Ct
7 Hereford Ho
8 Inverness Ct
9 Warwick Ho
10 York Ho
11 Suffolk Ho
12 Perth Ho
13 Norfolk Ho
14 Thanet Ct
15 Rutland Ct
16 Oxford Ct

89
A1 1 Avon Ct
2 Bromley Lo

3 Walter Ct
4 Lynton Terr
5 Acton Ho
6 Fells Haugh
7 Springfield Ct
8 Tamarind Ct
9 Lynton Ct
B1 1 Rosebank Gdns
2 Rosebank
3 Edinburgh Ho
4 Western Ho
5 Kilronan
B6 1 Fitzsimmons Ct
2 Bernard Shaw Ho
3 Longlents Ho
4 Mordaunt Ho
5 Wilmers Ct
6 Stonebridge Sh Ctr
D5 1 New Crescent Yd
2 Harlesden Plaza
3 St Josephs Ct

90
D1 1 Kelfield Ct
2 Downing Ho
3 Crosfield Ct
4 Robinson Ho
5 Scampston Mews
6 Girton Villas
7 Ray Ho
8 Walmer Ho
9 Goodrich Ho
10 Arthur Ct
11 Whitstable Ho
12 Kingsnorth Ho
13 Bridge Cl
14 Prospect Ho
15 Whitchurch Ho
16 Blechynden Ho
17 Waynflete Sq
18 Bramley Ho
D4 1 Westfield Ct
2 Tropical Ct
3 Chamberlayne Mans
4 Quadrant The
5 Queens Park Ct
6 Warfield Yd
7 Cherrytree Ho

91
A1 1 Malton Mews
2 Lancaster Lo
3 Manning Ho
4 Galsworthy Ho
5 Hudson Ho
6 Cambourne Mews
7 Camelford Ct
8 Camelford Wlk
9 Talbot Grove Ho
10 Clarendon Wlk
11 Kingsdown Cl
12 Lower Clarendon Wlk
13 Upper Clarendon Wlk
A2 1 Murchison Ho
2 Macaulay Ho
3 Chesterton Ho
4 Chiltern Ho
5 Lionel Ho
6 Watts Ho
7 Wheatstone Ho
8 Telford Ho
9 Golborne Mews
10 Millwood St
11 St Columb's Ho
12 Norfolk Mews
A3 1 Sycamore Wlk
2 Westgate Bsns Ctr
3 Buspace Studios
4 Bosworth Ho
5 Golborne Gdns
6 Appleford Ho
7 Adair Twr
8 Gadsden Ho
9 Southam Ho
10 Norman Butler Ho
11 Thompson Ho
12 Wells Ho
13 Paul Ho
14 Olive Blythe Ho

15 Katherine Ho
16 Breakwell Ct
17 Pepler Ho
18 Edward Kennedy Ho
19 Winnington Ho
A4 1 Slomon Ho
2 Stansbury Ho
3 Tilleard Ho
4 Selby Ho
5 Mundy Ho
6 Macfarren Ho
7 Mounsey Ho
8 Courtville Ho
9 Croft Ho
10 Batten Ho
11 Bantock Ho
12 Banister Ho
13 Symphony Mews
14 Bliss Mews
A5 1 Lancefield Ct
2 Verdi Ho
3 Wornum Ho
B1 1 Tavistock Mews
2 Silvester Ho
3 Melchester
4 Clydesdale Ho
5 Pinehurst Ct
6 Colville Sq Mews
7 Denbigh Ho
8 Golden Cross Mews
B2 1 Blagrove Rd
2 Tavistock Ho
3 Leamington Ho
B3 1 Western Ho
2 Russell's Wharf
B4 1 Boyce Ho
2 Farnaby Ho
3 Danby Ho
4 Purday Ho
5 Naylor Ho
6 St Judes Ho
7 Leeve Ho
8 Longhurst Ho
9 Harrington Ct
10 Mulberry Ct
11 Quilter Ho
12 Romer Ho
13 Kilburn Ho
B5 1 Claremont Ct
2 William Saville Ho
3 Western Ct
4 Bond Ho
5 Crone Ct
6 Wood Ho
7 Winterleys
8 Carlton Ho
9 Fiona Ct
C1 1 Shottsford
2 Tolchurch
3 Casterbridge
4 Sandbourne
5 Anglebury
6 Weatherbury
7 Westbourne Gr Mews
8 Rosehart Mews
9 Viscount Ct
10 Hereford Mans
11 Hereford Mews
C2 1 Ascot Ho
2 Ashgrove Ct
3 Lockbridge Ct
4 Swallow Ct
5 Nightingale Lo
6 Hammond Lo
7 Penfield Lo
8 Harvey Lo
9 Hunter Lo
10 Barnard Lo
11 Falcon Lo
12 Johnson Lo
13 Livingstone Lo
14 Nuffield Lo
15 Finch Lo
16 Polesworth Ho
17 Oversley Ho
18 Derrycombe Ho
19 Buckshead Ho
20 Combe Ho
21 Culham Ho
22 Dainton Ho
23 Devonport Ho
24 Hanwell Ho
25 Truro Ho
26 Sunderland Ho
27 Stonehouse Ho

28 Riverford Ho
29 Portishead Ho
30 Mickleton Ho
31 Keyham Ho
32 Moulsford Ho
33 Shrewsbury Mews
34 St Stephen's Mews
35 Westway Lo
36 Langley Ho
37 Brindley Ho
38 Radway Ho
39 Astley Ho
40 Willow Ct
41 Larch Ct
42 Elm Ct
43 Beech Ct
44 Worcester Ct
45 Union Ct
46 Leicester Ct
47 Kennet Ct
48 Oxford Ct
49 Fazerley Ct
C3 1 Westside Ct
2 Sutherland Ct
3 Fleming Cl
4 Hermes Cl
C4 1 Masefield Ho
2 Austen Ho
3 Fielding Ho
4 Park Bsns Ctr
5 John Ratcliffe Ho
6 Wymering Mans
7 Pavilion Ct
8 Nelson Cl
C5 1 Wells Ct
2 Cambridge Ct
3 Durham Ct
C6 1 Ryde Ho
2 Glengall Pass
3 Leith Yd
4 Daynor Ho
5 Varley Ho
6 Sandby Ho
7 Colas Mews
8 Bishopsdale Ho
9 Lorton Ho
10 Marshwood Ho
11 Ribblesdale Ho
12 Holmesdale Ho
13 Kilburn Vale Est
14 Kilburn Bridge
D1 1 Vera Ct
2 Alexander Mews
3 Gurney Ho
4 Burdett Mews
5 Greville Lo
6 Hatherley Ct
7 Bridge Field Ho
8 Ralph Ct
9 Peters Ct
10 Riven Ct
11 Cervantes Ct
12 Bishops Ct
13 Newbury Ho
14 Marlow Ho
15 Lynton Ho
16 Pembroke Ho
17 Pickering Ho
D3 1 Ellwood Ct
D5 1 Tollgate Ho
2 Regents Plaza
3 Royal Langford
D6 1 Farndale Ho
2 Birchington Ct
3 Greville Mews
4 Goldsmith's Pl
5 Remsted Ho
6 Bradwell Ho
7 Cheshunt Ho
8 Haliwell Ho
9 Braddock Ho
10 Philip Ho
11 Hillsborough Ct
12 Sandbourne
13 Wingreen
14 Toneborough
15 Silverthorn
16 Kington Ho
17 Marrick Ho
18 Broadoak Ho
18 Boadoak Ho

95

C4
1 Pimlico Wlk
2 Aske Ho
3 Hathaway Ho
4 Haberdasher Pl
5 Fairchild Ho
6 Burtt Ho
7 Enfield Cloisters
8 McGregor Ct
9 Royal Oak Ct
10 Hoxton Mkt
11 Bath Pl
12 Chapel Ct
13 Chapel Pl
14 Standard Pl
15 Cleeve Ho
16 Printing House Yd
17 Printing House Yd
18 Perseverance Works
19 Crooked Billet Yd
20 Drysdale Ho
21 Castlefrank Ho
22 School App
23 Basing House Yd
24 Mail Coach Yd

C5
1 Bracer Ho
2 Scorton Ho
3 Fern Cl
4 Macbeth Ho
5 Oberon Ho
6 Buckland Ct
7 Crondall Ct
8 Osric Path
9 Caliban Twr
10 Celia Ho
11 Juliet Ho
12 Bacchus Wlk
13 Malcolm Ho
14 Homefield St
15 Crondall Pl
16 Blanca Ho
17 Miranda Ho
18 Falstaff Ho
19 Charmian Ho
20 Myrtle Wlk
21 Arden Ho
22 Sebastian Ho
23 Stanway Ct
24 Jerrold St
25 Rosalind Ho
26 Cordelia Ho
27 Monteagle Ct
28 John Parry Ct
29 James Anderson Ct
30 Ben Jonson Ct
31 Sara Lane Ct
32 Walbrook Ct

C6
1 Portelet Ct
2 Trinity Ct
3 Rozel Ct
4 St Helier Ct
5 Corbiere Ho
6 Kenning Ho
7 Higgins Ho
8 Cavell Ho
9 Girling Ho
10 Fulcher Ho
11 Francis Ho
12 Norris Ho
13 Kempton Ho
14 Nesham Ho
15 Crossbow Ho
16 Catherine Ho
17 Strale Ho
18 Horner Hos
19 Stringer Hos
20 Whitmore Ho
21 Nightingale Ho
22 Fletcher Ho
23 Arrow Ho
24 Archer Ho
25 Meriden Ho
26 Rover Ho
27 Bowyer Ho
28 Longbow Ho
29 Tiller Ho
30 Canalside Studios
31 Bishopgate
32 Holburn
33 Fenchurch

D4
1 Gorsuch Pl
2 Strout's Pl
3 Vaughan Est
4 George Loveless Ho
5 Baroness Rd
6 James Brine Ho
7 Arthur Wade Ho
8 Robert Owen Ho
9 Sivill Ho
10 Georgina Gdns
11 Old Market Sq
12 Cuff Point
13 Bakers Rents
14 Leopold Bldgs
15 Dunmore Point
16 Wingfield Ho
17 Gascoigne Pl
18 Mandela Ho
19 Virginia Rd
20 Briggs Ho
21 Packenham Ho
22 Gowan Ho
24 Chambord Ho
25 Ducal St
26 Strickland Ho
27 Alliston Ho
28 Gibraltar Wlk
29 Equity Sq
30 Shacklewell St
31 Rochelle St
32 Sonning Ho
33 Culham Ho
34 Hurley Ho
35 Palissy St
36 Taplow Ho
37 Chertsey Ho
38 Sunbury Ho
39 Sunbury Workshops
40 Datchett Ho
41 Hocker St
42 Coll Sharp Ct
43 Marlow Studio Workshops
44 Marlow Ho
45 Shiplake Ho
46 Wargrave Ho
47 Iffley Ho

D5
1 Queensbridge Ct
2 Godwin Ho
3 Kent Ct
4 Brunswick Ho
5 Weymouth Ct
6 Sovereign Mews
7 Dunloe Ct
8 Cremer Bsns Ctr
9 James Hammett Ho
10 Allgood St
11 Horatio St
12 Cadell Ho
13 Horatio Ho
14 Shipton Ho

D6
1 Hilborough Ct
2 Scriven Ct
3 Livermere Ct
4 Angrave Ct
5 Angrave Pas
6 Benfleet Ct
7 Belford Ho
8 Orme Ho
9 Clemson Ho
10 Longman Ho
11 Lowther Ho
12 Lovelace Ho
13 Harlowe Ho
14 Pamela Ho
15 Samuel Ho
16 Acton Ho
17 Loanda Cl
18 Phoenix Cl
19 Richardson Cl
20 Thrasher Cl
21 Mary Secole Cl
22 Canal Path
23 Pear Tree Cl
24 Hebden Ct
25 Charlton Ct
26 Laburnum Ct
27 Mansfield Ct
28 Garden Pl
29 Amber Wharf

96

A1
1 Manningtree St
2 Whitechurch La
3 Morrison Bldgs
4 Mountford St
5 Mulberry St
6 Weyhill Rd
7 Fordham St
8 Myrdle Ct
9 Buckle St
10 Plough St
12 Goodman's Stile
13 Mitali Pas
14 Basil Ho
15 Hogarth Ct
16 Ropewalk Gdns
17 Golding Terr
18 Delafield Ho
19 Drewett Ho
20 Harkness Ho
21 Batson Ho
22 Danvers Ho
23 Bicknell Ho
24 Everard Ho
25 Philchurch Pl
26 Hadfield Ho
27 Kindersley Ho
28 Langmore Ho
29 Halliday Ho
30 Berner Terr
31 Victoria Yd

A2
1 Arthur Deakin Ho
2 Albert Cotts
3 Victoria Cotts
4 Boden Ho
5 Vollasky Ho
6 Daplyn St
7 Hobsons Pl
8 Hanbury St
9 Links Yd
10 Casson Ho
11 Ramar Ho
12 Greatorex Ho
13 Chicksand Ho
14 Spelman Ho
15 Tailworth St
16 Monthorpe Rd
17 Bloomfield Ho
18 Davenant Ho
19 Pauline Ho
20 Tannery Ho
21 Green Dragon Yd
22 King's Arms Ct
23 Fieldgate Mans
24 Mosque Tower

A3
1 Bentworth Ct
2 Kerbela St
3 Fuller Cl
4 Kinsham Ho
5 Menotti St
6 Barwell Ho
7 Grimsby St
8 Eckersley St
9 Stuttle Ho
10 McGlashon Ho
11 Fleet Street Hill
12 Bratley St
13 Weaver Ho
14 John Pritchard Ho

A4
1 Lygon Ho
2 Brabner Ho
3 Delta St
4 Tillet Way
5 Mullet Gdns
6 Elver Gdns
7 Cobden Ho
8 Lampern Sq
9 Jeremy Bentham Ho
10 Waring Ho
11 St James Ct
12 Hague St
13 Westhope Ho
14 Johnson Ho
15 Yates Ho
16 Simmons Ho
17 Swinton Ho
18 Eversley Ho
19 Rapley Ho
20 Dence Ho
21 Dickinson Ho
22 Hutton Ho
23 McKinnon Wood Ho
24 Satchwell Rd
25 Lorden Wlk

A5
1 London Terr
2 Sturdee Ho
3 Maude Ho
4 Haig Ho
5 Jellicoe Ho
6 Ropley St
7 Guinness Trust Bldgs
8 Ion Ct
9 Moye Cl
10 Morrel Ct
11 Courtauld Ho
12 Drummond Ho
13 Atkinson Ho
14 Gurney Ho
15 Halley Ho
16 Goldsmith's Sq
17 Ken Wilson Ho
18 Shahjalal Ho
19 Crofts Ho
20 April Ct
21 Sebright Ho
22 Beechwood Ho
23 Gillman Ho
24 Cheverell Ho
25 Besford Ho
26 Dinmont Ho
27 Wyndham Deedes Ho
28 Sheppard Ho
29 Mary James Ho
30 Hadrian Est
31 Blythendale Ho
32 George Vale Ho
33 Lion Mills
34 Pritchard Ho

A6
1 Broke Wlk
2 Rochemont Wlk
3 Marlborough Ave
4 Rivington Wlk
5 Magnin Cl
6 Gloucester Sq
7 Woolstone Ho
8 Marsworth Ho
9 Cheddington Ho
10 Linslade Ho
11 Cosgrove Ho
12 Blisworth Ho
13 Eleanor Ct
14 Wistow Ho
15 Muscott Ho
16 Boxmoor Ho
17 Linford Ho
18 Pendley Ho
19 North Church Ho
20 Debdale Ho
21 Broadway Market Mews
22 Welshpool Ho
23 Ada Ho

B1
1 Jacob Mans
2 Wicker St
3 Langdale St
4 Walford Ho
5 Welstead Ho
6 Peter Best Ho
7 Sly St
8 Barnett St
9 Kinder St
10 Richard St
11 Sarah Ho
12 Mellish Ho
13 Dickson Ho
14 Joscoyne Ho
15 Bridgen Ho
16 Wilton Ct
17 Silvester Ho
18 Greenwich Ct
19 Tylney Ho
20 Damien Ct
21 Siege Ho
22 Melwood Ho
23 Colstead Ho
24 Hungerford St
25 Burwell Cl
26 Chapman Ho
27 Tarling Ho
28 Sheridan St
29 Brinsley St
30 Dunch St
31 Luke Ho
32 Turnour Ho
33 Norton Ho

B3
1 Rochester Ct
2 Weaver Ct
3 Greenheath Bsns Ctr
4 Glass St
5 Herald St
6 Northesk Ho
7 Codrington Ho
8 Heathpool Ct
9 Mocatta Ho
10 Harvey Ho
11 Blackwood Ho
12 Rutherford Ho
13 Bullen Ho
14 Fremantle Ho
15 Pellew Ho
16 Ashington Ho
17 Dinnington Ho
18 Bartholomew Sq
19 Steeple Ct
20 Orion Ho
21 Fellbrigg St
22 Eagle Ho
23 Sovereign Ho
24 Redmill Ho
25 Berry Ho
26 Grindall Ho
27 Collingwood Ho

B4
1 Charles Dickens Ho
2 Adrian Bolt Ho
3 William Rathbone Ho
4 Southwood Smith Ho
5 Rushmead
6 William Channing Ho
7 John Cartwright Ho
8 Charles Darwin Ho
9 Thomas Burt Ho
10 John Fielden Ho
11 Gwilym Maries Ho
12 Joseph Priestley Ho
13 Wear Pl
14 John Nettleford Ho
15 Thornaby Ho
16 Stockton Ho
17 Barnard Ho
18 Gainford Ho
19 Stapleton Ho
20 James Middleton Ho
21 Kedleston Wlk
22 Queen Margaret Flats
23 Hollybush Ho
24 Horwood Ho
25 Norden Ho
26 Newcourt Ho
27 Seabright St
28 Viaduct Pl
29 Sunlight Sq

B5
1 Dinmont St
2 Marian St
3 Claredale Ho
4 Bradley Ho
5 Connett Ho
6 Winkley St
7 Temple Dwellings
8 Argos Ho
9 Helen Ho
10 Lysander Ho
11 Antenor Ho
12 Paris Ho
13 Nestor Ho
14 Hector Ho
15 Ajax Ho
16 Achilles Ho
17 Priam Ho
18 Peabody Est
19 Felix St
20 Cambridge Cres
21 Peterley Bsns Ctr
22 Beckwith Ho
23 Parminter Ind Est
24 Ted Roberts Ho
25 Cambridge Ct
26 West St
27 Millennium Pl
28 William Caslon Ho
29 Hugh Platt Ho
30 Mayfield Ho
31 Apollo Ho
32 Tanners Yd
33 Teesdale Yd

B6
1 Welshpool St
2 Broadway Ho
3 Regents Wharf
4 London Wharf
5 Warburton Ho
6 Warburton St
7 Triangle Rd
8 Warburton Rd
9 Williams Ho
10 Booth Cl
11 Albert Cl
12 King Edward Mans
13 Victoria Bldgs

C1
1 Woollon Ho
2 Dundalk Ho
3 Anne Goodman Ho
4 Newbold Cotts
5 Kerry Ho
6 Zion Ho
7 Longford Ho
8 Bromehead St
9 Athlone Ho
10 Jubilee Mans
11 Harriott Ho
12 Brayford Sq
13 Clearbrook Way
14 Rochelle Ct
15 Winterton Ho
16 Sheridan Ho
17 Brinsley Ho
18 Dean Ho
19 Foley Ho
20 Robert Sutton Ho
21 Montpelier Pl
22 Masters Lo
23 Steel's La
24 Swift Ho
25 Glastonbury Pl

C2
1 Fulneck
2 Gracehill
3 Ockbrook
4 Fairfield
5 Dunstan Hos
6 Cressy Ct
7 Cressy Hos
8 Callahan Cotts
9 Wexford Ho
10 Sandhurst Ho
11 Colverson Ho
12 Beckett Ho
13 Jarman Ho
14 Wingrad Ho
15 Armsby Ho
16 Miranda Cl
17 Drake Ho
18 Louise De Marillac Ho
19 Sambrook Ho
20 St Vincent De Paul Ho
21 Jean Pardies Ho
22 Clichy Ho
23 Le Moal Ho
24 Odette Duval Ho
25 Dagobert Ho
26 Charles Auffray Ho
27 Boisseau Ho
28 Paymal Ho

C3
1 William's Bldgs
2 Donegal Ho
3 Frederick Charrington Ho
4 Wickford Ho
5 Braintree Ho
6 Doveton Ho
7 Doveton St
8 Cephas Ho
9 Sceptre Ho
10 Bancroft Ho
11 Stothard St
12 Redclyf Ho
13 Winkworth Cotts
14 Ryder Ho
15 Hadleigh Ho
16 Hadleigh Cl
17 Amiel St
18 Stathard Ho
19 Barnanel Ho
20 Colebert Ho
21 Kenton Ho
22 Ibbott St
23 Stannard Cotts
24 Rennie Cotts
25 Rickman St
26 Rickman Ho
27 Pemell Cl
28 Pemell Ho
29 Leatherdale St
30 Gouldman Ho
31 Lamplighter Cl
32 Hamilton Lo
33 Cleveland Gr
34 Montgomery Lo
35 Bardsey Pl
36 Cromwell Lo
37 Colin Winter Ho
38 Allport Mews

C4
1 Mulberry Ho
2 Gretton Ho
3 Merceron Ho
4 Montfort Ho
5 Westbrook Ho
6 Sugar Loaf Wlk
7 Museum Ho
8 Burnham Est
9 Globe Terr
10 Moravian St
11 Shepton Hos
12 Mendip Hos
13 Academy Ho
14 Pepys Ho
15 Swinburne Ho
16 Moore Ho
17 Morris Ho
18 Burns Ho
19 Milton Ho
20 Whitman Ho
21 Shelley Ho
22 Keats Ho
23 Dawson Ho
24 Bradbeer Ho
25 Forber Ho
26 Hughes Ho
27 Silvester Ho
28 Rogers Est
29 Pavan Ct
30 Stafford Cripps Ho
31 Sidney Godley (VC) Ho
32 Butler Ho
33 Butler St
34 Thorne Ho
35 Bevin Ho

C5
1 Evesham Ho
2 James Campbell Ho
3 Thomas Hollywood Ho
4 James Docherty Ho
5 Ebenezer Mussel Ho
6 Jameson Ct
7 Edinburgh Cl
8 Roger Dowley Ct
9 Sherbrooke Ho
10 Calcraft Ho
11 Burrard Ho
12 Dundas Ho
14 Barnes Ho
15 Paget Ho
17 Maitland Ho
18 Chesil Ct
19 Reynolds Ho
20 Cleland Ho
21 Goodrich Ho
22 Rosebery Ho
23 Sankey Ho
24 Cyprus Pl
25 Royston St
26 Stainsbury St
27 Hunslett St
28 Baildon
29 Brockweir
30 Tytherton
32 Kingswood
33 Colville Ho

C6
1 Halkett Ho
4 Christ Church Sq
5 Swingfield Ho
6 Greenham Ho
7 Dinmore Ho
8 Anstey Ho
9 Weston Ho
10 Carbroke Ho
16 Bluebell Cl
17 Cherry Tree Cl
19 Georgian Ct
20 Park Cl
21 Regency Ct
22 Norris Ho

D1
1 Pattison Ho
2 St Thomas Ho
3 Arbour Ho
4 Bladen Ho
5 Antill Terr
6 Billing Ho
7 Dowson Ho
8 Lipton Rd
9 Chalkwell Ho
10 Corringham Ho
11 Ogilvie Ho

12	Edward Mann Cl
13	Lighterman Mews
D2 1	Roland Mews
2	Morecambe Cl
3	Stepney Green Ct
4	Milrood Ho
5	Panama Ho
6	Galway Ho
7	Caspian Ho
8	Darien Ho
9	Rigo Ho
10	Flores Ho
11	Taranto Ho
12	Aden Ho
13	Frances Grey Ho
14	Master's St
16	Diggon St
D3 1	Raynham Ho
2	Pat Shaw Ho
3	Colmar Cl
4	Withy Ho
5	Stocks Ct
6	Downey Ho
7	Bay Ct
8	Sligo Ho
9	Pegasus Ho
10	Barents Ho
11	Biscay Ho
12	Solway Ho
13	Bantry Ho
14	Aral Ho
15	Pacific Ho
16	Magellan Ho
17	Levant Ho
18	Adriatic Ho
19	Genoa Ho
20	Hawke Ho
21	Palliser Ho
22	Ionian Ho
23	Weddell Ho
D4 1	Stubbs Ho
2	Holman Ho
3	Clynes Ho
4	Windsor Ho
5	Gilbert Ho
6	Chater Ho
7	Ellen Wilkinson Ho
8	George Belt Ho
9	Ayrton Gould Ho
10	O'Brian Ho
11	Sulkin Ho
12	Jenkinson Ho
13	Bullards Pl
14	Sylvia Pankhurst Ho
15	Mary Macarthur Ho
16	Trevelyan Ho
17	Wedgwood Ho
18	Pemberton Ct
20	Walter Besant Ho
21	Barber Beaumont Ho
22	Brancaster Ho
23	Litcham Ho
D5 1	Kemp Ho
2	Piggott Ho
3	Mark Ho
4	Sidney Ho
5	Pomeroy Ho
6	Puteaux Ho
7	Doric Ho
8	Modling Ho
9	Longman Ho
10	Ames Ho
11	Alzette Ho
12	Offenbach Ho
13	Tate Ho
14	Norton Ho
15	St Gilles Ho
16	Harold Ho
17	Velletri Ho
18	Bridge Wharf
19	Gathorne St
20	Bow Brook The
22	Palmerston Ct
23	Peach Walk Mews
24	Lakeview
25	Caesar Ct

97

A1 1	Coltman Ho
2	Repton Ho
3	Causton Cotts

9	Darnley Ho
10	Mercer's Cotts
11	Troon Ho
12	Ratcliffe Ho
13	Wakeling St
14	York Sq
15	Anglia Ho
16	Cambria Ho
17	Caledonia Ho
18	Ratcliffe La
19	Bekesbourne St
20	John Scurr Ho
21	Regents Canal Ho
22	Basin App
23	Powlesland Ct
A2 1	Waley St
2	Edith Ramsay Ho
3	Andaman Ho
4	Atlantic Ho
5	Pevensey Ho
6	Solent Ho
7	Lorne Ho
8	Cromarty Ho
12	Greaves Cotts
13	Donaghue Cotts
14	Ames Cotts
A3 1	Formosa Ho
2	Galveston Ho
3	Arabian Ho
4	Greenland Ho
5	Coral Ho
6	Anson Ho
7	Lindop Ho
8	Moray Ho
9	Azov Ho
10	Sandalwood Cl
11	Broadford Ho
A5 1	Bunsen Ho
2	Bunsen St
3	Beatrice Webb Ho
4	Margaret Bondfield Ho
5	Wilmer Ho
6	Sandall Ho
7	Butley Ct
8	Josseline Ct
9	Dalton Ho
10	Brine Ho
11	Ford Cl
12	Viking Cl
13	Stanfield Rd
14	Ruth Ct
15	School Bell Cloisters
16	Schoolbell Mews
17	Medhurst Cl
18	Olga St
19	Conyer St
20	Diamond Ho
21	Daring Ho
22	Crane Ho
23	Exmoor Ho
24	Grenville Ho
25	Hyperion Ho
26	Sturdy Ho
27	Wren Ho
28	Ardent Ho
29	Senators Lo
30	Hooke Ho
31	Mohawk Ho
32	Ivanhoe Ho
33	Medway Mews
B1 1	Dora Ho
2	Flansham Ho
3	Gatwick Ho
4	Ashpark Ho
5	Newdigate Ho
6	Salmon St
7	Midhurst Ho
8	Redbourne Ho
9	Southwater Cl
10	Aithan Ho
11	Britley Ho
12	Cheadle Ho
13	Elland Ho
14	Butler Ho
15	Fitzroy Ho
16	Leybourne Ho
B2 1	Wearmouth Ho
2	Elmslie Point
3	Grindley Ho
4	Stileman Ho
5	Baythorne St
6	Wilcox Ho
7	Robeson St
8	Couzens Ho
10	Perley Ho
11	Whytlaw Ho

12	Printon Ho
13	Perkins Ho
14	Bowry Ho
15	Booker Cl
16	Tunley Gn
17	Callingham Cl
18	Tasker Ho
B4 1	Trellis Sq
2	Sheffield Sq
3	Howcroft Ho
5	Astra Ho
6	Byas Ho
7	George Lansbury Ho
8	Regal Pl
9	Coborn Mews
10	Cavendish Terr
11	Buttermere Ho
12	Tracy Ho
13	Hanover Pl
14	Coniston Ho
14	St Clair Ho
15	Verity Ho
16	Icarus Ho
17	Whippingham Ho
18	Winchester Ho
19	Hamilton Ho
20	Longthorne Ho
B5 1	Roman Square Mkt
2	John Bond Ho
3	McKenna Ho
4	Dennis Ho
5	McBride Ho
6	Libra Rd
7	Dave Adams Ho
8	Tay Ho
9	Sleat Ho
10	Ewart Pl
11	Brodick Ho
12	Lunan Ho
13	Mull Ho
14	Sinclairs Ho
15	Driftway Ho
16	Clayhall Ct
17	Berebinder Ho
18	Stavers Ho
19	Barford Ho
20	Partridge Ho
21	Gosford Ho
22	Gullane Ho
23	Cruden Ho
24	Anglo Rd
25	Dornoch Ho
26	Dunnet Ho
27	Enard Ho
28	Fraserburgh Ho
29	Forth Ho
30	Ordell Ct
31	William Pl
B6 1	Hampstead Wlk
2	Waverton Ho
3	Elton Ho
4	Locton Gn
5	Birtwhistle Ho
6	Clare Ho
7	Magpie Ho
8	Atkins Ct
9	Tait Ct
10	Ranwell Ho
11	Ranwell Cl
12	Tufnell Ct
13	Pulteney Cl
14	Vic Johnson Ho
C1 1	Landin Ho
2	Charlesworth Ho
3	Gurdon Ho
4	Trendell Ho
5	Menteath Ho
6	Minchin Ho
7	Donne Ho
8	Denison Ho
9	Anglesey Ho
10	Gough Wlk
11	Baring Ho
12	Hopkins Ho
13	Granville Ho
14	Gladstone Ho
15	Russell Ho
16	Pusey Ho
17	Overstone Ho
18	Stanley Ho
19	Old School Sq
C2 1	Bredel Ho
2	Linton Ho
3	Matthews Ho
4	Woodcock Ho
5	Limborough Ho
6	Maydwell Ho

7	Underhill Ho
8	Meyrick Ho
9	Ambrose Ho
10	Carpenter Ho
11	Robinson Ho
12	Bramble Ho
13	Bilberry Ho
14	Bracken Ho
15	Berberis Ho
16	Busbridge Ho
17	Metropolitan Cl
18	Invicta Cl
19	Bellmaker Ct
C3 1	Fairmont Ho
2	Healy Ho
3	Zodiac Ho
4	Buick Ho
5	Consul Ho
6	Bentley Ho
7	Cresta Ho
8	Daimler Ho
9	Riley Ho
10	Jensen Ho
11	Lagonda Ho
12	Ireton St
13	Navenby Wlk
14	Burwell Wlk
15	Leadenham Ct
16	Sleaford Ho
C4 1	Jarret Ho
2	Marsalis Ho
3	Lovette Ho
4	Drapers Almhouses
5	Mallard Point
6	Creswick Wlk
7	Bevin Ho
8	Huggins Ho
9	Williams Ho
10	Harris Ho
11	Marina Ct
12	Electric Ho
13	Matching Ct
14	Wellington Bldgs
15	Grafton Ho
16	Columbia Ho
17	Berkeley Ho
D1 1	Colebrook Ho
2	Essex Ho
3	Salisbury Ho
4	Maidstone Ho
5	Osterley Ho
6	Norwich Ho
7	Clarissa Ho
8	Elgin Ho
9	Shaftesbury Lo
10	Shepherd Ho
11	Jeremiah St
12	Elizabeth Cl
13	Chilcot Cl
14	Fitzgerald Ho
15	Vesey Path
16	Ennis Ho
17	Kilmore Ho
D2 1	Sumner Ho
2	Irvine Ho
3	David Ho
4	Brushwood Ho
5	Limehouse Cut
6	Colmans Wharf
7	Foundary Ho
8	Radford Ho
D3 1	Broxbourne Ho
2	Roxford Ho
3	Biscott Ho
4	Stanborough Ho
5	Hillstone Ct
D4 1	Bradley Ho
2	Prioress Ho
3	Alton Ho
4	Foxley Ho
5	Munden Ho
6	Canterbury Ho
7	Corbin Ho
8	Barton Ho
9	Jolles Ho
10	Rudstone Ho
11	Baxter Ho
12	Baker Ho
13	Insley Ho
14	Hardwicke Ho
15	Glebe Terr
16	Priory St
17	Sadler Ho
18	Ballinger Point
19	Henshall Point
20	Dorrington Point
21	Warren Ho
22	Fairlie Ct
23	Regent Sq

24	Hackworth Point
25	Priestman Point
26	Wingate Ho
27	Nethercott Ho
28	Thelbridge Ho
29	Bowden Ho
30	Kerscott Ho
31	Southcott Ho
32	Birchdown Ho
33	Upcott Ho
34	Langmead Ho
35	Limscott Ho
36	Northleigh Ho
37	Huntshaw Ho
38	Chagford Ho
39	Ashcombe Ho
40	Shillingford Ho
41	Patrick Connolly Gdns
42	Lester Ct
43	Franklin St
44	Taft Way
45	Washington Cl
46	Elizabeth Ho
47	William Guy Gdns
48	Denbury Ho
49	Holsworthy Ho

98

A1 1	Langdon Ho
2	Balfron Twr
3	Tabard Ct
4	Delta Bldg
5	Kilbrennan Ho
6	Thistle Ho
7	Heather Ho
8	Tartan Ho
9	Trident Ho
A2 1	Mills Gr
3	Duncan Ct
B1 1	Lansbury Gdns
2	Thesus Ho
3	Theseus Ho
4	Adams Ho
4	Jones Ho
5	Sam March Ho
6	Arapiles Ho
7	Athenia Ho
8	Jervis Bay Ho
9	Helen Mackay Ho
10	Gaze Ho
11	Ritchie Ho
12	Circle Ho
13	Dunkeld Ho
14	Braithwaite Ho
15	Rosemary Dr
16	Sorrel La
17	East India Dock Road Tunnel
C6 1	Barnby Sq
2	Barnby St
3	Brassett Point
4	David Lee Point
5	Worthing Cl
6	Bexhill Wlk
7	Old Borrowfield
8	Colmans Wharf
9	Stafford Morris Ho
10	Nina Mackay Cl
11	Lime Wlk
D1 1	Newton Point
2	Sparke Terr
3	Montesquieu Terr
4	Crawford Point
5	Rathbone Ho
6	George St
7	Emily St
8	Fendt Cl
9	Sabbarton St
D2 1	Radley Terr
2	Rathbone Mkt
3	Thomas North Terr
4	Bernard Cassidy St
5	Mary St
6	Hughes Terr
7	Swanscombe Point
8	Rawlinson Point
9	Kennedy Cox Ho
10	Cooper St
D6 1	Harris Cotts
2	Moorey Cl
3	Euro Bsns Ctr

4	Ladywell St
5	Caistor Ho
6	Redfern Ho

99

A2 1	Odeon Ct
2	Edward Ct
3	Newhaven La
4	Ravenscroft Cl
5	Douglas Rd
6	Ferrier Point
7	Harvey Point
8	Wood Point
9	Trinity St
10	Pattinson Point
11	Clinch Ct
12	Mint Bsns Pk
A3 1	Webb Gdns
2	Eric Shipman Terr
3	Warmington St
4	Jellicoe Rd
5	Frank St
6	Seaton Cl
7	Tabernacle Ave
8	Upland Rd
9	Clove St
10	Edward St
A4 1	Bob Anker Cl
2	Lea Ct
3	Third Ave
4	Suffolk Rd
A5 1	Lettsom Wlk
2	Ashburton Terr
3	Grasmere Rd
4	Dimsdale Wlk
5	Rawstone Wlk
6	Scott Ho
7	Willett Ho
8	James Cl
9	Cordwainers Wlk
10	Victoria Point
11	Settle Point
12	Middle Rd
A6 1	Royston Ct
B4 1	Barbers Alley
2	Grengate Lo
3	Augurs La
4	Surrey St
5	Dongola Rd W
6	Bemersyde Point
7	Rowntree Clifford Cl
C5 1	Wellby Ct
2	Bishop Wilfred Wood Ct
3	Castle Point
4	Moat Dr
C6 1	Queen's Mkt
2	Tolpuddle Ave
3	Crown Mews
4	Lilac Ct
5	Hamara Ghar
6	Greenleaf Rd
7	Massey Ct
8	Florence Rd
9	Sissulu Ct
10	Austin Ct
D2 1	Partridge Cl
2	Vanbrugh Cl
3	Meadowsweet Cl
4	St Michaels Cl
5	Long Mark Rd
6	Congreve Wlk
D5 1	Foxcombe Cl
2	Rochford Cl
3	Kylemore Cl
4	Stondon Wlk
5	Imperial Mews
6	Dominica Cl
D6 1	Oldegate Ho
2	Gaitskell Ho
3	Cabot Way

100

A1 1	Hadleigh Wlk
2	Hawksmoor Cl
3	Fraser Cl
4	Moncrieff Cl
5	Burlington Cl
6	Dundonald Cl
7	Oakley Cl
8	Ashwell Cl
A2 1	Orchid Cl
2	Bellflower Cl
3	Partridge Sq

109 C6 **415**

4	Larkspur Cl
5	Lobelia Cl
6	Stonechat Sq
7	Wintergreen Cl
8	Garnet Wlk
9	Mavis Wlk
10	Beacons Cl
11	Abbess Cl
12	Elmley Cl
13	Chetwood Wlk
14	Selby Cl
15	Denny Cl
16	Woodhatch Cl
A6 1	Oakwood Ct
2	Harrow Rd
3	Ray Massey Way
4	Madge Gill Way
5	Pilgrims Way
B1 1	Bowers Wlk
2	Barton Cl
3	Clayton Cl
4	Dixon Cl
5	Gautrey Sq
6	Wakerly Cl
7	Canterbury Cl
8	Goose Sq
9	Coventry Cl
10	Butterfield Sq
11	Winchester Cl
B2 1	Fleetwood Ct
2	Lymington Cl
3	Holyhead Cl
4	Bondfield Rd
5	Tulip Cl
6	Ambrose Cl
7	Sage Cl
8	Lindwood Cl
D1 1	Weymouth Cl
2	Founder Cl
3	Admirals Cl

101

A6 1	Wellington St
2	St Ann's Rd
3	Bamber Ho
B6 1	Jarvis Cl
2	Mayflower Ho
3	Westbury Ct
4	Millicent Preston Ho
5	Louise Graham Ho
6	Grange Ho
7	Basing Ho
8	Barnes Ho
9	Lexham Ho
10	Ripple Ct
11	Waldegrave Ct
12	Howard Ct

104

A6 1	Milburn Dr
2	Cousins Cl
3	Leacroft Cl

108

C5 1	Marlow Ct
2	Andrews Cl
3	Vine Cotts
4	Benjamin Ct
5	Broadway Bldgs
D5 1	Silverdale Cl
2	Burdett Cl
3	Hopefield
4	Maunder Rd

109

A5 1	Glastonbury Ct
2	Evesham Ct
3	Lacock Ct
4	Wigmore Ct
5	Melrose Ct
6	Brownlow Rd
7	Chignell Pl
8	Shirley Ct
9	Trojan Ct
10	Hatfield Rd
C6 1	Abbey Lo
2	Yew Tree Grange
3	Abinger Ct

110

A1
1 Burford Ho
2 Hope Cl
3 Centaur Ct
4 Phoenix Ct
A6
1 Watermans Mews
2 Hills Mews
3 Grosvenor Ct
4 Elton Lo
5 Hambledon Ct
C1
1 Surrey Cres
2 Forbes Ct
3 Haining Cl
4 Melville Ct
5 London Stile
6 Stile Hall Par
7 Priory Lo
8 Kew Bridge Ct
9 Meadowcroft
10 St James Ct
11 Rivers Ho
C5
1 Grosvenor Par
2 Oakfield Ct
3 Hart Grove Ct
4 Grosvenor Ct
D1
1 Churchdale Ct
2 Cromwell Cl
3 Cambridge Rd S
4 Oxbridge Ct
5 Tomlinson Cl
6 Gunnersbury Mews
7 Grange The
8 Gunnersbury Cl
D4
1 Cheltenham Pl
2 Beaumaris Twr
3 Arundel Ho
4 Pevensey Ct
5 Jerome Twr
6 Anstey Ct
7 Bennett Ct
8 Gunnersbury Ct
D5
1 Lantry Ct
2 Rosemount Ct
3 Moreton Twr
4 Acton Central Ind Est
5 Rufford Twr
6 Narrow St
7 Mount Pl
8 Sidney Miller Ct
9 Mill Hill Terr
11 Mill Hill Gr

111

A1
1 Arlington Park Mans
2 Sandown Ho
3 Goodwood Ho
4 Windsor Ho
5 Lingfield Ho
6 Ascot Ho
7 Watchfield Ct
8 Belgrave Ct
9 Beverley Ct
10 Beaumont Ct
11 Harvard Rd
12 Troubridge Ct
A2
1 Chiswick Green Studios
2 Bell Ind Est
3 Fairlawn Ct
4 Dukes Gate
5 Dewsbury Ct
6 Chiswick Terr
A3
1 Blackmore Twr
2 Bollo Ct
3 Kipling Twr
4 Lawrence Ct
5 Maugham Ct
6 Reade Ct
7 Woolf Ct
8 Shaw Ct
9 Verne Ct
10 Wodehouse Ct
11 Greenock Rd
12 Garden Ct
13 Barons Gate
14 Cleveland Rd
15 Chapter Cl
15 Carver Cl
16 Beauchamp Cl
17 Holmes Ct
A4
1 Belgrave Cl

2 Buckland Wlk
3 Frampton Ct
4 Telfer Cl
5 Harlech Twr
6 Corfe Twr
7 Barwick Ho
8 Charles Hocking Ho
9 Sunninghill Ct
10 Salisbury St
11 Jameson Pl
A5
1 Rectory Rd
2 Derwentwater Mans
3 Market Pl
4 Hooper's Mews
5 Cromwell Pl
6 Locarno Rd
7 Edgecote Cl
8 Harleyford Manor
9 Coopers Ct
B1
1 Chatsworth Lo
2 Prospect Pl
3 Townhall Ave
4 Devonhurst Pl
5 Heathfield Ct
6 Horticultural Pl
7 Merlin Ho
8 Garth Rd
C1
1 Glebe Cl
2 Devonshire Mews
3 Binns Terr
4 Ingress St
5 Swanscombe Rd
6 Brackley Terr
7 Stephen Fox Ho
8 Manor Gdns
9 Coram Ho
10 Flaxman Ho
11 Thorneycroft Ho
12 Thornhill Ho
13 Kent Ho
14 Oldfield Ho
C2
1 Chestnut Ho
2 Bedford Ho
3 Bedford Cnr
4 Sydney Ho
5 Bedford Park Cnr
6 Priory Gdns
7 Windmill Alley
8 Castle Pl
9 Jonathan Ct
10 Windmill Pas
11 Chardin Rd
12 Gable Ho
C3
1 Fleet Ct
2 Ember Ct
3 Emlyn Gdns
4 Clone Ct
5 Brent Ct
6 Abbey Ct
7 Ormsby Lo
8 St Catherine's Ct
C4
1 Longford Ct
2 Mole Ct
3 Lea Ct
4 Wandle Ct
5 Beverley Ct
6 Roding Ct
7 Crane Ct
D1
1 Miller's Ct
2 British Grove Pas
3 British Grove S
4 Berestede Rd
5 North Eyot Gdns
D2
1 Flanders Mans
2 Stamford Brook Mans
3 Linkenholt Mans
4 Prebend Mans
5 Middlesex Ct
D3
1 Stamford Brook Gdns
2 Hauteville Court Gdns
3 Ranelagh Gdns

112

A2
1 Hamlet Ct
2 Derwent Ct
3 Westcroft Ct
4 Black Lion Mews
5 St Peter's Villas
6 Standish Ho
7 Chambon Pl

8 Court Mans
A4
2 Victoria Ho
3 Lycett Pl
4 Kylemore Ct
5 Alexandra Ct
6 Lytten Ct
7 Becklow Mews
8 Northcroft Ct
9 Bailey Ho
10 Spring Cott
11 Landor Wlk
12 Laurence Mews
13 Hadyn Park Ct
14 Askew Mans
B2
1 Albion Gdns
2 Flora Gdns
3 Lamington St
4 Felgate Mews
5 Galena Ho
6 Albion Mews
7 Albion Ct
8 King Street Cloisters
9 Dimes Pl
10 Clarence Ct
11 Hampshire Hog La
12 Marryat Ct
B4
1 Westbush Ct
2 Goldhawk Mews
3 Sycamore Ho
4 Shackleton Ct
5 Drake Ct
6 Scotts Ct
B6
1 Abercrombie Ho
2 Bathurst Ho
3 Brisbane Ho
4 Bentinck Ho
5 Ellenborough Ho
6 Lawrence Cl
7 Mackenzie Cl
8 Carteret Ho
9 Calvert Ho
10 Winthrop Ho
11 Auckland Ho
12 Blaxland Ho
13 Havelock Cl
14 Hargraves Ho
15 Hudson Ct
16 Phipps Ho
17 Lawson Ho
18 Hastings Ho
19 Wolfe Ho
20 Malabar Ct
21 White City Est
21 Commonwealth Ave
22 Charnock Ho
23 Canning Ho
24 Cornwallis Ho
26 Champlain Ho
27 Grey Ho
28 Durban Ho
29 Baird Ho
30 Campbell Ho
31 Mitchell Ho
32 Denham Ho
33 Mackay Ho
34 Evans Ho
35 Daws Ho
36 Mandela Cl
C1
1 Bridge Avenue Mans
2 Bridgeview
3 College Ct
4 Beatrice Ho
5 Amelia Ho
6 Edith Ho
7 Joanna Ho
8 Mary Ho
9 Adela Ho
10 Sophia Ho
11 Henrietta Ho
12 Charlotte Ho
13 Alexandra Ho
14 Bath Pl
15 Elizabeth Ho
16 Margaret Ho
17 Peabody Est
18 Eleanor Ho
19 Isabella Ho
20 Caroline Ho
21 Chancellors Wharf
22 Sussex Pl
C2
1 Phoenix Lodge Mans
2 Samuel's Cl
3 Broadway Arc
4 Brook Ho

5 Hammersmith Broadway
C4
1 Verulam Ho
2 Grove Mans
3 Frobisher Ct
4 Library Mans
5 Pennard Mans
6 Lanark Mans
7 Kerrington Ct
8 Granville Mans
9 Romney Ct
10 Rayner Ct
11 Sulgrave Gdns
12 Bamborough Gdns
D3
1 Grosvenor Residences
2 Blythe Mews
3 Burnand Ho
4 Bradford Ho
5 Springvale Terr
6 Ceylon Rd
7 Walpole Ct
8 Bronte Ct
9 Boswell Ct
10 Souldern Rd
11 Brook Green Flats
12 Haarlem Rd
13 Stafford Mans
14 Lionel Mans
D4
1 Vanderbilt Villas
2 Bodington Ct
3 Kingham Cl
4 Clearwater Terr
5 Lorne Gdns
6 Cameret Ct
7 Bush Ct
8 Shepherds Ct
9 Rockley Ct
10 Grampians The
11 Charcroft Ct
12 Addison Park Mans
13 Sinclair Mans
D5
1 St Katherine's Wlk
2 Dorrit Ho
3 Pickwick Ho
4 Dombey Ho
5 Caranday Villas
6 Mortimer Ho
7 Nickleby Ho
8 Stebbing Ho
9 Boxmoor Ho
10 Poynter Ho
11 Swanscombe Ho
12 Darnley Terr
13 Norland Ho
14 Hume Ho
D6
1 Frinstead Ho
2 Hurstway Wlk
3 Testerton Wlk
4 Grenfell Wlk
5 Grenfell Twr
6 Barandon Wlk
7 Treadgold Ho
8 St Clements Ct
9 Willow Way
10 Florence Ho
11 Dora Ho
12 Carton Ho
13 Agnes Ho
14 Marley Ho
15 Waynflete Sq

118

A1
1 Alison Ct
2 West Point
3 Centre Point
4 East Point
5 Proctor Ho
6 Tovy Ho
7 Brettinghurst
8 Colechurch Ho
9 Harman Cl
10 Avondale Ho
11 Lanark Ho
12 George Elliston Ho
13 Eric Wilkins Ho
14 Archers Lo
15 Culloden Cl
16 Fallow Ct
17 Fern Wlk
18 Ivy Ct
19 Winter Lo
A2
1 Cadbury Way
2 Robert Bell Ho

3 Robert Jones Ho
4 William Rushbrooke Ho
5 Helen Taylor Ho
6 Peter Hills Ho
7 Charles Mackenzie Ho
8 Drappers Way
9 Abbey Gdns
10 Maria Cl
11 Windmill Cl
12 Townsend Ho
13 Mason Ho
14 Langdon Way
15 Hannah Mary Way
16 Kotree Way
17 Whittaker Way
A3
1 Rudge Ho
2 Spenlow Ho
3 Darnay Ho
4 Carton Ho
5 Giles Ho
6 Bowley Ho
7 Casby Ho
8 Sun Pas
9 Ness St
10 Voyager Bsns Est
11 Dockley Road Ind Est
12 Spa Ct
13 Discovery Bsns Pk
14 Priter Road Hostel
15 Salisbury Ct
16 William Ellis Way
17 John McKenna Wlk
18 Toussaint Wlk
19 Gillison Wlk
20 Bromfield Ct
21 Ben Smith Way
22 Major Rd
23 Old Jamaica Bsns Est
A4
1 Providence Twr
2 Springalls Wharf
3 St Saviours Ho
4 Providence Sq
5 Farthing Alley
6 Peter Butler Ho
7 Brownlow Ho
8 Fleming Ho
9 Dombey Ho
10 Copperfield Ho
11 Tapley Ho
12 Parkers Row
13 Wade Ho
14 Bardell Ho
15 Nickleby Ho
16 John Felton Rd
17 Pickwick Ho
18 Oliver Ho
19 Weller Ho
20 Weller Ho
21 Tupman Ho
22 Haredale Ho
23 Havisham Ho
24 Micawber Ho
25 Wrayburn Ho
26 Dartle Ct
27 Burnaby Ct
28 Waterside Cl
29 Wickfield Ho
30 Fountain Ho
31 Fountain Green Sq
A5
1 Trade Winds Ct
2 Spice Ct
3 Leeward Ct
4 Bridgeport Pl
5 Tamarind Yd
6 Cope Yd
7 Nightingale Ho
8 St Anthony's Cl
9 Stockholm Way
10 Miah Terr
11 Seville Ho
12 Douthwaite Sq
13 Codling Cl
14 Hermitage Ct
15 Capital Wharf
16 Cinnabar Wharf East
17 Cinnabar Wharf Central
18 Cinnabar Wharf West
19 Halcyon Wharf

A6
1 Conant Mews
2 Hanson Ho
3 Victoria Ct
4 Swan Pas
5 Royal Mint Pl
6 Flank St
7 Ensign Ct
8 Sapphire Ct
9 George Leybourne Ho
10 Fletcher St
11 Wellclose St
12 Noble Ho
13 Hatton Ho
14 Shearsmith Ho
15 Breezer's Ct
16 Pennington Ct
17 Onedin Point
18 Liberty Pl
B1
1 Hockney Ct
2 Toulouse Ct
3 Lowry Ct
4 Barry Ho
5 Lewis Ct
6 Gainsborough Ct
7 Renoir Ct
8 Blake Ct
9 Raphael Ct
10 Rembrandt Ct
11 Constable Ct
12 Da Vinci Ct
13 Gaugin Ct
14 Michelangelo Ct
15 Monet Ct
16 Weald Cl
17 Jasmin Lo
18 Birchmere Lo
19 Weybridge Ct
20 Florence Ho
21 Gleneagles Cl
22 Sunningdale Cl
23 Muirfield Cl
24 Turnberry Cl
25 St Andrews Cl
26 Kingsdown Cl
27 St Davids Cl
28 Galway Cl
29 Edenbridge Cl
30 Birkdale Cl
31 Tralee Ct
32 Woburn Ct
33 Belfry Cl
34 Troon Cl
35 Holywell Cl
B2
1 Market Pl
2 Trappes Ho
3 Thurland Ho
4 Ramsfort Ho
5 Hambley Ho
6 Holford Ho
7 Pope Ho
8 Southwell Ho
9 Mortain Ho
10 Radcliffe Ho
11 Southwark Park Est
12 Galleywall Road Trad Est
13 Trevithick Ho
14 Barlow Ho
15 Donkin Ho
16 Landmann Ho
17 Fitzmaurice Ho
18 Dodd Ho
B3
1 Perryn Rd
2 Chalfont Ho
3 Prestwood Ho
4 Farmer Ho
5 Gataker Ho
6 Gataker St
7 Cornick Ho
8 Glebe Ho
9 Matson Ho
10 Hickling Ho
11 St Andrews Ho
B4
1 Butterfield Cl
2 Janeway Pl
3 Trotwood Ho
4 Cranbourn Ho
5 Cherry Garden Ho
6 Burton Ho
7 Morriss Ho
8 King Edward The Third Mews
9 Cathay St
10 Rotherhithe St
B5
1 China Ct
2 Wellington Terr
3 Stevedore St

4 Portland Sq
5 Reardon Ho
6 Lowder Ho
7 Meeting House Alley
8 Farthing Fields
9 Oswell Ho
10 Park Lo
11 Doughty Ct
12 Inglefield Sq
13 Chopin's Ct
14 Welsh Ho
15 Hilliard Ho
16 Clegg St
17 Tasman Ho
18 Ross Ho
19 Wapping Dock St
20 Bridewell Pl
21 New Tower Bldgs
22 Tower Bldgs
23 Chimney Ct
24 Jackman Ho
25 Fenner Ho
26 Franklin Ho
27 Frobisher Ho
28 Flinders Ho
29 Chancellor Ho
30 Beechey Ho
31 Reardon Path
32 Parry Ho
33 Vancover Ho
34 Willoughby Ho
35 Sanctuary The
36 Dundee Ct
37 Pierhead Wharf
38 Scandrett St
39 St Johns Ct
B6
1 Newton Ho
2 Richard Neale Ho
3 Maddocks Ho
4 Cornwall St
5 Brockmer Ho
6 Dellow Ho
7 Bewley Ho
8 Artichoke Hill
C2
1 Damory Ho
2 Antony Ho
3 Roderick Ho
4 Pedworth Gdns
5 Beamish Ho
6 Gillam Ho
7 George Walter Ho
8 Richard Ho
9 Adron Ho
10 Westlake
11 McIntosh Ho
C3
1 Blick Ho
2 Neptune Ho
3 Scotia Ct
4 Murdoch Ho
5 Edmonton Ct
6 Niagara Ct
7 Columbia Point
8 Ritchie Ho
9 Wells Ho
10 Helen Peele Cotts
11 Orchard Ho
12 Dock Offices
13 Landale Ho
14 Courthope Ho
C4
1 Mayflower St
2 St Mary's Est
3 Rupack St
4 Frank Whymark Ho
5 Adams Gardens Est
6 Hatteraick St
7 Hythe Ho
8 Seaford Ho
9 Sandwich Ho
10 Winchelsea Ho
11 Kenning St
12 Western Pl
13 Ainsty St
14 Pine Ho
15 Beech Ho
16 Larch Ho
17 Seth St
18 Turner Ct
19 Risdon Ho
20 Risdon St
21 Aylton Est
22 Manitoba Ct
23 Calgary Ct

25 Irwell Est
26 City Bsns Ctr
27 St Olav's Sq
C5 1 John Rennie Wlk
2 Malay Ho
3 Wainwright Ho
4 Riverside Mans
5 Shackleton Ho
6 Whitehorn Ho
7 Wavel Ct
8 Prusom's Island
C6 1 Gosling Ho
2 Vogler Ho
3 Donovan Ho
4 Knowlden Ho
5 Chamberlain Ho
6 Moore Ho
7 Thornewill Ho
8 Fisher Ho
9 All Saints Ct
10 Coburg Dwellings
11 Lowood Ho
12 Solander Gdns
13 Chancery Bldgs
14 Ring Ho
15 Juniper St
16 Gordon Ho
17 West Block
18 North Block
19 South Block
D2 1 John Kennedy Ho
2 Brydale Ho
3 Balman Ho
4 Tissington Ct
5 Harbord Ho
6 Westfield Ho
7 Albert Starr Ho
8 John Brent Ho
9 William Evans Ho
10 Raven Ho
11 Egret Ho
12 Fulmar Ho
13 Dunlin Ho
14 Siskin Ho
15 Sheldrake Ho
16 Buchanan Ct
17 Burrage Ct
18 Biddenham Ho
19 Ayston Ho
20 Empingham Ho
21 Deanshanger Ho
22 Codicote Ho
D4 1 Schooner Cl
2 Dolphin Ct
3 Clipper Cl
4 Deauville Ct
5 Colette Ct
6 Coniston Ct
7 Virginia Ct
8 Derwent Ct
9 Grantham Ct
10 Serpentine Ct
11 Career Ct
12 Lacine Ct
13 Fairway Ct
14 Harold Ct
15 Spruce Ho
16 Cedar Ho
17 Sycamore Ho
18 Woodland Cres
19 Poplar Ho
20 Adelphi Ct
21 Basque Ct
22 Aberdale Ct
23 Quilting Ct
24 Chargrove Cl
25 Radley Ct
26 Greenacre Sq
27 Maple Leaf Sq
28 Stanhope Cl
29 Hawke Pl
30 Drake Cl
31 Brass Talley Alley
32 Monkton Ho
33 James Ho
34 Wolfe Cres
D5 1 Clarence Mews
2 Raleigh Ct
3 Katherine Cl
4 Woolcombes Ct
5 Tudor Ct
6 Quayside Ct
7 Princes Riverside Rd
8 Surrey Ho
9 Tideway Ct
10 Edinburgh Ct
11 Falkirk Ct
12 Byelands Cl
13 Gwent Ct
14 Lavender Ho
15 Abbotshade Rd
16 Bellamy's Ct
17 Blenheim Ct
18 Sandringham Ct
19 Hampton Ct
20 Windsor Ct
21 Balmoral Ct
22 Westminster Ct
D6 1 Barnardo Gdns
2 Roslin Ho
3 Glamis Est
4 Peabody Est
5 East Block
6 Highway Trad Ctr The
7 Highway Bsns Pk The
8 Cranford Cotts
9 Ratcliffe Orch
10 Scotia Bldg
11 Mauretania Bldg
12 Compania Bldg
13 Sirius Bldg
14 Unicorn Bldg
15 Keepier Wharf

119
A2 1 Trafalgar Cl
2 Hornblower Cl
3 Cunard Wlk
4 Caronia Ct
5 Carinthia Ct
6 Freswick Ho
7 Graveley Ho
8 Husbourne Ho
9 Crofters Ct
10 Pomona Ho
11 Hazelwood Ho
12 Cannon Wharf Bsns Ctr
13 Bence Ho
14 Clement Ho
15 Pendennis Ho
16 Lighter Cl
17 Mast Ct
18 Rushcutters Ct
19 Boat Lifter Way
A6 1 St Georges Sq
2 Drake Ho
3 Osprey Ho
4 Fleet Ho
5 Gainsborough Ho
6 Victory Pl
7 Challenger Ho
8 Conrad Ho
9 Lock View Ct
10 Shoulder of Mutton Alley
11 Frederick Sq
12 Helena Sq
13 Elizabeth Sq
14 Sophia Sq
15 William Sq
16 Lamb Ct
17 Lockside
18 Ionian Bldg
19 Regents Gate Ho
B1 1 Gransden Ho
2 Daubeney Twr
3 North Ho
4 Rochfort Ho
5 Keppel Ho
6 Camden Ho
7 Sanderson Ho
8 Berkeley Ho
9 Strafford Ho
10 Richman Ho
11 Hurleston Ho
12 Grafton Ho
13 Fulcher Ho
14 Citrus Ho
B2 1 Windsock Cl
2 Linberry Wlk
3 Lanyard Ho
4 Golden Hind Pl
5 James Lind Ho
6 Harmon Ho
7 Pelican Ho
8 Bembridge Ho
9 Terrace The
10 George Beard Rd
11 Colonnade The
12 Pepys Ent Ctr

B6 1 Hamilton Ho
2 Imperial Ho
3 Oriana Ho
4 Queens Ct
5 Brightlingsea Pl
6 Faraday Ho
7 Ropemaker's Fields
8 Oast Ct
9 Mitre The
10 Bate St
11 Joseph Irwin Ho
12 Padstow Ho
13 Bethlehem Ho
14 Saunders Cl
15 Roche Ho
16 Stocks Pl
17 Trinidad Ho
18 Grenada Ho
19 Kings Ho
20 Dunbar Wharf
21 Limekiln Wharf
C1 3 Hudson Ct
4 Shackleton Ct
5 Perry Ct
6 Maritime Quay
C2 1 Olympian Ct
2 Aphrodite Ct
3 Mercury Ct
4 Poseidon Ct
5 Neptune Ct
6 Artemis Ct
7 Hera Ct
8 Ares Ct
9 Cyclops Mews
10 Magellan Pl
11 Britannia Rd
12 Deptford Ferry Rd
13 Ironmonger's Pl
14 Radnor Wlk
15 Ashdown Wlk
16 Rothsay Wlk
17 Dartmoor Wlk
18 Ringwood Gdns
19 Dockers Tanner Rd
20 Apollo Bldg
21 Nova Bldg
C3 1 St Hubert's Ho
2 John Tucker Ho
3 Clare Grant Ho
4 Gilberton Ho
5 Bowsprit Point
6 Scoulding Ho
7 Cord Way
8 Cressall Ho
9 Alexander Ho
10 Kedge Ho
C4 1 Jefferson Bldg
2 Waterman Bldg
3 Pierpoint Bldg
4 Franklin Bldg
5 Bellamy Cl
6 Bosun Cl
7 Edison Bldg
8 Vanguard Bldg
C6 1 West India Ho
2 Birchfield Ho
3 Elderfield Ho
4 Thornfield Ho
5 Gorsefield Ho
6 Arborfield Ho
7 Colborne Ho
8 East India Bldgs
9 Compass Point
10 Salter St
11 Kelly Ct
12 Flynn Ct
13 Mary Jones Ho
14 Horizon Bldg
15 Berber Pl
D2 1 Brassey Ho
2 Triton Ho
3 Warspite Ho
4 Rodney Ho
5 Conway Ho
6 Exmouth Ho
7 Akbar Ho
8 Arethusa Ho
9 Tasman Ct
D6 1 Westcott Ho
2 Corry Ho
3 Malam Gdns
4 Devitt Ho
5 Leyland Ho
6 Wigram Ho
7 Willis Ho
8 Balsam Ho
9 Finch's Ct

10 Poplar Bath St
11 Lawless St
12 Storey Ho
13 Abbot Ho
14 Landon Wlk
15 Goodhope Ho
16 Goodfaith Ho
17 Winant Ho
18 Lubbock Ho
19 Goodwill Ho
20 Martindale Ho
21 Holmsdale Ho
22 Norwood Ho
23 Constant Ho
24 Woodall Cl

120
A2 1 Betty May Gray Ho
2 Castleton Ho
3 Urmston Ho
4 Salford Ho
5 Capstan Ho
6 Frigate Ho
7 Galleon Ho
8 Barons Lo
A3 1 Cardale St
2 Hickin St
3 John McDonald Ho
4 Thorne Ho
5 Skeggs Ho
6 St Bernard Ho
7 Kimberley Ho
8 Kingdon Ho
9 Lingard Ho
10 Yarrow Ho
11 Sandpiper Ct
12 Nightingale Ho
13 Robin Ct
14 Heron Ct
A4 1 Llandovery Ho
2 Rugless Ho
3 Ash Ho
4 Elm Ho
5 Cedar Ho
6 Castalia Sq
7 Walkers Lo
7 Antilles Bay
7 Alice Shepherd Ho
8 Oak Ho
9 Ballin Ct
10 Martin Ct
11 Grebe Ct
12 Kingfisher Ct
A6 1 Discovery Ho
2 Mountague Pl
3 Virginia Ho
4 Collins Ho
5 Lawless Ho
6 Carmichael Ho
7 Commodore Ho
8 Mermaid Ho
9 Bullivant St
10 Anderson Ho
11 Mackrow Wlk
12 Robin Hood Gdns
B2 1 Verwood Lo
2 Fawley Lo
3 Lyndhurst Lo
4 Blyth Cl
5 Farnworth Ho
6 Francis Cl
B6 1 Settlers Ct
2 Susan Constant Ct
3 Susan Constant Ct
4 Adventurers Ct
5 Bartholomew Ct
6 Atlantic Ct
7 Cape Henry Ct
8 Wotton Ct
9 Studley Ct
10 Wingfield Ct
C1 1 Bellot Gdns
2 Thornley Pl
3 King William La
4 Bolton Ho
5 Miles Ho
6 Mell St
7 Sam Manners Ho
8 Hatcliffe Almshouses
9 Woodland Wlk
10 Earlswood Cl
D1 1 Baldrey Ho
2 Christie Ho

3 Dyson Ho
4 Cliffe Ho
5 Moore Ho
6 Collins Ho
7 Lockyer Ho
8 Halley Ho
9 Kepler Ho

121
A1 1 Layfield Ho
2 Westerdale Rd
3 Mayston Mews
A5 1 Capulet Mews
2 Pepys Cres
3 De Quincey Mews
4 Hardy Ave
5 Tom Jenkinson Rd
6 Hanameel St
7 Kennacraig Cl
8 Gatcombe Rd
10 Badminton Mews
11 Holyrood Mews
12 Britannia Gate
13 Dalemain Mews
A6 1 Clements Ave
2 Martindale Ave
B1 1 Phipps Ho
2 Hartwell Ho
3 Nicholas Stacey Ho
4 Frank Burton Cl
B5 1 Beaulieu Ave
2 Charles Winchup Rd
3 Audley Dr
3 Julie Garfield Mews
4 Julia Garfield Mews
5 Rayleigh Rd
6 Pirie St
7 Rayleigh Rd
7 Hanameel St
8 Ramsgate St
9 West Mersea Cl
10 Hanameel St
11 Dunlop Point
11 Ramsgate St
12 Westwood Rd
C1 1 Ransom Rd
2 Linton Cl
3 Cedar Pl
4 Gooding Ho
5 Valiant Ho
6 Chaffey Ho
7 Benn Ho
8 Wellesley Cl
9 Gollogly Terr

122
A2 1 Harden Ct
2 Albion Ct
3 Viking Ho
4 Zealand Ho
5 Glenalvon Way
6 Parish Wharf
7 Elsinore Ho
8 Lelland Ho
9 Denmark Ho
10 Jutland Ho
11 Tivoli Gdns
12 Rance Ho
13 Peel Yates Ho
14 Rosebank Wlk
15 Paradise Pl
16 Woodville St
B2 1 Bowling Green Row
2 Sara Turnbull Ho
3 Brewhouse Rd
4 Red Barracks Rd
5 Marine Dr
6 Cambridge Ho
11 Hastings Ho
12 Cambridge Barracks Rd
13 Len Clifton Ho
14 Granby Ho
15 Milne Ho
16 Harding Ho
17 Rendlebury Ho
18 Rutland Ho
19 Townshend Ho
20 Mulgrave Rd
21 Murray Ho

22 Chatham Ho
23 Biddulph Ho
24 Carew Ho
25 Eleanor Wlk
C2 1 Preston Ho
2 Lindsay Ho
3 Fraser Ho
4 Pickering Ho
5 Watergate Ho
6 Grinling Ho
7 Glebe Ho
8 Slater Cl
9 Elliston Ho
10 Queensland Ho
11 Sir Martin Bowes Ho
12 Bathway
13 Limavady Ho
C5 1 Westland Ho
2 Queensland Ho
3 Pier Par
4 Woodman Par
5 Shaw Ho
6 Glen Ho
7 Brocklebank Ho
D1 1 Branham Ho
2 Ford Ho
3 Wilford Ho
4 Parker Ho
5 Stirling Ho
6 Twiss Ho
7 Hewett Ho
D2 1 Beresford Sq
2 Central Ct
3 Walpole Pl
4 Anglesea Ave
5 Troy Ct
6 Ormsby Point
7 Haven Lo
8 Green Lawns
9 Eardley Point
10 Sandham Point
11 Bingham Point

123
A1 1 Glenmount Path
2 Claymill Ho
3 George Akass Ho
B1 1 Bert Reilly Ho
C1 1 Fox Hollow Cl
2 Goldsmid St

124
B5 1 Rowntree Path
2 Macaulay Way
3 Manning Ct
4 Chadwick Ct
5 Simon Ct
B6 1 Beveridge Ct
2 Hammond Way
3 Leonard Robbins Path
4 Lansbury Ct
5 Raymond Postgate Ct
6 Webb Ct
7 Curtis Way
8 Lytton Strachy Path
9 Keynes Ct
10 Marshall Path
11 Cross Ct
12 Octavia Way
13 Passfield Path
14 Mill Ct
15 Besant Ct
C4 1 Binsey Wlk
2 Tilehurst Point
3 Blewbury Ho
4 Coralline Wlk
5 Evenlode Ho
C5 1 Kingsley Ct
2 Wilberforce Ho
3 Shaftesbury Ct
4 Hazlitt Ct
5 Ricardo Path
6 Nassau Path
7 Malthus Path
8 Bright Ct
9 Cobden Ct
D4 1 Oakenholt Ho
2 Trewsbury Ho
3 Penton Ho
4 Osney Ho
5 Jacob Ho
6 Masham Ho
7 St Helens Rd

8 Clewer Ho
9 Maplin Ho
10 Wyfold Ho
11 Hibernia Point
12 Duxford Ho
13 Radley Ho

125
A3 1 Harlequin Ho
2 Dexter Ho
3 Argall Ho
4 Mangold Way
5 Lucerne Ct
6 Holstein Way
7 Abbotswood Cl
8 Plympton Cl
9 Benedict Cl
B1 1 Shakespeare Ho
2 Tennyson Ho
3 Dickens Ho
3 Chestnuts The
4 Scott Ho
5 Lansbury Ho
6 Shaw Ho
C1 1 Stevanne Ct
2 Tolcairn Ct
3 Chalfont Ct
4 Alonso Ct
5 Ariel Ct
6 Miranda Ho
7 Prospero Ho
8 Laurels The
9 Camden Ct
10 Newnham Lo
11 Court Lo
12 Flaxman Ct
13 Hertford Wlk
14 Riverview Ct
C3 1 Cressingham Ct
2 Telford Ho
3 Kelvin Ho
4 Faraday Ho
5 Jenner Ho
6 Keir Hardy Ho
7 Lennox Ho
8 Mary Macarthur Ho
9 Elizabeth Garrett Anderson Ho
10 William Smith Ho
11 Baden Powell Ho
12 Baird Ho
13 Boyle Ho

129
D1 1 Heathwood Ct
2 Aldermead
3 Northumberland Ct

130
C4 1 Osterley Lo
2 St Andrew's Cl
3 Parkfield
4 Fairways
5 Granwood Ct
6 Grovewood Ct

131
A2 1 Brewery Mews Bsns Ctr
2 Tolson Ho
3 Percy Gdns
4 Wynne Ct
5 Wisdom Ct
6 Swann Ct
7 Shrewsbury Wlk
8 King's Terr
9 Gistelword Ho
D5 1 Galba Ct
2 Servius Ct
3 Maurice Ct
4 Leo Ct
5 Otho Ct
6 Nero Ct
7 Romulus Ct
8 Pump Alley
D6 1 Brockshot Cl
2 Westbury Pl
3 Braemar Ct
4 Brook Ct

418 **131 D6**

6 Clifden Ho
7 Cedar Ct
8 Cranbrook Ct
9 Somerset Lo
10 Alexandra Rd
11 Berkeley Ho

132

A1 1 St John's Gr
2 Michel's Row
3 Michelsdale Dr
4 Blue Anchor Alley
5 Clarence St
6 Sun Alley
7 Thames Link Ho
8 Benns Wlk
A6 1 Ferry Sq
3 Wilkes Rd
4 Albany Par
5 Charlton Ho
6 Albany Ho
7 Alma Ho
8 Griffin Ct
9 Cressage Ho
10 Tunstall Wlk
11 Trimmer Wlk
12 Running Horse Yd
13 Mission Sq
14 Distillery Wlk
B1 1 Towers The
2 Longs Ct
3 Sovereign Ct
4 Robinson Ct
5 Calvert Ct
6 Bedford Ct
7 Hickey's Almshouses
8 Church Estate Almshouses
9 Richmond International Bsns Ctr
10 Abercorn Mews
B4 1 Primrose Ho
2 Lawman Ct
3 Royston Ct
4 Garden Ct
5 Capel Lo
6 Devonshire Ct
7 Celia Ct
8 Rosslyn Ho
9 Branstone Ct
10 Lamerton Lo
11 Kew Lo
12 Dunraven Ho
13 Stoneleigh Lo
14 Tunstall Ct
15 Voltaire
C4 1 Clarendon Ct
2 Quintock Ho
3 Broome Ct
4 Lonsdale Mews
5 Elizabeth Cotts
6 Sandways
7 Victoria Cotts
8 North Ave
9 Grovewood
10 Hamilton Ho
11 Melvin Ct
12 Power Ho
13 Station Ave
14 Blake Mews
D1 1 Hershell Ct
2 Deanhill Ct
3 Park Sheen
4 Furness Lo
5 Merricks Ct

133

B2 1 Rann Ho
2 Craven Ho
3 John Dee Ho
4 Kindell Ho
5 Montgomery Ho
6 Avondale Ho
7 Addington Ct
8 Dovecote Gdns
9 Firmston Ho
10 Glendower Gdns
11 Chestnut Ave
12 Trehern Rd
13 Rock Ave
D3 1 Melrose Rd

2 Seaforth Lo
3 St John's Gr
4 Sussex Ct
5 Carmichael Ct
6 Hampshire Ct
7 Thorne Pas
9 Beverley Path

134

D1 1 Olivette St
2 Mascotte Rd
3 Glegg Pl
4 Crown Ct
5 Charlwood Terr
D6 1 Cobb's Hall
2 Dorset Mans
3 St Clements Mans
4 Bothwell St
5 Hawksmoor St

135

B3 1 Plato Pl
2 Mustow Pl
3 Laurel Bank Gdns
4 Ranelagh Mans
5 Churchfield Mans
6 Bear Croft Ho
7 Elysium Gate
8 Ethel Rankin Ct
9 Arthur Henderson Ho
10 William Banfield Ho
D3 1 Brightwells
2 Broughton Road App
3 Bulow Ct
4 Langford Rd
5 Elizabeth Barnes Ct
6 Snowbury Rd

136

A2 1 Molasses Ho
2 Molasses Row
3 Cinnamon Row
4 Calico Ho
5 Calico Row
6 Port Ho
7 Square Rigger Row
8 Trade Twr
9 Ivory Ho
10 Spice Ct
11 Sherwood Ct
12 Mendip Ct
13 Chalmers Ho
14 Coral Row
B1 1 Burke Ho
2 Fox Ho
3 Buxton Ho
4 Pitt Ho
5 Romsey Ho
6 Beverley Cl
7 Florence Ho
8 Linden Ct
9 Dorcas Ct
10 Johnson Ct
11 Agnes Ct
12 Hilltop Ct
13 Courtyard The
14 Old Laundry The
15 Oberstein Rd
16 Fineran Ct
17 Sangora Rd
18 Harvard Mans
B2 1 Benham Cl
2 Milner Ho
3 McManus Ho
4 Wilberforce Ho
5 Wheeler Ct
6 Sporle Ct
7 Holliday Sq
8 John Parker Sq
9 Carmichael Cl
10 Fenner Sq
11 Clark Lawrence Ct
12 Shaw Ct
13 Sendall Ct
14 Livingstone Rd
15 Farrant Ct
16 Jackson Ho
17 Darien Ho

18 Sheppard Ho
19 Ganley Ct
20 Arthur Newton Ho
21 Chesterton Ho
22 John Kirk Ho
23 Mantua St
24 Heaver Rd
B3 1 Archer Ho
2 White Ho
4 Powrie Ho
5 Morgan Ct
6 Fairchild Cl
7 Musjid Rd
C2 1 Kiloh Ct
2 Lanner Ho
3 Grifton Ho
4 Kestrel Ho
5 Kite Ho
6 Peregrine Ho
7 Hawk Ho
8 Inkster Ho
9 Harrier Ho
10 Eagle Hts
11 Kingfisher Ct
12 Lavender Terr
13 Temple Ho
14 Ridley Ho
15 Eden Ho
16 Hertford Ct
17 Nepaul Rd
C3 1 Meecham Ct
2 McKiernan Ct
3 Banbury St
4 Colestown St
5 Crombie Mews
6 Frere St
D3 1 Stevenson Ho
2 Ambrose Mews
4 Harling Ct
4 Southside Quarter
5 Latchmere St
6 Dovedale Cotts
7 Roydon Cl
8 Castlemaine
9 Wittering Ho
10 Berry Ho
11 Weybridge Point

137

A2 1 Shaftesbury Park Chambers
2 Selborne
3 Rush Hill Mews
4 Marmion Mews
5 Crosland Pl
6 Craven Mews
7 Basnett Rd
9 Woodmere Cl
10 Tyneham Cl
A3 1 Hopkinson Ho
2 Macdonald Ho
3 Rushlake Ho
4 Bishopstone Ho
5 Dresden Ho
6 Millgrove St
7 Farnhurst Ho
8 Walden Ho
9 Kennard St
10 Langhurst Ho
11 Kennard Ho
12 Voltaire Ct
13 Barloch Ho
B2 1 Turnchapel Mews
2 Redwood Mews
3 Phil Brown Pl
4 Bev Callender Cl
5 Keith Connor Cl
6 Tessa Sanderson Pl
7 Daley Thompson Way
8 Rashleigh Ct
9 Abberley Mews
10 Willow Lodge
11 Beaufoy Rd
B3 1 St Philip Sq
2 Montefiore St
3 Gambetta St
4 Scott Ct
5 Radcliffe Path
6 Moresby Wlk
C1 1 Polygon The
2 Windsor Ct
3 Trinity Cl
4 Hanscomb Mews
4 Studios The

5 Bourne Ho
C2 1 Clapham Manor Ct
2 Clarke Ho
3 Gables The
4 Sycamore Mews
5 Maritime Ho
7 Floris Pl
C3 1 Seymour Ho
2 Lucas Ho
3 Durrington Twr
4 Amesbury Twr
5 Fovant Ct
6 Allington Ct
7 Welford Ct
8 Ilsley Ct
D1 1 Kendoa Rd
2 Felmersham Cl
3 Abbeville Mews
4 Saxon Ho
5 Gifford Ho
6 Teignmouth Cl
7 Holwood Pl
8 Oaklands Pl
D2 1 Chelsham Ho
2 Lynde Ho
3 Greener Ho
4 Towns Ho
5 Hugh Morgan Ho
6 Roy Ridley Ho
7 Lendal Terr
8 Slievemore Cl
9 Cadmus Cl
D3 1 Haltone Ho
2 Surcot Ho
3 Kingsley Ho
4 Wood Ho
5 Dalemain Ho
6 Fallodon Ho
7 Dartington Ho
8 Esher Ho
9 Kneller Ho
10 Lostock Ho
11 Croxteth Ho
12 Donnington Ho
13 Farnley Ho
14 Hardwick Ho
15 Bradfield Ho
16 Brocket Ho
17 Colchester Ho
18 Clive Ho
19 Chessington Ho
20 Rushbrook Ho
21 Stanmore Ho
22 Newton Ho
23 Netherby Ho
24 Oakwell Ho
25 Rydal Ho
26 Rushton Ho
27 Harcourt Ho
28 Metcalfe Ho
29 Lydwell Ho
30 Raleigh Ho
31 Spencer Ho
32 Shipley Ho
33 Naylor Ho
34 Mordaunt Ho
35 Stanley Ho
36 Alderley Ho
37 Effingham Ho
38 Grant Ho
39 Wilson Ho
40 Fraser Ho

138

A1 1 Morris Ho
2 Gye Ho
3 Clowes Ho
4 Thomas Ho
5 Stuart Ho
6 Storace Ho
7 Bedford Ho
8 Ascot Ct
9 Ascot Par
10 Ashmere Ho
11 Ashmere Gr
12 Vickery Ho
13 Stafford Mans
14 Beresford Ho
A2 1 Callingham Ho
2 Russell Pickering Ho
4 Lopez Ho
5 Coachmaker Mews
A3 1 Barling Ct
2 Jeffrey's Ct
3 Brooks Ct

4 Dalmeny Ct
6 Fender Ct
7 Fishlock Ct
8 Bedser Ct
8 Gover Ct
9 Clarence Wlk
10 Barton Ct
11 Allom Ct
12 Garden Ho
13 Otha Ho
14 Hayward Ct
15 Surridge Ct
16 Knox Ct
17 Jephson Ct
18 Holmes Ct
19 McIntyre Ct
20 Richardson Ct
21 Cassell Ho
22 Packington Ho
23 Bain Ho
24 Enfield Ho
25 Fawcett Ho
26 Sidgwick Ho
27 Jowett Ho
28 Beckett Ho
29 Arden Ho
30 Pinter Ho
31 Barrington Ct
B1 1 Freemens Hos
2 Roger's Almshouses
3 Gresham Almshouses
4 Exbury Ho
5 Glasbury Ho
6 Dalbury Ho
7 Fosbury Ho
8 Chalbury Ho
9 Neilson-Terry Ct
10 Pavilion Mans
11 Daisy Dormer Ct
12 George Lashwood Ct
13 Marie Lloyd Ct
14 Trinity Homes
15 Lethaby Ho
16 Edmundsbury Ct Est
17 Regis Pl
18 Belvedere Pl
19 Alpha Ho
20 Beta Pl
21 Cedars Ho
B2 1 Turberville Ho
2 Thrayle Ho
3 Percheron Ct
4 Draymans Ct
B3 1 Maurice Ho
2 Thring Ho
3 Paton Ho
4 Huxley Ho
5 Morell Ho
6 Mary Ho
7 Beale Ho
8 Rosa Parks Ho
9 Birrell Ho
10 Waltham Ho
11 Burford Ho
12 Thornicroft Ho
13 Addington Ho
14 Goffton Ho
15 Redmayne Ho
16 Norton Ho
17 Aytoun Ct
18 Colwall Ho
19 Burrow Ho
20 Wynter Ho
21 Crowhurst Ho
22 Lidcote Gdns
23 Cumnor Cl
24 Park View Mews
C1 1 Electric Mans
2 Electric La
3 Connaught Mans
4 Clifton Mans
5 Hereford Ho
6 Chaplin Ho
7 Brixton Oval
8 Lord David Pitt Ho
9 Marcus Garvey Way
10 Montgo Cl
11 Bob Marley Way
12 Leeson Rd
C2 1 Buckmaster Cl
2 Albemarle Ho
4 Goodwood Mans
5 Angell Park Gdns

6 Fyfield Rd
7 Howard Ho
8 Harris Ho
9 Broadoak Ct
10 Burgate Ct
11 Witchwood Ho
12 Blacktree Mews
13 Chartham Ct
14 Chilham Ct
15 Northgate Ct
16 Westgate Ct
17 Dover Mans
C3 1 Norval Gn
2 Hilda Terr
4 Church Gn
5 Lord Holland La
6 Sorrell Cl
8 Burton Rd
9 Holles St
10 Leys Ct
11 Warwick Ho
12 Fairfax Ho
13 Wayland Ho
14 Dudley Ho
15 Denchworth Ho
16 Fitzgerald Ho
17 Lambert Ho
18 Chute Ho
19 Bedwell Ho
20 Ferrey Mews
21 Serenaders Rd
C4 1 Hector Ct
2 Jason Ct
3 Creon Ct
4 Hermes St
5 Argos Ct
6 Cadmus Ct
7 Appollo Ct
8 Mercury St
9 County Ho
10 Seasalter Ho
11 Downbarton Ho
12 Garlinge Ho
13 Maria Ho
14 Alvanley Ho
15 Woodchurch Ho
16 Durlock Ho
17 Hallam Ho
18 Whiteness Ho
19 Bromstone Ho
20 Penelope Ho
21 Melbourne Sq
22 Cloisters The
23 Cliffsend Ho
24 Sacketts Ho
25 Hanway Ho
26 Brickworth Ho
27 Redlynch Ho
28 Stodmarsh Ho
29 Kingsgate Ho
30 Chardin Ho
31 Annesley Ho
32 Knowlton Ho
33 Russell Gr
34 Eamann Casey Ho
C5 1 Swift Ho
2 Listowel Cl
3 Deal Wlk
4 Plover Ho
5 Aigburth Mans
6 Glencoe Mans
7 Glenshaw Mans
8 Cleveland Mans
9 Leda Ct
10 Jupiter Ct
11 Juno Ct
12 Healy Ho
13 Ashton Ho
14 Ramsey Ho
15 Annesley Ho
16 Cowley Rd
C6 1 Sherwin Ho
3 Kilner Ho
4 Read Ho
5 Lohmann Ho
6 Hornby Ho
7 Abel Ho
8 Blythe Ho
9 Key Ho
10 Lockwood Ho
11 Alverstone Ho
12 Blades Ho
13 Rothesay Ct
D1 1 Mahatma Ganhi Ind Est
2 Dylan Rd
3 Bessemer Park Ind Est
4 Pablo Neruda Cl

5 Langston Hughes Cl
6 Walt Whitman Cl
7 James Joyes Wlk
8 Alice Walker Cl
9 Louise Bennett Cl
10 Chadacre Ho
11 Burwood Ho
12 Pyrford Ho
13 Wangford Ho
14 Ashford Ho
15 Kenwood Ho
16 Moyne Ho
17 Elveden Ho
19 Carrara Wlk
20 Broughton Dr
21 Tilia Wlk
21 Angela Davis Ind Est
D2 1 Mallams Mews
2 Amberley Ho
3 Harper Ho
4 Leicester Ho
5 Station Ave
6 Wellfit St
7 Loughborough Ct
8 Belinda Rd
9 Higgs Ind Est
D3 1 Langport Ho
2 Iveagh Ho
3 Newark Ho
4 Edgehill Ho
5 Hopton Ho
6 Ashby Ho
7 Nevil Ho
D4 1 Fairbairn Gn
2 Hammelton Gn
3 Foxley Sq
4 Silverburn Ho
5 Butler Ho
6 Dalkeith Ho
7 Turner Cl
8 Bathgate Ho
9 Black Roof Ho
D6 1 Faunce Ho
2 Garbett Ho
3 Harvard Ho
4 Doddington Pl
5 Kean Ho
6 Jephson Ho
7 Cornish Ho
8 Bateman Ho
9 Molesworth Ho
10 Walters Ho
11 Cruden Ho
12 Brawne Ho
13 Prescott Ho
14 Chalmer's Wlk
15 Copley Cl

139

A3 1 Bergen Ho
2 Oslo Ho
3 Viking Ho
4 Jutland Ho
5 Norvic Ho
6 Odin Ho
7 Baltic Ho
8 Nobel Ho
9 Mercia Ho
10 Kenbury Gdns
11 Zealand Ho
12 Elsinore Ho
13 Norse Ho
14 Denmark Mans
15 Dane Ho
16 Canterbury Cl
17 York Cl
18 Kenbury Mans
19 Parade Mans
20 Winterslow Ho
21 Lilford Ho
22 Cutcombe Mans
23 Bartholomew Ho
24 Guildford Ho
25 Boston Ho
26 Hereford Ho
27 Weyhill Ho
28 Lichfield Ho
29 Lansdown Ho
30 Honiton Ho
31 Pinner Ho
32 Baldock Ho
33 Widecombe Ho
34 Nottingham Ho
35 Witham Ho

36 Barnet Ho
37 Empress Mews
A4 1 Bertha
   Neubergh Ho
2 Mornington
   Mews
3 Badsworth Rd
4 Sycamore Ct
5 Elm Tree Ct
6 Samuel Lewis
   Trust Dwellings
7 Valmar Trad Est
8 Keswick Ho
9 Mitcham Ho
A5 1 Boundary Ho
2 Day Ho
3 Burgess Ho
4 Carlyle Ho
5 Myers Ho
6 Thompson's Ave
7 Palgrave Ho
8 Winnington Ho
9 Brantwood Ho
10 Lowell Ho
11 Jessie Duffett
   Ho
12 Otterburn Ho
13 Crossmount Ho
14 Venice Ct
15 Bowyer St
16 Livingstone Ho
17 Gothic Ct
18 Coniston Ho
19 Harlynwood
20 Carey Ct
21 Finley Ct
22 Grainger Ct
23 Hayes Ct
24 Moffat Ho
25 Marinel Ho
26 Hodister Cl
27 Arnot Ho
28 Lamb Ho
29 Kipling Ho
30 Keats Ho
31 Kenyon Ho
32 New Church Rd
33 Sir John Kirk Cl
B1 1 Shaftesbury Ct
2 Mayhew Ct
3 Morris Ct
4 Swinburne Ct
5 Perth Ct
6 Tayside Ct
7 Matlock Ct
8 Hunter Ct
9 Turner Ct
B3 1 Selborne Rd
2 Hascombe Terr
B4 1 Joiners Arms Yd
2 Butterfly Wlk
3 Cuthill Wlk
4 Colonades The
5 Artichoke Mews
6 Peabody Bldgs
7 Brighton Ho
8 Park Ho
9 Peabody Ct
10 Lomond Ho
11 Lamb Ho
12 Kimpton Ct
13 Belham Wlk
14 Datchelor Pl
15 Harvey Rd
B5 1 Masterman Ho
2 Milton Ho
3 Pope Ho
4 Chester Ct
5 Marvel Ho
6 Flecker Ho
7 Landor Ho
8 Evelina Mans
9 Habington Ho
10 Langland Ho
11 Drinkwater Ho
12 Procter Ho
13 Shirley Ho
14 Drayton Ho
15 Bridges Ho
16 Cunningham Ho
17 Hood Ho
18 Herrick Ho
19 Dekker Ho
20 Sansom St
20 Houseman Way
21 Coleby Path
22 Jago Wlk
B6 1 Queens Ho
2 Arnside Ho
3 Horsley St

4 St Peter's Ho
5 St Johns Ho
6 St Marks Ho
7 St Stephens Ho
8 St Matthew's Ho
9 Red Lion Cl
10 Boyson Rd
11 Bradenham
C2 1 Harfield Gdns
2 Karen Ct
3 Seavington Ho
4 Appleshaw Ho
5 Birdsall Ho
6 Whitney Ho
7 Wheatland Ho
8 Wilton Ho
9 Walcot Ho
10 Whadden Ho
11 Melbrook Ho
12 Ledbury Ho
13 Tidworth Ho
14 Riseholme Ho
15 Ringmer Ho
16 Petworth Ho
17 Stagshaw Ho
18 Ivybridge Ho
19 Inwood Ho
20 Gatcombe Ho
21 Gatebeck Ho
22 Felbridge Ho
23 Cowdray Ho
C3 1 Springfield Ho
2 Craston Ho
3 Walters Ho
4 Edgecombe Ho
5 Fowler Ho
6 Rignold Ho
7 Chatham Ho
C4 1 Barnwell Ho
2 Brunswick Villas
3 St Giles Twr
4 Bentley Ho
5 Dawson Ho
6 Dryden Ho
7 Mayward Ho
8 Longleigh Ho
9 Fairwall Ho
10 Bodeney Ho
11 Sandby Ho
12 Vestry Mews
13 Netley
14 Lakanal
15 Racine
C5 1 Tower Mill Rd
2 Tilson Cl
3 Dorton Cl
4 Granville Sq
5 Tower Mill Rd
10 Farnborough
   Way
13 Hordle Prom W
15 Samuel Jones
   Ind Est
16 Dibden Ho
17 Marchwood Cl
18 Pilgrims
   Cloisters
19 Beacon Ho
20 Teather St
21 Stacy Path
22 Rumball Ho
23 Ballow Cl
24 Rill Ho
C6 3 Pearse St
4 Watling St
5 Gandolfi st
6 Andoversford Ct
8 Downend Ct
D1 1 Dulwich Mews
2 St James's
   Cloisters
D4 1 Colbert
2 Voltaire
3 Finch Mews
4 Charles Coveney
   Rd
5 Crane St
6 Curlew Ho
7 Mallard Ho
8 Tern Ho
9 Crane Ho
10 Falcon Ho
11 Bryanston Ho
12 Basing Ct
13 Marcus Ho
14 Sheffield Ho
D5 2 Whistler Mews
1 Painswick Ct
3 Sharpness Ct
3 Hordle Prom N
4 Mattingly Way

5 Calypso Cres
6 Samuel St
7 Hordle Prom S
8 Cinnamon Cl
9 Savannah Cl
10 Thames Ct
11 Amstel Ct
12 Danube Ct
13 Tilbury Cl
14 Hordle Prom E
15 Indus Ct
16 Oakcourt
17 Palm Ct
18 Rowan Ct
19 Blackthorn Ct
20 Pear Ct
21 Lidgate Rd
D6 1 Willsbridge Ct
2 Cam Ct
3 Quedgeley Ct
4 Saul Ct
5 Quenington Ct
6 Westonbirt Ct
7 Wickway Ct

140
A3 1 William Margrie
   Cl
2 Choumert Sq
3 Parkstone Rd
4 Atwell Rd
A4 2 Angelina Ho
3 Jarvis Ho
4 Richland Ho
5 Honeywood Ho
6 Wakefield Ho
7 Primrose Ho
8 Hardcastle Ho
9 Dunstall Ho
10 Purdon Ho
11 Flamborough Ho
12 Lambrook Ho
13 Witcombe Point
14 Yarnfield Sq
15 Winford Ct
16 Portbury Cl
17 Robert Keen Cl
A5 1 Thornbill Ho
2 Vervain Ho
3 Woodstar Ho
4 Tamarind Ho
5 Hereford Retreat
6 Haymerle Ho
7 Furley Ho
8 Applegarth Ho
9 Freda Corbett Cl
10 Rudbeck Ho
11 Henslow Ho
12 Lindley Ho
13 Collinson Ho
14 Sister Mabel's
   Way
15 Timberland Cl
16 Hastings Cl
17 Neville Cl
18 Sidmouth Ho
19 Budleigh Ho
20 Stanesgate Ho
21 Braemore Ho
22 Ely Ho
A6 1 Bowles Rd
2 Western Wharf
3 Northfield Ho
4 Millbrook Ho
5 Denstone Ho
6 Deerhurst Ho
7 Caversham Ho
8 Battle Ho
9 Cardiff Ho
10 Bridgnorth Ho
11 Exeter Ho
12 Grantham Ho
13 Aylesbury Ho
14 Royston Ho
B2 1 Tilling Ho
2 Goodwin Ho
3 Citron Terr
4 Cheam St
B3 1 Walkynscroft
2 Ryegates
3 Hathorne Cl
4 Pilkington Rd
5 Russell Ct
6 Heaton Ho
7 Magdalene Cl
B4 1 Willowdene
2 Pinedene
3 Oakdene
4 Beechdene

5 Hollydene
6 Wood Dene
8 Staveley Cl
9 Carnicot Ho
10 Martock Ct
11 Kendrick Ct
B5 1 Tortington Ho
2 Credenhill Ho
3 Bromyard Ho
4 Hoyland Cl
5 Willowdene
6 Ashdene
7 Acorn Par
8 Carlton Gr
9 Springall St
10 Harry Lambourn
   Ho
C3 1 Honiton Gdns
2 Selden Ho
3 Hathway Ho
4 Hathway St
5 Station Ct
C5 1 Ambleside Point
2 Grasmere Point
3 Windermere
   Point
4 Roman Way
5 Laburnham Cl
6 Romney Cl
7 Hammersley Ho
8 Hutchinson Ho
9 Hammond Ho
10 Fir Tree Ho
11 Glastonbury Ct
12 Highbridge Ct
13 Filton Ct
14 Chiltern Ct
15 Cheviot Ho
C6 1 Penshurst Ho
2 Reculver Ho
3 Mereworth Ho
4 Camber Ho
5 Chilam Ho
6 Otford Ho
7 Olive Tree Ho
8 Aspen Ho
9 Lewis Silkin Ho
10 Richborough Ho
11 Dover Ho
12 Eynsford Ho
13 Horton Ho
14 Lamberhurst Ho
15 Canterbury Ind
   Pk
16 Upnall Ho
17 Sissinghurst Ho
18 Rochester Ho
19 Leybourne Ho
20 Lullingstone Ho
D1 1 Laxton Path
2 Barlings Ho
3 Bayfield Ho
4 Coston Wlk
5 Coverham Ho
6 Gateley Ho
7 Dereham Ho
8 Greenwood Ho
9 Hilton Ho
10 Goodall Ho
11 Horsley Ho
12 Jordan Ho
D5 1 Richard
   Anderson Ct
2 Palm Tree Ho
3 Edward
   Robinson Ho
4 Antony Ho
5 Gerrard Ho
6 Palmer Ho
7 Pankhurst Cl
D6 1 Harrisons Ct
2 Grantley Ho
3 Sunbury Ct
4 Tilbury Ho
5 Graham Ct
6 Connell Ct
7 St Clements Ct
8 Henderson Ct
9 Jemotts Ct
10 Verona Ct
11 Heywood Ho
12 Francis Ct
13 Hind Ho
14 Donne Ho
15 Carew Ct
16 Burbage Ho
17 Newland Ho
18 Dobson Ho
19 Dalton Ho
20 Greene Ct

21 Redrup Ho
22 Tarplett Ho
23 Stunnell Ho
24 Gasson Ho
25 Bryce Ho
26 Barnes Ho
27 Barkwith Ho
28 Bannister Ho
29 Apollo Ind Bsns
   Ctr

141
A5 1 Batavia Ho
2 Marlowe Bsns
   Ctr
3 Batavia Mews
4 Woodrush Cl
5 Alexandra St
6 Primrose Wlk
7 Vansittart St
8 Granville Ct
9 Cottesbrook St
A6 1 Portland Ho
2 Phoenix Ct
3 Rainbow Ct
4 Hawke Twr
6 Woodpecker Rd
B5 1 Austin Ho
2 Exeter Way
3 Crossleigh Ct
4 Mornington Pl
5 Maple Ho
B6 1 Chester Ho
2 Lynch Wlk
3 Arlington Ho
4 Woodcote Ho
5 Cornbury Ho
6 Prospect Pl
7 Akintaro Ho
8 Mulberry Ho
9 Laurel Ho
10 Linden Ho
11 Ashford Ho
12 Wardalls Ho
13 Magnolia Ho
14 Howard Ho
15 Larch Cl
16 Ibis Ct
17 Merganser Ct
18 Wotton Rd
19 Kingfisher Sq
20 Sanderling Ct
21 Dolphin Twr
22 Mermaid Twr
23 Scoter Ct
24 Shearwater Ct
25 Brambling Ct
26 Kittiwake Ct
27 Guillemot Ct
28 Marine Twr
29 Teal Ct
30 Lapwing Twr
31 Cormorant Ct
34 Shelduck Ct
36 Eider Ct
39 Pintail Ct
40 Tristan Ct
41 Skua Ct
42 Rosemary Ct
43 Violet Cl
44 Diana Cl
45 Admiralty Cl
C4 1 Harton Lo
2 Sylvia Cotts
3 Pitman Ho
4 Heston Ho
5 Sandpiper Ct
C5 1 Flamingo Ct
2 Titan Bsns Est
3 Rochdale Way
4 Speedwell St
5 Reginald Pl
6 Fletcher Path
7 Frankham Ho
8 Cremer Ho
9 Wilshaw Ho
10 Castell Ho
11 Holden Ho
12 Browne Ho
13 Lady Florence
   Ctyd
14 Covell Ct
C6 1 Dryfield Wlk
2 Blake Ho
3 Hawkins Ho
4 Grenville Ho
5 Langford Ho
6 Mandarin Ct
7 Bittern Ct

9 Lamerton St
10 Armada St
11 Armada St
12 Benbow Ho
13 Oxenham Ho
14 Caravel Mews
15 Hughes Ho
16 Stretton Mans
D5 1 Finch Ho
2 Jubilee The
3 Gordon Ho
4 Haddington Ct
5 Maitland Cl
6 Ashburnham
   Retreat

142
A3 1 Ellison Ho
2 Pitmaston Ho
3 Windmill Cl
4 Hertmitage The
5 Burnett Ho
6 Lacey Ho
A4 1 Penn Almshouse
2 Jarvis Ct
3 Woodville Ct
4 Darnell Ho
5 Renbold Ho
6 Lindsell St
7 Plumbridge St
8 Trinity Gr
9 Hollymount Cl
10 Cade Tyler Ho
11 Robertson Ho
A5 1 Temair Ho
2 Glaisher St
3 Prince of
   Orange La
4 Lombard Ho
5 St Marks Cl
6 Ada Kennedy Ct
7 Arlington Pl
8 Topham Ho
9 Darnell Ho
10 Hawks Mews
11 Royal Pl
12 Swanne Ho
13 Maribor
14 Serica Ct
15 Queen Elizabeth
   College
A6 1 Greenwich Mkt
2 Turnpin La
3 Durnford St
4 Sexton's Ho
5 Bardsley Ho
6 Wardell Ho
7 Clavell St
8 Stanton Ho
9 Macey Ho
10 Boreman Ho
B6 1 Frobisher Ct
2 Hardy Cotts
3 Palliser Ho
4 Bernard Angell
   Ho
5 Corvette Sq
6 Travers Ho
7 Reade Ho
8 Maze Hill Lo
D5 1 Westcombe Ct
2 Kleffens Ct
3 Ferndale Ct
4 Combe Mews
5 Mandeville Cl
6 Heathway
7 Pinelands Cl

143
A5 1 Mary Lawrenson
   Pl
2 Bradbury Ct
3 Dunstable Ct
A6 1 Nethercombe Ho
2 Holywell Cl
C6 1 Warren Wlk
2 Wilson Ho
3 Priory Ho
4 Mar Ho
5 Langhorne Ho
6 Games Ho
7 Erskine Ho
8 Ducie Ho
9 Downe Ho
10 Bayeux Ho
11 Elliscombe
   Mount

147 C1 419

12 Harold Gibbons
   Ct
13 Mascalls Ct
14 Leila Parnell Pl
15 East Mascalls
16 Birch Tree Ho
17 Cherry Tree Ct
18 Elm Tree Ct
19 Cedar Ct
D5 1 Winchester Ho
2 Brentwood Ho
3 Shenfield Ho
4 Chesterford Ho

144
A4 1 Master Gunner's
   Pl
2 Nicholson Ho
3 Borgard Ho
4 Macleod Ho
5 Brome Ho
6 Ross Ho
7 Horne Ho
8 Pendlebury Gn
9 Dickson Ho
10 Roberts Ho
A5 1 Leyburn Ho
2 Greenwich Hts
3 Gardiner Ho
B4 1 Galton Ho
2 Florence Ho
3 Sidney Ho
4 Robertson Ho
5 Mennie Ho
6 Godwin Ho
7 Panbro Ho
8 Sutherland Ho
C6 1 Lawson Ho
2 Mabbett Ho
3 Petrie Ho
4 Memess Path
5 Ruegg Ho
6 Nile Path
7 Leslie Smith Sq
8 Spearman St
9 Siedle Ho
10 Watling Ho
11 O'Neill Path
12 Old Clem Sq
13 Jefferson Wlk
14 Millward Wlk
15 Wordsworth Ho
16 Fenwick Cl
D6 1 Acworth Ho
2 Griffiths Ho
3 Squires Ho
4 Cowen Ho
5 Turton Ho
6 Alford Ho
7 Boxshall Ho
8 Macallister Ho
9 Marvin Ho
10 Kelham Ho
11 Kimber Ho
12 Maxwell Ho
13 Woodford Ho
14 Penfold Ho

146
A2 1 Wellingfield Ct
2 Woodville Gr
3 Midwinter Cl
4 St Leonards Cl

147
A1 1 Woburn Ct
2 Arundel Ct
3 Longleat Villas
4 Upton Villas
B6 1 Bevercote Wlk
2 Boevey Path
3 Lullingstone
   Rd
4 Benjamin Ct
5 Charton Cl
6 Terence Ct
7 Renshaw Cl
8 Grove Rd
C1 1 Friswell Pl
2 Market Pl
3 Geddes Pl
4 Janet Ct
5 Broadway
   Shopping Ctr

420 **147 C1**

6 Mall The
7 Norwich Pl
8 Pincott Rd

148

A5 1 Stranraer Way
2 Deri Dene Cl
3 Lord Knyvetts Ct
4 Tudor Ct
5 Wessex Ct
6 Vanguard Ho
7 Shackleton Ct
8 Fleetwood Ct
9 Clifton Ct
10 Vickers Ct
11 Bristol Ct
12 Sunderland Ct

153

A3 1 Katharine Rd
2 Garfield Rd
4 Flood La
5 John Wesley Ct
6 King Street Par
7 Thames Eyot
A4 1 Perryn Ct
2 Ivybridge Cl
3 Brook Ho
4 Latham Cl
5 March Rd
6 Berkley Ct
7 Cole Court Lo
8 Cheltenham Ave
9 Railway App
A5 1 Greenways The
2 Cole Park View
B4 1 Melton Ct
2 Amyand Park
Gdns
3 Crown Ct
4 Burrell Ho
5 Owen Ho
6 Brentford Ho
7 Leeson Ho
8 Westbourne Ho
9 Orleans Ct
10 Lebanon Ct
B5 1 Grove The
2 Cumberland Cl
3 Westmorland Cl
4 Sussex Cl
5 Norfolk Cl
6 Nicol Cl
7 Old Lodge Pl
8 Kelvin Ct
9 St Margaret's Ct
10 Park Cotts
11 St Margarets
Bsns Ctr
12 Amyand Cotts
C5 1 Howmic Ct
2 Sefton Lo
3 Ravensbourne
4 Arlington Ct
5 Georgina Ct
6 Trevelyan Ho
7 Caradon Ct
8 Green Hedges
9 Old House Gdns
10 Queens Keep
11 Beresford Ct
12 Langham Ct
13 Poplar Ct
D5 1 Richmond
Bridge Mans
2 Heatherdene
Mans
3 Kenton Ct
4 Arosa Rd
5 Darling Ho
6 Turner Ho
7 Blanchard Ho
8 Ashe Ho
9 Bevan Ct
10 Lawley Ho
11 Leicester Ct
12 Roseleigh Cl
13 Beaulieu Cl
14 Richmond Mans
15 Mallard Ct
D6 1 Garrick Cl
2 Old Palace Yd
3 Wardrobe The
4 Maids of Honour
Row

5 Hunters Ct
6 Queensberry Ho
7 Green The
8 Old Palace Terr
9 Paved Ct
10 Golden Ct
11 Brewers La
12 Square The
13 Lower George St
14 St James's Cotts
15 Church Wlk
16 Victoria Pl
17 Castle Yd
18 Lewis Rd
19 Wakefield Rd
20 Church Terr
21 Warrington Rd
22 Ormond Ave
23 St Helena Terr
24 Whittaker Pl
25 Heron Sq
26 Northumberland
Pl
27 Church Ct
28 Holbrooke Pl

154

A5 1 Lancaster Cotts
2 Lancaster Mews
3 Bromwich Ho
4 Priors Lo
5 Richmond Hill Ct
6 Glenmore Ho
7 Hillbrow
8 Heathshot
9 Friars Stile Pl
10 Spire Ct
11 Ridgeway
12 Matthias Ct
A6 1 Lichfield Terr
2 Union Ct
3 Carrington Lo
4 Wilton Ct
5 Egerton Ct
6 Beverley Lo
7 Bishop Duppa's
Almshouses
8 Regency Wlk
9 Clearwater Ho
10 Onslow Avenue
Mans
11 Michels
Almshouses
12 Albany Pas
13 Salcombe Villas
B5 1 Chester Cl
2 Evesham Ct
3 Queen's Ct
4 Russell Wlk
5 Charlotte Sq
6 Jones Wlk
7 Hilditch Ho
8 Isabella Ct
9 Damer Ho
10 Eliot Ho
11 Fitzherbert Ho
12 Reynolds Pl
13 Chisholm Rd
B6 1 Alberta Ct
2 Beatrice Rd
3 Lorne Rd
4 York Rd
5 Connaught Rd
6 Albany Terr
7 Kingswood Ct
8 Selwyn Ct
9 Broadhurst Cl

155

D5 1 Allenford Ho
2 Swaythling Ho
3 Tatchbury Ho
4 Penwood Ho
5 Bramley Ho
6 Shalden Ho
7 Dunbridge Ho
8 Denmead Ho
9 Charcot Ho
10 Portswood Pl
11 Brockbridge Ho
12 Hurstbourne Ho

156

A3 1 Farnborough Ho
2 Rushmere Ho
3 Horndean Cl
4 Highcross Way

5 Timsbury Wlk
6 Foxcombe Rd
7 Ryefield Path
8 Greatham Wlk
9 Gosport Ho
10 Stoatley Ho
11 Milland Ho
12 Clanfield Ho
13 Fareham Ho
14 Grayswood Point
A4 1 Woodcott Ho
2 Lyndhurst Ho
3 Wheatley Ho
4 Allbrook Ho
5 Bordon Wlk
6 Chilcombe Ho
7 Vicarage Ct
8 Shawford Ct
9 Eastleigh Wlk
10 Kings Ct
A6 1 Theodore Ho
2 Nicholas Ho
3 Bonner Ho
4 Downing Ho
5 Johsen Ho
6 Fairfax Ho
7 Devereux Ho
8 David Ho
9 Leigh Ho
10 Clipstone Ho
11 Mallet Ho
12 Arton Wilson Ho
B3 1 Ramsdean Ho
2 Purbrook Ho
3 Portsea Ho
4 Blendworth
Point
5 Eashing Point
6 Hindhead Point
7 Hilsea Point
8 Witley Point
9 Buriton Ho
10 Grately Ho
11 Hascombe Ho
12 Dunhill Point
13 Westmark Point
14 Longmoor Point
15 Cadnam Point
C4 1 Cumberland Ho
2 Devonshire Ho
3 Cornwall Ho
4 Norfolk Ho
5 Leicester Ho
6 Warwick Ho
7 Sutherland Ho
8 Carmarthen Ho
9 Worcester Ho
10 Rutland Ho
C6 1 Inglis Ho
2 Ducie Ho
3 Warncliffe Ho
4 Stanhope Ho
5 Waldegrave Ho
6 Mildmay Ho
7 Mullens Ho
D3 1 Sandringham Cl
2 Eastwick Ct
3 Oatlands Ct
4 Banning Ho
5 Grantley Ho
6 Caryl Ho
7 Duncombe Ho
8 Chilworth Ct
9 Kent Lo
10 Turner Lo
11 Marlborough
12 Parkland Gdns
13 Lewesdon Cl
14 Pines Ct
15 Ashtead Ct
16 Mynterne Ct
17 Arden
18 Stephen Ct
19 Marsham Ct
20 Doradus Ct
21 Acorns The
22 Heritage Ho
23 Conifer Ct
24 Spencer Ho
25 Chartwell
26 Blenheim
27 Chivelston
28 Greenfield Ho
29 Oakman Ho
30 Radley Lo
31 Simon Lo
32 Admirals Ct
D4 1 Brett Ho
2 Brett House Cl
3 Sylva Ct

4 Ross Ct
5 Potterne Cl
6 Stourhead Cl
7 Fleur Gates
8 Greenwood
D5 1 Balmoral Cl
2 Glenalmond Ho
3 Selwyn Ho
4 Keble Ho
5 Bede Ho
6 Gonville Ho
7 Magdalene Ho
8 Armstrong Ho
9 Newnham Ho
10 Somerville Ho
11 Balliol Ho
12 Windermere
13 Little Combe Cl
14 Classinghall Ho
15 Chalford Ho
16 Garden Royal
17 South Ct
18 Anne Kerr Ct
19 Ewhurst
D6 1 Geneva Ct
2 Laurel Ct
3 Cambalt Ho
4 Langham Ct
5 Lower Pk
6 King's Keep
7 Whitnell Ct
8 Whitehead Ho
9 Halford Ho
10 Humphry Ho
11 Jellicoe Ho

157

A3 1 William Harvey
Ho
2 Highview Ct
3 Cameron Ct
4 Galgate Cl
5 Green Ho The
6 King Charles
Wlk
7 Florys Ct
8 Augustus Ct
9 Albert Ct
10 Hertford Lo
11 Mortimer Lo
12 Allenswood
13 Ambleside
A6 1 Claremont
2 Downside
3 Cavendish Cl
4 Ashcombe Ct
5 Carltons The
6 Draldo Ho
7 Millbrooke Ct
8 Coysh Ct
9 Keswick Hts
10 Lincoln Ho
11 Avon Ct
B6 1 Burlington
Mews
2 Cumbria Ho
3 St Stephen's
Gdns
4 Atlantic Ho
5 Burton Lo
6 Manfred Ct
7 Meadow Bank
8 Hooper Ho
C6 1 Pembridge Pl
2 Adelaide Rd
3 London Ct
4 Windsor Ct
5 Westminster Ct
6 Fullers Ho
7 Bridge Pk
8 Lambeth Ct
9 Milton Ct
10 Norfolk Mans
11 Francis Snary Lo
12 Bush Cotts
13 Downbury Mews
14 Newton's Yd
D6 1 Fairfield Ct
2 Blackmore Ho
3 Lancaster Mews
4 Cricketers Mews

159

A2 1 Upper Tooting
Park Mans
2 Cecil Mans
3 Marius Mans
4 Boulevard The

5 Elmfield Mans
6 Holdernesse Rd
A3 1 Heslop Ct
2 St James's Terr
3 Boundaries
Mans
4 Station Par
5 Old Dairy Mews
A4 1 Hollies Way
2 Endsleigh Ct
A5 1 Rayne Ho
2 St Anthony's Ct
3 Earlsthorpe
Mews
B3 1 Holbeach Mews
2 Hildreth Street
Mews
3 Coalbrook Mans
4 Hub Buildings
The
B4 1 Meyer Ho
2 Faraday Ho
3 Hales Ho
4 Frankland Ho
5 Graham Ho
6 Gibbs Ho
7 Anslie Wlk
8 Rokeby Ho
9 Caister Ho
10 Ivanhoe Ho
11 Catherine Baird
Ct
12 Marmion Ho
13 Devonshire Ho
C4 1 Limerick Ct
2 Homewoods
3 Jewell Ho
4 Glanville Ho
5 Dan Bryant Ho
6 Olding Ho
7 Quennel Ho
8 Weir Ho
9 West Ho
10 Neville Ct
C5 1 Joseph Powell
Cl
2 Cavendish Mans
3 Westlands Terr
4 Cubitt Ho
5 Hawkesworth Ho
6 Normanton Ho
7 Eastman Ho
8 Couchman Ho
9 Poynders Ct
10 Selby Ho
11 Valentine Ho
12 Gorham Ho
13 Deauville Mans
14 Deauville Ct
C6 1 Timothy Cl
2 Shaftsbury
Mews
3 Brook Ho
4 Grover Ho
5 Westbrook Ho
6 Hewer Ho
7 Batten Ho
8 Mandeville Ho
9 George Beare Lo
D3 1 Sinclair Ho
2 MacGregor Ho
3 Ingle Ho
4 St Andrews
Mews
D4 1 Riley Ho
2 Bennett Ho
3 White Ho
4 Rodgers Ho
5 Dumphreys Ho
6 Homan Ho
7 Prendergast Ho
8 Hutchins Ho
9 Whiteley Ho
10 Tresidder Ho
11 Primrose Ct
12 Angus Ho
13 Currie Ho
D5 1 Parrington Ho
2 Savill Ho
3 Blackwell Ho
4 Bruce Ho
5 Victoria Ct
6 Victoria Ho
7 Belvedere Ct
8 Ingram Lo
9 Viney Ct
10 Bloomsbury Ho
11 Belgravia Ho
12 Barnsbury Ho

160

A1 1 De Montfort Par
2 Leigham Hall
Par
3 Leigham Hall
4 Endsleigh Mans
5 John Kirk Ho
6 Raeburn Ct
7 Wavel Ct
8 Homeleigh Ct
9 Howland Ho
10 Beauclerk Ho
11 Bertrand Ho
12 Drew Ho
13 Dowes Ho
14 Dunton Ho
15 Raynald Ho
16 Sackville Ho
17 Thurlow Ho
18 Astoria Mans
A2 1 Wyatt Park Mans
2 Broadlands
Mans
3 Stonehill's Mans
4 Streatleigh Par
5 Dorchester Ct
A3 1 Beaumont Ho
2 Christchurch Ho
3 Staplefield Cl
4 Chipstead Ho
5 Coulsdon Ho
6 Conway Ho
7 Telford Avenue
Mans
8 Telford Parade
Mans
9 Wavertree Ct
10 Hartswood Ho
11 Wray Ho
A4 1 Picton Ho
2 Rigg Ho
3 Watson Ho
4 MacArthur Ho
5 Sandon Ho
6 Thorold Ho
7 Pearce Ho
8 Mudie Ho
9 Miller Ho
10 Lycett Ho
11 Lafone Ho
12 Lucraft Ho
13 Freeman Ho
14 New Park Par
15 Argyll Ct
16 Dumbarton Ct
17 Kintyre Ct
18 Cotton Ho
19 Crossman Hos
20 Cameford Ct
21 Parsons Ho
22 Brindley Ho
23 Arkwright Ho
24 Perry Ho
25 Brunel Ho
26 New Park Ct
27 Tanhurst Ho
A6 1 King's Mews
2 Clapham Court
Terr
3 Clapham Ct
4 Clapham Park
Terr
5 Queenswood Ct
6 Oak Tree Ct
7 Park Lofts
B1 1 Carisbrook Ct
2 Pembrook Lo
3 Willow Ct
4 Poplar Ct
5 Mountview
6 Spa View
B3 1 Charlwood Ho
2 Earlswood Ho
3 Balcombe Ho
4 Claremont Cl
5 Holbrook Ho
6 Gwynne Ho
7 Kynaston Ho
8 Tillman Ho
9 Regent Lo
10 Hazelmere Ct
11 Dykes Ct
B4 1 Archbishop's Pl
2 Witley Ho
3 Outwood Ho
4 Dunsfold Ho
5 Deepdene Lo
6 Warnham Ho
7 Albury Lo

8 Tilford Ho
9 Elstead Ho
10 Thursley Ho
11 Brockham Ho
12 Capel Lo
13 Leith Ho
14 Fairview Ho
15 Weymouth Ct
16 Ascalon Ct
17 China Mews
18 Rush Common
Mews
B6 1 Beatrice Ho
2 Florence Ho
3 Evelyn Ho
4 Diana Ho
5 Brixton Hill Ct
6 Austin Ho
7 Manor Ct
8 Camsey Ho
9 Romer Ho
10 Gale Ho
11 Byrne Ho
12 Farnfield Ho
13 Marchant Ho
14 Rainsford Ho
15 Springett Ho
16 Mannering Ho
17 Waldron Ho
C3 1 Valens Ho
2 Loveday Ho
3 Strode Ho
4 Ethelworth Ct
5 Harbin Ho
6 Brooks Ho
7 Godolphin Ho
8 Sheppard Ho
9 McCormick Ho
10 Taylor Ho
11 Saunders Ho
12 Talcott Path
13 Derrick Ho
14 Williams Ho
15 Baldwin Ho
16 Berkeley Ct
17 Churston Cl
18 Neil Wates Cres
19 Burnell Ho
20 Portland Ho
C4 1 Ellacombe Ho
2 Booth Ho
3 Hathersley Ho
4 Brereton Ho
5 Holdsworth Ho
6 Dearmer Ho
7 Cherry Cl
8 Greenleaf Cl
9 Longford Wlk
10 Scarlette Manor
Wlk
11 Chandlers Way
12 Upgrove Manor
Way
13 Ropers Wlk
14 Tebbs Ho
15 Bell Ho
16 Worthington Ho
17 Courier Ho
18 Mackie Rd
19 Hamers Ho
20 Kelyway Ho
21 Harriet Tubman
Cl
22 Estoria Cl
23 Leckhampton Pl
24 Scotia Rd
25 Charles Haller St
26 Sidmouth Ho
27 Hunter Ct
28 Onslow Lo
29 William Winter
Ct
30 Langthorne Lo
C5 1 Eccleston Ho
2 Scarsbrook Ho
3 Purser Ho
4 Rudhall Ho
5 Hardham Ho
6 Heywood Ho
7 Haworth Ho
8 Birch Ho
9 Lonsdell Ho
10 Lomley Ho
11 Laughton Ho
12 Bascome St
13 Dudley Mews
14 Herbert Mews
15 Blades Lo
16 Dick Shepherd
Ct

18 Charman Ho
19 Morden Ho
20 Bishop Ct
21 Blackburn Ct
22 Leigh Ct
23 John Conwey Ho
C6 1 Crownstone Ct
2 Brockwell Ct
3 Nevena Ct
4 St George's Residences
5 Hanover Mans
6 Fleet Ho
7 Langbourne Ho
8 Turnmill Ho
10 Cossar Mews
11 Carter Ho
D1 1 Thanet Ho
2 Chapman Ho
3 Beaufoy Ho
4 Easton Ho
5 Roberts Ho
6 Lloyd Ct
7 Kershaw Ho
8 Wakeling Ho
9 Edridge Ho
10 Jeston Ho
11 Lansdowne Wood Cl

161
B2 1 Coppedhall
2 Shackleton Ct
3 Bullfinch Ct
4 Gannet Ct
5 Fulmar Ct
6 Heron Ct
7 Petrel Ct
8 Falcon Ct
9 Eagle Ct
10 Dunnock Ct
11 Dunlin Ct
12 Cormorant Ct
C6 1 Velde Way
2 Delft Way
3 Arnhem Way
4 Isel Way
5 Kempis Way
6 Terborah Way
7 Steen Way
8 Deventer Cres
9 Nimegen Way
10 Hilversum Cres
11 St Barnabas Cl

162
A1 1 Tunbridge Ct
2 Harrogate Ct
3 Bath Ct
4 Leamington Ct
5 Porlock Ho
6 Cissbury Ho
7 Eddisbury Ho
8 Dundry Ho
9 Silbury Ho
10 Homildon Ho
11 Highgate Ho
12 Richmond Ho
13 Pendle Ho
14 Tynwald Ho
15 Wirrall Ho
16 Greyfriars
A6 1 Dorothy Charrington Ho
2 Keswick Ct
3 Kendall Ct
4 Halliwell Ct
B1 1 River Ho
2 Fordington Ho
3 Arbury Terr
4 Woodbury Ho
5 Gainsborough Mews
6 Forest Hill Ct
B2 1 Bromleigh Ct
2 Parfew Ct
3 Thetford Ct
4 Attleborough Ct
5 Dunton Ct
6 Frobisher Ct
7 Julian Taylor Path
8 Grizedale Terr
9 Worsley Ho
C1 1 Forest Lo
2 Sydenham Park Mans

3 William Wood Ho
C2 1 Fitzwilliam Hts
2 Taymount Grange
3 McLeod Ho
4 Featherstone Ave
5 Kingswear Ho
6 Salcombe Ho
C3 1 Harlech Ct
2 Angela Ct
3 Westwood Ct
4 New Belmont Ho
5 Pearcefield Ave
6 Waldram Pl
7 Horniman Grange
8 South View Ct
9 Heron Ct
10 Katherine Ct
D1 1 Standlake Point
2 Radcot Point
3 Newbridge Point
4 Northmoor
5 Kelmscott
6 Radnor Ct
7 Heathwood Point
8 Ashleigh Point
9 Deepdene Point
10 Rosemount Point
11 Woodfield Ho
12 Clairville Point
13 Trevenna Ho
14 Hyndewood
D2 4 Soper Cl

164
C4 1 Beaumont Terr
2 Littlebourne
3 Verdant Ct
D2 1 Kinross Ct
2 Montrose Ct
3 Rattray Ct
4 Rothesay Ct
D3 1 Edinburgh Ct
2 McMillan Ct
3 Rowallan Ct
4 Meridian Ct
5 Braemar Ct
6 Barrow Ct
7 Blair Ct
8 Darlington Ct
9 Hamilton Ct
10 Inverness Ct
11 Oak Cottage Cl
12 Willow Cl
13 Keswick Ct

165
A4 1 Swallow Ct
2 Honeysuckle Ct
3 Venture Ct
4 Cheriton Ct
5 Askham Lo
6 Syon Lo

166
A2 1 Portland Cres
2 Bourdillon Ct
3 Hillary Ct
4 Tenzing Ct
5 John Hunt Ct
6 Everest Ct
A6 1 Horsfeld Gdns
2 Foxhole Rd
C5 1 Roper St
2 Arcade The
3 Elm Terr
4 Imber Ct
5 Ashcroft Ct
6 Fairlands Ct
7 Brecon Ct
8 Newlands Ct
9 Harvard Ct
10 Garden Ct
11 Chiltern Ct
12 Fairway Ct

167
A2 1 Mervyn Stockwood Ho
2 Michael Marshall Ho

3 Keith Sutton Ho

168
A1 1 Ham Shades Cl
2 Aspen Ho
3 Medlar Ho
4 Cornel Ho
5 Stanton Ct
6 Hornbeam Ho
7 Beech Ho
8 Spindle Ho
9 Moat Ct
10 Hunters Lo
11 Edam Ct
12 Monica James Ho
13 Oak Ho
14 Crescent Ct
B5 1 Rochester Cl
2 Cobham Cl
3 Shorne Cl
4 Warne Pl

169
C4 1 Close The
2 Parkhurst Gdns
3 Chichester Ct
4 Pound Green Ct

171
D3 1 Bishops Ct
2 Ash Lo
3 Lime Lo
4 Oak Lo
5 Elm Ct
6 Willow Lo
7 Sycamore Lo
8 Priscilla Ho
9 Sunbury Cross Ctr
10 Isobel Ho

173
A6 1 Gabriel Cl
2 Metcalfe Wlk
3 Dunmow Cl
4 Burgess Cl
5 Chamberlain Wlk
C2 1 Sherbourne Ct
2 Somerset Ct
3 Jubilee Ho
4 Rushbury Ct
5 Hemming Cl
6 Ryedale Ct
7 Norman Ct
C4 1 Begonia Pl
2 Snowdrop Cl
3 Hyacinth Cl
4 Cyclamen Cl
5 Jonquil Gdns
6 Gladioli Cl
7 Daffodil Pl
8 Partridge Rd
D4 1 Acorn Cl
2 Wolsey Ho
3 Lytton Ho
4 Wren Ho
5 Faraday Ho

174
C5 1 Knaggs Ho
2 Keeling Ho
3 Elizabeth Ct
4 Oakhurst Cl
D5 1 Waldegrave Ct
2 Gresham Ho
3 Traherne Lo
4 Fishers Ct
5 Waterhouse Ct
6 Walpole Pl
7 Walpole Cres
8 Alice Mews
9 Bychurch End

175
A5 1 Cherrywood Ct
2 Cambridge Ho
3 Gleneagles Ct
4 Christchurch Ave
5 Hales Ct
6 Springfield Rd
D2 1 Wick Ho

2 Spinnaker Ct
3 Osiers Ct
4 Trent Ho
5 Arun Ho
6 Medway Ho
7 Avon Ho
8 Tyne Ho
9 Clyde Ho
10 Mersey Ct
11 Severn Ct
12 John Williams Cl
D6 1 Byron Ct
2 Coleridge Ct
3 Tennyson Ct
4 Herrick Ct
5 Spenser Ct
6 Marlowe Ct
7 Brooke Ct
8 Gray Ct
9 Shelley Ct
10 Pope Ct
11 Dryden Ct

176
A1 1 Cleave's Almshos
2 Parade The
3 Drovers Ct
4 Gough Ho
5 Eden Wlk
6 Alderman Judge Mall
7 Lady Booth Rd
8 Caversham Ho
9 Littlefield Cl
10 Bentall Sh Ctr The
11 Adams Wlk
12 Kingfisher Sports Ctr The
13 Greencoat Ho
A2 1 Regents Ct
2 Walter St
3 Canbury 2000 Bsns Pk
4 Sigrist Sq
5 Ashway Ctr
6 Warwick Ho
B1 1 Vicarage Ho
2 Rayleigh Ct
3 School Pas
4 Chippenham
5 Camm Gdns
B2 1 Onslow Ho
2 Dowler Ct
B3 1 McDonald Ho
2 Elm Ho
3 Dale Ct
4 York Ho
5 Florence Ho
6 Florence Rd
7 Roupell Ho
8 Delft Ho
C1 1 Wimpole Ct
2 Burwell
3 Caldecote
4 Fordham
5 Connington
6 Chesterton Terr
7 Westwick
8 Eureka Rd
9 Fulbourn
10 Comberton
11 Madingley
12 Grantchester
13 Cambridge Grove Rd
14 Oakington
15 Harston
16 Graveley
17 Croxton
18 Brinkley
19 Impington
20 Shelford
21 Duxford
C2 1 Farthings The
2 Brae Ct
3 Princeton Mews
4 Station App
C3 1 Queen's Ct
2 St George's Rd
3 Park Road Ho
4 Dagmar Rd
5 Tapping Cl
6 Arthur Rd
7 Borough Rd
8 Belvedere Ct
9 Braywick Ct
10 Dean Ct

1 Rowan Ct
2 Richmond Ct
3 Sunningdale Ct
4 Hawker Ho
5 Cromwell Ct
6 Kings Ct
D2 1 Trevallyn Lo
2 Chichester Ho
3 Beechcroft
4 Cedars The
5 Liddlesdale Ho W
6 Liddlesdale Ho E
7 Deerhurst
8 Brockworth
9 Alderton
D3 1 Bramley Ho
2 Abinger Ho
3 Thursley Ho
4 Ridge Ho
5 Clone The
6 Mount Ct
7 Hillside Ct
8 Hill Ct
9 Royal Ct
10 Lakeside
11 High Ashton
D4 1 Godstone Ho
2 Hambledon Ho
3 Kingswood Ho
4 Leigh Ho
5 Milton Ho
6 Newdigate Ho
7 Farleigh Ho
8 Ockley Ho
9 Effingham Ho
10 Dunsfold Ho
11 Pirbright Ho
12 Clandon Ho
13 Ripley Ho

178
C3 1 Roskeen Ct
2 Chimneys Ct
3 Rosemary Cotts
4 Victoria Lo
D2 1 Beaufort Ho
2 Kinnear Ct
3 Ranmore Ct
4 Lantern Ct
5 Crescent Ho
D3 1 Kings View Ct
2 Kingsdown
3 Wimbledon Cl
4 Beryl Harding Ho
5 Upton Ct
6 Marian Lo
7 Terraces The
8 Lanherne Ho
9 Cumberland Cl
10 Rathbone Ho
11 Princess Ct
12 Downs Ct
13 Ravenscar Lo
14 Haverley
15 Savona Cl
16 Beaumont Ct
17 Gordon Ct
D5 1 Lancaster Pl
2 Haygarth Pl
3 Allington Cl
4 Homefield Pl

179
A3 1 Mayfair Ct
2 Brunswick Ct
3 Pavilion Ct
A4 1 Walham Rise
2 Grosvenor Ct
3 Sovereign Ho
4 Holly Lo
5 Florence Ct
6 Linden Cotts
7 Sheep Walk Mews
B5 1 Lawns The
2 Prentice Ct
3 Catherine Ct
4 Woodlodge
5 Queen Alexandra's Ct
6 Lake Cl
7 Westwood Ct
8 Brambles The
9 Lismore
10 Rose Ct

11 Worcester Rd
C3 1 Ashbourne Terr
2 Sir Cyril Black Way
3 Downing Ho
4 Palmerston Gr
5 Gladstone Ct
6 Harefield Ct
7 Viscount Point
D2 1 Gilbert Cl
2 Becket Cl
3 Priory Cl
4 Hudson Ct
5 Ryder Ho
6 Eleanor Ho
7 Ramsey Ho
D3 1 Hamilton Road Mews
2 Dowman Cl

180
A2 1 Tanner Ho
2 May Ct
3 Marsh Ct
4 Lovell Ho
A3 1 Fiske Ct
2 Mellor Ct
3 Olive Rd
4 Allerton Ho
5 Victory Road Mews
6 Will Miles Ct
7 Vanguard Ho
8 Mychell Ho
9 Merton Pl
10 De Burgh Ho
11 Norfolk Ho
12 Hotham Road Mews
B1 1 Ripley Ct
2 Brooklands Ct
3 Horner La
C2 1 Linford Ct
2 Searle Ct
3 Gunnell Ct
C5 1 Robertson Ho
2 Dewar Ho
3 Jean Ho
4 Marion Ct
5 Gravenel Gdns
D1 1 Elms Cotts
2 Sibthorp Rd
3 Armfield Cotts

181
A1 1 Kennedy Cl
2 Pearce Cl
3 Mainwaring Ct
4 Coningsby Ct
5 Laburnum Ct
6 Beaumont Ct
7 Penfold Ct
8 Fitch Ct
A5 1 Osbourne Terr
2 Limetree Wlk
C5 1 Tyers Ho
2 Boothby Ho
3 Adams Ho
4 Burney Ho
5 Boswell Ho
6 Chesterfield Ho
7 Garrick Ho
8 Levett Ho
9 Shelburne Ho
10 Marchmont Ho
11 Ryland Ho
C6 1 Walmsley Ho
2 Chambers Ho
3 Fordyce Ho
4 Percy Ho
5 Langton Ho
6 Moorfields Ct
7 Hidaburn Ct
8 Salter Ho
D6 1 William Dyce Mews

182
C5 1 Belltrees Gr
2 Ash Ct
3 Alder Ct
4 Beech Ct
5 Acacia Ct
6 Blackthorn Ct
7 Cypress Ct
8 Hawthorn Ct
9 Hazel Ct

10 Sycamore Ct
11 Maple Ct
12 Laburnam Ct
13 Fern Lo
C6 1 James Boswell Cl
2 St Albans Ho
3 Suffolk Ct
4 Rockhampton Cl
5 Delphian Ct
D5 1 Woodcote Pl
2 Joe Hunte Ct
3 Cork Tree Ho
4 Lake Ho
5 Cedars Ho
6 Portobello Ho
7 Cooper Ho
8 Farnsworth Ho
9 Hook Ho
10 Crest The
11 Renshaw Ho
12 Ruscoe Ho
13 Sardeson Ho

183
A6 1 Moore Ho
2 Chaucer Ho
3 Bushell Ho
4 Bligh Ho
5 Hobbs Rd
6 Hogarth Ho
7 Goodbehere Ho
8 Astley Ho
9 Elder Gdns
10 Elderberry Gr
11 Pavement The
12 Dunkirk St
B6 1 Josef Perrin Ho
2 Jean Humbert Ho
3 Charles Staunton Ho
4 Violette Szabo Ho
5 Lilian Rolfe Ho
6 Odette Ho
7 Robert Gerard Ho
8 St Bernards Cl
9 Champness Cl
10 Pennington Cl
11 Queenswood Cl
C4 1 Northwood Way
2 High Limes
3 Valley Prospect
4 Plane Tree Wlk
5 City Prospect
6 Bankside Way
7 Ridge Way
8 Rochdale
9 Barrington Wlk
10 Gatestone Ct
11 Childs La
12 Carberry Rd
13 Norwood Heights Sh Ctr
C5 1 Oakdene
2 Thorsden Way
3 Oakfield Gdns
4 Georgetown Cl
5 Bridgetown Cl
6 Mountbatten Cl
7 Brabourne Cl
8 Alexandra Wlk
9 Compton Ct
10 Battenberg Wlk
11 Burma Terr
12 Wiseman Ct
C6 1 Linley Ct
2 Mellor Ho
3 Whitfield Ct
4 Michaelson Ho
5 Holberry Ho
6 Hovenden Ho
7 Huntley Ho
8 Telfer Ho
9 Markham Ho
10 Oldham Ho
11 Parnall Ho
12 Pierson Ho
13 Roper Ho
14 Roundell Ho
15 Sawyer Ho
16 Ransford Ho
17 Carmichael Ho

422 | **183 C6**

18 Bonne Marche Terr Mews
D3 1 Hetley Gdns
2 Claybourne Mews
3 Highland Lo
4 Mason Ct
5 Kendall Ct
6 High View

184

A3 1 Hanover Ct
2 Brunswick Ct
3 New Church Ct
6 Regency Ct
7 Owen Wlk
8 Bargrove Cl
9 Beaver Cl
B2 1 Dorset Ho
2 Collingwood Cl
3 Chartwell Way
4 Essex Twr
5 Appletree Cl
6 Ditton Pl
7 Kelvin Ct
8 Readman Ct
9 Glen Ct
10 Kingsbridge Ho
11 Carlton Ct
12 Benhurst Ct
13 Carole Ho
14 Dover Ho
15 Bettswood Ct
B5 1 Ragwort Ct
2 Firs The
3 Wingham Ho
4 Seath Ho
5 Ripley Ho
6 Lathwood Ho
7 Hurst Ho
8 George Ho
9 Browne Ho
10 Beacon Ho
11 Bailey Ho
12 Agate Ho
C2 1 Challin St
2 Rutland Ho
3 Pine Cl
C3 1 Watermens Sq
2 St John's Cotts
3 Gladstone Mews
6 Middlesex Ho
8 Bethesda Ct
9 Ospringe Cl
10 Goudhurst Ho
11 Walmer Ho
12 Strood Ho
13 Greatstone Ho
14 John Baird Ho
D3 1 Groombridge Ho
2 Provincial Terr
3 Smithers Ho
4 West Ho
5 Swallows Ct

185

A1 1 Clock House Ct
2 Blandford Ave
3 Old School Cl
4 Lynsted Ct
5 Florence Rd
A6 1 Paxton Ct
2 Kenton Ct
3 Grove Ct
4 Shirley Lo
B2 1 Ashton Ct
2 Coombe Ct
3 Fontaine Ct
4 Richfield Ct
5 Sheridan Way
C1 1 Christ Church Rd
2 Lea Rd
3 Stanmore Terr
C2 1 Erindale Ct
2 Bearsted Terr
3 Beck River Pk
4 Waterside
5 Station App
C3 1 Gardenia Ct

2 Brackendale Ct
3 Daniel Ct
4 Moliner Ct
5 Chartwell Lo
6 Randmore Ct
7 Dover Ho
8 Lucerne Ct
9 Malling Ho
10 Westerham Lo
11 Brasted Lo
12 Milton Ho
13 Bradsole Ho
14 Sandgate Ho
15 Adelaide Ct
16 Nettlestead Cl
17 Warren Ct
18 Alton Ct
19 Rockingham Ct
20 Camellia Ct
21 Sinclair Ct
22 Regents Ct
23 Minshull Pl
24 South Park Ct
D1 1 Parkside
2 Tudors The
3 Oakbrook
4 Tara Ct
5 Redlands The
6 Cambria
7 Hillworth
8 Kelsey Gate
9 Burrells
10 Lincoln Lo
11 Courtlands
12 Fairleas
13 Ashdown Cl
D2 1 Mayfair Ct
2 Clifton Ct
3 Fire Station Mews
D4 1 Warner Ho
2 Clifford Ho
3 Lloyd Ho
4 Thurston Ho
5 Byron Ho
6 Blake Ho
7 Keats Ho

186

A2 1 White House Ct
2 Hunters The
3 Sandringham Ct
4 Glenhurst
5 Copperfields
6 Westgate Ct
A6 1 Dedham Ho
2 Flatford Ho
3 Radley Ct
4 Langthorne Ct
5 Hoover Ho
6 Brunner Ho
7 Waterer Ho
8 Marriott Ho
9 Bourbon Ho
B5 1 Longford Ho
2 Ingrebourne Ho
3 Brent Ho
4 Darent Ho
5 Beverley Ho
6 Wandle Ho
7 Rythe Ho
8 Ember Ho
9 Crane Ho
10 Ravensbourne Ho
C1 1 Warwick Ct
2 Maplehurst
3 Mount Arlington
4 Arundel Ct
D2 1 Weston Gr
2 Gibbs Ho
3 Longfield
4 Hammelton Ct
5 Bracken Hill Cl
6 Townend Ct
7 Treversh Ct
8 Cameron Ho
9 Woodlands Ct
10 Blythwood Pk
11 Bromley Pk
D3 1 Homecoppice Ho
2 Kimberley Gate
3 Inglewood Ct

4 Mavery Ct
5 Glen Ct
6 Cawston Ct
7 Blendon Path

187

B2 1 Hansom Terr
2 Dainton Cl
3 St Timothy's Mews
4 Andringham Lo
5 Kendall Lo
6 Summerfield
7 Winston Ct
8 Laurels The
C1 1 Westland Lo
2 Dairsie Ct
3 Beechfield Cotts
4 Oasis The
5 Cromarty Ct
6 Silverstone Ct

188

A6 1 Beaconsfield Par
2 Cranley Par
3 Kimmeridge Gdns
4 King & Queen Cl
C1 1 Merewood Cl
2 Alpine Copse
C2 1 Ivybridge Ct
2 Greenbank Lo

190

A6 1 Minshaw Ct
2 Cyril Lo
3 Milton Lo
4 Glenwood Ct
5 Culverton Ct
6 Holmbury Manor
B1 1 Swanscombe Ho
2 Haverstock Ct
3 Arrandene Ho
4 Broomfield Ho
5 Headley Ho
6 Kenley Ho
7 Ladywell Ho
B6 1 Chudleigh
2 Wimborne
3 St John's Par
4 Holly Ct
5 Rectory Bsns Ctr

197

A2 1 Raleigh Ho
2 Leicester Ho
3 Gresham Ho
D2 1 Napier Ct
2 Darlington Ho
3 Charminster Ct
4 Mulberry Ct
5 Leander Ct
6 Clinton Ho
7 Hollingworth Ct
8 Gloucester Ct
9 Palmerston Ct
10 Redwood Ct
11 Hursley Ct
12 Westmorland Ct
13 Lawson Ct
14 Alexander Ct
15 Winton Ct
16 Sydenham Ho
17 Caroline Ct
18 Ellswood Ct
19 Masefield Ct

198

A1 1 Ash Tree Cl
2 Shrubbery The
3 Malvern Ct
4 Gate Ho
A3 1 Station App
2 South Bank Lo
3 Bramshott Ct
4 Pandora Ct
5 Wellington Ct
6 Glenbuck Ct
7 Leighton Ho
8 Oakhill Ct

9 Downs View Lo
10 Osborne Ct
A4 1 Effingham Lo
2 Maple Ho
3 Channon Ct
4 Falconhurst
5 Ferndown
6 Viceroy Lo
7 Frensham Ho
8 Kingsley Ho
9 Rannoch Ct
11 Stratton Ct
11 Moray Ho
12 Dulverton Ct
13 Westerham
14 Hill Ct
15 Assheton-Bennett Ho
16 Hatfield Ho
17 Oxford Ct
18 Pennington Lo
19 Austin Ho
20 Wentworth Ct
21 Priory The
22 Sheraton The
A5 1 Marquis Ct
2 Garrick Ho
A6 1 College Rdbt
2 Edinburgh Ct
3 Weston Ct
4 Grebe Terr
5 Heron Ct
6 Agar Ho
7 St James' Ct
8 Grove Ct
9 Springfield Ct
10 College Wlk
B3 1 Percy Ct
2 Holmwood
3 Middle Green Cl
B4 1 Woodleigh
2 Highcroft
3 Caernarvon Ct
4 Regency Ct
D1 1 Oakleigh Way
2 Chandler Ct

199

C2 1 Goodland Ho
2 Furzeland Ho
3 Oakcroft Ho
4 Meadcroft Ho
5 Newhouse
C4 1 Merryweather Ct
2 Roebuck Ct
3 Sable Ct
C5 1 Acacia Ho
2 Kingston Lo
3 Fairholme Ho
4 Marshall Ho
5 Norton Ho
6 Martin Ho

200

A1 1 Brookside Cres
2 Beverley Gdns
3 Purdey Ct
4 Avenue The
5 Briarwood Ct
6 Station App

202

D6 1 Fair Green Ct
2 Regal Ct
3 Lewes Ct
4 Esher Mews
5 Sibford Ct

205

B1 1 Tavistock Ct
2 Chartwell Cl
3 Speaker's Ct
4 Cumberland Ct
5 Viceroy Ct
6 Oriel Ct
7 Cherry Orchard Gdns
C1 1 Windmill Bridge Ho
2 Squire Ct
3 Houston Ct

9 St James's Lo
5 Kendal Ho
6 Warren Ct
7 Kendal Ct
D1 1 Hastings Pl
2 Grant Pl
3 Clive Ho
4 Havelock Ho
5 Bellmore Ct
6 Hereford Ct
7 Chequers Ct
8 Havelock Hall

206

A1 1 Farleycroft
2 Edgecumbe Ct
3 Wesson Ho
4 Sullivan Ct
5 Kenley Ho
6 Christopher Ct
7 Jayson Ct
D1 1 Cottongrass Cl
2 Oxlip Cl
3 Eyebright Cl

207

1 North Rd
2 Sussex Rd
3 Riverside Wlk
4 Christie Ho
5 Sherwood Ct
6 Wheatsheaf Par
D6 1 Linden Ct
2 Park Ct
3 Chilchester Ct
4 Iveagh Ct

208

A6 1 Overbury Ct
2 Wilton Pl
D1 1 Woodgrange Ct
2 Maycroft
3 Farnborough Cres
D4 1 Knowlton Gn
2 Speldhurst Cl
3 Bidborough Cl
4 Penshurst Wlk
D5 1 Wedgewood Ct
2 Birches The
3 Eccleshill
4 Tavistock Rd
5 Montpelier Ct

209

A5 1 Montague Terr
2 Chatsworth Ho
A6 1 Marina Cl
2 Cheveney Wlk
3 Bromley Manor Mans
4 Mall The
5 Westmoreland Pl

211

B1 1 Gleneagles Gn
2 Tandridge Pl
3 Springfield Wlk
4 Pinehurst Wlk
5 Cromer Pl
6 Oakmont Pl

214

A6 1 St Bernards Ho
2 Wentworth Ct
3 Sunningdale Cl
4 Arklow Mews
5 Edward Pinner Ct

215

D6 1 Kingsley Dr
2 Kingsley Ct
3 Mowat Ct
4 Squirrels Ct

216

A6 1 Lansdowne Copse
2 Lansdowne Ct

217

A2 1 Cheam Court Flats
2 Farnham Ct
3 Tabor Ct
C1 1 Lancaster Ct
2 Redclyffe Terr
3 Kenilworth Terr
4 Lincoln Terr
5 Garden Ct
6 Ashwood Pk
7 Lyndhurst Ct
8 Banbury Ct
9 Holly Ct
10 Castle Ho
11 Balmoral Ct
12 Hereford Ct
13 Lorac Ct
14 Camilla Ct
15 Midsummer Apmts
D1 1 Hadrian Ct
2 Magnolia Ct
3 Larchvale Ct
5 Alford Ct
6 Brockham Ct
7 Berrylands Ct
8 Camberley Ct
9 Dunsfold Ct
10 Courtlands
11 Leith Towers
12 Kingslee Ct

218

A1 1 Beauclere Ho
2 Melford Ct
3 Elmhurst Lo
4 Mansard Manor
5 Tranmere Ct
6 Beechcroft Lo
7 Savin Lo
8 Yew Tree Ct
9 Avondale Ct
10 Devonshire Ho
11 Hidcote Ho
12 Munstead Ct
13 Lodden Lo
14 Steetley Ct
15 Grampian Cl
A2 1 Grosvenor Ct
2 Forest Dene Ct
3 Cedar Ct
4 Vanborough Ct
A3 1 Goossens Cl
2 Cliffe Wlk
3 Marlins Cl
4 Clowser Cl
5 Montana Gdns

219

B2 1 Runnymede Ct
2 Dolphin Ct
3 Kings Ct
4 Cheyne Ct
5 Hendfield Ct
6 Ellerslie Ct
7 Embassy Ct
8 Chandler Ct
9 Hambledon Ct
10 Wallington Ct
11 Jasmine Ct
B4 1 Loraine Ho
2 Harcourt Lo
3 Coniston Ct
4 Alcester Ct
5 Friars Ct
6 Campbell Ho
7 Brodie Ho
8 Lesley Ct
9 Birch Ct
10 Airborne Ho
C2 1 Rossendon Ct
2 Mulberry Mews
3 Nairn Ct
4 Wallington Sq

5 Rosemount Towers
6 Connell Ho
7 Ashby Grange

221

A4 1 West Street Pl
2 Maple Ct
3 St Andrew's Rd
4 Albury Ct
5 Chestnut Ct
6 Elgin Ct
7 Beechfield Ct
8 Barham Ct
9 Whitstable Pl
10 Ledbury Pl
A5 1 Mann Cl
2 Halstead Ct
3 Fellmongers Yd
A6 1 Otterbourne Rd
2 Charrington Rd
3 Tamworth Pl
4 Priddy's Yd
5 Hospital of the Holy Trinity (Almshouses)
6 Bellhill
B4 1 Holmlea Ct
2 Garlands Ct
3 Coombe Ct
4 Deepdale Ct
5 Galloway Path
B6 1 Wellesley Court Rd
2 Norfolk Ho
3 Station App
4 Suffolk Ho
5 Cherry Orchard Gdns
6 Harrington Ct
D6 1 Cheyne Ct
2 Fourways
3 Princess Ct
4 Tierney Ct
5 Sinclair Ct
6 Guinness Ct
7 Mayfair Ct
8 Bishopscourt
9 Gloucester Lo
10 Beverley Hyrst
11 Melton Ct
12 Cecil Ct
13 Napier Ct

227

A3 1 Westfield
2 Farnborough Ct
3 Fern Hill Pl
4 Churchill Ct
5 Spencer Ct
6 Ladycroft Gdns
7 Crabbs Croft Cl
8 Clifton Ct
D2 1 Brittenden Cl
2 Wardens Field Cl
3 Winnipeg Dr
4 Superior Dr
5 Huron Cl
6 Manitoba Gdns
7 Lynne Cl
8 Flint Cl
9 Bakers Mews
D3 1 Osgood Gdns
2 Amberley Cl
3 Rawlings Cl
4 Beblets Cl
5 Fir Tree Cl
6 Raleigh Mews
7 King Henry Mews
D4 1 Healy Dr
2 Marsden Way
3 Taylor Cl
4 Strickland Way
5 Dryland Ave
6 Adcot Wlk
7 Lichlade Cl

✚ Hospitals with accident and emergency departments are highlighted in green

A

Acton Hospital W3 ..**110** C4

✚ **Ashford Hospital**
Stanmore Road, Ashford, Middlesex TW15 3AA ..**148** A2
☎ **01784 884488**

Athlone House (The Middlesex Hospital)
N6 ....**48** D1
Atkinson Morley Hospital
SW20 ....**178** B3

B

Barking Hospital IG11 **79** D1
Barnes Hospital
SW14 ....**133** C2
Beckenham Hospital
BR3 ....**185** B1
Bethlem Royal Hospital The
BR3 ....**207** C2
Blackheath Hospital
SE3 ....**142** C2
Bolingbroke Hospital The
SW11 ....**158** C6
Bowden House Hospital (Private) HA1 ....**64** C6
British Home and Hospital for Incurables SW16 **182** D5
✚ **Bromley Hospital**
Cromwell Avenue, Bromley, Kent BR2 9AJ **209** B5
☎ **020 8289 7000**
Brompton Hospital
SW3 ....**114** B1 **256** D2
BUPA Bushey Hospital
WD2 ....**8** D3

C

Carshalton, War Memorial Hospital SM5 .....**218** D2
Cassel Hospital
TW10 ....**175** D2
Castlewood Day Hospital
SE18 ....**144** C4
✚ **Central Middlesex Hospital**
Acton Lane, Park Royal, London, NW10 7NS **89** A4
☎ **020 8965 5733**
Central Public Health Laboratory NW9 .....**45** C6
Chadwell Heath Hospital
RM6 ....**58** B4
✚ **Charing Cross Hospital**
Fulham Palace Road, London W6 8RF (A&E entrance off St Dunstan's Road) **112** B3
☎ **020 8846 1234**
Charter Nightingale Hospital The
NW1 ....**92** C2 **237** B4
✚ **Chase Farm Hospital**
The Ridgeway, Enfield, Middlesex, EN2 8JL **4** C5
☎ **020 8366 6600**
Chelsea Hospital for Women SW3 **114** C1 **257** A2
✚ **Chelsea and Westminster Hospital**
369 Fulham Road, London SW10 9NH ..**136** A6 **266** B5
☎ **020 8746 8000**
Chingford Hospital E4 **20** A1
Chiswick Maternity Hospital
W4 ....**111** D1

Clayponds Hospital and Day Treatment Ctr TW8 .**110** A2
Clementine Churchill Hospital The HA1 ....**64** D5
Colindale Hospital
NW9 ....**45** C6
Connaught Day Hospital
E11 ....**54** C3
Coppetts Wood Hospital
N10 ....**30** D2
Cromwell Hospital
SW5 ....**113** D2 **255** C4

D

Devonshire Hospital
W1 ....**93** À2 **238** B4
Dulwich Hospital
SE22 ....**139** C1

E

✚ **Ealing Hospital**
Uxbridge Road, Southall, Middlesex UB1 3HW ..**108** B4
☎ **020 8574 2444**
East Ham Meml Hospital
E7 ....**77** D1
Eastman Dental Hospital
WC1 ....**94** B4 **240** C6
Edgware General Hospital
HA8 ....**26** D3
Elizabeth Garrett Anderson and Obstetric Hospital WC1 **93** C3 **235** B5

F

Farnborough Hospital
BR6 ....**226** C4
Finchley Memorial Hospital
N12 ....**30** A3
Fitzroy Nuffield Hospital
W1 ....**92** D1 **237** C2

G

Garden Hospital The
NW4 ....**46** C6
Goldie Leigh Hospital
SE2 ....**146** C6
Goodmayes Hospital
IG3 ....**58** A4
Gordon Hospital The
SW1 ....**115** D2 **259** C3
Great Ormond St Hospital for Children
WC1 ....**94** B3 **240** C5
✚ **Greenwich District Hospital**
Vanbrugh Hill, Greenwich, London, SE10 9HE ..**120** D1
☎ **020 8858 8141**
Grovelands Priory
N14 ....**16** A3
Guy's Hospital
SE1 ....**117** B5 **252** D2

H

Hackney Hospital E9 .**75** A3
Hamlet (Day) Hospital The TW9 ....**132** A2
✚ **Hammersmith Hospital**
Du Cane Road, London W12 0HS **90** B1
☎ **020 8383 1111**
Harrow Hospital HA2 .**64** C6
The Heart Hospital
W1 ....**93** B2 **238** C3
✚ **Hillingdon Hospital**
Pield Heath Road, Uxbridge, Middlesex UB8 3NN **82** B2
☎ **01895 238282**

✚ **Homerton University Hospital**
Homerton Row, E9 6SR ..**74** D3
☎ **020 8510 5555**
Hornsey Central Hospital
N8 ....**49** D4
Hospital for Tropical Diseases WC1 ....**232** C5
Hospital of St John and St Elizabeth
NW8 ....**92** B5 **229** C3

I

Inverforth House Hospital
NW3 ....**70** A6

J

Jewish Home and Hospital at Tottenham The N15 ....**51** D5

K

✚ **King George Hospital**
Barley Lane, Goodmayes, Ilford, Essex IG3 8YB ..**58** A4
☎ **020 8983 8000**
✚ **King's College Hospital**
Denmark Hill, (A&E in Ruskin Wing) SE5 9RS ...**139** B3
☎ **020 7737 4000**
Kings Oak Hospital (Private) The EN2 .....**4** C5
Kingsbury Hospital NW9 ....**44** C5
✚ **Kingston Hospital**
Galsworthy Road, Kingston-upon-Thames, Surrey KT2 7QB **176** D2
☎ **020 8546 7711**

L

Langthorne Hospital E11 ....**76** B5
✚ **Lewisham Hospital**
High Street, Lewisham, London SE13 6JH ...**163** D6
☎ **020 8333 3000**
Lister Hospital
SW1 ....**115** B1 **258** C1
London Bridge Hospital
SE1 ....**117** B5 **252** D4
London Chest Hospital
E2 ....**96** C5
London Clinic
NW1 ....**93** A3 **238** B5
London Foot Hospital
W1 ....**93** C3 **239** A5
London Hospital (Mile End) The E2 ....**96** D4
London Hospital (St Clements) The E3 ....**97** B4
London Independent Hospital The E1 .....**96** D2

M

Maida Vale Psychiatric Hospital W9 ..**92** A3 **236** B6
Manor House Hospital
NW11 ....**47** D1
Marlborough Day Hospital
NW8 ....**92** A5 **229** A4
Maudsley Hospital The
SE5 ....**139** B3
✚ **Mayday University Hospital**
Mayday Road, Thornton Heath CR7 7YE **204** D3
☎ **020 8401 3000**

Memorial Hospital
SE18 ....**144** C3
Middlesex Hospital
W1 ....**93** C2 **239** B3
Mildmay Mission Hospital
E2 ....**95** D4
Molesey Hospital
KT8 ....**195** C4
Moorfields Eye Hospital
EC1 ....**95** B4 **235** C1
Morland Road Day Hospital
RM10 ....**103** C6

N

National Hospital for Neurology and Neurosurgery N2 ....**48** C5
National Hospital The
WC1 ....**94** A3 **240** B5
National Physical Laboratory TW11 ..**174** C4
Nelson Hospital
SW20 ....**179** B1
New Cross Hospital
SE14 ....**140** C5
New Victoria Hospital
KT3 ....**177** C2
✚ **Newham General Hospital**
Glen Road, Plaistow, London E13 8SL **99** C3
☎ **020 7476 4000**
Normansfield Hospital KT8 ....**175** C4
North London Nuffield Hospital EN2 ....**4** C3
✚ **North Middlesex Hospital**
Sterling Way, Edmonton, London, N18 1QX **33** C5
☎ **020 8887 2000**
✚ **Northwick Park Hospital**
Watford Road, Harrow, Middlesex HA1 3UJ ...**43** A2
☎ **020 8864 3232**
Northwood Pinner and District Cottage Hospital HA6 ....**22** A4
Norwood Hospital
SE19 ....**183** B4

O

Orpington Hospital
BR6 ....**227** D4

P

Paddington Com Hospital W9 ....**91** C2
Penny Sangam Day Hospital
UB2 ....**107** B3
Plaistow Hospital E13 ....**99** C5
Portland Hospital for Women and Children The W1 ....**93** B3 **238** D5
Princess Grace Hospital The W1 ....**93** A3 **238** A5
Princess Louise Hospital W10 ....**90** C2
Priory Hospital The
SW15 ....**133** D1
Putney Hospital
SW15 ....**134** C2

Q

Queen Charlotte's Hospital W12 ....**90** B1
Queen Elizabeth Hospital for Children The E2 ..**96** A5
Queen Elizabeth Hospital SE18 ......**144** A5

✚ **Queen Mary's Hospital**
Frognal Avenue, Sidcup, Kent DA14 6LT **190** A4
☎ **020 8302 2678**
Queen Mary's Hospital
NW3 ....**70** A5
Queen Mary's Univ Hospital
SW15 ....**156** A5
Queen's Hospital CR0 **205** A3

R

Roding Hospital IG4 ...**55** D6
Royal Brompton and Nat Heart Hospital The
SW3 ....**114** C1 **257** A2
Royal Ear Hospital
WC1 ....**93** C3 **239** B5
✚ **Royal Free Hospital**
Pond Street, London NW3 2QG **70** C3
☎ **020 7794 0500**
Royal Hospital SW15 **157** A5
Royal London Homeopathic Hospital The
WC1 ....**94** A2 **240** B4
✚ **Royal London Hospital (Whitechapel)**
Whitechapel Road, London E1 1BB **96** B2
☎ **020 7377 7000**
Royal Marsden Hospital
SW3 ....**114** B1 **256** D2
Royal Masonic Hospital
W6 ....**112** A2
Royal National Orthopaedic Hospital
HA7 ....**9** C2
W1 ....**93** B3 **238** D5
Royal Nat TN&E Hospital The W5 ....**87** C2
WC1 ....**94** B4 **233** C2

S

St Andrew's Hospital E3 ....**97** D3
St Ann's General Hospital N4,N15 .....**51** A4
St Anthony's Hospital KT4 ....**200** D1
St Bartholomew's Hospital EC1 .**94** D2 **241** D3
St Charles' Hospital W10 ....**90** C2
St Christopher's Hospice SE26 ......**184** C5
✚ **St George's Hospital**
Blackshaw Road, London SW17 .....**180** B5
☎ **020 8672 1255**
St Giles Hospital SE5 **139** C4
✚ **St Helier Hospital**
Wrythe Lane, Carshalton, Surrey SM5 1AA **202** A1
☎ **020 8296 2000**
St Joseph's Hospice E9,E8 ....**96** B6
St Leonard's Hospital N1 ....**95** C5
St Luke's Hospital W1 .**93** C3 **239** A5
St Luke's Woodside Hospital N10 ....**49** A5
St Mark's Hospital EC1 .**94** D4 **234** D2
St Mark's Hospital HA1 ....**43** A4
St Mary's Cottage Hospital TW12 ....**173** B2
✚ **St Mary's Hospital**
Praed Street, Paddington W2 1NY **92** B1 **236** D2
☎ **020 7886 6666**

St Michael's Hospital EN2 ....**5** B4
St Pancras Hospital
NW1 ....**93** D6 **232** C5
✚ **St Thomas's Hospital**
Lambeth Palace Road, London SE1 7EH **116** B3 **260** C4
☎ **020 7928 9292**
St Vincent's Hospital
HA5 ....**39** D6
Samaritan Hospital for Women NW1 ..**237** C4
Shirley Oaks Hospital CR0 ....**206** C2
Sloane Hospital BR3 .**186** B2
South Western Hospital SW9 ....**138** B2
Southwood Hospital (Geriatric) N6 ....**49** A2
Springfield Hospital SW17 ....**158** C1
Stepney Day Hospital E1 ....**96** C1
Surbiton Hospital KT6 ....**198** A3

T

Teddington Memorial Hospital TW11 .....**174** C4
Thorpe Coombe Hospital E17 ....**54** A6
Tolworth Hospital KT6 ......**214** C6
Travel Clinic, Hospital for Tropical Diseases
WC1 ....**93** C3 **239** B5

U

✚ **University College Hospital**
A&E at Cecil Fleming House, Grafton Way, London, WC1E 3BG **93** C3 **239** B5
☎ **020 7387 9300**
Upton Day Hospital DA6 ....**147** A1

W

Wanstead Hospital E11 ....**55** B5
Wellington Hospital (North) NW8 .**92** B5 **229** D3
Wellington Hospital (South) NW8 .**92** B5 **229** D3
Wembley Hospital HA0 ....**65** D3
✚ **West Middlesex University Hospital**
Twickenham Road, Isleworth, Middlesex TW7 6AF ..**131** A3
☎ **020 8560 2121**
Western Hospital The NW1 ....**92** D2 **237** C4
✚ **Whipps Cross Hospital**
Whipps Cross Road, Leytonstone, London, E11 1NR **54** B3
☎ **020 8539 5522**
✚ **Whittington Hospital**
Highgate Hill, London, N19 5NF **71** C6
☎ **020 7272 3070**
Willesden Community Hospital The NW10 ..**68** A1
Winifred House Hospital
EN5 ....**11** D5

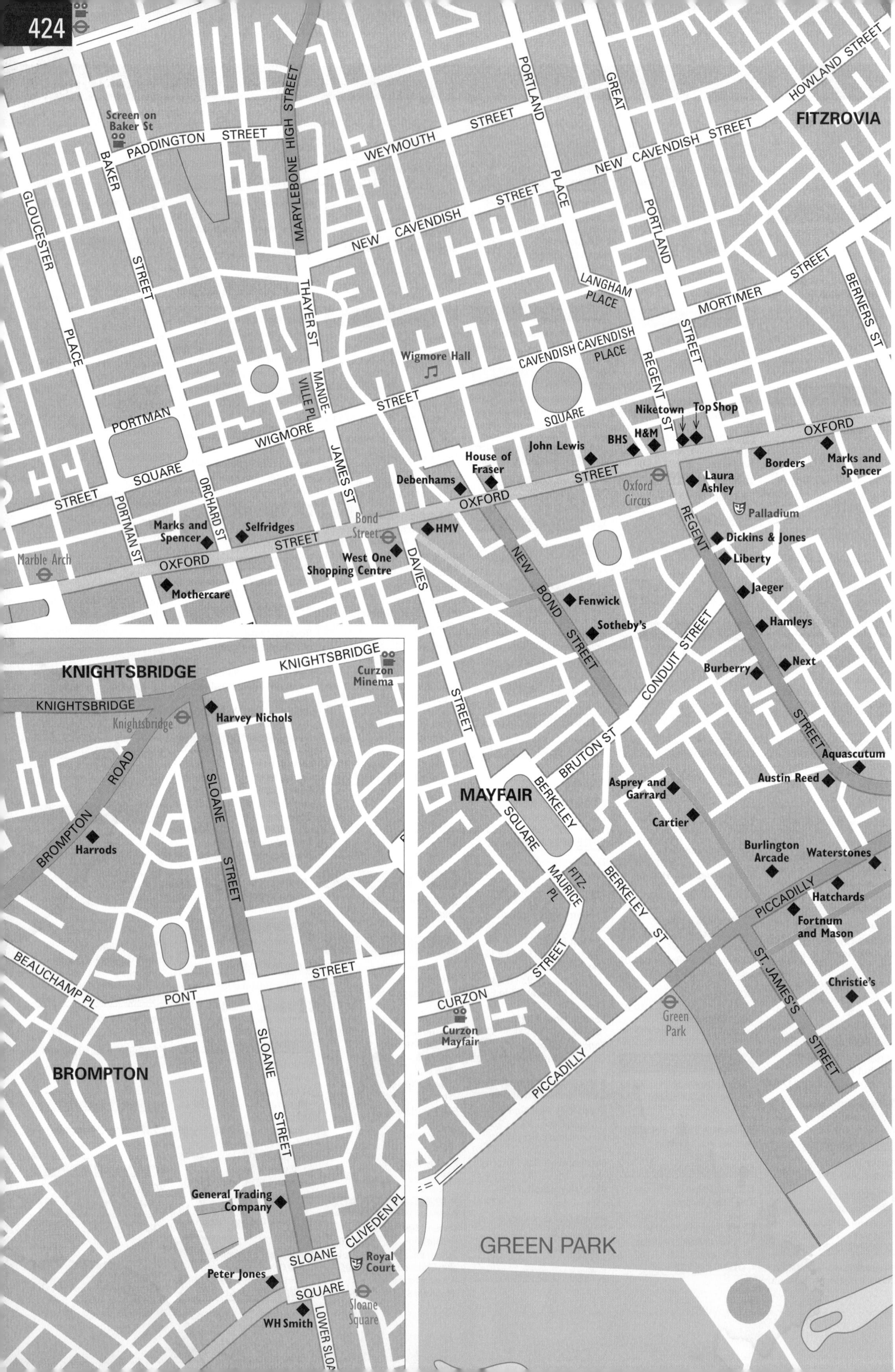

Screen on Baker St

FITZROVIA

BAKER STREET

PADDINGTON STREET

GLOUCESTER PLACE

MARYLEBONE HIGH STREET

THAYER ST

MANDE-VILLE PL

JAMES ST

ORCHARD ST

PORTMAN ST

WEYMOUTH STREET

NEW CAVENDISH STREET

NEW CAVENDISH STREET

PORTLAND STREET

GREAT

HOWLAND STREET

PORTLAND PLACE

LANGHAM PLACE

MORTIMER STREET

PORTLAND STREET

BERNERS ST

Wigmore Hall

CAVENDISH PLACE

CAVENDISH SQUARE

REGENT ST

WIGMORE STREET

Niketown

Top Shop

BHS

H&M

OXFORD

John Lewis

House of Fraser

Debenhams

OXFORD STREET

Oxford Circus

Laura Ashley

Borders

Marks and Spencer

Bond Street

HMV

Palladium

REGENT STREET

Dickins & Jones

Marks and Spencer

Selfridges

Liberty

PORTMAN SQUARE

OXFORD STREET

West One Shopping Centre

DAVIES STREET

Jaeger

Marble Arch

Mothercare

NEW BOND STREET

Fenwick

Hamleys

Sotheby's

Next

Burberry

CONDUIT STREET

KNIGHTSBRIDGE

KNIGHTSBRIDGE

Curzon Minema

Harvey Nichols

Knightsbridge

BROMPTON ROAD

SLOANE STREET

STREET

Harrods

BEAUCHAMP PL

PONT STREET

STREET

BROMPTON

SLOANE STREET

General Trading Company

CLIVEDEN PL

Peter Jones

SLOANE

SLOANE SQUARE

Royal Court

Sloane Square

LOWER SLOA

WH Smith

STREET

MAYFAIR

BERKELEY SQUARE

BRUTON ST

Asprey and Garrard

Cartier

Aquascutum

Austin Reed

Burlington Arcade

Waterstones

FITZ-MAURICE PL

BERKELEY ST

PICCADILLY

Hatchards

Fortnum and Mason

CURZON STREET

Curzon Mayfair

ST. JAMES'S STREET

Christie's

PICCADILLY

Green Park

GREEN PARK

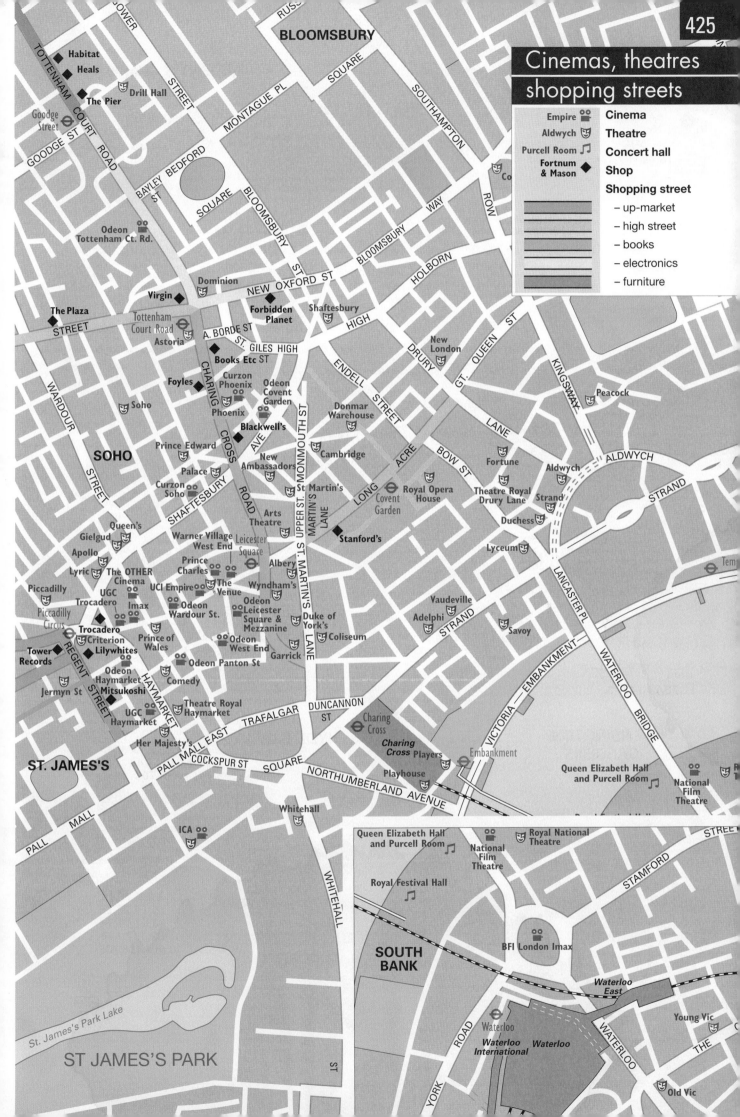

Cinemas, theatres shopping streets

Empire 📽️		Cinema
Aldwych 🎭		Theatre
Purcell Room ♫		Concert hall
Fortnum & Mason ◆		Shop
		Shopping street
		– up-market
		– high street
		– books
		– electronics
		– furniture

BLOOMSBURY

Habitat
Heals
The Pier
Drill Hall
Goodge Street
GOODGE ST
Odeon Tottenham Ct. Rd.
TOTTENHAM COURT ROAD
BAYLEY ST
MONTAGUE PL
BEDFORD SQUARE
BLOOMSBURY SQUARE
SOUTHAMPTON ROW
BLOOMSBURY WAY
HOLBORN
RUSSELL SQUARE

Dominion
NEW OXFORD ST
Virgin
Forbidden Planet
Shaftesbury
HIGH
New London
DRURY LANE
GT. QUEEN ST
KINGSWAY

The Plaza
STREET
Tottenham Court Road
Astoria
A. BORDE ST
ST. GILES HIGH ST
ENDELL STREET
Peacock

Books Etc
Foyles
Soho
Curzon Phoenix
CHARING CROSS ROAD
Odeon Covent Garden
Donmar Warehouse
LONG ACRE
BOW ST
Fortune
Aldwych
ALDWYCH
STRAND

SOHO
WARDOUR STREET
Phoenix
Blackwell's
Prince Edward
New Ambassadors
Cambridge
St Martin's
Covent Garden
Royal Opera House
Theatre Royal Drury Lane
Strand
Duchess
Lyceum

Palace
Curzon Soho
SHAFTESBURY AVE
UPPER ST MARTIN'S LANE
ST MARTIN'S LANE

Queen's
Gielgud
Apollo
Lyric
The OTHER Cinema
Piccadilly
UGC Trocadero
Piccadilly Circus
Warner Village West End
Leicester Square
Prince Charles
UCI Empire
Imax
The Venue
Odeon Wardour St.
Arts Theatre
Albery
Wyndham's
Stanford's
Vaudeville
Adelphi
STRAND
Savoy

Trocadero
Criterion
Tower Records
Lilywhites
Prince of Wales
REGENT STREET
Odeon Leicester Square & Mezzanine
Odeon West End
Garrick
Duke of York's
Coliseum

Odeon Haymarket
Jermyn St
Mitsukoshi
UGC Haymarket
HAYMARKET
Comedy
Odeon Panton St
Theatre Royal Haymarket
Her Majesty's
DUNCANNON ST
TRAFALGAR SQUARE
PALL MALL EAST
COCKSPUR ST
NORTHUMBERLAND AVENUE
Charing Cross
Charing Cross Players
Playhouse
Embankment
VICTORIA EMBANKMENT

ST. JAMES'S
PALL MALL
Whitehall
ICA
WHITEHALL
ST

Queen Elizabeth Hall and Purcell Room
National Film Theatre
Royal Festival Hall
SOUTH BANK
Royal National Theatre
BFI London Imax
STAMFORD STREET

Queen Elizabeth Hall and Purcell Room
National Film Theatre

ST JAMES'S PARK
St. James's Park Lake
YORK ROAD

Waterloo East
Waterloo
Waterloo International
Waterloo
Young Vic
WATERLOO
THE
Old Vic

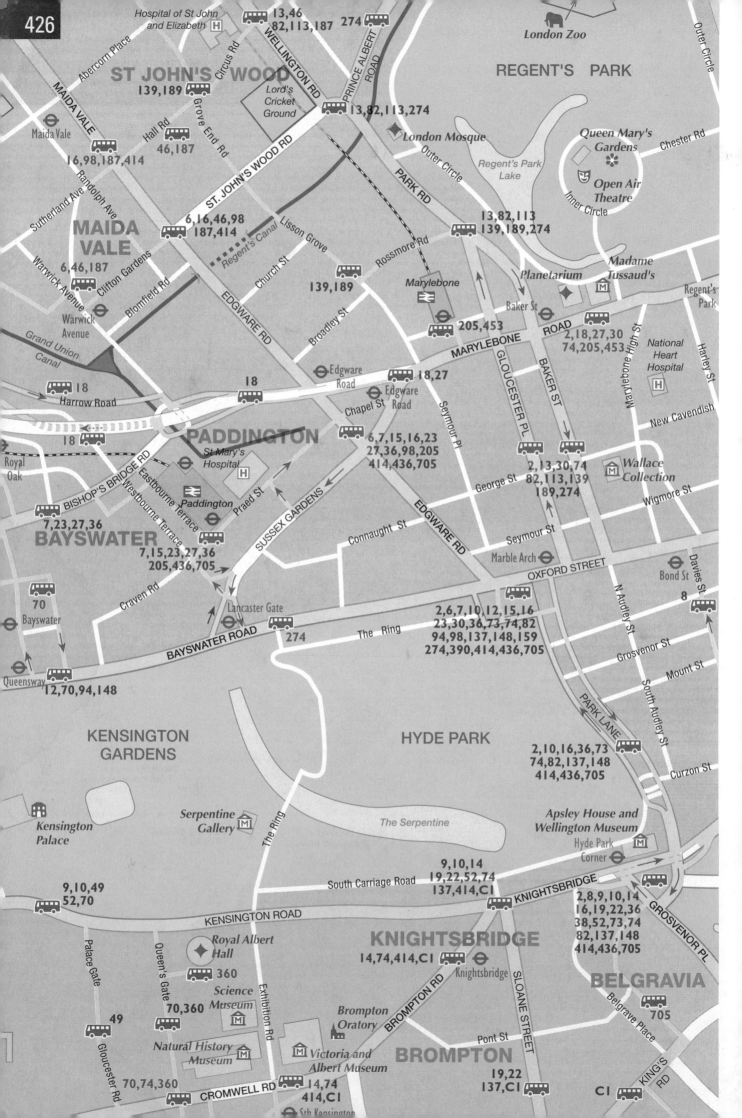

Hospital of St John and Elizabeth 🅷

13,46
82,113,187
274

London Zoo

ST JOHN'S WOOD

REGENT'S PARK

WELLINGTON RD

PRINCE ALBERT ROAD

Circus Rd

139,189

Lord's Cricket Ground

13,82,113,274

Queen Mary's Gardens

Chester Rd

Abercorm Place

MAIDA VALE

Maida Vale

Hall Rd

46,187

Grove End Rd

London Mosque

Regent's Park Lake

Open Air Theatre

16,98,187,414

ST. JOHN'S WOOD RD

PARK RD

Outer Circle

Inner Circle

Regent's Park

MAIDA VALE

Sutherland Ave

Randolph Ave

6,16,46,98
187,414

Regent's Canal

Lisson Grove

Rossmore Rd

13,82,113
139,189,274

Madame Tussaud's

Planetarium

6,46,187

Clifton Gardens

Church St

139,189

Marylebone

Baker St

2,18,27,30
74,205,453

National Heart Hospital

Warwick Avenue

Blomfield Rd

Broadley St

205,453

MARYLEBONE ROAD

BAKER ST

GLOUCESTER PL

Marylebone High St

Harley St

New Cavendish

Warwick Avenue

Grand Union Canal

18

18

Edgware Road

18,27

Seymour Pl

2,13,30,74
82,113,139
189,274

Wallace Collection

George St

Wigmore St

Harrow Road

18

18

PADDINGTON

Chapel St

Edgware Road

6,7,15,16,23
27,36,98,205
414,436,705

EDGWARE RD

Seymour St

Royal Oak

BISHOP'S BRIDGE RD

St Mary's Hospital 🅷

Praed St

Sussex Gardens

Marble Arch

2,6,7,10,12,15,16

Bond St

Davies St

8

Eastbourne Terrace

Paddington

Westbourne Terrace

7,23,27,36

BAYSWATER

Connaught St

EDGWARE RD

OXFORD STREET

7,15,23,27,36
205,436,705

Craven Rd

Lancaster Gate

23,30,36,73,74,82
94,98,137,148,159
274,390,414,436,705

N Audley St

Grosvenor St

Mount St

70

Bayswater

BAYSWATER ROAD

274

The Ring

South Audley St

PARK LANE

Queensway

12,70,94,148

KENSINGTON GARDENS

HYDE PARK

Curzon St

2,10,16,36,73
74,82,137,148
414,436,705

Serpentine Gallery

The Ring

The Serpentine

Apsley House and Wellington Museum

Kensington Palace

Hyde Park Corner

9,10,49
52,70

KENSINGTON ROAD

South Carriage Road

9,10,14
19,22,52,74
137,414,C1

KNIGHTSBRIDGE

2,8,9,10,14
16,19,22,36
38,52,73,74
82,137,148
414,436,705

Palace Gate

Queen's Gate

Royal Albert Hall

360

Science Museum

KNIGHTSBRIDGE

BROMPTON RD

Knightsbridge

SLOANE STREET

BELGRAVIA

Belgrave Place

705

Exhibition Rd

70,360

14,74,414,C1

Brompton Oratory

49

Natural History Museum

Victoria and Albert Museum

BROMPTON

Pont St

70,74,360

CROMWELL RD

14,74
414,C1

19,22
137,C1

KING'S RD

C1

Gloucester Rd

Sth Kensington

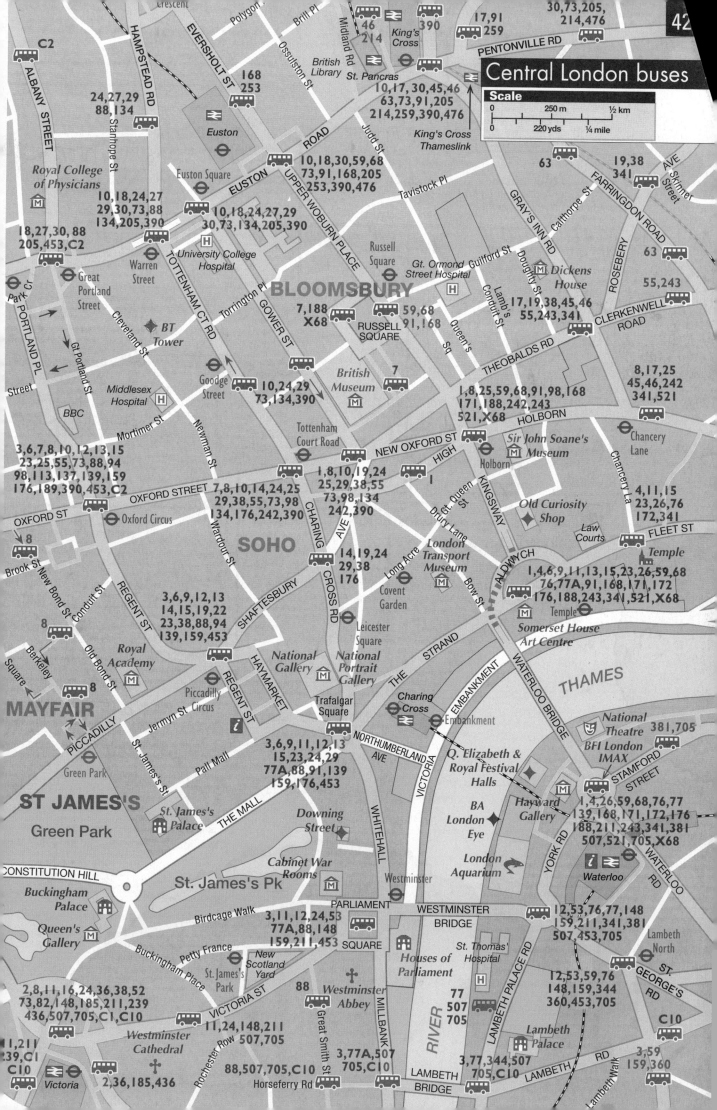

laces of interest

Central

West End

Admiralty Arch SW1 .....**249** D4
Apple Market WC2 . .**250** B6
Banqueting House
SW1 ....**250** A3
Big Ben SW1 ....**250** B1
British Library
WC1 ....**93** D4 **232** D2
British Museum
WC1 ......**94** A2 **240** A3
BT Tower W1 .**93** C2 **239** A4
Buckingham Palace
SW1 .....**115** C4 **249** A1
Cabinet War Rooms
SW1 .....**115** D4 **249** D2
Carnaby Street
W1 ....**93** C1 **239** A1
Cenotaph SW1 .....**250** A2
Changing of the Guard (site
of) SW1 ....**249** A1
Chinatown
W1 ....**115** D6 **249** D6
Clarence House
SW1 .....**115** C5 **249** B3
Cleopatra's Needle
WC2 .....**116** B5 **250** C5
Courtauld Galleries
WC2 ....**250** C6
Covent Garden
WC2 .....**116** A6 **250** B6
Dickens House Museum
WC1 .....**94** B3 **240** D5
Downing Street
SW1 ....**116** A4 **250** A2
Eros W1 .....**115** D6 **249** C5
Green Park
SW1,W1 ...**115** B4 **248** D2
Guards Museum
SW1 .....**115** C4 **249** B1
Holocaust Memorial Garden
W2 ....**114** D4 **247** D2
Horse Guards Parade
SW1 .....**115** D5 **249** D3
Houses of Parliament
SW1 ......**116** A3 **260** B6
Hyde Park
W2 ....**114** D5 **247** C3
Leicester Square
WC2 .....**115** D6 **249** D5
London Transport Museum
WC2 ....**250** B6
Marble Arch
W1 ....**114** D6 **247** D6
Methodist Central Hall
SW1 ......**115** D4 **249** D1
National Gallery
W1 ....**115** D6 **249** D5
National Portrait Gallery
W1 ....**115** D6 **249** D5
Nelson's Monument
WC2 ....**250** A4
New Scotland Yard
SW1 ......**115** D3 **259** C6
Parliament Square
SW1 ......**116** A4 **250** A1
Pepsi Trocadero
W1 ....**249** C5
Piccadilly Circus
W1 ....**115** D6 **249** C5
Queen Victoria Memorial
SW1 ....**249** A2
Queen's Gallery
SW1 ......**115** B4 **248** D1

Rotten Row
SW1 ....**114** D4 **247** C2
Royal Academy of Arts
W1 ....**115** C6 **249** A5
Royal Mews
SW1 ....**115** B3 **258** D6
Royal United Services
Museum SW1 ......**250** A3
St James's Palace
SW1 .....**115** C5 **249** B3
St James's Park SW1 **249** C2
Serpentine Gallery
W2 ....**114** B4 **246** D2
Soho W1 ....**93** D1 **239** C2
Somerset House
WC2 .....**116** B6 **250** D6
Speakers' Corner
W1 ....**114** D6 **247** D6
Tate Britain
SW1 ....**116** A2 **260** A3
Theatre
Museum WC2 .....**250** B6
Trafalgar Square
SW1 ....**115** D5 **249** D4
Tyburn Tree
(site of) W2 ......**247** C6
Wallace Collection
W1 ....**238** A2
Wellington Arch SW1 **248** B2
Wellington Museum
(Apsley House)
SW1 ......**115** A4 **248** B2
Westminster Abbey
SW1 ......**116** A3 **260** A6
Westminster Cathedral
SW1 ....**115** C3 **259** A5

City

Bank of England EC2 .**242** C1
Barbican Arts and
Conference Centre
EC2 ......**95** A2 **242** B4
Central Criminal
Court (Old Bailey)
EC4 ....**94** D1 **241** D2
Custom House
EC3 ....**117** C6 **253** A5
Dr Johnson's House
EC4 ....**241** B1
Gray's Inn WC1 **94** B2 **240** D4
Guildhall EC2 .**95** A1 **242** B2
Inner Temple EC4 ...**251** A6
John Wesley's House &
Museum EC1 ......**242** D6
Lincoln's Inn
WC2 ......**94** B1 **240** D2
Lloyd's Building
EC3 ......**95** C5 **243** A1
Mansion House EC4 .**242** C1
Merchant Taylors Hall
EC3 ....**242** D1
Middle Temple
EC4 ......**116** C6 **251** A6
Monument, The EC3 .**252** D6
Museum of London
EC2 ....**95** A2 **242** A3
Nat West Tower EC2 .**243** D2
National Postal Museum
EC1 ......**95** A1 **242** A2
Petticoat Lane Market
EC2 ....**95** D2 **243** C3
Public Record Office
Museum EC4,WC2 ...**241** A2
Royal Exchange EC3 .**242** D1
St Katharine Docks
E1 ....**117** D5 **253** D4

St Mary le Bow Church
EC2 ....**242** B1
St Paul's Cathedral
EC4 ....**95** A1 **242** A1
Sir John Soane's Museum
WC2 ....**94** B1 **240** C2
Spitalfields
Market E1 ..**95** D2 **243** C4
Stock Exchange EC2 .**242** D1
Tower Bridge
E1,EC3,SE1 ...**117** D5 **253** C4
Tower of London
EC3 ....**117** D6 **253** C5
Traitors Gate
EC3 ....**117** D5 **253** C4
Ye Olde Cheshire
Cheese EC4 ......**241** B2

Northern

Business Design
Centre N1 ..**94** C6 **234** B5
Camden Market
NW1 ....**93** B6 **231** D6
London Canal
Museum N1 ..**94** A5 **233** B4
London Central
Mosque NW8 .**92** C4 **230** B1
London Zoo
NW1 ....**93** A5 **231** A4
Lord's Cricket
Ground NW8 .**92** B4 **229** D2
Madame Tussaud's
NW1 ....**93** A3 **238** A5
Open Air Theatre,
Regent's Park NW1 .**231** A1
Planetarium
NW1 ....**93** A3 **238** A5
Primrose Hill
NW1 ....**92** D6 **230** C6
Queen Mary's
Gardens NW1 .....**231** A1
Regent's Park
NW1 ....**93** A4 **231** A3
St George's
Cathedral NW1 ....**231** D2
Sherlock Holmes Museum
NW1 ....**92** D3 **237** D5

Southern

Battersea Park
SW11 ......**137** A5 **268** A3
Battersea Power Station
SW8 ....**137** B6 **268** D6
Brompton Oratory
SW7 ....**114** C3 **257** A5
Bear Gardens Museum
SE1 ....**117** A5 **252** A4
Bermondsey
Market SE1 .**117** C3 **263** B8
Borough Market SE1 .**252** C3
Design Museum
SE1 ....**117** D4 **253** D2
Florence Nightingale
Museum SE1 .....**250** D1
Gabriel's Wharf SE1 .**251** A4
George Inn SE1 ...**252** C3
Globe Theatre SE1 ..**252** A5
Hayward Gallery
SE1 ....**116** B5 **250** D4
HMS Belfast SE1 ...**253** B4
Imperial War Museum
SE1 ....**116** C3 **261** B5
Lambeth Palace
SE1 ....**116** B3 **260** C5

London
Aquarium SE1 .....**250** C1
London Dungeon
SE1 ....**117** B5 **252** D4
London Eye
SE1 ....**116** B4 **250** C2
London Peace
Pagoda SW11 ....**267** D4
Millennium Bridge
SE1,EC4 ....**252** A5
Museum of Garden
History SE1 .....**260** C5
National Film
Theatre SE1 .....**250** D4
National Theatre
SE1 ....**116** B5 **250** D4
Old County Hall SE1 .**250** C2
Operating Theatre
Museum and Herb
Garret SE1 .**117** B5 **252** D3
Oxo Tower SE1 ....**251** B5
Royal Festival Hall
SE1 ....**116** B5 **250** D3
Saatchi Gallery SE1 .**250** C2
St George's RC Cathedral
SE1 ....**116** C3 **261** B6
Shakespeare's Globe
Theatre (site of)
SE1 ....**252** B4
Southwark Cathedral
SE1 ....**117** B5 **252** C4
Tate Modern
SE1 ....**116** D6 **251** D4
Vinopolis SE1 **117** B5 **252** C4

Western

Albert Memorial
SW7 ....**114** B4 **246** D1
Carlyle's House SW3 .**267** A5
Chelsea Barracks
SW1 ....**115** A1 **258** B1
Chelsea Physic Garden
SW1 ....**115** A1 **267** C6
Commonwealth Institute
W8 ....**113** C3 **255** A6
Geological Museum
SW7 ....**114** B3 **256** D5
Kensington Gardens
W2 ....**114** A5 **246** B3
Kensington Palace
W8 ....**113** D5 **245** D3
Leighton House
W14 ....**254** D6
Lindsey House SW10 .**266** D4
Little Venice
W9 ....**92** A2 **236** A4
London Toy and
Model Museum
W2 ....**114** A6 **246** A6
National Army Museum
SW3 ....**136** D6 **267** D6
Natural History Museum
SW7 ....**114** B3 **256** D5
Ranelagh Gardens
SW1 ....**115** A1 **258** B1
Royal Albert Hall
SW7 ....**114** B4 **246** C1
Royal Hospital
(Army Pensioners)
SW1 ....**115** A1 **258** A1
Science Museum
SW7 ....**114** B3 **256** C5
Victoria & Albert Museum
SW7 ....**114** B3 **256** D5

East

Bethnal Green Museum of
Childhood E2 .....**96** C4
Canary Wharf E14 ...**119** D5
Docklands
Museum E14 ....**119** D6
Epping Forest IG10 ...**21** B6
Geffrye Museum E2 ...**95** D5
London Docklands
Visitor Centre E14 ..**120** A4
London Gas Museum
E16 ....**98** B3
Museum of the Great
Eastern Railway E16 **122** C4
Queen Elizabeth's
Hunting Lodge
Museum E4 ....**20** D4
Ragged School
Museum E3 ....**97** A2
Vestry House
(Museum) E17 ....**53** D5
Whitechapel Art Gallery
E1 ....**95** D1

North

Alexandra Palace N22 **31** D1
Barnet Museum EN5 ..**1** A1
Battle of Britain
Museum NW9 ...**27** D1
Bruce Castle
Museum N17 ....**33** C2
Church Farm House
Museum NW4 ....**46** B6
Coppetts Centre N12 .**30** D3
Forty Hall EN2 ....**5** D6
Freud Museum NW3 ..**70** A2
Grange Museum of
Community History
NW10 ....**67** D4
Hampstead Heath
NW3 ....**70** B6
Harrow Museum &
Heritage Centre HA2 .**42** A6
Highgate Cemetery
N19 ....**71** B6
Kensal Green Cemetery
(All Souls) NW10 ...**90** C4
Kenwood House NW3 .**48** C1
Old Court (Museum &
Library) HA0 ......**65** C3
RAF Museum NW9 ...**28** A1
Ruislip Lido HA4,HA5 ..**39** B5
Ruislip Lido Railway
HA4 ....**39** B5
White Cube N1 .....**95** C4

South east

Blackheath SE3 ....**142** C4
Brockwell Park SE24 **160** D5
Cutty Sark SE10 ....**142** A6
Docklands Heritage
Museum SE16 .....**119** B5
Dulwich Picture Gallery
SE21 ....**161** C4
Eltham Palace SE9 ..**166** A4
Flamsteed
House SE10 ......**142** B5
Gipsy Moth IV SE10 .**142** A6
Greenwich Park SE10 **142** C5
Horniman Museum &
Gardens SE23 .....**162** B3
Livesey Museum
SE15 ....**140** B6

Meridian Building
SE10 ....**1**
Millennium Dome
SE10 ....**1**
National Maritime
Museum SE10 .....**1**
Old Royal Observatory
Greenwich SE10 ...**1**
Queen's House SE10 .**1**
Rotunda Museum
SE18 ....**1**
Scadbury Park Nature
Reserve BR7 ....**1**
South Norwood Count
Park SE25 ....**2**
Thames Barrier Visitor
Centre SE18 ......**1**
Well Hall Pleasaunce
SE9 ....**1**

South west

Barnes Common
SW13 ....**1**
Clapham Common
SW4 ....**1**
Fulham Palace SW6 .**1**
Hampton Court Palace
KT8 ....**1**
Kingston Museum
KT1 ....**1**
Wandsworth Museum
SW15 ....**1**
Wetland Centre SW13 **1**
Wimbledon Common
SW19 ....**1**
Wimbledon Lawn Tenn
Museum SW19 .....**1**
Wimbledon Windmill
Museum SW19 .....**1**

West

Chiswick House W4 ...**1**
Eel Pie Island TW1 ...**1**
Gunnersbury Park
Museum W3 ....**1**
Ham House TW10 ...**1**
Kew Bridge Steam
Museum TW8 .....**1**
Kew Gardens (Royal
Botanic Gardens)
TW9 ....**1**
Kew Observatory
TW9 ....**1**
Kew Palace TW9 ....**1**
London Butterfly
House TW8 ....**1**
Marble Hill TW1 ....**1**
Museum of
Richmond TW10 ....**1**
Musical Museum
TW8 ....**1**
Osterley Park TW7 ...**1**
Pitshanger Manor
Museum and
Art Gallery W5 ....**1**
Portobello Road Mark
W10 ....**1**
Richmond Park
TW10 ....**1**
Syon House TW8 ....**1**
Walled Garden TW16 **1**